An Encyclopedia of British Women Writers

An Encyclopedia of British Women Writers

REVISED AND EXPANDED EDITION

Edited by Paul Schlueter and June Schlueter

Rutgers University Press
New Brunswick, New Jersey, and London

First published by Garland Publishing, Inc., 1988
Revised and expanded edition published by Rutgers University Press, New Brunswick, New Jersey, 1998

Library of Congress Cataloging-in-Publication Data

Encyclopedia of British women writers / edited by Paul and June Schlueter. — Rev. and expanded ed.
p. cm.
Includes bibliographical references and index.
ISBN 0-8135-2542-X (alk. paper). — ISBN 0-8135-2543-8 (pbk. : alk. paper)
1. English literature—Women authors—Dictionaries. 2. Women authors, English—Biography—Dictionaries. 3. English literature—Women authors—Bibliography. 4. Women and literature—Great Britain—Bibliography. 5. Women and literature—Great Britain—Dictionaries. I. Schlueter, Paul, 1933– . II. Schlueter, June.
PR111.E54 1998
820.9'9287'03—dc21
[B] 97-48698
CIP

For the paperback cover, we gratefully acknowledge the following sources for permission to reprint photographs: Berg Collection of English and American Literature, The New York Public Library, Astor, Lenox and Tilden Foundations (Virginia Woolf); Portrait File, Miriam and Ira D. Wallach Division of Art, Prints and Photographs, The New York Public Library, Astor, Lenox and Tilden Foundations (Jane Austen, Elizabeth Barrett Browning, Charlotte Brontë); David Bishop Skillman Library, Lafayette College (Mary Shelley, Mary Wortley Montagu, George Eliot); and the Collection of the Earl of Pembroke, Wilton House, Wilton, England (Ephelia).

Manufactured in the United States of America

Dedicated to the Memory of
FREDERICK UNGAR
Publisher and Friend
(5 September 1898–16 November 1988)

When the column of light on the waters is glassed,
As blent in one glow seem the shine and the stream;
But wave after wave through the glory has passed,
Just catches, and flies as it catches, the beam:
So honors but mirror on mortals their light:
Not the man but the place that he passes is bright.

—Schiller (trans. Walter Scott)

Contents

Preface ix

Abbreviations of Reference Works xiii

Abbreviations of Periodicals xxi

The Encyclopedia 1

List of Contributors 701

Index 709

Preface

This volume has had an interesting if circuitous history. It was originally under contract with the distinguished independent firm of Frederick Ungar & Co. Mr. Ungar had supported the concept from its inception, partly because of other publishing projects we had worked on for his company, and partly so he would have such a work as companion to his four-volume *American Women Writers*, edited by Lina Mainiero (1979), which contained entries for 1,000 writers, and its two-volume abridgement, edited by Langdon Faust (1983). Though this work has necessarily changed in focus somewhat as it has progressed and changed publishers, it still owes its origin and direction to Frederick Ungar.

When Frederick Ungar & Co. was absorbed into Crossroad Continuum in 1987—Mr. Ungar was then eighty-nine and felt it was time to retire from publishing—our project yielded to a competing one. Garland Publishing expressed interest in the volume, saw it through production, and ended up with a critically praised book—*An Encyclopedia of British Women Writers* (1988)—that sold well. Garland generously arranged for a specially bound copy of the first edition to be sent to Mr. Ungar: He saw and admired it a few weeks before his death. That volume was the the sole book ever dedicated to him, and we remain appreciative of Garland's gesture, which recognized Frederick Ungar's distinguished place in publishing and in our lives.

We placed the present edition with Rutgers University Press following a reorganization at Garland that precipitated a change in that company's publishing plans. We are pleased at Rutgers's prompt acceptance of the project and are happy, finally, to see it in print, bringing to closure a volume that had, to say the least, a difficult gestation. In addition to the exigencies of the publishing world, our dealings with some 200 contributors involved the logistics of soliciting, receiving, editing, regularizing, and preparing for publication, on disk and on hard copy, a manuscript of major proportions. Throughout the process, we have been fortunate in being able to call again on most of the contributors to our first edition as well as a host of new contributors.

An Encyclopedia of British Women Writers is a massive project that makes readily available, in alphabetical sequence, some 600 biographical-critical entries on a range of women writers, from the early centuries of writing identified with England up to the present day, who have a claim to being "British." In part, the project was a recovery effort, validating the work of a large cast of women writers, many of whom wrote anonymously or under male pseudonyms or who, in their time, were for the most part neglected. Readers will recognize many familiar names of writers who have become canonical, but among these are also names that literary history has kept more obscure. Readers interested in finding patterns among British women writers may indeed do so; but so too will they find variety: in theme, style, output, and reception. The volume's contributors have carefully researched their subjects; many, in fact, are recognized authorities on their subjects and bring to these entries years of study and research. We trust that compiling these entries in one volume, which contains some 200 more entries than the first edition and includes updates for the entries that previously appeared, will prove a service to both the academic community and the general reader, and we hope that *An Encyclopedia of British Women Writers* will take its place among the more useful reference books in the library.

Assigning, assembling, and editing so substantial a volume has necessarily presented a challenge. But challenges existed even in the conceptual stage. What, for example, was the definition of a "British" writer? Need an author have been born in Britain to qualify, or might she simply have lived there—and for how long? By choosing the word "British" rather than "English," as we also did for the earlier edition, we indicated our desire to make the work as inclusive as possible rather than exclusive to one specific political entity. We found, even more now than previously, that we could not depend on place of birth as a criterion, since so much migration and movement has occurred both to and from the United Kingdom. If anything, we have broadened our sense of what "British" implies in this edition, for we have included a few additional writers who, though long resident in Great Britain, are also considered American. We felt similarly free to choose subjects usually identified with other nationalities when these authors resided in Great Britain fully as long as others about whom there is no question of nationality. This edition also includes a number of figures from other parts of the British Commonwealth or elsewhere, including some from Africa (e.g., Buchi Emecheta), the Caribbean (e.g., Valerie [Wright] Bloom, Amryl Johnson, Abena Musia, Grace Nichols), and Oceania (e.g., Anne Perry), who subsequently emigrated to Great Britain. Several native-English writers included in this work (e.g., Mina Loy, Jan Struther, Frances Wright) eventually emigrated to and lived in the United States for major portions of their lives; while some are also included in reference works devoted to American writers, it seemed legitimate to us to include them in a work on British literature as well. And reverse migration also applies, with some writers now included who are usually thought of as American but whose lives involved long periods of time in Great Britain (e.g., H. D., Sylvia Plath, Anne Stevenson). With Irish writers, we have drawn freely from those born before independence in 1922 and added a few born since that date (e.g., Edna O'Brien, Julia O'Faolain) because of their long residence in Great Britain, as well as more selected from earlier centuries.

Even though this volume is reasonably complete, there is no way it could accommodate all potential subjects. For one thing, some early figures are so shadowy or elusive or possibly fictional that little more than a name exists; these could include the possibly apocryphal Nossis (flourished in the third century B.C.), Liadain (flourished in the seventh century), and Gormlaith (died c. 947). Clearly nothing could be gained by including such writers, though we do include Juliana Berners, relatively well-known despite the fact that she probably never existed. We have tried to include as many medieval and Renaissance women writers as possible, even though little is generally known of their lives; their writing, given the circumstances under which they lived, usually consists only of journals or letters. The majority of entries are therefore from the eighteenth century and later, and we have assembled a rich array of twentieth-century writers, including some contemporary figures found in few if any other reference works. Even with the number of entries we include, however, practical problems prevented our including everyone we might have: In a few cases, the subject was assigned but we never received the entry; in other cases, we were unable to locate a scholar willing to accept the assignment; in still others, we simply overlooked particular writers.

For the entries we did secure, each contributor provided as complete a set of biographical data as possible; in the case of contemporary figures, our contributors often contacted the writers directly to corroborate biographical details and to clear up omissions and ambiguities. Hence, a number of entries are as definitive as possible because the subjects shared information with us and our contributors, information that often corrects data found in other reference works. Where significant data are omitted in a headnote, it should be assumed that the information is not available—or at least that despite imaginative searching, researchers have still been unable to locate the data. In some cases, even with living writers, there is simply no way of tracking down dates and places of birth or other information. Until Olivia Manning died, for example, no reference work even included a guess as to her year of birth; since her death in 1980, however, one now finds either 1911 or 1915 (both with a question mark) as her birth-year; any more precise information is still presumably inaccessible and will probably remain so.

An especially complex problem is the matter of how to list a particular author since some have a half-dozen or more pseudonyms, married names, or titles (e.g., Elizabeth von Arnim is listed under "Arnim," with cross-references including "von Arnim, Elizabeth," "Russell, Mary Annette Beauchamp," "Beauchamp, Mary Annette," "Cholmondeley, Alice," "Elizabeth," and "The Author of *Elizabeth and Her German Garden*"). In our previous edition, we merely listed cross-references in the index; in this edition, however, we include such variations both in the index and between alphabetically arranged entries to facilitate readers' locating particular authors. There seems to be no consistent pattern, even among reference volumes, as to the best ways to refer to some authors; thus we have had to be arbitrary, but this arbitrariness is not intended to suggest anything other than the need to solve a practical dilemma. In some cases, an author is listed under her family name (e.g., Sydney Owenson, Lady Morgan, is cited under "Owenson"; Margaret Cavendish, Duchess of Newcastle, is found under "Cavendish"; and Anne Kingsmill Finch, Countess of Winchelsea, is under "Finch"). In other cases, an author is found under her title (e.g., Elizabeth Percy, Duchess of Northumberland, is under "Northumberland"), as is the case with similar reference volumes. We yielded to the practical with the term "Anonymous": Given the substantial number of women writers who published without authorial attribution, we have not included the term "Anonymous" as a cross-reference.

We have tried, in short, to follow precedents, but when we lacked definitive sources we applied common sense in deciding how a particular woman is to be listed. We decided to make a few changes from our practice in our earlier volume when this seemed defensible; Lynne Reid Banks, for example, was previously listed under "Reid Banks," but now we have her under "Banks," with "Reid Banks" provided as a cross-reference. The reason is simple: Though she is cited in *Contemporary Authors* with a compound name (which derives from her father's hyphenated compound name), the British *Who's Who* (with information provided by the biographee) and the Library of Congress—guides we have decided are more definitive—use "Banks."

Even more complicated is the use of pseudonyms. While this presents no problem with major authors (e.g., George Eliot), it can be confusing for lesser figures. Again, we hope we have acted sensibly. Since all variations are cross-referenced, there should be no problem in determining whether a particular figure is included or not, even in those cases where four or five variants occur for a single writer. Hence, looking up a particular writer in the main alphabetical sequence of entries will often turn up an entry on a specific favorite whose name may not necessarily appear in the list of the volume's contents.

Each entry includes, in addition to headnote biographical information and the entry proper, as complete a list of primary works in book form through 1997 as we and our contributors could compile. We have excluded volumes edited by the subject except in those cases when the subject is known solely or primarily for such works, and we have similarly excluded periodical and other briefer writings by the subject except, again, when these amount to a subject's sole or primary publication record. We include a bibliography of books and important critical essays on the subject through 1997; we have excluded dissertations and theses and writings in languages other than English (though this does not preclude inclusion of essays written in English that appeared in journals or collections otherwise wholly written in another language). We include a sampling of major reference works that also list the subject, and "other references" that might deal, for example, with the subject's milieu or primary genre, that might include periodical reviews of the subject's writings, or that might simply serve as stimuli for further reading. We have necessarily kept all secondary lists as concise as possible by providing a brief version of critics' names and by abbreviating the names of reference works and periodicals when this has been possible; see the introductory comments to "Abbreviations of Reference Works" and "Abbreviations of Periodicals" for details. We similarly provide the year of publication for writings in journals rather than the volume and issue numbers and page numbers.

This kind of reference work could not have been produced in a vacuum; too many people have had a part in its compilation and success. Most important, of course, are the nearly 200 contributors whose entries and bibliographies constitute most of the book. The fact that almost all the contributors from our first edition elected to work with us on this revision is, of course, a matter for thanks. We have been continually grateful for our contributors' support, advice, suggestions of others who might be suitable as contributors, and encouragement. We wish in particular to recognize three contributors to the earlier edition who have died in the past decade and by so doing to say "thanks" to them once again:

Dorothy Allison
Angela Emanuel
Gail Kraidman

We have also had the continuing support of many connected with Skillman Library at Lafayette College in Easton, Pennsylvania. Lafayette's director of libraries, Neil McElroy, has uniformly excellent professionals on his staff, and we are pleased that we could draw on their expertise and knowledge. Theresa Weisser, Rani Sinha, Janice Masud, Robert Duncan, Dan Evans, Susanna Boylston, and above all Terese Heidenwolf have always responded quickly, professionally, and cheerfully to our need for bibliographic and biographic details. A former member of the Skillman staff, Richard Everett, also earns our thanks once again.

Nancy Williams, an assistant in the college provost's office, deserves much thanks for her heroic typing efforts, and Susan Castelletti, Mr. McElroy's secretary and assistant, repeatedly proved helpful. Our daughter, Greta Schlueter, also assisted with the typing and transcription, as did Lafayette College students Rachel Stanzioni, Nhat-Khai Do, and Tawney Williams.

Special thanks are reserved for Heather Braun, who was an indispensable part of the project over the last two years of its preparation. During that time, we came to trust her intelligence, perceptiveness, and judgment in many editorial tasks, and we felt fortunate to have had her assistance. Heather, who was an undergraduate when she began working with us and who is now studying for her advanced degrees in English, is as thoroughly a part of the book as any professional editorial assistant could have been.

We also thank the Modern Language Association of America, especially Karin E. McLaughlin, coordinator of acquisitions and the MLA *Directory of Periodicals*, for prompt, helpful answers to questions about the status of various journals cited in entries. The definitive computer printout of journals currently or formerly indexed in the MLA's *International Bibliography* proved particularly valuable.

Finally, we are grateful to the staff of Rutgers University Press, especially Leslie Mitchner, Assistant Director of the press, for support and advice in seeing this volume to publication. Her staff, notably Anne Hegeman, Production Editor, has been especially attentive to publication details. Above all, we are thankful to Sally M. Scott, our copyeditor, for her meticulous, imaginative, and perceptive editing. Sally has worked wonders to assure stylistic consistency, to emphasize bibliographic accuracy and completeness, and to eliminate potentially embarrassing errors of fact and interpretation. The book would be much the worse without her inspired efforts, and we are grateful.

Comments, criticisms, and corrections for this volume are welcome; please send them to us c/o Lafayette College, Easton, PA 18042 or, electronically, at schluetj@lafayette.edu.

P.S.
J.S.
Easton, PA
May 1998

Abbreviations of Reference Works

The following list of reference sources does not include all those cited in the volume but instead represents some of the most commonly cited: The list is intended to lead a reader to other brief critical assessments. Specifically omitted are such indispensable sources as the *Encyclopaedia Britannica*, in which entries for many of the writers can also be found.

ABYP — *Authors of Books for Young People*, ed. M. E. Ward (Metuchen, NJ: Scarecrow Press, 1964; 2nd ed., 1971; 3rd ed., 1990).

Adams — Adams, W. Davenport. *Dictionary of English Literature*, 2nd ed. (rpt.) (Detroit: Gale, 1966).

Allibone — *Allibone's Critical Dictionary of English Literature and British and American Authors*, ed. J. Foster Kirk (Philadelphia: Lippincott, 1858).

Allibone SUP — *Allibone's Critical Dictionary of English Literature and British and American Authors Supplement*, ed. J. Foster Kirk (Philadelphia: Lippincott, 1891).

ArtWW — *Articles on Women Writers: A Bibliography*, comp. Narda L. Schwartz (Santa Barbara, CA: ABC-Clio, 1977; vol. 2, 1986).

AWW — *American Women Writers*, 4 vols., ed. Lina Mainiero (New York: Ungar, 1979).

AWWW — *Authors and Writers Who's Who*, 6th ed., ed. J. V. Yates (Darien, CT: Hafner, 1971).

BAB1800 — *British Authors Before 1800: A Biographical Dictionary*, ed. Stanley J. Kunitz and Howard Haycraft (New York: Wilson, 1952).

Ballard — Ballard, George. *Memoirs of Several Ladies of Great Britain Who Have Been Celebrated for Their Writings or Skill in the Learned Languages* (Oxford, U.K.: W. Jackson, 1752; rpt. ed. Ruth Perry [Detroit: Wayne State University Press, 1985]).

BA19C — *British Authors of the Nineteenth Century*, ed. Stanley J. Kunitz and Howard Haycraft (New York: Wilson, 1936).

BCathA — *Book of Catholic Authors*, 5 vols., ed. W. Romig (Detroit: Romig, 1942–57).

BDA — *Biographical Dictionary of Actors, Actresses, Musicians, Dancers, Managers and Other Stage Personnel in London, 1660–1800*, 5 vols., 1973–87, ed. Philip H. Highfill, et al. (Carbondale: Southern Illinois University Press, 1978).

BDBF — *Biographical Dictionary of British Feminists*, ed. Olive Banks (New York: New York University Press, 1985).

BDIW — *Biographical Dictionary of Irish Writers*, ed. Anne M. Brady and Brian Cleeve (New York: St. Martin's Press, 1985).

BDLA — *Biographical Dictionary of the Living Authors of Great Britain and Ireland*, ed. John Watkins and Frederic Shober (London: H. Colburn, 1816; rpt. Detroit: Gale, 1966).

BDMBR — *Biographical Dictionary of Modern British Radicals*, ed. Joseph O. Bayler and Norbert J. Gossman (London: Harvester Press; Atlantic Highlands, NJ: Humanities Press, vol. 1, 1979; vol. 2, 1984).

BDWAEA — *Biographical Dictionary of Women Artists in Europe and America Since 1850*, ed. P. Dunford (Philadelphia: University of Pennsylvania Press, 1989; London: Harvester Wheatsheaf, 1990).

Bell — Bell, Maureen, et al. *A Biographical Dictionary of English Women Writers 1580–1720* (New York and London: Harvester Wheatsheaf; Boston: G. K. Hall, 1990).

BGEL — *Bloomsbury Guide to English Literature*, ed. M. Wynne-Davies (London: Bloomsbury, 1989; Englewood Cliffs, NJ: Prentice-Hall, 1990; 2d. ed., London: Bloomsbury, 1995).

BioIn — *Biography Index* (1946–).

Black — *Notable Women Authors of the Day*, ed. H. C. Black (Glasgow: D. Bryce, 1893).

Bloomsbury *Bloomsbury Guide to Women's Literature*, ed. Claire Buck (London: Bloomsbury, 1992).

Boase *Modern English Biography*, ed. Frederic Boase (London: Netherton & Worth, 1892–1921).

CA *Contemporary Authors* (Detroit: Gale, 1967–).

Cambridge *Cambridge Guide to Literature in English*, ed. Ian Ousby (Cambridge, U.K.: Cambridge University Press, 1993).

Carty *A Dictionary of Literary Pseudonyms in the English Language*, comp. T. J. Carty (London: Mansell; Chicago: Fitzroy Dearborn, 1995).

Cassell *Cassell's Encyclopedia of English Literature*, ed. S. H. Steinberg, rev. J. Buchanan-Brown (New York: Morrow, 1973).

CB *Current Biography* (New York: Wilson, 1940–).

CBD *Contemporary British Dramatists*, ed. K. A. Berney (London and Detroit: St. James Press, 1994).

CBEL *Cambridge Bibliography of English Literature*, ed. F. W. Bateson (Cambridge, U.K.: Cambridge University Press, 1941, 1957).

CD *Contemporary Dramatists*, ed. James Vinson (New York: St. Martin's Press, 1973, 1977, 1982, 1986).

CEMD *Concise Encyclopedia of Modern Drama*, ed. Siegfried Melchinger; trans. George Wellwarth, ed. Henry Popkin (New York: Horizon, 1964).

CHAL *Cambridge History of American Literature*, ed. William Peterfield Trent, et al. (New York: Putnam, 1917–21).

Chalmers *The General Biographical Dictionary: Containing an Historical and Critical Account of the Lives and Writings of the Most Eminent Persons in Every Land*, ed. A. Chalmers (London: Nichols, 1812).

Chambers *Chambers Cyclopaedia of English Literature*, ed. David Patrick (London: Chambers, 1890, 1902).

CHBP *Columbia History of British Poetry*, ed. Carl Woodring and James R. Shapiro (New York: Columbia University Press, 1994).

CHEL *Cambridge History of English Literature*, ed. A. C. Ward and A. R. Waller (Cambridge, U.K.: Cambridge University Press, 1907–33).

CinP *Childhood in Poetry*, 1st Supp., ed. John Mackay Shaw (Detroit: Gale, 1972).

CLC *Contemporary Literary Critics*, ed. Elmer Borklund (New York: St. Martin's Press, 1977, 1982).

CLR *Children's Literature Review*, ed. Gerard J. Senick (Detroit: Gale, 1976).

CN *Contemporary Novelists*, ed. James Vinson (New York: St. Martin's Press, 1972, 1976, 1986).

Collins *Collins Biographical Dictionary of English Literature*, ed. Antony Karmen (London: Collins, 1993).

ConSFA *Contemporary Science Fiction Authors*, ed. Robert Reginald (New York: Arno, 1975; previously published as *Stella Nova: Contemporary Science Fiction Authors* [Los Angeles: Unicorn & Son, 1970]).

CP *Contemporary Poets*, ed. James Vinson (New York: St. Martin's Press, 1970, 1975, 1980, 1985).

CSBD *Chambers Scottish Biographical Dictionary*, ed. R. Goring (Edinburgh and New York: Chambers, 1992).

CSLF *Critical Survey of Long Fiction* (English Language Series), ed. Frank N. Magill (Englewood Cliffs, NJ: Salem Press, 1983).

CWA *Cyclopedia of World Authors*, ed. Frank N. Magill (New York: Harper, 1958).

CWW *Checklist of Women Writers*, ed. R. C. Alston (Boston, G. K. Hall; London: British Library, 1990).

DAB *Dictionary of American Biography*, ed. American Council of Learned Societies (New York; Scribner, 1928–).

Dabundo *Encyclopedia of Romanticism: Culture in Britain, 1780–1850s*, ed. Laura Dabundo and Pamela Olinto (New York: Garland, 1992).

Daims *Toward a Feminist Tradition: An Annotated Bibliography of Novels in English by Women 1891–1920*, ed. Diva Daims and Janet Grimes (New York: Garland, 1982).

Darton *Children's Books in England*, F. J. Darton (Cambridge, U.K.: Cambridge University Press, 1932); 3rd ed., ed. Brian Alderson (Cambridge: Cambridge University Press, 1982).

DBA *Dictionary of British Artists Working 1900–1950*, ed. Grant M. Waters (Eastbourne, U.K.: Eastbourne Fine Art, 1975).

DBPP *Dictionary of Biography, Past and Present*, ed. Benjamin Vincent (London: Ward, Lock, 1877; rpt., Detroit: Gale, 1974).

DEA *Dictionary of English Authors, Biographical and Bibliographical*, ed. R. F. Sharp (London: Redway, 1897).

DIB *Dictionary of Irish Biography*, ed. Henry Boylan (Dublin: Gill and Macmillan; New York: Barnes & Noble, 1978).

DictEur *A Dictionary of European Literature Designed as a Companion to English Studies*, ed. Laurie Magnus (London: Routledge, 1927).

DIL *Dictionary of Irish Literature*, ed. Robert Hogan (Westport, CT: Greenwood Press, 1979, 2nd ed., 1996).

DIW *Dictionary of Irish Writers*, ed. Brian Cleeve (Cork, Ireland: Mercier, 1967).

DLB *Dictionary of Literary Biography* (Detroit: Gale, 1978–).

DLEL *Dictionary of Literature in the English Language from 1940 to 1970*, ed. Robin Myers (Oxford: Pergamon, 1978).

DNB *Dictionary of National Biography* (London: Macmillan, 1885–).

Dole *Bibliophile Dictionary*, ed. Nathan H. Dole, et al. (Detroit: Gale, 1966).

DVP *Dictionary of Victorian Painters*, ed. Christopher Wood (Woodbridge, U.K.: Antique Collectors' Club, 1971).

DWA *Dictionary of Women Artists: An International Dictionary of Women Artists Born before 1900*, ed. Chris Petteys (Boston: G. K. Hall, 1985).

EBH *Encyclopedia of British Humorists*, ed. Steven H. Gale (New York: Garland, 1996).

1890s *The 1890s: An Encyclopedia of British Literature, Art, and Culture*, ed. G. A. Cevasco (New York: Garland, 1993).

ECSTC *Eighteenth-Century Short Title Catalogue*, comp. Miriam Mandelbaum, 2 vols. (New York: New York Public Library, 1980).

ELB *Everyman's Dictionary of Literary Biography. English and American*, ed. D. C. Browning and J. W. Cousin (New York: Dutton, 1960; rev. 1969).

EMD *Encyclopedia of Mystery and Detection*, ed. Chris Steinbrunner and Otto Penzler (New York: McGraw-Hill, 1976).

EP *English Poetesses: A Series of Critical Biographies*, ed. E. S. Robertson (London: Cassell, 1883).

ESF *Encyclopedia of Science Fiction*, ed. John Clute and Peter Nicholls (New York: St. Martin's Press, 1993 [2d. ed. of *SFE*]).

Europa *Europa Biographical Dictionary of British Women*, ed. Anne Crawford, et al. (London: Europa, 1983).

EWLTC *Encyclopedia of World Literature in the 20th Century*, rev. ed., ed. Leonard Klein (New York: Ungar, 1981).

Feminist *Feminist Companion to Literature in English*, ed. Virginia Blair, et al. (New Haven, CT: Yale University Press, 1990).

Ferguson *First Feminists: British Women Writers 1578–1799*, ed. Moira Ferguson (Old Westbury, NY: Feminist Press; Bloomington: Indiana University Press, 1985).

GayLL *Gay and Lesbian Literature*, ed. Sharon Malinowski (New York: St. James Press, 1994).

Grimes *Novels in English by Women, 1891–1920: A Preliminary Checklist*, ed. Janet Grimes and Diva Daims (New York: Garland, 1981).

GWELN *Great Writers of the English Language: Novelists*, ed. James Vinson (New York: St. Martin's Press, 1979).

GWELP *Great Writers of the English Language: Poets*, ed. James Vinson (New York: St. Martin's Press, 1979).

Halkett *Dictionary of Anonymous and Pseudonymous English Literature*, ed. Samuel Halkett and John Laing (Edinburgh, U.K.: William Patterson, 1882–88).

Hickey *A Dictionary of Irish History Since 1800*, ed. D. H. Hickey and J. E. Doherty (Dublin: Gill and Macmillan, 1980).

IAWWW *International Authors and Writers Who's Who*, 9th ed., ed. Adrian Gaster (Cambridge, U.K.: International Biographical Centre, 1982).

IDBW *International Dictionary of Women's Biography*, ed. Jennifer Uglow (New York: Continuum, 1982; also published as *Macmillan Dictionary of Women's Biography* [London: Macmillan, 1982]).

Ireland *Index to Women of the World from Ancient to Modern Times*, ed. Norma Olin Ireland (Westwood, MA: Faxon, 1970; Metuchen, NJ: Scarecrow Press, 1988).

IWWW *International Who's Who of Women* (London: Europa, 1992).

Jackson *Romantic Poetry by Women: A Bibliography 1770–1835*, ed. J. R. Jackson (Oxford, U.K.: Clarendon Press, 1993).

JBA *Junior Book of Authors*, ed. Stanley J. Kunitz and Howard Haycraft (New York: Wilson, 1934, 1951).

LA *Living Authors*, ed. Stanley J. Kunitz (New York: Wilson, 1931).

Longman *Longman Companion to Twentieth Century Literature*, ed. A. C. Ward (London: Longman, 1970; 2nd ed., ed. Christopher Gillie [London: Longman, 1977]).

Mahl & Koon *The Female Spectator: English Women Writers Before 1800*, ed. Mary R. Mahl and Helene Koon (Old Westbury, NY: Feminist Press; Bloomington: Indiana University Press, 1977).

MAL *Modern American Literature*, 4th ed. ed. Dorothy N. Curley, et al. (New York: Ungar, 1969).

MAL SUP *Modern American Literature, Supplement I*, ed. Maurice Kramer and Elaine Kramer (New York: Ungar, 1976); *Supplement II*, ed. Paul Schlueter and June Schlueter (New York: Ungar, 1985).

Manly *Contemporary British Literature: Bibliographies and Study Outlines*, ed. John Matthews Manly and E. Rickert (New York: Harcourt Brace, 1921; 2nd ed., 1928; 3rd ed., 1935).

Marshall *Pen Names of Women Writers from 1600 to the Present: A Compendium of the Literary Identities of 2650 Women Novelists, Playwrights, Poets, Diarists, Journalists and Miscellaneous Writers, Fully Cross-Referenced*, comp. Alice Kahler Marshall (Camp Hill, PA: Marshall Collection, 1983).

MAWW *Modern American Women Writers*, ed. Elaine Showalter, et al. (New York: Scribner, 1991).

MBL *Modern British Literature*, ed. Ruth Z. Temple and Martin Tucker (New York: Ungar, 1966).

MBL SUP *Modern British Literature Supplement*, ed. Martin Tucker and Rita Stein (New York: Ungar, 1975).

MCL *Modern Commonwealth Literature*, ed. John H. Ferres and Martin Tucker (New York: Ungar, 1977).

MHEWB *McGraw-Hill Encyclopedia of World Biography: An International Reference Work* (New York: McGraw-Hill, 1973–89).

Miles *The Poets and the Poetry of the Century: Charles Kingsley to James Thomson*, ed. Alfred H. Miles (London: Hutchinson, 1891).

Millett *Contemporary British Literature: A Critical Survey and 232 Author-Bibliographies*, ed. Fred B. Millett; 3rd ed., ed. J. M. Manly and Edith Rickert (New York: Harcourt, 1935).

MJA *More Junior Authors*, ed. Muriel Fuller (New York: Wilson, 1963).

Moulton *Moulton's Library of Literary Criticism of English and American Authors through the Beginning of the 20th Century*, ed. Martin Tucker (New York: Ungar, 1966).

MWD — *Modern World Drama: An Encyclopedia*, ed. Myron Matlaw (New York: Dutton, 1972).

MWT — *Modern World Theatre: A Guide to Productions in Europe and the United States Since 1945*, ed. Siegfried Kienzle; trans. Alexander Henderson and Elizabeth Henderson (New York: Ungar, 1970).

NCBEL — *New Cambridge Bibliography of English Literature*, ed. George Watson (Cambridge, U.K.: Cambridge University Press, 1969).

NCHEL — *New Century Handbook of English Literature*, rev. ed., ed. C. L. Barnhart and William D. Halsey (New York: Appleton-Century-Crofts, 1967).

NCLC — *Nineteenth Century Literary Criticism*, ed. L. L. Harry, et al. (Detroit: Gale, 1981–).

NRGAL — *New Reader's Guide to African Literature*, ed. Hans M. Zell, Carol Bundy, and Virginia Coulon, 2nd ed. (New York: Africana Pub. Co.; London: Heinemann, 1983).

OCAL — *Oxford Companion to American Literature*, 5th ed., ed. James D. Hart (Oxford: Oxford University Press, 1983).

OCCL — *Oxford Companion to Children's Literature*, ed. Humphrey Carpenter and Mari Pritchard (New York: Oxford University Press, 1984).

OCEL — *Oxford Companion to English Literature*, rev. ed., ed. Margaret Drabble (New York: Oxford University Press, 1985).

OCIL — *Oxford Companion to Irish Literature*, ed. Robert Welch (Oxford and New York: Clarendon Press, 1996).

OCTCL — *Oxford Companion to Twentieth-Century Literature*, ed. Jerry Stringer (New York: Oxford University Press, 1996).

OxComp — *Oxford Companion to Twentieth-Century Poetry in English*, ed. Ian Hamilton (New York: Oxford University Press, 1994).

Oxford — *Oxford Guide to British Women Writers*, ed. Joanne Shattock (New York: Oxford University Press, 1993).

Palmer — *Who's Who in Shakespeare's England*, ed. A. Palmer and V. Palmer (Brighton, U.K.: Harvester; New York: St. Martin's Press, 1981).

PCEL — *Penguin Companion to English Literature*, ed. David Daiches (New York: McGraw-Hill, 1971).

PCWL — *Penguin Companion to World Literature*, 4 vols., ed. Malcolm Bradbury, et al. (New York: McGraw-Hill, 1969–71).

PHS — *Penguin Encyclopedia of Horror and the Supernatural*, ed. Jack Sullivan (New York: Viking Press, 1986).

Poole — *Poole's Index to Periodical Literature*, 3rd ed., ed. William F. Poole (Boston: Houghton Mifflin, 1882).

PPC — *The Poets and the Poetry of the Nineteenth Century*, ed. Alfred H. Miles (London: Routledge; New York: Dutton, 1905–1907).

RGTCW — *Reader's Guide to Twentieth-Century Writers*, ed. Peter Parker (New York: Oxford University Press, 1995).

RE — *Reader's Encyclopedia*, ed. W. R. Benet (New York: Crowell, 1948, 1965; London: Black, 1987).

RGCL — *Reader's Guide to Contemporary Literature, Being the First Supplement of the Best Books*, ed. William Swan Sonnenschein (New York: Putnam, 1895).

RGFMBP — *Reader's Guide to Fifty Modern British Poets*, ed. Michael Schmidt (London: Heinemann; New York: Barnes and Noble, 1979).

Roberton — *The Novel Reader's Handbook: A Brief Guide to Recent Novels and Novelists*, ed. William Roberton (Birmingham, U.K.: Holland, 1899).

Robinson — *Women Novelists, 1891–1920: An Index to Biographical and Autobiographical Sources*, ed. Doris Robinson (New York: Garland, 1984).

Rowton — *The Female Poets of Great Britain: Chronologically Arranged with Copious*

Selections and Critical Remarks [1853], ed. Frederic Rowton (Detroit: Wayne State University Press, 1981).

Sanders — *Celebrities of the Century: Being a Dictionary of Men and Women of the Nineteenth Century*, ed. L. C. Sanders (Ann Arbor, MI: Gryphon, 1971).

SATA — *Something About the Author*, ed. Anne Commire (Detroit: Gale, 1971–84).

SF&FL — *Science Fiction and Fantasy Literature*, ed. Robert Reginald (Detroit: Gale, 1979).

SFE — *Science Fiction Encyclopedia*, ed. Peter Nichols (Garden City, NY: Doubleday, 1979; 2d. ed. as *ESF*).

SFW — *Supernatural Fiction Writers: Fantasy and Horror*, ed. Everett F. Bleiler (New York: Scribner, 1985).

Stanford — *Stanford Companion to Victorian Fiction*, ed. John Sutherland (Stanford, CA: Stanford University Press, 1989).

STC — *A Short-Title Catalogue of Books Printed in England, Scotland, Ireland, and of English Books Printed Abroad, 1475–1640*, comp. A. W. Pollard and G. R. Redgrave (London: Bibliographical Society, 1926); followed by *A Short-Title Catalogue of Books Printed in England, Scotland, Ireland, Wales, and British America, and of English Books Printed in Other Countries, 1641–1700*, 3 vols., comp. A. W. Pollard (New York: Columbia University Press, 1945–51).

TCA — *Twentieth Century Authors: A Biographical Dictionary of Modern Literature*, ed. Stanley J. Kunitz and Howard Haycraft (New York: Wilson, 1942).

TCA SUP — *Twentieth Century Authors Supplement*, ed. Stanley J. Kunitz (New York: Wilson, 1955).

TCC&MW — *Twentieth Century Crime and Mystery Writers*, ed. John M. Reilly (New York: St. Martin's Press, 1980).

TCCW — *Twentieth Century Children's Writers*, ed. D. L. Kirkpatrick (New York: St. Martin's Press, 1983).

TCLC — *Twentieth Century Literary Criticism* (Detroit: Gale, 1978).

TCRGW — *Twentieth Century Romance and Gothic Writers*, ed. James Vinson and D. L. Kirkpatrick (New York: St. Martin's Press, 1982; rev. as *TCRHW*).

TCRHW — *Twentieth Century Romance and Historical Writers*, ed. Lesley Henderson (London: St. James Press, 1990).

TCSFW — *Twentieth Century Science Fiction Writers*, ed. Curtis C. Smith (New York: St. Martin's Press, 1981).

TCSSE — *Twentieth Century Short Story Explication: Interpretations, 1900–1975, of Short Fiction Since 1800*, ed. Warren S. Walker (Hamden, CT; Shoe String Press, 1977).

TCW — *Twentieth Century Writing: A Reader's Guide to Contemporary Literature*, ed. Kenneth Richardson (Levittown, NY: Transatlantic Arts, 1971).

ToddBWW — *British Women Writers: A Critical Reference Guide*, ed. Janet Todd (New York: Continuum, 1989).

ToddDBA — *A Dictionary of British and American Women Writers, 1600–1800*, ed. Janet Todd (Totowa, NJ: Rowman and Allanheld, 1985).

VB — *Victorian Britain: An Encyclopedia*, ed. Sally Mitchell (New York: Garland, 1988).

WA — *World Authors*, ed. John Wakeman (New York: Wilson, 1975).

WA SUP — *World Authors Supplement*, ed. John Wakeman (New York: Wilson, 1980).

W&D — *Wives and Daughters: The Women of Sixteenth Century England*, ed. K. L. Emerson (Troy, NJ: Whitston, 1984).

Warner — *Biographical Dictionary and Synopsis of Books, Ancient and Modern*, ed. Charles Dudley Warner (Detroit: Gale, 1965).

WD — *Writer's Directory* (London: St. James Press; New York: St. Martin's Press, 1983–).

WL17C — *Women and Literature of the Seventeenth Century: An Annotated Bibliography Based on Wing's Short-Title Catalogue*, ed. Hilda L. Smith and Susan Cardinale (Westport, CT: Greenwood Press, 1990).

WN — *Women Novelists 1891–1920: An Index to Biographical and Autobiographical Sources*, ed. D. Robinson (New York: Garland, 1984).

WNWC — *Webster's New World Companion to English and American Literature*, ed. Arthur Pollard (New York: World, 1973).

WWALA — *Who's Who Among Living Authors of Older Nations* (Los Angeles: Syndicate Pub. Co., 1931).

WWCL — *Who's Who of Children's Literature*, ed. B. Doyle (New York: Schocken, 1968).

WWHFF — *Who's Who in Horror and Fantasy Fiction*, ed. M. Ashley (London: Elm Tree; New York: Taplinger, 1977).

WWWAEEA — *Who Was Who among English and European Authors, 1931–1949: Based on Entries which First Appeared in the Author's and Writer's Who's Who and Reference Guide Originally Compiled by Edward Martell and L. G. Pine and In Who's Who among Living Authors of Older Nations Originally Compiled by Alberta Lawrence* (Detroit: Gale, 1978).

WWTCL — *Who's Who in Twentieth Century Literature*, ed. Martin Seymour-Smith (New York: Holt, 1976).

WWWiA — *Who Was Who in America, 1906–1934* (New York: Marquis, 1942–).

WWWiL — *Who Was Who in Literature 1906–1934* (New York: Marquis, 1990).

YA — *Yesterday's Authors of Books for Children*, ed. Anne Commire (Detroit: Gale, 1977).

Abbreviations of Periodicals

Periodicals cited in bibliographic entries are identified by acronyms if they are currently listed in the master list of periodicals in the annual bibliography of the Modern Language Association of America. Titles of periodicals that are not currently so indexed, whether or not they were previously indexed by the MLA, are given in full. The sole exceptions are selected American and British newspapers and book review publications, which are cited in abbreviated form and listed in a shorter grouping below.

A&E — *Anglistik & Englischunterricht*

ABR — *American Benedictine Review*

ABSt — *A/B: Auto/Biography Studies*

ADS — *Australasian Drama Studies*

AfricaR — *Africa Report*

AfrSR — *African Studies Review*

AJ — *Age of Johnson: A Scholarly Annual*

AJES — *Aligarh Journal of English Studies*

AJFS — *Australian Journal of French Studies*

AL — *American Literature: A Journal of Literary History, Criticism, and Bibliography*

ALS — *Australian Literary Studies*

ALT — *African Literature Today*

AmerS — *American Studies*

ANQ — *ANQ: A Quarterly Journal of Short Articles, Notes, and Reviews*

AntigR — *The Antigonish Review*

ANZSC — *Australian and New Zealand Studies in Canada*

AQ — *American Quarterly*

AR — *Antioch Review*

Arete — *Arete: The Journal of Sport Literature*

ArielE — *ARIEL: A Review of International English Literature*

ArkR — *Arkansas Review: A Journal of Criticism (Formerly Arkansas Quarterly)*

ArmD — *Armchair Detective: A Quarterly Journal Devoted to the Appreciation of Mystery, Detective, and Suspense Fiction*

ArQ — *Arizona Quarterly: A Journal of American Literature, Culture, and Theory*

AS — *American Speech: A Quarterly of Linguistic Usage*

ASch — *American Scholar*

ATQ — *American Transcendental Quarterly*

AUMLA — *Journal of the Australasian Universities Language and Literature Association: A Journal of Literary Criticism and Linguistics*

BB — *Bulletin of Bibliography*

BêteN — *Bête Noire*

BJA — *British Journal of Aesthetics*

BJRL — *Bulletin of the John Rylands University Library of Manchester*

BLR — *Bodleian Library Record*

BST — *Brontë Society Transactions*

BuR — *Bucknell Review: A Scholarly Journal of Letters, Arts and Sciences*

CahiersE — *Cahiers Elisabéthains: Late Medieval and Renaissance Studies*

CamObsc — *Camera Obscura: A Journal of Feminism, Culture, and Media Studies*

C&L — *Christianity and Literature*

CanL — *Canadian Literature*

CArts — *Critical Arts: A Journal of Cultural Studies*

CE — *College English*

CEA — *CEA Critic: An Official Journal of the College English Association*

CE&S	*Commonwealth Essays and Studies*
CentR	*The Centennial Review*
ChildL	*Children's Literature: Annual of The Modern Language Association Division on Children's Literature and The Children's Literature Association*
ChiR	*Chicago Review*
ChLB	*Charles Lamb Bulletin*
CJIS	*Canadian Journal of Irish Studies*
CL	*Comparative Literature*
CLAJ	*College Language Association Journal*
CLAQ	*Children's Literature Association Quarterly*
CLE	*Children's Literature in Education*
ClioI	*CLIO: A Journal of Literature, History, and the Philosophy of History*
ClQ	*Colby Quarterly*
Clues	*Clues: A Journal of Detection*
CollL	*College Literature*
CompD	*Comparative Drama*
ConL	*Contemporary Literature*
ContempR	*Contemporary Review*
CoRev	*The Commonwealth Review*
CQ	*The Cambridge Quarterly*
CRev	*The Chesterton Review: The Journal of the G.K. Chesterton Society*
Crit	*Critique Studies in Contemporary Fiction*
CritI	*Critical Inquiry*
CritQ	*Critical Quarterly*
CrSurv	*Critical Survey*
CVE	*Cahiers Victoriens et Edouardiens: Revue du Centre d'Etudes et de Recherches*
DHLR	*D. H. Lawrence Review*
DLN	*Doris Lessing Newsletter*
DownR	*Downside Review: A Quarterly of Catholic Thought*
DR	*Dalhousie Review*
DSA	*Dickens Studies Annual: Essays on Victorian Fiction*
EA	*Études Anglaises: Grande-Bretagne, États-Unis*
EAL	*Early American Literature*
EBC	*Etudes Britanniques Contemporaines: Revue de la Société d'Etudes Anglaises Contemporaines*
ECent	*Eighteenth Century: Theory and Interpretation*
ECF	*Eighteenth-Century Fiction*
ECLife	*Eighteenth-Century Life*
ECS	*Eighteenth-Century Studies*
ECW	*Essays on Canadian Writing*
EI	*Etudes Irlandaises: Revue Française d'Histoire, Civilisation et Littérature de l'Irelande*
EIC	*Essays in Criticism: A Quarterly Journal of Literary Criticism*
Eigse	*Eigse: A Journal of Irish Studies*
EinA	*English in Africa*
Eire	*Éire-Ireland: A Journal of Irish Studies*
EJ	*English Journal*
ELH	*English Literary History*
ELR	*English Literary Renaissance*
ELT	*English Literature in Transition (1880–1920)*
ELWIU	*Essays in Literature*
EMS	*English Manuscript Studies 1100–1700*
ERR	*European Romantic Review*
ES	*English Studies: A Journal of English Language and Literature*
ESA	*English Studies in Africa: A Journal of the Humanities*

ESC	*English Studies in Canada*
Expl	*Explicator*
FBS	*Franco-British Studies: Journal of the British Institute in Paris*
FForum	*Folklore Forum*
FolkH	*Folklore Historian: Journal of the Folklore and History Section of the American Folklore Society*
FS	*French Studies: A Quarterly Review*
FSt	*Feminist Studies*
GaR	*Georgia Review*
GHJ	*George Herbert Journal*
GL&L	*German Life and Letters*
GRAAT	*GRAAT: Publication des Groupes de Recherches Anglo-Américaines de l'Université François Rabelais de Tours*
GSJ	*Gaskell Society Journal*
HEI	*History of European Ideas*
HLB	*Harvard Library Bulletin*
HLQ	*Huntington Library Quarterly: A Journal for the History and Interpretation of English and American Civilization*
HR	*Hispanic Review*
HudR	*Hudson Review*
IFR	*International Fiction Review*
IowaR	*Iowa Review*
IUR	*Irish University Review: A Journal of Irish Studies*
JAmS	*Journal of American Studies*
JAS	*Journal of the Acoustical Society of America*
JCF	*Journal of Canadian Fiction*
JCL	*Journal of Commonwealth Literature*
JDECU	*Journal of The Department of English (Calcutta University)*
JDTC	*Journal of Dramatic Theory and Critism*
JEGP	*Journal of English and Germanic Philogy*
JENS	*Journal of the Eighteen Nineties Society*
JES	*Journal of European Studies*
JFA	*Journal of the Fantastic in the Arts*
JHI	*Journal of the History of Ideas*
JIWE	*Journal of Indian Writing in English*
JJQ	*James Joyce Quarterly*
JKSA	*Journal of the Kafka Society of America*
JLSTL	*Journal of Literary Studies/Tydskrif Vir Literaturwetenskap*
JML	*Journal of Modern Literature*
JNT	*Journal of Narrative Technique*
JPC	*Journal of Popular Culture*
JPRS	*Journal of Pre-Raphaelite Studies*
JRR	*Jean Rhys Review*
JRUL	*Journal of the Rutgers University Libraries*
JSSE	*Journal of the Short Story in English*
KJ	*Kipling Journal*
KN	*Kwartalnik Neofilologiczny*
KPR	*Kentucky Philological Review*
KR	*Kenyon Review*
KSJ	*Keats-Shelley Journal: Keats, Shelley, Byron, Hunt, and Their Circles*
L&H	*Literature and History*
L&P	*Literature and Psychology*
L&T	*Literature & Theology: An International Journal of Theory, Criticism and Culture (formerly Literature & Theology: An Interdisciplinary Journal of Theory and Criticism)*
L&U	*The Lion and the Unicorn: A Critical Journal of Children's Literature*
Lang&S	*Language and Style: An International Journal*

LB	*Leuvense Bijdragen: Contributions in Linguistics and Philology*
LCUT	*Library Chronicle of the University of Texas*
LeedsSE	*Leeds Studies in English*
LFQ	*Literature/Film Quarterly*
LIT	*Lit: Literature Interpretation Theory*
LJHum	*Lamar Journal of the Humanities*
LSE	*Lund Studies in English*
LWU	*Literatur in Wissenschaft und Unterricht*
Mallorn	*Mallorn: The Journal of the Tolkien Society*
M&L	*Music & Letters*
MAWAR	*MAWA Review*
MD	*Modern Drama*
Meta	*Meta: Journal des Traducteurs/Translators' Journal*
MFS	*Modern Fiction Studies*
MiltonS	*Milton Studies*
MinnR	*Minnesota Review*
MissQ	*Mississippi Quarterly: The Journal of Southern Culture*
MLN	*Modern Language Notes*
MLQ	*Modern Language Quarterly: A Journal of Literary History*
MLR	*Modern Language Review*
MLS	*Modern Language Studies*
MP	*Modern Philology: A Journal Devoted to Reserach in Medieval and Modern Literature*
MQ	*Midwest Quarterly: A Journal of Contemporary Thought*
MQR	*Michigan Quarterly Review*
MR	*Massachusetts Review: A Quarterly of Literature, the Arts and Public Affairs*
MRDE	*Medieval & Renaissance Drama in England: An Annual Gathering of Research, Criticism and Reviews*
MSE	*Massachusetts Studies in English*
MSEx	*Melville Society Extracts*
MSpr	*Moderna Språk*
MTJ	*Mark Twain Journal*
N&Q	*Notes and Queries*
NCC	*Nineteenth-Century Contexts*
NCF	*Nineteenth-Century Literature (formerly Nineteenth-Century Fiction)*
NConL	*Notes on Contemporary Literature*
NCS	*Nineteenth-Century Studies*
NCTR	*Nineteenth Century Theatre*
NEQ	*New England Quarterly: A Historical Review of New England Life and Letters*
NewC	*New Criterion*
NLH	*New Literary history: A Journal of Theory and Interpretation*
NLitsR	*New Literatures Review*
NTQ	*New Theatre Quarterly*
NWR	*Northwest Review*
NWRev	*New Welsh Review*
PAAS	*Proceedings of the American Antiquarian Society: A Journal of American History and Culture Through 1876*
PAPA	*Publications of the Arkansas Philological Association*
PBSA	*Papers of the Bibliographical Society of America*
Persuasions	*Persuasions: Journal of the Jane Austen Society of North America*
PLL	*Papers on Language and Literature: A Journal for Scholars and Critics of Language and Literature*
PLPLS-LHS	*Proceedings of the Leeds Philosophical and Literary Society, Literary & Historical Section*

PMLA	*Publications of the Modern Language Association of America*
PMPA	*Publications of the Missouri Philological Association*
PNR	*PN Review*
PoeticsJ	*Poetics: Journal for Empirical Research on Literature, the Media and the Arts*
PoetryR	*Poetry Review*
POMPA	*Publications of the Mississippi Philological Association*
PoT	*Poetics Today*
PQ	*Philological Quarterly*
PR	*Partisan Review*
Pretexts	*Pretexts: Studies in Writing and Culture*
PSt	*Prose Studies: History, Theory, Criticism*
PubHist	*Publishing History: The Social, Economic and Literary History of Book, Newspaper and Magazine Publishing*
PULC	*Princeton University Library Chronicle*
PURBA	*Panjab University Research Bulletin (Arts)*
QJS	*Quarterly Journal of Speech*
QQ	*Queen's Quarterly*
RAEI	*Revista Alicantina de Estudios Ingleses*
RAL	*Research in African Literatures*
R&L	*Religion and Literature*
RCF	*Review of Contemporary Fiction*
Reader	*Reader: Essays in Reader-Oriented Theory, Criticism, and Pedagogy*
RECTR	*Restoration and 18th Century Theatre Research*
Ren&R	*Renaissance and Reformation/Renaissance et Réforme*
RenD	*Renaissance Drama*
RenP	*Renaissance Papers*
RenQ	*Renaissance Quarterly*
RenSt	*Renaissance Studies: Journal of the Society for Renaissance Studies*
RES	*Review of English Studies: A Quarterly Journal of English Literature and the English Language*
RFEA	*Revue Française d'Etudes Américaines*
RJV	*Rheinisches Jahrbuch für Volkskunde*
RLC	*Revue de Littérature Comparée*
RMR	*Rocky Mountain Review of Language and Literature*
RMS	*Renaissance & Modern Studies*
RomN	*Romance Notes*
RQ	*Riverside Quarterly*
RR	*Romantic Review*
RRL	*Revue Roumaine de Linguistique*
RSSI	*Recherches Sémiotiques/Semiotic Inquiry*
SAD	*Studies in American Drama, 1945–Present*
SagetriebIO	*Sagetrieb: A Journal Devoted to Poets in the Imagist/Objectivist Tradition*
SALit	*Chu-Shikoku Studies in American Literature*
SAQ	*South Atlantic Quarterly*
SAR	*Studies in the American Renaissance*
SB	*Studies in Bibliography: Papers of the Bibliographical Society of the University of Virginia*
SBHC	*Studies in Browning and His Circle: A Journal of Criticism, History, and Bibliography*
SCen	*Seventeenth Century*
SCJ	*Sixteenth Century Journal*
ScLJ	*Scottish Literary Journal*
SCRev	*South Central Review: The Journal of the South Central Modern Language Association*

SDR	*South Dakota Review*
SECC	*Studies in Eighteenth-Century Culture*
SEEJ	*Slavic and East European Journal*
SEL	*SEL: Studies in English Literature, 1500–1900*
SELL	*Studies in English Language and Literature*
SFS	*Science-Fiction Studies*
ShawR	*Shaw: The Annual of Bernard Shaw Studies*
SHR	*Southern Humanities Review*
Signs	*Signs: Journal of Women in Culture and Society*
SIR	*Studies in Romanticism*
SlavR	*Slavic Review: American Quarterly of Russian, Eurasian and East European Studies (formerly Slavic Review: American Quarterly of Soviet and East European Studies)*
SLitI	*Studies in the Literary Imagination*
SLJ	*Southern Literary Journal*
SMy	*Studia Mystica*
SN	*Studia Neophilologica: A Journal of Germanic and Romance Languages and Literature*
SNew	*Sidney Newsletter & Journal*
SNNTS	*Studies in the Novel*
SoAR	*South Atlantic Review*
SoQ	*Southern Quarterly: A Journal of the Arts in the South*
SoR	*Southern Review*
SovL	*Soviet Literature*
SP	*Studies in Philology*
SPAN	*SPAN: Journal of the South Pacific Association for Commonwealth Literature and Language Studies*
SPAS	*Studies in Puritan American Spirituality*
SR	*Sewanee Review*
SRL	*Studies in Romance Languages*
SSEng	*Sydney Studies in English*
SSF	*Studies in Short Fiction*
SSL	*Studies in Scottish Literature*
SSr	*Spenser Studies: A Renaissance Poetry Annual*
SStud	*Swift Studies: The Annual of the Ehrenpreis Center*
StCS	*Studies in Contemporary Satire: A Creative and Critical Journal*
StHum	*Studies in the Humanities*
SVEC	*Studies on Voltaire and the Eighteenth Century*
SWR	*Southwest Review*
TCEL	*Thought Currents in English Literature*
TCL	*Twentieth Century Literature: A Scholarly and Critical Journal*
TDR	*Tulane Drama Review*
TDRev	*TDR: The Drama Review: A Journal of Performance Studies*
TexP	*Textual Practice*
Theoria	*Theoria: A Journal of Studies in the Arts, Humanities and Social Sciences*
THJ	*The Thomas Hardy Journal*
ThR	*Theatre Research International*
ThS	*Theatre Survey: The Journal of the American Society for Theatre Research*
TJ	*Theatre Journal*
TN	*Theatre Notebook: A Journal of the History and Technique of the British Theatre*
Topic	*Topic: A Journal of the Liberal Arts*
TPB	*Tennessee Philological Bulletin: Proceedings of the Annual Meeting of the Tennessee*

TPQ — *Text and Performance Quarterly*

TRB — *Tennyson Research Bulletin*

TSLL — *Texas Studies in Literature and Language*

TStL — *Tennessee Studies in Literature*

TSWL — *Tulsa Studies in Women's Literature*

TYDS — *Transactions of the Yorkshire Dialect Society*

UDR — *University of Dayton Review*

UES — *Unisa English Studies: Journal of the Department of English*

UMSE — *University of Mississippi Studies in English*

UtopSt — *Utopian Studies: Journal of the Society for Utopian Studies*

UTQ — *University of Toronto Quarterly: A Canadian Journal of the Humanities*

VLC — *Victorian Literature and Culture*

VN — *Victorian Newsletter*

VP — *Victorian Poetry*

VPR — *Victorian Periodicals Review*

VQR — *Virginia Quarterly Review: A National Journal of Literature and Discussion (Richmond, VA)*

VRev — *Victorian Review: The Journal of the Victorian Studies Association of Western Canada*

VS — *Victorian Studies: A Journal of the Humanities, Arts and Sciences*

VWM — *Virginia Woolf Miscellany*

W&L — *Women & Literature*

W&P — *Women & Performance: A Journal of Feminist Theory*

WascanaR — *Wascana Review of Contemporary Poetry and Short Fiction (formerly Wascana Review)*

WC — *Wordsworth Circle*

WF — *Western Folklore*

WL&A — *War, Literature, and the Arts*

WLT — *World Literature Today: A Literary Quarterly of the University of Oklahoma*

WLWE — *World Literature Written in English*

WS — *Women's Studies: An Interdisciplinary Journal*

WStu — *Weber Studies: An Interdisciplinary Humanities Journal*

WVUPP — *West Virginia University Philological Papers*

YES — *Yearbook and English Studies*

YJC — *Yale Journal of Criticism: Interpretation in the Humanities*

YR — *Yale Review*

YULG — *Yale University Library Gazette*

YWES — *Year's Work in English Studies*

ZAA — *Zeitschrift für Anglistik and Amerikanistik: A Quarterly of Language, Literature and Culture*

ZCP — *Zeitschrift für Celtische Philologie*

Abbreviations for selected U.S. and U.K. newspapers and book review publications.

AB — *Antiquarian Bookman*

ABR — *American Book Review*

BW — *Washington Post Book Week*

CSM — *Christian Science Monitor*

LJ — *Library Journal*

LonT — *[London] Times*

LonSunT — *[London] Sunday Times*

LonSunTBks — *[London] Sunday Times Book Review*

LonSunTMag — *[London] Sunday Times Magazine*

LonSunTS — *[London] Sunday Times Style Magazine*

LRB — *London Review of Books*

NYHTBR	*New York Herald-Tribune Book Review*
NYT	*New York Times*
NYTBR	*New York Times Book Review*
NYTMag	*New York Times Magazine*
NYRB	*New York Review of Books*
PW	*Publishers' Weekly*
TEdS	*[London] Times Educational Supplement*
THES	*[London] Times Higher Education Supplement*
TLS	*[London] Times Literary Supplement*
VV	*Village Voice*
VLS	*[Village] Voice Literary Supplement*
WRB	*Women's Review of Books*

An Encyclopedia of
British Women Writers

A. C.: See *Bacon, Ann*

Eliza Acton

BORN: 17 April 1799, Battle, Sussex.
DIED: 13 February 1859, Hampstead, London.
DAUGHTER OF: John Acton.

A., who is best known today for her contributions to culinary history, had a small reputation in her youth as a poet. Her *Poems* (1826) have the sound and feel of her better-known contemporaries of the Romantic movement. A.'s poems, however, are distinct from those luminaries' works in their imitation of Sapphic verse. Many of A.'s poems are addressed to women in the spirit of "romantic friendship."

A. was the eldest daughter of John Acton, a brewer of Hastings, and, later, Bramford Hall in Ipswich, where A. spent her childhood. Because of delicate health, she was taken abroad and lived some time in Paris. Many of her poems seem to have been written during this period when she was engaged to a French officer, whose integrity and probity her poems impugn.

Soon after her return to England, A. published, by subscription, 500 copies of her *Poems.* They include the Paris poems and the above-mentioned verses addressed to various women, in addition to poems on traditional romantic themes such as "Twilight," "The Grave," and "Venice." Her handling of these topics, however, is striking and often haunting. Some of the poems to women recall, in both situation and import, Sappho's poems to her beloved friends; both authors ask their subjects to remember former days now that the beloved women are separated, perhaps by marriage. Such a marked similarity strongly suggests A.'s familiarity with Sappho's work, either in Latin or other translation. At the same time, her lyrics, especially her descriptions of natural beauty, are reminiscent of William Wordsworth, showing her to have been a ready student of contemporary poetry. At their best, her poems keep company with the finest verse of the period, handling diction and verse form with a breathtaking grace.

A. published occasional verse in the decade following the publication of her *Poems.* In 1837, "The Two Portraits" appeared anonymously in the *Sudbury Pocket Book.* In 1838, she published "The Chronicle of Castel-Framingham" in the *Sudbury Pocket Book,* this time using her own name and identifying herself as the author of "The Two Portraits." In 1837, when she was living in Bordyke House, Tunbridge (where she is reported to have kept house for her mother), she presented Queen Adelaide with a panegyric praising her for her devoted nursing of her late husband, King William IV, on the occasion of the queen's visit there. *The Voice of the North* (1842) commemorated the first visit of Queen Victoria to Scotland.

A later collection of A.'s poems (now lost) was rejected by Longman, who suggested a cookbook instead; in 1845, that publisher brought out A.'s *Modern Cookery.* It was an instant success, reprinted five times in the first two years and many times thereafter through 1905. Unlike its early nineteenth-century predecessors that were better suited to the aristocratic household, this work was a truly useful guide for middle-class families where the "lady of the house" often found herself in the kitchen, at the stove. Indeed, A. said she tested all the recipes herself. The instructions are clear and practical, and she advocated high standards for English cooking. Following her move to Hampstead in the 1850s, A. contributed "Household Hints and Receipts" to Mrs. Jane Loudon's *Ladies Companion.* In 1857, A. produced *The English Bread-Book,* her last publication (though A. refers to another work in progress). One biographer calls it "an inspiring treatise on good bread." Her cookbooks were superseded by the legendary Mrs. Beeton's (who appropriated many of A.'s recipes, to her indignation), but they have remained popular and were last reprinted in 1990.

A. never married. Though she is reported to have died "after a long illness," she lived to be nearly sixty and was sufficiently well known at her death to be honored by a brief obituary notice in the *Gentleman's Magazine.*

WORKS: *Poems* (1826). "The Two Portraits," in *The Sudbury Pocket Book* (1837). "The Chronicle of Castel-Framingham," in *The Sudbury Pocket Book* (1838). *The Voice of the North* (1842). *Modern Cookery, in all its Branches: Reduced to a System of Easy Practice, for the use of Private Families* (1845). *The English Bread-Book: For Domestic Use, Adapted to Families of Every Grade; Containing the Plainest and Most Minute Instructions to the Learner; Practical Receipts for Many Varieties of Bread; With Notices of the Present System of Adulteration, and its Consequences; and of the Improved Baking Processes and Institutions Established Abroad* (1857).

BIBLIOGRAPHY: McKendry, M. *The Seven Centuries Cookbook: From Richard II to Elizabeth II* (1973). *The Best of Eliza Acton,* ed. E. Ray (1968).

For articles in reference works, see: *Boase. CinP. Companion to Scottish Literature. DNB. Europa. Feminist. IDWB* (under "Elizabeth Acton" [sic]). *Ireland. New Grove Dictionary of Music and Musicians. Oxford Companion to Music. Oxford.*

Kari Boyd McBride

Adam(s), Mrs. Jane: See *Adam(s), Jean*

Jean Adam(s)

BORN: 1710, Crawfordsdyke, Renfrewshire, Scotland.
DIED: 3 April 1765, Glasgow, Scotland.
WROTE UNDER: Mrs. Jane Adam(s).

The daughter of a shipmaster, A. became a poet, schoolmistress, and nursery governess. A's career began with opportunity and support. Orphaned young and employed as nursery governess and housemaid to a Mr. Turner, a clergyman, A. educated herself in the library of her employer. Here she wrote poems that were collected by a Mrs. Drummond of Greenock, who published *Miscellany Poems, by Mrs. Jane Adams, in Crawfordsdyke,* in

Glasgow in 1734. A. dedicated the collection to Thomas Crawford of Crawfordburn. Among the 154 subscribers to the indexed volume of religious poetry were clergy, merchants, and gentry.

Except for Archibald Crawford, who wrote the preface, critics have shown no interest in A.'s poetry in general. Her published poetry, mostly didactic and religious in tone, shows A.'s loving scrutiny of human nature. Of the power of refined and directed passion, she laments that anger might be directed at good instead of evil: "Why should a Virtue make it self a Lust?" Nor should grief be wasted: "It is a shame below our Kind to stoop, / More Glory 'tis to imitate the Top." The attribution of "There's nae Luck aboot the House" or "Song of the Mariner's Wife, " however, has at times been of interest. A.'s associates attributed this lyric poem, said to have been heard on the streets by Robert Burns, to her.

In the girls' school she founded at the quay head at Crawford's bridge, she was known for her emotive readings of Shakespeare. In spite of her pedagogical pyrotechnics, even swooning while reading *Othello,* A. closed her school for six weeks to walk to London to visit Samuel Richardson, whose *Clarissa* she admired.

Meanwhile, her poetry brought little profit; many copies, sent to Boston for distribution, have never been discovered. Finally, then, unable to depend on sales of her poetry, she closed the school and survived as a peddler for years. She died in the poorhouse in Glasgow in 1765.

WORKS: *Miscellany Poems, by Mrs. Jane Adams, in Crawfordsdyke* (1734). *The Works of the English Poets,* ed. A. Chalmers (1810). "Song of the Mariner's Wife," in *Select Scottish Songs, Ancient and Modern,* ed. R. H. Cromek (1810). *Songs of Scotland Prior to Burns,* ed. R. Chambers (1825). *Songs of Scotland,* ed. A. Cunningham (1825).

BIBLIOGRAPHY: Keddie, H. [pseud. Sarah Tytler] and J. L. Watson. *Songstresses of Scotland* (1871). *N&Q* (1866, 1869).

For articles in reference works, see: *Chalmers. Chambers. DNB. NCHEL. ToddBWW. ToddDBA.*

Mary Sauter Comfort

(Karen) Fleur Adcock

BORN: 10 February 1934, Papakura, near Auckland, New Zealand.
DAUGHTER OF: Cyril John Adcock and Irene Robinson Adcock.
MARRIED: Alistair Campbell, 1952; Barry Crump, 1962.

Born in New Zealand, A. spent the war years and some time afterward (1939–47) in Britain, where she attended a number of schools before returning to New Zealand. There she attended Wellington Girls' College before marrying, at the age of eighteen, the poet Alistair Campbell and studying classics at Victoria University (M.A., first class honors, 1955). Divorced in 1958, A. devoted more time to her childhood habit of writing verse while working as a librarian. The failure of a second marriage (to Barry Crump) led her to leave for Britain in 1963; she has lived there ever since, supporting herself and a son as a librarian until 1979, when she became a full-time writer. Today, A. is a well-known poet and a familiar presence in Britain, delivering talks on poetry for the BBC and readings at universities.

A. began to publish poems in journals and magazines while still living in New Zealand, but her first collection, *The Eye of the Hurricane,* was not published until 1964, the year after she emigrated. In 1967, her second volume of poems, *Tigers,* appeared; it reprinted many poems from the earlier collection along with some new poems written in Britain.

A.'s first two books present more than apprentice pieces. Time and again, to judge from the twenty-one poems reprinted in her *Selected Poems* of 1983, A. displays a developed ability to express strong feelings, particularly pain and loss, with restraint and discipline supplied by classical models. These first two collections are further distinguished by an economical deployment of formal and technical devices, an ability to craft an engaging first line (e.g., "All the flowers have gone back into the ground," "The room is full of clichés—'Throw me a crumb'"), and effective closure. The finest poem from these early collections is "Flight, With Mountains," a lovely, liquid, lyrical elegy for a fallen climber: This is a first-rate performance for a poet of any age, let alone one less than thirty at the time of its publication.

A.'s next collection, *High Tide in the Garden* (1971), gathers twenty-two poems; it is interesting to note that A. deleted but three (wisely, since they are flat-footed and cliché-ridden) for her *Selected Poems* of 1983. The poems in *High Tide* have to do mostly with terror in various forms (nightmare, departure, loss) and sex in two forms, heterosexual or solitary (as in her now famous "Against Coupling," which begins with pseudoclassical resonance, "I write in praise of the solitary act"). Where terror and sex intersect, A. writes the strongest poem of the collection, "Mornings After," a descent into the nightly netherworld of unconscious dreamscape. What A. does best here, in words taken from one of her own poems ("Clarendon Whatmough"), is to "display an emotion then anatomise it." Her verse is strongest when her lines hum with the conversational, with the breathed imperative or interrogative, as in "Afterwards" or "Being Blind." Her verse is weakest when she tackles subjects outside the realm of her experience and employs longer lines and longer forms unsuccessfully, notably in "Gas," a 350-plus-line excursus on multiple selves that may have been riveting narrative entertainment when A. read it on BBC Radio but is tortuously unsuccessful in poetic terms when read on the page.

As the title of A.'s fourth collection, *The Scenic Route,* indicates, the motif of the journey threads this collection of thirty-four poems together. It re-presents A.'s investigation of her maternal Northern Irish heritage and that journey "home" multiplies into others—to Italy, to Holland, to Nepal, and to New Zealand. Traditional forms dominate A.'s descriptions of physical and human landscapes; often these short poems are nothing more than clear-imaged snapshots that center a narrative; but, as in the case of "Richey" and "Acris Hiems," they can be moving poetic exercises nonetheless. Two other poems stand out here: "In Memoriam: James K. Baxter," an accomplished verse epistle demonstrating A.'s ability to handle longer forms on occasion, and "Kilpeck," an exploration of a Celtic ruin that becomes an assertion of the primary import of poetry in the life of the narrator.

In 1979, A. published *The Inner Harbour,* a collection of thirty-eight poems set in a four-part sequence ("Beginnings," "Endings," "The Thing Itself," "To and Fro"); it contains her strongest, most impressive work to date, and it received praise from prominent critics like Andrew Motion and Peter Porter. And, indeed, it is worthy of such praise: "The Ex-Queen among the Astronomers" is a remarkable exploration of sex and the ways of knowing; and "Letter from Highgate Wood" and "The Soho Hospital for Women" are clear-eyed, compassionate takes on a cruel, often brutish world. In "Poem Ended by a Death," the narrator declares, "This is my laconic style"; A. has not put her own laconic style to better effect than in this collection, not only in the several poems already mentioned but in the final sequence, "To and Fro," seven poems that comprise a compelling exercise in self-definition.

A.'s *Selected Poems,* published in 1983 and reissued in 1991, reprints poems from *The Eye of the Hurricane, Tigers, High Tide in the Garden, The Scenic Route,* and *The Inner Harbour.* In addition, it includes eleven poems from *Below Loughrigg,* a chapbook-journal of her year in the Lake District, courtesy of an Arts Council Creative Writing Fellowship, and twenty-six new poems as well. *Below Loughrigg* is the first of three "Bloodaxe Pamphlet Poets" books A. has published. This particular group of "Lake District poems" dwells on Romantic topography and figures; as the poet herself notes, "Wordsworthian locutions are carried on the winds in what I call my this year's home" ("Letter to Alistair Campbell"); and if she is perhaps a bit too much under the spell of the place, she does nonetheless articulate a believable sense of kinship with the spirits of the place. The "New Poems," critics noted, seemed somewhat experimental, but only to a degree. A. remains a poet of formal concerns, with an eye for the defining detail (e.g., "Shakespeare's Hotspur"), an ear for traditional rhyme ("Villa Isola Bella"), and an uninflected, cool-toned voice ("Influenza").

A.'s ninth volume, *The Incident Book,* appeared in 1986; this collection is quite literally a book of incidents from A.'s life. Time covered ranges from childhood and family life in New Zealand and the United Kingdom to Margaret Thatcher's Britain. A. treats particular scenes (the landscapes of childhood), themes (separation, loss), and episodes (traffic accidents, meeting an ex-lover), blending fictional and nonfictional into crafted poems animated by a now-familiar voice. What emerges are images of vulnerability and mutability of persons and worlds under clouds of diverse menace. A.'s preoccupations—art and language, death, counter-erotics—persist, and though she can indeed spin fascinating images (her unborn grandchild, "a pink tadpole, a promise of limbs and language" in "Tadpoles") and do a clever, witty take on Oscar Wilde's famous inversion of the "art imitates nature" dictum in "Leaving the Tate," A.'s poetry gets a bit thin in these forty-two poems.

Time Zones (1991), which incorporates the text of the Bloodaxe Poetry Pamphlet, *Meeting the Comet* (1988), might elicit a positive response from a first-time reader of A.'s verse; yet for anyone familiar with her previous collections, it rehearse familiar themes and remaps familiar territory (the domestic world; love, sex, and death) without freshness of form or insight. Occasionally, A.'s attempts at wit are merely smart and irritating ("Coupling," "Smokers For Celibacy"). *Time Zones* does present more political poems, on subjects ranging from antinuclear demonstrations to the American bombing of Libya to Romanian freedom fighters, but in each her politics and poetics diverge so radically that the result is unintentionally fractured verse. But some of the poems here are quite wonderful: "Toads," which begins, "Let's be clear about this: I love toads," and develops into a marvelous meditation on vision and mortality; "Under the Lawn," which begins, "It is hard to stay angry with a buttercup," and becomes a moving contemporary *memento mori.* But they serve more as a reminder of what A. can do at her best, and they do not redeem an unremarkable collection.

Judged as a whole, A.'s work was best described by Andrew Motion as moving "between high hopes and bad dreams, between fact and fantasy, between innocence and disillusionment, and between what can be observed and what can be imagined." On occasion, and with greater frequency in the work of mid-career, A. does this with wit, charm, clarity, and formal sheen; nevertheless, in her latest, original work A. seems to have reached something of a dead end. Perhaps her most recent work in translation will refresh her spirit and renew her poetic energies.

In addition to writing her own poetry, A. has done four books of translation: *The Virgin and the Nightingale: Medieval Latin Poems* (1983), *Orient Express: Poems by Grete Tartler* (from the Romanian, 1989), *Letters From Darkness: Poems by Daniela Crasnaru* (from the Romanian, 1991), and *Hugh Primas and the Archpoet* (from the medieval Latin, 1994). She has edited *The Oxford Book of Contemporary New Zealand Poetry* (1982), *The Faber Book of Twentieth-Century Women's Poetry* (1987), and *The Oxford Book of Creatures* (1995).

WORKS: *The Eye of the Hurricane* (1964). *Tigers* (1967). *High Tide in the Garden* (1971). *The Scenic Route* (1974). *Dragoncards Four* (1976). *In Focus* (broadside, 1977). (with G. Ewart) *A Morden Tower Reading* (1977). *New Poetry,* No. 4 (1978). *The Inner Harbour* (1979). *Below Loughrigg* (1979). (trans.) *The Virgin and the Nightingale: Medieval Latin Poems* (1983). *Selected Poems* (1983). *Hotspur: A Ballad* (1986). *The Incident Book* (1986). *Meeting the Comet* (1988). (trans.) *Orient Express: Poems by Grete Tartler* (1989). (trans.) *Letters from Darkness: Poems by Daniela Crasnaru* (1991). *Time Zones* (1991). (trans.) *Hugh Primas and the Archpoet* (1994). *Looking Back* (1997).

BIBLIOGRAPHY: Gregson, I. *English* (1993). Hulse, M. *Quadrant* (1984).

For articles in reference works, see *CA. CLC. DLB. Feminist. Oxford. ToddBWW.*

Other references: *CQ* (1984). *Encounter* (August 1979, March 1984). *English* (Spring 1968). *Landfall* (June 1980). *London Magazine* (October 1985). *LonT*

(27 October 1983). *New Review* (December 1974). *New Statesman* (8 June 1979, 13 January 1984). *NYTBR* (18 October 1987). *Observer* (9 September 1979). *Poetry* (December 1975). *Poetry Dimension* (1974). *PoetryR* (1984). *Stand* (1975–76). *TLS* (14 September 1967, 23 July 1971, 18 January 1980, 2 September 1983, 13 February 1987, 29 May 1987, 26 May-1 June 1989).

Robert Ellis Hosmer, Jr.

Cecilia Mary Ady

BORN: 28 November 1881, Edgcote, Northamptonshire.
DIED: 27 March 1958, Oxford.
DAUGHTER OF: Henry Ady and Julia Cartwright.

A. was a scholar and historian of the Italian Renaissance, following in the steps of her mother, Julia Cartwright, the renowned writer of many popular books on the art and history of the Italian Renaissance. In 1881, the year in which A. was born, her mother's first book on art, *Mantegna and Francia*, was published. As a young child, A. was taught her alphabet with, for example, the letter "D" representing the Italian writer Dante. In 1903, the year in which she took her first class honors degree in history at Oxford University, her mother's most successful book, *Isabella d'Este*, the biography of a Renaissance princess, was published.

Julia Cartwright had decided much earlier to earn enough money from her writing to pay for the formal education she envisaged for A., who was finally to gain a place at what was then known as St. Hugh's Hall, Oxford. The 1880s had seen a new statute for women's exams passed at Oxford. Lady Margaret Hall had been founded in 1878 and St. Hugh's in 1886. Her mother's aspirations for the intellectual development of her daughter were realized, and A. obtained her M.A. and a D.Lit., but she never married or had children. She became an academic, and as such she was one of the first women to be awarded her degree at Oxford University. Her work concentrated on the study of the Renaissance in Italy, and her main interest lay in the signorial families and their influence on politics and society during the fifteenth century. She thus depicted the Sforza, the Medici, the Bentivoglio, and the ascent of a Piccolomini to the papacy.

Her first book, which appeared in 1907, was *A History of Milan under the Sforza.* Her tutor, the historian Edward Armstrong, was then general editor of a series, *The States of Italy,* and encouraged her in this project. This book was followed in 1913 by *Pius II: The Humanist Pope.* Both these books remain of lasting value to scholars. In 1937, she published her most substantial book, *The Bentivoglio of Bologna,* and in 1955 she contributed *Lorenzo dei Medici and Renaissance Italy* to the *Teach Yourself History* series edited by A. L. Rowse. She also wrote sections for general history books such as *Italy, Mediaeval and Modern* (1917) and was invited to write a chapter in Volume VIII of the *Cambridge Modern History* (1930). Only one year prior to her death she contributed a chapter entitled "The Invasions of Italy" to the *New Cambridge Modern History,* Volume I.

A. had a fine reputation not only as a scholar but also as a teacher. She was tutor in modern history from 1909 to 1923 at St. Hugh's; her involvement in the problems at the college arising from the psychical experience recounted anonymously (1911) in *An Adventure* by the then principal, Miss Moberly, and the vice-principal, Miss Jourdain, however, led A. to leave her position. She then became tutor to the Society of Home Studies and only returned to her own college in 1929 as a research fellow, where on her retirement in 1951 she was elected to an honorary fellowship. She continued throughout her life to exert an influence on Italian studies, writing many articles as well as her books and giving many papers at conferences all over the world. Her paper on the "Manners and Morals of the Quattrocento" was delivered in the midst of the war as the annual lecture of the British Academy.

English students of Renaissance Italy invariably came under her influence, for she wrote reviews of most of the books published on her subject. Her style was admired for its clarity and precision. She enjoyed teaching, and her orderly yet humorous approach was of great benefit to her students. Both her parents were pious people, her father a rector. She remained throughout her life a devoted churchwoman and wrote a booklet, "The Role of Women in the Church" (1948). As a moderate Anglo-Catholic believing in the spiritual independence of the Church of England, she showed a great respect for English local custom, tempered always with her breadth of historical outlook. It was the latter quality for which she was particularly respected, and at her death the volume *Italian Renaissance Studies,* edited by E. F. Jacob, was dedicated to her memory.

WORKS: *A History of Milan under the Sforza* (1907). *Pius II (Aeneas Silvius Piccolomini): The Humanist Pope* (1913). *The Contribution of Women to History in Some Aspects of the Woman's Movement* (1915). (with others) *Italy, Mediaeval and Modern: A History* (1915). *Outlines of European History, Part 4: From 1494 to 1684* (1926). (trans.) *A History of Italy, 1871–1915,* by B. Croce (1929). *The Bentivoglio of Bologna* (1937). *Morals and Manners of the Quattrocento* (1942). *Lorenzo dei Medici and Renaissance Italy* (1955).

BIBLIOGRAPHY: *Italian Renaissance Studies: A Tribute to the Late Cecilia M. Ady,* ed. E. F. Jacob (1960). Trickett, R., in *St. Hugh's: One Hundred Years of Women's Education at Oxford,* ed. P. Griffin (1986).

Angela Emanuel
(updated by Benjamin G. Kohl)

Grace Aguilar

BORN: 2 June 1816, Hackney, London.
DIED: 16 September 1847, Frankfurt, Germany.
DAUGHTER OF: Emanuel Aguilar and Sarah Dias Fernandes.

In the thirty-one brief years of her life, A. wrote twelve books (seven published posthumously) and a large amount of poetry, essays, and articles in journals in England and America. Her literary reputation was so widespread that many of her works were translated into foreign languages. Today, however, almost no one has heard of her or her works, and the only public reminder of her existence is the 110th Street Branch of the New York Public Library, one of five branches of the defunct Aguilar Free Library Society, which provided free books to immigrants to help them become assimilated in America.

Certainly it was most appropriate to honor A. in this manner, because the earliest recognition given her work was as the popularizer of an alien culture. In a review of A.'s posthumous novel, *The Days of Bruce,* a historical romance, *Sharpe's Magazine* noted that while the book was "full of interest and the characters are well drawn . . . it is not equal to those productions of her pen, in which she is unrivalled because they illustrate a 'peculiar people.'" It was as a representative of that people that A. had first become known. Her religious writings were her first major works to be published, but her reputation grew with the publication of her novels.

A. was the first woman to write in English about Judaism, her religion and the faith of her ancestors; her maternal great-grandfather, Benjamin Dias Fernandes, wrote religious polemics, but A.'s religious writings were not polemical but rather explanatory. It was her desire to dispel prejudice and the mistrust of her people by providing accurate depictions of Judaic beliefs and practices to the English-reading public. She was particularly eager to provide this material in an era when Roman Catholicism was becoming more acceptable in England following Catholic Emancipation in 1830. Her fears of Catholicism and Catholic influence on fiction were informed by the legacy of suppression and the secret practice of Judaism handed down to her from the Marranos, Spanish and Portuguese Jews forced by the Inquisition to relinquish their faith or risk being burnt alive. Heiress to this colonial tradition, she was doubly marginalized by being a Jew in a Christian world and a woman in a world dominated by patriarchal ideology.

Her most popular domestic novels, *Home Influence* (1847) and its sequel, *The Mother's Recompense* (1851), promulgated the Victorian ideals of motherhood and the limited freedom of women. The details of her own life contain both this tradition of suppression of women's identities and the strong religious involvement that helped to promote this suppression.

A.'s early life was spent in London, where her father was a merchant and an important figure in the Sephardic Jewish community, and where her mother, with A.'s help, ran a small private school for young boys. Since both parents were plagued by ill health, the family spent many of A.'s early years away from London in Devonshire, where A. first became acquainted with British Protestantism by attending services in churches of many denominations. This was one of the few elements of her education that occurred outside the home, since both parents tutored her in the classics and history. The level of her erudition is astonishing in the light of what Charles Dudley Warner characterized as "her peculiar sheltered training."

Even when she had attained a wide literary reputation, she was not allowed to travel outside the family circle. Her father's death in 1845 made it necessary for the family to depend on her literary earnings for some of its support, while her two younger brothers, for whom she had written prayer books and who she tutored, were permitted to seek careers away from the home; one of her brothers was a musician and composer and was educated abroad, and the other had a career in the British navy. An archive of her letters in the Southern History Collection, University of North Carolina (available on microfilm through the American Jewish Archives), provides painful evidence of the confines within which she lived. Some of her mother's letters, also in this archive, show Sarah as the dominant influence on A.'s life. Like Mrs. Hamilton, the mother in *Home Influence* and *The Mother's Recompense,* Sarah Aguilar controlled her children's lives, the only socially acceptable use of power for women in the Victorian era.

A.'s final months were spent in Germany, where her mother had taken her to seek medical attention since she was always in frail health after having had the measles when she was twenty-one. At the end, she suffered violent spasms and lost all power of speech but continued to communicate by using her fingers, her last words being: "Though He may slay me, yet I will trust in Him."

WORKS: (Anon.) *The Magic Wreath* (1835). *The Spirit of Judaism* (1842). *Records of Israel* (1844). *Women of Israel* (1845). *The Jewish Faith* (1846). *History of the Jews in England* (1847). *Home Influence* (1847). *The Vale of Cedars* (1850). *The Mother's Recompense* (1851). *The Days of Bruce* (1852). *Women's Friendship* (1853). *Home Scenes and Heart Studies* (1853). *Sabbath Thoughts and Sacred Communings* (1853).

BIBLIOGRAPHY: Abrahams, B. Z. *Transactions of the Jewish Historical Society of England* (1948). Hall, S. C. *Art Union Journal* (1852). Zeitlin, L. G. *The Nineteenth Century Anglo-Jewish Novel* (1981).

For articles in reference works, see: *BA19C. Bloomsbury. DNB. Feminist. Oxford. ToddBWW.*

Gail Kraidman

Joan (Delano) Aiken

BORN: 4 September 1924, Rye, Sussex.
DAUGHTER OF: Conrad Aiken and Jessie MacDonald.
MARRIED: Ronald George Brown, 1945; Julius Goldstein, 1976.

The adjective most commonly used to describe A. is "prolific," not only because of her abundant production of works (nearly 100 books as of 1997, for both young readers and adults) but also because of her diverse genres. Her "well-written and enjoyable fiction" appears in the forms of stories, plays, and novels or are modeled into modern fairy tales for all ages. Her poems, for the most part, have been critically well received, but her nonfiction text, *The Way to Write for Children* (1982), has become the definitive guide for both prospective and experienced authors.

A.'s early educational and literary influences were initially provided by her Canadian mother—who maintained home-based instruction before A. attended Wychwood School, Oxford, 1936–40—and by her father, the American poet and novelist Conrad Aiken. He spent some time in England during the 1920s and early 1930s, where he was well respected as London correspondent for *The New Yorker.* An early exposure to a mix of classic and contemporary novels during the school years combined with her early career opportunities to influence the contents of her literary creations.

A.'s writing began at seventeen, when the BBC Children's Hour broadcast one of her short stories. She then worked for the BBC (1942–43) and eventually became information officer and librarian for the United Nations (1943–49). A. was sub-editor and features editor for *Argosy,* London (1955–60), and copywriter for advertising agency J. Walter Thompson, London (1960–61). It was during an interval as a professional reader of gothic and romantic fiction for Amalgamated Press that she finally expressed an interest in creating works of a similar nature.

When her husband died in 1954 and she was left a widow with a young son and daughter to support, her literary production increased, especially in adult romance and juvenile fiction. Several of her honors include the 1969 Guardian Award, the 1972 Mystery Writers of America–Edgar Allan Poe award, and being named runner-up for the Carnegie Award.

Even though A. professes being made aware—by her agent, Jean Leroy—of aspects of the novel *Jane Eyre* being a successful model combining gothic and romantic, her plots often develop through images created by a mixture of contemporary, sensual, formal, or informal phrasing often referred to as Dickensian. For example, in "Number Four Bowstring Lane," a "spooky tale" from a collection of short stories, *A Fit of Shivers,* A. vividly describes the ghostly town of Crowbridge with its "pointed red roofs, the Tudor chimney pots, the pantiles, wrought ironwork, and cobbled walks. . . . [It is populated by] a legacy of perturbed spirits who moan, squeak, gibber, jabber, rap, rattle, clank, wail, keen and scrabble every night . . . keeping up their cacophonous chorus until the formal signal of cock-crow calls a sudden halt to the racket."

Several of her early short stories appeared serially in periodicals (*Suspense* and *Everywoman*) until Doubleday purchased one of her children's books. The editor of the company's Crime Club requested she expand these serials into full-length novels. Of this particular period in her writing, A. says: "As the gothic market then began to be somewhat saturated I tried my hand at Regency romances, but I still prefer the classic gothic and wish it had not been so over-used. However as this is the case I propose to stick to domestic suspense for my next books."

Many of A.'s works highlight exceptional personalities ranging from the stereotypical comics in *The Dog on the Roof* to vicarious Luke, the hero of *Midnight is a Place,* who discovers himself through the others' ordeals. Another eccentric is whimsical but brooding Felix, the endearing traveler in *Go Saddle the Sea,* who narrates his tribulations as he wanders across nineteenth-century Spain and eventually seeks passage to England to locate his missing parents. Like the biblical Job, Felix expresses numerous asides to God that, although humorous, verbalize a search for answers, especially when he is in improbable situations. A.'s functional purpose for Felix's witty remarks thus seems to have a Gilbert and Sullivan charm: statements rendered as wry commentary carrying seemingly improbable, yet inevitable, solutions.

Identifying characters through clever name inventions has literary precedent. For example, certain characters suggest further Dickensian allusions: Miss Slightcarp and Mr. Grips, Mr. Grimshaw and Mrs. Shubunkin of *The Wolves of Willoughby Chase;* Abednego, Is, and Dodo Twight of *Is Underground;* and Squinting Edrica, Olive Findlater, and Gloria Baskin, three accused witches who are destroyed by fire in "The Shrieking Door."

Despite the pleasure A.'s unique language and imagery provide, one must not ignore her considerable regard for details and a "willingness to take risks," whether composing "contemporary gothics, historical romances," or "absurd" and "fantastically improbable" story lines. As one biographer aptly states, "At some point, in almost all of her books, she seems to skirt, or even fall over, the edge of absurdity."

The unique avoidance of a "simple narrative formula," extensive attention to medical minutiae, the employment of recurring characters, and considerable regard for her younger characters' predicaments combine to make A.'s works, though highly successful, difficult for some critics to categorize.

A.'s most successful works are those aimed at the adolescent audience, yet their appeal crosses over into adult readership. For example, *The Wolves of Willoughby Chase* (1962) is still popular more than thirty years after publication. *Time* considers it "one genuine small masterpiece . . . almost a copybook lesson in those virtues that a classic children's book must possess: a charm and style of its own." Part of that charm is the unexpected use of humor as relief from the "dreadful doings" in the plot, a technique she also employs in many of her other works. Over the years, this novel was designated the introduction to "The Wolves Chronicles," a series of fictions that expands the "rip-roaring adventure . . . both serious and thrilling fare young readers crave" while creating an "unhistorical" glimpse into an earlier England led by the last of the Stuart dynasty. In *Dido and Pa,* the reign is threatened by a Hanoverian conspiracy, but the plots also concern evil treatment of children. Dido's father, posing as a court orchestral conductor, discovers youngsters handled as slaves, who after each day of back-breaking toil have to sleep while dangling from ceiling hooks. Similarly, *Is Underground* (1992) concerns hundreds of children who have vanished from old London town, à la *The Pied Piper,* but, in reality, they have been kidnapped into working in vast underground coal mines, barely surviving abominable conditions.

Awareness of audience is a focal point of A.'s "practical approach to writing," and many budding authors are appreciative of her extensive advice on this topic in the definitive text, *The Way to Write for Children* (1982), although A. immediately challenges the title: "there is no *one* way in which to write for children." A. also stresses that a difference exists between writing *for* and writing *about* children, one that can be discovered by paying close attention to John Habberton's *Helen's Babies* and to Mark Twain's *Huckleberry Finn* (as well as to *Jane Eyre* and *David Copperfield*). A. states that these authors were creating "stories ostensibly intended for children but really meant for the diversion of adults."

Dual readership, however, has its hazards, A. cautions. While maintaining a pragmatic view of multiple types of readers, yet focusing the content onto one particular audience, authors may create poor reception or disapproval from the buying public: "If you try to write for children, but hope that adults will be reading the book, too, an element of archness or insincerity is almost certain to creep into your style. And if your book overlaps the two different areas, your publishers may not be sure who is going to buy it and so promotion and sales will suffer."

The Way to Write for Children, nevertheless, is more than a "how-to-do-it" text. It provides a history of juvenile literature, a discussion of various genres for young readers, quotes from numerous recognized authors, as well as advice—she humorously indicates—that has been given in other sources but carefully avoided.

A. notes that adults have an uncanny knack for rationalizing when emotions such as grief, fear, tragedy, or loneliness appear in a reading. Children, however, may be reading about these emotions for the first time, so it is the writer's obligation to "assume that his work may be read by an archetypal beginner . . . and should set its measure accordingly."

Paralleling the success of her juvenile works are her romantic and historical publications (1965–89), numerous short stories, nine theatrical and television plays, and a collection of verse, *The Skin Spinners* (1976). Included among these are her stories encompassing a fantastic, supernatural, and/or mythic curiosity. From *The Windscreen Weepers and Other Tales of Horror and Suspense* (1969) to (among others) *Give Yourself a Fright: Thirteen Tales of the Supernatural* (1989), she provides windows into the grotesque without giving an "overt moral message" or providing conspicuous violence, as the latter is "to easy [for readers] to imitate."

WORKS: *All You've Ever Wanted and Other Stories* (1953). *More Than You've Bargained for and Other Stories* (1955). *The Kingdom and the Cave* (1960). *The Wolves of Willoughby Chase* (1962). *Black Hearts in Battersea* (1964). *The Silence of Herondale* (1964). *The Fortune Hunters* (1965). *Nightbirds on Nantucket* (1966). *Trouble with Product X* (1966; in the U.S. as *Beware of the Bouquet*). *Hate Begins at Home* (1967; in the U. S. as *Dark Interval*). *The Ribs of Death* (1967; in the U.S. as *The Crystal Crow*, 1968). *Armitage, Armitage, Fly Away Home* (1968; as play, 1978). *The Necklace of Raindrops and Other Stories* (1968). *The Whispering Mountain* (1968). *A Small Pinch of Weather and Other Stories* (1969). *Night Fall* (1969). *The Whispering Mountain* (1969). *The Windscreen Weepers and Other Tales of Horror and Suspense* (1969; also published as *The Green Flash and Other Tales of Horror, Suspense, and Fantasy*, 1971). *Died on a Rainy Sunday* (1970). *The Embroidered Sunset* (1970). *Smoke from Cromwell's Time and Other Stories* (1970). *All and More* (1971). *The Cuckoo Tree* (1971). *Nightly Deadshade* (1971). *The Kingdom Under the Sea and Other Stories* (1971). *Arabel's Raven* (1971). *The Butterfly Picnic* (1972; in the U.S. as *A Cluster of Separate Sparks*). *The Green Flask and Other Tales of Horror, Suspense and Fantasy* (1972). *A Harp of Fishbones and Other Stories* (1972). *Winterthing: A Child's Play* (1972). *Arabel and the Escaped Black Mamba* (1973). *The Mooncusser's Daughter* (1973). *All But a Few* (1974). *The Bread Bin* (1974). *The Kingdom and the Cave* (1974). *Midnight is a Place* (1974; as play, 1977). *Not What You Expected: A Collection of Short Stories* (1974). *Voices in an Empty House* (1975). *A Bundle of Nerves* (1976). *Castle Barebane* (1976). *Dark Streets of Kimballs Green* (1976). *Mortimer's Tie* (1976). *The Skin Spinners* (1976). (trans.) *The Angel Inn*, by S. Segur (1976). *The Apple of Trouble* (1977). *The Faithless Lollybird and Other Stories* (1977). *The Far Forests: Tales of Romance, Fantasy, and Suspense* (1977). *Go Saddle the Sea* (1977). *Last Movement* (1977). *The Five-Minute Marriage* (1977). *Street* (1977). *Winterthing* (1977). *Mice and Mendelson* (1978). *The Smile of the Stranger* (1978). *Tale of a One-Way Street, and Other Stories* (1978). *Mortimer and the Sword Excalibur* (1979). *The Spiral Stair* (1979). *A Touch of Chill: Tales for Sleepless Nights* (1979). *The Lightning Tree* (1980; in the U. S. as *The Weeping Ash*). *The Shadow Guests* (1980). *The Stolen Lake* (1981). *Mortimer's Portrait on Glass* (1982). *The Mystery of Mr. Jones's Disappearing Taxi* (1982). *The Way to Write for Children* (1982). *A Whisper in the Night: Tales of Terror and Suspense* (1982). *The Young Lady from Paris* (1982; in the U. S. as *The Girl from Paris*). *Bridle the Wind* (1983). *Foul Matter* (1983). *The Kitchen Warriors* (1983). *Mortimer's Cross* (1983; includes *Mortimer's Portrait on Glass* and *The Mystery of Mr. Jones's Disappearing Taxi*). *Fog Hounds, Wind Cat, Sea Mice* (1984). *Mansfield Revisited* (1984). *Up the Chimney Down and Other Stories* (1984). *Mortimer Says Nothing* (1985). *The Last Slice of Rainbow, and Other Stories* (1985). *Dido and Pa* (1986). *Past Eight O'Clock* (1986). *Deception* (1987). *If I Were You* (1987). *The Moon's Revenge* (1987). *The Teeth of the Gale* (1988). *Voices* (1988; in the U. S. as *Return to Harken House*). *Blackground* (1989). *The Erl King's Daughter* (1989). *Give Yourself a Fright* (1989). *A Goose on Your Grave* (1989). *A Fit of Shivers: Tales for Late at Night* (1990). *Jane Fairfax* (1990). *A Foot in the Grave* (1991). *The Haunting of Lamb House* (1991). *The Shoemaker's Boy* (1991). *A Creepy Companion* (1993). *Is Underground* (1993). *The Midnight Moropus* (1993). *Eliza's Daughter* (1994). *Mortimer's Mine* (1994). *The Winter Sleepwalker and Other Stories* (1994). *Dark Interval* (1995).

BIBLIOGRAPHY: Apseloff, M. *CLAQ* (1994). Usrey, M., in *Proceedings of the Sixth Annual Conference of the Children's Literature Association, University of Toronto, March, 1979*, ed. P. A. Ord (1980).

For articles in reference books, see: *CA. CLR. DLB. SATA.*

Zelda R. B. Provenzano

Lucy Aikin

BORN: 6 November 1781, Warrington, Lancashire.
DIED: 29 January 1864, Hampstead, London.
DAUGHTER OF: John Aikin and Martha Jennings.
WROTE UNDER: Lucy Aikin; Mary Godolphin.

Born into a distinguished family of Dissenting clergy, writers, and educators, A. was brought up in an environment that encouraged intellectual pursuits in daughters and sons. Her grandfather, Dr. John Aikin, was a theologian and classicist at the Warrington Academy. A. grew up admiring her aunt, Anna Laetitia Aikin Barbauld, celebrated poet, essayist, editor, and writer of children's stories. A.'s father was a physician who wrote books on hymns, medicine, and poetry, and with Barbauld coauthored *Evenings at Home* (1792), essays and stories for children reprinted for more than 100 years. A. is known best for her historical biographies, letters, memoirs of her father and aunt, and works for children. A. was her parents' only daughter of five children; one brother, Charles, was adopted by their aunt Barbauld and her husband. Her father practiced medicine in Yarmouth and London, retiring to Stoke Newington in 1797 because of ill health. A., who never married, moved with her mother to Hampstead at her father's death in 1822. With the exception of a short period in Wimbledon, A. spent the rest of her life in Hampstead.

At Yarmouth, London, and Stoke Newington, the precocious and spirited A. received an advanced education from her parents at home. She learned history, the classics, science, French, Italian, and Latin. She knew her aunt's works intimately and was particularly inspired by the sense of the sublime in Barbauld's hymn poems for children. She recalled numerous moral lessons to teach her humility and charity. At Yarmouth, she learned to love the mystery of the sea and to cope, with her brothers, with the humiliations suffered because of her father's unpopular protests against the slave trade. Throughout her life, A. associated with distinguished authors, including Joanna Baillie, Harriet Martineau, and Elizabeth Benger. Among her correspondents was the Reverend William Ellery Channing, the noted leader in the American Unitarian Church. Their correspondence, lasting from 1826 until Channing's death in 1842, contained frank discussions of social and political issues, including Channing's dismay at the social class system in England and A.'s comparable dismay over slavery and inequality of women in the United States. The letters still provide a valuable lens into Anglo-American culture and politics of the period.

A. published her first piece, an article in the *Annual Register,* when she was seventeen. In her original and edited works for children, beginning with the anthology *Poetry for Children,* she celebrated poetry, considered more dangerous than facts in prose, as a liberating dimension for the child's pleasure and learning. Her *Epistles on Women,* considered a "bold and arduous" verse study of women's history, begins with Eve and Adam and ends with a seventeenth-century woman of letters, Lucy Hutchinson. A.'s first history, *Memoirs of the Court of Queen Elizabeth,* celebrating the intellectual and personal strength of the female monarch, was reprinted for more than a hundred years. Like A.'s other histories, it examines both the domestic and public affairs of its subject and was scrupulously researched. Her memoir of her illustrious aunt is insightful and laudatory but discreetly avoids confronting the insanity of Barbauld's husband, including odd compulsive behavior and attempts on his wife's life. At the end of her life, under the pseudonym "Mary Godolphin," A. shaped several literary classics, including Aesop's *Fables* and Defoe's *Robinson Crusoe,* to a series of "one syllable" publications for children. A. believed that the short sentences made the beauty, adventure, and morality of selected classics accessible to beginning readers. The works were published posthumously.

A.'s life and literary *oeuvre* reveal an educated, inquiring, and committed feminist of her time. Always working within an accepted ideology of woman as moral center, A. strove for the improvement of womankind and society at large.

WORKS: *Epistles on Woman* (1810). *Juvenile Correspondence* (1811). (trans.) *The Life of Ulrich Zwingli,* by J. Heim (1812). *Lorimer, a Tale* (1814). *Memoirs of the Court of Queen Elizabeth* (1818). *Evenings at Home [retold] in Words of one Syllable* (1819). *Memoirs of the Court of King James I* (1822). (trans.) *The Travels of Rolando,* by L. Jeuffret (1822). *Memoir of John Aikin* (1823). *Memoirs of the Court of King Charles I* (1833). *Life of Joseph Addison* (1843). *Memoirs, Miscellanies and Letters of the late Lucy Aikin,* ed. P. H. Le Breton (1864). *Correspondence of William Ellery Channing, D.D. and Lucy Aikin,* ed. P. H. Le Breton (1874).

BIBLIOGRAPHY: Apseloff, M. *CLAQ* (1984). Rodgers, B. *Georgian Chronicle: Mrs. Barbauld and Her Family* (1958). Smith, B. *American Historical Review* (1984). Usrey, M., in *Proceedings of the Sixth Annual Conference of the Children's Literature Association, Univ. of Toronto, March 1979* (1980).

For articles in reference books, see: *Bloomsbury. CA. Cambridge. CLR. Dabundo. DLB. DNB. Feminist. IAWWW. Oxford. SATA. ToddBWW. WD.*

Other references: Aiken, J. *Encounter* (May 1985).

Carol Shiner Wilson

A.J.V.: See *Vardill, Anna Jane*

A. L.: See *Locke, Anne Vaughan*

Mary Alcock

BORN: 1742.
DIED: 28 May 1798, Northamptonshire.
DAUGHTER OF: Denison Cumberland and Joanna Bentley.
MARRIED: John Alcock, Archdeacon of Raphoe.

Born into and surrounded by well-known families, A. was the youngest daughter of Denison Cumberland and Joanna

Bentley. Cumberland was the vicar of Stanwick, Northamptonshire, until he became Bishop of Clonfert in Ireland in 1763 and Bishop of Kilmore in 1772; Bentley was the daughter of Richard Bentley, celebrated classical scholar and Master of Trinity College, Cambridge, who became an object of satire in Jonathan Swift's *Battle of the Books*. A.'s brother, Richard Cumberland, was a dramatist whose literary friends included David Garrick, Joshua Reynolds, Oliver Goldsmith, Richard Brinsley Sheridan, and Lord George Sackville. She was active in literary circles, documented as a contributor to Lady Miller's poetry sessions in Bath in 1781. In reports of her death, she was described as the widow of Archdeacon Alcock, most probably John Alcock, Archdeacon of Raphoe. Notable subscribers to her collection of poems, published posthumously in 1799, included the Prince and Princess of Wales, William Cowper, John Kemble, Samuel Rogers, George Romney, and the noted women writers Elizabeth Carter and Hannah More.

Her niece and editor, Joanna Hughes, said of her, "She never held herself up as a writer; when she resorted to her pen it was either to amuse a leisure hour, to gratify an absent friend, or for the more sublime purpose of pouring out her heart in praise and thanksgiving to God." Despite this assertion, A.'s poetry comments upon political and cultural reform of the period, especially the revolutionary 1790s. She is allied with Romantic contemporaries such as William Blake in her ballad "The Chimney Sweeper's Complaint"; most interesting, however, are poems that satirize reform efforts in England. "Air Balloon; or The Flying Mortal" (1784), a seven-page poem that Lonsdale calls an "early reaction in verse to the current craze for aeronautics," clearly has a political component given A.'s Advertisement addressing those who "wish TO EVADE THE LAWS OF THEIR KING OR COUNTRY," thus allying radical reformers to those "AERIAL BEINGS" who try to escape the earth. "Instructions, Supposed to be Written in Paris, for the Mob in England" satirically invokes the revolutionary context by using the catchwords "freedom" and "rights" and includes specific allusion to both Thomas Paine and Mary Wollstonecraft: "Of Liberty, Reform, and Rights I sing, / Freedom, I mean, without or Church or King; / Freedom to seize and keep whate'er I can, / And boldly claim my right—The Rights of Man." "Modern Manners" mocks Romantic calls for freedom from cultural norms, especially marriage, in the character of Flirtilla who follows her free-thinking parents who "jeer and joke / at wedlock's galling chain," perhaps Wollstonecraft and William Godwin. "A Receipt for Writing a Novel" ridicules contemporary novels by ladies in the style of Jane Austen and Wollstonecraft. Although she is not well known, A. offers an interesting perspective on political, cultural, and aesthetic debates in the late eighteenth century.

WORKS: *The Air Balloon; or The Flying Mortal* (1784). *Poetical Writer,* ed. J. Hughes (1799; listed in some sources as *Poems*).

BIBLIOGRAPHY: *Eighteenth Century Women Poets,* ed. R. Lonsdale (1990). *Romanticism: An Anthology,* ed. D. Wu (1994).

For articles in reference works, see: *Feminist. ToddDBA.*

Other references: *Memoirs* (1808). Lonsdale, R., ed. *The New Oxford Book of Eighteenth Century Verse,* ed. R. Cumberland (1984).

Lisa Plummer Crafton

Alexander, Mrs.: See *Hector, Annie French*

Theodosia Alleine

BORN: probably after 1632, Ditcheat.
DIED: before 1685.
DAUGHTER OF: Richard Alleine.
MARRIED: Joseph Alleine, 1655; perhaps again after 1668.

A. is author of the largest portion of the hagiographic portrait of her husband, a dissenting clergyman, *The Life and Death of that Excellent Minister of Christ, Mr. Joseph Alleine* (1672). The volume was much reprinted throughout the seventeenth and eighteenth centuries and well into the nineteenth. A prefatory disclaimer to the book makes obligatory apology for A.'s unfitness as a writer. However, narrative details from the *Life* make it clear that she was a well-educated woman who provided significant support to her husband's ministry and to their common livelihood by running a school.

A. was born at Ditcheat, the daughter of the Reverend Richard Alleine. She was living in Batcombe (Somerset) where her father was rector, when she married her kinsman, Joseph Alleine. He had not originally intended to marry, an inclination that seems consonant with the portrait of a bookish and zealously religious man presented in much of the *Life*. A. herself acknowledges that early marriage was "contrary to his purpose," though they seem to have had an understanding from his days at Oxford. Their courtship was carried on at two-week intervals, when Joseph made the twenty-five mile journey to visit her in Batcombe. They married on 4 October 1655 at the urging of George Newton (the clergyman at Taunton to whom Joseph was assistant), for marriage was considered a useful if not essential ornament to Protestant ministry. The newlyweds lived with Newton for the first two years of their married life.

While the two seem to have grown in love toward one another, in their early life Joseph's zeal for holiness supplanted even ordinary expressions of conjugal tenderness. In a letter written from Oxford about a year before their marriage, his disgust for temptations of the flesh consumes the import of the letter. This language of corruption contrasts sharply with a letter written in the year of his death to an old friend (or perhaps a brother) styled "Pylades," in which Joseph ("Orestes") declares his love and desire in the imagery of the *Song of Songs*. He implies that "Pylades" is jealous of A., whom Joseph belittles in comparison to "Pylades." So while A. was his wife, Joseph's emotional (if not erotic) attachment was to another.

A. says of herself that she had been "alwayes bred to work," so it seemed most natural—and certainly financially necessary—to set up a school for "Tablers," "Schollars," and local children after the couple were settled in their own home in Taunton. Evidently she was a very successful teacher and businesswoman: She notes that her "Family" of boarded students was "seldome less than Twenty, and many times Thirty; My School usually [had] Fifty or Sixty of the Town and other Places." A. never had children of her own.

A.'s home and work life was altered by her husband's refusal to conform to the 1662 Act of Uniformity that required swearing loyalty to the Church of England. Instead, Joseph attempted to carry on his ministry privately, preaching and catechizing from house to house and town to town. These actions drew the ire of the authorities, forcing A. and her husband to sell all their goods in preparation for his imprisonment or possible emigration to "*China*, or some remote Part of the World." Joseph was ultimately tried, convicted, and imprisoned for his refusal to conform. Upon his release, he continued his preaching journeys while A. lived in Taunton. It is unclear whether she resumed teaching during this period. Joseph was soon arrested again and jailed. His health suffered because of the conditions of imprisonment; two trips to Bath failed to restore his health and he died there in 1668.

A. contributed her portion to the *Life* in 1672. There she paints an appropriately celestial portrait of her marriage to a saint. She values the respect he showed her in consulting her opinion: He would not "Manage any Affairs almost without Conversing with me." At the same time, she attests that he "was a faithful Reprover of anything he saw amiss in me." In his last sickness Joseph made a "Competent" (a will) that allowed what A. called "Comfortable provision for me." After Joseph's death, A. may have married again, either to a Taunton merchant or to another dispossessed clergyman.

WORKS: *The Life and Death of that Excellent Minister of Christ, Mr. Joseph Alleine, Late Teacher of the Church at Taunton, in Somersetshire, Assistant to Mr. Newton* (1672).

BIBLIOGRAPHY: Stanford, C. *Joseph Alleine: His Companions and Times* (1861). Wood, A. *Athenae Oxonienses* (1692) (under "Joseph Allein" [sic]). Wright, T. *Biographia Britannica*, Vol. 1 (1747–66) (under "Joseph Allein" [sic]).

For articles in reference works, see: *Bell. DNB* (under "Joseph Alleine"). Smith, H. and S. Cardinale *Women and the Literature of the Seventeenth Century* (1990).

Kari Boyd McBride

Allenby, G.: See *O'Malley, Mary Dolling (Sanders)*

Alleyn, Ellen: See *Rossetti, Christina*

Margery Allingham

BORN: 20 May 1904, London.
DIED: 30 June 1966, Colchester, Essex.
DAUGHTER OF: Herbert John Allingham and Emily Jane Hughes Allingham.
MARRIED: Philip Youngman Caret, 1927.

Although A. attended the Perse High School for Girls and the Polytechnic of Speech Training, her real education occurred at home. Since her father was a serial writer and hack journalist, as were many of his friends who continually visited the house, A. took writing as a profession for granted. Under her father's tutelage, A. began writing at the age of seven and produced her first published novel at sixteen. That hack work and serial writing could be vehicles for serious expression as well as a means of livelihood she also learned at an early age. Her father's friend, G.R.M. Hearne, who wrote both Robin Hood and Sexton Blake adventures, gave her the following axiom: "They never mind you putting all you've got into this sort of stuff. They never pay you any more for it, but they don't stop you."

A.'s books before 1930 are strictly in the thriller genre, in which she said the plot must contain "as many colorful, exciting or ingenious inventions . . . [and] incidents . . . as one [can] lay hands on" and must contain "a surprise every tenth page and a shock every twentieth." For most of her writing career her protagonist is mild-mannered Albert Campion, a character in the Robin Hood mode of the hero-outlaw. Like Dorothy Sayers and Agatha Christie, A. transcends the sentimental nostalgia adhering to such a hero by the use of comedy: irony, wit, whimsy, puns, jokes, absurdities, burlesques, slapstick, and zany Wodehousian repartee. Her mastermind criminals, for example, have names like Simister and Ali Fergusson Barber. Campion himself carries a water pistol rather than a gun; has a pet mouse named Haig; is always described as having an "idiotic" or "inane" expression; and permits his manservant, the ineffable and lugubrious Magersfontein Lugg, to answer the phone by announcing, "Aphrodite Glue Works."

With *Police at the Funeral* (1931), A. left the thriller behind and entered the world of the detective novel proper, which she continued to explore in her novels of the thirties, moving from international intrigue and mastermind criminals to domestic crime in mansions full of brooding atmosphere; from picaresque construction to Arthur Conan Doyle plots, replete with disguised clues; and leaving behind the exotic and the supernatural. The early humor remains, but it is muted and understated.

Toward the end of the decade, A. finally engaged the theme she had been avoiding, love, thus moving away from both the thriller and the detective tale toward the components of the serious novel: character, description, and analysis. With *The Fashion in Shrouds* (1938), A.'s fiction reached maturity by achieving a meld of the thriller, the detective story, and the psychological novel. After the war, during which she was engaged in war work, including a nonfiction work, *The Oaken Heart* (1941), she returned to this fusion in a series of delightful and considerable works of which the best is the Dickensian and ominous *The Tiger in the Smoke* (1952). Elegant writing coupled with wit, invention, and a sense of fun, in addition to serious interest in character and interpersonal relations, help A.'s work transcend its genres and endure.

WORKS: *Blackkerchief Dick* (1923). *Water in a Sieve: A Fantasy in One Act* (1925). *The White Cottage Mystery* (1928). *The Black Dudley Murder* (1929; in the U.K. as *Crime at Black Dudley*). *Mystery Mile* (1930). *Police at the Funeral* (1931). *The Gyrth Chalice Mystery* (1931; in the U.K. as *Look to the Lady*). *Kingdom of Death* (1933; in the U.K. as *Sweet Danger*). *Death of a Ghost* (1934). *Flower for the Judge* (1936). *The Case of the Late Pig* (1937). *Mr. Campion, Criminologist* (1937). *Dancers in Mourning* (1937; republished as *Who Killed Chloe?*, 1943). *The Fashion in Shrouds* (1938). *Black Plumes* (1940). *Traitor's Purse* (1941). *The Oaken Heart* (1941). *The Galantrys* (1943; in the U.K. as *Dance of the Years*). *Pearls Before Swine* (1945; in the U.K. as *Coroner's Pidgin*). *The Case Book of Mr. Campion* (1947). *Deadly Duo* (1949; in the U.K. as *Take Two at Bedtime*, 1950). *More Work for the Undertaker* (1949). *The Tiger in the Smoke* (1952). *No Love Lost: Two Stories of Suspense* (1954). *The Estate of the Beckoning Lady* (1955; in the U.K. as *The Beckoning Lady*). *Tether's End* (1958). *Hide My Eyes* (1958). *Crime and Mr. Campion* (contains *Death of a Ghost, Flowers for the Judge,* and *Dancers in Mourning* (1959). *Three Cases for Mr. Campion* (1961). *The China Governess* (1962). *The Mysterious Mr. Campion* (omnibus, 1963). *The Mind Readers* (1965). *Mr. Campion's Lady* (omnibus, 1965). *Mr. Campion's Clowns* (anthology, 1966). *The Mysterious Mr. Campion* (anthology, 1966). *Cargo of Eagles* (1967). *Mr. Campion and Others* (1967). *The Allingham Case-Book* (1969). *The Allingham Minibus* (1973). *The Fear Sign* (1976).

BIBLIOGRAPHY: Klein, K. G. *Great Women Mystery Writers* (1994). Martin, R. *Ink in Her Blood: The Life and Crime Fiction of Margery Allingham* (1988). Pike, B. A. *Campion's Career: A Study of the Novels of Margery Allingham* (1987). Thorogood, J. *Margery Allingham: A Biography* (1991).

For articles in reference works, see: *Bloomsbury. CA. Cambridge. EMD. Feminist. TCCM&W. ToddBWW.*

Other references: *Twentieth Century Suspense: The Thriller Comes of Age*, ed. C. Bloom (1990). Cox, J. *ArmD* (Winter 1982). Craig, P. and M. Cadogan, *The Lady Investigates* (1981). Gaskill, R. W. *And Then There Were Nine: More Women of Mystery*, ed. J. S. Bakerman (1985). Huey, T. *Clues* (1982). Mann, J. *Deadlier Than the Male* (1981). Panek, L. L. *Watteau's Shepherds: The Detective Novel in Britain, 1914–1940* (1979).

Carey Kaplan
(updated by Christina Root)

Alton, Delia: See *Doolittle, Hilda (H. D.)*

Andrews, Corinne: See *West, Rebecca*

Jane Anger

FLOURISHED: 1589

We know nothing for certain about this elusive Elizabethan personality apart from the contents of *Jane Anger, her protection for women*, a pamphlet published in London in 1589 by Richard Iones and Thomas Orwin, and written, says the title, by one Ia. Anger, Gent. Some have suggested that Jane Anger might not even be a woman since "Gent." was often employed as an abbreviation for "gentleman." The author herself insists that she is and that she is writing for women. There are also records of at least six Joan or Jane Angers who could have written the tract. Furthermore, even if Anger is a pseudonym, it may well hide a female author since, as the author's puns on the name indicate throughout, it is expressive of the writer's sentiment. In any case, although there has been no definite proof of her identity, there is also no proof that she is not what she says she is: a woman writing for women.

The position of women formed a recurrent theme in the popular literature of the sixteenth and seventeenth centuries, with pamphlets arguing pro and con appearing until the late 1600s in this continuation of the *querelle des femmes*. A.'s pamphlet was one such work. If she was a woman, and there is no hard evidence to refute her claim that she is, it is the first occurrence in English prose of a woman defending her own sex, and the *Protection* is the earliest example of a feminist pamphlet written by a woman. A. claims to have written her pamphlet in answer to another pamphlet containing the "Scandalous reportes of a Late Surfeiting Louer." Several books have been identified with this pamphlet, including *Eupheus his Censure to Philautus,* which was attributed to John Lyly but actually written by Robert Greene; the most likely is *Boke, his Surfeyt in love,* entered in the Stationer's Register for November 1588. Unfortunately, copies of the pamphlet are no longer extant; so although we have the response, we are not sure of the provocation.

In answering the lover, A. claims that men "have been so daintely fed with our good natures that like iades (their stomackes are grown so queasey), they surfeit of our kindnesse." Her protection, in the main, advises fellow women to beware of men's sexual trickery. "A goose," she writes, "standing before a rauenous fox is in as good case as the woman that trusted to a mans fidelitie." In addition to this practical caution, A. advances more elaborate defenses of her sex. She uses older theologically based defenses of women: that Eve was purer than Adam because she was made last and from his side rather than from the dirt, that Mary's role in salvation glorifies womankind. She also claims women are constant and chaste and that their services contribute greatly to their societies. She advises her readers to distrust men who speak slightingly of their sex. For A., as she makes clear in the prefatory letter, argues that men are the moral inferiors of women; in fact, she claims that men are given social superiority only to keep women from falling prey to pride. Yet A. lays many censures at the door of her fellow women as well, and she blames their vulnerability at various times on their own silliness, credulity, bashfulness, garrulity, and weakness of wit.

In many ways, the book speaks with two voices. There are in fact two prologues, one to women in general and one to gentlewomen. The latter is much less aggressive than its mate, the former much less restrained. A.'s tone is often witty and mocking; she attacks the men who write against women by criticizing their valuing of rhetorical technique over substantive thought. Yet she herself pulls from a deep bag of rhetorical tricks, so much so that at least one critic has suggested that the real target of A.'s attack is not men but false learning. The text is sprinkled with Latin quotations and the examples of famous women from classical and biblical traditions. There are three poems in the tract, playful puns on the "surfeiting lover" throughout, and an admission by A. herself that the lover's book came to hand because "as well women as men are desirous of nouelities." John Lyly's aureate style greatly influences much of the prose style. Yet the pamphlet is also strewn with numerous indications of an appeal to popular tradition. Proverbs, references to creatures from folk stories (the fox, for example), and at least one anecdote (the story of the wise man), a cross between a joke and a parable, impart a tough and realistic tone.

While A.'s pamphlet was the first of its kind to be written by a woman, several other women followed suit in the 1600s as the debate on the woman question intensified under the rule of James I (who was in favor of the suppression of women). Of these—Racheal Speght, Esther Sowerman, Constantia Mutanta, Mary Tattlewell, and Joan Hit-him-home—only Speght used her own name. A.'s pamphlet, in its bold tone, its vigorous defense, and spirited attacks, thus marks a landmark in the history of women writers in England. Its appearance in the Elizabethan popular press also gives witness to the new interest in woman as a social factor and to the seriousness with which women themselves were considering their social condition.

WORKS: *Jane Anger her protection for women. To defend them against Scandalous Reportes of a late Surfeiting Louer, and all other Venerians that complaine so to bee ouercloyed with womens kindnesse* (1589).

BIBLIOGRAPHY: Beilen, E. *Redeeming Eve* (1987). Ferguson, M. *First Feminists: British Women Writers 1578–1799* (1985). Henderson, K. and B. McManus. *Half Humankind: Contexts and Texts of the Controversy about Women in England, 1540–1640* (1985). Magnusson, A. *RenSt* (1993). Magnusson, A. *ESC* (1991). *The Women's Sharp Revenge: Five Women's Pamphlets from the Renaissance,* ed. S. Shepherd (1985). Travitsky, B. *The Paradise of Women* (1983). Warnicke, R. *Women of the English Renaissance and Reformation* (1983). Woodbridge, L. *Women and the English Renaissance* (1984). Wright, L. B. *Middle Class Culture in Elizabethan England* (1935).

For articles in reference works, see *Bloomsbury. Feminist. Oxford.*

Other references: *MLQ* (1947).

Glenda K. McLeod

Anne, Countess of Winchelsea: See *Finch, Anne Kingsmill, Countess of Winchelsea*

Anodos: See *Coleridge, Mary Elizabeth*

Anspach (Ansbach), Margravine of: See *Craven, Elizabeth (Berkeley)*

Anstruther, Joyce: See *Struther, Jan*

Anthony, C. L.: See *Smith, Dorothy (Dodie) Gladys*

Arblay, d', Frances Burney: See *Burney, Frances*

Arcasia: See *Boothby, Frances*

Ardelia: See *Finch, Anne Kingsmill, Countess of Winchelsea*

Aretina: See *Moody, Elizabeth*

Ariadne

FLOURISHED: 1696.

A. is the pseudonym of a playwright whose only known work is *She Ventures and He Wins*, a comedy staged at "the New Theatre in Little Lincoln's-Inn Fields" in September 1695 and published the following year. This "Young Lady," as she identifies herself on the title page, was the first woman to publish plays after Aphra Behn. The preface and prologue indicate that Behn's talent was both inspiring and confining for this self-deprecating woman. Very conscious of literary succession and of the harsh criticism that she could draw because she was female, A. comments in the preface, "The best Apology I can make for my Self and Play, is, that 'tis the Error of a weak Woman's Pen, one altogether unlearn'd, ignorant of any but her Mother-Tongue, and very far from being a perfect mistress of that too." It is this fear of criticism, Peter Anthony Motteux writes in the epilogue, that forces A. to hide her true identity. The epilogue concludes by suggesting that a good reception for this play might encourage the playwright to reveal her identity.

A conventional comedy of the late seventeenth century, *She Ventures and He Wins* weaves together two relatively unrelated love plots. In the main plot, which starred Mrs. Bracegirdle as Charlot in 1695, a young woman disguises herself as a man in order to study potential husbands. Knowing that men often flatter women and lie to them, she wants to observe men as they talk more naturally among themselves. Rather than treating the audience to an extended exploration of male duplicity, A. allows her heroine to find a suitable man very soon. Having identified Lovewell as loving and faithful, Charlot tests him by sending other women to flirt with him and by pretending to arrest him for debts that she has incurred in his name. When he passes all these tests, she marries him. The subplot involves a bumbling would-be philanderer, whose exploits are revealed to his ever-forgiving wife. The plots are linked only by their common concern for disguise, yet somehow all the characters end up in the same tavern at the end of the play. *She Ventures and He Wins* is more interesting for its portrayal of wise and powerful women than for clever dialogue or plotting. Although we have no record of how it was received by contemporary audiences at Lincoln's Inn Fields, certainly it did not earn enough praise to warrant the playwright's revealing her identity.

No other plays can be attributed to A. with any real assurance; it has been suggested that she also wrote *The Unnatural Mother,* staged at Lincoln's Inn Fields in 1697 and published in 1698, both anonymously.

WORKS: *She Ventures and He Wins* (1696).

BIBLIOGRAPHY:

For articles in reference works, see: *Bell. Feminist. ToddDBA.*

Tori Haring-Smith

Armytage, Mrs. G. or Armytage, R.: See *Watson, Rosamund Marriott*

Elizabeth von Arnim (pseudonym of Mary Annette Beauchamp Russell)

BORN: 31 August 1866, Sydney, Australia.
DIED: 9 February 1941, Charleston, South Carolina, United States.
DAUGHTER OF: Henry Beauchamp and Elizabeth "Louey" Lassetter Beauchamp.
MARRIED: Count Henning August von Arnim-Schlagenthin, 1891; John Francis Stanley, Lord Russell, 1916.
WROTE UNDER: The Author of *Elizabeth and Her German Garden;* Alice Cholmondeley; Elizabeth.

Considered one of the greatest wits of her day, A. found instant success with *Elizabeth and Her German Garden* (1898) and followed it with a body of work that sustained its themes of freedom in nature and rebellion against social tyranny. Her cumbersome pen-name, adopted initially to placate her first husband, became a necessity since her novels were often recognizably autobiographical. She frequently exorcised unhappy romances in her writing, avenging herself on the men involved: *Garden, The Caravaners* (1909), and *The Pastor's Wife* (1914) provide unflattering depictions of her first husband, while in *Vera* (1921) she portrays her notorious second husband as "the meanest man in fiction," as some critics described him. Throughout her life, A. devoted herself to exposing the unfairness of women's allotted role in a time when most took this for granted.

A. was born at her family's holiday residence in Australia but moved with her family to England in 1870, where she attended the Royal College of Music. After having been presented at court in 1890, she accompanied her parents on a European tour, during which she met the forty-year-old widower Count Henning von Arnim. They married the following year, and during what she wryly called her "wild career of unbridled motherhood" she bore him five children, whose tutors were to include E. M. Forster and Hugh Walpole. In 1897, they moved to Nassenheide, the family estate in Pomerania, which would be the setting for *Elizabeth and Her German Garden.*

This, her first book, was an instant best-seller and created widespread curiosity as to the identity of its anonymous author. With the exception of *Christine* (1917), which she wrote as "Alice Cholmondeley," the remainder of her books were to be signed "the Author of Elizabeth and Her German Garden" or, later, "Elizabeth." Widely criticized for its sentimentality (as some of her other works would be), *Garden* is primarily an account of A.'s love affair with her garden, but it also features the social satire that would become one of the most prominent themes in her work. Although more lighthearted than many of her subsequent books exploring the same ideas, her first novel introduces her recurring scrutiny of the ways in which women's liberty is countermanded. Even in this buoyant memoir, A. takes stabs at the outrageous chauvinism of her husband, "The Man of Wrath." A. also satirizes the German bourgeois mind and its complacently repressive expectations of women; anti-German feeling reappears in many of her later novels. In this and other early works, however, A.'s hostility toward the tyranny of marriage, motherhood, and society is still leavened by humor and optimism.

In 1899, Arnim was arrested on a false charge of embezzlement; A.'s novel *The Benefactress* (1901), based on his imprisonment, appeared in the same year in which he was acquitted. Arnim's financial situation worsened, however, and in 1908 they were forced to sell Nassenheide and move to England, while A. supported the family with her writing.

Following Arnim's death in 1910, A. embarked on a love affair with H. G. Wells. At this time she also began building the Chateau Soleil in Switzerland, where she wrote and reigned as hostess to a circle of admirers and literary figures. When war broke out in 1914, she fled to England. In the same year, she fell in love with convicted bigamist Francis, Lord Russell, whom she married in 1916. The marriage proved almost at once to be a disaster, and A. left him within a year to live in the United States; they separated formally in 1919. In 1921, she started an affair with twenty-four-year-old Alexander Frere, which inspired the bittersweet *Love* (1925), and would limp along in some degree until 1932. In 1929, A. moved to the south of France. At the outbreak of World War II, A. again left for the United Staes, where three of her children were living. Several years of deteriorating health ended with her death in 1941 at the age of seventy-five.

After Arnim's death, the tone of A.'s work became noticeably fiercer and darker, with the deliberate exception of the lighthearted *The Enchanted April* (1922); this, perhaps her most enduringly popular work, was filmed in 1992. The feminist perspective of her social criticism emerges more sharply in her later novels, particularly in *The Pastor's Wife* and *Vera,* generally considered to be her strongest works; in both, A. depicts the different forms of tyranny men exert on women. In *The Pastor's Wife,* the heroine attempts to gain control of her life from, respectively, her father, her husband, and her would-be seducer (a character based on H. G. Wells), each of whom enacts a different style of male domination. In *Vera,* the heroine marries a man who drove his eponymous first wife to suicide, and by the end of the novel the second wife faces the same fate.

Although many of her novels have been classified as romance, A.'s attitude toward marriage and motherhood in her later works is practical and unsentimental: in *The Pastor's Wife* and *Love,* she powerfully portrays the danger and physical devastation of childbearing. Passion is almost always relegated to male characters; women merely suffer the consequences of it without having, apparently, experienced any of the benefits. A.'s women are, in fact, often more passionate in regard to nature than to men. Only in her descriptions of the outdoors does A. completely abandon wit in favor of lyricism. Her great contemporary popularity as a writer was remarkable in that her commercial success did not preclude critical respect. Although her fame has been eclipsed by that of her cousin Katherine Mansfield, Hugh Walpole ranked her with Jane Austen for her deft style, and more recent critics have compared her favorably with Mansfield and Barbara Pym.

WORKS: *Elizabeth and Her German Garden* (1898). *The Solitary Summer* (1899). *The April Baby's Book of Tunes* (1900). *The Benefactress* (1901). *The Ordeal of Elizabeth* (1901). *The Pious Pilgrimage* (1901). *The Adventures of Elizabeth in Rugen* (1904). *Fraulein Schmidt and Mr. Anstruther* (1907). *The Caravaners* (1909). *The Pastor's Wife* (1914). *Christine* (1917). *Christopher and Columbus* (1919). *In the Mountains* (1920). *Vera* (1921). *The Enchanted April* (1922). *Love* (1925). *Expiation* (1929). *Father* (1931). *The Jasmine Farm* (1934). *All the Dogs of My Life* (1936). *Mr. Skeffington* (1939).

BIBLIOGRAPHY: de Charms, L. *Elizabeth of the German Garden* (1958). *The Letters of Katherine Mansfield,* ed. J. M. Murry (1945). Swinnerton, F. *Figures in the Foreground: Literary Reminiscences, 1917–1940* (1964). Usborne, K. *The Author of "Elizabeth and Her German Garden"* (1986). Wells, G. P. *H. G. Wells in Love* (1984).

For articles in reference works, see: *Europa. Feminist. Oxford. TCLC* (under "Elizabeth"). *TCRGW. Todd-BWW.*

Other references: *Book-of-the-Month Club News* (April 1940). *NYT* (10 February 1941). *Saturday Review* (19 April 1941, 10 February 1945). *TLS* (14 November 1986). *Wilson Library Bulletin* (February 1932).

Amanda DeWees

Anne Askew (Kyme)

BORN: 1521, Lincolnshire.
DIED: 16 July 1546, London.
DAUGHTER OF: Sir William Askew (Ayskough), of Kelsey, Lincolnshire.
MARRIED: Thomas Kyme.

Had A. (as she is generally known) been born fifty years after her actual date of birth, she would most probably have lived a quietly pious and uneventful life. As events did transpire, however, she fell victim to two current trends: the commonplace insensitivity of many sixteenth-century parents to their children's preferences in a marriage partner and the atmosphere of hysteria concerning deviations from the doctrines of the Henrician church.

Substituted by her callous father for her deceased older sister, who had been promised, on profitable terms, as the bride of Thomas Kyme, A. reportedly comported herself as a dutiful wife, bearing Kyme two children. However, her rejection of Roman Catholicism for Protestantism led to her husband's rejection of her and her eviction from their home. In London, where she settled herself, apparently to obtain a divorce, A. was brought up for questioning before Edmund Bonner in 1545, possibly at the instigation of her in-laws and possibly for the purpose of entrapping Katherine Parr and her sympathizers at court. She outwitted her examiners with apparent ease and was released (*The fyrst examinacyon . . .*, 1546).

Unhappily, the outcome of a second round of interrogation, detailed in *The lattre examinacyon . . .* (1547), was brutal and final. In 1546, she was rearrested, questioned twice, convicted as a heretic, and condemned to death. Heroically, she refused to recant her beliefs, even when, in her words, "my lorde Chancellor and master Ryche, toke paynes to racke me their own handes, tyll I was nygh dead." When she was burnt to death, on 16 July, she had to be brought to the stake in a chair and strapped to the stake for support because of the condition to which she had been brought. Since the torture of a gentlewoman was unheard of, as was the torture of an already condemned person, this mistreatment supports the idea that A.'s interrogators were attempting to implicate Katherine Parr and her coterie in heresy. A. was apparently caught in a net set for her superiors.

On the evidence of her *Examinacyons,* A.'s offenses seem to have arisen from her independent reading and interpretations of Scripture, which, by her own testimony, were disapproved of by the priests in her native Lincolnshire. A. left her husband, who had evicted her from their home, on the basis of 1 Cor. 7: "If a faythfull woman have an unbelevynge husbande, whych wyll not tarrye with her she may leave hym." However poignant her plight, these grounds were not accepted by the Henrician church; the annulment of the first marriage of King Henry VIII had been based on a claim of consanguinity. Finally, A. denied the doctrine of transubstantiation and the ritual of the mass. These independent positions were perceived as inherently subversive to both the political and social fabric of Henrician England. It is unlikely that they alone would have earned A. the crown of martyrdom if she had not been joined, as seems probable from both her own and Foxe's accounts, to the coterie of reformist women surrounding Katherine Parr, Henry's sixth and surviving queen.

After A.'s death, John Bale, the Bishop of Ossory, printed the records that she had composed of her examinations. Included with the second examination were a letter composed during her imprisonment, a confession of her faith, and a vivid ballad attacking the injustice and hypocrisy of her tormentors and affirming her beliefs ("The Balade whych Anne Askewe Made and Sange Whan She Was in Newgate"). These verses illustrate A.'s courage and independence, as the following excerpt demonstrates: "Fayth is that weapon strong / Whych wyll not fayle at nede / My foes therfor amonge / Therwith wyll I procede. // . . . Faythe in the fathers olde / Obtayned ryghtooysnesse / Whych makes me verye bolde / To feare no worldes distresse."

WORKS: *The fyrst examinacyon of Anne Askewe, lately martyred in Smythefelde, by the Romysh popes upholders, with the Elucydacyon of Johan Bale* (1546). *The lattre examinacyon of Anne Askewe, lately martyred in Smythfelde, by the wycked Synagogue of Antichrist, with the Elucydacyon of Johan Bale* (1547). Foxe, J. *Actes and monuments* . . . (1563; a major source of information about A.). *Writings of Edward VI, William Hugh, Queen Katherine Parr, Anne Askew, Lady Jane Grey, Hamilton and Balnaves* (1842). *Select Works of John Bale . . . and Anne Askewe* . . ., ed. H. Christmas (1849). *Anne Askew, The Examinations*, ed. E. Beilin (1996). *Anne Askew*, ed. J. N. King (1996).

BIBLIOGRAPHY: Bainton, R. H. *Women of the Reformation in France and England* (1973). Beilin, E., in *Silent but for the Word* . . ., ed. M. P. Hannay (1985). Beilin, E. *Redeeming Eve: Women Writers of the English Renaissance* (1987). Beilin, E., in *Contending Kingdoms* . . ., ed. M. L. Logan and P. L. Rudnytsky (1991). Hays, M. *Female Biography, or, Memoirs of Illustrious and Celebrated Women, of all Ages and Countries* (1803). Hogrefe, P. *Tudor Women: Commoners and Queens* (1975). King, J. N. *English Reformation Literature* . . . (1982). Levin, C. *International Journal of Women's Studies* (1980). McQuade, P. *L&H* (1994). Smith, L. B. *Henry VIII: The Mask of Royalty* (1971). Travitsky, B., ed. *Paradise of Women: Writings by Englishwomen of the Renaissance* (1981). Warnicke, R. M. *Women of the English Renaissance and Reformation* (1983). Webb, M. L. *The Fells of Swarthmoor Hall and their Friends: With an Account of Their Ancestor Anne Askewe, the Martyr: A Portraiture of Religious and Family Life in the 17th Century* (1865). Williams, J. *Literary Women of England* . . . (1861). Wilson, D. *Tudor Tapestry: Men, Women and Society in Reformation England* (1972).

For articles in reference works, see *Ballard. Bloomsbury. DNB. Europa. Feminist. IDWB. Oxford. ToddBWW.*

Betty Travitsky

Cynthia Asquith

BORN: 27 September 1887, Clouds, Wiltshire.
DIED: 31 March 1960, Oxford.
DAUGHTER OF: Hugo Charteris, Earl of Wemyss, and Mary Wyndham.
MARRIED: Herbert Asquith, 1910.

A. was a well-known anthologist of books for children and adults; she also wrote two novels, some short stories, a play, and several biographies. But she is best known today for the diaries she kept during World War I, which were published nine years after her death.

She was born into the aristocracy, with a distinguished ancestry that, according to one tradition, included Madame de Genlis. Her father, Lord Hugo Charteris, became Earl of Wemyss on his father's death; her mother, Mary Wyndham, came from an equally distinguished family. Marital infidelity among the upper class was common, and A. later in life had a lingering suspicion that she was, in fact, the daughter of Arthur James Balfour, who was for a time her mother's lover; her younger sister, Mary, was, in fact, the daughter of Wilfrid Scawen Blunt. A. was born at one of the family estates, Clouds, in Wiltshire, though most of her childhood was passed at Stanway, in Gloucestershire. She was educated primarily at home; one governess in particular, Charlotte Jourdain, influenced her greatly by instilling a respect for intellectual accomplishment. In accordance with the system of her class and time, a girl's education was not as rigorous as a boy's, but A. sought out greater challenges; she convinced her mother to allow her to have lessons in Greek, for example, though she had to agree to keep them a secret.

In 1903–04, she was sent to Dresden for "finishing," and there she met Herbert (Beb) Asquith; following a secret three-year engagement, they were married in 1910. Asquith's father was made prime minister in 1908, but the Asquiths were neither aristocratic nor particularly wealthy, and the young couple had to make do, by A.'s standards, with very little money; her social circle, however, did not change. They leased a house near Regent's Park, London, but when her husband entered the army the place had to be sublet, and A. began a long period of moving from one home to another—a practice she called cuckooing. When her grandfather died in 1914, she became Lady Cynthia Asquith, though the title brought with it no property. She visited the front in France in 1914 and saw first-hand the overcrowded hospitals full of wounded soldiers. Beb Asquith came home suffering from shell-shock, his ability to earn a living from the law severely impaired.

A.'s published diaries of 1915–18 are compelling reading, providing an inside picture of the lives of the aristocracy during the war. The leisured life of shopping and long visits to great houses is punctuated constantly by the news of the deaths of most of the young men she had known growing up, including two of her brothers, news that created a dazed sense of unreality among those on the home front. "Soon one will hardly remember who is alive and who is dead," she wrote in 1915. The diaries also provide insight into her own complex character; some readers have seen in them evidence of vanity and a triviality of mind, but writing in the diary was clearly a means for her to maintain some sense of normality amid the catastrophe of the war, and some of the comments about clothes, hairstyles, and mirror-gazing need to be read in that light. The diary entries are witty, often incisive, and often brilliantly expressed.

Her first son, John, was born in 1911, followed by Michael in 1914 and Simon in 1919. John developed from a somewhat unruly child into one with a severe behavioral problem and eventually became what would probably be diagnosed as autistic. Most references to John were expunged from the diaries as a subject too painful to confront, and in fact A. destroyed a separate diary she kept concerning him; he spent most of his life in institutions, dying in 1937.

In 1913, A. met D. H. Lawrence, who was intrigued by her. He wrote her long letters advising her on subjects from how to treat her son to how to live her life. His image of her was only a partial one, but he used it in a number of stories, including "The Thimble," "The Blind Man," and "The Ladybird"; the character of Lady Chatterley is modeled on her—though this was an identification she was eager to refute. She was not sexually active like Lady Chatterley or even like the members of her parents' generation, though she attracted a number of male admirers who proclaimed their love for her, including Charles Whibley, Harold Baker, and Desmond MacCarthy.

In 1918 she took a job as secretary to J. M. Barrie, who was one of the most important figures in her life until his death in 1937. Her secretarial role expanded until she was something of a mother, lover, nurse, and best friend to Barrie. At his death he left her £30, 000, which finally allowed her to enjoy financial security. She had turned to writing and editing shortly after the war, producing a number of anthologies for children and adults that enjoyed good sales; her many connections allowed her to call on some of the best writers to contribute work, as with Lawrence's "The Rocking-Horse Winner." She also produced a series of biographical books on the royal family, some for children and some for adults, that contributed to her reputation.

She published her first novel, *The Spring House,* in 1936; Barrie read and commented on the manuscript for her. While a competent and readable novel, its chief interest is in the light it sheds on the author. Its heroine, Miranda, from a social class much like the one in which A. grew up, struggles with her own vanity. The plots of both *The Spring House* and her next novel, *One Sparkling Wave* (1943), turn upon questions of illegitimate birth as major characters eventually learn their parents were not who they had believed them to be.

A.'s newfound financial independence allowed her and her husband to move out of the city and take a house in Sullington in rural Sussex from 1939 to 1946; here she enjoyed the company of old friends such as Viola Meynell, Enid Bagnold, and Gladys Huntington. After Beb died in 1947, she moved back to London. Barrie's nephew, James Barrie, approached her about writing her memoirs for his publishing house, and she produced *Haply I May Remember* in 1950 and *Remember and Be Glad* in 1952, both extremely valuable depictions of her life and times. She had become fascinated by the Countess Tolstoy, writing a play about her in the 1940s, and when A. died from meningitis in 1960 she had just completed a full-length biography, *Married to Tolstoy.*

A.'s significance as a writer may be small, but her diaries and memoirs leave us a rich portrait of a fascinating personality whose complexities and contradictions seem somehow very significant, somehow representative of her entire class. She had this effect on many during her lifetime, for she and her family figure not only in Lawrence's work but in that of Enid Bagnold, Angela Thirkell, and L. P. Hartley; her biographer argues that she is the model also for Virginia Woolf's Clarissa Dalloway.

WORKS: *The Child at Home* (1923). *Martin's Adventure* (1925). *The Ghost Book* (1926). *The Duchess of York* (1928). *The Married Life of the Duchess of York* (1933). *God Save the King* (1935). *The Spring House* (1936). *The King's Daughters* (1936). *The Family Life of Queen Elizabeth* (1936). *Queen Elizabeth: Her Intimate and Authentic Life* (1937). *One Sparkling Wave* (1943). *No Heaven for Me* (play, written 1943, produced 1946). *The Cynthia Asquith Book* (1948). *Haply I May Remember* (1950). *Remember and Be Glad* (1952). *Portrait of Barrie* (1954). *Married to Tolstoy* (1961). *Thomas Hardy at Max Gate* (BBC broadcast of 1956; published 1969). *Lady Cynthia Asquith: Diaries, 1915–1918,* ed. E. M. Horsley (1969).

BIBLIOGRAPHY: Beauman, N. *Cynthia Asquith* (1987).

For articles in reference works, see *Feminist. Longman.*

Other references: *ESC* (1983). *SSF* (1983). *TSWL* (1987).

Raymond N. MacKenzie

Emma Alice Margaret Tennant Asquith

BORN: 2 February 1864, Peeblesshire, Scotland.
DIED: 28 July 1945, London.
DAUGHTER OF: Charles Tennant and Emma Tennant.
MARRIED: Herbert Henry Asquith, 1894.
WROTE UNDER: Margot Asquith.

Vivacious, outspoken, and original, A. grew up in the Scottish countryside in a prosperous, lively family. As a child she developed a love of the natural world and cultivated her considerable talents as a rider to hounds. A. was taught by governesses, briefly attended finishing school, and completed her studies in Dresden, Germany.

Throughout her life, A. read widely and earnestly, although unsystematically. Her views on literature, like her opinions of her contemporaries, were characteristically pronounced, intelligent, and individual. In the 1880s, she became a leading member of the "Souls," a coterie that welcomed Liberals and Conservatives alike and occupied its time in fervent discussions of books, energetic recitations of poetry, and witty pencil games. In 1894, A. married H. H. Asquith (later Earl of Oxford and Asquith), who was to hold office as Liberal Prime Minister from 1908 to 1916. A. had a zealous interest in the political scene and in large part helped to promote her husband's career, although polite society frequently considered her behavior shocking, and not everyone found her candor charming.

A.'s distinction as an author rests on the claims of her *Autobiography* (1920). Although she wrote of herself that "my only literary asset is natural directness," the book at its best offers well-dramatized depictions of such events as her sister Laura's death, A.'s tempestuous early love affair with Peter Flower, and her prison visit to a female abortionist. In addition, it contains vivid portraits of notable acquaintances like Alfred Lord Tennyson and Benjamin Jowett and, overall, it paints an attractive picture of late Victorian and Edwardian high life undisturbed by too deep a concern for the social inequities and disruptions of the times. The virtues of A.'s work include an engaging, epigrammatic style and sensitive assessments of human nature; the *Autobiography* is least successful and most self-serving in its recurrent, unabashed quotations of letters and poems on the subject of A. herself.

Many readers disapproved of the *Autobiography's* frank descriptions of leading social figures and hitherto taboo subjects such as childbirth pains, but this did not prevent A. from writing *More Memories* (1933) and *Off the Record* (1943), further memoirs. She also completed *Places and Persons* (1925), an account of her travels; *Lay Sermons* (1927), a book of essays; and *Octavia* (1928), a novel of politics and hunting.

Although perhaps more memorable as a personality than as an author, A. displayed, in her writing, both verve and insight. Her *Autobiography* offers an entertaining if too complacent view of a vanished world.

WORKS: *A Little Journey in the Winter of 1897; and A Week in Glasgow, July 1892* (1892). *Margot Asquith: An Autobiography* (1920; abridged ed., ed. M. Bonham Carter, 1995). *Places and Persons* (1925). *Lay Sermons* (1927). *Octavia* (1928). *More Memories* (1933). *More or Less About Myself* (1934). *Off the Record* (1943).

BIBLIOGRAPHY: Bennett, D. *Margot: A Life of the Countess of Oxford and Asquith* (1984). *DNB*.

Other references: Cowles, V. *Edward VII and His Circle* (1956). Jenkins, R. *Asquith: Portrait of a Man and an Era* (1964). Leslie, A. *Edwardians in Love* (1972). *LonT* (30 July 1945).

Anne B. Simpson
(updated by Natalie Joy Woodall)

Mary Astell

BORN: 12 November 1666, Newcastle-on-Tyne, Northumberland.
DIED: 9 May 1731, Chelsea, London.
DAUGHTER OF: Peter Astell and Mary Errington Astell.
WROTE UNDER: Author of *The Proposal to the Ladies.*

An ardent feminist, A. wrote prodigiously concerning the education of women, religion, and politics. She was the daughter of a provincial middle-class family that was loyal to the Church of England and the monarch. Though A. was not formally educated, she did read widely on her own, and she knew a little French. A clergyman uncle may have taught her Latin, but her knowledge of it, along with Greek and Hebrew, was certainly not extensive, a fact of which she was painfully aware. She says in *The Christian Religion as Professed by a Daughter of the Church of England* (1705): "My ignorance in the sacred languages, besides all other disadvantages makes me incapable of expounding scripture with the learned."

Two years after her mother's death in 1684, A., aged twenty, went to Chelsea. Once there, she held court as the central focus of a group of progressive upper-class women, naturally assuming the role of teacher. Her friends included Lady Catherine Jones (to whom she dedicated some of her works), Lady Elizabeth Hastings, and, most famous of all, Lady Mary Wortley Montagu. A. carried on a lengthy correspondence with Hastings, but unfortunately all manuscripts were destroyed by Lady Elizabeth prior to her death. To A., Montagu was an exemplar of the brilliant woman envisioned in her writings, but this did not prevent A. from exhorting her to reject the vanities of upper-class life and attempting to persuade her of the truth of the immortality of the soul.

A.'s distinguished and often tempestuous career in controversial writing began in 1694 with the publication of *A Serious Proposal to the Ladies.* This work advanced the idea that a "monastery" or "religious retirement" should be established for women. In this sequestered institution, they would receive a program of religious and secular training, with the heaviest emphasis on religious study, because A. felt that religion was the primary aim of life. But A. also felt that women could fulfill their duty to God only by developing their full intellectual potential; therefore, secular training was crucial. In contrast to most of her contemporaries, who believed a woman's religious duty was always to obey her husband, being only a mere adjunct to him, A. believed that God intended women to develop their highest potential. They could not achieve this goal by remaining extensions of men. Through knowledge, women could also benefit society. Indeed, it was their express obligation to do so. A. felt strongly that the conventional upbringing of women served only to blunt their minds and make them dull company for themselves and others. In *A Serious Proposal to the Ladies: Part II* (1697), A. elaborated on her arguments in the first part.

The publication of *A Serious Proposal to the Ladies* provoked immediate attention, some of it favorable. Daniel Defoe approved of the program set forth by A. for her institution, but he had one reservation. He suggested that the emphasis should favor secular rather than religious training, thereby avoiding a dangerous resemblance to a Roman Catholic convent. A. also attracted the response of John Evelyn, who included her in his *Numismata* among women he felt should be known to fame. Unfortunately, most of A.'s contemporaries believed that she was advocating a return to Roman Catholicism; her "monastery" reminded them far too much of popery. Even feminist sympathizers, like Defoe, felt that the needs of women could not justify the establishment of such an institution; hence public support for A.'s ideas was not forthcoming.

In *Letters Concerning the Love of God* (1695), "by the author of the Proposal to the Ladies," A. set forth her position that mankind could best achieve an understanding of God through love. Though study and speculation have some relevance, we can only truly understand God through love, and when we love God, then we love one another. It is no wonder that A. vehemently rejected Deism, which injected too much reason into the understanding of God and asserted that He was indifferent to the affairs of humanity.

With the publication of *Some Reflections upon Marriage, Occasioned by the Duke and Duchess of Mazarine's Case* (1700), A. turned back to the subject of women. The acidity of A.'s tone might cause some to conclude that she was against marriage in general. A. was only against unwise marriage, and this she defined as obedience without love: "And if a woman can neither love nor honour, she does ill in promising to obey, since she is like to have a crooked rule to regulate her actions. A mere obedience, such as is paid only to authority, and not out of love and a sense of the justice and reasonableness of the command, will be of uncertain tenure." Again, unlike most of her contemporaries, A. was aware of the unhappy consequences of unwise marriage and the fact that women had no hope of remedying such a situation: "If therefore it be a woman's hard fate to meet with a disagreeable temper, and of all others the haughty, imperious, and self-conceited are the most so, she is as unhappy as anything in this world can make her. For when a wife's temper does not please, if she makes her husband uneasy, he can find entertainments abroad; he has a hundred ways of relieving himself, but neither prudence nor duty will allow a woman to fly out: her business and entertainment are at home; and though he makes it ever so uneasy to her, she must be content and make her best on't." A. realized it was virtually impossible for women to escape their tenuous position in society, for "what poor woman is ever taught that she should have a higher design than to get her a husband?"

With the publication of *Moderation Truly Stated, A Fair Way with the Dissenters, and Their Patrons,* and *An Impartial Enquiry into the Causes of Rebellion and Civil War in This Kingdom* (all 1704), A. became embroiled in political controversy. In these works, the loyalty to church and state that she was brought up with is evident. In *Moderation Truly Stated,* A. strongly contends that the true statesman must maintain loyalty to his monarch and not oppress his fellow subjects. He must be vigilant in the suppression of vice while encouraging "true religion." A. unequivocally states in *An Impartial Enquiry* . . . that those who dare to rebel turn "religion into rebellion" and "faith into faction." A king could only succumb to tyranny if he was seduced into it by ambitious courtiers, so A. effectively removed all blame for oppression from the monarch. In *A Fair Way with the Dissenters, and Their Patrons,* she forcefully attacked Defoe.

The Christian Religion as Professed by a Daughter of the Church of England summarized A.'s religious and educational theories (1705), and she continued her political involvement by opposing Shaftesbury in *Bart'lemy Fair or an Enquiry After Wit* (1709). From that date, A. was also involved in writing new prefaces to her works. She remained active in polemics by writing a letter to Henry Dodwell concerning the nonjuror debate and helped Dr. John Walker collect material for his work, *The Sufferings of the Clergy.* During this time, A. led a contemplative life and enjoyed religious meditation, but she was not the severe recluse tradition would have us believe. At the end of her life, A. very much wanted to establish the "monastery" for women made famous in *A Serious Proposal to the Ladies,* but since there was no public support for this, she instead formulated a plan for a charity school for the girls of Chelsea. Though Bishop Burnet dissuaded a prominent lady from donating £10,000 to the school, A. at least had the satisfaction of realizing that her plans would be carried out. The charity school was established in 1729, two years before A.'s death, by her old friends Lady Catherine Jones, Lady Elizabeth Hastings, Lady Ann Coventry, and others. Because of A.'s strong beliefs, which never wavered throughout her life, she experienced the isolation that the pioneer inevitably suffers, but it was precisely through her radical views that her readers could come to a better understanding of the social and educational problems facing women. Today, when the religious and political controversies of the eighteenth century have lost their potency, A. is mainly remembered for *A Serious Proposal to the Ladies* and *Some Reflections upon Marriage, Occasioned by the Duke and Duchess of Mazarine's Case.* It would be a mistake, however, to discount or separate religion from the corpus of her work, for religion was for A. the paramount direction of her life.

WORKS: *A Serious Proposal to the Ladies for the Advancement of Their True and Greatest Interest* (1694). *Letters Concerning the Love of God* (1695). *A Serious Proposal to the Ladies: Part II* (1697). *Some Reflections upon Marriage, Occasioned by the Duke and Duchess of Mazarine's Case* (1700). *Moderation Truly Stated* (1704). *A Fair Way with the Dissenters and Their Patrons* (1704). *An Impartial Enquiry into the Causes of Rebellion and Civil War in This Kingdom* (1704). *The Christian Religion as Professed by a Daughter of the Church of England* (1705). *Bart'lemy Fair or an Enquiry After Wit* (1709). *The First English Feminist: "Reflections on Marriage" and Other Writings,* ed. B. Hill (1986). *Astell: Political Writings,* ed. P. Springborg (1996). *A Serious Proposal to the Ladies,* ed. P. Springborg (1997).

BIBLIOGRAPHY: Perry, R. *The Celebrated Mary Astell: An Early English Feminist* (1986). Perry, R., in *Women and the Enlightenment,* ed. M. Hunt, et al. (1984). Rogers, K. M. *Before Their Time: Six Women Writers of the Eighteenth Century* (1979). Smith, F. M. *Mary Astell* (1916). Wallace, A. *Before the Bluestockings* (1929).

For articles in reference works, see: *Chalmers. DNB.*

Other references: Barash, C., in *Women, Writing, History: 1640–1799,* ed. I. Grundy and S. Wiseman (1992). Gallagher, C. *Genders* (1988). Perry, R., in *Sexuality in Eighteenth-Century Britain,* ed. P. G. Bouce (1982). Perry, R. *TLS* (20 August 1982). Rex, M., in

Proceedings of the Third Dakota Conference on Earlier British Literature (1995). Rudnik-Smalbraak, M., in *Between Dream and Nature: Essays on Utopia and Dystopia*, ed. D. Baker-Smith and C. C. Barfoot (1987). Schnorrenberg, B. *WS* (1982). Sharrock, C., in *Women, Writing, History: 1640–1799,* ed. I. Grundy and S. Wiseman (1992). Smith, H. L., in *Man, God, and Nature in the Enlightenment,* ed. D. C. Mell, Jr., T. E. D. Braun, and L. M. Palmer (1988). Thickstun, M. O. *SECC* (1991).

Anne Prescott

Astrea: See *Behn, Aphra*

Penelope Aubin

BORN: 1679, London.
DIED: 1731.

Known for the moral rehabilitation of the amatory fictions popularized by Eliza Haywood, A. produced poems, novels, plays, and translations, in all about three thousand pages of work between 1721 and 1729. Little is known about her life. Born in London, probably to an emigré French officer, she may have been Roman Catholic, although a 1729 reference to her career as an orator and lay preacher near Charing Cross suggests a more complex religious status. The death of her husband (whose name is unknown) sometime prior to 1722 and her friendship with Elizabeth Rowe may have prompted her to begin writing professionally.

Although she translated works such as *The History of Genghizcan the Great* (1722) from the French, and she wrote two odes to Queen Anne in 1707 and 1708, most of her publications have been categorized as "pious polemics," "religious romances," and, perhaps most accurately, "moral adventures." Her prefaces reveal a self-conscious combination of conventions drawn from the two best-selling novels of her day: Daniel Defoe's *Robinson Crusoe* and Haywood's *Love in Excess.* Unlike Haywood, however, she made morality rather than passion sell, altering the stereotypical characters of amatory fiction by attributing to them vigorously defended senses of honor. Such an advance in fictional technique led one eighteenth-century reader to praise the absence of anything in A.'s work with "the least tendency to pollute or corrupt." Her moral messages were made more palatable by association with what her booksellers called the "greatest variety of events that ever was publish'd, " events like broken legs, storms, cannibalism, kidnappings, the appearance of wild animals, and rampant piracy.

In her first fiction, *The Life of Madame De Beaumount* (1721), she emphasizes morality over calamity, suggesting that its "extraordinary" features lie in the heroine's virtue rather than in surprising adventures. Like most of A.'s works, though, *Madame De Beaumount* revels in odd events, including a shipwreck, a long-lost husband, and a fourteen-year stint of hermit-like seclusion in a cave in Wales. As is typical of her fiction, the story begins rather than ends with marriage, and the heroine's travails occur during an enforced separation from her husband.

Similarly, *The Noble Slaves* (1722) combines characteristics of amatory romance with a Defoe-like travel narrative, yet emphasizes moral rectitude throughout. Advocating against absolute monarchy and in favor of British liberty in the preface, A. submits that the enslaved lords and ladies of the title survive slavery, sickness, and bad seas because of their trust in God. The entertainment value of the novel lies in A.'s tendency to romp carelessly over an international geography; here one character easily roams from Canada to Peru to Japan to the coast of Mexico.

A.'s most integrated work, *The Life and Adventures of Lady Lucy* (1726), relies less on exotic settings and more on the workings out of the heroine's moral dilemmas. While demonstrating the consequences of irrational jealousy, the work also grapples with the heroine's inability to make public her interior life and suggests the tragic consequences of such a failure of communication.

Apparently neither morality nor exoticism was appropriate for the stage. A.'s one play, *The Merry Masqueraders: or, the Humourous Cuckold* (1733), a comedy in five acts modeled after Farquhar's *The Beaux' Stratagem,* failed quickly despite the author's delivery of an epilogue on the second night.

A.'s works, republished in a posthumous edition in 1739, remained popular after her death. In the introduction to the collected works, possibly written by Samuel Richardson, she was praised for delineating five essentials for good fiction: probability, purity of style and manners, universal benevolence, punishment of guilt, and reward for virtue.

WORKS: (trans.) *The Illustrious French Lover,* by Robert Challes (1720). *The Life of Madame De Beaumount, A French Lady* (1721). *The Strange Adventures of the Count De Vinevil and His Family* (1721). *The Life and Amorous Adventures of Lucinda, An English Lady* (1722). *The Noble Slaves* (1722). (trans.) *The History of Genghizcan the Great,* by Petis de la Croix (1722). (trans.) *The Life of the Countess de Gondez,* by Mme. de Beaucour (1722). (trans.) *The Life of the Prince of Clermont and Madam de Ravezan,* by Mme. de Beaucour (1722). *The Life of Charlotte du Pont, an English Lady* (1723). *The Life and Adventures of Lady Lucy* (1726). *The Life and Adventures of the Young Count Albertus* (1728). *The Merry Masqueraders: or, the Humourous Cuckold* (prod. 1730, pub. 1733). *A Collection of Entertaining Histories and Novels* (1739).

BIBLIOGRAPHY: Beasley, J. C., in *Fetter'd or Free? British Women Novelists, 1670–1815,* ed. M. A. Schofield and C. Macheski (1986). Dooley, B. *Penelope Aubin: Forgotten Catholic Novelist* (1959). London, A., in *Fetter'd or Free? British Women Novelists, 1670–1815,* ed. M. A. Schofield and C. Macheski (1986). McBurney, W. *HLQ* (1957). McBurney, W. H. *Mrs. Penelope Aubin and the Early Eighteenth-Century English Novel* (1957). McDermott, H. *Novel and Romance: The Odyssey to Tom Jones* (1989). Richetti, J. *Popular Fiction Before Richardson* (1969). Shugrue, M. F. *The Sincerest Form of Flattery: Imitation in the Early*

Eighteenth-Century Novel (1971). Spencer, J. *The Rise of the Woman Novelist* (1986). Turner, C. *Living By the Pen* (1992).

For articles in reference works, see: *Feminist. Oxford. ToddBWW. ToddDBA.*

Kathryn D. Temple

Aunt Belinda: See *Braddon (Maxwell), Mary Elizabeth*

Jane Austen

BORN: 16 December 1775, Steventon, Hampshire.
DIED: 18 July 1817, Winchester, Hampshire.
DAUGHTER OF: the Reverend George Austen and Cassandra Leigh Austen.

A "small square two inches of ivory" is the way A. once described her own work. Yet this same work, apparently being lightly dismissed, is among the most enduring and most popular literature of the nineteenth century. Categorized as novels of manners, the careful detail given to both setting and character in A.'s works has captivated readers for more than a century.

Born in 1775, A. was the seventh of eight children born to the rector of Steventon, Hampshire. A. began writing at about age eleven. Her notebooks containing "novels, " chiefly parodies of eighteenth-century sentimental novels, were passed around her family for their entertainment. A. and her family were, as she said, "great Novel-readers and not ashamed of being so."

A.'s writing and publishing history is somewhat confusing. Her writing falls into two groups of three novels with a "silent" decade between, yet her publishing history does not reflect this division. The following chronology shows the dates of composition, revision, and publication of A.'s novels: c. 1790–93: *Love and Freindship* [sic]; *Volume the First;* juvenilia. Before 1796: *Elinor and Marianne* (not extant); recast, 1797–99, as *Sense and Sensibility;* further revision, 1809–10; published 1811. 1792–96 (?): *Lady Susan;* survives in a fair copy of c. 1805 or later; first published in *Memoir* (Austen-Leigh) 2nd ed., 1871. 1796–97: *First Impressions* (not extant); rewritten, c. 1812, as *Pride and Prejudice* published 1813. 1797–98: *Susan* (not extant); recast and much expanded as *Northanger Abbey,* 1805; posthumously published 1818. 1803: *The Watsons* (a fragment); first published in *Memoir* (Austen-Leigh), 1871. 1811–13: *Mansfield Park;* published 1814. 1814–15: *Emma;* published late 1815 or, more probably, early 1816. 1815–16: *Persuasion;* published posthumously 1818. 1817: *Sanditon* (a fragment, given title by Austen family); first published, from manuscript, in 1925.

Many scholars believe that A.'s silent period was caused by discouragement after *First Impressions* was rejected unread and *Northanger Abbey* was picked up by a publisher in 1803 for a pittance but never issued, after which A. bought back the manuscript in 1816. Although she probably made some minor revisions, *Northanger Abbey* appears to be the earliest example of A.'s work. It is, however, a mistake to differentiate too sharply between the novels of the two periods, for the three of the first group were being revised while A. was writing the three of the second group. The most obvious influence occurs in the change of genre in *Sense and Sensibility* and *Pride and Prejudice;* in their original forms, *Elinor and Marianne* and *First Impressions* were both epistolary novels, a technique A. dropped in revision and never again employed.

According to A., "three or four Families in a Country Village is [the] very thing to work upon." She concentrated on a limited part of English society, provincial gentry and the aligning of the rural upper-middle class with the aristocracy. A. wrote about that with which she was familiar; when her niece sought her advice about a novel, A. advised her to "stick to Bath" where she was "quite at home."

A. herself resisted the temptation to stray from familiar ground, even when nudged by royalty. When the domestic chaplain to the Prince of Wales suggested that in her next novel she might delineate the character of a clergyman, A. realized that the hints he supplied were based on his own experiences. A. replied, somewhat mischievously, that she might be able to do "the comic parts of the characters" but "not the good, the enthusiastic, the literary."

Such an answer, with its somewhat stinging implications, was typical of A. Her satirical treatment of social standards and literary expectations in her novels and her acidic comments in her letters have earned A. a reputation for a sharp tongue. After A.'s death in 1817, her sister, Cassandra, burned many of A.'s letters, implying to some critics that the worst, the sharpest, of the letters were destroyed. But it is more likely that the more personal letters, the ones most likely to show the gentler side, were destroyed to protect A.'s privacy even after death. For it is important to realize how fiercely A. and her family guarded her privacy. All her novels were published anonymously and their authorship was a well-kept secret.

Nevertheless, much of A.'s personality, tastes, and interests can be discerned through her novels. In *Northanger Abbey,* for example, A. satirizes gothic romantic mysteries (Radcliffe's *Mysteries of Udolpho* in particular) and presents what was to become a recurrent theme: feminine self-delusion. A. picks up the latter theme again in *Sense and Sensibility* and *Pride and Prejudice* but demonstrates its pitfalls by contrasting the actions and reactions of two sisters. In *Sense and Sensibility,* the two sisters, Elinor and Marianne Dashwood, represent "sense" and "sensibility," respectively. Each is deserted by the young man from whom she has been led to expect a matrimonial offer. Reacting with sense, Elinor eventually untangles the complications surrounding her lover and they become engaged; Marianne, on the other hand, reacts with sensibility and impetuosity. She gradually comes to realize the foolishness of her love and see her real affection for another, a quieter and more serious lover. In *Pride and Prejudice,* the contrast between sisters is more subtle and further complicated by a parallel male pairing, Bingley and Darcy. One of the most popular of Austen's novels, *Pride and Prejudice* introduces many of the stylistic devices commonly associated with A.'s work: witty, cutting dialogue between couples; strong-willed heroines without a strong role model (her mother is either weak and ineffectual or dead); settings that reveal the underlying character of the male protagonist (in this instance, Pemberley); and an ironic undertone, often established in the opening lines of the novel ("It is a truth universally acknowledged that a single man in possession of a good fortune must be in want of a wife").

Mansfield Park marks a slight diversion from the pattern established in A.'s earlier novels, for here the heroine is an orphan adopted into her rich uncle's family. Despite being condescendingly treated as a poor relation, Fanny's honesty and modest disposition gradually make her an indispensable part of the household, particularly when her uncle is away on business for an extended period and the family's sense of discipline is relaxed. In this novel it is the male characters, particularly Edmund Bertram and Henry Crawford, who represent contrasting personalities, and it is Edmund who is self-deluded and eventually comes to see Fanny's virtues. To many critics *Mansfield Park* is one of A.'s lesser novels, perhaps because of her reversal of her usual male and female portrayals, a reversal she did not repeat.

In contrast, the novels that followed—*Emma* and *Persuasion*—are considered by many to be her best works. The heroine in *Emma* is again virtually alone in the world: her mother is dead, her father is absent-minded and ineffectual, and her governess-companion has left to be married. But unlike Fanny in *Mansfield Park,* Emma is not especially wise. In this novel A. again deals with the theme of feminine self-delusion, but the focus on a single, strong-willed character makes the impact stronger than in previous works. In *Persuasion,* A. returns to the contrasting of sisters but focuses primarily on the second of three (Anne Elliot). Anne is pretty, intelligent, amiable, but also malleable. She is persuaded by a trusted friend, Lady Russell, to break off a long-standing engagement despite her feelings for her lover. During the resulting confusion both lovers become entangled in other relationships but eventually realize that their affection for each other still exists. In this, A.'s last complete work, the satire and ridicule take a milder form, the tone is graver and tenderer, the interest lies in a more subtle interplay of characters. A. herself apparently recognized the difference in tone, for she wrote of Anne: "She is almost too good for me."

Although well received, A. was not immediately successful; few of her works reached a second edition during her lifetime. In fact, the collected edition of 1833 supplied the market until 1882. Attention began to increase during the 1890s as indicated by the appearance of biographies and critical pieces. Today, almost 175 years later, all of her books are in print and A. is one of the top-selling authors. Because one of the strongest elements in A.'s work is characterization, modern readers can still identify with her subtle rendering of recognizable emotional states and human relationships. Yet because much of her work depends on character analysis, many readers still identify with much of her work. Others are captivated by her style, her careful construction and use of the dramatic method where characters are introduced through dialogue before putting in an appearance. To some she is one of the greatest ironists who ever lived. And to most she is a challenge. As A. herself put it, "I do not write for dull elves who cannot think for themselves."

WORKS: *Sense and Sensibility* (1811). *Pride and Prejudice* (1813). *Mansfield Park* (1814). *Emma* (1815). *Northanger Abbey* (1818). *Persuasion* (1818). *Lady Susan* (1871). *The Watsons* (1871). Austen-Leigh, W. and R. A. Austen-Leigh, *Jane Austen: Her Life and Letters, a Family Record* (1913). *The Novels of Jane Austen,* ed. R. W. Chapman (1923). *Sanditon* (1925). *The Letters of Jane Austen,* ed. R. W. Chapman (1923). *Minor Works,* ed. R. W. Chapman (1954). *Letters 1796–1817,* ed. R. W. Chapman (1955). *Love and Freindship [sic], and Other Early Works,* ed. G. K. Chesterton (1922). *Letters,* ed. O. Le Faye (1995, 1997). *My Dear Cassandra,* ed. P. Hughes-Hallett (1990). *Collected Poems of the Austen Family,* ed. D. Selwyn (1996).

BIBLIOGRAPHY: Austen-Leigh, J. E. *A Memoir of Jane Austen* (1871). Babb, H. S. *Jane Austen's Novels: The Fabric of Dialogue* (1962). Butler, M. *Jane Austen and the War of Ideas* (1975). Burrows, J. F. *Computation into Criticism: A Study of Jane Austen's Novels and An Experiment in Method* (1987). Cecil, D. *Jane Austen* (1935). Cecil, D. *A Portrait of Jane Austen* (1978). Chapman, R. W. *Jane Austen, Facts and Problems* (1948). Chapman, R. W. *Jane Austen: A Critical Biography* (1953). *Cambridge Companion to Jane Austen,* ed. E. Copeland and J. McMaster (1997). Craik, W. A. *Jane Austen: The Six Novels* (1965). Duckworth, A. M. *The Improvement of the Estate: A Study of Jane Austen: Novels* (1994). Evans, M. *Jane Austen and the State* (1987). Fergus, J. *Jane Austen: A Literary Life* (1991). Firkins, D. W. *Jane Austen* (1920). Gilson, D. *A Bibliography of Jane Austen* (1982, 1997). Halperin, J. *The Life of Jane Austen* (1984). Honan, P. *Jane Austen: Her Life* (1987; 1997). Jenkins, E. *Jane Austen* (1949). Johnson, C. *Jane Austen and Politics* (1989). Kaplan, O. *Jane Austen Among Women* (1994). Lascelles, M. *Jane Austen and Her Art* (1939). Liddell, R. *The Novels of Jane Austen* (1963). Litz, A. W. *Jane Austen: A Study of Her Artistic Development* (1965). *Jane Austen and Discourses of Feminism,* ed. D. Looser (1995). McMaster, J. *Jane Austen The Novelist* (1995). Mudrick, M. *Jane Austen: Irony as Defense and Discovery* (1952). Myer, V. G. *Obstinate Heart: Jane Austen, A Biography* (1997). Nicolson, N. *The World of Jane Austen* (1997). Nokes, D. *Jane Austen* (1997). Roth, B. *An Annotated Bibliography of Jane Austen Studies 1984–94* (1996). Selwyn, D. *The Austen Family* (1997). Sourham, B. C. *Jane Austen's Literary Manuscripts* (1964). *Jane Austen: The Critical Heritage,* ed. B. C. Sourham (1968). Sulloway, A. *Jane Austen and the Province of Women* (1989). Tanner, T. *Jane Austen* (1987). Tomalin, C. *Jane Austen: A Life* (1997). Wallace, T. G. *Jane Austen and Narrative Authority* (1995). Williams, M. *Jane Austen: Ten Novels and Their Methods* (1986). Wright, A. *Jane Austen's Novels: A Study in Structure* (1953).

For articles in reference works, see: *Allibone. BA19C.*

Bloomsbury. Cambridge. Chambers. DLB. DNB. Feminist. Moulton. Oxford. ToddBWW.

Other references: Adams, T. D. *SNNTS* (1982). Auerbach, N. *W&L* (1983). Booth, W. C. *NCF* (1961). Booth, W. C. *Persuasions* (December 1983). Cohen, L. D. *NCF* (1953). Duckworth, A. M. *W&L* (1983). Duffy, J. M., Jr. *ELH* (1954). Elsbree, L. *NCF* (1960). Forster, E. M. *Olinger Harvest* (1936). Greene, D. J. *PMLA* (1953). Griffin, C. *ELH* (1963). Halperin, J. *MLQ* (1983). Harding, D. W. *Scrutiny* (1940). Karl, F. R. *Age of Fiction: The Nineteenth Century British Novel* (1964). Kelly, G. *ESC* (1984). Leavis, Q. D. *Scrutiny* (1941; 1942). McCann, C. J. *NCF* (1964). Millard, M. *Persuasions* (December 1980). Schorer, M. *KR* (1956). Shannon, E. F., Jr. *PMLA* (1956). Woolf, V. *The Common Reader* (1925). *TLS* (23 August 1996). Tennant, E. *Emma in Love: Jane Austen's "Emma" Continued* (1996).

Lynn M. Alexander
(updated by Linda Hunt Beckman)

Author of David Simple: See *Fielding, Sarah*

Author of Elizabeth and Her German Garden: See *Arnim, Elizabeth von*

Author of The Female Quixote: See *Lennox, Charlotte Ramsay*

Author of Frankenstein: See *Shelley, Mary Wollstonecraft*

Author of John Halifax, Gentleman: See *Craik, Dinah Maria Mulock*

Author of Lady Grace: See *Smedley, Menella Bute*

Author of The Ladies of Bever Hollow: See *Manning, Anne*

Author of Little Black Sambo: See *Bannerman, Helen Brodie Cowan Watson*

Author of Mary Powell: See *Manning, Anne*

Author of Mrs. Leicester's School: See *Lamb, Mary Ann*

Author of The Magic Lantern: See *Blessington, Margaret (Marguerite)*

Author of IX Poems by V: See *Clive, Caroline*

Author of Paul Ferroll: See *Clive, Caroline*

Author of Phyllis: See *Hungerford, Margaret Hamilton Wolfe*

Author of The Proposal to the Ladies: See *Astell, Mary*

Author of Sketches and Fragments: See *Blessington, Margaret (Marguerite)*

Avoos: See *Coleridge, Mary Elizabeth*

A. W., Mrs.: See *Weamys [Weamers], Anna [Anne]*

Aydy, Catherine: See *Tennant, Emma*

B.: See *Smedley, Menella Bute*

Ann Bacon

BORN: 1528, Gidea Hall, Essex.
DIED: August 1610, Gorhambury, Hertfordshire.
DAUGHTER OF: Sir Anthony Cooke and Ann Fitzwilliam Cooke.
MARRIED: Sir Nicholas Bacon, 1556–57 (?).
WROTE UNDER: A. C.; Lady Ann Bacon.

As a classicist, B. was unusual for her learning and influence. Typically, a well-to-do Renaissance woman had a limited number of interests, with her household, her family, and her faith most important. Unlike such notable women as Bess of Hardwick or Lady Anne Clifford, whose lasting accomplishments center on their administration of large households, B. achieved her reputation because her writing reflects her concern for her religion and for her two sons. Her translations and personal letters have survived; the translations are the more substantial achievement, while the letters are more human.

B. was able to translate from several languages because of her unusually thorough education. Although her mother, Ann Fitzwilliam Cooke, objected, her father, Sir Anthony Cooke, gave all five of his daughters the advanced training that had been advocated by some Tudor humanists, enabling his children to study Latin, Hebrew, Greek, Italian, and French. Despite maternal opposition to her education, B. dedicated her first published work to her mother: a translation into English of fourteen Italian sermons by Bernardino Ochino, a friar who had left the Roman Catholic Church and taken refuge in Canterbury. Published in around 1550, Ochino's sermons enjoyed a fair success, and an enlarged edition was published in 1570.

B.'s major achievement was her English version of Bishop John Jewel's *Apologia pro Ecclesia Anglicana* (1562), which she translated as *An Apologie or aunswer in defence of the Church of England* (1564). Jewel's great work describes the Church of England's doctrine, defends it from Roman Catholic charges of heresy, and attacks the doctrine of papal supremacy; today it remains a central document of the Anglican Church. After B. read Jewel's Latin text, she was so moved by what he said that she immediately essayed a translation that she sent to the Archbishop of Canterbury, Matthew Parker, as well as to Bishop Jewel. Both men approved her work, so Parker sent it into print without changes and without her knowledge, fearing her modesty would forbid its publication. It was popular, being issued again in 1600 and after her death. The quality of her work is high: her translation is concise, her diction is exact, and her style is close to the vernacular so that the work does not sound forced or foreign. As C. S. Lewis remarks, "If quality without bulk were enough, Lady Bacon might be put forward as the best of all sixteenth-century translators."

In addition to her scholarly work, a number of B.'s letters survive. Most of these are to her sons, Francis and Anthony, though others are to such noted men as Robert Devereaux, Earl of Essex, and to her brother-in-law, William Cecil, Lord Burghley. These letters offer a clearer view of her character. Her intense piety, her concern for her sons, and her dislike of Anthony's servant Lawson are topics that recur. Given the exalted reputation of Francis Bacon, one is amused to read a letter from B. scolding him for drinking at bedtime or the way he treats his tenants and sending him a basket of pigeons as a special treat. Irritable and loving in the same breath, she seems always convinced that both her sons are behaving injudiciously in London. Such letters provide welcome insight into the private life of a remarkable woman.

WORKS: *Fourteene Sermons of Barnardine Ochyne* (1550?, STC 18766). *Sermons Concerning the Predestinacion and Election of God* (1570?, STC 18768). *An Apologie or answer in defence of the Church of England* (1562, STC 14590). For B's letters, *The Works of Francis Bacon*, Vol. VII, ed. J. Spedding, et al. (1862), passim.

BIBLIOGRAPHY: Bainton, R. H. *Christianity and Spirituality* (1975). Barnes, S. *Essex Review* (1912). Hogrefe, P. *Women of Action in Tudor England* (1977). Hughey, R. *RES* (1934). Lamb, M. E., in *Silent but for the Word*, ed. M. Hannay (1985). Whiting, M. B. *ContempR* (1922). Whiting, M. B. *Hibbert Journal* (1931).

For articles in reference works, see: *Bell. Bloomsbury. DNB. Europa. Feminist. Oxford. Palmer.*

Other references: Beilin, E. *Redeeming Eve* (1987). Lewis, C. S. *English Literature in the Sixteenth Century, Excluding Drama* (1954). Travitsky, B. *The Paradise of Women* (1989).

Fran Teague

Enid Bagnold

BORN: 27 October 1889, Borstal Cottage, Rochester, Kent.
DIED: 31 March 1981, London.
DAUGHTER OF: Colonel Arthur Bagnold and Ethel Alger.
MARRIED: Sir Roderick Jones, 1919.

As the spirited eldest child of a well-to-do officer in the Royal Engineers, B. traveled extensively during her childhood and began writing poetry nightly at the age of nine while living in Jamaica, a habit she preserved throughout her youth. When the family returned to England in 1902, her father enrolled B. in an exclusive school administered by Mrs. Leonard Huxley (the mother of Aldous and Julian, the niece of Matthew Arnold, and the sister of Mrs. Humphrey Ward), where B.'s performance was unremarkable except for her poetic talent. At this time, B. recalls in her *Autobiography*, W. B. Yeats advised her: "never interest yourself in politics, welfare, or the conditions in which people live. Only in their aspect, their hearts and minds, and *what they are.*" Although B. made frequent literary forays into the world of political commentary, her best and most popular work was indeed produced when she heeded Yeats's advice.

From 1912 to 1919, B. lived in Chelsea, where her friends included Lovat Fraser, Henri Gaudier-Brzeska, Katherine Mansfield, John Middleton Murry, George Bernard Shaw, Max Beerbohm, Desmond MacCarthy, Bertrand Russell, and the Bibesco princes, among many others. B.'s first literary employment came from her first lover, Frank Harris, who hired her as a journalist for his new *Hearth and Home* magazine, and when that folded, for *Modern Society*, a glorified scandal sheet. B. became a shameless and self-confessed plagiarist for the magazine, often translating Maupassant stories and passing them off as her own. Although her work at this time was of poor quality, she did learn valuable skills such as editing, writing to deadlines, and researching, all of which provided a solid foundation for future projects.

During World War I, B. trained and worked as a nurse in London, keeping a journal of her experiences, which became her first published book, *A Diary Without Dates* (1918). Her journalistic training enabled her to compose a detailed and vivid impression, based on her close observation, of the horror and necessary cold-heartedness of a hospital system that was hopelessly unprepared for and overwhelmed by the casualties from France. Her descriptions of limbs piled in buckets and family members of the dying given callous treatment moved H. G. Wells to review the book favorably but also moved the hospital to fire her. Perhaps to balance the grotesqueness of her medical experience, B. also published her only volume of poems, *The Sailing Ships and Other Poems*, during the same year.

After the war, B. married into the working aristocracy in the person of Sir Roderick Jones, owner and head of Reuters, the news service. After her marriage, B. moved into high society, forming friendships with diplomats, peers, and such important literary figures as Vita Sackville-West, the Woolfs, Rudyard Kipling, Maurice Baring, and Rebecca West. The conversations, anecdotes, personalities, and intrigues of this circle would provide models and materials for her writing to come.

From journalism and poetry, B., now Lady Jones, turned to the novel, publishing three between 1920 and 1930, the most popular of which was *Serena Blandish: or the Difficulty of Getting Married*, which S.N. Behrman adapted as a play in 1929. In 1933, B. once again demonstrated the lack of political acumen that had gotten her into trouble with *A Diary Without Dates* by traveling to Nazi Germany and describing it somewhat favorably in an article for the *London Times,* for which she was severely attacked even by her friends. Two years later, she retreated into the safer and more familiar world of steeplechasing, producing her best-known work, *National Velvet,* for which B. drew from her own experiences. Characters were modeled closely on her servants and friends and plot situations upon her own daughter's love for horses and avid competitiveness.

Although she continued to write novels, B. became more and more drawn to the drama from the 1940s on, and it is perhaps as a playwright that she earned the greatest popularity and professional recognition. *Poor Judas,* a symbolic play that concerns a failed English writer who perseveres despite his lack of financial and popular success, won the Arts Theatre Prize in 1951. B.'s most famous play, *The Chalk Garden,* which received the Award of Merit for Drama from the American Academy of Arts and Letters in 1964, has as its protagonist Miss Madrigal, a woman with a questionable past who becomes governess to the spoiled pyromaniacal granddaughter of a selfish old dowager and who manages to introduce sanity, forgiveness, and love into the emotionally sterile household. Kenneth Tynan, reviewing the play for *The Observer,* called it "the finest artificial comedy to have flowed from an English (as opposed to an Irish) pen since the death of Congreve." B. continued to write successful plays until 1976, when *A Matter of Gravity* was published, taking time from drama to write her *Autobiography* in 1969. Written in B.'s typically light and flippant style, the *Autobiography* is a rather stream-of-consciousness reminiscence, lacking in facts and figures but rich in impressions and ideas. It is chiefly valuable for B.'s anecdotes of famous people and for the letters and drawings she reproduces.

B. felt that Henry James was a strong influence on her style, and many of her novels concern the same characters and ideas that James found fascinating. B., like James, is concerned with the shadings and gradations of truth and illusion as perceived from subjective individual perspectives, and consequently her work, in particular her plays, turn toward the symbolic, peopled with headstrong eccentrics who enact barbaric confrontations in exceedingly civilized syntax. Since most of her work is set in the ironic tone, it tends, paradoxically, to be highly comic while treating serious philosophical themes such as truth and illusion, the functions of art, the emotional relationships among families, and death. Her work is also highly autobiographical and reflects the interests and attitudes of the upper-class social circle in which she moved. *The Last Joke* is based upon the suicide of Prince Emmanuel Bibesco, the brother of another of B.'s lovers. B.'s own sentiments about herself as the clever but aging grandame form the basis for her own favorite play, *The Chinese Prime Minister,* an almost absurdist piece in which the butler dies three times, once giving formal notice.

B. considered herself, like Shaw, a writer of ideas and intricate language, but her work rarely considers the social or political issues with which Shaw was concerned. Her witty conversations and clever turnings of phrase are perhaps the best features of her writing and the features for which critics have continually praised her plays. Although tending toward the stylized, symbolic, and absurd rather than toward the realistic, the plays are in the Noël Coward style, full of repartée and carefully constructed dialogue, dedicated to characterizing and examining the manners and ideas of the sophisticated upper-classes, yet always providing an ironic or bizarre turn of plot or character to introduce the surreal into the finely drawn formal parlor.

WORKS: *A Diary Without Dates* (1918). *The Sailing Ships and Other Poems* (1918). *The Happy Foreigner* (1920). *Serena Blandish, or the Difficulty of Getting Married* (1924; adapted as a play by S. N. Behrman, 1929). *Alice and Thomas and Jane* (1930). *National Velvet* (1935; as a film in 1944, as a play in 1946). (trans.) *Alexander of Asia,* by M. Bibesco (1935). *The Door of Life* (1938). *The Squire* (1938). *Lottie Dundass* (1942). *Poor Judas* (1946). *The Loved and Envied* (1951). *Gertie* (1952). *The Chalk Garden* (1953). *The Last Joke* (1960). *The Chinese Prime Minister* (1964). *Call Me Jacky* (1968). *Enid Bagnold's Autobiography* (1969). *A Matter of Gravity* (1976).

BIBLIOGRAPHY: Friedman, L. *Enid Bagnold* (1986). Lebba, A. *Enid Bagnold: The Authorized Biography* (1986). Tyler, L. *CLAQ* (1993–94).

For articles in reference works, see: *CD. CN. DLB.*

Other references: Behrman, S. N., foreword to *Three Plays* (1934). Calder-Marshall, A., foreword to *The Girl's Journey* (1954). *New Statesman* (28 July 1951). *QJS* (October 1973). *TDRev* (December 1958). *Theatre Arts* (April 1952, January 1964). Weales, G., in *Laurel British Drama: The Twentieth Century,* ed. R. W. Corrigan (1965).

Suzanne Westfall

Grisell (Grizell) Hume Baillie

BORN: 25 December 1665, Berwickshire.

DIED: 6 December 1746, Berwickshire.

DAUGHTER OF: Sir Patrick Hume of Polwarth and Grisell Ker.

MARRIED: George Baillie, 1692.

B. was the author of at least two of the earliest poems of the Scottish ballad revival and of a diary that provides modern readers with insight into the daily life of an aristocratic Scottish woman of the eighteenth century. Her life itself, as paradoxically dramatic and ordinary as her writing, was romanticized by Joanna Baillie in *Metrical Legends* and gracefully remembered by her own daughter, Lady Grisell Murray, in her *Memoir.*

B. was born on Christmas Day, 1665, at Redbraes Castle in Berwickshire to a family whose Presbyterian politics had, by the closing years of the Stuart reign, made them subject to persecution. In 1685, her father came under suspicion of participating in the Ryehouse Plot to kill King James II; B., the oldest daughter among eighteen children, is reported to have saved him from the dreadful fate met by his friend Robert Baillie of Jerviswood by hiding him in the family vault and bringing him food and drink at night. When such tactics proved impossible to sustain, the Hume family fled its home for Utrecht. There, B. ran the household—cooking, cleaning, marketing, and caring for the younger children—sitting in only occasionally at her father's lessons.

Despite the hardships of her life in exile and her lack of formal education, B., according to her daughter, produced "a book of songs of her writing; many of them interrupted, half writ, some broke off in the middle of a sentence." Only two poems believed to be from the manuscript volume have survived. "Were ne my Hearts light I wad Dye" and a fragment, "The ewe butchin's bonnie," composed a century before Robert Burns' Scottish dialect *Poems,* recall the diction, rhythm, and themes of an ancient national tradition and are still considered among the best examples of the Romantic turn from neoclassicism to the natural melodies of Scottish folklore.

Upon the Revolution of 1688, B. traveled back to Britain with the Princess of Orange and was invited to become a maid of honor at the English court. She refused, for she had fallen in love with George Baillie, son of the martyred Robert Baillie and, like her brother, a soldier in King William's army. They were married in 1692, and B. happily gave her life over to managing her husband's and her father's restored estates in Scotland. The voluminous *Day Books* she kept for much of the remainder of her life contain household accounts, recipes, menus, and travel itineraries, and are totally prosaic, providing no indication of any further literary attempts. B. died in 1746, twenty years after the first anonymous publication of "Were ne my Hearts Light" in *Orpheus Caledonius,* a volume to which she, her brother, and her two daughters were subscribers.

WORKS: "Were ne my Hearts Light I wad Dye," *Orpheus Caledonius or a Collection of the Best Scotch Songs Set to Music,* by W. Thomson (1726). "The ewe butchin's bonnie" ["Absence"] (broadsheet, with music by Charles Sharpe, 1839). *The Household Book of Lady Griselle Baillie 1692–1733,* ed. R. Scott-Montcrieff (1911).

BIBLIOGRAPHY: Baillie, J. *Metrical Legends of Exalted Characters* (1821). *The Songs of Scotland Prior to Burns,* ed. R. Chambers (1862).*Scottish Poetry of the Eighteenth Century,* ed. G. Eyre-Todd (1896). *Kissing the Rod: An Anthology of Seventeenth-Century Women's Verse,* ed. G. Greer et al. (1988). Murray, G. *Memoirs of the Lives and Characters of the Right Honorable George Baillie of Jerviswood, and of Lady Grisell Baillie* (1822). Ramsay, A. *The Tea-Table Miscellany: A Collection of Choice Songs, Scots and English in Two Volumes* (1788). Warrender, M. *Marchmont and the Humes of Polwarth* (1894).

For articles in reference works, see: *Bell. DNB. Feminist. ToddBWW.*

Susan Hastings

Joanna Baillie

BORN: 11 September 1762, Bothwell, Lanarkshire, Scotland.
DIED: 23 September 1851, Hampstead.
DAUGHTER OF: James Baillie and Dorothy Hunter Baillie.

B., dramatist and poet, was descended from an ancient Scottish family that included in its lineage kinship with the patriot Sir William Wallace and the poet Lady Grizell Baillie. She spent her early childhood at Bothwell Manse, where her father was a clergyman. This rich historic environment impressed her deeply and is reflected in her poetic and dramatic works, but her home environment was stern and emotionally repressive. At ten, B. was sent to a school in Glasgow, where she excelled in vocal and instrumental music, demonstrated a talent for drawing, and enjoyed mathematics and the opportunity to use her argumentative powers. She was also distinguished for her skill in acting and composition, being especially facile in the improvisation of dialogue in character. In 1776, her father was appointed professor of divinity at the University of Glasgow, and the family took up residence in a home provided by the university.

But before B. could fully enjoy the academic environment, her father died (1778), and his widow and daughters retired to Long Calderwood in Lanarkshire, moving in 1784 to London. London provided B. with the opportunity to launch a literary career. In 1790, she published, anonymously, a small volume of miscellaneous poems entitled *Fugitive Verses,* which was favorably received. The first play she composed, *Arnold,* does not survive; in 1798, however, she issued the first volume of her *Plays on the Passions* in which each "passion" of the mind is the subject of a tragedy and a comedy. The work, also published anonymously, contained, for example, *Basil,* a tragedy on love, *Trial,* a comedy on love, and *De Monfort,* a tragedy on hatred. It was reviewed as the work of a man, with Sir Walter Scott at first suspected of being its author. It was through this work that B. met Scott, establishing a warm friendship that lasted till his death in 1832.

In her elaborate introduction to *Plays on the Passions,* B. explained her experimental venture. Having first shown that the study of human nature and its passions has an irresistible attraction for the individual, B. maintains that the sympathetic instinct is our best and most powerful instructor; it teaches us to respect ourselves and our kind and to dwell upon the noble, rather than the mean, view of human nature. Singularly Romantic in her view, B. also preferred a simplification of expression.

Such ideas required a restructuring of dramatic form. B. eliminated the patterns of Neoclassical diction, replacing them with more Anglo Saxon-like speech. Furthermore, she did not uphold the three unities, which were a mainstay of British Neoclassical drama. Finally, not being well versed in drama history, she tended to create works that were more dramas for the reader than for the stage and were consequently difficult to produce. Her plays were criticized for lack of event, as in Joseph

Campbell's remark, "If Joanna Baillie had known the stage practically, she would never have attached the importance she does to the development of single passions in single tragedies; and she would have invented stirring incidents to justify the passions of her characters." Instead of character, her main characters' passions "proceed from the wilful natures of the beings themselves."

Yet the plays attracted John Kemble, who decided to produce *De Monfort* at Drury Lane Theatre, with himself and Sarah Siddons as the main characters. Despite an elaborate, careful production, it failed to capture the public in its eleven-night run. Undeterred by adverse criticism, B. issued a second volume of *Plays on the Passions*, which included a comedy on hatred, a two-part tragedy on ambition, and a comedy on ambition. The comedy on hatred was produced at the English Opera House, but its tragic companion was considered too unwieldy for stage production. Shortly after the volume appeared, B., her sister, and her mother moved to Hampstead, where the mother died in 1806 and where the sisters lived till their deaths "in retirement" and B. later in life "in strict seclusion." This did not preclude their receiving visitors, including many friends eminent in letters, science, art, and society, such as Siddons, Scott, and their closest friend, Laetitia Barbauld.

In 1804, B. published *Miscellaneous Plays,* which included two tragedies, *Raynor* and *Constantine Paleologas,* constructed on traditional lines. The latter work, based on Gibbon's account of the Turkish siege of Constantinople, was produced at the Surrey Theatre as a melodrama and also in Liverpool, Dublin, and Edinburgh, in each case to large houses. In 1810, she produced *Family Legend,* based on a Highland feud; Scott wrote a prologue and sponsored its production in Edinburgh, and Henry Mackenzie, author of *The Man of Feeling,* wrote an epilogue. Its success led to a revival of *De Monfort.* In 1812, the third series of *Plays on the Passions* appeared; it contained two tragedies and a comedy on fear and a musical drama on hope. *Metrical Legends* appeared in 1821, a collection of poems suggested by her stay in Scotland the previous year with Scott. Sir William Wallace is the principal character in one poem and Grizell Baillie in another, and the volume also included dramatic ballads cast in "the ancient mould."

B. edited *Poetic Miscellanies* in 1823; contributors included Scott, Catherine Fanshawe, Felicia Hemens, herself, and others. *Martyr,* a drama, appeared in 1826, though it had been written earlier; this play presents the martyrdom of Cordenius Maro, an officer in Nero's imperial guard, who had converted to Christianity. B.'s Unitarian view of Jesus led to the publication when she was seventy of *A View of the General Tenor of the New Testament Regarding the Nature and Dignity of Jesus Christ.* In 1836, she published three volumes of *Miscellaneous Plays,* including a tragedy and comedy on jealousy and a tragedy on remorse.

B.'s inventiveness is great, and her blank verse possesses a notable dignity and sonorousness that cause her works to be ranked among English classical dramas, though they will never again be popular. Her minor works have beauty and delicacy, and some of her songs will doubtless live on. Her status currently is that of a virtual unknown, but renewed interest in literature written by women should reveal her to be an innovator whose efforts inspired both Scott and other Romantics to redefine the type of drama to appear on the English stage.

WORKS: *Fugitive Verses* (1790). *Plays on the Passions* (1798; second series, 1802; third series, 1812). *Miscellaneous Plays* (1804). *The Family Legend: A Tragedy* (1810). *The Beacon: A Serious Musical Drama in Two Acts* (1812). *Metrical Legends of Exalted Characters* (1821). *A Collection of Poems* (1823). *Martyr* (1826). *Complete Poetical Works* (1832). *A View of the General Tenor of the New Testament Regarding the Nature and Dignity of Jesus Christ* (1832). *Miscellaneous Plays* (1836). *Ahalya Bace: A Poem* (1849). *Dramatic and Poetical Works* (1851). *Poems* [1790] (1994).

BIBLIOGRAPHY: Burroughs, C. B. *Closet Stages: Joanna Baillie and the Theater Theory of British Romantic Women Writers* (1997). Carhart, M. S. *The Life and Work of Joanna Baillie* (1923, 1970). Purinton, M. *Romantic Ideology Unmasked* (1994).

For articles in reference works, see: *Allibone. BA19C. Bell. Bloomsbury. DLB. DNB. Europa. Feminist. Oxford. ToddBWW. ToddDBA.*

Other references: *Compar(a)ison* (1994). Curran, S., in *Romanticism and Feminism,* ed. A. K. Mellor (1988). Keddie, H. [pseud. S. Tytler] and J. L. Watson. *Friend: Comment on Romanticism* (October 1991–April 1992). McKerrow, M., in *Living by the Pen,* ed. D. Spender (1992). *RES* (1947). *Songstresses of Scotland* (1871). *WC* (1982; 1992).

Priscilla Dorr
(updated by Rebecca P. Bocchicchio)

Beryl (Margaret) Bainbridge

BORN: 21 November 1934, Liverpool.
DAUGHTER OF: Richard Bainbridge and Winifred Baines Bainbridge.
MARRIED: Austin Davies, 1954.

B. is a prolific novelist whose books derive from her childhood in working-class Liverpool; her many novels evoke a dull, unhappy world of lower-middle-class people whose lives are generally unrelieved by joy or hope. But these drab, dreary characters and their limited worlds are presented with such grotesque wit and savage irony, such skill in narrative and characterization, that B. has established a deserved reputation as an original writer.

Raised on the coast near Liverpool, B. was obsessed with writing from an early age. Her father, a sometime (but unsuccessful) salesman, and her mother, self-consciously aware of the family's low status and her own higher origins in a Britain obsessed with class differences, together stimulated B. to write of her own world. Her father opened the world of Charles Dickens to B. and her mother the world of the theater. B. began tap dancing in public at six, studied ballet while quite young, appeared on radio at ten, and acted with a repertory company at fifteen, continuing on stage until she was nearly forty. She briefly became a Roman Catholic in order to marry Austin Davies, a painter, and began writing during her children's early lives until her divorce in 1959.

B.'s first novels are explicitly based on her family memories. Though she had begun to write while only twelve (a melange of Dickens and Robert Louis Stevenson's *Treasure Island*), her first completed novel was submitted when she was barely seventeen and quickly rejected because of its "indecency." This first work was eventually published as B.'s third novel, *Harriet Said* (1972). Two schoolgirls, one the chubby thirteen-year-old narrator, the other the domineering Harriet, spy on a middle-aged man (including oedipally observing his lovemaking) and write lurid diary entries about him. After the narrator seduces him, she kills his wife (at Harriet's urging). Though some critics praised the book as a good specimen of the "corrupt childhood" novel and compared its grim psychological effects to those of Edgar Allan Poe, its incoherence and sensationalism struck others as reflective of its author's age at the time of writing.

Her first two books to be published, *A Weekend with Claud* (1967) and *Another Part of the Wood* (1968; revised 1979), differ considerably. The first is explicitly experimental: A photo prompts three stream-of-consciousness narratives about Claud's weekend a year previously with the unappealing, sloppy Maggie, her roomer, Norman, and a bag-lady, Shebah, ending with Claud's own recollections. Maggie's disorderly life constitutes the book's plotline, including Shebah's wounding and the various men in her life. Claud, though, is a type B. often writes about in later books, the man who ruthlessly takes advantage of and abuses women. The book was poorly received, and B. considers it a failure. The second novel, by contrast, derives from (and seems similar to) events at the end of her marriage: a divorced man takes several friends, as well as his lover and son, on a routine but awful vacation in the country, with the son's death resulting from his father's excessive expectations and cruelty. (B. subsequently revised the novel and republished it once she was able to gain a better perspective on her married life.)

The Dressmaker (1973; published in the U.S. as *The Secret Glass*) reverts to B.'s Liverpool life and is especially noted for its desperate working-class atmosphere and accuracy. Young Rita, living drearily with her two aunts, lusts after (and competes with one aunt for) a disgusting G.I. stationed nearby. After the other aunt kills the soldier, both aunts wrap up the body to keep Rita from noticing it. B.'s brief job in a bottling factory working with immigrants resulted in *The Bottle Factory Outing* (1974), an excellent novel, skillfully balancing humor and horror, about another pair of contrasting English women and their various relationships with Italian workers, both male and female, in such a factory. One woman, Freda, is brusque and gregarious compared to the other, Brenda, and the book moves inexorably from a funeral before the picnic to Freda's own death, following a series of morbid but comic incidents culminating in Brenda's disposing of the body by putting it in a barrel in the ocean.

In these first books, as in her numerous subsequent ones, B. is concerned with the common distinction between people's naïve expectations and the harshness of reality, between belief and truth. B. has been repeatedly criticized for a seemingly indifferent, even cruel attitude toward her often pathetic characters. Despite her skill at capturing proletarian people and surroundings, B.'s tone is admittedly narrowly focused and limited.

Sweet William (1975) did little to alter such conclusions, though it was commonly agreed that B.'s skill at characterization was superb. William, a charming though amoral male opportunist, woos Ann through his power of persuasion even though she is engaged to Gerald, only slightly William's better. Gerald beds Ann the night before he leaves for the United States, and her mother—another of B.'s string of such women—asserts her convictions about social propriety. William completely manipulates her life, seduces others in the apartment building, and Ann, pregnant and amazingly unaware of his inadequacies, moves away. When the child is born, it resembles Gerald, not William, with B.'s point being that none of her unlikable (though admittedly well-developed) characters really understands much about the nature of love.

A Quiet Life (1976) is explicitly autobiographical and also concerns a family with various emotional, even tragic, conflicts. B.'s narrator is a man who meets his sister to divide a small inheritance and who reflects on their unhappy childhood, along with touches of macabre humor in which death, for example, is described in the same passage and tone as locating clean bedding. Though B. often writes about such claustrophobic families, her control of her material and subtle characterization make this one of her best works. In *Injury Time* (1977), B. uses various narrative voices to offer alternative views of distinguishing truth from illusion. Though the forty-year-old Binny has a lover, Edward, the two only dimly understand each other, and when she persuades him to invite his friends for dinner, chaos, both real and imagined, results as assorted unsavory neighbors invade the dinner and escaping bank robbers try to take the group hostage. Small wonder that Binny thinks she is watching a television drama, so unreal is all of this for her.

B. visited Israel after writing *Injury Time* and, after reflecting on the Holocaust and reading a biography of Hitler, wrote *Young Adolf* (1978). Based on the premise of Hitler's secretly having visited Liverpool in 1910 to see his brother, this comic/prophetic novel features a deluded protagonist who, critics noted, sometimes seemed like Charlie Chaplin's *The Great Dictator.*

Winter Garden (1980) also combines wild comedy with earnest characterization. Based on B.'s visit to the Soviet Union as part of an exchange group, the novel focuses on Douglas Ashburner, who has also made such a visit and who plans an outing with his lover while telling his wife that he is going fishing. The inevitable confusion and complications occur: After both his luggage and lover mysteriously disappear and he is confused with both his lover's husband (a noted physician) and another man (an artist), Ashburner falls prey to B.'s complex plot, which satirizes both Soviet bureaucratic thinking and English conventionality. The novel's bleak, predictable conclusion offers little comedy or comfort.

Watson's Apology (1984), unlike most of B.'s works, is set in the past, specifically in 1872. An elderly retired headmaster pistol-whipped his wife to death and died in prison twelve years later, during which years he produced several impenetrable scholarly works as well as a curious, ambiguous note in Latin about the killing: "Often heretofore constant love has been injurious to the lover." B.'s novel re-creates courtship correspondence between Watson and his wife as well as scenes from their marriage; her instability contrasts with his genius and discipline. B.'s comic sense is somewhat daunted by this scenario, but it never flags; indeed, as with other books by B., one is never sure whether to laugh or cry, so effective is her character study.

In almost all of her fiction, her brilliant wit and imagination focus on luckless misfits from the post–World War II Liverpool she has known so well—people not quite tragic, certainly not intrinsically comic, but all, even the suicides and those doomed to continue living without hope, are seen with a clear, unsentimental eye and a highly original comic sense. B. has also written nonfiction (*English Journey, or, The Road to Milton Keynes,* 1984, a travel book based on J. B. Priestley's work with a similar title, and *Forever England North and South,* 1987, a study of social life and customs) in which the same sharp skill of observation is found, as well as other fiction (*Mum and Mr. Armitage: Selected Stories,* 1985, and another novel, *Filthy Lucre, or, The Tragedy of Ernest Ledwhistle and Richard Soleway,* 1986); thus far, though, her major talent has received relatively little substantial criticism.

WORKS: *A Weekend with Claud* (1967). *Another Part of the Wood* (1968, 1979). *Harriet Said . . .* (1972). *The Dressmaker* (1973; in the U.S. as *The Secret Glass,* 1974). *The Bottle Factory Outing* (1974). *Sweet William* (1975). *A Quiet Life* (1976). *Injury Time* (1977). *Young Adolf* (1978). *Winter Garden* (1980). *English Journey, or, The Road to Milton Keynes* (1984). *Watson's Apology* (1984). *Mum and Mr. Armitage: Selected Stories of Beryl Bainbridge* (1985). *Filthy Lucre, or, The Tragedy of Ernest Ledwhistle and Richard Soleway* (1986). *Forever England North and South* (1987). *Every Man for Himself* (1996).

BIBLIOGRAPHY: Lassner, P., in *Look Who's Laughing: Gender and Comedy,* ed. G. Finney (1994). Lassner, P. *Phoebe* (1991). Pickering, J. *Albion* (1979). Stamirowska, K. *KN* (1988). Wenno, E. *Ironic Formula in the Novels of Beryl Bainbridge* (1993). Yakovleva, V. *SovL* (1984).

For articles in reference works, see: *Bloomsbury. CA. Cambridge. CLC. CN. DLB. EWLTC. Feminist. Oxford. ToddBWW. WA.*

Other references: *Atlantic* (March 1979). *Books and Bookmen* (January 1974, December 1977, November 1978, February 1980, May 1984, August 1985, April 1987). *Encounter* (February 1975, February 1976, February 1985, May 1986). *HudR* (1977–78). *Listener* (13 December 1979, 20 November 1980, 5 December 1985). *London Magazine* (January 1978, April–May 1979). *LRB* (20 November to 3 December 1980). *New Leader* (2 September 1974, 5 May 1980). *New Republic* (28 September 1974, 24 May 1975, 25 March 1978). *New Statesman* (1 November 1974, 10 November 1978, 21 and 28 December 1979, 7 November 1980, 11 September 1981, 13 April 1984, 29 November 1985). *Newsweek* (12 August 1974). *NYRB* (1 May 1974, 15 July 1976, 5 April 1979, 17 July 1980, 25 October 1984). *NYTBR* (15 September 1974, 8 June 1975, 20 March 1977, 13 April 1980, 1 March 1981, 21 March 1982, 23 September 1984, 20 October 1985). *Spectator* (2 November 1974, 9 October 1976, 8 December 1979, 1 November 1980, 28 April 1984, 3 November 1984). *TLS* (28 September 1973, 1 December 1978, 2 February 1980, 31 October 1980, 11 September 1981, 5 October 1984, 20 December 1985, 17 October 1986, 24 April 1987). *YR* (1978).

Paul Schlueter

Isabella Varley Banks

BORN: 25 March 1821, Manchester.
DIED: 5 May 1897, Dalston, Cumbria.
DAUGHTER OF: James Varley and Amelia Daniels.
MARRIED: George Linnaeus Banks, 1846.
WROTE UNDER: Mrs. G. Linnaeus Banks; Isabella Varley.

A poet, journalist, and novelist, B. was the daughter of a Manchester chemist, smallware dealer, and amateur artist. She took charge of a school at Cheetham (near Manchester) when she was a teenager and taught for nine years. At the age of twenty-five, she married George Linnaeus Banks, a poet, journalist, editor, and orator from Birmingham. Despite her many pregnancies—she bore eight children, losing five of them—and ill health, she assisted her husband with his work and contributed to the periodicals he edited.

Her first published work, a poem entitled "A Dying Girl to Her Mother," was printed in the *Manchester Guardian* when B. was sixteen. B. continued to write poetry throughout her life, but she published only three books of poems: *Ivy Leaves* (1844), *Daisies in the Grass* (with her husband, 1865), and *Ripples and Breakers* (1878; 1893). These works are typical of the "popular" mediocre verse of the time.

B. evidenced an avid interest in social issues, such as corporal punishment, flogging, the status of women, treatment of servants, education of girls, and so forth. She publicized her views in writing and speaking, once lecturing on "Woman—as She Was, as She Is, and as She May Be" at the Harrogate Mechanics' Institute. Skilled as a designer, she created and published original fancy-work patterns every month for forty-five years. B. lived a difficult, sad life, moving frequently to follow her husband's work, enduring the deaths of five of her eight children, living with a drunken, raving husband threatening suicide, and suffering personal ill health. She died at Dalston on 5 May 1897.

B. turned from the pleasure of writing poetry to the serious task of writing prose as a practical necessity in 1863. Her husband was ill, and she needed money for food and education for her children. *God's Providence House* (1865) was the first of the many novels that she would write throughout her life. Called "meritorious" and obviously successful (a second edition was printed), the book is typical of B.'s novels, her style being relatively consistent. The characters, based on real persons, appear under their own names or in thinly disguised forms; incidents of family history within the framework are actual places of the late eighteenth century. B.'s style is almost cluttered with detail, making scenes and characters vivid and concrete. The emphasis in her works is on the characters rather than action; intelligence is subordinated to the heart and soul as the means for realizing happiness and success. Principal characters are reminiscent of the "Horatio Alger" type, and nearly all her works have a message of moral or social import, some almost to the point of didacticism. The terms "old-fashioned," "homey," "well-cooked," and "lovingly written" were often attributed to her style.

B. had to take on the male role of breadwinner even before the death of her husband, and her books present decided views about the prevailing attitudes toward women in her time. B. took responsibility, as did the characters Isobel Raines, Caroline Booth, Alice Latham, Edith, and Rosanna in her writings. She also deals with the unpopular theme of the illegitimate child and unwed mother in *Father and Daughter* and *Stung to the Quick*. Many stories focus on discrimination against women by individuals, law, and society.

B. was a constant contributor to magazines and Christmas annuals; she wrote many short stories and poems. Acknowledged as a minor nineteenth-century writer, commanding respect and interest, Banks was often called the "Lancashire novelist" because of her frequent use of the Manchester area as setting. Her best-known work is *The Manchester Man,* published in 1876. Its primary significance lies in the realistic depiction of social and industrial life in Manchester during the first quarter of the nineteenth century, including the riots of 1819. The conversational tone and profusion of literary detail are reminiscent of Daniel Defoe. It clearly exemplifies B.'s consummate interest as expressed in a letter to John Harland in December 1865, an interest in the "habits, customs, manners and daily life of the ancestors who have made us what we are."

WORKS: *Ivy Leaves: A Collection of Poems* (1844). (with G. L. Banks) *Daisies in the Grass: Songs and Poems* (1865). *God's Providence House* (1865). *Stung to the Quick* (1867). *The Manchester Man* (1876). *Glory: A Wiltshire Story* (1877). *Ripples and Breakers* (1878). *Caleb Booth's Clerk* (1878). *Wooers and Winners: Under the Scars* (1880). *More Than Coronets* (1881). *Through the Night: Short Stories* (1883). *Forbidden to Marry* (1883, as *Forbidden to Wed,* 1885). *Sibylla, and Other Stories* (1884). *In His Own Hand* (1885). *Geoffrey Ollivant's Folly* (1886). *A Rough Road* (1892). *Bondslaves* (1893). *The Slowly Grinding Mills* (1893). *The Bridge of Beauty* (1894).

BIBLIOGRAPHY: *Athenaeum* (9 May 1896). *Biograph* (1879). Burney, E. L. *Mrs. G. Linnaeus Banks* (1969). *Daily Graphic* (7 May 1896). Dorland, W. A. N. *The Sum of Feminine Achievement* (1917). *LonT* (6 May 1897). *Manchester Faces and Places* (December 1892). *Manchester Guardian* (6 May 1897). *The Manchester Man* (1876). *Men and Women of the Time,* 14th ed., ed. V. G. Plarr (1895).

For articles in reference works, see: *Allibone. Bloomsbury. CinP. DNB. Feminist. NCHEL.*

Phyllis J. Scherle

Lynne Reid Banks

BORN: 31 July 1929, London.
DAUGHTER OF: James Reid-Banks and Muriel Marsh Reid-Banks.
MARRIED: Chaim Stephenson, 1965.

B., the daughter of a physician and an actress, attended a convent boarding school in England before being evacuated to Canada during World War II. After returning to England, she acted in repertory theaters for several years, worked as a secretary, journalist, and television reporter, and was a scriptwriter for England's Independent Television News between 1955 and 1962. B.'s first published works were plays for stage, radio, and television. In 1960, B. traveled to Israel, where she taught English on a kibbutz and married an Israeli sculptor in 1965. B. returned to England with her family in 1972. She has written more than twenty novels for children and adults.

Of B.'s adult novels, the best known is *The L-Shaped Room* (1961), which was made into a film starring Leslie Caron in 1962, and the novel's two sequels, *The Backward Shadow* (1971) and *Two Is Lonely* (1974). The three novels trace the experiences of Jane Graham, a single mother; each book describes a crisis that requires her to reevaluate her beliefs and renew her life. The protagonist of *The L-Shaped Room* is a twenty-seven-year-old woman who moves to a seedy rooming house when she finds herself pregnant after a brief sexual relationship. As her pregnancy advances, the rooming house provides Jane with a community as her situation offers the other occupants a chance for emotional involvement. As in all of B.'s subsequent fiction, the narrative is straightforward and the style colloquial, without self-conscious stylistic flourishes. While the depiction of Jane's growing confidence and its renewing effect on the house prompted reviewer Jackson Burgess to retitle the book "Elsie Dinsmore Gets Pregnant," *The L-Shaped Room* displays B.'s talent for apt descriptive details and accurate dialogue and offers a vivid picture of London in the 1950s, with "teddy boys," "career girls," and jazz clubs. The novel is marred by some rather stereotypical minor characters, but the author takes a critical stance toward Jane's racist and antisemitic attitudes rather than making her anachronistically enlightened.

B.'s subsequent adult novels share the theme of renewal, depicting characters (often single women who must reconstruct their lives following some sort of personal catastrophe). B.'s heroines are typically ordinary, middle-class women, not exceptionally beautiful or gifted, who find in themselves the ability to face changing circumstances with courage and humor. Several of B.'s novels draw on her Israeli experiences. In *An End to Running,* the move from London to an Israeli kibbutz serves as a backdrop for the main character's emotional metamorphosis. A children's book, *One More River* (1973), describes a similar transformation when a wealthy, indulged adolescent moves from Saskatoon to the deprivations and rewards of kibbutz life. *Children at the Gate* depicts a bitter, disillusioned woman's spiritual reawakening when she becomes responsible for three children in the Arab section of a city in Israel. In *Two Is Lonely,* B. brought Jane Graham to Israel on the brink of the Six Day War.

B. achieved her greatest recognition for her juvenile and young adult fiction. Inspired by stories invented to entertain her own children, B.'s children's novels blend fantasy elements such as fairies and toys that come to life with grittily realistic contemporary settings and characters. In *The Indian in the Cupboard* (1980), *The Return of the Indian* (1986), *The Secret of the Indian* (1989), and *The Mystery of the Cupboard* (1993), an English boy encounters Native American culture and learns responsibility when miniature toy Indians are brought to life. *Melusine: A Mystery* (1988) incorporates fairy-tale elements into a depiction of sexual abuse. A less successful adolescent novel, *My Darling Villain,* is a conventional treatment of the relationship between a middle-class girl and her working-class boyfriend. *Dark Quartet: The Story of the Brontës* (1976) and *Path to the Silent Country: Charlotte Brontës Years of Fame* (1978) fictionalized the lives of Anne, Charlotte, and Emily Brontë, evoking the atmosphere of the Victorian era. B. has received more than fifteen awards for her children's books, and *The Indian in the Cupboard* was made into a film in 1995.

Each of B.'s works has met with mixed reviews. Critics have objected to the casual and at times predictable construction of her novels, stereotypical characters, and occasional heavyhanded moralizing. While these flaws may have kept B. from a position as a serious novelist, they are only minor irritations to B.'s readers, who enjoy her crisp phrases and memorable descriptions of specific places and times.

WORKS: (with V. Madden) *Miss Pringle Plays Portia* (1954). *It Never Rains* (1954). *All in a Row* (1956). *The Killer Dies Twice* (1956). *The L-Shaped Room* (1961, 1977). *Already It's Tomorrow* (1962). *An End to Running* (1962; in the U.S. as *House of Hope*). *The Gift* (1965). *Children at the Gate* (1969). *The Backward Shadow* (1971). *One More River* (1973). *Two Is Lonely* (1974). *Sarah and After: The Matriarchs* (1975; in the U.S. as *Sarah and After: Five Women Who Founded a Nation,* 1977). *The Adventures of King Midas* (1976). *The Farthest-Away Mountain* (1976). *Dark Quartet: The Story of the Brontës* (1976). *My Darling Villain* (1977). *Path to the Silent Country: Charlotte Brontës Years of Fame* (1978). *I, Houdini: The Autobiography of a Self-Educated Hamster* (1978). *Letters to My Israeli Sons: A Personal View of Jewish Survival for Young Readers* (1979). *The Indian in the Cupboard* (1980). *The Writing on the Wall* (1981). *Defy the Wilderness* (1981). *Torn Country: An Oral History of the Israeli War of Independence* (1982). *Maura's Angel* (1982). *The Warning Bell* (1984). *The Fairy Rebel* (1985). *Casualties* (1986). *The Return of the Indian* (1986). *Melusine: A Mystery* (1988). *The Secret of the Indian* (1989). *Travels of Yoshi and the Tea Kettle* (1991). *The Mystery of the Cupboard* (1993). *The Magic Hare* (1993).

BIBLIOGRAPHY:

For articles in reference works, see: *Bloomsbury. CA. CLC. CLR. CN. SATA. TCCW.*

Other references: *Books and Bookmen* (September 1968). *Commonweal* (11 November 1977). *ContempR* (1977). *Listener* (11 April 1974). *LonT* (13 August 1984). *New Statesman* (12 November 1960, 26 July 1968, 7 August 1970, 18 April 1975, 16 October 1981). *New Yorker* (8 June 1968). *NYTBR* (9 April 1961, 12 May 1968, 8 November 1970, 16 October 1977). *Observer* (9 August 1970, 7 April 1974). *Punch* (7 August 1968). *TES* (24 November 1978). *TLS* (22 March 1974, 10 December 1976, 2 October 1981).

Jane Weiss

Helen Brodie Cowan Watson Bannerman

BORN: 25 February 1862, Edinburgh, Scotland.
DIED: 13 October 1946, Edinburgh, Scotland.
DAUGHTER OF: the Reverend Robert Boog Watson and Helen Cowan Watson.
MARRIED: William Birney Bannerman, 1889.
WROTE UNDER: The Author of *Little Black Sambo*.

During a stressful period of her life, B. created a children's story that has received consistent recognition since its publication in 1899: *Little Black Sambo,* a work that provided humor, pleasure, and intrigue and changes in the publishing world. The little storybook, written and illustrated by B., has become a point of derision, but because of miscalculations and ironic distortions regarding the original work, she has become a victim rather than a literary icon.

Daughter of a minister/scientist, B. was born in Edinburgh after her father was invalided out as chaplain to the 93rd Highlanders fighting in the Crimea. B.'s roots to Edinburgh are strong; at one time she indicated that ties to the city exist because "everyone in the city was related to her," possibly because of the size of her mother's family (twenty sisters and brothers) and also because of her seven siblings.

After serving as a chaplain and scientist, B.'s father was given a post as minister to the Scots Church in Madeira, which provided B. with an education free from formal bonds since she and her sisters were educated by their father. Because of his interests, especially in the study of rocks and shells, B.'s instruction included a strong base in the sciences as well as an unprecedented fluency in various languages, among them Portuguese, French, Italian, German, and Latin. B. was also proficient in the "essential feminine accomplishments" of art and music, but her penchant for books remained prominent. Many years later, her first child told an interviewer that B. "could no more pass a bookshop than an alcoholic a pub." Since B.'s studies were not difficult, she filled her time writing stories and poems and drawing cartoons, her interest not financial but artistic and eventually expressive of her love for her family.

B. became friendly with her brother's schoolmate, Will Bannerman, whose family included the novelist Fanny Burney. When B. was nineteen, twenty-four-year-old Bannerman completed his medical studies. After accepting a junior hospital appointment, he passed the examinations for entry into the Indian Medical Service. When he proposed, B. accepted, but their marriage would not take place until he completed a five-year tour of duty in India. While he was away from Edinburgh, B. completed external studies in English, French, botany, and German, receiving her L.L.A. in 1887. Bannerman survived dangerous medical appointments in the mountainous areas of India, nearly losing his life to revolutionaries and to malignant malaria. Partially deaf, almost bald, and physically debilitated, he returned to marry B. in 1889.

B. and her husband then began his new appointment as regimental medical officer in Madras, where their first child was born. After two posts in remote areas, he left the military for a civilian job in the Indian Medical Service. In 1894, the family returned to Edinburgh for a year, then returned to India. It is at this time, when B.'s only interest was in keeping her children well, that her most acclaimed (yet controversial) work had its beginnings. *Little Black Sambo* is the story of a young man who takes a walk into the jungle and uses his four items of clothing and protection against the sun to save himself from the jaws of four tigers. When the tigers eventually meet and become envious of the shoes, pants, jacket, and umbrella each one owns, they angrily argue, eventually melting into a giant pool of clarified butter *(ghi),* which Sambo brings to his mother who puts it on their meal of delicious pancakes. Sambo eats 169 of them and reclaims his stolen possessions from the pool of melted tiger butter.

After she bound the story and sent it to her children, who had been sent to the hills during the unhealthy warmer weather, a friend, Alice M. E. Bond, suggested that she take it to London publishers. B. consented, but she wanted to be in control of any final agreements. The work was sold outright to the publisher because of the time it would have taken to communicate about the copyright. The little volume became a publishing and critical success.

B.'s name was on the cover, but never having desired nor having become accustomed to such renown and not wishing to embarrass her husband with unwanted notoriety, B.'s subsequent publications bore the disclaimer "By the author of *Little Black Sambo.*" Some critics found it "lively, colorful, well paced, charming and . . . authentic to India," although she really set the story in an unnamed land "far away and exotic." Its size was also a factor in its success. Predating the publications of Beatrix Potter's little books for children, this diminutive publication was just right for little hands to hold and to enjoy. Since B. had no rights to the story, more than fifty pirated editions appeared with different drawings or changes in the originals and no mention of the author's identity, but none of these factors could be contested. B. had no control over these pirated works, nor of the damage they brought (and are still bringing) to her original, loving material.

Both text and pictures in B.'s work and her following stories have been zealously studied, especially in light of political correctness. Papers have been written about the name of her characters, of the use of the work *black,* of the seemingly patronizing *little,* of the parental Mumbo and Jumbo, and of their lack of heritage—all considered, in many ways, as racist. Joseph Boskin, however, discusses the history of the name predating B.'s use: "As one of the earliest minority images to be translated into a cultural form, Sambo had become a multipublic figure by the eighteenth century, appealing across the social landscape." Boskin examines the evolution of the Sambo character, his humorous and cultural aspects, but finds a cultural distinction in B.'s text: "Helen Bannerman's *The Story of Little Black Sambo* was not . . . in the Sambo tradition. Its title had misled many a reader. The Indian youth is no buffoon. On the contrary, he uses his wits to defeat the tigers. But the wording of the title, as well as the illustrations in several editions, was in keeping with the stereotypical pose." Boskin mourns the censorship of the text, which rarely appears in American bookstores or libraries. The British, however, are more interested in the allusions to Indian versus African natives, yet these distinctions also have an effect on sales.

B. corresponded with her publisher about a second children's book, *The Story of Little Black Mingo.* Although the publisher seemed pleased to have another book, and he reassured her that the work would be anonymous, he would not agree to settle the copyright on the first work. B. changed publishers, the new firm issuing the story of a little black girl who has problems with the villain, a crocodile, which the author designates by the Indian word "mugger." This and other words—such as *chatty* for a water pot and *dhobi* for the man who washes the clothes—were debated but the contents remained unchanged because the accompanying pictures by B. leave no doubt as to what is meant.

B.'s drawings, an integral element of each story, seem influenced by *Punch* cartoons as much as by Punch and Judy and are carried over from the satirical cartoons in her personal letters, letters that also contain illustrations of a variety of humans, animals, and areas B. had visited or was impressed by. The weekly letters to her daughters in Edinburgh also contained colored illustrations that eventually filled seventeen bound volumes. Furthermore, other artists were influenced by B.'s illustrations, as is evident in the similarity of the little blond-haired girl holding an umbrella on the cover of *The Story of Little White Squibba* to the Morton Salt logo. The illustrations for this work, interesting enough, are by B.'s daughter, Janet.

Little Black Bobtail became the last of her children's books. Constantly writing for more than a decade, despite the pressures of her husband's career, her own infirmities, the needs of her children, and her other duties, she also increased her obligations on the Indian social scene. During World War I, her husband was unable to retire or bring his family home to Britain, and when their daughters visited them in India the war kept them from returning. Despite B.'s ill health, the family was happily reunited until the war had almost concluded. Eventually, at age fifty-five, after B. had spent more than thirty years in India, they sailed back to their beloved Edinburgh, arriving in London during the last air raid of the war.

B.'s stories differed from previous children's books in using "direct visual pictures and [lacked] an overt moral" or message. B. considered her works a depiction of close-knit families and their members' love for one another. Many attempts were made to have her create new stories or continuations of the originals, but she always refused. Eventually, her final publisher persuaded B. to create a special story for his children, and in 1937 *The Story of Sambo and the Twins* was published. It was received by most reviewers as a part of the collection, but one critic felt it "perpetuates the unconscious racism of its predecessors."

In 1939, on a trip to Lochinvar, while driving with her children, B. had a stroke that left her paralyzed. As one child states: "She had always hoped that when her time came, she would go quickly; but . . . it took seven years." Although she had been heartbroken at her husband's death in 1924 and never seemed to recover fully from that loss, her illness did not keep her from persevering to improve her condition, from reading, and from having numerous visitors. She died on 13 October 1946.

WORKS: *The Story of Little Black Sambo* (1899). *The Story of Little Black Mingo* (1901). *The Story of Little Black Quibba* (1902). *The Story of Little Degchiehead* (1903; in the U.S. as *The Story of Little Kettlehead*, 1904). *Pat and the Spider* (1905). *The Story of the Teasing Monkey* (1906). *The Story of Little Black Quasha* (1908). *The Story of Little Black Bobtail* (1909). *The Story of Sambo and the Twins* (1936). *The Story of Little White Squibba* (1966).

BIBLIOGRAPHY: Arbuthnot, M. H. *Children and Books* (1964). Boskin, J. *Sambo: The Rise and Demise of an American Jester* (1986). Hay, E. *Sambo Sahib* (1981). Kujoth, E. H. *Best Selling Children's Books* (1973). Larrick, N. *The All White World of Children's Books* (1964). McDonald, M. *Psycho-Analytic Study of the Child* (1973). Schiller, J. G. *Book Collector* (1974). Stokes, F. A., foreword to *The Jumbo Sambo* (1942). Yuill, P. *Little Black Sambo: A Closer Look* (1976).

For articles in reference works, see: *DLB. OCCL. SATA. TCCW. Todd BWW.*

Zelda R. B. Provenzano

Anna Laetitia Barbauld

BORN: 20 June 1743, Kibworth-Harcourt, Leicestershire.
DIED: 9 March 1825, Stoke-Newington, London.
DAUGHTER OF: John Aikin and Jane Jennings Aiken.
MARRIED: Rochemont Barbauld, 1774.

B., poet, editor, essayist, and writer for children, was one of four women to be cited (lines from two of her poems, "The Invitation" and "A Summer Evening Meditation") in the first edition of *Bartlett's Familiar Quotations* (1851). This honor most likely stemmed from B.'s popularity based on her widely known inspirational books for children. B.'s literary output, however, was not limited to children's books. She was active in the political and social circles of her day in spite of the problems she encountered in an unfortunate marriage.

At an early age, B. showed an uncanny talent and desire for learning. It was said that by the age of three she could read a book as well as any woman and that as a child she was acquainted with the best in English literature. She also mastered French and Italian very early, and through the special pleading of her mother she was allowed to expand her knowledge of languages by studying Greek and Latin even though her father discouraged such study.

B.'s life changed for the better, however, when her father was appointed tutor in 1758 at the newly opened Warrington Academy, established to give dissenters, who were shut out from Oxford and Cambridge, the benefits of a university education. B.'s brother, John Aikin, a physician with decidedly literary interests, encouraged her to publish, in 1773, her first volume of poems, which included "The Invitation," quoted by Bartlett, and "Corsica," a poem greatly admired by Mary Wortley Montagu. The book was an immediate success and went through four editions in the first year.

In the same year, B. also published, with her brother, *Miscellaneous Pieces in Prose,* also reprinted several times. Exact attribution of the essays is difficult since the authors did not sign all of their respective pieces, but B.'s known contributions include some of her best essays, notably on "Inconsistency in Our Expectations" and "On Romances." "On Romances" represents B.'s imitation of Samuel Johnson's style and method of reasoning, this type of imitation a frequent pastime of aspiring neoclassical writers. Of this essay Johnson observed: "The imitators of my style have not hit it. Miss Aikin has done it the best, for she has imitated the sentiment as well as the diction."

In the midst of these literary successes, B. married the Reverend Rochemont Barbauld, a student of the academy at Warrington, with whom she established a successful boys' school at Palgrave. While at Palgrave B. wrote her best-known work, *Hymns in Prose for Children* (1781), which went through many editions and was translated into several European languages. She also wrote her *Early Lessons for Children* (1781), which went through a number of editions as well and was translated into French. Her *Devotional Pieces, Composed from the Psalms and the Book of Job* (1775) was received respectfully by the literary community. B.'s literary fame and her devotion to the academy soon brought celebrity and success, and her home became an important gathering place for dissenters who aspired to prove themselves as intellectual, broad-minded, and skilled in the graces and amenities of social life as their Church of England contemporaries.

In 1785, due to her husband's declining mental condition, they closed the school and spent a year traveling abroad, settling a year later at Hampstead, where B. became close friends with Joanna Baillie and her sister. This new literary milieu inspired B. to write essays of a different kind. In 1791, B. wrote *Epistle to Mr. Wilberforce on the Rejection of the Bill for Abolishing the Slave*

Trade. In 1792, she published *Remarks on Mr. Gilbert Wakefield's Enquiry into the Expediency and Propriety of Public or Social Worship.* B., like many women of her time, was concerned with the social injustices and controversies of her days; her essays prefigure the kind of feminine social consciousness that was to blossom in the mid-nineteenth century into the novel of social reform. Also in 1792, B., in collaboration with her brother, published the first of six volumes of their best-known work, *Evenings at Home.* The book contributed to B.'s popularity and when read aloud provided evening entertainment for many British families, including the family of novelist Maria Edgeworth. B. is said to have contributed "fifteen papers" to this work, though the major part of the writing was done by her brother.

In 1804, she published *Selections from the Spectator, Tatler, Guardian, and Freeholder,* an edited work that reflected the interests of British readers who preferred serious books on religion and morality, essays of the *Spectator* and *Tatler* type. In the same year, she contributed a *Life of Samuel Richardson* to his *Correspondence,* which she edited. But her literary career was interrupted when her husband's mental health deteriorated to the point that he was forced to give up his pastoral work and eventually to be institutionalized. He died, insane, in London in 1808. Shortly after her husband's death, B. undertook an edition in fifty volumes of the best English novelists to which she prefixed a lengthy essay on the "Origin and Progress of Novel Writing," and she introduced the works of each author by short but complete biographical notices.

In 1811, B. "prepared for the use of young ladies, a selection, formerly well known and popular, of the best passages from English poets and prose writers," called *The Female Speaker.* Her greatest notoriety came from her criticism in this work of Samuel Taylor Coleridge's "The Rime of the Ancient Mariner." B. did not approve of this poem. She acknowledged its "queer, wizard-like quality," but she complained, characteristically, that it had no moral. Since the B. household was known not to be receptive to the romantic notions of progress and the emphasis on the imagination, a movement away from reason presented for B. and her circle an inadequacy in art. The same year she wrote a poem that again embroiled her in literary controversy, *Eighteen Hundred and Eleven.* Written at a time of the deepest national gloom, it was considered eloquent but too despondent. B. incurred much reproach by writing it because it prophesied that in some future day a visitor to London would be able to contemplate the ruin of St. Paul's Cathedral from a broken arch of Blackfriars Bridge. The poem evoked "a very coarse review" in *The Quarterly* by Robert Southey, who said later that he regretted the harshness of his review.

Though this was the last of B.'s published works, she continued to write both letters and minor pieces published after her death. Her letters show that "though her life was habitually retired she greatly enjoyed society." They record friendships formed or casual acquaintance made with Montagu, Hannah More, Joseph Priestley, Maria Edgeworth, Hester Chapone, Gilbert Wakefield, Walter Scott, Joanna Baillie, H. Crab Robinson, William Roscoe, William Wordsworth, W. E. Channing, Samuel Rogers, and Sir James Mackintosh, among others. All her work is characterized by a grace of style and lofty but not Puritanical principles.

WORKS: *Corsica: An Ode* (1768). *Poems* (1773). (with J. Aikin) *Miscellaneous Pieces in Prose* (1773). *Devotional Pieces, Composed from the Psalms and the Book of Job* (1775). *Hymns in Prose for Children* (1781). *Early Lessons for Children* (1781). *Lessons for Children, from Two to Three Years Old* (1788). *Lessons for Children, of Four to Five Years Old* (1788). *Lessons for Children of Four Years Old (Part 2)* (1788). *An Address to the Opposers of the Repeal of the Corporation and Test Acts* (1790). *Epistle to Mr. Wilberforce on the Rejection of the Bill for Abolishing the Slave Trade* (1791). *Letter to John Bull* (1792). *Remarks on Mr. Gilbert Wakefield's Enquiry into the Expediency and Propriety of Public or Social Worship* (1792). (with J. Aikin) *Evenings at Home, or, The Juvenile Budget Opened: Consisting of a Variety of Miscellaneous Pieces for the Instruction and Amusement of Young Persons,* 6 vols. (1792–95). *Civic Sermons to the People* (1793). *Sins of the Government, Sins of the Nation, or, A Discourse for the Fast, Appointed on April 19, 1793* (1793). *Essay on Akenside's Pleasures of the Imagination* (1795). *Essay on the Odes of Collins* (1797). *Gothic Stories* (1797). *Lessons for Children* (1798). *Poetic Gift; Containing Mrs. Barbauld's Hymns, in Verse* (1800). (with J. Aikin) *The Art of Life* (1802). *Selections from the Spectator* (1804). *The Female Speaker* (1811). *Eighteen Hundred and Eleven* (1812). *Lessons for Children* (1818). *Works,* ed. Aikin (1825). *Mrs. Barbauld's Little Stories for Children,* ed. J. Stephens (1830). *Things By Their Right Names, and Other Stories, Fables, and Moral Pieces, in Prose and Verse,* ed. S. J. Hale (1840). *A Memoir, Letters and a Selection from the Writings of Anna Laetitia Barbauld,* ed. G. A. Ellis (1874). *Letters of Maria Edgeworth and Anna Laetitia Barbauld,* ed. W. S. Scott (1953). *The Poems of Anna Letitia Barbauld,* ed. W. McCarthy and E. Kraft (1994).

BIBLIOGRAPHY: Ellison, J., in *Re-Visioning Romanticism: British Women Writers, 1776–1837,* ed. C. S. Wilson and J. Haefner (1994). Le Breton, A. L. *A Memoir of Mrs. Barbauld* (1874). Moore, C., in *Fetter'd or Free? British Women Novelists, 1670–1815,* ed. M. A. Schofield and C. Macheski (1986). Robbins, S. *L&U* (1993). Rogers, K. *SECC* (1991). Vallone, L. *L&U* (1991).

For articles in reference works, see: *Allibone. BA19C. Bloomsbury. Cambridge. DNB. Feminist. Oxford. ToddBWW.*

Other references: Brodribb, C. W. *ContempR* (1935). Darton, F. J. H. *Children's Books in English* (1932). Kramnick, M., preface to *Hymns in Prose for Children* (1977). *Eyes and No Eyes,* ed. M. V. O'Shea (1900). Thackeray, A. R. *A Book of Sibyls* (1883). Whiting, M. B. *London Mercury* (September 1932).

Priscilla Dorr
(updated by Carol Shiner Wilson)

Mary Barber

BORN: 1690 (?), probably Ireland.
DIED: 1757, Dublin, Ireland.
MARRIED: Jonathan Barber.
WROTE UNDER: Mary Barber; Sapphira.

Little is known of Mary Barber's life apart from references in the correspondence of her circle. We know that she lived in Dublin and had four children, the eldest of whom, Constantine, later became president of the Irish College of Physicians. In addition to acquaintance with the rich and powerful, she enjoyed the friendship of Jonathan Swift and his Dublin circle, including the other Irish women poets Constantia Grierson and Laetitia Pilkington. With Pilkington and Mrs. E. Sican, she made up what Swift called his "triumfeminate." It is generally agreed that she began writing to enliven her children's lessons while teaching them at home. Once persuaded to publish poems, she was introduced to Swift and discussed her poetry with him. She was lavishly praised by Swift as "our chief poetess," "a poeticall genius," and "the best poetess in both kingdoms." He and his friends offered comments on and amendments to her poetry. In the 1730s, it became normal for women to publish their verse by subscription, and, with the active support of Swift, B. went to England in 1730 to obtain subscriptions. In 1731, she was involved in a somewhat mysterious attempt to solicit the queen's support for her poetry, using Swift's forged signature. Swift ultimately forgave her. She spent some three years in England moving in fashionable circles at Tunbridge Wells, Bath, and London.

Poems on Several Occasions was published in 1734 and in each of the two following years; the 900 subscribers included the great and the good. The poems were well received, but their publication did not help B.'s poverty. She was now living very much apart from her husband, suffering (as she did throughout her life) from "gout" (i.e., that which we would now call arthritis). In 1734, B. was involved in another mysterious event when she was arrested with others in England for importing two scurrilous poems by Swift that were seen as an attack on the Walpole administration. She was eventually released and the matter dropped. Although some poetry on her gout appeared in *The Gentleman's Magazine* in March 1737 and a selection of her poems in *Poems by Eminent Ladies* in 1755, she wrote little poetry in her later years. In 1738, she became financially more secure by printing by subscription Swift's *Polite Convervation,* which he had given her. B. died in 1757.

Roger Lonsdale's *Eighteenth-Century Women Poets* has brought back into view the "forgotten" women poets of the eighteenth century. Until recently, few had remained in print—even in anthologies. Now that we can read the work of these poets, we can gain an alternative view of the century through domestic and everyday events. In a manner reminiscent of Swift, B. wrote caustically of love, sex, and marriage. She also, in common with other women poets of the period, underestimated her own performance.

A number of the poems in *Poems on Several Occasions* are clearly stated as having been written for specific reasons. These are wide ranging: a friend resenting advice, recovery from sickness, reading books, seeing pictures, apologies for various social events, behavior, marriage. This is in keeping with the pattern of much of the light verse of the early eighteenth century. B.'s poetry also contains references to political events, and there is also some criticism of Britain's treatment of Ireland. The poems of B. and her contemporaries offer us an introduction to the world of eighteenth-century women. They also help to balance the often frivolous and sometimes cynical view of women presented by the male poets until recently seen as the only poets writing at the time.

WORKS: *Poems on Several Occasions* (1734). *Poems by Eminent Ladies,* ed. G. Colman and B. Thornton (1755; rev. 1780). Brooke, H. *Brookiana* (1804). *Eighteenth-Century Women Poets,* ed. R. Lonsdale (1989).
BIBLIOGRAPHY: Doody, M. *YES* (1988). Tucker, B. *The Poetry of Mary Barber* (1992).

For articles in reference works, see: *BDIW. Feminist. Oxford. ToddDBA. Unveiling Treasures*, ed. A. O Weekes (1993).

Other references: Foxon, D. F. *English Verse, 1701–1750* (1975). *Hermathena* (1969). *LRB* (21 December 1989). *The Memoirs of Mrs. Laetitia Pilkington 1712–50* (1748–54). Swift, J. *Correspondence,* ed. H. Williams (1963–65).

Bernard Tucker

A[udrey]. L[ilian]. Barker

BORN: 13 April 1918, Kent.
DAUGHTER OF: Harry Barker and Elsie A. Dutton Barker.
WRITES UNDER: A.L. Barker.

B.'s best-received works are her short stories. Although all her fiction has some commitment to plot, that is, to tell a story, the primary impression of a B. story or novel is its surreal, detached aura of fiction itself. Indeed, some of her stories are called "ghost stories."

B.'s works do not spring from a highly specialized, formal education. She attended a county secondary school that she left at the age of sixteen, after which she found secretarial jobs in London offices and later as a subeditor in the Amalgamated Press. After World War II, she wrote for the BBC and freelanced. She has written screen adaptations of some of her stories.

The characters and plots of a B. story or novel seem to be everyday, but soon the situations become Kafkaesque. It is "as though we were continually being shown banal scenes but told original and disturbing things about them by some voice 'off camera'" (*Books and Bookmen,* May 1985). In *A Source of Embarrassment* (1974), for example, the novel's main character, Edith, is supposedly dying of a brain tumor. Ironically, her inability to communicate with her sister, daughter, and husband is the theme. It is left unclear whether the "source" of the embarrassment is Edith's bizarre actions that may be tumor induced or the lack of compassionate sympathy from those around her.

"The fictions of A. L. Barker are peopled with fantasists, liars, story-tellers and dreamers; the misfits and the self protecting, the mediocre and untalented are allowed to put their own cases in virtuoso monologues, presented with startling immediacy," the reviewer of *Zeph* said (*TLS*, 16 October 1992). Zeph, a young woman aspiring to become a writer "to learn the grammar of existence, burdened with an armful of platitudes and clichés," tells her own story. "I'll be classical, I'll be popular, I'll be the unintelligent woman's Iris Murdoch." These are the opening lines of *Zeph*, but because the reader has no clue from the title what the short novel is about and since the statement does not appear to be dialogue, there is a momentary confusion between a prologue and narration. Zeph is a short for Zephrine, the name of the young writer. As such, it is a *Kunstlerroman* in which the writer is struggling to establish herself in a weird world. While working on a book about Napoleon's exile—without doing any research—Zeph writes a poem, the first piece she has completed. She wants to organize an evening to present it to her writer community, a collection of pseudoartistic friends living with her. She "recited it to my Iris Murdochs" to get a serious discussion going. "I want to find out about Art, why we do it, what it is. . . . Art is the union of sensibilities. That was the biggest moment, absolute truth was raging out of me, I felt effulgent." Finally, through her search for the ultraliterary world and voice, she discovers Jamaican patterns picked up from her estranged father's girlfriend and tells imaginative, primal stories to her best friend's young son.

B. has found higher praise for her short stories than for her novels. Her collections have won awards: the Atlantic Award in Literature (1946), the Somerset Maugham Award for *Innocents* (1947), Cheltenham Festival Literary Award (1962), the Katherine Mansfield Short Story Prize (1984), the Macmillan Silver Pen Award for Fiction (1986 and 1989), and the Society of Authors' Traveling Scholarship (1988).

B.'s short story collections are frequently organized around a thematic concept. In *Any Excuse for a Party*, B. introduces the collection as a "kind of autobiography." Even this collection, which is taken from B.'s life work, suggests the variety of interests that inspired her: innocence versus adult sensibilities, supernatural occurrences, and, most of all, the world of "small domestic misunderstandings."

B.'s works have been termed off-beat, highly individual, precise, and controlled.

WORKS: *Innocents: Variations on a Theme* (1947). *Apology for a Hero* (1950). *Novelette, with Other Stories* (1951). *The Joy-Ride and After* (1963). *Lost upon the Roundabouts* (1964). *A Case Examined* (1965). *The Middling: Chapters in the Life of Elsie Toms* (1967). *John Brown's Body* (1969). *Femina Real* (1971). *A Source of Embarrassment* (1974). *A Heavy Feather* (1978). *Life Stories* (1979). *Relative Successes* (1984). *No Word of Love* (1985). *The Gooseboy* (1987). *The Woman Who Talked to Herself: An Articulated Novel* (1989). *Any Excuse for a Party* (1991). *A. L. Barker Omnibus: A Case Examined, John Brown's Body, and The Gooseboy* (1992). *Element of Doubt: Ghost Stories* (1992). *Zeph* (1992). *Seduction* (1994).

BIBLIOGRAPHY:

For articles in reference works, see: *CA*. *CN*. *DLB*. *IAWWW*. *TCA* and *SUP*. *TCSSE*. *WD*.

Other references: *Books and Bookmen* (September 1984, May 1985). *British Book News* (February 1982, October 1984). *Guardian Weekly* (16 September 1984). *Listener* (5 November 1981, 4 October 1984). *LonSunT* (12 August 1984, 22 October 1989, 17 March 1991, 22 November 1992). *New Statesman* (2 October 1981, August 1984, 31 May 1985). *Spectator* (26 September 1981, 10 August 1984). *TLS* (22 March 1974, 19 April 1974, 25 September 1981, 3 August 1984, 21 June 1985, 22 December 1989, 1 March 1991, 22 November 1992).

Marilynn J. Smith

Jane Barker

BAPTIZED: 17 May 1652, Blatherwicke, Northamptonshire.
DIED: 29 March 1732, Saint Germain-en-Laye, France.
DAUGHTER OF: Thomas Barker and Anne Connock.
WROTE UNDER: Mrs. Jane Barker; Fidelia; Galesia; A Young Lady.

B. was an artist who accepted the outward forms of convention without allowing them to restrict the originality of her work or its honest depiction of the life of an educated, unmarried woman in seventeenth-century England. In both her personal life and her writing, B. upheld the ideal of chastity that was urged upon all women of her time, but she was never easy with society's enforced separation of female sexuality and female intellect. Drawing upon her own experience, B. dramatized the conflict between a woman's conventional "public" role—that of a wife—and the "public" nature of writing. In all of B.'s novels, women are forced to choose between marriage and their intellectual pursuits, but B. rarely romanticizes the results of these choices and often denies her heroines the typical romance ending of a happy marriage. Yet she was unconventional not only in her willingness to depict the harsh demands that society placed on educated women but also in her innovative use of poetic and autobiographical techniques to shape the form of the novel itself.

Born in rural Northamptonshire to a Royalist family, B. was baptized into the Church of England on 17 May 1652. Her mother, Anne Connock, came from a Cornish family who were staunch supporters of the Stuarts, while her father, Thomas Barker, had taken up arms in defense of Charles I. B. spent most of her childhood in Wilsthorp, a tiny Lincolnshire village where her father was a tenant farmer of the Earl of Exeter. Despite the relative seclusion of her early years, B. secured the advantages of a good education through her brother, Edward, who assisted her in her studies of Latin and medicine. Nor was she denied access to the higher ranks of society. Years later in the dedication she wrote to the Countess of Exeter for her novel, *Exilius*, B. recalled that it was "Burleigh-house, with its Park, Shades, and Walks" that first inspired the bucolic setting of her romance.

In her later writing, B. makes it clear that her early poems received the approbation of her brother and his circle of friends at St. John's College, Oxford. B. recalled these years with nostalgia, and she portrayed them as a period of intellectual and emotional felicity when she was courted by young men and compared favorably with the acclaimed poet Katherine Phillips, known as the "Matchless Orinda." Yet B.'s early happiness and her contentment with her rural surroundings proved short lived. In the late 1670s, both her father and her beloved brother died, leaving her alone with her mother. The two women then moved to London where B. describes her sense of loneliness and estrangement through her semi-autobiographical character, "Galesia": "This was a new Life to me, and very little fitted the Shape of my Rural Fancy . . . I was like a Wild Ass in a Forest, and liv'd alone in the midst of this great Multitude, even the great and populous City of London."

After the death of her mother in 1685, B. remained a spinster, living on the income of the tenancy she had inherited from her father. The loss of so many family ties effectively left her independent, but her mature years were often lonely and filled with hardship. By this time, B. had either converted to the Roman Catholic faith or had ceased to conceal her family's Catholicism; as a penalty for her admission of her faith, she had to pay double tax, and her strong sympathies for the Catholic Stuart, James II, prompted her to follow his court-in-exile to France. She finally returned to England and began publishing her novels in 1713. In later years, B. suffered from cataracts, which she claims to have treated herself with some success, but her letters and manuscripts of unpublished poems offer little other information about her personal life. A letter from a relative refers to her serious illness in 1726; another letter mentions a projected trip to France in 1727. After that date nothing is known of B., nor of the circumstances of her death.

In fact, the best sources of information about B.'s personal life and literary ambitions consist of her largely autobiographical poems and novels. Through the persona of "Galesia," the "author" and heroine of many of her poems and novels, B. created an alter ego whose adventures cast her own experiences in a fictive setting. Several poems in *Poetical Recreations* (1688) that were written by B.'s admirers address her as "the incomparable Galesia" as well as the "ingenious Mrs. Barker," indicating that this was a longstanding pseudonym. By choosing to publish *Poetical Recreations* first, B. defined herself as primarily a poet, yet the collection also traces an autobiographical outline of her career, and these same poems would eventually form the "fabric" of her novel, *A Patch-work Screen,* in which they were interspersed with tales and commentary.

By 1688, B. had evidently begun writing a novel, since *Poetical Recreations* excerpts a poem from her novel *Exilius,* or the *Banish'd Roman,* which remained unpublished until 1715. Although its repetitive form and complex interweaving of plots may weary the reader, *Exilius* contains some of B.'s most imaginative episodes and exhibits an intriguing, often comic imposition of seventeenth-century sensibility upon the uninhibited, pagan world of Greek romance. In *Love Intrigues* (1713), B. begins her history of the semi-autobiographical "Galesia," recounting her unhappy love for her cousin, Bosvil, and her uneasy devotion to the Muses. B.'s title is an ironic one, for the novel offers little intrigue and its heroine appears to be betrayed not so much by love as by her own adherence to the Muses. The ending of the novel is unsettling since it offers no resolution of the heroine's troubles, while B.'s portrayal of Galesia's anguish and confusion demonstrate a rare psychological acuity by hinting at the rage and self-destructiveness that underlie Galesia's apparent passivity.

A Patch-work Screen (1723) and *The Lining of the Patch-work Screen* (1726) continue Galesia's history after her return from a sojourn in France. Galesia is by now a much older woman and the tone of these novels becomes progressively darker as she not only abandons her hopes of a happy marriage but also her poetic aspirations. In another dream sequence, Galesia attends the coronation of the "Matchless Orinda," her literary idol, yet in this vision she is merely a spectator and not the "Heiress of that Ladies Muse" as she had once claimed to be. Yet despite this shift in the narrator's tone, B.'s late novels are her most colorful and original works. By choosing the "patch-work screen" as a metaphor for her method of composition, B. defined the novel as a peculiarly feminine pursuit and justified the unusual form of her work by noting that "whenever one sees a Set of Ladies together, their *Sentiments* are as differently mix'd as the *Patches* in their Work."

From the perspective of Ian Watt's influential thesis of "formal realism" as the defining characteristic of the early English novel, B.'s refusal to observe conventional boundaries of form and genre has led some modern critics to disparage her work as "weak" and "incoherent." However, in more recent feminist and post-modern evaluations of the early English novel, criticism of B.'s work has taken on a more sympathetic cast; one feminist-Marxist critic describes *A Patch-work Screen* as "one of the most important, if ignored, works in women's literary history" (Donovan, 1991). B.'s experimental combinations of poetry, autobiography, and social commentary in her narratives serve as a reminder that the "novel" as we know it was still taking shape in the seventeenth century; they do not suggest a lack of stylistic control so much as B.'s determination to give the novel a peculiarly "feminine" form. By blending fact and fiction, B. consciously constructed an identity through her alter ego, Galesia, that was neither a fictive "character" nor a historical "person" but a self designed to communicate a wide range of female experience and to explore the conflict she and other women faced in attempting to reconcile the demands of social convention with their own personal desires and intellectual aspirations.

WORKS: *Poetical Recreations: Consisting of Original Poetry Songs, Odes & c. With Several New Translations* (1688). "A Collection of Poems refering to the times" (British Library MS. ADD 21, 621, c. 1700). "Poems on Several Occasions in three parts" (Oxford, Magdalen MS. 343, c. 1701). *Love Intrigues, or, The History of the Amours of Bosvil and Galeria: As Related to Lucasia, in St. Germains Garden* (1713, revised 1719; ed. J. Grieder, 1973). *Exilius, or, The Banish'd Roman: A New Romance: In Two Parts, Written after the Manner of Telemachus* (1715; ed. J. Grieder, 1973). (trans.) *The Christian Pilgrimage* (1718). *The Entertaining Novels of Mrs. Jane Barker* (1719). *A Patch-work Screen for the Ladies: or, Love and Virtue Recommended* (1723; ed. J. Grieder, 1973). *The Lining of the Patch-work Screen: Design'd for the Farther Entertainment of the Ladies* (1726). *The Galesia Trilogy and Selected Manuscript Poems of Jane Barker*, ed. C. S. Wilson (1997).

BIBLIOGRAPHY: Horner, J. *The English Women Novelists and Their Connection with the Feminist Movement 1688–1797* (1929). Kern, J., in *Fetter'd or Free? British Women Novelists, 1670–1815*, ed. M. A. Schofield and C. Macheski (1986). King, K., in *Anxious Power: Reading, Writing, and Ambivalence in Narrative by Women*, ed. C. J. Singley and S. E. Sweeney (1993). McCarthy, B. *Women Writers: Their Contribution to the English Novel 1621–1744* (1944). Morgan, C. *The Rise of the Novel of Manners* (1911). Reynolds, M. *The Learned Lady in England 1650–1760* (1920). Richetti, J. *Popular Fiction Before Richardson: Narrative Patterns 1700–1739* (1969). Spacks, P. M. *Imagining a Self: Autobiography and Novel in Eighteenth Century England* (1976). Spencer, J. *The Rise of the Woman Novelist: From Aphra Behn to Jane Austen* (1986). Williamson, M. *Raising Their Voices: British Women Writers, 1650–1750* (1990).

For articles in reference works, see: *Bloomsbury. DLB. Feminist. Oxford. ToddBWW. ToddDBA.*

Other references: Backscheider, P. *SNNTS* (1979). Burney, W. H. *PQ* (1958). Donovan, J. *Signs* (1991). Doody, M. A. *Genre* (1977). Gibbons, G. S. *N&Q* (1922). King, K. *ECent* (1994). McBurney, W. H. *PQ* (1958). Spencer, J. *TSWL* (1983).

Elizabeth Wahl and Carol Shiner Wilson

Anne Barnard

BORN: 8 December 1750, Fifeshire, Scotland.
DIED: 6 May 1825, London.
DAUGHTER OF: James Lindsay, fifth Earl of Balcarres, and Anne Dalrymple.
MARRIED: Andrew Barnard, 1793.

Little attention has been paid to the literary qualities of B.'s prose, and commentary on her brief poetic output even scanter. It seems that the definitive corpus of her work is yet to be established from among disparate, as yet unpublished manuscript sources. Nonetheless, her published epistolary collections and the fragments of her diaries ought to be of notable interest to scholars engaged in the study of social history, British imperial administration in South Africa, and the life of a well-to-do woman of letters who did not make a living from her own writing. She did enjoy being the central figure in her own literary salon.

Auld Robyn Gray is a fine ballad in the Scottish romantic tradition. It circulated for many years anonymously, suggesting the demure embarrassment of its author's having composed a poem set to the melody of a traditional bawdy song. Sir Walter Scott, in the introduction of the only complete published edition of the ballad, gives a warm account of his family's ties of friendship to B. and a brief character sketch of the author.

Had any of her letters made their way to newspapers or magazines of her day, they would have constituted an early form of journalistic foreign dispatches. Having found no evidence of periodical publication, she wrote solely to a well-chosen circle of personal friends and relatives.

Beyond the needs of the social historian in examining source documents from the upper echelons of British imperial circles or the needs of literary critics to perform rhetorical analysis in tracing the history of the epistolary tradition in English, there is nothing to suggest that B. is an author in need of being reclaimed by feminist scholarship.

WORKS: *Auld Robyn Gray. A Ballad*, ed. and intro. Sir Walter Scott (1825). *South Africa a Century Ago*, ed. William Henry Wilkins (1901; 2nd ed. 1924). *Lady Anne Barnard to Henry Dundas from the Cape and Elsewhere, 1793–1803*, ed. A. M. Lewin Robinson (1973).

BIBLIOGRAPHY: *Index to Lady Anne Barnard's South Africa a Century Ago*, comp. M. M. Boshoff (1967). Lenta, M. *EinA (1992)*. Lenta, M. *ArielE* (1991). Merwe, P. P. van der. *Current Writing* (1990).

For articles in reference works, see: *Chambers. CHEL. Personal Writings by Women to 1900. A Bibliography of American and British Writers*, ed. G. Davis and B. A. Joyce (1989). *Feminist. Jackson. Oxford.*

Nicolás Hernández, Jr.

Barrett, Elizabeth Barrett: See *Browning, Elizabeth Barrett*

Mary Bateson

BORN: 12 September 1865, Ings House, Robin Hood's Bay, near Whitby.
DIED: 30 November 1906, Cambridge.
DAUGHTER OF: William Henry Bateson and Anna Aikin.

As the daughter of the Master of St. John's College, Cambridge, B. lived in an atmosphere of committed liberalism. She was educated at the Misses Thornton's School, Cambridge; the Institut Friedlander, Baden; and the Perse School, Cambridge. In 1884, B. enrolled in Newnham College, Cambridge, a recently established college for women. Mandell Creighton, professor of ecclesiastical history at Cambridge, suggested that B. pursue a career as a professional historian. Her dissertation, "Monastic Civilisation in the Fens," won the college's historical essay prize. In 1888, after winning a first class in the historical tripod, she began a lifelong association with Newnham as teacher, member of the council, and liberal financial supporter. In 1903, she accepted a three-year research fellowship at Newnham.

As a protégé of Creighton, B. began her career as a student of medieval monasticism. In 1889, her first publication appeared, an edition of *The Register of Crabhouse Nunnery;* the next year she published a lengthy essay on the Pilgrimage of Grace in the *English Historical Review,* and she continued to publish articles and contributed numerous reviews, especially on medieval German urban history, in this journal. Her final contribution to monastic history was her important study "Origin and Early History of Double Monasteries" (1899).

Working closely with the great legal historian F. W. Maitland, Downing Professor at Cambridge, B. became a recognized authority in medieval English municipal history. She worked extensively in local history, publishing records on Cambridge as well as her monumental edition of sources on the Corporation of Leicester from the eleventh through the seventeenth centuries. Her painstaking editing brought to publication documents from many periods, including records of the Privy Council of the sixteenth century, letters of the Duke of Newcastle from the eighteenth century, a monastic library catalogue, and the poems of the fifteenth-century English writer George Ashby. Her finest achievement as editor came at the end of her life with the publication of her two-volume *Borough Customs* for the Selden Society.

B. demonstrated her capacity for historical popularization with her delightful *Mediaeval England, 1066–1350* (1903), a volume in the Story of Nations series and the first extensive social history of medieval England. Her flair for narrative enlivens her essay on the French in America written for the *Cambridge Modern History* (1903). By 1900, B. had contributed more than 100 entries on medieval figures to the *Dictionary of National Biography.* Her scholarly stature earned her, in 1906, appointment as one of the three editors of the projected *Cambridge Mediaeval History.* Her greatness as an historian (as opposed to an editor) is best demonstrated in her papers on "The Laws of Breteuil," where she proves convincingly that a large number of English towns based their institutions on the little Norman town of Breteuil, not on Bristol as previously thought.

B. died in Cambridge at the age of forty-one after a short illness. Her indefatigable labors in English urban history were matched only by her early interest and continuing activity for women's suffrage and women's emancipation. According to contemporaries, B. was generous, steady, hardworking, cheerful, and completely without pretense. She was, at the same time, according to Mrs. Creighton, writing in 1906, "one of the best, if not the best, women historical students that England has ever produced."

WORKS: (ed.) *The Register of Crabhouse Nunnery.* (ed.) *A Collection of Original Letters from the Bishops to the Privy Council, 1564* (1893). (ed.) *A Narrative of the Changes in the Ministry, 1765–1767,* by Thomas Pelham-Holles, Duke of Newcastle (1898). (ed.) *Catalogue of the Library of Synon Monastery* (1898). (ed.) *George Ashby's Poem, EETS* (1899). "Origin and Early History of Double Monasteries," in *Transactions of the Royal Historical Society* (1899). (ed.) *Records of the Borough of Leicester,* Vol. I (1899); Vol. II (1901); Vol. III (1905). "The Laws of Breteuil," *English Historical Review* (1900, 1901). "The French in America," in *Cambridge Modern History* (1903). (ed.) *Cambridge Guild Records* (1903). *Mediaeval England, 1066–1350* (1903). "The Scottish King's Household and Other Fragments," *Scottish History Society Miscellany* (1904). (ed.) *Borough Customs,* Selden Society, Vol. I (1904); Vol. II (1906).

BIBLIOGRAPHY:

For articles in reference works, see: *DNB.*

Other references: Maitland, F. W. *Collected Papers* (1911). Poole, R. L. *English Historical Review* (1907). *Who Was Who* (1920).

Judith C. Kohl

Henrietta M. Batson

BORN: 30 May 1859, Hamilton, Ontario, Canada.
DIED: 30 November 1943, Dorchester, Dorset.
DAUGHTER OF: Thomas John Mark Willoughby Blackman and Anne Gunn.
MARRIED: Alfred Stephen Batson, 1879.
WROTE UNDER: H. M. Batson; Mrs. Stephen Batson.

B. was a follower of Thomas Hardy. She set her novels in "Loamshire" and "Oakshire," modelled on her adopted county, Berkshire. Though she drew her subjects mostly from the gentry, she often refers to Wessex peasants. Her interest in their plight was sincere.

She spent her childhood in Canada, then moved with her parents to Froxfield, Wiltshire, in 1869. Two years later, her father took a curacy at Welford, Berkshire, which made possible B.'s attendance at a good school at Ramsgate. When her fiancé, Alfred Stephen Batson, succeeded to the rectorship at Welford, the two married, and B. entered that realm she often portrayed in her novels, the rectory. After publishing her first article in 1892, B. embarked on an eighteen-year literary career that included six novels and three books on gardening.

B. later spoke deprecatingly of her "spare time" literary endeavors as "books which . . . had no permanent value, except perhaps [the] volumes on gardening." She was too modest. Her novels both chart her development and chronicle changing Wessex ways. *Dark: A Tale of the Down Country,* a tale of love across class boundaries, has echoes of Eliot as well as Hardy. It is a rural tragedy, as is *The Earth Children.*

Her article "The Vogue of the Garden Book" (1900) signals awareness of both a change in contemporary gardening books and her desire to exploit this new form. The results were *The Book of the Country and the Garden* and two novels, *Adam the Gardener* and *A Splendid Heritage.* In the former, Adam Romaine, heir to a noble estate, chooses his lowly occupation to practice his socialist ideals and disguise his identity to study Wessex peasant life.

B. deserves recognition for temerity in following Hardy's lead, exploring various Wessex problems while developing her distinctive tragicomic voice. She was fascinated by the attitudes and values of country families in a region belatedly touched by progress. In their depiction of complex human problems in peaceful rural settings, her rural tragedies and social comedies show genuine talent.

WORKS: *Terrier and Inventory of Church Possessions in the Parish of Welford, Berks.* (1892). *Dark: A Tale of the Down Country* (1892). *Such a Lord is Love: A Woman's Heart Tragedy* (1893). *Adam the Gardener* (1894). *The Earth Children* (1897). *The Rubaiyat of Omar Khayyam [Fitzgerald's version] With a Commentary . . . by H. M. Batson* (1900). *A Book of the Country and the Garden* (1903). *A Concise Handbook of Garden Flowers* (1903). *The Summer Garden of Pleasure* (1908). *The Gay Paradines* (1909). *A Splendid Heritage* (1910).

BIBLIOGRAPHY: *CWW. WWWiL.*

W. Eugene Davis

Nina Bawden (Kark)

BORN: 19 January 1925, London.
DAUGHTER: Charles Mabey and Ellalaine Ursula May Cushing.
MARRIED: H. W. Bawden, 1946; Austen Steven Kark, 1954.

B. grew up in London and attended Somerville College, earning a B.A. in 1946 and an M.A. in 1951, and she pursued additional graduate studies at the Salzburg Seminar in American Studies in 1960. In addition to a prolific career as a novelist, B. worked as an assistant for a town-and-country planning firm and served as a justice of the peace for eight years. She has written in various fictional genres, including murder mysteries (*Who Calls the Tune,* 1953; in the U.S. as *Eyes of Green*), and *Change Here for Babylon,* 1955), a gothic romance (*The Solitary Child,* 1956), horror, and the bildungsroman. B. is best known, however, for her children's books and realistic adult novels exploring contemporary middle-class life. Her children's books have won many awards, and *Circles of Deceit,* an adult novel, was a Booker Prize nominee in 1987.

The majority of B.'s adult novels are domestic moral comedies, highlighting the fine shadings and repercussions of seemingly unimportant actions and casual decisions. Her perception of irony brightens her depiction of even potentially tragic situations, and she avoids bizarre characterization or overtly dramatic plotting. B. has stated that most of her novels "have an element of autobiography about them," and her fictions seeks to illuminate experiences or emotions common to her readers. "You take an event, a character, someone or something that until now you have observed only in passing, from the outside," B. wrote, "and examine it closely in order to turn it into a story, and it becomes much more complex, much richer than you had thought at first."

Family relationships and the responsibilities of parenthood are B.'s most frequent themes, addressed in nearly all her novels. *Anna Apparent* (1972) depicts an abused child; *George Beneath a Paper Moon* (1974) the title character's midlife crisis; *Familiar Passions* (1979) a woman's discovery of her father's identity. Based on B.'s own experiences as a lay magistrate, *Afternoon of a Good Woman* (1976) examines the antecedents and reverberations of one afternoon's activities in the life of a justice of the peace as she reflects on the cases she hears and on her own unhappy marriage. *Walking Naked* (1981) is similarly self-referential, describing a day in the life of a middle-aged novelist in order to reveal the process through which a fiction writer finds meaning in memories, even on trivial incidents. *The Ice House* (1983) describes the impact a revelation can have on seemingly secure, long-established relationships and conceptions of the past. *Circles of Deceit* (1987), which depicts a dishonest marriage, and *Family Money* (1991), satirizing the 1980s obsession with money and real estate, continue B.'s examination of deception and its effect on intimate relationships.

B. began writing children's books in 1962 with *The Secret Passage* (1963; in the U.S. as *The House of Secrets*) and has since written seventeen more, several of which have been dramatized for British television. Like her adult novels, B.'s children's books share as their themes family interactions and parental responsibility. Several of B.'s children's books depict neglected or abused children, including some written before such topics were usual in children's fiction. *The Witch's Daughter* (1966) describes a "wild child" who is feared by the people of the remote village in which she lives. *Squib* (1971) depicts the attempted rescue of an abused little boy by an adolescent who is herself lonely and isolated. B.'s most famous work, *Carrie's War* (1973), describes two children's wartime evacuation in the care of an unsympathetic guardian.

The settings of B.'s novels are typically contemporary and unromantic. However, B.'s style is lyrical and delicate in both her children's and her adult fiction, offering subtle imagery and vivid evocations of place and character. B. has been criticized for skimming too lightly over the moral issues her fiction raises and for the conventional resolutions with which many of the novels conclude. Other critics, however, appreciate B.'s affirmation of small daily satisfactions and the possibility of new beginnings within the limits of everyday life.

WORKS: *Who Calls the Tune* (1953; in the U.S. as *Eyes of Green*). *The Odd Flamingo* (1954). *Change Here for Babylon* (1955). *The Solitary Child* (1956). *Devil by the Sea* (1957). *Just Like a Lady* (1960; in the U.S. as *Glass Slippers Always Pinch*). *In Honour Bound* (1961). *Tortoise by Candlelight* (1963). *The Secret Passage* (1963; in the U.S as *The House of Secrets* (1964). *Under the Skin* (1964). *On the Run* (1964; in the U.S. as *Three on the Run* 1965). *The White Horse Gang* (1966). *The Witch's Daughter* (1966). *A Little Love, A Little Learning* (1966). *A Woman of My Age* (1967). *A*

Handful of Thieves (1967). *The Grain of Truth* (1968). *The Runaway Summer* (1969). *The Birds on the Trees* (1970). *Squib* (1971). *Anna Apparent* (1972). *Carrie's War* (1973). *George Beneath a Paper Moon* (1974). *The Peppermint Pig* (1975). *Afternoon of a Good Woman* (1976). *Rebel on a Rock* (1978). *The Robbers* (1979). *Familiar Passions* (1979). *William Tell* (1981). *Walking Naked* (1981). *Kept in the Dark* (1982). *St. Francis of Assisi* (1983). *The Ice House* (1983). *The Finding* (1985). *Princess Alice* (1986). *Circles of Deceit* (1987). *Keeping Henry* (1988; in the U.S. as *Henry*). *The Outside Child* (1989). *Family Money* (1991). *Humbug* (1992). *The Real Plato Jones* (1993). *In My Own Time: Almost an Autobiography* (1994). *Devil by the Sea* (1997). *A Nice Change* (1997).

BIBLIOGRAPHY:

For articles in reference works, see: *CA. Cambridge. CLR. CN. Feminist. Oxford. SATA. TCCW. TCC&MW. ToddBWW.*

Other references: *NYTBR* (5 June 1973). *TLS* (17 April 1981, 22 July 1983).

Jane Weiss

Ada Ellen Bayly

BORN: 25 March 1857, Brighton.
DIED: 8 February 1903, Eastbourne.
DAUGHTER OF: Robert Bayly and Mary Winter.
WROTE UNDER: Ada Ellen Bayly; Edna Lyall.

Youngest in a family of three daughters and one son, B. was left fatherless at age eleven and an orphan at fourteen. A delicate child, she was first educated at home, then later in the house of her guardian and uncle T. B. Winter, and finally in Brighton private schools. She describes her youth in *The Burgess Letters* (1902). After her education, she lived successively with her married sisters, both wives of clergymen. Until 1880, she lived in Lincoln with her older sister; from 1880 until her death she lived with her younger sister in London in 1881, in Lincoln from 1881 to 1884, and after 1884 in Eastbourne, where she became very involved in religious and charitable activities. She was an active supporter of the women's suffrage movement and the Women's Liberal Association.

By transposing the letters of her name, B. invented the pseudonym Edna Lyall under which she wrote her first book, *Won by Waiting* (1879), a girls' story that was not well received. Her second novel, *Donovan, A Modern Englishman* (1882), received much attention, in particular from Gladstone, with whom she began correspondence. The novel deals with the religious crisis of Donovan Farrant, a physician who becomes a member of Parliament and his conversion from atheism to Christianity. The novel also led to her correspondence with Charles Bradlaugh, with whom she shared many political beliefs. Although she did not agree with his atheism, her liberal views led her to campaign against his exclusion from the House of Commons. After Bradlaugh's death, B. based her next novel, *We Two* (1884), on his experiences. The book details the extraordinary relationship between the secularist Luke Raeburn and his daughter Erica, who eventually converts to Christianity. B. expounds openmindedness and attacks Christians for their intolerance toward religious unorthodoxy, though she was criticized by the *Church Quarterly* for being unfair, an absurd accusation since she was advocating what she considered basic Christianity.

B.'s first popular book was the novel *In Golden Days*, a well-written historical work on the seventeenth century and the last work read to Ruskin on his deathbed. Her popularity prompted false gossip about her that she describes in *Autobiography of a Slander.* In subsequent novels, she espoused her liberal support of the Irish cause and denounced the Boer War.

B.'s plots are always well constructed; her best characterizations are of women and young girls. Her prose is easy to read and is sprinkled liberally with quotations from Longfellow, Whittier, and Plato. In the long run, however, the militancy expressed in her novels far outweighs any esthetic quality they may contain. Her reputation rests on *Donovan, We Two,* and *In Golden Days.*

WORKS: (as Edna Lyall) *Won by Waiting* (1879). *Donovan: A Modern Englishman* (1882). *We Two* (1884). *In Golden Days* (1885). *Autobiography of a Slander* (1887). *Knight Errant* (1887). *Their Happiest Christmas* (1889). *Derrick Vaughn, Novelist* (1889). *A Hardy Norseman* (1890). *Max Hereford's Dream: A Tale* (1891). *To Right the Wrong* (1894). *Doreen: the Story of a Singer* (1894). *How the Children Raised the Wind* (1896). *Autobiography of a Truth* (1896). *Wayfaring Men* (1897). *Hope the Hermit* (1897). *In Spite of All* (1901). *Burgess Letters: A Record of Child Life in the 60's* (1902). *The Hinderers* (1902).

BIBLIOGRAPHY: Escreet, J. M. *Life of Edna Lyall* (1904). Payne, G. A. *Edna Lyall* (1903).

For articles in reference works, see: *Allibone. Bloomsbury. DNB. Feminist. Oxford. ToddBWW.*

Carole M. Shaffer-Koros

B. B.: See *Nairne, Baroness Caroline*

Beauchamp, Mary Annette: See *Arnim, Elizabeth von*

Sybille Bedford

BORN: 16 March 1911, Charlottenburg, Germany.
DAUGHTER OF: Maximillian von Schonebeck and Elizabeth Bernard.
MARRIED: Walter Bedford, 1935.

B. has published novels, biographies, and various works of reportage and memoirs, and she has been praised by Nancy Mitford, Evelyn Waugh, Aldous Huxley (she wrote a well-received biography of Huxley), Janet Flanner (Genet), and Christopher Sykes, among others, for her incisive, sharply defined fictional character portraits.

Born in Germany, she left that country while still quite young and was subsequently privately educated in France, Italy, and England, all countries in which—in addition to the United States—she has lived. Though she considered both the Sorbonne and Oxford for her university education and also considered studying law, she turned instead at age sixteen to writing, producing literary essays and several novels that were never published.

B. has also written widely for many British and American magazines on such topics as food, travel, and the law. She has written extensively about such trials as those of Jack Ruby in Dallas, Stephen Ward in London, the Auschwitz trials in Frankfurt, and the obscenity trials of D. H. Lawrence's *Lady Chatterley's Lover.* Her *The Best We Can Do: An Account of the Trial of John Bodkin Adams* (1958; in the U.S. as *The Trial of Dr. Adams*) has been praised as "an exposition of human justice at its careful best" and "a masterpiece of objective yet sensitive reporting." *The Faces of Justice* (1961) is a detailed analysis of criminal court procedures in England and four Continental countries; it was praised for being both objective and compassionate, winning special praise from British critics, who found its comparative approach helpful in understanding legal systems other than their own.

B.'s long, carefully researched and authorized *Aldous Huxley: A Biography* (1973) received less consistently favorable reception because of its "deficiencies of critical perception," as Diana Trilling called them, not its "affectionate compendiousness." She was able to bring Huxley's complex life and changing commitments into sharp focus, though she said little about his writing. As a longtime friend of Huxley's, she could hardly avoid suggestions of a lack of objectivity, though she did openly discuss Huxley's experiments with drugs; rather, the biography was criticized because of its faults in organization and style and, more importantly, for its lack of coherent judgment regarding her assessment of Huxley's life and accomplishments.

B.'s fiction has also received a mixed reception. *A Legacy* (1956), her first novel, tells of two wealthy families in pre-World War I Germany, one Roman Catholic, one Jewish, who reflect an entire era with all its conflicts. The book is witty, elegantly stylish in language, and vividly realized in its astonishing understanding of a society B. only dimly recalled, even though the book begins with the narrator describing a childhood in Charlottenburg. *A Favorite of the Gods* (1963), B.'s second novel, is a study of three women in Italian society in the late 1920s, one a rich American who married an Italian prince, her Italian daughter, and her English granddaughter. Also based on B.'s early life, the novel leisurely and sensitively explores B.'s nostalgic concern with a world of privilege and the role of free will in decision making. *A Compass Error* (1968), to complete the range of settings from B.'s early life, is set in a French town and concerns a shy, intellectual young woman who is lured into a lesbian relationship and eventually turns on her family and friends.

Though critics have been generous in praising B.'s precise descriptions, complex characterization, clear, graceful style, and knowledgeable detail, they have also been consistent in citing the brittle, superficial worlds of the anachronistic European aristocracy about which she writes, the irrelevant activities in which they are involved, and the contrived handling of such themes as sexual jealousy and betrayals. Her ability to link personal and political history is admittedly effective, but her sometimes self-conscious detail about food and wine, family intrigues and villas, and her stylized, contrived, witty plot manipulations increasingly strike critics as superficial and trivial.

WORKS: *The Sudden View: A Mexican Journey* (1953, 1963; also pub. as *A Visit to Don Otavio: A Traveller's Tale from Mexico*). *A Legacy* (1956). *The Best We Can Do: An Account of The Trial of John Bodkin Adams* 1958; in the U.S. as *The Trial of Dr. Adams,* 1959). *The Faces of Justice: A Traveller's Report* (1961). *A Favorite of the Gods* (1963). *A Compass Error* (1968). *Aldous Huxley: A Biography* (1973). *Last Trial of Lady Chatterley* (1973). *Jigsaw: An Unsentimental Education: A Biographical Novel* (1989). *As It Was: Pleasures, Landscapes, and Justice* (1990).

BIBLIOGRAPHY: Evans, R. O., in *British Novelists Since 1900,* ed. J. I. Biles (1987). Evans, R. O., in *Contemporary British Women Writers,* ed. R. E. Hosmer, Jr. (1993). Kimball, R. *NewC* (April 1994). Leavitt, D. *VLS* (June 1990).

For articles in reference works, see: *The Author Speaks* (1977). *Bloomsbury. CA. CN. Feminist. MBL. Oxford. ToddBWW. WA.*

Other references: Davenport, J. *New Statesman* (28 March 1953). Evans, R. O. *SLitI* (1978). Marcus, L. *TLS* (1 June 1984). Matthews, T. S. *NYT* (1 March 1959). *Nation* (4 May 1963). *New Statesman* (11 January 1963). *NYRB* (24 April 1969). Olney, J. *SAQ* (1975). Sale, R. *HudR* (1975). *Saturday Review* (9 February 1957). Sykes, C. *Encounter* (June 1956). *TLS* (24 October 1968). Waugh, E. *Spectator* (13 April 1956).

Paul Schlueter

Isabella Mary Mayson Beeton

BORN: 14 March 1836, London.
DIED: 6 February 1865, Grandhithe, Kent.
DAUGHTER OF: Benjamin and Elizabeth Jerram Mayson.
MARRIED: Samuel Orchart Beeton, 1856.

B.'s name is a household word literally as well as metaphorically, for she wrote *Mrs. Beeton's Book of Household Management,* a pioneering work in cookery and housewifery (1861), whose latest edition, a reprint of the original, appeared in 1984. More than any other woman in the nineteenth century, B. changed the nature of women's work in the home.

Married at the age of twenty to Samuel Orchart Beeton, the nineteenth century's most famous writer of Christmas annuals and a prolific publisher, B. intended no more than the usual wifely care of an active, demanding, and sickly husband. But her determination to learn cookery and household management in order to make life harmonious for him resulted in the famous *Book of*

Household Management (1861) and *Mrs. Beeton's Cookery Book* (1862).

The *Athenaeum* called *Household Management* "the most imposing work of all" advice-books for wives (19 July 1862). Embellished with colored plates printed by a new process that obviated handcoloring, it contained forty-six chapters covering (in addition to recipes) legal issues, the care of children and treatment of childhood diseases and injuries, anecdotes and homilies about food, quotations from Homer, Pinney, Linnaeus, Sir Humphry Davy, Erasmus, Darwin, and others, information on sanitation, reasonable wages for servants, etiquette, homemade cleansers and polishes, invalid cookery, and just about everything else a woman was likely to encounter in her daily life. Its helpful hints for housewives included "A place for everything, and everything in its place," and "Clear as you go," two immortal pieces of modern kitchen lore. B.'s direct, clear style and her chatty, almost personal tone makes *Household Management* as readable today as it was in 1861.

The cookery sections of both books were innovative in a number of respects. They offered an index and a cross-referencing system that made it easy to locate recipes, menus, and information. Within each section, recipes were listed alphabetically. Although by no means the first to write a cookbook (a popular one appeared in the early eighteenth century), B. was the first to list ingredients at the top of a recipe so the cook could easily assemble them; she was also the first regularly to indicate the amount of preparation and cooking time. Finally, B. believed in economical household management, and to this end she listed the approximate cost of each dish and indicated ways to utilize every sort of leftover. Herself a poor cook and unenthusiastic housewife, B. included in her books all the items she had been uncertain about in her early married life, thus making them accessible to the novice and the uneducated. In these books, B. established the modern cookbook format.

B. is also noted for setting up, with her husband, the first mail-order system for buying dress patterns from a pattern-book; she herself devised the dress pattern format we use today. B.'s various adaptations of *Household Management* served to elevate the housewife into an important family manager and placed the information and skills she needed at her fingertips for the first time. *Household Management* was reprinted in parts in the 1920s and has gone through fourteen complete editions. Its lively style, its timeless information, and its adaptability to a variety of formats have made "Mrs. Beeton" a household word for more than 125 years.

WORKS: *Mrs. Beeton's Book of Household Management* (1861). *Mrs. Beeton's Cookery Book* (1862). *Dictionary of Everyday Cookery* (1865). *Mrs. Beeton's House and Home Books* (1866–67). *Mrs. Beeton's All About Cookery* (1871). *Mrs. Beeton's How to Manage House, Servants, and Children* (1871). *Beeton's Every-Day Cookery and Housekeeping Book* (1872). *Mrs. Beeton's Cookery Book and Household Guide* (1890).

BIBLIOGRAPHY: Clausen, C. *ASch* (1993). Freeman, S. *Isabella and Sam: The Story of Mrs. Beeton* (1977). Hyde, H. *Mr. and Mrs. Beeton* (1951). North, G. *Mrs. Beeton: 150 Years of Cookery and Household Management* (1986). Spain, N. *Mrs. Beeton and Her Husband* (1948).

For articles in reference works, see: *Allibone SUP. Cambridge. Oxford. ToddBWW.*

Other references: *LonT* (11 February 1997).

Loralee MacPike

Aphra Behn

BORN: 1640 (?), Harbledown, Kent (?).
DIED: 16 April 1689, London.
DAUGHTER OF: Bartholomew Johnson and Elizabeth Denham Johnson (?).
MARRIED: Mr. Behn, 1665 (?).
WROTE UNDER: Astrea.

B.'s origins are uncertain, but recent evidence suggests that she was the Aphra Johnson christened in 1640 in Harbledown, Kent, although the yeoman status of her supposed father does not accord with her education, which is that of a gentlewoman. According to her novel *Oroonoko,* she traveled to Surinam in 1663–64 when she was a young woman. Tradition has it that upon her return to London she married a merchant named Behn, of Dutch extraction, who perhaps died of the plague in 1665; however, she never once refers to such a person. The earliest indisputable external evidence about her life is a series of letters documenting her employment in 1666 as a secret agent for the English government. She was sent to Antwerp to get information about exiled Cromwellians and to relay Dutch military plans. She used "Astrea" as her code name as a spy, later as her literary name. In the Netherlands, she ran into debt, and in 1667, when she returned home, she went briefly to debtor's prison. She was noted among a wide circle of friends and fellow writers for her beauty, wit, and generosity; Sir Peter Lely and Mary Beale painted portraits of her. Her strong Tory sentiments and personal loyalty to the royal family led to a political outspokenness that earned her enemies among some powerful Whigs. She satirized the Earl of Shaftesbury, the Whig leader, in *The City Heiress* (1682) but offended the king in the same year when she attacked the Duke of Monmouth in an epilogue, for which she was arrested. During her life, she was forced to fend off not only political and personal attacks but also attacks on her as a woman who wrote with the same freedoms as a man. In her last years, she suffered from poverty and a painful crippling disease, and her political hopes were crushed by the Revolution of 1688.

B. first achieved literary celebrity as a playwright, entering the theater in 1670 and producing seventeen extant plays; two more plays have been lost: *Like Father, Like Son* (1682) and *The Wavering Nymph* (1684). Four anonymous plays have been attributed to her: *The Woman Turned Bully* (1675), *The Debauchee* (1677), *The Counterfeit Bridegroom* (1677), and *The Revenge* (1680); these, however, may have been written by Thomas Betterton. B.'s dramatic specialty was the "Spanish" comedy of intrigue written in brisk, colloquial prose. She typically manipulates several sources into a complexly and wittily plotted play of expert stage craftsmanship. A number of couples—eluding the unwanted marriages arranged for them—meet, bed, and/or wed after innumerable intrigues, mistaken identities, duels, disguises, and practical jokes. Her plays abound in bedroom farce and scenes of comic lowlife with delightful portrayals of landladies, bawds, buffoons, and prostitutes. She provides spectacle in masquing, costuming, and dance and uses stage machinery and other technical resources to create special effects.

The best of B.'s intrigue comedies is *The Rover; or, The Banished Cavaliers* (1677), set at carnival time in Naples, where impoverished English cavaliers-in-exile become entangled with Spanish ladies and win their persons and fortunes. B.'s rover, Willmore, is her distinctive version of a favorite Restoration character, the wild gallant. *The Rover* stayed in the repertory until the middle of the eighteenth century, the role of the witty heroine being taken by such famous actresses as Elizabeth Barry, Anne Bracegirdle, Anne Oldfield, and Peg Woffington. Also among B.'s best plays is *Sir Patient Fancy* (1678), an amusing tangle of the amours of two neighboring London families. Her *Emperor of the Moon* was an instant success in 1687. A gay and extravagant combination of *commedia dell'arte*, operatic spectacle, sumptuous costuming, dance, song, satire, intrigue, and a bit of manners comedy, the play was performed for nearly a hundred years.

A number of her plays deal centrally with her most distinctive theme, her attack on forced marriage. She titled her first play *The Forced Marriage* (1670) and went on to write *The Town Fop* (1676) and *The Lucky Chance* (1686), respectively a sentimental and a harder treatment of the same subject. While New Comedy in general depicts the witty stratagems of young lovers who outwit their elders in order to marry according to their own choice, Behn goes beyond this to attack the arranged marriage as an institution. In doing so, she uses in distinctive ways two stock characters, the courtesan and the amazon. In *The Rover*, Parts I and II (1677; 1681), and *The Feigned Courtesans* (1679), B. uses the courtesan to suggest that marriage for money is a form of prostitution. In *The Young King* (1679) and *The Widow Ranter* (1689), the woman warrior in both romantic and comic versions provides a visual metaphor for the battle of the sexes and suggests the compatibility of lovers who are equals in wit and war.

B. was a versatile and sometimes distinguished poet. She wrote topical and witty prologues and epilogues for the theater. Her elegies and panegyrics in baroque pindarics for members of the royal family and the nobility were usually published in folio or quarto to celebrate a state occasion. Her elegies for the Earl of Rochester and the Duke of Buckingham display her personal affection and admiration for these two fellow wits. B. had a fine lyric gift; her elegant and sophisticated songs appeared both in her plays and in contemporary collections. Her best known song, "Love in Fantastic Triumph Sat," appeared in her one tragedy, *Abdelazer* (1676), and has often been reprinted.

B. made a number of miscellaneous translations from Latin and French in the latter part of her career, apparently for the money. She had no Latin and worked from a prose paraphrase of Ovid and Cowley; her French, however, was fluent, and she produced able, sometimes improved versions of Tallemant, La Rochefoucauld, Bonnecorse, Aesop, and de Fontenelle.

In the last years of her life, she also wrote fiction, producing more than a dozen novels, some of which were published posthumously. Her novels achieved great popularity: two were dramatized, and collections of her novels appeared throughout the eighteenth century; some continue to be reprinted. In her fictions B. pioneered in the transition from romance to novel by providing extensive circumstantial detail. Her two best tales—*The Fair Jilt* and *Oroonoko*—are based on events she herself witnessed. *Oroonoko*, the story of an African prince enslaved in Surinam, displays great originality in theme and structure and is perhaps her best-known work.

B. wrote ably in a number of genres. She is significant not only as an artist but also as the first professional woman writer and the first woman whose writing won her burial in Westminster Abbey. On her tombstone are these verses: "Here lies a proof that wit can never be / Defence enough against mortality."

WORKS: *The Forced Marriage* (1670). *The Amorous Prince* (1671). *The Dutch Lover* (1673). *Abdelazer* (1676). *The Town Fop* (1676). *The Rover* (1677; ed. F. Link, 1967). *Sir Patient Fancy* (1678). *The Feigned Courtesans* (1679). *The Young King* (1679). *The Second Part of the Rover* (1681). *The False Count* (1681). *The Roundheads* (1681). *Like Father, Like Son* (1682). *The City Heiress* (1682). *Poems upon Several Occasions* (1684). *Love Letters between a Nobleman and His Sister* (1684; modern ed., ed. M. Duffy, 1987). *The Wavering Nymph* (1684). *A Pindaric on the Death of Our Late Sovereign* (1685). *A Poem to Catherine Queen Dowager* (1685). *A Pindaric Poem on the Happy Coronation* (1685). *The Lucky Chance* (1686). *The Emperor of the Moon* (1687; in *Ten English Farces*, ed L. Hughes, 1948). *To Christopher, Duke of Albemarle* (1687). *To the Memory of George, Dole of Buckingham* (1687). *The Amours of Philander and Sylvia* (1687). *A Congratulatory Poem to Her Most Sacred Majesty* (1688). *The Fair Jilt* (1688). *A Congratulatory Poem on the Happy Birth of the Prince of Wales* (1688). *Oroonoko* (1688). *Agnes de Castro* (1688). *A Poem to Sir Roger L'Estrange* (1688). *To Poet Bavius* (1688). *A Congratulatory Poem to Queen Mary* (1689). *The History of the Nun* (1689). *The Lucky Mistake* (1689). *A Pindaric Poem to the Reverend Dr. Burnet* (1689). *The Widow Ranter* (1689). *The Younger Brother* (1696). *The Adventure of the Black Lady* (1698). *The Court of the King of Bantam* (1698). *The Nun* (1698). *The Unfortunate Happy Lady* (1698). *The Wandering Beauty* (1698). *The Dumb Virgin* (1700). *The Unhappy Mistake* (1700). *Works*, 6 vols., ed. M. Summers (1915). *The Works of Aphra Behn*, 7 vols., ed. J. Todd (1992–96). *Oroonoko, The Rover and Other Works*, ed. J. Todd (1992). *Oroonoko and Other Writings*, ed. P. Salzman (1994). *The Fair Jilt and Other Short Stories*, ed. J. Todd (1996).

BIBLIOGRAPHY: Armstrong, I., ed. *New Feminist Discourses* (1992). Campbell, E. *Kunapii* (1985). Cameron, W. J. *New Light on Aphra Behn* (1961). *Rhetorics of Order/Ordering Rhetorics,* ed. J. D. Canfield and J. P. Hunter (1989). Cotton, N. *Women Playwrights in England c. 1363–1750* (1980). Duffy, M. *The Passionate Shepherdess* (1977). *Teaching Eighteenth-Century Poetry,* ed. C. Fox (1990). Gallagher, C. *Nobody's Story* (1994). Goreau, A. *Reconstructing Aphra* (1980). *Women, Writing, History: 1640–1799,* ed. I. Grundy and S. Wiseman (1992). Guffey, G. *Two English Novelists* (1975). Hutner, H. *Rereading Aphra Behn* (1993). Link, F. *Aphra Behn* (1968). Loftis, J. *The Spanish Plays of Neoclassical England* (1973). O'Donnell, M. A. *Aphra Behn: An Annotated Bibliography of Primary and Secondary Sources* (1906). *The Discourse of Slavery,* ed. C. Plasa and B. J. Ring (1994). Sackville-West, V. *Aphra Behn* (1928). *Homosexuality in Renaissance and Enlightenment England,* ed. C. J. Summers (1992). *Renaissance Discourses of Desire,* ed. C. J. Summers and T. L. Pebworth (1993). Todd, J. *The Secret Life of Aphra Behn* (1996).*Women Writers of the Seventeenth Century,* ed. K. M. Wilson and F. J. Warnke (1989). Wiseman, S. J. *Aphra Behn* (1996). Woodcock, G. *The Incomparable Aphra* (1948). *Aphra Behn Studies,* ed. J. Todd (1996). *Shakespeare, Aphra Behn, and the Canon,* ed. W. R. Owens and L. Goodman (1996).

For articles in reference works, see: *Allibone. Bloomsbury. Cambridge. CinP. Feminist. Oxford. ToddBWW. ToddDBA.*

Other references: *ADS* (1991). *AL* (1993). Campbell, E. *Kunapipi* (1985). Day, R. A., in *Fetter'd or Free? British Women Novelists, 1670–1815,* ed. M. A. Schofield and C. Macheski (1986). DeRitter, J. *Restoration* (1986). *ECF* (1989, 1990, 1991). *ELWIU* (1989). *EMS* (1990). *FBS* (1990). *FS* (1992–93, 1993). *HLQ* (1993). Houston, B. *JNT* (1988). *L&P* (1986). *MLQ* (1946, 1951). *MLR* (1991). *MP* (1990). *N&Q* (1960, 1962, 1976, 1979, 1984, 1986, 1990, 1991, 1992, 1994). *NCF* (1984). *NLH* (1992). *PLL* (1978). *PMLA* (1913, 1934, 1936, 1960). *PoeticsJ* (1989). *RES* (1991). *Restoration* (1988, 1992, 1994). *RLC* (1989). *RQ* (1989). *SB* (1969). *SECC* (1989). *SEL* (1992, 1993, 1994). *SNNTS* (1988). *SP* (1962). *SVEC* (1992). *TLS* (1993). *TSLL* (1988). *TSWL* (1989). *W&L* (1977). *WS* (1980, 1988, 1991, 1992, 1993).

Nancy Cotton
(updated by Claudia Thomas Kairoff)

Bell, Acton: See *Brontë, Anne*

Bell, Currer: See *Brontë, Charlotte*

Bell, Ellis: See *Brontë, Emily*

George Anne Bellamy

BORN: 1731(?), Fingal, Ireland(?).
DIED: 16 February 1788, London.
DAUGHTER OF: John O'Hara, second Baron of Tyrawley; Mrs. Bellamy (née Seal).
MARRIED: West Digges, 1763 (the marriage was illegal).

B. was a popular eighteenth-century actress who claimed to have written *An Apology for the Life of George Anne Bellamy* (1785). In truth, this highly idealized "autobiography" was probably written by Alexander Bicknell, a historian, from material provided by B.; most reference works now list Bicknell as the editor for these volumes. Regardless of its authorship, this six-volume work offers valuable insights into eighteenth-century England and its theater.

Like her mother, B. was an actress who experienced one unhappy love affair after another and bore one illegitimate child after another (B. herself was illegitimate.) At the age of eleven or so, she defied her father, in whose custody she was living, and went to live with her mother. This relationship soon gave her access to the stage, where she played several small parts in the early 1740s and was introduced to the great actors and actresses of the day. Success came when she was playing Andromache in an informal staging of *The Distrest Mother.* John Rich was apparently enchanted with her and convinced James Quin, the manager of Covent Garden, to allow her a starring role in 1744. From that time until her last season in 1770, she was quite popular on the London, Dublin, and Edinburgh stages.

This popularity brought her the attentions of several men. She lived with but did not marry George Metham, John Calcraft, and West Digges, and she bore children to Metham and Calcraft. Although she went through a wedding ceremony with Digges, the ceremony was illegal since Digges had another wife still living. The only man with whom she seems to have lived happily was the great actor, Henry Woodward. Their relationship, which she claimed was platonic, lasted from 1767 until his death ten years later. Woodward was the only one of her many lovers to leave her large amounts of money in his will, a significant gesture because her taste for luxury left her continually in debt. But because she was unable to claim all of her inheritance from Woodward, her debts grew steadily worse after his death.

An Apology for the Life of George Anne Bellamy provides a mild and quite moralistic picture of her life, conveyed through letters written to the anonymous "Hon. Miss- ." The preface explains that she wrote the book to recover her reputation and to provide a morally instructive tale for young girls. In fact, the *Apology* omits many details from B.'s stage career and glosses over others in order to dramatize and tidy up her life. Although these volumes may today seem stilted and didactic, they were popular enough to be translated into French in 1799. Appended to the *Apology* is an angry letter to John Calcraft that she had intended to publish in 1767. Even though this letter did not appear until twelve years after Calcraft's death, certain portions of it were softened to protect his reputation and hers. In addition to the *Apology,* B. is credited with writing a single-volume narrative autobiography, *Memoirs of a Celebrated Actress* (1785?).

WORKS: *An Apology for the Life of George Anne Bellamy* (1785). *Memoirs of a Celebrated Actress* (1785?).

BIBLIOGRAPHY: Doran, J. *Annals of the English Stage from T. Betterton to E. Kean* (1888). Genest, J. *Some Account of the English Stage, 1660–1830* (1832). Hartmann, C. *Enchanting Bellamy* (1956). Wilkinson, T. *The Wandering Patentee* (1795).

For articles in reference works, see: *BDA. Cambridge. DNB. Oxford. ToddBWW.*

Tori Haring-Smith

Belloc Lowndes, Mrs.: See *Lowndes, Marie Adelaide Belloc*

Benedict, Peter: See *Pargeter, Edith Mary*

Elizabeth Ogilvy Benger

BORN: February 1778, Wells, Somerset.
DIED: 9 January 1827, London.
DAUGHTER OF: John Benger and Mary Long.
WROTE UNDER: Elizabeth Benger.

Biographer, poet, novelist, and feminist, B. was the only surviving child of a father who eventually became a purser in the navy. Starved for knowledge, B. read the open pages of publications in a bookseller's window daily. A family friend convinced B.'s mother to arrange for Latin lessons when B. was twelve. At thirteen, she published her first poem, "The Female Geniad," dedicated to Lady Champion de Crespigny, whom she had met through her uncle, Sir David Ogilvy. The work, which includes her name and age, praises literary foremothers like Sappho and contemporaries such as Laetitia Barbauld.

After her father's death in 1796 and until her own death, B. was virtually always financially insecure. In 1800, she and her mother moved to London. She began cultivating a circle of literary friends that included Barbauld, Lucy Aikin, Elizabeth Hamilton, Joanna Baillie, and the Lambs. Madame de Staël considered B. the most interesting woman she had met in England.

"A Poem, occasioned by the Abolition of the Slave Trade, in 1806" celebrates the end of that commerce after a long political struggle. In stately heroic couplets, the poem describes the plight of a noble African in exile and argues that the slave trade had disgraced England. By 1813, B. had anonymously published her only two novels: *Marian* and *The Heart and the Fancy, or Valsinore,* which was translated into French. Aikin and others considered B.'s later historical and biographical works as her finest achievements. The first, the *Memoirs of the late Mrs. Elizabeth Hamilton,* went quickly into a second edition. The biographies of Anne Boleyn and Mary, Queen of Scots, were reprinted frequently for more than fifty years. Other biographical subjects were John Tobin, dramatist and poet, and Elizabeth, Queen of Bohemia.

At the end of her life, in poor health and shabby surroundings, B. was collecting materials for a memoir of King Henri IV of France and receiving visitors. Much of her literary output and conversation over thirty-six years had celebrated the intellect of women.

WORKS: "The Female Geniad" (1791). "A Poem, occasioned by the Abolition of the Slave Trade, in 1806," in *Poems on the Abolition of the Slave Trade,* ed. J. Montgomery (1809; rpt. 1978). *Marian* (1812). *The Heart and the Fancy, or Valsinore* (1813). (trans.) *Klopstock and his Friends: A Series of Familiar Letters, Written Between the Years 1750 and 1803,* by F. G. Klopstock (1814). *Memoirs of the late Mrs. Elizabeth Hamilton* (1818). *Memoirs of John Tobin* (1820). *Memoirs of the Life of Anne Boleyn* (1821). *Memoirs of the Life of Mary, Queen of Scots* (1823). *Memoirs of the Life of Elizabeth Stuart, Queen of Bohemia* (1825).

BIBLIOGRAPHY: Aikin, L., in *Memoirs of the Life of Anne Boleyn,* 3rd ed. (1827).

For articles in reference works, see: *DNB. Feminist. ToddDBA.*

Carol Shiner Wilson

Anna [often miscalled Agnes] Maria (Evans) Bennett

BORN: c. 1750, Merthyr Tydfil, Glamorgan, Wales (or Bristol).
DIED: 12 February 1808, Brighton, Sussex.
DAUGHTER OF: David Evans, mother's name not known.
MARRIED: Mr. Bennett (?).

According to the *European Magazine* (1790), B.'s father and husband were customs officers and her brother a city lawyer of some repute. Her education was indifferent, giving cause for complaints about grammatical errors in her later works. According to other sources, though, her father was a Bristol grocer named David Evans and her husband a tanner at Brecknock with whom she moved to London. After leaving him, she worked as a shopkeeper of ready-made naval clothing, slopseller, workhouse matron, and "housekeeper" (i.e., mistress) to Admiral Sir Thomas Pye, the notoriously "ungainly" man whose nickname was "Nose-y" and whose name she gave to two children, Thomas and Harriet Pye Bennett. The legend is that the liaison began when he took shelter in her shop from the rain.

It is said that her first book, *Anna, or Memoirs of a Welch Heiress* (1785), dedicated to the Princess Royal, sold out in a day owing to her notoriety, readers probably hoping for some salacious revelations of her personal history. The readers were probably disappointed to find a strictly moral tale. It was published the same year that Pye died; though they had already separated after he sent her a letter intended for another woman, he left her a house and a cozy legacy.

B.'s fiction was probably autobiographical, at least to the extent that some of her own early struggles were reflected in the struggles of her low-born heroines who contended against morally inferior social superiors. She clearly projected herself into the heroine of *The Beggar Girl and her Benefactors* (1797). In the preface to *Ellen, or the Countess of Castle Howel* (1794), B. writes about "the greatest Distress, both of Mind and Circumstances," and of "mental derangement" or the struggle simultaneously to run and contest the lease of the Edinburgh theater on behalf of her daughter, Harriet Pye Esten, the noted beauty and actress. Harriet, whose stage debut she arranged in 1785, had a bigamous liaison with the Duke of Hamilton, by whom she had a child. In 1793, B. had to manage the cooling of the duke's relations with Harriet but lost control of the theater, then in the duke's gift, when she and Harriet returned to London. The preface states that writing fiction was an escape from such troubles. She was buried in London, and her funeral was attended by a throng of admirers.

Her other publications were *Juvenile Indiscretions* (1786), which was at first attributed to Frances Burney (whom B. resembles in style), the epistolary *Agnes de-Courci, a Domestic Tale* (1789), and *Vicissitudes Abroad, or, The Ghost of my Father: A Novel* (1806). One critic, I. Grundy, has termed *Juvenile Indiscretions* "Fieldingesque"; others, including M. Doody and P. Sabor, have called *Agnes de-Courci* "Richardsonian" as presumably modeled on *Clarissa. The Monthly Review* considered *Agnes de-Courci* "well-wrought" but lacking in "character." Another writer, J.M.S. Tompkins, has noted that *Anna* contains some elements of the Cinderella story, while *Ellen* probably resembles the story of Griselda's patience; however, B. also mocks the conventions of romance and fairy-tale endings in works such as *The Beggar Girl.* Her stories were sometimes thought to be based on real personages and activities, as she declared was true of some characters in *Juvenile Indiscretions.* She wrote five more novels, the first two published anonymously. According to one source (*Feminist*), *De Valcourt* (1800) and two by "Elizabeth B." are probably not her work.

She was devoted to the royal family and to an ideal of feminine propriety and piety that she did not always emulate in private life. Her most popular novel is probably *The Beggar Girl and Her Benefactors,* a satire on female Gothic novelists; it put her on the bestselling authors' list of the Minerva Press. Her last novel, *Vicissitudes Abroad,* reputedly sold two thousand copies on its first day of publication, even at the price of thirty-six shillings. She was popular and famous for a period—her name appears in Mary Robinson's roll of literary honor—largely due to the robustness and vividness of her characters' lives and struggles, since her characters ranged from the lower to the higher orders of society. She was also unhesitant in her satires of both classes of society and of sexual and economic exploitation of individuals, and her work depicted a range of female intellectuals and abandoned children, both perhaps "outcast" in that sense. Her novels were sprawling but witty and vivacious. According to Tompkins, her novels foreshadow the more broad-based nineteenth-century novel, especially in their pictures of society. Despite the decline in her fame due to the sexually explicit and daring nature of her work, Sir Walter Scott and Samuel Taylor Coleridge were enthusiastic about her books, and several were translated into French. Scott called *The Beggar Girl* "the best novel . . . since Fielding" and praised her and Jane Austen equally. The *Athenaeum's* obituary notice lists her as the equal of Fielding and Richardson.

WORKS: *Anna, or, Memoirs of a Welch Heiress, Interspersed with Anecdotes of a Nabob* (1785). *Juvenile Indiscretions: A Novel* (1786). *Agnes de-Courci, a Domestic Tale* (1789). *Ellen, or the Countess of Castle Howel, A Novel* (1794, 1805). *The Beggar Girl and Her Benefactors* (1797). *De Valcourt, A Novel* (1800). *Vicissitudes Abroad, or, The Ghost of My Father: A Novel* (1806).

BIBLIOGRAPHY: Blakey, D. *The Minerva Press 1790–1820* (1935). Fuller, J. F. *A Curious Genealogical Medley* (1913). Grundy, I., in *Samuel Richardson: Tercentenary Essays,* ed. M. Doody and P. Sabor, ed. (1989). Rogers, K. M. *Feminism in Eighteenth-Century England* (1982). Tompkins, J.M.S. *The Popular Novel in England, 1770–1800* (1932).

For articles in reference works, see: *Feminist. Oxford. ToddBWW. ToddDBA.*

Other references: Campbell, T. *A Gothic Bibliography* (1964). Coleridge, H. N. *Table Talk and Omniana of Samuel Taylor Coleridge,* ed. T. Ashe (1884). Coleridge, S. T. *Collected Letters of Samuel Taylor Coleridge,* ed. E. L. Griggs (1956–71). Lee Lewes, C. *Memoirs* (1805). Summers, M. *Life of Mrs. Siddons* (1834).

Nandini Bhattacharya

Stella Benson

BORN: 6 January 1892, Lutwyche Hall, Shropshire.
DIED: 6 December 1933, Honkai Tonkin, China.
DAUGHTER OF: Ralph Beaumont and Caroline Essex Cholmondeley Benson.
MARRIED: James O'Gorman Anderson, 1921.

B. wrote essays, short stories, poetry, and the novels for which she is best known. In her first three novels, especially, her personality as a writer shines through and her unique perception of the world is displayed with an imagination and a sympathy that can only be called humane. She satirizes her own British society, wherever she may find it—in London, in the West Indies, in China—with a voice that never forgets its own bent to occasional folly. She demonstrates a remarkable knack for combining reality and fantasy, criticism and compassion. Fanciful characters symbolize her feelings about serious social problems such as women's suffrage, imperial colonization, and World War I. She achieved popular success with her fifth novel, *The Far-Away Bride* (1930; in the U.K. as *Tobit Transplanted,* 1931), for which she won the Femina Vie Heureuse Prize and the A. C. Benson silver medal of the Royal Society of Literature in 1932.

B. was educated at home and in France, Germany, and Switzerland, and she continued to travel widely despite the fact that she suffered from weak lungs and was often plagued by ill health. She visited the West Indies, accumulating material for her first book. Home from the voyage, she worked from 1913 to 1917 in the East End of London, first serving in the Charity Organisation Society and then, disillusioned with their methods, helping the poor in her own way by opening a small store. She was active as a suffragist during this time, and, drawing on all her recent experiences, she wrote her first two novels. *I Pose* (1915) is a light-hearted feminist manifesto in which B. deals with woman's suffrage as an emotional, political, and economic concern. The novel centers on an unnamed suffragist whose adventures on the exotic Trinity Island and in the Brown Borrough of London illustrate the disheartening and sometimes fatal consequences of living in a world where "Oh, my dear, too killing" is the motto for women. *This Is the End* (1917) is also set in Brown Borrough and features a young woman, Jay, who has disowned her wealth, taken a job as a bus conductor, and escaped into the world of her own imagination. Jay's secret world is destroyed with the news that her brother and confidant, Kew, has been killed in France. The novel presents a cross section of attitudes toward World War I, ranging from the condescension of a pretentious Brown Borrough social worker to the logic of a pacifist Quaker to Kew's own nonchalance about his possible death.

B. lived in the United States from June 1918 to January 1920, supporting herself with various odd jobs while she wrote her third novel, *Living Alone* (1919). The setting is once again the Brown Borrough of London during World War I and draws on B.'s experiences with the Charity Organisation Society. This novel, written as B. herself said for "the magically-inclined minority," criticizes a society that does not temper charity with common sense. In January 1920, B. set out on an eighteen-month voyage to England by way of India and China. This journey included another series of various occupations. In China, she met James O'Gorman Anderson, a customs officer; they were married in London in September 1921, and their honeymoon was a trip to America, crossing the continent from east to west in a Ford.

Many of her experiences in the United States and in the Far East are captured in *The Little World* (1925), a collection of essays, and in *The Poor Man* (1922), her fourth novel. Except for occasional trips, the remainder of B.'s life, until her death from pneumonia in a hospital at Honkai Tonkin in December 1933, was spent in various regions of China where her husband was stationed. One of these places was Manchuria, the setting for her last-completed and best-known novel, *The Far-Away Bride* (1930). This unusual novel follows the outline of the legend of Tobit in the Old Testament Apocrypha, replacing the exiled families of ancient Israel with two families of White Russian refugees in Manchuria and Korea during the 1920s. Despite the novel's allegorical aspects, B. creates a realistic environment in which a complex and realistic tale of love and family conflicts is enacted. In *The Far-Away Bride* and *The Poor Man,* psychological characterization replaces the fanciful, humorous mode of B.'s earlier novels.

B.'s last novel, *Mundos* (published posthumously in 1935), is unfinished: Thirteen chapters were completed and revised; four, perhaps five, chapters remained unwritten. For this novel B. creates an island, Mundos, which is somewhat like the Trinity Island of her first novel. Surprisingly, in the descriptions of both these island worlds, B. falls prey to instances of what the contemporary reader would regard as blatant stereotyping and racial prejudice. Despite the way in which these unfortunate remarks date the novels, B.'s thought is still progressive and her goal is to observe the attendant ills and conflicts of what she terms, ironically, "liberal imperialistic thought."

In 1923, Joseph Collins wrote of B. in conjunction with Virginia Woolf, naming them as two of the most promising women writers in England at the time. B. visited Woolf on 16 July 1932, and Woolf wrote in her diary that B. talked of "making money by stories . . . in a sensible matter-of-fact way, like a working class woman." When Woolf heard of B.'s death the following year, she wrote, "I did not know her, but have a sense of those fine patient eyes: the weak voice; the cough; the sense of oppression. She sat on the terrace with me at Rodmell. And now, so quickly, it is gone, what might have been a friendship. . . . A very fine steady mind: much suffering; suppressed."

Though her life and literary career were cut short, both were characterized by a remarkable energy and love for life. Marked by her fresh, original, and irrefutable wit, her novels and essays convey the sensitivity noted by Woolf. B. achieves a careful balance between honest detachment from and empathetic involvement with her characters and readers, thus making her work a superb study of human identity, motive, instinct, and behavior.

WORKS: *I Pose* (1915). *This Is the End* (1917). *Twenty* (1918). *Living Alone* (1919). *Kwan-yin* (1922). *The Poor Man* (1922). *Pipers and a Dancer* (1924). *The Awakening, A Fantasy* (1925). *The Little World* (1925). *Goodbye, Stranger* (1926). *The Man Who Missed the Bus* (1928). *Worlds Within Worlds* (1928). *The Far-Away Bride* (1930; in the U.K. as *Tobit Transplanted,* 1931). *Hope Against Hope and Other Stories* (1931). *Christmas Formula and Other Stories* (1932). *Pull Devil, Pull Baker* (1933). *Mundos* (1935). *Poems* (1935). *Collected Short Stories* (1936).

BIBLIOGRAPHY: Battiscombe, G. *Nineteenth Century* (1947). Bedell, R. *Stella Benson* (1983). Bottome, P. *Stella Benson* (1934). Brandon, W. *MR* (1984). *Some Letters of Stella Benson, 1928–1933,* ed. C. Clarabut (1938). Collins, J. *The Doctor Looks at Literature* (1923). Gawsworth, J. *Ten Contemporaries: Notes Toward Their Definitive Bibliography* (1933). Grant, J. *Stella Benson: A Biography* (1987). Johnson, R., in *Some Contemporary Novelists (Women)* (1920). Mais, S.P.B. *Some Modern Authors* (1923). Mitchison, N. *You May Well Ask* (1979). Roberts, R. E. *Portrait of Stella Benson* (1939).

For articles in reference works, see: *Bloomsbury. CA. DLB. DNB. Europa. Feminist. Oxford. TCA. TCLC. WWTCL.*

Kitti Carriker

Phyllis Bentley

BORN: 19 November 1894, Halifax, Yorkshire.
DIED: 27 June 1977, Halifax, Yorkshire.
DAUGHTER OF: Joseph Edwin Bentley and Eleanor Bentley.

One of four children, only daughter of a textile manufacturer, B. was educated at Cheltenham Ladies College and obtained an external degree from London University. She began her career teaching in a boys' grammar school, but, unsuccessful at this, she remained at home. B.'s autobiography *O Dreams, O Destinations* (1962) tells of the dilemma of the educated woman living in the parental home in the early years of the twentieth century without income or independence. World War I provided the opportunity for B. to go to London to work as a clerk in the Ministry of Munitions, and when the war was over she returned to Yorkshire. After a librarian taught B. the Dewey Decimal System, she spent six years cataloguing books in local libraries and working on a series of short stories and her first novel, *Environment* (1922).

B. wrote primarily about her native West Riding and of the lives of men and women working in the textile trade. With *Inheritance* (1932), the story of the coming of the industrial revolution to Yorkshire, she came to prominence in Great Britain and the United States. The novel is a chronicle of a mill-owning family, the Oldroyds, in which B. delineated the rise and decline of the textile trade from the Luddite riots to the 1926 slump, and many of the events were based on the experiences of her own family. B. returned to the story of the Oldroyds in *The Rise of Henry Morcar* (1946) and ended their saga in *A Man of His Time* (1966).

Befriended by Winifred Holtby and Vera Brittain, who invited B. to stay with her in London, B. was introduced to the British literary world. From then on her horizons and opportunities expanded. Invited to the United States where her reputation as a regional novelist grew, she made two lecture tours in the 1930s.

B.'s only novel set outside Yorkshire, *Freedom, Farewell* (1936), was not a success. Describing the fall of the Roman republic, it was written as a protest against the rise of Hitler and Mussolini. B. was bitter that no one understood why she had written it.

B. continued to live at home in Yorkshire and helped to finance the family textile business during the Depression. World War II found her back in London working for the American Division of the Ministry of Information. In January 1941, braving the perils of submarines, B. crossed the Atlantic to lecture on wartime Britain. On her return she wrote *Here Is America* (1942), a booklet explaining America to the British. She returned to the United States in 1943, by air, to work with the British Information Services in New York. Her Atlantic wartime crossings and the rocket attacks on London provided material for *The Rise of Henry Morcar* (1946).

Following the war, B. nursed her mother devotedly for five years, during which time she was unable to write. Following her mother's death in 1949 she worked prodigiously, producing articles, reviews, broadcasts, books, and TV scripts. When the novel *Crescendo* (1958) was not a success, B. realized that her popularity was over as a result of changing times. The "angry young men," mostly Yorkshiremen, had taken over, and the working class had replaced the middle-class as material for novels.

An essay, "Yorkshire and the Novelist" (1968), discusses the phenomenon that so many English writers come from Yorkshire. B. believed that although the Yorkshire character had defects—little charm or grace—it had much humor and solidity. *The English Regional Novel* (1941) with special emphasis on Charlotte Brontë, George Eliot, Thomas Hardy, and Arnold Bennett, is a survey of English regional fiction that flowered between 1840 to 1940.

B. never married and believed she was unattractive to the opposite sex. This may explain why Henry Morcar was described by a *New York Times* reviewer as "A stilted lover who sounds as if his sentiments had been strained through the British Ministry of Information." She lived a restricted home life dominated by her mother, a beautiful woman in revolt against the sordidness of life. B. was thirty before she dared to use lipstick or smoke cigarettes. A solitary child and an inveterate daydreamer, she had difficulty with close relationships outside her family. The brotherhood of man became her creed. She believed that if she could present human beings in all their facets, she could promote better understanding between them.

B. wished to write a great novel but knew she had not succeeded. A *Manchester Guardian* reviewer described her as "a gifted and skilled practitioner in the art of fiction," and B. accepted this verdict on her work. She was awarded an honorary degree by the University of Leeds in 1949 and the Order of the British Empire in 1970.

WORKS: *Pedagomania: Or, the Gentle Art of Teaching* (1918). *The World's Bane and other Stories* (1918). *Environment* (1922). *Cat-in-the-Manger* (1923). *The Partnership* (1928). *The Spinner of the Years* (1928). *Sounding Brass: a Play in One Act* (1930). *Trio* (1930). *Inheritance* (1932). *A Modern Tragedy* (1934). *The Whole of the Story* (1935). *Freedom, Farewell* (1936). *Sleep in Peace* (1938). *The Power and the Glory* (1940). *Take Courage* (1940). *Manhold* (1941). *The English Regional Novel* (1941). *Here Is America* (1942). *The Rise of Henry Morcar* (1946). *Some Observations on the Art of Narrative* (1946). *Colne Valley Cloth from the Earliest Times to the Present Day* (1947). *Life Story* (1948). *The Brontës* (1950). *Quorum* (1950). *Panorama: Tales of the West Riding* (1952). *The House of Moreys* (1953). *Chain of Witnesses* (1954). *Noble in Reason* (1955). *Love and Money: Seven Tales of the West Riding* (1957). *Crescendo* (1958). *The New Apprentice* (1959). *Kith and Kin: Nine Tales of Family Life* (1960). *The Young Brontës* (1960). *A Mid-Summer's Night Crime* (1961). *Committees* (1962). *O Dreams, O Destinations* (1962). *Miss Phipps Discovers America* (1963). *Public Speaking* (1964). *Enjoy Books and Reading* (1964). *The Adventures of Tom Leigh* (1964). *Tales of the West Riding* (1965). *A Man of His Time* (1966). *Ned Carver in Danger* (1967). *Gold Pieces* (1968). *Ring in the New* (1969). *The Brontës and Their World* (1969). *Sheep May Safely Graze* (1972). *The New Venturers* (1973). *More Tales of the West Riding* (1974). (with J. Ogden) *Haworth of the Brontës* (1977).

BIBLIOGRAPHY:

For articles in reference works, see: *CA*. *EMD*. *Feminist*. *Longman*. *MBL*. *Oxford*. *TCA* and *SUP*. *TCC&MW*. *ToddBWW*.

Other references: *CSM* (16 April 1932, 28 November 1969). *KR* (1968). *New Yorker* (28 December 1946). *NYHTBR* (13 May 1962). *NYTBR* (18 September 1932, 15 December 1946, 22 December 1946).

TLS (7 April 1932, 25 May 1946, 13 April 1962, 10 March 1966, 25 May 1967).

Joan Ambrose Cooper

Benvolio: See *Seward, Anna*

Beran, J.: See *Doolittle, Hilda (H. D.)*

Anne Beresford

BORN: 10 September 1919, Redhill, Surrey.
DAUGHTER OF: Richard Beresford and Margaret Kent Beresford.
MARRIED: Michael Hamburger, 1951; remarried Hamburger, 1974.

B.'s poems are filled with literary allusions; for example, some titles are "Miranda," "Persephone," "Nicodemus," and "Eurydice and Andromeda." Yet her poetry is often based on daily life. She writes of the countryside, particularly the wild Suffolk landscape near her home. The nature she depicts is often threatening, as in these lines from "Leiston Abbey" describing a rabbit:

This is its sanctuary.
Nothing makes sense
with the heavy clouds spitting rain
onto the rabbit, its eyes obliterated
by the large swellings of diseased flesh.

One also gets frequent references to the past. Two repeated words in her volume *The Curving Shore* are "distance" and "mirror." These words suggest B.'s emphasis on the past and the reflective yet somehow detached nature of her poetry. "Passing Moment," for instance, begins,

As she brushed her hair
she'd looked in the mirror
and the strange woman peered back
curiously. Peering back
from a distance.

Her first volume of verse, the sixteen-page *Walking Without Moving*, is marked by a curious repetition throughout, as in "Against Hope": "I am willingly dragged / gladly brick on brick / pile up press down / just breath breath." A common theme is bittersweet love affairs ("The Falling," "Crows," "Autumn at Four," "Phrase Unanswered"). The conclusion of "Phrase Unanswered" serves as an example:

Why love
webbed in barbed wire?
A pineapple holds no more promises
Marzipan is not a luxury.
There is not love, nothing
but chrysanthemums.

B.'s poems can seem simple on first reading and occasionally sentimental, but her best work often is filled with drama and grotesque irony. As William Cookson states, B.'s "imagination is connected with humor and satire. Her irony succeeds because it is not obvious." This irony is demonstrated in "The Atlantic from a Liner." Here, as the passengers watch "legless birds" and "fried chickens," the speaker realizes that she, too, is "a legless bird / flying nowhere." The grim irony and stark landscapes help foster a generally melancholy mood in B.'s poetry.

In addition to her writing, B. has worked as a broadcaster for the BBC, a drama and poetry teacher, a musician, and an actress. She gives moving readings of her poetry. A sense of her busy life can be gleaned by reading *A Mug's Game*, memoirs by her husband, poet Michael Hamburger (even though she is rarely mentioned specifically).

WORKS: (with M. Hamburger) *Struck by Apollo* (1965). *Walking Without Moving* (1967). *The Lair* (1968). *The Villa* (1968). *Footsteps in Snow* (1972). *Modern Fairy Tale* (1972). *The Courtship* (1972). (trans.) *Alexandros: Selected Poems*, by Vera Lungu (1974). *The Curving Shore* (1975). (with M. Hamburger) *Words* (1977). *Unholy Giving* (1977). *The Songs of Almost from God's Country* (1980). *Songs a Thracian Taught Me* (1980).

BIBLIOGRAPHY: Levenson, C. *QQ* (1971).
For articles in reference works, see: *CA*. *CP*. *DLB*.
Other references: *TLS* (13 October 1972, 9 July 976).

Louis J. Parascandola

Juliana Berners (Barnes, Bernes)

Until about the end of the nineteenth century, "Lady Juliana Berners" was generally supposed to be the author or compiler of the work known as *The Boke of St Albans* (1486). This view has now been discarded, and it is clear that B. never existed.

The Boke of St Albans is the title given to the last product of the St Albans press (set up in 1479). It consisted of three separate manuals on hawking, hunting, and coat-armor. The collection has been rather doubtfully ascribed, again without any evidence, to a schoolmaster of St Albans.

When the collection was reprinted in London by Wynkyn de Worde in 1496, a manual on *Fishing with an Angle* was added, and this in fact proved to be the most important and durable part of the collection, since in both form and content it had considerable influence on one of the most widely read books in the English language, Izaak Walton's *The Compleat Angler, or, The Contemplative Man's Recreation* (1653).

The myth of B. derives from the colophon of the original treatise on hunting: "Explicit Dam Julyans Barnes in her boke of hunting." On this rather tenuous root, later scholars have cultivated an elaborate biography for B.—a noble lady, a nun, and a prioress associated with the gentle family of Berners and who had spent some time at court. All of this was certainly possible, but no single shred of evidence has been offered for any of it. Even the transformation of "Dam" into "Dame" is unsupported, though admittedly no alternative explanation has been offered.

This remarkable exercise in romantic historiography is fully discussed in John McDonald, *The Origins of Angling* (1963), which includes a facsimile of the treatise from the 1415 manuscript and a modernized text of the first printed version, together with other related documents and a full discussion of the legend of B. *English Hawking and Hunting in The Boke of St Albans,* edited by Rachel Hands (1975), is a facsimile edition of parts of the book, without a modernized text but with full discussion of the problems. *The Treatise on Coat-Armor,* however, has not received similar treatment since the facsimile edition of the whole work by William Blades (1881).

There has been no recent work on *The Boke of St Albans* since the section in *The New Cambridge Bibliography of English Literature* (1969; new edition forthcoming).

WORKS: *The Boke of St Albans by Dame Juliana Berners 1486,* ed. W. Blades (1881). Hands, R. *English Hawking and Hunting in The Boke of St Albans* (1975). McDonald, J. *The Origins of Angling* (1963).

BIBLIOGRAPHY:

For articles in reference works, see: *Bloomsbury. Cambridge. Feminist. Oxford.*

Leslie J. Workman

Mary Berry

BORN: 16 March 1763, Kirkbridge, Yorkshire.
DIED: 20 November 1852, London.
DAUGHTER OF: Robert Berry and Elizabeth Seaton Berry.

Editor, letter writer, and cultural historian, B. was best known in her youth as the dear companion of the aged Horace Walpole and in her old age as the gifted hostess of her intellectual salons. Her unique place in the London scene during the first half of the nineteenth century is reflected in these words written by Harriet Martineau shortly after B.'s death at the age of eighty-nine: "She was not only the woman of letters of the last century, carried far into our own—she was not only the Woman of Fashion who was familiar with the gaieties of life before the fair daughters of George III were seen abroad, and who had her own will and way with society up to last Saturday night: she was the repository of the whole literary history of four-score years; and when she was pleased to throw open the folding-doors of her memory, they were found to be mirrors of literature, from the mournful Cowper to Tennyson the Laureate."

B.'s origins hardly suggest the central role she was to play in London society. Her father, son of a tailor, took employment with his wealthy uncle, Robert Ferguson, a Scottish merchant. In 1762, when the youth married Elizabeth Seaton, a young lady with no dowry, Ferguson disinherited the newlyweds in favor of William Berry, the younger brother. A year after B.'s birth, a second daughter, Agnes, was born; three years later, Elizabeth Berry died in childbirth and the child also died. B. and her sister were then raised by her maternal grandmother. During these years both girls read widely and their lively, acquisitive minds more than compensated for their lack of formal education.

From her reading, B. developed a longing "to see that world of which [she] had been picking up all sorts of accounts." When her uncle William, now possessed of Ferguson's fortune, provided the Berrys with an income of £1000 a year, her longing became reality; and she, her father, and her sister traveled to Rotterdam in 1783. After three weeks in Holland, B. celebrated the experience in her journal: "I have always looked back to those three weeks as the most enjoyable and the most enjoyed of my existence, in which I received the greatest number of new ideas, and felt my mind, my understanding, and my judgment increase everyday, while at the same time my imagination was delighted with the charm of novelty in everything I saw or heard." As travel opened her mind, it also influenced her attitudes towards the future. For example, on arriving in Florence she wrote, "I began to feel my situation, and how entirely dependent I was on my resources for my conduct, respectability, and success." Recognizing her role in her small family, she stated "that I must be a protecting mother, instead of a gay companion, to my sister; and to my father a guide and monitor, instead of finding in him a tutor and protector."

In 1788, B. completely captured the affections of the seventy-one-year-old bachelor, Horace Walpole, the brilliant letter writer, art collector, and proud owner of Strawberry Hill in Twickenham. In a letter to Lady Ossory, Walpole described the sisters as "the best-informed and the most perfect creatures I ever saw of their age. They are exceedingly sensible, entirely natural and unaffected, frank, and, being qualified to talk on any subject, nothing is so easy and agreeable as their conversation." Although he referred to the sisters as his "twin wives," he seemed to feel a deeper affection for B. Not surprisingly, the more-than-four-decade age difference excited some humorous response in social circles, but Walpole never wavered in his devotion. In fact, shortly after their meeting he was inspired by the sisters to write one of his most charming books, *Reminiscences, Written by Mr. Horace Walpole in 1788, for the Amusement of Miss Mary and Miss Agnes Berry.* Rumors that he had proposed marriage to B. circulated from time to time, but no evidence exists to support this claim.

Yet there were problems. In 1796, B. became engaged to General Charles O'Hara, but when he was ordered to Gibraltar, she found reasons to delay their marriage and remain in England. Although they corresponded, the engagement ended in April 1797 and B. packed the O'Hara letters away. Forty-eight years later she reopened them and wrote, "This packet of letters relates to the six happiest months of my long and insignificant existence." She believed their problems could have been resolved "had we ever met for twenty-four hours." Another problem had arisen earlier, in 1791, when the Berrys made an extended European tour. Walpole was deeply distressed, especially when the family arrived in Paris, where they were exposed to the dangers of the Revolution. His letters, full of concern, followed them wherever they went.

Yet, on the whole, the relationship was the source of satisfaction to them all. The sisters were Walpole's constant friends and companions, and he responded by contributing to their material security in the form of a charming house called Little Strawberry Hill. Finally, when he died in 1797, in addition to the house, he provided each the interest from £4000, relieving them completely from financial worries. Most important was a wooden box containing "my own literary works as have been heretofore published or have been printed or still remain in manuscript." Although these were directed to Mr. Berry, it was B. who became Walpole's literary executor and published or republished his works.

The fifty-five years left to the sisters would center more in London than in Twickenham. Eventually, settled at 8 Curzon Street, they became the key figures in salons that attracted the most distinguished people in London. Lord Byron, Francis Jeffrey, Sydney Smith, Samuel Rogers, Thomas B. Macaulay, Thomas Malthus, Charles Dickens, and William M. Thackeray all dined and conversed under the watchful direction of the Berry sisters. The internationally famous Madame de Staël was a frequent visitor who believed B. was "by far the cleverest woman in England." The great actress Fanny Kemble was a favorite visitor during their last years.

B. did, however, leave behind a literary legacy; yet, aside from her correspondence, it receives little attention today. In 1798, she edited *The Works of Horatio Walpole* in five volumes, an edition that did not carry her name, and in 1810, she edited the letters of the Marquise du Deffand, part of the Walpole legacy. Nine years later, in 1819, B. published *The Life of Rachel, Lady Russell*, a biography consisting of letters and transitional remarks. Joanna Baillie described it as an "edifying example to the young women of the day, who consider religion as too exclusively connected with mystery."

Considered by her contemporaries to be her best work, *A Comparative View of the Social Life in England and France* was published in two parts in 1828 and 1831. In 1844, the two parts were published together in her collected works. Her success in managing such a broad topic is reflected in the unreserved praise of the critic for *The Quarterly Review*, who wrote, "she has presented us with a sketch of great power, the result of various and accurate learning, instinct with deep and sober reflection, ever exhibiting a love of justice and virtue, nor deformed by affectation any more than it is tinged with unworthy prejudice."

Yet, for today's reader, *Extracts of the Journal and Correspondence of Miss Berry, from the Year 1793 to 1852* has the greatest appeal. The seven decades, often recorded in considerable detail, of a life that touched so many important people during those many evenings in Richmond and London and during the many European tours provide a remarkable picture of English intellectual life in the first half of the nineteenth century; and then there are the memorable scenes when the sisters were received by royalty at home and by Napoleon in France. These experiences and more are mirrored for the reader in the three volumes edited by Lady Teresa Lewis.

B. has vanished from the pages of most literary accounts. Yet for more than half a century she was the center of intellectual life in London. Thackeray, a friend of her old age, wrote of her with affection: "I often thought, as I took my kind old friend's hand, how with it I held on to the old society of wits and men of the world."

WORKS: *The Works of Horatio Walpole, Earl of Oxford*, ed. M. Berry (1798). *The Fashionable Friends: A Comedy* (1802). *Letters of the Marquise du Deffand*, ed. M. Berry (1810). *Some Account of Rachel Wriothesley, Lady Russell, by the Editor of Madam Du Deffand's Letters. Followed by a Series of Letters of Mary Russell to Her Husband. . .*, ed. M. Berry (1819). *A Comparative View of the Social Life in England and France* (1828, 1831). *England and France: a Comparative View of the Social Conditions of Both Countries, from the Restoration of Charles the Second to the Present Time. To which are now first added: Remarks on Lord Oxford's Letters, the Life of the Marquise du Deffand, the Life of Rachel Lady Russell, Fashionable Friends, a Comedy* (1844). *Extracts from the journal and Correspondence of Miss Berry, from the Year 1783 to 1852*, ed. T. Lewis (1865).

BIBLIOGRAPHY: Adickes, S. *The Social Quest: The Expanded Vision of Four Women Travellers in the Era of the French Revolution* (1991). Byron, G. G. *Byron's Letters and Journals*, ed. L. A. Marchant (1973–82). Chorley, H. F. *Recollections* (1873). Ketton-Cremer, R. W. *Horace Walpole* (1940). Kimble, F. A. *Records of a Later Life* (1884). Martineau, H. *Biographical Sketches* (1885). Melville, L. [pseud. L. S. Benjamin]. *The Berry Papers: 1763–1852* (1914). Melville, L. [pseud. L. S. Benjamin]. *Regency Ladies* (1926). Moers, E. *Literary Women* (1976). Strachey, L. *Portraits in Miniature* (1931). *The Grace of Friendship: Horace Walpole and Misses Berry*, ed. V. Surtees (1995). Thackeray, W. M. *The Letters and Private Papers*, ed. G. N. Ray (1946). Walpole, H. *Horace Walpole's Correspondence with Mary and Agnes Berry. . .*, in *The Yale Edition of Horace Walpole's Correspondence* (1944). Walpole, H. *Memoirs of Horace Walpole and His Contemporaries*, ed. E. Warburton (1852).

For articles in reference works, see: *Adams. BA19C. DNB. Feminist. Index to Literary Biography*, ed. P. P. Harlice (1975). *IDWB. ToddDBA.*

Other references: *Edinburgh Review* (October 1865). *LonT* (23 November 1852). *N&Q* (August 1983). *Quarterly Review* (March 1845). Stenton, D. M. *The English Women in History* (1957).

Philip Bordinat

Berwick, Mary: See *Procter, Adelaide Anne*

Annie Wood Besant

BORN: 1 October 1847, London.
DIED: 20 September 1933, Adyar, India.
DAUGHTER OF: William Burton Persse and Emily (Morris) Wood.

MARRIED: Frank Besant, 1867.
WROTE UNDER: Annie Wood Besant; The Wife of a Beneficed Clergyman.

When B. was eight, her education was taken over by Miss Ellen Marryat with whom she resided for the next eight years and from whom she received a far better education than that of most nineteenth century girls. Soon after her education ended, B., deeply religious, married the Reverend Frank Besant, but from the beginning the marriage was far from a success. A series of disasters, including an almost fatal illness, led her to question her faith. Finally, unable to accept the doctrines of the Church of England, and more and more distraught over her marriage, she left her husband. While still under his roof, she had published three pamphlets, but now her writing became her means of financial support; for the rest of her life, she was never without a pen in her hand.

Thomas Scott and Moncure Conway, critics of orthodox Christianity, came to her rescue. When Scott published her religious pamphlets, such as *The Atonement, Mediation and Salvation, Eternal Torture,* and *The Religious Education of Children,* she declared herself a theist and soon she moved on to atheism. When Conway introduced her to Charles Bradlaugh, the leader of the National Secular Society and publisher of the *National Reformer,* B. joined the paper and from 1877 to 1887 served as coeditor. In addition, she played a major role in such other freethought periodicals as the *Secular Chronicle, Secular Review,* and the *Secularist.* B. began her speaking career in 1879, and she was considered the foremost woman orator in Britain.

In 1877, Bradlaugh and B. published a new edition of *Fruits of Philosophy,* a treatise on birth control written by an American physician and first published in 1832. Their ensuing arrest and trial for the publication of an obscene book caused a sensation; B. in defending herself was the first woman to speak out publicly in support of birth control, but both were found guilty. B. increasingly became concerned with the social problems of Victorian Britain. She began the publication of a monthly magazine, *Our Corner,* one of the first to publish George Bernard Shaw as well as other young aspiring writers. Her concern with social problems led her away from freethought and toward socialism. In 1884, she became a member of the Fabian Society and quickly undertook to speak and write pamphlets on its behalf. Since activism estranged her from Bradlaugh, she resigned her coeditorship of the *National Reformer.* She became increasingly active in the politics of social improvement and worked with a number of the social reformers of the period. One of these, the publisher W. T. Stead, introduced B. to her next enthusiasm, theosophy. In the meantime she served as editor of *Link,* the journal of the Law and Liberty League, organized by Stead.

During the late 1880s, B. delved into the occult and became a member of the Psychical Society, but since this experience failed to provide her with any spiritual insight, she was introduced to theosophy. Stead gave her a copy of *The Secret Doctrine* to review for his *Pall Mall Gazette* and also a letter of introduction to its author, Helena Petrovna Blavatsky. B. fell under her influence, converted to theosophy, and put her energies into speaking and writing on its behalf. After Blavatsky's death, B., first with Colonel Henry Steel Olcott and then alone, became head of the Theosophical Society.

From 1893 on, India was the center of her work, whether it was theosophy or Indian politics. Throughout this second half of her life, she edited many periodicals on both topics: *The Adyar Bulletin, Central Hindu College Magazine, Commonweal: Madras, Lucifer, New India, The Theosophical Review, Theosophist, United India, The Young Citizen.* She lectured repeatedly on almost yearly trips from India to England, frequently via the United States. From 1912 until 1920 her preoccupation with India and its role in the British empire was all-consuming. In 1917, she was elected president of the National Congress, the Indian political party whose platform at that time espoused home rule. She was the first non-Indian woman so honored. By 1920, however, Mohandas K. Gandhi and his policy of independence and nonviolence had become a stronger force than B.'s home rule and universal brotherhood. Until her death she continued to fight both in India and Britain for her views of the future of India.

Many of her publications, always of a philosophical or political nature, were written as speeches. They often had been delivered in diverse locations with only slight changes. Not an original mind, she was nonetheless an able popularizer of the ideas of the day.

WORKS: (By the wife of a beneficed clergyman) *On the Deity of Jesus of Nazareth: An Enquiry into the Nature of Jesus by an Examination of the Synoptic Gospels* (1873). (By the wife of a beneficed clergyman) *According to Saint John: On the Deity of Jesus of Nazareth, Pt. II* (1873). *Natural Religion versus Revealed Religion* (1874). *On the Atonement* (1874). *On Eternal Torture* (1874). *On Inspiration* (1874). *On the Religious Education of Children* (1874). *Essays by Mrs. Besant* (1875). *Euthanasia* (1875). *On the Mediation and Salvation of Ecclesiastical Christianity* (1875). *On the Nature and Existence of God* (1875). *On Prayer* (1875). *The Beauties of the Prayer-Book, Parts I, II, III* (1876). *Constructive Rationalism* (1876). *The Secular Song and Hymn Book* (1876). *The Freethinkers' Text-Book: Pt. II: Christianity: Its Evidences, Its Origin, Its Morality, Its History* (1877). *The Gospel of Atheism: A Lecture* (1877). *The Gospel of Christianity aand the Gospel of Freethought* (1877). *Giordano Bruno* (1877). (trans.) *The Idea of God in the Revolution,* by Emile Acollas (1877). *Is the Bible Indictable? Being an Enquiry whether the Bible Comes within the Ruling of the Lord Chief Justice as to Obscene Literature* (1877). *The Law of Population: Its Consequences, and Its Bearing upon Human Conduct and Morals* (1877). *My Path to Atheism* (1877). *Christian Progress* (1878). *English Republicanism* (1878). *The Fruits of Christianity* (1878). *In the High Court of Justice Queen's Bench Division, June 18, 1877. The Queen v. Charles Bradlaugh and Annie Besant* (1878). *Rushing into War* (1878). *Marriage As It Was, As It Is, and As It Should Be* (1879). *The Story of Afghanistan; or Why the Tory Government Gags the Indian Press: A Plea for the*

Weak against the Strong (1879). *The Ethics of Punishment* (1880). (trans.) *The Influence of Heredity on Free Will,* by Ludwig Büchner (1880). *Landlords, Tenant Farmers, and Labourers* (1880). (trans.) *Mind in Animals,* by Ludwig Büchner (1880). *England before the Repeal of the Corn Laws* (1881). *Free Trade versus 'Fair' Trade* (1881). *The History of the Anti-Corn-Law Struggle* (1881). *Labour and Land: Their Burdens, Duties, and Rights* (1881). *The Landlords' Attempt to Mislead the Landless* (1881). *Light, Heat, and Sound: a Hall of Science Manual* (1881). *Law Makers and Law Breakers* (1881). (trans.) *The Religion of Israel. A Study in Comparative Mythology,* by Jules Soury (1881). *Vivisection* (1881). *What Is Really Free Trade?* (1881). *Circulation* (1882) *Coercion in Ireland and Its Results. A Plea for Justice* (1882). *Digestion* (1882). *The English Land System* (1882). *Electricity Lectures I, II, III and IV* (1882). *Eyes and Ears, Six Chats on Seeing & Hearing* (1882). *Force No Remedy* (1882). *Henry Varley Exposed* (1882). *Organs of Digestion* (1882). *Physiology of Home* (1882). *Respiration* (1882). *The Christian Creed; or, What It Is Blasphemy to Deny* (1882). *Civil and Religious Liberty, with Some Hints Taken From the French Revolution* (1883). *The History of the Great French Revolution* (1883). *The Atheistic Platform* (1884–1888). *Biblical Biology. A Contribution to Religious Non-Science* (1884). *The Jesus of the Gospels and the Influence of Christianity on the World. A Two Nights' Debate between Annie Besant and the Rev. A. Hutchard* (1884). *Auguste Comte: His Philosophy, His Religion and His Sociology* (1885). *Autobiographical Sketches* (1885). *Gordon Judged Out of His Own Mouth* (1885). *Is Christianity a Success?* (1885). *The Legalization of Female Slavery in England* (1885). *Legends and Tales* (1885). *The Natural History of the Christian Devil* (1885). *The Political Status of Women* (1885). *The Redistribution of Political Power* (1885). *Sin and Crime: Their Nature and Treatment* (1885). *The Story of the Soudan* (1885). *Theological Essays and Debates* (1885). *Woman's Position According to the Bible* (1885). *A World Without God. A Reply to Miss Frances Power Cobbe* (1885). *A Burden on Labour* (1886). *A Creature of Crown and Parliament* (1886). *The Evolution of Society* (1886). *For the Crown and Against the Nation* (1886). *Life, Death and Immortality* (1886). *The Myth of the Resurrection* (1886). *The Sins of the Church* (1886). *Why I Am a Socialist* (1886). *The World and Its Gods* (1886). *Atheism and Its Bearing on Morals. A Debate between Annie Besant Atheist, and the Rev. G. F. Handel Rowe (of Halifax), Clergyman of the Church of England* (1887). *England's Jubilee Gift to Ireland* (1887). *Is Socialism Sound? Verbatim Report of a Four Nights' Debate between Annie Besant and G. W. Foote, at the Hall of Science, Old Street, London E.C., On February 2nd, 9th, 16th and 23rd 1887* (1887). *Radicalism and Socialism* (1887). *The Socialist Movement* (1887). *The Teachings of Christianity. A Debate between Annie Besant, Atheist, and the Rev. G. F. Handel Rowe, of Halifax, Clergyman of the Church of England* (1887). *Why I Do Not Believe in God* (1887). *Why I Became a Theosophist* (1889). *God's Views on Marriage as Revealed in the Old Testament* (1890). *Modern Socialism* (1890). *Socialism v. Individualism. Public Debate in the Mechanics' Hall, Nottingham, between Mrs. Annie Besant (of the Fabian Society) and Mr. Frederick Millar (of the Liberty and Property Defence League)* (1890). *The Trades Union Movement* (1890). *1875 to 1891. A Fragment of Autobiography* (1891). *In Defence of Theosophy* (1891). *Mrs. Annie Besant and Theosophy* (1891). *A Glossary of Theosophical Terms* (1891). *The Sphinx of Theosophy* (1891). *The Theosophical Society and H. P. B.* (1891). *Theosophy and Its Evidences* (1891). *Theosophy and the Law of Population* (1891). *The Influence of Alcohol* (1892). *The Place of Peace* (1892). *A Rough Outline of Theosophy* (1892). *The Seven Principles of Man* (1892). *Theosophy* (1892). *Theosophy and Christianity* (1892). *Theosophy and its Practical Application* (1892). *Why You Should Be a Theosophist* (1892). *Annie Besant in Ceylon* (1893). *An Autobiography* (1893). *An Exposition of Theosophy* (1893). *The Theosophical Society and H. P. Blavatsky* (1893). *Theosophy in Questions and Answers* (1893). *The Building of the C(K)osmos and other Lectures* (1894). *Indian Methods of Spiritual Self Culture* (1894). *An Introduction to Theosophy* (1894). *The Meaning and Use of Pain* (1894). *Vegetarianism in the Light of Theosophy* (1894). (trans.) *The Bhagavad Gita or the Lord's Song* (1895). *The Birth and Evolution of the Soul* (1895). *The Case Against W. Q. Judge* (1895). *Devotion and the Spiritual Life* (1895). *Eastern Castes and Western Classes* (1895). *First Steps in Occultism* (1895). *In the Outer Court* (1895). *Karma* (1895). *The Masters as Facts and Ideals* (1895). *Materialism Undermined by Science. A Lecture* (1895). *The Means of India's Regeneration* (1895). *The Pilgrimage of the Soul. A Lecture* (1895). *The Place of Politics in the Life of a Nation* (1895). *The Self and its Sheathes* (1895). *Theosophy and Its Teachings* (1895). *The Use of Evil. A Lecture* (1895). *Disestablish the Church; or, Sins of the Church of England* (1896). *The Future that Awaits Us* (1896). *Man and His Bodies* (1896). *Man, the Master of His Destiny. A Lecture* (1896). *The Path of Discipleship* (1896). *Four Great Religions* (1897). *Man's Place and Functions in Nature* (1897). *The Three Paths to Union with God* (1897). *The Atonement and the Law of Sacrifice* (1898). *Emotion, Intellect and Spirituality* (1898). *Esoteric Christianity* (1898). *The Hidden Side of Religions* (1898). *Individuality* (1898). *Natural and Spiritual Bodies, Resurrection and Ascension* (1898). *Occultism, Semi-Occultism and Pseudo-Occultism* (1898). *Sacraments and Revelation* (1898). *The Trinity: Divine Incarnation* (1898). *Dharma* (1899). *On Some Difficulties on the Inner Life* (1899). *The Story of the Great War* (1899). *Avataras* (1900). *Some Problems of Life* (1900). *Ancient Ideals in Modern Life* (1901). *Death—And After?* (1901). *Esoteric Christianity or the Lesser Mysteries* (1901). *Shri Rama Chandra, the Ideal King. Some Lessons for the Use of Hindu Students in the Schools of India* (1901). *Thought Power: Its Control and Culture* (1901). *Morning Thoughts for the Year. Adapted by a Student from Writings by Annie Besant* (1902). *Theosophy and Im-*

perialism (1902). *Against Vivisection. A Lecture* (1903). *Education as a National Duty* (1903). *England and India* (1903). *The Laws of the Higher Life* (1903). *Proofs of the Existence of the Soul. A Lecture* (1903). *The Education of Indian Girls* (1904). *Hindu Ideals. For the Use of Hindu Students in the Schools of India* (1904). *Is Theosophy Anti-Christian? An Explanation Addressed to the Bishop of London* (1904). *Life, and Life After Death* (1904). *Modern Science and the Higher Self. A Lecture* (1904). *The Necessity of Re-Incarnation* (1904). *The Pedigree of Man* (1904). *The Principle of Freethought* (1904). *Re-Incarnation, a Christian Doctrine* (1904). *The Secret of Evolution* (1904). *A Study of Consciousness. Contribution to the Science of Psychology* (1904). *Theosophy and the New Psychology* (1904). *The Value of Theosophy in the Raising of India. A Lecture* (1904). *When a Man Dies Shall He Live Again?* (1904). *The Indian Nation* (1905). (with C. W. Leadbeater) *Occult Chemistry* (1905). *Theosophy in Relation to Human Life* (1905). *Thought-Forms* (1905). *The Work of Theosophy in the World* (1905). *East and West and the Destinies of Nations* (1906). *Hints on the Study of the Bhagavad-Gita* (1906). *India's Awakening: A Lecture* (1906). *On Moods* (1906). *The Perfect Man* (1906). *H. P. Blavatsky and the Masters of Wisdom* (1907). *Last Days of the President-Founder [Colonel Olcott] and Mrs. Besant's Presidential Address* (1907). *London Lectures of 1907* (1907). *The Wisdom of the Upanishats* (1907). *Australian Lectures 1908* (1908). *Buddhist Popular Lectures* (1908). *An Introduction to Yoga* (1908). *The Changing World and Lectures to Theosophical Students 1909* (1909). *Questions on Hinduism with Answers* (1909). *The Religious Problem In India* (1909). *Popular Lectures on Theosophy* (1910). *Reincarnation* (1910). *Notes on The Science of the Sacred Word. Being a Summarised Translation of the Pranava-Vada of Gargayana by Bhagevan Das*, 3 vols. (1910–13). *The Emergence of a World Religion* (1911). *Essays and Addresses* (4 vols.) (1911–1913). *The Immediate Future and Other Lectures* (1911). *The Meaning and Method of Spiritual Life* (1911). *Psychology* (1911). *The Riddle of Life and How Theosophy Answers It* (1911). *The Future Socialism* (1912). *Gurus and Chelas. An Article by E. T. Sturdy and a Reply by Annie Besant* (1912). *The Ideals of Theosophy* (1912). *The Immediate Future* (1912). *Initiation: The Perfecting of Man* (1912). *An Introduction to the Science of Peace* (1912). *Islam in the Light of Theosophy* (1912). *The Law of Action and Reaction* (1912). *Man's Life in the Three Worlds* (1912). *The Masters and the Way to Them* (1912). *The Opening of the New Cycle* (1912). *A Sketch of Theosophy* (1912). *Social Problems: The Message of Theosophy* (1912). *The Spiritual Life* (1912). *A Study in Karma* (1912). *Theosophy* (1912). *The White Lodge and Its Messengers* (1912). *Communication between Different Worlds* (1913). *Evolution and Occultism* (1913). *Giordano Bruno: Theosophy's Apostle in the Sixteenth Century* (1913). *India* (1913). *An Introduction to Theosophy* (1913). *Investigation into the Super-Physical* (1913). *Man: Whence, How and Whither: A Record of Clairvoyant Investigation* (1913). *Man's Life in This and Other Worlds*, 3 vols. (1913). *The Spirit Who Is Man and the Spiritual Life* (1913). *Superhuman Men in History and Religion* (1913). *Theosophy and the Theosophical Society* (1913). *Wake Up, India* (1913). *The India That Shall Be* (1914?). *India and the Empire* (1914). *The Inner Purpose of the Theosophical Society* (1914). *Mysticiam* (1914). *The Reality of the Invisible and the Actuality of the Unseen Worlds* (1914). *Spiritual Life for the Man of the World* (1914). *Theosophical Ideals and the Immediate Future* (1914). *Women and Politics, The Way Out of the Present Difficulty* (1914). *A Word on Man, His Nature and His Power* (1914). *The Basis of Morality* (1915). *The Future of Young India* (1915). *How India Wrought for Freedom: The Story of the National Congress told from Official Records* (1915). *India, A Nation: A Plea for Self-Government* (1915). *The Law of Rebirth. From the Writings of Annie Besant* (1915). *The Political Outlook* (1915). *Reincarnation: Its Necessity* (1915). *Self-Government in India* (1915). *War Articles and Notes* (1915). *Whatsoever a Man Soweth. From the Writings of Annie Besant* (1915). *The Bearing of Religious Ideals on Social Reconstruction* (1916). *The Commonwealth of India Act* (1916). *Congress Work* (1916). *District Work* (1916). *The Garment of God. From the Writings of Annie Besant* (1916). *Home Rule and the Empire* (1916). *Home Rule. Articles from New India* (1916). *Preparation for Citizenship* (1916). *Psychic and Spiritual Development* (1916). *Social Service* (1916). *Theosophy and Life's Deeper Problems* (1916). *Under the Congress Flag* (1916). *A World Religion* (1916). *The Ancient Indian Ideal of Duty* (1917). *Apart or Together?* (1917?). *The Birth of New India* (1917). *Colonial Executive Councils and Cabinets* (1917). *The Coming Race* (1917). *Congress Speeches by Annie Besant* (1917). *Duties of the Theosophist* (1917). *The Indian Government* (1917). *Mrs. Besant's Farewell Message, To My Brothers and Sisters in India* (1917). *The Mysteries* (1917). *A Nation's Rights* (1917). *The Necessity for Home Rule* (1917). *The Case for India* (1918). *Criticisms of the Montagu-Chelmsford Proposals of Reform. Three Papers by Annie Besant and C. P. Ramaswami Aiyar* (1918). *India's Hour of Destiny* (1918). *The Masters* (1918). *Memories of Past Lives* (1918). *Nature's Finer Forces* (1918). *Notes on the Proposed Reforms* (1918). *The Place of Religion in National Life* (1918). *Principles of Education* (1910). *The Search for Happiness* (1918). *Coercion and Resistance in India* (1919). *Education for the New Era* (1919). *A Defense of Hinduism. A Booklet Written for Hindu Boys* (1919). *Is Belief in the Masters Superstitious or Harmful?* (1919). *Law* (1919). *Lectures on Political Science* (1919). *Life After Death* (1919). *Man's Life in Three Worlds* (1919). *Memory* (1919). *National Home Rule League, Why Founded and How* (1919). *The New Era* (1919). *Occultism* (1919). *The Problem of Indian Self-Government* (1919). *Problems of Reconstruction* (1919). *Study and Practice* (1919). *The War and Its Lessons on Equality* (1919). *The War and Its Lessons on Fraternity* (1919). *The War and Its Lessons on Liberty* (1919). *The War and the Builders of the Commonwealth* (1919). *Why India Wants Home Rule.*

A Reasoned Appeal (1919). *The Inner Government of the World* (1920). *The Paths of the Masters of Wisdom. Quotations from the Works of Annie Besant* (1920). *The Protestant Spirit* (1920). *[The First Reform Conference under the Auspices of the National Home Rule League, being the Malabar Conference 1921. Presidential Address by Annie Besant]* (1921). *Religion and Music. A Lecture* (1921). *Britain's Place in the Great Plan* (1921). *The Great Plan* (1921). *Karma and Social Improvement* (1921). *The Nature of Theosophical Proofs* (1921). *On Karma* (1921). *Reincarnation. Its Answers to Life's Problems* (1921). *Talks with a Class* (1921). *Theosophy: Its Meaning and Its Value* (1921?). *The War and Its Lessons* (1921). *What the Mystic Means by the "Eternal Now"* (1921). *Daily Meditations on the Path and Its Qualifications. From the Works of Annie Besant,* comp. E. S. Cooper (1922). *The Future of Indian Politics: A Contribution to the Understanding of Present-day Problems* (1922). *The Guild System as a Substitute for Trade Unionism* (1922?). (with C. Jinarajadasa, J. Krishnamurti, and G. S. Arundale) *Theosophy and World-Problems* (1922). *Brahmavidya (Divine Wisdom)* (1923). *Causes of the New Spirit in India* (1923). *India As She Was and As She Is* (1923). *Reaction of Autocracy in England* (1923?). (with C. Jinaraadasa and G. S. Arundale) *The Real and the Unreal* (1923). *What Is the National Conference?* (1923). *The Coming of the World Teacher* (1925). *Lives of Alcyone* (1925). *The Theosophical Society and the Occult Heirarchy* (1925). *India, Bond or Free?* (1926). *World Problems of Today* (1926). *The New Civilization* (1927). *A Selection of the Social and Political Pamphlets of Annie Besant,* ed. John Savant (1970).

BIBLIOGRAPHY: Besterman, T. *Mrs. Annie Besant: A Modern Prophet* (1934). Bright, E. *Old Memories and Letters of Annie Besant* (1936). Chandrasekhar, S. *"A Dirty, Filthy Book"* (1981). Dinnage, R. *Annie Besant* (1986). *The Annie Besant Centenary Book,* ed. J. Cousins (1947). Hollis, P. *Ladies Elect: Women in English Local Government, 1865–1914* (1987). Kumar, R. *Annie Besant's Rise to Power in Indian Politics, 1914–1917* (1981). Lutyens, Lady E. *Candles in the Sun* (1957). Lutyens, M. *Krishnamurti: The Years of Awakening* (1984). Nethercote, A. *The First Five Lives of Annie Besant* (1960). Nethercote, A. *The Last Four Lives of Annie Besant* (1963). Royle, E. *Radicals, Secularists and Republicans: Popular Freethought in Britain, 1866–1915* (1980). Taylor, A. *Annie Besant: A Biography* (1992). West, G. *The Life of Annie Besant* (1928). Williams, G. M. *The Passionate Pilgrim: A Life of Annie Besant* (1946).

For articles in reference works, see *DNB. 1890s. Feminist. Oxford. VB.*

Joanne Stafford Mortimer

Mathilda Betham-Edwards

BORN: 4 March 1836, Westerfield Hall, Ipswich, Suffolk.
DIED: 4 January 1919, Hastings, Sussex.
DAUGHTER OF: Edward Edwards and Barbara Betham.

Novelist, travel writer, essayist, journalist, poet, and autobiographer, B. grew up on her father's farm in Suffolk, one of six children. Her mother died when she was twelve. Her aunt was the poet and diarist Mathilda Betham, whose work she later celebrated in *Six Life Studies of Famous Women* (1884). Though largely self-educated, reading books from her father's library and from the Mechanic's Institute in Ipswich, B. attended a day school in Ipswich between the ages of ten and twelve. The school was run by a Miss Baker, who encouraged the young B. to become a pupil-governess at a boarding school in Peckham, which she disliked intensely.

Having a talent for language, B. was fluent in French, German, Italian, and Spanish, and she traveled regularly to France and Germany, writing articles about the France she knew so well for the British public. She edited Arthur Young's *Autobiography* (1898) and his *Travels in France During the Years 1787, 1788, 1789* (1890). In 1891, her writing about France was honored by the French government when she became the only Englishwoman to be made an *Officier de l'Instruction Publique de France.*

After their father's death, B. and her unmarried sister successfully ran the family farm for a year, an arrangement brought to an end when B.'s sister died. B. subsequently moved to Kensington, London, in 1865, where she met George Eliot, George Henry Lewes, Barbara Bodichon, and Charles Bradlaugh. She once attended a meeting at which Karl Marx presided and was both Nonconformist and antivivisectionist. Signing the 1866 petition for female suffrage, she was also a believer in women's equality.

B. was a prolific author during her sixty or so years of writing. She began her first novel, *The White House by the Sea* (1857), in her teens. It was set in Suffolk and became very successful and was reprinted for the next forty years. It was translated into several languages, and it was pirated in the United States. *The Lord of the Harvest* (1899) is usually seen as her best Suffolk novel, and the romantic best-sellers *Kitty* (1869), *Forestalled* (1880), and *Love and Marriage* (1884) were extremely popular, the latter two being B.'s personal favorites. The travel volumes *A Winter with the Swallows* (1866) and *Through Spain to the Sahara* (1867) describe her trips with Barbara Bodichon. B. published her own *Reminiscences* in 1898.

WORKS: *The White House by the Sea* (1857). *Now or Never* (1859). *Charles and Ernest or, Play and Work: A Story of Hazelhurst School* (1859). *Ally and her Schoolfellow: A Tale for the Young* (1861). *John and I* (1862). *Snow-Flakes and the Stories They Told the Children* (1862). *Scenes and Stories of the Rhine* (1862). *Doctor Jacob* (1864). *Lisabee's Love Story* (1865). *The Wild Flower of Ravensworth* (1866). *A Winter with the Swallows* (1866). *Through Spain to the Sahara* (1867). *Company's Courtship* (1868). *Kitty* (1869). *The Sylvesters* (1871). *Mademoiselle Joesphine's Fridays and Other Stories* (1874). *Bridget* (1877). *Forestalled, or the Life-Quest* (1880). *The Starry Blossom, and Other Stories for the Young*

(1881). *Poems* (1884). *Love and Marriage or, The Waiting on an Island, and Other Tales* (1884). *Six Life Studies of Famous Women* (1884). *Half-Way: An Anglo-French Romance* (1886). *The Parting of the Ways* (1888). *For One and the World* (1889). *A Dream of Millions and Other Tales* (1891). *A North-Country Comedy* (1891). *Two Aunts and a Nephew* (1891). *The Romance of a French Parsonage* (1892). *France of To-day* (1892–94). *A Romance of Dijon* (1894). (trans.) *Passages in the Life of a Galley Slave,* by J. Marteilhe (1895). *The Lord of the Harvest* (1899). *Reminiscences* (1898). *The Roof of France, or Travels in Lozere* (1899). *A Suffolk Courtship* (1900). *East of Paris* (1902). *Mock Beggars' Hall: A Story* (1902). *Barham Brockleback, M.D.* (1903). *Home Life in France* (1905). *Literary Rambles in France* (1907). *French Men, Women, and Books* (1910). *In French Africa* (1913). *From an Islington Widow: Pages of Reminiscent Romance* (1914). *Under the German Ban in Alsace and Lorraine* (1914). *Hearts of Alsace: A Story of Our Time* (1916). *Twentieth Century France* (1917). *War Poems* (1917). *Mid-Victorian Memories* (1919). (trans) *French Fireside Poetry,* ed. B. Miall.

BIBLIOGRAPHY:

For articles in reference works, see: *Bloomsbury. Feminist. Longman. NCHEL. ToddBWW.*

Jacqueline Dello Russo

L[ouisa]. S[arah]. Bevington

BORN: 1845, Battersea, London.
DIED: 1895, London.
DAUGHTER OF: Alexander Bevington and Louisa (De Hermes?).
MARRIED: Ignatz Guggenberger, 1883.
WROTE UNDER: L. S. Bevington; Louisa S. Guggenberger; Arbor Leigh.

B.'s father was from an old Quaker family; an ancestor of his was once confined with George Fox in Nottingham Gaol. B.'s parents instilled in her a strong social conscience, an ambitious intellect, and a love of nature that she sustained through her adulthood; however, the Christianity of her upbringing gave way to moral and metaphysical speculation and ultimately to agnosticism. From the 1870s through the mid 1890s, B. published poems and essays about contemporary life and evolutionary science. In her last decade, she was a well known spokesperson for anarchism.

B.'s first published verses were three sonnets that appeared in the *Friends' Examiner* in 1871; subsequently, Herbert Spencer had four more poems by B., published in the (U.S.) *Popular Science Monthly,* as "Teachings of a Day." In 1876, using the pseudonym "Arbor Leigh" (alluding to Elizabeth Barrett Browning's *Aurora Leigh*), B. published *Key Notes,* verses on evolution that were well received in intellectual and scientific circles. Charles Darwin, who had not read a volume of poetry in fifteen years, expressed satisfaction with this collection. In 1881, B. contributed an article to the *Fortnightly Review* defending evolutionary morality. In 1892, A. H. Miles summarized B.'s career this way: "She has discerned more accurately than many contemporaries, the immense poetical development which the acceptance of the evolutionary view has made possible for science, and her best poems are attempts . . . to bring out the poetic significance of scientific principles. She also has abundance of human feeling and passion." Indeed, B.'s commitments to evolutionism and to social justice were emotional and aesthetic as well as philosophical. The poems in her second volume, *Poems, Lyrics and Sonnets* (1882), convey strong personal feeling and are more polished and literary than in *Key Notes.* In 1883, B. married a Munich artist, Ignatz Guggenberger, and moved, briefly, to Germany. The marriage seems not to have lasted; she returned to London and associated herself with the international movement of atheists and anarchists. In the early 1890s, B. was contributing articles to anarchist and socialist journals such as *Freedom, Commonweal,* and *Liberty,* and she was lecturing on atheism and religion. The anarchists justified their cause by the many social ills of late Victorian England, including, for example, wife-beating and child sexual abuse, both of which B. addressed in poetry (see "Bees in Clover" and "One More Bruised Heart"). "The Poet's Tear" expresses her view that human suffering is the source of art. B.'s final book of poems, *Liberty Lyrics* (1895), was published by James Tochatti's anarchist Liberty Press. Her pamphlet "Why I Am an Expropriationist" (1894) was published in the same series as William Morris's "Why I Am a Communist." In her last essay, published posthumously in 1896, on "Anarchism and Violence," B. suggested that the utopian future she desired might have to be created by violent means.

When B. died at age fifty, *The Torch,* a radical political journal published by the children of William Michael Rossetti, reported that B.'s funeral had been conducted with no religious ceremonies. During her lifetime, B. had converted her passion for justice and her understanding of the universe from a religious to a humanitarian base. In the end, she gave political commitments more attention than poetry; yet one hundred years after her death, B.'s social essays remain uncollected, whereas her poems are finding a new audience.

WORKS: *Key Notes,* by Arbor Leigh (1876; reissued under L. S. Bevington, 1879). "Atheism and Morality," *Nineteenth Century* (October 1879). *Fortnightly Review* (August 1881). *Poems, Lyrics, and Sonnets* (1882). "Dogs in Germany," *Nineteenth Century* (1887). "Why I Am an Expropriationist" (1894). *Liberty Lyrics* (1895). "Anarchism and Violence" (1896).

BIBLIOGRAPHY: *The Torch of Anarchy* (18 December 1895). *Victorian Women Poets: An Anthology,* ed. M. Reynolds and A. Leighton (1995).

For articles in reference works, see: *Feminist. Miles. VB.*

Other references: Hickok, K. *Representations of Women: Nineteenth-Century British Women's Poetry* (1984). Hickok, K. *VP* (1995). Horowitz, I. L. *The An-*

archists (1964). Oliver, H. *The International Anarchist Movement in Late Victorian London* (1985).

Kathleen Hickok

Hester (Esther) Biddle

BORN: 1629.
DIED: 1696.
MARRIED: Thomas Biddle.

B. spent her youth in Oxford where she was brought up as an Anglican. In the 1640s, she moved to London and later became a Quaker. During this time, she married Thomas Biddle, a prosperous cordwainer, who was also a Quaker. Her first published tract arose from her fervent disapproval of the scholars at Oxford. In this broadside, *Wo to thee city of Oxford* (1655), B. delivers an emotional call to abandon the sins of pride and "voluptuousness." The following year, she issued a similar call to the inhabitants of Cambridge, *Wo to thee towne of Cambridge* (1656).

During the 1660s, she was imprisoned several times and, in 1662, arrested at a Quaker meeting and accused of preaching. While in prison, she wrote *The Trumpet of the Lord Sounded forth unto these three Nations,* in which she turned her "judgment" on the "sinners" of London who "spendeth God's creation on [their] lusts." She also condemns theaters, cards, dice, and ballad-singing.

B.'s writings were more sophisticated than mere polemic; she places her anguish over the sin of the individual alongside an articulate and moving call for social reform based on Christian principles: "did not the Lord make all men and women upon the earth of one mould, why then should there be so much honour and respect unto some men and women, and not unto others?" (*Trumpet*).

B. published nothing after 1662, although she was still an active speaker. Records show that in 1664 she was seized, punched, and imprisoned at Bridewell. And the following year she was sent to Newgate Prison for speaking in the street. She also had three sons between 1663 and 1668. Few details of her later life remain, although in 1694, only two years before her death, she visited France in order to meet King Louis XIV and plead for peace.

WORKS: *Wo to thee city* of *Oxford* (1655). *Wo to thee towne of Cambridge* (1656). *Oh! wo, wo, from the Lord* (1659). *To the inhabitants of the town of Dartmouth* (1659). *A Warning from the Lord God of Life and Power, unto Thee O City of London* (1660). *The Trumpet of the Lord God* (1662). *The Trumpet of the Lord Sounded Forth unto these three Nations* (1662).

BIBLIOGRAPHY: Hobby, E., in *Feminist Criticism: Theory and Practice,* ed. S. Sellers (1991). Hobby, E. *Virtue of Necessity: English Women's Writing 1649–88* (1988). Mack, P. *Visionary Women: Ecstatic Prophecy in Seventeenth-Century England* (1992).

For articles in reference works, see: *Bell. Feminist WL17C.*

Other references: *Friends Historical Society Journal* (1955). *Quaker History* (1955).

Jane Baston

Isabella Lucy Bird Bishop

BORN: 15 October 1831, Yorkshire.
DIED: 7 October 1904, Edinburgh.
DAUGHTER OF: the Reverend Edward Bird and Dora Lawson Bird.
MARRIED: John F. Bishop, 1881.
WROTE UNDER: Isabella L. Bird; Isabella Bird Bishop; Isabella L. Bishop; Mrs. J. F. Bishop.

B. was one of the most popular and prolific of the late nineteenth-century Victorian lady travelers. Throughout her early travels, which were motivated by a search for good health, she wrote to her sister Henrietta; these letters formed the basis for her first books. After the death of her sister in 1880 and of her husband in 1886, her travels centered on visits to missionaries and plans to endow various hospitals in memory of these relatives. The popularity of her travel books earned her membership in the Royal Scottish Geographical Society and later in the Royal Geographical Society. In addition to her eight major books, she wrote articles and pamphlets for British journals and religious societies, and she delivered several lectures.

B. was born in 1831 into a strongly religious family headed by the Reverend Edward Bird. Though troubled by chronic spinal problems, B. learned early to ride horses and walk long distances in the fresh air. Her first travels, which took her in 1854 to Prince Edward Island and then on to continental Canada and the United States, were recorded in *The Englishwoman in America* (1856). She returned to North America in 1857–58, where she studied the current religious revivals and described them in essays for *The Patriot,* later collected as *The Aspects of Religion in the United States of America* (1859).

After another trip to New York and the Mediterranean in 1871, B. embarked in 1872 on the first of her long, challenging expeditions. She was directed to Australia and New Zealand for her health, but these countries soon bored her, and she boarded a rickety steamer for the Sandwich Islands, now Hawaii. As always, she travelled without concern for the comforts of civilization, camping on the edge of volcanoes, riding horseback for hours on end, and sleeping and eating in the only accommodations available—frequently filthy, wet, and insect-ridden rattraps. She did not travel the well-worn routes of British aristocrats and colonists. This rustic existence did not bother her strong digestion, and she frequently withstood the rigors of travel better than her occasional travelling companions.

After leaving the Sandwich Islands, she sailed to California, the start of a lengthy tour in the Rocky Mountains. In the Rockies, she met Jim Nugent, known as

"Rocky Mountain Jim," a seasoned trapper and frontiersman with a violent history. She spent a month or so near him and grew very fond of him. Although this rough man frequently recounted for her his unsavory past, he was also very solicitous, showing her the land around Estes Park, Colorado. When he proposed to her, however, she realized, "He is a man any woman might love, but no sane woman would marry." At the conclusion of this eighteen-month trip, B. returned to England, where she published *The Hawaiian Archipelago* (1875) and *A Lady's Life in the Rocky Mountains* (1879). Her next trips took her to Japan, the Malay Peninsula, and Egypt in 1878–79 and resulted in the publication of *Unbeaten Tracks in Japan* (1880) and *The Golden Chersonese and the Way Thither* (1883).

Soon after she returned to England from these travels, B. suffered the first major personal tragedy of her life: the death of her sister Henrietta. Henrietta had served as her lodestar and her audience during all of her travels. Writing to Henrietta, she tried to make the scenery and people around her come alive with vivid description. Her later books have scattered passages that recall this style, but they are more didactic and dryly informative.

After Henrietta's death, B. married John F. Bishop, a physician who had proposed to her two years earlier. This marriage lasted only five years, however, until John's death in 1886. During her marriage, B. remained in England, was active in charity work, and studied nursing and first aid.

When her husband died, B. turned again to her travels, moving now almost compulsively around the globe on tours that defied both man and nature. In 1889–90, she travelled to India, Kashmir, and Tibet before crossing Asia to the Black Sea. This journey produced *Journeys in Persia and Kurdistan* (1891) and *Among the Tibetans* (1894). Four years later, she undertook a three-year jaunt through Canada, Japan, Korea, and China, writing her longest books, *Korea and her Neighbours* (1898) and *The Yangtze Valley and Beyond* (1899). These two books are of greater interest than her earlier works because of their subject matter, but their vivid descriptions of nature are frequently interrupted by statistics and moral reflections.

By this point, she was travelling more often by carrying chair than on horseback, but she frequently alighted for long walks in the fresh air. It is, however, extraordinary that although she was in her mid-sixties she was able to travel alone for fifteen months at a time across 8,000 miles of China. Her travels were also becoming emotionally more arduous. In her early letters and books, she repeatedly assured her reader that it was safe for a lady to travel alone. But in her last trip to China, she suffered antiforeign riots for the first time that forced her to reconsider this opinion. These experiences also led her to revise her earlier, Rousseauistic picture of the savage as noble.

When she returned to England after this lengthy expedition, she was restless and moved about a good deal, setting up one house only in time to pack and move on to a different one. Her last trip took her on horseback through Morocco at the age of seventy, but her growing illness restricted her to recording this travel only in articles. She died two years later in Edinburgh, still hoping for one more trip to China.

As well as being a valuable and accurate record of life in the United States and Asia in the late nineteenth century, B.'s work is a fascinating study of the late Victorian mind. Although she slept in filthy stables and ate maggotty food, B. insisted on retaining certain Victorian proprieties. She considered trousers unacceptable, for example, and asked her friend and publisher John Murray to defend her publicly when *The Times* reported that she wore "male habiliments" in the Rockies. Although she was not troubled by often being the only woman in a caravan, she always rode in an uncomfortable sidesaddle position when passing through inhabited areas. Her excellent memory and her love of nature that give life to her vivid narratives brought her well-deserved fame in her lifetime. As *The Spectator* said of *A Lady's Life in the Rocky Mountains*, "There never was anybody who had adventures so well as Miss Bird."

WORKS: *The Englishwoman in America* (1856). *The Aspects of Religion in the United States of America* (1859). *The Hawaiian Archipelago* (1875). *A Lady's Life in the Rocky Mountains* (1879). *Unbeaten Tracks in Japan* (1880). *The Golden Chersonese and the Way Thither* (1883). *Journeys in Persia and Kurdistan* (1891). *Among the Tibetans* (1894). *Korea and Her Neighbors* (1898). *The Yangtze Valley and Beyond* (1899). *Chinese Pictures* (1900).

BIBLIOGRAPHY: Campbell, J. *Women of Worth* (1908). Middleton, D. *Victorian Lady Travellers* (1965). Stoddart, A. M. *The Life of Isabella Bird* (1906). Williams, C. *The Story of Isabella Bird Bishop* (1909).

For articles in reference works, see: *BA19C. DNB.*

Tori Haring-Smith

Black, C[onstance]. C[lara].: See Garnett, Constance Clara Black

Blair, the Reverend David: See Fenwick, Eliza

Susanna Blamire

BORN: 1747 near Carlisle, Cumberland County.
DIED: 1794, Carlisle.
DAUGHTER OF: William Blamire.

B. was a poet and songwriter. "Highly esteemed in her own day," B. was known as the "Muse of Cumberland." She never married and lived a secluded life with relatives in Cumberland. She died at the age of forty-seven from "complications" of rheumatism.

B. received what little formal education she had at Raughton Head, the village school, and during her youth gave herself "completely up to her studies." She began early on to write poetry in imitation of her favorite authors. Her earliest known poem, "Written in a Churchyard, on seeing a number of cattle grazing in it," is written in imitation of Gray's "Elegy."

Her sister's marriage to a Colonel Graham of Gartmore (author of a popular song, "Oh tell me how to woo thee") allowed B. access to a circle of educated persons with literary tastes similar to her own, and, with her sister, B. made frequent trips to Scotland. Asked by a new acquaintance, Lord Tankerville, to write a poem about her rustic life, B. composed, in dialect, "Why, Ned, man, thou luiks sae down-hearted":

Wey, Ned, Man! thou luiks sae down-hearted,
Yen wad swear aw thy kindred were dead,
For sixpence, thy Jean and thee's parted,
What chen, man ne re bodder thy hedd!
There's lasses enow, I'll uphod te,
And t[h]ou may be suin as weel match'd
T[h]ou knows there's still fish in the river
As guid as has ever been catch'd.

Frederic Rowton, who included two of B.'s songs, "What ails this heart o' mine?" and "The Silver Crown," in his anthology *The Female Poets of Great Britain* (1853), described the characteristics of B.'s poetry as "considerable tenderness of feeling, very gracefully expressed, and a refined delicacy of imagination, which, whilst it never thrills, always pleases." Her songs, Rowton says, "though not without marks of elaboration, display great simplicity and force of feeling." B.'s most popular poem, "The Nabob" or "The Traveller's Return," is the poignant story of an Indian traveler's return home to his native village. Rowton refers to this poem as a "very affecting and delightful production," and, indeed, it is.

In modern terms, the value of B.'s poetry is that it re-creates, sympathetically as well as accurately, the language and customs of a remote section of eighteenth-century England. B.'s poem "Stoklewath, or the Cumbrian Village," written in imitation of Goldsmith's "The Deserted Village," gives a fascinating account of the daily lives of the rustic villagers who were B.'s neighbors. B. captures "the peculiar humor of the Cumbrian folk with admirable truth, and depicts it faithfully so far as was consistent with her own refinement."

B. wrote her songs and poems hastily, without plans for publication, although she did publish, anonymously, several poems in magazines. Unfortunately, none of her correspondence has survived. Nearly fifty years after her death, Patrick Maxwell, an Englishman living in India, began collecting B.'s work. In 1842, Maxwell and Henry Lonsdale, a physician from Carlisle, published an anthology of B.'s poems entitled *The Poetical Works of Miss Susanna Blamire, "The Muse of Cumberland," Now for the First Time Collected by Henry Lonsdale, M.D., with a Preface, Memoir, and Notes by Patrick Maxwell.*

WORKS: *The Poetical Works of Miss Susanna Blamire, "The Muse of Cumberland," Now for the First Time Collected by Henry Lonsdale, M.D., with a Preface, Memoir, and Notes by Patrick Maxwell,* ed. H. Lonsdale and P. Maxwell (1842). *Songs By Miss Blamire, together with Songs by Her Friend Miss Gilpin,* ed. S. Gilpin (1866).

BIBLIOGRAPHY: *The Female Poets of Great Britain,* ed. F. Rowton (1853; rpt. 1981).

For articles in reference works, see: *DNB. Songstresses of Scotland,* ed. Keddie, H. [pseud. Sarah Tytler] and J. L. Watson (1871).

Kay Beaird Meyers

Bland, E.: See *Nesbit, Edith*

Bland, Fabian: See *Nesbit, Edith*

Margaret (Marguerite) Blessington

BORN: 1 September 1789, Knockbrit, Tipperary, Ireland.
DIED: 4 June 1849, Paris, France.
DAUGHTER OF: Edmund Power and Ellen Sheehy Power.
MARRIED: Maurice St. Leger Farmer, 1804; Charles John Gardiner, first Earl of Blessington, 1818.
WROTE UNDER: The Author of The Magic Lantern; The Author of Sketcher and Fragments; Countess of Blessington.

When B. was fourteen, her father forced her to marry a brutal man. After three months, she left her husband and returned home. A few years thereafter, she began living with Captain Thomas Jenkins, and when she and the Earl of Blessington became interested in each other, the earl paid Jenkins to release her. B. was able to marry the earl when her husband died, at which time she changed her name from Margaret to Marguerite. As the Countess of Blessington, she became an important hostess to influential men. Their wives rebuffed her, though, because of her past. After the earl died, B. lived with the Count D'Orsay, the son-in-law of her second husband. They may have been lovers, or she may have assumed a maternal role. Whatever the relationship, London was outraged that they lived together. She spent her last years writing to support herself and the count. She died bankrupt in Paris.

B.'s most important literary contribution is *Conversations of Lord Byron* (1834). She wrote that when she met Byron in Genoa, Italy, in 1823, she found him to be less heroic-looking than she had imagined. She was also surprised to find him flippant rather than haughty. According to B., Byron loved to ridicule people, especially the English, for their cant and hypocrisy. The book is unnecessarily long and self-serving at times, but it is an accurate account of Byron.

B.'s other works are hastily constructed in a desperate effort to make enough money to pay her bills. These works include nonfiction as well as poetry and fiction. She is remembered primarily, though, as a victim of a patriarchal society and for writing a sustained account of one of the most important Romantic poets.

WORKS: *Journal of a Tour through the Netherlands to Paris* (1822). *The Magic Lantern* (1822). *Sketches and*

Fragments (1822). *Rambles in Waltham Forest* (1827). *Ella Stratford* (1830). *The Repealers* (1833). *Conversations of Lord Byron with the Countess of Blessington* (1834). *Two Friends* (1835). *The Confessions of an Elderly Gentleman* (1836). *Galeria* (1836). *Gems of Beauty* (1836) *The Honeymoon* (1837). *The Victims of Society* (1837). *The Works of Lady Blessington* (1838). *The Confessions of an Elderly Lady* (1838). *Desultory Thoughts and Reflections* (1839). *The Idler in Italy* (1839). *The Governers* (1839). *The Belle of a Season* (1840). *The Idler in France* (1841). *Veronica of Castille* (1842). *The Lottery of Life* (1842). *Meredith* (1843). *Strathern* (1844). *Etiquette of Courtship and Marriage* (1844). *The Memoirs of a Femme de Chambre* (1846). *Marmaduke Herbert* (1847). *The Book of Beauty or Regal Gallery* (1849). *Country Quarters* (1850). *Journal of the Correspondence and Conversations between Lord Byron and the Countess of Blessington* (1851), *One Hundred Valuable Receipts for the Young Lady of the Period* (1878). *The Blessington Papers* (1895). *Lady Blessington at Naples,* ed. E. Clay (1979).

BIBLIOGRAPHY: Connely, W. *Count D'Orsay, this Dandy of Dandies* (1952). Hickok, K. *Representations of Women: Nineteenth Century British Women's Poetry* (1984). Lovell, E. J. *Lady Blessington's Conversations with Lord Byron* (1969). Madden, R. R. *The Literary Life and Correspondence of the Countess of Blessington* (1855). Sadleir, M. *The Strange Life of Lady Blessington* (1933).

For articles in reference works, see: *Allibone. BA19C. Cassell. Feminist. NCHEL. ToddBWW.*

Margaret Ann Graham
(updated by Natalie Joy Woodall)

Mathilde Blind

BORN: 21 March 1841, Mannheim, Germany.
DIED: 26 November 1896, London.
DAUGHTER OF: Cohen Ettlinger and Friederike Ettlinger, adoptive father Karl Blind.
WROTE UNDER: Mathilde Blind; Claude Lake.

A free thinker and a feminist, B. sought, in her writings, to combine Shelleyean romanticism with Victorian political and scientific concerns. With a stepfather who was a well-known political writer, exiled from Germany for his revolutionary activities in the Baden insurrection of 1848, B. grew up in an environment that encouraged radical thinking. Her brother, Ferdinand, attempted an attack on Bismarck in 1866 and subsequently committed suicide in prison. In 1848, the family moved to England where their home became a meeting place for political refugees. There B. met Garibaldi, in 1864, and Mazzini, whom she particularly admired. Her upbringing, combining both the European and the English, led B. to be extremely independent. She traveled by herself in Switzerland at age eighteen. At the age of thirty, she moved out of her parents' house and lived on her own, traveling throughout England, the Continent, and even to Egypt.

B. admired the romantic poets. Her first known work was an "Ode to Schiller" (1859). And she was later to write introductions to editions of both Percy Bysshe Shelley (1872) and Lord Byron (1886). Her own work, after an initial book, *Poems by Claude Lake* (1867), was kindled by a trip to Scotland, which led to two books, *The Prophecy of St. Oran* (1881) and *The Heather on Fire* (1886), both noted for their descriptions of Scottish scenery, the second including a denunciation of indiscriminate highland evictions. Her only novel, *Tarantella* (1885), an imaginative romance, was unsuccessful, perhaps because it did not suit the tastes of the time. Her most ambitious work, *The Ascent of Man* (1889), is a romantic epic based on Charles Darwin's theory of evolution, a combination she had attempted earlier, in a public lecture entitled "Shelley's View of Nature Contrasted with Darwin's" (1886). She later wrote a series of poems based on her travels, *Birds of Passage: Songs of the Orient and Occident* (1896), and finally, during her stay at Stratford, a book of sonnets inspired by Shakespeare.

B.'s interest in feminism and women writers led her to translate *The Journal of Marie Bashkirtseff* (1892) and to write biographies of George Eliot (1883) and Madame Roland (1886) for the "Eminent Woman Series." B. was particularly motivated to write the second biography because it allowed her to return to her early Republican thinking and to Thomas Carlyle's *French Revolution.* At her death, B arranged to have the bulk of her money, a legacy from a stepbrother, given to Newnham College, Cambridge, in support of women's education.

B. is interesting as a figure because her concerns so closely parallel George Eliot's. B. even translated a work of David Friedrich Strauss's early in her career. B.'s contemporaries viewed her as more successful at getting her ideas across in conversation than in writing, but Vita Sackville-West has asserted that B.'s poetic gifts and vision of nature have been underestimated by critics.

WORKS: *Poems by Claude Lake* (1867). (trans.) *The Old Faith and the New,* by David Friedrich Strauss (1873). *The Prophecy of St. Oran* (1881). *George Eliot* (1883). *Tarantella: a Romance* (1885). *The Heather on Fire* (1886). *Madame Roland* (1886). *The Ascent of Man* (1889). *Dramas in Miniature* (1891). (trans.) *The Journal of Marie Bashkirtseff* (1892). *Songs and Sonnets* (1893). *Birds of Passage: Songs of the Orient and Occident* (1896). *A Selection from the Poems of Mathilde Blind,* ed. A. Symons (1897). *Poetical Works of Mathilde Blind,* ed. with a memoir by A. Symons (1897). *Romola,* by George Eliot (with a life of George Eliot by B., 1900). *Shakespeare Sonnets* (1900).

BIBLIOGRAPHY:, Hickok, K. *Representations of Women: Nineteenth-Century British Women's Poetry* (1984). Kaplan, C. *Salt and Bitter and Good: Three Centuries of English Women Poets* (1975).

For articles in reference works, see: *DNB* (under "Karl Blind"). *1890s. Feminist. ToddBWW. VB.*

Elsie B. Michie
(updated by Natalie Joy Woodall)

Valerie (Wright) Bloom

BORN: 1956, Clarendon, Jamaica.
DAUGHTER OF: parents' given names not known; family name: Wright.
MARRIED: Douglas Bloom.

A poet who incorporates the traditions of oral performance and folk narrative into her verse, B. speaks for Jamaican immigrants to England, voicing nostalgia for Caribbean culture, protest against racist attitudes, and celebration of black women's strength and wisdom. In much of her political poetry, the speaker criticizes the impact of British colonialism on Jamaica and attacks the contemporary racist government in Britain. In all her poetry, B. uses diction and syntax that deliberately re-create Jamaican speech patterns as a cultural alternative to the British literary tradition. One of the chief influences on her work has been the Jamaican poet and performer Louise Bennett. In most of her published poems, she chooses the rhymed iambic quatrain, which she handles as a monologue or dialogue. Contrasting with the angry tone of her political poems, her children's poems express joy and celebrate in precise, sensual detail the pleasures of life.

Born in Clarendon, Jamaica, she was educated in schools that taught British literary culture. She writes of being forced to memorize a poem a week, which she enjoyed, especially those by William Wordsworth. In addition, she began performing Bennett's poetry while she was still in primary school. She continued to perform during her school years, worked in Jamaica after graduation as a librarian and teacher, and wrote her own first poem only in 1978, winning a medal in the National Festival's Literary Competition. B. moved to England in 1979, when she was twenty-three. At the University of Kent, she earned a degree in English with African and Caribbean Studies. While living in London and Manchester, she taught dance, drama, poetry, and song as a Multicultural Arts Officer. B. has worked at the Ethnic Music Centre of Manchester, has performed on BBC radio and TV, and has recorded performances of her poetry. An active member of the black writers community around London, B. has written book reviews of other contemporary Caribbean poets publishing in the United Kingdom, most notably Grace Nichols, whom she praises for her "re-affirmation of the beauty and worth of black womanhood."

Most of B.'s poems are dramatic dialogues or monologues, and the title of her collection *Touch Mi! Tell Mi!* (1983) suggests the intimate conversation of gossip. B. begins with a humorous sketch of a character, a large woman who threatens to kill a "gal name Sue" for calling her a thief. To a listener, the character offers her own justification for being caught with the goods. But this boastful woman, when she sees Sue with her family coming to get her, cries out for mercy and a hiding place, and in the end she runs away ("mi gawn!"). The sudden revelation of her cowardice confirms the audience's suspicion that she was full of hot air and provokes laughter. The structure of the joke is classic, the character universal. By writing the poem in dialect, B. places her audience within the cultural community—if they understand the spoken language, they are rewarded by the joke.

B. focuses her audience's attention on the artificial conflict between Jamaican spoken English and standard English in the poem "Language Barrier." Although Jamaican phrases are translated into standard English, the speaker's perspective within the poem is clear: "Jamaica language sweet yuh know." The speaker had not even noticed how sweet her language was until a foreign friend said it sounded "queer." The foreigner, Hugh, searches for what the Jamaican phrases "really" mean, revealing his assumption that standard English is true and Jamaican dialect is incorrect. The speaker consistently uses the word "language" to describe her speech, comparing it to other languages: the Spanish say "burro" rather than "jackass"—her example implies that her foreign friend is an ass. From her perspective, if Jamaicans are "guilty" of speaking incorrect English, then "De French, Italian, Greek an Dutch, / Dem all guilty o' de crime." B. clearly expects her readers to learn the "patois" (a term she prefers to "dialect"), just as the speaker in this poem demands "Soh Hugh betta larn fe mime" (So Hugh better learn to [speak] mine).

In "Wat a Rain," the speaker narrates to her friend Miss Kate the story of rain that lasted a whole week, dripping through holes in her roof. She piles disaster upon catastrophe, comparing the house to "Noah Ark" with all the animals coming in for shelter. She is a resourceful and cheerful survivor, however, taking in the two chickens, the fish, the "ganda," and the goat that washed up to her house. She brags "Mi still mek likkle profit mam, / Outa de likkle rain." This speaker is a figure in the tradition of those who make do, or even triumph, with the little that they have. The audience delights in her brassy self-assurance as much as in her ability to rejoice over some gains, despite the trouble caused by the rain. There is music in the lines that accumulate the rain's disasters, the sound imitating the rain's patter. B. creates pleasure in form as well as theme.

"Vengeance" narrates, to an approving listener, "Miss Gatha," the joke the speaker played upon a proud and elegantly dressed "Mass Lijah," who not only refused to let him ride his horse but called him an unrepeatable name. Taking a stick in hand, the speaker causes the horse to swerve, throw off his rider, and run away, leaving Lijah in the mud, trousers ripped, top hat off, fancy leather boots up in a tree. The speaker, with great satisfaction, predicts that Lijah will never again call him that name. Like others in the tradition of trickster-figures, the person who is apparently powerless, who is disrespected and mistreated by a figure in power (this Master Elijah is on a horse and expensively dressed), suddenly overthrows the master and wins the freedom to laugh at him.

B.'s commitment to teaching young Jamaican immigrants to value their own culture is expressed not only in her career as a teacher of folk song, dance, and music but also in her poetry, especially in "Show Dem," which is "dedicated to all black children in British schools." In it, the speaker calls upon her brothers and sisters, reminding them that if they are cursed and shamed because of where they and their parents come from (across the water) and how much they want to achieve in their new land, they can show them what they know. The speaker encourages them proudly to assert their cultural identity: "yuh language different, / Different like yuh skin an hair, / Different like de place yuh spring from." Reminding them that different is not "wussar off," the speaker offers a metaphor: Although the leaf rides high on the tree, it needs a stem; so also the teachers, although they are in power, need to learn from the immigrant children. She calls for the children to show others the valuable lessons of Jamaican cultural tradition, and, in the same tone, she tells the children, the British teachers "know tings fe teach yuh to."

Several poems depict the racism and injustice of British immigration laws, notably "Rhodesia Result" and "Census Censure." In the first poem, the speaker comments on the biased news reports in Britain of the Rhodesian elections won by Robert Mugabe, prompting (according to the news report) the flight of white Rhodesians, and the speaker sarcastically says she will wait to see "If Mr Whitelaw gwine kip dem out / Wid im immigration policy." In the other poem, a Jamaican immigrant speaks with her friend while filling out the census form, wondering how the government will use this detailed information about where she and her family were born, her race, and her marital status. She fears trouble from the immigration law if she tells the truth, but she reads on the form the threat that failing to tell the truth will land her in jail. Trickster that she is, she creates true and evasive answers, thus fulfilling the letter of the census law while frustrating the racist intent of immigration law.

The pervasiveness of racism, which infects the schools, the census, the news reports, and the police, is illustrated in "Trench Town Shock (A Soh Dem Sey)." The speaker tells Miss May about a clash between the police and a boy who tried to sneak into the movies without paying and who was shot dead. As she narrates the tale, the first three lines of the quatrain tell the details that will be in the police report—that they warned him to stop, that he pulled a knife against their guns. The last line of each quatrain is the refrain "At leas' a soh dem sey"—casting doubt on the truth of what "they" say, exposing the destructive power of a repeated lie. Early in the poem, the repeated lies about black boys have judged this boy in advance: "di bwoy own fault." The victim is blamed for causing his own death.

The restrained tone of "Trench Town Shock" dissolves into explicit anger in "Gi' Dem Cake," which protests that poor people riot when they have no food for their children and their elected government lowers welfare payments and raises spending for nuclear armament. The poem's title suggests that the riots are comparable to the economic and political unrest that gave rise to the French Revolution.

The collection *Touch Mi! Tell Mi!* ends with a brief poem, "Yuh Hear About?" The speaker asks for news about arrests for racist murder, for police misconduct, for the failure of a Member of Parliament to protect his constituents from deportation. These are the acts that would correct social injustice. Cynically, bitterly, the speaker admits she has heard nothing about justice: "me neida." B. chooses to conclude this collection with a negative word, after beginning it with variations on the clever trickster who survives disaster and triumphs over his oppressors.

Her collection of children's poems, *Duppy Jamboree* (1992), presents a happier and more optimistic view of the future. Implicit in this collection is the hope B. displayed in the earlier poem, "Show Dem." The history of slavery and the present racism in society are present, but in these poems her audience is encouraged to triumph, to enjoy life, to know their own value.

B. claims affiliation with African oral traditions, rather than dub poetry or reggae, and her use of the trickster figure also connects her poetry with African culture. Her poems are occasioned by the present—by specific political events, by newspaper reports, by television broadcasts, and by her observations of people around her. For her, writing poetry is a vocation like that of the political or spiritual teacher, to help oppressed people. She fulfills her vocation sometimes by attacking the oppressor ironically, but often by reminding the people of their cultural roots.

WORKS: *Touch Mi! Tell Mi!* (1983). *Duppy Jamboree and Other Jamaican Poems* (1992). In anthologies: *News for Babylon*, ed. J. Berry (1984). *I Like That Stuff*, ed. M. Styles (1984). *Caribbean Poetry Now*, ed. S. Brown (1986). *Penguin Book of Caribbean Verse in English*, ed. P. Burnett (1986). *Angels of Fire*, ed. S. Paskin, J. Ramsay, and J. Silver (1986). *Facing the Sea*, ed. A.N.C. Walmsley (1986). *Watchers & Seekers*, ed. R. Cobham and M. Collins (1987). *From Our Yard*, ed. P. Mordecae (1987). *You'll Love That Stuff*, ed. M. Styles (1987). *Ain't I a Woman!*, ed. I. Linthwaite (1988). *Black Poetry*, ed. G. Nichols (1988). *Voiceprint*, ed. S. Brown, M. Morris, and G. Rohlehr (1989).

BIBLIOGRAPHY: Bakari, I., rev. of *Touch Mi! Tell Mi!*, in *Race Today Review* (August/September 1983). Johnson, L. K. intro. to *Touch Mi! Tell Mi!* (1983). Ncobo, L. *Let It Be Told: Essays by Black Women in Britain* (1987). Woodcock, B., in *Black Women's Writing*, ed. G. Wisker (1993).

For articles in reference books, see: *Bibliography of Women Writers from the Caribbean*, ed. B. Berrigan and A. Broek (1989). *Writers of the Caribbean and Central America 1*, ed. M. J. Fenwick (1992).

Other references: *TEdS* (7 February 1992).

Judith L. Johnston

Elizabeth Blower

BORN: 1763, Worcester.
DIED: after 1816.

By the time she turned twenty, B. was already the author of two novels and several published poems as well as being a Drury Lane actress. While she was in her teens, her father had become enmeshed in the notoriously violent Worcester political scene, supporting an unsuccessful independent candidate's run for Parliament. Whether this contributed to the decline of her family's finances is unclear; however, B. soon turned to writing to earn money. By seventeen, she had published her first novel, *The Parsonage House* (1780). In early 1782, she made her stage debut as Rosalind in *As You Like It* at Drury Lane. Despite positive reviews, she was not engaged by Drury Lane for the next season, and by fall 1782 she was in Ireland with her younger sister, where the two acted for the next five years. She apparently returned to London for her final season on stage, at Covent Garden in 1787–88.

B. continued to write during her stage career; she wrote four novels in all, and all by the time she was twenty-five: *The Parsonage House, George Bateman* (1782), *Maria* (1785), and *Features from Life; or, A Summer Visit* (1788). B.'s novels take virtuous heroines through various tests and tribulations: In *Features from Life,* the heroine must cope with a husband who has an affair with a society woman and then, after a deathbed reconciliation, leaves her widowed and grieving; *Maria's* orphaned heroine must negotiate a series of trials before attaining a properly suitable marriage. B. has been called "one of the most direct eighteenth-century predecessors of Jane Austen." Although lacking Austen's polish, B.'s novels are strong in characterization, and her sometimes moralizing tone is softened by deft satiric touches. Some change in B.'s circumstances likely occurred shortly after the publication of *Features from Life* and her final stage appearance in 1787, because no more is heard of her after that date; perhaps a marriage eased her financial needs.

WORKS: *The Parsonage House* (1780). *George Bateman* (1782). *Maria* (1785). *Features from Life; or, A Summer Visit* (1788).

BIBLIOGRAPHY:

For articles in reference works, see *BDA. Feminist. ToddDBA.*

Rebecca P. Bocchicchio

Enid Blyton

BORN: 11 August 1897, London.
DIED: 28 November 1968, London.
DAUGHTER OF: Thomas C. Blyton and Theresa Mary Harrison Blyton.
MARRIED: Hugh Pollock, 1924; Kenneth Darrell Waters, 1943.
WROTE UNDER: Enid Blyton; Mary Pollock.

B. has been called "the world's most successful children's writer," and the majority of British children since the 1930s have read at least one of her books. Her very prolific output from 1917 until her death includes at least 600 titles, which mostly comprise novellas and short stories but also include some verse and plays. Because she often published books in series with recurring characters, children would come back for more until they had read each one; this meant that libraries, especially during wartime, could hardly keep her work in stock.

Despite children's love for her work, B. has not always been approved by adults. Both her subject matter and her style have earned criticism since the 1950s; many libraries tried to limit or stop altogether the acquisition of new titles. Hostility to B.'s style derives from her simplistic vocabulary and limited plots; some critics have argued that these encourage children to read, but the majority claim that B.'s books may actually prevent reading skills from advancing. B.'s subject matter has been attacked for its class values, which tend to reflect upper-middle-class life, when families had maids and when class distinctions were precisely observed. More recently, charges of racism (for example, Noddy's treatment of golliwogs) and sexism (the boys have the adventures, the girls keep the cave clean) have emerged. Children, of course, do not notice these criticisms, and B.'s books are still popular among them.

Having qualified as a teacher, B. taught at a boys' school and then became a governess until 1924, when she married Hugh Pollock. Her first book was a collection of verse, *Child Whispers* (1922), but it was her short stories that initially made her famous. The first collection of these was *The Enid Blyton Book of Fairies* (1924), and from 1926 she edited the magazine *Sunny Stories for Little Folk,* which was renamed *Enid Blyton's Sunny Stories* in 1937. *The Adventures of the Wishing Chair* (1937), which represents a series of stories from the latter magazine, was especially popular; it documents the fantastic journeys of two children, Peter and Mollie, as they ride on a magic chair with Chinky the pixie. B. continued to publish stories in her magazines and in collections, but it was the different book series—the school stories, the Famous Five, the Secret Seven, the Adventure series, and the Noddy books—for which she is best remembered.

The school stories begin with *The Naughtiest Girl in the School* (1940), which describe Whyteleafe School, a progressive coeducational establishment. Later, B. concentrated on stories about girls' schools, producing two series: the six St. Clare's books (1941–45) and the six about Malory Towers (1946–51). The St. Clare's series focuses on the O'Sullivan twins, who arrive as disgruntled and obstinate new girls. Over the course of the series these two change and mature, until in the last book they are awarded the ultimate schoolgirl accolade of being made joint head-girls, an honor symbolic of their self-knowledge and wisdom as marriage might be in a book for adults. Their growth is attended by a recurring cast of characters such as the teacher, Miss Jenks, and Mam'zelle, the French mistress whose errors in language provide comic relief and who is the butt of constant practical jokes. New girls are introduced each term, some with personal problems who can be helped and guided, and others who bring drama, such as Claudine the French girl or Carlotta the former circus star. Although these stories, like the later Malory Towers series, which centers on the school career of Darrell Rivers, represent an idealized situation, they provide a moral didacticism in their representation of community living; the girls learn as much from each other about social obligations as they do from their school work.

The "Famous Five" series began in 1942 with *Five on a Treasure Island.* The Five are siblings Julian, Dick, and Anne, their cousin Georgina (a tomboy who is always called "George"), and Timmy, her dog. We usually see them without adults on a school vacation, either having to survive (on an island, for example), or to elude and possibly help apprehend spies or other adult villains. This series, with its rather cardboard characters, improbable situations, and attention to the nuances and language of social class, has been the target of much British satire. The last title, *Five Are Together Again,* was published in 1963. The "Secret Seven" series (1949–63) repeated the same kind of format with an emphasis on solving mysteries.

The character of "Noddy" became ubiquitous in the lives of young children because it was parlayed into toys, toothbrushes, wallpaper, and other consumer goods. Noddy is a toy rather like a pixie; he lives in Toyland with his friend Big Ears who resembles a garden gnome. Noddy has a little car with which he can help other toys and go on adventures. These stories (1949–68) are aimed at younger children, but their moral code seems facile and, at times, almost offensive to a postfeminist, racially enlightened adult reader. Thus the "Noddy" stories have provoked much criticism, although they were commercially very successful.

B. remains a crucially important figure in the history of children's literature. While much of her work seems very dated next to books by, for example, C. S. Lewis, R. M. Ballantyne, or Louisa May Alcott, she is still avidly read by many children. Certainly the hours of reading pleasure she has given over the years establish her as one of the great writers of children's fiction of her century.

WORKS: *Child Whispers* (1922). *Real Fairies* (1923). *Responsive Singing Games* (1923). *The Enid Blyton Book of Fairies* (1924). *Songs of Gladness* (1924). *The Zoo Book* (1924). *The Enid Blyton Book of Bunnies* (1925). *Reading Practice, 1–5, 8–9, 11* (1925–26). *Silver and Gold* (1925). *The Bird Book* (1926). *The Book of Brownies* (1926; as *Brownie Tales,* 1964). *A Book of Little Plays* (includes *The Princess and the Swineherd, Sing a Song of Sixpence, Fairy Prisoners, Robin Hood, Peronel's Paint,* (1926). *Tales Half Told* (1926). *The Animal Book* (1927). *The Play's the Thing* (includes *The Capture of the Robbers. Rag, Tag, and Bobtail, Rumpelstiltskin, The King's Jester, The Magic Apple, Merry Robin Hood, The King's Pocket Knife, In the Toyshop, The Cuckoo, The Rainbow Flowers, The Wishing-Glove, The Broken Statue,* 1927; as *Plays for Older Children* and *Plays for Younger Children,* 1940). *Aesop's Fables, Retold* (1928). *Let's Pretend* (1928). *Old English Stories, Retold* (1928). *Pinkity's Pranks and Other Nature Fairy Tales, Retold* (1928). *Tales of Brer Rabbit, Retold* (1928). *Nature Lessons* (1929). *Tarrydiddle Town* (1929). *The Knights of the Round Table* (1930). *Tales from the Arabian Nights* (1930). *Tales of Ancient Greece* (1930). *Tales of Robin Hood* (1930). *Cheerio! A Book for Boys and Girls* (1933). *Five [Fifteen, Twenty] Minute Tales* (1933–40). *Let's Read* (1933). *Letters from Bobs* (1933). *My First Reading Book* (1933). *Read To Us* (1933). *The Enid Blyton Poetry Book: Ninety-Six Poems for the Twelve Months of the Year* (1934). *The Old Thatch Series,* 20 vols. (1934–39). *The Red Pixie Book* (1934). *Round the Year with Enid Blyton: Spring, Summer, Autumn, Winter* (1934). *Stories From World History,* 4 vols. (1934). *Ten Minutes Tales: Twenty-Nine Varied Stories for Children* (1934). *The Children's Garden* (1935). *The Green Goblin Book* (1935; as *Feefo, Tuppeny, and Jinks,* 1951). *Hedgerow Tales* (1935). *Six Enid Blyton Plays* (includes *The Princess and the Enchanter, Robin Hood and the Butcher, The Enchanted Cap, A Visit to Nursery-Rhyme Land, The Squirrel's Secret, The Whistling Brownie,* 1935). *The Famous Jimmy* (1936). *The Yellow Fairy Book* (1936). *Adventures of the Wishing Chair* (1937). *The Adventures of Binkle and Flip* (1938). *Billy-Bob Tales* (1938). *Heyo, Brer Rabbit! Tales of Brer Rabbit and His Friends* (1938). *Mr. Galliano's Circus* (1938). *The Secret Island* (1938). *Boys' and Girls' Circus Book* (1939). *Cameo Plays, Book 4* (includes *The Making of a Rainbow, Poor Mr. Twiddle, The Three Wishes, The Donkey's Tail, Santa Claus Comes Down the Chimney, The Wind and the Sun, Brer Rabbit and Mr. Dog, The Little Green Imp,* 1939). *The Enchanted Wood* (1939). *How the Flowers Grow and Other Musical Plays* (includes *The Fairy in the Box, The Magic Ball, The Toys at Night-Time, Who Stole the Crown?, Santa Claus Gets Busy,* 1939). *Hurrah for the Circus! Being Further Adventures of Mr. Galliano and His Famous Circus* (1939). *Naughty Amelia Jane!* (1939). *The Wishing Bean and Other Plays* (includes *The Hole in the Sack, Spreading the News, The Queen's Garden, Sneezing Powder, The Land of Nursery Rhymes,* 1939; as *Six Plays for Schools,* 1939). (as Mary Pollock) *Children of Kidillin* (1940). (as Mary Pollock) *Three Boys and a Circus* (1940). *Birds of Our Gardens* (1940). *Boys' and Girls' Story Book* (1940). *The Children of Cherry Tree Farm* (1940). *The Little Tree-House, Being the Adventures of Josie, Click, and Bun,* 1940; as *Josie, Click, and Bun and the Little Tree House,* 1951). *Mr. Meddle's Mischief* (1940). *The Naughtiest Girl in the School* (1940). *The News Chronicle Boys' and Girls' Book* (1940). *The Secret of Spiggy Holes* (1940). *Tales of Betsy-May* (1940). *The Treasure Hunters* (1940). *The Adventures of Mr. Pink-Whistle* (1941). *The Adventurous Four* (1941). *The Babar Story Book* (1941). *Book of the Year* (1941). *A Calendar for Children* (1941). *Five O'Clock Tales* (1941). *The Further Adventures of Josie, Click, and Bun* (1941). *The Secret Mountain* (1941). *The Twins at St. Clare's* (1941). *The Children of Willow Farm* (1942). *Circus Days Again* (1942). *Enid Blyton Readers 1–7, 10–12* (1942–50). *The Further Adventures of Brer Rabbit, Being More Tales of Brer Rabbit and His Friends* (1942). *Happy Story Book* (1942). *Enid Blyton's Little Books: Brer Rabbit, Bed-time Stories, Jolly Tales, Ho-Ho and Too Smart, Tales of the Toys, Happy Stories,* 1942). *Five on a Treasure Island* (1942). *Hello, Mr. Twiddle* (1942). *I'll Tell You a Story* (1942). *I'll Tell You Another Story* (1942). *John Jolly at Christmas Time [by the Sea, on the Farm, at the Circus]* (1942–45). *The Land of Far Beyond* (1942). *Mary Mouse and the Doll's House* (1942). *The Naughtiest Girl Again* (1942). *The O'Sullivan Twins* (1942). *Shadow, The Sheep-Dog* (1942). *Six O'Clock Tales: Thirty-Three Short Stories for Children* (1942). *Tales of Babar* (1942). (as Mary Pollock) *Mischief at St. Rollo's* (1943). (as Mary Pollock) *The Secret of Cliff*

Castle (1943). (as Mary Pollock) *The Adventures of Scamp* (1943). (as Mary Pollock) *Smuggler Ben* (1943). *More Adventures on Willow Farm* (1943). *Bimbo and Topsy* (1943). *The Children's Life of Christ* (1943). *Dame Slap and Her School* (1943). *Five Go Adventuring Again* (1943). *The Magic Faraway Tree* (1943). *Merry Story Book* (1943). *More Adventures of Mary Mouse* (1943). *The Mystery of the Burnt Cottage* (1943). *Polly Piglet* (1943). *The Secret of Killimooin* (1943). *Seven O'Clock Tales: Thirty Short Stories for Children* (1943). *Summer Term at St. Clare's* (1943). *The Toys Come to Life* (1943). *At Appletree Farm* (1944). *Billy and Betty at the Seaside* (1944). *A Book of Naughty Children: The Mystery of the Disappearing Cat* (1944). *The Boy Next Door* (1944). *The Christmas Book* (1944). *Claudine at St. Clare's* (1944). *Come to the Circus* (1944). *The Dog That Went to Fairyland* (1944). *Eight O'Clock Tales* (1944). *Five Run Away Together* (1944). *The Island of Adventure*, 1944; as *Mystery Island*, 1945). *Jolly Little Jumbo* (1944). *Jolly Story Book* (1944). *Little Mary Mouse Again* (1944). *Nature Lover's Book* (1944). *Rainy Day Stories* (1944). *The Second Form at St. Clare's* (1944). *Tales from the Bible* (1944). *Tales of Toyland* (1944). *The Three Golliwogs* (1944). *The Blue Story Book* (1945). *The Brown Family* (1945). *The Caravan Family* (1945). *The Conjuring Wizard and Other Stories* (1945). *The Family at Red Roofs* (1945). *Fifth Formers at St. Clare's* (1945). *The First Christmas* (1945). *Five Go to Smugglers' Top* (1945). *Hallo, Little Mary Mouse* (1945). *Hollow Tree House* (1945). *The Mystery of the Secret Room* (1945). *Nature Readers, 1–30* (1945–46). *The Naughtiest Girl is a Monitor* (1945). *Round the Clock Stories* (1945). *The Runaway Kitten* (1945). *Sunny Story Book* (1945). *The Teddy Bear's Party* (1945). *The Twins Go to Nursery-Rhyme Land* (1945). *Amelia Jane Again* (1946). *The Bad Little Monkey* (1946). *The Castle of Adventure* (1946). *The Children at Happy House* (1946). *Chimney Corner Stories* (1946). *The Enid Blyton Holiday Book* (1946; 11 subsequent vols.) *First Term at Malory Towers* (1946). *Five Go Off in a Caravan* (1946). *The Folk of the Faraway Tree* (1946). *Gay Story Book* (1946). *Josie, Click, and Bun Again* (1946). *The Little White Duck and Other Stories* (1946). *Mary Mouse and Her Family* (1946). *The Mystery of the Spiteful Letters* (1946). *The Put-em-Rights* (1946). *The Red Story Book* (1946). *The Surprising Caravan* (1946). *Tales of Green Hedges* (1946). *The Train That Lost Its Way* (1946). *The Adventurous Four Again* (1947). *At Seaside Cottage* (1947). *Before I Go To Sleep: A Book of Bible Stories and Prayers For Children at Night* (1947). *Enid Blyton's Treasury* (1947). *Five on Kirrin Island Again* (1947). *The Green Story Book* (1947). *The Happy House Children Again* (1947). *Here Comes Mary Mouse Again* (1947). *The House at the Corner* (1947). *Jinky Nature Books*, 4 vols. (1947). *Little Green Duck and Other Stories* (1947). *Lucky Story Book* (1947). *More About Josie, Click, and Bun* (1947). *The Mystery of the Missing Necklace* (1947). *Rambles with Uncle Nat* (1947). *The "Saucy Jane" Family* (1947). *A Second Book of Naughty Children: Twenty-four Short Stories* (1947). *The Second Form at Malory Towers* (1947). *The Smith Family 1–3* (includes *At Home, At the Zoo, At the Circus*, 1947). *The Valley of Adventures* (1947). *The Very Clever Rabbit* (1947). *The Adventures of Pip* (1948). *The Boy with the Loaves and Fishes* (1948). *Bedtime Series* (1948). *Brer Rabbit and His Friends* (1948). *Brer Rabbit Book*, 8 vols. (1948–58). *Come to the Circus* (1948). *Five Go Off to Camp* (1948; as *Five on the Track of a Spook Train*, 1972). *How Do You Do, Mary Mouse* (1948). *Just Time for a Story* (1948). *Let's Garden* (1948). *Let's Have a Story* (1948). *The Little Girl at Capernaum* (1948). *Mister Icy-Cold* (1948). *More Adventures of Pip* (1948). *The Mystery of the Hidden House* (1948). *Nature Tales* (1948). *Now for a Story* (1948). *The Red-Spotted Handkerchief and Other Stories* (1948). *The Sea of Adventure* (1948). *The Secret of the Old Mill* (1948). *Six Cousins at Mistletoe Farm* (1948). *Tales After Tea* (1948). *Tales of the Twins* (1948). *They Ran Away Together* (1948). *Third Year at Malory Towers* (1948). *We Want a Story* (1948). *A Book of Magic* (1949). *Bluebell [Daffodil, Poppy, Buttercup, Snowdrop, Marigold, Foxglove] Story Book* (1949–55). *Bumpy and His Bus* (1949). *A Cat in Fairyland and Other Stories* (1949). *The Circus Book* (1949). *The Dear Old Snow Man* (1949). *Don't Be Silly, Mr. Twiddle* (1949). *The Enchanted Sea and Other Stories* (1949). *The Enid Blyton Bible Stories: Old Testament*, 16 vols. (1949). *The Enid Blyton Nature Plates*, 3 vols. (1949). *Good Morning Book* (1949). *Five Get into Trouble* (1949; as *Five Caught in a Treacherous Plot*, 1972). *Humpty Dumpty and Belinda* (1949). *Jinky's Joke and Other Stories* (1949). *Little Noddy Goes to Toyland* (1949). *Mr. Tumpy and His Caravan* (1949). *The Mountain of Adventure* (1949). *My Enid Blyton Bedside Book* (11 subsequent vols., 1949). *The Mystery of the Pantomime Cat* (1949). *Oh, What a Lovely Time* (1949). *The Rockingdown Mystery* (1949). *The Secret Seven* (1949; as *The Secret Seven and the Mystery of the Empty House*, 1972). *A Story Party at Green Hedges* (1949). *The Strange Umbrella and Other Stories* (1949). *Tales After Supper* (1949). *Those Dreadful Children* (1949). *Tiny Tales* (1949). *The Upper Fourth at Malory Towers* (1949). *The Astonishing Ladder and Other Stories* (1950). *Chuff the Chimney Sweep and Other Stories* (1950). *Five Fall into Adventure* (1950). *Hurrah for Little Noddy* (1950). *In the Fifth at Malory Towers* (1950). *The Magic Knitting Needles and Other Stories* (1950). *Mister Meddle's Muddles* (1950). *Mr. Pink-Whistle Interferes* (1950). *The Mystery of the Invisible Thief* (1950). *The Pole Star Family* (1950). *The Rilloby Fair Mystery* (1950). *Round the Year Stories* (1950). *Rubbalong Tales* (1950). *The Seaside Family* (1950). *Secret Seven Adventure* (1950; as *The Secret Seven and the Circus Adventure*, 1972). *The Ship of Adventure* (1950). *Six Cousins Again* (1950). *Tales About Toys* (1950). *The Three Naughty Children and Other Stories* (1950). *Tricky the Goblin and Other Stories* (1950). *We Do Love Mary Mouse* (1950). *Welcome Mary Mouse* (1950). *What an Adventure* (1950). *The Wishing Chair Again* (1950). *The Yellow Story Book* (1950). *Benny and the Princess and Other Stories* (1951).

Boody, the Great Goblin and Other Stories (1951). *The Big Noddy Book* (1951). *The Buttercup Farm Family* (1951). *Down at the Farm* (1951). *Father Christmas and Belinda* (1951). *Five on a Hike Together* (1951). *The Flying Goat and Other Stories* (1951). *Gay Street Book* (1951). *Hello Twins* (1951). *Here Comes Noddy Again* (1951). *Hurrah for Mary Mouse* (1951). *Last Term at Malory Towers* (1951). *Let's Go to the Circus* (1951). *The Little Spinning House and Other Stories* (1951). *The Magic Snow-Bird and Other Stories* (1951). *The Mystery of the Vanished Prince* (1951). *Noddy and Big Ears Have a Picnic* (1951). *Noddy and His Car* (1951). *Noddy Has a Shock* (1951). *Noddy Has More Adventures* (1951). *Noddy Goes to the Seaside* (1951). *Noddy Off to Rocking Horse Land* (1951). *Noddy Painting Book* (1951–57). *Noddy's House of Books* (1951). *A Picnic Party with Enid Blyton* (1951). *Pippy and the Gnome and Other Stories* (1951). *A Prize for Mary Mouse* (1951). *The Proud Golliwog* (1951). *The "Queen Elizabeth" Family* (1951). *The Runaway Teddy Bear and Other Stories* (1951). *The Six Bad Boys* (1951). *A Tale of Little Noddy* (1951). *"Too-Wise" the Wonderful Wizard and Other Stories* (1951). *Up the Faraway Tree* (1951). *Well Done, Secret Seven* (1951; as *The Secret Seven and the Tree House Adventure*, 1972). *Animal Lover's Book* (1952). *Bright Story Book* (1952). *The Circus of Adventure* (1952). *Come Along Twins* (1952). *The Enid Blyton Bible Stories: New Testament*, 16 vols. (1952–53). *Enid Blyton's Omnibus* (1952). *Five Have a Wonderful Time* (1952). *The Mad Teapot* (1952). *Mandy, Mops, and Cubby Again* (1952). *Mandy, Mops, and Cubby Find a House* (1952). *Mary Mouse and Her Bicycle* (1952). *Mr. Tumpy Plays a Trick on Saucepan* (1952). *My First Enid Blyton Book*, 3 vols. (1952). *My First Nature Book* (1952). *The Mystery of the Strange Bundle* (1952). *Noddy and Big Ears* (1952). *Noddy and the Witch's Wand* (1952). *Noddy's Colour Strip Book* (1952). *Noddy Goes to School* (1952). *Noddy's Ark of Book* (1952). *Noddy's Car Gets a Squeak* (1952). *Noddy's Penny Wheel Car* (1952). *The Queer Mystery* (1952). *The Rubadub Mystery* (1952). *Secret Seven on the Trail* (1952; as *The Secret Seven and the Railroad Mystery*, 1972). *Snowdrop Story Book* (1952). *The Story of My Life* (1952). *The Two Sillies and Other Stories* (1952). *The Very Big Secret* (1952). *Welcome Josie, Click, and Bun* (1952). *Well Done, Noddy* (1952). *Clicky the Clockwork Clown* (1953). *Enid Blyton's Christmas Story* (1953). *Five Go Down to the Sea* (1953). *Go Ahead Secret Seven* (1953; as *The Secret Seven Get Their Man*, 1972). *Gobo and Mr. Fierce* (1953). *Here Come the Twins* (1953). *Mandy Makes Cubby a Hat* (1953). *Mary Mouse and the Noah's Ark* (1953). *Mr. Tumpy in the Land of Wishes* (1953). *My Enid Blyton Story Book* (1953). *The Mystery of Holly Lane* (1953). *The New Big Noddy Book* (1953). *New Noddy Colour Strip Book* (1953). *Noddy and the Cuckoo's Nest* (1953). *Noddy at the Seaside* (1953). *Noddy's Cut-Out Model Book* (1953). *Noddy Gets Captured* (1953). *Noddy is Very Silly* (1953). *Noddy's Garage of Books* (1953). *The Secret of Moon Castle* (1953). *Snowball the Pony* (1953). *The Story of Our Queen* (1953). *Visitors in the Night* (1953). *Well Really Mr. Twiddle!* (1953). *The Adventure of the Secret Necklace* (1954). *The Castle Without a Door and Other Stories* (1954). *The Children at Green Meadows* (1954). *Enid Blyton's Good Morning Book* (1954). *Enid Blyton's Magazine Annual* (1954). *Five Go to Mystery Moor* (1954). *Friendly Story Book* (1954). *Fun with the Twins* (1954). *Good Work, Secret Seven!* (1954; as *The Secret Seven and the Case of the Stolen Car*, 1972). *How Funny You Are, Noddy* (1954). *Little Gift Books* (1954). *Little Strip Picture Books* (1954). *The Little Toy Farm and Other Stories* (1954). *Mary Mouse to the Rescue* (1954). *Merry Mister Meddle* (1954). *More About Amelia Jane* (1954). *The Mystery of Tally-Ho Cottage* (1954). *Noddy and the Magic Rubber* (1954). *Noddy's Castle of Books* (1954). *Noddy Gets into Trouble* (1954). *Noddy Giant Painting Book* (1954). *Noddy Goes to the Fair* (1954). *Noddy Pop-Up Book* (1954). *What a Surprise!* (1954). *Away Goes Sooty* (1955). *Benjy and the Others* (1955). *Bible Stories from the Old (and New) Testaments* (1955). *Bimbo and Blackie Go Camping* (1955). *Bobs* (1955). *Christmas with Scamp and Bimbo* (1955). *Favourite Book of Fables* (1955). *The Famous Five* (1955). *Finding the Tickets* (1955). *Five Have Plenty of Fun* (1955). *Gobo in the Land of Dreams* (1955). *The Golliwog Grumbled* (1955). *Holiday House* (1955). *The Laughing Kitten* (1955). *Little Bedtime Books* (includes *The Cloud Kitten, The Doll That Fell Out of the Pram, Silly Sammy, The Surprising Broom, Amanda Going Away, The Balloon Pipe, The Golliwog and the Wireless, The Wizard Who Was Really a Nuisance*, 1955–58). *Mandy, Mops, and Cubby and the Whitewash* (1955). *Mary Mouse in Nursery Rhyme Land* (1955). *Mischief Again* (1955). *Mother's Meeting* (1955). *Mr. Pink-Whistle's Party* (1955). *Mr. Sly-One and Cats* (1955). *Mr. Tumpy in the Land of Boys and Girls* (1955). *More Chimney Corner Stories* (1955). *Neddy the Little Donkey* (1955). *Noddy in Toyland* (1955). *Noddy Meets Father Christmas* (1955). *Playing at Home* (1955). *Ring o'Bells Mystery* (1955). *The River of Adventure* (1955). *Run-about's Holiday* (1955). *Secret Seven Win Through* (1955; as *The Secret Seven and the Hidden Cave Adventure*, 1972). *Sooty* (1955). *Trouble for the Twins* (1955). *The Troublesome Three* (1955). *Who Will Hold the Giant?* (1955). *You Funny Little Noddy!* (1955). *Be Brave, Little Noddy!* (1956). *Bom the Little Toy Drummer* (1956). *The Clever Little Donkey* (1956). *Colin the Cow-Boy* (1956). *A Day with Mary Mouse* (1956). *A Day With Noddy* (1956). *Animal Tales* (1956). *Noddy Play Day Painting Book* (1956). *Five on a Secret Trail* (1956). *Four in a Family* (1956). *Let's Have a Party* (1956). *The Mystery of the Missing Man* (1956). *Noddy and His Friends* (1956). *Noddy and Tessie Bear* (1956). *Noddy in Toyland* (play, 1956). *Noddy Nursery Rhymes* (1956). *The Noddy Toy Station Books* (1956). *The Rat-a-Tat Mystery* (1956). *Scamp at School* (1956). *A Story Book of Jesus* (1956). *Three Cheers Secret Seven* (1956; as *The Secret Seven and the Grim Secret*, 1972). *Bom and His Magic Drumstick* (1957). *Do Look Out, Noddy!* (1957). *Bom Painting Book* (1957). *Five Go to Billycock Hill* (1957).

Mary Mouse and the Garden Party (1957). *Mystery of the Strange Messages* (1957). *New Testament Picture Books* (1957). *Noddy and the Bumpy Dog* (1957). *Noddy's New Big Book* (1957). *Secret Seven Mystery* (1957; as *The Secret Seven and the Missing Girl Mystery,* 1972). *The Birthday Kitten* (1958). *Bom Goes Adventuring* (1958). *Bom Goes to Ho Ho Village* (1958). *Bom Annual* (1958–59). *Clicky Gets into Trouble* (1958). *Five Get into a Fix* (1958). *Mary Mouse Goes to the Fair* (1958). *Mr. Pink-Whistle's Big Book* (1958). *My Big-Ears Picture Book* (1958). *My Noddy Picture Book* (1958). *Noddy Has an Adventure* (1958). *The Noddy Shop Book* (1958). *Noddy's Own Nursery Rhymes* (1958). *Puzzle for the Secret Seven* (1958; as *The Secret Seven and the Case of the Music Lover,* 1972). *Rumble and Chuff* (1958). *The School Companion* (1958). *You're a Good Friend, Noddy!* (1958). *ABC With Noddy* (1959). *Bom and the Clown* (1959). *Bom and the Rainbow* (1959). *Hullo Bom and Wuffy Dog* (1959). *Mary Mouse Has a Wonderful Idea* (1959). *Noddy and the Bunkey* (1959). *Noddy Goes to Sea* (1959). *Noddy's Car Picture Book* (1959). *Ragamuffin Mystery* (1959). *Secret Seven Fireworks* (1959; as *The Secret Seven and the Bonfire Mystery,* 1972). *Adventure of the Strange Ruby* (1960). *Adventure Stories* (1960). *Bom Goes to Magic Town* (1960). *Cheer Up, Little Noddy!* (1960). *Clicky and Tiptoe* (1960). *Five on Finniston Farm* (1960). *Good Old Secret Seven* (1960; as *The Secret Seven and the Old Fort Adventure,* 1972). *Happy Day Stories* (1960). *Here Comes Bom* (1960). *Mary Mouse Goes to Sea* (1960). *Mystery Stories* (1960). *Noddy Goes to the Fair* (1960). *Noddy's One, Two Three Book* (1960). *Noddy's Tall Blue [Green, Orange, Pink, Red, Yellow] Book* (1960). *Old Testament Picture Books* (1960). *Tales at Bedtime* (1960). *Will the Fiddle* (1960). *The Big Enid Blyton Book* (1961). *Bom at the Seaside* (1961). *Bom Goes to the Circus* (1961). *Five Go to Demon's Rocks* (1961). *Happy Holiday, Clicky* (1961). *Mary Mouse Goes Out for the Day* (1961). *Mr. Plod and Little Noddy* (1961). *The Mystery of Banshee Towers* (1961). *The Mystery that Never Was* (1961). *Noddy's Toyland Train Picture Book* (1961). *Shock for the Secret Seven* (1961; as *The Secret Seven and the Case of the Dog Lover,* 1972). *A Day at School with Noddy* (1962). *Five Have a Mystery to Solve* (1962). *The Four Cousins* (1962). *Fun with Mary Mouse* (1962). *Look Out Secret Seven* (1962; as *The Secret Seven and the Case of the Missing Medals,* 1972). *Noddy and the Tootles* (1962). *Stories for Monday [and Tuesday]* (1962). *The Boy Who Wanted a Dog* (1963). *Brer Rabbit Again* (1963). *Five Are Together Again* (1963). *Fun for the Secret Seven* (1963; as *The Secret Seven and the Case of the Old Horse,* 1972). *Tales of Brave Adventure, Retold* (1963). *Enid Blyton's Sunshine Picture Story Book* (1964). *Happy Hours Story Book* (1964). *Mary Mouse and the Little Donkey* (1964). *Noddy and the Aeroplane* (1964). *Storybook for Fives to Sevens* (1964). *Storytime Book* (1964). *Tell-a-Story Books* (1964). *Trouble for the Twins* (1964). *The Boy Who Came Back* (1965). *Brer Rabbit's A Rascal* (1965). *Easy Reader* (1965). *Sunshine Book* (1965). *Treasure Box* (1965). *Learn to Count With Noddy,* 3 vols. (1965). *The Man Who Stopped to Help* (1965). *Noddy and His Friends: A Nursery Picture Book* (1965). *Noddy Treasure Box* (1965). *Tales of Long Ago, Retold* (1965). *Enid Blyton's Bedtime Annual* (1966). *Enid Blyton's Playbook* (1966). *The Fairy Folk Story Book* (1966). *Fireside Tales* (1966). *Gift Book* (1966). *The Happy House Children* (1966). *John and Mary* series (*The Great Big Fish, How John Got His Ducklings, The Dog Who Would Go Digging, The Wheel That Ran Away, The Three Sailors, The Kitten That Disappeared, The Little Brown Bear, Tim Gets a Chance, Granny's Lovely Necklace,* 1966–68). *Pixie Tales* (1966). *Pixieland Story Book* (1966). *Stories for Bedtime* (1966). *Stories for You* (1966). *Holiday Annual* [and *Magic, Pixie, Toy*] *Stories* (1967). *Noddy and His Passengers* (1967). *Noddy's Funny Kite* (1967). *Noddy and the Noah's Ark Adventure Picture Book* (1967). *Noddy in Toyland Picture Book* (1967). *Noddy's Aeroplane Picture Book* (1967). *The Playtime Story Book* (1967). *Adventures on Willow Farm* (1968). *Brownie Tales* (1968). *The Playtime Book* (1968). *Once Upon a Time* (1968). *A Basket of Surprises* (1970). *Noddy and the Magic Boots* (1979).

BIBLIOGRAPHY: Ray, S. *The Blyton Phenomenon: The Controversy Surrounding the World's Most Successful Children's Writer* (1982). Smallwood, I. *A Childhood at Green Hedges* (1989). Stoney, B. *Enid Blyton: A Biography* (1974).

For articles in reference works, see: *ABYP. CA. Europa. Feminist. IDWB. Longman. NCBEL. OCCL. SATA. TCCW. ToddBWW. WWCL.*

Other references: *CLE* (1974, 1975, 1982). *Encounter* (1958). *English in Education* (1980). *Library Association Record* (1960). *LonT* (24 January 1996). *New Society* (1974, 1979). *TEdS* (1994).

Helen Clare Taylor

Barbara Bodichon

BORN: 18 April 1827, London.
DIED: 11 June 1891, Scalands, near Robertsbridge, Sussex.
DAUGHTER OF: Benjamin Leigh Smith and Anne Longden.
MARRIED: Eugene Bodichon, 1857.
WROTE UNDER: Barbara Bodichon; Barbara Leigh Smith.

B., a leader of the Victorian feminist movement and the daughter and granddaughter of abolitionist members of Parliament, felt the stigma of illegitimacy: Her father, a Unitarian minister, had not married her mother, Anne Longden, a milliner's apprentice. At the age of twenty-one, B. received an annual income of £300 from her father; the resulting independence greatly shaped her life. In 1857, she married Eugene Bodichon, a radical humanitarian doctor who lived in Algeria. Thereafter she divided her time between Algeria and England until the last decade of her life when, partially paralyzed from a stroke, she remained in England.

B. was a painter throughout her life. She also established a progressive school in London for children of both sexes and different classes. In the 1850s she wrote a diary of a trip to America that was not published until 1972. An intimate friend of George Eliot, she guessed the identity of the author of *Adam Bede* simply from quotations in book reviews. In 1854, B. published a pamphlet titled *A Brief Summary in Plain Language of the Most Important Laws Concerning Women.* She organized a campaign to change the law preventing married women from owning property in their name, but the fight was not completely won until 1893, two years after her death. She argued that all professions be opened to women in the pamphlet *Women and Work* (1857). She also wrote articles on education for the *English Woman's Review.* In the 1860s she supported the fledgling movement for equality in two ways: by writing and by philanthropy. Her pamphlets on suffrage were widely circulated, and, with Emily Davies, she became a founder of Girton College.

In an 1866 pamphlet titled *Reasons for the Enfranchisement of Women,* B. argued that the status of non-voter contributed to the low self-esteem of women. She connected external barriers to a full life with the psychological harm caused by women's acceptance of those barriers. In another pamphlet the same year, *Objections to the Enfranchisement of Women Considered,* she challenged the powerful Victorian myth that gave women's influence in the home an almost mystical significance by noting that women at different times and in different places have assumed a variety of roles. More radically, she dismissed the notion that women should be moral guardians who could exert indirect influence on men and politics.

An American Diary, a series of letters to B.'s family in England, was based on a year of travel in 1857 and 1858. The work is valuable for its observations on slavery and women's rights and equally valuable for its self-portrait of an emancipated Victorian woman. In Boston at the end of her trip, B. met many women's-rights activists, and the sketch she gives of this circle anticipates the portrait drawn thirty years later by Henry James in *The Bostonians.*

One of the deepest expressions of B.'s feminism was her loving friendship with George Eliot. The many letters these women exchanged show a rare spiritual affinity. Apart from the light they shed on a particular friendship, their letters are valuable for all they reveal about the private lives of two public figures. Such friendships were especially important in the Victorian period, when intellectual or creative work by women was seen as odd and even unnatural. Each woman had felt the sting of ostracism: B. had been John Chapman's mistress before she married, and Eliot lived for twenty-five years with a man to whom she was not married.

Few women have been as successful as B. in work as varied as painting, politics, philanthropy, and writing. She was equally successful in her private life, living happily with her husband and happily away from him. One of the greatest writers of her time was her devoted friend for thirty five years. She described herself as "one of the cracked people of the world," adding that she was "never happy in an English genteel family life. I try to do it like other people, but I long always to be off on some wild adventure, or long to lecture on a tub in St. Giles, or go to see the Mormons, or ride off into the interior on horseback alone and leave the world for a month." B.'s complexity is revealed here: the wealthy woman attempting to be like others of her class; the artist needing isolation; and the reformer seeking a platform. Both B.'s fighting spirit and her independence are shown in her cartoon "Ye Newe Generation." Four women form a tableau on a mountain top. They hold a spear, a palette, a petition, and a pen.

WORKS: *A Brief Summary in Plain Language of the Most Important Laws Concerning Women* (1854). *Women and Work* (1857). *Reasons for the Enfranchisement of Women* (1866). *Objections to the Enfranchisement of Women Considered* (1866). *Barbara Leigh Smith Bodichon, An American Diary 1857–1858,* ed. J. Reed (1972).

BIBLIOGRAPHY: Bradbrook, M.C. *Barbara Bodichon, George Eliot, and the Limits of Feminism* (1975). Burton, H. *Barbara Bodichon 1827–1891* (1949). Davies, E. *The Papers of Emily Davies and Barbara Bodichon, from Girton College, Cambridge* (1985). *The George Eliot Letters,* ed. G. Haight (1954–55). Herstein, S.R. *A Mid-Victorian Feminist: Barbara Leigh Smith Bodichon* (1986). Hirsch, P. *Barbara Leigh Smith Bodichon and George Eliot: An Examination of Their Work and Friendship* (1992). *Barbara Leigh Smith and the Langham Place Group,* ed. C. A. Lacy (1987). *Barbara Leigh Smith Bodichon, An American Diary 1857–1858,* ed. and intro. J. Reed (1972). Spender, D. *Women of Ideas* (1982).

For articles in reference works, see: *Bloomsbury. Feminist. Oxford. ToddBWA. VB.*

Other references: Caine, B. *Victorian Feminists* (1992).

Margaret L. Cruikshank

(Amy) Maud Bodkin

BORN: 30 March 1875, Chelmsford, Essex.
DIED: 18 May 1967.
DAUGHTER OF: William Bodkin and Mrs. Bodkin.
WROTE UNDER: A. M. Bodkin; Maud Bodkin.

B.'s major work, *Archetypal Patterns in Poetry* (1934) is arguably one of the most important early uses of psychoanalysis in literary criticism. Her use of Freud and Jung for analysis of poetry's emotional depths is also historically important given the growing interest, from the 1960s into the 1980s, in the theories of French psychoanalyst Jacques Lacan and the *école freudienne.* In his 1947 study of the most important British and American literary critics, *The Armed Vision,* Stanley Edgar Hyman devotes an entire chapter to B. and psychological criticism because, he claims, her *Archetypal Patterns* is "probably the best use to date of psychoanalysis in literary criticism."

B. was the daughter of a physician, William Bodkin, and of a woman devoted to charity causes sponsored by the Congregational Church. Since his intellectual interests were extensive, William Bodkin spent all his leisure time reading philosophy. His interest in abstract questions of meaning was the major influence in B.'s life: "I have thought lately, turning the much marked and many times retread pages of my father's copy of William James' *Varieties of Religious Experience* that my life's quest has been, perhaps, a continuation of his" (*Twentieth Century Authors*). Along with Plato's *Dialogues,* B. believed that James's study was the most decisive influence on her career in teaching and psychology.

In 1901 she attended the University College of Wales, Aberystwyth, where she earned a B.A. and later an M.A. After leaving the university she began an eleven-year career as a lecturer in educational theory at a training college in Cambridge, where she concentrated on the pedagogical problems of communicating the perspectives of psychology to her students. During this time she spent a year in the United States to study methods of teaching educational psychology. She was dissatisfied with institutional answers to the problem of bringing psychology into the work of the schools and decided soon afterwards, influenced partly by health problems, to retire and study literary and philosophical questions on her own.

For several years during the 1920s B. studied Carl Jung's theories and attended one of his seminars for nonprofessional students of analytical psychology. He became the most important influence on her first book, *Archetypal Patterns in Poetry.* In this, her most influential work, B. draws on the definition of "archetypes" that Jung gives in his 1928 article "On the Relation of Analytical Psychology to Poetic Art." Jung argues that our emotional response in reading poetry can be attributed to primordial symbols or archetypes. These images result from numberless experiences that occurred not to the individual but to his ancestors, and that were inherited in the structure of the brain. Such a group of stories forms a "collective unconscious" that generates mythic heroes, fantasies, and recurring symbolism. In *Archetypes,* B. claims that such patterns and images are present in poetry and may be discovered there by "reflective analysis."

From the publication of *Archetypes* in the mid-1930s to her death in 1967, B. continued to write and lecture on the patterns and meaning of poetry. An article on the "philosophical novel," E.M. Forster's *A Passage to India,* appeared in the journal *The Wind and the Rain* in 1942. B. praises Forster's novel for its concern with the human relationships of love and understanding and with the impediments, what she calls the "goblin elements," that distort human communication between individuals and cultures. In *A Passage to India,* the Marabar Caves represent the frustrations and misunderstandings that can occur between two people or two groups of people.

B.'s second book, *The Quest for Salvation in an Ancient and a Modern Play* (1941), compares the pattern of redemption in Aeschylus's *Eumenides* with the pattern of personal salvation in T. S. Eliot's *Family Reunion.* In both plays the Furies are represented as ministers of revenge and primitive justice. The theme of both plays, B. argues, is that wisdom and salvation come through suffering. B.'s last work, *Studies of Type-Images in Poetry, Religion, and Philosophy* (1951), investigates types and patterns of thought that she regards as "God-given" and "clues to life's meaning" (*Twentieth Century Authors*). In this study she extends the argument of *Archetypes* by indicating that if collective patterns are operative in poetry, they may also be found in religious and philosophical writings concerning the origin and meaning of the human condition. B. argues that the true nature of God is not an omnipotent being but one of infinite wisdom. Human perversity does not originate in him but in humans themselves. God urges us beyond limited outlooks to the wisest courses. In her conclusion B. says that those who cannot believe in divine revelation must do without certainty but not without image-symbols, which give meaning to life and spiritual energy to our experience.

Although *Type-Images* was B.'s last book, she continued to write articles for the *British Journal of Medical Psychology,* the *British Journal of Psychology,* the *Hibbert Journal, Philosophy,* and *The Wind and the Rain.* Despite these substantial contributions to the role of psychology in literary criticism, B. is not well known either in Britain or the United States. *Archetypal Patterns in Poetry* received condescending reviews or was completely ignored until Hyman rehabilitated its reputation in the late 1940s. The reasons for B.'s obscurity are unclear, unless the lack of an academic degree in literature or professional training in psychoanalysis lessened her credibility for those who admired the recent increase in specialization. Possibly, her reliance on Jung brought her trouble since she did not challenge his ideas far enough. She did not, for example, explain the inadequacy of Jung's belief in archetypal patterns that are inherited biologically rather than culturally. Neither did she emphasize, although she herself avoided, the dangers that Jung posed for a mindless "glorification of the irrational." B. avoided all these questions about Jung by arguing in her later work for a faith in God as a kind of "ideal Statesman persuading men to the wisest course, in the interest of the whole that their conflicting self-interests and limited outlooks suffer them to accept" (*Type-Images*). Toward the end of her career, B. seemed to become a moral and theistic critic who moved away from psychoanalytic approaches to literature.

Although critics like Stanley Edgar Hyman believed B.'s moral and religious interests were outside the purview of the literary critic, her work deserves reconsideration at the end of the twentieth century as an important forerunner of the new school of literary critics who are once again using psychoanalysis as a heuristic device in looking at the literary canon. B. never made the mistake of seeing only patterns in literature; rather, she used Jungian psychology as one very innovative and creative perspective on literature.

WORKS: *Archetypal Patterns in Poetry: Psychological Studies of Imagination* (1934; with additional preface 1963). *The Quest for Salvation in an Ancient and a Modern Play* (1941). *Studies of Type-Images in Poetry, Religion, and Philosophy* (1951).

BIBLIOGRAPHY: Hyman, S. K. *The Armed Vision: A Study in the Methods of Modern Literary Criticism* (1947).

Knight, I. *The Wind and the Rain* (Autumn 1942). Lewis, C. Day. *The Poetic Image* (1947).

For articles in reference works, see: *CA. CLC. NCBEL. TCA SUP.*

Other references: *Folk-Lore* (June 1935). *Hibbert Journal* (January 1952). *Life and Letters* (January 1935). *Theology* (December 1951).

Laura Niesen de Abruña

Bogan of Bogan, Mrs.: See *Nairne, Baroness Caroline*

Eavan Aisling Boland

BORN: 24 September 1944, Dublin, Ireland.
PARENTS: Frederick Boland and Frances Kelly Boland.
MARRIED: Kevin Casey, 1969.

B. was born in Dublin in 1944 and attended secondary schools in both London and New York City. Following her graduation from Trinity College, Dublin, B. became a writer for *The Irish Times* as she worked on her poetry. After marrying, she moved to the Dublin suburbs and began a career as a fulltime mother and poet. She is considered one of Ireland's foremost contemporary poets, and she frequently contributes reviews and articles to *The Irish Times* while also lecturing at American and Irish universities.

B.'s first collection, *New Territory* (1967), while receiving little critical acclaim, exposes her considerable formal talent and training. The majority of critics view *The War Horse* (1975) as her transitional collection that introduces her major concerns regarding identities—specifically artistic, gender, and national identities. *The War Horse* explores the territory of the suburbs and the domestic world that she inhabits while also approaching the subject of violence in Northern Ireland. More importantly, in this volume she makes her first call for a "new" language that will actually describe and incorporate "lived" experience, a desire that becomes more apparent in later collections.

With *In Her Own Image* (1980), B. begins to experiment with what she calls "the anti-lyric" and to delve into subject matter more directly related to women's experiences (anorexia, mastectomy, menses, infanticide) and to present themes of entrapment, mutilation, and violence toward women. In doing so, her poetic voice emerges more confidently than in her previous collections as she strives to create a self-identity based upon actual female experience rather than on Western male myths, stereotypes, and images.

Night Feed (1982) and *The Journey* (1982) continue her interest in women's experiences and identities, delving not only into personal histories but also exploring the issues of nationalism and national identity in Ireland. *Night Feed* relies upon representations of women's personal experiences and the varying activities and responsibilities that create their lives. The collection is divided into three separate sections: The first details the mother-child relationship; the second explores artistic images of women and the effect of those images upon actual women; and the third revises the female image to present a new path toward determining women's identities. *The Journey* continues her exploration of public realities through domestic images and personal experiences. Furthermore, *The Journey* marks another transition in her career as she approaches the combined themes of nationalism and feminism in Ireland.

In *Outside History: Selected Poems* (1990) and *In a Time of Violence* (1994), B. proceeds to explore the complications of female identity and the conflict between the inherited images of the national and feminine for Irish women writers. The title sequence of *Outside History* investigates the issue of national identity; B. struggles to carve out a place for women in Ireland as she challenges the ways in which the Irish literary tradition has objectified and made ornaments out of women.

With *In a Time of Violence*, B. actively pleads that women be allowed to live inside and outside poems as subjects and authors. She calls for women to find ways to be subjects rather than objects and to be allowed by the Irish literary tradition to grow old and die in poems. Most significantly, she details how language captures Irish history and women's lives, creating immovable and unchanging images. Her poems, particular the lengthy poem "Anna Liffey," challenge those images, calling for women to create new, independent identities in art and in Ireland.

B. has moved from concern with the lyric and formal techniques to the domestic world to an overriding concern with how women can be independent, actual beings. Her discussion of the national and feminine brings her to call for actual action for women to become agents of change rather than elements of design in Ireland. B.'s poetry illustrates her belief in the need for poets to be responsible for the words they write so that they do not continue to inscribe dangerous and static images upon a page.

WORKS: *New Territory* (1967). (with Micheál Mac Liammóir) *W. B. Yeats and His World* (1971). *The War Horse* (1975). *In Her Own Image* (1980). *Introducing Eavan Boland* (1981). *Night Feed* (1982). *The Journey* (1982). *The Journey and Other Poems* (1987). *Selected Poems* (1989). *Outside History: Selected Poems 1980–1990* (1990). *In a Time of Violence* (1994). *Object Lessons: The Life of the Woman and the Poet in Our Time* (1995).

BIBLIOGRAPHY: Allen-Randolph, J. *ClQ* (1991). Baker, D. *KR* (1991). Conboy, S. *CJIS* (1990). Consuelo, D. M. *Studies* (1992). Hagen, P. L. and T. W. Zelman. *TCL* (1992). Henigan, R. *Concerning Poetry* (1985). *IUR* (1993, special B. issue). Klauke, A. *NWR* (1987). O'Connell, P. *Poets and Writers* (1994). Reizbaum, M. *ConL* (1989). Weekes, A. O. *BuR* (1994). Wills, C., in *Diverse Voices: Essays on Twentieth Century Women Writers in English*, ed. H. D. Jump (1991).

For articles in reference works, see: *CA. CLC. DLB.*

Jeannette E. Riley

Elizabeth Bonhote

BORN: 1744, Bungay, Suffolk.
DIED: July 1818, Bungay, Suffolk.
MARRIED: Daniel Bonhote.

B. was a conventional essayist and novelist. Little is known about her life beyond that which she mentions in the introductions to several of her works. She appears to have lived a generally uneventful life at Bungay and Bury in Suffolk. She and her husband, who was a solicitor, had several children, he died in 1804 in Bury at the age of fifty-six.

B.'s first work, *The Rambles of Mr. Friendly,* was published anonymously in 1772. It purported to describe various characters to be met in Hyde Park, but it was in fact a series of essays on the differing morality of town and country. It was translated into German in 1773.

B. published several novels between 1773 and 1796. All are very conventional gothic and romantic volumes. The plots are extremely elaborate, but there is very little delineation of character, time, or place. *Bungay Castle* (1796) is generally thought to be the best of B.'s novels, as it evokes more sense of place and atmosphere. She knew the castle well; local traditions of its role in the Wars of the Roses are part of the plot of the novel.

In 1788, B. brought out a series of essays on education, *The Parental Monitor;* the first edition was published by subscription; it was reprinted in 1796. She said she wrote the essays when in ill health, fearing she wouldn't to live to bring up her children. The work in two volumes, one for girls and one for boys, was to guide those who would be responsible for her family. Like her novels, this work is entirely conventional; its contents differ little from any standard conduct books of the day. Her final publication was *Feeling* (1810), a book of verse.

WORKS: *The Rambles of Mr. Friendly* (1772). *The Fashionable Friend* (1773). *Olivia* (1786). *The Parental Monitor* (1788). *Darnley Vale* (1789). *Ellen Woodley* (1790). *Bungay Castle* (1796). *Feeling* (1810).

BIBLIOGRAPHY:
For articles in reference works, see: *DNB. Feminist. Oxford. Todd BWW. Todd DBA.*

Barbara Brandon Schnorrenberg

Boole, Lily: See Voynich, Ethel Lilian Boole

Frances Boothby

FLOURISHED: 1669.
WROTE UNDER: "Arcasia"; F. Boothby.

If the pseudonymous "Ariadne" in her preface to *She Ventures and He Wins* (1695) styles herself one of the daughters of Aphra Behn, B might be considered, in one sense, Aphra's theatrical mother, in that her only known play *Marcelia: or the Treacherous Friend,* a tragicomedy first performed in 1669 by the King's Company, anticipated Behn's first play. Virtually nothing, however, is known of her life. *The London Stage* speculates that *Marcelia* might have first appeared in the summer of 1669, and the published text was licensed on 9 October 1669.

The play, an excerpt from which appears in *Kissing the Rod,* is highly conventional in its account of distressed virtue, and it is typical of its hybrid genre in intermixing verbal jousting and gender-oriented witticism. Before finally marrying her beloved Lotharicus—her virtue intact—Marcelia is tricked into suspecting the faithfulness of her lover, considers making herself a "heartless offering" to the king, and is betrayed by her own brother.

Along with Katherine Philips, whose *Horace* was also produced at the Theatre Royal, B. was a noteworthy forerunner of Behn's. Until more documentary evidence surfaces, however, her life remains a mystery.

WORKS: *Marcelia: or the Treacherous Friend* (prod. as "Arcasia,"1669; pub. under her own name, 1670).

BIBLIOGRAPHY: *Kissing the Rod: An Anthology of Seventeenth-Century Women's Verse,* ed. G. Greer et al. (1988). Langbaine, G. *Momus Triumphans* (1688).
For articles in reference works, see: *Bloomsbury. Feminist. ToddDBA.*

Richard C. Taylor

Phyllis Bottome

BORN: 31 May 1884, Rochester, Kent.
DIED: 22 August 1963, Hampstead, London.
DAUGHTER OF: William Macdonald Bottome and Mary Leatham Bottome.
MARRIED: A. E. Forbes-Dennis, 1917.

B. was a lecturer and a novelist known primarily for her romances—love affairs conducted against a backdrop of war and intrigue—and for her perceptive insight into the psychological motivations of her characters.

B.'s father was an American clergyman from New York City; her mother was a wealthy Englishwoman from Leatham, Yorkshire. Between the ages of nine and sixteen, B. lived in Jamaica, Queens, New York, where her father was minister of Trace Church. In 1901 the family returned to England, and B. entered an acting school. A few months later, a severe case of tuberculosis ended B.'s hopes for a career in the theater, and she turned to writing. Her first novel, *Raw Material* (1905), was completed when B. was only seventeen. During the first two years of World War I (1914–15), B. was a relief worker in Belgium. In 1916 she was hired by the British Ministry of Munitions as a writer of special public relations articles.

B. married A. E. Forbes-Dennis in 1917. When her husband was appointed Intelligence Officer at Marseilles and, later, Passport Control Officer in Vienna, B. traveled with him. In Vienna, B. became involved in postwar relief efforts and helped organize "food depots" for starving refugees. She lived in Austria until the Nazi occupation of that country made it necessary for her to return to England.

B. remained a life-long enemy of fascism. *The Mortal Storm* (1937), published shortly after B.'s return to England, is often credited with alerting the rest of the world to the "menace of Nazism." In 1938, B. wrote a pamphlet entitled "J'Accuse," modeled after Emile Zola's famous broadside, in which she accused the English government of ignoring the threat of fascism. Unable to find anyone in England who was willing to print the pamphlet, B., taking advantage of *The Mortal Storm's* popularity, began giving public lectures on the subject.

After World War II began, B. was made a lecturer for the British Ministry of Information and published several "patriotic" novels of love and war, including *The Mansion House of Liberty* (1941) and *London Pride* (1941). *Mansion House* is dedicated "To all those who love human beings better than they love power," and the foreword contains one of B.'s strongest antifascist statements:

> We must never forget that we are not only fighting against "Principalities and Powers" but against a Swastika—an empty cross with hooks, rather than a cross with a Human figure on it drawing us not by force but by love . . . the crux of what we are fighting for is the human spirit. Should the Nazis win, there would be a world without human spirits; a world of conscienceless State slaves . . . it is equally our duty now, and in the future, to give the utmost protection and fair play to those who are the victims of such force.

While living in Austria, B. developed a deep interest in psychiatry—and in the lives of psychiatrists. In the 1920s both B. and her husband became disciples of Alfred Adler, a Viennese psychiatrist who was president of the "Freudian circle" and editor of its *Psychoanalytical Journal;* B. studied with Adler until he moved to New York City in 1934. Shortly after Adler's death in 1937, B. published a highly complimentary biography, *Alfred Adler: Apostle of Freedom* (1939).

In *Within the Cup* (1943), B. tells the "true" story of Rudi von Ritterhaus, a Viennese psychiatrist and surgeon who was exiled to London in 1939. The book is particularly interesting in that, rather than simply telling the "life" of von Ritterhaus, B. tells the story through the doctor's "journal," in which he records his observations of English wartime living and contemplates the meanings of individual reactions to it.

Search for a Soul (1947) is the first of B.'s two autobiographical works. In it, she describes in detail the first eighteen years of her life, carefully psychoanalyzing herself according to Adlerian principles. The message of the work is that life rarely turns out as we, when we are young, assume that it will. B. concludes that "Our first choice of a self, since it is made in the dark spaces of early childhood . . . cannot be a very successful one and it is not perhaps surprising that we hardly like to be reminded of it." B.'s self-analysis continues in *The Challenge* (1953), her second autobiographical volume.

In 1944, B. moved to St. Ives, Cornwall. Her late work consists mainly of short-story collections such as the unusual *Man and Beast* (1954), in which the turning point of each "psychological tale" depends on the relationship between a human being and an animal.

WORKS: *Raw Material* (1905). *Broken Music* (1907). *The Dark Tower* (1909). *The Crystal Heart* (1911). *Old Wine* (1920) *Belated Reckoning* (1925). *Plain Case* (1928). *Strange Fruit* (1928). *Windlestraus* (1929). *Tatter'd Loving* (1929). *Wind in His Fists* (1931). *Devil's Due* (1931). *The Advances of Harriet* (1933). *Private Worlds* (1934). *Innocence and Experience* (1935). *Level Crossing* (1936). *The Mortal Storm* (1937). *Danger Signal* (1939; in the U.S. as *Murder in The Bud*). *Alfred Adler: Apostle of Freedom* (1939; in the U.S. as *Alfred Adler*). *The Heart of a Child* (1940). *Masks and Faces* (1940). *The Mansion House of Liberty* (1941). *London Pride* (1941). *Within the Cup* (1943; in the U.S. as *Survival*). *From the Life* (1944). *The Life Line* (1946). *Search for a Soul* (1947). *Under the Skin* (1950). *Fortune's Finger* (1950). *The Challenge* (1953). *Man and Beast* (1954).

BIBLIOGRAPHY:

For articles in reference works, see: *BioIn. CA. Feminist. Longman. MBL. Oxford. TCA* and *SUP. TCW. ToddBWW.*

Other references: *NYT* (23 August 1963, 24 August 1963). *PW* (9 September 1963). *Time* (28 August 1963).

Kay Beaird Meyers

Elizabeth (Dorothea Cole) Bowen

BORN: 7 June 1899, Dublin, Ireland.
DIED: 22 February 1973, London.
DAUGHTER OF: Henry Bowen and Florence Colley Bowen.
MARRIED: Alan Cameron, 1923.

Like two scissors blades working against one another, B.'s identification with the Anglo-Irish gentry and her sense of being an outsider to English culture sharpen her perception of social change during the twentieth century. Her characters fascinate and engage readers' imaginations, but her plots are sometimes improbable. Her elegant prose encompasses both the distortions of her characters' observations and the cold-eyed judgment of an authorial intelligence. Influenced by Marcel Proust, Henry James, and Jane Austen, B. utilized their technical narrative devices, but her fiction, rarely solemn, succeeds by exploiting the witty, satirical insights of moral comedy.

At the age of seven, B. was moved from Dublin to Folkestone, on the coast of Kent, and B. credits that split between her Irish heredity and her English childhood with making her a novelist. B. was raised by her mother alone after B.'s father certified himself insane. At the age of thirteen, B. lost her mother to cancer (B. herself later died of lung cancer), and B.'s aunt assumed responsibility for her niece's education and social training. B. transformed some of her schoolgirl experiences in *The Little Girls* (1964), and she set down her impressions of the Kentish resort town "Seale-on-Sea" in several of her novels. In 1917, B. left school to live with her recovered father, in Ireland, occupied by the British army since 1916. The Bowens, as members of the Anglo-Irish gentry, entertained the British officers, and B. was briefly engaged to a British lieutenant. Without a clear sense of vocation, B. attended a London school of art for two terms, quit, and began her literary career by showing some short stories to the established novelist Rose Macaulay, who offered both encouragement and introductions to the London literary circles. B.'s first collection of stories, *Encounters,* was published in 1923. That year also, B. married a British World War I veteran, Alan Cameron, with whom she lived until his death in 1952. The couple resided where his work as educational administrator took them, first to Northamptonshire, then to Oxford in 1925, and then to London in 1935; after spending World War II in London, they chose to retire in County Cork at Bowen's Court.

As the only child of an Anglo-Irish landowner, B. inherited Bowen's Court in 1930, and, as long as she was financially able, spent part of each year writing and entertaining at her Irish country estate. During 1921, B. had feared Bowen's Court would be burned down by Irish rebels; her nightmares prompted by that fear are recorded in her novel *The Last September* (1929). B. often retreated to Bowen's Court to write in solitude. Her love for the great house and her sense of being rooted there may be seen in the family history she wrote, *Bowen's Court* (1942).

B.'s first novel, *The Hotel* (1927) succeeds as a satirical comedy of a young woman, Sydney, attracted too suddenly to the sexuality of an older man. In the character of Mrs. Kerr, B. creates the first of many overly protective aunts and mothers who break off the young heroines' precipitous love affairs.

The Last September (1929), set during the Irish civil war, depicts the conflicting loyalties and hostilities felt by the Anglo-Irish gentry for their Irish tenants and their English guests. Lois, the heroine, loves the Irish great house, which closely resembles Bowen's Court, but she also loves an English soldier stationed in Ireland. In a lightly comic style, B. depicts the nineteen-year-old Lois's inexperience: "She could not remember, though she had read so many books, who spoke first after a kiss had been, not exchanged but—administered." Her aunt, Lady Naylor, discourages Lois's lover by suggesting, first, that Lois is too young, and, then, that the young man is too far below her class. Suddenly shifting to tragedy, B. has the English soldier killed and has Lady Naylor's great house burned by the Irish rebels.

B.'s novel *Friends and Relations* (1931) is a competent light comedy. B.'s sharply focused comic vision produced Elfrida's entrance: "Down the long shop, narrow and cumbered like the past, with its dull mirrors, she came very tall, *distraite,* balancing nervously in her speed like a ship just launched." *To the North* (1932) is a better novel, because B. makes her readers believe the naïve, humorless character of Emmeline, slow to make connections. When Markie almost apologizes for not wanting to marry her, saying, "Sorry. . . . But you knew I was always out for what I could get," Emmeline does begin to see, but, nevertheless, she compliantly continues their relationship. In an unconvincing and melodramatic conclusion, Emmeline drives with reckless speed, as if trying to escape the past, though Markie is her passenger in the car; as they crash, her final word to him is "Sorry."

In her next novel, *The House in Paris* (1935), B. explores the divided personality of Karen, who becomes a deceiver in order to carry on an illicit affair with Max. Less impressively, B. characterizes Max as a French-Jew, treating his rootlessness unsympathetically, and she ridicules his nervous fiancée, Naomi, because her eyes "start out of her head." In this history, "fate . . . creeps like a rat."

B.'s two finest novels, *The Death of the Heart* (1938) and *The Heat of the Day* (1949), depict characters who respond to contemporary moral problems. *The Death of the Heart* explores the cultural and psychological aftermath of World War I through the overly sensitive perceptions of an adolescent orphan, Portia, who has come to live in London with her brother, Thomas, and her sister-in-law, Anna. *The Heat of the Day* explores the psychological and moral problems of loyalty in the context of the wearing years of World War II.

B.'s lyrical, allusive descriptions of Regent's Park are an unmatched achievement in British fiction. While walking in Regent's Park, Anna, in *The Death of the Heart,* gradually thaws her frozen feelings and begins, painfully, to allow compassion a role in her life. In *The Heat of the Day,* the Londoners in wartime Regent's Park take refuge from and, paradoxically, wrestle with their moral choices. B.'s visual and psychological images make the locale emblematic of changes suffered by individuals caught in a particular historical moment.

Written as if history did not matter, *A World of Love* (1955) juxtaposes the passionate dreams of the adolescent Jane with the unsatisfied dreams of the adults around her in a shabby Irish great house. *The Little Girls* (1964) depicts three old women excavating their own childhood secrets. *Eva Trout* (1968) is a broad social comedy dominated by the wealthy, clumsy, troublemaking Eva, who is killed by her adopted child. These last three novels won public acclaim, but they are not as finely written as B.'s *The Death of the Heart* and *The Heat of the Day.*

B.'s development as a fiction writer is reflected in her short stories. *Encounters* (1923) and *Ann Lee's* (1926) offer mannered observations that are, as B. herself acknowledged, "a blend of precocity and naivete." In her stories of wartime London, collected in *The Demon Lover* (1945), B. skillfully captures the eeriness, the trauma, and the intensity she experienced during the Blitz. The melodramatic turns of plot that sometimes mar her novels succeed in the tighter shape of her short stories.

In her novels, B. sometimes failed to create credible plots, which proceed inevitably from actions taken by her characters. It does not seem possible, for example, that Stella, the sensible, self-controlled heroine of *The Heat of the Day,* would carry on an affair for months without knowing much about her lover, without suspecting that he feels no patriotic loyalty, and without having any information to verify or deny a charge that he is a traitor selling secrets to the Nazis. Nor is B. s explanation for the lover's behavior very credible: Robert betrays his country as part of his rebellion against a grasping, middle-class family who lacks a gentrified attachment to the land. Max, whom Karen loves in *The House in Paris,* hardly seems capable of fathering Karen's child or of committing suicide. Markie, in *To the North,* is such a complete cad that his desire for Emmeline cannot be comprehended. B. succeeds brilliantly, however, in her portrait of Portia's adolescent sensibility in *The Death of the Heart,* so that her disturbing behavior precipitates action.

B.'s reputation as a fiction writer rests on her creation of memorable characters, on her imaginative evocation of the atmosphere of a particular locale at a precise moment, and on her brilliant, mannered English prose.

WORKS: *Encounters* (1923). *Ann Lee's and Other Stories* (1926). *The Hotel* (1927). *The Last September* (1929). *Joining Charles* (1929). *Friends and Relations* (1931). *To the North* (1932). *The Cat Jumps* (1934). *The House in Paris* (1935). *The Death of the Heart* (1938). *Look at All Those Roses* (1941). *Seven Winters* (1942). *Bowen's Court* (1942). *English Novelists* (1942). *The Demon Lover* (1945; in the U.S. as *Ivy Gripped the Steps and Other Stories,* 1946). *The Heat of the Day* (1949). *Collected Impressions* (1950). *The Shelbourne* (1951). *The Early Stories* (1951). *A World of Love* (1955). *Stories by Elizabeth Bowen* (1959). *A Time in Rome* (1960). *Afterthought* (1962; in the U.S. as *Seven Winters and AfterThoughts*). *The Little Girls* (1964). *The Good Tiger* (1965). *A Day in the Dark and Other Stories* (1965). *Eva Trout* (1968). *Pictures and Conversations* (1975). *Collected Stories* (1981). *The Mulberry Tree: Writings of Elizabeth Bowen,* ed. H. Lee (1987).

BIBLIOGRAPHY: Austin, A. *Elizabeth Bowen* (1971). Bennett, A. and N. Royle. *Elizabeth Bowen and the Dissolution of the Novel* (1995). Blodgett, H. *Patterns of Reality: Elizabeth Bowen's Novels* (1975). Brooke, J. *Elizabeth Bowen* (1952). Glendinning, V. *Elizabeth Bowen* (1978). Halperin, J. *Eminent Georgians* (1995). Heath, W. *Elizabeth Bowen: An Introduction to Her Novels* (1961). Kenney, E. *Elizabeth Bowen* (1974). O'Toole, B., in *Across a Roaring Hill: The Protestant Imagination in Modern Ireland, Essays in Honour of John Hewitt,* ed. G. Daure and E. Longley (1985). Sellery, J. *Elizabeth Bowen: A Descriptive Bibliography* (1981). Lee, H. *Elizabeth Bowen: An Estimation* (1981).

For articles in reference works, see: *CA. CLC. DIL. DLB. EWLTC. Longman. MBL* and *SUP. TCA* and *SUP. TCW.*

Other references: Drabble, M. *Listener* (13 February 1969). Furbank, P.N. *TLS* (6 February 1981). Hall, J. *The Lunatic in the Drawing Room: The British and American Novel Since 1930* (1968). Hardwick, E. *PR* (November 1949). Kershner, R. B., Jr. *TSLL* (1986). Lassner, P. *Eire* (1986). Medoff, J. *MFS* (1984). Moss, H. *NYTBR* (8 April 1973). Partridge, A. C., in *Irish Writers and Society at Large,* ed. M. Sekine (1985).

Judith L. Johnston

Caroline Bowles

BORN: 7 October 1786, Lymington, Hampshire.
DIED: 20 July 1854, Buckland, Lymington, Hampshire.
DAUGHTER OF: Charles Bowles and Anne Burrard.
MARRIED: Robert Southey, 1839.
WROTE UNDER: Caroline Bowles; C.; Caroline Southey.

B. was the only child of a captain in the East India Company. Early in life she was badly scarred by small pox and developed a shy, retiring manner. Most of her life was spent in seclusion at Buckland Cottage, New Forest. B. received one proposal of marriage as a young woman, but her parents persuaded her to refuse it. Her mother died in 1816. B.'s literary career began in 1818 when she wrote Poet Laureate Robert Southey for an evaluation of her long poem *Ellen Fitzarthur,* a metrical tale about a runaway daughter, deserted by her husband, who remorsefully seeks the moonlit tomb of her mother. By the time B. died in 1854, she had published numerous Romantic tales in verse and prose, a poetical autobiography, and poems ranging from the humorous to the pathetic.

The success of *Ellen Fitzarthur,* published in 1820 by Longman's on Southey's recommendation, prompted B. to offer more poems for publication—chiefly lyrical ballads in the style of the Lake Poets and meditations upon the natural world. Some appeared in *Blackwood's* under the signature C.; *The Widow's Tale* (1822) and *Solitary Hours* (1826) collect these and other verses. *Tales of the Factories* (1833), an impassioned outcry against inhumane working conditions, anticipates *A Voice from the Factories* (1836) by Caroline Norton and "The Cry of the Children" (1843) by Elizabeth Barrett Browning.

B.'s best volume of poetry is *The Birthday* (1836). The title poem is both a nostalgic memoir of the poet's youth in the English countryside and a rueful feminist commentary on the upbringing of girls and the limited life opportunities for women in the early nineteenth century. Some poems in this volume, such as "The Hedgehog," strike a humorous note regarding modern life; others are more philosophical and melancholy. "The Churchyard," a Romantic ode, can be compared with Thomas Gray's "Elegy Written in a Country Churchyard" or with Percy Bysshe Shelley's "To a Skylark" or John Keats's "Ode to a Nightingale." Reviewing *The Birthday* for the *Quarterly Review,* Henry Nelson Coleridge pronounced B. "the Cowper of our modern poetesses."

B.'s prose tales include both sensational and pathetic narratives. Those published in *Blackwood's* were collected in two volumes in 1829 as *Chapters on Churchyards.* A. H. Miles referred to them as "pathetic novelettes" and pointed out that B.'s critical reputation dwindled during the Victorian period; however, he also declared that she "had a far better idea of the difference between true and false sentiment than most of the women poets of her time."

B.'s life and career are inevitably linked with Southey's. The two corresponded from 1818 until 1839, with Southey continuously offering B. advice and encouragement regarding her literary efforts. Their letters, about half of which were published in 1881, contain literary discussions and personal anecdotes; Southey's are much fuller and longer than B.'s. In 1839, Southey's first wife Edith died after a protracted invalidism from mental illness. Southey proposed to B., and she accepted, forfeiting a large annuity, and moved to Keswick. Aside from an unsuccessful attempt to collaborate with Southey on a poetical tale about Robin Hood, B. ceased writing after her marriage. Southey, who was sixty-five, soon began to fail, both physically and mentally; B. nursed him until his death in 1843. Her own health gave way as a result, and, resented by Southey's grown children, she returned to Buckland. In 1852 B. received a Civil List pension of £200, not as the widow of the Poet Laureate but as a literary artist in her own right.

WORKS: *Ellen Fitzarthur, A Metrical Tale* (1820). *The Widow's Tale* (1822). *Solitary Hours* (1826, 1839). *Chapters on Churchyards* (1829). *Tales of the Factories* (1833). *The Birthday, a Poem in Three Parts, to which are added, Occasional Verses* (1836). *Robin Hood: A Fragment, with Other Fragments and Poems by the late Robert Southey and Caroline Southey* (1847). *Select Literary Works* (1851). "The Smuggler" in *The Tale Book* (1859). *Poetical Works* (1867). *Harmless Johnny: or The Poor Outcast of Reason,* ed. D. Greenwell (1868). *The Correspondence of Robert Southey with Caroline Bowles,* ed. E. Dowden (1881).

BIBLIOGRAPHY: *Athenaeum* (5 August 1854). Coleridge, H. N. *Quarterly Review* (September 1840).

For articles in reference works, see: *BA19C. Feminist. NCHEL. Oxford. PPL.*

Other references: Ashfield, A. *Romantic Women Poets 1770–1830: An Anthology* (1995). Courtney, J. *The Adventurous Thirties: A Chapter in the Women's Movement* (1933, 1967). Hickok, K. *Representations of Women: Nineteenth-Century British Women's Poetry* (1984).

Kathleen Hickok

Elizabeth Boyd

FLOURISHED: 1727–45.
WROTE UNDER: Eloisa; Louisa.

In spite of her productivity, biographical details about the poet, novelist, journalist, and playwright are sketchy, a product largely of hints garnered from the Advertisement to B's novel *The Happy Unfortunate, or the Female Page* (1732). Clearly, though, she suffered persistent ill health and the ravages of poverty throughout her period of known literary output, 1727–1745.

She was already an accomplished poet, having written *Variety* in 1727 and a collection of poems dedicated to the king's birthday in 1730, when she published her only known novel in 1732, subscribers to which "raised me from the lowest condition of Fortune, and a worse state of Health." She assumes a conventionally apologetic stance in justifying herself as an author: "I never was ambitious of the Name of Author," but published with "a View to settling my Self in a Way of Trade, that may enable me to master those Exigencies of Fortune, which my long illness had for some time past reduc'd me to suffer." With the proceeds from her novel, she hopes to sell "Paper, Pens, Ink, Wax, Wafers, Black Lead Pencils, Pocket Books, Almanacks, Plays, Pamphlets and all manner of stationary [sic] goods" at her house near Leicester Fields.

"The Female Page" is a woman wearing breeches to be near the Duke with whom she is in love—a novelistic version of the late-seventeenth-century theatrical vogue. One critic, B. MacCarthy, argues that this work, which may have been a comic roman à clef, "united the picaresque and the tale of gallantry in a sorry concoction."

Her collection *The Humorous Miscellany* (1733) is probably most remarkable for its accounts of maternal suffering, the "soft mother's agonies" in the face of the death of a child.

Her persistent ill-health delayed her long-planned periodical publication *The Snail,* only one issue of which appeared in 1745. Her venture into playwrighting, *Don Sancho, or The Student's Whim* (1739), went unproduced.

WORKS: *Variety: A Poem* (1727). *Verses on the King's Birthday* (1730). *The Happy-Unfortunate; Or, The Female Page* (1732). *The Humorous Miscellany* (1733). *Don Sancho, Or The Student's Whim* (1739). *Truth* (1740). *The Snail* (1745).

BIBLIOGRAPHY: *Eighteenth-Century Women Poets,* ed. R. Lonsdale (1990). MacCarthy, B. G. *Women Writers: Their Contribution to the English Novel, 1621–1744* (1946). Reed, I. *Biographia Dramatica* (1782).

For articles in reference works, see: *Bloomsbury. Feminist. ToddDBA.*

Richard C. Taylor

Bradby, Anne: See *Ridler, Anne*

Mary Elizabeth Braddon (Maxwell)

BORN: 4 October 1835, London.
DIED: 4 February 1915, Richmond, Surrey.
DAUGHTER OF: Henry Braddon and Fanny White Braddon.
MARRIED: John Maxwell, 1874.
WROTE UNDER: Aunt Belinda; Mary Elizabeth Braddon; Babington White.

A prolific, controversial, and best-selling novelist, B. also wrote poetry, plays, and short fiction. In addition, she edited several magazines owned by her husband, the publisher John Maxwell, including *Belgravia* and *The Mistletoe Bough;* and she contributed to *Punch, The World,* and *Figaro.*

B.'s life was in ways as sensational as the fiction that became her trademark. Her father deserted the family while B. was still a child. To help support the family, she went on the stage at the age of nineteen under the name Mary Seyton. The financial support of an admiring Yorkshire squire named Gilby allowed her to leave the stage and finish *Garibaldi and Other Poems* (1861), "The Loves of Arcadia" (a comedietta produced at the Strand Theatre in 1860), and her first novel, *Three Times Dead* (1860), revised and released by Maxwell as *The Trail of the Serpent* (1861). By mid-1861 B. was living with Maxwell, whose actual wife, Mary Anne, remained in a Dublin insane asylum until her death in 1874. Only then did B. and Maxwell marry legally, after she had already borne him six children and helped raise the five from his first marriage. Maxwell's attempts to present B. as his lawful wife before 1874 were publicly refuted by his in-laws, leaving his and B.'s standing in society painfully ambiguous.

B.'s sufferings at the hands of smug Victorian respectability are reflected in the subtle undermining of social conventions that marks her most interesting novels. B. became adept at manipulating the intricately plotted suspense in everyday settings that had been popularized by Wilkie Collins' *Woman in White.* In *Lady Audley's Secret* (1862), the spectacular best-seller that defined the "sensation novel" of the 1860s, the blue-eyed, flaxen haired "angel in the house" turns bigamist in order to marry well and murders in order to protect her position; the insanity that constitutes her deepest secret metaphorically underlines her subversion of feminine stereotypes. The heroines of *Aurora Floyd* (1863) and *John Marchmont's Legacy* (1863) similarly confound convention by combining all the traits of the model woman with heinous villainy. In *The Lady's Mile* (1866) B. uses the circular bridal path in Hyde Park to represent the constriction of respectable female lives and the moral and social wilderness beyond it. Several of her novels during this period began as bloodthirsty serials turned out for magazines like *The Half-penny Journal* and *Belgravia,* some under the pen name "Babington White." B. herself maintained a wry distance from such work, joking in her frequent letters to Edward Bulwer-Lytton about "the amount of crime, treachery, murder, slow poisoning, and general infamy required by the half penny reader." Some of her experience as a potboiling journalist colors the portrait of Sigismund Smithin in *The Doctor's Wife* (1864), B.'s English version of *Madame Bovary. Birds of Prey* (1867) and its sequel, *Charlotte's Inheritance* (1868), offer the best examples of what B. referred to as writing of "the Balzac-morbid-anatomy school."

B.'s early novels came under attack for their "immorality" and "sensuality"—criticism that often carried innuendoes about her private life with Maxwell. B. learned to be more skillful in appearing to satisfy middle-class ideals while subtly satirizing them. In *Strangers and Pilgrims* (1873) and *Lost for Love* (1874) evangelical cant is her target. *Joshua Haggard's Daughter* (1876) was the first of many novels criticizing the irresponsibility and conspicuous consumption of the idle rich, among them *Vixen* (1879), *Just As I Am* (1880), *One Thing Needful* (1886), *Gerard* (1891), and *Rough Justice* (1898). B.'s interest in Emile Zola is reflected in the settings and detail of works like "Under the Red Flag" (1883), *Ishmael* (1884), and *Like and Unlike* (1887). She returned to the sensation novel with spectacular success in *The Fatal Three* (1888). B.'s contemporaries often appeared in fictional guise in her works: William Gladstone in *The One Thing Needful,* Gérard de Nerval in *Ishmael,* Oscar Wilde in *The Rose of Life* (1905). During the 1880s and 1890s B. also produced condensations of Sir Walter Scott's novels for the penny press, children's stories, short sentimental fiction, and several plays. *Dead Love Has Chains* (1907), like several novels in her final years, offers penetrating psychological studies of the sexual ambivalence of the nineties and beyond.

Although she may have tried out of deference to the advice of Bulwer-Lytton and Charles Reade to make her work more "serious" and "artistic," B. remained an unabashed popularizer. As she herself admitted, she was too often struck by the ridiculous side of things to be swayed much by the sentimental; she always maintained an ironic distance from the very stereotypes she was exploiting. Notwithstanding the unevenness of her work, B. stands out as a shrewd and skillful manipulator of plot, convention, and detail who earned the admiration of writers like William Makepeace Thackeray, Edward Bulwer-Lytton, Charles Reade, Robert Louis Stevenson, George Moore, Henry James, and others. Her tremendous success sprang from her ability to satisfy popular tastes, but her lasting interest derives from the skill with which she questioned and unsettled popular values.

WORKS: *Loves of Aracadia* (1860, unpublished). *Three Times Dead* (1860; republished as *The Trail of the Serpent,* 1861). *The Black Band* (1861) *Garibaldi and Other Poems* (1861). *The Lady Lisle* (1862). *Lady Audley's Secret* (1862). *Captain of the Vulture* (1863). *Aurora Floyd* (1863). *Eleanor's Victory* (1863). *John Marchmont's Legacy* (1863). *Henry Dunbar* (1864). *The Doctor's Wife* (1864). *Only a Clod* (1865). *Sir Jasper's Tenant* (1865). *The Lady's Mile* (1866). *Ralph the Bailiff and Other Tales* (1867). *Circe* (1867, by "Babington White"). *Rupert Godwin* (1867). *Birds of Prey* (1867). *Charlotte's Inheritance* (1868). *Run to Earth* (1868). *Dead Sea Fruit* (1868). *Fenton's Quest* (1871). *The Lovels of Arden* (1871). *Robert Ainsleigh* (1872). *To the Bitter End* (1872). *Milly Darrell* (1873). *Griselda* (1873, unpublished). *Strangers and Pilgrims* (1873). *Lucius Davoren* (1873). *Taken at the Flood* (1874). *Lost for Love* (1874). *A Strange World* (1875). *Hostages to Fortune* (1875). *Dead Men's Shoes* (1876). *Joshua Haggard's Daughter* (1876). *Weavers and Weft and Other Stories* (1877). *An Open Verdict* (1878). *Vixen* (1879). *The Cloven Foot* (1879). *Aladdin and Other Stories* (1880). *The Missing Witness* (1880). *The Story of Barbara* (1880). *Just as I Am* (1880). *Asphodel* (1881) *Mount Royal* (1882). *Flower and Weed* (1883). *The Golden Calf* (1883). *Phantom Fortune* (1883) *Ishmael* (1884). *Wyllard's Weird* (1885). *The Good Hermione* (1886, by "Aunt Belinda"). *One Thing Needful* (1886). *Under the Red Flag and Other Stories* (1886). *Cut by the County* (1886). *Mohawks* (1886). *Like and Unlike* (1887). *The Fatal Three* (1888). *The Day Will Come* (1889). *One Life, One Love* (1890). *Gerard* (1891). *The Venetians* (1892). *A Life Interest*

(1893, unpublished). *All Along the River* (1893). *The Christmas Hirelings* (1894). *Thou Art the Man* (1894). *Sons of Fire* (1895). *London Pride* (1896). *Under Love's Role* (1897). *In High Places* (1898). *Rough Justice* (1898). *His Darling Sin* (1899). *The Infidel* (1900). *The Conflict* (1903). *A Lost Eden* (1904). *The Rose of Life* (1905). *The White House* (1906). *Dead Love Has Chains* (1907). *Her Convict* (1907). *During Her Majesty's Pleasure* (1908). *Our Adversary* (1909). *Beyond These Voices* (1910). *The Green Curtain* (1911). *Miranda* (1913). *Mary* (1916).

BIBLIOGRAPHY: Hughes, W. *The Maniac in the Cellar* (1980). James, H. *Notes and Reviews* (1921). Michie, H. *Sororophobia: Differences Among Women in Literature and Culture* (1992). Morris, V. *Double Jeopardy: Women Who Kill in Victorian Fiction* (1990). Sadleir, M. *Things Part* (1944). Showalter, E. *A Literature of Their Own* (1977). Wolff, R. L. *Sensational Victorian* (1979).

For articles in reference works, see: *Allibone. BA19C. Bloomsbury. CA. Cassell. Chambers. DLB. DNB. ELB. Europa. Feminist. Women of the Day,* ed. F. Hays (1885). *IDWB. OCEL. Oxford. Men and Women of the Time,* ed. V. Plarr (1899). *RE. Todd-BWW. VB.*

Other references: *Bookman* (July 1912). Casey, E. M. *TstL* (1984). *New York Evening Post* (1915). Schroeder, N. *TSWL* (1988). *World* (25 April 1905).

Rosemary Jann

Bradley, Katharine Harris: See *Field, Michael (Katharine Harris Bradley)*

Anne Dudley Bradstreet

BORN: 1612, Northamptonshire.
DIED: 16 September 1672, Andover, Massachusetts.
DAUGHTER OF: Thomas Dudley and Dorothy Yorke.
MARRIED: Simon Bradstreet, 1628.
WROTE UNDER: A Gentlewoman from Those Parts.

Read almost constantly since her work was first published in 1650, B. is recognized as one of the most compelling poetic voices in colonial America. Early readers like Bathsua Makin praised B.'s verse for its edifying qualities, noble style, and political views. Today's readers value the more lyrical and personal poems and prose pieces that appeared in the second edition of her works, published posthumously: her account of the intensely examined life, important in Puritan tradition, in which she articulates her particular tensions as a female in this sober, conservative religious tradition; her identity in marriage and motherhood, including fear of death in childbirth and affection for her husband and children; and her sense of self as poetic artist.

Her parents were members of the gentry, and B. shared an early ancestor with the aristocratic poet, Sir Philip Sidney, author of the prose romance *Arcadia* (1590). Her father, known as an educated gentleman and called a "devourer of books" by Cotton Mather, wrote poetry; in 1619 he became steward to the fourth Earl of Lincoln, managing his estate at Sempringham. B. had five siblings: Samuel, Patience, Dorothy, Sarah, who also became a poet, and Mercy, who became a minister. B. received an excellent education from her mother and father, who taught her classical languages and natural science. She had free access to the extensive libraries at Sempringham and may have been taught by the tutors to the earl's children. Her intellectual and moral education were completed by the Puritan elite around her who valued reading, conversation, and serious investigation of religious and moral questions. Her reading included Sidney, Spenser, Milton, Bacon, Shakespeare, du Bartas, and the Geneva Bible.

After recovering from a case of smallpox at age sixteen, B. married the Cambridge-educated Simon Bradstreet, who had assisted her father with the management of Sempringham. Increasingly, King Charles I and the Church of England imposed painful contractions of religious and civil rights against Puritans and other nonconformists. In 1630, the Bradstreets and Dudleys, like many Puritans, fled persecution by establishing, through the Massachusetts Bay Company, settlements in the New World on their own terms.

After three months' passage marked by seasickness, scurvy, and other hardships, the company arrived to find the numbers and quality of life of earlier settlers ravaged by the harshness of frontier life. Although B.'s "heart rose" in protest against the grimness of the New World, she vowed to submit herself to God's will and the tests before her. The Dudleys and Bradstreets overcame these beginnings to become prosperous leaders of the Colony. Both Simon Bradstreet and Thomas Dudley prospered financially and eventually served as colonial governors; B.'s son Simon married a daughter of Governor Winthrop. The Dudleys and Bradstreets relocated several times, finally settling in Andover in 1645. Between 1633 and 1652, B. gave birth to eight children.

B.'s works, consistent with the genteel tradition of publication, were circulated in manuscript among family and friends. John Woodbridge, her brother-in-law, took a copy of her manuscript to England, where it was published in 1650, without B.'s name and possibly without her knowledge, as *The Tenth Muse, Lately Sprung Up In America.* The volume, listed in the 1658 *Catalogue of the Most Vendible Books in England,* was praised for its accomplished poetic form and intelligent handling of history, politics, and religion. Gratified by the public response to her work, B revised, corrected, and expanded the volume, which was published posthumously in 1678.

The first edition of *The Tenth Muse* reflects B.'s erudition, including an intimate knowledge of Renaissance English literature and Sylvestre's translation of the French Calvinist poet du Bartas; classical mythology; ancient history; and theories of the humors. Four long poems—"The Four Elements," "Of the Four Humours of Man," Of the Four Ages of Man," and "The Four Seasons"—follow commendatory material by others and her own dedication to her father and the prologue. The long poems, known as the quaternions, are followed by several shorter poems; most verse is in heroic couplets. In the "Dialogue between Old England and New" (1642), Mother England recounts, at the urging of her compassionate daughter, New England, the pain inflicted upon the mother's body by years of religious and political strife, intensified by bloody warfare in the Civil Wars and intrigues by the pope to restore idolatrous Roman Catholicism to England. "An Elegy upon Sir Philip Sidney" moves from her praise of the courtier's genius to her own desire for poetic achievement, cleverly manifest by Muses who drive her from Parnassus in "high disdain" at her impertinence. The ironic prologue contains the complaint of centuries of female artists that domesticity, manifest in the sewing needle, is valued over intellectual accomplishments that may masculinize and empower women: "I am obnoxious to each carping tongue / Who says my hand a needle better fits. . . . [I]f what I do prove well, it won't advance, / They'll say it's stoln, or else it was by chance." "In Honour of that High and Mighty Princess Queen Elizabeth of Happy Memory" (1643), however, presents a model of assertive womanhood: the wise, intelligent, politically shrewd, and bold monarch who "has wip'd off th'aspersion of her Sex."

The second edition of *The Tenth Muse,* with B.'s revisions and previously unpublished poems, was published posthumously as *Several Poems Compiled with Great Variety of Wit and Learning, Full of Delight* (1678). The added poems are grounded in realities of everyday life—childbirth, an absent husband, deceased parents, or illness—that become, in evocative and lyrical language, important reflections upon the nature of human existence and the tensions between the desire for earthly happiness and one's obligation to submit to the will of God, in fact or as interpreted by male religious authorities. The love poems to her husband, whose administrative and ecclesiastical obligations frequently took him away from home, sometimes at great length, reveal a companionate, affectionate, and passionate marriage. In "A Letter to Her Husband, Absent upon Public Employment," for example, B. compares herself with a female deer darting through the woods in search of her mate and a sad turtledove who mournfully coos for "her love and loving mate." She concludes the poem: "Let's still remain but one, till death divide, / Thy loving love and dearest dear, / At home, abroad, and everywhere." B.'s poem, with its powerful presence of desire, confirms Puritan suspicions that, although devoted marriages were proof of piety, earthly passion could eclipse the love for God that should transcend all. In the elegies for two of her grandchildren, Elizabeth and Simon, B. struggles between the attachment to the deceased children and her acceptance of God's will in taking them.

In 1867, John Harvard Ellis published B.'s complete works, adding her "Religious Experiences and Occasional Pieces" and "Meditations Divine and Morall" that she had entrusted to her son Simon in 1664. These later works depict the spiritual pilgrimage of a girl and then woman whose "straying soul" was, she felt, "too much in love with the world." Periodically, God chastened her love of this world and her temptation to atheism through lingering illnesses, loss of loved ones, the fire in which her goods and many of her manuscripts were destroyed, and other calamities. These trials, B argued in the Puritan tradition, were for her "spiritual advantage" and she should bear them, "not only willingly but joyfully" so she could return to the path of suffering that might, by God's grace, allow her access to eternal life. B., the "weary pilgrim" of her 31 August 1669 poem, bid farewell to the pains and sorrows three years later. Her literary work has secured her reputation as a compelling writer and an important female voice in the predominantly male Puritan tradition.

WORKS AND EDITIONS: *The Tenth Muse, Lately Sprung Up in America* (1650). Revised and enlarged as *Several Poems Compiled with Great Variety of Wit and Learning, Full of Delight* (1678). *The Works of Anne Dudley Bradstreet in Prose and Verse* (1867). *The Tenth Muse (1650) and, From the Manuscripts, Meditations Divine and Morall Together with Letters and Occasional Pieces by Anne Dudley Bradstreet* (rpt. 1965). *The Complete Works of Anne Dudley Bradstreet* (1981).

BIBLIOGRAPHY: Aldridge, A. *Proceedings of the Xth Congress of the International Comparative Literature Association* (1982). Arenal, E. *Reinventing the Americas* (1986). Boschman, R. *JAmS* (1992). Bush, S. *Wisconsin Academy Review* (1991–92). Caldwell, P. *Prospects* (1988). Campbell, H. *Anne Bradstreet and Her Time* (1891). *Critical Essays on Anne Bradstreet,* ed. P. Cowell and A. Stanford (1983). Craig, R. *SPAS* (1990). Derounian Stodala, K. *SPAS* (1990). Dolle, R. *Anne Bradstreet: A Reference Guide* (1990). Doriani, B. *Early American Literature* (1989). Dorsey, P. *Anne Bradstreet: Autobiography Studies* (1993). Dunham, M. *Anne Bradstreet: Young Puritan Poet* (1969). Eberwein, J. *EAL* (1973, 1981 and 1991). Hammond, J. *Sinful Self, Saintly Self: The Puritan Experience of Poetry* (1993). Hammond, J. *R&L* (1985). Hardy, B. *English* (1991). Hesford, W. *ELWIU* (1987). Hughes, W. *Engendering Men: The Question of Male Feminist Criticism* (1990). Kopacz, P. *EAL* (1988). Laughlin, R. *AL* (1970). Lerner, L. *BJA* (1992). Margerum, E. *EAL* (1982). Maragou, H. *EAL* (1988). Martin, W. *Shakespeare's Sisters* (1979). Martin, W. *An American Triptych: Anne Bradstreet, Emily Dickinson, and Adrienne Rich* (1984). McCay, M. *Dutch Quarterly Review* (1981). Nicolay, T. *Gender Roles, Literary Authority and Three American Women Writers: Anne Dudley Bradstreet, Mercy Otis Warren, Margaret Fuller Ossoli* (1995). Piercy, J. *Anne Bradstreet* (1965). Requa, K. *EAL* (1974). Richardson, R. *TSLL* (1967). Rosenfeld, A. *NEQ* (1970). Rosenmeier, R. *Puritan Poets and Poetics* (1985). Rosenmeier, R. *Anne Bradstreet Revisited* (1991). Salska, A. *EAL* (1984). Saltman, H., in *Critical Essays on Anne Bradstreet,* ed. P. Cowell and A. Stanford (1983). Sargent, R. *A Salzburg Miscellany* (1984). Schofer, Y. *Wisconsin Academy Review* (1991–92). Schweitzer, I. *EAL* (1988). Stanford, A. *NEQ* (1966). Stanford, A. *Anne Bradstreet: The Worldly Puritan* (1974). Stanford, A., in *Critical Essays on Anne Bradstreet,* ed. P. Cowell and A. Stanford (1983). Sweet, T. *EAL* (1988). Walker, C., in *Critical Essays on Anne Bradstreet,* ed. P. Cowell and A. Stanford (1983). Wharton, D., in *Critical Essays on Anne Bradstreet,* ed. P. Cowell and A. Stanford (1983). White, E. W.

Anne Bradstreet: The 'Tenth Musei' (1971). Yoshida, M. *SALit* (1983).

For articles in reference works, see: *AWW. Bloomsbury. Cambridge. Feminist. Oxford.*

Carol Shiner Wilson

Bramble, Tabitha: See *Robinson, Mary Darby (Perdita)*

Anna Eliza (Kempe) Bray

BORN: 25 December 1790, Newington, Surrey.
DIED: 21 January 1883, London.
DAUGHTER OF: John Kempe and Ann Arrow.
MARRIED: Charles Alfred Stothard, 1818; the Reverend Edward Atkyns Bray, c. 1823.

B. was a prolific, diversified writer; she published historical romances, children's tales, folklore, biographies, and travel accounts. As a child she had a fondness for art, and an early drawing, "Madonna and Child," served as the means for meeting the artist Thomas Stothard. Later, she planned to be an actress and was scheduled to appear at the Bath Theatre on 27 May 1815, but, becoming ill, she did not perform; circumstances did not provide another opportunity in the theater.

At the age of twenty-eight she married the artist Charles Alfred Stothard (son of Thomas), who devoted his talents to illustrating the sculptured monuments of England. After a journey to France with her husband, she published her first work, *Letters Written during a Tour through Normandy, Britanny and Other Parts of France*, in 1818. After her husband was killed on 28 May 1821, while making drawings of a stained-glass window for his book *The Monumental Effigies of Great Britain*, she decided, with the aid of her brother, Alfred John Kempe, to complete her husband's work. She published the work and a memoir to her late husband as well in 1823. This same early period of B.'s life provided information for a book about her father-in-law, *The Life of Thomas Stothard; with Personal Reminiscences* (1851).

A year or two after Stothard's death, B. married the Reverend Edward Atkyns Bray, vicar of Tavistock. During the following fifty years, she published more than a dozen novels. With the publication of one of them, *The Talba, or the Moor of Portugal*, she became acquainted with Robert Southey, whom she idolized throughout her life. Some of B.'s many novels dealt with foreign life, but the most popular ones were based on the history of the principal families of the counties of Devon and Cornwall. These writings were issued as a ten-volume set by Longmans in 1845–46 and reprinted in 1884 (twelve volumes) by Chapman and Hall, indisputable testimony to B.'s success as a writer.

After the death of her second husband, B. moved to London, where she edited some of his poetry and sermons before returning to her own original writing, focusing most of her efforts on historical subjects. B.'s final years were embittered by a report that she had stolen a piece of tapestry at Bayeaux in 1816. Ultimately, however, evidence on the subject presented through correspondence and articles in the *Times* cleared her name. B. died at the age of ninety-three.

B.'s most notable work is *The Borders of the Tamar and Tavy*. It is a series of letters written to Robert Southey on the legends and superstitions relating to the rivers Tamar and Tavy in the geographical area of Tavistock. Southey suggested the plan of the work, which contains anecdotes about the common people, describing their traditions and beliefs.

During her lifetime, B. was renowned as a writer of historical novels, contemporary critics citing her great powers of description, her ability to depict simple rural life and grandiose baronial halls as well as men and women of all classes. She was also highly commended for her ability to inspire moral purity indirectly through her novels, which could be recommended to sons and daughters with fullest confidence for entertainment and instruction in knowledge, men, and manners. Compared favorably with William Shakespeare in her ability to present human experience and emotions and with Daniel Defoe in her delineations of nature, she was also sometimes called "the female Walter Scott."

B. was an accomplished, versatile, and kindly woman; she was proud of her literary efforts. Her *Life of Thomas Stothard* remains a beautiful book, recording the artistry of Thomas Stothard through prints of his principal works and personal reminiscences of his life and art. A travel book, *The Mountains and Lakes of Switzerland* (1841), was apparently recognized as valuable at the time of publication when the country was not fully explored. Less significant are three books of French History: *The Good St. Louis and His Times* (1870), *The Revolt of the Protestants of the Cevennes* (1870), and *Joan of Arc* (1874), which suffer for lack of scholarly research.

WORKS: *Letters Written during a Tour through Normandy, Brittany and Other Parts of France* (1818). *Memoirs, Including Original Journals, Letters, Papers and Antiquarian Tracts of the Late C. A. Stothard; and Some Account of a Journey in the Netherlands* (1823). *Trials of Domestic Life,* (1823, 1848). *De Foix, or Sketches of the Manners and Customs of the Fourteenth Century* (1826). *The White Hoods* (1828). *The Protestant: A Tale of the Reign of Queen Mary,* (1828, 1833). *Fitz of Fitz-ford: A Legend of Devon,* (1830). *The Talba,* or *Moor of Portugal,* (1830). *Warleigh, or The Fatal Oak: A Legend of Devon,* (1834). *A Description of the Part of Devonshire Bordering on the Tamar and the Tavy in a Series of Letters to Robert Southey, Esq.*, (1836, 1838; as *Traditions, Legends, Superstitions and Sketches of Devonshire,* 1879; also as *The Borders of the Tamar and the Tavy*). *Trelawney of Trelawne,* or *The Prophecy: A Legend of Cornwall* (1837, 1845). *Trials of the Heart* (1839). *The Mountains and Lakes of Switzerland; with Descriptive Sketches of Other Parts of the Continent* (1841). *Henry de Pomeroy,* or *The Eve of St. John: A Legend of Cornwall and Devon* (1842, with *The White Rose: A Domestic Tale,* 1846). *Courtenay of Walreddon: A Romance of the West* (1844). *The Father's Curse and the Daughter's Sacri-*

fice: Two Tales (1848). *The Life of Thomas Stothard; with Personal Reminiscences* (1851). *A Peep at the Pixies: or Legends of the West* (1854). *Handel: His Life, Personal and Professional, with Thoughts on Sacred Music* (1857). *The Good St. Louis and His Times* (1870). *The Revolt of the Protestants of the Cevennes; with Some Account of the Huguenots in the Seventeenth Century* (1870). *Hartland Forest: A Legend of North Devon* (1871). *Roseteague: or The Heir of Treville Crewse* (1874). *Joan of Arc and the Times of Charles VII, King of France* (1874). *Silver Linings: or Light and Shade* (1880). *Autobiography of Anna Eliza Bray, to 1843* (1884).

BIBLIOGRAPHY: Boas, G. C. *Library Chronicle* (1884). Hamer, L. *FolkH* (1993). Maclean, J. *Parochial and Family History of the Deanery of Trigg Minor in the County of Cornwall* (1873). Southey. R. *Life and Correspondence* (1849–50). *Spectator* (1884).

For articles in reference works, see: *Bloomsbury. CBEL. Chambers. DNB. Feminist. NCBEL. Stanford. Warner.*

Phyllis J. Scherle

Angela Brazil

BORN: 30 November, 1869, Preston, Lancashire.
DIED: 13 March 1947, Helensburgh, Scotland.
DAUGHTER OF: Clarence Brazil and Angelica McKinnel.

B., who liked to pronounce her name in order to rhyme with "dazzle," was an author who would be mimicked by countless other writers in the early twentieth century who wanted to copy B.'s tremendous success as a popular novelist. Although her writing career did not begin until she was in her mid thirties when she wrote her first novel, *A Terrible Tomboy* (1904), B. made up for her late start by developing into a prolific writer, who typically churned out a few serial novels in a single year. The bulk of those books were schoolgirl novels, the formulaic works that were going to make B. famous. In forty-nine schoolgirl novels, Brazil honed her style, which was notable for its reliance on slang—a fact that caused her books to be condemned by some educators and to be loved by schoolgirls in many countries who read her translated work in Dutch, French, Polish, and German.

B.'s novels share many similarities; sometimes a later book will even recycle the plot or plot elements from a earlier novel. Her books focus on the pranks of a group of high-spirited young girls who live at a boarding school. Parents, conveniently, are rarely to be found in B.'s novels, making it possible for the girls to avoid interference. The girls, who have names like Lilias, Bulcie, Gowan, and Bertha, go to schools called Chilcombe Hall or the Turrets. In these imaginary locales, the girls experience a boarding-school life that anyone would envy. Schoolwork is rarely seen, but the novels are filled with sports, such as cricket and hockey, that the girls pursue avidly. A minor mystery or secret is added in order to add intrigue. And, of course, there is the slang: "Bosh!" "It's rather cheek," "I have to square Aunt Jessie." Although one might wonder whether any real schoolgirl ever talked this way, B. always insisted that she simply copied the slang of the schoolgirls she encountered.

One of the most important reasons for the tremendous success of B.'s books was their heroines—spunky, athletic girls who any reader might wish to emulate. Along with their athletic prowess, B.'s heroines are also able to get away with an amazing number of pranks directed at adults or fellow students. Through such activities, B.'s heroines show their rebellious side but do not challenge the status quo too greatly since they are "good girls" at heart who never cause any serious harm.

Typical of B.'s books is *The Madcap of the School* (1917), which is widely regarded as one of her better works. As do most of the author's works, the novel takes place in a boarding school, Marlowe Grange School, where the girls form a tight-knit community. Within the confines of the school, the girls learn, chiefly through interaction with one another, how to be better individuals and, even more importantly, how to be better members of the larger society. The all-female school community allows B.'s girls a degree of freedom that they never would have experienced in the world outside the school. Like most of B.'s books, *The Madcap of the School* follows a group of girls, "the Mystic Seven," through the adventures and mishaps that make up a single school term, adding a healthy dose of athletic games, midnight feasts, and other assorted hijinks to the book's excitement. These girls have a number of adventures, including capturing German spies, but most of their experiences are mild ones: going on a camping expedition or playing a prank on a classmate. B.'s books allowed their girl heroines freedom from gender stereotypes, which was one reason for the tremendous popularity of her formulaic stories. Girl readers could also be assured that one of B.'s novels would spirit them far away from their more mundane reality.

The endless schoolgirl heroines B. created in *The Madcap of the School* and her many other novels reflected her own personal interest in schoolgirl life. She herself always wished to remain a schoolgirl at heart. Whether she was writing novels, giving tea parties for young girls, or attending the sporting games of her young girl friends, B. insisted upon acting like a schoolgirl. Her novels perhaps fulfilled her fantasies about what school days should be like for girls; certainly in her years at Manchester High School and Ellerslie College B. had a less exciting career than the careers of her fictional schoolgirl heroines. Throughout her entire life, B. was never to abandon her fascination with the schoolgirl story, and, although her works became increasingly formulaic after 1935, she continued to write books until shortly before her death.

WORKS: *The Mischievous Brownie* (1899). *The Fairy Gifts* (1901). *Four Recitations* (1903). *The Enchanted Fiddle* (1903). *The Wishing Princess* (1904). *A Terrible Tomboy* (1904). *The Fortunes of Philippa* (1906). *The Third Class at Miss Kaye's* (1908). *Bosom Friends: A Seaside Story* (1909). *The Manor House School* (1910). *The Nicest Girl in the School* (1911). *A Fourth Form Friendship* (1911). *The New Girl at St. Chad's* (1911). *A Pair of Schoolgirls* (1912). *The Leader of the Lower*

School (1913). *The Youngest Girl in the Fifth* (1914). *The Girls of St. Cyprian's* (1914). *The School By the Sea* (1914). *The Jolliest Term on Record* (1915). *For the Sake of the School* (1915). *The Luckiest Girl in the School* (1916). *The Madcap of the School* (1917). *The Slap-Bang Boys* (1917). *A Patriotic Schoolgirl* (1918). *For the School Colours* (1918). *A Harum-Scarum Schoolgirl* (1919). *The Head Girl at the Gables* (1919). *Two Little Scamps and a Puppy* (1919). *A Gift from the Sea* (1920). *Loyal to the School* (1920). *A Popular Schoolgirl* (1920). *The Princess of the School* (1920). *Monitress Merle* (1922). *A Fortunate Term* (1923). *The School in the South* (1923). *The Khaki Boys and Other Stories* (1923). *Schoolgirl Kitty* (1923). *Captain Peggie* (1924). *My Own Schooldays* (1925). *Joan's Best Chum* (1927). *Queen of the Dormitory and Other Stories* (1926). *Ruth of St. Ronan's* (1927). *At School with Rachel* (1928). *St. Catherine's College* (1929). *The Little Green School* (1931). *Nesta's New School* (1932). *Jean's Golden Term* (1934). *The School at The Turrets.* (1935). *An Exciting Term* (1936). *Jill's Jolliest School* (1937). *The School on the Cliff* (1938). *The School on the Moor* (1938). *The New School at Scawdale* (1940). *Five Jolly Schoolgirls* (1941). *The Mystery of the Moated Grange* (1942). *The Secret of the Border Castle* (1943). *The School in the Forest* (1944). *Three Terms at Uplands* (1945). *The School on the Loch* (1946).

BIBLIOGRAPHY: Freeman, G. *The Schoolgirl Ethic: The Life and Work of Angela Brazil* (1976).

For articles in reference works, see: *CA. Cambridge. Feminist. Oxford. TCCW. ToddBWW.*

Sherrie A. Inness

Bridge, Ann: See *O'Malley, Mary Dolling (Sanders)*

Mary Golding Bright

BORN: 14 December 1857, Melbourne, Australia.
DIED: 12 August 1945, Ifield Park, Crawley, Sussex.
DAUGHTER OF: Captain John J. Dunne and Isabel George Bynon.
MARRIED: H.H.W. Melville, 1888 (the marriage was illegal); Egerton Clairmonte, 1891; Reginald Golding Bright, 1901.
WROTE UNDER: Mary Golding Bright; Mary Chavelita Dunne; George Egerton.

Writing under the name "George Egerton," B. is best remembered for a series of short stories she wrote in the 1890s, the theme of which is the difficulty in maintaining loving relationships between the sexes. Her style and substance shocked Victorian sensibilities; her technique and theme foreshadow twentieth-century concerns, and she is seen as a pioneering figure in both the refinement of the British short story and in her portrayal of female characters.

Born the daughter of an Australian sea captain, she was educated privately. She wanted to be an artist, before turning her attention to writing. In 1888, she eloped with her father's friend, H.H.W. Melville, a bigamist. They traveled widely together, but within two years he died, leaving her stranded in Norway. It is at this time that she had an affair with novelist Knut Hamsun. In 1891, she married Egerton Clairmonte, a penniless writer, and she turned to writing initially to support them both.

Keynotes (1893), her first work, was dedicated to Hamsun, and it created an immediate sensation; *Punch* parodied the work as "She-Notes." The first story, "A Cross-Line," is a keynote to the volume and all her work. She is interested in exploring "the eternal wildness, the untamed primitive savage temperament that lurks in the mildest, best women." For B., "the keynote of women's witchcraft and women's strength . . . may be concealed but is never eradicated by culture." The six stories are a study of female sexuality, much of which is autobiographical; the story "Now Spring Has Come" has its genesis in her relationship with Hamsun, and "Under Northern Sky" draws on her relationship with Melville in Norway. Although much of her fiction is personal and autobiographical, critics have noted that it does reflect the historical direction in which English fiction was moving and the literary climate of the 1890s. Her work is usually discussed in the context of the "New Woman" of the 1890s and influenced Thomas Hardy in his writing of *Jude the Obscure.*

Her second book of short stories, *Discords* (1894), continued similar themes. The story "Wedlock" offers a sympathetic portrait of female alcoholism. The story "Virgin Soil" protests the naïveté with which women approach marriage. In "Gone Under," she celebrates a more traditional role for women: motherhood. She writes that "the only divine fiber in a woman is her maternal instinct. Every good quality she has is consequent or coexistent with that. Suppress it, and it turns to a fibroid, sapping all that is helpful and good in her nature." In "Regeneration of Two," which closes the volume, however, she offers a more radical vision: "a colony of women managed by a woman, going their own way in the world in the face of opinion . . . this is the silver key to a golden casket." In general, her stories never become didactic and her characters are not mere mouthpieces for her ideas; instead, her characters and stories are introspective and psychologically astute.

Her realism was learned from her knowledge of Scandinavian literature; she had already begun work on translating Hamsun's *Hunger* before writing *Keynotes,* and she had read Ibsen, Strindberg, and other Scandinavian writers. Critics agree that from them she learned how to depict moments of private thought. Critics also agree that the originality of her technique is that she provides few details about a character's past; her style is stark. Her stories are often made up of distinct episodes with no direct links. Many of her stories were rapidly written; she described her style as "straight off." She sees characters and relationships in a constant state of transitions and flux; she does not provide a sense of permanence or closure, a staple of Victorian fiction.

Her fame rests on her first two collection of stories, which have been reprinted by Virago. Two subsequent collections, *Symphonies* (1897) and *Fantasias* (1898), are deemed less successful because she experimented with allegory and symbolism, whereas her talent was for psychological realism. With *The Wheel of God* (1898), B. began to use the novel form, yet her talent was for the shorter form; critics have seen this novel as three related stories concerning a young woman at three stages of her life: a young idealistic woman, a disillusioned woman who has her ideals shattered through two marriages, and a middle-aged woman dedicating herself to the lives of other women. She concludes: "The men we women today need, or who need us, are not of our time—it lies in the mothers to rear them for the women who follow us."

In 1901, P. and Clairmonte divorced and he soon died, leaving her widowed again. She then married Reginald Golding Bright, a theater critic (and subsequently a theatrical agent) fifteen years her junior. He persuaded her to shift her attention from fiction to drama and acted as her literary agent. Her theatrical activity brought her into the center of London's theater circle, and she numbered James Barrie, Somerset Maugham, Ellen Terry, and George Bernard Shaw among her acquaintances. She had no natural talent for the theater, however. Shaw felt that she lacked the ability to write dramatic dialogue, to recognize talent, or to take into consideration the practical aspects of theater productions; for her part, she felt that Shaw had ruined the drama in English and was "the most sterilizing influence on the theatre . . . in fifty years." Her knowledge of several languages and dialects served her well as she undertook a series of translations in her later life, outliving her much younger husband. In addition, she was interested in genealogy and was a founding member of the Irish Genealogical Research Society.

WORKS: *Keynotes* (1893). *Discords* (1894). *Young Olaf's Ditties* (1895). *The Africander: A Plain Tale of Colonial Life* (1896). *Symphonies* (1897). *Fantasias* (1898). *The Wheel of God* (1898). *Rosa Amorosa: The Love Letters of a Woman* (1901). *Flies in Amber* (1905). *His Wife's Family* (1908). *The Backsliders* (1910). (trans.) *La Rafale,* by H. Bernstein (1911). (trans.) *Daughter of Heaven* by P. Loti and J. Gautier (1912). (trans.) *The Attack* by H. Bernstein (1912). (trans.) *Wild Thyme* by R. deFlers and A. de Caillaret (1914). *Camilla States Her Case* (1925). (trans.) *Hunger,* by K. Hamsun (1926).

BIBLIOGRAPHY: Ardis, A. *New Women, New Novels* (1990). Cunningham, G. *The New Woman and the Victorian Novel* (1978). *A Leaf from the Yellow Book: The Correspondence of George Egerton,* ed. T. DeVere (1958). Dowling, L. *NCF* (1979). Fernando, L. *"New Women" in the Late Victorian Novel* (1977). Harris. W. V. *PMLA* (1968). Harris, W. V. *VN* (1968). *Transforming Genres,* ed. N. L. Manos and M. Rochelson (1994). Miller, J. E. *Rebel Women: Feminism, Modernism, and the Edwardian Novel* (1994). Showalter, E. *A Literature of Their Own* (1977). Showalter, E. *Sexual Anarchy* (1990). *Daughters of Decadence: Women Writers of the Fin de Siècle,* ed. E. Showalter (1993). Stoikes, J. *In the Nineties* (1989). Stott, R. *The Fabrication of the Late-Victorian Femme Fatale* (1992).

For articles in reference works, see: *Bloomsbury. Europa. Feminist. Oxford. ToddBWA. VB. Who Was Who.*

Other references: *Toward a Feminist Tradition,* ed. D. Daims and J. Grimes (1992). *TLS* (31 October 1958, 6 June 1995).

Tony Giffone

Vera Brittain

BORN: 29 December 1893, Newcastle-under-Lyme, Staffordshire.

DIED: 29 March 1970, London.

DAUGHTER OF: Thomas Arthur Brittain and Edith Mary Bervon Brittain.

MARRIED: George E. G. Catlin, 1925.

An ardent pacifist and feminist, B. wrote more than twenty-five books, which range from poetry to history and which discuss women's contribution to politics around the world. B. said that she wrote both of her famous autobiographies—*Testament of Youth* (1933) and *Testament of Experience* (1957)—to work through personal pain and to interpret history in terms of personal events. Her haunting and relentless spiritual self-evaluation has been compared to one of her major influences, the nonconformist John Bunyan, especially his *Grace Abounding to the Chief of Sinners* (1666).

The only daughter of a leisured provincial family, B. claimed that her life was molded by feminism and by her experience of World War I. While attending St. Monica's boarding school, B. read Olive Schreiner's *Woman and Labour* (1911), which made her a feminist, and convinced her reluctant parents to let her go up to Somerville College, Oxford, in 1914. After a year at Oxford, she became a Voluntary Aid Detachment nurse and went abroad to help the British effort in World War I. In *Testament of Youth,* B. describes the personal and sexual liberation involved in caring for wounded soldiers and prisoners of war. She says that she became a pacifist when she realized the absurdity of struggling to save the same soldiers her brother and his friends were trying to kill farther north. Through the deaths of her brother, her fiancé, and her closest friends, B. came to realize the way an entire society, particularly women, bears the emotional shock of war.

Returning from abroad, B. and other women who had served the war effort fought to gain degree status for women students at Oxford. B. also helped to edit a volume of *Oxford Poetry* (1920) that launched the careers of many students who would become prominent writers, including Robert Graves and Winifred Holtby. B. met Holtby in 1920 and they remained close friends, encouraging one another's political and creative writings, until Holtby's death in 1935. Using Elizabeth Gaskell's biography of Charlotte Brontë as its model, *Testament of Friendship* (1940) discusses the relationship between Holtby's family background and her writings, particularly the constant struggle faced by a woman who believes in numerous causes but who also requires time alone in order to write well. This struggle was B.'s as well.

After graduating from Oxford, B. settled in London with Holtby and committed her career to social and political change. She became a lecturer for the League of Nations Union in 1922, giving as many as four speeches a week, while contributing regularly to the *Manchester Guardian*, the *Nation*, and the feminist journal *Time and Tide* and completing her first published novel, *The Dark Tide* (1923).

While B.'s novels are more traditional in structure and tone than those of "modern" writers like Virginia Woolf and May Sinclair, the smooth nap of B.'s prose consistently explores those themes we have come to call feminist. From the frank discussion of women students and teachers at Oxford in *The Dark Tide* to the attempted rape in *Born 1925* (1948), B. builds her novels around the vastly different constraints and expectations that shape men's and women's lives. As with her friend Radclyffe Hall's *Well of Loneliness* (1928), B.'s *Honourable Estate* (1936) shows both the power of male and female homoerotic relationships and the ways in which those relationships are crippled by socially imposed distance and silence. *Honourable Estate*'s exposure of the need for more open attitudes toward homosexuality and abortion, as well as its portrayal of both old- and new-style marriages, are part of B.'s lifelong plea for the removal of double standards of sexual morality.

Between the wars, B.'s political energies were focused on feminist concerns. In the 1920s she was closely aligned with Lady Margaret Rhondda and the women writers who centered around *Time and Tide* and the *Six Point Group*. The group's goals—vast changes in human attitudes, a new concept of marriage, women's advancement to political and economic equality, improved social services for women, radical changes in sexual morality, and a new understanding of women's potential—formed the basis of her theoretical writing in *Women's Work in Modern England* (1928), *Halcyon* (1929), and *Lady into Woman* (1953). *Women's Work* encourages women to pursue their own careers as it exposes the legal obstacles that have prevented them from doing so in the past. B. was perhaps most original in *Halcyon*'s ideal of "semi-detached" marriage, a call for women's freedom to travel and to development of both emotional equality and independent careers. *Lady into Woman* brings feminist achievements from around the world to bear on the specific political situation of contemporary English women. During World War II, B. became vice-president of the Women's International League for Peace and Freedom, and she campaigned for improved Anglo-Indian relations.

Testament of Experience (1957) traces B.'s commitment to pacifism through the Peace Pledge Union and World War II. On behalf of world peace, B. wrote numerous pamphlets and contributed to hundreds of periodicals internationally. *Seed of Chaos, or What Mass Bombing Really Means* (1944) was the most widely known and scathing of these critiques. B.'s unpopular advocacy of peace made her an enemy of both the Home Office and the Gestapo during the war, and it obliterated the sale of her books in the United States. In the novel *Born 1925* (1948) B.'s experience of two wars is spread out among the three major characters.

B.'s marriage to political philosopher George Catlin was much like the ideal she described in *Halcyon* and *Lady into Woman*. She traveled internationally on behalf of peace and feminism and remained devoted to her women friends, particularly Winifred Holtby, who lived with B. for most of her married life. B. had two children, John Edward and Shirley (Williams), who was a Member of Parliament when her mother died in 1970. True to her diverse sympathies, B. was still participating in demonstrations and sit-ins and working on several books, including the final *Testament of Time*, when she died.

WORKS: *Verses of a V.A.D.* (1918). *The Dark Tide* (1923). *Good Citizenship and the League* (1924). *Not Without Honour* (1924). *Women's Work in Modern England* (1928). *Halcyon, or the Future of Monogamy* (1929). *Testament of Youth* (1933). *Poems of the War and After* (1934). *Honourable Estate* (1936). *Thrice a Stranger* (1938). *Testament of Friendship, the Story of Winifred Holtby* (1940). *War-Time Letters to Peace Lovers* (1940). *England's Hour* (1941). *Humiliation with Honour* (1942). *Law Versus War* (1944). *Seed of Chaos,or What Mass Bombing Really Means* (1944; in the U.S. as *Massacre by Bombing*). *Account Rendered* (1945). *Conscription or Cooperation?* (1946). *On Becoming a Writer* (1947; in the U.S. as *On Being an Author,* 1948). *Born 1925: A Novel of Youth* (1948). *Vera Brittain Writes on How Shall the Christian Church Prepare for the New World Order?* (194?). *In the Steps of John Bunyan* (1950; in the U.S. as *Valiant Pilgrim*). *The Story of St. Martin's: An Epic of London* (1951). *Search After Sunrise: A Traveller's Story* (1951). *Lady into Woman: A History of Women from Victoria to Elizabeth II* (1953). *Testament of Experience* (1957). (with G.E.W. Sizer) *Long Shadows* (1958). *The Women at Oxford: A Fragment of History* (1960). *The Pictorial History of St. Martin in-the-Fields* (1962). *Pethick-Lawrence: A Portrait* (1963). *The Rebel Passion: A Short History of Some Pioneer Peace-Makers* (1964). *Envoy Extraordinary: A Study of Vijaya Lakshmi Pandit and Her Contribution to Modern India* (1965). *Radclyffe Hall: A Case of Obscenity?* (1968). *Chronicle of Youth,* ed. A. Bishop (1981).

BIBLIOGRAPHY: Bailey, H. *Vera Brittain* (1987). Bennett, Y. A. *Atlantic* (1987). Berry, P., intro. to *Testament of Experience* (1979). Berry, P. and M. Bostridge *Vera Brittain: A Life* (1995). Bishop, A., in *Olive Schreiner and After,* ed. M. V. W. Smith and D. Maclenna (1983). *Selected Letters of Winifred Holtby and Vera Brittain (1920–1935),* ed. V. Brittain and G. Handley-Taylor (1960). Carlin, J. *Family Quartet: Vera Brittain and Her Family* (1987). Gorham, D. *Vera Brittain: A Feminist Life* (1996). Kennard, J. E. *Vera Brittain and Winifred Holtby: A Working Friendship* (1989). Layton, L., in *Behind the Lines: Gender and the Two World Wars,* ed. M. R. Higgonet, et al. (1987). Leonardi, S. J. *LIT* (1990). *McMaster University Library Research News* (November 1977 and December 1978). Mellown, M. *TSWL* (1983). Mellown, M. *Frontiers* (1985). Pickering, J. *WS* (1986). Shaw, M., in *The Representation of the Self in Women's Autobiography,* ed. V. Fortunati and G. Morisco (1993). *Feminist Theorists,* ed. D. Spender (1983).

For articles in reference works, see: *Biography and*

Genealogy Master Index. *CA*. *CLC*. *Longman*. *TCA* and *SUP*. *TCW*.

Other references: Adams, P. *Somerville for Women: An Oxford College 1879–1993* (1996). *Contemporary Statesman* (6 February 1960). *New Republic* (7 October 1957). *NYTBR* (2 March 1952). *SP* (24 August 1957).

Carol L. Barash

Anne Brontë

BORN: 17 January 1820, Thornton, Yorkshire.
DIED: 28 May 1849, Scarborough, Yorkshire.
DAUGHTER OF: Patrick Brontë and Maria Branwell Brontë.
WROTE UNDER: Acton Bell; Anne Brontë.

The youngest of the famous Brontë sisters, B. is often regarded as the least talented and therefore overlooked. Whether she deserves this reputation has been the subject of much debate. Her novels, *Agnes Grey: An Autobiography* and *The Tenant of Wildfell Hall*, for which she is best known, demonstrate her eye for detail and talent for storytelling, in addition to an unmistakably Brontëan taste for the unconventional. Although she wrote a great deal of poetry, it has, for the most part, been neglected; there has, however, been some recent interest in B.'s poems following the publication of Chitham's reliable edition in 1979.

B. escaped attending the Clergy Daughters' School at Cowan Bridge with her sisters because of her age. After the deaths of the two elder girls, Maria and Elizabeth, Charlotte and Emily returned home. During much of their childhood the four remaining Brontë children (including their brother Branwell) were allowed to roam and play freely in the Yorkshire moors. Such play encouraged extensive development of their imaginations.

The children created the Glass Town Confederacy—stories of twelve toy soldiers involving conquest, civil war, personal jealousies, loyalties, and loves. In 1831, Charlotte left for Miss Wooler's School at Roe Head, and at this point Emily and B. began chronicling the happenings of their own imaginary kingdom of Gondal, the setting for a series of poems characterized by romantic characters and language. Though Emily continued to be absorbed by this fantasy world, B. apparently lost interest during her late teens and early twenties, contributing Gondal poetry only under Emily's influence.

B. was initially educated at home by Charlotte and then spent two years as a student at Roe Head. In the spring of 1841, she was forced by economic need to find employment as a governess, as was Charlotte. Her experience at Blake Hall was brief and unhappy, and she soon returned home. B. then assumed a position at Thorpe Green, securing a job for her brother as well, but becoming shocked by Branwell's growing obsession with the mistress of the house. Ashamed of Branwell's behavior and in any case mentally exhausted, B. quit her position and returned home. Branwell's subsequent decline into madness is reflected in the writings of all his sisters but particularly in B.'s *The Tenant of Wildfell Hall*. In the course of time, B. would presumably have sought another teaching post, but the Brontë sisters began to explore other options. In 1844, they attempted to start their own school. The endeavor was not successful; they did not receive a single application.

Poems by Currer, Ellis and Acton Bell, a slim volume containing sixty-one poems, was published in May 1846. The Brontës selected male pseudonyms partly to protect themselves from prejudice against women writers and partly to meet Emily's demands for anonymity. Even before all the publication details had been completed, the sisters began working on novels, perhaps inspired by the ease with which their initial dreams of publication had become a reality. Publication did not mean success, however; by mid July only two copies of their poems had been sold, despite several complimentary reviews.

By the end of June 1846, the Brontë sisters had each finished a novel—Charlotte, *The Professor;* Emily, *Wuthering Heights;* and B. *Agnes Grey*—and were trying to locate a publisher who would offer the three novels as a triple decker. In July 1847 Thomas Cautley Newby accepted *Wuthering Heights* and *Agnes Grey* but refused *The Professor*. *Agnes Grey* appeared with *Wuthering Heights* in December 1847.

Newby promised early sheets of *The Tenant of Wildfell Hall* to an American publisher, with the statement that it was his belief that it was by the author of *Jane Eyre*. The resulting publicity caused problems with Charlotte's publishers, who had promised her next novel to a different American publisher. To straighten out the confusion and prove that the novels were the work of two authors, Charlotte and B. traveled to London to visit Messrs. Smith and Elder, Charlotte's publisher. Upon arriving in London the sisters were caught in a severe storm and B. developed a respiratory infection. When they returned home Charlotte and B. were faced with a series of domestic trials. Branwell died of consumption in September 1848. Emily's health then showed symptoms of collapse, but not until shortly before her death in December 1848 would she agree to see a doctor. After Emily's death B., who had never completely recovered from the illness caused by her soaking in London, quickly sickened. Consumption was soon obvious. On 24 May 1849 she left Haworth for Scarborough, dying there four days later. The poem "I hoped that with the brave and strong" was her last composition.

Most critics find B.'s work more conventional, and therefore less interesting, than that of her sisters. Still, more than her sisters, B. sought a realistic approach to fiction without sentimentalizing or romanticizing her characters. Charlotte's Jane Eyre marries far above her station, while B.'s Agnes Grey is allotted a thoroughly respectable though unglamorous clergyman. B. believed that her duty as a writer was to teach rather than entertain or fantasize.

As the last surviving Brontë, Charlotte greatly influenced the literary reputations of her sisters. Unfortunately, her condescending and apologetic attitude toward B.'s literary talent has set a precedent for much subsequent criticism. Critics note that B.'s attempt to portray the tedium of a governess's life in *Agnes Grey* results in many tedious passages. *The Tenant of Wildfell Hall* is often criticized for its weak structure, since the main body of the story is told through the protagonist's diary rather than by the character herself.

More recently, however, B.'s strategy of dual narrative in *The Tenant of Wildfell Hall* has been reappraised. The novel's innovative combination of form and perspective demonstrates B.'s originality; further, the novel's structure and subject suggests a critique of Emily's procedure and principles in *Wuthering Heights,* not to mention a response to Emily and Charlotte's Romanticism. In fact, B.'s independence of thought as artist calls into question Charlotte's picture of "gentle Anne." The vigor with which B. approached her subjects does not substantiate Charlotte's opinion. Of the three Brontë sisters, B. arguably had the greatest experience of the world beyond Haworth and the schoolroom, and her familiarity with some of the pressing social issues of her age is reflected in her novels. Many critics find merit in the presentation of the evils and fallacies of the double standard exercised in child-rearing in *Agnes Grey.* Her approach is similarly forthright in *The Tenant of Wildfell Hall* in which the heroine leaves her husband. These novels, with their feminist overtones, were considered immoral and sensational when originally published but will benefit from further study, particularly study of B.'s critique of Victorian mores.

WORKS: (as Acton Bell) *Poems by Currer, Ellis and Acton Bell* (1846; facsimile ed., 1985). (as Acton Bell) *Agnes Grey: an Autobiography* (1847). (as Acton Bell) *The Tenant of Wildfell Hall* (1848). *The Brontës' Life and Letters* (1908). *The Complete Poems of Anne Brontë* (1920). *The Poems of Anne Brontë: A New Text and Commentary,* ed. E. Chitham (1979).

BIBLIOGRAPHY: Alexander, C. and J. Sellars. *The Art of the Brontës* (1996). Barker, J. *The Brontës: A Life in Letters* (1995). Berry, E. H. *Anne Brontë's Radical Vision: Structures of Consciousness* (1994). Chitham, E. *A Life of Anne Brontë* (1991). Chitham, E. and T. Winnifrith. *Brontë Facts and Brontë Problems* (1983). Craig Bell, A. *The Novels of Anne Brontë: A Study and Reappraisal* (1992). Duthie, E. L. *The Brontës and Nature* (1986). Gordon, F. *A Preface to the Brontës* (1989). Langland, E. *Anne Brontë: The Other One* (1989). Liddell, R. *Twin Spirits: The Novels of Emily and Anne Brontë* (1990). McNees, E. *The Brontë Sisters: Critical Assessments* (1996). *The Brontës: Interviews and Recollections,* ed. H. Orel (1997). Prentis, B. *The Brontë Sisters and George Eliot: A Unity of Difference* (1987). Scott, P.J.M. *Anne Brontë: A New Critical Assessment* (1983). Stoneman, P. *Brontë Transformations* (1996). *The Brontës: Their Lives, Friendships and Correspondence,* ed. T. J. Wise and A. Symington (1932).

For articles in reference works, see: *Biographies of British Women* (1993). *Bloomsbury. Europa. Feminist. IDWB. Oxford. Stanford. ToddBWW. VB.*

Other references: Adlard, J. *N&Q* (1988). Berg, M. M. *VN* (1987). Davies, S. *CQ* (1985). Hirota, M. *SELL* (1988). Jackson, A. M. *ES* (1982). Jacobs, N. M. *JNT* (1986). Kostka, E. A. *Connecticut Review* (1992). Langland, E., in *Gender and Discourse in Victorian Literature and Art,* ed. A. H. Harrison and B. Taylor (1992). McGregor, C. *Dionysos* (1992). McMaster, J. *MLQ* (1982). Poole, R. *SEL* (1993). Shires, L. M., in *Rewriting the Victorians,* ed. L. M. Shires (1992). Thormahlen, M. *MLR* (1993). Villacanas-Paloma, B. *RAEI* (1993).

Lynn M. Alexander
(updated by LuAnn McCracken Fletcher)

Charlotte Brontë

BORN: 21 April 1816, Thornton, Yorkshire.
DIED: 31 March 1855, Haworth, Yorkshire.
DAUGHTER OF: Patrick Brontë and Maria Branwell Brontë.
MARRIED: Arthur Bell Nicholls, 1854.
WROTE UNDER: Currer Bell; Charlotte Brontë.

B. is recognized by literary historians for her contributions to the development of the novel. Her fame and influence rests on four novels and contributions to a single volume of poetry. Although much of her reputation is based upon the immediate success of *Jane Eyre* (1847) and the romantic appeal of her personal history, especially as presented by Elizabeth Gaskell (whose biography of B. is preeminent in its genre), B.'s real contribution was in the fictional exploration of emotional repression and of the female psyche. B.'s work introduced new depth and intensity to character development and the portrayal of emotion in fiction.

In 1824, her father, a Church of England clergyman, sent his two eldest daughters, Maria and Elizabeth, to the Clergy Daughters' School at Cowan Bridge, and in August of the following year he sent B. to join them. According to Brontë, "typhus fever decimated the school periodically, and consumption and scrofula in every variety of form, [which] bad air and water, and bad insufficient diet can generate, preyed on the ill-fated pupils." Both of B.'s sisters fell victim to consumption and returned home to die. B. was particularly close to Maria and later eulogized her in the portrait of Helen Burns in *Jane Eyre.*

After the deaths of his two eldest daughters, Mr. Brontë decided to educate his children at home. The children read Shakespeare, Milton, Bunyan, Dryden, Scott, Wordsworth, Byron, the *Arabian Nights,* and journals such as *Blackwood's Edinburgh Magazine.* Thrown upon their own resources, the children invented two kingdoms inhabited by twelve soldiers given to Branwell by Mr. Brontë: B. and Branwell created the kingdom of Angria, Emily and Anne the kingdom of Gondal, and the children wrote the histories and adventures of the characters inhabiting their kingdoms. In 1845, Emily and Anne were still devising plots for Gondal, but in 1839 B. consciously rejected Angria in order to free herself from what she felt to be an unhealthy obsession.

In January 1831, B. attended Roe Head, a small private school near Mirfield, where she stayed for a year and a half and returned in 1835 as an assistant teacher. Here B. made two lifelong friendships: Ellen Nussey and

Mary Taylor. The three women corresponded for more than twenty years, and B.'s periodic visits provided her with scenes and impressions upon which to draw when writing. In December 1837, B. returned to Haworth; however, financial circumstances soon forced her to seek employment once again, and in May 1839 she became a governess for three months and again in March 1841 for nine months, after which B. traveled to Brussels with Emily. The three Brontë sisters wished to open their own school, and in order to strengthen their credentials Emily and B. wished to spend a half-year in school on the Continent improving their foreign languages.

B. and Emily arrived at the Pensionnat Heger on 15 February 1842, but returned at the end of October when their aunt died. B. returned to Brussels towards the end of January 1843 and formed a passionate, but unrequited, attachment to Constantin Heger, her married instructor. Portraits of her relationship and feelings for Heger can be seen in *Villette* (1853) and *The Professor* (1857), and many scholars believe that Heger inspired the character of Fairfax Rochester in *Jane Eyre.* But by the end of the year, B.'s loneliness and homesickness became too much for her and she left Brussels on 1 January 1844. The sisters' plan to open a school proved to be fruitless; not one prospective pupil applied and by the close of the year the plan was abandoned.

Upon her return from Belgium, B. discovered that Emily and Anne, like herself, had been writing poetry. The three published, at their own expense, *Poems by Currer, Ellis, and Acton Bell,* assuming male pseudonyms to preserve secrecy and to avoid the patronizing treatment they believed critics accorded women. The book received few reviews and sold only two copies.

Their lack of success, however, did not deter the sisters; even before the appearance of the *Poems* they began working on fiction. Each wrote a short novel—*Wuthering Heights* by Emily, *Agnes Grey* by Anne, and *The Professor* by B.—intended to be one volume of a triple decker. Publication, however, proved to be elusive. The novels were rejected by half a dozen publishers before Thomas Cautley Newby agreed, in July 1847, to publish *Wuthering Heights* and *Agnes Grey* if the authors contributed £50 toward production costs. But Newby refused to include *The Professor.* The sisters agreed, and B. continued, unsuccessfully, her search for a publisher for *The Professor.* When one publishing house agreed instead to consider a lengthier, more exciting novel, B. immediately completed and submitted *Jane Eyre,* which she had begun several months earlier. The work, which appeared before that of her sisters, was an immediate success.

B.'s publisher, George Smith, was eager to follow up the success of *Jane Eyre* with another work, and in early 1848 she began working on what was to become *Shirley.* The composition of the novel was arrested half way through by a series of tragedies: B.'s brother and two sisters fell ill with consumption, and all died within the space of nine months. At thirty-three, B. was the sole survivor of the six Brontë children. Although grief-stricken, B. found solace in writing and pressed on with *Shirley,* completing it in August 1848. Although many scholars cite the subdued tone of the ending as a major weakness, *Shirley* nevertheless provides readers with one of B.'s most charming heroines: Caroline Helstone. Even though a somewhat passive victim, Caroline did make a plea for opportunities for women that was both novel and rousing:

> I believe single women could have more to do—better chances of interesting and profitable occupations than they do now possess. . . . The brothers of these girls are every one in business or in professions; they have something to do; their sisters have no earthly employment, but household work or sewing; no earthly pleasure but an unprofitable visiting; and no hope, in all their life to come, of anything better. This stagnant state of things makes them decline in health. . . . The great wish—the sole aim of everyone of them—is to be married, but the majority will never marry, they will die as they now live.

The protagonist of the novel, Shirley Keeldar, is an idealized portrait of Emily Brontë, but B.'s desire to eulogize her sister resulted in a character so saintly that she lacks substance. The plot of *Shirley* deals with the hardships of the Yorkshire unemployed and the bitter confrontations of masters and men. And it is by interweaving the stories of Caroline and Shirley with the theme of industrial conflict that B. can explore the failure of Victorian society to give women the opportunity to develop their abilities, realize their potential, and control their lives.

The publication of *Shirley* brought B. the friendship of Elizabeth Gaskell, Harriet Martineau, William Makepeace Thackeray, and other writers. And it was mainly at Gaskell's home that she wrote *Villette,* a novel which some critics feel is her richest and most completely integrated work, in the three years following *Shirley.* With *Villette,* B. returned to the autobiographical mode that had given *Jane Eyre* much of its coherence and conviction. But this time, unlike *The Professor,* she avoided an uncritical identification with her protagonist. Although Lucy Snowe embodies much of B.'s own experience and is in many respects a projection of her inner self, she is not simply an enactment of B.'s secret dreams and fantasies or a fictionalized expression of personal feelings. With *Villette,* B. comes full circle, returning to the fictionalized presentation of her experiences in Brussels first discussed in *The Professor.* But unlike the earlier portrayal, in *Villette* B. is able to distance herself from the character and present a stronger, more mature exploration of the experience.

In the year following the publication of *Villette,* B. married her father's curate. B. found married life congenial and satisfying, and her husband daily revealed qualities that won her respect and increased her attachment to him. But her happiness was short lived. In January 1855 she discovered she was pregnant. She suffered from extreme nausea and vomiting, conditions that her constitution, already weakened by incipient consumption, was unable to bear. She died on 31 March 1855, ten months after her marriage, one month before her fortieth birthday.

WORKS: (as Currer Bell) *Poems by Currer, Ellis and Acton Bell* (1846). (as Currer Bell) *Jane Eyre: An Autobiography* (1847). (as Currer Bell) *Shirley: A Tale* (1849). (as Currer Bell) *Villette* (1853). *The Professor: A Tale* (1857). *The Life and Works of Charlotte Brontë and Her Sisters* (1899–1900). *The Twelve Adventurers and Other Stories,* ed. C. K. Shorter and C. W. Hatfield (1925). *Legends of Angria: Compiled from the Early Writings of Charlotte Brontë,* ed. E. E. Ratchford and W. C. de Vane (1933). *Five Novelettes,* ed. W. Gerin (1971). *Complete Edition of the Early Writings of Charlotte Brontë, 1826–32. Vol. 1: The Glass Town Saga,* ed. C. Alexander (1987). *Unfinished Novels* (1994). *The Belgian Essays,* ed. and trans. S. Lonoff (1997).

BIBLIOGRAPHY: Alexander, C. *The Early Writings of Charlotte Brontë* (1983). Alexander, C. and J. Sellars. *The Art of the Brontës* (1995). *The Brontës: The Critical Heritage,* ed. M. Allott (1974). Barker, J. *The Brontës: A Life in Letters* (1995). Bentley, P. *The Brontës* (1947). Bentley, P. *The Brontës and Their World* (1969). Burkhart, C. *Charlotte Brontë: A Psychosexual Study of Her Novels* (1973). Chadwick, E. A. *In the Footsteps of the Brontës* (1914). Craik, W. A. *The Brontë Novels* (1968). Crump, R. W. *Charlotte and Emily Brontë, 1846–1913: A Reference Guide* (1982). Dry, F. S. *The Sources of Jane Eyre* (1940). Duthie, E. L. *The Foreign Vision of Charlotte Brontë* (1975). Eagleton, T. *Myths of Power: A Marxist Study of the Brontës* (1975). Ewbank, I.-S. *Their Proper Sphere: A Study of the Brontë Sisters as Early Victorian Novelists* (1966). Gaskell, E. C. *The Life of Charlotte Brontë* (1857). Gérin, W. *Charlotte Brontë: The Evolution of Genius* (1966). Gezari, J. *Charlotte Brontë and Defensive Conduct* (1997). Gordon, L. *Charlotte Brontë: A Passionate Life* (1994). Hanson, L. and E. M. Hanson. *The Four Brontës* (1949). *Approaches to Teaching Brontë's Jane Eyre,* ed. D. L. Hoevelar and B. Lau (1993). Knies, E. A. *The Art of Charlotte Brontë* (1969). Martin, R. B. *The Accents of Persuasion: Charlotte Brontë's Novels* (1966). Mitchell, J. *The Stone and The Scorpion: The Female Subject of Desire in the Novels of Charlotte Brontë, George Eliot, and Thomas Hardy* (1994). Myer, V. G. *Charlotte Brontë: Truculent Spirit* (1987). Nestor, P. *Charlotte Brontë* (1987). *The Brontës: Interviews and Recollections,* ed. H. Orel (1997). Peters, M. *Charlotte Brontë: Style in the Novel* (1973). Peters, M. *Unquiet Soul: A Biography of Charlotte Brontë* (1986). Prentis, B. *The Brontë Sisters and George Eliot: A Unity of Difference* (1987). Ratchford, F. E. *The Brontës' Web of Childhood* (1941). Shorter, C. K. *Charlotte Brontë and her Sisters* (1905). Shuttleworth, S. *Charlotte Brontë and Victorian Psychology* (1997). Stoneman, P. *Brontë Transformations* (1996). Tayler, I. *Holy Ghosts: The Male Muses of Emily and Charlotte Brontë* (1990). Tillotson, K. *Novels of the Eighteen-Forties* (1954). Winnifrith, T. *The Brontës and Their Background: Romance and Reality* (1973). Winnifrith, T. and E. Chitham *Charlotte and Emily Brontë* (1989). *The Brontës: Their Lives, Friendships, and Correspondence,* ed. T. J. Wise and J. A. Symington (1932). Yablon, G. A. and J. R. Turner. *A Brontë Bibliography* (1978).

For articles in reference works, see: *Allibone. BA19C. Bloomsbury. Cambridge. Chambers. DLB. DNB. Feminist. Moulton. Oxford. ToddBWW.*

Other references: Cecil, D. *Early Victorian Novelists* (1934). Chase, R. *KR* (1947). Freeman, J. H. *SEL* (1984). Heilman, R. B., in *From Jane Austen to Joseph Conrad,* ed. R. C. Rathburn and M. Steinmann, Jr. (1958). Heilman, R. B. *NCF* (1959). Heilman, R. B. *SNNTS* (1982). Homans, M., in *The Female Gothic,* ed. J. E. Fleenor (1983). Hunt, L. *CLQ* (1983). Kestner, J. *PLL* (1984). Scargill, M. H. *UTQ* (1950). Woolf, V. *The Common Reader* (1926).

Lynn M. Alexander

Emily Brontë

BORN: 30 July 1818, Thornton, Yorkshire.
DIED: 19 December 1848, Haworth, Yorkshire.
DAUGHTER OF: Patrick Brontë and Maria Branwell Brontë.
WROTE UNDER: Ellis Bell; Emily Brontë.

B.'s actual development as a writer began in 1831 when her sister Charlotte left for school at Roe Head. At this time B. and her sister Anne began to record the saga of Gondal. Previously they had helped with the Glasstown Confederacy, but Charlotte and their brother Branwell were the leaders in those creations.

Another factor in B.'s creative development was the freedom she and her siblings were allowed. Free to roam and play upon the moors as they wished, the girls expanded their imaginations beyond normal boundaries. Also contributing to their mental stimulation was the free access they had of their father's library, where they found histories, biographies, and poetry—including the complete works of Byron. B.'s writing shows the influence of the moors and the romanticism of writers such as Byron and Scott: The poetry of Gondal depends on landscape for its major effects and is filled with the reckless actions of outlaws and rebels fleeing from justice or from pursuing armies and sheltering in the hollows of rocks or down in the glens where their secret haunts were located.

On the eve of B.'s seventeenth birthday, she and Charlotte left for Roe Head School; Charlotte was to teach and B.'s acceptance as a pupil was partial payment of Charlotte's salary. B.'s stay lasted only three months, as she sickened physically and mentally while pining for the moors. Many years later, when preparing a memoir for B.'s publisher, Charlotte tried to explain her sister's strong reaction to the strictures of boarding school:

> Liberty was the breath of Emily's nostrils; without it, she perished. The change from her own home to a school, and from her own very noiseless, very secluded, but unrestricted and inartificial mode of life, to one of disciplined routine (though under the kindliest auspices) was what she failed in enduring. Her nature proved here too strong for her fortitude. Every morning when she woke, the vision of home and the moors rushed on her and darkened and saddened the day

that lay before her. Nobody knew what ailed her but me—I knew only too well. In this struggle her health was quickly broken; her white face, attenuated form, and failing strength threatened rapid decline. I felt in my heart she would die, if she did not go home, and with this conviction obtained her recall.

Anne was sent to Roe Head in her place, leaving B. without the companionship at home that she craved. At this same time Branwell returned home from his unsuccessful attempt to establish himself in London. Because both felt their attempts to confront the outside world to be steeped in failure, a new bond developed between Branwell and B. This period of close association lasted for two years, and it was during this time that her preoccupation with the themes of guilt and failure began to take root.

Abruptly, in the autumn of 1837, B. took a position as a teacher in a large school near Halifax. Exact details as to how and why are not known, but it is generally assumed that, while the position was secured by Charlotte, a desire to be near Branwell, who went to be an usher at a boys' school that autumn, was behind the decision. Although B. did not particularly enjoy her stay at Law Hill School—she once told a classroom of unruly girls that the only individual she liked in the whole establishment was the house dog—it was to have a lasting effect on her, for much of the salient features of the history of Law Hill found their way into *Wuthering Heights.* The evidence as to the length of B.'s stay at Law Hill is conflicting, but the discovery that a letter from Charlotte, complaining of the harsh conditions under which B. worked and dated by most biographers 2 October 1837, is clearly postmarked 2 October 1838, would seem to fix B.'s stay in the winter of 1838 to 1839.

Scholars regard B.'s stay at Law House as important because a nearby house, High Southerland Hall, is believed to be the model for the house known as Wuthering Heights, and it has been suggested that the kernel of the Heathcliff story was found in the recollections of a local Halifax man, Jack Sharp. The parallels are not exact, however, and there is another credible possibility for a model—Top Withens, near Haworth.

B. returned to Haworth in 1839 and remained there until February 1842 when she and Charlotte left for Brussels in order to study foreign languages and equip themselves to open their own school. Forced to return home by the death of their aunt in November 1842, B. decided to remain at Haworth when Charlotte returned to Brussels. It was at this time that B. wrote much of her poetry. By 1844 the three sisters' plan to start a school had foundered through lack of response, and the sisters found themselves in low spirits, trying to conceive of a way to earn their livings in a congenial manner.

It was at this point that Charlotte discovered a notebook of B.'s poetry, which she thought to be quite good. Anne soon admitted that she, too, had been writing poetry, as had Charlotte. Together the sisters published *Poems by Currer, Ellis and Acton Bell* (1846). The male pseudonyms were used at the insistance of B. to maintain anonymity and protect their privacy. Not even the publishers knew the actual identities of the authors.

The three sisters, perhaps inspired by the ease with which they were able to publish their poems, quickly decided to try their hand at writing fiction. By July 1846 each had written a novel—Charlotte, *The Professor;* Anne, *Agnes Grey;* and B., *Wuthering Heights.* The sisters wished to publish the three works as a triple decker, and after some searching a publisher, Thomas Newby, was found who would publish *Agnes Grey* and *Wuthering Heights,* but not *The Professor.* Charlotte wrote *Jane Eyre* in the interval and quickly found a publisher of her own. *Wuthering Heights* was published in two volumes and *Agnes Grey* in one volume in December 1847. Reviewers were baffled and shocked by *Wuthering Heights,* though some expressed admiration for its strange power. Even modern critics have difficulty dealing with the novel, tending either toward eccentricity or concentration on very small sections.

Setting the tone with the Yorkshire word "wuthering," an adjective referring to turbulent weather, B. created a novel of such intensity that it is the standard by which subsequent Gothic novels are measured. Heathcliff's violent obsession for Catherine and the almost incestuous nature of their relationship has fascinated critics and scholars since the novel's publication. The narrative itself is a stylistic challenge with its multiple narrators and the two Catherines, mother and daughter. The passionate tone of the novel was so shocking to Victorian readers that when it was revealed that the author was a woman, there was immediate speculation that Branwell had written it. Comparisons with extant juvenilia and poetry, however, leave no doubt that B. wrote *Wuthering Heights.*

It is not known what B. did after finishing *Wuthering Heights.* A letter from Newby, in an envelope addressed to Ellis Bell and referring to another novel, has been found; but Newby tended to confuse the sisters and the novel mentioned could be Anne's *The Tenant of Wildfell Hall* (published June 1848). It has also been suggested that B.'s time was taken up with expanding *Wuthering Heights* from one to two volumes. Whatever work B. might have done in the two years between the finishing of *Wuthering Heights* and her death, however, remains conjecture.

Branwell, who had been declining mentally and physically ever since he returned home in disgrace, died of consumption on 24 September 1848. His physical and spiritual welfare caused anxiety for all three sisters; and there are stories of B., the largest of the three, bearing the brunt of looking after him and carrying him about. Soon after his death B. was reported to have a cough and a cold, which quickly developed into consumption. B. struggled to continue her everyday tasks until almost the day of her death, refusing, according to most biographers, all medical assistance. She died suddenly on 19 December 1848.

B. remains enigmatic because so little is known about her, and what is known is often contradictory. Her life seems one of self-isolation and conformity; her writings seem designed to shock and outrage. B.'s defiance of rigid categories and her refusal to divide characters into obvious categories—good and bad, saints and sinners, aristocracy and servants—is very un-Victorian, but does not seem out of keeping with her temperament.

In the past several years, criticism has tended to deromanticize both B. and *Wuthering Heights.* Biographers have continued to revise myths about B.'s life; in some cases, this debunking has yielded an alternate appreciation of B.'s creativity inflected by feminist concerns or values. The power of *Wuthering Heights* has been explained, for example, through its revision of masculine Romantic norms and B's fierce independence and self-imposed isolation through reference to anorexia nervosa. Critics have often moved from searching for the definitive meaning of *Wuthering Heights's* archetypes to using this most unconventional of nineteenth-century novels—which "insists on contradictions" (Knoepflmacher, vii)—to demonstrate the vexed processes of reading. One of the book's most important functions, then, is its recognized status as an "open" text. One result of these recent treatments of *Wuthering Heights* has been to relinquish a bit of the eternal fascination with Heathcliff and Cathy and, instead, to give greater attention to the second half of the book, not only rescuing the intricate narrative structure of the novel but defining the interest and significance of the second generation as well. In addition, cultural studies of the novel have both sought the social contexts for the mythic figures of the two lovers and examined the significance of the novel in popular culture.

Finally, there has been a significant reappraisal of B.'s status as a poet. It is still possible to encounter conflicting evaluations such as "much of her poetry, largely unpublished in her lifetime, is commonplace" (*ToddBWW*); and "her poetry, only a fraction of which was published during her lifetime, has come to be recognized as some of the most original of the nineteenth century" (*Oxford*). However, there has undoubtably been far more critical interest in the poetry (beyond its relationship to *Wuthering Heights*), such interest attributable in part to new, inexpensive, and reliable editions, and in part to feminist criticism's project of reclaiming a women's tradition in Romantic/Victorian poetry. Critics have argued that one can find in the poetry a powerful aesthetic unity—especially in the non-Gondal poems—and important, original meditations on subjectivity and representation, meditations that constitute a rebellion against both the specific limitations of Victorian gender politics and the philosophical assumptions that helped bolster such ideologies.

WORKS: (as Ellis Bell) *Poems by Currer, Ellis and Acton Bell* (1846). (as Ellis Bell) *Wuthering Heights* (1847). *The Life and Works of Charlotte Brontë and Her Sisters* (1899–1900). *Poems of Emily Brontë* (1906). *The Complete Works of Emily Jane Brontë* (1906). *The Complete Poems of Emily Jane Brontë* (1924). "An Unpublished Verse by Emily Jane Brontë" (1934). *Two Poems: Love's Rebuke, Remembrance* (1934). *The Gondal Saga* (1934). *Gondal Poems, Now First Published from the Manuscript in the British Museum* (1938). *The Complete Poems* (1941). *Five Essays Written in French by Emily Jane Brontë* (1948). *The Complete Poems* (1951). *A Diary Paper* (1951). *Gondal's Queen: a Novel in Verse* (1955). *The Complete Poems of Emily Brontë,* ed. J. Gezari (1992). *Poems of Emily Brontë,* ed. B. Lloyd-Evans (1992). *Poems,* ed. D. Roper and E. Chitham (1996). *The Belgian Essays,* ed. and trans. S. Lonoff (1997).

BIBLIOGRAPHY: Alexander, C. and J. Sellars *The Art of the Brontës* (1995). Barker, J. *The Brontës: A Life in Letters* (1995). *CVE,* ed. A. Blayac and J. P. Farrell (1991). Davies, S. *Emily Brontë* (1988). Davies, S. *Emily Brontë, Heretic* (1994). Eagleton, T. *Myths of Power: A Marxist Study of the Brontës* (1976). Frank, K. *A Chainless Soul: A Life of Emily Brontë* (1990). Ghanassia, V. *Metaphysical Rebellion in the Works of Emily Brontë* (1994). Knapp, B. *The Brontës: Branwell, Anne, Emily, Charlotte* (1991). Knoepflmacher, U. C. *Emily Brontë: Wuthering Heights* (1989). Liddell, R. *Twin Spirits: The Novels of Emily and Anne Brontë* (1990). McNees, E. *The Brontë Sisters: Critical Assessments* (1996). Mengham, R. *Emily Brontë, Wuthering Heights* (1988). Miles, P. *Wuthering Heights* (1990). *The Brontës: Interviews and Recollections,* ed. H. Orel (1997). Peeck-O'Toole, M. *Aspects of Lyric in the Poetry of Emily Brontë* (1988). Pykett, L. *Emily Brontë* (1989). *Wuthering Heights: Emily Brontë,* ed. P. Stoneman (1993). Stoneman, P. *Brontë Transformations* (1996). Tayler, I. *Holy Ghosts: The Male Muses of Emily and Charlotte Brontë* (1990). Winnifrith, T. and E. Chitham. *Charlotte and Emily Brontë* (1989).

For articles in reference works, see: *Biographies of British Women: An Annotated Bibliography* (1993). *Bloomsbury. Cambridge. Europa. Feminist. IDWB. Oxford. Stanford. ToddBWW.*

Other references: Armstrong, N. *Genre* (1982). Barreca, R. *Sex and Death in Victorian Literature* (1990). Bersani, L. *A Future for Astyanax* (1976). Boone, J. *Tradition Counter-Tradition* (1987). Chichester, T. *VP* (1991). Gilbert, S. and S. Gubar. *The Madwoman in the Attic* (1979). Jacobs, C. *Uncontainable Romanticism* (1989). Jacobs, N. *JNT* (1986). Macovski, M. *ELH* (1987). McMaster, J. *VRev* (1992). Mellor, A. *Romanticism and Gender* (1993). Mermin, D. *CritI* (1986). Miller, J. H. *Fiction and Repetition* (1982). Newman, B. *PMLA* (1990). Oates, J. C. *CritI* (1982). Polhemus, R. *Erotic Faith* (1990). Rosebury, B. *Art and Desire* (1988).

Lynn M. Alexander
(updated by Robert P. Fletcher)

Charlotte Brooke

BORN: 1740, Rantavan, County Cavan, Ireland.
DIED: 29 March 1793, Longford, Gloucestershire.
DAUGHTER OF: Henry Brooke.

This neglected writer gets only four lines in Brady and Cleeve's *Biographical Dictionary of Irish Writers* (1985); but soon, as a subject of at least one doctoral dissertation and as a woman attractive to feminist critics, she may receive more of the attention she deserves, both as contributor to literature and representative of a kind of literary lady in the eighteenth century. Long ago, a critic said she "did an acceptable service to her country in rescuing from oblivion a few of the interesting remains of its ancient genius," for while her tragedy of *Belasarius* never saw print she did manage to collect, translate, and print some of the old Irish poetry that still survived, among the last of the wandering minstrels, in her time. All who value Ireland's literary heritage must honor her and wish there had been earlier and as dedicated persons in that field.

One of twenty-two children of the poet and playwright Henry Brooke (1703?–1783), who was famous in his day as the author of the novel published in five volumes (1766–1770) as *The Fool of Quality*, B. was brought up in a busy literary household. Her father's work was various. He wrote in addition to the novels some plays (*Gustavas Vasa* was banned in England but produced with great success on the Dublin stage as *The Patriot*), many political tracts (one of which was *The Interests of Ireland of 1759* and another *The Tryal of the Roman Catholics of 1761*), some poetry (Alexander Pope was said to have assisted him on his *Universal Beauty*, 1735), and miscellaneous publications of great charm for both children and adults. It was the father whose work came first in the household, the father who was so occupied with his literary efforts that his children were left more or less to their mother's care, and the father for whom B. (who never married) stayed home and cared for after the death of his wife and the dispersal of the rest of the family. Henry Brooke lived to be eighty; his daughter devoted her life to his care and turned to writing not only because of his example but because it was one of the few occupations that a woman in her circumstances could adopt to give some exercise to her lively mind.

When her mother died (1772), her father took the loss very hard. He had married his cousin when she was only fourteen and he only twenty, and they had been very close all their lives, so the death of his wife was crushing and there was even more need for B. to become "the child of his old age" in still another sense, taking care of him. Nonetheless, he published three volumes of *Juliet Grenville; or, The History of the Human Heart* (1774) with her support. Then he sank into senility, sitting (as B. confessed to her great friend Maria Edgeworth) staring at vacancy. She had to be full-time nurse and part-time writer.

The death of her father freed her from one burden but she had others, including loneliness and want. Her dashing cousin Captain Robert Brooke had long supported Henry Brooke's large family, but now his vast cotton mills were failing; he could no longer prevent her from becoming a pitiful "gentlewoman living in reduced circumstances." She was forced to try to get some pension from her late father's political friends or some advice from his literary ones. She begged from Bishop Thomas Percy, compiler of *Reliques of Ancient Poetry* (1765).

Bishop Percy may have given her something more than a little cash—the idea of saving some of Ireland's ancient literary treasures. In 1786, an anonymous translation by her of an Old Gaelic poem appeared in *Historical Memoirs of Irish Bards*. She rendered into English a poem ascribed to Turlogh (Terence) O'Carolan (1670–1738), one of the last of the romantic breed of blind, itinerant, harp-playing singers of the old songs. "Ossian"'s *Fragments of Ancient Poetry Translated from the Gaelic* (1760) and the epics *Fingal* (1762) and *Temora* (1763) may also have inspired her and helped to create a market. In 1789, she published for subscribers her own translations of heroic poems, odes, elegies, and lyrics, along with her "Thoughts on Irish Song" and an original "Irish Tale." She was encouraged by William Hayley (1745–1820), Blake's patron, a man of whom Poet Laureate Robert Southey said: "Everything about that man is good except his poetry." For her *Reliques* she went much farther back than Carolan, to "remotest antiquity." She sensed that Irish politics and Irish pride were intimately connected with Ireland as the center of Western Culture in remote times; she put her finger on what Douglas Hyde (speaking to the Irish National Literary Society in 1892) called the "de-Anglicising of Ireland," culturally and eventually politically, by stress on ancient glories and the Gaelic heritage.

In her day, Gaelic poetry was still being written. It was soon to fade. Had her *Reliques of Irish Poetry* not appeared and given impetus to other attempts to save the legacy, the older materials might have disappeared altogether. Her translations were generally adequate although never inspired, but she was very instrumental in keeping alive the old literature until the philologists got around to studying Old Irish (before the tenth century) in the middle of the nineteenth century and until the scholars and patriots such as Standish O'Grady and a host of others saw the practical use of revitalizing the myths and legends of ancient Ireland, creating an Irish Literary Renaissance and, in the long run, an Irish Republic.

Like so many of those who exalted the Irish past (and worked for political freedom for Roman Catholics and Protestants alike in Ireland), B. was Protestant, indeed the daughter of a clergyman of the Church of Ireland. Her work, however, was for all the Irish, as was (for example) the ballad-collecting by Sir Charles Gavan Duffy (*The Ballad Poetry of Ireland*). Her *Reliques of Irish Poetry* became one of Ireland's minor national treasures.

Where her father in his poem *Conrade*, which pretended to be a fragment of ancient Celtic saga, was fully in tune with "the poetic revival of Irish poetry exemplified by the Ossian controversy" but engaging in mere imitation, in *Reliques of Irish Poetry* B. translated and transmitted the "reliques" of the real thing. Her translations and other literary works were the "children" of this spinster.

WORKS: *Reliques of Irish Poetry* (1789; reprinted with intro. by L.R.N. Ashley and a memoir of the life of Charlotte Brooke, 1970). *Belisarius* (a tragedy, lost). "A Collection of Choice Irish Songs," *Balg an Tsohair; or, The Gaelic Magazine* (1795).

BIBLIOGRAPHY: Included in memoirs and biographical works on her father by C. H. Wilson (*Brookiana*, 1804); mentioned in editions of his works such as those by A. Chalmers (1810) and E. A. Baker (1906). Ashley, L.R.N. *EI* (1979). Hobart Seymour, A. C. *A Memoir of Miss Brooks* (1806; included in *Reliques of Irish Poetry*, ed. L.R.N. Ashley, 1970; adds to her translations of old Irish verse her own "Maon: An Irish Tale").

For articles in reference works, see: *BDIW*. Crone, J. H. *Concise Dictionary of Irish Biography* (1928).

DNB. History of the City of Dublin, ed. J. Warburton et al. (1818).

Leonard R. N. Ashley

Frances Moore Brooke

BORN: January 1724, Claypool, Lincolnshire.
DIED: 23 January 1789, Sleaford, Lincolnshire.
DAUGHTER OF: the Reverend Thomas Moore and Mary Knowles Moore.
MARRIED: John Brooke, 1756 (?).

B. is remembered by some chiefly as Canada's first novelist. In her own time, however, she was well known in England as a significant literary figure. Regularly reviewed in London literary periodicals, she was called "a female writer of very distinguished merit" in the *Catalogue of 500 Celebrated Authors of Great Britain Now Living* (1788) and frequently mentioned in *Gentleman's Magazine,* which also noted her death. She continued to be mentioned in bibliographical accounts and recorded in early listings of English novelists (such as those of Mrs. Barbauld, 1810, and Mrs. Elwood, 1843), in the *Encyclopaedia of Literary and Typographical Anecdote* (1842) and in various theatrical and literary directories until the early part of the twentieth century. During her lifetime, she was a friend of personalities from Samuel Johnson and Frances Burney to Tate Wilkinson and Mary Ann Yates.

The daughter of Mary Knowles Moore and the Reverend Thomas Moore, B. was born in Lincolnshire, where her father was curate. Both parents came from clerical families, with the Moores an old Lincolnshire family that had owned a local manor and clerical living from 1633 to 1744 and educated a long male line at Cambridge. B. was the oldest of three daughters, one of whom, Catherine, died in 1737; the other, Sarah, lived into old age and retained close connections with B. B.'s father died in 1727 while rector at Carlton Scroop, a post he received in 1726 following his father's death there in 1724. His mother moved with her daughters to her widowed mother's home in Pittsborough; within ten years, mother, daughter, and grandmother were dead and the two remaining Moore sisters were living at Tydd St. Mary with their aunt, Sarah Knowles Steevens, and her husband, the Reverend Roger Steevens.

Moore's will left yearly income to his two then-born daughters, B. and Catherine, as well as £1,000 to be raised and divided between the two when they reached twenty-one. In 1745, B. was twenty-one, and in 1748 her sister Sarah reached that age. By the end of 1748, B. had moved to London with the expressed desire of becoming a writer. There she met Samuel Johnson and his group, wrote a play, *Virginia,* met and married the Reverend John Brooke, a widower from Norfolk, and wrote and edited a newspaper, *The Old Maid,* from November 1755 to July 1756. By 1757, she was a familiar enough figure on the London literary scene to appear (as Caelia) in the second edition of John Duncombe's *Feminead.* A son, John Moore Brooke, was born 10 June 1757, the same year John Brooke was appointed acting chaplain to the British Army at Quebec. B. moved to Quebec in 1763. Already the author of one translation and a successful novel, she published three more novels after returning to England in 1768, completed two more translations, and became a successful playwright. From 1773 to 1778, she managed the King's Theatre in the Haymarket with her friend, noted actress Mary Ann Yates, Yates' husband, actor Richard Yates, and B.'s brother-in-law, James Brooke. In about 1785, B. moved to Sleaford, Lincolnshire, to live with her son, who was rector at Folkingham and vicar of Halpringham. She died there 23 January 1789, two days after her husband, and is buried at St. Denys Church, Sleaford.

B.'s first major success was *The History of Julia Mandeville* (1763), an epistolary novel of love and sensibility. It had multiple editions between 1763 and 1792 and was published in London, Dublin, and Philadelphia; there is one twentieth-century edition (1938). *The History of Emily Montague* (1769), similarly written in an epistolary format, is set in Quebec with extensive descriptions of the landscape, manners, and politics. Considered by some as the first Canadian novel, *Montague* has been translated into French and Dutch and has had four twentieth-century editions (1931, 1969, 1974, 1985). *The Excursion* (1777) created considerable controversy in London when it was published, due to its account of an innocent girl's life in that city, and it has had one twentieth-century edition (1996). *All's Right at Last; or, the History of Miss West* (1774), published by the London circulating library of Barnes and Noble, has been attributed to B. Her two-act comic operas *Rosina* (1783) and *Marion* (1788) had numerous productions.

WORKS: *Virginia: A Tragedy with Odes, Pastorals, and Translations* (1756). (trans.) *The Old Maid,* by Mary Singleton, Spinster (1756, 1764). (trans.) *Letters from Juliet, Lady Catesby, to her friend, Lady Henrietta Campley* (1760; ed. L. J. Burpee, 1931; ed. C. F. Klinck, 1969; ed. M. J. Edwards, 1985). *The History of Lady Julia Mandeville* (1763; ed. P. Poole, 1938.) *The History of Emily Montague* (1769). (trans.) *Memoirs of the Marquis de St. Forlaix* (1770). (trans.) *Elements of the History of England from Forlaix* (1770). (trans.) *Elements of the History of England from the Invasion of the Romans to the Reign of George the Second* (1771). *The Excursion* (1777; rev. 1785; ed. P. Backscheider, 1996). *The Seige of Sinope* (1781). *Rosina, a Comic Opera* (1783). *Marion, a Comic Opera* (1788). *The History of Charles Mandeville* (1790).

BIBLIOGRAPHY: Backscheider, P,. intro. to *The Excursion* (1996). McMullen, L. *An Odd Attempt in a Woman: The Literary Life of Frances Brooke* (1983). Todd, J. *The Sign of Angellica: Women, Writing and Fiction, 1660–1800.* (1989).

For articles in reference works, see: *DLB. DNB. Essays on Canadian Writers: Biographical Guide to Canadian Novelists* (1993). *ToddDBA.*

Other references: Benedict, B. *ArielE* (1992). Berland, K. J. H. *SECC* (1990). Boutelle, A. E. *WS* (1986). Blue, C. S. *Canadian Magazine* (1921). Carr, G. *ECW* (1987). Edwards, M. J. *ESC* (1981). Edwards, M. J., in *Beginnings: A Critical Anthology,* ed. J. Moss (1980).

McMullen, L. *JCF* (1977–78). McMullen, L. *Atlantis* (1980). McMullen, L. *CanL* (1980). McMullen, L. *WLWE* (1982). McMullen, L. *SVEC* (1989). Merrett, R. *CanL* (1992). Merrett, R. *RSSI* (1994). Moss, J. *Patterns of Isolation in English Canadian Fiction* (1974). New, W. H. *CanL* (1972). New, W. H. *JCF* (1973). Pacey, D. *DR* (1946–47). Rogers, K. M. *Genre* (1978). Rogers, K. M. *Feminism in Eighteenth-Century England* (1982). Sellwood, J. *CanL* (1993). Shohet, L., in *Beginnings: A Critical Anthology,* ed. J. Moss (1980). Spencer, J. *The Rise of the Woman Novelist from Aphra Behn to Jane Austen* (1986). Teague, F. *SVEC* (1992).

Elizabeth K. Larsen

Christine Brooke-Rose

BORN: 6 January 1923, Geneva, Switzerland.
DAUGHTER OF: Alfred Northbrook Rose and Evelyn Blanche Brooke.
MARRIED: Jerzy Peterkiewicz, 1953.

A novelist, poet, and critic, B. was professor of English language and literature at the University of Paris VIII, retiring in 1988. First appointed as lecturer at Vincennes in 1969 after she gave up freelance reviewing and journalism in London, B. is regarded as a "European intellectual." Daughter of an English father and a half-Swiss, half-American mother, B. was raised in Brussels, Belgium, and educated at Somerville College, Oxford (B.A. 1949; M.A. 1953) and University College London (Ph.D. 1954). Her doctoral thesis laid the foundation for her first important publication, *A Grammar of Metaphor* (1958), a study of metaphoric language in fifteen English poets from Geoffrey Chaucer to Dylan Thomas. Prior to her severe illness in 1962, B.'s fiction was light-hearted and witty. *The Languages of Love* (1957), her first novel, satirizes philologists, and B. has described *The Sycamore Tree* (1958), *The Dear Deceit* (1960) and *The Middlemen* (1961) as novels of "love-affairs, class-distinctions and one-upmanships or portraits of society." Dissatisfied with this early fiction and influenced by Sarraute, Beckett, and Robbe-Grillet, she has carried her linguistic interest into her more recent fiction. Heavily influenced by scientific writing, her new style incorporates chemical imagery in *Out* (1964), modeled after Robbe-Grillet's *La Jalousie* and set in Africa in the aftermath of nuclear war where the color problem has reversed itself; and astrophysics in *Such* (1966), a narrative that covers the three minutes before Lazarus, an astronomer, is revived from death. *Between* (1968) describes the life of a female simultaneous translator in terms of language; *Thru* (1975), again using linguistics and combining the theories of Barthes, Greimas, and Kristeva, is a *nouveau roman* that "progressively destroys itself" as B. plays "with the reader's habit of trusting the reliable narrator."

B.'s passionate concern with language influences her literary criticism. *A ZBC of Ezra Pound* (1971), written as an introductory text for students, explains Pound's technique of "repetition and echoes"; she acknowledges her debt to Pound's "attempt to make everything cohere through juxtaposition," a technical method she uses in *Thru,* and to his mixture of languages (B. herself speaks French, German, Spanish, and a little Polish, Portuguese, and Italian). B.'s *A Structural Analysis of Pound's Usura Canto* (1976), an application of Roman Jakobson's structuralist method to "Canto 45," has sparked critical discussion in *Paideuma,* the Pound journal on whose board she served as the associate for France. *A Rhetoric of the Unreal* (1981), a collection of essays, investigates the interaction of narrative techniques in the science fiction of Henry James, J.R.R. Tolkien, Kurt Vonnegut, and Joseph McElroy. In this collection B. continues her integration of narrative writing with critical theories, particularly of Barthes, Todorov, and Lodge.

Amalgamemnon (1985) begins B.'s recent series, which includes *Xorandor* (1986), *Verbivore* (1990), and *Textermination* (1991). These volumes, known as the "Intercom Quartet," warn of pressures brought by information-processing systems on the novel and everyday existence but suggest that these pressures will enhance the evolving role of the novel in modern civilization.

B. has contributed to *London Magazine, The Observer, The Times Literary Supplement, Modern Fiction Studies, Revue des Lettres Modernes* and *The Quarterly Review of Literature,* among others. She won the 1965 Society of Authors Travelling Prize for *Out* and the 1969 Arts Council Translation prize for her translation of Robbe-Grillet's *Dans le Labyrinthe.* She shared the 1967 James Tait Black Memorial Prize.

WORKS: *Gold* (1955). *The Languages of Love* (1957). *The Sycamore Tree* (1958). *A Grammar of Metaphor* (1958). (trans.) *Children of Chaos* by J. Goytisolo (1959). *The Dear Deceit* (1960). (trans.) *Fertility and Survival: Population Problems from Malthus to Mao Tse Tang* by J. Sauvy (1960). *The Middlemen* (1961). *Out* (1964). *Such* (1966). (trans.) *In the Labyrinth* by A. Robbe-Grillet (1968). *Between* (1968). *Go When You See the Green Man Walking* (1970). *A ZBC of Ezra Pound* (1971). *Thru* (1975). *A Structural Analysis of Pound's Usura Canto* (1976). *A Rhetoric of the Unreal: Studies in Narrative and Structure, Especially of the Fantastic* (1981). *Amalgamemnon* (1985). *Christine Brooke-Rose Omnibus* (1986; contains *Out, Such, Between,* and *Thru*). *Xorandor* (1986). *Verbivore* (1990). *Textermination* (1991). *Stories, Theories, and Things* (1991). *Remake* (1996).

BIBLIOGRAPHY: Birch, S. *Christine Brooke-Rose and Contemporary Fiction* (1994). *Utterly Other Discourse: The Texts of Christine Brooke-Rose,* ed. E. G. Friedman and R. Martin (1995). Hayman, D. and K. Cohen. *ConL* (1976). Little, J. *The Experimental Self: Dialogic Subjectivity in Woolf, Pym, and Brooke-Rose* (1996). Wolfe, G. K. *SFS* (1982).

For articles in reference works, see: *Bloomsbury. CA. Cambridge. CLC. CN. DLB. ESF. EWLTC. Feminist. IAWWW. MBL. OCEL. Oxford. TCSFW. TCW. WA. WD.*

Judith C. Kohl

Anita Brookner

BORN: 16 July 1928, London.
DAUGHTER OF: Newson Brookner and Maude Brookner.

B. was educated at James Allen's Girls' School; King's College, University of London; the Courtauld Institute; and in Paris. She was a visiting lecturer at the University of Reading from 1959 to 1964; later she was Slade Professor of Fine Arts at Cambridge (1967–68), the first woman to hold the position. A Fellow of New Hall, Cambridge, she retired as Reader at the Courtauld Institute in 1988 after a distinguished career of more than twenty years during which she trained a number of prominent scholars in European and American museums and universities. An internationally respected authority on eighteenth- and nineteenth-century French art, B. is the author of four specialized studies in the field: *Watteau* (1968), *The Genius of the Future: Studies in French Art Criticism: Diderot, Stendahl, Baudelaire, Zola, the Brothers Goncourt, Huysmans* (1971); *Greuze: The Rise and Fall of an Eighteenth-Century Phenomenon* (1972), and *Jacques-Louis David* (1980).

B.'s work in art history earned her the respect of colleagues, critics, and students. Her scholarly articles and texts are characterized by meticulous research, fluent expression, and extraordinary erudition. Her lectures showed the same careful attention to logic, detail, and style; B. is remembered as one of the Courtauld's finest tutors.

B. has also demonstrated considerable skill as a novelist and has published seventeen works of fiction thus far. *A Start in Life* (1981; published in the U.S. as *The Debut*) tells the story of Dr. Ruth Weiss, a quiet Balzac scholar who decides, at age forty, that literature has ruined her life: Balzac was right—the virtuous are passive victims doomed to unsatisfying lives. Temporarily freeing herself from clinging parents who are little more than spoiled, overgrown adolescents, she goes to Paris in search of a great romantic affair. Inevitably disappointed, she returns to London and ends up caring for her invalid, widowed father and is consumed anew by her study of virtue and vice in the fiction of Balzac.

Providence (1982) is the story of Kitty Maule, daughter of a long-deceased British army colonel and his French wife. A university lecturer who specializes in the Romantic tradition, Kitty delivers a series of presentations on Benjamin Constant's *Adolphe,* a short novel about failure. She lives in two worlds, one of her doting but demanding French grandparents, the other of British academe. Her perceptions clouded by fantasies, Kitty misreads the meaning of an affair with a colleague and retreats to a life of disappointment, unable to change, an intelligent heroine defeated.

B.'s third novel, *Look At Me* (1983), is a work of metafiction. Frances Hinton, cataloguer in an art library devoted to pictorial representations of medical illness, seems to crave companionship; living with an ancient housekeeper in a tomb-like flat, she catalogues and observes rather than experiences the people she meets. As an outsider with sensibilities too fine to allow her to develop the attributes she needs to survive in a social world, she returns, disappointed, to the bed in which her mother died in order to write the novel we read. Initially described as a "beggar at the feast," Frances ends up taking revenge, consuming her enemies while making literature a substitute for life.

Edith Hope, the protagonist of *Hotel du Lac* (1984), is a writer of romantic fiction sent into temporary exile after an "unfortunate lapse"; her scandalous behavior has caused her friends to banish her to Switzerland. At the elegant Hotel du Lac, she spends her time in genteel rituals with a number of interesting, eccentric characters, writing undelivered letters to her lover, and working on a new novel. In the course of her voluntary exile, Edith acquires some insight into her own predicament and chooses to reject a practical life of pragmatic arrangements in favor of returning to London and a life of romantic fiction.

In these four novels, B. presents several consistent concerns while demonstrating considerable technical advance: She portrays a woman of early middle age, often an exile or orphan, bound to, if not oppressed by, traditions, whether intellectual or social, and alienated. Lonely and inhibited, she nonetheless ventures, albeit timidly, into a love affair that will follow a preordained course: infatuation, disappointment, and failure, followed by accentuated isolation, with the whole experience transmuted to artistic creation of one sort or another. The B. heroine typically has yearnings for the romantic and the impossible, a desire for courtly love in Chelsea, as it were. Though she is perceptive and intelligent, she appears incapable of recognizing the impossibility of translating romantic fantasy into quotidian existence; when she does achieve some insight, as in the case of Edith Hope, she ignores it and returns to her customary life, incapable, or perhaps just unwilling, to change.

B.'s technical mastery has increased. The earlier novels showed a rather tentative hand outlining a plot perhaps more suited to a short story, a voice neither fully modulated nor smoothly inflected. In *Providence* and, to a greater extent, in *Hotel du Lac,* B. creates a developed plot of substance and breadth with well-paced events; sure wit and irony enrich a repertory of voices, and the prose is controlled, graceful, and evocative. B.'s style, described as "hyperliterate" and distinguished by references to Charles Dickens, Honoré de Balzac, Colette, and Henry James, holds a decided appeal for an audience both literate and literary. In a world rather carefully circumscribed, B. succeeds, particularly in *Providence* and *Hotel du Lac,* in depicting the plight of a twentieth-century woman with a comic richness deeply suggestive of more serious concerns.

Yet little in any of these novels prepared readers for *Family and Friends* (1985), a striking departure and an answer to those critics who claim that B.'s fiction is little more than transposed autobiography. *Family and Friends* chronicles the affairs of a wealthy Jewish family, the Dorns, during the late 1930s and 1940s. The story of a powerful matriarch, Sophia (Sofka), and her four children, Frederick, Alfred, Mimi, and Betty, this novel embraces not only a larger cast of characters but also a wider geography than the previous four. Transplanted to London in the hectic days preceding the outbreak of World War II, the family continues to prosper without their recently deceased patriarch. Sofka assumes his place and dominates the clan, openly favoring Frederick and Betty. B. traces the Dorn family from London to Paris and the Riviera to Hollywood, integrating new relations and acquaintances as she creates a densely populated narrative. *Family and Friends* is rich and robust, full-bodied and sparkling. The greater narrative breadth of this novel has enabled B. to portray characters of greater complexity and range than in her previous novels; they are so finely modelled, with such carefully limned sensibilities (and hungers), that these wonderful black-and-white family photographs described a half-dozen times in the novel actually come to life as full-color cinema.

In *Hotel du Lac,* Edith Hope frankly admits that in a world that can be divided according to Aesop's distinctions between the tortoise and the hare, she writes for the tortoise market; and indeed B.'s novels can be seen within the same context, for B. typically sets a tortoise-like woman at the center of her fictions. And she frequently sets a hare-like woman opposite her, launching not a dialectic so much as a narrative dynamics: a repressed, often infantilized woman, defined almost exclusively by functional relations to others and who desires both autonomy and connection, moves through a miasma of loneliness, disconnection, and disappointment, while the hare, a woman of childish greed, precocious sexuality, and vulgarian habits, seizes the day, the man, and some happiness.

In *A Misalliance* (1986), it is Blanche Vernon, a woman of considerable refinement, common sense, decorum, and good works who longs for warmth and light and whose attraction to the rapacious, glamorous world of the hares nearly does her in. We grasp the fullness of B.'s characterization in one sentence, the novel's first: "Blanche Vernon occupied most of her time most usefully in keeping feelings at bay." On the other side is the ironically named Mousie, a computer clerk described as an "emotional gangster," for whom Blanche's husband of twenty years deserts her, only to return at the novel's ambiguous end.

At the center of B.'s next novel, *A Friend from England* (1987), is Rachel Kennedy, a self-righteous youngish woman who leads a marginal, eventless life, self-condemned to solitude, until the appearance of Heather Livingstone, daughter of her accountant. Charged to guide Heather's entrance into life, Rachel's elegant passivity masks self-delusion and voyeurism. Here, as elsewhere, Darwinian politics predominate in a novel of such intense pessimism as to put readers off, perhaps deliberately.

Latecomers (1988), B.'s eighth novel, amplifies the Darwinian note of *A Friend from England:* Like its predecessor *Family and Friends* a family saga, *Latecomers* tells the story of two Jewish men, Fibich and Hartmann, who escaped Hitler's Germany to find financial success in postwar Britain. The novel is a moving study of emotional deprivation, cultural displacement, and personal dislocation as experienced by two men superficially similar but essentially different in their responses to experience. Bound by devotion to each other and to honor, they emerge triumphant, and so, too, does B.'s artistry.

In her ninth novel, *Lewis Percy* (1989), B. focuses on the male; but Percy is a B. tortoise-female in male clothing, for he is "modest and timid," inclined to fret about trivial matters, unable to act boldly, and bound to enervating relationships as he moves through the gray light of a typically Brooknerian cityscape. Marriage to Tissy, a feeble librarian, brings no improvement. Opportunity for life-enhancing adventure presents itself in the form of the other Brookner woman, the bold, grasping, pleasure-seeking hare, here named Emmy. Percy, decent and hapless as ever, departs for the United States in what might be an assertive move; but Percy is likely too dispirited to take advantage in the land of opportunity.

In her tenth novel, *Brief Lives* (1990), B. reverses Aubrey and gives us lives that are private, not public; uneventful, not eventful; and female, not male. The story of two women, Fay Langdon and Julia Morton—the former restrained, meek, vulnerable, yet longing for something vulgar ("blue carnations"); the latter reckless, selfish, flamboyant, exploitive—*Brief Lives* chronicles their parallel lives as recounted by Fay, an unwitting survivor who emerges as a narrator of Jamesian preciosity and judgment. B. creates a fiction about aging, class, and gender but ultimately more about fiction-making itself. *Brief Lives* is a study of articulate, self-conscious repression, denial, and containment and an elegant novel of manners at home with those of Jane Austen and Henry James. *Brief Lives* may well be B.'s most underrated novel to date.

A Closed Eye (1991) veers dangerously close to self-parody in laying out the story of Harriet Blakemore, a passive, terminally sad, aging English widow resident in Switzerland. Widowed by a man of her father's generation and predeceased by her only child, Harriet suffers from a typical B. malady, an inability to "pursue her own satisfaction" offered in the form of a handsome television journalist. As in *Latecomers,* parent and child represent the antithetical personality types essential to B.'s lack of narrative dynamics: Harriet is unassuming, virtuous, and repressed, while her daughter Imogen is beautiful, cruel, manipulative, and condescending. Though *A Closed Eye* can be read as a profound study of one woman's isolation that results from her decision to block out parts of experience, it seems so elegantly enervated, attenuated, and empty that it becomes unintentional self-parody.

Fraud (1992) marks a turning point of sorts for B., for here is a novel with what can be construed as a happy ending. Long-suffering Anna Durrant, brought up to believe that virtue brings happiness, cares for her widowed mother "like a daughter in a Victorian novel. *Little Dorrit.*" She loses the man her mother has marked out for her, a physician named Lawrence Halliday, to Vickie, a predatory, vulgar, and robustly sexual creature. Yet Anna comes to realize that she offers a fraudulent façade to the world, a mask she has spent years creating, and she realizes that she no longer knows the truth about herself.

B.'s thirteenth novel, *A Family Romance* (1993; in the U.S. as *Dolly,* 1994) is the moving story of Jane Manning, who describes herself as "a prig who needed a conscience." An unexpected relationship develops between Jane, a modest, retiring only child, and Dolly, her aunt by marriage, a voluptuous Middle-European woman with a perfumed mink coat, violent make-up, and predatory ways ("a true primitive"). B. is able to make her reader like, even care about, two narcissistic, rather disagreeable women.

A Private View (1994) presents the story of George Bland, a sixty-five-year-old, recently retired manager of a packaging company: Quiet, cautious, and reserved, Bland's retirement plans are dashed by the death of his closest friend, also recently retired. His quiet, ordinary, bored existence is soon threatened by the invasion of a young American woman who is both manipulative and seductive. Bland teeters on the edge of misbehavior (something "ancient, pagan, and selfish" has been aroused), but only briefly. The plot and characterization are vintage B.; the central character's gender links the novel to *A Private View, Family and Friends, Lewis Percy*, and *Latecomers* but leaves B. open to the charge of repetition without significant variation. A critic as eminent as Frank Kermode, however, observed that "the novel is as nearly perfect an instance of its genre as it is reasonable to ask."

Incidents in the Rue Laugier (1995) surprised some readers but it should not have done so; a long time ago B. confessed her faith in design, acknowledging that "form may be the only thing to save us." To a greater extent than ever before, B.'s fifteenth novel is about form. This story, told by a narrator named Maffy, a woman who declares at the outset, "Please accept me as an unreliable narrator . . . nothing is true," is a fantastic reconstruction of her mother Maud's one great passion, her subsequent marriage to an English bookseller, and her descent into a claustrophobic existence remembered for its utter absence of feeling. In illuminating this one great passion, B. creates two male characters who embody the received behavioral polarities that pervade her fiction, but they, like truth, give way to larger concerns. *Incidents* dramatically undercuts those readers and critics who persist in asserting that B. writes the same novel again and again, for here surface classicism masks a modernist, if not postmodernist, literary aesthetic. *Incidents in the Rue Laugier* sparkles with wit, elaborate linguistic play, irony, even elements of the carnivalesque; it ultimately becomes a Proustian meditation on time, memory, and reality and is B.'s most daring novel to date.

B. has emerged as one of this century's most distinguished and successful practitioners of the novel, or a certain version of it, a neorealist construction elegantly conservative in impulse and design, occasionally and faintly critical of politics, and only infrequently and ironically contemporary in its sentiments. Her novels of dislocation, displacement, constriction, repression, and unbearable sadness echo Virginia Woolf's lyric of mourning, with Woolf's fine-line description of material—food, clothing, fabric, interiors, and sentiment—but without her often explicit critique of political paradigms and ideologies. B. replaces Woolf's formal and technical strategies of subversion with an inscribing of a curiously disembodied female life story in an inherited male discourse. Like James and Proust, she seems to believe that the imposed order of art can displace the disorder of life and lead to salvation; once asked if writing novels was "a function of maladaption," she retorted, "It's a form of editing experience—getting it out in terms of form, because it is form that's going to save us all, I think, and the sooner we realize it the better." Too wise to believe that the meek can really inherit the earth, she nonetheless engineers the occasional triumph of the fictional tortoise in her race with the hare.

A number of criticisms can be leveled against her fiction, the most substantive of which may well be the overly facile division of womankind into the familiar madonna or whore categories, the sufferers and the seizers, the tortoises and the hares; as Alison Light has noted, her women are "the guardians and victims of respectability. And they rehearse the inevitable bourgeois question: can you have both passion and position?" But B.'s excellences set her alongside Austen as a novelist of manners: like Austen, B. crafts fiction that represents an artful editing of experience; like Austen, B. creates apparently unloved heroines; like Austen, B. works a deliberately circumscribed canvas with extraordinary facility, bringing whole worlds to life with precision, irony, restraint, and sympathy. Her *oeuvre* embodies that ultimate triumph of form over all obstacles, even reality.

WORKS: *An Iconography of Cecil Rhodes* (1956). (trans.) *Utrillo* (1960). (trans.) *The Fauves* (1962). (trans.) *Gauguin* (1963). *Watteau* (1968). *The Genius of the Future: Studies in French Art Criticism: Diderot, Stendahl, Baudelaire, Zola, the Brothers Goncourt, Huysmans* (1971, 1988). *Greuze: The Rise and Fall of an Eighteenth-Century Phenomenon* (1972). *Jacques-Louis David* (1980). *A Start in Life* (1981; in the U.S. as *The Debut*). *Providence* (1982). *Look At Me* (1983). *Hotel du Lac* (1984). *Family and Friends* (1985). *A Misalliance* (1986). *A Friend from England* (1987). *Latecomers* (1988). *Lewis Percy* (1989). *Brief Lives* (1990). *A Closed Eye* (1991). *Fraud* (1992). *A Family Romance* (1993; in the U.S. as *Dolly*). *A Private View* (1994). *Incidents in the Rue Laugier* (1995). *Altered States* (1996). *Soundings* (1997). *Visitors* (1997).

BIBLIOGRAPHY: Alexander, F. *Contemporary Women Novelists* (1989). Baxter, G. M. *English* (Summer 1993). Burchfield, R., in *The State of the Language*, ed. C. Ricks and L. Michaels (1995). Haffenden, J. *Novelists in Interview* (1985). Hosmer, R. E., Jr., in *Contemporary British Women Novelists: Texts and Strategies*, ed. R. E. Hosmer, Jr. (1993). Kenyon, O. *Women Novelists Today* (1988). Kenyon, O. *Women Novelists Talk* (1989). Lee, H. *New Yorker* (30 January 1995). Morrison, B., in *The Independent on Sunday* (19 June 1994). Sadler, L. V. *Anita Brookner* (1990). Skinner, J. *The Fiction of Anita Brookner: Illusions of Romance* (1992).

For articles in reference works, see: *Bloomsbury. Cambridge. CLC. DLB. Feminist. Oxford. ToddBWW.*

Other references: *Atlantic* (November 1985, September 1991). *Boston Review* (April/May 1985, August 1990). *Harper's* (April 1981, February 1984). *HudR* (Autumn 1993, Autumn 1994). *London Magazine* (December/January 1992, February/March 1993). *LonT* (16 June 1995). *LRB* (4 September 1986, 1 October 1987, 1 September 1988, 14 September 1989, 13 September 1990, 29 August 1991, 8 October 1992). *Nation* (9 September 1991). *New Republic* (26 March 1984). *New Statesman* (19 August 1988, 25 August

1989, 31 August 1990, 23 August 1991, 21 August 1992, 9 July 1993, 24 June 1994). *New Yorker* (10 March 1986, 1 May 1989, 23 April 1990, 27 April 1992, 22 February 1993, 11 April 1994). (*NYRB* 31 January 1985, 5 December 1985, 14 May 1992, 12 January 1995). *NYTBR* (22 May 1983, 18 March 1984, 3 February 1985, 26 October 1986, 29 March 1987, 31 January 1988, 20 March 1988, 1 June 1989, 12 April 1992, 3 May 1992, 10 January 1993, 28 March 1993, 6 June 1993, 5 December 1993, 30 January 1994, 20 February 1994, 5 June 1994, 29 January 1995). *Observer* (17 August 1986, 30 November 1986, 23 August 1987, 14 August 1988, 27 August 1989, 10 September 1989, 26 August 1990, 25 August 1991, 27 April 1992, 23 August 1992, 22 February 1993, 11 July 1993, 19 June 1994, 3 July 1994, 11 June 1995). *Spectator* (7 December 1985, 23 August 1986, 27 August 1987, 20 August 1988, 26 August 1989, 25 November 1989, 8 September 1990, 31 August 1991, 22 August 1992, 19 June 1993, 18 June 1994, 11 June 1995). *TLS* (28 May 1982, 25 March 1983, 29 August 1986, 21 August 1987, 12 August 1988, 25 August 1989, 23 August 1991, 21 August 1992, 25 June 1993, 17 June 1994, 2 June 1995). *VV* (25 June 1991). *VLS* (May 1987, April 1988). *WRB*. (July 1994).

Robert Ellis Hosmer, Jr.

Brigid Brophy

BORN: 12 June 1929, London.
DIED: 8 August 1995, Lincolnshire.
DAUGHTER OF: John Brophy and Charis (Grundy) Brophy.
MARRIED: Michael Levey, 1954.

An outspoken and often irreverent novelist and critic, B. embodied the values and even the hijinks of the 1960s to perfection. She made life and literature nearly inseparable, capturing the high excitability of a youth-driven era and giving expression to its iconoclasm. Her improprieties were decidedly indelicate and won her the pugnacious image she sought. A penchant for the bipolar—instinct and reason, eros and thanatos—the bedeviling dialectic of thrust and parry came to define her analytic framework. Fluent, sardonic, self-taught, B. was heir to a half-century of modernism and to such self-acknowledged masters as Sigmund Freud, James Joyce, and George Bernard Shaw, whose disturbing discoveries laid bare the compelling forces of life. Her sharp eye for the absurd, the pompous, and the second-rate oftentimes made her a perfect antidote to the self-intoxicated cant of the age.

Daughter of John Brophy, author of two novels, *The Bitter End* (1928) and *The Waterfront* (1934), B. appears to have inherited her instinct for nonconformity from her mother, the Chicago-born daughter of Liverpool's Irvingite bishop. B.'s education at St. Paul's Girls' School was interrupted during the war years, encouraging an autodidacticism that stood her in good stead. In 1947, she won a Jubilee Scholarship to St. Hugh's College, Oxford, to read classics, but boisterous behavior—drinking in chapel—resulted in her expulsion. After several years as a short-hand typist for a distributor of pornographic books, among others, she published *The Crown Princess and Other Stories* (1953), an apprentice work marred by didacticism. Her first novel, *Hackenfeller's Ape* (1953), published to critical acclaim, is a piquant melange of science fiction, fable, and fantasia in which an animal acquires a disconcerting set of human inhibitions. In 1954, she was awarded the Cheltenham Literary Festival prize for a first novel. *Hackenfeller's Ape,* originally planned as a narrative poem, was B.'s favorite work, exemplifying her contrapuntal style of composition. *The King of a Rainy Country* (1956), a witty and pointed naturalistic portrait of a bohemian girl, typified B.'s fascination with the erotic and the comic antiromance. Examination of this polymorphous theme was extended in *Flesh* (1962), a sharply satirical fable of London life, in which a diffident and retiring young man is transformed into a hedonistic dynamo. Going even a step further is *Finishing Touch* (1963), a mordant seriocomedy of a girl's boarding school on the French Riviera, which critics have conceded is a posthumous monument to Ronald Firbank. Writing at a rapid clip, B. sharpened her seriocomic touch in *The Snow Ball* (1964), a black comedy of manners that attempts to transcribe in literature the erotic angles and the marmoreal effects of a baroque tomb. This carefully contrived novella was dramatized on BBC television in 1964.

B.'s prolific criticism met with considerable ambivalence. A Freudian, she came in for the usual drubbing psychoanalysis has received at the hands of literary critics. *Black Ship to Hell* (1962) decries the suppression of instinct and imagination attendant upon the rise of reason. A longish meditation on the repercussions of a hypertrophied rationality, it was compared to Norman O. Brown's *Life Against Death.* Her love of the high speculative mode and her restless lurching for effect can tire the reader. Despite what has been called the "magazinish naturalism" of her prose and her penchant for erudite self-indulgence in miscellaneous arcane, her writing was never drearily slack.

Mozart the Dramatist (1964) lauded the classical composer for the perfection of design and the audacity of his plans. Arguing that Mozart's operas lifted "his genius to the highest and most sustained pitch," B. debunks the myth of his presumed serenity and imperturbability. Rather, she viewed him as a trailblazing psychologist sorting out the internal conflicts of an age renowned for its conservative exclusiveness. Her considerable erudition served to undo the "bogus, long-posthumous, idolatrous image of Beethoven" and replace it with the limpidity of Mozart.

In 1967, B. collaborated with husband Michael Levey, art historian and administrator, and Charles Osborne on a saucy dismissal of many of the revered classics entitled *Fifty Works of English and American Literature We Could Do Without.* Such puzzling and wrongheaded asseverations as "Melville is not a novelist: he is an annotator," "Hopkins' poetry is the poetry of a mental cripple," and "Whitman's so-called poetry ranges from a simpleton's idea of Shakespeare and the purpler passages of the Bible to sheer semi-literate sludge" have been widely dismissed for their obvious archness and tartness of tone and for an exasperatingly insistent need to be controversial and cute—a very 1960s-ish posture.

An admirer of the *fin de siècle* and its preciosity, B. wrote books on several of its most characteristic writers and artists. *Black and White: A Portrait of Aubrey Beardsley* (1968) was a detailed photographic essay on the artist whose hypertrophied decorativeness received popular acclaim. *Prancing Novelist: A Defence of Fiction in the Form of a Critical Biography in Praise of Ronald Firbank* (1973) demonstrated an exhaustive knowledge of the English novelist known as the "Beardsley in prose." B. articulated the precise contrapuntal nature of Firbank's mature style—his archness and his dismissal of the conventional novel's discursive and descriptive longuers—with an intense and concentrated zeal. B. took vigorous exception to those who dismissed the author of *Valmouth* as the "reductio ad absurdum of aestheticism."

B. was also known as a television personality, appearing on "Not So Much a Programme, More a Way of Life" in 1964 and 1965 and "The Book Programme" in 1974 and 1976. In 1969, she collaborated with the novelist Maureen Duffy on the preparation of a Pop-Art exhibition, consisting of polystyrene wigheads adorned with plastic carrots, toy drums, and masks.

B., who also tried her hand at drama, published *The Burglar* (1968), an account of a puritanical thief put out by the depravity of his social superiors, and a radio play, *The Waste Disposal Unit* (1964), a satirical portrayal of American life and language.

WORKS: *The Crown Princess and Other Stories* (1953). *Hackenfeller's Ape* (1953). *The King of a Rainy Country* (1956). *Flesh* (1962). *Black Ship to Hell* (1962). *The Finishing Touch* (1963). *Mozart the Dramatist* (1964). *The Snow Ball* (1964). *The Waste Disposal Unit* (1964; radio play). *Don't Never Forget: Collected Views and Reviews* (1966). (with Michael Levey and Charles Osborne) *Fifty Works of English and American Literature We Could Do Without* (1967). *The Burglar* (prod., 1967; pub. 1968). *Black and White: A Portrait of Aubrey Beardsley* (1968). *In Transit* (1969). *Prancing Novelist: A Defence of Fiction in the Form of a Critical Biography in Praise of Ronald Firbank* (1973). *Place without Chains* (1978). *Baroque 'n' Roll and Other Essays* (1987).

BIBLIOGRAPHY: *RCF*, ed. S. Moore (special B. issue, fall 1995). Stevenson, S., in *Feminism, Bahktin, and the Dialogic*, ed. D. M. Bauer and S. J. McKinstry (1991).

For articles in reference works, see: *Bloomsbury. CA. Cambridge. CLC. CN. DLB. EWLTC. Feminist. MBL. Oxford. ToddBWW. WA.*

Other references: *Atlantic* (February 1970). *LonT* (8 August 1995). *Saturday Review* (12 June 1954, 24 January 1970).

Michael Skakun

Rhoda Broughton

BORN: 20 November 1840, near Denbigh, North Wales.
DIED: 5 June 1920, near Oxford.
DAUGHTER OF: Delves Broughton and Jane Bennett Broughton.

B. was the author of almost thirty novels satirizing the mercenary marriages and idle young women of aristocratic England. She never married but passed her life first with her father in Staffordshire and, after his death in 1863, at Oxford with other relatives. One of four daughters of a Church of England clergyman who reportedly forbade her to read her own books, she was also the niece of Sheridan Le Fanu, the well-known Irish writer of suspenseful and supernatural tales. It was he who helped her begin her career when he serialized her first two novels, *Not Wisely, But Too Well* (1867) and *Cometh Up As a Flower* (1867), in the *Dublin University Magazine*, which he owned. He also introduced her to the London publisher Richard Bentley, the beginning of a mutually profitable relationship.

B. combined social satire with a toned-down version of the sensation novel (a form popular in the 1860s that often featured an adventuress anti-heroine, mysterious secrets, and shocking deeds). Her work was immediately successful and was considered as audacious as it was readable. (William Gladstone was once seen in Mudie's Circulating Library absorbed in a B. novel.) During her more than fifty years as an author she wrote with wit, wry humor, and a keen eye for the absurd social codes of the upper classes and their social-climbing relatives. In widely read works like *Belinda* (1883) and *A Waif's Progress* (1905), B. featured an engaging young woman who pays lip service to the ladylike ideal but is in reality mercenary and amoral. The spirited namesake of *Belinda*, for example, wearied in three days of a marriage of convenience to a pedantic Oxford don, Professor Forth, is ready to fly off with the romantic David Rivers. After lamentations about the boredom and drudgery of a proper marriage (complaints that must have echoed the sentiments of many female readers), Belinda is rescued from her own imprudence by a providential event: Professor Forth dies and she is free to wed again. Typically, B. both satirizes the high-minded ideal of feminine chastity and saves her flighty heroine's reputation.

In *A Waif's Progress*, the machinations of Bonnybell Ransome, a spiritual cousin of Mary Elizabeth Braddon's sensation heroine Lady Audley (*Lady Audley's Secret*, 1862), are the subject of B.'s satire on feminine duplicity and masculine gullibility. Bonnybell schemes to marry any wealthy man who will have her, a project in which, after some setbacks, she exuberantly succeeds. Almost wholly uneducated, Bonnybell is only skilled in prevarication, but she is more likable than the various prigs who attempt so unsuccessfully to control her.

George Bernard Shaw approvingly saw B.'s novels as trenchant comment on the miseducation of the English girl. There were other B. targets as well. Again in *A Waif's Progress*, B. lampoons the self-advertising piety of Bonnybell's "protector," the wealthy Mrs. Tancred, and the obsequiousness and materialism of her repressed young husband, Edward Tancred. The novel *Second Thoughts* (1880) includes a comic criticism of a fashionable young aesthete's maudlin poetry and narcissistic sensitivity. *Lavinia* (1902) has a hero who commits the double sin of opposing the Boer War and cultivating an interest in old lace.

B.'s books were considered improper reading for the

young lady so often invoked as the ideal audience of light fiction, and B. may have suffered for this reputation. Oxford mathematics don C. L. Dodgson (Lewis Carroll), for one, refused to dine out where he knew she had been invited. At one time she was friendly with Mark Pattison, Rector of Lincoln College, yet the friendship soured and she was ostracized for her caricature of him as Forth, the Professor of Etruscan in *Belinda.* Yet—a woman of intellect—she had enduring friendships with Henry James and Matthew Arnold.

B.'s reputation for "immoral" books all but disappeared as the twentieth century arrived, and recent critics have seen her work as little more than the tail end of sensation fiction. Her anti-heroines, tame compared to the tigresses of Wilkie Collins, usually salvage their reputations, especially in her early novels. The enduring value of B.'s work is her indictment of the emotional dishonesty of the upper classes. "How I hate shams!" remarks the narrator of *Not Wisely, But Too Well,* a credo to which B. remained faithful.

WORKS: *Not Wisely, But Too Well* (1867). *Cometh Up as a Flower* (1867). *Red as a Rose Is She* (1870). *"Goodbye, Sweetheart": A Tale* (1872). *Nancy: A Novel* (1873). *Tales for Christmas Eve* (1873). *Joan: A Tale* (1876). *Second Thoughts* (1880). *Belinda* (1883). *Doctor Cupid* (1886). *Alas!* (1890). (with E. Bisland) *A Widower Indeed* (1891). *Mrs. Bligh* (1892). *A Beginner* (1894). *Scylla or Charybdis?* (1895). *Dear Faustina* (1897). *The Game and the Candle* (1899). *Foes in Law* (1900). *Lavinia* (1902). *A Waif's Progress* (1905). *Mamma* (1908). *The Devil and the Deep Sea* (1910). *Between Two Stools* (1912). *Concerning a Vow* (1914). *A Thorn in the Flesh* (1917). *A Fool in Her Folly* (1920).

BIBLIOGRAPHY: Ardis, A. *New Women, New Novels* (1990). Beer, G. *TLS* (11 March 1994). DeMoor, M. *CVE* (1994). Lennox-Boyd, C. *Spectator* (10 December 1993). Wood, M. *Rhoda Broughton, 1840–1920: Profile of a Novelist* (1993).

For articles in reference works, see: *Bloomsbury. Cambridge. CBEL. 1890s. Feminist. Oxford. Todd-BWW. VB.*

Other references: *AQ* (1976). *Encounter* (April 1971). *Fortnightly Review* (August 1920). Sadleir, M. *Things Past* (1944). Showalter, E. *A Literature of Their Own* (1977). *TLS* (30 November 1940).

Laura Hapke

Browne, Felicia: See *Hemans, Felicia Dorothea Browne*

Elizabeth Barrett Browning

BORN: 6 March 1806, Durham, County Durham.
DIED: 30 June 1861, Florence, Italy.
DAUGHTER OF: Edward Barrett Moulton-Barrett and Mary Graham Clarke Moulton-Barrett.
MARRIED: Robert Browning, 1846.
WROTE UNDER: Elizabeth Barrett Barrett; Elizabeth Barrett Browning; EBB.

A celebrated nineteenth-century poet whose work has recently enjoyed an important feminist critical re-evaluation, B. was the oldest of twelve children. Educated at home by tutors, B. was endowed with a profound desire for knowledge and engaged herself in a remarkable curriculum of languages, classics, literature, and philosophy. Late in 1820 her father suffered financial losses; shortly thereafter B. was stricken with her first serious illness for which opium, which became a lifetime habit, was prescribed. Mrs. Barrett died in 1828, and in 1832 the Barretts left their beloved Hope End estate, settling first in Sidmouth, in Devonshire, then London.

By 1838, B. had published three volumes of poetry but had not yet earned any real critical attention. She moved that year with her favorite brother, Samuel, to the gentler climate of Torquay for her health, but returned to London two years later when he drowned, for B. a terrible and traumatic loss. Although *Poems* (1844) gained her a wide and admiring reading public, she lived a circumscribed life until her elopement with Browning in 1846.

The courtship of B. and Robert Browning, which resulted in volumes of letters and the famous *Sonnets from the Portuguese,* began with Browning's 1845 letter to the famous poetess in which he declared: "I do . . . love these books with all my heart—and I love you too." B. concealed the romance from her father, who opposed the marriage of any of his children. In September 1846, the couple was secretly married and shortly after left for the Continent, settling ultimately in Florence. The change of climate and mode of living vastly improved B.'s health, and in 1849 she gave birth to a son, Robert Wiedman Barrett-Browning (Pen). During the years 1850–59, the Brownings traveled a great deal, passing summers in England but always returning to Florence as their home. She never communicated with her father, who had disowned her upon her marriage, and in 1857 Mr. Browning died, never reconciled to his favorite daughter. In 1861, B. died and was buried in Florence. B.'s life, particularly her marriage to Robert Browning, has been the subject of many critical and romantic biographies. The last few years have witnessed several important studies that explore the influence of B. and Robert Browning on each other's work.

Today, her early poetry is neither widely read nor highly regarded; nonetheless, these volumes reveal her erudition and her passionate commitment to poetry. *The Battle of Marathon* (1820) and *An Essay on Mind* (1826) are long, didactic neoclassical poems in heroic couplets. *The Battle of Marathon* narrates the 490 B.C. battle between the Greeks and the Persians. *An Essay on Mind* is a metaphysical and epistemological enquiry that asserts the primary value of the imagination and poetry. Her earlier works also include a translation of Aeschylus' *Prometheus Bound* (1833) and *The Seraphim and Other Poems* (1838), a diverse collection of poems marked by a religious preoccupation and a certain morbidity.

Poems (1844) was B.'s first volume to draw wide attention. Although "Lady Geraldine's Courtship" was a favorite, she considered "A Drama of Exile" the best poem in the volume. "The Cry of the Children" is noteworthy, for it marks B.'s commitment to political and social issues, in this case the child labor system. B. became increasingly convinced that women writers must devote themselves and their work to pressing contemporary issues and injustices, a conviction that shapes her later poetry. Only in the last twenty years have critics addressed B.'s political commitment.

B.'s next major work was *Sonnets from the Portuguese*, published with *Poems* in 1850 but written several years earlier for Browning during their courtship. The title suggests translation but actually plays on a nickname Robert Browning used for B. Because of his fondness for B.'s poem "Catarina to Camoens," he often referred to B. as "the Portuguese." Thus, the sonnets are literally "from the Portuguese." *Sonnets,* which enjoyed enormous popularity, is a sequence of forty-four poems that traces the call of love, the attendant fears, doubts, and insecurities, and the final triumph of love. Several of these poems are considered masterful executions in the genre of amatory verse. Greater critical attention has recently been paid to *Sonnets,* a result of feminist revaluation of B.'s work and its place in the tradition of women's writing. Many critics also place the *Sonnets* alongside the other great sonnet sequences in English.

It is mainly B.'s later poetry, largely concerned with political and social issues, that has been the subject of feminist reconsideration. In 1851, she published *Casa Guidi Windows,* a well-crafted poem, which moves from optimism and hopefulness for the cause of Italian liberty to disillusionment. B.'s passionate commitment to Italian politics, which is just beginning to receive critical consideration, is also reflected in many of the poems in *Poems Before Congress* (1860). However, one poem in this volume, "A Curse for a Nation," is a condemnation of slavery in America. The poem embodies B.'s convictions about the power and responsibility of women to raise their voices in protest against injustice, claiming that "A curse from the depths of womanhood / Is very salt, and bitter and good."

Aurora Leigh (1857), a long epic poem, remains the most widely discussed poem of B.'s later years. In the narration of the trials, travels, and career of an independent woman poet, she explores feminist, political, and aesthetic issues. *Aurora Leigh,* which B. prefaced as the work "into which my highest convictions of work and art have entered," was admired by Algernon C. Swinburne, John Ruskin, and the Rossetti brothers, but received mixed, often highly critical reviews and was largely forgotten until Virginia Woolf urged reconsideration of the "stimulating and boring, ungainly and eloquent, monstrous and exquisite" poem that "commands our interest and inspires our respect" (*Second Common Reader*). The critical interest in the poem initiated by feminist criticism continues to produce fascinating and important psychoanalytic and feminist work on the poem. Recent criticism emphasizes the subversions and anger and gender conflicts in her poetry and relocates B. in a women's literary tradition. As a result, a greater degree of seriousness has become attached to her work, and a fuller portrait of this Victorian woman poet of deeply held convictions has emerged.

WORKS: *The Battle of Marathon: a Poem* (1820). *Essay on Mind, with Other Poems* (1826). *Prometheus Bound, Translated from the Greek of Aeschylus, and Miscellaneous Poems* (1833). *The Seraphim and Other Poems* (1838). *Queen Annelida and False Arcite,* in *The Poems of Chaucer Modernized* (1841). (with R. H. Home) *A New Spirit of the Age* (1844). *Poems* (1844). *Poems: New Edition* (1850). *Sonnets [or] Sonnets from the Portuguese,* in *Poems* (1850). *Casa Guidi Windows: a Poem* (1851). *The Cry of the Children,* in *Two Poems* (1854). *Aurora Leigh* (1857). *Poems Before Congress* (1860). *Last Poems* (1862). *Poetical Works* (1866). *Letters Addressed to R. Hengist Horn,* ed. S. R. T. Mayer (1877). *Poetical Works from 1826 to 1844,* ed. J. H. Ingram (1887). *Letters of Elizabeth Barrett Browning,* ed. F. G. Kenyon (1897). *Letters of Robert Browning and Elizabeth Barrett Browning 1845–1846* (1899). *Complete Works,* ed. C. Porter and H. Clarke (1900). *Poetical Works* (1904). *The Art of Scansion: Letters of E. B. Browning to Uvedale Price,* ed. A. Meynell (1916). *Letters of Elizabeth Barrett Browning to Robert Browning and Other Correspondents,* ed. T. J. Wise (1916). *Letters to Her Sister 1846–59,* ed. L. Huxley (1929). *Twenty-two Unpublished Letters of Elizabeth Barrett Browning and Robert Browning (to Her Sisters)* (1935). *From Robert and Elizabeth Browning: A Further Selection,* ed. W. R. Benét (1936). *Letters to B. R. Haydon,* ed. M. H. Shackford (1939). "Correspondence of Harriet Beecher Stowe and Elizabeth Barrett Browning" *Studies in English,* ed. H. Harrod (1948). "Twenty Unpublished Letters of Elizabeth Barrett to H. S. Boyd" *PMLA,* ed. B. Weaver (1950). "New Letters from Mrs. Browning to Isa Blagden" *PMLA,* ed. E. C. McAleer (1951). *Elizabeth Barrett to Miss Mitford: Unpublished,* ed. B. Miller (1954). "Unpublished Letters of Thomas de Quincey and E. B. Browning" *Auckland University College Bulletin,* ed. S. Musgrove (1954). *Elizabeth Barrett to Mr. Boyd: Unpublished Letters,* ed. B. P. McCarthy (1955). *Letters of the Brownings to George Barrett,* ed. P. Landis and R. E. Freeman (1958). *Diary of E. B. B.: The Unpublished Diary of Elizabeth Barrett Browning, 1831–1832,* ed. P. Kelley and R. Hudson (1969). *Elizabeth Barrett Browning's Letters to Mrs. David Ogilvy, 1849–1861,* ed. P. Heydon and P. Kelley (1974). *The Brownings' Correspondence, vols. I–XIII,* ed. P. Kelley and R. Hudson (1984–96). *The Browning Collections: A Reconstruction with Other Memorabilia,* ed. P. Kelley and B. Coley (1984). *Selected Poems of Elizabeth Barrett Browning,* ed. M. Forster (1992).

BIBLIOGRAPHY: Barnes, W. A. *Bibliography of Elizabeth Barrett Browning* (1967). Bidney, M. *Patterns of Epiphany* (1997). Cooper, H. *Elizabeth Barrett Browning, Woman and Artist* (1988). Cooper, H., in *Shakespeare's Sisters,* ed. S. Gilbert and S. Gubar (1979). David, D. *Intellectual Women and Victorian Patriarchy: Harriet Martineau, Elizabeth Barrett Browning, and George Eliot* (1987). Donaldson, S. *Elizabeth Barrett Browning: An Annotated Bibliography of the Commentary and Criticism, 1826–1990* (1993). Erickson, L. *Robert Browning: His Poetry and His Audiences* (1894). Forster, M. *Elizabeth Barrett Browning: a Biography* (1989). Gilbert, S., and S.

Gubar. *The Madwoman in the Attic: The Woman Writer and the Nineteenth Century Literary Imagination* (1979). Grylls, R. *Mrs. Browning: The Story of Elizabeth Barrett* (1980). Hayter, A. *Elizabeth Barrett Browning* (1965). Hayter, A. *Mrs. Browning: A Poet's Work in Its Setting* (1962). Hewlitt, D. *Elizabeth Barrett Browning* (1953). Hudson, G. W. *An Elizabeth Barrett Browning Concordance* (1973). Karlin, D. *The Courtship of Robert Browning and Elizabeth Barrett* (1985). Karlin, D. *Robert Browning and Elizabeth Barrett: The Courtship Correspondence, 1845–1846* (1989). Leighton, A. *Elizabeth Barrett Browning* (1986). Lewis, L. M. *Elizabeth Barrett Browning's Spiritual Progress: Face to Face with God* (1997). Lubbock, P. *Elizabeth Barrett Browning in Her Letters* (1906). Lupton, M. *Elizabeth Barrett Browning* (1972). Mermin, D. *Elizabeth Barrett Browning: The Origins of a New Poetry* (1989). Markus, J. *Dared and Done: The Marriage of Elizabeth Barrett and Robert Browning* (1996). Moers, E. *Literary Women* (1976). Radley, V. *Elizabeth Barrett Browning* (1972). Mermin, D., in *Mothering the Mind: Twelve Studies of Writers and their Silent Partners*, ed. R. Perry and B. M. Watson (1984). Stone, M. *Elizabeth Barrett Browning* (1995). Taplin, G. *The Life of Elizabeth Barrett Browning* (1958). Tomkins, J. M. S. *Aurora Leigh* (1962). Ward, M. *Robert Browning and His World: The Private Face* (1967). Woolf, V. *The Second Common Reader* (1932).

For articles in reference works, see: *Bloomsbury. Cambridge. DLB. DNB. Europa. Feminist. IDWB. NCBEL. NCLC. Oxford. ToddBWW. VB.*

Other references: Blake, K. *VP* (1986). *Browning Institute Studies* (1985). *BSNotes* (1977). *Durham University Journal* (1972). *ELH* (1981). Friedman, S. S. *TSWL* (1986). Gilbert, S., in *Textual Analysis: Some Readers Reading*, ed. M. A. Caws (1986). Mermin, D. *CritI* (1986). Mermin, D. *SEL* (1986). *PMLA* (1984). *Signs* (1978). *SBHC* (1979, 1981). *VP* (1983, 1984). *VS* (1983).

Patricia A. O'Hara
(updated by Virginia Zimmerman)

Mary Balfour Brunton

BORN: 1 November 1778, Island of Burra, Orkney.
DIED: 19 December 1818, Edinburgh, Scotland.
DAUGHTER OF: Colonel Thomas Balfour and Francis Ligonier Balfour.
MARRIED: the Reverend Alexander Brunton, 1798 (?).

B.'s life was essentially quiet, varied by travel, frequent socializing (especially after the authorship of *Self-Control* was revealed), and many philanthropic endeavors. She died shortly after giving birth to her stillborn child. B. wrote two novels: *Self-Control* (1811) and *Discipline* (1814). She left a third, *Emmeline,* unfinished when she died. B. also projected a series of moral tales, but these were never written. In 1819, her husband attached *Emmeline* to his *Memoir* of her life, along with some of B.'s religious musings, verse, and extracts from her letters and journals. Her husband commented in the *Memoir* that B.'s books "rose very fast into popularity, and their popularity seems to have as quickly sunk away." Nonetheless, Robert Colby noted that the popularity of *Self-Control,* at least, "appears to have been sustained well into the Victorian period to judge from its continuous appearance on Mudie's lists through 1884."

B., who is usually classed with the Scottish moral novelists, attempted in her writing to provide pleasantly couched moral lessons. *Self-Control* was written "to shew the power of the religious principle in bestowing self-command; and to bear testimony against a maxim as immoral as indelicate, that a reformed rake makes the best husband." *Discipline,* a companion piece to *Self-Control,* was "to shew the means through which when *Self-Control* has been neglected the mind must be trained for suffering ere it can hope for usefulness or for true enjoyment." *Emmeline's* text demonstrated "how little chance there is of happiness when the divorced wife marries her seducer." These central themes are explored within the context of a number of other concerns. As Margaret Bruce notes, she "drew on her experience as a minister's wife to comment on such subjects as poverty, philanthropy, and the treatment of the insane, while her interest in the situation of her own sex encouraged her to comment on love and marriage, the appropriate role for women, women's education, and the plight of the single woman."

Despite her avowed didacticism, B.'s novels have a freshness and a power that make them still quite readable. *Self-Control* was begun in secret, then continued under her husband's guidance. The heroine, Laura Montreville, rich in religious training but a novice in worldly matters, unwarily fell in love with the glib rake, Colonel Hargrave (probably named after a character in Samuel Richardson's *Sir Charles Grandison*). Shocked at Hargrave's attempt to seduce her, Laura conquers her love for him and eventually comes to love and marry Montague De Courcy, a Grandisonian paradigm. Before this, however, Hargrave has pursued Laura and repeatedly abducted her. Transported by him to America, she escaped in a canoe and managed to find her way back to Scotland. Hargrave, believing her dead, exonerates her and kills himself. This extravagant plot is redeemed somewhat by pungent character studies—most notably of the querulous and selfish Lady Pelham—and (albeit unintentionally) by the deliciously absurd portrayal of the New World. The novel drew gentle fire from Jane Austen, who described it as "an excellently meant, elegantly written Work, without anything of Nature or Probability in it."

Discipline, although even more earnest in its moral intent, is a better, tighter, and wittier novel. In an 1810 letter, B. wrote: "If ever I undertake another lady, I will manage her in a different manner. Laura is so decently kerchiefed . . . that to dress her is a work of time and pains. Her younger sister, if she ever have one, shall wear loose floating easy robes, that will slip on in a minute." Ellen Percy, this more credible younger sister, is spoiled as a child, then painfully schooled by the loss of fortune, friends, protection, and even, for a time liberty itself. The

Christian fortitude and charity that she ultimately attains earn her the hand of Henry Graham (alias Maitland), who has loved her from the beginning. The vigor and verisimilitude of the early part of *Discipline* suggests that it may well be autobiographical. *The Memoir* of B. hints that she, like Ellen, had been overly indulged as a child and given, at best, a fashionable and desultory education.

Whereas *Self-Control* reflects a Richardsonian model, *Discipline* recalls Fanny Burney's *Camilla.* The heroine's pride, strong feelings, imprudence, and reluctance to inflict pain on herself or on others lead her into one indiscretion after another until she becomes thoroughly entangled with the unscrupulous Lord Frederick de Burgh. Ironically, the ruin of her father's fortune and his subsequent suicide prevent her from eloping with Lord Frederick. Impoverished and driven abroad, Ellen weathers despair, illness, poverty, and repeated humiliation. Her mother's friend, Miss Mortimer, teaches her the principles of religion and guides her painful and gradual reformation. Ellen eventually recovers some of her fortune, meets Charlotte Graham, and accompanies her to the Highlands where she again encounters Henry.

In *Discipline,* Ellen tells her own story. The first retrospective, conjoined with the vivid portrayal of a young child, anticipates the Victorian novel and gives the work a richer flavor and stronger appeal than *Self-Control.* The London and Edinburgh sections of the novel, written in the Burney style, are enlivened with some very effective satirical figures. Best are the designing Julia Arnold (Ellen's fair-weather friend) and the jealous and indolent Mrs. Boswell, who hires Ellen as a governess. The novel is graced with wit, especially in the early pages. The Highlands section, however, freighted with long explanatory footnotes, is excessively sentimental. (There is, for instance, no such thing as adultery among the Highlanders.) B. notes with honest admiration and, perhaps, some chagrin, the inferiority of her Highland portraits to those of *Waverley,* which was published just as she was finishing *Discipline.*

B.'s novels bear clear evidence of her attempt—not always fully successful—to adhere to her own formula for an effective novelist: "Irish humour, Scotch prudence, and English sincerity,—the first, that his work may be read; the second, that it may be read without injury to himself; the third, that the perusal of it may be profitable to others."

WORKS: (Anon.) *Self-Control* (1811). *Discipline* (1814). (Anon.) *Emmeline, with Some Other Pieces* (1819).

BIBLIOGRAPHY: Alexander, B. *Memoir* (attached to the 1819 edition of *Emmeline* and the 1832 and 1849 editions of *Discipline*). Bruce, M. H. *Journal of Women's Studies in Literature* (1979). Elwood, Mrs. A. K. *Memoirs of the Literary Ladies of England* (1843).

For articles in reference works, see: *Allibone. BA19C. CHEL.* Ward, W. S. *Literary Reviews in British Periodicals, 1798—1820* (1973).

Other references: Baker, E. *The History of the English Novel* (1929). Colby, R. *Fiction with a Purpose* (1967). Moers, E. *Literary Women* (1976). Moler, K. *Jane Austen's Art of Allusion* (1968). Utter, R. and G. Needham *Pamela's Daughters* (1936).

Kathleen L. Fowler

Bryher (pseudonym of Annie Winifred Ellerman)

BORN: 2 September 1894, London.
DIED: 28 January 1983, Vevey, Switzerland.
DAUGHTER OF: Sir John Reeves Ellerman and Hannah Glover Ellerman.
MARRIED: Robert McAlmon, 1921; Kenneth Macpherson, 1927.

The first child of a shipping magnate, one of England's richest men, B. thoroughly rebelled against Victorian restrictions on women that thwarted her childhood desires—to go to sea as a cabin boy and then to inherit and operate her father's business and maritime empire. Her lifelong love of the sea, coasts, islands, and dangerous adventures began very early in her life, when, instead of being sent to school, she traveled abroad with her family. For her, travel was far more educational. It formed her artistic tastes and independent character as well as arousing the "geographical emotions," as she later described them, which motivate and permeate her historical novels, the writing for which she is best known.

With her parents, she wintered in Italy from 1901 to 1907 and in the south of France in 1908 and 1909. In that time, she also went twice to Egypt and once to Sicily, and she spent long periods in Paris. She taught herself to read at the age of four; she spoke French well—and a bit of Arabic—by the age of seven; and, resisting British insularity, she had, even before adolescence, formed the sense of herself as European, a feeling she never lost. Through travel she developed a large sense of time and space, and, having met all kinds of people, viewed all races and religions as worthy of respect. She considered as essential to her writing the fact that she had early been close to "poverty, fire, and death." Thus she developed a deep identification with the life of ordinary people in the stark milieux of ancient times, leading critics to feel in her work a vivid sense that the author was "somehow there," present at the events she recounts.

An experience decisive for B.'s literary future occurred when she was three years old: A nursery-maid read her *The Swiss Family Robinson.* Other important early literary influences were Shakespeare in E. Nesbit's retelling and Homer in W. C. Perry's *The Boy's Iliad,* which she read after a visit to the Colosseum in Rome in 1903 fired her interest in the Greco-Roman world. This interest grew as she read first G. A. Henty's *The Young Carthaginian,* then Gustave Flaubert's *Salammbô,* and later the Loeb Greek and Roman historians. When she was sixteen, B. took art lessons and wanted to be an artist; to prevent her, her family finally sent her to Queenwood School in Eastbourne, Sussex. School was "a violation of the spirit," she later said, but it strengthened rather than weakened her independence and intellectual bent. She pursued her own love of history, archaeology, and poetry and began to write. In 1914, she published *Region of Litany and Other Poems,* and in 1918 two books—a translation of Bion's *The Lament of Adonis* and *Amy Lowell: A Critical Appreciation.*

B.'s love of poetry brought about the most crucial event of her life. Early in 1919 she met the American poet H. D. (Hilda Doolittle), who was then pregnant, critically ill with pneumonia, and not expected to survive the birth of her child. Bryher saved H. D.'s life by providing personal support and medical care. After a daughter, Perdita, was safely born, the two women traveled together to the Scilly Isles, the name of one of which inspired the pseudonym "Bryher" when a year later B. published her first novel, *Development* (1920). Thus began a deep lifetime friendship that richly fed both literary careers. B., admiring H. D.'s work, committed herself to creating an environment in which her friend's poetic genius could flourish. However, after the unexpected success of *Development,* a candid reflection of her school days at Queenwood, B. was also able to think of herself as a professional writer. *Development* has a sequel in *Two Selves* (1923).

Late in 1920, B., H. D., and Perdita went to the United States, which B. hated, except for their meeting the American poet Marianne Moore, who from then on continually wrote to, praised, and encouraged B. as a writer. B.'s impressions of the United States, which she later modified, are recorded in *West* (1925). In New York City, B. also met Robert McAlmon, with whom she felt strong intellectual affinities, and in 1921 they married. They moved to Paris, with H.D. nearby. B. financed The Contact Press under McAlmon's editorship, publishing almost all of the modernist writers active in Europe between the wars, including James Joyce, Mina Loy, Gertrude Stein, Djuna Barnes, Ezra Pound, F. M. Ford, Ernest Hemingway, and Dorothy Richardson, whose work B. admired and promoted all her life. In this period, B. also subsidized The Egoist Press, which published McAlmon and H. D. among others.

Early in 1927, B. and McAlmon were divorced. In September 1927, she married Kenneth Macpherson, whose interest in filmmaking stimulated her to found Pool Productions, a film company that also put out the magazine *Close Up* from 1927 until 1933. With B.'s help, Macpherson made a film, *Foothills,* in 1927, starring H. D., and in 1931 the remarkable film *Borderline,* starring Paul Robeson, Robeson's wife, and H. D. B.'s interest in film took her to Vienna and Berlin, where in 1927 she met Dr. Hans Sachs, the psychoanalyst, and began the psychoanalysis that was key to the release of her literary creativity. Her book *Film Problems of Soviet Russia* (1929) shows her to be a fine film critic, but she never wrote on film again.

In 1930, B. made Switzerland her permanent residence, and she lived primarily at Kenwin, the home she built near Vevey—now a Bauhaus landmark—until the end of her life, although she and H. D. also shared an apartment in London from 1934 to 1946. In England from 1935 to 1950, she published the influential literary review *Life and Letters Today* and worked to rescue European intellectuals who were victims of Nazi persecution. She wrote little in the 1930s but continued her research; from 1940 to 1966 she had a period of high productivity in which she wrote ten novels and two volumes of autobiography, *The Heart to Artemis* (1962) and *The Days of Mars* (1972).

The first of the novels, *Beowulf,* depicting her London neighborhood during the bombings, appeared in France in 1948 but was not translated into English until 1956. Next she wrote *The Fourteenth of October* (1952), about the battle of Hastings, and *This January Tale* (1966), on the Norman Conquest. *Roman Wall* (1954) documents life in A.D. 298 on the borders of the Roman Empire as Germanic tribes invaded what is now Switzerland. *Ruan* takes place in B.'s beloved Cornwall as Christianity is infiltrating pagan Britain around A.D. 315. The events of *The Coin of Carthage* (1964) occur at the end of the Punic Wars (218–202 B.C.) at the time of Hannibal's death.

B.'s typical heroes are homeless young men or itinerant traders. Friendship and loyalty among men are dominant themes; sexual love and marriage are seldom mentioned. Although B. was an ardent feminist, her female characters are usually peripheral, although an exception is the Greek priestess Harmonia, heroine of *Gate to the Sea* (1958), whose courage saves her companions' lives in 326 B.C. when Poseidonia fell to Italian tribes after the death of Alexander.

While B.'s primary aim is to re-create the texture of ordinary lives of long ago, her themes also inevitably reflect the concerns of her contemporary world. She writes about past periods of social breakdown and upheaval, analogues of the chaos she saw created in Europe by two world wars. Her characters, itinerant and in danger, are prevented from establishing lasting human relations. Separations and deaths usually end her novels on a note of isolation and *tristesse,* yet often with meditative consolation. Valerius in *Roman Wall* says: "Things ended, and yet were continuous. . . . Creation sprang from eternity, but it also was transient; no second experience was exactly like the first." In times of cultural change and dissolution, she believed the old, true values could survive if individuals took the responsibility to incorporate, maintain, and carry them through war and destruction.

The strengths of B.'s writing are masterly documentation of historical fact, sensuous evocation of place, clarity of verbal description, and warmth of feeling for others. One critic called her "that very gifted, very human writer." She unremittingly upheld her belief in friendship and loyalty as primary virtues in human life. These virtues informed B.'s dual literary career as re-creator of history and as generous supporter of avant-garde arts, activities for which she remains important to this day.

WORKS: *Region of Litany and Other Poems* (1914). *Amy Lowell: A Critical Appreciation* (1918). (trans.) *The Lament for Adonis,* by Bion of Smyrna (1918). *Development, A Novel* (1920). (with others) *Arrow Music* (1922). *Two Selves* (1923). *West* (1925). *A Picture Geography for Little Children: Asia* (1925). *Civilians* (1927). *Film Problems of Soviet Russia* (1929). (with T. Weiss) *The Lighthearted Student* (1930). (with R. Herring and D. Bower) *Cinema Survey* (1937). *Beowulf, A Novel* (1948, 1956). *The Fourteenth of October* (1952). *The Player's Boy, A Novel* (1953). *Roman Wall* (1954). *Gate to the Sea* (1958). *Ruan* (1960). *The Heart to Artemis: A Writer's Memoirs* (1962). *The Coin of Carthage* (1964). *Visa for Avalon* (1965). *This January Tale* (1966). *The Colors of Valid* (1969). *The Days of Mars: A Memoir 1940–1946* (1972).

BIBLIOGRAPHY: Beach, S. *Shakespeare and Company* (1956). Ford, H. *Published in Paris: American and British Writers, Printers and Publishers in Paris 1920–1939* (1975). Guest, B. *Herself Defined: The Poet H. D. and her World* (1984). McAlmon, R. and K. Boyle. *Being Geniuses Together 1920–1930* (1968).

For articles in reference works, see: *Bloomsbury. CA. CN. Feminist. Oxford. ToddBWW.*

Other references: *BW* (6 November 1966). *Commonwealth* (30 May 1952, 20 August 1954, 12 October 1956, 10 October 1958, 2 December 1960). *NYTBR* (2 June 1963, 25 April 1965, 27 November 1966, 8 February 1970). *Observer Review* (7 January 1968). *Poetry* (February 1959). *San Francisco Chronicle* (10 June 1952). *Saturday Review* (1 September 1956, 12 November 1960). *Time* (21 June 1963).

Jane Augustine

Rosina Wheeler Bulwer-Lytton

BORN: 1802, Ballywire, County Tipperary, Ireland.
DIED: 1882, London.
DAUGHTER OF: Francis Massy Wheeler and Anna Doyle Wheeler.
MARRIED: Edward Bulwer-Lytton, 1827.
WROTE UNDER: Lady Bulwer-Lytton; Rosina, Lady Lytton.

A minor British novelist of the nineteenth century, often ridiculed and parodied in her own time, B. is now read chiefly for her revelations of upper-class Victorian women's lives. Scandals surrounded her separation from her aristocratic husband, novelist and member of Parliament Edward Bulwer-Lytton.

B., the second daughter, remembers being told about the wrath of her drunken father on learning that his wife had borne another girl. Later, a son was born, but only she and her sister survived infancy. B. remembers her mother reading the French philosophes and Mary Wollstonecraft on one couch while her mother's maiden sister, Bessie Doyle, read the sentimental novels of the Minerva Press on the other. B. tried to learn to draw and not bother them. The earlier published accounts of B.'s life blame her mother and her feminist ideas for B.'s later difficulties with her husband.

A falling-out with her mother in 1818 took her to London, where she eventually met Bulwer-Lytton. Their marriage, after a stormy courtship and over the objections of his mother, made them one of the most popular couples in London. She gave up writing to devote time to her husband's career and her family, giving birth to two children. The marriage broke up in 1836 because of her husband's much-publicized affairs and his violent physical attacks on her, and she lost custody of the children (as was usual). Divorce was not possible, even with the Divorce Act of 1857, because B. would not consent to being named the guilty party. At one point Bulwer-Lytton had her incarcerated in an insane asylum, but the resultant public outcry succeeded in freeing her after three weeks.

A poet before her marriage, B. turned to writing fiction after the separation as a way to make a living (her own inheritance having gone to her husband when she married) as well as to describe the vulnerability of Victorian women's legal and social position. Her first novel, *Cheveley, or the Man of Honour,* is dedicated to "the only man whose integrity I have found unimpeachable and whose friendship I have proved unvarying. . . . No One Nobody, Esq., of No Hall, Nowhere." Her best writing is in the historical novels *Bianca Cappello* and The *School for Husbands,* but others, even the *romans à clef* such as *Cheveley* and *Very Successful,* display ironic wit. Few copies of her novels remain extant, partly as a result of Bulwer-Lytton's pressure on reputable publishers not to publish his wife's work and partly because of the poor financial condition of some of the publishers she did use. She joked that her books were not published but "merely misprinted."

WORKS: *Cheveley, or the Man of Honour* (1839). *The Budget of the Bubble Family* (1840). *The Prince-Duke and the Page* (1841). *Bianca Cappello: An Historical Romance* (1843). *Memoirs of a Muscovite* (1844). *The Peer's Daughters* (1849). *Miriam Sedley, or The Tares and the Wheat* (1851). *The School for Husbands: or Molière's Life and Times* (1852). *Behind the Scenes* (1854). *Very Successful* (1856). *Lady Bulwer-Lytton's Appeal to the Justice and Charity of the English Public* (1857). *The World and His Wife, or a Person of Consequence: A Photographic Novel* (1858). *The Household Fairy* (1870). *Shells from the Sands of Time* (1876). (B. did not write *A Blighted Life,* which was published in her name in 1880.)

BIBLIOGRAPHY: Devey, L. *Life of Rosina, Lady Lytton* (1887). Sadleir, M. *Bulwer and His Wife, A Panorama* (1931).

For articles in reference works, see: *Ireland. NCBEL. ToddBWW.*

Other references: *HLQ* (1990). Shores, L. *MSE* (1978).

Margaret McFadden

Bunbury, Sarah: See *Lennox Bunbury Napier, Sarah*

Julie Burchill

BORN: 7 April 1960, Bristol.
DAUGHTER OF: Thomas William Burchill and Elizabeth Thomas.
MARRIED: Tony Parsons, 1980; Cosmo Landesman, 1985.

A hard-edged and uncompromising journalist, B. was originally associated with the punk movement in London in the late 1970s, when she left her home in Bristol at the age of seventeen and began working as a rock critic for the *New Musical Express.* Graduating to commentary on all areas of fashion, music, the youth scene, and popular culture in general, B. describes herself as an odd "combination of juvenile delinquent turned academic" and has earned a reputation in the London literary scene as a tough, ambitious, trendy iconoclast, the voice of a radical generation turned establishment martinet. "I write because speech is my second language," claims B.

She was born into a blue-collar, working-class family; her father, partially deafened by the noise of machinery, worked in a distillery, and her mother in a cardboard-box factory. Seeped in a proletarian background of trade-union activism and socialism, B. describes her political views as "New Rightism meets Communism." Having worked her way out of the rock-music press and into more mainstream publishing, she now writes for *The Spectator, New Society, The Literary Review, The Face, The Sunday Times, Taltler,* and *Cosmopolitan.* Her provocative, abrasive, and often controversial articles tend to deal with commercial and populist topics such as class and the proletariat, sex and sex scandals, teen idols, the record industry, fashion, contemporary politics, and Hollywood icons.

Her writing in the late 1970s, epitomized by *The Boy Looked at Johnny—The Obituary of Rock and Roll* (1978, with rock critic Tony Parsons, whom she married two years later), showed a cynical urgency in the way it demystified musical traditions and embraced new directions and fashions in youth culture. The 1980s witnessed B. broadening her journalistic horizons in texts such as *Love It or Shove It* (1985), a popular history of style, fashion, and music since World War II, and *Damaged Gods: Cults and Heroes Reappraised* (1986), an analysis of the failures of cults and cultures from the 1950s onwards. It was these two books that perhaps most clearly crystalized what has come to be recognized as B.'s particular journalistic trademark—an aggressive, controversial, catty prose style motivated (sometimes compulsively and self-consciously) to provoke and annoy, deliberately unpacking cultural preconceptions and taboos. Her writing is sometimes camp and throwaway, sometimes bitchy and insensitive, sometimes stylish and funny, but always fresh, fearless, and original. B. was characterized by the press in the 1970s and early 1980s as petulant and rebellious, a "downright bad influence." She has also been called "the cleverest woman of all time" (by Peter York), and the BBC has described her as "more influential than Kim Wilde, Vanessa Redgrave and the Princess of Wales rolled into one." By the late 1980s, the subject of her writing had broadened to cover not only popular and youth issues but television, literature, drama, art, and film, as well as most other areas of culture.

B.'s first novel, *Ambition* (1990), is the story of Susan Street, described by B. as "a simple, go-ahead girl who was out to get what she wanted by any means." Susan moves to London at a young age to become a brilliant and ambitious newspaper deputy whose path to the top is hindered by blackmail, scandal, the supernatural, and romance. Written in playful, earthy, and imaginative style, *Ambition* is a deliberate parody of the sex-and-shopping blockbuster, appropriating all the requisite scenarios to produce a deady and highly exaggerated fantasy of inordinate wealth, violent passion, cynical wit and cruel satire. The work received a great deal of critical acclaim, at least with British audiences, rising to no. 2 on the London *Times* bestseller list. Yet it was heavily criticized by reviewers for its erotic content, presented in a manner many critics claimed was inappropriate for a woman writer. Joseph Conelly of *The Times* attempted to explain this critical response by pointing out that "all the (mostly female) reviewers of B.'s work have either dismissed it contemptusously, or written at length about their shock, horror and disgust" over the book's subject matter. Conelly points out that other similar books of recent years—novels like Sally Beauman's *Destiny* and Judith Krantz's *Scruples*—also received negative reviews on their way to becoming highly successful sellers. B.'s follow-up novel, *No Exit* (1993), follows a similar path, this time employing a male protagonist: Gary First is an ambitious and hard-nosed foreign correspondent whose first big break comes with a World Service posting to Prague where he meets and falls in love with Maria, a political refugee with expensive tastes.

B. seems to be moving further and further away from popular journalism into the mainstream of elite culture. Two further novels appeared in 1996, *Century City* and *Happy Hour.* Her punk days well behind her, B. is also the founder and editor of *The Modern Review,* a precociously highbrow magazine/journal that takes both traditional and popular culture very seriously indeed.

WORKS: (with T. Parsons) *The Boy Looked at Johnny—The Obituary of Rock and Roll* (1978). *Love It or Shove It* (1985). *Damaged Gods: Cults and Heroes Reappraised* (1986). *Girls on Film* (1986). *Ambition* (1990). (with others) *The May Day Dialogues* (1990). *Prince* (screenplay, BBC-TV 1991). *Sex and Sensibility* (1992). *No Exit* (1993). *Debatable Land* (1994). *Century City* (1996). *Happy Hour* (1996).

BIBLIOGRAPHY: Hirschhorn, M. *Esquire* (September 1993). McAllister, N. *Melody Maker* (5 August 1989). *New Statesman* (11 June 1993). Schillinger, L. *New York* (19 June 1995). Wechsler, P. and R. D. Friedman. *New York* (31 July 1995). Wolcott, J. *Vanity Fair* (March 1992).

For articles in reference works, see: *CA. WD.*

Other references: *LonT* (28 July 1989, 20 February 1993).

Mikita Brottman

Katharine Penelope Burdekin

BORN: 23 July 1896, Spondon, Derbyshire.
DIED: 10 August 1963, Suffolk.
DAUGHTER OF: Charles James Cade and Mary Rowena Elizabeth Casterton Cade.
MARRIED: Beaufort Burdekin, 1915.
WROTE UNDER: Katharine Burdekin; Kay Burdekin; Murray Constantine.

Although she wrote in other genres of fiction, B.'s most distinctive contribution to twentieth-century literature is a series of utopian and dystopian novels. Like Charlotte Perkins Gilman and some contemporary feminist novelists, but unlike many other writers in these genres, B. incorporates acute analyses of gender relations in her utopian and dystopian imaginings. Her works of the 1930s provide highly innovative critiques of a Europe wracked by fascism, militarism, and "sex antagonism"; they also project potential futures based on B.'s prescient insights about the links between domination and gender hierarchy.

B. was the daughter of upper-middle-class English parents who did not honor her wish to attend Oxford as her brothers had. Her marriage to Australian barrister Beaufort Burdekin in 1915 took her to Sydney, where she began writing fiction. By 1922, B. had left her husband and returned to England with their two daughters. She eventually made a home with a female companion; they lived a quiet country existence together for the rest of B.'s life. During the 1920s and 1930s, B. wrote numerous novels, ten of which were published between 1922 and 1940. B. used the pseudonym "Murray Constantine" for four of these books; with great perseverance, scholar Daphne Patai uncovered the identity of the writer behind the pseudonym in the 1980s and has worked with the Feminist Press to begin republishing her novels and printing previously unpublished manuscripts.

Quiet Ways (1930) provides a fine example of B.'s more conventionally realistic work and demonstrates her political vision. This pacifist novel tells the story of a volunteer nurse, a reluctant soldier, and other characters "discontented with the way humanity orders itself"; they rebel against rigid gender and class stereotypes, heterosexuality, and war. Like many writers, B. distanced herself from pacifism when confronted with fascism, but her keen critique of the masculine culture of war continued through her significant utopian and dystopian works.

First in this group is *Proud Man* (1934), the most audaciously complex in narrative voice and scenario. The "Person" who narrates this novel returns via a dream to the England of the 1930s from a utopian world thousands of years in the future. The "Person" spends two years among what it perceives as "subhumans," "neither animal nor human, but in a transition state between the two." B. uses the form of a fictional anthropological report to defamiliarize and implicitly criticize many aspects of her society that her readers may have assumed were natural or inevitable.

Swastika Night (1937), as a Left Book Club selection, was B.'s most widely read novel. It presents a gruesome dystopian future created by seven centuries of "Hitlerian" rule. Written twelve years before *1984,* this novel incorporates many of George Orwell's themes, and Bonifas has made a case for its influence on this much more famous dystopia. B. again brings gender relations to the forefront in this work, portraying the glorification of masculinity at the heart of Nazism that is based on the subordination and "reduction" of women, who now live in communal cages and have lost all sexual and personal autonomy. B. also emphasizes ideological rather than military resistance to fascism; her fiction is an attempt to foster a "rebellion of disbelief" in Nazi principles. As such, the novel's plot remains somewhat skeletal; here and in her other works of this type, B.'s fictional mode tends to be expository and didactic rather than dramatic or focused on psychology in a modernist manner.

The End of This Day's Business (written 1930s, pub. 1989) reverses the gender coding of *Swastika Night* by presenting a feminist utopia in which women are dominant in a happy but hierarchical order that constrains men. The rebel in this novel is an artist who sees that the perfection of humanity can take place only if society moves beyond hierarchy, and she must die for her traitorous vision. B. here provides an analysis of power that anticipates feminist theories of much later in the century.

B. continued to write after World War II but stopped publishing her works. She moved away from directly political fiction and returned to concerns with religion and spirituality that had made their appearance in earlier novels. For example, *The Rebel Passion* (1929) provided an abbreviated history of the Western world in the visions of a monk filled with the passion of pity due to his having a woman's soul; *The Devil, Poor Devil* (1934) speculated on evil in the modern world through a hybrid plot of religious allegory and romance.

WORKS: *Anna Colquhoun* (1922). *The Reasonable Hope* (1924). *The Burning Ring* (1927). (as Kay Burdekin) *The Children's Country* (1929). (as Kay Burdekin) *The Rebel Passion* (1929). *Quiet Ways* (1930). (as Murray Constantine) *The Devil, Poor Devil* (1934). (as Murray Constantine) *Proud Man* (1934). (as Murray Constantine) *Swastika Night* (1937). (with M. Goldsmith) *Venus in Scorpio* (1940). *The End of This Day's Business* (written in the 1930s; published in 1989).

BIBLIOGRAPHY: Bonifas, G. *N&Q* (1987). Croft, A., in *Inside the Myth: Orwell, Views from the Left,* ed. C. Norris (1984). Crossley, R. *SFS* (1987). McKay, G. *SFS* (1994). Pagetti, C. *SFS* (1990). Patai, D., afterword to *The End of This Day's Business* (1989). Patai, D., foreword and afterword to *Proud Man* (1993). Patai, C., foreword to *Swastika Night* (1985). Patai, D., in *Rediscovering Forgotten Radicals: British Women Writers 1889–1939,* ed. A. Ingram and D. Patai (1993). Russell, E., in *Where No Man Has Gone Before: Women and Science Fiction,* ed. L. Armitt (1991). *Women's Studies International Forum* (1984).

For articles in reference works see: *ESF. SF&FL. SFE. WWWAEEA.*

Other references: Albinski, N. B. *Women's Utopias in British and American Fiction* (1988). Sargent, L. T. *British and American Utopian Literature, 1516–1985* (1988).

Loretta Stec

Barbara Burford

BORN: c. 1946.

There is little published biographical material on British-born B. In *A Dangerous Knowing* (1984), B. described herself as "a thirty-nine year old Black woman, an active feminist and the mother of a ten-year-old daughter. I am committed to my work in medical research. . . . I write science fiction, poetry, and prose." She has lived in London and in Kent.

B. has twelve poems in *A Dangerous Knowing: Four*

Black Women Poets. The book, also containing the work of Gabriela Pearse, Grace Nichols, and Jackie Kay, was the first collection of black women's poetry in Great Britain. The book's editors praise B.'s poems for their "subtle nuances and ironic humour and affirmative joy." B.'s keen sense of humor is demonstrated in "State of the Art," in which a woman claims she will change her life when she meets her ideal lover: "Then I'll ride my bike backwards, / Then I'll use mouthwash. / Eat red kidney beans. / dress on sundays." B.'s poems, however, do not lack for seriousness. In a particularly powerful piece, "Christine," a poor woman mourns the death of her unborn child. B.'s main focus is on women's strength, as demonstrated in such pieces as "In My Gift," "Daughters of Eve," "Women Talking," and "In Solitary." In this last poem, the narrator waits to "give birth to my own world."

Also in 1984, B. wrote a play, *Patterns,* which was commissioned by the Changing Women's Theatre. It was performed at the Drill Hall and at the Oval Theatre.

B.'s most significant work is *The Threshing Floor* (1986), consisting of six short stories and a novella. B's characters are often initially held down because of their gender, race, age, sexual preference, physical size, and/or economic situation, but ultimately they triumph, usually with the support of other women. One story, "The Pinstripe Summer," centers on an older woman, abused by those at work who take advantage of her experience without giving her any credit. She develops a close relationship with a woman at work and feels liberated. In another story, "He Said," a pregnant woman defies her father, her boyfriend, and her doctor and decides to keep her baby. Perhaps the most intriguing of the shorter pieces is "Miss Jessie," a chilling story of an elderly Jamaican cleaning lady who victimizes a vagrant in a ritualistic sacrifice. The long title piece is the lyrical story of Hannah, a young black woman, who grieves the death of her older, white female lover. Over time Hannah is comforted by and falls in love with a black woman.

The Threshing Floor received mixed critical reaction. The reviewer for *Publisher's Weekly* believes that "While the characters and the situation are of some interest, Burford's earnestness causes the story to drag." Jeanette Winterson states that in the title story "the sense of separation and loss that Burford achieves is extremely powerful—it is unfortunate, though that some of the power gets lost through having to sustain unnecessary characters." On the other hand, Sara Maitland writes that these are "stunning stories: magical realism firmly located in the political present and reverberating with both surprise and certainty." And Diane Bogus praises the book for showing "sanity, compassion, creativity and love."

B., along with Lindsay MacRae and Sylvia Paskin, edited *Dancing the Tightrope: New Love Poems by Women* in 1987. The editors look at love as being an act of revolution. The five poems by B. in the book generally convey a sense of sadness and separation. In "Scheherazade" the speaker, instead of being empowered by words, is "ensorcelled" by her lover. There is an absent lover in "Reflections," but although the lover is gone, it is said, "your voice, your scent, / the very taste of you, remain."

In her essay "The Landscapes Painted on the Inside of My Skin" (1987), B. points out the need to have more black British women writers in print. She reiterates this point in another essay, "' . . . and a star to steer her by'": "Black women writing in Britain at this moment share a commitment and a need to leave a legacy, an investment, for all those young Black people whose only experience is life in Britain." Unfortunately, B. may have fallen victim herself to the often exclusionary British publishing, editorial, and critical process. Despite showing much promise as a poet and fiction writer, she has had little published in recent years, mostly reviews in *The New Statesman* of works by authors such as bell hooks and Michele Wallace.

WORKS: (ed., with others, and contents in) *A Dangerous Knowing: Four Black Women Poets,* (1984). *Patterns* (1984). *The Threshing Floor* (1986). (ed., with others, and contents in) *Dancing the Tightrope: New Love Poems by Women* (1987).

BIBLIOGRAPHY: Bogus, S. *Small Pieces* (December 1988). Maitland, S. *New Statesman* (25 July 1986). *PW* (6 March 1987). Winterson, J. *TLS* (22 August 1986). Wisker, G., ed. *Black Women's Writing* (1994).

For articles in reference works, see: *Bloomsbury.*

Other references: "The Landscape Painted on the Inside of My Skin," in *Spare Rib* (June 1987). "' . . . and a star to steer her by,f" in *Charting the Journey: Writings by Black and Third World Women,* ed. G. Shabnam (1988).

Louis J. Parascandola

Elizabeth Burnet

BORN: 8 November 1661, Earontoun, Hampshire.
DIED: 3 February 1709, London.
DAUGHTER OF: Sir Richard Blake and Elizabeth Bathurst Blake.
MARRIED: Robert Berkeley, 1678; Bishop Gilbert Burnet, c. 1700.

B., devotional writer and benefactress, was born into a well-connected Hampshire family. At the age of seventeen, through the good offices of Dr. Fell, Bishop of Oxford, she met and married Robert Berkeley. Deeply religious, her convictions were soon tested by her mother-in-law, a devout Roman Catholic. To offset this powerful influence, B. became a determined student of her own religion. She finally journeyed to Holland with her husband to escape the pressures to renounce her faith. On her return to her husband's home in Spetchley in Worchestershire, she devoted her life to religious studies and charitable works.

During the years of her marriage until her husband's death in 1693, she gave freely of her time and money for the welfare of others. She attended the sick and dying, provided food and books for the clergy, and established schools for the children of the poor. At a time when education was available to only the privileged few, she paid for schooling for more than a hundred children. When her husband died, she implemented plans, liberally supported by his bequest, for a hospital for the poor in Worchester.

During the seven years following the death of her husband until she remarried, she continued her charitable work. Unlike many widows of the times, she was left wealthy by her husband, a blessing she shared freely with others less fortunate than herself. The practice she followed was to keep one-fifth of her income for herself and use the remainder for others. Though she gave liberally, she had the rare quality of not humiliating the recipients of her kindness. She was loved for her saintly ways by those who knew her.

In approximately 1700, she married Gilbert Burnet, Bishop of Salisbury, who is remembered for his *History of the Reformation* (1674–1714) and his *History of My Own Times* (1724–34). She took in hand the bishop's children from a previous marriage and raised them as her own. With the full support of her husband, she continued her charitable work for the remainder of her life. In 1707, she traveled to Spa, in Belgium, for her health. Somewhat recovered, she returned to England, but she again became ill and died in 1709 of pleuritic fever.

B.'s literary reputation depends on a single work of devotions, written for her own use during her seven years of widowhood. Reflecting the importance she placed on religion as a part of everyday experience, *A Method of Devotion* was designed, according to her preface, to achieve "The great End of all Religions and Devotions . . . to restore the depraved Nature of Men to its original Perfection" and to assist "weak young and ignorant Persons . . . to Purify their Hearts and Lives by Duties of Religion." She emphasizes that avoidance of "scandalous Vices" and repetition of prayers are not sufficient to achieve these goals. She apologizes for the repetitions that are explained by "Part . . . [having been] drawn up many years ago, and enlarged at several times." Adroitly, she turns weakness to advantage when she writes, "it is not thought worth while to correct those Repetitions, which might serve better to fix necessary truths in the Memory of young and ignorant Persons."

The work of nearly 400 pages is divided into two parts. The first part involves rules for living; the second, rules for worship. Part I provides schedules for prayer and directions for dealing with daily problems like eating, dressing, and working. Of principal importance is a concern for others, as the following directions on dress reveal: "Let your Cloathing be with a decent Frugality, the better to enable you to cloath the Poor." For B., the Bible was a practical guide in everyday affairs. For example, the Golden Rule is apparent in these directions regarding dealings with others: "In all your Transactions with your Neighbours, be it Friend or Enemy, do as you would be done to," or regarding employees, "Exact no more work of any than their Strength and Health enable them to Perform." Part II focuses on "Some Rules Relating to the Devotions" and surveys in its chapters a variety of subjects including days of fasting, humiliation, retirement, and contemplation. *A Method of Devotion,* with its clear, unaffected language, reflects in both style and content the saintly qualities of its author.

George Ballard recognized the unique nature of these qualities when he wrote of B., "Her design, indeed, was to render a strictness in religion as agreeable to all companies as was possible, and to show that it did not take off from that easiness and freedom which is the life of conversation, and few ever succeeded better in recommending it thus to the world than she did."

WORKS: *A Method of Devotion: or, Roles for Holy & Devout Living, with Prayers on Several Occasions, And Advices & Devotions For the Holy Sacrament. In Two Parts* (1708).

BIBLIOGRAPHY: *Biographica Britannica; Or, The Lives of the most Eminent Persons who have Flourished in Great Britain and Ireland,* 2nd ed., ed. A. Kippis (1778–93). Goodwyn, T. *Memorials and Characters of Two Hundred Eminent and Worthy Persons . . . of Great Britain* (1744; rpt. of "Some Account of Her Life," which accompanied the Second and Third Editions of *A Method of Devotion,* 1709 and 1713). Nichols, J. *Illustrations of the Literary History of the Eighteenth Century, Consisting of Authentic Memoirs and Original Letters* (1817–58).

For articles in reference works, see: *Ballard. DNB. Fifty Famous Women; Their Virtues and Failings, and the Lessons of their Lives* (n.d.). Ireland. *ToddDBA.*

Philip Bordinat

Frances (Fanny) Burney

BORN: 13 June 1752, King's Lynn, Norfolk.
DIED: 6 January 1840, London.
DAUGHTER OF: Charles Burney and Esther Sleepe Burney.
MARRIED: Alexandre Jean-Baptiste Piochard d'Arblay, 1793.

B. was the daughter of a music-master and organist later to gain renown as a historian of music and member of Samuel Johnson's circle. She was a shy and seemingly backward child but displayed an early talent for mimicry and a remarkably retentive memory. B.'s mother died in 1762, and five years later her father married Elizabeth Allen, a widow with a keen interest in literature. B. became a voracious reader and began extensive experimentation with writing. In 1767, her stepmother concluded that B. and her sister Susan were taking their writing too seriously, and the girls dutifully consigned their "scribblings"—including the draft of a novel by B., "Carolyn Evelyn"—to a bonfire.

In 1768, B. began keeping a detailed diary, and in 1778 her first novel, *Evelina, or a Young Lady's Entrance into the World,* was published. The novel was published anonymously, but the secret of its authorship quickly leaked out and B. found herself the center of a whirlwind of adulation. Samuel Johnson, Hester Thrale, Sir Joshua Reynolds, Richard Brinsley Sheridan, and others of the "best" people were effusive in their praise. B. quickly became the darling of the Streatham set and the special pet of Johnson.

B. next tried writing a comedy for the stage, but the project was dropped at the urging of her father and

Samuel "Daddy" Crisp, an old family friend. They apparently feared the play's sharp satire on female "wits" would offend the influential "bluestockings." Another novel, *Cecilia,* appeared in 1782. In 1784, B. lost three close and important friends. "Daddy" Crisp died that April. Then, that summer, the widowed Mrs. Thrale announced she would marry an Italian singing master. Her family and friends reacted with shocked disapproval, and she turned to B. for support. The very conservative and socially punctilious B. responded coldly, and the friendship ended. In December, Johnson died.

In 1785, B. was presented to King George III and Queen Charlotte and was soon offered the post of second keeper of the robes for Queen Charlotte, entering the royal service in July. She soon found the restrictive nature of her post disagreeable, and she resented the petty tyrannies of her immediate superior. In 1790, she voiced her discontent to her father, but he was reluctant to allow her to resign. The next year, though, her health began to fail, and she left the post in July 1791 with a pension of £100 a year. In January 1793, B. visited a friend at Norbury Park in Surrey and was introduced to a colony of French refugees who had rented nearby Juniper Hall. Among them was a former army officer, Alexandre d'Arblay, who had been adjutant general to the Marquis de Lafayette and accompanied Lafayette when he fled to Austria. A romance blossomed, and B. and d'Arblay were married on 28 July 1793. Their only child, Alexandre, was born on 18 December 1794.

Shortly after her marriage, B. wrote *Brief Reflections Relative to the Emigrant French Clergy,* a pamphlet encouraging charity toward Roman Catholic priests who had fled revolutionary France. March 1795 saw a performance at Drury Lane of *Edwy and Elgiva,* a tragedy written during her years at court. It was a dismal failure, withdrawn after one performance. *Camilla,* B.'s third novel, was published in 1796. A successful subscription sale made the novel a strong moneymaker, but critical reaction was mixed. In 1801, General d'Arblay returned to France to try to reclaim the property he had lost during the revolution, and B. joined him in 1802, intending to stay only a few months. But war broke out again, trapping her in France until 1812. B.'s last novel, *The Wanderer, or Female Difficulties,* appeared in 1814. It sold well, but it was seen as a pitiful example of the deterioration of a once-skilled writer's abilities. B. was surprised and hurt by the harsh criticism it received.

B. returned to France after the fall of Napoleon and was present there during the "Hundred Days." The d'Arblays returned to England in 1815 and settled in Bath, where the general died in 1818. B. moved to London and spent a quiet and retired old age. In 1832, she published the *Memoirs of Doctor Burney,* based on manuscript notes left by her father and fleshed out with her own anecdotes and recollections. The public found the work entertaining, but the critics condemned it roundly. B. became a recluse and died quietly at the age of eighty-seven.

B.'s fame as a novelist was initially based upon her first published work, *Evelina.* It is an epistolary novel, written in an easy and still-readable style, and the first important example of the domestic novel of manners. It combined a good-humored but sometimes biting social satire with a sentimentality much more appreciated in her age than in our own. In fact, the completely moral tone of B.'s works has been cited as an important influence in the establishment of the novel as a respectable literary genre.

In her second novel, *Cecilia,* discerning readers noted a disturbing change in B.'s style: a movement toward use of "elevated," more elegant language. This was so marked that there was widespread but unfounded speculation that Samuel Johnson had a hand in the novel's composition. B. had begun to lose her touch, and her style continued to decline into a stilted, pompous verbosity that makes *Camilla* seem tedious and *The Wanderer* almost unreadable to some; recent critics, however, have challenged this evaluation.Many factors have been advanced as the cause of this decline: a desire to imitate Johnson's style, a striving to enhance the respectability of her novels by elevating their tone, a loss of familiarity with the rhythms of English prose during her absence in France, a loss of spirit occasioned by the need to write for money rather than as purely creative expression, and a simple drying up of the creative juices. Some readers, however, see no evidence of this decline.

Although *Evelina* is the only one of Burney's novels to claim lasting readership, B. was not a "one-shot novelist." *Cecilia* and *Camilla,* too, were widely read and admired in their day. B. did much to make the novel a respectable literary form and novel writing an acceptable occupation for women. The influence of her works on Jane Austen has long been acknowledged, and traces of B.'s influence have been discerned in the works of Maria Edgeworth, Charlotte Smith, and others.

Conventional assessments of B.'s novels see her as fairly conservative in both form and content. They see little stylistic inventiveness in her work that draws on proven novelistic techniques. What is seen as fresh and engaging about *Evelina* is B.'s choice of a young heroine as the persona from whose viewpoint we observe the events of the plot—and her exceptional talent for depicting manners, social behavior, and conversation. B.'s heroines struggle, it is true, but (according to this view) their struggle is merely to regain their proper place in the social order, not to question the legitimacy of that order. Marriage with a socially acceptable partner is the desirable goal and its achievement a rightful cause for celebration at the end of the novel.

More recently, however, feminist critics have challenged these notions, finding a tension in B.'s works between an apparent conformity to social mores and a more rebellious subtext that attempts to challenge and subvert them. An undercurrent of protest against the conditions of female experience is seen in the imagery of confinement and violation, the presence of violence and cruelty, and the use of subterfuge as a feminine strategy that effectively undercuts the apparent acceptance of the status quo. The act of writing itself may serve to exorcise and at the same time contain anger and pain.

Public and private selves converge in the posthumous publication of B.'s *Diary and Letters* (1842–46), which assured her a place in literary history. In the *Memoirs of Doctor Burney,* she had provided fascinating glimpses of the famous figures of her day—unfortunately smothered in turgid prose. In her journals and letters, though, the characters stand out clearly and vividly. B. rivals James Boswell as a recorder of conversation, and her descriptions of people are much more lifelike. A keen observer, she gives detailed and animated portraits of her contemporaries; she is an excellent storyteller with plenty of stories to tell—especially about Johnson and the members of his circle, her days at Court, and her time in France during the Napoleonic Wars. In our own day, the ongoing edition of her voluminous journals provides fresh and compelling material on her family, her society, and her life and practice as a writer.

WORKS: *Evelina, or a Young Lady's Entrance into the World* (1778). *Cecilia* (1782). *Brief Reflections Relative to the Emigrant French Clergy* (1793). *Camilla* (1796). *Edwy and Elgiva* (staged 1795; ed. M. J. Benkovitz, 1957). *The Wanderer, or Female Difficulties* (1814). *Memoirs of Doctor Burney* (1832). *Diary and Letters of Madame d'Arblay*, ed. C. Barrett (1842–46). *The Journals and Letters of Fanny Burney (Madame d'Arblay)*, ed. J. Hemlow, et al. (1972–84). *Selected Letters and Journals*, ed. J. Hemlow (1987). *The Early Journals and Letters of Fanny Burney*, 3 vol., ed. L. E. Troide, et al. (1987–94). *The Complete Plays of Fanny Burney*, ed. P. Sabor, et al. (1995).

BIBLIOGRAPHY: Adelstein, M. E. *Fanny Burney* (1968). Devlin, D. D. *The Novels and Journals of Fanny Burney* (1987). Dobson, A. *Fanny Burney* (1903). Doody, M. A. *Frances Burney: A Life in the Works* (1988). Epstein, J. *The Iron Pen: Fanny Burney and the Politics of Women's Writing* (1989). Grau, J. A. *Fanny Burney: An Annotated Bibliography* (1981). Hahn, E. *A Degree of Prudery* (1950). Hemlow, J. *The History of Fanny Burney* (1958). Johnson, R. B. *Fanny Burney and the Burneys* (1926). Kilpatrick, S. *Fanny Burney* (1980). Lloyd, C. *Fanny Burney* (1936). Overman, A. A. *An Investigation into the Character of Fanny Burney* (1933). Rogers, K. M. *Frances Burney: The World of Female Difficulties* (1990). Simons, J. *Fanny Burney* (1987). Straub, K. *Divided Fictions: Fanny Burney and Feminine Strategy* (1987). Tourtellot, A. B. *Be Loved No More* (1938). White, E. *Fanny Burney, Novelist* (1960). Zonitch, B. A. *Familiar Violence: Gender and Social Upheaval in the Novels of Fanny Burney* (1997).

For articles in reference works, see: *Allibone. ArtWW. Bloomsbury. Cambridge. CBEL. Chambers. CHEL. DNB. ELB. Europa. Feminist. Moulton. NCBEL. NCHEL. OCEL. Oxford. RE. ToddBWW. ToddDBA.*

Other references: Bloom, L. D. and E. Bloom. *Novel* (1979). Brown, M. G., in *Fetter'd or Free? British Women Novelists, 1670–1815*, ed. M. A. Schofield and C. Macheski (1986). Cutting, R. M. *SEL* (1977). Epstein, J. L. *ECent* (1986). Epstein, J. *Representations* (1986). Henlow, J. *PMLA* (1950). Hemlow, J. *TLS* (23 August 1996). Newton, J. L. *Women, Power and Subversion: Social Strategies in British Fiction, 1778–1860* (1981). Spacks, P. M. *ECS* (1974). Spacks, P. M. *Imagining a Self: Autobiography and Novel in 18th Century England* (1976). Spencer, J. *The Rise of the Woman Novelist: From Aphra Behn to Jane Austen* (1986). Staves, S. *MP* (1976). Straub, K. *ECent* (1986). *TLS* (23 August 1996). *UTQ* (1950).

Joseph A. Grau
(updated by Lorna J. Clark)

Sarah Harriet Burney

BORN: 29 August 1772, King's Lynn, Norfolk.
DIED: 8 February 1844, Cheltenham, Gloucester.
DAUGHTER OF: Charles Burney and Elizabeth (Allen) Burney.

The youngest child of a talented family of musicians, artists, and writers, B. was daughter of the second marriage of musicologist Charles Burney and half-sister to the more famous novelist, Frances Burney (d'Arblay). She lived at home with her father until 1798, when she left to live with her half-brother, Captain James Burney, who had sailed around the world with Captain Cook. (Evidence suggests it was her father's difficult temper that inspired the move, not an incestuous relationship, as has been alleged.) After five years (in 1803), she became a governess, then returned home in 1807 to care for her elderly father, who nevertheless left her little provision in his will. After his death in 1814, she remained on at the Royal Hospital, Chelsea, until 1821–22 when she acted briefly as a paid companion and then took charge of two heiresses until 1829. Later that year, she traveled to Italy where she lived mostly in Florence before returning to England in 1833 to retire, first to Bath, then to Cheltenham, where she died in a boarding-house in 1844.

A spinster of narrow means, B. struggled all her life against social isolation and penury, yet retained a proud spirit and an unconventional character. Possessed of intelligence and an acerbic wit, she explicitly preferred male company as more stimulating; her friends included Henry Crabb Robinson, diarist and friend of Wordsworth, and Caroline Anne Bowles, the second Mrs. Southey. Her lively letters show a lifelong engagement with literature, whether as reader, self-styled critic, editor, or novelist. A voracious reader, she kept up with current literary trends; of contemporary writers, she admired the morality of Maria Edgeworth and the originality of James Fenimore Cooper, but reserved her enthusiasm for Sir Walter Scott and Jane Austen, whose genius she recognized immediately. Austen was also, it seems, an appreciative reader of B.

B.'s own novels, written for the most part in the genre of domestic novel of manners, were successful in their day, translated into French and printed abroad. After the third, *Traits of Nature* (1812), was an undoubted best-seller, she was offered a generous £100 a volume by the successful publisher, Henry Colburn. Her reputation has suffered (both inside and outside the family) by comparison with her sister novelist; even in her own day, she was taxed by reviewers with a family resemblance (although the first two novels were published anonymously, the identity of the author appears to have been an open secret).

Yet B.'s novels are not without interest of their own. In *Clarentine* (1796), a young orphan is courted by a fraternal sailor-figure against a background of comic characters. *Geraldine Fauconberg* (1808) features a fastidious hero and a Gothic sub-plot; the story unfolds through the letters of a sprightly confidante. *Traits of Nature,* her most successful, offers a mix of satire and romance in which the love interest is displaced by the heroine's quest for acceptance by her estranged father. *Tales of Fancy* (1816–20) contains "The Shipwreck," a tale of Crusoe-like castaways that borrows Shakespearian motifs; and "Country Neighbours," in which the narrative voice of a spinster-aunt comments on two families coming to terms with the sins of the past. Her last work, *The Romance of Private Life* (1839), is also split between "The Renunciation," in which the heroine rejects a life of imposture to seek her true identity, and "The Hermitage," a melodrama involving an unsolved murder.

B.'s fiction shows a recurrent and suggestive pattern of dysfunctional families—unnatural or absent mothers and tyrannical fathers afflicting the heroines with a sense of abandonment. Although she was self-deprecating about her work, which she attributed solely to financial motives, her pose is unconvincing. Her writing appears to have provided a welcome release that allowed her to transcend the restrictive conditions of her solitary life.

WORKS: *Clarentine* (1796). *Geraldine Fauconberg* (1808). *Traits of Nature* (1812). *Tales of Fancy* (1816–20). *The Romance of Private Life* (1839). *The Letters of Sarah Harriet Burney,* ed. L. J. Clark (1996).

BIBLIOGRAPHY: Clark, L. J. *Persuasions* (1995). Hemlow, J. *The History of Fanny Burney* (1958). Johnson, R. B. *Fanny Burney and the Burneys* (1926). Morley, E. J. *MP* (1941). Scholes, P. A. *The Great Dr. Burney* (1948). Zonitch, B. A. *Familiar Violence: Gender and Social Upheaval in the Novels of Fanny Burney* (1997).

For articles in reference works, see: *Allibone. ArtWW. Bloomsbury. DNB. Europa. Feminist. NCHEL. OGEWW. ToddDBA.*

Other references: Prance, C. A. *Companion to Charles Lamb: A Guide to People and Places 1760–1847* (1983).

Lorna J. Clark

Charlotte Bury

BORN: 28 January 1775, London.
DIED: 31 March 1861, London.
DAUGHTER OF: John Campbell, fifth Duke of Argyll, and Elizabeth Gunning, Duchess of Harni Hon, Duchess of Argyll.
MARRIED: John Campbell, 1796; Edward John Bury, 1818.

The daughter of the Duke and Duchess of Argyll, B. (née Campbell) nevertheless spent most of her life writing to support herself. Deeply religious, B. married twice for love rather than security: first, to her cousin John Campbell in 1796, with whom she had nine children; second, to the Reverend Edward John Bury in 1818, of whom those children strongly disapproved. This later marriage seems to have been particularly fulfilling in spite of its relative poverty. The Burys collaborated on *The Three Great Sanctuaries of Tuscanny* (1833), a series of poems about three Italian monasteries, written by B. and illustrated by Edward. Throughout her life, B. inhabited a world that was at once colored by Regency dissipation and dandyism, religious duty and resolve, and intellectual inspiration and interaction. She had been presented at court and was later called as a witness in the divorce proceedings of King George IV and Queen Caroline. She published a collection of prayers, *Suspirium Sanctorium* (1826). Close friends with Sir Walter Scott (who acted as a supportive reader and mentor), she reportedly introduced him to Matthew "Monk" Lewis.

B. is best known for a scandalous *Diary Illustrative of the Times of George the Fourth* (1838), in which she detailed her experiences as a lady in waiting for Princess Caroline (1809–10). The *Diary* in its time provoked much splenetic outrage, yet it reads as much more than a sensational tell-all: Included are portraits and assessments of the great figures of the Regency, as well as an analysis of the political successes and failures of George IV's reign. Although B. was a prolific novelist (eighteen books in addition to the poems, prayers, and diaries), she has been largely ignored and consequently forgotten by the present-day literary establishment.

Reaction to B. by both modern critics and her contemporaries is strikingly contradictory; she seems to elicit at once serious scholarly response and highly charged disparagement. Jacqueline Gray rightly applauds B.'s "ability to accurately portray relationships between women and to address the concerns of domestic violence, alcoholism, and economic powerlessness." In addition, she points out that *The Three Great Sanctuaries* was well received by the *Quarterly Review,* and Bruce Graver suggests strong evidence for the poem's influence on William Wordsworth's "The Cuckoo at Laverna." Edward White, however, dismisses B. as a "petty mind . . . [that] kept a diary, distinguished chiefly by incoherence and triviality." Scott admired her work, while William M. Thackeray subjected her religious poetry, her novel *Love* (1837), and the *Diary* to skillful lampooning, and identified B. herself as "a very silly and ridiculous person" (*The Times,* 11 January 1838).

The novels reflect the troublesome task of negotiating among the demands of the worlds of fashion, faith, and literature. Recurrent themes of "pure" sisterly and maternal love, wifely duty, and pious redemption suggest a certain limitation to B.'s "feminist" and literary visions. For readers accustomed to Jane Austen's wit and the Brontës' psychological insights, B.'s fiction can be read as superficial. For readers accustomed to George Eliot's complex questioning of moral duty and faith, and her articulation of a human religion, B.'s appeals to the wisdom of a higher power can wear thin. For readers accustomed to the view of the novel as power, and narrative as an instructing and disciplining force, the attribution of characters' fates to the will of God can feel positively contrived and evasive. But B.'s writing warrants consideration precisely because of these "problems" in her work. While her texts exhibit trials of faith, they do not obscure the social issues of her world. Indeed, B.'s attempts to manage the demands of faith and the social world may well be representative of the central struggle of her time.

WORKS: *Poems on Several Occasions* (1797). *Self Indulgence* (1812). *Conduct is Fate* (1822) *Suspirium Sanctorium* (1826). *"Alla Giornata" or To the Day* (1826). *Flirtation* (1828). *The Exclusives* (1830). *The Separation* (1830). *The Three Great Sanctuaries of Tuscanny* (1833). *The Disinherited and the Ensnared* (1834). *The Lady's Own Cookery Book, and New Dinner-Table Directory* (1835). *The Devoted* (1836). *The Divorced* (1837). *Love* (1837). *Diary Illustrative of the Times of George the Fourth* (1838). *A History of a Flirt* (1840). *Family Records; or, The Two Sisters* (1841). *The Manoeuvering Mother* (1842). *The Wilfullness of Woman* (1844). *The Roses* (1853). *The Lady of Fashion* (1856). *The Two Baronets* (1864).

BIBLIOGRAPHY: Graver, B. E. *PQ*. (1986). White, E. M. *RES* (1965).

For articles in reference works, see: *DLB*. *ToddDBA*.

Tracy W. Beck-Briggs

Abena P. A. Busia

BORN: 28 April 1953, Ghana.
DAUGHTER OF: Kofi Abrefa Busia and Naa-Morkor Busia.

B. is a professor, poet, short story writer, and critic whose work is informed by the central experience of exile across three continents since she spent her early childhood in Ghana, Holland, and Mexico before her family finally settled in England. Daughter of a former Ghanaian prime minister, B. was forced into exile amidst the turbulent political climate that characterized the postindependence era in Ghana. She completed her secondary and higher education in England where she earned a D.Phil. in social anthropology from St. Antony's College in 1984. B. began her teaching career in Oxford and has worked at several American universities in various capacities as post-doctoral fellow, visiting research scholar, and visiting lecturer. Since 1981, she has resided in the United States and teaches at Rutgers University in New Jersey.

B. has been published in journals in West Africa, Europe, and North America and in such anthologies as *Black Women's Writing: Crossing the Boundaries, Summer Fires, New Poetry for Africa, Mandela Amandla: A Seventieth Birthday Tribute to Nelson Mandela,* and *Daughters of Africa: Three Thousand Years of African Women's Writing.* Her volume of poems, *Testimonies of Exile,* was published in 1990. B. is best known for critical work on women's issues and black feminist theory. She is particularly concerned with the "double dispossession" of black women and with the idea of displacement from "home" which creates fractured identities. Like many other political exiles, B. knows the pain of displacement only too well. *Testimonies of Exile* reflects the autobiographical nature of her work.

The volume is divided into three sections: *Book I: Exiles, Book II: Incantations,* and *Book III: Altar Call.* The poetry contains themes of displacement, re-creation/rebirth, and the return of exiles to their homeland. *Book I: Exiles,* the strongest of the three sections, opens with "Calibari," which depicts the contradictions inherent in writing in a colonial language. As B. says, "this tongue that I have mastered has mastered me" but at the same time "has taught me curses," and the ultimate tragedy is her confession, "I speak this dispossession in the language of the master." As critic Tommie Jackson notes, B. "figuratively describes the exile as bound by a foreign language that produces the aberration of mongrelism comparable to that of the Shakespearean character for which the poem is named." The condition is common to all exiles, many of whom have crossed paths with each other but whose journeys never take them home. In "All my friends are exiles," B. declares the sad paradox of exile: "We have everywhere to go but home." Her poem "Migration" describes the class diversity among exile gatherings of "last warriors," "lost refugees," "the indentured," and "emigrés" trapped in "border camps" and in "strange cities."

B.'s language captures the "spirit of exiles, their struggles and their joys" (Courville). She speaks of the "unhealable rift," the yearning to return to "the places of our first heartbeat." Even the finality of death does not abate the agony of displacement. In "Exiles," B. laments, "Funerals are important, away from home we cannot lay our dead to rest, for we alone have given them no fitting burial."

In *Book II: Incantations,* B. focuses on the experience of exiled women. She treats the themes of birth and recreation of the exiled culture through memory. She begins with "Liberation," a testimony to the power of women and the use of language as a tool of liberation. She ends with a powerful, haunting poem, "Mawu/Mawo," which is written in her father's language, Twi, using "the nomenclature from her mother's language" and centered around the idea of women giving birth. *Book II* also includes testimonies of private, intimate encounters in "Roommates," "Illicit Passion," and "Dream Transformations." These poems, unfortunately, are too personal at times, which tends to weaken the political force of her testimonies.

Book III: Altar Call, is the weakest of the three. As Tanure Ojaide notes, "the poet might be proposing Christianity as an antidote to the loneliness of exile, but this is not effectively executed." "Trilogy for Azania" develops the theme of displacement/dispossession and return to the homeland. However, the sermonizing style of the poems in this last section appears anticlimactic to the vigor of *Books I* and *II*.

Despite its shortcomings, *Testimonies of Exile* "embraces the experiences of countless political exiles who have experienced the impact of colonialism, neocolonialism, liberation movements, coups and counter coups. . . . B.'s poetry dramatizes the threat of loss and the actual loss of political, social and cultural identity" (Courville).

B. has also dedicated a significant part of her career to black women's issues. She has written an impressive array of critical articles on what she calls "black feminisms," hence the title of a book that she edited with Stanlie James, *Theorizing Black Feminisms: The Visionary Pragmatism of Black Women* (1993), a collection of critical essays by and about black women on a wide range of issues including labor, the socioeconomic status across the diaspora, artists, rape, abortion, lesbianism, women's dress, and identity. In this collection, B. and her colleagues appeal to black women to speak out on all issues that affect their lives, especially racism and sexism, and to redefine themselves on their own terms in a world that has effectively silenced them.

In an essay entitled "Words Whispered Over Voids: A Context for Black Women's Rebellious Voices in the Novel of the African Diaspora" (1988), B. asserts that as a "doubly disenfranchised group," black women have had to write a different kind of narrative—one that is "transformational" and that becomes "a drive for self-definition and redefinition." In the final analysis, black women's works articulate "a narrative of the self, with a clear sense of one's sense of one's place among people, in an accepted or chosen location." B.'s other essays on black women's issues have appeared in a number of books and journals including *The Black Presence in English Literature,* ed. D. Dabydeen (1983), *Ngambika: Studies of Women in African Literature,* ed. C. B. Davies and A. A. Graves (1986), and *Changing Our Own Words,* ed. C. A. Wall (1989).

B. continues to be a prophetic voice among black feminists. Her experience of exile across three continents has fostered a breadth of vision that constantly invigorates her dedication to the struggles of black women.

WORKS: *Testimonies of Exile* (1990).

BIBLIOGRAPHY: Busia, A., in *Black Feminist Criticism and Critical Theory,* ed. H. Baker (1988). *Theorizing Black Feminisms: The Visionary Pragmatism of Black Women,* ed. A. Busia and S. James (1993). Courville, C. *Sage* (1990). Dabydeen, D. *The Black Presence in English Literature* (1985). Davies, B. and A. Graves. *Ngambika: Studies of Women in African Literature* (1986). Jackson, T. *AfrSR* (1993). Ojaide, T. *WLT* (1992). *Changing Our Own Words,* ed. C. Wall (1989).

Shondel J. Nero

Josephine (Elizabeth Grey) Butler

BORN: April 1828, Milfield, Northumberland.
DIED: 30 December 1906, Wooler, near Milfield, Northumberland.
DAUGHTER OF: John Grey of Dilston and Hannah Annett.
MARRIED: George Butler, 1852.

Regarded by Edwardian suffragists as "a great founding mother of modern feminism" (Walkowitz), B. is remembered chiefly for her leadership in the campaign to repeal the Contagious Diseases Acts (1870–86), which sought to regulate venereal diseases in prostitutes through registration, forced examination, and incarceration. For B., the Acts were a key example of the poor policies that result when women are excluded from legislative processes, and her work in the repeal campaign reflected the two main concerns of her life: the profound injustices associated with male control of women's sexuality and the development of a feminist theology, which she expounded through a prophetic persona.

The most influential person in B.'s early life was her father, whose devout Christianity underwrote his position against slavery and his support of the first Reform Bill (1832). A spiritual crisis at seventeen confirmed B.'s faith in a loving God, and twenty-four years later, in 1869, when she accepted leadership of the repeal movement (as head of the Ladies' National Association), B. believed she had received a divine call. The plight of prostitutes coupled with the problem in the 1860s of "surplus" women had resulted in B.'s first publication: *Education and Employment of Women* (1868) and *Woman's Work and Woman's Culture* (1869). With the repeal movement came her prophetic polemics.

Mixing stern exhortation with promises of divine compassion, B.'s numerous speeches and tracts combine the qualities of Old Testament prophecy and Victorian devotional literature. She repeatedly argues that women and men are spiritual equals and that middle- and upper-class women must break their silence about the sexual subjugation of their poorer sisters. In *The New Era* (1872), B. introduces her apocalyptic vision, wherein women's outcries against the injustices of men's licentiousness and women's sexual slavery represent the Holy Spirits's return to earth. In *Hour Before the Dawn* (1876), she comprehensively develops her feminist theology and vehemently assaults the men who hire prostitutes, blaming them for the evil of prostitution and the imminent destruction of Great Britain. B. contributed to the early feminist movement with these polemics, mainly by justifying women's public speech and by asserting their right to campaign against control of their sexuality.

B.'s biographies of saints are extensions of her prophetic message, in particular *Catharine of Siena* (1878), where B. makes thinly veiled comparisons between her challenges to Britain and Catharine's challenges to the Roman Catholic Church. She also expanded her crusade to the continent, the United States, and the colonies, and she attacked social and political policies besides the Contagious Diseases Acts. In "Our Christianity Tested by the Irish Question" (1887), she criticized British imperialism in Ireland, and in *Government by Police* (1888), she prophesied a police state in which state-sanctioned "espionage" would subvert Christian self-governance and tyrannize poor women.

Late in life, B. recorded the repeal campaign in *Personal Reminiscences of a Great Crusade* (1896) and wrote family biographies, notably *Recollections of George Butler* (1892), which describes her husband's unfaltering support. An organization named for B. continues her work to abolish prostitution.

WORKS: *The Education and Employment of Women* (1868). *Woman's Work and Woman's Culture* (1869). *Memoir of John Grey of Dilston* (1869). *Sursum Corda* (1871). *Vox Populi* (1871). *The Constitution Violated* (1871). *The New Era* (1872). *Some Thoughts on the Present Aspect of the Crusade* (1874). *The Hour Be-*

fore the Dawn (1876). *Catharine of Siena* (1878). *Social Purity* (1879). *Life of J. F. Oberlin* (1882). *The Salvation Army in Switzerland* (1883). *The Bright Side of the Question* (1883). *The Principles of Abolitionists* (1885). *The Work of the Federation* (1885). *Rebecca Jarrett* (1886). "Our Christianity Tested by the Irish Question" (1887). *Government by Police* (1888). *Recollections of George Butler* (1892). *St. Agnes* (1893). *The Present Aspect of the Abolitionist Cause in Relation to British India* (1893). *The Lady of Shunem* (1894). *A Doomed Iniquity* (1896). *Personal Reminiscences of a Great Crusade* (1896). *Truth Before Everything* (1896). *Some Lessons from Contemporary History* (1898). *Prophets and Prophetesses* (1898). *Native Races and the War* (1900). *Silent Victories* (1900). *In Memoriam Harriet Meuricoffre* (1901). *Josephine Butler: An Autobiographical Memoir,* ed. G. W. Johnson and L. Johnson (1909).

BIBLIOGRAPHY: Bell, E. M. *Josephine Butler: Flame of Fire* (1962). Boyd, N. *Three Victorian Women Who Changed Their World: Josephine Butler, Octavia Hill, Florence Nightingale* (1982). Butler, A. S. G. *Portrait of Josephine Butler* (1953). Caine, B. *Victorian Feminists* (1992). Fawcett, M. G. and E. M. Turner. *Josephine Butler: Her Works and Principles, and Their Meaning for the Twentieth Century* (1927). Petrie, G. R. *A Singular Iniquity: The Campaigns of Josephine Butler* (1971). Uglow, J., in *Feminist Theorists,* ed. D. Spender (1983). Walkowitz, J. R. *City of Dreadful Delight: Narratives of Sexual Danger in Late-Victorian London* (1992). Walowitz, J. R. *Prostitution and Victorian Society: Women, Class, and the State* (1980).

For articles in reference works, see: *BDBF. VB.*

Lucretia Anne Flammang

A[ntonia]. S[usan]. (Drabble) Byatt

BORN: 24 August 1936, Sheffield, Yorkshire.

DAUGHTER OF: John Frederick Drabble and Kathleen Marie (Bloor) Drabble.

MARRIED: Ian Charles Rayner Byatt, 1959; Peter John Duffy, 1969.

As a result of the international acclaim she received for *Possession* (1990), B. is generally recognized as a world-class author. In her fiction, B. examines the interplay between the smallest details of daily life and larger, existential issues that drive the superstructures of her characters' lives. B.'s novels are marked frequently by intellectual artifice, weighty symbolism, and characters with insular academic preoccupations. Influenced by D. H. Lawrence, E. M. Forster, and Iris Murdoch, B. returns frequently in her fiction to questions of the dynamics of family life, the demands of the artistic or literary life, and the social position of intellectual women in nineteenth- and twentieth-century Britain. The most powerful literary relationship in B.'s life involves her sister, the novelist Margaret Drabble, a relationship reflected in mutual influences, intense competition, and a recurring attention to the relationship between sisters in both writers' fiction.

Born in 1936, B. was the eldest of four children raised in wartime Britain, the daughter of a Yorkshire county-court judge. She was educated at the Newnham College, Cambridge; Bryn Mawr College in the United States; and Somerville College, Oxford. Best known for her novels, short stories, and literary criticism, B. has also worked as editor, script writer, and lecturer at University College London (from 1972 to 1983). When B. stopped teaching to concentrate fully on her writing, her decision resulted in a burst of productivity: five works of fiction (including *Possession*) and a collection of literary essays. B.'s work as a literary scholar is reflected by her novels' protagonists, many of whom are themselves engaged in writing fiction or scholarship. B.'s scholarly publications include two books on Iris Murdoch, a novelist to whom she has often been compared: *Degrees of Freedom: The Novels of Iris Murdoch* (1965) and *Iris Murdoch* (1976). With N. Warren, B. edited *The Selected Works of George Eliot,* for which she wrote the introduction; she has also edited Eliot's *The Mill on the Floss.*

In her first novel, *The Shadow of the Sun* (1964), B. traces the late adolescence of Anna Severell, who struggles to emerge from the shadow of her father, a novelist and visionary genius, by entering into a relationship, as a student at Cambridge, with one of her father's major critics. Anna never comes fully into her own, nor determines her own destiny. At the novel's crux, an unplanned pregnancy confronts her with decisions she is essentially unwilling and unprepared to make.

In *The Game* (1967), B.'s autobiographical interest in the relationship between sisters is most evident. Two sisters—Julia Corbett, a popular novelist, and Cassandra Corbett, an unmarried, introverted Oxford don—struggle as adults with the profound effects of the insular (rural, Quaker) home of their childhood, where they were immersed for a decade of their youth in a private imaginary game. Their father's death and the return of a mutual friend cause the sisters to reconsider their conflicting world views, but it also inspires Julia to write a novel based on her sister's inner life that forces the reader to consider the ethical problem of artistic freedom versus filial responsibility.

B. has completed the third novel of a quartet she began two decades ago. The first two novels chronicle the social and intellectual milieu of Britain in the 1950s, with special attention to the options available to women coming of age.

The Virgin in the Garden (1978), the first of these novels, follows the lives of adolescent siblings Stephanie, Frederica, and Marcus Potter during the summer of 1952, coinciding with the coronation of Elizabeth II. A historical novel in the European realist tradition, it concerns the production of Alex Wedderburn's play, "Astraea," about the first Elizabeth (the Virgin Queen), and compares the first and second Elizabethan ages.

In the second novel, *Still Life* (1985), B. attempted to impose on her narrative a visual, painterly aesthetic, which the first-person narrator observes is only partially successful. The art of painting figures prominently in the novel; Alex Wedderburn's play "Still Life" (about Vincent van Gogh's last years) parallels his play "Astraea" in *The Virgin in the Garden. Still Life* follows the lives of the Potters from 1954 to 1959: Stephanie, as curate's wife and mother; Frederica, in her intellectual and sexual pursuits as a Cambridge undergraduate; and Marcus, in his continued negotiation with a brilliance that borders on mental illness.

Babel Tower (1996), the third novel in the planned tetralogy, continues to focus on Frederica Potter, now a freelance writer in London and also a sometime adult-education and art instructor. After Stephanie's accidental death, Frederica has married Nigel Reiver, with whom she has a passionate if violent and intellectually limited relationship. In time, as an impoverished single mother, she moves to an undesirable part of London and suffers her young son's instability, the divorce court's judgements, and a lengthy trial for "obscenity" because of a novel-within-the-novel. Criticized for undeveloped subplots and useless didacticicism, *Babel Tower* nonetheless demonstrates B.'s skill in describing the same sort of fragmented self Doris Lessing explored in *The Golden Notebook* and *The Four-Gated City*.

Passions of the Mind: Selected Writings (1991) includes essays on B.'s own work as well as essays on the work and lives of Victorians Robert Browning and George Eliot and on vision and reality in the work of Samuel Taylor Coleridge and Vincent van Gogh. Seven essays on "The Female Voice?" consider twentieth-century authors Willa Cather, Elizabeth Bowen, Sylvia Plath, Toni Morrison, Georgette Heyer, Barbara Pym, and Monique Wittig.

B.'s first collection of stories, *Sugar and Other Stories* (1987), was also the first book-length publication following her decision to leave teaching to write full time. The stories reflect on aging and mortality, fear, the vagaries of memory, the construction of the family, and the presence of ghosts. B.'s often-anthologized "The July Ghost" is a kind of requiem for the untimely death of her own young son; "Precipice-Encurled" concerns Robert Browning and his biographer, clearly an early study for *Possession.* In *The Matisse Stories* (1993), B. examines the role of art in three carefully framed stories. "Medusa's Ankles" probes the effects of the male gaze on a woman anxious about aging. "Art Work" explores the persistence of class and racial stereotypes in modern British life and celebrates the public debut of a black woman's original textile art. In "The Chinese Lobster," B. exposes the personal and institutional conflicts raised by a graduate student's claim of sexual harassment and contrasts both sides of the harassment story by examining the differences in evaluation of Matisse's work that derive from gender and generation. B.'s latest collection of stories, *The Djinn in the Nightingale's Eye: Five Fairy Stories* (1994), includes two stories ("The Glass Coffin" and "Gode's Story") that appeared as subtexts of *Possession;* the novella-length "Djinn" raises questions of female self-definition, desire, autonomy, and aging.

Possession: A Romance (1990), B.'s most acclaimed novel to date, winner of the 1990 Booker Prize and the Irish Times-Aer Lingus International Fiction Prize, offers remarkable contrasts between the Victorian and modern worlds. The novel is a study of academic pursuit and scholarly detection by two literary scholars of the 1980s whose discovery of the love letters of two nineteenth-century poets contributes to the inception of their own romance. The nineteenth-century poets Christabel LaMotte and Randolph Henry Ash are clearly modelled on Christina Rossetti and Robert Browning.. B.'s tour de force in this novel is her successful layering of multiple narratives and seamless maneuvering among letter, diary, poetry, and straight narration. B.'s full-length poems, written in the style of Browning, Rossetti and Dickinson, merit serious attention in their own right.

Perhaps because she has written a book of criticism on Murdoch, B. is often compared with her. Indeed, faith in the power of the intellect is important to her vision; in *The Virgin in the Garden,* for instance, Elizabeth I is perceived as a ruler who prevailed because she used her intelligence, unlike her relative, Mary, Queen of Scots. However, although this work established B. as a writer of depth, it is also "donnish," carrying a great weight of literary and historical allusion. Like Drabble, B. often creates characters with literary or academic connections, as in *The Game.* One of the questions raised in this work about sister-rivals concerns the ethics of using real people as characters in fiction.

WORKS: *The Shadow of a Sun* (1964). *Degrees of Freedom: The Novels of Iris Murdoch* (1965). *The Game* (1967). *Wordsworth and Coleridge in Their Time* (1970). *Iris Murdoch* (1976). *The Virgin in the Garden* (1978). *Still Life* (1980). *Sugar and Other Stories* (1987). *Possession: A Romance* (1990). *Passions of the Mind: Selected Writings* (1991). *Angels and Insects* (1992; as film, 1995). *The Matisse Stories* (1993). *The Djinn in the Nightingale's Eye: Five Fairy Stories* (1994). *Babel Tower* (1996). (with I. Sodré) *Imagining Characters: Six Conversations about Women Writers,* ed. R. Swift (1997).

BIBLIOGRAPHY: Campbell, J. *SSF* (1991). Campbell, J. *Critique* (1988). Clutterbuck, C. *Southerly* (1993). Creighton, J. *Mosaic* (1987). Dusinberre, J. *Critique* (1982). Gitzen, J. *Critique* (1995). Giobbi, G. *JES* (1994). Holmes, F. M. *ESC* (1995). Hulbert, A., in *Contemporary British Women Writers: Narrative Strategies,* ed. R. E. Hosmer, Jr. (1993). Todd, R. A. S. *Byatt* (1996). Yelin, L. *VN* (1992).

For articles in reference works, see: *Bloomsbury. British Novelists Since 1960. CA. CLC. CN. DLB. Feminist. Oxford. ToddBWW. WA. WD.*

Other references: *Books and Bookmen* (4 January 1979). *Critique* (1982). *Encounter* (July 1968). *LonT* (6 June 1981, 15 January 1995). *Ms.* (June 1979). *New Statesman* (3 November 1978). *NYTBR* (26 July 1964, 17 March 1968, 1 April 1979). *TLS* (2 January 1964, 19 January 1967, 3 November 1968, 9 March 1984, 26 January 1996, 10 May 1996).

Angela G. Dorenkamp
(updated by Ann ter Haar)

Byrne, Charlotte Dacre: See *Dacre, Charlotte*

Byrne, Mrs.: See *Dacre, Charlotte*

C: See *Bowles, Caroline*

(Alice) Mildred Cable

BORN: 21 February 1878, Guildford, Surrey.
DIED: 30 April 1952, Shaftsbury, Dorset.
DAUGHTER OF: John C. Cable and Eliza Kindred Cable.

Attracted to a life of service in her adolescence, C. educated herself for foreign missions, qualifying as a Member of the Pharmaceutical Society in chemistry with training in anatomy, surgery, and midwifery. She intended to go to China with her fiancé, but when travel east was blocked for a time her fiancé broke off their engagement; yet she still determined to go to China.

C. joined Evangeline (Eva) French, as the Boxer Rebellion waned, in the China Inland Mission outreach to Chinese women and children. With French she reestablished the school in Shansi Province and ministered to the spiritual, social, and educational needs of the people. Known among her proselytes as the "Blue Lady" because of her love for Chinese blue clothing, C. was often as busy providing medical services as providing Bible services. When Francesca, Eva's younger sister, came to China upon the death of her mother, the "Two" became the "Trio" working in the region with a Confucian scholar and former opium addict Pastor Hsi, the "Paul" of Shansi Province. After thirty-five years in the area, the three women determined to extend the mission to the desert areas of northern China with its mix of ethnic groups. Writing individually or in collaboration with one or the other of the Frenches, C. chronicled their travels, the trials and successes of religious, educational, and social reform, and their own spiritual development. About half of these accounts were written in retrospect after being forced out of China in the 1936 Communist takeover. C. received the Lawrence Memorial Medal of the Royal Central Asian Society, and with the Frenches she received the Livingstone Medal of the Royal Scottish Geographical Society.

Coauthored with Francesca French, the biography of Henrietta Soltau, *A Woman Who Laughed* (1934), demonstrates the biography as novel. Relying heavily on Soltau's journals, diaries, and other papers, it traces the spiritual journey of one of the China Inland Mission's most dedicated members, who remained in England to care for candidates for the mission field. In contrast, C.'s *The Fulfillment of a Dream of Pastor Hsi's* (1917) is less a biography of the Chinese minister than a compilation of a series of incidents including demon possession, Boxer atrocities, miracles of provision, and conversions. This anecdotal style is more typical, and effective as well, of the journey and mission activities that comprise *Through the Jade Gate* (1927) and *The Gobi Desert* (1942). *China: Her Life and Her People* (1946) is a simple but eloquent overview of China's history, inhabitants, politics, socioeconomics, and geography. In this late book intended for "study-circles," church groups that support missions, C. offers less the European view of the East than a sincere and objective description of one who has lived in China for most of her life, becoming both an expert and a change agent.

WORKS: *The Fulfillment of a Dream of Pastor Hsi's: The Story of the Work in Hwochow* (1917). *Despatches from North West Kansu* (1925). *Through the Jade Gate and Central Asia: An Account of Journeys in Kansu, Turkestan, and the Gobi Desert* (1927). *Something Happened* (1933). *A Desert Journal: Letters from Central Asia* (1934). *A Woman Who Laughed: Henrietta Soltau* (1934). *The Making of a Pioneer: Percy Mather* (1935). *The Journey with a Purpose* (1935). *Ambassador for Christ* (1935). *The Story of Little Topsy, Little Lonely of Central Asia* (1937). *Grace, Child of the Gobi* (1938). *The Gobi Desert* (1942). *China: Her Life and Her People* (1946). *The Book Which Demands a Verdict* (1946). *George Hunter: Apostle of Turkestan* (1948). *The Wall of Spears: The Gobi Desert* (1951). *Why Not for the World: The Story of God Through the Bible Society* (1952).

BIBLIOGRAPHY: Allen, A. *Travelling Ladies—Victorian Adventuresses* (1980). Platt, W. *Three Women: Mildred Cable, Francesca French, Evangeline French* (1964). Thompson, P. *Desert Pilgrim* (1957). Tucker, R. *Guardians of the Great Commission* (1988). Warner, M., intro. to *The Gobi Desert* (1984).

For articles in reference works, see: *Feminist*. *ToddBWW*.

Sylvia McLaurin

Alice Mona Caird

BORN: 1858, Ryde, Isle of Wight.
DIED: 4 February 1932, Hampstead, London.
DAUGHTER OF: Hector (?).
MARRIED: A. Henryson-Caird, 1877.
WROTE UNDER: Mona Alison Caird; G. Noel Hatton.

Little is known of the life of this women's rights advocate, novelist, and antivivisectionist except that she was the daughter of an inventor named Hector, became the wife of A. Henryson-Caird in 1877, and was rather unhappy in her marriage to him.

She published her earlier novels, *Whom Nature Leadeth* (1883) and *One That Wins* (1887), under the pseudonym G. Noel Hatton. In their day, her novels were popular and controversial, but she is now chiefly remembered for her essays on marriage, the family, and women's relations to class and economic structure. She achieved notice when she published two articles, "Marriage" and "Ideal Marriage," in the August and November 1888 issues of the *Westminster Review*. The pieces created such controversy that she wrote further essays for the *Daily Telegraph*, collectively entitled "Is Marriage a Failure?" All of these essays were later included in her book *The Morality of Marriage* (1891).

The Morality of Marriage also took on one of the best-known conservative writers of the day, Eliza Lynn Linton, who called suffragists "the Shrieking Sisterhood" and feminists in general "social insurgents" and "wild women." C. rebutted Linton by denying that nature intended women only for motherhood, and she scorned Linton for everything from her inability to imagine female heroes to her pettiness in ridiculing the appearance of independent women whose views she disliked.

With such chapter headings as "The Lot of Women Under the Rule of Man," "Motherhood Under Conditions of Dependence," and "Suppression of Variant Types," *The Morality of Marriage* set forth the theory of adverse feminine social conditioning and the difficulties besetting the woman who rebels. C. praises Ibsen's Nora "who dared the terrors of the social torture-chamber" by bearing her children. C. also felt that woman's inequality was directly linked to the marriage state and the subordinate role of the wife. She argued that the way in which society defined marriage—and motherhood—as women's "proper spheres" fixated women on these goals and imprisoned them in thankless domestic routine, views that earned C. the reputation of an outspoken defender of the New Woman.

A Romance of the Moors (1891) was an exploration of these themes, using the story of a young woman who risks "losing her character" rather than submit to forcing a man to marry her and compromising her desire for an independent life. But it was in *The Daughters of Danaus* (1894) that C. truly harnessed the novel to her feminist aims. (The title is an allusion to the mythical Greek legend of the punishment of Danaus's fifty daughters, who unwillingly wed their suitors in a mass marriage, killed their husbands, and were forced in return to draw water from a sieve for eternity.)

The novel tells the story of Hadria Temperley, whose unhappy marriage to a conventional man illustrates C.'s theory of the limitations of wedlock. After an attempted rebellion and trip to Paris, where she tries to study music, Hadria bows to pressure and returns to England to the life of a middle-class matron. Rebelling again, she has an affair with another man that proves as unsatisfactory as her marriage. Ultimately, despite her belief in the power of ideas and her rather vacillating feminism, she is unable to find her way to a life of principle. The novel closes with her defeat as a lesson in the sacrifice of Talent to Convention.

C. was as passionate about injustice to animals as to women and was an early member of the antivivisectionist movement. Her works, with titles like *Legalized Torture* (n.d.) and *The Savagery of Vivisection* (1894–95), expressed her outrage. Only her travel books (she voyaged frequently on the Continent) seem without the spirit of polemic that characterized her other work. C. ceased writing a number of years before her death but remained active on behalf of the causes that appeared to be the ruling passions of her life.

WORKS: *Whom Nature Leadeth* (1883). *One That Wins* (1887). *For Money or for Love* (1889). *The Wing of Azreal* (1889). *A Romance of the Moors* (1891). *The Morality of Marriage and Other Essays* (1891). *The Daughters of Danaus* (1894). *Some Truths About Vivisection* (1894). *The Savagery of Vivisection* (1894–95). *A Sentimental View of Vivisection* (1894–95). *Beyond the Pale* (1896). *The Pathway of the Gods* (1898). *The Proposed Pasteur Institute at Chelsea Bridge* (189?). *The Stones of Sacrifice* (1915). *Legalized Torture* (n.d.). *Sacrifice, Noble and Ignoble* (n.d.).

BIBLIOGRAPHY: Calder, J. *Women and Marriage in Victorian Fiction* (1978). Cameron, A. *New Women, New Novels* (1990). Cunningham, G. *The New Woman and the Victorian Novel* (1978). Showalter, E. *A Literature of Their Own* (1977).

For articles in reference works, see: *BA19C. Bloomsbury. Chambers. Dole. 1890s. Feminist. Oxford. ToddBWW. VB.*

Laura Hapke

Margaret Steuart Calderwood

BORN: 1715.
DIED: 1774.
DAUGHTER OF: Sir James Steuart and Anne Dalrymple.
MARRIED: Thomas Calderwood, 1735.

In 1756, C. traveled from Scotland with her husband, sons, and servants to join her brother, Sir James Steuart, residing abroad because of his part in the Rebellion of 1745. During her journey through England, Holland, and what is now Belgium, C. sent a stream of letters back to her friends and daughter in Scotland. Settled briefly in Brussels, she revised and organized her writings into a continuous narrative, which circulated privately among her friends. C.'s "Volumes" are typical of eighteenth-century travel journals: She loads her account with facts about each place she visits, and some of the funniest passages of her account describe the mockery her continual petty questions incite. Her Scottishisms enliven violent attacks on the "papaists," carefully copied recipes and manufacturing details, and comic accounts of persons met along the way. C. criticizes the English heavily; at their best, they are not so "uptaking" as the Scots, and in Brussels the English women "are mostly what I call adventuresses."

The woman portrayed in the journals is forceful, energetic, and commonsensical. Despite her lack of French, C. slogged tenaciously about Brussels by herself until she managed to rent a house and place her sons in school. Back in Britain in December of 1756, she assumed the management of her husband's estates with great success. She tried her hand at novel writing, although *Fanny Roberts* never appeared in print, and she continued to write vigorous letters to her married daughter and friends. The persona presented in her journal in many ways prefigures the "splenetic" traveler Tobias Smollett was to create and Laurence Sterne to label, as when C. regrets that the "old Duchess of Aremberg is a-dying," since "on such occasions the bells ring so that you cannot hear what you are saying." Her journal balances two common forms of travel account, the guidebook and the more anecdotal narrative.

WORKS: *Letters and Journals in Coltness Collections* (1842). *The Adventures of Fanny Roberts* (unpublished). *Journal concerning the management of the Calderwood estates* (unpublished). *Letters* (unpublished).

BIBLIOGRAPHY: *Letters and Journals of Mrs. Calderwood of Polton*, ed. A. Fergusson (1884).

For articles in reference works, see: *DNB. Feminist.*

Marie E. McAllister

(Janet) Taylor Caldwell

BORN: 7 September 1900, Prestwich, Manchester.
DIED: 30 August 1985, Greenwich, Connecticut, United States.
DAUGHTER OF: Arthur Francis Caldwell and Anna M. Caldwell.
MARRIED: William Fairfax Combs, 1919; Marcus Reback, 1931; William E. Stancell, 1972; William Robert Prestie, 1978.
WROTE UNDER: Taylor Caldwell; Max Reiner.

C. is one of the world's most prolific and best-selling novelists; the Fawcett Publishing Company alone has published 25 million paperback editions of twenty-five novels. Most of her novels reached the best-selling lists, and several have been adapted for films. In addition, C. wrote essays, many of which were collected in one volume. Her last novel, *Answer as a Man* (1981), was her thirty-fifth. Shortly after she completed the manuscript in 1980, C. had a stroke that left her paralyzed and speechless. She had also been deaf for several years before her death in 1985.

C.'s parents left England and moved to Buffalo, New York, when she was six. They were never financially comfortable, so C. was required not only to do heavy chores around the house but also to quit school at the age of fifteen and work in a factory. She later finished high school at night, and she worked her way through college, graduating from the University of Buffalo in 1931.

Although her first published novel, *Dynasty of Death*, did not appear until 1938, C. had been writing and receiving rejections for twenty years. After the favorable reception of *Dynasty*, novels appeared nearly annually. She claimed, however, that her novels took her three to five years to write; *This Side of Innocence*, for instance, though published in 1946, was begun in 1927 and not finished until four years later.

C.'s novels are long, complicated historical tales, in which, as Richard Freedman said in 1981, "she loftily pretends the 20th century—at least in fiction—never happened." Her plots are complicated by several mysteries and mysterious characters, who often spend many agonizing moments debating both sides of an imposing social or moral issue with themselves. Martin Levin, for example, found *Captains and the Kings* (1972) to be "a jungle of a novel" in which secrets "grow like fungi." The fact is, the "literary establishment," as C. called academic and New York critics, dismissed her (in 1981) as a "shining exemplar of Grey Power." Nevertheless, C. had signed a $3.9 million contract for *Answer as a Man* and another yet-to-be-written novel.

The author of those "very long, very melodramatic" novels expressed such conservative and religious opinions in her novels that she received numerous awards for them. The John Birch Society gave her a plaque in 1975 for being a "great American Patriot and Scholar." Other honors were bestowed upon her by the Daughters of the American Revolution (1956) and Marquette University (1964).

While critics fault her novels as overwhelmingly verbose, C.'s essays are refreshingly charming and witty. Her accounts of people and events in her life are alive and endearing. The essays display the human contradictions of saying one thing and doing another. C. said, for example, that she was no "women's libber" in her collection *On Growing Up Tough* (1971), and yet she divorced her third husband in 1973, a few months after their marriage, because he thought a "woman was sort of a serf." In 1955, C. said, "I am not, and never was, a housewife. . . . I do not keep house." C.'s ideas about "manly men" and the "noisy and stupid Liberation Ladies" are the topics of two essays, "What Happened to American Men" and "Women's Lib." Her objections to polyester blends and food substitutes in "Plastic People" anticipate the later all-cotton, natural-food movement. In many ways dated, *On Growing Up Tough* recalls the dissensions of the late 1960s and early 1970s. Speaking in her own voice in this book, C. gives the most intriguing portrait of her colorful personality. In "T.L.C.—Keep Your Paws Off Me!" C. goes from the medical world to "practically every area of my life, with the exception of my family, of course." "As I am an enthusiastic hypochondriac, I had, a few years ago, worn to the very bone the local physicians and their catalogs of diagnoses. So, armed with brand-new symptoms, I went to another city which has a famous clinic, and entered its hospital for tests. I wasn't ill; I was simply curious to know what I had this time and if my own diagnosis would pay off to the discomfiture of my home doctors who had declared I was remarkably healthy."

Virtually no serious criticism, outside of reviews and interviews, has been written of C.'s works. The only possible exception is Jess Stearn's account of numerous hypnotic trances in which C. divulged the existence of thirty-seven separate former entities. Stearn was convinced that the medical knowledge displayed in *Dear and Glorious Physician* (1959) had to have come from practical experience that C. did not have. C. added her disclaimer to his book, but she left an element of acceptance: "I am a novelist, and . . . perhaps some or most of the material had lain fallow in my subconscious. . . . I still heartily reject the idea of reincarnation." The two most interesting characters she dealt with were George Eliot's scullery maid and Mary Magdalene's mother. In her life and in her works, C. has been entertaining.

WORKS: *Dynasty of Death* (1938; abridgement, 1957). *The Eagles Gather* (1940). *The Earth is the Lord's: A Tale of the Rise of Genghis Khan* (1941). (as Max Reiner) *Time No Longer* (1941). *The Strong City* (1942). *The Arm and the Darkness* (1943). *The Turnbulls* (1943). *The Final Hour* (1944). *The Wide Horse* (1945). *This Side of Innocence* (1946). *There Was a Time* (1947). *Melissa* (1948). *Let Love Come Last* (1949). *The Balance Wheel* (1951). *The Devil's Advo-*

cate (1952). *Maggie, Her Marriage* (1953). *Never Victorious, Never Defeated* (1954). *Tender Victory* (1956). *The Sound of Thunder* (1957). *Your Sins and Mine* (1959). *Dear and Glorious Physician* (1959). *The Listener* (1960). *The Man Who Listens* (1961). *A Prologue to Love* (1962). *Grandmother and the Priests* (1963). *To See the Glory* (1963). *The Late Clara Beame* (1963). *A Pillar of Iron.* (1965) *Wicked Angel* (1965). *No One Hears But Him* (1966). *Dialogues with the Devil* (1967). *Testimony of Two Men* (1968). *Great Lion of God* (1970). *On Growing Up Tough* (1971). *Captains and the Kings* (1972). *To Look and Pass (1973). Glory and the Lightning* (1974). *The Romance of Atlantis* (1975). *Ceremony of the Innocent* (1976). *I, Judas (1977). Bright Flows the River* (1978). *Answer as a Man* (1981).

BIBLIOGRAPHY: Stearn, J. *The Search for a Soul: Taylor Caldwell's Psychic Lives* (1973).

For articles in reference works, see: *Bloomsbury. CA. CLC. ESF. Encyclopedia of Parapsychology and Psychical Research*, ed. A. S. Berger and J. Berger (1991). *TCA* and *SUP. TCRGW.*

Other references: *American Novelists of Today*, ed. H. Warfel (1951). *Life* (7 April 1959). *Newsweek* (9 March 1959). *NYT* (2 September 1985). *NYTBR* (28 April 1946, 10 April 1949, 14 July 1963, 4 May 1972, 15 December 1974, 31 October 1976, 11 January 1977, 9 October 1977, 11 January 1981, 1 March 1981). *PW* (5 October 1976, 6 November 1981).

Marilynn J. Smith

Helen Maud Cam

BORN: 22 August 1885, Abingdon, Berkshire.
DIED: 9 February 1968, Orpington, Kent.
DAUGHTER OF: William Herbert Cam and Katherine Scott Cam.

C., a medieval historian and educator, was the first woman ever to hold a tenured professorship at Harvard University. She is particularly associated with studies of the hundred rolls and other documents of English local history during the thirteenth and fourteenth centuries.

The fourth of nine children, C. received an exceptionally good home education from her father (a schoolmaster and clergyman), her mother, and her maternal uncle (a classics scholar). She won a scholarship to Royal Holloway College, University of London, where she took a first class degree in history in 1907. She spent the following year as a fellow at Bryn Mawr College, in Pennsylvania. In 1909 she was awarded the M.A. degree from the University of London for the thesis that resulted from her Bryn Mawr studies, later published as *Local Government in Francia and England 768–1034* (1912).

C.'s teaching career began at Cheltenham Ladies' College (1909–12) and continued at Royal Holloway College. While teaching in London, she began research at the Public Record Office and was trained in paleography at the London School of Economics. In 1921, she went to Girton College, Cambridge, where she spent most of her career in various positions: Pfeiffer research fellow, lecturer in history, director of studies in history and law, and vice-mistress. She was named university lecturer in 1929 and served on Cambridge's Faculty Board of History from 1941 to 1948. In 1948, she was selected to hold the first Samuel Zemurray and Doris Zemurray Stone professorship for women scholars at Radcliffe College, and she enjoyed great popularity among history students at Radcliffe and Harvard until her retirement in 1954.

C.'s emphasis on the essential continuity of English legal traditions (apparent, for instance, in her 1950 textbook *England Before Elizabeth*) placed her in the historiographic camp of the Victorian constitutional scholar William Stubbs; she was most closely associated with the school of F. W. Maitland for both her focus on archival evidence and her conviction that legal studies could offer crucial insight into the attitudes and assumptions of ordinary people. Her most significant contributions to the history of medieval governance were *Studies in the Hundred Rolls: Some Aspects of Thirteenth-Century Administration* (1921) and *The Hundred and the Hundred Rolls: An Outline of Local Government in Medieval England* (1930). These works helped clarify the legal status of the rolls, or accounts of local administration, required by Edward I of every ward in England; from them C. extrapolated a portrait of local government in the late thirteenth century. Her continuing interest in county government in the Middle Ages also inspired the essays collected in *Liberties and Communities in Medieval England* (1944).

Both before and after her retirement from teaching, C. was an active member of her profession and distinguished herself in an overwhelmingly male field. She lectured frequently and was a regular contributor to journals such as *Speculum, History,* and the *English Historical Review;* several of her addresses were published separately as pamphlets, and some of her more significant short essays were collected in *Law-Finders and Law-Makers in Medieval England* (1963). She was a vice-president of the Royal Historical Society and member of the Medieval Academy and of the American Academy of Arts and Sciences. She was only the second woman (after Beatrice Webb) to be elected fellow of the British Academy and the first to deliver its Raleigh lecture (both in 1945). She served as president of the International Commission for the History of Assemblies of Estates from 1949 to 1960; upon her retirement scholars from more than thirteen nations honored her with a two-volume collection of studies, *Album Helen Maud Cam* (1960), which also includes a bibliography of her publications to 1960. A number of universities granted her honorary degrees, and she was appointed Commander of the British Empire in 1957.

C. combined formidable erudition with an infectious enthusiasm for the life of the past and a notable generosity to colleagues and students. Her commitment to English legal history sprang from her belief that the law represented the noblest expression of society's attempts to subject human relations to reason and to acknowledge citizens' mutual responsibility for one another's welfare. C.'s own dedication to the commonweal was apparent in her tireless efforts to raise scholarship funding for Royal

Holloway College, her assistance in founding Hillcroft College for working women, and her active involvement in the Y.W.C.A., the Cambridge Labour Party, and the Trades Council.

WORKS: *Local Government in Francia and England 768–1034* (1912). *Studies in the Hundred Rolls: Some Aspects of Thirteenth-Century Administration* (1921). (with A. S. Turberville) *A Short Bibliography of English Constitutional History* (1929). *The Hundred and the Hundred Rolls: An Outline of Local Government in Medieval England* (1930). *Liberties and Communities in Medieval England: Collected Studies in Local Administration and Topography* (1944). *The Legislators of Medieval England (Raleigh Lecture)* (1946). *England Before Elizabeth* (1950). *What of the Middle Ages is Alive in England Today? (Coffin Memorial Lecture)* (1960). *Historical Novels* (1961). *Law-Finders and Law-Makers in Medieval England* (1962). *Magna Carta: Event or Document? (Selden Society Lecture)* (1965). *The Eyre of London: 14 Edward II, A.D. 1321* (1968).

BIBLIOGRAPHY: Cheney, C. R. *Proceedings of the British Academy* (1969). Robbins, C., in *Album Helen Maud Cam* (1960).

For articles in reference works, see: *CA. CB. DNB. Europa. WWWAEEA.*

Other references: *Harvard University Gazette* (1968). *LonT* (12 February 1968). *NYT* (13 February 1968). *Time* (26 April 1948).

Rosemary Jann

Mrs. Patrick Campbell (Beatrice Stella Tanner Campbell Cornwallis-West)

BORN: 9 February 1865, Kensington, London.
DIED: 9 April 1940, Pau, France.
DAUGHTER OF: John Tanner and Maria Luigia Giovanna Romanini.
MARRIED: Patrick Campbell, 1884; George Cornwallis-West, 1914.

Although C., known as Stella or Mrs. Pat to her friends, was one of the most popular and successful actresses of the Victorian age, theater historians and critics still disagree about whether she was a genius or a charlatan. Reviews and eyewitness accounts indicate that her stage presence and acting talents were indeed formidable but also show that her performances were notoriously inconsistent. Her temperamental nature made her such a horror and pleasure to work with that George Bernard Shaw once suggested she title her autobiography "Why, Though I Was a Wonderful Actress, No Manager or Author Would Ever Engage Me Twice If He Could Possibly Help It."

If C. was indeed the genius that Shaw, W. B. Yeats, James Barrie, Arthur Pinero, Sarah Bernhardt, and many others thought her, the talent sprang from her own native intuition and instinct rather than from extensive theatrical training. Raised in poor gentility by her loving but profligate parents, C. was destined for a respectable career as a concert pianist but gave up a scholarship to the Leipzig Conservatoire to marry Patrick Campbell, who was, like her father, utterly unable to earn a living. In 1887, Patrick Campbell set off gold hunting in South Africa, and C., frail of health, broke, and with two young children to support, turned to the professional stage after some success in amateur productions.

Not until 1893 did C. establish herself undeniably as a major star, with the role of Paula Tanqueray in Pinero's *The Second Mrs. Tanqueray.* Capitalizing on her dark, sensuous beauty and rich contralto voice, C. became famous for her ability to sensitively play the "modern" heroine, a reformed woman with a shadowy past, rather than the helpless sentimental victim of the melodramatic stage. Although C. attempted Shakespeare's tragic heroines, she had neither the vocal dexterity nor technique to act the roles as Ellen Terry could and she wisely chose to forge her own style and make her mark with the contemporary English and continental authors. Her most famous roles included Pinero's *Notorious Mrs. Ebbsmith* (1895); Sardou's *Fedora* (which prompted Shaw's devastating review "Sardoodledom," 1895); Sudermann's *Magda* (1896); Maeterlinck's *Melisande* (1898; in 1904, with Bernhardt as her leading man); Bjornson's *Beyond Human Power* (1900); *Hedda Gabler* (1907); Yeats's *Deirdre* (1908); and *Eliza Doolittle* (1914). Shaw, Pinero, Barrie, and Yeats wrote plays for her, and she prided herself on her early recognition and frequent presentation of Henrik Ibsen's dramatic talents.

C. was partnered in her roles by some of the most famous actors of her age, including George Alexander, Herbert Beerbohm Tree, and Johnston Forbes-Robertson. Unfortunately, few actor-managers could either control her or put up with her inconsistencies in performance or in rehearsal. Consequently, she never became part of an acting team, as Ellen Terry and Henry Irving had been, and she was never able to form a long-term stylistic or personal relationship. This was, perhaps, fortunate for C. in the long run, for she became one of the first actress-managers, producing her own choice of plays, directing her own repertory company, and almost mismanaging herself into bankruptcy.

It is difficult to explain precisely what quality made C. so overwhelmingly attractive to audiences on stage and off, but C.'s writings provide evidence of her humor, warmth, and intellect. The most significant of these were her memoirs, *My Life and Some Letters* (1922) and the unfinished and unpublished *Chance Medley,* originally titled *Random Reminiscences* (1935), in the Shaw collection at Cornell University. These works contain invaluable anecdotes about the Victorian theatrical scene and the society in which C. moved, which included Oscar Wilde, Yeats, Edward Burne-Jones, Gilbert Murray, Bernhardt, and most of the literary and artistic luminaries of the late-nineteenth century. Combined with her annotated acting scripts (most at the Museum of London), C.'s memoirs demonstrate that she was not just a talented amateur; in spite of her reputation for impulsiveness, C. did in fact carefully consider her roles and devoted a great deal of thought to her technique. Two lecture tours, "Lectures on Diction and Dramatic Art" (London, 1927) and "Beautiful Speech and the Art of Acting" (New York City, Los Angeles, Chicago, and Toledo, in the United States, 1930), reinforce this conclusion. She also wrote three unproduced scenarios for films during her years in Hollywood, from 1933 to 1940.

It is for her voluminous letters, however, that C. is chiefly remembered. Her most famous correspondence was with Shaw, who was in love with her, perhaps platonically, for thirty years. Although she considered herself a mere "footnote" to his life, C. does not emerge the victim in the wit-battle of their letters. Shaw called her a "monster of illiteracy," and she called him a "literary tradesman" when he dared criticize her style, which was indeed fluid and impulsive. Her own comment that his "carnival of words" outshone her "poor whining beggars" is belied by the content of the correspondence. Shaw sent her galleys of his *Quintessence of Ibsenism* and incorporated C.'s critique in the final draft. He shared thoughts for and about his plays and discussed their work on *Pygmalion.* The letters range from pedestrian details to deep emotion, from adoration to anger on both sides, and are themselves entertaining and dramatic enough to have formed the play *Dear Liar,* compiled by Jerome Kilty in 1960.

Toward the end of her life, following an embarrassing failure in Hollywood, what had been artistic temperament dwindled into eccentricity and poverty, which caused her estrangement from her family, friends, and home. Her marriage to George Cornwallis-West (Patrick Campbell had died at war in 1900) had been brief and unhappy as well as financially ruinous. She fought bitterly with Shaw over the publication of their letters—he feeling that their intimate nature would hurt his wife, she desperately needing the notoriety and money they would bring. Unable to return to England because she refused to put her pet dog Moonbeam in quarantine, she died practically penniless in southern France at the age of seventy-five. As a final insult, Cornwallis-West remarried on the day of her memorial service.

The pathos of C.'s final years cannot, however, diminish the brightness of her earlier days as the darling of the English and American stage. She cannot have been talentless, for she was counted with Ellen Terry as one of the two finest actresses of her era, responsible for bringing many new works of realism from the Continent to the English theater. In spite of her reputation for being difficult to work with, she was in continuous demand and received glowing reviews. Her writing—ungrammatical, unpunctuated, and misspelled though it may be—reveals a keen intelligence, an exuberant wit, and a sensitivity that made her both a great actress and a woman of infinite variety.

WORKS: *My Life and Some Letters* (1922). *Chance Medley* (unpublished). *Bernard Shaw and Mrs. Patrick Campbell: Their Correspondence,* ed. Alan Dent (1952).

BIBLIOGRAPHY: Cornwallis-West, G. *Edwardian Hey-Days* (1931). Dent, A. *Mrs. Patrick Campbell* (1961). Peters, M. *Mrs. Pat: The Life of Mrs. Patrick Campbell* (1984). Shaw, G. B. *Our Theatre in the Nineties* (1931).

For articles in reference works, see: *IDWB. Longman.*

Suzanne Westfall

Mary Carey

BORN: c. 1610–12, Berwick, Sussex.
DIED: c. 1680s.
DAUGHTER OF: Sir John Jackson.
MARRIED: Pelham Carey; George Payler, c. 1643.

As a seventeenth-century woman writer, C. found a means, as did a large number of women of the era, of expressing her voice through spiritual autobiography. Her manuscript "Meditation and Poetry" blends the two genres and explores themes of marriage, family, motherhood, death, and religion.

C. was the daughter of Sir John Jackson of Berwick. Her first husband, Pelham Carey, was the son of Henry, fourth Lord Hunsdon; she gives few details of this marriage, but one child from this union is thought to have survived. Her second husband, George Payler, whom she married in around 1643, was paymaster of the parliamentary forces in the garrison at Berwick. Interestingly, C. never used Payler's last name except as "Mary Carey, alias Payler." C. traveled from garrison to garrison with her husband; she felt safer close to him during "these dividing times." Of this marriage, two children survived infancy.

C. began putting her meditations, prayers, and poetry together on 17 October 1653; the dedication, which begins the book, is dated that day, and reads, "To my Most loving, and dearly beloved Husband George Payler, Esq., My deare, the occation of my writing this following dialogue; was my apprehending I should dye on my fourth child." C.'s main composition, a meditation entitled "A dialogue betwixt the soule and the body" dated 11 February 1649, was written on the occasion of the imminent birth of her fourth child and follows the preface to her husband. Included are lines "written by my deare husband at the death of our 4th (at that time only) child Robert Payler, Covent Garden, on December 8, 1650." Following George Payler's brief poem is C.'s poem "written by me at the same time" on 10 December of that year. C.'s next poem was "written by me at the death of my 4th sonne and 5th child, Peregrine Payler," Grove Street, 12 May 1652, followed by "A meditation or commemoration of the love of God the Father, Son and Holy Ghost." The last poem included in the book is titled "upon the sight of my abortive birth, 31 of December 1657." C. does not mention her date of birth, but she does give a clue to her birthdate in one of her writings. In "A Meditation . . . of the love of God the Father" (MS. Rawl. D. 1308, pp. 180–214), she says at one point that she has "lived 45 yeares." Unfortunately this text carries no date of composition, but there are clues elsewhere. Another text refers to the death of her fifth child, Peregrine, on 12 May 1652, at which point, she says, all her children are dead. But by the date of "A Meditation . . ." two children (Bethia and Nathaniel) are still alive on 31

December 1657 when she produced a stillborn child. The dedication to the book, written on 17 October 1653, speaks of God having "removed" her children "from our present sight" and makes no mention of any pregnancy, so the earliest her next child could have been born would be mid-1654 and the second around mid-1655. So "A Meditation . . ." cannot have been composed much earlier than mid-1655 or be later than late 1657, which would place her year of birth between 1610 and 1612.

C.'s meditations contrast an early life spent following fashions and activities of her first husband's "frivolous set" with a later life during which she sought to follow God's will. In her meditations, she regrets that she spent much of her early life in "vaine Companye." Of her later life, however, she writes lovingly of her second husband, praises her parents, and thanks God for the blessings of two healthy surviving children. As the titles indicate, C.'s poems focus on the occasions of losing a child either in infancy or to miscarriage. The poems begin with questions, challenges, pleadings to God reminiscent of George Herbert. The speaker asks to understand why she must give up her child—her "hart's breth," her "love token." By the end of each of the poems, which also suggest Herbert's dialectical poems such as "The Collar," the challenges and pleadings melt into absolute acceptance of God's will—indeed, the speaker's intent is not only acceptance but joyful and patient attendance on that will. George Parfitt suggests that C. writes in "couplet stanzas in a minimalist manner" to convey simply her love of and faith in God even in extreme and intimate situations.

In her longest poem, "Upon ye Sight of my abortive Birth ye 31th: of December 1657," C. moves from grief over the loss of a child to happiness at following God's will. She speaks of the loss of the child; as she prays and meditates, she then hopes that her heart will not miscarry as did her womb, a spiritual, not physical, tragedy. The poem moves into an extended metaphor comparing the speaker to the bride of Christ, this union being her "only happynesse." As his Bride, her fruitfulness is not physical but spiritual. She will "Quicken" (Conceive) his word and his spirit, and the "delivered" fruits will be those of the spirit: "Love; Joy; peace; Gentlenesse; / long-suffering; goodnesse; faith; & / meeknesse." C.'s stance as mother/poet and her lamentations of lost children lead Germaine Greer to compare C.'s poems of loss to those of Anne Bradstreet. Greer also mentions that C.'s portrayal of herself as the Bride of Christ is similar to the "Eliza" of *Eliza's Babes.* George Parfitt compares C.'s simplicity and directness of style to George Herbert's *Temple.*

C.'s achingly personal tone and the theme of her meditations and poems reflect her concern for her religion and her family, and they become, as spiritual autobiography, models readers can follow as typical of a woman finding her voice in the expression of her beliefs.

WORKS: "Meditation and Poetry" (unpublished). *My Lady Carey's Meditation, & Poetry* (1681). *Meditations from the Notebook of Mary Carey, 1649–1657* (1917).

BIBLIOGRAPHY: *Kissing The Rod: An Anthology of Seventeenth-Century Women's Verse,* ed. G. Greer et al. (1988). Parfitt, G. *English Poetry of the Seventeenth Century,* 2nd ed. (1992).

For articles in reference works, see: *Bloomsbury. Feminist.*

Sonja Bagby

Rosa Nouchette Carey

BORN: 24 September 1840, Stratford-le-Bow, London.
DIED: 19 July 1909, Sandilands, Keswick Road, London.
DAUGHTER OF: William Henry Carey and Maria Jane Wooddill Carey.

C. was the eighth child (fourth daughter) of a shipbroker. She spent her early years at Hackney, being educated first at home and then at the Ladies' Institute, St. John's Wood. She was a "delicate" child, but she wrote little plays that her brothers and sisters performed. She also wrote poems and told stories to her siblings, especially one sister, as she worked needlework; thus the whole of *Nellie's Memories,* for example, she originated and told verbally, not writing it down until several years later (published in 1887). This novel brought fame, for it was very popular and was reissued in many editions. Although C. wrote thirty-nine novels during her lifetime, she first tried to quench her longing to write, believing it was impossible to combine her joy, that is, writing, with a useful domestic life. She continued to take her traditional role seriously throughout life, assuming the sole care of nieces and a nephew at a brother's death, even at the expense of her own writing. As Helen Marion Burnside, a contemporary writer of children's tales, related, "I do not think that I have known any author who has to make her writing—the real work of her life—so secondary a matter as has Rosa Carey. She has so consistently lived her religion, so to speak, that family duty and devotion to its many members have always come first" (Black, *Notable Women Authors).* Of her objectives in writing, C. stated, "My ambition has been to try to do good and not harm by my works, and to write books which any mother can give a girl to read" (Black). Orthodox and conventional, C. for years had a class for young girls and servants over fifteen years of age, formed in connection with the Fulham Sunday School. She wrote fine descriptions, but her style lacks distinction, her plots being similar, microcosms of a conventional society now obsolete.

C. was on the staff of the *Girl's Own Paper* and published several short stories in it. Many other short stories were published by the Religious Tract Society; a volume of brief biographies, *Twelve Notable Good Women of the Nineteenth Century,* appeared in 1899.

C. resided for about thirty-nine years at Hampstead, moving to Putney, where she resided for almost twenty years. She died on 19 July 1909 in London, and was buried in the West Hampstead cemetery.

WORKS: *Wee Wifie* (1869). *Wooed and Married* (1875). *Heriot's Choice: A Tale* (1879). *Esther: A Book for Girls* (1880). *Nellie's Memories, A Novel* (1880). *Queenie's Whim, A Novel* (1881). *Not Like Other Girls: A*

Novel (1884). *Robert Ord's Atonement: A Novel* (1884). *Barbara Heathcote's Trial* (1885). *For Lilias. A Novel* (1885). *Uncle Max* (1887). *Aunt Diana* (1888). *Only the Governess* (1888). *Merle's Crusade* (1889). *The Search for Basil Lyndhurst* (1889). *Averil* (1890). *Effie's Little Mother* (1890). *Lover or Friend* (1890). *"But Men Must Work"* (1891). *Mary St. John: A Novel* (1891). *Our Bessie* (1892). *Sir Godfrey's Grand-Daughters* (1892). *Little Miss Muffet* (1893). *Mrs. Romney* (1893). *Basil Lyndhurst* (1894). *The Old, Old Story; a Novel* (1894). *Uncle Max* (1894). *My Little Boy Blue* (1895). *Cousin Mona; a Story for Girls* (1896). *The Mistress of Brae Farm: A Novel* (1896). *Doctor Luttrell's First Patient* (1897). *For Love of a Bedouin Maid* (1897). *Other People's Lives* (1897). *Mollie's Prince* (1898). *My Lady Frivol* (1899). *Twelve Notable Good Women of the Nineteenth Century* (1899). *Life's Trivial Round* (1900). *Rue with a Difference* (1900). *Herb of Grace* (1901). *The Highway of Fate* (1902). *A Passage Perilous* (1903). *At the Moorings* (1904). *The Household of Peter: A Novel* (1905). *No Friend Like a Sister* (1906). *The Angel of Forgiveness* (1907). *The Sunny Side of the Hill* (1908). *The Key of the Unknown* (1909).

BIBLIOGRAPHY: Black, H. C. *Notable Women Authors of the Day* (1893). *LonT* (20 July 1909). Pratt, A. T. C. *People of the Period* (1897).

For articles in reference works, see: *DNB*. *Longman*.

Phyllis J. Scherle

Jane Welsh Carlyle

BORN: 14 July 1801, Haddington, Scotland.
DIED: 21 April 1866, Chelsea, London.
DAUGHTER OF: John Welsh and Grace Baillie Welsh.
MARRIED: Thomas Carlyle, 1826.

The only child of a respected country doctor, C. displayed a powerful intellect at an early age and distinguished herself at local schools. By the age of thirteen she had written a novel and a five-act tragedy, and she had convinced her parents that "like a boy" she ought to learn Latin. Edward Irving, a young clergyman and friend of Thomas Carlyle, was appointed C.'s tutor. C.'s father, to whom she was extremely devoted, died when she was eighteen, leaving her the estate of Craiggenputtock and a substantial income. Shortly later, she was introduced to Carlyle, who became not only her friend but her mentor.

C.'s intelligence and wit were complemented by a distinctive appearance; according to one description, she was "bright and beautiful with a certain star-like radiance and grace." She did not lack for suitors, many of whom are satirized in her letters, but only Irving, Carlyle, and the sculptor George Rennie appear to have been viewed seriously by her. C.'s meeting with Carlyle in 1821 was the beginning of a deep intellectual relationship with very little romance. In spite of the affectionate tone that develops in their correspondence until their marriage in 1826, there is very little passion. Later, the biographer J. A. Froude was to characterize their union as a "partnership not marriage," reflecting, among other things, the asexual element of their married life.

After spending two years in Edinburgh, the Carlyles moved to the remote estate of Craiggenputtock where Carlyle labored over *Sartor Resartus*. The six years spent there were among the worst of C.'s life; without society, C. had no outlet for her conversation and wit, and, what is worse, she had to contend with her husband's very changeable moods. In 1834, the Carlyles set up permanent residence at No. 5 Cheyne Row in Chelsea, London. Carlyle had emerged as an important literary figure and their home became something of a cultural center. Regular visitors at the Carlyles' evenings at home included Thomas Babington Macaulay, Charles Dickens, John Ruskin, and Alfred Lord Tennyson. Geraldine Jewsbury, who originally visited Cheyne Row to meet Carlyle, eventually became C.'s closest friend and regular correspondent.

C. was extremely attentive to the domestic concerns of Cheyne Row and supervised frequent renovations and redecorations, including the construction of the "quiet place," a room where Carlyle could work without having his fragile disposition disturbed. Insulating Carlyle from the daily activities of the world occupied much of C.'s time, and these efforts form the subject of many of her letters. Carlyle, she tells one correspondent, "dislikes nothing in the world so much as going into a shop to buy anything, even his own trowsers and coats; so that, to the consternation of cockney tailors, I am obliged to go about them." Elsewhere, in the journal she kept in 1855, C. provides a witty and biting description of the Tax Commissioners whom she sees on Carlyle's behalf (21 November 1855). As much as her writing sparkles when she writes of her domestic tasks, it is clear that they wore her down, particularly as she began to feel neglected by Carlyle.

C. was encouraged both by Carlyle and by friends to write a novel; while she may have started one, nothing of it remains. What emerges in her letters is a clear and simple style that draws strength from her canny sense of detail and her cynical wit. Occasionally her writing is much more subdued, and a tone of sadness and fatigue emerges. C. complained of a weak constitution and severe headaches throughout her life and was often depressed about Carlyle's inattention to her. Only after C.'s death, which though sudden appeared to be of natural causes, did Carlyle (after reading her letters) fully appreciate the stress she bore for his sake. Exactly how great a drain Carlyle was on C.'s spirit is not clear; by her own admission, she had recognized genius in Carlyle, had "married for ambition," and was prepared "to take the consequences."

WORKS: Froude, J. A. *Letters and Memorials of Jane Welsh Carlyle* (1883). Carlyle, A. ed. *New Letters and Memorials of Jane Welsh Carlyle* (1903). Carlyle, A., ed. *The Love Letters of Thomas Carlyle and Jane Welsh* (1909). *The Collected Letters of Thomas and Jane Welsh Carlyle*, ed. C. R. Sauders, et al. (1970–). *I Too Am Here: Selected Letters of Jane Welsh Carlyle*, ed. A. Simpson and M. M. Simpson (1977).

BIBLIOGRAPHY: Blunt, R. *The Carlyles' Chelsea Home* (1895). Clarke, N. *Ambitious Heights: Writings, Friend-*

ship, Love: The Jewsbury Sisters, Felicia Hemans and Jane Carlyle (1990). Drew, E. *Jane Welsh and Jane Carlyle* (1928). Hanson, L. and E. Hanson *Necessary Evil: The Life of Jane Welsh Carlyle* (1952). Rose, P. *Parallel Lives: Five Victorian Marriages* (1983). Surtees, V. *Jane Welsh Carlyle* (1986). Woolf, V. *The Second Common Reader* (1932).

For articles in reference works, see: *Allibone SUP. Bloomsbury. Cambridge. Feminist. Oxford.*

Other references: *British Quarterly Review* (July 1881). *Carlyle Newsletter* (1979). *Contemporary Review* (May 1883). *Cornhill Magazine* (March 1920). *Frontiers* (1979). Partridge, F. *Everything to Lose* (1985). *PSt* (2 September 1982).

Alan Rauch

Carr, Jolyon: See *Pargeter, Edith Mary*

Dora de Houghton Carrington

BORN: 29 March 1893, Hereford.
DIED: 11 March 1932, Ham Spray, Hampshire.
DAUGHTER OF: Samuel Houghton Carrington and Charlotte Houghton Carrington.
MARRIED: Ralph Partridge, 1921.

Immortalized as Mary Bracegirdle in Aldous Huxley's *Crome Yellow,* as Minnette Darrington in D. H. Lawrence's *Women in Love,* and as the petite sex therapist in Wyndham Lewis's *The Apes of God,* C.'s reputation rests primarily on her striking appearance and her tempestuous romantic liaisons. C.'s presence in the fiction of her contemporaries is not surprising, as her life reads like a novel. She was involved in an infamous *menage à trois* with Ralph Partridge (whom she married in 1921) and the homosexual writer Lytton Strachey (with whom she maintained a relationship until his death in 1932). C.'s unconventional lifestyle rivalled that of her friend Vanessa Bell, who also lived with a husband and homosexual lover. Finally, C.'s dramatic suicide (first attempting carbon monoxide from a car's exhaust, then more effectively with a shotgun) after Strachey's death assured that her life story would take precedence over her history as an epistolary, visual, and environmental artist.

Recently, however, scholars such as Jane Hill are turning their interests to the diverse artifacts C. produced. The last twenty-five years have witnessed the release of a major motion picture documenting her life (*Carrington,* directed by Christopher Hampton, with Emma Thompson as C. and Jonathan Pryce as Strachey), three exhibits of her art, publication of two overviews of her work and a biography, and, most importantly, a volume of her letters. C.'s letters are known primarily for their wit (she describes herself as "dead as a ducat"), humor, and charming illustrations. These letters prove compelling reading, chronicling her exploration of her gender and sexuality, her love affairs, and her relation to figures such as Virginia and Leonard Woolf, Augustus John, Henry Lam, John Meynard Keynes, Bertrand Russell, Ottoline Morrell, David Garnett, and Strachey. Besides offering insight into the cultural moment in which she lived, the letters also offer a vivid and often painful portrait of the artist as a young woman.

Moreover, like Dorothy Wordsworth's journals, C.'s letters have an immediacy and vibrancy in their descriptions of natural landscapes. As C.'s paintings illustrate, she had intimate relationships not only with individuals but also with her surroundings. This intimacy is reflected in her letters, which are as much about places as they are about the people that inhabit them. Her description of the downs at Hurtbourne Tarrant and the views from her Tidmarsh and Ham Spray homes are simple, yet strikingly beautiful.

As a painter, C. did not ascribe to any particular school. She was friends with Roger Fry, Clive Bell, Duncan Grant, and Vanessa Bell, but she appears to have ignored their call for "significant form" in painting. She studied with Fry and Stanley Spencer for three years at the Slade School of Art, winning awards for her drawing and oil painting, and her painting, like her letters, has a personal flavor to it. In fact, C. found her paintings so personal that she rarely exhibited and did not have a one-woman show until thirty-eight years after her death. While alive, she circulated her productions within a limited radius, painting familiar landscapes, portraits of friends and servants, and occasionally scenes from her travels. She also decorated the two homes she shared with Strachey (Tidmarsh and Ham Spray) and executed many commissions for friends. Her commitment to artworks as various as the letter, the painting, the mural, and the decorative arts makes her difficult to classify; as a result, C. is largely overlooked in art, historical, and literary studies. Though her fiction, poetry, and drama are less signfiicant than her correspondence, she is able to provide a rich perspective on Bloomsbury and elsewhere in England in the years before and after World War I.

WORKS: *Carrington: Letters and Extracts From Her Diaries,* ed. D. Garnett (1970). *Carrington: Paintings, Drawings, Decorations,* ed. N. Carrington (1978).

BIBLIOGRAPHY: Bell, C. *Old Friends* (1956). Bell, Q. *Virginia Woolf: A Biography* (1972). Caws, M. *Women of Bloomsbury* (1990). Duguid, L. *TLS* (29 September 1995). Gerzina, G. *Carrington: A Life* (1989). Gerzina, G. *Country Life* (March 1978). Hill, J. *The Art of Dora Carrington* (1994). Holroyd, M. *Lytton Strachey: A Critical Biography* (1968, 1994). Johnston, J. *Art in America* (February 1990). Partridge, F. *Love in Bloomsbury: Memories* (1981). Partridge, F. *Everything to Lose: Diaries 1945–1960* (1985). Seymour, M. *Ottoline Morrell: Life on the Grand Scale* (1992). Shone, R. *Bloomsbury Portraits* (1976). Strachey, J. and F. Partridge. *Julia: A Portrait of Julia Strachey* (1983). Wilson, J. J., in *Between Women,* ed. C. Scher and L. DeSalvo (1984).

For articles in reference works, see: *BioIn. DBA. DWA. Feminist. Oxford. ToddBWW.*

Other references: *LonT* (2 September 1995). *National Review* (31 December 1995). *New Republic* (4 December 1995). *New York Observer* (23 October 1995). *NYRB* (11 January 1996). *NYT* (13 October

1995). Partridge, F. *New Yorker* (18 December 1995). *TLS* (29 September 1995).

Geneviève Sanchis Morgan

Carroll, Susanna: See *Centlivre, Susanna*

Catherine Carswell

BORN: 27 March 1879, Glasgow, Scotland.
DIED: 18 February 1946, Oxford.
DAUGHTER OF: George MacFarlane and Mary Anne Lewis MacFarlane.
MARRIED: Herbert Jackson, 1904; Donald Carswell, 1915.

C. is today most often remembered for her 1932 biography of D. H. Lawrence, who was her good friend for almost two decades. But she also wrote a great deal of literary journalism, two remarkable novels, and two other biographies that deserve to be remembered.

C. was born into a Calvinist family but not a stereotypically dour one since her parents imbued their religion with great emphasis on works of charity and on tolerance of others. She spent two years studying piano in Frankfurt, Germany, and attended Glasgow University, where she studied English. In England, she met and fell in love with Herbert Jackson in September 1904; they were married the following month. It soon became evident that Jackson was seriously unstable, with a violent paranoiac disorder. When she announced her pregnancy to him in March 1905, he threatened her with a revolver; shortly thereafter he was committed to a mental hospital, where he spent the rest of his life. In May 1908, she successfully brought a case asking for an annulment of the marriage, the first such annulment ever granted in a case of mental illness, granted chiefly because she was able to prove that his illness had preceded the marriage. Their daughter, Diana, later contracted pneumonia and died in 1913.

In 1907, C. had become a reviewer for the *Glasgow Herald,* a post she held even after her 1911 move to London. In 1915, she married Donald Carswell, a writer for *The Times* who had been a friend during her university days in Glasgow, and their son John was born in 1918.

Shortly after the move to London, she began work on an autobiographical novel, *Open the Door!,* which went through numerous revisions before its publication in 1920. She had enthusiastically reviewed the early novels of D. H. Lawrence for the *Glasgow Herald,* and the two met in June 1914. Lawrence exhaustively critiqued the manuscript of her novel, finding many severe flaws but also giving her real encouragement to continue; she read and responded to his draft of *Women in Love.* They developed a strong friendship and continued to share manuscripts until his death in 1930.

Open the Door! was finally completed in 1918 and, though rejected by one publisher, it won a prize from Melrose, who put the book out in 1920. The novel's style is uneven and its plot wanders somewhat, but it is nonetheless an intriguing and significant female *Bildungsroman,* treating the sexual development of its main character, Joanna Bannerman, with remarkable openness and power; the flowering of Joanna's libido leads to considerable suffering. Many of the incidents and characters are directly drawn from C.'s experience, such as the painfully shy Lawrence Urquhart, who is Donald Carswell, and Joanna's Glasgow family, who are based on members of the author's own family. The novel's title refers to a hidden door in a particular Italian villa through which, in days past, a notorious woman's secret lovers entered; the door becomes a major symbol for Joanna.

C.'s next novel, *The Camomile,* is also strongly autobiographical, but it is superior in structure and in style. Much of the book is in the form of a journal-letter kept by Ellen Carstairs as she struggles to come to maturity as a writer and as a woman. The journal form allows Ellen to explore her inner self, but the fact that the journal is addressed to a London friend prevents the introspection from sacrificing pace and plot; the book's subtitle, *An Invention,* suggests C.'s interest in formal experimentation. Ellen's mother had been a writer, and her devotion to writing had led to negligence as a mother. Thus writing for Ellen presents itself as conflict between one's duties to others and to one's self; her journal includes much insightful commentary on writing as a challenge to women's familial roles. One role Ellen rejects is that of wife as she realizes that marriage to the young doctor Duncan Bruce will be stultifying. The novel ends on a triumphant note as Ellen, having worked through her conflicts and having found the right relationship between self and responsibility, leaves Glasgow for a free, adult life.

C. planned two more novels—one was to be written in collaboration with Lawrence—but they never came to be. Her next book was the biography of Robert Burns (the last manuscript of hers that Lawrence read). C. declares at the outset that "to lack sympathy with Burns is to lack sympathy with mankind," and she sees in him an honest and natural man. She freely, and sympathetically, depicted Burns's sexual adventures with an openness and detail that greatly offended many for whom the man had become a symbol of Scottish national pride. One reader sent her a threatening letter with a bullet enclosed (suggesting that she might use it), and the controversy continued for several years. Today it is difficult to see what so shocked contemporaries, since C.'s facts have mostly been well established by later biographers. Highly readable and often moving, the book remains one of the best available introductions to Burns. One of the book's major themes is Burns's developing awareness of the price of the fame he had sought: that when his poetry ceased to be local, social, and personal, it declined in literary value as it rose in the commercial scale. C.'s Burns is a modern hero, hardly without his faults but never losing hold of his profound integrity.

Lawrence's death in 1930 was a blow to C., and worsening things was the 1931 publication of John Middleton Murry's *Son of Woman,* which she and many others felt blackened Lawrence's name. She set to work immediately on her own memoir, *The Savage Pilgrimage,* which attacked Murry directly. Murry threatened a libel suit, and the publisher, Martin Secker, withdrew the book at the last minute; finally, Chatto and Windus published it. In 1933, Murry published his *Reminiscences of D. H.*

Lawrence, which included some eighty pages of attack on C.'s book. It is difficult to separate *The Savage Pilgrimage* from the controversy of which it formed a part, but it may be best to see it as a personal tribute to a friend rather than a biography as such; C.'s closeness to her subject, and the speed with which the book was composed, keep the book from being fully successful.

Her next book was also a biography, this time of Giovanni Boccaccio. *The Tranquil Heart* is lively and well written but also opinionated. Boccaccio is seen as a hero of sorts, the first writer to treat women as human beings rather than as symbols or ideals and the first to express a healthy view of sexuality. C. is also attracted to his distrust of princes and the ruling classes. The book brings Boccaccio to life and is very good on the labyrinthine politics of the Italian city-states, but it too often seems to force us to view the Renaissance through modernist lenses.

Both C. and her husband supported themselves primarily through literary piece-work and journalism; there is unfortunately no bibliography of the many reviews and essays the two produced. Donald died in an accident in 1940, after which C. worked intermittently on an autobiography, incomplete at her death, that was edited and published by her son John in 1950; it contains some of her very best writing and reflection. *Lying Awake,* as her son titled it, is fragmentary and contemplative, deliberately avoiding anything like a continuous narrative. It records her fatigue after a long life of writing and literary controversy: "I hope to attain heaven and the forfeit of verbal language where music, motion and the glance will say all there is to be said." The book contains an affectionate look back at her childhood home and friends and movingly ponders the change from youth to age. *Lying Awake* is often quietly powerful and is a fitting testament to a remarkable mind and personality.

WORKS: *Open the Door!* (1920). *The Camomile: An Invention* (1922). *The Life of Robert Burns* (1930). *The Savage Pilgrimage: A Narrative of D. H. Lawrence* (1932). *The Tranquil Heart: Portrait of Giovanni Boccaccio* (1937). *Lying Awake: An Unfinished Autobiography and Other Posthumous Papers* (1950).

BIBLIOGRAPHY: Carswell, J., intro. to *Lying Awake* (1950). Carswell, J. *Lives and Letters* (1978). Carswell, J., intro. to 1986 rpt. of *Open the Door!* Carswell, J., intro. to 1987 rpt. of *The Camomile.*

For articles in reference works, see: *DLB. Feminist. Longman. NCBEL. Oxford. TCA.*

Raymond N. MacKenzie

Angela (Olive Stalker) Carter

BORN: 7 May 1940, Eastbourne, Sussex.
DIED: 16 February 1992, London.
DAUGHTER OF: Hugh Alexander Stalker and Olive Farthing Stalker.
MARRIED: Paul Carter, 1960.

C. was born in Eastbourne, Sussex, and educated in Balham. She received a degree in English from the University of Bristol. After publishing her first three novels (two of them prize winning), she visited Japan from 1969 to 1972, by which time her marriage to Paul Carter, a photographer, had ended. In 1983, a son was born to her and Mark Pearce. C. was writer in residence in Australia in 1984 and subsequently a teacher at American universities for the next several years. Her last novel, *Wise Children,* was published in 1991, the year before she died of cancer.

At this point, several years after her death, C.'s literary status is high. She is valued as a postmodern writer with feminist interests and concerns. Critic Lorna Sage recently counted forty applications to write dissertations on C.'s fiction in England alone. *The Review of Contemporary Literature* devoted half of its Fall 1994 issue to a tribute to C. Criticisms of her work include the perception by some of her overly ornate style. John Bayley labeled her as "politically correct" and therefore faddish, and some feminists view her depiction of patriarchal structures as endorsements.

Three of C.'s novels—*Shadow Dance* (1966), *Several Perceptions* (1968), and *Love* (1971)—are set in contemporary England and reflect social realism despite some exaggerations and some gothic elements. In *Flesh and the Mirror,* Marc O'Day has called the three novels C.'s "Bristol trilogy." The three play with the borders of madness and theater. Fashionable young people reflect a counter-culture that is seedy, involved with second-hand things, and includes violence and death as part of the cultural mix.

The Bloody Chamber (1979) remains for some readers C.'s central work, a collection of fairy and folk tales often rewritten from a feminine point of view and usually anchored in a historical context, not in the timeless web of myth. The tales, while often presenting characters in grim situations, also offer transformation as a possibility and a choice. Various creatures such as Beauty's Beast and a lion and a vampire appear, but C. seems particularly fascinated with the figure of the wolf. Compared to other postmodern rewritings of fairy tales (even one by A. S. Byatt), C.'s have a depth and resonance that give them staying power, especially the title story, a Bluebeard retelling.

Margaret Atwood has analyzed the part that *The Sadeian Woman* (1979) played in C.'s thinking and writing. C. sheds light on de Sade's Justine, the female victim, and Juliette, the corresponding victimizer, interested in sexual pleasure and financial profit. Instead of these polar opposites, C. celebrates metamorphosis and flexibility.

Although it is set in contemporary England, *The Magic Toyshop* (1967) encompasses fantastic elements in the uncle's puppet theatre and the Irish aunt who does not speak. Sexual dangers including incest take place in the shadows, and childhood innocence is menaced. There is a Gothic atmosphere that surrounds the brother and sister when there are no parents to protect them.

In *Heroes and Villains* (1969), *The Passion of New Eve* (1977), and *The Infernal Desire Machines of Dr. Hoffman* (1972), C. has forsaken realism for popular forms like romance and the picaresque adventure story for the mode of fabulation or fantasy. *Heroes and Villains* reshapes the abduction romance plot while creating at least two vital three-dimensional women characters. *The Passion of New Eve* constructs gender and sexuality in unconventional ways, and *The Infernal Desire Machines of Dr. Hoffman* also plays with the dichotomy of actuality and possibility or imagination.

In *Nights at the Circus* (1984), C. combines disparate material and forms. The fiction concerns a variety of enchantments and the need to escape them with the aid of laughter. A major element in the plot is a romance between Fevvers, the winged woman, and Jack Walser, an American reporter who is seeking a story that proves Fevvers to be a fraud. Walser must undergo an initiation to prove his worth as Fevvers's love and mate. But Fevvers, tempted by greed, must also suffer and undergo a transformation. A section of the novel centering on clown-alley in St. Petersburg, Florida, is a descent into hell (like the scenes with the prostitutes in Rome in Joseph Heller's *Catch-22).* C. analyzes the brothel and the freak show as well as the circus. Unlike simplistic discussions of carnivalization, the world of the circus imprisons people as well as sets them free.

Wise Children (1991) is a novel that concerns the division of people into privileged and underprivileged, legitimate and illegitimate, with the two Chance sisters, Nora and Dora, as bastards in their family and in the tradition of the English stage. Shakespearean drama is the backdrop against which the twins' career in the music hall seems to be measured with their putative father, Melchior Hazard, a revered Shakespearean actor. Sets of twins and other doubling motifs fill the novel with exclusive legitimate families contrasted with found families, formed informally out of caring and mutual acceptance. It may be a wise child who knows his father, but even one's true mother may be a puzzle and a mystery if one insists on an official family tree. Wonder is part of the atmosphere of the novel, with the twins' uncle Peregrine making much of the magic for the girls, now celebrating their seventy-fifth birthdays. The novel encompasses romance, social criticism, and magic realism.

WORKS: *Shadow Dance* (1966; in the U.S. as *Honeybuzzard). Unicorn* (1966). *The Magic Toyshop* (1967). *Several Perceptions* (1968). *Heroes and Villains* (1969). *Miss Z, The Dark Young Lady* (1970). *The Donkey Prince* (1970). *Love* (1971, rev. 1987). *The Infernal Desire Machines of Dr. Hoffman* (1972; also pub. as *The War of Dreams,* 1977). *Fireworks* (1974, rev. 1987). *The Passion of New Eve* (1977). (trans.) *The Fairy Tales of Charles Perrault* (1977). *The Bloody Chamber* (1979). *The Sadeian Woman: An Exercise in Cultural History* (1979; also pub. as *The Sadeian Woman and the Ideology of Pornography). Martin Leman's Comic and Curious Cats* (1979). *Black Venus's Tale* (1980). *Moonshadow* (1982). *Nothing Sacred: Selected Writings* (1982, rev. 1992). (trans.) *Sleeping Beauty and Other Favourite Fairy Tales* (1982, 1989, 1991). *Nights at the Circus* (1984). *Black Venus* (1985). *Come Unto These Yellow Sands* (1985). *Saints and Strangers* (1986). *Images of Frida Kahlo* (1989). *Wise Children* (1991). *Expletives Deleted* (1992). *American Ghosts & Old World Wonders* (1993). *Burning Your Boats: The Collected Short Stories* (1995). *The Curious Room: Plays, Film Scripts and an Opera,* ed. M. Bell (1996). *Shaking a Leg: Journalism and Writings,* ed. J. Uglow (1997).

BIBLIOGRAPHY: Alexander, F. *Contemporary Women Novelists* (1989). Alvarez, A. *Meta* (September 1993). Anwell, M., in *The Female Gaze: Women as Viewers of Popular Culture,* ed. L. Gamman and M. Marshment (1988). Bayley, J. *NYRB* (23 April 1992). Bell, M. *GL&L* (1992). Blodgett, H. *RCF* (1994). Boehm, B. *RCF* (1994). Boehm, B. *Crit* (1995). Bonca, C. *RCF* (1994). Bradfield, S. *RCF* (1994). *The Infernal Desires of Angela Carter: Fiction, Femininity,* Feminism, ed. J. Bristow and T. L. Broughton (1997). Brown, S. R., in *Forked Tongues,* ed. A. Massa and A. Stead (1994). Bryant, S. *Criticism* (1989). Chedgzoy, K., in *New Essays on Hamlet,* ed. M. T. Burnett and J. Manning (1994). Christensen, P. *RCF* (1994). Clark, R. *WS* (1987). Claus, H. *RCF* (1994). Collick, J. *CrSurv* (1991). Coover, R. *RCF* (1994). Ducornet, R. *RCF* (1994). Duncker, P. *L&H* (1984). Falzon, A. *European-English Messenger* (1994). Ferrell, R., in *The Illusion of Life,* ed. A. Cholodenko (1991). Fowl, M. *CrSurv* (1991). Gass, J. *ArkR* (1995). Gass, J. *RCF* (1994). Goldsworthy, K. *Meanjin* (1985). Gorra, M. *HudR* (1991). Haase, D. *Proverbium* (1990). Hallab, M. *StCS* (1995). Hanson, C. *JSSE* (1988). Hardin, M. *RCF* (1994). Jacobson, L. *Antithesis* (1993). Johnson, H. *RCF* (1994). Jordan, E. in *Plotting Change,* ed. L. Anderson (1990). Jordan, E., in *New Feminist Discourses,* ed. I. Armstrong (1992). Jordan, E., in *Postmodernism and the Re-Reading of Modernity,* ed. F. Barker, P. Hulme, and M. Iversen (1992). Kaiser, M. *RCF* (1994). Katsavos, A. *RCF* (1994). Kendrick, W., in *Contemporary British Women Writers,* ed. R. E. Hosmer, Jr. (1993). Landon, B., in *Erotic Universe,* ed. D. Palumbo (1986). Lathers, M., in *Literature and the Bible,* ed. D. Bevan (1993). Ledwon, L. *JFA* (1993). Lewallyn, A., in *Perspectives on Pornography,* ed. G. Day and C. Bloom (1988). Lokke, K. *Frontiers* (1988). Makinen, M. *Feminist Review* (1992). Manlove, C., in *Twentieth-Century Fantasists,* ed. K. Filmer (1992). Martinsson, Y. *Eroticism, Ethics and Reading* (1996). Matus, J. *SSF* (1991). Meaney, G. *(Un)like Subjects* (1993). Mergenthal, S. *GRAAT* (1993). Michael, M. C. *ConL* (1994). O'Day, M., in *Flesh and the Mirror,* ed. L. Sage (1994). Palmer, P., in *Women Reading Women's Writing,* ed. S. Roe (1987). Punter, D. *The Literature of Terror* (1980). Punter, D. *Crit* (1984; reprinted in *The Hidden Script,* ed. D. Punter, 1985). Punter, D., in *The British and Irish Novel Since 1960,* ed. J. Acheson (1990). Robinson, S. *Engendering the Subject* (1991). Rose, E. C., in *The Voyage In,* ed. E. Abel, et al. (1983). Rosinsky, N. *Feminist Futures* (1982). Rubenstein, R. *TSWL* (1993). Sage, L. *Contemporary Writers: Angela Carter* (1990). Sage, L. *Granta* (Autumn 1992). Sage, L. *Women in the House of Fiction* (1992). Schmidt, R. *TexP* (1989). Snitow, A. *VLS* (June 1989). Steedman, C., in *Fin de Siècle/Fin du Globe,* ed. John Stokes (1992). Turner, R. *FForum* (1987). Vallorani, N. *SFS* (1994). Wilson, R. R., in *Past the Last Post,* ed. I. Adam and H. Tiffin (1990). Wisker, G. *Ideas and Production* (1985).

For articles in reference works, see: *Bloomsbury. CA. Cambridge. CD. CLC. CN. DLB. Feminist. TCSFW. ToddBWW.*

Kate Begnal

Elizabeth Carter

BORN: 16 December 1717, Deal, Kent.
DIED: 19 February 1806, London.
DAUGHTER OF: the Reverend Nicholas Carter and Margaret Swayne Carter.
WROTE UNDER: Eliza.

C. was the most learned lady in England during the eighteenth century. A poet, scholar, essayist, and translator, she achieved her erudition by remaining unmarried and devoting her life to scholarly and literary pursuits. A prominent member of the Bluestocking circle, C.'s friends included Samuel Johnson, Samuel Richardson, Sir Joshua Reynolds, Edmund Burke, and Horace Walpole. Her published letters present vivid and witty accounts of the eighteenth-century literary world and down-to-earth perceptions of women's lives. Her correspondents included Catherine Talbot, Elizabeth Vesey, and Elizabeth Montagu.

C.'s father was a schoolmaster, and she had a desire for learning from an early age. A frequently cited anecdote reveals that she spent many hours in serious study: "She read both late at night and early in the morning, taking snuff, chewing green tea, and using other means to keep herself awake. Beginning with Latin and Greek, she afterwards learned Hebrew, French, Italian, Spanish, and German. Later in life, she taught herself Portuguese and Arabic." In addition to languages, C. was interested in historical and scientific matters, such as ancient and modern history and ancient geography. As an eighteenth-century woman, she was expected to be accomplished in the "feminine" yearnings: She played both the spinet and German flute and sang, although by her own admission she did not sing well. She was an excellent needlewoman and a good cook. Johnson, one of her dearest friends, gave her this famous two-pronged compliment that exemplifies the position of women in eighteenth-century society and indicates the high quality of C.'s achievements. Upon hearing a lady commended for her learning, Johnson said, "A man is in general better pleased when he has a good dinner upon his table, than when his wife talks Greek. My old friend, Mrs. Carter," he added, "could make a pudding as well as translate Epictetus from the Greek; and work a handkerchief as well as compose a poem."

C.'s father was a friend of Edward Cave, the founder and publisher of the *Gentlemen's Magazine.* In 1734, in his magazine, C. published her first poem, an epigram, which was, following the conventions of her era for women writers, published under a pseudonym, "Eliza." As Eliza, she continued to contribute to the magazine for some years. In April 1758 her epigram caught the attention of Samuel Johnson, who had recently come to London, and he wrote a response to the epigram. At Johnson's request, Cave introduced the two, and they were friends until Johnson's death in 1784. In 1738, "Poems upon particular Occasions," a small pamphlet containing a collection of eight of her poems, was published by Cave. The anonymous publication included a translation of the poet Anacreon.

After meeting Johnson, C. contributed two articles to the *Rambler,* No. 44 on "Religion and Superstition" and No. 100 on "Modish Pleasures." In 1739, she published two anonymous translations: *Sir Isaac Newton's Philosophy Explain'd for the Use of Ladies,* translated from the Italian of Sig. Algarotti, and *An Examination of Mr. Pope's Essay on Man,* translated from the French of M. Crousaz. Humble about her literary accomplishments, C. "never willingly referred to" the translations after their publication. Her silence is most interesting when the fact is taken into account that the latter translation was for years misattributed to Johnson, and it was James Boswell who finally recognized that C., not Johnson, had done the work.

In 1741, C. made the acquaintance of Catherine Talbot, an aristocrat by birth, who lived in the household of Thomas Secker, the future Archbishop of Canterbury. Talbot became C.'s closest friend, and Secker became one of C.'s patrons. It was at their suggestion that C. undertook the translation of Epictetus, the Greek Stoic philosopher and emancipated slave who taught that man should wish for nothing that is not under his control. He advocated a serene life, free from unfulfilled desires and calm in the face of death.

C. began the translation in the summer of 1749, but she did not finish until December 1752. It was not originally intended for publication and was sent to Talbot in sheets as it was written. About the publication of the translation, Talbot wrote that it would "do honour to Epictetus, yourself, your country, and womankind." At the suggestion of Secker, C. added an introduction and notes to the manuscript, and in April 1758 it was published by subscription (by Samuel Richardson). It brought C. nearly £1000, with which she purchased her residence at Deal. The translation still is considered the standard one.

In 1762, C. published her second volume of poems, *Poetry on Several Occasions,* which went through four editions. Included in this volume was the poem "Ode to Wisdom," which had originally been published as part of Richardson's *Clarissa* in 1747. C.'s poetic style is delicate and restrained, and indicates her strong philosophic nature.

Established as an important member of the Bluestocking circle and a recognized female literary figure, C. spent the last forty years of her life in comfortable circumstances. In 1763, she visited France, Germany, and Holland, an interesting account of the trip being given in her letters to Talbot. From 1768 to 1774, many important friends died: her patron Archbishop Secker, her friend Catherine Talbot, her father. In 1782, she visited Paris for the last time, but she frequently traveled within England until her death in 1806.

C.'s letters comprise the largest segment of her works. Letters, considered the most appropriate type of expression for women during the eighteenth century, offer the biographer and historian great insight into the lives of these women whose public presence was restricted by stringent social codes but whose thoughts and ideas could be expressed in epistolary fashion. C.'s intellectual importance only now is beginning to receive critical attention. There is no contemporary biography, although her name is always included in women's histories of the time.

WORKS: *Poems Upon Particular Occasions* (1738). (trans.) *Sir Isaac Newton's Philosophy Explain'd for the Use of Ladies: in Six Dialogues on Light and Colours,* by F. Algarotti (1739). (trans.) *An Examination of Mr. Pope's Essay on Man,* by J.-P. de Crousaz (1739). (trans.) *All the Work of Epictetis, Which Are Now Extant, Consisting of His Discourses, Preserved by Arrian, in Four Books, the Enchiridion, and Fragments* (1752). *Poems on Several Occasions* (1762). *Memoirs of the Life of Mrs. Elizabeth Carter, with a New Edition of Her Poems. Including Some Which Have Never Appeared Before, to Which Are Added, Some Miscellaneous Essays in Prose, Together with Her Notes on the Bible, and Answers,* ed. M. Pennington (1807). *A Series of Letters Between Mrs Elizabeth Carter and Miss Catherine Talbot, from 1741 to 1770, to Which Are Added Letters from Mrs. Carter to Mrs. Vesey Between the Years 1763 and 1787,* ed. M. Pennington (1809). *Letters from Mrs. Carter to Mrs. Montagu, Between the Years 1755 and 1800, Chiefly Upon Literary and Moral Subjects* (1817). *Sketches in Biography* (1825). *Bluestocking Letters* (1926).

BIBLIOGRAPHY: Gaussen, A. and C. C. Gaussen. *A Woman of Wit and Wisdom: A Memoir of Elizabeth Carter* (1906). Martin, R. *PAPA* (1985). Rogers, K. M. *Feminism in Eighteenth Century England* (1982). Rowton, F. *The Female Poets of Great Britain* (1853). Spacks, P. M., in *The Private Self: Theory and Practice of Women's Autobiographical Writings,* ed. S. Benstock (1988). Thomas, C. *AJ* (1991).

For articles in reference works, see: *Allibone. BAB1800. DNB. Feminist. ToddBWW.*

Other references: Dobson, A. *Later Essays* (1921). Hampshire, G. *N&Q* (1972). Jones, H. P. *HLQ* (1978). Sena, J. F. *YES* (1971).

Priscilla Dorr
(updated by Natalie Joy Woodall)

Barbara Cartland

BORN: 9 July 1901.
DAUGHTER OF: Bertram Cartland and Mary Hamilton "Polly" Cartland.
MARRIED: Alexander McCorquodale, 1927; Hugh McCorquodale, 1936.
WROTE UNDER: Barbara Cartland; Barbara McCorquodale.

The most prolific romance novelist, according to *The Guinness Book of World Records,* and one of the top five best-selling authors of all time (long past the 100 million copy mark set in 1979), C. was also a playwright, biographer, journalist, pageant designer, decorator, glider pilot, county councillor, philanthropist, businesswoman, and world traveler.

C. ran her estate at Canfield and raised three children, a daughter, born during C.'s six-year marriage to Alexander McCorquodale, and two sons, born during her twenty-seven-year union with Alexander's cousin, Hugh. Each son manages either the financial affairs or the extensive corrections for each book.

C. began her career as a writer after World War I, when she was invited by publisher Lord Beaverbrook to contribute paragraphs of gossip to the *Daily News.* Insisting on anonymity for much of this material, as she "preferred to work behind the scenes," C. expanded the market for her columns to other newspapers: *Daily Mail, Daily Mirror,* and *Tatler.*

Her first novel, *Jigsaw* (1925), described as "Mayfair with the lid off," drew, in part, from C.'s own experiences and echoed the styles of favorite authors: Ethel M. Dell (especially *The Sheik*) and Elinor Glyn. *Jigsaw* has a freshness and charm rarely found in her later novels. It concerns the adventures of Mona Vivien, a "strikingly beautiful" young woman who has graduated from convent school and is ready to enter London society. Despite a brief fling with the mysterious, worldly half-brother of her "true love," a marquis, Mona recognizes that her source of future happiness depends on making the right decision and eventually accepts the marquis's proposal. Some criticisms of the novel were favorable, as in the statement that the book was "a dramatic conflict of emotions, written with zest," but not all concurred. Others bitingly commented that the writing was "amateurish" and one stated "If this is Mayfair, then let me live in Whitechapel." Critics notwithstanding, C.'s first work was published in six editions and five other languages, setting a precedent that has not ceased.

C.'s fictional formula rarely changed. A chaste heroine, whose name must end with the letter "a," meets the handsome, wealthy hero in an exotic nineteenth-century setting. Love blooms; obstacles are overcome; the couple marries; and only then do they give in to the passion that has beset them throughout the novel. Variations involve only the scene for each romance, as C.'s vast travels have inspired many of her stories. The conclusion of each work is relatively similar; lines or passages from one have even been found in other C. works.

C.'s lack of pornographic filigree has earned her more than 400 million readers. "I am their escape from the depression and boredom and lack of romance in modern life," she once explained to an interviewer. Each thin volume, usually no more than 60,000 words, was dictated to a series of secretaries. Scorning long paragraphs and complicated subplots, C. avoided lengthy explanations or needless descriptions.

C.'s literary strength was an insistence on thorough research. Attention to factual or epistolary evidence was most visible in several of her historical biographies, as was the added attraction of a "romantic angle." One such example is *Metternich: The Passionate Diplomat* (1964), which required thirty sources, including material from the Viennese Court and State Archives as well as numerous histories and biographies, in addition to C.'s own work on Josephine, Empress of France. The text centers on Metternich's political importance: his influence on the development of the Congress of Vienna and his ability to engage Austria in European affairs during the period 1815–48. But the ambivalent nature of the man is also pursued with an exposé of his relationships with three wives and four mistresses: "The loves of . . . Metternich, within the marital state or beyond it, softened the character of someone whose icy intellect produced a figure of superhuman coldness, objectivity, and brilliance," C. concludes in the text. C. had one film scenario to her credit (*The Flame Is Love*), which had 24 million viewers when shown in the United States in 1979.

Because of a serious illness, C. became interested in nutrition, especially proper diet and vitamins, and eventually created a series of books on the importance of good health on individual appearance (among them *Be Vivid, Be Vital,* 1956; *Look Lovely, Be Lovely,* 1958; and *Vitamins for Vitality,* 1959).

C. was known as "The Queen of Romance," an accolade that captured the writer's sincere desire to keep alive the fantasy her readers crave: the Cinderella story that ends "happily ever after." She "kept the faith" with her Regency novels, and her audience happily and constantly responded by demanding more works by C.

WORKS: *Blood Money* (1925). *Jigsaw* (1925). *Sawdust* (1926). *If The Tree is Saved* (1929). *For What?* (1930). *Sweet Punishment* (1931). *A Virgin in Mayfair* (1932). *Just Off Piccadilly* (1933). *Not Love Alone* (1933). *A Beggar Washed* (1934). *Touch the Stars* (1935). *Dangerous Experiment* (1936). *But Never Free* (1937). *Broken Barriers* (1938). *The Gods Forget* (1939). *Stolen Halo* (1940). *Now Rough, Now Smooth* (1941). *Ronald Cartland* (1942). *The Isthmus Years* (1943). *Yet She Follows* (1944). *The Years of Opportunity, 1939–1945* (1948). *A Duel of Hearts* (1949). *The Knave of Hearts* (1950; repub. as *The Innocent Heiress,* 1975). *Love Is an Eagle* (1951). *Love Is the Enemy* (1952). *The Passionate Pilgrim* (1952). *Elizabethan Lover* (1953). *Desire of the Heart* (1954). *The Fascinating Forties: A Book for the Over-Forties* (1954; rev. ed., 1973). *Love Me For Ever* (1954). *Wings on My Heart* (1954). *Bewitching Women* (1955). *The Kiss of the Devil* (1955). *Marriage for Moderns* (1955). *Be Vivid, Be Vital* (1956). *The Coin of Love* (1956). *The Outrageous Queen* (1956). *Polly, My Wonderful Mother* (1956). *The Caged Bird* (1957). *Love, Life and Sex* (1957). *The Scandalous Life of King Carol* (1957). *The Thief of Love* (1957). *Look Lovely, Be Lovely* (1958). *The Private Life of Charles II* (1958). *The Kiss of Silk* (1959). *The Private Life of Elizabeth, Empress of Austria* (1959). *Vitamins for Vitality* (1959). *Love Under Fire* (1960). *The Price Is Love* (1960). *Josephine, Empress of France* (1961). *The Messenger of Love* (1961). *Diane de Poitiers* (1962). *The Many Facets of Love* (1963). *Etiquette for Love and Romance* (1964). *The Fire of Love* (1964). *Living Together* (1964). *Metternich, The Passionate Diplomat* (1964). *Sex and the Teenager* (1964). *A Ghost in Monte Carlo* (1965). *Love Holds the Cards* (1965). *Love on the Run* (1965). *Woman—the Enigma* (1965). *A Virgin in Paris* (1966). *Danger by the Nile* (1967). *I Search for the Rainbow: 1946–1966* (1967; as *I Search for Rainbows,* 1973). *The Enchanting Evil* (1968). *Love Is Contraband* (1968). *The Youth Secret* (1968). *A Hazard of Hearts* (1969). *Love in Hiding* (1969). *Love is Dangerous* (1969). *The Unknown Heart* (1969). *The Unpredictable Bride* (1969). *Cupid Rides Pillion* (1970). *The Hidden Evil* (1970). *The Hidden Heart* (1970). *The Magic of Honey* (1970). *The Reluctant Bride* (1970). *Street Adventure* (1970). *We Danced All Night, 1919–1929* (1970). *After the Night* (1971). *Armour Against Love* (1971). *The Enchanted Waltz* (1971). *The Golden Gondola* (1971). *Health Food Cookery Book* (1971). *Husbands and Wives* (1971). *If We Will* (1971). *The Kiss of Paris* (1971). *The Little Pretender* (1971). *Out of Reach* (1971). *Stars in My Heart* (1971). *The Black Panther* (1972). *Book of Beauty and Health* (1972). *The Dream Within* (1972). *The Enchanted Moment* (1972). *Halo for the Devil* (1972). *The Irresistible Buck* (1972). *Lines on Life and Love* (1972). *Lost Enchantment* (1972). *Love is Mine* (1972). *No Heart Is Free* (1972). *Audacious Adventures* (1973). *Blue Heather* (1973). *The Coin of Love* (1973). *The Daring Deception* (1973). *The Leaping Flame* (1973) *A Light to the Heart* (1973). *Lights of Love* (1973). *The Little Adventure* (1973). *Love Forbidden* (1973). *Men Are Wonderful* (1973). *The Pretty Horse-Breakers* (1973). *Where Is Love?* (1973). *The Wicked Marquis* (1973). *Against the Stream* (1974). *The Bored Bride-groom* (1974). *The Castle of Fear* (1974). *The Cruel Count* (1974). *The Dangerous Dandy* (1974). *The Glittering Lights* (1974). *Journey to Paradise* (1974). *The Magnificent Marriage* (1974). *No Darkness for Love* (1974). *No Time for Love* (1974). *The Penniless Peer* (1974). *The Ruthless Rake* (1974). *An Arrow of Love* (1975). *As Eagles Fly* (1975). *Bewitched* (1975). *Call of the Heart* (1975). *Desperate Defiance* (1975). *The Devil in Love* (1975). *Fire on the Snow* (1975). *The Flame Is Love* (1975). *Food for Love* (1975). *A Frame of Dreams* (1975). *The Frightened Bride* (1975). *A Gamble with Hearts* (1975). *The Impetuous Duchess* (1975). *The Karma of Love* (1975). *A Kiss for the King* (1975). *Love Is Innocent* (1975). *The Mask of Love* (1975). *Say Yes, Samantha* (1975). *The Shadow of Sin* (1975). *A Sword to the Heart* (1975). *The Tears of Love* (1975). *Towards the Stars* (1975). *A Very Naughty Angel* (1975). *An Angel in Hell* (1976). *The Blue-Eyed Witch* (1976). *Conquered by Love* (1976). *The Disgraceful Duke* (1976). *The Dream and the Glory* (1976). *The Elusive Earl* (1976). *Escape from Passion* (1976). *The Golden Illusion* (1976). *The Heart Triumphant* (1976). *The Husband Hunters* (1976). *The Magic of Honey Cookbook* (1976). *Moon Over Eden* (1976). *Passions in the Sand* (1976). *The Slaves of Love* (1976). *Vote for Love* (1976). *The Wild Cry of Love* (1976). *A Duel with Destiny* (1977). *Kiss the Moonlight* (1977). *Look, Listen and Love* (1977). *Love and the Loathsome Leopard* (1977). *Love Locked In* (1977). *The Love Pirate* (1977). *Magic of Love* (1977). *The Marquis Who Hated Women* (1977). *No Escape from Love* (1977). *Recipes for Lovers* (1977). *A Rhapsody of Love* (1977). *The Saint and the Sinner* (1977). *A Sign of Love* (1977).

The Temptation of Torilla (1977). *A Touch of Love* (1977). *The Wild Unwilling Wife* (1977). *Alone in Paris* (1978). *Lessons in Love* (1978). *The Chieftain Without a Heart* (1978). *The Mysterious Maid-Servant* (1978). *Flowers for the God of Lore* (1978). *The Ghost Who Fell in Love* (1978). *The Irresistible Force* (1978). *I Seek the Miraculous* (1978). *The Judgement of Love* (1978). *The Light of Love: Lines to Live by Day by Day* (1978). *Love, Lords and Ladybirds* (1978). *Love and Lovers* (1978). *Magic or Mirage* (1978). *The Passion and the Flower* (1978). *A Princess in Distress* (1978). *The Problems of Love* (1978). *The Race for Love* (1978). *The Twists and Turns of Love* (1978). *The Captive Heart* (1979). *The Drums of Love* (1979). *The Duke and the Preacher's Daughter* (1979). *The Prince and the Pekingese* (1979). *Ashes of Desire* (1980). *Barbara Cartland* (1980). *Barbara Cartland's Scrapbook* (1980). *Bride to the King* (1980). *The Bridge of Kisses* (1980). *The Broad Highway* (1980). *Charles Rex* (1980). *The Dawn of Love* (1980). *Free from Fear* (1980). *A Gentleman in Love* (1980). *The Goddess and the Gaiety Girl* (1980). *The Great Moment* (1980). *Greatheart* (1980). *A Heart Is Stolen* (1980). *The Horizons of Love* (1980). *Imperial Splendour* (1980). *A Kiss of Silk* (1980). *Little White Doves of Love* (1980). *Lost Laughter* (1980). *Love at the Helm* (1980). *Love for Sale* (1980). *Love Has His Way* (1980). *Love in the Moon* (1980). *Lucifer and the Angel* (1980). *Money, Magic and Marriage* (1980). *My Brother, Ronald* (1980). *The Obstacle Race* (1980). *Ola and the Sea Wolf* (1980). *The Perfection of Love* (1980). *The Power and the Prince* (1980). *The Price of Love* (1980). *The Price of Things* (1980). *Pride and the Poor Princess* (1980). *The Prude and the Prodigal* (1980). *Punished with Love* (1980). *Rainbow in the Spray* (1980). *The Runaway Heart* (1980). *The Sequence* (1980). *Signpost to Love* (1980). *Six Days* (1980). *A Song of Love* (1980). *Son of the Turk* (1980). *The Sons of the Sheik* (1980). *The Sweet Enchantress* (1980). *The Waltz of Hearts* (1980). *Who Can Deny Love?* (1980). *Women Have Hearts* (1980). *Afraid* (1980). *The Amateur Gentleman* (1981). *The Complacent Wife* (1981). *Count the Star* (1981). *Dollars for the Duke* (1981). *Dreams do Come True* (1981). *Enchanted* (1981). *The Explosion of Love* (1981). *For All Eternity* (1981). *From Hell to Heaven* (1981). *A Gamble with Hearts* (1981). *Gift of the Gods* (1981). *The Heart of the Clan* (1981). *His Official Fiancée* (1981). *In the Arms of Love* (1981). *An Innocent in Russia* (1981). *The Kiss of Life* (1981). *The Lion Tamer* (1981). *The Lioness and the Lily* (1981). *Love at the Helm* (1981). *Love in the Dark* (1981). *Love Wins* (1981). *Lucky in Love* (1981). *A Night of Gaiety* (1981). *A Portrait of Love* (1981). *Pure and Untouched* (1981). *The River of Love* (1981). *Romantic Royal Marriages* (1981). *A Shaft of Sidelight* (1981). *Tether-stones* (1981). *Touch a Star* (1981). *Towards the Stars* (1981). *The Wild, Unwilling Wife* (1981). *Winged Magic* (1981). *The Wings of Ecstasy* (1981). *Wings on My Heart* (1981). *Written with Love: Passionate Love Letters* (1981). *Again This Rapture* (1982). *The Audacious Adventures* (1982). *Barbara Cartland Picture Romances* (1982). *Barbara Cartland's Book of Celebrities* (1982). *The Call of the Highlands* (1982). *Camfield Romances* (1982). *Caught By Love* (1982). *For All Eternity* (1982). *The Frightened Bride* (1982). *From Hate to Love* (1982). *The Incredible Honeymoon* (1982). *Keep Young and Beautiful* (1982). *A King in Love* (1982). *Kneel for Mercy* (1982). *Lies for Love* (1982). *Light of the Gods* (1982). *Looking for Love* (1982). *Love and the Marquis* (1982). *Love at the Helm* (1982). *Love Leaves at Midnight* (1982). *Love on the Wind* (1982). *Love Rules* (1982). *Love to the Rescue* (1982). *Love Wears a Veil* (1982). *A Marriage Made in Heaven* (1982). *A Miracle in Music* (1982). *Mission to Monte Carlo* (1982). *Moments of Love* (1982). *Music from the Heart* (1982). *The Naked Battle* (1982). *The Odious Duke* (1982). *Open Wings* (1982). *The Poor Governess* (1982). *The Power and the Prince* (1982). *The Secret Fear* (1982). *Secret Harbour* (1982). *The Smuggled Heart* (1982). *Touch a Star* (1982). *The Unknown Heart* (1982). *The Vibrations of Love* (1982). *Winged Victory* (1982). *Diona and a Dalmatian* (1983). *The Dragon and the Pearl* (1983). *The Duke Comes Home* (1983). *A Duke in Danger* (1983). *Free from Fear* (1983). *From Hate to Love* (1983). *Gypsy Magic* (1983). *A Heart Is Broken* (1983). *Help from the Heart* (1983). *In the Arms of Love* (1983). *Journey to a Star* (1983). *A King in Love* (1983). *The Kiss of Life* (1983). *Lies for Love* (1983). *Lights, Laughter and a Lady* (1983). *Love and Lucia* (1983). *Love in the Dark* (1983). *Love in the Wind* (1983) *Love to the Rescue* (1983). *The Magic of Honey* (1983). *The Magic of Love* (1983). *A Miracle in Music* (1983). *Riding to the Moon* (1983). *Tempted to Love* (1983). *The Unbreakable Spell* (1983). *Wish for Love* (1983). *Bride to a Brigand* (1984). *The Call of the Highlands* (1984). *A Dream from the Night* (1984). *The Duke Comes Home* (1984). *Etiquette for Love and Romance* (1984). *Fire in the Blood* (1984). *Getting Older, Growing Younger* (1984). *Help from the Heart* (1984). *Hungry for Love* (1984). *The Island of Love* (1984). *Journey to a Star* (1984). *Light of the Gods* (1984). *Little White Doves of Love* (1984). *Looking for Love* (1984). *Lord Ravenscar's Revenge* (1984). *Love Comes West* (1984). *Miracle for a Madonna* (1984). *Moonlight on the Sphinx* (1984). *The Peril and the Prince* (1984). *Princess to the Rescue* (1984). *A Rebel Princess* (1984). *Revenge of the Heart* (1984). *The Romance of Food* (1984). *The Unbreakable Spell* (1984). *Royal Punishment* (1984). *The Scots Never Forget* (1984). *Secrets* (1984). *The Storms of Love* (1984). *The Taming of Lady Lorinda* (1984). *Theresa and a Tiger* (1984). *The Unbreakable Spell* (1984). *The Unwanted Wedding* (1984). *White Lilac* (1984). *A Witch's Spell* (1984). *Alone and Afraid* (1985). *Barbara Cartland's Book of Health* (1985). *The Castle Made for Love* (1985). *The Devilish Deception* (1985). *Escape* (1985). *The Etiquette of Romance* (1985). *A Fugitive from Love* (1985). *Hungry for Love* (1985). *Look with Love* (1985). *Love Is a Gamble* (1985). *Love Is Heaven* (1985). *Love on the Wind* (1985). *The Outrageous Lady* (1985). *Paradise Found* (1985). *Polly: My Wonderful Mother* (1985). *The Proud Princess* (1985). *Safe at Last* (1985). *Temptation of a Teacher* (1985). *A Very Unusual Wife* (1985). *A Victory for*

Love (1985). *An Angel Runs Away* (1986). *Touch the Stars* (1986). *Crowned with Larva* (1986). *The Devil Defeated* (1986). *A Dream in Spain* (1986). *A Gentleman in Love* (1986). *The Golden Cage* (1986). *Haunted* (1986). *Helga in Hiding* (1986). *The Hell-Cat and the King* (1986). *Listen to Love* (1986). *Love Casts Out Fear* (1986). *Love Climbs In* (1986). *Love Joins the Clan* (1986). *The Love Trap* (1986). *Never Forget Love* (1986). *The Peril and the Prince* (1986). *The Secret of the Mosque* (1986). *A Serpent of Satan* (1986). *Terror and the Sun* (1986). *Bewildered in Berlin* (1987). *The Curse of the Clan* (1987). *Dancing on a Rainbow* (1987). *The Devlish Deception* (1987). *The Earl Escapes* (1987) *Escape* (1987). *For All Eternity* (1987). *Forced to Marry* (1987). *A Heart Is Stolen* (1987). *Journey to a Star* (1987). *Lies for Love* (1987). *Love and Kisses* (1987). *Love Casts Out Fear* (1987). *Love on the Wind* (1987). *The Love Puzzle* (1987). *Lovers in Paradise* (1987). *Never Laugh at Love* (1987). *The Perfume of the Gods* (1987). *Punishment of a Vixen* (1987). *A Runaway Star* (1987). *The Secret of the Glen* (1987). *Starlight Over Tunis* (1987). *Wanted: A Wedding Ring* (1987). *A World of Love* (1987). *An Adventure of Love* (1988). *Barbara Cartland's Year of Royal Days* (1988). *Caretaker of Love* (1988). *A Chieftain Finds Love* (1988). *The Goddess of Love* (1988). *The Herb for Happiness.* (1988). *Little Tongues of Fire* (1988). *Love is Invincible* (1988). *Love is a Maze* (1989). *The Lovely Liar* (1988). *Lovers in Lisbon* (1988). *Only a Dream* (1988). *Riding in the Sky* (1988). *Sapphires in Siam* (1988). *Saved by Love* (1988). *Secrets of the Heart* (1988). *The Bargain Bride* (1989). *A Circus for Love* (1989). *A Knight in Paris (1989). The Perfect Pearl* (1989). *Royal Lovers: A Collection of True Stories* (1989). *Solita and the Spies* (1989). *The Temple of Love: A New Camfield Novel of Love* (1989). *Heaven in Hong Kong* (1990). *The Marquis Wives* (1990). *Game of Love* (1991). *Seek the Stars* (1991). *Born of Love* (1992). *Drena and the Duke* (1992). *Hidden by Love* (1992). *Winged Magic* (1992). *The Angel and the Rake* (1993). *The Art of Love* (1993). *The Dangerous Marriage* (1993). *A Duel of Hearts* (1993). *A Duel of Jewels* (1993). *Good or Bad* (1993). *Love, Lies and Marriage* (1993). *Love at the Ritz* (1993). *Luck Logan Finds Love* (1993). *Peaks of Ecstasy* (1993). *The Queen of Hearts* (1993). *Terror from the Throne* (1993). *To Scotland and Love* (1993). *Walking to Wonderland* (1993). *The Waltz of Hearts* (1993). *The Wicked Widow* (1993). *The Dare-Devil Duke* (1994). *The Duke Finds Love* (1994). *The Duke's Dilemma* (1994). *The Eyes of Love* (1994). *Look with the Heart* (1994). *The Love Trap* (1994). *Never Lose Love* (1994). *A Royal Rebuke* (1994). *Running Away to Love* (1994). *Safe in Paradise* (1994). *Saved by a Saint* (1994). *The Spirit of Love* (1994). *This Is Love* (1994). *Beyond the Stars* (1995). *An Icicle in India* (1995). *The Incomparable* (1995). *I Reach for the Stars* (1995). *Love in the Ruins* (1995). *A Magical Moment* (1995). *Passage to Love* (1995). *The Patient Bridegroom* (1995). *The Protection of Love* (1995). *Running from Russia* (1995). *Someone to Love* (1995). *We Danced All Night* (1995). *The Wild Cry of Love* (1995). *Fascination in France* (1996). *The Ghost that Fell in Love* (1996). *The Innocent Imposter* (1996). *Love Casts Out Fear* (1996). *The Loveless Marriage* (1996). *Lovers in Paradise* (1996). *Love on the Wind* (1996). *Tempted to Love* (1996). *Three Days to Love* (1996).

BIBLIOGRAPHY: Cloud, H. *Barbara Cartland, Crusader in Pink* (1979). Robyns, G. *Barbara Cartland* (1985).

For articles in reference works, see: *CA*. *CB*. *TCR&GW*.

Other references: *Fifty Plus* (April 1979). *McCall's* (March 1982). *New Yorker* (9 August 1976, 9 May, 1983). *Saturday Review* (March 1981). *Vogue* (August 1984). *Writer's Digest* (June 1979).

Zelda R. B. Provenzano

Julia Cartwright

BORN: 7 November 1851, Edgcote, Northamptonshire.
DIED: 24 April 1924, Oxford.
DAUGHTER OF: Richard Aubrey Cartwright and Mary Fremantle.
MARRIED: Henry Ady, 1880.

C. was a Victorian writer whose work was primarily concerned with the art and history of the Italian Renaissance, and as such she made a considerable contribution to furthering the understanding and appreciation of Italian art and history in themainstream tradition of English Italophilia. It is interesting to perceive her view of women, as a woman historian, in history.

She published twenty-three books of art and history, including five major biographies on women. Of these, her biographies of the Italian Renaissance sisters Beatrice and Isabella d'Este (1899 and 1903) as well as her biography of Castiglione (1908) remain highly respected by modern scholars. She was a prolific writer and contributed regularly to the art magazines and journals of her time, including the *Art Journal* and the *Magazine of Art.* She also wrote for the *Manchester Guardian.* In her early days as an aspiring author, she published anonymously at least thirteen novels for the Society for the Promoting of Christian Knowledge (S.P.C.K.). For these, she was extremely well paid, and she relinquished this work only when she had begun to establish her more formal reputation as a scholar.

C. came from a family of English landed gentry. One of nine children with five sisters and three brothers, she was educated at home by a succession of tutors. She nevertheless knew French, German, and Italian by the age of sixteen and borrowed the textbooks of her brothers at Eton and Oxford to teach herself Latin. Extremely well read, it was her love of literature and poetry that above all inspired her life's interest in art.

The period in which she wrote witnessed a change in the taste for Italian art, with the emphasis gradually shifting from the medieval period to the Renaissance. A growing number of authors provided new literature for an expanding and eager public. C. and others like her provided serious works of scholarship that were nevertheless of popular interest.

C. was essentially a Victorian in her typically didactic approach. Her aim was educational and her emphasis on culture and learning the underlying thread of all her work. It is this aspect she emphasizes in her biographies of women and also in the two-volume biography of the Renaissance author of *The Courtier,* Baldassare Castiglione. Her own ideals and aspirations and those of many women of her class and background in England prior to the enfranchisement of women were for equal educational possibilities.

In 1880, C. married Henry Ady, the local rector; in 1881, the year her daughter Cecilia was born, her first book, *Mantegna and Francia,* was published. She continued to work. In the 1880s, apart from writing the introduction to a translation of La Motte Fouque's *Undine* (1888), she concentrated on articles and romantic stories like "Christabel" (1880), "The Fortunes of Hassan" (1880), "Una Creighton" (1882), and "Miss Judy" (1883). In 1893, she wrote *The Pilgrim's Way,* an account of the ancient walk from Winchester to Canterbury. The Adys were by then living in Charing in Kent, near Canterbury.

Her first successful biography, *Sacharissa* (1893), was an account of Dorothy Sidney, who had been the subject of Edmund Waller's seventeenth-century poem of the same name. With this and with *Madame* (1894), the story of Henrietta, the daughter of King Charles I who became the Duchess of Orleans, she established her reputation.

In 1894, she became friends with the English artist Edward Burne-Jones and wrote a very successful monograph: *Sir Edward Burne-Jones, His Life and Work* (1894). This was followed by a similar study of another living artist entitled *G. F. Watts, Royal Academician, His Life and Work* (1896), as well as a large volume about the recently deceased French painter *Jean François Millet, His Life and Letters* (1896).

In spite of this interest in English and French artists, it was the art of the Renaissance that remained C.'s most fervent love. She published several books on Raphael, on Botticelli, and on the Florentine painters, and she established herself as an Italian specialist. During this, her most prolific, period she frequented the artistic and literary milieux of her time and corresponded with Bernard Berenson, Roger Fry, and many others. With the publication of *Beatrice d'Este* (1899) and *Isabella d'Este* (1903), her reputation was secured and her advice often sought on matters pertaining to Italian art and history.

These two biographies of learned and cultivated women of the Renaissance and their environment of a courtly society were of particular significance in the historiography of the Renaissance. With them she secured for two women their place alongside the better-known names of popes and princes and introduced into the contemporary consciousness of the Renaissance a new and powerful exponent of politics and diplomacy as well as a great patron of the arts, Isabella d'Este.

C. strove for education and admired learning in others. She was determined to earn enough money to send her own daughter to Oxford and this she did. She became a serious and respected scholar without losing her passionate enthusiasm for her subject. She traveled extensively in Italy, which remained always for her "My dear land."

WORKS: *Mantegna and Francia* (1881). *The Children of Seelisberg* (1885). *Our Valley* (1877). *Rosebuds* (1878). *Christabel* (1880). *The Fortunes of Hassan* (1880). *King's Marden* (1881). *Una Creighton* (1882). *Miss Judy* (1883). *Nimrod Nunn* (1885). *Swanford Bridge* (1886). *Cecily's Birds* (1887). *Troy Farm* (1890). *The Pilgrim's Way* (1893). *Sacharissa* (1893). *Jules Bartien-Lepage* (1894). *Madame* (1894). *Sir Edward Burne-Jones, His Life and Work* (1894). *The Early Works of Raphael* (1895). *Raphael in Rome* (1895). *Jean François Millet, His Life and Letters* (1896). *G. F. Watts, Royal Academician, His Life and Work* (1896). *Christ and His Mother in Italian Art* (1897). *Beatrice d'Este* (1899). *The Painters of Florence* (1901). *Sandro Botticelli* (1903). *Isabella d'Este* (1903). *Raphael* (1905). *Baldassare Castiglione* (1908). *Hampton Court* (1910). *Christina of Denmark* (1913). *San Bernadino in Art* (1913). *Italian Gardens of the Renaissance* (1914). *The Diaries of Julia Cartwright 1851–1914, Art Critic and Historian of the Italian Renaissance,* ed. A. Emanuel (1988). *A Bright Remembrance: the Diaries of Julia Cartwright,* ed. A. Emanuel (1989).

BIBLIOGRAPHY: Emanuel, A. *Apollo Magazine* (October 1984). Emanuel, A. *Bulletin of the Society for Renaissance Studies* (October 1983). Emanuel, A. *Proceedings of Layard Conference in Venice* (1983).

For articles in reference works, see: (under "Mrs. Henry Ady") *Who Was Who,* Vol. 2 (1929). *Who Was Who in Literature* (1979).

Angela Emanuel
(updated by Benjamin G. Kohl)

Eleanor Mary Carus-Wilson

BORN: 27 December 1897, Montreal.
DIED: 1 February 1977, London.
DAUGHTER OF: Charles Ashley Carus-Wilson and Mary L. G. Petrie.

The most eminent student of the medieval English woollen industry and trade of her generation, C. was educated by three of the most influential women medievalists of the early twentieth century: Caroline Skeel and Dame Bertha Philpotts of Westfield College, University of London, and Eileen Power of the London School of Economics.

The youngest of three children, C. was born in Montreal, where her father was professor of electrical engineering at McGill University; soon, however, she was taken to England to reside in her mother's family home at Hanover Lodge, London. In 1917, having completed her education at Norland Place School and St. Paul's Girls' School, she entered Westfield College, which her grandfather Colonel Martin Petrie had helped to found and where her mother had briefly taught. Coming under the spell of the history mistress Caroline Skeel, C. early developed a love of medieval history and taste for long sessions of research in the British Museum. Earning her B.A. with second class honors from Westfield in 1921, C. taught for a decade at the girls' boarding school of Hayes Court in Kent, returning to London on weekends to conduct manuscript research in the British Museum and the Public Record Office. The first product of this research was a thesis on the Bristol Merchant Venturers for which she was awarded the M.A. with Honours from Westfield College in 1926. While in London, C. faithfully attended Eileen Power's seminar on medieval economic history at the London School of Economics and began to publish papers on the Bristol trade and medieval English cloth industry based on meticulous archival research. From 1936 to 1938, she held a Leverhulme Research Fellowship, which enabled her to begin study of the great cloth industry of medieval England and complete her first book, a collection of documents on *The Overseas Trade of Bristol in the Later Middle Ages* (1937). With the outbreak of war in the autumn of 1939, C. was made a temporary civil servant in the Ministry of Food, where she broke down the isolation of the several Commodity Divisions and accumulated unified data on food supply and resources.

At war's end, C. was appointed to a lectureship in medieval economic history at the London School of Economics; two years later she was made Reader, and from 1953 until her retirement in 1965 she held a chair as Professor of Economic History. Her authoritative synthesis on the woollen industry in medieval Europe was published in 1952 in Volume 2 of the *Cambridge Economic History*. Her essays on English medieval trade and cloth industry, which flowed from her pen from 1928 onwards, were collected in a volume of her papers entitled *Medieval Merchant Venturers* (1954).

Her major published work, done in collaboration with Olive Coleman and published in 1963, was a comprehensive study of *England's Export Trade 1275–1547*, which provides a very full collection of continuous statistics for wool and textile exports.

The invitation to give the Ford Lectures at Oxford in 1965 provided C. with opportunity to undertake a survey of the English cloth industry from Roman times to the sixteenth century. Though approached by several publishers, C., ever the perfectionist, was never able to finish the much-awaited book. Active on the Council and several committees of the Economic History Society, C. furthered her field by editing three volumes of indispensable *Essays in Economic History* (1954–63). She also took great interest in newer fields, contributing to the first volume of the journal *Medieval Archaeology* and serving as the president of the Society of Medieval Archaeology. In retirement, she presided over the Economic History Society from 1966 to 1969 and served as vice-chairman of the Westfield College Council from 1967 to 1974.

As C.'s historical scholarship won international acclaim, her honors multiplied. Early elected a Fellow of the Royal Historical society, in 1961 C. was made an Associate Fellow of the Royal Flemish Academy; in 1963 she was elected Fellow of the British Academy; and in 1968, on her only visit to the United States, she received an honorary doctorate from Smith College. In her later years she was tireless in her service to the Church of England and was devoted to the progress of historical studies in the United Kingdom and the welfare of Westfield College. C. developed an early appreciation for music and a love of mountains, delighting in attending concerts in London and wherever she traveled; it was said that even at seventy-eight she could outwalk younger friends in the Alps. Most of all, in her later years, she kept up with a wide circle of pupils, colleagues, and friends. Much beloved for her unfailing kindness and readiness to help younger scholars, C. was to have received a festschrift on cloth and clothing in medieval Europe at the International Economic History Conference in 1978. But she died suddenly of a heart attack in London on 1 February 1977, and the volume appeared in 1983, dedicated to her memory.

WORKS: (ed.) *Westfield College, University of London, 1882–1932* (1932). (ed.) *The Overseas Trade of Bristol in the Later Middle Ages* (1937). "The Woollen Industry," in M. M. Postan and E. E. Rich, ed. *The Cambridge Economic History II* (1952). *Medieval Merchant Venturers.* (1954) (with Olive Coleman) *England's Export Trade 1275–1547* (1963).

BIBLIOGRAPHY: *Cloth and Clothing in Medieval Europe, Essays in Memory of Professor E. M. Carus-Wilson*, ed. N. B. Harte and K. G. Ponting (1983; includes appreciation and bibliography). *PBA* (1982).

For articles in reference works, see: *CA*. *DNB*.

Judith C. Kohl

Anne and Lucy Cary

Anne

BORN: 1615, London.
DIED: 1671, Paris.
DAUGHTER OF: Sir Henry, Viscount Falkland, and Elizabeth Tanfield Cary, Lady Falkland.
WROTE UNDER: Dame Clementia (or Clementina), O.S.B.

Lucy

BORN: 1619, London (?).
DIED: 1 November 1650, Cambrai, Flanders.
DAUGHTER OF: Sir Henry, Viscount Falkland, and Elizabeth Tanfield Cary, Lady Falkland.
WROTE UNDER: Dame Lucy Magdalena (or Magdalena), O.S.B.

Daughters of the well-known dramatist, Elizabeth Cary, A. C. (a poet) and L.C. (a possible biographer), together with their sisters Elizabeth (b. 1617) and Mary (c. 1621–93), were professed at the English recusant Benedictine Abbey of Our Lady of Consolation (an abbey for English Roman Catholics who refused to attend Church of England services and were therefore guilty of a statutory offense), in Cambrai, Flanders. Their earlier lives in England can be found in the seventeenth-century biography of their mother, *The Lady Falkland: Her Life,* which dramatically tells of her and later of their religious conversions and how their mother managed to send them and their two younger brothers to the Continent in the care of the English Benedictine monks, narrowly escaping imprisonment herself for defiance of the penal laws against sending English children to live or study in a Roman Catholic country. Although the four girls did not know Helen Gertrude (Dame Gertrude) More, for she had died at the abbey in 1633, they lived and worked together with her sister Bridget More and cousins Anne and Grace (Dame Agnes) More. In 1652, A. C., who in England had been a lady-in-waiting to Queen Henrietta Maria, was sent with Bridget More and other Cambrai Benedictines to found our Lady of Good Hope, an affiliated abbey in Paris. The abbey succeeded with the assistance of Henrietta Maria, then in exile at the Court in Paris; and A. C. and Bridget More later died at the Paris abbey. The three other sisters remained Benedictines at Cambrai.

Several seventeenth-century records of the recusant English Benedictines, both at Cambrai and at Paris, as well as their Paris catalogue of books and manuscripts, note that A. C. wrote poetry and songs for the encouragement of the sick members of her religious community. The "3-Part" manuscripts of "Songs from the Psalms" fitting the now-printed descriptions in these records were discovered while researching the work of Dame Agnes More in the Departmental Archives at Lille; the "Songs" were recently published, with additional poems forthcoming.

During the French Revolution in 1789, books, manuscripts, and whatever could be carried had been taken from the abbeys at Cambrai and Paris (as well as many from elsewhere), and English recusant Religious were forced to flee to England, where by that time persecutions had ended. In later decades, some of the manuscripts on the Continent that had not been destroyed in the Revolution and subsequent Reign of Terror were deposited in government-run libraries or archives. Among the manuscripts from Cambrai found at Lille were handwritten seventeenth-century documents relating to L. C. and her characteristics, which indicate that she may have been the author of the cited biography of her mother, for the original seventeenth-century manuscript *Life* of Lady Falkland seems to have been placed with L. C.'s convent records in the seventeenth century (and under an erroneous heading in Bruchet's 1928 inventory of book manuscripts in the Lille, France, archives). Whether it is L. C. or one of her sisters who wrote the Falkland biography, the only manuscript's existence, with other manuscripts of the former Cambrai Abbey (now at an abbey at Stanbrook, Worcester), seems to indicate that it was one of the cloistered daughters who wrote and corrected it at the Cambrai Abbey. Thus, R. Simpson's 1861 statement that one of Lady Falkland's younger sons, who lived far from Cambrai, corrected some of the manuscript's facts (and there are few corrections) that he recalled more accurately than his sisters would seem to be unfounded.

WORKS: "Songs from the Psalms," in *"Glow-Worm Light," Writings of 17th Century English Recusant Women from Original Manuscripts,* ed. D. L. Latz (1989); in *"Recusant Literature," Collected Papers from the Recusant Sessions of the International Medieval Congress, 1990–1994, held at Western Michigan University,* ed. D. L. Latz (1996).

BIBLIOGRAPHY: Benedictines of Stanbrook Abbey *In A Great Tradition* (1956). *Répertoire Numérique: Archives departementales du nord, séries H., fonds Bénédictins and Cisterciens,* ed. M. Bruchet (1928). Gillow, J. *Publications of the Catholic Record Society* (1913). Guilday, P. *The English Catholic Refugees on the Continent, 1558–1798* (1914). Hansom, J. *Publications of the Catholic Record Society* (1911). Low, A. *Augustine Baker* (1970). McCann, J. and H. Connolly. *Publications of the Catholic Record Society* (1933). *The Lady Falkland: Her Life,* ed. R. Simpson (1861). Weller, B. and M. Ferguson. *The Tragedy of Mariam* (1994; contains the MS. biography of Lady Falkland with notes).

Other references: Gillow, J. *Bibliographical Dictionary of the English Catholics* (1885–1902).

Dorothy L. Latz

Elizabeth Cary, Viscountess Falkland

BORN: 1585 or 1586, Burford, Oxfordshire.
DIED: October 1639, London.
DAUGHTER OF: Lawrence Tanfield and Elizabeth Symondes Tanfield.
MARRIED: Henry Cary, 1602.

Only child and heiress of a wealthy Oxford lawyer, later Lord Chief Baron of the Exchequer, C. was a startlingly precocious child, teaching herself French, Spanish, Italian, Latin, Hebrew, and Transylvanian. By the age of twelve, she had incurred a debt of £100 to the servants for candles (forbidden by her parents) so that she could read late at night. At the age of fifteen or sixteen she was married to Henry Cary, ten years her senior, who later became a member of the Privy Council, a viscount, and Lord Chief Deputy of Ireland. They began living together about 1607 after Henry returned from military service abroad. C. lived with her husband for twenty years, during which she bore eleven living children, all of whom she nursed herself except her eldest son, Lucius, who was reared by her father. When C. mortgaged her dowry to advance her husband's career, her father disinherited her in favor of her eldest son. In 1626, C. converted to Roman Catholicism, damaging her husband's career as a courtier in a Protestant court. He responded by abandoning her, taking custody of her children, and stripping her house of the necessities of life. Her poverty and suffering caused her to appeal to the court for help. In 1627, the Privy council ordered Lord Falkland to support his wife, but seven months later he had not complied with the order. In her last years she kidnapped two of her sons and smuggled them to the Continent to become Catholics. Three of her daughters became nuns; one of these wrote a detailed biography of her mother, emphasizing her sufferings for her faith.

Widely and deeply read in many languages, C. early

turned her hand to translation. Between the ages of thirteen and fifteen she translated *Le Miroir de Monde,* an epitome of geography, and dedicated it to her great uncle, Sir Henry Lee. Later in life she translated the works of Jacques Davy Dupperon. One of these, *The Reply to the King of Great Britain,* published in 1630, was ordered publicly burned. Near the end of her life she was translating the writings of Blosius, a Flemish Benedictine monk.

She began writing poetry shortly after her marriage while living with her mother-in-law. When Lady Cary, angry at her son's wife for reading constantly, took away her books, C. "set herself to make verses" (*Life*). According to her daughter, the best thing C. wrote at this time was a life of Tamberlaine in verse; this and a tragedy set in Sicily are lost. During these same years, she also wrote *Mariam, The Fair Queen of Jewry,* a Senecan tragedy based on Josephus's *Antiquities.* The first of many English plays about Herod and Mariamne, *Mariam* is carefully researched and constructed, attentive to historical details; the absence of anachronisms is unusual in the period. In style and dramaturgy, the play is competent but conventional, with action discussed rather than dramatized and details of the execution left to a messenger. The play is written in quatrains with occasional couplets and sonnets inserted. For reasons not entirely clear, *Mariam* was published in 1613, some ten years after it was written, and C. thus became the first Englishwoman to publish a full-length original play.

C. began writing again after her separation from her husband. She wrote verse lives of several women saints and verses about the Annunciation. The only surviving creative work from this period, however, is a life of King Edward II, written, according to the author, to pass the "weary hours and a deep and sad passion."

Always of an intense and intellectual temperament, C. was phenomenally absent minded and profoundly eccentric; these characteristics were exacerbated by her painful circumstances. She was nonetheless social and generous, as evidenced by numerous friendships and dedications to her of the *Works of John Marston, of England's Helicon,* and of Michael Drayton's *England's Heroicall Epistles.* She was the subject of verses by William Basse and John Davies of Hereford. C. died peacefully of a lung disease and was buried in the chapel of the Catholic queen Henrietta Maria.

WORKS: *The Mirror of the World* (c. 1598–1602). (trans.) *Le Miroir da Monde,* by A. Ortellitis (c. 1602–1605, lost). *Mariam, The Fair Queen of Jewry* (c. 1602–1605; ed. B. Weller and M. W. Ferguson (1994). "Life of Tamberlaine" (c. 1602–1605, lost). *The History of Edward II* (1627). (trans.) *The Reply to the King of Great Britain,* by Cardinal J. Du Perron (1630). *Verse Lives of Mary Magdalen, St. Agnes, St. Elizabeth of Portugal* (c. 1630, lost). Trans. of Blosius (c. 1639, lost).

BIBLIOGRAPHY: *Privileging Gender in Early Modern England,* ed. J. R. Brink (1993). Cotton, N. *Women Playwrights in England c. 1363–1750* (1980). Dunstan, A. C. *Examination of Two English Dramas* (1908). Fullerton, G. *Life of Elizabeth, Lady Falkland* (1883). *Silent but for the Word,* ed. M. P. Hannay (1985). Haselkorn, A. M. and B. S. Travitsky. *The Renaissance English-Woman in Print* (1990). Howe, F. *Tradition and the Talents of Women* (1991). *Sexuality and Politics in Renaissance Drama,* ed. C. Levin and K. Robertson (1991). *Ambiguous Realities,* ed. C. Levin and J. Watson (1987). Lewalski, B. F. *Writing Women in Jacobean England* (1993). *Staging the Renaissance,* ed. D. S. Kastan and P. Stallybrass (1991). *The Witness of Times,* ed. K. Z. Keller (1993). Murdock, K. *The Sun at Noon* (1939). *The Lady Falkland: Her Life,* ed. R. Simpson (1861). Stauffer, D. A., in *Essays in Dramatic Literature: The Parrott Presentation Volume,* ed. H. Craig (1935). *Sexuality and Gender in Early Modern Europe,* ed. J. G. Turner (1993).

For articles in reference works, see: *Bloomsbury. CHBP. Feminist. Oxford.*

Other references: *BLR* (1988). *ECLife* (1988). *Gramma* (1993). *N&Q* (1986, 1994). *RenD* (1990). *TSLL* (1977). *TSWL* (1991).

Nancy Cotton
(updated by Claudia Thomas Kairoff)

Mary Cary

BORN: c. 1621.
DIED: after 1653.
WROTE UNDER: Mary Cary; Mary Rande.

Little is known about C.'s family background. Her description as a "gentlewoman" suggests that she was from a reasonably wealthy family. Although brought up as a Presbyterian, by the late 1640s she had joined the millennarian Fifth Monarchist sect. At the age of fifteen, C. began studying the scriptures, and her later writings are scholarly and soundly argued. Although her output was not huge, her prophecies follow a structure that attempts to critique and reform. Her prophecies call for social, educational, and religious reform and show concern for the betterment of women's lives.

In her earliest published pamphlet, *A Word in Season to the Kingdom of England* (1647), she warns her readers not to ignore the weak and oppressed and advises England's rulers on how to achieve "a happie and flourishing state" in which the poor will not be oppressed and prophets will not be silenced.

In her later work, *The Little Horn's Doom and Downfall* (1651), she appeals to a female audience by dedicating it to the wives of leading parliamentarians, Elizabeth Cromwell, Bridget Ireton, and Margaret Role—"the many pious, precious, prudent and sage matrons, and holy women, with which this commonwealth is adorned, as with so many precious jewels." In *A New and More Exact Mappe,* which was printed with *The Little Horn's,* C. continues with her appeal to and for women. She demands that women be permitted to prophesy and share their husbands' property rights. She also addresses the repeal of tithes, the sacking of lazy and corrupt church officials, democratization of universities, tolerance for papists and atheists, and concern for the idle poor.

In 1653, C. published *Twelve New Proposals* under the name of Mary Rande. Nothing is known of C. after this, but her articulate and closely argued calls for reform make her an important figure in the religiopolitical writings of the Civil War period and an original voice in the debate on the position of women.

WORKS: *A Word in Season to the Kingdom of England. Or, A Precious Cordiall for a distempered kingdom* (1647). *The Resurrection of the Witness; and England's Fall from The Mystical Babylon—Rome* (1648). *The Little Horn's Doom and Downfall: Or a Scripture Prophesie of King James, and King Charles* (1651). *A New and More Exact Mappe or Description of New Jerusalems Glory, When Jesus Christ and His Saints with Him Shall Reign on Earth a Thousand Years, and Possess all Kingdoms* (1651). (as Mary Rande) *Twelve New Proposals to the Supreme Governours of the Three Nations now assembled at Westminster* (1653).

BIBLIOGRAPHY: Berg, C. and P. Berry, in *1642: Literature and Power in the Seventeenth Century,* ed. F. Barker, et al. (1980). Capp, B. *The Fifth Monarchy Men: A Study in Seventeenth-Century English Millenarianism* (1972). Crawford, P. *Women and Religion in England 1500–1720* (1993). Hill, C. *The World Turned Upside Down: Radical Ideas during the English Revolution* (1972). Hinds, H., in *Gloriana's Face: Women, Public and Private, in the English Renaissance,* ed. S. P. Cerasano and M. Wynne-Davies (1992). Hobby, E. *Virtue of Necessity: English Women's Writing 1649–88* (1988). Lilley, K., in *Women, Texts & Histories 1575–1760,* ed. C. Brant and D. Purkiss (1992). Mack, P. *Visionary Women: Ecstatic Prophecy in Seventeenth-Century England* (1992).

For articles in reference works, see: *Bell. Feminist. WL17C.*

Other references: *FSt* (1982).

Jane Baston

Margaret Cavendish, Duchess of Newcastle

BORN: 1623, St. John's Abbey, Colchester, Essex.
DIED: 15 December 1673, Welbeck Abbey, Nottinghamshire.
DAUGHTER OF: Thomas Lucas and Elizabeth Leighton.
MARRIED: William Cavendish, 1645.

C. was among the most conspicuous and prolific female writers of the seventeenth century and the first to experiment with a broad variety of genres. During her lifetime, she wrote and published a dozen books of poetry, fiction, plays, orations, letters, philosophical treatises, biography, and autobiography, earning a reputation for genius and eccentricity that has endured for more than three hundred years.

The youngest child of Thomas Lucas, a wealthy landowner who died soon after her birth, and Elizabeth Leighton, who raised C. to be "virtuous . . . modest . . . civil . . . [and] honorable," C. passed an idyllic childhood in rural Essex, learning little more than the traditional accomplishments and otherwise devoting her time to the cultivation of her imagination. Upon the outbreak of the Civil War, she fled with her family to Oxford where in 1643 she became a maid of honor to Queen Henrietta Maria. Despite her painful shyness, she braved the loss of her protective family and the ridicule of the court to follow the queen into exile in Paris. There she met William Cavendish, Marquis of Newcastle, her brother Charles's commander and a Royalist hero of the siege of York. They were married in 1645 and, until the Restoration, lived in Paris, Rotterdam, and Antwerp.

Although William was a widower and thirty years older than she, C. never tired of rehearsing her husband's virtues: Sometime military hero, sometime poet and playwright, an amateur in philosophy and the natural sciences, William was the definitive romantic cavalier, his most serious work a study of the gentlemanly art of horsemanship. In the face of enormous debt, William maintained luxurious households on the Continent where he entertained the famous philosophers of the time, interpreting for his young wife the matter of their discussions. The father of five children from his first marriage, he apparently submitted to C.'s contempt for "breeding women" and encouraged only the growth of her intellect and imagination; in pride and gratitude for such an "Extraordinary Husband," C. wrote, "I cannot for my Life be so good a Huswife as to quit Writing . . . you are pleased to Peruse my Works and Approve of them so well, as to give me Leave to Publish them, which is a Favour few Husbands would grant their Wives. . . ."

Six years after their marriage, C. returned to England in an unsuccessful attempt to obtain money due on William's sequestered estates. During her eighteen-month stay, she composed her first book, *Poems and Fancies,* which was published in London in 1653. C.'s theory that, for her, poetry must be grounded in the rational "distinguishment" she had learned from the philosophers and the imaginative "similizing" retained from her childhood play was already apparent, but so too was her habitual dislike of revision: "There was more pleasure in making than mending," she later wrote, and more than once made the preponderance of thoughts in her head her excuse: "I did many times not peruse the copies that were transcribed, lest they should disturb my following conceptions." *Poems and Fancies* was followed within two months by *Philosophical Fancies,* like the first book an enchanting blend of fantasy and the popularization of current scientific inquiry, but, because of its uncontrolled leaps from the rational steps of evidence, division, and order into the realm of the imagination, an object of frequent derision. Aware of her shortcomings, C. had tried to apologize to her critics: "The Reason I write in Verse is Because I thought that Errors might better pass there, than in Prose, since poets write most Fiction and Fiction is not given for Truth but for pastime"; failing to convince them of the value of her work, but still encouraged by her husband and confident of her own "native wit," she turned to prose. During her remaining years in exile she published three books, which united her desire for personal fame with a growing feminist awareness.

The World's Olio (1655), a collection of essays compiled upon her return to Antwerp, concludes with a defense against charges of plagiarism, ironic because of the censure C. suffered but a theme already common in women's writing. In the dedication of her next book, *The Philosophical and Physical Opinions* (1655), to the universities of Oxford and Cambridge, C. straightforwardly attacked the customs that shut women out of education and power, using a familiar female image to "similize" her argument: . . . we are kept like Birds in Cages, to Hop up and down in our Houses, not Suffer'd to fly abroad, to see the several Changes of Fortune and the Various Humors, Ordained and Created by Nature, and wanting the Experience of Nature, we must needs want the Understanding and Knowledge." *Natures Pictures drawn by Fancies Pencil to the Life* (1655), a collection of tales of romantic heroines facing fantastic adversity, presented C.'s ideal woman in fiction, formless by modern standards and obviously the product of her vision of herself. The short autobiography attached to *Natures Pictures,* "A True Relation of my Birth, Breeding, and Life," is, however, charming in its "plain natural style," and like the *Life* of her husband she published twelve years later is as direct a portrait of personal experience as ever came out of that dramatic period of English history.

When, after the Restoration, King Charles II made William Duke of Newcastle and restored some of his property, C. and her husband retired to Welbeck Abbey. There, isolated from the distractions and criticisms of society, C. continued writing, producing within the next eight years a remarkable quantity and variety of works. The fourteen closet dramas included in her *Playes* were obviously modelled upon William's amateur attempts, but within their chaotic dramatic structures they present extraordinary women, skilled in the art of systematic public debate. "Female Orations," a section of *Orations of Divers Sorts,* C.'s next book, laid bare the customs and prejudices that had brought women to their current state of powerlessness. Even in its forthright feminist polemic, however, it could not escape the hallmarks of her "similizing" imagination: "The truth is, we live like bats or owls, labour like beasts, and die like worms." *CCXI Sociable Letters* and *Philosophical Letters* marked C.'s return to her most successful style: witty, enthusiastic, personal, and supremely confident that whatever she had to say was, for the moment, reasonable and right. *Observations upon Experimental Philosophy* was a return to her interest in science, but almost predictably rescinded her earlier opinions about experimentation; the science fiction story attached to it, *The Description of a new Blazing World,* combined C.'s passion for scientific speculation with her romanticized vision of the new woman. *The Life of the Thrice Noble, High and Puissant Prince William Cavendish* and a new book of *Playes* were the last of her original productions, yet her interest in writing seems never to have flagged. In the last years of her life she probably regretted the haste of her earlier composition; always proud of her work, she must have overseen its new editions and made the revisions she thought necessary to insure her fame.

In 1667, C. was an invited guest at the Royal Academy, honored for her scientific achievements that were not, after all, very much more implausible than those circulating during the period. Still, with her eccentric dress and her embarrassing habit of publishing her own writing, she was a curiosity for the Londoners who flocked to stare at her carriage. She returned to Welbeck Abbey after her triumphant visit, died in 1673, and was buried in Westminster Abbey. In 1676, William collected and published *Letters and Poems in Honour of the Incomparable Princess, Margaret Duchess of Newcastle,* a volume containing praise from Thomas Hobbes but also the sound criticism of Walter Charleton: "Your fancy is too generous to be strained, your invention too nimble to be fettered. . . . Hence it is that you do not always confine your sense to your verse, nor your verses to rhythm, nor your rhythm to the quantity and sounds of syllables." C. was hampered in her writing by her lack of disciplined intellectual training and in her philosophy by her necessary dependence upon the observations of others. Yet in her work, there is an inescapable exuberance that makes Virginia Woolf's judgment, "She has the irresponsibility of a child and the arrogance of a Duchess," seem more tribute than blame.

WORKS: *Poems and Fancies: Written by the Right Honourable, the Lady Margaret Countesse of Newcastle* (1653, 1664, 1668). *Philosophicall Fancies. Written by the Right Honourable, the Lady Newcastle* (1653). *The World's Olio. Written by the Most Excellent Lady the Lady M. of Newcastle* (1655, 1671). *The Philosophical and Physical Opinions, Written by her Excellency, The Lady Marchionesse of Newcastle* (1655, 1663, 1668). *Natures Pictures drawn by Fancies Pencil to the Life. Written by the thrice Noble, Illustrious, and Excellent Princess, the Lady Marchionesse of Newcastle. . . .* (1655, 1671). *Playes written by the thrice Noble, Illustrious and Excellent Princess, the Lady Marchionesse of Newcastle* (1662). *Orations of Divers Sorts, Accommodated to Divers Places. Written by the thrice Noble . . .* (1662, 1668). *CCXI Sociable Letters, Written by the thrice Noble . . .* (1664). *Philosophical Letters: or, Modest Reflections upon some Opinions in Natural Philosophy, maintained by several famous and learned Authors of this Age, expressed by way of Letters: By the thrice Noble. . . .* (1664). *Observations upon Experimental Philosophy. To which is added, the Description of a new Blazing World. Written by the thrice Noble . . .* (1666, 1668). *The Life of the thrice Noble, High and Puissant Prince William Cavendishe, Duke, Marquess, and Earl of Newcastle . . .* (1667, 1675). *Playes, never before Printed. Written by the thrice Noble . . .* (1668). *The Memoirs of Margaret, Duchess of Newcastle, written by Herself,* ed. E. Bridges (1814). *Sociable Letters*, ed. J. Fitzmaurice (1996).

BIBLIOGRAPHY: Bickley, F. *The Cavendish Family* (1914). Brown, S. *Critical Matrix* (1991). *Letters and Poems in Honour of the Incomparable Princess, Margaret Duchess of* Newcastle, ed. W. Cavendish (1676). Cotton, N. *Women Playwrights in England c. 1363–1750* (1980). Derry, S. *Persuasions* (1989). Ezell, M. *The Patriarch's Wife: Women Playwrights in England c.*

1363–1750 (1980). Ezell, M. *HLQ* (1988). Ferguson, M. *First Feminists: British Women Writers 1578–1799* (1989). *The Life of William Cavendish, Duke of Newcastle,* ed. C. Firth (1906). Fitzmaurice, J. *HLQ* (1990). Fitzmaurice, J. *PBSA.* Fitzmaurice, J., in *New Ways of Looking at Old Texts,* ed. W. Hill (1993). Fraser, A. *The Weaker Vessel* (1984). Gagen, J. E. *The New Woman. Her Emergence in English Drama, 1600–1730* (1954). Gagen, J. E. *Studies in Philosophy* (1959). Goreau, A. *The Whole Duty of a Woman: Female Writers in Seventeenth Century England* (1985). Goulding, R. W. *Margaret (Lucas) Duchess of Newcastle* (1925). Grant, D. *Margaret the First: A Biography of Margaret Cavendish, Duchess of Newcastle, 1623–1673. The Phanseys of William Cavendish, Marquis of Newcastle, Addressed to Margaret Lucas, and Her Letters in Reply,* ed. D. Grant (1956). *Kissing the Rod: An Anthology of Seventeenth-Century Women's Verse,* ed. G. Greer et al (1988). Hobby, E. *Virtue of Necessity: English Women's Writing 1649–88* (1989). Jones, K. *A Glorious Fame: the Life of Margaret Cavendish, Duchess of Newcastle* (1988). Kramer, A. *Women's History Review* (1993). *The Blazing World and Other Writings,* ed. K. Lilley (1994). *The Female Spectator: English Women Writers Before 1800,* ed. M. R. Mahl and H. Hoon (1977). Mendelson, S. *The Mental World of Stuart Women: Three Studies* (1987). Meyer, G. D. *The Scientific Lady in England 1650–1760* (1955). Mintz, S. I. *JEGP* (1952). Palomo, D. *WS* (1979). Payne, L. R., in *Curtain Calls: British and American Women and the Theatre 1660–1820,* ed. M. A. Schofield and C. Macheski (1991). Pearson, J. *TSWL* (1985). Pearson, J. *The Prostituted Muse: Images of Women & Women Dramatists 1642–1737* (1988). Perry, H. T. E. *The First Duchess of Newcastle and Her Husband as Figures in Literary History* (1918). Prasad, K., in *Essays Presented to Amy G. Stock,* ed. R. K. Kaul (1951). Reynolds, M. *The Learned Lady in England from 1650 to 1760* (1920). Ross, M. B., in *Women in the Middle Ages and the Renaissance: Literary and Historical Perspectives,* ed. M. B. Rose (1986). Rowton, F. *The Female Poets of Great Britain* (1853; ed. M. Williamson, 1981). Smith, H. L. *Reason's Disciples: Seventeenth-Century English Feminists* (1982). *The Women Poets in English,* ed. A. Stanford (1972). Stenton, D. M. *The English Woman in History* (1957). Stimpson, D. *Scientists and Amateurs* (1948). Todd, J. *The Sign of Angelica: Women, Writing, and Fiction, 1660–1800* (1989). Trease, G. *Portrait of a Cavalier: William Cavendish, First Duke of Newcastle* (1979). Truowitz, R. *TSWL.* Turberville, A. S. *A History of Welbeck Abbey and Its Owners* (1938). Whibley, C. *Essays in Biography* (1913). Wiseman, S., in *Women, Writing, History 1640–1740,* ed. I. Grundy and S. Wiseman (1992). Woolf, V. *The Common Reader* (1925).

For articles in reference works, see: *Ballard. Bell. Bloomsbury. Feminist. IDWB. ToddBWW. ToddDBA.*

Susan Hastings

C. C.: See *Cookson, Catherine Ann*

C. E.: See *Tonna, Charlotte Elizabeth*

Susanna Centlivre

BORN: 1667 (?).
DIED: 1 December 1723, London.
MARRIED: Joseph Centlivre, 1707.
WROTE UNDER: Susanna Carroll; Susanna Centlivre.

Accounts of C.'s life before 1700 are conjectural, but her frequent visits to Holbeach, Lincolnshire, support the tradition that she was born there. She first appeared in print in 1700 under the name Susanna Carroll; at this time, she was living in London and contributing fashionable correspondence to *Familiar and Courtly Letters* and similar collections. In 1707, she married Joseph Centlivre, a royal cook, and in 1713 the couple moved to Buckingham Court, where they lived the rest of their lives. C. was an ardent Whig, attracting a wide circle of friends among Whig writers; her politics and her anti-Catholicism were the main reasons for Alexander Pope including her in the 1728 *Dunciad.* C. is thought by some critics to be the model for Phoebe Clinket, the female playwright ridiculed by Pope, John Gay, and John Arbuthnot in *Three Hours After Marriage* (1717). Examination of theatrical satire of the woman dramatist shows, however, that Clinket, while embodying specific attacks on the Countess of Winchilsea, is a conventionalized comic figure in the tradition of the *femmes savantes.* C. was buried at St. Paul's, Covent Garden. An edition of her plays was advertised for 1732, but the first collected edition did not appear until 1760; her letters and incidental poems remain scattered in eighteenth-century periodicals and anthologies.

The best comic playwright in the early decades of the eighteenth century, C. wrote sixteen full-length plays and three short pieces. She typically wrote a farcical comedy of intrigue leading to the marriage of an honest hero (often a soldier) and a sensible heroine. Using a wide variety of sources in French, Spanish, and earlier English drama, her plays focused on fast-paced, witty situations rather than witty dialogue. She was an adroit stage technician who wrote for actors rather than for readers. Her four best comedies became stock repertory pieces.

The first of these, *The Gamester* (1705), a topical play about a major eighteenth-century vice, initiated a series of plays about gambling. The hero, Valere, faces ruin because of his addiction to gaming, but the rich and resourceful Angelica reclaims him by disguising herself as a man and winning his money, watch, ring, and finally her own portrait set with diamonds, a love token that he had solemnly sworn never to part with. When Valere is penitent, Angelica forgives and marries him. Ostensibly writing sentimental reform comedy, C. actually exploited audience interest in gaming. Valere's obsession is more convincingly portrayed than his reformation, and the liveliest scene in the play depicts the sharpers and dupes hot over the gaming table, absorbed in their own colorful jargon.

C.'s next success was *The Busy Body* (1709), a beautifully proportioned intrigue comedy in which two young couples outwit two comic old men. The special ingredient of the comedy is the character of Marplot, the busybody. In his impertinent but good-natured eagerness to discover his friends' secrets, Marplot repeatedly brings the young lovers near to disaster. The plot sets up a clever tension: The audience sympathizes with the lovers and at the same time with the idiotic Marplot. As the lovers must outwit not only their enemies but also their friend, the audience is in a continual state of anxious hilarity.

The Wonder (1714) is a masterpiece of comic theater. The action turns on Violante's promise to protect the secret of Isabella's runaway and romance. Although every event conspires to make Violante appear false, she keeps her friend's secret to the point of passionate quarrels with her beloved Don Felix. Delightful minor comic characters revolve around the central pair of lovers. Plot and dialogue are tightly packed so that a surprising turn occurs every few minutes. The role of Don Felix was one of David Garrick's triumphs, and he chose it for his farewell performance in 1776. C.'s last success, *A Bold Stroke for a Wife* (1718), is similarly fast paced and ingenious. The plot turns on a single premise. Colonel Fainwell, in order to marry Anne Lovely, must gain the consent of four amusingly different guardians—a beau, a virtuoso, a businessman, and a Quaker. He wins the lady by assuming five successive disguises, the last being an impersonation of the real Simon Pure (i.e., a character impersonating another in the play), adding that expression to the language. There is some social satire of the four types represented by the guardians, who are monomaniacal humor characters, but the tone is genial and lighthearted throughout, as it is always in the best of C.'s comedies.

Of these four comedies, the most popular in the eighteenth century was *The Busy Body*. *The Wonder* and *A Bold Stroke for a Wife* continued to grow in popularity; although *The Gamester* was replaced in the repertory by other plays about gambling, C.'s three later successes were performed regularly throughout the nineteenth century not only in England but also in the United States and Australia.

WORKS: *The Perjured Husband* (1700). *The Beau's Duel* (1702). *The Stolen Heiress* (1702). *Love's Contrivance* (1703). *The Gamester* (1705). *The Barrel Table* (1705). *Love at a Venture* (1706). *The Platonic Lady* (1706). *The Busy Body* (1709; rpt. 1949, intro. by J. Byrd). *The Man's Bewitched* (1709). *A Bickerstaff's Burying* (1710). *Marplot* (1710). *The Perplexed Lovers* (1712). *The Masquerade* (1713). *The Wonder* (1714). *A Poem Humbly Presented to His Most Sacred Majesty* (1714). *An Epistle to Mrs. Wallop* (1714). *The Gotham Election* (1715). *A Wife Well Managed* (1715). *The Cruel Gift* (1716). *An Epistle to the King of Sweden from a Lady of Great Britain* (1717). *A Bold Stroke for a Wife* (1718; ed. T. Stathas, 1968). *A Woman's Care* (1720). *The Artifice* (1722). *Works* (1760). *The Plays of Susanna Centlivre*, 3 vols., ed. R. Frushell (1982).

BIBLIOGRAPHY: Bateson, F. W. *English Comic Drama 1700–1750* (1929). Boas, F. S. *An Introduction to Eighteenth-Century Drama 1700–1780* (1953). Bowyer, J. W. *The Celebrated Mrs. Centlivre* (1952). Cotton, N. *Women Playwrights in England c.1363–1750* (1980). Lock, E. P. *Susanna Centlivre* (1979). *Curtain Calls: British and American Women and the Theatre 1660–1820*, ed. M. A. Schofield and C. Macheski (1991).

For articles in reference works, see: *Cambridge. Feminist. Oxford. ToddBWW. ToddDBA.*

Other references: *Book Collector* (1957, 1958, 1961). *MLN* (February 1928, February 1933). *MP* (1926). *N&Q* (September 1953). *PLL* (1986). *PQ* (1937). *RES* (1942).

Nancy Cotton
(updated by Claudia Thomas Kairoff)

Challans, Eileen Mary: See *Renault, Mary*

Mary Chandler

BORN: 1687, Malmsbury, Wiltshire.
DIED: 11 September 1745, Bath, Gloucestershire.
DAUGHTER OF: Henry Chandler and Miss Bridgman of Marlborough.

Daughter of a Dissenting minister, the poet C. received neither the traditional education of a marriageable young lady nor the formal education given her several brothers. Because of family reversal and a childhood accident that left her spine deformed, C. was raised to be a self-sufficient businesswoman. At around age eighteen, she opened a millinery shop in Bath Abbey Churchyard, which she tended for thirty-five years. Her social orbit included the Countess of Hertford, Lady Rachel Russell, Elizabeth Rowe, and Dr. William Oliver.

In her spare time, she read both modern and classical poetry to supplement her minimal education, and she wrote verse. She published "On Friendship" in James Ralph's *Poetry by Several Hands* (1729) and in February 1733 published her major work, the 322-line *A Description of Bath*. The Princess Amelia permitted C. to dedicate the revised second edition (1734) of the poem to her, a mark of social success. C.'s account, in polished heroic couplets, of Bath's natural history, architecture, commerce, and frivolous society saw eight editions in thirty-three years.

C.'s neoclassical verse, with its elegant and witty style, shows the influence of Alexander Pope and the Roman poet Horace. Pope visited her in Bath and "approved" of her satiric-encomiastic poem. She borrows Pope's form of the verse epistle and uses the end of his poem to Lord Burlington (1731) as a model when she apostrophizes Prior Park, the country house soon to be built by Ralph Allen, Bath's greatest citizen and Henry Fielding's model for Squire Allworthy.

The third edition of *A Description of Bath* (1736) includes seventeen additional poems, which C. published "to put an end to the troublesome employment of writing out copies." Most of them tackle conventional eighteenth-century topics: the joys of moderation, nature, solitude, and friendship. In general, C's verse addresses personal, not public, concerns: Mrs. Moor's fire screen, Mrs. Boteler's garden, the "romantic views" to be found at Mrs. Jacobs's Gloucestershire estate. She wrote primarily for friends, not for a general audience; several poems are on subjects inspired by conversations or visits with particular friends at their country houses. "A True Tale," added to the sixth edition (1744), recounts a visit by a wealthy gentleman who traveled eighty miles to propose marriage because he admired the sense in her poem, "The Wish." He received a refusal from a woman who found she could not bear "loss of liberty."

She died the following year, her health undermined by a severe vegetarian diet. According to the biography by her brother Samuel in *Lives of the Poets* (1753), C. left behind fragments of "a large poem on the being and attributes of God, which was her favourite subject." C. was one of the first to exploit Bath as a literary subject and to fuse Roman literary forms (country-house and town poems) with English forms (mediative local and satiric spa verse). However, satiric romps like Christopher Anstey's *The New Bath Guide* (1766) led to the social demise of C.'s poem, anapestic excess displacing tasteful moderation and restrained heroic couplets.

WORKS: *A Description of Bath: A Poem* (1733; rev. ed. 1734; with several poems added 1736, 1738, 1741; with "A True Tale" added 1744, 1755, 1767).

BIBLIOGRAPHY: Aubin, R. *Topographical Poetry in XVIIIth-Century England* (1936). Boyce, B. *The Benevolent Man* (1967). Case, A. *RES* (1926). Chandler, S., in *Lives of the Poets,* ed. T. Cibber and R. Shiels (1753). Doughty, O. *RES* (1925, 1926). Martin, P. *Pursuing Innocent Pleasures: The Gardening World of Alexander Pope* (1984). Thomas, C. *Alexander Pope and His Eighteenth-Century Women Readers* (1994). Troost, L., in *Pope, Swift, and Women Writers: Contemporary Essays in Criticism,* ed. D. Mell (1996).

For articles in reference works, see: *DNB. Feminist. ToddBWW. ToddDBA.*

Other references: Scott, M. *The Female Advocate* (1774).

Linda V. Troost

Vera Chapman

BORN: 7 May 1898, Bournemouth, Hampshire.
DIED: 14 May 1996, Croydon, Surrey.
DAUGHTER OF: John Frederick Fogerty and Kate Isabella Veronica Morse Fogerty.
MARRIED: Charles Sydney Chapman, 1924.

C. was educated at Lady Margaret Hall, Oxford, where she received a B.A. with second class honors in 1921. A member of the Church of England and resident of London, she served as student welfare officer in Her Majesty's Colonial Office for almost two decades after her two children, a son and a daughter, reached adulthood. In 1963, she left her position to become a full-time writer.

For a person who began her writing career at age sixty-five, C. was unusually prolific and successful. Her most notable publication was her "Damosel" trilogy based on Arthurian legend, consisting of *The Green Knight* (1975), *The King's Damosel* (1976), and *King Arthur's Daughter* (1978). The trilogy has been translated into Dutch, and *The Green Knight* was made into a noncommercial film by the West Surrey College of Art and Design. As fiction the trilogy was distinguished by its original handling of the legendary matter and by its focus on the point of view of its female protagonists.

The Green Knight was more than a retelling of the medieval tale. C. added to it an episode at Stonehenge, the figure of Merlin, and the story of the Loathly Lady. Part of the narrative was told by Bertilak's wife, Vivian. The events in *The King's Damosel* were related by Lynette, an appealing character who was developed from her tomboy childhood through her traumatic adolescence, when she was raped, to her later years, when she became a mystic seeker of the Grail. The final volume, *King Arthur's Daughter,* was narrated by the title character, Ursulet. In this concluding work, C. established her feminist perspective by stressing inheritance through the maternal line. The spirit of Britain was carried from mother to daughter, "by the line but not the name, by blood but not bloodshed, by the distaff, not the sword."

The "Damosel" trilogy was followed by an imaginative extrapolation from one of Chaucer's best-known characters in her novel *The Wife of Bath* (1978). C. also published the juvenile novel *Judy and Julia* (1977) and *Blaedud the Birdman* (1978). Her last work was *Miranty and the Alchemist* (1983), set in Elizabethan times and concerning the adventures of a young girl who, while left in the care of her alchemist uncle, was transported to fantastic realms inhabited by supernatural beings. In addition to her novels, C. contributed short stories to the magazine *Fantastic Imagination.*

Founder of the Tolkien Society, in which she assumed the name of Belladonna Took, C. was primarily a writer of fantasy and medieval adventure. Her fiction not only fulfilled her expressed intention to provide reading pleasure but also achieved added depth through inclusion of myth, philosophy, legend, and mysticism.

WORKS: *The Green Knight* (1975). *The King's Damosel* (1976). *King Arthur's Daughter* (1976). *Judy and Julia* (1977). *The Wife of Bath* (1978). *Blaedud the Birdman* (1978). *Miranty and the Alchemist* (1983).

BIBLIOGRAPHY:

For articles in reference works, see: *CA. SATA.*

Charlotte Spivack

Hester (Mulso) Chapone

BORN: 27 October 1727, Twywell, Northamptonshire.
DIED: 25 December 1801, Hadley, Middlesex.
DAUGHTER OF: Thomas Mulso and a Miss Thomas.
MARRIED: John Chapone, 1760.
WROTE UNDER: Hester Chapone; Hester Mulso.

C. was the only surviving daughter in a family of several children. Her first literary effort, a romance written when she was nine, met with maternal disapproval, possibly caused by jealousy at the child's talent. Only after her mother's death, when C. took over the management of her father's household, could she undertake a program of self-improvement, studying French, Italian, Latin, music, and drawing.

One of the Bluestockings, C. associated particularly with Elizabeth Montagu and Elizabeth Carter as well as with Samuel Johnson, Samuel Richardson, the naturalist Gilbert White, and Frances Burney d'Arblay. Richardson used her as a model for some of the "genteel characters" in *Sir Charles Grandison* (most likely Harriet Byron), and in 1783 the Earl of Carlisle's friends appealed to her when they needed someone to cajole Johnson into critiquing the earl's tragedy. Through Richardson, she met John Chapone, an attorney, whom she married after a long engagement; he died within ten months, leaving her in straitened circumstances.

Her first published work appeared in Johnson's *The Rambler* #10 (1750) and in Hawkesworth's *The Adventurer* #77–79 (1753). During these years, she also engaged in an epistolary debate with Samuel Richardson about *Clarissa* and filial obedience. In these letters C. argues that a daughter should not marry without the consent of the parents but could refuse anyone the parents might propose. Richardson's view was that children must obey parents in all things and accept their choices of spouses. According to Johnson, the friendship of C. and Richardson cooled because he objected to her allowing her verses to be read too publicly.

She wrote or translated poems on conventional subjects: friendship, the beauties of nature, the delights of solitude. For example, her poem to Susanna Highmore, "To Stella," plays with classical conventions while it discusses the superiority of platonic feminine friendship over romantic love. (In his 1755 dictionary, Johnson quoted from the then-unpublished poem to provide an example of a quatrain.) C. also composed a Pindaric ode on Epictetus for the preface to Carter's 1758 translation of that philosopher's work.

Letters on the Improvement of the Mind (1773), however, brought C. fame, if not fortune (she sold the copyright for £50). She wrote the educational letters for the benefit of her fifteen-year-old niece, but Montagu advised C. to publish them. One of the earliest in a long line of such treatises, *Letters* presents a detailed plan for educating girls and includes a list of recommended books. C. gives advice on reading the Bible, controlling one's temper, managing finances, and acquiring accomplishments. She recommends extensive reading in history, natural and moral philosophy, poetry, geography, and chronology. She also advises her niece to select a husband (one of whom her parents approved, of course) by listening to both heart and mind, but not to be "afraid of a single life."

In 1775, C. published *Miscellanies in Prose and Verse*, this time receiving £250. It contained her early verses, moral essays, and "The Story of Fidelia," first published in *The Adventurer.* Two years later, she brought out her last work, *A Letter to a New-Married Lady* (1777). After C. died in 1801, her relatives assembled a four-volume edition of her works that also reprinted her famous exchange with Richardson and her letters to Carter.

C.'s reputation rests on the *Letters on the Improvement of the Mind,* which went through dozens of editions in Great Britain, the United States, and France before its final one in 1851. It was one of the most influential works by the earlier generation of Bluestockings. The queen revealed to C. in 1778 (both were visiting C.'s uncle, the Bishop of Winchester) that even the Princess Royal's education had been guided by the *Letters.* As the clear, thoughtful style of C.'s writing illustrates, women can think rationally if motivated and instructed; nor do they have to abjure piety and emotion to do so.

WORKS: *Letters on the Improvement of the Mind, Addressed to a Young Lady* (1773). *Miscellanies in Prose and Verse* (1775). *A Letter to a New-Married Lady* (1777). *The Works of Mrs. Chapone: Now First Collected* (1807, with letters to Carter and Richardson, fugitive pieces, memoir by her family). *The Tenbury Letters,* ed. E. Fellowes and E. Pine (1943). *A Later Pepys,* ed. A. Gaussen (1904). *Bluestocking Letters,* ed. R. Johnson (1926).

BIBLIOGRAPHY: Cole, J., of Scarborough. *Memoirs of Mrs. Chapone* (1839). Elwood, A. *Memoirs of the Literary Ladies of England* (1843). Hemlow, J. *PMLA* (1950). Keymar, T. *Richardson's Clarissa and the Eighteenth-Century Reader* (1992). Marks, S. *Sir Charles Grandison* (1986). McKillop, A. *Samuel Richardson: Printer and Novelist* (1936). Myers, S. *The Bluestocking Circle* (1990). Wheeler, E. *Famous Bluestockings* (1910). Wilson, M. *These Were Muses* (1924).

For articles in reference works, see: *Bloomsbury. Cambridge. DNB. Feminist. Oxford. ToddBWW. ToddDBA.*

Other references: Duncome, J. *The Feminiad* (1754).

Linda V. Troost

Charlotte Cibber Charke

BORN: 1713.
DIED: 1760.
DAUGHTER OF: Colley Cibber and Katherine Cibber.
MARRIED: Richard Charke, c. 1729; possibly later married John Sacheverille.

C. failed at a number of careers (including pastrycook and manager, in 1745, of The Theatre-Royal in The Haymarket) but is remembered for an autobiography that tells all. Her father was Colley Cibber, actor, dramatist, manager of The Theatre-Royal in Drury Lane, and Poet Laureate. Cibber had ten children, but not even his obstreperous son Theophilus had a career as flamboyant as C.'s. Her father married her off to Richard Charke, a violinist at Drury Lane, in an attempt to curb her wildness; that did not work. Her life grew wilder. Her father's autobiography (*An Apology for the Life of Colley Cibber, Comedian,* 1740) shows that his eventful career was placid compared to the lurid reminiscences of her scapegrace life she put together for some much-needed cash as *A Narrative of the Life of Mrs. Charlotte Charke by Herself* (1755).

Having returned to London after extravagant adventures with, as she wrote, "only a single Penny in my pocket," she published her story in April 1755. First, she had tried to blackmail her father with the threat of embarrassment. He was adamant and would give her no money. As for her plight, his reply was: "You have made your own bed and therein you must lie," and he sent back her begging letter without any accompanying cash. In fact, it was said that in order to get anything out of her father she had to dress up as a highwayman (she often wore men's clothes) and accost Cibber on the road, forcing him to stand and deliver. When Cibber demanded of the "highwayman" why "he" had turned to a life of crime, "he" responded that "his" father was a tightwad who would not provide "him" with money on which to live.

C. made good use of her penchant for appearing in men's clothes during her theatrical career in London and her "nine Years peregrination" on the road. She was "valet" to a homosexual Irish peer for a while. She played Macheath in *The Beggar's Opera* on stage (as well as making the appearance as a "highwayman" already mentioned). She lived as a man and a farmer in the country. She passed as a doctor and an eligible bachelor. On one occasion there was a scheme to marry her off, as a male, to an heiress and seize the woman's fortune, but at the last minute C. (who had taken a liking to the girl) confessed the truth. The young lady would not believe C.'s confession; C. had, she tells us, to offer "ocular proof," whereupon the young girl fled. When Richard Charke ran off to Jamaica it really made little difference to C., because she had grown accustomed to supporting both herself and her daughter by whatever means were at hand.

Once there was hope C. would be a theatrical luminary. Cibber had made a star of his daughter-in-law, Susannah Maria Anne Cibber (Theophilus's wife), and Theophilus was also more or less successful on the stage; moreover, Cibber had connections. But he could not succeed with C., who made her debut as "a young gentlewoman who had never appeared before on any stage" in *The Provok'd Wife* on 8 April 1730. Characteristically, she had spent the previous day riding around London in a hired coach advertising the great event. By sheer nerve and persistence she came to replace the redoubtable Mary Porter in the next season; Mrs. Porter, famed for tragic roles, was to have appeared in Rowe's *Jane Shore* but fell and broke her leg. C. went on to play in *The Tender Husband, Orinooko,* by Aphra Behn, *Othello* (as Roderigo), *Pasquin* (as Lord Place), even to create a role in one of the two or three greatest hits of the eighteenth century, *George Barnwell; or, The London Merchant.* In female or male clothes, she played many parts under the theatrical management of her brother Theophilus and Cibber's partner Fleetwood. When London failed her, she turned to simple provincial tours and even penny gaffs. She acted on London stages (1730–37) and under the sleaziest provincial auspices, but she kept working. The money she made she spent recklessly on "the most idle and thoughtless extravagance" and in some respects her life resembled that of Daniel Defoe's fictional Moll Flanders.

That life ended in penury, though not for want of effort or invention in pennycatching schemes. She even ran a London puppet show. A second marriage her autobiography shrouds in silence; it cannot have lasted long. She got into trouble with creditors and with the police. And her family deserted her.

Near the end, Samuel Whyte (a sort of Irish publisher) and one H. Slater, Jr. (described as "a wary haberdasher of literature" in London's Grub Street) found C. in "a wretched hovel where it was usual at that time for the scavengers to deposit the sweepings of the streets." They bought from her a story called *The History of Henry Dumont, Esq.; and Miss Charlotte Evelyn* and gave her £10 for it. It went into a third printing, but that brought no more money to C., to her pet dog Fidele, or to her pet magpie in that hovel. She remained in dire poverty.

She also published *The Mercer; or, Fatal Extravagance* (around 1755) and *The Lover's Treat; or, Unnatural Hatred* (1758), both allegedly true stories. But neither those nor occasional theater pieces could feed her adequately. She perished in want and obscurity about 1760. The *British Chronicle* in that year published a brief obituary under the date of 16 April and called her "a gentlewoman remarkable for her adventures and misfortunes." Today she is remembered for the somewhat frighteningly indomitable courage she showed, for her dedication to rather riotous living, and for the unusual frankness of her autobiography.

WORKS: *The Art of Management* (1735). *The Carnival; or, Harlequin Blunderer ("intermix'd with songs, written by Mrs. Charke"), Tit for Tat; or, The Comedy and Tragedy of War* (1743). *A Narrative of the Life of Mrs. Charlotte Charke (Youngest Daughter of Colley Cibber, Esq.) Written by Herself* (1755). *The Mercer; or, Fatal Extravagance* (1755). *The Lover's Treat; or, Unnatural Hatred* (1758). *The History of Henry Dumont, Esq.; and Miss Charlotte Evelyn* (1758). *The History of Charley and Patty: or, The Friendly Strangers* (1760).

BIBLIOGRAPHY: Ashley, L. R. N. *Colley Cibber* (1968). Ashley, L. R. N., intro. to rpt. of *A Narrative* (1969). Friedl, L., in *Sexual Underworlds of the Enlightenment,* ed. G. S. Rousseau and R. Porter (1988). Mackie, E. *ELH* (1991). Morgan, F. *The Well-Known Troublemaker: A Life of Charlotte Charke* (1988). Robinson, M. *Memoirs of Mary Robinson* (1830). Rogers, P., in *Sexuality in Eighteenth-Century Britain,* ed. P. G. Bouce (1982). Waddell, H. *Spectator* (4 June 1937).

For articles in reference works, see: *DNB.*

Leonard R. N. Ashley

Charles, Gerda: See *Lipson, Edna*

Maria Charlesworth

BORN: 1 October 1819, Flowton, Suffolk.
DIED: 18 October 1880, Nutfield, Surrey.
DAUGHTER OF: the Reverend John Charlesworth.

Best known as the author of the children's novel *Ministering Children,* C. was born the daughter of the Reverend John Charlesworth, who was rector of Flowton, Suffolk, from 1814 to 1844. For a brief time, he was simultaneously rector at Blakenham Parva, near Ipswich, where C. was privately educated. From the age of six, she ministered among the poor in her father's parish. Later her father would have a small parish near St. Paul's in London, where C. became ill and would be confined to her room as an invalid. After her parents' death, she sometimes lived with her brother, the Reverend Samuel Charlesworth of Limehouse, though her permanent home was in Nutfield, Surrey, where she lived for the last sixteen years of her life. She never married.

Ministering Children is a didactic work whose aim was in "training the sympathies of children by personal intercourse with want and sorrow." It is an episodic series of adventures (some published separately) of good children who minister among the poor. Their actions are seen as admirable, and they are intended as role models. Helping the poor is seen as a necessary step towards spiritual salvation; personal sacrifice—even among the poor toward each other—is seen as an enobling experience. The work is strongly in the Evangelical children's book tradition; now seen as stylistically unsubtle in its didacticism and politically and socially ineffective in changing the ultimate plight of the impoverished, the work was widely successful in its day. It sold 170,000 copies in the United Kingdom and was also published in the United States, Sweden, Switzerland, France, and Germany. Its success led to the demand for a sequel, and it was influential in aspects of American prison reform. The popularity of the work in this century has waned, and it has not been in print since 1924. An excerpt, "The Story of Little Patience," is, however, included in the anthology *A Garland from the Golden Age* (1983), edited by Patricia Demers.

C.'s other works reveal similarly didactic purposes. Her first work, *The Female Visitor to the Poor* (1846), draws on her autobiographical experiences administering in her father's parish and in establishing a mission school in London. *Sunday Afternoons in the Nursery* (1853) is a retelling of "familiar narratives from the Book of Genesis." And *The Last Command of Jesus Christ* (1869) is subtitled "Plain Teaching on the Lord's Supper." C. was also interested in overseas mission projects as revealed in *African Mountain Valley* (1858), a biography of Augustine Johnson, a missionary to Sierre Leone. In it, she writes, "If the white man filled the cup of African slavery to the brim . . . the white man also, but with a heart far different, rose as Africa's deliverer, Africa's protection, Africa's blessing."

Though ultimately a minor figure, C.'s work sheds light on the mid-Victorian sensibility; her emotional excesses and appeal to religious sentiments are shared by several major figures.

WORKS: *The Female Visitor to the Poor* (1846). *A Book for the Cottage* (1848). *A Letter to a Child* (1849). *A Letter to a Friend Under Affliction* (1849). *The Light of Life* (1850). *Sunday Afternoons in the Nursery* (1853). *Ministering Children* (1854). *The Sabbath Given: The Sabbath Lost* (1856). *Africa's Mountain Valley* (1858). *India and the East* (1860). *England's Yeoman* (1861). *The Cottage and the Visitor* (1861). *The Sailor's Choice* (1862). *Beautiful Home and Other Letters to a Child* (1863). *A Sequel to Ministering Children* (1867). *The Last Command of Jesus Christ* (1869). *Where Dwellest Thou, or the Inner Home* (1871). *Oliver of the Mill: A Tale* (1871). *Eden and Heaven* (1872). *The Blind Man's Child* (1872). *Old Looking Glass* (1878). *Broken Looking Glass* (1880).

BIBLIOGRAPHY: Avery, G. *Childhood's Pattern* (1975). *Children and Their Books*, ed. G. Avery and J. Briggs (1989). Bratton, J. S. *The Impact of Victorian Children's Fiction* (1981). *A Garland from the Golden Age*, ed. P. Demers (1983). Grylls, D. *Guardians and Angels* (1978).

For articles in reference works, see: *Allibone SUP. DNB. Oxford. ToddBWW. WWCL.*

Other references: *TLS* (18 July 1980).

Tony Giffone

Charlotte, Elizabeth: See *Tonna, Charlotte Elizabeth*

Chesterton, Denise: See *Robins, Denise Naomi*

Chimaera: See *Farjeon, Eleanor*

Cholmondelay, Alice: See *Arnim, Elizabeth von*

Mary Cholmondeley

BORN: 8 June 1859, Hodnet, Shropshire.
DIED: 15 July 1925, London.
DAUGHTER OF: the Reverend Richard Hugh Cholmondeley and Emily Beaumont Cholmondeley.
WROTE UNDER: Mary Cholmondeley; Pax.

Although C.'s career covered the years from 1878 to 1921, the themes and execution of her fiction identify her as a nineteenth-century writer. Her novels, set in the closely circumscribed world of drawing rooms, estate houses, and country parsonages, are frequently compared to those of Jane Austen. In *Red Pottage* (1899), her finest novel, C. controls much of the melodrama and didacticism for which her critics have always taken her to task; nonetheless, her satiric wit, her carefully rendered characters, and her genuine affection for the pastoral splendor of the English countryside and for the grace and refinement of the genteel classes are evident in all of her novels.

Born the third of eight children to the rector of Hodnet in Shropshire, C. described herself as "a plain silent country girl, an invalid whom no one cared a straw about." Her mother died when she was sixteen, whereupon she assumed the responsibility of head of the household. The Cholmondeley family was of comfortable means, however, and C.'s youth was neither sheltered nor reclusive. The family journeyed to London and abroad and enjoyed the active social life one would expect for a family of their position in their community. Having achieved some measure of success with the publication of her first three novels, she moved to London with her father and two sisters in 1896. In a memoir, *Mary Cholmondeley: A Sketch from Memory,* Percy Lubbock recalls the Cholmondeley residence in London and the social gatherings there that included such guests as Howard Sturgis, Rhoda Broughton, and Lady Ritchie. The publication of the "scandalous" *Red Pottage* in 1899 made C. a celebrity, an occurrence she viewed with both amusement and bitterness. Her subsequent novels and stories were received with disappointment by her critics, and by the time she died in 1925 she was largely forgotten.

Although C. began writing when she was sixteen and published her first story anonymously when she was nineteen, she did not publish her first novel until she was twenty-eight. The first four novels she published—*The Danvers Jewels* (1887), *Sir Charles Danvers* (1889). *Diana Tempest* (1893) and *A Devotee: An Episode in the Life of a Butterfly* (1897)—were serialized in *Temple Bar.* Of these, *Diana Tempest,* the first novel published under her own name, was the best and most successful. The first two are mystery romances, marked by fine suspense, melodrama, and unlikely but exciting events. *Diana Tempest* is a tale of intrigue and romance, of guilt and retribution, and characteristically examines the irrevocable consequences of the actions of individuals. The female protagonist is an intelligent, independent woman, and her relationship with her lover is one of equality. In this novel, as in *Red Pottage,* C. condemns the loveless Victorian marriage of economic and social convenience.

Red Pottage, however, is C.'s best and most interesting novel. Published in 1899, the novel was enormously popular (one reviewer called it "the English novel of the year"), and its adultery, suicides, violent emotions, and satire of the country clergyman and his indolent, aristocratic parishioners caused, as Lubbock tells it, "quite a stir." More interesting, though, is the novel's angry protest against the marginalization, suppression, and, ultimately, silencing of the nineteenth-century woman writer, in particular the unmarried woman writer. For *Red Pottage* is a novel with two plots, and the tale of love and betrayal is but half the story. The second plot involves a woman novelist, Hester Gresley, and her struggle to complete her novel while residing with her antagonistic, self-righteous clergyman brother, himself a third-rate writer of religious pamphlets. Indignant about her satire of the clergy and her unorthodox religious views, he burns the completed manuscript, which has been accepted for publication and returned for revisions, in an act of monstrous destruction. Unlike the previous novels, *Red Pottage* presents an essentially tragic social vision. By novel's end, the selfish, powerful characters celebrate the triumphant marriage of one of their own, and Hester and her friend, Rachel, exile themselves to Australia.

After *Red Pottage,* C. published three novels: *Moth and Rust* (1902), *Prisoners (Fast Bound in Misery and Iron)* (1906), and *Notwithstanding* (1913); two collections of short stories: *The Lowest Rung* (1908) and *The Romance of His Life* (1921); a family memoir, *Under One Roof* (1918); and several contributions to periodicals. Although none of these is of the quality of *Red Pottage, Notwithstanding* offers an interesting examination of sexual mores and attitudes about women.

Many of the stories in C.'s last published work, *The Romance of His Life,* are concerned with the opposition between the values and scenes of the nineteenth century and the face of a modern world scarred by a world war. In one of the stories, "The Goldfish," C. returns to an examination of the fate of the female artist. A woman, a very talented artist, is married to a second-rate painter who rescued her from poverty and offered her the opportunity of advanced training. However, having become jealous of her superior ability, he makes her copy and enlarge his own canvasses. Convinced that she has betrayed her art, she drowns herself. Though flawed, "The Goldfish" remains compelling evidence of C.'s preoccupation with the various forms of violence imposed on women artists.

Today, only *Red Pottage* is available in reprint. Although her novels exhibit to varying degrees the flaws that characterize much popular fiction of the nineteenth century, she chronicles with wit and understanding the manners and mores of the Victorian upperclasses. The skillful and devastating protest against the subordination of the woman writer in the nineteenth century in *Red Pottage* render it a novel worthy of consideration.

WORKS: *The Danvers Jewels* (1887). *Sir Charles Danvers* (1889). *Diana Tempest* (1893). *A Devotee: An Episode in the Life of a Butterfly* (1897). *Red Pottage* (1899). *Moth and Rust; Together with Geoffrey's Wife and The Pitfall* (1902). *Prisoners (Fast Bound in Misery and Iron)* (1906). *The Lowest Rung With the Hand on the Latch, St. Luke's Summer and The Understudy* (1908; in the U.S. as *The Hand on the Latch,* 1909). *Notwithstanding* (1913; in the U.S. as *After All*). *Under One Roof: A Family Record* (1918). *The Romance of His Life and Other Romances* (1921).

BIBLIOGRAPHY: Ardis, A. L., in *Writing the Woman Artist: Essays on Poetics, Politics, and Portraiture,* ed. S. W. Jones (1991). Crisp, J. *Mary Cholmondeley, 1859–1925: A Bibliography* (Victorian Fiction Research Guides, 6) (n.d.). DeMoor, M. *CVE* (1994). Lubbock, P. *Mary Chomondeley: A Sketch from Memory* (1928). Rainwater, C. W. J. S. *PQ* (1992). Showalter, E. *A Literature of Their Own* (1977). Tindall, D., intro. to *Red Pottage* (rpt. 1968).

For articles in reference works, see: *Bloomsbury. DNB. Europa. Feminist. Longman. NCBEL. Oxford. VB.*

Other references: *Cornhill* (February 1935). *Edinburgh Review* (July 1900). *EIC* (1970). *National Review* (March 1900).

Patricia A. O'Hara
(updated by Virginia Zimmerman)

Agatha Christie

BORN: 15 September 1890, Torquay, Devon.
DIED: 12 January 1976, Wallingford, Berkshire.

DAUGHTER OF: Frederick Alvah Miller and an English mother.
MARRIED: Archibald Christie, 1914; Max Edgar Lucien Mallowan, 1930.
WROTE UNDER: Agatha Christie; Agatha Christie Mallowan; Mary Westmacott.

C.'s career—from *The Mysterious Affair at Styler* (1920), written in response to her sister's demand for a detective story not as easily solved by the reader as the popular fiction then in vogue, to *Curtain* (in which she finally disposed of her famous sleuth Hercule Poirot in 1975) and *Sleeping Murder* (serialized in a popular magazine in the year of her death, 1976)—was phenomenal. She wrote some 130 or 140 short stories, more than half that many novels, a score of radio and stage plays, a couple volumes of poetry, a travel book, and an autobiography. A film based on one of her novels (*Murder on the Orient Express,* based on *Murder on the Calais Coach,* one of more than a dozen films that brought her work to the screen) made more money than any other British film up to that date. A play (*The Mouse-Trap*), originating in her story "Three Blind Mice," opened in 1952 and is still running, having long since become the most successful play in the history of the English theater. Her books have sold hundreds of millions of copies and have been translated into more languages (more than 100) than has Shakespeare. "A Christie for Christmas" was for generations a British publishing tradition. Quite simply, she was the most famous British woman writer of her half a century or so of fame and the most commercially successful woman writer of all time.

All this production (she called herself "a perfect sausage machine") and practice did not make her an artistic writer. Her first novel was refused by a number of publishers before John Lane bought it for The Bodley Head. Some of the stories in *Poirot Investigates* (1924) and her very controversial novel *The Murder of Roger Ackroyd* (1926) are among her best work; she did not improve over fifty years, perhaps because she was quite good enough for her readers from the start and also perhaps because she was proud of the fact that "though I have given in to people on every [other] subject under the sun, *I have never given in to anyone over what I write.*"

Her skill was said to lie in ingenious plotting, but real invention was not really needed. She simply rang the inevitable changes on the conventions of the genre. She could not have "nobody did it" (suicide being a solution rejected by readers), but she could and did have "everybody did it," one of the "corpses" did it, the narrator did it—just about everything but satirist Stephen Leacock's crazy suggestion in his spoof on the red herrings and tortuous twists of mystery writing: He has the murder committed by two people who are just barely mentioned in the book—they are, in fact, the publishers, noted only at the bottom of the title page.

Julian Symons in his history of the crime novel, *Bloody Murder,* adds to the fact that "her skill was not in the tight construction of plot," that she did not often "make assumptions about the scientific and medical knowledge of readers," though her war work in pharmacies gave her a certain pride in the way she brought in poisons, playing (as she said) with "the phial" in her little "domestic murders." Nor were her characters or scenes especially well drawn. She created, actually, "never-never" world of fiction (as critic Edmund Crispin and others have noted) and seems to have had little interest in the world in which she lived. With characters that are "flat" and a rural English setting that had largely disappeared before she could write much about it, she moved from her early sensational claptrap (*The Seven Dials Mystery,* 1929, has been called "almost embarrassing" with its "bright young things, beautiful Balkan spies, and sinister anarchists") to her very own brand of upper-class twits gathered in the library of some country house (Styles, Chimneys, Nasse House, End House, and on and on) to hear the detective unravel the mystery. This is exactly the sort of thing that is spoofed at the start of the 1980 film version of her *The Mirror Crack'd,* which begins with the showing of *Murder at Midnight* in the village hall of St. Mary Mead, which all the world knows is the home of her eccentric but lovable Miss Marple (of *Murder at the Vicarage, The Body in the Library, A Caribbean Mystery, Nemesis,* and many more). Her world, like that of her contemporary P. G. Wodehouse, remained firmly that of times long past, before Labour lords with low-class accents; a time when garden fêtes and jumble sales, not socialism and common markets, were topics of discussion. In her novels, the action is in the library, not in the bedroom.

"What I'm writing is meant to be entertainment," C. told Francis Wyndham in 1966. As the creator of Tommy and Tuppence Beresford (*Partners in Crime,* etc.), Parker Pyne (*Parker Pyne Investigates,* etc.), Harley Quin (*The Mysterious Mr. Quin,* etc.), Superintendent Battle (*The Secret of Chimneys,* etc.), Col. John Race (*The Man in the Brown Suit,* etc.), Mark Easterbrook (*The Pale Horse*), Arthur Calgary (*Ordeal by Innocence*), Inspector Narracott (*The Sittaford Mystery*), and—most of all—the great Belgian detective Hercule Poirot, with his dapper little moustache, irritating little mannerisms (C.'s substitute for characterization), and "little grey cells," and as the basis for films such as *Witness for the Prosecution, And Then there were None,* and *Death on the Nile* (among others), C. was indubitably a genius at popular entertainment.

In a genre with magnificent milestones ever since Wilkie Collins' *The Moonstone* (1868), with Edgar Allan Poe and Arthur Conan Doyle and many more (including women such as Dorothy Sayers, Josephine Tey, P. D. James, and others whose work is not nearly as "abominably careless" as the *London Times* found, but truly literary), C. by sheer popularity and persistence carved herself out a lasting place that can be enjoyed as well as respected by everyone except the curmudgeons such as Edmund Wilson, who damned the whole detective fiction genre with the nasty question: "Who Cares Who Killed Roger Ackroyd?"

WORKS: *The Mysterious Affair at Styles: A Detective Story* (1920). *The Secret Adversary* (1922). *The Murder on the Links* (1923). *The Man in the Brown Suit* (1924). *Poirot Investigates* (1924; in the U.S., 1925). *The Secret of Chimneys* (1925). *The Murder of Roger Ackroyd* (1926). *The Big Four* (1927). *The Mystery of the Blue Train* (1928). *The Seven Deals Mystery* (1929).

Partners in Crime (1929). *The Underdog* (1929). *The Mysterious Mr. Quin* (1930; also as *The Passing of Mr Quin*). *The Murder at the Vicarage* (1930). (as Mary Westmacott) *Giants' Bread* (1930). *The Sittaford Mystery* (1931; in the U.S. as *The Murder at Hazelmoor*). *Blade Coffee* (produced 1931, published 1934). *Peril at End House* (1932). *The Thirteen Problems* (1932; in the U.S. as *The Tuesday Club Murders,* 1933; also as *Miss Marple and the Thirteen Problems*). *The Hound of Death and Other Stories* (1933; *Witness for the Prosecution,* produced 1953, published 1956). *Lord Edgware Dies* (1933; in the U.S. as *Thirteen at Dinner*). *Why Didn't They Ask Evans?* (1934; in the U.S. as *Boomerang Clue,* 1935). *Parker Pyne Investigates* (1934; in the U.S. as *Mr. Parker Pyne, Detective*). *The Listerdale Mystery and Other Stories* (1934). *Murder on the Orient Express* (1934; in the U.S. as *Murder on the Calais Coach*). *Murder in Three Acts* (1934; in the U.S. as *Three Act Tragedy,* 1935). (as Mary Westmacott) *Unfinished Portrait* (1934). *Death in the Clouds* (1935; in the U.S. as *Death in the Air*). *The ABC Murders: A New Poirot Mystery* (1936). (with F. Vosper) *Love from a Stranger* (1936; based on story, "Philomel Cottage"). *Cards on the Table* (1936). *Murder in Mesopotamia* (1936). *Death on the Nile* (1937; in the U.S., 1938; produced as *Murder on the Nile,* 1946). *Murder in the Mews and Other Stories* (1937; in the U.S. as *Dead Man's Mirror and Other Stories*). *Dumb Witness* (1937; in the U.S. as *Poirot Loses a Client;* also as *Murder at Littlegreen House* and *Mystery at Littlegreen House*). *Appointment with Death: A Poirot Mystery* (1938; produced and published as play, 1945). *Hercule Poirot's Christmas* (1938; in the U.S. as *Murder for Christmas: A Poirot Story,* 1939; also as *A Holiday for Murder*). *The Regatta Mystery and Other Stories* (1939; also as *Poirot and the Regatta Mystery*). *Murder Is Easy* (1939; in the U.S. as *Easy to Kill*). *Ten Little Niggers* (1939; in the U.S. as *And Then There Were None,* 1940; as play, 1945; produced in the U.S. as *Ten Little Indians,* 1946). *One, Two, Buckle My Shoe* (1940; in the U.S. as *The Patriotic Murders,* 1941). *Sad Cypress* (1940). *Evil Under the Sun* (1941). *N or M? The New Mystery* (1941). *The Body In the Library* (1942). *The Moving Finger* (1942; in the U.S., 1943). *Four Little Pigs* (1942; in the U.S. as *Murder in Retrospect;* produced and published as *Go Back for Murder,* 1960). *Death Comes as the End* (1942; in the U.S., 1945). *Towards Zero* (1944; with G. Verner, produced 1956; also as *Come and Be Hanged*) (as Mary Westmacott) *Absent in the Spring* (1944). *Sparkling Cyanide* (1945; in the U.S. as *Remembered Death*). *The Hollow: A Hercule Poirot Mystery* (also as *Murder After Hours*) (1946; produced as *The Hollow,* 1951, published 1952). *Come Tell Me How You Live* (1946). *The Labours of Hercules: Short Stories* (1947; in the U.S. as *Labors of Hercules: New Adventures in Crime by Hercule Poirot*). *Witness for the Prosecution and Other Stories* (1948). *Taken at the Flood* (1948; in the U.S. as *There Is a Tide*). (as Mary Westmacott) *The Rose and the Yew Tree* (1948). *Crooked House* (1949). *The Mousetrap and Other Stories* (1949; in the U.S. as *Three Blind Mice and Other Stories,* 1950; title story produced as *The Mouse-trap* (1952, published 1956; as radio play, 1952). *A Murder Is Announced* (1950). *They Came to Baghdad* (1951). *The Under Dog and Other Stories* (1951). *They Do It with Mirrors* (1952; in the U.S. as *Murder with Mirrors*). *Blood Will Tell* (1951; in U.S. as *Mrs. McGinty's Dead,* 1952). (as Mary Westmacott) *A Daughter's a Daughter* (1952). *After the Funeral* (1953; in the U.S. as *Funerals Are Fatal;* also as *Murder at the Gallop*). *A Pocket Full of Rye* (1953; in the U.S., 1954). *The Spider's Web* (produced 1954, published 1957). *Destination Unknown* (1954; in the U.S. as *So Many Steps to Death,* 1955). *Hickory, Dickory, Dock* (1955; in the U.S. as *Hickory, Dickory, Death*). *Dead Man's Folly* (1956). (as Mary Westmacott) *The Burden* (1956). (with G. Verner) *Towards Zero* (produced 1956, published 1957). *4:50 from Paddington* (1957; in the U.S. as *What Mrs. McGillicuddy Saw!,* 1961). *Ordeal by Innocence* (1958). *Verdict* (produced and published 1958). *The Unexpected Guest* (produced and published 1958). *Cat Among the Pigeons* (1959). *The Adventures of the Christmas Pudding, and Selection of Entrées* (1960). *Personal Call* (radio play, 1960). *Double Sin and Other Stories* (1961). *13 for Luck: A Selection of Mystery Stories for Young Readers* (1961; in the U.S. as *13 for Luck: A Selection of Mystery Stories,* 1966). *The Pale Horse* (1961; in the U.S., 1962). *The Mirror Crack'd from Side to Side* (1962; in the U.S. as *The Mirror Cracked,* 1963). *Rule of Three: Afternoon at the Seaside, The Patient, The Rats* (produced 1962, published 1963). *The Clocks* (1963; in the U.S., 1964). *A Caribbean Mystery* (1964; in the U.S., 1965). (as A. C. Mallowan) *Star over Bethlehem and Other Stories* (1965). *At Bertram's Hotel* (1965). *Surprize! Surprize!* [sic] *A Collection of Mystery Stories* (1965). *13 Clues for Miss Marple: A Collection of Mystery Stories* (1965). *Third Girl* (1966; in the U.S., 1967). *Endless Night* (1967; in the U.S., 1968). *By the Pricking of My Thoughts* (1968). *Halloween Party* (1969). *Passenger to Frankfurt* (1970). *Nemesis* (1971) *The Golden Ball and Other Stories* (1971). *Fiddlers Three* (produced 1971). *Elephants Can Remember* (1972). *Akhnaton* (1973). *Postern of Fate* (1973). *Hercule Poirot's Early Cases* (1974). *Curtain: Hercule Poirot's Last Case* (1975). *Sleeping Murder* (1976). *Best Detective Stories* (1986). *Remembrance* (1988). *Autobiography* (1991).

BIBLIOGRAPHY: Bargainner, E. F. *The Gentle Art of Murder: The Detective Fiction of Agatha Christie* (1981). Bargainnier, E. F. *JPC* (1987). Barnard, R. A. *A Talent To Deceive: An Appreciation of Agatha Christie* (1980). Barnard, R. and L. Barnard. *ArmD* (1985). Birns, N. and M. B. Birns, in *The Cunning Craft: Essays on Detective Fiction and Contemporary Literary Theory,* ed. R. G. Walker and J. M. Frazer (1990). Birns, M. B. *Clues* (1980). Borowitz, A. *ArmD* (1983). Carlson, M. *MD* (1993). DePaolo, R. *Clues* (1981). DeMarr, M. J., in *Commit Crime,* ed. E. F. Bargainnier (1987). Day, G., in *Twentieth-Century Suspense,* ed. C. Bloom (1990). Fitzgibbon, R. H. *An Agatha Christie Companion* (1980). Gerald, M. C. *The Poisonous Pen of Agatha Christie* (1993). Gesuato, S. *Versus* (1990). Gill, G. C. *Agatha Christie: The Woman and Her Mys-*

teries (1990). Grossvogel, D. I., in *Art in Crime Writing,* ed. B. Benstock (1983). Gwilt, P. R. and J. R. Gwilt. *Clues* (1980). Haining, P. *Agatha Christie: The Woman and Her Mysteries* (1990). Hardesty, S. M. *Clues* (1982). Hark, I. R. *LFQ* (1987). Hodges, R. R. *Clues* (1987). Keating, H. R. F., ed. *Christie: First Lady of Crime* (1977). Klein, K. G. *Great Women Mystery Writers* (1994). Knepper, M. S. *ArmD* (1983). Kroetsch, J. A. *CRev* (1986). Lane, T. D. *Clues* (1980). Lovitt, C. R., in *The Cunning Craft,* ed. R. G. Walker and J. M. Frazer (1990). Maida, P. D. and N. B. Spornick. *Murder She Wrote: A Study of Agatha Christie's Detective Fiction* (1982). McDiarmid, J. F. *Mid-Hudson Language Studies* (1982). Morgan, J. *TLS* (5 June 1981). Morgan, J. *Agatha Christie: A Biography* (1985). Morselt, B. *An A to Z of the Novels and Short Stories of Agatha Christie* (1986). Nickerson, E. A. *CentR* (1981). Osborne, C. *The Life and Crimes of Agatha Christie* (1983). Patterson, S. W. *ArmD* (1981). Ramsey, G. C. *Mistress of Mystery* (1946). Reed, J. V., Jr. *Clues* (1984). Reid, R. A. *RMR* (1992). *The Bedside, Bathtub & Armchair Companion to Agatha Christie,* ed. D. Riley and P. McAllister (1979; rev. 1987). Robertson, S. D. *Clues* (1982). Robyns, G. *The Mystery of Christie* (1978). Sanders, D. and L. Lovallo. *The Agatha Christie Companion: The Complete Guide to Agatha Christie's Life and Work* (1984). Shaw, M. and S. Vanacker. *Reflecting on Miss Marple* (1991). Singer, E. A. *WF* (1984). Slung, M., in *The Sleuth and The Scholar,* ed. B. A. Rader and H. G. Zettler (1988). Symons, J. *Bloody Murder* (1972). Vipond, M. *IFR* (1981). Wagoner, M. *Agatha Christie* (1986). Weinkauf, M. S. *Clues* (1980). White, W. *BB* (1983). Wilson, B. A. *Clues* (1987). Wren-Lewis, J. *CRev* (1993). Wynne, N. B. *An Agatha Christie Chronology* (1980).

For articles in reference works, see: *Bloomsbury. CA. Cambridge. CLC. DLB. Feminist. Longman. Oxford. TCA* and *SUP. TCC&MW. TCRGW. TCW. Todd-BWW.*

Other references: Ashley, L. R. N. *Literary Onomastics Studies* (1984). Culhane, J. *Reader's Digest* (October 1985). Fryxell, D. A. *Horizon* (November 1984). James, P. D. *TV Guide* (16 May 1981). James, P. D. *Writer* (February 1984).

Leonard R. N. Ashley

Caryl Churchill

BORN: 3 September 1938, London.
DAUGHTER OF: Robert Churchill and Jan Brown Churchill.
MARRIED: David Harter, 1961.

C. is a playwright, among the best now writing, who addresses social and political questions with audacity and wit. The talents of her political cartoonist father and her model-actress-secretary mother are extended in the style and substance of her plays. Born in London, she moved with her family to Canada in 1948, where she attended the Trafalgar School, Montreal. Returning to England in 1956 as a young adult gave her a shocked outsider's view of the class system despite her distant relationship to one of that system's staunchest defenders, Sir Winston Churchill. At Lady Margaret Hall, Oxford, she began to write plays. *Downstairs* and *Having a Wonderful Time* were produced there before she received her B.A. in English in 1960 and the Richard Hillary Memorial Prize in 1961.

After her marriage in 1961, she stayed at home raising three sons and writing more than a dozen plays for radio and television. Feeling isolated at home politicized her so that, although she dislikes labels, she now counts herself as a socialist and a feminist. In theme, her plays connect personal and political oppression, often expressed in conflicts about sexuality, mothering, and violence. In form, they are often Brechtian, using popular devices like song in a dance of ideas that emphasizes social rather than psychological conflicts.

In 1972, Michael Codron commissioned C. to write a play for the Royal Court, the theater that nurtured John Osborne, David Storey, and David Hare. C.'s play was *Owners,* on property values in mates, rowhouses, butcher's meat, infants, and senile mums. Edith Oliver found its American production promising, but, seconding C.'s own estimate of the influence of her father's cartoons, said that the characters talk like the captions in *Punch* cartoons or horror comics. The style reflects Joe Orton's savage mockery of cozy family life as a patriarchal butcher plans to murder his ambitious wife.

As resident dramatist at the Royal Court (1974–75), C. wrote a science fiction play, now called *Moving Clocks Go Slow,* and *Objections to Sex and Violence. Objections,* staged in 1975, puts a middle-class divorcee into a caretaker's job and involves her with terrorists, flashers, and pornography. In *Traps,* the next play she wrote, C. began to experiment with time and illusion. Four men, two women, and an infant explore the possibilities of change in a commune that is like a Möbius strip or an impossible Escher drawing. Their changing relationships form flexible traps like the traps that prevent the audience knowing whether the commune is in the city or the country, whether Syl has a child she doesn't want or wants a child she doesn't have. With one small hope for Utopia, the play ends as the characters bathe serially in an old wash tub, the most violent one bathing last, and smiling, in the deepest, dirtiest water of all. Although it was written early in 1976, *Traps* was first produced at the Royal Court Theatre Upstairs in January 1977.

Through *Traps,* C. had worked alone on plays about contemporary life. She then began to work with fringe theater workshops, a method that she found exhilarating, exhausting, and fruitful. With Monstrous Regiment, a feminist touring company, she wrote *Vinegar Tom* (1976), a play about witches with no witches in it. The play shows that the witchhunts of the seventeenth century used nonconforming women (old, poor, single, or skilled as healers) as scapegoats in a time of social unrest. Having finished a rough draft of *Vinegar Tom,* C. began work with the Joint Stock Theatre Group and its director, Max Stafford-Clark, on *Light Shining in Buckinghamshire* (1976). Ideas derived from improvizations enriched a play about the attempt of Diggers, Levellers, and Ranters to build a New Jerusalem in England's green and pleasant land in the 1640s. Both plays use a historical perspective to show that change can occur; both set groups of people in a political context; both are ensemble pieces without star roles; and both use short, self-contained scenes, interrupted by songs, to raise questions.

Floorshow (1977) was also worked out with Monstrous Regiment and with coauthors David Bradford, Bryony Lavery, and Michelene Wandor as sketches and lyrics for a cabaret about women and work. As C.'s career took off, some of her earlier radio plays were done as lunchtime plays in fringe theater. She wrote a television play called the *Legion Hall Bombing* (1978) on the trial without jury of Willie Gallagher in Northern Ireland but withdrew her name when the BBC censored it.

In a workshop on sexual politics with Joint Stock, C. developed *Cloud Nine* (1979), a satirical farce set in an African colony in 1880 and in a London park in about 1980. Through music hall devices and cross-sex casting, she connects colonial, sexual, and class oppression. In the first act, Clive, the Victorian patriarch, insists that his family and his Africans must live out his ideas. A male actor plays his wife, Betty, in an exaggerated stereotype of feminine compliance. Because he has assumed white values, a white actor plays African Joshua, for whom the walls of Empire finally come tumbling down. In exuberant farcical action, a white hunter tempts wife, son, and servant, but when he tempts Clive himself, he is forced to marry the lesbian governess.

In the second act of C.'s best-known play, the members of Clive's family are only 25 years older and they are no longer his. With new working-class characters, they meet in the public space of a London park and try out new arrangements in a quieter, tenderer questioning of class, gender, and homophobia oppression. *Cloud Nine* opened at the Royal Court in 1979; the 1981 New York production, which ran for two years, won three Obie awards.

Three More Sleepless Nights (1980), about two couples trying to change by changing partners, followed *Cloud Nine* but did not achieve its critical acclaim. Then *Top Girls* (1982) led Benedict Nightingale to rank C. as one of the half-dozen best contemporary dramatists. Its brilliant opening brings achieving women from the past millennium to a dinner celebrating Marlene's latest promotion. Of the top girls, only Dull Gret, from a Brueghel painting, has challenged the patriarchal hierarchy. Pope Joan, Lady Nijo, and the others, like Marlene, have sacrificed sexuality, maternity, and self-assertion in order to succeed in a man's world. In more naturalistic scenes in Marlene's employment agency and in her sister's working-class home, we see that nothing has changed at the bottom, although there are some places for women at the top.

Remembering *Top Girls,* several critics referred to C.'s next play as "Bottom Girls." *Fen* (1983) peoples a bleak East Anglia landscape with figures, five women and one man, in twenty-two roles on the potato farms. Designer Annie Smart filled the stage with furrowed earth and built the walls of a room around it so that one set serves for each brief scene. Fog steams from the fen to obscure distinctions between past and present, illusion and reality. If there is a heroine it is Val, torn between lover and children, unable, like the others, to give up and live. C. won the Susan Smith Blackburn prize for *Fen* in 1984.

In 1984, C. wrote a cabaret on crime and punishment called *Softcops.* A man of reason in nineteenth-century France tries to control crime with educational placards that explain how each punishment fits its crime. Vidocq, a robber who became chief of police, plays against Lacenaire, a glamorous criminal whose publicity distracts attention from genuine threats to authority. Its provocative structure and the music of a string quartet pleased some critics but most found the play too highbrow, too dependent on its inspiration in *Discipline and Punish* by French philosopher Michel Foucault. Also in 1984, she published *Midday Sun,* a script for a dance group at the Institute of Contemporary Arts. Four British tourists fantasize, experience, and then remember a holiday on a Moroccan beach and an encounter with an Arab beggar.

A Mouthful of Birds (1986), written with David Lan, is a relatively minor work loosely based on Euripides' *The Bacchae* that uses dance as well as dialogue to tell of the efforts of its seven characters to resolve the passions governing their lives. *Serious Money* (1987), one of C.'s more important plays and the winner of several major prizes, is a satiric attack on financial scandals, privatization, and deregulation in England during the Thatcher regime. To a large extent, its success is due to the fact that its targets found the work as comic as did its enthusiastic audiences; it was the first of C.'s plays to be staged in the West End. *Icecream* (1989) is even more blackly satiric in its probing into British-American relations as personified by an older middle-class American couple and a working-class British brother and sister; the play was combined with *Hot Fudge* (1989) in its American run. *Mad Forest* (1990), successful on both sides of the Atlantic, deals with the overthrow of the Romanian dictator Ceausescu.

The Skriker (1996) is a hallucinatory, highly cerebral, and demanding allegorical portrayal of modern-day London; the city is haunted by a supernatural being's predatory pursuit of two young women. *Hotel* (1997), written with Orlando Hough, combines two short plays, *Eight Rooms* and *Two Nights.* The first is a comic operatic work depicting various guests arriving in and departing from eight imaginary hotel rooms, and the second is a cryptic short work in which the characters sing the contents of a diary. *Blue Heart* (comprising *Heart's Desire,* a domestic farce, and *Blue Kettle,* a linguistically probing comic work about a con man) appeared in late 1997.

C. is an intellectual playwright, putting new ideas into new theatrical forms based on popular entertainment. In plays marked by beauty, anger, and generous humor, she continues to seek change and to challenge authority and centralized control.

WORKS: *Downstairs* (1958). *Having a Wonderful Time* (1960). *You've No Need to Be Frightened* (1960). *Easy Death* (1962). *The Ants* (1962). *Lovesick* (1967). *Identical Twins* (1968). *Abortive* (1971). *Not . . . not . . . not . . . not . . . not enough oxygen* (1971). *Henry's Past* (1972). *The Judge's Wife* (1972). *Schreber's Nervous Illness* (1972). *Owners* (1972). *Perfect Happiness* (1973).

Turkish Delight (1974). *Moving Clocks Go Slow* (1975). *Objections to Sex and Violence* (1975). *Save It for the Minister* (1975). *Light Shining in Buckinghamshire* (1976). *Vinegar Tom* (1976). *Traps* (1977). (with others) *Floorshow* (1978). *The After Dinner Joke* (1978). *Cloud Nine* (1979). *The Legion Hall Bombing* (1979). *Three More Sleepless Nights* (1980). *Crimes* (1981). *Top Girls* (1982). *Fen* (1983). *Softcops* (1984). (with others) *Midday Sun* (1984). (with D. Lan) *A Mouthful of Birds* (1986). (with J. Spink) *Fugue* (1987). *Serious Money* (1987). *Hot Fudge* (1989). *Icecream* (1989). *Mad Forest* (1990). *Lives of the Great Poisoners* (1991). *The Skriker* (1996). *Blue Heart* (1997). (with O. Hough) *Hotel* (1997).

BIBLIOGRAPHY: Diamond, E. *TJ* (October 1985). Itzin, C. *Stages in the Revolution: Political Theatre in Britain Since 1968* (1981). Keyssar, H. *Feminist Theatre* (1984). Kritzer, A. H., in *British Playwrights, 1956–1995: A Research and Production Sourcebook*, ed. W. W. Demastes (1996). Wandor, M. *Understudies* (1981). Wandor, M. *Carry On, Understudies* (1986). Wandor, M. *Look Back in Gender: Sexuality and the Family in Post War British Drama* (1987).

For articles in reference works, see: *Bloomsbury. CA. Cambridge. CD. CLC. DLB. Feminist. Oxford. ToddBWW.*

Other references: *NYT* (9 January 1983, 25 February 1984). *Vogue* (August 1983).

Mary R. Davidson

Sarah Jennings Churchill, Duchess of Marlborough

BORN: 29 May 1660, Holywell, near St. Albans.
DIED: 18 October 1744, London.
DAUGHTER OF: Richard Jennings (Jenyns) and Frances Thornhurst.
MARRIED: John Churchill, first Duke of Marlborough, 1678.
WROTE UNDER: Sarah, Duchess of Marlborough.

The last of nine children, C. became one of the most celebrated and notorious women of her time because of her court activities, her marriage, and her published explanation of her relationship with the queen.

C.'s association with Queen Anne began when both were children. James II's daughter by Anne Hyde, Princess Anne was six when she met the ten-year-old C. The future queen's admiration for C. began early, and it was, and continues to be, the subject of much speculation. Fueled by C's own statements, the girls' relationship even evoked an explanation from Winston Churchill, who wrote: "Very early . . . in these young lives did those ties of love, kindling into passion on one side and into affection on the other, grow deep and strong. . . . There was a romantic, indeed perfervid element in Anne's love for Sarah to which the elder girl responded warmly several years before she realised the worldly importance of such a relationship." Accused in later years of controlling and manipulating the queen for her own ends, C. wrote in her old age that the queen had "a person and appearance very graceful and something of majesty in her look. She was religious without affectation and certainly meant to do everything that was just" (*Blenheim Papers*). C. blames others, not the queen, for C.'s fall from favor.

That C. was influential with the young Princess Anne is clear from her history with the court. C. and her sister were placed in court as maids-of-honor to three future queens: the fifteen-year-old Duchess of York, Mary of Modena; her step-daughter, the eight-year-old Anne; and Anne's eleven-year-old sister Mary, who would later marry William of Orange and become Queen Mary II. Evidence of C.'s close relationship with the princess and the duchess appears early. In 1676, when but sixteen, C. persuaded the duchess to expel Mrs. Jennings, C.'s mother, from the court. Two years later, again with the duchess's help, C. secretly married John Churchill. One year later, C. bore the first of her eight children, only five of whom survived their infancy. During those years from 1679 to 1690, C. sustained a close and confidential relationship with Princess Anne, even using names of commoners so that their relationship would not be distanced by royal custom. To address one another as equals, C. became Mrs. Freeman and Princess Anne, Mrs. Morley. By 1685 C. became the First Lady of the Bedchamber and was at the height of her influence with the princess. C.'s husband's lot also continued to improve. From 1667, when he was commissioned ensign in the footguards to 1688 when he became an earl, John Churchill prospered and enjoyed court favor, too.

In 1702, C.'s influence reached its highest point, only to plummet in 1703. C.'s fall from favor came about in part as the result of the activities of Abigail Hill, C.'s cousin, an insignificant member of the court and a poor relation. Nonetheless, Abigail won, ousting C. and leaving C. to her second and enduring career—as writer and apologist. From 1722, after the death of John Churchill on June 16, to the end of her life, C. spent her time in quarrels. She was pugnacious, clever, and, depending upon the occasion, shrewd or wrongheaded. She completed the construction of Blenheim Palace, despite a long and bitter quarrel with its architect, Vanbrugh. She argued with two of her daughters: Henrietta, who was married to the Earl of Godolphin, and Mary, Duchess of Montagu. Among others, she quarreled with Lady Mary Wortley Montagu and Sir Robert Walpole.

In 1742, two years before she died, C. published her memoirs with the help of Nathaniel Hooke, who received £500 for his efforts. Even that task presented problems. When Hooke arrived at Blenheim, C. "caused herself to be lifted up, and continued speaking for six hours. Without the aid of notes she delivered her narrative in a lively and connected manner. Hooke resided in the house until the completion of the work. . . . During his residence with her she commissioned him to negotiate with [Alexander] Pope for the suppression, in consideration of the payment of three-thousand pounds, of the character of 'Atossa' in his 'Epistles'. . . . The duchess took a sudden dislike to Hooke because, finding her without religion, he attempted to convert her to popery" (Thompson Cooper, "Hooke," *DNB*). That, too, provoked a reply. This time, Henry Fielding defended her.

When she died, C. left a fortune to her heirs, but she also left £20,000 to Lord Chesterfield, £10,000 to William Pitt the Elder, and £500 each to two men to write the history of the Duke of Marlborough. Her own explanation of her life and her actions remains for posterity to read and debate. For some, like Sir Leslie Stephen, C. is "not an amiable woman." She is, instead, "spiteful and untrustworthy." Grudgingly, however, he notes that her writing is "frequently vigorous and shrewd" (*DNB*). Concerned about her name and her husband's reputation for future ages, C. wrote and generated even more words from others who attacked her. Among the many were Mary Manley and James Ralph who with wit and venom sought to discredit C. Years later, C. admitted, "Writting of books is looked upon as an Imployment not fit for our Sex: and if some have succeeded well in it, others have exposed themselves by it too much to Encourage a woman to venture on being an Authour: but it will appear more unusual for me to write so copiously, as I fear I may be forced to do, to tell my own Story, especially when it will seem to carry reflexions where one owes respect" (*Blenheim Papers*). In that spirit, C spent her last years writing to vindicate her name, justify her relationship to the queen, and celebrate her husband's ventures.

Only one work was published in her lifetime; the rest have survived either in others' editions of her works or in the *Blenheim Papers*. To read her words and to read of her impact on others is to learn of an amazing woman who dominated an age.

WORKS: *The Manuscript Cookery Book of Sarah Churchill, Duchess of Marlborough* (1738). *An Account of the Conduct of the Dowager Duchess of Marlborough, From her first coming to Court, To the Year 1710. In a Letter from Herself to My Lord* (1742). *The glorious memory of Queen Anne reviv'd: Exemplify'd in the conduct of her chief favourite the Duchess Dowager of Marlborough, from her first Coming to court, to the year 1710. In a letter from herself to Lord—[Nathaniel Hooke]* (1742). *Authentick memoirs of the life and conduct of Her Grace, Sarah, late dutchess of Marlborough, containing a genuine narrative of Her Grace's conduct, from her first coming to court, to the death of Her Royal Mistress Queen Anne, and from the demise of the Queen to Her Grace's death. Likewise all Her Grace's letters to the Queen and Her Majesty'a answers. To which is prefix'd, the last will and testament of Her Grace, from a true copy of the original, lodg'd in Doctor's Commons* (1744). *Some years of the life of the Duke and Duchess to Court, to the year 1710. Written by herself*, ed. N. Hooke (1817). *Private correspondence of Sarah, duchess of Marlborough, illustrative of the court and times of Queen Anne; with her sketches and opinions of her contemporaries, and the select correspondence of her husband John, duke of Marlborough* (1838). *Letters of Sarah, Duchess of Marlborough. Now first Published from the Original Manuscripts at Madresfield Court* (1875).

BIBLIOGRAPHY: Butler, I. *Rule of Three: Sarah, Duchess of Marlborough, and Her Companions in Power* (1967). Campbell, K. *Sarah, Duchess of Marlborough* (1932). Cecil, D. *Two Quiet Lives* (1948). Chancellor, F. *Sarah Churchill* (1932). Churchill, W. *Marlborough, His Life and Times* (2 vols., 1947). Cowles, V. *The Great Marlborough and His Duchess* (1983). *The Opinions of Sarah, Duchess-Dowager of Marlborough*, ed. D. Dalrymple (later Lord Hailes) (1788). Dobrée, B. *Sarah Churchill in Three Eighteenth-Century Figures* (1962). Fielding, H. *A Full Vindication of the Dowager Duchess of Marlborough* (1742). Green, D. *Sarah, Duchess of Marlborough* (1967). Harris, F. *A Passion for Government: The Life of Sarah, Duchess of Marlborough* (1991). *Memoirs of Sarah, Duchess of Marlborough, Together with Her Characters of Her Contemporaries and Her Opinions*, ed. W. King (1930). Kronenberger, L. *Marlborough's Duchess* (1958). Reid, S. *John and Sarah, Duke and Duchess of Marlborough* (1918). Rowse, A. L. *The Early Churchills* (1956). Rowse, A. L. *The Later Churchills* (1958). *Letters of a Grandmother, 1732–1735; Being the Correspondence of Sarah, Duchess of Marlborough with Her Granddaughter Diana, Duchess of Bedford*, ed. G. Thomson (1943). *The Blenheim Papers* from the British Library, London. The Papers of the 1st Duke of Marlborough. Sarah, Duchess of Marlborough, and the 3rd Earl of Sunderland (62 microform reels, 1987).

For articles in reference works, see: *BioIn. CHEL. DNB. Feminist. OCEL.*

Other references: Abbot, W. J. *Notable Women in History* (1913). Dorland, W. *The Sum of Feminine Achievement* (1917). *Fifty Famous Women* (1876). *Concise Universal Biography*, ed. J. A. Hammerton (1934). Schmidt, M. M. *400 Outstanding Women of the World, The Authors* (1953). Sitwell, E. *English Women* (1932). Speck, W. *ECLife*. Vance, A. *Fresh Reflections of Samuel Johnson: Essays in Criticism* (1987).

Sophia B. Blaydes

Clarinda: See Egerton, Sarah Fyge Field

Gillian Clarke

BORN: 8 June 1937, Cardiff, Wales.
DAUGHTER OF: Penri Williams and Ceinwin Evans Williams.
MARRIED: Peter Clarke, 1960.

A Welsh poet, editor, and essayist, C. is a writer whose subject matter centers upon family, the search for ancestral roots, and the connections between the natural world and society as well as Welsh culture and language. Known for her observational eye for detail and her imagery, C. relies upon the traditional Celtic metric and sound patterns while at the same time she is being conversational, minimal, and accessible. C. has worked as a BBC news researcher, freelance lecturer, broadcaster, and teacher of creative writing in primary and secondary schools. Her 1978 volume *The Sundial* won the poetry prize from the Welsh Arts Council, and she edited the *Anglo-Welsh Review* from 1975 to 1984.

C.'s first publication, *Snow on the Mountain* (1971), is a chapbook exploring the complex relationships that exist within the family unit. Her poems are based upon her own relationships with her children, husband, and the rural area of Wales in which she lives. *The Sundial* (1978), her first full-length volume of poetry, details her exploration of women's roles in Wales.

For BBC Radio Wales, C. wrote the poem "Letter From a Far Country" in 1981, which became the title poem for a subsequent collection published in 1982. Like *The Sundial, Letter From a Far Country* concerns itself with the role of women in Wales and the ways Welsh women live their daily lives. *Selected Poems* (1985) includes almost all of the poems C. published prior to 1985. Again, the collection focuses upon C.'s heritage as a woman and as a Welsh citizen. *Letting in the Rumour* (1989) explores her preoccupation with her ancestors and the connection that she feels to the past generation.

The King of Britain's Daughter (1993) also came about because of a commisioned poem. The title poem, based on Welsh legend, was commissioned as the text of an oratorio for the 1993 Hay-on-Wye Festival. Once again, C. returns to her recurring subject matter of Welsh legend, Welsh countryside, family history, women's lives, and birth as she explores the natural world in the context of war and environmental decline.

C.'s work continually returns to an examination of what it means to be a woman in Wales, particularly the rural Welsh countryside. She explores not only the sensibilities, experiences, and histories of Welsh women but also the strength she finds inherent in women. In doing so, she presents beautiful pictures of the Welsh landscape while also expressing a heartfelt understanding of the roles and lives of women in the context of place and history. Furthermore, C. tends always to move toward the future of Wales with a positive outlook, favoring final lines that enforce her sense of life that resounds throughout her poetry. C.'s concern with the identities of Welsh women and her portrayal of the country of Wales has moved her to the forefront of contemporary Welsh poets.

WORKS: *Snow on the Mountain* (1971). *The Sundial* (1978). *Letter From a Far Country* (1982). *Poems: Selections* (1985). *Letting in the Rumour* (1989). *The King of Britain's Daughter* (1993). *Collected Poems* (1997).

BIBLIOGRAPHY: Curtis, T. *Wales: The Imagined Nation: Studies in Cultural and National Identity* (1986). Hulse, M. *Quadrant* (1988). Matthias, J. *Another Chicago Magazine* (1986). Peach, L. *NWRev* (1988). Stevenson, A. *TLS* (15 July 1983). Wormald, M. *TLS* (29 September 1989).

For articles in reference works, see: *CA. CLC. DLB.*

Jeannette E. Riley

Mary Victoria (Novello) Cowden Clarke

BORN: 22 June 1809, London.
DIED: 12 January 1898, Genoa, Italy.
DAUGHTER OF: Vincent Novello and Mary Sabilla Novello.
MARRIED: Charles Cowden Clarke, 1828.

C. is remembered especially as a popularizer of William Shakespeare for nineteenth-century readers through her production of the first concordance to the plays, two editions of the plays, and many appreciations. The daughter of a popular organist, choirmaster, and music teacher, she received a musical as well as a sound general education at home and in France. Her well-read and vivacious mother was the most popular hostess in the Leigh Hunt–Charles Lamb circle and an author in her own right. The family had frequent evening parties attended by, among others, the Shelleys, with the widowed Mary Shelley continuing to visit after her return from Italy. In 1828, C. married Charles Cowden Clarke, a frequenter of these evening parties. He had been educated at his father's school at Enfield and was a staunch friend and beloved teacher of John Keats. Soon after their marriage, her husband, who had ventured into publishing, went bankrupt and began a new career in journalism, writing art, theater, and music reviews. C.'s father and her brother Joseph are known as the first in England to publish church music in popular editions, early English music from manuscript sources at Cambridge University, and the first full edition of Henry Purcell, for much of which C. provided translations and notes. C.'s talented family included, among her eight brothers and sisters who lived to adulthood, Clara Anastasia (1818–1908), who had a very successful musical career before marrying an Italian count, and Edward Petre (1813–34?), a precocious painter who exhibited successfully at the Royal Academy of Art.

At eighteen, C. published her first essays in William Hone's *Table Book* (1827) but established her reputation when, after fifteen years' work, *The Complete Concordance to Shakespeare* was issued in eighteen monthly parts and in complete editions in 1844–45. In the following years, mostly after their move in 1856 to Nice and then to Genoa, C. and her husband were to produce two major editions of Shakespeare's plays and poems and C. to produce many works of appreciation, thus keeping Shakespeare's popularity at fever pitch in the nineteenth century. Her *The Girlhood of Shakespeare's Heroines* (1851–52) provided a lead-in to the plays for generations of readers and is still in print. Charles Dickens cast her as Dame Quickly in his amateur production of *The Merry Wives of Windsor,* which played in London and in the provinces for a season to raise funds for the Shakespeare curator at Stratford. C. produced translations in Novello's theory of music series, a few children's stories, and several novels and volumes of verses. Her most valued work today is the body of reminiscences of the important literary figures with whom she and her husband were associated; most of these were included in *Recollections of Writers* (1878) and her autobiography, *My Long Life: An Autobiographic Sketch* (1896), and they have withstood the modern scholars' tests for accuracy.

Richard Altick describes C.'s style, modeled on Leigh Hunt's, as "cockney prose." It is characterized by overuse of compound epithets, of Latinisms, archaisms, and coinages. This style and an overwhelmingly sentimental tone are the reasons that C.'s work is little read today, although several titles are still in print. The style belies her spirited approach to a life, which included cold showers every morning, stiff walks in the mountains above Nice and Genoa, an egalitarian attitude toward her husband and their work, and a clear idea of the heroic woman.

WORKS: *The Complete Concordance to Shakespeare* (1844–45). *Shakespeare's Proverbs; or The Wise Saws of Our Wisest Poet Collected into a Modern Instance* (1847). *Kit Bam's Adventures, or, The Yarns of an Old Mariner* (1848). *The Girlhood of Shakespeare's Heroines in a Series of Tales* (1850–52). *The Iron Cousin, or, Mutual Influence* (1854). (trans.) *Treatise on Counterpoint and Fugue,* by Luigi Cherubini (1854). (trans.) *A Treatise upon Modern Instrumentation and Orchestration,* by Hector Berlioz (1855). *The Song of Drop o' Wather, by Harry Wandsworth Shortfellow* (1856). *World-Noted Women* (1858). *The Life and Labours of Vincent Novello* (1864). *The Trust and The Remittance: Two Love Stories* (1873). (with C. Clarke) *Recollections of Writers. With Letters of Charles Lamb, Leigh Hunt, Douglas Jerrold, and Charles Dickens* (1878). *Honey from the Weed, Verses* (1881). *Verse Waifs: Forming an Appendix to "Honey from the Weed"* (1883). *A Score of Sonnets to One Object* (1884). *Uncle, Peep, and I; a Child's Novel* (1886). *Centennial Biographic Sketch of Charles Cowden Clarke* (1887). *My Long Life: An Autobiographic Sketch* (1896). *Letters to an Enthusiast: Being a Series of Letters Addressed to Robert Balmanno, Esq., of New York, 1850–1861,* ed. A. U. Nettleton (1902).

BIBLIOGRAPHY: Altick, R. *The Cowden Clarkes* (1948). Ellis, R. *N&Q* (1984). Gross, G.C. *VS* (1972). Law, P. *SSEng* (1985).

For articles in reference works, see: *Bloomsbury. Cambridge. DNB. Feminist. NCHEL. Oxford. Todd-BWW.*

Eleanor Langstaff

Clementia (or Clementina), Dame: See *Cary, Anne*

Anne Clifford

BORN: 30 January 1590, Skipton Castle, Yorkshire.
DIED: 22 March 1676, Brougham Castle, Westmorland.
DAUGHTER OF: George Clifford, third Earl of Cumberland, and Lady Margaret Russell.
MARRIED: Richard Sackville, Lord Buckhurst and later third Earl of Dorset, 1609; Philip Herbert, fourth Earl of Pembroke and Montgomery, 1630.

Only three diaries survive that were kept by women who lived during the reign of Queen Elizabeth I. Of these, C.'s diary is the most interesting historically. Those by Margaret Hoby and Grace Mildmay concentrate on the routine of daily life and on religious faith; C. includes accounts of events such as Queen Elizabeth's death and funeral and talks with Queen Anne and John Donne as well as information about the history of her family. Her diary continues to hold our interest both because she led a remarkable life and because she wrote well, recording telling details. When she writes of her first presentation to King James I, for example, she comments that the fashion at court had certainly changed from Queen Elizabeth's time, for everyone in her party came away bitten by lice.

Her life had three stages. As a child, she was dutiful; as a wife, she was happy; as a widow, she came into her own. Her parents' marriage was troubled, and C.'s sympathies were with her mother, whom she adored. From her mother, she inherited a love of literature. C.'s reading ranged from works on religion to Ovid, Geoffrey Chaucer, and Ben Jonson. Lady Margaret Russell was one of Edmund Spenser's patrons and employed Samuel Daniel as her daughter's tutor; C., in turn, erected monuments to both of these poets and befriended Dianne and George Herbert. From her father, C. inherited troublesome lawsuits, for he willed the family lands to his brother rather than his child, and C. spent years suing to regain her estates.

When she married, C. probably hoped that her husband would help her in these suits, but instead Dorset tried to force her to stop the case because he thought settling it would provide him with ready money and please the king. After Dorset's death, C. rewed. Like Dorset, Pembroke was unfaithful and a spendthrift; unlike him, he sympathized with his wife's claims. Finally, in 1643, she received the property, and six years later she left her husband in London to go to her estates. Soon after she arrived, word came that Pembroke was dead.

The long lawsuit, with its frustration and unhappiness, probably led C. to begin writing. From 1605 until 1643, her time and energy had been engaged in lawsuits, and she wished to leave a careful account of what had happened for her two daughters. This desire, her interest in her family's history, and her pleasure in recording her daily activities led to a number of manuscripts: one in third person and another in first person that tell of her life, and others that summarize her family history. (The first-person autobiographical manuscript is referred to as C.'s diary.)

After the death of her second husband, C. spent the rest of her life as the industrious chatelaine of her property. She not only ran her large estates but also built or restored six castles, two almshouses, and seven churches and a chapel. As the *Dictionary of National Biography* remarks, "Her passion for bricks and mortar was immense." For nearly thirty years she built, administered, wrote, and pleased herself. Mildly eccentric (she pinned scraps of paper with sententiae all around her rooms) and extraordinarily generous, C. was a remarkable and influential woman. Her descendant David Clifford reports that after World War II plans were made to install electricity in the almshouses that C. had built, but the "proposal was politely declined, the reason being given that, 'Lady Anne would not have liked it.'"

WORKS: *Lives of Lady Anne Clifford and her Parents,* ed. J. P. Gilson (1916). *The Diary of Lady Anne Clifford,* ed. V. Sackville-West (1923). *Letters of the Sixteenth Century,* ed. A. G. Dickens (1962).

BIBLIOGRAPHY: Blodgett, H. *Centuries of Female Days* (1988). Costello, L. S. *Memoirs of Eminent Englishwomen, II* (1844). *Her Own Life,* ed. E. Graham et al. (1989). Holmes, M. *Proud Northern Lady* (1975). Lamb, M. E. *ELR* (1992). Lewalski, B. *YWES* (1991). Lewalski, B. *Writing Women in Jacobean England* (1993). Notestein, W. *Four Worthies* (1957). Sackville-West, V. *Knole and the Sackvilles* (1923). Spence, R. T. *Northern History* (1979). Spence, R. T. *Lady Anne Clifford, Countess of Pembroke, Dorset and Montgomery (1590–1676)* (1997). Walpole, H. *World* (5 April 1753). Williamson, G. *Lady Anne Clifford* (1992). Wilson, V. *Society Women of Shakespeare's Time* (1924).

For articles in reference works, see: *Bell. Bloomsbury. DNB. Europa. Feminist. IDWB. Oxford. Palmer.*

Fran Teague

Lucy Lane Clifford

BORN: 1855 (?), Barbados.
DIED: 21 April 1929, London.
DAUGHTER OF: John Lane.
MARRIED: William Kingdon Clifford, 1875.

Novelist, dramatist, and children's author, C. was born in Barbados. As an art student in London she met and in 1875 married W. K. Clifford, professor of mathematics and "delicious *enfant terrible,*" as William James called him, on the literary and scientific scene. Through her husband, C. became part of a circle that included Leslie Stephen, James Russell Lowell, and Henry and William James. She was one of the few women invited to George Eliot's Sunday afternoon parties at the Priory. When in 1879 C. was left a widow with two small daughters (one of whom, Ethel, later Lady Dilke, became a poet), Eliot helped C. to get a small Civil List pension and gave her the introductions that enabled her to augment it by writing articles for *The Standard.*

W. K. Clifford, who before his death at the age of thirty-four had made several contributions to mathematics, had also developed two philosophical concepts to which he gave the terms "mind-stuff" and the "tribal self" and which can be seen as themes in C.'s novels. The first concept asserts that the mind is the only reality but it defines "mind" as the elements—much like the atomic particles of physical matter—that form the mind, rather than the complex, conscious mind of common definition. The second, the "tribal self," posits a morality developed by the individual regulating his conduct to assure the "welfare of the tribe." These theories were explored fictionally in C.'s novels and tales. *Anyhow Stories* (1882), her first book, was so successful that an enlarged edition appeared in 1899. The literary fairy tale directed to an audience of all ages was popular in the latter part of the nineteenth century and provided a good vehicle for the exploration of "mind-stuff" and the "tribal self." A tale that has attracted recent critical notice, "Wooden Tony," is a plaintive exemplar of "mind-stuff," but also, Alison Lurie suggests, owes something to voodoo. Recent feminist freudian attention has been paid to "The New Mother," a fairy tale of "deeply resonant psychological power."

In the realm of fiction, *Mrs. Keith's Crime* (1885) explores the "tribal self" of a woman with an incurable, suffering child who decides that euthanasia is the solution. A sensational novel to reviewers and the public, it was much admired by Robert Browning and Thomas Hardy. *Aunt Anne* (1893), considered by some to be her best novel, recounted the process of the title character in establishing herself as the dominant power in a family—the tribe. Henry James, her friend from 1880 to his death in 1916, teasingly called her "Aunt Lucy" in reference to this work and her assertive but warm and friendly personality. They were perhaps closest when undergoing simultaneously the throes of seeing their plays staged. Of her writing, James wrote "you don't squeeze your material hard and tight enough . . . this is the fault of all fictive writing now" *(Letters* v. 4, 617).

WORKS: *Anyhow Stories* (1882; enlarged ed. 1899). *The Dingy House at Kensington* (1882). *Mrs. Keith's Crime* (1885; rev. ed. 1925). *A Grey Romance* (1890). *Love Letters of a Worldly Woman* (1891). *A Woman Alone* (1891; produced as a play, 1914). *The Last Touches and Other Stories* (1892). *Aunt Anne* (1892). *A Wild Proxy; a Tragic Comedy* (1893). *A Flash of Summer; the Story of a Simple Woman's Life* (1895). *Mere Stories* (1896). *The Dominant Note* (1897). *Marie May* (1900). *A Long Duel; A Serious Comedy in Five Acts* (1901). *The Likeness of the Night; a Modern Play in Four Acts* (based on *The Last Touches,* 1900). *Woodside Farm* (1902; also pub. as *Margaret Vincent*). *A Honeymoon Tragedy; a Comedy in One Act* (1904). *The Getting Well of Dorothy* (1904). *The Modern Way* (1906). *Proposals to Kathleen* (1908). *Mrs. Hamilton's Second Marriage* (1909). *Thomas and the Princess* (1909). *The Modern Way* (1909). *Sir George's Objection* (1910). *The Searchlight; A Play* (1913). *Two Company; A Play* (1915). *The House in Marylebone* (1917). *Mr. Webster, and Others* (1918). *Miss Fingal* (1919). *Eve's Lover* (1924).

BIBLIOGRAPHY: *American Imago* (1978). *Bookman* (1920). DeMoor, M. *CVE* (1994). Moss, A. *The Unicorn and the Lion* (December 1988). *NYRB* (11 December 1975). Shell, H. *Turn of the Century Women* (1990).

For articles in reference works, see: *TCA.*

Eleanor Langstaff

Elizabeth Knevet Clinton

BORN: 1574 (?), Charlton, Wiltshire (?).
DIED: 1630 (?), Great Grimsby, Lincolnshire (?).
DAUGHTER OF: Sir Henry Knevet and Anne Pickering Knevet.
MARRIED: Thomas Clinton, later eleventh Baron Clinton and third Earl of Lincoln, 1584.

Married very young, C. was a dutiful, aristocratic wife who, by her own account, bore her husband eighteen children. After his death in 1618, when she became countess dowager, she apparently concentrated her maternal attentions on the grandchildren born to her daughter-in-law, Brigit, and her son, Theophilus, who succeeded his father as earl in 1619.

As a token of her esteem for Brigit, the countess-dowager dedicated her 1622 tract on breastfeeding, *The Countesse of Lincolnes Nurserie,* to her daughter-in-law, who, unlike many noblewomen including the countess-dowager, breast-fed her children. C. publicly bewailed her own negligence in this matter, contending that putting a child out to nurse is a careless practice that often leads to physical neglect of the child as well as to harmful influences on it. In contrast, she writes, nursing by the child's natural mother is an important religious and maternal duty and privilege, prescribed by Holy Writ and incumbent on every mother who is physically able to suckle. "Think alwaies," the countess-dowager enjoins, "that having the child at your breast, and having it in your armes you have Gods blessing there. For children are Gods blessings. Thinke again how your babe crying for your breast, sucking hartily the milke out of it, and growing by it, is the *Lords owne instruction,* every houre, and every day, that you are suckling it, instructing you to shew that you are his new borne *Babes* by your earnest desire after his word, & the syncere doctrine thereof, and by your daily growing in grace and goodnesse therby, so shall you reape pleasure and profit."

Such thoughts echo the books aimed at Renaissance Englishwomen by both humanist and Protestant religious reformers. Although the countess-dowager styles her book, "the first work of mine that ever came in print," no other works by her survive.

WORKS: *The Countesse of Lincolnes Nurserie* (1622; English Experience Series, facsimile No. 7209, 1975). *Mothers' Advice Books,* ed. B. Travitsky (1997).

BIBLIOGRAPHY: Beilin, E. *Redeeming Eve: Women Writers of the English Renaissance* (1987). *Women as Mothers in Pre-Industrial England: Essays in Memory of Dorothy McLaren,* ed. V. Fildes (1989). Hays, M. *Female Biography, or, Memoirs of Illustrious and Celebrated Women, of All Ages and Countries* (1803). Klein, J. L. *Topic* (1982). Knyvett, T. *The Knyvett Letters, 1620–1644,* ed. B. Schofield (1949). McLaren, D., in *Women in English Society 1500–1800,* ed. M. Prior (1985). *The Female Spectator: English Women Writers before 1800,* ed. M. R. Mahl and H. Koon (1977). Poole, K. *SEL* (1995). Schnucker, R. V. *History of Childhood Quarterly* (1973–74). Sizemore, C. W. *South Atlantic Bulletin* (1976). Tebeaux, E. and M. Lay. *IEEE Transactions* (1992). Travitsky, B. *Bulletin of Research in the Humanities* (1979). Travitsky, B., in *Mothers and Daughters in Literature,* ed. C. N. Davidson and E. M. Broner (1979). *Paradise of Women: Writings by Englishwomen of the Renaissance,* ed. B. Travitsky (1981). Wall, W. *ELH* (1991). Walpole, H. *Royal and Noble Authors* (1806). Wayne, V., in *Women and Literature in England, 1500–1700,* ed. H. Wilcox (1996). Williams, J. *The Literary Women of England* (1861).

For articles in reference works, see: *Ballard. Europa. ToddBWW.*

Betty Travitsky

Caroline Clive

BORN: 30 July 1801, Shakenhurst, Worcestershire.
DIED: 12 July 1873, Whitfield, Herefordshire.
DAUGHTER OF: Edmund Meysey-Wigley and Anna Maria Watkins Meysey.
MARRIED: the Reverend Archer Clive, 1840.
WROTE UNDER: "The Author of *IX Poems by V*"; Mrs. Archer Clive; "The Author of *Paul Ferroll*"; V.

By her own testimony, life for C. as wife, mother, and recognized author was "the perfect prosperity of husband and children, place, fortune." However, until her marriage in 1840 to the Reverend Archer Clive, rector of Solihull, C.'s life was less than idyllic. Stricken by polio at age three, C. as a young woman was lame, plain, and solitary; yet she delighted in observing her own society, the landed gentry of Worcestershire. Her father was a member of the bar and a member of Parliament, her mother an heiress and the last of her ancient Norman family. C. had two brothers, Edmund and Meysey, and two sisters, Anna and Mary.

Her first volume of poetry, *IX Poems* (1841), written by "V.", received considerable critical acclaim by such notables as William Gladstone and Dugald Stewart; "V" stands for Vigolina, her husband's nickname for her. Her poetry, generally about mutability and death, seems predictable; yet lines in "At Llyncwmstraethy" and in "Written in Health" have a timeless sincerity. Among her longer poetic works, generally thought less effective than the shorter poems, *The Morlas* (1853) is considered the most notable. Other volumes of both poetry and satire, closely connected to her reading in the classics, brought her some celebrity status.

The publication of her most famous novel, *Paul Ferroll* (1855), however, prompted both praise and condemnation. She drew the hero of this rather "curiously modern" novel as an antihero, a man who, having killed his debauched wife, demonstrates charity, wisdom, and kindness throughout the rest of his life. In response to the controversy raised by the moral murkiness of *Paul Ferroll,* C. wrote different endings in subsequent editions, finally publishing a formal "answer" in a final rendering of the story, *Why Paul Ferroll Killed His Wife* (1860). With her death in 1873, her curious protagonist faded into obscurity.

Called a pivotal writer, she has been compared in the novel to Wilkie Collins and Charles Reade and in poetry to Matthew Arnold and Elizabeth Barrett Browning. She pulls together elements of both eighteenth-century and nineteenth-century literature through her combined elegance of phrase and forthrightness of content.

WORKS: *Essays on the Human Intellect* (1828). (by V.) *IX Poems* (1841). (by V.) *I Watched the Heavens* (1842). (anon.) *Saint Oldooman: A Myth of the Nineteenth Century* (1845). (by V.) *The Queen's Ball* (1847). *The Valley of the Rea* (1851). (by V.) *The Morlas* (1853). (by "The Author of *IX Poems by V.*") *Paul Ferroll* (1855). (by "The Author of *Paul Ferroll*") *Poems* (1856). (by "The Author of *Paul Ferroll*") *Year after Year* (1858). (by "The Author of *Paul Ferroll*") *Why Paul Ferroll Killed His Wife* (1860). (by "The Author of *Paul Ferroll*") *John Greswold* (1864). (by "The Author of *Paul Ferroll*") *Poems by V* (1872).

BIBLIOGRAPHY: Clive, M. *Caroline Clive: from the Diary and Family Papers of Mrs. Archer Clive 1801–1873* (1949). Partridge, E., intro. to *IX Poems by V* (1928). Partridge, E. *Literary Sessions* (1932). Sergeant, A. *Women Novelists of Queen Victoria's Reign* (1897).

For articles in reference works, see: *Feminist. Oxford. VB.*

Sylvia McLaurin

Catherine (Kitty) Clive

BORN: 1711.
DIED: 1785.
DAUGHTER OF: William Rafter and Mrs. Daniel.
MARRIED: George Clive, 1733.

Three of C.'s four afterpiece plays and her one prose polemic consistently allude to her personality and career. A brief sketch of both are, then, in order here. Coming to Drury Lane in 1728 while still in her teens, Kitty Rafter quickly became a favorite of the town by virtue of her operatic singing voice, vivacity, and gift for mimicry. Her voice was good enough to attract the attention of George Frideric Handel, who gave her the part of Delilah in his oratorio *Samson*. But her main vocal triumphs were in entr'acte songs and such specialty numbers as the Irish ballad "Elin aroon." Admired first as a singing actress, especially gifted in ballad farces, C. in 1731 showed her talents as a comic actress in the role of Nell in Charles Coffey's *The Devil to Pay*, one of over two hundred parts she mastered, including many "Miss Kitty" roles. She was often called for as Flora in *The Wonder*, Lady Bab in *High Life Below Stairs*, Lappet in *The Miser*, Catherine in *Catherine and Petracchio*, Mrs. Heidelberg in *The Clandestine Marriage*, and the Fine Lady in *Lethe*. Polly in *The Beggar's Opera* was also a favorite.

A star in an age of stage stars, C. was popular as comedienne and performer of prologues and epilogues, indicated by the frequency of her performances and long tenure at Drury Lane—she retired on 24 April 1769—and documented by the praise of Henry Fielding (see the preface to his farce *The Intriguing Chambermaid*), Arthur Murphy, Charles Churchill, David Garrick, Samuel Johnson, Oliver Goldsmith, Horace Walpole (who gave her his cottage on Strawberry Hill), fellow players, contemporary memoir writers, and audiences who admired—and defended—her. Henry Fielding and, later, James Miller wrote parts for her in their plays. The Prince and Princess of Wales were her patrons.

Johnson gives a balanced, just appraisal of C. the actress in James Boswell's *Life of Johnson* "What Clive did best she did better than Garrick; but could not do half so many things well; she was a better romp than any I ever saw in nature." The half she could not do well was tragedy roles, even though she insisted on playing Zara in *The Mourning Bride* and Ophelia in *Hamlet*. Her often-given burlesque of the role of Portia in *The Merchant of Venice* was never well received by audiences or critics, but the stubborn C. insisted on giving this rendering of Portia for many years. The half she could do well, according to her theater contemporary Thomas Davies, included chambermaid roles and roles of "country girls, romps, hoydens and dowdies, superannuated beauties, viragos, and humourists." She brilliantly satirized opera singers, burlettos, and excessiveness of several sorts. As Davies puts it, "Her mirth was so genuine that whether it was restrained to the arch sneer, the suppressed half-laugh, or extended to the downright honest burst of loud laughter, the audience was sure to accompany her."

Negligible as dramatic literature, C.'s farce afterpieces, written between 1750 and 1765, are, with the exception of the 1760 *Every Woman in Her Humour*, written in terms of her public personality and career. Indeed, topical and personal allusions largely constitute the play's subject matter. Most performances were in March, for her own "benefit," with C. playing the lead woman's part in all productions. Her first play, written and first performed in 1750 but nor printed until 1753, the two-act *Rehearsal; or, Bayes in Petticoats*, is in the "rehearsal" tradition begun by George Villiers', the Duke of Buckingham's, *Rehearsal* (1671). C.'s play, however, only borrows that earlier play's form, not its content. Her main satiric targets are would-be women dramatists (herself) and Italian opera singers (then in the mode), the latter called by her "squalling devils" and "a parcel of Italian bitches." In the play, Mrs. Hazard, who is the Bayes in Petticoats played by C. herself, has written a burletto, which of course never comes off.

The piece is a noteworthy showcase of C.'s public personality, including such pet peeves as playing conditions in the theater, her ill-treatment by Garrick, her penchant for a choice benefit night in March, and would-be women and men of fashion, to name a few. Her primary method of ridicule was to burlesque speech and demeanor, C. being one of the greatest mimics of the century. *The Rehearsal* shows how closely C. identified with Drury Lane theater, its denizens, its exigencies. Stories of her battles with Susanna Maria Anne Cibber, the actors Harry Woodward and Ned Shuter, and especially Peg Woffington have passed into the anecdotal record of the age's theatrical scuffles. Her satire either poked fun at her own habits and limitations in a straightforward way or presented herself opposite to what she really was, thereby making the context ironic. While most of C.'s ripostes are merely good fun and tonally light, she does clearly expose such poseurs as the play's Miss Giggle who enters to disrupt the rehearsal. C. is everywhere serious in her barbs aimed at those who do not take the theater seriously.

In the 1730s and 1740s, C. strenuously defended the acting profession and her own part in it. Although neglected today as such, C. is a significant eighteenth-century feminist, most properly viewed in the company of Aphra Behn and Susanna Centlivre. She was ever vigilant of women's artistic rights and freedom. The best indication of this and her thoroughgoing professionalism is her *The Case of Mrs. Clive Submitted to the Publick,* published in October 1744, by which time C. had established herself not only as first lady of comedy but also as a patriot of the acting profession and the Drury Lane company. In the 1733 theater dispute, C. and Charles Macklin, among the principal players, stayed with John Highmore, the unpopular, ineffective proprietor of Drury Lane, rather than join the players' revolt to the New Haymarket theater. She saw defection as disloyalty to her audiences, who were always her concern in matters of professional consequence.

But when Garrick and his Drury Lane colleagues felt their freedom and rights monumentally infringed in 1743, C. joined them. She published her *Case . . . Submitted to the Publick* to explain the unjust, oppressive situation in the two major London theaters, Drury Lane and Covent Garden, and her personal mistreatment by their managers, Fleetwood and Rich. Their cartel had the actors at its mercy in terms of hiring and salary, both abused against "custom," she charged.

C. was forced to seek a place in the Covent Garden company in the 1743–45 seasons, her only substantial time away from Drury Lane in her forty-year career, save for engagements in Ireland where she was a great favorite. C. considered her treatment at Covent Garden insulting for an actress of her stature. In the last third of her *Case,* she gives an affecting account of the personal costs of the Stage Licensing Act of 1737, which allowed the monopoly of Drury Lane and Covent Garden as the only two licensed theaters in London. November of the 1745–46 season, however, found her back at Drury Lane where she had remaining to her more than twenty years of triumphs, mostly under the management of her friend, colleague, and sometime antagonist, David Garrick.

C.'s second and most literarily ambitious play, the two-act *Every Woman in Her Humour* (1760), focuses on the ridiculousness of affectation. A "humours" play, *Every Woman* has C., who plays the role of Mrs. Croston, speak through her character only once, the opposite of her method in *The Rehearsal*. The comeuppance of the lying Sir Charles Freelove is the major plot, but central interest in the farce is centered on the low or humorous shenanigans of its women characters. A well-structured farce with some precise character writing, *Every Woman* had only one performance. While it has some correspondences to a mainpiece comedy, it was a failure on stage. Perhaps audiences wanted from C.'s pen a more self-regarding work, and this play is her least autobiographical. Too, C. had no talent for repartée or even the memorable phrase. There was little chance, then, that the piece would survive. Her earlier *Rehearsal*, by "literary" standards a lesser play, had fourteen mountings over a twelve-year period, surely because audiences wanted C.'s self-satire.

C.'s final plays, both farce afterpieces, are *The Sketch of a Fine Lady's Return from a Rout* (1763), whose title tells all, and *The Faithful Irish Woman* (1765), an enlarged and reworked version of *The Sketch.* In these plays, C. returned to the self-regarding technique of *The Rehearsal; or, Bayes in Petticoats.* She played the lead in both plays: *The Sketch* spoofs would-be fine ladies who love cards (as C. did) and "assemblies"; the final play, written only a few years before her retirement from the stage, allows C. to show her Irish patriotism as well as other facets of her celebrated public personality. Both plays are little more than *petite piéces* wherein she shows herself comically.

A very minor writer by literary standards, C. wrote revealing plays and one animated autobiographical prose piece, all directed to audiences who revered her as a supreme actress and sparkling personality.These works included common sense, loyalty, and unusual decency, all of which moved Samuel Johnson to say to his biographer: "Clive, Sir, is a good thing to sit by; she always understands what you say."

WORKS: *The Case of Mrs. Clive Submitted to the Publick* (1744). *The Rehearsal; or, Bayes in Petticoats* (1750). *Every Woman in Her Humour* (1760). *The Sketch of a Fine Lady's Return from a Rout* (1763). *The Faithful Irish Woman* (1765). Two plays, *The London 'Prentice* (1754) and *The Island of Slaves* (1761), are less surely from her hand. For the plight of the woman artist in society as well as glimpses of the C. known by Garrick, Walpole, and Jane Pope, C.'s successor in comedy at Drury Lane, see her letters in P. J. Crean (unpub. thesis, London, 1933), R. C. Frushell (1973), and especially *A Biographical Dictionary* below.

BIBLIOGRAPHY:

For articles in reference works see: Backscheider, P., F. Nussbaum and P. Anderson. *An Annotated Bibliography of Twentieth-Century Critical Studies of Women and Literature, 1600–1800* (1977). *Feminist.* Link, F. M. *English Drama, 1660–1800: A Guide to Information Sources* (1976). *Oxford. ToddDBA.*

Other references: Frushell, R. C. *N&Q* (1969). Frushell, R. C. *RECTR* (1970). Frushell, R. C. *DUJ* (1971). Frushell, R. C. *ThS* (1973). *The Case of Mrs. Clive Submitted to the Public,* ed. R. C. Frushell (1992). Highfill, P. H, Jr., K. A. Burnim, and E. A. Langhans, *A Biographical Dictionary of Actors, Actresses . . . in London, 1660–1800* (1975).

Richard C. Frushell

Clive, Mrs. Archer: See *Clive, Caroline*

Anne (Alice Andrée) Cluysenaar

BORN: 15 March 1936, Brussels.
DAUGHTER OF: John Cluysenaar and Sybil Fitzgerald Cluysenaar.
MARRIED: Walter Freeman Jackson, 1976.

C. is an Irish poet, long resident in Britain, whose lyric verse celebrates the role of communication, in particular the ways discourse enables her to explore her family's heritage and "the boundaries of self and others." She has published verse in a variety of journals (*Dublin, Poetry Review, Poetry Ireland, Hibernia, Stand, Poetry Nation Review,* and *Aberdeen University Review* among them) and anthologies. In addition, she has published several books of verse and some highly regarded theoretical studies.

After studying at Trinity College, Dublin (where she graduated with honors), and the University of Edinburgh (where she studied general linguistics), C. began a career teaching at the university level. She has taught at various English Irish, and Scottish universities and in 1987 was principal lecturer in English at Sheffield City Polytechnic, Sheffield.

C. published several volumes before her first notable work, *A Fan of Shadows,* in 1967. This is a relatively traditional collection of lyric verse, mostly in rhyme. In addition to the individual poems, often setting up syntheses of opposing forces or states of being, C. included notes in which she explained her intent in the explorations of the human predicament that she called "radiations from an occasionally moving centre." Little variety in subject, images, or words differentiates these poems, and several are little more than hackneyed explorations of the familiar, as with the several poems focused on the sea.

But C. has grown as a poet, and though she still favors landscapes, for example, more than the effects of setting on the poet's consciousness, many of her more recent poems are distinctive. *Double Helix,* written with Sybil Hewat (1982), is her most mature work. In it she mixes poetry with such family records as photographs, memoirs, drawings, and correspondence as a means of recording individual and family experience. She has stated that in this book she wants the focus to be on "communication rather than the language drawing attention to itself for its own sake," and to an extent she has succeeded. Her intent is, as she states, "to relate poetry very closely to life." Consequently, she moves easily from her family to forms of universal evil, politics, government policies, and the horrors of annihilation.

C.'s accomplishments in *Double Helix* relates directly to her formal interest in language. She teaches creative writing and linguistics because she finds aspects of writing that can be learned in group discussion and exercise; the formal study of language, she says, enables a person to approach a poem "with an understanding of language capable of matching that of the writer, both through some experience of practical 'thinking with words' and through theoretical understanding of how language works." In 1976, C. published *Introduction to Literary Stylistics: A Discussion of Dominant Structures in Verse and Prose* (published in the United States as *Aspects of Literary Stylistics*). In 1987, she continued this analysis in *The Missing Subject,* an outgrowth of a *Critical Quarterly* essay she published in 1984.

In the past few years, C. has returned to such traditional verse forms as the sonnet to encompass her commentaries on the future. A child in "Double," for example, serves C. as a means of contrasting simple diction and childish fears with complex social commentary; an infant's scream serves as the elemental parallel to the universal horrors of a possible future world. C.'s emotional range is not wide, nor is she especially well known; yet she commands a forcefulness in conception and sensitivity to language that distinguishes her verse.

WORKS: (trans.) *The Sonnets of Michelangelo* (1961, 1969). (with L. Durrell and R. S. Thomas) *Penguin Modern Poets I* (1962). *Recoveries: Poems* (1964). *Frost* (1964). *Christianity and Poetry* (1965; in the U.S. as *Christian Poetry*). *The Mind Has Mountains* (1966). *The Secret Brother and Other Poems for Children* (1966). *Collected Poems* (1967). *A Fan of Shadows* (1967). *The Animals' Arrival* (1969). *Nodes: Selected Poems, 1960–1968* (1969). *Lucidities* (1970). *Hurt* (1970). (with others) *Folio* (1970). *Relationships* (1972). *Growing-Points: New Poems* (1975). *Seven Men of Vision: An Appreciation* (1976). *Introduction to Literary Stylistics: A Discussion of Dominant Structures in Verse and Prose* (1976; in the U.S. as *Aspects of Literary Stylistics*). *Consequently I Rejoice* (1977). *After the Ark* (1978). *Moments of Grace: New Poems* (1979). *Selected Poems* (1979). *Winter Wind* (1979). *Moments of Grace* (1980). *A Dream of Spring* (1980). *Celebrations and Elegies* (1982). (with S. Hewat) *Double Helix* (1982). *Extending the Territory* (1985). *The Missing Subject* (1987). *In Shakespeare's Company* (1985). *Collected Poems, 1953–1985* (1986). *Timeslips* (1997).

BIBLIOGRAPHY: *Penguin Book of Contemporary Verse,* ed. K. Allott (1962). Byers, M., in *British Poetry Since 1960,* ed. M. Schmidt and G. Lindop (1972). MacCabe, C., in *Teaching the Text,* ed. S. Kappeler (1983). Morrison, B. *The Movement: English Poetry and Fiction of the 1950's* (1980). *The Poet Speaks,* ed. P. Orr (1966). Schmidt, M. *An Introduction to 50 Modern British Poets* (1979). Schofield, M. A. *NConL* (1983). Sturlz, E. Z., in *On Poetry and Poets, Fifth Series,* ed. J. Hogg (1983). Wheeler, M. *Hopkins Among the Poets: Studies in Modern Responses to Gerard Manley Hopkins* (1985).

For articles in reference works, see: *CA. CLC. CP. EWLTC. Feminist. MBL* and *SUP. TCW. WA.*

Other references: *British Book News* (May 1983). *Choice* (December 1976). *TES* (24 June 1983).

Paul Schlueter

Frances Power Cobbe

BORN: 4 December 1822, Newbridge, near Dublin.
DIED: 5 April 1904, Hengwrt, near Dolgelly, Wales.
DAUGHTER OF: Charles Cobbe and Frances Cobbe.

A feminist, suffragist, philanthropist, and antivivisectionist, as well as a prolific writer of pamphlets, articles, essays, and books on religion, philosophy, and social problems, C. was educated by private governesses at the home of her well-to-do family except for two years in a school at Brighton. Her reading was extensive; her preferences were history, astronomy, architecture, and heraldry. Aware of the inadequacies and waste of the female mind because of discrimination in education—her own father would not permit her brother to teach her Latin at home—C. advocated equal access to formal education for women, recommending the granting of university degrees. C. never married. She was deeply interested in theology during her life, becoming a heretic, a Christian, a theist, and finally a deist. Between 1852 and 1855 she wrote her first book, *The Theory of Intuitive Morals,* which she published anonymously to avoid the disapproval of her father.

After inheriting an income of £200 per year upon her father's death in 1857, C. began the first of many periods of foreign travel to Italy, Greece, Switzerland, and even Baalbec (in modern-day Lebanon). In 1864, she published the lively and fanciful *Italics: Brief Notes on Politics, People, and Places in Italy.* Between trips, she devoted much effort to improving conditions for juvenile delinquents, the destitute, and the sick. She was actively engaged in promoting women's suffrage and helped procure passage of the Married Women's Property Act. She was also an avid antivivisectionist. C. earned her livelihood working as a journalist for *The Daily News, Echo,* and *Standard,* publishing in the *Spectator, Economist, Quarterly Review, Fraser's Magazine, Macmillan's Magazine,* and others.

C. had personal contact with most of the major English figures of her day, such as Matthew Arnold, Robert Browning, John Stuart Mill, and Alfred Lord Tennyson (letters included in her autobiography); and several of her voluminous religious writings appeared in response to articles or statements by such writers. *The Hopes of the Human Race, Hereafter and Here* (1874) was an optimistic reply to Mill's "Essay on Religion." Her article "A Faithless World" (in *Nineteenth Century*) was written to counteract a remark by Sir Fitzjames Stephen that "we get on very well without religion" (she concluded that the absence of religion would change everything). C.'s *Darwinism in Morals and Other Essays* (1872), in its primary essay on Charles Darwin, which reviews his *Descent of Man,* argues that the moral history of mankind gives no support to Darwin's hypothesis that conscience arises from human development. Instead, C. asserts the validity of conscience as a divine transcript, reaffirming faith in a fixed and supreme law embodied in the will of God. *Broken Lights* (1864) also supports Christianity, defining its prospects and emphasizing Jesus's power in the world. Its sequel, *Dawning Lights* (1868), focuses on change in form and content in religion, (e.g., the method of theology, the idea of God and Christ, the doctrine of sin and concept of hell, and the approaches to happiness and death).

Although C.'s religious writings were popular, they are not original or profound. Typical of contemporary criticism are these words from the *Spectator* concerning *The Hopes of the Human Race, Hereafter and Here* (1874): "rather rhetorical lucubrations on the immortality of the soul, varied by a few not particularly original speculations regarding the conditions of the possible life of the future."

C. was most aggressive about women's rights. In her autobiography, she speculated concerning her grandfather's probable disapproval of her career; personally aware of the discrimination against women, she stated that she hoped to show in that book "how pleasant . . . and not altogether useless a life is open to women." In a similar vein, her most notable works, *Essays on the Pursuits of Women* (1863) and *The Duties of Women* (1881), focus on the roles of women. In *Essays,* she criticized the myth of "English domestic felicity," as evidenced by and in divorce courts; she analyzed the dilemma of the single woman, and she ridiculed the "dilettantish and ineffectual manner" of most upper-class women. *The Duties of Women* took immediate cognizance of the changes in society concerning women's attitudes, behavior, and status. Although C. approved of the new freedom of function of women, she noted also the difficulties inherent in contemporary concepts of right and duty. Advising caution, she advocated retention of the "old moral ideal" of motherhood, comparing mother-child love to that of God.

A social reformer, C. was more interested in substance than in literary style. She was an earnest, copious, and effective writer. She also edited the works of Theodore Parker, the American abolitionist and preacher.

WORKS: (Anon.) *The Theory of Intuitive Morals* (1855). *Essays on the Pursuits of Women* (1863). *Thanksgiving* (1863). *Religious Duty* (1864). *Broken Lights: An Inquiry into the Present Conditions and Future Prospects of Religious Faith* (1864). *The Cities of the Past* (1864). *Italics: Brief Notes on Politics, People, and Places in Italy in 1864* (1864). *Hours of Work and Play* (1867). *Dawning Lights, Secular Results of the New Reformation* (1868, 1984). *Darwinism in Morals and Other Essays* (1872). *Essays of Life and Death and the Evolution of Moral Sentiment* (1874). *The Hopes of the Human Race, Hereafter and Here* (1874). *False Beasts and True* (1876). *The Moral Aspects of Vivisection* (1875). *Re-Echoes* (1876). *The Duties of Women* (1881). *The Peak in Darien* (1882,1894). *The Scientific Spirit of the Age* (1888). *The Friend of Man: and His Friends, the Poets* (1889). *Health and Holiness* (1891). *Life, by Herself* (1894). Cobbe, F. *Life of Frances Power Cobbe,* ed. B. Atkinson (1904).

BIBLIOGRAPHY: Chappell, J. *Women of Worth* (1908). Hickok, K. *Representations of Women: Nineteenth-Century British Women's Poetry* (1984).

For articles in reference works, see: *Allibone. BA19C. BDBF. BDIW. Bloomsbury. Cambridge. CBEL. Chambers. CinP. DNB. Feminist. IDWB. Sanders. ToddBWW. VB. Warner.*

Other references: *Athenaeum* (12 October 1872, 28 November 1874). Frawley, M. H. *NCC* (1991). *LonT* (7 April 1904, 11 April 1904). *Men and Women of the Time,* 15th ed., ed. V. G. Pharr (1899). *Saturday Review* (1864). *Spectator* (1874, 1881, 1882).

Phyllis J. Scherle

Alicia (or Alison) Cockburn

BORN: 8 October 1713, Fairnalee, Selkirkshire, Scotland.
DIED: 22 November 1794, Edinburgh, Scotland.
DAUGHTER OF: Robert Rutherford.
MARRIED: Patrick Cockburn, 1731.

Known primarily during her lifetime for her sparkling wit, verse improvisations, and impromptu parodies, C. is now remembered for a ballad beginning "I've seen the smiling of Fortune beguiling," which shares the title (from the tune) "Flowers of the Forest" with a ballad written by Jean Elliot (1727–1805), who belonged to the Edinburgh legal circle C. joined after her marriage. The date of composition is not known, but it was before 1731, the year of her marriage to Patrick Cockburn of Ormiston, an Edinburgh lawyer.

Beautiful, vivacious, and intelligent, C. was a leader in Edinburgh aristocratic and legal circles for sixty years. Her charm was as legendary as her intelligence. Sir Walter Scott knew her as a relation and his mother's intimate friend; he described her, at six years of age, as "a virtuoso like myself." David Hume, the philosopher, frequently graced her drawing room, as did Lord James Burnett Monboddo, judge, anthropologist, and pre-Darwinian advocate of evolution. A staunch and outspoken Whig, C. lived through the 1745 uprising in Scotland and once was nearly apprehended by the Scottish guards with a comic attack on Prince Charles, "The Pretender's Manifesto," in her pocket.

The occasion for the composition of "Flowers of the Forest" is unclear. Custom has it that it was written to commemorate the financial ruin of neighbors in Selkirkshire; others attach it to the departure of a young man to whom C. was attached. Certainly it was written when C. was eighteen or younger, and it depicts a poignant sense of personal loss, which accounts for its survival; it has since been used, especially in reference to World War I, to describe the loss of gifted youth in battle, dying at the behest of "fickle Fortune." Scott says it is based on a fragment of an anonymous Border ballad commemorating the Battle of Flodden, which has long stood as a symbol of the weakening of society by destruction of its leading youth.

The authenticity of either the Elliot or the C. ballad was for a time a vexing question. Elliot's version, written in 1756, begins "I've heard them liltin' at the ewe-milkin'" and describes young peasant women, first happy in anticipation of their lovers' return and then grief-stricken at their loss. It is placed in the historical past and makes a direct political statement. C.'s, on the other hand, is a personal statement of individual loss with no overt political message other than that supplied by the melody. Possibly what accounts for the survival of the C. version is its literary quality and its more universal appeal. Comparing the last stanzas suggests the values of each: C.: "O fickle Fortune! / Why this cruel sporting? / O why thus perplex us, poor sons of a day? / Thy frown cannot fear me, / Thy smile cannot cheer me, / Since the Flowers of the Forest are a' wede away." Elliot's: "We'll hear nae mair liltin' at the ewe-milkin'; / Women and bairns are heartless and wae; / Sighin' and moanin' on ilka green loanin'— / The Flowers of the Forest are a' wede away."

WORKS: Three letters in *Letters of Eminent Persons Addressed to David Hume* (1749). "I've Seen the Smiling of Fortune's Beguiling," *The Lark* (1765), in *Letters and Memoirs, Felix, and Various Songs,* ed. T. Craig-Brown (1900). "Flowers of the Forest," in *Oxford Book of Eighteenth Century Verse* (1926) and *Book of Scottish Verse* (1983). "The Pretender's Manifesto," in *Love, Labour and Liberty: The Eighteenth Century Scottish Lyric,* ed. T. Crawford (1979).

BIBLIOGRAPHY: Crawford, T. *Society and the Lyric: A Study of the Song Culture of Eighteenth Century Scotland* (1979). Lockhart, J. *Memoirs of the Life of Sir Walter Scott* (1837–38). Scott, W. *Minstrelsy of the Scottish Border* (1802–1803).

For articles in reference works, see: *BAB1800. DNB. ELB. Feminist. NCHEL. Oxford Companion to Music,* 10th ed., ed. P. Scholes (1970). *ToddDBA.*

Eleanor Langstaff

Isabel Colegate

BORN: 10 September 1931, London.
DAUGHTER OF: Sir Arthur Colegate and Lady Colegate Worsley.
MARRIED: Michael Briggs, 1953.

Born into an aristocratic family, the daughter of a member of Parliament, C. has used a shrewd eye and acute ear to record the shifting relationships among the powerful, both titled and untitled, and not so powerful elements of English society at various times during the first half of the twentieth century. In a rather special sense, she is a historical novelist, a chronicler of life in England at critical times: In contrast to someone like Mary Renault who creates a language of legend from antiquity, C. explores the past, the English past, by integrating the idiom of genealogy within the language of fiction.

C., the youngest of four daughters, left school at the age of sixteen and chose not to go to university but to concentrate on writing. Her efforts resulted in a work as an assistant to Anthony Blond, a literary agent who turned publisher and printed C.'s first novel, *The Blackmailer,* in 1958. While all of her writing is concerned, to a greater or lesser extent, with the themes of money, class, power, and myth, their distinctions point to her evolution as a novelist. Indeed, they fall into clearly discernible groups: two trilogies (*The Blackmailer,* A *Man of Power,* and *The Great Occasion,* published separately but reissued as a trilogy by Penguin in 1984; and *Orlando King, Orlando at the Brazen Threshold,* and *Agatha,* also published separately but reissued as a trilogy by Penguin in 1984) and three novels that chronicle the impact of war on life among the upper classes of English society (*Statues in a Garden, News from the City of the Sun,* and *The Shooting Party*). C.'s most recent work includes a collection of short stories, *A Glimpse of Sion's Glory* (1985), something of a departure for her, and two novels, *Deceits of Time* (1988) and *The Summer of the Royal Visit* (1991).

In her foreword to the Penguin reprint of her first three novels, C. notes that "these three seem to me now to be the ones I wrote instinctively and without difficulty." From the reader's point of view, this is somewhat difficult to accept since narrative predictability, stylistic awkwardness, unimaginative character development, and, particularly in the case of *The Great Occasion,* an obvious and rather intrusive concern for technique create problems and sometimes diminish the pleasures of the text.

In *The Blackmailer,* C. tells the story of Judith Lane and Baldwin Rees. Judith, widow of Korean war hero Anthony Lane, keeps alive the myth of his valor in battle. Rees, who had served under Lane, confronts Judith with the "real" story: Lane had been a coward; now Rees's threat to sell the story to a newspaper provokes Judith to pay him off. Not satisfied, Rees returns for more money but soon the relationship changes and the blackmail stops. Rees has fallen in love with Judith, and for a time she is fascinated by him. Though somewhat tentative and afflicted with overwriting, syntactical awkwardness, and rather abrupt, implausible character changes, *The Blackmailer* introduces what will be dominant themes for C.—money, class, and power.

These same concerns appear in C.'s next novel, *A Man of Power,* a work reminiscent of Henry James's *The Awkward Age,* to which direct reference is made at one point. Here the upper-class young woman being educated is Vanessa, daughter of Lady Essex Cooper, who narrates the story of her mother's involvement with Lewis Ogden, "the man of power." Ogden divorces his wife in order to marry Essex, but his discovery of her with another lover in his own house terminates the relationship. C.'s use of Vanessa as the first-person narrator makes *A Man of Power* at once more assured and engaging than *The Blackmailer.*

C. regards her third novel, *The Great Occasion,* as her most technically successful effort. It is an ambitious autobiographical work as well, for C. tells the story of the five daughters of Gabriel Dodson, a wealthy but bland financier. Dodson's daughters mature in the England of the 1950s when traditional values and roles were just beginning to shift; within this context, each daughter searches for her own niche. The results are devastating: The eldest sacrifices herself to advance her husband's political career; the next suffers a mental breakdown; the third becomes a sexual athlete of sorts; the fourth abandons her own career as an artist to support her husband's; only the fifth seems, at novel's end, to be independent and functioning. Yet the sheer narrative weight of trying to trace the careers of one man and his five daughters through two decades of turbulent history burdens this novel; even if C. is given the benefit of the doubt, by suggesting that her focus on the life patterns of these six figures may be a means of exploring gender and class, she cannot handle such a trope deftly. At this stage of her career, such a task lay beyond the range of C.'s technical powers.

And, indeed, it seems that C. might have recognized this, for her next novel, *Statues in a Garden,* while related thematically to her first three, is a departure in stylistic terms. Here, C. focuses her attention on the Weston family during the fateful summer of 1914. Sir Aylmer Weston, a prominent Liberal politician and member of Anthony Asquith's cabinet, is married to Lady Cynthia, a stylish hostess who is the mother of his two children. They are very much a part of a gracious Edwardian world of power and privilege, but this world collapses when Aylmer's nephew and adopted son, Philip, seduces Cynthia. Aylmer kills himself, and Philip leaves Cynthia, who becomes an aging and pathetic sexual adventuress. Philip, who tried to join Aylmer's world of money and leisure by going to work for a shady financial speculator and by acquiring an aristocratic mistress, represents the role of business and new money. His rapaciousness is one powerful metaphor for those new forces that brought an end to a golden world.

With the three novels of the "Orlando Trilogy," C. returned to the best of her previous novels, combining extraordinarily perceptive character insight with richly atmospheric and identifiable historical context in order to craft a far more satisfying narrative. One critic, Ariel Swartley, has put it succinctly, and accurately, by calling the trilogy "Colegate's English Oedipal cycle . . . with Sophocles' Fate in a tweed toga." In *Orlando King,* the twenty-one-year-old protagonist, after a sheltered upbringing on an island off the coast of Brittany, establishes a brilliant business career for himself in the London of the 1930s. When asked, "Coming here as a stranger, did anything in particular strike you as a surprise?" Orlando answers, "The importance of class, I think, and the amount people talk about it," and thereby reveals the dominant concern in all of C.'s fiction. Unwittingly, Orlando marries his father's widow, Judith, whose failed attempt at suicide causes her complete breakdown. Orlando discovers his father's identity; partially blinded in the bombing of London, he forsakes his business and political careers and goes into exile.

C. details the last several months of Orlando's life in *Orlando at the Brazen Threshold,* enriching the narrative with interior monologue, flashback sequences, and precise delineation of diverse characters. Orlando returns to the island on which he had been brought up and penetrates some of the mysterious circumstances of his early life. In the course of the novel he is reunited with his daughter, Agatha, returns to London for a brief visit, and retires to Tuscany where he dies. Like its predecessor, which is set in 1951, *Agatha* has a precise temporal context; unlike that one, this novel's plot makes use of significant historical events.

All three novels in this trilogy are marked by a certain tentativeness and ambiguity, which, rather than being flaws, may well be understood as stylistic emblems for the difficulties of perception and determination in the modern world. More than the parts of the first trilogy, these three novels must be read together in order to appreciate fully the dynamics of character carefully set in motion by C. as she tells us that an awareness of the complexities of human behavior in the modern situation may be all we can hope for.

By mid-career a pattern of alternating between novels using history as setting and plot and novels using contemporary events to establish a grid for psychologically driven plots emerges. Her next novel, *News from the City of the Sun,* explores patterns of human activity within a specific historical context, this time England from 1931 until the early 1970s. Three brothers have established a kind of utopian community on the grounds of an unused abbey, gathering members who are distinctly representative of the times. A young female narrator, though participating in some of the novel's activities, remains essentially detached and clear sighted in presenting a story of class conflicts and power games played during these particularly volatile decades of English history.

C.'s most technically assured novel to date, *The Shooting Party* (1980), earned her not only the W. H. Smith Literary Award but also a wider audience when it became a movie with John Gielgud and James Mason. C. chronicles one weekend in autumn 1913 on the Oxfordshire estate of Sir Randolph Nettleby, with the guests, drawn from the ranks of the aristocracy and the affluent, assembled for a weekend of shooting, sherry, and sexual intrigue. The accidental shooting of one of the beaters (a member of the household staff who was to strike bushes and other ground cover in order to rouse game) changes the mood while providing the occasion for telling responses from each of the guests. Such a novel could easily become a static *Grand Hotel* or *Ship of Fools* piece were it not for C.'s ability to endow the narrative with psychological plausibility, technical finesse, and historical dimension.

C.'s next work, *A Glimpse of Sion's Glory,* a collection of three stories, represents neither consolidation of her powers nor real artistic growth. The stories are of uneven quality. The first, "The Girl Who Lived Among Artists," depicts a *menage à trois* consisting of Nancy, a young bohemian from a well-to-do family, and two laborers, Vere and Carley. Told years after their summer together in a boarding house, this tale of seduction and betrayal had the darkly appealing quality of a fairy tale, which makes it the only successful piece in the collection. With "Distant Cousins," a science fiction tale about a race of four-fingered humanoids, C. has offered a rather too familiar narrative weighted down by the trappings of unsuccessful parable. The title story, a parallel-lives' tale of Alison and Raymond, is an uninspired exercise tracing her youth and marriage and his crazy-quilt adventures after leaving Oxford. Raymond's career, narrated in a letter to Alison, follows the stereotypic "bright promise unfulfilled" scheme. As such, it might well serve as an appropriate metaphor for this collection.

Deceits of Time (1988), an elegant if perhaps over-crafted fiction that dwells typically on large questions of history, identity, class, and memory, takes as its ostensible subject the writing of biography. An undistinguished author with several thin volumes to her credit, Catherine Hillery, is the writer, and Neil Campion, World War I flying ace and undistinguished Conservative member of Parliament, is the subject. The trustees of the Campion estate have chosen Catherine because she is "conscientious and unprejudiced [and] . . . sound"; in sum, she is competent and safe to craft a bit of hagiography. As she searches for Campion's "real" life, Catherine investigates archives and interviews Campion's family, friends, and associates. In the process she becomes painfully aware of the unreliability of memory—others' and her own. Colegate's greatest technical strength in the novel, which is characteristically fine in its delineation of character within a richly developed historical context, is her subtle use of memory to link the writer's professional task with her own existential dilemma. The quest turns out to be dual, a search for the "real" Neal Campion and for the "real" Catherine Hillery. Though *Deceits of Time* is an imperfect fiction (the linking of major and minor plots depends too heavily on coincidence; minor characters, particularly Campion's widow, Effie, nearly steal the show), it is a brilliant illumination of what Anita Brookner has called "the flawed nature of England between the wars," an unpleasant truth that lives on in figures like Lord and Lady Sturmers who speak fondly of the Ribbentrops forty years after Auschwitz.

Ultimately, *The Summer of the Royal Visit,* with its deliberate allusion to John Fowles's *The French Lieutenant's Woman,* is an exercise in attempting to recapture a past that cannot—or will not—be recaptured. As the present-day narrator concludes, "There's seldom a single explanation for anything." What C. does in *The Summer of the Royal Visit* she has done before, and better, in *The Shooting Party;* nonetheless, her very considerable abilities shape this later novel into a moving meditation on history, narrative, cultural dislocation, and the fashioning of human identity.

WORKS: *The Blackmailer* (1958). *A Man of Power* (1960). *The Great Occasion* (1962). *Statues in a Garden* (1964). *Orlando King* (1968). *Orlando at the Brazen Threshold* (1971). *Agatha* (1973). *News from the City of the Sun* (1979). *The Shooting Party* (1980). *A Glimpse of Sion's Glory* (1985). *Deceits of Time* (1988). *The Summer of the Royal Visit* (1991). *Winter Journey* (1995).

BIBLIOGRAPHY: Averitt, B., in *Contemporary British Women Writers: Texts and Strategies,* ed. R. E. Hosmer, Jr. (1993). Lambert, A. *Independent* (25 September 1991).

For articles in reference works, see: *CA. CLC. CN. DLB. Oxford. ToddBWW.*

Other references: *BW* (13 July 1981, 3 September 1989, 8 February 1992). *CSM* (5 October 1984). *Guardian* (13 February 1981). *Harper's* (April 1966, May 1969). *HudR* (1984). *Listener* (27 August 1964, 30 May 1985). *London Magazine* (February-March 1974). *LRB* (18 July 1985). *LonT* (18 February 1980, 12 February 1981, 6 February 1985). *Los Angeles Times Book Review* (27 May 1984). *New Republic* (18 April 1981, 28 May 1984). *New Statesman* (4 May 1962, 21 August 1964, 20 September 1968, 13 July 1979, 12 September 1980, 25 October 1991). *New Yorker* (25 May 1981, 23 January 1989). *NYTBR* (11 December 1988, 8 March 1992, 5 February 1995). *Observer* (1 July 1969, 23 May 1971, 13 February 1981, 9 June 1985, 4 September 1988, 15 September 1991). *PW* (3 February 1984). *Saturday Review* (May 1981). *Spectator* (29 January 1960, 21 July 1979, 13 September 1980, 8 June 1985, 10 September 1988, 18 March 1989, 14 September 1991). Swartley, A. *VLS* (December 1985). *TLS* (28 October 1964, 19 September 1968, 20 May 1971, 5 October 1973, 4 December 1979, 12 September 1980, 25 April 1985, 21 June 1985, 2 September 1988, 13 September 1991). *VQR* (Autumn 1981).

Robert Ellis Hosmer, Jr.

Ann Raney Thomas Coleman

BORN: 5 November 1810, Whitehaven, Cumberland.
DIED: March 1897, Cuero, Texas.
DAUGHTER OF: John Raney.
MARRIED: John Thomas, 1833; John Coleman, c. 1848.

C. is known for her single autobiographical work. She was born to a well-to-do family in Whitehaven, Cumberland, and her early life was one of privilege. Her father was heir to £50,000 and her mother was the daughter of a rich merchant. C. attended "the best boarding schools" until her father's bankruptcy. Then she, her two brothers, and her sister went to live with their uncle and aunt who enrolled them in a neighborhood school in Newcastle.

C. and her mother later opened a genteel boarding house in Liverpool, where she became romantically attached to Henry Marks. Since Marks was Jewish, the romance was discouraged by C.'s relatives. However, C. showed the sort of courage that was to stand her in good stead later. She continued her close relationship with Marks until her departure for America, at which time he gave her a ring and "his picture in water colours on ivory."

C.'s father and one brother had emigrated to Texas earlier from Liverpool (her brother died shortly after their arrival). C. and her mother and sister sailed for Texas on the merchant vessel *St. George.* Off the coast of Cuba, they were accosted by pirates, who took all the ship's provisions. C. and her family hid in a closet during the raid and thus escaped the pirates' notice. The family arrived in Brazoria, Texas, shortly before the outbreak of the Texas War for Independence.

In 1832, the Battle of Velasco took place near Brazoria, and C. "sat the most of two nights and days moulding bullets and making bullet patches." Apparently C. also delivered the bullets to the combatants, because, in a letter to Governor Roberts, she says she took the bullets "on my horse 15 miles, to Mr. Bertrand's ranch for our men to come after them. I was pursued by two spies, but had the best horse and made my excape." The Texans were victorious in this opening skirmish of the Texas War for Independence, a war that was to force C. and her family to leave Texas.

C.'s parents died after the Battle of Velasco and she married John Thomas in "the first public wedding in Brazoria." A son was born before the family fled Texas in the wake of General Houston's retreat. They settled in Louisiana, where two more children were born. C.'s husband and both her sons died, and she subsequently married John Coleman, a local storekeeper. Coleman proved to be "unjust and cruel," and C. was very unhappy with her second marriage. The Colemans left Louisiana and moved back to Texas, settling near Matagorda. Later, C. returned to England to try to reclaim her father's estate, but the attempt failed. Upon her return to Texas, her husband became even more abusive. C. divorced him in September 1855 and for the rest of her life was self-supporting. She taught school for many years but was reduced to poverty in her old age. She wrote that she did not have the money to pay the expenses of paper and postage in order to send her memoirs to her niece.

Her memoirs are her only extant book, though C. does mention three other books that she had written for Mrs. Clara Stanton, who was apparently acting as her literary agent. She also wrote a journal of her first Atlantic crossing that she sent to Henry Marks. Though marred by phonetic spelling and inadequate punctuation, C.'s autobiography is a lively, and sometimes lyrical, account of the hardships and pleasures of the American frontier, where the women were as hardy and independent as the men.

WORKS: *A Victorian Lady on the Texas Frontier,* ed. C. R. King (1971). *A Victorian Lady on the Texas Frontier. Reminiscence of Ann Raney Thomas Coleman* (typescript at University of Texas, Austin; original manuscript at Duke University).

BIBLIOGRAPHY:

For articles in reference works, see: *BioIn.*

Sharon A. Winn

Mary Elizabeth Coleridge

BORN: 23 September 1861, London.
DIED: 25 August 1907, Harrogate, Yorkshire.
DAUGHTER OF: Arthur Duke Coleridge and Mary Anne Coleridge.
WROTE UNDER: Anodos; Avoos; Mary Elizabeth Coleridge.

C., the great-great niece of Samuel Taylor Coleridge, was called "the tail of the comet S.T.C." A somewhat enigmatic person, C. was shy and disliked meeting strangers, preferring to remain in her room and indulge her romantic imagination. Yet she was a close, loyal friend, easily overlooking people's flaws. Despite a sensitive, bookish nature, she had a merry disposition. While being educated at home, she learned Greek, French, Italian, German, and Hebrew. C. was fascinated with the age of chivalry and in her youth eagerly read Sir Walter Scott and Thomas Malory. By the age of thirteen, she began writing poetry; however, she paid little attention to her writing, instead choosing to concentrate on her painting. Although she enjoyed traveling, especially in Italy, C.'s home was the center of her life. She lived a quiet youth with her father, mother, sister, and aunt. Her father, clerk of the Assize to the Midland Circuit, entertained such guests as Alfred Lord Tennyson, Robert Browning, John Ruskin, Anthony Trollope, Frances Kemble, Jenny Lind, Henry Newbolt, Robert Bridges, and William Cory, who became her close friend and teacher.

C. began writing essays for *Monthly Review, Guardian,* and other periodicals when she was twenty. From 1902 until her death, she wrote articles for the *Times Literary Supplement.* As a critic, she could be prejudiced and become obsessed with details, but she praised Claude Monet, Auguste Renoir, and Henrik Ibsen before they became fashionable. She also wrote stories for *Cornhill Magazine.*

In 1893, she published *Seven Sleepers of Ephesus,* which describes seven young men's adventures. The novel, like much of her fiction, begins well but becomes bogged down near the middle. Robert Louis Stevenson was impressed with the book, although admitting halfway through it, "If she does get out, she is devilish ingenious." C.'s fiction is hampered by weak plot construction and improbable happenings; her interest is largely in dramatic action.

Bridges helped arrange the publication of *Fancy's Following* (1896), a thin volume of forty-eight short lyrics. This was followed by another volume of poetry, *Fancy's Gordon* (1897), which contained many of the poems in *Fancy's Following*. Her poems, now considered to be her greatest achievement, are restrained and dignified. As Bridges notes, they show a "delicate harmony," are "sincere and mysterious," and have a "natural and simple expression." He further states that she "brought to her poetry . . . a great literary appetite, knowledge, and memory—a wide sympathy, tenderness of feeling, and profound spirituality—and a humour which such seriousness and devotion of life as were hers can hardly be made palatable in literature." Walter de la Mare, whom she befriended, said her poems read "as though she hardly called before they answered."

However, it was *The King with Two Faces* (1897), a historical romance based on the life of King Gustav III of Sweden, that established her reputation during her lifetime. She followed this with a collection of essays, *Non Sequitur* (1900); a novel, *The Fiery Dawn* (1901); a romance, *The Shadow on the Wall* (1904), concerning the Duchess de Berri; and a novel, *The Lady on the Drawing-Room Floor* (1906). A biography, *Holman Hunt,* written at the artist's request, was published in 1908, after her death.

Despite claiming, "I hate Philanthropy," C. worked with the poor for several years, influenced by her reading of Leo Tolstoy. From 1895 on, she was a teacher at the Working Woman's College. Her dry wit can be seen in a lecture on Queen Elizabeth: "Queen Elizabeth, when first she saw the light of day, was a great disappointment. She was a girl—she ought to have been a boy." C. died of acute appendicitis in 1907. Her students were so fond of her that they disbanded on her death rather than accept a new teacher.

WORKS: *The Seven Sleepers of Ephesus* (1893). (as Avoos) *Fancy's Following* (1896). *The King with Two Faces* (1897). (as Anodos) *Fancy's Gordon* (1897). *Non Sequitur* (1900). *The Fiery Dawn* (1901). *The Shadow on the Wall* (1904). *The Lady on the Drawing-Room Floor* (1906). *Holman Hunt* (1908). *Poems,* ed. H. Newbolt (1908). *Gathered Leaves from the Prose of Mary E. Coleridge, with a memoir by E. Sichel* (1910; includes six unpublished poems). *The Collected Poems of Mary Coleridge,* ed. T. Whistler (1954).

BIBLIOGRAPHY: Bridges, R. *Cornhill Magazine* (November 1907; rpt. in *Collected Essays,* 1931). Gilbert, S. and S. Gubar. *Madwoman in the Attic: The Woman Writers and the Nineteenth Century Literary Imagination* (1979). Reilly, J. J. *Of Books and Men* (1942). Sichel, E. *Memoir in Gathered Leaves from the Prose of Mary Elizabeth Coleridge* (1910). Whistler, T., intro. to *The Collected Poems of Mary Coleridge* (1954).

For articles in reference works, see: *Feminist. Todd-BWW.*

Other references: *Nation* (12 September 1907).

Louis J. Parascandola

Sara Coleridge

BORN: 22 December 1802, Greta Hall, near Keswick, Cumberland.
DIED: 3 May 1852, Chester Place, Regent's Park, London.
DAUGHTER OF: Samuel Taylor Coleridge and Sarah Fricker.
MARRIED: Henry Nelson Coleridge, 1829.

The daughter of the distinguished poet and critic, C. spent her formative years in the presence of such famous literary men as Robert Southey, her uncle, and William Wordsworth, her father's intimate friend. She was celebrated by Wordsworth, along with Dora Wordsworth and Edith Southey, in his poem "The Triad"; she, in turn, dedicated her edition of the *Biographia Literaria* to Wordsworth, calling herself his "child in heart, and faithful friend" in the inscription.

C.'s first literary endeavor was a three-volume translation from the Latin of Martin Dobrizhoffer's *Account of the Abipones, an Equestrian People of Paraguay* (1822), published anonymously and initially conceived as a means of defraying her brother Derwent's college expenses. Her next work, published in 1825, was a translation of the "Loyal Servant's" memoirs of the Chevalier Bayard. In 1829, she married Henry Nelson Coleridge, her barrister cousin, by whom she had a son and a daughter. After her marriage, she turned briefly to original writing, although the scope of this work was influenced by her new domestic role as a mother. Her first creative production, *Pretty Lessons in Verse for Good Children* (1834), consisted of short pieces of poetry addressed to her children, partly for moral guidance and partly for instruction in Latin and other subjects. The fairy tale *Phantasmion,* her only work of fiction, followed in 1837.

With the death of her husband, C. turned her attention to the work he had begun as her father's literary executor—the collection, annotation, and publication of the literary remains of Samuel Taylor Coleridge. The last ten years of her life were devoted to this editorial enterprise, and the results included the *Biographia Literaria, Notes and Lectures Upon Shakespeare and Some of the Old Poets and Dramatists,* and *Essays on His Own Times.* Her learning and her energies were poured into the preparation of notes, prefaces, and appendices rather than into original productions. As her American correspondent and memoirist Henry Reed stated, in this labor dedicated to the memory of a father and a husband, she expended "an amount of original thought and an affluence of learning which, differently and more prominently presented, would have made her famous." The range of C.'s intellect, however, can be judged by a representative letter to Reed in which she discusses her editorial work, her daily domestic life, John Ruskin's aesthetic theories, the death of Sir Robert Peel, and the theological dogma of baptismal regeneration.

Although much of her work commemorates her father, C. reveals her remarkable creative powers in *Phantasmion.* The *Quarterly Review* praised it as "pure as a crystal in diction, tinted like an opal with the hues of an everspringing sunlit fancy." The fairy tale relates the adventures of Phantasmion, the young prince of Palmland, who loses his mother Queen Zalia and his father King Dorimant at an early age. The fairy Potentilla, the queen of the insect realm, watches over Phantasmion and invests him with a succession of insect-like attributes—from wings to feet with suction power—for his explorations of the hostile neighboring kingdom of Rockland. Potentilla also aids Phantasmion in his pursuit of Iarine, the beautiful daughter of the King of Rockland. She is also loved by Glandreth, a fearless but treacherous warrior, and Karadan, a youth who possesses the charmed vessel that controls her fate. The military and amatory exploits of the mortals are complicated by the intervention of good, evil, and fickle spirits—the water witch Seshelma; Feydeleen, the Spirit of the Flowers; Oloola, the Spirit of the Blast—who exist in a complex web of allegiances, counterallegiances, vows, and betrayals, not only to one another but also to the rival mortals.

Phantasmion reveals C.'s striking prose style. Its lush, luxuriant descriptions are replete with vivid, sensuous details and exotic, fantastical images. C.'s presentation of the water witch Seshelma expresses this combination of particularity and whimsey: "[Phantasmion] perceived a strange woman's form rising out of the waves, and gliding towards the beach: a wreath of living, moving flowers, like sea-anemones, clung round her head, from which the slimy locks of whitish blue hung down till they met the waters." The power and charm of *Phantasmion* lies in the fact that it is very much a fairy tale: It resists moralizing intrusions, and its fancifulness and inventiveness never succumb to allegory.

WORKS: (trans.) *Account of the Abipones, an Equestrian People of Paraguay,* by M. Dobrizhoffer (1822). (trans.) *The Right Joyous and Pleasant History of the Feats, Gests, and Prowesses of the Chevalier Bayard,* by "The Loyal Servant" (1825). *Pretty Lessons in Verse for Good Children* (1834). *Phantasmion* (1837). *Biographia Literaria,* by S. T. Coleridge prepared in part by H. N. Coleridge and completed by S. Coleridge (1847). *Notes and Lectures Upon Shakespeare and Some of the Old Poets and Dramatists,* by S. T. Coleridge, ed. S. Coleridge (1849). *Essays on His Own Times,* by S. T. Coleridge, ed. S. Coleridge (1850). *The Poems of Samuel Taylor Coleridge,* ed. D. Coleridge and S. Coleridge (1852).

BIBLIOGRAPHY: Broughton, L. N. *Sara Coleridge and Henry Reed* (1937). Cervo, N. *VN* (1990). *Memoir and Letters of Sara Coleridge,* ed. E. Coleridge (1873). Coleridge, J. D., preface to *Phantasmion* (1874). Lefebure, M., in *Coleridge's Imagination: Essays in Memory of Pete Laver,* ed. R. Gravil, et al. (1985). Mudge, B. K. *LCUT* (1983). Mudge, B. K. *WC* (1984). Mudge, B. K. *TSWL* (1986). Mudge, B. K. *W&L* (1988). Mudge, B. K. *Sara Coleridge, A Victorian Daughter: Her Life and Writings* (1989). Mudge, B. K., in *Women's Writing in Exile,* ed. M. L. Broe and A. Ingram (1989). Neverow-Turk, V. *VWM* (1990).

For articles in reference works, see: *BA19C. Bloomsbury. Cambridge. Feminist. Oxford. ToddBWW.*

Eileen Finan
(updated by Natalie Joy Woodall)

Mary Collier

BORN: 1690 (?).
DIED: 1762 (?).

The "Washer-Woman" turned poet, the self-described "Old Maid" who ran a farmhouse at Alton, in Hampshire, the defender of laboring-class women from the attacks of the notorious poet Stephen Duck, C. occupies a hazy but intriguing place in recent scholarly efforts to recuperate the contributions of working-class women writers. She offered a brief account of her "toilsome" life in an autobiographical sketch attached to *Poems on Several Occasions* (1762). After an upbringing of rural labor, she moved to Petersfield, in Hampshire. Her first published work, an epistle to Duck, defends the character of rural women against Duck's charges of "idleness." The advertisement attached to *The Woman's Labour* suggests that the "Novelty of a *Washer-Woman's* turning Poetess" might procure her financial reward. However, a washer-woman she remained until spending most of her sixties running a farmhouse. At about seventy, she retired to a "Garret" in Alton.

Donna Landry believes *The Woman's Labour* gives voice to "an emergent working-class consciousness with an emergent feminist critique of the misogynist tendencies embedded in that consciousness." Like other poets, such as Mary Leapor, who have recently received critical reevaluation, C. provides an early instance of working-class women taking on the dominant literary culture, in this case personified by the poet Duck—using established aesthetic forms to issue a radical protest against the oppression of working-class women. In *The Woman's Labour,* C. writes, "All the Perfections Woman once could boast, / Are quite obscur'd, and altogether lost." Hers is a fight against such obscurity, with the celebrated Duck her target: "And you, Great Duck, upon whose happy Brow / The Muses seem to fix their Garland now." C.'s conventional apologia for writing includes the facts of her personal hardship, but also the notion that her poem had attracted attention in manuscript form: "It soon Became a Town Talk," and she decided "to call an Army of Amazons to vindicate the injur'd Sex."

Landry also comments on the problem of learning as it is made manifest in C.'s poetry and in "Some Remarks of the Author's Life." Reading and writing are, for this single woman, virtually her sole source of recreation. The fact that women like C. were typically denied an education in itself seemed to exclude their validation, as C. suggests in "An Epistolary answer to an Exciseman, Who doubted her being the Author of the Washerwoman's Labour." Like many of her contemporaries, C. saw women's education as the key to social equality, yet her own faith in her writing, humble as her personae tend to be, remains assertive and hopeful.

Until the end of the twentieth century, the contest between C. and the "Great Duck" has been a literary-historical choice between obscurity and infamy, Duck becoming the embodiment of the failed poet. After two and a half centuries, though, it appears that C. is emerging triumphant: Duck's reputation will almost certainly never recover; C. on the other hand, has become a significant figure in the historiography of early British feminism.

WORKS: *The Woman's Labour: An Epistle to Mr. Stephen Duck* (1739). *Poems on Several Occasions* (1762).

BIBLIOGRAPHY: Ferguson, M. *First Feminists* (1985). Ferguson, M. *Eighteenth-Century Women Poets: Nation, Class, and Gender* (1995). Landry, D., in *The New Eighteenth Century*, ed. F. Nussbaum and L. Brown (1987). *Eighteenth-Century Women Poets*, ed. R. Lonsdale (1990).

Richard C. Taylor

Ann Collins

FLOURISHED: the mid-seventeenth century.

C.'s name is known through a single volume of poetry, *Divine Songs and Meditaciones* (1653), of which only one copy remains extant. What makes that volume particularly interesting is its biographical content. C. narrates a spiritual history that, by avoiding the more conventional disguises of persona or invented characters, is direct, immediate, and personal. As such, it gives us valuable insight into the spiritual experiences of seventeenth-century women. It also suggests, by implication, that the English meditative tradition in poetry is more varied, in form and content, than otherwise assumed.

In one of the few references to it, the volume, in the Huntington Library, has been noted as "so rare as to be probably unique" (Griffith), and it has been reprinted (in an Augustan Society reprint) in an abridged facsimile edition (1961). The rather undistinguished nature of the volume, a small octavo, about five by three inches, bound in thick, brown calf, with 102 pages of text, implies that the original seventeenth-century printing was probably a small one. It may have been commissioned either by C. herself or by a relative because C. makes clear in her dedicatory epistle, "To the Reader," that her purpose, not simply in writing but in publishing her verse, is her concern that her own spiritual autobiography serve "the benefit, and comfort of others Cheifly those Christians who are of disconsolat Spirits."

C. evidently knew something about what it was to be a "disconsolat Spirit," as she tells us that the stimulus for her writing was an acute physical illness that she probably suffered throughout her life. In the central poem, "The Discourse," C. says that "Even in my Cradle did my Crosses breed," and the depression and melancholy that resulted from that chronic illness were side effects that she struggled unsuccessfully to repress. "Of myself," she tells us, "I never could alay" her own depression. Evidently the emotional and spiritual consequences of her illness were even more acute than the physical pain.

C. describes in some detail the efforts she made to combat depression. Reading, even the seventeenth-century equivalent of escape literature that she describes as "plesant histories," was particularly frustrating as it promised a relief that she soon found to be only temporary. All such "mocions of delight" were brief: "they quickly were disperced every one. / Whereas my minde it self would much torment. / Vpon the rack of restless discontent."

What delivered C. from her torment was an unexpected religious experience, not, however, what we (or she) would describe as a conversion. Instead, by simply shifting from secular reading to the reading of scripture, an act which she describes as occurring through the gift of "grace," she began to find the peace she had been seeking. The reading of scripture, she tells us, at last supplied the "matter" for her soul to "feed" upon, and recovery was at hand.

This spiritual experience, while of life-saving import to C., might seem of small interest to us in the twentieth century. What makes C.'s volume fascinating, however, is the detail and range of emotion she brings to bear on that experience. She makes it quite clear, for example, that it is not enough simply to read scripture, her spiritual experience also compels her to write and rewards her for doing so. "The thing it self [i.e., writing poetry]," she tells her readers, "appeared to me so amiable, as that it enflamed my faculties, to put forth themselvs, in a practice so pleasing." The discipline of verse, then, is an absorbing mental exercise that she values. The published verse, in turn, suggests that she was evidently successful in teaching herself that discipline as the verse itself implies a practiced poet, particularly skillful in handling metric. Its metrical schemes vary from rhyme royal to a variety of stanzaic patterns, some innovative and some derived from the traditional forms associated with songs, ballads, and translations and imitations of the Psalms.

Additionally, C. makes it clear that her central purpose in publishing her poems is not simply to record a spiritual epiphany but rather to impress the reader fully with both the demanding and the fulfilling nature of the life she has chosen. It is this theme to which she gives her greatest sustained attention throughout the poems. What follows from faith is as important as faith itself because, as she points out, without hard work and close attention, spiritual ecstatic experience is no more lasting than its secular equivalents.

Each of the poems, then, details some facet of the spiritual life as experienced by a seventeenth-century woman faced with serious emotional and physical challenges. As such it is certainly of interest to historians since C.'s religious orientation is traditionally Protestant in its emphasis on scripture and on the application of the Word of God to the self, with a Calvinist emphasis on the doctrines of the elect and of total depravity. Nevertheless, C. backs away from too rigid an application of these harsh Calvinist doctrines by giving her greatest emphasis to grace and to the process of faith.

In the clarity and unmediated directness of her verse, C. offers us an alternative to the religious lyrics of the male writers of this period whom we may be more accustomed to reading. Her gifts of attention to her own spiritual state unmediated by a persona, to doctrine and scripture as viable and sustainable sources of emotional response, to modulations of tone from reflection to exaltation and back again, and to the role of metrics in the creation of such variations in tone—all extend the category of "the seventeenth-century religious lyric" in both form and content. Her verse is thus a tribute to what a writer working outside an inherited tradition can accomplish and a welcome supplement to what we already know of the powers of seventeenth-century meditative poetry.

WORKS: *Divine Songs and Meditacions* (1653).

BIBLIOGRAPHY: *Divine Songs and Meditacions,* ed. S. Stewart (1961).

Other references: *DLB* (1993). *Bibliotheca Anglo-Poetica,* ed. A. E. Griffith (1815). Graham, E., et al. *Her Own Life: Autobiographical Writings by Seventeenth-Century Englishwomen* (1989). *Kissing the Rod: An Anthology of Seventeenth-Century Women's Verse,* ed. G. Greer et al. (1988). *Women Poets in English,* ed. A. Stanford (1972).

Ann Hurley

Mary Mitchell Collyer

BORN: 1716–17.

DIED: December 1762 or January 1763, Islington, London.

MARRIED: Joseph Collyer.

C.'s few books were published anonymously, often "printed for" Joseph Collyer, her compiler/translator husband. From her translations of French and German texts and from the cleverness of her epistolary novel, we can guess that C. was well educated, though nothing is known of her early life.

As a contemporary of Samuel Richardson, C. offers intriguing possibilities of influence. Her first known publication, a translation of Pierre Marivaux's *La Vie de Marianne,* which Ronald Paulson dates from 1735, remained a standard English version well into the 1880s. C.'s preface to *The Virtuous Orphan* particularly recommends the novel in "English dress" to female readers, and it was perhaps with this audience in mind that she translated a mere third of Marivaux's text, adding a redemptive conclusion in which a penitent Valville marries Marianne. Richardson's *Pamela,* published five years later, was similarly sentimental, its servant girl also converting her would-be seducer to the respectability of "husband."

No source has been discovered for C.'s second "translation," *Memoirs of the Countess de Bressol* (1743), which may simply be a series of tales she connected with her own moralizing passages. If this is so, its formalistic shortcomings may have prompted her writing of *Felicia to Charlotte,* the first volume of which appeared in 1744.

C. published her epistolary novel three years after Richardson's *Pamela;* realizing there could be no more than one servant girl raised to high life, she chose her characters from polite society, anticipating Richardson's practice in *Clarissa* (1748) and *Sir Charles Grandison* (1753). The second volume of *Felicia to Charlotte* (1749) appeared one year after *Clarissa,* and, as Richardson's sequel continues Pamela's story after marriage, so C.'s novel presents the domestic life of her characters.

Quite apart from the teasing question of its relationship to Richardson's novels, *Felicia to Charlotte* not only is one of the better minor novels of its time but it also anticipates the pattern women's fiction was to take for the next several decades. The novel begins with Felicia's promise "to discover all the secret folds" of her heart in correspondence with her friend, Charlotte, who remains in London while Felicia pays a visit to her aunt in the country. The correspondence is largely one-sided, yet it maintains the semblance of a conversation, both in its familiar tone and in its response to the figured letters we do not see. Felicia's history in this first volume—the remove from home, courtship, and marriage—assumes a course many feminocentric novels (e.g., the Harriet Byron portion of *Sir Charles Grandison)* were to follow. The novelist's sensibility, her appreciation of nature, and her benevolent principles also seem precocious in the context of contemporary writers. The sequel, published one year after the birth of C.'s first and only child, may have biographic content, for Julius is "so unfashionably polite, as to consider the mother's suckling her own child, as one of the indispensable obligations of nature."

With the exception of a children's book (*The Christmas Box,* 1748–49) she mentions in *Felicia to Charlotte,* C. seems to have published nothing for the next twelve years. Her dedication to *The Death of Abel* (1761) admits that she translated Salomon Gessner's poem to support her family. The translation was so well received that C. wrote *The Death of Cain* (1762) in imitation. Her last work, a translation of Gottlieb Klopstock's *Messiah* (1763), was completed and published by Joseph Collyer after her death in 1763.

C.'s unwillingness to publish even her small literary corpus under her own name finds many parallels in the period. Yet as an intelligent, gifted writer, whose novel anticipated developing conventions and whose work may have influenced Richardson, C. deserves more critical attention than she has received.

WORKS: (trans.) *The Virtuous Orphan; or, the Life of Marianne, Countess of . . . ,* by P. Marivaux (1735; ed. R. Paulson, 1979). (trans.) *The Memoirs of the Countess de Bressol* (1743). *Felicia to Charlotte* (1744). *Letters from Felicia to Charlotte,* Vol. II (1749). *The Christmas Box* (1748–49). (trans.) *The Death of Abel,* by S. Gessner (1761). *The Death of Cain* (1762). (trans.) *Messiah,* by F. G. Klopstock (1763).

BIBLIOGRAPHY: Paulson, R., intro. to *The Virtuous Orphan* (1979).

For articles in reference works, see: *DLB. Feminist. Oxford. ToddBWW. ToddDBA.*

Other references: Hughes, H. S. *JEGP* (1916).

Katherine S. Green

Elizabeth Colville

BORN: late 1500s, Halhil, Scotland.

DIED: in 1600s.

DAUGHTER OF: Sir James Melvill.

MARRIED: John Colville, third Lord of Culross, before 1603.

WROTE UNDER: Eliz. Melvill; Gentelwoman in Culros; Ladie Culross yonger; M[istress]. M[elvill].

C.'s principal work is a long allegorical poem, "Ane Godlie Dreame," first published in 1603. None of C.'s other work survives, although a contemporary, Alexander Hume, wrote of her "delight in poesie" and claimed that she did "excel any of [her] sex in that art that ever I heard within this nation." Member of a prominent Scots family, C. remains a mystery, although much is known of the men around her: Her father, Sir James Melvill; her husband, John Colville; and her son, Alexander Colville, were all important figures in public life.

The 1603 version of "Ane Godlie Dreame" consists of fifty-five stanzas in *ottava rima.* In it the speaker laments the mortal world and, longing for release from life, falls asleep. In a dream, Jesus appears and leads the speaker on a long, dangerous journey to a gold and silver castle. Before entering it, the speaker must accompany Jesus to hell. In the course of their descent, the speaker seems to fall into the flames, then awakens. The poem's final section relates the speaker's thoughts about the dream and heaven. A later edition (1692) adds five extra stanzas in the last section as well as a separate, short religious lyric by Alexander Montgomerie.

C. is known to have been a pious woman to whom Alexander Hume dedicated a book of hymns. Certainly the poem gains strength from its emotional sincerity. Nevertheless, it would be a mistake for several reasons to regard the work as autobiographical: It may be based on a lost medieval dream poem; the first-person speaker in C.'s poem is urged to "Play the man"; and its details are more conventional than naturalistic.

The poem is interesting on historical and aesthetic grounds. First, it is written in Scots dialect and is one of relatively few works by Renaissance Scotswomen. And second, the description of the journey, particularly the vision of hell, uses forceful imagery and includes an interesting refutation of the concept of Purgatory.

WORKS: "Ane Godlie Dreame" (1603, STC 17811).

BIBLIOGRAPHY: Laing, D. *Early Metrical Tales* (1826). *N&Q* (1859).

For articles in reference works, see: *Bell. Bloomsbury. DNB. Europa. Feminist. Oxford.* Saunder, J. W. *Biographical Dictionary of Renaissance Poets and Dramatists, 1520–1650* (1983).

Other references: Beilin, E. *Redeeming Eve* (1987).

Fran Teague

Ivy Compton-Burnett

BORN: 5 June 1884, Pinner, Middlesex.
DIED: 27 August 1969, London.
DAUGHTER OF: James Compton-Burnett and Katharine Rees Compton-Burnett.

The eldest child of her father's second wife, Katharine, C. was raised with five older stepbrothers and sisters and six younger brothers and sisters in suburban Hove, in Sussex. Her father, a physician, wrote many books and pamphlets defending homeopathic medicine, which he practiced on his patients. C. received a classical education from the family tutor and took a degree in classics at Royal Holloway College, London, in 1902.

When C. became a young adult, a series of family disasters occurred. At her father's death in 1901, her mother went into formal mourning for two years. C. had a strong attachment to her younger brother, Guy, who died of pneumonia in 1905. In 1911, her mother died after a painful, lingering illness. C. became head of the household until her sisters rebelled and the family home was broken up in 1915. In 1916, her brother Noel was killed on the Somme. At the end of the year, her two youngest sisters, believed to be suicides, died of overdoses of veronal. C. herself nearly died in the influenza epidemic of 1918.

The turmoil seems to have ceased when in 1919 C. began to share living quarters with Margaret Jourdain, a writer and antiques expert, an arrangement that continued until Jourdain died in 1951. During this time, C. wrote the bulk of her novels.

C.'s first novel, *Dolores* (1911), with its self-sacrificing heroine, critics find to be immature, written in a crude style, without C.'s later distinctive irony. Her next, published fourteen years later, *Pastors and Masters* (1925), dealing with plagiarism, is the first novel in which C. realized her mature style and her characteristic fictional universe.

The idiosyncrasies of C.'s technique are noted by readers and critics. Her novels are set in the English countryside sometime between 1880 and 1910. The claustrophobic atmosphere derives from the self-enclosed society, composed of family, servants, and a few friends. No character escapes this milieu very far for very long. Intelligent and unsentimental, C. is said to have crossed Victorian domestic fiction with Greek tragedy.

C.'s novels are expressed predominantly in dialogue with only sketchy descriptions of the characters and with minimal authorial comment. Her reliance on dialogue elevates and abstracts the characters and their conflicts, revealing their moral and intellectual natures. Critic Nathalie Sarraute described C.'s dialogue as reflecting the fluctuating border between conversation and subconversation (what is almost said, *sotto voice,* on the tip of one's tongue). In the novels, children are continually reprimanded for this sub-conversation.

Egotism, power, and domination are C.'s typical themes. Her melodramatic devices—wills destroyed, conversations overheard, or illegitimate children belatedly claimed—reveal the secret lives of her characters. Frederick Karl complains that these recognition scenes do not lead to reformation or salvation as in Greek tragedy or Christian comedy; instead, the characters try to hush up the scandal and carry on. Other critics also bemoan the lack of poetic justice. Some label C. amoral because her wicked characters flourish and her good continue to suffer. A realist, C. depicts family life where love and hate meet most intensely. Family is home, the ground. For it to break apart would be an unthinkable, primal disaster.

The comedy of C.'s writing contains other contradictions. Critics find her dialogue witty, brilliant, and epigrammatic. Some call her a creator of great humorous characters such as parasites and busybodies. All find her ironic. But, like Harold Pinter's, her comedy is dark comedy, laughter from shock at the outrageous. As in Freud's theory of the joke, we laugh at the emperor's nakedness, at authority denuded.

WORKS: *Dolores* (1911). *Pastors and Masters* (1925). *Brothers and Sisters* (1929). *Men and Wives* (1931). *More*

Women than Men (1933). *A House and Its Head* (1935). *Daughters and Sons* (1937). *A Family and a Fortune* (1939). *Parents and Children* (1941). *Elders and Betters* (1944). *Manservant and Maidservant* (1947; in the U.S. as *Bullivant and the Lambs*). *Two Worlds and Their Ways* (1949). *Darkness and Day* (1951). *The Present and the Past* (1953). *Mother and Son* (1955). *A Father and His Fate* (1957). *A Heritage and Its History* (1959; dramatized by Julian Mitchell, 1965). *The Mighty and Their Fall* (1961). *A God and His Gifts* (1963). *The Last and the First* (1971). *Collected Works* (1972).

BIBLIOGRAPHY: Baldanza, F. *Ivy Compton-Burnett* (1964). Burkhart, C. *The Art of I. Compton-Burnett* (1972). Burkhart, C. *Herman and Nancy and Ivy* (1977). Crecy, S., in *Lesbian and Gay Writing*, ed. M. Lilly (1990). Doan, L., in *Old Maids to Radical Spinsters*, ed. L. Doan (1991). Johnson, P. H. *I. Compton-Burnett* (1951). Karl, F. *A Reader's Guide to the Contemporary Novel* (1971). Kiernan, R. F. *Frivolity Unbound: Six Masters of the Camp Novel* (1990). Liddle, R. *The Novels of I. Compton-Burnett* (1956). Lively, P., intro. to *Manservant and Maidservant* (1983). Nevius, B. *Ivy Compton-Burnett* (1970). Powell, V. *A Compton-Burnett Compendium* (1973). Sprigg, E. *The Life of Ivy Compton-Burnett* (1973). Spurling, H. *The Life of Ivy Compton-Burnett* (1984). Spurling, H., in *The Troubled Face of Biography*, ed. E. Homburger and J. Charmly (1988). Tristram, P., in *British Novelists Since 1900*, ed. J. I. Biles (1987).

For articles in reference works, see: *Bloomsbury. Cambridge. CLC. DLB. DNB. IDWB. Oxford. ToddBWW.*

Other references: Anan, G. *NYRB* (20 December 1984). Bellringer, A. W. *Durham University Journal* (1992). *ES* (1991). Cross, N. *New Statesman* (15 June 1984). Hendriksen, J. *Durham University Journal* (1992). Hurst, M. J. *Lang&S* (1987). Kemp, P. *Listener* (7 June 1984). Lees-Milne, J. *Books and Bookmen* (1984). Mobilio, A. *VLS* (September 1990). Morton, B. *TES* (8 June 1984). Oates, J. C. *NYTBR* (9 December 1984). Spackman, W. M. *BW* (9 December 1984). Stewart, J. I. M. *LRB* (19 July).

Kate Begnal

Constantine, Murray: See *Burdekin, Katharine Penelope*

Eliza Cook

BORN: 24 December 1818, London.
DIED: 23 September 1889, Wimbledon, Surrey.
DAUGHTER OF: Joseph Cook.

A self-made woman from a working-class background, C. wrote feminist essays about women and work, sentimental verses on domestic and nationalist themes, poems of social protest, and satiric treatments of middle-class Victorian smugness and conventional gender arrangements. She was praised in the nineteenth century as a poet "who sang for the people and was comprehended of the people," and her verses were sometimes set to music.

C. was the youngest of eleven children of a brazier from Southwark in London who retired to a farm in Horsham, Sussex, when C. was nine. Entirely self-educated, C. escaped the conventional socialization of middle-class girls. As an adult, she defiantly dressed in a way perceived to be masculine, displayed a passionate attachment to the actress Charlotte Cushman, and published essays and poems criticizing the restrictions society placed upon middle-class women's lives. C. published her first volume of verses, *Lays of a Wild Harp*, at the age of seventeen; its favorable reception led her to submit poems to the *Weekly Dispatch*, the *Metropolitan Magazine*, the *Literary Gazette*, and the *New Monthly Magazine*. Her most famous poem, "The Old Arm Chair," was a sentimental tribute to her mother, who died when C. was about fifteen; it appeared in the *Dispatch* in 1837. This and many other poems on the subject of her mother's death expressed a grief that contemporary readers were likely to share.

Melaia and Other Poems (1838), with its witty satires and poignant protest poems, was a great success in both England and America. "Our Father," like Elizabeth Barrett Browning's "The Cry of the Children," was written in response to R. H. Horne's 1842 government commission report exposing the horrendous conditions of children working in English factories. "Song for the Workers" resembles the labor anthem "Bread and Roses."

Eliza Cook's Journal, which C. wrote and edited virtually single-handedly from May 1849 to May 1854, was a miscellany of sketches, reviews, social essays, and verses intended to improve the lives of middle-class women by entertaining and informing them and by contributing a feminist voice to contemporary debates about women's proper role in society. In this journal, C. particularly addressed the difficulties and despair of English working women, whether governesses, seamstresses, factory workers, or servants. She attacked the interpretation of English law that allowed husbands to "discipline" their wives physically, she defended "old maids," and she criticized the superficiality of English girls' education. The journal ceased publication after five years because of C.'s failing health and poor business management. A large portion of the contents of the journal was reissued in 1860 as *Jottings from My Journal*.

In 1863, C. was awarded a Civil List pension of £100 per year. *New Echoes, and Other Poems* (1864) was her last book of new poetry; a collection of aphorisms, *Diamond Dust* (1865), was her last book of prose. For the final twenty-five years of her life, C. was an invalid. She died at the age of seventy-one, having outlived her popularity as a poet but not her reputation as a radical feminist.

WORKS: *Lays of a Wild Harp* (1835). *Melaia and Other Poems* (1838). *Poems*, second series (1845). *Eliza Cook's Journal* (1849–54). *I'm Afloat: Songs* (1850?). *Jottings from My Journal* (1860). *New Echoes, and Other Poems* (1864). *Diamond Dust* (1865). *Poetical Works* (1870). *The Old Armchair* (1886).

BIBLIOGRAPHY: For articles in reference works, see: *BA19C. DNB. Europa. Feminist. Notable Women of Our Own Times* (1883). *OCEL. Oxford. PPC. VB.*

Other references: Faderman, L. *Surpassing the Love of Men: Romantic Friendship and Love between Women from the Renaissance to the Present* (1981). Hickok, K. *Representations of Women: Nineteenth-Century British Women's Poetry* (1984). *Victorian Women Poets: An Anthology*, ed. A. Leighton and M. Reynolds (1995). Mitchell, S. *The Fallen Angel: Chastity, Class, and Women's Reading 1835–1880* (1981). Woodring, C. *Victorian Samplers: William and Mary Howitt* (1952).

Kathleen Hickok

Catherine Ann Cookson

BORN: 20 June 1906, Tyne Dock, South Shields, County Durham.
DIED: 11 June 1998, Newcastle-upon-Tyne.
DAUGHTER OF: A "gentleman" and Catherine Fawcett.
MARRIED: Thomas Henry Cookson, 1940.
WROTE UNDER: C. C.; Catherine Cookson; Catherine Marchant.

C. was a prolific writer of historical and gothic romances, juvenile fiction, and autobiography, memoirs, and personal meditations. More than 90 million copies of her works have been sold worldwide, attesting to her overwhelming success as interpreter of popular imagination. Several of her works were written under the pseudonym "Catherine Marchant." The daughter of an unnamed "gentleman" and Catherine Fawcett, a domestic servant and alcoholic whom C. believed to be her sister for most of her childhood, C. went into service at the age of fourteen, later working as a checker in a workhouse laundry before managing a laundry until her marriage in 1940 to Thomas Henry Cookson, a teacher. It was not until after the age of forty that C. began to write, and she published more than eighty popular novels, many set in the towns of northern, industrialized England from the early 1800s through the 1970s. C. was awarded the Winifred Holtby Prize for a regional novel for her *The Round Tower* (1968).

Her romance fiction heroines typically tend to be spirited, strong-minded, and determined to attain respectability, often overcoming numerous harsh obstacles, violence, and tragedy. The popular Mary Ann series (1954–67) depicts a farmer's daughter who saves her father from alcoholism. C.'s plots complicate familial relations almost incestuously, as in the Trotter series (1978–82), where the heroine, Tilly, marries the oldest son of the man to whom she is mistress. In *The Tide of Life* (1976), Emily seeks happiness from the former husband of the wife of the man to whom Emily is mistress.

C.'s first novel, *Kate Hannigan* (1950), drew on her own difficult childhood experiences, yet her prodigious body of works ranges from an historic account of the landed gentry in the Mallen Trilogy (1973–74) to an examination of local superstition and witchcraft in the Tilly Trotter novels. The Mallen series enacted a typical C. female fantasy of a heroine, Anna Grigmore, a lady of reduced circumstances who enters the Mallens' Highbanks Hall as governess. She subsequently becomes mistress to Thomas Mallen, then adoptive mother to his children from his rape of a niece; governess to Harry Bensham's children at the Hall in order to support Mallen's niece; wife to Bensham; and finally sole mistress of Highbanks Hall. Billed as a "dark tale of passion," this family saga was adapted for television in 1979–80. Other novels were adapted for film (*The Cinder Path*, 1978; *The Black Velvet Gown*, 1984), stage (*The Fifteen Streets*, 1952), and radio (*The Dwelling Place*, 1971).

C. wrote extensively of her life in the autobiographical *Our Kate* (1969) and again in *Catherine Cookson Country* (1986). *Let Me Make Myself Plain* (1988) is a personal anthology of poems and meditations stemming from her televised broadcasts of weekly epilogues. She lived in Northumberland; she was awarded the Order of the British Empire in 1985 and made Dame of the British Empire in 1993. Thirty of her manuscripts are collected at Boston University.

WORKS: *Kate Hannigan* (1950). *The Fifteen Streets* (1952). *Colour Blind* (1953). *Maggie Rowan* (1954). *A Grand Man* (1954, retitled as screenplay *Jacqueline*, 1956). *The Lord and Mary Ann* (1956). *Rooney* (1957). *The Menagerie* (1958). *The Devil and Mary Ann* (1958). *Fanny McBride* (1959). *Slinky Jane* (1959). *Fenwick Houses* (1960). *Love and Mary Ann* (1961). *Life and Mary Ann* (1962). *The Garment* (1962). *The Blind Miller* (1963). *Heritage of Folly* (1963). *The Fen Tiger* (1963). *House of Men* (1963). *Hannah Massey* (1964). *Marriage and Mary Ann* (1964). *Evil at Roger's Cross* (1965 in the U.S.; in the U.K. as *The Iron Façade*, 1976). *Mary Ann's Angels* (1965). *Matty Doolin* (1965). *The Long Corridor* (1965). *The Unbaited Trap* (1966). *Katie Mulholland* (1967). *Mary Ann and Bill* (1967). *The Round Tower* (1968). *Joe and the Gladiator* (1968). *The Nice Bloke* (1969). *Our Kate: An Autobiography* (1969, repub. as *Our Kate: Catherine Cookson—Her Personal Story*, 1974). *The Glass Virgin* (1970). *The Nipper* (1970). *The Invitation* (1970). *The Dwelling Place* (1971). *Feathers in the Fire* (1971). *Blue Baccy* (1972). *Pure as the Lily* (1972). *The Mallen Streak* (1973). *Our John Willie* (1974). *The Mallen Girl* (1974). *The Mallen Litter* (1974). *The Invisible Cord* (1975). *The Gambling Man* (1975). *Miss Martha Mary Crawford* (1975). *The Tide of Life* (1976). *The Slow Awakening* (1976). *Mrs. Flannagan's Trumpet* (1976). *The Girl* (1977). *Go Tell it to Mrs. Golightly* (1978). *The Cinder Path* (1978). *The Man Who Cried* (1979). *Tilly Trotter* (1980). *Tilly Trotter Wed* (1981). *Lanky Jones* (1981). *Nancy Nuttal and the Mongrel* (1982). *Tilly Trotter Widowed* (1982). *The Whip* (1983). *Hamilton* (1983). *The Black Velvet Gown* (1984). *Goodbye Hamilton* (1984). *A Dinner of Herbs* (1985). *Harold* (1985). *Catherine Cookson Country* (1986). *The Moth* (1986). *Bill Bailey* (1986). *The Parson's Daughter* (1987). *Bill Bailey's Lot* (1987). *The Cultured Handmaiden* (1988). *Bill Bailey's Daughter* (1988). *Let Me Make Myself Plain* (1988). *The Harrogate Secret* (1989). *The Black Candle* (1989). *The Wingless Bird* (1990). *The Gillyvors* (1990). *My Beloved Son* (1991). *The Rag Nymph* (1991). *The House of Women* (1992). *The Maltese Angel* (1992). *The Year of the Virgins* (1993). *The Golden Straw* (1993). *Justice Is a Woman* (1994). *The Tinker's Girl* (1994). *A Ruthless Need* (1995).

BIBLIOGRAPHY: Goodwin, C. *To Be a Lady: The Story of Catherine Cookson* (1994).

For articles in reference works, see: *Bloomsbury. CA. Feminist. IAWWW. International Who's Who. International Who's Who of Women* (1992). *Major Twentieth-Century Writers* (1991). *Oxford. SF&FL. SATA. TCRGW. ToddBWW. WD. Who's Who. Who's Who in America.*

Other references: *Catholic World* (June 1955). *NYT* (7 January 1955). *NYTBR* (20 October 1974). *LonT* (15 August 1983). *TLS* (7 January 1955, 19 June 1969, 24 July 1981).

Eve M. Lynch

Cooper, Edith Emma: See *Field, Michael*

Elizabeth Cooper

FLOURISHED: 1730s.
WROTE UNDER: Mrs. Cooper.

A critic, compiler, playwright, and actress, C. is one of the early anthologizers of English poetry. Her collection *The Muses' Library; or a Series of English Poetry from the Saxons to the Reign of King Charles II* (1737) provides a sort of canon of early modern British verse, complete with critical commentary and brief biographies of writers from Edward the Confessor to Samuel Daniel.

C. was also the author of two plays, one of them, *The Rival Widows*, a highly successful comedy. It opened 22 February 1735 and enjoyed six initial performances at Covent Garden, with C. herself playing the principal role (Lady Bellair) on her benefit nights. A second play, *The Nobleman*, apparently closed after a single performance at the Haymarket on 17 May 1736; no copies are extant.

WORKS: *The Rival Widows, or the Fair Libertine* (1735). *The Nobleman; or, The Family Quarrel* (1736). *The Muses' Library; or a Series of English Poetry from the Saxons to the Reign of King Charles II* (1737).

BIBLIOGRAPHY: Genest, J. *Some Account of the English Stage* (1832). *British Women Poets 1660–1800: An Anthology*, ed. J. Fullard (1990).

For articles in reference works, see: *DNB. Feminist. ToddDBA.*

Richard C. Taylor

Jilly Cooper

BORN: 21 February 1937, Hornchurch, Essex.
DAUGHTER OF: W. B. Sallitt and Mary Elaine Whincup.
MARRIED: Leo Cooper, 1961.

Beginning her career as a reporter on the *Middlesex Independent* in Brentford from 1957 to 1959, C. occupied a variety of positions in the literary world, including copy writer, publisher's reader, typist, and model before attaining widespread public recognition for her popular columns in the *Sunday Times* (1969–82) and *The Mail on Sunday* (1982–85), which she has described as "part domestic comedy and part reporting events like a royal wedding or a vets conference." Adopting the persona of a hopeless, scatty, and sometimes coquettish housewife, the column's anecdotes of married life, ribald merrymaking, country society, and behavior of the British upper-middle classes also form the basis of C.'s commercially successful trilogy *Riders* (1985, televised 1993), *Rivals* (1988), and *Polo* (1991), farcical tales of upper-class jealousies, gin drinking, love affairs, domestic antics, and highly charged sexual rivalries among the social and sporting elite of Gloucestershire. *Polo*, a typical example of these sexy popular entertainments, centers mainly on the adventures of the "ravishing" Perdita, who invariably takes on the men in the otherwise almost exclusively male domain of polo; she "finds herself" at the end of the book, after a variety of sporting and sexual adventures both on and off the polo field, when she finally realizes what has been going wrong with her life, discovers true love, and lives happily ever after.

C. is best known as an affectionately satirical observer of human relations and a romantic novelist, although she has also written historical and juvenile fiction. Other notable commercial successes include *Class* (1981), an affectionately humorous observation of the behavior of the British classes in courtship, their choice of furnishings, appetites, and ambitions; and her first book, *How to Stay Married* (1969), an antidote to 1960s feminism that now appears grimly ironic in the light of constant media gossip concerning her husband Leo Cooper's widely reported six-year affair with a publishing house colleague. Also highly popular are her series of short, light-hearted romantic novelettes *Emily* (1975), *Bella* (1976), *Harriet* (1976), *Octavia* (1977), *Imogen* (1978), *Prudence* (1978), and *Lisa & Co.* (1982). C.'s most recent success, *The Man who Made Husbands Jealous* (1993), is set in the fictional county of Rutshire. It is the typically light-hearted romantic tale of Lysander Hawkley, who combines "breathtaking good looks" with "the kindest of hearts" and decides that the wife of the world-famous conductor Rannaldini needs rescuing.

C. has stated that her aim as a writer is "to cheer people up and occasionally, amid the laughs, to make a serious point." Her helpless, kittenish persona has made her a favorite with British television and press, among many other long-standing and stalwart admirers of her telling observations and light, witty prose—a fluent and familiar punning style that forms the basis for a quite prodigious output of fruity romances, humorous, lighthearted bestsellers, affectionate observations about the reserve of the British middle classes, and coffee-table books about dogs and horses. "I think I started off a very flip, brittle writer because I was frightened of sentimentality," admits C., "but gradually, I think, I'm putting my heart into my writing." Her school-day reminiscences, tales of coming-out parties, and anecdotes about shopping and flirting expose a hearty, jolly, universally affable personality, humanized by the occasional touch of snobbery or coterie backbiting.

C.'s unending fascination with the daily round of upper-middle-class life, housekeeping, weekend guests, lunching out, embarrassing moments, celebrity friends, and the onset of middle-age has led to her being described by Polly Toynbee as a "lost soul of a writer, unable to set aside her friendly persona of self-deprecating fluffiness and bubble-headed daffiness," wasting her talents on "best-selling piffle." Nevertheless, C.'s raunchy, sensational tales have become massive sellers. Others have described them as "highly entertaining," "acerbic and wickedly observant," "enormously readable," and "very funny." She is currently Britain's best-read writer; the inevitable popular success of her novels testifies to a huge following for her own particular blend of satire, humor, innuendo, and romance.

WORKS: *How to Stay Married* (1969). *How to Survive from Nine to Five* (1970). *Jolly Super* (1971). *Men and Supermen* (1972). *Jolly Super Too* (1973). *Women and Superwomen* (1974). *Emily* (1975). *Jolly Superlative* (1976). *Bella* (1976). *Harriet* (1976). *Octavia* (1977). *Imogen* (1978). *Prudence* (1978). *Superjilly* (1978). *The British in Love* (1979). *Class* (1981). *Little Mabel* (1980). *Supercooper* (1980). *Violets and Vinegar* (1981). *Intelligent and Loyal: A Celebration of the Mongrel* (1981). *Little Mabel's Great Escape* (1981). *Jolly Marsupial Down Under and Other Scenes* (1982). *Lisa & Co.* (1982). *Little Mabel Wins* (1982). *Animals in War* (1983). *The Common Years* (1984). (with Patrick Lichfield) *Hot Foot to Zabrieski Point—The Unipart Calendar Book* (1985). *Riders* (1985, televised 1993). *Leo & Jilly Cooper on Cricket* (1985). *Little Mabel Saves the Day* (1985). *Leo and Jilly Cooper on Horse Mania* (1986). *How to Survive Christmas* (1986). *Turn Right at the Spotted Dog* (1987). *Rivals* (1988). *Angels Rush In* (1990). *Polo* (1991). *Love and Other Heartaches* (1991). *Araminta's Wedding* (1993). *The Man Who Made Husbands Jealous* (1993). *Huskies* (1994). *Appassionata* (1996).

BIBLIOGRAPHY:

For articles in reference works, see: *CA*. *TCRGW*. *WD*. *Who's Who*.

Other references: *LonSunT* (2 May 1993, 30 April 1994, 2 April 1996). *LonSunTMag* (27 April 1996).

Mikita Brottman

Cordelia, John: See *Underhill, Evelyn*

Marie Corelli (pseudonym of Mary Mackay)

BORN: 1 May 1855, Perth, Scotland.
DIED: 21 April 1924, Stratford-on-Avon, Warwickshire.
DAUGHTER OF: Charles Mackay (?) and Mary Elizabeth Kirtland Mackay (?).
WROTE UNDER: Marie Corelli.

The storytelling of C., world-famous novelist of late Victorian England, extended to her own life. To some, she claimed to have been adopted at birth by literary man Charles Mackay, her real parents being an Italian father and a Scottish clairvoyant mother. To others, she said she was Mackay's stepdaughter; however, rumor had it that she was actually his illegitimate daughter. Whether her adoptive, legitimate, or natural father, Charles Mackay provided the young Mary with a useful model of literary endeavor. He was a lyricist, essayist, poet, war correspondent, editor of the *London Illustrated News,* and author of *Popular Delusions and the Madness of Crowds.* Mackay's literary connections helped his convent-bred, musically inclined daughter with publication of her early work.

Changing her name to Corelli in her attempt at a concert recital career, she had some initial successes. But with the publication of her first novel, *A Romance of Two Worlds* (1886), when she was only twenty-two, she became a best-selling author. So she remained for the rest of the century and into the next, half of her more than thirty novels selling a then-impressive 100,000 copies.

Most literary people concurred with Arnold Bennett that "if Joseph Conrad is one pole [of artistic talent], Marie Corelli is the other." She was the subject of much critical derision, including an unflattering special issue of the *Westminster Review.* Yet she was also the favorite novelist of Queen Victoria and was admired by William Gladstone, Herbert Henry Asquith, Oscar Wilde, Italian queens, Indian potentates, circulating libraries, and an enthusiastic lower- and middle-class following.

Her immensely popular *Romance of Two Worlds,* an entertaining and original tale of occultism and clairvoyance, features a heroine of great appeal to Victorian audiences, the neurasthenic girl seeking a meaning to existence. In this novel, the heroine is providentially rejuvenated by the Electric Principle of Christianity, the control of magnetic force emanating from a celestial Electric Ring. The novel features a mysterious mesmerist, Dr. Casimir, and his exotic sister Sara, who is thirty-eight but looks sixteen as a result of the blessings of spiritual electricity. Also intriguing are the opulent interiors with secret light sources and herbal opiate-induced visions of angels. The novel obviously catered to Victorian fascination with spiritualism (though C. claimed to scorn the spiritualists of the day) and ingeniously combined pseudoscientific theory and Christianity.

C. followed up her first success with a number of novels combining romance, religion, and social criticism, notably *Barabbas: A Dream of the World's Tragedy* (1893), her treatment of the Crucifixion, and *The Murder of Delicia* (1896), a novel condemning marital infidelity. However, *The Sorrows of Satan* (1895)—whose initial sale was greater than that of any prior English novel—was her landmark success. It concerns a Faustian pact between one Geoffrey Tempest and the Devil who, in a clever twist of characterization, is weary of sinners and sorrowed at the evil of man. Typically, C. used the novel to criticize the loose morality of wealthy women and aristocratic men-about-town. She urged a return to Christian living, embodied by Mavis Clarke, a young woman novelist who is Geoffrey's savior and bears a marked resemblance to C. herself. Despite C.'s self-promotion, the novel was so popular that it was in its sixtieth edition by the time of her death. It even supplemented the Bible as the text of many sermons. What readers perhaps liked better than its evangelism, however, were its florid descriptions of the haunts and sins of the rich.

A child of her time, C. united a desire for moral uplift—she did passionate battle against what she termed "the evils of nineteenth-century cynicism and general flippancy of thought"—with prodigious industry. In addition to fiction, her almost forty books included verse and social criticism, and she wrote numerous articles for the popular papers of the day. A woman of drive and egotism (she published fan letters in a reissue of *Romance of Two Worlds*), she railed against the "marriage market" for upper-class women but opposed suffrage because she considered it unladylike.

Though her works are still in print and she has been praised by twentieth-century writers as diverse as Rebecca West, Leonard Woolf, and Henry Miller, some of her own biographers have ridiculed her, accusing her of wooden characterization, purple prose, and endless moralizing. Whether she is guilty of the besetting sins of Victorian fiction is debatable. What is not debatable is her brilliant understanding of the public's need for fictions combining sinful excitement with spiritual exhortation. She was a literary phenomenon created by her own shrewdness and the rise of a mass market, a readership whose opinions continue to enshrine such artists as C. who give imaginative expression to its own longings and beliefs.

WORKS: *A Romance of Two Worlds* (1886). *Vendetta, or the Story of One Forgotten* (1886). *Thelma: A Society Novel* (1887). *Ardath: The Story of a Dead Self* (1889). *My Wonderful Wife: A Study in Smoke* (1889). *Wormwood: A Drama of Paris* (1890). *The Silver Domino* (1892). *The Soul of Lilith* (1892). *Barabbas: A Dream of the World's Tragedy* (1893). *The Sorrows of Satan* (1895). *The Murder of Delicia* (1896). *The Mighty Atom* (1896). *Cameos* (1896). *Zisha: The Problem of a Wicked Soul* (1897). *Jane: A Social Incident* (1897). *Boy: A Sketch* (1900). *The Master Christian* (1900). *A Christmas Greeting of Various Thoughts, Verses and Fancies* (1901). *"Temporal Power": A Study in Supremacy* (1902). *The Vanishing Gift* (1902). *The Plain Truth of the Stratford-on-Avon Controversy* (1903). *God's Good Man: A Simple Love Story* (1904). *The Strange Visitation of Josiah McNason: A Christmas Ghost Story* (1904). *Free Opinions Freely Expressed on Certain Phases of Modern Social Life and Conduct* (1905). *The Treasure of Heaven: A Romance of Riches* (1906). *Woman or Suffragette? A Question of National Choice* (1907). *Holy Orders* (1908). *The Devil's Motor* (1910). *The Life Everlasting: A Reality of Romance* (1911). *Eyes of the Sea* (1917). *The Young Diana: An Experience of the Future* (1918). *My Little Bit* (1919). *The Love of Long Ago* (1920). *The Secret Power* (1921). *Love and the Philosopher* (1923). *Open Confession to a Man from a Woman* (1925). *Poems*, ed. B. Vyver (1925).

BIBLIOGRAPHY: Bigland, E. *Marie Corelli: The Woman and the Legend* (1953). Carr, K. *Miss Marie Corelli* (1901). Casey, J. G. *ELT* (1992). Kershner, R. B., in *Transforming Genres: New Approaches to British Fiction of the 1890s*, ed. N. L. Manos and M. J. Rochelson (1994). Kowalczyk, R. L. *MP* (1969). Kowalczyk, R. L. *JPC* (1974). Magalaner, M., in *Modern Irish Literature: Essays in Honor of William York Tindall*, ed. R. J. Porter and J. D. Brophy (1972).Masters, B. *Now Barabbas Was a Rotter: The Extraordinary Life of Marie Corelli* (1978). Scott, W. S. *Marie Corelli: The Story of a Friendship* (1953). Vidan, I. *JML* (1990). Vyver, B. *Memoirs of Marie Corelli* (1930).

For articles in reference works, see: *Bloomsbury. Cambridge. 1890s. Feminist. Oxford. ToddBWW. VB.*

Other references: *Bookman* (February 1918). *N&Q* (April 1943). *Strand* (1898). *Westminster Review* (December 1906).

Laura Hapke

Corinna: See *Thomas, Elizabeth*

Frances Crofts Darwin Cornford

BORN: 30 March 1886, Cambridge.
DIED: 19 August 1960, Cambridge.
DAUGHTER OF: Francis Darwin and Ellen Crofts Darwin.
MARRIED: John M. Cornford, 1909.

In the course of her long career as a poet, C. developed her poetic themes and images in response to her contemporary experience of the English countryside, motherhood, war, and loss. Her reputation links her to the Georgian period in poetry because of her pastoral images and her friendships with Edward Marsh and with Rupert Brooke. Her poems express both sorrow at the transitoriness of mortal life and wry amazement at the brevity of human pleasures. Occasionally, they hope for transcendence of death through the artistic imagination or through scholarly knowledge. An agnostic, she nevertheless reveals a belief in the continuity of human history and in the eternal forces of nature.

She began writing poetry in 1902, when she was sixteen, and her career as a poet continued until her death in 1960. Raised in Cambridge, in a family for whom intellectual pursuits were the norm, C. was the granddaughter of Charles Darwin. C.'s mother died when she was seventeen, and C., an only child, lived in the household of her father, a university professor. She was educated at home, but she had many university friends, including the anthropologist Jane Harrison, who introduced her to the classics scholar John Cornford, a lecturer at Trinity College, Cambridge. C. married him in 1909, published her first and second volumes of poetry in 1910 and 1912, and gave birth to five children between 1913 and 1924. Her experience as a mother who nursed her babies and who comforted her children when they awoke frightened at night is often reflected in the imagery of poems she collected into four volumes and published in 1915, 1923, 1928, and 1934. C.'s second child, a son, John, was also a poet; they exchanged their draft poems for one another's comments, and their letters honestly debate their political and literary differences. John died fighting in Spain in 1936. Deeply affected by this loss, C. did not publish her own poems again until 1948. When she resumed her public career as a poet, she demonstrated a firm commitment to her work, publishing four more books of poetry during her sixties and seventies. In 1959, she was honored by the Queen's Medal for Poetry. Her two posthumously published books of poetry (1960 and 1976) were edited by her son Christopher.

That C. wrote sentimental pastoral poems need not blind readers to her other poems, which reveal a variety of styles and a wry, sometimes bitter, but very dry wit. In her 1910 volume of poetry, an unsentimental triolet portrays a woman who has isolated herself from life's sensual pleasures. This poem, "To a Fat Lady Seen from the Train," does not dismiss the subject with cold scorn but views her with a compassion that is distanced by the observer's sense of the woman's absurd behavior. In a realistic poem, "London Streets," with an epigram from her agnostic grandfather Charles Darwin, C. proclaims a bitter indictment of the life of the urban poor, who are exhausted and in pain. C.'s sentimental tone is heard, however, in the poem "Youth"; this is frequently and mistakenly quoted as if it were written as an elegiac tribute to her blond friend, the poet Rupert Brooke, who died in 1915 during World War I, five years after this volume was published. The youth is praised as a golden-haired Apollo, "Magnificently unprepared / For the long littleness of life."

C.'s tribute to those who died suddenly in World War I is dated April 1915 and entitled "No Immortality?" in *Autumn Midnight* (1923). In a later collection, she retitled it "Contemporaries." Although the fact of death is awful, so is the realization that the survivors, even if they strive to remember, will forget the "timeless beauty" and the specific details of the dead: "Time destroys." No matter how beloved, the dead will dissolve in human memory.

The emphasis on life's limited span of years is a recurrent theme throughout C.'s career, but she suggests that some people have insight denied to other human beings. The collection *Spring Morning* (1915) contains "In Dorset," depicting an eerie encounter with two old gypsy women, who remain silent as they meet the eyes of the wandering poet, out for a walk in the rainy and muddy countryside. The long journey on foot symbolizes life's journey, and the gypsies have more direct experience than the poet, whose walks outside are only occasional.

C. frequently personifies female power. In "Autumn Midnight," the title poem of the 1923 collection, the moon is a cold killer, a "Queen" whose light kills the summer flowers, especially the sun's eye, the daisy. A child, awakened by the moonlight at midnight, is frightened by death. In "Better," an antithetical female power is evoked, a life-affirming mother, who rises at dawn on a spring morning, who with a touch of her hand seems to awaken life in the flower buds. This gladness she shares with her daughter. In both "Autumn Midnight" and "Better," powerful female figures are associated with seasonal change, and both reveal the significance of nature's transitions to a child. The mother and child also appear in an earthy, funny poem, "The New-Born Baby's Song," in which the baby's voice declares selfish indifference to the sensual stimuli of nature poetry—no heard melodies, no pastoral beauty seen, no tactile pleasure.

In *Different Days* (1928), the poem "At Night" depicts a mother addressing her child in bed but certainly thinking also of herself as a child. The speaker compares sleep to a "nursing mother" and to the sea, describing the underwater movements of the waves and the passing fish in a way that suggests the poet's familiarity with psychoanalytical explanations of the unconscious mind. This poem affirms the power of dreams, explaining that fantasies during sleep feed the imagination and allow one to face the "chaos of day." *Different Days* celebrates many eras of artistic creativity, including that of the Renaissance composer John Dowland (in "Words for Music"), John Milton (in "A Glimpse"), and a modern Hungarian poet killed in World War I ("Feri Bekassy"). In these poems, the timeless achievement of their artistic creation or scholarly work is contrasted with C.'s awareness of mortality and of aging. A less solemn tone is heard in other poems. "Mediterranean Morning" echoes Cambridge scholar Gilbert Murray's translation of Aristophanes' *The Frogs* in the opening word "brekekoax," and "The Woman with the Baby to the Philosophers" mocks a pompous sage by reminding him that his mother saw him as the baby "who put your toes inside your mouth."

In *Mountains and Molehills* (1934), C.'s "Ode on the Whole Duty of Parents" professes a respect for the child's independence and necessary freedom; the parent's role is that of the rooted tree to which the child returns for comforting shelter and for the fruits of wisdom. "Cambridge Autumn" reassures and comforts with a vision of "sun-receiving fields" even though dark storm clouds of death loom.

C.'s poetic world, however, is not always envisioned through a golden haze. "On August the Thirteenth" is a poem that offers little comfort regarding the sudden departure (death) of one who delighted in the ordinary pleasures of "the tea and tray." Although this one lived a life whose rhythm seemed untouched by "modernity," death when it comes is "unseemly, seemly." To suggest the disruption, she, like other modernist poets, employs free verse, irregularly rhymed, with alliteration, and she alludes nostalgically to classical myths. In "After the Eumenides," alluding to the poetic curse of the vengeful Furies (Eumenides) after Orestes kills his mother Clytemnestra, C. expresses an agonized hope that the song of poetry might somehow ease the pain of those who desire peace in a war-cursed world. Unlike her son John, who chose to fight, C. in the 1930s chose pacifism; his death and her husband's death affected the themes in her subsequent poems.

The collection *Travelling Home* (1948) contains many short lyrics, most set in Cambridge or the surrounding countryside, and they reflect a longing to find a place within a stable tradition, including the tradition of English poets. Other poems in this collection are imagist gems, such as "Autumn Blitz," which brilliantly juxtaposes "the human chaos of the night" with "calmly yellow, gently falling leaves." Her compassionate pacifism is heard in "Soldiers on the Platform," which recognizes them as alienated, burdened victims, with "young, bare, bullock faces."

C.'s poetic tone ranges from the resigned to the joyous, and her themes and poetic forms reflect both the tragic loss in the modern era and the comic celebration of nature and maternal love.

WORKS: *Poems* (1910). *Death and the Princes: A Morality* (1912). *Spring Morning* (1915). *Autumn Midnight* (1923). *Different Days* (1928). *Mountains and Molehills* (1934). (trans., with E. P. Salaman) *Poems from the Russian* (1943). *Travelling Home, and Other Poems* (1948). (trans., with S. Spender) *Le Dur desir de durer*, by Paul Eluard (1950). *Collected Poems* (1954). *On a Calm Shore* (1960). *Fifteen Poems from the French* (1976).

BIBLIOGRAPHY: Anderson, A. *A Bibliography of the Writings of Frances Cornford* (1975). Cornford, J., in *Understand the Weapon, Understand the Wound: Selected Writings of John Cornford with Some Letters of Frances*

Cornford, ed. J. Galassi (1976). Delaney, P. *The Neo-Pagans* (1987). McFadden, G. *Discovery of the Comic* (1982). Raverat, G. *Period Piece* (1952). Stansky, P. and W. Abraham. *Journey to the Frontier* (1966).

For articles in reference works, see: *Avenel Companion to English & American Literature. Bloomsbury. CBEL. Literary Britain: A Reader's Guide to Its Writers and Landmarks* (1980).

Other references: *LonT* (22 August 1960).

Judith L. Johnston

Cory, Annie Sophie: See *Cory, Victoria*

Victoria Cory (pseudonym of Annie Sophie Cory)

BORN: 1 October 1868, Punjab, India.
DIED: 2 August 1952, Milan, Italy.
DAUGHTER OF: Arthur Cory and Elizabeth Fanny [or Fanny Elizabeth] Griffin Cory.
WROTE UNDER: Bal Krishna; V. C. Griffin; Victoria Cory; Victoria Cross(e); Vivian Cory; Vivien Cory.

Notorious as the "Noël Coward of the early Nineties" and one of the most daring of the "New Woman" writers, C. adopted her pseudonym, and inaugurated her career, by publishing "Theodora: A Fragment" in the *Yellow Book* in 1895. This story—a first-person account in male persona of a young archaelogist's passionate attraction to a brusque, boyish, cigar-smoking heiress—was condemned as part of a trend towards sexual sordidness and literary degeneracy. She subsequently published twenty-six volumes of fiction, all dealing with sexual love, generally set in exotic locations (among them Italy, India, Hungary, Egypt, Utah, and Alaska), sometimes across boundaries of race, religion, convention, and law. Her books were adapted for the stage and screen, reviewed world-wide, and translated into French, Norwegian, and Italian; *Anna Lombard* (1901), *Life's Shop-Window* (1907), and *Five Nights* (1908) appeared in multiple editions. Her productivity declined in the 1920s and 1930s, as did the sales of her books. Her themes remained consistent: sexual love as the summit of material and spiritual values; the triumph of individual ambition over social circumstances; the crucial importance of setting one's course—in love and in work—and allowing nothing to deflect steady progress in the direction of one's goals. Her narrative situations are imaginative and surprising.

Born in India, where her father was an army officer, she selected as a pseudonym the name of a military decoration, as if to imply that she too had engaged in combat and displayed valor. The initials "V. C." corresponded to "Victoria Cross," a name she used instead of her birth name, and suggested double meanings: the frankness of her fiction would cross (Queen) Victoria, or make Victoria cross. Her first heroine, Theodora, appeared to cross lines of gender, adopting male assertiveness and mobility and, ultimately, male attire. Her later fiction depicts a variety of transgressions. *Anna Lombard* contrasts a woman's physical passion for a Pathan with her intellectual attraction to an Englishman, along with the motivations that lead her to murder her child, with an author's understanding and sympathy, to claim her own future. In the continuation of "Theodora," *Six Chapters of a Man's Life* (1903), the heroine saves her lover's life by yielding sexually to a group of Egyptian men. C.'s interest in colorful settings, particularly India, reflects not only the years she spent there but also an enthusiasm she shared with her older sister Adela Florence "Violet" Cory Nicolson, who lived many years in India and who wrote, under the name "Laurence Hope," several volumes of love lyrics, including *The Garden of Kama* and *Indian Love*.

C.'s perspective, like her name, frequently appears to be a disguise. Her first novel, *The Woman Who Didn't* (1895), was marketed by her publisher, John Lane, as a rejoinder to Grant Allen's *The Woman Who Did*, which had appeared earlier that year in the "Keynotes" series. Allen's novel, condemned in the company of Thomas Hardy's *Jude the Obscure* as shocking and repulsive, deals with a woman's decision to live with a romantic partner in free union, without legal or religious sanction: From this perspective, all married women, by definition, are women who didn't do what his heroine did. *The Woman Who Didn't* has as its subject a much narrower topic: not the legitimacy of marriage itself, but the allegiance to a pre-existing tie. In *The Woman Who Didn't*, a married woman declines the affections of a distinctly charmless man. Although the title of this novel may have led some readers to assume that the writer was attempting to defend convention, a careful reading of the novel showed otherwise. *The Woman Who Didn't* is a character study masquerading as a polemic; it is far from a defense of conventional marriage.

Marriage for C. was sometimes a convenience, occasionally a suitable accompaniment to love, but never a necessity or a significant obstacle to extramarital passion. In *Hilda against the World* (1914), a loveless marriage takes place for practical reasons, and love follows thereafter; the chief characters in *Self and the Other* (1911) are unmarried lovers; in *Daughters of Heaven* (1920), husbands are repeatedly condemned for interfering with the freedom of wives whose affections they have forfeited. *Life's Shop-Window* (1907) and *Five Nights* (1908) contrast the religious, legal, spiritual, and psychological bases of monogamy.

Several novels depict the price of artistic success. *Paula: A Sketch from Life* (1896) portrays an aspiring playwright, intensely ambitious, who marries a man she does not love in exchange for his producing her first play. She experiences the glow of artistic fulfillment and fame and goes on to achieve romantic fulfillment when she saves the life of the man she loves through a transfusion of her blood. In *Over Life's Edge* (1921), a writer abandons fame for the privacy of a deserted cavern, allowing herself to be assumed dead. The writer's name, Violet Cresswell, suggests an identification with C. herself, who isolated herself from the post-1890s literary world, concealed information about her private life, and lived—generally in Italy, Colorado, and Switzerland—with her maternal uncle Heneage Griffin.

C.'s late fiction returns to her earliest themes. *Martha Brown, M.P.: A Girl of Tomorrow* (1935) is a utopian fantasy set in a thirtieth-century England in which women are the dominant sex. Although women have assumed male garb, mannerisms, and privileges, there has been no noticeable improvement in the ability of men and women to understand each other across the persistent, if reversed, gender boundaries. At the end, Martha flies off—over her husband's dead body—to the United States, where men remain dominant. The perspective is ambivalent: Although Martha perceives her departure as necessary and desirable, she also perceives it as a form of death; the novel's vision of her cheerful activity, in the world she leaves behind her, is compelling, to her and to the reader.

Although C.'s novels have not been reissued since the 1930s, "Theodora" is included in *Daughters of Decadence* (1993). In the 1890s, her name was familiar enough to figure in one of Oscar Wilde's witticisms: "If one could only marry Thomas Hardy to Victoria Cross, he might have gained some inkling of real passion to animate his little keepsake pictures of starched ladies." More recently, her intense passion, ingenious plots, and speculative tendencies have received critical attention.

WORKS: "Theodora: A Fragment," *Yellow Book* (1895; rpt. in *Daughters of Decadence: Women Writers of the Fin-de-Siècle*, ed. E. Showalter, 1993). *The Woman Who Didn't* (1895; also published as *A Woman Who Did Not*). *Paula: A Sketch from Life* (1896). *A Girl of the Klondike* (1899). *Anna Lombard* (1901). *Six Chapters of a Man's Life* (1903). *To-morrow?* (1904). *The Religion of Evelyn Hastings* (1908). *Life of My Heart* (1905). *Six Women* (1906). *Life's Shop-Window* (1907). *Five Nights* (1908). *The Eternal Fires* (1910). (as Bal Krishna) *The Love of Kusuma: An Eastern Love Story* (1910). *Self and the Other* (1911). *The Life Sentence* (1912). *The Greater Law* (1914; also published as *Hilda against the World*). *Daughters of Heaven* (1920). *Over Life's Edge* (1921). *The Beating Heart* (1924). *Electric Love* (1929). *The Unconscious Sinner* (1930; also published as *The Innocent Sinner*). *A Husband's Holiday* (1932). *The Girl in the Studio: The Story of Her Strange, New Way of Loving* (1934). *Martha Brown, M.P.: A Girl of Tomorrow* (1935). *Jim* (1937).

BIBLIOGRAPHY: Ardis, A. *New Women, New Novels: Feminism and Early Modernism* (1991). Beauman, N. *A Very Great Profession: The Woman's Novel 1914–39* (1983). Calder, J. *Women and Marriage in Victorian Fiction* (1976). Cunningham, G. *The New Woman and the Victorian Novel* (1978). Fernando, L. *"New Women" in the Late Victorian Novel* (1977). Knapp, S. M., in *Rediscovering Forgotten Radicals: British Women Writers 1889–1939,* ed. A. Ingram and D. Patai (1993). Knapp, *News-Stead* (1993, 1994). Mix, K. L. *A Study in Yellow: The Yellow Book and its Contributors* (1960). Patai, D. *Extrapolation* (1982). Stead, W. T. *Review of Reviews* (1901). Stokes, S. *Pilloried!* (1928).

For articles in reference works, see: *DLB. 1890s. Grimes. Oxford. Who Goes There: A Bibliographic Dictionary,* ed. J. A. Rook. *WN.*

Other references: *Academy and Literature* (5 December 1896, 11 February 1899). *Athenaeum* (17 October 1896, 25 February 1905). *Blackwood's Edinburgh Magazine* (June 1895), *Contemporary Review* (April 1895). *Critic* (25 July 1896). *Fortnightly Review* (1 April 1895). *Literary Review* (2 April 1921). *Literary World* (5 October 1895). *Literature* (4 March 1899). *Mirror* (26 May 1910). *Nineteenth Century* (April 1895). *Review of Reviews* (1895, 1904, 1905). *NYTBR* (1 June 1901, 23 July 1904, 15 December 1906, 9 February 1907, 15 June 1907, 24 October 1908, 4 June 1922). *Saturday Review* [London] (21 September 1895, 17 October 1914). *Sunday Express* (11 October 1953). *TLS* (12 January 1906, 18 January 1907, 12 January 1911, 12 December 1912). *Westminster Review* (June 1895).

Shoshana Milgram Knapp

Priscilla Cotton

DIED: 1664.
MARRIED: Arthur Cotton.

C., a Quaker pamphleteer associated with southern England, Cornwall, and particularly Plymouth, wrote two notable pamphlets during the 1650s. The first, *To the Priests and People of England,* 1655, coauthored by Mary Cole, was written from Exeter prison. (She was imprisoned because, as a Quaker, she refused to identify with the Church of England.) In this tract she argues against the biblical injunctions preventing women from preaching. She does this by defining the word "woman" as "weakness" and suggests that "the woman or weakness whether male or female, is forbidden to speak in the church." Conversely, those who are spiritually inspired, whether male or female, are led by the "light within" and have the right both to preach and to govern.

In a later tract, *A Brief Description by way of Supposition* (1659), C. turns to political theory. In this, she envisions a utopian society marked by religious toleration and universal education. Her last published pamphlet, *A Visitation of Love unto all People* (1661) is a call to all religions to become reunited as followers of Christ. Her earlier magnanimity towards other faiths appears to have waned as she urges Turks, Jews, and others to renounce "idolatry, covetousness, and all uncleanness."

WORKS: (with Mary Cole) *To the Priests and People of England* (1655). *As I was in the Prison-house* (1656). *A Brief Description by way of Supposition* (1659). *A Visitation of Love unto all People* (1661).

BIBLIOGRAPHY: Hobby, E. *Virtue of Necessity: English Women's Writing 1649–88* (1988). Mack, P. *Visionary Women: Ecstatic Prophecy in Seventeenth-Century England* (1992).

For articles in reference works, see: *Bell. Feminist. WL17C.*

Jane Baston

Cowden Clarke, Mary Victoria: See *Clarke, Mary Victoria (Novello) Cowden*

Hannah Parkhouse Cowley

BORN: 1743, Tiverton, Devon.
DIED: 11 March 1809, Tiverton, Devon.
DAUGHTER OF: Philip Parkhouse.
MARRIED: Thomas Cowley, c. 1768.

Although not as well-known as Aphra Behn or Susanna Centlivre, C. warrants attention for her thirteen plays. She may have been influenced by the fact that her father, Philip Parkhouse, was a bookseller who could trace his heritage to John Gay. At the age of twenty-five, she married Captain Thomas Cowley of the East India Company. On visiting the playhouse with her husband, she declared that she could do better than the playwright being staged. This enthusiasm caused her to write her first play, *The Runaway,* which was successfully produced by David Garrick at Drury Lane on 15 February 1776. Later she was to write of the play "that it was one of the most profitable Plays, both to the Author and Manager, that appears in the records of the *Treasury Books* at either house."

For eighteen years, she wrote plays, chiefly comedies, her most successful being *Who's the Dupe?* (1779), *The Belle's Stratagem* (1781), and *A Bold Stroke for a Husband* (1783). She twice ventured into the world of tragedy and twice failed. C.'s first tragedy, *Albina,* produced an unpleasant confrontation with Hannah More, whom she accused of plagiarism. Puzzled at production delays, C. later wrote in her preface to the play, "I learnt with great surprise, that it [More's *The Law of Lombardy*] bore a resemblance to *Albina.*" The argument that followed carried over into an unpleasant exchange of articles in the newspapers, none of which helped the play, which was relegated to unprofitable summer production at the Haymarket. Her other tragedy, *The Fate of Sparta* (1788), which Leigh Hunt described as hackneyed in its sentiments, was not revived after its initial run of eight performances at Drury Lane.

Yet C. is best remembered for her comedies of manners, which depend on lovely heroines, who through clever intrigues, inspired by the love of virtue and the goal of an ideal marriage, triumph over attractive but superficial males. *The Belle's Stratagem* reveals C. at her best. The play opens with Doricourt contracted to marry Letitia Hardy, an English "country cousin" whom he has not met, and who, he is sure, lacks the vitality of "the restless charmers of Italy and France." Beautiful, modest Letitia, realizing that she will be doomed to a loveless marriage, plots to make Doricourt dislike her on the assumption "that it is easier to convert a sentiment to its opposite than to transform indifference to a tender passion." She then alienates Doricourt by becoming a parody of the "country cousin"; later, at a masquerade, she uses all her English charms and conquers him completely. Finally, using the further intrigue of a false marriage, she wins him. The play ends with Doricourt's praising English women, with their innate modesty, above their Continental counterparts.

The effectiveness of *The Belle's Stratagem* undoubtedly resides in the character of Letitia Hardy, which was a favorite role of Mrs. Jordan and which was to appeal to fine actresses for the next century—including Fanny Davenport, Ada Rehan, and Ellen Terry, who acted the part opposite Henry Irving's Doricourt. In this century, the play was presented at the Royal Court in 1913.

Most of the comedies had limited stage histories of from one to sixteen performances over one- to two-year spans. The exceptions, in addition to *The Belle's Stratagem,* were *The Runaway, Which Is the Man?, A Bold Stroke for a Husband,* and *Who's the Dupe?* These were frequently revived during the last two decades of the eighteenth century, and *A Bold Stroke for a Husband* was revived in 1872 at New York's Fifth Avenue Theater, where Fanny Davenport played Donna Olivia. The critic for the *New York Times* paid tribute to the actors and the playwright when he expressed the wish that "modern writers would more frequently strive to catch something of the briskness and rapidity of their dialogue and the fun and contrast of their characters."

C.'s nondramatic work includes a number of long, sentimental romances and a poetic correspondence between Anna Matilda (C.) and Della Crusca (Robert Merry), which was attacked by William Gifford in his satire *The Baviad* (1794).

C.'s best plays reflect clever plots, sound characterization, and lively dialogue, qualities that make them good reading today. Her *Works* (1813), published in three volumes, contain eleven plays and most of the poems.

WORKS: *The Runaway* (1776). *Who's the Dupe?* (1779). *Albina, Countess Raymond* (1779). *The School for Eloquence* (1780). *The Maid of Arragon; a Tale* (1780). *The Belle's Stratagem* (1781). *The World as It Goes; or a Party at Montpellier* (1781; also titled *Second Thoughts Are Best*). *Which Is Man?* (1782). *A Bold Stroke for a Husband* (1783). *More Ways Than One* (1784). *A School for Greybeards, or The Mourning Bride* (1786). *The Scottish Village, or Pitcairne Green* (1786). *The Poetry of Anna Matilda* (1788). *The Fate of Sparta, or The Rival Kings (1788). A Day in Turkey: or the Russian Slaves* (1792). *The Town Before You* (1795). *The Siege of Acre: An Epic Poem* (1801). *The Works of Mrs. Cowley: Dramas and Poems,* 3 vols. (1813). *The Plays of Hannah Cowley,* 2 vols., ed. F. M. Link (1979).

BIBLIOGRAPHY: Baker, D., et al. *Biographica Dramatica,* 2nd rev. (1812). Donkin, E., in *Curtain Calls: British and American Women and the Theater, 1680–1820,* ed. M. A. Schofield and C. Macheski (1991). Gagen, J. *UMSE* (1990). "Life of Mrs. Cowley," in *Works of Mrs. Cowley. . . . ,* Vol. I (1813). Norton, J. E. *Book Collector* (1958). Rhodes, R. C. *RES* (1929).

For articles in reference works, see: *Bloomsbury. DLB. DNB. OCEL. Oxford. ToddBWW. ToddDBA.*

Philip Bordinat

Pearl Craigie

BORN: 3 November 1867, Chelsea, Massachusetts, United States.
DIED: 13 August 1906, London.
DAUGHTER OF: John Morgan Richards and Laura Arnold Richards.

MARRIED: Reginald Craigie, 1887.
WROTE UNDER: Pearl Craigie; John Oliver Hobbes.

C. was born to a wealthy American businessman and his wife, who moved to London when she was one year old. She was educated in London and at a finishing school in Paris, though much of her education resulted from her omnivorous readings as an adolescent of most of the important authors writing in English and from regular attendance at many of London's theaters. In 1887, she married Reginald Craigie, a banker with whom she was badly matched because of his interest in other women and in alcohol; she separated from him in 1891, taking her son, John, with her, and divorced him in 1895. She studied Greek and Latin at University College, London, and published a successful first novel, *Some Emotions and a Moral* (1891). In 1892, she converted from her family's Nonconformist variety of Protestantism to the more mystical Roman Catholicism, which thereafter pervaded her life to a degree that precluded any subsequent liaisons or marriage.

C., in addition to writing well-received novels during her relatively short career, also turned to playwriting, becoming friends with actress Ellen Terry and novelist-playwright George Moore, whose fascination with C. endured in his memoirs, letters, and fiction. Her first comedy, *Journeys End in Lovers' Meeting,* appeared in 1894; Prime Minister William Gladstone requested that she personally read the play to him as he recuperated from cataract surgery. She became president of the Society of Women Journalists in 1895, lectured widely, and reported from India for several newspapers in 1903.

Her health, never strong, diminished after her travels, sometimes requiring bedrest for several weeks at a time in the family home, at which times she dictated her novels to a secretary. She attempted a trip to the United States in 1905, but returned home early because of poor health, suffered a mild heart attack in March 1906, and died on 13 August. Though Moore encouraged a rumor that she had died of a drug overdose, the official verdict was heart failure. Lord George Nathaniel Curzon, who had been among her suitors following her divorce, dedicated a memorial plaque to her in University College.

C. is best remembered for her novels and her comedies, Wildean in nature, though she also wrote well-received stories, essays, and lectures. Aside from two stories published when she was only ten, her career began with *Some Emotions and a Moral,* which was recommended to her publisher, T. Fisher Unwin, by Edward Garnett, Unwin's reader. She created "John Oliver Hobbes" from the names of her father and son, from Cromwell, and from the seventeenth-century rationalist philosopher. The best-selling novel is a humorous tale of young love and marriage in fashionable English society, a tale that ends in violence and melodrama. She rapidly, almost annually, churned out a number of successful if weakly plotted novels, including *The Sinner's Comedy* (1892), *A Study in Temptations* (1893), *A Bundle of Life* (1894), *The Gods, Some Mortals, and Lord Wickenham* (1895), *The Herb Moon* (1896), and *The School for Saints* (1897), as well as a one-volume collection of four novellas, *The Tales of John Oliver Hobbes* (1894).

C.'s plays were even more popular than her novels. Her first effort, written in collaboration with Moore, was a fragmentary first act entitled *The Fool's Hour* that appeared in the first issue of *The Yellow Book* (April 1984). That same year they collaborated on *Journeys End in Lovers' Meeting,* a play that, though immensely popular for many years, has been described as "charming froth," its three characters merely stereotyped figures but its theme offering unusual insight into love and marriage and its wit making it a distinctly modern social comedy. In 1898, her year of greatest success, she wrote *The Ambassador,* a four-act social comedy that was immensely popular in London and elsewhere in England as well as in the United States, followed rapidly by *Osborn and Ursyne* (1898), *A Repentance* (1899), and *The Wisdom of the Wise* (1901). *The Ambassador* was almost immediately compared favorably to the plays of Oscar Wilde, though modern readers or audiences might also identify it with works by George Bernard Shaw and Noël Coward. *A Repentance,* a one-act tragedy set in Spain in 1835, perplexed many theatregoers. She wrote *Osborn and Ursyne,* a more mythically oriented tragedy, in a little more than two weeks; this verse drama was not produced in England but appeared solely in printed form, though it received a student production in New York in 1899. She collaborated with Murray Carson on *The Bishop's Move: A Comedy in Three Acts* (1902), which was successful in England though considerably less so in the United States because of the work's "superficial" theme and characters; her sole later play was a Molière-style comedy, *The Flute of Pan* (1904; subsequently issued as a novel in 1905).

C. had a wide circle of friends, including Jennie Churchill, William Archer, Lord George and Lady Mary Curzon, Ellen Terry, and others, and she corresponded with such figures as Thomas Hardy and Edmund Gosse. She distinguished herself in several genres and moved easily in such disparate worlds as end-of-the-century English society, journalism, literature, theater, politics, and religion, among others. She once wrote to a friend: "If my true story could be written, it would be the history of an air-bird in the water. I must keep, somehow, long enough in the air not to suffocate under the sea." Her plays have long since ceased reflecting this "air-bird" quality, but her novels continue to appeal because of their contrast between faith and passion, their wit, their appealing style, their substantial philosophic content.

WORKS: *Some Emotions and a Moral* (1891). *The Sinner's Comedy* (1892). *A Study in Temptations* (1893). *A Bundle of Life* (1894). (with George Moore) *Journeys End in Lovers' Meeting* (1894). (with George Moore) *The Fool's Hour* (1894). *The Gods, Some Mortals, and Lord Wickenham* (1895). *The Tales of John Oliver Hobbes* (1895). *The Herb Moon* (1896). *The School for Saints* (1897). *The Ambassador: A Comedy in Four Acts* (1898). *Osborn and Ursyne* (1898). *A Repentance* (1899). *Robert Orange* (1900). *The Wisdom of the Wise* (1901). *The Serious Wooing* (1901). *Tales About Temperaments* (1902). (with Murray Carson) *The Bishop's Move: A Comedy in Three Acts* (1902). *Love and the Soul Hunters* (1902). *Imperial India: Letters from the East* (1903). *Letters from a Silent Study* (1904). *The Flute of Pan* (prod., 1904; pub. as novel, 1905). *The Vineyard* (1904). *The Artist's Life* (1904). *The Dream and the Business* (1906).

BIBLIOGRAPHY: Archer, W. *Real Conversations* (1904). Churchill, Lady R. *Reminiscences* (1908). Churchill, P. and J. Mitchell. *Jennie: Lady Randolph Churchill* (1974). Clarke, I. C. *Six Portraits* (1935). Colby, V. *The Singular Anomaly: Women Novelists of the Nineteenth Century* (1970). Courtney, W. L. *The Feminine Note in Fiction* (1904). Curzon, G. *Subjects of the Day* (1915). Dilks, D. *Curzon in India* (1970). Harding, M. D. *Air-Bird in the Water: The Life and Works of Pearl Craigie (John Oliver Hobbes)* (1996). Hone, J. *The Life of George Moore* (1936). Leslie, S. *Studies in Sublime Failure* (1932). Maison, M. *John Oliver Hobbes: Her Life and Works* (1976). Martin, R. G. *Jennie: The Life of Lady Randolph Churchill* (1969). Mosley, L. *The Glorious Fault: The Life of Lord Curzon* (1960). Nicolson, N. *Mary Curzon* (1977). Richards, J. M. *The Life of John Oliver Hobbes Told in her Correspondence with Numerous Friends* (1911). Ronaldshay, Earl of (L. J. L. Dundas). *The Life of Lord Curzon* (1927). Rose, K. *Superior Person: A Portrait of Curzon and His Circle in Late Victorian England* (1969). Weintraub, S. *The London Yankees* (1979).

For articles in reference works, see: *Bloomsbury. Cambridge. Feminist. Oxford. ToddBWW.*

Other references: *The Reinterpretation of Victorian Literature*, ed. J. E. Baker (1950). Baring, M. *Have You Anything to Declare?* (1936). Brown, W. F. *Through Windows of Memory* (1946). Chesterton, G. K. *Heretics* (1905). Clark, B. H. *Intimate Portraits* (1951). Edel, L. *Stuff of Sleep and Dreams: Experiments in Literary Psychology* (1982). Edwards, O. *LonT* (15 December 1966). Gerber, H. E. *George Moore in Transition* (1968). Howells, W. D. *North American Review* (1906). Jackson, H. *The Eighteen Nineties* (1913, 1966). Maison, M. *Listener* (28 August 1969). Mitchell, S. *George Moore* (1916). Procter, Z. *Life and Yesterday* (1960). Stetz, M. D. and M. S. Lasnor. *England in the 1880s* (1989). Sutton, E. *Dublin Review* (1927). Terry, E. *The Story of My Life* (1908). Weintraub, S. *Beardsley* (1969). Williams, H. *Modern English Writers* (1919).

Paul Schlueter

Dinah Maria Mulock Craik

BORN: 20 April 1826, Stoke-on-Trent, Staffordshire.
DIED: 12 October 1887, Shortlands, Kent.
DAUGHTER OF: Thomas Mulock and Dinah Mellard Mulock.
MARRIED: George Lillie Craik, 1865.
WROTE UNDER: Author of *John Halifax, Gentleman;* Dinah Maria Craik; Mrs. Craik; D.M.M.; Dinah Maria Mulock; Miss Mulock.

C.'s literary estimation has varied widely. In 1856, when she published *John Halifax, Gentleman,* she was a respected novelist, frequently compared to the Brontës and George Eliot. The huge popularity of *John Halifax,* while ensuring her literary fame and financial success, by its very success doomed her to critical dismissal: She was promptly labeled a women's novelist and her work thereafter treated with condescension. At the time of her death she was widely considered a successful but second-rate writer whose works catered to middle-class Victorian tastes, and her work came to represent the worst clichés of Victorian fiction: complacency, sermonizing, and sentimentality. Only recently have feminist critics begun to consider her work seriously, noting that C. encouraged a closer look at women's place in Victorian society while advocating greater self-reliance and independence for women.

C.'s life indicates that she lived by the principles she championed. Her father was an evangelical preacher whose undependable support forced C.'s mother to open a day school at home during one of his frequent absences. Then thirteen, the precocious C. dropped out of Brampton House Academy to help her mother teach Latin. In 1839, Mrs. Mulock inherited money and the family moved to London, where they remained until 1844. When her mother died in 1845, her father, ever a sporadic provider, abandoned his children entirely. C., who had begun publishing poetry signed "D. M. M." in 1841, chose to support herself by writing. During her career she would produce children's stories, poems, translations, and nonfiction, as well as novels.

The older of her two brothers, Tom, died in 1847, after which she and her brother Ben shared lodgings in London, where C. began to move in literary circles. Her first novel, *The Ogilvies,* appeared in 1849. When Ben departed for Australia in 1850, C. set up house with another young single woman, Frances Martin, and lived an unconventional latch-key life, acting as mentor to many other ambitious young woman. In 1864, she was awarded a Civil List pension, which she always used to help less successful writers.

Some time in the early 1860s, George Lillie Craik, nephew of the historian and writer of the same name, spent several weeks convalescing at C.'s cottage in Hampstead. They were married in 1865, when C. was thirty-nine, Craik twenty-eight. In 1869, they adopted an infant girl, whom she named Dorothy. C. continued to write prolifically after her marriage and to support struggling writers and young career women. She helped to design Corner House at Shortlands, where she and Craik lived after its completion in 1869. She died of heart failure in 1887 while preparing for Dorothy's wedding.

John Halifax, Gentleman, the novel that made her name, has never been out of print since its first appearance. In this rags-to-riches fable, the titular hero's rise from orphan to "gentleman," through hard work and Christian virtue, embodies the Protestant ethic and prefigures the principles of Samuel Smiles' *Self-Help* (1859). Called by contemporary critics a modern *Pilgrim's Progress,* it is also a historical allegory depicting the rise of the British middle class and the advent of industrialization. The narrator, Phineas Fletcher, is one of a long line of crippled characters in C.'s works and, like Prince Dolor in her perennially popular children's book *The Little Lame Prince (1875),* has been considered by recent critics to represent women's restricted role in Victorian society.

C. addressed the question of women's role most directly in *A Woman's Thoughts on Women and Plain Thoughts* (1857). In these essays, she urges women to become financially and emotionally independent, thus earning self-respect as well as self-reliance. She also advocates a sense of unity and sisterhood among women, encouraging disregard of class boundaries and empathetic understanding toward "fallen" women. Although she feels that marriage and motherhood represent the most satisfying goal women can attain, she notes that they should be prepared to support themselves should this destiny not fall to their lot. She also maintains that such training in self-reliance will be useful even for women who marry, for it can only earn the respect of their husbands and make them more useful wives and mothers. She does not call for revolutionary change; the careers she proposes—in teaching and the arts—are those traditionally accessible to women. But she accepts as universal women's need for independent, meaningful lives and accords respect to women's emotional as well as financial needs.

Her novel *A Life for a Life* (1859) expresses much of her philosophy, positing a single moral standard for men and women and suggesting that an unwed mother can nevertheless be a useful member of society. Some other novels of social purpose are *King Arthur* (1886), a propaganda novel in favor of adoption; *A Brave Lady* (1870), which advocates the Married Women's Property Act; and *Hannah* (1871), which criticizes the marital restrictions placed on in-laws. Most of her novels, however, follow *John Halifax* in enacting a traditional romantic formula in a domestic setting, and her later works in particular are prone to sentiment and preachiness. While C.'s movement toward the subversion of contemporary ideology is always restrained by conventional values, her work both initiates and contributes to a fresh assessment of women's position.

WORKS: *Michael the Miner* (1846). *How to Win Love; or, Rhoda's Lesson* (1848). *Cola Monti; or, the Story of a Genius* (1849). *The Ogilvies* (1849). *Olive* (1850). *The Half-Caste: An Old Governess's Tale* (1851). *Alice Learmont: A Fairy Tale* (1852). *Bread Upon the Waters; A Governess's Life* (1852). *The Head of the Family* (1852). *Agatha's Husband* (1853). *Avillion and Other Tales* (1853). *A Hero: Philip's Book* (1853). *The Little Lychetts* (1855). *John Halifax, Gentleman* (1856). *A Woman's Thoughts About Women and Plain Thoughts* (1857). *Nothing New* (1857). *Domestic Stories* (1859). *A Life for a Life* (1859; rev. ed., 1860). *Poems* (1859). *Romantic Tales* (1859). *Our Year: A Child's Book in Prose and Verse* (1860). *Studies from Life* (1861). *The Fairy Book* (1863). *Mistress and Maid* (1863). *Christian's Mistake* (1865). *A New Year's Gift to Sick Children* (1865). *A Noble Life* (1866). (trans.) *M. de Barante, A Memoir*, by F. P. G. Guizot (1867). (trans.) *A French Country Family*, by H. DeWitt (1867). *Two Marriages* (1867). *The Woman's Kingdom* (1869). *A Brave Lady* (1870). *The Unkind Word and Other Stories* (1870). *Fair France: Impressions of a Traveller* (1871). *Little Sunshine's Holiday* (1871). *The Adventures of a Brownie, as Told to My Child* (1872). *Hannah* (1872). *My Mother and I: A Girl's Love-Story* (1874). *The Little Lame Prince and His Travelling Cloak* (1875). *Sermons out of Church* (1875). *Songs of Our Youth* (1875). *The Laurel Bush: An Old-Fashioned Love Story* (1877). *A Legacy* (1878). *Young Mrs. Jardine* (1879). *Miss Letty's Experiences* (1880). *Thirty Years: Being Poems New and Old* (1880; also published as *Poems*, 1888). *Children's Poetry* (1881). *His Little Mother and Other Tales and Sketches* (1881). *Children's Poetry* (1881). *Plain Speaking* (1882). (trans.) *A Christian Woman*, by H. deWitt (1882). *An Unsentimental Journey Through Cornwall* (1884). *Miss Tommy* (1884). *About Money and Other Things* (1886). *King Arthur: Not a Love Story* (1886). *An Unknown Country* (1887). *Fifty Golden Years* (1887). *A Christmas Carol* (1888). *Concerning Men and Other Papers* (1888). *A Friend Stands at the Door* (1888). Christina Rossetti, "Maude," and Dinah Mulock Craik, "On Sisterhoods" and "A Woman's Thoughts on Women," ed. E. Showalter (1993).

BIBLIOGRAPHY: Brantlinger, P. *The Spirit of Reform: British Literature and Politics, 1832–1867* (1977). Foster, S. *Victorian Women's Fiction* (1985). Hickok, K. *Representations of Women: Nineteenth-Century British Women's Poetry* (1984). Mitchell, S. *Dinah Mulock Craik* (1983). Oliphant, M. *Macmillan's Magazine* (1887). Parr, L. *The Author of John Halifax, Gentleman: A Memoir* (1898). Showalter, E. *FSt* (1975). Showalter, E. *A Literature of Their Own* (1977).

For articles in reference works, see: *Allibone SUP. BA19C. BDBW. Bloomsbury. Cassell. DLB. ELB. Europa. Feminist. GWELN. JBA. NCHEL. NCLC. OCCL. OCEL. Oxford. SATA. ToddBWW* (under "Mulock"). *VB.*

Other references: Hutton, P. H. *North British Review* (1858). Martin, F. *Athenaeum* (October 1887). Miles, A. *The Poets and the Poetry of the Nineteenth Century* (1891). Parr, L. *Women Novelists of Queen Victoria's Reign* (1897).

Amanda DeWees
(updated by Natalie Joy Woodall)

Elizabeth (Berkeley) Craven, Baroness Craven, afterward Margravine of Anspach (Ansbach)

BORN: 17 December 1750, Spring Garden, Middlesex.
DIED: 12 January 1828, Naples, Italy.
DAUGHTER OF: Augustus, fourth Earl of Berkeley, and Elizabeth (Drax), Countess of Berkeley.
MARRIED: William Craven, 1767; Christian Frederic, Margrave of Anspach (Ansbach), 1791.

C. was a playwright, novelist, translator, librettist, and musician whose learning, alliances, travels, and memoirs earned her an international audience for fifty years. The occasional nature of her most popular writings meant that their vogue did not much outlast their author. C.'s idiosyncrasies led to the jaundiced viewpoint of later biographers, such as George Paston, who wrote a classic hatchet job in *Little Memoirs of the Eighteenth Century*.

Her Ladyship, who is said to have been an admirable *raconteur* in society, had a dull and incoherent prose style; and was so engrossed by the contemplation of her own beauty, virtues, and accomplishments, that it is necessary to sift her autobiography and letters very carefully in order to extract a few grains of amusement, or even of truth.

Such criticism misses much that is attractive about C.'s work and life.

Not expected to survive at birth, C. had a delicate childhood. Despite her poor health and negligent mother, C. developed intellectually at an early age. When she married the nephew and heir of Lord Craven at the age of seventeen, C. had already gained a reputation as a linguist, wit, and beauty. Her social circle came to include Horace Walpole, Samuel Johnson, David Garrick, and Sir Joshua Reynolds. Johnson thought she talked too much; Reynolds began but never finished a portrait of her. Walpole was an early champion of her work, either because of a toadying impulse or a genuine crush. He had her play *The Sleep-Walker* printed at his own Strawberry Hill Press in 1778.

C. worked comfortably in French, German, Latin, and Italian (by no means unparalleled accomplishments for a woman of her rank), but C. was unusual in the extent to which she used her wide reading in these languages as a basis for stories and plays. Her *oeuvre* reflects the tastes of the times: private theatricals, light opera, "humors" comedy, and sentimental drama. *The Sleep-Walker* was the first work of Count de Pont deVesle's to be translated; *The Statue Feast* (1782) was a translation of Molière's *Le Festin de Pierre; The Robbers* (1799) was a version of Schiller's *Die Rauber.* Her short novel *Modern Anecdotes of the Ancient Family of the Kinkvervankotdarsprackingatchderns* (1780) was popular enough to see five editions; a play based on it was written by Miles Andrews and performed at the Theatre Royal in Haymarket in 1781. Though C. intended most of her plays as private entertainments, some, like *A Miniature Picture* and *The Silver Tankard,* had public runs.

A pivotal event both in her life and her literary career was C.'s separation from Lord Craven in 1780. He had taken a mistress quite publicly and was surprised to find out that C. knew. She resisted an effort by Craven's family to silence her, and she seems to have triumphed over the standard counter-rumor of her own intrigues with a servant. Her response to the separation was to depart for the Continent and travel through Greece, Turkey, Austria, Russia, and what is now Romania. While in Ansbach, she visited and became the mistress of Christian Frederic, Margrave of Ansbach. Their correspondence was published in London in 1786 under the title *Journey through the Crimea to Constantinople.* Partly because of C.'s scandalous reputation, this mélange of travel sketches, opinions, and reflections on customs became an international success; it was published in France in 1789 and in Vienna in 1800.

In September 1791, Lord Craven died; a little more than a month later, C. and the margrave were married. They moved to England the next year and purchased Brandenburgh House in Hammersmith and Benham House in Berkshire; both houses became sites of theatricals and feasts for the rest of the decade. C.'s most popular book, her *Memoirs,* appeared in 1826, two years before her death.

Far from being dull, her prose, especially *Journey* and *Memoirs,* bears out her reputation for wit, storytelling, and cattiness (for example, she met and was unimpressed by the Empress Catherine, who had "the remains of a fine skin"). Her by-the-way opinions are often as interesting as the subject at hand. As for incoherence, she clearly wrote at great speed without looking back—but then, she was neither the first nor the last memoiriste with that failing.

For a woman who enjoyed a form of emancipation, she is ambivalent about the place of women. "Through every age and every country we shall find women adored and oppressed," she writes. Further, she defends the adeptness and versatility of the feminine intelligence: "Whenever women are indulged with any freedom, they polish sooner than man." Nevertheless, when actually comparing the roles of women and men, C. reverts to a standard defense of male domination—the idea that biology is destiny.

Intellectual powers respond to the destination of nature: Men have penetration and solid judgment to fit them for governing; women have sufficient understanding to make a respectable figure under good government; a greater proportion would excite a dangerous rivalship. Still, C. was very conscious of being both a writer and a woman of rank. Some of the prefaces to her plays plead for the same critical openness accorded to male authors.

C. was much more comfortable with comedy than with serious drama. Of her comedies, *The Sleep-Walker* is quite good, as is *A Miniature Picture.* Moralism and the urge to sentimentalize weigh down action, character, and dialogue in her noncomic plays. The range of her female characterizations reflects the split in her thinking: Her female characters are either stereotypes or women who exploit the little freedom they can find within their social niches. Eliza of *The Georgian Princess* (1799), who gains an advantageous marriage through disguise and gender-role reversal, ends the play by saying, "Ladies, I trust you will adopt my plan / and only wear the dress to gain the man." The marriage game is itself a form of role playing that the resourceful woman can work to her own advantage.

Her reading, if not always deep, was promiscuous. She preferred contemporary authors to ancient ones (she once censured Johnson for having precisely the opposite taste) and continental authors to her English countrymen. She prescribed Henault, Fontenelle, Buffon, and Montesquieu as the beginnings of any serious library. C. was certainly not averse either to demonstrating her learning or to talking about herself ("My taste for music and my style of imagination in writing . . . were great sources of delight to me"). C.'s literary persona is so open and unself-conscious that her frequent discussions of herself do not seem like mordant conceit but rather more as Walpole himself recognized: "There is such an integrity and frankness in her consciousness of her own relents, that she speaks of these with a naïveté as if she had no property in them, but only wore them as gifts of the gods." Walpole, not a faithful friend, revised his opinion later into a sort of bitchy condemnation. C.'s writings, however, present her as a learned, ingenuous, authentically accomplished writer.

WORKS: *A Christmas-Box* (1773). (trans.) *The Sleep-Walker,* by P. deVesle (1778). *Modern Anecdotes of the Ancient Family of Kinkvervankotdarsprackingatchderns. A Tale for Christmas 1799* (1780). *A Fashionable Day* (1780).

A Miniature Picture (1780). *The Point at Portsmouth, or The Silver Tankard* (1781). *La Folie du four* (1781). (trans.) *The Statue Feast,* by Molière (1782). *The Arcadian Pastoral* (1782). *A Journey through the Crimea to Constantinople* (1786). *Le Philosophe Moderne* (1790). *The Yorkshire Ghost* (1799). (trans.) *The Robbers,* by F. von Schiller (1799). *The Georgian Princess* (1799). *Puss in Boots* (1799). *Love Rewarded* (1799). *Nourgad* (1803). *Love in a Convent* (1805). *Memoirs* (1826). *The Beautiful Lady Craven* (memoir, 1913). *Three Songs by Lady Elizabeth Craven,* ed. C. Lloyd-Morgan (1992).

BIBLIOGRAPHY: For articles in reference works, see: *Annual Biography and Obituary* (1828). *Biographica Dramatica* (1812). *DNB.* Genest, J. *History of the Stage* (1832).

Other references: Franke, W. *N&Q* (1973). Nicoll, A. *A History of Late Eighteenth Century Drama* (1927). Paston, G. *Little Memoirs of the Eighteenth Century* (1901). Rogers, K. M. *Feminism in Eighteenth-Century England* (1982). *SECC* (1986). Walpole, H. *Letters* (1857–1859).

John Timpane

Bithia May (or Mary) Croker

BORN: c. 1849, Kilgefin, County Roscommon, Ireland.
DIED: 20 October 1920, London.
DAUGHTER OF: the Reverend William Sheppard, Rector of Kilgefin.
MARRIED: Lieutenant-Colonel John Croker.

C., the "talented wife" of Colonel Croker, was "known to the world through her delightful novels of Indian life and experiences" (Black). She was the eldest daughter of the writer and controversialist the Reverend William Sheppard of Kilgefin or Gilgefin, and came of old Puritan stock on both sides of the family. Her father died when she was only seven. Educated at Rockferry, Cheshire, and Tours, France, she spent all her childhood leisure hours in reading, but she was also a famous horsewoman. Her educational records demonstrate her early belletristic gifts, her penchant for descriptions of people and places, her love of history, geography, languages, and poetry, and her repugnance for mathematical subjects. On her return from France, she married John Croker of the twenty-first Royal Scots Fusiliers and traveled to Burma and India with him. She and her husband lived in India and the Far East for fourteen years but later returned to live in London and Bray, in Berkshire.

She started writing in 1880, supposedly to overcome the heat and ennui of life in India; her early works, *Proper Pride* (1882) and *Pretty Miss Neville* (1883), were written for the enjoyment of a select band of bored friends. Initially, *Proper Pride* was rejected by an English publisher in 1881 because the publisher felt that "'The story had no pretensions whatsoever to style or interest, and would not obtain even a passing notice from the public . . .'" (Black). When published, *Proper Pride* had good reviews, three editions in six weeks, and twelve by 1896; it was thought to be a man's work. Eventually her works enjoyed much popularity, were translated into German, and were reprinted through the 1920s and 1930s during the height of her popularity. She was a prolific writer of novels and short stories; her works span over forty volumes.

C.'s "delightful tales from India" are supposedly products of her own observation and experience. The treacheries of the native Indian population and the British woman's trials in a strange land and an unfavorable marriage-market form pervasive themes of her works, such as *"To Let"* (1893), *Diana Barrington* (1888), and *Mr. Jervis* (1894). Her own two favorite works were *A Bird of Passage* (1886) and *Diana Barrington.* Her tales and novels often skillfully weave the themes of female growth, self-realization, and romance with those of the snares and pitfalls infesting the choice of a partner for life.

Her novels sometimes showed the punishment of the heroine, such as in *Proper Pride* where the heroine's pride and distrust separates her from her husband. According to *The Feminist Companion to Literature in English, The Road to Mandalay* (1917) was "full of upright men and calculating women." Some of her works, such as *Mr. Jervis* and *Diana Barrington,* however, showed a keen understanding of the ambivalence and anxiety surrounding the role of the colonial daughter, wife, or mistress in British India. *The Road to Mandalay* was later made into a film. Other novels by her dealt with upper-class life in Ireland, where she and her husband returned to live in retirement.

WORKS: *Proper Pride* (1882). *Pretty Miss Neville* (1883). *Some One Else* (1885). *A Bird of Passage* (1886). *Diana Barrington* (1888). *Two Masters* (1890). *Interference* (1890). *A Family Likeness* (1892). *"To Let"* (1893). *A Third Person* (1893). *Mr. Jervis* (1894). *Married or Single* (1895). *Village Tales and Jungle Tragedies* (1895). *In the Kingdom of Kerry and Other Stories* (1896). *The Real Lady Hilda* (1896). *Beyond the Pale* (1896). *Miss Balmaine's Past* (1898). *Peggy of the Bartons* (1898). *Infatuation* (1899). *Jason and Other Stories* (1899). *Terence* (1899). *Angel; A Sketch in Indian Ink* (1901). *A State Secret, and Other Stories* (1901). *The Cat's Paw* (1902). *Her Own People* (1903). *Johanna* (1903). *The Happy Valley* (1904). *A Nine Days' Wonder* (1905). *The Old Cantonment, With Other Stories of India and Elsewhere* (1905). *The Youngest Miss Mowbray* (1906). *The Company's Servant; A Romance of Southern India* (1907). *The Spanish Necklace* (1907). *Katherine the Arrogant* (1909). *Fame* (1910). *Babes in the Wood; Romance of the Jungles* (1910). *A Rolling Stone* (1911). *The Serpent's Tooth* (1912). *In Old Madras* (1913). *Lismoyle: An Experiment in Ireland* (1914). *Quicksands* (1915). *Given in Marriage* (1916). *The Road to Mandalay* (1917). *A Rash Experiment* (1917). *Bridget* (1918). *Blue China* (1919). *Odds and Ends* (1919). *Jungle Tales* (1919). *The Pagoda Tree* (1919). *The Chaperon* (1920). *The House of Rest* (1921).

BIBLIOGRAPHY: Black, H. *Pen, Pencil, Baton and Mask: Biographical Sketches* (1896). Maher, H. *Roscommon Authors* (1978).

For articles in reference works, see: *BDIW. Feminist. VB.*

Nandini Bhattacharya

Richmal Crompton (Lamburn)

BORN: 15 November 1890, Bury, Lancastershire.
DIED: 11 January 1969, Farnborough, Kent.
DAUGHTER OF: the Reverend Edward John Sewell Lamburn and Clara Lamburn.

Famous as the creator of the "William" stories, writing under the name Richmal Crompton, C. was the middle child of three born to a priest of the Church of England and his wife. C. was given the odd forename "Richmal" after her mother's sister; the name had been used in the family since the seventeenth century.

C.'s father was a teacher at Bury Grammar School in Lancashire, and she attended Elphin's School (for the daughters of clergymen) in Dareley Dale, Derbyshire. Her family's finances were small, but with a founder's scholarship she attended Royal Holloway College (London) in 1911, where she had a university scholarship (1912) and the Driver scholarship in classics (1914)., After graduating from the University of London (1914), she taught classics in Darley Dale (1915–17) and Bromley (Kent) High School for Girls (1919–24). Stricken with polio in 1923, she lost the use of her right leg, gave up teaching, and began a writing career. She did not complain about her disability. Indeed, in later life she said she had led "a much more interesting life" because she had become a writer than she would have done as a schoolmistress.

Her writing began with stories, based on her younger brother and her nephew, and on her own tomboy days. They centered on William Brown, a pubescent, anarchic, and charming brat. He offered little challenges to the Establishment but no real threat, for C. was a staunch conservative in both politics and religion and never condoned antisocial behavior. Her little hero was much like her brother: William Brown was John Lamburn as a child, a boy with scraped knees and messed clothes. In those days, little girls like C. envied boys for their freedom from restrictions placed upon proper little ladies. William first appeared in *Home Magazine* in February 1919. Monthly tales followed in that periodical and later in the *Happy Magazine* and were collected for two books in 1922: *Just William* and *More William.* When polio struck C., the success of the "William" stories was already established. That encouraged her to become a professional writer, though she missed dealing directly with children as a schoolteacher. From then until the end of her life, C. imitated Agatha Christie's self-description as "a sausage machine": the "William" books came out with great regularity and the titles illustrate how she stayed with the eleven-year-old but kept up with the times.

C. also tried a somewhat younger and less iconoclastic little hero in *Jimmy* (1949) and *Jimmy Again* (1951), but a dedicated public much preferred William Brown. Unlike the American writer Edward L. Stratemeyer (1862–1930), who used several pen names and ran an amazing number of successful series (*Bound to Win, The Rover Boys, The Bobbsey Twins, Tom Swift, The Motor Boys, The Boy Hunters,* etc.), C. stuck with "Richmal Crompton" and wrote books categorized basically as "William" books and "others."

Since she preferred to be known as a more serious writer of fiction, she assiduously produced nonjuvenile short story collections and popular novels. The short fiction was a better-than-average quality and appeared, chiefly in the late 1920s, from Hutchinson (London) and other important publishers: *Kathleen and I and, Of Course, Veronica* (1926), *A Monstrous Regiment* (1927) *Enter, Patricia* (1927), *Mist, and Other Stories* (1928), *The Middle Things* (1928), *Felicity Stands By* (1928), *Sugar and Spice* (1929), *Ladies First* (1929), *The Silver Birch, and Other Stories* (1931), and *First Morning* (1936). The novels ran from *The Innermost Room* (1923) to *The Inheritor* (1960). Typical are such as *Abbot's End* (1929), *The Odyssey of Euphemia Tracy* (1932), and *Narcissa* (1941). The most remembered, if any are, may be *Dread Dwelling* (in The U.K. as *The House)* 1926, a tale of the Crofton family, gay and debonnaire, who move into an old house whose evil atmosphere poisons them all and, after awful occurrences, is burned down by Donald Crofton to break its hold. The *Literary Review* dismissed it as "an ineffectual variation on the theme of the old house with a sinister influence over its inmates," and the *Saturday Review of Literature* said the family (especially a good mother who comes to a bad end) was done in in rather lively fashion but added "It is in the tragic episodes for which the malevolent house is blamed that the story weakens."

C.'s life in Kent, at Bromle and later at Chiselhurst, gave her some backgrounds for tales. She made little of her wartime experience, 1939–45, as a fire warden, though her amusement at bureaucracy slips into some works. Her style remained redolent of the 1920s even as she kept subject matter wedded to events experienced by her readers over the decades.

Her works of fiction would today be little recalled were it not for the "William" books. They may now look somewhat formulaic and old-fashioned but in their day had an avid following. William Brown endeared himself to a generation or two of readers. He is as much a part of British literature as, say, Tom Swift or The Hardy Boys are of American literature—no Huck Finn or Holden Caulfield but worth notice. "Tough and resilient, " wrote Mary Cadogan in the *Dictionary of National Biography,* "he became typical of the outdoor, nonbookish child. His author's insight, acute observation, and engaging irony assured his appeal." The irrepressible William was translated into about a dozen languages and sold some 9 million copies worldwide.

WORKS: *Just William* (1922). *More William* (1922). *William Again* (1923). *The Innermost Room* (1923). *William the Fourth* (1924). *The Hidden Light* (1924). *Anne Morrison* (1925). *The Wildings* (1925). *Still William* (1925). *Kathleen and I and, Of Course, Veronica* (1926). *David Wilding* (1926). *Dread Dwelling* (1926; in the U. K. as *The House*). *William the Conqueror* (1926). *William in Trouble* (1927). *A Monstrous Regiment* (1927). *Enter, Patricia* (1927). *Millicent Dorrington* (1927). *Leadon Hill* (1927). *William the Outlaw* (1927). *Mist, and Other Stories* (1928). *The Middle Things* (1928). *Felicity Stands By* (1928). *The Thorn Bush* (1928). *Roofs Off!* (1928). *William the Good* (1928). *The Four Graces* (1929). *Sugar and Spice* (1929). *Ladies First* (1929). *Abbot's End* (1929).

William (1929). *William the Bad* (1930). *Blue Flames* (1930). *Naomi Godstone* (1930). *William's Happy Days* (1930). *Portrait of a Family* (1931). *The Silver Birch, and Other Stories* (1931). *William's Crowded Hours* (1931). *The Odyssey of Euphemia Tracy* (1932). *The Marriage of Hermione* (1932). *William the Pirate* (1932). *William the Rebel* (1933). *The Holiday* (1933). *Chedsdey Place* (1934). *William the Gangster* (1934). *William the Detective* (1935). *The Old Man's Birthday* (1934). *Quartet* (1935). *Caroline* (1936). *First Morning* (1936). *Sweet William* (1936). *William the Showman* (1937). *There Are Four Seasons* (1937). *Journeying Wave* (1938). *William the Dictator* (1938). *William's Bad Resolution* (1939; originally as *William and the A.R.P.*). *Merlin Bay* (1939). *Steffan Green* (1940). *William and the Film Star* (1940; originally as *William and the Evacuers*). *William Does His Bit* (1940). *William and the Film Star* (1940). *Narcissa* (1941). *William Carries On* (1942). *Mrs. Frensham Describes a Circle* (1942). *Weatherly Parade* (1944). *William and the Brain Trust* (1945). *Westover* (1946). *The Ridleys* (1947). *Family Roundabout* (1948). *Just William's Luck* (1948). *Jimmy* (1949). *William the Bold* (1950). *Frost at Morning* (1950). *Jimmy Again* (1951). *Linden Rise* (1952). *William and the Tramp* (1952). *William and the Moon Rocket* (1954). *The Gypsy's Baby* (1954). *Four in Exile* (1955). *Matty and the Dearingroydes* (1956). *William and the Space Animal* (1956). *Blind Man's Bluff* (1957). *William's Television Show* (1958). *Wiseman's Folly* (1959). *The Inheritor* (1960). *William the Explorer* (1960). *William and the Treasure Trove* (1962). *William and the Witch* (1964). *William and the Pop Singers* (1965). *William and the Masked Anger* (1966). *William the Superman* (1968). *William the Lawless* (1970).

BIBLIOGRAPHY: Craig, P. and M. Cadogan. *LonSunT* (6 February 1977). Doyle, B., ed. *Who's Who in Children's Literature*. *NYT* (13 January 1969).

For articles in reference works, see: *CA*. *Cambridge*. *DNB*. *Feminist*. *Longman*. *Oxford*. *SATA*. *ToddBWW*. *TWCCW*.

Leonard R. N. Ashley

Cronwright-Schreiner, Olive: See *Schreiner, Olive Emilie Albertina*

Cross(e), Victoria: See *Cory, Victoria*

Catherine Anne Crowe

BORN: 1800 (?), Borough Green, Kent.
DIED: 1876, Folkestone, Kent.
DAUGHTER OF: John Stevens.
MARRIED: Lieutenant-Colonel John Crowe, 1822.

Novelist and writer on the supernatural, C. enjoyed wide popular success and the friendship of many prominent people during the mid-nineteenth century. Between 1841 and 1854, she produced five novels, a play, a book of short stories, an anthology of writings on the supernatural, tales for children, an adaptation of *Uncle Tom's Cabin*, and a translation. In Edinburgh, where she had moved after her marriage, she was welcomed in intellectual and artistic circles. Her friends included astronomer John Pringle Nichol, chemist Samuel Brown, painter David Scott, writer Thomas DeQuincey, and the founder of the *Edinburgh Review*, Francis Jeffrey. She met Charles Dickens and Ralph Waldo Emerson on their visits to Edinburgh, and when she went to London, she called on the Carlyles and dined with William MakepeaceThackeray and Charlotte Brontë. In 1854, she suffered a serious breakdown. According to Dickens, she was seen "walking down her own street in Edinburgh, not only stark mad but stark naked too"—on the instruction of "spirits." After her recovery, she published a Christmas book, a treatise on spiritualism, and more stories for children, but she did not receive serious attention. The last years of her life are obscure.

C.'s fiction gives little evidence of learning or literary self-consciousness; her other writing suggests eclectic reading. *Aristodemus* (1838), C.'s first work, suggests that she had some knowledge of classical tragedy, but she used historical legends of the Messenian king not to analyze the end of a dynasty but rather to assert the primacy of domestic virtue: Her king falls because he denies his family. C. was fluent enough in German to translate the *Seeress of Prevorst* (1845). In *Spiritualism and the Age We Live In* (1859), she identifies herself as a disciple of Scottish phrenologist George Comber; inspired by his work, she studied phrenology, physiology, and spiritualism. That she was regarded as a person of considerable learning willing to speak boldly on controversial issues can be deduced from the fact that *Vestiges of the Natural History of Creation*, which Robert Chambers published anonymously in 1844, was often attributed to her; that she was overly eager to have the intellectual respect of her contemporaries might be assumed by her reluctance to undeceive them.

C.'s first novel, *Adventures of Susan Hopley; or, Circumstantial Evidence* (1841), is, according to one of the characters, a picture of "real life and human nature," an experiment in disclosing "the exact truth with all its detail." It was followed by four more novels—*Men and Women; or, Manorial Rights* (1843), *The Story of Lilly Dawson* (1847), *Adventures of a Beauty* (1852), and *Linny Lockwood* (1854)—and by stories in such periodicals as *Household Words* and *Chambers' Journal*. *Susan Hopley* became "a great hit" at the circulating libraries, and like many of her later works quickly went into cheap editions. Nineteenth-century readers regarded C. as a realist because she set her novels in ordinary surroundings and chose working people—merchants, lawyers, even servants—for her characters. Susan Hopley is a housekeeper; Lilly Dawson works as a nurse, milliner's assistant, and maid. When Jane Carlyle compared her life to a C. novel—"futile in the extreme, but so full of plot that the interest . . . has never been allowed to flag"—she caught the prevailing response of Victorian readers. As one reviewer said, C. liked to cram her novels with "scheming and cross-scheming, ravelling and unravelling, plot and counter plot." Even the *Westminster Review* described C. as a "conjurer who can make a card fly out of the pack into a gentleman's pocket or a lady's reticule, and restore it to its proper place with a wave of his wand." Although the plots are marked by melodrama, lurid intrigue, and violent incidents—what novelist Susan

Ferrier called "bad doings and bloody murders"—malefactors are punished in the end; hence C. acquired a reputation for conveying "good moral instruction in an exceedingly pleasing form." Moreover, since her novels upheld the importance of "homely duties, faithful attachment, and domestic happiness," they were regarded as safe reading in the turbulent 1840s. Even in cheap editions, her novels were fit "for the perusal of all classes."

Although C. does not undertake a sustained criticism of English society, her novels do express discontent regarding the status of women. In *Lilly Dawson*, she claims that nature intended woman "to play a noble part in the world's history, if man would but let her play it out and not treat her like a full-grown baby to be flattered and spoilt on the one hand and coerced and restricted on the other, vibrating between royal rule and slavish serfdom." C.'s women frequently find themselves in trouble because their education has not provided them with practical skill or sound judgment. The most interesting characters deviate from conventional literary roles. The brave and stalwart Susan Hopley chooses to remain single. "Husbands and lovers have great power over women, and can not only oblige them to do as they please, but very often can make them see with their eyes, and hear with their ears," she observes. C.'s fallen women are not punished for "sins" that are the result of economic circumstances. Instead of dying, they live to raise their children, help their parents, or, at worst, enter convents. The heroine of *Linny Lockwood* (1854), who has been deserted by her husband, forms a close emotional bond with his mistress and assists at the birth of their illegitimate child, whom she promises to raise.

In her writings about the supernatural, C. was influenced by physician and poet Justinus Kerner, whose study of the somnambulist and clairvoyant Frederike Hauffe she translated as *The Seeress of Prevorst.* C. scorned the rationalism of the eighteenth century and the orthodox religions of the nineteenth. In *The Night Side of Nature; or, Ghosts and Ghost Seers* (1848), she set out to explore "all that class of phenomena which appears to throw some light on our psychical nature, and on the probable state of the soul after death." Drawing heavily on French and German authorities, she filled two volumes with enthusiastic accounts of dreams, trances, presentiments, wraiths, *Doppelgängers,* spectral lights, haunted houses, and poltergeists. Despite disorganization and occasional fits of stylistic incoherence, the book was very popular; in 1921, Richard Garnett could still describe *The Night Side of Nature* as "one of the best collections of supernatural stories in our language."

WORKS: *Aristodemus* (1838). *Adventures of Susan Hopley; or, Circumstantial Evidence* (1841). *Men and Women; or, Manorial Rights* (1843). (trans.) *The Seeress of Prevorst,* by Frederike Hauffe (1845). The *Story of Lilly Dawson* (1847). *Pippie's Warning; or, Mind your Temper* (1848). *The Night Side of Nature; or Ghosts and Ghost Seers* (1848). *Light and Darkness; or, Mysteries of Life* (1850). *Adventures of a Beauty* (1852). *The Cruel Kindness: A Romantic Play* (1853). *Linny Lockwood* (1854). *Ghosts and Family Legends* (1859). *Spiritualism and the Age We Live In* (1859). *The Story of Arthur Hunter and his First Shilling* (1861). *The Adventures of a Monkey* (1862).

BIBLIOGRAPHY: Clapton, G. T. *MLR* (1930). Dalziel, M. *Popular Fiction 100 Years Ago* (1957). Keegan, P. Q. *Victoria Magazine* (1879). Mitchell, S. *The Fallen Angel: Chastity, Class and Women's Reading, 1835–1880* (1981). Sergeant, A. *Women Novelists of Queen Victoria's Reign* (1897).

For articles in reference works, see: *Allibone. BA19C. Boase. CBEL. DNB. Europa. Feminist. NCBEL. Oxford.*

Robin Sheets

Culross Yonger, Ladie: See *Colville, Elizabeth*

Nancy Cunard

BORN: 10 March 1896, Nevill Holt, Leicestershire.
DIED: 16 March 1965, Paris, France.
DAUGHTER OF: Sir Bache Cunard and Lady Maud Burke Cunard.
MARRIED: Sidney Fairbairne, 1916.

C. was born into the British upper class and spent her childhood at the family estate, Nevill Holt. Her mother, a wealthy American socialite who later changed her name to "Emerald," was a patron of the arts, and C. grew up surrounded by artists, musicians, and writers. One of her closest companions during her formative years was her mother's friend, George Moore. C. was educated at home by a governess until the age of fourteen, when she and her mother moved to London so Lady Cunard could be near her lover, the conductor Sir Thomas Beecham. She then attended private schools in London, Germany, and Paris.

C. preferred the company of her friends, who called themselves the Corrupt Coterie, to the fashionable society world. C., Iris Tree, Diana Manners, Augustus John, Osbert Sitwell, Ezra Pound, and Wyndham Lewis spent their evenings in 1914 at the Cafe Royal or the Eiffel Tower Restaurant discussing politics and poetry. Also during that period, C. began writing poetry, most of which was conventional in theme and style. Her first poems were published in 1915 in the *Eton College Chronicle,* and in 1916 she contributed several poems to the *Wheels* anthology edited by Edith Sitwell.

After World War I, C. spent most of her time in Paris, where she became involved in the newest movements in art and literature—Dada, Surrealism, Modernism. She became more dependent on alcohol and also started to experiment with drugs. In 1920, C. began a lengthy affair with Michael Arlen, a novelist who would later use C. as the model for Iris March, the main character in his novel *The Green Hat.* In 1922, C. had a brief liaison with Aldous Huxley. The relationship ended badly, and Huxley made C. the basis for Lucy Tantamount, his ultimate femme fatale, in *Point Counter Point.*

Outlaws, C.'s first volume of poetry, was published in 1921. In general, it received kind reviews, even though much of the poetry was melodramatic. *Sublunary,* a volume of mostly autobiographical poetry, appeared in 1923. Although this book, too, received only mediocre reviews, one poem, "To the Eiffel Tower Restaurant," is interesting for its nostalgic view of C.'s past: "Those old nights of drinking, / Furtive adventures, solitary thinking . . . / I think the Tower shall go up to heaven / One night in a flame of fire, about eleven." C.'s best book of poems, *Parallax,* was published in 1925 by the Hogarth Press of Virginia and Leonard Woolf. It records the thoughts of a young poet as he travels around Europe contemplating youth and ambition, love and friendship. Although the poetry is often imitative of *The Waste Land,* it is introspective and self-revealing: "Think now how friends grow old— / Their diverse brains, hearts, faces, modify; . . . / Am I the same? / Or a vagrant, of other breed, gone further, lost. . . . " The reviewer for the *Times Literary Supplement* declared that *Parallax* "seems to be the creation of a resilient mind; it has a complexity and grasp of reality which is so frequently lacking from women's poetry."

In 1927, C. bought an old farmhouse at Reanville, outside Paris, where she set up the Hours Press. Reacting against the conservatism of British publishers who refused to print anything innovative or controversial, C. published works by both new and well-established authors who could not get their material into print elsewhere. C. printed *A Draft of Cantos* by Ezra Pound because it would be "the first printing of all the thirty cantos ready at that date." She was the first person to print work by Samuel Beckett, a long poem called *Whoroscope.* The Hours Press also featured stories, poetry, and essays by Moore, Norman Douglas, Laura Riding, Roy Campbell, Robert Graves, Brian Howard, and Havelock Ellis.

Hours Press survived for only four years, as C.'s attention was diverted, in 1930, to what she considered a more important cause, the civil rights movement in the United States. C. had been romantically involved since 1928 with Henry Crowder, a black American musician, and she had become an avid collector of African art and jewelry. In fact, C. had become so renowned for her collection of ivory bracelets that both Cecil Beaton and Man Ray had photographed her wearing them, her arms covered in ivory bangles. Through Crowder, C. learned about America's problems with segregation and racism. Always in favor of the underdog, C. decided to create a record of the history of the American Negro. She spent more than two years collecting poetry, stories, and essays by and about blacks, and many of C.'s friends contributed to the anthology; both Samuel Beckett and William Carlos Williams were very much involved in the project. C. made two trips to New York City to gather work from black writers, but because she stayed in Harlem with a black man, she received hundreds of obscene letters and death threats, many of which she boldly printed in *Negro. Negro* was finally published in 1934, at C.'s expense. The book was a failure commercially and was often called "communistic" because of its leftist slant. C. and her coworkers put thousands of hours and thousands of dollars into creating a history of the American black that would stand as a reminder of the evils of hatred and prejudice. *Negro* also enabled writers such as Langston Hughes, Claude McKay, and Zora Neale Hurston to find an outlet for their work.

During the Spanish Civil War, C. worked as a freelance writer/correspondent. She lived most of the years 1936–39 in Madrid with the poet Pablo Neruda. In 1937, she printed a pamphlet entitled "Poets of the World Defend the Spanish People," which included poems by Neruda, Louis Aragon, Tristan Tzara, Federico García Lorca, Brian Howard, and the first printed version of W. H. Auden's controversial poem, "Spain." At the same time, she circulated a questionnaire among several hundred writers in England, Scotland, Ireland, and Wales, asking them: "Are you for, or against, the legal government and the People of Republican Spain? Are you for, or against, Franco and Fascism?" *The Left Review* published the 148 responses in a special issue called *Authors Take Sides on the Spanish War.*

C. spent the last years of World War II in London. In 1944, inspired by Stephen Spender and John Lehmann's *Poems for Spain,* C. put together another anthology, *Poems for France.* The contents were highly diversified in style (both Vita Sackville-West and Hugh MacDiarmid, for example, were included) but were unified in celebrating France and her people. This anthology, combined with C.'s antifascist activities in Spain, earned her a place on Adolph Hitler's enemies list. When she returned to Reanville in 1945, C. was devastated to find that nearly all her books and personal papers, jewelry, artwork, and furnishings had been stolen or desecrated by the Germans.

C.'s last years were spent traveling, visiting friends, and writing. C. published *Grand Man: Memories of Norman Douglas* in 1954 and *GM: Memories of George Moore* in 1956. Her own memoir, *These Were the Hours,* was published posthumously in 1969. C. died, alone and penniless, in the public ward of a Paris hospital in 1965.

WORKS: *Outlaws* (1921). *Sublunary* (1923). *Parallax* (1925). *Poems (Two) 1925* (1930). *Black Man and White Ladyship: An Anniversary* (1931). (with G. Padmore) *The White Man's Duty* (1942). *Relève in Manquis* (1944). *Man-Ship-Tank-Gun-Plane* (1944). *Grand Man: Memories of Norman Douglas* (1954). *Thoughts About Ronald Firbank* (1954). *GM: Memories of George Moore* (1956). *These Were the Hours: Memories of My Hours Press, Reanville and Paris, 1928–1931* (1969), ed. H. Ford.

BIBLIOGRAPHY: Benstock, S. *Women of the Left Bank: Paris 1900–1940* (1986). Burkhart, C. *Herman & Nancy & Ivy: Three Lives in Art* (1977). Chisholm, A. *Nancy Cunard* (1979). Fielding, D. *Emerald and Nancy: Lady Cunard and Her Daughter* (1968). *Nancy Cunard: Brave Poet, Indomitable Rebel, 1896–1965,* ed. H. Ford (1968).

For articles in reference works, see: *BioIn. Bloomsbury. Feminist.*

Other references: Flanner, J. *London Was Yesterday, 1934–1939* (1975). Ford, H., intro. to *Negro: An Anthology,* ed. N. Cunard (rpt. 1970). Green, M. *Children of the Sun: A Narrative of "Decadence" in England After 1918* (1976).

Kay Beaird Meyers

Mary (Montgomerie) Lamb Singleton Currie, Lady Currie

BORN: 24 February 1843, Beauport, Littlehampton, Sussex.
DIED: 13 October 1905, Harrogate, Yorkshire.
DAUGHTER OF: Charles James Saville Montgomerie Lamb and Anna Charlotte Grey.
MARRIED: Henry Sydenham Singleton, 1864; Sir Philip Henry Wodehouse Currie, later Baron Currie of Hawley, 1894.
WROTE UNDER: V; Violet Fane.

A versatile writer of novels, verse, essays, and a single drama, C. combines graceful ease with language, a relish of gentle satire, and an ironic sense of romance. She took the pseudonym "Violet Fane" from Benjamin's Disraeli's *Vivian Grey* to hide her authorship from her family. Nonetheless, she became well-known in London society and appears as "Mrs. Sinclair . . . a sort of fashionable London Sappho" in W. H. Mallock's *New Republic* (1877), which is also dedicated to her. Descendant of John Wilmot, Earl of Rochester and acquaintance of Oscar Wilde (who printed several of her poems and reviewed *The Story of Helen Davenant* in *Woman's World*), C. is in the tradition of urbane, ironic writers who make fun of the very conventions they employ. Critics of her day both categorized her simply as "a flippant writer of graceful *vers-de-societé*" and attempted to correct such a dismissive evaluation. Her poetry was well known in its time, and some of it was set to music, notably "For Ever and For Ever," by Paolo Tosti.

C. wrote poetry from an early age, despite her father's disapproval. In a late newspaper interview, she reported that as a child she had trouble sleeping and would lie awake at night reciting to herself ballads from Percy's *Reliques of Ancient English Poetry,* an exercise that she credited with giving her "that metrical sense," as *The Lady* put it, "which is so manifest in her poetry." Several years after her marriage in 1864 to Henry S. Singleton, an Irish landowner, she began to publish the steady mix of prose and verse that characterized her career.

In January 1894, ten months after Singleton's death, C. married Sir Philip Henry Wodehouse Currie and accompanied him to Constantinople and then Rome, where he held positions as ambassador. Two books of poetry resulted from her experiences in Constantinople. After her husband's retirement, C. lived at Hawley, Hampshire, where she gardened and raised dogs. After an illness of two months' duration, she died of heart failure on 13 October 1905 at the Grand Hotel, Harrogate, while her husband was ill at home in Hampshire.

After an early collection of romantic verse, C. published perhaps her most distinctive work, *Denzil Place* (1875), an interesting novel in verse sometimes likened to Elizabeth Barrett Browning's *Aurora Leigh.* Both of these long poems analyze contemporary society, but whereas *Aurora Leigh* is narrated by its passionate heroine over the course of her life, *Denzil Place* is told by a detached, witty, third-person narrator who provides ironic perspective on the sentimental story she tells and helps her reader distinguish the tenor of this narrative from the romantic verses that form epigraphs to each of its nine books. The story of a young woman's early marriage to an older, wealthy man and a subsequent temptation to adultery, *Denzil Place,* a rather self-conscious "fairy tale," rescues its heroine with the convenient death of the husband but then reflexively comments on the improbability of a little rabbit felling Sir John from his horse. The story snatches away the romantic ending, though, as Constance dies in childbirth and only her daughter (by her young lover) and stepson are allowed to live happily ever after.

The *Collected Verses* (1880) are also characterized by such a double voice, offering both romance and its subtle undermining. In "A Reverie," a female speaker traverses hope, despair, and cynicism about her future life, only to have that potentially subversive meditation give way to hope again as a handsome neighbor's collie happens by and she muses about its owner. "Divided" poses the question of the relative importance of professional ambition and love through the story of a woman poet married to a politician. In "Killed at Isandula," the lament of a dead soldier's wife against "the fierce black man, / Who has murdered our lovers, and darkened our lives!" is countered by the narrator's wish for the "wider wisdom, higher hope / [of] The hearts of nations warring against War!" The two collections published while she was in Constantinople, however, are characterized by the contradictory treatment of the Asian "Other" that Edward Said has called Orientalism. "In a Turkish Lane" (from *Under Cross and Crescent,* 1896), for instance, affirms the speaker's fidelity to England and imagines Turkey as a mysterious woman whose veil cannot be lifted, while Turkish women are pictured as mindless beasts.

C.'s novels evidence both the ironic perspective on romance and the taste for exoticism found in her poetry. As a story of a woman who falls in love with a military man in a railway carriage, loses him, and then pursues him, *Thro' Love and War* (1886) enjoys reflecting on the nature of its own bold protagonist: To become a heroine of romance, "cockney, middle-class Lucy Barlow must pass through and become purified in the furnace of affliction," which for her includes being pursued herself by the Pecksniffian character Podmore. *The Story of Helen Davenant* (1889) blends Gothicism, mesmeric hypnotism, a gruesome murder, diplomatic intrigue, and a heroine with a mad husband in the attic (actually, in an asylum). The eponymous heroine loses her mother in the first pages and later imagines herself in a dalliance with the "fatherly" man who eventually turns out to have been her mother's lover and her actual father.

Commentators have most praised C.'s witty social sketches. She satirizes late Victorian absurdities through a comic ethnography in the essays entitled *The Edwin and Angelina Papers* (1878). "Myself"—"a cynical and eccentric foreigner"—anatomizes English religion, courtship and *marriage à la mode,* make-up, the fashion for skating, and the idea of a woman's club, to name a few topics, and spends a few papers skewering flighty Angelina's attempts at female authorship. In his farewell, "Myself" reveals himself to be Japanese and provides a list of those things English he will take back to his country, each custom duplicated twice over in its Japanese incarnation: "by thus imitating and exaggerating everything and everybody that we have ever beheld in any other country on the globe, we shall be certain in time of obtaining the respect and admiration of our neighbours." In a more serious vein, "Two Moods of a Man" (1901) examines gender differences and heterosexual love relationships, arguing that the "indissoluble trinity" of passion, truth, and tenderness might last longer in marriages if men were more given to "sentimental retrospection," a valuable reconstructive memory that serves primarily women, she claims, as an interpretive frame for the present.

C.'s facility in prose and verse has been acknowledged since her day, and her wit has been attested to by those who encountered her at London parties, but the fine ironic effects she achieves in her writing, whether her subject be adulterous love in Victorian England or Muslim-Christian conflicts in Turkey, should be singled out for praise and deserves further study.

WORKS: *From Dawn to Noon: Poems* (1872). *Denzil Place: A Story in Verse* (1875). *The Queen of the Fairies and Other Poems* (1876). *Anthony Babington: A Drama* (1877). *The Edwin and Angelina Papers, Essays by "V" Reprinted from the World* (1878). *Collected Verses* (1880). *Sophy; or the Adventures of a Savage* (1881). *Thro' Love and War* (1886). *The Story of Helen Davenant* (1889). *Autumn Songs* (1889). *Poems* (1892). (trans.) *Memoirs of Marguerite de Valois, Queen of Navarre* (1892). *Under Cross and Crescent: Poems* (1896). *Betwixt Two Seas: Poems and Ballads Written at Constantinople and Therapia* (1900). *Two Moods of a Man, with Other Papers and Short Stories* (1901). *Collected Essays* (1902).

BIBLIOGRAPHY: Miles, A. H., ed. *The Poets and Poetry of the Century* (1891–97, rev. and enlarged, 1905–1907). Interview with V. Fane, *The Lady* (29 December 1904).

For articles in reference works, see: *DLB. DNB. Feminist. Oxford. Stanford. VB.*

Other references: Hickok, K. *Representations of Women: Nineteenth-Century British Women's Poetry* (1984). Reynolds, M. *Victorian Women Poets: An Anthology* (1995).

Robert P. Fletcher

Curtin, Philip: See *Lowndes, Marie Adelaide Belloc*

Olive Custance

BORN: 7 February 1874, Weston, Norfolk.
DIED: 12 February 1944, Hove, East Sussex.
DAUGHTER OF: Colonel Frederick Hambelton Custance and Eleanor Custance Jolliffee.
MARRIED: Lord Alfred Douglas, 1902.
WROTE UNDER: Olive Custance; Opals.

C. was a well-known and well-liked poet who initiated her career with contributions to the *Yellow Book*. She was especially lauded by John Gray, Aubrey Beardsley, Richard Le Gallienne, and Lord Alfred Douglas, who considered her one of the most talented poets of the period.

Shortly after her first volume of poetry, *Opals,* was published in 1897, she became a close friend of Douglas, with whom romantic involvement in the manner of the Brownings followed. Douglas became her "Prince," C. his "Page." After they eloped in 1902, they lived at first on the Continent in a glow of happiness. Upon their return to England, they reconciled with C.'s father. Colonel Custance, however, continued to regard his daughter's marriage to the Marquess of Queensbury's son (who had been so intimately linked with Oscar Wilde) as a disaster.

C. was pitied by her family and friends, but she and Douglas managed to live together for almost ten years. Their son, Raymond, who had been born during the first year of their marriage, helped keep them united. Then, after a series of legal maneuvers in 1911 and 1912, C. separated from her husband, who lost custody of his son. Despite their separation, they did their best to live on amicable terms, and since Douglas resided in a nearby flat, he visited almost every day. "I have often been unhappy with him," C. complained to Douglas's mother, but added, "I love him above everything."

To what extent Douglas's relationship with Wilde and his relationships with others in the Wilde Circle contributed to the breakup of C.'s marriage makes for interesting speculation. Certainly their marriage was damaged severely by Douglas's many legal disputes and subsequent financial difficulties. Douglas's imprisonment for six months in 1924 for libeling Winston Churchill further damaged his relationship with C., yet they did their utmost to remain respectful of each other over the balance of their lives. C. died at the age of seventy, one year before Douglas.

C.'s poetry is somewhat soft and neither distinguished nor profound, though in her own time she appealed to a select group of readers. Many of her best efforts are autobiographical. In one of her early poems, "Ideal," for example, she wrote

You were indifferent . . . and I may forget
Your profound eyes, your heavy hair, your voice
So clear, yet deep and low with tenderness
That lingered on my ears like a caress
And roused my heart to make a futile choice.
O! Poet that clamoured unto God in song!
How should I lose you thus you lack regret?

The subject of the above lines is John Gray, whom she had met in 1890 when she was sixteen and he was several years her senior. An extremely beautiful girl, she fell deeply in love with the prototype of Oscar Wilde's Dorian Gray. Her "Prince of Poets" read her lines with appreciation. Gray, however, came to experience a deep and lasting metanoia, and after he "clamoured unto God in song" went off to Rome to qualify for the Roman Catholic priesthood. In another poem, "Reminiscences," she lamented, "Is it regret / I lost a friend so sweet / That stings my heart to tears?" At first, she hoped Gray would not persevere; when he did, however, she became reconciled to the fact. Only after his ordination in 1901 and his appointment to an Edinburgh parish did she agree to marry Douglas.

C. published her early poems under the pseudonym

"Opals," but published her later works under her family name.

WORKS: *Opals* (1897). *Rainbows* (1902). *The Blue Bird* (1905). *The Inn of Dreams* (1911).

BIBLIOGRAPHY: Cevasco, G. A. *John Gray* (1982). Croft-Cooke, R. *Bosie* (1963). Sewell, B. *Like Black Swans* (1982). C.'s diaries are in the Berg Collection, New York Public Library.

For articles in reference works, see: *1890s. ToddBWW.*

G. A. Cevasco

Charlotte Dacre

BORN: 1772 (?).
DIED: 7 November 1825, London.
DAUGHTER OF: Jonathan King and Deborah King.
MARRIED: Nicholas Byrne, 1806.
WROTE UNDER: Charlotte Dacre Byrne; Charlotte King; Rosa Matilda.

Best remembered for her novel *Zofloya* (1806), D. was a well-known Gothic novelist in her time who, at the end of the twentieth century, has begun to attract critical interest. D., who went by the pseudonym "Rosa Matilda," was the daughter of the famous Jewish self-made banker, writer, blackmailer, and supporter of radical causes, Jonathan King ("Jew King"), known by William Godwin, Lord Byron, and P. B. Shelley. D. wrote in the "school of horror" made famous by M. G. Lewis, and D.'s contemporaries were struck by her work's resonance with Lewis's; one reviewer commented that her *Zofloya* had "the same lust—the same infernal agents—the same voluptuous language" as *The Monk.* But because it is the heroine of *Zofloya* who enacts the same infernal and murderous desires as the male protagonist of *The Monk,* D.'s novel offers an unique portrait of transgressive female subjectivity rarely seen in her times or ours.

Along with her sister Sophia King (later Fortnum), also a novelist and poet, D. first published *Trifles of Helicon* (1798), which the two sisters dedicated to their infamous father by name. D.'s poems reappeared in her *Hours of Solitude* (1805). According to marriage records, Charlotte King, "spinster," married the editor of *The Morning Post,* Nicholas Byrne, in 1815, and thus it appears that "Dacre" was itself a pseudonym; but a mystery persists, for the 1806 Longman accounts ledger for *Zofloya* show that a thousand copies were printed for "Mrs. Byrne." D. had three children, William, Charles, and Mary in 1806, 1807, and 1809, respectively, who were all baptized much later, in 1811; this implies that her children were born while Nicholas Byrne was married to his first wife, Louisa. D. died in 1825 at the age of fifty-three, thus placing her birth in 1771 or 1772, ten years earlier than her prefatory remarks indicated in *Hours of Solitude* (1805), when she gave her age as twenty-three.

D.'s *Zofloya,* or *The Moor* was very popular in its day, was pirated in a chapbook in 1810, and was translated into French and German. P. B. Shelley was "enraptured" by *Zofloya,* and D.'s novel influenced his own Gothic romances. In *Zofloya,* D. revised Lewis's *The Monk* to create a unique female antiheroine, Victoria, whose shocking descent into multiple murder and lust rivals that of any satanic romantic hero or Sadean libertine. The Sadean undertones of *Zofloya* and of Victoria herself were noted by A.C. Swinburne, who admired D.'s "remarkable romance" for its spectacular "vivisection of virtue" and likened her character to the Marquis de Sade's Justine and Juliette. Victoria is thus unique in women's fiction of the period, for no traditional heroine could say, as she does "with a fierce malignant smile," that "there is certainly a pleasure . . . in the infliction of prolonged torment."

D. had acknowledged her debt to Lewis's school of horror in her first novel, *Confessions of the Nun of St. Omer* (1805), which she dedicated to Lewis. *Confessions,* which went into three editions by 1807, consists of memoirs narrated by Cazire, whose illicit sexual relationships lead to pregnancy, debtor's prison, and madness, and her lovers to death and suicide. Cazire's own debt-ridden father established this pattern when he abandoned her mother and began a liaison with a countess, much as D.'s own father had done in 1785 when he divorced his Jewish wife Deborah and married an English countess. In 1805, D. also published a two-volume collections of Romantic poems, *Hours of Solitude,* some of the poems reprinted from *Trifles of Helicon. Solitude* contains many passionate poems in the effusive Della Cruscan style, which have inspired comparisons to Byron's *Hours of Idleness* as well as to many supernatural poems such as "The Skeleton Priest, or the Marriage of Death," "To the Shade of Mary Robinson," and "The Mistress to the Spirit of Her Lover."

D.'s third novel, *The Libertine* (1807), went into three editions by 1809 and was translated into French in 1816. The libertine Angelo, after repeatedly betraying his unmarried lover Gabrielle for three volumes, sends her to an early grave and nearly seduces his own daughter whom he does not recognize. Robbed by his own son, who has become a highwayman, Angelo unwittingly delivers him into the hands of the executioner and finally shoots himself in despair. The heroine, Gabrielle, is a conventional long-suffering one who endured the multiple betrayals of her lover with such excessive and vocal selflessness that the conflation of proper femininity with martyrization and masochism becomes painfully clear.

The Passions (1811), D.'s last novel, like *Zofloya,* presents a unique and flamboyantly destructive female character, the Countess Appollonia Zulmer, who also undertakes a vicious and carefully planned vivisection of virtue, embodied in the Rousseauesque Julia. *Passions* makes its critique of J.-J. Rousseau's construction of femininity explicit: Appollonia declares war on the passionless "idyllic" marriage of Julia and Weimar, clearly modeled on the couple in *La Nouvelle Héloïse,* and begins their downfall by initiating Julia into illicit sexual passion by giving her Rousseau's novel. The aftermath of this proliferation of passion destroys every character in the novel save the least interesting, the passionless Weimar. Described throughout in Luciferan, Promethean, and Wollstonecraftian terms, Appollonia is a fascinating femme fatale of the same rank as Victoria in *Zofloya.* D.'s works continue to challenge our models of "female Gothic" and "feminine Romanticism," and for this reason she continues to be of value to any gendered study of the Gothic or of Romanticism.

WORKS: (with Sophia King) *Trifles of Helicon* (1798). *Confessions of the Nun of St. Omer* (1805). *Hours of Solitude* (1805). *Zofloya; or the Moor: A Romance of the Fifteenth Century* (1806; ed. A. Cracium, 1997). *The Libertine* (1807). *The Passions* (1811). *George the Fourth* (1822). *School for Friends, or Domestic Tale* (18??).

BIBLIOGRAPHY: Craciun, A. *ERR* (1995). Hughes, A. M. D. *MLR* (1912). Jones, A. H. *Ideas and Innovations: Best-sellers of Jane Austen's Age* (1986). Miles, R. *Gothic Writing 1750–1820, A Genealogy* (1993). Summers, M. *Essays in Petto* (1928; rpt. 1967).

For articles in reference works, see: *Feminist. Oxford.*

Other references: Frank F. *The First Gothics* (1987). McGann, J., in *Byron: Augustan and Romantic*, ed. A. Rutherford (1990). Summers, M. *The Gothic Quest* (1965). Tracy, A. *The Gothic Novel 1790–1830* (1981).

Adriana Craciun

Dame Clementia (or Clementina): See *Cary, Anne and Lucy*

Dame Lucy Magdalena: See *Cary, Anne and Lucy*

Clemence Dane (pseudonym of Winifred Ashton)

BORN: 21 February 1888, Greenwich, London.
DIED: 28 March 1965, London.
DAUGHTER OF: Arthur Charles Ashton and Florence Bentley.

Winifred Ashton, born in Greenwich (London), used the pseudonym "Clemence Dane" (suggested by the church of St. Clement's Dane in The Strand) to disguise the sex of the unimportant actress "Diana Portis" when she wrote some popular plays, screen plays, and radio plays. It was more importantly the name under which she turned out a score or more of well-received fictions. A male pseudonym was perhaps understandable in the light of the disdain in critical circles for the title of her first novel, *Regiment of Women* (1917), and the attitudes of the male Establishment toward some women writers. Also, London had a literary jungle, which she portrayed in her third novel, *Legend* (1919). Eventually, she triumphed in it. She made "Clemence Dane" as famous a pseudonym as "George Eliot" or at least "Acton Bell," and she showed the public that women could write something besides detective fiction, low-brow sentimental novels, and middle-brow historical fiction, at that period the major products of the many women in the literary marketplace.

Raised in a late-Victorian suburb, she showed some rebelliousness in becoming an art student (at The Slade 1904–1906 and in Dresden 1906–1907), a teacher far from home (in Geneva 1903 and in Ireland 1907–13), then a mildly successful young actress in London under the name "Diana Portis" (1913–15). Then she tried her hand at writing.

Her life as a teacher was drawn upon to some extent for her first novel, *Regiment of Women;* it involves a complex but not very sensational relationship between a couple of teachers. Her second novel, *First the Blade* (1918), described in a subtitle as "a comedy of growth," was less autobiographical, but also well received. She returned to her own experience for her third novel, *Legend* (1919), in which the "legend" of the career of a minor novelist is cattily dissected on the night of her death by a few of her friends (or perhaps one ought to say "associates"). The cat-eat-cat world of backbiting and blatant careerism among types that the British have now come to call "pseuds" is beautifully illustrated in this study of the London writing world just after World War I.

Some of the denizens of London's Bohemia in her work might have been even more vividly shown had she drawn on her personal life as a struggling actress and written of the theater back-stage. But she determined to write for the stage, rather than act on it, so maybe she needed not to annoy the powers that were. In 1921, she began as a playwright with *A Bill of Divorcement*, a piece of the sort Sir Arthur Wing Pinero had firmly established, one that asks a question of supposed social importance (but in theatrical terms) and answers it with equal theatricality. The question in *A Bill of Divorcement* may sound odd today: Should a marriage be annulled on grounds of insanity? Still, the play is finely crafted and has several effective moments, though *coups de théâtre* is too strong a term for them. The same year saw *The Terror* (a minor effort) and an ingenious short play, *Will Shakespeare* (a charming "invention" concerned with his affair with Anne Hathaway). She was off to a fast start as playwright.

Her dramatic career seldom lagged. She adapted *Legend* for the stage (1923), followed with a couple of "plays for boys" (*Shivering Shocks*, 1923, *Mr. Fox*, 1927), some commercial West End fare (*Naboth's Vineyard*, 1925, *Granite*, 1926, *Mariners*, 1927, *A Traveller Returns*, 1927, etc.), some musicals with Richard Addinsell (*Adam's Opera*, 1928, *Come of Age*, 1934), some adaptations (*L'Aiglon*, from Rostand, 1934; *The Happy Hypocrite*, from Max Beerbohm, 1936; *Herod and Mariamne*, from Hebbel, 1936; *Alice's Adventures in Wonderland and Through the Looking-Glass*, from Lewis Carroll, with music by Richard Addinsell, 1943, 1948), and many pleasant entertainments for matinees (such as *Gooseberry Fool*, 1929; *Wild Decembers*, 1933; *Moonlight Is Silver*, 1934; *England's Darling*, 1940' *Cousin Muriel*, 1940; *The Golden Reign of Queen Elizabeth*, 1941; *The Lion and the Unicorn*, 1943; *Call Home the Heart*, 1947; *Eighty in the Shade*, 1958; *The Godson*, 1964, etc.). In an era when theatre was the ordinary middle-class way of ending or highlighting a day in town after sightseeing or shopping, the West End theaters produced many plays like these. They were not world-shaking, nor were they meant to be. They were (by modern standards) inexpensive to mount and to attend. The woman who took her name from a building standing right in the middle of The Strand could just as conspicuously establish herself in London's commercial theater. She understood playwriting and the theater market. She was able to supply that market with contemporary drawing-room plays such as *The Way Things Happen* (1923) (from *Legend* and life) or costume pieces on familiar subjects (the

Brontës in *Wild Decembers,* Alfred in *England's Darling, The Golden Reign of Queen Elizabeth,* etc.) or musical entertainments on romantic figures (the young son of Napoleon in *L'Aiglon,* the young eighteenth-century poet Thomas Chatterton in *Come of Age*). She could be serious when required, as in *Granite* or *Eighty in the Shade.* Predictably, the "serious" dramas were considered her best work. *Granite* (1926) long endured, a tragedy much appreciated by repertory and amateur players in its day, though for our day the dialogue is too heavy. The stars of the original *Granite,* Dame Sybil Thorndike and Sir Lewis Casson, also appeared years later in D.'s last work for the stage, *Eighty in the Shade,* a play long since eclipsed by David Storey's powerful play with a similar setting, *Home.*

A critically neglected aspect of D.'s work is her significant contribution to radio, television, and cinema drama. She worked with others on the BBC serial of *The Scoop* (1931) and wrote *The Saviors: Seven Plays on One Theme for Radio* (1940–41), as well as adapting for radio Shakespeare's *Henry VIII* (1954) and Schiller's *Don Carlos* (1955). Her last radio play was *Scandal at Coventry* (1958), and that same year *Till Time Shall End* (based on the life of Elizabeth I) was televised. That was included in the first (and only) volume of her *Collected Plays* (1961). Elizabeth I was also the focus (magisterially played by Dame Flora Robson) of the film script *Fire over England* (1937), in which Sir Alexander Korda hoped to repeat the success of *Henry VIII.* D. wrote it with Sergei Nolbandov.

Other film scripts were *The Tunnel* (also called *Transatlantic Tunnel*) and *Anna Karenina* (starring Greta Garbo and Basil Rathbone), both 1935; *The Amateur Gentleman* (from Jeffrey Farnol's novel of the Regency), written with Edward Knoblock (1936); *Farewell Again* (also called *Troopship*), written with Patrick Kirwin (1937); *St. Martin's Lane* (in the U.S. as *Sidewalks of London*), 1938; *Salute John Citizen* (written with Elizabeth Baron), 1942; *Perfect Strangers* (in the U.S. as *Vacation from Marriage,* written with Anthony Pelissier), 1945; *Bonnie Prince Charlie,* 1948; *Bride of Vengeance* (written with Cyril Hume and Michael Hogan), 1949; and *Angel with a Trumpet* (written with Karl Hartl and Franz Tassie), 1950. Unfortunately, neither Leslie Halliwell nor Ephraim Katz, leading encyclopedists of the movies, think D. is worth a mention. Even the fiction she wrote in collaboration (with Helen Simpson) gets a mention in some places, but film collaborations and original scripts seem quickly forgotten. Actually, her film writing is better than average, and *Fire over England* is a classic.

D. was active in the Society of Women Journalists (president in 1941) and was the author of critical studies of literature and a book about gardening; she also edited Lord Nelson's letters, and even *The Shelter Book* during the war. She was made a Commander of the Order of the British Empire in 1953.

She was never much of an actress, but one ought to mention acting in any discussion of D. She debuted in H. V. Esmond's best sentimental comedy, *Eliza Comes to Stay* (1913), and probably would have continued in similar light parts had not *A Bill of Divorcement* changed her direction. She was sometimes lucky in the leads for her own plays: Katherine Cornell played in *A Bill of Divorcement;* the casts of *Fire over England* on the screen and *Wild Decembers* on stage were extraordinary (the Brontës were played by Diana Wynyard, Beatrix Lehmann, and Emlyn Williams). But her own experience as "Diana Portis" onstage and her own observation of theater permitted her to give to actors, as much as she gained from them; her plays are eminently considerate of actors, even generous to them. She deserves a better place in theater history than she has, if not a bust in the lobby of The Theatre-Royal in Drury Lane, where now is hung her excellent portrait of Ivor Novello, who was no more important a theater personality than herself. Her plays may be dated but they were part of the London theater of her time, if not always as typical of her talent as the novel *The Moon Is Feminine* (1938) and the nine stories of *Fate Cries Out* (1935). The career in fiction that stretched from *Regiment of Women* (1917) to her last novel, *Bonfire* (1981), published posthumously, is notable by any standard; it is as a playwright whose work ranged from drawing-room comedy and Lady Godiva (*Scandal at Coventry*) to murder on Lundy Island (*Granite*) and seven generations of an acting family (*Broome Stages*), however, that D. has the most secure place in history.

WORKS: *Regiment of Women* (1917). *First the Blade* (1918). *Legend: A Comedy of Growth* (1919). *A Bill of Divorcement* (produced and pub. 1921). *The Terror* (1921). *Will Shakespeare* (produced and pub. 1921). *The Way Things Happen* (from *Legend,* 1923; pub. 1924). *Shivering Shocks; or, The Hiding Place* (1923). *Wandering Stars, with the Lover* (1924). *Naboth's Vineyard* (1925). *The Woman's Side* (1926). *Granite* (produced 1926, pub. 1927). *The Dearly Beloved of Benjamin Cobb* (1927). *Mariners* (produced and pub. 1927). *Mr. Fox* (1927). *A Traveller Returns* (1927). *Adam's Opera* (produced and pub. 1928). *The Baylons: A Family Chronicle* (1928). (with H. Simpson) *Enter Sir John* (1928). *The King Waits* (1929). *Tradition and Hugh Walpole* (1929). *Gooseberry Fool* (produced 1929). (with H. Simpson) *Printer's Devil* (1930; also as *Author Unknown*). *Broome Stages* (1931). (with others) *The Scoop* (broadcast 1931). (with H. Simpson) *Re-Enter Sir John* (1932). *Recapture* (1932). *Wild Decembers* (pub. 1932, produced 1933,). *Come of Age* (pub. 1933, produced 1934). *L'Aiglon* (adapted from Rostand; produced 1934, pub. 1934). *Moonlight Is Silver* (produced 1934, pub. 1934). *Fate Cries Out: Nine Tales* (1935). (with K. Siodmak and L. D. Peach) *The Tunnel* (screenplay, *Transatlantic Tunnel,* 1935). *Anna Karenina* (adapted from Tolstoy; screenplay, 1935). (with E. Knoblock) *The Amateur Gentleman* (screenplay, 1936). *The Happy Hypocrite* (adapted from M. Beerbohm; pub. 1936). (with P. Kirwan) *Farewell Again* (screenplay, *Troopship,* 1937). (with S. Noblandov) *Fire over England* (screenplay, 1937). *St. Martin's Lane* (1938; in the U.S. as *Sidewalks of London*). *Herod and Mariamne* (adapted from Hebbel; produced and pub. 1938). *The Moon Is Feminine* (1938). *The Arrogant History of White Ben* (1939). *Trafalgar Day 1940* (1940). *England's Darling* (1940). *Cousin Muriel* (produced and pub. 1940). *The Saviours: Seven Plays on One Theme* (broadcast 1940–41; pub. 1942). *The Golden Reign of Queen Elizabeth* (produced and pub. 1941). (with E. Baron) *Salute John Citizen* (1942). *The Lion and the Unicorn*

(1943). *Alice's Adventures in Wonderland and Through the Looking Glass* (adapted from Lewis Carroll; produced 1943, pub. 1948). *He Brings Great News* (1944). (with A. Pelissier) *Perfect Strangers* (in the U.S. as *Vacation from Marriage;* screenplay, 1945). *Call Home the Heart* (produced and pub. 1947). *Bonnie Prince Charlie* (screenplay, 1948). (with C. Hume and M. Hogan) *Bride of Vengeance* (screenplay, 1949). (with K. Hartl and F. Tassie) *Angel with a Trumpet* (1950). *The Flower Girls* (1954). *Henry VIII* (adapted from Shakespeare; broadcast 1954). *Don Carlos* (adapted from F. von Schiller; broadcast 1955). *Scandal at Coventry* (broadcast 1958; in *Collected Plays,* 1961). *Eighty in the Shade* (produced 1958, pub. 1959). *Till Time Shall End* (broadcast 1958; in *Collected Plays,* 1961). *Approaches to Drama* (1960). *Collected Plays I* (1961). *The Godson: A Fantasy* (1964). *London Has a Garden* (1964). *Bonfire* (1981).

BIBLIOGRAPHY: Mais, S.P.B. *Some Modern Authors* (1923). Sutton, C. *Some Contemporary Dramatists* (1924). Tydeman, W. M., in *Great Writers of the English Language: Dramatists,* ed. J. Vinson (1979).

For articles in reference works, see: *Bloomsbury. CA. Cambridge. CD. Feminist. MBL. Oxford. TCA. TCW. Library of Literary Criticism,* ed. R. Z. Temple and M. Tucker (1966). *ToddBWW.*

Leonard R. N. Ashley

Sarah Daniels

BORN: 21 November 1956, London.
DAUGHTER OF: Frank James Daniels and Otome Daniels.

During the 1980s, D. became one of the most provocative and influential feminist playwrights writing in Britain. Many of her works were developed and premiered at the Royal Court Theatre in London, where D. received encouragement for her first script. D. won the George Devine Award in 1982 and served as writer-in-residence at the Royal Court in 1984. She has collaborated with significant women directors and companies, including Jules Wright, the Women's Playhouse Trust, and Clean Break Theatre Company, composed of women ex-prisoners. She has also written scripts for radio and television.

D.'s plays address the social, sexual, and political pressures that affect contemporary women. Her heroines struggle to speak honestly about their experiences within a patriarchal hierarchy that often judges them ridiculous, hysterical, or insane. Many of the social issues of the 1980s and 1990s have emerged in D.'s work. *Beside Herself* (1990) describes the crippling legacy of childhood sexual abuse and subsequent denial. *Masterpieces* (1983), D.'s most notorious play, takes a harrowing look at pornography and industrialized violence against women. *Neaptide* (1986) was the first play to be produced at the Royal National Theatre that overtly addressed lesbian motherhood and family life.

D.'s acerbic wit and whimsical imagination enliven a political dramaturgy that might otherwise become polemical. She has stated that she is "always trying to be funny" and uses fantasy to lift her work "out of a 'social play for today' slot." *Ripen Our Darkness* (1981) transports a housewife from her suicide (her note to her husband reads, "your dinner and my head are in the oven") into a feminist heaven, complete with a Holy Hostess. A wise-cracking angel appears to one of the inmates of a psychiatric institution in *Head-Rot Holiday* (1992), and *Beside Herself* begins with a fantastic, Churchillesque prologue in which Eve, Delilah, Mary, and Lot's Wife meet in a supermarket and discuss their biblical fates. Realism, however, is the dominant mode of D.'s complex collages. Her episodic plots juxtapose contrasting scenes and characters to create the hyperrealistic effect of a documentary. D.'s keen ear for dialogue captures the rhythms and idioms of contemporary Britain while cleverly underscoring the classist and sexist assumptions that permeate the everyday speech of her characters.

While most of D.'s plays are set in the present, several make intriguing use of specific historical contexts. In *Byrthrite* (1986), her most Brechtian work, D. draws explicit comparisons between the witch-hunts of her seventeenth-century setting with contemporary political arguments over reproductive healthcare. *The Gut Girls* (1988), a play about slaughterhouse workers, looks at class relations at the turn of the twentieth century from a feminist perspective.

D.'s woman-centered plays have been criticized for their unflattering representation of men, particularly by the male theater critics in the mainstream British press, but D. is unrepentant. She has commented, "What I am doing is presenting women's experience of male oppression and my writing of men has been heavily criticized, but I have just as much validation from women who identify those characters in their husbands, boyfriends, fathers or friends." Perhaps because of this uneasy relationship with the theater press, D.'s work is more often staged in alternative or studio theaters than in large, popular venues. Nonetheless, D.'s work commands international attention, and two volumes of her plays have been published in the Methuen World Classics series.

WORKS: *Ripen Our Darkness* (1981). *Ma's Flesh is Grass* (1981). *Penumbra* (1981). *Masterpieces* (1983). *The Devil's Gateway* (1983). *Neaptide* (1986). *Byrthrite* (1986). *The Gut Girls* (1988). *Beside Herself* (1990). *Head-Rot Holiday* (1992). *The Madness of Esme and Shaz* (1994). *Plays: One* (1991). *Plays: Two* (1994).

BIBLIOGRAPHY: Aston, E. *An Introduction to Feminism and Theatre* (1995). Aston, E. *TJ* (1995). Goodman, L. *Contemporary Feminist Theatres: To Each Her Own* (1993). Haedicke, S. C. *JDTC* (1994). Keyssar, H. *Feminist Theatre and Theory* (1996). Minwalla, F. *Theater* (1990). Remnant, M. *Plays By Women: Volume 6* (1987).

For articles in reference works, see: *CA. CD. CBD. Feminist. WD.*

Other references: *Drama* (1984). *New Statesman* (1990).

Julia Matthews

Daphne: See *Hands, Elizabeth; Robinson, Mary Darby (Perdita)*

d'Arblay, Francis Burney: See *Burney, Frances*

Darby, Mary: See *Robinson, Mary Darby (Perdita)*

Ella D'Arcy

BORN: 1856 or 1857, London.
DIED: 5 September 1937, London.
DAUGHTER OF: Anthony D'Arcy and Sophia Anne Byrne.
WROTE UNDER: Ella D'Arcy; Gilbert H. Page.

A short-fiction writer, D. is known primarily for her association with the "decadent" literary magazine *The Yellow Book* (1894–1897). Like many in the Yellow Book circle, D.'s work reflects the influence of French realists and naturalists such as Guy de Maupassant and Emile Zola. Her stories, which contain harsh depictions of the relations between the sexes, have often been criticized for their portrayals of scheming, grasping women who ensnare men. Such portraits, it has been argued, contrast sharply with "New Woman" writers of the 1890s, who typically represented women as the victims of brutal men. But D. viewed men and women as equally capable of selfishness, and she produced many stories about men treating women badly. In her work, D. studied human psychology and explored the role that contemporary social forces played in shaping gender relations of the fin-de-siècle.

Biographical information about D. is meager and conflicting. Commonly agreed-upon facts include her birth in London to Irish parents, either in 1856 or 1857, and her schooling in Germany and France. During her childhood, she and her family spent substantial periods of time in the Channel Islands, where she later set several stories. She studied at the Slade School of Art in London, hoping to become a painter; however, problems with her eyesight caused her to turn to writing instead.

The recollection of those who knew D. as an adult reveal two significant facts about her: First, while she never married, she was romantically involved with a number of men, including the science fiction writer Matthew Phipps Shiel; and second, she was a procrastinator. It is this latter detail that seems to account for the modest size of D.'s canon; although she lived until she was eighty, she disappointed her literary admirers by producing only two short story collections, one novella, and one translation.

D. first attracted attention as an author when she published her story "Irremediable" in *The Yellow Book,* edited by Henry Harland. While several magazines had rejected the tale because of its stark treatment of courtship and marriage, Harland and his set—Hubert Crackenthorpe, George Moore, George Gissing, and publisher John Lane, among others—welcomed D.'s realism. Her stories appeared in ten of the thirteen volumes of *The Yellow Book,* and she served as its secretary and unofficial subeditor. During the same time as her *Yellow Book* association, the London *Argosy* published several of her stories under the pseudonym Gilbert H. Page. A decade later, she contributed four stories to Ford Madox Ford's *The English Review.*

D. reissued several of her stories in *Monochromes* (1895), which John Lane—the publisher of *The Yellow Book*—released in his Keynotes series. Reviewers reacted positively to the collection, singling out for praise three psychological studies: "Irremediable," "The Pleasure Pilgrim," and "Poor Cousin Louis." The last of these, a horror story in which an old man is terrorized into his grave, is particularly powerful. Each of the characters is "involved entirely in his own egotisms"—none less so than Cousin Louis's physician. When Dr. Owen leaves the old man at the mercy of his servants, Owen thinks only of the condolence call he will soon pay on Louis's heir and the social benefits Owen will gain from that acquaintance.

The short fiction collected in *Modern Instances* (1898)—also issued as part of the Keynotes series—was previously published in *The Yellow Book.* "At Twickenham" is an example of a story that is often cited as evidence of the author's negative views of her own sex. In it, a young woman named Letty manages to extract a marriage proposal from a local doctor. When he breaks the engagement on the grounds of incompatibility, he explains to a friend, "Like most other girls she's a victim of her upbringing." Rather than condemning women, this line suggests that middle- and upper-class women who are encouraged to be idle and to think only of catching a husband cannot be blamed for failing to become the intellectual equals of men.

D. did not always fault society for her characters' flaws; nor did she always cast a woman as the villain. Several stories in *Modern Instances* present heartless characters—both male and female—who are motivated by greed and self-interest. "A Marriage," told from the point of view of an ailing young husband, seems to indict his wife for cruelty. But he is far from blameless in bringing about his miserable situation. Moreover, his belief that "women require to be kept under, to be afraid of you, to live in a condition of insecurity" implies that he would be just as brutal to her were he in better health. In "An Engagement," Dr. Owen of "Poor Cousin Louis" reappears to break the heart of Agnes, a simple Channel Island girl. When he discovers that she cannot advance his climb up the social ladder, he jilts her. Crushed by his public snubbing of her, Agnes catches a chill and dies. These stories and others demonstrate D.'s general pessimism about humanity; they do not suggest a particular hostility to her sex.

The Bishop's Dilemma (1898), a novella that again depicts egotistical characters of both sexes, was the last book D. published except for a translation of André Maurois' *Ariel: The Life of Shelley* (1924). Although she wrote a biography of the French Symbolist poet Arthur Rimbaud, which contained translations of his poems, she could never find a publisher for it; apparently Rimbaud was considered too avant-garde. She wrote other works that went unpublished as well, perhaps because she was easily discouraged by criticism. According to Katherine Mix, when Arnold Bennett asked to see one of D.'s manuscripts, she refused because a publisher had already rejected it.

D. lived most of her final years in Paris. She died in London in 1937.

WORKS: *Monochromes* (1895). *Modern Instances* (1898). *The Bishop's Dilemma* (1898). (trans.) *Ariel: The Life of Shelley,* by A. Maurois (1924).

BIBLIOGRAPHY: Anderson, A. *Ella D'Arcy: Some Letters to John Lane* (1990). Beckson, K. *Henry Hartland: His*

Life and Work (1978). Fitzgerald, P. *Charlotte Mew and Her Friends* (1988). Mix, K. L. *A Study in Yellow: "The Yellow Book" and its Contributors* (1960). Syrett, N. *The Sheltering Tree* (1939).

For articles in reference works, see: *DLB. 1890s. Feminist. Oxford. 1890s. ToddBWW.*

Other references: Fisher, B. F. IV. *ELT* (1992). Fisher, B. F. IV. *ELT* (1994). Fisher, B. F. IV. *UMSE* (1992). *PULC* (Winter 1990).

Bette H. Kirschstein

Margaretta Ruth D'Arcy

BORN: 14 June 1934, Dublin, Ireland.
MARRIED: John Arden, 1957.

Playwright and critic D. grew up in Dublin where she developed her lifelong political commitment; the themes of anti-imperialism, socialism, and feminism have persisted throughout her prolific career. As a young actress, D. began working in Britain in the early 1950s. At the Royal Court Theatre in London, D. met the young playwright John Arden in 1955. She has commented, "Our attraction to one another was based on our obsession with the theatre—also our dissatisfaction with it. We promised each other we would change it." D. and Arden married in 1957 and have four sons. They have collaborated on numerous works in pursuit of their vision of a theater based in the life and rituals of a community, a theater unconstrained by orthodox ideology or mainstream commercial aesthetics.

In the small Somerset village of Brent Knoll, D. and Arden created *The Business of Good Goverment* (1960), a Christmas play to be performed by local residents and children in the village church. In this early play, the dramatists consciously revive the conditions and conventions of medieval mystery plays, including fluid theatrical space, improvised costumes and properties, and amateur performers, who address the audience directly with song and verse as well as prose. In her directing as well as her writing, D. has continued to use these "folk" techniques.

In their next home in Kirkbymoorside, North Yorkshire, D. and Arden developed their communal vision with free public entertainments in their home and children's drama in the community. They created *Ars Longa, Vita Brevis* (1964), a savage fable in which a controlling art teacher joins the Territorial Army and is killed. D. rehearsed the Kirkbymoorside Girl Guides in the play, while Peter Brook directed it for the Royal Shakespeare Company's famous "Theatre of Cruelty" season.

With *The Ballygombeen Bequest* (1972), D. and Arden turned to Ireland, where they had lived for some years, and dramatized a local eviction case. The play explores the complex net of conflicts between England and Ireland, rich and poor, north and south, and men and women, all driven by capitalist greed. The play employs such Brechtian devices as titles announced directly to the audience, such as "SENTIMENTAL IDEALISM CONFOUNDED WITH SHORT-SIGHTED ECONOMIC CONFUSION." *The Ballygombeen Bequest* was first produced in the Falls Road, Belfast, at the height of the Troubles, and then toured by the British company 7:84. The landlord in the Galway eviction case sued D. and Arden for libel, however, and the play was withdrawn. The libel charge was settled out of court in 1977, and *The Ballygombeen Bequest* was rewritten as *The Little Gray Home in the West* (1978).

The Island of the Mighty: A Play on Traditional British Themes in Three Parts (1972) also aroused contention. The three plays present Arthurian legends as chronicles of social and cultural change. D. and Arden were greatly influenced by their 1970 trip to India and employed a "stage-upon-the-stage," a raised platform on which to perform presentational songs and dances in the manner of Indian folk-plays. The Royal Shakespeare Company produced a truncated version of *The Island of the Mighty* in 1972, but differences over interpretation escalated to the point at which D. and Arden, as members of the Society of Irish Playwrights, a regular trade union, went on strike and picketed the production. Despite the legal controversies surrounding the two plays, D. and Arden received an award from the Arts Council in 1974 for *The Ballygombeen Bequest* and *The Island of the Mighty*.

D. and Arden's twenty-six hour extravaganza, *The Non-Stop Connolly Show: A Dramatic Cycle of Continuous Struggle in Six Parts* (1975), is their most ambitious and far-reaching work. This work uses the life of socialist leader James Connolly (1868–1916) to examine the international complexities of the socialist movement. The plays were first produced in Liberty Hall, an important trade union hall in Dublin, at Easter 1975, by a heterogeneous cast of professionals, students, members of the Workers' Cultural Group, and children, for a left-wing audience of union members. The plays comprised improvization, dialogue, songs, masks, placards, banners, verse, and emblems. Although some mainstream critics condemned the work as mere propaganda, others have praised *The Non-Stop Connolly Show* as a vital, inventive breakthrough in political theater that springs from the populist aesthetic of its audience.

From the late 1960s, D. became increasingly involved in Irish politics, frequently damaging her artistic reputation in the eyes of British critics. After protesting the H Block at the 1978 Belfast Arts Festival, she was imprisoned at Armagh Gaol and became more radical in her actions against political oppression. Her book *Tell Them Eveything* (1981) describes her experience in prison, and her essays in *Awkward Corners* (1988, with Arden) further articulate her political philosophy. In the late 1980s, D. and Arden were once again exploring the claims of ritual on the political life of a people; their nine-part script about the formation of the early Christian church, *Whose Is the Kingdom?*, was dramatized by BBC Radio in 1988.

D. is only beginning to receive critical attention for her large body of work. Critics in the 1960s and 1970s frequently attributed collaborative works to Arden alone, and after *The Island of the Mighty* debacle, Arden and D. moved away from mainstream, professional theaters and critics. In the relative obscurity of community-based productions, however, they have had the freediom to experiment with dramatic structure, performance techniques, and local political concerns. Their commitment and confident vision have produced some of the most complex and innovative political drama of modern Britain and Ireland.

WORKS: (with John Arden) *The Happy Haven* (1960). (with Arden) *The Business of Good Government* (1960). (with Arden) *Ars Longa, Vita Brevis* (1964). (with Arden) *Friday's Hiding* (1966). (with Arden) *The Royal Pardon: or, the Soldier Who Became an Actor* (1966). (with Arden) *Vietnam Carnival* (1967). (with Arden) *Harold Muggins Is a Martyr* (1968). (with Arden) *The Hero Rises Up* (1968). (with Arden) *Granny Welfare and the Wolf* (19671). (with Arden) *My Old Man's a Tory* (1971). (with Arden and Roger Smith) *Two Hundred Years of Labour History* (1971). (with Arden) *Rudi Dutschke Must Stay* (1971). (with Arden) *The Ballygombeen Bequest* (1972; rev. as *The Little Gray Home in the West*, 1978). (with Arden) *The Island of the Mighty: A Play on Traditional British Themes in Three Parts* (1972). (with Arden) *Keep Those People Moving!* (1972, for radio). (with Arden) *The Henry Dubb Show* (1973). (with Arden) *Portrait of a Rebel* (1973, for television). (with Arden) *The Devil and the Parish Pump* (1974). (with Arden) *The Non-Stop Connolly Show: A Dramatic Cycle of Continuous* Struggle in Six Parts (1975). (with Arden) *The Crown Strike Show* (1975). (with Arden) *Sean O'Scrudu* (1976). (with Arden) *The Hunting of the Mongrel Fox* (1976). (with Arden) *No Room at the Inn* (1976). (with Arden) *Mary's Name* (1977). (with Arden) *To Present the Pretence: Essays on the Theatre and Its Public* (1977). (with Arden) *A Pinprick of History* (1977). (with Arden) *Silence* (1977). (with Arden) *Blow-In Chorus for Liam Cosgrave* (1977). (with Arden) *Vandaleur's Folly* (1978). *Irish Women's Voices* (1978). *The Trial and Imprisonment of Countess Markievicz* (1979). *Tell Them Everything: A Sojourn in the Prison of Her Majesty Queen Elizabeth II at Ard Macha (Armagh)* (1981). (with Arden) *The Manchester Enthusiasts* (1984, for radio). (with Arden) *Whose Is the Kingdom?* (1988, for radio). (with Arden) *Awkward Corners* (1988). (with Arden) *Arden/D'Arcy, D'Arcy/Arden Plays: One* (1991).

BIBLIOGRAPHY: Chambers, C. and M. Prior. *Playwrights' Progress: Patterns of Postwar British Drama* (1987). Etherton, M. *Contemporary Irish Dramatists* (1989). Itzin, C. *Stages in the Revolution: Political Theatre in Britain Since 1968* (1980). King, K. *Twenty Modern British Playwrights: A Bibliography, 1956 to 1976* (1977). Page, M. *Arden on File* (1985). Rosen, C. *Plays of Impasse* (1983). Wilke, J. *John Arden and Margaretta D'Arcy: A Casebook* (1995). Winkler, E. H. *The Function of Song in Contemporary British Drama* (1990).

For articles in reference works, see: *CA. DLB*.

Other references: *Educational Theatre Journal* (1967). *Guardian* (5 December 1972). *New Statesman* (1979). *LonT* (9 December 1972, 16 December 1972).*TDR* (1966). *Theatre Research International* (1990).

Julia Matthews

Darmesteter, A.M.F. (Mary): See *Robinson, Agnes Mary Frances*

Dart, Helga: See *Doolittle, Hilda (H. D.)*

D'Arusmont, Frances Wright: See *Wright, Frances*

D'Arusmont, Madam: See *Wright, Frances*

Elizabeth Daryush

BORN: 5 December 1887, London.
DIED: 7 April 1977, London.
DAUGHTER OF: Robert Bridges and Monica Waterhouse.
MARRIED: Ali Akbar Daryush, 1923.

Robert Bridges was poet laureate of England, a friend of Gerard Manley Hopkins, and an idiosyncratic, patrician, philosophic, technical virtuoso both very advanced as a poet and quite out of touch with poetic currents of the time. He once wrote, "What has led me to poetry was the inexhaustible satisfaction of form."

D., his daughter, inherited that taste for form, and she carved out a direction all her own in English poetry. She, too, ignored the poetic practices of her day, insisting that poetry was basically conventional ("found beside the worn road," as she put it), and writing poems invested with traditional imagery and the dramatic personification of abstractions. What is amazing is that she forged some excellent poems from these practices.

Living most of her life at or near her father's home at Boar's Hill, Oxford, D. grew up among writers, artists, and academics. While studying Persian literature at Oxford, she met her husband, with whom she lived in Persia for three years before moving back to a house on Boar's Hill. Her personal life was almost reclusive, and she tended to avoid public and professional notice.

She wrote her best poems in the 1930s. Anguish, both personal and universal, became a constant theme. She insisted that poetry must deliver the truth, clearly, precisely, and without sentiment. Life for her was characterized by what she called the "stubborn fact" of tragedy, to which we must respond with determination and strength but absolutely without self-pity. At her best moments, as in "Song: Throw Away the Flowers," she achieves a direct, stately and original voice, somber, unyielding, and spare: "Throw away the flowers, / fetch stubborn rock: / build for the hours / of terror and shock."

Yvor Winters praised her "ability to imbue a simple expository statement of a complex theme with a rich association of feeling, yet with an utterly pure and unmannered style." Her style, however, was anything but "unmannered" and took on more manner as she grew older. D. can use a somewhat archaic vocabulary at times, echoing Renaissance (or at least Georgian echoes of Renaissance) poetry, but this habit should not obscure her strengths. A resolute clarity of mind is one of them. A quiet courage in the face of inevitable sufferings is another. A will to maintain identity in a universe whose disorder threatens anything enduring is yet another.

From her father she inherited a devotion to traditional craft alongside an interest in syllabic verse. Her handling of the latter is assured and striking, as in these lines from "Still-Life":

She comes over the lawn, the young heiress,
from her early walk in her garden wood,
feeling that life's a table set to bless
her delicate desires with all that's good,
that even the unopened future lies
like a love-letter, full of sweet surprise.

She is probably one of the best practitioners of syllabic verse in the twentieth century.

Just as Bridges had attempted to do in his long philosophical poem *The Testament of Beauty,* D., as she grew older, evolved a personal philosophy that emphasized the renunciation of illusions in favor of a clear view of life and its sufferings. Perhaps her most spectacular single poem is "Air and Variations," in which she explores some of these ideas—along with the astounding technical feat of reproducing the stanzaic form of Gerard Manley Hopkins's "Wreck of the Deutschland." In one of her last poems, "Song of a Pentecostal Summer," she made a final attempt to sum up her view:

Again, again
Must mortal truth return.
Shrink to a self, less blindly then
Striving, its fault discern.
Content is death: to live is only this:
Each hour the anguish of remorse to earn,
To feel defeat, refuse each longed-for armistice
World without end—Amen.

Scrupulousness, integrity, a refusal to compromise: these are the hallmarks of D.'s work. She was a severe critic who could show scorn for immaturity and lack of craft in other writers. Of modern fashions in poetry she once wrote, "Most modern poetic form, as I see it, is a kind of open prison, without the disciplines of either the cells or the workshop, or perhaps I should rather describe it as the weedy garden of instant verse!" But she was most severe with herself: In preparing the last edition of her *Collected Poems* (1976), she cut out half of her poetry. Her work searches unceasingly for moral clarity, for the truth of things. Her virtues, very much like those of Winters, are those of the very fine minor poet. What saves her from being a pathetic, isolated figure is, first, that she refuses self-pity so gracefully, and, second, that her best poems achieve a disciplined elegance—albeit an odd, out-of-date elegance—most poets can only hope for, combined with something profound and lasting to say.

WORKS: *Charitessi 1911* (1912). *Verses* (1916). *Sonnets from Hafez and Other Verses* (1921). *First Book Verses* (1930). *Second Book Verses* (1932). *Third Book Verses* (1933). *Fourth Book Verses* (1934). *Selected Poems* (1935). *The Last Man and Other Verses (Fifth Book Verses)* (1936). *Sixth Book Verses* (1938). *Selected Poems,* with an intro. by Y. Winters (1947; rev. and enlarged, 1972). *Seventh Book Verses* (1971). *Collected Poems,* with an intro. by D. Davie (1976).

BIBLIOGRAPHY: *American Review* (1937). Finlay, J. *SoR* (1978). *Poetry* (1974). Schreiber, J. *SoR* (1973). Stanford, D. E. *SoR* (1977).*TLS* (9 April 1977).

For articles in reference works, see: *Bloomsbury. CA. Cambridge. CLC. Feminist. Oxford. RGFMBP. Todd-BWW.*

John Timpane

Eleanor Audeley Davies (Douglas)

BORN: 1590, Ireland.
DIED: 5 July 1652.
DAUGHTER OF: George Touchet, Baron Audeley, and Lucy (Mervin).
MARRIED: Sir John Davies, 1609; Sir Archibald Douglas, 1627.
WROTE UNDER: Eleanor Audeley, Reveale O Daniel; The Lady Eleanor.

D.'s prophetic career spanned the years between 1625 and 1652. During that time, she published some sixty-nine treatises, spent years in jail, and made astonishing predictions on subjects ranging from the coming of the apocalypse to the death of her first husband. Viewed as both an inspired seer and a mad "ladie" by her contemporaries, D. has recently received a great deal of scholarly attention, not least of all because of her densely allusive and complex prose style.

D. was born in 1590 to George Touchet, Baron Audeley, and his wife, Lucy, but little is known about her upbringing and education. Her biographer, Esther S. Cope, appeals to the content of her writings to speculate that she may have had training in Latin in addition to exposure to classical and modern authors. In 1609, she married the poet and prominent barrister Sir John Davies, to whom she bore three children. Of her children, only her daughter, Lucy, survived into adulthood.

Her prophetic career began in 1625 with the publication of *A Warning to the Dragon and all his Angels.* An exegetical treatise on the prophecies of Daniel, *Warning* predicted that "the day of Judgement" would occur "nineteene yeares and a halfe" from 28 July 1625. (Her later texts identified the execution of William Laud, Archbishop of Canterbury, in January of 1645 as ringing the "day of Judgement.") In *Warning,* D. also introduced the anagram "Eleanor Audeley, Reveale O Daniel" that would appear as her signature in many of her treatises and through which she attempted to assert that her family name possessed hidden properties that linked her to the prophet Daniel.

Preoccupied with his own career ambitions, her husband discouraged her in the beginning stages of her prophetic career and burned one of her early treatises. She responded by telling Sir John "within three years to expect the mortal blow," and he died shortly thereafter in 1626. When her second husband, the soldier, Sir Archibald Douglas, burned her prophetic writings, she cryptically predicted that "worse then death should befal" him. By her account, this prediction was fulfilled when, during church services, Sir Archibald was "strooken bereft of his sences, in stead of speech made a noice like a Brute creature."

In 1633, she traveled to Amsterdam to find a printer willing to produce her treatises. Once she returned to England and began to distribute her newly printed tracts, Archbishop Laud ordered them burned. Beyond destroying her books, Laud oversaw her trial before the Commission for Causes Ecclesiastical at which the judges determined that her writings "much unbeseemed her Sex." Her two years in prison did not deter her, and she was jailed again in 1637 for banding with a group of women to protest the "Romish" rituals practiced at the Cathedral of Lichfield. The spectacular nature of her defiance—she occupied the bishop's throne, declared herself "primate and metropolitan," and defaced the cathedral's tapestries—only served to reenforce earlier accusations of her madness and resulted in her being committed to the Hospital of St. Mary of Bethlehem, or Bedlam.

In terms of her literary output, D.'s most productive years came between 1641 and 1652 when she published sixty-six of her sixty-nine treatises. Although the easing of censorship restrictions in this period clearly enabled her to publish with greater freedom, she continued to encounter official rebuke and found herself in and out of jail in the years between 1646 and 1651. She died on 5 July 1652.

WORKS: *A Warning to the Dragon and all his Angels* (1625). *All the Kings of the Earth* (1633). *Woe to the House* (1633). *Her Appeale* (1641). *Samsons Fall* (1642). *To the High Court* (1642). *Samsons Legacie* (1643). *Amend, Amend* (1643). *Star to the Wise* (1643). *Restitution of Reprobates* (1644). *Apoc. J.C.* (1644). *Her Blessing* (1644). *Prayer* (1644). *Discovery* (1644). *Sign* (1644). *Prophetia* (1644). *I am the First* (1645). *Word of God* (1645). *As not Unknowne* (1645). *Brides Preparation* (1645). *Great Brittains Visitation* (1645). *For Whitsontyds* (1645). *Second Coming* (1645). *Of Errors* (1645). *Prayer* (1645). *Prophesie* (1645). *For the Blessed Feast* (1645). *Day of Judgment* (1646). *Her Appeal* (1646). *Je le tien* (1646). *Revelation Interpreted* (1646). *Gatehouse Salutation* (1647). *Mystery of General Redemption* (1647). *Ezekiel the Prophet* (1647). *Ezekiel, cap. 2* (1647). *Excommunication out of Paradise* (1647). *Reader* (1648). *And without Proving* (1648). *Writ of Restitution* (1648). *Apoc. chap. 11* (1648). *Of the Great Days* (1648). *Remonstrance* (1648). *Given to the Elector* (1648). *Appeal from Court to Camp* (1649). *Blasphemous Charge* (1649). *Crying Charge* (1649). *New Jerusalem* (1649). *Prayer* (1649). *Sions Lamentation* (1649). *Strange and Wonderful* (1649). *For Gerbier* (1649). *For the States* (1649). *Sign* (1649). *Discovery* (1649). *Everlasting Gospel* (1649). *New Proclamation* (1649). *Arraignment* (1650). *Bill of Excommunication* (1650). *Appearance* (1650). *Before the Lords Second Coming* (1650). *Elijah the Tishbite* (1650). *Her Jubilee* (1650). *Hells Destruction* (1651). *Of Times* (1651). *Serpents Excommunication* (1651). *Benediction* (1651). *Dragons Blasphemous Charge* (1651). *Given to the Elector* (1651). *Restitution of Prophecy* (1651). *Tobits Book* (1652). *Bethlehem* (1652). *Prophetic Writings of Lady Eleanor Davies*, ed. E. S. Cope (1996).

BIBLIOGRAPHY: Cope, E. S. *Handmaid of the Holy Spirit* (1992). Feroli, T. *Criticism* (1994). Feroli, T. *WS* (1994). Fraser, A. *The Weaker Vessel* (1984). Hindle, C. J. *Edinburgh Bibliographical Society Transactions* (1936). Mack, P. *Visionary Women* (1992). Matchinske, M. *ELH* (1993). Nelson, B. *Women's Studies Internationl Forum* (1985). Spencer, T. *Harvard Studies and Notes in Philology and Literature* (1938). Wright, S. G. *Bodleian Quarterly Record* (1932–34).

For articles in reference works, see: *Bloomsbury* (under "Douglas"). *DNB* (under "Sir John Davies"). *Feminist* (under "Douglas"). *ToddBWW* (under "Douglas").

Other references: *Criticism* (1994). *Edinburgh Bibliographical Society Transactions* (1936). *ELH* (1993). Powicke, F. M. *HLQ* (1938). Spencer, T. in *Harvard Studies and Notes in Philology and Literature* (1938). *Women's Studies International Forum* (1985). Wright, S. G., in *Bodleian Quarterly Record* (1932–34). *WS* (1994).

Teresa Feroli

Emily Davies

BORN: 22 April 1830, Southampton, Hampshire.
DIED: 13 July 1921, Hampstead, London.
DAUGHTER OF: the Reverend John Davies and Mary Hopkinson Davies.

Feminist, educator, and polemicist, D. founded Girton College in 1869, determined to make it "a college like a man's," with the same curriculum and examination standards as Cambridge. A skillful rhetorician, she wrote in support of the women's issues that occupied her life: women's employment, suffrage, and education.

The fourth of five children, D. was educated at home by her mother and sister. She and her sister had lessons in French, Italian, and music, and she learned "a little Latin" from her brothers' tutor. Her writing skill may be traced to the weekly compositions she wrote under the direction of her father, John Davies, an evangelical clergyman and author. As a young woman, D. was influenced by her brother Llewelyn, a supporter of F. D. Maurice in his efforts to improve the education of governesses at Queen's College.

Friendship with Barbara Bodichon and the women working at Langham Place helped D. to understand her "feeling of resentment at the subjection of women" and to take a leading part in feminist activities of the mid-nineteenth century. The substance and style of D.'s essays are best understood in the context of the reforms she accomplished. She used language for practical purposes, whether she was speaking at the National Association for the Promotion of the Social Sciences, a reform organization open to women; undertaking an extensive letter-writing campaign; or editing the *Englishwoman's Journal* (1862) and *Victoria Magazine* (1864). D. founded an employment society for women and, in her determination to help Elizabeth Garrett Anderson become a physician, became a strong advocate of medical education for women. She and Anderson delivered the first petition for women's suffrage to John Stuart Mill in 1866; during 1866–1867 she acted as secretary to the first women's Suffrage committee.

Her most important achievements were in education.

D. persuaded the Schools Inquiry Commission of 1864 to include girls' secondary schools in its epoch-making study. To provide the schools with an external standard of measurement, she campaigned for the admission of girls to the Cambridge Local Examinations. D. founded the London Schoolmistresses' Association in 1866 and served on the London School Board from 1870 to 1873. For more than forty years, she was the practical force behind Girton College, raising money, supervising construction, setting policy. As the first women's college to follow the university model, Girton provided an opportunity for women to demonstrate their intellectual equality with men.

D.'s educational philosophy is contained in *The Higher Education of Women* (1866), a book praised by Matthew Arnold and Frances Power Cobbe. Unlike many other reformers, D. did not base her argument for higher education on the necessity of providing single women with a way to support themselves. The "education of a lady" ought to be considered irrespective of "any specific uses to which it may afterwards be turned"; education "ought to mean the highest and the finest culture of the time." Thus D. made liberal education a good in itself rather than a solution to a dilemma. Then she did something even more radical: She pronounced the question of its "womanliness" to be irrelevant. According to D., theories of woman's "special" nature were factually unfounded and contrary to religious principle. She built her educational philosophy on the "deep and broad basis of likeness" between the sexes. Rejecting prevailing systems of "womanly" education, she urged her students to pursue classics and mathematics and to compete with men in the demanding university examinations. Eager to see both sexes transcend the conventional limitations of their assigned spheres, she foresaw husbands and wives working together as physicians, ministers, and artists. In the present, she regarded a liberal education "as a means of bringing men and women together, and bridging over the intellectual gulf between them."

In addressing the public, D. found that two issues were especially controversial: the use of examinations and the creation of a residential college. Many Victorians objected to taking women out of the home: Novelist Charlotte Yonge warned D. that when girls were brought together they "always hurt one another in manner and tone if in nothing else." D. maintained that a residential college located in the country was necessary to protect women from the demands of domestic routine and social propriety. D. wanted each student to have "a small sitting room to herself where she will be free to study undisturbed, and to enjoy at her discretion the companionship of friends of her own choice." Only a residential college could offer women the unique combination of personal privacy and sympathetic support. While physicians, parents, and professors predicted that testing would cause undue stress and competition among the students, D. argued that university examinations would provide students and teachers with an exciting challenge, a communal goal, and public evidence of their ability.

In the controversial area of women's education, D. carefully anticipated objections to her argument. With well-chosen quotations, she shows her opponents contradicting themselves or finds support in unexpected places. She uses metaphors from nature to undermine society's promised land and is a pragmatic strategist. She can be witty about the inconsistencies in Victorian society while remaining polite toward her detractors. Her persona is cautious, reasonable, and willing to qualify her assertions ("perhaps" and "probably"). Gestures of sympathy for her opponents are often followed by quietly incontrovertible assertions of her own ("No doubt they honestly believe . . . but the fact is . . ."). Her prose, which might be studied in conjunction with Arnold's and Mill's, is clear, logical, and understated, her voice, controlled. She told Barbara Bodichon, "Men cannot stand indignation, and tho' of course I think it is just, it seems to me better to suppress the manifestation of it." Such tactical accommodations to her audience should not obscure the radical implications of D.'s thought.

WORKS: *The Higher Education of Women* (1866). *Thoughts on Some Questions Relating to Women* (1910). *The Papers of Emily Davies and Barbara Bodichon from Girton College, Cambridge* (1985).

BIBLIOGRAPHY: Bradbrook, M. C. *"That Infidel Place": A Short History of Girton College* (1969). Forster, M. *Significant Sisters: The Grassrools of Active Feminism, 1839–1939* (1984). Murray, J. H. *Strong-Minded Women and Other Lost Voices from Nineteenth-Century England* (1982). McWilliams-Tullberg, R. *Women at Cambridge: A Men's University—Though of a Mixed Type* (1975). Stephen, B. *Emily Davies and Girton College* (1927). Vicinus, M. *Independent Women: Work and Community for Single Women, 1850–1920* (1985).

For articles in reference works, see: *BDBF. DNB. Europa. VB.*

Robin Sheets

Davies, Gordon: See *Mackintosh, Elizabeth*

Davies, P.: See *Godden, (Margaret) Rumer*

Daviot, Gordon: See *Mackintosh, Elizabeth*

Mary Davys

BORN: 1674, Ireland.
DIED: 1731, Cambridge.
MARRIED: Peter Davys.

Little is known about the life of the Irish playwright and novelist D. She corresponded with Jonathan Swift; she married the Dublin schoolmaster Peter Davys, who died in 1698; and she lived for some time thereafter in York. She later kept a coffeehouse in Cambridge, where she died. W. H. McBurney credits her with being "one of the first writers before Fielding to exploit extensively the English scene," and J. Spencer puts her "at the beginning of a long line of women writers who create coquettish heroines and lover-mentors to reform them."

Her first comedy, *The Northern Heiress,* was performed in 1716 at the New Theatre in Lincoln's Inn Fields. The preface to the published text hints at its reception: "The first Night, in which lay all the Danger, was attended with only two single Hisses. This one was a Boy, and not worth taking Notice of, the other a Man who came prejudiced." In spite of the relative lack of hissing, receipts fell off drastically for the second performance, and the play closed. Her collected miscellany (1725) included an unperformed second play, *The Self-Rival,* "as it should have been acted at the Theatre Royal in Drury Lane."

On her playwrighting career, D. observed wryly, "The two plays I leave to fight their own battles, and I shall say no more than I never was so vain as to think they deserved a place in the first rank, or so humble as to resign them to the last."

Her first work of prose fiction, *The Reform'd Coquet,* was published in 1724, followed by *The Accomplish'd Rake* (1727), which purported to be "An Exact Description of the Conduct and Behavior of a Person of Distinction." The novel relies heavily on theatrical conventions; it is similar in plot and tone to Farquhar's *The Beaux' Stratagem* and, as McBurney points out, is "an intricate mosaic of borrowings" from Etherege, Cibber, and other playwrights. It is, however, a well-crafted novel, and D. succeeds in her attempt to "order accidents beter than Fortune will be at the pains to do, so to work upon the reader's passions, sometimes keep him in suspense betwen fear and hope, and at least send him satisfied away."

WORKS: *The Northern Heiress, or the Humors of York* (1716). *The Reform'd Coquet, or the Memoirs of Amoranda* (1724). *The Works of Mrs. Davys* (1725). *The Accomplish'd Rake, or the Modern Fine Gentleman* (1727).

BIBLIOGRAPHY: *DNB.* McBurney, W. H. *Four Before Richardson: Selected English Novels, 1720–1727* (1963). Spencer, J. *The Rise of the Woman Novelist* (1986).

Richard C. Taylor

E. M. Delafield (pseudonym of Edmée Elizabeth Monica de la Pasture)

BORN: 9 June 1890, Hove, Sussex.
DIED: 11 December 1943, Kentisbeare, Devon.
DAUGHTER OF: Comte Henri du Carel de la Pasture and Elizabeth Lydia Rosabelle Bonham de la Pasture.
MARRIED: Arthur Paul Dashwood, 1919.
WROTE UNDER: E. M. D.; E. M. Delafield

Although her first novel, *Zella Sees Herself,* was published in 1917, it was not until the 1930s that D. became one of Britain's best-loved novelists and humorists. In that decade, her satirical sketches appeared regularly in *Punch* and in the feminist periodical *Time and Tide.* She is best known today for *The Diary of a Provincial Lady* (1930), which was originally published in the latter periodical in installments. Such was its popularity that three other volumes followed. These books, like much of D.'s fiction, focus on the quiet struggles of middle-class women faced with the strictures of the social system (the right schools, domestic help, and entertaining, all on a limited budget) and with unresponsive and reserved husbands. With sympathetic irony, D. creates comedies of manners that implicitly question social mores.

D.'s background was romantic; her father was a French nobleman whose family had left France for England after the Revolution, and her mother was a socialite and novelist ("Mrs. Henry de la Pasture"). Despite, or perhaps because of, these colorful beginnings, D. passed an unhappy childhood that culminated in an unhappier period as a debutante. She entered a convent in Belgium in 1911—thinly and painfully fictionalized in *Consequences* (1919)—but left in 1913. After her marriage, she spent two years in Singapore (although none of her fiction is set there), returning to settle into provincial life in Devon where she combined duties as a Justice of the Peace and as a pillar of the Women's Institute with a full schedule as a writer. In the 1930s, her success in print took her to both the United States and the Soviet Union; these experiences produced *The Provincial Lady in America* (1934), and *Straw Without Bricks* (1937). She died of cancer at home at the age of fifty-three.

D. began writing reviews for *Time and Tide* in 1922 and soon graduated to articles and comic pieces, becoming a director of the journal in 1930. Her output for *Time and Tide* and *Punch* was regular and prolific; she missed only a week, for example, after her son's death in 1940. Her characteristic genre was the comic sketch, in which she deftly probed and punctured social absurdities. This satiric vision also informs her novels, some of which treat specific issues in a serious manner: *Faster, Faster* (1936) explores life in a family where the mother is a dedicated career woman, while *Nothing Is Safe* (1937) examines the deleterious effects of divorce on children. D.'s earlier novels, while still dealing with social issues, often employ a lighter tone. In *The Way Things Are* (1927), Laura Temple, faced with a less-than-inspiring family life, falls in love with her sister's friend Duke Ayland, who tries to persuade her to run off with him. Torn between her "duty" in the provinces and the new sexual freedom that seems to be sweeping London, Laura finally decides she must abandon Duke and submit to "the way things are." D. both satirizes the frivolity of city life and evokes its blandishments. "Good" women like Laura, she seems to be saying, must endure the status quo even through clenched teeth.

The Diary of a Provincial Lady (1930) delineates a similar social scene; in fact, both these novels seem autobiographical in their settings. Arthur Watts's illustrations were actually modelled by D. and her husband, which increased the public's identification of author with character. The unnamed narrator of *The Diary* records conflicts with servants, nasty encounters with the snobbish Lady Boxe, and conversations with "Our Vicar's Wife" in an elliptical, almost shorthand, first-person style whose breathless quality renders provincial life comic and poignant. The narrator, at the end of a troubling day, posits questions regarding the puzzling or predictable behavior of herself or others and sets down the response, "Answer comes there none," a phrase that was taken up into the popular slang of the 1930s. After the first volume, the narrator's horizons expand with the acquisition of a London flat in *The Provincial Lady Goes Further* (1932). The new setting allows the narrator to contrast her life as a writer in the metropolis with the mundaneness of her life at home. *The Provincial Lady in America* (1934) extends D.'s satiric gaze across the Atlantic, while *The Provincial Lady in Wartime* (1939) documents the effects of the blackout, evacuation policies, and preparations for blanket bombing in both rural and city communities. All four volumes present the provincial lady as a comic but sympathetic character who accepts life's banana skins with fortitude.

In her novels, journalism, and plays, D.'s social comedy exposes the pressures on ordinary women. She has often been likened to Jane Austen in her style and her subject matter, although she is more broadly comic in her tone. D.'s work tells us much about life for women in the 1920s and 1930s, yet her humor and satiric wit prevent her work from being too dated. She is an important figure in twentieth-century women's fiction.

WORKS: *Zella Sees Herself* (1917). *The War Workers* (1918). *The Pelicans* (1918). *Consequences* (1919). *Tension* (1920). *The Heel of Achilles* (1920). *Humbug* (1921). *The Optimist* (1922). *A Reversion To Type* (1923). *Messalina of the Suburbs* (1923). *Mrs. Harter* (1924). *The Chip and the Block* (1925). *The Entertainment* (1926). *Jill* (1926). *The Way Things Are* (1927). *What is Love* (1928; in the U.S. as *First Love*). *The Suburban Young Man* (1928). *Women Are Like That* (1929). *Diary of a Provincial Lady* (1930). *To See Ourselves* (1930). *Turn Back the Leaves* (1930). *Challenge to Clarissa* (1931; in the U.S. as *House Party*). *Thank Heaven Fasting* (1932; in the U.S. as *A Good Man's Love*). *The Provincial Lady Goes Further* (1932; in the U.S. as *The Provincial Lady in London*). *Gay Life* (1933). *General Impressions* (1933). *The Glass Wall* (1933). *The Provincial Lady in America* (1934). *The Balzagettes* (1935). *The Brontës* (1935). *The Mulberry Bush* (1935). *Faster! Faster!* (1936). *As Others Hear Us* (1937). *Ladies and Gentlemen in Victorian Fiction* (1937). *Nothing Is Safe* (1937). *Straw Without Bricks* (1937; in the U.S. as *I Visit The Soviets*). *The Provincial Lady in Wartime* (1939). *Three Marriages* (1939; in the U.S. as *When Women Love*). *People You Love* (1940). *Love Has No Resurrection* (1941). *No One Will Know* (1942). *Late And Soon* (1943).

BIBLIOGRAPHY: McCullen, M. *E. M. Delafield* (1987). Powell, V. *The Life of a Provincial Lady* (1988). Roberts, D. K. *Titles To Fame* (1937).

For articles in reference works see: *CA. Cambridge. DLB. Europa. ELB. Feminist. Longman. MBL. NCBEL. NCHEL. OCEL. RE. RGCL. TCA. TCRGW. TCW. ToddBWW. WWALA. WN.*

Helen Clare Taylor

Shelagh Delaney

BORN: 25 November 1939, Salford, Lancashire.
DAUGHTER OF: Joseph and Elsie Delaney.

"To talk as we do about popular theatre, about new working class audiences, about plays that will interpret the common experiences of today—all this is one thing, and a good thing, too. But how much better even, how much more exciting, to find such theatre suddenly here, suddenly sprung up under our feet! This was the first joyful thing about Theatre Workshop's performance of *A Taste of Honey.*" So Lindsay Anderson wrote during the summer of 1958 about the first play of a nineteen-year-old girl from a working-class family from the north of England. With the critical and popular success of *A Taste of Honey,* D. was catapulted into prominence as an extraordinarily promising and precocious writer of the New Drama. Although in 1960 she produced a second play, *The Lion in Love,* the hopes of many exuberant early supporters for a bountiful body of writing from her has not been rewarded.

D. was raised in Salford, an industrial suburb of Manchester that serves as background setting for both of her plays. She left school at the age of seventeen and found employment variously as a salesgirl, a milk depot clerk, and usher at a local cinema. She had an ambition to write, however, and had begun work on a novel at the time she was working as an usher. The novel was transformed to playscript when, upon going to the theater one evening and seeing a touring production of Terence Rattigan's bourgeois entertainment, *Variations on a Theme,* she was so disgusted by the febrile character of Rattigan's tea-tinkling conventions that she became convinced she could do better herself. When she completed the script, D. sent a copy to Joan Littlewood, director of the Theatre Workshop at the Theatre Royal Stratford-East, expecting only, perhaps, some helpful criticism. Within two weeks, *A Taste of Honey* was in rehearsal with Littlewood directing.

Set in a "comfortless flat," *A Taste of Honey* examines the misfortunes of Jo, a sensitive and awkward teenager who defends herself with a sometimes caustic tongue and hardened outer shell of indifference to the general squalor of life that surrounds her. The play, written in two acts, progresses by examining Jo's relationships within the context of a sordid environment she can never fully overcome, with her sluttish mother, a lover, and a new-found friend. In turn, Jo is abandoned by each of them. Her mother agrees to marry a current lover and leaves Jo to fend for herself. Her lover, a black seaman, ships out, leaving her with an engagement ring from Woolworth's and a child in her womb. Her friend Geof, a spirited homosexual lad, helps Jo during her pregnancy and, by drawing her away from being overwhelmed by hate and self-pity, introduces her to the joy of simple affection (the taste of honey). Geof proposes marriage to Jo and is refused. He also departs when the prodigal mother returns, her own fling at marriage in ruin, to reclaim rudely the territory.

Audiences and critics alike were impressed by the unaffected honesty of character and relationships. What may have been the material of clichéd melodrama came off with such vitality and directness that the pathos of situation was illuminated all the more clearly by the brightness of the ironic humor found in Joan Littlewood's glowing production—performed in a style blending elements of modern naturalism with the presentational openness of the traditional music hall. Indeed, some suggested that Littlewood (widely known for her success at shaping theatrically effective productions out of unlikely sources) had substantially rewritten the script during the course of rehearsal. However, John Russell Taylor's examination of the original typescript (provided by Littlewood) determined that "The dialogue throughout has been pruned and tightened—rather more, evidently, than is usual in rehearsal—but most of the celebrated lines are already there . . . and the character of Jo, the play's raison d'être, is already completely created and unmistakably the same. . . . The play is obviously much superior in the final version, but it is not so different, and the only modifications which one might find out of keeping are very minor."

The *eclat* that accompanied *A Taste of Honey's* 1958 premiere brought its then-nineteen-year-old author international attention. The play was produced in New York City in 1960 and received enthusiastic critical acclaim as well as the New York Drama Critics Award for "Best Foreign Play." D.'s screenplay for the 1962 cinema adaptation, written with the film's director Tony Richardson, brought her a British Film Academy Award and the Robert Flaherty Award for "Best Screenplay."

Some observers of the theater scene, inclined to categorize D. as the "Angry Young Woman" of the new drama, were cautioned in a program note for the original production that because D. "knows what she is angry about," she may well be the antithesis of the so-called Angry Young Men. Unlike Jimmy Porter in John Osborne's *Look Back in Anger,* Jo does not account for her situation in terms of bitter denunciations directed against the government of socioeconomic injustice. In dramatic situations where she might be moved to anger, Jo's commentary is colored by statements like, "I hate love!" Lindsay Anderson, in his 1958 review of *A Taste of Honey,* compares Jo to Holden Caulfield of J. D. Salinger's *A Catcher in the Rye.* "Like Holden, Josephine is a sophisticated innocent," notes Anderson. "Precious little surprises her; but her reactions are pure and direct, her intuitions are acute, and her eye is very sharp. . . . But Josephine is luckier than Holden in some ways: she is tougher, with common-sense, Lancashire working-class resilience that will always pull her through. And this makes her different too from the middle-class angry young man, the egocentric rebel. Josephine is not a rebel, she is a revolutionary." Rather than being a social philosopher who deliberately tries to move an audience with didactic messages, D. is a careful and compassionate observer of life; her audiences are moved to ponder the implications of what they see.

D.'s second (and, to date, only other) play, *The Lion in Love,* was originally presented in September 1960 at the Belgrade Theatre, Coventry, for a run outside London before moving to the Royal Court in late December. The script draws its title from an Aesop fable that moralizes, "Nothing can be more fatal to peace than the ill assorted marriages into which rash love may lead." Naturalistic in style, the play examines a strained marriage, problems and difficulties of each generation in search of what it wants, and the "waywardness of life itself." Unlike *A Taste of Honey,* the play incorporates a large cast, a complex interweaving of story-lines, and direct statements of social-consciousness by a number of the characters. It was not a popular success and received mixed critical reactions. Although most reviewers considered it verbose, poorly constructed, and thematically unfocused, Kenneth Tynan found the realistic qualities of the piece to have "authenticity, honesty, restraint and . . . a prevailing sense of humor." John Russell Taylor found some merit in the characterization, particularly the mature perspicuity of one of the play's young females, but hoped *The Lion in Love* would eventually prove only a transitional work.

Since her heralded arrival, D. has produced new work sporadically. In 1963, D. published a collection of autobiographical short shories entitled *Sweetly Sings the Donkey.* Reviewers thought the writing uneven, but, at its best, composed "in that same arresting voice," in Marion Magid's words, "without literary pretension, honest to the point of brutality, that made Miss Delaney's first work so striking." Since 1963, she has written screenplays for a handful of films—*The White Bus* (1966) and *Charlie Bubbles* (1968)—and several scripts for television including "The House That Jack Built" (1977), which was performed without accolade in 1979 as a stage production Off-Broadway; a couple of radio plays—including *Don't Worry about Matilda* (1983), which was staged in London in 1987; and an adaptation of a novel by Jennifer Johnston, *The Railway Station Man* (1992), for a BBC-produced television film starring Julie Christie and Donald Sutherland. In 1985, she generated a remarkable screenplay, in collaboration with director Mike Newall, for a critically celebrated film, *Dance With a Stranger,* based on the true story of a marginalized, underclass nightclub hostess who falls for an upper-class gent. When she is abandoned by him, she murders him and is hanged for it. The film captured the Prix Populaire at the Cannes Film Festival in 1985. D. was honored the same year by being named a Fellow of the Royal Society of Literature.

WORKS: *A Taste of Honey* (1958; screenplay 1961). *The Lion in Love* (1960). *Sweetly Sings the Donkey* (1963). *The White Bus* (1966). *Charlie Bubbles* (1968). "Did Your Nanny Come from Bergen?" (1970). "St. Martin's Bummer" (1974). "The House That Jack Built" (1977). "Find Me First" (1981). "So Does the Nightingale" (1981). *Don't Worry about Matilda* (BBC radio, 1983). (with Mike Newall) *Dance with a Stranger* (1985). *The Railway Station Man* (1992).

BIBLIOGRAPHY: Anderson, L. *Encore* (July-August 1958). Clurman, H. *The Naked Image.* (1966). Ippolito, G. J. *Drama Survey* (1961). Kerr, W. *The Theatre in Spite of Itself* (1963). Kitchin, L. *Mid-Century Drama* (1962). Lindroth, C., in *British Playwrights, 1956–1995: A Research and Production Sourcebook,* ed. W. W. Demastes (1996). Lumley, F. *New Trends in 20th Century Drama* (1972). MacInnes, C. *Encounter* (April 1959). Magid, M. *NYHT* (18 August 1963). *New Theatre Voices of the Fifties and Sixties,* ed. C. Marowitz, T. Milne, and T. Hale (1965). Noel, J. *RLV* (1960). Oberg, A. K. *ConL* (1966). Simon, J. *HudR* (1961). Taylor, J. R. *Anger and After* (1962; rev. 1963; rev. as *The Angry Theatre: New British Drama,* 1969). Tynan, K. *Tynan Right and Left* (1968). Wandor, M. *Look Back in Gender: Sexuality and the Family in Post-War British Drama* (1987). Wellwarth, G. *The Theatre of Protest and Paradox* (1964).

For articles in reference works, see: *CA. CD. Crowell's Handbook of Contemporary Drama* (1971). *McGraw-Hill Encyclopedia of World Drama* (1972). *MWT. Oxford. WD.*

Paul D. Nelsen

Mary Granville Pendarves Delany

BORN: 14 May 1700, Iston, Wiltshire.
DIED: 15 April 1788, Windsor.
DAUGHTER OF: Bernard Granville.
MARRIED: Alexander Pendarves, 1718; Patrick Delany, 1743.
WROTE UNDER: Mrs. Delany; Mary Granville; M. Pendarves.

When the adolescent D. was being courted by a man of whom her parents disapproved, they sent her to live with an aunt and uncle, Lord Lansdowne, who arranged the marriage of D. to Alexander Pendarves, sixty-eight, a wealthy Cornish landholder. After the marriage in 1718, the couple lived mostly in Cornwall. At her husband's death in 1725, D. moved to London where she earned the affection and enjoyed the society of the court. While visiting Jonathan Swift in Ireland, she met Patrick Delany, a widower, an Irish Anglican clergyman, and Dean of Down, whom she married. When Delany died in 1768, D. again established residence in London, this time as a member of the Bluestocking circle with Elizabeth Montagu, Frances Boscawen, and others. She met Fanny Burney at this time and became her patron. The paper mosaics she cut during this period, evidence of her patience, skill, and artistry, remain in the British Library. A constant associate of the members of the royal family, D. received a pension and lived in a "grace and favour" house at Windsor.

Acquainted with Edmund Burke, George Frideric Handel, and Jean-Jacques Rousseau, D. wrote often to Swift and to her sister Ann and other relatives and friends. Her letters show the concerns and occupations of privileged women of the eighteenth century. She criticizes women who waste their time playing cards and urges women to appreciate attentive and honest husbands. Swift noted that D.'s "want of ignorance" did not make her affected and generalized his admiration: "To say the truth, the ladies in general are extremely mended both in writing and reading since I was young." Like Horace Walpole and Mary Wortley Montagu, D. was aware of the literary quality of a fine letter. Of her sister Ann's letter "dated Easter Eve," D. says, "You never wrote a better; I cannot say more in its praise." Her own letters to her sister are sometimes instructive, as when she offers advice on learning French: "Wherever you go take some French book with you, and the dictionary, and read for every day half an hour." D.'s candidness lightens descriptive passages; "I have [a garden] as big as your parlour at Gloucester," she boasts to her sister, "and in it groweth damask-roses, stocks variegated and plain, some purple, some red, pinks, Philaria, some dead some alive; and honeysuckles that never blow. But when you come to town to weed and water it, it shall be improved after the new taste, but till then it shall remain dishevelled and undress."

WORKS: *A Catalogue of Plants Copyed from Paper Mosaics, Finished in the Year 1778, and Disposed in Alphabetical Order, According to the Generic and Specific Names of Linnaus* (1778). *Letters from Mrs. Delany from the Year 1779 to the Year 1788 to Mrs. Frances Hamilton* (1820). *Autobiography and Correspondence* (ed. A.W.H. Llanover, 1861; rev. and ed. A.W.H. Llanover and S. Coolidge, 1879). *Mrs. Delany at Court and Among the Wits, Being the Record of a Great Lady of Genius in the Art of Living,* ed. R. B. Johnson (1925). *Aspasia: The Life and Letters of Mary Granville, Mrs. Delany (1700–88),* ed. C. E. Vulliamy (1935).

BIBLIOGRAPHY: Dewes, S. *Mrs. Delany* (1904). Dobson, A. *Side-walk Studies* (1902). Hayden, R. *Mrs. Delany, Her Life and Her Flowers* (1980). Symonds, E. M. *Mrs. Delaney (Mary Granville), a Memoir (1700–1788)* (1900).

For articles in reference works, see: *Allibone. ArtWW. BAB1800. BA19C. Cambridge. DBPP. Dictionary of Women Artists,* ed. C. Pettys (1985). *DLEL. DNB. Feminist. Literature Criticism from 1400 to 1800,* ed. J. Person (1984). *Ireland. Longman. NCBEL. NCHEL. OCEL. OPEL. ToddBWW. ToddDBA.*

Mary Sauter Comfort

Dering, Anna: See *Locke, Anne Vaughan*

Monica Dickens

BORN: 10 May 1915, London.
DIED: 24 December 1992, Reading.
DAUGHTER OF: Henry Charles Dickens and Fanny Runge Dickens.
MARRIED: Roy Stratton, 1951.

As became the great-granddaughter of Charles Dickens, D. was a prolific writer of fiction and social observation. Her literary career began with an autobiographical work in 1939 (*One Pair of Hands*), and her later works included nonfiction or autobiography (*Cape Cod,* 1972, *An Open Book,* 1978), but the majority of her extensive production lay in fiction written either for adults or for children.

A Roman Catholic, she was educated at St. Paul's School for Girls and traveled abroad before joining a dramatic school. After her presentation at Court in 1935, she rebelled against life of the privileged by seeking employment as a maid and cook in private homes in London for two years. These experiences formed the basis of *One Pair of Hands,* which was immediately popular for its deft, witty social observations.

During World War II, D. worked both as a nurse and as a mechanic in an aircraft repair factory. *One Pair of Feet,* about her experiences in a London hospital, made it impossible for her to obtain another hospital position for some time, her candor having incurred the displeasure of hospital administrators.

After the war, D. worked as a local reporter for the *Hertfordshire Express,* gathering material for *My Turn to Make the Tea* (1950) and contributing a popular regular column to *Woman's Own* magazine. She later married a retired U.S. naval officer, a writer of detective fiction, and moved to Cape Cod, Massachusetts, where she remained until his death in 1985. She then retired to a cottage in Brightwalton, Berkshire. D. is survived by two adopted daughters.

D.'s rejection of her social upbringing is reflected particularly in her later works, both fiction and nonfiction, which are often concerned with such social ills as urban poverty, alcoholism, the treatment of the aged, and the making of a mass murderer. *Kate and Emma* (1964), which focuses chiefly on child abuse, was the result of much research among social workers and attendance at juvenile courts.

The problems of suicide formed the principal center of interest for D. during her latter years. Once in England for research purposes, she was impressed by the work of the Samaritans, a group of trained volunteers who take phone calls and "listen" to those contemplating suicide. Her novel *The Listeners* (in the U.S. as *The End of the Line,* 1970) concerns characters who tend the phones and engage in the stressful task of attempting to save the despairing from suicide, connecting them whenever possible with professional assistance. D. founded the American branch of this remarkable international organization in Boston, Cape Cod, and Providence, Rhode Island, and continued to be profoundly involved in mental health issues. D.'s late-life interests centered on the problems of critically ill children and their families.

While D. was obviously devoted to the writing profession, her success has been limited in terms of positive critical response to her adult fiction. It is probable that she will be primarily remembered for her compassionate, penetrating social work and for her enormously popular "Follyfoot" children's series about horses and farming communities, which was serialized for television.

WORKS: *One Pair of Hands* (1939). *The Moon Was Low* (1940). *One Pair of Feet* (1942). *Edward's Fancy* (1943). *Thursday Afternoons* (1945). *The Happy Prisoner* (1946). *Joy and Josephine* (1948). *Flowers on the Grass* (1949). *My Turn to Make the Tea* (1950). *The Nightingales Are Singing* (1953). *The Winds of Heaven* (1955). *The Angel in the Corner* (1956). *Man Overboard* (1958). *Cobbler's Dream* (1963). *Kate and Emma* (1964). *The Room Upstairs* (1966). *My Fair Lady* (1967). *The Landlord's Daughter* (1968). *The Great Fire* (1970). *The Listeners* (in the U.S. as *The End of the Line,* 1970). *The Great Escape* (1971). *Summer at World's End* (1971). *Follyfoot* (1971). *World's End in Winter* (1972). *Cape Cod* (1972). *Talking of Horses* (1973). *Follyfoot Farm* (1973). *Spring Comes to World's End* (1973). *An Open Book* (1978). *Miracles of Courage* (1985). *Enchantment* (1989). *One of the Family* (1993).

BIBLIOGRAPHY:

For articles in reference works, see: *Bloomsbury. BCathA. CA. CN. Feminist. Longman. NCHEL. Todd-BWA. WA.*

Miriam Quen Cheikin
(updated by Nancy E. Schaumburger)

Dimant, Penelope: See Mortimer, Penelope Ruth

Ella Nora Hepworth Dixon

BORN: 1857, London.
DIED: 12 January 1932, London.
DAUGHTER OF: William Hepworth Dixon and Marian MacMahon Hepworth Dixon.
WROTE UNDER: Ella Hepworth Dixon; Margaret Wynman.

D. was a successful London journalist and critic who also published many short stories and an excellent novel. Because she earned her own living and had protofeminist views of women's experiences and the gender bias they faced, Edmund Gosse and others aptly called her a "New Woman."

D. was born in London and lived there for most of her life. Privately educated in London and Heidelberg, Germany, she briefly attended art school in Paris. She exhibited her paintings at the Royal Society of British Artists between 1877 and 1883, but she gave up art for journalism in the mid-1880s. As the daughter of William Hepworth Dixon, the editor of the *Athenaeum* from 1853 to 1869, she gained easy access to Fleet Street. She had a flair for journalism, however, and did not need to depend on family connections for long. One of her first jobs was at the short-lived *Women's World,* edited by Oscar Wilde. In the course of her career, she wrote for many of the major London newspapers, including *The Daily Mail, The Daily Telegraph, The St. James Gazette, The Westminster Gazette,* and Arnold Bennett's *Woman.*

As a journalist, D. undertook a variety of topics, genres, and roles. Her fashion articles included "Women on Horseback" and "On Cloaks," while in essays like "Is Marriage a Failure?" and "Are Young Men Decadent?" she debated controversial social issues of the day. She also contributed travel articles and gossip columns and reviewed art exhibitions, concerts, and books. Her literary criticism earned her a seat on the Femina Vie Heureuse and Northcliffe Prizes committee, which gave awards for French and English books of outstanding merit; she became its vice president in 1930. Moreover, between 1895 and 1900, she served as the first and only editor of *The Englishwoman,* an illustrated magazine that included employment notices for women in its columns.

Under the pseudonym "Margaret Wynman," D. published *My Flirtations* (1892), a group of linked sketches depicting the humorous adventures of a young woman and a series of idiosyncratic "beaus." Two years later, D. produced her only novel, the grimly realistic *The Story of a Modern Woman* (1894). While W. T. Stead discussed this book in *The Review of Reviews* under the heading "The Novel of the Modern Woman"—along with works by Schreiner, Caird, Grand, Egerton, and other "New Woman" writers—some critics disagreed with Stead's label. They rightly viewed the heroine, Mary Erle, as too conventional to be a "modern" woman but failed to see the radicalism of other aspects of the novel. In it, D. unmasks the sexual double standard and criticizes society for failing to educate women to lead productive lives in case they find themselves without money or male protection. Moreover, Mary's friend Alison makes a plea for what the author called "a kind of moral and social trades-unionism among women." Alison tells Mary never to harm another woman, adding: "If only we [women] were united, we could lead the world." Thus, when Mary is tempted into an affair with the man who jilted her—and whom she still loves—she refuses to succumb to her passion out of deference to his wife rather than out of respect for conventional morality.

As Kate Flint points out, contemporary reviewers were not wrong to make distinctions between *The Story of a Modern Woman* and other "New Woman" novels. In particular, D. avoided the sensationalism of writers such as Caird and Grand. At the end of *The Story of a Modern Woman,* Mary has no hope of marriage but resigns herself to her fate as a self-supporting woman rather than killing herself, murdering the man who betrayed her (as Viola does in Caird's *The Wing of Azrael),* or having a nervous breakdown (as Evadne does in Grand's *The Heavenly Twins).* The realism of D.'s denouement and her close attention to social detail link her with English Naturalists such as George Gissing.

In 1904, D. compiled several of her previously published stories in *One Doubtful Hour and Other Side-Lights of the Feminine Temperament.* These tales, which range from the tragic to the comic, depict the various ways in which women of different ages, classes, and outlooks cope with the vicissitudes of life. While most of the collection merits rediscovery, the title story is the most affecting. It recounts the last days of a woman who, unlike Mary Erle, commits suicide at the age of thirty-one when she fails to obtain the marriage proposal she so desperately wants.

D.'s last book-length work, *As I Knew Them* (1930), was a collection of her reminiscences about her friends and acquaintances, many of them celebrated writers, artists, playwrights, diplomats, and socialites. Among those she recalled were W. B.Yeats, H. G. Wells, Alice Meynell, Max Beerbohm, May Sinclair, John Singer Sargent, James Whistler, Edward Burne-Jones, Sir Arthur Wing Pinero, and David Lloyd George. She also recollected her former editor, Oscar Wilde, who had made several fictionalized appearances in her previous works—as Val Redmond in *My Flirtations,* as Beaufort Flower in *The Story of a Modern Woman,* and as Gilbert Vincent in the story "The World's Slow Stain" (1904). While D. satirized Wilde in her fiction, her remarks about him in *As I Knew Them* were, as Margaret Stetz comments, "softened by [the] distance and nostalgia" of advanced age.

D. rejected the label "New Woman" in *As I Knew Them;* but the reminiscences themselves tell a different story. She strongly supported the suffragists and took the unusual step of cofounding a dining club that admitted both male and female members. Whereas the fictional Mary Erle fails to find happiness outside of marriage, *As I Knew Them* suggests that D. was satisfied with her life as a single woman. In addition to forging a lucrative and successful career, she acquired many friends and earned the respect of her colleagues.

WORKS: *My Flirtations* (1892). *The Story of a Modern Woman* (1894). *One Doubtful Hour and Other Side-Lights on the Feminine Temperament* (1904). *The Toy-Shop of the Heart* (1908). *As I Knew Them* (1930).

BIBLIOGRAPHY: Flint, K., intro. to *The Story of a Modern Woman* (1990). Mix, K. L. *A Study in Yellow: The Yellow Book and its Contributors* (1960).

For articles in reference works, see: *DVP. 1890s. Feminist. WWWAEEA.*

Other references: Croft, A. *New Statesman* (13 July 1990). Stead, W. T. *Review of Reviews* (1894). Stetz, M. *TCW* (Winter 1984).

Bette H. Kirschstein

D. M. M.: See *Craik, Dinah Maria Mulock*

Hilda Doolittle (H. D.)

BORN: 10 September 1886, Bethlehem, Pennsylvania, United States.

DIED: 27 September 1961, Zurich, Switzerland.

DAUGHTER OF: Charles Leander Doolittle and Helen Eugenia Wolle Doolittle.

MARRIED: Richard Aldington, 1913.

WROTE UNDER: Delia Alton; J. Beran; Helga Dart; Helga Doorn; Edith Gray; H. D.; John Helforth; D. A. Hill; Rhoda Peter.

The past two decades of feminist, psychoanalytic, biographical, and bibliographical criticism have secured D.'s position as a major modernist. Research into her acting, film criticism, translation, verse drama, novels, essays, memoirs, and poetry has expanded D.'s reputation beyond her early fame as an Imagist poet. Publication of works suppressed during her life and study of her letters and manuscripts have documented her contributions to modernism, for she not only participated in major movements of her lifetime—Imagism cinema, psychoanalysis, and modernism—she also shaped their history. Her treatment of memories, visions, and unconscious material at times follows Freudian principles. Even more presciently, D.'s treatment of lesbian, bisexual, and matrifocal relationships anticipates recent French and other psychoanalytic feminist theory on a central and powerful maternal principle. Most important, her visionary gift transformed the cultural traditions she inherited to create a female-centered artistic identity and mythology.

The Doolittles moved from Bethlehem to Philadelphia in 1895, when D.'s father became professor of astronomy and director of the observatory at the University of Pennsylvania. D.'s later mysticism and visionary writing preserved her mother's family's Moravian beliefs as she expanded the Wolle family tradition of European travel to include visits to Greece and Egypt and residence in London and Switzerland. Early exposure to fairy tales, myths, and religious stories set the pattern for her lifelong search for illumination through the supernatural, mystical, and unconscious, with more conventional education coming later. In 1901, D. met Ezra Pound, a student at the University of Pennsylvania, the first of her male "initiators" into poetic and psychic quests, and her mentor in classical studies; as a result, she became thoroughly grounded in classics, and Greek culture became a sustaining influence and inspiration throughout her life. Her friendship with William Carlos Williams, then in medical school, also began at this time. When she entered Bryn Mawr College in 1905, she became informally engaged to Pound; in 1906, she withdrew from college after a failing mark in English and continued her studies at home and in the College Course for Teachers at the University of Pennsylvania. In London in 1911, Pound introduced her to F. S. Flint, Ford Madox Ford, Wyndham Lewis, May Sinclair, W. B. Yeats, Richard Aldington, and Dorothy Shakespear, who soon became engaged to Pound herself.

D.'s first publications (1909–13) were for children in syndicated and Presbyterian papers. Three of D.'s first Imagist poems appeared in *Poetry* in 1913; Pound had edited them and abbreviated her name to initials, after which he added "Imagiste." The inclusion of six of her poems in *Des Imagistes* in 1914, publication of *Sea Garden* (1916), the *Vers Libre Prize* from the *Little Review*, and Amy Lowell's praise in a volume of criticism (both 1917) established D. as a poet and as the purest of the Imagists. Through concrete, sensual presentation, Imagist poems evoke immediate intuitive apprehension rather than analysis; D.'s later poetry and fiction retain these emphases, expanding sensory, especially visual, appeal into a visionary and the intuitive moment into glimpses of a wise "overmind" or "inspirational mind."

D.'s friendship with Frances Gregg (1910) deepened into a romance and, when Gregg became involved with Pound, into a triangulated liaison that awakened intertwined erotic and artistic energies for D. She kept her contact with Gregg alive into the 1930s. Their affair inspired D. to write Gregg love poetry modeled on Theocritus and provided the basis for several novels written in the 1920s.

D. married fellow Imagist Richard Aldington in 1913, thus gaining British citizenship. With him, Pound, and Flint, D. formulated the principles of Imagism. During her years with Aldington, D. became friends with D. H. and Frieda Lawrence (fictionalized in *Bid Me to Live,* 1960), Marianne Moore (who sent poems to *The Egoist,* where Aldington was assistant editor), John Cournos, and John Gould Fletcher. She wrote the poems in *Hymen* (1921) and *Heliodora* (1924) and translated *Iphigeneia in Aulis and the Hippolytus of Euripides* (1919); *Euripides'* lyricism and what she saw as his feminine traits drew her to his poetry. Of D.'s early "initiators," Pound was to remain influential, while Aldington and Lawrence dwindled in importance. Each involved with other partners, Aldington and D. separated in 1918.

Also in 1918, D. met Bryher (Annie Winifred Ellerman), who provided invaluable emotional, social, and economic support for D.'s personal and artistic welfare and who helped save D. and Perdita, her unborn baby (by Cecil Gray), from near-fatal pneumonia. Bryher's fidelity as Perdita's "other parent" freed D. to write and to live in relative freedom from domestic tasks. After an intense affair, both had other partners but remained committed to each other. Tall, gifted, and striking, D. was always fortunate in attracting artists and analysts who inspired and supported her; of these, Bryher remained her most sustaining relationship.

D.'s early career culminates in the positive reception of her *Collected Poems* (1925); a second phase dominated by fiction begins with *Palimpsest* (1926). A *Kunstlerroman*-like *Hedylus* (1928), *Palimpsest* thematically links stories about three women, using layering techniques to reveal universal patterns. D.'s Madrigal cycle, written next during this period, includes *Paint it Today* (1986), *Asphodel* (unpub.), *HERmione* (1981), and *Bid Me To Live* (1960). These novels, probably suppressed for their depictions of same-sex love and published posthumously, recount D.'s turn from the marriage plot to a quest for artistic identity. *HERmione,* probably the most successful of the four, uses stream of consciousness, repetition, flashback, and classical allusion to explore themes of love, bisexuality, betrayal, and breakdown. Its protagonist's name, Her, emphases women's usual object status to carry over the book's thematic reversals to name and syntax. *Red Roses for Bronze* (1931), confusing readers of her poetry, marked a transition between D.'s "crystalline" early poems and her greatest and revisionary poetic works.

In her forties, D. turned to the occult, acting and cinema, and psychoanalysis, because of their access to the unconscious. In 1927–30, D. became intensely involved with film, writing about it and acting in several productions, including *Borderline* with Paul Robeson, and falling in love with its director, Kenneth Macpherson. He edited *Close-Up,* the first film journal in English, with Bryher and published D.'s poems and articles. Bryher's marriage of convenience with Robert McAlmon, who owned a publishing company, ended in 1927, after which she married Macpherson, then D.'s lover, to keep him near D. D.'s relationship with Macpherson appears in *Kora and Ka* (1934) and *Nights* (1935); his affairs with men and estrangement from D. overlap with her turn from film back to writing and to the psychoanalytic process.

Sigmund Freud was the most influential "initiator" of midlife healing and creativity for D., but was far from D.'s only experience with the new science. Vulnerable throughout her life to breakdowns, D. used the support of analysts at periods of stress and because of intellectual and artistic interest in its methods. D. applied to Freud to help her "root out [her] personal weeds, strengthen [her] purpose, reaffirm [her] beliefs, canalize [her] energies."

Freud's associative method and archeological metaphors had much in common with D.'s mythologizing. In her fundamental impulse of looking to the past, whether of myth, history, or her own life, D.'s method was to return to an earlier moment in order to reconstruct, revise, and transform painful experience into generative and curative visions. *Tribute to Freud* (1956) eloquently recounts her three months in 1933 and five weeks in 1934 in Vienna as analysand and student. With Freud, D. focused on her dreams and visions, artistic process, and "war phobia," traumatic fears amplified by World War I. *Tribute,* both memoir and autobiography, makes obvious her belief that "the Professor was not always right." Their interpretation of her 1920 visions at Corfu differed greatly; Freud labelled such "hallucinations" potentially dangerous symptoms while D. and Bryher found them profoundly significant. Strikingly, D.'s finest mature works, *Trilogy* (published as three poems, 1944–46) and *Helen in Egypt* (1961), both close with a vision of a woman newly created from religious stories and myths. References to Isis and Osiris underscore D.'s role of priestess in gathering and reassembling fragments.

The mythologizing impulse that influenced most of D.'s works culminated in her finest poetic works and recognition for them. The decade of D.'s fifties included the translation of Euripides' *Ion* (1937), psychoanalysis with Walter Schmideberg, study of the hermetic tradition, and spiritualism, and at the end, three major poems. In 1938, D. received the Levenson Prize from *Poetry* and her divorce from Aldington. In the early 1940s, D. wrote the three poems published together posthumously as *Trilogy* (1973). These poems find in World War II not only the terror of World War I but also an occasion for assimilation and regeneration. "The Walls Do Not Fall" connects images of bombed London with ruins at Karnak; "Tribute to the Angels" explores a method of double seeing as a means to spiritual wisdom and beauty; and "The Flowering of the Rod" culminates with a vision inscribing woman at the center of myth and generation.

D. resided in Switzerland, either in hotels or at a sanitorium, for the rest of her life. In 1946, a breakdown from ill health, the strains of the war, and rejection by spiritualist Lord Hugh Dowding took her to Klinik Brunner near Zurich. Norman Holmes Pearson, her executor, was D.'s frequent visitor before this and later her correspondent, literary advisor, and editor. Eric Heydt, physician in the Klinik at Kusnacht where she stayed in 1953–4 and lived from 1956 to1960, provided intellectual companionship for her. Journalist Lionel Durand inspired D.'s last romance, but it proved one of her irresistible but injurious affairs.

Helen in Egypt, D.'s last and greatest work, transforms the story of a Greek Helen into an Egyptian one, recreating the plot of *Pallinode* by Stesichorus of Sicily and incorporating Freud as Theseus. Guided by him, Helen emerges as capable of transforming not only family romance but also the forces of war. Such forays into myth and consciousness provided D. with strategies for creating a place and voice for herself as a woman artist.

The 1950s crowned D. with honors, among them a *Selected Poems of H.D.* in 1957, the Harriet Monroe Memorial Prize from *Poetry* in 1958, and the Brandeis University Creative Arts Award for Poetry in 1959. In 1960, the year *Bid Me to Live* appeared, D., who had regained American citizenship, was the first woman to receive the Award of Merit Medal for Poetry from the American Academy of Arts and Letters in her last trip to the United States. *Hermetic Definitions* (1972) contains D.'s last poems and celebrates Helen's maternal and poetic creations. A stroke prevented D. from reading *Helen in Egypt* (1961) before she died on 27 September 1961. Barbara Guest reports that D. wrote to Norman Pearson, "[she] did get what [she] was looking for in art and in life."

WORKS: *Sea Garden* (1916). *Choruses from Iphigeneia in Aulis* (1916). *The Tribute and Circe: Two Poems* (1917). *Choruses from Iphigeneia in Aulis and the Hippolytus of Euripides* (1919). *Hymen* (1921). *Heliodora and Other Poems* (1924). *Collected Poems* (1925). *H.D.* (1926). *Palimpsest* (1926, re. 1968). *Hippolytus Temporizes* (1927). *Hedylus* (1928). *Narthex* (1929). *Red Roses for Bronze* (1931). *Kora and Ka* (1934). *The Usual Star* (1934). *Nights* (as John Helforth) (1935). *The Hedgehog* (1936). (trans.) *Euripides' Ion* (1937). *What Do I Love?* (1950). "The Walls Do Not Fall" (1944). "Tribute to the Angels" (1945). "The Flowering of the Rod" (1946). *By Avon River* (1949). *Tribute to Freud* (1956). *Selected Poems* (1957). *Bid Me To Live (A Madrigal)* (1960). *Helen in Egypt* (1961). *Two Poems* (1971). *Hermetic Definitions* (1971). *Temple of the Sun* (1972). *Trilogy* ("The Walls Do Not Fall," "Tribute to the Angels," "The Flowering of the Rod") (1973). *Advent* (in *Tribute to Freud*) (1974). *The Poet and The Dancer* (1975). *The Mystery* (in *Images of H. D.*) (1976). *Ends to Torment: A Memoir of Ezra Pound* (1979). *HERmione [Her]* (1981). *The Gift* [abridged] (1982). *Notes on Thought and Vision and The Wise Sappho* (1982). *Vale Ave* (1982). *Collected Poems, 1912–1944* (1983). *Priest and a Dead Priestess Speaks* (1983). *Hippolytus Temporizes* (1985). *Ion: A Play after Euripides* (1986). *Nights* (1986). *Paint It To-Day* [chapters 1–4] (1986). *H.D.* (as Delia Alton) (1986). *Selected Poems* (1988). *The Hedgehog* (1988). *Within the Walls* (1990). *By Avon River* (1990). *Richard Aldington and H. D.: The Later Years in Letters*, ed. C. Zilboorg (1995).

BIBLIOGRAPHY: Boughn, M. *H. D.: A Bibliography 1905–1990* (1993). Burnett, G. *H. D. Between Image and Epic: The Mysteries of Her Poetics* (1990). Dodd, E. C. *The Veiled Mirror and the Woman Poet: H. D., Louise Bogan, Elizabeth Bishop, and Louise Glück* (1990). DuPlessis, R. B. *H. D.: The Career of The Struggle* (1986). Edmunds, S. *Out of Line: History, Psychoanalysis, & Montage in H. D.'s Long Poems* (1994). Friedman, S. S. *Psyche Reborn: The Emergence of H. D.* (1981). Friedman, S. S. *Penelope's Web: Gender, Modernity, H. D.'s Fiction* (1990). *Signets: Reading H. D.*, ed. S. S. Friedman and R. B. DuPlessis (1990). Fritz, A.D. *Thought and Vision: A Critical Reading of H. D.'s Poetry* (1988). Guest, B. *Herself Defined: The Poet H. D. and Her World* (1984). Holland, N. *Poems in Persons* (1973). Hollenberg, D. K. *Poetics of Childbirth and Creativity* (1991). *H. D.: Woman and Poet*, ed. M. Kind (1986). Kloepfer, D. K. *The Unspeakable Mother: Forbidden Discourse in Jean Rhys and H.D.* (1989). Laity, C. *H. D. and The Victorian Fin de Siècle* (1996). Mathis, M. S. *H. D.: An Annotated Bibliography, 1913–1986* (1991). Quinn, V. *Hilda Doolittle* (1967). Robinson, J. S. *H. D.: The Life and Work of an American Poet* (1982). Swann, T. B., *The Classical World of H. D.* (1962). *Richard Aldington and H. D.*, ed. C. Zilboorg (1995).

For articles in reference works, see: *AWW. Bloomsbury. CA. Cambridge. CLC. DLB. EWLTC. Longman. TCA* and *SUP. TCW.*

Other references: *Agenda* (special issue on H. D., 1987–88). Benstock, S. *Women of the Left Bank, Paris, 1900–1940* (1986). *ConL* (special issues on H. D., 1969, 1986). Coffman, S. K., Jr. *Imagism—A Chapter for the History of Modern Poetry* (1951). DuPlessis, R. B. *Writing Beyond the Ending: Narrative Strategies of Twentieth Century Women Writers* (1985). Gelpi, A. *A Coherent Splendour: The American Poetic Renaissance, 1910–1950* (1987). Gilbert, S. M. and S. Gubar. *No Man's Land: The Place of the Woman Writer in the Twentieth Century* (1990). Gould, J. *American Women Poets: Pi-*

oneers of Modern Poetry (1980). *IowaR* (1986). Levertov, D. *Poetry* (Special Issue on H. D., 1962). Lowell, A. *Tendencies in Modern American Poetry* (1917). Ostriker, A. *Writing Like a Woman* (1983). *Poesis* (special issue on H. D., 1985). Revell, P. *Quest in Modern American Poetry* (1981). Rosenmeier, R., in *Notable American Women: The Modern Period*, ed. B. Sicherman, et al. (1980). *Sagetrieb* (special issue on H. D., 1987). *San Jose Studies* (special issue on H. D., 1987). Watts, E. S. *The Poetry of American Women from 1632–1945* (1977).

Elizabeth M. Fox

Doorn, Helga: See Doolittle, Hilda (H. D.)

Anne Dowriche

BORN: before 1560, Mount Edgcumbe, Cornwall.
DIED: after 1613.
DAUGHTER OF: Sir Richard Edgcumbe and Elizabeth Tregian Edgcumbe.
MARRIED: Hugh Dowriche, 1580.

As a committed west-country Puritan, D. contributed a 2,400–line poem, *The French Historie* (1589), to the religious and political struggle of the "godly." Both D. and her husband, a Puritan minister, were committed to the Puritan cause. Hugh Dowriche published one of his sermons, *The Jailor's Conversion* (1596), for which D. wrote commendatory verses echoing the doctrine of her poem: "And all that haps to His elect, / Is always for the best."

D.'s account of the French civil wars of the previous thirty years is a profoundly partisan narration of the heroic attempts of French Protestants—the Huguenots—to win tolerance and a political voice from a demonized Roman Catholic monarchy. Satan actually appears in the poem as an advisor to Queen Catherine de Medici and as instigator of the St. Bartholomew's Day Massacre, an event powerfully narrated in the third part of the poem.

In her dedication to "the right worshipful her loving brother, Master Pearse Edgecombe," D. urges him to appreciate the importance of her subject, although she deprecates her style as "base and scarce worth the seeing." Like other early women poets, she apologizes for her sex: "If you find any thing that fits not your liking, remember I pray, that it is a woman's doing." However, she is quick to claim pleasure in "collecting and disposing" her history and insists on the significance of her mission to bring her readers to "care, watchfulness, zeal, and ferventness in the cause of God's truth." In her preface, D. identifies her historical source as "the French Commentaries"; indeed, she worked closely with Thomas Tymme's *Three Parts of Commentaries Containing the Whole and Perfect Discourse of the Civil Wars of France* (1574), a translation from the Latin history of Jean de Serres, also written from a strongly Protestant perspective. Perhaps representing her sources, D.'s two narrators are an exiled Frenchman and an Englishman who encounters the lamenting Huguenot in the woods; the poem is the Frenchman's account of his country's recent history. As she transformed the prose chronicles to a narrative poem in poulter's measure (couplets of iambic hexameter and heptameter), D. elaborated certain dramatic moments with invented orations by Protestant martyrs as well as by her Catholic villains and even by Satan himself.

The three parts of the poem focus on three key events: the arrest of Protestants in the rue St. Jacques in Paris in 1557; the execution of the Protestant senator, Anne Du Bourg, in 1559; and the St. Bartholomew's Day Massacre in 1572. D.'s version of each event exposes the politics of religious persecution; her integration of scriptural parallels emphasizes the providential framework within which she places the Huguenot martyrs, all of whom are God's "elect." In the poem, the persecution of the French Protestants derives politically from an evil Catholic monarchy committed to eradicating "Lutherans," but also providentially from a divine plan. Influenced by current anti-Catholic propaganda, which was particularly strong in Puritan circles, and by Huguenot antimonarchical politics, D. emphasizes heroic resistance to tyranny, particularly in her depiction of Anne Du Bourg and those who oppose the order to massacre Protestants. Du Bourg "very boldly and freely uttered his mind" in the Senate, defying Henri II: "If Truth do conquer kings, if Truth do conquer all, / Then leave to love these Popish lies; let whorish Babel fall." In the third part of the poem, the Huguenots are pitted against Catherine de Medici, a "scholar" of Machiavelli and Satan, who advocates violent repression. The antithesis to Catherine appears to be Elizabeth I, praised as the "chiefe Pastor" of English Protestantism; she is, however, warned to "hunt with perfect hate / The Popish hearts of fained frends before it bee too late."

The implication that England was in grave religious and political danger aligns D. with other Puritans who argued that the English Reformation was incomplete and that it was threatened from within by Catholics and the Elizabethan settlement.

WORKS: *The French Historie* (1589, STC 7159).

BIBLIOGRAPHY: Beilin, E. *Redeeming Eve: Women Writers of the English Renaissance* (1987). *Women, Writing, and the Reproduction of Culture*, ed. M. Burke, et al. (1996). Davis, N. Z., in *Beyond Their Sex*, ed. P. H. Labalme (1984). Edgcumbe, W. H. *Records of the Edgcumbe Family* (1888). *MLQ* (1990). Trease, G. E. *Devon and Cornwall Notes and Queries* (1974).

For articles in reference works, see: *Bloomsbury. DLB. Feminist. Oxford.*

Elaine V. Beilin

Margaret Drabble

BORN: 5 June 1939, Sheffield, Yorkshire.
DAUGHTER OF: John Frederick Drabble and Kathleen Marie Bloor Drabble.
MARRIED: Clive Swift, 1960; Michael Holroyd, 1982.

Widely read and well received by both critics and the general audience, D. plays a lively role in British culture. In addition to several novels, she has written stories, screenplays, and a biography of Arnold Bennett. She has written or edited several books on literary subjects and scores of reviews and other pieces for journals, newspapers, and magazines. She writes on popular and literary topics for both schoolchildren and adults, for both scholars and laymen. Frequently interviewed and photographed, the subject of several feature articles as well as much critical commentary, she also appears on televised literary programs, participates on governmental councils and Arts Council tours, and teaches adult education one day a week at Morley College in London.

D. went from The Mount, a Quaker boarding school in York, to Newham College, Cambridge, on scholarship, receiving a brilliant starred First in English literature. While her fiction is located within, enriched by, and played off against the literary language, traditions, and characters she knows so well, D. deliberately chooses not to be a high-culture artist disengaged from day-to-day realities. Eminently accessible and readable, she is attuned to herself and to ordinary experience, vividly rendering the ordinary with intelligence and learning, insight, and humor. Her informal, intimate, personal voice seems to speak directly for a whole generation of readers, particularly women, in Great Britain, the United States, and other countries.

The protagonists of D.'s novels have followed the course and concerns of her own life: young women leaving university, getting married and separated, birthing children, having affairs, raising progressively older children, reaching midlife, and wondering what next. The surface lucidity of D.'s early novels and the seeming candor of her first-person narrators have misled some readers into assuming that little critical distance separates the author and her narrators. In fact, the tension between surface and meaning gives to D.'s work an unresolved, exploratory quality quite different from the popular women's fiction it deceptively resembles. D.'s fiction at its best is a virtual "double-voiced discourse" exemplifying the tension that many women experience as they struggle to define themselves within a patriarchal frame of reference. She examines with subtlety and moral acuity the very tissue and structure of women's lives. From her first comparatively slight novel, *A Summer Bird-Cage* (1963), D.'s first-person characterizations grow in depth and subtlety, reaching their culmination in the portrait of Jane Gray in her most technically experimental narrative, *The Waterfall* (1969). Whereas each of these narrators lives in a solipsistic world and uses her body as a decorative front and self-protective retreat from external realities, *The Waterfall* records Jane Gray's orgasmic breaking out of the constrictions of female identity. The significance of this experience is equivocally examined by Jane, as are the lives and experiences of the narrators who proceed her.

The third-person novels of D.'s middle period move further out of the solipsistic spaces of the early novels. They record a more graphic exodus from the constricting world of childhood: its geography, class-bound values, moral outlook. Northern landscapes are rejected in each novel for the cosmopolitan environment of London, duplicating the journey D. herself made from Sheffield to London. While born into a liberal, professional, middle-class family (her sister is the writer A. S. Byatt), D. draws from her family's rural, working-class roots in her fiction, dramatizing particularly the "need to escape" from oppressive provincial limitations. "By will and by strain," her characters create new selves and new worlds out of preconceived "golden" fantasies: a golden Jerusalem, a Bunyanesque holy city, realms of gold. Literary influence continues to be important: *Jerusalem the Golden* (1967) was, D. admits, "profoundly affected" by Bennett and by his character Hilda Lessways. *The Needle's Eye* (1972) is characterized by its skillful adaptation of Jamesian central intelligence and its probing psychological and moral complexities. The interconnected network of characters, images, literary allusions, and levels of reference of *The Realms of Gold* (1975) initiates D.'s more expansive later style.

While these novels link up to the sociomoral tradition of the English novel—which D. outspokenly values over modernist experiments—they, like her earlier work, continue to be in many ways double-voiced and equivocal, mediating between traditional realistic humanism and modern perspectives. "Omniscience has its limits," the narrator of *The Realms of Gold* candidly admits, calling attention to the fictionality of this carefully constructed world. Similarly, character is not at all stable, and perhaps not knowable. Because the characters' lives are such a composite of psychological determinism and willful self-creation, the boundaries between the real and the imagined are equivocal for characters and readers alike. Furthermore, D.'s use of houses and landscapes as objective correlatives of mental states lends considerable subtlety and depth to these works, dramatizing her intense preoccupation with the "effect of landscape upon the soul." Where D. is resolutely traditional is her liberal belief that the individual must link up to something larger than the self—a place, a community, shared values, the past. All of her work is about the conflict between free will and determinism, between the search for free feeling and the desire for some measure of control and judgment. The search for a suitable moral and human habitation is the compelling genesis of her art. The tension within these middle novels resides in the apparent freedom of the individual to create a new self coupled with his or her necessary circumspection within geographical, communal, and historical contexts.

In her novels *The Ice Age* (1977) and *The Middle Ground* (1980), D. focuses on the commonly shared contexts and experiences of urban middle-class life, detailing the texture, the trends, and the trappings of mass culture. The most vividly memorable passages of both books depict the dehumanized, noisy, dirty, ugly, and graffiti-ridden world that is modern urban Britain. The environment in which characters live is largely shaped from without. The individual may be, like Anthony Keating in *The Ice Age*, no more than a "weed upon the tide of history," doomed to enact a drama that differs only in particulars from other members of his or her generation.

Like their author, the characters, successful in their professional lives, are now experiencing a midlife reappraisal of self. The characters are less obsessed with the past than they are with the quality and significance of the lives they are now leading, lives that strikingly resemble those of their associates. D.'s characters crave connection, and in midlife the connection they seek is increasingly social and metaphysical. What is happening to individuals reflects, in turn, what is happening to the British nation as a whole, which is getting older, tired, staid, facing crises, going through some strange and disorienting metamorphosis. *The Ice Age* is highly controlled, a visibly plotted work, and so too are the lives of the characters it chronicles, whereas *The Middle Ground* is plotless and shapeless; the novel's structure is open to contingency just as are the lives of its characters.

Because D. refuses to stay in the same spot, her fiction is constantly nourished by her own personal development. As a result, D., perhaps more than any other contemporary British woman novelist, has the opportunity to produce a distinctively female work that surpasses gender limitations. Her mediating position between "male" and "female" concerns and traditions, literary and popular issues and perspectives, the literary and the real, the traditional and the modern, gives equivocal resonance and strength to her fiction. Her attempt to "only connect" these diverse strains is the generating energy of her work.

WORKS: *A Summer Bird-Cage* (1963). *The Garrick Year* (1964) *The Millstone* (1965). *Wordsworth* (1966). *Jerusalem the Golden* (1967). *The Waterfall* (1969). *The Needle's Eye* (1972). *Virginia Woolf: A Personal Debt* (1973). *Arnold Bennett: A Biography* (1974). *The Realms of Gold* (1975). *The Ice Age* (1977). *For Queen and Country: Britain in the Victorian Age* (1978). *A Writer's Britain: Landscape in Literature* (1979). *The Middle Ground* (1980). *The Tradition of Women's Fiction: Lectures in Japan* (1982). *The Radiant Way* (1987). *A Natural Curiosity* (1989). *Stratford Revisited: A Legacy of the Sixties* (1989). *Safe as Houses* (1990). *The Gates of Ivory* (1991). *The Garrick Year* (1994). *Angus Wilson: A Biography* (1995). *The Witch of Exmoor* (1996).

BIBLIOGRAPHY: For the most extensive listing of primary and secondary sources, see "A Margaret Drabble Bibliography," by J. S. Korenrnan, in *Critical Essays on Margaret Drabble*, ed. E. C. Rose (1984). Creighton, J. V. *Margaret Drabble* (1985). Hannay, J. *The Intertextuality of Fate: A Study of Margaret Drabble* (1986). Moran, M. H. *Margaret Drabble: Existing Within Structures* (1983). Myer, V. G. *Margaret Drabble: Puritanism and Permissiveness* (1974). Rose, E. C. *The Novels of Margaret Drabble: Equivocal Figures* (1980). Roxman, S. *Guilt and Glory: Studies in Margaret Drabble's Novels, 1963–1980* (1981). Sadler, L. V. *Margaret Drabble* (1986). *Margaret Drabble: Golden Realtor*, ed. D. Schmidt (1982).

For articles in reference works, see: *Bloomsbury. CA. Cambridge. CLC. CN. EWLTC. Feminist. MBL. Oxford. WA. ToddBWW.*

Other references: Bromberg, P. S. *JNT* (1986). Olshanskaya, N. I. *ZAA* (1986).

Joanne Creighton

Duchess, The: See *Hungerford, Margaret Hamilton Wolfe*

Duclaux, Mary: See *Robinson, Agnes Mary Frances*

Lucie Duff-Gordon

BORN: 24 June 1821, London.
DIED: 14 July 1869, Cairo, Egypt.
DAUGHTER OF: John Austin and Mary Taylor.
MARRIED: Sir Alexander Cornwall Duff-Gordon, 1840.

A woman of strong temperament, independent mind, and uncommon munificence, D. achieved renown as a travel writer. Her *Letters from Egypt* (1865) record with moving sympathy Arab customs and manners, and especially the indigence of the fellahin (peasants) who came to esteem her as "Sitt el Kebeer," the great lady. This superb transcript is marked not only by the vigor of her commentary but also by a rare regard for her subject, a point noted by George Meredith who wrote in his preface to the 1902 edition of her travel letters, "Hers was the charity which was perceptive and embracing." Nettled by the colonial arrogance of some of the English, D., who confessed that "my heart is with the Arabs," asked pointedly, "Why do the English talk of the beautiful sentiment of the Bible and pretend to feel it so much and when they come and see the same life before them, they ridicule it?"

Praised widely for her statuesque and majestic beauty, D. was the model for Alfred Lord Tennyson's poem "The Princess." A personal friend of Heinrich Heine, William Makepeace Thackeray, Charles Dickens, and Alexander W. Kinglake, she became during the mid-nineteenth century a cultural figure of scintillating brilliance. Her home in London and then at "Gordon Arms" in Esher, Surrey, was one of England's acclaimed salons to which Guizot fled across the Channel after the Revolution of 1848. Kinglake, the famed traveler to the Levantine who entranced her with his rich vein of reminiscence, spoke for many of her admirers when he wrote, "But she was so intellectual, so keen, so autocratic, sometimes even so impassioned even in speech, that nobody, feeling her powers, could well go on feebly comparing her to a mere Queen or Empress."

The breadth of her interests and the charm of her personality are partly products of a roving childhood. At the age of five, D. traveled to Bonn with her parents, mastering German with great alacrity. In later years, she was known for her enviable ability to out-talk Thomas Carlyle on German literature, a not-inconsiderable achievement. While still a youngster, she met Heinrich Heine at Boulogne who remembered her at the end of his life when she came to visit him in his "mattress grave" in Paris. D. has left a moving account of the great German lyrical poet in Lord Houghton's *Monographs Personal and Social* (1873).

Her literary career began in 1839, appropriately with a translation of Barthold Georg Niebuhr's *Studies of Ancient Grecian Mythology.* While yet a child, she heard the respected German classical scholar recount these tales to his son while she was in Bonn with her parents. In 1844, she translated W. Meinhold's *Mary Schweidler, the Amber Witch,* a narrative with derivations from a seventeenth-century chronicle, followed by *Narrative of Remarkable Criminal Trials,* by Anselm Ritter von Feuerbach, father of the famous theologian and philosopher, Friedrich von Feuerbach, whose theory of religious anthropomorphism was a major precursor of Marxism. In collaboration with her husband, Sir Alexander Cornwall Duff-Gordon, whom she married in 1840, she translated *Memoirs of the House of Brandenburg* by Leopold von Ranke, a much-respected historian who numbered among the illustrious figures to visit her in London.

The Duff-Gordons diffused such charm that their democratic hospitality included the humble and undistinguished as much as those of reputation and rank. Even abroad, D. was a glowing star, drawing luminaries into her orbit. When she lived in the rue Chaillot in Paris in 1857, she was befriended by a roster of French geniuses including Victor Cousin, Alfred de Viguy, Barthelmy St. Hilaire, Auguste Comte, and Leon de Wailly, whose *Stella and Vanessa* she had translated and published in 1850. The life of ideas inspired by these associations enhanced a social conscience already brought to an extraordinary level of acuity.

Her health, always frail—she had nearly died of consumption in 1849 after the birth of a son, Maurice—declined vertiginously around 1860, forcing her to abandon England for the more clement weather of the Cape of Good Hope. There she made many loyal friends among the Malays who had originally been brought across the Indian Ocean as slaves by the Dutch East India Company and who had been set free under the British Slave Emancipation Act of 1834. Here, as later in Egypt, she was to champion the downtrodden and win their hearts by a concern and tenderness of sympathy atypical for a Westerner of the period. Her sharply etched observations of her South African sojourn are recorded in *Letters from the Cape,* which were printed in Francis Galton's edited volume, *Vacation Tourists,* during 1862–63.

The aggravation of her consumption forced her removal to the dry climate of Egypt. A good many of her seven years of residence in the nominally Turkish province were spent at Luxor in an old house built over an ancient Egyptian temple. She took an avid interest in the multicolored life and manners of the natives and filled her famed *Letters from Egypt* with ethnological remarks on the differences between the Arabs and the Turks, the kindness of the Copts, the calligraphic beauty of Arab art, and the pictorial complexity and splendor of its architecture. Despite the widely regarded despotism of the East, she argued that in the Levant "social equality" existed to a greater degree than elsewhere. Ever amazed at the expanse and depth of Egypt, she wrote, "This country is a palimpsest in which the Bible is written over Herodotus, and the Koran over that. In the town the Koran is most visible, in the country Herodotus."

D. died of consumption in 1869 and lies buried in the English Cemetery in Cairo. Her *Letters from Egypt* are the most memorable of her productions, indicative of a preternatural acuity of observation and judgment, and for a while boasted a considerable circulation among the English literati and orientalists. Her trenchant commentary and her open distaste for colonialism give much of her writing a contemporary ring.

WORKS: (trans.) *Studies of Ancient Grecian Mythology,* by B. G. Niebuhr (1839). (trans.) *Mary Schweidler, the Amber Witch,* by W. Meinhold (1844). (trans.) *Narrative of Remarkable Criminal Trials,* by A. R. von Feuerbach (1844). (trans.) *Memoirs of the House of Brandenburg,* by L. von Ranke (1849). (trans.) *Stella and Vanessa,* by L. de Wailly (1850). (trans.) *History of Prussia; Ferdinand I and Maximilian II of Austria; State of Germany after the Reformation,* by L. von Ranke (1853). *Letters from the Cape* (1863). *Letters from Egypt* (1865). *Last Letters from Egypt* (1875). *Lady Duff-Gordon's Letters from Egypt* (1902).

BIBLIOGRAPHY: Etherington-Smith, M. and J. Pilcher, *The "It" Girls: Elinor Glyn, Romantic Novelist, and Lucy, Lady Duff-Gordon. Lucile, the Courtriére* (1986). Frank, K. *A Passage to Egypt: The Life of Lucie Duff-Gordon* (1994). Gendron, C. *ArielE* (1986). Norton, C. *Macmillan's Magazine* (1869).

For articles in reference works, see: *Feminist. ToddBWW. VB.*

Michael Skakun
(updated by Natalie Joy Woodall)

Carol Ann Duffy

BORN: 23 December 1955, Glasgow, Scotland.
DAUGHTER OF: Francis Duffy and Mary Black Duffy.

D. has been acclaimed as one of the most penetrating and original poets of Britain's New Generation. In less than a decade she published five collections of poems, *Standing Female Nude* (1985), *Selling Manhattan* (1987), *The Other Country* (1990), *Mean Time* (1993), and *Selected Poems* (1994). She began writing plays in college and launched her career with two plays staged at the Liverpool Playhouse. Humor, wit, voice, and dramatic play of first-person monologues characterize her lines and produce an impressive range of styles. An American audience might deem her intention part performer, part practiced stand-up comedienne, and part talk-show host, because of her timing and dramatic mimicry. In her lines conversations persist to reveal character, while monologues resonate with class inflections. What had been repressed is said and speakers are often surprised by thought. Readers (as listeners) may be shocked by recognition of shared inhibitions; shame is an epicenter for speech as her characters reveal their thoughts and feelings in self-expressed true registers of demotic sounds. Her lines capture a "character's" syntax as well as apt diction and cadences of speech, including the rhythms of London's street speech.

D. was born in Glasgow but moved in 1964 when she was nine to Staffordshire. A charged image in the childhood poems helps to identify wariness, the child's feeling of helplessness, the ubiquitousness of being lost in the adult world. It is an image that expands throughout her first four collections to become a motif of foreignness, an outsider's stance. ("Imagine living in a strange, dark city for twenty years. / There are some dismal dwellings on the east side / and one of them is yours. On the landing, you hear / your foreign accent echo down the stairs. You think / in a language of your own and talk in theirs," from "Foreign.") This liminal point of view operates as a theme in D.'s political consciousness, one of the marks of the New Generation of English poets to emerge in the 1980s. A political correctness, not a borrowed and banal journalistic phrase but a new pluralism, regionalism, the rise of working-class voices, performance poetry, and street-speak cohere in a global consciousness. D.'s fresh perspective penetrates these issues in hopes of transforming and globalizing language, making it less provincial. Paul Muldoon's postmodernism of European influences is current in D.'s words, along with shared themes of isolation and intensity, wit and shifting visual frames of reference producing visual puns. Critic Peter Forbes noticed in her vigor, directness, and psychological insight an almost Larkinesque nostalgia and pathos in the collection *Mean Time:* "She writes poems for our times of great generality. 'Translating the English, 1989' is a monologue which holds up a hideous distorted mirror to English society. The voice is that of an atrocious interpreter-cum-tout, and what it is saying is too concentrated an essence of sleaze to be true . . . but is is."

She dramatizes scenes of childhood, adolescence, and adult life that do not waver because setting informs character. In "Standing Female Nude," her first collection of poems, D. includes famous and infamous voices. There is the prostitute model for Seurat's painting, Franz Schubert, as well as immigrant schoolchildren and war photographers.

Humor and wit, voice and dramatic play, first person monologues in writerly narration condense and shape. "Mean Time" combines the measures of voice with conscience and reflects on the nature of loss and on the variable setting of time and change. Commenting on the poems in "Mean Time," D. has said of her title that the effects of time can be mean and that "mean" can mean average: "The events in the poems can happen to the average woman or man. The dwindling of childhood. Ageing. The distance of history. The tricks of memory and the renewal of language. The end of love. Divorce. New love. Luck. And so on. In the last book, *The Other Country,* I had begun to write more personal, autobiographical poems; and this switch from the dramatic monologue dominated stance of earlier collections is intensified in *Mean Time*" (*Poetry Review,* 1994). She depicts scenes that are current and contemporary as well as historical, which her poetry then deconstructs; throughout, she offers moments of consolation through love, memory, and discoveries of language.

D. generates generous drama from voice to voice, but the subjects of longing and desire reside in the poet's voice in many lyrics, especially in those from *The Other Country.* She writes as though discovering the knowledge of love for the first time, found in lovers' steps toward sexuality revealing lesbian love ("Girlfriends"), or lover separated from lover who alone must confront anxieties of violence that may be allayed only by mantras ("safety, safely, safe home") since "Too many people being gnawed to shreds," under an ozoneless sky, where "loveless men and homeless boys . . . out there and angry . . . and Nightly people end their lives in the shortcut" ("Who Loves You"). "The Way My Mother Speaks" echoes lyrically in the poet's memory while on a train. In "River," the metonym widens into a language of interpretation as "water crosses the border," translates itself, but words stumble, fall back, and there "nailed to a tree is proof. A sign /in a new language."

Liam McIlvanney, reviewing *New Scottish Writing,* notes that, of the new generation of poets (Kate Clanchy, Carol Ann Duffy, Don Paterson, Robin Robertson, and Kathleen Jamie), it is D. who "is the pick of the younger poets." Typical of her charged, sensual dynamism that can be heard in the description of the Notre Dame bells in "Mrs. Quasimodo's Divorce": "Their generous bronze throats / gargling, then chanting slowly," is her accretion of imagery. Irony accrues as she echoes the movie icon, here humorously commenting on marriage and divorce.

D. noted in a biographical entry that she is a satirist; and her words, like all satire, work to conserve, an irony but a label to be understood in the political climate of the 1980s as revisions of the welfare state became a dismantling. Like other recent poets, she indicts modernism in a crusade for social justice, for diversity and equality. Many of her themes emerge from the single voice—the woman who has no identity except as Mummy stereotyped by culture: She elicits the artist's need by comparing the kinds of hunger each feels, the artist and the prostitute-model. Her knowledge ridicules the "bourgeoisie" who "will coo / at such an image of a river-whore" while recognizing that "both poor, we make our living how we can," depicting poor model and poor artist as allies.

How does she accomplish so much in so few words? From angular surfaces, D. often crosscuts to make a collage-like double life for each speaker where small dramas occur. She makes an interior of rhythm, both sound and pause, to capture her speaker's wit in verbal gesture or idiom; she uses slant rhyme well to enhance the pause, and she seems to hear slang as an inflex of dialect. Speech rhythms and cadences, in other words, help to identify speakers by shorthand while cross-reference to pop icons does the work of narration, further suppressing narrative logic. D.'s subjects transcend political rhetoric because of their deft psychological acuity. No stereotypical victims, no slack, no labels to slap on the poor, only their own testimony in ugly and grisly details that reveal not only their habit of mind but universal ones. Voices of conscience, poems of the oppressed, live familiarly in the landscape of Margaret Thatcher's sprawling urban centers. When you feel you understand their range, something more disturbs. What you hear are selves, heard through their jangling delusions, heard as though for the first time, unique, individual, and rare.

WORKS: *Fleshweathercock* (1973). *Fifth Last Song* (1982). *Take My Husband* (1982). *Cavern of Dreams* (1984). *Standing Female Nude* (1985). *Little Women, Big Boys* (1986). *Loss* (BBC radio, 1986). *Thrown Voices* (1986). *Selling Manhattan* (1987, 1994). *The Other Country* (1990). *William and the Ex-Prime Minister* (1992). *Mean Time* (1993). *Selected Poems* (1994). *Grimm Tales* (1995).

BIBLIOGRAPHY: Allen-Randolph, J. *WRB* (May 1995). Fiennes, W. *TLS* (3 March 1995). McIlvanney, L. *TLS* (20 December 1996). *PoetryR* (1994). *New Scottish Writing,* ed. H. Richie (1996). Samson, I. *LRB* (6 July 1995). Thomas, J. E. *BêteN* (1989). Warner, M. *TLS* (6 January 1995).

For articles in reference works, see: *Bloomsbury. Cambridge. Feminist.*

Other references: McAllister, A. *BêteN* (1988). *TLS* (19 November 1993).

Brett Averitt

Maureen Duffy

BORN: 21 October 1933, Worthing, Sussex.
DAUGHTER OF: Cahia P. Duffy and Grace Wright.

Raised in an impoverished London family, D. began writing seriously at the age of thirteen, and when asked to "Say us a piece" by family visitors, often successfully passed off her own poetry as "real" writing. Her autobiographical first novel, *That's How It Was* (1962), described the grinding poverty of her childhood as well as the positive influence of her mother's love and encouragement. D. was educated at state schools and at King's College, London (B.A., honors, 1956), and taught school for five years. She has published ten novels, five plays (all produced), a television play, six books of poetry, and three nonfiction works; in addition, she has edited, translated, and written reviews of nonfiction and music for *The New Statesman.* Active on various British arts councils that have increased funding for authors, she is also deeply involved in the antivivisection cause.

The main characters of her novels are often outsiders: a writer who has left his family to spend a bitter winter alone on a houseboat (*The Paradox Players,* 1967); a wealthy, precocious and Oedipal adolescent (*The Love Child,* 1971); a group of lesbians who frequent a bar in London (*The Microcosm,* 1966); a convict released from prison by a group of anti-vivisectionists so that he can free animals from their cages (*All Heaven in a Rage,* 1973); and a half-human, half-gorilla child (*Gor Saga,* 1981). D. describes herself as a writer for whom the most poignant image is "the nose pressed against the glass. The very curious sort of flattening that happens and the way you see things inside as though under water and both more attractive and more frightening. This whole image is just not there for people who haven't spent their childhoods waiting outside pubs." Frequent themes in her novels are education, "social engineering," and love as a redeeming force; however imperfect our world—and she registers those imperfections with a deadly accurate eye—D.'s novels warmly suggest that since this is the only world we have, we must try to look at it not only clearly but constructively.

D. has always been acknowledged for the excellence of her writing, especially for her ability to imagine compellingly specific moments of her characters' lives. Criticism has been directed at her allowing consciously learned sections to interrupt her story (*Love Child*) and for an awkward mix of literary styles (*The Microcosm*). The most common criticism has been of a lack of focus in some of her works. Her novels seem to have moved toward a smooth blend of her proletarian background—"What you escaped from feeds you," she believes—her knowledge of philosophy, and her facility with literary forms. In *Housespy* (1978), an espionage thriller, and *Gor Saga,* she has achieved that blend and a place as one of the few British novelists who is rooted in the England of ordinary people, with the versatility needed to portray that reality in compelling and intelligent ways.

WORKS: *Josie* (1961). *The Lay Off* (1962). *That's How It Was* (1962). (trans.) *A Blush of Shame,* by D. Rea (1963). *The Single Eye* (1964). *The Microcosm* (1966). *The Silk Room* (1966). *The Paradox Players* (1967). *Lyrics for the Dog Hour* (1968). *Wounds* (1969). *Rites* (in *New Short Plays 2,* 1969). *Solo, Olde Tyme* (1970). *The Venus Touch* (1971). *The Love Child* (1971). *The Erotic World of Faery* (1972). *Actaeon* (1973). *I Want to Go to Moscow: A Lay* (in the U. S. as *All Heaven in a Rage,* 1973). *A Nightingale in Bloomsbury Square* (1973; in *Factions,* 1974). *Evesong* (1975). *Capital* (1975). *The Passionate Shepherdess: Aphra Behn, 1640–1689* (1977). *Housespy* (1978). *Memorials of the Quick and the Dead* (1979). *Inherit the Earth: A Social History* (1980). *Gor Saga* (1981). *Collected Poems* (1985). *Change* (1987). *An Introduction to the Joint Commission* (1988). *First Born* (1989). *Five Plays* (1990). *Illuminations* (1992). *Occam's Razor* (1993). *A Thousand Capricious Chances* (1989). *Henry Purcell* (1994).

BIBLIOGRAPHY: Interview with D. Barber. *Transatlantic Review* (Spring 1973). Bode, C. *Anglistik* (1995). Brimstyone, L., in *Lesbian and Gay Writing,* ed. M. Lilly (1990). Hersh, A. *MD* (1992). Lassner, P. *Phoebe* (1991). Newman, J., in *Where No Man Has Gone Before: Women and Science Fiction,* ed. L. Armitt (1991). Rule, J. *Lesbian Images* (1982). Sizemore, C. W. *A Female Vision of the City: London in the Novels of Five British Women* (1989). Winkler, E. H., in *Madness in Drama,* ed. J. Redmond (1993).

For articles in reference works, see: *Bloomsbury. CA. Cambridge. CD. CN. CP. DLB. Feminist. Oxford. Todd-BWW. WA. WWTCL.*

Katherine A. Allison

Daphne du Maurier

BORN: 13 May 1907, London.
DIED: 19 April 1989, Parr, Cornwall.
DAUGHTER OF: Gerald du Maurier and Muriel Beaumont.
MARRIED: Lieutenant-General Sir Frederick Browning, 1932.

D. is the granddaughter of George [Louis Pamella Busson] du Maurier (1834–96), author of *Peter Ibbetson, Trilby,* and *The Martian,* and daughter of the actor-manager Sir Gerald [Hubert Edward] du Maurier (1871–1934) and his costar in *The Admirable Crichton* in 1902, Muriel Beaumont (1881–1957). She has done much to preserve the reputation of her colorful forebears (whom one critic in *The New Statesman* in 1937 said she regards "on the whole, with much kindliness and some condescension") and to build a fame of her own as a novelist, playwright, and short-story writer.

She began writing in about 1928; her first published novel, *The Loving Spirit* (1931), already indicated the direction she was to take and exhibited (according to Helen Grosse) a talent "full of promise." She followed with *I'll Never Be Young Again* (1932) and *The Progress of Julius* (1933) and hit her stride with the romantic adventures of *Jamaica Inn* (1936). Then came perhaps her best known work: *Rebecca* (1938), called by some "the twentieth-century *Jane Eyre,* and by *TLS* as "a lowbrow story with a middlebrow ending."

In *Rebecca,* D.'s talent for well-researched and melodramatic atmosphere and romantic settings, her deft way with an inventive and mysterious plot embroiling innocent heroine and moody hero, her characters conflicted by dual natures or sudden forced changes of circumstance—in fact, all the armamentarium of the modern Gothic novel—is at the peak. Though *Rebecca* has been accused of plagiarism because of its fairly close resemblance to Carolina Nabuco's *A Sucesora* (a novel in Portuguese about a second wife) and Edwina Macdonald's "I Planned to Murder My Husband" and *Blind Windows,* it really simply partakes of the basic material of the romantic genre. The moping hero melancholy mad is as old as the Byronic Hero (or older), the distressed heroine right out of the melodramas of the Victorian theater, the mysterious mood as ancient as Walpole, Holcroft, Collins, Radcliffe, Mary Shelley, and others. Within this format, even the *Times Literary Supplement* had to admit, D. is "extraordinarily bold and confident, eloquent and accomplished" and "merits genuine respect."

In Menabilly (her own manor house at Par in Cornwall), D. created commercial family sagas (such as *The Loving Spirit* and *Hungry Hill* (1943), for which she also wrote the screenplay), thoroughly reliable and exciting historical novels (such as *The King's General,* 1946, set in the English Civil War, and *The Glass Blowers,* 1963, set in the French Revolution), plays (*Rebecca,* 1940, *The Years Between,* 1944–45, *September Tide,* 1948), a screenplay (*Hungry Hill,* 1947, with Terence Young and Francis Crowdry), a television play (*The Breakthrough,* 1976), novels warmly received by book clubs (*Frenchman's Creek,* 1941, *Rule Britannia,* 1976, etc.) and Hollywood (*Rebecca, My Cousin Rachel,* 1951), macabre stories, and more.

D. has perhaps not received the praise she deserves for her short fiction, eclipsed by her blockbuster best-sellers, but she is the author of *Happy Christmas* (1940), *Come Wind, Come Weather* (1940), *Escorts* (1942), *Nothing Hurts for Long* (1943), *Consider the Lilies* (1943), *Spring Picture* (1944), *Leading Lady* (1945), *London and Paris* (1945), *Early Stories* (1954), *The Breaking Point: Eight Stories* (1959; as *The Blue Lenses and Other Stories,* 1970), *The Treasury of Du Maurier Stories* (1960), *Not After Midnight* (1971, in the U. S. as *Don't Look Now,* 1971), *Echoes from the Macabre: Selected Stories* (1976), *The Rendezvous and Other Stories* (1980), the short novel *The Apple Tree* (with other stories, 1952), and *Kiss Me Again, Stranger: A Collection of Eight Stories Long and Short* (1953). She has also edited an anthology of the short story. Had she never written *The Parasites* (1949), *Mary Anne* (1954), *The Scapegoat* (1957), completed Sir Arthur Quiller-Couch's novel *Castle Dor* (1962), or written any of her better-known novels, her short fiction alone would earn her a respected place in any guide to women writers. Especially in those stories in which she can concentrate her ability to evoke the eerie, so often a part of her longer works, she is masterful. While novels such as *The Parasites* may be (as Antonia White remarked) "not, unfortunately, a work of art" in the best sense, her stories are seldom ineffective and often memorable. They do not often depend upon the incredible, as do some of her novels (in *The Scapegoat* an Englishman passes himself off as a Frenchman and the Frenchman's intimates do not even notice the deception), but they do exploit the mysterious.

The best of D.'s novels have, at least while one is engrossed in them, a powerful charm and exciting and well-managed plots. *My Cousin Rachel* is typically melodramatic and essentially hollow. Sober literary critics may well find Rachel Ashley, unknown even to herself, too trite a bundle of contradictions and Gothic claptrap, but the market for transpontine melodrama, which did not end with the Victorian era, continues to be in vogue today; one cannot really say that after half a century D. is out of date.

D. is also notable as family biographer (*Gerald: A Portrait,* 1934; editor of the letters of *The Young Du Maurier,* 1951; and chronicler of *The Du Mauriers,* 1937) and autobiographer (*Growing Pains,* 1977; in the U.S. as *Myself When Young,* and *The Rebecca Notebook and Other Memories,* 1980). She has also written about *The Infernal World of Branwell Brontë* (1960) and the dashing Sir Francis Bacon (*Golden Lads,* 1975, is about Sir Francis and his brother Anthony, *The Winding Stair,* 1978, about Sir Francis himself). All of these are solid, readable, commendable.

"Every book is like a purge," D. told the eager fans in *Ladies' Home Journal* (November 1956), "at the end of it one is empty . . . like a dry shell on the beach, waiting for the tide to come in again." But for many years and with great reliability, the tide kept coming in for her, so she gave her adoring readers book after book that could excite and entertain. Whether she gave them something approaching science fiction (*The House on the Strand*) or fantasy (*Rule Britannia* involves Britain threatened with an American invasion), whether she made her readers feel that they were drenched with Italian sunlight or the mists of the Cornish coast, she knew how to spin a yarn that kept adolescents from their play and matrons from their bridge tables. Frequently, she gave them more than they sought in escapist fiction. She inherited her grandfather's pictorial sense and her father's theatrical sense and made good use of both in her own version of the arena in which both of her ancestors had made a name for themselves: popular entertainment. Her work, or some of it, is likely to live longer than theirs.

WORKS: *The Loving Spirit* (1931). *I'll Never Be Young Again* (1932). *The Progress of Julius* (1933). *Gerald: A Portrait* (1934). *Jamaica Inn* (1936). *The du Mauriers* (1937). *Rebecca* (1938; as play, produced London 1940, New York 1945, published 1943). *Happy Christmas* (1940). *Come Wind, Come Weather* (1941). *Frenchman's Creek* (1941). *Escorts* (1942). *Hungry Hill* (1943; as screenplay 1947). *Nothing Hurts for Long* (1943). *Consider the Lilies* (1943). *Spring Picture* (1944). *The Years Between* (produced Manchester 1944, London 1945, published 1945). *Leading Lady* (1945). *London and Paris* (1945). *The King's General* (1946). *September Tide* (produced Oxford and London 1948, published 1949). *The Parasites* (1949). *My Cousin Rachel* (1951). *The Apple Tree: A Short Novel and Some Stories* (1952). *Early Stories* (1954). *Mary Anne* (1954). *The Scapegoat* (1957). *The Breaking Point* (1959; as *The Blue Lenses and Other Stories,* 1970). *The Treasury of du Maurier Stories* (1960). *The Infernal World of Branwell Brontë* (1960). *Castle Dor*

(1962). *The Glass Blowers* (1963). *The Flight of the Falcon* (1965). *Vanishing Cornwall* (1967). *The House on the Strand* (1969). *Not After Midnight* (1971; in the U. S. as *Don't Look Now,* 1971),. *Golden Lads: Sir Francis Bacon, Anthony Bacon, and Their Friends* (1975). *Rule Britannia* (1976). *The Breakthrough* (1976). *Echoes from the Macabre: Selected Stories* (1977). *Growing Pains: The Shaping of a Writer* (1977; in the U.S. as *Myself When Young,*). *The Winding Stair: Francis Bacon, His Rise and Fall* (1978). *The Rebecca Notebook and Other Memories* (1980). *The Rendezvous and Other Stories* (1980). *Classics of the Macabre* (1987). *Letters from Menabilly: Portrait of a Friendship*, ed. O. Malet (1994).

BIBLIOGRAPHY: Bakerman, J. S., in *And Then There Were Nine . . . More Women of Mystery*, ed. J. S. Bakerman (1985). Forster, M. *Daphne du Maurier* (1993). Kelly, R. *Daphne du Maurier* (1987). Lloyd-Smith, A. *PoT* (1992). Nollen, E. M. *Clues* (1994). Schroder, G. *LWU* (1987). Williams, T. *NConL* (1996).

For articles in reference works, see: *CA. CLC. CN. Longman. MBL. TCA* and *SUP. TCC&MW. TCRGW. TCW.*

Other references: Auerbach, N. *CritI* (1981). Banta, M. *SLitI* (1983). Bromley, R. *L&H* (1981).

Leonard R. N. Ashley

Nell Dunn (pseudonym for Nell Mary Sandford)

BORN: 1936, London.
MARRIED: Jeremy Sandford, 1956.

"In 1959 Nell Dunn, a Chelsea heiress, crossed the Thames and went to live in Battersea, a working-class district of London." So noted the *Library Journal* in first introducing its readers to an eyebrow-raising literary study of slum life produced by a young writer of middle-class background. D.'s experiences with and observations of the indigenes, particularly the women, of the blue-collar ghetto formed the foundation of her writing career. "There is a lot of observation in what I write," she has stated. "I don't make very much up. What I do, really, is listen for about two years, and then, with what I've heard and what I've thought, I make something."

D.'s first book was a collection of short sketches, *Up the Junction* (1963), about life around the Clapham Junction commercial center of Battersea. The vignettes are candid pictures of routines among the denizens of Clapham: girls putting on their makeup for a night out; sexual flirtations at the local pub; life around a home for unwed mothers; and bawdy conversations and unthinking chit-chat among women who work in a small candy factory. The author's "coolly observant narrative" endeavors to document the character of their existence, finding stories in the little struggles that color their lives, without shrinking from the vulgarity of the milieu of which she writes.

Up the Junction's most effective writing, according to D.A.N. Jones in *The New Statesman,* conveys a "miserable comment on English class relations"; Edgar Z. Friedenberg praised D.'s successful "use of ethnology" in her accounts of "lower-depths poverty." Many critics, however, accused her of "slumming" and snubbed the book as more spectacularly coarse than socially illuminating. "In this underworld of varicose veins and sleazy plastic," wrote James R. Frakes, "where nobody is frightened of death since 'you can't get hurt when yer dead' and the ultimate compliment you can pay a bird is 'you smell as if you never sweated in yer life,' the dawn that slides over the gasworks illuminates only a junkyard landscape of total hopelessness, pop culture at its most rancid." *Up the Junction* won the John Llewellyn Rhys Memorial Prize for a short-story collection in 1964, was adapted for a feature film, and in 1966 received its first publication in the United States.

Talking to Women, a 1965 collection of interviews, and *Poor Cow,* a novel published in 1967, are also outgrowths of her Battersea "research." In these works, D. focuses on the struggles and passions of working-class women, quoting the brutal dialect with which they try to communicate, revealing obscenity and preoccupation with indelicate matters of sex as simple verities of a complex stratum of British society. Like *Up the Junction, Poor Cow* is a loosely assembled series of sketches but with the difference of a pervasive central character—a bawdy adventuress named Joy.

Although *Punch* dismissed D.'s effort as "just taking the lid off a slum and leaving it at that," V.S. Pritchett considered *Poor Cow* an accurate picture of "the exposed, unsupported, morally anonymous condition of people who have nothing that can really mean much to them except the vagaries of the sexual itch, what the telly says, and what is lit up in the supermarkets and pubs." "Based on the kind of true confessions that Nell Dunn collected in her *Talking to Women,*" wrote the *Times Literary Supplement,* "this is a serious and moving little book, but it is scarcely a novel nor, quite, an original substitute for one." *The New Yorker* praised *Poor Cow* saying, "Whether [this] is a novel . . . does not matter. What does matter is that this young writer is possessed of a high degree of talent, and, beyond that, that there is something unforgettable about her work—some quality so individual and gentle that her writing is irresistible." At a time before feminism had become a popular movement, D., based on personal observations of exploited women of the working class, had written three works—representing sometimes startling, feminist points of view—that provoked critical interest in her blend of candor and compassion.

During the next dozen years, D. wrote or collaborated on a half-dozen books as well as a screenplay, with director Kenneth Loach, for a film adaptation of *Poor Cow.* With Susan Campbell she produced a book for children in 1969, and in 1971 she published another novel, *The Incurable.* The following year a collaboration with Adrian Henri was published as *I Want.* From 1974 through 1978, Dunn completed three more books—*Tear His Head off His Shoulders,* a novel; *Living Like I Do,* a documentary work; and another novel, *The Only Child.* None of these works received the critical attention of her early books nor the international praise that came in 1981 with the production of her first play, *Steaming.*

D.'s only prior link to the stage was through her maternal grandfather, the Earl of Rosslyn, who had owned a

London theater. Weary of "scribbling away by herself in a tiny upstairs workroom," she decided to write a play to force her out of her "cocoon" and "spent about a year going to plays and reading them" in order to learn the craft of the playwright. *Steaming* opened July 1 at the famous fringe playhouse, Theatre Royal Stratford East, drew immediate and nearly universal acclaim from the press, and by the end of August was playing to enthusiastic audiences at The Comedy Theatre in the West End.

In *Steaming,* D. follows the pattern of her early work and "listens in" on a group of women talking. The setting is the "Turkish Lounge" of dilapidated public baths in the East End of London, a place of escape where the play's five principal characters meet to relax and share their troubles. "As they take off their clothes," notes Sylviane Gold, "they also shed their inhibitions, and they compare notes on men, on sex, on what matters most in their lives. Although their accents range from genteel to Cockney, their concerns, it turns out, are not all that different. And Miss Dunn unites the characters politically as well, when the baths are threatened with demolition."

Some critics complained that the play's feminist polemics were superficially represented; other observations focused on the "creaky theatrical devices" and transparent plot contrivances employed by an inexperienced playwright to structure the work. Nevertheless, the popular success of *Steaming,* in America and Australia as well as in England, reflected the charm of its "lively, ribald humor" and "homely sincerity." D. was awarded the 1981 Susan Smith Blackburn Prize, a highly regarded award given to a female writer for "a work of outstanding quality for the English-speaking theatre." In an interview for the *New York Times* at the time *Steaming* opened in New York in December 1982, D. stated that she found drama to be a stimulating medium and suggested that her next writing venture would also be for the stage.

WORKS: *Up the Junction* (1963). *Talking to Women* (1965). (with Kenneth Loach) *Poor Cow* (1967; screenplay, 1968). (with Susan Campbell) *Freddy Gets Married* (1969). *The Incurable* (1971). (with Adrian Henri) *I Want* (1972). *Tear His Head off His Shoulders* (1974). *Living Like I Do* (1976). *The Only Child* (1978). *Steaming* (1981). *Every Breath You Take* (1988). *The Little Heroine* (1988). *Grandmothers* (1991). *My Silver Shoes* (1996).

BIBLIOGRAPHY: *LJ* (1 November 1966). *New Statesman* (22 November 1966). *New Yorker* (11 November 1967). *NYRB* (18 May 1967). *NYT* (12 and 13 December 1982). *NYTBR* (6 November 1966). *Punch* (26 April 1967). *TLS* (4 May 1967). *YR* (1968).

For articles in reference works, see: *Bloomsbury. CA. CD. CN. Feminist. OCEL. Oxford. ToddBWW. Women Dramatists.*

Paul D. Nelsen

Dunne, Mary Chavelita: See *Bright, Mary Golding*

Susan Du Verger

BORN: before 1625.
DIED: after 1657.
WROTE UNDER: Susan Du Vergeere; S. Du Verger.

Not much is known about D. other than the information we can glean from the printed works she left behind. The subject matter of her books, her didicatory letters to Roman Catholic aristocrats, and her rhetorically sophisticated prose style tell us that D. was likely a well-educated and well-connected English Catholic who supported the Catholic cause in England just before the Civil War. She published two works between 1639 and 1641. *Admirable Events* (1639) was a translation of a collection of moralized romance tales written in French by Jean Pierre Camus, a Catholic bishop. *Diotrephe* (1641) was also a translation of Camus, this time of a single romance novella.

Previous research on D. has overlooked the possibility that she may have been the author of *DuVergers Humble Reflections* (1657), an original work defending Catholicism and monastic life against the criticism published by Margaret Cavendish, the Duchess of Newcastle, in her 1655 work, *The World's Olio.*

Admirable Events and *Diotrephe* were published at a time when Catholicism and prominent Catholics in England were increasingly under attack by both Puritan divines and members of Parliament who were stirring up popular fears of "popery" and foreign invasion by Catholic forces of the pope. At such a highly charged historical moment, translating and publishing the works of a charismatic French Catholic bishop were inherently political acts. D.'s Catholic and royalist politics are made even clearer by the dedication that prefaces the works. *Admirable Events* is dedicated to Henrietta Maria, the devoutly Catholic queen of England's Protestant king, Charles I, and the daughter of Henry IV of France. *Diotrephe* is dedicated to Lady Herbert, Elizabeth Somerset Powis, a zealous and active Catholic, and her husband, William Herbert Powis, one of the leaders of the Catholic aristocracy. Both works are moral romances that tell tales of love but with a strong lesson about the pitfalls of lustful or immoderate sexual behavior. Because this genre was extremely popular in sixteenth- and seventeenth-century England, D. may have been trying, through the publication of these familiar and unthreatening tales, to undermine the portrayal of Catholicism as foreign and menacing.

There is some debate over whether D. was the author of *DuVergers Humble Reflections;* Smith and Cardinale, for example, attribute the work to a French male author. However, there is significant textual evidence that the author is a Catholic Englishwoman: In the introductory letter from the author to Margaret Cavendish, the author aligns herself with Cavendish by referring to the "honor of *our nation, and sex*" (emphasis added). It seems extremely likely that D., an English woman with two other published works connected to the Catholic cause, was also the author of the *Humble Reflections.* The work responds directly and at length to a specific number of passages in Cavendish's *Olio* that malign Catholicism. The long period between the publication of *Diotrephe* in 1641 and

Humble Reflections in 1657 may suggest that D. had to leave England during the Interregnum because of her Catholic and royalist symphathies, possibly living in France where the *British Library Catalogue* believes the *Humble Reflections* was printed.

WORKS: (trans.) *Admirable Events: Selected out of foure bookes, Written in French by the Right Reverend, John Peter Camus, Bishop of Belley* (1639; fascimile reprint ed. J. Collins, 1995). (trans.) *Diotrephe of A History of Valentines, Written in French by the Right Reverend John Peter Camus, Bishop and Lord of Belley* (1641). *DuVergers Humble Reflections upon some passages of the right Honorable the Lady Marchioness of Newcastles Olio* (1657).

BIBLIOGRAPHY: *Women and the Literature of the Seventeenth Century*, ed. H. Smith and S. Cardinale (1990). *Paradise of Women*, ed. B. Travitsky (1981).

For articles in reference works, see: *Feminist*.

Other references: Arber, E. *Transcript of the Stationers' Register* vol. 5 (rpt. 1950).

Jane Collins

Elizabeth Rigby, Lady Eastlake

BORN: 17 November 1809, Norwich.
DIED: 2 October 1893, London.
DAUGHTER OF: Dr. Edward Rigby and Anne Palgrave Rigby.
MARRIED: Sir Charles Lock Eastlake, 1849.
WROTE UNDER: The author of "Letters from the Baltic"; Lady Eastlake; Elizabeth Rigby.

Best known to modern readers for her acerbic attack on the author of *Jane Eyre* in the *Quarterly Review*, E. was a well-informed art critic, travel writer, translator, social commentator, and occasional author of fiction. She was the fifth child and one of twelve children of Edward Rigby, a prominent obstetrician, and his second wife, Anne Palgrave. When she was eight years old, E. began to draw: Art became a life-long love. Although E. lacked a formal education—an omission E. regretted as an adult—her father entertained educated visitors and encouraged his children to read broadly. Dr. Rigby died in 1821, when E. was eleven, and in 1827, E., her mother, and her sisters settled in Heidelberg, Germany, for two and a half years because of E.'s health. E.'s foreign experience and her education in German provided her with the cultural vision and language skills she would rely on in her later writing.

In 1830, E. returned to England and published her first work, a short tale for *Fraser's Magazine* entitled "My Aunt in a Salt Mine," as well as a translation of Johann David Passavant's work on British art collections. E. went to London in 1832 and spent a year studying literature and art in the British Museum and the National Gallery. In 1835, she returned to Germany, and in 1838 she traveled to Russia to visit a married sister for two years. E. recounted her experiences of Russian life in letters to her mother; these letters were collected and published as *A Residence on the Shores of the Baltic* in 1841. The collection was popular with the public, requiring a second edition in a few months, and established its author's reputation in London's publishing circles. E. was invited to write an article for the *Quarterly Review* and became a frequent contributor to that periodical. In her lifetime, E. wrote close to fifty art and literature reviews and social commentaries for the *Quarterly Review* and other periodicals, most published anonymously. She made a brief foray into fiction with a series of tales based on her Baltic experience: *The Wolves* and *The Jewess* were both published separately before appearing with a third story, *The Deponent*, in a collection entitled *Livonian Tales* (1846).

In 1842, E.'s mother took the family to Edinburgh, where E. became popular in intellectual circles for her conversational ability, her attractiveness, and her height (E. was 5'11" and bore the nickname "Lofty Lucy"). Throughout the 1840s, E. continued to travel, taking a second journey to Russia and another to Germany and writing accounts of art, architecture, and politics upon her returns to England and Edinburgh. In 1848, she produced her infamous reviews of *Jane Eyre*, *Vanity Fair*, and the 1847 report of the Governesses' Benevolent Institution. If E. reveals the limits of her upper-middle-class vision in her comments on what she saw as the revolutionary aspects of Brontë's novel, on the one hand, and, on the other, her certainty that the author was a man or, if a woman, one who had "long forfeited the society of her own sex," her discussion of the plight of governesses highlights for the modern reader the moral and class dimensions of an acknowledged Victorian social problem.

E.'s marriage in 1849 to Charles Lock Eastlake, R.A., President of the Royal Academy and eventual Director of the National Gallery, gave her entrance into the Victorian art world, a world she was more than competent to join as amateur artist and reviewer. Her view that art has its own language independent of the character of the artist necessitated her opposition to the age's most visible spokesperson for the artist as moralist, John Ruskin. In fact, E. disagreed with Ruskin both personally and professionally: She privately supported Ruskin's wife Effie Gray in her estrangement and eventual divorce from her husband even as she publicly criticized the first three volumes of *Modern Painters* in the *Quarterly Review* (1856).

Despite having to endure the sorrow of giving birth to a stillborn child in 1851, E.'s marriage was a happy one; upon the death of Eastlake in 1865, E. wrote a pamphlet anonymously to confront her grief that won the approval of Queen Victoria. Entitled *Fellowship: Letters Addressed to My Sister Mourners* (1868), this work provides a sensible study of grief and how to respond to it; running through the text is the suggestion of the mourner's reliance on and belief in women's sympathy. E. continued to travel and write until the year of her death; her work—from art review to biography to history to social commentary—is characterized by a flair for the apt phrase, a penchant for the lively detail and the strong opinion, and a capacity for storytelling.

While E.'s fiction, written early in her career, lacks sophistication of plotting and narrative style, its blend of factual reporting and imaginative re-creation productively influenced her later journalism. Of those early tales, *The Deponent* (i.e., a bailiff) is the most sophisticated in its delineation of character and its narrative control. Both *The Deponent* and *The Jewess* are interesting for their representation of a strong woman's vision. In *The Deponent,* E. criticizes the practice of arranged marriages, developing the plot out of an arrangement gone awry. The protagonists' accumulating troubles are removed by the heroine's resolve to confront the Russian patriarchal system and its corruption. Similarly, in *The Jewess,* the English heroine finds a common bond of womanly sympathy with the title character, Rose: The maternal nature of both women enables their heroism. As a whole, E.'s work tends to be characterized by a paradoxical combination of class and national prejudice (which frequently takes the form of political and social conservatism) and what may be termed a feminist vision of women's moral power.

WORKS: (trans.) *Tour of a German Artist in England: With Notices of Private Galleries, and Remarks on the State of Art,* by J. M. Passavant (1831). *A Residence on the Shores of the Baltic, Described in a Series of Letters* (1841). *The Jewess: A Tale from the Shores of the Baltic* (1843). (trans.) *Treasures of Art in Great Britain,* by G. F. Waagen (1845–47). *Livonian Tales* (1846). *Music and the Art of Dress: Two Essays* (1852). (trans.) *The Schools of Painting in Italy,* by F. T. Kugler (1857). *The History of Our Lord as Exemplified in Works of Art* (begun by Mrs. A. Jameson, completed by E., 1864). *Fellowship: Letters Addressed to my Sister Mourners* (1868). *Contributions to the Literature of the Fine Arts by Sir C. L. Eastlake* (completed by E., with a memoir of Eastlake written by E., 1870). *Life of John Gibson R. A.* (1870). *Mrs. Grote: A Sketch* (1880). *Five Great Painters,* (1883). (trans.) *S. T. Coleridge and the English Romantic School,* by A. Brandl (1887). *Journals and Correspondence,* ed. C. E. Smith (1895).

BIBLIOGRAPHY: Layard, A. H., ed. and intro. to *The Schools of Painting in Italy,* 5th ed. (1887). Lochhead, M. *Elizabeth Rigby, Lady Eastlake* (1961). Lutyens, M. *The Ruskins and the Grays* (1972). *Women in the Victorian Art World,* ed. C. C. Orr (1995). Poovey, M. *Uneven Developments: The Ideological Work of Gender in Mid-Victorian England* (1988). Robertson, D. *Sir Charles Eastlake and the Victorian Art World* (1978).

For articles in reference works, see: *Allibone. Biographies of British Women,* ed. P. Sweeney (1993). *DNB. Feminist. NCBEL. Oxford. Stanford. ToddBWW. VB.*

Other references: Johnson, W. S. *VN* (1964). Robertson, D. *Gazette of the Grolier Club* (1970).

LuAnn McCracken Fletcher

EBB: See *Browning, Elizabeth Barrett*

Echo: See *Robinson, Mary Darby (Perdita)*

Emily Eden

BORN: 3 March 1797, London.
DIED: 5 August 1869, Richmond, Surrey.
DAUGHTER OF: William Eden and Eleanor Elliot Eden.

E. lived her life in the aristocratic surroundings she depicts in her two novels. She was the twelfth child and seventh daughter of the 1st Baron Auckland, a commissioner in America after the Revolutionary War, chief secretary in Ireland, Minister-Plenipotentiary to Versailles, and ambassador to both Spain and Holland. E.'s uncle, Robert Eden, was the last colonial governor of Maryland. Her family's descendants were equally illustrious: novelist Eleanor (Lena) Eden was her niece; Violet Dickinson, friend of Virginia Woolf and Vita Sackville-West, was her great-niece; and Prime Minister Anthony Eden was her great-great nephew.

E. was well educated by governesses and then by the same tutor who taught her brother Robert. She was conversationally at ease amid topics of Whig politics and foreign affairs. E. never married, a personal choice rather than an effect of the growing surplus of women over men as the nineteenth century advanced. She and her sister Frances (Fanny) lived with her brother George (later Lord Auckland), first in London, where he was first lord of the Admiralty, and then, from 1835 to 1842, in India, where George was governor general and E. and Fanny served as his "first ladies." Two of her books describe this experience. *"Up the Country": Letters Written to her Sister from the Upper Provinces of India* (1866), is an account of E.'s two-and-one-half-year tour of India. Although she was largely unconscious of her brother's role in initiating the nadir of British rule in India through his mismanagement of the First Afghan War, E. does give an accurate contemporary glimpse into the life of the British in India, including a sympathetic comprehension of the Indian dislike of British arrogance and self-righteousness. *Up the Country* was E.'s most popular work and has continued to be of interest to contemporary travelers to India, with modern reprintings in 1930, 1978, and 1983.

Portraits of the Princes and People of India (1843) is a beautifully printed volume of E.'s sketches and watercolors, which elicited praise for her as "one of the most accomplished amateur artists in India in the early nineteenth century." Her drawings were highly enough regarded that they received a showing by the viceroy of India in 1916, and some 200 of them are still on display in the Victoria Memorial in Calcutta. Her portrait of Ranjit Singh has influenced subsequent portraitists.

It is for her novels, however, that E. is most enduringly remembered. *The Semi-Detached House* (1859) and *The Semi-Attached Couple* (1860) have both been readily available since their initial publication, most recently in Virago Press editions. In them E. shows an Austenesque love-and-marriage market among the very rich. In *House,* young Lady Blanche Chester awaits the birth of her son, establishes herself as a force in country society, and comes to know the Hopkinsons and to help promote the marriages of Janet and Rose, thwarting meanwhile the snobbery of Baroness Sampson. The semi-detachment of the house reflects E.'s democratic belief in human worth and relatedness despite class differences. *Couple* details the difficulties a young married couple face in learning to know one another; romance takes a back seat to very real differences of upbringing, sensitivity, and activity, as Lord Teviot's hearty loving frightens young Helen. In addition, the houseguests, hunting, and ambassadorial duties incumbent upon their lifestyle make it impossible for the couple to become intimate. In the midst of a borough election, Helen learns both how to yield and how to stand up for herself, and Teviot sees the roughness of his prideful ways. In both books the dry drollery of E.'s presentation remains as fresh and captivating as it was over a century ago. She is aptly characterized as a minor Jane Austen.

WORKS: *Portraits of the Princes and People of India* (1843). *The Semi-Detached House* (1859). *The Semi-Attached Couple* (1860). *The Journals and Correspondence of William, Lord Auckland,* ed. G. Hogge (1861–62). *"Up the Country": Letters Written to Her Sister from the Upper Provinces of India* (1866; rpt. as *Letters From India,* 1872). *Catalogue of Exhibition of Paintings by the Hon. Miss Eden* (at Victoria Memorial Exhibition, Belvedere, Calcutta, 1916). *Miss Eden's Letters,* ed. V. Dickinson (1919).

BIBLIOGRAPHY: Archer, W. G. *Paintings of the Sikhs* (1966). Dunbar, J. *Golden Interlude: The Edens in India 1836–1842* (1955).

For articles in reference works, see: *DNB. Feminist. ToddBWW.*

Other references: Cornillon, S. K. *Images of Women in Fiction: Feminist Perspectives* (1972).

Loralee MacPike
(updated by Natalie Joy Woodall)

Maria Edgeworth

BORN: 1 January 1768, Black Bourton, Oxfordshire.
DIED: 22 May 1849, Edgeworthstown, Ireland.
DAUGHTER OF: Richard Lovell Edgeworth and Anna Maria Elers Edgeworth.

In the "General Preface" to his *Waverley Novels,* Sir Walter Scott wrote: "Without being so presumptuous as to hope to emulate the rich humor, pathetic tenderness, and admirable tact which pervade the work of my accomplished friend, I felt that something might be attempted for my own country, of the same kind with that which Miss Edgeworth so fortunately achieved for Ireland." E.—an Anglo-Irish novelist, short-story writer, dramatist, and educational essayist—is known chiefly for her work in the tradition of the novel of manners, although she is also remembered for her contributions to educational theory. Her reputation as a novelist has suffered from inevitable comparisons to Jane Austen; however, literary historians have long acknowledged her many innovations to English fiction.

Much of E.'s work was inspired and motivated by her father, a politician, inventor, and educator. Married four times, he fathered twenty-two children. Besides her responsibilities as agent and secretary of the family estate (Edgeworthstown, Ireland, where she lived from age fifteen until her death), E. had control of her father's ever-increasing family. To entertain them she composed stories, first on a slate and then, if they approved, in ink. In this manner E. perfected her skills as a storyteller.

E.'s first major publication was *Letters for Literary Ladies* (1795), a spirited defense of female education. In the following year a collection of didactic children's stories, *The Parent's Assistant,* appeared. Going through numerous editions in England, Ireland, and the United States, as well as being translated into French, the collection was available well into the mid-nineteenth century. E.'s interest in children's literature continued throughout her career, with collections of stories, such as *Early Lessons* (1801) and *Popular Tales* (1804), interspersed among her novels and tales for adults. These collections went through multiple editions, usually with one or two of the original stories supplemented by a variety of new tales.

Formal collaboration between E. and her father occurred on only two books, most notably *Practical Education* (1798), which espouses many ideas on education taken from Jean-Jacques Rousseau, but her father's hand is noticeable in almost all her work. Not only did he urge her to write moralistic and didactic stories, but he edited her manuscripts, deleting and inserting, rearranging and rewriting to his own taste. Most critics agree that his presence within E.'s work is more of a hindrance than a help. Yet some maintain that the dichotomy of highly imaginative fiction with extreme pragmatism creates an interesting puzzle.

Castle Rackrent: An Hibernian Tale (1800) is considered by most to be E.'s best work. Written while her father was traveling, the novel is free from the overt didacticism of much of E.'s other works. Although surpassed in many of her efforts by later writers, E. implemented several new narrative techniques in *Castle Rackrent.* Of major importance is her narrator, Thady Quirk. Not only is he active rather than passive, but the narrative is presented from his perspective (a narrative device later adopted by Austen). The first regional novel, *Castle Rackrent* depicts speech, mannerisms, and activities of a specific group—a technique that greatly influenced Scott as well as others, such as William Thackeray, and James Fenimore Cooper. Ivan Turgenev said that his *Sportsman's Sketches* were also influenced by *Castle Rackrent* in their full development of lower-class characters.

E.'s other Irish tales are also considered to be worthy of note. Included in this group are *The Absentee,* published as part of *Tales of Fashionable Life* (1812) and detailing another enterprising landed family; *Ennui* (1809); and *Ormond* (1817). Concerned with social and economic problems and showing great understanding for Irish culture, these are generally grouped among E.'s best works. Other novels focused on contemporary English society. *Belinda* (1801), also regarded as one of E.'s major achievements, is a picture of society at the close of the eighteenth century and is commented on by Austen in *Northanger Abbey. Leonora* (1806), *Patronage* (1814), and *Helen* (1834) also center around English society.

Thus, because of her innovations to narrative technique in the English novel, her sensitivity to local atmosphere, and her sympathetic portrayal of national character, E. influenced some of England's best-known authors (most notably Austen and Scott) and is an important figure in the history of the English novel.

WORKS: *Adelaide and Theodore* (1783). *Letters for Literary Ladies* (1795). *The Parent's Assistant* (1796). (with R. L. Edgeworth) *Practical Education* (1798). *Castle Rackrent: An Hibernian Tale* (1800). *Early Lessons*

(1801). *Moral Tales* (1801). *Belinda* (1801). *The Mental Thermometer* (1801). *Essay on Irish Bulls* (1802). *Popular Tales* (1804). *The Modern Griselda* (1805). *Leonora* (1806). (with R. L. Edgeworth) *Essays on Professional Education* (1809). *Tales of Fashionable Life* (1812). *Patronage* (1814). *Continuation of Early Lessons* (1814). *Comic Dramas* (1817). *Harrington, a Tale;* and *Ormond, a Tale* (1817). *Roramond: A Sequel to Early Lessons* (1821). *Frank: A Sequel to Frank in Early Lessons* (1822). *Harry and Lucy Concluded: Being the Last Part of Early Lessons* (1825). *Thoughts on Bores, Janus* (1826). *Little Plays for Children* (1827). *Garry-Owen* (1829). *Helen, a Tale* (1834). *Orlandino* (1848). *The Most Unfortunate Day of My Life* (1931).

BIBLIOGRAPHY: Butler, M. *Maria Edgeworth: A Literary Biography* (1972). Harden, E. *Maria Edgeworth* (1984). Hare, A. J. C. *The Life and Letters of Maria Edgeworth* (1894). Kowaleski-Wallace, E. *Their Fathers' Daughters: Hannah More, Maria Edgeworth, and Patriarchal Complicity* (1991). *Family Chronicles: Marie Edgeworth's "Castle Rackrent,"* ed. C. Owens (1987).

For articles in reference works, see: *Allibone. BA19C. Cassell. CBEL. Chambers. CinP. DIL. DLEL. DNB. Longman. NCHEL. NCLC. OCEL. Oxford.*

Other references: Atkinson, C. B., and J. Atkinson. *Eire* (1984). *Reading and Writing Women's Lives: A Study of the Novel of Manners,* ed. B. K. Bowers and B. Brothers (1990). Croghan, M. J. *IUR* (1990). Dunleavy, J. E., in *Reading and Writing Women's Lives,* ed. B. K. Bowers and B. Brothers (1990). Fitzgerald, L. *SVEC* (1992). Kirkpatrick, K. J. *ECF* (1993). *Studies in Anglo-Irish Literature,* ed. H. Kosok (1982). Mortimer, A. *EI* (1984). Myers, M. *L&U* (1989). Myers, M., in *Romanticism and Children's Literature in Nineteenth Century England,* ed. J. H. McGavrah, Jr. (1991). Myers, M., in *The Idea of The Novel in The Eighteenth Century,* ed. R. W. Uphaus (1988). NiChuilleanain, E. *Irish Women: Image and Achievement* (1985). Ohogain, D., in *Family Chronicles: Maria Edgeworth's "Castle Rackrant,"* ed. C. Owens (1987). Ragussis, M. *CritI* (1989). Richie, A. T. *A Book of Sibyls* (1883). Saito, Y. *Shiron* (1991). *Fetter'd or Free? British Women Novelists, 1670–1815,* ed. M. A. Schofield and C. Macheski (1986). Umasreiter, R., in *Functions of Literature,* ed. U. Broich et al. (1984). Woolf, V. *The Common Reader* (1925).

Lynn M. Alexander

"The editor of The Phoenix": See *Reeve, Clara*

Edmonds, Helen Wood: See *Kavan, Anna*

Amelia Ann Blanford Edwards

BORN: 7 June 1831, London.
DIED: 15 April 1892, Weston-super-Mare, Somerset.

E. was well known as a novelist, short-story writer, journalist, Egyptologist, and travel-writer. She was the daughter of a retired army officer turned London banker and was educated at home by her mother, a theater-loving Irishwoman, who early recognized E's talents. She sent her seven-year-old's poem, "The Knights of Old," to a penny weekly where it was published. At the age of nine, E. won a prize for a temperance story. Her second published work, "The Story of a Clock," was written when she was twelve and republished in the January 1893 *New England Magazine.* E. was also adept at music and drawing. A manuscript she sent to George Cruikshank for *The Omnibus* had such impressive pencillings on the back that he called on its author and was stunned to find these caricatures the work of a fourteen-year-old girl.

She began her career as a journalist after sending a story to *Chambers' Journal* for which she was paid. Thereafter she wrote regularly for *Household Words* and *All the Year Round,* often supplying the ghost story for the Christmas issues. In fact, she contributed a number of ghost stories to the leading periodicals of the day. E. was also a member of the staffs of *Saturday Review* and *Morning Post,* sometimes contributing the lead articles and often music, drama, or art reviews. She wrote for the *Graphic* and the *Illustrated News* as well.

Once established as a journalist, E. began to write longer works, mainly romantic novels and historical portraits. Her first, *My Brother's Wife: A Life History,* was published in 1855. In 1857, she followed with another novel, *The Ladder of Life: A Heart-History.* Her earliest popular success, however, did not come until she published *Barbara's History* (1864), which went through three editions, was published in the American magazine *Harper's,* and was translated into German, French, and Italian. The novel (very colorful and vivid) was full of historical and topographical information. In 1865, she published *Miss Carew,* a collection of tales, and her own *Ballads,* and edited a collection of poetry, *Home Thoughts and Home Themes.* She edited a second anthology of poetry, *A Poetry-Book of Elder Poets* (1879). Some of her tales, such as "The 4.15 Express" (1867) and "The Tragedy in Bardello Place" (1868) were very popular. *Half a Million of Money* (1865), *Debenham's Vow* (1870) and *In the Days of My Youth* (1873), were well received. Her most widely read novel was *Lord Brackenbury* (1880), a work about English country life, which originally came out in the *Graphic* with illustrations by Luke Fildes based on her own water-color sketches. The novel, her last, ran through fifteen editions and was translated into Italian, French, German, and Russian.

During this time, she also wrote nonfiction. Her interest in history is reflected not only by the research she did for her novels but also by the summaries of English and French history she wrote in *A Summary of English History: from the Roman Conquest to the Present Time* and *The History of France from the Conquest of Gaul by the Romans to the Peace of 1856* (both published in 1856); she continued her summary of French history with *The History of France from the Conquest of Gaul by the Romans Continued to the Death of the Prince Imperial* (1880). She turned to writing travel books as well, publishing *Sights and Stories: Being Some Account of a Holiday Tour through the North of Belgium* (1862) and *A Night on the Borders of the Black Forest* (1874). A third travel book, *Untrodden Peaks and Unfrequented Valleys: A Midsummer Ram-*

ble in the Dolomites (1873), was published with illustrations from her own sketches.

Her excursion to Egypt in the winter of 1873–74 instilled a life-long passion for the Middle East that altered the course of her life. Her interest in travel writing was transformed into scholarship on ancient Egyptian civilization as she learned to decipher hieroglyphics and evolved into England's foremost Egyptologist. *A Thousand Miles up the Nile* (1877) became a popular guide book, with a second edition in 1889, and a third thereafter. The book included facsimiles of hieroglyphic inscriptions, plans, maps, and more than eighty of her own illustrations. Alarmed by the irresponsible destruction of antiquities in Egypt, she worked to further the scientific excavation and preservation of ancient Egyptian monuments and artifacts. In 1882, E. founded the Egypt Exploration Fund, whose purpose was to prevent the destruction of antiquities, with herself and Reginald Stuart Poole as joint honorary secretaries; the Fund sponsored annual expeditions to Egypt for excavations. E. was active in the organization until her death in 1892. From 1882, on, E. wrote about Egypt for many journals and newspapers. She contributed more than 100 scholarly articles on Egypt to the *Academy* alone, and she wrote frequently on the subject for *The Times* as well as various journals, both scholarly and popular. Her article "Lying in State in Cairo," published in *Harper's Magazine* (July 1882), describes in detail the discovery of the royal mummies at Thebes.

E. attended the Orientalist Congress in Leyden, in Holland, in 1884, where she read a paper, later published as a pamphlet, titled "On a Fragment of Mummy-Case," with her illustrations. At the Orientalist Congress in Vienna the following year, she read a paper on "The Dispersion of Antiquities," a subject that greatly concerned her and that was again the topic of her paper in 1886. In 1888, she presented an important paper detailing the contents of private and provincial collections of antiquities in England. She lectured on Egyptological topics in Britain and toured the United States in 1889, the trip marred by an accident in which she broke her arm and from which she never fully recovered. The lectures she delivered in the United States were published two years later under the title *Pharoahs, Fellahs and Explorers.* She earned an honorary doctorate from Columbia University.

E. is credited with introducing the general public to the wonders of Egyptian history and culture. Her Egyptological writing was valued and admired for its accessibility to the general reader as well as for its reliability as careful scholarship. She was a member of the Bible Archaeological Society and of the Society for the Promotion of Hellenic Literature, and she was vice-president of a society promoting women's suffrage.

She died a few months after the passing away of the friend with whom she had shared her home for twenty-eight years. She bequeathed her Egyptological library and antiquities to University College London, with an endowment to found a chair of Egyptologies, the only such chair in England. Most of her books, however, she bequeathed to Somerville Hall, Oxford. A marble bust by Percival Ball, sculpted in Rome in 1873, was bequeathed to the National Portrait Gallery, London. Her photograph provides the frontispiece of "The Queen of Egyptology," a biographical sketch by W.C. Winslow first published in *The American Antiquarian Magazine.*

WORKS: *My Brother's Wife: A Life History* (1855). *A Summary of English History: from the Roman Conquest to the Present Time* (1856). *The History of France from the Conquest of Gaul by the Romans to the Peace of 1856* (1856). *The Ladder of Life: A Heart-History* (1857). *The Young Marquis* (1857). *Hand and Glove* (1858). (trans.) *A Lady's Captivity Among the Chinese Pirates,* by F. Loviot (1858). *Sights and Stories: Being Some Account of a Holiday Tour through the North of Belgium* (1862). *The Story of Cervantes, who was a Scholar, a Poet, a Soldier, a Slave Among the Moors, and the author of "Don Quixote"* (1863). *The Eleventh of March* (1863). *Barbara's History: A Novel* (1864). *Ballads* (1865). *Half a Million of Money* (1865). *Miss Carew: A Novel* (1865). *The Four-Fifteen Express* (1867). *Debenham's Vow* (1870). *Untrodden Peaks and Unfrequented Valleys: A Midsummer Ramble in the Dolomites* (1873). *In the Days of My Youth* (1873). *Monsieur Maurice: A New Novelette and Other Tales* (1873). *A Night on the Borders of the Black Forest* (1874). *A Thousand Miles up the Nile* (1877). *Lord Brackenbury: A Novel* (1880). *The History of France from the Conquest of Gaul by the Romans Continued to the Death of the Prince Imperial* (1880). (trans.) *Egyptian Archeology,* by G. C. C. Maspero (1887). *Pharohs, Fellahs, and Explorers* (1891). (trans.) *Julia Kavanagh,* by K. S. Macquoid (1897). (trans.) *Manual of Egyptian Archeology,* by G. C. C. Maspero (1902).

BIBLIOGRAPHY: Macquoid, K. *Amelia Blandford Edwards* (1897). Rees, J. *Writings on the Nile: Harriet Marineau, Florence Nightingale, Amelia Edwards* (1995). *Women Novelists of Queen Victoria's Reign,* ed. A. Sergeant (1897). Winslow, W. C. *American Antiquarian Magazine* (November 1892).

For articles in reference works, see: *Bloomsbury. DNB. Europa. Feminist. Oxford.*

Other references: *Maiden Voyages: Writings of Women Travelers,* ed. M. Morris (1993).

Gale Sigal

Egerton, George: See *Bright, Mary Golding*

Sarah Fyge Field Egerton

BORN: 1669–72, London.
DIED: 13 February 1722, Winslow, Buckinghamshire.
DAUGHTER OF: Thomas Fyge and Mary Fyge (née Beecham or Beacham).
MARRIED: Edward Field, 1687 (?); Thomas Egerton, 1690s.
WROTE UNDER: Clarinda; Mrs. Egerton; Mrs. Field; S. F. E.

Jeslyn Medoff writes of E.: "She is only one of a number of women poets of the Restoration and early eighteenth century who published their work, achieved a measure of notoriety, and then, except for sporadic resurfacings, disappeared. An examination of Sarah Fyge's life and works reveals a woman representative of her time and exceptional in all times." E. was one of six daughters of Thomas Fyge and Mary Beecham Fyge; Fyge was a physician and a city councilor descended from a land-owning family in Winslow, Buckinghamshire, while Mary Beecham came from Seaton, Rutlandshire. Her father wrote commendatory verse on works by his friend John Heydon, a physician, which suggests that he knew people interested in Rosicrucianism and Hermeticism; E.'s arcane learning as depicted in her poems may have come from such early associations.

E. was banished from her father's home because she wrote, at about the age of fourteen, *The Female Advocate; Or, An Answer to a Late Satyr* (1686), printed anonymously with a preface signed "S. F."; this was a verse reply to Robert Gould's misogynist *Love Given O're; or, A Satyr against the Pride, Lust and Inconstancy etc. of Woman* (1682). The second expanded edition, with significant changes, appeared in 1687; its success prompted her father to send her to live with relatives in Buckinghamshire. She records her feelings of grief on that occasion in the poem "On my Leaving London, June the 29" (*Poems on Several Occasions,* 1703). After an abortive engagement (identified only as "Philaster" in *Poems*), she was married against her will to Edward Field ("Amintor" in her verses), a lawyer who died in the mid-1690s leaving her a wealthy, childless widow. Field may have been supportive of E.'s work, but she was not very appreciative of his qualities. On his death, however, she wrote about her strong feelings in explicitly visual and sensual detail in "The Gratitude."

She then became enamored of Henry Pierce, her husband's married friend and legal clerk, her poems' "Alexis." Her infatuation continued throughout her second marriage at the age of thirty to Thomas Egerton ("wealthy Strephon" in her *Poems*), rector of Adstock in Buckinghamshire and her distant cousin, who had several grown children. She wrote more than 120 love letters to "Alexis" "expressive of the most violent and outrageous love" (according to "M. J." writing in *The Gentleman's Magazine,* March 1781) and made him occasional gifts of money, though her feelings were probably unrequited. Her marriage with Egerton was possibly coerced by her parents and was an acrimonious battle. In 1703, the couple engaged upon a highly public and bitter but unsuccessful divorce suit. Though the marriage and the marital relations of the Egertons became something of a public joke, with Delariviere Manley—E.'s estranged friend—satirizing it mercilessly in her *The New Atlantis* (1709) and a broadside published about it in 1711, the Egertons remained married until 1720. Manley writes that in marrying E., Egerton had hoped that she would help him with his sermons, but that he found her a "new woman" and very ambitious. She was engrossed in her literary pursuits, he found, mocked Deists, and loved scandal. She appears to have been well read and to have known some points of law. E. died in 1723, leaving the church at Winslow some plate and a bequest of one pound per annum to the parish poor, a bequest never executed by her corrupt executor.

E. laid claim to some acquaintances in literary circles; she knew John Dryden, John Norris, Matthew Prior, and the first Earl of Halifax. She was also known as "Clarinda" or "Mrs. Field" to belletristic women such as Mary Pix, Elizabeth Thomas, and Susanna Centlivre. She published *Luctus Britanicci; or The Tears of the British Muses* (1700) and contributed three poems to *The Nine Muses; or, Poems Written by Nine Several Ladies Upon the Death of the Late Famous John Dryden* (1700), edited by Manley. She knew other literary and theatrical personalities of the day, such as John Froude, Joshua Barnes, Nahum Tate, and Elizabeth Bracegirdle. Her pastoral "The Fond Shepherdesse" (1703; in *Poems*) was dedicated to William Congreve. Her literary reputation was primarily based on *The Female Advocate,* as was her name as a protofeminist. In "To the Lady Campbell, with a Female Advocate" (*Poems on Several Occasions*). E. claimed that she wrote *The Female Advocate* in fourteen days. The work was part of a literary battle of the sexes that raged for twenty years and was mainly carried on by Robert Gould and Richard Ames, both of whom occasionally wrote as women. E., therefore, literally fell in between these two not very exalted satirists (Medoff). The poem's couplets are somewhat slow and ponderous, but the poem is a perceptive and rationalist critique of the fears of misogynists. In her 1686 edition of *The Advocate,* Egerton had been incautious enough to claim her own volition as the motive for publishing her poem. By 1687, however, the bold assertion of volition gave place to a more apologetic preface whereby she made the more "feminine" claim of not having had complete control over the poem's publication. She also wrote that she revised the text to omit things that were more fitting for a private eye than for public perusal. In the second edition, her poetry was in some ways better, but her general points remained the same: Women could not be blamed for the fall; Mary had brought salvation to humankind; women were not inconstant and lustful, though men were; women had saved men's lives in the past; and marriage was not the only destiny for all women. Cuts in the 1687 edition included references to specific instances of male profligacy and references to women's defiance of their seducers or rapists.

E. seemed particularly aggrieved at the injunctions upon women to be uneducated as well as unobtrusive. In "The Liberty" (*Poems on Several Occasions*), for instance, she refers to "Tyrant Custom" or society's mandates as "fetters," "gyves," and "manacles." She also began to present herself as a tragic victim of fate and gender whose artistic sensibilities and intelligence were misunderstood by her contemporaries. Though she was significantly influenced by the platonic tradition of self-development promulgated by Mary Astell, in her work there is a sense of little reliance on, even some impatience for, such palliatives for the female condition and the tyranny of custom. According to H. Smith, she came perhaps closer to Sylvia Plath than to some of her contemporaries in her feminist polemic.

Her poems such as "The Liberty" and "The Extasy" also contain references to occult matters, minerals, necromancy, mythology, magic, and metaphysics, and they exemplify elements of Rosicrucian discourse. Her poetry includes pastoral, elegy, panegyric, song, love lyric, the irregular or Cowleyan ode, and rural retirement verse. Her characteristic metrical form is the heroic couplet. She is also open about sexual passion, a quality that some have linked to Aphra Behn's tradition. Her poems include both feminist critique and saddened self-portraits. Her last known poem was the unpublished "The Essay, Address'd to the Illustrious Prince and Duke of Marlbrow after the Long Campaigne 1708" (1708; Huntington Library MS. EL 8796). Medoff writes that "E.'s work, as a whole, will never establish her as anything more than a minor literary figure. . . . *The Poems* are alternately forceful in their claims for women's rights, and plaintive in their depiction of S. E. as a tragic victim of fate, a misunderstood, intellectual woman of artistic sensibilities."

WORKS: *The Female Advocate: Or, An Answer to A Late Satyr Against the Pride, Lust and Inconstancy of Woman. Written by a Lady in Vindication of her Sex* (1686; preface signed "S. F."). "An Ode, On the Death of John Dryden, Esq.; By a Young Lady," signed "S. F.," in *Luctus Britannici;* or The Tears of the British Muses (1700). Three elegies to Dryden "By Mrs. S. F."—"Erato," "Euterpe," and Terpischore"—in *The Nine Muses: Or, Poems Written by Nine Several Ladies Upon the Death of the Late Famous John Dryden* (1700); reprinted in *Poems on Several Occasions, Together with a Pastoral; By Mrs. S. F.* (1703); reissued as *A Collection of Poems on several Occasions . . . by Mrs. Sarah Fyge Egerton* (1706), with a dedication signed "S. F. E."

BIBLIOGRAPHY: Ferguson, M. *The First Feminists: British Women Writers 1578–1799* (1985). *The Gentleman's Magazine* (December 1780, March 1781, October 1781). Hobby, E. *Virtue of Necessity: British Women Writers 1640–1688* (1988). Medoff, J. *TSWL* (1982). Smith, H. *Reason's Disciples: Seventeenth Century English Feminists* (1982).

For articles in reference works, see: *Bell. Feminist. Oxford. ToddBWW. ToddDBA.*

Other references: Anderson, P. B., in *MP* (1935). *Kissing the Rod: An Anthology of Seventeenth-Century Women's Verse,* ed. G. Greer et al. (1988). Nussbaum, F. *The Brink of All We Hate: English Satires on Women 1660–1750* (1983). Nussbaum, F., in *Satires on Women, Augustan Reprint Society no. 180* (1976).

Nandini Bhattacharya

E. H.: See *Haywood, Eliza Fowler*

George Eliot (pseudonym of Mary Ann Evans)

BORN: 22 November 1819, South Farm, Arbury, Warwickshire.
DIED: 22 December 1880, London.
DAUGHTER OF: Robert Evans and Christiana Pearson Evans.
MARRIED: John Walter Cross, 1880.
WROTE UNDER: George Eliot.

One of the greatest of Victorian novelists, E. was born Mary Ann Evans (alternatively spelled Mary Anne, Marianne, and Marian), third child, second daughter, of a second marriage, in a farm house on the Arbury estate where her father was land agent. Her older brother Isaac was the "dominating passion of her childhood" (Haight). Her youth was marked by strong religious conviction: first through family teaching; then through schooling, starting at the age of nine, at a school taught by Maria Lewis; then, at the age of thirteen, schooling by two daughters of the minister of the Baptist Chapel, where the tone was Calvinistic. During this time, she studied the Bible intensively; she read widely in English literature; excelled in French; and studied Latin, German, and Italian. Her education was largely self-acquired.

After her mother's death in 1836, E. and her father moved, in 1841, to Foleshill, near Coventry. Here she met and became close friends with Charles Bray, a wealthy ribbon manufacturer, philanthropist, and freethinker, his wife, Cara, and his sister-in-law, Sara Hennell. Their influence, plus that of Sara's brother, Charles Hennell, who published *An Inquiry Concerning the Origins of Christianity* (1838), was pivotal in shaking E.'s faith in formalized religion. For a time, she refused to attend church with her father, precipitating a crisis; a compromise was reached when she agreed to attend but reserved the right to think as she pleased.

Her career as an author began in 1846 with publication of her translation of D. F. Strauss's *Life of Jesus, Critically Examined,* although her name did not appear. She also contributed to the *Coventry Herald,* purchased by Bray in 1846. After her father's death in 1849, she visited Europe with the Brays and returned to their home, Rosehill, in Coventry, where she was introduced to the handsome and ambitious London publisher, John Chapman, soon to become editor and publisher of the influential quarterly *The Westminster Review.* At his invitation she reviewed R. W. Mackay's *The Progress of the Intellect* and soon moved to London to pursue a writing career. She boarded with Chapman, whose wife and mistress also lived in the house, and she became emotionally attracted to him, causing intolerable emotional complexities that drove her back to Coventry after two months. Chapman needed E. to help him edit the *Westminster,* however, so she returned to London to help him; she wrote book reviews, edited articles, and was editor in all but name for ten issues between January 1852 and April 1854. She met many of the leading intellectuals of the day, both English and American, including Herbert Spencer, to whom she also became emotionally attached.

Through her work on the *Westminster,* she also met George Henry Lewes, a prolific contributor to the *Review,* destined to be her life-companion. With his press passes they were able to attend London's many cultural entertainments—theater, concerts, the opera, the galleries—and gradually decided fate had determined they should be together for life. This was a momentous decision because Lewes was a married man who, under the law of the day, could not obtain a divorce because he earlier had condoned his wife's adultery; it also caused a permanent breach with her beloved brother, Isaac, who refused henceforth to communicate. However, E. and Lewes each regarded their union as a solemn moral commitment that they honored scrupulously until his death in 1878.

On 20 July 1854, they traveled together to Germany, partly so Lewes could work on his *Life of Goethe* (1855) and partly to avoid the storm of scandal their unorthodox union would cause. Earlier in the same month E.'s translation of Ludwig Feuerbach's *Essence of Christianity* was published. Lewes was a man of many parts: In addition to being a versatile journalist who wrote on a wide range of topics, he had published five books, including two novels and a history of philosophy; he was active in the theater world, he was a good friend of Charles Dickens, and he had lived a bohemian life. He brought an intellectual sophistication into E.'s life at the same time that she offered him domestic stability so he was free to accomplish the more serious work that lay ahead for him.

Soon after their arrival in Germany, E. began work on a translation of Spinoza's *Ethics* (never published), and gradually Lewes encouraged her to try her hand at fiction. In January 1857, "The Sad Fortunes of Amos Barton" appeared in *Blackwood's Magazine,* followed later the same year by "Mr. Gilfil's Love Story" and "Janet's Repentance," the three stories that would later appear as *Scenes of Clerical Life* (1858) and signed "George Eliot," the pseudonym she henceforth adopted. Each was the story of a country parson, each set in a country parish, each marked by depiction of simple country people and intimate description of the English countryside. The stories were instantly popular, and there was much speculation about the identity of the author, a mystery not solved until 1859 when the truth became generally known.

Adam Bede (1859), set at the end of the eighteenth century, is the story of a brave and stalwart carpenter, who loves Hetty Sorrel, a pretty but vain country lass seduced by the young squire, Arthur Donnithorne. In her ignorance and desperation, she commits infanticide and is sentenced to transportation, rather than death, through the efforts of the chastened squire. Hetty's cousin, Dinah Morris, a Methodist preacher, comforts her in jail, eventually marries Adam, and makes him a worthy wife. The novel is noted for the humorous and realistic picture of the Poyser family, particularly Mrs. Poyser and her dairy, and for the realism and sympathy of its portrayal of country life and virtues. As with most of E.'s fiction, the carefully drawn minor characters add much interest to the book. *Adam Bede* was instantly successful with the reading public and established Eliot as an important novelist.

The Mill on the Floss (1860) is the story of total devotion between a brother, Tom, and sister, Maggie, despite a conflict of temperaments, he being narrow, unimaginative, and unintellectual, while she was emotional and intelligent but rebellious and frustrated in seeking a purpose in life. Their father, Mr. Tulliver, is the honest but ignorant owner of Dorlcote mill. Maggie seeks companionship from the hunchbacked Philip Wakem, son of the town lawyer and a talented artist, a relationship that is broken off by Tom, after his father quarrels with Lawyer Wakem. To escape, Maggie goes to visit her cousin, Lucy Deane, who is engaged to Stephen Guest. Maggie and Stephen are attracted to one another, but during a river picnic they row out too far and are unable to return until morning. Maggie is totally compromised and ostracized in the small community. Despite having quarreled with Tom, Maggie goes to rescue Tom when there is a flood, but they drown in each other's arms. As usual, minor characters add much interest and veracity to the story, particularly Mrs. Tulliver and her three sisters, narrow-minded and domineering women. The instantly successful novel is notable for its portrayal of childhood, nature, and country life and for its accurate characterization.

Silas Marner (1861), often referred to as a moral allegory, is the story of a linen-weaver, driven from his home in a small religious community, Lantern Yard, by a false charge of theft. He relocates in Raveloe, where he is an outsider and practices his trade in isolation, only taking consolation in the gold he hoards. This bag of gold is stolen by the evil Dunstan Cass and he is bereft. In a parallel plot, Dunstan's brother, Godfrey Cass, loves Nancy Lammenter, but he is secretly and miserably married to a lower-class woman in the next village, by whom he has a child. She brings the child to Raveloe on New Year's Eve but unfortunately dies in the snow, while the child, Eppie, finds her way to Silas's cottage. He learns to love her and raises her; many years later Dunstan's body is found, with the gold, at the bottom of a pond. Local color is added by the rustic travelers at the Rainbow Inn. The deceptively simple tale is really an inquiry into the conditions of human happiness, love, and community as opposed to isolation and secrecy.

Perhaps least successful of E.'s novels is *Romola* (1863), a story set in fifteenth-century Florence, despite the fact that she researched the period in detail before and following a visit to Italy. The city is in upheaval following the expulsion of the Medici, the expedition of Charles VIII, and the preaching of Savonarola. The story is of the purification by trials of the noble-hearted Romola, daughter of the old, blind scholar, Dino de Bardi. After she marries a young Greek, Tito Melema, he betrays her by selling off her father's library. She leaves him but is turned back by Savonarola and instead works during famine and pestilence in Florence. She learns of Tito's mistress, Tessa, and two of his children. She leaves Florence again, but later returns, finds Tessa and the children, and they all live together in the house of her elderly cousin, Monna Brigida.

In *Felix Holt* (1866), E. returns to English soil, a setting with which she was more familiar. Set in Treby Magna, a typical market town, in the year 1832, immediately before passage of the Reform Bill, it provides an excellent view of the agitation of the times. Harold Transome returns to inherit the family estate after his elder brother's death and startles his family by standing as a Radical candidate. His views are not sincere, however, and he is contrasted with Felix Holt who, although educated, is idealistic, passionate, and austere and has deliberately chosen the life of an artisan, a watch-maker, in order to imbue his fellow workers with a sense of their own worth.

Esther, the heroine, thinks she is the daughter of the Reverend Rufus Lyon but later proves to be the rightful heiress to the Transome fortune. Holt rebukes Esther for her frivolous and self-indulgent ways. In the end, she must choose between Harold Transome and Holt and chooses the latter in spite of his having been jailed for being innocently involved in a riot. The novel has a complex and not entirely believable plot, relying greatly on coincidence to move the action. It is remarkable in evoking the tension and emotional atmosphere prevailing during passage of the Reform Bill, depicting the rioting and rowdiness of the elections, and describing conditions prevailing in the absence of a secret ballot. It has been said that *Felix Holt* is not a great book but that portions of it are great.

E.'s reputation reached its height with *Middlemarch* (1871–72). Not only was she now a revered artist but she was also wealthy and known and loved world-wide. Middlemarch is a provincial town in the years preceding the Reform Bill. The book is composed of multiple plots. The main thread concerns Dorothea Brooke, an intelligent, idealistic young woman who marries Mr. Casaubon, an elderly, unpleasant pedant. She wants to help him in his life's work, "a Key to all Mythologies," and to share in his intellectual life. After a disastrous honeymoon in Rome, she realizes neither desire will ever be possible and the marriage is intensely unhappy. Dorothea turns to Casaubon's cousin, Will Ladislaw, for companionship, which angers the scholar who leaves a codicil to his will disinheriting Dorothea if she marries Will; when he dies, Dorothea chooses Ladislaw over fortune. Other plot threads involve characters such as Fred and Rosamond Vincy, Mary Garth, Caleb Garth, Mr. Featherstone, Tertius Lydgate, and Mr. Bulstrode. Subthemes in the book include the social and political upheavals of the time, the Tories versus the Reform advocates, and the importance of marital loyalty, duty, and personal renunciation.

E.'s last novel, *Daniel Deronda* (1876), is a book with two main plots: the story of Gwendolyn Harleth, and of Deronda himself. Gwendolyn, beautiful, selfish, and badly spoiled, marries Henleigh Grandcourt, a cruel and arrogant man possessing both wealth and position; she marries so as to save her mother and sisters from destitution, despite having met Lydia Glasher, his mistress and knowing about his illegitimate son and three daughters. Grandcourt wants absolute control over Gwendolyn, and as he becomes more unbearable she turns for comfort to Deronda, an intelligent, compassionate young man of mysterious parentage with whom she later falls in love. A ruthless Grandcourt takes her on a boat on the Mediterranean intending to drown her, but instead he is swept away.

Meanwhile, Deronda rescues a young Jewish girl, Mirah, from suicide and places her for safe care with Mrs. Meyrick, later reuniting her with her consumptive brother Mordecai, who has given his all to his vision of a united Israel. It is gradually revealed that Deronda is the grandson of a great Jewish patriot, paving the way for Deronda to marry Mirah, who will wed only a Jew. The two plots are united by a letter from Gwendolyn on Deronda's wedding day saying "it shall be better with me because I have known you." As a minor character, there is a chilling portrait of Deronda's mother, a cold and proud woman, who has cast him out of her life in order to pursue an operatic career. This is a richly textured book and the first effort by a serious novelist to deal with the themes of Jewish society.

Less well known is E.'s poetry: "Oh, May I Join the Choir Invisible" (1867), *The Spanish Gypsy* (1868), "Agatha" (1869), *Brother and Sister* (1869), "Armgart" (1871), and *Legend of Jubal* (1874). She published two short stories, "The Lifted Veil" (1859) and "Brother Jacob" (1864). Her last published work was *The Impressions of Theophrastus Such* (1879), a collection of eighteen essays, the author's persona taking the form of a bachelor son of a Midlands parson, a Tory, reflecting on assorted subjects and including a vigorous defense of Jewish nationalism.

On 30 November 1878, Lewes died from intestinal cancer, leaving E. understandably bereft, their working and their personal lives having been so intertwined. One of the great unsolved mysteries of her life occurred on 9 April 1880, when she agreed to marry John Walter Cross, twenty years her junior, a man known to both E. and Lewes since 1869 as manager of their investments. Some have suggested that it was the temptation to be a legitimately married woman that prompted her decision. It also re-established relations with her estranged brother, Isaac, who wrote to congratulate her on the nuptials after a silence of twenty-two years. In any case, it was a short relationship because less than a year later, on 22 December 1880, she died. She and Lewes lie in adjacent plots in Highgate Cemetery, London.

WORKS: (trans.) *Life of Jesus, Critically Examined,* by D. F. Strauss (1846). (trans.) *Essence of Christianity,* by L. Feuerbach (1854). *Scenes of Clerical Life* (1858). *Adam Bede* (1859). *The Mill on the Floss* (1860). *Silas Marner* (1861). *Romola* (1863). *Felix Holt, The Radical* (1866). *The Spanish Gypsy* (1868). *Brother and Sister* (1869). *Middlemarch* (1871–72). *The Legend of Jubal* (1874). *Daniel Deronda* (1876). *The Impressions of Theophrastus Such* (1879). *The George Eliot Letters* 9 vols., ed. G. S. Haight (1954–78). *George Eliot: A Writer's Notebook, 1854–1879,* ed. J. Wiesenfarth (1981). *Selections from George Eliot's Letters,* ed. G. S. Haight (1985). *George Eliot. Selected Critical Writings,* ed. R. Ashton (1992). *George Eliot's "Daniel Deronda" Notebooks,* ed. J. Irwin (1996).

BIBLIOGRAPHY: Ashton, R. *G. H. Lewes, A Life* (1991). Ashton, R. *George Eliot: A Life* (1996). Beer, G. *George Eliot* (1986). Bennett, J. *George Eliot: Her Mind and Her Art* (1948). *Approaches to Teaching "Middlemarch,"* ed. K. Blake (1990). Bodenheimer, R. *The Real Life of Mary Ann Evans: George Eliot, Her Letters and Fiction* (1994). Carroll, D. *George Eliot: The Critical Heritage* (1971). *George Eliot: Critical Assessments,* ed. S. Hutchinson (1996). Haight, G. S. *George Eliot and John Chapman* (1940; 2nd ed., 1969). Haight, G. S. *A Century of George Eliot Criticism* (1965). Haight, G. S. *George Eliot: A Biography* (1968). *George Eliot: A Centenary Tribute,* ed. G. S. Haight and R. T. Van Arsdel (1982). Hardy, B. *The Novels of George Eliot: A Study in Form* (1959). Hartnoll, P. *Who's Who in George Eliot* (1977). Harvey, W. J. *The Art of George Eliot* (1971). *George Eliot: Critical Assessments,* ed. S. Hutchinson (1996). Karl, F. R. *George Eliot, Voice of a Century: A Biography* (1995). Leavis, F. R. *The Great Tradition: George Eliot, Henry James, Joseph Conrad* (1948). *An Annotated Critical Bibliography of George Eliot,* ed. G. Levine and P. O'Hara (1988). Martin, C. A. *George Eliot's Serial Fiction* (1995). Pinion, F. B. *A George Eliot Miscellany* (1982). Uglow, J. *George Eliot* (1987).

For articles in reference works, see: *Allibone SUP. BA19C. Bloomsbury. Cambridge. DLB. Feminist. IDWB. Oxford. ToddBWW. VB.*

Rosemary T. Van Arsdel

Eliza: See *Carter, Elizabeth; Moody, Elizabeth*

Elizabeth: See *Arnim, Elizabeth von*

Elizabeth, Charlotte: See *Tonna, Charlotte Elizabeth*

Elizabeth I (Elizabeth Tudor)

BORN: 7 September 1533, Greenwich.
DIED: 24 March 1603, Richmond, Surrey.
DAUGHTER OF: King Henry VIII and Anne Boleyn.

Known more for her rule of England during its literary Renaissance than for her own writings, E. nonetheless produced speeches and letters, a book of prayers, verse and prose translations from at least four languages, and six to eight extant original poems. Much of this output relates to her personal and political circumstances.

Her earliest recorded original verses, written on a wall and window during her imprisonment at Woodstock under her sister Mary's reign, treat the deception of appearances and the instability of fortune. These themes reappear in her poems even after she became queen in 1558. E. does not complain about fortune but reveals her determination to surmount her troubles: "wit me warns to shun such snares as threaten mine annoy," she claims in "The Doubt of Future Foes." "On Monsieur's Departure," which differs from her other poems in relying on Petrarchan conventions, laments unrequited love from the position of a royal woman.

E.'s speeches and letters more clearly deal with her political predicaments, but their directness varies. The surviving speeches, while expressing her love for her people generally, often evade the specific issues at hand, such as her proposed marriages or the execution of Mary, Queen of Scots. In particular, the early speeches rely on an obfuscating style and elaborate metaphors. Her two most famous orations—the rallying of her troops in the face of the 1588 Spanish invasion and her final, "Golden" speech to Parliament—show unusual dramatic boldness, though the former is of uncertain authenticity. E.'s numerous letters, penned in her roles as princess and queen, suit their style to the particular situations and correspondents. Sometimes she abruptly rebukes her courtiers or even other monarchs; sometimes she hides her feelings with high diction and philosophical platitudes.

Her translations may be the least political of her writings. She was proud of her linguistic ability, inculcated under Protestant humanist educators like William Grindal and Roger Ascham. She compiled *A Book of Devotions* in Greek, Latin, French, Italian, and English, but even these private prayers show her as conscious of her political image. She also produced English translations from various languages throughout her long life, turning Marguerite de Navarre's *Le Miroir de l'âme pécheresse* into prose as *The Mirror* [or *Glass*] *of the Sinful Soul* when only eleven and versifying part of Horace's *Art of Poetry* at sixty-five. Her lines from Petrarch's *Triumph of Eternity* have the most polish among her translations, but her lengthy verses rendering Boethius's *The Consolation of Philosophy* (1593) and Plutarch's "On Curiosity" from the *Moralia* (1598) suffer from raggedness. A 270-line translation into French in her hand, a meditation appropriate to her royal position but from an unknown source, has also recently surfaced. In many of these works, the alliteration, irregular lines, and Latinate word-order sound awkward, and there are some mistranslations, but E. translated at great speed. The devotion of time to such tasks amid the affairs of state is remarkable; however, even these pieces often treat her recurring topics of deceptive appearances and unstable fortune.

After a precarious youth, E. in her reign brought England a long period of relative peace, defensive military success, and enhanced political importance. Her popularity, often high, fluctuated with the unsteady economy, but she won elaborate literary tributes from writers of the period, including John Lyly, William Shakespeare, Ben Jonson, and, most notably, from Edmund Spenser in *The Faerie Queene.* She also won sometimes grudging respect from allies and enemies abroad, not only for her political astuteness but also for her learning.

WORKS: (trans.) *The Consolation of Philosophy,* by Boethius (1593). (trans.) "On Curiosity," *Moralia,* by Plutarch (1598). (trans.) *Mirror of the Sinful Soul,* by M. de Navarre, ed. P. Ames (1897). *Queen Elizabeth's Englishings of Boethius . . . Plutarch . . . Horace,* ed. C. Pemberton (1899, rpt. 1973). *The Letters of Queen Elizabeth,* ed. G. Harrison (1935). Rice, G. *The Public Speaking of Queen Elizabeth* (1951). *The Poems of Queen Elizabeth I,* ed. L. Bradner (1964). "Ah silly pugge," in L. Black, *TLS* (23 May 1968). *A Book of Devotions Composed by Her Majesty Elizabeth R.*, trans. A. Fox and intro. J. Hodges (1970). *Proceedings in the Parliaments of Elizabeth I,* ed. T. Hartley (1981). *Elizabethan England and Europe: Forty Unprinted Letters,* ed. E. Kouri (1982). *Elizabeth's Glass with "The Glass of the Sinful Soul" (1544) by Elizabeth I,* ed. M. Shell (1993). "The French Verses," ed. and trans. S. May and A. Prescott, *ELR* (1994).

BIBLIOGRAPHY: Bassnett, S. *Elizabeth I: A Feminist Perspective* (1988). Erickson, C. *The First Elizabeth* (1983). Frye, S. *Elizabeth I: The Competition for Representation* (1993). Hageman, E. *ELR* (1984, updated in *Women in the Renaissance,* ed. K. Farrell, E. Hageman, and A. Kinney, 1990). Hibbert, C. *The Virgin Queen* (1990). Hodges, J. *The Nature of the Lion* (1962). Hopkins, L. *Queen Elizabeth I and Her Court* (1990). Jenkins, E. *Elizabeth the Great* (1958). Johnson, P. *Elizabeth I: A Study in Power and Intellect* (1974). Levin, C. *"The Heart and Stomach of a King": Elizabeth I and the Politics of Sex and Power* (1994). Levine, J. *Great Lives Observed: Elizabeth I* (1969). May, S. *ELR* (1993). Neale, J. *Queen Elizabeth* (1934). Neale, J. *Elizabeth I and her Parliaments* (1953–57). Plowden, A. *The Young Elizabeth* (1971). Ridley, J. *Elizabeth I: The Shrewdness of Virtue* (1987). Somerset, A. *Elizabeth I.* Ziegler, G. *ELR* (1994).

For articles in reference works, see: *Ballard. Bloomsbury. DLB. Europa. Feminist. IDWB. Mahl and Koon. Oxford. Rowton. ToddBWW.*

Other references: Beilin, E. *Redeeming Eve* (1987). Brooke, T. *HLQ* (1938). Crane, M. *SEL* (1988). Frye, S. *SCJ* (1992). Gallagher, L. *Medusa's Gaze* (1991). Haugaard, W. *SCJ* (1981). Heisch, A. *Signs* (1975). Heisch, A. *Feminist Review* (1980). Kastan, D. *N&Q* (1974). Marcus, L., in *Women in the Middle Ages and the Renaissance,* ed. M. Rose (1986). May, S. *The Elizabethan Courtier Poets* (1991). *N&Q* (1985). Nevalinna, S., in *Proceedings from the Third Nordic Conference for English Studies . . . 1986,* ed. I. Lindblad and M. Ljung (1987). Prescott, A. in *Silent But for the Word,* ed. M. Hannay (1985). Teague, F., in *Gloriana's Face: Women, Public and Private, in the English Renaissance,* ed. S. Cerasano and M. Wynne-Davies (1992).

Sayre N. Greenfield

Elizabeth of York

BORN: 11 February 1465, Westminster Palace, London.
DIED: 11 February 1503, Tower of London.
DAUGHTER OF: Edward IV and Elizabeth Woodville.
MARRIED: Henry VII, 1486.

In an age of bitter struggle over dynastic succession, E., daughter of King Edward IV, was a figure of central importance. She was first promised to George Nevill in 1469, but when his father turned against the king the match was cancelled. Next, her marriage to the French Dauphin was a condition of peace between Edward and Louis XI, but this too was called off. While engaged to the dauphin she was also offered to Henry Tudor, then Earl of Richmond, as a ploy to lure him into Edward's control. Henry, then a refugee in Brittany, did not take the bait. When the king died in 1483, the family entered Westminster for sanctuary from Richard, Duke of Gloucester, where they remained for ten months. When they left, E. was treated so well at court that rumors spread concerning herself and Richard III. After Richard was killed at the Battle of Bosworth Field, Henry became King Henry VII and married E. on 18 January 1486. She was crowned queen on 25 November 1487.

As a youth, she read widely from among the books William Caxton was printing at Westminster Abbey—books of history, philosophy, theology, and literature. She could read and write French and Spanish. Although none of E.'s writing survives, her letters appear to have played an important role in politics. In a letter reported by Sir George Buck in the seventeenth century (the document has not been seen by anyone else), she encourages Richard III in the hope that he may marry her after his queen dies. Though the letter cannot be verified, it is true that rumors of Richard's intentions were so widespread that in April 1485 he made a dramatic public denial of them before the Lord Mayor and aldermen of London.

A group of letters was sent to Henry, Earl of Richmond, while E. was staying at Sheriff Hutton Castle in Yorkshire, still under Richard's guard. According to the popular "Song of the Lady Bessy" by Humphrey Brereton (a servant of Lord Stanley), E. hated Richard and sent messages to Henry encouraging him and promoting his uprising. She sent a letter with a ring to Henry in Brittany, and Henry pledged himself to her at Vannes Cathedral on Christmas Day 1483.

In 1492, King Henry VII invaded France and laid siege to Boulogne. Bernard Andreas, the royal historiographer, indicates that E. sent numerous letters to Henry in France and had no small influence on his decision to return to England.

All indications are that their married life was a happy one. She is said to have been beautiful, with a fair complexion and golden hair. She appears to have enjoyed music, dancing, cards, dice, and hunting. Of her seven children, three died as infants. The oldest son, Prince Arthur, died in 1502, causing both parents such grief that it is said to have led to E.'s death after the birth of her last child, Catherine, in 1503. Her daughter Mary became queen of Louis XII of France, and her second son became King Henry VIII of England. Sir Thomas More wrote an elegy on her death.

WORKS: none surviving.

BIBLIOGRAPHY: Harvey, N. L. *Elizabeth of York: Tudor Queen* (1973). Leland, J. *De Rebus Britannicus Collectanae* (1770). Nicolas, N. H. *Privy Purse Expenses of Elizabeth of York* (1830). Strickland, A. *Lives of the Queens of England* (1863).

For articles in reference works, see: *DNB*. Routh, C. R. N. *Who's Who in History* (1964).

Richard Poss

Ellerman, Annie Winifred: See *Bryher*

Ellis, John Fanshawe: See *Wilde, Jane Francesca*

Sarah Stickney Ellis

BORN: 1799 (?), Holderness, Yorkshire.
DIED: 16 June 1872, Hoddesdon, Hertfordshire.
DAUGHTER OF: William Stickney and Esther Richardson Stickney.
MARRIED: William Ellis, 1837.
WROTE UNDER: Mrs. Ellis; Sarah Ellis; Sarah Stickney Ellis; Sarah Stickney.

E. wrote scores of novels, poems, and moral tales, but she achieved her greatest success with *The Women of England* (1839) and other conduct manuals. In many ways, her life approaches the Victorian ideal of womanhood that her books disseminated. Raised a Quaker on her father's farm in East Riding, she learned the duties of the sickroom by nursing her sisters and numerous other relatives through their fatal illnesses. Instead of getting to "act the bride," she plunged into the "trials, perplexities, and hard work" of marriage at the age of thirty-eight when she became the second wife of author and missionary William

Ellis (1794–1872). An admirer of Elizabeth Fry, E. performed the good deeds appropriate for middle-class women: She ran bazaars, visited the poor, and directed a Sunday school. Yet her letters reveal the discrepancy between prescription and practice. Although her advice books warned against vanity, E. delighted in having her portrait done. She advised women to conceal their gifts (talent, she wrote, is "a jewel which cannot with propriety be worn"), but she became acquainted with her husband by submitting poetry to an annual he edited; he encouraged her work and relied on her editorial assistance, especially after his health began to fail. E. recommended deference to male authority but resisted much of her husband's advice about religion and writing. In her books, women are sheltered from economic competition; letters show she kept a keen eye on sales and resented relatives who tried to borrow money. She exhorted women to make the home pleasant for others; in her house, she wanted a room of her own for painting and other art projects.

As a writer, E. intended to inculcate truth and earn money. E. admired William Shakespeare, John Milton, Lord Byron, Alfred Lord Tennyson, Margaret Oliphant, and Harriet Beecher Stowe; she felt that Charlotte Brontë, another Yorkshire writer, had a special hold upon her. Since sales for *The Negro Slave* (1830) and other privately printed early works were disappointing, she followed the advice of her friend Mary Howitt and contacted Thomas Pringle in 1832. When he made her a good offer to write for the circulating libraries, she quickly agreed, provided she could include "a certain degree of moral or religious sentiment." An experienced portrait painter, she often supervised the illustrations for her books. Apart from friendship with Mary Howitt and Mary Sewell, E. had little contact with other writers. Despite her husband's interest in her work, E. suspected that literary achievement and marital happiness were antithetical: The Howitts offered a hopeful model for literary marriage, but the unhappy situation of Anna Brownell Jameson suggested that there was "no luck with authoress-wives." When E. became a formidable figure in the mid-century marketplace, she still complained about "the bondage of writing." Preferring to spend her time on educational endeavors, she founded a school at Rawdon House (1845), where she lectured for twenty years; she spoke frequently to women's groups; and at the age of seventy-one she wrote with enthusiasm about setting up new classes for young women.

E. helped turn the novel away from romance and toward domestic realism. Her "Apology for Fiction" is contained in her first collection of tales, *Pictures of Private Life* (1833–37). Anticipating religious objections, she cited allegory and scripture as evidence that fiction could be used "as a means of reproof and conviction." "Fiction," she said, "may be compared to a key, which opens many minds that would be closed against a sermon." E. endorsed "lawful" fictions, "drawn from the scenes of every-day life, animated with our feelings, weak with our frailties, led into our difficulties, surrounded by our temptations, and altogether involved in a succession of the same causes and effects which influence our lives." Virtue must be flawed according to the demands of realism, but it must also be rewarded. Thwarting the reader's expectations for romantic endings, E. tries to create ideal goodness in the midst of everyday life. The heroine of "The Hall and the Cottage" overcomes vanity, ambition, and desire, but she meets "no belted knight, no steel-clad warrior, no prince in disguise"; instead she ends her days as a "respectable old maid" exuding "unbounded benevolence" in humble surroundings. Later novels, such as *The Brewer's Family* (1863), describe the dreadful consequences of drinking and parental neglect. *Home; or The Iron Rule* (1836) is a lesson to fathers who make their children's obedience a matter of compulsion rather than a choice of the heart. *The Mother's Mistake* (1856) is a warning to mothers lest they misread their children's characters and channel their energies in the wrong directions.

Addressing her conduct manuals to "women" rather than "ladies," E. attacks the "false notions of refinement" that were making modern women "less influential, less useful, and less happy" than in the past. E. urges the reader to be content with her proper sphere, to practice the "art of accommodation," to make prudent use of material resources. Laying aside "her very self," and putting away "all personal feeling," the Christian woman should dedicate herself to making time "pass pleasantly and profitably for others." The charm—and indeed, the moral duty—of "the true English woman" is found in "diffusing happiness, without appearing conspicuously as the agent of its diffusion." E. did not advocate unlimited sacrifices for irresponsible husbands, but she did maintain that women's interests were best served by ministering to men.

E.'s work is fraught with contradiction. Women are said to constitute the "fabric of society," but they are rendered silent and invisible as their identities are submerged in others. E. believed that women should establish intimate bonds with one another through the shared suffering of their lives, but she instructed them to shape their education, conversation, and conduct to men's needs. The enormous popularity of *The Women of England* and its sequels indicates how well E. understood the needs of middle-class women to redefine their roles in a newly industrialized and very competitive society. Driven by religious zeal, some writers on women's influence would soon argue for rebellion and reform. But as the debate on the woman question evolved, E. remained loyal to existing social and economic structures, limiting her advice to "the minor morals of domestic life."

WORKS: *The Negro Slave* (1830?). *The Poetry of Life* (1835). *Pictures of Private Life* (1833–37). *Home; or, The Iron Rule* (1836). *Pretension* (1837). *The Women of England* (1839). *The Sow of the Soil* (1840). *Summer and Winter in the Pyrenees* (1841). *The Daughters of England* (1842). *Family Secrets* (1842). *The Mothers of England* (1843). *The Wives of England* (1843). *The Irish Girl and Other Poems* (1844). *Look at the End* (1845). *Temper and Temperament* (1846). *The Island Queen* (1846). *Prevention Better than Cure* (1847). *Social Distinction* (1848). *Fireside Tales for the Young* (1848). *Pique: A Tale of the English Aristocracy* (1850). *Family Pride* (185–?). *Self-Deception* (1851). *The Education of Character* (1856). *The Mother's Mistake* (1856). *Friends at Their Own Fireside; or, Pictures of the Private Life of the People Called Quakers* (1858). *The Mothers of Great Men* (1859). *The Widow Green and the Three Nieces*

(1859). *Janet: One of Many* (1862). *The Brewer's Family* (1863). *William and Mary* (1865). *Share and Share Alike* (1865). *The Beautiful in Nature and Art* (1866). *Northern Roses* (1868). *Education of the Heart* (1869). *The Brewer's Son* (1881).

BIBLIOGRAPHY: Colby, V. *Yesterday's Woman: Domestic Realism in the English Novel* (1974). Davidoff, L. and C. Hall. *Family Fortunes: Men and Women of the English Middle Class, 1780–1850* (1987). Langland, E. *Nobody's Angels: Middle-Class Women and Domestic Ideology in Victorian Culture* (1989). Shuttleworth, S., in *Rewriting the Victorians: Theory, History, and the Politics of Gender,* ed. L. M. Shires (1992). *The Home Life and Letters of Mrs. Ellis Compiled by Her Nieces* (1893).

For articles in reference works, see *Allibone. Boase. CBEL. DNB. Europa. Feminist. NCBEL. Oxford. VB.*

Robin Sheets

Una Mary Ellis-Fermor

BORN: 20 December 1894, London.
DIED: 24 March 1958, London.
DAUGHTER OF: Joseph Turnley Ellis-Fermor and Edith Mary Katherine Ellis-Fermor.
WROTE UNDER: U. M. Ellis-Fermor; Una Ellis-Fermor; Una Mary Ellis-Fermor; Christopher Turnley.

E., one of the most versatile literary critics of the writers of the English Renaissance, wrote the majority of her work during the 1930s and 1940s. Major contributions were her analysis of Christopher Marlowe's satanic overreachers, her analysis of the literary history of Jacobean drama, and her research on William Shakespeare's use of imagery and characterization. Her long writing career, beginning in 1927 with *Christopher Marlowe,* was honored in 1946 when she was invited to become general editor for *The Arden Shakespeare* editions of the plays, a role she filled until her death in 1958. Although E.'s criticism placed too much emphasis on characterization, especially in her discussions of Elizabethan and Jacobean drama, her contributions to the study of drama have not been sufficiently acknowledged. Few people are able to write about such a wide range of literary topics as Marlowe, Shakespeare, Henrik Ibsen, and the early twentieth-century Irish dramatic movement.

E. was so careful a scholar as to edit, meticulously, the 1930 edition of Marlowe's *Tamburlaine (Parts One and Two);* but she could also write theoretically in *The Frontiers of Drama* (1945), where she questions the generic limits of the drama's subject matter and type of conflict. She was also able to translate several of Ibsen's plays and to speculate, in *Masters of Reality* (1942), on the value of imagination in controlling one's life. She was a poet who wrote two collections, *Twenty-Two Poems* (1938) and *Sharpness of Death* (1939), under the pseudonym Christopher Turnley, a combination of Christopher Marlowe and Joseph Turnley Ellis-Fermor. Surprisingly, given all of her talent and achievements, few of the standard British or American reference works carry articles about her work. The reason her work was neglected is unclear, unless her emphasis on character as revealing the author's personality was already suspect when she was writing.

E. began her study of drama at Somerville College, Oxford, where she received the B. Litt. and M.A. degrees, and at the University of London where she received the D. Litt. Aside from a position at Manchester University, most of her career was spent at Bedford College, University of London, first as Reader in English Literature and, from 1947 until her death, as Hildred Carlile Professor of English. She spent several years in the United States, first as Rose Sidgwick Fellow at Yale and Columbia Universities (1922–23), then as a Fulbright scholar in 1951. She also received the Rose Mary Crawshay Prize for Literature in 1930.

In E.'s first work, *Christopher Marlowe* (1927), she attempts to trace the development of Marlowe's art as revealed in his surviving work and to draw some conclusions about his personality. She considers Marlowe's early translations, *Tamburlaine, Faustus, The Jew of Malta, The Massacre at Paris, Edward II,* and *Hero and Leander,* arguing that in most of his plays Marlowe was interested in large questions concerning the nature of man and his part in the universe. *Tamburlaine,* for example, embodies a vision of the power of the human will, and *Faustus* records the loss of harmony between a man's mind and the forces surrounding him. All of Marlowe's work, she concludes, investigates man's relationship not to other men but to God and the universe. She places perhaps too much emphasis on Marlowe's personality in determining his characters' ambitions.

One of E.'s lasting contributions is her in-depth study of the plays and lives of the major Jacobean dramatists. *The Jacobean Drama: An Interpretation* (1936) attempts to consider the outstanding plays during the years 1598 to 1625 that share literary and dramatic techniques. Her book treats Chapman, Marston, Jonson, Dekker, Middleton, Tourneur, Webster, Greville, Beaumont and Fletcher, and Ford. Writing in very general terms, E. argues that the mood of the drama during 1598 to 1625 passed through three phases: (1) worship of the vitality, the expansion and elation of the mind, (2) a sense of defeat, and (3) much apprehension in social and political life after Elizabeth's death—a sense of futility in man's achievements and a preoccupation with death.

With some trepidation, E. next investigates the drama, in *The Irish Dramatic Movement* (1939), of the early twentieth-century movement in Ireland begun by William Butler Yeats, Lady Gregory, John Millington Synge, and the group who supported and followed them at the Abbey Theatre. The book is, however, more concerned with Yeats than any other member of the movement. E.'s major interest in this drama was its ability, she argued, to bring back high poetry to English-language literature. She believed that poetic drama, which had been in decline since Jacobean times, was restored by the Irish Dramatic Movement to the living theater. The leaders' Irish revival was made in large terms; it was not limited to one country. For E., Yeats was the movement's fountainhead of poetic ideals.

Imagination became the pre-eminent human faculty for E. in her speculative *Masters of Reality* (1942). The book describes the functions of the imagination in the daily lives of the English people. She asserts that the use of the imagination, far from being an irresponsible escape, may be a determining factor for the survival of civilization itself. In England, she argues, there is an unfortunate valuation of the unimaginative and suppressed. Such habits of mind, when combined with over-reliance on machines, lead to passivity and fatalism, indifference and dullness. Beset by machines, we lose our capacity for wonder; our need for stimulation becomes more and more exaggerated.

In her only theoretical study, *The Frontiers of Drama* (1945), E. examines plays whose themes and subject matter defy common beliefs in what is appropriate for the theater. Although she believes that the drama imposes some inevitable limits, she is interested in the very few plays that manage to transcend these limitations. Attempts at religious drama have usually had disastrous results because religious emotion, what she calls "beatitude," is a condition free from conflict, upon which drama depends.

Shakespeare the Dramatist (1961) is a volume of E.'s critical essays. Kenneth Muir, who edited this collection and compiled a careful bibliography, believed that her work on Shakespeare was E.'s greatest contribution to literary criticism. She believed that the specifically dramatic qualities in Shakespeare's art were passion, thought, and a poetic imagination that "irradiates" the mind of the poet. Fullest expression of the drama comes from within the characters, and Shakespeare is able to speak from within all of his characters; his art is the most consistently dramatic of English dramatists.

Although some of E.'s observations about Shakespeare's characterization were familiar to her audience, she wrote intelligently and perceptively about the ways in which Shakespeare, and the other dramatists, presented characters to the audience. Her greatest contribution as a literary critic was her work on drama, especially her two excellent introductory guides, one to the Jacobean plays and another to the Irish Dramatic Movement.

WORKS: *Christopher Marlowe* (1927). *The Jacobean Drama: An Interpretation* (1936; 2nd ed., 1947; 3rd ed., 1953; 4th ed., 1958). *Some Recent Research on Shakespeare's Imagery* (1937). (as Christopher Turnley) *Twenty-Two Poems* (1938). *The Irish Dramatic Movement* (1939; 2nd ed., 1954). (as Christopher Turnley) *Sharpness of Death* (1939). *Masters of Reality* (1942). *The Frontiers of Drama* (1945; 2nd ed., 1946; 3rd ed., 1948). *The Study of Shakespeare* (1948). (trans.) *Three Plays*, by H. Ibsen (1950). (trans.) *The Master Builder and Other Plays*, by H. Ibsen (1958). *Shakespeare the Dramatist and Other Papers*, ed. K. Muir (1961).

BIBLIOGRAPHY: Muir, K. *A Select List of the Published Writings of Una Ellis-Fermor*, in *Shakespeare the Dramatist and Other Papers*, ed. K. Muir (1961).

For articles in reference works, see: *Biography Master Index. NCBEL. NCHEL. Who Was Who. WWWAEEA.*

Other references: *Books and Bookmen* (August 1965). *British Book News* (October 1981). *Choice* (March 1965, April 1968). *Observer* (30 July 1967). *RenQ* (1975). *Reprint Bulletin Book Reviews* (1978). *Saturday Review* (1982). *Spectator* (9 October 1965). *TLS* (30 December 1965).

Laura Niesen de Abruña

Eloise: See *Boyd, Elizabeth*

Elizabeth Elstob

BORN: September 1683, Newcastle-on-Tyne, Northumberland.
DIED: 30 May 1756, Bulstrode.
DAUGHTER OF: Ralph Elstob and Jane Elstob.

E. is the first (known) female scholar of Anglo-Saxon. Her father, a merchant in Newcastle, died when she was three; her mother, whom E. herself described as "a great admirer of learning, especially in her own sex," began to teach her daughter Latin, but she died when E. was eight. We do not know precisely how the "Anglo-Saxon nymph," as she was dubbed in her own day, subsequently acquired her remarkable learning. After her mother's death she was raised by an uncle, a Prebendary of Canterbury, who like most men of his time objected to the education of women. Her brother William was a student and later Fellow of University College, Oxford; biographers speculate that E. may have joined him at Oxford, and in fact one tradition has it that she was the "first home student" there. In any case, she was certainly her brother's companion in London from 1702 (when E. was nineteen) until the time of his death in 1715. William presumably trained E. in Anglo-Saxon at some point, and her scholarly writings all date from the latter half of her days in London (1708–15).

E.'s first work was an anonymous translation of Mlle. de Scudery's *Essay Upon Glory.* A year later (1709) she published her first work in Anglo-Saxon, an edition of an Old English sermon, titled in full *An English-Saxon Homily on the Birthday of St. Gregory: Anciently Used in the English-Saxon Church. Giving an Account of the Conversion of the English from Paganism to Christianity.* In a lengthy preface to this pioneering edition, E. defends both her right as a woman to learning and the importance of her subject matter (which was at the time often ridiculed as too arcane), as well as its theological interest. Despite criticism of her work—or more likely of its apparatus—as a "Farrago of Vanity," E.'s edition was apparently well enough received to encourage her to plan the publication of a "Saxon homilarium," a much larger project including most of Aelfric's sermons. In the early eighteenth century, scholarly editions of this sort were funded by subscribers, and E. published preliminary plans and appeals for subscription in pamphlet form in 1713. The Homilarium, however, was never completed, though proofs of the first few pages survive in the British Museum. In 1715, E.'s final scholarly publication appeared, the first grammar of Old English written in modern English, entitled *The Rudiments of Grammar for the English-Saxon Tongue.* Modern readers will again be interested, as in the case of the *English-Saxon Homily,* in E.'s discursive notes and in the Preface, which is noteworthy for two reasons. First, E. explicitly addresses her work to a female audience. She says that she was motivated to write the text after meeting with an unnamed "young lady" in Canterbury who wanted to become her pupil and that she writes her grammar "considering the

Pleasure I myself had reaped from the Knowledge I have gained from this Original of our Mother Tongue, and that others of my own Sex might be capable of the same Satisfaction." Second, E. defends the validity of Anglo-Saxon studies, this time attacking, among other detractors, Jonathan Swift, whose *Proposal for Correcting, Improving, and Ascertaining the English Tongue* criticizes English for its tendency to become monosyllabic and disparages the study of the language's history and development. E.'s defense of her philological work against "Pedagogues who huff and swagger in the height of their arrogance" has been called by one modern scholar "a bravura display of vast learning and wide reading."

In the same year in which E.'s grammar was published, personal disaster struck, and the precariousness of the female scholar's career becomes evident. E.'s brother William died, and so did her most important scholarly supporter, George Hickes. For almost two decades afterwards, E. virtually disappears from the record. There is some evidence that she remained in London for two or three years after her brother's death, attempting to carry on her work and publish her Homilarium; then, to avoid debtor's prison, she was forced to leave the city, perhaps heading north, changing her name, and becoming a domestic servant. She re-emerges in the 1730s as a careworn schoolmistress in Evesham. With the help of a few friends (including Mary Pendarves Delany, who was Swift's friend and later Fanny Burney's patroness), the unsuitability of E.'s position was finally brought to the attention of Queen Caroline, who intended to patronize E. but died in 1737. After various trials and failures, E. became a governess in 1739 in the house of the Duchess of Portland, where she remained until her death in 1756.

In 1738, at the request of her friend George Ballard, tailor and author of *Memoirs of Learned Ladies* (1752), E. wrote a brief, still unpublished memoir. Through the efforts of Ballard and a few others, she was not completely forgotten by antiquarians and scholars in her own day, but her work as governess for seventeen years afforded her no more scope and time for renewed scholarly activities than did the years in which she vanished from society. She appears to have been fond and proud of her noble young pupils but told friends that "my acquaintance and interest is reduced to a very narrow compass." She wrote to Ballard, advising him against the notion of compiling a book about female scholars, "For you can come into no company of Ladies and Gentlemen where you shall not hear an open and vehement exclamation against Learned Women, and by those women who read much themselves, to what purposes they know best." One material reminder of E.'s career survives: Oxford University Press still owns punches and matrices of an Anglo Saxon type known as the "Elstob" font, presumably used in the printing of her English-Saxon Grammar.

WORKS: (trans.) *Essay upon Glory,* by Mlle. de Scudery (1708). *An English-Saxon Homily on the Birthday of St. Gregory: Anciently Used in the English-Saxon Church. Giving an Account of the Conversion of the English from Paganism to Christianity.*(1709). *Some Testimonies of Learned Men, in Favour of the Intended Edition of the Saxon Homilies* (1713). *The Rudiments of Grammar for the English-Saxon Tongue* (1715; facsimile ed., 1968).

BIBLIOGRAPHY: Collins, S. H., in *Anglo-Saxon Scholarship: The First Three Centuries,* ed. C. T. Berkhout and M. Gatch (1982). Delany, M. *Autobiography and Correspondence* (1861–62). E.'s memoirs in Ballard MSS., Bodleian Library). Hearne, T. *Remarks and Collections* (1885–1921). Hughes, S. F. D., in *Anglo-Saxon Scholarship: The First Three Centuries,* ed. C. T. Berkhout and M. Gatch (1982). "Memoirs of the Learned Saxonists Mr. Wm. Elstob and His Sister," in *Bibliotheca Topographica Britannica,* ed. J. Nichols (1790). Morton, R. *SECC* (1990). Thoresby, R. *Diary and Correspondence* (1832).

For articles in reference works, see: *Bloomsbury. Feminist. Oxford. ToddBWW.*

Other references: Ashdown, M. *MLR* (1925). Green, M. E. in *Female Scholars: A Tradition of Learned Women Before 1800,* ed. J. R. Brink (1980). Morton, R. *SECC* (1990). Reynolds, M. *The Learned Lady in England, 1650–1750* (1920). Wallas, A. *Before the Bluestockings* (1929).

Elaine Tuttle Hansen

E. L. V.: See *Voynich, Ethel Lilian Boole*

E. M. D.: See *Delafield, E. M.*

(Florence Onye) Buchi Emecheta

BORN: 21 July 1944, Yaba, Nigeria.
DAUGHTER OF: Jeremy Nwabudike Emecheta and Alice Okwuekwu Emecheta.
MARRIED: Sylvester Onwordi, 1960.

E., a Nigerian immigrant now residing in London, is a complete storyteller, having learned this art at her aunt's knee as she told stories nightly to all the village children. E., because of her schooling and immigration to England, wrote her stories down and has become a prolific writer with fourteen novels, an autobiography, and several children's stories and television plays.

E., born in Yaba, a small village near Lagos, was orphaned as a young child. Her need for independence asserted itself early, as she insisted on being educated at a missionary high school until she was sixteen, at which time she married Sylvester Onwordi to whom she had been betrothed since she was eleven. In 1962, at the age of eighteen, with two children, E. emigrated to England with her husband, a student. After giving birth to three more children and after suffering physical and emotional abuse from her husband, culminating in his burning of her first manuscript, she separated from him in 1966. She supported herself and her five children on public assistance and from scrubbing floors. Later, she became a librarian at the British Museum and a teacher, and she earned an honors degree in sociology, all the time writing her stories early in the morning before the children were awake.

She tells of this time in her autobiographical *Head above Water,* written in 1986, but more poignantly and simply in her first semi-autobiographical novels, *In the Ditch* (1972) and *Second-Class Citizen* (1974). *In the Ditch,* originally a series of columns in the *New Statesman,* finds the heroine, Adah, living in the Pussy Cat Mansions, a council housing estate for problem families (on the dole, often African or West Indian, and usually single mothers). *Second-Class Citizen* speaks of Adah's emigration to London and her oppression because of sex, race, and class but especially the sexual discrimination she experiences in her marriage.

Though not reviewed much at the time, these books have been extensively critiqued and praised as her most accomplished books. A critic, R. Bray, states: "Both books are simply told, bearing the mark of painful authenticity even before you know they're autobiographical. She wrote them to rid herself of rage at a society and a man who could not accept her independent spirit."

Her autobiography, *Head above Water,* continues E.'s story as a single parent, getting a degree in sociology, publishing her first books, buying a house, and becoming a full-time writer. It also describes one of her jobs as a social worker with black teenagers, thus exploring social conditions in London.

The Bride Price (1976) is set in Lagos and Ibuza in the 1950s and is concerned with victims of caste structure. Aku-nna falls in love and runs away with her schoolteacher, a descendant of slaves who should not marry her, a freeborn and wealthy woman. She dies in childbirth because her bride price was not paid.

The Slave Girl (1977), next in a series of novels about women in Nigeria, ia again historical as Objeta is sold into slavery when her parents die in the 1918 influenza epidemic. She enters the modern world and becomes a Christian and literate. She is freed to marry an educated man but in essence belongs to him now, the caste of marriage. E. won the Jock Campbell Award for literature after her first three books in 1978 and was also selected Best Black British Writer in the same year.

The Joys of Motherhood (1979) is probably E.'s best-known and loved book. Again it is set in historical Nigeria from the 1930s to just before independence. The many social, economic, and political changes greatly affect the women who struggle to survive poverty and cultural taboos. Nnu Ego must also contend with losing her status as wife when a second wife is brought in. Writing about these Nigerian novels, Bray acknowledges that "Between the rock of African traditions and the hard place of encroaching Western values, it is the women who will be caught."

Destination Biafra (1982) was published to mixed reviews as E. tried to take on a larger topic, that of the Nigerian Civil War. In her descriptions of the war's impact on the people, particularly the killing of civilians, she is, however, most convincing.

E. lectured at various universities in the United States, England, and Nigeria from 1972 through 1982 and then began to run the Ogwugwu Afor Publishing Company. With branches in London and Ibuza, Nigeria, this company published her next books, *Double Yoke* (1982), the story of Nko, a university student and wife who is forced to prostitute herself to her professor to get her degree, and the *Rape of Shavi* (1983), which was called "an allegory about the relationship between Europe and Africa" in the *Dictionary of Literary Biography.* A group of Englishmen flee a nuclear attack and crash in a desert, where the Shavian people live a simple life herding cattle. Their society is ultimately devastated by the greed of Western civilization. In 1983, after these books were published, E. was selected as one of the Best British Young Writers.

E.'s latest novels, *Gwendolen* (1989) and *Kehinde* (1994), return to London locales. In *Gwendolen* the theme is incest and the blaming of an innocent child. Kehinde, however, seems to have more power but does not use it until she refuses to accept second-class status (second to her husband's new wife in Nigeria), and returns to London to complete her education. As she says, "Claiming my right does not make me less of a mother, not less of a woman. If anything it makes me more human."

E. has also written children's books with the help of her daughters, Alice and Christy. In fact, *Head above Water* is dedicated to her daughter Chiedu (Christy), who died in 1984. E. has also put some of her London experiences into television plays such as *A Kind of Marriage, The Juju Landlord, Family Bargain,* and *Tanya, A Black Woman.*

Critics seem to be drawn to her novels and debate endlessly her critique of African culture and her feminism. She is seen sometimes as being a traitor to her culture by misrepresenting Igbo society, although she has said that "The main themes of my novels are African society and family. I always try to show that the African male is oppressed and he too oppresses the African women." On the other hand, though she refuses to be called a feminist, her feminism shows in all her stories since a woman is always at the center. Whether in London or in Nigeria, this woman is fighting to survive, fighting for her independence, for her children in these African and English cultures that put the needs of men first. E. always insists on "education and middle-class values as means of female emancipation." The *Dictionary of Literary Biography* emphasizes that E. "represents a new and vigorous departure in fiction about women in and from Africa." As E. says, "Women are born storytellers. We keep the history."

WORKS: *In the Ditch* (1972). *Second-Class Citizen* (1974). *The Bride Price* (1976). *The Slave Girl* (1977). *Titch the Cat* (1979). *The Joys of Motherhood* (1979). *Nowhere to Play* (1980). *The Moonlight Bride* (1980). *The Wrestling Match* (1980). *Our Own Freedom* (1981; photographs by M. Murray, intro. and comments by E.). *Naira Power* (1982). *Double Yoke* (1982). *Destination Biafra* (1982). *Adah's Story* (1983). *The Rape of Shavi* (1983). *Head above Water* (1986). *A Kind of Marriage* (1986; produced 1987). *Family Bargain* (produced 1987). *Gwendolen* (1989). *Kehinde* (1994). *The Juju Landlord. Tanya, A Black Woman.*

BIBLIOGRAPHY: Allan, T. J. *Womanist and Feminist Aesthetics* (1995). Barthelemy, A. *Callaloo* (Summer 1989). Bruner, C. *AfrSR* (1986). Davis, C. *CE&S* (1990). Fishburn, K. *Reading Buchi Emecheta: Cross-Cultural Conversations* (1995). Frank, K. *WLWE* (1982). Palmer, E. *ALT* (1983). Sougou, O. *Crisis and Creativity in the New Literatures in English: Cross/Cultures* (1990). Taiwo, O. *Female Novelists of Modern Africa* (1984).

Umeh, M. *Ngambika: Studies of Women in African Literatures* (1986).

For articles in reference works, see: *CA. CLC. DLB. BW.*

Other references: Andrade, S. *RAL* (Spring 1990). Bazin, N. T. *The Tragic Life: Bessie Head and Literature in Southern Africa* (1990). Bazin, N. T. *Black Scholar* (May-July 1989). Birch, E. L. *Black Women's Writing* (1993). Bray, R. *VLS* (June 1982). Brown, L. W. *Women Writers in Black Africa* (1981). Christian, B. *Black Feminist Criticism* (1985). Cosslett, T. *WS* (1991). Dooley, T. *TLS* (20 April 1990). Emenyonu, E. N. *JCL* (1988). Ezenwa, O. *CE&S* (Autumn 1990). Gardner, S. *WRB* (November 1994). Haraway, D. *Inscriptions* (1980). Hunter, E. *ESA* (1987). Katrak, K. H. *JCL* (1987). Kemp, Y. *Obsidian II* (Winter 1988). King, B. *The British and Irish Novel Since 1960* (1991). Mason, D. *HudR* (Winter 1992). McKnight, R. *NYTBR* (29 April 1990). Newman, J. *CollL* (February 1995). Nwankwo, C. *Ufahamu* (1988). Osborne, L. B. *BW* (25 September 1983). Palmer, E *NLitsR.* (November 1982). Phillips, M. *R&L* (Winter 1994). Porter, A. M. *IFR* (Summer 1988). Ravell-Pinto, T. *SAGE* (Spring 1985). Sandmann, A. L. *CE* (March 1993). Solberg, R. *ES* (1983). Topouzis, D. *AfricaR* (May-June 1990). Umeh, D. and M. Umeh *BaShiru: A Journal of African Languages and Literature* (1985). Updike, J. *New Yorker* (23 April 1984). Walker, A. *Ms.* (January 1976). Ward, C. *PMLA* (January 1990).

Jacquelyn Marie

Ephelia

FLOURISHED: c. 1660s–early 1680s, London.
WROTE UNDER: Ephelia; A Gentlewoman (in 1678).

E., a poet-playwright-songwriter of Restoration London, is a famous and reputedly impenetrable case in the annals of English pseudonyms. Persistent interest in this intriguing figure centers on her concealed authorship, saucy feminism, and powerful connections to the Stuart court. While there has been a longstanding inquiry into the E. subject dating from the seventeenth century, the closing decades of the twentieth century have witnessed a resurgence of critical activity, culminating in a first scholarly edition, critical reassessments, and graduate theses, and the inclusion of E. in course syllabi and new reference works and anthologies on early women writers.

E.'s problematic identity has excited continuing scholarly debate on the attribution and authenticity of her work. To date, hypotheses consist of delicate shards of circumstantial and internal evidence. Research on E.'s authorship has produced a thicket of multiple traditions: (1) E. is an utterly invented poet and hoax, constructed by Sir George Etherege and a playful cabal of Restoration writers (Ebsworth, 1883; Greer, 1989, 1993); (2) E. is one Joan Phillips (Wheatley, *Dict.*, 1885), the traditional, though undocumented, attribution, which Edmund Gosse in 1897 glossed incorrectly as a daughter of poet Katherine Philips; (3) E. "both is and is not Cary Frazier, Countess of Peterborough" (Greer, 1989); (4) E. "could have been Anne Phillips Proud (Prowde) of the Proud-Milton-Phillips line, an attractive speculative candidate" (Mulvihill, 1992); (5) E. exists principally as a voice within the poetry, as artifice and persona (Chernaik 1995); (6) E. may have been courtesan Elizabeth ("Betty") Felton (Hardman, 1996); and, the most forceful candidate to date, (7) E. appears to have been Mary ("Mall") (Stuart *née* Villiers), Duchess of Richmond and Lennox (1622–85), the *grande dame* and "Butterfly" of the Restoration court ("by making herself the dedicatee of her own book, clever Lady Villiers hid in plain sight and also executed the genius stroke that assured her pseudonymity and kept researchers fumbling these three centuries" (Mulvihill, *Restoration*, 1995; Mulvihill, *ANQ*, 1996).

E.'s present canon (sixty-eight verses) displays a rich variety of poetry: political broadside, elegy, verse-essay, verse-epistle, satiric verse-drama, female complaint, song, and acrostic. The lyric dominates her *oeuvre,* and E.'s characteristic form is the heroic couplet. Her acknowledged literary models, in her collection *Female Poems . . . by Ephelia* (1679, 1682), are Abraham Cowley, John Dryden, Katherine Philips, and Aphra Behn. Other influences are Sir Philip Sidney, John Donne, and, possibly, Louis Labé of Lyons. E. exercises her muse in several poetic traditions (Petrarchan, Ovidian, Cavalier, modified libertine, *précieuse*), and she marks occasions public and private. Her amatory lyrics display impressive poetic range and emotional complexity, the best being Ovidian love-epistles (or complaints) to deceitful lovers. She also produces coterie verse to selected individuals of the Restoration court. Settings of her amorous and pastoral songs, by court composers Thomas Farmer, Moses Snow, and William Turner, appeared in contemporary song books published by the Playfords. In the current century, one of her best lyrics, "To One That Ask'd Me Why I Lov'd *J. G.*," was set by Cecil Armstrong Gibbs of the Royal College of Music. E. is also a thinking poet. Her longest poem, "Wealth's Power" (eighty-two lines), is an important early verse-essay on cultural materialism, and her rousing broadsides of 1678 and 1681 address volatile affairs of state and identify E. as a passionate royalist. Yet the Stuarts could stir her satiric temper, as in E.'s play, "The Pair-Royal of Coxcombs," probably a burlesque-farce against King Charles II and his brother, James, Duke of York. Finally, she leaves us some juvenilia, four acrostics to women friends. Researchers who hear an authentic female voice in E.'s work (Hobby, Mulvihill, Page, Williamson, and others) point to a continuity in the poems' voice, *ethos,* thematic material, grammar, syntax, and poetic habits (imagery, rhyme-words).

E. makes important contributions to Restoration poetry and to developing traditions of women's literature. Her political broadsides of 1678 and 1681 serve as an early and rare instance of a woman writer's public engagement with serious state affairs. "On Wealth" (*Female Poems,* 1679) is distinctive as an early model of a woman writer's attempt in the philosophical verse-essay; and this lengthy piece serves as possible parent-text of Anne Killigrew's "Invective Against Gold" (*Poems,* 1686) and sections of Sarah Egerton's "Extacy" (*Poems,* 1703). E.'s play, "The Pair-Royal of Coxcombs," judiciously excerpted in *Female Poems* and "damn'd" by critics according to its Epilogue, raises useful questions of writerly protocols, censorship, and royalist satire. Her elegant octavo, *Female Poems . . . by Ephelia,* doubtless a small printing in view of its rarity, is the first secular pseudonymous poetic collection by an English woman writer; with the single exception of Lady Mary Wroth's (suppressed) *Urania* (1621), E.'s is the first collection of verse in English produced from an explicitly "female" perspective, as its title boldly asserts. But chief among E.'s contributions is her work in lyric. E.'s "female poems" valuably reaffirm the lyric strain in English poetry at a time when the national literature was dominated by political, antifeminist, and cynical material. Her best work reconstructs obsessive states of unrequited love. The textural quality and tension in her amorous poems, resulting from the interplay of memory, desire, and feminist pride, are expertly managed in the large "*J. G.*" cluster in *Female Poems,* and masterfully so in her signature poem to "*Bajazet*" (familiarly, "*Ephelia's* Lamentation"), occasioned by the "Mall" Kirke–Lord Mulgrave scandal of 1675. This famous lyric, a ventriloquial *tour de force,* depicts the E. poet doubly masked as she assumes the persona of an abandoned mistress addressing a deceitful lover. The "Lamentation," which circulated in manuscript c. 1677 ("Wit & Learning . . . , 1677," Beinecke Library), is a classic reconstruction on the Ovidian model of a *naif*'s initiation in duplicitous love. It begins with the well-turned question, "How far are they deceiv'd, that hope in vain / A lasting Lease of Joys from Love t' obtain?" Its longstanding attribution to Etherege has been vigorously contested (Mulvihill, *ANQ,* 1996). John (Wilmot), Earl of Rochester's prompt reply to E.'s poem was an immediate success, and the two poems were published together as companion pieces in poetry collections for the next two centuries. Finally, much of E.'s coterie and romantic verse challenges the libertine and misogynistic vogues of the day by showing that it is man, not woman, who is unfaithful in love. In fact, by Restoration standards, E. is rather prudish. Her poem "Maidenhead" in *Female Poems* is unfinished because she cannot sustain a libertine persona; E. unfashionably respects monogamy and marriage, as in "To a Lady who [tho Married] . . . ," and "To a Gentleman that had left a Vertuous Lady. . . . " When she hears of "*J. G.*"'s marriage to a younger woman in Tangier, E. accepts his new status and promptly removes the cad from her roster.

A clash of cultures animates E.'s best work. Her concern with proper deportment between the sexes, in "To *Coridon,* on shutting his Door . . ." and "To One That Affronted the Excellent *Eugenia,*" suggests a morality of an earlier time. E.'s is often the scolding voice of a genteel dowager, especially in her railing rimes to boorish gallants, dishonest suitors, and sneering critics. She holds contemporaries to a higher aristocratic code of conduct than she observes at the decadent court of Charles II. Her obvious familiarity with Sidney, Donne, and Cowley, as well as with Cavalier and *précieuse* verse (not to mention her acrostics and old-fashioned phrasing), date E. to the more refined culture of the pre-Restoration Stuarts.

WORKS: *A Poem To His Sacred Majesty. On The Plot. Written by a Gentlewoman* (licensed broadside, 1678). *Female Poems On Several Occasions. Written by Ephelia* (octavo, 1679; eleven known extant copies; reprints, with significant titular variant, the anonymous broadside. of 1678). *The Pair-Royal of Coxcombs* (c. 1679), a lost play, four selections in *Female Poems. Advice To His Grace (Monmouth), signed Ephelia* (broadside., c. 1681). "A funerall Elegy on Sir Thomas Isham Barronet," signed Ephelia (c. August 1681) (Portland MS. PwV 336, Nottingham), a working draft with marginal brackets, catchword, authorial revision, and armorial watermark (cf. Heawood 821). *Female Poems . . . by Ephelia. The Second Edition, With Large Additions* (1682) (text of first ed. and thirty new poems, by Rochester, Lady Rochester, Dryden, Philips, Behn, Scroope, D'Urfey, Lee, et al.). Modern edition: *Poems by Ephelia, Circa 1679. The Premier Facsimile Edition of the Collected Manuscript and Published Poems. With a Critical Essay and Apparatus,* ed. M. E. Mulvihill (1992, 1993). Anthologies with selections: *Tixall Poetry,* ed. A. Clifford (1813). *Prologues & Epilogues,* ed. P. Danchin (1978). *Roxburghe Ballads IV,* ed. J. W. Ebsworth (1883). *Seventeenth-Century Verse,* ed. A. Fowler (1991). *British Women Poets,* ed. J. Fullard (1990). *Whole Duty of a Woman,* ed. A. Goreau (1984). *Kissing the Rod: An Anthology of Seventeenth-Century Women's Verse,* ed. G. Greer et al. (1988). *Penguin Book of Restoration Verse,* ed. H. Love (1997). *Rare Poems of the Seventeenth Century,* ed. L. B. Marshall (1936). *Poems On Several Occasions,* compiled and contrib., John (Wilmot), Earl of Rochester, et al. (1680). *New Meridian Anthology,* ed. K. Rogers and W. McCarthy (1987). *Cavalier Poets,* ed. R. Skelton (1970). *Women Poets,* ed. A. Stanford (1972). *Triumph of Wit* (1688, 1692, 1707). "Wit and Learning . . . 1677" (MS. collection, Beinecke Library, Yale University).

BIBLIOGRAPHY: Barash, C. *English Women's Poetry* (1996). Burghclere, W. *Villiers* (1903). D'Aulnoy, M. *Memoires* (1695). Gosse, E. *Seventeenth-Century Studies* (1885). Greer, G. *Behn* (1989). G. Greer *TLS* (25 June 1993). Hardman, S. J. *Sir Anthony Van Dyck's Portraits of Lady Mary Villiers* (1976). Hardman, S. J. *Lord Poulett's Paintings in Georgia* (1978). Hobby, E. *A Virtue of Necessity* (1988). Kerrigan, J. *Motives of Woe* (1991). Lipking, L. *Abandoned Women & Poetic Tradition* (1988). Page, J. A. *Fashioning an Identity of the Libertine Woman in "Female Peoms . . . by Ephelia"* (1995). Rahir, E. *Elzevier* (1896) (*cf.* fleuron no. 203 with t.p. device of *Female Poems,* 1679). Rothstein, E. *Restoration & Eighteenth-Century Poetry* (1981). Thorpe, J. *Rochester* (1950). *Etherege,* ed. J. Thorpe (1963). Vieth, D. M. *Attribution in Restoration Poetry* (1963). Wheatley, H. B., in *Dict. Anon. and Pseud. Eng. Lit.,* ed. Halkett and Laing (1885). Williamson, M. *Raising Their Voices* (1990).

For articles in reference works, see: *Feminist.* Reynolds, M. *The Learned Lady in England, 1650–1760* (1920). *ToddBWW. ToddDBA.*

Other references: Barber, G. G. *BJRL* (1985). Chernaik, W. *PQ* (1995). Heller, J. R. *Belles Lettres* (1996). John, G. *Fortnightly* (1920). Lamoine, G. *EA* (1996). Milhous, J. and R. Hume. *HLB* (1977; lists E.'s "lost" play). Mulvihill, M. E. *ANQ* (1996). Mulvihill, M. E. *Restoration* (1987; 1995; 1997). Mulvihill, M. E. *Scriblerian* (1989). Mulvihill, M. E. *SECC* (1992). Mulvihill, M. E. *TLS* (3 September 1993). Mulvihill, M. E.

Women's Writing (1995). Page, J. A. *Texture Press* (1992). Schneller, B. E. *Eighteenth Century: A Current Bibliography* (forthcoming). Skerpan, E. P. *Quarterly Journal of Ideology* (1994). Wilson, K. *ANQ* (1997). Grolier Club, New York. *Engraved Portraits of Women Writers, Sappho to George Eliot* (exhibition catalogue, 1895; "Ephelia" frontis., exhibit 259). *Female Poems . . . by Ephelia* was exhibited at The Grolier Club, New York, in 1895, and at The Small Press Center, New York, in 1994.

Maureen E. Mulvihill

Eusebia: See *Hays, Mary*

Evans, Mary Ann: See *Eliot, George*

Mary Evelyn

BORN: 1 October 1665, Wotton, Surrey.
DIED: March 1685, Deptford, Wiltshire.
DAUGHTER OF: John Evelyn and Mary Brown Evelyn.

Although she died of smallpox when only nineteen years old, E. is recognized as a literary figure because of her father. After his daughter's death, Sir John Evelyn, the royalist diarist, found among her effects manuscripts of poems, prayers, and personal letters. Five years later, in 1690, he published anonymously her poem *Mundus Muliebris,* a burlesque of the "women's world." He included with it a preface and a fop-dictionary of terms peculiar to the late seventeenth century's world of feminine fashion along with an antifeminist warning:

Whoever has a mind to abundance of trouble.
Let him furnish himself with a Ship and a Woman.
For no two things will find you more Employment.
If once you begin to rig them out with all their Streamers.

Some have suggested that the preface and dictionary may have been written by Evelyn himself, not E. In either case, the work was reprinted three times that year and again in 1790. Since then the poem has been reprinted frequently and is often included in volumes of his work. More recently, two facsimile editions have been published, one of the first edition by the Toucan Press in 1978 and the other of the second edition by the Costume Society in 1977.

Like other bright young women of her day, E. was curious and educated herself beyond the usual limits afforded women. In her father's library, she studied French, Italian, music, history, and poetry, both ancient and modern. Perhaps because of her father's wish that she model herself on Margaret Godolphin, for whom he had written a hagiographic memorial on her death at the age of twenty-five in 1678, E. apparently followed his rules of conduct and his wish that she dedicate her time to religious devotion. Noted for her charm and conversational gifts, E. spent one summer with the court at Windsor.

A delightful satire, *Mundus Mulliebris* displays E.'s maturity and her lethal powers of observation. In hudibrastic couplets, she confidently examines the woman and her toilette:

Behind the Noddle every Baggage
Wears bundle *Choux,* in *English* Cabbage . . .
All which with *Meurtriers* unite.
And *Creve-Coeurs* silly Fops to smite,
Or take in Toil at *Park* or *Play.*
Nor Holy *Church* is safe, they say,
Where decent Veil was wont to hide
The modest Sex Religious Pride . . .

No detail is too small just as no cosmetic is too slight to women in the world E. describes. Along with the toilette, the poem satirizes women's vanity and criticizes their superficial reading, theatergoing, and modes of entertainment. The rollicking mock-heroic poem testifies to E.'s wit, her interest in music, and her conservative outlook.

Most of the manuscripts of E.'s work may be found at Christ Church, Oxford, including "Rules for Spending my Pretious Tyme Well." Some of her letters are in Oxford, and others are held by the British Museum in its manuscript collection.

WORKS: *Mundus Muliebris, or, The Ladies Dressing-Room Unlock'd, and Her Toilets Spread. In Burlesque. Together with the Fop-Dictionary, compiled for the Use of the Fair Sex* (1690; reissued as *The Ladies Dressing-Room Unlock'd, and Her Toilette Spread Together, with a Fop-Dictionary and a Rare and Incomparable Receipt to Make Pig, or Puppidog-Water for the Face,* 1700).

BIBLIOGRAPHY:

For articles in reference works, see: *Bell. BGEL. Feminist. ToddBWW.*

Sophia B. Blaydes

Everett, Mary Anne: See *Green, Mary Anne Everett Wood*

Juliana Horatia Ewing

BORN: 3 August 1841, Ecclesfield, Yorkshire.
DIED: 13 May 1885, Bath, Somerset.
DAUGHTER OF: the Reverend Alfred Gatty and Margaret Gatty.
MARRIED: Major Alexander Ewing, 1867.
WROTE UNDER: Juliana Horatia Ewing; J. H. Ewing; J. H. G.

A storyteller, poet, and illustrator, E. is best known for the stories she wrote for children. Eldest daughter of the noted children's author Margaret Gatty, E. began her storytelling career entertaining her younger siblings in the nursery. Her first published story, "A Bit of Green," appeared in July 1861 in Charlotte Yonge's *Monthly Packet.* When Mrs. Gatty launched *Aunt Judy's Magazine* in 1866, E. began contributing stories to that magazine and took over as editor with her sister after their mother's death in 1873. Nearly all of E.'s stories were published first in *Aunt Judy's* before being collected into separate volumes.

In 1867, E. married Major Alexander Ewing and traveled with him to New Brunswick, Canada. The couple returned to England in 1869, living subsequently in Aldershot (Hampshire), Manchester, York, and Taunton (Somerset). E. often accompanied her husband on temporary overseas assignments until her health deteriorated and she died prematurely of cancer in 1885. Many of E.'s letters have been published since her death, including those she wrote when she and her husband were stationed overseas. She wrote that she liked the works of Sir Walter Scott and especially William Shakespeare, but she did not fully admire important Victorian writers. She found Charles Dickens and Henry James imperfect writers although interesting, and she criticized George Eliot for her limited imagination and unnatural characters.

During her married life, E. continued to write as a pastime and to pay off debts. *Mrs. Overtheway's Remembrances* (1869) is a charming collection of stories about daily family life from a child's perspective. E.'s best-known works include *Jackanapes* (1884), *The Story of a Short Life* (1884), and *The Brownies and Other Tales* (1870). This latter colletion, with original illustrations by George Cruikshank, is best remembered for providing the name for the junior section of the Girl Guide Movement. "Jackanapes," illustrated by Randolph Caldecott, tells the story of a young soldier who sacrifices his own life to save a friend. Similarly, "The Story of a Short Life" describes a dying boy's last days that he chooses to spend among soldiers. The story emphasizes the importance of patriotism even in the face of death. Many of E.'s stories draw on her memories of childhood and her overseas military life. E. preferred to write stories with an explicit moral and believed modern fairy tales should reflect the oral tradition of older fairy tales. To this end, "The Brownies" and "Amelia and the Dwarfs" are moralistic tales with a character who acts as storyteller. One of the keys to E.'s popularity among young readers was her ability to write with the voice and perspective of a child while still addressing serious themes.

E.'s best-known stories include "The Story of a Short Life" and "Jackanapes," but the former is too rambling and saccharine for modern tastes. Because the tone and structure of "Jackanapes" are more controlled, it is a better work of art. As E. stated in the conclusion of "Jackanapes," the hero shows the importance of patriotism. To the modern reader, the moral is less interesting than the characterization of Jackanapes, an impish orphan, who grows up to face death fearlessly.

Though E.'s style today seems sometimes unduly religious, patriotic, and saccharine, she remains an important figure in the history of children's literature as one of the earliest authors to break for the traditional didacticism characteristic of that genre to evoke a less sentimental realism about the world of the young. Where E.'s stories contain a strong social or moral comment, she weaves this message skillfully into the plot and lightens it with humor. A popular writer in her day, E. was a favorite of such contemporaries as children's author Edith Nesbit and the younger Rudyard Kipling.

WORKS: *Melchior's Dream and Other Tales* (1862). *Mrs. Overtheway's Remembrances* (1869). *The Brownies and Other Tales* (1870). *Lob Lie-by-the Fire* (1874). *A Very Ill-Tempered Family* (1874–75). *Six to Sixteen* (1876). *Jan of the Windmill* (1876). *Master Fritz* (188–?). *Old-Fashioned Fairy Tales* (188–?). *A Flat Iron for a Earthing* (1880). *We and the World* (1880). *Brothers of Pity* (1882). *Blue and Red* (1883). *A Week Spent in a Glass Pond* (1883). *A Soldier's Children* (1883). *The Blue Bells on the Lea* (1884). *Daddy Darwin's Dovecot* (1884). *Jackanapes* (1884). *The Story of a Short Life* (1884). *Dandelion Clocks and Other Tales* (1887). *The Peace Egg and a Christmas Mumming* (1887). *Mother's Birthday Review and Seven Other Tales in Verse* (1888). *Snap-Dragons* (1888). *Works* (1890). *Jackanapes and Other Tales* (1890). *Last Words* (1891). *Lob Lie-by-the-Fire, Jackanapes, Daddy Darwin's Dovecot and Other Stories* (1893). *Verses for Children and Songs for Music* (1895). *A Great Emergency* (1897). *The Trinity Flower and Other Stories* (1897). *The Land of the Lost Toys* (1900). *Mary's Meadow* (1900). *Madam Liberality* (1901). *Juliana Horatia Ewing's Works* (1909). *Jackanapes and the Story of a Short Life* (1909). *Jackanapes and Other Stories*, ed. S. C. Bryant (1917). *Stories by Juliana Horatia Ewing* (1920). *Jackanapes and the Peace Egg* (1928). *The Ewing Book*, ed. E. M. Allsopp (1930). *Three Christmas Trees* (1930). *Timothy's Shoes and Two Other Stories* (1932). *The Brownies and Other Stories* (1954). *Canada Home*, ed. M. H. Blom and T. E. Blom (1983).

BIBLIOGRAPHY: Avery, G. *Mrs. Ewing* (1961). Avery, G. *Nineteenth Century Children* (1965). Eden, H. K. (Gatty). *Juliana Horatia and Her Books* (1885). Hall, D. E. *CLAQ* (1991). Laski, M. *Mrs. Ewing, Mrs. Molesworth, and Mrs. Hodgson Burnett* (1950). Maxwell, C. *Mrs. Gatty and Mrs. Ewing* (1949). Mills, C. *CLAQ* (1989). Plotz, J., in *The Child and the Family*, ed. S. R. Gannon (1989). Plotz, J., in *Romanticism and Children's Literature in Nineteenth-Century England*, ed. J. H. McGavran, Jr. (1991). *Women Novelists of Queen Victoria's Reign*, ed. A. Sergeant (1897).

For articles in reference works, see: *BA19C. Cassell. Children's Authors and Illustrators. Europa. ELB. Feminist. OCCL. OCEL. Oxford.*

Other references: *CLAQ* (Summer 1989, Summer 1991). *CLE* (December 1989).

Margaret Ann Graham
(updated by Karen Castellucci Cox)

Exploralibus: See *Haywood, Eliza Fowler*

Ruth Fainlight

BORN: 2 May 1931, New York City, United States.
DAUGHTER OF: Leslie Alexander Fainlight and Fanny Nimhauser Fainlight.
MARRIED: Alan Sillitoe, 1959.

F. was educated in America and England before attending Birmingham and Brighton Colleges of Arts and Crafts.

Except for travels to France, Spain, Morocco, Israel, and Majorca, she has lived most of her adult life in London, where she married the novelist and poet Alan Sillitoe. Best known as a poet, she is also a short-story writer, translator, and adapter of dramas. Her claim to literary accomplishment, however, rests with a series of poetry collections published steadily since 1958.

F.'s poetry is most often characterized by a sense of quietness. Her rhythms are smooth, her language measured, and her voice controlled, all of which is surprising, given the nature of her subjects. Like Sylvia Plath, who dedicated "Elm" to F., her poems are often about death, suicide, madness, imprisonment, and the frustrations of housewives. She also shares Plath's interest in children, the English countryside, gardening, and the Nazi Holocaust, and in her earlier books her poetry has a particularly Plathian sound: "I am the seer who reads her own entrails: / I search for signs of what the future means / in the past's hot reek," or "Perhaps I'll bleed to death. / Appropriate, if I still seek a role. / Then I will be / As clean as any animal / My family eats." Her affinity for the sort of subjects that attracted Plath is indicated in such titles as "The Vampire Housewife," "The Screaming Baby," and "The Infanticide," all from *Cages* (1966).

F.'s earlier books often have a brooding quality, an obsession with death, guilt, and anxiety over growing old without having had one's say. Her recent books, however, although meditations on similar themes, replace an earlier measured despair with a more subtle sense of strength. As the title poem of her fourth collection attests, she wishes "To See the Matter Clearly," even when the matter is intense self-preoccupation. Instead of being "overwhelmed by giant agony," she remains a survivor, not by avoiding the anguish of life but by her ability to "turn down the sound."

As a result, her later poems, while continuing to echo some of Plath's subjects, create a sense of control, even as her poetic forms become more proselike. In "Hospital Flowers," for instance, she writes: "Unless the nurses take them / away, day after day they wilt in regulation / vases or commandeered drinking glasses, reminders / of the friends who brought them, and that fear / which, though omnipresent, looms clearer here / than in the world outside, the place where / flowers are forced especially for this purpose." The first half of *Sibyls and Other Poems* is taken up with a series of variations on the theme of the sibyl, a series that echoes the mixture of Jewish and Christian prophecy common to both *Sibyls* and to F.'s family origins in Austro-Hungary, England, and America.

Eventually, a series of personal subjects emerge from the body of her work: She is particularly drawn to the moon, hair, mirrors, babies, allusions to classical mythology, and, as she continues to write, to an uneasy acceptance of age and rural life, lyrically rendered in poems that find relief in the cyclical pattern of nature and in the victory of natural death over suicidal impulses.

Although some reviewers see F.'s voice as being too restrained, others have applauded her tone, her determination to examine a personal situation that in many ways parallels Plath's. Like her more famous friend, F. is an expatriate American living in England, struggling to write poetry while fulfilling the difficult role of wife of a well-known British author and mother of young children. F., who wrote in a poem titled "Unseemly," "I left my race and family / To learn about myself," has managed to survive her situation and to find a home for herself within it. The result is a body of poetry centered around the major problems of twentieth-century women, expressed in a voice that commands our attention, despite its quietness, a voice "Between fineness and toughness," qualities she called "my own special markings."

WORKS: *A Forecast, A Fable* (1958). *Cages* (1966). (trans. and adapted with A. Sillitoe) *18 Poems from 1966*, ed. E. Lucie-Smith (1967). (trans.) *All Citizens Are Soldiers*, by Lope de Vega (1967). *To See the Matter Clearly and Other Poems* (1968). (with A. Sillitoe and T. Hughes, 1971). *Poems. Daylife and Nightlife* (1971). *The Region's Violence* (1973). *Twenty One Poems* (1973). *Another Fall Moon* (1976). *Two Fire Poems* (1977). *The Function of Tears* (1979). *Sibyls and Other Poems* (1980). (trans.) *Coral*, by Sophia de Mello Breyner Andresen (1982). *Climates* (1983). *Fifteen to Infinity* (1983).

BIBLIOGRAPHY:

For articles in reference works, see: *CA. Cambridge. CP. Feminist. ToddBWW.*

Other references: *Letters Home by Sylvia Plath*, ed. A. S. Plath (1980). *New Statesman* (12 March 1976, 9 May 1980). *Poetry* (1978). *TLS* (8 April 1977, 23 May 1980).

Timothy Dow Adams

Fairfield, Cicily Isabel: See *West, Rebecca*

Anna Maria Falconbridge

FLOURISHED: Bristol, 1790–94.
MARRIED: Alexander Falconbridge, 1790; Isaac Dubois, 1793.

Most information about F. comes from her 1794 *Narrative of Two Voyages to Sierra Leone During the Years 1791–2–3*. In 1790, she married Alexander Falconbridge, a former slaveship surgeon turned antislavery author. His abolitionist activities led them in 1791 to West Africa, where he was employed in an attempt to reestablish a small antislavery colony. Her husband succeeded in arranging a new site for the colony, and F.'s narrative is lively and cheerful as she describes her visits to African villages, the royalty she meets, the strange animals and insects, the scenery, her liking for African food, and even the privations and illnesses of the colonists. Keeping herself out of the account at most times, she is factual and detailed, quick with sarcasm, and careful to blend observations with interesting anecdotes.

Five months later the F.s returned to England after a three-month voyage marked by storms, disease, and near starvation. The Sierra Leone Company promoted her husband to commercial agent and persuaded F. to return to Sierra Leone with him. In Africa, F. noted desperate shortages and daily death tolls, but her husband had to answer to a self-important council whose members did little to encourage agriculture or provide land for a group of new colonists, black American loyalists who had removed to Nova Scotia because of the Revolution. From company letters we know that her husband was impossible: His "hot, rash, and impetuous" temper, lack of commercial qualifications, and habitual drunkenness finally forced the company to replace him. F. defended his actions but had few regrets at his subsequent death: "his conduct to me for more than two years past was so unkind (not to give a harsher term) as long since to wean every spark of affection or regard I ever had for him."

F.'s account becomes increasingly critical as she describes the deteriorating conditions in the colony. She scorns the company's stress on religious idealism at a time when the necessities of life were often lacking in the colony. Shortly after her husband's death, she married Isaac Dubois, a town planner, and several months later they left for Jamaica, which she compares unfavorably to Sierra Leone. In Jamaica, however, the treatment of the slaves seems better to her than that of "three fourths" of Africans under tribal rule, and she finds her former circle "bigoted for the abolition."

From Jamaica, F. and Dubois returned to England, where she fought for money due her at her first husband's death. The last section of her account protests the company's broken promises to the black colonists and to herself, and she appends a letter urging her rights. With the exception of a month of journal entries, the rest of the *Narrative* is epistolary. F. says it was written for publication, and she could have heard through colony Governor Clarkson of the remunerative vogue for travel accounts. The detail and clarity with which she records events and registers her opinions make the *Narrative* a delight to read as well as an important historical resource.

WORKS: *Narrative of Two Voyages to Sierra Leone During the Years 1791–2–3* (1794; also excerpted in Ingham, E. G. *Sierra Leone After a Hundred Years,* 1894).

BIBLIOGRAPHY: Clarkson, R. N. *Sierra Leone Studies* (1927). Ferguson, M. *Subject to Others* (1994). Mackenzie-Grieve, A. *The Great Accomplishment* (1953). Pratt, M. L. *Imperial Eyes* (1992).

For articles in reference works, see: *DNB. Feminist. ToddDBA.*

Marie E. McAllister

Falkland, Viscountess: See *Cary, Elizabeth*

Fane, Violet: See *Currie, Mary (Montgomerie) Lamb Singleton, Lady Currie*

Anne Fanshawe

BORN: 25 March 1625, London.
DIED: 30 January 1680, Ware, Hertfordshire.
DAUGHTER OF: Sir John Harrison and Margaret Harrison.
MARRIED: Sir Richard Fanshawe, 1644 or 1645.

F.'s *Memoirs* are her only literary legacy. Originally intended as both a family history and as an ethical guide for her last surviving son, the work has since been estimated as a "charming" collection of "remarkable actions and accidents" revealing a wife and mother "of conjugal devotion, of maternal excellence, and of enduring fortitude under calamities."

According to her chronicles, F. initially enjoyed a privileged and pleasant childhood as the daughter of a devoted Royalist until unfavorable consequences of the Civil War forced the family to move from St. Olan's Hart Street, London (her birthplace), to a poor baker's house in Oxford. The series of reverses continued with the death of F.'s mother in 1650 and the loss of William, the second of three brothers, as a result of injuries sustained during a skirmish with the Earl of Essex's retinue. F.'s father, having refused a baronetcy "on the grounds of poverty," was subsequently arrested and confined as a political prisoner. Marriage to Sir Richard Fanshawe, a career diplomat and integral member of the Prince of Wales's assemblage, only served to increase opportunities for privation and danger, which she describes in detail throughout her *Memoirs.*

F.'s writings trace her husband's loyalty to the royal family with vivid accounts of her family's jaunts to each of Sir Richard's diplomatic posts. F.'s admiration for her husband at this time is only exceeded by her endurance and strength: F.'s fourteen pregnancies were often jeopardized by constant changes of residence, and only five children survived.

Each account of F.'s adventures is depicted in gentle, gracious tones. Scenes of deprivation or tragedy have a matter-of-fact quality, as if almost anyone else could claim similar experiences. One particular event seems almost operatic. From 13 September to 28 November 1651, Sir Richard was imprisoned at Whitehall. Every day, at 4 A.M., F. spoke with him under the cell window. Daily she demanded from his keepers a certificate of ill health, which she finally received and used to petition council for his release.

Sir Richard died during his last post as ambassador to Madrid, Spain. Refusing the queen mother's generous offers of wealth, honor, and a permanent residence if she embraced the Roman Catholic faith, F. sold many possessions to bring her children and the body of her husband back to England.

In addition to fulfilling her original intentions, the *Memoirs* serve several other functions. They elicit the essentials required of a public servant, unrequited obedience and unfailing dedication to duty; they present "lively and entertaining" asides on personal and national history; and they serve as a treatise on the conditions in court after the Restoration (which F.'s publisher considers "the most disgraceful in the annals of [England]" in his addition to a later printing). The *Memoirs* also added to the "evidence which exists of the total want of principle which characterised the court of Charles the Second."

There are variations in dates within the notations, as the inaccuracies were difficult for the publisher to correct "because the Authoress sometimes used the old and sometimes the new style, and now and then speaks of things out of the order in which they happened." An amended addition, including excerpts from Lord Fanshawe's correspondence, was published in 1829 and edited by Sir N. Harris Nicolas. A further reprint appeared in 1907 from an original manuscript possessed by a descendant of the family.

The dedication in the initial printing indicates the family's appreciation of their mother's nobility. F.'s son, Charles, addresses the Duchess of Clarence and notes the Fanshawe heritage of loyalty and courage: "These qualities still animate the hearts and steel the hands . . . 'Like men to conquer, or like Christians fall.'"

WORKS: *Memoirs of Lady Fanshawe; Wife of the Right Hon. Sir Richard Fanshawe, Bart.; Ambassador from Charles the Second to the Court of Madrid in 1665,* ed. Sir N. Harris Nicolas (1829).

BIBLIOGRAPHY:

For articles in reference works, see: *BAB1800. Chambers. CHEL. DNB.*

Zelda R. B. Provenzano

Eleanor Farjeon

BORN: 13 February 1881, Hempstead, London.
DIED: 5 June 1965, Hempstead, London.
DAUGHTER OF: Benjamin Leopold Farjeon and Margaret Jefferson Farjeon.
WROTE UNDER: Chimaera; Eleanor Farjeon; Tom Fool

F. was a prolific writer whose best-known works were children's short stories and poems written for the most part between the two world wars. These numerous works share an interest in children's fantasy and a deep-seated belief in the essential goodness of humanity. These traits have led many commentators to compare her work with that of her contemporary and friend, Walter de la Mare. Her work, which has been translated into twelve European languages as well as Hebrew and Japanese, is now known mainly through anthologies.

F. grew up in a thoroughly literary family, her father being a prolific novelist and her mother the daughter of Joseph Jefferson, a celebrated American actor. Two of her brothers became writers, and the third taught music at the Royal Academy. F. educated herself by reading widely in the family library and listening to the conversations among writers, musicians, and actors who were frequent guests in her home. As she explains in *A Nursery in the Nineties* (1935), her early life, filled with fantasy games, was essential to her development as a person and as a writer. These fantasy games were so realistic that it became second nature for her to create and inhabit worlds of her own.

Although she wrote stories and poems as a child, her serious career as a writer began when her father died in 1903. At first, she wrote humorous or topical verse for *Punch, The Daily Herald* and *Time and Tide.* At this time, she was also beginning to publish stories and verse, first *Dream-Songs for the Beloved* (1911) and then *The Soul of Kol Nikon* (1914). This early work was completed with the encouragement and guidance of the poet Edward Thomas and his wife.

After Thomas's death in 1917, she rented a cottage in Sussex for two years, during which time she wrote *Martin Pippin in the Apple Orchard* (1921), one of her best-known works. This collection of tales was intended for an adult audience, but reviewers read it as a children's book, and it was reissued as such in 1952. By 1925, she was writing her first stories intended for children; by 1930, she was fully established as a writer. From 1930 to 1944, she wrote plays, musicals, and humorous verse in collaboration with her brother Herbert, as well as publishing many collections of retold tales such as *Tales from Chaucer* (1930).

The 1950s marked another productive period for her, a time when much of her earlier work was reissued. During that time, she published her major collections of poetry as well as her award-winning story collection, *The Little Bookroom* (1955). This collection earned the Carnegie Medal and the Hans Christian Andersen Medal in 1956.

F.'s work is diverse and uneven. Certainly her best works are her short stories, notably the two collections centering on the minstrel character of Martin Pippin, *Martin Pippin in the Apple Orchard* (1921) and *Martin Pippin in the Daisy-Field* (1937), the latter of which includes her famous story "Elsie Piddock Skips in Her Sleep." This simple story is typical of F.'s work in that its fairy-tale plot demonstrates the triumph of good over evil, freedom over restriction. In the story, a man threatens to build a factory on the children's playground, but he allows one last skipping-rope contest to be held there. He will not break ground, he says, until the last jump-rope skipper has stopped. In order to save the playground, an old woman, Elsie Piddock, skips endlessly with the aid of her fairy jump rope. Many of F.'s other story collections, like *Jim at the Corner* (1934), are strung together by a single theme or a single character. Her most famous story collection is *The Little Bookroom* (1955), which contains twenty-seven stories, including "The Glass Peacock" and "I Dance Mine Own Child," two of her more successful realistic tales. In addition to these original stories, F. published several new versions of old tales, including *Tales from Chaucer* (1930), *Ten Saints* (1936), and *The Wonders of Herodotus* (1937).

F.'s poems are collected in several volumes, including *Silver-Sand and Snow* (1951), *The Children's Bells* (1957), and *Then There Were Three* (1942). In addition, *Nursery Rhymes of London Town* (1912) reproduces all her poems from *Punch* (which she later set to music), and *Kings and Queens* (1932) and *Heroes and Heroines* (1933) are farcical poems on historical subjects that she wrote in collaboration with her brother Herbert. With Herbert, she also wrote several plays including *The Glass Slipper* (1946), a rendition of the Cinderella story.

Not all of her books were for children, however. She wrote several novels and collections of stories for adults including *Ladybrook* (1931), *Humming Bird* (1936), *Miss Granby's Secret* (1940), and *Ariadne and the Bull* (1945). But more interesting are her two autobiographical memoirs that paint vivid pictures of life in Victorian and Edwardian England. The first, *A Nursery in the Nineties* (1935), includes biographies of her parents and recounts her life until her father's death in 1903. The second volume, *Edward Thomas: The Last Four Years* (1958), was intended as the first in a series of autobiographical works and covers her early writing career and her relationship with Thomas.

F. will probably be best remembered as a writer of children's books that present fascinating characters in fully realized fantasy worlds. In recognition of this work, she was awarded the American Regina medal in 1959. But she is also a fascinating study of the female writer. Indeed, most books about F. address her personal rather than her literary merits. In her memory, the Children's Book Circle in England awards the Eleanor Farjeon award each year for "distinguished service to children's books."

WORKS: *Floretta* (1894). *The Registry Office* (1900). (with H. Farjeon) *A Gentleman of the Road* (1903). *Pan-Worship and Other Poems* (1908). *Dream-Songs for the Beloved* (1911). *Nursery Rhymes of London Town* (1912). *The Soul of Kol Nikon* (1914). *Trees* (1914). *More Nursery Rhymes of London Town* (1917). *All the Way to Alfriston* (1918). *Sonnets and Poems* (1918). (with H. Farjeon) *A First Chaphook of Rounds* (1919). (with H. Farjeon) *A Second Chapbook of Rounds* (1919). *Singing Games for Children* (1919). *Gypsy and Ginger* (1920). *Martin Pippin in the Apple Orchard* (1921). *Songs for Music and Lyrical Poems* (1922). (trans.) *Four Comedies*, by C. Goldoni (1922). *Tunes of a Penny Piper* (1922). *All the Year Round* (1923). *The Soul of Kol-Nikon* (1923). *The Country Child's Alphabet* (1924). *Mighty Men* (1924). *The Town Child's Alphabet* (1924). *Faithful Jenny Dove and Other Tales* (1925). *Songs from 'Punch' for Children* (1925). *Tom Cobble* (1925). *Young Folk and Old* (1925). *Italian Peepshow and Other Tales* (1926). *Joan's Door* (1926). *Nets and May* (1926). *Singing Games from Arcedy* (1926). *Come Christmas* (1927). *King's Barn* (1927). *Mill of Dreams* (1927). *The Wonderful Knight* (1927). *Young Gerard* (1927). *ABC of the B.B.C.* (1928). *An Alphabet of Magic* (1928). *Kaleidoscope* (1928). *Open Winkins* (1928). *A Bad Day for Martha* (1928). *A Collection of Poems* (1929). *The King's Daughter Cries for the Moon* (1929). *The Perfect Zoo* (1929). *The Tale of Tom Tiddler* (1929). *Tales from Chaucer* (1930). *Westwoods* (1930). *Ladybrook* (1931). *The Old Nurse's Stocking-Basket* (1931). (with H. Farjeon) *Kings and Queens* (1932). *The Fair of St. James* (1932). *Katy Kruse at the Seaside* (1932). *Perkin the Pedlar* (1932). *Ameliaranne and the Magic Ring* (1933). (with H. Farjeon) *Heroes and Heroines* (1933). *Ameliaranne's Prize Packet* (1933). *Over the Garden Wall* (1933). *Pannychis* (1933). *Ameliaranne's Washing Day* (1934). *The Clamber Pup* (1934). *Jim at the Corner* (1934; also issued as *The Old Sailor's Yarn Box*). *And I Dance Mine Own Child* (1935). *A Nursery in the Nineties* (1935; in the U.S. as *Portrait of a Family*). (with H. Farjeon) *The Two Bouquets* (1936). *Humming Bird* (1936). *Jim and the Pirates* (1936). *Ten Saints* (1936). *Martin Pippin in the Daisy-Field* (1937). *Paladins in Spain* (1937). *The Wonders of Herodotus* (1937). *One Foot in Fairyland* (1938). (with H. Farjeon) *Songs of Kings and Queens* (1938). *Sing for Your Supper* (1938). *Grannie Gray* (1939). *A Sussex Alphabet* (1939). *Miss Granby's Secret* (1940). *Brave Old Woman* (1941). *Magic Casements* (1941). *The New Book of Days* (1941). *Cherrystones* (1942). *Then There Were Three* (1942). *The Fair Venetian* (1943). *Golden Coney* (1943). *Ariadne and the Bull* (1945). *Dark World of Animals* (1945). *The Mulberry Bush* (1945). *A Prayer for Little Things* (1945). (with H. Farjeon) *The Glass Slipper* (1946). *First and Second Love* (1947). *Love Affair* (1947). *The Two Bouquets* (1948). *The Starry Floor* (1949). *Mrs. Malone* (1950). *Poems for Children* (1951). *Silver-Sand and Snow* (1951). (with R. F. Birch) *Roundelay* (1952). (with H. Farjeon) *Aucassin and Nicolette* (1952). *The Silver Curlew* (1953). *The Little Bookroom* (1955). *The Children's Bells* (1957). *Elizabeth Myers* (1957). *Edward Thomas: The Last Four Years* (1958). *Mr. Garden* (1966). *Around the Seasons* (1969).

BIBLIOGRAPHY: Blakelock, D. *Eleanor: Portrait of a Farjeon* (1966). Cameron, E. *The Green and Burning Tree* (1967). Colwell, E. *Eleanor Farjeon* (1961). Farjeon, A. *Morning Has Broken: A Biography of Eleanor Farjeon* (1986). Greene, E. P., in *The Child and the Story*, ed. P. Ord (1983). Greene, E. *CLAQ* (1986).*A Book for Eleanor Farjeon: A Tribute to Her Life and Work, ed. N. Lewis* (1966).

For articles in reference works, see: *CA*. *DNB*. *Longman*. *TCA* and *SUP*. *TCCW*. *TCW*.

Tori Haring-Smith

Farrell, M. J.: See *Keane, Molly*

Eliza Fay

BORN: 1756, perhaps at Blackheath, Worcestershire.
DIED: September 1816, Calcutta, India.
MARRIED: Anthony Fay, late 1770s.

Though very little is known of her life, F.'s *Original Letters from India—1779–1815* contributes to our record of the British in Calcutta in the late eighteenth century. As the new bride of Anthony Fay, an advocate at the Supreme Court, F. went to India in 1779 via France, Italy, and Egypt. After her husband failed at law and fathered an illegitimate child, they divorced; F. returned to England in 1782. She took up business schemes of her own based on mantua-making and the cloth trade and eventually returned to Calcutta in 1784, 1796, and 1816. Each time, her financial plans went awry. After she died in debt in 1816, the administrator of her estate published her letters, which she had been gathering for the press in hopes of paying off her creditors. The letters were published in Calcutta in 1817, reprinted in 1821, and re-edited there in 1908. The 1908 edition came to the attention of E. M. Forster, who found it troublesome because both prose and punctuation had been altered by the Reverend W. R. Firminger. Forster restored the original text and wrote the introduction and notes to the 1925 edition.

F.'s one great Indian adventure, which required her impressive resourcefulness and mettle, came when she first arrived in India and was imprisoned for fifteen weeks by Hyder Ali at Calicut [Calcutta]. All in all, however, her letters have relatively little to do with India; indeed, her attitude towards Indians and Indian customs is often disdainful. Her canvas is Anglo-Indian life—setting up house; going to dinners, balls, the races, and the theater; sorting out marital and financial difficulties; the long journeys to and from India. Her unstated theme is how to surmount life's adversities with good grace and even verve. Her style, so admired by E. M. Forster, is piquant and self-confident.

Barbara Hofland's 1834 novel, *The Captives in India*, draws on F.'s travel experiences. In 1986, in response to renewed interest in travel literature and the Raj, Forster's edition of *Original Letters from India* was re-issued with a new introduction by M. M. Kaye.

WORKS: *Original Letters from India—1779–1815* (1817, 1821, 1908, 1925, 1986).

BIBLIOGRAPHY: Beyer, K. C. *AJES* (1983). Dyson, K. K. *A Various Universe* (1978). Forster, E. M. *Egyptian Gazette* (5 and 16 April, 11 May 1917; rev. and rpt. in *Pharos and Pharillon,* 1923). Forster, E. M. *Cornhill Magazine* (May 1924). Grundy, I. *SECC* (1992). Hofland, B. *The Captives in India, A Tale* (1834).

For articles in reference works, see: *Feminist.*

Other references: Robinson, J. *Wayward Women: A Guide to Women Travellers* (1990).

Kathleen Collins Beyer

Elaine Feinstein

BORN: 24 October 1930, Bootle, Lancashire.
DAUGHTER OF: Isidore Cooklin and Fay Compton Cooklin.
MARRIED: Arnold Feinstein, 1957.

A poet, translator, writer of fiction, television playwright, biographer, and editor, F. has published a dozen books of her own verse in addition to well-received translations of poetry by Russian writers, notably Marina Tsvetayeva, and she has won a number of prizes for both fiction and poetry. She began writing poetry in the 1960s when she taught at Essex University. She was, she says, consciously influenced by such American poets as William Carlos Williams, Wallace Stevens, Emily Dickinson, and Robert Creeley, "at a time when the use of line, and spacing, to indicate the movement of poetry was much less fashionable than it is now among young British poets." She also states that her translations of Tsvetayeva gave her her "true voice as a poet" and that the Russian made her "attend to a strength and forward push, against and within a formal structure."

Though raised in the same period as "the angry young men" and others of the 1950s who felt socially displaced and guilt-ridden, she knew little of the anxieties of the time because of her cultural background. F. received her B.A. and M.A. from Newnham College, Cambridge. She took law examinations, worked as an editor for Cambridge University Press, taught at several schools, worked as a journalist, and in 1957 married a biochemist specializing in immunology.

Her Cambridge experience enabled her to meet Donald Davie, a well-known poet, and when he moved to Essex University she taught there as well. She first read Russian literature at Essex and was part of a poetry group that included Ed Dorn, a group that planned, unsuccessfully, to be similar to the Black Mountain group in the United States. Their support and criticism helped her and enabled her to become more conscious of her non-British roots.

She published her first book of verse, *In a Green Eye,* in 1966, and her first two novels, *The Circle* and *The Amberstone Exit,* in the early 1970s. These works relate to each other because of F.'s similar techniques: wide spaces between groups of words, unusual syntax, and similar attempts to imitate actual speech rhythms and pauses. Her first two novels use language economically as a means of expressing the constricted lives of her characters. In *The Circle,* through Lena and other women and their children, F. suggests the fragmented existences of the characters and their variously successful abilities to find their own niches or "private worlds" in life. *The Amberstone Exit,* similarly, describes a woman seeking her own "space," as she tries, only partially successfully, to find security in London as she reflects on her earlier life in the small town of the title.

The Magic Apple Tree (1971) like most of F.'s verse, uses imagery, color, speech rhythms, and, again, broken syntax to capture the vivid patterns of everyday life; her emphasis on the visual can be seen in the title poem (based on a painting), in "Out" (citing Buster Keaton), "West" (hinting at Mae West), and "I Have Seen Worse Days Turn" (the weather), as well as in echoes of earlier poets, such as in "Our Vegetable Love Shall Grow" (an echo of Andrew Marvell's "The Garden"). *At the Edge* (1972) continues F.'s exploration of personal discovery, as does the long title poem in *The Celebrants and Other Poems* (1973), which not only considers love, religion, and poetry as forces governing human survival, but moves into new territory as well, a more somber tone and touches of mordant humor.

In 1973, F. published *The Glass Alembic,* titled *The Crystal Garden* in the United States. Written after a year's stay in Switzerland, the novel is set in Basel and focuses on the drug culture of the 1960s as this contrasts with the more traditional Swiss society. The central characters, Matthew and Brigid and their teenage son and daughter, experience a variety of sexual and familial disappointments before the near death from drugs of one of Matthew's laboratory colleagues, and hovering always are the "ghosts" of such earlier residents of Basel as Erasmus and Paracelsus.

Although descended from Russian immigrants from Odessa, F. was not particularly aware of Jewishness. Her gradual interest in her heritage, both Jewish and Russian, grew after her parents' deaths in 1973, resulting first in *Children of the Rose* (1975), about Polish Jews who survived World War II and were financially successful but who subsequently lived in different countries: The insatiable Alex lives an emancipated life in France, while the troubled Lalka lives in London and learns to live with the past by revisiting Poland.

F.'s next two novels are satiric attempts to use the conventions of such popular genres as science fiction and fantasy while still centering on her Jewish heritage and the search for roots. *The Ecstasy of Dr. Miriam Garner* (1976) is a wildly absurdist foray into a woman's psychic "journey" to medieval Spain, when Jews, Arabs, and Christians lived easily with each other, unlike the situation she, as a specialist in Islam, finds in the modern world. *The Shadow Master* (1978) is similarly farcical while exploring a serious situation—a new messiah comes to modern Istanbul—but the novel's metaphysical framework gets bogged in excessive digressions, in both geography and character. It is less successful than its predecessor.

F.'s other collections of verse include *Some Unease and Angels* (1977), which attempts a synthesis between incompatible human and natural forces through the use of poetic language, and *The Feast of Euridice* (1980), which uses myth—as in the poems about Dido and Aeneas—to contrast mortal and immortal love; in both collections F. experiments with longer verse forms than she did in her earlier collections. In 1980, F. published her only collection of stories, *The Silent Areas;* the shorter form, like her verse, enabled her to avoid the relative lack of focus and control the more expansive novel led to in *The Shadow Master.*

It is F.'s translations, however, that have brought her the greatest degree of recent critical attention. Her *Three Russian Poets: Margarita Aliger, Yunna Moritz, Bella Akhmadulina* (1979) was noted for its idiomatic accuracy, but *The Selected Poems of Marina Tsvetayeva* (1971, 1987), as well as her *A Captive Lion: The Life of Marina Tsvetayeva* (1987), have given her a much wider audience than any of her own poetry or fiction. Tsvetayeva's poetry has been called "incredibly difficult to translate" because of its syntactical and linguistic complexity; F.'s translation is considered the standard. The biography, however, has been welcomed for its obvious love for its subject but criticized severely for its lack of scholarship and awareness of recent work on Tsvetayeva.

F. has grown as a writer, particularly as a poet and translator of poetry by others, but her work in a number of genres suggests her versatility, talent, and willingness to consider new alternatives for her creative impulses.

WORKS: *In a Green Eye* (1966). *The Circle* (1970). *The Magic Apple Tree* (1971). (trans.) *The Selected Poems of Marina Tsvetayeva* (1971, 1986). *At the Edge* (1972). *Matters of Chance* (1972). *The Amberstone Exit* (1972). *The Celebrants and Other Poems* (1973). *The Glass Alembic* (1973; in the U.S. as *The Crystal Garden,* 1974). *Children of the Rose* (1975). *The Ecstasy of Dr. Miriam Garner* (1976). *Some Unease and Angels: Selected Poems* (1977). *The Shadow Master* (1978). (trans.) *Three Russian Poets: Margarita Aliger, Yunna Moritz, Bella Akhmadulina* (1979). *The Feast of Euridice* (1980). *Masters of Chance* (1980). *The Silent Areas: Stuart Stories* (1980). *The Survivors* (1982). *The Border* (1984). *Bessie Smith* (1985) *Badlands* (1986) *Mother's Girl* (1987). (trans.) *First Poems,* by Nika Turbina (1987). *A Captive Lion: The Life of Marina Tsvetayeva* (1987). *Selected Poems* (1995). *Lady Chatterley's Confession* (1995). *Daylight* (1997).

BIBLIOGRAPHY: Mitchell, D., in *British Poetry Since 1970: A Critical Survey,* ed. P. Jones and M. Schmidt (1950). Tavis, A. *SlavR* (1988).

For articles in reference works, see: *Bloomsbury. CA. Cambridge. CN. CP. DLB. Feminist. Oxford. ToddBWW.*

Other references: *Books and Bookmen* (January 1977, September 1984, January 1986). *Encounter* (September 1984). *Harper's* (June 1974). *Listener* (10 August 1972, 21 June 1973, 24 April 1975, 28 September 1978, 28 February 1980, 11 March 1982, 21 June 1984, 5 December 1985). *New Statesman* (4 August 1972, 11 April 1975, 4 June 1976, 22 September 1978, 15 February 1980, 26 February 1982, 8 June 1984, 15 November 1985). *NYT* (25 February 1974, 21 August 1987). *NYTBR* (19 May 1974, 4 November 1979, 20 September 1987). *Observer* (20 August 1972, 13 May 1973, 27 May 1973, 10 March 1974, 20 April 1975, 30 May 1976, 10 September 1978, 3 February 1980, 28 February 1982, 10 June 1984, 3 November 1985). *Spectator* (5 June 1976, 24 September 1977, 23 September 1978, 16 June 1979, 9 February 1980). *TLS* (11 August 1972, 29 June 1973, 7 December 1973, 25 April 1975, 4 June 1976, 6 October 1978, 22 February 1980, 18 January 1980, 26 February 1982, 8 June 1984). *WLT* (Spring 1980).

Paul Schlueter

Margaret Fell

BORN: 1614, Marsh Grange, near Dalton, Lancashire.
DIED: 1702.
DAUGHTER OF: John Askew.
MARRIED: Thomas Fell, 1632; George Fox, 1669.
WROTE UNDER: Margaret Fell; Margaret Fox.

F., frequently referred to as the "Mother of Quakerism," played a central role in the formation of the early Quaker movement. An advocate of women's right to preach, F. spent much of her life boldly confronting the various powers that be (whether the Protector, Oliver Cromwell, or the monarch, Charles II) with her pleas for the end of the persecution of the Quakers.

F. was born in 1614 at Marsh Grange near Dalton (Lancashire). Her father, John Askew, was a gentleman who gave the estate, Marsh Grange, and £3,000 to his daughter as part of her dowry. In 1632, she married Thomas Fell, who was then a barrister and later became a Lancashire judge. She gave birth to nine children, only one of whom died in infancy.

In 1652, she was converted to Quakerism by the sect's founder and leader, George Fox. Later, she recalled that at the moment of her conversion she had cried to the Lord, "We are all thieves; we are all thieves; we have taken Scriptures in words, and know nothing of them in ourselves." While F.'s seven daughters followed their mother into Quakerism, her son and husband did not convert. Nevertheless, Fell supported his wife's Quakerism by permitting her to hold meetings at their home, Swarthmoor Hall, and by using his authority to intervene on behalf of persecuted Friends. He died in 1658.

As the author of some twenty-four religious and political treatises, F. actively participated in the two distinctive facets of early (1652–80) Quaker life—pleading for the end of her sect's persecution and proselytizing. Outraged by the vicious tortures inflicted on Friends by civil authorities, F. addressed letters to Oliver Cromwell and, later, to King Charles II, urging them to pursue policies of religious toleration. In a particularly compelling passage from *A Declaration and an Information* (1660), she describes the sorts of tortures the Friends have stoically withstood: "we have suffered under, and been persecuted by them all; Even some persecuted & prisoned till death; others their bodies bruised till death; stigmatized; bored thorow the tongue, gagged in the mouth, stockt, and whipt thorow Towns & Cities, our goods spoiled, our bodies two or three years imprisoned, with much more that might be said." Typical of many millenarian sects of the period, the Quakers sought to bring about the conversion of the Jews, and F. pursued this work by directing five of her books to Jews. Scholars believe that two of these books—*For Manasseth Ben Israel* (1656) and *A Loving Salutation to the Seed of Abraham* (1656)—may have been translated into Hebrew, for circulation among Jews in Amsterdam, by Benjamin Spinoza.

Of her many literary works, F. is perhaps best known among modern students as the author of *Womens Speaking Justified* (1666, 1667). In this text, she demonstrates that both the Hebrew and Christian Bibles, including what are conventionally seen as the misogynous Pauline letters to the Corinthians and to Timothy, advocate the right of women to prophesy in public. F. identified herself with female Friends not only through her writings but also through her participation in women's meetings. In 1671, as part of a move toward greater structure and organization that would ultimately ensure the sect's survival, the Quakers established a system of women's quarterly and monthly meetings. Through these meetings, female Friends became responsible for dispensing social services, censuring the activities of disorderly Quakers, and supervising marriages. Phyllis Mack argues that while the women's meetings served to limit women's roles, they also formalized female authority. This was significant because, "in the matter of female authority, [the Quakers'] contemporaries were far more concerned with form than with substance." While women might manage "businesses or estates . . . they did these things informally, as surrogates for men."

In 1669, F. married the Quaker leader and her longtime friend, George Fox. Fox died in 1691, and she outlived her second husband by eleven years, dying in 1702.

WORKS: *False Prophets* (1655). *A Loving Salutation to the Seed of Abraham* (1656). *For Manasseth Ben Israel* (1656). *A Testimonie of the Touchstone* (1656). *Concerning Ministers Made by the Will of Man* (1659). *A Paper concerning such as are made Ministers* (1659). *To the General Councel* (1659). *To the Generall Councell of Officers of the English Army* (1659). *To the General Council of Officers. The Representation* (1659). *The Citie of London Reprov'd* (1660). *A Declaration and an Information* (1660). *An Evident Demonstration from God's Elect* (1660). *This is to the Clergy* (1660). *This Was Given to Major General Harrison* (1660). *A True Testimony from the People of God* (1660). *To the Magistrates and People of England* (1664). *Two General Epistles to the Flock of God* (1664). *A Call to the Universal Seed of God* (1665). *A Letter Sent to the King from M. F.* (1666). *Womens Speaking Justified* (1666; 2nd ed., 1667). *The Standard of the Lord Revealed* (1667). *A Touch-stone, or, a Perfect Tryal* (1667). *A Call unto the Seed of Israel* (1668). *The Daughter of Sion Awakened* (1677). *A Brief Collection of Remarkable Passages and Occurrences Relating to the . . . Eminent Servant of the Lord, Margaret Fell* (1710).

BIBLIOGRAPHY: Dailey, B. R. *SCen* (1987). Ezell, M. J. M. *Writing Women's Literary History* (1993). Kunze, B. Y. *Margaret Fell and the Rise of Quakerism* (1994). Mack, P. *Visionary Women* (1992). Ross, I. *Margaret Fell: Mother of Quakerism* (1949). Thickstun, M. O. *SECC* (1991).

For articles in reference works, see: *DNB*. *ToddBWW*. *ToddDBA*.

Teresa Feroli

Fellowes, Anne: See *Mantle, Winifred Langford*

Eliza Fenwick

BORN: 1 February 1766, Cornwall.
DIED: 8 December 1840, Providence(?), Rhode Island.
DAUGHTER OF: Thomas Jago and Elizabeth Jago.
MARRIED: John Fenwick, c. 1788.
WROTE UNDER: the Reverend David Blair (?).

The primary source on F. is her extensive correspondence with Mary Hays (1798–1828), edited by A. Webb as *The Fate of the Fenwicks* (1927). Otherwise, there are only scattered references in letters, biographies, and memoirs of contemporaries like Charles Lamb, Thomas Holcroft, H. C. Robinson, William Godwin, and Mary Wollstonecraft. With Hays and a servant, F. nursed Wollstonecraft in her final days and then cared for a time for the infant Mary. Other friends included Jane and Anna Porter, Elizabeth Benger, Mary Darby Robinson, and Frances Place. This scanty biographical material has been interpreted and expanded by I. Grundy's excellent introduction to the 1994 edition of F.'s *Secresy* (1795). The present entry is indebted to Grundy, who has identified much of F.'s bibliography and most of the biographical data in the headnote.

Little information exists on F. prior to her marriage to John Fenwick, a member of the London Corresponding Society, who visited the National Convention in France in 1793 and whose radical publications, alcoholism, and affinity for debts put himself and his family at risk. After bearing him two children, F. separated from him in 1800 and subsequently worked constantly to raise her children. She ran schools, served as a governess in London and in Ireland, did extensive hack writing, ran Godwin's juvenile library for a time, and sewed costumes for her actress daughter, Eliza Ann. She accompanied Eliza Ann's tour to Ireland and eventually (with her son, Orlando) followed her to Barbados, where Eliza Ann had become a successful (although often miserable) actress. Eliza Ann had written her mother in 1812: "Players are certainly the condemned of Heaven. Some of them deserve and all of them suffer every misery that grows upon this earth." Now a mother of four, Eliza Ann, like her mother, had been forced to abandon an alcoholic husband and to fend for herself. Both women suffered illnesses and misfortunes in the next years in the West Indies, and Orlando died there of yellow fever. F. moved with her daughter, four grandchildren, and some boarding school pupils to the United States, where, when her daughter died, she soon found herself again responsible for raising children alone. F. died in 1840 in Rhode Island, where she had been living with her granddaughter, Elizabeth.

F.'s letters, fascinating, often moving and evocative, say little of her writings, except to hint at the relentless demands of writing numerous children's works. Only some of these have been identified. Grundy notes that a "new edition" of *Lessons for Children,* a sequel to Anna L. Barbauld's children's books, was published in 1811. Since *The European Magazine* reviewed *Lessons* in 1809, this probably hails its initial appearance: "These volumes contain a collection of tales calculated to attract the attention of children and foster the expansion of their minds: they are told in language plain and comprehensive."

Secresy, the only novel we know that F. wrote for adults, is a complex, psychologically compelling, powerfully written study of a friendship between two young women. One is Sibella, raised by a peculiar Rousseauistic system designed to make her eventually fall in love with her uncle Valmont's ward, Clement. Clement is sent out into society to be "matured" into a worldly cynicism his guardian believes will make him happy with the sequestered—and, as far as Clement knows, forbidden—Sibella. Sibella, hidden away from all society, must instantly obey her uncle's will without questioning. The outspoken and daring Caroline Ashburn intervenes: "though you have denied me the charm of associating with your niece, you will not also refuse me her correspondence? A letter, Sir, cannot waft down your drawbridges; the spirit of my affection breathed therein cannot disenchant her from the all-powerful spell of your authority. No. And you surely will not forbid an indulgence so endearing to us, while unimportant to yourself. Already I feel assured of your consent; and, with my thanks, dismiss the subject."

Caroline, of course, is disingenuous. The correspondence does undermine the drawbridges, precipitating, unwittingly, the inevitably tragic but startingly intricate consequences of Valmont's machinations. The book, while drawing on all the conventions of the period and making use of many of the popular genres, is a unique achievement, repeatedly catching the reader off-guard. Grundy contends:

> As a novel of ideas, *Secresy* is a heavy-weight. It intervenes in multiple psycho-socio-political debates of the 1790s, offering a distinctive blend of gender and class analysis which derives from Fenwick's friend Wollstonecraft. . . . None of the available labels—epistolary, gothic, sentimental, radical, novel of manners, or novel of social conscience—can package this stunning single work.

After initial mixed reviews of *Secresy* and some brief acclaim for F., she largely dropped out of literary history until C. Tomalin's 1977 edition of F.'s children's book, *Visits to the Juvenile Library* (1805), and J. Todd's 1989 edition of *Secresy.* Grundy (1989) analyzes F.'s debts to Samuel Richardson, and recent encyclopedia articles have supplemented what little material exists on *Secresy.* Unquestionably, more extensive attention to this extraordinary novel is warranted.

WORKS: *Secresy, or the Ruin Upon the Rock* (1795). *Mary and Her Cat* (1804). *The Life of Carlos, the Famous Dog of Drury Lane Theatre* (1804). *Presents for Good Boys* (1805). (as the Rev. David Blair, a pseudonym used for a number of works, some of which may also be F.'s) *Visits to the Juvenile Library, or Knowledge Proved to Be the Source of Happiness* (1805; ed. C. Tomalin, 1977). *The Class Book; or, Three hundred sixty-five reading lessons adapted to the use of schools* (1806). *The History of the Little Old Woman, Who Found a Silver Penny* (1806; attributed to F. by C. Tomalin). *Simple Stories in Verse* (1809). *Lessons for Children: or Rudiments of Good Manners, Morals and Humanity* (1809?). *Infantine Stories Composed Progressively, in Words of One, Two, and Three Syllables* (1810, 1815). *Rays from the Rainbow: Being an Easy Method for Perfecting Children in the First Principles of Grammar without the Smallest Trouble to the Instructor* (1812).

BIBLIOGRAPHY: Castle, T. *TLS* (22 February 1995). *The Fate of the Fenwicks: Letters to Mary Hays* (1798–1828), ed. A. T. Webb (1927). Grundy, I. *Samuel Richardson: Tercentenary Essays,* ed. M. L. Doody and P. Sabor (1989). Grundy, I., intro. to *Secresy* (1994). Todd, J., intro. to *Secresy* (1989). Tomalin, C., intro. to *Visits to the Juvenile Library, or Knowledge Proved to Be the Source of Happiness*

For articles in reference works, see: *Allibone. Feminist. ToddBWW.*

Other references: *Analytical Review* (1795). *British Critic* (1795). *Critical Review* (1795). *English Review* (1795). *European Magazine* (1809). *Monthly Review* (1795). *Providence Daily Journal* (9 December 1840).

Kathleen L. Fowler

Ferguson, Helen: See *Kavan, Anna*

Susan Edmonstone Ferrier

BORN: 7 September 1782, Edinburgh, Scotland.
DIED: 5 November 1854, Edinburgh, Scotland.
DAUGHTER OF: James Ferrier and Helen Coutts Ferrier.

The tenth and last child of James Ferrier, writer to the signet (clerk in the Secretary of State's office), and Helen Coutts Ferrier, F. never married, although John Leyden, the Oriental scholar, may have proposed. F. wrote three novels—*Marriage* (1818), *The Inheritance* (1824), and *Destiny: or the Chief's Daughter* (1831)—and numerous letters, later collected by her grandnephew John Ferrier. As B. Hardy notes, the letters are "sprightly, clever, intelligently and fluently communicative, arch and facetious." F. teases a fellow writer: "You have but one serpent; I shall have nine. Yours can only speak (which they could do in the days of Adam); mine shall sing and play on the harp and waltz."

Many of F.'s Scottish acquaintances appear, thinly disguised, in her novels, although F. found identification attempts largely amusing. "*Everybody* knows who the characters are, but no two people can agree about them. I have heard of 5 or 6 Lord Rossvilles and as many Miss Pratts." However, N. Bushnell notes F.'s near panic at the unexpected publication of the "reminiscences" of an acquaintance she had caricatured. F.'s self-portrait (*Marriage*'s Lady Emily's) confides: "[M]y talent lies fully as much in discovering the ridiculous as the amiable . . . it is much easier to hit off the glaring caricature lines of deformity than the finer and more exquisite touches of beauty."

F.'s literary acquaintances included Matthew "Monk" Lewis, Henry Mackenzie, Mme. de Staël, Robert Burns, Sir Walter Scott, Robert Blair, and John Gibson Lockhart. F. established a friendship and literary relationship with Charlotte Clavering (the Duke of Argyle's niece). While differing tastes and styles precluded joint authorship, Clavering contributed a chapter (properly acknowledged) to *Marriage*. Her main value to F., though, was as a keen and thoughtful critic.

F. has been regularly grouped with Scottish didactic novelists (Mary Balfour Brunton, Elizabeth Hamilton), novelists of manners (Jane Austen, Fanny Burney) and the regionalists (John Galt, Jane Porter, Scott, Maria Edgeworth). Certainly F. admired most of these writers. Hamilton's McLartys are "the most exquisite family group imaginable"; Brunton's *Discipline* "one of the very few novels I think fit for family use." Austen's *Emma* is "excellent" ("characters all so true to style and the style so piquant"), and F. famously rewrites Austen in *The Inheritance:* "It is a truth universally acknowledged, that there is no passion so deeply rooted in human nature as that of pride." F. playfully uses Scott's *Guy Mannering* to paralyze Uncle Adam in *The Inheritance;* he can neither put the book down nor admit to such an embarrassing occupation as novel reading. Scott assisted F. in the publication of *Destiny* and she visited him at Abbotsford. Still, while such connections help locate F. and identify many key cross-fertilizations, it is F.'s own considerable merits that have ensured her continued vitality.

Animated by sprightly dialogue and a keen dramatic instinct, F.'s novels of Scottish society are pointedly witty, rather acerbic, and sometimes farcical They are closer to Tobias Smollett, or, as W. Parker suggests, to William Hogarth than to Austen. Tendentious moralizing sometimes dampens her prose, but as F. Hart urges, "there is no point in lamenting the submergence of F. the satirist in F. the Christian moralist: they are inseparable."

F. describes the origin of *Marriage:* "I do not recollect ever to have seen the sudden transition of a high-bred English beauty, who thinks she can sacrifice all for love, to an uncomfortable solitary Highland dwelling among tall red-haired sisters and grim-faced aunts" (*Memoir,* 76). F.'s realization of this encounter is brilliant. The squeamish Lady Juliana boggles at the eccentric aunts (Nicky, Grizzy, and Jacky) and the five "great purple" sisters, not to mention neighbor Lady MacLaughlan, described by *Macmillan's* Gwynn as "the pink of all rough, rude, dogmatical, snuff-taking, doctoring, intolerable old viragos." Lady Juliana flees to London to spoil one of her twins (Adelaide), leaving the other (Mary) in the Highlands with predictably different results, although, as M. Cohen demonstrates, each twin "mirrors" and "extends" a portion of her mother's life.

The Inheritance offers the engaging history of the headstrong but good-hearted Gertrude St. Clair, who despite her extravagant lifestyle is hemmed in, exploited, tricked, and forced into compromising secrecy in a way that is psychologically convincing, even terrifying. Learning she is not the rightful heir, Gertrude honorably repudiates wealth and title, and her false lover deserts. Gertrude gradually matures, and regains position and wealth, helped by cantankerous but kindly Uncle Adam (possibly modeled on F.'s father) and by her true lover. Mercifully, F. confines her moral message to a few chapters, while the remainder sparkles with spirited dialogue and lively eccentrics like Lady Betty—a horror-novel addict like her creator—and the irresistible bore, Miss Pratt (well-meaning, tiresome and ubiquitous), who mortifies Lord Rossville to death when she arrives during a snowstorm in the hearse of a brewer.

Destiny was written after F.'s life had been increasingly narrowed by the loss of many of her siblings and by her own long confinement with her ill father. Critics generally maintain that, as W. Craik puts it, "the sands of inspiration are running out." The novel is precisely articulated, almost too symmetrical. Providence appropriately accounts for the remarkable coincidences of the book, but they remain difficult to digest. Nonetheless, the great comic clergyman, Mr. McDow, atones for pages of overly sentimental prose, and F.'s unromanticized portraits of the petty, selfish, irascible Glenroy, fiercely proud of his heritage and unforgivably blind to his daughter, are strikingly original. J. G. Lockhart, a novelist, critic, biographer, and Walter Scott's son-in-law, comments that "the age of lucre-banished chieftains dwindled into imitation squires . . . the euthanasia of kilted aldermen and steam-boat pilbrochs was reserved for Miss Ferrier."

Although F. repeatedly implies that an unmarried woman can devote herself only to piety and good works to be happy and worthy, F.'s views on women are largely progressive. N. Paxton, for instance, sees *Marriage's* Mary as a Wollstonecraftian feminist heroine. F.'s class politics are more conservative; she criticizes class arrogance and especially targets Major Waddell, the nabob in *The Inheritance,* but she does not seem fundamentally to challenge contemporary imperial policies or existing class divisions. L. Fletcher contends that F.'s alternative "is not democratic division of land and wealth but rather a Christian *contemptuo mundi.*" F.'s working-class and peasant portraits are generally unattractive and her notions of appropriate philanthropy rather disquieting. Lady Alicia Douglas is praised for improving her estate and the poor by employing small children to keep up the grounds. F. is even less conscious of racist and antisemitic intonations that jar painfully with her Christian messages. A single line can illustrate: "Gertrude . . . was . . . the bitter drop in her cup—the black man in her closet—the Mordecai at her gate!"

Other than rare trips to London about her failing vision, F.'s final years were almost entirely homebound. While declining to write another novel, F. did revise her works for Bentley's *Standard Novels* (1841), and she continued to read, to think, and to grow. As late as 1852, F. became involved with the Ladies Abolition Society of Edinburgh and reported on *Uncle Tom's Cabin:* "I was never so stirred by any book and I'm glad to hear the whole world is the same" (quoted by Grant).

WORKS: *Marriage* (1818). *The Inheritance* (1824). *Destiny, or the Chief's Daughter* (1831). *Memoir and Correspondence of Susan Edmonstone Ferrier,* ed. J. Ferrier and J. A. Doyle (1898, rpt. 1970).

BIBLIOGRAPHY: Alston, R., intro. to *Marriage* (1986). Bushnell, N. S. *SSL* (1968). Cohen, M., in *Significances of*

Sibling Relationships, ed. J. S. Mink and J. D. Ward (1993). Craik, W., in *Scott: Bicentenary Essays,* ed. A. Bell (1973). Craik, W. *GSJ* (1995). Cohen, M., in *The Significance of Sibling Relationships in Literature,* ed. J.-A.S. Mink and J. D. Ward (1992). Cullinan, M. *Susan Ferrier* (1984). Douglas, G. *The Blackwood Group* (1897). Fletcher, L., *ScLJ* (1989). Foltinek, H., intro. to *Marriage* (1971). Grant, A. *Susan Ferrier of Edinburgh: A Biography* (1957). Johnson, R. B., intro. to *The Novels of Susan Ferrier* (1918, rpt. 1972). Parker, W. *Susan Ferrier and John Galt* (1965). Paxton, N. *W&L* (1976).

For articles in reference works, see: *Bloomsbury. Cambridge. Dabundo. Feminist. Oxford. ToddBWW.*

Other references: Birrell, A. *More Obiter Dicta* (1924). Colby, V. *Yesterday's Women* (1974). Graham, H. *Parties and Pleasures: The Diaries of Helen Graham, 1823–26,* ed. J. Irvine (1957). Gwynn, S. *Macmillan's Magazine* (April 1899). Hamilton, C. J. *Women Writers* (1892). Hardy, B. *TLS* (7 June 1985). Hart, F. R. *The Scottish Novel* (1978). Kestner, J. *WC* (1979), Leclaire, L. A. *A General Analytical Bibliography of the Regional Novelists* (1954). Lindsey, M., in *A Companion to Scottish Culture,* ed. D. Daiches (1981). MacCarthy, B. G. *Later Women Novelists* (1947). *Macmillan's Magazine* (June 1818). Mellor, A. *Romanticism and Gender* (1993). *Edinburgh Review* (1942). Sackville, Lady M., intro. to *Marriage, The Inheritance,* and *Destiny, or the Chief's Daughter,* in *The Works of Susan Ferrier* (1929; rpt. 1970). Saintsbury, G. *Collected Essays and Papers* (1883). Williams, M. *Women in the English Novel 1800–1900* (1984).

Kathleen L. Fowler

Fidelia: See *Barker, Jane*

Michael Field

Katharine Harris Bradley

BORN: 27 October 1846, Birmingham.
DIED: 26 September 1914, Richmond, Surrey.
DAUGHTER OF: Charles Bradley and Emma Harris.
WROTE UNDER: Michael Field; Arran Leigh.

Edith Emma Cooper

BORN: 12 January 1862, Kenilworth, Warwickshire.
DIED: 13 December 1913, Richmond, Surrey.
DAUGHTER OF: James Robert Cooper and Emma Bradley.
WROTE UNDER: Michael Field; Isla Leigh.

B. and C. were constant companions from 1865, when B., at eighteen years of age, joined the household of her invalid older sister, C.'s mother, and assumed the care and tutelage of her four-year-old niece. B. had attended Newnham College, Cambridge, and the College de France in Paris. Between 1875 and 1880, she corresponded with John Ruskin; however, she and C. found they disagreed with the "speckled silliness in Ruskin's dealings with women." In 1878, the two women attended the University College in Bristol, where they participated in women's suffrage organizations, debate societies, and antivivisectionist activities. By the time C. was twenty years old, the two women had sworn "Against the world, to be / Poets and lovers evermore." For the remainder of their lives, they lived together, traveled abroad together, and collaborated on more than twenty-five tragic dramas on classical and historical themes and eight volumes of lyric poetry. In private life, B. called herself "Michael," and C. was "Field" or, more often, "Henry." After their deaths, their journal *Works and Days* revealed the great joy they had found in the life they led.

The first volume issued under the pseudonym "Michael Field" was a pair of tragic dramas, *Callirrhoë* and *Fair Rosamund* (1884). Like most of B. and C.'s plays, these were never performed, but the book was hailed by the popular press as the work of a promising new writer, comparable in some respects to William Shakespeare. When it was revealed that the author was not a man ("some avatar of Waring"), but a spinster aunt and her spinster niece, public acclaim quickly subsided. Nevertheless, praise from Robert Browning, George Meredith, Arthur Symons, and various late-century poets (e.g., W. B. Yeats, Vernon Lee, George Moore) encouraged B. and C. to continue writing. Their many plays, mostly verse dramas, are slow and stiff, though well researched and often at least mildly feminist in theme. The only one that was ever performed, *A Question of Memory* (1893), failed immediately. That they were able to publish so many was attributable to their private income from their fathers' mercantile interests. B. and C.'s close friends, Charles Ricketts and Charles Shannon, privately printed elegant illustrated editions of *Fair Rosamund, The World at Auction* (1898), *The Race of Leaves* (1901), and *Julia Domna* (1903) for them at the Vale Press.

B. and C.'s poetry, on the other hand, is comparable to that of Oscar Wilde and George Meredith (both of whom they knew) in its turn-of-the-century aestheticism. *Long Ago* (1889), for example, is a collection of intense and sensuous verses based on Sappho; this volume also contains "Tiresias," a passionate appreciation of feminine "receptivity of soul" and "the mystic raptures of the bride." Although B. wrote many of the poems in *Underneath the Bough* and in *Mystic Trees* (1913) and C. wrote *Poems of Adoration* (1912), the majority of their work, including the journal *Works and Days,* was a joint effort.

Near the end of their lives, fearing the separation of death, the two women converted to Roman Catholicism, with its promise of everlasting life together. When C. subsequently developed cancer, B. nursed her until her death; she herself died of the same illness within six months. Their relationship has been cited as an example of the "romantic friendships" common among women in the nineteenth century. Recent critics, attending to the erotic and Sapphic elements of their poetry, have claimed it for the growing canon of lesbian literature. *Works and Days,* originally written for a personal rather than a public audience, was entrusted to T. Sturge Moore, who was asked to open it at the end of 1929 and publish whatever seemed fitting; he did so. The journal offers many insights into the complex self-definitions and self-concepts of two talented and mutually devoted women artists who stood together at the crossroads of the nineteenth and twentieth centuries.

WORKS: (as Arran Leigh) *The New Minnesinger and Other Poems* (1875). (as Arran and Isla Leigh) *Bellerophon and Other Poems* (1881). *Callirrhoë* and *Fair Rosamund* (1884). *The Father's Tragedy; William Rufus; Loyalty or Love* (1885). *Brutus Ultor: A Play in Verse* (1886). *Canute the Great; The Cup of Water* (1887). *Long Ago* (1889). *The Tragic Mary* (1890). *Stephania: A Trialogue* (1892). *Sight and Song* (1892). *Underneath the Bough: A Book of Verses* (1893). *A Question of Memory: A Play in Four Acts* (1893). *Attila, My Attila: A Play in Verse* (1898). *The World at Auction: A Drama in Verse* (1898). *Noontime Branches* (1899). *Anna Ruina: A Drama in Verse* (1899). *The Race of Leaves* (1901). *Julia Domna: A Drama in Verse* (1903). *Borgia: A Period Play* (1905). *Queen Mariamne: A Play* (1908). *Wild Honey from Various Thyme: Poems* (1908). *The Tragedy of Pardon; Diane* (1911). *The Accuser; Tristan de Léonois; A Messiah* (1911). *Poems of Adoration* (1912). *Mystic Trees* (1913). *Dedicated: An Early Work of Michael Field* (1914). *Whym Chow, Flame of Love* (1914). *Deirdre; A Question of Memory; Ras Byzance* (1918). *In the Name of Time: A Tragedy of Love* (1919). *The Wattlefold: Unpublished Poems* (1930). *Works and Days: Extracts from the Journals of Michael Field*, ed. T. S. Moore and D. C. Moore (1934).

BIBLIOGRAPHY: *Some Letters from Charles Ricketts and Charles Shannon to "Michael Field" (1894–1902)*, ed. J. G. P. Delaney (1979). Leighton, A. *Victorian Women Poets* (1992). Moore, T. S., in *A Selection from the Poems of Michael Field* (1923). Ricketts, C., in *Michael Field*, ed. P. Delaney (1976). Sturgeon, M. *Studies of Contemporary Poets* (1920). Sturgeon, M. *Michael Field* (1922).

For articles in reference works, see: *BA19C*. *The Distaff Muse: An Anthology of Poetry Written by Women*, ed. D. Bax and M. Stewart (1949). *1890s*. Faderman, L. *Chloe Plus Olivia: An Anthology of Lesbian Literature from the Seventeenth Century to the Present* (1994). *Feminist*. *Victorian Women Poets: An Anthology*, ed. M. Reynolds and A. Leighton (1995). Moriarty, D. J., in *Nineteenth Century Women Writers of the English-Speaking World*, ed. R. B. Nathan (1986). *Oxford*. *PPC*. *The Women Poets in English: An Anthology*, ed. A. Stanford (1982).*VB*.

Other references: *Writing*, ed. J. Bristow (1992). Faderman, L. *Surpassing the Love of Men: Romantic Friendship and Love between Women from the Renaissance to the Present* (1981). Foster, J. *Sex Variant Women in Literature* (1956). Hickok, K. *Representatives of Women: Nineteenth-Century British Women's Poetry* (1984). Laird, H. *VP* (1995). Locard, H. *JENS* (1979). Prins, Y. *YJC* (1995). White, C., in *Sexual Sameness: Textual Differences in Lesbian and Gay Writers*, ed. J. Bristow (1992). White, C. *TexP* (1990).

Kathleen Hickok

Field, Mrs.: See Egerton, Sarah Fyge Field

Sarah Fielding

BORN: 1710, East Stour, Dorset.
DIED: 9 April 1768, Bath, Somerset.
DAUGHTER OF: Edmund Fielding and Sarah Gould Fielding.
WROTE UNDER: The Author of David Simple; A Lady.

F. spent her girlhood as a middle child in a family of six children. Their mother died when F. was seven and a half, and her father's remarriage caused a breach in the family that resulted in F.'s grandmother, Lady Gould, concerned about inheritance rights and the children's upbringing, filing a Bill of Complaint in the Court of Chancery. The five younger children subsequently lived with their grandmother in Salisbury, with Henry (the oldest) joining them on holidays from Eton. F. and her three sisters attended a boarding school in Salisbury, "in order to be educated and to learn to work and read and write and to talk French and Dance and be brought up as Gentlewomen" F.'s reading was extensive, as is indicated by frequent allusions in her novels to William Shakespeare, John Milton, Horace, Virgil, Alexander Pope, and Montaigne. During this girlhood, F. met Jane Collier, the daughter of a family acquaintance, who became her lifelong friend.

When Lady Gould died in 1733, F., who was then twenty-three, remained in the house with her sisters for several years, with an aunt as chaperone. In 1737, the family estate at East Stour was sold and the income from the sale divided among the six children. Off and on during the 1740s, F. lived with Henry, helping him care for his children. By 1754, she appears to have settled in the vicinity of Bath, in a house provided by Ralph Allen (Squire Allworthy of Henry's *Tom Jones*).

In 1742, F. likely wrote the Letter from Leonora to Horatio in Henry's *Joseph Andrews*, and one year later she seems to have written Ann Boleyn's story for Henry's *Journey from this World to the Next*. In May 1744, when she was thirty-four years old, F. published her first novel, *The Adventures of David Simple . . . by a Lady*, which she preceded with this note: "Perhaps the best Excuse that can be made for a Woman's venturing to write at all, is that which really produced this Book—Distress in her Circumstances, which she could not so well remove by any other Means in her Power. If it should meet with Success, it will be the only Good Fortune she ever has known." Immediately popular, the novel came out in a second edition that autumn, in a form "revised and corrected" by Henry.

F.'s innovative genius, political consciousness, and interest in psychology are reflected in her seven novels, each of which experiments with the form of fiction in order to examine the damage to the human psyche incurred by the mid-eighteenth-century system of patriarchal capitalism. Her fictional experiments include writing the first children's novel and first British fictional autobiography, as well as creating a new genre she called "dramatic fable." In the 1744 *David Simple*, she experiments with urban picaresque as a vehicle for apologue, and in the completion of this novel, *Volume the Last* (1753), she draws her apologue to its dark conclusion through the use of domestic tragedy. She uses satire throughout, its light stroke in the 1744 work sharpening to a painful edge in the last volume. She condemns the system we know as patriarchal capitalism for the greed and mistrust it fosters in families and communities and through such professionals as lawyers and financiers. In particular, she depicts the insidious effects of internal oppression, damning the supposed feminine virtues of innocence, passivity, and privacy for the illness and failure they allow to fester unto death.

In 1746, F. likely wrote a story for the March 18–25 issue of her brother's journal, *The True Patriot.* One year later, she published her epistolary collection. *Familiar Letters Between the Principal Characters in "David Simple";* her children's novel, *The Governess; or, The Little Female Academy,* was published in 1749 after readings in manuscript by both Samuel Richardson and Jane Collier, with a second edition the same year. Using formal realism in combination with such modes as fable, fairy tale, and parable, *The Governess* illustrates the connection of womanly community to female identity. In the female academy, young girls learn to bring their own powers of analysis to everyday situations and to tell their own stories as a way of articulating identity. Also in 1749, F. seems to have published the pamphlet *Remarks on Clarissa, Addressed to the Author,* and in 1752, she likely contributed two pieces to Henry's *Covent-Garden Journal, Numbers 63 and 64.* During this time, she must also have been writing *The Adventures of David Simple: Volume the Last.* Grief for the deaths of her three sisters, who had died within eighteen months of each other, in 1750–51, may have inspired the dark vision of *Volume the Last,* in which despair for a healthy society is emphasized through repeated illnesses and deaths of innocent people.

At this same time, F. and her friend Jane Collier were at work on *The Cry: A New Dramatic Fable,* which they published in 1754. *The Cry* is a work of metafiction, examining parameters of responsibility and dialogue between author and audience and focusing on woman's effort to define herself in a world that demands her self-effacement. Assuming "a certain freedom in writing, not strictly perhaps within the limits prescribed by rules," F. and Collier here shape a unique genre, one that employs the essay form as well as drama and fable, a shifting angle of vision, narrative within narrative, and frequent satiric/comic sallies.

In 1757, F. published by subscription *The Lives of Cleopatra and Octavia,* a fictional autobiography in which F. employs the device of paired women in order to illustrate internal oppression and its various corruptions of the female psyche. In writing *Cleopatra and Octavia,* F. drew upon her knowledge of classical history and literature and told the story of these parallel lives through the use of epistolary fiction, first-person narration, and fantasy set in the underworld.

The History of the Countess of Dellwyn was published in 1759. Employing satire and domestic tragedy, F. here tells the devastating story of a woman whose corruption by the marriage market is such that she becomes goods-for-sale, even to herself. Her outward humiliation, culminating in the shame of a public divorce, is petty compared to the spectacle of her total loss of self and consequent inability to love. *The History of Ophelia,* published in 1760, experiments with a Richardsonian plot, the Gothic, and satire of a type that looks forward to Fanny Burney and Jane Austen. Opening with bitter condemnation of the sexual oppression of women, the novel explores the effects of the feminine "virtues" in perpetuating female sexual vulnerability.

Although F. worked to earn her own way, all her life she was a needy gentlewoman, and the plight of others like herself is a theme in her novels. In *The Countess of Dellwyn,* she offers a solution, a community of women. In January 1768, when she was fifty-eight, F. was invited by her friends Elizabeth Montagu and Sarah Scott to join just such a household, which they were planning to establish, but by then she was too ill to leave her cottage and in April she died.

WORKS: *The Adventures of David Simple: Containing an Account of his Travels thro' the Cities of London and Westmister, in the Search of a Real Friend. By a Lady* (1744). *The Adventures of David Simple . . . The Second Edition revised and corrected, with Alterations and Additions; and a Preface by Henry Fielding Esq.* (1744, 1775 [abridged]). *Familiar Letters between the Principal Characters in David Simple, and some others . . . To which is added, A Vision. By the Author of David Simple* (1747). *The Governess; or, Little Female Academy* (1749). *Remarks on Clarissa, Addressed to the Author* (1749). *Attributions: The History of Charlotta Summers* (1749). *The History of Betty Barnes* (1753). *The Adventures of David Simple, Volume the Last* (1753). *The Cry: A New Dramatic Fable* (1754). *The Lives of Cleopatra and Octavia* (1757). *The History of the Countess of Dellwyn* (1759). *The History of Ophelia* (1760). *The Histories of Some of the Penitents in the Magdalen House* (1760). (trans.) *Xenophon's Memoirs of Socrates* (1762).

BIBLIOGRAPHY: *The Adventures of David Simple,* ed. and intro E. A. Baker (1904). Burdan, J. F. *CLAQ* (1994). Burrows, J. F. *ECS* (1988). Cross, W. *The History of Henry Fielding* (1918). Dudden, F. H. *Henry Fielding: His Life, Work, and Times* (1952). Grey, J. E., ed. and intro. *The Governess* (1968). *Sarah Fielding: 1710–1768,* ed. and intro. J. E. Grey (1968). *The Lives of Cleopatra and Octavia,* ed. and intro. R. B. Johnson (1928). *The Adventures of David Simple,* ed. and intro. M. Kelsall (1969). Kern, J. B., in *Fetter'd or Free? British Women Novelists, 1670–1815,* ed. M. A. Schofield and C. Macheski (1986). McKillop, A. D. *Samuel Richardson, Printer and Novelist* (1936). MacCarthy, B. *The Female Pen. Vol 1: Women Writers: Their Contribution to the English Novel, 1621–1744* (1944). Schellenberg, B. A. *SVEC* (1992). *The Cry,* ed. and intro. M. A. Schofield (1986). Wilner, A. F. *SECC* (1995). Woodward, C., in *Transactions of the Samuel Johnson Society of the Northwest* (1984).

For articles in reference works, see: *Bloomsbury. Cambridge. DNB. Feminist. OCEL. Oxford. ToddBWW. ToddDBA.*

Other references Barker, G. A. *MLS* (1982). Battestin, M. C. *Novel* (1979). Black, C. *Gentleman's Magazine* (1888). Downs-Miers, D. *CLAQ* (1985). Downs-Miers, D., in *Fetter'd or Free: British Women Novelists, 1670–1815,* ed. M. A. Schofield and C. Macheski (1986).

Horner, J. M. *Smith College Studies in Modern Languages* (October 1929). Hunting, R. S. *Boston University Studies in English* (1957). Johnson, R. B. *TLS* (11 April 1929). McKillop, A. D. *MP* (1934). Reynolds, M. *The Learned Lady in England* (1929). *TLS* (4 April 1929). Utter, R. P. and G. B. Needham, *Pamela's Daughters* (1937). Watt, I. *The Rise of the Novel* (1965).

Carolyn Woodward

Celia Fiennes

BORN: 1662, Newton Toney, near Salisbury, Wiltshire.
DIED: 1741, Hackney, London.
DAUGHTER OF: Colonel Nathaniel Fiennes and Frances Whitehead Fiennes.

Like many women writers, F. is not recognized for her contribution to literature for her unusual travel book. Instead, her limited fame has been garnered by the historical and sociological importance of her observations. Born in the manor house at Newton Toney of a prominent Puritan family, and christened Cecilia, F. began her travels in 1685 when she was about twenty-three. At first, her "great journey" was with her mother, but later she traveled by coach, sometimes alone, sometimes with two other women, and sometimes with two servants. Her longest journeys were on horseback between 1697 and 1698. By 1712, when she finished her travels, she had visited every county in England, Scotland, and Wales and had become the first woman to record her experiences. Unfortunately, no record of her life survives beyond the account of her travels, even though she lived about thirty more years.

Most of the men in her family served in the Parliamentary forces during the Civil War. Her grandfather, William Fiennes, First Viscount Say and Sele, opposed King Charles I in Parliament; her father, the second son of the viscount, was an officer in the parliamentary army; her mother was the daughter of Colonel Richard Whitehead of the parliamentary forces; and three uncles of the immediate family along with five uncles by marriage fought against the king.

Although she took her longest trips in 1697, F. wrote most of her journal from notes in 1702. She began her travels twenty-five years after the Restoration of the monarchy "to regain my health by variety and change of aire and exercise." She wrote of her journeys to encourage others to "spend some of their tyme in Journeys to visit their native Land." She thought it of special concern for members of Parliament who "are ignorant of anything but the name of the place for which they serve." During her travels, F. visited London, where she witnessed the coronations of James II, William and Mary, and Anne. She saw and then vividly described towns, inns, orchards, country houses, and local customs.

Through F., we learn that life even for the privileged traveler was fraught with problems. On one occasion, she and her two servants lost their bed linens between Durham and Darlington. On another she notes that they needed six hours to travel nine miles. At crowded inns, she notes that "sometymes . . . three must ly in a bed." She writes with distaste and propriety of filth, highwaymen, and anti–Roman Catholicism. In the process she opens a window on life in the late seventeenth century from the perspective of a young Puritan woman.

Although Robert Southey quoted from the first draft of the book in 1812, F.'s book was not printed until 1888, when her descendant, Emily Griffiths, found the manuscript and published most of it as *Through England on a Side Saddle in the Time of William and Mary.* G. M. Trevelyan found the Griffiths's text had historical value and included it in his *English Social History.* Not until 1947, when Christopher Morris published his edition, however, did it receive scholarly treatment. He divided the work into four parts: "The Early Journeys in the South (c. 1685–96)," "The Northern Journey and the Tour of Kent (1697)," "My Great Journey to Newcastle and to Cornwall (1698)," and "London and the Later Journeys (c. 1701–1703)." Highly praised by Trevelyan, the edition became an important source of economic and social history. Today, F.'s diary should be revisited, for, like Samuel Pepys's diary, it is often naïve and rarely thoughtful but constantly curious, informative, and entertaining.

WORKS: *Through England on a Side Saddle in the Time of William and Mary,* ed. E. Griffiths (1888). *The Journeys of Celia Fiennes,* ed. C. Morris (1947).

BIBLIOGRAPHY: *The Journeys of Celia Fiennes,* ed. J. Hillaby (1983). Parkes, J. *Travel in England in the Seventeenth Century* (1925). Thomas, P. R. and D. S. Thomas. *Papermaking in Seventeenth-Century England* (1990). Willy, M. *Three Women Diarists: Celia Fiennes, Dorothy Wordsworth, Katherine Mansfield* (1964).

For articles in reference works, see: *Bell. BioIn. Bloomsbury. CBEL. DNB. Feminist. Index to Women of the World (Supplement). ToddBWW. Who Was Who in World. Exploration.*

Sophia B. Blaydes

Eva Figes

BORN: 15 April 1932, Berlin, Germany.
DAUGHTER OF: Emil Eduard Unger and Irma Cohen Unger.
MARRIED: John George Figes, 1954.

Born to affluent, German-Jewish parents in Berlin shortly before Hitler assumed power, F. lived her first seven years in Germany before escaping, with her parents and brother, to England in 1939. There she excelled in studies and won a scholarship to read literature at Queen Mary College, London, from which she received a B.A. (with honors) in 1953. From 1952 until 1967, she worked as an editor for several publishing houses; during that time she married John George Figes (1954) and had two children. The breakup of her marriage led to her writing her first novel, *Equinox* (1966). Her second novel, *Winter Journey* (1967), won the Guardian Fiction Prize. A number of additional novels and several scholarly studies, including *Patriarchal Attitudes: Women in Society* (1970), *Tragedy and Social*

Evolution (1976), *Sex and Subterfuge* (1982), and an autobiography, *Little Eden* (1978), followed.

F.'s fiction is experimental, intricate, sometimes obscure, and often challenging; for some readers it is simply inaccessible while for others it is singularly unsatisfying. *Patriarchal Attitudes: Women in Society* is a classic historical study, convincing in its presentation of how men have sought to subjugate women. Her opposition to traditional sexual stereotypes runs parallel to her pronounced dissatisfaction with traditional forms of fiction. Because of this dissatisfaction, F.'s fiction is marked by three sometimes troubling qualities: lack of traditional, identifiable plot structure; an often unreliable narrator/protagonist; and a prose style that is frequently dense, allusive, and obscure—and sometimes deliberately manipulative.

Winter Journey is a short, 119–page novel narrated by a confused, failing elderly man, Janus Stobbs. The story of one day in his life, the novel succeeds in depicting an old man's pain-wracked efforts just to keep moving. *Konek Landing* (1969) reveals F.'s debt to Franz Kafka: A stateless orphan suffers through a complex series of interior monologues and nightmares in an often incomprehensible struggle; a Central European Jew who narrowly escaped the Nazi Holocaust, F. here expresses a profound sense of survivor's guilt in an attempt to make some sense of this ghastly period of human history. *B.* (1972), a metafictional experiment documenting the creative angst of an alienated writer, received a cool critical reception. Likewise, *Days* (1974), a stream-of-consciousness tale told by a nameless female narrator lying in a hospital, lacks convincing narrative unity and is marred by heavy-handed allegorizing. And in *Nelly's Version* (1977), F.'s fondness for ambiguity pervades a tale of lost identity. The narrator, a middle-aged female amnesiac, functions as a video/audio cassette recording the people and places of typical English landscapes. The novel shows the influence of Harold Pinter and Samuel Beckett as well as Kafka; read as a thriller, it invites comparison with Alfred Hitchcock's films.

In two of her recent novels, F. has realized a stunning poetic lyricism. *Waking* (1981) chronicles that hazy period between sleep and full awakening at seven times in the life of an unnamed female narrator whose interior monologues reveal her as intensely preoccupied with self, a woman who feels herself defiled by contact with others. *Light* (1983), a 91–page novella limning one day in the life of Claude Monet, offers an integrated, more traditional narrative. F.'s poetic prose, impressionistic and sensuous, perfectly matches the subject with an evocative power sufficient to make light the chief character of this work as it was in Monet's.

In somewhat oversimplified fashion, we might divide F.'s novels into two groups: the first includes *Equinox, Winter Journey, Konek Landing, B., Days,* and *Nelly's Version;* the second includes *Waking* and *Light.* The novels of the first group are essentially fables of identity, whether personal, racial, or artistic, with unreliable, fallible narrators wandering in space and time. They live in constricted worlds of social isolation, weighted down by the past. Oppression, the product of political and sexual forces, abounds. *Waking,* while taking its subject matter from these previously explored areas of identity and structure, is organized chronologically. F.'s powerful lyric language delineates a woman-in-process; here, Virgina Woolf's rhythmic rendering of character finds new expression.

In *Light,* F.'s preoccupations with time, identity, and creativity merge. Though creativity and identity have intersected before (*B.*), they've never met forcefully, nor could they, except in the person of Monet, a consummate artist who sought to capture fugitive light before time stole it from him. Likewise, F. attempts to capture light and time in her creation. Her pointillist, poetic language embraces the experience of time: We live with and through Monet, as well as the members of his household, for twenty-four hours. *Light* seems to point in a new direction, for F. Monet is an isolated, rather than alienated, figure. He moves freely away from and back toward his family and household at Giverny. His excursions on the water are nearly solitary; though accompanied by a sleepy boyhood friend, he is, for all intents and purposes, surrounded by silence and light as he paints. His individual perceptions are transmuted into art; a canvas, temporarily finished, is laid aside, until another day, and the painter returns to his small, vital human community. *Light* is a poetic distillation of F.'s probing not only inner consciousness but the unconsciousness, where the springs of creativity swirl. This is F.'s finest novel to date.

While some critics have asserted that F.'s ninth novel, *The Seven Ages* (1986), is "a new sort of historical novel, a remarkable blend of history, folklore, and the poetic imagination; a narrative progression of intense beauty," it falls short of the mark. This is a novel of seven individualized female voices, each speaking from a different historical time period—early medieval, Chaucerian, Renaissance, Puritan, eighteenth-century, Victorian/Edwardian, contemporary—and linked by common experiences of childbirth and patriarchal oppression. Such exploration constitutes valid and interesting material for a novel, yet this feminist counterpoint to William Shakespeare's "seven ages of man," flawed by triteness, hyperbole, confused and confusing chronology, repetition, and excessive use of coincidence, never achieves coherence. Is it a novel, a series of short stories, a diatribe, or a catalogue of folk medicines and herbal lore? It could well be all of these, but F.'s failure to assert some greater aesthetic control—as she did so splendidly in *Waking* and *Light*—fragments the text and leaves the reader wanting.

Ghosts (1988) is likewise a flawed exercise; a self-consciously "aesthetic" and autoderivative work, its center assumed by an anonymous, late-middle-aged female narrator who lives on the margins of death, *Ghosts* is a sustained, often lyrical, monologue on loss, darkness, fear, death, and absence. F. has set her narrative on a carefully constructed four-part grid of the seasons; in the one year covered by the novel, the narrator spends most of her time inventorying her losses (childhood, father, children, lover) before dealing with present matters. Typically, F.'s skills render another classic expression of age-induced alienation, and this novel may be, for some, the luminous "prose poem" its blurb proclaims; but for others it will be found wanting: an irritating overuse of paradox ("is, and is not"; "am, and am not"), an overabundance of white space to punctuate text, and an altogether too-obvious attempt to universalize the narrator's experience weaken the novel. Moreover, in a novel rather too literary for its own good (ghosts of Shakespeare, James Joyce, Thomas Hardy, and Henrik Ibsen, of course), the ending with its contrived echoes of the *Tempest* proves yet another irritation.

F.'s eleventh novel, *The Tree of Knowledge* (1990), is an eight-part dramatic monologue delivered by Deborah, daughter of John Milton; this woman, denied the opportunity for education given to her male cousins, made servant to her father's "genius," and further abused by a stepmother who inherited nearly all Milton had to leave, lives as a poor widow who has lost seven of her ten children. Though not consumed by bitterness (she says that she has long since forgiven her father, though she cannot forget his harshness), Deborah feels more than the loss of parental affection. Men eager to know more of her father call and she recounts details from his life while telling more and more of her own; her narrative reveals the tragedy of a very considerable intelligence never given ample room for development. Nonetheless, she has achieved remarkable insight into a world where women lack opportunity for fulfillment and are little more than servants to men.

The Tree of Knowledge is revisionist history, a remarkable feminist rereading of Milton and his times from which overt hostility and bitterness have been purged. The last chapter, the eighth monologue, is a tour-de-force, a brilliant evocation of the dying Deborah's thoughts in which the threads of memory connect and disconnect in light and darkness as she wanders in and out of consciousness: Her recognition that the tree of knowledge and the tree of life are one and the same is succeeded by a glorious vision of daylight promise. In the process of telling Deborah's story, F. portrays England after the utopian hopes unleashed by Oliver Cromwell have been dashed, a world in which few still subscribe to a notion of providential history evolving toward grand fulfillment. F.'s triumph here lies in creating a vividly truthful portrait of a great poet and the damage done by his genius, set within the richly rendered context of enormous sociocultural change; and more: F. has inscribed the story of many women while bringing to life a richly complex and sympathetic individual woman whose voice echoes down through the ages.

The Tenancy (1993) tells the story of Edith Johnson, a middle-aged woman living in a contemporary, unnamed city—presumably London. Edith has had an unhappy life: Bullied by an insulting mother who always preferred Edith's sly brother, Robert, Edith, who has no visible means of support, lives without husband, lover, or children. Freed at last from responsibility for the care of her mother, who is taken off to a nursing home, Edith seems to hover at the edge of freedom and a new life, but things fall apart rapidly; unexplained catastrophes occur in the decaying building inhabited by Edith: The water is turned off; the pipes freeze; uncollected garbage litters the stairwells. A final conflagration scorches all possibility. The essential problem with *The Tenancy* is one of genre and intention. Is this a novel, a fantasy, a fable, a parable? Edith is simply not rich or deep enough to sustain a novel; her story lacks the freshness and originality essential to engaging a reader's enduring interest. The other tenants, who are types more than characters, the dark menacing forces that come to control Edith's building, the darkness and essential sparseness of the narrative, and the unmistakable echoes of Kafka would seem to establish the dynamics for a parable. If so, of what might *The Tenancy* be a parable? If not, and that seems to be the case, this novel remains, nonetheless, a gripping, if unresolved, tale of one contemporary woman's powerless existence within a context of social collapse and urban terror.

F. has recently edited and published *Women's Letters in Wartime, 1450–1945* (1993), a collection that covers a time period from the Wars of the Roses to World War II. F.'s introduction makes clear the links between her fiction and nonfiction: She notes that she collated these letters because of her curiosity "about the nature and content of lost lives." The collection includes nearly 200 letters written by twenty-six women, including Queen Victoria, Florence Nightingale, Lord Nelson's wife, Frances, and his mistress, Emma Hamilton. As absorbing as letters written by these well-known figures are, even more fascinating and affecting are those written by unknown women like Isabel Gore, who went to South Africa to be with her husband during the Boer War, and Ellie Rendel, who served as a nurse in Russia and the Balkans during World War I. All letters inscribe longing in poignant and powerful terms.

The list of F.'s works includes a number of translations as well as several books for children (*The Musicians of Bremen*, 1967, *The Banger*, 1968, and *Scribble Sam: A Story*, 1971). F. has also written radio plays: *Time Regained* (1980), *Days* (1981), *Dialogue Between Friends* (1982). *Punch-Flame and Pigeon-Breast* (1983), *The True Tale of Margery Kempe* (1985).

WORKS: (trans.) *The Gadarene Club*, by M. Walser (1960). *Equinox* (1966). *The Musicians of Bremen* (1967). *Winter Journey* (1967). (trans.) *He and I and the Elephants*, by B. Grzimek (1967). (trans.) *Little Fadette*, by G. Sand (1967). *The Banger* (1968). *Konek Landing* (1969). (trans.) *Family Failure*, by R. Rasp (1970). *Patriarchal Attitudes: Women in Society* (1970). *Scribble Sam: A Story* (1971). (trans.) *The Deathbringer*, by M. von Contra (1971). *B.* (1972). *Days* (1974). *Tragedy and Social Evolution* (1976). *Nelly's Version* (1977). *Little Eden* (1978). *Time Regained* (1980). *Days* (1981). *Waking* (1981). *Light* (1982). *Dialogue Between Friends* (1982). *Sex and Subterfuge: Women Novelists to 1850* (1982). *Punch-Flame and Pigeon-Breast* (1983). *The True Tale of Margery Kempe* (1985). *The Seven Ages* (1986). *Little Eden: A Child at War* (1987). *Ghosts* (1988). *The Tree of Knowledge* (1990). *The Tenancy* (1993). *The Knot* (1996).

BIBLIOGRAPHY:

For articles in reference works, see: *Bloomsbury*. *CA*. *CLC*. *CN*. *DLB*. *DLEL*. *Feminist*. Kenyon, O. *Women Writers Talk* (1989).

Other references: *BW* (11 November 1984, 13 October 1985, 31 May 1987, 23 September 1990, 7 April 1991). *Commonweal* (2 April 1971, 27 April 1986, 24 April 1987). *Guardian* (27 October 1993). *LRB* (10 February 1994). *Ms.* (November 1991). *Nation* (31 December 1983, 7 January 1984, 25 September 1987, 13 May 1988). *New Statesman* (25 September 1987, 13 May 1988). *New Yorker* (8 June 1968). *NYRB* (22 July 1971, 12 May 1982). *NYT* (23 February 1982). *NYTBR* (28 April 1968, 28 February 1982, 16 October 1983, 22 February 1987, 25 September 1988, 16 June 1991). *Ob-*

server (9 April 1967, 15 May 1988, 23 September 1990, 26 March 1993, 27 November 1994)). *RCF* (Summer 1988). *Spectator* (30 June 1977). *TLS* (24 April 1967, 31 July 1970, 23 January 1981, 26 August 1983, 3–9 June 1988, 19 October 1990, 26 March 1993). *YR* (January 1984).

Robert Ellis Hosmer, Jr.

Anne Kingsmill Finch, Countess of Winchelsea

BORN: April 1661.
DIED: 5 August 1720, London.
DAUGHTER OF: William Kingsmill and Anne Kingsmill.
MARRIED: Heneage Finch, 1684.
WROTE UNDER: Anne, Countess of Winchelsea; Ardelia; A Lady.

The best thing that ever happened to F., or more precisely to her poetry, was the deposition of King James II in 1688. She and her husband, Heneage Finch, had held positions in James's court, he as gentleman of the bedchamber, she as maid of honor to Mary of Modena. With the exile of James, those at court were required to take an oath of allegiance to William and Mary. This the Finches could not do, meaning that their public lives were over.

Heneage Finch was the uncle of the Earl of Winchelsea. When in 1690 the Earl invited F. and husband to the family seat in Kent, F. found an environment conducive to poetry: a circle of literate and literary friends (she knew Nicolas and Elizabeth Rowe as well as John Gay, Alexander Pope, and Jonathan Swift, all of whom wholly recognized her talents); the devotion and encouragement of a loving husband (Heneage became Earl of Winchelsea when his nephew died in 1712); beautiful natural surroundings; alternation between London and Kent with the social season; and plenty of free time.

This is not to suggest that her way was completely smooth. F. had the inner tensions that produce good poetry; some of these had to do with the fears and frustrations of a woman who wishes to enter the male-dominated world of literature. It is true that as a woman of rank she was exempt to some extent from real critical calumny, but even a cursory reading of her work reveals her deep wish to be taken seriously. Many ruling-class women of her time dabbled in verse, but F. set herself apart with a genuine desire, not to say need, to write. Writing was literally her life, all the more so after the Finches left court. If we can believe her poem "Ardelia to Melancholy," her writing was therapy for and a retreat from recurrent bouts of depression. She herself, however, considered her poetry far more than therapy. F. kept informed of the major intellectual and artistic currents of the Augustan age, and her poetry shows genuine poetic sensibility together with a keen interest in ideas.

There are essentially three divisions of F.'s work. The first are the occasional poems, devotionals, and songs that she wrote between 1680 and 1700. These she either kept private out of fear of ridicule or published anonymously in anthologies. During this period she wrote "The Spleen" (1701), a fine Augustan Pindaric ode and one of the best meditations on melancholy in English.

Many of these early poems appeared in *Miscellany Poems on Several Occasions, Written By a Lady* (1713). This book marks a second division in F.'s work because her decision to publish was in itself remarkable. On the one hand, she was shy and retiring; her fear of ridicule was not the convention it may appear to be in some of her poems. She genuinely abhorred the labels of female versifier or dilettante scribbler. In "The Introduction" F. writes that the prospect of facing the critical establishment, intimidating enough to any writer, must appear worse still to a woman: "So strong the opposing faction still appears, / The hopes to strive can ne'er outweigh the fears." Her next line might well be taken as her personal and literary credo: "Be cautioned then, my Muse, and still retired."

Miscellany Poems indeed does show the work of a cautioned muse. Here, F.'s poems steer clear of confrontation and controversy; rather, they are public poems, showing her talent and versatility in many of the popular Augustan modes, including dramatic verse, fables, meditations, and odes. In this volume she is already an accomplished poet, with a flexible line, a sensitive ear, and the knack for disposition that other writers strove for in this age of "rational" poetic utterance.

There is also a distinctive sensibility striving to be expressed that is most apparent in the manuscript of poems she left for posthumous publication, the third division in F.'s work. Here, she felt freer to condemn the exclusion of women from public life, the male contempt for women poets, and (in the poem "The Unequal Fetters") the unjust double standard that makes marriage the end of a woman's life and only an intermittent obligation for a man. Although individual poems from this collection did appear in print, the entire manuscript was not published until 1903.

In this manuscript, F. largely writes from the feminine perspective, which in itself would be enough to set her apart. She writes of her relation to other women and other women writers, of her quite happy marriage, and of the rigors of writing. "Ardelia's Answer to Ephelia" is the only Augustan poem to attempt a serious moral judgment of women; F. satirizes the empty-headed followers of fashion as women without much inner content, and, perhaps most exciting, she portrays the ideal of woman as rational and moral. Such a thing had certainly never been done by any of her contemporaries, and only seldom, if at all, before then. F.'s models were mostly by, for, and about the ideal man, and thus she may be said to have been writing without precedent.

Miscellany Poems had been prefaced by "Mercury and the Elephant," a conventional poem of self-effacement. We need only compare it to the later "Introduction" to measure the difference in the two volumes. The first twenty lines of "The Introduction" are a list of the stock criticisms leveled at the woman writer, culminating with the bitter words "the dull manage of a servile house / Is held by some our utmost art and use." This poem is F. at her most tough minded. Yer there is a note of despair at the end, a fear that her poems may never have been meant for the "laurel groves" of established literature.

F. cannot be said to have had much of a reputation for the rest of the century, for her real poetic career began when William Wordsworth rediscovered her. When we read "A Nocturnal Reverie," we can see why Wordsworth felt she was a kindred spirit. She had anticipated by almost a century the paradigm of the Romantic meditation on nature. The poet finds a solitary spot one evening, and, by devoting rapt attention to the reality of nature, discovers ease, release, and, ultimately, the desire "to seek / Something, too high for syllables to speak." F.'s meditation is different, however, from Shelleyan ecstasy or Byronic fury. She emphasizes that the speaker's spirit feels a "sedate content" and that the soul discovers a "solemn quiet." This is not the spontaneous overflow of Wordsworth, though the emotions revealed are indeed powerful. Still, it is remarkable that F. anticipated so much of the Romantic program in this and in other poems (such as "The Petition for an Absolute Retreat," in which the poet seeks isolation in nature for meditation). And in "A Nocturnal Reverie" we may feel that F. observes nature far more precisely than some Romantics did: At twilight, "a paler hue the foxglove rakes / Yet checkers still with red the dusty brakes"; odors "through temperate air uninterrupted stray"; in a startlingly modern line, "swelling haycocks thicken up the vale." In the end, F. may have been right. Her poems, so Augustan, were not for the Augustan age but for later readers, better equipped with the open mind needed to appreciate them.

New interest arose in F.'s work with the rise of feminist and post-structuralist ways of reading. Some have tried to portray her as deeply frustrated, unhappy, and unfulfilled—and she definitely did chafe at male efforts to circumscribe and discount the poetic powers of women. But such efforts may obscure what truly drove F. What she wanted most was to write and to be recognized as a worthy thinker and writer. Recognition has come three centuries too late, but at least it has definitely come. The more people read her, the more they have come to appreciate that she belongs among the significant poets in English.

WORKS: *Miscellany Poems on Several Occasions, Written By a Lady* (1713). *The Poems of Anne Countess of Winchelsea,* ed. M. Reynolds (1903). *Selected Poems of Anne Finch, Countesse of Winchelsea,* ed. K. M. Rogers (1979). "Poems by Anne Finch," ed. E. Hampsten, *WS* (1980). *Selected Poems,* ed. D. Thompson (1987). *The Wellesley Manuscript Poems of Anne Countess of Winchelsea: From an Unpublished Manuscript* (1988).

BIBLIOGRAPHY: Brower, R. A. *SP* (1945). Chavis, J. A. S. *Aphra Behn and Anne Finch: Uncommon Women* (1986). Ellis D'Alessandro, J. *When in the Shade—Imaginal Equivalents in Anne the Countess of Winchelsea's Poetry* (1989). Hinnant, C. *The Poetry of Anne Finch: An Essay in Interpretation* (1994). Lewis, J. *The English Fable: Aesop and Literary Culture, 1651–1740* (1996). McGovern, B. *Anne Finch and Her Poetry: A Critical Biography* (1992). Messenger, A. *ESC* (1980). Messenger, A. *Restoration: Studies an English Literary Culture, 1660–1700* (1981). *Gender at Work: Four Women Writers of the Eighteenth Century,* ed. A. Messenger (1990). Rogers, K. M. *Shakespeare's Sisters,* ed. S. Gilbert and S. Gubar (1979). Sena, J. F. *YES* (1971). Thompson, D. *PNR* (26 June 1982).

For articles in reference books, see: *Bloomsbury. Cambridge. Feminist. Oxford. ToddBWW.*

Other references: Barash, C. *HLQ* (1991). Bonnell, T. F., in *Teaching Eighteenth-Century Poetry,* ed. C. Fox (1990). Brashear, L. *Explicator* (1981). Greer, G., in *The Nature of Identity,* ed. W. Weathers (1981). Hinnant, C. *SEL* (1991). Hinnant, C. *ECent* (1992). Johnston, L. *Explicator* (1983). Messenger, A. *Restoration* (1981). Mermin, D. *ELH* (1990). Rogers, K. M. *Mosaic* (1989). Thompson, D. *PNR* (1982).

John Timpane

Penelope (Knox) Fitzgerald

BORN: 17 December 1916, Lincoln.
DAUGHTER OF: Edmund Valpy Knox and Christina Hicks.
MARRIED: Desmond Fitzgerald, 1941.

F.'s family was distinguished by achievement in letters and religion. Her father was the editor of *Punch* and his brother, her uncle, Monsignor Ronald Knox, the acclaimed biblical scholar. At Somerville College, Oxford, she read English and received a degree with first-class honors in 1939. She has worked as a journalist, a programmer for the BBC, a book shop proprietor, and a tutor. Before her first work of fiction, written at the age of sixty-one and published in 1977, she wrote two biographies, one of Edward Burne-Jones, the other of her uncles, the four Knox brothers. She has also written *Charlotte Mew and Her Friends* (1979) and edited *The Novel on Blue Paper* (1981), an incomplete work by William Morris.

The author of ten novels to date, F. has enjoyed popular and critical success, not only in England but also in the United States where nearly all her novels have been published as well. In all her writing, F. demonstrated a remarkably fluent, evocative prose style, consistently favoring, by her own acknowledgment, the virtues of economy and compression. Without oversimplifying or undervaluing her fiction, we might say that her work is characterized by several telling qualities: careful illumination of a small world; unsentimental, though not unsympathetic, delineation of characters, particularly the young and the aged; a concern for articulating sound moral values; and finally, a decided comic richness that unifies character, language, and narrative.

The Golden Child, a thriller set "in the great hive of the [unnamed] Museum with the Golden Treasure at its heart," presents the stifling world of that museum with its competing personalities of varying backgrounds and interests as a metaphor for society. F.'s characters, with the exception of only a few, most notably Sir William Livingstone Simpkin, are detached from ordinary human concerns, viewing the museum as a kind of secret treasure chest, open only when absolutely necessary to viewing by outsiders. Simpkin, with his sympathy for the crowds of cold children queued up around the building, waiting for admission to the exhibition of the golden child, is the humane and moral center of gravity for the novel. Knowing that the golden treasures are fakes, he shuns any role in the commercial spectacle and dies when crushed between two steel shelves in the Museum's library. In an explosive climax, the glass case containing the golden child breaks and "reveals the ancient royal child as an undernourished, recently deceased African child."

Likewise, in *The Bookshop* (1978), the focus falls on an individual of courage and conviction living within a world of competing forces. Here the social context is nearly as static as the Department of Funerary Art at the museum: the town of Hardborough is a depressed area, victim to the hard times that hit Britain in the late 1950s. Florence Green decides to open a bookshop in the Old House, a damp, haunted structure at the atrophied heart of the town. From the outset, physical setting, economic conditions, and social context collaborate against her, yet their victory is no quick conquest. Old Mr. Brundish and young Christine Gipping lend considerable, though ultimately ineffectual, support to Florence. In her unsentimental depiction of these three characters, F. creates a carefully localized drama of individual courage and determination assaulted by inhospitable natural forces and knowing political powers. Mr. Brundish dies after pleading Florence's case; Christine's work at the shop may have caused her poor showing on her exams; Florence loses her bookshop and leaves town. Flecked with wonderfully comic episodes and a poetic recreation of land- and seascape, *The Bookshop* is a novel about the oppression imposed by divisions of class, education, and individual consciousness.

In her third novel, *Offshore* (1979), for which she won the Booker Prize, F.'s powers of specificity and richly atmospheric description enable her to present a whole world in the space of only 133 pages. Set in 1961 within a kind of utopian community of houseboat dwellers, a classless cast of characters living on the tidal Thames at Battersea Reach, the novel presents these men and women living in a divided world, half the time mired in the mud, half the time drifting. As in her depiction of Florence Green, F. is interested in the ways in which human beings live within particular contexts; some succeed, some do not, and once again F. is particularly successful at creating children who are knowing survivors in an adult world. But F. gathers rather too many characters on board to keep things afloat with her typical buoyancy. *Offshore* ends neither at sea nor on dry land but in ceaseless flux, subject to the threat of cruel tides on the one hand and gelatinous mud on the other.

Human Voices (1980) is perhaps F.'s least engaging novel. This time the fictional microcosm is the BBC's Records Programmes Department (RPD); the time is summer and autumn, 1940. Very much like the museum of *The Golden Child,* the department is a hive of power games and territorial intrigue, and here, too, there is "the pride and bitter jealousy which is the poetry of museum-keeping," though rhetorical concerns are naturally of greater moment in this context. Dialogue, which comprises the bulk of the novel, etches character and delineates conflict; silence emphasizes and amplifies. More than in any other F. novel, style functions as content; in her use of both speech and silence, in her attempts to capture the nuances and peculiarities of human communication, F. has extended the range of her own voice, but it is open to question whether her attempt to broaden the meaning and relevance of her miniature set-piece, the BBC's RPD, succeeds.

With the delightful *At Freddie's* (1982), F. returned to the world of aged eccentrics and knowing children, in this case the Temple Stage School, founded and run by Miss Freddie Wentworth, a snappy, Kate Hepburn–type character. For nearly forty years, she has trained child actors for the London theater; the roguish band of children studying at Freddie's in 1964 comprises talented characters who are professional but not prematurely adult. A crisis occurs when the government decides to establish a national Stage School; realizing that she will be out of business, Freddie orchestrates a letter-writing campaign to *The Times.* In the end, though the government's plans are shelved, the savvy Freddie decides that she will henceforth train her charges for television commercials. Like Florence Green, Freddie is a survivor; unlike her, she is a successful survivor. This novel is marvelously entertaining, seamless in construction, knowing in character development, and brightly human, though not Pollyannish in its optimistic outlook.

With F.'s next novel, intensity of interest in the human condition remains the same, but the geography shifts: *Innocence* (1986), set in 1950s Florence, tells the story of the Ridolfi family, descended from sixteenth-century midgets. The old count, Giancarlo, lives in the Piazza Limbo with his sister, Maddalena, widow of an English bird-watcher, and his eighteen-year-old daughter, Chiara, the central figure in the narrative. In another departure, F. has written a novel in allegory, and from that as well as her typically skillful illumination of character and period context derives extraordinary resonance and considerable pleasures. F. casts her gaze on a multiplicity of innocences here, plotting the development of love between Chiara, fresh from an English convent school, and Salvatore, a neorologist, within this baffling predicament called human life. F.'s characteristic, tender understanding of all that is human enables her to explore the mysteries of life and love with a sympathy and grace that led one reviewer, Francis King, to describe *Innocence* as "a work of moral, intellectual, and emotional richness."

F.'s seventh novel, *The Beginning of Spring* (1988), displays the scholarly precision and readability of her biographies. Set within the vividly realized detail of Russia in 1913, F. tells the story of Frank Reid, born in Russia to English expatriate parents, now supervising the operations of the family-owned printing company. The plot of the novel is carefully circumscribed: Reid's wife has deserted him, leaving three children in his care. Natural questions about why she has left, where she has gone, and when she might return are never answered. Rather, F. crafts a comedy of manners with a small but rich cast of characters, including the company accountant, Selwyn Crane, a disciple of the only recently deceased Leo Tolstoy, and various Russian peasants and officials. F.'s eye for the details of life—samovars, church bells, trams, streets choked with slush and mud, disaffected students and protesters, venal police—enables her to do more than create rich period atmosphere: She brings pre-Revolutionary Moscow so alive that it becomes a character. As in her previous novels, F.'s focus remains cast on the peculiar dynamics of human relationships; here, in plotting the evolution of human relationships, she suggests that the way such relationships "work" is as mysterious as the unexplained return of Frank Reid's wife in the novel's last line. *The Beginning of Spring* invites favorable comparision with E.M. Forster's novels of expatriate experience on the Continent; indeed, in major ways, it is superior to his.

The Gate of Angels (1990) concerns itself essentially with mystery as well, though here mystery assumes greater resonance. The novel begins as a "who-done-it?": Fred Fairly, a junior fellow at the fictitious Cambridge college, St. Angelicus ("Angels"), and Daisy Saunders collide after being struck by an unlit cart driven by an unknown figure. The unraveling of this rather more minor mystery takes place against the backdrop of a greater mystery (the composition of light) and greater issues (women's fight for equal rights). Once again, F. deftly depicts a particular historical context—here Cambridge University before World War I—within which eminently human drama develops. Within Fred's academic world, observation and measurement are privileged; his chance collision with Daisy intensifies his sense that purely rational, "scientific" inquiry and academic discourse are inadequate ways of representing, let alone understanding, the fullness of human experience. *The Gate of Angels* pulsates with intellectual life: When F. traces Fred's studies in physics, she brings alive the world of Cambridge University during a golden age, when groundbreaking research on particle physics was underway while figures like Bertrand Russell, John Maynard Keynes, and G. H. Hardy were academic stars; and the novel throbs with real human life, particularly in the figure of the working-class Daisy, a young woman whose assertive spirit has enabled her to claim a place of her own as a trained nurse. It is a mark of F.'s extraordinary gifts as a novelist that she can create an engaging narrative about some of the oldest polarities, paradoxes, and tensions (faith/reason, science/religion, appearance/reality) without ever falling into clichés or losing her reader's interest.

In 1795, at the age of twenty-three, Friedrich von Hardenberg, the nineteenth-century romantic poet and philosopher later known as "Novalis," fell in love with Sophie von Kuhn, a dull and inarticulate twelve-year-old girl who seemed to embody all his yearnings. To information gleaned from papers, letters, and diaries of Friedrich and scraps of Sophie's diaries, F. has added the detailed knowledge of a social or cultural historian: once again, an historical time and place spring to life. The result, F.'s ninth novel, *The Blue Flower* (1995), is a deeply human portrait of a genius in love, an awkward young man possessed by the mysterious power of love. As rich and diverting as the novel's context is—J. W. Goethe and Friedrich von Schiller appear—it characteristically serves the higher end of illuminating the eminently human drama that takes place within it. F.'s seamless narrative takes its cue from her epigraph, quoted from Novalis himself: "Novels arise out of the shortcomings of history." Certainly *The Blue Flower* prompts renewed reflection on the nature of history, biography, and fiction, as well as their interrelationships; but it never ceases to be a thoroughly enjoyable, entertaining story.

Readers of F.'s fiction must resist the temptation to dismiss her elegantly economical narratives as mere light entertainment. While perhaps not expressive of the serious, metaphysical concerns presented by Muriel Spark, to whom she is often compared, F.'s work is distinguished by undeniable excellences of style, by sharply focused insights into character, and by a consistent, humane concern for the moral dimension of human existence. Too wise to manipulate elements of fiction to create a fablelike world in which good always wins, F., like Florence Green, knows full well that the world is divided into exterminators and exterminatees, but unlike her she knows that comedy is therapeutic and ultimately triumphant. In all her work, F. displays a keenly intelligent and analytical insight into human thought and behavior and a sharply moral calibration of that behavior; matched to a remarkable and extraordinary sympathy for the foibles and failures of humankind and a rare originality, these gifts have given twentieth-century British fiction an individual voice of clarity and integrity. Critical recognition of her work may have come late, but it has been considerable: Three of her novels-*The Bookshop, The Beginning of Spring,* and *The Gate of Angels*—were shortlisted for the Booker Prize; and one, *Offshore,* won Britain's most prestigious literary prize.

WORKS: *Edward Burne-Jones: A Biography* (1975). *The Knox Brothers* (1977). *The Golden Child* (1977). *The Bookshop* (1978). *Offshore* (1979). *Charlotte Mew and Her Friends* (1979). *Human Voices* (1980). *William Morris: The Novel on Blue Paper* (1981). *At Freddie's* (1982). *Innocence* (1986). *The Beginning of Spring* (1988). *The Gate of Angels* (1990). *The Blue Flower* (1995). *Heat Wave* (1996).

BIBLIOGRAPHY: Bawer, B. *NewC* (March 1992; rpt. in B. Bawer. *The Aspect of Eternity,* 1993). Sudrann, J., in *Contemporary British Women Writers: Texts and Strategies,* ed. R. E. Hosmer, Jr. (1993).

For articles in reference works, see: *Bloomsbury. CA. Cambridge. CLC. CN. DLB. Feminist. ToddBWW. Who's Who.*

Other references: *Books and Bookmen* (December 1979). *BW* (13 September 1985, 12 July 1987). *Contemporary Review* (April 1978). *Encounter* (January 1981, June–July 1982). *Independent* (25 August 1990). King, F. *Spectator* (13 September 1986). *Listener* (23 November 1978, 2 October 1980, 23 August 1990). *London Magazine* (February 1980, October 1986, September 1990). *LonSunT* (28 March 1982, 17 September 1995). *LRB* (20 November-4 December 1980, 9 October 1986, 12 November 1987, 13 October 1988, 13 September 1990, 5 October 1995). *New Statesman* (7 October 1977, 7 September 1979, 24 August 1990). *NYRB* (17 July 1997). *NYTBR* (1 April 1979, 7 February 1988, 7 August 1988, 7 June 1989, 13 August 1989, 25 July 1993). *Observer* (2 September 1979, 28 March 1982, 25 September 1994). *Spectator* (27 March 1982, 1 October 1988, 1 September 1990). *TLS* (17 November 1978, 23 November 1979, 26 September 1980, 18 October 1985, 24–30 August 1990, 23 September 1994, 15 September 1995, 5 October 1995, 17 November 1995). *VLS* (September 1993).

Robert Ellis Hosmer, Jr.

Fool, Tom: See *Farjeon, Eleanor*

Margaret Forster

BORN: 25 May 1938, Carlisle, Cumberland.
DAUGHTER OF: Arthur Gordon Forster and Lilian Hind Forster.
MARRIED: Hunter Davies, 1960.

After her upbringing in the northern English city of Carlisle, F. won an open scholarship to Somerville College, Oxford, graduating with a degree in history. She married writer Hunter Davies in 1960 and became the mother of two daughters and a son. Primarily a novelist, F.'s published works to date include twelve novels and three historical-biographical volumes. In addition, F. served from 1977 to 1980 as the chief nonfiction reviewer for the London *Evening Standard* and has contributed to *Punch*. In 1966, one of F.'s early novels, *Georgy Girl*, was turned into a successful film for which she coauthored the script with Peter Nichols.

Perhaps because her manner is realistic, her storytelling apparently straightforward, F.'s writing has attracted no critical attention more extensive than reviews. Yet her writing has been consistently published in the United States as well as in England and has been, for the most part, favorably reviewed. Auberon Waugh, for example, in a *Times Literary Supplement* (22 January 1971) assessment of F.'s *Mr. Bone's Retreat*, remarked that "she has become as good as anyone writing in the English language."

The four earliest novels (*Dame's Delight*, 1964, *Georgy Girl*, 1965, *The Bogeyman*, 1965, and *The Travels of Maudie Tipstaff*, 1967), and some of the later ones (*Miss Owen-Owen Is at Home*, 1969, *The Seduction of Mrs. Pendlebury*, 1974), delineate exceptionally strong-willed and not particularly attractive characters. The writing in *Dame's Delight* and *Georgy Girl* is clinical and sharply satirical; while this style continues as an element, the later novels, from *Bogeyman* onward, display a more complex vision of the human condition. F.'s monsters have human needs and motivations; her conventional characters act, on occasion, as compulsively as the strong-willed.

A few generalizations can be made about F.'s fiction. She is primarily a novelist of character. Her stories deal with their characters' response to modern life. The books' scale is small, usually limited to the relationships of a single group of people brought closely together by marriage, by physical proximity (neighbors in *The Seduction of Mrs. Pendlebury*), or by an organizational bond (the country high school in *Miss Owen-Owen*). Their time, with the exception of *Fenella Phizackerly* (1970), is concentrated.

These generalizations fail to account for readers' perceptions of both strength and variety in F.'s fiction. F. experiments with form, from the tight patterning of the nonetheless realistic *Maudie Tipstaff*, to the mock fairytale of *Fenella Phizackerly*, to the overt romance of *The Bride of Lowther Fell* (1980), to the complex realistic structure of *Mother, Can You Hear Me?* (1979). F. also explores an unusually varied range of protagonists, from young or middle-aged middle-class women to the elderly of every class and both sexes.

F.'s nonfiction has received mixed reviews. *The Rash Adventurer* has been praised as the best biography of Bonnie Prince Charlie, though the later years of the prince's life were exceptionally dull and the biography cannot enliven them. In *Memoirs of a Victorian Gentleman* (1978), F. imitates William Makepeace Thackeray's voice in a pseudoautobiography, an experiment some readers appreciated and others heartily disliked. *Significant Sisters* offers rather tame though well-told lives of several illustrious women, including Florence Nightingale, Elizabeth Cady Stanton, and Emma Goldman. The book's intention was to make these formidable women accessible; in doing so, it somewhat dims their fires.

F.'s works are pleasing, astute, skilled, and powerful enough to deserve the careful critical assessment they have not yet received.

WORKS: *Dame's Delight* (1964). *Georgy Girl* (1965; filmscript, 1966). *The Bogeyman* (1965). *The Travels of Maudie Tipstaff* (1967). *The Park* (1968). *Miss Owen-Owen Is at Home* (1969; in the U.S. as *Miss Owen-Owen*). *Fenella Phizackerly* (1970). *Mr. Bone's Retreat* (1971). *The Rash Adventurer: The Rise and Fall of Charles Edward Stuart* (1973). *The Seduction of Mrs. Pendlebury* (1974). *William Makepeace Thackeray: Memoirs of a Victorian Gentleman* (1978). *Mother, Can You Hear Me?* (1979). *The Bride of Lowther Fell* (1980). *Marital Rites* (1981). *Significant Sisters: The Grassroots of Feminism 1839–1939* (1984). *Mother's Boys* (1994). *Hidden Lives: A Family Memoir* (1995). *Shadow Baby* (1996). *Rich Desserts and Captain's Thin: A Family and Their Times, 1831–1931* (1997).

BIBLIOGRAPHY:

For articles in reference works, see: *Bloomsbury. Feminist. Oxford. ToddBWW. Who's Who. WD.*

Other references: Adams, P. *Somerville for Women: An Oxford College 1879–1993* (1996). *LonSunT* (27 August 1995, 27 July 1996).

Ellen Laun

Jessie Fothergill

BORN: June 1851, Cheethem Hill, Manchester.
DIED: 28 July 1891, Berne, Switzerland.
DAUGHTER OF: Thomas Fothergill and Anne Coultate Fothergill.
WROTE UNDER: Jessie Fothergill; J. F.

Eldest child of a cotton-industry businessman, F. resided in the Manchester area for most of her life. She was educated first in a small private school in Bowdon (Cheshire), later studying several years at a boarding school in Harrogate (Yorkshire). When F. was a child, the death of her father brought financial hardship, and the family moved to a house near a cotton mill in Littleborough. F. suffered from a chronic lung complaint throughout her life. Her later years were spent abroad in such places as Germany, Italy, Switzerland, and America, often for health reasons.

F.'s father was a Yorkshireman, a yeoman, and a Quaker; this last fact influenced F. even though her father had left the church when he married. F.'s first book, *Healey* (1875), and a later work, *Kith and Kin* (1881), present sympathetic portraits of the Quakers and their lifestyle. Her Quaker background surfaces also in the austerity of many of her protagonists, reminiscent of her own lifestyle, and in her inherent distrust of characters who love luxury and need material comforts.

After finishing her studies at Harrogate, F. returned to her family. An early nonconformist, she turned aside from the pursuits of conventional young ladies. She read omnivorously, wandered about the Tadmorden Valley, studied the lives of the people at the cotton mill, and wrote stories in her attic. Several of her works relate to this period of her life: *The Lasses of Leverhouse* (1888), narrated by a literary-minded adolescent, is the tale of an impoverished, boisterous family; *Healey* (1875) and *Probation* (1879) focus on the cotton industry and the lives of its people. The latter is especially noteworthy for its vivid and sympathetic portrayal of the lives of the workers; it also covers the cotton famine of 1862.

F.'s most popular novel, *The First Violin* (1877), was published anonymously (although later editions bore her name)—presumably because her Quaker family may have been unhappy with the author's excessive romanticism and the nonjudgmental handling of a married woman's involvement with another man. The novel, narrated by a naïve English girl observing life in Düsseldorf, Germany, is melodramatic. The protagonist, Eugen Courvoisier, hiding under an assumed name, has accepted disgrace and exile to shield another's guilt. F. began this work during a fifteen-month sojourn in Düsseldorf with her sister and two friends, and the book is filled with her impressions. All subsequent novels generally included episodes reflecting her interest in Germany and its music.

Although *The First Violin* went through many editions and brought F. fame, it is an uneven romantic work. It is, however, still readable and, of course, because of its extreme popularity, is particularly interesting to scholars of the period.

Unlike the imaginative and clearly fictional *The First Violin,* F.'s other novels are realistic, focusing mainly on the scenes, situations, and people in the Manchester area. Her settings are those of her ancestors and her family: the Yorkshire moors and the manufacturing towns. Littleborough is Hamerton in *Healey and The Lasses of Leverhouse;* Rochedale is Thanshope in *Probation;* Manchester is Darkinford in *Peril* (1884) and Irkford in *Kith and Kin.*

The author's characters, too, are substantive, endemic to their milieu, universal in nature. Wilfred Healey (*Healey*) is a mill owner; Godfrey Noble (*A March in the Ranks,* 1890) is a medical man like her grandfather. Through him F. exposes the charlatanism of a hydropathic establishment, the popular contemporary "rest cure." (One may assume that F.'s chronic ill health would have led her to such institutions.)

F.'s heroines are not as believable as their male counterparts, possibly because they often personify the "dream" rather than the "actual," the exception rather than the standard, for most Victorian women. Frequently "masculine" by the conventions of the time, these heroines are interested in political and social issues; they work at "men's" work: Katherine Healey (*Healey*) helps run her brother's business; Alison Blundell (*A March in the Ranks*) manages the estate and affairs of her invalid brother. Reality for the Victorian woman was often frustrating, however, whatever the achievement; more in keeping with the truth is Helena Spenceley in *Probation,* evidencing the stress and revolt experienced by women of ability and strength restricted by established, inferior roles.

Overall, F.'s protagonists are strong and independent. They lean toward agnosticism, and her laxness concerning religion offended some of her reviewers. Politically, they were liberal, even radical.

It is in this vivid and concrete depiction of the people she knew and observed in her immediate area that F.'s literary strength lies. Contemporary reviewers criticized her weak plots, but modern readers may construe that weakness constructively: F. centered her attention on a particular human situation, such as an individual struggling against the restraints of class, poverty, or tradition, or lovers defying barriers of status, money, or previous commitments. F., like Anton Chekhov, focused on internal rather than external tension. At her best F. can be favorably compared—as she was—with other regional writers such as the Brontës and Elizabeth Gaskell.

WORKS: *Healey* (1875). *Aldyth* (1877). *The First Violin* (1877). *Probation* (1879). *The Wellfields* (1880). *Kith and Kin* (1881). *Made or Marred* (1881). *Peril* (1884). *Borderland: A Country-town Chronicle* (1886). *The Lasses of Leverhouse* (1888). *From Moor Isles. A Love Story* (1888). *A March in the Ranks* (1890). *Oriole's Daughter* (1893).

BIBLIOGRAPHY: Black, H. C. *Notable Women Authors of the Day* (1906). Crisp, J. *Jessie Fothergill* (Victorian Fiction Research Guides 11) (1980). De la Mare, W., in *The Eighteen-Seventies,* ed. H. Granville Barker (1929). Fothergill, C., preface to *Aldyth* (1891). Gardiner, L. *Novel Review* (1892). O'Conor, W. A. *Manchester Quarterly* (1883).

For articles in reference works, see: *Allibone. New Century Cyclopedia of Names,* ed. C. L. Barnhart (1954). *DNB. Dictionary of Biographies of Authors,* ed. R. Johnson (1927). *NCHEL. Century Cyclopedia of Names,* ed. B. Smith (1894). *Stanford.*

Other references: *Athenaeum* (1 August 1891). *Critic* (New York) (29 August 1891). Gettmann, R. A. *A Victorian Publisher: A Study of the Bently Papers* (1960). *Illustrated London News* (8 August 1891). *LonT* (31 July 1891). Speight, H. *Romantic Richmondshire* (1897). Wright, M. B. *Literary World* (Boston) (1891).

Phyllis J. Scherle

Fox, Margaret: See *Fell, Margaret*

Frances: See *Griffith, Elizabeth*

Pamela Frankau

BORN: 3 January 1908, London.
DIED: 8 June 1967 Hampstead, London.
DAUGHTER OF: Gilbert Frankau and Dorothea Drummand (Black) Frankau.

MARRIED: Marshall Dill, Jr., 1945.
WROTE UNDER: Pamela Frankau; Eliot Naylor.

Journalist, novelist, short-story writer, World War II major in the Auxiliary Territorial Service, lecturer, broadcaster, F. was the youngest child of her father's first marriage. Her early years were spent in Windsor with her mother and sister, Ursula. After graduating from Stapleton with first scholastic honors and being forced to forgo entrance to Cambridge due to financial shortages stemming from her mother's severe illness, F. began her literary career at the age of eighteen as a member of the London staff of the *Woman's Journal.* She later advanced to feature writer for the *Daily Sketch* and the *Mirror.* Though eventually regretting this practical decision, one which almost alienated F. from her father's influence and affection, she used the time spent traveling to and from work in a third-class rail carriage to create her first novel, *Marriage of Harlequin* (1927), reputedly using a scarlet pen on paper taken from the office supply. *The New York Herald Tribune* considered this semi-autobiographical novel, about a sophisticated debutante and a wily fortune hunter in post–World War I London, almost "too well written" for one so young.

With the publication of her first work, F. became the third member of her family to achieve literary recognition. Grandmother Julia, as "Frank Denby," wrote *Pigs in Clover* (1903) and other well-received fiction. F.'s father, though considered "an admirable novelist for ordinary people," was acclaimed during his lifetime as one of the world's best-selling authors.

F.'s next few novels reflected her strong admiration for Michael Arlen's fiction, with its development of breezy, energetic characters in "smart," unconventional settings. *Three* (1929), for example, concerns the adventures of Janet James. While engaged to an English officer, she enjoys a prolonged vacation on the Italian Riviera where she meets and falls in love with Count Fermi. After a year's liaison, she finally rejects romance for security and returns to her fiancé.

Another novel, *Born at Sea* (1932), involves a wealthy but neurotic egotist determined to succumb to the sea while on a South African voyage, but his despair is alleviated by three female passengers. Though criticized as somewhat superficial, it signals the onset of more mature and complicated plots somewhat removed from the Arlen influence.

F.'s most commended work, *The Willow Cabin* (1949), represents the culmination of her early period. Its plot deals with a twenty-two-year-old British woman's rejection of a promising career when she becomes the mistress of a journalist twice her age. At his death, she insists on meeting her former lover's estranged wife to untangle inevitable emotional complexities. The writing is sharper, more precise, and more highly polished and earned accolades from *The New York Times.*

Perhaps the most important influence was F.'s father. After her parents' divorce, F.'s novels contained several villains whose careers and philosophies mocked the older novelist, but in *Pen to Paper* (1961), her second autobiography, she includes a posthumous apology "for all the times we had worn masks in each other's company." When they weren't at odds, F. often consulted her father on a particular turn of a plot or argued with him about a character's motivation and occasionally took his well-intended advice.

In 1942, F. converted to the Roman Catholic Church. Three years later, she married Marshall Dill and moved to the United States. Their only child died soon after birth. Despite her religious convictions, F. divorced her husband in 1961. Other forms of writing included essays, newspaper articles, serial fiction, and short stories. She also read manuscripts and wrote reviews for the Book Society. F. carefully avoided any form of pleasure that might deter her from writing at least 3,000 words a day.

An interest in psychic phenomena pervaded F.'s later fiction. A trilogy, *The Clothes of a King's Son* (1963–1967), provided a distinctive creative experience. Its protagonist, Thomas Weston, is given the ability to discover the differences between good and evil through the use of extrasensory perception. *Slaves of the Lamp,* the second volume, is an exercise in manipulation, as she manages to keep myriad plots moving while highly articulate characters—almost artificial, some critics claimed—infuse the narrative with their upper-class morality.

F.'s thirty-first and last novel, *Colonel Blessington,* edited by her cousin, Diana Raymond, and published posthumously, involves the disappearance of the leading character. F. died as she was completing this work, her most complicated mystery, but Raymond's attention to F.'s notes produced a worthy member of the author's prolific library.

WORKS: *Marriage of Harlequin* (1927). *Three* (1929). *She and I* (1930). *Letters from a Modern Daughter to Her Mother* (1931). *Born at Sea* (1932). *Women Are So Serious* (1932). *I Was the Man* (1932). *Walk into My Parlor* (1933). *The Foolish Apprentices* (1933). *Tassel-Gentle* (1934). *Fly Now, Falcon* (1934). *I Find Four People* (1935). *Villa Anodyne* (1936; in the U.S. as *Laughter in the Sun*). *Fifty-Fifty and Other Stories* (1936). *Some New Planet* (1937). *Jezebel* (1937). *No News* (1938). *The Devil We Know* (1939). *A Democrat Dies* (1939). *Appointment with Death* (1940). *Shaken in the Wind* (1948). *The Willow Cabin* (1949). (as Eliot Naylor) *The Off-Shore Light* (1952). *The Winged Horse* (1953). *To the Moment of Triumph* (1953). *A Wreath for the Enemy* (1954; also as *The Duchess and the Smugs*). *The Bridge* (1957). *Ask Me No More* (1958). *Road Through the Woods* (1960). *Pen to Paper: A Novelist's Notebook* (1961). *Sing for Your Supper* (*Clothes of a King's Son,* Part I, 1963). *Slaves of the Lamp* (*Clothes of a King's Son,* Part II, 1965). *Over the Mountains* (*Clothes of a King's Son,* Part III, 1967). (completed and ed. D. Raymond) *Colonel Blessington* (1968).

For articles in reference works, see: *BCathA. CA. DLB. Feminist. Longman. TCA. TCW. ToddBWW.*

Other references: *NYT* (9 June 1967). *Saturday Review* (1 January 1966).

Zelda R. B. Provenzano

Antonia Fraser (Lady Antonia Pinter)

BORN: 27 August 1932, London.
DAUGHTER OF: Seventh Earl of Longford and Countess of Longford (Frank and Elizabeth Harmon Pakenham).
MARRIED: Rt. Hon. Sir Hugh Charles Fraser, 1956; Harold Pinter, 1980.
WRITES UNDER: Antonia Fraser; Antonia Pakenham.

F. received her university degree from Lady Margaret Hall, Oxford, in 1953; she grew up in Oxford where her father was an Oxford don before his elevation to the peerage. It is no surprise, therefore, that the family is popularly known as the "literary Longfords." Lord Longford wrote the first biography of John F. Kennedy to be published in Great Britain, but he is better known by the nickname of "Lord Porn" for his exhaustive inquiries into pornography. F.'s mother, Elizabeth Longford, has written successful biographies of Queen Victoria and Lord Wellington, and two sisters and a brother are also published authors. F., however, maintains that her family was not the only factor in determining her career. In *Maclean's* she says, "I don't say it very often, but I began to write to help support our family [the children she had with Fraser]. There's no better inspiration than that." Although her first work, *King Arthur and the Knights of the Round Table,* was published in 1954, F.'s distinction as a biographer was established with *Mary, Queen of Scots* (1969), which won the James Tait Black Memorial Prize for biography. In addition to her outstanding biographies, F. has written a succession of well-received mysteries. Her literary prestige has earned her invitations to serve as a member of The Arts Council of Great Britain, 1970–1972, English PEN, 1979– , and the Crimewriters' Association, 1980– .

F. has written four biographies of prominent historical figures: *Mary, Queen of Scots* (1969), *Cromwell Our Chief of Men* (1973), *King James: VI of Scotland, I of England* (1974), and *King Charles II* (1979), also published as *Royal Charles.* On the basis of these four works, F.'s literary reputation has been labeled "ambiguous" by one critic, and Mel Gussow in the *New York Times Magazine* says that "her work receives respectful reviews for her impressive research and readability. Her primary strength is her sense of narrative. At the same time some professional historians consider her approach a storybook view of history." F. does spend an impressive amount of time in research. She devoted three years to *Mary, Queen of Scots* and four years to *Cromwell.* Almost every reviewer calls attention to the amount of exact detail that F. includes. Her most valuable contribution seems to be in the mass of detail concerning Mary Stuart's health, which F. uses to explain many of the charges relating to the queen's scandalous behavior. Although F. invested the same quantity of energy in the biography of Cromwell, it met with more mixed critical reaction. F.'s intention is to make her subjects seem more human, and this she does very well. For example, Paul Johnson comments that this book went "a long way to redress the distortion from which Cromwell has suffered." It is this "humane" approach, however, that bothers critics the most. Jane Majeski remarks that F.'s "emphasis on Cromwell as a typical country gentleman leaves one with the implausible impression that he stumbled on the throne of England by accident." Even Johnson charges that F.'s treatment of the political situation is "skimpy" and "cursory."

Although the two biographies of kings, *James VI* and *Charles II,* were best sellers, F. did not spend as much time in research, and neither book is as extensive as the two earlier works. Once again critical reaction is mixed. Alden Whitman writes that *King James VI* is "thoroughly readable as a character study" and that "on superficial levels . . . [F.] has cleared away some of the unjust accusations leveled against James that have persisted over the years." Jane Majeski claims that the book "lacks the thorough research and depth" of the earlier biographies. With *Cromwell,* critics—Majeski in particular—had charged F. with failing to deal adequately with the political situation; in contrast with *King James VI,* these same critics comment that F. "would have done better to have written a thorough analysis of James's character . . . and to have left aside the political complications."

King Charles II has elicited the same diverse response. Writing in the *Economist,* one critic says that "Antonia Fraser's greatest achievement is her dissection and reconstruction of the king's political and personal character." On the other hand, Peter Prescott in *Newsweek* calls the book "a revisionist work, a highly intelligent but partisan reinterpretation." F.'s contribution in biography has been to investigate highly controversial historical figures, dispel many of the myths surrounding these figures, and produce immensely readable, provocative best sellers.

With the 1977 publication of her first mystery novel, *Quiet as a Nun,* F. introduced Jemima Shore, investigator. Frequently referred to as an adult Nancy Drew or a new Miss Marple, Jemima, a reporter for Megalith Television, finds herself investigating mysteries surrounding the subjects she has been assigned to cover. Using settings familiar to her, F. places *Quiet as a Nun* in a Roman Catholic convent similar to the one where F. attended school. *Wild Island* (1978) is set in the Scottish Highland retreat of the Fraser family, and *Oxford Blood* (1985) is in F.'s childhood home of Oxford. Continuing to draw upon her own experiences, *Cool Repentance* (1982) is set amid a group of actors in a provincial drama festival. The conflicts and tensions among the festival group certainly mirror those she has encountered as the wife of playwright Harold Pinter. T. J. Binyon notes that the novels have an "unobtrusive *roman à clef* element." In addition, the description of the victim in *A Splash of Red* (1981) could also be of F. herself. Chloe Fontaine had looks that "hid a considerable talent as a novelist" and "there had been a series of admirers, lovers, and husbands. . . . Her friends sometimes remarked on the odd contrast of her disorderly private life and the careful formality of her work." Although critics found her early mysteries too predictable, all five novels have been best sellers. *Quiet as a Nun* was a "Mystery!" presentation on PBS in 1982 (having been produced by Thames Television in Britain), and another television series based on the Jemima Shore stories has been produced.

As a result of her research on the biographies, as well as a feeling of affinity for the people of the seventeenth century, F. wrote *The Weaker Vessel* (1984), an exploration into the position of women in that century. Christopher Lehmann-Haupt in *The New York Times* says that "it appears to gather up almost everything one could possibly think of to ask about women in the century that began with the death of Queen Elizabeth in 1603 and ended with the accession of Queen Anne in 1702." In this book, which could be classified biography, history, or even women's studies, F. recounts actual experiences of women from the alehouse to the palace, from the church, the academy, and the prison. Referring to the work as a "breakthrough" for F., Mel Gussow says that this is the first time F. "has dealt foursquare with feminist issues and the first time that she has felt a kind of missionary zeal." Summing up her investigations in the epilogue, F. notes that despite a rise in women's stature in the middle decades, at the end of the century it was back on the same level it had been at the death of Queen Elizabeth. F. comments, "This cyclical pattern . . . is perhaps worth bearing in mind; as with all forms of liberation, of which the liberation of women is only one example, it is easy to suppose in a time of freedom that the darker days of repression can never come again."

In spite of the notable scholarly quality of her biographies, F.'s lively presentation of what could be dull historical fact has attracted a large reading public. Her creation of the contemporary, racy, liberated Jemima Shore is not a contrast to her earlier work but an obvious extension. F.'s work has the possibilities of joining the ranks of writers such as Dorothy L. Sayers, someone whom F. greatly admires.

WORKS: (as Antonia Pakenham) *King Arthur and the Knights of the Round Table* (1954). (trans.) *Martyrs in China*, by Jean Monsterleet (1956). *Robin Hood* (1957). (trans.) *Dior by Dior: The Autobiography of Christian Dior* (1957). *Dolls* (1963). *A History of Toys* (1966). *Mary, Queen of Scots* (1969). *Cromwell Our Chief of Men* (1973, also published as *Cromwell, The Lord Protector*). *Mary, Queen of the Scots, and the Historians* (1974). *King James: VI of Scotland, I of England* (1974). *Quiet as a Nun* (1977). *The Wild Island* (1978). *King Charles II* (1979, also as *Royal Charles*). *A Splash of Red* (1981). *Cool Repentance* (1982). *The Weaker Vessel* (1984). *Oxford Blood* (1985). *Jemima Shore's First Case and Other Stories* (1987). *Faith and Treason* (1996).

BIBLIOGRAPHY: Klein, K. G. *Great Women Mystery Writers* (1994).

For articles in reference works, see: *CA. DLEL. Feminist. TCC&MW. ToddBWW. WA. WD.*

Other references: Binyon, T. J. *TLS* (5 May 1978). *Economist* (29 September 1979). Gussow, M. *NYTMag* (9 September 1984). Johnson, P. *New Statesman* (8 June 1973). Lehmann-Haupt, C. *NYT* (14 November 1984). Majeski, J. *Saturday Review* (23 October 1979). Prescott, P. *Newsweek* (12 November 1979). Whitman, A. *NYT* (30 March 1975).

Alice Lorraine Painter

Mary Crawford Fraser

BORN: 8 April 1851, Rome, Italy.
DIED: 7 June 1922.
DAUGHTER OF: Thomas Crawford and Louisa Cutler Ward Crawford.
MARRIED: Hugh C. Fraser, 1874.
WROTE UNDER: Mrs. Hugh Fraser.

Like the writings of a number of other Victorian women writers, among F.'s earliest literary efforts were sentimental novels, which according to contemporary reviews were generally unremarkable. *A Maid of Japan* (1905) is termed much like *Madame Butterfly*, *A Little Grey Sheep* (1901) as a tale of endangered virtue is "conventional," and *The Looms of Time* (1898) replete with stolen gold mine is "melodramatic." Yet even through these runs her skill as a keen observer of the sites, people, and cultures through which she moved as the wife of a British diplomat, and it is her travel writings that earn for her a literary reputation as an adept chronicler of life and times. F.'s works are not travelogues in the usual sense, however. Instead, she rather intimately acquaints the reader with real people, both the famous and powerful figures of the area and the less well known. She introduces their families, their joys, their difficulties, in rich and involved descriptions of place that become integral to the unfolding vignettes and stories. Interspersed are historical anecdotes that provide links between the living and the deceased, the latter becoming as real as the former.

Her style is uniform, moments of life that are strung on the narrative of her own experience like beads on a cord, but F. sublimates her own voice, becoming a minor character, to focus on the primary actors in her descriptions. Because she moved in privileged circles, she was acquainted with prelates, royalty, government officials, and the wealthy merchant class, yet her commentaries often offer castigating details about men and women living unhappy lives in the midst of power and plenty. In accordance with the perceptions of the people she describes and her own fascination with the unusual, her accounts include ghostly apparitions, unexplained coincidences, even legends and lore as fact.

Typical of her travel writings is a two-volume work, *A Diplomatist's Wife in Many Lands* (1901). F. begins with her own family. Her mother, an heiress to considerable money, was the sister of Julia Ward Howe and was related by marriage to the Jacob Astors and to Joseph Bonaparte. Her father was a successful artist. Her brother, Francis Marion Crawford, later became an editor of an Indian periodical and a writer of novels. Though returning at intervals to the United States, F. spent much of her childhood traveling about Europe as her father studied and found patronage. She writes of her memories of such people as Louis I of Bavaria, for whom her father sculpted, and his inamorata Lola Montez; of Elizabeth Barrett Browning; of U.S. Civil War generals Grant, Sherman, and McClellan who toured Italy; and of Henry Wadsworth Longfellow. Volume II recounts the early years of her marriage to Hugh Fraser, son of Sir John Fraser, and their move to Peking,

China. She describes the court intrigue surrounding the Dowager Empress and her own life in the British Legation Compound. Returning to Rome after four years, F. moved to Vienna, Austria, with her husband, who was appointed Secretary of the Embassy.

F. subsequently lived in Chile and in Japan, but did not offer her writing for publication until after the death of her husband in 1894. As a gypsy told her, "You have eaten your bread in many lands," so she offers the reader a generous sampling of her remarkable feast.

WORKS: *Dora Murray's Ideal and How It Came to Her* (1896). *Palladia* (1896). *A Chapter of Accidents* (1898). *The Looms of Time* (1898). *The Splendid Porsenna* (1899). *A Diplomatist's Wife in Japan* (1899). *A Little Grey Sheep: A Novel* (1901). *Marna's Mutiny* (1901). *A Diplomatist's Wife in Many Lands* (1901). *The Stolen Emperor, A Tale of Old Japan* (1903). *A Maid of Japan* (1905). *In the Shadow of the Lord: A Romance of the Washingtons* (1906). *The Heart of a Geisha* (1908). *Giannella* (1909). *A Diplomatist's Wife in Italy* (1910). *Reminiscences of a Diplomatist's Wife* (1912). *Italian Yesterdays* (1913.) *Seven Years on the Pacific Slope* (1914). *Storied Italy* (1915). (trans.) *The Patrizi Memoirs: A Roman Family under Napoleon, 1796–1815,* by the Marchesa Maddalena Patrizi (1915).

BIBLIOGRAPHY: Barr, P. *Cornhill Magazine* (Summer 1971). C. Blacker, *TLS* (23 September 1982). *Novels in English by Women, 1891–1920,* ed. J. Grimes and D. Daims (1981). *A Diplomat's Wife in Japan: Sketches at the Turn of the Century,* ed. H. Cortazzi (1982). Tobias, R. *Bibliographies of Studies in Victorian Literature 1975–1984* (1991).

For articles in reference works, see: *Feminist.*

Sylvia McLaurin

Gillian Freeman

BORN: 5 December 1929, London.
DAUGHTER OF: Jack Freeman and Freda Davids Freeman.
MARRIED: Edward Thorpe, 1955.
WROTE UNDER: Gillian Freeman; Eliot George; Elaine Jackson.

F.'s career, which extends through the second half of the twentieth century, is characterized by a variety of genres (novels, screenplays, ballet scenarios, and criticism) and a multiplicity of settings (including Nazi Germany, nineteenth-century United States, and a contemporary England imagined as a potential fascist dystopia); several novels contain double plots, with events in different time periods and cultures. She herself retrospectively identifies a thematic unity in her fiction; although story-telling was her conscious purpose, her writing reveals a central concern: "the problems of the individual seen in relation to society and the personal pressures brought to bear because of moral, political or social conditions and the inability to conform." Better known in Great Britain than abroad, she has earned respect for her narrative craft, for her moral seriousness, and for the courage to experiment with multiple narrative perspectives and sensitive subject matters. Although various themes—freedom and its enemies, maternity and its discontents, class boundaries and their blurring—recur in F.'s novels, she does not repeat herself.

Educated in literature and philosophy at the University of Reading, she worked as a copywriter, teacher, and literary secretary before publishing *The Liberty Man* in 1955, the year she married Edward Thorpe, then an actor and subsequently a novelist and critic. A compassionate, gentle treatment of a romance between a sailor and a middle-class teacher, *The Liberty Man* uses the difference in class to develop the characters, not to define them; they are not reducible to class stereotypes. The same is true in her second novel, *Fall of Innocence* (1956), in which a middle-aged man has a brief love affair with a friend of his adolescent daughter. The encounter—far from the stock situation of exploitation and betrayal—is inconsequential for the young woman (who is far from innocent) and redemptive for the genuinely innocent widower, whose devotion to his children had blinded him to his capacity for personal happiness.

Under the pseudonym "Eliot George," F. wrote the novel (and later the screenplay) *The Leather Boys* (1961), another unlikely love story. Two lower-class young men—one married and one single, neither self-identified as homosexual—suddenly find themselves lovers, as their friendship catches fire. Unfolding against the background of a motorcycle gang, their relationship allows them to grow in wisdom even as they test their bonds with their families and friends and with the legal and cultural institutions that surround them. The violent resolution is tragic and somber but not melodramatic or sententious.

The Leader (1965) is the first of F.'s novels to foreground politics while retaining an interest in characterizations that transcend typing. Vincent, a bank clerk who is frustrated by the dullness of his work and smothered by his solicitous mother, attempts to lead a neo-Nazi movement in Britain. He recruits schoolboys, wastrels, and the discontented middle class by appealing to various collectivist prejudices (against Jews, blacks, "foreigners"). He is, however, not only a defensive crank but also a young man yearning to rise above his roots. Vincent believes that what matters is not "social origins or physical appearance, but one's vision, one's determination, one's conception of the future." He disintegrates psychologically and descends into paranoia: He accuses his close supporters of treachery, arranges pointless demonstrations, attempts suicide, and ultimately is reduced to dependence on his mother. F.'s novel, while in part spotlighting the ironic impotence of power-seekers, also explores the challenge and the tragedy of the wish to change oneself and one's world.

Several of F.'s later novels juxtapose two or more story lines. On the one hand, these serve to emphasize parallels between situations separated in time and place; on the other hand, the very parallels highlight differences: People try to join together, but they remain apart. *The Alabaster Egg* (1970) contrasts two doomed love affairs: a Jewish woman's fascination with an attractive opportunist who becomes a Nazi, abandoning her and her child, and the passion her husband's uncle had experienced, years earlier, for "mad" King Ludwig of Bavaria. *The Marriage Machine* (1975), chronicling an American-British mismatch, shuttles back and forth from the present (a journey by boat to England) to the distant past (a first trip to the United States) to a more distant past (the war years) and a more recent past (the central period of the marriage). *An Easter Egg Hunt* (1981) deals with the discovery, years later, of the circumstances of a young woman's disappearance from school; the narrative is pieced together from three stories submitted, years apart, for magazine publication, and accounts of the present and past alternate. In *Termination Rock* (1989), a contemporary protagonist, made infertile by cancer, experiences apparent memory flashes of a previous life as a woman who gave up a son for adoption; her memories intensify when she and her husband spend a sabbatical year in the United States, where she "recalls" having traveled as her alter ego.

F. wrote *The Undergrowth of Literature* (1967), an illustrated study of the literature of sexual fantasy, with chapters on flagellation, rubber, transvestitism, lesbianism, and other subjects. She assumes that the reading audience is curious but uninformed. Her approach throughout is detached, humorous, brisk, and specific; she reports, for example, on the recommendations given in specialty magazines for the care of leather equipment and clothing. The cool approach to a potentially inflammatory topic is neither condescending nor condemnatory; her book, she has said, illustrates her "interest in and compassion for those unable to conform to the accepted social mores," a theme throughout her fiction. She subsequently dealt with this subject matter in her screenplays *Girl on a Motorcycle* (1968) and *I Want What I Want* (1972).

F.'s other nonfiction work includes a biography of Albert Einstein, written for children; *The Schoolgirl Ethic: The Life and Work of Angela Brazil* (1976), a study of the novelist known for describing the friendships and rivalries of girls in Edwardian boarding schools (i.e., the environment F. portrays in *An Easter Egg Hunt*); and *Ballet Genius* (1988), coauthored with her husband, twenty sketches of dancers from Nijinksy to Baryshnikov. She has also created several ballet scenarios—including *Mayerling* (1978)—for Kenneth MacMillan and others and has adapted books for the screen.

Love Child (1984), published under the pseudonym "Elaine Jackson," is a suspense thriller. It deals with characteristic elements (a problematic marriage, class boundaries, travel between England and the United States) and a modern situation: a surrogate mother who wishes to keep the child she has been hired to conceive. Although the surrogate mother is initially presented as essentially passive and the couple as primarily sympathetic, F. complicates the perspective through which the reader sees the three main characters; the final plot twist, although apparently inevitable in retrospect, comes as a shock.

Described by Brigid Brophy in 1963 as "one of the most purely *novelist*" of recent writers, F. constructs plots that force characters—from schoolgirls to leather boys, from artists to Nazis—to confront and extend their limits.

WORKS: *The Liberty Man* (1955). *Fall of Innocence* (1956). *Jack Would Be a Gentleman* (1959). *The Story of Albert Einstein* (1960). (as Eliot George) *The Leather Boys* (1961; screenplay, 1963). *The Campaign* (1963). *The Leader* (1965). *The Undergrowth of Literature* (1967). *Girl on a Motorcycle* (X-rated version known as *Naked under Leather,* co-written with Ronald Duncan, from a novel by André Pieyre de Mandiargues, 1968). *That Cold Day in the Park* (based on a novel by Richard Miles, 1969). *The Alabaster Egg* (1970). *I Want What I Want* (based on a novel by Geoff Brown, 1972). *The Marriage Machine* (1975). *The Schoolgirl Ethic: The Life and Work of Angela Brazil* (1976). *The Confessions of Elisabeth Von S.* (1978, also published as *Nazi Lady*). *Mayerling* (1978). *Isadora* (1981). *An Easter Egg Hunt* (1981). (as Elaine Jackson) *Love Child* (1984). *Day after the Fair* (based on a story, "On the Western Circuit," by Thomas Hardy, 1987).(with Edward Thorpe) *Ballet Genius* (1988). *Termination Rock* (1989).

BIBLIOGRAPHY: Brophy, B. *London Magazine* (May 1963). Brophy, B. *New Statesman* (27 August 1965). Brophy, B. *Don't Never Forget* (1966). Dick, K. *Friends and Friendship* (1974).

For articles in reference works, see: *CA. CN. DLEL. Feminist. IAWWW. WD.*

Other references: *A.L.A. Booklist* (1 June 1971). *British Book News* (July 1987). *Economist* (10 July 1976). *Listener* (7 August 1975, 24 June 1976, 7 May 1981). *LRB* (6 July 1989). *LonT* (28 May 1981). *Manchester Guardian* (2 September 1965, 4 July 1976). *Ms.* (June 1982). *New Statesman* (17 November 1967, 16 October 1970, 11 July 1975). *Newsweek* (9 October 1978, 12 October 1981). *New York* (9 June 1969). *New Yorker* (28 September 1981). *NYTBR* (18 April 1971). *TLS* (2 September 1965, 16 November 1967, 16 October 1970, 4 July 1975, 16 July 1976, 22 May 1981, 25 August 1989). *VQR* (1982). *VS* (1979). *VV* (25 September 1978).

Shoshana Milgram Knapp

French, Ashley: See *Robins, Denise Naomi*

F.R.H.: See *Havergal, Frances Ridley*

Friend, A: See *Lennox, Charlotte Ramsay*

Friend to Humanity, A: See *Robinson, Mary Darby (Perdita)*

Anne Fuller

FLOURISHED: late eighteenth century.

The author of at least two, and probably three, novels, F. left few traces of her history behind. Her death in 1790 of consumption near Cork, Ireland, is the only recorded fact of her life beyond her books.

Alan Fitz-Osborne (1786), the story of a knight of Henry III, and *The Son of Ethelwolf* (1789), which recounts King Alfred's resistance to the Danes, are both subtitled "an historical tale"; in the preface to *Alan Fitz-Osborne,* however, F. explains that she will serve truth through fiction: "I mean not to offend the majesty of sacred truth by giving her but a secondary place in the following pages." The murder, bloody dagger-bearing ghosts, and druidic priests of these two novels suggest F. has indeed given "fiction the pre-eminence." The very different tone of *The Convent, or the History of Sophia Nelson* (1786), written by "a young lady," has caused some to question its attribution to F. In this epistolary novel, two young women exchange their views on the world. They are particularly harsh on women who, "having no ideas of their own . . . get a little consequence in the world by adopting those of other people." The gothic creeps into even this work, however, with one of the book's lovers having escaped a domineering aristocratic father to live in a secret cave. The critics of the day were not kind to F.; the *Monthly Review* bluntly characterized *The Son of Ethelwolf* as "prose gone mad."

WORKS: (Anon.) *Alan Fitz-Osborne: An Historical Tale* (1786). *The Convent, or the History of Sophia Nelson* (1786). *The Son of Ethelwolf: An Historical Tale* (1789).

BIBLIOGRAPHY:

For articles in reference works, see *Feminist. Todd-DBA.*

Rebecca P. Bocchicchio

Monica Furlong

BORN: 17 January 1930, Harrow, Middlesex.
DAUGHTER OF: Alfred Gordon Furlong and Freda Simpson Furlong.
MARRIED: William John Knights, 1953.

F. is a prolific Christian feminist writer of poetry, of essays and books exploring Christian issues, of novels, both for adults and children, and of biographies. She chaired the Movement for the Ordination of Women from 1982 to 1985 and has been a pioneer in exploring many of the issues that confound and divide the Christian church, especially those touching women and sexuality.

F. was born in Harrow, near London, and educated at Harrow County Girls' School and at University College London. From her early childhood she was "puzzled" about the subordinate status of women. She married William John Knights in 1953, by whom she had a son and a daughter; the marriage was dissolved in 1977. Beginning in 1956, F. worked as a journalist, writing for many publications including the Anglican *Church Times, The Guardian,* and *The Daily Mail.* She also worked as a producer for the BBC from 1974 to 1978.

F.'s earliest works explored twentieth-century challenges to the polity and spirituality of the Christian church, particularly those issues that affected the Anglican Communion. Her first pieces looked at a wide range of issues: her contribution to *Ourselves Your Servants* (1967), for instance, explores "The Parson's Role Today"; *Christian Uncertainties* (1976) collects a series of articles earlier published by *The Church Times* addressing issues from the seven deadly sins, prayer, and suffering to abortion, homosexuality, and pornography.

Her attention has turned increasingly over the past two decades to women and sexuality in the church; she has been a strong voice in the Anglican Church for the ordination of women to the priesthood and for the acceptance of homosexuality and other extramarital expressions of sexuality. Her *Shrinking and Clinging* (1981) explores the attitudes of the Society of Friends to homosexuality, and she contributed "Sexuality and the Church: On Trying to Speak the Truth" to the *Launch Conference Papers* (1990) for the Institute for the Study of Christianity and Sexuality. In 1984, she edited *Feminine in the Church,* a selection of various Christian denominations' statements supporting the ordination of women. Her more recent *A Dangerous Delight* (1991) traces the history of rising feminist consciousness within the church from the nineteenth century and provides a detailed chronicle of the recent debate within the Church of England on the ordination of women. (The Church of England voted in favor of the ordination of women priests in November 1992.) F. has also been active in supporting feminist liturgical reform, overseeing the publication of *Women Included: A Book of Services and Prayers* (1991), which makes available liturgies and prayers developed by women of the St. Hilda Community. F.'s most recent publication in this area, *Bird of Paradise* (1995), continues her exploration of women and the Christian life.

In addition, her knowledge and experience of the religious life has made her an intelligent and sensitive biographer of those very mystical and religious figures who most perplex the secular world. *Puritan's Progress* (1975) examines the remarkable life of John Bunyan, the working-class artist whose religious ideas influenced the quarrels of his own time and whose *Pilgrim's Progress* modelled the Christian life for generations who came after, particularly those who defined the American religious spirit. *Merton: A Biography* (1980) traces life from lonely childhood through frantic young manhood to tortured monk struggling to reconcile his writing self with his religious self in a monastic context whose busy-ness drove him to seek out the life of a hermit. *Genuine Fake* (1986) explores the life and times of Alan Watts, English-born devotee of high Anglican spirituality, brilliant student of Zen, Episcopal priest, iconoclast, and friend of Jack Kerouac and Timothy Leary. F. sees Watts as an icon of the explosive experimentation of the 1960s and as a holy trickster figure whose life was filled with "disgrace" as well as "grace." F.'s *Thérèsa of Lisieux* (1987) looks at this symbol of Christian womanhood whose life modeled "the favourite moulds of traditional female sanctity, the mould of virginity, of suffering, of drastic self-abnegation." F. uses the exploration of Thérèsa's life as a lens through which to view the history of Christianity's attitudes to women.

Like her nonfiction writings, F.'s novels, *The Cat's Eye* (1976) and *Cousins* (1983), explore the place of women in society and the means they use to negotiate the tangles of sexuality and relationship. F.'s children's novels often reexamine the myths of English history and culture. *Wise Child* (1987) and *Juniper* (1991), two books in a series about a seventh-century witch woman, redeem that archetypal symbol of female evil, the witch. Her recent

Robin's Country (1995) presents the Robin Hood legend from a mute orphan boy's point of view.

WORKS: *With Love to the Church* (1965). (with S. Evans and B. S. Moss) *Ourselves Your Servants* (1967). *Traveling In* (1971). *Contemplating Now* (1971). *The End of Our Exploring* (1973). *God's A Good Man, and Other Poems* (1974). *Puritan's Progress: A Study of John Bunyan* (1975). *Christian Uncertainties* (1976). *The Cat's Eye: A Novel* (1976). *Burrswood, Focus of Healing* (1978). *Merton: A Biography* (1980). *John Bunyun's [sic] Pilgrimage* (1981). (with E. F. Vere and D. Blamires) *Shrinking and Clinging* (1981). *Divorce: One Woman's View* (1981). *Cousins: A Novel* (1983). *Genuine Fake: A Biography of Alan Watts* (1986; in the U.S. as *Zen Effects: The Life of Alan Watts,* 1986). *Thérèsa of Lisieux* (1987). *Wise Child* (1987). *Mirror to the Church: Reflections on Sexism* (1988). *A Year and a Day* (1989). *A Dangerous Delight: Women and Power in the Church* (1991). *Juniper* (1991). *Going Under: Preparing Yourself for Anesthesia* (1994). *Bird of Paradise* (1995). *Robin's Country* (1995). *The Flight of the Kingfisher* (1996).

BIBLIOGRAPHY:

For articles in reference works, see: *Feminist. Who's Who.*

Kari Boyd McBride

Gabrieli: See *Meeke, Mary*

Galesia: See *Barker, Jane*

Helen Louise Gardner

BORN: 13 February 1908, London.
DIED: 4 June 1986, Oxford.
DAUGHTER OF: Charles Henry Gardner and Helen Mary Roadnight Cockman Gardner.

G. was a distinguished literary critic and scholar who has, during the past fifty years, deeply influenced many readers' perceptions of British poetry, especially of the late sixteenth and early seventeenth centuries. She is particularly credited for her careful interpretive and textual work in preparing several editions of John Donne's poetry and prose: *The Divine Poems* (1952, 2nd. ed. 1978), *Selected Prose* (1967), and *The Elegies and the Songs and Sonnets* (1965). An important T. S. Eliot scholar as well, G. wrote three critical studies on this twentieth-century poet, who also had the major influence on her own criticism: *The Art of T. S. Eliot* (1949), *T. S. Eliot and the English Poetic Tradition* (1966), and *The Composition of "Four Quartets"* (1978), which analyzes both the drafts of *Four Quartets,* especially as marked by John Hayward, and Eliot's process of textual emendation. G. also wrote on John Milton and on William Shakespeare's tragedies.

G.'s critical methodology brought an impeccably well-informed and sensitive mind to a literary work and was eclectic, ignoring neither a work's historical context, the author's personal habits of mind, the relationship of a work to its time, nor the meaning we can logically deduce from the relationship of the parts of a work to its whole structure. In two works, *The Business of Criticism* (1959) and *In Defense of the Imagination* (1982), G. stated that her twenty-five and then fifty years of experience with literature formed her belief in the critic's responsibility to elucidate a work's meaning and its relationship to a historical context, and, inevitably, to make a judgment of its value.

G.'s literary education began at North London Collegiate School. She received the B.A. in 1929 from St. Hilda's College, Oxford, where she was granted the M.A. in 1935. Although she had begun a thesis on the medieval mystic writer Walter Hilton, she took a job as an assistant lecturer at the University of Birmingham in 1930, remaining at Birmingham until 1941, when Oxford offered her the position of tutor in English literature at her alma mater, St. Hilda's College. She was a Fellow of St. Hilda's from 1942 to 1966 and University Reader in Renaissance English Literature, Oxford University, from 1954 to 1966. She became Merton Professor of English Literature and a Fellow of Lady Margaret Hall, Oxford, both from 1966 to 1975. She became an Honorary Fellow of Lady Margaret Hall and St. Hilda's College. Beginning in 1954 with an invited lectureship at the University of California, Los Angeles, G. lectured throughout the United States; at Harvard University, she delivered the 1979–80 Charles Eliot Norton Lectures (later published as *In Defense of the Imagination*). She was a member of the Royal Academy, the American Academy of Arts and Sciences, and the Royal Society of Literature.

In the two works in which she examines her beliefs about literature and the role of the critic, *The Business of Criticism* and *In Defense of the Imagination,* G. explained her purpose in writing. G. eschewed any attempt to measure the amount of poetic value or to rank one poem as more valuable than another. The critic's task, or judgment, is to uncover the meaning the author intended the work to embody and to read the poem in that light. But the critic does not create readings for her audience; she simply assists other readers to read for themselves. Her strategy, similar to T.S. Eliot's "impersonal" theory of poetry, was to divest one's reading from the biases of personal prejudices and emotion.

G. also argued for the necessity of an historical approach to works of literature, which places the poem in the context of its time period. Yet we cannot simply equate a specific work's meaning with an idea that was historically popular, both because of the illogicality of such a simplistic equation and the possibility of the writer's opinions being unusual or exceptional for that time. The modern critic must recognize the historical nature of his or her own approach: It, too, is conditioned by the time period, about which we have no balanced perspective.

In her work *In Defense of the Imagination,* G. reviewed her positions, professional regrets, and achievements, and gave her opinion of recent literary theories and the state of the profession. In the essay "Present Discontents," G. expressed dissatisfaction with the "new New Criticisms" that had arisen during the previous twenty years, usually in France. She found that the work of structuralists, deconstructionists, and psychoanalytic theorists is damaging to the reader's pleasure in experiencing a work of the imagination. She foumd that modern criticism is insecure about the worth of its own activity; she linked this both to the disease of the time and to the emphasis universities now place on publication. Both tempt young scholars to do something to the text rather than elucidate it for students or other interested readers who may not know the jargon of literary theorists. She recommended that universities lessen the "over-production" of scholarly publications by shifting their focus to good teaching, which to G. was the ability to elucidate a text and to add to students' enjoyment of literature. Despite her long and varied bibliography, G. considered herself, even after fifty years of publishing and teaching, primarily a teacher: "I would wish to be considered as a teacher or as nothing."

Since G. did not write about her own teaching, or on pedagogy, she will be remembered by most for her sensitive and careful scholarship on Donne, Shakespeare, Milton, and Eliot. Some critics have been uneasy with her insistence on "judgements" in analyzing literary works; and others have criticized her admitted belief that the concerns of Shakespearian tragedy are often "Christian." In the 1990s, we might have hoped for a more discriminating analysis of recent critical theories than she admits in "Present Discontents." But using G.'s own tenet of consistency, one finds her position a logical outgrowth of her insistence on the integrity and impersonality of a poem. The value of her scholarship will endure.

WORKS: *The Art of T. S. Eliot* (1949). *The Limits of Literary Criticism: Reflections on the Interpretation of Poetry and Scripture* (1956; rpt. in *The Business of Criticism,* 1959). *The Business of Criticism* (1959). *Edwin Muir* (1961). *Reading of Paradise Lost* (1965). *T. S. Eliot and the English Poetic Tradition* (1966). *King Lear* (1967). *Literary Studies* (1967). *Religion and Literature* (1971). *Poems in the Making* (1972). *The Waste Land* (1972). *The Composition of "Four Quartets"* (1977, 1978). *In Defense of the Imagination* (1982). *The Divine Poems* (1982). *A Nocturnal upon St. Lucy's Day* (1982). *The Metaphysical Poets* (1985). *The Noble Moor* (1990).

BIBLIOGRAPHY: *English Renaissance Studies Presented to Dame Helen Gardner in Honour of Her Seventieth Birthday,* ed. J. Carey (1980). Gardner, H. "Apologia Pro Vita Mea," in *In Defense of the Imagination* (autobiographical essay, 1982).

For articles in reference works, see: *CA. CLC. Todd-BWW. WA. Who's Who.*

Other references: *Choice* (November 1978). *Commonwealth* (12 May 1972). *New Statesman* (27 August 1971, 5 May 1978). *New Yorker* (21 October 1950). *NYT* (27 October 1972). *NYTBR* (15 October 1972). *Observer* (11 April 1969). *Poetry* (October 1950). *TLS* (6 April 1967, 13 July 1967, 17 August 1967, 1 September 1972).

Laura Niesen de Abruña

Constance Clara Black Garnett

BORN: 1862, Brighton, Sussex.
DIED: 18 December 1946, Edenbridge, Kent.
DAUGHTER OF: David Black and Clara Patten Black.
MARRIED: Edward Garnett, 1889.
WROTE UNDER: C[onstance]. C[lara]. Black; Constance Garnett.

Wife of critic and scholar Edward Garnett, mother of novelist and autobiographer David Garnett, G. is now the most famous of her eminently literary family. Her translations into English of important Russian novels, plays, and tales filled seventy volumes and greatly promoted the appreciation of Russian literature in England and the United States. G. inherited part of her interest in things Russian: Her grandfather, Peter Black, had served as Naval Architect to Tsar Nicholas I, and her father had grown up in Russia before studying law in London, living briefly in Canada, and settling in Brighton, where he became coroner. G.'s mother—devoted to her eight children and domestic duties—was the daughter of Prince Albert's portrait-painter-in-ordinary and had been accustomed before her marriage to travel in intellectual and artistic circles.

G. owed much of her early education to her mother and her older siblings. Like the typical middle-class Victorian girl, however brilliant, G. was kept at home as a child; because she had contracted tuberculosis of the hip (which was cured by the time she was seven), her family regarded her as particularly delicate. She managed nevertheless to master mathematics, basic science, geography, French, German, and Latin before reaching her teens. G.'s formal education began inauspiciously with a brief stay at a boarding school, where she was suicidally depressed by her isolation: Her characteristic shyness was compounded by the school's policy of separating G. from the other girls in class because she was so intellectually advanced, as well as separating her from them in their dormitories because—a lifelong atheist—she refused to say her prayers.

Fortunately, after her unhappy experience at this boarding school, G. entered Brighton High School for Girls, which had just opened its doors in 1876, when she was fourteen. An example of the kind of public schools that were set up in the late-Victorian period to reform the education of girls, Brighton High had Edith Creak, who was only twenty-one when she took her post, as its headmistress; one of the first five female students to attend Newnham College, Creak seems to have been an important role model for her students, running the school in an easygoing yet rigorous way. Her methods appear to have been effective: Seven girls from Brighton High School distinguished themselves in Cambridge Senior Local exams in 1878; G. gained a distinction in English, and her marks overall were higher than those of any of the other 3,000 girls who sat for the examination in England. Because the Black family lived in Brighton, G. may have resided at home, but she was a full participant in the educational and social activities of the high school, becoming good friends with Amy Levy (the poet and novelist) who, like G., was to go on to Newnham College in 1879. In that year, at the age of seventeen, she won a scholarship to Newnham, where she was ecstatically happy. Although Cambridge granted no degrees to women until 1947, G. took first-class honors on her final examination, the Classical Tripos, in 1883.

When her studies were complete G. lived in London, first with two of her sisters, then alone in the East End. She became librarian at the People's Palace, joined the Fabian Society, married Edward Garnett in 1889, and supported his literary endeavors with the income from her library job for the next three years, when she resigned to have a child. While G. was pregnant with David, her only child, she began to learn Russian, under the encouragement of Felix Volkhovsky, a house guest who had recently escaped imprisonment in Siberia. To alleviate the postpartum depression resulting from a particularly difficult birth, G. worked in 1892 on her first translation, I. Goncharov's *A Common Story*. She proceeded to an essay of Leo Tolstoy's and then to the works of Ivan Turgenev, whom—as one of her very favorite authors—she later regretted having tackled at so early and inexperienced a stage in her career. For more than thirty-five years, G. worked constantly on translations of Russian texts, never once publishing an original composition.

G. associated with several Russian revolutionaries in exile, among them N. Tchaykovsky, Prince Peter Kropotkin, Prince Tcherkessov, and Sergey Stepniak. At Stepniak's urging, she traveled alone to Russia in 1894, officially to deliver famine-relief funds that had been raised in England but actually to deliver letters from the exiles to fellow revolutionaries. Though she had personal ties to proponents of the revolution, as well as philosophical leanings to socialism, G. never became a communist. She believed that *Das Kapital* held only very limited truth and ultimately she had no respect at all for the Bolsheviks. When G. returned to Russia with her son in 1904, her enthusiasm was waning; in 1907, when she met Joseph Stalin, V. I. Lenin, and Leon Trotsky at the Russian Social Democratic convention in England, she declined even to serve as interpreter for Lenin's public address.

Her devotion to Russian literature, however, remained fervent. She translated continuously, even though her always-weak eyesight was permanently impaired by her unstinting work on *War and Peace.* In later years, she would dictate her English translations to an assistant who read the Russian originals aloud to her. G.'s major translations included thirteen volumes of Anton Chekhov's tales and two volumes of his plays, seventeen of Turgenev, thirteen of Feodor Dostoyevsky, six of Nikolay Gogol, four of Tolstoy, and six of A. J. Herzen, as well as scattered volumes of Goncharov and A. Ostrovsky. G.'s translations are not now universally accepted as definitive; G.'s theory of translating required that she render the language in a style appropriate to the period of the author, which somewhat dates her works. But as the most authoritative and comprehensive (not, in every case, the first) English translations of major Russian works in her day, they played an enormous role in influencing modern British and American writers.

WORKS: (trans.) *A Common Story,* by I. Goncharov (1894). (trans.) *The Kingdom of God Is Within You,* by L. Tolstoy (1894). (trans.) *The Complete Works* (13 vols.), by I. Turgenev (1894–99). (trans.) *The Storm,* by A. Ostrovsky (1899, 1917). (trans.) *Anna Karenina, The Death of Ivan Ilyitch and Other Stories,* and *War and Peace,* by L. Tolstoy (1901–1904). (trans.) *Twenty-six Men and a Girl,* by M. Gorky (1902). (trans.) *The Revolt of the "Potemkin,"* by K. Feldman (1908). (trans.) *The Brothers Karamazov,* by F. Dostoevsky (1912). (trans.) *The Idiot,* by F. Dostoevsky (1913). (trans.) *Letters from the Underground,* by F. Dostoevsky (1913). (trans.) *The Possessed,* by F. Dostoevsky (1914). (trans.) *Crime and Punishment,* by F. Dostoevsky (1914). (trans.) *The House of the Dead,* by F. Dostoevsky (1915). (trans.) *The Insulted and Injured,* by F. Dostoevsky (1915). (trans.) *A Raw Youth,* by F. Dostoevsky (1916). (trans.) *The Tales of Chekhov* (13 vols.), by A. Chekhov (1916–22). (trans.) *Stories* (4 vols.), by F. Dostoevsky (1917–20). (trans.) *Letters: to His Family and Friends,* by A. Chekhov (1920–26). (trans.) *Christianity and Patriotism,* by L. Tolstoy (1922). (trans.) *The Works of Gogol* (6 vols.), by N. Gogol (1922–26). (trans.) *The Cherry Orchard and Other Plays,* by A. Chekhov (1923). (trans.) *Three Sisters and Other Plays,* by A. Chekhov (1923). (trans.) *The Memoirs* (6 vols.) by A. J. Herzen (1924–27).(trans.) *Letters to Olga Leonardovna Knipper,* by A. Chekhov (1926).

BIBLIOGRAPHY: Black, C. C. [Garnett] and O. Dymmond. *Catalogue of the Books in the Library of the People's Palace for East London* (1889). Garnett, D. *The Golden Echo* (1954). Heilbrun, C. G. *The Garnett Family* (1961). Garnett, R. *Constance Garnett: A Heroic Life* (1991). Muchnic, H. *Smith College Studies in Modern Languages* (1939). Rubinstein, R. *Colorado Quarterly* (1974).

For articles in reference works, see: *DNB. Europa. Oxford. ToddBWW.*

Other references: *New Republic* (6 January 1947). *Time* (30 December 1946). *TLS* (2 January 1954, 30 April 1954, 16 July 1954).

Robyn R. Warhol
(updated by Linda Hunt Beckman)

Elizabeth Gaskell

BORN: 29 September 1810, London.
DIED: 12 November 1865, Holybourne, Hampshire.
DAUGHTER OF: William Stevenson and Elizabeth Holland Stevenson.
MARRIED: William Gaskell, 1832.
WROTE UNDER: Mrs. Gaskell; Cotton Mather Mills, Esq.

In November 1865, when reporting her death, *The Athenaeum* rated G. as "if not the most popular, with small question, the most powerful and finished female novelist of an epoch singularly rich in female novelists." Today G. is generally considered a lesser figure in English letters, remembered chiefly for her minor classics *Cranford* (1853) and *Wives and Daughters: An Every-Day Story* (1866). G.'s early fame as a social novelist began with the 1848 publication of *Mary Barton: A Tale of Manchester Life,* in which she pricked the conscience of industrial England through her depiction and analysis of the working classes. Many critics were hostile to the novel because of its open sympathy for the workers in their relations with the masters; the high quality of writing and characterization were undeniable, however, and critics have compared *Mary Barton* to the work of Friedrich Engels and other contemporaries in terms of its accuracy in social observation.

The later publication of *North and South* (1855), also dealing with the relationship of workers and masters, strengthened G.'s status as a leader in social fiction.

G.'s fiction was deeply influenced by her upbringing and her marriage. The daughter of a Unitarian clergyman who was a civil servant and journalist, G. was brought up after her mother's death by her aunt in Knutsford, Cheshire, a small village that served as the prototype not only for Cranford but also for Hollingford in *Wives and Daughters* and the settings of numerous short stories and novellas. In 1832, she married William Gaskell, a Unitarian clergyman in Manchester in whose ministry she actively participated and with whom she collaborated to write the poem "Sketches Among the Poor" in 1837.

"Our Society at Cranford," now the first two chapters of *Cranford,* appeared in Charles Dickens's *Household Words* on 13 December 1851 and was itself a fictionalized version of an earlier essay, "The Last Generation in England." Dickens so liked the original episode that he pressed G. for more; at irregular intervals between January 1852 and May 1853 eight more episodes appeared.

Two controversies marred G.'s literary career. In 1853, she shocked and offended many of her readers with *Ruth,* an exploration of seduction and illegitimacy prompted by anger at moral conventions that condemned a "fallen woman" to ostracism and almost inevitable prostitution—a topic already touched on in the character of Esther in *Mary Barton.* The strength of the novel lies in its presentation of social conduct within a small Dissenting community when tolerance and rigid morality clash. Although some element of the "novel with a purpose" is evident, G.'s sensitivity in her portrayal of character and, even more, her feel for relationships within small communities and families show a developing sense of direction as a novelist. Although critics praised the soundness of the novel's moral lessons, several members of G.'s congregation burned the book, and it was banned in many libraries. Even G. admitted that she prohibited the book to her own daughters, but she nevertheless stood by the work.

The second controversy arose following the 1857 publication of *The Life of Charlotte Brontë.* The biography's initial wave of praise was quickly followed by angry protests from some of the people dealt with in the work. In a few instances, legal action was threatened; however, with the help of her husband and George Smith, editor of *Cornhill* magazie and the publisher of the *Dictionary of National Biography,* the problems were resolved without recourse to law. The most significant complaint resulted from G.'s acceptance of Branwell Brontë's version of his dismissal from his tutoring position (he blamed it on his refusal to be seduced by his employer's wife) and necessitated a public retraction in *The Times,* withdrawal of the second edition, and the publication of a revised third edition, the standard text. Despite the initial complications and restrictions necessitated by conventions of the period (G. did not, for example, deal with Brontë's feelings for Constantin Heger), *The Life of Charlotte Brontë* has established itself as one of the great biographies; later biographies have modified but not replaced it.

During 1858 and 1859, G. wrote several items, mainly for Dickens, of which two are of particular interest. *My Lady Ludlow,* a short novel cut in two by a long digressive tale, is reminiscent of *Cranford,* yet the setting and social breadth anticipates *Wives and Daughters.* The second work, *Lois the Witch,* is a somber novella concerning the Salem witch trials that prefigures G.'s next work, *Sylvia's Lovers* (1863), by its interest in morbid psychology. *Sylvia's Lovers* is a powerful if somewhat melodramatic novel. The first two volumes are full of energy; they sparkle and have humor. The ending, however, shows forced invention rather than true tragedy. Regarded by G. as "the saddest story I ever wrote," *Sylvia's Lovers* is set during the French Revolution in a remote whaling port with particularly effective insights into character relationships.

Most critics agree that *Cousin Phillis* (1864) is G.'s crowning achievement in the short novel. The story is uncomplicated; its virtues are in the manner of its development and telling. *Cousin Phillis* is also recognized as a fitting prelude for G.'s final and most widely acclaimed novel, *Wives and Daughters: An Every-Day Story,* which ran in *Cornhill* from August 1864 to January 1866. The final installment was never written, yet the ending was known and the novel as it exists is virtually complete. The plot of the novel is complex, relying far more on a series of relationships between family groups in Hollingford than on dramatic structure. Throughout *Wives and Daughters* the humorous, ironical, and sometimes satirical view of the characters is developed with a heightened sense of artistic self-confidence and maturity.

G. was hostile to any form of biographical notice of her being written in her lifetime. Only months before her death, she wrote to an applicant for data: "I disapprove so entirely of the plan of writing "notices" or "memoirs" of living people, that I must send you on the answer I have already sent to many others; namely an entire refusal to sanction what is to me so objectionable and indelicate a practice, by furnishing a single fact with regard to myself. I do not see why the public have any more to do with me than buy or reject the ware I supply to them" (4 June 1865). After her death, the family sustained her objection, refusing to make family letters or biographical data available.

Critical awareness of G. as a social historian is now more than balanced by awareness of her innovativeness and artistic development as a novelist. While scholars continue to debate the precise nature of her talent, they also reaffirm the singular attractiveness of her best works.

WORKS: *Mary Barton: A Tale of Manchester Life* (1848). *Lizzie Leigh: A Domestic Tale* (1850). *The Moorland Cottage* (1850). *Cranford* (1853). *Ruth* (1853). *Lizzie Leigh and Other Tales* (1855). *North and South* (1855). *The Life of Charlotte Brontë* (1857). *My Lady Ludlow* (1858). *Right at Last and Other Tales* (1860). *Lois the Witch and Other Tales* (1860). *Sylvia's Lovers* (1863). *A Dark Night's Work* (1863). *Cousin Phillis: A Tale* (1864; rpt. as *Cousin Phillis and Other Tales,* 1865). *The Grey Woman and Other Tales* (1865). *Wives and Daughters: An Every-Day Story* (1866). *The Letters of Mrs. Gaskell,* ed. J. A. V. Chapple and A. Pollard (1996).

BIBLIOGRAPHY: d'Albertis, D. *Dissembling Fictions: Elizabeth Gaskell and the Victorian Social Text* (1997). Bonaparte, F. *The Gypsy-Bachelor of Manchester: The Life of Mrs. Gaskell's Demon* (1992). Brodetsky, T. *Elizabeth Gaskell* (1986). *Private Voices: The Diaries of Elizabeth*

Gaskell and Sophia Holland, ed. J. A. V. Chapple and A. Wilson (1996). Chapple, J. A. V. *Elizabeth Gaskell: The Early Years* (1997). Colby, R. B. *"Some Appointed Work to Do": Women and Vocation in the Fiction of Elizabeth Gaskell* (1995). Craik, W. A. *Elizabeth Gaskell and the English Provincial Novel* (1975). Easson, A. *Elizabeth Gaskell* (1979). Ffrench, Y. *Mrs. Gaskell* (1949). Ganz, M. *Elizabeth Gaskell: The Artist in Conflict* (1969). Gerin, W. *Elizabeth Gaskell: A Biography* (1976). Hopkins, A. B. *Elizabeth Gaskell: Her Life and Work* (1952). Lansbury, C. *Elizabeth Gaskell: The Novel of Social Crisis* (1975). Nestor, P. *Female Friendships and Communities: Charlotte Brontë, George Eliot, Elizabeth Gaskell* (1985). Pike, E. H. *Family and Society in the Works of Elizabeth Gaskell* (1994). Pollard, A. *Mrs. Gaskell: Novelist and Biographer* (1966). Rubenius, A. *The Woman Question in Mrs. Gaskell's Life and Works* (1950). Sanders, G. D. *Elizabeth Gaskell* (1929). Schor, H. M. *Scheheregarde in the Marketplace: Elizabeth Gaskell and The Victorian Novel* (1992). Selig, R. L. *Elizabeth Gaskell: A Reference Guide* (1977). Sharps, J. G. *Mrs. Gaskell's Observation and Invention: A Study of Her Non-Biographic Work* (1970). Spencer, J. *Elizabeth Gaskell* (1993). Stoneman, P. *Elizabeth Gaskell* (1987). Unsworth, A. *Elizabeth Gaskell: An Independent Woman* (1996). Welch, J. *Elizabeth Gaskell: An Annotated Bibliography 1929–75* (1977). Weyant, N. S. *Elizabeth Gaskell: An Annoted Bibliography of English-Language Sources, 1976–1991* (1994). Wright, E. *Mrs. Gaskell: The Basis for Reassessment* (1965). Wright, T. *Elizabeth Gaskell: "We Are Not Angels"* (1996).

For articles in reference works, see: *Allibone. Bloomsbury. Cambridge. DLB. DNB. Feminist. Oxford. Todd. BWW. VB.*

Other references: Buchanan, L., in *Joinings and Disjoinings,* ed. J. S. Mink (1991). Davis, D. L. *Signs* (1992). Dolin, T. *VS* (1993). Gallagher, C. *The Industrial Reformation of English Fiction 1832–1867* (1986). GSJ (1987–present). *Gaskell Society Newsletter* (1986–present). Lucas, J. *Tradition and Tolerance in Nineteenth-Century Fiction: Critical Essays on Some English and American Novels* (1966). Mews, H. *Frail Vessels: Woman's Role in Women's Novels from Fanny Burney to George Eliot* (1969). Minto, W. *Fortnightly Review* (1 September 1878). Schor, H. *DSA* (1990). Shorter, C. K. *Bookman* (June 1896). Warhol, R. R. *PMLA* (1986). Webb, R. K., in *Dickens and Other Victorians,* ed. J. Shattock (1988).

Lynn M. Alexander

Margaret Gatty

BORN: 3 June 1809, Burnham, Essex.
DIED: 4 October 1873, Ecclesfield, Yorkshire.
DAUGHTER OF: Alexander John Scott and Mary Frances Ryder Scott.
MARRIED: Alfred Gatty, 1839.

G. was a popular writer of children's literature and a talented amateur naturalist and collector. The whimsical combination of moral allegory and scientific instruction in her best-known work for children, *Parables from Nature* (1856–71), is characteristic of her writing. Her literary work embodied a distinctly Victorian emphasis on useful information and moral improvement, and her enthusiasm for scientific study was animated by a secure, pre-Darwinian faith in the divine ordering of nature.

After her mother's early death, G.'s father encouraged his daughters to share his own enthusiastic but eclectic love of books and learning. As a young girl, G. became an avid student and translator of Italian and German literature. She also developed her considerable artistic skill by copying in the British Museum print-room and by mastering the techniques of calligraphy, illumination, and etching. After bearing ten children (eight of whom survived) as the wife of the Reverend Alfred Gatty, vicar of Ecclesfield Church, G. took up writing seriously in her forties as a means of supporting her large household. Her first book, coauthored with her husband, was a memoir of her father, chaplain to Lord Nelson: *Recollections of the Life of the Rev. A. J. Scott, D. D.* (1842). After trying her hand at children's literature in *The Fairy Godmothers, and Other Tales* (1851), she found her most successful formula in the first of five series of *Parables from Nature* (1855). In the typical parable, anthropomorphized plants, animals, and elements demonstrate the functioning of the natural world while allegorically rendering religious truths or illustrating the value of conservative morals like obeying authority or accepting one's ordained place in life. G.'s anti-Darwinian sentiments are made explicit in "Inferior Animals," which satirizes the argumentative methods of the *Origin of Species,* and in "The Cause and the Causer," which stages an insect inquest into the death of a moth in order to demonstrate the superiority of divine design over natural selection as an explanation for instinct and adaptation. The *Parables* were frequently reprinted and illustrated by various prominent Victorian artists.

G.'s other most successful children's book was *Aunt Judy's Tales* (1859); *Aunt Judy's Letters* followed it in 1862. The "Aunt Judy" in both was a fictionalized version of the Gatty children's favorite story-teller, their sister Juliana. Encouraged by her publisher, George Bell, G. started *Aunt Judy's Magazine* for children in 1866. It included a lively and eminently didactic blend of stories, serials, poems, songs, reviews, drawings, and historical and scientific information. G. also used the magazine to solicit endowments for cots in the Great Ormond Street Hospital for Sick Children. *Aunt Judy's Magazine* frequently included translations from continental authors such as Hans Christian Andersen; it also featured contributions by Lewis Carroll and provided Juliana Gatty Ewing with her own start as a children's writer. G.'s lifelong interest in emblems led her to include them in many issues; these were later collected in *A Book of Emblems* (1872). After G.'s death, her daughter Horatia continued the popular magazine (with assistance from Juliana) until 1885.

According to Juliana Ewing, her mother viewed her literary work as gainful employment and her scientific pursuits as leisure. G.'s avid interest in seaweeds and zoophytes originated when she was sent to Hastings for several months in 1848 to recover her health after the birth of her seventh child. Her studies introduced her to experts like

William Henry Harvey and George Johnston, under whose tutelage she eventually published her own well-regarded *History of British Seaweeds* (1863). Both men later honored her scientific work by naming new discoveries after her. Notwithstanding her antievolutionary sentiments, G.'s enthusiasm for what she viewed as practical kinds of scientific progress led her to encourage the use of chloroform and homeopathy.

The paralysis that would eventually end G.'s life began to impair her physical ability to write from the early 1860s, forcing her to rely increasingly on her daughters as secretaries and editors. In a later age or more prosperous circumstances, a woman with her intellectual gifts might have become an artist or scientist or rivaled the success of children's writers like Charlotte Yonge. Instead, like many Victorian women, she subordinated her intellectual work to a life of ceaseless domestic industry and duty to others. After her death, a stained glass "Parable Window" was erected in her honor in Ecclesfield Church; it was later joined by a marble plaque donated by juvenile subscribers to *Aunt Judy's Magazine,* a fitting memorial to a writer whose best work charmingly captured a child's view of the natural world and shaped it to the ends of Christian edification.

WORKS: (with Alfred Gatty) *Recollections of the Life of the Rev. A. J. Scott, D. D.* (1842). *The Fairy Godmothers, and Other Tales* (1851). *Parables from Nature,* 5 vols. (1856–71). *Worlds Not Realised* (1856). *Proverbs Illustrated* (1857). *The Poor Incumbent* (1858). *Legendary Tales* (1858). *Aunt Judy's Tales* (1859). *The Human Face Divine, and Other Tales* (1860). *Old Folks from Home, or, a Holiday in Ireland* (1862). *Aunt Judy's Letters* (1862). *History of British Seaweeds,* 2 vols. (1863). *Domestic Pictures and Tales* (1866). *Waifs and Strays of Natural History* (1871). *The Mother's Book of Poetry* (1872). *A Book of Emblems, with Interpretations Thereof* (1872). *The Book of Sundials* (1872).

BIBLIOGRAPHY: Ewing, J. *Aunt Judy's Magazine* (1874). Katz, W. *The Emblems of Margaret Gatty: A Study of Allegory in Nineteenth-Century Children's Literature* (1993). Knoepflmacher, U. C. *NCF* (1983). Maxwell, C. *Mrs. Gatty and Mrs. Ewing* (1949). Moss, A. *L&U* (1988).

For articles in reference works, see: *Allibone. Bloomsbury. Cambridge. DNB. Feminist. OCCL. Oxford. ToddBWW. VB. WWCL.*

Other references: *Athenaeum* (11 October 1873). Avery, G. *Nineteenth Century Children* (1965). Beer, G. *Darwin's Plots* (1983). *Illustrated London News* (18 October 1873).

Rosemary Jann

Pam Gems

BORN: 1 August 1925, Bransgore, Hampshire.
DAUGHTER OF: Jim Price and Elsie Mabel Annetts Price.
MARRIED: Keith Gems, 1949.

G. is a prolific and frequently produced playwright whose best-known plays, *Dusa, Fish, Stas and Vi* (1976), *Queen Christina* (1977), *Piaf* (1978), and *Camille* (1985), show that neither generosity, majesty, talent, nor beauty can free women from the special choices imposed by gender roles. Finding women "very funny, coarse, subversive," G. provides major roles for actresses that reveal women's changing lives with intelligence and compassion for both sexes. G. rejects an extremist feminist position, asserting that her work is an argument for a new society "more suited to both sexes."

G. was the first child of working-class parents. Her mother brought up her daughter and two younger sons alone after their father's death in a workhouse in 1929. G. won a scholarship to Brockenhurst County Grammar School in Hampshire but left school to join the Women's Royal Naval Service (WRENS) in World War II. She describes her war years on the south coast of England as "all sex and high adrenalin" because of the risk, particularly for the men, of being killed. Her war service provided the means for attending Manchester University, where she took a degree (with honors) in psychology in 1949. That same year, she married Keith Gems, a model manufacturer. Living at first in Paris and then on the Isle of Wight, the family moved to London after the birth of their fourth child.

Though G.'s life experiences include work as a charwoman, model, sheet metal worker, and actress, she has declared, "I never wanted to be a writer. I always was. And it was always plays." She had worked briefly for the BBC after the birth of her first two children, writing three plays for television, of which only *A Builder by Trade* (1961) was produced. Once all four children were in school, G. began to sell her plays. Living in London, G. began to work with lunchtime theaters and with the feminist movement. In 1973, she wrote *My Warren* (about aging and sexuality) and *After Birthday* (about infanticide) for Al Berman's Almost Free Theatre and *The Amiable Courtship of Miz Venus and Wild Bill* for Almost Free's Women's Season.

Dusa, Fish, Stas and Vi (1976), her first play to reach the West End, was originally called *Dead Fish* when produced at Edinburgh. It details the attempts of four strong women to live without men. Rich and radical Fish shares her flat with Dusa, who is searching for the children her ex-husband has kidnapped; Stas, who works as a physiotherapist by day and a party girl by night; and Vi, who revels in anorexia. Warm and tough, the women support each other, but they cannot overcome Fish's depression when her lover, and fellow radical organizer, leaves her to marry a more submissive woman. Fish ends her masochistic obsession by poisoning herself, an act discovered, ironically, just as the women's joint efforts have recovered Dusa's children. The women have no positive relationship with men: Dusa's husband takes her children; Fish's lover envies her skills as a speaker; Stas's johns give her gonorrhea along with the money she wants for graduate study; and Vi would rather starve. Fish's suicide note recognizes that it will be harder to change male-female relations than to change women's lives: "We don't do as they want any more, and they hate it. What are we to do?" Fish models herself on Rosa Luxemburg, another middle-class socialist, and is partly modeled, according to Colin Chambers, on Buzz Goodbody, the brilliant young director of the Royal Shakespeare Company's Other Place, who killed herself in 1975. *Dusa, Fish, Stas, and Vi,* G.'s first major commercial success, was produced in Los Angeles in 1978.

The Other Place in Stratford produced G.'s *Queen Christina* in 1977 after the Royal Court had turned it down because it was "too sprawly, expensive, and slanted toward women." It is the first of a number of plays centered on historical figures and marks the beginning of a discernible curve of development in G.'s work. G. has consistently reacted to received notions about historical personages, rescripting the life in each case so that the play illuminates the flesh-and-blood person who became a cultural icon. In nearly every instance, G. creates dramatic irony by juxtaposing myth—romantic, cultural, spiritual—and reality, exposing, in the process, the crushing power of patriarchy and privilege.

Christina of Sweden (1626–89), brought up to rule as a man, learns that only power is respected and abdicates rather than accept her woman's duty to provide an heir. She travels south to Rome, where she embraces Roman Catholicism and tries to persuade a cardinal to become her lover. Finally, offered military power as a surrogate male, she feels cheated of her woman's life and refuses further violence. Christina's transformation shows her that women's lives produce bread and children rather than power and corpses and shows her that she was wrong to despise women. Yet Irving Wardle praised the play, ironically, as "a most masculine performance" in its "energy, fair-mindedness and bold construction." What Christina wanted, but could not achieve with all her brilliance and power, was scope for her "masculine" talents and energy, and for her emotions. The point is not that she made the wrong choice but that she should not have had to choose between achievement and nurturing. *Queen Christina,* like *Piaf, Camille,* and *The Blue Angel* that would follow, foregrounds female character and contextualizes obstacles of gender and birth set before attractive women (G. is fascinated by beautiful women and says her own ordinariness explains the fascination); each central figure, while superficially glamorous, stands revealed without the protective covering of sentimentality.

In 1977, G. produced a one-act play called *Franz into April* about the director of a mental health institute and a repressed Englishwoman. The following year, the Royal Shakespeare Company produced *Piaf,* the first full-length play she wrote (1973), her second play to reach the West End, and her first to cross the Atlantic to Broadway, in 1981. It played to sold-out houses in London, but its reception in the United States was less enthusiastic. As Edith Piaf, the Parisian streetwalker who became a cabaret star without denying her background, Jane Lapotaire was funny and desperate, vulgar and elegant, addicted to morphine and to a series of lovers. Piaf's only lasting relationship is with her woman-friend Toine, from the same background. G. considers the play "partly . . . a feminist document celebrating an extraordinary woman." *Piaf* displays G.'s characteristic difficulties with form. In structure, the play is deliberately episodic, joined by songs, to the satisfaction of London critics but not of New Yorkers ("inept," said Brendan Gill; "cartooned archetypes," opined Frank Rich). Lapotaire, however, received a Tony award for her role.

While *Piaf* was running, G.'s adaptations of Anton Chekhov's *Uncle Vanya* and Henrik Ibsen's *A Doll's House* were produced. In 1982, *The Treat,* set in a French brothel, portrayed the cruel enactments of male fantasies with grotesque humor. The gentler fantasies of literary male transvestites enliven *Aunt Mary* (1982). A television producer who would exploit them on her show as a cage of odd birds is defeated by the campy, anarchic, generous community of writers.

1984 was a landmark year for G.: *Loving Women* was produced at the Arts Theatre; her version of Chekhov's *The Cherry Orchard* appeared; and the Royal Shakespeare Company mounted her *Camille.* Returning to the Parisian floating world, a century earlier than *Piaf,* G.'s version of Alexandre Dumas's *Camille* was first produced at The Other Place in Stratford in 1984, then at the Comedy in London, and in 1986 at the Long Wharf in New Haven, Connecticut. Her Camille first gives up her livelihood for love, threatening her circle of dependents, and then gives up her lover when his father promises to educate her son for a place in the secure class. In England, the play provided a vehicle for Frances Barber to temper passion with pragmatism; and in New Haven, for Kathleen Turner to create an alternative Camille.

G.'s *The Danton Affair* (1986) was adapted from the stage chronicle by Stanislawa Przybyszewska and produced at the Barbican by the Royal Shakespeare Company. A very large cast acts out bread riots and faction fights that lead Danton to challenge Robespierre. In contrast to the better-known play by Georg Büchner, *Danton's Death,* G. makes the sea-green incorruptible Robespierre more admirable than Danton, whose credibility on her stage is undercut by his forced attentions to his peasant-born child-bride. Several critics praised Ian McDiarmid as Robespierre, but few liked the three-hour play. Still, G. has brought her concern for the complex connections between private and public lives from lunchtime theater to the main stage of the Barbican.

In 1991, G.'s *The Blue Angel,* an adaptation of Heinrich Mann's novel *Professor Unrat,* debuted in a Royal Shakespeare production at Stratford; typically, the director, Trevor Nunn, received more attention than the playwright. The subject matter, the story of a staid professor whose life is complicated, even ruined, by his obsession with a night club singer, Rosa (renamed Lola when Josef von Sternberg made the 1930 film with Marlene Dietrich as Lola). G.'s adaptation, divested of romantic elements, is a study of arrogance and raw power.

Deborah's Daughter (1995) is a postmodern feminist work, though G. would object to such a label. Long fascinated by the myth of Demeter, Pluto, and Persephone as represented in a grammar school poem by the Victorian poet Jean Ingelow, G. has deconstructed the old myth and constructed a new one of her own in which Persephone assumes an autonomy—both personal and verbal—that in turn becomes a metaphor for the condition of muted Others. G.'s concerns here are broader than gender, incorporating issues of culture, age, class, and race. *Deborah's Daughter,* while certainly a text receptive to a number of contemporary critical approaches, avoids polemic and provides a vigorous, dramatic confrontation of ideas and ideologies.

In another turn, G.'s latest performed play, *Stanley* (1996), takes a man as its central character: Sir Stanley Spencer, sometimes described by art historians as "the wayward genius of modern British painting," but largely unknown outside academic circles. G. has a longstanding interest in Spencer's work, and when she investigated the life she found the stuff of theater. Certainly, any man who declares "Why can't I have two wives if that's what I need?" offers what is needed. And so, the messy entanglements of art and sex become the play, with figures famous (Augustus John) and relatively unknown (Spencer's wife, Hilda) careening across the stage. Spencer himself emerges a tragic figure, bent on a frustrating quest for the unattainable; yet it is clear from the text that only in the hands of a gifted actor like Antony Sher, who took the role in the Royal National Theatre production, can *Stanley* become really engaging drama.

Most recently, G. has finished a new work, a one-woman play about Marlene Dietrich, written for Sian Phillips and yet to be staged.

In something of a departure, G. has published two novels: *Mrs Frampton* (1989) and *Bon Voyage, Mrs Frampton* (1990). G. has said that she turned to novel writing, a less complex task than playwriting, after a difficult year trying to mount a Broadway production of *Camille* with Kathleen Turner. May Frampton, an awkward, angry, rather frumpy character—a far cry from the superficially glamorous women of the plays—has retired to Marbella with husband Vic. Contrary to her own expectations, May thrives in the Spanish sun, finding new life in her friendship with a wealthy Asian widow, while Vic plays golf and dallies with amorous French widows. His slapstick death releases May into greater freedom. A robust, episodic comedy, *Mrs Frampton* is, like G.'s plays, more than entertainment; it examines marriage and female friendship as well as issues of personal independence and self-definition. *Bon Voyage, Mrs Frampton* picks up May's story and moves her quickly from Spain to France to Florida, from widowhood to marriage with a millionaire. While G. does not ignore the vicissitudes and pain of aging, she is relentlesslessly hopeful about opportunities and possibilities. Humor and zest for living imbue *Bon Voyage, Mrs Frampton* with high spirits. Both novels have bounce, optimism, and a fairytale quality that set them apart from G.'s drama; yet like the plays, the novels display a fast-paced, freewheeling looseness of structure that some find disconcerting.

Writing about *Dusa, Fish, Stas and Vi* in *The Independent* (31 January 1996), Georgina Brown may have best summed up G.'s achievement to date: Brown notes that it was "her earthy directness, racy pungent turn of phrase, her robust humour and astute awareness of feminine as well as feminist issues that impressed." Revision, rescripting, and retelling are integral, cognitive activities in G.'s theater. Revision—understood in Adrienne Rich's terms as reentering a text or life and seeing it from a different angle—is central. G. rejects polemic. Lives, most often female but occasionally male, are examined analytically. G. has observed that she so often begins with someone from history, thus creating expectations, then "pull[s] the rug, [and] play[s] another game." The game is part of the contract between playwright and audience; it can be intellectual, but it must be entertaining.

WORKS: *A Builder by Trade* (television, 1961). *Betty's Wonderful Christmas* (1972). *My Warren* (1973). *After Birthday* (1973). *The Amiable Courtship of Miz Venus and Wild Bill* (1973). *Sarah B. Divine!* (1973). *Go West, Young Woman* (1974). *Up in Sweden* (1975). *The Project* (1976). *Dead Fish* (later called *Dusa, Fish, Stas and Vi*, 1976). *Guinevere* (1976). *My Name is Rosa Luxemburg* (adapted from play by M. Auricoste; 1976). *The Rivers and Forest* (adapted from play by M. Duras; 1976). *Queen Christina* (1977; rev. 1982). *Franz into April* (1977). *Piaf* (1978). *Sandra* (1979). *Ladybird, Ladybird* (1979). *Uncle Vanya* (adapted from play by A. Chekhov; 1979; rev. 1992). *We Never Do What They Want* (television, 1979). *A Doll's House* (adapted from play by H. Ibsen; 1980). *The Treat* (1982). *Aunt Mary* (1982). *The Cherry Orchard* (adapted from play by A. Chekhov; 1984). *Loving Women* (1985). (lyrics by G. and P. Sand, music by Sand) *Pasionaria* (1985). *The Danton Affair* (adapted from play by S. Przybyszewska; 1986). *Camille* (adapted from play by A. Dumas fils; prod. 1984, pub. 1985). *Mrs Frampton* (1989). *Bon Voyage, Mrs Frampton* (1990). *The Blue Angel* (adapted from novel by H. Mann; 1991). (with T. Yates) *Yerma* (adapted from play by F. García Lorca, 1993). *Ghosts* (adapted from play by H. Ibsen; 1993). *The Seagull* (adapted from play by A. Chekhov; 1994). *Deborah's Daughter* (1995). *Stanley* (1996).

BIBLIOGRAPHY: Bassnett-McGuire, S. E., in *Semiotics of Drama and Theatre: New Perspectives in the Theory of Drama and Theatre,* ed. H. Schmidt and A. Van Kesteren (1984). Betsko, K. and R. Koenig. *Interviews with Contemporary Women Playwrights* (1987). Burkman, K., in *British and Irish Drama Since 1960,* ed. J. Acheson (1993). Carlson, S. L. *Drama, Sex and Politics* (1985). Cody, G.-H. *Theater* (Fall/Winter 1987). Itzin, C. *Stages in the Revolution: Political Theatre in Britain Since 1968* (1980). Keyssar, H. *Feminist Theatre* (1985). Passnett-McGuire, S. E., in *Semiotics of Drama and Theatre: New Perspectives in the Theory of Drama and Theatre,* ed. H. Schmidt and A. Van Kesteren (1984). Reinelt, J. *W&P* (1989). Rudolph, S. J., in *British Playwrights, 1956–1995: A Research and Production Sourcebook,* ed. W. W. Demastes (1996). Sakellaridou, E. *Women Studies International Forum* (September–December 1995). Wandor, M. *Understudies* (1981). Wandor, M. *Carry On, Understudies* (1986). Wandor, M. *Look Back in Gender: Sexuality and the Family in Post-War British Drama* (1987). Worth, K., in *Feminine Focus: The New Woman Playwrights,* ed. E. Brater (1989).

For articles in reference works, see: *Bloomsbury. CA. CD. DLB. Feminist. ToddBWW. WD. Who's Who in the Theatre,* 17th ed. (1981).

Other references: *British Book News* (February 1986). Chambers, C. *Drama* (1986). *Guardian* (30 April 1992). *Independent* (31 January 1996). *Listener* (8 June 1989, 4 October 1990). *LonSunT* (12 December 1976, 23 January 1977, 18 September 1977, 20 January 1980, 3 February 1980). *New Yorker* (16 February 1981). *NYT* (5 August 1979, 6 February 1981, 5 February 1981, 10 May 1993, 19 February 1996). *Observer* (14 May 1989, 7 October 1990). *Other Spaces* (1980). *Plays & Players* (June 1984, March 1985, April 1985, January 1986, September 1986). *TJ* (October 1985, October 1987). *TLS* (9 July 1982, 16 February 1986, 6 September 1991).

Mary R. Davidson
(updated by Robert Ellis Hosmer, Jr.)

Gentleman on His Travels, A: See *Scott, Sarah*

Gentlewoman, A.: See *Ephelia*

Gentlewoman from Those Parts, A: See *Bradstreet, Anne Dudley*

Gentlewoman in Culros: See *Colville, Elizabeth*

George, Eliot: See *Freeman, Gillian*

Grace Norton Gethin

BORN: 1676, Abbots Leigh, Somerset.
DIED: 11 October 1697.
DAUGHTER OF: Sir George Norton and Lady Frances Freke Norton.
MARRIED: Sir Richard Gethin.

After G. died in October 1697 in her twenty-first year, a monument to her memory was erected in the south aisle of Westminster Abbey. Within two years, writings taken from her commonplace book were published as *Reliquiae Gethinianae, or Misery Is Virtu[']s Whetstone,* probably at the instigation of her mother, Lady Frances Norton. The book begins with "A Poem in Praise of the Author" by W. C., very likely William Congreve, and is followed by brief essays, generally no longer than a page, on various subjects, such as "Of Friendship," "Of Love," and "Of Gratitude." Only later was it discovered that most of these essays originated in the works of earlier writers and were mistakenly thought to be written by G., who must simply have copied them for her own edification, occasionally adding brief comments. In spite of its derivative nature, *Reliquiae Gethinianae* went through three editions in four years, and in the 1703 edition there is a second elegant poem, this time signed by Congreve, "Sacred to the Memory of Grace Lady Gethin."

A collation of *Reliquiae Gethinianae* with Bacon's *Works* shows that many passages are indeed taken from the *Essays;* another source is probably Bishop Hall, as suggested in the eighteenth-century marginalia of the first edition (British Library copy, 12269.bbb.17).

G. was survived by her husband as well as her parents, but it was her mother, Lady Frances Norton, described by one eighteenth-century writer (Ballard, *Learned Ladies*) as "a lady of great piety and uncommon abilities," who seems to have grieved most over her daughter's death. Although one cannot be certain, it is perhaps true that Lady Frances was unaware that her daughter's writings were not original and, ironically enough, had *Reliquiae Gethinianae* published as a tribute to G.'s integrity. On the other hand, it is just as plausible that Lady Frances—who seems to have been responsible for her daughter's moral education—wished to use the commonplace book as an example of how a virtuous education can be based on ethical readings.

But there were other memorials. In 1700, came a funeral sermon for G. (printed after being preached in Westminster Abbey) and a third edition of *Reliquiae Gethinianae* in 1703. More remarkable, Lady Frances, at the age of sixty-five, had two additional books published. Both of these volumes, *Applause of Virtue* and *Memento Mori, or Meditations on Death,* are mostly quotations on ethical subjects from the Bible, several church fathers, and ancient classical writers. Thus, she became a compiler, if not a writer, of two books under her own name, perhaps to mitigate her sorrow for her recently deceased daughter, G. Before Lady Frances's death at the age of ninety-one, she had outlived three husbands and three children, and she left three books compiled on the subject of "virtuous living and holy dying."

WORKS: *Reliquiae Gethinianae* (1699, 1700, 1703).

BIBLIOGRAPHY: Birch, P. *Sermon Preached at Westminster Abbey on 28 Mar 1700.* Collinson, J. *History of Somersetshire* (1791). *DNB.* Stanley, A. P. *Historical Memorials of Westminster Abbey,* 5th ed. (1882).

For articles in reference works: *Ballard. Feminist. ToddDBA.*

Susan Garland Mann and David D. Mann

Stella Gibbons

BORN: 5 January 1902, London.
DIED: 19 December 1989, London.
DAUGHTER OF: Telford Charles Gibbons and Maud Williams Gibbons.
MARRIED: Allan Bourne Webb, 1933.

If G.'s name is recognized at all today, it is usually for her comic novel *Cold Comfort Farm* (1932), whose good-natured parody of the pastoral novel of the early twentieth century has created for her a small but staunch cult following. In fact, G. was the author of twenty-five novels, three volumes of short stories, and four volumes of poetry—most of them refreshing, original, and good enough to reward rereading.

Cold Comfort Farm, G.'s first novel, won the Femina Vie Heureuse Prize for 1933 and, according to *Choice,* "belongs in any collection of modern British fiction." In it, Flora Poste opens the mental as well as physical doors of a gloomy Surrey farm, dispels the family ghosts, and sends everyone off to his or her own happiness. The somewhat disappointing sequel, *Conference at Cold Comfort Farm* (1949), brings a married Flora back to the farm sixteen years later, where she presides over a comic conference of Independent Thinkers. She also once again saves the farm, which had been bought out by the National Trust and renovated into a nightmare of cuteness, and brings the seven Starkadder brothers back from South Africa to restore Cold Comfort Farm to its primal brutality.

In her other novels, G. proved herself a careful chronicler of the modern era. She wrote of young love with that mixture of sensibility and romance unique to those who lived through both world wars; *Nightingale Wood* (1938) rewards the naive honesty of a shopgirl by a fairy-tale marriage to a rich and handsome landowner. Nancy Leland in *The Wolves Were in the Sledge* (1964) and Nell Sely in *Here Be Dragons* (1956) show the utter surrender possible only to romantics with hope, while Margaret Steggles in *Westwood* (1946) and Una Beaumont in *The Weather at Tregulla* (1962) deal with the failure of romance. G. also showed the condition—it is not dire enough to be called a plight—of middle-aged women with uncertain financial futures in *Bassett* (1934), *Miss Linsey and Pa* (1936), and *The Charmers* (1965). (G.'s married, middle-class, middle-aged women, such as Lucy in *The Swiss Summer,* 1951, and Alda in *The Matchmaker,* 1949, often turn out to be petty and unlikable.)

G.'s work is particularly valuable because it provided an intimate and detailed chronicle of life during World War II. *White Sand and Grey Sand* (1958) unravels the mystery of a Belgian foundling raised during the war. *The Bachelor* (1944) and *The Matchmaker* (1949), set in the war-torn British countryside, capture England's grim winter existence during the last years of the war. G. at her best describing the painful ordinariness of life under siege, and her war novels offered a fine supplement to historical accounts.

Several of G.'s works ventured into the occult. Most unusual is *Starlight* (1967), which begins as a sympathetic portrayal of elderly London slum dweller and ends with a startling exorcism; in *The Shadow of a Sorcerer* (1955), the eerily charming hero just might be the devil himself.

In spite of her attentiveness to the details of contemporary life, G. was not a "problem" novelist. As she said of her novelist character Amy Lee in *My American* (1939), her novels contained "no deep psychological problems or social analysis." What they do contain is an extremely fine cast of charming, nice people who linger in the reader's mind long after her often weak plots are forgotten. She had a rare ability to enter into the feelings of the uncommunicative and to bring to life the emotions of the unremarkable. Her comic genius, too, was recognized both in the timeless popularity of *Cold Comfort Farm* and in the reissue of *Ticky* (1943) in 1984 as part of Sutton's "Classics of Humor" series. *Cold Comfort Farm* was made into a Broadway musical, "Something Nasty in the Woodshed," in 1965, was adapted for television in 1968, and was made into a film in 1996.

G.'s shorter works do not match the quality of her novels. The short stories present a *tranche de vie* much in the style of Katherine Mansfield but too often without Mansfield's incisive characterization. Her poems are slight lyrics, describable in her own words (from *Conference at Cold Comfort Farm*) as "show[ing] a nice nature but technically weak." They tend toward classic, even archaic, diction, and only occasionally do they show flashes of the novels' wit. *The Untidy Gnome* was her lone sally into children's stories.

Before beginning her forty-year career as a novelist and poet, G. was a cable decoder for British United Press and a journalist in London, most notably for the *Evening Standard* (1920–30). She was elected a Fellow of the Royal Society of Literature in 1950.

WORKS: *The Mountain Beast* (1930). *Cold Comfort Farm* (1932). *Bassett* (1934). *The Priestess* (1934). *The Untidy Gnome* (1935). *Enbury Health* (1935). *Miss Linsey and Pa* (1936). *Roaring Tower* (1937). *Nightingale Wood* (1938). *The Lowland Venus* (1938). *My American* (1939). *Christmas at Cold Comfort Farm* (1940). *The Rich House* (1941). *Ticky* (1943). *The Bachelor* (1944). *Westwood* (1946). *Conference at Cold Comfort Farm* (1949). *The Matchmaker* (1949). *Collected Poems* (1950). *The Swiss Summer* (1951). *Fort of the Bear* (1953). *Beside the Pearly Water* (1954). *The Shadow of a Sorcerer* (1955). *Here Be Dragons* (1956). *White Sand and Grey Sand* (1958). *A Pink Front Door* (1959). *The Weather at Tregulla* (1962). *The Wolves Were in the Sledge* (1964). *The Charmers* (1965). *Starlight* (1967). *The Snow Woman* (1969). *The Woods in Winter* (1970).

BIBLIOGRAPHY: English Study Group, Centre for Contemporary Cultural Study, Birmingham. "Thinking the Thirties," in *Practices of Literature and Politics,* ed. F. Barker (1979). Jacqueline, A. *Review of International English Literature* (1978). Vickers, J. *N&Q* (1993).

For articles in reference works, see: *Bloomsbury. CA. Cambridge. CN. EBH. Feminist. TCA. ToddBWW.*

Other references: *Books of Today* (May 1949). *Leader* (28 April 1945). *PW* (May 1934). *Saturday Review* (1946).

Loralee MacPike

Penelope Gilliatt

BORN: 25 March 1932, London.
DAUGHTER OF: Cyril Conner and Mary Douglas Conner.
MARRIED: R. W. Gilliatt, 1954; John Osborne, 1963.

Novelist, short story writer, critic, and playwright, G. has established a considerable reputation as a woman of letters. G. grew up in Northumberland, the daughter of a prominent barrister and his Scots wife. G.'s education, divided as it was between Queen's College, University of London (1942–47) and Bennington College in Vermont (1948–49), foreshadowed her transatlantic career, for she continues to divide her time between England and the United States. She worked for several magazines in London, most prominently *Vogue,* becoming features editor there, and for the *Observer,* for which she served as film critic (1961–64) and drama critic (1964–67). After a stint as guest film critic for *The New Yorker* in 1967, G. became regular film critic for that magazine, taking six-month turns with Pauline Kael until 1979, when she resigned. Since then, G. has continued to write, concentrating her energies on stories and profiles for *The New Yorker* and novels, though an opera libretto and other pieces have appeared as well.

G.'s first major publication, a novel, *One by One,* appeared in 1965. It would be the first of four; *A State of Change* (1967), *The Cutting Edge* (1978), and *Mortal Matters* (1983) followed. The first three show striking similarities, while the fourth is a departure of sorts. Each of these novels is concerned with establishing those coping mechanisms necessary to integrate the past and order the present; G.'s sense of this finds clearest expression in a letter from one brother to another in *The Cutting Edge:* "Oh to have the Lord's capacity of language and themes, and to reduce the bickering world to order with each stroke of the keys." Memory is an essential adjunct as well; somehow, in G.'s scheme of things, memory is a repository of values for survival and language a means of activating those values.

One by One focuses attention on a trio of characters: Joe, married to Polly, and Coker, Joe's lifelong friend. Set in contemporary London during a fictional plague that provides G. with ample opportunity to offer political commentary, the novel documents the disintegration of Joe's and Polly's marriage and his descent into a madness that results in suicide. While G.'s talent for limning characters with telling psychological accuracy manifests itself here with haunting precision, her mixing of elements from allegory and parable as she layers conflicts of all sorts—emotional, physical, social, and political—produces a narrative altogether too tentative and diffuse.

A State of Change likewise dwells on a relationship among three characters: Kakia, a Polish cartoonist who comes to London in the 1950s; Don Clancy, a BBC star; and Harry Clopton, a physician. Kakia seeks political and artistic freedom but is caught in the paradox of trying to maintain that while bound in a cramping relationship with Harry. Like an avant-garde drama, *A State of Change* offers minimal plot; indeed, three-quarters of the novel seems to be conversation, bright but brittle word games, with characters and scenes functioning as mere props.

In *The Cutting Edge* we meet Peregrine and Benedick Corbett, brothers so deeply attached that by novel's end each has altered his physical appearance to resemble the other. Born and brought up in the Northumbrian border country, they live their whole lives on the edge, both geographically and existentially. The inevitable third person is Joanna, sometime wife to Benedick, who becomes Peregrine's mistress; rather than severing the brothers' relationship, this *ménage à trois* only joins Peregrine and Benedick more significantly. Here, too, G. shows an acute ear for dialogue and an infectious enthusiasm for words as exchanges sparkle with wit and as letters, diaries, and journals become large slices of narrative.

Mortal Matters concerns the life of Lady Averil Corfe, widow of a shipping magnate and central character. In a novel of eleven chapters, the first and last are set in the present while those in between constitute an elaborate flashback sequence to Averil's years in Northumberland as a child, wife, and mother, chronicling her mother's, as well as her own, involvement in the social/political struggle for women's rights. G. has incorporated substantial historical research to make this an evocative portrait of an extraordinary woman and her age. While *Mortal Matters* illuminates the role of the past in shaping the present, in personal as well as social and political terms, and while it displays G.'s characteristic verbal virtuosity, this novel marks a departure with its focus on one pivotal character and its optimistic conclusion.

Though this last novel may be a more satisfying effort, G. is not a novelist of the first rank. While Anthony Burgess has rightly praised her as "intelligent, economical poignant, highly contemporary, and innovative," he has, in noting that G. likes "to shunt plot elements to a perfunctory margin and allow the characters to play word games," discerned something that, if not a weakness, is certainly an indication of fiction for a very special taste.

The short story, a literary form calling for economy, intensity, and narrowed focus, suits G.'s talents far better. All five of her collections demonstrate those virtues that have earned her a reputation for being the quintessential *New Yorker* writer; indeed, of the forty-eight collected stories, thirty-eight originally appeared in that magazine.

The nine stories in *What's It Like Out?* (1968), published in the United States as *Come Back If It Doesn't Get Better* (1969), are character studies that show G.'s interest in the workings of the disintegrating human psyche. The eight stories and one play in *Nobody's Business* (1972) follow suit, both in concentration on character and in mood. The stories of Frank, the "Family Robot Adapted to the Needs of Kinship," Izolska, the little girl whose connection with the world is limited to a telephone hooked to a computer, and Max, Peg, and Abberly, three aging patients immobilized and attached to electrocardiograph machines, are typical of the collection. Characters in all these stories struggle with the dehumanizing forces of technocracy. Each story's focus on a particular situation imparts a static quality only slightly relieved by verbal sophistication, humor, and an uncanny choice of the most revealing remark or exchange.

Splendid Lives (1977) contains nine stories, virtually all about the last years of aged characters, none more memorable than the Bishop of Hurlingham, aged ninety-two, of the title story. This "cousin three times removed of Queen Victoria," who spent some of his early years going to jail with suffragists, is now obsessed by the problem of his racehorse being off his feed. The bishop's involvement in anti-Vietnam and anti-Rhodesia protests illustrates a political dimension prominent in nearly all the stories in *Splendid Lives,* and strikes, riots, and unemployed workers figure in some of the stories.

Quotations from Other Lives (1981), with its eleven stories and one play, continues G.'s examination of lives in contemporary England and the United States. Many are tales of lovers, whether young, vital, and displaced or geriatric and fixed; all share a desire to escape from pervasive loneliness, but none is particularly memorable. (G.'s stock of plots has been depleted; she repeats not only names and jokes but even remarks.)

They Sleep Without Dreaming (1985), a collection of ten stories and one play, breaks no new ground. There are tales of mental imbalance, for example, "The Purse," which features an upper-middle-class bag lady with a son who is a Fellow of All Souls, Oxford; of irreconcilable character types in exile ("The Hinge"); and of adults overcoming painful childhoods to make considerable names for themselves ("The Windchild Factor" and the title story).

Reading all the novels and collected short stories of G. brings an awareness of deficiencies as well as excellences. The flaws become obvious and irritating. An essential emptiness of plot, while less noticeable in a short story, is fatal in a novel. Then, too, G. is given to repetition, not just of theme but of devices and descriptions. She borrows not only from herself but from other writers, and to little point. Moreover, a reader seeking emotional engagement must look elsewhere, for G.'s writing is rather cerebral entertainment. Her excellences are mainly stylistic: flashing remarks, witty conversation, and language that is economical, evocative, and precise enough to sketch important characters with rhetorical flourish.

The best story in each of G.'s last four collections turns out to be a play, and, given her talent for description, dialogue, and close-up analysis, that is not surprising. The world of film and theater engages her sensibilities and employs her skills best, whether in original work or criticism. Certainly her finest creative work produced the screenplay *Sunday Bloody Sunday* (1971), which treats the lives of a trio of characters: Daniel Hirsh, a homosexual Jewish physician; Alex, a divorced businesswoman; and Bob, a young artist who is lover to both. While little happens in *Sunday Bloody Sunday,* for it is simply the story of Bob leaving Daniel and Alex behind to go to the United States, the juxtaposition of carefully rendered personalities and the shifting dynamics of their interaction make for riveting drama.

G.'s critical writing about film and theater spans her entire professional career. She has published two collections of reviews, *Unholy Fools: Wits, Comics, Disturbers of the Peace: Film and Theater* (1973) and *Three-Quarter Face: Reports and Reflections* (1980). The first is a gathering of short, lively pieces ranging from reviews of Royal Shakespeare Company productions to profiles of great comics like Buster Keaton, Charlie Chaplin, and Harold Lloyd to pieces on the film version of the *Tales of Beatrix Potter* and new films from Poland and Czechoslovakia. Two of the profiles in this volume became full-length studies: *Jean Renoir: Essays, Conversations, Reviews* (1975) and *Jacques Tati* (1976). Both demonstrate that, though G. does not ignore technical matters, she is clearly more interested in the film as fictional narrative. The keen biographical interest shown in *Renoir* and *Tati* emerges again in *Three-Quarter Face,* essentially a study of two dozen or so directors and entertainers. G. seeks to uncover that one-quarter face of the artist hidden from public view because she believes it is essential to understanding the work.

WORKS: *One By One* (1965). *A State of Change* (1967). *What's It Like Out?* (1968; in the U.S. as *Come Back If It Doesn't Get Better,* 1969) *Sunday Bloody Sunday* (1971). *Nobody's Business* (1972). *Unholy Fools: Wits, Comics, Disturbers of the Peace: Film and Theater* (1973). *Jean Renoir: Essays, Conversations, Reviews* (1975). *The Western* 1975). *The Method* (1975). *Living on the Box* (1975). *The Flight Fund* (1975). *Jacques Tati* (1976). *Splendid Lives* (1977). *The Cutting Edge* (1978). *In the Unlikely Event of an Emergency* (1978). *Three-Quarter Face: Reports and Reflections* (1980). *Property* (1980). *In Trust* (1980). *Quotations from Other Lives* (1981). *Beach of Aurora* (1981). *Mortal Matters* (1983). *They Sleep Without Dreaming* (1985). *22 Stories* (1986). *A Woman of Singular Occupation* (1988). *Lingo* (1990). *To Wit: In Celebration of Comedy* (1990; in the U.S. as *To Wit: Skin and Bones of Comedy*).

BIBLIOGRAPHY: Hodgson, M. *GrandS* (1989).

For articles in reference works, see: *CA. CLC. CN. DLB. Feminist. Oxford. ToddBWW. WA.*

Other references: *BW* (18 July 1965, 21 January 1979). *London Magazine* (February 1979). *New Statesman* (30 April 1965, 27 October 1978). *New Yorker* (7 November 1983). *NYT* (15 June 1969, 3 October 1971). *NYTBR* (25 April 1965, 10 September 1972, 29 January 1978, 21 January 1979). *Observer* (25 April 1965, 24 September 1972, 6 November 1983, February 1985). *Spectator* (30 April 1965, 7 January 1984). *TLS* (29 April 1965, 20 August 1982, 29 November 1985).

Robert Ellis Hosmer, Jr.

Hannah Glasse

BORN: 1708, Holborn, London.
DIED: 1770, Newcastle, Northumberland.
DAUGHTER OF: Isaac Allgood and Hannah Allgood.
MARRIED: John (Peter?) Glasse, 1725.
WROTE UNDER: Hannah Glasse; A Lady.

G.'s father was the son of the Reverend Major Allgood, rector of Simonburn, in Northumberland; her mother was the daughter of Isaac Clark, a London vintner. She and her husband, son of a Scotswoman and an Irishman, had six or eight children, half of whom died in infancy. G.'s half-brother Lancelot Allgood (1711–82) was knighted in 1760. G. may be the "Hannah Glass of St. Paul's Co. Garden" on the 1754 bankruptcy list in the *Gentleman's Magazine.* The author of *The Compleat Confectioner* and *The Servant's Directory,* G. is best known for *The Art of Cookery, Made Plain and Easy.* First published in 1747 as "by a lady" and claimed in the fourth edition in 1751 by G. identifying herself as "Habit Maker to Her Royal Highness the Princess of Wales, in Tavistock Street, Convent Garden," the cookbook first bore G.'s name in 1788, by which time it had appeared in more than ten editions and had become popularly associated with her. While some questioned her originality and others accused her of extravagance, the book was generally acclaimed for its clarity and its organization. Listing 200 subscribers in 1747, it had appeared in twenty-six editions, two in America, by 1812.

Although she promises not to be so "pertinent" as to "direct a Lady how to set out her Table," her advice frequently goes beyond measurements and ingredients as she urges cooks to consider economy, to be flexible, and to attend to the appearance of their dishes. French cooks and cookery often appear as the negative examples of kitchen economy. She warns, "If Gentlemen will have *French* Cooks, they must pay for *French* Tricks." While one French cook "used six Pounds of Butter to fry twelve Eggs," G. reminds her readers, "Every Body knows, that understands Cooking, that Half a Pound is full enough." Although she offers specific instructions, she recognizes the need to make changes based on variations in ingredients. "The strength of your Beer must be according to the Malt you allow more or less, there is no certain Rule." Similarly, times for roasting a pig cannot be specified exactly: "If just kill'd, an Hour; if kill'd the Day before, an Hour and a Quarter." For all pigs, however, "the best Way to judge is when the Eyes drop out." Cooks must prepare food to be admired as well as eaten. Pickled red cabbage is a "Pickle of little Use, but for garnishing of Dishes, Sallats and Pickles, tho' some People are fond of it." To make a tart, "fill it with what Fruit you please, lay on the Lid, and it is done; therefore if the Tart is not eat, your Sweetmeat is not the worse, and it looks genteel."

Although G. recommends that a few eels stewed in broth may remedy "weakly and consumptive constitutions," she does not, as do many authors of eighteenth-century cookbooks, emphasize medicinal uses of food. Nor does she flippantly ignore the exigencies of her recipes with the advice, long attributed to her, that the cook "First Catch your Hare."

WORKS: (as "a lady") *The Art of Cookery, Made Plain and Easy; Which Far Exceeds Anything of the Kind Ever Yet Published, etc.* (1747). *The Complete Confectioner: or, the whole art of confectionary made plain and easy* (c. 1760). *The Servants Directory, or house-keeper's companion wherein the duties of the chamber-maid, nursery-maid, house-maid, laundry-maid, scullion or under-cook . . . to which is annexed . . . directions for keeping accounts. etc.* (1760).

BIBLIOGRAPHY: Aylett, M. and O. Ordish. *First Catch Your Hare: A History of the Recipe-Makers* (1965). Hope, M. *Archeologia Aeliana* (1938). Willan, A. *Great Cooks and Their Recipes: From Taillevent to Escoffier* (1977).

For articles in reference works, see: *DNB. Feminist. IDWB. NCHEL. OCEL. ToddBWW. ToddDBA.*

Other references: Drake, T. G. H. *Journal of the American Dietetic Association* (1952) (cf. notes on "Glasse, Hannah"). Heal, A. *N&Q* (1938). *A Short Title Catalogue of Household and Cookery Books Published in the English Tongue 1701–1800* (1981).

Mary Sauter Comfort

Caroline Glyn

BORN: 27 August 1947.
DIED: 1981.
DAUGHTER OF: Sir Anthony Glyn and Lady Susan Rhys Williams Glyn.

Great-granddaughter of Elinor Glyn (prolific author of *Three Weeks, It,* and other novels and screenplays), G. became, at age fifteen, the *Wunderkind* of the 1960s with the publication of her first novel, *Don't Knock the Corners Off* (1963). Encouraged by parents who were similarly gifted (Sir Anthony, a writer; Lady Susan, an artist), G. began writing short stories and poetry at the age of six. At nine, she was recognized for another talent when one of her designs received an award from *Good Housekeeping.* Other, unique honors followed: Poem-Tilling First Prize, 1959, and second prize, "Jeune Espoir," for a painting, France, 1964. G. worked as a teenage correspondent for the color supplement of *The Observer,* and her poems were published in numerous journals, including *Cornhill.* She and her mother together penned an article for *Stained Glass* concerning their familial and artistic relationships. One of her more enjoyable occupations was working as a long-distance telephone operator in London. The position enabled G. to have financial freedom while she completed her novels. G. also enjoyed traveling and visited the United States with members of her family.

Don't Knock the Corners Off was, for the most part, a critical success. Astonished at G.'s talent for unselfconscious narration, many reviewers went overboard in their praise; one even cited it as "the best novel by a fifteen-year-old ever written," and it received the La Libra Belgique award for best foreign novel. Using the first-person, G.'s narrator, Antonia Rutherford, a somewhat aloof, shy, and clever young girl, describes her grammar and primary-school experiences, especially the indignities she suffers as the brunt of her peers' taunting behavior. Antonia tries to resolve the differences between her somewhat relaxed home environment and the structured, middle-class conformities deemed necessary for survival in a scholastic atmosphere. At novel's end, the narrator's acceptance into an art school presents hope for a much-needed escape: "Art students still have their corners on. . . . Everything's going to be all right after all," Antonia concludes.

When sixteen, G. followed her parents to Paris and was admitted into the Ecole Supérieure des Arts Moderns. Here, she literally dogged the footsteps of her more financially privileged classmates, at first admiring their independence, then despairing over their pretentiousness. Winston Hosanna, the black West Indian who is the hero of G.'s second novel, *Love and Joy in the Mabillon* (1966), also attempts to enter a society of wealthy young artists whose world-weary existence is lightened by visits to sidewalk cafés like the Mabillon. Winston is disheartened as his natural longings (love and joy) are declined by an upper-class "ice princess." He finally realizes that he will only be marginally permitted into the farthest perimeters of their blasé lives. Once more, G. was able to reproduce conflicting views of a particularly youthful, yet deplorable, society. The novel was runner-up for the Society of Authors award to young writers in 1966.

While completing her third novel, *The Unicorn Girl* (1966), G. explained to an interviewer that the teen-aged heroine would also become the leading character in two other, related works, *Heights and Depths* (1968) and *The Tree* (1969). She also promised to take a more optimistic tone, and the results indicated that she focused on a less-despairing philosophy.

G. also created sufficient material for several one-woman art shows in England and France. When asked about her interest in these varied forms of expression, she stated that her "painting and writing complement each other, and I could not live without either. I paint trees, stars, and religious abstracts, and my books come into being while I am about it."

In 1979, G. revealed that William Wordsworth and William Blake were important influences, "believing in the redemption of the earth—as it undergoes visible destruction—by the visionary principle in man, true imagination. By this power, which is love, the world is being remade, a spiritual world, in which all is restored. All my books are on this theme and I like to think that, by writing them, I have shared in the great work."

WORKS: *Dream Saga* (1962). *Don't Knock the Corners Off* (1963). *Love and Joy in the Mabillon* (1965). *The Uni-*

corn Girl (1966). *Heights and Depths* (1968). *The Tree* (1969). *The Tower and the Rising Tide* (1971). *The Peacemakers* (1974). *In Him Was Life* (1975). *A Mountain at the End of the Night: Stories of Dream and Vision* (1977). *Poems from The Dark* (1982).

BIBLIOGRAPHY: Glyn, S. *SMy* (Winter 1981).

For articles in reference works, see: *CA*. *DLEL*. *IAWWW*.

Other references: *Life* (13 May 1966). *New Statesman* (19 September 1969, 8 July 1977) *NYTBR*. (5 January 1964). *Observer* (21 September 1969, 11 July, 1971, 7 August 1977). *Saturday Review* (4 January 1964). *Seventeen* (July 1964). *Stained Glass* (Fall 1983). *Time* (3 January 1964).

Zelda R. B. Provenzano

Elinor Glyn

BORN: 17 October 1864, Jersey, Channel Islands.
DIED: 23 September 1943, London.
DAUGHTER OF: Douglas Sutherland and Elinor Saunders Sutherland.
MARRIED: Clayton Glyn, 1892.

G. was a prolific novelist who wrote more than twenty books, several of which were made into silent films starring such legendary performers as Gloria Swanson, Clara Bow, John Gilbert, and Rudolph Valentino. She was raised by her mother after her father died of typhoid fever when G. was only a few months old, received only the minimal education available in local schools, and in 1892 married Clayton Glyn, a wealthy entrepreneur.

In 1899, G. published her first book, *The Visits of Elizabeth*, an epistolary novel. This book, published anonymously and serialized in *The World*, was quite successful. According to her biographer, her grandson Anthony Glyn, G. got great pleasure from listening to her friends trying to guess the name of the author, especially the friend who declared that G. could not be the author because "a really clever person must have written these letters." With her earnings, G. traveled to Italy, France, and Egypt. The style of G.'s second novel, *Reflection of Ambrosine* (1902), is similar to that of *Visits of Elizabeth*. This book is the "autobiography," written in diary form, of Ambrosine Eustasie, Marquise de Galincourt, who was guillotined in 1793. In *Reflections*, G. exhibits considerable historical knowledge as well as great empathy for her protagonist. Now proud of her success as a novelist, G. includes a note at the front of *Ambrosine* stating that she will no longer write anonymously: "Everything I write will be signed."

Among G.'s most unusual books is *The Damsel and the Sage: A Woman's Whimsies* (1903), a series of witty exchanges between a "fun-loving" Damsel and a misanthropic Sage who hates women and lives in a cave, contemplating the mysteries of the universe. The two eventually fall in love, and the Damsel convinces the Sage to leave his cave and "Remember the tangible now." *The Damsel and the Sage* is clever in that the characters debate whether to "seize the day" in much the same way as Christopher Marlowe's Shepherd and Sir Walter Raleigh's Nymph, but the male and female roles are reversed and the Damsel wins the debate.

G.'s most popular book nearly ended her writing career. *Three Weeks* (1907) was called too "sensational" and was viciously attacked by nearly every London critic. The love scenes, tame by modern standards, were too explicit for what was still a Victorian press. Thought by Anthony Glyn to be partly autobiographical, *Three Weeks* is the story of Lady Henrietta, who marries for money, falls in love with a man she meets in Egypt, has a son by her lover (whom she passes off as her husband's child), and spends her life helping her child succeed. By 1916 more than 2 million copies had been sold, and *Three Weeks* had been translated into virtually every European language. The financial success of *Three Weeks* was fortunate for G. because her husband had lost all his money by 1908, making G. the sole support of her family.

During 1907 and 1908, G. toured the United States, dividing her time between New York City and the mining areas of Colorado, Nevada, and California. As a result of her travels, G. wrote another epistolary novel, *Elizabeth Visits America* (1909), that she illustrated herself. G. hoped to regain her reputation with the critics by returning to the style of her first novel, but she was only moderately successful.

His Hour (1910) was the result of six months G. spent in St. Petersburg and Moscow, Russia, as the guest of the Grand Duchess Vladimir. This novel, which finally restored G. to the critics' favor, is the story of an English widow, Tamara Loraine, who, while traveling in Egypt, falls in love with Prince Gritzko Milaslavski. She follows him to St. Petersburg, where, after overcoming numerous obstacles, they eventually marry. Probably because of G.'s first-hand knowledge of St. Petersburg and the customs of the Russian Imperial Court, *His Hour* suffers from none of what M. Crosland calls the "effusive vagueness" of most romance novels.

After G.'s husband died in 1915, she increased the volume of her work and in 1917 signed a lucrative contract with William Randolph Hearst for the American rights to her novels. G. and Hearst became close friends despite an "artistic disagreement" over *The Career of Katherine Bush* (1916). According to Anthony Glyn, Hearst asked G. to make her heroine "more lovable." G. steadfastly refused, and Hearst eventually gave in.

G.'s career as a filmwriter began in 1920, when Famous Players–Lasky asked her to write the screenplay for *The Great Moment*, starring Gloria Swanson. G.'s own novel *Beyond the Rocks* (1906) was filmed in 1922 and featured Gloria Swanson and Rudolph Valentino. G.'s other film credits include *Three Weeks* (1924), *His Hour* (1924), *Man and Maid* (1925), *The Only Thing* (1925), *Love's Blindness* (1926), and *Ritzy* (1927). *Ritzy*, based on G.'s short story "It" in which she gave her own definition of "personal magnetism," led to Clara Bow, the star of the film, being known forever after as the "It Girl." G. left Hollywood in 1929 after the failure of her only nonsilent film, *Such Men Are Dangerous*.

During the 1930s, G. lost most of her money in a failed attempt to start her own film production company. Both of the movies she produced (and financed), *Knowing Men* and *The Price of Things,* were financial disasters. She returned to writing full-time and continued publishing novels until her death in 1943.

WORKS: *The Visits of Elizabeth* (1900). *Reflections of Ambrosine* (1902; in the U. S. as *The Seventh Commandment*). *The Damsel and the Sage: A Woman's Whimsies* (1903). *Beyond the Rocks* (1906; as screenplay, 1922). *Three Weeks* (1907; as screenplay, 1923). *The Sayings of Grandmama and Others* (1908). *Elizabeth Visits America* (1909). *His Hour* (1910; in the U. S. as *When His Hour Came,* 1915; screenplay, with K. Vidor and M. Fulton, 1924). *The Reason Why* (1911). *Halcyone* (1912; in the U. S. as *Love Itself,* 1924). *The Sequence* (1913; in the U.S. as *Guinevere's Lover*). *The Contract and Other Stories* (1913). *Letters to Caroline* (1914; in the U.S. as *Your Affectionate Godmother*). *The Man and the Moment* (1914; as screenplay, with A. C. Johnson and P. Perez, 1929). *Three Things* (1915). *The Career of Katherine Bush* (1916). *Destruction* (1918). *The Price of Things* (1919; in the U.S. as *Family,* as screenplay, 1930). *Points of View* (1920). *The Philosophy of Love* (1920). (with M. M. Kaeterjohn) *The Great Moment* (screenplay 1921; book, 1923). *Man and Maid—Renaissance* (1922; in the U.S. as *Man and Maid,* 1922; as screenplay, 1925). *The Elinor Glyn System of Writing* (1922). (with C. Campbell and G. Bertholon) *The World's a Stage* (screenplay, 1922). *The Philosophy of Love* (1923; in the U. K. as *Love—What I Think of It,* 1928). *Six Days* (1924). (with C. Wilson) *Three Weeks* (1924; also pub. as *The Romance of a Queen*). (with D. Z. Dory and G. Carpenter) *How to Educate a Wife* (1924). *Letters from Spain* (1924). *This Passion Called Love* (1925). *The Only Thing* (1925). *Love's Blindness* (1926; as screenplay, 1926). (with others) *Ritzy* (1927). (with others) *It* (screenplay, 1927). *It and Other Stories* (1927). *The Wrinkle Book: or, How to Keep Looking Young* (1927; in the U.S. as *Eternal Youth,* 1928). (with others) *Three Week-Ends* (screenplay, 1928). (with E. Vajda) *Such Men Are Dangerous* (screenplay, 1930). (with E. Knoblock) *Knowing Men* (screenplay, 1930). *The Flirt and the Flapper* (1930). *Love's Hour* (1932). *Glorious Flames* (1932). *Sooner or Later* (1933). *Did She?* (1934). *Saint or Satyr? and Other Stories* (1933; in the U. S. as *Such Men Are Dangerous*). *Romantic Adventure* (1936). *The Third Eye* (1940).

BIBLIOGRAPHY: Crosland, M. *Beyond the Lighthouse* (1981). Etherington-Smith, M. and J. Pitcher *The "It" Girls: Elinor Glyn, Romantic Novelist, and Lacy, Lady Duff Gordon, Lucile, the Couteriere* (1986). Glyn, A. *Elinor Glyn: A Biography* (1955). Haskell, M. *From Reverence to Rape: The Treatment of Women in the Movies* (1974).

For articles in reference works, see: *Cambridge. CB. Chambers. DNB. Feminist. Longman. Oxford. TCA and SUP. TCRGW. TCW. ToddBWW.*

Other references: Bennett, A. *Books and Persons* (1917). Davson, G. *Good Housekeeping* (April 1955). Mosley, L. O. *Curzon: The End of an Epic* (1960).

Kay Beaird Meyers

(Margaret) Rumer Godden

BORN: 10 December 1907, Sussex.
DAUGHTER OF: Arthur Leigh Godden and Katherine Hingley Godden.
MARRIED: Laurence S. Foster, 1934; James Haynes Dixon, 1949.
WRITES UNDER: P. Davies; Rumer Godden.

G. is a child of England and of India, and her sixty-plus-year career as a novelist and writer of children's books reflects this dual influence. G. was born in Sussex, but as a small child she lived on the banks of India's greatest river, which, according to *Twentieth-Century Authors,* she preferred to the "dull and colorless life in a cold South Coast town." In the 1930s, G. founded and operated a children's dancing school in Calcutta and began her long career with a book about a Chinese man and a Pekingese dog called *Chinese Puzzle,* published under the pseudonym of P. Davies in 1936.

Three themes seem predominant in G.'s world. First, she writes about the vulnerability and fragility of children and about their innate toughness and spunk. *An Episode of Sparrows* (1955), for instance, is the story of Lovejoy Mason, deserted by her man-hungry actress mother in a London slum. Lovejoy is a feisty, determined tomboy who battles both the natural elements and the slum's inhabitants in her efforts to create a beautiful garden in a bombed-out churchyard. *The Greengage Summer* (1958) describes the more amusing (but sometimes bittersweet) adventures of five English siblings on their own in the unfamiliar world of a French pension. There are similarities in the thematic structure of these and other G. novels about children. The youngsters are always initially bereft and cut off from adult authority and strength, but they are, finally, resourceful, courageous, and competent. The English children in *Breakfast with the Nikolides* (1942), saddled with a neurotic, unhappy mother and an angry but idealistic father, prove to be more insightful than either parent. The English children in *The Battle of the Villa Fiorita* (1963) are determined to extricate their forty-two-year-old mother from her romance with an Italian film director. In league with the director's young daughter, Pia, they force the lovers apart, which leaves the reader with a sense of surprise and disappointment.

G., a Roman Catholic, has produced several books that deal with the lives of cloistered nuns. *Black Narcissus* (1939) is about an Anglican sisterhood in India. *In This House of Brede* (1969) and *Five for Sorrow, Ten for Joy* (1979) both deal with women who become nuns in their middle years. In the first of these, Philippa Talbot, an English superwoman type, is a widowed executive who speaks Japanese, has mastered the intricacies of both the commercial and real estate markets, and enters Brede, an enclosed convent of upper-middle-class Benedictine nuns. This novel is an encyclopedia of details about first clothings, simple and solemn professions, discipline, prayer, and politics in an English convent. Lise Ambard (in *Five for Sorrow, Ten for Joy*), a thirty-seven-year-old ex-prostitute, also chooses "enclosure" at Saint Etienne and

Bethanie in France, as do the nuns in *The Dark Horse* (1981), set in India. G. seems to be fascinated with walls and with both the enervating and invigorating effects of limits. Her houses and hotels protect, but they often imprison as well.

G.'s third theme is the contrast of divergent cultures. She is particularly gifted in pointing out both the confusion of multilingual and multiethnic India, a land of many religions and an entrenched caste system. But her India is also wise and accepting, beautiful and vibrant. As Paul Zimmerman of *Newsweek* has pointed out, "Rumer Godden remains among the last British novelists to be influenced by the colonial experience in India," and her books reflect "the enlightenment and catholic vision acquired from those early years along the banks of the great accepting rivers of the sub-continent."

G. has written more than twenty books for children, many of which have dolls as their protagonists. The most famous are *The Doll's House* (1947) and *Impunity Jane* (1954), in which a doll falls into the hands of a gang of boys. *The Mousewife* (1951), based on an entry in Dorothy Wordsworth's *Journal*, is the story of a friendship between a caged dove and a mouse.

At least six of G.'s novels have been made into successful films for TV or the movies because she is, in the final analysis, a perceptive and sympathetic teller of tales. Her novels will remain popular because they are about basic human nature in England, India, and elsewhere.

WORKS: (as P. Davies) *Chinese Puzzle* (1936). (as P. Davies) *The Lady and the Unicorn* (1938). *Black Narcissus* (1939). *Gypsy, Gypsy* (1940). *Breakfast with the Nikolides* (1942). (as P. Davies) *Rungli-Rungliot* (1944). *Bengal Journey 1939–1945* (1945). *Take Three Tenses: A Fugue in Time* (1945). *The River* (1946). *The Doll's House* (1947). *A Candle for St. Jude* (1948). *In Noah's Ark* (1949). *A Breath of Air* (1950). *The Mousewife* (1951). *Kingfishers Catch Fire* (1953). *Impunity Jane: The Story of a Pocket Doll* (1954). *Hans Christian Andersen: a Great Life in Brief* (1954). *An Episode of Sparrows* (1955). *The Fairy Doll* (1956). *Mooltiki* (1957). *Mouse House* (1957). *The Story of Holly and Ivy* (1958). *The Greengage Summer* (1958). *Candy Floss* (1960). *St. Jerome and the Lion* (1961). *Miss Happiness and Miss Flower* (1961). *China Court: The Hours of a Country House* (1961). *Prayers from the Ark* (1962). *The Creatures' Choir* (1962). *Little Plum* (1963). *The Battle of the Villa Fiorita* (1963). (with J. Godden) *The Feather-Duster: A Fairy-Tale Musical* (1964). *Home Is the Sailor* (1964). *Two Under the Indian Sun* (1966). (with M. Bell) *Round the Day: Poetry Programmes for the Classroom or Library* (1966). (with M. Bell) *The World Around: Poetry Programmes for the Classroom or Library* (1966). *The Kitchen Madonna* (1967). (with M. Bell) *A Letter to the World: Poems for Young People* (1968). *Mrs. Wanders' Cook Book* (1968). *Gone: A Book of Stories* (1968). *Operation Sippacik* (1969). *In This House of Brede* (1969). *The Raphael Bible* (1970). *The Tale of Tales: The Beatrix Potter Ballet* (1971). *Shiva's Pigeons* (1972). *The Old Woman Who Lived in a Vinegar Bottle* (1972). *The Diddakoi* (1972). *Mr. McFadden's Hallowe'en* (1975). *The Peacock Spring* (1975). *The Rocking Horse Secret* (1977). *The Butterfly Lions: The Story of the Pekingese in History, Legend and Art* (1978). *Five for Sorrow, Ten for Joy* (1979). *The Dark Horse* (1981). *Thursday's Children* (1987). *A Time to Dance, No Time to Weep* (1987). *Fu-dog* (1989). *A House with Four Rooms* (1989). *Indian Dust* (1989). *Mercy, Pity, Peace, and Love* (1989). *Coromandel Sea Change* (1991). *Great Grandfather's House* (1992). *Listen to the Nightingale* (1992). *Mouse Time: Two Stories* (1993). *Pippa Passes* (1994). *Cockcrow to Starlight* (1996). *Premlata and the Festival of Lights* (1996). *Cromartie v. the God Shiva* (1997).

BIBLIOGRAPHY: Evans, G. *CLAQ* (1949). Frey, J. R. *JEGP* (1947). Prescott, O. *In My Opinion* (1952). Simpson, R. G. *Rumer Godden* (1973). Smaridge, N. *Famous British Women Novelists* (1967). Tindall, W. Y. *EJ* (1952).

For articles in reference works, see: *CA. CN. DEL. Longman. MBL. NCHEL. TCA SUP. TCCW. TCW.*

Other references: *Atlantic* (October 1969). *Books and Bookmen* (December 1967, August 1968, December 1971). *Book Week* (29 September 1963). Boyd, J. D. *New Catholic World* (July–August 1985). *Commonweal* (10 November 1978). *Economist* (20 December 1975, 26 November 1983). *Harper's* (May 1968). Hardey, L. *Makfil: A Quarterly of South Asian Literature* (1966). *Listener* (12 July 1979, 24 September 1981). *New Republic* (24 November 1979, 23 June 1982). *New Statesman* (2 June 1972, 10 November 1972, 19 May 1978, 2 December 1983). *Newsweek* (30 September 1963, 4 April 1976, 6 December 1982, 9 December 1985). *NYHTBR* (18 December 1949, 8 October 1950). *NYTBR* (9 July 1939, 7 February 1965, 12 June 1966, 7 January 1968, 30 June 1968, 1 June 1969, 21 September 1969, 13 February 1972, 7 May 1972, 4 June 1972, 5 November 1972, 25 April 1976, 29 April 1979, 16 December 1979, 15 November 1981, 24 June 1982, 18 November 1984). *Observer* (2 October 1966, 14 July 1968, 2 November 1969, 25 April 1971, 28 May 1972, 28 September 1975, 23 November 1975, 7 December 1975, 6 February 1977, 21 December 1980, 17 January 1982, 1 December 1985, 16 December 1984). *Progressive* (May 1980). *PW* (10 November 1969). *Saturday Review* (3 December 1955, 4 October 1969, 17 June 1972). Sharma, V. *Indian P.E.N.* (1975). *Spectator* (3 November 1967, 13 November 1971, 11 November 1972, 4 October 1975, 6 December 1975, 17 October 1981). *Time* (17 July 1939, 12 August 1940, 11 October 1963, 14 November 1969, 19 April 1976). *TLS* (30 November 1967, 3 April 1969, 12 May 1972, 14 July 1972, 3 November 1972, 5 December 1975, 30 January 1976, 16 December 1977). *Washington Post* (29 November 1969, 3 December 1979).

Mickey Pearlman
(updated by Abby H. P. Werlock)

Godolphin, Mary: See *Aikin, Lucy*

Godwin, Mary: See *Wollstonecraft, Mary Godwin*

Catherine Grace Frances Moody Gore

BORN: 1800, London.
DIED: 29 January 1861, Linwood, Lynhurst, Hampshire.
DAUGHTER OF: C. Moody.
MARRIED: Charles Arthur Gore, 1823.
WROTE UNDER: Mrs. Gore; Albany Poyntz.

When G. died in 1861, the *London Times* praised her as "the best novel writer of her class and the wittiest woman of her age." She was known throughout novel-reading Britain, particularly among women, as the author of more than sixty "fashionable novels," works that portray the manners, romances, and scandals of high society. Yet G. also published plays, poems, short stories, literary sketches, songs, and even a gardener's manual on roses. Among those who knew her personally, including Mary Russell Mitford, William Thackeray, and Charles Dickens, she was renowned for her learned and clever conversation.

Raised in East Retford, Nottinghamshire, and in London, G. began writing at an early age and published her first novel, *Theresa Marchmont, or The Maid of Honour*, in 1824, a year after her marriage: 1829 saw the appearance of her *Hungarian Tales*, narratives blending fact and fiction. But it was in 1830, with the publication of *Women As They Are, or Manners of the Day*, that G. joined the ranks of the "Silver-Fork School" of novelists; she ultimately became its most prolific, and possibly most popular, writer. In *Women As They Are* and dozens of subsequent novels of fashion, G. depicts the gay leisure class of Regency England, complete with strutting dandies, arrogant parvenus, scheming mamas, and hopeful girls decked out in the family jewels. G.'s novels appealed both to the fashionables about whom she wrote and to middle-class readers. The romances portrayed in her works often play out the middle-class female daydream of marrying into aristocracy, and her pages are crowded with the minute details about shops, dress, and etiquette craved by those themselves struggling to rise in society. However, G. also brought to her novels a sharp wit and keen insight into the pretensions and absurdities of the fashionable world; in fact, one reviewer cautioned her not to be too reckless in her exposure of hypocrisy.

Following the appearance of *Women As They Are*, G. turned out work at an astonishing rate, producing six books and several plays in 1831 and 1832 alone. Toward the end of this period, she published *The Fair of May Fair* (1832), a collection of short stories. It was not well received, and G.'s correspondence indicates she was stung by the bad reviews, particularly by suggestions that she was wasting her talents. G. had privately referred to herself as a writer of "rubbish," but in the face of public criticism, she fiercely defended the fashionable novel, contending that "every picture of passing manners, if accurate, is valuable from the drawing room to the alehouse." However, when she published *A Sketchbook of Fashion* anonymously, in 1833, G. requested that the book be given no notice at all and confessed to her publisher that she had grown rather ashamed of her novels of fashion. Hoping to redeem her name and remind readers of her earlier success at a more serious form of literature, G. also produced a collection of historical stories in 1833 and announced them as *"Polish Tales, by the authoress of Hungarian Tales."*

In 1832, the Gores had moved to Paris, where G. presided over a Sunday salon frequented by literary and political personalities. She published little more until 1836, when a flurry of novels appeared, occasioned, most likely, by a financial crisis. Years later, G. expressed her belief that "even from an iron intellect the sparks are only elicited by collision with the flints of this world." In G.'s case, however, necessity tended to result in the frivolous novels for which she was famous rather than the serious work to which she sporadically returned.

By 1841, the Gores had returned to England, and G. published her best-known novel: *Cecil: or Adventures of a Coxcomb.* At her insistence, the novel was published anonymously to encourage readers in the belief that an exciting new talent had appeared: It created just the sensation G. had hoped for. Purporting to be the autobiography of a dandy, a friend and companion of Lord Byron, *Cecil* displays an intimate acquaintance with London clubs as well as a greater knowledge of Greek and Latin than would ordinarily be attributed to a woman. Hence, no one imagined it had been written by G., who probably got her information about the clubs from her friend William Beckford. Throughout the novel, G. mercilessly satirizes dandyism, although she also uses Cecil's travels to show off her own acquaintance with Parisian manners, cuisine, and politics.

In the same year that *Cecil* appeared, G. began a series of articles in *Bentley's Miscellany* under the pseudonym "Albany Poyntz." In one of the earliest of these articles, "The Children of the Mobility versus the Children of the Nobility," G. bitterly contrasts the "freedom" of poor children with the "deprivations" and discomforts supposedly suffered by the gaudily dressed children featured in the currently popular "Portraits of the Nobility." The Albany Poyntz articles also include a series of satirical sketches of members of the upper-class entourage—"The Standard Footman," "The Lady's Maid," and so on—but even in some of these, G. reveals an understanding of and compassion for the hardships of the poor.

G.'s efforts at playwriting met with considerably less success than her novels and sketches. Although *The School for Coquettes* was a hit in 1831, G.'s most highly publicized play, *Quid Pro Quo, or The Day of the Dupes*, was a theatrical disaster. The play won a lucrative prize in 1844 as the best comedy of British life and manners, but when it was produced the play was hooted off the stage and assailed by the press.

In 1846, G.'s husband died, and four years later she received an inheritance from another family member that allowed her to relax her demanding pace. G. had regularly turned out novels over the previous decade, but none had met with the same success as *Cecil*—not even its sequel, *Cecil, A Peer* (1841), or *Adventures in Borneo* (1849), another fictional autobiography, this time in the style of *Robinson Crusoe.* Interest in the fashionable novel was waning; when G. fell victim to a bank scandal in 1855, she cunningly reissued her 1843 novel about a corrupt banker, *The Banker's Wife, or Court and City*—omitting, of course, the appreciative dedication she had made, ironically enough, to her own trusted banker, who later involved her funds in the scandal; 1855 also saw the appearance, fittingly, of G.'s *Mammon, or The Hardships of an Heiress.* G. published her last novel in 1858. Her eyesight began to fail and she died in 1861.

Comparing G.'s life and work produces some odd contradictions: She courted high society even as she satirized it, and despite her own financial hardships and hard-headed business sense, her novels celebrate the virtue of womanly submission and chronicle the disastrous consequences of women's attempts at independence. G. herself alternately disparaged and defended her fashionable writing. Had she not been driven by financial necessity, she might have produced works of more lasting stature; still, her *oeuvre* provides a revealing portrait of the follies of her era.

WORKS: *Theresa Marchmont, or The Maid of Honour: A Tale* (1824). *The Bond: A Dramatic Poem* (1824). *Richelieu, or the Broken Heart* (1826). *The Lettre de Cachet: A Tale, with The Reign of Terror: A Tale* (1827). *Hungarian Tales* (1829). *Romances of Real Life* (1829). *Women As They Are, or The Manners of the Day* (1830). *The Historical Traveller* (1831). *The School for Coquettes* (1831). *Pin Money: A Novel* (1831). *The Tuileries: A Tale* (1831). *Mothers and Daughters: A Tale of the Year 1830* (1831). *The Opera: A Novel* (1832). *The Fair of May Fair* (1832). *The Sketchbook of Fashion* (1833). *Polish Tales* (1833). *The Hamiltons, or The New Era* (1834). *The Maid of Croissey, King O'Neil,* and *The Queen's Champion,* in *Webster's Acting National Drama* (1835). *The Diary of a Désennuyée* (1836). *Mrs. Armytage, or Female Domination* (1836). (trans.) *Picciola, or Captive Creative,* by X. B. Saintine (1837). *Memoirs of a Peeress, or the Days of Fox,* ed. C. Bury (1837). *Stokeshill Place, or The Man of Business* (1837). *The Rose Fancier's Manual* (1838). *Mary Raymond and Other Tales* (1838). *The Woman of the World: A Novel* (1838). *The Cabinet Minister* (1839). *The Courtier of the Days of Charles II, with Other Tales* (1839). *A Good Night's Rest, or Two O'-Clock in the Morning,* in *Duncombe's British Theatre* (1839). *Dacre of the South, or The Olden Time: A Drama* (1840). *The Dowager, or The New School for Scandal* (1840). *Preferment, or My Uncle the Earl* (1840). *The Alley and Other Tales* (1840). *Greville, or a Season in Paris* (1841). *Cecil, or The Adventures of a Coxcomb: A Novel* (1841). *Cecil, a Peer* (1841). *Paris in 1841* (1842). *The Man of Fortune and Other Tales* (1842). *The Ambassador's Wife* (1842). *The Money Lender* (1843). *Modern Chivalry, or A New Orlando Furioso* (1843). *The Banker's Wife, or Court and City: A Novel* (1843). *Agathonia: A Romance* (1844). *Marrying for Money,* in *Omnibus of Modern Romance* (1844). *The Birthright and Other Tales* (1844). *Quid Pro Quo, or The Day of the Dupes: A Comedy* (1844). *The Popular Member: The Wheel of Fortune* (1844). *Self* (1845). *The Story of a Royal Favourite* (1845). *The Snowstorm: A Christmas Story* (1845). *Peers and Parvenus: A Novel* (1846). *New Year's Day: A Winter's Tale* (1846). *Men of Capital* (1846). *The Debutante, or The London Season* (1846). *Sketches of English Character* (1846). *Castles in the Air: A Novel* (1847). *Temptation and Atonement and Other Tales* (1847). *The Inundation, or Pardon and Peace: A Christmas Story* (1847). *The Diamond and the Pearl: A Novel* (1849). *Adventures in Borneo* (1849). *The Dean's Daughter, or The Days We Live In* (1853). *The Lost Son: A Winter's Tale* (1854). *Transmutation, or The Lord and the Lout* (1854). *Progress and Prejudice* (1854). *Mammon, or The Hardships of an Heiress* (1855). *A Life's Lessons: A Novel* (1856). *The Two Aristocracies: A Novel* (1857). *Heckington: A Novel* (1858).

BIBLIOGRAPHY: Adburgham, A. *Silver Fork Society* (1983). Anderson, B. *JPC* (1976). Farrell, J. F. *LCUT* (1986). Gettman, R. A. *A Victorian Publisher: A Study of the Bentley Papers* (1960). *A New Spirit of the Age,* ed. R. H. Horne (1872). Hughes, W. *NCF* (1995). Kadas, J. *Neohelicon* (1990). Rosa, M. W. *The Silver-Fork School: Novels of Fashion Preceding Vanity Fair* (1936).

For articles in reference works, see: *Allibone. BA19C. Bloomsbury. Boase. Chambers. CHEL. DEA. DLEL. DNB. ELB. Feminist. NCBEL. NCHEL. OCEL. Oxford. VB* (under "Silver-Fork Novel").

Other references: *Archives of Richard Bentley and Sons 1829–1898, Part Two* (Somerset House microfilm, reel 32, 1977). *Illustrated London News* (16 February 1861). *London Athenaeum* (9 February 1861, 16 February 1861). *New Monthly Magazine* (June 1833, March 1837, June 1852). *LonT* (4 February 1861).

Cynthia A. Merrill

Eva Gore-Booth

BORN: 22 May 1870, Lissadell, County Sligo, Ireland.
DIED: 30 June 1926, London.
DAUGHTER OF: Sir Henry Gore-Booth and Georgina Hill.

The Irish Literary Revival, the British movement for Woman's Suffrage, and the Women's Peace Crusade during World War I all fed G.'s imagination as a political writer, a poetess, and a dramatist.

Born in the shadow of "Knocknarea," the legendary burial cairn of Queen Maeve, G. spent her childhood learning about the people and legends of Connaught. In addition to this familiarity with the Irish, she was tutored in German, English, and French literatures and led a typical Anglo-Irish girlhood, preparing to enter aristocratic society with a strong background in the arts. Her father, Sir Henry Gore-Booth, who accompanied A. H. Markham on an expedition to the North Pole in 1879 as a scientist and who showed an equally active social conscience in that same year by generating aid for County Sligo's severe famine, was unprecedented in his concern as a landlord for the needs of the local Irish peasantry. G.'s early travels outside Ireland included a voyage to the Caribbean and North America with Sir Henry in 1894. In the following year, the father and daughter made the traditional tour of the European Continent that carried them from the Wagner Festival at Bayreuth to the theater in Oberammergau (both in Germany) to northern Italy's cathedrals and museums.

G. and her sister, Constance, attracted a circle of literary acquaintances during the 1890s. W. B. Yeats often visited the ancestral Gore-Booth estate, "Lissadell," Irish for "the Court of the Blind Man"; in the thirteenth century, it had been the home of a famous blind piper whose prominence in legend, along with the reputed beauty of the Gore-Booth sisters, may have attracted Yeats from his nearby home. G. also socialized with the novelist Julian Sturgis, who introduced her to Andrew Lang. It was through Lang that her early poems reached the editor of *Longman's Magazine,* where her work first appeared. G.'s first, slim book of verse entitled *Poems* appeared in 1898. Yeats wrote to her of its final four lines as being "really magical" and concluded, "I think it is full of poetic feeling and has great promise." In addition, *The Irish Homestead, The New Irish Review, The Nineteenth Century, The Yellow Book,* and *The Savoy* published poems by G. before the close of the 1890s.

In 1903, George Russell (A. E.) anthologized poems by G. in *New Poems: A Lyric Selection* by A. E., with poetry from seven others, among whom were Padraic Colum and Katherine Tynan. Russell's preface to the collection speaks of the "new ways the wind of poetry listeth to blow in Ireland today." By this time, G. had entered into the spirit of the Celtic Twilight, a spirit generated by images of ethereal "winds" whose composers saw themselves as prophets taking up the role left them by ancient, mystical Irish bards. G.'s best-known work, "The Little Waves of Breffny," invokes this spirit: "the haunted air of twilight is very strange and still, / And the little winds of twilight are dearer to my mind," treating this vague and airy "twilight" as a romantic symbol of Ireland's occult past. In 1904, James H. Cousins remarked, in a letter to Yeats, of the awkwardness involved in staging one of G.'s plays because "difficulties of stage management, such as getting a crow to fly across the stage, and a fog to enter and condense into a human figure, were too much even for our enthusiasm."

G.'s adult life was divided between participation in the Irish Literary Revival and her political activities in Britain. In 1896, she met Esther Roper, with whom she lived in northern England and for whom she joined as a joint secretary to the Women's Textile and Other Workers' Representation Committee. From 1896, G. was engaged in protesting British trade union policies, which excluded women from joining unions and exploited women by hiring them to replace the more expensive, organized male workers. She organized, wrote, and spoke in all parts of England, submitting deputations to cabinet ministers and to members of Parliament. She edited a paper called *The Women's Labour News* and acted as a representative of the women workers to the Manchester Education Committee. She ran reading classes for workers as well as dramatic societies. G. sustained her literary career simultaneously with her political activities. In 1906, she published *The Egyptian Pillar,* assimilating the imagery of her politics to Christian and Islamic themes; "The Good Samaritan," for example, seems to indicate her respect for the proletariat: "Stone-breakers resting from their toil / Have poured out wine and oil. / The miner hurrying from his mine / Has seen a flash of light divine, / And every tired laborer / Has given a helping hand . . ." Another book of poems, *The Agate Lamp,* appeared in 1912, with more variations upon Irish themes; another play, *The Death of Fionovar,* was substantially revised in 1916.

G.'s plays treated themes from Ulster's *Red Branch Cycle.* Her dramatic skit "The Death of Cuchulain," from her book *Unseen Kings* (1904), was performed at the Abbey Theatre. Her sister, Constance, produced a version of the entire *Unseen Kings* for the Independent Theatre Company in January of 1912. Constance was also an enthusiast of G.'s drama *The Buried Life* of *Deirdre* (1908), which G. rewrote and illustrated while Constance was being tried and imprisoned in 1916 for her part in the Easter Uprising. She was sentenced as Constance Markievicz (the wife of a Polish count) to a life term in prison; her male counterparts were executed. G.'s focus upon peace allowed her a closeness to her sister regardless of their differences. Although G. supported her sister's cause of Ireland's independence from Britain, she remained a pacifist throughout World War I, the Anglo-Irish War, and the Irish Civil War. Politically opposed to Constance's militarism, G. nonetheless devoted the same zealous energy to defending her sister against the British courts and prison policies. G. was an activist committed to the fundamental human rights of conscientious objectors who refused to participate in wars. While G. was traveling widely in Britain attending courts marshal and tribunals on behalf of pacifists, she was also carrying on a campaign of letter writing and parliamentary appeal in support of her sister, one of the founders of the Irish Republican Army. Constance was released from Kilmaianham Jail in Dublin due to G.'s efforts. The needs of Dublin's poorest communities, particularly the health issues of the women, consumed what remained of Constance's life. She died in 1927.

Christian ideals consumed G.'s interests during the 1920s. *A Psychological and Poetic Approach to the Study of Christ in the Fourth Gospel* was published in 1923 while she was studying Latin and Greek to become closer to the Scriptures. *The Shepherd of Eternity* was a book of poetry that followed in 1925. *The Inner Kingdom* (1926) and the unfinished, final book, *The World's Pilgrim* (1927), were both published posthumously. G. died on 30 June 1926, writing poetry and promoting peace to her final day.

G. is probably best known through W. B. Yeats' elegy, "In Memory of Eva Gore-Booth and Con Markievicz." Yeats summons images of a pastoral Lissadell, and G.'s youthful beauty is described as that of a "gazelle" only to be contrasted with the later image of her, "withered old and skeleton gaunt, / An image of such politics."

WORKS: *Poems* (1898). *Unseen Kings* (1904). *The One and the Many* (1904). *The Three Resurrections and the Triumph of Maeve* (1905). *The Egyptian Pillar* (1906). *The Sorrowful Princess* (1907). *The Buried Life of Deirdre* (1908). *The Agate Lamp* (1912). *The Death of Fionovar* (1916). *Broken Glory* (1918). *The Sword of Justice* (1918). *The Psychological and the Poetic Approach to the Study of Christ in the Fourth Gospel* (1923). *The Shepherd of Eternity* (1925). *The House of Three Windows* (1926). *The Inner Kingdom* (1926). *The World's Pilgrim* (1927). *Poems of Eva Gore-Booth* (1926).

BIBLIOGRAPHY: Chandran, K. N. *ANQ* (1994). Fox, R. M. *Rebel Irishwomen* (1935). VanVorris, J. *Constance de Markievicz: In the Cause of Ireland* (1967).

For articles in reference works, see: *DIL. Longman. The Modern Irish Drama: A Documentary History,* ed. R. Hogan and J. Kilroy (1976).

John Lavin

Elizabeth (de Beauchamp) Goudge

BORN: 24 April 1900, Wells, Somerset.
DIED: 1 April 1984, near Henley-on-Thames, Oxfordshire.
DAUGHTER OF: Henry Leighton Goudge and Ida de Beauchamp Collenette.

Novelist, playwright, artist, and teacher of handicrafts, G. was a prolific and popular, though somewhat old-fashioned, writer of books for both adults and children. She was especially recognized for her precise ability to depict the English countryside and for her characterization. The best known of her nearly fifty books—*Green Dolphin Country* (1944; published in the U. S. as *Green Dolphin Street*), *The Little White Horse* (1947), *Gentian Hill* (1949), and *The Child from the Sea* (1970)—have been compared favorably to Victorian novels; like most of her work, they are explicitly religious, reflective of G.'s active Anglicanism. After studying art, she taught design and applied art from 1922 to 1932 in Ely (where her father became a canon in 1911) and Oxford (where her father become Regius Professor of Divinity in 1923) and lived with her parents until her father died in 1939 and her mother in 1944.

Her first works were plays, including one about the Brontës that was produced in London when she was thirty-two; when she was advised to try writing fiction, she succeeded with her third effort, *Island Magic,* published in 1934. She thereafter wrote stories for such periodicals as *The Strand* and continued writing plays (which she preferred) and novels. In the mid-1930s she had a nervous breakdown; after her mother's death, she moved to Henley-on-Thames, where she lived till her death in 1984.

G. wrote in a variety of forms, including historical fiction, children's works, nonfiction works on religion, and, most often, novels celebrating particular locales. *Island Magic,* for example, told of her maternal grandparents' lives on Guernsey in the Channel Islands and was the first of a number of works dealing with specific British locations. Several works are set in cathedral towns including *A City of Bells* (1936), a contemporary novel set in Wells (but called "Torminster"); *Towers in the Mist* (1938), set in sixteenth-century Oxford; and *The Dean's Watch* (1960), set in nineteenth-century Ely (in Cambridgeshire).

Her best-known adult novel, the long historical romance *Green Dolphin Country,* is again about a member of her family, in this case a great-uncle, also from Guernsey, who emigrated to New Zealand; he writes home for a wife but because of confusion over her name gets her sister instead. The novel won several awards, was bought for $125,000 by M.G.M., and was made into a popular motion picture under its American title. Other historical novels include *Gentian Hill,* set in the Napoleonic era, and *The Child from the Sea,* about Lucy Waters, the secret wife of Charles II.

G. wrote a series of novels set in Devon about the several generations of the Eliot clan of Damerosehay; these emphasized family and spiritual values. G.'s favorite, *The Bird in the Tree* (1940), depicts the matriarch of the clan, Lucilla, trying to persuade her actor grandson, David, to end his affair with his uncle's ex-wife, Nadine, so she can return to her family. *The Herb of Grace* (1948), about an inn of that name, shows how Nadine finally renounces David and he returns to the family home. David is also the focus of *The Heart of the Family* (1953), in which he learns to forgive the actions of others through the intervention of a concentration-camp survivor; David had participated in the 1945 bombing of Hamburg, in which the survivor's family was killed, and after their encounter David can be fully restored to his family as Lucilla's heir.

G.'s children's books—which she started writing, unsuccessfully, even before entering art school (*The Fairies' Baby and Other Stories,* 1919)—gave her more pleasure, she said, than anything else she wrote, even though they now seem excessively sentimental. Most of these books, both novels and collections of stories, appeared relatively early in her career, as with the best-known, *Henrietta House* (1942; in the U. S. as *The Blue Hills*) and *The Little White Horse* (1947), but she maintained her interest up to 1971 (*The Lost Angel*). In addition, G. wrote numerous explicitly religious works, including *God So Loved the World* (1951), a biography of Jesus, and *Saint Francis Assisi (1959; in the U.S. as My God and My All),* a biography of Francis of Assisi, as well as others on prayer, peace, Christmas, and faith.

G. has often been criticized for her reliance on happy endings, didacticism, and sentimentality. She once stated that though such endings are "inartistic," they are the only kinds she can write; given the amount of tragedy in life, she said, "we don't want it in the story books to which we turn when we are ill or unhappy." She acknowledges that her books are escapist, and she knows that she writes primarily for the old, the young, and the sick. Her explicitly Christian emphasis assumes a hierarchical, planned universe in which everyone—even evil people—works toward the good. Yet at her best her works show a remarkable insight into character (again, especially the young and the old) and place, and her children's works, along with one or two adult historical novels, are likely to remain popular.

WORKS: *The Fairies' Baby and Other Stories* (1919). *Island Magic* (1934). *The Middle Window* (1935). *A City of Bells* (1936). *A Pedlar's Pack and Other Stories* (1937). *Towers in the Mist* (1938). *The Sister of the Angels: A Christmas Story* (1939). *Three Plays: Naomi, The Brontës of Haworth, and Fanny Burney* (1939). *Smoky House* (1940). *The Bird in the Tree* (1940). *The Golden Skylark and Other Stories* (1941). *The Well of the Star* (1941). *The Castle on the Hill* (1941). *Henrietta House* (1942; in the U.S. as *The Blue Hills*). *The Ikon on the Wall and Other Stories* (1943). *Green Dolphin Country* (1944; in the U.S. as *Green Dolphin Street*). *The Elizabeth Goudge Reader,* ed. R. Dobbs (1946; in the U. K. as *At the Sign of the Dolphin: An Elizabeth Goudge Anthology,* (1947). *The Little White Horse* (1947). *Songs and Verses* (1947). *The Herb of Grace* (1948; in the U. S. as *Pilgrim's Inn*). *Gentian Hill* (1949). *Make-Believe* (1949). *The Reward of Faith and Other Stories* (1950). *The Valley of Song* (1951). *God So Loved the World: A Life of Christ* (1951). *White Wings: Collected Short Stories* (1952). *The Heart of the Family* (1953).

David, the Shepherd Boy (1954). *The Rosemary Tree* (1956). *The Eliots of Damerosehay* (1957). *The White Witch* (1958). *Saint Francis of Assisi* (1959; in the U. S. as *My God and My All: The Life of St. Francis Assisi). The Dean's Watch* (1960). *The Scent of Water* (1963). *Linnets and Valerians* (1964). *Three Cities of Bells* (1965). *The Chapel of the Blessed Virgin Mary, Buckler's Hard, Beaulieu* (1966). *A Christmas Book* (1967). *I Saw Three Ships* (1969). *The Ten Gifts* (1969). *The Child from the Sea* (1970). *The Lost Angel* (1971). *The Joy of the Snow: An Autobiography* (1974). *Pattern of People* (1976). *A Book of Faith* (1989). *A Book of Peace* (1989). *A Vision of God; A Selection* (1990). *A Diary of Prayer* (1991). *Linnets and Valerians* (1992).

BIBLIOGRAPHY: Leasor, J. *Author by Profession* (1952).

For articles in reference works, see: *CA. CB. Feminist. Longman. Oxford. SATA. TCA and SUP. TCCW. TCRGW. TCW. ToddBWW. WD.*

Other references: *Books and Bookmen* (May 1972). *Christian Century* (3 November 1976). *CSM Magazine* (8 June 1940). Dobbs, R., intro. to *The Elizabeth Goudge Reader,* ed. R. Dobbs (1946). *LonT* (3 April 1984). Marsden, M., in *Images of Women in Fiction: Feminist Perspectives,* ed. S. K. Cornillon (1972). *New Statesman* (27 September 1974). *NYHTBR* (7 October 1951). *NYT* (27 April 1984). *Observer* (8 September 1974, 21 July 1985). *Scholastic* (4 March 1939). *TES* (14 December 1979). *Time* (4 September 1944). *TLS* (6 April 1973).

Paul Schlueter

Graham, Maxtone: See *Struther, Jan*

Graham, Viva: See *Somerville and Ross*

Sarah Grand (pseudonym of Frances Elizabeth [Clarke] McFall)

BORN: 10 June 1854, Donaghadee, County Down, Northern Ireland.

DIED: 12 May 1943, Calne, Wiltshire.

DAUGHTER OF: Edward John Bellenden Clarke and Margaret Bell Sherwood Clarke.

MARRIED: David Chambers McFall, 1870.

One of five children, G. was born in Ireland of English parents, but when her father, a naval officer, died in 1861, her mother moved the family back to England. G. was educated at home until she was fourteen, when she was sent to boarding school for more discipline. She escaped from school at sixteen by marrying a naval surgeon twenty-three years her senior, apparently an unhappy match. After *Ideala* (1888) was published, she moved from her husband and son to live in London, where her career flourished; when her husband died in 1898, G. joined the Women Writers' Suffrage League and became active in the women's suffrage movement in Tunbridge Wells, Kent. In 1922, two years after moving to Bath, she became that city's mayoress for six years. She died in 1943 in Calne, where she had moved for safety during World War II.

One of the "New Women" writers of the 1890s who criticized the oppression of women, G. used her ample experience and acute observation, as well as her travels to the Far East, in writing her novels, which can be read as arguments for the need to reform society's treatment of women, the way women themselves behave, and the economic system. Besides her novels, G. wrote many short stories and articles for women's magazines, such as "Is It Ever Justifiable to Break Off an Engagement?" and "Should Irascible Old Men Be Taught to Knit?"

G.'s first successful novel, *Ideala,* forms a trilogy with *The Heavenly Twins* (1893) and *The Beth Book* (1897). *Ideala,* a first-person narrative about Ideala by a male friend, examines a number of social problems as well as the question of the proper goal for women: to be or to act. In G.'s first best-seller, *The Heavenly Twins,* she experiments with her narrative voice, producing some disconcerting breaks. Otherwise, the novel is well worth reading since it introduces many of G.'s themes. The inadequacy of women's education and its disastrous effects are graphically revealed in this novel, which does, however, show some characters rising above and conquering the hardships society has given them. The title refers to the twins Angelica and Diavolo, female and male, and their upbringing, but the novel actually focuses on Evadne, a highly intelligent and self-educated woman who, through being kept in ignorance by her parents, inadvertently marries a brutish man with a sordid past. This is also a novel within a novel, and plots and subplots abound, intertwining with each other to produce a complete world in which many young people join to improve society.

The Beth Book (1897) is G.'s best novel, primarily because of the strong, fascinating character of Beth and the detailed description of the Victorian upbringing of a young girl. Based loosely on G.'s own life, the first half of the novel deals with Beth's life from birth through adolescence (one reason the novel was scorned by critics when it was first published), but instead of being a pathetic, sentimental account of the oppression of female children, the novel presents Beth refusing to submit, a refreshing change from conventional novels of the day. Indeed, G.'s heroines often succeed in spite of society rather than succumbing to their oppressors. But *The Beth Book* does have problems. Besides occasional over-explanation, the problems are mainly accounted for by the narrative point of view. Sometimes G. creates awkward scenes when she tries to develop other characters while retaining Beth's point of view. In one scene, for example, Beth trails her corrupt Uncle James around his estate, unseen yet close enough to hear his conversations, for an unbelievably long time. On the other hand, the absence of a sense of time in the passages from Beth's early childhood seems similar to the experiments with point of view of modern writers such as Faulkner.

Although G. had a social purpose for writing, her characters are not stereotypes. In fact, she goes so far in her attempts to portray even minor characters as complex individuals that inconsistencies sometimes develop, such as the abrupt change in Mr. Caldwell, Beth's father, from a harsh, domineering, and critical husband ("not to disturb him was the object of everybody's life") to a patient, appreciative, and understanding father to Beth shortly before his death. The advice he gives Beth is necessary for the continuation of the novel, but the change in his personality is explained only perfunctorily in a few hasty scenes in the garden. Nevertheless, G.'s short character descriptions and pithy statements are honed with irony and truth.

Unlike her trilogy, *Singularly Deluded* (1893) caused little controversy and was even praised for its vivid description of a fire at sea; unfortunately it is much less interesting than the other novels and offers little satisfaction besides finding out how it ends. G.'s next two major novels, *Adnam's Orchard* (1912) and *Winged Victory* (1916), deal with the problem of land reform. In these novels, G. branches out to focus for the first time on characters who are not all members of nobility. In doing so, G. considers at length what makes a person "noble." How much is heredity and how much environment? In *Adnam's Orchard*, we see a land laid waste by its unambitious noble landowners, the workers and their families either out of work or scraping by in substandard housing. The absurdity of the landowners' raising the rent as soon as tenants make any improvements in the property is apparent. *Winged Victory* follows the life of Ella Banks, a character in *Adnam's Orchard*, and her attempts to improve the lives of women workers in the sweatshops.

G. is intelligent enough not to prescribe one path for everyone. She accepts individuality and wants only a society that also recognizes individuality in its members instead of forcing them all, both men and women, into preordained roles. Her novels provoked controversy. Although critics severely criticized both subject matter and style, G.'s novels were very popular among readers and were praised by, among others, Mark Twain and George Bernard Shaw. Indeed, she has lapses; yet when read today, her novels resound with common sense.

WORKS: *Two Dear Little Feet* (1880). *Ideala: A Study From Life* (1888). *A Domestic Experiment* (1891). *Singularly Deluded* (1892). *The Heavenly Twins* (1893). *Our Manifold Nature* (1894). *The Beth Book* (1897). *The Modern Man and Maid* (1898). *Babs the Impossible* (1900). *Emotional Moments* (1908). *Adnam's Orchard* (1912). *Winged Victory* (1916). *Variety* (1922).

BIBLIOGRAPHY: Cunningham, G. *The "New Woman" and the Fiction of the 1890's* (1978). Hudleston, J. *Sarah Grand: A Bibliography* (1979). Mangum, Teresa, in *The Significance of Sibling Relationships in Literature*, ed. J. S. Mink and J. D. Ward (1992). Senf, C. A., intro. to *The Heavenly Twins* (1992).

For articles in reference works, see: *Bloomsbury. Feminist. Oxford. TCA. ToddBWW.*

Other references: *Journal of Women's Studies in Literature* (1979). *MTJ* (Summer 1972). *MD* (December 1971). *Turn-of-the-Century Women* (Winter 1987).

Carol Pulham

Anne MacVicar Grant

BORN: 21 February 1755, Glasgow, Scotland.
DIED: 7 November 1838, Edinburgh, Scotland.
DAUGHTER OF: Duncan MacVicar and Catherine Mackenzie.
MARRIED: James Grant of Laggan, 1779.

Often referred to by contemporaries as Mrs. Grant of Laggan, G. was best known for her imaginative re-creations of her earlier experiences. She was also a leading authority on Scottish folklore, which she introduced to a wide public through her works. Though praised by such authorities as Sir Walter Scott and Francis Jeffrey of the *Edinburgh Review*, who also respected G. as a critic, her work lapsed into obscurity in the latter nineteenth century.

G.'s father came from a rural Highland Scots family. In 1757, he secured a commission in the army and sailed for North America. He was stationed near Albany, New York, where he was joined in 1758 by his wife and daughter. The family became especially friendly with the Dutch patron Schuyler family. When MacVicar went on the Ticonderoga campaign in the French and Indian War, his wife and daughter remained in the Schuylers' care. They stayed there until MacVicar retired from the army and took up a land grant in eastern Vermont in 1765. The family left North America abruptly in 1768; MacVicar went first to Glasgow and then became barrackmaster at Fort Augustus. In 1779, G. married James Grant, chaplain at the fort and minister of the nearby parish of Laggan.

G. became a model minister's wife. She was interested in her Highland parishioners, learning Gaelic and collecting stories and information about their way of life. In long and lively letters to various friends and relations she described her life, activities, and neighbors. G. and her husband had twelve children, of whom eight survived their father, who died in 1801; only one son survived G. Her husband's death left G. with no income except a small chaplain's pension. Like many other women of literary bent, she had long written brief poems on various topics. These were published in 1802 with a subscription list of three thousand names.

G. moved to Stirling in 1803 to provide better opportunities for her children. In 1806, she published selections from her Laggan correspondence in three volumes under the title *Letters from the Mountains*, a work that was immediately popular with a wide variety of readers, for the pictures of Highland life and culture appealed to many who had been introduced to Scotland by Scott. Others enjoyed her comments on literature, the role and duties of women, and contemporary events. G., not a radical or a feminist, took a conventional view of the nature of women, but she did not undervalue their abilities to cope with everyday problems, as she herself continued to do. In 1810, she moved to Edinburgh where she took young women into her household to be introduced to the pleasures of urban life and the intellectual circles of the northern capital. Most of these young women were daughters of wealthy families; their stay with G. finished their education and provided her with an income. A pension was secured for her in 1826, which added to the comfort of her last years.

In 1808, G. published *Memoirs of an American Lady*, a biography of Mrs. Philip Schuyler, her mentor from New York days, enlarged by G.'s recollections of late colonial life. The book was widely read in both the United States and Great Britain. The line between fact and invention in this work is often unclear; it is probably better read as G.'s memoirs than Schuyler's.

A posthumous collection of G.'s letters was published with a memoir by her son, J. P. Grant, in 1844. These letters are sometimes more chatty about her personal life than her earlier collection, but they too are full of her comments on literature and life.

WORKS: *Poems* (1803). *Letters from the Mountains* (1806). *Memoirs of an American Lady* (1808). *Essays on the Superstitions of the Highlands of Scotland* (1811). *Eighteen Hundred and Thirteen: a Poem* (1814). *Memoir and Correspondence of Mrs. Grant of Laggan*, ed. J. P. Grant (1844).

BIBLIOGRAPHY:

For articles in reference works, see: *DNB. Feminist. GER. Oxford.*

Barbara Brandon Schnorrenberg

Granville, Mary: See *Delany, Mary Granville Pendarves*

Gray, Edith: See *Doolittle, Hilda (H. D.)*

Gray, Harriet: See *Robins, Denise Naomi*

Mary Anne Everett Wood Green

BORN: 19 July 1818, Sheffield, Yorkshire.
DIED: 1 November 1895, London.
DAUGHTER OF: Robert Wood.
MARRIED: George Pycock Green, 1846.
WROTE UNDER: Mary Anne Everett; Mary Anne Everett Wood Green.

Lauded repeatedly by contemporary critics for diligent research, extraordinary pains, zealous pursuit of the truth, and careful attention to detail, G. was unique in nineteenth-century scholarship: she was universally acclaimed a scholar who happened to be a woman rather than a woman who was condescendingly labeled a "lady-scholar."

G. was born into a family of Methodist ministers, and her early life was passed in Non-Conformist parishes her father served in Yorkshire and Lancashire. She received all her education at home until the family moved to London in 1841. Residing near the British Museum, G. soon discovered the Reading Room and embarked upon a passionate, life-long study of history, especially as it pertained to royal ladies. The novelty of a reigning queen produced several historical works on queens, the most famous of which was Agnes Strickland's *Lives of the Queens of England* (1840–48), published by Colburn. Before Strickland's study appeared, G. approached Colburn with her own plan to publish a book on the princesses of England. Colburn approved of the project but deferred publishing it until Strickland's was completed. While waiting for this to occur, G. brought out *Letters of Royal and Illustrious Ladies of Great Britain, from the Commencement of the Twelfth Century to the Close of the Reign of Queen Mary* (1846), the only work she published under her maiden name. From 1849 to 1855, six volumes of *Lives of the Princesses* were brought out, eliciting consistently congratulatory and laudatory reviews in the periodicals. One of the *Lives*, that of Elizabeth of Bohemia, was later republished separately by G.'s niece, Sophia Crawford Lomas (1909).

In 1853, G. accepted an invitation from Lord Romilly to become an editor of calendars of state papers, a task that occupied her for forty years and that produced forty-one volumes of text, a staggering achievement since each calendar contained 600 to 800 pages of material. G. described the papers she calendared rather than merely indicating the contents. Her meticulous dating, ability to read several languages, and skill as a paleographer all contributed to volumes that, according to one biographer, "serve[d] hundreds of English historians during and since her time" (Van Eerde).

G. somehow found time to edit two texts for the Camden Society and, according to an item in the *Athenaeum* (12 May 1855), another was projected though apparently never completed. Those she did finish plainly show the extent of her learning and research skills. Careful annotations remark upon discrepancies between the diary entries and documents seen in the Public Record Office. Her historical notes reveal a close familiarity with both the Tudor and the Stuart periods. G.'s skill as an original researcher is further revealed in the 1909 edition of Elizabeth, Electress Palatine and Queen of Bohemia, where Lomas lists her aunt's sources, written in English, French, Latin, German, Dutch, and Italian: "On it [this text] the author lavished unstinted time and indefatigable research . . ." (Lomas). Lastly, *The Letters of Queen Henrietta Maria* (1857) reveal G. as a first-rate cryptographer.

In 1846, G. married George Pycock Green, a painter whose pastel portrait of his wife today hangs in the National Portrait Gallery. For the first two years of their marriage, they lived in Paris and Antwerp, Belgium, where he pursued his artistic work and she continued her historical studies. The couple returned to London and lived at 7 Gower Street from 1849 to 1864 and then at 100 Gower until her death in 1895. They became members of the Society of London Nonconformity, a charitable and philanthropic organization. G.'s husband died in 1893. She continued her researches in the Public Record Office until shortly before her death.

WORKS: *Letters of Royal and Illustrious Ladies of Great Britain, from the Commencement of the Twelfth Century to the Close of the Reign of Queen Mary*, 3 vols. (1846). *Lives of the Princesses of England, from the Roman Conquest*, 6 vols. (1849–55). (ed.) *Diary of John Rous* (1856; rpt. 1968). (ed.) *Letters of Queen Henrietta Maria* (1857). *Calendar of State Papers, Domestic Series, of the Reign of James I*, 4 vols. (1857–59). *Calendar of State Papers, Domestic Series, of the Reign of Charles II*, vols. 1–7 (1860–66). (ed.) *Life of William Whittingham* (1870; rpt. 1968). *Calendar of State Papers of Elizabeth*, vols. 3–8, 12 (1867–72). *Calendar of the Commonwealth*, 13 vols. (1875–85). *Calendar of the Proceedings of the Committee for the Advance of Money*, 3 vols. (1888). *Calendar of the Committee for Compounding with Delinquents*, 5 vols. (1889–92). *Calendar of the State Papers of the Reign of Charles II*, vols. 8–10 (1893–95). *Elizabeth, Electress Palantine and Queen of Bohemia* (1855; in *Lives*, new ed., ed. S. C. Lomas, 1909).

BIBLIOGRAPHY:

For articles in reference works, see *Allibone* and *SUP. BA19C. Boase. CHEL. DNB. Europa. NCBEL. Who Was Who.*

Other references: *Athenaeum* (16 June 1852, 24 July 1852, 31 July 1852, 7 August 1852, 12 May 1855, 9 November 1895). *LonT* (5 November 1895). *Gentleman's Magazine* (April 1858). Van Eerde, K. *Victorians Institute Journal* (1984).

Natalie Joy Woodall

Kate Greenaway

BORN: 17 March 1846, Hoxton, London.
DIED: 6 November 1901, Hampstead, London.
DAUGHTER OF: John Greenaway and Elizabeth Jones Greenaway.
WROTE UNDER: Kate Greenaway; K. G.

Primarily known for her illustrations of children's books, G. wrote verse and other texts as well. Her children's rhymes and drawings of children and English gardens were very popular in Europe and in the United States. G.'s parents recognized her budding talent at the age of twelve and provided art lessons for her, but her formal education alternated between visiting tutors and girls' schools. Her first published works, in 1868, were designs for Christmas and Valentine cards. She soon began illustrating little books and continued this work throughout her life.

G.'s writings alone would not have gained entry into the publishing world, however. Her writings fall into five categories: illustrated verses, datebooks, nonfiction, correspondence, and miscellaneous poetry. Her popular illustrated verses still have a special innocent charm, and the almanacs and datebooks brought her some notoriety. G. also illustrated texts for art lessons and game rules.

The only two children's rhyme books that G. both wrote and illustrated were *Under the Window* (1879) and *Marigold Garden* (1885); they were both very successful. *Under the Window* is a series of outside scenes spotlighting Victorian emerging ladies and gentlemen, reflecting in words and images the whimsy and innocent fantasy of childhood. The rhyme is sing-songy, and the theme is a combination of fantasy and etiquette.

In recent years, Victorian art has been examined for more realistic and autobiographical elements, and G.'s work also shows such links. The drawings have been connected to real gardens and farms from G.'s childhood, and dresses of her art children were drawn from models she stitched herself. Indeed, G.'s mother, a professional seamstress, opened a small factory and shop to produce and sell clothes designed from G.'s popular books.

Marigold Garden is said to be G.'s favorite work and is still primarily valued for the well-crafted watercolor pictures that accompany her verses. Scenes with young curly-headed girls with bonnets and simple sashed dresses are in carefully tended gardens or fantasy places such as the "Bright Green Tower in the Middle of the Sea," where "The Four Princesses" live, each looking out her compass point in the tower and each so pretty "You could not tell which was the prettiest." There is nothing in the verse that explains why each pretty princess lives in a tower so small that each stands touching shoulders on their look-out, or why the most profound question is who is prettiest. Other rhymes have a fantasy song feeling, but not without stated ironic humor: In "The Cats Have Come to Tea," the question is asked: "What should she do—oh, what should she do? / What a lot of milk they would get through; / For here they were with 'Mew—mew—mew!' / —She didn't know—oh, she didn't know, / If bread and butter they'd like or no; / They might want little mice, oh! oh! oh!" The original water color painting with the young little lady in front of the carefully shaped shrub, surrounded by approaching cats, hangs in the Royal Library in Windsor Castle.

Many of the rhymes in *Marigold Garden,* however, are the verbal counterpoint to the lush floral images depicted, each little gem meant to be savored for its little beauty in its entirety. The assembly of maidens "Under Rose Arches" will always arrive in "Rose Town on the top of the hill; / For the Summer wind blows and music goes, / And the violins sound shrill," singing "Twist and twine Roses and Lilies; / And little leaves green, / Fit for a queen; / Twist and twine Roses and Lilies."

These works' popularity was a reflection of the Victorian age of which G. was certainly a part. In many ways, the innocence and beauty of G.'s children, who in no way resemble the chimneysweeps and other poor waifs then on the streets, are directly influenced by the Pre-Raphaelite movement. G. admired the paintings of John Everett Millais, Dante Gabriel Rossetti, and Holman Hunt and was a disciple of John Ruskin. The Ruskin–G. correspondence extended from 1880, when he wrote about the *Under the Windows* exhibition, to 1900, when he died; he wrote about 500 letters, and she wrote 1,000 or more. Ruskin, the authoritarian art critic, offered advice and friendship and devoted a lecture to G. called "Fairyland" on 30 May 1883. Feeling that G. was wasting much effort on her illustrations and datebook art, he encouraged G. to paint larger works, which she did. G. subsequently illustrated more than twenty books written by others. In addition to a collection of cat poems edited by Ruskin, *Dame Wiggins of Lee and Her Seven Wonderful Cats* (1885). G.'s best known collaborators were Bret Harte (*The Queen of the Pirate Isle,* 1886) and Robert Browning (*The Pied Piper of Hamelin,* 1888).

G.'s unpublished poems fill up four volumes of manuscripts, though several were subsequently published in a biography. Most of her poems are unpolished and amateurish, and G. was never satisfied with them. They are not, however, nursery rhymes. They are lyrics, some in sonnet form, on a number of different themes, many serious and sad, and many other verses are about love.

The artist described by her biographers was "sincere, modest, patient, intelligent, bighearted, sensitive, forgiving, and humorous," and Ruskin said that G. was able to "re-establish throughout gentle Europe the manners and customs of fairyland."

WORKS: *Under the Window: Pictures and Rhymes for Children* (1879). *Art Hours: After K. Greenaway* (1882). *Steps to Art: After Kate Greenaway* (1882). *Kate Greenaway's Almanac for 1883–95, 1897,* 14 vols. (1882–96).

Language of Flowers (1884). *Kate Greenaway's Alphabet* (1885). *Marigold Garden: Pictures and Rhymes* (1885). *An Apple Pie* (1886). *Kate Greenaway's Book of Games* (1889). *Kate Greenaway's Pictures from Originals Presented by Her to John Ruskin and Other Personal Friends* (1921). *The Kate Greenaway Treasury: An Anthology of the Illustrations and Writings of Kate Greenaway,* ed. E. Ernest and P. Lowe (1967). *The Birthday Book* (1975). *The Kate Greenaway Book,* ed. B. Holme (1976). *Kate Greenaway's Mother Goose* (1984, 1987, 1988). *Book of Games* (1989). *Kate Greenaway's Nursery Rhyme Classics* (1990).

BIBLIOGRAPHY: Engen, R. *Kate Greenaway* (1976). *The Kate Greenaway Treasury,* ed. E. Ernest (1967). Holme, B. *The Kate Greenaway Book* (1976). Moore, A. *A Century of Kate Greenaway* (1946). Ruskin, J. *Works,* ed. E. Cook (1903–12). Spielmann, M. and G. Layard, *Kate Greenaway* (1905). Tarbox, A. *Magic Land of Kate Greenaway* (1968). Taylor, I. *The Art of Kate Greenaway: A Nostalgic Portrait of Childhood* (1991).

For articles in reference works, see: *Authors of Books for Young People 3. BDWAEA. BGEL. CA. CL. DLB. DNB. Illustrators of Children's Books, 1744–1945,* ed. B. Mahony (1947). *NCHEL. OCEL. Oxford. Stanford. VB. Who's Who of Children's Literature,* ed. B. Doyle (1968). *Yesterday's Authors of Books for Children,* ed. A. Commire (1978).

Other references: Dooley, P., in *Touchstones: Reflections on the Best in Children's Literature,* ed. P. Nodelman (1989). Hearn, M. *ConL* (August 1980). Lundin, A. *L&U* (June 1993). Schuster, T. *Book Collector* (1988).

Marilynn J. Smith

Dora Greenwell

BORN: 6 December 1821, Greenwell Ford, Lanchester, Durham.
DIED: 29 March 1882, Clifton, near Bristol.
DAUGHTER OF: William Thomas Greenwell and Dorothy Smales.

G.'s life and career exhibit spiritual commitment and social conscience as well as artistic ambition. From 1848 until 1877, she published poetry and prose marked by religious and mystical inspiration. Besides hymns, devotionals, and Christian theological essays, G. also wrote lyrics, ballads, dramatic monologues, biographies, and social essays. She was friends with social reformer Josephine Grey Butler and with Christina Rossetti, William Bell Scott, Jean Ingelow, and Margaret Hunt.

G. grew up at Greenwell Ford in County Durham, where her father was Deputy Lieutenant; when the family estate was sold to pay his debts, G. and her parents moved first to Ovingham Rectory and then to Golbourne Rectory (the homes of G.'s two brothers, both Anglican clerics). When the father died in 1854, G. and her mother moved to Durham, where they remained until the mother's death in 1871. Afterwards, G. spent more time in London, moving to Westminster in 1874. In 1881, an accident ended her self-sufficiency and she joined her brother Alan at Clifton, near Bristol. Always in frail health, G. had become addicted to opium in her late fifties; about a year after her accident, she died.

G.'s career as a poet began out of financial need in 1848 with *Poems,* followed in 1850 by *Stories That Might Be True.* Her 1861 volume containing new poems was enlarged in 1867 and dedicated to the memory of Elizabeth Barrett Browning, from whom G. drew inspiration. While nearly all of G.'s poems reflect her religious orientation, many of the most popular concerned secular subjects. "Home," considered her most memorable poem, celebrates sentimental Victorian ideas of the home as a refuge and marriage as a union of spirits. On the other hand, some of G.'s poems are at least incipiently feminist (e.g., "Bring Me Word How Tall She Is: Woman in 1873," and "Christina," a dramatic monologue of a fallen woman, comparable to Augusta Webster's "A Castaway"). In "The Broken Chain" and "The Sunflower," G. explores the psychology of submission and dependence.

Like her friend Christina Rossetti, Greenwell turned mostly to religious poetry in her later years, with *Songs of Salvation* (1873), *The Soul's Legend* (1873), and *Camera Obscura* (1876). Alexander Japp thought *Songs of Salvation* showed "an exceptional power of uniting a high religious teaching with a kind of dramatic realism of portraiture of simple characters by monologue and dialogue." Japp also noted that, like George MacDonald, whose story "The Wow O'Rivven, or The Idiot's Home" she edited in 1868, G. had a tendency to allegorize. Her insistence upon "translating everything into a text for religious truth," Japp speculated, "has operated against the popular acceptance of her poetry as a whole."

G.'s prose works, like her poetry, do not easily divide into the secular and the religious. However, several of her most powerful and influential essays on secular subjects appeared in the *North British Review,* including "Our Single Women" (February 1862) and "On the Education of the Imbecile" (September 1868). G., a self-declared "liberal," wrote about slavery, war, child labor, matchworkers, poverty, women's suffrage, girls' education, women's right to work, animals' rights (vivisection), and the plight of mentally disabled children and adults. In 1867, she edited a volume to raise funds for the Royal Albert Insane Asylum and related causes: refuges for "idiots" and a hospital for insane children. In 1868, she edited *Harmless Johnny, or the Poor Outcast of Reason,* by the late Caroline Bowles Southey.

G.'s other prose publications include biographies of Henri Lacordaire, a Dominican friar (1867), and John Woolman, a Quaker (1871). A devout Anglican, G. was nevertheless broad-minded and sympathized with Methodists, Quakers, and Roman Catholics. Carl Woodring calls G. "the keenest—if not the only—theologian among nineteenth-century Englishwomen." Among the theological problems she addressed was the tension between Hebraism and Hellenism, duty and beauty, the moral and the aesthetic. If this accounts for the high moral tone of her poetry, it also explains the lyricism of her religious prose. G.'s devotional volumes include *A Present Heaven* (1855), letters on the Gospel; *The Patience of Hope* (1860), a spiritual treatise dedicated to Josephine Butler; *Two Friends* (1862), a spiritual dialogue dedicated to G.'s publisher and friend Thomas Constable, and its sequel *Colloquia Cru-*

cis (1871); and, most notably, *Carmina Crucis* (1869), which along with lyrical prose meditations contains some of G.'s most distinguished poetry.

WORKS: *Poems* (1848). *Stories That Might Be True, with Other Poems* (1850). *A Present Heaven* (1855; in 1867 as *The Covenant of Life and Peace*). *The Patience of Hope* (1860; with preface by J. G. Whittier, 1862). *Poems* (1861, 1867). *Two Friends* (1862, 1867; ed. C. L. Maynard, 1926, 1952). *Home Thoughts and Home Scenes,* in *Original Poems,* by J. Ingelow, D. Greenwell, et al. (1865). *Essays: Our Single Women; Hardened in Good; Prayer; Popular Religious Literature; Christianos ad Leones* (1866). *Lacordaire* (1867). *Carmina Crucis* (1869; ed. C. L. Maynard, 1906). *Colloquia Crucis: A Sequel to Two Friends* (1871). *John Woolman: A Biographical Sketch* (1871). *Songs of Salvation* (1873). *The Soul's Legend* (1873). *Liber Humanitatis* (1875). *Camera Obscura* (1876). *A Basket of Summer Fruit* (1877). *Poems,* ed. and intro. W. Dorling (1889). *Poems* (1904). *Selected Poems,* ed. C. L. Maynard (1906). *Selections from the Prose of Dora Greenwell,* ed. W. G. Hanson (1952).

BIBLIOGRAPHY: *Academy* (12 August 1905). Bett, H. *Studies in Literature* (1929). Bett, H. *Dora Greenwell* (1950). Dorling, W. *Memoirs of Dora Greenwell* (1885). Japp, A. H., in *The Poets and the Poetry of the Nineteenth Century: Joanna Baillie to Jean Ingelow,* ed. A. H. Miles (1907). Maynard, C. L. *Dora Greenwell: A Prophet for Our Own Times on the Battleground of Our Faith* (1926).

For articles in reference works, see: *Feminist. NCHEL. Oxford. ToddBWW. VB.*

Other references: Armstrong, I. *Victorian Poetry: Poetry, Poetics and Politics* (1993). Hickok, K. *Representations of Women: Nineteenth-Century British Women's Poetry* (1984). Kaplan, C. *Salt and Bitter and Good: Three Centuries of English and American Women Poets* (1975). Leighton, A., in *New Feminist Discourses: Critical Essays on Theories and Texts,* ed. I. Armstrong (1992). Leighton, A. *Victorian Women Poets: Writing Against the Heart* (1992). *Victorian Women Poets: An Anthology,* ed. A. Leighton and M. Reynolds (1995). Sandars, M. F. *The Life of Christina Rossetti* (1930). Woodring, C. *Victorian Samplers: William and Mary Howitt* (1952).

Kathleen Hickok

Germaine Greer

BORN: 29 January 1939, near Melbourne, Australia.
DAUGHTER OF: Eric Reginald Greer and Margaret May Mary Lanfrancan (in some sources Lanfrank) Greer.
MARRIED: Paul de Feu, 1968.

G. is a feminist, teacher of literature, media personality, and Shakespearean scholar. G. is the oldest of three children (she has a sister, Alida Jane, and a brother, Barry John). Her upbringing was tainted by her father's voluntary departure for military service in World War II and his return in 1944 suffering from anxiety neurosis, and by her mother's physical and mental abuse of G. and G.'s siblings.

When she was twelve, G. won a scholarship to the Star of the Sea convent school in a Melbourne suburb. Despite her reputation as a difficult student, the nuns supported her scholarly ambitions, and she credits them for her not going "to secretarial school and marrying a stockbroker."

A versatile linguist, G. is fluent in German, French, and Italian; she attended Melbourne University on a scholarship, graduating with a B.A. in 1959 with honors in English and French literature. In 1961, she earned an M.A. in English at the University of Sydney. She won a Commonwealth scholarship to study at Newnham College, Cambridge University, where she received a Ph.D. in 1967 with a dissertation on Shakespeare's early comedies. She then become a lecturer at the University of Warwick.

During this time, G. began developing the outrageous public personality for which she is still known. She appeared on television talk shows and wrote articles for the *Listener* and the *Spectator;* she was also a "supergroupie" to rock stars, and she appeared in a British situation comedy. As such she became a member of Britain's counterculture. She wrote regularly for *Oz,* an underground newspaper published by Australian expatriates, and she was cofounder of *Suck,* an Amsterdam-based, erotic, radical magazine.

Her transcontinental fame was initiated when a literary agent urged her to write a book on women's liberation. *The Female Eunuch* (1970), a bestseller in both the United Kingdom and the United States and translated into many languages, argues that women are castrated by societal demands to accept the characteristics of the eunuch: "Timidity, plumpness, languor, delicacy and preciosity." G. further argues that femininity means "without libido" and that women must reject that definition. She sees the nuclear family as an isolating form of social control. A woman wishing to be liberated, in G.'s view, should never marry, or, if married, should live in a commune where mothers can jointly rear children and fathers can visit. She assails the women's liberation movement as addressing only the middle class. Her contention that "The castration of our true female personality is not the fault of men but our own, and history's" led the popular media in the United States to embrace her, as *Life* magazine declared on its May 1971 cover, as the "Saucy Feminist that Even Men Like." G. participated in the media blitz in the United States, highlighted by her debate that year with self-identified chauvinist writer Norman Mailer in New York City.

G.'s phenomenal success with *The Female Eunuch* enabled her to give up teaching, and she spent the subsequent eight years combing museums and art galleries in Europe to research her next book, *The Obstacle Race: The Fortunes of Women Painters and Their Work* (1979). The intention of this massive discussion of dead women artists, G. writes in the introduction, is "To show women artists not as a string of over-rated individuals but as members of a group having much in common, tormented by the same conflicts of motivations and the same practical difficulties, the obstacles both external and surmountable, internal and insurmountable of the race for achievement." Her study of the works and lives of these women concludes, "There is . . . no female Leonardo, no female Titian, no female Poussin. . . . The reason is simply that you cannot make great artists out of egos that have been damaged, with wills that are defective, with libidos that have been driven out of reach and energy diverted into neurotic channels."

The subjects of *Sex and Destiny: The Politics of Human Fertility* (1984) are wide-ranging, including a comparison of western and third-world attitudes toward childbirth and child rearing. G. takes on customs and methods of childbirth, attitudes toward sexuality, histories of eugenics, and birth control. G. argues that less-advanced societies are more satisfying for women than the West because the western societies have an "anti-child" attitude. She claims that natural forms of population control are superior to the technological forms that she accuses the West of foisting on unwilling peoples. G. concludes that the world is overpopulated only in the sense that it cannot afford more people living at the western standard. The book was not universally well received by feminists, who responded that G. wanted women barefoot and pregnant. G. believed that her argument was misunderstood: "They decided that *The Female Eunuch* told people to [have sex]. Then they decided that *Sex and Destiny* told them to stop. Wrong on both counts."

Further indications of G.'s wide-ranging interests and talents are her short book, *Shakespeare* (1986), a discussion of the playwright's works, philosophy, and life, and a volume on British elections reported to have been completed in 1987 but never published. She also helped to edit an anthology of seventeenth-century women's verse, *Kissing the Rod.*

Her next major work, published in 1989, reveals the most about the woman herself. *Daddy, We Hardly Knew You* is the feminine version of the "journey of the hero—the spiritual quest." The quest is for her father's roots, and the book is both his biography and a record of her journey through her homeland of Australia to find herself through records of her father's past. She is frustrated and diverted many times in her search, and she eventually finds that the father who never loved her enough, who never read a word that she wrote, who never watched her on television, stricken by active duty in World War II with "anxiety neurosis," was in fact a fraud himself, and "Greer" was not even his birth name. Kennedy Fraser of the *New Yorker* opines that "under all the commotion is the voice of a woman who seems to need reassurance that she herself is not a fraud."

In her next major publication, *The Change: Women, Aging and Menopause* (1992), G. returns to the subject of women. In a comprehensive volume on menopause, which she calls "the climacteric," G. presents a multidisciplinary overview of allopathic, traditional, and alternative treatment approaches to menopause and describes physical symptoms and psychological responses as well; she discusses postmenopausal sex and argues that cronelike behavior is expected of middle-aged women, so "you might as well act dreadful." G. believes that women can find freedom, joy, serenity, and power in that stage of life, and she suggests that the middle-aged woman take a cue from her invisibility to society and become invisible to herself, to shuck off her desire to please, her endless obsession with her own skin, lips, breasts, and buttocks, and to "take in the theatre of life, to be agog, spellbound." G. coins the term "anophobia"—"hatred and fear of older women"—and insists that it is central to the mythos of menopause. This book rounds out G.'s outspoken body of work on women.

G. spends her time between her homes near London's Hyde Park, near Cambridge, and in Tuscany, Italy. She lives alone but has frequent visitors, having spent only three weeks living with Paul de Feu, her former husband. De Feu is an English construction worker and an occasional contributor to the underground press who was the first male to pose for a nude centerfold in the British edition of *Cosmopolitan;* he later married the writer Maya Angelou. G. attributes the breakup of her marriage to male chauvinism, though du Feu has published his own account. An accomplished cook and gardener, G. enjoys shopping, especially for her eccentric wardrobe. She continues to write and hopes one day to establish a center for women's literature at Cambridge University.

WORKS: *The Female Eunuch* (1970). *The Obstacle Race: The Fortunes of Women Painters and Their Work* (1979). *Sex and Destiny: The Politics of Human Fertility* (1984). *Shakespeare* (1986). *Daddy, We Hardly Knew You* (1989). *The Change: Women, Aging and Menopause* (1992).

BIBLIOGRAPHY: Angier, N. *NYTBR* (11 October 1992). Boxer, S. *NYTBR* (11 October 1992). Carroll, M. *Book List* (1 September 1992). Ehrnereich, B. *Time* (26 October 1992). Fraser, K. *New Yorker* (16 April 1990). Lewin, T. *NYTBR* (28 January 1990). *Life* (7 May 1971). *LonSunTMag* (3 March 1996). *LonT* (21 September 1995, 3 March 1996, 10 September 1995). *TLS* (13 October 1995, 14 December 1995).

For articles in reference works, see: *Bloomsbury. CA. CB. Feminist. Oxford. ToddBWW.*

Anne-Marie Ray

Augusta Gregory

BORN: 15 March 1852, Roxborough, Ireland.
DIED: 22 May, 1932, Coole Park, Ireland.
DAUGHTER OF: Dudley Persse and Frances Barry.
MARRIED: Sir William Gregory, 1880.

A playwright, director, folklorist, historian, translator, biographer, and cofounder of the Irish national theater, G. was an important figure in the Irish Literary Renaissance of the early twentieth-century. Although born into and married within the Protestant land-owning ascendancy, she developed early in life an interest in the Irish Roman Catholic peasantry, which, along with her goal of literary nationalism, exerted the formative influence on her large and varied oeuvre.

Educated privately and probably first made aware of Irish peasant life by her Irish Catholic nurse, G. was married once, in 1880, to Sir William Gregory, with whom she traveled extensively. He died in 1892. Her literary use of Irish peasants and their dialect formally began with her study of Gaelic in 1894. Excited by the growing interest in folklore, she began visiting the peasants around her estate, listening to and recording their oral poems and stories. W. B. Yeats, whom she met in 1896 and who became a close friend, encouraged her work; in 1902, she published her translations of some of the native Irish epics in *Cuchulain of Muirthemne.* She went on to translate other works from the Gaelic, some of which influenced important Irish writers of the time. In 1920, she published her serious folklore study, *Visions and Beliefs in the West of Ireland,* which earned her the epithet "mother of folklore" from Thomas Wall of the Irish Folklore Commission.

G. later used her study of folklore and dialect to full advantage in her plays. A cofounder of the Abbey Theatre (its name and location were her suggestions), she was one of the theater's most important playwrights, contributing more plays than any other author in the group and serving, with John Millington Synge and Yeats, as one of the three major directors in the theater. She collaborated with both Yeats and Douglas Hyde on several plays, including Yeats's *Cathleen ni Houlihan* (1902). Writing alone, she primarily composed one- and two-act plays and tried her hand at a number of modes: tragic, comic, and farcical. It is generally felt that her true gift was for light-hearted comedies, as her plays *Spreading the News* (1932), *The Jackdaw* (1909), and *The Gaol Gate* (1906) demonstrate. However, her later plays, such as *The Golden Apple* (1916) and *Aristotle's Bellows* (1921), are also interesting experiments combining fantasy and realism in a single, theatrical form. She eventually wrote twenty-seven plays, among which are found peasant plays, folk history plays, and a passion play; she translated one play from Goldoni; and she adapted four from Molière. Like Synge, she generally wrote in the distinctive English of the peasants of western Ireland, a dialect rich in concrete images and metaphors and odd grammatical constructions.

G.'s plays are characterized by her rich gift for dialogue, her ear for the character-revealing saying, and her skill in creating taut dramatic plots from simple stories. She often created comic effects by writing dialogue as two monologues and was talented at raising a story from the particular to the universal. In plays like *Kincora* (1905), *Dervorgilla* (prod. 1907), and *Grania* (1912), she also gave intriguing studies of frustrated women, in the last presenting the Irish counterpart to the Deirdre figure used by Synge and Yeats in their plays.

An advocate of home rule and a defendant of free speech (she defended Synge's *Playboy of the Western World* on opening night, although she did not care for the play), G. also evinced political and national concerns in her own works, such as *Canavans* (1906), *The Wrens* (1914), and *The Deliverer* (1911). Her role in confronting and fighting English censorship of the plays at the Abbey Theatre is only now being fully appreciated. After her son's death in World War I, she turned her talents to children's plays, fairy plays, and a biography of her nephew, Hugh Lane. Her passion play, *The Story Brought by Bridget* (1924), was written following the Irish Civil War and treats the futility of hatred as a motivating force. Her memoirs of the Abbey's history, *Our Irish Theatre* (1913), still serve as an important historical source. G.'s last act at the Abbey was her direction of Sean O'Casey's *The Plough and the Stars.* In her last years, G. lived on at her estate at Coole Park, where she died in 1932.

Long recognized for the help she offered other writers, G. is now being appreciated for her own creative works. In her plays, folklore collections, biographies, memoirs, essays, and translations and in her efforts to establish the Abbey as a successful theater, she was, she said, "a beggar at many doors." But her work left some of the finest one-act plays in English, provided material other writers drew upon for their works, and introduced many English readers to the Irish sagas and native literature. Her "series of enthusiasms," only begun when she was forty-four, has left the Irish nation and all of us with a rich and varied literary heritage.

WORKS: *Arabi and His Household* (1882). *Over the River* (1888). *A Phantom's Pilgrimage, or Home Ruin* (1893). *Ideals in Ireland* (1901). *Cuchulain of Murithemne* (1902). *Poets and Dreamers* (1903). *Gods and Fighting Men* (1904). *Kincora* (1905). *A Book of Saints and Wonders* (1906). *Canavans* (1906). (trans.) *The Doctor in Spite of Himself,* by Molière (1906). *The Gaol Gate* (1906). *Dervorgilla* (1907). (trans.) *The Rogueries of Scapin,* by Molière (1908). (trans.) *Teja,* by H. Sudermann (1908).*The Jackdaw* (1909). *The Kiltartan History Book* (1909). (trans.) *The Miser,* by Molière (1909). *Seven Short Plays* (1909). *The Kiltartan Wonder Book* (1910). *The Kiltartan Molière* (1910). (trans.) *Mirandolina,* by C. Goldoni (1910). *Grania* (1912). *Irish Folk History Plays,* first and second series (1912). *Our Irish Theatre* (1913). *Comedies* (1913). *The Full Moon* (1913). *The Wrens* (1914). *The Golden Apple* (1916). *The Kiltartan Poetry Book* (1919). *Visions and Beliefs in the West of Ireland* (1920). *The Dragon* (1920). *Aristotle's Bellows* (1921). *Hugh Lane's Life and Achievement* (1921). *The Image and Other Plays* (1922). *Three Wonder Plays* (1923). *Mirandolina* (1924). *The Story Brought by Bridget* (1924). (trans.) *The Would-Be Gentleman,* by Molière (1924). *A Case for the Return of Hugh Lane's Picture to Dublin* (1926). *On the Race Course* (1926). *Three Last Plays* (1928). *My First Play: Colman and Guaire* (1930). *Coole* (1931). *Spreading the News* (1932). *Collected Plays I: The Comedies* (1970). *Collected Plays II: The Tragedies and the Tragi-Comedies* (1970). *Collected Plays III: The Wonder and Supernatural Plays* (1970). *Collected Plays IV: The Translations and Adaptations* (1970). *Seventy Years: Being the Autobiography of Lady Gregory* (1976). *Journals,* ed. D. J. Murphy, Vol. I (1978); Vol. II (1987). *Theatre Business: The Correspondence of the First Abbey Theatre Directors: W. B. Yeats, Lady Gregory, and J. M. Synge,* ed. A. Saddlemeyer (1982). *Selected Writings,* ed. L. McDiarmid and M. Waters (1996). *Diaries, 1892–1902,* ed. J. Pethica (1996).

BIBLIOGRAPHY: Adams, H. *PMLA* (1957). Adams, H. *Lady Gregory* (1973). Benilde, M. *Irish Renaissance Annual* (1982). Butler, G. *Eire* (Winter 1987). Clement, W. M. *CLQ* (1978). Coxhead, E. *A Literary Portrait* (1961). Foster, J. *Fictions of the Irish Literary Revival* (1987). Knapp, J. *Macropolitics of Nineteenth-Century Literature: Nationalism, Exoticism, Imperialism* (1991). Kohfeldt, M. *Lady Gregory: The Woman Behind the Irish Renaissance* (1985). Kopper, E. A. *Lady Isabella Persse Gregory* (1970). Kopper, E. A. *Explicator* (Spring 1989). Kopper, E. A. *Lady Gregory: A Review of the Criticism* (1991). Krause, D. *The Profane Book of Irish Comedy* (1982). *Shaw, Lady Gregory, and the Abbey: A Correspondence and a Record,* ed. D. Laurence and N. Grene (1993). Leersen, J. *History and Violence in Anglo-Irish Literature,* ed. J. Duytschaever and G. Lernout (1988).

McHugh, R. *JJQ* (1970). McCurry, J. *ClQ* (March 1992). McDiarmid, L. *PMLA* (1994). Mikhail, E. H. *Lady Gregory: An Annotated Bibliography of Criticism* (1982). Murphy, M. *ClQ* (March 1991). Pihl, L. *IUR* (1991). Pratt, L. *Eire* (Winter 1989). Romine, S. *ArkQ* (Spring 1993). Saddlemyer, A. *In Defense of Lady Gregory, Playwright* (1966). *Lady Gregory: Fifty Years After,* ed. A. Saddlemyer and C. Smythe (1987). Weygandt, C. *Irish Plays and Playwrights* (1913).

For articles in reference works, see: *Bloomsbury. DIL. Europa. Feminist. IDWB. Longman. MBL. MWD. Oxford.*

Other references: Ayling, R. *ShawR* (1961). *Birmingham Post* (16 May 1970). Gregory, A. *Me and Nu: Childhood at Coole* (1966). *Hibernia* (26 June 1970). Howarth, H. *The Irish Writers: 1880–1940* (1959). *MD* (1965). *ShawR* (10 December 1967). Saddlemyer, A., in *Myth and Reality in Irish Literature,* ed. J. Ronsley (1972). Stevenson, M. L. *JRUL* (1978).

Glenda K. McLeod

Constantia Grierson

BORN: 1706 (?), Graiguenamanagh, County Kilkenny, Ireland.
DIED: 2 December 1732 (?), Dublin, Ireland.
DAUGHTER OF: Mr. and Mrs. Crawley(?) or Phillips(?).
MARRIED: George Grierson, 1726 (?).

G. was born into a poor family but seems to have been singled out at an early age as a possible genius. She later wrote that she "had received some little instruction from the minister of the parish, when she could spare time from her needlework, to which she was closely kept by her mother." At the age of eighteen, she was apprenticed to Laetitia Pilkington's father to learn midwifery; she had probably become acquainted with Pilkington in 1721. The dates surrounding her birth and early life are in dispute: Her birth is variously given as 1704, 1705 and 1706; the date of her death is usually agreed as 1732 or 1733. There are also questions about her erudition. Pilkington described her prodigious learning: "She was Mistress of Hebrew, Greek, Latin and French and understood the Mathematics as well as most men. . . ." In their preface to *Poems by Eminent Ladies* (1755), George Colman and Bonnell Thornton described her as "a most excellent scholar, not only in Greek and Roman literature, but in history, divinity, philosophy and mathematics." However, a modern scholar, A. C. Elias, argues that Laetitia Pilkington's claims for her friend must be mitigated by her own self-admitted ignorance of all foreign and classical languages. He also points out that Mary Glanville doubted the Hebrew and that Mary Barber, describing G.'s learning, omitted mention of Hebrew and French but added history, divinity and philosophy. G. translated Latin classics that were published by her husband, who was the king's printer in Ireland: *Virgil* in 1724, *Terence* in 1727, and *Tacitus* in 1730. Edward Harwood, the classical bibliographer, said about her *Tacitus:* "I have read it twice through, and it is one of the best edited books ever delivered to the world. Mrs Grier, who was a lady possessed of singular erudition, and had an elegance of taste and solidity of judgment which justly rendered her one of the wonderful, as well as amiable of her sex."

Like Pilkington and Barber (with whom she is often compared), G. moved in the Dublin literary circle of Jonathan Swift, Thomas Sheridan, and Patrick Delaney. She had two sons, one of whom died young; the other became the king's printer in 1753–55, was a friend of Samuel Johnson, and died at the age of twenty-seven.

Few of her poems have survived. Three appear in Pilkington's *Memoirs* (1748–54) (although the accuracy of these may be questioned since she is recalling them after some two decades); and six were published in Barber's *Poems on Several Occasions* (1734). Seven poems praising friends are collected in Colman and Thornton's *Poems by Eminent Ladies* (1755). One poem, "The Art of Printing," appears in C. H. Wilson's compilation of writings by Henry Brooke from 1804. More recently, A. C. Elias has discovered a manuscript book that results in a virtual doubling of her extant poems; the poems in this manuscript book show three of the six G. poems in *Poems on Several Occasions* and the poem on her baby son's death "Unhappy Child to early Sorrows born."

Little has been written about G.'s poetry since the majority of her poems tend to be polished examples of occasional polite verse, often addressed to a friend or acquaintance. One of her best known poems, "To the Hon. Mrs. Percival on her desisting from the Bermucan Project," makes a brief reference to the state of Ireland: "Let others still near Albion's court reside, / Who sacrifice their country to their pride, [13–14] / Our gold may flow to Albion with each tide-, [23]." Her other well-known poem ("On the Art of Printing") has been widely anthologized over the years (but not, it seems, in the twentieth century).

G., together with Barber and Pilkington, represent an important group of poets from the early eighteenth century who have, until recently, been ignored at the expense of the "major" (and male) poets.

WORKS: (trans.) *Virgil* (1724). (trans.) *Terence* (1727). (trans.) *Tacitus* (1730). Barber, M. *Poems on Several Occasions* (1734). Pilkington, L. *The Memoirs of Mrs Laetitia Pilkington 1712–50. Written by Herself* (1748–54, rpt. 1928). *Poems by Eminent Ladies,* ed. G. Colman and B. Thornton (1755, rev. 1780). *The Art of Printing* (n.d., 1732?), in Brooke, H. *Brookiana,* ed. C. H. Wilson (1804). *Eighteenth-Century Women Poets,* ed. R. Lonsdale (1989). *The Poetry of Laetitia Pilkington (1712–1750) and Constantia Grierson (1706–1733),* ed. B. Tucker (1996).

BIBLIOGRAPHY: Doody, M. *YES* (1988). Elias, A. C. *SStud* (1987). Tucker, B. *ISRev* (1994).Tucker, B., ed. and intro. *The Poetry of Laetitia Pilkington and Constantia Grierson* (1996).

For articles in reference works, see: *Allibone. Ballard. DNB. Feminist. OCIL. Oxford. ToddBWW. ToddDBA. Unveiling Treasures,* ed. A. O. Weekes (1993).

Bernard Tucker

Griffin, V. G.: See *Cory, Victoria*

Elizabeth Griffith

BORN: 11 October 1727, Dublin, Ireland.
DIED: 5 January 1793, Millicent, County Kildare, Ireland.
DAUGHTER OF: Thomas Griffith and Jane Foxcroft Griffith.
MARRIED: Richard Griffith, 1752.
WROTE UNDER: Frances; Mrs. Elizabeth Griffith; Mrs. Elizabeth Griffiths.

A playwright and novelist, G. wrote primarily for the support of her family. She married Richard Griffith secretly in 1752 after guiding him toward marriage for six years (he was no relation). Over the next three years, G. appeared on the stage in Dublin and London. She began to write plays in 1765 and in 1769 succeeded in attracting the attention of David Garrick, who successfully produced two of her plays and to whom she dedicated her longest work, *The Morality of Shakespeare's Drama Illustrated* (1775). From 1764, G. lived in London while her husband spent much time in Ireland. After many years of marriage, her husband seduced a wealthy young woman with whom he lived until his death. G. died in 1793 at her son Richard's house in County Kildare.

G.'s original plays and translations enjoyed success in her day, but none have been produced subsequently. Although they lack originality, all show her characteristic delicacy of feeling. She believed that gentleness and magnanimity are the best equipment for life and that marriage should be founded upon love and esteem. *The School for Rakes* (1769; translated, at Garrick's suggestion, from Beaumarchais's *Eugénie*) shows G.'s characteristic delicacy. Although the heroine has already been tricked into a sham marriage by the hero, the couple refuse a forced marriage because they love each other. In *The Platonic Wife* (1765; adapted from Marmontel's *L'Heureux Divorce*), the falsely suspected wife is virtuous; in *A Wife in the Right* (1772), the husband proves he loves only his wife; in *The Times* (1780; adapted from Goldoni's *Berry Bienfaisant*), the wife's extravagance is cured when she realizes the damage it has done her husband.

G.'s first publication was *A Series of Genuine Letters Between Henry and Frances* (1757), a selection from her correspondence with her husband before their marriage. Though overly sentimental, it is perceptive on books, men, and manners. Encouraged by the moderate success of this production, the couple published later correspondence in four more volumes. G. also wrote three epistolary novels, each of which links several slightly related stories to a main plot. In *The Delicate Distress* (1769), a companion novel to her husband's *The Gordian Knot* (1770), the husband's former mistress almost recaptures him, but his wife's selfless nursing of him through a fever, even after she knows of his divided affections, makes him realize his love for her. *The History of Lady Barton* (1771) and *The Story of Lady Juliana Harley* (1776), less well constructed and more melodramatic, revolve around forced and loveless marriages. G. also edited *A Collection of Novels* (1777), by Aphra Behn, Eliza Haywood, and Penelope Aubin, and *Novellettes* (1780), which included thirteen of her stories. Her last work, *Essays Addressed to Young Married Women* (1782), contains thoughts on the education of the young, affection for a husband, and the wife's necessary fortitude, charity, economy, and accomplishments.

Although marred by excessive sensibility as well as loose structure and derivative plotting, G.'s work offers a broad and generous moral perspective, common sense, and distinctive and humorously drawn characters.

WORKS: *A Series of Genuine Letters Between Henry and Frances* (1757). (trans.) *Memoirs of Ninon de l'Enclos* (1761). *Amana: A Dramatic Poem* (1764). *The Platonic Wife* (adapted from J.-F. Marmontel; 1765). *The Double Mistake* (1766). (trans.) *The School for Rakes,* by P.-A. Beaumarchais (1769). *The Delicate Distress* (1769). (trans.) *Memoirs, Anecdotes, and Characters of the Court of Lewis [sic] XIV,* by Marie M. de V. Caylus (1770). (trans.) *The Shipwreck and Adventures of Monsieur Pierre Viaud* (1771). *The History of Lady Barton* (1771). *A Wife in the Right* (1772). (trans.) *The Fatal Effects of Inconstancy: or, Letters of the Marchioness de Syrce, the Count of Mirbeele [sic: Mirbelle] and Others,* by C. J. Dorat (1774). *The Morality of Shakespeare's Drama Illustrated* (1775). *The Story of Lady Juliana Harley* (1776). (trans.) *The Barber of Seville,* by P.-A. Beaumarchais (1776). (trans.) *A Letter from Monsieur Desenfans to Mrs. Montague* (1777). (trans.) *The Princess of Cleves,* by Segrais [Mme. M. de la Fayette] (1777). (trans.) *Zayde, A Spanish History,* by Segrais [Mme. M. de la Fayette] (1780). *The Times* (adapted from C. Goldoni, 1780). *Essays Addressed to Young Married Women* (1782).

BIBLIOGRAPHY: MacCarthy, B. G. *Later Women Novelists, 1744–1818* (1947). Whitmore, C. H. *Women's Work in English Fiction* (1910).

For articles in reference works, see: *BDA. Chalmers. DNB. Feminist. Oxford. ToddBWW.*

Kate Browder

Sarah Lynes Grubb

BORN: 13 April 1773, Wapping, London.
DIED: 16 March 1842, Sudbury, Suffolk.
DAUGHTER OF: Mason Lynes and Hannah Holdway Lynes.
MARRIED: John Grubb, 1803.

An active minister in the Society of Friends for more than fifty years, including several stints as an itinerant evangelist, G. had a wide acquaintance all over the British Isles. After her death, an autobiographical sketch and some 566 of her letters were edited for publication by two of her surviving children. Some sermons and addresses also survive.

She grew up as one of seven children in a devout Quaker home. Her father, a craftsman in the shipbuilding trade, died when she was about six. Two years later, she began attending the Friends' school in Clerkenwell. At fourteen, she left home to live as a nanny with Sarah Pim Grubb, a widow with four young children, who was carrying on her husband's milling business in the vicinity of Clonmel, Ireland, and whose sister-in-law, the minister and writer Sarah Tuke Grubb, was also active in the Clonmel meeting.

Already Sally Lynes, as she was called, had begun to feel a call to ministry. She first spoke in meeting when she was seventeen; "the gift grew," she states; and by the age of nineteen she was speaking in Cork, Dublin, and other Irish towns. Here, too, she began open-air preaching in markets and prison visiting, practices that were distinctive aspects of her ministry for the next ten years, a period spent mostly in traveling to various towns in England, Scotland, and Wales. She preached at the Pump Room in Bath, hired the theater in Yarmouth for a public meeting, had a confrontation with the mayor in Leicester, and interrupted a Christmas service in St. Paul's Cathedral. In 1797, she left Mrs. Grubb's service and became a member of Gracechurch Street Meeting, London, which supported her itinerant ministry. When not traveling, she lived with her mother, helped "in keeping school, and [took] in a little needlework."

In 1803, she accepted a proposal of marriage from her employer's husband's cousin, John Grubb, who had waited for six years because he recognized her call to a traveling ministry. He too was a Friends minister, as well as having a grocery business. They settled in Clonmel, but eight months after the birth of their first child they left together for an itinerant ministry in England and Scotland that occupied most of early 1808. Records for the next ten years are spotty, but at least from 1812 through 1816 she was on the road much of the time, leaving John at home. In 1818, she persuaded him to sell his business and move permanently to England, where they continued their labor as leaders in the Society of Friends. John's eyesight started to fail in about 1834 and he died in May 1841; she, though now "feeble," nevertheless continued to minister in Ireland and across southern England until January 1842, when her final illness began.

G. was active in the society's annual convention—the London Yearly Meeting—across more than forty years. Her regular theme was warning against what she regarded as the drift of Quakerism from its earliest principles. In the factional strife of the 1820s and 1830s, she sided with the Quietists against those who, in her view, would replace individual spiritual inspiration with "head-knowledge" and a dogmatic, rationalized orthodoxy based on the authority of Scripture. At the 1837 Yearly Meeting, she bitterly opposed the credentialing of Joseph Gurney for ministry in America.

Contemporary accounts allow no simple characterization of her style. She could preach extemporaneously for more than two hours nonstop, with "elegance of language" and "persuasive energy" as well as "sweet humility." Her address (by permission) to a men's meeting was described by one listener as "intimidatory and denunciatory," but others on different occasions found her "strengthening, consoling, and deeply instructive," noting her "remarkably emphatic and deliberate" delivery and the "weightiness" of "her words, often so few in number"; she herself claimed to "dread . . . a *wordy* ministry . . . interrupting the silence of our assemblies by *words without life.*" A schoolgirl remembered her as "like some weird prophetess, very forbidding and gaunt, who even eschewed a white lining to her Friends' bonnet." In private, she was "highly humorous."

Her published *Letters* include letters to her children, numerous letters of spiritual counsel and comfort, some travel descriptions and social observation, and much on her ministry and spiritual struggles ("deep wading"). One letter tells of her vision for world unity, and many express great concern for the state of Quakerism. References to God are often by circumlocution; "Heavenly Parent" is a favorite. The frequent embedding of Scripture quotations is a mark of her style; also prominent are proverbs and references to her reading—John Woolman, William Cowper, and various seventeenth-century religious authors (she studied French in order to read Fénelon and Madame Guyon in the original).

The autobiography incorporates some extracts from her journals, but most of these she had destroyed, according to her editors, and in the latter half of her life she did not keep a journal.

WORKS: *Letter to Henry Hull,* 1834 (single sheet, c. 1845). *Extracts from Memoranda by the late Sarah (Lynes) Grubb* (single sheet, 184–?). Selected sermons and letters, in *The British Friend* (1844, 1845) and *The Friend* (1845, 1848). *A Selection from the Letters of the Late Sarah Grubb (formerly Sarah Lynes),* ed. H. Grubb and J. Grubb (1848; abridged 1864, with more letters added).

BIBLIOGRAPHY: Andreasen, T. *The Famine: or, The State of the Society of Friends at the Present Day* (1890). (Anon.) *A Brief Account of the Life and Religious Labours of Sarah Grubb (formerly Sarah Lynes)* (extracts from the 1848 *Letters,* with commentary, 1863). Beck, W., et al. *Biographical Catalogue [of] the London Friends' Institute* (1888). *The British Friend* (1843, 1852). Rickman, R. *Private Testimony Concerning Sarah Grubb, late of Sudbury* (single sheet, 1844). Society of Friends. *Testimonies concerning Deceased Ministers* (1843). Walton, J. *Brief Biographies of Some Members of the Society of Friends,* enlarged ed. (190–?).

For articles in reference works, see: *British Library Catalog* (conflated with Sarah Tuke Grubb). Davis, G. and B. A. Joyce. *Personal Writings by Women to 1900: A Bibliography of American and British Writers* (1989). Smith, J. *Descriptive Catalogue of Friends' Books* (1867).

Other references: *Annual Monitor* (1844). Cockin, R., et al. *Pen Pictures of London Yearly Meeting 1789–1833* (1929–30). Friends Historical Library of Swarthmore College. *Catalog of the Book and Serial Collections* (1982). Grubb, G. W. *The Grubbs of Tipperary* (1972). Grubb, J. *Extracts from the Letters of John Grubb,* ed. J. F. Carroll and O. C. Goodbody (1966). Hewitt, N. *Witnesses for Change: Quaker Women over Three Centuries,* ed. E. P. Brown and S. M. Stuard (1989). Hodgson, W. *The Society of Friends in the Nineteenth Century* (1875). Isichei, E. *Victorian Quakers* (1970). Jones, R. M. *The Later Periods of Quakerism* (1921). *Journal of the Friends Historical Society* (1917–21, 1923, 1926, 1930, 1950, 1954, 1988). *London Yearly Meeting during 250 Years* (1919). Swift, D. E. *Joseph John Gurney* (1962).

Charles A. Huttar

Sarah Tuke Grubb

BORN: 20 June 1756, York.
DIED: 8 December 1790, Cork, Ireland.
DAUGHTER OF: William Tuke and Elizabeth Tuke.
MARRIED: Robert Grubb, 1782.

G.'s father and stepmother, William and Esther (her mother Elizabeth having died before G. was five), were leaders in the Quaker community in York and provided her a "watchful and religious education." When John Woolman's 1772 tour of England brought him, already stricken with smallpox, to York, Esther Tuke was his chief nurse, assisted by the sixteen-year-old G., who received his dying blessing. Spiritual sensitivity is evident in her earliest surviving letters, dating from this time.

At the age of twenty-two, she began a career in ministry, would involve extensive traveling over the next twelve years to visit Quaker congregations in Britain and like-minded communities on the Continent, encouraging the faithful and arousing the negligent. From April 1780 to March 1781, she made several such trips throughout northern England, sometimes accompanied by her stepmother and sometimes by a cousin, Tabitha Hoylake. In April 1782, she married Robert Grubb; in contemporary accounts, the name often used for her is Sarah R[obert]. Grubb. Marriage did not interrupt her career, however. Two weeks later, with Mary Proud as companion, she began a journey in Scotland and Cumberland that lasted some ten weeks. During this time, Robert returned briefly to Ireland, word having come of his father's death, and in November they visited Ireland together. For five years, they lived in Foston, a village near York, and G. continued her traveling ministry with visits in Yorkshire, Lincolnshire, Norfolk, most of the western counties, Wales, and Ulster. The latter journey was marked by storm, seasickness, and stench, but what she had heard (from Woolman?) about the suffering on slave ships put her own "small trials" in perspective. She attended London Yearly Meeting and served at least twice as clerk for the women's sessions running concurrently with the men's. When not traveling, G. devoted much energy to education. She assisted in the girls' school in York that her father had founded and that Esther Tuke directed; there and at nearby Ackworth School, she helped to shape the regulations; and in Clonmel, Ireland, she founded (with her husband) a finishing school for girls, Suir Island boarding school, and served as its headmistress.

In 1787, the Grubbs moved to Robert's home town of Clonmel, County Tipperary. From February to August 1788, with five other Friends, they visited sister churches in the Low Countries, the Rhineland, Switzerland, and southern France, covering 2,500 miles, and in 1790 they made a similar trip to a community in northern Germany. G. and three others in October sent a joint letter to King Leopold II of Hungary on behalf of the Quietists in that part of Europe. Late in 1790, she died unexpectedly, aged thirty-four. She was eulogized for "a solid and weighty spirit," judgment and discernment beyond her years, and humility; many, it was said, would remember her as "a nursing Mother" in the faith.

Extracts from her journals and from more than 100 letters, set in an anonymous and sketchy biographical framework, were published in 1792 as *Some Account of the Life and Religious Labours of Sarah Grubb,* with three writings on education and 163 more letters appended. By 1796, there were four more editions, including two in American cities (Wilmington, Delaware, and Trenton, New Jersey); it was reprinted in Belfast in 1837 and, without the supplementary letters, in Philadelphia in 1848. The tract on education, *Observations* [alternatively, *Remarks*] *on Christian Discipline,* was reprinted many times separately, at least until 1842, not always with attribution.

She wrote a clear prose, devoted largely (in the extracts that have been preserved) to narrating her travels and encounters, but also sometimes playful, sometimes intense in its introspection and spiritual longing, often appropriating biblical phraseology. She also wrote some verse, including two pieces in the appendix of the *Life and Labours.* Her work in hymnlike meters is little better than doggerel, but a sixty-three-line poem in blank verse beginning "Though clothed now with ease" is a reflective and moving account of the anguish and consolation found in her spiritual pilgrimage.

WORKS: Metrical version of the Twenty-third Psalm (single sheet, c. 1786, rpt. 1848). *A Serious Meditation: or, A Christian's Duty Fully Set Forth* (single sheet, c. 1790; titles vary—the first four words are sometimes omitted, "briefly" may be substituted for "fully," and "stated" may be substituted for "set forth"). *Some Account of the Life and Religious Labours of Sarah Grubb. With an Appendix containing an Account of the Schools at Ackworth and York, Observations on Christian Discipline, and Extracts from Many of Her Letters* (1792; many copies with alternate title *Journal* on the binding; rpt. in *Friends' Library,* 1848 [*Life and Observations* only]). *Some Remarks on Christian Discipline, as It Respects the Education of Youth* (extract from the above, 1795; rpt. in part in A. Frank, *Brief Remarks on an important Subject,* 1820, together with J. Woolman's "On Schools"). *A Letter to the Monthly Meeting of Old Meldrum, Scotland* (1866; rpt. from the *Journal*).

BIBLIOGRAPHY: Beck, W., et al. *Biographical Catalogue [of] the London Friends' Institute* (1888). Cockin, R., et al. *Pen Pictures of London Yearly Meeting 1789–1833* (1929). Society of Friends. *Testimonies Concerning Ministers* (1791).

For articles in reference works, see: *Allibone. British Library Catalog* (conflated with Sarah Lynes Grubb). Davis, G. and B. A. Joyce. *Personal Writings by Women to 1900: A Bibliography of American and British Writers* (1989). Matthews, W. *British Diaries: An Annotated Bibliography* (1950). Smith, J. *Descriptive Catalogue of Friends' Books* (1867).

Other references: Bevan, *J. G. Piety Promoted . . . the Tenth Part* (1810). Cadbury, H. J. *John Woolman in England* (1931). *The Life of Mary Dudley, including . . . Extracts from her Letters,* ed. E. Dudley (1825). Frank, A. *Brief Remarks on an Important Subject* (1820). Friends Historical Library of Swarthmore College. *Catalog of the Book and Serial Collections* (1982). Grubb, G. W.

The Grubbs of Tipperary (1972). Grubb, I. *Quakers in Ireland 1654–1900* (1927). Grubb, S. L. *A Selection from the Letters* (1848). Hill, R. *Letters of Doctor Richard Hill and His Children* (1854). Jones, R. M. *The Later Periods of Quakerism* (1921). *Journal of the Friends Historical Society* (1905, 1910, 1915, 1916, 1918, 1919, 1928, 1955, 1958, 1964). *London Yearly Meeting during 250 Years* (1919). Moulton, P., intro. to *Journal and Major Essays of John Woolman*, ed. P. Moulton (1971). Tylor, C. *The Camisards* (1893). Williams, C. *New Christian Year* (1941).

Charles A. Huttar

Elizabeth Grymeston or Grimston

BORN: Before 1563, North Erpingham, Norfolk.
DIED: 1603, London(?).
DAUGHTER OF: Martin and Margaret Flint Bernye.
MARRIED: Christopher Grymeston or Grimston, 1584.

A recusant Roman Catholic (i.e., an English Catholic who refused to attend Church of England services and therefore was guilty of a statutory offense), G. published only one work, *Miscelanea. Meditations. Memoratives.* A series of short essays interspersed with poetry, this work follows the Boethian tradition of theodicy, borrowing directly from the work of another Norfolk recusant, Robert Southwell (1561–95), as well as from *Englands Parnassus* (1600). Published posthumously, the work had four editions between 1604 and 1618 [?]; the later editions have six additional chapters of meditation and prayer on such subjects as the cross, murder, and the role of judges. The earlier editions, which may come closer to the author's intention in their structure, begin with a fascinating letter from G. to her son, Bernays Grymeston, that explains the circumstances of composition and gives personal advice. This opening letter is followed by chapters that consider death, affliction, and God's role in human affairs; other chapters are interior monologues by such characters as Dives and Heraclitus. Chapters XI–XIII offer religious poetry by others with G.'s meditations on their verse. The final chapter is a collection of moral maxims.

The literary quality of G.'s work does not lie in its originality, for, like others who wrote meditative literature, she borrows extensively, practicing the tradition of *imitatio*. Instead, its strength is the vivid development she gave to the ideas of others and the emotional intensity of her style. The work moves us because of G.'s situation. Her life was difficult; not only was she persecuted as a recusant, she also watched eight of her nine children die and fought bitterly with her mother. Writing to Bernays from her sickbed, G. knew she was dying and believed that her mother's "undeserved wrath so virulent" had fatally aggravated the consumption that was killing her. Furthermore, she thought that her mother had tried repeatedly to murder her husband, Christopher.

Despite her troubles, G. writes with good sense, affection, and humor, urging Bernays to marry wisely and live temperately. In the essays that follow the letter, she turns to her own fate and that of all humans, regarding pain and affliction without discouragement and death without fear. Given her suffering and the nearness of her end, her sincerity and self-possession work with her rhetorical skills to make *Miscelanea. Meditations. Memoratives* a fine example of meditation literature.

WORKS: *Miscelanea. Meditations. Memoratives.* (1604, STC 12407).

BIBLIOGRAPHY: Fletcher, B. Y. and C. W Sizemore. *The Library Chronicle* (1981). Hughey, R. and P. Hereford. *The Library* (1934–35). Mahl, R. and H. Koon. *The Female Spectator* (1977).

For articles in reference works, see: *Bloomsbury. DNB. Feminist. Oxford. ToddBWW.*

Fran Teague

Charlotte E. B. Guest

BORN: 19 May 1812, Uffington House, Lincolnshire.
DIED: 15 January 1895, Canford Manor, Dorset.
DAUGHTER OF: Albemarle Bertie, ninth Earl of Lindsey, and Charlotte Layard.
MARRIED: Sir Josiah John Guest, 1833; Charles Schreiber, 1855.
WROTE UNDER: Lady Charlotte Guest; Lady Charlotte E. Guest; Lady Charlotte Elizabeth (Bertie) Guest; Lady Charlotte Schreiber; Lady Charlotte Elizabeth Schreiber.

G. is usually remembered for her scholarly, annotated translation of *Mabinogion* into English. An avid collector of china, fans, and playing cards, she made extensive contributions from her collections to the holdings of the Victoria and Albert Museum and to the British Museum. She produced several catalogues containing detailed descriptions of her collections. G. also kept a journal from 1822 until 1891 in which she recorded events in her daily life along with her impressions of contemporary political, social, and economic issues.

G. recorded that her childhood was an unhappy one due to the death of her father in 1818 and her mother's remarriage in 1821 to her tyrannical cousin, the Reverend Peter William Pegus. It was only after G.'s marriage in 1833 to the wealthy ironmaster Josiah Guest, by whom she had ten children, that she had the freedom to indulge her varied interests. She studied ancient and modern European and Middle Eastern languages, taking an especial interest in Welsh and translating the *Mabinogion* from 1838 until 1846. Her three-volume edition, with notes and the original Welsh text, was published in 1849, and a second abridged edition, which omitted the Welsh text, appeared in 1877. In 1881, she published *The Boy's Mabinogion; Being the Earliest Welsh Tales of King Arthur in the Famous Red Book of Hergest*.

Besides languages, G. studied music and art. She was an accomplished pianist, harpist, and etcher on copper plate. Her interest in Welsh culture led her to work on various projects for the improvement of the living conditions of Welsh workers, including the founding of several schools for the poor. She also took an active part in the administrative affairs of her husband's ironworks at Dowlais in Wales, acting as his private secretary and completely taking over the management of the works upon his death in 1852.

In 1855, she married Charles Schreiber, a member of Parliament for Cheltenham (Surrey) and Poole (Dorset). It was during her second marriage that she became less actively involved with business and reform activities, although she gave much support to the Turkish Compassionate Fund between 1877 and 1880, the period in which her son-in-law, Sir Austen Henry Layard, was ambassador to Turkey. Her chief interest throughout the second half of her life was her art collections, and it was in 1865 that she began to collect china, frequently traveling throughout Europe in search of rare pieces. She later developed an interest in collecting playing cards and fans.

It was upon the death of her second husband in 1884 that she presented her collection of English china and Battersea enamels in his memory to the South Kensington Museum, which is now the Victoria and Albert Museum. She catalogued the 2,000 pieces in the Schreiber collection in the same year, and her catalogue was printed in 1885. She also published two folio volumes entitled *Fans and Fan Leaves Collected and Described by Lady Charlotte Schreiber.* The first volume was published in 1888, contains 161 illustrations, and describes her English fans. The second volume appeared in 1890, contains 153 illustrations, and describes her foreign fans. She presented her collection to the British Museum in 1891, the same year she was presented with the freedom or franchise of the Fanmakers' Company. A catalogue of her fan collection was printed in 1893. In 1892, she published the first volume of her *Playing Cards of Various Ages and Countries,* the same year in which she received the honorary freedom of the Company of Makers of Playing Cards. Her first volume presents English, Scottish, Dutch, and Flemish cards, her second volume (1893) French and German cards, her third volume (1895) Swiss and Swedish cards. She grew blind during her work on the volumes of fans and playing cards and died on 15 January 1895, leaving to the British Museum those cards in her collection for which the museum did not already have specimens.

Lady Charlotte Schreiber's Journals: Confidences of a Collector of Ceramics & Antiques Throughout Britain, France, Holland, Belgium, Spain, Portugal, Turkey, Austria and Germany from the Year 1869 to 1885 was edited by her son, Montague J. Guest, and published in 1911 in two volumes that contain more than 100 illustrative plates of objects from her collections. *Lady Charlotte Guest: Extracts from Her Journal, 1833–1852* and *Lady Charlotte Schreiber: Extracts from Her Journal 1853–1891* were published in 1950 and 1952, respectively, by the Earl of Bessborough. Together, her published entries form a valuable picture of life in Victorian England, covering everything from workers' strikes to political economy to Whig controversies to society dinner parties to social mores. G.'s style is often florid and sentimental, as was typical of her age. The entry she made on the day of her wedding to Josiah Guest begins, "A Journal! Again dare I commence a journal, and with what hope of continuing it?" Yet the incidents she recorded reveal an energetic personality consisting of equal parts romantic emotionalism and hard-headed business practicality. Upon concluding business affairs left unresolved by the death of her first husband, she wrote that she clasped his marble bust for some minutes and kissed its cold lips. A few months later she quelled a pending workers' strike at Dowlais.

It is not for her political or business activities that G. is remembered, however, or for her immense journal, but for her work as a translator and collector. Although inaccuracies have been pointed out in her translation, such as her incorrect use of *mabinogion* as the plural of *mabinogi,* and her incorrect application of the term to the entire contents of the Red Book of Hergest, contemporary scholars still refer to her work. Her collections are still being held in the Victoria and Albert Museum and in the British Museum.

WORKS: *The Mabinogion: From the Llyfr Coch o Hergest, and Other Ancient Welsh Manuscripts, with an English Translation and Notes, by Lady Charlotte E. Guest,* 3 vols. (1849). *The Boy's Mabinogion: Being the Earliest Welsh Tales of King Arthur in the Famous Red Book of Hergest* (1881). *Catalogue of English Porcelain, Earthenware, Enamels, &., Collected and Described by Charles Schreiber, Esq., M.P., and the Lady Charlotte Elizabeth Schreiber, and Presented to the South Kensington Museum in 1884* (1885). *Fans and Fan Leaves Collected and Described by Lady Charlotte Schreiber,* 2 vols. (1888–90). *Playing Cards of Various Ages and Countries, Selected from the Collection of Lady Charlotte Schreiber,* 3 vols. (1892–95). *Lady Charlotte Schreiber's Journals: Confidences of a Collector of Ceramics and Antiques Throughout Britain, France, Holland, Belgium, Spain, Portugal, Turkey, Austria & Germany from the Year 1869 to 1885,* 2 vols., ed. M. J. Guest (1911). *Lady Charlotte Guest: Extracts from Her Journal, 1833–1852,* ed. the Earl of Bessborough (1950). *Lady Charlotte Schreiber: Extracts from Her Journal, 1853–1891,* ed. the Earl of Bessborough (1952).

BIBLIOGRAPHY: *The Mabinogion,* trans. G. Jones and T. Jones (1974).

For articles in reference works, see: *DNB.*

Karen Michalson
(updated by Natalie Joy Woodall)

Guggenberger, Louisa S.: See *Bevington, Louisa Sarah*

Susannah Minifie Gunning

BORN: 1740, Fairwater, Somersetshire.
DIED: 28 August 1800, London.
DAUGHTER OF: the Reverend James Minifie.
MARRIED: Captain, later Lieutenant-General, John Gunning, 1768.
WROTE UNDER: Mrs. Gunning; Miss Minifie.

The "Miss Minifies" (G. and her sister, Margaret) were well known as the authors of four novels, all published before G.'s marriage in 1768. With the initiative that marks G.'s entire career, she and her sister arranged for their first effort, *The Histories of Lady Frances S— and Lady Caroline S—*, to be published by subscription in 1763. Subsequent collaborations, *Family Pictures* (1764), *The Picture* (1766), and *The Cottage* (1769), were printed by commercial publishers. These early novels were poorly constructed, markedly sentimental and conventional in plot. G. published her first independent work, *Barford Abbey* (1768), the year of her marriage to Captain John Gunning, and its improvement over the earlier works may derive from autobiographic content.

It is tempting to compare Miss Warley's marriage to Lord Darcey in *Barford Abbey* with G.'s marriage to the son of a viscount's daughter. The epistolary story begins when Miss Warley's "mother" dies, leaving her the ward of Lady Mary, whose directions she receives from a German "spaw." During a visit to Lord and Lady Powis, the heroine attracts the attentions of Lord Darcey, their ward, whom Lord Powis is determined to marry prudently. The opposition between love and patrilineal prudence is resolved when Lord Powis's estranged son returns; the father/guardian blesses both the Lord Darcey-Miss Warley match and his son's clandestine marriage. But before the denouement can be settled, a set of contradictions must be resolved. Miss Warley, still in doubt about Lord Darcey's intentions, leaves to meet Lady Mary in France and is thought to have been lost in a shipwreck. Meanwhile, a birth mystery unravels by which she is discovered to be Mr. and Mrs. Powis's daughter, heiress to Lord and Lady Powis. Miss Warley found safe and restored to her family, and the novel concludes in marriage.

After the publication of *The Cottage* (1769), *The Hermit* (1770), and a second edition of *Barford Abbey* in 1771, it was 1783 before G. published her next novel, *Coombe Wood*. Read biographically, the novel bears evidence of G.'s own marital difficulties, for marriage, rather than an ideal denouement, has become a target for satire.

The scandal for which the Gunnings became famous began when their daughter Elizabeth was accused of forging a letter that forwarded her own schemes of marriage with her cousin, the Marquis of Lorne. G.'s response was a public letter, in 1791, to the marquis's father denying her daughter's guilt. With societal approval, General Gunning ejected his wife and daughter, only to become embroiled in his own scandal when he was fined £5,000 for "criminal conversation" with his tailor's wife. His response was also literary, his *Apology* (1792)—written in exile from Naples—boasting of many conquests. Five years later, however, a letter from Elizabeth prompted him to change his will, leaving his £8,000 estate to her and her mother.

For the next several years, G. turned these family details to good use in her fiction. The novels *Anecdotes of the Delborough Family* (1792) and *Memoirs of Mary* (1793) and the poem *Virginius and Virginia* (1792) are particularly susceptible of biographic interpretation. *Memoirs of Mary*, probably the best of G.'s novels, had achieved a third edition by 1794.

Much like Fanny Burney's *Evelina*, *Memoirs of Mary* begins with a history of the heroine's early life as her grandmother's ward on a country estate. An interpolated tale explains her parents' courtship and death; after a secret marriage, Mary's father served briefly with a regiment in America. Mary's social life begins when she is sent to live with the Duke and the Duchess of Cleveland. A cousin who envies her inheritance connives against Mary's impending marriage with Henry Lexington, nephew and heir of the Duke of Cleveland. Eventually, the plot resolves in Mary's favor, but not before G. has exposed the dissipations of fashionable life.

The novel combines biographical allusions and elements of gothic. G.'s canvas foregrounds the courtship story, it is true, yet the attendant family squabbles and plottings form a much broader backdrop than the typical woman's novel of the period. For analogues, one must look back to Samuel Richardson or forward to Maria Edgeworth and Jane Austen. Another stroke of originality is Mary's suitor, who not only is developed more fully than the usual ancillary hero but is allowed to be witty. *Memoirs of Mary*, a cleverly written epistolary novel that relieves the stasis of letters with idiomatic expressions and clever plotting, is one of the better minor novels of its period.

In 1796, G. turned away from the family scandal to write *Delves*, a picaresque tale set in Wales, and *The Forester*, an "adaptation" from the French. With *Love at First Sight* (1797) and *Fashionable Involvements* (1800), G. returned to the novel, but these late efforts were less successful, hackneyed tales of manners. At her death in 1800, G. left unfinished *The Heir Apparent* (1802), which her daughter Elizabeth (later Plunkett) revised, augmented, and published.

WORKS: *The Histories of Lady Frances S— and Lady Caroline S—* (1763). *Family Pictures* (1764). *The Picture* (1766). *Barford Abbey* (1768). *The Cottage* (1769). *The Hermit* (1770). *Coombe Wood* (1783). *A Letter from Mrs. Gunning, addressed to . . . the Duke of Argyll* (1791). *Anecdotes of the Delborough Family* (1792). *Virginius and Virginia* (1792). *Memoirs of Mary* (1793). *Delves* (1796). *The Foresters* (1796). *Love at First Sight* (1797). *Fashionable Involvements* (1800). (completed by E. Gunning) *The Heir Apparent* (1802).

BIBLIOGRAPHY: Todd, J. *SVEC* (1983). Todd, J. *The Sign of Angellica* (1989).

For articles in reference works, see: *Europa*. *Feminist*. *Oxford*. *ToddDBA*.

Katherine S. Green

Anne (or Anna) Murray Halkett

BORN: 4 January 1622, London.
DIED: 22 April 1699, probably in Scotland.
DAUGHTER OF: Thomas Murray and Jane Drummond.
MARRIED: Sir John Halkett, 1656.
WROTE UNDER: Anne Lady Halkett; Lady Halkett.

A Royalist and a writer on religious subjects, H. left more than twenty volumes of manuscripts at her death. In 1701, a volume of her religious meditations was published along with her autobiography that she had written a quarter of a century earlier.

H. came by her Royalist enthusiasms naturally. Her father, the Earl of Tullibardin, had been appointed by James I to be preceptor to his son, Charles I. Until his death in 1625 when H. was three years old, her father was provost of Eton College. Her mother, who was related to the noble family of Perth, was governess to the Duke of Gloucester and to Princess Elizabeth, the children of King Charles I. Both H. and her sister Jane were educated by their mother, who, as H. wrote, "paid masters for teaching my sister and me to write, speak French, play on the lute and virginals, and dance, and kept a gentlewoman to teach us all kinds of needlework." In her autobiography, H. noted that her mother oversaw their religious training: They read the Bible and attended "divine service at five o'clock in the morning in summer and six o'clock in the winter." In keeping with the noblewoman's lot, H. studied physic and surgery to help the poor. Her success at treating the sick was legendary. She drew patients not only from England but from the Continent as well.

In 1644, when she was twenty-two, H. quarrelled with her mother, who discouraged a match with Thomas Howard, the eldest son of Edward, Lord Howard, because H. was without a fortune. Reluctantly submitting to her mother's wishes that she never see Howard again, H. insisted she would marry no one else. In a way, she kept her promise: When she said goodbye to Howard, who was sent off to relatives in France, she wore a blindfold. So distressed was she that she asked her cousin who was a consul in Holland whether she could enter a Protestant nunnery there. The cousin gave his answer to H.'s mother, who was again angry with her daughter. H. explains: "Since I found nothing would please her that I could do, I resolved to go where I could most please myself, which was in a solitary retired life." That same year, Howard not only privately married Lady Elizabeth Mordaunt, a much richer woman, substantiating the expectations of the age, but he also publicly humiliated H. She writes: "Is this the man for whom I have suffered so much?" While her mother laughed at her despair, H. was sad and indignant. Looking back on those events, H. writes in her memoir that Howard's wife "miscarried several children before she brought one to the full term, and that one died presently after it was born; which may be a lesson to teach people to govern their wishes."

In 1647, during the Civil War, H. met Joseph Bampfield who enchanted and influenced her for the next nine years. In a dramatic moment, H. had women's clothing made to fit the fourteen-year-old Duke of York for the boy's escape to the Continent. H. met the future king at the water's edge and helped him dress. She also provided him with some food and cake. Later, Bampfield enlisted her help as a courier to carry his letters to the king. Their dangerous activities united them so that Bampfield's proposal of marriage was not a surprise. His duplicity was: When he proposed he explained that his wife was dead. Not until 1649 did she learn the truth—that his wife was alive. It was about that time, too, that she learned that Bampfield had been arrested. Sickened almost to death by the news of Bampfield's wife and his arrest, H. did not recover until she heard of his escape. In 1650, she traveled to Scotland to recover a part of her inheritance. Reaching Edinburgh on 6 June, she found that Bampfield was already there. About that time, she met Charles II, encountered wounded soldiers after the battle of Dunbar, and spent a few days at Kinross attending them. At Perth, the king thanked her and gave her £50. For the next two years she remained in Aberdeenshire where she treated the sick and the wounded who came to her.

In 1652, H. returned to Edinburgh where she tried to recover the portion left to her by her mother. She also assisted Bampfield in Royalist plots until he left for the north. News reached H. that Bampfield's wife was in London. By 1653, H. met Sir James Halkett, who convinced her to take charge of his two daughters and to promise to marry him. In 1654, when H. visited London, Bampfield called on her and asked if she were married to Halkett. With extraordinary efforts to be honest, "She said, 'I am' (out loud), and secretly said 'not.'"

Married on 2 March 1656 at her sister's house in Charleton, H. and her husband returned to Scotland. It was there that H. wrote her first tract. She was understandably fearful of childbirth; she was, after all, thirty-four years old. H. wrote "The Mother's Will to her Unborn Child," while she was pregnant with her first child. H. wrote a tract during each of her subsequent pregnancies providing a Mother's Instructions to be used in the chance that she died.

After the Restoration, H. received £500 in recognition of the £412 annual interest that she had lost after the death of King Charles I. In addition she received £50 from the Duke of York. In 1676, her husband died, leaving her without enough income to provide for their children. She began to teach upper-class children in her home, and in 1685 King James II provided her with £100 annually because of her help to him during the Civil War.

Her devotional writing is tied closely to events in her life. She lost three or four children in their infancy, and her prayers and meditations reflect her grief and her loss. Her twenty volumes contain material that is of interest to the historian as well as the biographer of women of the seventeenth century. Her work is personal and vivid. According to James Sutherland, H. could have provided Samuel Richardson "with all the material he could possibly need for another novel; for Lady Halkett, intelligent, lively, resourceful, far from indifferent to moral and religious scruples, and yet placed in an equivocal position by her love for an adventurer, was the sort of heroine Richardson could not have failed to appreciate. To her own friends, Colonel Bampfield may never have appeared to be anything better than a Lovelace, but she herself continued to believe in his integrity." Sutherland finds that her work is not only of historical interest but of considerable human value.

WORKS: Bound in one volume entitled by the binder as *Lady Halket* are the following works, all dated 1701: "Instructions for Youth . . . For the use of those young noblemen and gentlemen whose education was committed to her care" (18 pp.). "Meditations and Prayers, upon the first; with observations on each day's creation: and considerations of the seven capital vices, to be opposed: and their opposite vertues to be studied and practiced" (50 pp.). "Meditations on the twentieth and fifth Psalm. By one who had found how beneficial it was to have the soul continually placed upon divine objects, and therefore made choice of this Psalm to raise her contemplations" (48 pp.). "The Life of the Lady Halkett" (64 pp.). *Meditations upon the seven gifts of the Holy Spirit mentioned Isaiah XL 2, 3, as also meditations upon Jabez, his request, I Chron. IV, 10, together with sacramental meditations on the Lord 's Supper and prayers, pious reflections and Observations* (1702). *Meditations on the 25th Psalm . . . wrote in the year 1651–2. By a Lady* (1771). *The Autobiography of Anne Lady Halkett*, ed. by J. G. Nichols (1875 by Camden Society, N. S. XIII). *The Memoirs of Anne, Lady Halkett, and Ann, Lady Fanshawe*, ed. with an intro. by John Loftis (1979 rpt. of Nichols's 1875 ed.).

BIBLIOGRAPHY: Bottrall, M. S. *Personal Records: A Gallery of Self-Portraits* (1961). Cumming, L. M. *Blackwood's Magazine* (November 1924). Fraser, A. *The Weaker Vessel* (1984). Reynolds, M. *The Learned Lady in England, 1650–1760* (1920). Stenton, D. M. *English Women in History* (1957). Sutherland, J. *English Literature of the Late Seventeenth Century* (1969).

For articles in reference works, see: *Bloomsbury. CBEL. DNB. Feminist. Oxford. ToddBWW. ToddDBA.*

Sophia B. Blaydes

Anna Maria Fielding Hall

BORN: 6 January 1800, Dublin.
DIED: 30 January 1881, Devon Lodge, East Moulsey, Surrey .
DAUGHTER OF: Sarah Elizabeth Fielding.
MARRIED: Samuel Carter Hall, 1824.
WROTE UNDER: Mrs. S. C. Hall.

H. is known primarily for Irish sketches and novels; she also wrote short stories, plays, and children's books. She was born in Ireland, residing for most of her first fifteen years in the house of her step-grandfather, George Carr of Craigie, Wexford, her mother being left a widow. In 1815, H. and her mother came to England, becoming permanent residents. At the age of twenty-four she married Samuel Carter Hall. She published her first work, "Master Ben," five years later and continued to write until her death.

"Master Ben" was the first of a series of Irish sketches based on the author's recollection of areas and persons familiar during her early years in Ireland, later offered in one volume, *Sketches of Irish Character.* Although H. presented the Irish milieu, she was never popular in Ireland, for she did not identify solely with either of the political factions, the Orangemen or the Roman Catholics, impartially commending and criticizing both.

She devoted much time in beneficent efforts, being instrumental in establishing the Hospital for Consumption at Brompton, the Governesses' Institute, the Home for Decayed Gentlewomen, and the Nightingale Fund. She worked for women's rights, the friendless, and the fallen, and for temperance causes. She was known for her friendliness toward street musicians. Ironically, although she remained a dedicated and devout Christian throughout her entire life, she embraced spiritualism with equal fervor. *Marian* (1840), often considered the best of her nine novels, displays a knowledge of Irish character comparable in quality to the writings of Maria Edgeworth, her contemporary; *Midsummer Eve, A Fairy Tale of Love* (1848) has been touted as her most beautiful book.

Several of H.'s tales were dramatized rather successfully: "The Groves of Blarney," first published as one of a series under the title *Lights and Shadows of Irish Life* in *New Monthly Magazine* (ed. by H.'s husband), ran for a whole season at the Adelphi in 1938 (adapted especially for Tyrone Power). Other productions were *The French Refugee*, running for ninety nights at the St. James's Theatre in 1836, and *Mabel's Curse*, featuring John Pritt Harley (same theater). The sole copy of one of her dramas, *Who's Who*, was lost at sea in 1841.

H.'s works contain fine rural descriptions; they are delicately humorous and have a high moral tone. She often contributed to the publications her husband edited and was herself an editor of the *St. James Magazine* from 1862 to 1863.

WORKS: *Sketches of Irish Character* (1829; 2nd. series, 1831). *Chronicles of a School-Room* (1830). *The Buccaneer* (1832). *The Outlaw* (1835). *Tales of a Woman's Trials* (1835). *Uncle Horace* (1837). *St. Pierre, the Refugee* (1837). *Lights and Shadows of Irish Life* (1838). *The Book of Royalty: Characteristics of British Palaces* (1839). *Tales of the Irish Peasantry* (1840). *Marian, or a Young Maid's Fortunes* (1840). *The Hartopp Jubilee* (1840). (with S. C. Hall) *A Week at Killarney* (1843). (with S. C. Hall) *Ireland, Its Scenery, Characters &c* (1841–43). *The White Boy, a Novel* (1845). (with J. Foster) *Stories and Studies from the Chronicles and History of England* (1847). *Midsummer Eve, A Fairy Tale of Love* (1848). *The Swan's Egg, a Tale* (1850). *Pilgrimages to English Shrines* (1850). *Stories of The Governess* (1852). (with S. C. Hall) *Handbooks for Ireland* (1853). *The Worn Thimble, a Story* (1853). *The Drunkard's Bible* (1854). *The Two Friends* (1856). *A Woman's Story* (1857). *The Lucky Penny and Other Tales* (1857). *Finden's Gallery of Modern Art, with Tales by Mrs. S. C. Hall* (1859). (with S. C. Hall) *The Book of the Thames* (1854). *The Boy's Birthday Book* (1859). *Daddy Dacre's School* (1859). (with S. C. Hall) *Tenby* (1860). (with S. C. Hall) *The Book of South Wales* (1861). *Can Wrong be Right? A Tale* (1862). *The Village Garland: Tales and Sketches* (1863). *Nelly Nowlan and Other Stories* (1865). *The Playfellow and Other Stories* (1866). *The Way of the World and Other Stories* (1866). *The Prince of the Fairy Family* (1867). *Alice Stanley and Other Stories* (1868). *Animal Sagacity* (1868). *The Fight of Faith, A Story* (1869). *Digging a Grave with a Wineglass* (1871). *Chronicles of a Cosy Nook* (1875). *Boons and Blessings: Stories of Temperance* (1875). *Annie Leslie and Other Stories* (1877). (with S. C. Hall) *A Companion to Killarney* (1878). *Grandmother's Pockets* (1880).

BIBLIOGRAPHY: *Colburn's New Monthly Magazine* (August 1838). *Dublin University Magazine* (August 1840). *Fraser's Magazine* (June 1836). *Hale's Woman's Record* (1855). Hall, S. C. *A Book of Memories* (1876). Hall, S. C. *Retrospect of a Long Life* (1883). Howitt, M. B. *An Autobiography* (1889). *Illustrated London News* (12 February 1881). *Illustrated News of the World* (1861).

LonT (1 February 1881). Thomas, J. *Universal Pronouncing Dictionary of Biography and Mythology* (1901).

For articles in reference works, see: *BA19C. BDIW. Cambridge. DIB. DIL. Dole. Feminist. VB.*

Phyllis J. Scherle

Radclyffe Hall

BORN: 1886, Bournemouth, Hampshire.
DIED: 11 October 1943, London.
DAUGHTER OF: Radclyffe Radclyffe-Hall and Mary Jane Diehl Radclyffe-Hall.

H., christened Marguerite Hall, was the daughter of Radclyffe-Hall, whom she barely knew but who left her a large inheritance when she turned seventeen. H. was raised by her flighty mother and a moody Italian stepfather, parents who often subjected her to emotional and even physical abuse.

H. started her writing career at age three when she wrote her first poem. Between 1906 and 1915, she published five volumes of poems. Her work improved in the later volumes though becoming increasingly personal, and the poems' lyrical qualities enabled several composers, including Coleridge Taylor, Liza Lehmann, Woodesforde Finden, Mrs. George Batten, and Coningsby Clarke, to set them to music.

In 1907, H. became the lover of Mabel Veronica Batten, who was almost twice H.'s age. Batten, known as "Ladye," encouraged H. to write and introduced her to William Heinemann, who would publish her fiction. H. met Batten's cousin, Lady Una Troubridge, in 1915 and began a relationship with her that would last the remainder of H.'s life.

Her first novel, *The Forge*, was a brief social comedy published in 1924, followed by *The Unlit Lamp* later the same year. This latter work hints at incest and the subject of lesbianism, which she returned to in *The Well of Loneliness,* but the treatment is so muted that the book attracted little public notice. Nevertheless, the writing is powerful in its bleakness. H. published *A Saturday Life,* a novel dealing with the life of an artist and the subject of reincarnation in 1925. Another novel, *Adam's Breed,* was published the next year. Although *Adam's Breed* is overly sentimental, the protagonist, Gian-Luca, a headwaiter, again demonstrates a character struggling against conforming to society's demands. The story is presented with H.'s usual honesty and won several prizes, including the Feminia Vie Heureuse Award and the James Tait Memorial Prize.

In 1928, H. published her famous novel of "sexual inversion," *The Well of Loneliness.* The novel became a *cause célèbre* as people either defended or condemned the book, which was banned in England because, said the magistrate, it portrayed "unnatural and depraved relationships." The novel, which tells the story of the androgynous Stephen Gordon and her lover, Mary, received mixed critical reactions. Psychologist Havelock Ellis claims in a preface to the book that it shows "poignant situations . . . set forth so vividly." Yet Leonard Woolf and Rebecca West, both of whom fought for its publication, consider the work flawed. Woolf states that the characters "appear to be the creation of the intellect, and for the reader they have no emotional context." West is even harsher in her remarks, saying it is "not a very good book. . . . A novel which ends a chapter with the sentence 'And that night they were not divided' cannot redeem itself by having 'they' mean not what it usually does." West's complaint underlies the fact that despite its subject matter, the novel is still encased in Victorian trappings. Regardless of its flaws, however, the work is important because, as Jane Rule says, it "remains the lesbian novel," a courageous book that profoundly affected many people's lives and influenced a host of later writers.

H. was a devout Christian, although maintaining a strong interest in psychic research, and this became the topic of her next novel, *The Master of the House* (1932). Christopher Benedit is the son of a carpenter, Jouse, has a mother named Marie, and has a cousin, Jan. The parallel to the Holy Family is obvious; though some critics questioned the propriety of modernizing Jesus' life, H. considered this to be her finest work.

In 1934, she published *Miss Ogilvy Finds Herself,* a collection of five stories. The title story again speaks of lesbianism. Her last novel, *The Sixth Beatitude,* was published in 1936. The protagonist, Hannah Bullen, a servant, is an unwed mother of two children by different fathers, who, nevertheless, is presented, as the title implies, as being pure of heart. The novel, like much of H.'s better fiction, is grim and unrelenting.

In 1933, H. met Evguenia Souline, a Russian nurse hired to care for Troubridge during an illness The three women formed a *ménage à trois* until 1942, when H. died of cancer in London. The novel on which she had been working was destroyed, as she had requested, by Troubridge.

WORKS: *'Twixt Earth and Stars* (1906). *A Sheaf of Verses* (1908). *Poems of the Past and Present* (1910). *Songs of Three Counties, and Other Poems* (1913). *The Forgotten Island* (1915). *The Forge* (1924). *The Unlit Lamp* (1924). *A Saturday Life* (1925). *Adam's Breed* (1926). *The Well of Loneliness* (1928). *The Master of the House* (1932). *Miss Ogilvy Finds Herself* (1934). *The Sixth Beatitude* (1936). *Your John: The Love Letters of Radclyffe Hall,* ed. J. Glasgow (1996).

BIBLIOGRAPHY: Baker, M. *Our Three Selves: The Life of Radclyffe Hall* (1985). Brittain, V. *Radclyffe Hall: A Case of Obscenity?* (1969). Castle, T. *Noël Coward and Radclyffe Hall: Kindred Spirits* (1996). Cline, S. *Radclyffe Hall: A Woman Called John* (1997). Dickson, L. *Radclyffe Hall at the Well of Loneliness: A Sapphic Chronicle* (1975). Ellis, H., intro. to *The Well of Loneliness* (1928). Omrod, R. *Una Trowbridge: The Friend of Radclyffe Hall* (1985). Pritchett, V. S. *New Statesman* (15 December 1961). Radford, J., in *The Progress of Romance: The Politics of Popular Fiction,* ed. J. Radford (1986). Rule, J. *Lesbian Images* (1975). Troubridge, U. *The Life of Radclyffe Hall* (1961). West, R. *Ending in Earnest: A Literary Log* (1931). Woolf, L. *Nation* (4 August 1928).

For articles in reference works, see: *Bloomsbury. CA. Cambridge. Feminist. Longman. MBL. Oxford. TCA. TCLC. ToddBWW.*

Louis J. Parascandola

Elizabeth Hamilton

BORN: 25 July 1758, Belfast, Ireland.
DIED: 23 July, 1816, Harrogate, Yorkshire.
DAUGHTER OF: Charles Hamilton and Katherine Mackay Hamilton.

H. is primarily known for her regional novel, *Cottagers of Glenburnie,* and for her satiric renditions of the radical philosophers. M. Butler calls her "the most amusing of the anti-jacobins." H. also wrote poems, a popular song ("My Ain Fireside"), and educational treatises. Her literary friends included Joanna Baillie and Maria Edgeworth. While religiously conservative and not feminist, H. strongly supported Thomas Clarkson's abolitionism, defended Warren Hastings, and advocated Roman Catholic emancipation. She believed deeply in the power and moral responsibility of authors and educators: "[B]ooks are the chief, and in some cases the only medium, through which we derive the knowledge that enlightens the understanding, and the sentiments that rectify and improve the heart."

As an infant, H. was separated from her older sister, Katherine, and brother, Charles, when their father died in 1759. Their mother died in 1767. Raised on a Stirlingshire farm by her aunt, she read voraciously, attended a coeducational school, and acquired the usual "female accomplishments."

Meeting her brother in 1772, she began what she termed "a second education." After Charles sailed for India, H. visited the Highlands, producing a journal (published locally), began a novel on Arabella Stuart, and published an essay in *The Lounger.*

On Charles' return, H. assisted him with his translations, enthusiastically absorbing Indian culture. She began a lifelong reflective journal. She lived in London with Katherine and Charles until Charles died in 1792. *Hindoo Rajah* (1796), in the tradition of Oliver Goldsmith's *Citizen of the World,* portrays Charles as Captain Percy and herself as Charlotte. Echoing Goldsmith's *Citizen,* Rajah Zaarmilla criticizes English mores. H. satirizes English imperialism: "To disseminate the love of virtue and freedom, they cultivated the trans-Atlantic isles"; she adds, more soberly, "unhappy negroes are torn from their friends and families, for no other purpose, but to cultivate the sugar-cane." She wittily skewers modern philosophers who "reject whatever has the sanction of experience and common sense." Vapour lampoons William Godwin, while Miss Julia Ardent, a fervent feminist and devotee of sensibility, is helplessly impractical. Sir Caprice trains sparrows to swarm like bees, causing his sister to declaim: " . . . by a proper course of education, a monkey may . . . be a minister of state, or a goose, Lord Chancellor of England."

H. renewed her assault in the anonymous *Memoirs of Modern Philosophers* (1800), probably, Macarthy suggests, in response to Mary Hays's *Emma Courtnay.* Ugly and foolish Bridgetina Botherim—maliciously depicting Hays—fawns on Vallaton (a vicious Rousseau caricature), and Glib (Godwin again). H. brilliantly renders her targets ridiculous by distorting their own words. Glib praises Bridgetina's flight from home: "That's the way to perfectibility! What is it but loving one's own child, or one's own mother, or one's own wife, better than other people's, that obstructs the progress of morals? Leave them all. Let them all shift for themselves." Curiously, as V. Colby notes, H. praises Mary Wollstonecraft despite her "overzealousness." Memoirs contends that society's rules for women are essential protections, rather than undesirable restraints. The novel begins lightly but quickly congeals into sententious moralizing, Juvenalian satire, and bathos. Perhaps H.'s gout, interrupting the book's composition, explains this shift in tone. Still, at Bath for her health, H. found herself lionized for *Memoirs.*

Letters on . . . Education (1801–1803), based on experiential testing of H.'s educational theories, maintains that observation and experience are as vital as reading. H. raises religious objections to sexual inequality: Contempt for women leads men to suspect religion as a feminine value. Boys and girls should be educated equally, not "for an equality of employments and avocations, founded on the erroneous idea of a perfect similarity of powers," but for "an equality of moral worth."

Despite periodic illness, H. traveled through Wales and Scotland and then settled in Edinburgh in 1804, where she was awarded a royal pension. She carefully researched her *Agrippina* (1804) to illustrate her educational principles through biography and helped to establish a House of Industry for which she composed *Exercises in Religious Knowledge* (1804). *Letters Addressed to the Daughter of a Nobleman* (1806) followed six months as a governess.

H.'s comic novel, *Cottagers of Glenburnie* (1808), was written to combat ignorance and laziness among her Scottish neighbors. The pious, garrulous narrator, Mrs. Mason, fails to overcome the indolence ("I canna be fashed") and parental indulgence of the MacClartys, but the school she establishes inculcates cleanliness, piety, and industry, thus reforming the village. Tobin likens *Cottagers* to the works of Hannah More and Mary Leadbeater: "These women writers were confident that women of the middling classes, who had mastered the microtechnologies of self-regulation, could change the habits of the poor, teaching them to accept with humility and gratitude their place in the paternal order." Today's reader might reject *Cottagers'* sentimentality and side with the MacClartys's resentment of Mrs. Mason, but Sir Walter Scott, among other contemporaries, praised its fine character sketches and dialectical humor. Lord Francis Jeffrey raved: "This contains as admirable a picture of the Scottish peasantry as [Edgeworth's] do of the Irish and rivals them. . . . Our cottagers are reading and reasoning animals; and are more likely to be moved from their old habits by hints and suggestions which they themselves may glean up from a book, than by the more officious and insulting interference of a living reformer."

Popular Essays (1813) "is an attempt to deduce, from a consideration of the nature of the human mind, proofs that revealed religion offers the only effectual means of improving the human character." *Hints* (1815) proposes a partial adoption of Pestalozzi's educational system. V. Colby praises H.'s psychological insights: "In the first half of the nineteenth century . . . her writings on the education of children and the psychology of learning were very influential." Nonetheless, only *Cottagers* and *Memoirs* have reappeared in the twentieth century, and H. has yet to receive any extended scholarly analysis.

WORKS: *The Lounger,* No. 46 (December 17, 1785). *Translation of the Letters of a Hindoo Rajah* (1796). *Memoirs of Modern Philosophers* (1800). *Letters on the Elementary Principles of Education* (1801–1803). *Memoirs of the Life of Agrippina, the wife of Germanicus* (1804). *Exercises in Religious Knowledge* (1804). *Letters Addressed to the Daughter of a Nobleman* (1806). *The Cottagers of Glenburnie* (1808). *Rules of the Annuity Fund for the Benefit of Governesses* (1808). *Popular Essays Illustrative of Principles Connected with the Improvement of the Understanding, the Imagination and the Heart* (1813). *Hints Adressed to Patrons and Directors of Schools* (1815).

BIBLIOGRAPHY: Benger, E. *Memoirs of the Late Mrs. Elizabeth Hamilton* (1818). Jeffrey, F. *Edinburgh Review* (1808). Luria, G., intro. to *Cottagers of Glenburnie* (1974).

For articles in reference works, see: *Allibone. BA19C. BDLA. Cambridge. CBEL. DLB. DNB. Feminist. ToddBWW. ToddDBA.*

Other references: Baker, E. *History of the English Novel* (1929). Black, F. *The Epistolary Novel in the Late Eighteenth Century* (1940). Blakey, D. *The Minerva Press* (1939). Butler, M. *Jane Austen and the War of Ideas* (1975). Colby, R. *Fiction with a Purpose* (1967). Colby, V. *Yesterday's Woman* (1974). Elmwood, A. K. C. *Memoirs of the Literary Ladies of England* (1843). Findlay, J. *Stirling Natural History and Archaeological Society* (1932, 1939–54). Hamilton, C. J. *Women Writers: Their Works and Ways* (1892). Heilman, R. *America in English Fiction* (1937). Henderson, T. F. *Scottish Vernacular Literature* (1910). MacCarthy, B. *The Later Women Novelists* (1947). Mews, H. *Frail Vessels* (1969). Moers, E. *Literary Women* (1976). Moler, K. *Jane Austen's Art of Allusion* (1968). Renwick, W. *English Literature, 1789–1815* (1963). Tobin, B. *Superintending the Poor: Charitable Ladies and Paternal Landlords in British Fiction* (1993). Tompkins, J. M. S. *The Popular Novel in England* (1900). Wilson, M. *Jane Austen and Some Contemporaries* (1938).

Kathleen L. Fowler

Hamilton, Hervey: See *Robins, Denise Naomi*

Elizabeth Hands

FLOURISHED: 1789, Coventry, Warwickshire.
DIED: After 1789.
MARRIED: a blacksmith, 1785 (?).
WROTE UNDER: Daphne; E. H.

As a domestic servant, H. wrote a witty and skillful volume of poetry that satirizes popular conceptions of the rural poor, reworking pastoral verse forms to question social conventions and parody traditional poetic forms. Accounts of H.'s life are slim, and what is known of her stems largely from her sole published volume of verse, *The Death of Amnon. A Poem. With an Appendix: containing Pastorals, and other Poetical Pieces* (1789). The Preface of her book states that she was "born in obscurity . . . never emerging beyond the lower station in life." A domestic servant for many years to the Huddesfords of Allesly, near Coventry, H. married a blacksmith at Bourton, near Rugby, and gave birth to a daughter, celebrated in her poem "On the Author's Lying-In, August, 1785." She published some pieces as "Daphne" in *Jopson's Coventry Mercury,* and with the help of "some particular friends," including dramatist Bertie Greatheed (1759–1826) and the headmaster of Rugby, Thomas James, she acquired a substantial subscription list including Anna Seward; Dr. and Mrs. Loveday, the patrons of Mary Latter; and Samuel Blencowe and his wife, of the family that served as patrons to Mary Leapor.

H.'s volume of poetry reveals her working-class resistance to popular conceptions of the rural poor and laborers, as in her two poems that expose the arch conventions of domestic employers, "On the Supposition of an Advertisement in a Morning Paper, of the Publication of a Volume of Poems by a Servant Maid" and "On the Supposition of the Book having been published and read." Writing in a pastoral mode, H. portrays a countryside and village life that attests to a dignity and independence of rural labor, with shepherdesses mediating pastoral debates and milkmaids deflating amorous advances from clumsy swains. Her mock-heroic poem, "Written, originally extempore, on seeing a Mad Heifer run through the Village where the Author lives," defies traditional pastoral images of blithe and cheerful picturesqueness, instead showing a cow's unruly intrusion in a village decaying at the political and economic margins of late eighteenth-century agrarian society. Her lengthy poem "The Death of Amnon" reworks biblical narrative to de-emphasize woman's victimization and seek reassurance in a domestic sphere ordered by honorable mastery and loyal servitude. In "Critical Fragments, on some of the English Poets," H. imitates the styles of several great male poets, ignoring chronology and authoritative sequence in a brilliant romp through poetic precursors.

With only one volume as evidence of her literary achievements, H.'s work attests to the sustained difficulties faced by women writers emerging from the working classes in the late eighteenth century. Her versatile skills and social acuity position her work with writers such as Mary Collier, Ann Yearsley, and Mary Leapor, laboring-class women poets whom Donna Landry has demonstrated ventriloquize and thus challenge the verse forms and values of mainstream culture as a mode of resistance to the master's texts.

WORKS: *The Death of Amnon. A Poem. With an Appendix: containing Pastorals, and other Poetical Pieces* (1789).

BIBLIOGRAPHY: *Women Romantic Poets 1785–1832,* ed. J. Breen (1992). Landry, D. *The Muses of Resistance: Laboring-Class Women's Poetry in Britain, 1739–1796* (1990). *Eighteenth-Century Women Poets: An Oxford Anthology,* ed. R. Lonsdale (1989).

For articles in reference works, see: *Allibone. BDLA. Feminist. ToddDBA.*

Eve M. Lynch

Mary Ann(e) Hanway

BORN: Mary Ann Vergy (?) 1755–59(?).
DIED: 1823–25(?), London.
MARRIED: Hanway Balack Hanway, 1788.
WROTE UNDER: Mary Ann Hanway; Mary Anne Hanway; A Lady.

H. has been entirely neglected by the critics, and little is known of her life other than her own reports that she was petite, not "saturnine" in her disposition, and often unwell. A contemporary reviewer in the *European Magazine* identifies her husband as nephew to Jonas Hanway, the eighteenth-century English philanthropist. Actually, Hanway Balack Hanway was his great-nephew and partial heir. Hanway Hanway's will (proved in 1840) indicates that he died childless and mentions his late wife, a sister of hers (Jenny Cromer), and a niece (Louise Maria Ann Cooke). A handwritten inscription (apparently by the author) in Yale University's copy of *Falconbridge Abbey* mentions another niece, Mrs. Hitchcock.

As a very young woman, apparently, H. wrote the anonymous *Journey to the Highlands of Scotland* (1776). Her authorship seems confirmed by internal evidence. Considerably later, H. wrote four novels: *Ellinor* (1798), *Andrew Stuart* (1800), *Falconbridge Abbey* (1809), and *Christabelle* (1814). She may have written other unidentified anonymous works. The preface to *Andrew Stuart* identifies *Ellinor* as the first work to which she put her name.

Journey provides a fairly typical account of travels through the Highlands, praising the noble Scots, although complaining about their excessive family pride. It observes that the "wise acts" of England over the preceding decades had done much "to improve Scotland." *Journey* is most notable for its long diatribe against Samuel Johnson. Written in the form of familiar letters, it was allegedly published at the behest of a learned lady of the author's acquaintance.

H.'s novels, while heavily didactic, are closer to the sentimental/romantic novel than to the usual moralizing style of the day. *Ellinor,* especially in the early volumes, is a Burneyesque novel of manners, although it becomes increasingly romantic, improbable, and sentimental as it progresses. The reviewer of the *British Critic* notes with quiet approval: "This performance certainly does not want incident, the narrative is neat and simple; and the whole makes an agreeable publication." Like *Evelina, Ellinor* relates the story of a young woman in quest of her identity (and incidentally her ideal mate). Frequently witty and generally well written, if overly long, it offers a wonderful character study in Lady John Dareall, the outspoken feminist who protects Ellinor.

The next novel, *Andrew Stuart,* is a grabbag of unintegrated stories, written in a florid and sentimental style. *The Anti-jacobin Review* could not resist parodying its pretentious vocabulary: "The wrongs of the gentle hearted Isabella incarcerated in a castellated mansion intenerated not our rigid feelings." Even in this book, however, H. occasionally exhibits a pointed and skillful satiric style and consistently maintains an urgent moral tone. The book recounts the adventures of Stuart the Northern Wanderer, who, having run off to sea as a child, later rescues Isabella Newton from her tormenting sister. On the morning of their wedding day, Isabella is abducted and Stuart is shipped off in chains to India. Stuart wins his freedom there and falls in love with his cousin; Isabella is rescued and falls in love with her new savior. The novel, whose moral is "To Be Good is To be Happy," ends with weddings all around and appropriately bitter ends for the wicked.

Falconbridge Abbey represents a new level of achievement for H. Although the longest of all her works, this novel is relatively tight, often clever, and largely effective. It is a study of the havoc wrought among the noble Falconbridges, Berenvilles, and Glenallens by two unscrupulous Elizas (mother and daughter). These women (especially the younger) are splendidly selfish, ruthless, and ambitious. They anticipate Thackeray's Becky Sharp in their Machiavellian talent for manipulating words, people, and situations. A number of other convincing characters and a greatly improved sophistication in style and figuration make this a readable and at points even powerful work.

H. repeatedly praised verisimilitude in writing and maintained that she herself was faithful to human nature, society, probability, and even to facts. *Christabelle,* however, while subtitled "A Novel Founded on Facts," suffers no taint of realism. It is thoroughly romantic in its notions and its style and relies heavily on elaborate plot contrivances. Virtuous characters are veritable paradigms, villainous ones innocent of any redeeming qualities. *Christabelle,* set in the French Reign of Terror, swarms with gothic devices: anarchists, revolution, imprisonment and peremptory trials, miraculous interventions, a determined ravisher who repeatedly (and unsuccessfully) abducts the heroine, a sea capture, and the like. H.'s favorite themes are the folly of family pride, the failure of parents (in myriad forms), and the inevitable triumph of virtue. Intermingled with these principal concerns are her abhorrence of slavery, war, and dueling; her admiration for liberty, religious tolerance, individual merit, and education; and her profound ambivalence toward women. While H. urges proper conduct, especially for young women—her heroines are all faultless—she clearly delights in racy, energetic older women like Lady John, who not only advocate women's rights but live by them. None of H.'s novels were reissued until Gina Luria reprinted *Ellinor* in 1974. *Ellinor* and *Falconbridge Abbey* are well worth reading, however, and *Christabelle* is a fascinating document in the study of England's response to the French Revolution.

WORKS: *A Journey to the Highlands of Scotland With Occasioned Remarks on Dr. Johnson's Tour, by a Lady* (1776). *Ellinor, or the World as It Is: A Novel in Four Volumes* (1798). *Andrew Stuart, or the Northern Wanderer: A Novel in Four Volumes* (1800). *Falconbridge Abbey: A Devonshire Story in Five Volumes* (1809). *Christabelle, the Maid of Rouen: A Novel Founded on Facts in Four Volumes* (1814).

BIBLIOGRAPHY: *BDLA*. Copeland, E. *MLS* (1979). Gregory, A. *The French Revolution and the English Novel* (1915). Luria, G., intro. to *Ellinor* (1974). Ward, W. S. *Literary Reviews in British Periodicals 1789–1797: A Bibliography* (1979).

For articles in reference works: see: *BDLA*.

Kathleen L. Fowler

Barbara Hardy

BORN: 27 June 1924, Swansea, Wales.
DAUGHTER OF: Maurice Nathan and Gladys Nathan.
MARRIED: Ernest Dawson Hardy, n.d.

H., one of Britain's foremost literary critics, is a teacher, critic, poet, and professor of English. After receiving her bachelor's and master's degrees at the University of London, she held visiting teaching positions at Northwestern, Princeton, Dijon, and Stockholm universities and since 1965 has been a professor of English at Royal Holloway and Birkbeck colleges at the University of London. She is an honorary member of the Modern Language Association and the Welsh Academy and has lectured at universities in Japan, the Soviet Union, France, Canada, the United States, and Scandinavia.

H.'s scholarly work has been primarily concerned with arguing theoretical and generalized views of narrative form and genre through textual analysis. Her early books modified and revised then-current concepts of fictional form, and she has continued to elaborate and extend analysis to lyric poetry and Shakespearian drama. She has also examined the sociological and moral imagination of writers, especially William Makepeace Thackeray and Jane Austen as well as William Shakespeare and Henry James. Narrative is emphasized in all her writing, though in greatest detail in *Tellers and Listeners: The Narrative Imagination* (1975), in which H. discusses such forms of narrative as jokes, daydreams, gossip, memoirs, and boasting, among others, as these serve to make up longer narrative patterns.

Her most significant body of work is her analysis of nineteenth-century writers, notably Thomas Hardy, George Eliot, Thackeray, Austen, and Charles Dickens. Her *The Moral Art of Dickens* (1970) has been praised for its incisive treatment of Dickens's "moral transformation" in his novels. *The Exposure of Luxury: Radical Themes in Thackeray* (1972) was similarly cited for H.'s perceptive handling of Thackeray's psychological insights.

Her first book, *The Novels of George Eliot: A Study in Form* (1959), remains one of her most distinguished. In addition to H.'s thorough knowledge of Eliot's work, H. demonstrates a wide-ranging familiarity with numerous influences on Eliot, in particular such problems of the day as education, Positivism, and political reform. H. also draws parallels to and applies a wide variety of writers to Eliot, including Dickens, Sigmund Freud, Shakespeare, William Wordsworth, and Henry James.

H. is especially concerned with interpreting Eliot's concern with "form" in a broad sense to include everything that helps the reader to see how Eliot's work reflects both a coherent, disciplined structure and a profound understanding of human nature. Indeed, "form" was a recurrent emphasis in H.'s writings, from her second book, more specifically on novelistic structure, *The Appropriate Form: An Essay on the Novel* (1964), through *Forms of Feeling in Victorian Fiction* (1985).

In addition to the many books she has written or edited, H. has also contributed to numerous journals, including *The New Statesman, The Guardian, Times Literary Supplement, Essays in Criticism, Furman Studies, Victorian Studies,* and *George Eliot–George Henry Lewes Studies.* Her verse has appeared in *Poetry Wales, New Poets, Critical Quarterly,* and *London Review of Books,* among others. She has written on a broad range of authors—including James Joyce, W. H. Auden, Elizabeth Gaskell, John Donne, W. B. Yeats, Emily Brontë, John Berryman, D. H. Lawrence, William Empson, and Virginia Woolf—for various collections, symposia, and journals, as well as on the craft of fiction in general.

Recent publications include *Swansea Girl* (1994), a recollection of the childhood and adolescence of H. and her brother Bill, concentrating on the years 1924–42. H.'s maternal grandfather came from a Devon family, some of whom migrated to South Wales and the late-Victorian industries. *London Lovers* (1995), as Lorna Sage noted in the *Times Literary Supplement* (29 December 1995), is a continuation of *Swansea Girl* in the "form of a 'novel,' in which the names have been changed to protect the men in [H's] life" and with her own name changed to Florence Jones. Sage also notes that, although the book contains H.'s "humour, intelligence, energy and inspired greed that took her from working-class South Wales to a life of academic distinction and amorous adventure," it also contains a bland, unpersuasive set of characters whose identities are barely hidden.

H.'s latest book, *Shakespeare's Storytellers: Dramatic Narration* (1997), is a compilation of some of her earlier essays and is a valuable companion to her volumes on other writers.

WORKS: *The Novels of George Eliot: A Study in Form* (1959). *The Appropriate Form: An Essay on the Novel* (1964). *Charles Dickens: The Later Novels* (1968). *The Moral Art of Dickens* (1970). *The Exposure of Luxury: Radical Themes in Thackeray* (1972). *Tellers and Listeners: The Narrative Imagination* (1975). *A Reading of Jane Austen* (1975). *The Advantage of Lyric: Essays on Feeling in Poetry* (1976). *Particularities: Readings in George Eliot* (1982). *Forms of Feeling in Victorian Fiction* (1985). *Narrators and Novelists: The Collected Essays of Barbara Hardy* (1987). *Swansea Girl: A Memoir* (1994). *London Lovers* (1995). *Shakespeare's Storytellers: Dramatic Narration* (1997).

BIBLIOGRAPHY:

For articles in reference works, see: *CA. CLC.*

Other references: *Encounter* (July 1977). *LRB* (4 February 1996). *New Statesman* (24 October 1975). *NYRB* (8 October 1970). *NYTBR* (11 September 1977). *TLS* (18 January 1968, 5 February 1970, 25 December 1970, 6 October 1972, 23 April 1976, 16 January 1976, 29 December 1995). *VQR* (Summer 1971, Winter 1973). *Washington Post* (30 December 1970).

JoAnna Stephens Mink

Brilliana Harley

BORN: 1600, Brill, Holland.
DIED: October 1643, Brampton Bryan, Herefordshire.
DAUGHTER OF: Sir Edward Conway and Dorothy Tracy.
MARRIED: Sir Robert Harley, 1623.

H. remains a paradoxical figure. Known in her own time for the successful military defense of Brampton Bryan castle during the Civil War, for which she became something of a hero to the Roundheads, she is principally remembered today for her extraordinary letters to her son, which present her as an attentive mother consumed with domestic activities.

She was named after Brill, the town in Holland where she was born; her father, Sir Edward Conway, was then Lieutenant-Governor of the Netherlands, and the family returned to England in 1606. H. received an unusual education; she was well read and knew both Latin and French. She married Sir Robert Harley in 1623, his third wife, and bore seven children between 1624 and 1634. Her husband served in parliament under James I and Charles I. Both she and her husband were Calvinist and sided with the parliamentary forces during the Civil War. After her marriage and until her death she resided principally at Brampton Bryan castle in Herefordshire, which she successfully held against royalist forces in 1643. In December 1642, shortly after hostilities had begun, the royalist governor, knowing her Puritan sympathies, demanded that she surrender the castle to the king's forces, to which request she refused.

H. wrote numerous letters, none of which were published in her lifetime. In the 1850s, however, a descendant, Lady Frances Vernon Harcourt, discovered a cache, which included 205 letters, mainly to her son Ned, subsequently published as *Letters of the Lady Brilliana Harley* in 1854. The first letter is dated 30 September 1625, and the last 9 October 1643, shortly before her death. Eight letters—the first in the collection—are to her husband, the remainder to her son. They provide vivid information about the daily life of an upper-class family of the period. While not as intense as the letters of Madame de Sevigne to her daughter, written a few decades later, they nevertheless evince considerable maternal affection. Often she sends him folk medicinal recipes, such as: "beare boyled with licorisch; it is a most excelent thinge for the kidnee" (12 December 1638). Or: "It is an excelent thinge to carry a littell peece of meer in your mouth, to keep you from any infection" (19 April 1641). She comments regularly on various members of the household receiving bloodlettings. Occasionally, she sends him pies, cakes, and cheeses; he, in turn, sends her books. One, a copy of "The Man in the Moune," she finds "some Line to Donqueshot" [Don Quixote] (30 November 1638), an indication of the breadth of her own reading. In short, the letters are an important document of social history, giving us a rare and charming glimpse of a seventeenth-century woman at ease, relaxed and in conversation.

The final letters record her anxieties about the siege. On 25 August she wrote: "The gentill men of this cuntry have . . . [brought] an army against me." And in her last letter she remarked, "I have taken a very greete coold, which has made me very ill thees 2 or 3 days, but I hope the Lord will be mercifull to me" (9 October 1643).

WORKS: *Letters of the Lady Brilliana Harley*, ed. T. T. Lewis (1854).

BIBLIOGRAPHY: Fraser, A. *The Weaker Vessel* (1984). Lewis, T. T., intro. and notes to *Letters of the Lady Brilliana Harley* (1854).

For articles in reference works, see: *Bloomsbury. DNB. Feminist.*

Josephine Donovan

Harper, Edith: See *Wickham, Anna*

Jane Ellen Harrison

BORN: 9 September 1850, Cottingham, East Yorkshire.
DIED: 15 April 1928, London.
DAUGHTER OF: Charles Harrison and Elizabeth Hawksley Nelson Harrison.

"Jane Harrison is truly . . . the great lady who found Greece marble and left it living flesh." So wrote Stanley Edgar Hyman about the classical scholar who was pre-eminent in revolutionizing the study of classical literature in the early twentieth century.

H., the third daughter in the family, lost her mother very early. She was educated by governesses, one of whom became her stepmother. H. early showed an aptitude for languages and, with the assistance of a sympathetic governess, began her study of Latin, Greek, German, and Hebrew. By the end of her life, she had studied fourteen languages "and read cunieform for relaxation" (Hyman). Her stepmother, a very religious woman, brought H. up in an atmosphere of strict Evangelicalism: At the age of twelve, H. was teaching two classes of Sunday School and playing the organ for two services. The effect of this confining, restrictive climate was to cause the young girl eventually to rebel altogether against organized religion and to become an agnostic. She was a life-long member of and lecturer for the Rationalist Association.

At the age of fifteen, H. was sent by her stepmother to Cheltenham Ladies' College for the purpose of being "finished" before entering the marriage market. H., however, had other ideas. Having won a scholarship, she persuaded her father to allow her to attend the newly opened Newnham College, Cambridge. H. studied classics from 1874 to 1879, with the encouragement of Professor Henry Sidgwick. She placed first in the second class in the Classical Tripos in 1879, the highest rank attained by a woman thus far. H. next moved to London to study archaeology at the British Museum under the direction of Sir Charles Newton. From 1880 to 1898 she lectured on Greek art at the museum and also at local boys' schools, the latter activity raising a few conservative eyebrows. She then returned to Newnham College as a lecturer in Greek archaeology. Recorded accounts by former students indicate that she was a brilliant lecturer and compassionate instructor. According to F. M. Cornford, "She was never happier than when teaching the rudiments of Greek or other languages to beginners, whose co-operation she easily won by her infectious enthusiasm" (*Dictionary of National Biography*).

H. was called "the cleverest woman in England" when still in her twenties (Hyman), and her stature as a classicist was permanently established in 1882 with the publication of her first book, *Myths of the Odyssey in Art and Literature.* Influenced by Sir James Frazer's *The Golden Bough* and the excavations at Troy by Heinrich Schliemann and at Athens by Wilhelm Dörpfeld, among others, H. began to question what lay beneath the surface of the Greek literary legacy, especially as it applied to religion. In *Prolegomena* (1903), the first of her great scholarly trilogy, she wrote: "Homer represents, not a starting point, but a culmination, a complete achievement. . . . Beneath this splendid surface lies a stratum of religious conceptions, ideas of evil, of purification, of atonement. . . . It is this substratum of religious conception, at once more primitive, and more permanent, that I am concerned to investigate." *Themis* (1912), her second great work, continues her investigation, exploring the concept of mystery-religions. Lastly, her *Epilegomena* (1921) provides a summation and clarification of earlier claims.

H.'s work incorporated the new sciences of anthropology, archaeology, and, later, psychology. She freely acknowledged her indebtedness not only to Emile Durkheim and Henri Bergson but also to Sigmund Freud and Carl Jung. As a pioneer, however, she was frequently attacked for her ideas. Critics accused her of poor scholarship and failure of attention to detail. The greatest objection came from mainstream colleagues who could not comprehend and thus resisted the necessity of bringing the new sciences into the realm of classical literature. John Wilson sums up contemporary feeling best: "What a way to teach classics! Imagine if every teacher of classics had to know all these things?" H., however, lived to see her theories vindicated. In 1927, she could write: "Perhaps I was prejudiced, for I found to my joy that most of my own old heresies that had seemed to my contemporaries so 'rash' were accepted by the new school, almost as postulates . . . the real delight was to find that these notions which for me, with my narrow classical training, had been, I confess, largely *a priori* guesses had become for the new school matter of historical certainty, based on definite facts, and substantiated by a touch-and-handle knowledge and a sort of robust common-sense to which I could lay no claim. To find myself thus out-dated was sheer joy."

If H. caused a stir in the classical world, she effected a tornado when she began to question Christian theology by employing the same principles she had formerly used when investigating Greek religion. She was, for example, denounced by the Provost of King's College for suggesting that primitive myth was the foundation for the story of John the Baptist's head (Todd).

H. supported the women's suffrage movement. In 1913, she wrote "Homo Sum: Being a Letter to an Anti-Suffragist from an Anthropologist" in which she stated that woman's claim to humanity was the reason behind the struggle. She campaigned to force Cambridge University to admit women. She was also a pacifist, and when World War I broke out, she left England for Paris where she lived until the conflict ended. There, she and Hope Mirrlees, her "ghostly daughter," studied Russian together. They went back to England in 1917. H. resumed her teaching position at Newnham, where she lectured on Russian literature until her retirement at the age of seventy-two. In 1926 H. and Mirrlees published *The Book of the Bear,* a series of twenty-one tales translated from Russian.

H. was awarded honorary degrees from the University of Aberdeen and the University of Durham. She was vice-president of the Hellenic Society from 1889 to 1896 and was a corresponding member of the Institute of Archives in Berlin. She was one of the first women elected justice of the peace in the borough of Cambridge. After she retired, she divided her time between London and Paris.

WORKS: *Myths of the Odyssey in Art and Literature* (1882). *Introductory Studies in Greek Art* (1885). *Itys and Aedon: A Panaitios Cylix* (1887). *Manual of Ancient Sculpture* (1890). *Manual of Mythology in Relation to Greek Art* (1890). (with M. de G. Verrall) *Mythology and Monuments of Ancient Athens: Being a Translation of a Portion of the "Attica" of Pausanias* (1890). *Primitive Athens as Described by Thucydides* (1906). *Heresy and Humanity . . .* (1908). *Prolegomena to the Study of Greek Religion* (1903). *The Religion of Ancient Greece* (1905). *Douris and the Painters of Greek Vases* (1908). *Themis: A Study of the Social Origins of Greek Religion* (1912, 1927). *Ancient Art and Ritual* (1914). *Alpha and Omega* (1915). *Peace with Patriotism . . .* (1915). *Russia and the Russian Verb: A Contribution to the Psychology of the Russian People* (1915). *Aspects, Aorists, and the Classical Tripos* (1919). *Rationalism and Religious Reaction* (1919). *Epilegomena to the Study of Greek Religion* (1921). *The Life of the Archpriest Avvakum* (1924). (1890). *Mythology* (1924). *Reminiscences of a Student's Life* (1925). (with H. Mirrlees) *The Book of the Bear* (1926). *Myths of Greece and Rome* (1927).

BIBLIOGRAPHY: Hyman, S. E. *Standards: A Chronicle of Books for Our Time* (1966). Macmillan, S. J. G. *Jane Ellen Harrison* (1959). *LonT* (17 April 1928). Murray, G., in *Jane Ellen Harrison: The Mask and the Self,* ed. S. J. Peacock (1988). Phillips, J. K. *JML* (1991). Stewart, J. G. *Jane Ellen Harrison: A Portrait from Letters* (1959). Torgovnick, M., in *Revisioning Edwardian and Modernist Literature,* ed. C. Kaplan (1996). Wilson, J. *Epilegomena* (1962).

For articles in reference works, see: *Allibone SUP. DNB. NCBEL. ToddBWW. VB. Who Was Who.*

Other sources: Cuddy-Keane, M. *PMLA* (1990). Maika, P. *Virginia Woolf's Between the Acts and Jane Harrison's Conspiracy* (1987). Shattuck, S., in *Virginia Woolf and Bloomsbury: A Centenary Celebration,* ed. J. Markus (1987).

Natalie Joy Woodall

Mary St. Leger (Kingsley) Harrison

BORN: 4 June 1852, Eversley, Hampshire.
DIED: 27 October 1931, Tenby, Wales.
DAUGHTER OF: Charles Kingsley and Frances Grenfell Kingsley.
MARRIED: William Harrison, 1876.
WROTE UNDER: Lucas Malet.

The youngest daughter of Charles Kingsley, eminent Christian Socialist clergyman, novelist, and poet, H. became a popular and controversial novelist. At Eversley the rectory was filled with celebrities—intellectuals, royalty, creative spirits—and during H.'s years of growing up with her two brothers, Maurice and Genville, and her elder sister, Rose, the Kingsley children found themselves in an atmosphere where individualism and learning were equally emphasized. When the Prince of Wales came to tea, H. stayed away, for she had determined that it was not appropriate to curtsy to another human. H. attended the Slade School to study art; although she was considered to show exceptional promise, she abandoned this career in 1876 when she married her father's curate, William Harrison, and went with him to North Devon, where he had been appointed rector of Clovelly. Unhappy in her marriage, H. later legally separated from her husband and began a writing career. Not wishing to trade too heavily on the fame of her father and uncle, Henry Kingsley, H. chose as her pen name two family names, so that it was as "Lucas Malet" that she made her mark in English letters, although her identity was no secret.

Her first novel, *Mrs. Lorimer: A Sketch in Black and White* (1882), attracted little attention, but her second, *Colonel Enderby's Wife* (1885), established her reputation, which was strengthened by *The Wages of Sin* (1891). These novels, based on her experiences in Devon and in London's artistic circles, were considered somewhat daring and unpleasant by some critics. Another novel, *The Carissima: A Modern Grotesque* (1896), was even more shocking as it details, in a somewhat Jamesian style, the trauma of a young man who fails to prevent a dog from eating a baby and his continuing obsession with the event.

A handsome woman and brilliant conversationalist, she was friend to Henry James and the critic W. L. Courtney and, during her years on the Continent, of Romain Rolland. When her husband died in 1897, H. bought a house in Eversley, adopted her cousin Gabrielle Vallins, and spent most of her time in France and Switzerland with yearly visits to England. It was on such a visit that she died in 1931. H. became a Roman Catholic in 1902 and revised her early novels, but her postconversion writings continue to puzzle, shock, or enrage critics. Her middle and late novels focused on one or more moral dilemmas inherent in relations between men and women and often contained elements of the gothic. Some, such as *The Gateless Barrier* (1900), in which the heroine is a ghost endeavoring to bring her former lover to self-knowledge, and *The Tall Villa* (1920), which concerned ancestral ghosts and their effect on the living, were more gothic than psychological.

H. inherited Charles Kingsley's literary remains, although she did not obtain possession of them for sixteen years. Finding a fragment of a novel, *Alcibiades,* she completed it, prefaced it with an essay in which she discusses her theory of fiction, comparing it to that of her father, and published it as *The Tutor's Story* in 1916.

It is in her novels describing the effects of a moral dilemma in naturalistic terms but coming to a religioromantic conclusion that she made a major impact. *Sir Richard Calmady* (1901) is an ambitious attempt to explore the different relationships that three women have with the same man, somewhat shocking in the early twentieth century for the outspoken, but not explicit, sexual nature of these relationships. *Adrian Savage* (1911) developed a triangle of widow, daughter, and young poet, which ends with the suicide of the daughter. A critic in the *Times Literary Supplement* called it "ugly and brutal." *Damaris* (1916) and *Deadham Hard* (1919) tell the story of Damaris from age five to eighteen. In the first, Damaris's father wants his mistress to bring up the child, and in the second, Damaris learns to cope with the knowledge that she has an illegitimate half-brother. In these dark-toned novels, women trained to be toys from childhood both suffer and cause suffering to others. Despite the seeming naturalism of the subject matter, critics describe H. as romantic in approach and like George Meredith in style. It seems, however, that H. herself saw her fiction as more than entertainment, rather as a forum for discussing humanity's hard choices.

WORKS: *Mrs. Lorimer: A Sketch in Black and White* (1882). *Colonel Enderby's Wife* (1885). *A Counsel of Perfection* (1888). *Little Peter: A Christmas Morality* (1888). *The Wages of Sin* (1891). *The Carissima: A Modern Grotesque* (1896). *The Gateless Barrier* (1900). *The History of Sir Richard Calmady: A Romance* (1901). *The Far Horizon* (1906). *The Score* (1909). *The Golden Galleon* (1910). *Adrian Savage* (1911). *The Tutor's Story: An Unpublished Novel by Charles Kingsley, Revised and Completed by Lucas Malet* (1916). *Damaris* (1916). *Deadham Hard, A Romance* (1919). *The Tall Villa* (1920). *Da Silva's Widow and Other Stories* (1922). *The Survivor* (1923). *The Dogs of Want: A Modern Comedy of Errors* (1924). *The Private Life of Mr. Justice Syme* (1932; completed by G. Vallins).

BIBLIOGRAPHY: Archer, W. *Real Conversations* (1904). Chitty, S. *The Beast and the Monk* (1974). Collums, B. *Charles Kingsley: The Lion of Everlley* (1975). Courtney, W. L. *Feminine Notes in Fiction* (1904). *Charles Kingsley, His Letters and Memories of His Life, Edited by His Wife,* ed. F. Kingley (1877). Pope-Hennessy, U. *Canon Charles Kingsley* (1948). Thorp, M. F. *Charles Kingsley, 1819–1875* (1937).

For articles in reference works, see: *Bloomsbury. Cambridge. DNB. Dictionary of Catholic Biography,* ed. J. J. Delaney and J. E. Tobin (1961). *1890s. Feminist. Oxford. ToddBWW. WN.*

Other references: *LonT* (29 October 1931). *NYT* (6 July 1885).

Eleanor Langstaff

Harvey, Caroline: See *Trollope, Joanna*

Haswell, Susanna: See *Rowson, Susanna*

Hatton, G. Noel: See *Caird, Alice Mona*

Frances Ridley Havergal

BORN: 14 December 1836, Astley, Worcestershire.
DIED: 3 June 1879, Swansea, Wales.
DAUGHTER OF: the Reverend William Henry Havergal and Jane Head Havergal.
WROTE UNDER: F.R.H.; Frances Ridley Havergal; Sabrina; Zoide.

A prolific poet and writer of religious tracts and children's books, H. is remembered chiefly for her hymns and her saintly life. This reputation, strongest among Evangelicals, has unjustly obscured her stature as a minor Victorian poet. She wrote some seventy-five hymns, also composing tunes for many of them, and had a hand in editing three books of hymns and tunes. A dozen or so of her hymns, such as "Consecration Hymn" ("Take my life") and "A Worker's Prayer" ("Lord, speak to me"), are still in use. But her collected verse, running to some 850 pages, includes sonnets, odes, mottoes, epigrams, narrative poems, a cantata, translations from the German, meditations, some political verse, and various other forms.

The quality of her work is uneven. Too much of it tries too hard to teach a lesson or achieve still more utilitarian ends, such as fund raising for one of her many causes. She wrote verse fluently, starting at the age of seven, and verse became her natural vehicle to commemorate birthdays and other family events, stirring mountain scenery, memorable experiences, and the like; and she would usually try to honor anyone's request for a poem on a given theme. Writings of this sort she herself tended to dismiss as containing "not a spark of poetry." Take them all away, however, and sparks enough remain—her intense appreciation of nature; her flashes of gentle wit, as in "Evening Song," which occasionally relieve the sometimes overwhelming earnestness; her eye for the apt metaphor and, often, the allegorical application that rings true; her strong intellect organizing the movement of thought in a poem; her attention to technical detail.

Thanks to the technical discipline, very little of what H. wrote—even if uninspired, even the floral greeting-card verse for which she was much sought after—can be called mere doggerel or cliché. Though her themes invited sentimental treatment, at her best the artistry firmly controlled the emotion. Besides the hymnlike stanza forms that predominate, she used the "Locksley Hall" meter, acrostics, blank verse, and other patterns. "Yesterday, To-day, and for Ever" is "a Greek acrostic, thrice tripled"—nine triplets, each an acrostic on the word AEI, "always." She sometimes changed meter within a poem and speculatively linked the aesthetic effect of doing so with key modulation in music. "Her musical ear," wrote the novelist Charlotte Yonge, "enabled her to write verses of much sweetness of rhythm" (Bodleian Library MS. Eng.misc.d.1096, quoted by permission).

Music in fact played an important part in her artistic life. One poem, "The Moonlight Sonata," includes a quite creditable verbal description and imitation of Beethoven's composition; the ode "Threefold Praise" is inspired equally by a Prayer Book text and by oratorios of Haydn, Mendelssohn, and Handel. A satire, "To the Choir of Llangryffyth," criticizes practices in church music. Of a distinguished musical family—her father and brother were composers and the former, an Anglican clergyman, pioneered the revival of older English church music—she published several compositions of her own; the listing below includes only a sampling. She was also a talented pianist and singer who gave up a promising concert career to devote her talents entirely to God's service. The lines "Take my voice, and let me sing / Ever, only, for my King" ("Consecration Hymn") she meant quite literally. Vocation was a frequent theme in early poems—such as "The Ministry of Song," where music is implicitly a metaphor for poetry, and "The Poet's Zenith"—and a continuing struggle later in recurrent periods of failed inspiration. "Poetry is not a trifle, / Lightly thought and lightly made," she wrote ("Making Poetry"); "the songs that echo longest" must be written "with your life-blood." Requisite is "suffering before you sing."

Other prominent themes in H.'s poetry are the praise of God, his goodness, trust in his providence despite affliction, seeking God's will and obeying it—her favorite terms for him are "king" and "master"—and the certainty of eternal things as opposed to the evanescence of the temporal. To be sure, H. dashed off dozens of occasional verses whether based on a holy day (Christmas, New Year's, Easter) or on a text used as a starting point for meditation. Yet as the early poem "Our Hidden Leaves" suggests, as well as the title of her second collection, *Under the Surface* (1874), she strove to penetrate beyond the obvious and probe true feelings and motivations. She brooded on the extreme difficulty of revealing or even knowing one's inner self ("Autobiography," "How Should They Know Me?").

Yet her writings reflect a remarkable depth of spiritual insight, gained both from introspection and from the Scriptures that she studied incessantly. The youngest of six children in an Evangelical vicarage, she experienced a spiritual awakening at the age of fourteen, and much later, after years of intense activity in teaching and personal evangelism, she made a more profound act of surrender to God (see her booklet *Such a Blessing*, 1873). Her mysticism has been likened to that of St. Teresa of Avila. Despite repeated long illnesses, she had a remarkable cheerfulness and buoyancy, and her pastimes included mountaineering in Switzerland, which furnished some of her best imagery.

H.'s many text-based poems—often taking a phrase from Scripture and applying it personally in allegorical fashion—owe much to her seriousness as a scholar. She committed several books of the Bible to memory, including most of the New Testament. Though her classroom schooling, including the Luisenschule in Düsseldorf, Germany, totaled less than two years, she knew several modern languages—she dashed off one poem in French—and she habitually used the Hebrew and Greek texts in Scripture study. The typological method had an especial attraction for her. She had a high regard for the English seventeenth-century poets and divines, and glimpses of Robert Herrick, George Herbert, John Milton, and John Bunyan may be seen in her work.

Much of H.'s time in her last decade, beyond the demands of an immense correspondence, was given to writing prose books and leaflets. She bought an "American typewriter"—only recently invented—for professional use. Viewing her supreme calling as ministry to others, she devoted her writing talent to that end. Her causes included circulating Irish-language Bibles in Ireland (*Bruey*, 1872), keeping Bible studies in the English curriculum (*An Educated Topsy*, 1873; verse satire), furthering the Young Women's Christian Association (*Holiday Work*, 1873; *All Things*, 1880), and promoting devotional exercises through daily and weekly guides (*My King*, 1877; the "Royal" series followed by *Loyal Responses*, 1878; *Starlight through the Shadows*, 1881, for invalids; *Little Pillows* and *Morn-*

ing Bells, both 1874, for children). *The Four Happy Days* (1873) is a story for children to which she added songs of her own composition; other children's stories appeared posthumously in *Ben Brightboots* (1883). *Kept for the Master's Use* (1879), a line-by-line prose commentary on her "Consecration Hymn," has maintained its place in evangelical devotion down to the present.

Such works enjoyed immense popularity, as did articles and poems published separately in magazines and leaflets, some with a combined circulation close to half a million. After her death the demand continued: More than sixty posthumous anthologies of extracts from her writings have been published (of which the list below contains only a selection), and many single poems have appeared in lavishly illustrated format. Translations were made into numerous African, Asiatic, and European languages. At the end of the twentieth century, in addition to hymns, five works by H. were still in print.

An autobiographical sketch written at the age of twenty-two is incorporated in her sister's *Memorials,* and letters—many of them replete with theological insight and spiritual counsel—are included there and in other biographies. Later journals and autobiography are extant in manuscript, as are notes on her life by the contemporary novelist Charlotte Yonge.

WORKS: *The Ministry of Song* (1869; reprinted 1879 in *Life Mosaic*). *Sacred Songs for Little Singers* (1870). *Scotland's Welcome* (1871). *Bruey: A Little Worker for Christ* (1872). *An Educated Topsy* (1873). *The Four Happy Days* (1873). *Holiday Work* (1873). *Such a Blessing* (1873). *Hints for Lady Workers at Mission Services* (1874?). *Little Pillows; or, Good-Night Thoughts for the Little Ones* (1874). *Morning Bells or, Waking Thoughts for the Little Ones* (1874). *Under the Surface* (1874, in the U.S. as *Our Work and Our Blessings;* reprinted 1879 in *Life Mosaic*). *Twilight Voices* (1876). *My King; or, Daily Thoughts for the King's Children* (1877). *Royal Bounty; or, Evening Thoughts for the King's Guests* (1877). *Royal Commandments; or, Morning Thoughts for the King's Servants* (1877). *Loyal Responses; or, Daily Melodies for The King's Minstrels* (1878; rev. ed. with music by H., 1881). *The Royal Invitation; or, Daily Thoughts on Coming to Christ* (1878). (with C. W. Ashby) *Talitha Cumi, and Other Verses,* ed. M. Havergal (1878). *Advent Verses* (1879). *Echoes from the Word for the Christian Year* (1879). *Kept for the Master's Use* (1879; abridged as *Meet for the Master's Use,* 1945). *Life Mosaic* (1879). (musical setting) *Loving All Along,* by S. G. Prout (1879). *Morning Stars; or, Names of Christ for His Little Ones* (1879). *Red-Letter Days: A Register of Anniversaries and Birthdays* (2d. ed., 1879). *Royal Grace and Loyal Gifts* (1879). *Songs of Peace and Joy* (2d. ed., 1879). *Under His Shadow: the Last Poems,* ed. M. Havergal (1879). *All Things* (1880). *Life Chords* (1880). *Most Blessed for Ever,* ed. M.V.G. Havergal (1880). *My Bible Study: for the Sundays of the Year,* ed. H. Bullock (1880). *Daily Text-Book: Scriptures and Verses* (1881; reprinted as *The Havergal-Murray Daily Text-book,* 1927). *Messages for Life's Journey,* ed. J. Peck (1881). *Poems* (1881). *Specimen Glasses for the King's Minstrels: Papers on Modern Hymn Writers,* ed. C. Bullock (1881). *Starlight through the Shadows and Other Gleams from the King's Word,* ed. M. Havergal (1881). *Swiss Letters and Alpine Poems,* ed. J. M. Crane (1881). *Ben Brightboots and other True Stories, Hymns and Music,* ed. M.V.G. Havergal (1883). *Life Echoes,* ed. M.V.G. Havergal (1883). (with C. W. Ashby) *Lilies and Shamrocks,* ed. M. Havergal (1883). *Ivy Leaves,* ed. F. A. Shaw (1884). *Poetical Works,* 2 vols., ed. F. A. Shaw and M. V. G. Havergal (1884). *Letters,* ed. M.V.G. Havergal (1885). *Treasure Trove: Extracts from Unpublished Letters and Bible Notes,* ed. E. P. Shaw (1886). *Seven Songs for Eastertide* (1886). *Streamlets of Song for the Young,* ed. J. M. Crane (1887). *Blossoms from a Believer's Garden* (1888). *Birthday Blessings: A Havergal Birthday Book* (1904). *Gems from Havergal* (1912; *Poetry,* ed. F. A. Shaw; *Prose,* ed. B. H. Shaw). *Opened Treasures,* comp. W. J. Pell (1962).

BIBLIOGRAPHY: Bullock, C. *The Crown of the Road* (1884). Bullock, C. *The Sisters: Reminiscences and Records of Active Work and Patient Suffering* (1890). Bullock, C. *Near the Throne: Frances Ridley Havergal, Sweet Singer and Royal Writer* (1902). Darlow, T. H. *Frances Ridley Havergal: A Saint of God. A New Memoir, with a Selection of Extracts from Her Prose and Verse* (1927). Davies, E. *Frances Ridley Havergal: A Full Sketch of Her Life, with Choice Selections from Her Prose and Poetical Writings* (1884). Duffield, S. W. *English Hymns* (1886). Enock, E. E. *Frances Ridley Havergal* (1929). Fairchild, H. N. *Religious Trends in English Poetry* (1957). Grierson, J. *Frances Ridley Havergal: Worcestershire Hymnwriter* (1979). Havergal, M. *Frances Ridley Havergal: The Last Week* (1879). Havergal, M. *Memorials of Frances Ridley Havergal* (1880). Wrenford, J. T. *A Brief Memorial of One of the King's Daughters* (1879). Yonge, C. M. "Frances Ridley Havergal" (Bodleian Library MSS. Eng.misc.d.1096 and Eng.misc. e.1125).

For articles in reference works, see: *Allibone. BA19C.* Baptie, D. *Handbook of Musical Biography* (1883). *Boase. British Library Catalogue.* Brown, J. D. and S. S. Stratton *British Musical Biography* (1897). *Catalogue of Printed Music in the British Library to 1980* (1984). Claghorn, G. *Women Composers and Hymnists: A Concise Biographical Dictionary* (1984). Davis, G. and B. A. Joyce *Personal Writings by Women to 1900: A Bibliography of American and British Writers* (1989). Davis, G. and B. A. Joyce *Poetry by Women to 1900: A Bibliography of American and British Writers* (1991). *DNB. Europa. Feminist. Ireland.* Julian, J. *A Dictionary of Hymnology* (1891). Matthews, W. *British Autobiographies: An Annotated Bibliography* (1955). *Miles. NUC. Oxford.* Routley, E. *An English-Speaking Hymnal Guide* (1979). Routley, E. *A Panorama of English Hymnody* (1979). *Shaw* and *SUP. ToddBWW.*

Other references: *Christianity Today* (1979). Coombe, E. M., in *Footprints,* ed. C. Bullock (1882). *Historical Companion to Hymns Ancient & Modern,* ed. M. Frost (1962). Houghton, E. *Christian Hymn-Writers* (1982). *The Oxford Book of English Mystical Verse,* ed. D.H.S. Nicholson and A.H.E. Lee (1916). Prescott, J. E. *Christian Hymns and Hymn Writers* (1886).

Charles A. Huttar

(Jessie) Jacquetta (Hopkins) Hawkes

BORN: 5 August 1910, Cambridge.
DIED: 18 March 1996, London.
DAUGHTER OF: Sir Frederick Gowland Hopkins and Jessie Anne Stephens Hopkins.
MARRIED: Christopher Hawkes, 1933; J. B. Priestley, 1953.

Professional archeologist and popularizer of the science, novelist, poet, playwright, and biographer, H. was a writer in many genres whose hallmark was a successful blending of her fields. In particular, she brought science and literature together, creating in the process what the London *Times* in her obituary called "a new literary genre," one that "brought to a period of burgeoning science and technology a welcome and articulate artistry." There was also, in her best work, again according to the *Times,* yet another kind of blending: a "fusion of commonsense and uncommon vision."

H.'s heritage provided a nurturing environment for extraordinary achievement, both scientific and literary. She was born into an academic family in Cambridge, the younger daughter of Sir Frederick Gowland Hopkins, a professor of biochemistry who shared the 1929 Nobel Prize in physiology and medicine and a first cousin of the poet Gerard Manley Hopkins. When she entered Newnham College at Cambridge, she was the first woman to take the Archaeological and Anthropological Tripos, where she earned a first-class honors degree and a scholarship that enabled her to work at Stone Age sites in Palestine. She continued her research in prehistory at excavations in France, Ireland, and Britain and wrote her first book on the prehistory of the Channel Islands. In 1940, she was elected a Fellow of the Society of Antiquaries, and in 1943, in collaboration with the archeologist Christopher Hawkes, whom she had married in 1933 and by whom she had one son, she published a survey of early British history, *Prehistoric Britain. Early Britain,* written entirely in her own name, followed in 1945.

In 1941, with Britain besieged, H. had already entered wartime civil service, first in the Postwar Reconstruction Secretariat, then in the Ministry of Education, and finally as secretary of the U.K. National Commission for UNESCO. While working with UNESCO, she became acquainted with the playwright J. B. Priestley, whom she married in 1953 after divorcing Hawkes, and with whom, as she had with Hawkes, she collaborated in writing. The results were a play, *The Dragon's Mouth* (1952), and *Journey Down a Rainbow* (1955).

Even though she left the civil service in 1949 with the intent of devoting herself full-time to creative writing—she had published a book of verse, *Symbols and Speculations,* the preceding year and followed it with *Fables,* a collection of stories, in 1953, and a novel, *King of the Two Lands,* in 1966—H. still continued to perform important official functions, and as archeological correspondent for *The Observer* and the *Sunday Times* traveled widely to excavation sites. She also contributed to many learned journals, and in 1951 published A *Guide to the Prehistoric and Roman Monuments in England and Wales* (in the U.S. as *History in Earth and Stone*) for publication in the United States. She also served as vice president of the Council for British Archaeology (1949–52) and as governor of the British Film Institute (1950–55). But it was out of that crowded agenda, particularly from her role as archeological advisor for the 1951 Festival of Britain—for which she was awarded the Order of the British Empire—that her most creative writing developed. Her vivid presentation and interpretation of Britain's past in that exhibition led almost effortlessly, it seemed, to her award-winning, and still most-loved book, *A Land* (1951).

"In this book," H. begins her preface to *A Land,* "I have used the findings of the two sciences of geology and archaeology for purposes altogether unscientific. I have tried to use them evocatively, and the image I have sought to evoke is of an entity, the land of Britain, in which past and present, nature, man, and art, appear all in one piece." Illustrated with photographs of Henry Moore–like rocks and fossils, the book also includes two color plates by Moore in which "his lines follow Life back into the stone"; it is this fusing of biological life and stone, together with the life of the mind represented in the words and images of British poets and artists, that gives the book its extraordinary character.

The thesis already suggested in *A Land,* that human life is intimately and perhaps purposefully connected with geological and cosmic processes, was further developed in later books, *Man on Earth* (1954) and *Man and the Sun* (1962)—an anti-Darwinian position that could have given her trouble in conventional academic circles. Fortunately for her, H. was an independent thinker and writer, free to be idiosyncratic or not as she chose. In works such as the first volume of the *UNESCO History of Mankind* (1963), written with Sir Leonard Woolley, she chose a more conformist approach, as she did in her introduction and notes to the two-volume *The World of the Past* (1963), an account of some of the world's greatest archeological discoveries in the words of those who made or interpreted them. Equally "respectable" was her study of Bronze Age Greece, *Dawn of the Gods* (1968), although in her preface to *Dawn* she suggested that her contrast of the feminine and masculine personalities of Minoan and Mycenaean cultures might be provocative for some readers.

In her 1972 John Danz Lecture at the University of Washington, *Nothing But or Something More,* H. chose a more subversive course. Following scholars like Julian Huxley and Fred Hoyle in this lecture series on "the impact of science and philosophy on man's perception of a rational universe," she invoked both Noam Chomsky's theories of language structure and C. G. Jung's archetypes to combat the possibility of a random universe or the development of civilization from natural selection. She noted that her own approach to the subject, a "mixture of intuition and commonsense," was "of the kind most rightly deplored by science," but, again, it was precisely that mixture that gave her work its distinctive quality.

Choosing a less-controversial role once again, in the 1970s H. published several scholarly books that still appealed to the lay reader—*The First Great Civilizations* (1973), *Atlas of Ancient Archaeology* (1974), and *The At-*

las of Early Man (1976)—and in the next decade a well-received biography of a long-time friend, *Mortimer Wheeler: Adventurer in Archaeology* (1982), and, with Paul Bahn, *The Shell Guide to British Archaeology* (1986). During those years, she was awarded an honorary doctorate (University of Warwick, 1986) and appointed to such honorary posts as member of the UNESCO Cultural Advisory Committee (1966–79) and life trustee of the Shakespeare Birthday Trust (1985). But her distinctive "commonsense" nevertheless surfaced spectacularly, with "devastating" effect, according to her *London Times* obituary, over the question of whether the megalith builders of prehistoric Europe actually carried out precise measurements and astronomical observations, as a renowned Oxford professor claimed to have determined. Relying on that "commonsense" as well as her scientific training, H. demonstrated the imprecision of the professor's data and eventually found herself vindicated, with general acceptance of an astrological rather than astronomical use of the megaliths.

About H.'s *Quest of Love* (1980), it is true, many reviewers complained that her customary "commonsense" had given way to mysticism. Half novel, half autobiography, the book recounts the experiences of a woman, apparently H. herself, as her "long body" lives through successive reincarnations from earliest prehistory to the present. "What is an old admirer to make," asked Katha Pollitt in a *New York Times* review, "of this humorless rambling document . . . in which autobiography and antifeminist lectures are interleaved with chapters of imagined past incarnations?" Yet the "long body" of H.'s work as a whole is not diminished by this single aberration, if indeed it was such. A brilliant scientist, she is best remembered as a brilliant popularizer, in whose writing two seeming opposites came together: once again in the words of the *London Times*–"the precision of science" with the "intuition of the poet."

WORKS: *The Archaeology of the Channel Islands* (1928, 1938). *The Archaeology of Jersey* (1939). (with C. Hawkes) *Prehistoric Britain* (1943). *Early Britain* (1945). *Symbols and Speculations* (1949). *A Guide to the Prehistoric and Roman Monuments in England and Wales* (1951; in the U.S. as *History in Earth and Stone,* 1952). *A Land* (1951). *Discovering the Past* (1951). (with J. B. Priestley) *Dragon's Mouth: A Dramatic Quartet in Two Parts* (1952). *Fables* (1953; in the U.S. as *A Woman as Great as the World and Other Fables*). *Man On Earth* (1954). (with J. B. Priestley) *Journey Down a Rainbow* (1955). *Providence Island: An Archaeological Tale* (1959). *The Aborigines of Australia* (1961). *Man and the Sun* (1962). *Women Ask Why: An Intelligent Woman's Guide to Nuclear Disarmament* (1962). (with L. Woolley) *History of Mankind,* Vol. 1, Part l (1963). *The World of the Past* (1963). *Pharaohs of Egypt* (1965). *King of the Two Lands* (1966). *Dawn of the Gods* (1968). *Nothing But or Something More* (1972). (with A. Voysey) *The Why of Our Farms* (1972). *Why the Past Is Always Present* (1972). *The First Great Civilizations* (1973). *Atlas of Ancient Archaeology* (1974). *The Atlas of Early Man* (1976). *A Quest of Love* (1980). *Mortimer Wheeler: Adventurer in Archaeology* (1982). (with P. Bahn) *The Shell Guide to British Archaeology* (1986).

BIBLIOGRAPHY: Bahn, P. *British Archaeology* (May 1996). Collins, D. *Time and the Priestleys: The Story of a Friendship* (1994).

For articles in reference works, see *CA. OCEL. OCTCL. TCA. ToddBWW. Who's Who.*

Other references: *LonT* (20 March 1996). *NYT* (21 March 1996).

Elizabeth Huberman

Laetitia Matilda Hawkins

BORN: 1759, London.
DIED: 1835, Twickenham, Middlesex.
DAUGHTER OF: Sir John Hawkins and Sidney Storer.

H., a didactic novelist, earnest intellectual, and conservative prose-writer now largely unknown, grew up amid a rich if demanding intellectual environment in Twickenham and London. Her father, a magistrate, writer, and editor, supervised her education and employed her as his assistant. H.'s *Anecdotes* (1823), describing her father's life, provides vivid insights into events like the Wilkes and Gordon riots and figures like Henry Fielding, Samuel Johnson, Angelica Kauffman, Voltaire, Mary Darby Robinson, and Lady Elizabeth Hamilton. *Anecdotes* also offers brief personal insights. H. reports writing several anonymous novels (still unidentified) "when I had no time but what I could purloin, and was writing 6 hours in the day for my father, and reading aloud to my mother nearly as long. . . . I learnt Italian and extracted from every book that came in my way; I made . . . my clothes . . . ; I worked muslin; I learnt botany; and I was my mother's storekeeper." Among other tasks, H. provided reviews of Johnson's works for her father's biography and corrected his manuscript as well as Sir John's edition of Izaak Walton's *Compleat Angler.*

H.'s parents restricted her reading, forbidding frivolous books (including *Clarissa*). When H. began reading novels, her taste ran to Hannah More's *Coelebs* ("an epoch in moral fiction") and Adelaide O'Keeffe's "elegant work of moral instruction."

In 1793, H. answered Helen Maria Williams's radical *Letters from France* with an openly antifeminist, proslavery treatise, *Letters on the Female Mind.* "Whatever has a tendency to render women confident is . . . highly injurious to the delicacy of their tempers, as well as to their manners. . . . Let us then, if we do not love darkness, be very careful to do nothing to provoke our superiors to take away the lamp they had allowed us." On slavery, she writes: "I am inclined to believe, that slavery is not in itself a state of misery; that it is not universally felt as such; and that there are at this moment many negroes . . . to whom liberation would be a most cruel dereliction." Citing Dr. John Hunter's racialist anatomy, H. concluded, "they are by nature fitted, though perhaps not without exception, to only the more sordid purposes of life." H. does suggest restraints for cruel planters and particularly condemns female brutality: "There is no slaveholder as a woman." She urges women to exercise moral suasion: "Let us endeavour to infuse into the minds of all, over whom we have either authority or influence, the best principles of humanity."

In 1806, H. translated from the German J. M. Miller's *Siegwart,* adding a critical introduction. After her father's death, she published the autobiographical *The Countess and Gertrude* (1811), which "has for its basis so much truth that it must not pretend to rank with efforts of invention. . . . Such a mode of discipline as that of Gertrude Aubrey was practised. . . . She is an existing being." Gertrude, raised by cold, selfish Lady Luxmore, is trained and employed by the stern taskmaster, Mr. Stirling. The models he sets for Gertrude suggest the kind of reading H. had undergone: "Bacon, Hooker, Barrow, Browne, Osborne, Clarendon, Bentley, Clarke, Warburton, Johnson . . . The Whole Duty of Man, Hawkesworth, Sir Wm. Temple, and Walton." H.'s determinedly didactic work is laden with numerous anecdotal footnotes, some more interesting than the desultory narrative. H. advocates firm discipline of children and strong governance of servants: "The lower classes can always understand justice, but seldom fail to mis-use indulgence." Her views on women, however, seem to have moderated. She is openly sympathetic to Gertrude and advocates marital equality and shared responsibility as described by her model character, Montague Sydenham: "The interests of our family make it a point of conscience with us to maintain our own opinions till we are convinced we may do better; we are both trustees for our infants; and we act, I hope, conscientiously." H. even advocates educating a small percentage of girls: "There have been and are, women who ought to follow the impulse of attainment to its utmost limits; it seems designed by providence that they should; they are eminently gifted, and they should be pre-eminently diligent."

Here and in *Rosanne* (1814), H. bluntly raises the spectre of child abuse and its reverberations through generations. Lady Luxmore's neglect of Gertrude hearkens back to her mother's miserable childhood: "She was beaten and horsewhipt for doing mischief, which if she had had the will she had not the power to perpetrate." In *Rosanne,* Frank Eugene's weak character derives from his guardian's immorality and from his father's earlier capriciousness: "The cane, the horsewhip, the any thing at hand, were reason, argument, reprehension" atoned for by excessive indulgence.

H. remained politically reactionary, praising a "parody of a thorough-German tragedy in the 'Anti-Jacobin,' one of those invaluable productions, which, while they made us laugh, contributed to save us as a nation from revolution." She comments acidly: "There were English ladies . . . at this period, who made no scruple of avowedly wishing for a revolution. It is a pity they were not indulged with a private exhibition." *Rosanne's* plot (the conversion of an atheist father by his Christian daughter) ultimately sags under H.'s moralizing, although the *British Critic* was kind: "If the reader can find resolution sufficient to be jolted through the first seven or eight chapters, he will be amply repaid by the remainder." More readable and less preachy, *Heraline* (1821) revolves on a bizarre plan of Heraline's father using all sorts of clever but indirect maneuvers to prevent her marrying a particular man. Heraline, wanting to oblige but forced to act in ignorance, marries the very man she was to avoid. H.'s last novel, *Annaline* (1824), following the engaging *Anecdotes,* is a genuine surprise: an outright romance extravagantly plotted, which H. declined to acknowledge. This most entertaining of her novels suggests a potential that H. sadly never seems to have quite fulfilled.

WORKS: *Letters on the Female Mind: Its Powers and Pursuits* (1793). (trans.) *Siegwart, A Tale from the German,* by J. M. Miller (1806). *The Countess and Gertrude, or Modes of Discipline* (1811). *Rosanne, or Father's Labour Lost* (1814). (with H. Hawkins) *Sermonets* (1814). *Heraline, or Opposite Proceedings* (1821). *Anecdotes, Biographical Sketches and Memoirs* (1823). *Annaline, or Motive Hunting* (1824). *Old Bedford or the Silent (?): Gossip About Dr. Johnson and Others, Being Chapters from the Memoirs of Miss Laetitia Matilda Hawkins,* ed. F. H. Skrine (1920). *Memoirs* (selections) (1978).

BIBLIOGRAPHY: *Anti-Jacobin Review* (1813). *British Critic* (1812, 1815, 1821, 1824). *Critical Review* (1812, 1815). *Literary Chronicle* (1824). *Monthly Critical Gazette* (1824). *New Monthly Magazine* (1821). *Universal Review* (1824). *Western Luminary* (1824).

For articles in reference works, see: *Feminist. ToddDBA.*

Kathleen L. Fowler

Mary Hays

BORN: 1760, Southwark.
DIED: 1843, London.
WROTE UNDER: Eusebia.

H. achieved contemporary recognition as a novelist and feminist writer. She was a member of the radical London circle that included the publisher Joseph Johnson, William Godwin, and Mary Wollstonecraft. Conservatives condemned her as the leading disciple and propagator of Wollstonecraft's dangerous feminist ideas.

H. came from a dissenting family in Southwark, where she grew up. At the age of eighteen, she fell in love with John Eccles, also a dissenter. Although he returned her affection, the match was opposed by both sets of parents. Parental approval was finally won in 1780, but Eccles died unexpectedly shortly thereafter. H. turned to study and reading for consolation. She came under the guidance of Robert Robinson, a rational dissenter who later became a Unitarian. Through him, she was introduced to many leading radicals. She attended lectures at the Hackney dissenting academy in the late 1780s. Her first publication was a reply to Gilbert Wakefield's attack on dissenting public worship. This pamphlet, published under the name Eusebia, brought her into the radical circle of Joseph Johnson.

H. was much moved by Wollstonecraft's *Vindication of the Rights of Woman* (1792). She asked Wollstonecraft to read her *Letters and Essays, Moral and Miscellaneous* before publication and gladly received the advice not to make excuses for being female. H. is usually credited with reintroducing Wollstonecraft and Godwin in 1796, a meeting that resulted in their marriage. *Memoirs of Emma Courtney,* H.'s first novel, was published in 1796. Like H.'s other novels, it was partly autobiographical. Her portrayal of a passionate woman whose proffered love was refused was regarded as shocking at the time. It also laid H. open to all sorts of gossip and stories about possible affairs. In the mid-1790s, H. was also writing for periodicals, especially the *Monthly Magazine.* She wrote an important obituary of Wollstonecraft for that periodical, as well as one for *Annual Necrology 1797–1798.* By the late 1790s, the radicals were being attacked on all sides. H. was mercilessly caricatured by such authors as Elizabeth Hamilton and Richard Polwhele. *Appeal to the Men of Great Britain in Behalf of Women* was published anonymously by Johnson in 1798; it was then and later ascribed to H. Its ideas are very similar to those of Wollstonecraft's *Vindication,* though it emphasizes religious teachings far more.

After 1800, H. retreated from her most radical feminist position. She lived for several years outside London, teaching school and undertaking charitable projects. She continued to be concerned about the plight of women trapped in the expectations of society. Her later works concentrated more on moral and spiritual support, but always with the assumption that women should have a proper education and some means of supporting themselves.

WORKS: *Cursory Remarks on an Enquiry into the Expediency and Propriety of Public or Social Worship* (1792). *Letters and Essays, Moral and Miscellaneous* (1793). *Memoirs of Emma Courtney* (1796; ed. E. Ty, 1996). *Appeal to the Men of Great Britain in Behalf of Women* (1798). *The Victim of Prejudice* (1799). *Female Biography; or, Memoirs of Illustrious and Celebrated Women, of all Ages and Countries* (1802). *Harry Clinton; or A Tale of Youth* (1804). *Historical Dialogues for Young Persons* (1806–1808). *The Brothers; or Consequences* (1815). *Family Annals; or The Sisters* (1817). *Memoirs of Queens, Illustrious and Celebrated* (1825). *The Love Letters of Mary Hays (1779–1780),* ed. A. F. Wedd (1925).

BIBLIOGRAPHY: Adams, M. R. *Studies in Literary Background of English Radicalism* (1947). Kelly, G. *Women, Writing, and Revolution 1790–1827* (1993). Luria, G. *Signs* (1977). Pollin, B. R. *EA* (1971). *The Fate of the Fenwicks: Letters to Mary Hays (1798–1828),* ed. A. F. Wedd (1927).

For articles in reference works, see: *BDMBR. Europa. Dabundo. Oxford. ToddDBA.*

Barbara Brandon Schnorrenberg

Eliza Fowler Haywood (or Heywood)

BORN: 1693, London.
DIED: 25 February 1756, London.
DAUGHTER OF: a London shopkeeper and his wife.
MARRIED: the Reverend Valentine Haywood, c. 1710; separated by 1719; widow (?) by 1728.
WROTE UNDER: E. H.; Exploralibus; E. Haywood; Eliza Haywood (or Heywood); Mrs. Eliza Haywood; R. Justicia (?); Mira; T. B.

Recent scholarship has unearthed a wealth of new biographical information about H., unsettling longtime clichés about her life and writing. Author of more than seventy novels, plays, translations, conduct books, and periodicals, H. was a major figure in the rise and growth of the popular novel in eighteenth-century England. H.'s career spans nearly half a century; her works reflect both the changing demand for fiction in the eighteenth century and her consistent concern for the economic and educational constraints faced by women in this period.

H. occasionally appealed to readers' generosity on the basis of her limited education (and her need to earn a living by writing) but more often claimed to be better educated than the average woman. She left her parents' home to become an actress and appeared as Chloe in a production of *Timon of Athens; or, the Man-Hater* in Dublin in 1715. Although she continued to write plays through the 1720s and 1730s—including several for Henry Fielding's experimental (and politically oppositional) "Little Theatre" in Haymarket—she turned to writing novels, she said, because her plays proved only moderately successful.

H. lived a life of intrigue and adventure, and she knew many political and literary figures. She was married only briefly; her husband, Valentine Haywood, was neither the father of her two children, who were born out of wedlock, nor an important figure in her life. She was lover with the poet Richard Savage and the actor-playwright Richard Hatchett, with whom she later worked in her own publishing business.

H. launched her highly successful career as a novelist in 1719 with the bodice-ripping romance, *Love in Excess; or, the Fatal Enquiry.* In her numerous short novels of the 1720s, H. created a form that combined the expansive, emotionally rich texture of seventeenth-century French romances with the day-to-day problems and dangers of eighteenth-century English women. H.'s characters often derive from songs and ballads of the period and from stories available in the new mass journalism. By using available popular forms, H. was able to appeal to a wide audience. At the same time, she manipulated romance conventions to explore and develop the emotional side of women's economic and sexual vulnerability, an emphasis that became central to the epistolary fiction of the 1740s.

H.'s novels often contrast the experience of several heroines, suggesting the range of women's needs and desires and their different experiences of pleasure and danger in love. In *The British Recluse* (1722), Cleomira and Belinda meet and share their stories of betrayal; they end the novel living together in the country seeking "revenge" on the world of love that has betrayed them. Similarly, by way of accident or abandonment, H.'s upper-class heroines often travel to remote parts of the world, where, in order to survive, they must dress as men or as peasant women. In *Philidore and Placentia* (1727), such a period of wandering and disguise allows the heroine's emotional education and eventual ability to negotiate her own marriage settlement. Although most of H.'s plots end either in a happy marriage or in a series of tragic deaths, they often maintain the possibility of other sexual arrangements—bigamy, homosexuality, celibacy—right up to the end. This fantasy structure continues to inform popular romances by and for women and H. was crucial in developing explicitly erotic popular narrative for women.

We have much less information about H.'s writing in

the 1730s because the bulk of it was published anonymously. In 1725, she began a series of direct stabs at the ruling elite with the politically scandalous *Memoirs of a Certain Island,* based on Delariviere Manley's *The New Atlantis* (1709), *Memoirs of a Certain Island* presents thinly veiled contemporary figures in a series of sexual and political exploits. H.'s funny but deadly serious political satires were probably part of what incited Alexander Pope's wrath and his damning her as a half-naked woman surrounded by illegitimate children in *The Dunciad* (1728). Her best political satire, the anti-Walpole *Adventures of Eovaii, Princess of Ijaveo* (1736), is dedicated to the Duchess of Marlborough and calls itself a "Pre-Adamitical History." Here, H. indicts everything from spying to the sexual inequities built into language and firmly advocates republicanism and sexual freedom instead.

During the 1730s, H. also acted in, wrote, and collaborated on several plays including *The Opera of Operas* (1733). After the Licensing Act closed Henry Fielding's "Little Theatre" in Haymarket, effectively silencing political and satirical theatrical performances, H. returned to writing fiction. In 1741, she published *Anti-Pamela; of Feign'd Innocence Detected,* one of numerous parodies of Samuel Richardson's best-selling novel *Pamela* (1740). Appealing to the advocates as well as the opponents of the new conduct literature, H. wrote a number of her own conduct books and periodicals. These range from *A Present for a Servant-Maid* (1743), which suggests how to fend off a master's sexual advances, to the highly successful and decorous *Female Spectator* (1744–46), the first English periodical specifically addressed to a female audience. Although the *Female Spectator* is organized around a ladies' discussion circle, it was written entirely by H.

The very different kinds of writing—one that advocates proper female conduct and one that satirizes and subverts it—come together in H.'s later novels, especially in the delightful *History of Miss Betsy Thoughtless* (1751). Betsy Thoughtless is one of the great naughty heroines of all time, "thoughtless" because she repeatedly ignores her own danger as well as others' concerns in pursuing her own freedom and experience. Betsy is nearly raped several times and only learns how vulnerable she is—both sexually and economically—by her disastrous marriage to the cruel and selfish Munden. In *Betsy Thoughtless* and again in *The Wife* (1756), H. suggests that because divorce was all but legally impossible, women should leave, if necessary, in order to free themselves of bondage within marriage. A writer of incredible range, passion, and political insight, H. is one of the major writers of the eighteenth century, one whose works were known and imitated by Richardson, Fielding, and others.

WORKS: *Love in Excess; or, the Fatal Enquiry* (1719–20; rpt. 1994). (trans.) *Letters from a Lady of Quality to a Chevalier,* by E. Boursault (1721). *The Fair Captive: a Tragedy* (1721). *The British Recluse; or, the Secret History of Cleomira, Suppos'd Dead* (1722). *The Injur'd Husband; or, the Mistaken Resentment* (1723). *Idalia; or, the Unfortunate Mistress* (1723). *Lasselia; or, the Self Abandoned* (1723). *A Wife to be Lett: A Comedy* (1728). *The Rash Revolver; or, the Untimely Discovery* (1724; rpt 1973). *The Arragonian Queen: A Secret History* (1724). *The Fatal Secret; or, Constancy in Distress* (1724). *A Spy upon the Conjurer* (1724). *The Surprise; or, Constancy Rewarded* (1724). (trans.) *La Belle Assemblee; or, the Adventures of Six Days,* by Mme. deGomez (1724–26). *The Tea-Table; or, a Conversation between Some Polite Persons of Both Sexes, at a Lady's Visiting Day* (1724). *The Masqueraders; or, Fatal Curiosity* (1724). *The Works of Mrs. Eliza Haywood* (1724). *The Memoirs of Baron de Brosse* (1725). *Memoirs of a Certain Island Adjacent to the Kingdom of Utopia* (1725; rpt. 1972). *The Unequal Conflict; or, Nature Triumphant* (1725). *Mary Stuart, Queen of Scots: Being the Secret History of her Life, and the Real Cause of her Misfortunes* (1725). *Bath Intrigues* (1725). *Secret Histories, Novels and Poems* (1725). *The Mercenary Lover; or, the Unfortunate Heiresses* (1726). *The City Jilt; or, the Alderman Turn'd Beau* (1726). *Secret History of the Present Intrigues of the Court of Caramania* (1727; rpt. 1972). *Letters from the Palace of Fame* (1727). *The Fruitless Enquiry* (1727). *Cleomelia; or, the Generous Mistress* (1727). *The Life of Mme. Villesache* (1727). (trans.) *Love in its Variety,* by M. Bandello, (1727). *Philidore and Placentia, or L'Amour trop delicat* (1727; rpt. 1963). *The Agreeable Caledonian; or, Memoirs of Signiora di Morella, a Roman Lady* (1728). *Irish Artifice; or, The History of Clarina* (1728). *Persecuted Virtue, or the Cruel Lover* (1728). *The Perplex'd Dutchess; or, Treachery Rewarded* (1728). *Frederick, Duke of Brunswick Lunenburgh: A Tragedy* (1729). *The Fair Hebrew* (1729). *Love-Letters on All Occasions Lately Passed between Persons of Distinction* (1730). *Secret Memoirs of the Late Mr. Duncan Campbell* (1732). *The Opera of Operas; or, Tom Thumb the Great* (1733). (trans.) *L'Entrien des Beaux Esprits: Being the Sequel to La Belle Assemblee by Mme. deGomez* (1734). *The Adventures of Eovaii, Princess of Ijaveo* (1736; rpt 1972). *Anti-Pamela; of Feign'd Innocence Detected* (1741; rpt., 1975). *The Virtuous Villager; or, Virgin's Victory* (trans., 1742; rpt. 1975). *A Present for a Servant-Maid; or, The Sure Means of Gaining Love and Esteem* (1743). *The Fortunate Foundlings: Being the Genuine History of Colonel M—rs and His Sister, Madam du P—y* (1744; rpt. 1974). *The Female Spectator* (1744–46; rpt. 1929). *The Parrot* (1746). *Life's Progress Through the Passions; or, the Adventures of Natura* (1748; rpt. 1974). *Epistles for the Ladies* (1749–50). *The History of Miss Betsy Thoughtless* (1751; rpt. 1986). *The History of Jemmy and Jenny Jessamy* (1752; rpt. 1974). *The Invisible Spy* (1754). *The Wife* (1756). *The Husband, In Answer to the Wife* (1756). *The History of Miss Leonora Meadowson* (1788). *Plays of Eliza Haywood,* ed. V. Rudolph (1983). *Four Novels of Eliza Haywood* (1983). *Masquerade Novels,* ed. M. A. Schofield (1986). *Three Novellas: The Distress'd Orphan, The Double Marriage, The City Jilt,* ed. E. A. Wilputte (1995). *Popular Fiction by Women, 1660–1730,* ed. P. Backscheider and J. Richetti (1996). *Eliza Haywood, Plays and Fiction,* ed. P. Backscheider (1996). *Selections from the Female Spectator,* ed. P. Spacks (1996).

BIBLIOGRAPHY: Backscheider, P. *Spectacular Politics* (1993). Ballster, R. *Seductive Forms: Women's Amatory Fiction from 1684 to 1740* (1992). Beasley, J. *Novels of the 1740s* (1982). Blouch, C. *SEL* (1991). Blouch, C. *Eliza Hay-*

wood: Questions on the Life and Works (1992). Bowers, T. *The Politics of Motherhood* (1996). Craft-Fairfield, C. *Masquerade and Gender* (1993). *Compendious Conversations: The Method of Dialogue in the Early Enlightenment,* ed. K. L. Cope (1992). Craft, C. A. *MLR* (1991). Doody, M. A. *A Natural Passion* (1974). Eaves, T. C. D. and B. D. Kimpel. *Samuel Richardson* (1971). Fields, P. S., in *Compendious Conversations: The Method of Dialogue in The Early Enlightment,* ed. K. L. Cope (1992). Gallagher, C. *Nobody's Story* (1994). Green, K. *The Courtship Novel, 1740–1820* (1991). Horner, J. M. *The English Women Novelists and Their Connection with the Feminist Movement (1688–1797)* (1930). Kern, J. B. *SECC* (1981). Kishi, E. *TCEL* (1980). MacCarthy, B. G. *Women Writers: Their Contribution to the English Novel (1621–1744)* (1944). McDowell, P. *The Women of Grub Street* (1998). Messenger, A. *His and Hers* (1986). Nester, D. J. *SEL* (1994). Reeve, C. *The Progress of Romance* (1785). Richetti, J. *Popular Fiction Before Richardson: Narrative Patterns 1700–1739* (1969). Richetti, J. *SNNTS* (1987). *Cambridge Companion to the Eighteenth-Century Novel,* ed. J. Richetti (1996). Rogers, K. *Feminism in Eighteenth-Century England* (1982). Schofield, M. A. *Quiet Rebellion: The Fictional Heroines of Eliza Fowler Haywood* (1982). Schofield, M. A. *CEA* (1981). Schofield, M. A. *SECC* (1983). Schofield, M. A., in *Fetter'd or Free: British Women Novelists, 1670–1815,* ed. M. A. Schofield and C. Macheski (1986). Shrevelow, K. *Reader* (1985). Spencer, J. *The Rise of the Woman Novelist* (1986). Todd, J. *The Sign of Angellica* (1989). Whicher, G. F. *The Life and Romances of Mrs. Eliza Haywood* (1913). Williamson, M. *Raising Their Voices* (1990).

For articles in reference works, see: *Bloomsbury. Cambridge. DLB. DNB. Feminist. GWELN. Oxford. ToddBWW. ToddDBA.*

Other references: *CEA* (1981). *Columbia History of the British Novel* (1994). *HLQ* (1978). *MLR* (1991). *N&Q* (1973, 1983, 1989, 1991, 1995). *PQ* (1989). *RomN* (1969). *SECC* (1981, 1983). *SEL* (1991, 1994). *SNNTS* (1987). *SP* (1973). *TSLL* (1964).

Carol L. Barash

H. D.: See *Doolittle, Hilda*

Annie French Hector

BORN: 23 June 1825, Dublin, Ireland.
DIED: 10 July 1902, London.
DAUGHTER OF: Robert French and Anne Malone.
MARRIED: Alexander Hector, 1858.
WROTE UNDER: Mrs. Alexander; Annie French Hector.

The only daughter of a Dublin barrister, H. was educated under governesses and was widely read. After some financial difficulties, her family left for Liverpool and after much moving about finally settled in London; H. returned only once to Ireland. She established many literary friendships in London, notably with Eliza Lynn and W.H. Wills, editor of *Household Words.* It was in this magazine that she first attracted attention with an article, "Billeted in Boulogne" (1856). She had previously written two novels that went unnoticed.

After her marriage to an ambitious explorer and merchant, H. wrote little since her husband thought it unwomanly. After his health began to fail, however, she published *Which Shall It Be?* (1866), and shortly before he died in 1875, she published her best-known novel, *The Wooing O't,* which had appeared in installments in *Temple Bar* in 1873 and as a three-volume work under her pseudonym, Mrs. Alexander. The story is a wholesome Cinderella-like tale of a thoroughly good but poor young girl who marries well at the end of the novel.

Left alone with three daughters and a son, H. began to write in earnest to support her family. They lived for six years in Germany and France, an experience reflected in her novels; after three years in St. Andrews, they moved in 1885 to London where H. occupied herself with writing. *The Saturday Review* had judged *The Wooing O't* to be "a book of healthy tone and pleasant feeling, womanly but not sentimental," but her many later novels were judged to be "dry" and "without life." For example, *Her Dearest Foe* (1876) reads now as a rather hackneyed story of a young widow's struggle to regain her husband's property from a gentleman with whom she falls in love and eventually marries.

A number of H.'s novels were popular in America as well as in Britain, and eleven were printed in second editions. *The Freres* (1882) was translated into Spanish, *By Woman's Wit* (1886) into Danish, and *Mona's Choice* (1887) into Polish. Her final novel, *Kitty Costello* (1904), describing an Irish girl's experience in England, contains autobiographical details. Perhaps the most outstanding characteristic of H.'s novels is their blandness, which makes them pleasant and light entertainment.

WORKS: *Agnes Waring* (1854). *Kate Vernon* (1855). *Which Shall It Be?* (1866). *The Wooing O't* (1873). *Ralph Wilton's Weird* (1875). *Her Dearest Foe* (1876). *The Heritage of Langdale* (1877). *Maid, Wife or Widow* (1879). *A Peep at Presburg and Perth* (1879). *The Australian Aunt* (1882). *At Bay* (1882). *The Freres* (1882). *Look Before You Leap* (1882). *Valerie's Fate* (1882). *The Admiral's Ward* (1883). *The Executor* (1883). *Second Life* (1883). *Beaton's Bargain* (1884). *Mrs. Vereker's Courier Maid* (1884). *By Woman's Wit* (1886) *Forging the Fetters* (1887). *Mona's Choice* (1887). *A Life Interest* (1888). *A Crooked Path* (1889) *False Scent* (1889). *Blind Fate* (1890). *A Woman's Heart* (1890). *Mammon* (1891). *Well Won* (1891). *What Gold Cannot Buy* (1891). *The Snare of the Fowler* (1892). *For His Sake* (1892). *Found Wanting* (1893). *Broken Links* (1894). *A Choice of Evil* (1894). *A Ward in Chancery* (1894). *A Fight with Fate* (1896). *A Winning Hazard* (1896). *Barbara, Lady's Maid and Peeress* (1897). *A Golden Autumn* (1897). *Mrs. Chrichton's Creditor* (1897). *V. C. Brown* (1899). *The Cost of Her Pride* (1899). *A Missing Hero* (1900). *The Step Mother* (1900). *Through Fire to Fortune* (1900). *The Yellow Fiend* (1901). *Stronger than Love* (1902). *Kitty Costello* (1904).

BIBLIOGRAPHY: Black, H. *Notable Women Authors of the Day* (1893).

For articles in reference works, see: *BDIW. DNB.*

Carole M. Shaffer-Koros

Helforth, John: See *Doolittle, Hilda (H. D.)*

Felicia Dorothea Browne Hemans

BORN: 25 September 1793, Liverpool.
DIED: 16 May 1835, Dublin, Ireland.
DAUGHTER OF: George Browne and Felicity Wagner Browne.
MARRIED: Captain Alfred Hemans, 1812.
WROTE UNDER: Felicia Browne; Felicia Hemans; Mrs. Hemans.

The most popular woman poet of the nineteenth century, H. spent most of her life in Wales, where her family moved after her father's business failures. A beautiful, precocious child, she was educated at home under her mother's direction. She studied French, Spanish, Italian, Portuguese, German, and Latin. She read Shakespeare at the age of six, began writing poetry at eight, and published her first volume at fourteen—dedicated to the Prince of Wales and listing more than 900 subscribers, including her future husband. Her marriage lasted less than six years. Shortly before the birth of their fifth son, Captain Hemans went to Rome "for the sake of his health," and was never seen again. Pursuing "uninterrupted domestic privacy," she devoted herself to her sons and mother. American writer Lydia Sigourney attributed H.'s success to the influence of "maternal culture": "By her prolonged residence under the maternal wing, she was sheltered from the burden of those cares which sometimes press out the life of song." The mother's death in 1827 seems to have marked the beginning of her own decline. H. died of tuberculosis at age forty-two, mourned by William Wordsworth as "that holy Spirit, / . . . who, ere her summer faded / Has sunk into a breathless sleep."

H. produced numerous volumes of poetry, songs, translations, and some periodical essays. Her five-act tragedy, *The Vespers of Palermo* (1823), failed at Covent Garden but was produced more successfully in Edinburgh with the assistance of Sir Walter Scott. H. read, and often quoted, Shakespeare, Petrarch, Lope de Vega, Tasso, Gibbon, Schiller, Novalis, Goethe, Byron, Shelley, and Mme. de Staël. *Corinne*, she said, "has a power over me which is quite indescribable. Some passages seem to give me back my own thoughts and feelings, my whole inner being." She corresponded with Joanna Baillie and Mary Howitt, and in 1829, she visited Scott at Abbotsford. At the instigation of Maria Jewsbury, she also became acquainted with Wordsworth, whom she visited in 1830 at Rydal.

Although she set most of her long poems in exotic places—Moorish palaces, Carthaginian ruins, Spanish castles—and invoked stories of political rebellion and war, her real concerns are domestic. Her chosen themes are, in Sigourney's words, "the loveliness of nature, the endearments of home, the deathless strength of the affections, the noble aims of disinterested virtue, the power of that piety which plucks the sting from death." Maternal love is a prevailing concern, especially in *The Records of Woman* (1828), poetical tales written shortly after her mother's death.

H. provides insight into the critical values and popular taste of the nineteenth century. She was acclaimed by such prominent reviewers as Francis Jeffrey and recommended for study in the schools by Matthew Arnold (her poems, he said, "have real merits of expression and sentiment"). In America, where H. was the most frequently anthologized English writer in the gift books and annuals, critics Andrews Norton and Andrew Peabody ranked her work above Milton's and Homer's. Essay after essay defines her as the perfect lady poet.

Assuming that the "nature of this poetess is more interesting than her genius, or than its finest productions," reviewers evaluate the poetry in terms of her personality. She is applauded for living in retirement and maintaining proper "feminine reserve." Readers note her "tremulous sensibility," "delicate organization," and "intense susceptiveness," but conclude that she keeps her feelings under control. "The calm mistress of her stormiest emotions," H. exudes the right amount of melancholy and reveals "no unsatisfied cravings." Moreover, she has little sense of artistic self-consciousness. As Sigourney said, "Sympathy, not fame, was the desire of her being." H. proclaimed that she was determined not to become "that despicable thing, a woman living upon admiration!" In "Properzia Rossi," a celebrated woman sculptor decries her fame as "worthless" because her statue has no effect on the knight she adores.

Being "a genuine woman, and, therefore, a true Christian," H. is commended for dispensing religious and moral sentiments. According to William Michael Rossetti, she had "that love of good and horror of evil which characterize a scrupulous female mind." Her favorite poem, "The Forest Sanctuary," concerns a sixteenth-century Spaniard who flees to North America in search of religious freedom; "The Sceptic," a poem arguing for the necessity of deism, infuriated Lord Byron ("too stiltified & atmospheric—& quite wrong"), but most readers saw it as appropriate for women to act as "natural guardians of morality and faith."

Women also praised H. in extravagant terms. Author Maria Jewsbury idolized her as "a Muse, a grace, a variable child, a dependent woman, the Italy of human beings." George Eliot, who quoted "our sweet Mrs. Hemans" frequently during the early 1840s, called *The Forest Sanctuary* "exquisite!" Elizabeth Barrett Browning and Letitia Landon wrote elegies for H., while Sigourney and other American "poetesses" claimed her as their precursor. Indeed, it has been suggested that H. "ought to be read at length before trying any of the great woman poets of the nineteenth century." Despite an awkward situation that left her living without her husband, H. proved that it was possible to be a poet, a lady, a mother, and a great popular success. But the gushing praise for her poetry reveals a double critical standard that would limit the aspirations and diminish the achievements of women poets throughout the century.

WORKS: *Poems* (1808). *England and Spain, or Valour and Patriotism* (1808). *Domestic Affections, and Other Poems* (1812). *The Restoration of the Works of Art to Italy* (1816). *Modern Greece, a Poem* (1817). *Translations from Camoens and Other Poets* (1818). *Tales and Historic Scenes, in Verse* (1819). *Wallace's Invocation to Bruce: a Poem* (1819). *The Sceptic* (1820). *Stanzas to the Memory of the late King* (1820). *Dartmoor, a Poem* (1821). *Welsh Melodies* (1822). *The Vespers of Palermo* (1823). *The Siege of Valencia, a Dramatick Poem. The Last Constantine, With Other Poems* (1823). *The Forest Sanctuary, and Other Poems* (1825). *Lays of Many Lands* (1825). *The Poetical Works* (1825). *Hymns for Childhood* (1827). *The Records of Woman, with Other Poems* (1828). *Casabianca* (1828). *Songs of the Affections, with Other Poems* (1830). *Poetical Works of Hemans, Heber and Polock*, ed. J. Crissy and G. Goodman (1831). *Hymns on the Works of Nature for the Use of Children* (1833). *Hymns for Childhood* (1834). *National Lyrics and Songs for Music* (1834). *Scenes and Hymns of Life, with Other Religious Poems* (1834). *Poetical Remains* (1836). *Works (with Memoir by her Sister)*, 7 vols. (1839). *Early Blossoms, With a Life of the Authoress* (1840). *Selected Poetical Works* (1865). *Poems*, ed. R. Griswold (1875). *Favorite Poems* (1877). *The Hemans Birthday Book* (1884). *Selections* (1911).

BIBLIOGRAPHY: Chorley, H. F. *Memorials of Mrs. Hemans* (1836). Clarke, N. *Ambitious Heights: Writing, Friendship, Love: The Jewsbury Sisters, Felicia Hemans, and Jane Welsh Carlyle* (1990). Courtney, J. E. *The Adventurous Thirties: A Chapter in the Women's Movement* (1933). Cruse, A. *The Victorians and Their Reading* (1935). Hale, S. *Woman's Record, or Sketches of All Distinguished Women* (1870). Harding, A. J., in *Romantic Women Writers: Voices and Countervoices*, ed. P. Feldman and T. Kelley (1995). Helsinger, E., R. Sheets, and W. Veeder. *The Woman Question: Literary Issues* (1983). Hickok, K. *Representations of Women: Nineteenth-Century British Women's Poetry* (1984). Hughes, H. M. B. *Memoir of the Life and Writings of Mrs. Hemans* (1839). Jeffrey, F. *Edinburgh Review* (1829). Kaplan, C. *Salt and Bitter and Good* (1975). Leighton, A. *Victorian Women Poets: Writing Against the Heart* (1992). Lootens, T. *PMLA* (1994). Mack, A. *MLQ* (1993). McGann, J. *The Poetics of Sensibility: A Revolution in Literary Style* (1996). Reiman, D. H., intro. to *Poems* (1978). Ritchie, A. T. *Blackstick Papers* (1908). Robinson, E. S. *English Poetesses* (1883). Rossetti, W. M., "Prefatory Notice" in *The Poetical Works of Mrs. Felicia Hemans* (1837). Rowton, F. *The Female Poets of Great Britain* (1853). *A Short Sketch of the Life of Mrs. Hemans* (1835). Sigourney, L. H., "An Essay on Her Genius," in *The Works of Mrs. Hemans* (1840). Sweet, N., in *At the Limits of Romanticism: Essays in Cultural, Feminist, and Materialist Criticism*, ed. M. Favret and N. Watson (1994). Trinder, P. W. *Mrs. Hemans* (1984). Walford, L. B. *Twelve English Authoresses* (1893). Walker, C. *The Nightingale's Burden: Women Poets and American Culture before 1900* (1982). Williams, I. A. *London Mercury* (1922). Wolkson, S., in *Revisioning Romanticism: British Women Writers, 1776–1837*, ed. C. S. Wilson and J. Haefner (1994).

For articles in reference works, see: *Allibone. Bloomsbury. CBEL. DNB. Europa. Feminist. IDWB. NCBEL. OCCL. Oxford. ToddBWW.*

Other references: Cochran, P. *TLS* (21 July 1995).

Robin Sheets

Hemans, Mrs.: See *Hemans, Felicia Dorothea Browne*

Henrietta Maria

BORN: 12 November 1609, Paris.
DIED: 21 August 1669, Colombes (near Paris).
DAUGHTER OF: Henry IV and Marie de Medici.
MARRIED: Charles I, 1625 (by proxy).

Queen consort of King Charles I; mother of Charles II and James II; and grandmother of Mary II, William III, and Queen Anne—H. devoted herself to her husband and to her religion, the latter of which exacerbated the hostilities between Charles and Parliament that led to the English Civil Wars. The sixth child of the French king Henry IV and Marie de Medici, H. grew up in the royal nursery at Saint-Germain-en-Laye, France, in the company of both legitimate and illegitimate children of Henry IV. Her education focused primarily on religion, though her beautiful voice may have led to some voice training. She grew up in a court accustomed to participating in theatrical performances, and she imported this custom to the English court after her marriage to Charles by proxy in 1625. Her marriage became a love-match after the assassination in 1628 of the Duke of Buckingham, the king's closest confidant, and was the center of the masques that shaped court culture during the 1630s. The sumptuous aesthetic beauty of the masques combined with their inclusion of women as actresses and their proselytizing undercurrents irritated some, most notably William Prynne, whose *Histriomastix* (1633) was interpreted, in part, as a direct attack on H.'s active role in shaping court culture.

While H.'s active Roman Catholicism made her unpopular in England, it was her expedition to Holland in 1642 to pawn and sell crown jewels in order to raise money for arms and ammunition for the royalist army that led the House of Commons to charge her with treason in June 1643. Despite parliamentary plans to capture her on her return, she rejoined her husband at the displaced court at Oxford, where Margaret Lucas (later Margaret Cavendish, Duchess of Newcastle) attended her as a maid of honor and fled with her into exile in France in 1644. From France, H. continued to advise Charles on military, economic, religious, and political matters, but she was never to see him again. After his beheading in 1649, she devoted herself increasingly to monastic life, establishing a convent at Chaillot. She lived in England after the Restoration but returned to France in 1665, where in 1669 she died at her chateau at Colombes, near Paris.

The significance of her letters lies in their portrait of her active pursuit of religious, political, and military interests during the English Civil Wars. Recent work by Erica Veevers calls attention to the intertwining of her religious and aesthetic interests, casting new light on H.'s patronage of court masques and revealing her influence on writers like Inigo Jones and Walter Montagu.

WORKS: *Letters of Queen Henrietta Maria,* ed. Mary Anne Everett Green (1857; see also *Mémoires de Madame de Motteville,* 1869, parts of which were dictated by H.).

BIBLIOGRAPHY: Bone, Q. *Henrietta Maria* (1972). Oman, C. *Henrietta Maria* (1936). Peacock, J., in *The Court Masque,* ed. D. Lindley (1984). Veevers, E. *Images of Love and Religion: Queen Henrietta Maria and Court Entertainments* (1989).

For articles in reference works, see: *DNB.*

Other references: *EHR* (1978). *ELR* (1983) *SN* (1970).

Anna Battigelli

Herbert, Mary: See *Sidney, Mary*

Herring, Geilles: See *Somerville and Ross (Edith Œnone Somerville)*

Georgette Heyer

BORN: 16 August 1902, London.
DIED: 4 July 1974, London.
DAUGHTER OF: George Heyer and Sylvia Watkins Heyer.
MARRIED: George Ronald Rougier, 1925.
WROTE UNDER: Georgette Heyer; Stella Martin.

H., the eldest of three children and the only daughter of George and Sylvia Heyer, was privately educated and did not attend university. When H. was seventeen, she wrote a story, as she said, "to relieve my own boredom, and my brother's." Although she had written merely to entertain her brother Boris while he was recovering from an illness, her father, who himself had written several articles for *Punch,* liked the story and encouraged her to work on it for publication. She did, and in 1921 H.'s first novel, *The Black Moth,* was published.

Despite her early success, she cared little for publicity. Throughout her writing career of more than fifty years, she made no appearances and never granted an interview, even in the interest of increasing book sales. She used the pseudonym Stella Martin for her third book but thereafter retained the name of H. That she was an early success would, however, prove to be especially important in 1925. When her father died, she became the principal means of financial support for her mother and two younger brothers.

In 1925, she married a mining engineer; in 1927, she joined him in Africa, but he was unhappy with his job and H. was unhappy with their travels, so in 1929 they returned to England. There, with his wife's encouragement, he began studying to be a barrister, something he had long wished for; H.'s writing was now providing the basic financial support not only for her mother's family but also for her own.

H. was a prolific writer. Best known for her Regency novels, her publishers noted that she "worked quickly . . . and made few corrections, soaking herself in the Regency Period—becoming an expert on the history and manners of that time." Indeed, she kept copious notes and sketches of Regency life and fashion. This attention to detail did not encumber her style, which is marked by a verve and wit that at times has been compared to that of Jane Austen. Instead, the details of dress and use of Regency slang lend a viable sense of scene to these novels in which the functions of social class, manners, and romance figure predominantly. A 1948 *New York Times* review captured the tone of these novels when the reviewer said of H. that she "writes cheerful and highly unorthodox historical novels, set in Regency England, in which people never lose their lives, their virtue, or even their tempers."

Such a novel is *The Nonesuch* (1962), in which Sir Waldo Hawkridge comes to Broom Hall, setting the countryside in a turmoil as families rush to entertain him with the most stylish and engaging parties, mothers and daughters concoct matchmaking schemes, and the young men of the town try desperately to emulate this paragon of style known as the "Nonesuch." The story contains common elements of the romance genre. The hero suddenly appears in a small town, unknown but by his reputation, and falls in love with Ancilla Trent, governess of the feisty and coquettish Miss Tiffany Wield. Tiffany, "a most accomplished flirt," determines to charm the Nonesuch and at least capture the heart of the young Lord Julian. Yet in the end, it is the "very gentle" but courageous Miss Patience Chartley who takes Lord Julian's heart.

H., here as in many of her Regency romances, relieves the potential melodrama of these situations with humor, wit, and a refreshing use of common sense. Characters are well defined and even the most annoying Tiffany is likeable. H. develops the potential of the genre by mirroring characters and relationships—the Nonesuch and Ancilla Trent with the young Lord Julian and Patience Chartley, the coquette with the gentle beauty, fashion with foppery. The humorous romantic complications are enlivened by the overriding satire of the society that busies itself in frenzied albeit always clumsy attempts to marry off the Nonesuch or to imitate his fashion and skill. Good manners, "tradition, and upbringing" are the measure of the nobility of character in these novels that exemplify the best elements of the romance genre right up to the climax when the runaway Tiffany must be rescued and finally taught a lesson by the Nonesuch.

While H. is best known for these Regency novels, she also published a dozen mysteries, the first being *Footsteps in the Dark* (1932). Her husband, while studying for the bar, frequently collaborated with her on these novels by helping with the plot. The wit, clear characterization, and closely defined social scene that marked her Regency novels were also important elements of her detective novels. Two of H.'s characters—Scotland Yard detectives Superintendent Hannasyde and Inspector Hemingway—make return appearances in eight of these novels as they frequently confront eccentric characters whose humor enlivens both the investigation and the novel.

While H. at times criticized her own work as not being "real" literature, she summarized many readers' responses as she noted that "it's unquestionably good escapist literature . . . its period detail is good . . . and . . . I will say that it is very good fun."

WORKS: *The Black Moth* (1921). *The Great Roxhythe* (1922). (as Stella Martin) *The Transformation of Philip Jettan* (1923). *Instead of the Thorn* (1923). *Simon the Coldheart* (1925). *These Old Shades* (1926). *Helen* (1926). *The Masqueraders* (1928). *Beauvallet* (1929). *Pastel* (1929). *The Barren Corn* (1930). *The Conqueror* (1931). *Footsteps in the Dark* (1932). *Devil's Cab* (1932). *Why Shoot a Butler?* (1933). *The Unfinished Clue* (1934). *The Convenient Marriage* (1934). *Death in the Stocks* (1935). *Regency Buck* (1935). *Behold, Here's Poison!* (1936). *The Talisman Ring* (1936). *They Found Him Dead* (1937). *An Infamous Army* (1937). *A Blunt Instrument* (1938). *Royal Escape* (1938). *No Wind of Blame* (1939). *The Spanish Bride* (1940). *The Corinthian* (1940). *Envious Casa* (1941). *Faro's Daughter* (1941). *Penhallow* (1942). *Friday's Child* (1944). *The Reluctant Widow* (1946). *The Foundling* (1948). *Arabella* (1949). *The Grand Sophy* (1950). *Duplicate Death* (1951). *The Quiet Gentleman* (1951). *Detection Unlimited* (1953). *Cotillion* (1953). *The Toll-Gate* (1954). *Bath Tangle* (1955). *Sprig Muslin* (1956). *April Lady* (1957). *Sylvester: or The Wicked Uncle* (1957). *Venetia* (1958). *The Unknown Ajax* (1959). *Pistols for Two and Other Stories* (1960). *A Civil Contract* (1961). *The Nonesuch* (1962). *False Colours* (1963). *Frederica* (1965). *Black Sheep* (1966). *Cousin Kate* (1968). *Charity Girl* (1970). *Lady of Quality* (1972). *My Lord John* (1975).

BIBLIOGRAPHY: Bargainier, E. F. *Clues* (1982). Devlin, J. P. *ArmD* (1984). Glass, E. R. and A. Mineo, in *La Performance del Testo*, ed. F. Marucci (1984). Hodge, J. A. *The Private World of Georgette Heyer* (1984). Pall, E. *NYTBR* (30 April 1989).

For articles in reference works, see: *CA*. *Feminist*. *Oxford*. *TCC&MW*. *ToddBWW*.

Other references: *NYT* (6 June 1974). *NYTBR* (21 March 1948).

Paula Connolly

Emily Henrietta Hickey

BORN: 12 April 1845, Macmine Castle, County Wexford, Ireland.
DIED: 9 September 1924, St. John's Wood, London.
DAUGHTER OF: Canon John Stewart Hickey and [given name unknown] Newton-King Hickey.

Called a "brilliant essayist, the erudite student of early English texts, [and] the spoiled child of the Victorian versemakers" by her biographer, Enid Dinnis, H.'s literary career began when her poem, "Told in the Firelight," was published in *Cornhill Magazine* before she was twenty-one years old. From this modest beginning grew a bibliography encompassing a novel, several volumes of poetry, numerous critical and biographical essays, and short stories.

H., whose ancestry was Anglo-Irish and Scots, was born at the home of Pierce Newton-King, her maternal grandfather, and passed her childhood in the rectory at Goresbridge, Co. Kilkenny, and later at Clonmulsh, Co. Carlow. Her paternal grandfather, the Reverend William Hickey, was famous for the political and agricultural treatises he wrote under the pseudonym "Martin Doyle." The second daughter in the family, H., who learned to read when very young, was first educated at home. At the age of ten she attended a day school, and at thirteen she was sent to a boarding school for several years. Here her limited exposure to literature was broadened by Madame Stuart, her teacher and lifelong friend.

Encouraged by the success of her first poem, H. soon envisioned a career in writing, ultimately moving to London where she found work as a secretary, companion, and governess. She actively participated in the Charity Organisation Society, a group dedicated to bettering the lot of working women through higher education. H. attracted the attention of Frederick Furnivall when he heard her give a lecture on Shakespeare's *Measure for Measure*. He advised her to obtain a teacher's certificate through a correspondence course from Cambridge University. She received a first class honors certificate and was subsequently employed at the London Collegiate School for Girls for eighteen years. Ill health necessitated a sabbatical leave, which was spent on an extended trip to Europe. During this time, inspired perhaps by her friend Harriet Hamilton-King, H. experienced a religious epiphany that resulted in her conversion to Roman Catholicism in 1901. While personally satisfying, H.'s decision cut her off from many associates. She became an editor for the Catholic Truth Society and wrote numerous articles for *The Catholic World* while slowly being forgotten by mainstream readers.

H. and Furnivall cofounded the Browning Society in 1881. H. was elected the first honorary secretary, and minutes of the meetings included in Browning Society Papers reveal that she took an active role in the sessions. She also contributed to Furnivall's *Bibliography of Robert Browning* (1881). She was friendly with Browning, whom she defended in biographical and critical essays. Correspondence between the two is still extant.

H.'s work may be divided into "creative and educative" texts (Dinnis). She edited Browning's *Strafford* (1884) for use by schoolchildren, wrote critical essays on English blank verse, Milton, Spenser, and Shakespeare, and published a book on the Roman Catholic background of English literature. She was the author of many biographical essays and even translated Victor Hugo's poetry. H.'s creative output was equally as impressive. Her *Verse-Tales, Lyrics, and Translations* (1889) included several Old English poems she had translated herself. She translated the Middle English romance *Havelok the Dane* (1902). H.'s important narrative poems include *A Sculptor* (1881), which deals with an artist's neglect of his wife to concentrate on his career, with disastrous results; *Michael Villiers, Idealist* (1891), in which the protagonist, the nephew and heir of a prosperous Irish landowner, personally confronts the Irish Problem; and "The Ballad of Lady Ellen" (1896), in which the heroine sells her soul to the Devil to provide food for her country's starving population. As a lyric poet, H. is best remembered for "Beloved, It is Morn,"

"A Sea Story," "To Miranda Asleep," and "At Eventide," which, at her request, was published posthumously. Following her conversion, her texts consisted primarily of religious subjects, a significant factor in the decline of her popularity as a poet. In the area of prose fiction, H. wrote the short story, "Billy Boy: The Story of a Country Lad" (1889), retold an Irish epic in "The Story of the Táin Bo Coolney" (1915), and published a novel, *Lois* (1908). This little-known (and hard to obtain) novel, the tale of a woman's spiritual odyssey from a nominal adherence to Anglicanism to a real and fervent embrace of Roman Catholicism, contains many interesting autobiographical nuances.

Pope Pius X presented H. with the Cross *Pro Ecclesia et Pontifice* (1912). Contemporary photos show her wearing the medal, which she highly prized. She was also awarded a Civil List pension near the end of her life for her literary and educational endeavors. She was almost totally blind when she died, although her last work was in press at the time of her death.

WORKS: *A Sculptor and other Poems* (1881). *Verse-Tales, Lyrics, and Translations* (1889). *Michael Villiers, Idealist, and Other Poems* (1891). *Poems* (1896). *Ancilla Domini: Thoughts in Verse on the Life of the Blessed Virgin Mary* (1898). *Our Lady of May and Other Poems* (1902). (trans.) *Havelok the Dane: An Old English Romance Rendered into Later English* (1902). (trans.) *The Dream of the Holy Rood* (1903). *Thoughts for Creedless Women* (1905). *Lois* (1908; originally serialized in *The Month*, July 1906–June 1907). *The Catholic Church and Labour* (1908). *Our Catholic Heritage in English Literature* (1910). *Litanies of the Most Holy Rosary* (1910). *George Leicester, Priest* (1910). *Prayers from the Divine Liturgy* (1910). *Later Poems* (1913). *Devotional Poems* (1922). *Jesukin and Other Christmastide Poems* (1924).

BIBLIOGRAPHY: Dinnis, E. *Catholic World* (1925). Dinnis, E. *Emily Hickey: Poet, Essayist, Pilgrim* (1927). *LonT* (9 September 1924).

For articles in reference works, see: *Feminist*. *NCBEL*. O'Donoghue, D. J. *The Poets of Ireland* (1912). *Poole*. *Who Was Who, 1916–1928*.

Other references: *Browning Society, London Papers* (1881). *New Letters of Robert Browning*, ed. W. C. DeVane and K. L. Knickerbocker (1950). *A Bibliography of Robert Browning from 1833–1881*, ed. F. Furnivall (1881). Hull, E. *Catholic World* (1916). *Irish Monthly* (February 1892). Knight, H. [H. J. Arden]. *Bookman* (1914). Leslie, J. B. *Ferns Clergy and Parishes* (1936). Leslie, J. B. *Unpublished Biographical Succession List of the Clergy of Diocese of Leighlin* (n.d.). *Poets and Poetry of the Nineteenth Century*, ed. A. Miles (1907). *Athenaeum* (1884). Willis, G. *Unpublished Addenda to Leslie* (n.d.).

Natalie Joy Woodall

Hill, D. A.: See *Doolittle, Hilda (H. D.)*

Hill, James: See *Jameson, Storm*

Octavia Hill

BORN: 3 December 1838, Wisbech, Cambridgeshire.
DIED: 12 August 1912, London.
DAUGHTER OF: James Hill and Caroline Southwood Smith Hill.

H. was a social reformer whose writing and work centered primarily on the reform of urban housing for the poor and the improvement of the quality of urban life. She developed the principles of social casework and of enlightened housing management. H. was the first woman invited to sit on a Royal Commission and played a large role in framing British housing legislation. She is primarily remembered today as one of three original founders of the National Trust.

The eighth of eleven children (thus her name), H. was educated at home by her mother, Caroline Southwood Smith, a teacher and educational theorist. Her father, James Hill, was a corn merchant and banker who was an activist on behalf of civil rights, social reform, and education, and who made several attempts—mostly unsuccessful—at a political career. H.'s mother began early in the 1830s to publish articles on educational theory in *Monthly Repository*. Her ideas were influenced by the new theories of the Swiss educator, J. H. Pestalozzi, who asserted that observation (as opposed to endless repetition, memorization, and rote learning) was the only sure basis for learning. Her articles so impressed one of her readers that he visited her and offered her the position of governess to his children. That man was James Hill, a recent widower who shared her views and became her husband several years later (in 1835). H. was Caroline's third child, James's eighth.

When H. was born in December 1838, her father's fortunes were beginning to decline. The family left Wisbech, moving first to Hampstead, then Gloucestershire, and later to Leeds, in Yorkshire. By the time they settled in Leeds, James Hill had suffered a severe mental breakdown from which he never fully recovered. The family split up, never to live together again, and some of the children went to live with relatives. H. had little contact with her father from this time on. Sometime later, Caroline and her daughters moved to Finchley, a country village north of London. As a child, H. met Robert Browning, Barbara Leigh Smith (later Bodichon), Charles Dickens, William Wordsworth, and Hans Christian Andersen, all visitors to or friends of her maternal grandfather.

At the age of fourteen, H. began attending meetings of the Christian Socialists where she met the Reverend F. D. Maurice and became a follower. She was offered her first post at that age in another Christian Socialist venture, taking charge of the "ragged children," girls employed in a toy-furniture-making operation. H. handled all aspects of the operation, from bookkeeping to designing and quality control. Her first article, published in *Household Words* (1856), was an account of the lives of the poverty-stricken toymakers.

H.'s success at teaching the toymakers led Maurice to employ her to teach arithmetic at the newly established classes for working women at his Working Men's College. The

Ladies' Cooperative Guild failed in 1856, and Maurice, director of the Working Men's College since 1854, offered her a salaried post as secretary to the women's classes.

In the early 1860s, H. became friends with two women who were to make medical history: Elizabeth Garrett, the first British woman physician, qualifying in Paris in 1870; and Sophia Jex-Blake, then a mathematics teacher, who later founded the Edinburgh School of Medicine for Women and who qualified as a physician in Berne and Dublin, registering in Britain in 1877. In 1862, the Hills started a school for girls at their new home in Nottingham Place that thrived for thirty years. H. and her sister Emily managed the school, with H. acting as headmistress and teacher. The school participated, along with several others, in spearheading an ultimately successful campaign for the extension of University Examinations and places to girls. H. also became involved with the nonsectarian Working Women's College, which opened in 1864; among its teachers was Elizabeth Garrett. H. received her certificate in mathematics from Queen's College in 1864.

During her early work at the Ladies' Guild, H. met John Ruskin, whose works she greatly admired. In 1855, he started to train H. as a copyist. H. copied pictures for *Modern Painters*, the Society of Antiquaries, and the National Portrait Gallery. During the time she worked at the Working Men's College, H. continued drawing for Ruskin. The association proved fruitful not only because she received artistic training but also because Ruskin assisted her in her most important venture, which launched her life-long career and in which she found her true vocation: housing reform. Her earlier work with the "Ragged School" girls familiarized her with the appalling housing conditions endured by the poor; she was convinced that landlords would never countenance improvement on the scale required. To support H.'s scheme, Ruskin purchased in 1865 three tenanted slum-houses in Paradise Place (now Garbutt Place), a street in the Marylebone section of London known colloquially as "Little Hell." H. planned to manage and improve these properties, seeking to secure her tenants' trust, repairing buildings and establishing clubs, classes, and savings banks for their benefit. In return, regular rent payments were demanded; in her view, financial accountability was a moral and practical necessity if independence and self-reliance were to be encouraged among the tenants. In her aim to combine housing and character reform, she urged self-respect and communal responsibility. Also in 1865, H.'s eldest sister, Gertrude, married Charles Lewes, the son of G. H. Lewes and stepson of Marian Evans (George Eliot). As a result, H. met Evans, who offered her support in H.'s housing schemes. In 1865, H. also became involved in the founding of the London Association for the Prevention of Pauperization and Crime, designed to combat indiscriminate and demoralizing alms giving.

As H.'s first scheme succeeded, she turned the profits to improvements suggested by the tenants and gradually rehabilitated both living quarters and their occupants. In 1866, Ruskin supported a further scheme by purchasing a row of cottages in Freshwater Place for H. to manage; later that year, she had four more dilapidated houses placed in her increasingly competent management. Her success was due to her knowledge of building, finances, rates and legal matters combined with her idealism. Her first article specifically about the work at Paradise Place and Freshwater Place appeared as "Cottage Property in London" in the *Fortnightly Review* (November 1866) and was followed by a series of others on the same subject.

In June of 1869, the Reverend W. Freemantle invited H. to join his Marylebone District Committee. In January 1870, he asked her to take charge of the very poor Walmer Street District in his parish, in which resided about 200 families, the poorest in Freemantle's parish, under the Charity Organisation Society's auspices. Undirected charity was abolished while volunteer visitors were employed to seek out and assist the deserving. Doles of any kind, gifts of money, or tokens for groceries or coal were eliminated and in their place H. offered work for everyone who needed it. In 1872, H. wrote an account of the Walmer Street experiment, asserting that her plan succeeded beyond her best hopes (*Further Account of the Walmer Street Industrial Experiment,* 1872.) Her successful management led to more and more similar undertakings, and her reputation as an expert on property management grew. In 1875, H. became a member of the Central Council of the Charity Organisation Society. With the demands of her property management growing, she found it necessary to train workers to whom she could delegate her increasing responsibilities. Also in 1875, five of her articles were collected into a book and published in America under the title *Homes of the London Poor.* This work, translated into German by Princess Alice of Hesse-Darmstadt, Queen Victoria's third child, led to the founding of the "Octavia Hill Verein" in Berlin.

By 1884, H. had become a figure of international repute, with regular correspondents in Germany, Holland, Paris, Sweden, Denmark, Russia, and America. Housing schemes were established on H.'s principles in New York City and Boston. In 1896, the Octavia Hill Association of Philadelphia was established. The Women's House Property Management Society was formed after her death in 1912 by her fellow-workers, offering training for women. By January 1928, more than 28,600 dwellings had been built on H.'s system.

H.'s concern for the quality of urban life inspired her alarm at the disappearance of public open spaces. She successfully fought to preserve Swiss Cottage Fields, an area that formed the slope to the west of Hampstead and Highgate and was the nearest available green space and open countryside to Marylebone and Paddington. H. joined the Commons Preservation Society and became a member of its Executive Council; her sister Miranda proposed a "Society for the Diffusion of Beauty," which was officially constituted in 1876 as the Kyrle Society, to obtain "small open spaces for out-door sitting-rooms for people in various parts of London"—in other words, to improve the quality of life for the poor by creating urban parks and gardens, by converting disused burial grounds into public spaces, by introducing color and beauty wherever possible. In 1881, the Metropolitan Open Spaces Act was passed, which facilitated the transfer of gardens and burial grounds to public authorities. It was largely due to H.'s efforts that £70,000 was raised to purchase the threatened Parliament Hill Fields (acquired in 1889), extending and securing Hampstead Heath for public use. In addition, she set up a campaign against smoke pollution and steadily fought for the maintenance of rights of way and commons. In 1877, H. published a collection of essays on open spaces, *Our Common Land.*

In 1881, she bought Paradise Place from Ruskin. H. gave evidence to the Royal Commission on Housing in 1884 and in that year accepted the Ecclesiastical Commissioners' invitation to manage forty-eight Deptford houses, with more following later that year in Southwark. The Ecclesiastical Commissioners also held extensive property (some 4,000 slum houses) in South London, which she was asked to manage. In 1887, she was honored as one of three women who had most influenced the course of Victorian Britain by being given a distinguished seat in Westminster Abbey for the Queen's Golden Jubilee, along with Josephine Butler and Florence Nightingale. In 1890, she was invited to an audience with Queen Victoria herself.

In 1889, H. joined the Committee of the Southwark Women's University Settlement, a settlement in which educated single women volunteers lived and worked in poor districts; it offered a thorough training in social work intended to qualify the residents for either a career or voluntary service. Southwark Women's University Settlement attracted an international following, including Jane Addams, founder of Hull House, Chicago.

She is also remembered for her vital part in the founding of the National Trust (1895), an outgrowth of the Kyrle and Commons Preservation Societies, to be "general trustee for all property intended for the use and enjoyment of the nation at large." So respected and trusted was H. that no National Trust appeal failed in her lifetime.

Preferring voluntary to official schemes, she refused to join the Royal Commission on Housing in 1889, but she did become a member of the Royal Commission on the Poor Laws, along with the young Beatrice Webb, from 1905 to 1908. This work, which H. regarded as serious and important, occupied a great deal of her time and included much travel throughout Great Britain.

A strong supporter of individual rights and limited government, H. favored private initiative over state-supported socialism and local reforms over large-scale subsidized housing. Although she never married, H. thought highly of traditional family life. She believed that the feminine domestic instinct was universal, transcending class barriers. Though she herself was a public servant, her program for housing reform was centered in her belief in the redeeming power of home life. She opposed female suffrage, fearing that it would undermine women's commitment to practical service in favor of nebulous political activity. Her ideal social worker was an educated woman who fostered mutual sympathy between the classes by living and working among the poor as a voluntary professional. She died from lung cancer at the age of seventy-five.

WORKS: *Further Account of the Walmer Street Industrial Experiment* (1872). *Letter to My Fellow-Workers Accompanying the Account of Donations Received for Work Amongst the Poor During 1872–1911* (1873–1912). *Homes of the London Poor* (1875). *District Visiting* (1877). *Our Common Land and Other Short Essays* (1877). *Colour, Space and Music for the People* (1884). *An Open Space for Deptford: An Appeal* (1892). "Preservations of Commons: Speech at a Meeting for Securing West Wickham Common." Kent and Surrey Committee of the Commons Preservation Society (1892). *Memorandum on the Report of the Royal Commission on the Poor Laws and Relief of Distress* (1909). *Report of an Attempt to Raise a Few of the London Poor Without Gifts* (n.d.).

BIBLIOGRAPHY: Bell, E. M. *Octavia Hill* (1942). Boyd, N. *Three Victorian Women Who Changed Their World: Josephine Butler, Octavia Hill, Florence Nightingale* (1982). Darley, G. *Octavia Hill* (1990). Hill, W. T. *Octavia Hill, Pioneer of the National Trust and Housing Reformer* (1956). Lewis, J. *Women and Social Action in Victorian and Edwardian England* (1991). Maurice, C. E. *Life of Octavia Hill as Told in Her Letters* (1913). *Octavia Hill, Early Ideals,* ed. E. S. Maurice (1928). *Extracts from Octavia Hill's "Letters to Fellow-Workers," 1864–1911,* ed. E. S. Ouvry (1933). Owen, D. *English Philanthropy 1660–1960* (1964). *Society of Housing Managers Quarterly Journal,* Vol. 8 (special H. issue, October 1962). Tabor, M. E. *Pioneer Women: Octavia Hill* (1927). Wohl, A. S. *Journal of British Studies* (1971). Wohl, A. S. *The Eternal Slum* (1977). Woodroofe, Kathleen. *From Charity to Social Work in England and the United States* (1974).

For articles in reference works, see: *DNB. Europa. IDWB. VB.*

Other references: Cockburn, J. *Quarterly Review* (1939). Jardine, [White], E. *Women of Devotion and Courage* (1925). Kent, M. *Cornhill Magazine* (1928). Lee, M. *Cornhill Magazine* (1936). Malpass, P., in *Founders of the Welfare State,* ed. P. Barker (1984).

Gale Sigal

Susan Hill

BORN: 5 February 1942, Scarborough, Yorkshire.
DAUGHTER OF: R. H. Hill and Doris Hill.
MARRIED: Stanley Wells, 1975.

In 1985, H. was first seen on American television rather than in bookshops in her own dramatization—for *Masterpiece Theatre*—of "A Bit of Singing and Dancing," the title story of a collection she published in 1973. It is typical of H.'s emphasis: the plight of an abused, proud, gullible person suddenly released from responsibilities (parental, economic) late in life and therefore willing, even eager, to avoid loneliness even if it means accepting "second best." Typically choosing seaside resorts, H. follows in the footsteps of two novelists she admires, Elizabeth Bowen and Elizabeth Taylor, whose spas are lined with respectable older folk and not so respectable day trippers. Esme in "A Bit of Singing and Dancing" accepts a mysterious lodger after her mother finally dies, a Mr. Amos Curry, who appears very "right" in dress and manner, the perfect gentleman lodger for her "part of town." In fact, Esme, one day weeks later, stumbles on him poignantly reliving his earlier music-hall profession at a busy intersection of the seafront: There he is tap dancing and singing, a cap for coins at his feet, coins that eventually, she realizes, pay her rent.

H. has produced television and radio plays, reviews, talk shows, chatty columns in literary papers, in 1983 a chilling ghost story the length of *The Turn of the Screw*—called *The Woman in Black*—and a number of novels for adults and young people that have resulted in the showering of literary prizes and favorable reviews. H.'s novels are kept in print, while many of her contemporaries disappear after a season in the sun.

She chooses as characters people outside the usual list of friends and relations. They are often very young boys, sometimes deaf and dumb, often maimed in some way. They can be at the other end of life, too: elderly but alone, retired, their isolation making them nearly pathological. But H., in her spare, economic way, never treats her folk like psychotics: She instills in them an isolated dignity that borders on the heroic whatever their age (the boy victim in *I'm the King of the Castle,* 1970). They are the misfits, the disadvantaged, to be sure, but they are also the ones who care and think about others; they possess a sense of value absent around them. Put in political terms, they are the minority group just barely tolerated by the majority, the normal, the confident. In *The Bird of Night* (1972), older, gifted men (a scientist, a poet) seek refuge from the world in each other, one overfastidious, the other paranoid, almost "mad." The possibility of their abnormal relationship is vaguely assumed but not developed. It is what society has done to them, how society has isolated them, that concerns H. She is also concerned with the inexpressible pain of loss a woman feels, newly married, at the sudden death of her husband. The only person in the community who understands her is a youngster, her brother-in-law. As in so many of her novels and stories, the isolated central character turns to nature, even to animals and birds, for solace.

A limit is met in the most extraordinary story of all, "The Albatross" (1971). A terrible burden is placed on a rather simple son by a dominant mother who issues commands from her wheechair. Set again on the seashore of a northern fishing village, the sea and the elements become almost a character in the story. Duncan, the son, finally discovers the possibility of relief: escape to become apprenticed to Ted Flint, a fisherman, a strong, important person in the pub and in the town. Ted quite casually lets Duncan know he, Duncan, is a person. Indeed, the setting reminds one of a Benjamin Britten opera: the boats, the sea, the life of the villages reduced to survival through fishing. The sea pounds the shore, pounds the village; the mother's words pound at the consciousness of the child. The intensity reaches a screaming point, and we nearly rejoice when Duncan puts his mother in her wheechair in the middle of the night and pushes her over the end of the jetty. The language H. chooses to use is understated, quiet. The matter-of-factness of the murder provides a catharsis in its almost atonal cadence.

It might be argued that the controlled tension H. generates in her long stories is more appropriate than when applied to the novel. *I'm the King of the Castle,* a sadomasochistic story of two youngsters, becomes almost unbearable in its later pages: Its passionate factual development of hate becomes suffocating. The gothic quality becomes an end in itself rather than a reference to a more substantial generalization. That generalization seems to surface in "The Albatross" and in some of the earlier radio plays.

Finally, the attachment H. obviously has for birds and for the countryside reminds one of Thomas Hardy, whose stories she has edited. At her best, she integrates the setting with the plight of the characters. She is both off-beat and concerned, gothic but humane. Antiheroes in many instances, these off-center folk are not scarecrows because they are so deeply felt. We see them vividly; we sympathize with them.

WORKS: *The Enclosure* (1961). *Do Me a Favour* (1963). *Gentleman and Ladies* (1963). *A Change for the Better* (1969). *I'm the King of the Castle* (1970). *Miss Lavender Is Dead* (1970). *Taking Leave* (1971). *The End of Summer* (1971). *Lizard in the Grass* (1971). *Strange Meeting* (1971). *The Albatross and Other Stories* (1971). *The Custodian* (1972). *The Bird of Night* (1972). *The Cold Country* (1972). *A Bit of Singing and Dancing* (1973). *White Elegy* (1973). *Consider the Lilies* (1973). *In the Springtime of the Year* (1974). *A Window on the World* (1974). *Strip Jack Naked* (1974). *Mr. Proudham and Mr. Sleight* (1974). *The Cold Country and Other Plays for Radio* (1975; includes *The End of Summer, Lizard in the Grass, Consider the Lilies, Strip Jack Naked*). *The Elephant Man* (1975). *On The Face of It* (1975). *The Summer of The Giant Sunflower* (1977). *The Ramshackle Company* (1981). *Chances* (1981). *The Magic Apple Tree: A Country Year* (1982). *The Woman in Black: A Ghost Story* (1983). *Go Away, Bad Dreams!* (1984). *One Night at a Time* (1984). *Mother's Magic* (1986). *Through the Garden Gate* (1986). *Lanterns Across the Snow* (1987). *The Lighting of the Lamps* (1987). *Can It Be True?* (1988). *The Spirit of the Cotswolds* (1988). *Family* (1989). *Shakespeare Country* (1989). *Suzy's Shoes* (1989). *I Won't Go There Again* (1990). *Stories from Codling Village* (1990). *Through the Kitchen Window* (1990). *Air and Angels* (1991). *The Glass Angels* (1991). *Friends Next Door* (1992). *The Mist in the Mirror* (1992). *Pirate Poll* (1992). *Septimus Honeydew* (1992). *Beware, Beware* (1993). *King of Kings* (1993). *Mrs. de Winter* (1993). *The Christmas Collection* (1994). *Reflections from a Garden* (1995). *Listening to the Orchestra: Four Stories* (1996).

BIBLIOGRAPHY: Hofer, E. H., in *Contemporary British Women Writers: Narrative Stategies*, ed. R. E. Hosmer, Jr. (1993). Ireland, K. P. *JNT* (1983). Jackson, R., in *Twentieth-Century Woman Novelists,* ed. T. F. Staley (1982). Low, D. A., in *British Radio Drama,* ed. J. Drakakis (1981). Muir, K., in *The Uses of Fiction: Essays on the Modern Novel in Honour of Arnold Kettle,* ed. D. Jefferson and G. Martin (1982). Olshanskaya, N. L. *ZAA* (1986). Reed, M. J. *EJ* (April 1983). Schubert, M., in *English Language and Literature: Positions and Dispositions,* ed. J. Hogg *et al.* (1990).

For articles in reference works, see: *Bloomsbury. CA. Cambridge. CD. CLC. CN. DLB. DNB. Feminist.*

Other references: *Listener* (11 February 1971, 14 September 1972, 29 March 1973, 24 January 1974, 15 May 1975, 22 September 1983, 29 November 1984). *LRB* (17 November 1983). *New Statesman* (28 October 1983, 7 December 1984). *NYTBR* (30 March 1969,

27 May 1973, 10 June 1973, 2 December 1973, 5 May 1974, 17 May 1985). *Observer* (21 September 1969, 21 December 1969, 6 September 1970, 14 February 1971, 17 October 1971, 17 September 1972, 1 April 1973, 20 January 1974, 8 February 1976). *Spectator* (16 September 1972, 19 May 1973, 15 May 1982, 29 October 1983, 5 November 1983). *TLS* (25 September 1969, 30 October 1970, 5 March 1971, 29 October 1971, 15 September 1972, 30 March 1973, 25 January 1974, 30 November 1984).

Ernest Hofer

Hobbes, John Oliver: See *Craigie, Pearl*

Margaret Hoby

BORN: 1571, Linton, East Riding, Yorkshire.
DIED: 1633, Hackness, Yorkshire.
DAUGHTER OF: Arthur Dakins and Thomasine Guy or Gye.
MARRIED: Walter Devereux, 1589; Thomas Sidney, 1591; Thomas Posthumous Hoby, 1596.

The author of one of the first diaries written by an Englishwoman, H. was the only heir of a prosperous Yorkshire landowner. Raised in the household of Henry Hastings, third Earl of Huntingdon, H. was thoroughly inculcated into Puritan beliefs and practices. Also raised in this household was her first husband, Walter Devereux, the younger brother of Robert Devereux, Earl of Essex, a favorite courtier of Elizabeth I. After her first husband's death in a skirmish in France, H. married Thomas Sidney, a ward of Henry Hastings who had also spent time in the Huntingdon household. Thomas Sidney was the brother of Philip Sidney and Mary Herbert, Countess of Pembroke. After Thomas Sidney's death in 1595, H. at first rejected Thomas Posthumous Hoby's suit. D. Meads speculates that a threatened lawsuit over her ownership of Hackness after the death of the Earl of Huntingdon played a role in her decision to marry Hoby, son of Elizabeth Cooke Russell and a man with well-connected friends. C. Cross claims that H. was swayed by the dying earl's appeal to set up a Puritan household in Catholic Yorkshire. After her marriage to Hoby, H. resided primarily at their estate in Hackness, Yorkshire, with visits to her mother in Linton and to London. She died in 1633.

Covering the years 1591 to 1605, H.'s *Diary* begins three years after her marriage to Hoby. H.'s diary primarily enacts a religious exercise to search her life for signs of assurance of her election. Especially in the first few years, she keeps a meticulous account of her devotional activities, such as praying alone, with household members, or with her chaplain; reading the Bible or devotional writings by such writers as William Perkins and Richard Greenham; and writing in her commonplace book, her testament book, her sermon book, and her table book. H. expresses special concern with the liveliness of her faith. Inattention at sermons, for example, signified the "buffets" of Satan, and she sometimes interpreted physical ailments as God's correction of her faults. H.'s diary also provides accounts of the activities of ordinary country living: tending to the sick, walking with her husband, bowling and fishing, visiting and receiving visits, and making trips to her mother's house at Linton and to London.

While H.'s diary does not often record her thoughts or her deepest feelings, it remains a highly significant document for its insights into the life of an early modern Reformation subject.

WORKS: *The Diary of Lady Margaret Hoby*, ed. D. Meads (1930). *Paradise of Women*, ed. B. Travitsky (1981). Blodgett, H. *"Capacious Hold-All": An Anthology of Englishwomen's Diary Writings* (1991). *English Women's Voices: 1540–1700*, ed. C.F. Otten (1991).

BIBLIOGRAPHY: Blodgett, H. *Centuries of Female Days* (1988). Cross, C. *The Puritan Earl* (1966). Meads, D., intro. to *The Diary of Lady Margaret Hoby* (1930). Mendelson, S. H., in *Women in English Society 1500–1800*, ed. M. Prior (1985). Perry, E. *Van de Bempde Papers* (n.d.). Stone, L. *Crisis of the Aristocracy* (1965). Warnicke, R. *Women of the English Renaissance and Reformation* (1983). Wilcox, H., in *Gloriana's Face*, ed. S. P. Cerasano and M. Wynne-Davies (1992).

For articles in reference works, see: *Bell. Bloomsbury. Feminist.*

Mary Ellen Lamb

Molly Holden

BORN: 7 September 1927, London.
DIED: 5 August 1981, Bromsgrove, Worcestershire.
DAUGHTER OF: Conor Henry Gilbert and Winifred Farrant Gilbert.
MARRIED: Alan W. Holden, 1949.

Although H. wrote several novels and children's books, she is best known for her nature poetry. H. was an atheist, but a sense of power and order prevails in her truthful, unsentimental portrayal of nature. She especially admires its toughness. In "Pieces of unprofitable land," it is asserted that "their vigour justifies all wastes and weeds." Nature's fierceness and heroism are demonstrated in poems such as "Hare":

> But he is no more than flesh and blood
> living all his speedy life with fear,
> only oblivious of constant danger
> at his balletic time of year
> when spring skies, winds, the greening furrows
> overcome hunger, nervousness, poor sight,
> fill him with urgent, huge heroics,
> make him stand up and fight.

It is this tenacity that most attracts H. It is why the speaker in "Giant decorative dahlia" says of the "unnamed tuber, offered cheap" that "I could not deny it love if I tried."

H.'s poems show similarities to the verse of Edward Thomas, John Clare, and Thomas Hardy (though without his sense of irony). H. was aware of these influences and proudly acknowledged them, as in her poem for Hardy,

"T.H." She praises the wariness of the author who "saw everything he needed / about his fellow-men and the world, marking it all / upon the full-mapped country of his mind and memory." In fact, her poems often contain literary and artistic references. The influence of earlier writers may account for the great number of poems using rhyme, as, for example, in the volume *To Make Me Grieve* (1968). This rhyme often has a startling simplicity. The conclusion of "Every May" is one example: "But now and then I notice / in May's sweet cold, / the comfortable heat of humans. / I grow old."

H. was disabled by multiple sclerosis in 1964, ironically at the same time her poetic powers ripened. Her affliction is sometimes the subject of her work, for instance, "Illness" and "Adjustment," but she is never self-pitying. She rejects the temptation to "raise my voice and howl / at what has been done to me." In "Hospital" we see that religion is no comfort for her sickness. She is "seeking inside not out for a human grace / that would give me a strength and a courage for enduring / against great odds in a narrow place." The comfort must come from an inner strength, much like the force that runs through her nature poetry. For this reason, it is not surprising that in such poems as "The seven bushes" there is a oneness between the speaker and nature: "We share this soil with mutual wariness."

H. possesses a strong narrative sense, but there can be a certain uniformity of tone in her work. Regardless of this possible flaw, she has been one of England's greatest nature poets of this century. Her poems have a quiet, subtle distinctiveness. As John Cotton asserts, H.'s poems "steadily grow on you." Before her death in 1981, she was awarded the Arts Council Award in 1970 and the Cholmondeley Award in 1972.

WORKS: *The Bright Cloud* (1964). *To Make Me Grieve* (1968). *The Unfinished Feud* (1971). *Air and Chill Earth* (1971). *A Tenancy of Flint* (1971). *White Rose and Wanderer* (1972). *Reivers' Weather* (1973). *The Speckled Bash* (1974). *The Country Over* (1975). *Selected Poems, with a memoir by A. Holden* (1988).

BIBLIOGRAPHY: Byers, M., in *British Poetry Since 1960*, ed. M. Schmidt and G. Lindop (1972). Holden, A. "Memoir," in M. Holden, *Selected Poems* (1988).

For articles in reference works, see: *CA. Cambridge. CP. DLB. ToddBWW.*

Other references: Alma, R. *Poetry Nation* 2 (1974). *Observer Review* (19 January 1969). *New Statesman* (28 February 1969). *London Magazine* (July 1969).

Louis J. Parascandola

Catherine Holland

BORN: 1637, Quidenham (?), Norfolk.
DIED: 6 January 1720, Bruges, Flanders.
DAUGHTER OF: Sir John Holland and Alethea Sandys Holland.

H. is known for her autobiography, which is written as a dramatic narrative and with passages of poetic prose. It recounts her suspenseful adventures in "seeking liberty of conscience" during the English Civil War and its aftermath, and, in the genre of spiritual autobiography, it parallels the thought, structure, and metaphors of St. Augustine's *Confessions*, which she knew well. Apart from its literary value, H's work gives a detailed account of aristocratic social and family conditions in England during her era. H.'s life was closely controlled, even at the age of twenty-four, although arranged marriages were beginning to be publicly challenged by her contemporaries, such as Mary Astell.

Born to a Puritan father and a Roman Catholic mother (who, H. writes, was married for her wealth and permitted to keep her religion although her children were not allowed to do so), H. relates how she both loved and feared her father and how she constantly suffered from the harshness of his tutelage and his attitude of crushing her high-spirited personality and independent thinking. Sir John Holland held increasingly prominent places in government, becoming advisor at the courts in both England and Holland, where he sent his family to live during the English Civil War. The family traveled frequently between the two countries, and H. was constantly in the privileged social milieu of both courts. She relates her love of pleasure: music, dancing, cards, "farces and sportive fooleries." She also tells of her deeper philosophical questioning on the meaning of life and of her theological readings, and when the family spent three years in Bruges, Flanders, c. 1652–55, she surreptitiously (for fear of her father's discovery) frequented Roman Catholic churches and became acquainted with the way of life of the English recusant (i.e., Roman Catholics who refused to attend Church of England services) Canonesses Regular of St. Augustine at Nazareth Monastery (for historical background, see entry for Elizabeth Shirley). H. returned to England with her father in 1657, went back to Holland in 1659 to be with her family, and the entire family returned from Holland to reside in London a few years later.

H's narrative tells of her years of failed attempts to convince her father that she should be given "liberty of conscience" to convert to Catholicism, but this resulted only in her loss of freedom since she was then carefully watched in all of her visits and associations. H. tells how she then made successful contact by letter with the prioress at Nazareth Monastery in Bruges and with the latter's friends in London, despite her father's opening of her letters (she was then twenty-four), and she tells dramatically of her plans to escape to Bruges even when nearby Jesuits refused to help her because of her father's high position. H. describes how, entirely alone, she successfully traveled incognito across the Channel, narrowly evading government officials who knew her, and how, arriving at the enclosed monastery at Bruges in August 1662, she was welcomed and later professed as a religious. She wrote her narrative there in 1664 at the request of superiors so that, she says, her community would understand her background.

In the monastery, H. translated devotional works into English from French and Dutch and wrote dramatic sketches (now lost) for the nuns. In independence of thought and in her written and publicly expressed urging of "liberty of conscience" as a right, H. was in advance of her times.

Two other English women writers were professed as canonesses at H's monastery: Lady Lucy Herbert (b. 1669 in England, d. 1744 in Bruges), daughter of William, first Earl and titular Duke of Powis, and Elizabeth Somerset Herbert; and Grace Birnand Babthorpe (b. 1570[?] in Yorkshire, d. 1635 in Bruges), daughter of William Birnand of York and widow of Sir Ralph Babthorpe of Yorkshire. Herbert wrote devotions and meditations published in several volumes from 1722 to 1791 (see *DNB* and Gillow). Babthorpe wrote *Another Narrative of the Lady Babthorpe* (the first was lost), recounting the persecution she and her family suffered as recusants in Yorkshire, and published in John Morris, *Troubles of Our Catholic Forefathers*, Vol. I (1872) (see Gillow).

WORKS: Most of H.'s 1664 narrative is in Durrant, C. S. *A Link Between the Flemish Mystics and English Martyrs* (1925). Critical edition of MS. edited by the Canonesses Regular of St. Augustine (Windesheim), Bruges, Belgium, in progress. "A Method to Converse with God," H.'s translation from French (c. 1682), also in progress.

BIBLIOGRAPHY: Guilday, P. *The English Catholic Refugees on the Continent, 1558–1798* (1914). Hamilton, A., ed. *The Chronicle of the English Augustinian Canonesses Regular at St. Monica's, Louvain* (includes Bruges), 2 vol. (1904, 1906). Latz, D. L., in *"Recusant Literature," Collected Papers from the Recusant Sessions at the International Medieval Congress, 1990–1994, held at Western Michigan University*, ed. D. L. Latz (1996).

Other references: Gillow, J. *A Bibliographical Dictionary of the English Catholics* (1885–1902).

Dorothy L. Latz

Holt, Jane: See *Wiseman, Jane*

Winifred Holtby

BORN: 23 June 1898, Rudstone, Yorkshire.
DIED: 25 September 1935, London.
DAUGHTER OF: David Holtby and Alice Holtby.

H., novelist and essayist, was a prolific writer on numerous subjects. Born to a father who worked as a farmer and a mother who served as alderman of East Riding, Yorkshire, H. was a precocious child, publishing a volume of poems, *My Garden and Other Poems*, at the age of thirteen. Her schoolmistress encouraged her parents to send her to Somerville College, Oxford, where she was an exceptional student. Her studies were interrupted for a year during World War I while she served in a post of the signals branch of the Women's Auxiliary Army Corps.

After she graduated, H. joined Lady Margaret Rhondda as an editor of *Time and Tide*, eventually (after 1926) serving as director. She traveled extensively throughout Europe, lecturing for the League of Nations Union. In London, she lived with Vera Brittain, whom she had met at Oxford; their friendship was to endure until H.'s death at the age of thirty-seven. When Brittain married, H. shared her home, caring for Brittain's children as her own. Though H. never married, she had an extended relationship that culminated with her engagement on her deathbed. Both overwork and heart disease have been cited as responsible for her early death. Indeed, H., dedicated to her writing even when she knew death was imminent, barely completed her best-known novel, *South Riding*, working rapidly during her last four weeks of life.

At her death, H. had published six novels, two volumes of stories, a book of verse, two volumes of satire, a study of Virginia Woolf, a book about women, and a play that she saw produced. Moreover, she was an active journalist, turning out many articles for such publications as the *Manchester Guardian*, the *News Chronicle*, and *Time and Tide*, and she campaigned actively for blacks' rights in South Africa. Though her talents as a critic and essayist are often noted, it is as a novelist that she is remembered today.

H.'s best novels are usually considered to be *Poor Caroline* (1931), *Mandoa! Mandoa!* (1933), and *South Riding* (published posthumously in 1936). *Poor Caroline* tells of the Christian Cinema Company and especially of its founder, Caroline Denton-Smyth, a vigorous but self-deluded woman who tackles projects that have no hope of being completed. A heavily ironic story, it describes especially well how Denton-Smyth and her company affect others who depend on them for their livelihoods. *Mandoa! Mandoa!* is even more heavily satiric; in it, an aggressive British travel agency attempts to advertise and market a small isolated community in Africa, with H. in the process offering thoughtful, barbed comments about the contrasts between an industrial civilization and a less-developed one.

South Riding: An English Landscape is considerably more complex, suggesting H.'s likelihood of achieving even more significant fiction had she lived. It is set in H.'s native Yorkshire, with the title a reference to a fictional part of the county (Yorkshire has only north, east, and west "ridings," or administrative divisions) and with H.'s mother's experiences as a member of the County Council especially relevant. The county, gradually becoming urbanized, is reflective of England in its contrasts between country and city, older ways of thinking versus the newer, and traditional ways contrasted with more innovative. The County Council, in its "apparently impersonal" (Brittain's term) deliberations and decisions, affects the lives of all local citizens; as H. wrote in her preface (addressed to her mother), "The complex tangle of motives prompting public decisions, the unforeseen consequences of their enactment of private lives, appeared to me as part of the unseen pattern of the English landscape."

In *South Riding*, H. shows how the conservative councillor, Robert Carne, and the relatively unconventional new teacher, Sarah Burton, necessarily clash in their differing approaches to education and to life. Carne comes to love Burton, but no liaison occurs because of his heart condition. H. offers numerous lesser though equally dramatic vignettes, such as those involving a bright, impoverished girl who must quit school to care for her family, a dying woman who tries to protect her husband from the truth about her condition, a councillor who fears tuberculosis, a woman who dreads death in childbirth, and a shopkeeper whose wife withholds sexual activity and who is blackmailed by his lover.

The book has been compared favorably to the work of

Arnold Bennett and other writers, with the *Literary Digest* calling it a "magnificent epitaph" for H. and with Brittain comparing it to Henrik Ibsen's *An Enemy of the People.* Without any doubt, H. was growing in skill and confidence, thus making her death—at an earlier age, as Brittain noted, than George Eliot, John Galsworthy, or George Bernard Shaw had been before they had accomplished anything of note—especially premature. Her diverse interests, balanced as they were between her public life, including her friends and their families, and her need for time alone in order to write, made for a remarkably full and varied life. Though she focused on Yorkshire, her work has had remarkable success in both England and the United States, with a motion picture version of *South Riding* (1938) contributing to her reputation.

WORKS: *My Garden and Other Poems* (1911). *Anderby Wold* (1923). *The Land of Green Ginger* (1928). *Eutychus; or, The Future of the Pulpit* (1928). *Poor Caroline* (1931). *Virginia Woolf, A Critical Study* (1932). *The Astonishing Island* (1933). *Mandoa! Mandoa!* (1933). *Truth Is Not Sober and Other Stories* (1934). *Women and a Changing Civilization* (1934). *The Frozen Earth and Other Poems* (1935). *South Riding: An English Landscape* (1936). *Pavements at Anderby: Tales of South Riding and Other Regions* (1937). *Letters to a Friend* (1937). *The Crowded Street* (1938). *Take Back Your Freedom* (1939). *Women* (1941). *The Letters of Winifred Holtby and Vera Brittain, 1920–1935,* ed. V. Brittain and G. Handley-Taylor (1960). *Testament of a Generation: The Journalism of Vera Brittain and Winifred Holtby,* ed. P. Berry and A. Bishop (1985).

BIBLIOGRAPHY: Albinski, N. B. *UtopSt* (1987). Baurley, G. L. *TYDS* (1989). Brittain, V. *Testament of Friendship* (1940). Handley-Taylor, G. *Winifred Holtby: A Concise and Selected Bibliography Together with Some Letters* (1955). Kennard, J. E. *Vera Brittain and Winifred Holtby: A Working Partnership* (1989). Leonardi, S. J. *LIT* (1990). Oram, A. *Women's History Review* (1992). Shaw, M., in *Women's Writing: A Challenge to Theory,* ed. M. Monteith (1986). White, E. *Winifred Holtby as I Knew Her* (1938).

For articles in reference works, see: *Bloomsbury. Cambridge. Feminist. MBL. Oxford. TCA* and *SUP. TCW. ToddBWW.*

Other references: Adams, P. *Somerville for Women: An Oxford College 1879–1993* (1996). *Christian Century* (30 October 1935). Gray, J. *On Second Thought* (1946). Green, M. *A Mirror for Anglo-Saxons* (1950). Heilbrun, C., intro. to V. Brittain. *Testament of Friendship* (1981). *Literary Digest* (11 April 1936). *Ms.* (June 1986). O'Faolain, S. *London Mercury* (April 1936). *PW* (12 October 1935). *Punch* (25 November 1981). *Scholastic* (22 January 1938). Scott-James, V. *London Mercury* (May 1937). *Spectator* (6 February 1982). *TLS* (25 December 1981, 18 July 1986). *VLS* (May 1986). *Wilson Library Bulletin* (April 1934, November 1935).

Paul Schlueter

Home, Cecil: See *Webster, (Julia) Augusta Davies*

Homespun, Prudentia: See *West, Jane*

Hope, Laurence: See *Nicolson, Violet (Adela Florence)*

Susanna Harvey Hopton

BORN: 1627.
DIED: 12 July 1708, Hereford, Herefordshire.
DAUGHTER OF: [given name unknown] Harvey, of an old Staffordshire family, and [given name unknown] Wiseman, of an Essex family.
MARRIED: Richard Hopton.

H., devotional writer and benefactress, was born in 1627 to a family of ancient Staffordshire stock. In her youth, she converted to Roman Catholicism; after a careful analysis of the opposing arguments advanced by Roman Catholic writers and by Anglican authorities, however, she returned to the Anglican faith. She married Richard Hopton of Kington, Herefordshire, a barrister and judge, with whom she lived happily until his death in 1696. They were childless. She died in Hereford at the age of eighty-one and was buried next to her husband at Bishop's Frome.

She was known for her charity to those in need both near her home in Kington and in distant places, as evidenced by the letters of gratitude found among her papers. Her executor, William Brome, writes concerning her good work that "she was charitable to the poor in the highest degree, and hospitable to her friends in a generous manner." Her dedication to her church is revealed in her bequest of £800 to suffering clergymen.

Her devotion to God's work extended to the conduct of her own spiritual life, which was both demanding and disciplined. Each day, she awakened at four in the morning for the first of her five worship sessions, a course of devotions she maintained throughout most of her life. Her extraordinary commitment included the world of learning; for, although she had little formal education, she read deeply in the devotional books in her own library and conversed at length with "the best Divines" so that "she attained," according to her friend and editor Nathaniel Spinckes, "to a very considerable knowledge in Divinity; and has been a Benefactress to the Age, by the religious and instructive Works she has left behind her."

Her literary survivals are all of a religious nature. Her *Daily Devotions,* published in 1673, consists of thanksgivings, confessions, and prayers, which she describes in "The Preface to the Reader" as "Rational, Comprehensive, and Emphatical." Even a brief passage like the following reveals her vigorous, straightforward style: "Shake the earth of my Heart with terror at the approach of every sin that I may die rather than commit one known wilful sin against thee more." Less dramatic, yet quietly powerful, is her Prayer for the Ninth Hour, which closes with these words: "O by this death of shine, have mercy upon me, let it kill, crucifie, and destroy all sin in me, let me die unto the World, and live henceforth only unto thee."

Devotions in the Ancient Way of Offices, published in 1700, was "reformed" by H. for the use of Anglicans from the earlier work of the same title by John Austin, a Roman Catholic, originally published in Paris in 1668. The work provides psalms, hymns, and prayers "for every Day of the Week" and "for our Saviour's Feasts," "the Holy Ghost," "the Saints," and "the Dead." George Hickes, editor of the work, fails to identify H. as the reformer; however, the description in "To the Reader," with its reference to self-education and to a successful book of devotions, fits H. In addition, in his Preface to *Controversial Letters* (1710), Hickes attributes the work to her.

A letter to Father Henry Turbeville, published by Hickes in 1710 in his *Second Collection of Controversial Letters,* is a carefully reasoned argument justifying her return from the Church of Rome to the Church of England. Spinckes, in describing the letter, writes that she "gave such reasons for her return, as not only will justify it before all intelligent and impartial persons, but may be of very good use to others."

In 1717, Spinckes published *A Collection of Meditations and Devotions, in Three Parts* which consisted of H.'s *Hexaemeron, or Meditations on the Six Days of Creation and Meditations and Devotions on the Life of Christ,* and another edition of *Daily Devotions.* In *Hexaemeron,* she reveals in her discussion of the six days of creation how God made man in his likeness, endowed him with the gifts of reason and understanding, and brought him into a world that was provided with all necessities for subsistence, comfort, delight, and ultimate salvation. She raises the question, How, in view of such kindness, could man fail to give thanks? *Meditations . . . on the Life of Christ* is a logical sequel to *Hexaemeron* in its examination of God's gifts, including the Son and the nature of the sacrifice.

Although H.'s works are not readily available except in research libraries, they do warrant attention because they reflect a sensitive, dedicated woman's overcoming the lack of formal education and recording her thoughts in clear, powerful prose. In addition, she herself is important as a seventeenth-century woman who managed to get her books published and who impressed religious thinkers like George Hickes and Nathaniel Spinckes with her superior qualities of mind and spirit.

WORKS: *Daily Devotions Consisting of Thanksgivings, Confessions, and Prayers* (1673). *Devotions in the Ancient Way of Offices* (1700). *Letter to Father Turbeville,* in *Second Collection of Controversial Letters,* ed. G. Hickes (1710). *Hexaemeron, or Meditations on the Six Days of the Creation and Meditations and Devotions on the Life of Christ,* in A Collection of *Meditations and Devotions, in Three Parts,* ed. N. Spinckes (1717).

BIBLIOGRAPHY: Ballard, G. *Memoirs of Several Ladies of Great Britain* (1752; ed. R. Perry, 1985). Hickes, G., preface to *Linguarum Vetterum Septentrionalium Thesaurus* (1705). Hickes, G. prefaces to *Daily Devotions* (1673); *Devotions in the Ancient Way of Offices* (1700); *Second Collection of Controversial Letters* (1710). Jordan, R. D. *YES* (1982). Smith, J. J. *N&Q* (June 1991). Spinckes, N., preface to S. Hopton, *A Collection of Meditations and Devotions,* 1717; in Wilford, J. *Memorials and Characters of Two Hundred Eminent and Worthy Persons . . . of Great Britain* (1741).

For articles in reference works, see: *DNB. Feminist. Ireland.* Stenton, D. M. *The English Woman in History* (1957). *ToddDBA.*

Philip Bordinat

Elizabeth Jane Howard

BORN: 26 March 1923, London.
DAUGHTER OF: David Liddon Howard and Katharine Margaret Somervell Howard.
MARRIED: Peter Scott, 1942; James Douglas-Henry, 1960; Kingsley Amis, 1965.

Educated privately at home, H. later studied acting at the London Mask Theatre and in the Scott Thorndyke Student Repertory; she also performed at Stratford-upon-Avon and in repertory theater in Devon. During World War II, she served as an air raid warden, and at the same time she worked in radio and television broadcasting and as a model. Writing was a secret "vice" from the age of fourteen; however, she did not enter the literary profession until the 1950s, when her novels began to appear. She also worked as an editor for London publishing houses.

Known for both her long and short fiction, H. considers herself to be "in the straight tradition of English novelists." Her fiction deals with character and manners in elegant, irreverent, witty, lightly satirical prose. H.'s milieu is the carefully described, devastatingly detailed world of the middle class in which she deftly delineates the often tacit but nonetheless excruciating conflicts among family members: husbands and wives, siblings, children and parents, grandparents and grandchildren. Her central characters are frequently alienated young women or men whose internal sense of emptiness and inadequacy spill over into other lives, disrupting and complicating them, particularly as the young people seek through these others the elusive chimeras of love and security.

Occasionally striving too hard for resolution, H. provides cheerful endings inappropriately, but her most serious studies, especially the gem of black comedy, *Odd Girl Out* (1972), conclude more ambivalently. Because even H.'s most substantial novels are comic and unpretentious, she has not received the critical attention she deserves. Auberon Waugh comments about *Odd Girl Out,* "she may not have written a highbrow novel, to be approved of by the tiny and extraordinarily unintelligent untalented circle of people in London who like to think of themselves as highbrow, but she has written a thunderingly good novel."

H. says, "I write about 300 words a day with luck and when I am free to do so. I do it chiefly because it is the most difficult thing I have tried to do." Her recent novels, *Light Years* (1990), *Marking Time* (1992), and *Confusion* (1994), which together comprise *The Cazalet Chronicles,* have been well received. In their historical sweep and their attention to the lives within a family over generations, *The Cazalet Chronicles* have been favorably compared to John Galsworthy's *The Forsyte Saga.*

WORKS: *The Beautiful Visit* (1950). (with R. Aickman) *We Are for the Dark: Six Ghost Stories* (1951). *The Long View* (1956). (with A. Helps) *Bettina: A Portrait* (1957). *The Sea Change* (1959). *After Julius* (1965). *Something in Disguise* (1970). *Odd Girl Out* (1972). *Mr. Wrong* (1975). *Getting It Right* (1982). (with T. Maschler) *Howard & Maschler on Food* (1987). *The Light Years* (1990). *Marking Time* (1992). *Confusion* (1994). *Casting Off* (1995).

BIBLIOGRAPHY:

For articles in reference works, see: *CA. CLC. CN. Feminist. MBL* and *SUP. SF&FL. ToddBWW. WA.*

Other references: Becker, A. *NYTBR* (July 1992). *LonT* (3 November 1995). *New Statesman* (21 September 1957, 11 July 1975). *Newsweek* (29 December 1975). *NYT* (9 January 1966). *NYTBR* (22 February 1976). Pearlman, M. *The Anna Book: Searching for Anna in Literary History* (1992). Rubin, M. *CSM* (July 1994). *Spectator* (8 April 1972, 26 July 1975). *TLS* (20 November 1959, 24 March 1972).

Carey Kaplan
(updated by Christina Root)

Henrietta Hobart Howard

BORN: c. 1688, Bickling, Norfolkshire.
DIED: 26 July 1767, Twickenham, Middlesex.
DAUGHTER OF: Sir Henry Hobart and Elizabeth Maynard Hobart.
MARRIED: Charles Howard, 1706; George Berkeley, 1735.

H., later the Countess of Suffolk, was a letterwriter, courtier, and mistress to George II of England. She was born in about 1688 in Bickling, Norfolkshire, the first daughter of Sir Henry Hobart, Baronet, and Elizabeth Maynard, whose grandfather had been commissioner of the great seal under William III. In 1706, while still in her teens, H. married the Hon. Charles Howard, who twenty-five years later would become the ninth Earl of Suffolk. Seeing few opportunities for immediate advancement in England, the young couple traveled to Hanover, Germany, where they came to the attention of Prince George Augustus and Princess Caroline of Ansbach, who, on the death of Queen Anne of England in 1714, would become the Prince and Princess of Wales. In October of 1714, Princess Caroline appointed H. as one of the women of the bedchamber, commencing a relationship that would continue until H. retired in 1734. During many of these years that she served Caroline, H. served the husband as well. Horace Walpole, the close friend of her twilight years, writes of H.'s relationship to the king that she diverted "the channel of his inclinations to herself." Indeed, she became the prince's mistress and continued the liaison after he became king. He visited her in her lodgings at the same time each day and spent hours walking and talking with her in the gardens of St. James and Richmond, where she resided at Richmond Lodge.

After a number of years, the king financed the construction for her at Twickenham of an elaborate villa, Marble Hill, which was completed in 1724. Her neighbor, Alexander Pope, helped design the gardens. Here was the perfect setting for entertaining the monarch when they were away from St. James and for conversing with her many friends, among them some of the most exciting personalities from the worlds of English letters, politics, and society. Yet the pleasures of such encounters were sometimes marred by tensions arising from ambitions and jealousies. For example, ambitious to gain royal patronage, Jonathan Swift, John Gay, and Aaron Hill sought to use the friendship of H. to their advantage. Although Gay received small favors and Swift had an audience with Queen Caroline, when he spoke vigorously for his own and for Ireland's welfare, the material results of such appeals were insignificant. Unfortunately, H.'s lack of success on Swift's behalf spoiled their friendship. The "Character of Mrs. Howard," written in 1727, reflects in characteristic Swiftian tones his bitterness. Although Swift achieved a measure of vengeance for what he believed to be H.'s disloyalty, her friends, including Gay and Pope, defended her, recognizing, no doubt, that though she had the ear of royalty she had little real influence.

When the eighth Earl of Suffolk died without an heir in 1731, Charles Howard succeeded to the title, a development that allowed H. to be called Lady Suffolk; at this time she was appointed Groom of the Stole to the Queen, a position with a stipend of £800 a year. Two years later, on 28 September 1733, her husband died, and the following year she petitioned the king and queen to be allowed to retire. The queen, referring to her as the best of servants, insisted that H. take a week to reconsider. However, H., now in her mid-forties and quite deaf, stood by her decision and left the royal service.

Although she had severed her royal connections, H., during the more than three decades of life that remained to her, continued to entertain important people at Marble Hill and in her London residence at 27 Saville Street, now Saville Row. In 1735, she married the Hon. George Berkeley, who was described by Lord Hervey as "neither young, handsome, healthy, nor rich." Yet their marriage was apparently happy, being marked by frequent visits from their many friends, among them Pope, until his death in 1744, young William Pitt, at the start of his illustrious career, and Horace Walpole, after H.'s husband died in 1746.

H.'s modest place in literature depends on her correspondence, which was published in two volumes in 1824 under the title *Letters to and from Henrietta, Countess of Suffolk, and her Second Husband, the Hon. George Berkeley; from 1712 to 1767.* The work was edited anonymously by John Wilson Croker, who is remembered chiefly for his devastating attack on Keats's *Endymion.* Croker acquired the manuscripts of the letters from Lord and Lady Londonderry, who could trace their family back to H. Croker provides a representative selection from the five folio volumes of Suffolk papers that currently reside in the British Library (Add. MS. 22, 625–29).

The edition opens with the editor's biographical notice, followed by Swift's character of H. and Pope's poem "To a Certain Lady at Court." The preliminaries conclude with a poem by the Earl of Peterborough, who exclaims, "O wonderful creature!" The letters, chronologically arranged and copiously annotated, span more than half a century, from 1712 to 1767. Only 30 of the nearly 250 were written by H. The others were usually directed to her by her friends who were involved in literature, politics, and society. Swift, Gay, Pope, Arbuthnot, Chesterfield, Pitt, Glenville, Peterborough, Bolingbroke, and Horace Walpole were among the men, and the Duchesses of Buckingham, Marlborough, and Queensbury were among the women who corresponded with the countess. The cumulative effect upon the reader is involvement in the social milieu. One must look elsewhere for comment on the major issues of the times.

For the reader who would arrive at an independent assessment of the merits of H.'s correspondence, the task is complicated because there has been no edition since Croker's in 1824, although in 1924 Lewis Melville reprinted in *Lady Suffolk and Her Circle* a considerable number of the letters plus some not previously printed. Fortunately, the reader can sample the correspondence in modern editions of the letters of Walpole, Pope, Swift, and the Earl of Chesterfield.

A reading of H.'s correspondence provides access to the social worlds of the eighteenth-century English court and of the English aristocracy. In the process, the reader encounters key figures in literature, politics, and society as they touched the life of one of the fascinating women of the times. The portrait of H. that emerges is intrinsically interesting. Her characteristic qualities are captured by comments made over forty years apart by two of her dearest friends. In approximately 1725, Pope wrote of her, "I know a Reasonable Woman Handsome and witty, yet a Friend"; and in 1767, shortly after her death, Walpole wrote, "I never knew a woman more respectable for her honour and principles and have lost few persons in my life whom I shall miss so much."

WORKS: *Letters to and from Henrietta, Countess of Suffolk, and Her Second Husband, the Hon. George Berkeley; from 1712 to 1767. With Historical, Biographical, and Explanatory Notes,* ed. J. W. Croker (1824).

BIBLIOGRAPHY: Aitken, G. *The Life and Works of John Arbuthnot* (1892). Arkell, R. L. *Caroline of Ansbach: George the Second's Queen* (1939). Brightfield, M. F. *John Wilson Croker* (1940). *Burke's Peerage* (1970). Chesterfield, Earl of *The Letters of Philip Dormer Stanhope, Earl of Chesterfield* (1845). *Edinburgh Review* (March 1824). *Gentleman's Magazine* (July 1767). Kippis, A. *Biographica Britannica* (1778). *LonT* (18 August 1992). Melville, L. [pseud. L. S. Benjamin]. *Lady Suffolk and Her Circle* (1924). Pope, A. *Minor Poems* (1954). Pope, A. *Correspondence* (1956). *Quarterly Review* (January 1824). Quennell, P. *Caroline of England: An Augustan Portrait* (1939). Quennell, P. *Architectural Digest* (1987). Salmon, F. E. *RES* (1991). Swift, J. *Prose Writings.* (1962). Swift, J. *Correspondence* (1963). Walpole, H. *Memoirs of the Reign of King George the Second* (1846). Walpole, H. *Memoirs* (1852). Walpole, H. *Correspondence* (1961). Walpole, H. *Selected Letters* (1973).

For articles in reference works, see: *DNB.*

Other references: Dobree, B. *English Literature of the Early Eighteenth Century* (1959). Ireland, N. O. *Index to Women of the World* (1957). Melville, L. [pseud. L. S. Benjamin]. *Maids of Honour* (1917). Sherman, R. *World's Great Love Letters* (1917). Stenton, D. M. *The English Woman in History* (1957).

Philip Bordinat

Susan Howatch

BORN: 14 July 1940, Leatherhead, Surrey.
DAUGHTER OF: George Sturt and Ann Watney Sturt.
MARRIED: Joseph Howatch, 1964.

H. is a popular novelist whose work is noted for attention to characterization, for pressing the boundaries of genres, and, especially in the last few years, for its intellectual depth. Her career has developed in several distinct stages.

Born early in World War II (her father was killed in the war), she attended schools in Surrey. She took a law degree at King's College, London, in 1961 and clerked for a year. But writing was her chief interest—she had been writing novels since the age of twelve—and, unable to get her work published in Britain, she emigrated in 1964 to the United States, working in New York City as a secretary. Soon after, her first novel was accepted, and over the next six years she published six short romantic mysteries. The trade labeled them gothics, but she said (in a 1974 article in *The Writer*) that "realism" better described her intentions. In the third and fourth of these novels she experimented with first-person narration, and in the fourth with a historical setting (the Napoleonic era); both techniques were to be hallmarks of all her more substantial works.

During this book-per-year period, she was also engaged in a larger project—the reinvention of the "family saga" genre that had declined since its heyday early in the twentieth century under John Galsworthy. *Penmarric* was published in 1971; it is an epic spanning two generations (1890–1945) of a landed family in Cornwall, arranged in five books that are each centered on a different major character and told from that person's viewpoint. It was followed, at about three-year intervals, by four more sagas of similar structure. *Cashelmara* (1974)—another work titled after the mansion that both motivates and symbolizes the fluctuating family fortunes—centers on Ireland in the period following the potato famine (1859–91) but is set partly in New York and Boston. In *The Rich Are Different* (1977), the mystique of a decayed stately home in Norfolk counterpoints the nouveau-riche ethos of the New York–based international banking house about which the action revolves. It covers only the years 1922–40, but its story is continued to 1967 in *Sins of the Fathers* (1980). *The Wheel of Fortune* (1984) returns to a stately home setting, this time in southwest Wales, to trace the effects of domestic violence and guilt across five generations. It ends with the posthumous publication of a murder victim's prize manuscript—a family saga ("he . . . wanted to prove he could do something better than *The Forsyte Saga*"), which is scorned by English publishers but taken up in America with great success. H. here fictionalizes her own experience and reveals her ambition to outdo Galsworthy.

Penmarric was serialized on BBC television in 1978, and all five family sagas were reissued in 1989–90. Still present in these works are the mystery and romance of her earlier novels, with greater attention to sex, both "normal" and otherwise, and to physical violence, but there is a deeper concern with other themes. H. deals in these novels with the pain of tangled relationships and the emotional effects of growing up burdened by the tangled relationships of one's forebears. Her first-person technique, with five or six of the central characters taking their turns as narrators in each novel so that sometimes parts of the same story are told from different viewpoints, is designed, H. says, to "put the reader in the place of God" (personal interview, 1995) in knowing more about the characters than they do themselves. The technique also serves to expose the subjectivity of all reporting of events—a condition that is crucial in the genre of mystery as well as that of history. H. is concerned with accuracy of historical detail in her settings and especially with social history and social observation. Ethnic and national differences (Irish, Welsh, English, American) loom large in her sagas, as does the impact of the English class system.

Her interest in history further appears in the attempt to make the relationships in each novel parallel those of a historical family. *Penmarric* is based on the lives of King Henry II and his two families, legitimate and illegitimate, as its epigraphs amply show. After the three Edwards in *Cashelmara,* H. went back to Roman history for the next two novels (Julius Caesar, Cleopatra, Mark Antony, and Augustus's daughter Julia; Rome and Greece/Egypt paralleled respectively by America and Britain), though H.'s scheme was obscured by the publisher's suppression of her epigraphs. For *The Wheel of Fortune,* the framework is, loosely, the English royal family of the fourteenth and early fifteenth centuries. The progenitor of the family is a pedophile, and later generations include the brothers Lionel, John, and Thomas; John's son, Harry, who kills his cousin to secure his usurpation of the estate; and Harry's son, Hal.

Other kinds of intertextuality increasingly mark the later sagas. *The Wheel of Fortune* takes its title and most of its epigraphs from Boethius, and other substantial allusions range from Cicero and the Bible to Anthony Hope's *The Prisoner of Zenda.* The literature of doubles informs H.'s treatment of the relationship between Harry and his cousin Kester, the visionary Richard II figure.

H. describes *The Wheel of Fortune* as a "bridge" to the next stage of her career. Something of that quality may be seen in its exploration of the theme of forgiveness and, toward the end, in Hal's religious conversion. By the time it was published in 1984, H. had herself become disillusioned about the lifestyle of affluent hedonism celebrated in her novels and made possible for her personally by their success. She had left the United States in 1976 and, after four years' residence in Ireland, moved back to England, living in an apartment in the precincts of Salisbury Cathedral. She turned from writing to intensive reading, mainly in theology and church history, and gradually became a Christian convert. Researching for her next novel in the life of the Liberal statesman H. H. Asquith, she found the ecclesiastical background of the Edwardian era more absorbing than the political, and she conceived a series of six novels with a cathedral setting and interlocking plots and characters. The first of these was published in 1987 and the last seven years later.

H.'s Starbridge novels—set, like the cathedral novels of Anthony Trollope, in a fictionalized Salisbury—successfully challenge Trollope's dominance of this subgenre. She lacks Trollope's satiric gift but, with her technique of first-person narration, excels in the ability to get inside her characters. To a Trollopian interest in the irony of a worldly church, as shown in the social and political maneuverings and rivalries of clergymen and their wives, she adds concern for the spiritual dimension of her characters' experience and for the intellectual issues that have challenged the Church from the mid-1930s to the late 1980s, the time frame of the series.

Though a "bold departure" from H.'s earlier work, the new series is not altogether discontinuous. As in the family sagas, ambition and sex are still driving motivations ("I wanted to write about clergymen with balls"), as are the need to dominate and control others or to free oneself from oppressive memories or from the English class system. But her characters' conflicts are now heightened by the genuineness of their religious commitment. Furthermore, her stories continue to be firmly anchored in contemporary historical events, and the clergy of Starbridge represent something of the range—conservative, liberal, mystic, evangelical, charismatic, gay—of the Established Anglican Church.

As in all her writing, mystery maintains suspense. The first of the series, *Glittering Images* (1987), is narrated by Charles Ashworth, who has been sent to Starbridge by the archbishop to investigate rumors about a curious ménage involving the bishop, his wife, and his young, attractive housekeeper-manager, a situation modeled on actual circumstances in Durham at the time. In *Mystical Paths* (1992), the narrator sets himself to learn whether the disappearance at sea of Oxford don Christian Aysgarth (son of Neville, whose troubled life twenty years before dominates *Ultimate Prizes,*1989, and whose affair with a young heiress is the plot of *Scandalous Risks,* 1990—modeled on the real-life story of Asquith and Venetia Stanley) was accident, suicide, murder, or a well-plotted escape into a different identity.

With enough variations to make each novel interesting, H. usually follows this pattern: A clergyman of great gifts and promise faces an inner crisis that threatens to undermine his life; he meets a sympathetic pastor/counselor/healer who sees through the sham and enables the protagonist to get past the distortions in his view of things, distortions resulting from flawed relationships, perhaps long past, especially with father or mother or both; and finally, through this new self-understanding and through divine grace, manifested most importantly in the ability to forgive, he is freed to follow the calling that is defined by his unique gifts.

H.'s counselors combine psychological expertise (often but not exclusively Jungian) with a theological understanding of the human predicament, drawing especially on the medieval mystics. She is equally at ease with the vocabulary of both schools, "self-realization" and "salvation." One of the recurrent themes in *Mystical Paths,* in fact, is language itself, the complementary validity of scientific and religious codes for describing psychological disorder. In *Mystical Paths,* with its 1960s setting and its accounts of psychic powers, demon possession, and exorcism, H.

again foregrounds the occult as she had in *The Devil on Lammas Night* (1970) but now includes a rational questioning of the phenomena that, paradoxically, makes them more convincing.

This novel and its predecessor, *Scandalous Risks* (awarded the Winifred Mary Stanford prize in 1991), differ from the other four in being narrated by members of the younger generation. Both capture well the "death of God" thinking and the ethical permissiveness of the 1960s; the epigraphs in *Scandalous Risks* are taken from Bishop J.A.T. Robinson, author of the controversial *Honest to God,* and his critics. In the last of the series, *Absolute Truths* (1994)—focusing again on Ashworth, now the bishop—H. continues to wrestle with the theological issues raised by Robinson. She treats all such issues in a balanced fashion and with due regard for their complexity.

In five of the six Starbridge novels, the central consciousness is that of a clergyman; only *Scandalous Risks* focuses on a woman narrator (as *The Shrouded Walls,* 1968, and sections of the sagas had done). H. handles both female and male characters with insight but rejects classification as a women's novelist. "The real truth about human beings lies beyond gender," she believes; "in the basic things [such as forgiveness and wholeness] men and women think alike."

By 1993, H.'s aggregate sales had passed 20 million copies. In that year, she gave an endowment of £1 million to establish the Starbridge Lectureship in Theology and Natural Science at the University of Cambridge. She considers science and theology to be "complementary, two aspects of one truth" but faults writers in each discipline (e.g., Jurgen Moltmann and Stephen Hawking) for their naïveté about the other. In 1994 she edited, with substantial introductions, the eight-volume "Library of Anglican Spirituality,"a reprint edition of twentieth-century classics.

Another novel appeared in 1997. Set in contemporary London, *A Question of Integrity* (in the U. S. as *The Wonder Worker*) explores the phenomenon of healing and its border with the paranormal.

WORKS: *The Dark Shore* (1965). *The Waiting Sands* (1966). *Call in the Night* (1967). *The Shrouded Walls* (1968). *April's Grave* (1969). *The Devil on Lammas Night* (1970). *Penmarric* (1971). *Cashelmara* (1974). *The Rich Are Different* (1977). *A Susan Howatch Treasury,* 2 vols. (containing the first six novels, 1978). *Sins of the Fathers* (1980). *The Wheel of Fortune* (1984). *Glittering Images* (1987). *Glamorous Powers* (1988). *Ultimate Prizes* (1989). *Scandalous Risks* (1990). *Mystical Paths* (1992). *Absolute Truths* (1994). *A Question of Integrity* (1997; in the U.S. as *The Wonder Worker*).

BIBLIOGRAPHY: Alderson, K. *LonT* (interview; 19 March 1993). Bridgwood, C., in *The Progress of Romance,* ed. J. Radford (1986). Maitland, S. *Books and Religion* (Summer 1990). McCollough, D. *Christianity Today* (28 October 1991). Smith, A. *PW* (interview; 16 October 1987).

For articles in reference works, see: *Authors in the News* (1976). *CA. IAWWW. IWWW. Ireland SUP. SF&FL.* Seymour-Smith, M. *Novels and Novelists* (1980). *TCRGW* (1982). *TCRHW* (1994).

Other references: Bernikow, L. *Cosmopolitan* (November 1988). Edwards, O. C. *Anglican Theological Review* (1991). Fowler, B. *The Alienated Reader: Women and Romantic Literature in the Twentieth Century* (1991). Hinckley, K. and B. Hinckley. *American Best Sellers: A Reader's Guide to Popular Fiction* (1989). *LJ* (June 1991). *LonT* (7 May 1994). *Tablet* (27 March and 7 August 1993). *THES* (19 March 1993). Thurmer, J. *Seven: An Anglo-American Literary Review* (1994).

Charles A. Huttar

Mary Botham Howitt

BORN: 12 March 1799, Coleford, Gloucestershire.
DIED: 30 January 1888, Rome, Italy.
DAUGHTER OF: Samuel Botham and Ann Wood Botham.
MARRIED: William Howitt, 1821.

A prolific author, producing, sometimes in collaboration with her husband, more than 110 books and scores of articles, H. was a novelist, nature writer, children's book author, editor, and translator. She was the daughter of strict Quaker parents; along with her sister Anna, eighteen months older, she was first educated at home, until both girls were sent to a school run by neighbor Mary Parker. Samuel Botham required, however, that his daughters sit apart from the other girls lest they acquire un-Quaker-like ideas and habits. In 1809 the two girls attended a Society of Friends school in Croydon until their mother's illness caused them to return to Uttoxeter, in Staffordshire. Study at a Friends school in Sheffield in 1811 was followed by a brief period of instruction from tutors at home in 1812, after which H. was left to self-education. Because Samuel Botham was a firm believer in the Quaker prohibition against art and literature, the Botham daughters had to study both secretly. In 1818 H. met fellow Quaker William Howitt, who shared her interest in literature and in writing. They were married in a Quaker ceremony at Uttoxeter on 16 April 1821. William worked briefly in his own chemist's shop, but soon the couple depended on writing, translating, and editing for their income. Their first works, *The Forest Minstrel, and Other Poems* (1823) and *The Desolation of Eyam, and Other Poems* (1827), began a collaboration that continued throughout their lives. Like much of their subsequent work, these poems show the influence of the Romantics of whom they were early popularizers. H. and her husband became friends with William Wordsworth, and they also admired John Keats and Lord Byron, defending the latter against detractors after his death.

One of their early joint editing ventures was *Howitt's Journal,* which began 2 January 1847 but lasted only a year and a half because of financial difficulties. H. was a friend of Elizabeth Gaskell, whose earliest stories were published in *Howitt's Journal* under the pseudonym "Cotton Mather Mills." H. and her husband also encouraged Gaskell in her first novel, *Mary Barton,* working to arrange its publication. H. was also a friend of Fredrika Bremer and was the first to translate her Swedish novels into English, starting with *Neighbours* in 1842. She also translated Hans Christian Andersen's stories and the work of several German authors, and with her husband produced a history of Scandinavian literature, *The Literature and Romance of Northern Europe* (1852). Her children's stories include *The Children's Year* (1847) and *Our Cousins In Ohio* (1849), based on letters from her younger sister Emma, who had moved to the United States. She wrote for most of the major and minor periodicals of Victorian England, including *Athenaeum, Household Words, and All the Year Round.*

Her reputation during her lifetime was considerably stronger than it has been since; in the United States she was especially well regarded for her poems, a collection of which appeared in an American edition along with the work of Keats and Henry Hart Milman. Most of her work has been out of print in the twentieth century except for her *Autobiography* (1889) and her Bremer translations.

Her life reflects the struggles and concerns common to Victorians and to women. She supported the 1856 proposal for a Married Women's Property Act, working with friends such as Barbara Leigh Smith Bodichon and Octavia Hill, with whom H. pasted together the signed petitions. She also had a lifelong concern for social, educational, and political reform and for the peace movement. In addition to writing, translating, and editing, H. managed a family that included five children who survived infancy; four of them reached adulthood. Family responsibilities and the need to earn a living undoubtedly affected the quality of her work; she anticipated Virginia Woolf's *A Room of One's Own* by more than seventy-five years, regretting in 1848 that a new house gave her "no little working-room to myself," but that she could "bear interruptions" better than other members of her family (*Autobiography,* II, 46). Her life also reflected the crisis of faith experienced by many Victorians: Having been raised in the Society of Friends, she later became involved in Unitarianism and spiritualism and in her old age joined the Roman Catholic Church (26 May 1882).

Her *Autobiography* remains one of her most readable works, the record of an energetic and thoughtful woman, a keen observer of nature, a writer who worked for the rights of working people and women, for copyright reform, for broader educational opportunities, and for peace.

WORKS: (with W. Howitt) *The Forest Minstrel, and Other Poems* (1823). (with W. Howitt) *The Desolation of Eyam; The Emigrant, a Tale of the American Woods: and Other Poems* (1827). *The Seven Temptations* (1834). *Sketches of Natural History* (1834). *Tales in Prose* (1836). *Tales in Verse* (1836). *Wood Leighton; or, A Year in the Country* (1836). *Hymns and Fire-Side Verses* (1839). *Hope On, Hope Ever!* (1840). *Strive and Thrive* (1840). *Sowing and Reaping; or, What Will Come of It?* (1841). *Little Coin, Much Care; or, How Poor Men Live* (1842). *Which Is the Wiser; or, People Abroad* (1842). *Work and Wages; or, Life in Service* (1842). (trans.) *The Neighbours: A Story of Every-Day Life,* by F. Bremer (1842). *Alice Franklin* (1843). *Love and Money* (1843). *No Sense Like Common Sense; or, Some Passages in the Life of Charles Middleton* (1843). (trans.) *The Home: or, Life in Sweden.,* by F. Bremer (1843). *My Uncle the Clockmaker* (1844). *The Two Apprentices* (1844). (trans.) *The Rose of Tistelon,* by E. Carlen (1844). (trans.) *The H. Family,* by F. Bremer (1844). (trans.) *New Sketches of Every Day Life,* by F. Bremer (1844). (trans.) *The Picture of the Virgin,* by J. C. von Schmid (1844). (trans.) *The Child's Picture and Verse-Book,* by O. Spektor (1844). (trans.) *The Curate's Favourite Pupil,* by K. Stober (1844). *Fireside Verses* (1845). (trans.) *The Improvisatore,* by H. C. Andersen (1845). (trans.) *Only a Fiddler!,* by H. C. Andersen (1845). (trans.) *O. T. or Life in Denmark,* by H. C. Andersen (1845). *Who Shall Be Greatest?* (1845). *My Own Story; or, The Autobiography of a Child* (1845). (trans.) *Wonderful Stories for Children,* by H. C. Andersen (1846). (trans.) *The Citizen of Prague,* by T. Thyrnau (1846). (trans.) *A Diary; the H—Family, etc.,* by F. Bremer (1846). (trans.) *The Neighbours . . . and Other Tales,* by F. Bremer (1846). (trans.) *The President's Daughter, including Nina,* by F. Bremer (1846). *The Heir of Wast-Waylan* (1847). *Ballads and Other Poems* (1847). (trans.) *The True Story of My Life,* by H. C. Andersen (1847). (trans.) *Genevieve: A Tale,* by A. de Lamartine (1847). (trans.) *Pictures of Life,* by A. Stifter (1847). *The Children's Year* (1847; rev. 1864; rev. as *The Story of a Happy Home; or, The Children's Year, and How They Spent It,* 1875). (trans.) *Brothers and Sisters,* by F. Bremer (1848). *The Childhood of Mary Beeson* (1848, 1870). *The Steadfast Gabriel* (1848). (trans.) *The Peasant and His Landlord,* by S. M. von Knorring (1848). *Our Cousin in Ohio* (1849). (with W. Howitt) *Stories of English and Foreign Life* (1849). (trans.) *The Midnight Sun . . . .,* by F. Bremer (1849). *How the Mice Got Out of Trouble and Other Tales* (1850). (trans.) *An Easter Offering,* by F. Bremer (1850). (with W. Howitt) *The Literature and Romance of Northern Europe* (1852). *The Dial of Love* (1852). (trans.) *Jacob Bendixen, the Jew,* by M. A. Goldschmidt (1852). (trans.) *The Homes of the New World,* by F. Bremer (1853). *Birds and Flowers and Other Country Things* (1855). *The Picture Book for the Young* (1855). (trans.) *Trust and Trial,* by B. M. Bjornson (1858). (trans.) *Hertha . . .,* by F. Bremer (1859). *Marion's Pilgrimage: A Fire-Side Story, and Other Poems* (1859). (trans.) *Father and Daughter,* by F. Bremer (1859). *A Popular History of the United States of America, from the Discovery of the American Continent to the Present Time* (1859). *The Blackbird, the Parrot, the Cat, and Other Stories* (1861). *Adventures of Jack and Harry* (1861). (trans.) *Two Years in Switzerland and Italy,* by F. Bremer (1861). (with Mrs. S. C. Hall) *The Favourite Scholar and Other Tales* (1861). *Lillieslea; or, Lost and Found* (1861). *Little Arthur's Letters to His Sister Mary* (1861). *A Treasury of New Favourite Tales for Young People* (1861). (with W. Howitt) *Ruined Alleys and Castles of Great Britain* (1862). (trans.) *Travels in the Holy Land,* by F. Bremer (1862). *The Poet's Children* (1863). (trans.) *Greece and the Greeks,* by F. Bremer (1863). *The Story of Little Cristal* (1863). (with W. Howitt) *The Wye: Its Ruined Abbeys* (1863). *The Cost of Caergwyn* (1864). *Stories of Stapleford* (1864). *Mr. Rudd's Grandchildren* (1864). (with W. Howitt) *The Ruined Abbeys of the Border* (1865). (with W. Howitt) *The Ruined Abbeys of Yorkshire* (1865). *Our Four-Footed Friends* (1867). (trans.) *Behind the Counter [Handel and Wandell],* by J. W. Hackländer (1867). *John Oriel's Start in Life* (1868). *Pictures from Nature* (1869). *Vignettes of American History* (1869). *A Pleasant Life* (1871). *Birds and Flowers*

(1871). *Birds and Their Nests* (1872). *Natural History Stories* (1875). *Tales for All Seasons* (1881). *Tales of English Life* (1881). *An Autobiography* (1889).

BIBLIOGRAPHY: de Groot, H. B. *Blake Studies* (1971). Duncliff, J. *Mary Howitt: Another Lost Victorian Writer* (1992). Lee, A. *Laurels and Rosemary: The Life of William and Mary Howitt* (1955). Paston, G. [E. M. Symonds]. *Little Memoirs of the Nineteenth Century* (1902). Walker, M. H. *Come Wind, Come Weather: A Biography of Alfred Howitt* (1971). Woodring, C.A. *HLB* (Spring 1951).Woodring, C. R. *Victorian Samplers, William and Mary Howitt* (1952).

For articles in reference works, see: *BA19C. DNB. Europa. Feminist. Oxford. ToddBWW. VB.*

Other references: *AS* (Fall 1992). Butler, J. A. *ELN* (1975). *Country Life* (30 April 1981).

Carol A. Martin

Anna Hume

FLOURISHED: 1644.
DAUGHTER OF: David Hume of Godscroft (c. 1560–c. 1630).

H. was a poet, a translator of Latin and Italian verses, and the editor of her father's history of Scotland. She was born to a scholarly family and received a classical education. Her father was a champion of Scottish language and history, a learned essayist, and the author of two collections of Latin poems including *Lusus Poetici* (1605). Her brother was a mathematician and medical doctor and also the author of prose romances and poetry. H. herself was called "the learned and worthy gentlewoman" of a "pregnant and rare . . . wit" by William Drummond of Hawthornden, who praised her original verse, now lost.

Nothing more is known of H.'s life outside her published works. Her translations of Petrarch's *Triumphs of Love: Chastitie: Death* (1644) come at the end of a long tradition of translating the Italian poet's works into English. Many versions of the *Triumphs* circulated widely in manuscript for more than fifty years before H.'s translation was printed, but H. claims never to have seen *The Triumphs* except in Italian. The book is dedicated to Elizabeth of Bohemia, niece of King Charles I. H.'s connection with the royal family is unclear, but her dedication of the *Triumphs* to the princess underscores H.'s fealty to the Stuart monarchy.

H.'s lively and able translations do not follow Petrarch's *terza rima* but rather turn the original into iambic pentameter couplets. Her wide learning is apparent in the notes explaining classical references that follow each chapter. In a postscript to her reader, H. vows to translate the other three "triumphs" if the first three "afford thee either profit or delight," but the promised book never appeared. Nonetheless, H.'s incomplete translations of *The Triumphs* were deemed fine enough to be reprinted as part of the "Bohn's Illustrated Library" series in *The Sonnets, Triumphs, and Other Poems of Petrarch. Now First Completely Translated into English Verse by Various Hands* (1859).

Why Evan Tyler, the publisher, decided to put out a seemingly superfluous translation of Petrarch's works in 1644, long after their wide dissemination throughout Britain, may perhaps be explained by Tyler's publication of David Hume's *History of the Houses of Douglas and Angus* in the same year; perhaps the two books were part of an arrangement made between H. and the publisher. David Hume's *History* was controversial because of the volatile political atmosphere surrounding questions of royal houses and Scottish connections in the 1640s and because of the opposition of William Douglas, eleventh earl of Angus, to the use Hume's book made of family archival material. Nowhere in the *History* is H. named as the promoter of the work, but she is probably the "gentlewoman" so named in a letter of Drummond of Hawthornden. Hume himself had died in 1630, but H. seems to have supervised the editing of his work, translating her father's Latin poems contained therein, venturing her "whole fortune" on the project, and finally succeeding in bringing it to publication.

WORKS: (trans.) *The Triumphs of Love: Chastitie: Death: Translated out of Petrarch by Mrs. Anna Hume* (1644). (ed.) *The History of the Houses of Douglas and Angus* (1644; also titled *A Generall History of Scotland, Together With a Particular History of the Houses of Douglas and Angus*).

BIBLIOGRAPHY:

For articles in reference works, see: *Bell. Bloomsbury. DNB. Feminist.* Goring, R. *Chambers Scottish Biographical Dictionary* (1992). *Kissing the Rod: An Anthology of Seventeenth-Century Women's Verse,* ed. G. Greer et al. (1988).

Kari Boyd McBride

Margaret Hamilton Wolfe Hungerford

BORN: c. 1855, Cork, Ireland.
DIED: 24 January 1897, Bandon, Ireland.
DAUGHTER OF: Canon Fitzjohn Stannus Hamilton, Vicar-Choral of St. Faughman's Cathedral and Rector of Ross Co., Ireland.
MARRIED: Edward Argles, 1872; Thomas Henry Hungerford, 1882.
WROTE UNDER: The Author of Phyllis; The Duchess; Mrs. Hungerford.

Eldest daughter of an old and distinguished family, H. began writing as a young child and won many prizes in composition at school. She enjoyed telling her friends fairy tales and ghost stories, which she made up; and she decided to write seriously at eighteen, publishing her first novel, *Phyllis,* in 1877. Typical of the many novels that followed, the work is light and full of wit, humor, and pathos. It focuses on the affairs of the human heart and ends happily.

H. wrote more than forty-six works. Her best-known novel is *Molly Bawn* (1878), the tale of a frivolous, petulant Irish girl, a flirt, who arouses her lover's jealousy and naïvely ignores social conventions.

H.'s works deal with conventional stories and situations. Slighting plot, she wrote of the country society almost exclusively on the level of landlords, ignoring the peasant class. She did not analyze character; her common subject is romantic love and the frivolous interplay between couples in love before marriage. H. conveyed these trivial incidents of passion and turmoil largely through dialogue. She provided interest with flirtations and delicate love scenes (never offensive even to the most prudish). She did not pursue political issues or social concerns, and, unlike some of her contemporaries, she was not didactic. She did have a sensitive ear for language, sometimes using dialect as well as slang. With artistic skill she included vivid descriptions of nature as in *Moonshine and Marguarites* (1883) and *A Week in Killarney* (1884). Her occasional movement from prose to verse often distracts rather than intensifies the tone.

Although largely superficial, sentimental, and clearly lacking in serious intent, H.'s works are still readable, even somewhat entertaining. Adept at re-creating the social milieu of her day, H. has imaginatively recorded the small-talk of her fashionable contemporaries residing at country estates like St. Brenda's, where she had lived with her second husband till her death from typhoid fever in 1897.

WORKS: *Phyllis: A Novel* (1877). (as "By the Author of *Phyllis*") *Molly Bawn* (1878). *Airy Fairy Lilian* (1879). *Beauty's Daughters* (1880). *Mrs. Geoffrey* (1881). *Faith and Unfaith* (1881). *Portia* (1882). *Moonshine and Marguerites* (1883). *Monica* (1883). *Loijs, Lord Beresford, and other Tales* (1883). *Rossmoyne* (1883). *Doris* (1884). *A Week in Killarney* (1884). *The Witching Hour* (1884). *Sweet Is True Love* (1884). *O Tender Dolores* (1885). *A Maiden All Forlorn, and other Stories* (1885). *Mildred Trevanich* (1885). *In Durance Vile and Other Stories* (1885). *Lady Branksmere* (1886). *A Mental Struggle* (1886). *Lady Valworth's Diamonds* (1886). *Her Week's Amusement* (1886). *Green Pastures and Gray Grief* (1886). *A Modern Circe* (1887). *The Duchess* (1887). *Undercurrents* (1888). *Marvel* (1888). *Hon. Mrs. Vereker* (1888). *A Born Coquette* (1890). *Life's Remorse* (1890). *A Little Irish Girl* (1891). *Nor Wife Nor Maid* (1892). *The Hoyden* (1894). *The O'Connors of Ballynainch* (1894). *The Coming of Chloe* (1897). *Nora Creina* (1903).

BIBLIOGRAPHY: Black, H. C. *Notable Women Authors of the Day* (1893). Dorland, W. A. N. *The Sum of Feminine Achievement* (1917). Showalter, E. *A Literature of Their Own* (1977). *The Englishwoman* (April 1897).

For articles in reference works, see: *Allibone*. *BDIW*. *Biographical Dictionary and Synopsis of Books Ancient and Modern*. *BA19C*. Brown, S. J. *Ireland in Fiction: A Guide to Irish Novels, Tales, Romances, and Folklore* (1969). *DIW*. *Dole*. *Ireland*. Roberton, W. *The Novel Reader's Handbook* (1899). *Robinson*. *Warner*.

Other references: *Athenaeum* (31 August 1878). *Illustrated London News* (30 January 1897). *LonT* (25 January 1897). *NYT* (25 January 1897). *Spectator* (1855, 1878). *Strand Magazine* (October 1893).

Phyllis J. Scherle

Violet Hunt

BORN: 28 September 1862, Durham, County Durham.
DIED: 16 January 1942, South Lodge, Campden Hill.
DAUGHTER OF: Alfred William Hunt and Margaret Raine Hunt.
WROTE UNDER: I[sobel]. V[iolet]. Hunt; Violet Hunt.

Her mother a novelist and her father a famous Pre-Raphaelite painter, H. has been remembered more for the company she kept in youth and adulthood than for her novels, biographies, and autobiography. Growing up in a family where Robert Browning, John Everett Millais, Edward Burne-Jones, John Ruskin, and the Rossettis were familiar visitors, H. studied painting from her earliest years to please her father, who hoped she would become an artist. H. was ultimately more influenced by the literary side of her background; she sought Christina Rossetti's reaction to her earliest poems.

At the age of twenty-eight, H. published her first book, "a novel in dialogue," *The Maiden's Progress* (1894). A modest experiment in narrative technique, the novel includes passages of interior monologue as well as stage-comedy banter. Its light-hearted reliance on slang and formula jokes (e.g., "illusions, like wisdom teeth, are last to come and first to go") typifies H.'s early work and, though genuinely amusing, is probably responsible for the general appraisal of her writings as dated and superficial. Parodying novels of initiation, it traces the social successes of eighteen-year-old Moderna, who, an admirer says, can "take the impress of every passing wave of modern thought and yet preserve [her] individuality." Moderna likes playing practical jokes and rebuffing suitors; still unmarried at twenty-seven, she begins to worry that she may have "no heart." The flamboyantly happy ending rewards her with a man she had rejected at eighteen: This time, he announces, "I simply take you."

The traditional woman's reward that H. gave her first heroine was never to become her own. Though H. did not marry, her famous liaison with novelist Ford Madox Ford (then Ford Madox Hueffer) lasted from 1909 to 1919, indelibly marking her life and work. H. had renewed her acquaintance with Ford (who shared her Pre-Raphaelite roots) when he published an early story of hers in his *English Review*. When their affair began, Ford's wife refused to divorce him. H. went so far as to travel with Ford to Germany in 1911 and return calling herself "Mrs. Hueffer"; when various London newspapers referred to H. by that name, Ford's wife sued, bringing the affair to the scandalized attention of the public. Eventually Ford was estranged from H. when he fell in love with one of her younger friends. H.'s bitterness over their hostile parting is openly expressed in her unpublished diary of the period (now at the Pennsylvania State University Library), and colors her autobiography, *The Flurried Years* (1926; published in America as *I Have This to Say*).

Before and during her time with Ford, H. achieved her own fame for her weekly columns for the *Pall Mall Gazette*; her parties in London and at her country home, South Lodge, and her fiction, especially the occult and bizarre

Tales of the Uneasy (1911). She raised funds for women's suffrage. She worked for Ford's Review and shares with him the credit for "discovering" D. H. Lawrence, whose career they promoted by publishing his early poems. In 1916, she and Ford collaborated on *Zeppelin Nights*, a frankly patriotic collection of framed tales (explicitly comparing itself to the *Decameron*) that concludes that even poets must "do something" for the war effort by enlisting.

White Rose of Weary Leaf (1907), often considered H.'s best novel, is the long and melodramatically sad story of Amy Stevens, "a common person's child—a unit of no particular value." Showing the influence of Ford's literary circle, the novel emphasizes the importance of early impressions: The unfortunate Amy's childhood memories include images of a prison, a paralyzed woman, and a crucifix. Her story plays out these obvious symbols of frustration, helplessness, and martyrdom as she strives to support herself in occupations as diverse as secretary, actress, and director of a boys' home. Unconventional and unattached, she is known as an "adventuress" but manages at last to find a permanent situation as companion in a family where she inevitably falls in love with the father. Unconsummated for years, their affair consists of intellectual but intimate conversations, described in narration that is—surprisingly—not at all ironic in tone: "'Learn that men are brutes,' said her master gently." Their ménage collapses under the pressure of his wife's jealousy; when at last Amy becomes pregnant, she disappears to begin a new, solitary life. Optimistic, she enjoys her independence and the comfort of not having broken up her lover's family. When her lover learns in the extravagantly tragic last scene that Amy has died in childbirth, he commits suicide. The novel holds up very little hope for the fate of the resourceful but unattractive single woman who has neither money nor position of her own.

H. may have come to see herself as a similarly tragic figure. Her last book, a biography called *The Wife of Rossetti* (1932), reveals her bitterness. According to Thomas C. Moser, H. "identifies wholly with the barbarously treated Lizzie Siddal." As a younger, successful novelist she may have been, as Ford called her, "cheerfully heartless," but her later work still reflects Moderna's private fear that a woman without a man—a woman, perhaps, without a heart—cannot find fulfillment. The recent scholarship of Marie and Robert Secor promotes appreciation of H.'s literary accomplishments as well as treating her experiences from H.'s own point of view rather than from that of the man who so much affected her perspective.

WORKS: *The Maiden's Progress* (1894). *The Celebrity at Home* (1894). *A Hard Woman* (1895). *The Way of Marriage* (1896). *Unkissed, Unkind!* (1897). *The Human Interest: a Study in Incompatibilities* (1899). *Affairs of the Heart* (1900). (trans. by H. and A. Farley) *The Memoirs of Jacques Casanova de Seingalt* (1902). (trans.) *The Heart of Ruby*, by B. Tosti (1903). *Sooner or Later: the Story of an Ingenious Ingenue* (1904). *The Cat* (1905). *The Workaday Woman* (1906). *White Rose of Weary Leaf* (1907). *The Wife of Altamont* (1910). *Tales of the Uneasy* (1911). *The Doll: A Happy Story* (1911). *The Governess* (begun by H.'s mother, Margaret Hunt; finished by H. and F. M. Hueffer, 1912). *The Desirable Alien* (with a preface and two chapters by F. M. Hueffer, 1913). *The Celebrity's Daughter* (1913). *The House of Many Mirrors* (1915). *Their Lives* (1916). (with F. M. Hueffer) *Zeppelin Nights* (1916). *The Last Ditch* (1918). *Their Hearts* (1921). *The Tiger Stein* (1924). *More Tales of the Uneasy* (1925). *The Flurried Years* (in the U.S. as *I Have This to Say*, 1926). *The Wife of Rossetti* (1932).

BIBLIOGRAPHY: Adcock, A. St. J. *The Glory That Was Grub Street* (1928). Belford, B. *Violet* (1990). Goldring, D. *South Lodge: Reminiscences of V. Hunt, etc.* (1943). Hardwick, J. *An Immodest Violet* (1990). Miller, J. E. *PULC* (1990). Patmore, B. *My Friends When Young* (1968). Richards, G. *Memories of a Misspent Youth* (1932). Secor, M. *ELT* (1976). Secor, M. and R. Secor. *W&L* (1978). Secor, M. and R. Secor. *The Pre-Raphaelite Review* (1979). Secor, R. and M. Secor. *The Return of the Good Soldier: Ford Madox Ford and Violet Hunt's 1917 Diary* (1983). Secor, R. *Browning Institute Studies in Victorian Literary and Cultural History* (1979). Secor, R. *TSLL* (1979). Secor, R. *JML* (1986). Sinclair, M. *English Review* (1922). Wiesenfarth, J. *Persuasions* (1989). Works on F. M. Ford that discuss H.: Goldring, D. *The Last Pre-Rapaelit* (1948). Goldring, D. *Trained for Genius* (1949). Judd, A. *Ford Madox Ford* (1990). MacShane, F. *The Life and Work of F. M. Ford* (1965). Mizener, A. *The Saddest Story* (1971). Moser, T. C. *The Life in the Fiction of F. M. Ford* (1980).

For articles in reference works, see: *Cambridge. 1890s. Feminist. Longman. Oxford. PHS. RE. TCA. TCLC. ToddBWW. WWHFF.*

Other references: *Bookman* (October 1931, June 1932). *LonT* (19 January 1942). *The Windmill* (1947).

Robyn R. Warhol
(updated by Bette H. Kirschstein)

Huntley, Frances E.: See *Mayne, Ethelind Frances Colburn*

Lucy Apsley Hutchinson

BORN: 29 January 1620, London.
DIED: after 1675.
DAUGHTER OF: Sir Allen Apsley and Lucy St. John.
MARRIED: John Hutchinson, 1638.

Along with her contemporary, Margaret Cavendish, the Duchess of Newcastle, H. is one of the first significant women prose writers in English. She was born 29 January 1620 in the Tower of London, where her husband was later imprisoned in 1663. H.'s father, Sir Allen Apsley, was Lieutenant of the Tower at the time of her birth, and her mother, Lucy St. John, was Apsley's third wife. They had ten children; H. was the fourth, following three boys.

Though she is best known for her biography of her husband, the *Memoirs of the Life of Colonel Hutchinson*, her most interesting extant piece is an autobiographical fragment: *The Life of Mrs. Hutchinson Written by Herself.*

This work gives a rare inside glimpse into the lives of upper-class young women in the early seventeenth century. It opens with a grim prefiguration of what was to be the central historical event in the lives of her and her husband—the English Civil War: "The land was then at peace [at the time of her birth] . . . if that quietness may be called a peace, which was rather like the calm and smooth surface of the sea, whose dark tomb is already impregnated with a horrid tempest." This statement is a fairly typical example of H.'s style, which, despite her Puritan inclinations, retained a Latinate sophistication, derived no doubt from the strong classical training she received as a child.

That education, very unusual for a woman at that time, H. received partly because she was very precocious and partly because her mother doted on her. Having had three sons, her mother "received me with a great deal of joy" and learning that the child might not live "became fonder of me." H. was taught French and English simultaneously by a French "day-nurse" and could read English by the age of four. She had an excellent memory and recited sermons verbatim, much to the delight of the adults. By the age of seven she had eight tutors in such fields as languages, music, dancing, writing, and needlework, but her bent was already toward serious reading. Her mother feared that her zeal for studies would "prejudice" her health, but even during periods of prescribed play, "I would steal into some hole or other to read." In Latin she "outstripped" her brothers who were at school, even though her tutor was a "pitiful dull fellow." "Play among other children I despised," and she neglected the traditional feminine accomplishments: "and for my needle I absolutely hated it."

H.'s mother met her father when he was forty-eight and she was sixteen. After their marriage they lived in the Tower, where Mrs. Apsley became active in caring for prisoners. She funded "experiments" in "chemistry" done by Sir Walter Raleigh (then in prison) and others, "Partly to comfort and divert the poor prisoners, and partly to gain the knowledge of their experiments, and the medicines to help such poor people as were not able to seek physicians. By these means, she acquired a great deal of skill." She evidently taught some of her medicinal knowledge to her daughter, who ministered to the enemy wounded during the Civil War despite criticism by one of her husband's fellow officers. H.'s sympathy for the poor and disabled was clearly a factor in her support of the Puritan cause. In the *Memoirs* she notes with enthusiasm how under the Republic her husband, as a member of the Council of State (1649–51), was able to take "such courses that there was very suddenly not a beggar left in the country, and all the poor [were] in every town so maintained and provided for, as they were never so liberally . . . before nor since."

The interest in the *Memoirs of Colonel Hutchinson* lies in the anecdotes that illuminate the social life of the time as well as the character of the actors in the drama she unfolds. For example, we learn that on the day of her engagement she came down with smallpox. Despite the fact that "all that saw her were affrighted," her fiancé stood by her, the marriage took place, and "God recompensed his justice and constancy by restoring her . . . as well as before."

Much of the *Memoirs*, however, is a rather dry exposition of the events of the Civil War in which her husband was personally involved, such as the defense of Nottingham against the royalists, a strategic battle that preserved the north-south passage for the forces of parliament. H. clearly sees herself as writing military history and rejects temptations to elaborate romantic episodes. The work was written in the third person, ostensibly to recount her husband's life to her children and not intended for publication. She proposed that "a naked, undressed narrative speaking the simple truth of him, will deck him with more substantial glory, than all the panegyrics [of] the best pens." However, the weakness in the work lies in its relentless enthusiasm for her husband's improbably impeccable character. As a follower of Oliver Cromwell, Hutchinson was out of favor during the Restoration and in 1663 was arrested; he died in prison eleven months later. H. wrote the *Memoirs* shortly thereafter, probably between 1664 and 1671. It was not published until 1806, but thereafter reprinted several times, remaining one of the most popular of the Civil War memoirs.

Its author herself lived into the late 1670s, having presented a translation of Lucretius' *De Rerum Natura* in 1675, which had been written much earlier. The dedication to that work is largely a recantation of having committed "the sin of amusing myself with such vain philosophy" as Epicureanism. She asserts, however, that she did the translation only as a diversion: "I did not employ any serious study . . . for I turned it into English in a room where my children practiced . . . with their tutors, and I numbered the syllables of my translation by the threads of the canvas I wrought in"—a further glimpse into the early milieu of the woman writer. She also completed a partial translation of the *Aeneid* and wrote two treatises on religion: *On the Principles of Christian Religion,* written for her daughter, and *On Theology,* which were published in 1817. An earlier manuscript narrative of the events of her husband's life remains in the British Museum, and some additional writings on moral and religious subjects were still privately owned in the early 1900s.

WORKS: (trans.) *De Rerum Natura,* by Lucretius (1675). *Memoirs of the Life of Colonel Hutchinson to which is Prefixed The Life of Mrs. Hutchinson Written by Herself* (1806). *On the Principles of the Christian Religion; Addressed to Her Daughter; and on Theology* (1817).

BIBLIOGRAPHY: Barbour, R. *RenP* (1994). Cook, S. *CrSurv* (1993). Findley, S. and E. Hobby, in *1642: Literature and Power in the Seventeenth Century,* ed. F. Barker et al. (1981). Firth, C. H., intro. to *Memoirs of the Life of Colonel Hutchinson* (1906, rpt.). Handley, G. M. *Notes on the Memoirs of Colonel Hutchinson* (1905). Narveson, K. *N&Q* (1989).

For articles in reference works, see: *Bell. Bloomsbury. Cambridge. DNB. Feminist. Oxford. ToddBWW. ToddDBA.*

Other references: *Contemporary Review* (1949). *Evangelical Quarterly* (1959). MacCarthy, B. *Women Writers: Their Contribution to the English Novel* (1944). *N&Q* (1955).

Josephine Donovan

Elspeth Josceline Grant Huxley

BORN: 23 July 1907, London.
DIED: 10 January 1997, Tetbury, Gloucestershire.
DAUGHTER OF: Major Josceline Grant and Eleanor Lillian Gosvenor.
MARRIED: Gervas Huxley, 1931.

A biographer, memoirist, broadcaster, novelist, crime and suspense writer, travel writer and journalist, H. moved to British East Africa (now Kenya) with her parents in 1913 at the age of five. Raised on their coffee farm near Thika, she was educated in European schools in Nairobi, thirty-five miles away. She recounts this life, especially of her family's interaction with the Kikuyu and Masai, in her most popular book, *The Flame Trees of Thika* (1959), which she labelled as "half fiction, half true." She continued her account of her family's life in Kenya in *On the Edge of the Rift* (1962). In both these books, H. beautifully describes her enchantment with the unspoiled veld and bush prior to the industrialization brought to Kenya by Europeans.

Although her mother did not leave their up-country farm until 1965, H. returned to England at eighteen and attended Reading University, where she earned a diploma in agriculture in 1927. She then attended Cornell University in the United States for a year before joining the Empire Marketing Board as assistant press officer in London. Her student days are described in *Love Among the Daughters* (1968).

In 1931, H. married Gervas Huxley, cousin of Aldous and Julian. They had one child, Charles Grant. Because of her husband's position as a tea commissioner, they traveled extensively. H. claimed she took up mystery writing on board ship to avoid playing bridge. Her early mysteries, such as *Murder at Government House* (1937) and *Murder on Safari* (1938), are set in colonial Africa and rely on the standard detective story techniques. But these and later mysteries, such as *The Incident at the Merry Hippo* (1964), reveal her acknowledged sensitivity to African cultures, as does the novel *Red Strangers* (1938), which describes a Kikuyu family caught up in colonial East Africa under the impact of what H. called the "arrogant European."

During World War II, H. served in the BBC London news department. From 1952 to 1954, she served as a broadcaster for the BBC on "The Critics" program and also as an expert on African matters as a member of the general advisory council. After the war, H. and her family settled in Wiltshire, where H. was able to continue her broadcasting and freelance journalism. From 1946 until 1977, she served as justice of the peace for Wiltshire. She also served on the Monckton Advisory Commission in Central Africa. *Gallipot Eyes: A Wiltshire Diary* (1975) covers a year in her farming village of Oaksey, the Wiltshire village that became her permanent home. *The African Poison Murders* (1986) also discusses farming, but in colonial East Africa. *Brave New Victuals* (1965) looks into modern food production. Membership in such organizations as the Royal Society for the Protection of Birds, the World Wildlife Fund, Rhino Rescue, and the Woodland Trust reflects her lifelong interest in preservation and wildlife.

H.'s other writings suggest additional interests, especially in biography and travel. Her first publication, the two-volume *White Man's Country: Lord Delamere and the Making of Kenya* (1935), combined her interest in biography with her deep understanding of Kenya. *Last Days of Eden* (1984) is illustrated with photographs of Kenya by Hugo van Lawick. During the 1970s, H. wrote and edited several biographies including *Livingstone and His African Journeys* (1974) and *Scott of the Antarctic* (1977); she also edited a biographical anthology of the Kingsleys (1973). Her travel writings included her own experiences in The Challenge of Africa (1971) as well as those of M. H. Kingsley, whose *Travels in Africa* (1976) she edited. Her last book was *Peter Scott: Painter and Naturalist* (1993).

In 1962, H. was awarded the Commander of the British Empire. One of her last visits to Kenya was to view the 1980 filming of *The Flame Trees of Thika* for the television serialization (shown in the United States on Masterpiece Theater). Her papers are held by Rhodes House Library, Oxford.

WORKS: *White Man's Country: Lord Delamere and the Making of Kenya* (1935). *Murder at Government House* (1937). *Murder on Safari* (1938). *Red Strangers* (1938). *Atlantic Ordeal* (1941). *East Africa* (1941). *Race and Politics in Kenya: A Correspondence Between Elspeth Huxley and Margery Perham* (1944). *The Walled City* (1948). *The Sorcerer's Apprentice* (1948). *I Don't Mind if I Do* (1951). *Four Guineas* (1954). *A Thing to Love* (1954). *The Red Rock Wilderness* (1957). *The Flame Trees of Thika* (1959). *A New Earth* (1960). *On the Edge of the Rift* (1962; in the U.K. as *The Mottled Lizard* (1962). *The Merry Hippo* (1963; in the U. S. as *The Incident at the Merry Hippo*). *Forks and Hope: An African Notebook* (1964). *A Man From Nowhere* (1964). *Back Street New Worlds* (1964). *Brave New Victuals* (1965). *Their Shining Eldorado: A Journey Through Australia* (1967). *Love Among the Daughters* (1968). *The Challenge of Africa* (1971). *Livingstone and His African Journeys* (1974). *Florence Nightingale* (1975). *Gallipot Eyes: A Wiltshire Diary* (1975). *Scott of the Antarctic* (1977). *Whipsnade: Captive Breeding for Survival* (1981). *The Prince Buys the Manor* (1982). (with H. van Lawick) *Last Days of Eden* (1984). *Out in the Midday Sun: My Kenya* (1985). *The African Poison Murders* (1986). *Nine Faces of Kenya* (1990). *Peter Scott: Painter and Naturalist* (1993).

BIBLIOGRAPHY: Cross, R. and M. Perkin *Elspeth Huxley: A Bibliography* (1996). Russell, S., in *Introduction to Mysteries of Africa*, ed. E. Schleh (1991).

For articles in reference works, see: *Bloomsbury. CA. DLB. DLEL. EMD. Feminist. IAWWW. Longman. SATA. TCC&MW. TCW. WA. WD. Who's Who. Wilson Library Biography* (January 1961).

Other references: *Atlantic* (July 1967). *BW* (3 November 1968, 22 March 1987). *Daily Telegraph* (13 January 1997). *Economist* (12 November 1977). *Encounter* (October 1976). Giffuni, C. *Clues* (1991). *Guardian* (13 January 1997). *Independent* (13 January 1997). Knipp, T. *SoAR* (1990). *LonT* (13 January 1997). *Nature* (3 August 1935). *NYT* (18 January 1997, 18 March 1987).

NYTBR (22 September 1968). *Observer* (21 May 1967, 29 September 1969). *Punch* (19 July 1967, 9 October 1968). *Spectator* (6 February 1982). *TLS* (2 December 1965, 25 May 1967, 29 October 1982, 31 January 1987).

Judith C. Kohl

Elizabeth Simpson Inchbald

BORN: 15 October 1753, Stanningfield, Suffolk.
DIED: 1 August 1821, Kensington, London.
DAUGHTER OF: John Simpson and Mary Rushbrook Simpson.
MARRIED: Joseph Inchbald, 1772.
WROTE UNDER: Elizabeth Inchbald; Mrs. Inchbald.

I. was eighth in a family of nine. She ran away from home at the age of nineteen to seek her fortune on the London stage, but, as an attractive woman with a pronounced stammer, she faced formidable obstacles in her aspirations. The stammer she could control when delivering carefully rehearsed lines, but her beauty prompted advances from such unscrupulous actors as James Dodd, who attempted to molest her when she applied to him for help.

The experience of independence was so thoroughly frightening that, three months after her arrival in London, I. accepted the marriage proposal of Joseph Inchbald, a fellow actor whom she had earlier rejected. Seventeen years her senior, Joseph provided I. the security of a marriage with a fellow Roman Catholic as well as automatic access to the stage. Ironically, or perhaps intentionally, I.'s Bristol debut as Cordelia to Joseph's Lear capitalized on their age difference; it was a role she was to repeat many times. For the first four years of their marriage, I. served an apprenticeship in the regional theaters of England and Scotland, but finally, in July 1776, Joseph having quarreled with the Edinburgh audience, they moved to Paris, where he tried to earn a living by his avocation, painting, and she tried writing comedies; they returned to Brighton in September. It was at this low period that the Inchbalds befriended Sarah Siddons and her brother, John Philip Kemble, and I. fell in love with the latter. Though her husband died in 1779, Kemble never proposed, and I. never remarried.

One of I.'s earliest known literary efforts was an outline of *A Simple Story,* which she circulated among friends in 1777. By 1779, I. had completed the first version of the novel, which she offered for publication several times over the next ten years. Meanwhile, she began to succeed in her dramatic writing, earning 100 guineas from the sale of her first play, *The Mogul Tale, or The Descent of the Balloon,* which played for ten days at the Haymarket in 1784. After this first success, inspired by the French craze for ballooning, I. received consistently high fees for subsequent plays, most of which were produced and printed. I.'s humanitarian interests were revealed in her most popular plays. Under the guise of a light summer comedy, *I'll Tell You What* (1786) raised questions about marriage and divorce. *Such Things Are* (1788), which brought her £900, probed social issues by portraying, in the character Haswell, the prison reformer John Howard. Today I.'s best-known play may be *Lover's Vows,* a rendering of a Kotzebue play that scandalizes Fanny Price in Jane Austen's *Mansfield Park.*

Although her first gainful writing was for the theater, I. is better known for her novels *A Simple Story* (1791) and *Nature and Art* (1796). When she failed to locate a publisher for her early version of *A Simple Story,* I. began a second novel in 1779, yet it was not until she combined the plots ten years later that she succeeded in selling the book to a publisher for £200. *A Simple Story,* well received by the public, went into a second edition within months. Ultimately, I.'s earnings for the two novels exceeded £1000.

Praised for its realism and its dramatic qualities, *A Simple Story* may be read autobiographically, the Dorriforth–Miss Milner relationship reminiscent of I.'s infatuation with Kemble (another Roman Catholic who studied for the priesthood). I. subverted the usual vilification of her religion by depicting a sympathetic Catholic priest whose tender and virtuous relationship with his ward ripens into love. Dorriforth is torn between his "prospect of futurity" in heaven and his earthly love for Miss Milner, between his recognition of her moral weakness and his desire to reform her. The struggle is resolved when he inherits an earldom and, forgiven his priestly vows, is encouraged to marry as a family duty. In the second part of the novel (set some sixteen years later), however, Dorriforth's first instincts are proven correct when his wife, still bent on testing the extent of his tolerance, slips into an affair in his absence. Although she dies shortly thereafter with a deathbed repentance, Dorriforth continues to prosecute the sins of the mother in their daughter until the shock of her near abduction effects a reconciliation.

Nature and Art, frankly revolutionary in tone, is less psychologically acute and thought less successful now, though I.'s contemporaries praised it highly. The story begins with two brothers who make their way after their father's death. Henry, a fiddler, supports William until the latter has risen to a deanship; the resentment he receives in return prompts him to leave England for Africa. Later, Henry's "naturally" educated son, also named Henry, returns to live under his uncle's protection in England and there meets his cousin, William, whose "artificial" education has molded him in the image of his own calculating father. The opposition between the two persists as William seduces a virtuous woman and later (as judge) sentences her for the prostitution he forced on her, and Henry first delivers his father from exile and then marries his faithful Rebecca.

I. continued writing for the London stage until 1805, her last production being the comedy *To Marry, or Not to Marry* (1805). Having contributed twenty plays—farces, comedies, and adaptations included—in 1805 I. turned to editorial work, writing a series of 125 biographical and critical prefaces for *The British Theatre* (1806–1808), a twenty-five volume collection published by Longman. She then selected plays for a seven-volume *The Modern Theatre* (1811). I. also wrote articles and reviews for the *Edinburgh Review* and the *Artist,* but she declined other offers to write for the *Quarterly Review* and to edit *La Belle Assemblée.* I. lived the last two years of her life in Kensington House, a Roman Catholic residence for women, dying there on 1 August 1821.

Self-tutored and remarkably successful, I. achieved an unusual degree of recognition for a professional woman writer of her period. She was an active playwright for more than twenty years, earning the respect of Oliver Goldsmith, who commissioned *The Wedding Day* (1794). Her first novel, *A Simple Story*, praised by her contemporaries, has continued to be reissued since its publication.

WORKS: *The Mogul Tale, or The Descent of the Balloon* (1784). *Appearance Is Against Them* (1785). *I'll Tell You What* (1786). *The Widow's Vow* (1786). *Such Things Are* (1788). The Mogul's Tale (1788). *Animal Magnetism* (1788). *A Simple Story* (1791; ed. J.M.S. Tompkins and Jane Spencer, 1988; ed. P. Clemit, 1997). *The Massacre* (1792). *Everyone Has His Fault* (1793). *The Wedding Day* (1794). *Nature and Art* (1796; 1994). *Wives as They Were, and Maids as They Are* (1797). *Lovers' Vows* (1798, adapted from A. Kotzebue; ed. J. Wordsworth, 1990). *To Marry, or Not to Marry* (1805). (ed.) *The British Theatre*, 25 vols. (1808). *Remarks for the British Theatre, 1806–09*, ed. C. Macheski (1991).

BIBLIOGRAPHY: Boaden, J. *Memoirs of Mrs. Inchbald* (1833). Joughin, G. I. *UTSE* (1934). Littlewood, S. R. *Elizabeth Inchbald and Her Circle* (1921). McKee, W. *Elizabeth Inchbald, Novelist* (1935). Manvell, R. *Elizabeth Inchbald: England's Principal Woman Dramatist* (1988).

For articles in reference works, see: *BAB1800*. *Bloomsbury*. *DLB*. *Europa*. *Feminist*. *IDWB*. *Oxford*. *ToddDBA*.

Other references: Castle, T. *Masquerade and Civilization* (1986). Cauwels, J. *PBSA* (1978). Jordan, E. *Novel* (1987). Kelly, G. *The English Jacobin Novel, 1780–1805* (1976). Conger, S. *SP* (1988). Lott, A. *SEL* (1994). Macheski, C. *Transactions of the Samuel Johnson Society of the Northeast* (1980). Patterson, E. *EA* (1976). Rogers, K. M. *ECS* (1977). Scheuermann, M. *Her Bread to Earn* (1993). *Curtain Calls: British and American Women and the Theatre, 1660–1820*, ed. M A. Schofield and C. Macheski (1991). Sigl, P. *N&Q* (1982). Sigl, P. *TN* (1989). Sigl, P. *TN* (1990). Taylor, P. *N&Q* (1978). Turner, C. *Living by the Pen* (1992). Ty, E. *Unsex'd Revolutionaries* (1993).

Katherine S. Green

Jean Ingelow

BORN: 17 March 1820, near Boston, Lincolnshire.
DIED: 20 July 1897, London.
DAUGHTER OF: William Ingelow and Jean Kilgour Ingelow.
WROTE UNDER: Jean Ingelow; Orris.

I. has been called a "lost Pre-Raphaelite." Her poetry and prose, published during the second half of the nineteenth century, exhibit the form, style, and subject matter characteristic of Pre-Raphaelite art. I. and her numerous brothers and sisters were educated at home by their mother, who encouraged their creativity; together they produced a family periodical in which I. first saw her poems "in print." However, it was financial exigency that prompted her to begin publishing in earnest, in the 1850s: mostly children's tales, under the pen name "Orris" (these were illustrated by John Millais), and an anonymous book of poems.

Her second volume of poetry, published in 1863, went through thirty editions. Many of her best poems appeared in this book, including "Songs of Seven" and "Divided," a wistful tale about a couple walking on opposite sides of a streamlet that becomes ever wider and faster until it divides them absolutely and forever. The natural descriptions and the emotional authenticity in this poem made it one of her best-loved and most-quoted pieces. It is comparable in content, style, and quality to Christina Rossetti's "An Echo from Willow-Wood."

"Divided" led I.'s biographer, Maureen Peters, to conclude that in her youth I. must have lost a sweetheart herself. It is true that I. never married; a spinster aunt Rebecca who was against marriage may have influenced I.'s opinions on the subject. And though she was essentially conservative, in many of her poems I. expressed reservations about marriage: "Katherine of Aragon to Henry VIII" (1850), "Brothers, and a Sermon" (1863), and "Wedlock" (1867). On the whole, however, her numerous narratives of love, courtship, and marriage are more similar to Coventry Patmore's *The Angel in the House* than, say, to George Meredith's *Modern Love*.

The High Tide on the Coast of Lincolnshire, 1571 (1883), a ballad about a sixteenth-century disaster, was her most popular poem. Contemporary readers were also moved by her poems about childhood deaths; the best of these is probably "Katie, Aged Five Years," written for her friend (and first editor) the Reverend Edward Harston, who had lost three children in rapid succession. In her later years, I. wrote mostly fiction, including several novels—*Off the Skelligs* (1872) and *Sarah de Berenger* (1879)—and numerous children's tales. Her most successful children's story is *Mopsa the Fairy* (1869), written in a graceful, Pre-Raphaelite style reminiscent of George MacDonald or William Morris and in a fantasy mode comparable to *Alice in Wonderland* or *"Goblin Market."*

I. was on friendly terms with John Ruskin, Henry Wadsworth Longfellow, and Alfred Lord Tennyson, as well as Christina Rossetti and Jane and Ann Taylor of Ongar. When Tennyson died in 1892, I. was mentioned as a candidate for the poet laureateship, though she was actually better known in the United States than in England. Some people believed it was I.'s popularity in America, combined with her female gender, that prompted Queen Victoria to offer the laureateship to Alfred Austin instead.

WORKS: *A Rhyming Chronicle of Incidents and Feelings*, ed E. Harston (1850). *Allerton and Drieux; or the War of Opinion* (1857). *Tales of Orris* (1860). *Poems* (1863). *Studies for Stories* (1864). *Stories Told to a Child* (1865). *Home Thoughts and Home Scenes* (1865). *Songs of Seven* (1866, 1881). *The Wild Duck Shooter and I Have a Right* (1867). *A Story of Doom and Other Poems* (1867). *A Sister's Bye-Hours* (1868). *Mopsa the Fairy* (1869). *The Little Wonder-Horn* (1872). *Off the Skelligs* (1872). *Fated to be Free* (1875). *One Hundred Holy Songs, Carols and Sacred Ballads* (1878). *Sarah de Berenger* (1879). *Poems* (1880). *Don John: A Story* (1881). *The High Tide on the Coast of Lincolnshire, 1571* (1883). *Poems: Third Series* (1885, 1888). *Poems of the Old Days and the New*

(1885), *John Jerome, His Thoughts and Ways: A Book Without Beginning* (1886). *Very Young and Quite Another Story* (1890). *A Motto Changed* (1894). *The Old Man's Prayer* (1895).

BIBLIOGRAPHY: (Anon.) *Some Recollections of Jean Ingelow and Her Early Friends* (1901). Lewis, N. *TLS* (8 December 1972). Peters, M. *Jean Ingelow, Victorian Poetess* (1972). Stedman, E. A. *An Appreciation* (1935). Symons, A. *Saturday Review* (1897).

For articles in reference works, see: *BA19C. Black. EP. Europa. Feminist. Our Living Poets,* ed. H. B. Forman (1871). *Oxford. PPC. VB.*

Other references: *Athenaeum* (24 July 1897). Attebury, B. *Extrapolation* (1987). Auerbach, N. and U. C. Knoepflmacher. *Forbidden Journeys: Fairy Tales and Fantasies by Victorian Women Writers* (1992). Green, R. *Tellers of Tales* (1946). Hall, W. *Manchester Quarterly* (1931). Hearns, L., in *Appreciations of Poetry,* ed. J. Erskine (1916). Hickok, K. *Representations of Women: Nineteenth Century British Women's Poetry* (1984). Johnson, H. *VP* (1995). King, H. D. *N&Q* (1952). Leighton, A. and M. Reynolds, ed. *Victorian Women Poets: An Anthology,* ed. A. Leighton and M. Reynolds (1995). *LonT* (21 July 1897). Mermin, D. *Godiva's Ride: Women of Letters in England, 1830–1880* (1993). Singers-Biggers, G. *English* (1940). Wagner, J. *VP* (1993).

Kathleen Hickok

Iron, Ralph: See *Schreiner, Olive Emilie Albertina*

Jackson, Elaine: See *Freeman, Gillian*

P[hyllis]. D[orothy]. James (White)

BORN: 3 August 1920, Oxford.
DAUGHTER OF: Sidney Victor James and Dorothy Amelia Hone James.
MARRIED: Ernest Conner Bantry White, 1941.
WRITES UNDER: P. D. James.

J.'s formal education ended at the age of sixteen in 1937 after she attended Cambridge High School for Girls. Although J. wanted to attend college, her father, a tax officer, did not believe in educating girls. J. first worked in a tax office and then as assistant stage manager of the Cambridge Festival Theatre until her marriage in 1941. After her husband returned home following World War II, he began to suffer from a mental illness and was confined to psychiatric hospitals until his death in 1964. J. was consequently forced to return to work in 1949 in order to support herself and her two daughters. She took a job with the National Health Service and worked her way up to principal administrative assistant of the North West Metropolitan Regional Hospital Board in London, moving in 1968 to the Home Office Criminal Policy Department.

At the age of forty, she decided to fulfill her long-time dream of becoming a writer, and to this day J. has never received a rejection slip. In addition, many of her novels have won awards, such as The Silver Dagger of the British Crime Writers Association; *Innocent Blood, The Skull Beneath the Skin,* and *A Taste for Death,* all written in the 1980s, have been best sellers; and several—e. g., *Death of an Expert Witness, A Shroud for a Nightingale, A Taste for Death, Devices and Desires*—have been made into television serials. J. was granted an OBE (Order of the British Empire) award in 1983.

In the classic detective novel tradition, J. has created two major central detective characters: Adam Dalgliesh and Cordelia Gray. Dalgliesh, a professional policeman who rises through the ranks during the course of the novels, is an intelligent, sensitive individual and a published poet. Cordelia Gray, the central character in *An Unsuitable Job for a Woman* and *The Skull Beneath the Skin,* is more of an amateur because her career as a private detective is just getting started. In fact, Gray finds herself suddenly thrust into running the agency on the unexpected death of her mentor and boss. Throughout *An Unsuitable Job for a Woman,* Adam Dalgliesh remains in the background, quietly guiding Gray through her first case.

In reviewing *Cover Her Face* (1966), J.'s first novel, Anthony Boucher writes that the novel is "modeled firmly upon the detective story of thirty years ago at its dullest. No forward plot, nothing but 80,000 words of relentless (and non-procedural) investigation leading to the final assembly of all characters and the unbelievable confession. . . . When I keep urging a return to the formal detecive story, this is *not* what I mean." J. is sometimes criticized for following the detective novel canon, but other critics find no fault with this. For example, Jean White, reviewing *An Unsuitable Job for a Woman,* comments that this novel "honorably carries on in the tradition of the classic English mystery—literate, intelligent, with shrewdly observed characters and sound plotting." J. herself, in an October 1987 interview on National Public Radio (NPR), cheerfully admitted that she writes to a formula. She stated that working within the formula allows her creative imagination to develop realistic characters and to focus on socially relevant themes.

Most of J.'s novels are set in a closed society. In several, the setting is a village and, in addition, in the conventional "country house." *Cover Her Face* is in the village of Chadfleet near London, *Unnatural Causes* in a village in Suffolk, and *An Unsuitable Job for a Woman* in the Callender Laboratory and Summertrees—a country house near Cambridge. As an outcome of her hospital and police experiences, J. sets *A Mind to Murder* in the Steen Psychological Clinic in London, *Shroud for a Nightingale* in Nightingale Hospital and House, *Black Tower* in a nursing home for victims of multiple sclerosis, and *Death of an Expert Witness* in the Hoggatt Forensic Laboratory. The action in *Devices and Desires* is centered around the Larksoken Nuclear Power Station and the village of Lydsett in Norfolk, and *A Certain Justice* takes place in the law courts of London.

One of the reasons J. always rejects the comparison made between her novels and those of Agatha Christie is the difference in the treatment of death. In her NPR interview, J. maintained that Christie's corpses were just blood-splattered bodies lying on a floor. She stated that she herself was interested in how the person died, but that Christie was only interested in the puzzle created by the death. It is J.'s characterization that has so often drawn favorable critical comment. In reviewing *Death of an Expert Witness,* Barbara Bannon writes that J.'s "insight into sexual fears and needs . . . is profound, and she makes of even her murderers and his victims, human beings whom one can, in the end, deeply pity."

Another break with tradition occurs with J.'s focus on illness and dying. In *Cover Her Face,* the father of the family is terminally ill and in a coma; in *Unnatural Causes,* one of the characters is a paraplegic; many of the characters in *Black Tower* suffer from multiple sclerosis; and in *A Mind to Murder,* the mother of the victim had been mentally ill for years and had been treated by the medical director of the clinic. Even when the critics find her novels disappointing, as many did with *Black Tower,* they praise her compassionate and perceptive handling of such difficult themes.

J.'s movement outside the traditional confines of the detective novel, *Innocent Blood,* has received the most widely divergent critical comment. *Innocent Blood* was J.'s first best seller, became a Book-of-the-Month Club main selection, and made the writer financially secure. On the other hand, critics such as Julian Symons charge that the book "shows among other things the risks of too much ambition. . . . And judged by its characters . . . is strikingly implausible." Writing in the (London) *Times Literary Supplement,* Paul Bailey says, "There are two novels fighting for dominance within the covers of *Innocent Blood.*" One, he says, "conveys something of the messiness involved in being human," and the other "look[s] at crime through a dusty lorgnette. For most of the book, the two go their separate ways, but every so often they merge—with embarrassing consequences."

Innocent Blood is the story of Philippa Palfrey's search for her real parents. During the course of the novel, there is strangulation, death by automobile and cancer, suicide, rape of a child, a child battering, incest, and revenge. In addition, the novel ends happily. Writing in the *New York Times,* Christopher Lehmann-Haupt says that J.

> has burst the bounds of her territory . . . she has gone far beyond the conventional limits of the whodunnit . . . and written a novel that is subtle, rich, allusive and positively Shakespearean in its manipulation of such symbols as blindness, bastardy and flowers, and in its preoccupation with Guilt and Innocence, Good and Evil, Justice and Revenge, and the competing claims of Blood and Environment.

Although the elements of the detective story are present, for Palfrey does follow certain clues, *Innocent Blood* can be more easily compared with the psychological novels of Ruth Rendell, whom J. often reviews. With an ending more hopeful than many of Rendell's, J.'s main character learns to love and forgive while exploring the extremes of happiness and disappointment in a human relationship. It is interesting to note that J. followed *Innocent Blood* with *The Skull Beneath the Skin,* the second Cordelia Gray novel. Gray and Palfrey have a number of characteristics in common, notably their wish to be strong, determined women.

J. compares her novels to those of Dorothy L. Sayers and Margery Allingham, and there is no doubt in her reader's mind that her novels carry on in that same tradition. It is for J., however, to continue to take the mystery novel on to greater triumphs. In an article in *The Writer,* J. says that she has used "the setting to fulfill all the functions of place in detective fiction." She concludes the article by saying,

> And it is surely the power to create this sense of place and to make it as real to the reader as is his own living room—and then to people it with characters who are suffering men and women, not stereotypes to be knocked down like dummies in the final chapter—that gives any mystery writer the claim to be regarded as a serious novelist.

This J. has accomplished.

WORKS: *Cover Her Face* (1966). *A Mind to Murder* (1967). *Unnatural Causes* (1967). *Shroud for a Nightingale* (1971). (with T.A. Critchley) *The Maul and the Pear Tree: The Ratcliffe Highway Murders, 1811* (1971). *An Unsuitable Job for a Woman* (1973). *The Black Tower* (1975). *Death of an Expert Witness* (1977). *Innocent Blood* (1980). *The Skull Beneath the Skin* (1982). *A Taste for Death* (1987). *Bad Language in Church* (1989). *Devices and Desires* (1989). *The Children of Men* (1992). *Murder in the Dark* (1994). *Original Sin* (1994). *Tales of Obsession* (1994). *A Certain Justice* (1997).

BIBLIOGRAPHY: Baker, S., in *Acting Funny,* ed. F. Teague (1994). Bakerman, J. S. *Clues* (1984). Benstock, B., in *Twentieth Century Women Novelists,* ed. T. F. Staley (1982). Campbell, S. E. *MFS* (1983). Campbell, S. E., in *Feminism in Women's Detective Fiction,* ed. G. Irons (1995). Harkness, B., in *Art in Crime Writing: Essays on Detective Fiction,* ed. B. Benstock (1983). Heilbrun, C., in *Reading and Writing Women's Lives,* ed. B. K. Bowers and B. Brothers (1990). Hubley, E. *Clues* (1982). Hubley, E. *MFS* (1983). Joyner, N. C., in *Ten Women of Mystery,* ed E. F. Bargainnier (1981). Klein, K. G. *Great Women Mystery Writers* (1994). Maxfield, J. F. *Crit* (1987). Nixon, N., in *Feminism in Women's Detective Fiction,* ed. G. Irons (1995). Salwak, D. *Clues* (1985). Siebenheller N. *P. D. James* (1982) Sizemore, C. W. *A Female Vision of the City* (1989). Smyr, R. I. *Clues* (1982).

For articles in reference works, see: *Bloomsbury. CA. Cambridge. CLC. Feminist. Oxford. TCC&MW. Todd-BWW.*

Other references: Craig, P. *TLS* (5 June 1981). Herbert, R. *ArmD* (1986). Kotker, J. G., in *Women Times Three,* ed. K. G. Klein (1995). Leonard, J. *AUMLA* (1995). *LonT* (4 October 1997). Majeske, P. K. *Clues* (1994). Mosebach, A. *A&E* (1994). Owens, J. T. *POMPA* (1988).

Alice Lorraine Painter

Anna Brownell Jameson

BORN: 19 May 1794, Dublin, Ireland.
DIED: 17 March 1860, London.
DAUGHTER OF: Denis Brownell Murphy.
MARRIED: Robert Sympson Jameson, 1825.

Art historian, social and cultural critic, author of a novel and many essays, J. helped shape the popular taste of Victorian England and America. As a child, she lived in a world of dreams, which she later denounced as "unhealthy." "I was always a princess heroine in the guise of a knight, a sort of Clorinda or Britomart, going about to redress the wrongs of the poor, fight giants, and kill dragons; or founding a society in some far-off solitude or desolate island . . . where there were to be no tears, no tasks, and no laws—except those which I made myself." She loathed the religious stories of Hannah More, and the illustrations to *Pilgrim's Progress* gave her nightmares. J. liked nature poetry, fairy tales (especially "The Arabian Nights"), and Shakespeare. She read books, not for their "contents, but for some especial image or picture I had picked out of them and assimilated to my own mind and mixed up with my own life." J. wrote her earliest tales to amuse her sisters and asked her father, an Irish miniature painter, to comment on her poems. She became a governess at the age of sixteen and remained in the employment of wealthy families until her ill-fated marriage in 1825.

J. was encouraged to seek publication by her husband, barrister Robert Jameson. Her novel, *The Diary of an Ennuyee* (1826), was based on journals of a European tour she had begun in 1821 after her engagement to Jameson was temporarily broken off. Situating her text in relationship to John Evelyn's *Diary,* Madame de Staël's *Corrine,* and Lady Morgan's *Italy,* the narrator records her responses to the beauties of Italian art and broods about a mysterious passion that eventually kills her.

J.'s early essays are biographical sketches of women who have been immortalized in poetry, like Petrarch's Laura, and queens, like Cleopatra and Catherine II. Writing for ladies who are "fair, pure-hearted, delicate-minded, and unclassical," J. is timid, self-deprecating, and reluctant to criticize. She gained confidence in addressing a general audience with the favorable reception of *Characteristics of Women* (1832), an analysis of Shakespeare's heroines based on the assumption that the characters are "complete individuals" who "combine history and real life."

Winter Studies and Summer Rambles in Canada (1838) resulted from J.'s 1836 trip to Canada. She went hoping to resolve differences with her husband, who was soon to be appointed Vice-Chancellor of Upper Canada; she returned with an allowance of £300 a year, a guarantee that she could live separately from her husband, and material for one of the century's most interesting travel memoirs. *Winter Studies* contains essays on German culture; *Summer Rambles* recounts her strenuous journey to Sault Ste. Marie. "The woman of the bright foam," as the Indians called her, was exhilarated by new friends, such as Indian authority Henry Schoolcraft and his Chippewa wife, and by the wild beauty of the land. "O how passing lovely it was," she said of Mackinaw, "how wondrously beautiful and strange." Realizing that she had been thrown "Into relations with the Indian tribes, such as few European women of refined and civilised habits have ever risked, and none have recorded," J. described clothing, agricultural implements, religious rituals, stories, and songs. Having set out "to see, with my own eyes, the condition of women in savage life," she soon took issue with the accounts of Indian women prepared by "gentlemen travellers." The squaw performed heavy physical labor, but by "providing for her own subsistence and the well-being of society," she attained dignity. J. argued that "the woman among these Indians holds her true natural position relatively to the state of the man and the state of society; and this cannot be said of all societies." Chastity was not highly valued among the Indians, but prostitution was unknown. Given the lack of real property and the absence of class divisions, Indian life offered a kind of rough equality. Indeed, J. observed that the squaw's life was "gracious" in comparison with that of a factory girl or servant in London.

As a social critic, J. was particularly concerned with women's need for employment. J. believed that women's work, including writing, was necessitated by men's failure to provide them with financial and emotional support. When she knew her own marriage was failing, she observed, "Only in the assiduous employment of such faculties as we are permitted to exercise, can we find health and peace, and compensation for the wasted or repressed impulses and energies more proper to our sex." The government's 1842 report on factories and mines prompted J. to take a broader perspective on the consequences of industrialization. Women forced into such exhausting and degrading work could not fulfill their domestic responsibilities. "'Woman's mission,' of which people talk so well and write so prettily, is irreconcilable with woman's position, of which no one dares to think, much less to speak," she charged. She called for better education, here and in a 1846 pamphlet in support of the Governesses' Benevolent Association. She encouraged the founding of *The Englishwoman's Journal,* and she made her home a gathering place for young feminists—her "adopted nieces." In the 1850s, she lectured on "sisterhoods," Protestant communities that would provide women with training in nursing and social service. J.'s feminism assumes sympathetic understanding between the sexes. "At the core of all social reformation, as a necessary condition of health and permanence in all human institutions, lies the working of the man and the woman together, in mutual trust, love, and reverence." Invoking the family model, she argues for the extension of "motherly and sisterly" influence into the state.

Between 1840 and 1860, she wrote primarily about art. J. wanted to introduce the English public "to that many-sided and elevated spirit in criticism with which the Germans have long been familiar." Showing increased professionalization and a greater awareness of herself as a specialist, she produced several important guidebooks and a very influential account of early Italian art. In *Poetry of Sacred and Legendary Art* (1848), the first part of her tetralogy, she set out to interpret the symbolism of Christian art in historical rather than religious terms. Her *Legends of the Madonna* (1852) constitutes the "first extensive study of the imagery of the Virgin in the literature of art."

An energetic and emotionally impulsive traveler, J. had a wide range of friends. She sought Fanny Kemble's advice on Shakespeare, supported Ottilie von Goethe through the birth of her illegitimate child, participated in Lady Byron's intrigues, joined the Brownings on their honeymoon trip, gave Elizabeth Gaskell advice about her novels, and at the age of sixty-eight toured with Hawthorne around Rome. Despite the popularity of her books, she was often under financial pressure. When her husband's retirement and death left her in precarious straits, friends secured pensions for her. Her works, said Harriet Martineau, "will remind a future generation that in ours there was a restless, expatiating, fervent, unreasoning, generous, accomplished Mrs. J."

WORKS: (selected): *The Diary of an Ennuyee* (1826). *The Loves of the Poets* (1829). *Memoirs of Celebrated Female Sovereigns* (1831). *Characteristics of Women* (1832). *Visits and Sketches at Home and Abroad* (1834). *Winter Studies and Summer Rambles in Canada* (1838). *Memoirs of the Early Italian Painters* (1845). *Memoirs and Essays* (1846). *The Poetry of Sacred and Legendary Art* (1848). *Legends of the Monastic Orders* (1850). *Legends of the Madonna* (1852). *A Commonplace Book of Thoughts, Memories, and Fancies* (1854). *Sisters of Charity* (1855). *The Communion of Labour* (1856). *History of Our Lord* (1864). *Memoirs of Anna Jameson*, ed. G. MacPherson (1878). *Anna Jameson: Letters and Friendship, 1812–1860*, ed. B. Erskine (1915). *Letters of Anna Jameson to Ottilie von Goethe*, ed. G. Needler (1939).

BIBLIOGRAPHY: Buss, H., in *Essays on Life Writing: From Genre to Critical Practice*, ed. M. Kadar (1992). Desmet, C., in *Women's ReVisions of Shakespeare*, ed. M. Novy (1990). Friewald, B., in *A Mazing Space: Writing Canadian, Women Writing*, ed. S. Newman and S. Kamboureli (1986). Gilley, S., in *The Church and the Arts*, ed. D. Wood (1992). Holcomb, A., in *Women as Interpreters of the Visual Arts*, ed. C. Sherman (1981). Holcomb, A. *Art History* (1983). Johnson, J. *VPR* (1994). Johnston, J. *Anna Jameson: Victorian, Feminist, Woman of Letters* (1997). Killham, J. *Tennyson and "The Princess": Reflections of an Age* (1958). Slights, J. *ESC* (1993). Thomas, C. *Love and Work Enough: The Life of Anna Jameson* (1967). York, L. M. *Mosaic* (1986).

For articles in reference works, see: *BA19C. BDBF. DNB. Europa. Feminist. IDWB. Oxford. VB.*

Robin Sheets

Storm Jameson

BORN: January 1891, Whitby, Yorkshire.
DIED: 30 September 1986, Cambridge.
DAUGHTER OF: William Storm and Hannah Margaret Jameson.
MARRIED: Charles Douglas Clarke, 1913; Guy Patterson Chapman, 1926.
WROTE UNDER: James Hill; Storm Jameson; William Lamb.

Although she wrote more than fifty novels, J. asserted in her autobiography, *Journey from the North* (1969–70), "novels, for the intense pains taken with them—are not serious, not worth a tear." She often deprecated her work, most often being too hard on herself (her work does vary somewhat in quality). J. also spoke often of her hatred of settled domestic life, passed down, she felt, from her mother, who often accompanied her sea-captain husband on his travels. She continued this practice after J.'s birth and settled down only after the number of children made travel cumbersome. When she settled, she chose the seaport of Whitby, in Yorkshire, where the Jameson ancestors had lived and where J. had been born. Whitby had been a fishing and shipbuilding port but was reduced by the time of J.'s birth to a minor harbor on the North Sea. J. endured a poor yet ambitious childhood. Her own intense desire for an education and her mother's support led her to earn a rare county scholarship, which enabled her to attend Leeds University. There she took first class honors in English language and literature in 1912. Granted a research scholarship to University College London, she transferred to King's College—which she felt was more interesting than the pedantic University College—where she earned an M.A. in 1914, writing her thesis (later published) on modern drama in Europe.

True to her dislike of settled life, J. traveled and moved around a great deal. Her first marriage gave her a son whom she loved deeply and a husband unsuited to her. Her husband found a way of life he loved while in the army during World War I, as J. painfully separated herself from her child in order to take jobs. She began to publish her novels, work as a copywriter for an advertising agency, and edit the *New Commonwealth*, a weekly. She met her second husband, Guy Chapman, while working for the Alfred A. Knopf publishing company as their English representative. Her relationship with Chapman lasted until his death in 1972.

J. was an active member of P.E.N. International and president of its English Centre from 1938 to 1945. This work took her over much of Europe aiding refugee writers. As a result, her own work was banned by the Nazis. Her later novels reflect this interest and atmosphere. A book unlike most of her work, *In the Second Year* (1936), is a futuristic story of the takeover of England by fascists. In the late 1930s, J. lost many of her friends as her pacifist stand gave way to support for England's war effort against Nazism.

J. wrote furiously most of her life. Many of her novels are set in Yorkshire and deal with families involved in shipbuilding or sailing. Her *Triumph of Time* and *Mirror of Darkness* series cover four generations of Yorkshire families. The three books in *The Triumph of Time* and the three in *The Mirror of Darkness* are realistic in every detail of setting and character. Mary Hervey, the main character of *The Triumph of Time* trilogy—*The Lovely Ship* (1927), *The Voyage Home* (1930), and *A Richer Dust* (1931)—is head of a shipbuilding firm; the story covers her life from 1841 to 1923 and follows shipbuilding from sail to steam to turbines to war boom. *The Mirror of Darkness* saga—*Company Parade* (1934), *Love in Winter* (1935), and *None Turn Back* (1936) —centers on Mary Hervey Russell, granddaughter of the *Triumph of Time* protagonist and a character close to J. herself in many ways. J. used transcripts of arguments between herself and her first husband for dialogue in some of these works.

Her two-volume autobiography, *Journey from the North* (1969–70) is possibly her best work and an excellent preparation for a study of her fiction. In it, she describes her eyes as "a darker clouded grey-blue: I fit badly into my skull, and while my eyes are taking you in my brain is trying to guess what you are thinking and what will keep you at a safe distance." She tells of her hatred of domesticity and her decision to write novels: "I have a strong, patient brain, but it is myopic and slightly mad. It reminds me of a young horse I once rode, which was blind in one eye and under the delusion that it could jump walls." The autobiographical narrative of J.'s life reads as lively as any of her novels or short stories as it explores, with a relentless truthfulness few are capable of, the forces that formed her.

Aware that she was writing too quickly, midway through her *Mirror of Darkness* series J. took on two successive male pennames in an attempt to change her pace and direction in a way that was not really successful. Much of her work is criticized for being too socially motivated and pedantic, while her stories of the Yorkshire families remain the most popular. Much of J.'s later work, such as *Cousin Honoré* (1940) and *Europe to Let* (1940), is set in Europe. In 1974, she was awarded the English Centre of International P.E.N. award for *There Will Be a Short Interval* (1973).

J. worked in several genres other than that of the novel. She translated Guy de Maupassant, and she wrote such nonfiction as *The Georgian Novel and Mr. Robinson* (1929), *The Decline of Merry England* (1930), *The Soul of Man in the Age of Leisure* (1935), *The Novel in Contemporary Life* (1938), *The Writer's Situation and Other Essays* (1950), and *Speaking of Stendhal* (1979), a work of literary criticism. She worked as editor with her second husband on his autobiography, *A Kind of Survivor* (1975), as well as producing short stories and television plays.

J. is only now beginning to gain the kind of popularity she had in her heyday, due partly to reprints of her major works.

WORKS: *The Pot Boils* (1919). *The Happy Highays* (1920). *Modern Drama in Europe* (1920). *The Clash* (1922). *The Pitiful Wife* (1923). *Lady Susan and Life: An Indiscretion* (1924). (trans.) *Mont-Oriol,* by G. de Maupassant (1924). (trans.) *Horla and Other Stories,* by G. de Maupassant (1925). *Three Kingdoms* (1926). *The Lovely Ship* (1927; *The Triumph of Time* I). *Farewell to Youth* (1928). *The Georgian Novel and Mr. Robinson* (1929). *Full Circle* (1929). *The Decline of Merry England* (1930). (trans., with E. Boyd) *88 Short Stories,* by G. de Maupassant (1930). *The Voyage Home* (1930; *The Triumph of Time* II). *A Richer Dust* (1931; *The Triumph of Time* III). *The Single Heart* (1932). *That Was Yesterday* (1932). *A Day Off* (1933). *Women Against Men* (1933; includes *A Day Off, The Delicate Monster,* and *The Single Heart*). *No Time Like the Present* (1933). *Company Parade* (1934; *Mirror of Darkness* I). *The Soul of Man in the Age of Leisure* (1935). *Love in Winter* (1935; *Mirror of Darkness* II). *In the Second Year* (1936). *None Turn Back* (1936; *Mirror of Darkness* III). *The Delicate Monster* (1937). *Moon Is Making* (1937). (as William Lamb) *The World Ends* (1937). (as James Hill) *Loving Memory* (1937). (as James Hill) *No Victory for the Soldier* (1938). *The Novel in Contemporary Life* (1938). *Here Comes a Candle* (1938). *A Civil Journey* (1939). *Farewell Night, Welcome Day* (1939; in the U.S. as *The Captain's Wife*). *Europe to Let: The Memoirs of an Obscure Man* (1940). *Cousin Honoré* (1940). *The End of This Year* (1941). *The Fort* (1941). *Then We Shall Hear Singing: A Fantasy in C Major* (1942). *Cloudless May* (1943). *The Journal of Mary Hervey Russell* (1945). *The Other Side* (1946). *Before the Crossing* (1947). *The Black Laurel* (1947). *The Moment of Truth* (1949). *The Writer's Situation and Other Essays* (1950). *The Green Man* (1952). *The Hidden River* (1955). *The Intruder* (1956). *A Cup of Tea for Mr. Thorgill* (1957). *A Ulysses Too Many* (1958). *Days Off: Two Short Novels and Some Stories* (1959). *Last Score; or, The Private Life of Sir Richard Ormston* (1961). *Morley Roberts: The Last Eminent Victorian* (1961). *The Road from the Monument* (1962). *A Month Too Soon* (1963). *The Aristide Case* (1964; in the U.S. as *The Blind Heart*). *The Early-Life of Stephen Hind* (1966). *The White Crow* (1968). *Journey from the North* (1969–70). *Parthian Words* (1970). *There Will Be a Short Interval* (1973). *Speaking of Stendhal* (1979).

BIBLIOGRAPHY: Burdett, O. *English Review* (May 1935). Gindin, J. *CentR* (1978). *"S.O." English Review* (January 1921). Taubman, R. *New Statesman* (26 January 1962).

For articles in reference works, see: *CA. CN. DLB. MBL. SF&FL. TCA* and *SUP. TCW.*

Other references: *Books and Bookmen* (May 1970). *CSM* (29 September 1937, 19 July 1969). *New Republic* (13 March 1971). *NYHTBR* (8 April 1962). *NYTBR* (9 May 1971). *Spectator* (25 October 1969).

Jan Calloway-Baxter

(Patricia) Ann Jellicoe

BORN: 15 July 1927, Middlesborough, Yorkshire.
DAUGHTER OF: John Andrea Jellicoe and Frances Jackson Henderson.
MARRIED: C. E. Knight-Clarke, 1950; David Roger Mayne, 1962.

During the decade or so that followed the momentous 1956 arrival of John Osborne's *Look Back in Anger* at London's Royal Court Theatre, J. achieved critical recognition as one of a group of young playwrights whose innovative works were revitalizing British drama. Although J.'s reputation is associated almost exclusively with the success in 1961 of her eccentric comedy, *The Knack* (particularly Richard Lester's 1965 film adaptation of the script), her distinctive contribution to the "New Drama" generation may be more broadly related to nonliterary elements she includes within the body of her scripts—a factor clearly rooted in J.'s interest and experience with directing. These script notes may suggest opportunities for actors to improvise; they may describe specific visual action or rhythmic noises and nonverbal vocalization and often evoke a feeling of ritual or mystical ambiguity. "These are not loose effects," J. comments. "They are introduced to communicate with the audience directly through their senses to reinforce the total effect of the play, and they are always geared to character and situation." Nevertheless, readers of J.'s early plays must be prepared to employ the imagination of a stage director, thus conjuring a *mise-en-scène* in their heads, in order to comprehend fully the character of the drama she creates.

Because J. boldly colors her scripts with elements integral to her training and ambitions as a director, critic John Russell Taylor describes her writing as "certainly exotic, and perhaps unique among the younger dramatists" writing scripts at the time her first full-length play, *The Sport of My Mad Mother* (1958), made its debut on the stage of The Royal Court. In contrast with Osborne, John Arden, Arnold Wesker, Shelagh Delaney, Harold Pinter, even the significant tradition of British playwriting, "Jellicoe was trying," Taylor observes, "to make her play primarily something which happened in front of an audience and made its effect as a totality, rather than a piece of neatly carpentered literary craftmanship which would 'read well' and work largely by way of its dialogue's appeal to the mind." Her influence as an individual playwright cannot be measured precisely, but the nonliterary emphasis of her style of script composition anticipated a trend in works for the stage that took hold in the early 1960s throughout Europe and the United States and that remains today a recognizable genre of dramaturgy.

J. was born in the north of England; her parents were separated when she was eighteen months old. "My childhood," she has stated,

> was rather unpleasant [and] spent mostly at boarding school which, as I now realise, is a system designed to make children conform, to mould them into a standard pattern. At the time I could never understand why I was so unpopular, unhappy and out of step. I thought they were right and I was wrong, and I tried very hard to be like everyone else. To some extent I succeeded and after I left school it took me more than ten years to discover what sort of person I really was, and what my ideas were.

From 1943 to 1947, J. studied acting in war-ravaged London at the Central School of Speech and Drama, winning most of the prizes for which she was eligible. When she completed her studies, she traveled extensively through Europe and discovered in herself a facility for learning languages—an ability that would serve her later when she completed translations and adaptations of plays by Ibsen and Chekhov—and so, she explains, "earned the time and independence to write my own work."

In 1950, she became the founding director of the Cockpit Theatre Club in London as an extension of a commission she had received to develop a study of the relationship between theater practice and theater architecture. "For the first time in my life," she has commented, "I began to think deeply about the nature of theatre; this led to an interest in the open stage (audience on three sides) and I founded a theatre club to experiment with the form." After more than two years of intensive work at the Cockpit, which included production of a one-act play and two translations of her own, J. returned in 1953 to the Central School of Speech and Drama to teach and direct; she remained there until 1955. "When I left it was chiefly because you were never free to concentrate on trying to achieve an absolute work of art. . . . About this time *The Observer* newspaper organised a playwriting competition; the conditions of entry showed they wanted something new and different. . . . I saw that if I didn't write a play now I never would, so I sat down and wrote *The Sport of My Mad Mother,* which won third prize and was produced at the Royal Court in 1958. So I became a playwright."

Kenneth Tynan described *The Sport of My Mad Mother* as "a tour de force that belongs in no known category of drama. It stands in the same relationship to conventional play-making as jazz does to conventional music: in an ideal production it would have the effect of spontaneous improvisation, or of a vocal *danse macabre* that makes up its own rules and language as it goes along." The play portrays a London street gang of Teddy-boys led by Greta, an earth-mother figure associated with the Indian goddess Kali, force of destruction and creation (the play's title is based on a Hindu hymn: "All creation is the sport of my mad mother Kali"). The essentially unstructured plot progresses in waves of unmotivated violence where word and cries are repeated, evolving into ritualized manifestations of abstract menace. Its original production was codirected by J. and George Devine (founding director of the English Stage Company) and was curtly dismissed by all but a few critics with a taste for the avant-garde. J. wrote her next play on commission from the Girl Guides' Association, providing them with a spectacular pageant-like fantasy entitled *The Rising Generation* (1960). The piece envisioned a fabulous creature called Mother who decries the crimes of men, proclaims that the best of life is rooted in the spirit of womankind—"Shakespeare was a woman; Milton was a woman; . . . Newton was a woman . . ."—and devises to reform the ills of life by invoking the spirit of open-mindedness and cooperation to carry a select group of girls and boys into outer space to colonize a braver, newer world. The Girl Guides declined producing the provocative work, but this feminist pageant did finally reach the stage of the Royal Court in 1967, nearly a decade after its original commission, and was "warmly received."

"With her next play, *The Knack,*" notes John Russell Taylor, "Ann Jellicoe scored one of the most resounding popular successes of the New Drama." The play was first presented by the English Stage Company at the Arts Theatre, Cambridge, in October 1961; made its Royal Court premiere the following March, with J. codirecting; and saw its New York debut in May 1964 in an off-Broadway production with Brian Bedford and George Segal in a cast directed by Mike Nichols. The title alludes to the focus of the play's driving spirit-the obsession of young men with the knack of seducing women. Within a loosely structured whirligig of often zany antics, the action develops around three male housemates—Tom, Tolen, and Colin—representing a wide range of sexual résumés, and their competition to win the favor of Nancy, an apparently innocent young woman who stops at the window of their domicile, seeking directions to the Y.W.C.A. In the most frequently cited scene of the play, Tom and Colin charm Nancy into a fantasy game in which they pretend the bed is a Bechstein piano and "play it" in a wild incantation of "pings" and "plongs" to the tune of "The Blue Danube" waltz. Beneath the surface ebullience of the action, however, one senses the anxieties and frustrations of young innocents in a maze of sexual bewilderment. The climactic images of the play involve a ritualized chase scene, accompanied by the cacophonous clang of pot covers and repeated howls of "Rape," where games and rivalries resonate with undertones of primal violence. Although events are stopped short of brutality, these final movements, when well performed, hold the potential of being immensely stirring.

The plays that have followed *The Knack* have met with little critical enthusiasm. In *Shelley; Or, The Idealist* (1965), J. offers "an almost documentary account," in conventional dramaturgical form, of the poet's life. *The Giveaway* (1968) playfully examines the goings-on in a family that has just won a ten-year supply of corn flakes. *London Times* critic Irving Wardle saw it as "an honest and logical effort to extend her work into popular territory" but, nonetheless, did not find the piece rewarding comedy. *You'll Never Guess,* another attempt at reviving the distinctive zaniness of her early work, opened in London in 1973 under J.'s direction to poor notices. A handful of short plays she has written since have been similarly disappointing and, in the words of John Russell Taylor, who was among the first critics to celebrate her work, "rather give the impression of marking time. Now perhaps we may hope that she will return to a subject within the center of her most personal style and range—that area where she is just not at all like anyone else."

WORKS: *Rosmersholm* (adaptation of play by H. Ibsen, 1952; rev. 1959). *The Sport of My Mad Mother* (1958; rev. 1964). *The Rising Generation* (1960). *The Lady from the Sea* (adaptation of play by H. Ibsen, 1961). *The Knack* (1961). (with A. Nicolaeff) *The Seagull* (adaptation of play by A. Chekhov, 1964). (trans.) *Der Freischutz,* libretto by F. Kind, music by C. M. Weber, 1964). *Shelley, Or, The Idealist* (1965). *Some Unconscious Influences in the Theatre* (1967). *The Giveaway* (1968). *You'll Never Guess* (1973). *Two Jelliplays: Clever Elsie, Smiling John, Silent Peter and A Good Thing or a Bad Thing* (1974). (with R. Mayne) *Devon: A Shell Guide* (1975). *The Reckoning* (1978). *The Tide* (1980). *Community Plays: How to Put Them On* (1987). *Changing Places* (1992).

BIBLIOGRAPHY: *New Theatre Magazine* (1960). *New Theatre Voices of the Fifties and Sixties,* ed. C. Marowitz, et al. (1965). *NYT* (30 June 1965). Oliver, J., in *British Playwrights, 1956–1995: A Research and Production Sourcebook,* ed. W. W. Demastes (1996). Taylor, J. R. *Anger and After* (1962). Tynan, K. [London] *Observer* (2 March 1958). *VV* (5 June 1967).

For articles in reference works, see: *CA. CD. Crowell's Handbook of Contemporary Drama* (1971). *At the Royal Court,* ed. R. Findlater (1981). *McGraw-Hill Encyclopedia of World Drama* (1972). *Modern World Theatre* (1970). *WA.*

Paul D. Nelsen

Elizabeth (Joan) Jennings

BORN: 18 July 1926, Boston, Lincolnshire.
DAUGHTER OF: Henry Cecil Jennings.

J. was born into a Roman Catholic physician's family and grew up in Oxford (where she still lives), graduating from St. Anne's College at Oxford with honors in English. She wrote her first meaningful poem when she was thirteen, after reading a work by G. K. Chesterton, and found rhythm and alliteration "exciting" enough to try writing poetry herself. Her uncle suggested that she avoid "writing [about] experiences one has never had," and the encouragement he offered led to a simple honesty in her verse throughout her career as poet, critic, and translator. She acknowledges the influence of W. H. Auden and T. S. Eliot and is fond of Edwin Muir, Wallace Stevens, and especially W. B. Yeats.

During the eight years she worked as a librarian, her first published efforts appeared: *Poems* (1953) and *A Way of Looking* (1955), both of which won prizes. These volumes were criticized as somewhat monotonous, limited in scope, and imitative of Eliot's free verse, though her admitted power in creating verse of a meditative nature was readily acknowledged by critics. She subsequently published several other volumes in the 1950s and the early 1960s, most of which reflected her involvement with a short-lived group of poets identified with Robert Conquest's *New Lines* collection; while others in the group, such as Philip Larkin, Thom Gunn, and Kingsley Amis subsequently diverged from the group's emphasis on understated emotion, J. has continued to write with an ostensible lack of feeling while actually demonstrating controlled though subdued power.

J.'s breakdown and attempted suicide in the early 1960s led to hospitalization, psychotherapy, and the writing of *Recoveries* (1964) and *The Mind Has Mountains* (1966), which also won a literary prize. The poems in the latter collection (with a title from a poem by Gerard Manley Hopkins) deal primarily with such phenomena as suicide, hysterical behavior, and madness and are as understated as her previous volumes. The self-conscious poems in this volume reflect the struggle of a troubled soul for enlightenment, but they are not self-pitying, only restrained, searching, and ultimately triumphant in celebrating J.'s overcoming depression. When her *Collected Poems* appeared in 1967, it not only enabled readers and critics to see her career to that date at a glance but even more to evaluate her strengths. Terry Eagleton noted that, in this collection, J.'s mind "works in exact congruence with the poetic structure she uses, so that this pared, precise, aesthetic yet morally sensitive structure seems to reproduce the structure of her thinking and feeling"; this "congruence" serves as both her strength and her weakness since the lack of tension results in a "passive, abstract and energyless verse." Her limited emotional range was frequently noted, as was the genuineness of her convictions. She frequently writes about Roman Catholic saints (St. John of the Cross, St. Teresa of Avila, St. Catherine, St. Augustine) and biblical figures and events (Jesus, Mary, the Annunciation, the Visitation), as well as various artists (Rembrandt, Rouault, Cézanne, and, especially, van Gogh).

In addition to other volumes of verse for both adults

and children, J. has written various works of criticism, including *Let's Have Some Poetry* (1960), for children; *Poetry Today* (1961), an overview of contemporary British poetry; books taking a religious approach to literature, *Every Changing Shape* (1961) and *Christianity and Poetry* (1965; in the U.S. as *Christian Poetry*); a biography of Robert Frost; a well-received translation of *The Sonnets of Michelangelo* (1961, 1969); and *Seven Men of Vision: An Appreciation* (1976), about Yeats, D. H. Lawrence, Lawrence Durrell, St.-John Perse, David Jones, Antoine de St. Exupery, and Boris Pasternak, among many other books.

J. has found that as an insecure, solitary person, poetry can help her relate to the larger world and is in fact a form of prayer for her; even her poems of exaltation and celebration reflect her concern with isolation and the effects of the passing of time on "the mind," a term she uses frequently. Her quiet, mystical poems suggest, in their metrical formality and precise, understated diction, an admittedly subdued voice, but one with equally acknowledged emotional conviction and spiritual power.

WORKS: *Poems* (1953). *A Way of Looking: Poems* (1955). *A Child and the Seashell* (1957). *A Sense of the World* (1958). *Let's Have Some Poetry* (1960). *Every Changing Shape* (1961). *Poetry Today 1957–60* (1961). *Song for a Birth or a Death and Other Poems* (1961). (trans.) *The Sonnets of Michelangelo* (1961, 1969). (with L. Durrell and R. S. Thomas) *Penguin Modern Poets 1* (1962). *Recoveries: Poems* (1964). *Frost* (1964). *Christianity and Poetry* (1965; in the U.S. as *Christian Poetry*). *The Mind Has Mountains* (1966). *The Secret Brother and Other Poems for Children* (1966). *Collected Poems* (1967). *The Animals' Arrival* (1969). *Lucidities* (1970). *Hurt* (1970). (with others) *Folio* (1970). *Relationships* (1972). *Growing Points: New Poems* (1975). *Seven Men of Vision: An Appreciation* (1976). *Consequently I Rejoice* (1977). *After the Ark* (1978). *Moments of Grace: New Poems* (1979). *Selected Poems* (1979). *Winter Wind* (1979). *A Dream of Spring* (1980). *Celebrations and Elegies* (1982). *Extending the Territory* (1985). *In Shakespeare's Company* (1985). *Collected Poems, 1953–1985* (1986). *Every Changing Shape: Mystical Experience and the Making of Poems* (1997). *In the Meantime* (1997).

BIBLIOGRAPHY: *Penguin Book of Contemporary Verse*, ed. K. Allott (1962). Byers, M., in *British Poetry Since 1960*, ed. M. Schmidt and G. Lindop (1972). Eagleton, T. *Stand* (1968). *The Poet Speaks*, ed. P. Orr (1966). Schmidt, M. *An Introduction to 50 Modern British Poets* (1979). Schofield, M. A. *NConL* (1983). Sturzl, E. A., in *On Poetry and Poets, Fifth Series*, ed. J. Hogg (1983). Wheeler, M. *Hopkins Among the Poets: Studies in Modern Responses to Gerard Manley Hopkins* (1985).

For articles in reference works, see: *CA*. *CLC*. *CP*. *EWLTC*. *MBL* and *SUP*. *TCW*. *WA*.

Other references: *Books and Bookmen* (December 1972, February 1980). *Encounter* January 1980). Fraser, G. S. *The Modern Writer and His World*, rev. ed. (1964). *Listener* (23 July 1964, 22 March 1973, 30 October 1975, 13 October 1977, 31 January 1980, 5 May 1986). *London Magazine* (February 1962, November 1964). *Mademoiselle* (January 1955). *New Statesman* (13 October 1967, 29 September 1972, 30 May 1975, 2 November 1979, 15 November 1985). *Observer* (27 April 1975, 1 September 1985). *Poetry* (December 1956, November 1959, March 1977). *PoetryR* (Spring 1967). *Spectator* (1 December 1979, 19 October 1985). *TES* (24 November 1978, 30 July 1982). *TLS* (4 July 1975, 30 December 1977, 1 February 1980, 16 July 1982, 28 November 1986). *WLT* (Spring 1979). *YR* (Summer 1959).

Paul Schlueter

Geraldine Ensor Jewsbury

BORN: 22 August 1812, Measham, Derbyshire.
DIED: 23 September 1880, London.
DAUGHTER OF: Thomas Jewsbury.

A popular and controversial novelist, journalist, reviewer, and promoter of women's causes, J. was six when her mother died in 1818; she was raised, along with her three brothers, by her sister Maria Jane, twelve years her elder. Maria Jane managed in spite of her housekeeping responsibilities to write to great critical acclaim, publishing her first book in 1825. This stimulating literary environment, which included visits to and from literary notables both English and American, continued until 1833 when Maria Jane married and sailed for India and J. assumed the responsibilities of the household until her father's death in 1840.

J.'s two great philosophical mentors were George Sand and Thomas Carlyle. J. discovered Carlyle's writings, notably *Past and Present*, at a time of spiritual crisis; they affected her so profoundly that she wrote to him, perhaps following the example of her sister, who had early been encouraged by William Wordsworth and other influential literary critics and writers but who had died in 1833 in India. Perhaps J. felt she must take up her career where her sister's had ended, but instead of following the Wordsworthian example, J. proposed a woman's right to full equality, especially independence and equal education, sexual freedom, and secular thinking as themes for her writing.

In 1841, she visited Thomas and Jane Carlyle in Cheyne Row and began a lifelong friendship with both of them that was at times tempestuous. Although demanding the support of the Carlyles, J. refused to be wholly guided by them, disgusting Carlyle by her enthusiasm for George Sand. She returned to Lancashire to keep house for her favorite brother, Frank, and there wrote her first novel, *Zoe* (1845). J. spent the next decade in Lancashire, housekeeping, entertaining visiting writers such as Ralph Waldo Emerson and George Henry Lewes, and writing. "Faith and Scepticism" was sent to the *Westminster Review* by Lewes on her behalf in 1849 and made a strongly favorable impression in certain literary circles. In 1854, she moved to Chelsea to be near the Carlyles and continued to write for periodicals and to produce novels until 1859. In 1866, after the death of Jane Carlyle, she moved to Kent where she lived in retirement but continued to read for the publishing house of Bentley and Sons and to review for the *Athenaeum*. Illness forced her back to London, where she died in 1880.

J. enjoyed a full career as a journalist, but her true influence over the course of English reading was as a reader for Bentley and Sons from 1858 to 1880 and as a reviewer of more than 1,800 books for the *Athenaeum.* While history sees J. as a writer of popular fiction, she saw herself as a serious writer of social novels although she spent only twelve years of a long career producing them. The hero's conflict between religion and love in *Zoe* is used as a means to question the validity of organized religion and made the book an instant success. While the development of the hero was influenced by J.'s interest in the Oxford Movement, the heroine was an exploration of passion along George Sand lines. *The Half-Sisters* (1848) showed a woman rising above her illegitimate birth and lack of social standing to a respected place in society. *Marian Withers* (1851) discussed women's education and society's requirement that a woman establish herself by an appropriate marriage. George Henry Lewes described it, to J.'s annoyance, as a reply to Elizabeth Gaskell's *Mary Barton. Constance Herbert* (1855) details the fate of a woman who chooses power over other possible human relationships. *The Sorrows of Gentility* (1856) explores society's approbation of a husband's exploitation of his wife. In *Right or Wrong* (1856), J.'s last novel, she returns to religion in a denunciation of priestly celibacy in the Roman Catholic Church. In all her novels the pace is brisk, the characters well drawn, the descriptions vivid, and the tone didactic. George Eliot criticized her for making all women heroines and all men villains as she espoused the cause of unmarried women. J. also wrote two children's books, *The History of an Adopted Child* (1853) and *Angelo; or, The Pine Forest in the Alps* (1855), as well as numerous children's stories in *Juvenile Budget* and *Household Words.* Selections of her letters to Jane Welsh Carlyle have been published, and Virginia Woolf has written of their friendship.

WORKS: *Zoe: The History of Two Lives* (1845). *The Half-Sisters: A Tale* (1848). *Marian Withers* (1851). *The History of an Adopted Child* (1853). *Constance Herbert* (1855). *Angelo; or, The Pine Forest in the Alps* (1855). *Right or Wrong* (1856). *The Sorrows of Gentility* (1856). *Selections from the Letters of Geraldine Ensor Jewsbury to Jane Welsh Carlyle Prefaced by a Monograph on Miss Jewsbury, by the Editor*, ed. A.E.N. Ireland (1892).

BIBLIOGRAPHY: Cary, M. *Research Studies* (1974). Clarke, N. *Ambitious Heights: Writing, Friendship, Love; The Jewsbury Sisters, Felicia Hemans, and Jane Carlyle* (1990). Fahnestock, J. R. *NCF* (1973). Fryckstedt, M. C. *Geraldine Jewsbury's Athenaeum Reviews: A Mirror of Mid-Victorian Attitudes Toward Fiction* (1986). Griest, G. L. *Mudie's Cirulating Library and the Victorian Novel* (1970). Howe, S. *Geraldine Jewsbury, Her Life and Errors* (1935). Mercer, E. *Manchester Quarterly* (1898). Thomson, P. *George Sand and the Victorians: Her Influence and Reputation in Nineteenth-Century England* (1977). Woolf, V. *Collected Essays*, vol. 2 (1967).

For articles in reference works, see: *Bloomsbury. Cambridge. DLB. Feminist. Oxford. ToddBWW. VB.*

Eleanor Langstaff

Maria Jane Jewsbury

BORN: 25 October 1800, Measham, Derbyshire.
DIED: 4 October 1833, Poona, India.
DAUGHTER OF: Thomas Jewsbury.
MARRIED: William Kew Fletcher, 1833.

Vivacious friend of William Wordsworth and his daughter, Dora, J. received some early formal education at Mrs. Adams' School, Shenstone, but returned home for health reasons at the age of fourteen. At eighteen, upon the death of her mother and the family's move to Manchester, she took charge of her younger sister Geraldine and her three brothers, one an infant. In spite of her intellectual isolation, she burned to achieve a literary career, writing to Felicia Hemans that "the ambition of writing a book, being praised publicly and associating with authors, seized me."

Alaric A. Watts, editor of the *Manchester Courier,* encouraged her in her ambition and sponsored her first book, *Phantasmagoria, or Sketches of Life and Character,* published at Leeds in 1825 with a dedication to Wordsworth, whom she did not as yet know. The resulting correspondence began a lifelong friendship with the Wordsworth family, especially with Dora Wordsworth. Wordsworth appreciated J. as an accurate observer of simple people. After reading "The Young Gleaner and His Cousin," he urged her to abandon poetry and write about life and manners, advice that she took to heart.

The youthful, lively, satirical tone of *Phantasmagoria* was generally faulted by the reviewers even while assuring their attention. A poem written at the same time, "Song of the Hindoo Women While Accompanying a Widow to the Funeral," reflects the love of exoticism of the period as well as a universal approach to the "woman question."

After J. fell very ill in the summer of 1826, the tone of her work became less satirical and more serious and religious. *Letters to the Young* (1828), a meditative work, discusses belief in God, intellectual snobbery, and "the true end of education." Its popularity required a second edition in 1829 and a third in 1832. *Lays of Leisure Hours* appeared in 1829 and *The Three Histories* in 1830; subtitled *The History of an Enthusiast, the History of a Nonchalant, the History of a Realist,* the latter work is considered by modern scholars to owe much to Mme. de Staël's *Corrine, ou l'Italie.*

She was praised for her eloquent style by Letitia Landon and Christopher North, and her work appeared frequently in the *Atheneum* from 1830 to 1832. In keeping with her new seriousness and religious fervor, however, she married William Kew Fletcher, a chaplain for the East India Company, in August 1833. As a closing to her life in English letters (though she kept a diary of her trip to India, parts of which were later published), she wrote to Hemans that she regretted her early reputation and desire for premature publication. She died of cholera in October 1833 in Poona, India, without seeing Wordsworth's "Liberty," which he had dedicated to her and of which she was the subject.

WORKS: *Phantasmagoria, or Sketches of Life and Character* (1825). *Letters to the Young* (1928). *Lays of Leisure*

Hours (1829). *The Three Histories: The History of an Enthusiast, the History of a Nonchalant, the History of a Realist* (1830). Extracts from her journal of her voyage and early days in India were published in *Lancashire Worthies*, ed. F. Espinasse (1874).

BIBLIOGRAPHY: Clarke, N. *Ambitious Heights: Writing, Friendship, Love: The Jewsbury Sisters, Felicia Hemens, and Jane Carlyle* (1990). Fryckstedt, M. C. *BJRL* (1984). Howe, S. *Geraldine Jewsbury, Her Life and Errors* (1939). Levin, S. M. *PSt* (1987). Wilkes, J. *Persuasions* (1991).

For articles in reference works, see: *DNB. Feminist. Oxford. ToddBWW.*

Eleanor Langstaff

J. F.: See *Fothergill, Jessie*

Ruth Prawer Jhabvala

BORN: 7 May 1927, Cologne, Germany.
DAUGHTER OF: Marcus Prawer and Leonora Cohn Prawer.
MARRIED: Cyrus S. H. Jhabvala, 1951.

J. has lived major portions of her life in four countries. Born in Cologne in 1927 to a Polish Jewish lawyer and his German Jewish wife, J. fled from Germany to England in 1939 with her parents and brother. In 1951, after graduating from the University of London with an M.A. in English literature, she married Cyrus Jhabvala, an Indian architect, and moved with him to Delhi, India. There the Jhabvalas raised three daughters. For both professional and personal reasons and with her husband's encouragement, J. left India in 1975 and moved to the United States. The personal reasons that caused J. to leave are presented in a powerful essay, reprinted as the introduction to *An Experience of India (1971)*. Essentially India, so exhilarating at first, had become oppressive to J. She uses the image "living on the back of an animal" to represent her irritation at India's extreme and inescapable poverty and her inability either to affect or to overlook it.

J. chose New York City because its pressures and variety somehow drew together for her the experiences of the Europe of her youth and the India of her adulthood. She also chose it because it was the home of her cinematic collaborators, James Ivory and Ismail Merchant. Ivory, an American director, and Merchant, an Indian producer, had come to India in 1961 to ask J. to write the filmscript for her novel, *The Householder*, published in 1960. Since that time the team has produced eighteen films, including two based on J.'s novels. J., Merchant, and Ivory are personal friends as well as colleagues, all living in the same apartment building. J.'s 1980 story "Grandmother," and novel, *In Search of Love and Beauty* (1983), explore this friendship.

To date, J.'s writings on India, along with her screenplays, constitute the main body of her work. Of her novels, *In Search of Love and Beauty* is one of the few that do not have an Indian setting. In India, J. is often considered with others writing about India in English, such as Kamala Markandaya. Indian reviews are not always favorable, finding J.'s writing able but unsympathetic.

In fact, J.'s earliest novels, *To Whom She* Will (1955; in the U.S. as *Amrita)* and *The Nature of Passion* (1956), while comic and satiric, present Indian life with considerable delight. The mood of *Esmond in India* (1958), J.'s third novel, however, is darker. In it, a pretty, naïve Indian heroine, much like her counterparts in the earlier novels, feels modern enough to make her own matrimonial choices. But her story, unlike theirs, does not close happily: At novel's end she is left pursuing a damaging affair with Esmond, a selfish Englishman already married to an Indian woman who had made a similar choice. The bitterness of *Esmond* lies less in the Indian life depicted than in the effects of the intersection of Indian and Western ways. The next novel, *The Householder*, returns to more purely Indian life. There Western figures appear but only as exotic yet finally irrelevant interlopers. J.'s last novel concerned mainly with Indian family life and told from an Indian point of view is *Get Ready for Battle* (1962). In mood it is closer to the first novels than to *Esmond*.

The next three novels, *A Backward Place* (1965), *A New Dominion* (1973; in the U.S. as *Travelers*), and *Heat and Dust* (1975), reflect J.'s declaration in *An Experience of India* that she is no longer interested in India but in herself (as symbolic of the westerner) in India. The central characters in these novels are westerners who have come to India for varied reasons. Judy, of *A Backward Place*, is an English girl married to an Indian actor. Because she has come without an agenda—neither to find herself as Lee of *Travelers* wishes to do, nor to have India give up its secrets, as Olivia of *Heat and Dust* wants—Judy remains healthy and becomes more assimilated into India than any of the other westerners. Yet Judy, J. suggests, is not a complicated girl, and other westerners, because of their natures, are more likely to become trapped by India's sensuality or its mystical religions (as do Lee and Olivia). Or they may be unable to leave their western background behind enough to enter into Indian life. The true meeting of East and West, J.'s fiction suggests, is a rarity, and the path to that meeting is fraught with danger to travelers in either direction. *A New Dominion* is similar in its emphasis on the efforts of westerners to survive in India.

J.'s more recent books, like *In Search of Love and Beauty* (1983), focus increasingly on non-Indian characters and situations, not always to critical acclaim. *Three Continents* (1987) is J.'s attempt to explain her feelings as an alienated foreigner in India, but J. has not completely severed her fictional ties to India. *Poet and Dancer* (1993), for example, is transitional in that it is non-Indian in setting and theme but some characters are Indian; it is an exploration of the Manichean split between good and evil as explored in the mutually corrosive relationship between two romantically involved cousins.

Shards of Memory (1995) is a complicated fictional consideration of exile and estrangement in several generations of a family that could also have been called "three continents." Set primarily in New York City but with scenes harkening back to India as well as London, the novel uses J.'s cinematic experience to create interwoven flashbacks in which she cuts back and forth in time and space among her characters, some of whom tell their own stories. This book, like others by J., also focuses on a self-styled guru, in this case called "the Master," whose outrageous claims include single-handedly ending World War II.

Recently J. has written more screenplays than novels, for she reports that writing for the screen is less taxing. Writing for film, however, has definitely influenced her novels, for the later books tend to be written in distinct scenes with sharp cuts between people and places; a similar change has taken place in her short fiction. J.'s later work, then, seems more modern than her earlier, but it is also colder and more distancing, reflecting perhaps J.'s increasing sense of her own rootlessness. Predicting her future direction, however, is difficult because she continues to deal occasionally with Indian subjects and characters, as well as with European and American settings and characters.

WORKS: *To Whom She Will* (1955; in the U.S. as *Amrita,* 1956). *The Nature of Passion* (1956). *Esmond in India* (1958). *The Householder* (1960; as filmscript, 1963). *Get Ready for Battle* (1962). *Like Birds, Like Fishes* (1964). *A Backward Place* (1965). *Shakespeare Wallah* (1965). *A Stronger Climate* (1968). *The Guru* (1969). *Bombay Talkie* (1970). *An Experience of India* (1971). *A New Dominion* (1973; in the U.S. as *Travelers*). *Heat and Dust* (1975; as screenplay, 1983). *Autobiography of a Princess* (1975). *How I Became a Holy Mother and Other Stories* (1976). *Roseland* (1977). *Hullabaloo over Georgie and Bonnie's Pictures* (1978). *The Europeans* (1979). *Jane Austen in Manhattan* (1980). *Quartet* (1981). *In Search of Love and Beauty* (1983). *A Room with a View* (1985; screenplay). *Out of India: Selected Stories* (1986). *The Courtesans of Bombay* (1987). *Three Continents* (1987). (with J. Schlesinger) *Madame Sousatzka* (1988; screenplay). *Esmond in India* (1990). *Mr. and Mrs. Bridge* (1990; screenplay). *The Bostonians* (1991; screenplay). *Silence, Exile, and Cunning* (1991). *Howards End* (1992; screenplay). *Poet and Dancer* (1993). *The Remains of the Day* (1993; screenplay). *Jefferson in Paris* (1995; screenplay). *Shards of Memory* (1995). *Surviving Picasso* (1997; screenplay).

BIBLIOGRAPHY: Agerwald, R. G. *Ruth Prawer Jhabvala: A Study of Her Fiction* (1990). Bawer, B. *NewC* (1987). Chadha, R. *Indian English Fiction: An Analysis of the Novels of Ruth Prawer Jhabvala and Kamala Markandaya* (1988). Chakravarti, A., in *Margins of Erasure,* ed. J. Jain and A. Amin (1995). *Passages to Ruth Prawer Jhabvala,* ed. R. J. Crane (1991). Crane, R. J. *Ruth Prawer Jhabvala* (1992). Dhar, T. N. *PURBA* (1990). Dudt, C., in *Faith of a (Woman) Writer,* ed. A. H. Kessler and W. McBrien (1988). Gooneratne, Y. *WLWE* (1979). Gooneratne, Y. *Language and Literature in Multicultural Contexts* (1983). Gooneratne, Y. *Silence, Exile and Cunning: The Fiction of Ruth Prawer Jhabvala* (1983). Gooneratne, Y. *Westerly* (December 1983). Gooneratne, Y. *ArielE* (1984). Gooneratne, Y., in *International Literature in English: Essays on the Major Writers,* ed. R. L. Ross (1991). Gooneratne, Y. in *Westerly Looks to Asia,* ed. B. Bennett, et al. (1993). Gooneratne. Y. in *Still the Frame Holds,* ed. R. Roberts and Y. P. Tevis (1993). Hayball, C. *JIWE* (1981). Jha, R. *The Novels of Kamala Markandaya and Ruth Prawer Jhabvala* (1990). Kandala, N. R. *JES* (1978). King, B. A. *New English Literatures* (1981). Lenta, M. *ArielE* (1989). McDonough, M. *San Francisco Review of Books* (Spring 1987). Newman, J. *MFS* (1994). Rai, S., in *Margins of Erasure,* ed. J. Jain and A. Amin (1995). Rao, R. K. *JES* (1982). Rubin, D. *MFS* (1984). Rutherford, A., and K. N. Peterson. *WLWE* (1976). Shahane, V. A., in *Aspects of Indian Writing in English.* ed. M. K. Naik (1980). Shahane, V. A. *Ruth Prawer Jhabavala* (1976). Shahane, V. A. *JCL* (1977). Shepherd, R. *CoRev* (1990–91). Singh, B., in *Major Indian Novels: An Evaluation,* ed. N. S. Pradhan (1986). Singh, R. H. *The Indian Novel in English: A Critical Study* (1977). Souza, E., in *Awakened Conscience,* ed. C. V. Narasimhaiad (1979). Sucher, L. *The Fiction of Ruth Prawer Jhabvala* (1989). Williams, H. M. *TCL* (1969). Williams, H. M. *The Fiction of Ruth Prawer Jhabvala* (1973).

For articles in reference works, see: *CA. CLC. CN. NCHEL. TCW. WA.*

Other references: Bell, P. K. *NYTBR* (4 April 1976). Grimes, P. *NYT* (30 October 1977). Kaplan, J. *Commentary* (November 1973). King, B. A. *Saturday Review* (Winter 1977). *Midstream* (March 1974). Nott, K. *Encounter* (February 1983). Pritchett, V. S. *New Yorker* (16 June 1973). Weingarten, R. *Midstream* (March 1974). Weintraub, B. *NYTMag* (11 September 1983).

Ellen Laun

J. H. G.: See *Ewing, Juliana Horatia*

Elizabeth Jocelin

BORN: 1596, Norton, Chester.
DIED: 21 October 1622, Cambridgeshire.
DAUGHTER OF: Sir Richard Brooke and Joan Chaderton Brooke.
MARRIED: Tourell Jocelin, 1616.

J.'s only work was a popular advice book, *The Mothers Legacie to Her Unborne Childe* (1624). Between 1624 and 1625, it had three editions and other English editions followed; a Dutch translation appeared by 1699 and a German one by 1748. The chief interest of this book is the contrast between the education that J. suggests is appropriate for her child and the education that J. herself had.

In an essay prefixed to *The Mothers Legacie,* Thomas Goad makes it clear that J. had an unusually thorough education for a Renaissance woman. As a consequence of her parents' separation, J. was reared in the household of her grandfather, William Chaderton, bishop of Lincoln, where she studied religion, history, and languages. In particular, Goad praises her memory for both English and Latin; she seems to have had almost total recall of the sermons she heard in church.

When she became pregnant with her first child, J. feared she would die in childbirth. She therefore wrote *The Mothers Legacie,* giving advice about the education of her unborn child. The actual schedule that she suggests draws no distinction between what is appropriate for a son or daughter: The morning and evening are given to meditation, study, and prayer, while the afternoon is spent in discourse and social pursuits. In advice to her husband, however, J. urges him to allow a son formal study, which, she hoped, would lead him to the ministry. A daughter, however, was to have a limited education. A girl should be literate so she might read the Bible, and to learn "good housewifery . . . and good workes: other learning a woman needs not." This advice, of course, is inconsistent with J.'s own experience.

One can account for this inconsistency by noting that J. praises educated women who are also humble. She may have urged a limited education for her daughter to protect the child from pride, which J. regarded as the most dangerous of sins. Furthermore, J. wrote in a period of intense misogyny, when such women as Lady Mary Wroth and Rachel Speght were under attack for their writing, so *The Mothers Legacie* may reflect an awareness of this antifeminist bias.

On 12 October 1622, J. gave birth to a healthy daughter, Theodora; nine days later, J. died.

WORKS: *The Mothers Legacie to Her Unborne Childe* (1624, STC 14624).

BIBLIOGRAPHY: Clarke, S. *The Lives of Sundry Eminent People* (1683). Feroli, T. *ELH* (1994). Sizemore, C. W. *SAB* (1976). Sizemore, C. W. *UDR* (1981).

For articles in reference works, see: *Bloomsbury. DNB. Europa. Feminist.*

Other references: Beilin, E. *Redeeming Eve* (1987). Travitsky, B. *The Paradise of Women* (1989).

Fran Teague

Amryl Johnson

BORN: 1944, Trinidad, West Indies.

A poet and fiction writer, J. writes passionately about the intersection of contemporary and historical exploitation of black people, reflecting on her own double exile from Africa and Trinidad and celebrating the inventive imagery of Creole speakers.

J. was born in Trinidad, raised by her grandmother, and joined her parents in London when she was eleven. Her education continued in London schools and in Paris during her one year living as an *au pair.* At the University of Kent, she completed a degree in African and Caribbean Studies. While researching the history of slavery for a novel in progress (which was rejected by publishers), J. began to write poetry, completing "Midnight Without Pity" in 1977. Angered by racism in the United Kingdom, and especially by the 1981 New Cross massacre, she wrote the poem "Shackles," in which the speaker cries out angrily, "I choke / on the dregs / of my ancestry." She self-published her first collection of twenty-two poems, *Long Road to Nowhere* (1982). After visits to Trinidad in 1982 and to several Caribbean islands in 1983, she returned to the United Kingdom, when Virago Press invited her to submit her writing for publication. Thirty-one poems influenced by her recent experiences in the Caribbean, but written in England, were published under the same title: *Long Road to Nowhere* (1985). An autobiographical prose narrative of her Caribbean journey was published under the title *Sequins for a Ragged Hem* (1988), a nonfiction account of the people she met, emphasizing equally the beautiful creativity ("sequins") and the painfully ugly behavior ("ragged hem") that remains from the rape of slavery. J. has published other poems and stories in various anthologies, and she works as a writer and as an arts educator.

In 1985, J. wrote about her choice to return to the United Kingdom. "The journey would need to begin again . . . the road begins right here and now." The cultural journey envisioned in her poetry and prose involves both a personal awakening and a connection to history. In many different contexts, her writing depicts sudden recognition of how individuals live now under the shadows of slavery, colonialism, and past acts of racist violence.

The exile returned to the Caribbean for a visit has much to learn. In "Panorama from the North Stand," she is both welcomed and reproved: "But girl eat, nah! Yuh go get tin!" The voice criticizes her thinness and gives her "a lesson in living." In "Panorama" and many other poems, J. uses the metaphor of a swimmer struggling in a strong, powerful ocean current: She is pulled away from "the beach of self-awareness," and, unable to "pull against the tide," she "must go down and drink deeply" from this experience. In the poem "And Sea," she is "baptized" into the culture. The ocean that enslaved Africans crossed unwillingly in their transportation to the new world she now crosses willingly, flying from England to the Caribbean to rediscover her cultural roots.

J.'s metaphors for the exile's transformation from observer to participant are powerful and startling. For example, in "Papillon," describing a gaudily beautiful butterfly that parades its colors until exhausted, and in "River," describing the flow of brilliant but turbulent color, both poems conclude with the observer immersing herself passionately. The butterfly and river, however, are not images of nature; they are cultural. The poems' titles refer to Carnival bands (Papillon in the 1982 and River in the 1983 Carnival). By joining in the Carnival bands' parades, she enacts symbolically her desire to connect emotionally with West Indian culture.

She understands the appeal of Carnival in the context of a history of slavery and continuing economic oppression. In "King of the Band," the child who becomes the Carnival King, dancing in sequins and feathers, knowing that all eyes and video cameras are watching him, is proud: "today / you are king / you have the world at your feet." The exhilaration is enhanced by the fact that the Carnival is an escape from the everyday poverty and powerlessness. In addition to the escape, however, J. offers a sudden revelation on the symbolism of the Carnival: The changing fiery colors of the parade suggest the "separation, absorption and expulsion" that is the cultural history of the Caribbean.

The rhythms of calypso are echoed in her poem "J'Ouvert (we ting)," which celebrates the independence of spirit ("De mood is yours to do what yuh please") and the connection between personal and political: "Dis abandon to pleasure is drawin' we / to one conclusion of unity / Freedom was bought wit' dis in min'." No external power can take away this joy and liberty because it is internal.

The stubborn independence of a proud individual is depicted fondly and comically in "Granny in the Market Place," which also illustrates the linguistic creativity of Creole speakers. In a verbal competition clearly won by "Granny," she pronounces elaborate insults about the fish, mangoes, yams, figs, and oranges offered for sale. The poem breaks off with the undefeated Granny beginning the next exchange of insults. That she does not give up symbolizes the indomitable spirit of the Caribbean people.

Visiting the Caribbean islands, J. wrote in her introduction to *Sequins for a Ragged Hem* that she felt haunted by ghosts of the ancestral past. These are evident in several of her poems, notably "How Do You Feed the Ghosts?"—which evokes the hunger, the feeling of loss, the pain, and the imagined sounds of memory. This poem has no answers, only questions. Questions arise out of historical knowledge in the poem "The Wheel," which recalls the history of enslaved African people, brought to the islands to work in the sugar cane industry—the rusting wheel was part of a sugar mill—but the wheel still stands, just as the emancipated people still struggle within the socioeconomic hierarchy that remains from the old plantation system. For some questions about the past, the speaker realizes "you may never / find / answers," and she remains imprisoned (in the poem "Qu'est-ce qu'elle Dit?"). After such knowledge of the past, what can she say?

Similar connections between past and present are made in "Spices and Guns," which is dated "Grenada—March 1983" and recalls the old violent history of the spice trade in nutmegs and cloves. The opening line quotes Miranda's amazed remark from *The Tempest:* "Brave New World," initially resonating with bitterness, in the context of the new world seized and scarred in the seventeenth century by the Europeans, who, in 1983, are still invading in "khaki and / boots." The tone gradually shifts, however, to one of cautious optimism for the determined native people of the island, "those gentle people / with their friendly ways." This poem, however ironically, expresses hope.

Passivity is not the response J. can accept. In "The Loaded Dice," a speaker urges her to "Throw de dice, girl, throw." While remembering that European colonial powers once divided up Africa, with the legacy that some black people blame the unfairly weighted dice, the history of oppression, for current misery, the speaker nevertheless begs her to "Leave de pas' behind"—not to forget it, but rather "let de memory give we de strength to push / fuh wha we want." These "loaded dice" are not only weighted against her, but her decision to throw them is also weighted with significance. The voice pleads with her to "fin' de will to free" ourselves, to reject blaming the past, to "Throw de dice . . . out de dam' window."

This defiant embrace of the painful past in order to break out of the prison concludes the self-awakening in the final poem of the collection, "Long Road to Nowhere," which is set in London. On a Saturday, the shopping day, while strutting down Kentish Town Road, she saw a black man walking on his strong arms at the crossing of painted white lines on the black pavement, and she heard the racist hatred expressed against him, mocking him as a gorilla crossing the zebra. Beginning with the "I" who wants to exclude a stranger from her consciousness, because he threatens her "emptiness," she discovers that she cannot exclude him; she cannot remain simply the angry but distant observer to British racism. The poem shifts from first person inside her mind to an external voice addressing her as "you," accusing her of wanting to ignore him, and shifts back again to an internal voice realizing that the stranger like a ghost haunts "me." The personal and the political are connected; a link is forged between understanding the past and being able to act in the present. After his and her eyes meet, she begins to turn her anger to a positive determination: "put his load on me." She accepts that "now he shares / my brain." She, too, is trapped in the prison bars of racism, of the zebra crossing. She decides to bend the bars to let both of them escape from the cage, and, fighting racism, she accepts her complicity in his violence "this gun / . . . / will serve / us / both."

J.'s poetry and prose expresses, in powerful visual images and memorable metaphors, the anger that is first recognized, then investigated and defined, and finally translated into commitment. It is a personal and political journey of an exile who rediscovers her cultural and historical roots and who then begins the new journey of self-transformation in the urban world she has chosen.

WORKS: *Long Road to Nowhere* (1982; new collection 1985). *Sequins for a Ragged Hem* (1988) (contrib.) *Ambit,* ed. M. Bax (1982). (contrib.) *News for Babylon,* ed. J. Berry (1984). (contrib.) *Facing the Sea,* ed. A. Walmsey and N. Caistor (1986). (contrib.) *Watchers & Seekers,* ed. R. Cobham and M. Collins (1987). (contrib.) *Voiceprint,* ed. S. Brown, M. Morris, and G. Rohlehr (1989). (contrib.) *Caribbean New Wave,* ed. S. Brown (1990). (contrib.) *Creation Fire,* ed. R. Espinet (1990).

BIBLIOGRAPHY: Gohrisch, J. *Hard Times: Deutsch-Englisch Zeitschrift* (Fall 1994). Pearn, J., in *Let It Be Told: Essays by Black Women in Britain,* ed. L. Ngobo (1988).

For articles in reference works, see: *Bibliography of Women Writers from the Caribbean,* ed. B. Berrian and A. Broek (1989). *Bloomsbury. Feminist.* Fenwick, M. J. *Writers of the Caribbean and Central America* (1992). *OxComp.*

Other references: *TLS* (1 April 1988).

Judith L. Johnston

Esther ("Stella") Johnson

BORN: 13 March 1681, near Richmond, Surrey.
DIED: 28 January 1728, Dublin, Ireland.
DAUGHTER OF: Edward Johnson and Bridget Johnson.
MARRIED: Jonathan Swift, 1716 (?).

The mysterious character of the liaison between J. and Jonathan Swift, much speculated about when they were alive, has inspired meticulous but inconclusive scholarly activity ever since. It is certain that Swift met J. at Moor Park, the country home of Sir William Temple, when J., the housekeeper's daughter, was only eight and Swift, Temple's newly engaged secretary, twenty-two. It is also established that Temple was fond of both, offering each preferential treatment over others associated with his household staff. The theory that J. and Swift were both illegitimate children of their benefactor, however, seems to have lost prestige in the most recent biographical research.

In 1701, two years after Temple's death, Swift helped arrange for the nineteen-year-old J. to establish herself permanently in Ireland with her life-long companion Rebecca Dingley. The motive was, as Swift to the end insisted, to ease the women's financial difficulties by enabling them to live where goods and services could be had for much better prices than were then current in England. Several scholars, however, interpret the move as evidence of a pact or a promise or perhaps even a type of engagement in some way preliminary to marriage or to something like it. The arguments cast complex patterns of light and shadow upon our understanding of Swift the lover and Swift the writer.

Despite the paucity of extant proofs of her talents, Swift scholars all acknowledge J. as a writer meriting notice in her own right. They see J.'s role in relation to Swift as a telling one. They point out that Swift himself recognized her talent on numerous occasions. Indirect evidence, they also argue, suggests that her skill in writing, as in conversation, must have been quite considerable to have sustained Swift's respect through a relationship (sometimes painfully stressful) lasting nearly forty years. All speculation aside, the facts stand as a stark challenge to literary historians: Only one poem by J. and only one letter from J. to Swift remain. Some idea of her characteristic style may be garnered from phrases Swift appears to attribute to her from 1710 to 1713 in his *Journal to Stella.* The rest of what she wrote is lost, destroyed perhaps by Swift himself. Whatever the case, the extant letter (a perfunctory thank you note) can hardly be called witty. Dated 25 May 1723, it is conventionally polite, almost exaggeratedly humble and grateful, only hinting at strengths of character in the measured emphatics of "to be sure you did exstreamly right to give a receipt in full of all demands." The log Swift kept of letters received from J. is nothing more than a tantalizingly long list of postmark dates.

On the other hand, the poem "Stella to Dr. Swift on his Birth-day, November 30, 1721" handsomely repays close reading in the light of scholarly research because the gratitude J. expresses is laced through with a saucy piquancy that might well escape the casual reader but that comports with Swift's otherwise mystifying practice of addressing J. as "Sirrah" and of teasing her with such sobriquets as "Admirable Bitch." E. Hardy identifies the quality in J. that Swift could not do without once he had cultivated it in her: "a certain hardness . . . to combat his egotism." Other women (J. writes in her poem, with evident self-satisfaction) must eventually lose their place in Swift's regard and come "tumbling down Time's steep hill, / While Stella holds her station still." Rich in gallantry, J.'s captious lines to Swift ("My early and my only guide") are slender evidence of her power over him but strong evidence of her rapier wit: "O! turn your precepts into laws, / Redeem the women's ruin'd cause, / Retrieve lost empire to our sex / That men may bow their rebel necks."

If Swift had anything to do with the eradication of J.'s *oeuvre,* might these two pieces by J. have survived because they express gratitude for his attentions, but not too much gratitude? They do not, in any case, contradict the spirit of Swift's elegiac prose piece *On the Death of Mrs. Johnson,* which he wrote the night of J.'s death.

WORKS: "To Dr. Swift, on his Birth-day, November 30, 1721," in *The Poems of Jonathan Swift,* 2nd. ed., ed. H. Williams (1958).

BIBLIOGRAPHY: Byrn, R. F. M. *SStud* (1988). Davis, H. J. *Stella: A Gentlewoman of the Eighteenth Century* (1942). *Jonathan Swift: A Critical Anthology,* ed. D. Donoghue (1971). Ehrenpreis, I. *Swift, the Man, His Works, and the Age,* 3 vols. (1962, 1967, 1983). Gold, M. B. *Swift's Marriage to Stella: Together with Unprinted and Misprinted Letters* (1937). Hardy, E. *The Conjured Spirit, Swift: A Study in the Relationship of Swift, Stella, and Vanessa* (1949). Le Brocquy, S. *Swift's Most Valuable Friend* (1968). Nokes, D. *Jonathan Swift: A Hypocrite Reversed, A Critical Biography* (1985). Peake, C., in *Proceedings of the First Munster Symposium on Jonathan Swift,* ed. H. J. Real and J. J. Vienken (1985). Real, H. J. *SStud* (1986). Swift, J. *Journal to Stella,* ed. H. Williams, (1948). Swift, J. *Stella's Birth-Days: Poems,* ed. S. Le Brocquy (1967). Woods, M. L. *Transactions of the Royal Society of Literature of the U.K.* (1914). Woolley, J. *SStud* (1989). Woolley, J., in *Swift and His Contexts,* ed. J. I. Fischer, et al. (1989).

For articles in reference works, see: *DNB* (under "Jonathan Swift"). *Europa. ToddDBA.*

R. Victoria Arana

Pamela Hansford Johnson

BORN: 29 May 1912, London.
DIED: 18 June 1981, London.
DAUGHTER OF: Reginald K. Johnson and Amy Howson Johnson
MARRIED: Gordon Neil Stewart, 1936; C. P. Snow, 1950.
WROTE UNDER: Pamela Hansford Johnson; Nap Lombard (with Neil Stewart).

The novels of J.'s second husband, centrally concerned as they are with questions of might and right, paradoxes in the corridors of power, decisions and machinations in hierarchies and bureaucracies, are better known than hers. Where he writes of the political environment, she writes of the psychological. She is concerned with decision and dilemma, too, but her focus is upon the individual rather than the institution and how he or she reacts to the moral questions. This is true of all her career, from her very first novel, *This Bed Thy Centre* (1935), written when she was just twenty-two.

The Last Resort (1956), for instance, contrasts ordinary people with saints and martyrs, and writing of the book Anthony Burgess has summed it up as "they commit themselves to the big terrible decisions, we hold back." In *The Humbler Creation* (1959) we see the struggle of an Anglican clergyman with an unhappy married life, which drives him, rather unwillingly, into adultery that he is hardly equipped to revel in. In *An Error of Judgement* (1962), a highly successful doctor examines his innermost heart and admits to himself that it was sadism that determined his choice of profession. He gives it up and turns to altruism: He will help delinquent youth. Then he encounters a "worthless" little monster, a boy who has committed a ghastly crime, got away with it, feels no remorse whatever, and is not unlikely to do worse in the future. The doctor kills the boy and we are left to decide whether it was "an error" or not, to judge him but also to keep firmly in mind that this is not a world of black and white, that circumstances alter facts, and that good deeds can be done for bad reasons as well as bad ones for good reasons. If Snow's series *Strangers and Brothers* shows us a very complicated world of power, J.'s works show us one of no less complexity, no more cut and dried motivations.

The picture she gives us of modern people caught up in a struggle of good and evil, between us, within us, perplexed by the challenges of morality and ethics in situations as doubtful and diverse as those in her novels *The Family Pattern* (1942), *A Summer to Decide* (1948), *Catherine Carter* (1952), *An Impossible Marriage* (1954), and *The Unspeakable Skipton* (1959), definitely places her in that select group of modern writers of fiction such as Graham Greene, William Golding, Anthony Burgess, P. H. Newby, and Patrick White, who address the large issues of theology as they affect moral dilemmas. In her best-known novel, the "unspeakable" writer Skipton lives by his wits and amuses us by his audacity, but even he raises (as do more sober characters in other novels from her pen) touchy questions of amorality and immorality. Some people struggle with private demons. Some are trapped in incomplete or "impossible" marriages. Some are baffled by the problems of hopeless affairs (as in *The Sea and the Wedding*, also titled *The Last Resort*, 1957). Avoiding both unnecessary complexity or popular easy answers, J. tackles questions quite as serious as her husband, actually more serious than the jockeying for a university position of power in *The Masters.* Though J.'s insights are often startling, her characters are usually ordinary. It is the predicament they may be in, seen both in their own terms and also against a standard of judgment that may be said to be more objective (or more middle-class orthodox), that engages our attention, even sympathy.

Before her marriage to Snow, she wrote the play *Corinth House* (1950), and after her marriage she collaborated with him on plays such as *The Supper Dance, Family Party, Spare the Rod, To Murder Mrs. Mortimer, The Pigeon with the Silver Foot, Her Best Food Forward* (all published in 1951), and *The Public Prosecutor* (adapted from Georgi Dzhagarov; produced 1967, pub. 1969). With Kitty Black she did *The Rehearsal* (adapted from Jean Anouilh, produced 1961), and she authored half a dozen "reconstructions" for radio of characters from Marcel Proust. All her plays show her interest in middle-class mores and her skill with dialogue. None is exceptionally good but all are adequate.

She and Snow edited *Winter's Tales 7* (1961; modern Russian short stories), and she wrote *Personalia* (1974), a charming and intelligent book about things "important" to her personally. Her novels, however, are the real basis for her literary reputation. Americans will wince at *Night and Silence, Who Is Here?* (1963), a novel set in New Hampshire on a college campus and worthy to rank with those acerbic pictures of academia drawn with a certain malice by such authors as Mary McCarthy, Randall Jarrell, and Anthony Burgess. Belgians will appreciate the Belgian settings of *Too Dear for My Possessing* (1940), *The Holiday Friend* (1972), and *The Unspeakable Skipton* (in which a "Baron Corvo" sort of ne'er-do-well is resident not in Venice but in Bruges). Londoners will applaud the accuracy of the settings of *This Bed Thy Centre, The Survival of the Fittest* (1968), and the truly nasty but hilarious send-up of London literary life in her "novel in bad taste," *Cork Street, Next to the Hatter's* (1965).

After she wrote *Too Dear for My Possessing* (1940), she briefly collaborated with her then husband (Neil Stewart) on *Tidy Death* (1940) and *Murder's a Swine* (1943; also published as *The Grinning Pig*). Then, after her own *The Family Pattern* (1942), *Winter Quarters* (1943), and *The Trojan Brothers* (1944), she added to *Too Dear for My Possessing* two more novels to make a trilogy: *An Avenue of Stone* (1947) and *A Summer to Decide* (1948). Margaret Willy makes the point that the narrator of the trilogy is a man—*The Unspeakable Skipton, The Survival of the Fittest, The Good Listener,* and so forth also have male central characters—and writes:

> Pamela Hansford Johnson has a talent, comparatively rare among women novelists, for subtle and convincing depiction of the viewpoints, thought-processes, and emotional responses of the opposite sex. Indeed her whole breadth of subject and treatment is peculiarly masculine in its detachment, expressing a shrewd yet compassionate acceptance of many aspects of human frailty.

Men and women speak differently, however, and the male characters in J., however keenly observed and central, speak an oddly non-"masculine" prose, male dialogue as written by someone who cannot speak or reproduce the male language, just as most males cannot write like women. All readers can agree, however, that J. masters plot with careful construction and involves readers with moral dilemmas.

WORKS: *Symphony for Full Orchestra* (1934). *This Bed Thy Centre* (1935). *Blessed Above Woman* (1936). *Here Today* (1937). *World's End* (1937). *The Monument* (1938). *Girdle of Venus* (1939). *Too Dear for My Possessing* (1940). (as Nap Lombard, with N. Stewart) *Tidy Death* (1940). *The Family Pattern* (1942). *Winter Quarters* (1943). (as Nap Lombard, with N. Stewart) *Murder's a Swine* (1943; also published as *The Grinning Pig*). *The Trojan Brothers* (1944). *An Avenue of Stone* (1947). *A Summer to Decide* (1948). *The Duchess at Sunset* (1948). *Hungry Milliner; An English Critical Appraisal of Thomas Wolfe* (1948). *The Philistines* (1949). *Corinth House* (1950). *Ivy Compton-Burnett* (1951). (with C. P. Snow) *The Supper Dance* (1951). (with C. P. Snow) *Family Party* (1951). (with C. P. Snow) *Spare the Rod* (1951). (with C. P. Snow) *To Murder Mrs. Mortimer* (1951). (with C. P. Snow) *The Pigeon with the Silver Foot* (1951). (with C. P. Snow) *Her Best Foot Forward* (1951). *Catherine Carter* (1952). *An Impossible Marriage* (1954). *Madame de Charles* (1954). *Albertine Regained* (1954). *Saint-Loup* (1955). *The Last Resort* (1956; in the U. S. as *The Sea and the Wedding*, 1957). *A Window at Montjarrain* (1956). *Proust Recaptured* (collecting the radio plays based on M. Proust; 1958). *The Humbler Creation* (1959). *The Unspeakable Skipton* (1959). (with Kitty Black) *The Rehearsal* (adapted from J. Anouilh, 1961). *An Error of Judgement* (1962). *Night and Silence, Who Is Here?* (1963). *Cork Street, Next to the Hatter's* (1965). *On Iniquity: Some Personal Reflection Arising out of the Moors Murder Trial* (1967). *The Survival of the Fittest* (1968). (with C. P. Snow) *The Public Prosecutor* (from G. Dzhagarov, 1969). *The Honours Board* (1970). *The Holiday Friend* (1972). *Important to Me: Personalia* (1974). *The Good Listener* (1975).

BIBLIOGRAPHY: Franks, M. M. *BB* (1983). Halperin, J. *C. P. Snow: An Oral Biography Together with a Conversation with Lady Snow (Pamela Hansford Johnson)* (1983). Lindblad, I. *Pamela Hansford Johnson* (1982). Quigly, I. *Pamela Hansford Johnson* (1968).

For articles in reference works, see: *CLC. CN. GWELN. LLC. Longman. MBL* and *SUP. TCA SUP. TCW.*

Other references: Allen, W. *Tradition and Dream* (1964; in the U.S. as *The Modern Novel in Britain and the United States*). *AS* (Fall 1971). *Atlantic* (November 1965, July 1968). *Books and Bookmen* (October 1965, July 1968, March 1969, October 1970, February 1973, May 1975, January 1978). Borowitz, A. *Innocence and Arsenic: Studies in Crime and Literature* (1977). Brophy, B. *Mosaic* (1968). *Commonweal* (11 February 1966). *ContempR* (May 1967). Dick, K. *Friends and Friendship: Conversations and Reflections* (1974). *Harper's* (November 1965, April 1967). *Listener* (16 May 1968, 16 March 1967, 13 August 1970, 26 October 1972, 19 June 1975, 3 October 1974, 26 October 1978, 7 May 1981). *Nation* (19 August 1968). Newquist, R. *Counterpoint* (1964). *New Republic* (25 March 1967). *New Statesman* (1 October 1965, 17 May 1968, 24 March 1967, 14 August 1970, 27 October 1972,20 September 1974, 4 July 1975). *Newsweek* (27 May 1968). *NYTBR* (14 November 1965, 7 July 1968, 20 September 1970, 28 September 1975, 14 September 1975). *Observer* (3 October 1965, 19 May 1968, 16 August 1970, 29 October 1972, 22 September 1974, 22 June 1975, 22 October 1978, 19 April 1981). Rabinowitz, R. *The Reaction Against Experiment in the English Novel, 1950–60* (1967). Raymond, J. *The Doge of Dover* (1960). *Spectator* (1 October 1965, 10 March 1967, 17 January 1969, 15 August 1970, 4 November 1972, 21 June 1975, 30 May 1981). *Saturday Review* (9 October 1965, 3 August 1968, 15 April 1967, 24 October 1970). *Time* (19 November 1965, 7 April 1967, 28 September 1970). *TLS* (30 September 1965, 16 May 1968, 14 August 1970, 27 October 1972, 20 June 1975, 3 January 1975, 2 May 1975, 3 November 1978, 1 May 1981). *Vogue* (1 March 1961). Willy, M. *Great Writers of the English Language: Novelists* (1979).

Leonard R. N. Ashley

Jennifer Johnston

BORN: 12 January 1930, Dublin, Ireland.
DAUGHTER OF: Denis Johnston and Shelah Richards.
MARRIED: Ian Smyth, 1951; David Gilliland, 1976.

Daughter of one of Ireland's foremost playwrights and a noted actress-director-producer, J. has received wide praise and a number of awards for her novels, several of which have also been produced as television dramas. Her novels are all set in the Republic of Ireland or Northern Ireland (where she lives) and are chiefly concerned with differences in class, religion, or politics. She has also consistently been sensitive to the gradual ability of an adolescent to understand old age and the corresponding indifference and cruelty of adults. Her protagonists often find themselves in situations in which their social, political, or religious restrictions become a source of confrontation and growth.

J. uses multiple points of view in her fiction, with diary entries as well as shifting perspectives in voice and time supporting her interest in the effects of the historical past upon the present. Her use of these techniques to apply to Ireland's periods of Troubles enables her novels, according to the *Times Literary Supplement,* to "convey more about her country than whole volumes of analysis and documentation."

Her first completed novel, *The Gates,* was rejected because publishers considered it too short; after the success of her first published work, *The Captains and the Kings* (1972), however, *The Gates* was accepted and published in 1973. *The Captains and the Kings* won several prizes as best first book. It focuses on the decay of the Anglo-Irish "Big House" tradition in the years prior to the Irish Rebellion. The elderly Charles Prendergast, whose youth and marriage were emotionally empty, finds the past impinging on the present; haunted by memories he cannot control, he limits himself to one bare room of his home. Prendergast befriends a local youth, who is coerced into accusing Prendergast of sexual abuse, but just as the police come to arrest the innocent old man, he dies. The novel opens with the guards leaving the police station to make the arrest and closes with their arrival.

The Gates also uses a complex structure to show how sixteen-year-old Minnie McMahon, daughter of a Communist journalist, reluctantly learns the importance of living in Ireland. J. shows that Minnie's misplaced affections and near escape from a derelict existence like that she sees around her results from youthful idealism and romanticism, not overwhelming conviction. Through the use of diary entries to open each chapter, followed by an omniscient narrative perspective and dialogues between Minnie and a ghost or other people, J. offers a sometimes confusing but incisive account of the dilemma the young in Ireland face; a subplot concerned with the stealing of manorial gates suggests again the decline of the Anglo-Irish estates.

Though part of the action of *How Many Miles to Babylon?* (1974) occurs on such an estate, the emphasis is not on the decline of the "Big House." The novel is set during World War I and vividly depicts front-line horrors, but the emotional desperation surpasses the physical in its treatment of Alexander Moore. Moore shot his only friend, a lower-class Irish youth, to save him from execution for desertion; he now awaits his own death, offering a first-person narrative of his simultaneous coming-of-age and death. The book was widely praised for its handling of war scenes and was compared favorably to work by writers ranging from Stephen Crane to Siegfried Sassoon and Wilfred Owen.

Shadows on Our Skin (1977) is set in contemporary Londonderry (where J. lives); it centers on Protestant-Catholic relations, in this case through a young woman teacher, a Protestant, and a twelve-year-old Roman Catholic boy who wishes to write poetry. The boy's older brother, active in the Irish Republican Army, at first believes himself in love with the teacher, but after learning that she plans to marry a British soldier, he and his I.R.A. friends attack her as a means of persuading her to leave the country. But the boy himself and his attempt to use poetic language as a means of overcoming the political and religious divisiveness in the outside world are J.'s primary concerns.

J. returns to Ireland in the 1920s in *The Old Jest* (1979), with her viewpoint again shifting between diary entries and a third-person narrator and with another adolescent nearing adulthood as protagonist. Nancy Gulliver, age eighteen, reflects through her diary on her grandfather's one-time greatness in the Boer War and his subsequent senility as well as on her friend, an Irish terrorist who is killed by the British. Nancy, another would-be writer, confuses love with emotional security, knowing she cannot endure the pain of the adult world. After the terrorist's death, she is better able to make adult decisions.

The Christmas Tree (1981), set in contemporary Dublin, focuses on Constance Keating, age forty-five and dying of leukemia less than a year after bearing an illegitimate child. She reflects on her unsatisfactory life and her desire to write, but other narrative viewpoints are also brought in, including a servant's comments after her death and flashbacks; her life thus becomes the novel she wishes she could have written.

In *Fool's Sanctuary* (1987), J. returns to the "Big House" theme and again has an adolescent protagonist, Miranda, who cannot envision life away from the estate—or, for that matter, life ever changing. Her father knows that independence is imminent and wishes to make amends for his family's centuries of abuse. Miranda's love, a Dublin student, talks of fighting rather than love, and her brother, a British soldier, even more fervently advocates violence. At novel's end, Miranda stays in the house, emotionally unable to leave or to accept her own limited maturity as she herself approaches death. Based on a play titled *Indian Summer* (produced in Belfast in 1983), the novel in most respects returns in emphasis and technique to J.'s earlier works.

It has been frequently noted that J.'s novels offer bleak conclusions. *The Railway Station Man* (1984) is typical of these in its focus on a middle-aged widow whose husband has been killed in fighting in Derry between Protestants and Roman Catholics and who finds painting to be a means of achieving a degree of inner peace in the midst of violence. *The Invisible Worm* (1991), a work that J. told Paddy Wordworth was one she had always "wanted to write," is concerned with incest. Laura Quinlan, the protagonist, daughter of a Protestant mother and Catholic father, spends years attempting to escape recollections of sexual abuse by her father; among other things, she burns down the "Big House" in which the family lived.

The Illusionist (1995) is concerned with a mismatched marriage, in this case focusing on Stella, an Irish woman who meets Martyn (the illusionist of the book's title) on a train, marries him, and ever after regrets the match because of her husband's secretive and tyrannical ways. Their daughter Robin, however, clearly takes her father's side, considering him a great man because he has taught her to think only about herself, not others. Stella gradually realizes that her own mother, with whom she has had a close relationship, has seemed distant and silent about Stella's marriage, for the mother clearly sees Martyn's evil nature. When Stella tries to find herself through writing, for example, Martyn throws her typewriter out the window and destroys her manuscript. Martyn is eventually killed by a bomb and Robin becomes even more alienated from her mother. J. suggests, though, that Robin, also an illusionist of sorts, may eventually accept the truth about her father.

At her best, J. constructs her novels carefully and methodically, and her skill at handling several narrative points of view simultaneously is excellent. She is also able to develop character superbly, especially in her fully drawn characters' ability to grapple with both their own and their country's struggles for identity. She continually shows how the past, personally as well as nationally, impinges upon the present, thus making her fiction considerably more effective than would be the case were it merely historical fiction. Though character types and incidents of which she has limited personal knowledge have sometimes been criticized as little more than unrealistic caricature, at her best her compact, tightly structured novels are powerful and deeply realized.

WORKS: *The Captains and the Kings* (1972). *The Gates* (1973). *How Many Miles to Babylon?* (1974). *Shadows on Our Skin* (1977). *The Old Jest* (1979). *The Christmas Tree* (1981). *The Railway Station Man* (1986). *Fool's Sanctuary* (1987). *The Invisible Worm* (1991). *The Illusionist* (1995). *The Desert Lullaby: A Play in Two Acts* (1996).

BIBLIOGRAPHY: Benstock, S., in *Twentieth Century Women Novelists*, ed. T. F. Staley (1982). Burleigh, D., in *Irish Writers and Society at Large*, ed. M. Sekine (1985). Connelly, J. *Eire* (1986). Deane, S. *Ireland Today* (February 1985). Dunleavy, J. E. and R. Lynch, in *The British Novel Since 1960*, ed. J. Acheson (1991). Hargreaves, T., in *Cultural Contexts and Literary Idioms in Contemporary Irish Literature*, ed. M. Kenneally (1988). Imhof, R. *EI* (1985). Kearney, E. *ClQ* (1991). Lanters, J. *Dutch Quarterly Review* (1988). Lanters, J., in *The Clash of Ireland: Literary Contrasts and Connections*, ed. C. C. Barfoot and T. D'haen (1989). Lubbers, K., in *Ancestral Voices: The Big House in Anglo-Irish Literature*, ed. O. Rauchbauer (1992). O'Toole, B., in *Across a Roaring Hill: The Protestant Imagination in Modern Ireland: Essays in Honour of John Hewitt*, ed. G. Dawe and E. Longley (1985). Perrick, P. *LonSunT* (24 February 1991). Stewart-Liberty, N. *An Droichead: The Bridge* (1986). Wilmer, S. *NTQ* (1991). Woodworth, P. *Irish Times* (23 February 1991).

For articles in reference works, see: *Bloomsbury*. *CA*. *Cambridge*. *CLC*. *DIB*. *DIL*. *DLB*. *Feminist*. *ToddBWW*.

Other references: *Cosmopolitan* (November 1980). *Irish Times* (3 March 1973). *New Statesman* (19 January 1973, 15 March 1974, 15 April 1977). *NYTBR* (27 October 1974, 12 January 1975, 26 March 1978, 16 March 1980). (London) *Observer Magazine* (26 October 1975). *Spectator* (29 January 1972). *TLS* (26 January 1973, 1 March 1974, 15 April 1977, 18 September 1981, 1 May 1987). *YR* (1975).

Paul Schlueter

Jenefer Ruth Joseph

BORN: 7 May 1932, Birmingham.
DAUGHTER OF: Louis Joseph and Florence Joseph.
MARRIED: Tony Coles, 29 April 1961.
WRITES UNDER: Jenny Joseph.

After graduating with honors from St. Hilda's College, Oxford, in 1953, J. worked as a reporter, first for the *Bedfordshire Times* and later for the *Oxford Mail*. She went to South Africa in 1957 as a reporter for Drum Publications. She also taught for a short time at Central Indian High School, Johannesburg, returning to England in 1959. From 1969 to 1972 she ran a pub in London with her husband. In 1972, she accepted a post at West London College to teach English as a foreign language; she also taught adult education classes for the Workers Education Association. She has been a guest broadcaster for BBC-TV and a contributor to the *London Magazine* and other periodicals.

J.'s literary career, begun in the 1950s, gained recognition with the publication of *The Unlooked-For Season* (1960). This collection of poems, which won the Eric Gregory Award in 1961, is heavily influenced by her stay in South Africa. Running through the poems are the themes of loss, exile, desertion, and death. In many of the poems, winter forms the background while summer is the "unlooked-for season" that will alleviate the negativity connoted with winter.

Rose in the Afternoon (1974) focuses more on the "oddities of normal everyday life" (*Contemporary Poets*). The eponymous poem examines a cut rose that delivers pleasure to the narrator even as it is dying. In 1975, J. received the Cholmondeley Award for this haunting poem. "The Warning," perhaps J.'s most famous poem, also appears in this collection. A humorous text, its ostensible purpose is to admonish the reader that the narrator intends to "make up for the sobriety of my youth" by doing such things as "wear[ing] purple / and a red hat which doesn't go" once her responsibilities as wife and mother have been completed. At the end, however, the narrator hints that rebellion is actually imminent: "But maybe I ought to practice a little now? / So people who know me are not too shocked and surprised / When suddenly I am old and start to wear purple" (in Janeczko).

Between her first and second collections of adult poetry, J. collaborated with Katharine Hoskyns on a series of children's poetry entitled *Nursery Series* (1966–68), a collection of six separate books of poetry.

In 1986, J. was awarded the James Tait Black Memorial Award for Fiction for her *Persephone* (1984), a reworking in poetry and prose of the ancient myth. According to Jo-Ann Goodwin in the *Times Literary Supplement*, J.'s text "provides an elaboration of the despair and abandonment felt by all parents whose children must eventually grow up and leave." J.'s principal characters, Demeter, Hades, and Persephone, tell their stories in verse. The prose pieces deal with the themes of the text. Commenting on *Persephone*, J. once stated: "The tone of the particular literary style chosen is meant to reflect the personality of the voice and so be part of the meaning" (*Contemporary Poets*).

J.'s work has moved from the formal language found in *The Unlooked-For Season* to a more colloquial style seen in *Rose in the Afternoon*. As has been remarked, she seldom overlooks her "reporter's skill of homing in on the human detail" (*Oxford Companion*). She admits to a fascination with language and languages: "I am interested in the use of the speaking voice, not merely to provide a 'realistic' character for dramatic monologue, but as material, recognizable straight away on one level to the reader, in the musical use of language." She believes that poetry—while a unique genre—should be capable of incorporating elements of the novel, the play, music, and even philosophic inquiry (*Contemporary Poets*).

WORKS: *The Four Elements* (1950). *The Unlooked-For Season* (1960). (with K. Hoskyns) *Nursery Series* (1966–68) [*Boots* (1966). *Wheels* (1966). *Water* (1967). *Wind* (1967). *Tea* (1968). *Sunday* (1968).] *Tim and Terry* (1967). *Judy and Jasmin* (1967). *Rose in the Afternoon* (1974). *The Thinking Heart* (1978). *Beyond Descartes* (1983). *Persephone* (1984). *First Spring Dawn* (1989). *The Four Elements* (1989). *The In-Land Sea* (1989). *First Spring Dawn* (1989). *Highwayman* (1990). *Warning* (1990). (with L. Larsen) *When I am an Old Woman* (1990). *Jennie Joseph* (1991). (with R. Mitchell) *Beached Boats* (1991). *Sunlight on Ice* (1991). *Upside Down* (1991). *Selected Poems* (1992). (with S. McRae) *Fair Warning: A Testament to Independence in Old Age* (1993). *Ghosts and Other Company* (1995). *Extended Similes* (1997).

BIBLIOGRAPHY:

For articles in reference works, see *CA*. *CP*. *DLB*. *IAWWW*. *OxComp*.

Other references: Goodwin, J. A. *TLS* (29 August 1986). Janeczko, P., ed. *Going Over to Your Place* (1987).

Natalie Joy Woodall

Julia: See *Robinson, Mary*

Julian of Norwich

BORN: 1343.
DIED: after 1416.

One of the outstanding theological and mystical writers of the Roman Catholic church, J. composed two versions of her book in sixteen chapters (or showings), *Revelations of Divine Love* (1670). The first version was probably written shortly after she experienced her sixteen visions, and the longer, more theological text some twenty years later.

J. evidences familiarity with mystical texts both from England and the Continent as well as a thorough knowledge of the Vulgate and of the writings of St. Gregory and

St. Augustine. She is also remarkably original and at times controversial in her de-emphasis on man's proclivity for sin and the gloomy results of Adam's fall from grace. Hers is a loving and forgiving God full of compassion. She was also recognized for her talents at spiritual counseling, as is evident from Margery Kempe's account of their meeting. Well-educated, erudite, and blessed with remarkable intellectual skills, J. not only recorded but also interpreted her visions. Unlike the bourgeois (and uneducated) Margery Kempe, whose revelations are nonanalytic, J. explained her mystical experiences in clear theological terms.

Like most medieval mystics, J. strove for the perfect union through love with the Godhead. Concerned with the spiritual welfare of her readers and intent upon sharing her message of hope, she emphasized the limitless nature of divine love and compassion by contemplating the motherhood of God. "God as Mother," or rather, Christ, the creative force of the Trinity, the nature creatrix, is eulogized by J. as the ultimate (because tender and self-sacrificing in love) embodiment of true love:

> The Mother may tenderly lay her child to her breast, but our Mother, Jesus, may familiarly lead us into His blessed breast by His Sweet open side. . . . This fair and lovely word, Mother, is so sweet and so kind in itself that it may not truly be said of anyone but Him and Him Who is the very life of all things. To the property of motherhood belong nature, love, wisdom, and understanding and it is God.

J. has earned an eminent and well-deserved place in the history of Roman Catholic mysticism; in her we have a visionary of remarkable literary and imaginative powers and a compassionate, fascinatingly complex human being. Her spirituality is essentially optimistic; her message is one of hope in divine benevolence; her revelations are theologically and analytically sound, and her style is memorable.

WORKS: (modern editions) *A Shewing of God's Love: The Shorter Version of Sixteen Revelations by Julian of Norwich,* ed. S. A. Reynolds (1958). *Revelations of Divine Love,* ed. J. Walsh (1961). *Revelations of Divine Love,* ed. C. Walters (1966). *Revelations of Divine Love,* ed. M. Glasscoe (1976). *A Book of Showings to the Anchoress Julian of Norwich,* ed. E. Colledge and J. Walsh (1978).

BIBLIOGRAPHY: Bradley, R. *DR* (1986). Clay, R. M. *The Hermits and Anchorites of England* (1914). Colledge, E. *The Mediaeval Mystics of England* (1961). Colledge, E. and J. Walsh. *Medieval Studies* (1976). Foss, D. A. *DR* (1986). Knowles, D. *The English Mystical Tradition* (1961). Krantz, M. D. F. *The Life and Text of Julian of Norwich* (1997). *The Book of Margery Kempe,* ed. S. B. Meech and H. E. Allen (1940). Molinari, P. *Julian of Norwich: The Teaching of a Fourteenth-Century Mystic.* (1958). Nowakowski, D. N. *Julian of Norwich's Showings: From Vision to Book* (1994). Panichelle, D. S. *DR* (1986). Reynolds, F. *LeedsSE* (1952). Reynolds, F., in *Pre-Reformation of English Spirituality,* ed. J. Walsh (1966). Riehle, W., in *The Middle English Mystics,* ed. W. Riehle, trans. B. Standring (1981). Siegmund Schultze, D. *ZAA* (1986). Stone, R. K. *Middle English Prose Style: Margery Kempe and Julian of Norwich* (1970).

For articles in reference works, see: *Allibone. Bloomsbury. Cambridge. Cassell. Feminist. Oxford. ToddBWW.*

Katharina M. Wilson

Justicia: See *Haywood, Eliza Fowler*

Juvenal, Horace: See *Robinson, Mary Darby (Perdita)*

Kane, Julia: See Robins, Denise Naomi

Katherine of Sutton

FLOURISHED: 1360–76.

K., abbess of the Barking nunnery, near London, from 1363 to 1376, is the first known woman playwright in England. She composed her liturgical plays for ardently religious and pragmatically didactic reasons. She wished to dramatize the Easter offices, she says, in order to "dispel the sluggish indifference of the faithful" and to increase devotion, interest, and piety among people attending the services. Her adaptations in Latin of the traditional liturgical ceremonies at Easter are recognized to constitute a far more impressive effort in the way of dramatic realism than do other contemporary ventures. K.'s *Depositio Crucis,* celebrated at the close of the Matins, contains such animated and realistic details as the removal of Christ's figure from the cross and the cleansing of his wounds with wine and water by Joseph and Nicodemus. Her adaptation of the *Elevatio Hostiae* contains a representation of the *Harrowing of Hell* whereby members of the convent (representing the patriarchs in Hell awaiting the coming of Christ) wait behind closed doors at the chapel of Mary Magdalene and come forth, carrying palm leaves, after the priest (representing Christ) had knocked on the door three times.

K.'s *Visitatio Sepulchri* also contains several inventions. The three Marys, for example, are played by nuns and not, as was usual, by clerics; Mary Magdalen converses with a second angel after the other two Marys had entered the tomb; and the three Marys engage in a dialogue with the clergy representing the disciples. In her copious rubrics preceding the play, K. gives directions for the three nuns representing the three Marys to be dressed, confessed, and absolved by the abbess before the play.

K.'s imaginative adaptations are especially noteworthy for their attempt at representation (though not quite impersonation) and her elaboration of and addition to the speeches by the characters of her plays.

WORKS: (modern editions): *The Ordinale and Customary of the Benedictine Nuns of Barking Abbey,* ed. J.B.L. Tolburst (1977–78). Young, K. *Transactions of the Wisconsin Academy of Sciences, Arts and Letters* (1910).Young, K. *The Drama of the Medieval Church* (1933).

BIBLIOGRAPHY: Cotton, N. *Women Playwrights in England c. 1363–1750* (1980). Young, K. *The Drama of the Medieval Church* (1933).

For articles in reference works, see: *Bloomsbury. Oxford. ToddBWW.*

Katharina M. Wilson

Anna Kavan (Helen Woods Edmonds)

BORN: 10 April 1901, Cannes, France.
DIED: 5 December 1967, London.
DAUGHTER OF: Claude Charles Edwards Woods and Helen Eliza Bright.
MARRIED: Donald Ferguson, c. 1920; Stuart Edmonds, c. 1930.
WROTE UNDER: Helen Ferguson; Anna Kavan.

K.'s experimental novels and short stories place her in the realm of literary modernism. During her sixty-seven years she wrote eighteen books, worked as an assistant editor for *Horizon* magazine and as a military psychiatric worker, raised bulldogs, and designed houses; she was also an accomplished painter. Her writings, many of them cryptic and symbolic, have been called "before their time" in both technique and content. As an author, K. exhibits skill in description and a penchant for unusual narrative designs. She employs a variety of forms such as dreams, parables, allegories, and tales. Her style is characterized by economy, clarity, and concreteness. Her most successful novel, *Ice* (1967), presents a futuristic vision of the end of the world by ice and a man's harrowing search for a thin helpless blonde girl as the ever-encroaching ice gets closer and closer. This work, sometimes classified as science fiction, is told in a narrative of fluctuating reality where the distinctions between reality and unreality have become blurred.

As a child K. was financially but not emotionally well provided for. Her father committed suicide when K. was quite young, and her mother felt K.'s birth to be an intrusion on her privacy and an embarrassment to her youth. She both dominated and neglected the child, leaving her with relatives and strangers and then reappearing to whisk her off on a cross-continental or cross-Atlantic excursion that could last for months before returning her to England again. K. was educated in a Church of England school, by private tutors, and in California, New York, and France. She enjoyed being physically active and showed a talent for both writing and painting.

When she was in her late teens, to escape her mother's dominance and to gain independence, K. married a wealthy Scotsman, Donald Ferguson, who was in the foreign service. K. went to Burma with him in the early 1920s, but it was not a happy marriage. By 1926, she had returned to England with her two-year-old son, Brian. According to her unpublished diaries, she felt nothing but hatred for the father of her child. In this same year she began an emotional affair with Englishman Stuart Edmonds, whom she subsequently married in around 1930. Edmonds encouraged K. to enroll in the Central Academy of Art in London. K. believed that creativity and productivity were essential to existence, and so she was eager to select her lifework. She considered herself to be a failure, however, as she had already tried "medicine, writing, and marriage" and was a success at none.

By 1929, she was able to publish her first novel, *A Charmed Circle,* which examines the problem of two sisters attempting to achieve independence and self-fulfillment in a hostile environment of familial disapproval and cultural disarray. She published this book and the five subsequent ones under her first married name, Helen Ferguson. These early works, including *Let Me Alone* (1930), *The Dark Sisters* (1930), *A Stranger Still* (1935), *Goose Cross* (1936), and *Rich Get Rich* (1937), represent a particular segment of K.'s career; these books, exploring the subject of "suburban neurosis," are written in a conventional manner with named characters and logical plots. They reflect the author's interest in descriptive and lyrical writing, psychological representation, and social issues.

K.'s marriage to Edmonds was happy at first, but as he went through a transformation from bohemian artist to successful real estate agent and Sunday painter, she began to be bored with him. As they drew farther apart, K. lapsed into mental illness. She had begun using drugs during the late 1920s, mostly for the treatment of insomnia, and her drug use, combined with a suicidal tendency, manifested itself into a series of mental breakdowns and two incarcerations. After her second period in a mental institution, following the dictum of the surrealist, André Breton, "Changez la vie!," K. died her hair blonde, grew very thin, and changed her name to Anna Kavan. She also registered herself with the British authorities as a drug addict, which enabled her to receive heroin by prescription. Divorcing Edmonds sometime in the late 1930s, K. assumed her previous lifestyle and spent much of her time traveling. She went to New York and New Zealand and then returned to London where she worked for a year in a military psychiatric unit taking case histories. In 1943, she was hired as an editorial assistant on the avant-garde literary magazine, *Horizon,* edited by Cyril Connolly.

K., who had taken her name from one of her own characters in *Let Me Alone* and *A Stranger Still,* published five books during the 1940s, a period marking the beginning of her mature style. As she changed from suburban characters to inmates in a mental institution, she sharpened the narrative focus on internal psychological processes. *Asylum Piece* (1940) and *I Am Lazarus* (1945) are collections of short stories that robe the psyches of the mentally ill and the emotionally disturbed.

K.'s main concern during this period was the importance of the individual's rights to maintain dissenting views in a rapidly changing British society. Having gained the reputation as an expert on psychological methods, K. was also critical of certain psychological treatments such as insulin shock therapy, the effects of which she portrays in her story "I Am Lazarus," published in *Horizon* in 1943. Some of K.'s other fictional interests include natural history and the presentation of dreams. These two elements come together in her masterly two-page short story "The Gannets" in *I Am Lazarus,* a gruesome nightmarish vision of the tragic post-war world.

In 1948, K. published *Sleep Has His House,* an experimental novel that attempts to delineate the existence of "a nighttime world" and a character whose predominant existence is in the world of dreams. This book's lack of critical success was a disappointment for K., so, other than a brief collaboration with her friend and doctor, K. T. Bluth, on a short novel, *The Horse's Tale,* K. spent her time traveling to Switzerland and South Africa and considered a return to painting as her profession.

In 1956, her publishing connections in a bad state, she partially subsidized a small press to publish *A Scarcity of Love,* an exploration of the effects on personality development of the absence of genuine affection. The book received a favorable review by Edwin Muir in the London *Sunday Times,* but before it could be distributed the publisher went bankrupt and the book was pulped. In 1957, K. published the first of the three novels that are her best work, *Eagle's Nest.* With strong undertones of Franz Kafka, K. creates a nightmare vision of confusion and misfortune. This dream technique was used again in her 1963 novel, *Who Are You?,* which is actually a rewrite of the early work *Let Me Alone.* Her final dream work, *Ice,* brought her literary recognition since it was published in both England and the United States and translated into French and Italian.

The increased interest in modernist writing by women has created a new interest in K.'s works. Her elliptical narratives seem to baffle more than please critics, but K.'s carefully constructed tales and visions yield an excellent but gloomy commentary on the state of the twentieth-century world.

WORKS: (as Helen Ferguson) *A Charmed Circle* (1929). (as Helen Ferguson) *Let Me Alone* (1930). (as Helen Ferguson) *The Dark Sisters* (1930). (as Helen Ferguson) *A Stranger Still* (1935). (as Helen Ferguson) *Goose Cross* (1936). (as Helen Ferguson) *Rich Get Rich* (1937). *Asylum Piece and Other Stories* (1940). *Change the Name* (1941). *I Am Lazarus* (1945). *Sleep Has His House* (1948). (with K. T. Bluth) *The Horse's Tale* (1949). *A Scarcity of Love* (1956). *Eagle's Nest* (1957). *A Bright Green Field* (1958). *Who Are You?* (1963). *Ice* (1967). *Julia and the Bazooka* (1970). *My Soul in China,* ed. R. Davies (1975). *The Parson* (1995).

BIBLIOGRAPHY: Crosland, M. *Beyond the Lighthouse* (1981). Davies, R., preface to *Let Me Alone* (1975). Davies, R., intro. to *Julia and the Bazooka* (1970). Owen, P., preface to *Asylum Piece* (1972). Seymour, M. *TLS* (16 June 1995).

For articles in reference works, see: *CA. CSLF. Feminist. SLF. ToddBWW. WA.*

Other references: Aldiss, B. *Billion Year Spree: The True History of Science Fiction* (1973). Byrne, J. *Extrapolation* (Spring 1982). Centing, R. *Under the Sign of Pisces* (Summer 1970). Gornick, V. *VV.* (2–8 December 1981). Muir, E. *LonSunT* (5 April 1956). Nin, A. *The Novel of the Future* (1968). Seymour, M. *TLS* (16 June 1995).

Priscilla Dorr

Julia Kavanagh

BORN: 1824, Thurles, Ireland.
DIED: 28 October 1877, Nice, France.
DAUGHTER OF: Peter Morgan Kavanagh.

Novelist and biographer, K. lived much of her early life in France, the scene of many of her novels. Settling in London in 1844, she began her writing career partially as a support for her invalid mother, partially because of her interest in social amelioration. Her family life was not very satisfactory. Although a lifelong invalid requiring a daughter's constant supervision, her mother survived her by a decade; her father, himself a writer and self-styled philologist, damaged her growing literary reputation in 1857 by passing off a poor novel of his own, *The Hobbies,* as one of hers.

K.'s third book, *Madeleine* (1848), based on the life of a peasant girl of Auvergne, brought her to the notice of critics and public alike. K. continued to utilize her detailed knowledge of France in a collective biography, *Woman in France During the Eighteenth Century* (1850) and in many of her novels. Charlotte Brontë praised *Nathalie* (1850), whose heroine—small, defenseless, deprived of compatible intellectual companionship—possibly suggested Brontë's Lucy Snowe in *Villette.* Rose, the heroine's sister, Brontë thought to be autobiographical. *Nathalie,* set in a girls' school in northern France, addresses itself to the question of whether experience is self-fulfillment or the expiation for sin that it is seen to be in a convent where young women are taught to submit to the rules of society.

Although her fresh French material gave K. her first hearing, the condition of England, rather than the exotic landscape of France, seized her imagination as she became acclimatized to England as an adult. In *Rachel Grey: A Tale Founded on Fact* (1856), she depicted, through the eyes of an orphaned working girl, how relentless striving for success affected both the workers and managers who were driven by the standard of success imposed upon them. Rachel departs from the typical stereotype of the Victorian heroine by learning to work well with her male relations and outsiders. Although George Eliot's review faulted the novel as narrative, *Rachel Grey* is considered to have influenced her own work. Having elected to set the novel in a part of England Eliot knew well, K. is justifiably criticized by an expert for not being at home with the speech and folkways of her characters.

Whether set in England or on the Continent, K.'s novels reached a large audience as serialized in periodicals or published as multivolume novels. She figured prominently in the Tauchnitz series of British novel reprints; although considered a woman's novelist and thus meant only to entertain, K. nonetheless addressed herself consistently to the problems of women in an unreformed but reformable society.

WORKS: *The Montyon Prizes* (1846). *The Three Paths: A Story for Young People* (1848; in the U.S. as *Saint-Gildes; or, The Three Paths,* 1856). *Madeleine: A Tale of Auvergne* (1848). *Nathalie: A Tale* (1850). *Woman in France During the Eighteenth Century* (1850). *Women of Christianity Exemplary for Acts of Piety and Charity* (1852). *Daisy Burnbs: A Tale* (1853). *Grace Lee: A Tale* (1855). *Rachel Grey: A Tale Founded on Fact* (1856). *Adele: A Tale* (1858). *A Summer and Winter in the Two Sicilies* (1858). *Seven Years and Other Tales* (1860). *French Women of Letters: Biographical Sketches* (1863). *English Women of Letters: Biographical Sketches* (1863).

Queen Mab: A Novel (1863). *Beatrice: A Novel* (1865). *Sybil's Second Love: A Novel* (1867). *Dora: A Novel* (1868). *Silvia* (1870). *Bessie: A Novel* (1872). *John Dorrien: A Novel* (1875). *The Pearl Fountain and Other Fairy Tales* (1876). *Two Lilies: A Novel* (1877). *Forget-me-not* (1878).

BIBLIOGRAPHY: Colby, R. *Fiction with a Purpose* (1967). Foster, S. *EA* (1982).

For articles in reference works, see: *Bloomsbury. Cambridge. DNB. Feminist. Oxford. ToddBWW. VB.*

Eleanor Langstaff

Sheila Kaye-Smith

BORN: 4 February 1887, St.-Leonard's-on-the-Sea, Sussex.
DIED: 14 January 1956, near Rye, Sussex.
DAUGHTER OF: Edward Kaye-Smith.
MARRIED: Theodore Penrose Fry, 1924.

K. was a popular, prolific regional novelist between the world wars who continued writing, though less successfully, to the end of her life. Most of her forty-six books are novels. She also collaborated on two studies of Jane Austen and wrote various other volumes, including autobiographical and bibliographical works, poetry, and stories. She was raised in Sussex (the area about which she wrote most frequently), the daughter of a country physician and a French Huguenot whose parents had emigrated from France. A bright child, she wrote from childhood on, publishing her first novel, *The Tramping Methodist* (1908), when she was twenty-one. From the beginning, she was compared favorably to Thomas Hardy and Maurice Hewlett, who also wrote about rural England. Though raised in a Protestant family, she became first an Anglo-Catholic and then, with her husband, a Church of England clergyman, a convert to Roman Catholicism.

K. published six additional novels (mostly melodramatic and sentimental) before succeeding with *Sussex Gorse* (1916), still considered one of her finest books. After this work K. avoided the sentimental, strove for greater realism, and began to emphasize regionalism and stronger characterization of the rural men and women who peopled her novels. She depicts Reuben Backfield, a nineteenth-century landowner, as being so obsessed with developing his land that he becomes hateful and isolated; once his plan succeeds, however, with all his family and friends having deserted him, he dies at age eighty-five, a happy man. *Sussex Gorse* received consistent high praise, despite some critics' feeling that Sussex was too limited a source for fiction.

With *Joanna Godden* (1921), K. wrote her first book with a strong female protagonist, about a tenacious woman who must take control of her dead father's prosperous farm. Her success exceeds her expectations, making the property more valuable than ever (despite other, male, farmers' efforts) and simultaneously maintaining a complicated personal life. Joanna Godden is presented vividly and memorably, and despite defeats and heartbreaks she prevails. *The End of the House of Alard* (1923) was K.'s first best seller and focused on her Anglo-Catholicism. Set immediately after World War I, the novel concerns class conflicts on hereditary estates as well as conflicts between Low Church and High Church Anglicanism. Her rather stereotyped characters in this novel tended toward flatness, as L. P. Hartley noted, and the "painful" book seemed to him to be based on a false assumption about a family's living so "steadfastly and stupidly in the past" that K.'s superb handling of the clashes, not the issues themselves, dominate. As the Alard family dies out, the void is filled by previously declassé people who look to the future, not the past.

Shortly after she converted to Roman Catholicism, K. wrote *The History of Susan Spray, the Female Preacher* (1931), about a woman raised in a free-church religious tradition derived from Calvinism who serves as an itinerant preacher, presumably by inspiration of God but actually, at first, as rationalization for her unwillingness to work at physical labor. So persuaded is she of her inspiration, though, that she eventually achieves high status as a prophet as well as enduring personal complications. Her behavior may be hypocritical, or it may be based on true conviction; either way, she is successful and uses her talents effectively.

Rarely did K. permit her personal religious convictions to intrude into her fiction, other than in *The End of the House of Alard* and, to a lesser extent, in *Gallybird* (1934) and *Superstition Corner* (1934), both of which use her Roman Catholicism to suggest the progressive decline in the sixteenth and seventeenth centuries of the same Alard family whose end she wrote about previously. K. eloquently defended her use of her Catholicism as foundations for her fiction (in her autobiographical *Three Ways Home,* 1937). None of her more than a dozen novels after *Gallybird* and *Superstition Corner* were as eloquent a defense, nor did any make much of an impact as fiction.

K. wrote a number of nonfiction works as well, notably *Talking of Jane Austen* (1943; in the U. S. as *Speaking of Jane Austen,* 1944) and *More About Jane Austen* (1949; in the U. K. as *More Talk of Jane Austen,* 1950), both written in alternating chapters with G. B. Stern and both charming, conversational sets of impressions, quizzes, and analyses of characters. She also wrote *John Galsworthy* (1916), *Anglo-Catholicism* (1925), *Mirror of the Months* (1931), *The Weald of Kent and Sussex* (1953), and *All the Books of My Life: A Bibliography* (1956).

It is for her novels, however, for which K. is best remembered; despite her occasional two-dimensional characters with their explicitly doctrinaire religious views and excessive ambitions, her excessively detailed settings, and her dependence on overly complicated plots, she is at her best a natural storyteller who writes about her native Sussex with obvious affection and knowledge. Like Hardy, she is a fine regionalist and social historian, even if she lacks much of the tragic element that makes Hardy's novels so enduring. Still, three or four of her many novels are likely to endure as accurate, moving portraits of life in provincial England before the encroachment of the modern world.

WORKS: *The Tramping Methodist* (1908). *Starbrace* (1909). *Spell Land: The Story of a Sussex Farm* (1910). *Isle of*

Thorns (1913). *Willow's Forge and Other Poems* (1914). *Three Against the World* (1914; in the U.S. as *The Three Furlongers*). *John Galsworthy* (1916). *Sussex Gorse: The Story of a Fight* (1916). *The Challenge to Sirius* (1917). *Little England* (1918; in the U.S. as *The Four Roads*, 1919). *Tamarisk Town* (1919). *Green Apple Harvest* (1920). *Joanna Godden* (1920). *Saints in Sussex* (1923). *The End of the House of Alard* (1923). *The George and the Crown* (1924). *Anglo-Catholicism* (1925). *The Mirror of the Months* (1925). *Joanna Godden Married and Other Stories* (1926). *Iron and Smoke* (1928). *The Village Doctor* (1929). *Sin* (1929). (with J. Hampden) *Mrs. Adis, and The Mock-Beggar* (1929). *Shepherds in Sackcloth* (1930). *Songs Late and Early* (1931). *The History of Susan Spray, the Female Preacher* (1931; in the U.S. as *Susan Spray*). *The Children's Summer* (1932; in the U.S. as *Summer Holiday*). *The Ploughman's Progress* (1933; in the U.S. as *Gipsy Wagon: The Story of a Ploughman's Progress*). *Gallybird* (1934). *Superstition Corner* (1934). *Selina Is Older* (1935; in the U.S. as *Selina*). *Rose Deeprose* (1936). *Three Ways Home* (1937). *Faithful Stranger and Other Stories* (1938). *The Valiant Woman* (1938). *Ember Lane: A Winter's Tale* (1940). *The Hidden Son* (1941; in the U.S. as *The Secret Son*, 1942). (with G. B. Stern) *Talking of Jane Austen* (1943; in the U.S. as *Speaking of Jane Austen*, 1944). *Tambourine, Trumpet and Drum* (1943). *Kitchen Fugue* (1945). *The Lardners and the Laurelwoods* (1947). *The Happy Tree* (1949; in the U.K. as *The Treasure of the Snow*, 1950). (with G. B. Stern) *More About Jane Austen* (1949; in the U.K. as *More Talk of Jane Austen*, 1950). *Mrs. Gailey* (1951). *Quartet in Heaven* (1952). *The Weald of Kent and Sussex* (1953). *The View from the Parsonage* (1954). *All the Books of My Life: A Bibliography* (1956).

BIOLOGRAPHY: Allen, W. G. *Irish Ecclesiastical Record* (1947). Doyle, P. A. *ELT* (1972, 1973, 1974, 1975). Hopkins, R. T. *Sheila Kaye-Smith and the Weald Country* (1925). Walker, D. *Sheila Kaye-Smith* (1980).

For articles in reference works, see: *Bloomsbury*. *BCathA*. *CA*. *Cambridge*. *CN*. *CWA*. *DLB*. *Feminist*. *MBL*. *Oxford*. *TCA* and *SUP*. *TCLC*. *TCW*. *ToddBWW*.

Other references: Adcock, A. St.-J. *Gods of Modern Grub Street: Impressions of Contemporary Authors* (1923). Alexander, C. *The Catholic Literary Revival: Three Phases in Its Development from 1845 to the Present* (1935). Anderson, R., intro. to *Joanna Godden* (rpt. 1983). Bowen, R. O. *Renascence* (Spring 1955). Braybrooke, P. *Some Goddesses of the Pen* (1927). Braybrooke, P. *Some Catholic Novelists: Their Art and Outlook* (1931). Cavaliero, G. *The Rural Tradition in the English Novel, 1900–1939* (1977). Cowley, M. *The Dial* (February 1920). Daiglish, D. N. *Contemporary Review* (January 1925). Drew, E. A. *The Modern Novel: Some Aspects of Contemporary Fiction* (1926). George, W. L. *Literary Chapters* (1918). Hartley, L. P. *Spectator* (15 September 1923). Johnson, R. B. *Some Contemporary Novelists (Women)* (1920). Kernahan, C. *Five More Famous Living Poets: Introductory Studies* (1928). Lawrence, M. *The School of Femininity* (1936). *LonT* (16 January 1956). Mackenzie, M. *Thought* (June 1931). Malone, A. E. *Living Age* (1924). Malone, A. E. *Fortnightly Review* (2 August 1926). Mansfield, K. *Athenaeum* (12 September 1919). Montefiore, J., intro. to *The History of Susan Spray: The Female Preacher*(rpt. 1983). *North American Review* (December 1916). *NYT* (16 January 1956). *NYTBR* (5 February 1922). O'Brien, J. A. *The Road to Damascus* (1949). Pendry, E. D. *The New Feminism of English Fiction: A Study in Contemporary Women-Novelists* (1956). Quigley, J. *Fortnightly Review* (1 October 1923). Roberts, R. E. *Bookman* (London) (March 1923). Smaridge, N. *Famous British Women Novelists* (1967). *Saturday Review* (London) (3 May 1930), Stack, M. *Commonweal* (18 January 1935). Stern, G. B. *YR* (October 1925). Stern, G. B. *And Did He Stop and Speak to You?* (1958). Swinnerton, F. *The Georgian Literary Scene, 1910–1935* (1935; rev. 1969).

Paul Schlueter

Molly Keane (Mary Nesta Skrine Keane)

BORN: 4 July 1904, County Kildare, Ireland.
DIED: 22 April 1996, Ardmore, County Waterford, Ireland.
DAUGHTER OF: Walter Clarmont Skrine and Agnes Shakespeare Higginson Skrine.
MARRIED: Robert Lumley Keane, 1938.
WROTE UNDER: M. J. Farrell; Molly Keane.

K., one of five children born to Anglo-Irish gentry, had a successful, though intermittent, literary career as both novelist and playwright; that career can be divided into two periods: 1928–61 (eleven novels, four plays); and 1981–96 (three novels, two nonfiction works). During the first period, K. wrote under the pen name "M. J. Farrell," in order, she says, "to hide my literary side from my sporting friends." Her novels were favorably received by press and public alike. Her first two plays, *Spring Meeting* (1938) and *Ducks and Drakes* (produced 1941), written with John Perry and directed by John Gielgud, prompted comparison with Noël Coward's bright, sophisticated comedies; *Guardian Angel* (1944) and *Treasure Hunt* (1952) confirmed that estimate.

The death of her husband at the age of thirty-six and the failure of her fifth play, *Dazzling Prospect* (1961), led to her withdrawal from the world of letters for a time. Nearly three decades after the publication of her eleventh novel, *Treasure Hunt* (1952), K. appeared with a new novel, *Good Behaviour* (1981), quickly followed by *Time After Time* (1983). Her last novel, *Loving and Giving*, appeared in 1988; it was published in the United States as *Queen Lear* (1989).

The world of K.'s early years is the world of her novels: the Ireland of stately, if decaying, houses, interminable hunts, and high-spirited horses. Reared in an atmosphere of benign neglect by a father impervious to cold and pain and a mother more interested in poetry than children, K. and her four siblings developed close, lasting relationships. Their lives revolved around the pleasures of the hunt and of a social life circumscribed by class and culture with a particular code dictating good behavior.

K.'s first novel, *The Knight of Cheerful Countenance* (1926), written at the age of seventeen, establishes the ground she would work in all her fiction: a story of broken hearts and reputations set among the landed Anglo-Irish gentry who live in the big-house world of hunting and dancing. K. displays precocious gifts for storytelling, psychological insight, and social comment. *The Knight of Cheerful Countenance* disappeared for decades, but was rediscovered in 1992 in the British Library and reprinted by Virago in 1993.

Young Entry (1928), a Gothic tale of two young women entering the adult world, displays K.'s sharp eye for description, particularly of landscape and animal life, keen insight into character, and acute ear for dialogue. *Taking Chances* (1929) offers a witty comedy of manners: four key characters and a fifth, who ruins the lives of all, trade love and venom in an Irish countryside of dogs, horses, fox hunting, and martinis. In *Mad Puppetstown* (1931), place is dominant: Puppetstown, a wild and romantic Irish country house belonging to the Chevingtons, is the central character, exerting magnetic force to the plot. Likewise, *Conversation Piece* (1932; in the U.S. as *Point-to-Point*) is light on plot and character; it is really a study of the savage, brutal appeal of blood sport among the Anglo-Irish gentry.

Both *Devoted Ladies* (1934) and *Full House* (1935) demonstrate K.'s acid wit; with satiric edge she attacks the pseudoliterary and artistic world of London, creating a memorable rogues' gallery of characters in the process. The emphasis in *Full House* is also on satire: locale recedes as character occupies center stage in this novel, which studies inherited insanity. In *The Rising Tide* (1937), K. traces the fortunes of the French-McGrath family during the first two decades of this century, telling a poignant tale of power and pain.

K.'s current reputation rests on her three recent novels. She began this second literary career after widowhood and the marriage of her daughters because, she says, "I had time on my hands and a lack of money . . . and a wish to write again and prove myself." *Good Behaviour*, shortlisted for the Booker Prize in 1981, is a black comedy that opens with a chilling death scene. Miss Aroon St. Charles, the obese, unmarried, only surviving child of an Anglo-Irish family, kills her mother by feeding her rabbit quenelles. The rest of the novel, a flashback told by Aroon, a naïve and unreliable narrator, details life at Temple Alice, the family house, with a philandering amputee of a father, an elegant, malicious mother, a homosexual brother, and a cast of roguish retainers. The death of the brother and the father's stroke rearrange the household; Aroon, though victimized and dominated by her mother, takes charge, vindicated in the end when her father leaves Temple Alice to her, not to her mother. Consistently misinterpreting most events, Aroon nonetheless practices the "good behaviour" expected by her narrow social world, deluded into believing that "all my life so far I have done everything for the best reasons and the most unselfish motives."

Time After Time returns to the same basic plot structure of *Taking Chances:* four characters whose lives are ruined by the actions of a fifth. April, May, June, and Jasper Swift, aged Irish siblings living at Durraghglass, are visited by their blind Jewish cousin Leda. Each of the Swifts is disfigured in some way: April, deaf, vain, and addicted to exotic diets; May, a kleptomaniac with a deformed hand; June, mentally slow and dyslexic; Jasper, blind in one eye from a childhood mishap. Confined in their once-grand country house, the four survive in malicious balance by torturing each other with petty cruelties. Even their various dogs and cats reflect their owners' love-hate dependency. But it is spiritual, not physical, deformity that makes each of these characters so repulsive. K. catalogues their sins, foibles, and shortcomings; in some ways the chaos, filth, and decay of their house are metaphors for the states of their souls. K. spins a narrative with perfect timing, carefully revealing the shameful secret each Swift harbors and bringing everything to a head in a wonderfully vicious "true confessions" scene orchestrated by Leda at breakfast one morning. These two dark comedies, frequently called modern classics by contemporary critics, are illuminated by K.'s poetic descriptions of the world of nature. Her specialty is the use of the unreliable narrator, a technique that invites the reader to discover truths about the characters and events in her novels that the characters themselves are unable (or unwilling) to see. In these two novels K. tells her story with renewed wit, devastating irony, and comic detachment, her novelist's powers undiminished.

K.'s last novel, *Loving and Giving* (1988), stays within familiar territory: the story of Nicandra Forester, daughter of Anglo-Irish gentry, married to Andrew Bland and subsequently divorced from him, the novel is a typical mix of pungent social comedy, satire, and serious issues, all set around another grand Irish country house, Deer Forest. Two elements seem amplified here, however: a subtle concern for demonstrating the impact of childhood social trauma on subsequent development, and a tone pervaded more by relief at a world well lost than by wistful regret.

K. has also written nonfiction. In *Molly Keane's Nursery Cooking* (1985), K. offers a collection of recipes almost incidental to the rich narrative of a child's life in the familiar world—upstairs and downstairs—of the big house in Ireland. The brief memoir of her childhood K. contributed to *Portrait of the Artist As a Young Girl* (ed. J. Quinn, 1987), while it covers some of the same territory, makes more pointed criticism of her upbringing. Her foreword to Sybil Connolly's *In An Irish House* (1988) succinctly captures the grandeur and decay of these domestic monuments. K. and her daughter Sally Phipps compiled *Molly Keane's Ireland* (1993), a seductive anthology of prose, poetry, and drama, judiciously chosen to represent the extraordinary range of Irish literature from earliest anonymous lyric to classic texts from James Joyce, William Butler Yeats, Seamus Heaney, Brian Friel, and others. The volume offers an evocative experience of Ireland, described by K. as "the country that owns me." Well into her tenth decade, K. continued to write, occasionally reviewing books for the British press from her house in County Waterford, a carefully restored Georgian structure featured in *Architectural Digest* (January 1986). She died in 1996.

Today K. deserves greater recognition for her ability to portray scenes from a vanished way of life; though her canvas is small, she renders all her subjects, whether human or animal, with attention to detail and considerable zest.

WORKS: *The Knight of Cheerful Countenance* (1926). *Young Entry* (1928). *Taking Chances* (1929). *Mad Puppetstown* (1931). *Conversation Piece* (1932; in the U.S. as *Point-to-Point*). *Red-Letter Days* (1933). *Devoted Ladies* (1934). *Full House* (1935). *The Rising Tide* (1937). (with J. Perry) *Spring Meeting* (1938). *Two Days in Aragon* (1941). (with J. Perry) *Ducks and Drakes* (1941). *Guardian Angel* (1944). *Treasure Hunt* (1952). *Loving Without Tears* (1951; in the U.S. as *The Enchanting Witch*). *Dazzling Prospect* (1961). *Good Behaviour* (1981). *Time After Time* (1983). *Molly Keane's Nursery Cooking* (1985). *Loving and Giving* (1988; in the U.S. as *Queen Lear*, 1989).

BIBLIOGRAPHY: Blackwood, C. *Harper's & Queen* (November 1985). Boylan, C., in *Contemporary British Women Writers: Texts and Strategies*, ed. R. E. Hosmer, Jr. (1993). Cahalan, J. *The Irish Novel: A Critical History* (1988). Devlin, P., in *Writing Lives: Conversations Between Women Writers*, ed. M. Chamberlain (1988). Elliott, M., in *The Big House in Ireland, Reality and Representation*, ed. J. Genet (1991). Hargreaves, T., in *Cultural Contexts and Literary Idioms in Contemporary Irish Literature*, ed. M. Kenneally (1988). Hildebidle, J., *Five Irish Writers* (1989). Imhof, R., in *Ancestral Voices: The Big House in Anglo-Irish Literature*, ed. O. Rauchbauer (1992). Kreilkamp, V. *MR* (1987). O'Toole, B., in *Across a Roaring Hill: The Protestant Imagination in Modern Ireland. Essays in Honour of John Hewitt*, ed. G. Dawe and E. Longley (1985). *Portrait of the Artist As a Young Girl*, ed. J. Quinn (1987). Parkin, A., in *Cultural Contexts and Literary Idioms in Contemporary Irish Literature*, ed. M. Kenneally (1988).

For articles in reference works, see: *Bloomsbury. CA. CLC. CN. Feminist.* Higginson, A. H. *British and American Sporting Authors* (1949). *Oxford.*

Other references: *Harper's* (January 1984). *LonSunT* (11 September 1988). *Newsweek* (15 January 1984). *New Republic* (6 June 1981, 30 January 1984). *New York* (16 January 1984). *New Yorker* (13 October 1986). *NYRB* (12 April 1984). *NYT* (10 January 1981). *NYTBR* (10 March 1929, 16 February 1930, 19 June 1932, 9 April 1933, 10 June 1934, 27 October 1935, 9 August 1981, 22 January 1984). *Observer* (18 September 1988; 12 November 1989). *Saturday Review* (London) (12 February 1938). *Spectator* (24 September 1988). *TLS* (22 March 1928, 25 July 1929, 10 September 1931, 9 October 1981, 9 September 1988, 13 July 1991).

Robert Ellis Hosmer, Jr. and Marjorie Podolsky

Adelaide Kemble

BORN: c. 1814, London.
DIED: 4 August 1879, Warsash House, Hampshire.
DAUGHTER OF: Charles Kemble and Marie Thérèse (Maria Theresa) De Camp Kemble.
MARRIED: Edward John Sartoris, 1843.
WROTE UNDER: Adelaide Sartoris.

During her lifetime, K. achieved public recognition primarily as a dramatic vocalist; her career as an author was secondary to and perhaps brought about by experiences related to her life as an opera singer. She was the younger daughter of famous parents, both actors with long careers and important reputations. Her sister, Frances Anne (Fanny), was an extremely popular actress who later published three volumes of reminiscences. She had two brothers, neither of whom was involved in theater: John Mitchell, a poet and archaeologist, and Henry, who was in the military until he was declared insane and institutionalized. Her mother was born in Vienna to a family of musicians and dancers.

Fanny Kemble later wrote of her sister that she had an "unquenchable musical genius" that alone sustained her "timid disposition" through her early years of vocal training, since their mother was critical of her efforts. Consequently, she was taught by her Aunt Adelaide ("Dal"), who was a patient teacher. K. sang professionally for the first time at a concert of ancient music on 13 May 1835 and at the York Festival the following September. She toured Germany and then Italy, where she met and studied with Guidetta Pasta, the great Italian singer for whom Vincenzo Bellini composed *Norma;* K. introduced that opera to England after her return in 1841, where it was met with great enthusiasm. K. received critical acclaim for her operatic talent, based not so much on the quality of her voice as on the nature of her personality and her sensitivity as an interpreter of dramatic roles. She was said to be the "greatest though not the best English singer of the century." Her musical career over after 1842, she married and raised her children. She sang frequently on social occasions but never returned to the stage, and she began directing her creative energy instead to writing. She is known to have written some songs, but none were published.

Her first literary work, *A Week in a French Country House*, appeared in *Cornhill Magazine* and was published as a book in 1867. Described by its author as "more than a sketch and less than a story," it is said to have attained popularity in its time because of the portraits of the celebrities it contained. Her reputed lighthearted personality and sensitivity are evidenced by the book's lively representation of nineteenth-century family life, social customs, furnishings, and food. English readers are taught about the rituals of the hunt in France, including the costumes, technique, and terminology. The characters are full of anecdotes interestingly and realistically related. K. was correct, though, in her assessment of the work as falling short of a real novel; while Bess, the first-person narrator, and her fiancé of eleven years finally manage to obtain the financial means to marry, there is no true plot. The details of that romance are essential to the entire work but are not the primary focus of the book, however; woven into the story as a kind of cautionary tale is the case of a couple who did not marry: Ursula and René. Although Bess is the narrator, it is the spirited Ursula who most resembles K. The two women together represent K.'s divided feelings about leaving her career to marry and raise children. René, a flamboyant individualist, confides to Bess that women adore the "masculine element" in Ursula but predicts that men will never adore her. He professes a desire for a weak, dependent, "feminine" woman, which Bess so obviously is, and then proposes to Ursula, who refuses. By speaking in Bess's voice, K. indicates that she had indeed given up those "early adventurous times," expressing her ambivalence over the prospect of doing so through the yet-untamed Ursula.

K.'s second book, *Medusa and Other Tales* (1868), is a collection of short pieces and was republished in 1880 with additions, which included some poetry, under the title *Past Hours,* with a preface by K.'s daughter. *Medusa,* the most strongly developed piece in the collection, is a novella, smoothly and gracefully written. It is a strange, absorbing tale containing Gothic elements and further develops K.'s ambivalence about women's roles, focusing on aberrant styles of mothering.

The story, whose protagonist is Edward Saville, a wealthy, idle man of twenty-nine, is filled with a variety of mothers. "Good" mothers come in strange shapes and are difficult to recognize. Mrs. Hausmann, initially described by Edward as "Medusa," is subsequently revealed to be an extraordinary mother. She had raised the mysterious Wanda, with whom Edward is in love, among her own children. Mrs. Hausmann fiercely mothers not only her own children but also Wanda, whose madness burdens her with special requirements. An unlikely mother is Harty, Edward's thirty-nine-year-old cousin, who lived twenty years in a childless marriage with William Brande, twenty-two years her senior. She had married William because he was "dear and good," "excellently kind," and "so perfect for mamma." William is not affected by their childlessness, but Harty attempts throughout to mother Edward. A tragic mother is Wanda's Brontë-esque mother, also named Wanda, who, as a dowerless girl of seventeen had been given to a sinister fifty-five-year-old count by her parents. After a difficult pregnancy and labor, she gives birth not to the son and heir the count expects but to a frail baby girl. In a rage, the count takes the baby from her, giving it to Mrs. Hausmann to raise, and Wanda becomes mad, prefiguring her daughter.

The younger Wanda gives birth to a son and through a "most remarkable and powerful development of maternal instinct" experiences a "decided reawakening of her intellect." Her respite from madness is short lived; again in a rage, her father wrenches the child from her, and the details of the story suggest that Wanda murders the child rather than part from it. Wanda's madness is treated by a specialist who, observing her behavior with a two-year-old boy she loves, advises that marriage and children would cure her. Incapable of caring for herself, Wanda proves a remarkable mother, redeemed by a powerful, selfless maternal act; as she attempts to rescue the young boy, she drowns.

The story, like other Gothic stories, raises questions about women's domestic responsibilities and the roles and values of those roles that women are expected to play in society. Motherhood is a paradox. It is a tragic experience that may cause a woman to lose her mind, yet it has the power to redeem. Women who do not have children, however, may impose the patriarchal imperative of childbearing on themselves by seeking children to mother. A "good" mother is complicated to define because she is so difficult to recognize; indeed, "good" mothers may not even be known to themselves. Madness is a metaphor for what society considers the deviant behavior of women who fail to bear children, and the cure, of course, is a family. Madwomen who cannot control the destinies of their children must relinquish authority to the patriarchy once the biological process is complete. Their alternative is to become child-destroying mothers.

Medusa continues the discourse on marriage begun in *A Week in a French Country House.* It continues to wonder why and whom women marry and reflects on the consequences—motherhood. In both works, feminist ideas are nestled among witty conversations and sparkling repartee. Both provide a space for K. to reflect on her decision to abandon her career to devote herself to her family and to consider the cost of becoming a mother.

WORKS: *A Week in a French Country House* (1867). *Medusa and Other Tales* (1868; rpt. with additions as *Past Hours,* 1880).

BIBLIOGRAPHY: Butler, F. K. *Records of a Girlhood* (1830). Butler, F. K. *Records of a Later Life* (1846). Chorley, H. F. *Thirty Years of Musical Recollections* (1862). Gordon, M. E., preface to *Past Hours.* Ritchie, A. T., preface to 1903 ed. of *A Week in a French Country House.*

For articles in reference works, see: *DNB. Feminist. Oxford. ToddBWW.*

Dolores De Luise

Fanny (Frances Anne) Kemble

BORN: 27 November 1809, London.
DIED: 15 January 1893, London.
DAUGHTER OF: Charles Kemble and Marie Thérèse (Maria Theresa) De Camp Kemble.
MARRIED: Pierce Butler, 1834.
WROTE UNDER: Fanny Kemble; Mrs. Kemble.

Born into England's first family of the theater, K. exemplifies what was possible for talented, assertive nineteenth-century women. Remembered chiefly for her incomparable readings of Shakespeare in England and America, she also received attention for her inspired acting and for her literary output. Her writings, spanning the Victorian era, include journals, poetry, letters, essays, historical dramas, and one novel, as well as translations of works by Friedrich Schiller and Alexandre Dumas, *père.*

K. was the third generation of Kembles to work in the theater, although she always preferred writing to acting. Niece of John Philip Kemble and Sarah Siddons and daughter of the actor-proprietor of Covent Garden and an actress, K. made her acting debut as Juliet in 1829 at Covent Garden, at the urgings of her family, to help stave off debt. Though she was an instant success, her efforts did not save her father from bankruptcy, and in 1832, father and daughter left for a two-year American theatrical tour to recoup funds. K. was wildly successful in America, but she most ardently desired a literary career like that of Sir Walter Scott, Lord Byron, or John Keats. In April 1834, she gladly rejected a stage career in favor of marriage to Pierce Butler, an American who had avidly pursued her since seeing her act in Philadelphia two years before. As K. later wrote to Anna Brownell Murphy Jameson nearly five months after her wedding, "In leaving the stage, I left nothing that I regretted."

Two years after their marriage, Butler inherited a Georgia plantation that made him one of the state's largest slaveholders, and he and K. went to live briefly at Sea Islands. This sojourn began the inexorable destruction of their marriage and, ironically, also provided the impetus for the work her admirer Henry James was to call her best prose work, *Journal of a Residence on a Georgian Plantation in 1838–1839*. The book, based on K.'s 100 days in Georgia, was not published until 1863, when it joined the debate over slavery at a crucial juncture in the North's will to triumph. Though K. wished only to bury her past, she was impelled to publish the journal to counteract the British interest in entering the American Civil War. Her book undoubtedly contributed to that decision, but it came too late to play the decisive role her biographers have attributed to it. Though subsequently neglected, the work deserves to be read as an important document in American cultural history. It argues passionately against slavery and includes many brutally realistic passages describing conditions on a southern plantation before the Civil War. It is also noteworthy for its fascinating insights into the life and mind of a talented Victorian personality.

Noting in 1839 that she had been ignorant of her husband's "dreadful possessions," K. found herself increasingly unable to overlook his values or unconventional lifestyle, though it is clear during these years that she most valued and passionately desired an intact family, especially after the birth of her two daughters. She moved away from her concern with abolition to fight to keep her family whole, but her effort failed in 1849, when Butler sued for divorce and won custody of their children until the girls came of age. Emotionally wounded by the sensational court case, K. returned to England, where she filled the next decade of her life by writing *A Year of Consolation* (1847) and returning to the stage. After appearing in several plays, K. settled into an extremely lucrative career staging readings of Shakespeare in England and America that won her universal praise and a secure financial future.

After her antislavery journal was published in 1863, K. lived for thirty more years, deriving satisfaction from closeness to her daughters and their families. Her first grandchild, Owen Wister, Jr., was later to continue the literary tradition of his grandmother by writing *The Virginian*. K. read Shakespeare on stage; she enjoyed the company of literary greats such as Robert Browning, Henry Wadsworth Longfellow, Henry James, and Edward FitzGerald; and she published a play, poems, and her autobiographical *Records of a Girlhood* (1878–79) and *Records of Later Life* (1882). James, her friend in old age, called these journals "one of the most animated autobiographies in the language." At eighty, she became a novelist for the first time, publishing *Far Away and Long Ago* (1889), a curious work that correlates with her earliest expressions of desire for a life of love and adventure. Though not carried off as she had wished in girlhood—"The death I should prefer would be to break my neck off the back of a good horse at a full gallop on a fine day"—she did manage to live life to the fullest, in good Romantic fashion, ranging over England and America in stage performance and trying her hand at numerous genres.Her active life as mother, writer, actress, and political activist correctly entitles her to an early biographer's subtitle, "a passionate Victorian." Both her life and literary works await definitive scholarly study.

WORKS: *Francis the First: An Historical Drama* (1832). *Journal of F. A. Butler* (1835). *The Star of Seville, A Drama in Five Acts* (1837). *Poems* (1844). *A Year of Consolation* (1847). *Journal of a Residence on a Georgian Plantation in 1838–1839* (1863). (trans.) *An English Tragedy, Mary Stuart,* by F. Schiller. (trans.) *Mademoiselle de Belle-Isle,* by A. Dumas, *père* (1863). *Poems* (1866). *Records of a Girlhood: An Autobiography* (1878–79). *Notes upon Some of Shakespeare's Plays* (1882). *Records of Later Life* (1882). *Adventures of John Timothy Homespun in Switzerland: A Play Stolen from the French of Tartann de Tarearcon* (1889). *Far Away and Long Ago* (1889). *Further Records, 1848–1883* (1890). *Fanny, The American Kemble: Her Journals and Unpublished Letters,* ed. F. K. Wister (1972). *Journal of a Young Actress,* ed. M. Gough and E. Fox-Genovese (1990). (with F. A. Butler-Leigh) *Principles and Privilege: Two Women's Lives on a Georgia Plantation* (1995).

BIBLIOGRAPHY: Allmendinger, B. *MissQ* (1988). Armstrong, M. *Fanny Kemble: A Passionate Victorian* (1938). Bobbe, D. *Fanny Kemble* (1931). Booth, A. *VS* (1995). Buckmaster, H. *Fire in the Heart* (1948). Byerly, A. *BuR* (1990). Clinton, C. *Frontiers* (1987). Driver, L. *Fanny Kemble* (1933). Fellini, T. *CQ* (1990). Furnas, J. C. *Fanny Kemble: Leading Lady of the Nineteenth Century Stage* (1982). Gibbs, H. *Affectionately Yours, Fanny: Fanny Kemble and the Theatre* (1945). Juncker, C., in *Rewriting the South,* ed. L. Honnighausen, et al. (1993). Kahan, G. *ThS* (1983). Marshall, D. *Fanny Kemble* (1977). Mulvey, C., in *Views of American Landscapes,* ed. M. Gigley and R. Lawson-Peebles (1989). Sanders, V. *PSt* (1986). Stevenson, J. *The Ardent Years* (1960). Taylor, M. A., in *The Image of the Child,* ed. S. P. Iskander (1991). *Fanny, The American Kemble: Her Journals and Unpublished Letters,* ed. F. K. Wister (1972). Wright, C. C. *Fanny Kemble and the Lovely Land* (1972).

For articles in reference works, see: *American Authors, 1600–1900. AWW. BA19C. Bloomsbury. Cambridge. DAB. DLB. Feminist. Library of Southern Literature. Notable American Women. Oxford. ToddBWW. VB.*

Other references: James, H. *Essays in London and Elsewhere* (1893). Lee, H. *Atlantic* (May 1893). McMahon, E. *Living Age* (1983). Miles, A. *The Poets and the Poetry of the Nineteenth Century* (1891). Pope-Hennessey, U. *Three English Women in America* (1929). Scott, J. A., ed. and intro. to *Journal of a Residence on a Georgian Plantation in America in 1838–1839* (1984).

Rhoda Flaxman
(updated by Natalie Joy Woodall)

Margery Kempe

BORN: c. 1373, Bishop's Lynn (today King's Lynn), Norfolk.
DIED: c. 1439.
DAUGHTER OF: John Brunham or Burnham.
MARRIED: John Kempe, c. 1393.

Often labeled "fanatic" and "hysterical," K. is perhaps one of the most immediate, personal, and fascinating religious mystics in England. Illiterate, she dictated her autobiography, *The Book of Margery Kempe,* in old age to an amanuensis, probably a priest. *The Book of Margery Kempe* is the first vernacular autobiography in England, and it relates K's life, sufferings, conversion, and subsequent conversations (dalliances) with God the Father, Christ, the Holy Spirit, the Virgin Mary, St. Catherine, St. Bridget, and other saints in great and lively detail. Throughout the book K. refers to herself almost invariably in the third person as "this creature" in apposition to God her Creator, whose glorification is ultimately the purpose of her book. K.'s visions are characterized by their vivid conciseness and are accompanied by sensual experiences (smells, sounds, and other sensations).

In her autobiography, K. reveals herself as a headstrong, determined woman. Her first vision of Christ came at the end of a long period of tribulations: an apparently difficult confinement and birth was followed by hallucinations in which devils threatened and tortured her and Christ came to her aid, consoling, calming, and healing her. This experience triggered her religious enthusiasm and initiated her path of piety, which, though interrupted at the onset by worldly ambitions and self-doubts, culminated in lively dalliances with Christ and His saints.

Having failed in several commercial ventures (brewing, milling), which she interpreted as God's punishment for her ostentation and worldly cares, she focused all her energies and determination on her religious experience. Her frequent fits of uncontrollable cryings, sighs, and lamentations not only in church but on pilgrimages and other public places as well earned her much scorn and criticism, occasionally even the accusation of hypocrisy. Nevertheless, firm in her faith (though not always sure of the genuineness of her revelation) and encouraged, too, by her confessors and spiritual counselors, Philip Repyngdon, bishop of Lincoln, and the Anchoress Julian of Norwich, among them, she pursued her religious career with a dogged determination and unfaltering decisiveness.

In 1413, as a result of her long insistence, she and her husband took vows of mutual continence and shortly thereafter she set out for the first of her long series of pilgrimages abroad and in England. Her travel to the Holy Land, beset with trials and difficulties but rich, too, in excruciatingly intense visionary experiences, is particularly informative. Accused more than once of Lollardy, because her brand of popular pietism smacked of heresy to the clerical class, she was vindicated every time as orthodox.

What makes *The Book of Margery Kempe* an invaluable literary and historic document are her uncompromising honesty even toward herself and her exuberantly vivid, clear style, devoid of theological and philosophical reflections but abounding in physical and psychological details; they make K. and her world come alive even to today's readers.

WORKS: *The Book of Margery Kempe,* ed. S. B. Meech and H. E. Allen (1940). *The Book of Margery Kempe: A Modern Version,* ed. W. Butler-Bowden (1944). *The Book of Margery Kempe,* ed. T. Triggs (1994).

BIBLIOGRAPHY: Atkinson, C. W. *Mystic and Pilgrim: The Book and World of Margery Kempe* (1983). Beckwith, S., in *Medieval Literature: Criticism, Ideology, and History,* ed. D. Aers (1986). Boyd, B. *Mystics Quarterly* (1986). Collis, L. *The Apprentice Saint* (1964). Collis, L. *Memoirs of a Medieval Woman* (1995). Cross, C., in *Medieval Women,* ed. D. Baker (1978). Goodman, A., in *Medieval Women,* ed. D. Baker (1978). Knowles, D. *The English Mystical Tradition* (1961). Provost, W., in *Medieval Women Writers,* ed. K. M. Wilson (1984). Staley, L. *Margery Kempe's Dissenting Fictions* (1994). Stone, R. K. *Middle English Prose Style: Margery Kempe and Julian of Norwich* (1970).

For articles in reference works, see: *Allibone. Bloomsbury. Cambridge. Cassell. Feminist. Oxford. ToddBWW.*

Katharina M. Wilson

Margaret Moore Kennedy

BORN: 23 April 1896, London.
DIED: 31 July 1967, Adderbury, Oxfordshire.
DAUGHTER OF: Charles Moore Kennedy and Elinor Marwood Kennedy.
MARRIED: David Davies, 1925.
WROTE UNDER: Margaret Kennedy.

K. was a lifelong writer, beginning before she could read or write with a "play" performed with other children, and including five novels and three plays (all destroyed) written before she entered Somerville College, Oxford. In her half-century of active writing as an adult, she wrote a textbook on modern European history as well as some thirty novels, plays, memoirs, and other nonfiction, in addition to film scripts (such as *The Little Friend,* written with Christopher Isherwood in 1936). From the start, she was known as a writer who was able to combine the major social issues and developments of her era with excellent storytelling talents.

K.'s first published novel, *The Ladies of Lyndon* (1923), was set in post–World War I England; it is a conventional, though perceptive, account of a "decorative" woman raised to be merely a suitable wife for a man; set on an English estate, the novel analyzes upper-class British society through the lives of a materialistic family. *The Constant Nymph* (1924; adapted for the stage, with Basil Dean, two years later) is also about an unhappy love affair, in this case about the naïve daughter, Tessa Sanger, of a composer (ostensibly based on the artist Augustus John) thrown into emotional chaos when her father dies and she has to fend for herself in her love for a musician: K.'s most popular novel, it was made into a 1943 film starring Charles Boyer and Joan Fontaine.

Red Sky at Morning (1927) also reflects an essentially romantic view of elegant life: A Victorian housekeeper keeps her dead husband's reputation alive, though he was little more than a hack writer, as she cares for her own children and their cousins, who, unlike her husband and her offspring, reflect greater talent, imagination, and freedom. K.'s somewhat contrived romantic relationships and maudlin conclusion make the novel less convincing as art but still valuable as social commentary.

The Fool of the Family (1930) is also about Tessa Sanger's family, in this case about two of her brothers, one a great artist, the other honest but dull. The two compete for the same woman, who is herself incapable of understanding love. An artist and his craving for success is also the subject of *Return I Dare Not* (1931), but this is generally considered too serious a handling of essentially comic material, as the playwright-protagonist desperately appeals for support from party-goers. The same privileged world is the setting for *The Midas Touch* (1938), *Troy Chimneys* (1952), and *The Heroes of Clone* (1957; in the U.S. as *The Wild Swan*), among K.'s other books, suggesting that her range in both setting and subject changed little over her career. K. often wrote of artists, particularly those who are misunderstood by society or who try to nurture wealthy benefactors.

K.'s last books suggest a certain sense of loss, not only of the England she had known as a young woman, but also of the values she herself knew. Her allegorical novel about the "seven deadly sins" (*The Feast,* 1950) was her first since 1938. Most of those that followed had flat characters and anachronistic viewpoints, only occasionally heightened by a sense of understanding of the modern world; in *The Forgotten World* (1961), for example, she sensitively describes the plight of a woman no longer needed by her family and who tries, not wholly successfully, to find a life of her own.

K.'s novels are characterized by excessively romantic situations and characters and by widely divergent settings (Greek islands, the Austrian Alps, Welsh country houses, a woman's college). Though her ostensible subject is the ability to survive in the modern world, she often hearkens to a simpler era. She was never in any particular literary group, though she had attended college with Vera Brittain and Dorothy L. Sayers, was friends with L. P. Hartley and Elizabeth Bowen, and was related to Joyce Cary. Her work was popular and respected during her lifetime but has not retained much popularity since.

WORKS: *A Century of Revolution, 1789–1920* (1922). *The Ladies of Lyndon* (1923). *The Constant Nymph* (1924; as play, with B. Dean, 1926). *A Long Week-End* (1927). *Red Sky at Morning* (1927). *Dewdrops* (1928). *The Game and the Candle* (1928). (with B. Dean) *Come With Me* (1928). *The Fool of the Family* (1930). *Return I Dare Not* (1931). *A Long Time Ago* (1932). *Escape Me Never! A Play in Three Acts* (1934). (with C. Isherwood) *The Little Friend* (1936). *Together and Apart* (1936). *The Midas Touch* (1938). (with G. Ratoff) *Autumn* (adapted from L. Surgochev, 1940). *Where Stands a Winged Sentry* (1941). *The Merchanized Muse* (1942). *Who Will Remember?* (1942). *The Feast* (1950). *Jane Marten* (1950). *Lucy Carmichael* (1951). *Troy Chimneys* (1952). *The Oracles* (1955; in the U.S. as *Act of God*). *The Heroes of Clone* (1957; in the U.S. as *The Wild Swan*). *The Outlaws on Parnassus* (1958). *A Night in Cold Harbors* (1960). *The Forgotten World* (1961). *Not in the Calendar: The Story of a Friendship* (1964). *Women at Work* (1966).

BIBLIOGRAPHY: Beauman, N., intro. to *The Ladies of Lyndon* (1981). Birley, J., intro. to *Together and Apart* (1981). Powell, V. *The Constant Novelist* (1983).

For articles in reference works, see: *Bloomsbury. CA. Cambridge. CLC. DLB. DNB. Feminist. MBL. MWD. Oxford. TCA* and *SUP. TCR&GW. TCW. WA* and *SUP.*

Other references: *Antiquarian Bookman* (28 August 1967). *Arts and Decoration* (May 1925). *Bookman* (October 1925). *Books Abroad* (Spring 1968). *Life* (10 February 1941). Mackenzie, C. *Literature in My Time* (1933). *NYHTBR* (5 August 1951). *NYT* (1 August 1967). *NYTBR* (19 March 1950). *Time* (11 August 1967). *TLS* (24 June 1955).

Paul Schlueter

K. G.: See *Greenaway, Kate*

Anne Killigrew

BORN: 1660, London.
DIED: 16 June 1685, London.
DAUGHTER OF: Dr. Henry Killigrew.

K., a poet and a painter, was a member of a family "prominent in the court of Charles II." Her father was a theologian and Master of the Savoy; her uncle Thomas, a playwright, was "court wit" and author of *The Parson's Wedding.* K. (as did Anne Finch) served as a Maid of Honour to Mary of Modena, Duchess of York.

K. received, according to George Ballard, a "polite education," indicating that she was taught the "accomplishments" necessary to a woman of her social situation. Evidently, however, she did learn something of the classics as her paintings demonstrate a knowledge of Greek and Roman mythology and literature. Germaine Greer asserts that "Her scenes with sacred groves and nymphs and satyrs are allegorical as well as fantastic: her understanding of their function raises her above the throng of the King's artisans."

John Dryden admired K.'s paintings and praised them in the prefatory poem he composed for a posthumous collection of her poems: "Her Pencil drew, what e'er her Soul design'd, / And off the happy Draught surpass'd the Image in her Mind." In the same poem, Dryden describes K.'s landscape paintings, which are now lost. Myra Reynolds believes that if the paintings were as "truly English" in subject and tone as Dryden said, K. could be placed "at the very inception of English landscape art."

K.'s poetry has often been dismissed as imitative, a criticism perpetuated by a probably well-intentioned remark in Dryden's prefatory poem: "Such Noble Vigour did her Verse adorn, / That it seem'd borrow'd, where 'twas only born." In actuality, K. was simply following the seventeenth-century conventions she observed in the work of other poets, not an unusual technique for any beginning writer. Unfortunately, K. did not live long enough to develop a distinctive style of her own.

More interesting than her "style," however, is the subject matter of K.'s poetry. Reynolds accurately describes K. as pessimistic, scornful, rather hard and drastic in her judgments, an "anomaly." Although K. was an active participant in the festive life surrounding the court of Charles II, she learned early on that "all this world has to offer will turn to dust and ashes in the mouth." Her poetry usually included "invectives" against greed, ambition, unbridled love, atheism, and war. She often seemed to long for death, as in her poem "On Death":

Tell me thou fastest End of all our Woe,
Why wreched Mortals do avoid thee so:
Thou gentle drier o' th' afflicteds Tears
Thou noble ender of the Cowards Fears
Thou sweet Repose to Lovers sad dispaire
Thou Calm t' Ambitions rough Tempestuous Care.

K. herself encapsulated the meaning of her life and work in "An Epitaph on her Self": "When I am Dead, few Friends attend my Hearse, / And for a Monument, I leave my VERSE."

K. died of smallpox on 16 June 1685 at the age of twenty-five. K.'s father published a memorial edition of her collected works as *Poems* (1686). The small volume, to which an engraving of K.'s self-portrait is prefixed, contains the prefatory ode by Dryden, "To the Pious Memory of the Accomplisht Young LADY Mrs. Anne Killigrew Excellent in the two Sister-Arts of Poesie, and Painting," as well as a memorial tribute in verse ("On the Death of The Truly Virtuous Mrs. Anne Killigrew") signed by E. E., assumed to be Edmund Elys, a scholarly poet and writer of theological pamphlets.

WORKS: *Poems* (1686). Morton, R., intro. to *Poems: A Facsimile Reproduction* (1967).

BIBLIOGRAPHY: Bernikow, L. *The World Split Open* (1974). Greer, G. *The Obstacle Race: The Fortunes of Women Painters and Their Work* (1979). Reynolds, M. *The Learned Lady in England 1650–1760* (1920; rpt. 1964). Rowton, F. *The Female Poets of Great Britain* (1853; rpt. 1981).

For articles in reference works, see: *Ballard. Bloomsbury. CBEL. DNB. Feminist. Oxford. ToddBWW. ToddDBA.*

Other references: Bryan, M. *Bryan's Dictionary of Painters and Engravers* (1903–1905). Clayton, E. *English Female Artists* (1867). Costello, L. *Memoirs of Eminent Englishwomen*, vol. 3 (1844). Fine, E. *Women and Art* (1978). Hale, S. J. *Woman's Record* (1855; rpt. 1970). Hays, M. *Female Biography; or Memoirs of Illustrious and Celebrated Women* (1807). Hope, A. *SoR* (1963). *PQ* (1964). Stanford, A. *The Women Poets in English: An Anthology* (1972). Straub, K. *TSWL* (1987). Waters, C. *Women in the Fine Arts, From the Seventh Century B.C. to the Twentieth Century A.D.* (1904).

Kay Beaird Meyers

Anne King

BORN: 1621.
DIED: after 1684.
DAUGHTER OF: John King, Bishop of London, and Joan Freeman King.
MARRIED: John Dutton, 1648; Sir Richard Grobham Howe, before 1671.

K., the youngest of nine children, was only five weeks old at her father's death. She grew up in a clerical and poetical family that suffered for their support of the royalist cause. She was especially close to her eldest brother, the poet Henry King (1592–1669), Bishop of Chichester. Family friends included Ben Jonson, John Donne, and Izaak Walton. In 1648, K. married John Dutton, who was twenty-eight years her senior and among the richest men in England until he was fined heavily for his support of the Stuarts.

In 1643, K.'s brother Henry was ejected from Chichester when it was seized by the parliamentary forces. K., Henry, other family members, and John Hales, who had been ejected from another ecclesiastical position, took refuge at the home of Lady Salter, where they established a sort of college for "praying the church prayers [and] rec[eiving] the Sacram[en]t," according to Izaak Walton. While there she wrote one of only two poems that can with certainty be attributed to her, "Under Mr. Hales Picture" (1656), a verse that accompanied her drawing of Hales (now lost). The poem (which survives in Walton's notes for a projected "Life of John Hales," never published) plays cleverly on the woman writer's obligatory apology for her unfitness to write. Readers, K. says, will pardon the inadequacy of both the poem and the picture "when they understand / the lines were figur'd by a womans hand."

K.'s other poem survives because it is part of a monument she erected for her older sister, Dorothy, in 1684, twenty-six years after her death. The "Inscription on monument of Dorothy, Lady Hubert at Langley, Buckinghamshire," shows mastery of the learning, wit, and conceit that distinguished the Jacobean poets. In K.'s poem, the monument becomes a "field of Marble" where "Death and Love Contend." The tears of the poet and the reader embalm the corpse, which lies "Living and fresh" until Death (here personified as a woman) dies; the tears themselves become "both the Dead's, and Living's Monument."

K.'s first husband died in 1657, leaving her £500, the silver and household goods she had brought to her marriage, and all his coaches and coach horses. That same year, Henry King's collected poems were published (along with those of other, unnamed, writers) as *Poems, Elegies, Paradoxes, and Sonnets;* some of the poems may have been by K. One of the poems by Henry, entitled "To my sister Anne King, who chid me in verse for being angry," argues that he would willingly display his faults if he could always be so wittily corrected "with a Quill so sage / It Passion tunes, and calmes a Tempest's rage."

The loss of K.'s poems is made more poignant by the fact that so many of her contemporaries praised her abilities. Walton called her "a most generose and ingenious lady." Jasper Mayne, archdeacon of Chichester, praised her poetic ability in "On Mrs. Anne King's Table-Book of Pictures." James Howell, in a letter of 1637, commented that the poetic genius of the King family "diffuseth itself also among the sisters." After reading an epitaph and an anagram by K., he composed a poem "For the admitting of Mrs Anne King to be the Tenth Muse."

K. was remembered in her brother Henry's will, the recipient of "one guilt cup and cover" and a "great french Bible with prints" that had belonged to John Donne. Izaak Walton left her a ring in his will of 1683. In her nephew's will of 1671, she is called "the Lady How," that is, wife of Sir Richard Grobham Howe (1621–1703). She is buried with him at Great Wishford near Salisbury.

WORKS: "Under Mr. Hales Picture" (1656); Corpus Christi College, Oxford (Fulman MS., Vol. 10, ff. 79, 80; printed in J. Butt, "Izaak Walton's Collections for Fulman's Life of John Hales," *MLR,* 1934). "Inscription on monument of Dorothy, Lady Hubert at Langley, Buckinghamshire" (1684), in *Kissing the Rod: An Anthology of Seventeenth-Century Women's Verse,* ed. G. Greer et al. (1988).

BIBLIOGRAPHY: Berman, R. *Henry King and the Seventeenth Century* (1964). Butt, J. *MLR* (1934). Crum, M. *The Poems of Henry King* (1965). *Kissing the Rod: An Anthology of Seventeenth-Century Women's Verse,* ed. G. Greer et al. (1988). *Poems and Psalms by Henry King,* ed. J. Hannah (1843).

For articles in reference works, see *Bell.*

Kari Boyd McBride

King, Charlotte: See *Dacre, Charlotte*

Mary Henrietta Kingsley

BORN: 13 October 1862, Islington.
DIED: 3 June 1900, Simonstown, South Africa.
DAUGHTER OF: Dr. George Kingsley and Mary Bailey.

K. was a celebrated traveler, ethnologist, and naturalist whose two trips to West Africa yielded three books as well as numerous articles and lectures. Of the Victorian lady travelers, she was among the most political, firmly opposing many missionary activities, the common patronizing attitude toward the Africans, and the Crown Colony system of governing West Africa. Her writings are notable for their unusual combination of vivid poetic description, self-deprecating humor, and cool scientific prose.

K.'s first thirty years were spent in relative isolation, running the house for her mother and brother while her father traveled as personal physician to a number of English noblemen. Although her brother was given an education at Cambridge, she was self-educated. In her father's library, she found delight in scientific writings (many of them amusingly archaic), travel tales, eighteenth-century picaresque novels, and the writings of Charles Dickens and Mark Twain. Except for one brief visit to Paris, she did not travel until after her parents died within a few months of each other in 1892.

A combination of professional and personal concerns moved her to travel, and she went to one of the few continents not visited by her father. Her first trip to West Africa began in August 1893 in the company of British traders. During this voyage, she learned the habits of traders and Africans alike and became an accomplished naturalist. She left no record of this trip, although it is alluded to in letters and in her later writings. Her second trip to Africa, begun in December 1894, took her through rarely traveled areas, brought her in close contact with several tribes, some of which were cannibalistic, and concluded with an ascent of Mungo Mah Lobeh, a 13,760-foot mountain.

Throughout these travels, she firmly adhered to the dress codes and etiquette of an English lady even as she forded leech-filled swamps up to her neck in muck or tumbled into fifteen-foot deep animal traps. Her travel books are filled with accounts of taking tea in the most unlikely of places. But she carried little else from England with her as she waded through malarial swamps, faced aggressive crocodiles and gorillas, and slept in filthy huts. She learned how to trade in rubber and oil and partially supported herself by this commerce. Her preference for traveling in native fashion suited her meager means, and she announced at one point that one of her most prized accomplishments was learning to paddle a native canoe.

When she returned from her second trip, she found that she was quite a celebrity, and she lectured and wrote extensively before the publication of her two major books, *Travels in West Africa* (1897) and *West African Studies* (1899). She intended to return to West Africa but became embroiled in political discussions about appropriate forms of government for that area. Although she did not oppose colonization, she firmly objected to a system of rule that violated African culture and interfered with trade in the area. Instead of rule from Whitehall, she proposed a system of colonial government administered by traders and based on existing tribal politics. Her books, articles, and lectures consistently depict the Africans as a wise and rational people, different from whites more in kind than in degree.

Her political involvement and her devotion to her brother kept her in England until early in 1900, during which time she completed a short narrative history of West Africa, *The Story of West Africa* (1899), and completed her brother's aborted attempts at editing her father's *Notes on Sport and Travel* (1900). In March 1900, she traveled to South Africa, nominally to collect more specimens of African wildlife but in fact to nurse soldiers from the Boer War. After only two months of work in a hospital, she herself died from enteric fever and, in accordance with her wishes, was buried at sea.

Her first book, *Travels in West Africa,* combines a travel narrative with the presentation of scientific information about Africa. Although her lack of education made her unsure about her writing ability, she resisted editing the final manuscript heavily because she wanted her voice to sound natural. And indeed it did. Her colloquial tone and rambling, episodic narrative recall the style of Twain and the structure of the picaresque novels that she loved. She described her method as showing the reader "a series of pictures of things" in the hope that the reader would divine from them "the impression which is the truth." Addressing both the scientific community and the public at large, the persona in the book shifts rapidly from a professional naturalist to a self-abnegating female traveler to a confident and even aggressive seaman. She assigned herself both male and female gender, calling herself a "trading man" and then, a few sentences on, insisting on her femininity. In addition to concerns about her style, K. worried about whether she would be credible as a scientist, and so she avoided sensationalism and omitted accounts of her outstanding bravery from this narrative.

Clearly, one underlying purpose in this book and her second, more scholarly *West African Studies* was to depict the humanity that the Africans and Europeans shared. She consistently identified herself with Africa, calling herself a "firm African." By explaining African customs by analogy to British manners, she strongly combatted the notion that Africans are naïve or childlike. She described her friendship with the Africans saying, "We recognized that we belonged to that same section of the human race with whom it is better to drink than to fight. We knew we would each have killed the other, if sufficient inducement were offered, and so we took a certain amount of care that the inducement should not arise." This passage is typical of the fine, understated humor that pervades K.'s work. The many articles that K. published in journals like *The National Review* and *Cornhill Magazine* made her an influential figure in late nineteenth-century-colonial politics and earned her the designation of "new woman," a title that she disliked as strongly as she opposed female suffrage.

K.'s dry wit, warm humanity, and poetic description make her travel books stand out among those of her contemporaries. Although her political stance is complex and outdated, her stories of human interaction are timeless.

WORKS: *Travels in West Africa* (1897). *West African Studies* (1899). *The Story of West Africa* (1899).

BIBLIOGRAPHY: Blunt, A., in *Writing Women and Space*, ed. A. Blunt and G. Rose (1994). Campbell, O. *Mary Kingsley* (1957). Dobrzycka, I. *KN* (1988). Frank, F. *A Voyager Out: The Life of Mary Kingsley* (1986). Gwynn, S. *The Life of Mary Kingsley* (1933). Howard, C. *Mary Kingsley* (1957). Hughes, J. *Invincible Miss* (1968). *Travels in West Africa*, ed. E. Huxley (1992). Middleton, D. *Victorian Lady Travellers* (1965). Shearman, J. *KJ* (1987). Srebrnik, P., in *Muscular Christianity*, ed. D. E. Hall (1994). Stevenson, C. B. *Victorian Women Travel Writers in Africa* (1982). Thiesmeyer, L. *Japan Women's University Studies in English and American Literature* (1991). Thiesmeyer, L., in *Transforming Genres*, ed. N. L. Manes and M. J. Rochelson (1994). Wallace, K. *This Is Your Home* (1956).

For articles in reference works, see: *Bloomsbury. Cambridge. DNB. Feminist. Oxford. ToddBWW.*

Tori Haring-Smith

Ellis Cornelia Knight

BORN: 27 March 1758, Westminister, London.
DIED: 18 December 1837, Paris, France.
DAUGHTER OF: Sir Joseph Knight, Rear Admiral of the White, and Lady Phillipina Deane Knight.

Linguist, poet, novelist, and classical scholar, K. was educated briefly in a school run by the Mesdames Thompets, by M. Petitpierre, a Swiss pastor, then privately by various clergymen. Most of K.'s early education, however, was gained by her association with her mother's friend Frances Reynolds, the sister of Sir Joshua Reynolds, who painted K.'s portrait, and with Samuel Johnson and members of his circle. Her mother was also a close friend of Anna Williams, Johnson's blind housekeeper, and Elizabeth Carter, the translator of Epictetus. When her father died in 1775, her mother's unsuccessful attempt to gain a pension forced them to relocate abroad in the interest of saving money. Lady Knight and K. lived mostly in Rome and Naples, with frequent sojourns in Paris. It was on the Continent that K. refined her skills in modern languages and pursued her interest in Roman history.

Tall and exceedingly proper, almost priggish, K. remained her mother's companion as they ingratiated themselves with aristocratic society. At Naples they became well acquainted with Sir William and Lady Emma Hamilton. At the death of Lady Knight in 1799, K. returned to England under the protection of Emma Hamilton. Lord Nelson, who accompanied them, was celebrated in verses composed by K. Her Pindaric ode "The Battle of the Nile," among other poems, told of Nelson's naval victories and earned her the honor of being known as his poet laureate. Nevertheless, her embarrassment at and disapproval of the intimate relationship between Admiral Nelson and Emma Hamilton caused her to remove herself from their circle. In her autobiography, K. attempts to finesse her priggishness: "Most of my friends were very urgent with me to drop the acquaintance; circumstanced as I had been, I feared the charge of ingratitude," a charge that K., who had been protected and brought back to England free of expense by Hamilton, indeed faced.

Now safely in England, K. re-established herself with the prim elements of polite society, especially Lady Aylesbury, a Lady of the Bedchamber to Queen Charlotte. It was through Aylesbury's efforts that K. became attached to the household of Queen Charlotte; later K. escaped the controlling queen and her boring household to become companion to the adolescent Princess Charlotte in 1813. In 1814, Princess Charlotte refused to marry her father's choice, the Prince of Orange, and fled to the protection of her mother, Caroline of Brunswick. In his anger, the regent dismissed K. from her service to the princess. Although K. maintained ties with England, she retumed to the Continent, where she died in Paris on 18 December 1837. K.'s autobiography and journals provide valuable information on the court history of the Regency.

K. is read today, if at all, for her association with Johnson and his circle. *Dinarbas* (1790), her presumptuous continuation of Johnson's "Rassalas," was a philosophical tale intended to counter the pessimistic tone of "Rassalas." K., however, wrote a romance that fails to engage the essential wisdom of Johnson's writing. She stressed a notion of human happiness that runs counter to Johnson's idea that in life "there is much to be endured and little to be enjoyed." Her other important work, *Marcus Flaminius* (1793), written in a series of dry letters, described a political, military, antisocial view of Augustan Age life. Nevertheless, historians find that her autobiography offers insights into the court life and politics of the Regency.

WORKS: *Dinarbas, A Tale; being a Continuation of Rasselas, Prince of Abyssinia* (1790). *Marcus Flaminius, or a View of the Military, Political, and Social Life of the Romans* (1793). *A Description of Latium, or La Campagna di Roma* (1805). *Chronological Abridgement of the History of Spain* (1809). *Chronological Abridgement of the History of France* (1811). *Translations from the German, in Prose and Verse* (1812; rpt. as *Prayers and Verse*, ed. E. Harding, 1832). *Autobiography*, ed. J. W. Kaye and J. Hutton (1861). *Miscellaneous Poems*, by K. W. R. Spencer, S. Rogers, and others (1932). *Sir Guy de Lusignan: A Tale of Italy (1933).*

BIBLIOGRAPHY: Boswell, J. *The Life of Samuel Johnson* (1791). Luttrell, B. *The Prim Romantic: A Biography of Ellis Cornelia Knight, 1758–1837* (1965). Messinger, A. *Ellis C. Knight* (1993). Osgood, C. G. *PULC* (1943). Rawson, C. J., in *Bicentenary Essays on "Rassalas,"* ed. M. Wahba (1959).

For articles in reference works, see: *Cambridge. DNB. Feminist. ToddDBA.*

James Reibman

Krishna, Bal: See *Cory, Victoria*

L.: See *Landon, Letitia Elizabeth*

Lactilla: See *Yearsley, Ann Cromartie*

Ladie Cubross yonger: See *Colville, Elizabeth*

Lady, A: See *Fielding, Sarah; Finch, Anne Kingsmill, Countess of Winchelsea; Glasse, Hannah; Hanway, Mary Ann*

Lady Ann Bacon: See *Bacon, Ann*

Lady Eleanor: See *Davies (Douglas), Eleanor Audeley*

Lady Stepney: See *Stepney, Lady Catherine*

Lake, Claude: See *Blind, Mathilde*

Caroline Lamb

BORN: 13 November 1785, London.
DIED: 24 January 1828, London.
DAUGHTER OF: Sir Frederick, third Earl of Bessborough, and Henrietta Spencer Ponsonby.
MARRIED: William Lamb, later Lord Melbourne, 1805.

L., an aristocratic novelist and poet of the early nineteenth century, is chiefly remembered as the flighty married woman who fell in love with Lord Byron and who ungraciously accepted his decision to terminate their liaison. Brought up in a social class in which titled family connections and elegance ruled, L. was given no formal education because a doctor had advised that she "should not be taught anything or placed under any restraint." When she married William Lamb at the age of twenty, L. was described as a model of fashion and of pale, delicate complexion.

The liaison with Byron flourished under the system of literary soirées in which the evening's amusement is to complete verses for a partner. L. met Byron in 1812 shortly after the success of his *Childe Harold.* She met him at a ball, exchanged gifts and letters, and appeared in public with him for about nine months. As the relationship slowly and tortuously died before L.'s eyes, Byron married Anne Isabella Milbanke on 2 January 1815. His marriage ended in scandal when Lady Byron signed separation papers; he subsequently left England for good. There are numerous references to L. in his correspondence.

Meanwhile, L.'s in-laws were plotting to separate her legally from William by having her declared insane. During this period she secretly wrote *Glenarvon,* a *roman à clef* about her affair with Byron. She published it anonymously in 1816, but the particulars were immediately well discovered. As a novel, its chief interest is to Byron scholars. The complicated plots and "innumerable subsidiary characters" make the book confusing, Elizabeth Jenkins, one of L.'s biographers, said. There are some scenes that bring a scene or emotion to life, but basically it was L.'s "sole comfort" during a time when she and her husband were ostracized. The parallels between her life and her novel are easily drawn. Calantha, young, ingenuous, and irresponsible, falls in love with Lord Avondale and marries him. Over time, Calantha's wild behavior and Avondale's negligence create a weak marriage. She associates with several London society ladies, all easily recognizable to L.'s contemporaries. While Avondale is away to quiet a political disturbance, Calantha meets Glenarvon, a stranger who has appeared to lay claim to some property. This stranger Edward Bulwer-Lytton later described as a "beautiful monster—half demon, and yet demigod" (1883). The two are attracted to each other and exchange gifts and letters. After numerous calamities Glenarvon marries and leaves.

Her second novel, *Graham Hamilton* (1820), is not as complicated or emotionally charged as her first; consequently, little attention has been given to it. Her third novel, *Ada Reis,* finished in 1823, was inspired by exotic Eastern tales such as *Vathek* (by William Beckford, 1786) and was well received in its day. Jenkins says that Ugo Foscolo, the exiled Italian writer, encouraged her to write something that "would not offend." Ada Reis becomes a pirate, settles in Arabia, and meets Kabarra, a spirit of darkness, who becomes his mentor. L. also wrote a few poems, mostly autobiographical, that are generally technically stilted and cliché-ridden, as, for example, "William Lamb's Return from Paris, Asking Me My Wish."

Always of delicate health, her final years were relatively quiet. In 1824, however, she happened to pass the cortege carrying Byron's body, and popular legend reports that L.'s emotional stability broke as a result. Actually, she reports having been troubled at the sight, but what caused her the most pain was the biography of Byron written by Thomas Medwin shortly after the poet's death. In it, according to Jenkins, she had to "endure . . . the new anguish of seeing herself for the first time as she had been held up to the scorn of Byron's friends, and now to that of the public." Even her obituary notice in the *London Gazette* could not allow her liaison with Byron to sink into oblivion: "The world is very lenient to the mistresses of poets, and perhaps not without justice, for their attachments have something of excuse; not only in their object but in their origin, they arise from imagination, not depravity." Other writers she knew intimately were Benjamin Constant and Mme. de Staël, and, beginning in 1825, the young Edward Bulwer-Lytton.

WORKS: (Anon.) *Glenarvon* (1816; reissued as *The Fatal Passion,* 1865). *Verses from Glenarvon; To Which is Pre-*

fixed the Original Introduction (1816). (Anon.) *A New Canto* (1819). (Anon.) *Graham Hamilton* (1820). (Anon.) *Ada Reis: A Tale* (1823). *Fugitive Pieces and Reminiscences of Lord Byron with Some Original Poetry*, ed. I. Nathan (1829).

BIBLIOGRAPHY: Blyth, H. C. *Caro: The Fatal Passion* (1972). Cecil, D. *The Young Melbourne and the Story of His Marriage with Caroline Lamb* (1939). Green, A. *PQ* (1878). Hofkosh, S., in *Romanticism and Feminism*, ed. A. K. Mellor (1988). Jenkins, E. *Lady Caroline Lamb* (1932). Manchester, S. *Mad, Bad and Dangerous to Know: The Life of Lady Caroline Lamb* (1992). Mayer, S.R.T. *Temple Bar* (1878). Paston, G. *Cornhill Magazine* (1934). Paul, C. *William Godwin: His Friends and Contemporaries* (1876). Sadleir, M. *Life of Bulwer-Lytton* (1931). Smiles, S. *A Publisher and His Friends* (1891). Strickland, M. *The Byron Women* (1974).

For articles in reference works, see: *BA19C*. *Biographie Universelle* (1870). *DLB*. *DNB*. *ENE*. *Feminist. Guide to the Gothic* (1984). *Lives of the Georgian Age*, ed. W. Gould (1978). *NCLC*.

Other references: *ArielE* (October 1981). *Byron Journal* (1991). *IUR* (1980). *KSJ* (1991). *N&Q* (1974). *SEEJ* (1992). *WC* (1979).

Marilynn J. Smith

Mary Ann Lamb

BORN: 3 December 1764, London.
DIED: 20 May 1847, London.
DAUGHTER OF: John Lamb and Elizabeth Field Lamb.
WROTE UNDER: The Author of Mrs. Leicester's School; M. B.; Sempronia..

L. is known chiefly as the sister of Charles Lamb, a writer of the early Romantic period. Despite having intermittent bouts with mental illness throughout her adult years, she worked on several publishing projects to help support herself and Charles. Of the works attributed to Charles, L. was responsible for fourteen of the twenty tales in their children's Shakespeare book, all but three of the stories in *Mrs. Leicester's School*, and a third of the poems in a small volume of children's poems. In addition, she wrote an article addressing the issue of the role of women in nineteenth-century England.

L. had two brothers: Charles, born when she was eleven, and John, one year her senior, who left home early on and who apparently did not involve himself in their literary pursuits. The family spent many years living in quarters in the Temple, property once owned by the Knights Templar, where their father was a factotum of a prominent lawyer, Samuel Salt, who had chambers in the Temple. Through Salt, John and Charles received scholarships to attend Christ's Hospital, where Charles met Samuel Taylor Coleridge. L.'s only formal schooling was briefly at William Bird's Day School.

The adolescent L. had to assist her parents by taking care of young Charles and doing needlework. Then, as her parents declined in health, she nursed them at home. On 27 September 1796, at the age of thirty-two, exhausted from the physical and emotional strain of caring for her aging parents, L. became hysterical. In a knife-wielding charge against a young apprentice, L. stabbed her mother, who was trying to stop the fracas. The wound killed Mrs. Lamb, but it was several days before L. remembered the incident at all. Declared a lunatic, she stayed in an asylum until the following April, when she was placed under Charles's guardianship and moved to a private home, not returning home until the death of her father in 1799. From the day of the collapse she was never able to discuss the incident of her mother, and she experienced occasional upsets, some of which necessitated hospital care.

Upon release from the hospital in 1797, L. joined her brother in new lodgings. They regularly received their friends at Wednesday evening parties and developed their writing interests. They visited regularly with Coleridge, the Wordsworths, and the Hazlitts; later they knew Leigh Hunt and Robert Southey. One association that prepared L.'s literary career was with the Godwins. She did not know William Godwin before the death of his first wife, Mary Wollstonecraft, but she did know his second wife, Mary Jane Godwin, who began publishing and selling juvenile books. She commissioned L. to write *Tales from Shakespear*, which appeared in 1807. L. wrote fourteen comedies and histories, and Charles did the six tragedies, but only Charles's name appeared on the title page. The prose tales taken from some of Shakespeare's plays have been well received and are probably the best-known work of the Lambs.

Mrs. Godwin also published two other collaborations in 1809: *Mrs. Leicester's School* and *Poetry for Children*. Although unverified, approximately a third of the poems may have been L.'s and all but three of the stories were L.'s. This time, the title page listed no author; the stories are "autobiographical" accounts told by different girls at the school. The book was well received, running into eight editions by 1823.

L.'s article "On Needlework," appearing in *The British Lady's Magazine* in April 1815, addressed the issue of women's duties and how best to meet them. L. proposes ways that a woman, within the framework of her feminine world, can add to the comfort and income of her household. Noting that "women have of late been rapidly advancing in intellectual improvement" and that "workwomen of every description were never in so much distress for want of employment," L. recommends selling the needlework that so many women do to fill leisure hours. Her idea of feminine duty is to "be accounted the helpmates of men; who, in return for all he does for us, expects, and justly expects, us to do all in our power to soften and sweeten life." "After many years of observation and reflection," L.'s view of men's "engrossing to themselves every occupation and calling . . . cannot well be ordered otherwise." By selling needlework, work done traditionally by women in the home, women can earn money and still not "encroach upon some employment now engrossed by men." Thus, by doing needlework for money, "so much more nearly will woman be upon an equality with men as far as respects the mere enjoyment of life." A. Gilchrist suggested that L.'s attitude about "woman's work" might have been wiser during a later period. L.'s demonstrated use of Latin and ability to understand difficult concepts are clearly seen in those works that were published out of financial necessity; when Charles began making more money from his essays, however, L. stopped writing altogether.

WORKS: (with C. Lamb) *Tales from Shakespear* (1807; L. wrote "The Tempest," "A Midsummer Night's Dream," "The Winter's Tale," "Much Ado About Nothing," "As You Like It," "The Two Gentlemen of Verona," "The Merchant of Venice," "Cymbeline," "All's Well that Ends Well," "The Taming of the Shrew," "The Comedy of Errors," "Measure for Measure," "Twelfth Night," and "Pericles, Prince of Tyre"). (Anon.) *Mrs. Leicester's School; or the History of Several Young Ladies, Related by Themselves* (1809; L. wrote "Elizabeth Villiers," "Louisa Manners," "Ann Withers," "Elinor Forester," "Margaret Green," "Emily Barton," "Charlotte Wilmot"). (by the author of *Mrs. Leicester's School*) *Poetry for Children* (1809). *Ulysses* (1809). *Mary and Charles Lamb: Poems, Letters, and Remains*, ed. W. Hazlitt (1874). *The Works of Charles and Mary Lamb*, ed. E. V. Lucas (1903–1905). *The Works of Charles and Mary Lamb*, ed. T. Hutchinson (1924). *The Letters of Charles and Mary Lamb*, ed. E. W. Marrs, Jr. (1975–78).

BIBLIOGRAPHY: Aaron, J., in *Romanticism and Feminism*, ed. A. K. Mellor (1988). Aaron, J., in *Revealing Lives: Autobiography, Biography, and Gender*, ed. S. Bell (1990). Aaron, J. *A Double Singleness* (1991). Anthony, K. *The Lambs: A Story of Pre-Victorian England* (1945). Courtney, W. *Young Charles Lamb: 1775–1802* (1982). Frend, G. *The Lambs, Fanny Kelly and Some Others* (1926). Gilchrist, A. *Mary Lamb* (1883). Hazlitt, W. *Mary and Charles Lamb* (1874). Wilson, C., in *Re-Visioning Romanticism: British Women Writers*, ed. C. S. Wilson and J. Haefner (1994). Wolfson, S., in *Women's Re-Visions of Shakespeare*, ed. M. Novy (1990).

For articles in reference works, see: *BA19C*. *Bloomsbury*. *CHEL*. *DLEL*. *DNB*. *Feminist*. *New Moulton*. *OCCL*. *OCEL*. *SATA*.

Other references: Aaron, J. *ChLB* (July 1987). Aaron, J., in *PSt* (September 1987). Courtney, W. *ChLB* (January 1987). Craik, T. W. *ChLB* (January 1987). Marsden, J. I. *Annual of the MLA Division on Children's Literature* (1989). Misenheimer, C. *ChLB* (July 1989, April 1990). Misenheimer, C. *New Rambler* (1991/1992). Nabholtz, J. R. *ChLB* (April 1989). *SAQ* (January 1948). *Transactions of the Royal Society of Canada* (1928). *TLS* (21 August 1924, 20 September 1947). Wilson, D. G. *ChLB* (January 1985). Woof, R. *ChLB* (January 1984).

Marilynn J. Smith

Lamb, William: See *Jameson, Storm*

Letitia Elizabeth Landon

BORN: 14 August 1802, Chelsea, London.
DIED: 15 October 1838, Cape Coast Castle, Ghana.
DAUGHTER OF: John Landon.
MARRIED: George Maclean, 1838.
WROTE UNDER: L.; L.E.L.

L. is a memorable figure in British literary history for various reasons. First, her poetry perfectly illustrates the standards of popular taste for women's verse in the nineteenth century in subject matter, style, and tone. Second, the years of her greatest popularity correspond exactly to the hiatus in English poetry between the Romantic and Victorian eras. Finally, her career illustrates the vicissitudes of fame and fortune for an aspiring literary woman in nineteenth-century England.

L.'s prolific output of verse was marked by a constant tone of melancholy and sentimentalism, although in person, by all accounts, she was quite a cheerful and pragmatic young woman. In a preface to her *Poetical Works*, L. explained, "Aware that to elevate I must first soften, and that if I wish to purify I must first touch, I have ever endeavored to bring forward grief, disappointment, the fallen leaf, the faded flower, the broken heart, and the early grave. . . . [As to] my frequent choice of Love as my source of song, I can only say that, for a woman, whose influence and whose sphere must be in the affections, what subject can be more fitting than one which it is her peculiar province to refine, spiritualize, and exalt?"

Educated at the same school in Chelsea as Mary Russell Mitford and Lady Caroline Lamb, L. was considered a child prodigy. When William Jerden ran across some of her early poems, he was so impressed that in 1820 he launched her career in his *Literary Gazette*. L. was just eighteen years old. Her verses were so well received that she went on to publish five full volumes of poetry between 1821 and 1828: *The Fate of Adelaide* (1821), *The Improvisatrice* (1824), *The Troubadour* (1825), *The Golden Violet* (1827), and *The Venetian Bracelet, The Lost Pleiad, A History of the Lyre, and Other Poems* (1828). Her work was acclaimed by contemporary critics and awaited eagerly by readers who romanticized the life of the mysterious L. in accord with the recurrent subjects of her poems. She was hailed as a female Byron, raising expectations that she could never fulfill.

The immense popularity of L.'s poetry has been explained by critic Lionel Stevenson as a function of her success in capturing the "surface characteristics" of Romanticism at a time when all the great Romantic writers had died or had lost their poetic vitality and of her anticipation of the emerging moralism of Victorian verse. Equally significant, however, was the extent to which her continual characterizations of self-sacrificing femininity captured the new social ideal of womanhood. Regarding L., *Blackwood's* "Tickler" asked in 1825, "Does she not throw over her most impassioned strains of love and rapture a delicate and gentle spirit from the recess of her own pure and holy woman's heart?" Answered Lord North, "She does."

Yet L. thought of herself as a professional writer, motivated by the financial need of her family. Thus, in addition to half a dozen volumes of poetry, five novels, and a book of moral tales, she also published numerous fugitive pieces in various annuals and periodicals, including the *Drawing-Room Scrapbook*, *Keepsake*, and *Friendship's Offering*. A few of these she edited or coedited with the Countess of Blessington and others.

Her unguarded professional relationships with editors William Jerdan and William Maginn damaged her personal reputation and may have caused biographer John

Forster to break off his engagement to marry her. To the astonishment of her friends, she responded by secretly marrying George Maclean, the governor of Cape Coast Castle, in Ghana, and setting sail with him for a three-year term in Africa despite rumors that Maclean already had an African wife. A few months later, she was found dead in her room with a bottle of prussic acid in her hand. Whether she died by accident, suicide, or murder was never determined.

The extensive recognition accorded to L. in her teens encouraged her to conceive of writing as a spontaneous, improvisatory act rather than as a conscious discipline. Consequently, she wrote effusively and seldom revised; the sublime effect she aimed for often collapsed into triteness and sentimentality. In "Erinna" (1826), however, abandoning her usual rhymed couplets for blank verse, she wrote a truly autobiographical poem. In this dramatic monologue on the subject of the ancient "poetess," L. revealed her own frustrations as a woman writer. Finally, in a poetical fragment found among her papers after her death, L. lamented, "Alas! that ever / Praise should have been what praise has been to me— / The opiate of the mind." Sadly, L.'s untimely death forestalled whatever maturation of her talents might have followed from this revelation.

WORKS: *The Fate of Adelaide: A Swiss Romantic Tale, and Other Poems* (1821). *The Improvisatrice and Other Poems* (1824). *The Troubadour* (1825). *The Golden Violet* (1827). *The Venetian Bracelet, The Lost Pleiad, A History of the Lyre, and Other Poems* (1828). *Romance and Reality* (1831). *Frances Carrara* (1834). *The Vow of the Peacock, and Other Poems* (1835). *Traits and Trials of Early Life* (1836). *Ethel Churchill, or The Two Brides* (1837). *A Birthday Tribute, Addressed to the Princess Alexandrine Victoria (1837). Duty and Inclination: A Novel, Edited by Miss Landon* (1838). (with Lady Blessington and T. H. Bayley) *Flowers of Loveliness* (1838). *The Easter Gift: A Religious Offering (1838). The Zenana, and Minor Poems of L. E. L., with a Memoir by E. Roberts* (1839). *Life and Literary Remains of L. E. L.*, ed. S. L. Blanchard (1841). *Lady Anne Granard: or Keeping Up Appearances* (1842). *Poetical Works, with a Memoir of the Author* (1850). *Poetical Works*, ed. W. B. Scott (1853). *Complete Works* (1854). *The Gift of Friendship, with Contributions by L. E. L.* (1877). *Selected Writings*, ed. J. J. McCann and D. M. Riess (1997).

BIBLIOGRAPHY: Ashton, H. *Letty Landon* (1951). Courtenay, J. *The Adventurous Thirties* (1933). Enfield, D. L. *A Mystery of the Thirties* (1928). Sheppard, S. *Characteristics of the Genius and Writings of L. E. L.* (1841). Stephenson, G. *Letitia Landon: The Woman Behind L. E. L.* (1995). Stevenson, L. *MLQ* (1947).

For articles in reference works, see: *Allibone. EP. Feminist. OCEL. Oxford. PPL.*

Other references: Armstrong, A. *Victorian Poetry: Poetry, Poetics and Politics* (1993). Armstrong, A., in *Romantic Women Writers: Voices and Countervoices*, ed. P. Feldman and T. Kelley (1995). Bethune, G. *The British Female Poets* (1848). *Blackwood's* (August 1824, September 1825). Blain, V. *VP* (1995). Curren, S., in *Romanticism and Feminism*, ed. A. K. Mellor (1988). Elwin, M. *Victorian Wallflowers* (1934). Elwood, A. K. *Memoirs of the Literary Ladies of England* (1843). Greer, G. *TSWL* (1982). Hall, S. C. and A. M. Hall *Atlantic* (March 1865). Hickok, K. *Representations of Women: Nineteenth-Century British Women's Poetry* (1984). Jerdan, W. *Autobiography of William Jerdan* (1852–53). Mellor, A. K. *Romanticism and Gender* (1993). *New Monthly Magazine* (December 1831). Stephenson, G. *VP* (1992). Stephenson, G., in *ReImagining Women: Representations of Women in Culture*, ed. S. Neuman and G. Stephenson (1993).

Kathleen Hickok

Lang, Frances: See Mantle, Winifred Langford

Leonora Blanche Alleyne Lang

BORN: 12 July 1851, Clifton, Bristol.
DIED: 10 July 1933, London.
DAUGHTER OF: Charles Thomas Alleyne.
MARRIED: Andrew Lang, 1875.

The daughter of a younger son of a family of planters in Barbados, L. passed most of her childhood in Clifton, Bristol, and was privately educated. She lived into her eighties and was wont to describe herself in later years as having lived a repressed childhood, scrabbling up what education she could and escaping into an early marriage. This romantic statement—she was not a child bride but twenty-four when she married—suggests that she resented the limitations imposed on someone of her sex and class, especially as her father was in his mid-fifties when she was born and likely to have been old-fashioned in his ideas of female education. Moreover, she showed an aptitude for languages, translating from Russian and Polish as well as the more common European ones, and she worked as a censor of Russian materials during the World War I. Her ambition was to write and to become a popular London hostess, and in a certain measure she achieved both by marrying Andrew Lang, the folklorist, writer, and poet. As a wife to a prolific writer who soon became a household name, L. adopted his interests as her own. She proofread for him and undertook the research and verification tasks for his many publications.

She was a competent writer, frequently seeing articles in print that were collected in *Men, Women, and Minxes* (1912) and producing at least one novel, *Dissolving Views* (1884). In it the ideal woman is developed in Eleanor, who is shown as tough-minded and discerning, yet fated to suffer. She strives for a mental attitude of independence while yearning for romantic love and a nuclear family. Eleanor finds she lacks the energetic attack and the glad acceptance of life her guardian exhibits. Many of the novel's details reflect the interests L. shared with her husband: knowledge of and interest in anthropological artifacts and concepts, enthusiasm for book collecting, and folk songs and customs. Catalogs of heroes and heroines in the text are multicultural and multiracial. An episode early in the novel wherein a hapless student is forced to the summit of a mountain of stools is an Andrew Lang childhood experience, and it suggests the degree of involvement he had in L.'s writing. L. seems to have returned to other forms of writing after this one novel.

Much of her time was spent in the production of a wide variety of children's books, usually anthologies of legends, short biographies, and the like. While Lang edited with invisible scholarship the fairy tales books for which he is remembered, L. provided him with translations from French, German, Italian, and Catalan sources. Yet to the public she was "Mrs. Andrew Lang," and the impression that she was riding on her husband's reputation was stronger than it should have been. There was a demand for the kind of children's books she produced, whose subjects were heroes and princesses and brave animals. After Lang's death in 1912 and her war service, L. undertook the editing of his poetry, often republished but never collected. The four-volume work that appeared in 1923, however, omitted some two hundred poems, and the arrangement was topical, with no dates of writing or first publication supplied. It was a book for browsing and enjoying but a disaster for the scholar.

Andrew Lang's reputation today rests with his fairy books because these renditions have become known as relatively pure versions of the tales today, when many collections are available. L.'s contribution Lang described in his preface to *The Lilac Fairy Book* (1910): "My part has been that of Adam, according to Mark Twain, in the Garden of Eden. Eve worked, Adam superintended. I also superintend. I find out where the stories are, and advise, and in short superintend."

WORKS: (trans.) *The History of Russia from the Earliest Times to 1877,* by A. N. Rambaud, 2 vols. (1879). *A Geography, Physical, Political and Descriptive, for Beginners,* 3 vols. (1881–83). *Dissolving Views. A Novel.* 1884. (trans.) *Memoirs of an Old Collector,* by Count M. Tyszkiewicz (1898). *The Gateway to Shakespeare for Children, Containing a Life of Shakespeare by Mrs. Andrew Lang, a Selection from the Plays, and from Lamb's "Tales"* (1908). *The Book of Princes and Princesses* (1908). *All Sort of Stories Book* (1911). *The Book of Saints and Heroes* (1912). *Men, Women, and Minxes. Essays* (1912). *The Strange Story Book* (1913). (ed.) *The Poetical Works of Andrew Lang,* 4 vols. (1923).

BIBLIOGRAPHY: Green, R. L. *RES* (1944). Green, R. L. *Andrew Lang: A Critical Biography* (1946). Langstaff, E. *Andrew Lang* (1978). Saintsville, G., in *The Eighteen-Seventies,* ed. H. Granville-Barker (1929). *Concerning Andrew Lang: Being the Andrew Lang Lectures Delivered Before the University of St. Andrews, 1927–1937,* ed. A. B. Webster (1949). Weintraub, J. *ELT* (1975).

For articles in reference works, see: *Allibone SUP. DLB.*

Eleanor Langstaff

Langford, Jane: See *Mantle, Winifred Langford*

[A]emelia Lanier (Lanyer)

BORN: 1569, Bishopsgate, near London.
DIED: 1645.
DAUGHTER OF: Baptista Bassano and Margaret Johnson.
MARRIED: Alphonso Lanier, 1592.

Born in the London suburb of Bishopsgate, L. was the daughter of a court musician. Her father died when she was seven, leaving his family with financial problems but providing L. a dowry of £100. A dedicatory poem to L.'s *Salve Deus Rex Judaeorum* reveals that Susan Bertie, countess dowager of Kent, was the "Mistris of my youth"; L. probably received training as she served the household in some capacity. L. was also present, probably as a companion or attendant, in the household of Margaret Clifford, Countess of Cumberland, at some point after the birth of Anne Clifford in 1589, according to "The Description of Cookeham"; this represents L.'s participation in the "former sports" of Anne while she was a "sweet youth." At about the age of eighteen, L. became the mistress of Henry Cary, Lord Hunsdon, Lord Chamberlain to Queen Elizabeth. When L. became pregnant, she was married to Alphonso Lanier, musician to Queen Elizabeth. Shortly afterwards, she gave birth to a son, named Henry after Lord Hunsdon. After her marriage, she visited the magician Simon Forman several times, and his diary records her complaint that her husband had spent the money she had brought with her into her marriage; Forman also reports that she asked him to predict whether she would rise to the rank of a lady. In 1598, she gave birth to a daughter, Odillya, who died nine months later. In 1604, the Lanier finances prospered when King James granted Alphonso Lanier a patent for weighing hay and corn. When Lanier died in 1613, this patent became subject to litigation with L.'s in-laws and her fortunes again declined. From 1617 until 1619 she kept a school in a London suburb where, according to a Chancery petition, she educated "the children of divers persons of worth and understanding." In 1633, her son, Henry Lanier, died, leaving her several grandchildren. S. Woods notes that at her death in 1645, the parish record described her as a "pensioner" with a dependable income.

L.'s *Salve Deus Rex Judaeorum* is divided into three parts: (1) prefatory dedications to women patrons, (2) the *Salve Deux Rex Judaeorum,* and (3) "The Description of Cookeham." While L. tailored single copies of the work with various combinations of dedications, taken together all the dedications compose a substantial one-third of the published text. In addition to representations of early modern women readers, these poems provide insights into the patronage system as L. experienced or manipulated it. The *Salve Deus Rex Judaeorum* itself is composed primarily of a graceful meditation on the stations of the cross, designed to move pious readers to a lively compassion for Jesus's suffering. Within this meditation, L. abruptly inserts a defense of Eve that reaches the radical conclusion that since men's sin of crucifying Christ so far outweighs Eve's sin, men should hold no sovereignty over women, and men and women should be equals. Finally, "The Description of

Cookeham" pays tribute to an estate owned by the family of the Countess of Cumberland. Portraying the creatures of Cookeham joyfully preparing to greet the Countess and then dolefully mourning her departure, "The Description of Cookeham" represents L.'s own nostalgia for a place and perhaps for a way of life. Predating Ben Jonson's "To Penshurst," "The Description of Cookeham may be the first English country house poem.

WORKS: *Poems of Shakespeare's Dark Lady: Salve Deus Rex Judaeorum by Aemilia Lanier,* ed. A. L. Rowse (1978). Travitsky, B. *Paradise of Women* (1981). *The Poems of Aemilia Lanyer: Salve Deus Rex Judaeorum,* ed. S. Woods (1993).

BIBLIOGRAPHY: Beilin, E. V. *Redeeming Eve* (1987). Coiro, A. *Criticism* (1993). Hutson, L., in *Women, Texts and Histories 1575–1760,* ed. C. Brant and D. Purkiss (1992). Krontiris, T. *Oppositional Voices* (1992). Lerner, G. *Creation of Feminist Consciousness* (1993). Lewalski, B., in *Silent But for the Word,* ed. M. Hannay (1985). Lewalski, B. *YES* (1991). Lewalski, B. *Writing Women in Jacobean England* (1993). McGrath, L. *LIT* (1991). McGrath, L., *WS* (1992). Powell, B. J. *C&L* (1996). Rowse, A. L. *Shakespeare the Man* (1973). Wall, W. *The Imprint of Gender* (1993). Wall, W., in *Anxious Power,* ed. C. J. Singley and S. E. Sweeney (1993).

For articles in reference works, see *Bell. DLB. ToddBWW. ToddDBA.*

Mary Ellen Lamb

Marghanita Laski

BORN: 24 October 1915, London.
DIED: 6 February 1988, Dublin, Ireland.
DAUGHTER OF: Neville J. Laski and Phina Gaster Laski.
MARRIED: John Eldred Howard, 1937.
WROTE UNDER: Marghanita Laski; Sarah Russell.

L. left Somerville College, Oxford, with an M.A. in 1936. After growing up under the influence of her maternal grandfather, Moses Gaster, who was the chief rabbi for the Portuguese and Spanish Jews in England, and an uncle, Harold Laski, a well-known English liberal, L. tried careers in fashion design and philological research before turning to writing in 1944. With a varied background and working life—dairy farming, nursing, publishing, intelligence, and radio and television broadcasting—it does not seem strange that L.'s journalistic career should also reflect diverse interests. Having established a reputation as novelist, critic, and journalist, L. held positions on several prestigious committees: the Annan Committee of Inquiry into the Future of Broadcasting, the Arts Council of Great Britain, Chairman of the Literature Advisory Panel, and Chairman of the Arts and Films Committees. She was also named an Honorary Fellow of Manchester Polytechnic.

L.'s novelistic career began with two works of fantasy. *Love on the Supertax* (1944), L.'s first novel, is a science-fiction account of an England altered by war. In her third novel, *Tory Heaven* (1948), also published as *Toasted English,* L. satirizes government by creating a mock utopia based upon the caste system. Emmett Dedmon in the *Chicago Sun* comments that L.'s satire is "in the tradition of Jonathan Swift, that is to say literate, enjoyable and with a purpose." Similarly, Charles J. Rolo in the *Atlantic* praises the book as "a scorching indictment of a hierarchical society." The critical response to L.'s satire is not unanimous, however. Writing in the *Christian Science Monitor,* Ruth Chapin charges that "Miss Laski is betrayed by her own system. . . . Her satirical intent has been blurred by her sheer delight in reconstructing the mores of the Victorian upper classes."

Little Boy Lost (1949), L.'s first serious novel, is set against a background of France after World War II and involves a father's search through a wilderness of orphanages for his missing son. By the end of the novel, the father has also found himself. As with *Toasted English,* critical reaction ranges from Sylvia Norman's favorable comment in the *Spectator* that *"Little Boy Lost* has a simplicity like that of a Blake poem—less naïve than ultimate. . . . Character, action, and atmosphere are as one here," to Elizabeth Jenkins' conflicting opinion in the *Manchester Guardian* that "the ring is false" although "the writing is always accomplished."

L. returns to her earlier theme of class consciousness in *The Village* (1952). In this humorous novel, the author depicts two lovers from different social classes in a small English village battling the snobbery of their parents. Written during a period when English society was undergoing pressure for reform, the novel, according to Robert Riley in *Catholic World,* is "a most perceptive comedy of manners in the English tradition" and that "it delineates . . . the quiet but implacable social revolution which is now taking place within that tradition."

In *The Victorian Chaise-Longue* (1953), L.'s last adult novel, she turns from humor to terror. After falling asleep on an antique chaise, a young woman suffering from tuberculosis has a nightmare during which she finds herself changed into the chaise's original owner, a Victorian lady dying of the same disease. Antonia White in the *New Statesman and Nation* says that this "device enables Miss Laski to create an authentic sense of terror and frustration" and gives "one a genuine feeling of nightmare." Called "a little jewel of horror" by J. H. Jackson in the *San Francisco Chronicle,* this suspense novel can certainly be favorably compared to those of more recent psychological-thriller writers such as Ruth Rendell.

After establishing herself as primarily a writer of fiction, L. turned to other fields. With the publication of *Mrs. Ewing, Mrs. Molesworth, and Mrs. Hodgson Burnett* (1950), *Jane Austen and Her World* (1969), and *George Eliot and Her World* (1973), critics now consider L. a capable biographer and critic. The first volume is a study of three Victorian writers of children's books, another area of her literary interest. It is the work on Jane Austen that established her reputation as biographer, however. Writing in the *Times Literary Supplement,* a critic remarks that "readers of this book will put it down knowing almost everything there is to know about Jane Austen. Miss Laski has written a scholarly and immensely readable account of Jane Austen's life, her family friends, and surroundings. No short biography could be better done." In addition, a reviewer in the *New Yorker* comments that L.'s book "brings the first fully enduring English novelist into a reasonably satisfactory focus."

With two books on the same scientific study, *Ecstasy: A Study of Some Secular and Religious Experiences* (1961) and *Everyday Ecstasy* (1980), L. turns to an exploration into the way in which intense human experiences are triggered, how they affect society, and whether or not they should be approved. The conclusions in the earlier volume came as a result of a questionnaire sent to sixty-three people, with their responses then compared to various literary and religious examples. The critical reaction, as with most of her work, is diverse. Frances O'Brien, writing in *Saturday Review,* particularly calls attention to L.'s use of her own criteria and original terminology as well as her controversial use of the word "trigger" to include nature, art, and sexual love. Maurice Richardson in the *New Statesman* refers to the book as "a useful descriptive catalogue" that deserves a place in the library with William James. On the other hand, Alan Brien in the *Spectator* maintains that "by the end of the book, the reader is still not convinced that the patterns may not be accidental, or illusory, because he cannot be certain that the minimum laboratory conditions for any kind of scientific study have been observed."

The later work, *Everyday Ecstasy,* is a published series of lectures given at Kings College, London. In these lectures, L. explores the effects of ecstasy on society. In the *Times Literary Supplement,* Mary Warnock refers to the "paradoxes" that "mar the book." One paradox, Warnock charges, is L. herself, whom Warnock calls "the most rational, anti-enthusiastic, unsentimental, conventional person . . . to explore the subject of ecstasy." The worst paradox, however, according to Warnock, concerns the style. L. fails to treat her subject "with gentleness and subtlety," and by the end of the work "there is a terrible sense that the concept of pleasure has somehow been irrevocably lost."

In addition to her major works, L. also wrote a three-act play, *The Offshore Island* (1959); edited several anthologies for young people: *The Patchwork Book* (1946), *Stories of Adventure* (1947), and *A Chaplet for Charlotte Yonge* (1965); contributed to *Survivors: Fiction Based on Scientific Fact*, published by the Campaign for Nuclear Disarmament (1960); wrote a children's novel, *Ferry the Jerusalem Cat* (1983); and edited a book of reviews, *From Palm to Pine* (1987).

Although not widely known outside her own country, L.'s reputation as writer, critic, and lecturer has continued to grow in Great Britain since the 1940s. Until her death, she continued to be a contributor of articles and reviews to books, periodicals, and newspapers, including the *London Times* and the *Oxford English Dictionary.*

WORKS: *Love on the Supertax* (1944). (as Sarah Russell) *To Bed with Grand Music* (1946). *Stories of Adventure* (1947). *Tory Heaven* (1948; also as *Toasted English*). *Little Boy Lost* (1949). *Mrs. Ewing, Mrs. Molesworth, and Mrs. Hodgson Burnett* (1950). *The Village* (1952). *The Victorian Chaise-Longue* (1953). *The Offshore Island* (1959). *Ecstasy: A Study of Some Secular and Religious Experiences* (1961). "The Secular Responsibility" (Conway Memorial Lecture) (1967). *Jane Austen and Her World* (1969). *George Eliot and Her World* (1973). *Everyday Ecstasy: Some Observations on the Possible Social Effects of Major and Minor Ecstatic Experiences in our Daily Secular Lives* (1980). *Ferry the Jerusalem Cat* (1983).

BIBLIOGRAPHY: Lassner, P., in *Look Who's Laughing: Gender and Comedy*, ed. G. Finney (1994). Schmitt, N. C. *CompD* (1994).

For articles in reference works, see: *CA. CB. Longman. MBL. TCA.*

Other references: *AS* (Summer 1976). *Books and Bookmen* (August 1973). Chapin, R. *CSM* (5 May 1949). *CSM* (5 September 1986). Dedmon, E. *Chicago Sun* (25 December 1949). *Economist* (19 May 1973, 26 November 1983). *KR* (1977) *Listener* (29 May 1980, 3 November 1983). *MLR* (April 1974). *New Statesman* (25 July 1969). *New Yorker* (1 August 1977). *NYT* (26 April 1978). *NYTBR* (27 July 1986). *Observer* (12 August 1973, 11 May 1980, 22 March 1987). Rolo, C. J. *Atlantic* (May 1949). *Spectator* (16 August 1980). *TES* (25 July 1980, 10 June 1983). *TLS* (28 August 1969, 29 June 1973, 6 June 1980, 5 June 1987, 29 December 1989).

Alice Lorraine Painter

Laura: See *Robinson, Mary Darby (Perdita)*

Laura Maria: See *Robinson, Mary Darby (Perdita)*

Mary Lavin

BORN: 11 June 1912, Walpole, Massachusetts, United States.
DIED: 25 March 1996, Dublin, Ireland.
DAUGHTER OF: Thomas Lavin and Nora Mahon Lavin.
MARRIED: William Walsh, 1942; Michael MacDonald Scott, 1969.

Author of many volumes of short stories and recipient of numerous literary awards, L. is one of Ireland's foremost writers of short fiction. The only child of Irish emigrants, she spent the first ten years of her life in Walpole, Massachusetts. In 1921, L. and her mother returned to her mother's family's home in Athenry, and when her father returned in the following year the family settled in Dublin. As a young woman, L. attended the Loretto Convent, then University College Dublin, where her M.A. thesis on Jane Austen was awarded high honors. She started a dissertation on Virginia Woolf but abandoned the project to devote herself to writing fiction. She published five volumes of short stories and two novels before her first husband's death in 1954, leaving L. with three young children to raise and a farm to manage. After several difficult years, a Guggenheim Fellowship for 1959–61 provided L. with time and support for writing, and the next two decades were productive years. She served as writer-in-residence at the University of Connecticut in 1967 and 1971, and in 1969 she married a close friend from her college days.

Throughout the 1970s, L. lived at the center of Irish literary life. In the early 1980s her health deteriorated, and she moved to a nursing home in 1990, after her second husband's death. She died six years later at the age of eighty-three.

Although she wrote two novels as well as two books for children, the short story is L.'s genre. Her stories examine the often-troubled relationships of families, friends, and lovers and the conflicts arising from strictures and conventions of class, religion, and society. In her narration of the seemingly ordinary and insignificant events surrounding the lives of her predominantly Irish middle-class characters, L. dramatizes and explores the loneliness and isolation, the regrets and sorrows, of common experience. Characteristically, the stories are told in the third person from the point of view of a central consciousness; more than half are told from a female perspective. In the most effective stories, her technique is one of inconclusiveness, implication, and suggestion, and the complexity of experience and emotion is evoked with sympathy and understanding.

Her career began in 1939 when *Dublin Magazine* published her first story, "Miss Holland," the first of three to appear in that periodical. These stories drew attention and support, and in 1942 her first volume of short stories, *Tales from Bective Bridge,* was published with a preface by Lord Dunsany; the following year it was awarded the James Tait Black Memorial Prize. Two of the stories from this period—"A Cup of Tea" (*The Long Ago,* 1944) and "A Happy Death" (*The Becker Wives,* 1946)—are among her best. In "A Cup of Tea," a mother anticipates and prepares for her daughter's return from college. The awaited evening ends, however, in anger and bitter silence between them, a result of the mother's resentment toward her husband and the daughter's inattentiveness to the mother. The father never appears in the story, and the couple's incompatibility is revealed through the thoughts and exchanges of mother and daughter. "A Happy Death," a long, beautifully crafted story, moves between present and past to unfold the story of a failed marriage and of broken dreams, of youthful love that yielded to smoldering resentment and misunderstanding. The need for husband and wife to know and to empathize with each other separates the two even at the moment of the husband's death. His peaceful vision of the two of them in the carefree days of their youthful love brings to the husband a happy death; to his wife it brings remorse over his failure to turn his thoughts to eternal salvation.

Of the stories that L. wrote in the 1950s, many are generally considered to be flawed by intrusive authorial commentary and by excessively artificial contrivances, a frequent criticism of her novels as well. Revised versions of some of these stories, however, reveal the author's awareness of these flaws.

During the 1960s and 1970s, L. published nine volumes of short stories, became a regular contributor to the *New Yorker,* and won the Katherine Mansfield Prize for the title story of *The Great Wave and Other Stories* (1961). Several stories in these volumes have widows for their central characters and explore the isolation and loss as well as the determination and endurance of the woman suffering through the death of her husband. The title story of *In the Middle of the Fields and Other Stories* (1967) portrays a widow so terrified of the darkness that she retreats upstairs every evening at nightfall. She is, at the same time, sufficiently assertive and self-assured to demand a fair deal from a local workman and to fend off his bumbling, though threatening, advances. "The Cuckoo's Spit," from the same volume, offers scenes from the encounters of a widow and a much younger man to dramatize difficulties of their developing intimacy.

The stories of widows have obvious autobiographical overtones. However, in one story, "Tom" (*The Shrine,* 1977), L. presents a completely autobiographical narration, a first-person reminiscence of her father and "the gold spikes of love with which he pierced me to the heart." In this story, a series of evocative recollections, she speaks of the "not happy marriage" of her parents and recounts a trip that she and her father made to his native Roscommon. As is the case with much of L.'s fiction, the effectiveness of "Tom" lies in her power to suggest and reveal a great deal more than appears in a few scenes, dialogues, and details.

Only since the mid-1970s has L.'s fiction received full-length critical treatment. Unlike many Irish writers, she rarely treats the issue of nationalism (the story "The Patriot Son," in the book with the same title, is an exception). She depicts with precision the social and physical settings inhabited by her Irish characters but her works belong to a larger literary context. In his preface to *Tales from Bective Bridge,* Lord Dunsany compared her stories to the works of the great Russian writers. Of tradition and influence L. herself has said: "Anything I wanted to achieve was in the traditions of world literature. . . . As for influences perhaps I owed most to Edith Wharton, the pastoral works of George Sand, and especially to Sarah Orne Jewett." Indeed, in both Jewett's and L.'s fictions, one finds embodied in the local and ordinary the universal endurance of the human spirit and the courage of the individual. Perhaps the best statement of these qualities comes from one of L.'s characters in "A Tragedy" (*The Patriot Son,* 1956). Of the victims of an air crash, the character reflects: "not one of them . . . but would fling back, if he could, his mantle of snow and come back to it all: the misunderstandings, the worry, the tensions and cross-purposes." It is this affirmation of life and experience that underlines L.'s fiction.

WORKS: *Tales from Bective Bridge* (1942). *The Long Ago and Other Stories* (1944). *The House in Clewe Street* (1945). *The Becker Wives* (1946). *At Sallygap* (1947). *Mary O'Grady* (1950). *A Single Lady and Other Stories* (1951). *The Patriot Son and Other Stories* (1956). *A Likely Story* (1957). *Selected Stories* (1959). *The Great Wave and Other Stories* (1961). *The Stories of Mary Lavin,* Vol. I (1964). *In the Middle of the Fields and Other Stories* (1967). *Happiness and Other Stories* (1970). *Collected Stories* (1971). *The Second Best Children in the World* (1972). *A Memory and Other Stories* (1972). *The Stories of Mary Lavin,* Vol. II (1973). *The Shrine and Other Stories* (1977). *A Family Likeness* (1985).

BIBLIOGRAPHY: Asbee, S. *JSSE.* (1987). Bowen, Z. *Mary Lavin* (1975). *Anglo-Irish and Irish Literature: Aspects of Language and Culture,* ed. B. Bramsback and M.

Croghan (1988). Burnham, R. *CCEI* (1977). Dunleavy, J. E., in *The Uses of Historical Criticism,* ed. R. H. Canary, C. Huffmann, and H. Kuzicki (1974). Hawthorne, M. *SSF* (1994). *IUR* (special L. issue) (1979). Kelly, A. A. *Mary Lavin: Quiet Rebel* (1980). *The Irish Short Story: A Critical History,* ed. J. Kilroy (1984). Kosok, H., ed. *Studies in Anglo-Irish Literature* (1982). Meszaros, P. *Crit* (1982). Murray, T. J. *Eire* (1972). O'Connor, F. *The Lonely Voice: A Study of the Short Story* (1963). Peterson, R. F. *MFS* (1978). Peterson, F. *Mary Lavin* (1978). Pritchett, V. S., intro. to *Collected Stories* (1971). Schumaker, J. *SSF* (1995).

For articles in reference works, see: *Bloomsbury. BCathA. CA. CLC. CN. DIL. DLB. DLEL. Feminist. Longman. MBL SUP. NCHEL. TCA SUP.*

Other references: *Eire* (1968, 1972). *Kilkenny Review* (Spring 1965). *LonT* (26 March 1996). *NYT* (27 March 1996). *St. Stephen's* (1967). *Studies* (Winter 1963).

Patricia A. O'Hara
(updated by Virginia Zimmerman)

Emily Lawless

BORN: 17 June 1845, County Kildare, Ireland.
DIED: 19 October 1913. Surrey.
DAUGHTER OF: Edward Lawless, third Lord Cloncurry, of Lyons House, County Kildare, and Elizabeth Kirwan of Castle Hackett, County Galway.

Little attention has been paid to L.'s broad and rich literary output, though it would be inappropriate to speak of the Irish Renaissance and omit L. Her prose spans the novel, the fake travel diary as historical novel (*With Essex in Ireland,* 1890; this had a title page that gave 1599 as its publication date and listed L. as the editor and author of the introduction), and literary biography (*Maria Edgeworth,* 1904), a classic of literary biography and a monument of feminist scholarship at the turn of the century. Her poetry, an equally deep expression of her historical and living vision of Ireland, is worthy of a reappraisal.

With the Wild Geese (1902) presents the combined worldviews of Irishmen who, forced into economic and political exile, had fought on the Continent for France, Spain, and Austria from 1691 on. "After Aughrim" serves as an introduction to the theme of Ireland as a mother who casts her sons away from her. Ireland speaks in the poem. Through all their vicissitudes, the soldiers continue to love their island-mother. "Clare Coast, circa 1720" is narrated by soldiers about to embark for the Continent; they range from the youthful excitement of boys about to go to war as if it were child's play to the wizened rancor of the forgotten veteran: "So, cold island, we stand / Here tonight on your shore, / Tonight, but never again, / Lingering a moment more."

L.'s work deserves serious reconsideration beyond Irish adulation or rejection. She and her writing must be seen in their milieu. A number of critics have indicated that in verse she is a precursor to William Butler Yeats. Her prose, especially her character sketches and depiction of place and ambiance, are echoed by James Joyce in *Dubliners* and in *Portrait of the Artist as a Young Man. Grania* (1892), *Maelcho* (1894), and, especially, *With Essex* contain powerful echoes of Sydney Owenson (Lady Morgan) in sentiment and message, if not in the same mordant, disarming anti-English wit.

WORKS: *A Chelsea Householder* (1882). *A Millionaire's Cousin* (1885). *Hurrish. A Study* (1886). *With Essex in Ireland* (1890). *Grania. The Story of an Island* (1892). *Maelcho: A Sixteenth Century Narrative* (1894). *Major Lawrence, F.L.S.* (1897). *Traits and Confidences* (1898). *Garden Diary* (1901). *With the Wild Geese* (1902). *Maria Edgeworth* (1904). *The Point of View* (1909; completed by S. F. Bullock). *The Race of Castlebar* (1913). *The Inalienable Heritage* (1914). *Poems of Emily Lawless,* ed. P. Fallon (1965).

BIBLIOGRAPHY: Brewer, B. W. *Eire* (Winter 1983). Calahan, J. M. *ClQ* (1991). Grubgeld, E. *Turn-of-the-Century Women* (Winter 1986).

For articles in reference works see: *BDIW. Bloomsbury.* Brady, A. *Women in Ireland. An Annotated Bibliography* (1988). *Chambers. CHEL. DIL. Feminist. OCEL. Oxford.*

Nicolás Hernández, Jr.

Frieda (von Richthofen) Lawrence

BORN: 11 August 1879, Metz (Lorraine), Germany.
DIED: 11 August 1956, Taos, New Mexico, United States.
DAUGHTER OF: Baron Friedrich von Richthofen and Anna Marquier.
MARRIED: Ernest Weekley, 1899; D[avid]. H[erbert]. Lawrence, 1914; Angelo Ravagli, 1950.

An editor, correspondent, and memoirist, L. is best known as the "noble, healthy, fertilizing influence" on the work of her second husband, D. H. Lawrence. Her three marriages divided her career into distinct phases; she did not begin personal writing until the 1930s. Raised in the German garrison town of Metz and surrounded by admiring young soldiers, L. early displayed her inexhaustible capacity for enjoying life. Following her youthful marriage to and three children by Ernest Weekley, a professor of romance languages at University College, Nottingham, she grew restless; under Weekley's encouragement, she edited Schiller's *Secret Ballads* (1902) and *Bechstein's Märchen* (1906) for Blackie's Little German Classics.

In 1912, L. ran off with Lawrence and, as the fertilizing influence on his work, led a passionate, peripatetic life for the next eighteen years. L. accompanied Lawrence on his search for the "life experience," which took them throughout Europe, India, Australia, Mexico, and the United States, where they lived on a farm near Taos, New Mexico. During this period, L. did not write, but her letters to friends and Lawrence's editors are filled with astute criticism of the novelist's work. Lawrence himself claimed that what was creative in his work sprang from L. as much as from himself.

L.'s writing began shortly after Lawrence's death in 1930. In an effort to clarify for others her life with Lawrence, she wrote *"Not I, But the Wind . . ."* (1934), the title taken from one of his poems. Of their marriage, she wrote of "the certainty of the unalterable bond between us, and the everpresent wonder of the world around us." Most poignant is L.'s account in "Nearing the End" of Lawrence's death and burial in Vence, France.

In 1931, L. returned to Kiowa Ranch near Taos with Angelo Ravagli, an Italian soldier and former landlord whom she married in 1950. Here, L. began her memoir. In "And the Fullness Thereof . . . ," using pseudonyms for herself, family, and friends, L. recalled Christmas celebrations in Metz, her adolescence, her English marriage, and an account of her first year with Lawrence, which records her anguish at being separated from her beloved children. She also wrote of the present, as she recorded life and travels with "Angelino." Although never finished, the memoir is, according to E. W. Tedlock, "a complete record of her adventure, and constitutes an important human and literary document. Like her speech, the writing is simple, candid, and forceful, rising to climaxes of intense feeling and characteristic wit. Through it run the elemental force and the fierce honesty with which she responded to everyday experience and the crises of her life."

L.'s wide circle of friends and correspondents included literati from two continents, among them Edward and David Garnett, Bertrand Russell, Lady Cynthia Asquith, S. S. Koteliansky, Witter Bynner, Rhys Davies, Mabel Dodge Luhan, Dorothy Brett, William York Tindall, John Middleton Murry, Katherine Mansfield, Harry T. Moore, Richard Aldington, and Aldous Huxley. She died on her seventy-seventh birthday and is buried on Kiowa Ranch in front of the shrine she and Ravagli built for Lawrence's ashes.

WORKS: *Not I, But the Wind* (1934). (intro. to D. H. Lawrence) *The First Lady Chatterley* (1973). *The Memoirs and Correspondence*, ed. E. W. Tedlock (1964). *D. H. Lawrence's Manuscripts: The Correspondence of Frieda Lawrence, Jake Zeitlin and Others*, ed. M. Squires (1991).

BIBLIOGRAPHY: Bynner, W. *Journey with Genius: Recollections and Reflections Concerning the D. H. Lawrences* (1953). Byrne, J. *A Genius for Living: The Life of Frieda Lawrence* (1995). Delavenay, E. *DHLR* (1975). Green, M. *The von Richthofen Sisters: The Triumphant and the Tragic Modes of Love. Else and Frieda von Richthofen, Otto Gross, Max Welter and D.H. Lawrence, in the Years 1870–1970* (1974). Lawrence, D. H. *Look! We Have Come Through* (1917). Lawrence, D. H. *Letters*, ed. J. T. Boulton (1979–93; 7 vols.). Lawrence, D. H. *Mr. Noon* (1984). Lucas, R. *Frieda Lawrence: The Story of Frieda von Richthofen and D. H. Lawrence* (1973). Moore, H. T. *The Intelligent Heart: The Story of D. H. Lawrence* (1960). Moore, H. T. and D. B. Montague. *Frieda Lawrence and Her Circle: Letters From, To and About Frieda Lawrence* (1981). Worthen, J. *D. H. Lawrence: The Early Years, 1885–1912* (1991).Worthen, J. *Cold Hearts and Coronets: Lawrence, the Weekleys, and the von Richthofens, or the Right and Romantic versus the Wrong and Repulsive* (1995).

For articles in reference works, see: *IDWB*. *Longman*. *RE*.

Other references: Cohn, R. *Tennessee Williams Review* (1993). Delavenay, E. *DHLR* (1975). Hills, S. J. *TLS* (6 September 1985). *LonT* (13 and 16 August 1956). *NYT* (12 August 1956). Rudnick, L. P. *DHLR* (1981). Turner, J., C. Rumpf-Worthen, and R. Jenkins, *DHLR* (1990).

Judith C. Kohl

Jane Ward Lead[e]

BORN: March 1623, Norfolk.
DIED: 19 August 1704, London.
DAUGHTER OF: Schildknap Ward of Norfolk.
MARRIED: William Leade, c. 1644.

A religious mystic, L. had her first religious experience at the age of fifteen when she heard a voice whispering to her during the Christmas revels at her father's house. L., who had at least a rudimentary education, lapsed into a melancholic state, which abated when she was eighteen due to a vision of "a pardon with a seal on it" which absolved her from a trifling lie she had told earlier in her life. At twenty-one, she married a distant relative, William Leade, with whom she lived happily for twenty-seven years. They had at least one daughter, Barbara, who lived to adulthood. William Leade died in February of 1670, and L. devoted the remainder of her life to religion, becoming "a widow of God."

In 1663, L. met Dr. John Pordage, a follower of Jakob Böhme, and the acquaintance may have solidified her belief in the value of mystic revelation. Her mystical experiences increased until, in 1670, she had almost nightly visions, which are recorded in her journal, *A Fountain of Gardens* (1696–1701). In 1681, L.'s first book, *The Heavenly Cloud Now Breaking*, was published and excited a great deal of interest in both Holland and Germany. Her second book, *The Revelation of Revelations*, was published in 1683; the Dutch and German editions, translated by Loth Fischer of Utrecht, were published in 1694 and 1695. Dr. Francis Lee, an Oxford scholar, heard of L. in Holland and visited her upon his return to England. The visit developed into a lifelong friendship between the two. L. later adopted Lee as a son, and he married her daughter, allegedly as the result of a divine order.

In 1694, Lee and L. inaugurated the Philadelphian Society, which was partially financed by Baron Knyphausen of Germany. Richard Roach, also an Oxonian, joined them, and he and Lee published the society's monthly periodical, *Theosophical Transactions by the Philadelphian Society*. The Philadelphians were adamant that they were not a group of Dissenters, and they stressed the fact that they were in complete agreement with the authorities and were not religious revolutionaries. Nevertheless, they aligned themselves with those movements that stressed an increase in spiritual life.

L., with the help of Lee and Roach, was the center of the Philadelphian Society, receiving her directions from God. Though she originally kept accounts of her visons for her own edification, she began publishing them when commanded by God to do so. Due to L.'s blindness in her later years, many of her works were dictated to Lee and are chiefly remarkable for complex sentence structure, strained metaphors, and lengthy titles. Her talent for transforming her thoughts into concrete images not only secured her position as head of the Philadelphian Society but likely contributed to the elaborate images that distinguish her prose.

L. died in 1704, "in the 81st year of her age and 65th of her vocation to the inward life," and was buried in Bunhill Fields. After her death, Lee wrote *The Last Hours of Jane Lead, by An Eye and Ear Witness* (1704), which, along with her own writings, gives a full account of L.'s life and beliefs. L.'s importance lies less in the artistry of her work than in her position as head of the English contingent of Behmenists, a subgroup illustrative of the religious controversy of the seventeenth century.

WORKS: *The Heavenly Cloud Now Breaking. The Lord Christ's Ascension-Ladder sent down* (1681). *The Revelation of Revelations* (1683). *The Enochian Walks with God, Found out by a Spiritual Traveller, Whose Face Towards Mount Sion Above was Set. With an Experimental Account of What Was Known, Seen, and Met Withal There* (1694). *The Laws of Paradise Given Forth by Wisdom to a Translated Spirit* (1695). *The Wonders of God's Creation manifested in the variety of Eight Worlds, as they were made known experimentally unto the Author* (1695). *A Message to the Philadelphian Society whithersoever dispersed over the whole Earth* (1696). *The Tree of Faith, or the Tree of Life springing up in the Paradise of God, from which all the Wonders of the New Creation must proceed* (1696). *The Ark of Faith, a supplement to the Tree of Faith* (1696). *A Fountain of Gardens watered by the Rivers of Divine Pleasure, and springing up in all the Variety of Spiritual Plants, blown up by the Pure Breath into a Paradise, sending forth their Sweet Savours and Strong Odours for Soul Refreshing* (1696–1701). *A Revelation of the Everlasting Gospel Message* (1697). *The Ascent to the Mount of Vision* (n.d.). *The Signs of the Times: forerunning the Kingdom of Christ, and evidencing when it is to come* (1699). *The Wars of David and the Peaceable Reign of Solomon* (1700). *A Second and Third Message to the Philadelphian Society* (n.d.). *A Living Funeral Testimony, or Death overcome and drowned in the Life of Christ* (1702). *The First Resurrection in Christ* (1704).

BIBLIOGRAPHY: *British Quarterly Review* (July 1873). *Dawn: A Journal of Social and Religious Progress* (December 1862). *N&Q* (17 December 1870). Lee, F. *The Last Hours of Jane Lead, by an Eye and Ear Witness* (1704). Reynolds, M. *The Learned Lady in England* (1964). Smith, C. P., in *Poetic Prophecy in Western Literature*, ed. J. Wojcik and R. J. Frontain (1984). Thune, N. *The Behmenists and The Philadelphians* (1948).

For articles in reference works, see: *Bloomsbury. DNB. Feminist. Oxford. ToddBWW.*

Sharon A. Winn

Mary Leadbeater

BORN: December 1758, Ballitore, County Kildare, Ireland.
DIED: 27 June 1826, Ballitore, County Kildare, Ireland.
DAUGHTER OF: Richard Shackleton and Elizabeth Carleton.
MARRIED: William Leadbeater (Leadbetter), 1791.
WROTE UNDER: Mary Leadbeater; The Quaker Authoress.

This modest "Quaker authoress" and post-mistress of Ballitore, County Kildare, distinguished herself as a prolific chronicler of late eighteenth- and early-nineteenth-century Irish rural history and culture. In her diverting moral tales, sketches, and dialogues, L. also proved to be an effective educator of the Irish peasantry. Her literary career spanned thirty-four years (1790–1824), during which time she produced a formidable corpus of published work: didactic tales, sketches, dialogues, secular and religious poetry, Quaker biographies, an extensive correspondence with Irish and English contemporaries, and moral anecdotes for the improvement of youth. Like most successful Irish writers of her day, L. published in English, not Irish; yet her vivid reconstructions of Irish rural life valuably preserved the speech and "old ways" of an ancient culture. Her work circulated in the literary centers of Dublin, London, and Philadelphia, and her publishers included three forceful bookmen: Richard David Webb, a patriotic and learned Irishman; Joseph Johnson, a prominent London publisher and promoter of Mary Wollstonecraft; and Samuel R. Fisher, Jr. of South Fourth Street, Philadelphia. While most of L.'s work recounts events in her own Quaker village of Ballitore, she also recorded important moments in Irish history such as the United Irishman's Rising of 1798 and 1800, as well as (Robert) Emmet's Rising of 1803. With the exception of a brief trip to London with her father in 1784 and frequent visits to the public library in County Limerick, whose collection she significantly expanded, L. wrote in the relative seclusion of small-town Ballitore. Through a vigorous correspondence, however, she wisely cultivated a broad literary network, which included Edmund Burke (her unofficial patron and career mentor), Sir Joshua Reynolds, George Crabbe, and Irish writers Melesina Trench and especially Maria Edgeworth ("the gem of our Emerald Isle"), who visited L. in Ballitore.

L.'s memoir, which she maintained from the age of eleven, provides a window on her early beginnings, education, and literary influences. She was born in December 1758 in the small village of Ballitore, County Kildare, to well-educated parents. Paternally, she descended from a line of Quaker teachers. Her father, Richard Shackleton, was a schoolmaster and the keeper of the boarding-school founded by his father, Abraham Shackleton (Edmund Burke's schoolmaster). L.'s mother, Elizabeth Carleton, was Shackleton's second wife. Literate at the age of four, L. was home educated. Her zeal for learning (especially literary texts) received good direction from one Aldborough Wrightson, an elderly scholar of Ballitore.

In 1784, at the age of twenty-six, L. had her first important exposure to literary professionals and the literary life when she visited London, accompanied by her father. She also saw Yorkshire and Beaconsfield at this time. During her London visit, L. met Burke (who had ties to Ballitore), Reynolds, and Crabbe. In 1791, at the age of thirty-three, she married one of her father's students, William Leadbeater, a farmer and landowner, whose family were Huguenots of Le Batre. The couple settled in Ballitore, and L.'s husband soon converted to Quakerism. Theirs was reportedly a happy union of thirty-five years.

In 1790, L. began her literary career with a variety of verse published in the second volume of Joshua Edkins's *Poems.* She next had an anonymous piece published in Dublin, targeted to the juvenile market, *Extracts & Original Anecdotes for the Improvement of Youth* (1794). This inaugural publication was a success owing to L.'s method: Her anecdotes were not only taken from real life but their style and content were a welcome respite from the humorless didacticism of most children's literature of the day. Her *Extracts* also included a brief overview of "the people called Quakers" as well as some secular and "divine odes." L.'s best work appeared in her ongoing prose reconstructions, the "Annals of Ballitore," which valuably transmit the character of rural Irish life and, of special value, the outbreak of the Irish Rising of 1798 and its tumultuous effects on the life of her village. L.'s reconstructions vividly recount the general mayhem of this moment, when Ballitore was occupied and sacked by insurgents. L. and her husband narrowly escaped with their lives. The horrors of the Rising deeply affected L., who admitted to experiencing acute distress and repeated nightmares. "Everyone seemed to think that safety and security were to be found in my brother's house," L. wrote of the Rising, "but thither the insurgents had brought their wounded and suffering prisoners . . . It was an awful sight to behold. All dreaded to see the door open, lest some new distress or horrors might enter. We knew not what one day might bring forth."

With the success of her early work, L. began to publish under her own name. In 1808 she brought out her *Poems,* a miscellany of some seventy verses consisting of religious odes; a metrical translation of her husband's prose translation of Virgil's thirteenth book of the *Aeneid;* and personal poems on family, friends, the Ballitore spa, and so forth. Next came L.'s popular *Cottage Dialogues among the Irish Peasantry,* which she sold to London publisher Joseph Johnson for £50 in 1811. This work was a humorous and valuable collection of anecdotes inspired by contemporary rural Irish life. L.'s cottagers discuss a broad range of subjects, such as Irish wakes, cooking, dress, fairs, spinning matches, and marriage. The educative goal of the exchanges is patent, and the informal dialogue-design of the *Dialogues* was suggested to L. by William P. Le Fanu (1774–1817). L.'s *Cottage Dialogues* received a great boost from her good friend, Irish novelist Maria Edgeworth, who contributed both preface and notes to the first edition. Within three years on the market, *Cottage Dialogues* saw a fourth edition in 1814; and it continued to sell well in Dublin, London, and Philadelphia after L.'s death in 1826.

Following the broad success of *Cottage Dialogues,* L.'s productivity accelerated, with the publication of *The Landlord's Friend* (1813), *Tales for Cottagers* (1814), *Cottage Biography* (1822), *Memoirs & Letters of Richard & Elizabeth Shackleton* (her parents) (1822), *Biographical Notices of Members of the Society of Friends who were Resident in Ireland* (1823), and *The Pedlars. A Tale,* written for the Kildare Street Education Society (1824). L.'s mother collaborated in some of these works; and one of L.'s several children, Lydia Jane Leadbeater (later Fisher), also took up the pen and went on to establish herself as the muse of Irish writer Gerald Griffin and his literary circle. Surrounded by her husband, children, and other relatives, L. died in her native Ballitore on 27 June 1826 at the age of sixty-eight. She was buried in the village Quaker cemetery.

The best of L.'s work, her "Annals of Ballitore" (prose reconstructions of Irish rural culture and civil war, 1766–1823), was gathered and published posthumously in two volumes in 1862 by Irish printer Richard Davis Webb under the title *The Leadbeater Papers.* L.'s manuscripts have been preserved in Irish, English, and American collections. In Ireland: Trinity College, Dublin; National Library of Ireland, Dublin; Religious Society of Friends, Dublin; Royal Irish Academy, Dublin; Kildare County Library; University College Library, Cork. In England: Society of Friends Library, London; British Library, London; Northamptonshire Record Office, Northamptonshire; Sheffield Archives, Sheffield; John Rylands University Library, Manchester; Christ Church Library, Oxford; Wordsworth Museum, Grasmere. In the United States: University of California, Santa Barbara; Historical Society of Pennsylvania, Philadelphia. A microfilm copy of L.'s *Ballitore Papers* is in the collection of the National Library of Ireland, Dublin.

WORKS: (contrib.) *Collection of Poems,* Vol. II, ed. Joshua Edkins (1790). (Anon.) *Extracts & Original Anecdotes for the Improvement of Youth* (1794, 1820). *Poems* (1808).*Cottage Dialogues among the Irish Peasantry* (1811). *The Landlord's Friend* (1813). (with E. Shackleton) *Tales for Cottagers, Accommodated to the Present Condition of the Irish Peasantry* (1814). *Cottage Biography; being A Collection of Lives of the Irish Peasantry* (1822; rpt. 1987). *Memoirs & Letters of Richard & Elizabeth Shackleton* (1822, 1849). *Biographical Notices of Members of the Society of Friends who Were Resident in Ireland* (1823). *The Pedlars: A Tale* (1824). *Leadbeater Papers,* ed. R. D. Webb (1862; rpt. 1987).

BIBLIOGRAPHY: *Field Day Anthology of Irish Writing, vol. 4: Women,* ed. S. Deane (1997). *British Women Poets of the Romantic Era,* ed. P. Feldman (1997). Gandy, C. *W&L* (1975). Hamilton, C. J. *Notable Irishwomen* (1904). O'Neill, K. *Friends and Neighbors: Mary Shackleton-Leadbeater and the Village of Ballitore, 1769–1826* (forthcoming). O'Neill, K., in *Visualizing Ireland,* ed. A. Dalsimer (1993). O'Neill, K., in *Chattel, Servant or Citizen,* ed. M. O'Dowd and S. Wichert (1995). O'Neill, K., in *The Women of '98,* ed. D. Keogh (forthcoming). Young, M. *Journal of the County Kildare Archaeological Society* (1916).

For articles in reference works, see: *DIL. DNB. Feminist.*

Other references: *Eighteenth-Century Short-Title Catalogue* (ESTC). Elmes, R. M. *Catalogue of Engraved Irish Portraits in the Joly Collection, National Library of Ireland* (1937). *The Orlando Project: An Integrated*

History of Women's Writing in the British Isles (U. of Alberta, Canada, forthcoming). Sutton, D. C. *Location Register of English Literary Manuscripts & Letters* (1995).

Maureen E. Mulvihill

Mary Leapor

BORN: 16 February 1722, Marston St. Lawrence, Northamptonshire.
DIED: 12 November 1746, Brackley, Northamptonshire.
DAUGHTER OF: Philip Leapor and Anne Leapor.

The daughter of Judge John Blencowe's gardener, L. is thought to have been either a cook or a cookmaid in a gentleman's family. She was educated by her mother and showed an early aptitude for poetry, which was encouraged by her parents for a while and then discouraged because they felt the pursuit would cause unhappiness in her station in life. L. persisted in writing poetry, however, exhibiting a keen admiration for the works of Alexander Pope. She acquired a library of seventeen books, which included the works of both Pope and John Dryden; her own poems are primarily imitations of Pope.

L. was described as being "courteous, obliging to all, cheerful, good-natured, and contented in the Station of Life in which providence had placed her." Her poetry is remarkable for its tolerant humor, though her satire was sometimes as pointed as Pope's. She apparently was sensible but vivacious and quick-witted and showed remarkable talent for one so young.

L.'s book *Poems Upon Several Occasions* was published by subscription in 1748, two years after her death. The list of subscribers is liberally sprinkled with members of the nobility, including several earls, dukes, and countesses, and David Garrick is said to have written the prospectus. The poems reveal Pope's influence but are definitely written from a female point of view. "Dorinda at her Glass," written in heroic couplets, is a delightful comment on aging belles. "The Fox and The Hen" is apparently influenced by Geoffrey Chaucer, and "The Ten-Penny Nail" is a dream vision reminiscent of "The Dream of the Rood." The nail, however, is not a religious object but an emblem of workaday life and as such it admonishes the poet to stop dreaming and get on with her work. L.'s criticism of elegant dress in "The Sow and The Peacock" is much more pointedly satirical than her other poems, and her essays on friendship, happiness, and hope are rather inferior imitations of Pope. The volume also contains several pastorals, one of which, "Damon and Strephon. A Complaint," is a pastoral elegy on the death of a great poet, presumably Pope, who died in 1744. A second volume, containing letters to patrons, a tragedy in blank verse entitled "The Unhappy Father," and a few acts of another drama, was published in 1751. L.'s poems also predominate in *Barber's Poems By Eminent Ladies*, published in 1755.

L. died of measles at the early age of twenty-four, two days after the death of her mother. Most of her poems are satires in the Horatian vein, and they are so good natured and cheerful that they succeed where more spiteful satire might have failed. L.'s witty comments on the social foibles of her day should secure her a place among the minor satirists of the eighteenth century.

WORKS: *Poems Upon Several Occasions, I & II* (1748, 1751). *The Unhappy Father, a Tragedy* (1751).

BIBLIOGRAPHY: *DNB*. Blunden, E. *Journal of the Northamptonshire Natural History Society* (1936). Green, R. *Mary Leapor: A Study in Eighteenth-Century Women's Poetry* (1993). Hays, M. *Female Biography*, (1803). Potts, J. *An Impertinent Voice: The Poetry of Mary Leapor* (1994). Reynolds, M. *The Learned Lady in England* (1964). Rizzo, B. *AJ* (1991).

Sharon A. Winn

Q[ueenie]. D[orothy]. Leavis

BORN: 7 December 1906, London.
DIED: 17 March 1981, Cambridge.
MARRIED: Frank Raymond Leavis, 1929.
WROTE UNDER: Q. D. Leavis.

A respected literary critic, L. was widely regarded as an educator of sensibilities, an amaneunsis of the great tradition of English literature, and a stout defender of standards much reduced by the coarsening of mass culture. Coeditor of the quarterly review *Scrutiny*, founded by her husband and collaborator Frank Raymond Leavis, she sought to stem the floodtide of dinginess sweeping across the world of letters. Her unerring vigilance led to an elitist view of culture with *Scrutiny* serving, in the words of one American commentator, as "the graveyard of a thousand literary reputations, ancient as well as modern, incorruptible guardian of standards in a decadent culture, upholder of seriousness in a frivolous age."

Cambridge educated, L. accepted in toto Ford Madox Ford's position that modern industrial civilization would of necessity restrict high culture to a select few who were to be conscious of the privilege of their station and the responsibility with which they were invested. Her small output was marked by a strong ethical impulse or, as some of her detractors came to term it, a moral fastidiousness. Although an admirer of Edith Wharton's sharp wit and lancing style, she faulted the American "literary aristocrat" for lacking "the natural piety, that richness of feeling and sense of moral order, of experience as a process of growth, in which George Eliot's local criticisms are embedded and which give the latter her large stature." Sensitive to every leap of the mind, L. was most attuned to the moral poise that she found at the center of all great writers.

Dismissive of cheap psychologizing and haute vulgarization equally endemic on both sides of the Atlantic, she hoped to find in the critical idiom a restoration of values. *Fiction and the Reading Public* (1932) bemoans the division between writers and the public, the apparently impassible gulf between sensibility and self-indulgence. The gross multiplication of inferior genres (in L.'s words, the cinema, the circulating library, the magazine, the newspaper, the dance hall) keep the majority jovially impervious to taste, quality, and depth. Her views are congruent with those of T. S. Eliot, who came to regard romanticism as a demoralizing and ultimately degenerating literary phenomenon.

Far from retreating to a sterile classicism, L. sought meaning in the confluence of character and narrative that served as the spawning ground for the kind of creative force that lends itself to genius. Taking the broad view, she esteemed Charles Dickens as a force to contend with. Disagreeing vividly with Edmund Wilson, who viewed the Victorian novelist as a misfit and disaffected with the moral obliquity of his age, the Leavises in their joint effort, *Dickens the Novelist* (1970), insisted on a corrective optic that "will enforce . . . the conviction that Dickens was one of the greatest of creative writers, that with the intelligence inherent in creative genius, he developed a fully conscious devotion to his art, becoming a popular and fecund but yet profound, serious and wonderfully resourceful practicing novelist."

For her, the past was never dead, and in the capacious pocket of her beautifully educated memory there was a special place for writers who could dramatically resolve moral equivocations. Although never slighting the importance of sociological themes in the novels she elevated into critical consideration, L. preferred the complexity of character delineation in which narrative reaches its most passionate pitch of perfection. In "A Fresh Approach to *Wuthering Heights*," an essay addressed to an American audience during her visit to the United States in 1966, she sought to turn attention to "the human core of the novel, to recognize its truly human centrality" while never forsaking its firm moral effect. In this novel of hopeless, tragic renunciation, L. professed to see the resolution of the highest moral principles not by didactic instruction but rather by the subtle art of indirection, through such technical instrumentalities as contrast and parallelism. *Wuthering Heights* obtains a Leavisian imprimatur precisely because of its sustained complexity and textural richness, which adds dimension to historical portraiture. She makes her point by contrasting Emily Brontë's novel with Henri-Pierre Roche's popular but lesser work, *Jules et Jim* (1953), which falls prey to that "moral vacuum in which the characters merely exhibit themselves."

Accused of fostering a kind of cultural mandarinism in which the great works of literature succeed each other as if engraved in a splendid frieze, L. regarded her often severe principles of consideration as tending to a new "social and ethical hygiene." To obtain a completeness of response, the signature of a *Scrutiny* critic, called for a vigorous abstention from mystic rapture or self-absorption. Her anxious pursuit of moral rigor created unhappiness in circles where aesthetic appreciation received greater sympathy; her obdurate disregard for the sensuous in language, a perhaps too unyielding espousal of high thinking and plain living to the exclusion of literature's mellower pleasures, has led to a loss in her reputation.

L.'s standing has been hurt by charges that her writing lacks bite and originality. F. W. Bateson has lamented "the curious absence in the typical *Scrutiny* critic of creative talent." Although literary criticism provided her, much as it did her husband, with the test for life and sheer concreteness—ultimately attaining the status as the "central organon for humanistic studies"—it never escapes the patriarchalism of the very conscious moral intention.

WORKS: *Fiction and the Reading Public* (1932). (with F. R. Leavis) *Lectures in America* (1969). (with F. R. Leavis) *Dickens the Novelist* (1970).

BIBLIOGRAPHY: Annan, N., in *Virginia Woolf and Bloomsbury: A Centenary Celebration*, ed. J. Marcus (1987). Fernandez, J. R. D. *RAEI* (1994). Greenwood, E. *F. R. Leavis* (1978). Kinch, M. B., et al. *F. R. Leavis and Q. D. Leavis: An Annotated Bibliography* (1989). Lyons, D. *NewC* (1991). MacKillop, I. *F. R. Leavis: A Life in Criticism* (1995). Robertson, P. J. M. *The Leavises on Fiction: An Historic Partnership* (1981). Robertson, P. J. M. *Novel* (1983). Singh, G. *AJES* (1984). *The Leavises: Recollections and Impressions*, ed. D. Thompson (1984). Walsh, W. *F. R. Leavis* (1980).

For articles in reference works, see: *CA*. *CLC*.

Other references: *LonSunT* (6 August 1995).

Michael Skakun

Harriet Lee

BORN: 1757, London.
DIED: 1 August 1851, Clifton, Bristol.
DAUGHTER OF: John Lee and Anna Sophia Lee.

L.'s father was a moderately successful actor in the shadow of David Garrick and a less successful theater manager. Little is known about her mother other than the fact that she bore five other children, including author Sophia Lee, and that she died young. L. helped Sophia run a school for girls in Bath, and she turned down William Godwin's proposal of marriage.

In her life, L. was regarded more as a novelist than as a dramatist, though she produced significant work in both genres. L. wrote the five-volume *The Canterbury Tales* (1797–1805) with Sophia. She is possibly better known, however, for the fact that Lord Byron based his *Werner, or the Inheritance* (1822) on *Kruitzner* (from the *Tales*) and acknowledged his debt in his preface, for which acknowledgment L.'s advertisement for her play *The Three Strangers* (1875) expresses her feeling of flattery. *Kruitzner*, however, is the superior work: It has a skillfully developed plot with a decided sense of rhythm, and the reader is drawn into the story less because of the work's gothic adornments than because of the strong tension that occurs in the work's resolution. *The Three Strangers*, which received four performances at Covent Garden, calls to mind Miguel de Cervantes's motivation in publishing the second part of *Don Quixote*—namely, to kill off his hero lest another author like Avellaneda could steal his literary glory.

Her earlier play, *The New Peerage, or Our Eyes May Deceive Us*, was performed nine times at Drury Lane in 1787. It is a comedy in which a nobleman and a rich merchant switch identities upon their return to England after having been sent on a tour of the Continent by their respective guardian and father. They are able to fool their elders some of the time, but the women they seek are not as gullible. At the end, all is well and class distinction does not prevent future happiness. Pierre Marivaux's *Le jeu de l'amour et du hasard* (1730) may be a possible model, but L. attempts a virtuosity of diction that lacks the *élan* and *ésprit* of the theater of customs.

L.'s major contribution to the development of the English novel is tied in with the work she and Sophia wrote, *The Canterbury Tales,* which includes *Kruitzner,* and specifically regarding narrative technique and the shape of the plot. *The Canterbury Tales,* which contains no direct references to Geoffrey Chaucer's work, has parallels with Cervantes's *Exemplary Novels* (1613). If this is the case, an exploration of the novella—of what Cervantes and his peninsular contemporaries would have called *novelas de corte italiano*—is an avenue of scholarship that could prove useful in filling in the landscape of the genre of the novel in England. *Kruitzner,* for example, conforms more closely to the Italianate model that Cervantes used in *Exemplary Novels* than to the English romances of, say, Eliza Haywood.

The introduction to the 1857 two-volume edition of *Canterbury Tales* explains that the collection, with no direct reference to Chaucer, is based on the lives of Mrs. Dixon's boarders. Mrs. Dixon produces a manuscript that was written by her former lodger, a man sought by Mr. Atkinson, "proving old stories are proverbially called Canterbury Tales, and therefore mine claim that title."

WORKS: *The Errors of Innocence* (1786). *The New Peerage, or Our Eyes May Deceive Us* (produced and pub. 1787). (with S. Lee) *The Canterbury Tales* (five vols., 1797–1805; two vols., 1857, containing all of L.'s novellas: *The Landlady's Tale—Mary Lawson; The Friend's Tale—Stanhope; The Wife's Tale—Julia; The Traveler's Tale—Montford; The Poet's Tale—Arundel; The Old Woman's Tale—Lothaire; The German's Tale—Kruitzner; The Scotman's Tale—Claudine; The Frenchman's Tale—Constance;* and *The Officer's Tale—Cavendish*). *The Mysterious Marriage, or the Heirship of Roselva* (1798). *The Three Strangers. A Play in Five Acts* (produced and pub. 1825). *The German's Tale: Kruitzner* (1848).

BIBLIOGRAPHY: Punter, D. *The Literature of Terror* (1980). Rogers, K. *Feminism in Eighteenth Century England* (1982). Summers, M. *The Gothic Quest* (1938). Tompkins, J. M. S. *The Popular Novel in England 1770–1800* (1932).

For articles in reference works, see: *Bloomsbury. Chambers. Feminist. OCEL. Oxford. RPW. ToddBWW. ToddDBA.*

Nicolás Hernández, Jr.

Sophia Lee

BORN: 13 May 1750, London.
DIED: 13 March 1824, Clifton, Bristol.
DAUGHTER OF: John Lee and Anna Sophia Lee.

The eldest of six children born to acting parents, L. was nineteen when her mother died, leaving her in charge of her siblings, John Alexander, Charlotte, Harriet, George Augustus, and Anne. While her father was imprisoned for debt in the King's Bench prison, she wrote her first drafts of *The Chapter of Accidents* (1780), a comic play that became the foundation of her literary and financial success. The play's composition was influenced by L.'s reading of Diderot's *Le Père de Famille,* but its genesis was long and convoluted, involving many revisions and drastically different forms—including that of an opera—over seven years before it was ultimately produced by George Colman at the Little Theatre in the Haymarket on 5 August 1780. It was published in the same year and was translated into French and German.

Using the profits from this stage success, in January 1781 L. and her sisters opened a school for girls in Bath, where her father managed the Orchard Street Theatre. This school was called Belvidere House; among the students it attracted were the youngest daughter of the actress Sarah Siddons and the daughter of the poet Richard Tickell. The daily life of the school is described in *The Memoirs of Susan Sibbald* (1926; ed. F. P. Hett). Until its closing in 1803, when L. decided to retire, Belvedere House provided the Lee sisters with a stable home and community that also placed them within the most artistic and intellectual circles in Bath society.

Also in 1781, L. worked on an operatic version of Frances Sheridan's *Nourjahad,* but this work did not immediately appear on the stage. In 1783, L.'s early affinity for the theater and music gave way to efforts in prose when she published the first volume of the groundbreaking historical novel *The Recess, or a Tale of Other Times.* The second and third volumes appeared in 1785; this novel spawned a series of imitators and paved the way for the historical novels of Walter Scott. A year later, L. published *Warbeck, a Pathetic Tale,* a translation of Baculard D'Arnaud's *Varbeck,* which, like *The Recess,* blended historical fact with sentimental fiction. *A Hermit's Tale,* a ballad in 156 stanzas, followed in 1787 and featured a story line concerning frustrated love in the Borders region of England. L. returned to the theater in 1796 with her second play, a tragedy in blank verse called *Almeyda; Queen of Granada;* Drury Lane manager Richard Brinsley Sheridan paid L. the exceedingly high price of £450 for the right to produce this play. Although *Almeyda* was not a popular success, it received positive critical reviews and served as a vehicle for Sarah Siddons. L. also contributed two lengthy stories to her sister's story collection, *The Canterbury Tales* (1797–1805). These stories, "The Young Lady's Tale—The Two Emilys" and "The Clergyman's Tale—Pembroke," together comprised one and one-half volumes of the total five volumes. The events described in "The Two Emilys," although fantastic by modern standards of credibility, were entrancing to contemporary readers, including Hester Lynch Piozzi; due to its popularity, this tale was subsequently republished in a separate edition. "The Clergyman's Tale" is set in Wales and clearly reflects the vogue of the picturesque, which L. and her sisters enjoyed in their own sojourns in Wales. Published in 1804, L.'s epistolary novel *The Life of a Lover* actually constitutes her earliest literary effort; this novel verged on scandal in its presentation of vivid love scenes between a young woman and a married man. L.'s final work, the comedy *The Assignation,* was produced at Drury Lane in 1807, but it was unfavorably received due to its supposed satirical treatment of Admiral Horatio Nelson and Emma, Lady Hamilton.

L.'s contemporary literary reputation rests upon *The Recess,* one of the earliest and most influential examples of historical gothic writing. Although this literary genre was pioneered by Thomas Leland's *Longsword, Earl of Salisbury* (1762), it was *The Recess* that inaugurated a lengthy train of successors. This work is set during the reign of Queen Elizabeth I, who figures as one of the major characters, along with Sir Philip Sidney, Sir Francis Drake, Lord Burleigh, and Lady Pembroke. The plot is as convoluted and labyrinthine as the subterranean recess that gives the novel its name. Briefly, *The Recess* tells of the extended sufferings of two fictitious daughters of Mary, Queen of Scots, by a clandestine marriage to Thomas, fourth Duke of Norfolk. The two daughters, Ellinor and Matilda, are raised in secrecy in a subterranean recess within the precincts of an abandoned abbey. Their retirement ends abruptly with the entrance of the Earl of Leicester, his secret marriage to Matilda, and the removal of both sisters from seclusion to court. There Ellinor falls in love with the Earl of Essex, but their union is thwarted. The rest of the narrative recounts the persecution both sisters undergo at the hands of a villainous Elizabeth, who discovers in their noble birth a threat to the security of her own throne.

L.'s novel clearly is indebted to the English Gothic writers Sir Horace Walpole and Clara Reeve as well as the French writers of historical romance, Abbé Prevost and Baculard D'Arnaud. Like Reeve and Walpole, L. presents herself as the editor, rather than the author, of an authentic and antique manuscript that chronicles a bygone era. Like Prevost and D'Arnaud, L. interweaves fictitious and factual events with a free hand; like them, she casts over this concoction a distinctly Gothic gloom, employing such standard Gothic themes as death, incest, and madness and conventions like subterranean vaults, trapdoors, and monastic ruins. In *The Recess* history affords a basis for suggestion rather than knowledge, and dates are confused or ignored, perhaps by design, perhaps by accident. Neither L. nor her readers seem disturbed by a rewriting of history that places the Armada invasion (1588) before the execution of Mary, Queen of Scots (1587). The explanation behind historical events is shown to be personal and private rather than political and public (for example, love controls Essex's behavior in Ireland and causes Sidney's death at Zutphen). L. deflates the grand panoramic sweep of history and brings it within the comprehension of her contemporary reading public. She reveals this intention in the novel's advertisement: "History, like painting, only perpetuates the striking features of the mind, whereas the best and worst actions of princes often proceed from partialities and prejudices, which live in their hearts and are buried with them." The narrative seeks to demonstrate not only the intensely personal motives comprising history but also the subjectivity inherent in our interpretations of history. The narrative is made up of two long letters, one by each sister, each bringing to bear strikingly different viewpoints on essentially similar occurrences.

In its own time, *The Recess* was well received, with four editions by 1792, a fifth in 1804, an Irish edition in 1791, and various printings and abridgements in 1800, 1802, 1824, 1827, and 1840 as well as French and Portuguese versions. The German play *Maria Stuart* (1784) by actor and romanticist Christian Heinrich Spiess owed its inspiration to L.'s novel. The writing of historical romances flowered after the publication of *The Recess,* and a number of works clearly took L.'s book as their model: Mrs. Harley's *St. Bernard's Priory* (1786), Anne Fuller's *Alan Fitz-Osborne, an Historical Tale* (1787), and Rosetta Ballin's *The Statue Room* (1790). The art of Sir Walter Scott and Ann Radcliffe also bear the impress of L.'s achievement. Her use of the rationally explained supernatural reached its perfection in Radcliffe, and the strain of historical romance that L. inaugurated culminated in Scott's novels.

L. lived for the last twenty years of her life with her sister Harriet in Clifton, near Bristol, where she remained active in literary-social circles that included Mrs. Piozzi; the industrialists Matthew Boulton and James Watt, Jr.; Sarah Siddons; and the president of the Royal Academy, Sir Thomas Lawrence. Upon her death at age seventy-three, L. left to her sister Harriet a personal estate valued at over £7,000; Harriet survived L. by twenty-six years. Some of L.'s correspondence is preserved in the New York Public Library, The Beinecke (Yale University), The Bodleian (Oxford University), and elsewhere. Her poetic efforts, unpublished except for *A Hermit's Tale,* are still in the family's possession.

WORKS: *The Chapter of Accidents* (1780). *The Recess, or a Tale of Other Times* (three vols., 1783–1785). (trans.) *Varbeck,* by Baculard D'Arnaud (as *Warbeck, a Pathetic Tale,* 1786). *A Hermit's Tale, Recorded by His Own Hand and Found in His Cell* (1787). *Almeyda; Queen of Granada* (1796). (with H. Lee) *The Canterbury Tales* (five vols., 1797–1805; *The Young Lady's Tale—The Two Emilys,* and *The Clergyman's Tale—Pembroke*). *The Life of a Lover* (1804). *The Assignation* (stage performance only, 1807).

BIBLIOGRAPHY: Alliston, A. *YJC* (1990). Backscheider, P. *Spectacular Politics* (1993). Foster, J. *History of the Pre-Romantic Novel* (1949). Lewis, J. E. *ECF* (1995). MacCarthy, B. G. *The Female Pen* (1946). Punter, D. *The Literature of Terror* (1980). Roberts, B. *MSE* (1979). Spencer, J. *The Rise of the Woman Novelist* (1986). Stanton, J. P., in *Curtain Calls,* ed. M. A. Schofield and C. Macheski (1991). Summers, M. *The Gothic Quest* (1938). Tompkins, J. M. S. *The Popular Novel in England 1770–1800* (1932). Varma, D., ed. and intro. to *The Recess* (1972).

For articles in reference works, see: *BAB1800. Feminist. ToddBWW.*

Other references: Spender, D. *Mothers of the Novel* (1986).

Eileen Finan
(updated by Steven J. Gores)

Lee, Vernon: See *Paget, Violet*

Rosamond Lehmann

BORN: 3 February 1901, Bourne End, Buckinghamshire.
DIED: 14 March 1990, London.

DAUGHTER OF: Rudolph Chambers Lehmann and Alice Marie Davis Lehmann.
MARRIED: Leslie Ruciman, 1923; Wogan Philipps, 1928.

Born into an unusually intellectually and artistically gifted family, L. fit in well with her younger sister, Beatrix, who became a well-known actress, and her youngest brother, John, who became a critic, poet, founder of *New Writing*, and, for a time, manager of Leonard and Virginia Woolf's Hogarth Press. L.'s father, an editor of *Punch* and a regular contributor of verse and prose to that magazine, also entertained many literary figures at his home. Educated privately, L. went to Girton College, Cambridge, in 1919 to study modern languages, returning home in 1922.

Partly because most of her important work was published by 1947, L.'s reputation does not live up to early expectations that ranked her with Elizabeth Bowen and Virginia Woolf, although she has consistently enjoyed critical esteem. Those who have objected to aspects of her writing have chided her for confining herself to the world of "feminine sensibility" in which, in technically impeccable but mannered and highly charged emotional prose, women and girls are faced with disillusionment, loss of innocence, and betrayal by love and life.

Despite these problems, L.'s novels profoundly and lyrically investigate aspects of women's lives that are frequently ignored, for example, lesbian relations, infidelity, suicide, hatred, and power manipulations. In her first highly acclaimed novel, *Dusty Answer* (1927), published a year before Radclyffe Hall's *Well of Loneliness*, L. treated the theme of adolescent lesbianism with sensitivity and candor, using her own college experiences. *A Note in Music* (1930) and *The Weather in the Streets* (1936) both deal with the drabness and disillusionment accompanying unfulfilled middle age, an accomplishment especially in an era when there were even fewer novels than there are today depicting lives of women over thirty. *The Ballad and the Source* (1945) is L.'s best-known and most critically acclaimed novel. Stylistically breathtaking and structurally complex, full of Jamesian experimentation with point of view, the book presents a charismatic but egomaniacal central character, the aging Mrs. Sybil Anstey Herbert Jardine, who comes to dominate the consciousness of a progressively disillusioned adolescent, Rebecca Landon, who learns variations of the story of Mrs. Jardine's life—a tale encompassing adultery, madness, suicide and hatred—from four people who knew her. A theme introduced in this novel that remains important in L.'s later writing is that of the mystical and transcendent influence of the self on others. Many critics have praised L.'s ornate, romantic, lyrical prose. L. said of herself that she wrote in a "halftrance," experiencing herself as "a kind of preserving jar in which float fragments of people and landscapes, snatches of sound, [but] there is not one of these fragile shapes and serial sounds but bears within it the explosive seed of life."

After her daughter's death of poliomyelitis in 1958, L. turned increasingly to spiritualism, which she discusses in *The Swan in the Evening* (1967), a disquieting, even embarrassing but moving personal memoir.

WORKS: *Dusty Answer* (1927). *A Note in Music* (1930). *Letter to a Sister* (1932). *Invitation to the Waltz* (1932). *The Weather in the Streets* (1936). *No More Music* (1945). *The Ballad and the Source* (1945). *The Gipsy's Baby and Other Stories* (1947). *The Echoing Grove* (1953). (with W. Tudor Pole) *A Man Seen Afar* (1965). *The Swan in the Evening: Fragments of an Inner Life* (1967). (with Cynthia Hill Sandys) *Letters from Our Daughters* (1972). *A Sea-Grape Tree* (1977). *Lehmann's Album* (1985).

BIBLIOGRAPHY: LeStourgeon, D. *Rosamond Lehmann* (1965). Siegel, R. *Rosamond Lehmann: A Thirties Writer* (1989). Simons, J. *Rosamond Lehmann* (1992).

For articles in reference works, see: *Bloomsbury. CA. Cambridge. CN. DLB. EWLTC. Feminist. Oxford. TCA SUP. ToddBWW.*

Other references: Blodgett, H. *UMSE* (1992). Broughton, P. *SCRev.* (1984). *ConL* (1974). Kaplan, S. *TCL* (1981). Pfaltz, K. *EBC* (1992). *Virginia Woolf Quarterly* (Spring 1973).

Carey Kaplan
(updated by Christina Root)

Leigh, Arbor: See *Bevington, Louisa Sarah*

Leigh, Arran: See *Field, Michael (Katherine Harris Bradley)*

Dorothy Kempe Leigh

FLOURISHED: 1616.
DAUGHTER OF: Robert Kempe (or Kemp), Esq. of Spainshall, and Elizabeth, daughter of Sir Clement Higham of Barrowhall, Suffolk.
MARRIED: Ralph Leigh (or Lee).

An English gentlewoman of the middle class, L. authored one work, *The Mothers Blessing*, for her three sons. Little is known of L.'s life or that of her family except that she was pious, a Puritan, and a dedicated mother. She is not listed in the *Dictionary of National Biography.* She was born in Finchingfield, Essex, and married Ralph Leigh (or Lee), a Cheshire gentleman and soldier under the Earl of Essex at Cadiz; they had three sons, George, John, and William. Her son William may have become Rector of Groton near Hadleigh, appointed by John Winthrop.

The Mothers Blessing is a fine example of the advice book, a genre then in vogue. It is evident that L.'s advice book reflects the results of both the humanist and religious advocates of education for women. In fact, her book forwards their attitudes as she urges her sons to educate their wives and servants, stressing knowledge of the Bible and practical skills. It is divided into four sections. The first is a dedication to Princess Elizabeth who is asked to serve as "protectoresse" of the work. Part II is a letter to her sons explaining her reasons for writing. The third section is an Introductory Epistle, which is composed in an eight-line stanza. The epistle is controlled and indicates some poetic merit. Possibly as a reflection of her country life, L. employs images of nature, such as bees and flowers, which are then incorporated into a parable of the busy bee wherein L. urges her sons to model themselves after the busy rather than the idle bee. Part IV is the longest section of the work, presenting in forty-five brief chapters L.'s concerns with personal behavior, choice of wife, and education. Her advice to her sons, though practical, is primarily religious. Each of the chapters opens with a biblical quotation.

The book was extremely popular as evidenced by the publication of seventeen editions between 1616 and 1640 and its continued printing into the last quarter of the century. Although popular, the book did not seem to have much literary influence, though it may have had social influence. It did, however, presage John Milton, also a Puritan, in its attitude toward education, especially of women, and in the belief that a wife functions chiefly as a companion.

WORKS: *The Mothers Blessing* (1616, STC 15402).

BIBLIOGRAPHY: Beilin, E. V. *Redeeming Eve* (1987). Sizemore, C. *South Atlantic Bulletin* (1976). Sizemore, C. *UDR* (1981). Travitsky, B., in *The Lost Tradition: Mothers and Daughters in Literature,* ed. E. M. Broner and C. N. Davidson (1979). *The Paradise of Women: Writings by English Women of the Renaissance,* ed. B. Travitsky (1981).

For articles in reference works, see: *Feminist.*

Marcia M. Davis

Leigh, Isla: See *Field, Michael (Edith Emma Cooper)*

L. E. L.: See *Landon, Letitia Elizabeth*

Charlotte Ramsay Lennox

BORN: c. 1729–32, Gibraltar or America (?).
DIED: 4 January 1804, London.
DAUGHTER OF: Captain James Ramsay, of Dalhousie, Scotland, and Catherine Ramsay.
MARRIED: Alexander Lennox, 1747.
WROTE UNDER: "Author of the Female Quixote"; "A Friend": Charlotte Lennox; Charlotte Ramsay Lennox; Parthenissa; Perdita; Penelope Spindle; Mrs. Trifler; "A Young Lady."

According to Andrew Millar, L.'s primary publisher, "Nothing is more public than her writings, nothing more concealed than her person." This statement would seem to be true, for although she wrote novels, poetry, literary criticism, and plays and she published a periodical as well as several translations, little is known about her life. Even the date and place of her birth are disputed; however, the consensus seems to be that she was born in 1729 or 1730, either in Gibraltar or in America. As a young person, L. spent several years in America while her father was stationed there. According to Philippe Séjourné, the biographer of L.'s life in America, she resided there from April 1739 to March 1742.

Because large portions of L.'s first and last novels take place in America, she has often been hailed as the "first American novelist." On 10 March 1742, her father, James Ramsay, died. Soon after, L. was sent to England to live with a rich aunt (Mrs. Lucking of Messing Hall, in Essex) who offered to care for her in order to give Mrs. Ramsay some financial relief. Upon L.'s arrival in London, however, she learned that her aunt was insane and/or dead. Left unprotected and alone in London at the age of thirteen, L. served as a companion/governess in the home of the Marchionness of Rockingham, a member of the circle that included Lady Isabella Finch and the Duchess of Newcastle. M. R. Small writes that L. served as a companion/governess in the Rockingham home until something happened that offended her protectress. Various contemporary references suggest that L.'s offense (or that the offense against her) was sexual. L. also become a member of the Samuel Johnson/Thomas Birch circle, and Birch may have served as her tutor, and possibly as her first publisher. "The Dream, An Ode by Mrs. Ramsey at 15," a poem by L., formed part of his *Poetical Fragments,* a collection of manuscript poems that was never actually published but that might have circulated among friends and acquaintances. L.'s friendship with Johnson lasted throughout his life.

L.'s ode appeared in her first published book, *Poems on Several Occasions* (1747), published in the same year as her marriage to her publisher's assistant; in December 1750 Johnson hosted a celebration for her first novel, *The Life of Harriot Stuart.* Her second novel, *The Female Quixote; or, The Adventures of Arabella,* which followed in 1752, received much acclaim. Henry Fielding praised it highly: "Upon the whole, I do very earnestly recommend it, as a most extraordinary and most excellent Performance. It is indeed a Work of true Humour, and cannot fail of giving a rational, as well as very pleasing, Amusement to a sensible Reader, who will at once be instructed and very highly diverted."

L.'s most famous, controversial work was *Shakespear Illustrated; or The Novels and Histories, on which the Plays of Shakespear are founded, Collected and Translated from the Original Authors with Critical Remarks* (1753–54), L. claims William Shakespeare misread the romances he turned into plays and criticizes him for not doing women justice; she finds the original superior to the revisions. Margaret Doody concludes that L."is the first woman to produce a scholarly work on English literature, and the first feminist critic of a major author."

L.'s periodical, *The Lady's Museum*—a witty compendium of history, natural science, poetry, fiction, and translations of moral and philosophical works—went through eleven numbers in 1760–61. Using a panoply of personac—"Parthenissa," "Perdita," "Penelope Spindle," and the journal's editor ("Mrs. Trifler," the self-proclaimed daughter and granddaughter of triflers)—L. produced a series of ironic reflections on women in society. While the explicit text suggests that women are naturally triflers and happiest when they submit to their natural inclination to trifle, the subtext argues that women sometimes want to be taken seriously and that perhaps even the Trifler herself—despite her claims to Trifler-hood—has purposes other than merely to divert and please her readers.

L.'s attack on Shakespeare was probably one of the main causes for her failure as a dramatist. Her first play, *The Sister,* was withdrawn after its opening performance at

Covent Garden on 18 February 1769 because it was "treated so badly by the audience." Unfortunately, the play was never performed again. L. did not produce another play until 1775; *Old City Manners,* an adaptation of Ben Jonson's *Eastward Ho,* fared much better, running through seven performances. L.'s translations include *Memoirs of Maximilian de Bethune, Duke of Sully* (1755), *The Memoirs of the Countess of Berci* (1756), *Memoirs for the History of Madame de Maintenon and of the Last Age* (1757), and *The Greek Theatre of Father Brumoy* (1760).

L.'s life was difficult. Her daughter died at the age of sixteen or seventeen. Her son, who showed much promise and even published some poetry, escaped to America to avoid criminal prosecution. Toward the end of her life, she was separated from her husband, who was improvident throughout most of his life. In the last years of her life, she was supported by the Royal Literary Fund.

WORKS: (by "A Young Lady") *Poems on Several Occasions* (1747). (by "herself") *The Life of Harriot Stuart* (1750; ed. S. K. Howard, 1995). *The Female Quixote; or, The Adventures of Arabella* (1752). *Shakespear Illustrated; or The Novels and Histories, on which the Plays of Shakespear are founded, Collected and Translated from the Original Authors with Critical Remarks* (1753–54; 3 vols.). (trans.) *The Memoirs of the Countess of Berci* (1756). (trans.) *Memoirs of Maximilian de Bethune, Duke of Sully* (1756). (trans.) *Memoirs for the History of Madame de Maintenon and of the Last Age* (1757). *Henrietta* (1758). *Philander, a pastoral* (1758). (trans.) *The Greek Theatre of Father Brumoy* (1759). *The Lady's Museum* (1760). *Sophia* (1762). (by "A Friend") *The History of Eliza* (1767). *The Sister* (1769). (trans.) *Meditations and Penitential Prayers, written by the celebrated Dutchess De La Valliere* (1774). *Old City Manners* (1775). *Euphemia* (1790).

BIBLIOGRAPHY: (Anon.) "Memoir of Mrs. Lennox" *Edinburgh Weekly Magazine* (1783). *Lady's Monthly Museum* (1813). Maynadier, G. H. *The First American Novelist?* (1940). Séjourné, P. *The Mystery of Charlotte Lennox: First Novelist of Colonial America (1727?–1804)* (1967). Small, M. R. *Charlotte Ramsay Lennox: An Eighteenth Century Lady of Letters* (1935).

For articles in reference works, see: *Allibone. Biographia Dramatica. Cambridge. DNB. Eighteenth-Century Vignettes, Literary Anecdotes. Oxford. ToddDBA.*

Other references: Barbauld, A. L. preface to *The Female Quixote* (1820). Craft, C. A. *MLR* (1991). Doody, M. A. *SNNTS* (1987). Gallagher, C. *MLQ* (1992). Gray, J. *MP* (1985). Green, S., in *Cultural Readings of Restoration and Eighteenth-Century English Theater,* ed. J. D. Canfield and D. E. Payne (1995). Grundy, I. *AJ* (1987). Howard, S. K. *ECF* (1993). Isles, D. *New Rambler* (1967). Isles, D. *HLB* (1970–71). Kramnick, J. B. *MLQ* (1994). Langbauer, L. *Novel* (1984). Lynch, J. J. *ELWIU* (1987). McNeill, D., in *TransAtlantic Crossings: Eighteenth-Century Explorations,* ed. D. W. Nichol (1995). Marshall, D. *ECF* (1993). Ross, D. *SEL* (1987). Shevelow, K. *TSWL* (1982). Spacks, P. M., in *Fetter'd or Free? British Women Novelists, 1670–1815,* ed. M. A. Schofield and C. Macheski (1986). Spacks, P. M. *MP* (1988). Spencer, J., in *Contexts of Pre-Novel Narrative,* ed. R. Eriksen (1994). Thomson, H. *Living by the Pen* (1992). Warren, L. E. *SECC* (1982).

Temma F. Berg

Sarah Lennox Bunbury Napier

BORN: 25 February 1745, London.
DIED: 26 August 1826, London.
DAUGHTER OF: Charles Lennox, second Duke of Richmond, and Sarah Cadogan.
MARRIED: Sir Thomas Charles Bunbury, 1762; George Napier, 1781.

L. is best known for her letters and her unconventional life. The fourth and youngest surviving daughter of the second Duke of Richmond, she was orphaned at the age of five. Brought up by her older sisters, Lady Caroline Fox, Emily, Duchess of Leinster, and Lady Louisa Conolly, L. blossomed as a wit and flirt at an early age. Though not regarded by contemporaries as equal in looks to her sisters, she surpassed them in vivacity and unconventionality.

Introduced at court in 1759, she made an immediate impact, especially on George, the Prince of Wales. The romance seemed serious, but her self-confessed "wild & giddy spirits," the disapproval of his mother, Princess Augusta, and her status as a commoner posed insurmountable obstacles. George became King George III in 1760 and in the following year married Charlotte of Mecklenburg. L. wrote that she was disappointed in the king's behavior toward her, characterizing it as that of "a man who has neither sense, good nature, nor honesty." Nevertheless, she wrote, "I have almost forgiven him; luckily for me I did not love him, & only liked him, nor did the title weigh anything with me."

In 1762, L. married Sir Thomas Charles Bunbury, but the marriage was not a success. Bunbury devoted himself to his horses and L. to society. Her letters for this period are mostly chronicles of social and family news. Besides her sisters, her main correspondent was her cousin, Lady Susan Fox-Strangways, who in 1764 eloped with William O'Brien, an Irish actor. These letters told of fashions, the theater, and the latest marriages and divorces in society. L. took several lovers including Lord William Gordon, whose child she bore in 1768. Her subsequent elopement with Gordon brought her marriage to an end; it was dissolved by Act of Parliament in 1776.

L. lived in seclusion with her daughter on the family estate at Goodwood for several years. In 1781, she married the Hon. George Napier, an army officer of noble birth but modest circumstances. They had five sons and three daughters. Several of the Napier sons became distinguished generals. Her happy second marriage ended with his death in 1804. L., who was granted a royal pension after her husband's death, became blind in her later years but never lost her wit or charm.

After her separation from Bunbury, L.'s letters took on a more serious tone, partly explained by her exclusion from society and family involvement in politics. She took great pride in her nephew, Charles James Fox, though she was well aware of his faults. In 1783, she commented that "I am sure greatness pursues him to be Minister, can he avoid it?" After the first major attack of George III's debilitating illness, she reflected on what might have been, observing "I still rejoice I was never Queen, . . . I always preferred my own situation, sometimes happy, sometimes miserable, to what it would have been." Her last letters were increasingly elegaic, for she had outlived not only her husband but also her siblings, her daughters, and many of her nephews and nieces.

The Lennox sisters remained close throughout their lives. Important political connections, wide social contacts, and wealth made them and their families a part of the establishment. They corresponded with each other regularly; many of their letters have been preserved and published. L. was a most perceptive observer; her correspondence provides valuable insights into the politics and personalities of Whig Britain in the reign of George III.

WORKS: *The Life and Letters of Lady Sarah Lennox 1745–1826*, ed. Countess of Ilchester and Lord Stavordale (1902).

BIBLIOGRAPHY: Curtis, E. R. *Lady Sarah Lennox: An Irrepressible Stuart, 1745–1826* (1946). *Correspondence of Emily Duchess of Leinster* (1731–1814), ed. B. Fitzgerald (1949–1957). Tillyard, S. *Aristocrats: Caroline, Emily, Louisa, and Sarah Lennox 1774–1832* (1994).

For articles in reference works, see: *ToddDBA* (under "Bunbury").

Barbara Brandon Schnorrenberg

Doris Lessing

BORN: 22 October 1919, Kermanshah, Persia.
DAUGHTER OF: Alfred Cook Tayler and Emily McVeagh Tayler.
MARRIED: Frank Wisdom, 1939; Gottfried Lessing, 1944.
WRITES UNDER: Doris Lessing; Jane Somers.

When L. entered the literary scene in 1950 with the conventionally realistic *The Grass Is Singing*, she began a career devoted to exploring the psychic wholeness missing in the "fragmented" modern world. In her novels, as well as in numerous stories and work in other genres, L. has been for many readers a kind of Cassandra or conscience of the modern age. L. has produced fiction of many forms, including a multivolume *Bildungsroman*, works focusing on characters seeking inner knowledge or independence, a "space fiction" series, books about a young terrorist, a career woman working in the world of fashion, and an evil child—in short, a wide literary canvas peopled with earnest characters who have had considerable impact on intelligent readers around the world.

L.'s first novel, *The Grass Is Singing*, published after L. emigrated from Rhodesia to London, is set in and clearly deeply concerned with the colonial world L. knew as a child. Mary Turner is seen in flashback as incapable of adjustment to white "superiority" on the impoverished farm she and her husband run, and her cruelty and insecurity result in her being killed by her black houseboy. Africa is also the setting for four of the five parts of L.'s "Children of Violence" series (1952–69); Martha Quest is depicted from adolescence to old age and death, from colonial expectations during World War II through failed marriages and child raising, political and social involvement, emigration to England, and psychic complexities in a world hurtling rapidly toward destruction (in *The Four-Gated City*, 1969) at the end of the twentieth century.

The Golden Notebook (1962) is by common consent L.'s masterpiece. More overtly concerned with the fragmented soul than any of L.'s other books, this novel shows how Anna Wulf divides her life into notebook narratives (black for her life in colonial Africa, red for her life as a Communist, yellow about an alter ego, and blue a factual diary), all of which culminate in a golden one serving as therapy and reconciliation of her various "selves." In addition, several "Free Women" sections comprise a short conventional novel, also about Anna Wulf but "written" by her as counterpoint to her "real" life. Erroneously considered by some critics to be L.'s own "confessions," the novel is instead a rich, multilayered, endlessly rewarding account of a woman's search for wholeness through Jungian therapy as well as through sex, marriage, dreams, politics, writing, and incessant analysis of news reports and of herself.

L.'s forays into "inner space" continued with *Briefing for a Descent into Hell* (1971), a claustrophobic work somewhat indebted to Scottish psychiatrist R. D. Laing in its concern with mental imbalance and psychic phenomena. Charles Watkins, one of the few male protagonists in L.'s novels, is a classics professor who "travels" psychically to a gathering of Greek deities (hence the book's title, with "hell" equated with earth), to World War II Yugoslavia (where he fights with partisans), and, most startling, to a raft on the ocean that lands him in a prehistoric city where strange species of animals fight and from which he escapes to "reality." After the amnesiac Watkins is found wandering in London, he is hospitalized, able to recall his various "existences" but not his "real" life; after therapy, he is restored to "sanity," but not to wholeness, freedom, and human harmony.

Restoration of psychic health is also L.'s concern in *The Summer Before the Dark* (1973) and *Memoirs of a Survivor* (1974). The first is a realistic, somewhat clichéd account of Kate Brown's gradual awakening at the age of forty-five into a self-conscious "liberation"; she goes away from home and family for a series of experiences one summer that culminate in her returning, chastened and reconciled, to her routine life. The latter work, though, is an important study of a woman's solitary survival following the ultimate war; inexplicably, she must care for a preadolescent girl who rapidly matures into a sexually liberated woman and who, with her lover and a strange hybrid pet, pioneers in helping other survivors endure the end of civilization. Most impressive in the book, however, are those passages in which the narrator "walks" through a wall to "see" a series of tableaux about her own earlier life by which she rids herself of behavior and thinking invalid in her world.

L.'s five-volume series of "space fiction" narratives, "Canopus in Argos: Archives," depicts earth's history as a battleground for opposing forces of ageless beings. *Shikasta* (1979) is a prolix sequence of documents, reports, and records presenting earth's history from a cosmic perspective; as allegory, the work shows how humanity flounders helplessly from catastrophe to catastrophe, but as a novel it is unconvincing. *The Marriages Between Zones Three, Four and Five* (1980), however, is a fascinating fable that, although allegorical, also offers a convincing love story and psychological analysis of the rise and fall of civilizations. *The Sirian Experiments* (1981) contains many documents about earth's early history, but it also offers a female demigod who slowly changes as she understands the "group mind" that runs the universe and the effects this has on and for earth. *The Making of the Representative for Planet 8* (1982) concerns the freezing death of a world whose inhabitants must prepare for their promised removal to another planet; even the "Overlords," though, are subject to inexorable cosmic forces that radically diminish earthly concerns with nationalism and historical pride. Finally, *Documents Relating to The Sentimental Agents in the Volyen Empire* (1983) again includes various documents but is also an ineffectual attempt at satire regarding the debasement of language as mere "rhetoric" in the rise and fall of societies.

In 1983, L. attempted a hoax by publishing *The Diary of a Good Neighbour* under the name "Jane Somers," and *If the Old Could* . . . under the same name the year after; her intent in the experiment was to see whether novels could be published on their merits instead of on an author's name and reputation. But neither realistic book—one focusing on a fashion magazine editor's relationship with a dying older woman, the other on a nonconsummated love affair and a woman's relationship with her niece—is very good: Characters are banal, plots are sentimental, and insights into any larger world view are limited. It seems as if L. had both a narrower purpose and a more unquestioning attitude toward human behavior in these pseudonymous works than in her ealier books.

The Good Terrorist (1985) is a return to a realistic approach; it concerns a young insecure middle-class woman who works with (and supports) a gang of would-be terrorists; they prefer to fight the "system" through parasitic behavior and endless discussions and demonstrations while she works as a drudge cleaning up after them, abusing her own parents, and, through misguided idealism, taking the revolution into her own hands. Topical though the book is, it lacks emotional liveliness and compelling characters.

L. continued to experiment in her fiction with *The Fifth Child* (1988), her first foray into the horror genre. L.'s interests in anthropology led to this harrowing moral fable in which a conventional English couple, David and Harriet Lovatt, have four "normal" children. But their "fifth child," Ben, who is variously presented as a Neanderthal, a troll, or (L.'s term) a goblin, is shown to be an amoral (or premoral) creature that gradually destroys the family's life. As Ben grows up, he demonstrates sadistic behavior toward siblings, pets, and parents until, as an adolescent, he joins with other antisocial youths in organized terror. L. has denied in an interview that Ben is evil, "just out of the right place," of a "different race of being that's landed . . . in our . . . complicated society."

L. has produced more nonfiction than fiction in recent years. In 1995 she published *Playing the Game,* a slight "graphic novel," a few hundred words of text accompanied by colorful science-fiction illustrations. *Love, Again* (1996), L.'s only novel since *The Fifth Child,* is close to *The Summer Before the Dark* in its focus on an older woman who is seeking meaning in life. The long, self-analytical narrative centers on Sarah Durham, manager of a small theater company that plans to produce the story of Julie Vairon, a nineteenth-century quadroon from Martinique who survives as an artist and composer in France before killing herself. The novel is especially good in capturing Durham's emotional struggles, such as her sense of life's unfairness, the need for sacrifice, the complexities of aging, and her ambiguous feelings toward family, colleagues, and lovers.

L's recent nonfiction is impressive, especially her various volumes of autobiography. *African Laughter* (1992) describes four visits to Zimbabwe between 1982 and 1992 and combines the political with the personal, as when she tells of her racist brother's views and subsequent death. Her picture of Zimbabwe's future is bleak, given its decline and chaos, but she is hopeful that the country can mature and survive.

Under My Skin (1994) covers her life from childhood in Rhodesia (Zimbabwe) until 1959, when she migrated to England. The work necessarily compares her early fiction with the facts of her life and is candid about her views, though she is less revealing about her two marriages and affairs. The book captures colonial African physical and emotional life well; it is unsentimental, candid, and enthralling. *Walking in the Shade* (1997), another volume of autobiography, covers the period until 1962 and the publication of *The Golden Notebook.* L. is less concerned in this volume with childhood memories, at which she excels, and is more concerned with her struggle to survive in her adopted London with fellow writers, publishers, and assorted lovers. It is concerned most of all with her years as a Communist, which she explains in terms of her idealistic years in Africa and her need for a cause. She is especially good in describing her subsequent disillusionment with Communism, but she only hints at her later retreat into mysticism. The book is valuable for its comments on the writing process but less so regarding precise details about children, lovers, and friends.

In addition to these volumes of autobiography, L. and composer Philip Glass have collaborated on operatic adaptations of two her novels: *The Making of the Representative for Planet 8* (1988) and *The Marriages Between Zones Three, Four and Five* (1997). Neither has been staged since their initial productions; the former was performed by four major opera houses in the United States and Europe to generally respectful reviews, but the latter was performed solely in one provincial German house to generally negative reviews.

L.'s work has obviously changed radically over the years, especially as she has taken chances in trying new approaches and subjects. Her high prophetic seriousness (as reflective of her interest in Sufism) and relative lack of a sense of humor have often been noted, but at her best, when she focuses on a solitary, compulsive person (usually a woman) who has been forced to a moment of crisis, she effectively dramatizes a revaluation of personal identity.

Though her fiction is often repetitive and didactic, her depth of character presentation and sense of character commitment have secured her place among the most powerful and compelling writers of the century.

WORKS: *The Grass Is Singing* (1950). *This Was the Old Chief's Country* (1951). *Martha Quest* ("Children of Violence" I) (1952). *Five: Short Novels* (1953). *A Proper Marriage* ("Children of Violence" II) (1954). *Retreat to Innocence* (1956). *The Habit of Loving* (1957). *Going Home* (1957). *A Ripple from the Storm* ("Children of Violence" III) (1958). *Each His Own Wilderness*, in *New English Dramatists: Three Plays*, ed. E. M. Browne (1959). *Fourteen Poems* (1959). *In Pursuit of the English: A Documentary* (1960). *Play with a Tiger* (1962). *The Golden Notebook* (1962). *A Man and Two Women* (1963). *African Stories* (1964). *Landlocked* ("Children of Violence" IV) (1965). *Particularly Cats* (1967). *The Four-Gated City* ("Children of Violence" V) (1969). *Briefing for a Descent into Hell* (1971). *The Story of a Non-Marrying Man and Other Stories* (1972; in the U.S. as *The Confessions of Jack Orkney and Other Stories*). *The Singing Door*, in *Second Playbill Two*, ed. A. Durband (1973). *The Summer Before the Dark* (1973). *Memoirs of a Survivor* (1974). *A Small Personal Voice: Essays, Reviews, and Interviews*, ed. P. Schlueter (1974). *Collected Stories* (1978; in the U.S. as *Stories*). *Shikasta* ("Canopus in Argos: Archives" I) (1979). *The Marriages Between Zones Three, Four and Five* ("Canopus in Argos: Archives" II) (1980). *The Sirian Experiments* ("Canopus in Argos: Archives" III) (1981). *The Making of the Representative for Planet 8* ("Canopus in Argos: Archives" IV) (1982). *Documents Relating to the Sentimental Agents in the Volyen Empire* ("Canopus in Argos: Archives" V) (1983). (as Jane Somers) *The Diary of a Good Neighbour* (1983). (as Jane Somers) *If the Old Could . . .* (1984). *The Good Terrorist* (1985). *Prisons We Choose to Live Inside* (1986). *The Wind Blows Away Our Words* (1987). *The Doris Lessing Reader* (1988; U.S. edition with same title but different contents). (with music by P. Glass) *The Making of the Representatives for Planet 8* (opera, 1988). *The Fifth Child* (1988). *Particularly Cats and More Cats* (1989; in the U.S. as *Particularly Cats . . . and Rufus*, 1991). *African Laughter: Four Visits to Zimbabwe* (1992). *London Observed: Stories and Sketches* (1991; in the U.S. as *The Real Thing: Stories and Sketches*, 1992). *Under My Skin* (1994). *Conversations*, ed. E. G. Ingersoll (1994; in the U.K. as *Putting the Questions Differently: Interviews*, 1996). *Playing the Game* (1995). *Love, Again* (1996). *Play with a Tiger and Other Plays* (1996). *Walking in the Shade* (1997). (music by P. Glass) *The Marriages Between Zones Three, Four and Five* (opera, 1997).

BIBLIOGRAPHY: *Doris Lessing*, ed. E. Bertelsen (1985). Budhos, S. *The Theme of Enclosure in Selected Works of Doris Lessing* (1987). Cederstrom, L. *Fine-Tuning the Feminine Psyche: Jungian Patterns in the Novels of Doris Lessing* (1990). Chown, L. *Narrative Authority and Homeostasis in the Novels of Doris Lessing and Carmen Martín Gaite* (1990). Draine, B. *Substance Under Pressure: Artistic Coherence and Evolving Form in the Novels of Doris Lessing* (1983). Fahim, S. S. *Doris Lessing and Sufi Equilibrium* (1994). Fishburn, K. *The Unexpected Universe of Doris Lessing: A Study in Narrative Technique* (1985). Galin, M. *Between East and West: Sufism in the Novels of Doris Lessing* (1997). Gardiner, J. K. *Rhys, Stead, Lessing, and the Politics of Empathy* (1989). Greene, G. *Doris Lessing: The Poetics of Change* (1994). Hite, M. *The Other Side of the Story* (1989). Holmquist, L. *From Society to Nature: A Study of Doris Lessing's "Children of Violence"* (1980). King, J. *Doris Lessing* (1989). Knapp, M. *Doris Lessing* (1984). Labowitz, E. K. *The Myth of the Heroine: The Female Bildungsroman in the Twentieth Century* (1986). Maslen, E. *Doris Lessing* (1994). Morris, R. K. *Continuance and Change: The Contemporary British Novel Sequence* (1972). Pickering, J. *Understanding Doris Lessing* (1990). *Doris Lessing: Critical Studies*, ed. A. Pratt and L. K. Dembo (1974). Rose, E. C. *The Tree Outside the Window: Doris Lessing's Children of Violence* (1976). Rowe, M. M. *Doris Lessing* (1994). Rubenstein, R. *The Novelistic Vision of Doris Lessing* (1979). Sage, L. *Doris Lessing* (1983). *Woolf and Lessing: Breaking the Mold*, ed. R. Saxton and J. Tobin (1995). Schlueter, P. *The Novels of Doris Lessing* (1973). Seligman, D. *Doris Lessing: An Annotated Bibliography of Criticism* (1981). Spiegel, R. *Doris Lessing: The Problem of Alienation and the Form of the Novel* (1980). *Critical Essays on Doris Lessing*, ed. C. Sprague and V. Tiger (1986). Sprague, C. *Rereading Doris Lessing: Narrative Patterns of Doubling and Repetition* (1987). St. Andrews, B. *Forbidden Fruit: On the Relationship Between Women and Knowledge in Doris Lessing, Selma Lagerlof, Kate Chopin, Margaret Atwood* (1986). Steele, M. C. *Children of Violence and Rhodesia: A Study of Doris Lessing as Historical Observer* (1974). *Notebooks/Memoirs/Archives: Reading and Rereading Doris Lessing*, ed. J. Taylor (1982). Thorpe, M. *Doris Lessing* (1973). Thorpe, M. *Doris Lessing's Africa* (1978). Whittaker, R. *Doris Lessing* (1988).

For articles in reference works, see: *Bloomsbury. CA. Cambridge. CD. CN. DLB. Feminist. MBL* and *SUP. Oxford. TCW. ToddBWW. WA.*

Other references: Ahearn, M. *Proceedings of the Fifth National Convention of the Popular Culture Association* (1976). Barnouw, D. *ConL* (1973). Bazin, N. T. *MFS* (1980). Balling, D. *ConL* (1973). Burkom, S. *Crit* (1969). Cederstrom, L. *Mosaic* (1980). Christ, C. *Diving Deep and Surfacing: Women Writers on Spiritual Quest* (1980). Drabble, M. *Ramparts* (February 1972). Draine, B. *MFS* (1980). Eder, D. L. *ConL* (1973). Fishburn, K., in *The Lost Tradition: Mothers and Daughters in Literature*, ed. C. N. Davidson and E. M. Brown (1980). Gindin, J. *Postwar British Fiction* (1962). Hardin, N. S. *ConL* (1973). Hinz, E. and J. Teunissen. *ConL* (1973). Hynes, J. *IowaR* (1973). Kaplan, S. J. *Feminine Consciousness in the Modern Novel* (1975). Kaplan, S. J., in *Twentieth Century Women Novelists*, ed. T. F. Staley (1982). Karl, F. J. *ConL* (1972). Karl, F. J., in *Old Lines, New Forces: Essays on the Contemporary British Novel, 1960–1970*, ed. R. K. Morris (1976). McDowell, F. P. W. *ArQ* (1965). Magie, M. *CE* (1977). Mulkeen, A. M. *SNNTS* (1972). Pickering, J. *MFS* (1980). Porter, N. *WLWE* (1973). Rigney, B. H. *Madness and Sexual*

Politics in the Feminist Novel (1978). Schlueter, P., in *Contemporary British Novelists,* ed. C. Shapiro (1965). Schweichkart, P. C. *MFS* (1985) Showalter, E. *A Literature of Their Own: British Women Novelists from Brontë to Lessing* (1977). Sprague, C. *MFS* (1980). Stimpson, C. in *The Voyage In: Fictions of Female Development,* ed. E. Abel and M. Hirsch (1983). Vlastos, M. *PMLA* (1976). Watson, B. B., in *Old Lines, New Forces: Essays on the Contemporary British Novel, 1960–1970,* ed. R. K. Morris (1976).

Paul Schlueter

Ada Leverson

BORN: 10 October 1862.
DIED: 30 August 1933.
DAUGHTER OF: Samuel Henry Beddington and Zillah Simon Beddington.
MARRIED: Ernest Leverson, 1881.

Oscar Wilde once referred to L. as "a poem and a poet in one, an exquisite combination of perfection and personality which are the keynotes to modern art." That he admired her is obvious, and he knew the feeling was mutual. They took to each other at their first meeting early in the 1890s and quickly became good friends. The wit of the "Sphinx" (as he dubbed her) was often equal to his own, and he even worked several of her epigrams into his plays. She in turn did good-natured parodies of him for *Punch.*

Aware of Wilde's homosexuality, she became an understanding confidante. In 1895, she displayed her loyalty when she sheltered Wilde during his trials. Upon his release from prison two years later, she was one of a limited number of friends who greeted him. L.'s friendship with and continued kindness to Wilde tend to overshadow her own literary achievements.

L. was the eldest of eight children of a prosperous Jewish wool-merchant. She inherited a passion for music from her mother, a gifted pianist, and three of her sisters were talented vocalists; one of them, Violet, married the writer Sydney Schiff ("Stephen Hudson") and was a friend of Marcel Proust, T. S. Eliot, and Katherine Mansfield, and another, Sybil Seligman, was a close friend of Giacomo Puccini.

Though her parents marked her out for a musical career, L. expressed a greater interest in literature. Her understanding parents engaged a governess to instruct her in the classics and French and English literature. She delighted in Honoré de Balzac, Gustave Flaubert, Charles Dickens, and William Makepeace Thackeray and for diversion read Lewis Carroll, Francis Burnand, and Anthony Hope.

Late in her teens, she was introduced to Ernest Leverson, the son of a wealthy diamond merchant, whom she married after a proper courtship more from thoughts of independence than from dreams of everlasting love. Shortly after their marriage they realized their serious mistake. Bored by her husband's sportsminded and gambling acquaintances, L. sought the company of those with whom she could share her wit and love for literature. Among her friends were Wilde, Lord Alfred Douglas, Aubrey Beardsley, Max Beerbohm, George Moore, Robert Ross, Reginald Turner, G. S. Street, John Gray, and André Raffalovich. When Brandon Thomas, the actor-songwriter married to one of Ernest's cousins who wrote the phenomenally successful *Charley's Aunt* (1892), encouraged L. to write, she contributed stories and sketches to various periodicals. In 1892, she began a ten-year association with *Punch,* where she published brilliant sketches of society life that reflected a Wildean indifference to nature and played upon concepts of artifice. Her periodical pieces are witty and observant, full of epigrams and paradox. Most of her characters, precious young aesthetes, are cynical and flippant and epitomize *fin de siècle* ennui. The most memorable of them, Cecil Carington, narrates her two *Yellow Book* stories, "Suggestion" (1895) and "The Quest of Sorrow" (1896).

When John Gray published *Silverpoints* in 1893, L. was moved to comment. Drawn to the elegance of the tall and slender volume (11 × 22 cm), which was bound in green cloth and adorned with wavy gold lines running from top to bottom, with sixty-six flamelike golden blossoms, she praised Gray's poems but, calling attention to the wide expanse of white on each page of handmade Von Gelder paper that framed each poem, she quipped: "There was more margin; margin in every sense and I remember when I saw the tiniest rivulet of text meandering through the very largest of the meadow of the margin, I suggested to Oscar Wilde that he should go a step further; that he should publish a book all margin, full of beautiful unwritten thoughts."

Other critics also had their say about Gray's *Silverpoints,* but none could match L.'s cleverness, though Robert Hichens made a special effort to do so. In *The Green Carnation* (1894), his sparkling satire of the period and of Wilde, Douglas, and others in their circle who had publicly worn carnations dyed green, Hichens put all sorts of quasi-aesthetic gibberish into the mouths of Esmé Amarinthe (Wilde) and Lord Reggie Hastings (Douglas); but he left it to Mrs. Windsor, the ideal society hostess (based on L.) to comment on Gray's poetry. *"Silverpoints,"* Mrs. Windsor pontificates, "was far finer literature than Wordsworth's *Ode to Immortality* or Rossetti's *Blessed Damozel,"* for her proclivity was for preciosity and obscurity in verse.

The more L.'s fame increased, the more her marriage foundered. When Ernest went to Canada, L. remained in London and earned her living by journalism. She then turned her attention to the writing of fiction and produced six novels, lightly plotted love stories distinctive for their combination of frivolity with a profound grasp of human nature.

Populating her major works of fiction are absurd but formidable eccentric characters reflective of those in Wilde's best plays. A few of her most notable characters were drawn from real life, such as Mabel Beardsley and Somerset Maugham in *The Limit* (1911).

At the height of her success, she became ill and suffered depression. Shortly after meeting Osbert Sitwell, she recovered physically and emotionally and began to spend time in Florence with the Sitwells and to champion their vast output. Though the Sitwells' Modernism caught her fancy, she still hearkened to the 1890s. Though she was hardly a relic, Wyndham Lewis lampooned her as one—"The Sib"—in his *Apes of God* (1930).

When she was close to seventy, she wrote her last book, a memoir of Wilde, *Letters to the Sphinx from Oscar Wilde, with Reminiscences of the Author* (1930)—the most read of all her works.

WORKS: *The Twelfth Hour* (1907). *Love's Shadow* (1908). *The Limit* (1911). *Tenterhooks* (1912). *Bird of Paradise* (1914). *Love at Second Sight* (1916). *Letters to the Sphinx from Oscar Wilde, with Reminiscences of the Author* (1930).

BIBLIOGRAPHY: Burkhart, C. *Ada Leverson* (1973). Sitwell, O. *Noble Essences* (1950). Wyndham, V. *The Sphinx and Her Circle: A Biographical Sketch of Ada Leverson* (1963).

For articles in reference works, see: *Cambridge. 1890s. Feminist. Oxford. ToddBWW.*

G. A. Cevasco

Amy Levy

BORN: 10 November 1861, London.
DIED: 10 September 1889, London.
DAUGHTER OF: Lewis Levy and Isabelle Levin.

Born to an upper-middle-class Jewish stockbroker, L. was apparently allowed to read freely and to entertain "advanced ideas" as a precocious child. At the age of thirteen she reviewed Elizabeth Barrett Browning's *Aurora Leigh* for a children's publication, at fourteen she published a poem in the feminist magazine *The Pelican,* and while in her teens she wrote "Xantippe," a monologue in which Socrates's maligned wife expresses her view of their marriage.

She attended Brighton High School for Girls when it opened in 1876; this school was a product of the struggle to reform secondary education for women, with its headmistress, Edith Creak, one of the first five women to attend Newnham College (one of Cambridge University's two earliest women's colleges). L. and her Brighton high school friend Constance Black (Garnett), later the famous translator of Russian literature, attended Newnham in 1879, but L. left Newnham without taking her exams. This was possibly, as suggested by two stories, "Leopold Leuniger: A Study" (unpublished) and "Cohen of Trinity" (1889), because of anti-semitism; possibly because of her ambivalence about Cambridge; and possibly, as suggested by her unpublished stories "Between Two Stools" and "Lallie," because of the strain of being a pioneering student.

Though L. returned to her parents' home, she was independent, she traveled extensively through Germany and Italy, and she maintained an active social and professional life. With such friends as Olive Schreiner, Eleanor Marx, Beatrice Potter Webb, and Clementina Black (her closest friend, a suffragist and trade-unionist), she frequented the British Museum's Reading Room, a former male bastion, resulting in complaints by male scholars. L. satirized such attitudes in "The Recent Telepathic Occurrence at the British Museum" (1888). Despite her political friendships, L. appears to have been more closely connected to the aesthetic subculture; from 1881 to 1885 she belonged to the "Men and Women's Club," which discussed both politics and the arts.

In the 1880s, L. published three volumes of poetry, three novels, and many stories and essays. She often critiqued bourgeois society, as in her story "Wise in Her Generation" (1890), which, like her most important novel, *Reuben Sachs* (1888), links women's plight in a sexist society to that society's excessive individualism. Her "New Woman" novel *The Romance of a Shop* (1888) focused on four sisters who open a photography business after their father's death in defiance of conventional expectations. L.'s beautifully written if conventional novel *Miss Meredith* (1889), as well as several of her finest stories, appeared posthumously.

L. ignored her Jewish identity until 1886, when she wrote several articles for the *Jewish Chronicle* on middle-class Jewish women's difficulties, Jewish humor, Jews in fiction, and the Florence ghetto, all of which may have led to *Reuben Sachs,* about life in the affluent Anglo-Jewish community. The novel tells of the relationships between the Sachs and Leuniger families, and specifically of a rising lawyer who loves and then rejects his cousin Judith in favor of a more politically and socially advantageous marriage. L. gives the novel a feminist focus by emphasizing Judith's predicament in Jewish society, which views marriage, even more than does mainstream culture, as a woman's sole legitimate destiny. Another protagonist from the same society is the idealistic Leo Leuniger, who appears in the early unpublished story and L.'s last published short story, "Cohen of Trinity"; he is offended by gentile materialism but fails to see that his aristocratic gentile friends seek status and money more than do Jews. Indeed, *Reuben Sachs,* though praised by gentile reviewers, was excoriated by Jews who failed to see that its multiple, contradictory perspectives were not wholly negative.

Because L. committed suicide in 1889, the year after the novel appeared, speculation suggested that the controversy was a factor. Her surviving letters, though, show that L. battled depression throughout her adult life despite many friends, capacity for high spirits, and sense of humor. Richard Garnett, who (with his wife, Constance) was a close friend, understood that her problem was deep rooted; his entry on L. in the *Dictionary of National Biography* notes that "She was indeed frequently gay and animated, but her cheerfulness was but a passing mood that merely gilded her habitual melancholy, without diminishing it by a particle, while sadness grew upon her steadily, in spite of flattering success and the sympathy of affectionate friends."

L.'s "habitual melancholy" is most apparent in her poetry. Eleven of her poems are lyrics addressed to women. While some critics, including Melvyn New, have assumed that in these she is using a male persona, this seems unlikely since passion for men is all but absent in the poems and the intense, often erotic feeling in the ones addressed to women is strikingly authentic. Moreover, in the lyrics not explicitly addressed to women, the beloved's gender is virtually always unspecified, so these too are probably homoerotic. "To Vernon Lee," one of the best and most sensuous, expresses L.'s feeling for her friend the aesthetician, scholar, and novelist Violet Paget (Vernon Lee), known as a lesbian in the 1880s. L.'s letters to Lee, however, suggest a rather formal relationship characterized more by admiration than intimacy.

Her gifts and promise were recognized by prominent

literary figures, such as Oscar Wilde (in whose *Woman's World* some of her stories and essays had appeared), who noted in his obituary his regret that "the world must forego the full fruition of her power." A recent resurgence of interest in L., however, has resulted in a 1993 republication of all three of her novels as well as a selection of her poetry and stories, which may, along with renewed critical interest, serve to rescue her from obscurity.

WORKS: *Xantippe and Other Verse* (1881). *The Unhappy Princess* (1883). *A Minor Poet and Other Verse* (1884). *The Romance of a Shop* (1888). *Reuben Sachs* (1889). *Miss Meredith* (1889). *A London Plane-Tree* (1900). *The Complete Novels and Selected Writings of Amy Levy, 1861–1889,* ed. M. New (1993).

BIBLIOGRAPHY: Cheyette, B. *Jewish Historical Society of England Transactions* (1985). Garnett, R. *Constance Garnett: A Heroic Life* (1991). Hunt, L. *SNNTS* (1994). Kapp, V. *Eleanor Marx* (1976). Lask, B. Z. *Jewish Society of England Transactions* (1926). Modder, M. F. *The Jew in the Literature of England* (1939). Nord, D. *Signs* (1990). Oppenheim, J. *"Shattered Nerves": Doctors, Patients and Depression in Victorian England* (1991). Rochelson, M. *WS* (1995). Showalter, E. *A Literature of Their Own* (1977). Wagenknecht, E. *Daughters of the Covenant* (1983). Zatlin, L. G. *The Nineteenth Century Anglo-Jewish Novel* (1981).

For articles in reference works, see: *Bloomsbury. BA19C. DNB. Feminist. Stanford. ToddBWW. VB.*

Gail Kraidman
(updated by Linda Hunt Beckman)

Eliza Lynn Linton

BORN: 10 February 1822, Cumberland.
DIED: 14 July 1898, London.
DAUGHTER OF: the Reverend James Lynn and Charlotte Lynn.
MARRIED: William James Linton, 1858.

L., a prolific writer and social critic, wrote twenty-four novels, thirteen other books, and scores of journal articles, essays, and reviews. Her novels were often thinly cloaked polemics centering primarily on moral conflicts, the theme of class consciousness, or the Woman Question. An outspoken, energetic writer, she was an observant chronicler of her age. She earned notoriety for her iconoclastic attacks on Victorian respectability. Although she herself was an independent woman, she is best known for her virulent opposition to women's rights.

L. was the sixth daughter, the twelfth and last child of Charlotte and James Lynn. Her mother died when L. was five months old, and her childhood was lonely and unhappy. L. was self-educated, since her father, an Anglican clergyman, disapproved of learning for girls; she taught herself French, German, Spanish, and Italian as well as some Latin and Greek. L. developed a passion for religion in her late teens, assuming austere habits, but she rebelled after suffering a total loss of faith.

Leaving her family home in the Lake District in 1845, she set out to earn a living in London as a writer, receiving a year's support from her father. She spent that year living in poverty, reading in the British Museum, and writing her first novel, *Azeth the Egyptian* (1846), an erudite historical romance that she published at her own expense with Newby and that received some favorable reviews. Her second novel, *Amymone: A Romance of the Days of Pericles* (1848), whose heroine was a learned and independent Greek woman, received favorable reviews by, among others, Walter Savage Landor, whom she soon met and who wrote a poem for the *Examiner* entitled "Eliza Lynn on her *Amymone.*" On the basis of her article, "Aborigenes," which she submitted to the *Morning Chronicle,* she was hired as a salaried staff writer. Thus L. became the first Englishwoman to receive a regular salary as a journalist.

Between August 1849 and February 1851, when she left the *Chronicle,* L. wrote at least eighty articles and thirty-six reviews. During this time, she became very close to Landor, whom she regarded as a second father; through him she began to move in literary circles, meeting Charles Dickens and John Forster. She sold the house she inherited from her father, Gad's Hill (Kent), to Dickens. She joined a radical free-thinking group through which she met G. H. Lewes. She also wrote for *All the Year Round* during this time.

In 1851, she published her third novel, *Realities,* which she dedicated to Landor. A graphic documentary about the way young girls were destroyed by patriarchal middle-class mores, *Realities* deprecated double sexual standards, urged the relaxation of divorce laws, and argued for the entry of learned women into male professions. L. had difficulties finding a publisher, this time because of the daring subject matter; once again she resorted to using her own money to finance publication. Lewes, in "The Lady Novelists," called *Realities* "a passionate and exaggerated protest against conventions, which failed of its intended effect because it was too exaggerated, too manifestly unjust." In fact, *Realities* proved to be a disaster, dashing L.'s hopes of becoming an esteemed novelist. L. harbored resentment toward Lewes and his partner Marian Evans (George Eliot) for the rest of her life. Shortly after the publication of *Realities,* she was dismissed from the *Morning Chronicle.* The failure of her work was a turning point in L.'s writing career: She did not attempt another novel for fourteen years, and she curtailed her advocacy of women's rights.

Humiliated by the dismal reception of *Realities,* she left for the Continent and lived in Paris from 1852 until 1854, taking the post of correspondent for *The Leader* and writing freelance for periodicals such as Dickens' *Household Words.* On her return to England in the spring of 1854, she contributed essays and short stories to numerous periodicals. She published an essay in praise of Mary Wollstonecraft in *The English Republic,* the monthly run by her future husband, William James Linton. Soon thereafter, however, she wrote an essay in the opposite vein, the kind of essay by which she would acquire her long-sought fame and success: the "Rights and Wrongs of Women." This essay expressed strong views against "the emancipated woman" whom she called an "amorphous monster."

Rather than continue to write feminist essays for the *English Republic,* L. married its founder, Linton, in 1858.

He was a Chartist engraver, writer, and reformer, and he was a recent widower with seven children. In 1864, L. collaborated with her husband on *The Lake Country,* writing the text for his illustrations. His difficulty finding steady employment as an engraver and his sloppy handling of finances forced L. to work exceptionally hard at her writing, and the burden of raising stepchildren, running a large household, and supporting the family economically proved too heavy; the marriage collapsed. She and William lived apart from 1865 on, although they remained life-long friends. William emigrated to the United States in 1866 where he achieved success as an engraver. The couple never divorced, and L. retained her husband's name. The addition of "Mrs." to her name gave L. the respectability she desired.

In 1866, she was hired as a freelance book reviewer and essayist for the *Saturday Review,* at the time England's most influential weekly; it was edited by John Douglas Cook, the same man who had fired her from the *Morning Chronicle* in 1851. The *Saturday Review* expressed conservative views, including opposition to women's emancipation. Among the thirty-three articles she contributed to the *Saturday Review* in 1868 is the one for which she became best known, her anonymous but sensational "Girl of the Period" (14 March 1868; it was distributed as a pamphlet in 1868 and reprinted in book form in 1883). Although she had formerly championed women's education and rights, and although at the time she had established herself as a professional writer, personally and economically independent, L. vehemently attacked the idea of female emancipation. She argued pointedly against what she characterized as the frivolity and vulgarity of the advanced woman, arguing in favor of the ideals of feminine charm and domesticity. Attacking the "new woman" as "hard, unloving, mercenary, ambitious, without domestic faculty and devoid of healthy natural instincts," she accused the modern woman of masculine aggressiveness and "hysterical" materiality and saw the women's movement as "a pitiable mistake and a grand national disaster." She decried the overriding selfishness and immorality of the "girl of the period," a member of the "Shrieking Sisterhood" whose concern with fashion, cosmetics, and luxury L. likewise denounced. The essay created a sensation; as a result of this and later similar pieces, L. became the *Saturday Review*'s most profitable and indispensable writer. Ironically, whereas her feminist novel, *Realities,* was viewed as indecent and sold poorly, her sensationalist and often contradictory antifeminist diatribes earned L. a steady income as well as credibility and respect as a social critic. She continued writing for the *Saturday Review,* contributing about twenty-four articles a year over the next ten years.

In addition to writing regularly for the *Saturday Review* and for other journals, she also published *Ourselves: Essays on Women* (1869), in which she continued attacking women's emancipation. She was critical of the generation that succeeded hers and voiced antifeminist views for the next thirty years both in periodicals and such novels as *The Atonement of Leam Dundas* (1877), *The Rebel of the Family* (1880), and *The One Too Many* (1894). Despite her criticism of the "Girl of the Period," however, L. supported divorce reform, arguing in favor of economic and legal rights for married and divorced women. Writing such pieces until her death, L. became the accepted mouthpiece of conservative views on "feminine nature" and women's roles. And although her views won her enemies among her own sex, they secured her financial success as a writer.

From 1865 until her death in 1898, L. published a novel a year in addition to countless articles and reviews. These novels are more accomplished and realistic than her earlier, more sentimental, novels. In *Grasp Your Nettle* (1865) and *Lizzie Lorton* (1866), she criticized village life; *Lizzie Lorton,* set in L.'s native Cumberland, received high praise. These novels, in addition to *Sowing the Wind* (1864) and *The Mad Willoughbys and Other Tales* (1875), confront the problems of women.

Forster's *The Life of Landor* came out in 1869; it slighted her importance in Landor's life, so L. wrote a scathing review and published an article on Landor herself. In 1872, L. published *Joshua Davidson,* her most popular novel. An adaptation of the gospel story to the conditions of modern life, it attacked Christian morality and the position of the Church of England. Her next novel, *The Atonement of Leam Dundas,* was among her favorite works but but it was one of her least commercially successful and was harshly reviewed. For the next several years, L. traveled on the Continent, turning out a stream of articles as well as writing several novels—*The World Well Lost* (1877); *Under Which Lord?* (1879), an attack on ritualism in the Church; *The Rebel of the Family* (1880); *Within a Silken Thread* (1880), a three-volume collection of long short stories; and *My Love* (1881). In 1883, she published *Ione,* a novel dedicated to Algernon Swinburne; in that year her "Girl of the Period" essays were published under her own name as *The Girl of the Period and Other Social Essays.* Although this two-volume work gave her lasting fame, it did not sell well at the time and produced numerous counterattacks, including Sarah Grand's "The Man of the Moment."

In 1885, she published another notable work, the one she considered her best, a thinly veiled autobiography in three volumes, *The Autobiography of Christopher Kirkland.* Although the novel depicts her own childhood surroundings, she gave the role of protagonist to a male persona, Christopher Kirkland. Focusing on the Woman Question, the novel was neither a popular nor critical success. In that year, she also published "The Higher Education of Women," in which she argued against "education carried to excess, and [the] exhausting anxieties of professional life." Before the end of the year, she also published a short novel, *Stabbed in the Dark,* contributed an essay on George Eliot to *Temple Bar,* and wrote other articles. In 1886, she published *Paston Carew, Millionaire and Miser,* a work she had begun in 1884. In 1889, she came out with *Through the Long Night.* During the next years, L. continued writing social criticism as well as novels. Her public prominence is apparent in the fact that in 1890 she was one of the three contributors to a symposium on *Candour in English Fiction* in the *New Review;* the other two contributors were Walter Besant and Thomas Hardy.

L. skillfully articulated the fears of social change shared by many of her contemporaries. By the 1890s, she had become so extreme that she was often satirized, and her last novels did not achieve the popularity of those of her middle years. In 1891, she published *An Octave of Friends,* and one of her best essays, "Our Illusions," was published in the *Fortnightly Review. One Too Many,* another virulent attack against female emancipation and higher education for women (the cult of the so-called Girton girl), was serialized in the *Lady's Pictorial* in 1893 and published as a book the next year. Also in 1893, Helen Black published a collection of interviews with "Notable Women Authors," and L., at the age of seventy-one, was the first woman interviewed for the series. *In Haste and at Leisure* (1895) further condemned the "new woman."

In 1896, L. was elected to the Society of Authors; ironically, she accepted the honor of being the first woman invited to serve on its committee. She was still steadily contributing essays on the relations between the sexes, asserting in the January 1896 issue of *Woman at Home* the impossibility of platonic friendships between man and woman as well as women's inferiority and weakness. Early in 1897, she wrote an "appreciation" of George Eliot for a series entitled *Women Novelists of Queen Victoria's Reign* (edited by Hurst and Blackett). Her piece was a mean-spirited assessment of Eliot's literary genius and a scathing indictment of her personal life and character as well as Lewes's. Eliot, according to L., was a flawed artist who "suffered from unmeasured adulation" and exhibited "profound learning tarnished by pedantry." In that year, she began work on her last novel, *The Second Youth of Theodora Desanges,* which was published posthumously in 1899, as was her final work, a collection of reminiscences, *My Literary Life.*

WORKS: *Azeth the Egyptian* (1846). *Amymone: A Romance of the Days of Pericles* (1848). *Realities: A Tale* (1851). *Witch Stories* (1861). (with W. J. Linton) *The Lake Country* (1864). *Sowing the Wind* (1864). *Grasp Your Nettle* (1865). *Lizzie Lorton of Greyrigg* (1866). *Modern Women and What is Said of Them* (1868; repub. 1886). *Ourselves: Essays on Women* (1869). *The True History of Joshua Davidson* (1872). *Patricia Kemball* (1875). *The Mad Willoughbys, and Other Tales* (1875). *The Atonement of Leam Dundas* (1877). *The World Well Lost* (1877). *A Night in the Hospital* (1879). *Under Which Lord?* (1879). *The Rebel of the Family* (1880). *Within a Silken Thread and Other Stories* (1880). *My Love* (1881). *Ione* (1883). *The Girl of the Period and Other Social Essays* (1883). *Stabbed in the Dark: A Tale* (1885). *The Autobiography of Christopher Kirkland* (1885). *Paston Carew, Millionaire and Miser* (1886). *The Philosophy of Marriage* (1888). *Through the Long Night* (1889). *Was He Wrong?* (1889). *About Ireland* (1890). *An Octave of Friends with Other Silhouettes and Stories* (1891). *About Ulster* (1892). *Freeshooting: Extracts from the Work of Mrs. Lynn Linton* (1892). *The One Too Many* (1894). *In Haste and at Leisure: A Novel* (1895). *Twixt Cup and Lip: Tales* (1896). *Dulcie Everton* (1896). *My Literary Life* (1899). *The Second Youth of Theodora Desanges* (1900).

BIBLIOGRAPHY: Anderson, N. F. *Eliza Lynn Linton and the Woman Question in Victorian England* (1973). Anderson, N. F. *Women Against Women in Victorian England: A Life of Eliza Lynn Linton* (1987). Bellflower, J. *The Life and Career of Elizabeth Lynn Linton 1822–1898* (1967). Layard, G. S. *Mrs. Lynn Linton, Her Life, Letters and Opinions* (1901). Smith, F. B. *Radical Artisan: William James Linton* (1973). Van Than, H. *Eliza Lynn Linton: The Girl of the Period* (1979).

For articles in reference works, see: *Bloomsbury. DNB. IDWB. Feminist. Oxford. VB.*

Other references: Aria, B. *My Sentimental Self.* Bevington, M. *Saturday Review 1855–1868* (1941). Black, H. C. *Notable Woman Authors of the Day* (1893). Buller, G. *George Eliot* (1947). Carr, J. *Some Eminent Victorians* (1908). Clodd, E. *Memories* (1916). Cockran, H. *Celebrities and I* (1902). Crow, D. *The Victorian Woman* (1971). Edel, L. *Henry James: The Conquest of London 1870–1933* (1962). Elwin, M. *Landor: A Replevin* (1958). Gettman, R. A. *A Victorian Publisher: A Study of the Bentley Papers* (1960). *The Eighteen-Seventies,* ed. H. Granville-Barker (1929). Haight, G. S. *George Eliot* (1968). *The Socialist Novel in Britain: Towards the Recovery of a Tradition,* ed. H. G. Klaus (1982). Linton, W. J. *Memories* (1895). *The Girl's Own: Cultural Histories of the Anglo-American Girl, 1830–1915,* ed. C. Nelson and L. Vallone (1994). Paget, W.E.H. *In My Tower* (1924). Royle, E. *Victorian Infidels* (1974). Spencer, H. *Autobiography* (1904). Swinburne, A. *Letters,* ed. E. Gosse and T. J. Wise (1927). Thomson, P. *The Victorian Heroine* (1956). Yates, E. *Recollections and Experiences* (1884).

Gale Sigal

Edna Lipson

BORN: 14 August 1914, Liverpool.
DIED: November 1996.
DAUGHTER OF: Gertrude Lipson.
WROTE UNDER: Gerda Charles.

L. was the author of five novels and a number of short stories, published under the pseudonym "Gerda Charles." Although she received critical attention in the early 1960s—when L. and her contemporaries, Brian Glanville and Frederick Raphael, were classed as Anglo-Jewish writers—today her work is largely overlooked. This is due primarily to her seriousness, her traditional moral vision, an outdated interest in the minutiae of life, and the suffering and survival of ordinary individuals rather than the extraordinary achievements of heroes and heroines. In fact, L.'s work has more in common with nineteenth-century fiction than it does with modern writing and has been compared favorably with that of Charlotte Brontë. L.'s stories and literary reviews have appeared in such publications as the *Daily Telegraph, Jewish Chronicle, New Statesman, New York Times, Quest,* and *Vanity Fair.* In 1978–79, she was television critic for the *Jewish Observer* and *Middle East Review.*

Born in Liverpool, L. developed a loathing for the provinces that is evident throughout her work. Her father died when L. was one year old; her mother raised her only child in poverty and loneliness, without family support. Mother and daughter moved regularly while Gertrude Lipson took unskilled work and ran boarding houses. L. had attended nine different schools by the age of fifteen, when she completed her formal education without writing the School Certificate examination. L. and her mother lived together until 1981, when Gertrude Lipson died following a lengthy decline.

After leaving school, L. helped her mother run boarding houses while she pursued her interest in writing. An essay entitled "Forgotten Books," first published in the Morley College magazine and reprinted in *Books,* the house magazine of the National Book League, attracted the attention of literary agent and novelist Paul Scott. Scott encouraged L., and she went on to become a writer, publishing her first novel, *The True Voice,* in 1959. Hoping to avoid the humiliation of failure, she chose to publish her novel under a pen name: Gerda is a combination of Gertrude and Edna, and Charles is a family name.

Lindy Frome, the narrator of *The True Voice* who yearns to better herself, is a recurring character in L.'s fiction. Frustrated, bright, but inarticulate, Lindy wants desperately to leave Staveley Park, a stultifying milieu that she despises. Although her experiences in the larger world do not provide the escape she seeks, the novel concludes on a hopeful note. L.'s second and best book, *The Crossing Point* (1960), is a third-person story of marriage that centers on Rabbi Leo Norberg and two sisters, Sara and Essie Gabriel. Rather than marry Sara, who loves him, Norberg makes a practical choice and proposes to a woman he does not love. Sara's oppression and pain represent Jewish suffering, a theme that L. explores in her subsequent work.

L.'s novel in epistolary form, *A Slanting Light,* won the James Tait Black Memorial Prize in 1963. In letters sent from London to her husband in Liverpool, Ruth writes of herself and her employer, Bernard Zold, a Jewish-American playwright. The dramatist, despite his achievements, and his housekeeper are both isolated individuals. Through her peripheral involvement with the family, however, Ruth comes to value Zold's moral vision and character over the superficial appeal of success. In *A Logical Girl* (1966), which takes place in a seaside town in wartime 1943, the narrator, Rose Morgan, is enchanted with the American servicemen who assemble at Peach Bay. In the end, however, she is unwilling to conform to societal expectations of marriage and rejects a proposal from her boyfriend.

The Destiny Waltz, which won the Whitbread Fiction Award in 1971, describes in third-person narration the making of a television documentary about a fictitious poet, Paul Salomon. The project brings together the director, Georges, critic Michele Sandburg, and Salomon's closest friend, Jimmy Marchant. Since he no longer requires their assistance once the work is completed, Georges increasingly avoids his partners. By the novel's conclusion, however, Michele and Jimmy have fallen in love. L. was working on a sixth novel about the Six-Day War when she died in 1996.

Although the response to L.'s work has been mixed, critics are united in their appreciation of her adroit characterization and her fine evocation of detail. The landscape of L.'s fiction is "the region of everyday hurt." As she has said, her novels are concerned "with the job of maintaining sanity, dignity, and order. They advocate the unfashionable virtues of delicacy, tact, and generosity of heart within the context of day-to-day life."

WORKS: *The True Voice* (1959). *The Crossing Point* (1960). *A Slanting Light* (1963). *A Logical Girl* (1966). *The Destiny Waltz* (1971).

BIBLIOGRAPHY: Baron, A. *Jewish Quarterly* (Summer 1971). Winegarten, R. "The World of Gerda Charles," *Jewish Quarterly* (Summer 1967).

For articles in reference works, see: *CA. CN. DLB. DLEL. WA.*

Other references: Gardner, M. *CSM* (27 July 1967). Hodgart, P. *Illustrated London News* (20 May 1967). McDowell, F. P. W. *Crit* (1964–65). *Nation* (2 October 1967). Price, R.G.G. *Punch* (24 May 1967).

Ruth Panofsky

Anne Lister

BORN: 3 April, 1791, Yorkshire.
DIED: 22 September, 1840, Koutalis, Russia.
DAUGHTER OF: Captain Jeremy Lister and Rebecca Battle.

Known primarily as a diarist and traveler, L. was the eldest surviving child of an upper-class Yorkshire family. As a result of the early deaths of her four brothers, she inherited Shibden Hall in Halifax, West Yorkshire, where she lived from 1815 onward with her unmarried aunt and uncle.

L. was frequently bored with country life and deemed many in her social circle beneath her; as a result, she set for herself a rigorous plan of study, learning mathematics, philosophy, languages, and literature, sometimes engaging a tutor, sometimes studying on her own. Her goal ultimately was to attain a man's education so that she could write articles on various subjects for publication. She read widely, supported local schools and libraries, and became the first woman elected to the Halifax branch of the Literary and Philosophical Society.

Her journal, which she kept from 1817 until her death and which is written partly in code, details L.'s plans for study and musical training, her literary ambitions, her travels, and her sometimes tumultuous and painful love affairs with women. L. was an extraordinary personality; while she held conservative political opinions and tended to be a snob, especially in regard to class and manners, she maintained a fierce independence, insisting on living on her own unconventional terms. Her journal is fascinating for the detail it provides about daily aristocratic life (the visiting rounds, petty gossip, and local politics) and about the early effects of the Industrial Revolution on the countryside. Moreover, L.'s frank discussion of sexuality, which includes flirtations and sexual encounters with local women, offers a valuable insight into lesbian experience in the nineteenth century.

Rejecting traditional marriage for herself, L. longed for a life-partner and spent several years waiting for her lover, Marianne Lawton, to extricate herself from an unhappy marriage to a jealous husband. The journal records L.'s sense of betrayal at Lawton's marriage, her frustration at their (often forced) separation, and her hopes for the future. She gave up those hopes around 1824, after having waited for more than seven years, when it became apparent that Lawton would not separate from her husband.

When her uncle died in 1826, L. took over full responsibility for managing the estate. Keenly interested in the new agricultural technologies that were emerging during this time, she undertook to improve the farms and to develop coal mining on the estate, often supervising the labor herself. Because of her active role in management and business, she was called "Gentleman Jack" by the local townspeople.

The inheritance of Shibden Hall also provided L. with financial independence, which allowed her to fulfill her ambition of traveling. She spent some time in France but wished to see more of the world. On her return to England, she met Anne Walker, an heiress from Yorkshire, and the two entered into the sustained emotional and financial partnership that L. had been desiring since her relationship with Lawton had cooled. In 1839, she and Walker traveled together through Russia and Persia, observing and commenting on local customs and industries. Often going without the relative comforts that their class and station would have afforded them, they opted at times to travel on foot—hiking, and climbing mountains, including Mount Ararat.

The journal ends abruptly, however, as it was during these travels, in Koutalis, Georgia, that L. contracted *fièvre chaude* and died soon afterwards. She was forty-nine. Her obituary in the *Halifax Guardian* remembers her "public spirit" and her generosity toward local organizations and likens her adventurousness to that of Lady Mary Wortley Montagu and Lady Hester Stanhope.

WORKS: *I Know My Own Heart: The Diaries of Anne Lister, 1791–1840,* ed. H. Whitbread (1988). *No Priest But Love: Excerpts from the Diaries of Anne Lister, 1824–1826,* ed. H. Whitbread (1992). *Miss Lister of Shibden Hall: Selected Letters (1800–1840),* ed. M. M. Green (1992).

BIBLIOGRAPHY: Castle, T. *The Apparitional Lesbian: Female Homosexuality and Modern Culture* (1993). Ramsden, P. M. *Transactions of the Halifax Antiquarian Society* (6 January 1970).

For articles in reference works, see: *DNB. Feminist.*

Other references: Batts, J. S. *British Manuscript Diaries of the Nineteenth Century: An Annotated Listing* (1976). *Books* (February 1988). *Belles Lettres* (September 1993). *ContempR* (March 1988). *Lambda Book Report* (May 1992, May 1993). Lesbian History Group. *Not a Passing Phase: Reclaiming Lesbians in History, 1840–1985* (1989). *LRB* (4 February 1988). *Ms.* (May 1993). *Punch* (19 February 1988). *WRB* (January 1989).

Samantha Webb

Ivy (Low) Litvinov

BORN: 4 June 1889, Maidenhead, Berkshire.
DIED: 16 April 1977, Hove, Sussex.
DAUGHTER OF: Walter Low and Alice Baker Low.
MARRIED: Maxim Litvinov, 1916.

L., author of three novels and a number of short stories, was among the first group of young writers to fall under the spell of D. H. Lawrence, who was a major influence. She spent much of her life in Stalinist Russia with her diplomat husband, Maxim Litvinov, returning to England only in her seventy-first year.

L.'s father, a literary scholar who was a close friend of H. G. Wells, was of Hungarian Jewish descent; her mother, an Anglo-Indian, was unconventional and outspoken, telling the young L. that she should be proud she was conceived out of wedlock. In 1890 the family set up house in West Kensington, in London, where a small circle of progressive intellectuals met and two more daughters were born. L. developed a close, almost adoring relationship with her father, and his sudden death from pneumonia in 1895 was traumatic. Matters worsened in 1896 when her mother married John Alexander (Sandy) Herbert and the family moved to Harrow. L. became a rebellious and unhappy child and resented for the rest of her life what she saw as her mother's betrayal of her dead father. Under the guise of enhancing her marriageability, her mother weakened her self-confidence by teaching her to feel ambivalence about her Jewish heritage and to worry that she wasn't feminine enough; at her mother's insistence, L. had all her teeth extracted at age seventeen so as to improve her appearance.

After attending Maida Vale High School, she took a job as a clerk at the Prudential insurance company. During this period, she read the early novels of Viola Meynell and wrote her an admiring letter; the two became friends, and L. frequently spent time with the Meynell family both in London and at their country home in Greatham, Sussex. L. also developed a close friendship with her aunt Edith and her husband, David Eder, one of England's earliest exponents of Freudian psychology.

Meynell's example and encouragement led L. to write her first novel, *Growing Pains* (1913), which depicts many of the details of her early life. In some respects a conventional *Bildungsroman,* the novel is nonetheless remarkable for its frank treatment of the developing sensuality of its heroine, Gertrude Wilson. Her earliest passion is for an older girl at school, Madge Chambers, who returns her friendship but not her love. Gertrude is introspective and confused about her identity and passes successively through episodes of obsession with high-church religion and sexual affairs with young men until she finally finds happiness with an older artist, George Lacey.

The issue of women's suffrage comes up a number of times in *Growing Pains,* but Gertrude (and, implicitly, the author) rejects it, Gertrude saying, "I don't want a vote." Yet Gertrude's story proclaims the ideal of the strong, independent, assertive woman who makes her own informed choices in life, even if those choices are often in direct conflict with social convention. Gertrude is an only slightly idealized version of the author herself, though there was no George Lacey figure as yet in her life. *Growing Pains* received favorable reviews, including one by Catherine Carswell, with whom L. became close friends. In 1913, L. had read Lawrence's *Sons and Lovers* and was determined to meet the author. She traveled to Tuscany to meet him, but her evident infatuation with him was a sore point with Frieda Lawrence, and the visit ended abruptly.

Lawrence's views on sexuality found a receptive soul in

L., and her next novel, *The Questing Beast* (1914), reflects the influence. The title refers to the animal-like sexuality that the heroine detects in herself and a number of young men she encounters, a sexuality that fascinates and ultimately liberates her. The novel is even more explicit in its treatment of sexual issues than *Growing Pains;* when its heroine, Rachel Cohen, finds herself pregnant, she decides to forgo a loveless marriage in favor of raising her child alone. L. includes many autobiographical touches: Rachel's Jewishness, her concern over what she believes to be her mediocre appearance, and her work at a company very much like the Prudential.

At David Eder's house in 1914, L. met a young Russian exile, Maxim Litvinov, whom she married in 1916 and with whom she had two children. Litvinov's political activities on behalf of the Bolsheviks, however, led to his deportation in 1918, and L. soon followed him to the new Soviet Union. Her husband rose in Joseph Stalin's bureaucracy, eventually becoming Soviet Foreign Ambassador and, later, Ambassador to the United States. L. wrote little during these years; although she had a sound marriage, she indulged in some sexual experimentation with both men and women. She taught basic English in Sverdlovsk from 1936 to 1938 and lived in Washington, D.C., with her husband from 1941 to 1943. In Washington, she became something of a celebrity and wrote sketches and gave interviews for a number of magazines. She revised a detective tale she had written in 1930 and published it as *The Moscow Mystery*. While well paced and readable, as a novel it lacks the depth and interest of her two earlier works.

Her husband died in 1951, but it was not until 1960 that she decided to return to England. In her later years, she began writing short stories, collected under the title *She Knew She Was Right* (the title echoes the novel by Anthony Trollope, one of her literary idols). Some with Russian, some with English settings, these are among her very best work. Her style is mature enough that though some of the stories are simply reminiscences, they exhibit powerful concentration and pace. Some of them, particularly the title story, depict her mother and with precision and comedy trace the kind of tensions L. felt her mother created in those around her. "Call It Love" is a warm portrayal of her early meetings with Litvinov.

Though she must be considered a minor writer, L. lived a long and fascinating life, and the works she left vividly trace her strange path from a Victorian childhood to life under Stalin. Both her life and her works show us a woman who was warm, enthusiatic about life, independent, and unafraid of risks.

WORKS: *Growing Pains* (1913). *The Questing Beast* (1914). *The Moscow Mystery* (1930). *She Knew She Was Right* (1971).

BIBLIOGRAPHY: Carswell, J. *The Exile: A Life of Ivy Litvinov* (1983).

For articles in reference works, see: *CA. TCC&MW.*

Raymond N. MacKenzie

Penelope Lively

BORN: 17 March 1933, Cairo, Egypt.
DAUGHTER OF: Roger Vincent Low and Vera Reckett Greer Low.
MARRIED: Jack Lively, 1957.

L.'s literary production has been prolific, varied, and acclaimed since the publication of her first book in 1970. Her works include novels for children and adults, short stories, a personal memoir, an introduction to landscape history, and literary reviews. Most of her literary productions blur generic boundaries and are profound examinations of the elastic and ambiguous connections, rather than separation, of past and present, personal and public, myth and history, imaginative and actual. Her writing is graceful, marked by vivid description of people and places, and by a mixture of serious, witty, and ironic passages. Her awards include the Carnegie Medal for Children's Literature (1973), the Whitbread Award (1976), the Southern Arts Literature Prize (1978), the National Book Award (1979), and the Booker Prize (1987). She was named to the Order of the British Empire (O. B. E.) in 1991.

L., an only child, spent the first twelve years of her life in Cairo, where her father was a manager in the National Bank of Egypt. In *Oleander, Jacaranda: A Childhood Perceived* (1994), she recalls the Englishness of her surroundings: the furniture, gardens, whiskies and soda, patriotism, and paternalism toward Egyptians. She also remembers her isolation from her parents, particularly her mother, and her intense attachment to Lucy, her English nurse. L. was educated at home, using the strict content, timetable, and repetition methodology of the English Parents National Educational Union (PNEU) program. A voracious reader, L. often read aloud, taking turns with Lucy. She recalls that her first attempt at serious writing was at age seven, with a book begun—and soon abandoned—on Egypt.

When L. was eleven, her parents divorced and her father was granted custody of his daughter. She moved to England, where she lived with her paternal grandmother until her father's return in 1945. She was then sent to Seaford, the English boarding school where, detesting the emphasis on sports rather than intellect, she spent "five wretched years and learned little except endurance." She read history at St. Anne's College, Oxford, taking her B.A. in 1954. In 1957, she married Jack Lively, a research assistant at St. Antony's College, Oxford, and later professor of politics. They had two children, Josephine and Adam. Motherhood and an intense reading schedule filled the years before her first novel.

What she calls the "palimpsest" quality of historical pasts and present, a defining and increasingly sophisticated feature of L.'s work, is evident in her earliest fiction for children. In *The Ghost of Thomas Kempe* (1973), the ghost of a Jacobean sorcerer, frustrated by the oddities of twentieth-century science and modern life, enlists the help of a little boy to set things right. Discovering a cache of old letters and diaries, the little boy also bridges time to another ten-year-old who had been plagued by the same sorcerer in the nineteenth century. In *The Road to Lichfield* (1977),

L.'s first novel for adults, a woman discovers in the papers of her dying father the story of his adultery that reflects her own adulterous relationship. In *A Stitch in Time* (1976), a woman discovers a strange set of connections with the little girl who, a hundred years before, worked a sampler hanging in the summer house she visits. Numerous characters in L's fiction are historians or archeologists who literally dig away layer after layer of the past. In most L. works, the contemplation of a place or material object—an orchid patch, a sampler, a painting, one's own hand, the childhood home visited forty years later—leads to an understanding of one's personal past and a past embracing all those, either private or public figures, connected to the place. That vision is always provisional and subjective, and the world is made up of thousands of such perceptions. At times, the vision may simultaneously complicate and illuminate tangled family relationships, as in *The Road to Lichfield* and *Passing On* (1989), or the nature of evil and the "darkness out there," as in the short story of the same name and *The Wild Hunt of Hagworthy* (1971). In an unpublished lecture, "Fiction and Religion," she argues that fiction can provide the coherence and enlightenment to face such darkness in a world where the power of traditional religion has diminished.

Moon Tiger (1987), drawing on her first visit to Egypt since childhood, exemplifies in structure, theme, and character L.'s vision of truth and history. In a complex movement of flashbacks, philosophical reflections, and multiple points of view, a seventy-six-year-old woman dying of cancer reconstructs her past. Unconventional and assertive throughout her life, Claudia Hampton worked as a historian and journalist in an era when such careers were dominated by men. Her popular histories, which weave together personal lives and public events, have been scorned by "dessicated don[s]." She rejects the linear notion of time and history, arguing rather that the "kaleidoscope" of moments, everything happening simultaneously at many layers, is more truthful to human experience. She also argues that objectivity in history is impossible, for the history one sees and writes about is conditioned by the writer's own sociological, psychological, and ideological identities. Claudia also realizes that the body carries the memory of prehistoric humankind and millenia of descendents. She decries the modern imitations of history, such as the fake ducal chateau at a NATO conference she covers. In her personal memory, Claudia returns to one of the richest moments of her own life: her love affair with a tank commander in World War II Egypt, his death in action, and her miscarriage of the child they would have loved together.

In *Oleander, Jacaranda*, her memoir of her childhood in Egypt, L. articulates her conviction, familiar in Romantic literature, that the freshness and wisdom of childhood are irretrievably lost as the child grows, conditioned by adult expectations and language. Like William Wordsworth's "spots of time" or Marcel Proust's "madeleine," the "pictures of the mind" are moments of glimpsing the mysterious, connecting truth of one's own childhood perceptions and attempting to turn it into language accessible to the adult mind and experience. One such epiphany for L. was seeing, at an archeological dig in the desert near Cairo, an ancient skeleton in a fetal position. Enthralled by this glimpse of life and death so long ago, she claims: "I do not know what it is that I have seen, but I understand that it is of significance." As a teenager on tour of country churches in England, she felt suddenly connected to the beings represented by stone effigies on tombs in old country churches in England—"one of those Virginia Woolf–like moments of vision."

WORKS: *Astercote* (1970). *The Whispering Knights* (1971). *The Wild Hunt of Hagworthy* (1971). *The Driftway* (1972). *The Ghost of Thomas Kempe* (1973). *The House in Norham Gardens* (1974). *Boy Without a Name* (1975). *Going Back* (1975). *A Stitch in Time* (1976). *The Stained Glass Window* (1976). *Fanny's Sister* (1976). *The Presence of the Past: An Introduction to Landscape History* (1976). *The Road to Lichfield* (1977). *The Voyage of QV 66* (1978). *Nothing Missing but the Samovar* (1978). *Fanny and the Monsters* (1979). *Treasures of Time* (1979). *Fanny and the Battle of Potter's Piece* (1980). *Judgement Day* (1980). *The Revenge of Samuel Stokes* (1981). *Next to Nature, Art* (1982). *Perfect Happiness* (1983). *According to Mark* (1984). *Dragon Trouble* (1984). *Corruption* (1984). *Uninvited Ghosts and Other Stories* (1984). *Pack of Cards* (1986). *Debbie and the Little Devil* (1987). *A House Inside Out* (1987). *Moon Tiger* (1987). *Passing On* (1989). *City of the Mind* (1991). *Judy and the Martian* (1992). *Cleopatra's Sister* (1993). *The Cat, the Crow and the Banyan Tree* (1994). *Oleander, Jacaranda: A Childhood Perceived* (1994). *Good Night, Sleep Tight* (1995). *Heat Wave* (1996). *Beyond the Blue Mountains* (1997).

BIBLIOGRAPHY: Cameron, E. *CLAQ* (1984). Chater, A. *Ispoda* (1988).,Dukes, T. *WL&A* (1991). El-Sadda, H., in *Images of Egypt in Twentieth-Century Literature*, ed. H. Gindi (1991). LeMesurier, N. *NWRev* (1990). Moran, M. H. *Frontiers* (1990). Raschke, D. *ArielE* (1995). Rees, D. *Horn Book* (1975). Rees, D. *The Marble in the Water* (1979). Ryan, J. *Mallorn* (1988). Smith, L. *CLAQ* (1985). Townsend, J. *A Sounding of Storytellers: New and Revised Essays on Contemporary Writers for Children* (1979). Yvard, P. *JSSE* (1989).

For articles in reference works, see: *Bloomsbury. CA. Cambridge. DLB. Feminist. IAWWW. Oxford. ToddBWW. TWCCW.*

Carol Shiner Wilson

Liz Lochhead

BORN: 26 December 1947, Motherwell, Lanarkshire, Scotland.

DAUGHTER OF: John Lochhead and Margaret Forrest Lochhead.

MARRIED: Tom Logan, 1987.

L., Scots poet, playwright, and performer, was born and brought up in an industrial and fiercely Protestant environment; her father was a local government official. She was educated at Newarthill Primary School and Dalziel High School, where she abandoned the academic program and chose instead to study drawing and painting at Glasgow School of Art, taking a diploma in 1970. She began writing poems in art school and was recognized almost immediately, winning the BBC Radio Scotland poetry prize in 1971 and, in 1972, the Scottish Arts Council Award for her first book of poems, *Memo for Spring*.

L. taught art in various high schools for eight years after receiving her diploma and traveled with her partner, Tarik Okyay, who died young of cancer. She has cited him as a strong influence on her life and poetry. In 1978, she published a second book of poems, *Islands*, and left teaching to accept the first Scottish/Canadian Writer's Exchange Fellowship.

Also in 1978, another turning point in her life was her collaboration with Marcella Evaristi in *Sugar and Spite*, a performance that used costumes, props, and music to make poetry readings intelligible and entertaining. In this production, L. developed her trademark performance style of rhythmic rap-like speech and began her work in the theater. She continues to write revues and pantomimes, alone and in collaboration. L. is a popular and lively actress in her own revues and reader of her own poetry, sometimes performing on behalf of the Rape Crisis Centre and women's shelters.

In the 1980s, she filled a number of writer-in-residence posts, at Duncan of Jordanstone College, the Tattenhall Centre, the University of Edinburgh, and the Royal Shakespeare Company. As a poet she came into her own with the witty and spirited deconstructions of tales in *The Grimm Sisters* (1981); the poems reconstruct the women's roles in fairy tales and play with clichés in new and unexpectedly resonant contexts. She continued this style in *Dreaming Frankenstein* (1984), which also contains some love poems of real power. In her poetry, as in her performances, L. creates a variety of personae speaking in direct living cadences; her tales show a strong narrative sense. Situating woman as subject rather than object, her poems have been widely anthologized in feminist collections as well as poetry anthologies in both Scotland and England.

L.'s plays have been performed on stage, radio, and television. Her three major stage plays dramatize stories of subversive female physicality and power. *Blood and Ice*, a consideration of Mary Shelley as mother and artist, exists in a number of versions: an early one-act play *Mary and the Monster* (1981), differing full-length versions in 1982 and 1984, and a 1990 radio play. The sheer physicality of miscarriage and childbirth, the physical tie to the child that can be abandoned by Percy Shelley and Lord Byron but not by Mary Shelley, reappear in her monster-myth of scientific, masculine creation. L.'s *Dracula* (1985) similarly reconstructs the tale of womanhood and monstrosity in a completely new dramatization of Bram Stoker's novel. Although the play has a certain naïveté in its sense of discovery that *Dracula* is about sexuality, the remarkable poetry of both language and visual image in the play shows an advance over *Blood and Ice*. In 1987, L. wrote *Mary Queen of Scots Got Her Head Chopped Off*, choosing a subject from Scots history that is as mythologized as Mary Shelley and tales of vampires. The play uses a Brechtian perspective on Mary and Elizabeth I grappling with rule and gender roles, with political power and the power of female sexuality. Again, the staging and language are memorable, particularly the eclectic and poetic sixteenth-century Scots dialect L. devised.

She used Scots dialect with great effect also in her adaptations of Molière: *Tartuffe* (1986) and *Patter Merchants* (1989), based on *Les Précieuses Ridicules*. Continuing her work as an adaptor, L. rendered the *York Cycle* (a series of forty-eight plays from the fourteenth century performed in York, which treat biblical stories from creation to the Last Judgment) into northern speech for a 1992 performance. In 1993, her *Magic Island* rewrote Shakespeare's *The Tempest* from Miranda's point of view. L.'s plays, like her poems, explode the clichés of history and traditional tales by repositioning woman as subject, using language that is dense, vivid, and witty.

WORKS: *Memo for Spring* (1972). *Now and Then* (1972). (with M. Evaristi) *Sugar and Spite* (1978). *Islands* (1978). *Goodstyle* (1980). *The Grimm Sisters* (1981). *Mary and the Monster* (1981). *True Confessions* (1981). (with others) *Tickly Mince* (1982). *Disgusting Objects*. (1982). *Blood and Ice* (1982, 1984). (with others) *A Bunch of Fives* (1983). (with others) *The Pie of Damocles* (1983). *Shanghaied* (1983). *Red Hot Shoes* (1983). *Dreaming Frankenstein & Collected Poems* (1984). *Same Difference* (1984). *Rosaleen's Baby* (1984). *Sweet Nothings* (1984). *Dracula* (1985). *Tartuffe* (adapted from Molière) (1986). (with others) *Nippy Sweeties: The Complete Alternative History of the World Part I* (1986). *Fancy You Minding That* (1986). *Mary Queen of Scots Got Her Head Chopped Off* (1987). *The Big Picture* (1988). (with A. Owens) *Them Through the Wall* (1989). *Patter Merchants* (adapted from Molière) (1989). (with G. Mulgrew) *Jock Tamson's Bairns* (1990). *Mozart and Salieri* (1990). *Quelques Fleurs* (1991). *Bagpipe Musak* (1991). (adapt.) *York Cycle* (1992). *The Story of "Frankenstein"* (1992). *The Magic Island* (1993).

BIBLIOGRAPHY: The most extensive listing of primary and secondary sources, compiled by Hamish Whyte, appears in *Liz Lochhead's Voices*, ed. R. Crawford and A. Varty (1993). Koren-Deutsch, I. *MD* (1992). Koren-Deutsch, I., in *British Playwrights, 1956–1995: A Research and Production Sourcebook*, ed. W. W. Demastes (1996). McDonald, J., in *Novel Images: Literature in Performance*, ed. P. Reynolds (1993).

For articles in reference works, see: *Bloomsbury*. *CA*. *Cambridge*. *CD*. *CP*. *Feminist*. *OxComp*. *WD*.

Other references: *LonT* (2 February 1993). *MD* (1995).

Nancy Cotton

Anne Vaughan Locke

BORN: early 1530s.
DIED: after 1590.
DAUGHTER OF: Stephen Vaughan and Margaret Gwynneth (Guinet) Vaughan.
MARRIED: Henry Locke (Lok), 1552 (?); Edward Dering, 1572 (?); Richard Prowse (Prouze), before 1583.
WROTE UNDER: A. L.; Anna Dering; Anne Prowse.

Poet, translator, and a leading figure in the Elizabethan Protestant community, L. is the probable author of the first English sonnet sequence.

Her connection with the Reformation was lifelong. Her father, a mercer who handled several diplomatic missions under King Henry VIII, tried to use his influence to stop William Tyndale's execution; later, he was a member of Parliament. Her mother was a silkwoman to Queen Anne Boleyn; her stepmother had been the widow of Henry Brinkelow, the Protestant printer; and her tutor was involved in printing radical texts. Left a minor at Stephen Vaughan's death in London in the winter of 1549–50, she married a year or two later Henry Locke, a cloth merchant belonging to another prominent Protestant family. The first of her six children (two of whom lived to adulthood) was born in 1553.

Shortly before this time she first met the Scottish reformer John Knox, who was in London as one of the chaplains of King Edward VI; they became close friends, and the Lockes took Knox into their home. To escape persecution under Queen Mary, Knox fled to the Continent early in 1554. In 1556, established as English pastor in Geneva, he wrote to persuade L. to join the colony of exiles there. She arrived the next spring, with children and a servant; her husband's business interests presumably kept him in London or elsewhere on the Continent. She remained in Geneva for nearly two years; she then rejoined Henry in 1559, probably in Frankfurt, and returned to London, where she took a prominent role among the returned exiles. Her correspondence with Knox continued until at least 1562, but only Knox's letters have survived. In them, he entrusted her with messages for the Puritan community, requests for books and money, news of the progress of reformation in Scotland, and a manuscript copy of an unpublished treatise.This she eventually was able to have printed in London, though the printer was fined for it (STC 15068).

Widowed in 1571, L. married, perhaps as early as 1572, the rising (and controversial) Puritan preacher Edward Dering, who died of consumption at the age of thirty-six in 1576. Her third husband was Richard Prowse, a well-to-do draper and member of a prominent Exeter family, who served terms as sheriff, mayor, and member of Parliament. She remained active in evangelical affairs in the west country.

L. was the mother of the minor Elizabethan poet Henry Lok, who in his turn published several hundred religious sonnets. The date of her death is unknown, but in Richard Prowse's will of 1607 she is not mentioned. She may well have died before 1595, when Prowse had her son Henry arrested for a debt.

During her residence in Geneva, L. heard, or saw in manuscript, four sermons on chapter thirty-eight of Isaiah, preached by John Calvin in the fall of 1557. She translated these into English, publishing the translation soon after returning to London—two years ahead of the printing in Geneva of the original French version. She translated closely—"I haue rendred it so nere as I possibly might, to the very wordes of his text, and that in so plaine Englishe as I could expresse"—but in a vigorous, colloquial style. The work was popular, requiring at least two more editions.

Appended to this text, she published *A Meditation of a Penitent Sinner: Written in maner of a Paraphrase vpon the 51. Psalme of Dauid,* a sequence of twenty-six sonnets. (The identification of L. as author is ambiguous, but there is no serious rival candidate.) The first five sonnets form a "preface" comprising the penitent's first-person psychological narrative; the rest are expansions in meditative fashion on the successive verses of the psalm. The work displays sophisticated craftsmanship in its handling both of prosody and of rhetorical figures, and a variety of verbal devices link one sonnet to the next.

Printed as marginal glosses are the verses of Psalm 51 in a form that matches no other known English prose translation. This, too, appears to be L.'s work. Surprisingly, it contains several echoes of the Latin Vulgate version.

In 1590, L. published another translation from French, a tract first addressed to persecuted Protestants in the Netherlands, now "augmented by the Author" and chosen by L., no doubt, for its applicability to the circumstances of English Puritans. A popular work, L.'s translation was reprinted at least seven times over the period 1591 to 1634. As a topically apt appendix L. contributed a 124–line poem in quatrains, "The necessitie and benefit of Affliction."

Also extant, in a manuscript from around 1572, is a Latin epigram by L.

WORKS: (trans.) *Sermons of John Calvin, vpon the songe that Ezechias made after he had bene sicke, and afflicted by the hand of God* (1560, from French; facsimile rpt. with notes by L. Lupton, 1973; facsimile rpt. with intro. by E. Beilin, 1998). (trans.) *Of the markes of the children of God, and of their comforts in afflictions,* by Jean Taffin (1590, from French; facsimile rpt. with intro. by E. Beilin, 1998). *A Meditation of a Penitent Sinner,* ed. K. Morin-Parsons (1997). *Collected Works,* ed. S. M. Felch (1998).

BIBLIOGRAPHY: Collinson, P. *Godly People* (1983). Felch, S. *SCJ* (1995). Felch, S. *Ren&R* (1996). Felch, S. *Reformation* (1997). *Silent but for the Word,* ed. M. P. Hannay (1985). Hannay, M. P. *R&L* (1991). Hannay, M. P. *ANQ* (1992). Hannay, M. P., in *Privileging Gender in Early Modern England,* ed. J. Brink (1993). Huttar, C. *Modern Philology* (1998). Knox, J. Letters to Locke, in *Works*, ed. D. Laing (1846–64). Lupton, L. *A History of the Geneva Bible,* Vol. 4 (1972); Vol. 8 (1976). Roche, T. P. *Petrarch and the Sonnet Sequences* (1989). Schleiner, L. *Tudor and Stuart Women Writers* (1994). Spiller, M.R.G. *The Development of the Sonnet* (1992). Woods, S. *ANQ* (1992). Woods, S. *The New Seventeenth Century,* ed. A. Boesky and M. Crane (1998).

For articles in reference works, see: *Allibone* (under Prowse). *Blain. DNB* (under Henry Lok). Emerson, K. L. *W&D. Europa. Feminist. Ireland SUP.*

Other references: Bainton, R. H. *Women of the Reformation from Spain to Scandinavia* (1977). Beilin, E. *Redeeming Eve: Women Writers of the English Renaissance* (1987). Brigden, S. *London and the Reformation* (1989). Frankforter, A. D. *Journal of the Rocky Mountain Medieval and Renaissance Association* (1985). Greene, R. *Post-Petrarchism* (1991). Krontiris, T. *Oppositional Voices* (1992). Labalme, P. H. *Beyond Her Sex* (1980). Muir, E. *John Knox* (1929). Richardson, W. C. *Stephen Vaughan* (1953). Ridley, J. *John Knox*

(1968). Stevenson, R. L. *Familiar Studies of Men and Books* (1882).

Charles A. Huttar

Elizabeth (Pakenham née Harman), Countess of Longford

BORN: 30 August 1906, London.
DAUGHTER OF: Nathaniel Bishop Harman and Katherine Chamberlain.
MARRIED: Frank Pakenham, later seventh Earl of Longford and K.G., 1931.
WROTE UNDER: Elizabeth Pakenham (until 1961); Elizabeth Longford (after her husband's elevation to the peerage).

As Frances Makower shows in the first authorized biography of L. (1997), the unusual life of this broadly talented and prolific writer resulted from a confluence of forces: intelligent parents and mentors, a supportive husband and family, astute agents and publishers, and influential connections throughout the British establishment. Unlike the majority of British historians and biographers, L.'s prestigious contacts effectively gave her full and, in most cases, immediate personal access to the essential archival materials that shaped her research and culminated in her many books. In a lifespan of more than nine decades, L. has achieved broad success as a journalist, Labour Party activist (in the 1930s), and award-winning biographer. Her record as the author of sixteen monographs and the editor of five collections is handsomely balanced by dedication to family and marriage. L.'s husband of more than sixty years, a self-described "Catholic Irishman in English politics," has been a strong ally in his wife's public ambitions. In *Five Lives* (1964), he writes that L. "always had priceless literary assets: she has been steeped in good literature since a girl; and she has a natural gift of observing everything—people, houses, furniture, nature . . . there is nothing she looks forward to more than a long distracted 'write.'" L. mentions in her memoir, *The Pebbled Shore* (1986), that the axis of her life and career has been the large united family front of Harmans, Bishops, Chamberlains, and Pakenhams. The mother of eight children, L. has been an inspiring role model for her family, whom she often involves in various projects, such as *The Pakenham Party Book* (1960). Her eldest daughter, Lady Antonia Fraser Pinter, and Lady Antonia's daughter, Flora Fraser, both successful authors, seldom pass up an opportunity to acknowledge the wise direction of the family's premier woman writer.

Though not born into the peerage, L. enjoyed a privileged upper-middle-class upbringing. Both of her parents were medical doctors by training, though only her father practiced. In addition to his career in ophthalmic surgery, L.'s father was an inventor and poet. Her mother was a cousin of Prime Minister Neville Chamberlain; from her maternal line, L. cultivated an abiding interest in politics, which dominated her activities in the 1930s.

L. received a private education, first at the Francis Holland Church of England School for Girls, and, later, in the 1920s, at the Headington School for Girls outside Oxford. During this period, she developed what would later become a life-long passion for history and biography, crediting Lytton Strachey's *Queen Victoria* as an early influence. Her budding talent was acknowledged by various school prizes, and L. was a contestant in the 1925 *Spectator* poetry competition. When her plans to matriculate at Oxford University failed to work out, L. sought the education of a traveler and spent more than a year abroad. In Grenoble, France, she completed a course of intensive study, which ultimately led to acceptance at Oxford and an open scholarship in English Literature at Lady Margaret Hall. Her circle at Oxford included family relatives as well as Frank Pakenham, Hugh Gaitskell, and such Oxford aesthetes as Evelyn Waugh and John Betjeman. Her principal mentor, Maurice Bowra, Dean of Wadham College, convinced her to change her major field from literature (considered a predictably feminine pursuit) to Classics. The great thrill of her Oxford years, however, was a national poetry prize, presented to her by John Masefield. Her college's publication, *Isis,* described L. as "Artistic, beautiful, cultured, decorative, enigmatic, fashionable, even headstrong. If in full womanhood she fulfills the wide promise of her brilliant maidenhood, she will take her place in the honoured band of female worthies."

After Oxford, in the 1930s, L. began to develop radical socialist sympathies. Under the tutelage of Frank Pakenham, whose aristocratic family ties involved him with Lady Astor and Winston Churchill, L. joined the Labour Party. Pakenham, whom L. married in 1931 at the age of twenty-five, introduced her to the Worker's Educational Association (WEA). Appreciating her gifts, he thrust her into its program, first as a tutor in the poor outlying counties of England. In 1935, in Cheltenham, L. became something of a *cause célèbre* when she publicly derided the House of Lords ("rotten with decay"). Her political zeal was given further exposure at this time, though from a wholly different perspective, when Pakenham accepted a fellowship in politics at Christ Church College, Oxford. For fourteen continuous years, 1930–44, L. was an ardent (and active) supporter of England's Labour Party.

In the 1940s, L. and Pakenham converted to Roman Catholicism; and, with a growing family, L. curtailed her political activities. Trading the soapbox for the pen, she began to express her political views as a journalist; her opinions and engaging style resulted in regular columns, as "Elizabeth Pakenham," for several Catholic newspapers. In the 1950s, L. continued her journalistic writings for the *Daily Express, News of the World,* and the Sunday *Times.* She was also a popular visitor to English television and radio panels and "chat shows." Her specialties were largely domestic and moral subjects ("progressive Catholic views on the modern family and child-rearing"). Anthony Hern, features editor at the *Daily Express,* convinced L. to publish her advice pieces, and *Points for Parents* appeared in 1954 (revised edition, 1970). The following year, she edited *Catholic Approaches to Modern Dilemmas and Eternal Truths* (1955).

It was a long newspaper strike in the mid-1950s that precipitated L.'s return to literature and history. A reunion aboard a Hellenic cruise with Bowra and former college friends redirected L. to scholarly research and history writing. Always attracted to large, charismatic personalities, L.'s first subject was her great-uncle, Joseph Chamberlain. After roughing out three long chapters on a defining episode in his life (the Jameson Raid, 1895–96), L. accepted her husband's advice to submit the manuscript as a monograph on this important incident alone. In 1960, *Jameson's Raid* was published to rave reviews. Critics judged L.'s first major book a penetrating portrait of a statesman, with credible delineation of character and psychology.

With her husband's elevation to the peerage in 1961, L. became Countess Longford and was warmly received in aristocratic circles. Unsurprisingly, her politics from this time forward became increasingly more conservative, and L.'s choice of subjects reflected this shift. Her second biography was a modern view of Queen Victoria. L.'s goal was to supersede Lytton Strachey's biography (1921) with a more faithful reconstruction of Victoria as a fully rounded, complex personality. On the strength of her first biography, she was permitted to conduct research in the Round Tower of Windsor Castle, where she immersed herself in state documents, private journals, and royal correspondence. "To enter into another human life," L. wrote, "I must follow as far as possible in his or her footsteps, look at the houses, gardens, scenery they knew. I must follow in her personality the tensions of family and public life." In Queen Victoria, L. found a multilayered subject (ruler, wife, mother), whose total personality had not been fully revealed by historians and biographers. *Victoria R.I* was published in 1964; when this book won the 1964 James Tait Black Prize for biography, L. achieved a new level of celebrity and respect.

For roughly the next ten years, L. prepared her third biography, a two-volume study of the Duke of Wellington, judged the most consummate and best work in her long career. (Conveniently, her new subject was also a relative of her husband's family.) L.'s research was significantly aided by Gerald, seventh Duke of Wellington, also an historian, who gave L. open access to his collection of Wellington's extant papers. Her research extended to more than two years, at Apsley House, Picadilly, and at the Wellington family country seat at Stratfield Saye; L. also traveled to the Continent to immerse herself in the sites of her subject's great battles. Part I of her study, *Wellington: The Years of the Sword,* appeared in 1969, and *Wellington: Pillar of State,* in 1973. Reviewers praised L.'s new book, judging her incisive portrait of Wellington more richly contextualized than her previous subjects and finding in the book a reliable record of an entire age.

Only three years after her *Wellington,* L. produced a literary biography of the poet Lord Byron in 1976. As in her management of Queen Victoria and especially Wellington, L.'s Byron is a credible individual. Her goal in this new book was essentially threefold: to dispel longstanding perceptions of Byron as an extravagant romantic figure; to explain his perceived greatness in literary history; and to address readers' continuing fascination with him. For L., Byron's life and poetry were indistinguishable: one became (indeed, was) the other. Her biography includes, in an appendix, A. E. Houldsworth's notes on the opening of Byron's vault in June 1938.

Maintaining a prolific schedule, L. next produced a second literary biography. Her new subject was Wilfrid Scawen Blunt, a controversial diarist, poet, traveler, horse breeder, and politician. When Blunt's secret diaries were opened at the Fitzwilliam Museum in Cambridge in 1972, Michael Jaffé, one of the trustees, suggested Blunt to L. as a new subject. Her authorized biography appeared in 1979 under the title *A Pilgrimage of Passion: The Life of Wilfrid Scawen Blunt.* Though blessed with a certain genius, L.'s new subject never attained greatness in any of his many pursuits. The monotony of his lust and womanizing, L. wrote, were happily relieved by his liberal politics. Blunt was an enthusiastic champion of national freedom, with special interests, like those of the Longfords, in Egypt, India, and Ireland.

L. has also produced biographies on the royal Windsors and others of the English establishment, including *The Royal House of Windsor* (1974), *Winston Churchill* (1974), *The Queen Mother: A Biography* (1981), and *Elizabeth R: A Biography* (1983). Her memoir, *The Pebbled Shore,* appeared in 1986. Of particular interest are her contributions to S. Raven's *Women of Achievement* (1981) and to J. Meyers' *The Craft of Literary Biography* (1985).

In 1965 L. was elected fellow of the Royal Society of Literature, and in 1974 she was appointed a Commander of the Order of the British Empire.

The prediction about the young L. in Oxford University's *Isis* has been (manifestly) fulfilled: "If in full womanhood she fulfills the promise of her brilliant maidenhood, she will take her place in the honoured band of female worthies."

WORKS: (as Elizabeth Pakenham) *Points for Parents* (1954, 1970). *Catholic Approaches to Modern Dilemmas and Eternal Truths* (1955). (as Elizabeth Pakenham) *Jameson's Raid* (1960). (as Elizabeth Pakenham) *The Pakenham Party Book* (1960). *Victoria R.I* (1964). *Wellington: The Years of the Sword* (1969). *Wellington: Pillar of State*(1973). *Piety in Queen Victoria's Reign* (1973). *The Royal House of Windsor* (1974). *Winston Churchill* (1974). *Byron's Greece* (1975). *Byron* (1976; in the U. S. as *The Life of Byron*). *A Pilgrimage of Passion: Wilfrid Scawen Blunt* (1979). *Images of Chelsea* (1980). *Eminent Victorian Women* (1981). *The Queen Mother: A Biography* (1981). *Elizabeth R: A Biography* (1983). *The Pebbled Shore* (1986).

BIBLIOGRAPHY: Makower, F. *Elizabeth Longford* (1997).

For articles in reference works, see: *CA. DLB. DLEL. IAWWW. WA. WD.*

Other references: Holroyd, M. "E. Longford" (Eighteen Nineties Society, 1997). Pakenham, F. *Born to Believe* (1953). Pakenham, F. *Five Lives* (1964). Pakenham, F. *The Grain of Wheat* (1974).

Maureen E. Mulvihill

Jane Wells Webb Loudon

BORN: 19 August 1807, Birmingham.
DIED: 13 July 1858, London.
DAUGHTER OF: Thomas Webb.
MARRIED: John Claudius Loudon, 1830.

L., made a name for herself first as a novelist and then as a popularizer of horticulture and gardening in England. Her early fame as author of *The Mummy!* (1827) brought her to the attention of John Claudius Loudon, already widely known for his landscape architecture and encyclopedias of gardening. With Loudon, she become part of the rapidly expanding knowledge industry. Her own works ranged widely, from her early *Conversations Upon Comparative Chronology* (1830) to *Domestic Pets* (1851), but she is still primarily remembered for her horticultural works, including *The Ladies' Companion to the Flower Garden* (1841), which sold more than 20,000 copies in nine editions. Whether it was in *The First Book of Botany* (1841) or *The Lady's Country Companion* (1845), L.—like her husband—found a strong if not always profitable market for horticultural knowledge.

L. was the daughter of a prosperous businessman in Birmingham. Shortly after the death of her mother, the twelve-year-old L. and her father traveled to the Continent. Upon returning to Birmingham, Thomas Webb suffered financial reverses and retired with his daughter to a country estate at Kitwell House in Bartley Green until his death in 1824. Orphaned at the age of seventeen, L. found herself alone, with little means of financial support. While the details of her life are sketchy at this time, it is clear that she had some connections in London. She spent a good deal of time at the home of John Martin, the Romantic painter, who often entertained the London literati, including Thomas Hood, William Godwin, George Cruikshank, and Harrison Ainsworth. She was also friends with William Jerdan, the writer and journalist, who had taken an active interest in the careers of Lady Blessington, Anna Maria Fielding Hall, and Eliza Cook.

L. turned to fiction in order to earn a living. In 1827, Martin's friend Henry Colburn, whose firm had recently produced Mary Shelley's *The Last Man* (1826), published *The Mummy! A Tale of the Twenty Second Century.* The novel, which draws on London's recent craze for Egyptian antiquities, also reflects the influence of Shelley's prior work, particularly *Frankenstein. The Mummy!* describes the political circumstances of a technologically advanced England in the year 2126. Ruled by a matrilineal monarchy of virgin queens, England (now Roman Catholic) is about to succumb to corruption and political infighting. L. restores order and peace, through the actions of the reanimated mummy, Cheops, who pays the debt for his own past corruption by restoring moral and political strength to Great Britain. It is a work full of humor and vision that is compelling in its insistence on moral standards.

L.'s vision of science and technology in the twenty-second century is striking. In her future world, electricity is used to generate rainstorms, compressed air is stored for balloons, documents are written on asbestos paper, "steamboats" travel at sixty miles an hour, and women's hats are illuminated by "streams of lighted gas . . . in capillary tubes." In the midst of this confidence about the ability of science and technology to improve the quality of life, however, there is a genuine concern for the decline of moral responsibility. The popular response to the work resulted in a second edition; it had, as *The London Literary Journal* noted in 1851, "made a great noise in its day for the daring flights of invention which it exhibited." *The Mummy!* was, of course, written before L. herself became immersed in scientific popularizing, but although not yet a part of the knowledge industry, she was clearly concerned with the role of knowledge in society. *The Mummy!* reveals an author who was both attracted to, and apprehensive of, the transformative power of knowledge.

The Mummy, though apparently successful, did not reverse L.'s financial difficulties. In 1829, apparently in poor health, she applied to the Royal Literary Fund (an agency set up to help struggling authors) for assistance, and received £25. *The Mummy's* most sympathetic reviewer was John Claudius Loudon, who praised the work for its insight and innovation. In fact, Loudon was so taken by the novel that he insisted on being introduced to the anonymous author. Expecting to meet a young man, Loudon was surprised, and obviously impressed, by the twenty-three-year-old woman. Later that year, on 14 September 1830, they were married. Literary receptions were common at the Loudon household at No. 3 Porchester Terrace in Bayswater, although it is clear that they were generally modest evenings. In 1832, L. gave birth to a daughter, Agnes, who subsequently appeared as a character in some of Loudon's books for children. Agnes took to writing while young and published *Tales for Young People* (1846) in her teens.

The remainder of L.'s career, from the late 1830s to her death in 1858, revolved around the popularization of knowledge for children and for women. L. was, without question, one of most important and popular botanical writers in the nineteenth century. When her husband died in 1843, he left behind some substantial debts. L.'s later years were thus marred by financial troubles in spite of a £100 per annum civil pension. L. also suffered from chronic respiratory problems, which eventually took her life in 1858. She is buried in Kensal Green Cemetery near her husband; her daughter, Agnes Loudon Spofforth, died five years later in 1863.

WORKS: *Prose and Verse.* (1824). (Anon.) *The Mummy!: A Tale of the Twenty Second Century* (1827). *Stories of a Bride* (1829). *Conversations Upon Comparative Chronology* (1830). *Agnes: The Little Girl Who Kept Her Promise* (1839). *The Young Naturalist's Journey: or the Travels of Agnes Merton with her Mama* (1840). *Gardening for Ladies* (1840) *The Ladies' Flower Garden,* Vol. I (1840); Vol. II (1841); Vol. III (1843); Vol. IV (1848). *The First Book of Botany* (1841). *The Ladies' Companion to the Flower Garden* (1841). *Botany for Ladies* (1842; 2nd ed., *Modern Botany,* 1851). *The Entertainining Naturalist* (1843) *Glimpses of Nature During a Visit to the Isle of Wight* (1843). *The Lady's Country Companion; or How to Enjoy a Country Life Rationally* (1845). *British Wild Flowers* (1846). *The Amateur Gardener's Calendar* (1847; rev. ed., W. R. Robinson (1869). *Facts From the World of Nature: Animate and Inanimate* (1848). *Domestic Pets: Their Habits and Management* (1851). *Tales About Plants* (1853). *My Own Garden; or the Young Gardener's Year Book* (1855).

BIBLIOGRAPHY: Alkon, P. *The Origins of Futuristic Fiction* (1987). Howe, B. *Lady with Green Fingers: The Life of Jane Loudon* (1961). Loudon, J. C. *In Search of English Gardens: The Travels of John Claudius Loudon and his Wife Jane*, ed. P. Boniface (1988). Macleod, D. *Down-to-Earth Women: Those Who Care for the Soil* (1982). Rauch, A., intro. to *The Mummy! A Tale of the Twenty-Second Century* (1994). Shteir, A. B. *Cultivating Women, Cultivating Science: Flora's Daughters and Botany in England 1760–1860* (1996). Simo, M. L. *Loudon and the Landscape: From Country Seat to Metropolis* (1988).

For articles in reference works, see: *DNB*. Desmond, R. *Dictionary of British and Irish Horticulturalists* (1977).Ogilvie, M. B. *Women in Science: Antiquity through the Nineteenth Century* (1986).

Other references: *Cottage Gardner and Country Gentleman* (27 July 1858).

Alan Rauch

Louisa: See *Boyd, Elizabeth; Robinson, Mary Darby (Perdita)*

Marie Adelaide Belloc Lowndes (Mrs. Belloc Lowndes)

BORN: 1868, La Celle Saint Cloud, France.
DIED: 14 November 1947, Eversley Cross, Hampshire.
DAUGHTER OF: Louis Belloc and Bessie Parkes Belloc.
MARRIED: Frederic Sawrey A. Lowndes, 1896.
WROTE UNDER: Philip Curtin; Mrs. Belloc Lowndes; Elizabeth Rayner.

Born late in life to an English mother and a French father, L. was the sister of the well-known Roman Catholic writer Hilaire Belloc and the great-great-granddaughter of Joseph Priestley. L. and her brother were born in France, where she spent large portions of her young life. Her adolescent and married life was spent primarily in England. Fluent in French, she confessed to a life-long attachment to France and her French family. L.'s father died at forty-two and left her mother to raise the two children alone. Bessie Parkes Belloc moved her family back to England, where she made a bad investment, and the family had to live on a modest income.

Although L.'s education was somewhat untraditional (she had only two years of formal education at a convent school), she was drawn to writing. At the age of sixteen, L. decided to make writing her career. She obtained her first writing job in 1888 when she was made a part author of a guide to the Paris Exhibition of 1889 by W. T. Stead, editor of the *Pall Mall Gazette.* Between 1889 and 1895, she continued to write for the *Gazette* and a number of other publications, and her life during this period, according to her accounts, was a relatively free and liberated one for a woman of that time. During those early writing years, she made numerous trips to France and met many French literary figures, including Edmond de Goncourt, Paul Verlaine, Alphonse Daudet, Anatole France, Emile Zola, and Jules Verne. She was also quite interested in the French theater of the time.

Throughout her life, L. was a prolific writer. Her publications begin in the 1890s and continue through the 1940s, though a few works were published posthumously, including *The Young Hilaire Belloc* (1956). Among her numerous publications were articles, sketches, memoirs, biographies and autobiographies, and plays. Her greatest production, however, was in fiction, both short stories and novels.

L. wrote more than forty novels, mostly mysteries or novels of crime—*The Lodger* (1913) (involving the story of Jack the Ripper) and *The Chink in the Armour* (1912) are probably her best known—and several short-story collections. She also wrote two works under pseudonyms—*Noted Murder Mysteries* by Philip Curtin (1914) and *Not All Saints* by Elizabeth Rayner (1914). Her daughter in the Foreword to the *Diaries and Letters of Marie Belloc Lowndes, 1911–1947* notes that L. "did not consider it to be the business of a novelist to inculcate moral lessons . . . [but] believed that 'who breaks, pays.' Her novels depict the reactions of ordinary persons to sudden violence in their own circle. . . . The reader soon knows who is guilty, and so watches the reactions of the people in the story, with an ever deepening sense of horror and suspense." Her settings are varied and her topic is people, people involved in love, mystery, crime, the supernatural, and life. Her strengths are plot, character, and the ability to hold the interest of the casual mystery reader. Her weakness for the modern reader may be her slant toward the melodramatic and her somewhat sanitized view of crime.

WORKS: (trans. and comp. L. and M. Shedlock) *The Life and Letters of Charlotte Elizabeth, Princess Palatine* (1889). *Edmond and Jules De Goncourt, with letters and Leaves from Their Journals* (1894). *King Edward the Seventh* (1898). *The Philosophy of the Marquise* (1899). *T. R. H. The Prince and Princess of Wales* (1902). *The Heart of Penelope* (1904). *Barbara Rebell* (1905). *The Pulse of Life* (1908). *The Uttermost Earthing* (1908). *Studies in Wives* (1909). *When No Man Pursueth* (1910). *Jane Oglander* (1911). *The Chink in the Armour* (1912). *Mary Pechell* (1912). *The End of her Honeymoon* (1913). *The Lodger* (1913). *Studies in Love and in Terror* (1913). (as Philip Curtin) *Noted Murder Mysteries* (1914). (as Elizabeth Rayner) *Not All Saints* (1914). *Good Old Anna* (1915). *Price of Admiralty* (1915). *Lilla, a Part of Her Life* (1916). *The Red Cross Barge* (1916). *Told in Gallant Deeds: A Child's History of the War* (1916). *Love and Hatred* (1917). *Out of the War (Gentleman Anonymous)* (1918). *From the Pasty Deep* (1920). *The Lonely House* (1920). *What Timmy Did* (1921). *Why They Married* (1923). *The Terriford Mystery* (1924). *Bread of Deceit* (1925). *Some Men and Women* (1925). *What Really Happened* (1926). *Thou Shalt Not Kill* (1927). *The Story of Ivy* (1927). *Cressida, No Mystery* (1928). *Love's Revenge* (1929). *One of Those Ways* (1929). *The Second Key, Possibly The Key: A Love Drama in Three Acts* (1930). *With All John's Love* (1930). *Why Be Lonely* (1931). *The House by the Sea* (1931) (in the U.S. as *Vanderlyn's Adventure*). *Letty Lynton* (1931). *Jenny Newstead* (1932; in the U.S. as *An Unrecorded Instance)*. *Love is a Flame* (1932). *The Reason Why* (1932). *Duchess Laura, Certain Days of Her Life* (1933). *Duchess Laura, Farther Days of Her Life* (1933). *Another Man's Wife* (1934). *The Chianti Flash* (1934). *Who Rides on a Tiger* (1935). *And Call It Accident* (1936). *Her Last Adven-*

ture (1936). *The Second Key* (1936). *The Marriage Broker* (1937; in the U.S. as *The Fortune of Bridget Malone*). *The Empress Eugenie* (1938). *Motive* (1938; in the U.S. as *Why It Happened*). *The Injured Lover* (1939). *Lizzie Borden* (1939). *Reckless Angle* (1939). *The Diamond* (1940). *Before the Storm* (1941). *I, Too, Have Lived in Arcadia* (1941). *What of the Night* (1943). *Where Love and Friendship Dwelt* (1943). *The Merry Wives of Westminster* (1946). *A Passing World* (1948). *She Dwelt with Beauty* (1949). *The Young Hilaire Belloc* (1956).

BIBLIOGRAPHY: Klein, K. G. *Great Women Mystery Writers* (1994). Lowndes, S., ed. *Diaries and Letters of Marie Belloc Lowndes, 1911–1947* (1971). Mansfield, K. *Novels and Novelists* (1930).

For articles in reference works, see: *NCBEL*. *NCHEL*. *TCA*.

Other references: *Baker Street Journal* (1978). *TLS* (1 October 1971). *Toward a Feminist Tradition: An Annotated Bibliography of Novels in English by Women*, ed. D. Daims and J. Grimes (1982).

Evelyn A. Hovanec

Mina Loy

BORN: 27 December 1882, London.
DIED: 25 September 1966, Aspen, Colorado, United States.
DAUGHTER OF: Sigmund Lowy and Julia Bryan Lowy.
MARRIED: Stephen Haweis, 1903; Arthur Cravan (Fabian Avenarius Lloyd), 1918.

L., a painter and designer as well as poet, wrote a relatively small amount of poetry that had a significant influence on modern poetic technique. Although she deprecated herself and deliberately chose obscurity toward the end of her life, she was a major force in introducing the ideas of pre–World War I European writers and artists to the United States. She was formally uneducated except for art classes where she excelled; she was extraordinarily intelligent, sensitive, and bold, her intellect stimulated by and challenging to Futurist artists Marinetti, Papini, and others in Mabel Dodge Luhan's circle in Florence, where L. lived and painted from 1906 to 1916.

After the end of her marriage to Stephen Haweis, she lived intermittently in New York City and Paris from 1916 to 1923; she designed lampshades, painted, modeled, acted in dadaist plays, frequented literary salons, and, famous for her talent and beauty, was a center of attraction in avant-garde artistic circles, wittily recorded in "O Marcel . . . Otherwise I Also Have Been to Louise's." Critics praised her poems, which appeared in magazines such as *Rogue*, *Others*, and *Contact*. In 1918, she married dadaist artist Arthur Cravan, nephew of Oscar Wilde, in Mexico, where Cravan disappeared late that year; she never got over his loss. Their daughter, Fabi, was born in 1919. In 1923, L. returned to Paris and for the next seven years was in contact with modernist writers there—James Joyce, André Breton, Gertrude Stein, and others—although an increasing sense of isolation besieged her. In the 1930s, she published only two poems but worked on her painting and prose; in 1936, she returned to the United States, where she lived in New York City and Aspen, near her daughters, until her death.

L.'s first poems, published from 1914 on and collected in *Lunar Baedecker* [sic] in 1923, shocked her early readers. She refused rhyme and fixed meter, used extremely short uncapitalized lines, and made explicit sexual references, pioneering in techniques that are now familiar in twentieth-century poetics. In 1918, Ezra Pound commented that L.'s verse, like Marianne Moore's, is "a dance of the intelligence among words and ideas . . . a mind cry rather than a heart cry." In this review, Pound also said, evidently ignorant of L.'s English parentage, that her work was "distinctly American in quality." Her poems are more accurately seen as international modernist in style, not tied to any one national culture, in their tight construction, sharp satiric thrust, punning word-play, and references to other arts and artists.

An early poem, "Apology of Genius," contains an artistic manifesto similar to James Joyce's; L. says: "In the raw caverns of the Increate / we forge the dusk of Chaos / to that imperious jewelry of the Universe /—The Beautiful—." In another poem, "Der Blinde Junge," she sees a war-blinded beggarboy on the streets of Vienna, "drowned in dumfounded instinct," as an emblem and warning: "Listen! / illuminati of the coloured earth / How this expressionless 'thing' / blows out damnation and concussive dark / Upon a mouth-organ."

Excessive alliteration—excess for L. is a virtue—always characterizes her work, creating the effect of intense involvement startlingly combined with unsentimentalized distance. "Lunar Baedeker," the poem that first brought her literary notice, mocks romanticism's treatment of the moon, indicating a new irrationality and colder view of both love and art: "in the oxidized Orient / Onyx-eyed Odalisques / and ornithologists / observe / the flight / of Eros obsolete" and concludes: "Pocked with personification / the fossil virgin of the skies / waxes and wanes." In "The Black Virginity," her cubist visualization of young priests strolling in a park—"Fluted black silk cloaks / Hung square from shoulders / Truncated juvenility"—expresses her antiauthoritarianism and hatred of religious hypocrisy.

L. was also a feminist. Even as a child in England, she rejected the traditional feminine dress and behavior urged on her because of her physical beauty and chose to leave home as soon as possible for the artist's life abroad. Although she said that contact with Marinetti's vitality "added twenty years to my life," she broke with the Futurists in 1915 and wrote: "What I feel now are feminist politics." "The Effectual Marriage," "At the Door of the House," and "Parturition" reflect these concerns. Her "Feminist Manifesto," now collected with other prose in *The Lost Lunar Baedecker* (1982), shows her ahead of her time: "there is nothing impure in sex except the attitude toward it." She advises women: "Leave off looking to men to find out what you are not. Seek within yourselves to find out what you are."

A continual seeker and thinker, she scrutinized the sources of her own independent intellect and creativity in the remarkable long autobiographical poem, *Anglo-Mongrels and the Rose*. Published in segments between 1923 and 1925, it describes her Jewish father, a tailor, called in the poem Exodus; her mother, the English rose, called Ada; and herself, Ova. She sees herself at birth as a "mystero-chemico Nemesis / . . .The isolate consciousness / projected from back of time and space / pacing its padded cell" and records the genesis of this consciousness through the baby's visual impressions. She saw her parents as "armored towers"; the green of a cat's-eye brooch associated with ivy taught her the link between the color and the word "green"—an essential moment in the artist's development.

The growing child suffers from the indifference of her angry antisexual mother and from the cruelty of her father. She is moved by a housemaid's story of Gentle Jesus and is later impressed by a church crucifix with its feet "wounded with red varnish." Her religious feelings mature into the Swiftian antitheology of the poem's last segment, in which a post-God deity, the Tailor, remakes the human race: "conscience / disappears / in utter / bifurcate dissimulation / leaving / only those inevitable yet more or less circumspect / creasings / in the latest in trouserings." Thus, we see that L.'s forms unite with content deep in her consciousness. The literary roots of her poems may lie in the French "art for art's sake," but she goes beyond that position while never denying the integrity of the artist. Her compression and formal innovation spring from the passionate conviction that no other mode will serve to penetrate intellectually and philosophically as far as she wants to go.

Later poems, written after she moved to the United States, such as "Property of Pigeons," "On Third Avenue," "Idiot Child on a Fire-Escape," and "Mass Production on 14th Street," record her fascination with the American scene. Her theological concerns continue, with more emphasis on death under the shadow of World War II, as in "Aid of the Madonna": "Skies once ovational / with celestial oboes . . . / are skies in clamor / of deathly celerities— / the horror of diving obituaries / under flowers of fire." For years she lived on the Bowery in New York City; in "Hot Cross Bum" she looks ruthlessly at the derelicts there yet strangely identifies with them. Coinages, witty puns, and powerfully condensed images continue to enliven her work: "a dull-dong" bell / thuds out admonishment / . . . waylaying for branding / indirigible bums / with the hot-cross / of ovenly buns." As she saw the blind beggarboy in Vienna long before, so she sees the bum as emblematic of a degraded world and loss of the genuine, yet with some unironic remnant of hope in his imitation of love: "he's lovin' up the pavement / —interminable paramour / of horizontal stature / Venus sans-vulva—/ A vagabond in delirium / aping the rise and fall / of ocean / of inhalation / of coition." From what she early called "civilized wastes" and from the most unpromising materials, L. reclaims moments of hope and vitality without sacrificing truth through her combination of humane vision and brilliant language.

WORKS: *Auto-Facial Constructions* (1919). *PsychoDemocracy* (1920). *Lunar Baedecker [sic]* (1923). *Lunar Baedeker and Time-Tables: Selected Poems of Mina Loy* (1958). "Constructions" (gallery exhibit statement, 1959). *The Lost Lunar Baedecker* (1982; rev. and updated 1996, ed. R. L. Conover). *Insel* (novel, written c. 1933–35, published 1991, ed. E. Arnold).

BIBLIOGRAPHY: Augustine, J. *Mid-Hudson Language Studies* (1989). Benstock, S. *Women of the Left Bank: Paris, 1900–1940* (1986) Burke, C. *WS* (1980). Burke, C. *PoeticsJ* (1984). Burke, C., in *Silence and Power,* ed. M. L. Broc (1985). Burke, C., in *Coming to Light: American Women Poets in the Twentieth Century,* ed. D. W. Middlebrook and M. Yalom (1985). Burke, C. *FSt* (1985). Burke, C. *AQ* (1987). Burke, C. *Becoming Modern: The Life of Mina Loy* (1996). Bryan, T. J., in *Gender, Culture and the Arts,* ed. R. Dotterer and S. Bowers (1993). Conover, R. L., intro. to *The Lost Lunar Baedecker* (1996). Guggenheim, P. *Out of This Century* (1946). Gunn, T., in *On Modern Poetry: Essays Presented to Donald Davie,* ed. V. Bell and L. Lerner (1988; also in *Shelf Life,* 1983). Hunting, C. *Sagetrieb* (Spring 1983). Johnston, S. *A Reading of Mina Loy's Love Songs* (1981). Kinnahan, L. *Poetics of the Feminine* (1994). Kouidis, V. *Boundary 2* (1980). Kouidis, V. *Mina Loy: American Modernist Poet* (1980). Kreymborg, A. *A History of American Poetry: Our Singing Strength* (1934). Pound, E. *The Little Review* (March 1918). Powell, J. *ChiR* (1990). Schaum, M. *MSE* (1986). Winters, Y. *Yvor Winters: Uncollected Essays and Reviews,* ed. Francis Murphy (1973).

For articles in reference works, see: *CA* (although this work erroneously lists Loy's birthname as Lowry instead of Lowy). *CLC*. *DLB*.

Other references: *AL* (1981). *Contact Collection of Contemporary Writers* (1925). *ConL* (1961). *HOW(ever)* (1985). *JAS* (1981). *Los Angeles Times Book Review* (22 August 1982). *MP* (1982). *Nation* (27 May 1961). *New York Evening Sun* (13 February 1917). *NYTBR* (16 November 1980, 16 May 1982). *RFEA* (1994). *Saturday Review* (1967).

Jane Augustine

Lucy Magdalena, Dame: See *Cary, Lucy*

Joanna (Jane) Fitzalan Lumley

BORN: 1537 (?), presumably in Sussex.

DIED: 1576 (or 1577), presumably in the Fitzalan family home on the Strand.

DAUGHTER OF: Henry Fitzalan, twelfth Earl of Arundel, and Katherine Grey Fitzalan.

MARRIED: John, first Baron Lumley, of the Second Creation, c. 1549.

L., the older of the two unusually learned daughters of Henry Fitzalan, Earl of Arundel, may have been highly educated with the expectation that she would marry into the royal family, but was married at around age twelve to John Lumley, her brother's classmate at Cambridge. She was fortunate in being matched to a man of a very learned turn, who, like her father, became high steward of Oxford, a member of the Elizabethan Society of Antiquities, and an amasser of a noteworthy library. It is possible that Lord and Lady Lumley worked at similar study, side by side. The combined Fitzalan and Lumley libraries became part of the Royal Library after Lumley's death, and it is in this collection, now in the British Library, that L.'s manuscript compositions (MS. Reg. 15. A. ix.) are preserved.

It is not surprising that her translations from Greek and Latin literature were not printed, since even highly educated Tudor "prodigies" hesitated to put their writings into print; those brave women who did so overwhelmingly produced religious translations. The chief of L.'s productions is her abridged prose translation of about 1550 of Euripides's *Iphigenia at Aulis,* first printed, by the Malone Society, in 1909. Although it is not a polished translation, it is a remarkable achievement, since, in England, Renaissance scholarship was concentrated heavily on Latin materials; the remaining translations by L. in the quarto volume containing the *Iphigenia* are from Latin. Her translation of Euripides is the earliest known translation from Greek to English of a Greek drama.

WORKS: (trans.) "The Tragedie of Euripides called Iphigenia translated out of Greke into Englisshe" (British Library MS. Reg. 15. A. ix.; rpt. Malone Society, ed. H. H. Child, 1909).

BIBLIOGRAPHY: Beilin, E. V. *Redeeming Eve: Women Writers of the English Renaissance* (1987). Cotton, N. *Women Playwrights in England c. 1363–1750* (1980). Crane, F. D. *CJ* (1944). Greene, D. H. *CJ* (1941). Hays, M. *Female Biography, or, Memoirs of Illustrious and Celebrated Women, of All Ages and Countries* (1803). Hogrefe, P. *Tudor Women: Commoners and Queens* (1975). Reynolds, M. *The Learned Lady in England, 1650–1760* (1920). Stenton, D. *English Women in History* (1957). Warnicke, R. M. *Women of the English Renaissance and Reformation* (1983). Williams, J. *Literary Women of England* (1861).

For articles in reference works, see: *Ballard. Bloomsbury. DNB* (under "Henry Fitzalan, twelfth Earl of Arundel [1511–1580]"). *Feminist. Oxford. ToddBWW.*

Betty Travitsky

Lyall, Edna: See *Bayly, Ada Ellen*

(Emilie) Rose Macaulay

BORN: 1 August 1881, Rugby, Warwickshire.
DIED: 30 October 1958, London.
DAUGHTER OF: George Macaulay and Grace Macaulay.

The second of seven children, M. was a tomboy who believed she would grow up to be a man; in her early twenties, she still hoped to join the Navy. This sense of gender ambiguity, both playful and serious, pervades her fiction. In 1887, the Macaulays left Rugby, where M.'s father was an assistant master, and moved to Italy. In the seacoast town of Varazze, the children led an exciting and undisciplined life before the family returned to England in 1894. M. attended Oxford High School and later Somerville College, Oxford, where she read modern history. After graduating in 1903, she lived with her parents, first in Aberystwyth, Wales, and afterwards in Cambridge. By late 1905, she had had several poems published and was at work on her first novel, *Abbots Verney* (1906).

M.'s early novels combine a witty, aphoristic style with themes of loss and isolation from society. *The Lee Shore* (1912) concludes by urging philosophical detachment from failure and the "lust to possess": "The last, the gayest, the most hilarious laughter begins when, destitute utterly, the wrecked pick up coloured shells upon the lee shore." After the success of this novel (which won first prize and £1,000 in a competition organized by its publisher), M. moved to London where she mingled with writers and intellectuals. In 1914, during "this pre-war golden age," as she once called it, M. published *The Making of a Bigot,* a comic novel about the necessity of compromising the "many-faced Truth" in order to get on in the world, and her first book of poems, *The Two Blind Countries,* which reflects the influence of Walter de la Mare and other Georgians but succeeds in registering her own peculiar sense of the instability of institutions and social structures, which she figures as "the transient city."

M. worked as a nurse for part of World War I and in 1916 became a civil servant in the War Office, dealing with exemptions from service and conscientious objectors. In *Non-Combatants and Others* (1916), the heroine, Alix, comes to realize that her pacifist mother, Daphne—one in a series of exuberant, confident, worldly women in M.'s fiction—is right in campaigning for a "positive" peace, "a young peace, passionate, ardent, intelligent, romantic, like poetry, like art, like religion." The novel also contains an early and sensitive study of the psychological effects of trench fighting. Early in 1918, M. was transferred to the Ministry of Information. Here, she met and fell in love with Gerald O'Donovan, a married novelist with whom she had a relationship that lasted until his death in 1942. His stimulus and criticism were of much importance to her career.

During the 1920s, M. established her reputation for trenchant, clear-eyed social satire. Her first best-seller, *Potterism* (1920)—an attack on the popular press and the muddleheaded emotionalism it exploits—is dedicated to "the unsentimental precisians in thought, who have, on this confused, inaccurate, and emotional planet, no fit habitation." In *Crewe Train* (1926), London society and its malicious gossip are exposed through the silent, anarchic figure of Denham who, much against her husband's will, prefers to live alone in a Cornish cottage and explore the caves beneath it. But "Life" is too strong for her; her self-sufficiency gives way to social and marital pressures. She relinquishes her cottage and the cave of her own and returns to her husband.

In the 1930s, M. became increasingly absorbed in the study of the seventeenth century and wrote a refreshing, informed biography of John Milton. More important is her historical novel *They Were Defeated* (1932), set in the early 1640s and featuring the poet Robert Herrick. M. restricted the characters' vocabulary to words known to have existed at the period, and the dialogue is remarkably credible and fluent. The novel elegizes the Cavalier tradition and movingly portrays Herrick, whose verses celebrating simple rural joys go unheeded in a world where Donnian "conceit" is all the rage. Most poignant are the "defeats" involving women. A harmless old eccentric is hunted down as a witch; and Julian Conybeare, a brilliant and poetically gifted girl, becomes the mistress of the poet John Cleveland only to discover that he wants her to give up ideas and poetry and assume her proper role in life. Her protest,

"It makes no differ, being a maid," does not avail. The story ends with her tragic, absurd death. In *Crewe Train* M. had described Denham as "the Silent Woman"; Julian might be called "the silenced woman."

M. visited Portugal and Spain and produced two works of great learning and wit based on her travels, *They Went to Portugal* (1946) and *Fabled Shore* (1949). In 1948, M. began writing *The World My Wilderness* (1950), her first novel in almost a decade. The central symbol—the London Blitz ruins—is a variation of the cave motif used in *Crewe Train.* Barbary, a girl resembling Denham in many ways, leaves her home in a tiny French port to live in "civilized" London. But her earlier life and her participation in the French Resistance have made her unfit for all this, and she is at home only in the bombed-out buildings of the city. Here, the "cave" is more a symbol of widespread moral decline than an image of personal freedom.

M. was fascinated by religious questions, and much of her work reflects this. She had stopped receiving Communion in 1922 because of her involvement with the married O'Donovan. Yet she always considered herself an "Anglo-Agnostic," and in 1950 she began exchanging letters with her cousin, an Anglican priest named H. C. Johnson. M.'s letters to him fill two books, *Letters to a Friend* (1961) and *Last Letters to a Friend* (1962), and trace her return to the Anglican Communion under his guidance.

In 1956, M. published *The Towers of Trebizond,* which John Betjeman considered "the best book she has written, and that is saying a lot." Partly inspired by a trip to Turkey in 1954, the novel is a masterful and picaresque compendium of M.'s beliefs and interests, written in what she called a "rather goofy, rambling prose style." This allows her to sketch a scene swiftly or digress at length (e.g., on the history of mistresses). The eccentric Father Chantry-Pigg, along with an insane camel and a trained ape, provide hilarity, but the work also reflects, in part, M.'s crisis of faith. The narrator, Laurie—who does not reveal herself to be a woman until the end—yearns for the Byzantine city of Trebizond, which symbolizes the church, but her adulterous relationship prevents her from making "the pattern and the hard core" of the city her own. At the end, she is still outside the city.

"Ignorance, vulgarity, cruelty" were M.'s "three black jungle horrors." In contrast, her work consistently offers a voice that is civilized, ironic, playful, canny, and sane. Her satire is sometimes accused of flippancy, but this is because her narrative "mimicry" and use of authorial voice are not yet properly understood. Nor are her feminism and her play on gender expectations fully appreciated. What Katherine Mansfield called "her offhand, lightly-smiling manner" thinly disguises intense commitment to difference and eccentricity and equally intense religiosity. Her pluralistic mind, like the Anglican Church as she describes it in *The Towers of Trebizond,* was "very wonderful and comprehensive." M. was made a Dame Commander of the British Empire in 1958.

WORKS: *Abbots Verney* (1906). *The Furnace* (1906). *The Secret River* (1909). *The Valley Captives* (1911). *Views and Vagabonds* (1912). *The Lee Shore* (1912). *The Two Blind Countries* (1914). *The Making of a Bigot* (1914). *Non-Combatants and Others* (1916). *What Not: A Prophetic Comedy* (1919). *Three Days* (1919). *Potterism: A Tragifarcical Tract* (1920). *Dangerous Ages* (1921). *Mystery at Geneva* (1922). *Told by an Idiot* (1923). *Orphan Island* (1924). *A Casual Commentary* (1925). *Crewe Train* (1926). *Catchwords and Claptrap* (1926). *Keeping Up Appearances* (1928; in the U.S. as *Daisy and Daphne*). *Staying with Relations* (1930). *Some Religious Elements in English Literature* (1931). *They Were Defeated* (1932; in the U.S. as *The Shadow Flies*). *Going Abroad* (1934). *Milton* (1934). *The Minor Pleasures of Life* (1934). *Personal Pleasures* (1935). *An Open Letter to a Non-Pacifist* (1937). *I Would Be Private* (1937). *The Writings of E. M. Forster* (1938). *And No Man's Wit* (1940). *Life Among the English* (1942). *They Went to Portugal* (1946). *Fabled Shore: From the Pyrenees to Portugal* (1949). *The World My Wilderness* (1950). *Pleasure of Rains* (1953). *The Towers of Trebizond* (1956). *Letters to a Friend: 1950–1952* (1961). *Last Letters to a Friend: 1952–1958* (1962). *Letters to a Sister* (1964).

BIBLIOGRAPHY: Babington Smith, C. *Rose Macaulay* (1972). Bensen, A. *Rose Macaulay* (1969). Crosland, M. *Beyond the Lighthouse: English Women Novelists of the Twentieth Century* (1981). Mansfield, K. *Novels and Novelists* (1930). Monro, H. *Some Contemporary Poets* (1920). Sherman, S. *Critical Woodcuts* (1926). Sturgeon, M. *Studies of Contemporary Poets* (1919). Swinnerton, F. *The Georgian Literary Scene* (1935).

For articles in reference works, see: *Bloomsbury. CA. Cambridge. DLB. Feminist. Longman. MBL. Oxford. TCA. TCW. ToddBWW.*

Other references: Adams, P. *Somerville for Women: An Oxford College 1879–1993* (1996). *Bookman* (May 1927). Fromm, G. G. *NewC* (October 1986). Nicholson H. *Observer* (6 May 1949). Nicholson, H. et al. *Encounter* (March 1959). Swinnerton, F. *KR* (November 1967). *TLS* (12 May 1950).

Robert Spoo

McCorquodale, Barbara: See *Cartland, Barbara*

McFall, Frances Elizabeth [Clarke]: See *Grand, Sarah*

Medbh McGuckian

BORN: 12 August 1950, Belfast, Northern Ireland.
DAUGHTER OF: Hugh Albert McCaughan and Margaret Fergus McCaughan.
MARRIED: John McGuckian, 1977.

M. (her first name is pronounced "Maeve") currently resides in northern Belfast and is associated with the Ulster poets. The critical views of M.'s work range from beautiful and erotic to difficult and esoteric. Yet, while many view her poetry as obscure and dense, her themes, once discovered, are universal. She explores issues such as the female psyche, the historic position of women in visual arts, relations among different generations in a family, motherhood, the role of the poet in Ireland, and the influence of Irish history upon the present, among many others. M.'s primary influences are Seamus Heaney, who taught her at Queen's University in Belfast, and fellow Ulster poet Paul Muldoon, as well as Roman Catholic rituals and faith. Her imagery revolves around concrete experiences and the natural world as well as imaginative experiences within the self. M.'s preferred technique is to juxtapose concrete experiences with imaginative experiences in order to expose some truth about the female psyche.

M.'s first full-length collection, *The Flower Master* (1982), was hailed for well-turned-out, styled, and formed poems. The collection serves to introduce her primary subject of womanliness through an exploration of the subject positions of women in the visual arts and the value of decorative arts, such as embroidery, by women. M. argues that women displayed as models and disregarded as artists have something important to contribute to Ireland and the world in general. As in *The Flower Master,* the subject of womanhood reigns throughout her second collection, *Venus and the Rain* (1984). The voice of Venus, represented by the moon, sisterhood, and motherhood, is placed in a post-scientific universe. Once there, Venus exists in the present while also visiting the past through nostalgic remembrances such as her love affair with Mars. Thus, M. effectively juxtaposes myth and science where, according to some critics, she manages to recombine the two and create poetry out of scientific theory.

On Ballycastle Beach (1988), a volume based upon the theme of desire, struggles to regain the power of imagination and, through imagination, sensuality. Critics believe that M.'s Romantic tendencies (influenced by John Keats and Percy Bysshe Shelley) appear most strongly here as she plays upon and desires freedom of emotion and imagination. By playing upon these desires, M. questions women's inner lives and the boundaries that define women. Such questioning leads to an exploration of the stability, or lack of stability, of such boundaries.

Marconi's Cottage (1991), M.'s fourth volume, employs domestic scenes in order to explore one's inner being. Furthermore, images based upon domesticity, motherhood, and birth, for example, also serve to respond to the political troubles found in Belfast, marking a new political edge to her poetry. *Captain Lavender* (1994) expands upon M.'s recurring themes of womanhood, motherhood, women's inner lives, as well as continuing to employ Roman Catholic images of resurrection, faith, love, ceremony, and ritual. The epigraph to the volume indicates M.'s growing belief, also seen in *Marconi's Cottage,* that while her previous collections avoid explicit discussion of the Troubles in Northern Ireland, these Troubles are becoming increasingly difficult to avoid in the images of her poetry.

While M. has been both praised and criticized for her ambiguous and esoteric verse, she remains one of Northern Ireland's premier contemporary poets. Her work is gaining gradual international recognition as well as increased recognition in her own country. Furthermore, her themes of womanhood and the female psyche remain universal and, as of now, with room for added exploration and introspection.

WORKS: *Portrait of Joanna* (1980). *Single Ladies* (1980). *The Flower Master* (1982). *Venus and the Rain* (1984). *On Ballycastle Beach* (1988). *Marconi's Cottage* (1991). *The Flower Master and Other Poems* (1993). *Captain Lavender* (1994). *Selected Poems, 1978–1994* (1997).

BIBLIOGRAPHY: Beer, A. *CJIS* (1992). Bendall, M. *AR* (1990). Cahill, E. *IUR* (1994). Docherty, T., in *The Chosen Ground: Essays on the Contemporary Poetry of Northern Ireland,* ed. N. Corcoran (1992). Gray, C., in *Learning the Trade: Essays of W. B. Yeats and Contemporary Poetry,* ed. D. Fleming (1993). O'Brien, P. *CQ* (1992). Porter, S. *CJIS* (1989). Salier, S. S. *MQR* (1993). Wills, C. *T&C* (1988).

For articles in reference works, see: *CLC. CP. DLB.*

Jeannette E. Riley

Mackay, Mary: See *Corelli, Marie*

Shena Mackay

BORN: 6 June 1944, Edinburgh, Scotland.
DAUGHTER OF: Benjamin Carr Mackey and Morag Carmichael Mackey.
MARRIED: Robin Francis Brown, 1964.

M., a contemporary British novelist and short-story writer, is admired for her superb portrayals of humor, satire, and realism. Born in Edinburgh in 1944, she was educated at Tonbridge Girls' Grammar School in Kent and Kidbrooke Comprehensive School in London. In her teens, she discovered the family name was originally Mackay, so she changed her last name from Mackey to that spelling. In 1964, she married Robin Francis Brown; they divorced in 1981. M. worked at a variety of jobs before becoming a full-time writer. She lives in London, where she is working on her current projects. She has three daughters and one grandson.

A prolific writer, M. wrote her first two novellas, *Dust Falls on Eugene Schlumburger* (1964) and *Toddler on the Run* (1964), when she was a teenager. Her novellas were followed by the publication of the novels *Music Upstairs* (1965), *Old Crow* (1967), *An Advent Calendar* (1971), *A Bowl of Cherries* (1984), and *Redhill Rococo* (1986), which received the 1987 Fawcett Fiction Prize. Her novel *Dunedin* (1992) and her collection of short stories *The Laughing Academy* (1993) were awarded Scottish Arts Council Book Awards.

A Bowl of Cherries, Redhill Rococo, and *Dunedin* are M.'s best-known novels. *A Bowl of Cherries* concerns Daisy Beaumont, her husband Julian, and her parents, Daphne and Rex. The plot involves Rex's illegitimate son, who meets his father's dysfunctional family for the first time. The son's presence influences the family tremendously, and the ending leaves hope for the family's recovery.

Redhill Rococo, set in the outskirts of Surrey, reflects suburban desolation. The novel contrasts the lifestyles of a bourgeois Redhill family with a genteel Reigate family, whose children attend the same school. The Redhill family consists of Pearl Slattery, who works in a candy factory, her common-law husband Jack, who is in prison, and their children. The Reigate family, Helen Headley-Jones, Jeremy, and their children, live a sophisticated lifestyle. Whereas Helen wears *Guardian* jogging suits and buys her husband personalized golf tees because she needs a unique gift for a man who has everything, Pearl has slugs under her bathtub and cannot afford a decent iron. Both women recognize the differences between their life-styles. Helen says, "We're turning into the Slatterys," explaining to her daughter that she has become rough, rude, and graceless. Likewise, Pearl holds animosities toward Helen, calling her "the Weasel." Through her brilliant use of black humor and other techniques, M. demonstrates that members of both social strata live isolated, lonely lives but for different reasons. In the end, Pearl and Helen discover a unique friendship because of their common dilemma, representing hope for both of them.

Dunedin represents M.'s superb portrayal of plot, management of characterization, and depiction of the Realist tradition, characteristics that are compared with Charles Dickens's techniques. *Dunedin,* set in Southeast London, involves generations of the Mackenzie family told through a framing device. The novel begins and ends in 1909, with the portrayal of Jack Mackenzie. The generation of Jack Mackenzie's grandchildren during the 1980s is portrayed in the encased story, where the primary plot of the novel is revealed.

M. is also a distinguished short-story writer, recognized for her poetic language, strong use of vivid imagery, and her humor. *Dreams of Dead Women's Handbags: Collected Stories,* contains thirty-one stories: the three short-story collections *Babies in Rhinestones, Dreams of Dead Women's Handbags, The Laughing Academy,* and two previously unpublished stories. Many of M.'s stories concern the frustrations of working-class people, who are often lonely and isolated. In most of her stories, M. portrays realistic life situations, written in the traditional short story structural mode. In other stories, such as "Perpetual Spinach" and "Dreams of Dead Women's Handbags," M. takes a surrealistic approach. "Dreams of Dead Women's Handbags" concerns a mystery writer who recalls a murderous childhood experience. Boundaries between the protagonist's dreams, memories, and fictional material are blurred. In "Babies in Rhinestones," two lonely people, the proprietor of a fine arts school and the proprietress of a dance school, discover each other. Unusual circumstances and chance meetings bring the characters together in a relationship where they share their mutual animosity. "Other People's Bathrobes" offers a serious look at ways people are sometimes misunderstood. A woman's hidden past is examined, viewed through the eyes of her live-in boyfriend, who discovers secrets about her by looking at an old photograph album. M.'s short story "The Most Beautiful Dress in the World" was adapted for a BBC-2 television film in 1993, and many of her stories have been broadcast on the radio.

Before she turned twenty, M. was considered a prodigy with the publication of *Dust Falls on Eugene Schlumburger* and *Toddler on the Run.* While she has received little serious critical attention, her works are generally reviewed favorably both in England and in the United States.. American publisher Moyer Bell has reprinted several of M.s works, an indication that she is gaining international attention. Her satire, wit, and ability to capture contemporary British bourgeois life provides her a permanent place among British novelists and short-story writers.

WORKS: *Dust Falls on Eugene Schlumburger* (1964). *Toddler on the Run* (1964). *Music Upstairs* (1965). *Old Crow* (1967). *An Advent Calendar* (1971). *A Bowl of Cherries* (1984). *Redhill Rococo* (1986). *Dunedin* (1992). *Babies in Rhinestones* (1983). *Dreams of Dead Women's Handbags* (1987). *The Laughing Academy* (1993). *Dreams of Dead Women's Handbags: Collected Stories* (1994).

BIBLIOGRAPHY:

For articles in reference works, see: *AWWW. CA.*

Laurie Champion

Elizabeth Mackintosh

BORN: 25 June 1896, Inverness, Scotland.
DIED: 13 February 1952, London.
DAUGHTER OF: Colin Mackintosh and Josephine Horne Mackintosh.
WROTE UNDER: Gordon Daviot; Josephine Tey.

M. is best known as the author, as Josephine Tey, of several extraordinary novels of detection. More extensive, however, and in her own estimation more central to her career as a serious writer, was her output of fiction, plays, and biography under the pseudonym Gordon Daviot.

Born in Inverness, Scotland, she attended the Royal Academy there but declined to go on to university or art school ("I balked, too, at art—my talent is on the shady side of mediocre"). Instead, she studied three years at Anstey Physical Training College, Birmingham, worked briefly as a physical therapist, and taught physical education at schools in Scotland and England. Called home in 1923 to attend her dying mother, she remained in Inverness, living with her father. She took long annual holidays in England and developed some friendships in London theatrical circles but shunned publicity and was generally reclusive. She continued her work through the year of illness that preceded her early death. Found among her papers were two novels and thirteen plays, since published. Two collections of Jesephine Tey novels later appeared and were Book-of-the-Month Club alternates.

The career of "Gordon Daviot" began in about 1925 with contributions to magazines and continued in 1929 with two novels, including a detective story, *The Man in the Queue.* M. then turned to drama but, on the rejection of her first effort, reworked it as a romantic novel, *The Expensive Halo* (1931). Finally, in 1932, came *Richard of Bordeaux;* running in London for more than a year, starring John Gielgud, as well as in New York City, this remained M.'s most successful play. In Gielgud's opinion, "she improved on Shakespeare . . . by giving [King] Richard [II] a sense of humour." *Richard* was followed by twelve other full-length plays, five of which were produced in her lifetime (Laurence Olivier played Bothwell in *Queen of Scots*), and thirteen shorter plays, including several radio broadcasts. Nearly half her plays retell stories from history or the Bible—Sarah and Hagar, Joseph (*The Stars Bow Down,* produced at the 1939 Malvern Festival), Moses, Rahab. The latter group should not be considered religious plays. It was the story that interested M., and her reading of it typically was nonsupernaturalist. Romantic themes appear occasionally in her plays; more prominent is a vein of tart satire, especially of politicians. M. also wrote two historically based prose works—a biography of the seventeenth-century Scottish royalist Viscount Dundee (*Claverhouse,* 1937) and a novel about the pirate Henry Morgan (*The Privateer,* 1952).

The pseudonym "Josephine Tey" first appeared in 1936 with *A Shilling for Candles,* and M. reserved it for detective fiction, which she deprecated as her "yearly knitting." From 1947 to 1952, indeed, one Tey novel did appear each year. These works, exhibiting M.'s skill in dialogue (honed by writing for the stage) and attention to characterization, not only rank high in classic "golden age" detective fiction but also belong to the mainstream of the novel. Exploration of character is M.'s chief interest. Insight into motive and the perception of such typically "criminal" character traits as vanity are always, for her, key elements in detection; when her detectives err, as often happens, it is by suppressing such insight and trusting more traditional, apparently objective, kinds of evidence. (One oddity in M.'s presentation of character is the obsessive notion that it can be read infallibly in trivial details of facial features and expression. Her Scotland Yard inspector Alan Grant relies heavily on this method, applying it no less accurately with photographs or portraits than in the flesh. But curiously, M. hardly ever describes Grant himself.) Thematically, M. develops love interests in some of the Tey novels, though avoiding the clichés of romance, and, with delightful asperity of tone, she makes fun of the vanity and shallow life-style of the theater and arts crowd. Another serious theme uniting these works is that of identity, ranging from initial difficulty in identifying the corpse (*The Man in the Queue, The Singing Sands*) through the morally neutral effort of a prodigal to escape disgrace by resuming his old name (*A Shilling for Candles*), to imposture (a teenage harlot posing as innocent victim in *The Franchise Affair,* 1948; a foundling cousin posing as heir in *Brat Farrar,* 1949; and a transvestite disguise in *To Love and Be Wise,* 1950).

Moreover, M. feels free to depart from golden-age formulas, often in ways suggesting a more skeptical postmodern sensibility. Only half of the eight novels have corpses; in two no one dies, and in two long-closed cases are reopened. Especially remarkable is *The Daughter of Time* (1951), in which a bedridden detective conducts an academic investigation into the fate of the young princes in the Tower and concludes that King Henry VII, not Richard III, had them murdered. Here and twice more (*Miss Pym Disposes,* 1947; *The Franchise Affair*), M. ends not with order satisfyingly restored by justice but with innocence suffering and society powerless to punish the wrongdoers adequately if at all.

Among the sufferers are M.'s detectives, who may be physically (*Daughter of Time*) or emotionally (*The Singing Sands*) ill, prone to play God—hence the title *Miss Pym Disposes*—but inept, or themselves involved in crime though fundamentally honest (*Brat Farrar*). For all M.'s favorable, even sympathetic treatment of him, Grant is unusually fallible. He wastes time chasing the wrong suspect, and sometimes (*Shilling, Franchise*) it takes an amateur detective to correct his errors. Three cases (*Queue, Pym,* and *Sands*) are solved by the murderer's confession, not the detective's sleuthing; in the last, however, to do Grant justice, the confession merely anticipates his independent solution. In *The Daughter of Time,* the verdict against King Henry inherently must lack the external corroboration standard for the genre.

If the police have trouble drawing the right conclusions, all the more easily is the general public hoodwinked. M.'s skepticism on this score unites the Tey and the Daviot *oeuvres.* Frequently, she attacks gullibility in the face of fraudulent piety, whether that of the rogue "monk" in *A Shilling for Candles* or that of the Covenanters in *Claverhouse.* Misled public opinion drives an innocent into exile in *The Franchise Affair* (a fictionalized version of an eighteenth-century case) and, in the one-act play *Leith Sands* (1946), hangs a man for a murder that never occurred. Much of Grant's case in *The Daughter of Time* consists of questioning the reliability of accepted "evidence" and citing parallel instances of historians' naïve credulity. This book is M.'s best known in academic circles, being used as a textbook for raising questions on historical method. M. handled the same story in dramatic form in *Dickon.* She especially enjoyed rehabilitating characters vilified by history (Dundee, Morgan, Richard III) and, in fiction, portraying the character type of the honest rogue (*Kif, Brat Farrar*).

Other links between Tey and Daviot are an interest in biblical archetyes (note, for example, the motifs from the Joseph story in *Brat Farrar*), consistent patterns in the treatment of women and a cinematic quality in M.'s writing. She loved movies, habitually attending twice weekly, and several of her novels have been dramatized in film (e.g., Hitchcock's *Young and Innocent* in 1937) or television.

WORKS: (as Gordon Daviot) *The Man in the Queue* (1929, rpt. 1953 as by Josephine Tey). (as Gordon Daviot) *Kif: An Unvarnished History* (1929). (as Gordon Daviot) *The Expensive Halo* (1931). (as Gordon Daviot) *Richard of Bordeaux* (produced 1932, pub. 1933). (as Gordon Daviot). *The Laughing Woman* (1934). (as Gordon Daviot) *Queen of Scots* (1934). (as Josephine Tey) *A Shilling for Candles* (1936). (as Gordon Daviot) *Claverhouse* (1937). (as Gordon Daviot) *The Stars Bow Down* (1939). (as Gordon Daviot) *Leith Sands* [broadcast 1941] *and Other Short Plays* (1946). (as Josephine Tey) *Miss Pym Disposes* (1947). (as Josephine Tey) *The Franchise Affair* (1948). (as Josephine Tey) *Brat Farrar* (1949). (as Josephine Tey) *To Love and Be Wise* (1950). (as Josephine Tey) *The Daughter of Time* (1951). (as Josephine Tey) *The Singing Sands* (1952). (as Gordon Daviot) *The Privateer* (1952). (as Gordon Daviot) *Plays,* 3 vols. (1953–54; foreword by J. Gielgud; *The Pen of My Aunt,* rpt. in *Eight Short Plays,* 1965; *Dickon,* rpt. with intro., historical commentary, and notes by E. Haddon, 1966). *Three by Tey* (*Miss Pym Disposes, The Franchise Affair, Brat Farrar*) (1954; intro. by J. Sandoe). *Four Five and Six by Tey* (*The Singing Sands, A Shilling for Candles, The Daughter of Time*) (1958).

BIBLIOGRAPHY: Champion, L., in *A Fair Day in the Affections: Literary Essays in Honor of Robert B. White, Jr.*, ed. J. Durant and M. Hester (1980). Light, A., in *The Progress of Romance*, ed. J. Radford (1986). Mann, J. *Deadlier Than the Male* (1981). Martin, C. R. *Studies in Scottish Literature* (1996). Mitchell, D. *LFQ* (1997). Rollyson, C. *Iowa State Journal of Research* (1978). Roy, S. *Josephine Tey* (1980). Talburt, N. E. *10 Women of Mystery*, ed. E. Bargainnier (1981). Vickers, A., in *Great Women Mystery Writers: Classic to Contemporary*, ed. K. Klein (1994). Yost, C. W. *The Researched Novel* (1982).

For articles in reference works, see: Barzun, J. and W. H. Taylor. *A Cataloger of Crime* (1971). *Bloomsbury. CA. Cambridge. DLB. DLEL Chaucer to 1940* (1970). *EMD. Europa. Feminist.* Herman, L. and B. Stiel. *Corpus Delicti* (1974). *Ireland. NCBEL* (under "Daviot"). *NCHEL. Oxford. PCEL* (1971). *RE.* Seymour-Smith, M. *Novels and Novelists* (1980). *TCA. SUP. TCC&MW. TCLC. TCW. ToddBWW. Who's Who* (under "Daviot," 1936 through 1952).

Other references: *ArmD* (Summer 1977, Fall 1977, Spring 1981, Fall 1987). *BW* (21 December 1980). Charney, H. *The Detective Novel of Manners* (1981). *Clues* (Fall–Winter 1980, Spring–Summer 1991). Morley, F. *Literary Britain* (1980). *New Republic* (14 March 1934, 20 September 1954). *New Statesman* (5 November 1949). *Newsweek* (7 September 1953). *Saturday Review* (16 September 1933). Symons, J. *Bloody Murder* (1972).

Charles A. Huttar

May McKisack

BORN: 30 March 1900, Belfast, Northern Ireland.
DIED: 14 March 1981, Oxford.
DAUGHTER OF: Audley John McKisack and Elizabeth McCullough.

An eminent scholar and teacher of medieval English history, M., having studied under several distinguished women historians, published three major books and influenced the lives and careers of undergraduates, research students, and scholars in both Europe and the United States.

Widowed early, M.'s mother moved her two children, M. and her brother Audley, knighted in 1958, from Belfast to Bedford, in Bedfordshire, where M. studied with Agnes Sandys at the highly regarded Bedford School for Girls (1910–19). M. continued her studies as the Mary Ewart Scholar at Somerville College, Oxford, as a pupil of Maude Clarke, earning her B.A. with Second Class Honors and Final Honors in the School of Modern History in 1922. For the next two years, M. remained at Somerville as Mary Somerville Research Fellow, completing her B.Litt., *Parliamentary Representation of the English Boroughs in the Middle Ages;* this was later published as a volume in the Oxford Historical Series (1932). After teaching history for a year in high school, she served as lecturer in medieval history at Liverpool University from 1927 to 1935. In 1936, she returned to Somerville, where she remained for the next two decades. During this period, the Oxford tutorial system enabled her to develop close ties with her students while she continued her research in medieval English political history. In 1955, M. was installed as professor of history at Westfield College, University of London. Her inaugural lecture, *History As Education*, reveals her love not only of the subject but also of those who study it. As Professor of History at Westfield, M. exercised the same concern and leadership in department and college matters that had served so many students at Somerville. Her sure hand guided Westfield through a period of rapid growth while she instituted in the London Honours Program a new special subject on the reign of Richard II. Retirement from Westfield allowed M. to accept a visiting professorship of history at Vassar College in New York in 1967–68, where she again brought medieval topics and people alive for undergraduates and forged new friendships with American colleagues. M. retired to Oxford where she made her home with Dame Lucy Sutherland and was often visited by friends and former pupils.

M.'s distinguished teaching career was highlighted by several influential publications. In 1932, her *Parliamentary Representations of the English Boroughs in the Middle Ages* challenged current interpretations of the topic and established her reputation as a careful researcher. In this volume she argued that representation of boroughs did not decrease for the fourteenth century and showed an increase in the fifteenth century. Her research corrected the view that burgesses did not attend Parliament and argued that burgesses were not as subordinate to knights as was generally thought by modern historians.

M.'s most widely read work, *The Fourteenth Century*, appeared in 1959 as volume five of the *Oxford History of England.* The great strength of this balanced and detailed survey was its clear presentation of institutional developments and political events. Revising current interpretations, she suggested that the aristocracy did not expand dangerously during this period. The volume has remained the most authoritative treatment of fourteenth-century England.

In 1971, M. published her third book, *Medieval History in the Tudor Age.* Using manuscripts in the royal, diocesan, and university collections, she documented England's awakening interest in its medieval past during the sixteenth century. In the same year, she was honored by a volume of essays from her former pupils and colleagues on the reign of King Richard II. She died in 1981.

WORKS: *Parliamentary Representation of the English Boroughs* (1932). *History as Education, an Inaugural Lecture* (1956). *The Fourteenth Century* (1959). *Medieval History in the Tudor Age* (1971).

BIBLIOGRAPHY: *The Reign of Richard II: Essays in Honour of May McKisack*, ed. F.R.H. Du Boulay and C. M. Barron (1971).

Other references: Barron, C. *Somerville College Report and Supplement* (1981). *IAWWW. Annual Obituary 1981*, ed. J. Podel (1982). *Who's Who. Who Was Who.*

Judith C. Kohl

Mary MacLeod

BORN: c. 1615, Rodel, Harris, Scotland.
DIED: c. 1706, Dunvegan, Scotland.
DAUGHTER OF: Alasdair Ruadh na Droighnich.

Mairi nighean Alasdair Ruaidh (Mary the daughter of Red Alasdair), as she was known to her contemporaries, was perhaps the finest of the Gaelic bards of her era. M. lived and worked during the period of transition from classic to modern Scottish poetry; indeed, she was the first to compose court poetry using popular versification and vernacular diction. Attached to the lords of the MacLeod clan for the greater part of her life, M. composed many of her poems during the chaotic period from the reign of Charles I through the Restoration of Charles II; during the period of Oliver Cromwell's rule, the Scottish clans suffered debilitating loss of life and property by virtue of their loyalty to the Stuart monarchy. The MacLeods in particular suffered extensively for their support of Charles I. Thus, her poetry records formal laments for the deaths of MacLeod noblemen as well as provides glimpses of daily life in those Highland courts so far removed from the better-documented European capitals of the era.

Nineteenth-century sources, including the *Dictionary of National Biography*, record M.'s dates incorrectly as 1569–1674, making her an unlikely 105 years old at her death. Even the corrected dating gives her ninety-one years, a prodigious age for the era. Strong tradition holds that M. was born on the Outer Hebrides, in the village of Rodel, Harris. She describes her father's house as one in which were found "venison and bones of the deer"—a nobleman's household. In another poem, M. says that she was "reared / On the breast-milk / of white-palmed women" in Ullinish, a village on the Isle of Skye. By the time she was ten or eleven, she had been placed in the household of the MacLeod chief, Sir Roderick Mór, at Dunvegan in Skye. There she served as nurse to his family, later enjoying the prestige of a court bard or "harper" once her poetic gifts emerged. She became fiercely devoted to Sir Roderick's third son, Sir Norman of Bernera, who was honored for his dangerous missions on behalf of Charles II to Frederick III of Denmark. It was for Sir Norman that M. wrote three of her extant poems, two of them lamenting his death. There is no record of her ever marrying, though a poem entitled "Jealousy" chides an Islay woman for seducing M.'s sweetheart, and "A Satiric Song" chastises "Tricky Margaret" who spread the false rumor that M. was pregnant by "honest Calum." A widely held tradition notes her fondness for snuff and whiskey.

Sometime during her stay in Dunvegan, M. was exiled from the court, probably one of many court dependents expelled under the "anglified regime" of Roderick, the seventeenth chief, though other theories have been advanced. Her exile certainly came after the Restoration, probably as late as the 1690s and near the end of her life. She seems to have been peripatetic during her exile, moving among the barren islands around Skye and ending up in Mull. Upon the death of Sir Roderick and the accession of her beloved Sir Norman, she was recalled to the latter's court near her birthplace on the Outer Hebrides. He gave her a house nearby whose remains were still visible in the earlier part of this century. Tradition holds that she was buried face down—by her own request—in the south transept of St. Clement's church there.

Though M. ultimately held the position of a learned bard, she was never formally educated in that tradition. Her poems do, however, show detailed affinity with bardic verses and conventions. She composed during a renaissance in Gaelic language and literature when those native forms were as yet largely untouched by the English tradition. There are but a few English words in M.'s poems and, more significantly, the poems recall the world of those "loud shouting hero[es] of tough stern wounding swordblades" in the great halls of the medieval north rather than the cavaliers of seventeenth-century European courts. But while her subject matter is quite traditional—almost entirely limited to praise of noble heroes and their military exploits and to laments and eulogies for those who have died—her imagery and ornamentation, her voice and tone are fresh and wholly hers.

M.'s poems, sixteen of which survive, formed part of an oral poetic tradition and were not published during her lifetime. Rather, M.'s poems were passed down through generations of MacLeods and were still being sung in the mid-nineteenth century. Resurgent interest in national literature led to these few of M.'s poems being recorded, beginning in the late eighteenth century.

WORKS: Mackenzie. J. *The Beauties of Gaelic Poetry and Lives of the Highland Bards* (1907). Watson, J. C. *Gaelic Songs of Mary MacLeod* (1934).

BIBLIOGRAPHY: Mackenzie, A. *History of the MacLeods* (1889).

For articles in reference works, see: *CSBD. DNB.*

Kari Boyd McBride

Candia McWilliam

BORN: 1 July 1955, Edinburgh, Scotland.
DAUGHTER OF: Colin Edgar McWilliam and Margaret Henderson.
MARRIED: Quentin Wallop, the Earl of Portsmouth, 1981; Fram Eduljee Dinshaw, 1986.

Her pervasive and sometimes unsettling stories have earned M. a reputation for an arcane and disturbing interest in "the edge of things." The crafted architecture of her parallel plots is peopled by singular, eccentric, and oddly motivated characters viewed from alternating perspectives. M. is compared most frequently to Iris Murdoch in her reputation for "verbal exhibitionism and extreme cleverness," her meticulous literariness, her multiclaused sentences, and her use of an uncommon, styled vocabulary. Her appropriation of crafted, eclectic tropes has caused her work to be seen as deliberately and sometimes awkwardly literary. "The avoidance of easy solutions and formulas is important to me," writes M. "Also of importance are the vivid conveyance of physical sensations and the incidental jokes and tragedies which suddenly illuminate a seemingly random tangle of events and perceptions, the mysteriousness of people to each other, and the question of what has filled the gap left by lost faith."

M. was born in Edinburgh, daughter of an architectural historian and a textile designer. After a formal, classical Scottish education at Sherborne School (during which time she won first prize in the *Vogue* talent contest for 1971), she graduated from Girton College, Cambridge, in 1976 with a First in English. Initially considering remaining in academia to work for a Ph.D. on dis-syzygy in Scottish literature, she chose to write for *Vogue* (between 1976 to 1979), then went to a London advertising agency from 1979 to 1981. At twenty-six, she married Quentin Wallop, later Earl of Portsmouth, by whom she had two children; she began writing her first novel after separating from her husband. She now lives with her second husband, an Oxford academic by whom she has a third child, in North Oxford.

M.'s first novel, *A Case of Knives,* was published to great acclaim in 1988 and was joint winner of the 1988 Betty Trask Award. Through the use of four narratives, the novel tells the story of Lucas Salik, a middle-aged surgeon in obsessive control of his patients' lives, and his closest friend, Anne Cowdenbeath. Salik, clandestinely involved in the homosexual underworld, falls in love with Hal Darbo, a young man who finds delight in hurting people. Salik accepts this pain as an aspect of his love. When Darbo aspires to marriage, Salik and Cowdenbeath engage in a series of emotional experiments on an awkward young girl, Cora, who is looking for a husband to help raise her child. The various machinations and manipulations engineered by the quartet of strange, obsessive, and sometimes vicious characters results in unforeseeable and violent consequences. A structure of parallel narratives reveals just how little each of the four characters knows about each other and how the significance of any action depends wholly upon the observer.

Her second novel, *A Little Stranger* (1989), is an intricately woven tale of domestic horror that tells the story of two women losing their minds in deft parallel, their madness threatening their own lives and the future of a child. This tautly imaginative tale is set in motion by the arrival of a vulgar but indispensable nanny, Margaret, for the four-year-old son of a wealthy couple, Daisy and Solomon. The narrative explores the relationship from the perspective of Daisy, a woman given to recollections of her past as a desirable beauty, who allows herself to be pushed to the limit even at the expense of her home, her husband, her children and her life. Daisy's husband Solomon holds Margaret in rather higher regard, and the novel culminates in a surprising revelation. The work has been taken up wrongly, claims M., as a story about the child-care dilemma. *A Little Stranger* was very favorably received by reviewers, such as Thomas M. Disch in the *New York Times Book Review,* who deemed it "short but pungent," contending that the writing was "descended from the work of Jane Austen." *London Times* reviewer Elaine Feinstein expressed similar praise, describing M.'s prose as "spare and elegant throughout."

M.'s *Debatable Land* (1994), a novel with a far broader scope than her previous narratives, sees her returning for her subject matter to her native Scotland's eerie magnetism. *Debatable Land* is the tale of six characters, three of whom are Scottish, sailing in a yacht from Tahiti to New Zealand. As they sail from island to island, each of them begins to come to terms with precisely what it means to be colonized, both geographically and psychologically. *Debatable Land* won the Guardian Fiction Prize for 1994.

M. is frequently described in terms of her success as a Scottish writer, as a woman writer, or as one of Britain's new generation of writers. Since her later works have witnessed similar critical acclaim to that awarded to *A Case of Knives,* however, M. is increasingly acknowledged, for her short-story writing and her journalism as well as for her novels, as one of the most complex and intelligent writers working in Britain today.

WORKS: *A Case of Knives* (1989) *A Little Stranger* (1989). *Debatable Land* (1994). *Wait Till I Tell You* (1997).

BIBLIOGRAPHY:

For articles in reference works, see: *CA. WD.*

Other references: *Independent Magazine* (4 June 1994). *LonSunT* (6 May 1994). *LonT* (22 January 1988, 13 January 1989, 19 January 1989). *LRB* (4 August 1994). *New Yorker* (25 December 1995). *NYT* (6 July 1989). *NYTBR* (16 July 1989). *TLS* (22 January 1988, 27 January 1989).

Mikita Brottman

Madam D'Arusmont: See *Wright, Frances*

Sara Maitland

BORN: 27 February 1950, London.
DAUGHTER OF: Adam Maitland and Hope Maitland.
MARRIED: Donald Hugh Thomson Lee, 1972.

M. is the second of six children, raised in London and Scotland. Educated privately, she went on to attend St. Anne's College, Oxford. M. has worked as a freelance academic researcher, journalist, writer, and lecturer. As a feminist socialist, M. has been involved with the Women's Liberation Movement since 1970 and has been active in various campaigns such as the Women's Lobby, Women's Aid, and the Christian Feminist Network. She has also lectured on feminist theology, women's history, and contemporary literature in England and the United States. In 1972, M. married an Anglican priest and spent a number a years in an East London vicarage with their two children. Most recently, M. moved to Northhamptonshire with her family. She has converted to Roman Catholicism.

M.'s first novel, *Daughter of Jerusalem* (1978), won the Somerset Maugham Award in 1979. The novel's nine chapters, an ironic parallel with the nine months of pregnancy, describe the protagonist's obsessive desire to bear a child. When Elizabeth and her husband Ian are unable to conceive after five years of marriage, she turns to a medical specialist. The dichotomies of heart and mind, soul and body, come under close scrutiny because the specialist insists that Liz, reluctant to become a "Real Woman" by embracing a stereotypical definition of femininity, psychologically represses ovulation. The novel depicts how Liz's obsession with child bearing pervades every aspect of her life, compelling her to view her promiscuous past as punishment for her present barrenness, to rethink her feminist principles, and to reassess personal relationships (marriage with a gay man, parental relations, and friendships with various members of a feminist discussion group). Narrative devices, such as the abrupt fluctuation from present to past through flashbacks or from an objective third-person to inner thoughts, give the novel a claustrophobic intensity. *Daughter of Jerusalem* establishes the sorts of themes that M. will explore again: fatherly approval and self-doubt, patriarchal authority, and feminist disobedience. M. incorporates her continuing interest in Christianity and feminism by concluding each chapter with the retelling of Biblical stories, feminist rereadings, for instance of Sarah and Abraham, Samson and Delilah, or Mary and Joseph.

Virgin Territory (1984), M.'s second novel, opens with the rape of a American Roman Catholic nun, which functions as the catalyst for protagonist Sister Anna's nervous breakdown. Anna eventually arrives in London (to perform research on another sort of rape, the plunder and enslavement of native tribes by the Conquistadors) where, as a motherless daughter, she confronts the omnipresent voice of the Fathers. M. both invokes and subverts the standard pattern of enclosure and escape, and the intense third-person narrative renders Anna's extended struggle with these inner voices all the more violent and disturbing. Anna's relationships with Karen (a lesbian to whom she is attracted) and with Cara (a brain-damaged child who serves as another mouthpiece for patriarchal authority) sustain her through a painful search for an authentic female identity. In juxtaposing two seemingly different sorts of women's communities, lesbians and nuns, M. expands the meaning of virgin territories to portray female sexuality in depth.

M.'s first published writings appear in *Tales I Tell My Mother* (1978), an anthology of short stories and essays by the members of a feminist collective (including Zoë Fairbairns, Valerie Miner, Michèle Roberts, and Michelene Wandor). M. is fascinated with the act of writing and the process of writing as a feminist collective. In examining the impact of the women's movement and the way that it affects the outlook of both women and men, M. argues that "art is a way of organizing experience in order to clarify it." M. tests definitions of female and feminists by using a variety of literary forms and techniques, inner dialogue, letters, and myths. In *Telling Tales* (1983), a collection of her own short stories, M. rewrites myths and tales of the past to challenge the patriarchal view of women's place in history while focusing, at the same time, on present issues that concern contemporary women. *Weddings and Funerals,* cowritten with Aileen La Tourette, shows her continuing interest in writing as a collective experience and in the short-story form as a means to present ideas in a concentrated way.

In addition to fiction, M. has written two important, distantly related works of nonfiction. The first, *A Map of the New Country: Women and Christianity* (1983), is an impressive analysis of the predicament the church poses for Christian feminists (this very phrase an oxymoron to some members of each respective group). The study includes an overview of the history of women and the church, communities of religious women, women's ordination, women in the church hierarchy, and a critique of sexism in religious language and spirituality. M. argues that feminism offers a unique "way forward, a way of healing our dangerous divisions and a way back to the Christian truth of service, equality, justice, and the renunciation of power through love." In combining systematic research and a coherent argument with a subjective voice and personal interviews collected in Britain and the United States, M. not only fills a gap in religious and women's studies but further demonstrates the potential for a specifically feminist scholarly approach that avoids the preferred objective voice of traditional scholarship.

The second work of nonfiction, M.'s biography of *Vesta Tilley* (1986), is a contribution to the Virago Pioneers series, an ambitious feminist history project designed to introduce and reassess women of the past and examine their lives and contributions from a feminist perspective. Vesta Tilley (1864–1952), actress, singer, and male impersonator, was a fascinating figure of the Victorian music hall who used maleness to attain a higher social position. Such an "extraordinary woman," M. writes, "deserves a brassy book," and M.'s narrative style is a perfect match. The biography blends careful research with a relaxed and jovial narrative style, and, perhaps most importantly, M. uses the opportunity of telling Tilley's life to probe larger questions on gender and culture.

M.'s most recent books include ventures into memoirs and feminist theology as well as other nonfiction genres. *Very Heaven: Looking Back at the 60s* (1988) is a volume of reflections about the decade of M.'s teenage years. *A Big-Enough God: A Feminist's Search for Joyful Theology* (1995) sees the world as a gift from God and existence as a means of praising that gift. With L. Appignanesi, she coedited a volume of material on the controversies surrounding Salman Rushdie, *The Rushdie File* (1989).

Her fiction continues to explore themes and settings similar to some of her nonfiction interests. *Home Truths* (1993; in the U.S. as *Ancestral Truths*) focuses on the Kerslake family—seven siblings and their spouses, children, and parents—while all are vactioning in Scotland. Other works of fiction include *Three Times Table* (1990), *Women Don't Fly When Men Aren't Watching* (1993), *Angel and Me: Short Stories for Holy Week* (1995), and *Angel Maker: The Short Stories of Sara Maitland* (1996).

In "A Feminist Writer's Progress" (in *On Gender and Writing,* ed. M. Wandor, 1983), M. characterizes her development as a writer in terms of a mock-quest in which the heroine must discover suitable companions (the Feminist Writers' Group), negotiate perilous straits between great writing and politics, and find the voice of the wise animal (her daughter). Though incomplete, this pseudoquest identifies the special difficulties faced by the feminist writer and encapsulates M.'s principal themes and concerns. By retelling the old stories, whether mythic or biblical, M. works effectively to resolve the tension that arises when the patriarchy collides with a feminist sensibility. Within M.'s determination to explore the possible and important connections between the seemingly irreconcilable, especially between feminism and Christianity, both the strengths and limitations of her writing are evident.

WORKS: *Introduction 5* (1973). *Daughter of Jerusalem* (1978; in the U.S. as *Languages of Love*, 1981). (with others) *Tales I Tell My Mother* (1978). *A Map of the New Country* (1983). *Telling Tales* (1983). (with A. La Tourette) *Weddings and Funerals* (1984). *Virgin Territory* (1984). *Vesta Tilley* (1986). (with others) *More Tales I Tell My Mother* (1987). *A Book of Spells* (1987). (with M. Wandor) *Arky Types* (1987). *Very Heaven: Looking Back at the 60s* (1988). *Three Times Table* (1990). *Home Truths* (1993; in the U.S. as *Ancestral Truths*). *Women Fly When Men Aren't Watching* (1993). *Angel and Me: Short Stories for Holy Week* (1995). *A Big-Enough God: A Feminist's Search for a Joyful Theology* (1995). *Angel Maker: The Short Stories of Sara Maitland* (1996).

BIBLIOGRAPHY: Alexander, F. *Contemporary Women Novelists* (1989). *Plotting Change: Contemporary Women's Fiction*, ed. L. Anderson (1990). *ContempR* (October 1983). Duncker, P. *Sisters and Strangers: An Introduction to Contemporary Feminist Fiction* (1992). *Harper's* (April 1981). Jordan, S. *Sojourner* (October 1986). Martin, R. *ABR* (July–August 1985). *New Statesman* (4 March 1983, 1 July 1983, 21 December 1984, 23 May 1986, 4 September 1987). *NYTBR* (29 June 1986). Palmer, P. *Contemporary Women's Fiction: Narrative Practice and Feminist Theory* (1989). *TLS* (1 December 1978, 15 April 1983, 9 November 1984).

For articles in reference works, see: *Bloomsbury. CA. CLC. Feminist.*

Other references: Guerin, C. *L&T* (1992). *Listener* (16 November 1978, 17 September 1987). Muchnick, L. *VLS* (March 1994).

Laura L. Doan

Bathsua Reginald Makin

BORN: 1608 (?) Southwick, Sussex.
DIED: 1675 (?).
DAUGHTER OF: Henry Reginald.
MARRIED: Richard Mackin[g], 1621.

Until 1991, when J. R. Brink discovered otherwise, M. was identified as the daughter of John Pell and the sister of Thomas Pell, a "gentleman of the bedchamber" to Charles I. Brink's research indicates, however, that M. was actually the daughter of Henry Reginald, a schoolmaster in St. Mary Axe parish, and John Pell's sister-in-law. Although no record exists of M.'s ever having attended a school, she apparently knew Greek, Latin, Hebrew, Spanish, French, Italian, and mathematics.

M. published her first book of poems, *Musa Virginea*, in 1616, making her, according to Brink, "one of the first middle-class women to publish her poetry in England." During some part of the 1640s, M. served as the tutor of Princess Elizabeth (1635–50), the daughter of King Charles I. In fact, Princess Elizabeth's expertise with languages was much admired throughout Europe, and, as her teacher, M. became known as the "most learned English woman of her day." At around this same time. M. began corresponding with Anna Marie van Schurman (Dutch, 1607–78), whom Brink refers to as the "most famous woman scholar of her time in Europe"; she knew not only Latin, Greek, and Hebrew but also Syriac, Arabic, Chaldee, and Ethiopic, and she had studied geography, philosophy, mathematics, the sciences, and religion. Proficiency in Greek was rare among women at that time, yet two letters written in Greek and signed by M. were found among Schurman's papers.

Only sketchy information has been uncovered about the events of M.'s later life. According to Brink, M.'s marriage to Richard Makin[g] was recorded on 4 March 1621 in the parish register of St. Andrew Undershaft, where the birth of M.'s daughter Hanna was recorded in February 1622. Research by V. Salmon shows that M. probably had two other children, a son, Richard, born in 1626, and another daughter, Bathsua, born in 1628. M. was, according to the *Dictionary of National Biography*, keeping "schools or colleges of the young gentlewomen" at Putney in 1649. In that same year, M. wrote the first of two poems now held in the Hastings Collection of the Huntington Library, a Latin elegy on the death of Henry, Lord Hastings, the son of M.'s friend and patron, Lucy Hastings, the Countess of Huntingdon. On 2 May 1664, M. wrote the second poem, an elegy on the death of the countess's daughter entitled "Upon the much lamented death of the Right Honourable, the Lady Elizabeth Langham." In the letter accompanying that poem, M. described herself as a widow; in another letter, dated 24 October 1668, M. indicated that she had a son.

In 1673, while she was mistress of a school at Tottenham High Cross, M. published her most important work, *An Essay to Revive the Ancient Education of Gentlewomen*, a piece of writing that M. Reynolds calls "admirable propaganda," a document that "tossed off the unmeaning arguments of opponents with . . . contemptuous ease." The essay, dedicated to "all Ingenious and Virtuous Ladies, more especially to her Highness the Lady Mary, the eldest daughter to his Royal Highness of Duke of York," is prefaced by two (probably fictitious) letters, the first written by a man who is supportive of women's education, the second by a man who says educating women is "preposterous." M. begins *An Essay* by listing the names of many learned women who have made contributions to the arts and sciences. The list is followed by such comments as: "Had God intended women only as a finer sort of cattle, He would not have made them reasonable. Brutes, a few degrees higher than . . . monkeys . . . might have better fitted some men's lust, pride, and pleasure; especially those that desire to keep them ignorant to be tyrannized over." M. specifies the subjects in which women should be educated, such as grammar and rhetoric, logic, physic, languages (especially Greek and Hebrew), mathematics, geography, and the arts (music, painting, poetry). She says that "women thus instructed" will be of profit to themselves, to their relations, and to the nation. M. concludes the essay by calling on all who read it to "Let a generous resolution possess your minds, seeing men in this age have invaded women's vices, in a noble revenge, reassume those virtues which men sometimes unjustly usurped to themselves, but ought to have left them in common to both sexes."

WORKS: *Musa Virginea* (1616). "Upon the much lamented death of the Right Honourable, the Lady Elizabeth

Langham" (1664). *An Essay to Revive the Antient Education of Gentlewomen* (1673; rpt. 1980).

BIBLIOGRAPHY: Brink, J. R. *International Journal of Women's Studies* (1978). Brink, J. R. *Female Scholars, A Tradition of Learned Women Before 1800* (1980). Brink, J. R. *HLQ* (1991). Hobby, F. *Virtue of Necessity: English Women's Writing, 1646–1688* (1988). *The Female Spectator: English Women Writers Before 1800,* ed. M. Mahl and H. Koon (1977). Reynolds, M. *The Learned Lady in England 1650–1760* (1920; rpt. 1977). Salmon, V. *Pelliana* (August 1965). Stenton, D. *The English Woman in History* (1957; rpt. 1977). Teague, F. *Bathsua Makin, Woman of Learning* (1997). *Women Writers of the Seventeenth Century,* ed. K. Wilson and F. Warnke (1989).

For articles in reference works, see: *Bell. Bloomsbury. DNB. Europa. Feminist. ToddBWW.*

Other references: van Beek, P. *Dutch Crossing* (Summer 1995). Gardner, D. *Girlhood at School* (1929). *Kissing the Rod: An Anthology of Seventeenth-Century Women's Verse,* ed. G. Greer et al. (1989). Helm, J. *CahiersE* (1993). Myers, M. *SECC* (1985). Reep, D. *SCN* (1982). Teague, F. *SCN* (1986).

Kay Beaird Meyers

Malet, Lucas: See *Harrison, Mary St. Leger (Kingsley)*

Mallowan, Agatha Christie: See *Christie, Agatha*

Judith Man

FLOURISHED: 1640s.
DAUGHTER OF: Peter Man.

M., the little-known translator of John Barclay's *Argenis,* seems to have been a part of a barely perceptible community of reading and writing women. M. may have been educated with the children of Thomas Wentworth, later first Earl of Strafford, as was Alice Thornton. If so, her education would have been more deliberate than that of most women of her class, for Wentworth employed a writing tutor especially for his two daughters (educating his son separately), wrote to them often when absent, and seems to have valued their letters to him. Their affectionate stepmother wrote poetry, none of which has yet been discovered. Since the Wentworth daughters spent much of their childhood in Ireland, however, M.'s interactions with the family would have been irregular since her father would have been based at the Wentworth estate in Yorkshire. M. may have also seen herself as subscribing to a larger community of writing women since she refers to Mary Wroth's *Urania* in her preface as a justification for her translation.

M.'s one known work, *An Epitome of the History of Faire Argenis and Polyarchus* (1640), belongs to the genre of political/allegorical romance, as described by Paul Salzman, a genre that emerged as a vehicle for Royalist discussions of the Civil War. Barclay first wrote *Argenis* (1621) as a *roman à clef* in order to gain the favor of King James I. A popular work, three translations of Barclay precede M.'s; Ben Jonson translated it at the request of James I, but it was destroyed before it was published. Two later published translations include keys to the *roman à clef,* multiplying the work's political currency.

Although little is known about M. herself, her translation of Nicolas Coëffeteau's (1574–1632) French version of the work was a politicized act. She dedicates her translation to Anne Wentworth, whose father had just been created the first Earl of Strafford, a social elevation that caused resentment among the members of Parliament who less than one year later clamored for his execution; M. alludes to the controversy in her preface. Since evidence in Wentworth's letters show that he considered Peter Man privy to many of his family arrangements, it is likely that Peter Man constrained his daughter to publish her translation in celebration of his employer's new title. Barclay's Royalist position in the story of *Argenis* also reflects Wentworth's ardent commitment to the monarchy. Because of the fame of her father's employer, further information about M. and her writing may have been preserved in family papers.

WORKS: (trans.) *An Epitome of the History of Faire Argenis and Polyarchus by N. Coëffeteau,* by John Barclay (1640; STC 1396).

BIBLIOGRAPHY: Salzman, P. *English Prose Fiction, 1558–1700* (1984).

For articles in reference works, see: *Bell. Feminist.*

Kathryn Coad Narramore

(Mary?) Delariviere Manley

BORN: 6 or 7 April 1663 (?) or 1667–72, Jersey.
DIED: 11 July 1724, London.
DAUGHTER OF: Sir Roger Manley and Margaret Manley.
MARRIED: John Manley, c. 1688.

Much is problematic about the early years of M., including whether Mary was her first name and where she was born. Her own testimony, given in thinly fictionalized autobiographical narratives, is unreliable; and the little remaining documentary evidence is ambiguous. We do know that she was born in the latter part of the seventeenth century in England, possibly on the island of Jersey, or possibly at sea between Jersey and Guernsey, the daughter of Sir Roger Manley, who was lieutenant-governor of Jersey, a Stuart sympathizer, and an author of histories. Her mother died in M.'s youth and her father in about 1688, apparently leaving her the ward of a cousin, John Manley, who later married her under false pretenses (he was already wed) and abandoned her with a son. This "bigamous marriage," which M. recounts in *The New Atlantis* (1709) and *The Adventures of Rivella* (1714), seriously damaged her social reputation.

Shortly thereafter, she became the companion of Barbara Palmer, the Duchess of Cleveland, who figures in various M. works. They soon parted over M.'s alleged flirtation with the duchess's son, and M. retired to Exeter, having discovered, as she put it in *The Adventures of Rivella,* that "her Love of Solitude was improved by her Disgust of the

World." In Exeter, she wrote the first of her works: two plays—*The Lost Lover* (1696), a comedy, and *The Royal Mischief* (1996), a tragedy—and an epistolary proto-novel entitled *Letters Written by Mrs. Manley* (1696; retitled *A Stage Coach Journey to Exeter* in 1725). At about this time, she had an affair with Sir Thomas Skipworth, who produced her plays in London in 1696. *The Lost Lover,* presented at Drury Lane in about March 1696, had little success, but the tragedy, which appeared a month or so later at Lincoln's Inn Fields, helped to establish M.'s reputation and yielded her a financial profit. Both plays were preceded by important feminist prefaces. Only "prejudice against our Sex," she maintained, prevented the plays from receiving a more enthusiastic reception

Partly as a response to these statements, Drury Lane shortly thereafter exposed M. and other women playwrights of the period to public ridicule by presenting a burlesque of the production of *The Royal Mischief* entitled *The Female Wits.* Whether this play had a chastening effect on M. is unclear, but she gave up writing (or at least publishing) for nearly a decade. During this period, she became romantically involved with John Tilly, who was married and the warden of the Fleet Street prison. Tilly was the great love of her life, but she gave him up after several years to allow him to make a financially advantageous liaison with a rich widow.

It was shortly after this (1702) that M. began producing her most celebrated works, a series of fictionalized satires written partly to vindicate herself, partly to promote her Tory political interests, and partly to make money. The first of these, which most scholars attribute to her, is *The Secret History of Queen Zarah, and the Zarazians* (1705). It includes an important theoretical preface, which provides a critique of the then-popular heroic romance. *Queen Zarah* has the distinction of being the first *roman à clef* written in English. The work is a political satire in the form of a picaresque romance, directed against Sarah Churchill, the Duchess of Marlborough, who with her husband was an influential Whig member of the court of Queen Anne. In *Queen Zarah,* Churchill is portrayed as ambitious, cruel, greedy, rude, and guilty of various sexual improprieties. Perhaps because of the explicitness of the latter descriptions, the book was both extraordinarily popular, selling several thousand copies, and influential—"Zarah" and "Zarazians" were soon popular names for the duchess and her followers. In 1706, M. produced another play, *Almyna,* considered her best tragedy.

M.'s most celebrated work, *Secret Memoirs and Manners . . . from the New Atlantis,* appeared in 1709. Like *Queen Zarah,* this satire is a kind of *roman à clef* that recounts political intrigue and sexual scandal, mainly among members of the Whig aristocracy. The work includes scenes of homosexual, as well as heterosexual, orgy, drunkenness, rape, and incest, which have given it a sensationalist reputation. The second volume, for example, opens with a piece on the New Cabal, a group of wealthy lesbians. M. was arrested for libel on 29 October 1709 but was released under the new *habeas corpus* writ on 5 November, and the case was eventually dropped in 1710. As in all M.'s works, *The New Atlantis* reveals the author's talent at realistic description, of dress, manners, and psychological motivation, as well as her wry, sarcastic wit. The last of M.'s political works, *Memoirs of Europe,* appeared in 1710, and *Court Intrigues,* in 1711. During this period, M. published *The Female Tatler,* a journal of political satire, and in 1711 succeeded Jonathan Swift, a fellow Tory, as editor of *The Examiner.*

Probably of most interest to the modern reader is M.'s *Adventures of Rivella* (1714), which remains an important early precursor to the novel. Essentially autobiographical, Rivella's (M.'s) story is narrated by Sir Charles Lovemore to a Chevalier d'Aumont, who is an admiring Rivella/M. reader. Like many later novels, the central character is presented as an innocent victim of circumstances—mainly financial—and of prejudice against women. M. is particularly exercised by the double standard: "*If she had been a Man, she had been without Fault:* But the Character of that Sex being much more confin'd than ours, what is not a Crime in Men is scandalous and unpardonable in Woman." In addition to a feminist perspective, the work expresses a kind of cynicism reminiscent of la Rochefoucauld (whom, indeed, Rivella reads) that contributes to the growing tradition of realism in literature. The world is portrayed as a decidedly unromantic jungle where people operate primarily according to self-interest.

Her final works included a play, *Lucius, the First Christian King of Britain,* produced at Drury Lane in 1717, *The Power of Love: in Seven Novels* (1720), and *Bath Intrigues* (1725), published posthumously; the last may not be hers.

Her contribution lies in having forged an authentically feminist realism, in creating vigorous true-to-life characters whose psychological behavior is finely tuned, and in having braved the negative currents that opposed women's entrance into the field of dramatic and fictional literature. She is one of the pioneers of women's literature in English, but only in recent years has her work begun to receive the serious critical attention it deserves.

WORKS: *Letters Written by Mrs. Manley* (1696; rpt. as *A Stage Coach Journey to Exeter,* 1725). *The Lost Lover; or, the Jealous Husband* (1696). *The Royal Mischief* (1696). *The Secret History of Queen Zarah, and the Zarazians* (1705). *Almyna; or the Arabian Vow* (prod., 1706; pub., 1707). *Secret Memoirs and Manners of Several Persons of Quality of Both Sexes, from the New Atlantis, an Island in the Mediterranean* (1709). *Memoirs of Europe, toward the Close of the Eighth Century* (1710). *Court Intrigues, in a Collection of Original Letters from the Island of the New Atlantis* (1711). *The Adventures of Rivella; or, the History of the Author of the Atlantis by Sir Charles Lovemore* (1714). *Lucius, the First Christian King of Britain* (1717; rpt. 1989). *The Power of Love: in Seven Novels* (1720). (attributed to M.) *Bath Intrigues* (1725). *The Novels of Mary Delariviere Manley,* ed. and intro. P. Köster (1971). *New Atlantis,* ed. R. Ballaster (1991).

BIBLIOGRAPHY: Ballaster, R. *Seductive Forms: Women's Amatory Fiction from 1684–1740* (1992). Clark, C. *Three Augustan Women Playwrights* (1986). Finke, L. A. *Restoration* (1984). Kern, J. B. *SECC* (1981). Jerrold, W. *Five Queer Women* (1929). Lock, F. P. *Woman in the Eighteenth Century and Other Essays,* ed. P. Fritz and R. Morton (1976). MacCarthy, B. *Women Writers: Their Contribution to the English Novel* (1944). *A Woman of*

No Character: An Autobiography of Mrs. Manley, ed. F. Morgan (1986). Richetti, J. J. *Popular Fiction Before Richardson: Narrative Patterns 1700–1739* (1969). Todd, J. *The Sign of Angellica* (1989).

For articles in reference works see: *BAB1800. Bell. Bloomsbury. Cambridge. DLB. DNB. EWW. Feminist. FCL. IDWB. Oxford. ToddBWW. ToddDBA.*

Other references: *Bookman's Journal* (1925). *ECent* (Spring 1994). *ECLife* (1977). London, A., in *Fetter'd or Free? British Women Novelists, 1670–1815,* ed. M. Schofield and C. Macheski (1986). *HLQ* (1948–49, 1951). *MP* (1930, 1931, 1936, 1937, 1984). *PQ* (1934, 1936, 1973). *PMLA* (1937). *RES* (1978). *Restoration* (1984). *Transactions of the Samuel Johnson Society of the Northwest* (1971). Turner, C. *Living by the Pen* (1992). *W&L* (1978). *WS* (1979, 1988).

Josephine Donovan
(updated by Rebecca P. Bocchicchio)

Manners, Mrs.: See *Stepney, Lady Catherine*

Ethel Mannin

BORN: 11 October 1900, London.
DIED: 5 December 1984, Devon.
DAUGHTER OF: Robert Mannin and Edith Gray Mannin.
MARRIED: J. A. Porteous, 1920; Reginald Reynolds, 1938.

M. wrote more than 100 books in her fifty-year literary career: novels, travel books, autobiographies, and memoirs as well as works on education, religion, politics, and morality. She was a woman with definite views. "A writer's business," she wrote, "is essentially with truth, to interpret life in its infinite complexity, to illuminate, to communicate."

From the outset, M. believed in the importance of the individual and the inadequacy of the existing social system. During the 1920s, she was concerned with freedom of the individual; during the 1930s, she became involved in political movements that promised to change society; by the 1940s, she was the champion of an unpopular view, upholding the individualist creed of "pacifist-anarchist," a view she maintained. Her immense canon is a detailed document of her personal growth and a record of the changes in the world around her. "I am one of those who believe that the writer should concern himself with current affairs, be of his time, concerned with its problems, social and political," she said.

M. was born to working-class parents of Irish descent (her father was a post office sorter), and from her early life she drew a belief in the value of the working-class point of view. Educated at state school, she began writing at the age of seven, left school at age fifteen, and got a job in an advertising agency as a stenographer. By age seventeen, she was editing inhouse publications and the *Pelican,* a theatrical and sporting paper. In 1920, she married J. A. Porteous, by whom she had a daughter, Jean. At first, she established herself as a freelance journalist by writing for the women's market. Her first serious literary recognition came with the publication of her third novel, *Sounding Brass* (1926), a satire of the advertising world. It created a stir on Fleet Street because the hero of the novel was thought to be her former employer.

Her literary career underway, M. in 1928 was "emancipated from marriage into independence" by divorcing Porteous. In the late 1920s and early 1930s, M. mingled with the Jazz Age crowd, traveling to America where she encountered A. S. Neill, going frequently to the Continent, especially Paris and Vienna, "because running around Europe was the vogue with the young intelligentsia of the period," and writing more than a dozen books in damp hotels and dismal flats as well as in her "Very Jazz Age" decorated suburban cottage. Her first important book of this period was *Confessions and Impressions* (1930), an autobiography and memoir, called by the author (in retrospect) a "rash and brash account" of the 1920s scene. It contains sketches and portraits of "people who have interested me," including Osbert Sitwell, Tamara Karsavina, D. H. Lawrence, Bertrand Russell, and A. S. Neill.

Neill's progressive ideas on child education had a profound effect on M. When she went to America in 1926, she sent her six-year old daughter to his school. M. wrote about Neill's school in her 1928 novel, *Green Willow,* and, in 1931, wrote her first book on child education, *Common-sense and the Child,* for which Neill wrote the preface; M. also wrote two other books in this series: *Common-sense and the Adolescent* (1937) and *Common-sense and Morality* (1942), which also included a preface by Neill.

For M., the end of her twenties was important in terms of personal development. During the years 1929–30, she began her regular rhythm of literary output: a novel and a nonfiction book each year. In the early 1930s, M., like other members of her generation, became involved in political movements. This change in focus is evident in the kinds of novels M. wrote during this decade, such as *Linda Shawn* (1932) and *Venetian Blinds* (1933), both of which are concerned with social rather than romantic themes. In 1933, she joined the International Labour Party (ILP), which was Marxist by ideology. One of the major tenets of the ILP was "critical support of the Soviet Union." *Cactus* (1935) and *The Pure Flame* (1936) are the culmination of M.'s Marxist sympathies, portraying the struggle of the classes against the forces of imperialism. In 1934, when she toured a Soviet commune, she was very impressed with the progress of the Communist project. When she returned to the Soviet Union in 1935, however, an unguided trip to the collective at Samarkand proved to be a disillusioning experience. She found that the Soviet experiment was riddled with the power interplay that she was rejecting in her own country as an opponent of imperialism and capitalism. Her disappointment was portrayed in the travel book *South to Samarkand* (1936) and the novel, *Comrade, O Comrade; or, Low-Down on the Left* (1947).

The involvement with the ILP coincided with M.'s association with the pacifist movement. It was at an ILP meeting that she met her future husband, Reginald Reynolds, a Quaker pacifist and former student of Mohandas K. Gandhi. With him, she participated in nonviolent activities, speaking at public meetings, writing articles, raising funds, and distributing literature for freedom groups. At the end of the decade, as an opponent of fascism, M. was involved with fund-raising activities for the Spanish anarchists and Emma Goldman. M.'s *Women and the Revolution* (1939) discusses the involvement of women in the anarchist experiment in Catalonia, Spain, and *Red Rose* (1941) is a slightly romanticized and highly readable novel about the life of Emma Goldman.

When World War II broke out in England, M. and her husband declared themselves pacifists and refused to take part in the war effort. This unpopular view prevented M. from acquiring a travel permit, so she spent the war years in England and continued her amazing productivity. One of her most interesting political books was *Bread and Roses: An Utopian Survey and Blue-Print* (1944), which outlines a program for a Utopian world based on the political philosophy of anarcho-syndicalism, "the practical expression of anarchism." The basic concept, which organized each trade and industry into syndicates controlled by the workers, had been put into practice in Catalonia and was eventually crushed by the forces of power operative in the Spanish Civil War. M. was convinced that "man must find a new way of living or perish," which must have seemed self-evident in London during the war. This new way of living was to come to the pacifist-anarchist conclusion that a revolution must occur in the mind of man that would enable him to seek out a world controlled by the ideals of brotherhood. The object of political striving then was to construct a new culture with man living harmoniously with man in a free ungoverned society. The book, however, was at first difficult to publish and then when in print received little notice. It is a singular document, laying down in clear but idealized language the dreams of this philosophical view. It serves as an indicator of M.'s creed, which was not to change for the next thirty years of her writing.

In the post-war world, M. continued to be involved in international political issues. Traveling to Germany and Austria to observe hunger problems there, for example, resulted in *German Journey* (1948), a travel book, and *Bavarian Story* (1949), a novel. She also wrote *The Dark Forest* (1946), about the invasion of a neutral country. In order to publish it, M. had to modify the epilogue, which suggested that one occupying army in a neutral country was very like another. M. and her husband also traveled to India, Morocco, Burma, and Japan. Each of these journeys resulted in a travel book in which M. not only told of her experiences but also informed the public of the living conditions, from a liberal perspective, in the various countries. M. and Reynolds were not extremely popular for their views, which included supporting the Arab cause as opposed to the Jewish Palestinian one and sponsoring the independence of India. Each of these journeys also produced a novel such as *The Living Lotus* (1956), *The Road to Beersheba* (1964), *The Night and Its Homing* (1966), *The Midnight Street* (1969, and *Mission to Beirut* (1973) as well as several travel books.

In 1958, Reynolds died of a cerebral hemorrhage while on a journey to Australia. M.'s *Brief Voices* (1959) ends with a discussion of his death and how she never expected the book to end that way. The immediacy of her life to her writing is evident from the ending of the book. After Reynolds' death, M. continued her literary career. She continued to travel, to write of her travels, and to write more novels. In 1971, she wrote *Young in the Twenties*, which serves as a commentary on her first piece of autobiography, *Confessions and Impressions.* She also wrote *Stories from My Life* (1973) and, in 1977, published *Sunset over Dartmoor: A Final Chapter of Autobiography.* During the same twenty-year period, she wrote fourteen novels, four juvenile books, travel books on Japan, Egypt, Jordan, the United States, and two on England. She also wrote books on the revolt of the individual, loneliness, and the human phenomenon of love. M. lived in Devon until her death.

M.'s books are highly readable and informative, and she is always concerned with presenting the prevailing view, tempered by her own liberal attitude. She has received little critical attention, perhaps due to her radical politics, highly individualized manner, and working-class status. An author of diverse talents and interests, M.'s most important achievement is as a chronicler of the experiences of the twentieth century.

WORKS: *Martha* (1923; rev. 1929). *Sounding Brass* (1926). *Green Willow* (1928). *Confessions and Impressions* (1930; rev. 1936). *Common-sense and the Child: A Plea for Freedom* (1931). *Green Figs* (1931). *The Tinsel Eden and Other Stories* (1931). *Bruised Wings and Other Stories* (1931). *Ragged Banners: A Novel with an Index* (1931). *All Experience* (1932). *Linda Shawn* (1932). *Venetian Blinds* (1933). *Dryad* (1933). *Men Are Unwise* (1934). *Forever Wandering* (1934). *The Falconer's Voice* (1935). *Cactus* (1935; rev. 1944). *The Pure Flame* (1936). *South to Samarkand* (1936). *Common-sense and the Adolescent* (1937; rev. 1945). *Women Also Dream* (1937). *Rose and Sylvie* (1938). *Darkness My Bride* (1938). *Women and the Revolution* (1939). *Privileged Spectator: A Sequel to "Confessions and Impressions"* (1939; rev. 1947). *Julie: The Story of a Dance-Hostess* (1940). *Red Rose: A Novel Based on the Life of Emma Goldman* (1941). *Christianity—or Chaos? A Re-Statement of Religion* (1941). *Common-sense and Morality* (1942). *Captain Moonlight* (1942). *The Blossoming Bough* (1943). *No More Mimosa* (1943). *Bread and Roses: An Utopian Survey and Blue-Print* (1944). *Proud Heaven* (1944). *Lucifer and the Child* (1945). *The Dark Forest* (1946). *Selected Stories* (1946). *Comrade, O Comrade; or, Low-Down on the Left* (1947). *Connemara Journal* (1947). *German Journey* (1948). *Late Have I Loved Thee* (1948). *Every Man a Stranger* (1949). *Bavarian Story* (1949). *Jungle Journey* (1950). *At Sundown the Tiger*... (1951). *The Fields at Evening* (1952). *The Wild Swans and Other Tales Based on the Ancient Irish* (1952). *Moroccan Mosaic* (1953). *So Tiberius* (1954). *Land of the Crested Lion: A Journey Through Modern Burma* (1955). *The Living Lotus* (1956). *Fragrances of Hyacinths* (1958). *Brief Voices: A Writer's Story* (1959). *The Flowery Sword: Travels in Japan* (1960). *Sabishisa* (1961). *Curfew at Dawn* (1962). *A Lance for the Arabs: A Middle East Journey* (1963). *Rebels' Ride: A Middle East Journey* (1964). *The Road to Beersheba* (1964). *The Burning Bush* (1965). *The Lovely Land: The Hashemite Kingdom of Jordan* (1965). *Loneliness: A Study of the Human Condition* (1966). *The Night and Its Homing* (1966).

The Lady and the Mystic (1967). *An American Journey* (1967). *England for a Change* (1968). *Bitter Babylon* (1968). *The Midnight Street* (1969). *Practitioners of Love: Some Aspects of the Human Phenomenon* (1969). *England at Large* (1970). *Free Pass to Nowhere* (1970). *Young in the Twenties: A Chapter of Autobiography* (1971). *The Curious Adventure of Major Fosdick* (1972). *Stories from My Life* (1973). *Mission to Beirut* (1973). *Kildoon* (1974). *An Italian Journey* (1974). *Sunset over Dartmoor: A Final Chapter of Autobiography* (1977).

BIBLIOGRAPHY: Croft, A., in *Rediscovering Forgotten Radicals,* ed. A. Ingram and D. Patai (1993). O'Rourke, R. *L&H* (1988).

For articles in reference works, see: *CA. CN. DIL. Longman. TCA* and *SUP.*

Other references: *Bookman* (August 1926). *BW* (30 August 1964). *Commonweal* (12 November 1948). *LonT* (8 January 1985). *New Statesman* (10 January 1932). *NYT* (20 June 1926, 7 October 1928, 26 June 1932, 16 June 1935, 25 July 1937, 10 October 1948, 1 September 1957). *Saturday Review* (24 July 1926, 13 October 1928, 15 July 1950). *TLS* (13 November 1924, 27 April 1933, 12 September 1936, 2 April 1938, 3 August 1967, 14 May 1970, 25 August 1972). *Washington Post* (10 December 1984).

Priscilla Dorr

Anne Manning

BORN: 17 February 1807, London.
DIED: 14 September 1879, Tunbridge Wells, Kent.
DAUGHTER OF: William Oke Manning and Joan Whatmore Gibson Manning.
WROTE UNDER: The Author of The Ladies of Bever Hollow; The Author of Mary Powell; Anne Manning; erroneously identified with Hannah Mary Rathbone.

M. can be included among those Victorian writers whose works were castigated by critics as "spurious antiques." Her novels of this sort employ the epistolary style and are characterized by the language and typographical conventions of the period in which they are supposed to have been composed.

The eldest child of a Lloyd's of London insurance agent, M. spent the early part of her life in Chelsea. Later, she lived at Norbury Priory in Mickleham, then at Reigate Hill, and finally at Tunbridge Wells, where she resided with her sisters, Lydia and Frances, until her death. Her mother was largely responsible for the good education M. and her siblings received. At an early age, M. began reading history, a custom she practiced throughout her life. Her first published work, *A Sister's Gift* (1826), was composed as an educational tool for the younger brothers and sisters she was commissioned to teach. The only book M. published under her own name was *Stories From the History of Italy* (1831). Her literary reputation was ensured with the serialization of *The Maiden and Married Life of Mary Powell, Afterwards Mistress Milton* (1849). So popular was this novel that M. needed only to identify herself as "The Author of Mary Powell" on subsequent works. An intensely private person, M. revealed little of herself in her writings. *Family Pictures* (1861) is a vague chronicle of important events in her family's history, but its only allegedly autobiographical section is singularly uninformative about M. herself. Her "Passages in an Authoress's Life," serialized in *Golden Hours* (1872), is much more informative, although due to ill health, she never finished it. In the last installment M. advises would-be authors to choose their subjects wisely, to refrain from offending, and to ignore detractors.

M.'s talents were not limited to literature. While yet a child, she won three gold medals for her paintings, including one from the Royal Academy for her copy of Murillo's painting, "The Flower Girl." She was competent in several languages and cultivated an interest in botany.

Although M.'s health began to decline in the mid-1850s, she published at regular intervals. Only near the end of her life, when afflicted with failing eyesight and paralysis, did she discontinue writing. Her bibliography includes more than fifty novels, but none is so well known as *Mary Powell,* which was translated into German and French. This sympathetic "her-story," written as a journal by the heroine, describes the unusual circumstances surrounding Mary's hasty marriage to John Milton, their quick separation, and their ultimate reconciliation. The novel's subtle attack on women's educational opportunities revealed M.'s feminist leanings. M. examined the relationship between Milton and his daughters in *Deborah's Diary* (1858), giving a voice to these young women who are only known through others' words. M. also attempted to unravel the mysteries surrounding Milton's *A Maske* in her own *The Masque at Ludlow* (1866). A series of letters by various "hands," including one in Latin by John Milton *ad patrem,* humorously retells the events leading up to the celebration on Michaelmas and offers a solution to the question of Milton's possible participation in the production. Many of her novels are based on historical events or personalities, such as *Cherry and Violet: A Tale of the Plague* (1853), which is set in the time of the Great Plague of London, and *The Chronicle of Ethelfled* (1861), which focuses on the sister-in-law of Alfred the Great, a powerful woman who was marginalized by ecclesiastical chroniclers. A novel nearing the popularity of *Mary Powell* was *The Household of Sir Thomas More* (1851), narrated by Margaret Roper, More's daughter. The uses and advantages of female education, topics explored in *Mary Powell,* are again examined here. While many of M.'s texts are historically based, others reveal her astute and often amusing observations of rural life. Among these are *Village Bells* (1838) and *The Ladies of Bever Hollow* (1858).

M. contributed to contemporary periodicals such as *Living Age* and *Macmillan's.* In the latter she published, among others, "Mary Russell Mitford: An Epitome" (1870), a sympathetic biographical essay. Five works, serialized in *Golden Hours,* were never released as full-length novels: "Madame Prosni and Madame Bleay" (1868), "Rosita" (1869), "On the Grand Tour" (1870), "Octavia Solara" (1871), and "Illusions Dispelled" (1871).

M. never married. L. B. Walford, a contemporary, records, however, that a proposal was made. Because M.'s response was accidentally not mailed, the young man left England thinking she had rejected him.

WORKS: *A Sister's Gift: Conversations on Sacred Subjects* (1826). *Stories From the History of Italy, from the Invasion of Alaric to the Present Time* (1831). *Village Bells* (1838). *The Maiden and Married Life of Mary Powell, Afterwards Mistress Milton* (1849). *The Household of Sir Thomas More* (1851). *Queen Philippa's Golden Rule* (1851). *The Colloquies of Edward Osborne, Citizen and Cloth Worker of London* (1852). *The Drawing Room Table Book* (1852). *Cherry and Violet: A Tale of the Plague* (1853). *The Provocations of Madame Palissy* (1853). *Chronicles of Merry England* (1854). *Claude the Colpasteur* (1854). *Jack and the Tanner of Wymondham* (1854). *The Hill Side: Illustrations of Some of the Simplest Terms Used in Logic* (1854). *Some Account of Mrs. Clarinda Singlehart* (1855). *Stories from the History of the Caliph Haroun al Raschid* (1855). *A Sabbath at Home* (1855). *The Old Chelsea Bun House: A Tale* (1855). *Tasso and Leonora: The Commentaries of Ser Pantaleone degli Gambacorti* (1856). *The Week of Darkness: A Short Manual for the Use and Comfort of Mourners* (1856). *Helen and Olga: A Russian Story* (1857). *Lives of Good Servants* (1857). *The Good Old Times: A Tale of Auvergne* (1857). *Deborah's Diary* (1858). *The Year Nine: A Tale of the Tyrol* (1858). *The Ladies of Bever Hollow* (1858). *Poplar House Academy* (1859). *Autobiography of Valentine Duval* (1860). *Town and Forest* (1860). *The Day of Small Things* (1860). *The Chronicle of Ethelfled* (1861). *Family Pictures* (1861). *The Cottage History of England* (1861). *A Noble Purpose Nobly Won* (1862). *Bessy's Money: A Tale* (1863). *Meadowleigh* (1863). *The Duchess of Trajetto* (1863). *An Interrupted Wedding* (1864). *Belfast: A Tale* (1865). *Selvaggio: A Tale of Italian Country Life* (1865). *Miss Biddy Frobisher: A Saltwater Story* (1866). *The Lincolnshire Tragedy: Passages in the Life of the Faire Gospeller, Mistress Anne Askewe, Recounted by Nicholas Moldwarp* (1866). *The Masque at Ludlow and Other Romanesques* (1866). *Diana's Crescent* (1868). *Jacques Bonneval* (1868). *The Spanish Barber: A Tale* (1869). *Margaret More's Tagebuch* (1870). *One Trip More* (1870). *Compton Friars* (1872). *The Lady of Limited Income* (1872). *Passages in an Authoress's Life* (1872). *Lord Harry Bellair* (1874). *Monk's Norton* (1874). *Heroes of the Desert: The Story of the Lives of Moffat and Livingstone* (1875). *An Idyll of the Alps* (1876).

BIBLIOGRAPHY:

For articles in reference works, see: *Allibone SUP* (under Mrs. Anne Rathbone [Manning]," 1891, 1965). *BA19C. Boase. DNB. Feminist. NCBEL. Oxford. Poole's.* Sadleir, M. *XIX Century Fiction: A Bibliographical Collection* (1951, 1969). *Stanford. ToddBWW. VB.*

Other references: Mrs. Batty, *Englishwoman's Review* (1880). *Fraser's* (1855). Miller, L. *MQ* (1977). *N&Q* (6 July 1895). Simmons, J. C. *ANQ* (1971). Simmons, J. C. *VN* (1972). Swaim, K. and M. Culley. *MQ* (1976). Walford, L. B. *Memories of Victorian London* (1912). Yonge, C. *Women Novelists of Queen Victoria's Reign* (1897).

Natalie Joy Woodall

Mary Manning

BORN: 30 June 1906, Dublin, Ireland.
DAUGHTER OF: FitzMaurice Manning and Susan Bennett Manning.
MARRIED: Mark DeWolfe Howe, Jr., 1935; Faneuil Adams, 1980.

M.'s career as a playwright, novelist, and drama critic began at Ireland's historic Abbey Theatre and extends to the present day. She has lived primarily in the United States since the 1930s, but her close ties to Ireland and its literary heritage are apparent in her work. M. was a founding member of Poets' Theater in Cambridge, Massachusetts, and her stage adaptation of James Joyce's *Finnegans Wake* was premiered by that company in 1955. Her best-known novel, *The Last Chronicles of Ballyfungus* (1978), is a black comedy about the battle between a local entrepreneur and eccentric residents over a planned development in "enchanted" Balooly Woods. In typical M. fashion, the story charts the hypocrisies and harsh compromises of Irish society and ends unhappily.

M., whose father worked in the British colonial service, was raised as part of Dublin's genteel Protestant middle class. She attended Morehampton House School and Alexandra College, where she acted in a production of W. B. Yeats' *Countess Cathleen.* She went to the Abbey School of Acting after graduation and later joined the Abbey Theatre Company. She joined the Gate Theatre when it was founded in 1930 and began writing in addition to acting. She also edited the Gate's magazine, *Motley*, in 1932–33. The Gate produced M.'s first play, *Youth's the Season—?* (1931), as well as M.'s less-successful and unpublished works *Storm Over Wicklow* (1933) and *Happy Family* (1934). At its premiere, *Youth's the Season—?*, a black drawing-room comedy about a group of young Irish people teetering on the cusp of adulthood, was hailed as a well-crafted first effort notable for its witty dialogue. The play is also noted for the character of Horace Egosmith, a silent *Doppelgänger* figure, whose presence M. attributed to a suggestion from playwright Samuel Beckett.

M. first visited the United States in 1924 to study art in Boston. When she returned in 1934 to scout locations for a possible Gate Theatre tour, she met and married Mark DeWolfe Howe, Jr., a Harvard Law School professor. She remained active in drama after her move to Cambridge, working with local troupes as well as becoming drama director for Radcliffe College in 1942. In 1950, she helped found Poet's Theater, a group devoted to encouraging poets to write for the stage. M. also published two novels during this period, *Mount Venus* (1938), a darkly comic look at the Troubles, and *Lovely People* (1953), a satire of Boston society.

In the 1950s and 1960s, M. shifted her dramatic focus to adaptation of Irish literature for the stage. Her partial adaptation of Joyce's *Finnegans Wake* is considered by some to be a masterful effort to make the *Wake* intelligible and remain true to Joyce's linguistic flow, by others to be an unacceptable reduction. *Finnegans Wake* was produced at the Abbey in 1963 and won the Drama Festival Prize. Mary Ellen Bute adapted the play for film, and it won a prize at the Cannes International Film Festival in 1965. M. also wrote her adaptations of Joyce's "Ivy Day in the Committee Room" (1967) and Frank O'Connor's "The Saint and Mary Kate" (1968) during this time.

Following her husband's death in 1967, M. returned to Dublin and for the next ten years wrote acerbic drama criticism for *Hibernia, The Irish Times,* and *The Independent.* She also wrote sketches of Irish life for the *Atlantic,* eventually publishing them as *The Last Chronicles of Ballyfungus.*

In 1979, M. met Faneuil Adams and returned with him to the United States. M. has remained in Cambridge since then, nearer to her three children, writing plays and occasional pieces. Her version of *Ivy Day* was awarded a prize for Best Artistic Merit and Inspiration at the Festival of International Plays in Washington, D.C., in 1993. *Go, Lovely Rose,* a short play about the girlhood of Rose Fitzgerald, appeared in *The Massachusetts Review* in 1989 with the first lengthy biographical portrait of M. At the present time, little critical assessment of M.'s work exists outside reviews, and no collected edition of her plays has been published. While her novels are out of print but available, most of her plays are difficult to find even in typescript.

WORKS: *Youth's the Season—?* (1931). *Storm Over Wicklow* (1933). *Happy Family* (1934). *Mount Venus* (1938). *Castle Irish* (1938). *Lovely People* (1953). *Finnegans Wake* (also called *Passages from Finnegans Wake* or *The Voice of Shem,* 1955). *Ivy Day in the Committee Room* (1967). *The Saint and Mary Kate* (1968). *Ah Well It Won't Be Long Now* (1972). *The Last Chronicles of Ballyfungus* (1978). *Go, Lovely Rose* (1989). *The Widow's Pique* (n.d.).

BIBLIOGRAPHY: Abramson, D. *MR* (1989). Finke, L. A. *Restoration* (1984). *James Joyce's Finnegans Wake: A Casebook,* ed. J. Harty III (1991). Kern, J. B. *SECC* (1981).

For articles in reference works, see: *Bell. BDIW. Bloomsbury. Cambridge. Plays of Changing Ireland,* ed. C. Canfield (1936). *DIL. DIW. DLB. Feminist.* Geisinger, M. and P. Marks. *Plays, Players, and Playwrights* (1975). *Oxford. ToddBWW. Who's Who of American Women* (1958).

Other references: Kenny, H. A. *Literary Dublin, A History* (1974).

Jennifer Poulos Nesbitt

Olivia Manning

BORN: 1911(?) or 1915(?), Portsmouth, Hampshire.
DIED: 23 July 1980, Isle of Wight.
DAUGHTER OF: Oliver Manning and Olivia Manning.
MARRIED: Reginald Donald Smith, 1939.

Though best known for her novels, particularly *The Balkan Trilogy* (1965), M. also wrote stories, humor, history, travel essays, and other works as well as numerous essays and reviews for the *London Times* and such journals as *Horizon, Spectator, Punch,* and *New Statesman.* Little biographical information is available for her, and until her death even an approximate year of her birth was unknown. Her father was a commander in the Royal Navy and her husband a BBC drama producer. She served in the press office in the U.S. embassy, Cairo, Egypt (1942); in the Public Information Office, Jerusalem, Palestine (1943–44); and in the British Council Office, Jerusalem (1944–45). She was also a painter; indeed, Walter Allen once noted that she had a "*painter's* eye for the visible world" that "enabled her to render particularly well the sensual surface of landscape and places."

M.'s first novel, *The Wind Changes* (1938), dealt with the Irish uprising but differs from most other fictionalized accounts of the Troubles in its focus on the conflicts within the central characters, a woman and two men, rather than on larger political and social issues. Her insightful handling of mental states was praised for its clarity and careful pacing, and her style, especially dialogue, was compared favorably to the work of Ernest Hemingway. The characters, however, were said to be indistinguishable in mood or act simply because of her emphasis on thought processes.

M.'s precise observation and description seemed to limit her efforts to present people and their actions adequately. Though her other early novels (*Artist Among the Missing,* 1949; *School for Love,* 1951; and *A Different Face,* 1953) were respectfully received, none made any appreciable impact. Yet all seem in retrospect to be leading, through her acknowledged gifts of humor, precision of language, sweeping sense of history, and keen appreciation of place, toward her *Balkan Trilogy. School for Love* is set in Jerusalem during World War II as experienced by a stranded sixteen-year-old boy. *A Different Face,* by contrast, is set on the English coast and concerns a man who discovers that his investment in a school has disappeared. In both cases, these early novels reflect M.'s skill at dramatizing essentially pessimistic, even hopeless, situations with a sharp eye for the telling detail, the vivid phrase, the ironic perspective, even though her dispassionate distance from her subjects sometimes displeased both readers and critics.

Each of these works was deservedly praised for its broad canvas, juxtaposition of individual fates against the backdrop of great European conflicts, and careful placement of characters in particular historical contexts; yet here, too, M.'s handling of her central characters came in for repeated criticism. Her acknowledged skill in penetrating the male psyche was often noted, but the individual, male or female, seemed wholly overwhelmed by the sheer magnitude of world events, so much so, in fact, that readers sometime found the books more persuasive as historical documents than as fiction.

The Balkan Trilogy includes *The Great Fortune* (1960), *The Spoilt City* (1962), and *Friends and Heroes* (1965). *The Great Fortune* (the title presumably refers to life itself) presents a husband and wife (Guy and Harriet Pringle) in Bucharest, Romania, who see how the older world is doomed but who, of course, are incapable of altering the inevitable. The cosmopolitan Guy (as seen through Harriet's eyes) is considered one of the most complex, appealing, full-bodied characters in all of modern literature; Anthony Burgess considers him a "kind of civilization in himself." Bucharest is the "spoilt city" of the second novel; in this work, Guy tries to save the city during its occupation by the Germans, though he is scarcely able to save himself and can never wholly fathom the radical changes he is witnessing. The same emphasis on the uncertainty of events is found in *Friends and Heroes,* in which the Pringles, now in Athens, Greece, find themselves still surrounded by flux and discord; M. seems to suggest that never again will Europe—or the world—be able to experience the previous world of stability and order.

M. subsequently completed an additional three volumes about World War II. Also considered a fine example of the *roman fleuve* (series or sequence novel), the *Levant Trilogy* (made up of *The Danger Tree,* 1977; *The Battle Lost and Won,* 1978; and *The Sum of Things,* 1980) continues the story of the Pringles, now stranded in Egypt and soon to wander through Palestine and Syria. M.'s excellent sense of atmosphere continues to dominate her characters' perceptions, though critics noted her more conventional reliance on routine descriptions and incidents as they experience the sharp contrast between England and Egypt, the rich and the poor. The soberly realistic Middle East descriptions avoid the poetic or exotic temptations of, say, Lawrence Durrell's *Alexandria Quartet* ,as M. dryly, wittily captures the world of military hospitals, markets, religious shrines, and cafés.

M.'s other novels include *The Rain Forest* (1974), set on an island in the Indian Ocean, again focusing on the gradual dissolution of a colonial way of life. She necessarily utilizes details of a steamy, oppressive climate as she contrasts incompetent British authority and the forbidden forest of the title. Her protagonists are a married couple who after struggling against both humans and nature are able to go on together, while other characters find the forest itself a primeval refuge.

M.'s talent was widely recognized, and her ambitious series novels are likely to endure as her most important works. Her concern was not with shifting political loyalities or historical topicality, despite the specific settings of her best novels, so much as with a quiet but vivid sense of the effects of setting on sensitive characters' awareness of the dissolution of empires.

WORKS: *The Wind Changes* (1938). *The Remarkable Expedition: The Story of Stanley's Rescue of Emin Pasha from Equatorial Africa* (1947; in the U.S. as *The Reluctant Rescue*). *Growing Up: A Collection of Short Stories* (1948). *Artist Among the Missing* (1949). *The Dreaming Shore* (1950). *School for Love* (1951). *A Different Face* (1953). *The Doves of Venus* (1955). *My Husband Cartwright* (1956). *The Great Fortune* (1960, *The Balkan Trilogy,* I). *The Spoilt City* (1962, *The Balkan Trilogy,* II). *Friends and Heroes* (1965, *The Balkan Trilogy,* III). *A Romantic Hero and Other Stories* (1967). *Extraordinary Cats* (1967). *The Play Room* (1969; as screenplay, 1970; in the U.S. as *The Camperlea Girls*). (with others) *Penguin Modern Stories 12* (1972). *The Rain Forest* (1974). *The Danger Tree* (1977, *The Levantine Trilogy,* I). *The Battle Lost and Won* (1978, *The Levantine Trilogy,* II). *The Sum of Things* (1980, *The Levantine Trilogy,* III). *The Weather in the Streets* (1986).

BIBLIOGRAPHY: Allen, W. *Tradition and Dream: The English and American Novel from the Twenties to Our Time* (1964; in the U.S. as *The Modern Novel in Britain and the United States,* 1965). Burgess, A. *The Novel Today* (1963; in the U.S. as *The Novel Now: A Guide to Contemporary Fiction,* 1967). Martin, G. C. *BB* (1989). Mooney, H. J., in *Twentieth Century Women Novelists,* ed. T. F. Staley (1987). Morris, R. K. *Continuance and Change: The Contemporary British Novel Sequence* (1972). Morris, R. K., in *British Novelists Since 1900,* ed. J. I. Biles (1987).

For articles in reference works, see: *Bloomsbury. CA. Cambridge. CLC. CN. Feminist. MBL* and *SUP. Oxford. TCW. ToddBWW. WA.*

Other references: *Books and Bookmen* (August 1971). *British Book News* (January 1981). *CSM* (9 April 1979). *Encounter* (May 1960). *John O'London's* (18 February 1960). *Listener* (25 September 1980). *London Magazine* (October-November 1974). *Manchester Guardian* (17 May 1962). *New Statesman* (11 April 1969, 5 April 1974, 17 November 1978, 26 September 1980). *NYTBR* (3 April 1938, 9 October 1977). *Saturday Review* (London) (9 April 1938). *Saturday Review* (New York) (17 November 1956). *Time and Tide* (22 December 1956, 29 January 1960, 24 November 1978, 19 September 1980).

Paul Schlueter

Katherine Mansfield

BORN: 14 October 1888, Wellington, New Zealand.
DIED: 9 January 1923, Fontainebleau, France.
DAUGHTER OF: Harold Beauchamp and Annie Dyer Beauchamp.
MARRIED: George C. Bowden, 1909; John Middleton Murry, 1918.

M., born Katherine Mansfield Beauchamp, is generally recognized as a major modernist, particularly for her experimentation with the short-story form. In addition to the half-dozen collections of short fiction published during her lifetime, she wrote numerous reviews of contemporary writers, published a number of poems, and, with S. S. Koteliansky, translated Maxim Gorki's *Reminiscences of Leonid Andreyev* (1928) from the Russian. Critics have traced the influence of Anton Chekhov and Oscar Wilde on M.'s writing; naturalists Frank Norris and Emile Zola were influential as well. Since M.'s death from tuberculosis in 1923, at the age of thirty-four, a number of her early writings, unpublished stories and journals, and four volumes of letters have appeared posthumously.

The fourth daughter of a successful Wellington merchant, M. grew up in colonial, rural New Zealand, which serves as a setting for more than half of her short stories. M. attended Queens College in London between the ages of fifteen and eighteen (1903–1906), returned unwillingly to New Zealand for two years, then left New Zealand definitively at the age of twenty to reside again in England. M. never returned to New Zealand, living in England, Germany, France, and Switzerland. Her one-day marriage in 1909 to George Bowden ended in annulment; M. was pregnant at the time, though not with Bowden's child. M. went alone to Germany to have the child, although the pregnancy ended in miscarriage.

Some of M.'s first stories appeared from 1910 to 1912 in the Fabian-Socialist magazine *The New Age.* There she published sharp, satirical sketches, literary parodies, feminist polemics, and the "Bavarian Sketches," later collected under separate cover as *In A German Pension* (1911). She established a new periodical called *Rhythm* with J. M. Murry, whom she married in 1918, and through her work for *Rhythm* met D. H. Lawrence and Leonard and Virginia Woolf. She was involved briefly with Francis Carco, a popular French novelist, after her marriage to Murry; the liaison with Carco inspired M.'s story "Je ne parle pas français." A relationship with L. M. (Ida Baker, renamed Lesley Moore by M.) that began as a schoolgirl friendship lasted until her death and competed with her relationship with Murry. Diagnosed with tuberculosis in 1918, M. sought cures in Switzerland and France and in her last years lived less in England than abroad. Her deteriorating relationship with Murry, whose work and discomfort with M.'s illness kept him in England while M. lived abroad, produced a significant correspondence between the two. M. died in Fontainebleau in the winter of 1923 while living under the harsh regime of the Gurdjieff Institute. The four-volume *Collected Letters* reflect the frequency and intensity of M.'s correspondence with Murry during her last years and stand as a literary achievement in their own right.

M.'s stories are often cited as representative of the quintessential modern format, with conscious epiphanies serving as focal points for the portrayal of internal crisis. Among her favorite devices are interior monologues, parallelisms, contrasts, flashbacks, and daydreams. In the Burnell-Sheridan sequences, M. experimented with the short-story cycle in which separate stories are linked by character, setting, and repeated images and motifs. Among M.'s favorite themes were the flowering of the self, sexual corruption, the terrors of childhood, the female artist, solitude, and death. From her symbolist roots, she also inherited a keen interest in expanding the poetic potentials of the prose genre; and many of the short stories are written in a lyrical prose employing rhythm, image, and sound as aids to convey meaning.

In a German Pension, M.'s first, highly autobiographical collection of short stories, dating from her experiences living in Germany, is told from the perspective of a female British protagonist who desires solitude and independence even as she satirizes the foibles of her fellow female travelers. In later stories like "The Garden Party," "The Doll's House," and "The Daughters of the Late Colonel," M. satirized the social norms of the New Zealand petty bourgeoisie. Her range of expression can be seen in a number of widely anthologized stories that are less easily classifiable, such as "Bliss" and "The Fly," stories that demonstrate M.'s expertise in evoking an atmosphere or mood created through a network of concrete images and the power of the idealizing imagination.

While M.'s stories have often been compared to well-wrought lyrics in their sensitivity, unity, and controlled form, recent criticism focuses less on these "feminine" qualities in M.'s writing, considering instead stories that are less well contained and more dramatic in their subject matter. Certainly in stories such as "The Woman at the Store" (1912), "The Little Governess" (1915), "Je ne parle pas français" (1918), and "The Married Man's Story" (1920), M. explored the darker themes of desire, fear, betrayal, desertion, estrangement, and death. M.'s skill in presenting social contexts and their often harsh realities is evident here.

M.'s most sustained narrative project was in the New Zealand stories, family sequences featuring the Sheridans and Burnells. In 1916, M. completed "The Aloe" (which was published in 1930), revised as "Prelude" in 1918, a story patterned largely after M.'s own early days in New Zealand; it explores the fates of four generations of Burnell women, including M.'s autobiographical portraits of herself as a child (Kezia) and young woman (Beryl). "At the Bay" (1922) continued the family narrative. M.'s focus on the New Zealand family sequences during her last years has also been a source of critical debate. Some critics claim that her imminent death evoked a need for reconciliation with her prodigal past, which was achieved through the New Zealand narratives. Others claim that the stories explain and celebrate her escape from a family cycle that would have doomed her creatively.

Modern readers may be confused by the available "selected" and "collected" compilations of M.'s writing. While most of the original collections of M.'s stories are no longer available, neither has a really definitive or chronologically accurate collection yet been produced. Worth mention is I. Gordon's *Undiscovered Country: The New Zealand Stories of Katherine Mansfield* (1974), a useful catalogue of her New Zealand stories, particularly in its coherent groupings of the family-sequence Burnell and Sheridan stories.

WORKS: *In a German Pension* (1911). *Prelude* (1918). *Je ne parle pas français* (1918). *Bliss, and Other Stories* (1920). *The Garden-Party, and Other Stories* (1922). *The Dove's Nest, and Other Stories* (1923). *Poems* (1923; rev. 1988). *Something Childish, and Other Stories* (1924; in the U.S. as *The Little Girl, and Other Stories*). *Journal,* ed. J. M. Murry (1927). (trans., with S. S. Koteliansky) *Reminiscences of Leonid Andreyev,* by M. Gorki (1928). *Letters,* ed. J. M. Murry (1928). *The Aloe* (1930; rev. 1985, ed. V. O'Sullivan). *Novels and Novelists,* ed. J. M. Murry (1930). (trans., with S. S. Koteliansky and L. Woolf) *Reminiscences of Tolstoy, Chekhov and Andreyev,* by M. Gorki (1934). *The Scrapbook,* ed. J. M. Murry (1939). *Collected Stories* (1945). *Letters to John Middleton Murry,* ed. J. M. Murry (1951). *Undiscovered Country: The New Zealand Stories,* ed. I. A. Gordon (1974). *The Letters and Journals of Katherine Mansfield, A Selection,* ed. C. K. Stead (1977). *The Complete Stories of Katherine Mansfield* (1978). *The Urewara Notebook,* ed. I. A. Gordon (1978). *Collected Letters, Vols. I–IV,* ed. V. O'Sullivan and M. Scott (1984, 1987, 1993, 1996). *Critical Writings,* ed. C. Hanson (1987). *Dramatic Sketches* (1989).

BIBLIOGRAPHY: Alpers, J. *The Life of Katherine Mansfield* (1980). Baker, Ida (L. M.; Leslie Moore) *Katherine Mansfield: The Memories of L. M.* (1971). Berkman, S. *Katherine Mansfield: A Critical Study* (1951). Burgan, M. *Illness, Gender and Writing: The Case of Katherine Mansfield* (1994). Daly, S. R. *Katherine Mansfield* (1965). Fullbrook, K. *Katherine Mansfield* (1986). Gordon, I. A. *Katherine Mansfield* (1971). Gunsteren, J. van.

Katherine Mansfield and Literary Impressionism (1990). Hankin, C. *Katherine Mansfield and Her Confessional Stories* (1983). Hanson, C. and A. Gurr. *Katherine Mansfield* (1981). Kaplan, S. J. *Katherine Mansfield and the Origins of Modernist Fiction* (1991). Kobler, J. F. *Katherine Mansfield: A Study of the Short Fiction* (1990). Magalaner, M. *The Fiction of Katherine Mansfield* (1971). Meyers, J. *Katherine Mansfield: A Biography* (1978). Moore, J. *Gurdjieff and Mansfield* (1980). Moran, P. *Word of Mouth: Body/Language in Katherine Mansfield and Virginia Woolf* (1996). Morrow, P. D. *Katherine Mansfield's Fiction* (1993). Murry, J. M. *The Autobiography of John Middleton Murry: Between Two Worlds* (1936). *Critical Essays on Katherine Mansfield*, ed. R. B. Nathan (1993). Robinson, R. *Katherine Mansfield: In From the Margin* (1994). Rohrberger, M. *The Art of Katherine Mansfield* (1977). Tomalin, C. *Katherine Mansfield: A Secret Life* (1987). Tomalin, C. *The Winter Wife* (1991).

For articles in reference works, see: *CA*. *GayLL*. *MBL* and *SUP*. *MCL*. *TCA* and *SUP*.

Glenda K. McLeod
(updated by Ann ter Haar)

Winifred Langford Mantle

BORN: 15 February 1911, Merry Hill, Staffordshire.
DIED: 13 November 1983, Wolverhampton, Staffordshire.
DAUGHTER OF: Joseph Langford Mantle and Florence Fellows Mantle.
WROTE UNDER: Jan Blaine; Anne Fellowes; Frances Lang; Jane Langford; Winifred Mantle.

M. was a prolific writer of romance novels and juvenile fiction from the 1950s to the early 1980s. Her juvenile fiction, particularly the Jonnesty books and the four novels featuring the Westcott and Lester children, was her most successful work. Most of M.'s adult fiction squarely fits the conventions of mass-market romance produced during the 1950s and 1960s. Her 1961 novel, *A Pride of Princesses*, written as by Frances Lang, was awarded the Romantic Novelists' Association prize for best historical novel, but this and later books conform to genre requirements in plot, characterization, and sexual content.

Born near Wolverhampton, Staffordshire, in 1911, M. was the daughter of a lecturer at a technical college. She attended Lady Margaret Hall, graduating with first class honors and later completing an M.A. Her first post was as a lecturer in French at St. Katharine's Training College, Liverpool (1938–41), after which she became assistant lecturer in French at St. Andrew's College, Scotland (1941–46).

M. published her first novel, *Happy is the House*, in 1951. This novel is not a typical romance in that the heroine, Stella, never marries, and M. shows a young intelligent woman both fascinated by and critical of conventions of romance and marriage. But M. soon began writing for the surging romance market, producing as many as three books per year through the 1960s.

M. became a full-time writer in 1957, returning to the Staffordshire countryside that forms the backdrop of many of her children's books. She published her first children's novel, *The Hiding Place*, in 1962, inaugurating a series of holiday adventure stories with the Westcott and Lester children. These stories typically feature absent parents, evil or obtuse adults, and mysteries based on events from British and French history. The books are didactic and reinforce gender and racial stereotypes, but M. deftly weaves the anxieties of the struggling genteel middle class into intelligent plots and realistic child characters. These stories reaffirm the traditions of England, but they also depict anxiety over career choices for young men and the difficulties of keeping up an estate in the post-war era.

Since her death in 1983, M.'s work has largely been ignored, despite the praise her children's literature received on publication. Her books are out of print and her romance fiction is largely unavailable. Since M. wrote to meet the requirements of a publishing industry increasingly interested in marketing a well-defined product to an identified audience, her fiction tends to follow the conventions of her genres, but her children's fiction captures the concerns of the professional middle class in post-war England.

WORKS: (as Winifred Mantle) *Happy is the House* (1951). (as Winifred Mantle) *Country Cousin* (1953). (as Jane Langford) *Haste to the Wedding* (1955). (as Jane Langford) *The Secret Fairing* (1956). (as Jane Langford) *King of the Castle* (1956). (as Jane Langford) *Half-Way House* (1957). (as Jane Langford) *Promise of Marriage* (1957). (as Anne Fellowes) *The Morning Dew* (1957). (as Jane Langford) *One Small Flower* (1958). (as Jane Langford) *Strange Adventure* (1958). (as Jane Langford) *Green Willow* (1958). (as Anne Fellowes) *The Keys of Heaven* (1958). *Five Farthings* (1958). (as Jane Langford) *Change of Tune* (1959). *Kingsbarns* (1959). *Lords and Ladies* (1959). (as Jane Langford) *Happy Return* (1960). (as Frances Lang) *Marriage of Masks* (1960). (as Frances Lang) *A Pride of Princesses* (1961). (as Frances Lang) *The Sun in Splendour* (1962). (as Winifred Mantle) *The Hiding Place* (1962). (as Winifred Mantle) *Griffin Lane* (1962). (as Frances Lang) *The Leaping Lords* (1963). (as Winifred Mantle) *Sandy Smith* (1963). (as Winifred Mantle) *Bennet's Hill* (1963). (as Winifred Mantle) *Tinker's Castle* (1963). (as Winifred Mantle) *The Chateau Holiday* (1964). (as Winifred Mantle) *The River Runs* (1964). (as Winifred Mantle) *A View of Christowe* (1965). (as Winifred Mantle) *The Painted Cave* (1965). (as Frances Lang) *Blind Man's Buff* (1965). (as Frances Lang) *The Marrying Month* (1965). (as Winifred Mantle) *The Same Way Home* (1966). (as Winifred Mantle) *The Penderel House* (1966; in the U.S. as *The Penderel Puzzle*). *Summer at Temple Quentin* (1967). (as Frances Lang) *The Well-Wisher* (1967). (as Frances Lang) *The Duke's Daughter* (1967). (as Winifred Mantle) *The Admiral's Wood* (1967). (as Winifred Mantle) *Winter at Wycliffe* (1968). (as Frances Lang) *The Malcontent* (1968). (as Winifred Mantle) *Piper's Row* (1968). (as Winifred Mantle) *The May Tree* (1969). (as Winifred Mantle) *A Fair Exchange* (1970). (as Frances Lang) *Double Dowry* (1970). (as Frances Lang) *The Tower of*

Remicourt (1971). (as Winifred Mantle) *The House in the Lane* (1972). (as Winifred Mantle) *Jonnesty* (1973). (as Frances Lang) *Milord McDonald* (1973). (as Frances Lang) *The Prince's Pleasure* (1974). (as Winifred Mantle) *The Inconvenient Marriage* (1974). (as Winifred Mantle) *Jonnesty in Winter* (1975). (as Frances Lang) *The Marquis's Marriage* (1975). (as Frances Lang) *Stranger at the Gate* (1975). (as Winifred Mantle) *The Beckoning Maiden* (1976). (as Frances Lang) *The Baron's Bride* (1978). (as Frances Lang) *The Vanishing Bridegroom* (1980). (as Frances Lang) *The Filigree Bird* (1981). (as Frances Lang) *Fortune's Favourite* (1981). (as Frances Lang) *To Be a Fine Lady* (1982).

BIBLIOGRAPHY:

For articles in reference works, see: *AWWW. IAWWW. CA. WD.*

Other references: Crouch, M. *The Nesbit Tradition: The Children's Novel in England 1945–1970* (1972). Hunt, P. *An Introduction to Children's Literature* (1994). Radway, J. A. *Reading the Romance* (1984).

Jennifer Poulos Nesbitt

Marchant, Catherine: See *Cookson, Catherine Ann*

Marie de France

BORN: 1140 (?); probably French by birth.
DIED: 1215 (?).

In the epilogue to her fables, M. says: "Marie ai num, s'-suis de France," generally interpreted to mean that she was of the Ile de France, though she spent most of her life in England. Several attempts have been put forth to identify her: She may have been the abbess of Shaftesbury (the illegitimate daughter of Geoffrey of Anjou); the abbess of Reading; or Marie de Meulan, daughter of Count Waleron de Beaumont. M. wrote at or for the English court of King Henry II and Eleanor of Aquitaine. Her works enjoyed popularity in the Middle Ages: Denis Piramus mentions her in his *Vie Seint Edmund le Rey* (c. 1170–80), saying that she was one of the most popular authors with lords and ladies, and her lais were translated into various languages during the Middle Ages.

M. is the first known woman writer to compose vernacular narrative poetry; she is often praised as the author of the best short vernacular fiction before Boccaccio. Her trademark, as has been repeatedly observed, is her sophisticated use of symbolic creatures or artifacts around which the lais' action revolves. Functioning almost as leitmotives, these symbolic entities enable M. to craft multidimensional, often ambiguous narratives that explore the nature of love, fidelity, loyalty, and sacrifice. Her themes center on the need for self-fulfillment both for men and women and the unlimited power of the imagination and of love to make one's wish and desire come true.

Her twelve lais, all in octosyllabic couplets, range in length from 118 lines ("Chevrefoil") to 1,184 lines ("Eliduc") and were probably intended for oral recitation. Based on Celtic tales and transmitted orally by Breton bards, they were composed between 1160 and 1199. "Guigemar" depicts the psychological and sexual growing up of the protagonist in a fairy-tale setting. The young hero, oblivious to the attractions of women, is wounded by a deer and can be healed only by a woman's love. "Le Fresne" concerns the selfless love of an abandoned girl, which is ultimately rewarded by recognition by her parents and marriage to her beloved. "Bisclavret," M.'s tale of a werewolf, centers on betrayal and loyalty, and "Lanval" presents the ennobling effects of love in the tale of a noble knight and his fairy sweetheart set against the ignoble court of Arthur and his lascivious and cruel queen. "Les Deus Amanz," a tragic tale, celebrates the all-embracing joy of true love, while "Yonec" paints a virtuous lady's escape from her marital prison through her imagination, manifested in her bird-knight-lover. "Milun" tells of long-lasting love and of a father's encounter with his unknown son, while "Chaitivel" recounts the sad story of an indecisive lady who loses all her lovers. "Equitan," the most didactic of the lais, explores the nature of reciprocal responsibilities and loyalties. "Laustic" is the tragic story of a lady deprived of all joy in her marriage, and "Eliduc" is the classic triangle story of a man caught between two women and two lords.

M.'s fables, translated into French from English, are all characterized by a sense of social obligations and justice and compassion for the oppressed. Yet M. does not fall prey to over-simplifications: Wickedness is sometimes committed by the oppressed as well as the oppressor, and corruption is not the exclusive domain of the rich and the powerful. *L'Espurgatoire Saint Patrice,* finally, is a translation from Latin into French depicting the otherworldly journey of the Irish knight Owein. Having witnessed the pain and suffering of the souls in purgatory as well as the bliss of earthly paradise, he returns to earth to lead an exemplary life.

M.'s strength lies with her lively style, psychological astuteness, and economy of expression. Throughout her works, she avoids easy generalizations. She is an exciting, intense, suggestive, and talented storyteller, able to present archetypal themes in engaging contemporary guise.

WORKS: *The Lais of Marie de France,* ed. J. M. Ferrante and R. W. Hanning (1978). *Fables,* ed. and trans. H. Spiegel (1987). *Les Lais de Marie de France,* ed. P. Rychner (1983).

BIBLIOGRAPHY: Boland, M. *Architectural Structure in the Lais of Marie de France* (1994). Burgess, G. S. *Marie de France: An Analytical Bibliography* (1977); *Supplement I,* ed. G. S. Burgess (1986). Burgess, G. *The Lays of Marie de France* (1987). Clifford, P. *The Lays of Marie de France* (1982). Freeman, M. *PMLA* (1984). Kinoshita, S. *RomN* (1993–94). Le Mee, K. W. *A Metrical Study of Five Lais of Marie de France* (1978). Malvern, M. M. *TSWL* (1983). *In Quest of Marie de France,* ed. C. Marechal (1992).

For articles in reference works, see: *Bloomsbury. Cambridge. Cassell. Feminist.*

Katharina M. Wilson

Marinda: See *Monck, Mary*

Beryl Markham

BORN: 26 October 1902, Westfield House, Ashwell, Rutland.
DIED: 3 August 1986, Nairobi, Kenya.
DAUGHTER OF: Charles Baldwin Clutterback and Clara Alexander.
MARRIED: Alexander Laidlow "Jock" Purves, 1919; Mansfield Markham, 1927; Raoul Schumacher, 1942.

A noted horse trainer and pioneer aviator, M.'s most famous writing is *West with the Night* (1942), her account of her early life near Nairobi in British East Africa, now Kenya, where she lived from the age of four with her father, a famous horse trainer and ex-officer of the King's Own Scottish Borderers, her mother having returned to England with her brother after only a year in Africa.

On Green Hill Farm, a series of governesses were unable to prevent the young M. from going barefoot (a lifelong habit) or adventuring after lions in the bush with her African friends; after two and a half years, M. was expelled from her only formal school. By 1919, when she married "Jock" Purves, M. had developed considerable skill with horses; as a result, in 1921, after her father emigrated to Peru, she was granted a horse trainer's license, the first awarded to a woman in Kenya. After the breakup of her stormy first marriage and a brief visit to England, a friend's financial assistance enabled her to return to Kenya, where she established herself as a horse trainer. Eventually, M. became known as "Memsahib Wa Farasi" (Lady of the Horses). A year after her marriage to Mansfield Markham in 1927, M. was presented at court, but the couple returned to Kenya in time to participate in the safaris organized for the Prince of Wales and Prince Henry, Duke of Gloucester, with whom M. became involved. Years later, M.'s biographer revealed that the palace settled an annuity on M. to prevent scandal. Soon after her son Gervase was born in February 1929, M. sent him to her mother-in-law; thereafter, they had little contact.

Adventuresome and influenced by Denys Finch Hatton, M. commenced flying lessons in April 1930 under the tutelage of Tom Campbell Black, who became a close friend. On 11 June 1931, M. completed her first solo flight from Wilson Airport, Nairobi. It was five minutes long and recorded in M.'s logbook, which she kept throughout her flying career; on 13 July, she passed her license test. In September 1932, after flying to England and obtaining her commercial B license in Nairobi, M. began a freelance flying business, often acting as big-game scout by spotting from her flimsy biplane. In 1936, she flew from Nairobi to London and became chief pilot for Air Cruisers Ltd., a position she forsook to fly *The Messenger,* the plane in which, on 4 September 1936, after several delays, she took off to fly trans-Atlantic from east to west. After 2,656 miles in twenty-one hours, twenty-five minutes, she became the first woman and first person to make a non-stop solo flight east to west. She recounts this period in *West with the Night.*

Now a heroine, M. spent five months in the United States and sailed to Africa after unsuccessful movie tests; she returned to Hollywood in 1939 as technical adviser for *Safari,* a film starring Douglas Fairbanks, Jr. Upon the urging of Antoine de Saint-Exupery, she drafted an outline for *West with the Night;* by 1941, she had signed a contract, and by publication in 1942 had married Raoul Schumacher, who is thanked for his editorial assistance in the book's dedication to her father. A series of short stories followed, some written by M., some co-authored by M. and Schumacher, and some, based on M.'s knowledge, by Schumacher, in *Ladies' Home Journal, Collier's Magazine, Saturday Evening Post,* and *Cosmopolitan.* Years later, a controversy would brew concerning M.'s authorship of some of the stories as well as of *West with the Night.*

Always on the brink of financial disaster, M. left California alone to return to Africa in 1949; Lord Delamere provided her fare. Destitute in Nairobi, she became the legal secretary to Charles Bath-Hurst Norman but gradually returned to horse training. By 1958, M. won the Kenya St. Leger horse race, and she and jockey Ryan "Buster" Parnell set the standards for racing in Kenya as M. enjoyed a second brilliant career. Over the next decade she trained horses in Kenya, South Africa, and Rhodesia, finally returning to Thika. In 1977, M. was the guest of honor at the fiftieth anniversary of the Aero Club of East Africa. By 1978, M. had trained numerous classic winners; during her best season, her horses won forty-six races.

Although less active, M. continued as a presence and horse trainer in Kenya. However, her habitual inability to manage her financial affairs prompted Jack Couldrey, a Nairobi solicitor, to establish a subscription fund for her and to manage her finances until her death. She was living in a small cottage at the Nairobi race track when *West with the Night* was republished in 1983. Journalists sought her out because of her role in the life of Karen Blixen (Isak Dinesen), and finally, the documentary *World Without Walls* was released in 1986 shortly before her death in August from injuries sustained in a fall.

WORKS: *West With the Night* (1942, 1983). *The Splendid Outcast,* ed. M. S. Lovell (collected short stories, 1987). *The Illustrated West With the Night* (1994).

BIBLIOGRAPHY: Lovell, M. S. *Straight On Till Morning* (1987). SGH Productions. *World Without Walls* (1986). Trzebinski, E. *The Lives of Beryl Markham* (1994).

For articles in reference works, see: *Annual Obituary* (1986). *CA. CB. CWA. Explorers and Discoverers of the World. IDWB.*

Other references: Fox, J. *Observer Magazine* (30 September 1984). Huxley, E. *White Man's Country* (1935). Knipp, T. *SoAR* (1990). Petry, A. H. *Hemingway Review* (1985). Smith, S., in *De-Colonizing the Subject: The Poliitics of Gender in Women's Autobiography,* ed. S. Smith and J. Watson (1992). Thurman, J. *Isak Dinesen: The Life of Karen Blixen* (1982). Zoghby, M. *Chattahoochee Review* (1991).

Judith C. Kohl

Marlborough, Sarah, Duchess of: See *Churchill, Sarah Jennings, Duchess of Marlborough*

Florence Marryat

BORN: 9 July 1837, Brighton.
DIED: 27 October 1899, St. John's Wood, London.
DAUGHTER OF: Frederick Marryat and Catherine Shairp.
MARRIED: T. Ross Church, 1854; Francis Lean, 1890.

M., the sixth daughter of Captain Frederick Marryat, the celebrated writer of sea adventures, was a prolific popular novelist of Victorian England. Early in life she displayed an interest in writing, and she published her first novel, *Temper* (1859), at the age of twenty-two. She scored a success six years later with *Love's Conflict* (1865), written to distract herself while nursing her children who had come down with scarlet fever.

She married young, wedding Colonel T. Ross Church of the Madras Staff Corps when she was sixteen. Her extensive travels with him in India resulted in *"Gup": Sketches of Anglo-Indian Life and Character* (1868) ("Gup" is Hindustani for "gossip"). While emerging as a popular fiction writers of the 1870s, she also found time to publish her father's correspondence (the two-volume *Life and Letters of Captain Marryat,* 1872), to which she contributed a biographical portrait, and to edit the monthly periodical *London Society* (1872–76).

In the 1880s and 1890s, M. added drama and spiritualism to her growing interests, writing and starring in a comedy, *Her World* (1881), and producing among other such works *There is No Death* (1891), a detailed account of seances and interviews with mediums. By 1890, when, as a widow, she married Colonel Francis Lean of the Royal Marine Light Infantry, there seemed no end to her accomplishments: She was an operatic singer, entertainer, public speaker, and manager of a school of journalism.

M. is remembered as a practitioner of the "sensation novel," a semi-Gothic literary form of the 1860s and 1870s featuring sinister family secrets and daring anti-heroines. Her novel *Love's Conflict* (1865) employs these elements in the story of Helen Du Broissart, a social climber and the daughter of an adulteress, who marries into the wealthy Treherne family only to be murdered by her former lover. Like her fellow sensationalists Mary Elizabeth Braddon and Mrs. Henry Wood, M. both paid fascinated attention to the fallen woman and prudently punished her by the end of the story. M. treated another favorite character, the cynical aristocrat who skirts immortality, in *The Confessions of Gerald Estcourt* (1867), one of a string of popular works.

Many of M.'s almost sixty novels were widely read in the United States and translated into a number of languages, including Swedish and Russian. Her fluid style (such sentences as "The affections will be their own judges" came effortlessly to her narrators), sharp eye for social pretension, and travel writer's observation of place earned her a certain success with a readership avid for details of aristocratic houses and the *mesalliances* that occurred in them.

WORKS: *Temper* (1859). *Love's Conflict* (1865). *Woman Against Woman* (1865). *Too Good for Him* (1865). *For Ever and Ever: A Drama of Life* (1866). *The Confessions of Gerald Estcourt* (1867). *"Gup": Sketches of Anglo-Indian Life and Character* (1868). *Nelly Brooke* (1868). *Veronique* (1869). *The Girls of Feversham* (1869). *Petronel* (1870). *The Prey of the Gods* (1871). *Her Lord and Master* (1871). *Life and Letters of Captain Marryat* (1872). *Mad Dumaresq* (1873). *Sybil's Friend, and How She Found Him* (1874). *No Intentions* (1874). *Open! Sesame!* (1875). *Fighting the Air* (1875). *My Own Child* (1876). *Hidden Chains* (1876). *Her Father's Name* (1876). *A Harvest of Wild Oats* (1877). *Christmas Leaves* (1877). *Our Villas* (1877). *Written in Fire* (1878). *A Little Step-son* (1878). *Her World Against a Life* (1879). *A Star and a Heart* (1879). *Out of His Reckoning* (1879). *The Poison of Asps* (1879). *A Scarlet Sin* (1880). *The Root of All Evil* (1880). *The Fair-Haired Alda* (1880). *Her World* (1881). *With Cupid's Eyes* (1881). *My Sister the Actress* (1881). *Phyllida, a Life Drama* (1882). *How They Loved Him* (1882). (with Sir C. L. Young) *Facing the Footlights* (1882). *A Moment of Madness, and Other Stories* (1883). *Peeress and Player* (1883). *The Heir Presumptive* (1886). *The Master Passion* (1886). *Tom Tiddler's Ground* (1886). *A Crow of Shame* (1888). *Mount Eden* (1889). *The Nobler Sex* (1890). *A Fatal Silence* (1891). *Gentleman and Courtier* (1891). *The Risen Dead* (1891). *There is No Death* (1891). *How Like a Woman* (1892). *The Spirit World* (1894). *A Bankrupt Heart* (1894). *A Hampstead Mystery* (1894). *The Beautiful Soul* (1895). *The Heart of Jane Warner* (1895). *The Strange Transfiguration of Hannah Stubbs* (1896). *A Rational Marriage* (1899). *The Folly of Allison* (1899).

BIBLIOGRAPHY: *Athenaeum* (4 November 1899). Hays, F. *Women of the Day* (1885). *LonT* (28 October 1899). MacFie, S., in *Subjectivity and Literature from the Romantics to the Present,* ed. P. Shaw and P. Stockwell (1991). Plarr, V. *Men and Women of the Time* (1895). Showalter, E. *A Literature of Their Own* (1977). Williams, A. S. *The Lifted Veil: The Book of Fantastic Literature by Women, 1800–World War II* (1992).

For articles in reference works, see: *Allibone. Bloomsbury. DNB. Feminist. Oxford. ToddBWW. VB.*

Laura Hapke

Marsh, Anne: See *Marsh-Caldwell, Anne*

Marsh, Mrs.: See *Marsh-Caldwell, Anne*

Ngaio Marsh

BORN: 23 April 1899, Christchurch, New Zealand.
DIED: 18 February 1982, Christchurch, New Zealand.
DAUGHTER OF: Henry Edmund Marsh and Rose Elizabeth Seager Marsh.

In the mid-1930s, when M. came on the literary scene with a detective novel, the appearance of a woman writer in the genre was not unusual. In the 1920s, for instance, readers of the kind of fiction that stretched back to Edgar Allan Poe and Wilkie Collins, Sir Arthur Conan Doyle, and the rest had been introduced to Agatha Christie (*The Mysterious Affair at Styles,* 1920), Lord Peter Wimsey of

Dorothy L. Sayers (*Whose Body?*, 1923), Albert Campion of Margery Allingham (*The Crime at Black Dudley,* 1929), and more. But soon, especially with *Death in a White Tie* (1938) and *Overture to Death* (1939), it was clear that M. was going to carve herself a special place in this field of popular literature.

While some critics (such as Edmund Wilson) attacked detective fiction, the public on the whole loved it, and they loved the work of M. Wilson might say authoritatively that M., even Sayers, padded books and mangled prose, but readers did not care, and they strongly resented Wilson for describing her prose as "unappetizing sawdust" or her characters in *Overture to Death* as "faked-up English country people who are even more tedious than those of [Sayers's] *The Nine Tailors.*" The fact is that M.'s prose is subliterary, but with Christie in competition that will hardly be noticed. Moreover, though she does "fake-up" her characters, at least her detectives (such as Inspector Alleyn) are ordinary, not blind, fat, foreign, or otherwise odd. Most of all, as with Christie, no one reads M. for the syntax or the psychology; people read her for the plot.

Though it is true that the plot may hinge on a gun being rigged up inside a piano to kill someone who pushes down a pedal, and though it is also true that *Death in a White Tie* has a story that can politely be described as intricate, such is M.'s talent that it works and reading the novels is a distinct pleasure. M. can do more than make a mere puzzle; she can make an entertaining detective story.

M. was not a scholar like Sayers (who translated Dante, *The Song of Roland,* and other literature), but she received a D.Litt. from the University of Canterbury (New Zealand); was awarded first a C.B.E. (Commander of the British Empire) in 1948 and then a D.B.E. (Dame of the British Empire) in 1966; became a Fellow of the Royal Society of Arts; won various prizes (such as the coveted Grand Master Award from the Mystery Society of America, 1978); and retired to her native land having won the hearts of Britain, the United States, and the whole English-speaking world.

Born in New Zealand, she was educated there and went into the theater as actress, producer, and writer. She was in London as an interior designer in 1928–32 and dabbled in writing. So well was her work received early on that she decided to write professionally. But "full-time" to a woman of her energy left plenty of time for wartime service with the Red Cross, post-war theatrical producing, lecturing, and many other activities. In her autobiography, *Black Beech and Honeydew* (1965), M. has a busy story to tell and in fact stresses not her detective-story writing but her theater work. She is the author not only of detective novels but also of books on play production (1946 and 1960), on New Zealand (1942, 1960, 1964), some plays (often from her own novels), a couple of juvenile entertainments (*The Christmas Tree,* 1962, *A Unicorn for Christmas,* 1965), a television play (*Evil Liver,* 1975), and so forth.

It is, however, for thirty novels, from *A Man Lay Dead* (1934) to *Light Thickens* (1983), that she is famous. Some, such as *Colour Scheme* (1943), do not really qualify as detective fiction, but most are centered on crimes solved by Inspector Roderick Alleyn, a sleuth who combines the aristocracy of such as Lord Peter Wimsey with the practicality featured in more recent "police procedurals." As Doyle's Sherlock Holmes had his Dr. Watson, so Inspector Alleyn often has Inspector Fox, his friend Nigel Bathgate, or his wife Troy; they act as foils. Neither they nor M.'s central character are as deliberately peculiar as Christie's Hercule Poirot or Miss Marple or the strange detectives that other writers place in pathology labs, wheelchairs, and so on.

M. puts her solid Inspector Alleyn and other characters into settings that are often vivid, some coming from M.'s personal experience as actress, theatrical producer, or playwright (as in *Opening Night,* also published as *Night at the Vulcan,* 1951). If only a few of her detective stories give evidence of life as she knew it in New Zealand, it may be because her readership has always been primarily British and American.

M. once said that "intellectual New Zealand friends tactfully avoid all mention of my published work" and that it was pleasant for her to appear on British radio and be asked about detective-story writing as "a tolerable form of reading by people whose opinion one valued." Maybe, as she told *The Writer* (April 1977), she fell into detective-story writing pretty much as James Fenimore Cooper fell into writing (he read a book and announced he could do better than that); but that day in 1933 when M. put down her reading (she tactfully refuses to say whether it was Christie, Sayers, or another mistress of mystery) was a bright one for her and her countrymen and for the readers everywhere of detective stories. Her first novel she constructed on the plan of the popular parlor game of the time called "Murder." For forty years afterwards she wrote essentially the same kind of book, and each one of them was welcomed and enjoyed by the public, so that (as the *Spectator* said on 4 May 1974) she has really "now reached that classic state where she is almost above criticism."

WORKS: *A Man Lay Dead* (1934). *Enter a Murderer* (1935). *Artists in Crime* (1936). (with H. Jellett) *Nursing Home Murder* (1936). *Vintage Murder* (1937). *Death in Ecstasy* (1937). *Death in a White Tie* (1938). *Overture to Death* (1939). *A Wreath for Riviera* (1940; also published as *Swing, Brother, Swing*). *Death at the Bar* (1940). *Death of a Peer* (1940; also published as *Surfeit of Lampreys,* 1941). *Death and the Dancing Footman* (1942). (with R. M. Burden) *New Zealand* (1942). *Colour Scheme* (1943). *Died in the Wool* (1945). *A Play Toward: A Note on Play Production* (1946). *Final Curtain* (1947). *Night at the Vulcan* (1951; also published as *Opening Night*). *Spinsters in Jeopardy* (1953). *Scales of Justice* (1955). *Death of a Fool* (1956). *Singing in the Shrouds* (1958). *False Scent* (1959; as play, 1961). *Play Production* (1960). *Perspectives: New Zealand and the Visual Arts* (1960). *The Christmas Tree* (1962). *Hand in Glove* (1962). *Dead Water* (1963). *New Zealand* (1964). *A Unicorn for Christmas* (1965). *Killer Dolphin* (1966). *Black Beech and Honeydew: An Autobiography* (1965). *Clutch of Constables* (1968). *When in Rome* (1970). *Murder Sails at Midnight* (1972). *Tied Up in Tinsel* (1972). *Black as He's Painted* (1973). *Evil Liver* (1975). *Last Ditch* (1977). *Grave Mistake* (1978). *Photo Finish* (1981). *Light Thickens* (1983).

BIBLIOGRAPHY: Acheson, C. *JPC* (1985). *Return to Black Beech: Papers from a Centenary Symposium on Ngaio Marsh,* ed. C. Acheson and C. Lidgard (1996). Bargainner, E. F. *ArmD* (1978). Bargainner, E. F. *Ten Women of Mystery* (1981). "Birth of a Sleuth." *The Writer* (April 1977). Dooley, A. C. and L. J. Dooley, in *Art in Crime Writing,* ed. B. Benstock (1983). Gibbs, R. and R. Williams. *Ngaio Marsh: A Bibliography* (1990). Harding, B. *ANZSC* (1992). Klein, K. G. *Great Women Mystery Writers* (1994). Lewis, M. *Ngaio Marsh: A Life* (1991). McDorman, K. *Ngaio Marsh* (1991). Rahn, B. J. *ArmD* (1995). *Ngaio Marsh: The Woman and Her Work,* ed. B. J. Rahn (1995). *Spectator* (4 May 1974). Weinkauf, M. S. *Murder Most Poetic: The Mystery Novels of Ngaio Marsh* (1994).

For articles in reference works, see: *CA. CLC. CN. TCA* and *SUP. TCC&MW. TCW.*

Leonard R. N. Ashley

Anne Marsh-Caldwell

BORN: 1791, Linley Wood, Staffordshire.
DIED: 5 October 1874, Linley Wood, Staffordshire.
DAUGHTER OF: James Caldwell and Elizabeth Stamford Caldwell.
MARRIED: Arthur Cuthbert Marsh, 1817.
WROTE UNDER: Anne Marsh; Mrs. Marsh; Anne Marsh-Caldwell.

M., a mid-nineteenth-century domestic novelist, launched her literary career under the direction of Harriet Martineau. Daughter of a Staffordshire landholder and lawyer, wife of a failed banker, and mother of seven children, she had often written stories for her own amusement. When Martineau came to visit, M. read her "The Admiral's Daughter," a story of a young woman's adultery. After a fit of crying, Martineau expressed her amazement and admiration; after rereading the manuscript at home, she agreed to help M. find a publisher. The author's name was withheld from the public at the direction of her husband. "A father of many daughters," explained Martineau, "did not wish their mother to be known as the author of what the world might consider second-rate novels." Although "The Admiral's Daughter" was a sensational success, M. continued to publish anonymously. Some reviewers knew her name; others simply referred to her as "the authoress." Very little is known about the circumstances of her life. Although some attributions are still in doubt, she seems to have produced more than twenty novels, two books of stories, a history of the Protestant Reformation in France, and some translations from French. When her brother died in 1858, she succeeded to her family's property at Linley Wood and resumed the surname of Caldwell. She died on the estate where she was born, "lady of the manor, landholder, like her father," said the *Athenaeum* obituary.

M.'s best-known works were "The Admiral's Daughter" and *Emilia Wyndham* (1846). As Margaret Oliphant observed, "Her first and most ambitious work is not addressed to her audience of young ladies." Its protagonist, a beautiful woman of Spanish descent, drifts into an illicit affair with her husband's friend. She is, therefore, a "worm," "an empty casket," a "worthless withered rose." Ridden with guilt, she can no longer feel comfortable in attending church or caring for their children. She must face a duel, her husband's fatal injury, and her lover's suicide. In contrition and love, she disguises herself as a nurse to attend her dying husband; dressed as a governess, she supervises her daughters' education. No book produced "more solemn silent showers than that heartrending story," said one paper. While Harriet Martineau believed that "the singular magnificence of that tale was not likely to be surpassed," most readers preferred the pure and patient heroines of her later novels.

In *Emilia Wyndham,* for example, "the charm of the story is the character of its heroine—her trials—her patience—her fidelity." Emilia dreams "of Una and her lion—or Clarinda and her lance," but she must follow her mother's instructions and achieve heroism in "the heavy, wearying every-day evils of every-day actual life . . . combining patience, perseverance, endurance, gentleness, and disinterestedness." "A highminded, devoted girl," she does not err; she rescues others. M. dedicated the novel to William Wordsworth in recognition of "the fine influence of his poetry" and prefaced it with an essay on domestic realism. The indisputable quality of the novel, she argued, is "that it should convey the sense of reality—that the people we read of should be to us as actual beings and persons—that we should believe in them." Without overstepping the bounds of easy probability, the novelist should bring "causes and their consequences into obvious connexion."

Like other domestic novelists, M. sometimes criticized the way men abused their power within the family. In *Emilia Wyndham,* she took issue with Douglas Jerrold's characterization of the nagging wife in *Mrs. Candle's Curtain Lectures,* a series of satirical sketches in *Punch.* "Any vulgar penny-a-liner can draw Mrs. Candle, and publish her in a popular journal; and with such success that she shall become a by-word in families, and serve as an additional reason for that rudeness and incivility that negligent contempt, with which too many Englishmen still think it their prerogative, as men and true-born Britons, to treat their wives." Her heroine must confront a tyrannical father who torments his daughter and wife. At the end of the novel she asks, "Is it not just possible, think you, that some of the discomforts of married life—a very small proportion, of course—might be ameliorated, if husbands now and then received a lesson in their turn, and learned to correct themselves as well as their wives?" *Punch* retaliated with a parody.

At a time when fiction was still regarded with considerable suspicion, M. seemed safe. She "writes as an English gentlewoman should write and what is better still, she writes what English gentlewomen should read," said James Lorimer, having commended her for avoiding metaphysical precipices, moral volcanos, and "the odours of the workhouse." She was, according to Oliphant, "orthodox and proper beyond criticism." Indeed, one conservative journal saw her popularity as evidence of the nation's moral integrity. But if she helped make fiction respectable, she also made it dull: She and her heroines were "a wee, wee bit prosy." Moreover, she was not able to sustain her early achievements. Writing in 1855, Oliphant concluded, "She has taken to making books rather than to telling stories, and has perceptibly had the printing-press and certain editorial censors before her." A modern literary historian theorizes that M.'s situation was typical of many other popular women writers of the time: Working in isolation and drawing upon her own fantasies, she produced one book of considerable promise; entering the literary world and receiving suggestions from editors and readers, she lapsed into a formulaic fiction.

WORKS: *The Old Men's Tales: "The Deformed" and "The Admiral's Daughter"* (1834). *Tales of the Woods and Fields* (1836). *The Triumphs of Time* (1844). *Mount Sorel: Or, The Heiress of the de Peres* (1845). *Father Darcy* (1846). *Emilia Wyndham* (1846). *Norman's Bridge: Or, The Modern Midas* (1847). *The Protestant Reformation in France: or, The History of the Hugonots [sic]* (1847). *Angela* (1848). *Mordant Hall: or, A September Night* (1849). *Tales of the First French Revolution* (1849). *Lettice Arnold* (1850). *The Wilmington* (1850). *Ravenscliffe* (1851). *Time the Avenger* (1851). *Castle Avon* (1852). *The Longwoods of the Grange* (1853). *Aubrey* (1854). *The Heiress of Houghton: or, The Mother's Secret* (1855). *Woman's Devotion* (1855). *Margaret and Her Bridesmaids* (1856). *The Rose of Ashurst* (1857). *Mr. and Mrs. Ashton* (1860). *The Ladies of Lovel-Leigh* (1862). *Chronicles of Dartmoor* (1866). *Lords and Ladies* (1866).

BIBLIOGRAPHY: Colby, V. *Yesterday's Woman: Domestic Realism in the English Novel* (1974). Cruse, A. *The Victorians and Their Reading* (1936). Martineau, H. *Autobiography* (1877). Mitchell, S. *The Fallen Angel: Chastity, Class and Women's Reading, 1835–1880* (1981).

For articles in reference works, see: *Allibone. Boase. CBEL. DNB. Feminist. NCBEL. Oxford. VB.*

Robin Sheets

Martin, Stella: See *Heyer, Georgette*

Martin, Violet Florence: See *Somerville and Ross (Violet Florence Martin)*

Harriet Martineau

BORN: 12 June 1802, Norwich.
DIED: 27 June 1876, Birmingham.
DAUGHTER OF: Thomas Martineau and Elizabeth Rankin Martineau.

The study of M.'s life affords the student of nineteenth-century English and American society a view not only of an exceptional woman but also of the transformations taking place during this era in politics, views of child rearing and education, and the strain inherent in a woman's life if that woman happens to defy convention by following a calling beyond her designated sphere. Although M.'s discerning eye and prolific ease with the written word earned her the respectful title of "the first sociologist," her accomplishments were at times threatened by debilitating disease, conflicting feelings regarding family responsibilities, and the volatile reaction of her readers on the many controversial issues she deigned to explore and popularize in her fifty-year literary career.

M. was described as a delicate and difficult child, the latter adjective a result perhaps of her mother's seeming indifference to her sixth child. M.'s experience, however, was like that of many in the early 1800s when scrupulous attention was paid to material and educational needs while emotional and nurturing components were virtually ignored. Early bouts with digestive and nervous disorders and the partial loss of hearing justify the term "delicate."

Rather than letting her past embitter or impede her personal development as an adult, M. used her own childhood experiences (described in detail in *Household Education*, 1849, and *Autobiography, with Memorials, by Maria Weston Chapman*, 1877), as a catalyst for a lengthy and impassioned articulation of the deficiencies of early-nineteenth-century beliefs on children and childhood education; in so doing, M. became an early popularizer of the theories of John Locke and David Hartley. Other examples of M.'s use of personal experience as a basis for broad social texts are *Life in the Sickroom* (1844), a description of invalidism, common among women in the nineteenth century, a book that also reads like a home-care nursing manual; and *Our Farm of Two Acres* (1865), which describes M.'s brief venture into rural living.

Much of M.'s writing appeared in journals and newspapers such as the *Edinburgh Review, Westminster Review, National Anti-Slavery Standard,* and, most especially, the *Monthly Repository.* In 1864, her essays published in the *Daily News* were compiled into a book, *Biographical Sketches,* many of which are formal obituaries of historical personages of her time. These miniature biographies eulogize such women as Amelia Opie, Charlotte Brontë, Mary Wordsworth, and Jane Marcet, and, as such, offer contemporary readers historical and biographical information regarding other women, known and unknown, of this era.

M.'s first pieces, "On Female Education" and "Female Writers on Practical Divinity," published in 1823 and 1827, reflect a constant theme of her work, that is, that any discrepancy in women's and men's capabilities was due to a disparity in education; although M. believed that educating women would certainly enhance women's status in their domestic sphere, she in no way believed that women should be relegated to that area.

Women were indeed an important subject in M.'s most noted work, *Society in America* (1837). Her keen observations regarding the status of women in a nation professing freedom of opportunity for all was certainly one of the main factors in the mixed reaction of her readership in both countries. *Society in America* as well as *Retrospect of Western Travel* (1838), a more readable tract of her observations during her two-year visit to America, and *How to Observe: Morals and Manners* (1838) are considered some of the earliest instances of the science of comparative sociology and as such won her the distinction of innovator in a field previously uncharted. Besides remaining one of the best sources of descriptive information regarding the early years of the American republic, *Society in America* is also an honest chronicle of one woman's discovery of the discrepancies between political theory and the actualities of people's lives within any social system.

M.'s reputation as a writer, which preceded her coming to America in 1834, was based principally on her *Illustra-*

tions of Political Economy. In this series, written between 1832 and 1834, she defined and illustrated, in rather stilted story form, the unfolding principles of *laissez-faire* capitalism and the concepts of progress and opportunity based on ability rather than ancestry. These popular works were originally written as separate booklets and were directed specifically at the working class in England, though they were read widely by all. Her idealistic enthusiasm regarding the mutually beneficial relationship possible between labor and capital interests was based in part on her belief that if all members of such a system understood the principles of political economy, corruption within the system was less apt to occur.

M. was first and foremost a natural journalist, never editing or changing her thoughts once they were committed to the page. This resulted in a prolific legacy (more than fifty books and pamphlets) on a surprising range of subjects and in many styles; she is considered at her best with social descriptions and at her worst with fictional accounts. *The Hour and the Man* (1841), an example of her fiction, re-creates the life of a black Haitian revolutionary and that nation's struggle for freedom from white domination. Fiction also offered a "respite" from her usual journalistic style, said M., in describing *Deerbrook* (1839), a three-volume love story.

People responded to the mature M. in extremes, from intense dislike, as was the case with George Eliot, to the devoted admiration of Maria Weston Chapman, her first biographer. Her passionate dual personality and frankness caused the loss of many friendships throughout the years, as did her association with such controversial issues as abolition, women's rights, and nontraditional forms of healing. M. remained, however, a teacher in the broadest sense of the word, an activist early called to share her observations and experiences with others through the written word. She never married but rather developed into a happily independent woman, consumed not by relationships but by her work.

WORKS: *Devotional Exercises* (1823). *Addresses, with Prayers and Original Hymns* (1826). *Principles and Practice. The Orphan Family* (1827). *Mary Campbell, or The Affectionate Granddaughter* (1828). *The Turn Out. A Tale* (1829). *Traditions of Palestine* (1830; in the U.S. as *The Times of the Saviour,* 1831). *The Essential Faith of the Universal Church* (1831). *Five Years of Youth, or Sense and Sentiment* (1831). *Sequel to Principle and Practice* (1831). *Illustrations of Political Economy,* 9 vols. (1832–34). *Prize Essays* (1832). *Poor Laws and Paupers* (1833). *Christmas Day or The Friends* (1834). *Illustrations of Taxation* (1834). *Letter to the Deaf* (1834). *The Hamlets* (1836). *Society in America,* 3 vols. (1837). *The Guide to Service* (1838). *How to Observe* (1838). *My Servant, Rachel* (1838). *Retrospect of Western Travel,* 3 vols. (1838). *Deerbrook* (1839). *The Hour and the Man,* 3 vols. (1841). *The Playfellow (The Settlers at Home; The Prince and the Peasant; Feats on the Fiord; The Crofton Boys* (1841; also pub. separately). *Life in the Sickroom* (1844). *Dawn Island. A Tale* (1845). *Letters on Mesmerism* (1845). *The Billow and the Rock* (1846). *Game Law Tales* (1846). *Eastern Life, Past and Present,* 3 vols. (1848). *The History of England during the Thirty Years' Peace,* 2 vols. (1849). *Household Education* (1849). *Two Letters on Cow-Keeping* (1850). *Introduction to the History of the Peace* (1851). *Letters on the Laws of Man's Nature and Development* (1851). *Letters from Ireland* (1852). (trans.) *The Positive Philosophy of Auguste Comte,* 2 vols. (1853). *A Complete Guide to the English Lakes* (1855). *The Factory Controversy* (1855). *A History of the American Compromises* (1856). *Sketches from Life* (1856). *British Rule in India* (1857). *Suggestions towards the Future Government of India* (1858). *Endowed Schools for Ireland* (1859). *England and her Soldiers* (1859). *Health, Husbandry and Handicraft* (1861). *Our Farm of Two Acres* (1865). *Biographical Sketches* (1869). *Autobiography, with Memorials, by Maria Weston Chapman,* 3 vols. (1877). *Harriet Martineau's Letters to Fanny Wedgewood,* ed. E. Arbuckle (1983). *Harriet Martineau on Women,* ed. G. G. Yates (1985). *Harriet Martineau: Selected Letters,* ed. V. Sanders (1990). *Women, Emancipation and Literature: The Papers of Harriet Martineau 1802–1876, From the Birmingham University Library: A Listing and Guide to the Microfilm Collection* (1991). *Harriet Martineau in the London Daily News; Selected Contributions,* ed. E. S. Arbuckle (1994).

BIBLIOGRAPHY: *Science and Sensibility: Gender and Scientific Enquiry 1780–1945,* ed. M. Benjamin (1991). Bosenquet, T. *Harriet Martineau: An Essay in Comprehension* (1927). David, D. *Intellectual Women and Victorian Patriarchy: Harriet Martineau, Elizabeth Barrett Browning, and George Eliot* (1987). Heanue, K. *No Space For the History of a Woman's Life: The Autobiography of Margaret Oliphant, Harriet Martineau and Beatrice Webb* (1991). Hoecker-Drysdale, S. *Harriet Martineau: First Woman Sociologist* (1991). Hoecker-Drysdale, S. *Harriet Martineau: A Vocational Life* (1992). Hunter, S. *Harriet Martineau: The Politics of Moralism* (1995). Miller, F. B. *Harriet Martineau* (1884). Neville, J. *Harriet Martineau* (1943). *Harriet Martineau: The Woman and Her Work,* ed. V. Pichanick (1980). Rees, J. *Writing on the Nile: Harriet Martineau, Florence Nightingale, Amelia Edwards* (1995). Sanders, V. *Reason Over Passion: Harriet Martineau and the Novel* (1986). Shackleton, J. R. *Two Early Female Economists: Jane Marcet and Harriet Martineau* (1988). Thomas G. *Harriet Martineau* (1985). Vittorio, D. *These Remarkable Little Books: A Study of the Fiction of Harriet Martineau, 1827–1840* (1987). Webb, R. K. *Harriet Martineau: A Radical Victorian* (1960). Weiner, G., in *Feminist Theorists,* ed. D. Spender (1983). Wheatley, V. *The Life and Work of Harriet Martineau* (1957). *The Slaughter-house of Mammon: An Anthology of Victorian Social Protest,* ed. S. A. Winn and L. Alexander (1992). Wong, A. *Wollenstonecraft and Martineau: The Legacies of a Pioneer Feminist and a Founding Sociologist* (1993).

For articles in reference works, see: *Allibone* and *SUP. BANC. Bloomsbury. Cassell. Chambers. DLB. Feminist. JBA. Moulton. NCHEL. OCEL. Oxford. With Women's Eyes: Visitors to the New World, 1775–1918,* ed M. Tinling (1993). *YA.*

Other references: Broughton, T. L. *L&H* (1993). Collins, K. and A. M. Cohn. *MP* (1982). Colson, P. *Vic-*

torian Portraits (1932). Culver, M. *N&Q* (1984). Dentler, R. *Midcontinent American Studies Journal* (1962). Frawley, M. H. *VN* (1992). Hobart, A. *VS* (1994). Home, R. H. *A New Spin of Age* (1844). Lever, T. *BST* (1974). Lohrli, A. *SSF* (1983). Mineka, F. E. *The Dissidence of Dissent: "The Monthly Repository," 1806–1838* (1944). Morley, J. *Critical Miscellanies* (1909). Myers, M., in *Women's Autobiography: Essays in Criticism*, ed. E. C. Jelinek (1980). Pichanick, V. *WS* (1977). Richardson, B. *PLL* (1984). Sanders, V. *N&Q* (1983). Thavenet, D. J. *Michigan Historical Review* (1993).

Valerie Kim Duckett

Mary I (Mary Tudor)

BORN: 18 February 1516, Greenwich.
DIED: 17 November 1558, London.
DAUGHTER OF: King Henry VIII and Catherine of Aragon.
MARRIED: Philip II of Spain.
WROTE UNDER: Mary Tudor.

The reign of M. is one of the shortest in English history and one of the most tragic. Fraught with civil and religious dissension, her five-year reign focused almost entirely on reuniting England with Rome. Although she is not considered one of the more popular English monarchs, she was certainly one of the most educated, having received a classical training under the careful eye of Juan Luis Vives. Fluent in several languages, M. used her intellect to produce translations of many popular religious treatises, although only one was published during her lifetime.

M., the only surviving child of King Henry VIII and his first wife, Queen Catherine of Aragon, daughter of King Ferdinand II of Aragon and Queen Isabella of Castile, was reared under the strict hand of her Roman Catholic mother and never wavered from her belief that Roman Catholicism was the one true religion. As a child and adolescent, M. spent little time with her father, who in 1533 sued her mother for divorce and married Anne Boleyn. After the birth of their daughter, Elizabeth, in 1533, the title of princess was taken from M. and given to Elizabeth. The succession act of 1534 declared her illegitimate.

Before the death of Henry in 1547, his sixth wife, Katherine Parr, a close friend of M.'s, encouraged him to include both M. and Elizabeth in a new "Act of Succession." He eventually consented to the changes, and upon his death Edward (son of Henry's third wife, Jane Seymour) was declared king, with M. to succeed him should he die without an heir. King Edward VI's reign was short (1547–53), and he usurped his father's will by signing a new act of succession that made his cousin, Lady Jane Grey, successor.

In retaliation, M. mounted an army and regained her throne on 19 July 1553. In her first parliamentary session, she legitimized her mother's marriage to Henry and began a vigorous campaign to reinstate papal authority in England, an endeavor that led to the blatant and often violent persecution of Protestants. By the time of her death, she had burned more than 300 "heretics," hence the name "Bloody Mary." Her reign, however, was not always so violent. She was also known for acts of kindness toward her subjects and for sparing the lives of many conspirators who, under any other monarch, would have met with the executioner.

Shortly after her accession, against the wishes of Parliament, M. wed her cousin, Philip II of Spain, son and heir of Holy Roman Emperor Charles V (1500–58). At the time of their marriage, she was thirty-eight years old and Philip was twenty-seven. Politically, her reign was unremarkable, and on 17 November 1558 she died at St. James Palace without an heir. Her half-sister, Elizabeth, succeeded her.

Reared entirely in England, M.'s education was strictly implemented by her mother, who believed that her daughter's education should serve to render her a more virtuous woman. A supporter of both Spanish and English intellectual thought, Catherine sought the advice of her friend and fellow Spaniard, Vives, who personally developed a master educational plan for the princess. Prior to Vives, Thomas Linacre, founder of the College of Physicians and Surgeons, oversaw M.'s education. During her many years of study, M. was able to master several languages, including Spanish, Latin, Greek, Italian, and French. She also studied the early Greek poets as well as other classical writers. In addition, she was well read in the Old and New Testaments and in the writings of the Patristic Fathers. Geography, mathematics, astronomy, music, history, and politics—especially the works of Cicero, Seneca, Plutarch, Plato, Erasmus, and Sir Thomas More—were also emphasized. By the time she reached adulthood, M. was known as one of the most educated women on the Continent; she was described by Venetian ambassador Michiel Giovanni in the following manner: "[B]esides the facility and quickness of her understanding, which comprehends whatever is intelligible to others, even to those who are not of her own sex (a marvelous gift for a woman), she is skilled in five languages, not merely understanding, but speaking four of them fluently."

Because instructors of classical languages commonly used translations as a teaching tool, it would not have been unusual for M. to have produced a number of translations as part of her education. What is unusual, however, is that one was published during her lifetime. Due largely to the prodding of the queen, Katharine Parr, M. undertook the translation of Erasmus's *Paraphrase of the Gospel of St. John*, a dense and complicated document that was completed with the help of Francis Malet. Although encouraged to use her own name, M. chose to publish anonymously. M.'s translation was incorporated into a larger project initiated by Queen Katherine that included translations of Erasmus's paraphrase on St. Mark and St. Luke by Thomas Key and Nicholas Udall, respectively, and St. Matthew and Acts by anonymous translators; the Queen may have used her skills as a translator to help bring them to completion. The entire text, entitled *The First Tome or Volume of the Paraphrases of Erasmus Upon the Newe Testamente*, was published in 1548 as a guide for Protestant theological thought. All English churches were required to purchase a copy; it is not certain whether the text was actually used by clergy and/or church officials, but a second, expanded version was published the following year.

WORKS: (trans.) *Translation of the Paraphrase of the Gospel of St. John,* in *The First Tome or Volume of the Paraphrases of Erasmus Upon the Newe Testamente,* ed. N. Udall (1548).

BIBLIOGRAPHY: Devereux, E. J. *A Checklist of English Translations of Erasmus to 1700* (1968). Devereux, E. J., in *Collected Works of Erasmus,* vol. 42, ed. R. D. Snider (1984). Erickson, C. *Bloody Mary: The Remarkable Life of Mary Tudor* (1978). Loades, D. *Mary Tudor: A Life* (1989). Perry, M. *The Word of a Prince: A Life of Elizabeth I from Contemporary Documents* (1990). *The Paradise of Women: Writings by Englishwomen of the Renaissance,* ed. B. Travitsky (1989). Waldman, M. *The Lady Mary: The Biography of Mary Tudor 1516–1558* (1972). Williams, C. H., in *English Historical Documents 1485–1558,* ed. D. C. Douglas (1967).

For articles in reference works, see: *Bloomsbury.*

Annemarie Koning Whaley

Mary, Queen of Scots (Mary Stuart)

BORN: 1542, Linlithgow Palace, Scotland.
DIED: 8 February 1587, Fotheringay Castle, Scotland.
DAUGHTER OF: James V of Scotland and Mary of Guise.
MARRIED: François, Dauphin of France, later François II, 1558; Henry Stuart, Lord Darnley, 1565; James Hepburn, Earl of Bothwell, 1567.

A center of controversy in her lifetime, M. has remained an enigma to later ages. Queen of Scotland from the sixth day of her life, she was, when a young child, sent by her mother, the queen regent, to the French court; there she was raised with the children of King François I in a scintillating, somewhat corrupt Roman Catholic atmosphere. After the death of her young husband, François II, M. elected to return to Scotland, a relatively rude, semi-feudal kingdom that was staunchly Protestant, foregoing the luxury—and the difficult intrigues—of the French court but entering tumultuous waters in Scotland. Her marriage to Darnley, her cousin, strengthened her claim to the English throne and incurred the suspicion of Queen Elizabeth I and her advisers, for in 1565 Elizabeth was still quite insecure on her throne and fearful of sedition by Roman Catholic subjects for whom M. was a rallying point. On the other hand, M. was most unappealing as a ruler to the Scottish reformed church, and her position in Scotland was also undermined by Darnley, from whom she became increasingly alienated. The birth of their son, later King James VI of Scotland and James I of England, on 19 June 1566, did not strengthen her position; Darnley refused to attend the child's christening.

It is probably impossible to determine the truth concerning M.'s involvement in the most serious of the crimes attributed to her: the murder of Darnley by the Scottish nobles, led by James Hepburn, Earl of Bothwell, on 10 February 1567. It is also impossible to be certain what her feelings for Bothwell were: whether she feared him or was passionately in love with him. What is known is that she and Bothwell were married, in a Protestant ceremony, on 15 May 1567; that the event followed a supposed kidnapping of M. by Bothwell's forces; and that it led to open, tumultuous outcries against her.She was separated forcibly from Bothwell by alienated noblemen and forced to abdicate her throne in favor of her son, James, on 24 July 1567. James, also separated from her, was raised by her enemies in the Protestant faith.

Imprisoned by her nobles in Lochleven, M. escaped and raised an army but was defeated at Langside. She then decided to throw herself on the protection of Elizabeth, her cousin and sister-queen, a political blunder that she never overcame. M. was kept in varying conditions of captivity by Elizabeth for nineteen years but finally was recognized by her cousin as a grave threat, tried for various political intrigues in which she had been embroiled, and condemned to death. She was executed in Fotheringay Castle on 8 February 1587 and interred in Petersborough. On 11 October 1612, her body was reinterred in Westminster, by order of her son.

A product of the high Renaissance in France, M. was educated by outstanding French writers. She composed occasional verse and prose at critical moments throughout her life. As George Ballard has noted, her verses have never been accorded serious attention as literature: "The many writers of her history," he states, "have been so full in their accounts of her misfortunes and tragical end, and so warmly engaged either in heightening or depressing her reputation in regard to her conduct in life, that they have almost all forgot to transmit to posterity an account of her education and what part she bore in the republic of letters." Nonetheless, her writings are indeed worthy of attention. M. did not publish them herself, but many of her pieces appeared in works by her contemporaries and others were collected after her death and printed in several collections, the most important of which are noted below.

Of her writings, the so-called casket letters and sonnets, produced at her first English trial as evidence of her complicity in the murder of Darnley, are the most contested. While the letters do speak of the assassination and may be open, therefore, to the suspicion of having been manufactured as evidence against her, the sonnets, which are truly great poems, do not implicate her in the crime but merely attest to her feelings for Bothwell. On that account, they may be more readily recognized as her own work, and they constitute a unique group of passionate love sonnets in a woman's voice. That they can easily be related to the course of M.'s association with Bothwell adds to their poignancy. Her other poetry ranges from a mourning dirge for François II to appeals to Elizabeth and a moving type of poetry of resignation and acceptance.

WORKS: *Letters, Transcripts, and Papers Relating to Mary, Queen of Scots* (1544). *The Genuine Letters of Mary, Queen of Scots* (1726). *Letters Now First Published from the Originals, Collected from Various Sources, Private as well as Public, with an Historical Introduction and Notes,* ed. A. Strickland (1843). *Recueil des Lettres et Memoires de Marie Stuart,* ed. Prince A. Labanoff (Lobanov-Rostovski) (1844).*Letters* (1845). *Latin Themes of Mary Stuart,* ed. A. de Montaignon (1855). *Poems of*

Mary Queen of Scots, ed. J. Sharman (1873). *Queen Mary's Book, A Collection of Poems and Essays by Mary Queen of Scots*, ed. Mrs. P.S.M. Arbuthnot (1907). *Last Letter of Mary Queen of Scotland Addressed to her brother in law Henry III King of France on the night before her execution at Fotheringay Castle 8th February 1587* (1927). *Collection de Manuscrits, Livres Estampés et Objects d'art relatifs à Marie Stuart, Reine de France et D'Ecosse* (1931). *Poems of Mary Queen of Scots, to the Earl of Bothwell* (1932). (supposed author) *Silver Casket: Being Love-Letters and Love-Poems Attributed to Mary Stuart, Queen of Scots*, ed. and trans. C. Bax (1946). *Bittersweet Within My Heart: The Collected Poems of Mary, Queen of Scots*, ed. R. Bell (1992).

BIBLIOGRAPHY: Angus, D. *Review of Scottish Culture* (1987). Fraser, A. *Mary, Queen of Scots* (1969). Hays, M. *Female Biography* (1807). Strickland, A. *Life of Mary Stuart, Queen of Scots* (1907). Tannenbaum, S. *Elizabethan Bibliographies. X. Marie Stuart* (1946). Thomson, G. M. *The Crime of Mary Stuart* (1967). *Paradise of Women*, ed. B. Travitsky (1981). Warnicke, R. M. *Women of the English Renaissance and Reformation* (1983). Williams, J. *Literary Women of England* (1861). Wormald, Jenny. *Mary Queen of Scots A Study in Failure* (1988).

For articles in reference works, see: *Ballard. Bloomsbury. DNB. Europa. IDWB.*

Betty Travitsky

Damaris Masham

BORN: 1658.
DIED: 1708.
DAUGHTER OF: Ralph Cudworth and Damaris Cradock Cudworth.
MARRIED: Sir Francis Masham, 1685.

M., the daughter of Cambridge Platonist Ralph Cudworth, carried on a spirited theological debate with Mary Astell and played the roles of correspondent, friend, and biographer to John Locke. An early friendship with John Norris, another English Platonist, gradually melted away as M. grew closer to Locke's pragmatism, and her critiques of Astell's theories defended women's education and women's rights in her discussions of theology.

Despite a lack of formal schooling, M. seems to have been taught by her father, and Locke also offered some guidance in her studies. M. met Locke in 1681, and they carried on an extensive correspondence that ranged from playful flirtations to discussions of domestic matters to theoretical debates, in a series of letters between "Philoclea" and "Philander." Locke wrote of M. that she was "so well versed in theological and philosophical studies, and of such an original mind, that you will not find many men to whom she is not superior in wealth of knowledge and ability to profit by it." Ironically referring to herself as "your Governess," M. exchanged books and recommendations with Locke, and they debated some of the ideas that Locke would eventually publish in his *Essay Concerning Human Understanding*. In his letters to M., Locke teases her, calling her an "Enthusiast," and she questions his attacks on enthusiasm. Although their letters sometimes seem romantic, there is no evidence that their relationship was more than a platonic friendship. In 1685, M. married Sir Francis Masham, a widower and father of nine children, and she gave birth to one son, Francis Cudworth Masham. By 1691, she had convinced Locke to move to Oates, the Masham estate; he lived there until his death in 1704, taking an active role in M.'s finances and family life. After Locke's death, M. wrote a short biography of her friend, which was published in the *Great Historical Dictionary*.

In 1690, John Norris of Bemerton dedicated his "Reflections upon the Conduct of Human Life" to M., with whom he corresponded for several years. They grew less intimate as M. came under the influence of Locke, however, and M. was to attack what she saw as the high-flown idealism of Norris and Astell. In a battle between hidden adversaries, Astell and M. exchanged critiques as they developed their ideas about religion, reason, and women's philosophy. They never named each other in their assaults on each other's ideas, and both were at times uncertain of the other's identity. Paradoxically, Astell's *A Serious Proposal to the Ladies* (1694) was at first attributed by many to M. In 1696, M. anonymously published *A Discourse Concerning the Love of God*, in which she attacked the published letters between Norris and Astell. M. criticized their abstract ideas, which she said ignored the real world. Astell returned the fire with *Christian Religion as Profess'd By a Daughter of the Church* (1705), addressed mainly to Locke, whom she believed was the author of *Discourse*. In *Occasional Thoughts in Reference to a Vertuous or Christian Life* (written in 1700, published in 1705), M. replies with her own, more down-to-earth version of a woman's proper Christian philosophy. She defends Locke on government, education, and reason and advises women to educate themselves while they educate their children. At the same time, M. criticizes the lack of women's education and society's double standards for men and women. M.'s strong feelings about the way men oppressed women are evident in a poem she earlier sent to Locke. M. wrote that she hoped relations between the sexes would change in heaven: "And our weake sex I hope will then / Disdaine yt stupid ignorance/wch was at first impos'd by men / their owne high merits to inhance."

WORKS: *A Discourse Concerning the Love of God* (1696). *Occasional Thoughts in Reference to a Vertuous or Christian life* (1705). Biography of John Locke in *La Bibliothèque universelle* (MS at University of Amsterdam, n.d.).

BIBLIOGRAPHY: *The Correspondence of John Locke II*, ed. E. S. DeBeer (1976). Laslett, P. *History Today* (1953). O'Donnell, S., in *Mothering the Mind: Twelve Studies of Writers and Their Silent Partners*, ed. R. Perry and M. Watson Brownley (1984).

For articles in reference works, see: *Ballard. DNB. Europa. Feminist.*

Other references: Cranston, M. W. *John Locke: A Biography* (1957). O'Donnell, S. *SECC* (1978). Perry, R. *The Celebrated Mary Astell* (1986).

Jennie Dear

Matchless Orinda: See *Philips, Katherine*

Matilda, Rose: See *Dacre, Charlotte*

Ethelind Frances Colburn Mayne

BORN: 7 January 1865, Johnstown, County Kilkenny, Ireland.
DIED: 30 April 1941, Torquay, Devon.
DAUGHTER OF: Charles Edward Bolton Mayne and Charlotte Emily Henrietta Sweetman Mayne.
WROTE UNDER: Frances E. Huntley (1895–97, in the *Yellow Book* and *Chapman's Magazine*); Ethel Colburn Mayne.

Short-story writer, novelist, translator, biographer, literary critic, journalist, and editor, M. has not been well remembered for any of her myriad professional roles. Perhaps her best-known work, a two-volume biography of Lord Byron once lauded by reviewers as "superseding all others," has itself been long since supplanted. Widely respected in her day for the distinctive quality of her translations, M. was nevertheless obliged to pitch suggestions to publishers assiduously in order to guarantee herself a living. Indeed, although her first major translation, *Confessions of a Princess* (1906), became a bestseller, M. received only the standard modest fee for it; she even had to press the publisher repeatedly for the complimentary copies to which she was entitled. (She also received no credit for the translation because she declined to have her name on the title page of such a risqué work.) Possibly the most significant oversight of literary history, however, has been its failure to note M.'s association with "the most important and notorious" of the avant-garde literary periodicals of the *fin de siècle*, the *Yellow Book*. Not only were three of her short stories published in its pages (a fourth that had been accepted never appeared), but in 1896 M. also worked as an assistant editor for Henry Harland, the *Yellow Book*'s literary editor, replacing Ella D'Arcy, "who had hitherto acted in that capacity," when D'Arcy left England "for a stay in France."

To be fair, M. did not help to promote or even preserve herself for posterity. Unlike her close friend Violet Hunt, whose beauty and scathing wit supplemented her talents as a writer, M. was instead rather plain, quiet, and reserved. Whereas Hunt achieved notoriety for her scandalous liaison with Ford Madox Ford, M. steered clear of intrigues, living most of her life with her sister and never marrying. And in practical terms, from the standpoint of the literary historian, M. did not even leave a will when she died, much less the diaries, notes, and detailed instructions for their disposition that Hunt so shrewdly left behind. As a result, her memory is largely derived from the handful of memoirs by literary figures in which she is mentioned, most of which describe her relatively late in her career, when she had already produced a solidly respectable body of work in both fiction and nonfiction. She ultimately became friendly with a number of more famous writers, from her own generation and that of "*les jeunes*," including from the former group such eminent figures as Lady Ottoline Morrell and Marie Belloc Lowndes and from the latter the novelist Hugh Walpole and the dramatist Clifford Bax.

Though it may have been true that her one "grand passion" was Byron (as some have alleged), M. held an almost worshipful lifelong regard for her mentor, Henry Harland, with whom she first became acquainted through a vigorous correspondence begun in 1895 following his acceptance of her story, "A Pen-and-ink Effect," for the *Yellow Book*. When, later that year, he offered her the opportunity to assist him in "what he called the 'derisory' post of his sub-editor," M. accepted his invitation with understandable enthusiasm. She arrived in London in January 1896, but stayed only until June, due to D'Arcy's (unexpected) return.

Despite the brevity of their working relationship, Harland had a lasting impact on M.'s work. The title of her first volume of short stories, *The Clearer Vision* (1898), is taken from a phrase of Harland's describing the object of his quest for excellence in writing: "the newly-minted phrase or word . . . coming of itself to the 'clearer vision' of a consciousness humbly alive to its waiting presence." She also shared Harland's reverence for Henry James—"the Master"—causing more than one reviewer to note James's influence on her style (particularly in her short stories), most notably in the subtlety of its psychological insights and the manner of the dialogue. In addition, her appreciation for the poetry of Robert Browning could not have helped but be enhanced by Harland's constantly quoting from *The Ring and the Book*. In the preface to her 1913 literary study, *Browning's Heroines*, M. fondly recalled "the editor of that golden Quarterly reading, declaiming, quoting, almost breathing Browning! . . . A hundred Browning verses sing themselves around my memories of the flat in Cromwell Road."

M. published her first novel, *Jessie Vandeleur*, in 1902, and left Ireland for London with her younger sister in 1905. Although it received positive reviews, the novel was not a commercial success, a fact that caused M. both to blame its publisher, George Allen, and to despair of ever writing anything the public would like. She supported herself with journalism and translations while working on her next novel, *The Fourth Ship* (1908). Originally titled "Miss," it offers a dark psychological study of Josie, an "unintellectual" woman who is thwarted in love and life, the apparent antithesis of the eponymous protagonist of *Jessie Vandeleur*, whom one reviewer had called a "take-all-I-can-get-from-life kind of heroine." Despite its less-than-upbeat storyline, *The Fourth Ship* received critical praise and fared well with the public—better, in fact, than either M. or her publisher, Chapman and Hall, had dared to hope. It was soon followed by M.'s second collection of stories, *Things That No One Tells* (1910), which won less notice despite its more titillating title.

Not unlike the work of a number of female authors at the time—and of their immediate predecessors, the New Women writers of the 1890s—M.'s novels and short stories deal primarily with such bleak and "morbid" topics as the bitterness of women abandoned by their lovers and the futility of trying to renew lost love as well as such hotly debated issues as the imbalance of power between the sexes and the injustices inherent in social conventions. The heroines of M.'s other two novels, *Gold Lace: A Study of Girlhood* (1913) and *One of Our Grandmothers* (1916), are similar, respectively, to the first two. In *Gold Lace,* Rhoda is seen by some (readers and characters alike) as cold and heartless, by others as strong and independent minded, much as Jessie was viewed; both women might be called "feminists," but at that time the term could be meant pejoratively. In *One of Our Grandmothers,* Millie might be pitied for being thrown over by her lover or admired for her nobility of character, just as Josie was. In each case, the element of undecidability is integral to the narrative.

Although M.'s last novel was published in 1916, she produced four more collections of short stories between 1917 and 1925 and two biographies and eight translations between 1925 and 1939. Several of her stories also appeared in such periodicals as *The Transatlantic Review* and *Life and Letters,* and they were reprinted in a number of contemporary anthologies, including *Georgian Stories* (1922, 1926, and 1927), *The Best British Short Stories* (1923 and 1931), *Great Short Stories of Detection, Mystery, and Horror* (1928), and *The Faber Book of Modern Stories* (1937); in addition, "A Pen-and-ink Effect" was included in the more recent anthology *Femmes de Siècle* (1990). It is unfortunate that, despite the range and extent of M.'s output, the only works that have much opportunity of being read today are these few anthologized stories (and possibly her biographies of Byron and Lady Byron), which can still be found at least in many university libraries. If, however, one should undertake to locate and read any of M.'s other work, her uncommonly sensitive and nuanced style promises to more than repay the effort.

WORKS: *The Clearer Vision* (1898). *Jessie Vandeleur* (1902). (trans.) *Confessions of a Princess* (1906). (trans.) *The Diary of a Lost One,* by "Thymian," ed. M. Bohme (1907). (trans.) *Louise de la Vallière and the Early Life of Louis XIV,* by Jules Lair (1908). *The Fourth Ship* (1908). *Enchanters of Men* (1909). *The Romance of Monaco and Its Rulers* (1910). *Things That No One Tells* (1910). (trans.) *The Lessons of Raoul Pugno,* by Raoul Pugno (1911). (trans.) *Casanova and His Time,* by Edouard Maynial (1911). *Byron* (1912). (trans.) *My Friendship with Prince Hohenlohe,* by Alexandrine von Hedemann (1912). (trans.) *The Department Store,* by M. Böehme (1912). *Browning's Heroines* (1913). *Gold Lace: A Study of Girlhood* (1913). (trans.) *Letters of Fyodor Michailovitch Dostoevsky to His Family and Friends* (1914). *One of Our Grandmothers* (1916). *Come In* (1917). *Blindman* (1919). *Nine of Hearts* (1923). *Inner Circle* (1925). (trans.) *Madame de Pompadour,* by Marcelle Tinayre (1925). (trans.) *Kaiser Wilhelm II,* by Emil Ludwig (1926). (trans.) *Goethe: The History of a Man, 1749–1832,* by Emil Ludwig (1928). (trans., with J. F. Muirhead) *Selected Poems of Carl Spitteler* (1928). *The Life and Letters of Anne Isabella, Lady Noel Byron: From Unpublished Papers in the Possession of the Late Ralph, Earl of Lovelace* (1929). (trans.) *The Forest Ship: A Book of the Amazon,* by Richard Bermann (1930). (trans.) *Philip Eulenburg, the Kaiser's Friend,* by Johannes Haller (1930). (trans.) *Three Titans,* by Emil Ludwig (1930). (trans.) *Byron and the Need of Fatality,* by Charles du Bos (1932). *A Regency Chapter: Lady Bessborough and Her Friendships* (1939).

BIBLIOGRAPHY: Bullett, G. *Modern English Fiction: A Personal View* (1926). Ford, F. M. *Thus to Revisit . . . Some Reminiscences* (1921). Gould, G. *The English Novel of To-Day* (1924). Hunt, V. *I Have This to Say* (1926). Mix, K. L. *A Study in Yellow: The Yellow Book and Its Contributors* (1960). Stetz, M. and M. S. Lasner. *The Yellow Book: A Centenary Exhibition* (1994). Swinnerton, F. *Background with Chorus* (1956). West, R. *Ending in Earnest: A Literary Log* (1931).

For articles in reference works, see: *Daims. ELB. Grimes. Longman. Manly. Millett. NCHEL. TCA.*

Susan Waterman

M. B.: See *Lamb, Mary Ann*

Meade, Mrs.: See *Pilkington, Laetitia*

Mary Meeke

DIED: 1816, Staffordshire.
MARRIED: the Reverend Francis Meeke.
WROTE UNDER: Gabrielli; Mary Meeke.

During her lifetime, M. was a prolific and successful writer of Gothic fiction; one of the most popular of the Minerva Press writers for twenty years, she wrote thirty-four books and translations. Despite her best-selling status, little is known of her life. The widow of the Reverend Francis Meeke (d. 1801) is recorded as having died at Staffordshire in 1816, and this woman was probably the novelist. It has been suggested that her frequent pseudonym, "Gabrielli," was her maiden name and thus indicative of M.'s Italian origin; no biographical facts, however, substantiate this claim.

M.'s first novel, *Count St. Blancard, or the Prejudiced Judge* (1795), established the plot pattern that would dominate her novels. In it, the talented but untitled Dr. Dubois is prevented from courting his true love by the difference in their ranks; by the end of the novel, however, various plot twists have revealed the young doctor to be the son of President de Ransal, a man of rank and wealth. Dubois ends the novel happily united with his love. This story is typical of M.'s novels, as Thomas Babington Macaulay, an admirer of M., commented in a letter to his sister: "My tastes, I fear, are incredibly vulgar," he admits; her books are "one just like another, turning on the fortunes of some young man in a very low rank of life who eventually proves to be the son of a duke."

The second of M.'s novels to be published under "Gabrielli," *The Mysterious Wife* (1797), adds a twist to this story: Here it is not the hero but the heroine who discovers her impressive true heritage. Despite the minor variations in plot and the introduction of exotic locales, the formulaic nature of M.'s works may have led to her critical devaluation in this century. The *Dictionary of National Biography* comments that "her plots are commonplace, and her literary style poor, and her characters only faintly reflect contemporary manners"; the editors of *British Authors of the Nineteenth Century* can only offer that "her work is pure trash of the commercial variety." Indeed, in the introduction to *Midnight Weddings* (1802), she suggests that aspiring authors ought to consult their publishers regarding popular taste to ensure commercial success. Today, of all her works, only *Count St. Blancard* has been reprinted, and that in a facsimile edition.

WORKS: (as Gabrielli) *Count St. Blancard, or the Prejudiced Judge* (1795; facsimile, 1977). *The Abbey of Clugny* (1795). (as Gabrielli) *The Mysterious Wife* (1797). *Palmira and Ermance* (1797). (as Gabrielli) *The Sicilian* (1798). *Ellesmere* (1799). (as Gabrielli) *Harcourt* (1799). (as Gabrielli) *Anecdotes of the Altamont Family* (1800). *Which is the Man?* (1801). (as Gabrielli) *Mysterious Husband* (1801). *Midnight Weddings* (1802). (as Gabrielli) *Independence* (1802). *A Tale of Mystery, or Celina* (1803). *Amazement!* (1804). *The Nine Days' Wonder* (1804). (as Gabrielli) *Something Odd* (1804). *The Old Wife and the Young Husband* (1804). (trans.) *Lobenstein Village*, by Augustus La Fontaine (1804). *The Wonder of the Village* (1805). (as Gabrielli) *Something Strange* (1806). (trans.) *Julian, or My Father's House*, by Ducrai Dumenil (1807). *There is a Secret, Find It Out!* (1808). (as Gabrielli) *Laughton Priory* (1809). (trans., as Gabrielli) *The Unpublished Correspondence of Madame du Deffand with d'Alambert, Montesquieu, etc.* (1810). (as Gabrielli) *Strategems Defeated* (1811). *Matrimony, the Height of Bliss, or the Extreme of Misery* (1812). *Conscience* (1814). (trans.) *Elizabeth, or the Exiles of Siberia*, by Sophie Cottin (1814). (trans.) *Paul et Virginie*, by Jacques Henri Bernardin de Saint-Pierre (1814). (trans.) *Solyman and Almena*, by John Langhorne (1814). *The Spanish Campaign; or, The Jew* (1815). *The Veiled Protectress; or, the Mysterious Mother* (1819). *What Shall Be, Shall Be* (1823). *The Parent's Offering to a Good Child: A Collection of Interesting Tales* (c. 1825). *The Birthday Present, or Pleasing Tales of Amusement and Instruction* (1830).

BIBLIOGRAPHY: Blakey, D. *The Minerva Press 1790–1820* (1939). Frank, F. *The First Gothics* (1987). Garrett, J., intro. to *Count St. Blancard* (1977). Summers, M. *The Gothic Quest* (1938). Varma, D. P. *The Gothic Flame* (1951). Varma, D. P. *The Evergreen Tree* (1972).

For articles in reference works, see *BA19C. DLB. DNB. Feminist. Oxford. ToddBWW. ToddDBA.*

Rebecca P. Bocchicchio

Melvill, Elizabeth: See *Colville, Elizabeth*

Charlotte Mew

BORN: 15 November 1869, London.
DIED: 24 March 1928, London.
DAUGHTER OF: Frederick Mew and Anna Kendall Mew.

The life of M. lacked outward event, but her inner life possessed enormously complex vitality and intensity of feeling. Incompatible emotions warred within her, as the personae in her writings reveal. Whenever sexual desire arises, religious or moral renunciation blocks its expression. Obsession with death dominated everything she wrote. For none of her deepest longings could she find satisfying outlets in her life; she could find them only in her writing. Erotic love, religion, and death are the three great irreconcilable themes that create almost unbearable tensions in her poetry and prose. Although her output is quantitatively small—sixty-eight poems, eighteen stories, and thirteen essays—it is of the highest quality, utterly genuine and moving, deserving the praise it won from writers and critics in her lifetime and after. If she had written nothing but the seventeen poems of *The Farmer's Bride*, Louis Untermeyer commented, they "would have been sufficient to rank her among the most distinct and intense" of modern poets.

The bare facts of M.'s biography do little to explain her accomplishments. Her father, Frederick Mew, an architect, married his partner's daughter: of their seven children, two died in infancy, one died at the age of five, and two finished their lives in mental institutions. M. grew close to her remaining sister, Anne, four years her junior. Believing their siblings' insanity to be hereditary, they both pledged not to marry lest their offspring inherit the family madness. This pledge must have been costly to M., for her writing shows an appreciation and enjoyment of children and also a profound intuition of the human need for sexual intimacy. Her inner religious standards, high and severe, must, however, ultimately account for her constricted life.

M. began writing short stories in the 1890s. She published the first of these, "Passed," in *The Yellow Book* in 1894 and between 1900 and 1912 also published some poetry. In 1913, she met the novelist May Sinclair, who admired and encouraged her work;she also met Alida Monro, wife of Harold Monro, owner of the Poetry Bookshop and later the publisher of her collection, *The Farmer's Bride* (1916). The volume received discriminating critical notice and made a strong impression on such writers as Virginia Woolf, Hugh Walpole, the poet laureate Robert Bridges, and especially on Thomas Hardy, who invited M. to visit him at Max Gate. Hardy was the one writer who, of all her contemporaries, she most admired and to whose work her own is most often compared.

M.'s mother and sister both became ill early in the 1920s and, as caring for them absorbed all her energies, she wrote very little from then on. Their financial situation was desperate until 1922 when Hardy, John Masefield, and Walter de la Mare procured for M. a Civil List pension of £75 a year. Her mother died in 1923 and her sister in 1927. In 1928, M. entered a nursing home for treatment of neurasthenia; there, apparently fearing that she, too, was losing her mind, she committed suicide by drinking half a bottle of Lysol.

Death following renounced or thwarted love is a predominant motif in all her work. Sometimes religious principle causes the renunciation, as in the stories "An Open Door" and "In the Curé's Garden." Sometimes, as in the stories "The China Bowl," "A Wedding Day," and "White World," parental love jealously opposes marital love; only death brings resolution. Missed opportunity is an abiding theme, as in "Passed" and "The Bridegroom's Friend."

Even in the fairy tale "The Smile," the struggling heroine dies as she reaches the goddess of happiness, for the goddess happened not to be watching the struggle and so could not reward it, a paradigm of M.'s life.

Irreconcilable conflict between sexual desire and spiritual aspiration is also a principal theme of her poems, which are excellently crafted, economical in language, and usually in the form of rhymed odes. Often the poem is an interior monologue expressing the intense subjectivity of a persona clearly not the poet herself. These personae are often drawn from the fishing villages of England or France, since M. was deeply attracted to French literature and to Roman Catholic France, as is seen in the essay "Notes in a Brittany Convent" and the poem "The Little Portress (St. Gilda de Rhuys)." Although Christian in her thinking, she never became a Roman Catholic.

Rural settings also enabled her to express her profound love of the natural world, which she described in her essay, "A Country Book." The long poem "Madeleine in Church," the interior monologue of a prostitute, a modern Mary Magdalen, expresses M.'s doubts concerning God's forgiveness and eternal life. The motif of "really seeing," of the intense look, recurs frequently in M.'s work. The eyes of two beings meet in passionate contact to express boundless emotions beyond speech, as in "Ken," a poignant poem about an idiot-madman taken to an institution. The intense look also often signals falling in love, as in "The Fête," the monologue of an enamoured adolescent boy who feels "half-hidden, white unrest" watching a circus performer.

Sexual love is characteristically linked to and countermanded by its inevitable contrary, religious feeling. Sexual love is by no means always the debased activity of a Madeleine or a Pecheresse. Often, it is a sublime ideal of union precluded by death, as in the moving poem, "In Nunhead Cemetery." This interior monologue is spoken by a male persona, a husband to a dead wife, but, as Nunhead Cemetery is the actual burial-place of M.'s brother Henry, the emotions in it may be seen as transmutations of her own. Here, as often in M., grief is mixed with and heightened by sexual longing put in terms of burning. Burning suggests flames, the color red, and the red rose, all of which she uses with the traditional symbolism of sexual passion, as in "The Quiet House," a poem that she described as "perhaps the most subjective to me" of the poems in *The Farmer's Bride.* The female persona, a daughter kept home to care for an ailing father, muses: "When you are burned quite through you die. / Red is the strangest pain to bear; / . . . A rose can stab you across the street / Deeper than any knife: / And the crimson haunts you everywhere—." M. once said of herself: "I have a scarlet soul." Here the *persona* continues: "I think that my soul is red / Like the soul of a sword or a scarlet flower: / But when these are dead / They have had their hour. / I shall have had mine, too, / For from head to feet, / I am burned and stabbed half through, / And the pain is deadly sweet." The oxymoron of "deadly sweet pain" sums up M.'s being. The poem's final words convey her strange premonitory self-understanding and read almost as an epitaph:"No one for me—I think it is myself I go to meet; / I do not care; some day I shall not think; I shall not be!"

WORKS: *The Farmer's Bride* (1916). *Saturday Market* (1921). *The Rambling Sailor* (1929). *Collected Poems,* ed. A. Monro (1953). *Collected Poems and Prose,* ed. V. Warner (1981).

BIBLIOGRAPHY: Fitzgerald, P. *Charlotte Mew and Her Friends* (1988). Hedberg, J. *MSpr* (1974, 1989). *Friends of a Lifetime: Letters to Sydney Carlyle Cockerell,* ed. V. Meynell (1940). Mizejewski, L. *TSLL* (1984). Monro, A., intro. to *Collected Poems of Charlotte Mew* (1953). Monro, H. *Some Contemporary Poets* (1920). Moore, V. *Distinguished Women Writers* (1934). Schmidt, M. *A Reader's Guide to Fifty Modern British Poets* (1979). Swinnerton, F. *The Georgian Literary Scene, 1910–1935: A Panorama* (1950). Untermeyer, L. *Modern British Poetry* (1962). Warner, V., intro. to *Charlotte Mew: Collected Poems and Prose* (1981). Williams-Ellis, A. *An Anatomy of Poetry* (1922).

For articles in reference works, see: *CP. OCEL. TCA. TCLC.*

Other references: *American Book Review* (1989). *ASch* (1988). *Bookman* (May 1928). *Bulletin of the New York Public Library* (1970, 1971). *Bulletin of Research in the Humanities* (1978). *Encounter* (June 1954). *ELT* (1989). *LRB* (1982). *Nation* (8 July 1916). *NYRB* (1987). *NYTBR* (19 June 1921, August 1988). *TLS* (19 October 1984, 28 April 1995).

Jane Augustine

Alice Meynell

BORN: 11 October 1847, Barnes, Surrey.
DIED: 17 November 1922, London.
DAUGHTER OF: Thomas James Thompson and Christiana Weller.
MARRIED: Wilfred Meynell, 1877.
WROTE UNDER: Alice Meynell; A. C. Thompson.

Though M.'s literary output also included essays, art history, travel writing, literary criticism, translations, anthologies, and editorial work, it was primarily her poetry that brought her fame in her day. A prominent late Victorian, Edwardian, and mid-Georgian writer, her reputation, along with that of Christina Rossetti, whose aesthetic and religious interests she generally shares, suffered eclipse in the twentieth century. Critical admiration for her restrained, stylistically simple, and rhythmically disciplined verse is now returning, and her *oeuvre* is ripe for re-evaluation.

In recent years, feminist literary critics have become increasingly drawn to the story of M.'s life as an example of an "early superwoman" who successfully fused a marriage of equal partners with a family (seven living children) and career while working on women's issues such as suffrage and peace. A woman of passionate attachments to male mentors—most prominently, a Father Augustus Dignam (her early spiritual guide), Francis Thompson (no relation), Coventry Patmore, and George Meredith—she managed to maintain her marriage, busy social life, and maternal obligations while turning out a large and varied body of writing.

The daughter of independently wealthy, culturally enlightened parents, M. was educated by daily tutorials and a life lived, in alternate seasons, in northern Italy and England. Brought up among adults and books, she wrote poems as early as seven years old and resolved to be a poet. Her famous protest, written in her diary at the age of eighteen, signals her seriousness of purpose: "Of all the crying evils in the depraved earth . . . the greatest, judged by all the laws of God and humanity, is the miserable selfishness of men that keeps women from work." But her diaries also reveal her struggle to balance her dedication to work with an equal interest in an active life among people.

Converting to Roman Catholicism at the age of twenty, she caught the eye of Aubrey de Vere, and, through his interest, of Patmore, Alfred Lord Tennyson, and Henry King, who admired her work. *Preludes* (1875), her first book of poems, earned praise from John Ruskin, Christina Rossetti, George Eliot, and others, placing her as a late-Romantic of notable stylistic economy. Her poetic themes in this first volume foreshadow her consistent poetic interests throughout her life: love, time, process, religious faith, poetic inspiration, and nature.

Her marriage to Wilfred Meynell in 1877 presages the shift in her attention from poetry to journalism, piece work against deadlines that she evidently found most compatible with raising seven children, including the novelist and short-story writer Viola Meynell. The Meynells established and co-edited the short-lived *Pen: A Journal of Literature* (1880); in 1881, her husband became owner and editor of *The Weekly Register,* a stable source of income for the next eighteen years. In addition, he founded *Merry England,* a literary magazine. M. wrote for these journals as well as for *The Spectator, The Saturday Review, The Scots* (later *The National*), *The Observer, The Tablet,* and *The Pall Mall Gazette.* Turning to prose writing in the 1880s and 1890s, she suspended poetry publishing until 1896.

When her husband sold *The Weekly Register* in 1899, M. began to travel again, lecturing across the United States in 1901–1902, the date of her *Later Poems.* She remained an active writer for the rest of her life. Between 1903 and 1911, her literary output included brief essays on Wordsworth, Tennyson, Robert and Elizabeth Barrett Browning, Shelley, Keats, Herrick, Coleridge, Cowper, Arnold, Rossetti, Ingelow, and Blake for Blackie's *Red Letter Library. Poems* (1913) contained reissued poems as well as several new ones. In spite of her busy family life, she published four books of poetry during World War I. Though in failing health, she wrote twenty-five new poems in the last three years of her life, dying in 1922 at the end of a long and productive literary, social, and family life.

Modern critics fault M.'s essays for humorlessness, overprecious satirical slant, and impressionistic and underdeveloped ideas. Most of her essays, composed to fit the format of the editorial column, lack elaborately reasoned arguments. Yet it was just these qualities that earned her the praise of contemporaries as one of the first successful female literary critics and popular essayists, one who never overwrote and who left room for the reader's interpretation.

The key to both her life and art lies in the word "discipline." Among her elegant, austere lyrics, her religious poems have earned special attention for their highly controlled expression of moral, rather than mystical, religious consciousness and their lack of sentimentality. Her poetic ideas about religion emphasize a life of renunciation and understated stoicism, and she was regarded as one of England's most important Roman Catholic poets of her day.

M.'s important ties to many of the famous writers of her period occasion her biographer's description of her as a woman paradoxically surrounded by friends and admirers, yet solitary at the core. Contemporary accounts suggest that no one in her circle really felt he or she knew M. She was somewhat of an enigma to those closest to her, both welcoming relationships and protecting her privacy. In the midst of an unusually rich and interesting private life among gifted writers, she produced her highly disciplined poems and economical essays that shield as much as they reveal.

WORKS: (as A. C. Thompson) *Preludes* (1875). *The Poor Sisters of Nazareth* (1889). (with F. W. Farrar) *William Holman Hunt, His Life and Work* (1893). *Poems* (1893, 1896). *The Rhythm of Life and Other Essays* (1893, 1896). (trans.) *Lourdes: Yesterday, To-Day and To-Morrow,* by D. Barbe (1894). *The Colour of Life and Other Essays on Things Seen and Heard* (1896). *Other Poems* (1896). *The Children* (1897). *London Impressions* (1898). *The Spirit of Place and Other Essays* (1899). *John Ruskin* (1900). (trans.) *The Madonna,* by A. Venturi (1901). *Later Poems* (1902). *Children of the Old Masters: Italian School* (1903). (trans.) *The Nun,* by R. Bazin (1908). *Ceres' Runaway and Other Essays* (1909). *Mary, the Mother of Jesus* (1912, 1923). *Childhood* (1913). *Poems* (1913). *Essays* (1914). *The Shepherdess and Other Verses* (1914). (trans.) *Pastoral Letter of His Eminence Cardinal Mercier, Archbishop of Malines, Primate of Belgium* (1915). *Ten Poems* (1915). *Poems on the War* (1916). *Hearts of Controversy* (1917). *A Father of Women and Other Poems* (1917). *The Second Person Singular and Other Essays* (1921). *The Last Poems of Alice Meynell* (1923). *The Poems of Alice Meynell, Complete Edition* (1923). *Essays of To-day and Yesterday* (1926). *Wayfaring* (1929). *Selected Poems of Alice Meynell,* ed. F. Meynell (1930). *The Poems of Alice Meynell,* ed. F. Page (1940). *The Poems of Alice Meynell, 1847–1923, Centenary Edition,* ed. F. Meynell (1947, 1955). *Alice Meynell: Prose and Poetry, Centenary Edition,* ed. F. Page, V. Meynell, O. Sowerby, and F. Meynell (1947). *The Wares of Autolycus: Selected Literary Essays,* ed. P. M. Fraser (1965).

BIBLIOGRAPHY: Alexander, C. *The Catholic Literary Revival* (1935). Anson, J. S. *SMy* (1986). Badeni, J. *The Slender Tree: A Life of Alice Meynell* (1981). Brégy, K. *The Poets Chantry* (1912). Burnett, A. D. *N&Q* (1984). *Alice Meynell: Centenary Tribute, 1847–1947,* ed. T. L. Connolly (1948). Crisp, S. J. *Explicator* (1991). Dixon, E. *As I Knew Them* (1930). Mais, S.P.B. *Books and Their Writers* (1920). *The Letters of George Meredith to Alice Meynell, 1896–1907* (1923). Meynell, F. *Alice Meynell, 1847–1922: Catalogs of the Centenary Exhibition of Books, Manuscripts, Letters and Portraits* (1947). Meynell, V. *Alice Meynell: A Memoir* (1929). Meynell,

V. *Francis Thompson and Wilfred Meynell, A Memoir* (1952). Noyes, A. *Some Aspects of Modern Poetry* (1924). Sedelak, V. F. *MAWAR* (1982). Sewell, B. *CRev* (1982). Smulders, S. *ELT* (1993). Tuell, A. K. *Mrs. Meynell and Her Literary Generation* (1925).

For articles in reference works, see: *DLB. 1890s. Feminist. ToddBWW. VB.*

Other references: Bluen, H. *Aryan Path* (May 1966). Evans, I. *English Poetry in the Later Nineteenth Century* (1933). Fairchild, H. N. *Religious Trends in English Poetry* (1962). Meynell, F. *My Lives* (1971). Moore, V. *Distinguished Women Writers* (1934). Schlack, B. A. *WS* (1980).

Rhoda Flaxman
(updated by Natalie Joy Woodall)

Viola Meynell

BORN: 15 October 1885, London.
DIED: 27 October 1956, Greatham, Sussex.
DAUGHTER OF: Wilfrid Meynell and Alice Thompson Meynell.
MARRIED: John Dallyn, 1922.

M., whose works have been unfairly neglected since her death, was a novelist and short-story writer with a considerable reputation for fiction that combined beauty of language with acute psychological analysis.

One of seven children of the poet Alice Meynell (to whom she was especially devoted) and the journalist Wilfrid Meynell, she grew up in a literary and Roman Catholic atmosphere in London, where she attended the nearby school of the Sisters of Sion as a day student. Her first novel, *Martha Vine* (1910), is an effective blend of love story and tale of spiritual rebirth; in later life, it remained the only one of her early novels that she valued. *Cross-in-Hand Farm* (1911) and *Lot Barrow* (1913) are naturalistic stories of village life that reveal the influence of George Eliot and Thomas Hardy but are marked by her own Roman Catholic sensibility, with emphasis on moral transgression and redemption.

After her father bought property near Greatham, Sussex, in 1911, she increasingly divided her time between the country and London. One of many literary visitors at Greatham was D. H. Lawrence, who stayed with the family for six months in 1915; M. helped him type the manuscript of *The Rainbow.* That same year, Lawrence published a story about the family, "England, My England," which the Meynells felt treated them unfairly, thus ending their friendship.

The novels M. wrote during World War I show an ever-widening scope and an increasing depth. The most popular of them were *Modern Lovers* (1914) and *Second Marriage* (1918), in which her moral and spiritual themes receive their most effective development; to these themes she also wedded deft satire of small-town life. *Columbine* (1915) and *Narcissus* (1916), though less commercially popular, are powerful narratives that reveal her increasingly Augustinian view of a flawed and sinful human nature. Her ability to combine this theme with realistic narrative is remarkable; only in *Antonia* (1921) does the strain show: The least successful of her novels, both critically and aesthetically, it verges throughout on melodrama.

She was engaged twice—to the painter Charles Stabb and to her publisher Martin Secker—but in both cases she broke it off. In 1921, she became engaged to a neighboring farmer in Greatham, John Dallyn; they were married in 1922 and had one child, Jacob. But they were not well matched since Dallyn was neither literary nor Roman Catholic, so the marriage developed into a permanent separation. The death of her mother in 1922 was a severe blow, and she increasingly devoted herself to caring for her father till his death in 1948. Her prolific output of fiction slowed considerably after her mother's death. She later wrote two fine memoirs about her parents that reveal her closeness to them and, in a sense, her continuing dependence upon them.

As early as 1918, she had begun writing short stories, having become fascinated with the short fiction of Chekhov, and she produced a number of distinguished volumes in the genre. Her short stories appeared in many periodicals (including, shortly before her death, *The New Yorker*), and won her many new readers. Her stories tend to be ironic and tightly focused, leading her characters up to a moment of psychological epiphany; few of them reveal anything like the theological preoccupations of her novels. The 1927 novel *A Girl Adoring* was originally a short story, and it is noticeably thinner, thematically, than her earlier novels; she experimented in this work, however, with an oblique style and an emotional distance from her characters that make the book unique among her novels. She only returned to a full-scale novel in 1935 with *Follow Thy Fair Sun,* which received strong reviews and good sales. Its theme is the impossibility of fulfillment in love, played out through the tragically mismatched temperaments of its two protagonists; as in some of her earlier work, the novel uses religious allusion and imagery to give its simple story an almost epic scope.

In her later years, she turned to literary journalism and editing, while her own creative work slowed to a trickle; in a letter to her friend, the poet George Rostrevor Hamilton, she said "I sometimes think we women have a shorter season." From 1937 to her death, she maintained an especially close friendship with the scholar and curator Sydney Carlyle Cockerell and edited two collections of letters to him. Her last novel, *Ophelia* (1951), brilliantly orchestrates her major themes of duty, sin, and redemption one last time, complicated by the circumstance of a mother and daughter who are rivals for the same man.

In the last decade of her life, she was plagued by health problems, including a degenerative nerve disease that left her unable to walk; periods of severe depression worsened things for her, as did bouts with eye trouble and pleurisy. In the days before her death, she was working on a new volume of collected stories, which was published a few months later. She was buried in a village churchyard not far from Greatham.

She had little interest in the Modernist movement and, except for the brief friendship with Lawrence, little contact with it. This and her increasing seclusion from the London literary world no doubt worked against her, allowing her once wide popularity to dwindle. Taken as a whole, her fiction reveals both a continuity with late Victorian themes—like moral duty and the purgative effects of suffering—and realist narrative structures, as well as an incisive analysis of twentieth-century psychology; her mastery of language makes the combination powerful and unique in modern fiction.

WORKS: *Martha Vine* (1910). *Cross-in-Hand Farm* (1911). *Lot Barrow* (1913). *Modern Lovers* (1914). *Columbine* (1915). *Narcissus* (1916). *Julian Grenfell* (1917). *Second Marriage* (1918). *Verses* (1919). *Antonia* (1921). *Young Mrs. Cruse* (1924). *A Girl Adoring* (1927). *Alice Meynell: A Memoir* (1929). *The Frozen Ocean and Other Poems* (1930). *Follow Thy Fair Sun* (1935). *Kissing the Rod and Other Stories* (1937). *Lovers* (1944). *First Love and Other Stories* (1947). *Ophelia* (1951). *Francis Thompson and Wilfrid Meynell: A Memoir* (1952). *Louise and Other Stories* (1954). *Collected Stories* (1957).

BIBLIOGRAPHY: Bogan, L., in *Literary Opinion in America*, ed. M. D. Zabel (1937). Gould, G. *The English Novel of Today* (1924). Johnson, R. B. *Some Contemporary Novelists (Women)* (1920). Maguire, C. E. *Renascence* (1959), Meynell, F. *My Lives* (1971).

For articles in reference works, see *Longman. DLB. Feminist. NCBEL. TCA.*

Raymond N. MacKenzie

Elizabeth Middleton

FLOURISHED: 1630s.
MARRIED: perhaps George Warburton of Arley, Chester (d. 1676).

M. was the author of the poem "The Death and Passion of our Lord Jesus Christ; As it was Acted by the Bloodye Jewes, & Registered by The Blessed Evangelists." The poem exists in a unique Bodleian Library manuscript dated 1637 and is sandwiched between an unattributed and undated Calvinist prose tract, "A Soveraign Antidote agayst [sic] Despayre fitt to be taken of all those who are afflicted eyther outwardlye in Boddy or Inwardly in Mynde, or both," and an incomplete (ninety-line) version of William Austin's "Ecce Homo" (written before 1628). While the subject matter of the manuscript is wholly religious, and all of the authors expound at length on the guilt of the Jews, the poems range widely between the extremes of Roman Catholic and Protestant piety.

M.'s identity remains a mystery; Germaine Greer argues that M. is one of the Middletons or Myddeltons of Denbighshire in Wales. Though allied with the Puritans, they had contacts with English Catholic exiles on the Continent and with the London literary community that included the Jesuit Robert Southwell, whose poetry M. quotes at length. However, the large number of Elizabeth Middletons of that family who might have written around 1637 makes it impossible to identify the author with certainty. Greer suggests the daughter of Sir Thomas Myddelton (1586–1666), who was both leader of the Parliamentary forces and, later, supporter of the restoration of Charles II. He seems to have provided his daughters with an education, as another daughter, Mary (d. 1639), was noted for "her singular piety and learning, her judiciousness in and studiousness about the best thinges." Sir Thomas himself wrote poetry and was interested in the Jesuits. The Elizabeth Middleton who was daughter of Sir Thomas was born in 1619, one of thirteen children, and married George Warburton by whom she had four daughters and two sons.

The poem, composed of 173 six-line stanzas, is dedicated to Mrs. Sara Edmondes (who may have been the sister of Sir John Harington of Exton, a tutor to Princess Elizabeth). The work opens with a dedicatory acrostic sonnet, the first twelve lines of which begin with the letters that spell out Edmondes's name. Part of the poem (st. 145–47) quotes from "Saint Peter's Complaint" by the Jesuit martyr Robert Southwell (1561–95). His work circulated in manuscript after his arrest in 1592, and this poem in particular was widely published following his execution.

M.'s poem seems to have been written with reference to a Jesuit edition of Southwell's poetry and to the Rheims-Douai (Roman Catholic) Bible. M.'s poem is one of many contemporary meditations on the Passion and consists of paraphrases of the Gospel accounts, followed by sections that depict various characters' emotional responses to the events described. The poem makes wide use of mercantile imagery in a singularly negative light—Judas is portrayed as an "Unhappy merchant" marketing Jesus to the "bloody Merchaunte" Jewish priests—a feature that would be doubly interesting if M. were the daughter of Sir Thomas, whose family's fortune came through commerce, banking, and moneylending.

WORKS: "The Death and Passion of our Lord Jesus Christ; As it was Acted by the Bloodye Jewes, & Registered by The Blessed Evangelists" (1637; Bodleian Library, Oxford [Bod. Don. e.17, 16v-17v]).

BIBLIOGRAPHY: *Bell. DNB* (under "Sir Thomas Myddelton"). *Feminist. Kissing the Rod: An Anthology of Seventeenth-Century Women's Verse*, ed. G. Greer et al. (1988).

Kari Boyd McBride

Grace Sherrington Mildmay

BORN: 1553, Laycock Abbey, Wiltshire.
DIED: July 1620, Apethorpe, Northamptonshire.
DAUGHTER OF: Sir Henry Sherrington and Lady Sherrington.
MARRIED: Sir Anthony Mildmay, 1567.

Few journals kept by Elizabethan women survive; M.'s is the longest of these surviving journals. M. began keeping the journal when she was about seventeen, three years after her marriage to Anthony Mildmay, and she continued to keep it until a few years before she died at age sixty-seven. In it, she recorded meditations, advice, and autobiography.

The autobiographical sections suggest M.'s compliant nature. One of three daughters, M. was reared by her mother and by a much-loved governess, Mrs. Hamblyn. As in many Renaissance households, her mother believed in education by beating and "never so much as for lying." M. herself felt that corporal punishment was a sign of love and concern that led her to value the truth for its own sake. Under this tutelage M. learned the usual Elizabethan accomplishments: needlework, the lute, household management, and good behavior. In her journal M. has much to say on this last topic, explaining how she was taught that a woman should always be quiet, modest, and industrious.

Her father was a Protestant (he had been associated with Thomas, Baron Seymour of Sudeley, who served as King Edward VI's Lord High Admiral and wooed Elizabeth), and as a consequence of his faith his daughters were taught to be devout—and literate—Anglicans. This circumstance has two consequences for M.'s work. First, because M. was taught to read and write so that she could study her Bible, she was predisposed to value education, including education for women. Second, she concentrated on her religious faith in her journal.

M.'s marriage, a very good match, was arranged, and her husband's interests included hunting and war; nor was he intellectually negligible, if we can judge from a successful speech he made at Peterhouse, Cambridge, during Queen Elizabeth's visit in 1564. Like M., her husband came from a Protestant family that valued education; his father had served as Chancellor of the Exchequer under Elizabeth and had founded the Puritan Emmanuel College, Cambridge. Nevertheless, Sir Anthony was unwilling to marry until his father assured him of financial support. The early years of M.'s marriage were not happy ones; the couple had little money and Sir Anthony was often away on diplomatic business. When he was home, he seems to have been often harsh. During these years, M., prompted both by her respect for her father-in-law and by her education in obedience, "could not find it in [her] heart to challenge him for the worst worde or deede which ever he offered [her] in all his lyfe." Instead, she withdrew into herself, studying religious books, writing down household remedies and recipes, or educating her one child, Mary. As the years passed, M.'s life grew happier. Her husband's affection for her increased, their financial position improved, and her daughter made a brilliant marriage to Sir Francis Fane, later the Earl of Westmorland. M. concerned herself more and more with her beloved grandchildren as well as with the household and her charitable works.

The journal gives details of M.'s life, but her writing also suggests that she combined spiritual and practical interests. The bulk of her journal is a series of Protestant meditations, interrrupted from time to time by her notes on her life. In addition to the journal, M. collected cures and recipes; some occur in her household books and others were copied after her death by her daughter. The picture M.'s writing presents is one of a quiet, devout, and useful life.

WORKS: *Lady Grace Mildmay's Journal and Papers* (1570–1617, unpublished; Northampton Public Library).

BIBLIOGRAPHY: Pollock, L. *With Faith and Physic* (1993). Warnicke, R. *SCJ* (1989). Wiegall, R. *Quarterly Review* (1911).

For articles in reference works, see: *Bell. Bloomsbury.* Bush, D. *English Literature In the Earlier Seventeenth Century, 1600–1660* (1962). *Europa. Feminist.*

Other references: Travitsky, B. *The Paradise of Women* (1989).

Fran Teague

Harriet Hardy Taylor Mill

BORN: 8 October 1807, London.
DIED: 3 November 1858, Avignon, France.
DAUGHTER OF: Thomas Hardy and Harriet Hurst Hardy.
MARRIED: John Taylor, 1826; John Stuart Mill, 1851.

M. was an intellectual woman who spent her life energies in dialogue with a famous male philosopher but who herself gained almost no recognition. Born into a wealthy, contentious London doctor's family, she had little formal education and married a London druggist when she was eighteen. Knowledge of the young M. is sketchy since her life before she married John Stuart Mill has not been of importance to scholars. Her first husband was well-to-do and of a liberal (radical) persuasion; he attended the Unitarian South Place Chapel, where her friend William Johnson Fox, the preacher, became the trustee of the Flower sisters, Eliza and Sarah, in 1829, with Eliza ultimately becoming his housekeeper and common-law wife. The resultant scandal forced Fox to spend less time in the church and to put more effort into his political and journalistic endeavors. He was the owner and editor of the *Monthly Repository,* the Unitarian radical journal; the intellectual coterie surrounding that journal was the center of M.'s life before and for several years after she met Mill.

M. was twenty-three when Fox brought Mill to dinner at the Taylors' house in 1830; she had been married four years and had two sons. Many stories are told of that first meeting (including reminiscences by Harriet Martineau, also a dinner guest that night), but it is certain that the two were drawn to each other.

M. was already writing poetry after her daughter, Helen, was born in 1831, and soon her contributions—both poetry and reviews—began appearing in the *Monthly Repository.* Her most prolific year was 1832; after that time she published little under her name. Since her relation with Mill was becoming intense, she and Taylor agreed to a trial separation in 1833; they agreed at the end of six months that she would both continue to live with Taylor and keep on seeing Mill. Mill and M. continued this intellectual romantic arrangement for nearly twenty years, until Taylor's death (1849); two years later, they were married. M. always insisted that Mill was her *Seelefreund* (soul mate), implying that they were never physical lovers. For Victorians, this arrangement was certainly possible, although the couple's outward behavior even before marriage—they worked together, traveled abroad together, wrote daily love letters when apart, dined together, and appeared socially together—did little to keep scandal from appearing.

From the beginning, M. spent her best energies on Mill's intellectual projects, and many of his works are coproduced with her. He acknowledges her influence and her help, detailing the kind of editorial and compositional assistance she made—sometimes her ideas, sometimes her wording, sometimes whole sentences—but she has never been given co-authorship credit for *On Liberty,* the *Autobiography,* or any other of Mill's works. Only "The Enfranchisement of Women," first published in 1851, was acknowledged to be, in fact, written by M. There are differences between M.'s ideas and Mill's. M. was always much less tentative than Mill, more certain, in some ways more rational. A correspondence exists, for example, between Mill and Auguste Comte in which Mill takes Comte to task for his stand against women's rights. In the ensuing discussion, however, Mill is almost apologetic in his position. M., in going over this series with him in 1844, castigated him for this tendency, and Mill determined, as a result, not to publish the letters at all.

Two early pieces, one by Mill and one by M. (first published in 1951), suggest more specific differences. M. argues that there should be no marriage laws at all, that a woman should simply take responsibility for her own children, thus removing the child custody problem from divorce issues. Mill calls for a postponement of childbearing so that couples could determine if their choice of a mate was a good one. In the case of the divorce of parents with children, Mill advocated a kind of joint custody within a supportive community. A second and more striking difference is found in their attitude toward increased education for women. For M., women should be well educated so that all occupations will be open to them, but her husband cautiously argued that woman's education had the goal of creating a better wife and mother, that only in exceptional cases (single women, widows) should women enter the labor force at all. M. wanted education for its own sake for women; he wanted women's education for men.

M. continued to do her own intellectual work through Mill even after they were married. She suggested that he write on religion (*Three Essays on Religion*, 1874), and she wrote a long outline of what should be in that work. She suggested and then added the chapter "On the Probable Future of the Labouring Classes" in *Political Economy* (1848), a chapter emphasizing the domestic slavery of women and stressing working women's need to be freed from that double burden. *On Liberty* (1859) was evidently a joint venture from its very conception, with M. writing, revising, and suggesting throughout its creation. The *Autobiography,* not published until many years later (1873), was actually written and revised while M. was still alive (during 1853–54); many conversations and letters attest to the detailed care that she gave to that work.

On Liberty, Mill's most famous and enduring work, is also the one on which M. did the most work; according to Mill, it should be considered a "joint production," since this essay packed all the "intellectual pemican" that the couple thought liberal thinkers might need for posterity. The concept of political freedom was translated into individual, everyday situations, and the basic tenet of "liberal conservatism" was enunciated: The liberty of an individual can only be interfered with if it constitutes a danger to society or to other individuals; otherwise, the individual is sovereign. The book is a balanced, rational argument against tyranny. Great stress was placed on women and children as the two groups most tyrannized and least protected by law. The essay strongly advocates a system of universal education for all children (both boys and girls) to be required and provided by the parents, the State only paying the costs for those who cannot afford it. Examinations should be confined to factual matters, and great care must be exercised to assure that the State's bias on politics and religion not be determining factors.

Although the couple had continued to work on the essay for several years, refining concepts, changing words or sentences, it had not yet been completed to their satisfaction at the time of M.'s death. After that time, Mill could not bring himself to make any further changes and published it as it was as a kind of memorial. In the next few years, Mill wrote *The Subjection of Women,* attributing most of the inspiration and ideas of the essay to M. (although he did not publish it until 1869, when, he said, the climate of opinion was more favorable). Like many women, M.'s creative and intellectual efforts were spent in assisting a man. Although Mill did not hesitate to give her credit, for more than a century a doubting and suspicious world has refused to take his tributes seriously.

WORKS: "On Marriage and Divorce" (1832). (with J. S. Mill) *Principles of Political Economy* (1848). "The Enfranchisement of Women" (1851). (with J. S. Mill) *On Liberty* (1859). (with J. S. Mill) *The Autobiography* (1873). (with J. S. Mill) *Letters* (in F. A. Hayek, *John Stuart Mill and Harriet Taylor: Their Friendship and Subsequent Marriage,* 1951).

BIBLIOGRAPHY: Bell, S. G. *Revealing Lives: Autobiography, Biography, and Gender* (1990). Hayek, F. A. *John Stuart Mill and Harriet Taylor: Their Friendship and Subsequent Marriage* (1951). Himmelfarb, G. *On Liberty and Liberalism* (1974). Kamm, J. *John Stuart Mill in Love* (1977). Mill, J. S. and H. Mill *Essays on Sex Equality,* ed. A. Rossi (1970).

For articles in reference works, see: *DNB. IDWB.*

Other references: *AntigR* (1973). Jacobs, J. E. *Hypatia* (1994). Pugh, E. L *Canadian Journal of History* (1978). *QQ* (1966). Spender, D. *Women of Ideas* (1983). *WS* (1992).

Margaret McFadden

Anna Riggs Miller

BORN: 1741.
DIED: 24 June 1781, Hot-Wells, Bristol.
DAUGHTER OF: Edward Riggs and Margaret Piggott.
MARRIED: John Miller, 1765.

Best known in her own day as the socialite who introduced poetical contests to England, M. remains important as the founder of a genre new in the eighteenth century: women's Grand Tour accounts. A wealthy heiress, M. married a poor Irish ex-military man who adopted her maiden name with his own. She became Lady Riggs Miller when her husband was created an Irish baronet in 1778. Using M.'s fortune, the couple built an elegant villa outside Bath and entertained lavishly until money ran short. Prompted by the knowledge that life was cheaper on the Continent, M. set out on an early family version of the traditionally male Grand Tour of education. The first stop was Paris, where M. left her mother-in-law, her newborn son, and her daughter, who later enchanted Fanny Burney by begging that she "be so good as to tell me where Evelina is now." M. and her husband then proceeded to Italy, visiting most of the principal tourist stops of the day.

Letters from Italy, M.'s account of the tour, was published anonymously in 1776. Horace Walpole, M.'s wittiest critic, declared that M.'s head had been completely turned by her travels and so was unimpressed by the *Letters* themselves: "The poor Arcadian poetess does not spell one word of French or Italian right through her three volumes of travels." Despite such comments, the book was reasonably successful. It was praised and extracted in the *Analytical Review, Gentleman's Magazine,* and *London Magazine,* and it appeared in a second "corrected" edition the next year.

M.'s travel book adapts the male-dominated genre of travel writing in a variety of fascinating ways. The book quickly establishes a plot—the tour will end at Vesuvius—and offers readers the kind of effusive scenic description associated with later travel writers like Ann Radcliffe. M. distinguishes herself clearly from her published male predecessors in France and Italy: Although she has caught them in many an error, she travels merely for her own amusement, not as a professional guidebook writer. Nonetheless, she provides a wealth of detailed information about Italian art, architecture, medicine, costume, archaeology, and more. Although sometimes tiresome to a modern reader, such detail forcefully establishes her credentials as an eighteenth-century commentator. More than typically aware of the traveler's voyeuristic role, M. draws attention to her own status as tourist, noting for instance that the Swiss make their famous butter solely for English visitors. M. also pays particular attention to women in the countries she visits, whether remarking on a translation of the *Female Spectator* in the Turin library, interpreting the romantic intrigues of Venetian ladies for her readers, or praising the usefulness of a portable cook stove and other kitchen accoutrements found at Herculaneum. Like many of her male compatriots, she expresses indignation at the French convent system; unlike them, she gently hints at a parallel between domineering men and lesser animals: In France, dirt for agricultural terracing is brought up "in baskets fastened to the backs of women and children, the mountain being too steep for an ass or mule to ascend."

Upon her return, M. established a sort of dilettante literary salon at Batheaston, featuring poetical contests in which guests dropped *bouts-rimés* (short verses incorporating an assigned set of rhyming words) into an antique marble vase found at Frascati and declared by M. to come from Cicero's villa. Submissions were read aloud and judged, with wreaths of myrtle awarded to the winners. The participants included a wide range of visitors to Bath, among them enduring figures like David Garrick, Hester Thrale Piozzi, and Anna Seward, the last of whom began her poetic career under M.'s auspices. M. periodically collected the winning entries into a volume, the proceeds of which went to benefit the Bath Pauper-Charity. Seven poems of her own appear in the first volume; Walpole claimed they had "no fault but wanting meter."

Although the contests were widely mocked by the literary world, they were extremely popular among visitors to Bath; contemporaries speak of seeing fifty carriages lined up along the drive to the Batheaston villa and of recognizing as many as four different duchesses in the crowds. M. herself was alternately praised for her good nature and ridiculed for her pretensions; Burney said that "while all her aim is to appear an elegant woman of fashion, all her success is to seem an ordinary woman in very common life, with fine clothes on. Her manners are bustling, her air is mock-important, and her manners very inelegant." M. has been suggested as the model for Charles Dickens's Mrs. Leo Hunter in *The Pickwick Papers;* her own contemporaries intimated that her gatherings were too easy of access but flocked to them by the thousands. M. died suddenly in 1781, and Bath society turned to other amusements. Her obituary stressed not only her social conquests but also her care for the poor; her monument depicts the famous marble vase, surrounded by the figures of Liberality and Genius.

WORKS: (contrib. and ed.) *Poetical Amusements at a Villa Near Bath* (1775; additional volumes 1776, 1777, 1781). *Letters from Italy, Describing the Manners, Customs, Antiquities, Paintings, of that Country, in the Years MDCCLXX and MDCCLXXI* (1776; second ed., 1777). *On Novelty: and On Trifles, and Triflers* (1778).

BIBLIOGRAPHY: *Edinburgh Magazine* (April 1782, September 1785). *Gentleman's Magazine* (June 1781). Hesselgrave, R. A. *Lady Miller and the Batheaston Literary Circle* (1927).

For articles in reference works, see: *Bloomsbury. DNB. Feminist. ToddDBA.*

Other references: Burney, F. *Early Journals and Letters,* ed. L. E. Troide (1994). Piozzi, H. *The Piozzi Letters,* ed. E. A. Bloom and L. D. Bloom (1989–96). Walpole, H. *Letters,* 16 vols., ed. P. Toynbee (1903–1905).

Marie E. McAllister

Florence Fenwick Miller

BORN: 5 November 1854, London.
DIED: 24 April 1935, Hove, Sussex.
DAUGHTER OF: Captain John Miller and Eleanor Fenwick.
MARRIED: Frederick Alfred Ford.
WROTE UNDER: Florence Fenwick Miller; Philomena.

M.'s career was notable because she was a woman pioneer in all that she did: the study and practice of medicine; advocacy of women's rights, including suffrage; sitting on the London School Board; lecturing from the platform; and pursuing journalism as a professional woman.

M. was born on the day of the Battle of Inkerman in the Crimea and was named for Florence Nightingale, giving rise to her later use of "Philomena" as a pseudonym. After being privately educated in London, at the age of sixteen and a half she joined the second wave of pioneering women, led by Sophia Jex-Blake, at the University of Edinburgh, seeking the necessary education to qualify to practice medicine. When they were unsuccessful, she entered the fledgling Ladies' Medical College, London, graduated at the top of her class, and briefly practiced obstetrics from her home.

In 1876, she was elected to the London School Board for the Borough of Hackney, the first elective office open to women in England, and served three three-year terms.

At the same time, she was a pioneer among "platform women." She lectured widely for women's suffrage, not only in London but also in Ireland, Scotland, Manchester, Birmingham, and the provinces. She also gained renown as a lecturer at the London Dialectical Society and the Sunday Lecture Society, appearing at the latter eleven times between 1873 and 1883, pioneer work at a time when women did not usually speak in public. M. married Frederick Alfred Ford, a stockbroker's clerk, but because she was already well established as a public figure, she kept her own name, becoming simply Mrs. Fenwick Miller.

During her medical school days, she began contributing to periodicals; it was the field of journalism in which she was to gain her most lasting reputation. At a time when women reporters were rare, she contributed regularly to such journals as *Fraser's Magazine*, Lett's *Illustrated Household Magazine, Belgravia,* and the *Governess.* In March 1886 she began to write "Ladies' Notes" for the *Illustrated London News,* a post that she occupied continuously for thirty-three years and from which she exerted her influence in favor of women's issues. She also wrote for the *Lady's Pictorial, Women's World,* the *Young Woman,* and the *Echo.* She was editor of three periodicals, *Outward Bound* (1890–95), *Homeward Bound* (1892), and the influential *Woman's Signal* (1895–99).

M.'s work for women took her to the United States as a delegate to the Colombian Exposition, the Chicago world's fair in 1893, where she appeared numerous times as a featured speaker. She returned to the United States in 1902 to become a founding member and first treasurer of the International Council of Women. She was a close associate of such international figures as Susan B. Anthony, Elizabeth Cady Stanton, Carrie Chapman Catt, Frances Willard, and Lady Henry Somerset.

M. died 24 April 1935 at her home in Hove.

WORKS: *House of Life* (1878). *An Atlas of Anatomy* (1879). *Lynton Abbott's Children* (1879). *Animal Physiology for Elementary Schools* (1882). *Readings in Social Economy* (1883). *Harriet Martineau* (1884). *Hughes's Natural History Readers* (1884). *In Ladies' Company* (1892).

BIBLIOGRAPHY: *Allibone SUP. BDBF. DNB.* VanArsdel, R. T. *VPR* (1982). VanArsdel, R. T. *Bulletin of the History of Education Society* (1986). *Who Was Who* (1940). *Women of the Day,* ed. F. Hays (1885).

Rosemary T. Van Arsdel

Mills, Cotton Mather, Esq.: See *Gaskell, Elizabeth*

Minifie, Miss: See *Gunning, Susannah Minifie*

Mira: See *Haywood, Eliza Fowler*

Miss A. M.: See *Porter, Anna Maria*

Miss G.: See *Moody, Elizabeth*

Miss Minifie: See *Gunning, Susannah Minifie*

M[istres] M[elvill]: See *Colville, Elizabeth*

Naomi Mitchison

BORN: 1 November 1897, Edinburgh, Scotland.
DAUGHTER OF: John Scott Haldane and Kathleen Trotter Haldane.
MARRIED: Gilbert Richard Mitchison, 1916.
WRITES UNDER: Naomi Mitchison; Naomi Margaret Mitchison; Naomi Haldane Mitchison.

From the 1920s onward, M. wrote on an astonishing variety of subject—from classical antiquity to contemporary African politics, from birth control to Byzantine historiography, from the oil and herring industries in Scotland to her own girlhood in the Edwardian Age. A prolific professional author known for her crystalline expository prose, M. is also recognized in Great Britain as a playwright, a poet, and, perhaps especially, as a novelist with a flair for historical fiction.

M. has related the most important incidents of her life in a series of autobiographies. These convey a sense of life lived to the fullest: In them, she recalls Edwardian grandmothers and country places; describes the health hazards of serving as a volunteer nurse during World War I; analyzes her life as the young wife of a Labour Party member of Parliament; narrates the circumstances of her research in Botswana; remembers her friendships with such people as Aldous Huxley, W. H. Auden, and D. H. Lawrence; characterizes both the Socialists and the Nazis she met in Vienna in the 1930s; evokes images of herself watching the natives in Beirut, Karachi, the Kalahari, Arkansas, and the Soviet Union; and gives an account of her participation in local Scottish political life after World War II as a member of the Argyll County Council. Many of these experiences found their way into book-length essays, novels, and books for children.

M.'s evident thirst for an understanding of human life in the twentieth century led her to engage in a sustained study of African history and cultures; her research and personal observations culminated in one of the best general introductions to the continent ever written (*The Africans,* 1970) as well as in a number of local histories and folklore anthologies.

Over the long course of her career as a writer, M. also edited a number of literary projects aimed at synthesizing up-to-date reports on the current state of human knowledge (for example, *An Outline for Boys and Girls,* 1932, and *What the Human Race Is Up To,* by F. Bartlett, 1962) that included many contributions by such brilliant thinkers as J. B. S. Haldane (her brother) and W. H. Auden. "Our ideas . . . are . . . on the move," wrote M. by way of introduction to her encyclopedic *What the Human Race Is Up To.* A progressive at heart, M. devoted her long writing career to the building of bridges—bridges between western and third-world cultures, between the elder and the younger generations, between scientists and humanists, between businesses and community interests.

In recognition of her nearly two decades of service and friendship, the Bakgatla tribe of Botswana honored M. in 1963 by bestowing on her the honorific title "Tribal Mother." Characteristically, in 1980, M. returned the compliment by publishing a collection of stories entitled *Images of Africa.* "To my mind, much of the communication between Europe and Africa is either superficial or has been deflected by a clash of values," she wrote, adding that only "imagination bridges differences." A poetic work, *Images of Africa* offers parables of race relations and cultural history from the African point of view, based on stories borrowed from the Kgatleng, the Bushmen of the Kalahari, and the people of Botswana and Zambia.

The principal quality of M.'s more than eighty book-length publications—the lively candor with which she addresses human experience—has been spilling over refreshingly from work to work for more than seven decades. Whatever her topic or genre, her writing radiates a joyful recognition of human potential and a clear-eyed awareness of human frailty. Her attitude is far from sentimental. M. has repeatedly voiced the need for active responsibility, creative intelligence, and ultimate hopefulness.

WORKS: *The Conquered* (1923). *When the Bough Breaks and Other Stories* (1924). *Cloud Cuckoo Land* (1925). *The Laburnum Branch* (1926). *Black Sparta: Greek Stories* (1928). *Nix-Nought-Nothing: Anna Commena* (1928). *Four Plays for Children* (1928). *Barbarian Stories* (1929). *Comments on Birth Control* (1930). *The Hostages and Other Stories for Boys and Girls* (1930). *Boys and Girls and Gods* (1931). *The Corn King and the Spring Queen* (1931). (with L. E. Gielgud) *The Price of Freedom* (1932). *The Powers of Light* (1932). *The Delicate Fire: Short Stories and Poems* (1933). *The Home and a Changing Civilization* (1934). *Naomi Mitchison's Vienna Diary* (1934). *Beyond This Limit* (1935). *We Have Been Warned* (1935). *The Fourth Pig* (1936). (with R. H. S. Grossman) *Socrates* (1937). *An End and a Beginning and Other Plays* (1937). *The Moral Basis of Politics* (1938). *The Kingdom of Heaven* (1939). (with L. E. Gielgud) *As It Was in the Beginning* (1939). *The Blood of the Martyrs* (1939). *Not By Bread Alone* (1943). *The Bull Calves* (1947). (with D. Macintosh) *Men and Herring* (1949). *The Big House* (1950). *The Corn King* (1950). (with D. Macintosh) *Spindrift* (1951). *Lobsters on the Agenda* (1952). *Travel Light* (1952). *Graeme and the Dragon* (1954). *The Swan's Road* (1954). *To the Chapel Perilous* (1955). *The Land the Ravens Found* (1955). *Little Boxes* (1956). *The Far Harbour* (1957). *Behold Your King* (1957). *Other People's Worlds* (1958). *Five Men and a Swan* (1958). *Judy and Lakshmi* (1959). *The Rib of the Green Umbrella* (1960). *Karensgaard: The Story of a Danish Farm* (1961). *Presenting Other People's Children* (1961). (with G.W.L. Paterson) *A Fishing Village on the Clyde* (1961). *The Young Alexander the Great* (1961). *The Young Alfred the Great* (1962). *Memoirs of a Space Woman* (1962). *The Fairy Who Couldn't Tell a Lie* (1963). *Alexander the Great* (1964). *Henny and Crispies* (1964). *Ketse and the Chief* (1965). *When We Become Men* (1965). *Friends and Enemies* (1966). *Return to the Fairy Hill* (1966). *Highland Holiday* (1967). *The Big Surprise* (1967). *African Heroes* (1968). *Don't Look Back* (1969). *The Family at Ditlabeng* (1969). *The Africans* (1970). *Sun and Moon* (1970). *Cleopatra's People* (1972). *The Danish Teapot* (1973). *Sunrise Tomorrow: A Story of Botswana* (1973). *Small Talk: Memories of an Edwardian Childhood* (1973). *A Life for Africa: The Story of Bram Fischer* (1973). *Oil for the Highlands?* (1974). *All Change Here: Girlhood and Marriage* (1975). *Sittlichkeit* (1975). *Solution Three* (1975). *Snake!* (1976). *The Brave Nurse and Other Stories* (1977). *The Two Magicians* (1978). *The Cleansing of the Knife* (1979). *Images of Africa* (1980). *You May Well Ask* (1980). *The Vegetable War* (1980). *Mucking Around: Five Continents over Fifty Years* (1981). *What Do You Think Yourself?* (1982). *Margaret Cole 1883–1990* (1982). *Not by Bread Alone* (1983). *Among You Taking Notes: Wartime Diary 1939–45* (1985). *Saltire Self-Portraits: Naomi Mitchison* (1986). *Early in Orcadia* (1987).

BIBLIOGRAPHY: Benton, J. *Naomi Mitchison: A Century of Experiment in Life and Letters* (1990). Calder, J. *New Statesman* (16 December 1994). Calder, J. *The Nine Lives of Naomi Mitchison* (1997). Dickson, B. *Chapman* (1987). Lefanu, S., in *Utopian and Science Fiction by Women,* ed. J. L. Doawerth and C. A. Kolmertan (1994). Mirksky, J. *New Statesman* (13 May 1983). Murray, I., in *The History of Scottish Literature,* ed. C. Craig (1987). Nellis, M. K. *Studies in Medievalism* (Fall 1983). Smith, A. *Chapman* (1987).

For articles in reference works, see: *Bloomsbury. CA. Cambridge. CN. ConSFA. Feminist. Longman. MBL. Oxford. TCSFW. TCA* and *SUP. ToddBWW.*

Other references: *Horn Book* (June 1961). *LonT* (31 October 1997). *NYT* (28 October 1923). *NYTBR* (28 May 1961). *TLS* (5 June 1980, 24 July 1981).

R. Victoria Arana

Jessica Mitford

BORN: 11 September 1917, Batsford Mansion, Gloucestershire.

DIED: 23 July 1996, Oakland, California, United States.

DAUGHTER OF: David Bertram Ogilvy Freeman-Mitford and Sydney Bowles Freeman-Mitford.

MARRIED: Esmond Romilly, 1936; Robert E. Treuhaft, 1943.

The daughter of the Earl of Redesdale, Jessica—or "Decca"—Mitford grew up in one of the most intellectual, artistic, eccentric, and notorious families in the contemporary British peerage. As an adult, however, she distinguished herself largely as a social and political critic of American culture since her emigration in 1939.

Although M.'s family included politicians, writers, and historians, she (like her sister, Nancy, the novelist and biographer) received no formal education. Instead, they were educated privately—and idiosyncratically—at home. M.'s five other siblings included Diana, who married the fascist Sir Oswald Mosley, and Unity, who became a disciple of Adolph Hitler. Of opposite political leanings than those two sisters, M. ran off to join the Loyalist cause in Spain with her second cousin, Esmond Romilly, in 1936. For several years, the young couple traveled and took various employments. In Spain, they worked as journalists; in England, M. was a market researcher for an advertising agency; in the United States, they did odd jobs along the East Coast. After Romilly's plane was lost flying a Royal Canadian Air Force mission over the North Sea in 1941, M. held a position in the Office of Price Administration in Washington, D.C., for two years. There she met her future husband, a lawyer in the same office.

M. married Robert E. Treuhaft, who shared her progressive views and her activism, in 1943, and became a naturalized U.S. citizen the following year. She then relocated with her husband to Oakland, California, where she lived until her death. In the half-century after becoming an American citizen, she made a name for herself as one of America's hardest-hitting, funniest, and most versatile investigative journalists. A self-proclaimed "muckraker," she tackled topics ranging, literally, from birth to death—from the maternity industry to the funeral business. She was also known for her involvement in civil rights issues, her twenty-year membership in the Communist Party, her teaching at San Jose State University, her work for a commission investigating police brutality, and her articles in magazines and newspapers including *The Nation, Life, Esquire,* and the *San Francisco Chronicle.*

M.'s writing can be divided broadly into two categories: autobiographical/biographical works about herself, her family, and other British subjects; and exposés of American life and culture. *Daughters and Rebels* (1960) provided her American audience with a humorous peek into the doings of the British upper classes, telling the story of her youth and first marriage. (It was published under the title *Hons and Rebels* in England.) Three years later, M. published her first work of investigative journalism, *The American Way of Death* (1963), which not only excoriated the funeral business for its predatory commercialism but also caused a sensation that ultimately forced reforms. Meticulously researched and brilliantly satiric, the book was later made into a television documentary. M.'s next work, *The Trial of Dr. Spock, The Reverend William Sloane Coffin, Jr., Michael Ferber, Mitchell Goodman, and Marcus Raskin* (1969), made an eloquent plea for dissent through her account of the trial of the "baby doctor" and four codefendants for conspiring to subvert the draft during the Vietnam War. The following year, M.'s article in *The Atlantic,* "Let Us Now Appraise Famous Writers," took a scathing look at the Famous Writers School in Westport, Connecticut. In 1973, she turned her attention toward prison reform with *Kind and Usual Punishment: The Prison Business,* which criticized sentencing, the parole system, and the use of prisoners for medical, psychiatric, and pharmaceutical research.

In 1977, M. returned to autobiographical writing with *A Fine Old Conflict,* a witty and unblinking memoir of her membership in the U.S. Communist Party from World War II through the "Red Menace" days of the House Un-American Activities Committee. Included as an appendix is *Lifeitselfmanship,* M.'s first book—a satire of Party jargon that she originally published privately in 1956 and that became an underground mimeographed classic. *Poison Penmanship: The Gentle Art of Muckracking,* a collection of seventeen of her journalism pieces, appeared in 1979, followed in 1984 by *Faces of Philip: A Memoir of Philip Toynbee* and in 1989 by *Grace Had an English Heart,* a biography of Grace Darling, who became a British heroine for her role in the rescue of shipwreck survivors off the Northumberland coast in 1838.

In 1992, M. returned to the subject of American culture with *The American Way of Birth,* an indictment of the role of politics, money, and the medical establishment in the business of giving birth. After looking back at the circumstances of the births of M.'s own four children (the first with Romilly, the others with Treuhaft), the book examines the mistreatment and exclusion of midwives since the Middle Ages, the Victorian customs of birth, and the gradual takeover of the birth process by the medical model—whether through anesthesia, technology, or "natural" methods.

In both her writing and her life, M. showed an unflagging commitment to social justice. Her body of work not only demonstrates the uses of satire for investigative reporting but also ranks among the very best in American journalism.

WORKS: *Lifeitselfmanship* (1956). *Daughters and Rebels* (1960; in the U.K. as *Hons and Rebels*). *The American Way of Death* (1963). *The Trial of Dr. Spock, The Reverend William Sloane Coffin, Jr., Michael Ferber, Mitchell Goodman, and Marcus Raskin*(1969). *Kind and Usual Punishment: The Prison Business* (1973). *A Fine Old Conflict* (1977; includes *Lifeitselfmanship*). *Poison Penmanship* (1979). *Faces of Philip: A Memoir of Philip Toynbee* (1984). *Grace Had an English Heart* (1989). *The American Way of Birth* (1992).

BIBLIOGRAPHY: *Mother Jones* (November–December 1992). *Daughters and Rebels* (1960). *A Fine Old Conflict* (1977).

For articles in reference works, see: *AWW* (1988). *CA. Oxford. WA. WD.*

Other references: Cockburn, A. *Nation* (12 August 1996). Degnan, J. P. *Change* (May–June 1994). Murphy, S. *The Mitford Family Album* (1985). *NYT* (24 July 1996). Weir, L. and C. Martin. *Nation* (May 1990).

Paula Harrington

Mary Russell Mitford

BORN: 16 December 1787, Alresford, Hampshire.
DIED: 10 January 1855, Swallowfield, near Reading, Berkshire.
DAUGHTER OF: Dr. George Mitford and Mary Russell.

The author of *Our Village* was born into relatively favored circumstances; her mother was an heiress and her father a physician. Because of her father's profligacy, however, M. spent much of her life on the edge of poverty. Indeed, it was a desperate need for money that prompted her profuse literary production, which began in the 1820s: historical dramas and the "sketches" of rural life that made her famous.

A precocious only child, M. could read by the age of

three. Her mother's fortune had already been dissipated by her father by the time M. was six or seven, so because of their straitened financial situation, the Mitfords moved first to London and later to Reading. While in London (in 1797), M. herself won a lottery prize of £20,000, which put the family back on a sound financial track for some years. The following year, she matriculated at a "ladies' school" in London, St. Quintin, run by a French emigré; there she won various prizes. Throughout her life she remained a voracious reader; she was conversant in French and knew some Italian and Latin. She studied at the school for more than four years, after which she returned to live with her parents.

Her first publications were a collection of poems in 1810, followed by several longer poetic works. *Christina,* which concerned a romance that developed in the wake of the mutiny on the *Bounty,* appeared in 1811 and was very popular, especially in the United States, and went through several editions. *Blanch of Castile* followed in 1812 and *Narrative Poems on the Female Character* in 1813. These years are documented in a series of letters M. wrote, some to her parents, most to Sir William Elford, a dilettante painter who became a kind of mentor. They now comprise the first volume of her collected letters, published in 1869, a mine of information on nineteenth-century manners and attitudes. The first volume reveals M. to have a lively, frank intelligence, given to irreverent humor, whose talent for moving descriptions of rural life is apparent early in her life. The conversational mode that M. used in her letters became the hallmark of her fictional style, about which she once wrote: "we are free and easy in these days, and talk to the public as a friend . . . we have turned over the Johnsonian periods . . . to keep company with the wigs and hoops"—an indication that M. saw herself as part of the democratization of art that was a central aspect of Romantic literary theory.

M., however, remained ambivalent about the works of her Romantic contemporaries, William Wordsworth, Samuel Taylor Coleridge, and Lord Byron, though she reveled in Wordsworth's and Coleridge's praise of her work. Her preference, not surprisingly (given the similarity between their work and hers), was for the prose fiction of Maria Edgeworth and Jane Austen; her other major influence was Washington Irving. In 1824, as the first series of *Our Village* was about to be published, she explained that the book "will consist of essays and characters and stories, chiefly of country life, in the manner of the 'Sketch Book,' but without sentimentality or pathos—two things which I abhor." Throughout her correspondence, M. iterates her distaste for romantic sentimentalism and her preference for realism. That she herself occasionally indulged in sentimentalism reflects the romantic cast of the era but may also be due to her need to appeal to popular taste.

By 1820, the family, reduced to near destitution, had to move to humbler quarters in Three Mile Cross, a small village near Reading where M. was to live for more than thirty years and that she was to endow with international celebrity as the site of "our village." The first of these sketches appeared in the *Lady's Magazine* in 1819. At the same time, M. turned her hand to a completely different literary form, tragedy. Her first attempt at drama, *Fiesco,* was not accepted, but shortly thereafter *Julian* was presented at Covent Garden on 15 March 1823 with William Charles Macready, an eminent actor, in the title role. It ran for eight performances and evidently received much sexist criticism.

Foscari, her second work, was completed in 1821 but not produced until 4 November 1826, when it ran for fifteen performances at Covent Garden with Charles Kemble in the lead. Coincidentally, Byron had put forth a tragedy on the same subject in 1821, which caused M. considerable consternation. Her most successful play was *Rienzi,* another romantic historical tragedy set in Renaissance Italy and concerning rival noble families who contend for power and containing a "Romeo and Juliet" subplot. Critics consider this her best play, and audiences evidently agreed, for it had thirty-four performances in London in the fall of 1828 and was very successful on the road in the United States, where Charlotte Cushman played the lead female role. M.'s other dramatic works include *Inez de Castro* (1831), *Mary, Queen of Scots* (1831), *Charles the First* (1834), and an opera, *Sadak and Kalasrade* (1836).

Meanwhile, M. had begun publishing *Our Village,* the work that was to establish her as an international celebrity, in five volumes published in 1824, 1826, 1828, 1830, and 1832. She described it as "not one connected story, but a series of sketches of country manners, scenery, and character, with some story intermixed, and connected by unity of locality and of purpose." This is in fact an accurate description of the work, which did not fit into traditional notions of genre but instead created a new form, "village fiction," and provided the basis for a dominant nineteenth-century women's literary tradition, that of the local-color writers. Particularly strong in the United States, it included such writers as Caroline Kirkland, Harriet Beecher Stowe, Rose Terry Cooke, and Sarah Orne Jewett—all of whom were directly influenced by M. She also had an effect on American writer Catherine Sedgwick, with whom she corresponded, Irish writer S. C. Hall (*Sketches of Irish Character*), and Elizabeth Gaskell, whose *Cranford* is a direct descendant of *Our Village.*

Our Village is narrated by a persona who guides the reader through the streets of her town, describing in detail the surrounding vegetation, housing, and landscape as well as the various "characters" who inhabit the village. Their stories are sketched in, as well, which provides what little plot *Our Village* may be said to have. Writing in the heyday of Romanticism, it is not surprising that M. saw the rural world as a kind of pastoral Utopia that nurtured authentic people who spoke truths born of their intimate experience of nature. She favors such characters and their eccentricities and resists any sign of encroaching urban homogenization. *Our Village* became a popular rage. M. was for years besieged by visitors and correspondents wanting to see or learn more about the original model for such characters. Children were named after them, and flowers were named after M. herself.

M. continued her studies of rural life with *Belford Regis* (1834), *Country Stories* (1837), and *Atherton* (1854). In 1836, she met Elizabeth Barrett (later Browning), with whom she was to form a strong friendship; numerous letters between them are extant. Despite her industrious literary production, M. remained impoverished in the latter years of her life, finally forced to move to a small cottage in Swallowfield, also near Reading, where she died. A charming stylist and a pioneer of an important direction in women's literature, M.'s current obscurity is undeserved.

WORKS: *Poems* (1810). *Christina, the Maid of the South Seas; a Poem* (1811). *Blanch of Castile* (1812). *Narrative Poems on the Female Character, in Various Relations of Life* (1813). *Julian* (1823). *Our Village: Sketches of Rural Character and Scenery,* 5 vols. (1824, 1826, 1828, 1830, 1832). *Foscari* (1826). *Dramatic Scenes, Sonnets, and Other Poems* (1827). *Rienzi, A Tragedy* (1828). *Mary, Queen of Scots* (1831). *Inez de Castro* (1831). *Charles the First, an Historical Tragedy* (1834). *Belford Regis, or Sketches of A Country Town* (1835). *Sadak and Kalasrade; or the Waters of Oblivion* (1836). *Country Stories* (1837). *The Works of Mary Russell Mitford: Prose and Verse* (1841). *Recollections of A Literary Life* (1852). *Atherton and Other Tales* (1854). *The Dramatic Works of Mary Russell Mitford* (1854). *The Life of Mary Russell Mitford . . . Related in a Selection from Her Letters to Her Friends,* ed. A.G.K. L'Estrange (1869). *Letters of Mary Russell Mitford,* ed. H. Chorley (1872). *Correspondence with Charles Boner and John Ruskin,* ed. E. Lee (1914).

BIBLIOGRAPHY: Agate, J. E. *Mary Russell Mitford* (1940). Austin, M. *Mary Russell Mitford: Her Circle and Her Books* (1930). Hill, M. C. *Mary Russell Mitford and Her Surroundings* (1920). Horn, P. *Hatcher Review* (1986). Hunter, S. *Victorian Idyllic Fiction: Pastoral Strategies* (1984). Idol, J. L., Jr. *SoAR* (1983). Johnson, R. B. *The Women Novelists* (1919). Jones, C. M. D. *Miss Mitford and Mr. Harness* (1955). *The Friendships of Mary Russell Mitford as Recorded in Letters from Her Literary Correspondents,* ed. A.G.K. L'Estrange (1882). *Elizabeth Barrett to Miss Mitford: Unpublished Letters,* ed. B. Miller (1954). Pigrome, B. *ChLB* (1989). Roberts, W. J. *Mary Russell Mitford* (1913). Watson, V. *Mary Russell Mitford* (1949).

For articles in reference works, see: Martineau, H. *Biographical Sketches* (1877). *DNB. Europa. Feminist. Oxford. ToddBWW.*

Other references: Agress, L. *The Feminine Irony: Women on Women in Early-Nineteenth-Century English Literature* (1978). *BJRL* (1957). *British Museum Quarterly* (1965). *SB* (1959). *SSF* (1968). *SoAR* (1983).

Josephine Donovan
(updated by Karen Castellucci Cox)

Nancy Mitford

BORN: 28 November 1904, London.
DIED: 30 June 1973, London.
DAUGHTER OF: David Bertram Ogilvy Freeman-Mitford and Sydney Bowles Freeman-Mitford.
MARRIED: Peter Rodd, 1923.

M. was the oldest of the Earl of Redesdale's seven children. Though she came from a family of writers, as well as politicians and historians, her parents were convinced she needed no education, and so she (like her writer sister Jessica) got none. This contributed to her independent nature and perhaps to a certain eccentricity. She did not, however, become a fascist like two of her five sisters (one of whom married Sir Oswald Mosley, who led the British Union of Fascists). Her amusement at her family's odd behavior is reflected in her entertaining novel *The Pursuit of Love* (1945), where she treats her relatives as almost Dickensian caricatures; they were also the "hons and rebels" Jessica wrote about.

M.'s most familiar novels are probably *Love in a Cold Climate* (1949), *The Blessing* (1951), and *Don't Tell Alfred* (1960), but she was also the author of fiction of the 1930s: *Highland Fling* (1931), *Christmas Pudding* (1932), and *Wigs on the Green* (1935). They were appreciated in their day for a witty style and a facile, sometimes farcical, humor; today they are read because of the fame of her later work.

In *Highland Fling* a huntress, Jane Dacre, goes after Albert Gates, despite the fact that when he invited her to see his etchings he was really thinking about art. In *Christmas Pudding* we have "one of those houses which abound in every district of rural England, and whose chief characteristic is that they cannot but give rise, on first sight, to a feeling of depression." In the house, however, is the lively young lady, Philadelphia Bobbin, in search of romance. In *Wigs on the Green,* Poppy St. Julien knows that Jasper Aspect has neither propects nor scruples—which makes him irresistible to her. Reissued in the 1970s (with *Pigeon Pie* of 1940, in which a bored sophisticate, Sophia Garfield, is out to cheer up the dreariness of wartime with a skirmish in the war between the sexes), these early novels are a little dated but still have some charm.

Especially dated is *Pigeon Pie,* written at the time of the "phony war" at the beginning of World War II and joking about such things as espionage, sabotage, and propaganda, which were soon to become serious matters. But the intrigue of the book is, in fact, like the country house and the London "smart set" backgrounds of the other books, truly incidental. Essentially the books are all satires of the Sweet Young Things, now called The Beautiful People. "Cracks in the upper crust," ran a blurb on the Penguin edition of one of M.'s novels, were "almost Nancy Mitford's private literary domain."

M. knew the upper crust. As the wife of the son of a former British ambassador to Italy, M. lived in Paris and reported the social life there for the *London Sunday Times.* She set *Love in a Cold Climate* and some other work in Parisian diplomatic circles: Alfred in *Don't Tell Alfred* is the British ambassador to France. Most undiplomatically, Fanny, the narrator and Alfred's wife, is really M. herself and writes (as Norman Collins said in the *Observer*) "of the heart with a most engaging heartlessness." Fanny/Nancy satirizes the surfaces of life, at least in the upper echelons (said a critic in the *Spectator*), "with more truth, more sincerity, and more laughter than a year's output of novels in the bogus significant style."

M. had no desire to attempt the "bogus significant" and knew she was not penetrating, that she was clever but not profound. She never gets very deeply into characters; she is at her best with eccentrics such as the couple in *The Blessing.* She is Grace Allingham, who has lived with her dashing husband only ten days in seven years and nonetheless adores him. He is a French marquis who loves her—

and any other beautiful women he can get his hands on. Another writer might make a tragedy of this material, but M. plays it for laughs. She lacks the bite that makes serious satire better (if bitter); she is content to jest about aristocratic friends and foes and their horrible children and their trendies and toadies.

Horsemanship and French, she said, was all the knowledge her parents' weird ideas about education gave her to work with. The French she used to make *The Little Hut* (1951) out of André Roussin's pleasant little play and to research solid studies of *Madame de Pompadour* (1954, revised 1968), *Voltaire in Love* (1957), and *The Sun King: Louis XIV at Versailles* (1966). She also translated Mme. de Lafayette's classic *The Princess of Cleves* (1950). She educated herself widely and was able to write the essays in *The Water Beetle* (1962), a popular biography of *Frederick the Great* (1970), and *Noblesse Oblige: An Enquiry into the Identifiable Characteristics of the English Aristocracy* (1956), which made her widely known in connection with the differences between "U" (upper-class) and "nonU"(non–upper-class) speech. She edited the letters of Maria Josepha, Lady Stanley of Aderley, and her daughter-in-law (Henrietta Maria Stanley) as *The Ladies of Aderley* and *The Stanleys of Aderley* (both 1938), throwing interesting sidelights on Victorian women. Like many self-educated persons, however, in all her work she seems attracted to curious detail rather than the large picture, to gossipy anecdotes, to flash and filigree, to peculiarities rather than profundities. At the same time she is nobody's fool, and she can always limn a character deftly when she wants to or conjure up the costumes and scenery of a bygone age convincingly.

M. lacked not so much education as malice. She would have been a better writer had she some of the nastiness of, say, Evelyn Waugh. As it is, her satire is never scathing and one wonders if there is enough salt in it to preserve it for posterity. The "hons and rebels" are fast fading. There was a time, M.'s mother once said, that whenever she saw "Peer's Daughter" in a sensational banner headline she knew it was "going to be something about one of you children." Today, Unity (with her fascination with the Nazis) and some of the other Redesdale brood (one of whom married royalty) are far less likely to ring a bell in memory than M. Whether the interest in her pre-war world and her post-war eccentrics will last, or whether M. herself will continue to be of interest because of the autobiographical elements in *The Pursuit of Love,* remains to be seen.

One hopes M.'s fun will not be forgotten. There was more to the 1930s than strikes and depression and, though one might not know it from reading most modern fiction, not all the world is lower class or middle class.

WORKS: *Highland Fling* (1931). *Christmas Pudding* (1932). *Wigs on the Green* (1935). *The Stanleys of Aderley* (1938). *The Ladies of Aderley* (1938). *Pigeon Pie* (1940). *The Pursuit of Love* (1945). *Love in a Cold Climate* (1949). (trans.) *The Princess of Cleves,* by Mme. de Lafayette (1950). *The Blessing* (1951). *The Little Hut* (1951). *Madame de Pompadour* (1954, 1968). *Nancy Mitford Omnibus* (1956). *Noblesse Oblige: An Enquiry into the Identifiable Characteristics of the English Aristocracy* (1956). *Voltaire in Love* (1957). *Don't Tell Alfred* (1960). *The Water Beetle* (1962). *The Sun King: Louis XIV at Versailles* (1966). *Frederick the Great* (1970). *A Talent to Annoy: Essays, Journalism and Reviews,* ed. C. Mosley (1968). *Selima Hastings* (1985). *The Letters of Nancy Mitford and Evelyn Waugh,* ed. C. Mosley (1996).

BIBLIOGRAPHY: Acton, H. *Mitford: A Memoir* (1975). Clemens, A. V. *DR* (1982). Hastings, S. *Nancy Mitford: A Biography* (1986). Hastings, S., in *Essays by Divers hands: Being the Transactions of the Royal Society of Literature,* ed. R. Faber (1988). Parise, M. P. *BB* (1989).

For articles in reference works, see: *CA. GWELN. Longman. MBL. TCA SUP. TCW.*

Other references: Amis, K. *Spectator* (28 October 1960).

Leonard R. N. Ashley

Mlle. V. P.: See *Paget, Violet*

Deborah Moggach

BORN: 28 June 1948, Lake District, London.
DAUGHTER OF: Richard Alexander Hough and Charlotte Woodyat Hough.
MARRIED: Anthony Moggach, 1971.

A novelist, journalist, and critic, M. was born to literary parents—her mother a children's author and illustrator, her father the writer of more than seventy historical books. M. graduated with honors in English from Bristol University and then married and moved to Pakistan with her husband, Anthony Moggach, a publisher. In Pakistan, M. launched her journalism career and continued to write after the couple's return to England. Divorced in 1985, M. now lives in North London with her two teenage children. Her companion of nearly ten years, the cartoonist Mel Calman, died in February 1994. M. has written for magazines and newspapers, and she won the Young Journalist award from the Westminster Arts Council in 1975. Working variously as a journalist, book reviewer, and movie critic, M. began to feel she was not being taken seriously as a novelist, so she has concentrated most of her energy on her book writing since the early 1980s. To date M. has written ten novels and two short-story collections. Her work has been adapted for television, and a screenplay for her 1991 novel *Stand-In* is in the works. M. hopes eventually to work in Hollywood and has confessed that she wrote the latter novel with such a purpose in mind.

Many of M.'s books focus on domestic relationships, some drawn from real-life experiences. As Valentine Cunningham has stated in the *New Statesman,* M.'s books represent "family life most achingly bared." Her first novel, *You Must Be Sisters* (1978), is a somewhat autobiographical account of the growing pains of a middle-class adolescent girl living in London. *Close to Home* (1979), written after the birth of M.'s two children, is an intense examination of the wondrous if sometimes claustrophobic world of new motherhood. In the subtle novel *A Quiet Drink* (1980), the split narrative follows two characters, Claudia in the painful days following her marriage's break-up and Steve in the year his young marriage began to lose its charm. The plot—built around small daily events and quiet drinks in pubs—is held together by the inevitability of the two characters meeting and discovering their compatibility. This tension is delayed for much of the novel, with the *dénouement* that is realistic if not storybook perfect.

M.'s fourth novel, *Hot Water Man* (1982), draws on her expatriate life in Pakistan, exploring the frustrations of the British outsider during the 1970s in a shifting post-colonial world. Still dominated by the joys and woes of domestic relationships, the book follows one middle-aged business man through a tumultuous and disastrous affair with a modern Pakistani woman, while a young and somewhat estranged couple newly moved to the country seek in separate pilgrimages a past and a future that will cement their love for each other.

In later books, M. is not afraid to tackle more controversial issues. *Porky* (1983) is the disturbing story of a daughter's growing alienation from her incestuous father. Told from the daughter Heather's viewpoint as she puts words to her horror for the first time over the period of one long night, the narrative tries to make sense of the father's abuse and Heather's own self-destructive behavior as an adult. Unsettling in its stark, unsentimental images, the novel also explores an interracial relationship between Heather and a Pakistani man who loves and tries to reach her, only to be tragically wronged and subsequently abusive himself.

Exploring another serious contemporary issue, *To Have and To Hold* (1986) looks at the critical questions surrounding surrogate motherhood. M. has said that the material for the novel came from her own experience when, many years ago, she agreed to have a baby for her infertile sister. While the sisters did not go through with the plan, the novel was successful and M.'s first to be dramatized as a TV mini-series.

In recent novels, M. has reached beyond the domestic arena to examine, for example, in *Stand-In* (1991), the obsessive jealousy of a serious British actress relegated to the part of body double for a less-talented American until rage and paranoia overtake her. Continuing to enjoy popularity among British readers, M. hopes to extend her talents to the silver screen and continues to publish a new book every few years.

WORKS: *You Must Be Sisters* (1978). *Close to Home* (1979). *A Quiet Drink* (1980). *Hot Water Man* (1982). *Porky* (1983). *To Have and To Hold* (1986). *Smile and Other Stories* (1987). *Driving in the Dark* (1988). *Stolen* (1990). *Stand-In* (1991). *The Ex-Wives* (1993). *Changing Babies and Other Stories* (1995). *Close Relations* (1997).

BIBLIOGRAPHY:

For articles in reference works, see: *CA*. *Feminist*.

Other references: Cunningham, V. *New Statesman* (17 February 1978). *Guardian* (1 June 1994). *LonTMag* (13 April 1996). *LonT* (5 July 1996). *PW* (28 June 1991). *TLS* (17 February 1978, 23 May 1980, 30 April 1982, 3 June 1983, 8 July 1988, 19 April 1991).

Karen Castellucci Cox

Martha Molesworth (Moulsworth)

BORN: 10 November 1577, probably in or near Oxford.

DIED: Autumn 1646, probably in Hoddesdon, Hertfordshire.

DAUGHTER OF: Robert Dorsett.

MARRIED: Nicholas Prynne, 1598; Thomas Thorowgood, 1605; Bevill Molesworth, 1619.

M. is important for having written one of the earliest autobiographical poems (certainly one of the earliest by a woman) in the English language, and also for having expressed one of the earliest protests against educational inequality. Indeed, in her poetic "Memorandum" (1632), she calls explicitly for founding a women's university and confidently asserts that educated women would not only equal but far surpass men in intellectual achievements. Her sophisticated poem offers a complex overview of the life of a Renaissance Englishwoman. It expresses complicated attitudes toward M.'s multiple roles as daughter, wife, mother, and widow, revealing an intriguing combination of deference and defiance, love and self-assertion, devout submission and feisty self-regard. Deeply religious, M. nonetheless possessed a mind of her own.

"The Memorandum of Martha Moulsworth / Widdowe," written in November 1632, when M. was fifty-five, is transcribed at the end of a volume of political documents owned by M.'s extended family. The poem, now at the Beinecke Library at Yale University, was first published in 1993; since then, much new information about M. has been uncovered, and the poem itself has attracted a great deal of serious critical attention.

M.'s father, Robert Dorsett, taught at Christ Church College, Oxford, serving as a tutor to Sir Philip Sidney. He seemed headed for a distinguished ecclesiastical career when he died in 1580, while M. was still an infant. Her poem expresses great reverence for her father, claiming he encouraged her interest in learning and Latin. Her father's learned reputation probably influenced her claims; of her mother (who died within a year of Dorsett), M.'s poem says nothing, perhaps because she knew little about her. In any case, Germaine Greer has established that M.'s mother left her children in the care of her own mother and stepfather, Helena and Ralph Johnson. Whether M. was raised solely by them is unclear.

M., at the age of twenty-one, married Nicholas Prynne, a London goldsmith. Her poem says that many considered this a late marriage, but, in this matter and others, M. seems satisfied with her choice. She gave birth to a son (Richard) in 1602 and was pregnant with a daughter (Martha) when her husband died in late 1603 or early 1604; both the son and daughter had apparently died by the time M. wrote her poem. M. then married Thomas Thorowgood, a London draper from Hoddesdon, a small town about twenty miles north of London on the main road to Cambridge. M. seems to have spent her time both there and in London until Thorowgood's death in 1615. In 1619, M. married Bevill Molesworth, a London goldsmith with a residence in Hoddesdon, about whom she spoke with glowing affection. Although they married when she was forty-two and he was sixty-five, they had a son (Bevill), who died while still a boy; Molesworth died in 1631.

M.'s "Memorandum," penned in November 1632, reviews the most important events and figures in her life up to that point. In 110 lines (one couplet for each of her fifty-five years), she discusses her birth and baptism, her father and early education, her frustration with the marriage market and with the limits on women's learning, the happiness of her three marriages, the deaths of her husbands, her confidence in their resurrection, her thoughts about her relations with them in heaven, and her final resolution not to remarry.

The "Memorandum" reveals a learned woman, a fact confirmed by a funeral sermon that mentions her love of reading and note taking. It seems highly likely that she did other writing, although no other literary text definitely by her has yet turned up. Her will survives, as do her husbands' wills, which confirm many details from the poem and provide interesting insights into M.'s life and social circle. Other documents from Hoddesdon mention her repeatedly; she seems to have been a wealthy, well-regarded citizen. She was very active in local religious affairs, championing one priest to the annoyance of his neighboring rival. When the latter took her to court, she triumphed, a fact that lends added point to her contemporaneous insistence (in the "Memorandum") on the need to fight to maintain the Christian religion.

M. seems to have enjoyed very loving relations with her extended family, especially with her stepdaughter by Thorowgood. This daughter's husband was a prominent royalist during the Civil War, although M. herself was also godmother to the famous Puritan radical, William Prynne, whom she remembers in her will. The funeral sermon preached by her favorite priest (following her painful illness) complements the self-portrait offered in the "Memorandum."

The poem itself is rich in rhetorical and thematic balances and is also numerologically sophisticated. It effectively blends tones of wit, humor, sarcasm, piety, pragmatism, worldliness, spirituality, prophetic fervor, and subtle understatement to offer an extremely nuanced insight into the mind of a thoughtful, lively, but ultimately serene and confident woman.

WORKS: *"The Memorandum of Martha Moulsworth / Widdowe"*, in *"My Name Was Martha": A Renaissance Woman's Autobiographical Poem,* ed. R. Evans and B. Wiedemann (1993; offers a detailed close reading of the poem, plus essays on its historical, autobiographical, and feminist contexts) and in *"The Muses Females Are": Martha Moulsworth and Other Women Writers of the English Renaissance,* ed. R. Evans and A. Little (1995; provides both old- and modern-spelling texts, plus notes, documents, a facsimile of the manuscript, and biographical and critical essays by G. Greer, I. Grundy, A. Low, A. L. Prescott, M. E. Lamb, J. A. Roberts, C. Perry, J. T. Shawcross, F. Teague, J. R. Brink, and E. S. Cope).

BIBLIOGRAPHY: R. Evans. *YULG* (1995).

Robert C. Evans

Mary Monck (Monk)

BORN: 1678 (?).
DIED: 1715, Bath.
DAUGHTER OF: Robert Molesworth, Viscount Molesworth, and Letitia, daughter of Richard, Lord Coote of Colooney, Ireland.
MARRIED: George Monck.
WROTE UNDER: Marinda.

Posthumously published in an edition of poetry dedicated by her father to Carolina, Princess of Wales, M. displayed her skill as poet and translator of Latin, Italian, and Spanish verse. The daughter of the author and politician Viscount Molesworth, she married George Monck, an Irish member of Parliament from 1703 to 1713. The letters of Viscount Molesworth indicate a probable source of M.'s eventual estrangement from her husband in the year or so before she died: George's apparent physical and mental illness in the years 1712–14. She took up lodging, with her children, in Bath, where she produced the poems her father called "the product of the leisure Hours of a Young Gentlewoman lately Dead" who wrote "without any Assistance but that of a good Library" while charged with "the daily Care due to a large Family."

"On a Romantic Lady" from *Poem and Translations* shows her skill in taking up one of the most popular themes of eighteenth-century satire: young women, in this case a servant girl, falling victim to the influence of romantic fiction. In snappy tetrameter couplets, M. portrays a deluded "Mistress Betty" who has transformed herself imaginatively into a romantic heroine and so, in the manner of Charlotte Lennox's *Female Quixote,* making herself useless to herself and others. M.'s poem actually appears quite early in the long eighteenth-century tradition of pseudo-serious warnings of the dangers attendant upon reading romances.

"Verses written on her Death-bed at Bath to her Husband in London," published and attributed forty years after her death, is somewhat puzzling, given her marital turmoil. The poem, written in heroic couplets, attempts to reconcile a dying woman to her fate and to her absent husband. It is a conventional mutability lament, with an apostrophe to her husband, her "unwearied friend," that asks him not to grieve for her, "thy faithful wife." The poem's poignancy is muted, implicit in the fact that she is alone and that she must ask "should'st thou grieve that rest is come at last?," not knowing if he is even aware of her fate.

The erudition, wit, and skillful prosody that M.'s poems reveal, along with the extraordinary biographical circumstances that attended their composition, make her one of the most intriguing, if still virtually unknown, figures of the early eighteenth century.

WORKS: *Poems and Translations upon Several Occasions* (1716). *Poems by Eminent Ladies,* ed. G. Colman and B. Thornton (1755).

BIBLIOGRAPHY: *British Women Poets 1660–1800: An Anthology,* ed. J. Fuller (1990).). *Eighteenth-Century Women Poets,* ed. R. Lonsdale (1990). Jacob, G. *His-*

torical Account of the English Poets (1720). Shiels, R. *The Lives of the Poets of Great Britain and Ireland* (1753

For articles in reference works, see: *Allibone. Ballard. Bloomsbury. DNB. Feminist. ToddDBA. Todd BWW* (under "Monk").

Richard C. Taylor

Elizabeth Montagu

BORN: 2 October 1720, York.
DIED: 25 August 1800, London.
DAUGHTER OF: Matthew Robinson and Elizabeth Drake Robinson.
MARRIED: Edward Montagu, 1742.

Essayist and Shakespearean critic M. was also a prolific letter writer. Her witty and vividly descriptive correspondence, spanning two-thirds of the eighteenth century, recreates the diverse activities in which she excelled, from the London establishment of scholarly forums to the management of Berkshire farmlands and Northumberland collieries. Additionally, the letters reveal her political interests, such as her concern for the welfare and advancement of women and her discomfort with the ethical implications of the century's newly developing capitalism. Finally, her letters tell the story of her more private life—her relationship with her husband and her several intimate and steadfast friendships.

M. was the fourth child and first daughter in a large family that was wealthy, socially prominent, and well educated. In her adolescence, she was energetic and gregarious, and when she was twenty-two, she married Edward Montagu, nearly thirty years her senior. Shortly after his death in 1775, M. adopted her young nephew, Matthew Robinson (later Montagu), as her heir; after her death he became custodian of her correspondence, bringing out collections of her letters in 1809 and 1813.

M.'s first published work consisted of three dialogues she contributed anonymously to her friend Lord Lyttelton's *Dialogues of the Dead* (1760), with the delightful "Dialogue between Mercury and a modern Fine Lady" influenced by Elizabeth Carter's "Modish Pleasures" (*Rambler*, 2 March 1751). Also during 1760, M., with Carter's encouragement, began a second project, an extended essay in response to Voltaire's attack on Shakespeare in his *Dictionnaire philosophe*. In 1768, M. wrote to Carter, "Between attending Mr. Montagu in his very infirm state, domestic Orders for the regulation of a family consisting of about thirty persons, letters of business, and my authorlike duties, I have sometimes a great hurry, and I have also some sick patients for whom I am obliged to make up Medicines, that being in some cases not to be trusted to another; poor Shakespear is last served." But she persevered, and in 1769 her *Essay on the Writings and Genius of Shakespeare* was published anonymously. Her identity almost immediately known, M. became highly esteemed as a Shakespearean critic. The *Essay* went to several editions and was translated into French and Italian.

Besides spending time in Berkshire and Northumberland, M. traveled in Scotland, the Rhineland, and the Low Countries, and she often visited France. An enthusiastic patron of the arts, she supported many writers, architects, and painters. Among the women writers she assisted were Sarah Fielding, Hester Chapone, and Hannah More. At one point, she proposed the establishment of a women's college, and in 1767 she and her sister Sarah Scott were working on a plan to provide a home for unmarried gentlewomen. Among M.'s several close female friends, Elizabeth Carter may have been the most important. The two exchanged many letters, sometimes traveled together, often visited one another, and planned to share a home in later life. But although M. settled a pension on Carter immediately after her husband's death, the two friends never lived together. Affectionate friendship marked the Bluestocking women, that group of London ladies with perhaps M. at the center, which created a forum for social, literary, artistic, and intellectual interests. The Bluestockings looked to one another for intellectual support, and in their self-sufficiency demonstrated the strengths of womanly community. Through her Bluestocking parties, M. brought together women and men of diverse backgrounds, interests, and beliefs to share ideas: "I have always pitied a certain set of people who some years ago called themselves the 'little world,' it is so much better to be of the general world . . . to be able to converse with ease, and hearken with intelligence to persons of every rank, degree and occupation."

WORKS: (anon.), in Lyttelton, G. L. *Dialogues of the Dead*, 3rd ed. (1760). *Letters of Mrs. Elizabeth Montagu, with Some of the Letters of Her Correspondents*, ed. M. Montagu (1809–13). *An Essay on the Writings and Genius of Shakespeare, Compared with the Greek and French Dramatic Poets*, 6th ed, corrected, to which are added *Three Dialogues of the Dead* (1810). *Letters from Mrs. Elizabeth Carter to Mrs. Montagu Between the Years 1755 and 1800*, ed. M. Pennington (1817). Gaussen, A. C. C. *Later Pepys: The Correspondence of Sir W. W. Pepys 1758–1825, with . . . Mrs. Montague . . . and Others* (1904). *Elizabeth Montague, the Queen of the Bluestockings: Her Correspondence from 1720 to 1761*, ed. E. J. Climenson (1906). *Mrs. Montagu, "Queen of the Blues,"* ed. R. Blunt (1923). Anson, E. and F. *Mary Hamilton at Court and at Home* (1925; contains letters from M.). *Bluestocking Letters*, ed. R. B. Johnson (1926).

BIBLIOGRAPHY: Busse, J. *Mrs. Montagu, Queen of the Blues* (1928). Doran, J. *A Lady of the Last Century* (1893). *The Tenbury Letters*, ed. E. H. Fellowes and E. Pine (1943). Halsband, R., in *The Lady of Letters in the Eighteenth Century*, ed. I. Ehrenpreis and R. Halsband (1969). Hornbeak, K. G. *The Age of Johnson: Essays Presented to C. B. Tinker* (1949). Huchon, R. L. *Mrs. Montagu and Her Friends, 1720–1800* (1907). Hufstader, A. A. *Sisters of the Quill* (1978). Jones, W. P. *HLQ* (1952). Ross, I. *HLQ* (1965). Scott, W. S. *The Bluestocking Ladies* (1947). Tinker, C. B. *The Salon and English Letters* (1915). West, R., in *From Anne to Victoria*, ed. B. Dobree (1937). Wheeler, E. R. *Famous Bluestockings* (1910).

For articles in reference works, see: *DNB. ToddDBA.*

Other references: Beatty, J. M., Jr. *MLN* (1926). Boulton, J. T. *Burke Newsletter* (1961–62). de Castro, J. P. *N&Q* (1941). Harmsen, T. G. *N&Q* (1958) Hegeman,

D. V. *Kentucky Foreign Language Quarterly* (1957). Hufstader, A. A. *Musical Quarterly* (1961). Jones, C. E. *N&Q* (1946). Jones, W. P. *N&Q* (1958). Larson, E. S. *SECC* (1986). Phillips, G. L. *RES* (1949). *TLS* (20 September 1941).

Carolyn Woodward

Mary Wortley Montagu

BORN: 1689, London.
DIED: 21 August 1762, London.
DAUGHTER OF: Evelyn Pierrepont and Lady Mary Fielding.
MARRIED: Edward Wortley Montagu, Esq., 1712.
WROTE UNDER: MWM, M. Wortley Montagu, Mary Wortley Montagu.

After their mother died in 1693, M. and three siblings were left to the care of paternal grandparents and a governess, who, says M., "took so much pains from my infancy to fill my head with superstitious tales and false notions, it was none of her fault I am not at this day afraid of witches and hobgoblins, or turned Methodist." Educated in part by tutors, M. was largely self-taught and began writing poetry when she was twelve. In 1712, she eloped with Edward Wortley Montagu, appointed Ambassador Extraordinary to the Court of Turkey in 1716. Journeying with her husband to Constantinople, M. began to write the letters that would establish her reputation as an author. The couple returned to England in 1718 and, encouraged by Alexander Pope, M. settled at Twickenham with their two children, Mary, who later married John Stuart and became Lady Bute, and Edward, whose marriages and profligate spending constantly embarrassed his family. Resuming her travels in 1739, in part at the invitation of the Italian Count Algarotti, M. resided first at Avignon and then at Lovere; she returned in January 1762, after the death of her husband and at the request of her daughter, and died in August.

A vigilant observer of human nature in society and politics, M.'s poetry, essays, and letters show her concerns as a feminist and as a moralist. As a *bel esprit*, M. eschewed publication, but she circulated much of her writing in manuscript, and both the pirated printings and the unpublished works met with acclaim from contemporaries, including her friend Lord Hervey, Pope, Horace Walpole, Samuel Johnson, and Robert Burns. Contemporary publication of M.'s works, therefore, was sporadic and not authoritative, but her literary reputation was firmly established during her lifetime. Her varied works include *A Comedy/Simplicity*, a translation and adaptation of *Le Jes de glamour et du hasard*, a play written by Pierre de Marivaux.

In her essays, some of which she published anonymously, she often started by exposing a fashionable error, an intellectual misstep. A longing for honesty and integrity in all human relationships frequently underlies her focus on specific public personalities. The voice and intention of her persona are defined in an essay from 24 January 1738: "I keep up to the character I have assum'd, of a Moralist, and shall use my endeavors to relieve the distress'd, and defeat vulgar prejudices whatever the event may be." On 28 July 1714, M.'s essay justifying the light-heartedness of some widows appeared in the *Spectator*. In *The Nonsense of Common-Sense*, a series of nine essays published as a weekly newspaper from December 1737 to March 1738, M. defends Walpole against attacks in the Opposition paper, *Common Sense*. On 3 January 1738, justifying Walpole's attempts to tax wine and tobacco, she writes, "The highest Perfection of Politicks, they say, is to make the Vices of the People contribute to the Welfare of the State." In her poetry, M.'s Augustan forms and her consistently satiric tone attest to her respect for the models of her contemporaries, but her opinions and insights shape her poems, frequently occasioned by personal and public events.

Written in 1715 during a literary liaison with Pope and John Gay, three of her *Court Eclogues* were printed anonymously without her permission by Edmund Curll in 1716 as *Court Poems*. In 1718, Pope presented M. with his autograph copy of her manuscript of the eclogues, and Walpole printed an annotated edition of all six eclogues in 1747. The subject of the third eclogue, "The Drawing Room," shows the wisdom of M.'s decision to circulate poetry only among friends, for in it she criticizes the morality of Princess Caroline's court: "A greater miracle is daily view'd, / A virtuous Princess with a court so lewd."

M. is best known for her letters. Most famous are her Embassy letters, the value of which was recognized by Mary Astell, whose preface shows her characteristic encouragement and admiration of M. and identifies the unique quality of M.'s voice:

> "To how much better purpose the Lady's Travel than their Lords. . . . A Lady has the skill to strike out a New Path and to embellish a worn-out Subject with variety of fresh and elegant Entertainment . . . besides that Purity of Style for which it may justly be accounted the Standard of the English tongue, the Reader will find a more true and accurate Account of the Customs and Manners of the several Nations with whom the Lady Convers'd than he can in any other Author. . . . Her Ladyship's penetration discovers the inmost follys of the heart, . . . treating with the politeness of a Court and gentleness of a Lady, what the severity of her Judgment cannot but Condemn.

In addition to the descriptive letters themselves, M. brought back from Turkey an enthusiastic and convincing tale of inoculation against smallpox. In a letter to Sarah Chiswell, in which she recalls her discovery, she shows her disdain for professional irresponsibility and betrays her own desire to be more assertive. "I should not fail to write to some of our doctors very particularly about it if I knew any one of 'em that I thought had virtue enough to destroy such a considerable branch of their revenue for the good of mankind, but that distemper is too beneficial to them not to expose to all their resentment the hardy wight should undertake to put an end to it. Perhaps if I live to return I may, however, have courage to war with 'em. Upon this occasion, admire the heroism in the heart of your friend."

In her letters to her sister Frances, the Countess of Mar, M. creates whimsical sketches of her social life. Similar subjects become polished commentary in letters to the

Countess of Oxford and the Countess of Pomfret. Although they differ in their views on morality and propriety, M. and Lady Bute correspond openly on issues of feminism and child raising. M. gracefully defends having emphasized domestic training for her own daughter and then urging scholarly training for her granddaughter. "The ultimate end of your education was to make you a good wife . . .; hers ought to make her happy in a virgin state." M.'s individualized feminism takes its direction from the status quo: "I have heard it lamented that boys lose so many years in mere learning of words: this is no objection to a girl, whose time is not so precious: she cannot advance herself in any profession, and has therefore more hours to spare." M.'s evaluation only lightly conceals an ironic complaint about women's limited options, but her *carpe diem* response, based on practicality and preference, precludes bitterness.

Letters to Lady Bute lament "the general want of invention which reigns amongst our writers." She wonders if England "has not sun enough to warm the imagination." Only William Congreve and Henry Fielding, M. concludes, show originality, but, because they must publish in order to make a living, they fall short of their potential genius. "The greatest virtue, justice, and the most distinguishing prerogative of mankind, writing, when daily executed do honor to human nature, but when degenerated into trades are the most contemptible ways of getting bread." And although she participates herself in a literary battle with Pope, she insists that authors should, instead of "stigmatizing a Man's name, . . . confine their censure to single Actions . . . [instead of] Satyrs and Panegyricks."

In her practical feminism, M. urges readers to consider that reform benefits the oppressor as well as the oppressed. She writes, "Amongst the most universal Errors I reckon that of treating the weaker sex with a contempt, which has a very bad Influence on their conduct, who, many of them, think it excuse enough to say, they are Women, to indulge any folly that comes into their Heads, and also renders them useless members of the common wealth, and only burdensome to their own Familys." It is little wonder that with a pen so merciless in exposing folly, M.'s friends' and family's responses varied from profound affection to violent antagonism. Modern audiences discover in M.'s writing a sensitive and sensible response to significant issues of the eighteenth-century.

WORKS: *Six Token Eclogues. With some other Poems*, ed. H. Walpole (1747). *A Collection of Poems* (printed for R. Dodsley, 1748). *Works*, ed. J. Dallaway (1803). *Letters and Works*, ed. Lord Wharncliffe (1837). *Letters and Works*, ed. W. Moy Thomas (1861). *The Nonsense of Common Sense*, ed. R. Halsband (1947). *Complete Letters of Lady Mary Wortley Montagu*, 3 vols., ed. R. Halsband (1965–67). *Essays and Poems and Simplicity, A Comedy*, ed. R. Halsband and I. Grundy (1977). *Court Eclogs, Written in the Year Seventeen Sixteen: Alexander Pope's Autograph Manuscript*, ed. R. Halsband (1977). *The Best Letters of Lady Mary Wortley Montagu* ed. T. Octave (1978). *Turkish Embassy Letters*, ed. M. Jack (1993). *Romance Writings*, ed. I. Grundy (1996).

BIBLIOGRAPHY: Barry, I. *Portrait of Lady Mary Montagu* (1928). Gibbs, L. *The Admirable Lady Mary* (1949). Halsband, R. *The Life of Lady Mary Wortley Montagu* (1957). Huchon, R. *Mrs. Montagu & Her Friends, 1720–1800* (1907; rpt. 1983). Leslie, D. *A Toast to Lady Mary* (1968). Lowenthal, C. *Lady Mary Wortley Montagu and the Eighteenth-Century Familiar Letter* (1994). Melville, L. *Lady Mary Wortley Montagu: Her Life and Letters* (1925). Paston, G. *Lady Mary Wortley Montagu and Her Times* (1907).

For articles in reference works, see: *Allibone. AWW. BAB1800. BCE. Bell. Biographical and Bibliographical Dictionary of English Literature. Biographical Dictionary of English Women Writers, 1580–1720. Cambridge. Cassell. Chambers. CinP. DBPP. Dictionary of English Authors. Dictionary of European Literature. DLEL. DNB. Dole. EDL. Feminist. GWELP. IDWB. Ireland. Literature Criticism from 1400 to 1800. Moulton. NCBEL. NCHEL. OCEL. RE. Penguin Book of Women Poets. PCWL. ToddDBA. Warner.*

Other references: *AR* (1981). *BLR* (1981). Bradford, G. *Portrait of Women* (1916). Ehrenpreis, I. *The Lady of Letters in the Eighteenth Century* (1969). *GaR* (1983). Holmes, W. *Seven Adventurous Women* (1953). Melville, L. *Maids of Honour* (1917). *N&Q* (1958). *New Statesman* (1958). *PMLA* (1965). *PQ* (1965, 1966). *RES* (1972). *Before Their Time: Six Women Writers of the Eighteenth Century*, ed. K. Rogers (1979). Rubenstein, J. *PrS* (1986). *SB* (1958). Thomson, K. *The Queens of Society* (1861).

Mary Sauter Comfort

Elizabeth Moody

BORN: April 1737, Kingston, Surrey.
DIED: 10 December 1814, Turnham Green, London.
DAUGHTER OF: Edward Greenly and Mary Shepherd Greenly.
MARRIED: the Reverend Christopher Lake Moody.
WROTE UNDER: Aretina; Eliza; Miss G; Elizabeth Moody; Mrs. Moody; The Muse of Surbiton; Sappho.

In his review of M.'s collected poems in the *Monthly Review* (Sec. Ser., 1798), publisher Ralph Griffiths enrolls her in the list of England's distinguished poetesses. Today, while contemporaries Anna Barbauld, Helen Maria Williams, and Mary Robinson are the focus of renewed critical attention, M. remains an elusive figure.

The daughter of a wealthy Hereford lawyer, M. grew up amidst a witty Thames-side milieu of lawyers, politicians, and courtiers. She read voraciously and from an early age belonged to a literary circle of neighboring family and friends. A key figure in this circle was the Reverend Richard Wooddeson, master of the Kingston grammar school attended by M.'s brother Edward; also contributing to M.'s development were two other Wooddeson pupils. One was her poetic mentor, Edward Lovibond, with whom she engaged in spirited verse dialogues as "Sappho" and "Miss G." Lovibond's 1785 *Poems on Several Occasions* (which M. may have helped edit) contains examples of these exchanges. The other was judge/philanthropist George Hardinge, an early admirer and lifelong correspondent. Several of M.'s poems, as well as many addressed to and about her, appear in his 1818 *Miscellaneous Works in Prose and Verse.*

In 1777, M., aged forty, married the twenty-three-year-old Reverend Christopher Lake Moody, a literary man and dissenting minister from Hampshire. Unlike M.'s coterie-mates, her husband was highly publication-oriented and seemingly nudged his diffident wife into print. Shortly after their marriage, her poems began appearing occasionally in such periodicals as the *General Evening Post* and *Gentleman's Magazine.* In 1788, he joined his friend Ralph Griffiths and others as a partner in the thrice-weekly *St. James's Chronicle* and in doing so provided M. with a crucial "familial" forum for her writing: Over a fifteen-year period she published more than fifty poems and several letters in the *Chronicle.* Internal evidence suggests that both Moodys had an editorial hand in the paper's "Poet's Corner," in which M. was celebrated as the "Muse of Surbiton" (the Surrey village where the couple lived).

In 1789, M. began her tenure as the *Monthly Review's* first regular female reviewer. During the years 1789–91 and 1800–1808, she published thirty critiques of novels, nonfiction, and verse, occasionally in collaboration with her husband, one of the *Monthly's* most prolific critics. M.'s reviews are ironic and self-reflexive; she takes obvious delight in her anonymous male-reviewer persona. Donning a female persona to voice her antiwar sentiments, M. published her poem "Anna's Complaint" in George Miller's 1796 tract, *War, a System of Madness and Irreligion.*

M.'s *Poetic Trifles,* a collection that included several dozen of her periodical poems as well as a large selection of previously unpublished verse, was published in 1798. Typical of coterie verse, M.'s *Trifles* poems are occasional and dialogic; among the collection are poems addressed to public figures Joseph Priestley, Erasmus Darwin, Sarah Trimmer, and lawyer Thomas Erskine. M.'s friends characterized her work as *jeux d'esprit* and *vers de société* (both species of light verse), and the book's six reviewers concurred, one of them dubbing the poems "trifles of a better order" (*British Critic* 14, 1799). The reviewers describe M.'s verse as an imaginative blend of sensibility and sense, never mentioning that her primary mode is satiric. M.'s poem "The Housewife, or the Muse Learning to Ride the Great Horse Heroic" exemplifies the mock-heroic strain that pervades her work and often expresses the contradictions inherent in her role as wife and writer.

While M. published infrequently after 1800, when she and her husband became Griffiths' neighbors at Turnham Green, she continued to exchange verse and letters with a wide circle of correspondents, including new friend Elizabeth Inchbald, the playwright and novelist. Although few of M.'s personal letters are available today, those that survive lend support to her obituarist's claim that "they had a variety of talent in that branch of written eloquence, which has been seldom equalled in our language by either sex" (*Gentleman's Magazine,* 1814).

In styling herself a writer of playful trifles, M. was able to exercise her inveterate critical bent and remain a "proper lady." Her lightweight *oeuvre,* her equivocal attitude toward publicity, and the ephemerality of the media in which she published help explain the present invisibility of this intelligent, engaging "semi-public" writer.

WORKS: *Poetic Trifles* (1798).

BIBLIOGRAPHY:

For articles in reference works, see *Feminist.*

Jan Wellington

Agnes More

BORN: 1591, Bampton County, Oxon (?).
DIED: 14 March 1656, Cambrai, Flanders.
DAUGHTER OF: John More of Bampton County, Oxon.
WROTE UNDER: Dame Agnes More (or Moor).

M. translated a French work of her contemporary, Jeanne de Cambry, Augustinian nun in Flanders, into English. A work of mystical theology written in (and translated into) poetic prose, Cambry's volume was originally entitled *La ruine de l'amour propre et batiment de l'amour divin* (*The Ruin of 'Self-Seeking' Love and Building of Divine Love*) but was modifed by M., who excludes the first and more negative part of the work, the "Ruin," and, as the seventeenth-century English manuscript states, the M. translation therefore is simply entitled *The Building of Divine Love.* The English manuscript also points out that M. translated the work from Cambry's expanded second edition, printed at Tournai in 1627.

Little is known of M.'s early life in England. A great-great-granddaughter of Sir Thomas More and a cousin of John Donne, in 1623 M. entered the recusant English Benedictine Abbey of Our Lady of Consolation at Cambrai (i. e., an abbey for English Roman Catholics who refused to attend Church of England services and were therefore guilty of a statutory offense), together with her first cousins, Helen Gertrude More and Anne More. The abbey had been financially endowed by M.'s uncle, Cresacre More; under the aegis of one of the abbey's chaplains, the now-well-known Augustine Baker, it soon became a center where the nuns collected, preserved, transcribed, translated, and wrote in emulation of the writings of the English medieval mystics (often banned in England) as well as of many of the continental medieval and sixteenth-century spiritual writers. Cambry's work was influenced by the work of Bernard de Clairvaux, Catherine of Genoa, St. Augustine, Teresa of Avila, and John of the Cross, among others. The seventeenth-century English manuscript states it is written "with a mystic explication of the Canticle of Canticles of Solomon." The volume is similar in structure to the work of Teresa of Avila insofar as it sets forth the "Purgative, Illuminative and Unitive ways" of the spiritual life—that is, the "purification of the senses and the intellect"—so that the higher powers of the contemplative soul become strengthened and self-seeking becomes transformed into selflessness through divine love and charity towards others. Cambry states that the volume is written for all: men and women, laity and religious. Its theme revolves quite originally on "The Four Seasons of Life," which become extended metaphors and symbolic of stages of the spiritual life. The work is replete with figurative language easily recognized by readers of the seventeenth-century English metaphysical poets: the microcosm (the individual) in the macrocosm (the larger world or universality), the eternal circle as Alpha and Omega, darkness and sunlight as reflections of the Divine, and other neoplatonic and Augustinian metaphors and symbols. M.'s fine and subtle translation of the original poetic prose illustrates seventeenth-century recusant knowledge of English and Continental spiritual traditions and helps to answer questions concerning Continental influences on seventeenth-century English literature.

It is not known if M. translated or wrote other books.

WORKS: (trans.) *The Building of Divine Love As Translated by Dame Agnes More, Transcribed from the 17th Century Manuscript* (MS. of the Archives du Departement du Nord, Lille; intro. and ed., D. L. Latz, 1992).

BIBLIOGRAPHY: Benedictines of Stanbrook Abbey. *In A Great Tradition* (1956). Gillow, J. *Publications of the Catholic Record Society* (1913). Guilday, P. *The English Catholic Refugees on the Continent, 1558–1798* (1914). Latz, D. L., in *"Glow-Worm Light . . ." Writings of 17th Century English Recusant Women*, ed. D. L. Latz (1989). *Neglected English Literature, 16th–17th Century Recusant Writings: Collected Papers from the Recusant Sessions of the International Medieval Congress, Western Michigan University, 1990–1994*, ed. D. L. Latz (1997). Low, A. *Augustine Baker* (1970). McCann, J. and H. Connolly, *Publications of the Catholic Record Society* (1933). Norman, M. *Recusant History* (1975–76). Underhill, E. *Mysticism* (1911).

Other references: Gillow, J. *Bibliographical Dictionary of the English Catholics* (1885–1902). For J. de Cambry, see *Dictionnaire de Spiritualité*, Vol.II (1953).

Dorothy L. Latz

Hannah More

BORN: 2 February 1745, Stapleton, Gloucestershire.
DIED: 7 September 1833, Windsor Terrace, Clifton, Bristol.
DAUGHTER OF: Jacob More and Mary Grace More.
WROTE UNDER: Will Chip; Hannah More; Z.

M. lived through two eras, a fact that both defined and curtailed her impact as a writer. Born in the century of Samuel Johnson, she died at the end of the Romantic age. Toward the close of her life she was a celebrated anachronism, refusing to accept the fundamental social and philosophical changes that followed the French and Industrial Revolutions. Yet in her own way she had encouraged change just as surely as she had tried to ignore it. Too conscientious to ignore things as they were, M. was too conventional to opt for radical transformation. Ultimately, her attempts to preserve the status quo while modifying it for the better helped lay the groundwork for the English system of reform.

One of five sisters who ran a boarding school in Bristol, M. as a young woman was engaged to a wealthy landowner for six years. Jilted repeatedly by her fiancé, she finally ended their relationship in 1773. Thereafter forswearing marriage, she sublimated her feelings into her religion, her work, her sisters, and her friends.

While recovering from the stress of the broken engagement, M. visited London. There David Garrick and his wife became her patrons. Already a Bristol playwright, M. first worked with Garrick when he wrote the epilogue to her play *The Inflexible Captive* (1774). Her next drama, *Percy* (1777), a tragedy, was the triumph of its season largely because of Garrick's editing and promotion. On its own, *Percy* is neither poetic nor dramatic, merely a bland imitation of the tragic mode. After Garrick's sudden death in 1779, M. lost interest in the stage, eventually repudiating it altogether. She did produce another play, *The Fatal Falsehood* (1779); her *Sacred Dramas* (1782), a set of biblical stories done as closet drama, was of greater significance to her future, however.

Even without Garrick, M.'s renown grew. Over her lifetime she made some £30,000 as an author, tangible proof of her ability to communicate equally well with the great and the unknown. An acknowledged Bluestocking, she became a friend of Samuel Johnson and, later, of Horace Walpole. Her literary coterie delighted in her poem "The Bas Bleu" (1782), in which M. saluted London's female intelligentsia. Ironically, M. herself was turning away from fashionable poetry.

Instead, she turned to a series of prose works in which she exhorted her readers to embrace true Christianity, by which she meant an Evangelical form of Anglicanism. M. became gradually convinced that Christians must demonstrate their relationship with God in their every action. Thus, in *Thoughts on the Importance of the Manners of the Great to General Society* (1788), she urged the aristocracy to exemplify their religion for the rest of society in basic matters such as respecting the sabbath. In *An Estimate of the Religion of the Fashionable World* (1790), she held that Christianity must be embraced in its entirety rather than in part. In *Strictures on the Modern System of Female Education* (1799), she suggested that women should be trained as circumstances require and as a Christian society demands.

William Cobbett once called M. an "old bishop in petticoats," and so she was. She was as well, however, a parson to the poor. Following William Wilberforce, she worked for the abolition of slavery, a cause she championed in her poem "Slavery" (1788); and with her sisters, she established a string of Sunday schools for the neglected rural poor. Yet she remained a staunch Tory who despised the French Revolution. In 1792, she wrote *Village Politics*, a tract that used the simple language of a chapbook to justify the English system and revile the French. Much praised, this anti-Jacobin propaganda led to the *Cheap Repository Tracts* (1795–98), distributed by the rich to the poor in an effort to quell unrest. A prime mover in this cause, M. wrote almost fifty of these tracts. Their success as an antidote to the "French poison" is debatable; what is certain is their wide circulation among a people whose grievances subsequently led to reform rather than revolution.

Critical of feminists like Mary Wollstonecraft and disdainful of Jacobins, M. nonetheless promoted the rudiments of equity in society's treatment of women and the working classes. Her outspoken activism inevitably alarmed the more suspicious of her fellow Anglicans, whose misgivings culminated in the Blagdon Controversy (1800–03), whereby M. was indirectly accused of Methodism. Something of a political squabble disguised as a doctrinal dispute, Blagdon left M. troubled but unbowed. She continued her mission in 1805 with *Hints Towards Forming the Character of a Young Princess,* an instructional guide for Princess Charlotte that was well received by both the public and the queen. In 1808, M. published her only novel, *Coelebs in Search of a Wife,* as an alternative to the romances then in fashion. This alternative was another huge success, running to dozens of editions in both England and America. Like most of M.'s work, *Coelebs* is too didactic to be good reading now. Ostensibly the story of a bachelor's quest for true—and sanctified—love, the book is in fact a general lecture on M.'s favorite subjects: women, education, children, charity, and above all piety.

After *Coelebs,* the old "female bishop" wrote several other pious works, each continuing her earlier themes. Everything sold well, but M.'s personal influence had dwindled. The Romantic mentality now dominated England, and though Romanticism was more than revolution, its unrestrained emotion and complex metaphysics were distasteful to an aged Tory. Romantics such as Samuel Taylor Coleridge and Thomas De Quincey found M. equally distasteful. Among their peers, only William Wordsworth appealed to M., for he shared her concern for ordinary people and—increasingly—her conservative perspective. After M.'s quiet death, even her literary reputation faded, relegating her works to the status of artifacts. What did not fade, however, was the heritage of social concern she had helped to create. By that heritage, M. found a place in the continuum of those who work for the welfare of humanity.

WORKS: *The Search After Happiness* (1773). *The Inflexible Captive* (1774). *Essays for Young Ladies* (1777). *Percy* (1777). *The Fatal Falsehood* (1779). *Sacred Dramas* (1782). *Florio, and the Bas Bleu* (1786). *Slavery* (1788). *Thoughts on the Importance of the Manners of the Great to General Society* (1788). *An Estimate of the Religion of the Fashionable World* (1790). *Village Politics* (1792). *Cheap Repository Tracts* (1795–98). *Strictures on the Modern System of Female Education* (1799). *Hints Towards Forming the Character of a Young Princess* (1805). *Coelebs in Search of a Wife* (1808). *Practical Piety* (1811). *Christian Morals* (1813). *An Essay on the Character and Practical Writings of St. Paul* (1815). *Stories for the Middle Ranks, and Tales for the Common People* (1819). *Moral Sketches; with Reflections on Prayer* (1819). *Bible Rhymes* (1821). *The Spirit of Prayer* (1825). *Works* (8 vols., 1801; 19 vols., 1818–19; 11 vols., 1830; 6 vols., 1834; 2 vols., 1840). *Poems* (1816, 1829). *Letters to Zachery Macauley* (1860). *Letters* (1925). "Village Politics" (1793, with "The Shepherd of Salisbury Plain," c. 1820), ed. R. B. Johnson (1995). *Selected Writings,* ed. R. Hole (1996).

BIBLIOGRAPHY: Collingwood, J. and M. Collingwood. *Hannah More* (1990). Demers, P. *The World of Hannah More* (1990). Ford, C. H. *Hannah More: A Critical Biography* (1996). Hopkins, M. A. *Hannah More and Her Circle* (1947). Jones, M. G. *Hannah More* (1952). Knight, H. C. *Hannah More* (1862). Kowaleski-Wallace, E. *Their Fathers' Daughters: Hannah More, Maria Edgeworth, & Patriarchal Complicity* (1991). Meakin, A. M. B. *Hannah More* (1911). More, M., in *Mendip Annals,* ed. A. Roberts (1859). Roberts, W. *Memoirs of the Life and Correspondence of Mrs. Hannah More* (1834). Thompson, H. *Life of Hannah More* (1838). Yonge, C. M. *Hannah More* (1888).

For articles in reference works, see: *CHL. DLB. DNB. Europa. Feminist. Oxford. ToddBWW. ToddDBA.*

Other references: Brown, F. K. *Fathers of the Victorians* (1961). Cole, L. *ELH* (1991). Demers, P. *HLQ* (1993). Donkin, E., in *Curtain Calls: British and American Women and the Theatre, 1660–1820,* ed. M. A. Schofield and C. Macheski (1991). Evans, M. J. C. *Transactions of the Eighth International Congress on the Enlightenment* (1992). Forster, E. M. *New Republic* (16 December 1925). Kelly, G., in *Man and Nature,* ed. K. W. Graham and N. Johnson (1987). Kowaleski-Wallace, B. *FSt* (1986). Myers, M., in *Fetter'd or Free? British Women Novelists, 1670–1815,* ed. M. A. Schofield and C. Macheski (1986). Pedersen, S. *Journal of British Studies* (1986). Pickering, S. *SSF* (1975). Poovey, M. *The Proper Lady and the Woman Writer* (1984). Walpole, H. *Correspondence,* ed. W. S. Lewis, et al., Vol. 31 (1961).

Mary Pharr

Helen Gertrude More

BORN: 25 March, 1606, Low Leyton, Essex.
DIED: 17 August, 1633, Cambrai, Flanders.
DAUGHTER OF: Cresacre More and Elizabeth Gage More.
WROTE UNDER: Dame Gertrude More.

Great-great-granddaughter of Sir Thomas More and a cousin of John Donne, M. was an accomplished poet as well as a spiritual writer and was described by Evelyn Underhill as "a remarkable and neglected mystic." We know that she had a happy early life in England and was especially devoted to her father, her mother having died when she was five. As did many of More's descendants and associates, the family had remained in England as long as their safety permitted, but the penal laws following renewals of the Oath of Allegiance first promulgated by Henry VIII, as well as the religious Uniformity Act and the Treason Act and statutes, finally caused M.'s family members to settle on the Continent to practice their religion in freedom. Together with her first cousins Anne and Agnes More and later joined by her younger sister Bridget, M. became a nun at the recusant English Benedictine Abbey of Our Lady of Consolation, financially endowed by her father, at Cambrai, Flanders.

M. was a particularly loyal follower of the ideas of one of the abbey's chaplains, the Benedictine don Augustine Baker (1575–1641), now well known for his preservation and collection of the writings of English medieval mystics, including *The Cloud of Unknowing* (from the latter half of the fourteenth century), and for his transcriptions, modernizations, and commentaries on them, as well as for his collections and translations of the Continental medieval and sixteenth-century mystics. In her 1657 work, M. includes a list of "readings fit for a contemplative spirit," and among many others she names Walter Hilton, Jan van Ruysbroeck, Heinrich Suso, Johann Tauler, Bennet de Canfield (Joseph Fitch), Catherine of Siena, Teresa of Avila, and John of the Cross. Julian of Norwich was later first published from manuscript at Paris by one of Baker's Benedictine followers. Through Baker's influence, the Cambrai Abbey became a center for copying, transcribing, studying, and even imitating the manuscripts and medieval spiritual books that he had collected from England (where many were banned) during his incognito travels back and forth across the Channel. His collection of M.'s writings—prose interspersed with poetry—was published by his follower Serenus Cressy in Paris in 1657 and 1658 and was presented to M.'s sister Bridget, who at that time was abbess at the English Benedictine Abbey of Our Lady of Good Hope, an affiliation of the Cambrai Abbey.

M.'s spiritual writings follow Baker's thought, which was Augustinian with a pre–Council of Trent emphasis upon the interior life and contemplative prayer as divine love, divine illumination, and direct inspiration from God, with consequent freedom of conscience. This was not a predominant emphasis in M.'s and Baker's era after the Council of Trent, when more methodical meditation was preferred, and differences from Protestantism were stressed rather than a shared Judeo-Christian heritage. Baker was questioned about his orthodoxy by some members of his order but was completely vindicated within his and M.'s lifetime, for it was evident his thoughts and writings followed those of the recognized medieval mystics. M.'s writing is best seen in the 1657 and 1658 editions of her work; subsequent editors have selected, revised, modernized, and omitted paragraphs from her prose and have either neglected or changed her poetry according to the preferences of their respective eras, when often both her mysticism and her poetic style were ignored.

At the age of twenty-seven, M. died of smallpox at the abbey during a raging epidemic in Flanders.

WORKS: *The Holy Practises of a Divine Lover or the Sainctly Ideots Devotions* (1657). *The Spiritual Exercises of . . . D. Gertrude More. She called them Amor ordinem nesat and Ideot's Devotions. Her only spiritual father and director the Ven. Father Baker stiled them Confessiones Amantis, A Lover's Confessions* (1658; rev. and abridged eds. by H. Collins, 1907–1909; H. L. Fox, 1909; and B. Weld-Blundell, 2 vols., 1910, 1911; rpt. 1937). *Neglected English Literature, 16th–17th Century Recusant Writings: Collected Papers from the Recusant Sessions of the International Medieval Congress, Western Michigan University, 1990–1994,* ed. D. L. Latz (1997).

BIBLIOGRAPHY: Benedictines of Stanbrook Abbey. *In A Great Tradition* (1956). Gillow, J. *Publications of the Catholic Record Society* (1913). Guilday, P. *The English Catholic Refugees on the Continent, 1558–1798* (1914). Latz, D. L., in *"Glow-Worm Light . . . " Writings of 17th Century English Recusant Women,* ed. D. L. Latz (1989). Low, A. *Augustine Baker* (1970). McCann, J. and H. Connolly, *Publications of the Catholic Record Society* (1933). Norman, M. *Recusant History* (1975–76). Underhill, E. *Mysticism* (1911).

Other references: Gillow, J. *Bibliographical Dictionary of the English Catholics* (1885–1902).

Dorothy L. Latz

Morgan, Lady: See *Owenson, Sydney*

See *Owenson, Sydney*

Penelope Ruth Mortimer

BORN: 19 September 1918, Rhyl, Flint, Wales.
DAUGHTER OF: A.F.G. Fletcher and Amy Caroline Fletcher.
MARRIED: Charles Dimont, 1937; John Clifford Mortimer, 1949.
WRITES UNDER: Penelope Dimant; Penelope Mortimer; Ann Temple.

In her poetic autobiography, *About Time* (1979), M. reveals important insights into growing up in rural England between the two world wars, as well as chronicling her parents' lives, both of whom were born in the last quarter of the nineteenth century. M., the younger of two children, was reared as an only child, since her brother, four years older, was sent away to school at four.

Her novels, following *Johanna* (1947), which was unsuccessful, have built her reputation solidly as one of Britain's finest living writers. In 1979, she received the Whitbread Award for nonfiction. M. has also written short stories and screenplays and was a critic-journalist and former lonely hearts columnist for London's *Daily Mail,* where she used the pseudonym Ann Temple. From 1967 to1970, she was movie critic for *The Observer.*

Throughout her novels, she uses the lives of women as a metonym of human vulnerability. In women's roles—as daughters, mothers, mistresses, wives, sisters—the shabby shelters of the self seem most tentative. M. chooses again and again the image of the house to convey the structure of self emblematic of women's roles, as suggested by her titles: *The Villa in Summer, The Bright Prison* ("shades of the prison house falls upon the growing boy"), *Cave of Ice, The Pumpkin Eater, My Friend Says It's Bullet-Proof, The Home, Long Distance* (from home), and *The Handyman* (the role of a man around the house). The image of architecture and the sound of voice identified in nursery rhymes and fairy tales carry her themes.

In 1972, she wrote: "The canvas of my fiction is narrow—domestic, mainly concerned with sexual and parental relationships—but I hope makes up in depth what it lacks in breadth. So far, I am almost entirely concerned with individuals' motives and the development of their personalities from an early age (*Pumpkin Eater* and *The Home,* particularly). Rather obviously (though not necessarily) I write through the eyes and ears of a woman. My men, I think, are getting better, and maybe I will someday venture to try to put myself inside a man's head and write from there. I believe that comedy is absolutely essential to tragedy, and I hope my books are almost as funny as they are (I'm told) sad or depressing. I would like to enlarge my scope, but not if it's at the expense of depth." In many of M.'s plots, the self is threatened in its relationships, feels captured, shelled, shelved, eaten. The depth of the heroine's mind is plumbed to reveal that the "I" is lost in its "we" relationships and that power flows from men. The lyric self of childhood memories and egoism is lost in the passage of time, and love cannot rescue it. M.'s stories and novels explore the conflict and theme of identity in transition.

About Time: An Aspect of Autobiography (1979) discloses the origins of M.'s lyric self, the persona of the novels. M.'s voice recounting her girlhood is fond, bemused, and deadly honest in its portrayal of her parents and their siblings, even when the truth is difficult and painful. For example, she reports her father's pitiful attempts to seduce her at eight and her own provocative behavior toward him when she turned sixteen. This incestuous and competitive relationship is reported in a truly disinterested voice. Her gentleness and independence serve her well in investigating her parents' generation. Many scenes drawn from memory recur in the fiction and are memorable; her uncle's rope factory and the dance with Mr. Fox, who was "at least forty-five, heavily married, and had a nasty little black mustache." Yet more indelible than the drawing of character, later caricatured in comedy, is M.'s disclosure of the details of provincial life that improbably represent the full range of human emotion in her fiction.

Her three early novels, *A Villa in Summer* (1954), *The Bright Prison* (1956), and *Daddy's Gone A-Hunting* (1958) center on the case of the emotionally overcommitted woman caught in a failing marriage: He withdraws, she frantically pursues. Adultery is a symptom of betrayal within the self. M. is interested not in the war between the sexes but in the war within the self. Two individuals may never become one in marriage, but each may romantically count on becoming one whole person. This failed dream sets up the blaming that turns the plot in all three. Marriage is the "bright" prison, the confining institution that hosts children's birthday parties and sexual infidelities. In *Daddy's Gone A-Hunting*, guilt for her part in the couple's failure to find unity in sexual fidelity paralyzes the heroine. She suffers but cannot change her own plight or, more damaging, protect her daughter from her "hunter"-husband, Rex.

The Pumpkin Eater (1962), M.'s best-known novel, was adapted as a film by Harold Pinter and starred Anne Bancroft and Peter Finch. After three marriages end in divorce, the heroine meets and falls in love with Jake, who welcomes marriage and family life, embracing the many children of his new wife. To say that purpose for the unnamed heroine amounts to having babies shows how M. simplifies a narrative of desire to its fairy-tale structure. To keep Jake happy and fed, to keep her own sanity that is linked to his happiness, she must terminate her last pregnancy. For her, it is the murder of desire and sanity. An abortion and sterilization are prescribed to remedy her depression. The displacement of motive and the manipulation of wills foment madness whose horror is simulated in the novel's fragmentation and dissolution.

My Friend Says It's Bullet-Proof (1967) demonstrates how "comedy is absolutely essential to tragedy" and how the novelist deepens her themes of isolation and identity by genre exploration. Comedy integrates character through change. In *Bullet-Proof* and *The Home* (1971), the heroines face their dissolving marriages and de-selved roles with comic verve. They are obsessed with recording their loss. Rather than finding a recognizable self in the record, a new self emerges in the recording.

If *Bullet-Proof* is comedy and *The Home* realism, then M.'s eighth novel, *Long Distance* (1974), is allegory and fabulation, the journey into the past by way of madness. Again, the "I" of *Long Distance*, like Jake's wife in *The Pumpkin Eater*, has no given name; she speaks directly to a "you" who seems to be the eternal judging and deserting male. Read as a sequel to *The Pumpkin Eater*, the "action" follows the nightmare of shock treatments, drugs, and psychoanalytic therapy after her breakdown. M. has been criticized for her mishandling of fantasy and the fantastic landscape, but the image of the woman as a lost child, a long distance from home, making her escape to the gardener's shed to confess her incestuous love to this gardener-father is a terrifying Alice with her trick looking-glass. The novel attempts to render the terrors of madness by poetically concentrating the familiar and customary roles in erotic associations. All characters are figments of her mind and, therefore, highly stylized: for example, the old witch-sibyl-mother, the gardener-seducer-father, and her young dream lover, Simon, her son in reality.

John Updike called M.'s novel *The Handyman* (1985) a "lovely book—fierce in its disillusion, poetic and carefree in its language, comic and horrifying and deeply familiar all at once." The novel tells the story of Phyllis Muspratt, who in her middle sixties is thrust into change and choice after her husband, Gerald, suddenly dies of a heart attack. Muspratt has an optimistic nature and life-long energetic habits that allow her to cope with her grown children and enjoy her grandchildren, especially her adored grandson. She is a woman who relies on traditional wisdom and roles. When she moves to the country, it is as though the civilized past is left behind because citizenship has been perverted into an underworld or an underground economy. It feels like a ruthless cowboy economy run by hired bullies with one strong-man leader, Wainwright, calling the shots.

Technically, M. works like a poet, reinforcing brevity of plot and episode with character density and depth. Her language is deft, hinting at associations with imagery, allusive discourse, tracing details. In the early books, the vulnerable self is identified with women's roles whenever and wherever they serve others: lovers, wives, mothers. The creative self in her early novels is covert: the voice of the mad housewife. In *The Handyman*, the traditional woman and the independent woman—little Phyllis Muspratt of private life and Rebecca Broune of public life—are allowed to speak. Neither is lesser. What we hear are two original voices of spirit, dignity, and courage, noble heroines, both, in a splendid, notable novel.

WORKS: (as Penelope Dimont) *Johanna* (1947). *A Villa in Summer* (1954). *The Bright Prison* (1956). (with J. Mortimer) *With Love and Lizards* (1957). *Daddy's Gone A-Hunting* (1958; in the U.S. as *Cave of Ice*, 1959). *The Renegade* (1961). *Saturday Night with the Brownings* (1960). *The Pumpkin Eater* (1962). (with J. Mortimer)

Bunny Lake Is Missing (1965). *Ain't Afraid to Dance* (1966). *My Friend Says It's Bullet-Proof* (1967). *The Home* (1971). *Three's One* (1973). *Long Distance* (1974). *About Time: An Aspect of Autobiography* (1979). *The Handyman* (1985). *Queen Elizabeth: A Life of the Queen Mother* (1986; also pub. as *Queen Mother: An Alternative Portrait of Her Life and Times,* 1995). *Portrait of a Marriage by Nigel Nicolson* (1989).

BIBLIOGRAPHY: Rubenstein, R. *Boundaries of the Self: Gender, Culture, Fiction* (1987).

For articles in reference works, see: *CA*. *CN*. *TCW*. *WA*.

Other references: *BW* (1 September 1985). *Listener* (14 July 1983). *London Journal* (August 1985). *LonT* (13 March 1986, 6 November 1995). *LRB* (21 July 1983). *New Statesman* (20 May 1983). *NYTBR* (19 August 1979, 1 December 1985, 29 June 1986). *Observer* (22 May 1983). *TLS* (20 May 1983, 4 April 1986).

Brett Averitt

Patricia Moyes

BORN: 19 January 1923, Bray, Ireland.
DAUGHTER OF: Ernst Pakenham-Walsh and Marion Boyd Pakenham-Walsh.
MARRIED: John Moyes, 1951; John S. Haszard, 1962.

Although born in Ireland, M. was educated in Northamptonshire, England. She served in the British Women's Auxiliary Air Force from 1940 to 1945. Her early occupations included being an aide to Peter Ustinov and assistant editor for *Vogue,* London. She translated *Time Remembered* by Jean Anouilh into English (1955) and wrote a filmscript, *School for Scoundrels* (1960), before publishing mysteries. In 1951, M. married John Moyes, a photographer; they were divorced eight years later. In 1962, she married John S. Haszard, who served as an official of the International Court of Justice. M. resided in the Netherlands for a time and then in the British Virgin Islands; she has set several of her mysteries in each of these settings.

M.'s detective stories are categorized as classic British mysteries, "cozy" rather than hard-boiled. Her detective is Henry Tibbett, an inconspicuous-looking police inspector who becomes superintendent. Tibbett's "nose" or intuition informs him when something is not right in a situation in which a death has been accepted as an accident or suicide. M.'s mysteries are not police procedurals such as those in the *Prime Suspect* series, with action in the squad room and interest in the interaction of a group of detectives. Instead, Tibbett is often on vacation or in a private capacity when he encounters a mystery to be solved.

Involved in all his cases is his wife Emmy, who supports him and contributes to the solutions, especially in *Johnny Under Ground* (1965), a case that begins with the reunion of her Royal Air Force comrades. In *The Curious Affair of the Third Dog* (1973), when Emmy visits her sister for a fortnight, a case of vehicular homicide turns out to be a gang slaying. Emmy brings the case to Henry's attention, and she and her sister smuggle him out of a hospital to deceive the master criminal and help capture him.

In most of the detective novels, the central characters and central consciousnesses are the Tibbetts. One exception is *Falling Star* (1964), in which the central consciousness, who functions as a narrator, is Pudge, the moneyman and executive producer of a film. Tibbett is an acquaintance of his to whom Pudge makes known the death of the leading actor from a seeming accidental fall down a flight of stairs into the path of a train. Like Dr. Watson in relation to Sherlock Holmes, Pudge's deductions are often wrong, and other characters deceive him. In contrast, Tibbett's reasoning shines. Other works in which Tibbett is not the central character include *Season of Snows and Sins* (1971), which has three narrators, including Emmy; *Who is Simon Warwick* (1978), in which the story is told partly through the eyes of Ambrose Quince, a solicitor trying to solve the mystery of which of two claimants for an inheritance is the real heir; and *Twice in a Blue Moon* (1993), in which the role of the Tibbetts' young friend Susan Gardiner is much like that of Pudge.

More recent mystery writers often specialize in one milieu, such as Dick Francis, whose mysteries involve horses, or Tony Hillerman, whose mysteries concern Native Americans in the Four Corners area of the United States. M. varies the milieu in her fictions from skiing in *Dead Man Don't Ski* (1959) to sailing in *Down Among the Dead Men* (1961) and *Angel Death* (1980) to fashion in *Murder à la Mode* (1963) to dog racing in *The Curious Affair of the Third Dog. A Six Letter Word for Death* (1983) involves the creation of crossword puzzles as well as a group of mystery writers who try to outwit and embarrass Tibbett in setting him a puzzle to be solved. M. has written that the puzzle element and the characterization are equally important to her and to the fictions' success.

M.'s detective novels enjoy sustained popularity, are still in print, and continue selling in the United States. They are only recently beginning to attract serious critical analysis, however.

WORKS: (trans.) *Time Remembered,* by Jean Anouilh (1955). *Dead Men Don't Ski* (1959). (with others) *School for Scoundrels* (1960; filmscript). *Down Among the Dead Men* (1961; in the U. K. as *The Sunken Sailor). Death on the Agenda* (1962). *Murder à la Mode* (1963). *Falling Star* (1964). *Johnny Under Ground* (1965). *Murder by 3's* (*Dead Men Don't Ski, Down Among the Dead Men, Falling Star*) (1965). *Murder Fantastical* (1967). *Death and the Dutch Uncle* (1968). *Helter-Skelter* (1968). *Many Deadly Returns* (1970; in the U. K. as *Who Saw Her Die?*). *Season of Snows and Sins* (1971). *The Curious Affair of the Third Dog* (1973). *After All, They're Only Cats* (1973). *Black Widower* (1975). *The Coconut Killings* (1977; in the U.K. as *To Kill a Coconut*). *Who Is Simon Warwick?* (1978). *How to Talk to Your Cat* (1978). *Angel Death* (1980). *A Six-Letter Word for Death* (1983). *Night Ferry to Death* (1985). *Black Girl, White Girl* (1989). *Twice in a Blue Moon* (1993).

BIBLIOGRAPHY: Albert, W. *Detective and Mystery Fiction* (1985). Breen, J. L. *What About Murder? 1981–1991* (1993). Brobera, J. *Korsforhor* (1976). Burback, S. K. *Writing Mystery and Crime Fiction* (1985). Charney, H. *The Detective Novel of Manners* (1981). *Cops and Constables,* ed. G. N. Dove and E. F. Bargainnier (1986).

100 Great Detectives, ed. M. Jakubowski (1991). La Cour, T. and H. Mogensen. *The Murder Book* (1971). McDorman, K. S. *Ngaio Marsh* (1991). *Cooking with Malice Domestic,* ed. J. M. McMillen and R. McMillen (1991). Oleksiw, S. *A Reader's Guide to the Classic British Mystery* (1988). Wynn, D. *Murderess Ink* (1979).

For articles in reference works, see: *CA. TCC&MW. WD.*

Other references: Barzun, J. and W. H. Taylor, intro. to *Johnny Under Ground* (1966). Boucher, A., intro. to *Murder by 3's* (1965). Moyes, P. *The Writer* (April 1970, October 1976). Interviews in *Ellery Queen Mystery Magazine* (June 1982, July 1982).

Kate Begnal

Mrs. Alexander: See *Hector, Annie French*

Mrs. Bogan of Bogan: See *Nairne, Carolina, Baroness*

Mrs. Bryne: See *Dacre, Charlotte*

Mrs. Ellis: See *Ellis, Sarah Stickney*

Mrs. K. P.: See *Philips, Katherine*

Mrs. Manners: See *Stepney, Lady Catherine*

Mrs. Meade: See *Pilkington, Laetitia*

Mrs. Piozzi: See *Piozzi, Hester Lynch Salusbury Thrale*

Mrs. Robinson: See *Robinson, Mary Darby (Perdita)*

Mrs. Rowson of the New Theatre, Philadelphia: See *Rowson, Susanna*

Mrs. S. C.: See *Schreiner, Olive Emilie Albertina*

Mrs. Tighe: See *Tighe, Mary*

M. S.: See *Smedley, Menella Bute*

M. T.: See *Tighe, Mary*

Willa (Wilhelmina or Williamina) Johnstone Anderson Muir

BORN: 13 March 1890, Montrose, Scotland.
DIED: 22 May 1970, London.
DAUGHTER OF: Peter Anderson and Elizabeth Pray Anderson.
MARRIED: Edwin Muir, 1918.
WROTE UNDER: Willa Muir; Agnes Neill Scott.

As a writer, M. is most widely known today for her part—in fact the major part—in the husband-wife team of Willa and Edwin Muir, the original English translators of Franz Kafka, Hermann Broch, and other European writers. But M. also translated independently and she published two novels of her own; essays on what she saw as the special role of women; a study of ballads; a memoir, *Belonging;* and a few poems. An almost equal amount of unpublished material testifies to her lifelong commitment to the writer's art. That translating should be the work to gain her most recognition seemed assured from her childhood. Because her family had come from the Shetlands, Shetland was the language spoken at home and the first that M. learned. When neighborhood children teased her about her speech, however, her response, even though she was barely three, was an immediate mastery of both "broad Montrose" and English. That, she says in her memoir, "was why I became good at Greek and Latin as I grew up."

She did become "good at Greek and Latin." Excelling at Board School, she was given a scholarship to Montrose Academy and then another to the University of St. Andrews. Graduating with a first in Classics, she was offered a scholarship to the British School in Rome to work for a Ph.D., with the prospect of a distinguished academic career. But she was not only a brilliant linguist; she was ardently romantic. For the sake of "true love," she threw away this "chance of a lifetime" because she did not want to leave her current rugby-playing sweetheart. Two years later, now an independent woman teaching in England, she ended the relationship equally dramatically by throwing his diamond and sapphire ring into the sea.

But "true love" for M. was more than a romantic gesture. It arose from a deep sense, described in her memoir, of "Belonging to the Universe": a sense of being somehow in tune with an essential rightness in things. With this deeper meaning, "true love" once more intervened in her life when she abandoned a secure position as lecturer in psychology and vice-principal of a training college in London for marriage to Edwin Muir and an uncertain financial future. For Edwin, an Orkneyman who had been forced to leave school at the age of fourteen, had nevertheless just won some recognition as a writer and wanted to escape the drudgery of his clerking job in a Glasgow shipbuilding firm for a literary life. And because the head of M.'s college considered Edwin's book a godless volume, she had to quit her post for marrying him. Providentially at this point, a new American weekly, *The Freeman,* offered to pay Edwin for one or two articles a month; with this sudden fortune in hand, the two of them left London for a European adventure, beginning with Prague, Czechoslovakia. In the process, M. of course added more languages to her Greek and Latin, with Edwin following suit. At the same time, his dark Glasgow memories dissolved, freeing him at last to become the poet he essentially was. But when in March 1924 *The Freeman* suspended publication and left them penniless, neither his poetry nor the sketches of European life that she tried to market offered a means of survival. Instead, there was translation. Unexpectedly, a request arrived from a New York publisher asking them to translate three plays by Gerhart Hauptmann. And that, says Edwin in his *Autobiography,* "was the beginning of a period when we turned ourselves into a sort of translation factory," as together they put often multiple works of more than a dozen authors into English and she independently completed particularly sensitive translations of four Hans Carossa novels.

As their translations gained recognition, however, they were able to suggest titles that they themselves found important. In 1929, they persuaded a publisher to commission translations of a writer hitherto unknown in English who was to provide a name for some of the twentieth-century's nightmares: Franz Kafka. Beginning with *The Castle* (1930), they translated six of his books, finding an appropriate but clear English style for his distinctive German. Another major triumph was their translation of Hermann Broch's massive trilogy, *The Sleepwalkers;* during this time they engaged in such a warm correspondence with Broch, who was still changing and completing his text as the translation proceeded, that they became friends. M. and Edwin visited him in Vienna during one of their European excursions, and later, after the Austrian *Anschluss,* were able to help him escape to refuge with them in St. Andrews.

In all of this, although the fact was not always recognized, M. had the major role. She was the better linguist. "Edwin's interpretations tended to be wild and gay," she noted. She also sacrificed more time taken from her own work to the task. Yet they developed a basic partnership, on Kafka particularly, dividing the books in two, with each translating a half, then going over each other's translation "as with a fine-tooth comb." By the time they put the two halves together, "the translation was like a seamless garment," she wrote, and each volume recognized as a work of art. Today, more than sixty years later, their *The Castle, The Trial,* and *Selected Short Stories* are still in print.

Still, somehow they also managed to produce their own writing. Because she deferred to what she considered his greater genius, she voluntarily, though not always happily, tried to assure him uninterrupted hours for his poetry, reviews, and novels. She was, too, more involved than he in household business, especially after their son Gavin was born in 1927, and thus had far less time for her own work. Even so, she published several essays on women, including *Women: An Inquiry* (1925), in which she argued that women's minds, working in circles, both complemented and corrected male linearity. Two imperfect but strongly imagined novels followed—*Imagined Corners* (1931) and *Mrs. Ritchie* (1933). She also finished two unpublished novels, the last, in 1952, based on their postwar experience in Prague, when Edwin was director of the British Institute. After her 1936 essay, *Mrs. Grundy in Scotland,* however, there were no more publications, aside from a few translations and an essay on translating, until after Edwin's death in 1959.

Before his death, Edwin had received a grant from the Bollingen Foundation to do a study of ballads, but he had written nothing. Now she readily took up the task. She called her book *Living with Ballads* (1965) because, like Edwin, she had lived with ballads in her youth and witnessed their emergence from the "underworld of feeling" into the life of a community. Then in her seventies, she wrote *Belonging* (1968), a loving memoir of a marriage in which both partners belonged inseparably together, and a testament to her lifelong sense of belonging to the universe. Finally, nearing seventy-nine, she published her last little book, "a kind of farewell" to her friends, called *Laconics, Jingles and Other Verses* (1969). But although some of the verses are undoubtedly jingles, others are true poems, and among these the most moving are farewells, not to friends, but to Edwin.

WORKS: *Women: An Inquiry* (1925). (trans., with E. Muir) *Dramatic Works,* Vol. 8, by G. Hauptmann (1925). (trans, with E. Muir) *The Island of the Great Mother,* by G. Hauptmann (1925). (trans., with E. Muir) *Jew Süss,* by L. Feuchtwanger (1926; in the U.S. as *Power*). (trans., with E. Muir) *The Ugly Duchess,* by L. Feuchtwanger (1927). (trans., with E. Muir) *Two Anglo-Saxon Plays,* by L. Feuchtwanger (1928). (trans., with E. Muir) *Class of 1902,* by E. Glaeser (1929). (trans., with E. Muir) *War,* by L. Renn [pseud. A.F.V. von Golssenau] (1929). (trans., as A. N. Scott) *A Roumanian Diary,* by H. Carossa (1929). (trans., with E. Muir) *The Life of Eleanora Duse,* by E. A. Reinhardt (1930). (trans., as A. N. Scott) *A Childhood,* by H. Carossa (1930). (trans., with E. Muir) *Success,* by L. Feuchtwanger (1930). (trans., with E. Muir) *The Castle,* by F. Kafka (1930). (trans., with E. Muir) *After War,* by L. Renn [pseud. A.F.V. von Golssenau] (1931). *Imagined Corners* (1931). (trans., as A. N. Scott) *Boyhood and Youth,* by H. Carossa (1931). (trans.) *Five Songs from the Auvergnat* (1931). (trans., with E. Muir) *The Sleepwalkers,* by H. Broch (1932). (trans., with E. Muir) *Josephus,* by L. Feuchtwanger (1932). (trans., with E. Muir) *The Inner Journey,* by K. Heuser 1932; in the U.S. as *The Journey Inward*). (trans, with E. Muir) *Three Cities,* by S. Asch (1933). *Mrs. Ritchie* (1933). (trans., with E. Muir) *The Great Wall of China,* by F. Kafka (1933). (trans., with E. Muir) *Little Friend,* by E. Lothar (1933). (trans., as A. N. Scott) *Doctor Gion,* by H. Carossa (1933). (trans., as A. N. Scott) *The Child Manuela,* by C. Winsloe [Baroness Hatvany] (1933). (trans., with E. Muir) *Salvation,* by S. Asch (1934). (trans., with E. Muir) *The Jew of Rome,* by L. Feuchtwanger (1934). (trans., with E. Muir) *The Hill of Lies,* by H. Mann (1934). (trans., with E. Muir) *The Mills of God,* by E. Lothar (1935; in the U.S. as *The Loom of Justice*). (trans., with E. Muir) *Mottke the Thief,* by S. Asch (1935). (trans., with E. Muir) *The Unknown Quantity,* by H. Broch (1935). (trans., as A. N. Scott) *Life Begins,* by C. Winsloe [Baroness Hatvany] (1935; in the U.S. as *Girl Alone*). (trans., with E. Muir) *Night Over the East,* by E. M. von Kuhnelt-Leddihn (1936). (trans., with E. Muir) *The Queen's Doctor,* by R. Neumann (1936). (trans., with E. Muir) *The Call of Paper,* by S. Asch (1936; in the U.S. as *The War Goes On*). *Mrs. Grundy in Scotland* (1936). (trans., with E. Muir) *The False Nero,* by L. Feuchtwanger (1937; in the U.S. as *The Pretender*). (trans., with E. Muir) *The Trial,* by F. Kafka (1937). (trans., with E. Muir) *The Enigmatic Czar,* by G. M. Paleologue (1938). (trans., with E. Muir) *A Woman Screamed,* by R. Neumann (1938). (trans., with E. Muir)

America, by F. Kafka (1938). (trans., with E. Muir) *Richelieu,* by C-J. Burckhardt (1940). (trans., with E. Muir) *Through a Woman's Eyes,* by Z. Harsanyi (1940). (trans., with E. Muir) *Lover of Life,* by Z. Harsanyi (1942). (trans., with E. Muir) *Parables in German and English,* by F. Kafka (1947). (trans., with E. Muir) *In a Penal Settlement,* by F. Kafka (1948). *Living with Ballads* (1965). *Belonging* (1968). *Laconics, Jingles, and Other Verse* (1969).

BIBLIOGRAPHY: Butter, P., in *Edwin Muir: Centenary Assessments,* ed. C.J.M. MacLachlan (1990). Butter, P. *Chapman* (1993). Butter, P., in *Scotland and the Slavs,* ed. P. Henry, et al. (1993). Caird, J. *Chapman* (1992). Huberman, E. *MAL* (1989). Huberman, E., in *Edwin Muir: Centenary Assessments,* ed. C.J.M. MacLachlan (1990). Mandel, U. M. *Journal of the Kafka Society of America* (1990). Mudge, P. R. *Chapman* (1992). Murray, I. *Scottish Literary Journal* (1994). Soukup, C. *Chapman* (1992). Soukup, L. *Chapman* (1992). Soukup, L. *The Wider Europe* (1992).

For articles in reference works, see: *Feminist.*

Other references: Butter, P. *Edwin Muir* (1962). Butter, P. *Edwin Muir, Man and Poet* (1966). *Selected Letters of Edwin Muir, ed. P. Butter* (1974). Huberman, E. *The Poetry of Edwin Muir* (1971). Mellown, E. W. *Edwin Muir* (1979).

Elizabeth Huberman

Mulock, Dinah Maria: See *Craik, Dinah Maria Mulock*

Mulock, Miss: See *Craik, Dinah Maria Mulock*

Mulso, Hester: See *Chapone, Hester Mulso*

Constantia Munda

FLOURISHED: early 1600s.

M. wrote *The Worming of a mad Dogge: Or, A Soppe For Cerberus The Jaylor of Hell. No Confutation but A sharpe Redargution of the bayter of Women,* printed in 1617, the third response to Joseph Swetnam's very popular 1615 pamphlet, *The Araignment of Lewde, idle, froward, and unconstant women: Or the vanitie of them, choose you whether.* The pseudonym "Constantia Munda" means "Moral Constancy."

M. identifies herself as a woman, and Rachel Speght in *Mortalities Memorandum, With A Dreame Prefixed* confirms this by referring to M. as "she." M. dedicates *Worming* to "The Right Worshipful Lady her most deare Mother, the Lady Prudentia Munda," to whom she offers "her writing hand" that penned this pamphlet "in recompence" for the "pangs of sorrow you sustain'd / In child-birth."

M. demonstrates a knowledge of the law and many Greek, Latin, and Italian texts in *The Worming,* which is unusual for a woman, but she does establish her persona as the daughter of a lady, which could account for her learned references. Her ranting language ("your turbulent mind is defecated"), however, is unusual for a lady.

The Worming is more of an attack on Swetnam and the popular press than a defense of women. M. describes Swetnam as "an ill-favoured hunks" and accuses the press of having "become the receptacle of every dissolute Pamphlet." According to M., the public theater attracts "every fantasticke Poetaster," who "strive[s] to represent unseemely figments imputed to our sex."

One of M.'s most unusual arguments is her response to Swetnam's statement that he thinks it strange that men and women should love each other because they are so different: Men love war and drums, women love sweet music. M. contends that the purpose of war is peace and that the difference between men and women in terms of war is constructed, not an intrinsic attribute of each sex.

The Worming was printed for Laurence Hayes by G. Purslowe, the same printer who produced the second edition of *The Araignment.*

WORKS: *The Worming of mad Dogge: Or, A Soppe For Cerberus The Jaylor of Hell. No Confutation but A sharpe Redargution of the bayter of Women* (1617, STC 18257); ed. S. Shepherd (1985); facsimile with intro. by S. O'Malley (1995).

BIBLIOGRAPHY: Beilin, E. *Redeeming Eve* (1987). *ELR* (1984). Jones, A. R., in *The Renaissance Englishwoman in Print,* ed. A. Haselkorn and B. Travitsky (1990). Shepherd, S. *Amazons & Warrior Women* (1981). Speght, R. *Mortalities Memorandum, With A Dreame Prefixed* (1621). Woodbridge, L. *Women and the English Renaissance* (1984).

Susan Gushee O'Malley

(Jean) Iris Murdoch

BORN: 15 July 1919, Dublin, Ireland.
DAUGHTER OF: Wills John Hughes Murdoch and Irene Alice Richardson Murdoch.
MARRIED: John O. Bayley, 1956.

Born of Protestant Anglo-Irish parents in Dublin, M. grew up in London but retained an active interest in Ireland, especially as setting for some of her novels. She studied classics, ancient history, and philosophy at Oxford before World War II, worked during the war for the British government, and later helped refugees for the United Nations. She continued her study of philosophy at Cambridge after the war and subsequently became a fellow at Oxford. She married John Bayley, poet, critic, novelist, and also a fellow at Oxford, in 1956.

In addition to specialized papers on linguistic analysis and existentialism, she has written a number of less technical works on ethics, aesthetics, and similar moral issues, including *Sartre: Romantic Rationalist* (1953), *The Sovereignty of Good* (1970), *The Fire and the Sun: Why Plato Banished the Artists* (1977), and *Acastos* (1986). Though she has tried to keep her philosophic work distinct from her literary output (more than twenty novels as well as stories and plays), her philosophic bent is immediately evident in her fiction.

M.'s fiction is characterized by a remarkable sense of humor, particularly wit and word play, farce (including wild chases), burlesque, dependence on split-second timing, and unforeseen plot twists. Her sense of parody and satire is less obvious, but her balance among various comic modes, including gentle satiric thrusts, combined as these are with serious, even polemical concerns, makes her work considerably more complex than it first appears.

She has repeatedly stated that she identifies with the tradition of George Eliot. Though she has acknowledged Henry James's influence, she has also stated that she prefers the non-Jamesian "open" novel (a spontaneous gathering of eccentric characters engaged in casual, seemingly uncontrolled activities), a claim not wholly borne out by her tightly structured books. She has used the term "transcendental realism" (in her essay "Against Dryness: A Polemical Sketch") to apply to her fiction, a term suggesting an initial acceptance of conventional concepts of plot, character, and setting with a subsequent explosion of absurd, wildly outrageous, and richly unconventional occurrences and "messy" characters. Despite the seemingly anarchic tone and nature of her novels, M. is evidently pessimistic about transient humanity's chances of survival in a formless, directionless universe.

M.'s fiction, consequently, focuses on individuals who are required by some circumstance (possibly violent or absurd) to ponder the nature of personal freedom and commitment. They must then realize that they can know neither love nor freedom unless they accept the radical "contingency" and ultimate pointlessness of existence as prerequisite to relations with others. M.'s first novel, *Under the Net* (1954), for example, offers a protagonist, Jake Donaghue, who discovers the sheer joy and unknowable wonder of life through some wildly comic adventures involving continual misunderstanding of other people. *The Flight from the Enchanter* (1956), a more complex, original novel, contrasts the fascinating but amoral Mischa Fox, who uses other people, with Rosa Keepe, who barely escapes his influence.

The Bell (1958), commonly considered (with *A Severed Head,* 1961) the best of M.'s earlier works, follows a variety of ordinary characters who retreat to a monastery to escape human limitations and failure, especially at love. Unable to live either in the world or out of it, they individually work out their destinies. *A Severed Head* is a remarkably effective comic account of the same efforts to understand the nature of human freedom; one of M.'s familiar clumsy male protagonists, Martin Lynch-Gibbon, reluctantly learns about love and sex in a series of wildly incongruous sexual couplings.

Following *A Severed Head,* M. published seven novels in quick succession. *An Unofficial Rose* (1962) is a family chronicle about an elderly man's reflections on his past and his desires for his son's future; *The Unicorn* (1963) is a slight though heavily philosophical work concerned with the ambiguity of relationships, especially sexual ones; *The Italian Girl* (1964) is a short, more Gothic work set in a Scottish household; *The Red and the Green* (1965) is a historical work set in Dublin during the 1916 Easter uprising; *The Time of the Angels* (1966), M.'s "God is dead" novel closely related to *The Unicorn* in its concern with metaphysical concepts, is a fascinating, sensational, Gothic exploration into the nature of evil; *The Nice and the Good* (1968) is a return to M.'s earlier concern with the conflicts inherent in spiritual and sexual love; and *Bruno's Dream* (1969) is a somewhat surrealistic account of an old man's dying thoughts as he feebly attempts to understand the world and death.

In the 1970s, M. continued her rapid production, with *A Fairly Honourable Defeat* (1970) an appropriate name for the position many of her characters accept in their metaphysical quest. Though this novel breaks no new ground for M., she is more detailed in her evident knowledge of cuisines and cultural allusions, and this and several of her subsequent works are more expansive in scope and bulk. *An Accidental Man* (1971) focuses on the contrast between the search for love and the search for power through a kind of parallel novel-within-a-novel. *The Black Prince* (1973) is more experimental in its obsessive handling of a middle-aged man's lust for a twenty-year-old woman and with other sexual pairings reminiscent of *An Accidental Man. The Sacred and Profane Love Machine* (1974) is also about a man obsessed, in this case with his two loves, his wife (the sacred) and his mistress (the profane); this book, by far M.'s most violent, raises numerous moral questions but resolves few of them satisfactorily. The protagonist in *A Word Child* (1975) discovers that his adultery has been indirectly responsible for the deaths of two others and that his past is returning to haunt him; desperate to touch and love others, he eventually tries to purge his guilt by contacting the man he cuckolded.

The more thoughtful *Henry and Cato* (1976) focuses on two men who attempt individually to reconcile private impulses, especially the need for love: One, a self-exile in the United States until his brother's death, returns to England and echoes of his earlier life; the other, his boyhood friend turned Anglican priest, wrestles with forbidden love. Both men are complicated, both have muddled emotional lives, and both learn about pure evil in the forms of "fallen angels" who tempt them. *The Sea, The Sea* (1978) has been compared by Margaret Drabble to *The Tempest* and to Homer; it deals with a theater director who retires to the seashore but who slowly entraps his old circle of friends in his sexual obsessiveness.

The 1980s and 1990s showed a continuation of M.'s prolific productivity, with no diminution of her philosophical interests but with greater abstraction in characterization. The first word of *Nuns and Soldiers* (1980) is "Wittgenstein," who has frequently been invoked in analyses of M.'s work; the speaker, dying on Christmas Eve, hosts an entourage of friends who later intrude possessively between would-be lovers, the widow, and one of the friends. *The Philosopher's Pupil* (1983) presents an overly didactic allegorical struggle between good and evil, even to the point of identifying the narrator by an initial; similarly, *The Good Apprentice* (1985) is both allegorical and muddled, though it is much more emphatic about the protagonist's suffering through personal irresponsibility toward a friend.

M.'s "novels of ideas" have continued to intrigue readers and critics in recent years, though her production has diminished; she retired in 1993 as Warton professor of English at Oxford University. The revelation early in 1997 that she suffers from Alzheimer's disease, with its concomitant forgetfulness that manifested itself in such minor ways as M. losing her way when visiting friends and forgetting the titles of her books and in such serious ways as her inability to organize an entire novel, suggests that her writing may have ended. Ironically, *The Message to the Planet* (1989) itself deals with an influential writer/thinker, Marcus Vallar, who has disappeared but who is required to rescue an impoverished poet who is dying of a disease. Other aspects of this novel, of course, are less parallel to M.'s own life, such as a "miraculous" cure for the poet, but M.'s familiar philosophic explorations, in this case into the possibilities of genius tinged with madness, remains paramount.

Jackson's Dilemma (1995), M.'s twenty-sixth and possibly last novel, is also intellectually tantalizing as well as broadly humorous, a "mystic farce," as the critic for the *Times Literary Supplement* called it, as well as a psychological thriller. The eponymous Jackson is a butler, in the line of such indispensable servants as Jeeves and Crichton, who arrives unannounced at a fashionable home on the eve of a wedding between two troubled young people in a houseful of upper-class twits. Jackson is possibly divine; he is surely able to bring order into the complex relationships in the home. The novel is inescapably funny in a broad, eccentric manner, though as usual M. offers a complex, convoluted set of relationships to suggest more profound underlying levels of meaning.

M.'s books have steadily grown longer and more turgid, though with greater concern with her character's experiential growth and breadth. She has often written about her characters' sexuality, even promiscuity, and she has dealt with such sexual taboos as incest. As her books have grown more abstract and philosophical, they have also sometimes grown less interesting as fiction, with recent characters less memorable than those of the 1960s.

She remained a fertile writer, with undiminished vigor and productivity, with meticulous detail, and above all with dense, austere, unromantic, and pessimistic perspectives on her characters' lives until the onset of Alzheimer's. Her characters are not tragic, just pathetic or terrible, and comedy helps the reader to see how enslaved they are, trapped by the ideas M. forces them to bear. At her best she is both entertaining and intellectually challenging; at her worst, she is abstract to the point of obscurity. She deals primarily with concepts such as love, freedom, and power, and the "morality" she offers through her characters is limited in part by their own limitations, in part by the opposition of a host of authority figures, but almost always by some form of love and moral commitment.

WORKS: *Sartre: Romantic Rationalist* (1953, 1980). *Under the Net* (1954). *The Flight from the Enchanter* (1955). *The Sandcastle* (1957). *The Bell* (1958). *A Severed Head* (1961; as play, with J. B. Priestley, 1964). *An Unofficial Rose* (1962). *The Unicorn* (1963). *The Italian Girl* (1964; as play, with J. Saunders, 1968). *The Red and the Green* (1965). *The Time of the Angels* (1966). *The Nice and the Good* (1968). *Bruno's Dream* (1969). *A Fairly Honourable Defeat* (1970). *The Sovereignty of Good* (1970). *The Servants and the Snow* (1970). *An Accidental Man* (1971). *The Three Arrows* (1972). *The Black Prince* (1973). *The Sacred and Profane Love Machine* (1974). *A Word Child* (1975). *Henry and Cato* (1976). *The Fire and the Sun: Why Plato Banished the Artists* (1977). *The Sea, the Sea* (1978). *A Year of Birds* (1978). *Nuns and Soldiers* (1980). *Art and Error* (1980). *The Philosopher's Pupil* (1983). *The Good Apprentice* (1985). *Acastos* (1986). *Above the Gods* (1987). *The Book and the Brotherhood* (1987). *The Message to the Planet* (1989). *Metaphysics as a Guide to Morals* (1993). *The Green Knight* (1994). *Jackson's Dilemma* (1995). *Existentialists and Mystics: Writings on Philosophy and Literature,* ed. P. Conradi (1997).

BIBLIOGRAPHY: *Iris Murdoch and the Search for Human Goodness*, ed. M. Antonaccio and W. Schwelker (1996). Baldanza, F. *Iris Murdoch* (1974). Begnal, K. *Iris Murdoch: A Reference Guide* (1987). Bove, C. B. *A Character Index and Guide to the Fiction of Iris Murdoch* (1986). Byatt, A. S. *Degrees of Freedom: The Novels of Iris Murdoch* (1965). Conradi, P. J. *Iris Murdoch: The Saint and the Artist* (1986). Dipple, E. *Iris Murdoch: Work for the Spirit* (1982). Gerstenberger, D. *Iris Murdoch* (1975). Gordon, D. J. *Iris Murdoch's Fables of Unselfing* (1995). Hague, A. *Murdoch's Comic Vision* (1979). Hawkins, P. S. *The Language of Grace: Flannery O'Connor, Walker Percy, and Iris Murdoch* (1983). Heusel, B. S. *Patterned Aimlessness: Iris Murdoch's Novels of the 1970s and 1980s* (1995). Johnson, D. *Iris Murdoch* (1987). Kane, R. C. *Iris Murdoch, Muriel Spark and John Fowles: Didactic Demons in Modern Fiction* (1988). Rabinovitz, R. *Iris Murdoch* (1968). Ramanathan, S. *Iris Murdoch: Figures of Good* (1990). Todd, R. *Iris Murdoch: The Shakespearian Interest* (1979). Todd, R. *Iris Murdoch* (1986). Tucker, L., ed. *Critical Essays on Iris Murdoch* (1992). Wolfe, P. *The Disciplined Heart: Iris Murdoch and Her Novels* (1966).

For articles in reference works, see: *Bloomsbury. CA. Cambridge. CD. CLC. CN. DLB. EWLTC. Feminist. MBL* and *SUP. Oxford. TCR. WA.*

Other references: Bellamy, M. *ConL* (1977). Biles, J. L. *SLITI* (1978). Blum, L. A. *Philosophical Studies* (1986). Bradbury, M. *Possibilities: Essays on the State of the Novel* (1973). Brans, J. *SWR* (1985). *ChiR* (Autumn 1959). Conradi, P. J. *CritQ* (1981). Culley, A. *MFS* (1969). Drabble, M. *Saturday Review* (6 January 1979). *Encounter* (January 1961). Jaidev. *PURLA* (October 1985). Jefferson, D., in *The Uses of Fiction: Essays on the Modern Novel in Honour of Arnold Kettle,* ed. D. Jefferson and G. Martin (1982). Moss, H. *GrandS* (1986). *PR* (1959). *The Nature of Metaphysics,* ed. U. F. Pears (1957). Sage, L. *CritQ* (1977). Scholes, R. *The Fabulators* (1967; rev. as *Fabulation and Metafiction,* 1979). Tucker, L. *ConL* (1986). Widman, R. L. *Crit* (1967). Widmer, K., in *Twentieth Century Women Novelists,* ed. T. F. Staley (1982). *YR* (1959).

Paul Schlueter

MWM: See *Montagu, Mary Wortley*

Carolina, Baroness Nairne

BORN: 16 August 1766, Gask, Perthshire, Scotland.
DIED: 27 October 1845, Gask, Scotland.
DAUGHTER OF: Laurence Oliphant and Margaret Robertson.
MARRIED: William Nairne, 1806.
WROTE UNDER: B. B.; Mrs. Bogan of Bogan.

Raised by ardent Jacobites and named for Prince Charles Stuart, N. spent her early life listening to tales of her Jacobite kin—the Robertsons, Murrays, Drummonds, and Graemes—and learning the music that was a particular pleasure to her upper-class family. Her paternal grandfather was a veteran of the rebellion of 1715; both he and her father were veterans of the 1745 rebellion; and her maternal grandfather was Duncan Robertson, chief of the clan Donnochy. Such distinguished lineage no doubt influenced the young woman, as did the music that played an important part in her homelife from early childhood when the children would sing a song before going to bed. N. and her two sisters were all able to play musical instruments and often entertained at social gatherings. This background provided the inspiration when "pretty Miss Car" began writing Jacobite songs as a young woman.

She enthusiastically welcomed the poetry of Robert Burns and persuaded her brother, Laurence, to subscribe to an edition of his poems that was published in 1786. N. was interested in Burns's method of providing new lyrics for old Scottish tunes because she felt that some of the old lyrics were too earthy. In 1792, she persuaded her brother to present her own anonymous version of "The Ploughman" or "The Pleuchman" to a group of his tenants. It became very popular, and in succeeding years N. wrote a number of humorous and patriotic songs, among which were "John Tod," "Jamie the Laird," and "The Laird o' Cockpen." In 1798, N. sent a copy of "The Land o' the Leal" to her friend Mrs. Campbell Colquhoun when the latter's child died. The song, a lament for a dead child that promises a better life in heaven, was for many years thought to be Burns's deathbed song because N. insisted on anonymity with regard to her lyrics.

In 1806, N. married her kinsman William Murray Nairne, who was heir to a peerage but whose lands and title were forfeit under the Act of Attainder. The couple had one son. N. continued writing lyrics as part of a committee of women dedicated to purifying the national minstrelsy; the committee published *The Scotish Minstrel* (1821) with N. contributing to the collection under the name of Mrs. Bogan of Bogan. Her songs were signed B. B., and even the publisher did not know her true identity because she disguised herself as an old gentlewoman when she held interviews with him. Though she admired Burns, she thought some of his songs "tended to inflame the passions," and she asked to have his "Willie brewed a peck o'maut," a drinking song, removed from *The Scotish Minstrel.* At this time, she was composing Jacobite songs for her aged uncle, the Chief of Strowan, and songs of the working classes for Nathaniel Gow, son of the famous Perthshire fiddler Neil Gow; among the latter was "Caller Herrin," about a Newhaven fishwoman. The tune of the song represents the chimes of Iron Church in Edinburgh.

N.'s husband was restored to the peerage by King George IV in 1824, and N. became Baroness Nairne. Lord Nairne died in 1830, after which N. took her ailing son to Ireland where she wrote several songs, the best known of which is "Wake, Irishmen, Wake," a political protest against the oppressiveness of the Roman Catholic Church in Ireland. N.'s son died in 1837 in Brussels, Belgium; from that time on, she often commented on her joy in the rapid passing of time so she could rejoin her husband and son in the afterlife.

At the age of thirty-one, when she had a mystical experience, N. became very devout. Disapproving of the lyrics of the old Scottish songs, she resolved to rewrite them in a more modest vein. Her efforts, though welcomed in her own time, have been criticized by modern commentators as mere contributions to the sentimental pietism and the genteel falsification of the working-class that overtook Scottish culture in the early nineteenth century. Such a charge may be leveled at "The Land o' the Leal" and perhaps "Caller Herrin," but it is not valid with regard to N.'s patriotic airs. "Will ye no' come back again?" beautifully expresses the desolation of the Jacobites at the exile of their prince, and "The Hundred Pipers," though apocryphal, is a thoroughly rousing portrayal of the crossing of the Esk by Scottish troops.

Before her death, N. agreed to have her songs published anonymously, and the book was in preparation at her death. With the approval of her sister, the songs were subsequently published in 1846 as *Lays from Strathearn* by Carolina, Baroness Nairne, and N.'s lifelong secret was at last revealed. N.'s songs, some of which rival Burns's best, are important reminders of the humor, the piety, and the patriotism of the Scottish nation.

WORKS: *Land o' the Leal and Other Songs* (1800). *The Scotish Minstrel* (1821). *Lays from Strathearn* (1846). *The Life and Songs of the Baroness Nairne: with a Memoir and Poems of Caroline Oliphant the Younger,* ed. C. Rogers (1869). *Will Ye No Come Back Again* (1900). *Caller Herrin': from Lays & Lyrics of Scotland* (1900). *The Songs of Lady Nairne* (1912). *Charlie is My Darling: Jacobite Songs* (1930). *The Laird o' Cockpen* (1981).

BIBLIOGRAPHY: Crichton, A. *"The Land o'the Leal": Who Wrote It, Lady Nairne or Burns?* (1919). Henderson, G. *Lady Nairne and Her Songs* (1906). Keddie, H. [pseud. Sarah Tytler] and J. L. Watson. *Songstresses of Scotland* (1871). *New Moulton's Library of Literary Criticism, Early Victorian* (1989). Redpath, J. *Songs of Lady Nairne* (1986). Simpson, M. S. *The Scottish Songstress, Caroline Baroness Nairne* (1894).

For articles in reference works, see: *DNB. PCWL. ToddBWW.*

Other references: Montgomerie, W. *Scottish Studies* (1957, 1959).

Sharon A. Winn

Napier, Sarah Lennox Bunbury: See Lennox Bunbury Napier, Sarah

Naylor, Eliot: See Frankau, Pamela

Edith Nesbit

BORN: 15 August 1858, London.
DIED: 22 April 1924, Dymchurch, Kent.
DAUGHTER OF: John Callis Nesbit and [given name unknown] Alderton.
MARRIED: Hubert Bland, 1880; Thomas Terry Tucker, 1917.
WROTE UNDER: E. Bland; Fabian Bland; E. Nesbit; Edith Nesbit.

N. was the youngest of four surviving children born to an agricultural chemist and the principal of an agricultural college in Kennington, a rural suburb of London, who died when N. was only three. Her widowed mother managed the college for a time but then decided to take her family abroad. This was an unsettled time for N., who hated the continental schools so much that she ran away from one of them. Her one happy time was in Brittany, where she stayed with a French family who had a daughter her own age. When she was thirteen, her family returned to England and settled in a large country house in Kent, which she loved; her mother soon ran out of money, however, necessitating a move to London.

When N. was twenty, she met Hubert Bland, a bank clerk, whom she married a year later. When her husband became ill with smallpox and his partner absconded with his funds, the family was left penniless. N., who had been publishing verse occasionally, was forced to support her children by selling poems and stories. The Blands both became socialists and were founders of the Fabian Society. They were the center of a literary salon, entertaining friends in Bohemian but intellectual gatherings. In spite of her domestic responsibilities with four children to support, N. was a prolific writer, publishing many short stories and other hack work. Her well-known books for children, which distinguished her career as a fiction writer, were not written until her forties. In 1899, she became famous for *The Story of the Treasure Seekers,* a collection of short pieces about the Bastable family, which had appeared in *Pall Mall* and *Windsor* magazines. This success also brought her prosperity and a new period of happy life at Well Hall in Kent, a moated sixteenth-century house. The second Bastable book, *The Wouldbegoods,* appeared in 1901.

The best-known of her children's novels, still popular today, are *Five Children and It* (1902), *The Phoenix and the Carpet* (1904), and *The Story of the Amulet* (1906). In *Five Children and It,* the children discover the Psammead, or sandfairy, which grants them wishes every morning and revokes the effects each evening at sunset. In *The Phoenix and the Carpet,* children find a phoenix egg rolled up in a carpet. Both magical creatures, the testy, cynical Psammead and the haughty, pompous phoenix, are memorable creations. *The Story of the Amulet* is a well-researched novel in which the quest for a missing half of an amulet takes the children on a series of time travels to ancient civilizations. Unlike most of her predecessors, N. was not didactic in her novels for children. Not concerned with moral issues, she rather took delight in the sheer variety of experience, particularly the comic and the fantastic. Influenced by Charles Dickens, whom she greatly admired, and by Victorian fantasist F. Anstey (Thomas Anstey Guthrie), N. in turn has influenced modern children's writers, including Edward Eager, who praised and imitated her technique of introducing magic into ordinary daily life.

In spite of her tremendous output—fifteen novels for children, nine novels for adults, and more than forty other books—N. continued to be in financial straits. Her husband's death in 1914 left her desolate, though she was awarded a modest civil pension in 1915 for her literary achievement. In 1917, she remarried and settled with her new husband, a widowed, retired marine engineer and an old friend, in a bungalow on the Kent coast, where she died in 1921 at the age of sixty-five.

N. regarded herself as one of those who remain children in a grown-up world. This quality of perceiving life from a child's point of view clearly influenced her effective portrayal of children and her convincing excursions into the realm of fantasy.

WORKS: *Lays and Legends,* 2 vols. (1886, 1892). *The Lily and the Cross* (1887). *The Star of Bethlehem* (1887). *The Better Part and Other Poems* (1888). *By Land and Sea* (1888). (with C. Brooke) *Easter Tide: Poems* (1888). *Landscape and Song* (1888). *Leaves of Life* (1888). *The Message of the Dove: An Easter Poem* (1888). (with C. Brooke and others) *The Time of Roses* (1888). (with H. J. Wood) *The Lilies Round the Cross: An Easter Memorial* (1889). (as Fabian Bland, with H. Bland) *The Prophet's Mantle* (1889).(with others) *Life's Sunny Side* (1890). *Songs of Two Seasons* (1890). *Sweet Lavender* (1892). *The Voyage of Columbus, 1492: The Discovery of America* (1892). (as E. Bland, with H. M. Burnside and A. Scanes) *Flowers I Bring and Songs I Sing* (1893). *Grim Tales* (1893). (with others) *Listen Long and Listen Well* (1893). *Our Friends and All About Them* (1893). *Something Wrong* (1893). (with others) *Sunny Tales for Snowy Days* (1893). (with others) *Told By Sunbeams and Me* (1893). (with O. Barron) *The Butler in Bohemia* (1894). (with others) *Fur and Feathers: Tales for All Weathers* (1894). (with others) *Hours in Many Lands: Stories and Poems* (1894). (with others) *Lads and Lassies* (1894). (with others) *Tales That Are True, for Brown Eyes and Blue* (1894). (with others) *Tales to Delight from Morning to Night* (1894). *Doggy Tales* (1895). (with T. Gift and Mrs. W. Bliss) *Dulcie's Lantern and Other Stories* (1895). (with N. Gale and R. Le Gallienne) *Holly and Mistletoe: A Book of Christmas Verse* (1895). *A Pomander of Verse* (1895). *Pussy Tales* (1895). *Rose Leaves* (1895). *Tales of the Clock* (1895). (with others) *Treasures from Storyland* (1895). *As Happy as a King* (1896). *In Homespun* (1896). *The Children's Shakespeare* (1897). *Dinna Forget* (1897). *Royal Children of English History* (1897). *Tales Told in Twilight: A Volume of Very Short Stories* (1897). (with A. Guest and E. R. Watson) *Dog Tales, and Other Tales* (1898). *Songs of Love and Empire* (1898). *Pussy and Doggy Tales* (1899). *Secret of the Kyriels* (1899). *The Story of the Treasure Seekers, Being the Adventures of the Bastable Children in Search of a Fortune* (1899). *The Book of Dragons* (1900). *Nine Unlikely Tales for Children* (1901). *Thirteen Ways Home* (1901). *To Wish You Every Joy* (1901). *The Wouldbegoods, Being the Further Adventures of the Treasure*

Seekers (1901). *Five Children and It* (1902). *The Red House* (1902). *The Revolt of the Toys and What Comes of Quarreling* (1902). *The Literary Sense* (1903). *Playtime Stories* (1903). *The Rainbow Queen and Other Stories* (1903). (with R. Bland) *Cat Tales* (1904). *The New Treasure Seekers* (1904). *The Phoenix and the Carpet* (1904). *The Story of the Five Rebellious Dolls* (1904). *Oswald Bastable and Others* (1905). *Pug Peter: King of Mouseland, Marquis of Barkshire, D. O. G., P. C. 1906, Knight of the Order of the Gold Dog Collar, Author of Doggerel Lays and Days . . .* (1905). *The Rainbow and the Rose* (1905). *The Incomplete Amorist* (1906). *Man and Maid* (1906). *The Railway Children* (1906). *The Story of the Amulet* (1906). *The Enchanted Castle* (1907). *Twenty Beautiful Stories from Shakespeare: A Home Study Course* (1907). *Ballads and Lyrics of Socialism 1883–1908* (1908). *The House of Arden* (1908). *Jesus in London* (1908). *The Old Nursery Stories* (1908). *Cinderella* (1909). *Daphne in Fitzroy Street* (1909). *Harding's Luck* (1909). *Salome and the Head: A Modern Melodrama* (1909). *These Little Ones* (1909). *Fear* (1910). *The Magic City* (1910). *Ballads and Verses of the Spiritual Life* (1911). *Dormant* (1911). (with G. Manville Fenn) *My Sea-Side Book* (1911). *The Wonderful Garden, or The Three C.'s* (1911). *Children's Stories from Shakespeare* (1912). *Garden Poems* (1912). *The Magic World* (1912). *Our New Story Book* (1913). *Wet Magic* (1913). (with D. Ashley) *Children's Stories from English History* (1914). *The Incredible Honeymoon* (1916). *The New World Literary Series, Book Two* (1921). *The Lark* (1922). *Many Voices* (1922). *To the Adventurous* (1923). *Five of Us—And Madeline,* ed. Mrs. C. Sharp (1925). *Long Ago When I Was Young* (1966). *Fairy Stories,* ed. N. Lewis (1977).

BIBLIOGRAPHY: Bell, A. *Edith Nesbit* (1960). Briggs, J. *A Woman of Passion: The Life of Edith Nesbit, 1858–1924* (1987). Carpenter, H. *Secret Gardens: The Golden Age of Children's Literature* (1985). Moore, D. L. *Edith Nesbit: A Biography* (1933, rev. ed. 1966). Streatfeild, N. *Magic and the Magician: Edith Nesbit and Her Children's Books* (1958).

For articles in reference works, see: *MJA* (1963). *OCCL*. *TCCW*.

Other references: *LonT* (2 November 1987). Manlove, C. *The Impulse of Fantasy Literature* (1984).

Charlotte Spivack

Newcastle, Duchess of: See Cavendish, Margaret

Grace Nichols

BORN: 18 January 1950, Georgetown, Guyana.
DAUGHTER OF: Peter Nichols and Iris Nichols.

As an Afro-Caribbean, postcolonial poet, novelist, and children's writer, N. spares no opportunity to celebrate her black womanhood and criticize her colonial past. Born and raised in Guyana, a former British colony, N. attended St. Stephen's Scots school, the Progressive and Preparatory Institute, and the University of Guyana, where she earned a Diploma in Communications. She worked in various capacities as teacher (1967–70), reporter for the Georgetown *Chronicle* (1971–73), freelance writer, and as an information assistant for the Government Information Services before migrating to Britain in 1977. She lives in Lewes, East Sussex, with her partner, poet John Agard, and her two daughters. N. has published several volumes of poetry for children and adults, numerous short stories, one adult novel, and one novel for children. Her poems have been published in journals such as *Frontline, City Limits, Ambit, Poetry Review, Artrage,* and *Third Eye.*

N.'s first and most celebrated cycle of poems, *i is a long memoried woman,* which won the 1983 Commonwealth Poetry Prize, traces the life of an unknown black woman through a series of stages. The volume is divided into five sections, each characterizing a stage of the woman's life. Together, the five sections describe the history of a black woman from her capture in Africa to the brutality of her life as a slave in the Caribbean. The woman mourns for her African past, embodied in her ancestors, her gods, and her "Mother." Eventually, in the course of time and history, she acquires a new identity bound up closely with a new language. But N.'s black woman is no victim. She resists, rebels, resolves, and ultimately rallies. She does this by maintaining her African traditions and believing in change and in her own potential power. N. uses a language of resistance and resilience to depict her defiant black woman. She fuses creole and standard English and defies traditional uses of punctuation. The seemingly erratic layout of her poems conveys not only the freedom to express oneself on one's own terms but also an outright refusal to subscribe to western writing conventions, which is part of a colonial experience. N.'s *long memoried woman* is a successful collection for its originality and effective play with language.

N.'s next volume was *The Fat Black Woman's Poems* (1984), a collection that she claims came out of a sheer sense of fun, but which brings into being a new image—one that questions the acceptance of the "thin" European model as the ideal figure of beauty. Writing in a postcolonial era, N. uses her fat black woman to challenge deeply internalized European standards by taking a satirical, tongue-in-cheek look at the world. The fat black woman is brash, loves herself, and charts her own future. She poses tough questions to politicians, lovers, and to a white world that is still oppressive. N.'s language is economical yet vivid. Gwendolyn Brooks says there is an "earthy honesty" to the fat black woman.

N.'s only adult novel, *Whole of a Morning Sky* (1986), is a lyrical evocation of her Guyanese childhood. Set in a less-than-idyllic Guyana in the last days of colonial rule, the story begins in the coastal village of Highdam where teacher Archie Walcott and his family prepare to move to the capital, Georgetown. By an effective accumulation of ordinary detail, N. re-creates the texture of everyday life in Highdam and in the slums of Georgetown. The days in Georgetown are punctuated by strikes, arson, looting, interracial riots between blacks and Indians, and grim talk of American and British destabilization in the final hours of colonial rule. Each chapter is preceded by a poetical passage expressing the feelings of Archie's eleven-year-old daughter, Gem, the protagonist. In a clear, unforced style, N. shows how the forces of disintegration experienced by Gem come from outside of the family. The aspiration of a middle-class family are thwarted by local and global politics. But the greatest strength in the writing is the alternation between Gem's first-person voice, filled with what Liz Heron calls the "secret intensities of childhood perceptions," and the third-person authorial flow, giving an undercurrent of memory, expectancy, and unresolved experience to the story. The novel ends with the family preparing to move again, this time to an unknown location—symbolic of the migratory nature and uncertain future of colonized people.

N. takes time out from more serious issues to muse in her collection of laid-back, sensuous, witty poems, *Lazy Thoughts of a Lazy Woman* (1989). The poems encompass a range of thoughts—sexuality, white male power, Caribbean migration, sorcery. The writing is funny, sometimes raw, but many of these poems "fail to refresh the language" (Crawford). N.'s attempts to capture the "laissez-faire" disposition of the "lazy woman" disrupts her usual effective manipulation of language.

Among her children's poetry, the best-known volume is *Come on into My Tropical Garden* (1988), which paints a portrait of a fun-filled Caribbean childhood. The illustrations by Caroline Binch capture the beauty of a tropical landscape, the people, and their customs and contribute to the celebration of island life.

N. remains a forceful voice among post-colonial black women writers. She continues to reject the stereotype of the "long-suffering black woman." Her scathing critique of slavery and colonialism is balanced by a remarkable ability to celebrate the various black, female experiences. She continues to pose questions, challenge authority, and defy socially embedded norms through her writing. Her poems and prose still resonate with a rich imagination and an acute sensitivity to language.

WORKS: *Trust you, Wriggly* (1981). *i is a long memoried woman* (1983). *The Fat Black Woman's Poems* (1984). *Leslyn in London* (1984). *A Dangerous Knowing: Four Black Women Poets* (1984). *Whole of a Morning Sky* (1986). *Come on into My Tropical Garden* (1988). *Lazy Thoughts of a Lazy Woman* (1989). *Poetry Jump Up* (1989). *Give Yourself a Hug* (1995).

BIBLIOGRAPHY: Crawford, R. *LRB* (December 1989). *Caribbean Women Writers: Essays from the First International Conference,* ed. S. Cudgoe (1990). Davies, C. *Black Women Writing and Identity (1994).* Heron, L. *Listener* (August 1986). Ngcobo, L. *Let It Be Told: Essays by Black Women in Britain* (1987). *Black Women's Writing: Insights,* ed. G. Wisker (1993).

For articles in reference works see: *Bloomsbury. Feminist.*

Other references: *BB* (July 1986). *Book List* (May 1990). *British Book News* (March 1986, September 1986). *Children's Book Review Service* (April 1990). *CSM* (July 1990). *Horn Book* (January 1990). *Kirkus Reviews* (March 1990). *LRB* (7 August 1986). *Observer* (London) (13 July 1986). *SLJ* (April 1990). *TLS* (22 August 1986).

Shondel J. Nero

Ni Chonaill, Eibhlin Dubh: See *O'Connell, Eileen*

(Violet) Adela Florence Nicolson

BORN: 9 April 1865, Stoke Bishop, Gloucestershire.
DIED: 4 October 1904, Madras, India.
DAUGHTER OF: Arthur Cory and Elizabeth Fanny [or Fanny Elizabeth] Griffin Cory.
MARRIED: Malcolm Hassels Nicolson, 1889.
WROTE UNDER: Laurence Hope.

Among the most popular poets of the Edwardian period, widely admired for her exotic, largely fictitious "translations" of Indian love lyrics, N. has long been unduly neglected by literary historians. Perhaps the only Anglo-Indian woman poet to achieve widespread acclaim, she "succeeded where most modern poets have failed," James Elroy Flecker wrote in 1907: "She has created for herself a world of admirers, a multitude of initiants—a Public." Thomas Hardy attributed the popularity of her poems to "their tropical luxuriance and Sapphic fervour." Some of the lyrics reflected the poet's experiences in various regions of India, North Africa, and the Far East; some have an air of veiled autobiography or confession; and others may be read as oblique reflections on the position of women in the British Empire. In many poems, the exotic offers a site for an often-transgressive exploration of sexual themes: submission and domination, obsession, female desire, violent sexuality. In her most famous poem, "Kashmiri song," the speaker pines for the "Pale hands I loved beside the Shalimar," concluding, "I would have rather felt you round my throat / Crushing out life, than waving me farewell!" Although her brief literary career was abruptly brought to a close by her suicide in 1904 (less than three years after the publication of her first volume), her work continued to grow in popularity in the following decades.

The second of three Cory daughters, N. was born Adela Florence Cory in England while her father, then a captain in the Bombay Army stationed at Lahore, was on furlough. She was raised by relatives in England and educated in Richmond and abroad. When she arrived in Lahore at the age of sixteen, her stay was cut short by the illness of her father, then co-editor of the *Civil and Military Gazette;* after his recovery in England the family returned to India, where Colonel Cory took up the editorship of the *Sind Gazette* in Karachi (his former position in Lahore having been filled by Rudyard Kipling). She and her sisters Isabell and Victoria (later the novelist Victoria Cross) assisted their father with the newspaper. In 1889, at twenty-three, she married Colonel Malcolm Hassels Nicolson, forty-six, of the Bombay Army, commander of a native regiment, veteran of the Second Afghan War, and an expert linguist. After several years of regimental duty in various regions of northwest India, he was promoted in 1895 to general and for the next five years served as C.O. of Mhow, the headquarters of the Western Command, where much of N.'s verse was written.

The Garden of Káma, N.'s first collection of verse, was

published in 1901 under the name "Laurence Hope." (The Nicholsons had returned to England the previous year.) Reviewers were uncertain about the authenticity of the translations. Some attacked the book on moral grounds, but the male pseudonym and pretense of translation protected N. from the worst of these charges. Spurred by the success of Amy Woodforde-Finden's musical arrangements of "Four Indian Love Lyrics" in 1902, *The Garden of Káma* went through dozens of printings.

In 1903, returning to London after a sojourn in North Africa, she was drawn briefly into the circle of Blanche Crackanthorpe, at whose home she met Thomas Hardy, who became an admirer of her work. A second volume, *Stars of the Desert*, was completed and published in September 1903. It contained additional Indian poems as well as more recent verses set in North Africa and a few set in the Far East. Shortly thereafter, the Nicolsons again left England, this time for southern India. In August 1904, her husband died during a routine prostate operation; N., prone to depression since childhood, poisoned herself two months later in Madras. She was thirty-nine.

The 1905 posthumous collection, *Indian Love*, revealed the poet's gender (which, along with her true identity, had been published by the *Critic* as early as 1902) in a photographic portrait. The dedication of the volume to her late husband in a poetic "suicide note," which alluded to the "vain . . . regret / That pours my hopeless life across thy grave," invited the reader to view her death as a kind of *sati;* despite the dedication's disclaimer that "I, who of lighter love wrote many a verse, / Made public never words inspired by thee," readers detected a confessional note, intriguing to some, distasteful to others. Again, the volume sold well but failed to garner public recognition from established poets. (A preface to the volume by Thomas Hardy, who had written an anonymous obituary for the *Athenaeum*, was rejected by Heinemann.)

A volume of juvenilia appeared in 1907, and different illustrated editions of *The Garden of Káma* appeared in 1909 and 1914. Two films, *Less than the Dust* (1916, with Mary Pickford and David Powell) and *The Indian Love Lyrics* (1923), attest to the continuing popularity of the poems and their musical adaptations over the course of several decades. N.'s son edited *Selected Poems, published* in 1922, and *Complete Love Lyrics* appeared in 1929.

The scarcity of letters and other biographical materials has inhibited scholarly studies of N. and her work. Lesley Blanch's biographical essay, compiled with the aid of material provided by N.'s son, remains the most important published study to date.

WORKS: *The Garden of Káma, and Other Love Lyrics from India, Arranged in Verse by Laurence Hope* (1901; in the U. S. as *India's Love Lyrics*). *Stars of the Desert* (1903). *Indian Love* (1905; in the U. S. as *Last Poems*). *Laurence Hope's Poems* (1907). *Selected Poems from the Indian Love Lyrics of Laurence Hope,* ed. M. J. Nicholson (1922). *Complete Love Lyrics* (1929).

BIBLIOGRAPHY: Blanch, L. *Under a Lilac-Bleeding Star* (1963). Bruce, H. *East and West* (1906). Flecker, J. E. *Monthly Review* (1907). Garnett, R. *Bookman* (1905). [Hardy, T.] *Athenaeum* (29 October 1904). Hooker, B. *Bookman* (1909). Jacob, V. *Diaries and Letters from India, 1895–1900.* Johnson, A. *PoetryR* (1913). Macmillan, M. *Women of the Raj* (1988). Payne, W. M. *Dial* (1903). Perkins, D. *A History of Modern Poetry* (1976). Rothfeld, O. *Indian Dust* (1909). Thomas, E. M. *Critic* (1902). Williams, H. H. *Modern English Writers* (1918).

For articles in reference works, see: *DNB. 1890s. Feminist. TCA.*

Edward Marx

Florence Nightingale

BORN: 12 May 1820, Florence, Italy.
DIED: 13 August 1910, London.
DAUGHTER OF: William Edward Nightingale and Frances Smith Nightingale.

"I had so much rather live than write; writing is only a supplement for living," N. told a friend. "I think one's feelings waste themselves in words; they ought all to be distilled into actions, and into actions which bring results." N. won her place in history through her heroic actions during the Crimean War, but her reasons for rebelling against society's expectations for women, her religious justification of her conduct, and her proposals for reforming health care and sanitation are all formulated in words: diaries, letters, government reports, journal articles, addresses to nursing students, and more than two hundred books and pamphlets. For N., writing was a means to self-knowledge and an instrument for social change.

Educated at home by their wealthy, well-bred father, N. and her older sister Parthenope studied history, philosophy, mathematics, and classics; they also wrote weekly compositions. At the urging of classical scholar Benjamin Jowett, she prepared an anthology of writings by medieval mystics prefaced with the statement, "This reading is good only as a preparation for work." N. objected to writers who failed to understand the importance of work: poets who ignored poverty and disease in order to celebrate "the glories of this world"; "female ink-bottles" who spewed out pages of useless polemics; novelists who lured young women into fantasies of romantic love. Without action, the imagination could be dangerously self-indulgent. Dreaming, which N. regarded as an all-consuming activity for many women, was a sign of despair and frustration, an alternative rather than a prelude to accomplishment.

Writing served a therapeutic function in N.'s private life. Early journals describe her anger and frustration with the idle life of an upper-class Englishwoman. N. believed she had a call from God to undertake a life of heroic service, while her family asked her to write letters, play the piano, and entertain company; writing enabled her to break with her family and begin her work in nursing. She told her father, "I hope now I have come into possession of myself." "Cassandra," an autobiographical fragment from this period, criticizes Victorian family structure, analyzes the ways women's time and talents are wasted, and prophesies the coming of a female Christ who will arise in the midst of suffering and complaint. Although the work remained unpublished during N.'s lifetime, John Stuart Mill incorporated some of her criticism of domestic routine into *The*

Subjection of Women. N. continued to write "spiritual meditations" throughout her life: confessions of guilt, apologies for her self-obsession, communings with God.

Suggestions for Thought (1860), the work from which "Cassandra" is derived, is, according to Elaine Showalter, "a major document of Victorian religious thought, which should be studied alongside Newman's *Apologia Pro Vita Sea.*" In 1852, N. declared, "I have remodeled my whole religious belief from beginning to end. I have learnt to know God. I have recast my social belief; have them both written for use, when my hour is come." Rejecting Anglicanism, Roman Catholicism, Protestantism, and Positivism, N. argued that the laws of God could be discovered by experience, research, and analysis. God is the Universal Being who is Law, "a Being who, willing only good, leaves evil in the world solely in order to stimulate human faculties by an unremitting struggle against every form of it." N. tried to impose order—digests with elaborate divisions and subdivisions, running titles, marginal glosses—but the massive manuscript is marred by rambling digressions and repetitions. N. sent her jumbled "Stuff," as she called it, to Mill, who advised publication, and Jowett, who called for extensive revision. Although N. had a few copies privately printed in 1860, she lost interest in revising the book for a general audience. *Suggestions* had served its purpose: She had formulated a theological justification for her commitment to self-development and public service.

In the public sphere, N. wrote her way into positions of power. Although N. was a public idol when she returned from the Crimea in 1856, she had no official standing with the military or governmental agencies investigating British losses in the war. She had also become an invalid. Arrogant, manipulative, and almost demonically energetic, she used her pen to attack the administrative chaos and poor sanitary conditions in the British army. When a report was omitted from the government's publication, she paid to have 500 copies printed in the form of a parliamentary blue book and circulated among her influential acquaintances. *Notes on Matters Affecting the Health, Efficiency, and Hospital Administration of the British Army* (1858) resulted in the establishment of a Royal Commission and passage of many of N.'s recommendations. Recognizing her brilliant analytic skills and knowledge of statistics, government leaders frequently sought N.'s advice, especially on matters of public health in India. When necessary, N. could organize tremendous public support through adroit use of the press.

Notes on Nursing: What It Is, and What It Is Not (1860) was N.'s most popular book, selling 15,000 copies in a few months and receiving scores of enthusiastic reviews; according to Harriet Martineau, it was "a work of genius." N.'s advice on domestic hygiene was intended for a wide audience, for she defined a nurse as anyone who has responsibility for another's health. N.'s belief that all disease is "more or less a reparative process" meant that the nurse must "put the patient in the best condition for nature to act upon him." The doctor's duties were diminished by N.'s adamant opposition to the germ theory and her conviction that "nature alone cures." N.'s prose is clear, concrete, often epigrammatic in style, and occasionally satiric in tone; through related image patterns, she fuses moral fervor and scientific authority.

N. carefully cultivated her image as the noble, self-sacrificing "lady with the lamp," but she also identified with Jesus, Joan of Arc, Correggio's Magdelen, and Queen Victoria. A skilled mythmaker, she made the nurse into a figure of epic proportions. "Una and the Lion" (1868) invokes Spenser's *Faerie Queene* to eulogize Agnes Jones, a woman who died while nursing in a workhouse, as "Una in real flesh and blood—Una and her paupers, far more untameable than lions." In actuality, N. thought Jones was inept; in print, she saw an opportunity to satisfy her own ego needs and win converts to Christian service.

N. was reluctant to align herself with women, perhaps because of unresolved conflicts with her mother and sister. She supported married women's property rights, but she resisted Mill's appeals for help in the suffrage campaign, remarking that she herself exerted more influence on government than if she "had been a borough returning two M.P.'s." Having money, position, and great personal strength, N. claimed to be "brutally indifferent to the wrongs or rights of my sex." But even as she urged readers to keep clear of "both jargons"—the jargon about women's rights, "which urges women to do all that men do," and the jargon about woman's mission "which urges women to do nothing that men do"—she set an example and gave advice that enabled many women to set out upon independent lives: "Oh, leave these jargons, and go your way straight to God's work, in simplicity and singleness of heart."

WORKS: *The Institution of Kaiserswerth on the Rhine for the Practical Training of Deaconesses* (1851). *Letters from Egypt* (1854). *Suggestions of a System of Nursing for Hospitals in India* (1856). *Statements Exhibiting the Voluntary Contributions Received by Miss Nightingale for the Use of the British Hospitals in the East, with the Mode of their Distribution* (1857). *Construction of Hospitals, the Ground Plan* (1858). *Lunatic Asylums* (1858). *Notes on Matters Affecting the Health, Efficiency, and Hospital Administration of the British Army. Founded Chiefly on the Experience of the Late War* (1858). *Report of the Commissioners Appointed to Inquire into the Regulations Affecting the Sanitary Condition of the Army* (1858). *Subsidiary Notes as to the Introduction of Female Nursing into Military Hospitals in Peace and in War* (1858). *A Contribution to the Sanitary History of the British Army during the Late War with Russia* (1859). *Notes on Hospitals* (1859). *Notes on Nursing: What It Is, and What It Is Not* (1860). *Suggestions for Thought to the Searchers after Truth among the Artizans of England,* 3 vols. (1860). *Directions for Cooking by Troops, in Camp and Hospital* (1861). *Notes on Nursing for the Laboring Classes* (1861). *Observations on the Sanitary State of the Army in India* (1861). *Army Sanitary Administration and Its Reform under the Late Lord Herbert* (1862). *Hospital Statistics and Hospital Plans* (1862). *Observations on the Evidence Contained in the Stational Reports Submitted to Her by the Royal Commission on the Sanitary State of the Army in India* (1863). *How People May Live and Not Die in India* (1863). *Sanitary Statistics of Native Colonial Schools and Hospitals* (1863). *Organization of Nursing* (1865). "Una and the Lion" (1868). *Introductory Notes on Ly-*

ing-in Institutions. Together with a Proposal for Organising an Institution for Training Midwives and Midwifery Nurses (1871). *Life or Death in India* (1874). *On Trained Nursing for the Sick Poor* (1876). *Miss Florence Nightingale's Addresses to Probationer-Nurses in the "Nightingale Fund" School at St. Thomas's Hospital and Nurses who Were Formerly Trained There* (1872–1900). *The People of India* (1878). *The Dumb Shall Speak and the Deaf Shall Hear* (1883). *Heroines* (1883). *Our Indian Stewardship* (1883). *Infection* (1882). *Health and Local Government* (1894). *Rural Hygiene: Health Teachings in Towns and Villages* (1894). *The Eclectic Family Physician* (1895). *The Lady of the Lamp* (1900). *Florence Nightingale to Her Nurses* (1914). *Notes of Nursing* (1914). *Letters from Miss Florence Nightingale on Health Visiting in Rural Districts* (1917). *Indian Letters. A Glimpse into the Agitation for Tenancy Reform. Bengal 1878–82*, ed. P. Sen (1937). *Selected Writings*, ed. L. R. Seymer (1954). *Cassandra*, ed. M. Stark (1979). *Letters from Egypt: A Journey on the Nile, 1849–1850*, ed. A. Sattin (1987). *Ever Yours, Florence Nightingale: Selected Letters*, ed. M. Vicinus and B. Nergaard (1989). *Letters from the Crimea, 1854–1856*, ed. S. M. Goldie (1997).

BIBLIOGRAPHY: Bishop, W. J. and S. Goldie. *A Bio-Bibliography of Florence Nightingale* (1962). Boyd, N. *Three Victorian Women Who Changed Their World: Josephine Butler, Octavia Hill, and Florence Nightingale* (1982). Bullough, B. et al., in *Florence Nightingale and Her Era: A Collection of New Scholarship*, ed. V. Bullough, et al. (1990). Cook, E. T. *The Life of Florence Nightingale* (1914). Forster, M. *Significant Sisters: The Grassroots of Active Feminism, 1839–1939* (1984). Holton, S. *Social Analysis* (1984). Jenkins, R. *Reclaiming Myths of Power: Women Writers and the Victorian Spiritual Crisis* (1995). Landow, G., in *Victorian Sages and Cultural Discourse: Renegotiating Gender and Power*, ed. T. Morgan (1990). Poovey, M. *Uneven Developments: The Ideological Work of Gender in Victorian England* (1988). Pugh, E. L. *Journal of British Studies* (1982). Quinn, V. and J. Press. *Dear Miss Nightingale: A Selection of Benjamin Jowett's Letters to Florence Nightingale, 1860–1893* (1987). Rees, J. *Writings on the Nile: Harriet Martineau, Florence Nightingale, Amelia Edwards* (1995). Roberts, J. and T. Group. *Feminism and Nursing* (1995). Rosenberg, C. E., in *Healing and History*, ed. C. E. Rosenberg (1979). Showalter, E. *Signs* (1981). Showalter, E., in *Tradition and the Talents of Women*, ed. F. Howe (1991). Smith, F. B. *Florence Nightingale: Reputation and Power* (1982). Snyder, K., in *The Politics of the Essay: Feminist Perspectives*, ed. R. Joeres and E. Mittman (1993). Vicinus, M. *Independent Women: Work and Community for Single Women, 1850–1920* (1985). Vicinus, M., in *Florence Nightingale and Her Era: A Collection of New Scholarship*, ed. V. Bullough, et al. (1990). Woodham Smith, C. *Florence Nightingale* (1950).

For articles in reference works, see: *BDBF. DNB. Europa. Feminist. IDWB. Oxford.*

Other references: Adams, P. *Somerville for Women: An Oxford College 1879–1993* (1996). *LonT* (18 January 1996).

Robin Sheets

Duchess of Northumberland (Elizabeth Percy)

BORN: 26 November 1716.
DIED: 5 December 1776, Alnwick Castle.
DAUGHTER OF: Algernon (Seymour), Baron Percy, seventh Duke of Somerset, and Frances Thynne.
MARRIED: Sir Hugh Smithson, 1740.

In her own day a leading figure in English society, N. remains interesting to political and social historians, students of architectural and landscape history, and connoisseurs of travel writing. With her husband, N. supported the arts, worked to institute reforms on their estates, and campaigned against John Wilkes during the 1767 Westminster elections. A friend of Horace Walpole and a correspondent of James Boswell, N. served as Lady of the Bedchamber to her friend Queen Charlotte until the queen took umbrage, Walpole says, at N.'s parading "before the Queen with more footmen than her Majesty."

From 1752 to 1776, N. kept detailed diaries of political and social events and of her visits to country houses, a principal entertainment even when ill health forced her to spend increasing amounts of time on the Continent. N. made her own country house, Syon, into England's finest, and kept a list of more than 150 with which she noted the details of estates she visited. The descriptions she kept have helped scholars identify architects, flesh out their knowledge of vanished houses, and trace the tastes of the century, including N.'s own liking for gothic.

A Short Tour (1775), taken from the travel diaries, may have been unauthorized; neither the author's nor the publisher's name appears in the volume. The excerpt is unremarkable, revealing N.'s eye for detail but little of her sharp wit. Other portions of the diaries describe her two years in Ireland, where the then Earl of Northumberland served as Lord Lieutenant; her many journeys to the Continent; and a brief visit to Voltaire, whom she found "like all the busts," but plumper.

A minor versifier, N. contributed what Walpole labeled "bouts rimés on a buttered muffin" to a miscellany by Bath socialite and travel writer Anna Riggs Miller. Samuel Johnson, while defending the right of "a lady of her [N.'s] high rank" to do anything she pleased, also scorned the book.

N's style in the diaries sometimes founders under the weight of innumerable details, but she can be direct, gossipy, or stingingly clever. A new acquaintance is "the biggest puppy I ever met" and on a country visit she must kiss "an ugly Cousin and a sweaty Brother of Lord Belhaven." In France, she has "the advantage of a reeking Dunghill under the Window" of her inn; "I really thought I should have hanged myself." She revels in pomp, enthuses over scenery, and delights in news of Lady Harriet eloping with her footman or Madame de Boufflers' husband being "so complaiscent as to dye" shortly before rumors that her lover, the Prince de Conti, planned to marry her.

No complete edition of N.'s works has yet appeared. J. Grieg's edition contains excellent notes but concentrates on the social and political, omitting most of N.'s architectural descriptions and the common events of her days.

WORKS: *Diaries and Notebooks* (unpublished). *A Short Tour Made in the Year 1771* (1775, extracts). "The pen, which now I take and brandish." *Poetical Amusements at a Villa Near Bath,* ed. A. R. Miller) (1775). *Diaries of a Duchess,* ed. J. Grieg; intro by the Duke of Northumberland (1926).

BIBLIOGRAPHY: Hesselgrave, R. *Lady Miller and the Batheaston Circle* (1927). Percy, V. and G. Jackson-Stops *Country Life* (31 January 1974, 7 February 1974, 14 February 1974).

For articles in reference works, see: *DNB* (under "Hugh Percy"). *ToddDBA.*

Other references: Boswell, J. *Life of Johnson* (1791). Walpole, H. *Letters,* 16 vols., ed P. Toynbee (1903–1905).

Marie E. McAllister

Frances (Freke) Norton

BORN: 1640, Hannington, Wiltshire.
DIED: 20 February 1731, Somerset.
DAUGHTER OF: Ralph Freke and Cecili Colepepper (Culpepper).
MARRIED: Sir George Norton, c. 1672; Colonel Ambrose Norton, 1718; William Jones, 1724.

The third daughter of Ralph and Cecili Freke of Hannington, Wiltshire, N. was a devotional writer and poet who was familiar with Latin and Greek and wrote verses of extraordinary piety. N. was so acclaimed that on her death she was buried in Westminser Abbey. Her life, however, was fraught with the pain and melancholy that seemed the lot of so many women of her time. Apparently married first in about 1672 to Sir George Norton, knight of Abbots Leigh, Somerset, N. gave birth to three children: George and Elizabeth, who died young, and Grace, afterwards Lady Gethin. It was said of Norton that he had concealed Charles II in his home during the battle of Worcester. The marriage between N. and her Royalist husband survived the first few years, but just barely. N. left her husband after Grace was born. Grace died in 1697, and two years later N. published her daughter's manuscripts in a volume called *Misery's Virtues Whetstone.* Praised by critics such as William Congreve and later Edmund Gosse, the volume was reprinted in 1700 as *Reliquiae Gethinianae.* In 1705, N. published two of her own works in small quarto volumes: *The Applause of Virtue,* in four parts, and *Memento Mori, or Meditations on Death.* So affected was she by the death of her daughter, N. explains in the preface, that her essays served as "melancholy divertisement." Each of the works is a collection of quotations on moral lessons from ancient and modern writers.

After her first husband's death on 26 April 1715, N. married again on 3 April 1718, possibly to Colonel Ambrose Norton (cousin of Sir George), who died in 1723, and in 1724 she probably married William Jones. In 1714, she produced her *Miscellany of Poems,* religious poems that she also preserved in needlepoint, which she signed.

WORKS: *The Applause of Virtue. In four parts. Consisting of several divine and moral essays towards the obtaining of true virtue* (1705). *Memento Mori, or Meditations on Death* (1705). *Miscellany of Poems* (1714).

BIBLIOGRAPHY: Collison, J. *History of Somersetshire* (1791).

For articles in reference works, see: *Ballard. Bell. BioIn. DNB. Feminist. Fifty Famous Women* (n.d). *ToddDBA.*

Sophia B. Blaydes

Kathleen (Cecilia) Nott

BORN: 1909 (?), London.
DAUGHTER OF: Philip Nott and Ellen Nott.
MARRIED: Christopher Bailey, 1927.

N., poet, translator, critic, philosopher, and novelist, has written in many genres but considers herself primarily a poet. She studied philosophy extensively, especially ethics and aesthetics, at the universities of London and Oxford. She was a social worker among poor Jews in London's East End during the 1930s, and out of her experiences she wrote her first novel, *Mile End* (1938). She has since written numerous volumes of verse, fiction, philosophy, and criticism, the best known of which is *The Emperor's Clothes* (1953), an attack upon the "dogmatic orthodoxy" of such writers as C. S. Lewis, T. S. Eliot, and Dorothy Sayers. In addition, N. has written for many newspapers and journals, including the *Times Literary Supplement, Observer, Spectator,* and *Time and Tide.* She has long been active with P.E.N., as editor of one of its publications and in various executive positions.

Mile End, N.'s longest novel, attempts to span three generations of East London Jews torn between their own heritage and the demands of the larger, non-Jewish world. This work was criticized for its common first-novel excesses, both in style and in length, as well as for N.'s repeated reliance on philosophizing rather than on action, but it successfully captures the dilemmas faced by her characters. Her conclusion—that neither set of rigid orthodoxies is preferable—leads to her characters simply opting for "Life."

The Dry Deluge (1947) and *Private Fires* (1960) are generally considered lesser fictional efforts because of problems with narrative perspectives as well as continued reliance on authorial commentary. *The Dry Deluge* describes the creation of an underground socialistic Utopia, run by an eccentric but charismatic professor and devoted to planning for and practicing immortality; *Private Fires* focuses on various unusual characters in London immediately after World War II. In neither case are N.'s characters fully dimensional or believable, nor are her contrived conclusions convincing.

N.'s fourth novel, *An Elderly Retired Man* (1963), is by common consent her best, primarily because N. seems in greater control of materials. Her title character, Roden Cluer, a civil servant, attempts belatedly to resolve his lifetime of doubts and uncertainties; for the first time he realizes the necessity—and painful difficulty—of accurately assessing his marriage, friends, and loyalties, especially as he contemplates the ways in which his one deeply emotional attachment affects his and his wife's situation. Unlike her earlier novels, in which N. tried to force the reader's conclusions, this one is perceptive, convincing, and moving.

The Emperor's Clothes was N.'s attempt to expose the "New Philistinism" represented by the religious and cultural orthodoxy of Eliot, Lewis, Graham Greene, Walter Allen, and, by implication, others who also show what N. perceives as hostility to and inability to grasp the meaning of science. Vigorously defending the "humanism" that has dominated Western thought for the past 300 years, N. defends such writers as Jacob Bronowski and Bertrand Russell while criticizing those she called "Augustinian novelists." N. is fully as dogmatic in rejecting Christian orthodoxy as are those she attacks, and her sometimes sarcastic tone serves less to defend the "Two Cultures" concept of C. P. Snow and more to suggest a certain closemindedness. *Philosophy and Human Nature* (1970), by contrast, is a more balanced assessment of the various philosophies (including existentialism and Eastern thought) that appeal to modern men and women, with N.'s own allegiance to logical positivism (and the linguistic analysis of A. J. Ayer) clearly uppermost in her mind.

N.'s other works in philosophy include *Objections to Humanism* (1963; written with others); *A Soul in the Quad* (1969), which she describes as what she conceives "the relations of poetry and philosophy to be" in an "autobiographical and intellectual-social setting"; and *The Good Want Power: An Essay in the Psychological Possibilities of Liberalism* (1977).

N.'s poetry reflects her philosophical tendencies; she regards poetry as a "special language and an existential one," the "language of beings of rather peculiar physiological and psychological organization," and the "most favourable . . . highly authentic personal vision." Her four volumes of verse have been noted for their rhythm more than for their use of conventional forms, and they have been criticized for their imprecise and forced diction and confused resolution of the ideas prompting the poems.

Most likely, N. will be remembered as a writer on philosophical topics rather than as a poet or novelist, with her most contentious work, *The Emperor's Clothes,* especially prominent—primarily because of her target's lasting reputations rather than her own persuasive observations.

WORKS: *Mile End* (1938). *The Dry Deluge* (1947). *Landscapes and Departures* (1947). (trans.) *Northwesterly Gale*, by L. Chauvet (1947). *The Emperor's Clothes: An Attack on the Dogmatic Orthodoxy of T. S. Eliot, Graham Greene, Dorothy Sayers, C. S. Lewis and Others* (1953). *Poems from the North* (1956). (trans.) *Son of Stalin*, by R. Baccelli (1956). (trans.) *The Fire of Milan*, by R. Baccelli (1958). *Creatures and Emblems* (1960). *Private Fires* (1960). *A Clean Well-Lighted Place: A Private View of Sweden* (1961). *An Elderly Retired Man* (1963). (with others) *Objections to Humanism* (1963). (with others) *What I Believe* (1966). *A Soul in the Quad* (1969). *Philosophy and Human Nature* (1970). *The Good Want Power: An Essay in the Psychological Possibilities of Liberalism* (1977). *Elegies and Other Poems* (1981).

BIBLIOGRAPHY: Holloway, J. *The Colours of Clarity: Essays on Contemporary Literature and Education* (1964).

For articles in reference works, see: *Bloomsbury. CA. CN. CP. Feminist. SFE. WA.*

Other references: Sayers, D. "A Debate Deferred: (I) The Dogma in the Manger; (II) Notes towards a Reply [reply by N.]" *Seven* (1982). *TLS* (3 December 1938, 24 May 1947, 7 June 1947).

Paul Schlueter

Oberon: See *Robinson, Mary Darby (Perdita)*

Edna O'Brien

BORN: 15 December 1930, Tuamgraney, County Clare, Ireland.

DAUGHTER OF: Michael O'Brien and Lena Cleary O'Brien.

MARRIED: Ernest Gebler, 1951.

O., an Irish expatriate, has been sexually candid in her works. These attributes, plus the fact that she is a woman, have added to her appeal to her reading public, especially in the United States, where she has had to endure the peculiar fate of a woman writer criticized as much as she is celebrated. Her professional readers and critics are, it seems, on the lookout for the least echo of James Joyce, the least emotional excess, the least indication of derivative lyricism or self-indulgence. Scrutiny has been even more intense because she writes so well so often.

O. writes best about what she knows, and much of her best writing draws from her personal experience. Therefore, she writes better stories about Ireland than she does about London, better stories about village life than city life, and best about women facing and abandoning a Roman Catholic, Irish heritage for a secular, passionate life in search of what O. is never ashamed to call "true love." The word "girl" surfaces and resurfaces in her writing, evoking the pain involved in young girls' coming to maturity. For many of her women, this abandoned heritage remains in the psyche and the flesh forever; one never stops being an Irish Catholic, a daughter, a village girl.

Thus, O. has forged a body of work parallel to her real life. The *Country Girls* trilogy (*The Country Girls,* 1960; *The Lonely Girl,* 1962; *Girls in Their Married Bliss,* 1964), begun shortly after O. had moved to London, deals with growing up, breaking ties, and learning about (and failing in) love. Her novels of the late 1960s, especially *August Is a Wicked Month* (1965) and *Casualties of Peace* (1966), address the consequences of marriage's collapse. (O. herself was divorced in 1964.) In 1977, she published *Johnny I Hardly Knew You,* which she has said was an exploration of the older woman's attraction for younger men, a search to re-establish the unambiguous mother-son relationship through the ambiguous medium of sex. That book may also take revenge on males in general when the heroine murders her handsome younger lover.

By the 1980s, O. was ensconced in a large house in Maida Vale, a largely Irish residential district in London. Her expatriation appears in two ways in her fiction: in the less successful stories about urban life collected in *A Fanatic Heart* (1984) and an exploration of things Irish in her nonfiction, including *Mother Ireland* (1976), *James and Nora* (1981), and *Returning* (1982).

O. is famous for writing well (and frequently) about sex. She has taught women writers how to write lyrically and honestly about physical and emotional intimacy, but she has been most convincing when she portrays sex as part of a woman's total existence, something involving her education, her childhood, her hopes, even her career. Her depictions of sexual relations in stories such as "The Love Object" and "Paradise" are less convincing than those in "A Rose in the Heart of New York," "A Scandalous Woman," or in novels such as *Country Girls* or *Night* (1972); the latter emphasize the passion involved with intimacy more concretely and in greater detail.

O. explores human emotions through a richly lyrical confessional prose. Perhaps the height of her lyric mode was reached in the interior monologues of Mary Hooligan in *Night.* Lyricism and confessionalism arise from the Irish narrative tradition as does her very Irish sensibility: She is looking for the rhythms of the human soul and the rules of life. There is an intoxication with the dangers at hand for any Irish writer: sentimentality, maudlin self-absorption, facile lyricism, blather, blarney. And if she sometimes succumbs to these temptations—"That night their lovemaking had all the sweetness and all the release that earth must feel with the longawaited rain'—there are riches that more than balance the lapses.

The *Country Girls* trilogy is, as a whole, quite successful, even if there is a loss of energy and descent into pessimism in the last novel, the too-obviously-titled *Girls in Their Wedded Bliss.* Kate and Baba of the *Country Girls* books are perhaps O.'s best-known characters. Kate, one of her most sympathetic and frustrating creations, is, quite simply, a victim of romance; as we watch her mature, we follow her through a series of amorous disappointments and disasters, realizing that her unrealistic expectations of love disqualify her for happiness. Her friend and opposite, Baba, a reckless ironist, prospers in the ironic world of intimacy. True love fails for Baba, too, but she is resilient and hard enough to settle for a series of nongenuine attachments, culminating in a marriage to a rich man she does not love. One of the rewards of the *Country Girls* books is that O. as author identifies ideals in which she passionately wishes to believe—and allows them to fail. By the end of the trilogy, none of these ideals are left standing. Kate fails because of her devotion to the love ideal, and Baba succeeds because of a complete absence of ideals.

Of her stories, the two best are possibly "Sister Imelda" and "A Rose in the Heart of New York." "Sister Imelda" describes a nun and her schoolgirl pupil, both obsessed with the quest for purity, who fall in love with each other and with the intensity of their quest. One of O.'s best moments occurs when the girl realizes she must turn away from her mentor and toward a worldly future. "Rose," also about turning away, is a careful tracing of the relation of mother and daughter. If there is a single best moment in O.'s fiction, it may well be the moment when the daughter discovers some money her dead mother has left for her.

O. has also written successfully in other genres. She has written screenplays for film versions of her novels, including *The Girl with Green Eyes* (1964), and *X, Y, and Zee* (1971). Her play *Virginia* (1981) is a successful study of Virginia Woolf. She is also an excellent essayist, having published extensively on such subjects as Ireland, the relations between the sexes, autobiographical reflections, international affairs, and, most impressively, on writing itself.

O.'s fame (and productivity) rose to new heights during the late 1980s and the 1990s. She wrote not only novels and stories but also travelogues, books on contemporary Irish history, political op-ed pieces, and essays. Sought out as a spokesperson for Ireland, she held fast to the notion that all sides wanted peace but that all face huge obstacles, mostly those of inbred prejudice. She continues to claim Ireland as one of the last bastions of truly spiritual literature—even as she acknowledges the rapid changes shoving Ireland into the next century.

After years of avoiding the topic of political strife in Northern Ireland in her fiction, O. published *The House of Splendid Isolation* (1993), in which an aging single woman finds herself at the mercy of an IRA terrorist. This widely admired novel discusses the issues of terrorism and the future of Ireland—while also being about an older woman and a younger man. *The House of Splendid Isolation* speaks of politics within a limited, human frame, avoiding the explicit sermon in favor of truths that arise between man and woman.

O.'s independent mind has put her at odds with other women writers who have expected her to be a spokesperson for the feminist viewpoint. "I don't feel strongly about all the things they feel strongly about," she has said. "I feel strongly about childhood, truth or lies, and the real expression of feeling." She has insisted on a real difference between the sexes. Especially unfeminist is her conviction that there is "both a conscious and an unconscious degree of submission in a woman"; O. feels, however, that women can and must fight this submissiveness. O. has said that her goal is to create a truly great female character. She wishes not only to match the best of literature's women (ironically, created mostly by male authors) but also to create a truly believable heroine, a "woman who succeeds," if only to show that success is possible. Above all, she remains devoted to her quest for what she calls "real feeling."

WORKS: *The Country Girls* (1960). *The Lonely Girl* (1962; rpt. as *The Girl with Green Eyes,* 1964; screenplay, 1964). *A Cheap Bunch of Nice Flowers,* in *Plays of the Year,* ed. J. C. Trewin (1963). *Girls in Their Married Bliss* (1964). *August Is a Wicked Month* (1965). *Casualties of Peace* (1966). (with D. Davis) *Time Lost and Time Remembered* (screenplay, from O.'s story "A Woman at the Seaside," 1966). *Three into Two Won't Go* (screenplay, from the novel by A. Newman, 1968). *The Love Object* (1969). *A Pagan Place* (1970). *Zee & Co.* (screenplay for the film *X, Y, and Zee,* 1971). *Night* (1972). *A Pagan Place* (1973). *The Gathering* (1974). *A Scandalous Woman and Other Stories* (1974). *Mother Ireland* (1976). *Johnny I Hardly Knew You* (1977; in the U.S. as *I Hardly Knew You,* 1978). *Arabian Days* (1978). *The Collected Edna O'Brien* (1978). *Mr. Reinhardt and Other Stories* (1978). *A Rose in the Heart* (1979). *James and Nora* (1981). *Virginia: A Play* (1981). *Returning* (1982). *A Fanatic Heart* (1984). *The Country Girls Trilogy and Epilogue* (1986). *Vanishing Ireland* (1986; photos by R. Fitzgerald). *Tales for the Telling* (1988). *The High Road* (1988). *On the Bone* (1990). *Lantern Slides* (1990). *Time and Tide* (1992). *The House of Splendid Isolation* (1993). *An Edna O'Brien Reader* (1994). *Down by the River* (1996).

BIBLIOGRAPHY: Carlson, J. *Banned in Ireland: Censorship and the Irish Writer* (1994). "Edna," in *Talking to Women*, ed. N. Dunn (1965). Eckley, G. *Edna O'Brien* (1974). Heffron, J. *The Best Writing on Writing* (1994). Kiely, B., in *Conor Cruise O'Brien Introduces Ireland*, ed. O. Edwards (1969). King, K. *Ten Irish Playwrights* (1979). "Dialogue with Edna O'Brien," in *Under Bow Bells: Dialogues with Joseph McCulloch* (1974). O'Brien, D., in *Twentieth Century Women Novelists*, ed. T. F. Staley (1982).

For articles in reference works, see: *Bloomsbury. CA. Cambridge. CLC. CN. DIL. DLB. Feminist. MBL. Oxford. TCW. ToddBWW. WA. WD.*

Other references: Alexander, F., in *The Comic Tradition in Irish Women Writers*, ed. T. O'Connor (1996). *Bookviews* (January 1978). Cahalan, J. M. *ClQ* (1995). Carpenter, L., in *Essays on the Contemporary British Novel*, ed. H. Bock and A. Wertheim (1986). Carriker, K. *NMIL* (1989). *Eire* (1967, 1977). Gramich, K. *Swansea Review* (1994). Hargreaves, T., in *Cultural Contexts and Literary Idioms in Contemporary Irish Literature*, ed. M. Kenneally (1988). Haule, J. M. *ClQ* (1987). Herman, D. *Style* (1994). *IUR* (1977). *JJQ* (1966). *Nation* (14 May 1973). *New Republic* (7 January 1985, 30 June 1986). *New Yorker* (12 February 1972). Nicolson, N. et al. *VWM* (1981). *NYT* (7 April 1976, 11 October 1977, 27 June 1978, 12 March 1984, 12 November 1984, 3 October 1985, 6 December 1987, 5 November 1989, 1 February 1993, 14 February 1993). *NYTBR* (1 January 1978, 18 November 1984). O'Brien, P. *MR* (1987). *Observer* (18 January 1981). O'Hara, K. *SSF* (1993). Pelan, R. *CJIS* (1993). *Saturday Review* (1 February 1979). Shumaker, J. R. *SSF* (1995). *TLS* (23 April 1982). *VV* (1 July 1986).

John Timpane

Kate O'Brien

BORN: 3 December 1897, Limerick, Ireland.
DIED: 13 August 1974, Faversham, Kent.
DAUGHTER OF: Thomas O'Brien and Catherine Thornhill O'Brien.
MARRIED: Gustaaf Renier, 1923.

O. was an Irish novelist and playwright, who, unlike most Irish writers of her time (who wrote about the poor and the working class), concentrated her work on the cultured Irish middle class and the emotional tensions created for them by the "puritanism" of the Roman Catholic Church in Ireland. O.'s work is, according to Eavan Boland, "our only link in literature" with

> an Ireland of increasing wealth and uneasy conscience, where the women wore stays and rouged their cheeks, had their clothes made by Dublin dressmakers and tried to forget the hauntings of their grandparents. This was Catholic Ireland; it was never nationalist Ireland. Its citizens were wealthy merchants, and it perished overnight when the ghosts of their ancestors walked again in their hunger and their anger.

In 1903, when O. was five, her mother died. O. was sent to school at the Laurel Hill Convent, Limerick, where she lived for twelve years. In 1915, she won a scholarship to study arts at University College, Dublin. During World War I, O. moved to England and worked as a journalist in Manchester and London; she then spent a year in Spain, employed as a governess. She married Gustaaf Renier, a Dutch journalist, in 1923, but the marriage lasted only a few months. Afterward, she devoted her time to writing short stories and plays. O.'s reputation as a playwright was established with the success of her first play, *Distinguished Villa*, in 1926. Her second play, *The Bridge*, was produced in 1927.

The first of O.'s nine novels, *Without My Cloak* (1931), was highly praised, and for it she won both the Hawthornden and the James Tait Black prizes for literature. *Without My Cloak* is set in a fictional town called "Mellick" (probably Limerick), also the setting of O.'s second novel, *The Ante-Room* (1934), considered one of O.'s best works; it tells a story of love and marriage among the Irish-Catholic bourgeoisie of the early twentieth century. O., as Boland points out, views "the world of her birth with the eyes of an exile." By doing so, Boland says, O. manages "to make us love these selfish merchant souls. They are dross. We know they are dross. But by the end of the book we have spent such golden hours in their company that they look different."

O. spent the early 1930s working as a journalist in Bilbao, Spain, but returned to England at the start of the Spanish Civil War. Three of O.'s books, *Mary Lavelle* (1936) and *That Lady* (1946), both novels, and *Farewell Spain* (1937), a "romanticized" travel book, are based on her experiences in Spain. *Mary Lavelle* is the story of a young Irishwoman spending a year as a governess in Spain before marrying her childhood sweetheart in Mellick. Mary falls in love, predictably, with the married son of her employer, but there is no sentimental happy ending. What makes *Mary Lavelle* an important book is O.'s sympathetic portrayal of a lesbian character, Agatha Conlon, who falls in love with Mary. Both *Mary Lavelle* and O.'s later book, *The Land of Spices* (1941), in which the protagonist discovers that her father is homosexual, were banned in Ireland for "immorality."

That Lady (1946; in the U.S. as *For One Sweet Grape*), is an historical novel based on the relationship between Ana de Mendoza, the Princess of Eboli, and Philip II of Spain, a story O. discovered in the letters of St. Teresa of Avila, about whom she would later publish a monograph (1951). In its concern with an illicit love affair, *That Lady* exemplifies what Tamsin Hargreaves calls the "unorthodox" nature of O.'s work:

> Kate O'Brien's novels are unorthodox; her heroines are driven by personal need and they struggle to reach modes of behaviour and thought which are true to themselves, even if, at times, this means going against the teaching of the Catholic Church. All Kate O'Brien's major novels describe love . . . which in orthodox terms

is illicit and forbidden and which is therefore deeply problematic.

For Ana de Mendoza, human love comes to mean less "than her own spirituality"—a spirituality that includes personal freedom. Ultimately, she enters a convent and finds peace by isolating herself from "the passions of human loving." Although the book was very successful, both a play (1949) and a movie (1955) based on the story failed.

In addition to her plays and novels, O. also wrote several nonfiction pieces, of which *English Diaries and Journals* (1943), a combination of history and criticism, is one of the most interesting. O. examines the diaries of many famous people as well as those of relatively obscure historical figures, including Samuel Pepys, John Evelyn, John Wesley, Fanny Burney, Queen Victoria, Sir Walter Scott, and Katherine Mansfield. O.'s comments on Burney are quite perceptive: "We cannot but wonder why she never took herself in hand and became a great novelist, as great as Jane Austen." The reason may have been Burney's "benevolent" but "rather foolish" father.

In 1947, O. was elected to the Irish Academy of Letters and was made a Fellow of the Royal Society of Literature. She lived most of her life at Roundstone, County Galway, but moved in 1961 to Faversham, in Kent. She published *My Ireland,* a travel book, in 1962, and *Presentation Parlour,* her autobiography, in 1963.

WORKS: *Distinguished Villa* (1926). *The Bridge* (1927). *Without My Cloak* (1932). *The Ante-Room* (1934). *Mary Lavelle* (1936). *Farewell Spain* (1937). *Pray for the Wanderer* (1938). *The Land of Spices* (1941). *The Last of Summer* (1943). *English Diaries and Journals* (1943). *That Lady* (1946; in the U.S. as *For One Sweet Grape*). *Teresa of Avila* (1951). *The Flower of May* (1953). *As Music and Splendour* (1958). *My Ireland* (1962). *Presentation Parlour* (1963).

BIBLIOGRAPHY: Boland, E., preface to *The Ante-Room* (rpt. 1982). Dalsimer, A. M. *Eire* (1986). Hargreaves, T., preface to *Mary Lavelle* (rpt. 1984). Reynolds, L. *Kate O'Brien: A Literary Portrait* (1987).

For articles in reference works, see: *AWWW. BDIW. Bloomsbury. CA. CBEL. DIL. DLB. Feminist. Longman. Oxford. TCA* and *SUP. ToddBWW.*

Other references: *Literature and the Changing Ireland,* ed. P. Connolly (1982). Kiely, B. *HC* (1992). Lawrence, M. M. *The School of Feminism, or We Write as Women* (1930). Nathan, G. J. *Theatre Book of the Year, 1949–1950* (1950). Quiello, R. *Eire* (1990). Walshe, E. *Ordinary People Dancing* (1993). Zach, W. and H. Kosok, ed. *Literary Interrelations: Ireland, England, and the World,* ed. W. Zach and H. Kosok (1987).

Kay Beaird Meyers

Eileen O'Connell

BORN: c. 1743, Derrynane, County Kerry, Munster, Ireland.
DIED: c. 1800.
DAUGHTER OF: Maire Ni Dhonnchadha and Domhnall Mor ("Big Dan") O'Connell.
MARRIED: O'Connor of Firies, County Kerry, 1758; Art (Arthur) O'Leary, 1767.
WROTE UNDER: Eibhlin Dubh Ni Chonaill ("Dark" Eileen O'Connell); Eileen O'Leary.

To "Dark" O. of Derrynane, County Kerry, Munster, Ireland, is attributed a classic of Irish literature, the *Caoineadh Airt Ui Laoghaire* (*Keen for Art O'Leary*) (1773). This lamentation of more than 400 lines was extemporized, in the passionate chanting style of the ancient Celtic keen, over the body of a husband shot dead on 4 May 1773. The tradition of keening for a departed beloved, usually by female relatives, is an ancient, secular ritual of bereavement, dating from about A.D. 1200. The keen is a legitimate literary subgenre whose precedents reach back to secular sources: Irish sagas, Fenian ballad poetry, Scottish ballads, and Scots-Gaelic keens, such as those of Mary Macleod of Dunvegan (c. 1615–1706). The domain of the keen is exclusively female; it was women, including professional female mourners hired for Irish wakes, who evolved and expanded the genre over the centuries. Scholars and commentators agree that O.'s lament is a masterpiece of its kind and the climax in the development of a particular type of ceremonial oral verse in the rich repertoire of Ireland's literary genius. Seamus Deane judges the *Keen for Art O'Leary* the greatest love poem in Irish.

O. was born into the prosperous and educated O'Connell family of Derrynane, County Kerry, in the 1740s. Her father, Domhnall Mor O'Connell ("Big Dan" O'Connell, d. 1770), who extended Derrynane House, descended from hereditary constables of the 1350s seated at Ballycarbery Castle, Chirciveen, County Kerry. O.'s mother, Maire (Mary) Ni Dhonnchadha of Glenflesk (1702–95), was daughter and heiress of Daniel O'Donoghue of the "Dark" O'Donoghue line of landowners at Anwyss, Killarney, County Kerry, Munster. Their sobriquet ("Dark" or *dubh*) derived from their intense, passionate temperament, though some commentators attribute this description to the brunette coloration of many of the "black Irish" male O'Donoghues. Maire and O. were reportedly fair haired and light eyed. Maire, mother of twenty-two children (twelve of whom lived to adulthood), was a strong-minded, talented woman with special gifts in Gaelic poetry and old Irish folklore. She and most of her kin were keepers of the old ways, and they resisted the encroaching anglicization of rural Ireland. A close relation of the literary Ferriter line, Maire served as a sort of patroness to Irish poets, such as Egan O'Rahilly, through her generosity and hospitality; she also preserved their work by including it in her own oral repertoire of verse.

The folklore culture of the O'Connell line, studied by Diarmid O Muirithe and O. descendant Maurice R. O'Connell, suggests that O. and her siblings profited from the advantages of both a tutor and the rich oral traditions of earlier centuries, which were typically preserved through regular recitation and storytelling. O., an aunt of the famous Irish hero Daniel O'Connell, inherited her mother's vivacity and love of Gaelic verse; and, as her famous *Keen* to her dead husband shows, she also resisted the new anglicized ways. In 1758, at about the age of fifteen, O. was married off by her family to an elderly neighbor, one O'Connor of Firies, County Kerry, who died six months later. Though unshaken (it seems) by his death, she nonetheless composed an elegy, long remembered in the local culture. Following her mother, O. was probably one of the last members of the older school of Gaelic Irish poets, which still survived in remote places of Kerry and environs. In about 1767, during a visit to her twin sister, O. caught a glimpse of the charismatic Captain Art O'Leary, recently returned from service in the Austrian Army. A bold, assertive Roman Catholic, O'Leary enjoyed provoking Protestants in his native Cork. Ignoring her family's opposition to the volatile O'Leary, she soon eloped with him and settled in the home he built in Rath Laoich, Macroom. Theirs was a felicitous though brief union (six years) that produced two sons. (As her poem states, O. was pregnant with a third child at the time of her husband's murder.)

Most accounts of her tragedy fail to address the broader contexts that precipitated her husband's murder. The traditional line mentions a personal vendetta between O'Leary and one Abraham Morris, a local anti-Catholic Protestant and a former high sheriff. Angry that his horse lost to O'Leary's glorious chestnut mare at the Macroom races and jealous of O'Leary's local popularity, Morris insulted O'Leary by invoking the old Penal Law and offering O'Leary a mere £5 for his horse. (An unsubstantiated though credible rumor claimed that O'Leary had been enjoying a liaison with Morris's wife and that more than the price of a horse was involved in O'Leary's downfall.) When O'Leary refused, a series of disputes, challenges, and threats ensued. As documented in the *Cork Evening Post* (October 1771), O'Leary soon became a wanted man and outlaw. Surprised by Morris's bodyguard, O'Leary was shot dead at Carriganima, County Cork. Morris, a magistrate, was tried for murder in September 1773 but acquitted. O. curses Morris in her lament, and he in fact died shortly after the trial (shot, according to one reconstruction, by O'Leary's brother). Again, O. would compose an epitaph for a dead husband. On the headstone of O'Leary's grave, in the family burial place inside Kilcrea Abbey, is O.'s last homage, tendered in a sparse Augustan couplet: "Lo! Art O'Leary, generous, handsome, brave, / Slain in his bloom, lies in this humble grave. // Died May 4th, 1773, Aged 26 years." Shedding fresh light on the lament, L. M. Cullen shows that the poem is an extraordinary social document with explicit political and religious contexts. O'Leary's perceived brashness and recklessness with Morris, Cullen suggests, was actually prompted less by ego than by Catholic defiance of the local establishment's virulent anti-Catholicism.

The famous keen by O. that marked this tragic incident has inspired a substantial body of scholarship and commentary. As Denis Donoghue aptly observed, "Scholars take particular care of a literature when it is on the edge of being lost" (*We Irish*, 1986). O.'s lament draws upon a traditional meter (*rosc*) and several generic characteristics, which originate in oral Irish literature of the Middle Ages and, possibly, in classical Greek funereal rites. Investigations into the poem's backgrounds explain that the *Keen* was initially preserved in Irish oral tradition by the retentive memory of Irish-speaking farmers and cottiers in Kerry and in Cork, who faithfully preserved its narrative, imagery, and language. These unremarkable people then served as important conduits for local scribes, who took down the poem from their recitation. By the nineteenth century, the *Keen* had circulated in several Irish manuscript versions. Its prominence in the literature of old romantic Ireland was immediate. A much-consulted manuscript of the poem, preserved at University College Dublin (Ferriter MS. No.1:ff.298–306), is a transcription (c. 1889) by Patrick Ferriter, Tralee, County Kerry, of a manuscript of the poem, written down by Domhnall Mac Caba of Bantir, County Cork, from the recitation of the poem by Nora Ni Shindile (Norry Singleton), a professional keener, who lived with her brother, Domhnall, a piper, near Millstret, Macroom, County Cork, until her death in about 1870. Another manuscript, based on Shindile's recited text, is preserved in the private collection of Donnchadh O Mathghamhna. Scholars agree that the gist of the *Keen*—the lamenter's reconstruction of joyful moments in her marriage, poignantly juxtaposed with exclamations of deep, moving grief—was extemporized by O. in the recitative style of the whining keen-wake. Yet no manuscript has surfaced, to date, that is contemporaneous with the events themselves. As L. M. Cullen explains, the poem is best appreciated as a living text: first memorized by cottiers and villagers, then expanded and altered over time by events occurring after the murder of O'Leary and by popular, local commentary. Some scholars suggest that O., her father, or a scribe expanded the original text of the *Keen* to reflect events that occurred after the bloody incident of 4 May 1773.

The history of this rhapsodic piece continues to hold special interest for textual scholars and folk literature specialists, for it serves as a remarkable model of four discrete stages in the transmission and evolution of a famous literary text: spontaneous lyrical utterance, communal memory, scribal manuscript, and print. When this *Keen* of 1773 reached print in 1892, in Mrs. Morgan John O'Connell's *Last Colonel of the Irish Brigade,* it found a second, modern audience. In the twentieth century, it has found a third. Several published translations, old and new, have been undertaken. Sean O Tuama's Irish-language edition (1961), with its thorough apparatus, is the most scholarly treatment to date. The poem has recently received particular attention from enthusiasts in Irish women poets, Irish folk tradition, and Gaelic Irish poetry. When Seamus Heaney won the Nobel Prize in 1995, Irish verse, with its rousing mix of the sentimental and the political, received fresh international attention. O., never an obscure figure for Irish readers, has benefitted handsomely from this renaissance.

O.'s words are rooted in her native culture. The form and character of her *Keen* invoke not the Christian Fathers or St. Patrick but bardic Irish heroes of yore: Oisin, Cuchulain, Niamh. She gives to Art O'Leary a hero's genealogy: "My friend and my pet! / O Art O'Leary, / Son of Conor, son of Caedac, / Son of Laoiseac O'Leary." And he is a power, even abroad on foreign ground: "My love, so steadfast! / When you walked through the / Occupied, fortified cities, / The wives of the merchants / Bowed to the ground to you / Knowing well in their hearts / What a good bed-fellow you were, / A great front-rider, / A father of children." In the ancient folk tradition of the keen, O. would have intoned her words in an inspired, trance-like state, with closed eyes, marking the measure of her words with graceful movement: "My love so steadfast! The day I first saw you, / By the market-house gable, My eye took a note of you, / My heart took a shine to you, I eloped from my father with you, / Far from home with you, And never regretted it." A controversial section of the poem involves the widow drinking the blood of her dead husband, but J. F. Killeen has located precedents for this sensational image in early Scottish ballads and in the Irish keens of Emer for Cuchulain and Deirdre for the Sons of Uisneach.

O.'s *Keen for Art O'Leary* testifies to the improbable survival of an ancient form of Irish poetry into the late eighteenth century. Though its existence as literature may be vestigial, it remains a classic in the extensive oral tradition of an ancient and proud people.

WORKS: *Caoineadh Airt Ui Laoghaire* (1773). *Epitaph for husbands O'Connor of Firies, Co. Kerry* (1758) and *Art O'Leary of Macroom, Co. Cork* (1773) (both published in Mrs. Morgan John O'Connell, *The Last Colonel of the Irish Brigade: Count O'Connell and Old Ireland at Home and Abroad,* 2 vols. [1892, 1977]). Versions and translations: Bergin, O. *The Gaelic Journal* (1896). *Penguin Book of Women Poets,* ed. C. Cosman et al. (1978). Ni Dhonnchadha, M. *History Ireland* (1993). Dillon, E. *IUR* (1971). O Croinin, D. A. *Danta Ard-Teistimeireachte* (school version, 1949–50). O Mathghamhna, D. *An Musgraidheach* (MS. version, from Nora Ni Shindile, 1944). Singleton, N., from her recitation, in O'Connell, M. J. *The Last Colonel of the Irish Brigade* (1892, 1977). Modern editions: *Lament for Art O'Leary,* ed. M. McCormick (dual-language edition, 1994). *Caoine Airt Ui Laoghaire,* ed. S. O Cuiv (1923). *Caoineadh Airt Ui Laoghaire,* ed. S. O Tuama (definitive Irish-language edition, 1961).

BIBLIOGRAPHY: Arensberg, C. *The Irish Countryman* (1931). Bourke, A. *Caoineadh na Tri Maire* (*Lament of the Three Marys*) (1983; in *Ballad Research,* ed. H. Shields, 1986; in *Feminist Messages,* ed. J. N. Radner, 1993). *Penguin Book of Women Poets,* ed. C. Cosman et al. (1978). Crofton, C. *The Keen of the South of Ireland* (1844). Cullen, L. M. *Emergence of Modern Ireland 1600–1900* (1981). Deane, S. *Short History of Irish Literature* (1986). *Irish Poems: From Cromwell to the Famine,* ed. J. T. Keefe (1977). *Pillars of the House: Anthology of Verse by Irish Women, 1690 to Present,* ed. A. A. Kelly (1988). *New Oxford Book of Irish Verse,* ed. T. Kinsella (1986). Levi, P. *The Lamentation of the Dead* (1984). *Herself, Long Ago,* ed. M. McCormick (1991). Murphy, G., in *O'Connell,* ed. M. Tierney (1949). O'Connell, M. J. *The Last Colonel of the Irish Brigade* (1892, 1977). O'Connell, M. R. *Irish Politics and Social Conflict in the Age of the American Revolution* (1965, 1976). O'Connell, M. R. *Daniel O'Connell: The Man and His Politics* (1990). O Muirithe, D., in *O'Connell,* ed. M. R. O'Connell (1985). Watson, J. C. *Gaelic Songs of Mary Macleod* (1934).

Other references: Bourke, A. *Women's Studies International Forum* (1988). Bromwich, R. *Eigse* (1947). "Caoineadh Airt Ui Laoghaire" *Comhar* (1986). Collins, J. T. *Journal of the Cork Archaeological and Historical Society* (1949). Cullen, L. M. *History Ireland* (1993). Donoghue, D. *We Irish* (1986). *Graph* (1989). *Journal of Women's Studies,* ed. J. Hoff and M. Coulter (1995; useful bibliography of Irishwomen's verse). Killeen, J. F. *ZCP* (1991). McDiarmid, L. *NYTBR* (1995). Murphy, G. *Eigse* (1943). Ni Dhomhnaill, N. *NYTBR* (1995). O'Connell, M. R. *SECC* (1976). *Orlando Project: An Integrated History of Women's Writing in the British Isles* (U. of Alberta, Canada, forthcoming).

Maureen E. Mulvihill

Julia O'Faolain

BORN: 6 June 1932, London.
DAUGHTER OF: Sean O'Faolain and Eileen O'Faolain.
MARRIED: Lauro Martines.

Writer of fiction, translator, editor, and reviewer, O. is most accomplished in the short story, the form that won her father international recognition. She was educated in Dublin by Sacred Heart nuns, graduated from University College, Dublin, and continued her schooling in Rome and Paris. She is married to the American historian, Lauro Martines, and maintains residences in London and Los Angeles.

Although many of her works reflect her Irish heritage, O.'s fiction has an international scope, as many of her stories and novels are set on the Continent and in the United States. A writer with definite feminist sympathies, O. poses questions about the role of women in society and delineates the repression of women in a male-dominated world. Her fiction deals honestly, sometimes almost brutally, with sexual and religious hypocrisy; the toughness and frankness of her prose has been the object of both critical acclaim and disapproval. A more compassionate humanity and refined sense of humor, however, have surfaced in some of her more recent works.

The stories in O.'s first collection, *We Might See Sights* (1968), introduce concerns that are to reappear throughout her subsequent fiction. The Irish stories, in which O. reveals little sympathy for her homeland, explore such subjects as adolescent sexuality and suppression of the passions. The softer Italian stories center on the intricate links between the past and present and on the sadness of loneliness and old age.

O.'s first novel, *Godded and Codded* (1970), received a mixed critical response. The work, entitled *Three Lovers* in the United States, recounts the sexual initiation of a young Irishwoman in Paris during the Algerian troubles. While the characterizations tend to be shallow, O. shows talent as a caricaturist of Left Bank life and convincingly conveys the protagonist's victimization by men. In 1973, O. published *Not in God's Image: Women in History from the Greeks to the Victorians,* which she edited with her husband. In their efforts to study the subjection of women in western civilization, the editors compiled selections from a variety of primary sources, ranging from diary entries to excerpts from literary works, accompanied by commentary. Termed by one critic as "in a class quite of its own," this volume was especially praised for its scholarship.

The vast array of problems besetting individuals as they attempt to deal with sexuality dominate the stories of *Man in the Cellar* (1974). Serious social concerns inform some pieces, such as the title story, in which a battered wife locks her husband in their cellar, thus gaining revenge and regaining a sense of identity. In other selections, O. reveals a gift for black comedy.

Women in the Wall (1975) constitutes O.'s most ambitious, and, perhaps, most successful achievement to date. Basing her novel on the historical account of Queen Radegund, patron saint of prisoners and captives, who founded the monastery of the Holy Cross with St. Agnes, O. has transformed original manuscript material into a vivid recreation of life in sixth-century Gaul. Ingunda, the fictional daughter of St. Agnes and a poet-priest, walls herself up to expiate her parents' sin, but the title has implications that reach far beyond this act. The figurative "walling up" of the characters' intellects, spirits, and individuality are caused by the blend of violence, politics, and mysticism pervading the novel's world. O.'s concern with the powerful force of sexuality and the buried life of women brings to the novel a strong sense of contemporaneity.

The positive and negative features of Irish politics, from the Troubles through the 1970s, are the subject of O.'s third novel, *No Country for Young Men* (1980). As she shifts between past and present throughout the novel, she studies the changes that Ireland has undergone since gaining its independence. While the work has been commended for its apprehension of the political reality of Ireland, it has been criticized for an uncertainty of purpose, a looseness of form, and a tendency toward melodrama.

In The Obedient Wife (1982), O. places her Italian heroine, Carla, in a contemporary Los Angeles, California, suburb. Carla emerges as an admirable, sensitive, and stable force in a world that is permeated with moral, sexual, and religious disintegration and hypocrisy. O. explores the obsessive and frequently destructive powers of the passions in her critically acclaimed collection of stories, *Daughters of Passion* (1982). She often reveals sympathy for her characters, though she examines with critical distance the degree to which their passions have enslaved them.

A major voice in British letters, O. has produced works of intellectual and imaginative complexity, notable for their understanding of human nature and their attention to significant contemporary social issues.

WORKS: *We Might See Sights and Other Stories* (1968). *Godded and Codded* (1970; in the U.S. as *Three Lovers*, 1971). *Man in the Cellar* (1974). *Women in the Wall* (1975). *Melancholy Baby and Other Stories* (1978). *No Country for Young Men* (1980). *The Obedient Wife* (1982). *Daughters of Passion* (1982). *The Irish Signorina* (1984). *The Judas Cloth* (1992).

BIBLIOGRAPHY: Burleigh, D. *Irish Writers and Society at Large*, ed. M. Sekine (1785). Weekes, A. *Eire* (1986).

For articles in reference works, see: *Bloomsbury*. *CA*. *CLC*. *DIL*. *DNB*. *Feminist*.

Other references: *Economist* (17 February 1973). *New Republic* (10 May 1975). *NYTBR* (9 May 1971). *Spectator* (1 January 1983). *TLS* (23 January 1969, 16 August 1974, 23 July 1982).

Peter Drewniany

Oland, John: See *Wickham, Anna*

Old Acquaintance of the Public, An: See *Piozzi, Hester Lynch Salusbury Thrale*

O'Leary, Eileen: See *O'Connell, Eileen*

Olinda: See *Taylor, Elizabeth (Wythers)*

Margaret Oliphant

BORN: 4 April 1828, Wallyford, near Musselburgh, Midlothian, Scotland.
DIED: 25 June 1897, Eton.
DAUGHTER OF: Francis Wilson and Margaret Oliphant.
MARRIED: Francis Oliphant, 1852.

The last of several children born to cousins, O. spent her early years in Lasswade, near Edinburgh. Her two much older brothers, the only other surviving children of the family, went to school in Edinburgh, and for much of the time O. was the focus of her mother's attentions. Her mother, descended from the Oliphants of Kellie Castle in Fife, was an excellent storyteller and a dedicated reader and was one of the major influences on O.'s literary tendencies.

When O. was six years old, the family moved to a large and gloomy house in Glasgow. The lugubrious surroundings and the lack of social contacts increased her voluminous reading; Q. D. Leavis notes that at "seven or eight [O.] was already a confirmed novel-reader," and what Henry James called her "immensity of reading" led naturally to an "easy flow" of writing. This "easy flow" led to an output both prodigious and varied. She published more than 100 books of fiction, criticism, translations, travel guides, and biography. In addition, the articles and essays she produced for many periodicals, chiefly *Blackwood's*, amount to at least another hundred volumes.

The first of her published works, *Passages in the Life of Mrs. Margaret Maitland* (1849), was written while the family was living in Liverpool, where her father had a position in the Customs House. During this period, O. became engaged to a young man who was going to America for three years, after which they were to have been married, but the engagement was broken following a year of quarrelsome letters. In her *Autobiography* (1899), O. refers to this time as one of "depression and sadness." It was also a time when her mother became ill and O. sat silently at her mother's bedside and began to write in order to amuse herself. Her brother, living in London, took the manuscript of her first book to the publishing firm of Colburn, where it was accepted for publication.

The £150 O. earned for the novel financed her first trip to London, where she had gone to await its publication and to look after her eldest brother, who was perpetually in debt. Thus began the pattern of her life—ceaseless literary labors in the support of her male relatives. Ironically, it was at this time that she became acquainted with her cousin Francis Oliphant, whom she would marry in 1852. He was an artist who had designed the stained-glass windows in the Houses of Parliament, but, like her father, brothers, and sons, he was never as financially successful as she was to become.

On the morning of her wedding, she received the page proofs of her novel *Katie Stewart*, published by Blackwood, an association that was to last forty-five years until her death in 1897. Her marriage to Francis Oliphant, however, lasted only seven years and ended with his death in Rome in 1859. The Oliphants had gone to Italy in search of a more healthful climate for Francis, who was suffering from consumption. The family, which by this time included a daughter and a son, settled in Florence where the weather was cold and damp, but Francis's health did not improve. The preceding years had been difficult for O.; she had given birth to four children, only two of whom survived, and her mother, her greatest source of strength and support, had died shortly after the second child. Throughout this tragic time, she published dozens of articles for *Blackwood's* and at least two or three novels each year. Her third child was born six weeks after the death of her husband.

She returned to Scotland and continued with her writing, beginning what was perhaps her most famous series of novels, *The Chronicles of Carlingford*. The first two, *The Rector and the Doctor's Family* and *Salem Chapel*, were published in 1863; *The Perpetual Curate* (1864) and *Miss Marjoribanks* (1866) continued the series. The latter is considered by most critics to be her best work and the one that was most influential upon the work of other writers. Ironic, satirical, and comedic, the novel was written following the death of her twelve-year-old daughter Margaret. The success of the Carlingford series had enabled her to travel again to Italy, where the child succumbed to an attack of fever.

O. returned to England and lived near Eton, where she had enrolled her sons. The expenses of their education and the support of her brother Frank and his family necessitated an unending literary output, notably the concluding volume in the Carlingford series, *Phoebe, Junior* (1876). The last years of her life were as unfortunate personally as the earlier ones had been. She outlived both of her sons, who had never fulfilled her hopes for them. Her nephew, whom she had educated, showed promise as an engineer but died of typhoid in India.

The tragedies of her personal life have tended to obscure her unique accomplishments as a writer. The first writer to note the "feminine cynicism" in Austen's novels, she was an original and perceptive critic. Her work is unusually realistic for her period: She believed a "happy ending" was simply "a contemptible expedient." And, while she was conservative regarding sexual ethics and critical of what she termed the "Anti-Marriage League" of writers such as Mary Elizabeth Braddon and Thomas Hardy, O.'s fiction tends to portray marriage as problematic. The heroines of her novels do not conform to the usual Victorian stereotypes; they are practical, clever, and articulate, and they work (as O. herself had always done), often in direct defiance of the wishes of their husbands, brothers, or fathers. For example, Catherine in *Hester* (1883) runs the family bank, while the heroine of *Kirsteen* (1890) escapes from home to set up a successful dressmaking shop.

Her last major work, the first two of the three-volume *Annals of a Publishing House* (1897), a history of Blackwood (the third volume was written by Mrs. G. Porter), remains as one of the most detailed, accurate, and engaging works of its kind. Her last journal article for *Blackwood's*, "'Tis Sixty Years Since," published in May 1897, honored the long reign of Queen Victoria in anticipation of the Queen's Jubilee, which was to be held in June. When she had completed the article, her doctor told her she was dying. With typical Scottish fortitude, she clung to life until two days after the celebration. She died as she had lived, pleasing others through the efforts of her pen but never totally satisfying her own desires.

WORKS: *Passages in the Life of Mrs. Margaret Maitland* (1849). *Caleb Field* (1851). *Merkland: A Story of Scottish Life* (1851). *Memoirs and Resolutions of Adam Graeme of Mossgay* (1852). *Katie Stewart* (1853). *Harry Muir: A Story of Scottish Life* (1853). *Quiet Heart* (1854). *Magdalen Hepburn: A Story of the Scottish Reformation* (1854). *Lilliesleaf: Conclusion of Margaret Maitland* (1855). *Zaidee: A Romance* (1856). *The Athelings, or The Three Gifts* (1857). *The Days of My Life* (1857). *Sundays* (1858). *The Laird of Nordlaw* (1858). *Orphans: A Chapter in Life* (1858). *Agnes Hopetoun's Schools and Holidays* (1859). *Lucy Croften* (1860). *The House on the Moor* (1861). *The Last of the Mortimers* (1862). *The Life of Edward Irving* (1862). *The Rector and the Doctor's Family* (1863). *Salem Chapel* (1863). *Heart and Cross* (1863). *The Perpetual Curate* (1864). *Agnes* (1866). *Miss Marjoribanks* (1866). *A Son of the Soil* (1866). *Madonna Mary* (1867). *The Brownlows* (1868). *Francis of Assisi* (1868). *The Minister's Wife* (1869). *Historical Sketches of the Reign of George II* (1869). *John: A Love Story* (1870). *The Three Brothers* (1870). *Squire Arden* (1871). *At His Gates* (1872). *Memoirs of the Count de Montalembert* (1872). *Ombra* (1872). *May* (1873). *Innocent: A Tale of Modern Life* (1873). *A Rose in June* (1874). *For Love and Life* (1874). *The Story of Valentine and His Brother* (1875). *Whiteladies* (1875). *The Curate in Charge* (1876). *Dress* (1876). *The Makers of Florence: Dante, Giotto, Savanarola, and Their City* (1876). *Phoebe, Junior* (1876). *Young Musgrave* (1877). *Dante* (1877). *Mrs. Arthur* (1877). *Carita* (1877). *The Primrose Path* (1878). *Within the Precincts* (1878). *The Two Mrs. Scudamores* (1879). *Moliere* (1879). *The Greatest Heiress in England* (1879). *A Beleaguered City* (1880). *Cervantes* (1880). *He That Will Not When He May* (1880). *Harry Joscelyn* (1881). *In Trust* (1882). *A Little Pilgrim in the Unseen* (1882). *Hester* (1883). *It Was a Lover and His Lass* (1883). *Literary History of England in the End of the Eighteenth and Beginning of the Nineeenth Century* (1882). *Sheridan* (1883). *The Ladies Lindores* (1883). *Sir Tom* (1884). *The Wizard's Son* (1884). *Two Stories of the Seen and Unseen* (1885). *Madam* (1885). *Oliver's Bride* (1886). *A Country Gentleman and His Family* (1886). *Effie Ogilvie* (1886). *The Makers of Venice: Doges, Conquerors, Painters, and Men of Letters* (1887). *A House Divided Against Itself* (1887). *The Son of His Father* (1887). *The Land of Darkness* (1888). *Joyce* (1888). *Memoir of the Life of John Tulloch* (1888). *The Second Son* (1888). *Cousin Mary* (1888). *Neighbours on the Green* (1889). *A Poor Gentleman* (1889). *Lady Car: The Sequel of a Life* (1889).

Kirsteen (1890). *Royal Edinburgh: Her Saints, Kings, Prophets, and Poets* (1890). *The Duke's Daughter and the Fugitives* (1890). *Sons and Daughters* (1890). *The Mystery of Mrs. Blencarrow* (1890). *Jerusalem: Its History and Hope* (1891). *Memoirs of the Life of Laurence Oliphant, and Alice Oliphant, His Wife* (1891). *The Railway Man and His Children* (1891). *Janet* (1891). *The Cuckoo in the Nest* (1892). *Diana Trelawny* (1892). *The Marriage of Elinor* (1892). *The Heir Presumptive and the Heir Apparent* (1892). (with F. R. Oliphant) *The Victorian Age of English Literature* (1892). *The Sorceress* (1893). *Lady William* (1893). *Thomas Chalmers, Preacher, Philosopher, and Statesman* (1893). *A House in Bloomsbury* (1894). *Who Was Lost and Is Found* (1894). *The Prodigals and their Inheritance* (1894). *A Child's History of Scotland* (1895). *Two Strangers* (1895). *Sir Robert's Fortune* (1895). *The Makers of Modern Rome* (1895). *The Unjust Steward, or the Minister's Debt* (1896). *The Two Marys* (1896). *Old Mr. Tredgold* (1896). *Jeanne d'Arc: Her Life and Death* (1896). *The Lady's Walk* (1897). *The Sisters Brontë* (1897). *Annals of a Publishing House: William Blackwood and His Sons, Their Magazine and Friends* (1897). *A Widow's Tale and Other Stories* (1898). *That Little Cutty; and Two Other Stories* (1898). *Autobiography and Letters of Mrs. Margaret Oliphant*, ed. A.L.W. Coghill (1899). *Selected Short Stories of the Supernatural*, ed. M. K. Gray (1986).

BIBLIOGRAPHY: Calder, J., in *History of Scottish Literature*, ed. D. Gifford and C. Craig (1988). Clarke, I. C. *Six Portraits* (1935). Clarke, J. S. *Margaret Oliphant: A Bibliography* (1986). Colby, V. and R. Colby. *The Equivocal Virtue: Margaret Oliphant and the Victorian Literary Marketplace* (1966). Craik, W. *GSJ* (1995). Harris, J. H. *MLQ* (1986). Haythornthwaite, J. *Bibliotheck* (1990). Haythornthwaite, J. *PubHist* (1990). James, H. *Notes on Novelists, with Some Other Notes* (1914). Jay, E. *Caliban* (1994). Jay, E. *Mrs. Oliphant: "A Fiction to Herself"* (1995). Johnson, R. B. *The Women Novelists* (1918). Leavis, Q. D., intro. to *Autobiography and Letters of Mrs. Oliphant*, ed. A.L.W. Coghill (reprint, 1974). O'Mealy, J. H. *SNNTS* (1991). O'Mealy, J. H., in *The New Nineteenth Century: Feminist Readings of Underread Victorian Fiction*, ed. B. Harriman and S. Meyer (1996). Ritchie, A. T. *From the Porch* (1913). Rubik, M. M., in *A Yearbook of Studies in English Language and Literature, 1985/86*, ed. O. Rauchbauer (1986). Rubik, M. *The Novels of Mrs. Oliphant* (1994). Sanders, V. *PSt* (1986). Tintner, A. R. *AB/Bookman's Weekly* (22 April 1985). Trela, D. J. *CAnn* (1990). *Margaret Oliphant: Critical Essays on a Gentle Subversive*, ed. D. J. Trela (1995). Williams, M. *Margaret Oliphant: A Critical Biography* (1986).

For articles in reference works, see: *BA19C*. *Bloomsbury*. *Cambridge*. *Europa*. *Feminist*. *Oxford*. *ToddBWW*.

Other references: Clark, J. S. *N&Q* (1981). Moore, K. *Victorian Wives* (1974). Showalter, E. *A Literature of Their Own* (1977). Stebbins, L. P. *A Victorian Album: Some Lady Novelists of the Period* (1946). Williams, M. *N&Q* (1995).

Gail Kraidman
(updated by Kirsten T. Saxton)

Mary Dolling (Sanders) O'Malley

BORN: 11 September 1889, Shenley, Hertfordshire.
DIED: 9 March 1974, Oxford.
DAUGHTER OF: James Harris Sanders and Marie Louise Day.
MARRIED: Sir Owen St. Clair O'Malley, 1913.
WROTE UNDER: G. Allenby; Ann Bridge; Mary O'Malley.

A writer of what she styled "modern historicals" under the pseudonym of "Ann Bridge," O.'s contributions to literature are her earlier works, which deal with key themes in modern history—the forging of a modern Turkey, the Spanish Civil War, the fierce conservatism of Albania. The first novels, on the cultural impact of China upon the West, brought her early critical acclaim, but she reached her greatest readership with the romantic thrillers she wrote later in life. She was reviewed by the most prominent of reviewers but somehow always just failed to pass muster. Graham Greene, for instance, found her too bound by good form but liked some of the characters she presented. The application of feminist criticism to this seemingly traditionalist matter would be of value to the modern reader.

O.'s reputation today is somewhat blurred by the Julia Probyn series of romantic espionage novels of her later career in which the reader is regaled with a picture of upper-class British life lived in exotic settings. These late novels capitalized on the vogue for this innocent genre of the romantic thriller and were written with an eye on providing a comfortable retirement. Nevertheless, because O. traveled widely and with a discerning eye and wrote with a strong sense of place, her novels have preserved pictures of worlds that have since disappeared—the China of *Peking Picnic* (1932) and *The Ginger Griffin* (1934); anglophile aristocratic domestic life in early twentieth-century Italy of *Enchanter's Nightshade* (1937); precommunist Hungary of *A Place to Stand* (1953), *The Tightening String* (1962), and *The Portuguese Escape* (1958); the Balkans of *Illyrian Spring* (1935); and possibly her most historically valuable work, *The Dark Moment* (1961), based on oral histories of Turkish women who lived, loved, and worked during the Kemal Ataturk revolution. Another contender for her best work is *Frontier Passage* (1942), set in France and Spain during the Spanish Civil War, a novel that reads with fresh impact in the post-Vietnam era and that includes a wonderful treatment of an unusual teenager's rite of passage.

O. was forced, as she said, to begin to earn a living at the age of twenty-two, during which time she also followed a course of studies at the London School of Economics. She was conscious of being less well educated than her eldest sister, who had received a double first at Oxford, and less adventurous than another sister who went to Russia as a governess before World War I and stayed on through the Revolution. O. used in her writing what she had gained from excellent private tutoring, travel, and her passion for mountain climbing. She later said that she would have been a first-rate novelist had she had a university education.

For three years, O. worked as a secretary of the Charity Organisation Society in London until her marriage to Owen O'Malley, a diplomat at the Foreign Office.

O'Malley's first posting was Peking in 1925. During the early years of their marriage, he worked in London and later researched for Winston Churchill, who was then engaged in writing his multivolume history of World War I. O'Malley was knighted in 1930 and served as ambassador to Mexico, Portugal, and Poland, with other intervening assignments. His training and career had been designed to lead him to the upper reaches of the Foreign Office, but his early role as scapegoat in the Zenoviev Affair and his later ill-timed paper on the Katyn Wood massacre inconveniently implicating the Russians kept him out in the field and ended in a fairly early retirement. O. brought her energies to bear on the social side of diplomacy, an aspect that did not appeal to her husband. This type of diplomat was echoed in the characters of Mr. Leroy in *Peking Picnic* and Mr. Grant-Howard in *The Ginger Griffin.* Her first long work, a narrative account of her husband's disgrace and reinstatement in the diplomatic service and the role she played in this reinstatement, was published in 1971, years after her husband's retirement. *Permission to Resign: Goings On in the Corridors of Power* received a long and thoughtful review in the *Times Literary Supplement* as a contribution to modern diplomatic history but was not published in the United States.

With great energy, O. ran Bridge End, the picturesque and inconvenient medieval house they rented in the country, where she raised two daughters and a son and organized several income-producing projects—raising, killing, and plucking fowls for her husband to deliver to colleagues at the Foreign Office. With her family past infancy, O. began writing for publication in 1928 with such articles as "The Invalid Child," "The Child at Sea," and "The Child Abroad" for *The Nursery World* and a short story in *Cornhill,* "The Buick Saloon," under the name "Mary O'Malley." Poetry was published in the *Spectator* under "G. Allenby." "Ann Bridge" was born at the behest of the Foreign Office when her first novel, *Peking Picnic,* received the *Atlantic Monthly* Prize in 1932; now that her career as a novelist was launched, she needed to distance her writing life from her diplomatic life.

Peking Picnic recounts the adventures of a group of British and American characters exposed to and vigorously attempting to understand the culture of China as manifested in the brigand armies of the 1920s and the tourist sights of Peking. Inevitably compared to E. M. Forster's *A Passage to India,* it was never intended to be so culturally confrontational. Two other novels with Chinese settings were published, *The Ginger Griffin* and *Four-Part Setting* (1939). This last is a searing study of the discipline required of persons who aspire to intellectual integrity, with the two protagonists coming to an understanding of their fates, Rose by forgiving the unforgivable and Anastasia by moving from the contemplative world to one of action.

O. published six novels in the 1930s. Besides the Chinese novels, *Illyrian Spring* is credited with making Yugoslavia a tourist destination for English-speaking travelers, though critics were embarrassed at the theme of regeneration of a fortyish woman. *Enchanter's Nightshade* renders the downfall of an emancipated and comfortably middle-class Englishwoman in her encounter with the Italian aristocracy of 1905. The setting is based on O.'s family visits as a young child and is rich in the kind of detail a precocious child would retain over the years.

O. used her talents in both world wars. In the first, newly married, she was a member of a team of code breakers, recruited through her membership in the Ladies Alpine Club. These experiences provided the personal relationships updated for the Probyn books and convinced her that amateurs were better at espionage than professionals. Because of her Chinese novels, O.'s name was well known in the United States in the early 1940s, and she was used as a public speaker, arguing for support of the English against Hitler's Germany. She worked as British Red Cross representative in Hungary (1940–41) and with the Polish Red Cross in England in 1944–45. During these years she wrote several novels and published *Frontier Passage,* whose theme dealt with the effect of the Spanish Civil War on civilians. It indicted both the French and the English governments for their callous treatment of the civilian population, giving details available only to an eyewitness. This novel was translated into Spanish immediately on publication in English.

Two works of the latter period are of interest. *The Selective Traveller in Portugal* (1949), written with Susan Lowndes (Mrs. Luiz Marguez), the daughter of Mrs. Belloc Lowndes, is a popular guide to Portugal for the English speaking and went through several editions. *Portrait of My Mother* (1955), an account of O.'s American mother's family, was well received, critics appreciating the family stories set in New Orleans, Louisiana, during Civil War and Reconstruction times. Published in 1955, the year of her husband's retirement to Ireland, it marked the end of her serious fiction writing, although she would publish eight more novels.. O.'s writing is very much in the French Roman Catholic tradition of François Mauriac, whom she admired, and is an exploration of the way in which women, despite the defects of their virtues, measure their lives against objective standards and strive to meet them, usually at great personal cost.

WORKS: *Peking Picnic* (1932). *The Ginger Griffin* (1934). *Illyrian Spring* (1935). *The Song in the House* (1936). *Enchanter's Nightshade* (1937). *Four-Part Setting* (1939). *Frontier Passage* (1942). *Singing Waters* (1945). *And Then You Came* (1948). (with S. Lowndes) *The Selective Traveller in Portugal* (1949; rev. 1958). *The House at Kilmartin* (1951). *A Place to Stand* (1953). *Portrait of My Mother* (1955; in the U. S. as *A Family of Two Worlds: A Portrait of Her Mother). The Lighthearted Quest* (1956). *The Portuguese Escape* (1958). (with S. Lowndes) *The Numbered Account* (1960). *The Dark Moment* (1961). *The Tightening String* (1962). *The Dangerous Islands* (1963). *Emergency in the Pyrenees* (1965). *The Episode at Toledo* (1966). *Facts and Fictions: Some Literary Recollections* (1968). *Malady in Madeira* (1969). *Moments of Knowing; Some Personal Experiences beyond Normal Knowledge* (1970). *Permission to Resign: Goings On in the Corridors of Power* (1971). *Julia in Ireland* (1973).

BIBLIOGRAPHY: Cadogan, M. and P. Craig. *Women and Children First: The Fiction of Two World Wars* (1978). Lammers, D. *CentR* (1992). *LonT* (11 March 1974).

For articles in reference works, see: *CA. Feminist. Longman. TCA. TCC&MW. TCRGW.*

Eleanor Langstaff

Opals: See Custance, Olive

Amelia Opie

BORN: 12 November 1769, Norwich, Norfolk.
DIED: 2 December 1853, Norwich, Norfolk.
DAUGHTER OF: James Alderson and Amelia Briggs.
MARRIED: John Opie, 1798.

A novelist who brought heightened pathos and mournful tenderness to the domestic novel and a small gift to poetry, O. reached the apogee of her fame in the three-volume *Adeline Mowbray,* a tale suggested in part by the colorful history of William Godwin and Mary Wollstonecraft. High spirited, convivial, with a self-acknowledged love of society and luxury, in later years she came to recoil from the sumptuary side of life, devoting her best energies to befriending the mentally ill, developing republican sympathies, and ultimately turning to the asceticism of the Quakerism of her native Norwich. She found favor with prominent English radicals and won the admiration of Kosciusko, Benjamin West, and Maria Edgeworth. In Paris, the *illustrati* of the day applauded her as much for the strength of her compassionate instincts as for her literary achievements. Although not nearly as subtle and steady a reader of character as Jane Austen, her near contemporary, O. achieved a limited mastery over style and setting. Twentieth-century critical estimations have been harsh, ranking her far beneath the realm of the distinguished.

As a child, she imbibed the radical politics and utilitarianism of her father, a physician and the grandson of a dissenting minister. Her education was brief but richly supplemented by reading and the graces of French and dancing. Her juvenilia include poems and a tragedy, "Adelaide" (1787), mounted for the amusement of her local friends. At the age of fifteen, becoming mistress of her father's house upon the death of her mother, she entered local society, regaling it with wit and song. Acting as hostess to such famous visitors as William Godwin and James Macintosh matured her political awareness and gave her a larger sense of life.

Part of her fame can be attributed to the numerous portraits painted of her by her husband, John Opie, often referred to as the English Rembrandt. Sir Joshua Reynolds thought his numerous court commissions and such genre canvases as "Cornish Beggar" were representative of a talent of "Caravaggio and Velásquez in one." After his marriage to O. in 1798, his work, it is commonly agreed, was enhanced by a certain grace it lacked before. Indeed, it was John Opie who encouraged O. to take up the pen, for he hoped thus to wean her of her love of society. Her first acknowledged work appeared three years after her marriage. *Father and Daughter* (1801) achieved a certain fame as a moral tale, leading Sir Walter Scott to confess shedding tears upon reading it. Once she assumed the role of author, she became steadfast at her craft, putting in eight- to ten-hour days at her writing desk. She remained devoted to John Opie; after his death in 1807, she prepared a memoir later prefixed to her edited version of his *Lectures on Painting,* which are acknowledged to be among the most brilliant and original presented at the Royal Academy.

O.'s renown in her day, since greatly diminished, resulted from her inclusion in the orbit of William Godwin's circle. Inspired by the radical beliefs of the French *philosophes,* Godwin was an inveterate system builder and espouser of radical politics. O. first met Godwin in 1793 at Norwich, and the most extreme of British revolutionary philosophers took a pronounced liking to her. Her most important novel, *Adeline Mowbray* (1804), is based on the career of the proto-feminist, Mary Wollstonecraft, author of *A Vindication of the Rights of Women,* who lived with Godwin. Harriet Westbrook gave this multivolume work to Percy Bysshe Shelley in a successful bid to convince him to undertake the vows of marriage.

O.'s literary career came to a halt in 1825 when she was formally inducted into the Society of Friends. The renewal of her early acquaintance with Joseph John Gurney, "the Quaker pope," gave definite shape to her hitherto amorphous religious beliefs and convinced her to renounce novel writing.

Her last novel, *Madeline,* was published in two volumes in 1822. When O. donned the grey habit of the Friends, she declined to finish *The Painter and his Wife,* which was under contract. Her last work, *Lays for the Dead* (1833), poems in memory of departed relatives and friends, was entirely different in character, devotional and elevating. It was in keeping with her daily round of visiting hospitals, ministering to the poor, and helping ameliorate workhouse conditions. Every consideration gave way to the imperative claim of her newfound religious convictions. Complete self-abnegation, however, was beyond her reach, for she entertained the love of society and its pleasures too much to effect a complete and irreparable break. Not surprisingly, Harriet Martineau noted in 1839 that O. could not resist "a spice of dandyism" in the demure peculiarity of her dress. During the socially restricted years of her Quakerism, she still continued to meet such notables as the Marquis de Lafayette, Benjamin Constant, Georges Cuvier, Comtesse Sophie de Ségur, and Mme. Félicité de Genlis.

Although she accepted the renunciation of her craft with philosophic calm, her old habits were not so easily dismissed. Even when invested in the full canonicals of her newfound calling, O. could not bow to all the strictures of Quakerism, certainly not those that would darken her vivacity and irrepressible wit. Her social conscience remained with her to the last, for injustice was a conception her mind refused to admit. She was active in antislavery circles, and in her advanced years, when she had long abandoned the life of the writer, she attended the London Antislavery Convention of 1840 as a Norwich delegate.

Dismissed by her peers as too "lachrymose" a novelist and too sentimentally gushing a poet, O. remained a sympathetic and congenial personality of her age, extending the dominion of the domestic novel by perfecting the tone and timbre of social dialogue. Her poetry, although not of the first order except possibly for "Elegy to the Memory of the Late Duke of Bedford" (1801), possesses a warbling persuasiveness and sweetness that lend it charm and color.

WORKS: "Adelaide" (1787). *Father and Daughter* (1801). "An Elegy to the Memory of the Duke of Bedford" (1801). *Adeline Mowbray* (3 vols., 1804). *Simple Tales* (1806). *The Warrior's Return and Other Poems* (1808). *Temper, or Domestic Scenes* (1812). *Tales of Real Life* (1813). *Valentine's Eve* (1816). *Tales of the Heart* (1820). *Madeline* (1822). *Lays for the Dead* (1833).

BIBLIOGRAPHY: Brightwell, C. L., ed. *Memorials of the Life of Amelia Opie* (1854). Eberle, R. *SNNTS* (1994). Fergus, J. *SECC* (1987). Howells, W. D. *Heroines of Fiction* (1901). Kelly, G. *ArielE* (1981). Macgregor, M. E. *Smith College Studies in Modern Language* (1933). Ra'ad, B. *MSEx* (1991). Ritchie, A.I.T. *A Book of Sibyls: Mrs. Barbauld, Miss Edgeworth, Mrs. Opie and Miss Hasten* (1883). Wilson, A. M. *Amelia: The Life of a Plain Friend* (1937).

For articles in reference works, see: *Allibone. BA19C. DNB. Feminist. ToddBWW.*

Other sources: Agress, L. *The Feminine Irony: Women on Women in Early-Nineteenth-Century English Literature* (1978). Spender, D. *Mothers of the Novel* (1986).

Michael Skakun
(updated by Natalie Joy Woodall)

Emma Magdalena Rosalia Maria Josefa Barbara Orczy

BORN: 23 September 1865, Tarna-Ors, Hungary.
DIED: 12 November 1947, London.
DAUGHTER OF: Baron Felix Orczy and Emma Wass Orczy.
MARRIED: Montague Barstow, 1894.

Due to agricultural unrest and violence in Hungary, O.'s family abandoned their country estate and moved to Budapest; they then moved to Brussels, Paris, and finally to London, where O. arrived at the age of fifteen, knowing no English. Her father, a talented amateur musician, moved in a cosmopolitan society of musical, social, and theatrical celebrities. This milieu inspired O. with the desire for a career in the arts; finding no success in music, she pursued painting at the West London School of Art and the Heatherley School of Art, where she met Montague Barstow, an illustrator and painter. Married shortly after, they had one child, a son, in 1899. After World War I, they bought the Villa Bijou in Monte Carlo, Monaco, where they lived for the rest of their lives; they also made long visits to England and lived occasionally in a villa they purchased in Italy until the rise of fascism became intolerable. During World War II, they remained in occupied Monte Carlo, where Barstow died in 1943, after which O. remained alone in spite of bombing raids.

In 1895, O. translated and edited Hungarian fairy tales, sometimes illustrated by Barstow. She also began writing stories for magazines in the late 1890s when the couple found themselves in narrowed circumstances. Her first novel, *The Emperor's Candlesticks* (1899), was not a success, but editors continued to buy her stories and serials.

Her second novel, *The Scarlet Pimpernel* (1905), however, introduced the character for whom she is best known and made her famous. According to her autobiography, *Links in the Chain of Life* (1947), she wrote the novel in five weeks, thinking of it in theatrical scenes as she did so, and she and Barstow adapted it for the stage. The novel was rejected by a dozen publishers, and the play had several provincial tryouts over the next few years. Finally, in 1905, *The Scarlet Pimpernel* appeared as a novel and a play simultaneously, and both achieved success. The play, starring Fred Terry, ran for years, sometimes in London, sometimes on tour, until Terry died in 1933. The novel had been translated into sixteen languages by the time O. wrote her autobiography and was filmed in 1934 with Leslie Howard in the title role. More recently, *The Scarlet Pimpernel* was dramatized in a television series. Small wonder that the title entered the language as a term to indicate one who rescues others from mortal danger by smuggling them over a border.

Reasons for the success of *The Scarlet Pimpernel* are not hard to determine. A historical romance set in England and France immediately after the French Revolution, the novel offers adventure, romance, and mystery embodied in the person of the title character. Both countries are agog over the exploits of the daring and ingenious Pimpernel, who rescues French aristocrats from the guillotine by means of bold and ingenious stratagems and disguises, always alerting the French by means of his signature, the little scarlet flower whose name provides his *nom de guerre.* Only the small band of equally daring young English aristocrats who assist in his exploits know that the Scarlet Pimpernel is Sir Percy Blakeney, a seemingly foolish fop, the richest man in England, and a favorite of the Prince of Wales. Even his wife, the beautiful and accomplished Marguerite St. Just, does not know of Sir Percy's double life because of their estrangement arising out of misconceptions about her earlier life as a French actress and republican sympathizer.

The novel also appeals to patriotic sentiment, for the befuddled French authorities as well as the ignorant French mobs are always more than a few steps behind the clever and elusive Pimpernel. Like Thomas Carlyle and Charles Dickens before her, O. denigrates the French Revolution and idealizes the independent English commoner who is content with his place in a free and prosperous country.

O.'s lifetime output of novels, plays, short stories, essays, biography, and an autobiography was prodigious. Among the dozens of titles, it is worth pointing out *Lady Molly of Scotland Yard* (1910), in which she created an early woman detective, and her "old man in the corner" series, which portrays one of the earliest armchair detectives. Her popular *The Laughing Cavalier* (1914) was inspired by Frans Hals's painting and provided an appropriate ancestor for Sir Percy Blakeney.

The Scarlet Pimpernel, still a page turner, continues in print (in several editions) nearly 100 years after its initial publication, as do the other nine novels and two volumes of short stories that O. wrote about the adventures of Sir Percy Blakeney and his band. That these and other works continue to entertain attests to O.'s skills as a contriver of dramatic and ingenious narratives.

WORKS: *The Emperor's Candlesticks* (1899). *The Scarlet Pimpernel* (novel and play, 1905). *The Case of Miss Elliott* (1905). *By the Gods Beloved* (1905). (with M. Barstow) *The Sin of William Jackson* (1906). *A Son of the People* (1906). *I Will Repay* (1906). *In Mary's Reign* (1907). *The Tangled Skein* (1907). *Beau Brocade* (novel and play, 1907). *The Elusive Pimpernel* (1908). *The Nest of the Sparrowhawk* (1909). *The Old Man in the Corner* (1909). *Lady Molly of Scotland Yard* (1910). *Petticoat Government* (1910). *A True Woman* (1911). *The Duke's Wager* (1911). *Meadowsweet* (1912). *Fire in the Stubble* (1912). *The Traitor* (1912). *Two Good Patriots* (1912). *Eldorado* (1913). *Unto Caesar* (1914). *The Laughing Cavalier* (1914). *A Bride of the Plains* (1915). *The Bronze Eagle* (1915). *Leatherface* (1916, also adapted as a play). *The Old Scarecrow* (1916). *A Sheaf of Bluebells* (1917; also adapted as a play, *The Legion of Honour,* 1917). *Lord Tony's Wife* (1917). *Flower o' the Lily* (1918). *The Man in Grey* (1918). *The League of the Scarlet Pimpernel* (1919). *His Majesty's Well-Beloved* (1919). *The First Sir Percy* (1920). *Castles in the Air* (1921). *Nicolette* (1922). *The Triumph of the Scarlet Pimpernel* (1922). *The Old Man in the Corner Unravels the Mystery of the Khaki Tunic* (1923). *The Old Man in the Corner Unravels the Mystery of the Pearl Necklace* (1924). *The Honourable Jim* (1924). *The Old Man in the Corner Unravels the Mystery of the Russian Prince* (1924). *Pimpernel and Rosemary* (1924). *A Question of Temptation* (1925). *The Old Man in the Corner Unravels the Mystery of the White Carnation* (1925). *The Old Man in the Corner Unravels the Mystery of the Fulton Gardens Mystery* (1925). *The Miser of Maida Vale* (1925). *Unravelled Knots* (1925). *The Celestial City* (1926). *Sir Percy Hits Back* (1927). *Blue Eyes and Gray* (1928). *Skin o' My Tooth* (1928). *Adventures of the Scarlet Pimpernel* (1929). *Marivosa* (1930). *In the Rue Morgue* (1931). *A Child of the Revolution* (1932). *A Joyous Adventure* (1932). *The Way of the Scarlet Pimpernel* (1933). *The Scarlet Pimpernel Looks at the World* (1933). *A Spy of Napoleon* (1934). *The Uncrowned King* (1935). *The Turbulent Duchess: H.R.H. Madame la Duchesse de Berri* (1935). *Sir Percy Leads the Band* (1936). *The Divine Folly* (1937). *No Greater Love* (1938). *Mam'zelle Guillotine* (1940). *Pride of the Race* (1942). *Will-o'-the-Wisp* (1947). *Links in the Chain of Life* (1947).

BIBLIOGRAPHY: Hughes, H. *The Historical Romance* (1993). Klein, K. *Great Women Mystery Writers* (1994).

For articles in reference works, see: *CA. Cambridge. DNB. Feminist. OCEL. Oxford. TCRGW. ToddBWW.*

Other references: *ArmD* (1981).

Nancy Cotton

Orinda: See *Philips, Katherine*

Orris: See *Ingelow, Jean*

Dorothy Osborne

BORN: 1627, Chicksands Priory, Bedfordshire.
DIED: January 1695, Moor Park, Surrey.
DAUGHTER OF: Sir Peter Osborne and Dorothy Danvers.
MARRIED: Sir William Temple, 1655.

Included in the *Dictionary of National Biography* in the entry for her husband, O. began to receive attention in her own name after extracts from forty-two of her letters were printed in T. P. Courtenay's *Memoirs of . . . Sir William Temple* in 1836. Containing "personal rather than literary charm," according to the *Dictionary of National Biography,* the letters appealed to Thomas Babington Macaulay, whose enthusiasm sparked the Honourable Judge E. A. Parry to edit them in a separate volume in 1888. Since then Parry's edition has been reprinted frequently, and other editions have followed.

The appeal of the letters extends beyond the limits suggested by the *Dictionary of National Biography,* providing for readers today insights into the life of an intelligent seventeenth-century woman who could re-create a period for readers centuries later through a scene or a character. Not designed for publication, the letters were written for O.'s future husband, and they contain intimate details and descriptions of the Interregnum not found elsewhere. Exhibiting the literary qualities and immediacy of the diaries of Samuel Pepys and John Evelyn, the letters focus upon the dilemmas of a young Royalist woman whose affections have been captured by a Puritan.

O.'s father was the Royalist governor of Guernsey who had defended the Castle Cornet. Sir William Temple's father, however, was a Puritan who sat in the Long Parliament. The couple met by chance in 1648 at the Isle of Wight when Temple was on his way to a diplomatic assignment in France. After O.'s brother wrote some anti-Puritan graffiti on a window, Temple watched as O., upon being arrested by Puritans, confessed that she did it. Courageously, O. trusted that the Puritan officer was gallant enough that he would not punish a young woman for such a prank. She was right. All who had been arrested, including O., were released. The incident occurred when O. was twenty-one and Temple, twenty. Their courtship, a long and unlikely one, had begun.

For the next seven years, the two corresponded, Temple from the Continent, O. in England. Both families objected to their union, and both urged more advantageous matches; yet O. remained constant. She was considered to be a good match and was courted by others, even though her father was an impoverished Royalist. One of the suitors she rejected was Oliver Cromwell's fourth son, Henry. Her account to Temple of Henry's attempt to woo her by giving her a greyhound is both informative and amusing. Young Cromwell did not mourn; within a few months after he had been rejected by O., he was married to another. O.'s family, especially her youngest brother, Henry, urged her to break her vow with Temple and to marry another man. In her letters, O. writes of her isolation and her unhappiness; despite her misery, she remains stoical and patient, writing secretly to her future husband. When the marriage finally did take place, O. was severely scarred by smallpox. Married in 1655 by a justice of the peace at St. Giles, Middlesex, the couple left that year for Ireland, not returning to England until 1663. In 1666, Temple became a baron.

The letters cover only the first years of their courtship. The rest of O.'s life remains in the shadow cast by her husband's more evident achievements. He continued his distinguished diplomatic career, negotiating for the monarchs. Through his essays, romances, and histories, he secured his reputation as a writer. Adding to his subsequent importance in the literary history of England was his secretary, his cousin, Jonathan Swift.

Throughout her life, O. remained deeply attached to Temple, apparently coping with a more dominant figure in the household, her sister-in-law, Lady Giffard. Through her letters and events later in her life, O. is revealed as a gentle, unpretentious woman who actively helped her husband, and who, once again, on a voyage from Ireland to England in 1671 (*Calendar of State Papers, Domestic* 1670–71), exhibited the unusual courage that Temple had admired years earlier.

Only O.'s letters to Temple written from 1652 to 1654 have survived. Even though they give only half of the correspondence, the letters are valuable. Preserved by Temple and the couple's descendants, the letters are reflective, witty, and informative. They demonstrate O.'s belief that "All Letters mee thinks should bee free and Easy as ones discourse, not studdyed, as an Oration, nor made up of hard words like a Charme." Katharine M. Rogers has noted that O.'s letters reveal the seventeenth-century woman's lack of education. By the eighteenth century those elements that are problematic in O.'s letters improved, especially the spelling, punctuation, sentence structure, and paragraphing.

Despite errors and problems with composition, the letters remain part of that personal literature that arose in the seventeenth century. O. richly describes everyone, not just herself. Her commentaries on her family, her friends, and her views of her future husband are illuminating, sympathetic, and delightful. As Douglas Bush suggested, one would need to go "far to find another such individual mixture of Juliet, Rosalind, and Jane Austen." Through the letters we see an intimate view of a young woman in an unsettled age. O. writes of people she knew, of the books she read, and, perhaps most important to her, of love, marriage, and filial duty. It is through O. that we learn of the reception of the Duchess of Newcastle's first book, published in 1653, and of the horror with which society viewed a woman who published; it is through O. that we discover the aversion that well-bred young women had of passion, "that whereso'ever it comes destroys all that entertain it"; and it is through O. that we learn how Royalists sought refuge from the chaos of England in the 1650s.

WORKS: *Memoirs of . . . Sir William Temple*, ed. T. P. Courtenay (1836). *Letters from Dorothy Osborne to Sir William Temple, 1652–54*, ed. E. A. Parry (1888, rev. and enlarged 1903). *The Love Letters of Dorothy Osborne to Sir William Temple, 1652–54,* ed. E. A. Parry (1901). *The Love Letters of Dorothy to Sir William Temple, Newly Edited from the Original Manuscripts,* ed. I. Gollancz (1903). *Martha, Lady Giffard, Her Life and Correspondence (1664–1722), A Sequel to the Letters of Dorothy Osborne*, ed. J. G. Longe, with preface by Judge Parry (1911). *The Letters of Dorothy Osborne to William Temple*, ed. G. C. Moore Smith (1928). *The Letters of Dorothy Osborne to Sir William Temple, 1652–54*, ed. K. Hart (1968).

BIBLIOGRAPHY: Bush, D. *English Literature in the Earlier Seventeenth Century* (1945). Cecil, D. *Two Quiet Lives* (1948). Hewlett, M. *Last Essays* (1924). Irvine, L. L. *Ten Letter Writers* (1932). Lerch-Davis, G. S. *TSLL* (1978). Lucas, F. L. *Studies French and English* (1934). Marburg, C. *Sir William Temple: A Seventeenth Century "Libertin"* (1932). Reynolds, M. *The Learned Lady in England 1650–1760* (1920). Rogers, K. M. *Feminism in 18th Century England* (1982). Woolf, V. *The Second Common Reader* (1932).

For articles in reference works, see: Balch, M. *Short Biographies* (1945). Bottrall, M. S. *Personal Record* (1962). *DNB*. *ELB*. Stenton, D. M. *English Women in History* (1957).

Other references: Donovan, J. *Women and Language in Literature and Society* (1980). Wade, R. *ContempR* (1986).

Sophia B. Blaydes

Ouida: See *Ramée, Maria Louisa de la*

Jane Owen

FLOURISHED: After 1617 and before 1634.

DAUGHTER OF: Unknown. Related to Sir George Owen of Godstow, Oxfordshire.

O.'s only known work is the *Antidote against Purgatory,* published in 1634 at St. Omer, then in Spanish-held Flanders. The title page of the book indicates that O. had already died by that date, and it identifies her simply as Jane Owen, a "learned lady" of Godstow, Oxfordshire, an estate originally awarded to Sir George Owen (d. 1558), physician to King Henry VIII, King Edward VI, and Queen Mary I.

From the book's content, it is evident that O. is a Roman Catholic recusant (i. e., someone who refused to attend Church of England services and therefore was guilty of a statutory offense) who lived many years in England, although it is not known if she also lived in exile abroad later in life. In the *Antidote,* O. translated part of the Latin work of Robert Bellarmine, *De Gemitu Columbae,* first printed at Rome in 1617; therefore, she was alive at that date. It is also known that John Owen, a great-grandson of George Owen and grandson of Richard and Mary Chamberlain Owen, was living at Godstow when he was imprisoned for Catholic recusancy in 1615; subsequently he was exiled to Spain, where a brother of his grandmother had also been an exiled recusant. He later married in Spanish-held Flanders, where his son, George Chamberlain, became the Bishop of Ypres.

In her work, O. gives many reasons why the more wealthy Catholic recusants in England should give alms to support the impoverished seminaries, religious orders, schools, and convents established abroad—particularly in Flanders—and she states that such charity, together with prayer, would atone for one's sins and help one to avoid purgatory. She also urges her fellow Roman Catholics to send their children to study in Catholic countries abroad. In her plea, she gives details of the daily lives of seventeenth-century families in England, and thus the work gives a rare view of social history and customs of the time. In her comments on the work by Bellarmine, O. expands on his repetition of medieval legends on the concrete "fires" and "tortures" in purgatory, a concrete "place"; these were imaginative and superstitious legends that the Council of Trent had specifically stated were not representative of theological teaching and were to be avoided by the church in its sermons and teachings. Internal evidence, therefore, may point to O.'s having remained in England where she would not have been well instructed in her faith; it would seem from her vivid descriptions of recusant situations abroad, however, that she might have crossed the Channel surreptitiously for visits or to deliver the alms collected in England since it is known that many recusants did so by traveling incognito on business or by hiring private boats. Her reference to herself as a woman "preaching" might also indicate that she was one of the secret followers Mary Ward had placed in England to help in sending Catholic children abroad to be educated, in defiance of the penal laws. (O. should not be confused with Jane Morris Owen, mother of the epigrammatist John Owen [d. 1622], whose family members were not of Godstow and not recusants, or with other seventeenth-century "Jane Owens.")

WORKS: *Antidote Against Purgatory.* (1634; STC No. 18984, microfilm of copy in Bodleian Library; facsimile edition in Scolar Press Series, ed. P. Cullen and B. Travitsky, intro. D. L. Latz, 1996).

BIBLIOGRAPHY: Guilday, P. *The English Catholic Refugees on the Continent 1558–1798* (1914).

Other references: *DNB* (under "George Owen and descendants"). Gillow, J. *A Bibliographical Dictionary of the English Catholics* [Chamberlain, Bp. of Ypres] (1885–1902).

Dorothy L. Latz

Sydney Owenson, Lady Morgan

BORN: 25 December 1776–78 (?), on the Irish Sea.
DIED: 14 April 1859, Pimlico, London.
DAUGHTER OF: Robert MacOwen and Jane Hill MacOwen.
MARRIED: Charles T. Morgan, 1812.
WROTE UNDER: Lady Morgan.

O. was the first financially successful professional woman writer. A fast, prolific producer of what Sir Walter Scott praised (and imitated in *Waverley*) as "national and picaresque fiction," as well as travel books, history, and essays, O. was a celebrated social, literary, and political figure for half a century. In 1837, she became the first woman to receive a pension (£300 a year) "in acknowledgment of the services rendered by her to the world of letters."

The eldest child of actors, O. claimed to have been born on board a ship on the Irish Sea. She was educated at various schools in Dublin and was employed as a governess from 1798 to 1800. After her third novel, *The Wild Irish Girl* (1806), made her famous, she rose quickly in Dublin society and became a member of the household of the Marquis of Abercorn. Here she met Charles Morgan, their physician, whom she married in 1812. He supported her literary endeavors throughout a long, childless, and happy marriage. After he died, in 1843, she remained a force in London literary society until her death in 1859.

O.'s first two novels, *St Clair, or the Heiress of Desmond* (1803) (an imitation of Goethe's *Werther*) and *The Novice of St Dominick* (1806), were popular enough to procure her a £300 advance on her third, *The Wild Irish Girl* (1806), which went into seven editions in two years. Her fresh, original tone and lively powers of description were praised; her carelessness and her sometimes bombastic style were criticized. The book created a political controversy due to its nationalistic sentiments, its sympathy for the dispossessed heirs of the ancient rulers of Ireland, and its extensive, well-documented passages on Irish history, legend, and art. Glorvina, the heroine, is an Irish princess whose natural grace and refinement have not been corrupted by erroneous education.

O.'s other patriotic Irish novels include *O'Donnel* (1814), an attempt to describe "the flat realities of life" in Ireland; *Florence Macarthy* (1818), best remembered for its satire of John Wilson Croker (one of the most vicious of the critics who had attacked *O'Donnel* in the pages of the *Quarterly Review*); and *The O'Briens and the O'Flahertys* (1827). All were undertaken to promote the emancipation of the Catholics of Ireland. O. initiated the genre of the political romance, a mixture of sensibility, nationalism, the sublime, and the picturesque. She defended the use of fiction for political ends in the preface to *O'Donnel:* "A novel is specially adapted to enable the advocate of any cause to steal upon the public."

O.'s other novels include *Woman, or Ida of Athens* (1809), *The Missionary* (1811, revised and re-issued as *Luxima the Prophetess,* 1859), and *The Princess* (1835). *France* (1817) was very popular; in 1818, O. traveled through Italy to write *Italy* (1821), for which she had received an offer of £2,000 and which Lord Byron called "fearless and excellent." O. also published essays (*Absenteeism* [1825]) and verse on Irish subjects.

WORKS: *Poems by a Young Lady between the Age of 12 and 14* (1801). *Deep in Love* (1802). *St. Clair, or The Heiress of Desmond* (1803). *A Few Reflections* (1805). *The Novice of St. Dominick* (1806). *The Wild Irish Girl* (1806). *Patriotic Sketches of Ireland Written in Connaught* (1807). *The First Attempt* (1807). *The Lay of an Irish Harp, or Metrical Fragments* (1807). *Woman, or Ida of Athens* (1809). *The Missionary: An Indian Tale* (1811). *O'Donnel: a National Tale* (1814). *France* (1817). *Florence Macarthy: an Irish Tale* (1818). *Italy* (1821). *The Life and Times of Salvatore Rosa* (1824). *Absenteeism* (1825). *The O'Briens and the O'Flahertys: a National Tale* (1827). *The Book of the Boudoir* (1829). *France in 1829–30* (1830). *Dramatic Scenes from Real Life* (1833). *The Princess, or The Beguine* (1835). *Woman and Her Mas-*

ter: a History of the Female Sex from the Earliest Period (1840). *Book Without a Name* (1841). *Letter to Cardinal Wiseman in Answer to His Remarks on Lady Morgan's Statements Regarding St. Peter's Chair* (1951). *Luxima the Prophetess. A Tale of India* (1859). *An Odd Volume: Extracted from an Autobiography* (1859). *Lady Morgan's Memoirs: Autobiography, Diaries and Correspondence* (1862).

BIBLIOGRAPHY: Campbell, M. *Lady Morgan: The Life and Times of Sydney Owenson* (1988). Fitzpatrick, W. J. *Lady Morgan* (1860). Jones, A. *Ideas and Innovations: Best Sellers of Jane Austen's Age* (1986). Kavanagh, J. *English Women of Letters* (1863). Newcomer, J. *Lady Morgan the Novelist* (1990). Spender, D. *Mothers of The Novel* (1986). Stevenson, L. *The Wild Irish Girl* (1936). Whitmore, C. *Women's Work in English Fiction* (1910). Wilson, M. *These Were Muses* (1924).

For articles in reference works, see: *Bloomsbury. Cambridge* (under "Morgan"). *DNB. Feminist. Oxford* (under "Morgan"). *ToddBWW.*

Other references: *CJIS* (December 1987). *KSJ* (1990). *Dutch Quarterly Review* (1989). *Historical Studies* (1987). *N&Q* (December 1989). *NCF* (December 1982, June 1985).

Kate Browder

Isobel Pagan

BORN: c. 1742, Scotland.
DIED: 1821, Scotland.

One of many song lyricists who flourished in Scotland in the eighteenth and nineteenth centuries, P. remains a shadowy but interesting figure. Two well-known lyrics are attributed to P., "Ca' the Yowes to the Knowes" and "The Crook and the Plaid," although her authorship of both lyrics has been disputed. Henry Grey Graham (1908) doubts that P. wrote the two often-anthologized poems, offering for proof his opinion that her other poems are "doggerel." He is referring to *A Collection of Songs and Poems on Several Occasions*, by Isabel [sic] Pagan, published in Glasgow in 1803. That volume's first poem, "Account of the Author's Lifetime," reveals that P. was born "near four miles from Nith-head" and that she learned to read the Bible with the help of a "good old religious wife."

Although few details are known about P.'s family and the major events of her life, nineteenth-century anthologists formed rather vivid impressions of the woman. In *The Songs of Scotland* (n.d.), the editor writes of P. that she was a "contemporary of Burns," a "strange compound of woman and devil," who "subsisted partly by charity, but principally by selling whisky (without a licence) to drouthy neighbors and visitors," adding that she possessed singing ability, wit, bad manners, and a wicked temper. Whereas P. was thought to have been "well connected," James Paterson, another anthologist, asserts that her relatives kept their distance from the poet, whom he describes unflatteringly: "She squinted with one of her eyes—had a large tumour on her side—and was so deformed in one of the feet as to require crutches when walking" (1840). Unfortunately, more attention seems to have been paid to her appearance and way of life than to her poetry.

Paterson, who included P.'s song lyric "Ca' the Yowes" in his collection *The Contemporaries of Burns*, believes that the last verse was added by Burns, whom he credits with "pruning" the poem; nevertheless, Paterson gives credit for the original lyric to P., citing as evidence "the assertion of Burns, who wrote in 1797, that the air or words were never before in print." George Eyre-Todd, in *Scottish Poetry of the Eighteenth Century* (1896), argues that Burns did not know P. had written "Ca' the Yowes" and may not have even "known of her existence." Eyre-Todd calls this a "fine song," stating that Burns wrote the final verse; he also reminds us that Burns wrote his own version of the song. The lyric celebrates common themes of folk song: the pastoral life, love, the enduring natural world, and the milieu of working-class people. The female narrator's materialism, however, challenges the romantic tone: She does not accept the shepherd until promised finery, and he, not she, declares undying love.

In "The Crook and Plaid" (which also exists in versions by other authors), P. celebrates the life of the shepherd, the beauty of nature, and the love between the narrator and the shepherd, in pleasant and conventional language, except for the revelation that the shepherd "reads in books of history that learns him meikle skill" and the cozy image of the lad hiding a bonnie lass "in his plaidie," his tartan cloak.

If P. in fact wrote these two lyrics, she has made a contribution to Scottish song. Her 1803 *Collection of Songs and Poems,* though not the complete doggerel derided by Graham, contains no songs of equal value.

WORKS: *A Collection of Songs and Poems on Several Occasions* (1803). "Ca' the Yowes" and "The Crook and the Plaid" (in various anthologies).

BIBLIOGRAPHY: Eyre-Todd, G. *Scottish Poetry of the Eighteenth Century* (1896). Graham, H. G. *Scottish Men of Letters in the Eighteenth Century* (1908). Paterson, J. *The Contemporaries of Burns* (1840). *The Songs of Scotland Chronologically Arranged With Introduction and Biographical Notes* (n.d.).

For articles in reference works, see: *Feminist.*

Anita G. Gorman

Page, Gilbert H.: See *D'Arcy, Ella*

Louise Page

BORN: 7 March 1955, London.

Playwright P. completed her degree in drama and theatre arts at the University of Birmingham in 1976, and her short play *Want-Ad* was given a reading at the Royal Court Theatre that year. At that time, P. says, she had never seen a play by a woman. Since then, P. has matured into a sophisticated writer, well aware of the complexity and contradictions of feminism and feminist theater.

In her plays, P. explores a wide range of subjects and theatrical styles, from naturalistic family dramas to documentary collages to unabashed fantasy, yet women's experiences usually take priority. P.'s dramatic strategy is often to confound popular stereotypes about the feminine: Her characters often chafe in their social roles and compete with one another for power, driven by a most unladylike ambition.

P.'s early impressionistic play *Tissue* (1978) describes a young woman's encounter with breast cancer. In a series of fifty brief scenes, Sally moves back and forward through time, associating the discovery, breast surgery, and recuperation with her childhood acculturation into female sexuality. One man and one woman play all the secondary roles in Sally's world: doctors, nurses, parents, siblings, friends, lovers. Inexorably, the play begins to confront the nature of sexuality and the fetish of the female breast; is it "only a bit of tissue," as one voice contends, or is it female identity?

Several of P.'s plays explore the relationships between mothers and daughters, with their complicated power struggles, envies, and regrets. *Hearing* (1979) dramatizes the conflicts between a deaf young woman and her guilty, over-protective mother. *Salonika* (1982), P.'s best-known work, follows an eighty-four-year-old woman and her retired daughter on their holiday. Although the women have come to Salonika to visit the grave of their husband and father, a World War I soldier who appears to them as a ghost, the energy of the play lies in the unbroken bond between mother and daughter and the threats of mortality and marriage that compromise their relationship. Enid, the daughter, envies her mother's sexuality and her septuagenarian suitor and regrets the dreams she has deferred: "I've never had a life of my own. I wouldn't know what to do with it." Charlotte, her mother, relishes the prospect of love and independence before death but is constrained by Enid's lonely future. Their fractious, dependent relationship provides the dramatic tension in a dreamlike beach setting that includes the soldier ghost and a somnolent, nude young man who mysteriously dies at the end of the play. As in *Tissue,* memories become a palpable force, and in P.'s leisurely structure time ebbs away from the characters like the tide on the beach.

P. reconstrues the mother-daughter relationship in a much more realistic mode in *Real Estate* (1984), in which a daughter returns to the mother she left twenty years before. Jenny, now thirty-eight and pregnant, seeks support from her mother, Gwen, now a successful career woman. As Jenny moves into her mother's house, family, and office, Gwen realizes that she is unwilling to provide the kind of unconditional care that Jenny (and the audience) expects from mothers. Their twenty-year separation has scarred the relationship, and Gwen ultimately chooses her independence over a new familial life. P. has commented that *Real Estate* is a subversive play in that it says that the mother should be free to live her own life and not bring up the grandchild. Although the liberation from social expectations is a feminist concept, P. prods at simple assumptions of female solidarity by emphasizing the mother's liberation from her manipulative daughter.

P. says that the "great strength of feminism is its contradictions," and her plays investigate the ambiguity of female independence and ambition. *Golden Girls* (1984), first produced by the Royal Shakespeare Company, follows five British women athletes training for international competition in the hundred-meter relay. Not only are the five women competing for the four slots on the relay team, but their corporate sponsor is pushing them for increased sales and their team doctor gives them a placebo drug to boost their confidence. The most ambitious athlete independently seeks out the real drug and is caught in a scandal. In this ethically complex world, P. shows the power and satisfaction of female ambition alongside its corruptibility and ruthlessness. The sprawling script encompasses racism, sexual jealousy, paternal anxiety, and scandal mongering; despite its flaws, *Golden Girls* is one of P.'s most adventurous works.

Diplomatic Wives (1989) shows a more fatalistic side of P.'s feminism. Chris, the intelligent woman who gives up her own impressive diplomatic career for her frustrating marriage, no longer believes her mother's promise that "when you were grown up, you would be able to do whatever you wanted." P. describes *Diplomatic Wives* as "a play about the fatigue of the feminist movement," which has "inevitably become tired of fighting and battling and constantly having to explain."

P. has written several works for younger audiences, both children and teenagers. Her adaptation of *Beauty and the Beast* (1985) was commissioned by the Women's Playhouse Trust; *Toby and Donna* (1989) treats the subject of date rape; and her more recent *Royal Blood Bath 3* (1992) is an adaptation of Sophocles's *Antigone.*

Since completing her post-graduate course at the University of Wales, Cardiff, in 1977, P. has taught at the Universities of Birmingham and Sheffield, and she continues to lecture and teach internationally. Her work has been recognized with the George Devine Award (1981) and the first J. T. Grein Prize from the Critics' Circle (1985). She served as writer in residence at the Royal Court in 1982–83 and has worked with many of Britain's most innovative theater companies.

P.'s subtle, ambiguously subversive plays continue to fascinate audiences with their revelation of the uncomfortable subcurrents beneath what appears to be acceptable female behavior.

WORKS: *Want-Ad* (1977; rev. 1979). *Glasshouse* (1977). *Tissue* (1978; in *Plays by Women 1,* ed. M. Wandor, 1982). *Saturday, Late September* (radio, 1978). *Lucy* (1979). *Hearing* (1979). *Flaws* (1980). *Agnus Dei* (radio, 1980). *Housewives* (1981). *DIY in Venice* (television, 1982). *Salonika* (1982). *Falkland Sound/Voces de Malvinas* (1983). *Armistice* (radio, 1983). *Legs Eleven* (television, 1984). *Real Estate* (1984). *Golden Girls* (1984). *Beauty and the Beast* (1985). *Goat* (1986). *Birds' Heads and Fishes' Tails* (television, 1986). *Working Out* (radio, 1988). *Peanuts* (television, 1988). *Diplomatic Wives* (1989). *Toby and Donna* (in *They Said You Were Too Young,* ed. R. Robinson, 1989). *Plays: One* (*Tissue, Salonika, Real Estate, Golden Girls,* 1990). *Adam Was a Gardener* (1991). *Like to Live* (1991). *Hawks and Doves* (1992). *Royal Blood Bath 3* (1992).

BIBLIOGRAPHY: Betsko, K. and R. Koenig. *Interviews with Contemporary Women Playwrights* (1987). Eisen, K., in *British Playwrights, 1956–1995: A Research and Production Sourcebook,* ed. W. W. Demastes (1996). Griffiths, T. R. and M. Llewellyn-Jones. *British and Irish Women Dramatists since 1958: A Critical Handbook* (1993). Wandor, M. *Drama Today: A Critical Guide to British Drama 1970–1990* (1993).

For articles in reference works, see: *CA. CBD. CD. CLC. Feminist. WD.*

Other references: *Drama* (1985). *Forum Modernes Theater* (1990). *Guardian* (4 May 1984). *Independent* (21 August 1991). *NTQ* (1990). *NYT* (6 December 1987). *Plays & Players* (September 1983). *THES* (29 November 1985). *TLS* (10 January 1986). *WRB* (1986).

Julia Matthews

Violet Paget

BORN: 14 October 1856, Boulogne-sur-Mer, France.
DIED: 13 February 1935, San Gervasio, Italy.
DAUGHTER OF: Henry Hippolyte Ferguson Paget and Matilda Adams Lee-Ferguson.
WROTE UNDER: Mlle. V. P.; Vernon Lee.

From the Victorian to the modern period, P. wrote consistently about aesthetics and the arts. A figure of importance to the artists who surrounded her, she is mentioned in Robert Browning's poem "Asolando" (1889) and Anatole France's *Le Lys Rouge* (1894), as well as having been commented on by Walter Pater, Henry James, Edith Wharton, Wyndham Lewis, I. A. Richards, Bernard Shaw, Aldous Huxley, and H. G. Wells, among others.

Brought up on the Continent, where her family traveled from one watering place to another, P. first lived in Germany, later Italy, where the family visited in 1868 and eventually settled. Rome at that time was, as depicted in *The Marble Fawn,* a center for artists; P. began there a lifelong interest in the arts, fostered by her acquaintance with the family of John Singer Sargent, a childhood friend, whose painting of P. is in the Tate Gallery. P.'s acquaintance with the artistic community in Italy led, when she finally started visiting England in 1881, to her being immediately introduced to a circle of writers including Henry James, Oscar Wilde, Walter Pater, and others. In England, which she visited yearly while residing in Florence, P. was to become a kind of *enfant terrible.* Wearing a black tailor-made dress and Gladstone collar, her hallmark, she expressed her opinions freely and aggressively on all subjects. Henry James described her as having a "monstrous cerebration" and as being a "tigercat." She repeatedly gave offense through her outspokenness, right up to the end of her life when her unpopular public statements on pacifism during World War I made her new enemies. P. never married but had longlasting friendships with women artists, first with Mary Robinson and later with Kit Anstruther-Thomson; both relations caused her intense pain when they were broken off.

P.'s first piece of writing, "Les Aventures d'une Piece de Monnaie" (1870), appeared when she was thirteen and is characteristic of her later interests. It describes in first person from a coin's point of view its history from Hadrian's time to the Victorian era, a device that allows P. to explore imaginatively various cultures and time periods. P.'s first serious work, *Studies of the Eighteenth Century in Italy* (1880), a book of essays on music and literature, began a series of such works, including *Euphorion* (1884), which contains an essay on Shakespeare and Renaissance Italy, and *Renaissance Fancies and Studies* (1895). Work on the separate branches of the arts led P. to aesthetics in general, about which she was to write a series of books beginning with *Belcaro* (1881), which examines the relation of artistic form to pleasure. In *Juvenilia* (1887), P. moved to the Tolstoyan question of art's use for the lower classes; in *Beauty and Ugliness* (1912) and *The Beautiful* (1913) to the overall question of the psychological response of the viewer; and, finally, in *Music and Its Lovers* (1932) to interviewing a series of listeners about why they loved music. These books, though stylistically difficult, introduced ideas that were taken very seriously by critics of the time, as, for example, by I. A. Richards who disagrees with P. in *Principles of Literary Criticism.*

P. was less successful with her fiction. *Miss Brown* (1884), a satire against the aestheticism of the Pre-Raphaelites, and *Vanitas* (1892) offended London literary society, particularly Henry James, who was represented in the second, because the fictional characters were easily identifiable as real figures. P. seems to have been unaware of the offensiveness of these works as she wrote them. Described as "better with place than with people," she was more successful with her play, *Ariadne in Mantua* (1903), a lyric drama about concepts of love that evokes the atmosphere of Italy, and her essays on travel, *Genius Loci* (1899), perhaps her two best-known works. Her satiric allegory about the need for peace, *Satan the Waster* (1920), is also effective polemical writing.

The range of P.'s intelligence was her most impressive characteristic. Henry James said of her that "the vigour and sweep of her intellect are most rare and her talk superior altogether," Walter Pater that if she could overcome the difficulties of her style, she would stand "among the very few best critical writers of all time."

WORKS: *Studies of the Eighteenth Century in Italy* (1880). *Tuscan Fairy Tales* (1880). *Belcaro: Being Essays on Sundry Aesthetical Questions* (1881). *The Prince of the Hundred Soups* (1883). *Ottilie: An Eighteenth Century Idyll* (1883). *Euphorion: Being Studies of the Antique and the Medieval in the Renaissance* (1884). *The Countess of Albany* (1884). *Miss Brown* (1884). *Baldwin: Being Dialogues on Views and Aspirations* (1886). *A Phantom Lover: A Fantastic Story* (1886). *Juvenilia: Being a Second Series of Essays on Sundry Aesthetical Questions* (1887). *Hauntings: Fantastic Stories* (1892). *Vanitas: Polite Stories* (1892). *Althea: A Second Book of Dialogues on Aspirations and Duties* (1894). *Renaissance Fancies and Studies: Being a Sequel to "Euphorion"* (1895). *Limbo, and Other Essays* (1897). *Genius Loci: Notes on Places* (1899). *Ariadne in Mantua* (1903). *Penelope Brandling: A Tale of the Welsh Coast* (1903). *Pope Jacynth, and Other Fantastic Tales* (1904). *Hortis Vitae: Essays on the Gardening of Life* (1904). *The Enchanted Woods, and Other Essays* (1905). *Sister Benvenuta and the Christ Child* (1906). *The Spirit of Rome: Leaves from a Diary* (1906). *The Sentimental Traveler: Notes on Places* (1908). *Gospels of Anarchy, and Other Contemporary Studies* (1908). *Laurus Nobilis: Chap-*

ters on Art and Life (1909). *Vital Lies: Studies of Some Varieties of Recent Obscurantism* (1912). (with C. Anstruther-Thomson) *Beauty and Ugliness, and Other Studies in Psychological Aesthetics* (1912). *The Beautiful: An Introduction to Psychological Aesthetics* (1913). *Louis Norbert: A Two-fold Romance* (1914). *The Tower of Mirrors: And Other Essays on the Spirit of Places* (1914). *The Ballet of Nations: A Present-day Morality* (1915). *Satan the Waster: A Philosophical War Trilogy* (1920). *The Handling of Words: And Other Studies in Literary Psychology* (1923). *The Golden Keys, and Other Essays on the Genius Loci* (1925). *Proteus: Or the Future of Intelligence* (1925). *The Poet's Eye* (1926). *For Maurice: Five Unlikely Stories* (1927). *A Vernon Lee Anthology*, ed. I. C. Willis (1929). *Music and Its Lovers* (1932). *Letters*, intro., I. C. Willis (1937). *The Snake Lady, and Other Stories*, intro., H. Gregory (1954). *Supernatural Tales*, intro., I. C. Willis (1955). *Pope Jacynth and More Supernatural Tales* (1956).

BIBLIOGRAPHY: Baring, M. *The Puppet Show of Memory* (1922). Colby, V. *The Singular Anomaly: Women Novelists of the Nineteenth Century* (1970). Gardner, B. *The Lesbian Imagination (Victorian Style): A Psychological and Critical Study of "Vernon Lee"* (1987). Gunn, P. *Vernon Lee: Violet Paget 1856–1935* (1964). Lewis, P. W. *The Lion and the Fox* (1927). Licht, M., in *A Literary Miscellany Presented to Eric Jacobsen*, ed. G. D. Caie and H. Norgaard (1988). Mannocchi, P. F. *ELT* (1983). Mannocchi, P. F. *WS* (1986). Markgraf, C. *ELT* (1983). Richards, I. A. *Principles of Literary Criticism* (1922). Robbins, R., in *Fin de Siècle/Fin du Globe: Fears and Fantasies of the Late Nineteenth Century*, ed. J. Stokes (1992). Sinha, A. *JDECU* (1981–82). Tintner, A. *TCW* (1985). Tintner, A. *SSF* (1991).

For articles in reference works see: *Allibone. Bloomsbury. CA. Cambridge. DLB. DNB. 1890s. Feminist. GayLL. OCEL. Oxford. PHS. RE. TCLC. ToddBWW. VB. WNWC. WWHFF.*

Other references: Caballero, C. *VS* (Summer 1992). Christensen, P. G. *StHum* (1989). *PMLA* (1953, 1954). *RES* (1982).

Elsie B. Michie
(updated by Bette H. Kirschstein and Natalie Joy Woodall)

Pakenham, Antonia: See *Fraser, Antonia*

Pakenham, Elizabeth: See *Longford, Countess of, Elizabeth (Pakenham née Harman)*

Palmer, H.: See *Stannard, Henrietta Eliza Vaughn Palmer*

Emmeline Goulden Pankhurst

BORN: 14 July 1858, Manchester, Cheshire.
DIED: 14 June 1928, London.
DAUGHTER OF: Robert Goulden and Jane Quinn.
MARRIED: Richard Marsden Pankhurst, 1879.

P. was one of eleven children born to ardent abolitionists who provided both a loving home and a model for the life of political activism she led. After her marriage in 1879 to an extremely liberal activist barrister, she and her husband raised a family and fought for suffrage and other social reform. After her husband died in 1898, P. became the registrar in Rushholme, a working-class district in Manchester.

P. received her education in Paris under the direction of Mlle. Marchef-Girard, returning to Manchester at eighteen to begin a lifelong commitment to public office, political and social militancy, and motherhood. P. and her daughter Christabel frequently spoke publicly, marched in rallies, and were arrested and imprisoned together. P.'s first arrest was in 1908, and she chose jail over a fine and then went on a hunger strike. In part in response to her actions, the government in 1913 passed the Prisoners' Temporary Discharge for Ill-Health Act, known as the Cat and Mouse Act. It allowed hunger-striking prisoners to be temporarily released until they regained strength. P. was rearrested thirteen more times. P. reported that, after meeting Susan B. Anthony in 1902, Christabel declared, "It is unendurable to think of another generation of women wasting their lives begging for the vote. We must not lose any more time. We must act."

Act they did. The Pankhurst name is inextricably linked to the fight for suffrage in England as well as to reform for laborers, poor and unemployed persons, children, prisoners, indeed all powerless and disenfranchised groups. P. was a Fabian Socialist, a member of the Manchester school board, founder of the Women's Social and Political Union (WSPU), originator of the Women's Parliament of 1907, member of the Chorlton Board of Guardians, and founder of a Committee for the Relief of the Unemployed. The WSPU encouraged and employed militancy in their tactics. She was a part of every reform movement of her time; as she states in the opening of her autobiography, "those men and women are fortunate who are born at a time when a great struggle for human freedom is in progress. . . . I am glad and thankful that this was my case."

P.'s ability as an orator was well known. She also wrote a number of pamphlets to attempt to persuade men and women to support her cause. Her autobiography, *My Own Story* (1914), documents her participation in public speeches, rallies, marches, and addresses to Parliament as well as two trips to the United States to meet American feminists. She reports incidents of police brutality and deplorable imprisonment during which she was force fed and subjected to political ridicule. She responded always with incredible strength throughout the physical suffering and with determination, placing the struggle for votes for women above all else. Tried for conspiracy, P. declared, "Women of intelligence, women of training, women of upright life, have for many years ceased to respect the laws of this country" and "It is the government that is our enemy; it is not the MPs, it is not the men of the country, it is the Government in power that can give us the vote."

For a short time following her husband's death in 1898, P. retired from public militancy. Upon receiving the position of registrar of births and deaths, however, she was brought back into public life; in 1909, when her friend and comrade James Keir Hardie (1856–1915) was re-elected to Parliament, her political activity was revived and continued till her death in 1928, the year British women received the vote.

WORKS: *The Importance of the Vote* (1908). *The Causes of the Revolt of the Women in England* (1909). *Verbatim Report of Mrs. Pankhurst's Speech Delivered November 13, 1913 at Parsons' Theatre, Hartford, Conn.* (1913). *Why We Are Militant: A Speech Delivered by Mrs. Pankhurst in New York, October 21, 1913* (1914). *My Own Story* (1914).

BIBLIOGRAPHY: Cromwell Films Ltd. *Emmaline Pankhurst and the Suffragettes* (1994). Felder, D. *The 100 Most Influential Women of All Time* (1996). Mack, J. *The Rhetoric of the Pankhursts: Militant Suffragettes of Great Britain* (1995). Marcus, J. *Suffrage and the Pankhursts* (1987). Mitchell, D. *The Fighting Pankhursts* (1966). Pankhurst, E. S. *The Suffragette Movement: An Intimate Account of the Persons and Ideas* (1930). Pankhurst, E. S. *The Life of Emmeline Pankhurst* (1935). Rolka, G. *100 Women Who Helped Shape History* (1994). Smith, H. *British Feminism in the Twentieth Century* (1990). Spacks, P. M., in *Women's Autobiography: Essays in Criticism,* ed. E. C. Jelinek (1980). Vicary, T. *Mrs. Pankhurst* (1993).

For articles in reference works, see: *Bloomsbury. Feminist. Longman. WHEWB.*

Anne-Marie Ray

Estelle Sylvia Pankhurst

BORN: 5 May 1882, Manchester, Cheshire.
DIED: 27 September 1960, Addis Ababa, Ethiopia.
DAUGHTER OF: Richard Marsden Pankhurst and Emmeline Goulden Pankhurst.

As one of the Pankhurst family's three daughters, P. encountered early in life the cause of organizing feminism's political causes. That encounter was both a personal and a public process of solidarity. Her mother, Emmeline Goulden Pankhurst, founded the Women's Social and Political Union (WSPU). Under the influence of their mother, P. and her sisters, Adela and Cristabel, worked with the WSPU and other movements to establish voting rights for women in the United Kingdom. P.'s father, Richard Pankhurst, a lawyer who had earned a doctorate in jurisprudence at the University of London, had drafted Britain's first unsuccessful women's suffrage bill in the late 1860s.

James Keir Hardie (1856–1915), Scottish labor leader and member of Parliament, a friend of her father's who became P.'s lover, was first elected to Parliament in 1892 and helped to found Britain's Labour Party the following year, the same year her parents founded the Independent Labour Party.

In 1900, P. won a scholarship to Manchester School of Art and in 1902 traveled to Venice to study art. In 1903, she decorated the hall that the Independent Labour Party erected to the memory of her father. In that year, P. participated in the first "Women's Parliament" at Caxton Hall and joined a deputation to the House of Commons that the police broke up brutally. P. was arrested and imprisoned.

When H. H. Asquith became British prime minister in 1908 and declared his opposition to women possessing the right to vote, P. became active on many levels. She planned and marched in demonstrations in Hyde Park and elsewhere in England. In 1910, she toured the United States to lecture on the women's suffrage movement in England. By 1912, she had become intensely involved in the women's campaign in the East End of London. P.'s political life reached a dramatic peak in 1913 when she went on a hunger and thirst strike while in prison under charges of sedition.

In 1914, P. launched the *Workers' Dreadnought,* a newspaper that took the shape of a chronicle for P.'s activism on behalf of women, pacifists, the poor, and the unemployed. As its editor, she threatened to continue her hunger and thirst strike to the point of death unless Asquith would receive a deputation of London's East End women. Asquith relented and met the deputation. P. opposed World War I and concentrated her efforts on her literary and social work in the East End during the war years.

In 1919, P. joined Silvio Corio, an Italian socialist, and declared herself a Bolshevik, rechristening her East End Federation the "Communist Party." In 1924, she opened a café with Corio at the Red Cottage, Woodford; in 1927, she gave birth to their son, Richard Keir Pethick Pankhurst.

P.'s mother died in 1928, the same year in which the act was passed to give British women full adult suffrage. A summary of the roles played by women's groups, labor unions, and community activists in the struggle to achieve women's suffrage appears in P.'s book *The Suffragette Movement* (1930). In 1932, P.'s book on World War I was published under the title *The Home Front.*

When Mussolini invaded Ethiopia in 1936, P. espoused the Ethiopian cause. In 1939, she opposed the Fascist powers in Italy and Germany and expressed her support for the war declared by Britain and its Allies. Both her political activism and her artistic sensibilities are pervasive in her books on Ethiopia: *Education in Ethiopia* (1946), *The Ethiopian People: Their Rights and Progress* (1946), and *Ethiopia and Eritrea* (1953). After World War II, P. settled in Ethiopia, where her son, Richard, joined her in researching and writing about that country's history and culture. When P. died in Addis Ababa in 1960, Emperor Haile Selassie attended her funeral.

WORKS: *The Suffragette* (1911). *Education of the Masses* (1921). *Soviet Russia as I Saw It* (1922). *The Life of Emmeline Pankhurst* (1935). *The Suffragette Movement: An Intimate Account of the Persons and Ideas* (1930). *The Home Front: A Mirror to England* (1932). *Education in Ethiopia* (1946). *The Ethiopian People: Their Rights and Progress* (1946). *Ethiopia and Eritrea* (1953).

BIBLIOGRAPHY: Benn, C. *Keir Hardie* (1992). Bullock, I. *Sylvia Pankhurst: From Artist to Anti-Fascist* (1992). Castle B. *Sylvia and Cristabel Pankhurst* (1987). Dodd, K. *A Sylvia Pankhurst Reader* (1993). Francini, S. *Sylvia Pankhurst—1912–1924. Dal Suffragismo alla Rivoluzione Sociale* (1980). Marcus, J. *Suffrage and the Pankhursts* (1987). Mitchell, D. *The Fighting Pankhursts*

(1966). Pankhurst, C. *Unshackled* (1959). Pankhurst, E. *My Own Story* (1914). Pankhurst, R. *Sylvia Pankhurst: Artist and Crusader* (1979). Pethick-Lawrence, E. *My Part in a Changing World* (1938). Romero, P. E. *Sylvia Pankhurst: A Portrait of a Radical* (1986). Winslow, B. *Sylvia Pankhurst: Sexual Politics and Political Activism* (1996).

For articles in reference works, see: *Feminist. IDWB. Longman. ToddBWW.*

John Lavin

Julia Pardoe

BORN: 1804 (?), Beverley, Yorkshire.
DIED: 26 November 1862, London.
DAUGHTER OF: Major Thomas Pardoe and Elizabeth Pardoe.
WROTE UNDER: Miss Pardoe.

A popular writer in her lifetime, P.'s reputation has waned in this century. Known for her travel literature, her many novels, and her collections of tales, she did much to create the favorable attitudes toward Hungary held by her British contemporaries.

The second daughter of Major Thomas Pardoe, an officer in the Royal Wagon Train (later, the Transport Corps), and his wife Elizabeth, P. was baptized at St. John Parish in Beverley, Yorkshire, on 4 December 1804; the exact date of her birth is unknown, and most sources incorrectly give the year of her birth as 1806. When she was thirteen, she dedicated to her uncle her first published volume of poetry, a book that enjoyed a second edition. In 1829, she published her first novel, *Lord Morcar of Hereward: A Romance of the Times of William the Conqueror.* P.'s alleged "consumptive symptoms" (alluded to in the anonymous memoir accompanying the 1887 edition of *The Court and Reign of Francis the First, King of France*) precipitated curative travel to warmer climates; there she found material for both her novels and travel literature. *Traits and Traditions of Portugal* (1833), the first of her writings to interest the public, was dedicated to the Princess Augusta, who had encouraged her efforts. The author of the unsigned biography included in P.'s *The Court and Reign of Francis the First* (1887 edition) alludes to *Traits and Tradition*'s "charm of freshness and enthusiasm"; a twentieth-century reader may also see in it the author's characteristically ornate style and a condescension toward its subject.

In 1835, P. traveled with her father to Istanbul, Turkey, a site of literary inspiration for her as well as of danger: She visited during an outbreak of cholera. *The Dictionary of National Biography*, echoing the memoir in *The Court and Reign of Francis the First,* states that P. and Lady Mary Wortley Montagu (writing in the previous century) knew more about Turkey than any other women writers. *The City of the Sultan and Domestic Manners of the Turks* (1837) was favorably reviewed in the *London Atlas* and was reprinted as a three-volume work in 1838, 1845, and 1854. P.'s appreciation for the Islamic culture of Turkey surpasses her earlier, lukewarm appreciation of Roman Catholic Portugal; her descriptions of dervishes, harems, baths, mental hospitals, and slaves still command interest. *The Beauties of the Bosphorus* (1838), another work inspired by her trip to Turkey and reprinted later under the title *Picturesque Europe* (1854), praises the "true charm of the Bosphorus" and "its endless variety of perspective."

A trip to the south of France resulted in *The River and the Desart, or Recollections of the Rhône and the Chartreuse* (1838). In the preface, P. calls attention to the book's spontaneity and confronts those who had earlier criticized her "ornate and ambitious style."

In *The City of the Magyar; or Hungary and Her Institutions* (1840), P. mixes travelog with comments on Hungarian politics and society. According to Judit Kadar (1990), P. was one of the originators of the generally positive nineteenth-century view of Hungary held by the British. During this period, P. translated Guido Sorelli's poem *La Peste* (1834) and also produced novels and collections of tales, including *Speculation* (1834), *The Mardens and the Daventrys* (1835), *The Romance of the Harem* (1839), and *The Hungarian Castle* (1842), published in the United States as *Hungarian Tales and Legends.*

Fatigued from work, P. left London in about 1842 and went to live with her parents on Perry Street, near Gravesend, and later at Northfleet in Kent. Nevertheless, other works of fiction followed, including *The Confessions of a Pretty Woman* (1846), *The Rival Beauties* (1848), *Flies in Amber* (1850), *Reginald Lyle* (1854; in the U.S. as *The Adopted Heir,* 186?, and later as *The Rich Relation,* 1862), *The Jealous Wife* (1855), *Lady Arabella* (1856), and *A Life-Struggle* (1859; in the U.S., after P.'s death, as *The Earl's Secret,* 1865). P. continued to produce nonfiction works during this period, among them *Louis the Fourteenth, and the Court of France in the Seventeenth Century* (1846), *The Court and Reign of Francis the First* (1849), *The Life of Marie de Medicis, Queen of France, Consort of Henry IV, and Regent of the Kingdom Under Louis XIII* (1852), and *Episodes of French History* (1859). In 1850, P. edited Anita George's *Memoirs of the Queens of Spain* (in the U.S. as *Annals of the Queens of Spain*). *Pilgrimages in Paris* (1857), a collection of tales, includes some description of the French capital. In 1857, P. wrote the introduction to *The Thousand and One Days: A Companion to the Arabian Nights;* the book was republished in the United States in 1860 as *Hassan Abdallah: or, The Enchanted Keys, and Other Tales: A Companion to the Arabian Nights.*

Many of P.'s books were originally serialized. She wrote for a number of British and American periodicals, including the *Dublin University Magazine,* the *New Monthly Magazine, Fraser's Magazine,* and the *Foreign and Colonial Quarterly Review,* which in 1844 published P.'s thoughtful analysis of the Haitian Revolution, "Hayti, its Past and Present State."

In January 1860, P. was given a civil list pension "in consideration of thirty years' toil in the field of literature, by which she has contributed both to cultivate the public taste and to support a number of helpless relations." She died on 26 November 1862.

J. Cordy Jeaffreson, in *Novels and Novelists, from Elizabeth to Victoria* (1858), writes of his contemporary that "Miss Pardoe has shown herself capable of constructing ingenious plots, of charming by lively, and at times, gorgeously coloured narrative, and of giving an attractive and novel exposition of history." *The Dictionary of National Biography* calls P. "a warm-hearted woman, singularly bright and animated; a capital raconteuse, and, notwithstanding her literary talents, learned in the domestic arts." Her portrait, drawn by J. Lilley in 1849 and engraved by Samuel Freeman, appears in the second edition of *The Court and Reign of Francis I* (1887). Sarah J. Hale, compiler of *Woman's Record: or, Sketches of all Distinguished Women from the Creation to A.D. 1868* (1870), writes of P. that "she has never been a favourite in our reading republic. There seems to us something wanting in her writings; her works of fact want historic truth in details, those of fiction want impassioned truth in sentiment." Whereas Mrs. Hale asserts that British reviewers generally admired P.'s work, P. herself was sensitive to negative criticisms of her books, as Lola L. Szladits (1955) demonstrates by alluding to a letter P. wrote to Sir John Philippart about her novel *The Jealous Wife:* "All reviews have hitherto been most favorable, except the *Athenaeum* which has its usual snarl at me as a matter of course." In fact, at her death, the *Athenaeum* declared, "The City of the Sultan" had in its day "a certain share of success, but neither that nor any of its fellows had the strong quality which keeps a book alive."

WORKS: *Poems* (1818?). *The Nun: A Poetical Romance, and Two Others* (1824; attributed to P. by S. Halkett and J. Laing, *Dictionary of Anonymous and Pseudononymous Literature*, 1882–88). *Lord Morcar of Hereward: A Romance of the Times of William the Conqueror* (1829). *Traits and Traditions of Portugal Collected During a Residence in That Country* (1833). *Speculation: A Novel* (1834). (trans.) *La Peste,* by Guido Sorelli (1834). *The Mardens and the Daventrys* (1835). *The City of the Sultan, and Domestic Manners of the Turks in 1836* (1837). *The River and the Desart, or Recollections of the Rhône and the Chartreuse* (1838). *The Beauties of the Bosphorus* (1838; republished as *Picturesque Europe,* 1854). *The Romance of the Harem* (1839). *The City of the Magyar, or, Hungary and Her Institutions in 1839–40* (1840). *The Hungarian Castle* (1842; published in the U. S. as *Hungarian Tales and Legends*). *The Confessions of a Pretty Woman* (1846). *Louis the Fourteenth, and the Court of France in the Seventeenth Century* (1846). *The Rival Beauties: A Novel* (1848). *The Court and Reign of Francis the First, King of France* (1849, 1887). *Flies in Amber* (1850). *The Life of Marie de Medicis, Queen of France, Consort of Henry IV, and Regent of the Kingdom Under Louis XIII* (1852). *Reginald Lyle* (1854; in the U.S. as *The Adopted Heir,* 186?, and as *The Rich Relation,* 1862). *Louise de Lignerolles: A Tragic Drama in Five Parts,* adapted from the French of Prosper Denaux and Ernest Legouvé (1854). *The Jealous Wife* (1855). *The Wife's Trials: A Novel* (1855). *Lady Arabella, or, The Adventures of a Doll* (1856). *Abroad and At Home: Tales Here and There* (1857). *Pilgrimages in Paris* (1857). *The Poor Relation* (1858). *Episodes of French History During the Consulate and the First Empire* (1859). *A Life-Struggle* (1859; in the U.S. as *The Earl's Secret,* 1865).

BIBLIOGRAPHY: Hale, S. J. *Woman's Record: or, Sketches of all Distinguished Women from the Creation to A.D. 1868* (1870). Jeaffreson, J. C. *Novels and Novelists, from Elizabeth to Victoria* (1858). Kadar, J. *Neohelicon* (1990). *London Athenaeum* (13 December 1862). Szladits, L. L. *Biblion* (1955).

For articles in reference works, see: *Allibone. BA19C. BioIn. DNB.*

Anita G. Gorman

Edith Mary Pargeter

BORN: 29 September 1913, Horschay, Shropshire.
DIED: 14 October 1995, London.
DAUGHTER OF: Edmund Valentine Pargeter and Edith Hordley Pargeter.
WROTE UNDER: Peter Benedict; Jolyon Carr; Edith Pargeter; Ellis Peters; John Redfern.

P., born and bred in Shropshire, the site of many of her novels, including her best-known detective stories, attended a Church of England elementary school and an all-girl county high school before becoming a pharmacist's assistant in 1933, a job she held for seven years. During World War II, from 1940 to 1945, she served in the Women's Royal Naval Service, reaching the rank of petty officer. For her work in the communications department, she received the British Empire Medal from King George VI. At the same time, P. began writing and publishing fiction, her first novel *Hortensius, Friend of Nero,* appearing in 1936. She published five more novels before she was discharged from military service. During the war, having met some Czechs serving in the Royal Air Force and feeling anguish over the West's betrayal of Czechoslovakia at Munich, she became interested in Czechoslovakia and taught herself Czech. She visited the country frequently and translated some fifteen books from the Czech.

Her work as English translator of Czech poetry and prose was only a minor part of her work as a writer who published more than fifty novels and numerous short stories: historical fiction, including two multivolume works (*The Brothers of Gwynedd,* 1989, a four-volume tale about the thirteenth-century Welsh Prince Llewelyn, and the trilogy *The Heaven Tree,* 1960, about a thirteenth-century English stone carver, mason, and architect, Harry Talvace); contemporary fiction; and detective fiction. Whatever the critical and popular reception of her work, P. believed that *The Heaven Tree,* dealing as it does with art and imagination, is "the work that came nearest what I wanted it to be," as she explained in the introduction to the 1993 American edition.

Nevertheless, P. is best known for her detective fiction. She began writing mysteries about contemporary police officer George Felse and his wife Bunty and son Dominic in 1959 under the pseudonym of "Ellis Peters" to distinguish these stories from her other work. As she told *Publisher's Weekly* in 1991, "When I wrote my first deliberate mystery novel, it was like giving myself a holiday from the straight novel, and I found I liked it very much. I liked the feeling of getting into a different world. I found I could go to a far country, as long as I was acquainted with it."

P. had her greatest success with her medieval detective

series about the Welsh monk Brother Cadfael, which began with *A Morbid Taste for Bones* (1977) and continued to the twentieth volume, *Brother Cadfael's Penance* (1994). Although her series is often, and foolishly, compared to Umberto Eco's *The Name of the Rose,* the resemblances are superficial. Brother Cadfael appeared four years before Eco's Brother William and the re-creation of a mid-fourteenth-century Benedictine abbey in Northern Italy. Her stories contain no word games, intellectual puzzles, or long philosophical disquisitions. Novelist Andrew M. Greeley claims that "she is a far better storyteller than Umberto Eco." What attracts him and millions of other readers to these medieval whodunits is the warm and wise Brother Cadfael, who loves young people as much as his creator did (children, teenagers, and young adults always appear in her fiction) and who frequently bent the rules of the Abbey of Saint Peter and Saint Paul at Shrewsbury to help those in trouble. In Brother Cadfael, P. provided readers with a modern-day Good Samaritan. And her simple re-creation of England in the mid-twelfth century during the reign of Stephen and his wars with his cousin, the Empress Maud, provided verisimilitude. The political situation was always backdrop, if not anchor, for her stories, most of which begin with a date and an update on where things stood in England and whose star was in the ascendancy.

Brother Cadfael, who supports King Stephen, is the abbey's apothecary and herbalist. He knows the world well. He joined the Benedictines only in middle age; he spent his early years fighting in the Crusades and loving several women. The most important, Mariam, a Saracen widow of Antioch, bore a son whom Cadfael meets in *The Virgin in Ice* (1982), the sixth and one of the most satisfying of all twenty volumes. Cadfael's regard and respect for women distinguish him from the other men in and out of the abbey. As P. told *Publisher's Weekly* in trying to account for the success of her mysteries, "We've both got an incurable weakness for young people. And, of course, Cadfael's very unmonastic in the fact that he likes a nice attractive girl, takes pleasure in her company. Well, why not?"

Like many detective novels, the Brother Cadfael whodunits follow a formula, often that of young lovers kept apart by foolish or greedy adults and whom the monk relishes in helping. The good and the deserving come out on top; the wicked are suitably punished. Although P.'s romantic views of twelfth-century life bothered some critics and book reviewers who prefer gritty realism, P. was not dismayed or deterred by the criticism. For her, the unforgivable sin is destruction of the innocent and the good to take pleasure in evil and despair.

In 1961, P. received the Edgar Allan Poe award for best mystery novel (her Inspector Felse story, *Death and the Joyful Woman*) and in 1981 the Crime Writers Association award for the Brother Cadfael mystery *Monk's Hood.* She also received the gold medal from the Czechoslovak Society for International Relations (1968). Many of P.'s earlier novels are now being reprinted; omnibus editions of her two mystery series have been published; and Brother Cadfael stories starring Derek Jacobi have been filmed for television. Thanks to her success, medieval whodunits are now an established subgenre within detective fiction.

WORKS: (as Ellis Peters) *Hortensius, Friend of Nero* (1936). *Iron-Bound* (1936). (as Peter Benedict) *Day Star* (1937). *The City Lies* (1938). (as Jolyon Carr) *Murder in the Dispensary* (1938). *Foursquare* (1939). *Freedom for Two* (1939). *Death Comes by Post* (1940). *Masters of the Parachute Mail* (1940). (as John Redfern) *The Victim Needs a Nurse* (1940). *Ordinary People* (1941; in the U.S. as *People of My Own*). *She Goes to War* (1942). (as Ellis Peters) *The Eighth Champion of Christendom* (1945). (as Ellis Peters) *Reluctant Odyssey* (1946). (as Ellis Peters) *Warfare Accomplished* (1947). *The Fair Young Phoenix* (1948). *By Firelight* (1948; in the U.S. as *By this Strange Fire*). (as Ellis Peters) *The Coast of Bohemia* (1950). *Fallen Into the Pit* (1951). (as Ellis Peters) *Lost Children* (1951). (as Ellis Peters) *Holiday with Violence* (1952). *This Rough Magic* (1953). *Most Loving Mere Folly* (1953). (as Ellis Peters) *The Soldier at the Door* (1954). *A Means of Grace* (1956). (trans.) *Tales of the Little Quarter,* by J. Neruda (1957). (trans.) *Don Juan,* by J. Toman (1958). *Leaves* (1958, anthology). (as Ellis Peters) *Death Mask* (1959). (as Ellis Peters) *The Will and the Deed* (1960; in the U.S. as *Where There's a Will*). *The Heaven Tree* (3 vols., 1960). (as Ellis Peters) *Death and the Joyful Woman* (1961). (trans.) *The Abortionists,* by V. Styblova (1962). (as Ellis Peters) *Funeral of Figaro* (1962). (as Ellis Peters) *The Green Branch* (1962). (trans.) *Granny,* by B. Nemcova (1962). (trans.) *The Terezin Requiem,* by J. Bor (1963). (as Ellis Peters) *The Scarlet Seed* (1963). (as Ellis Peters) *Flight of a Witch* (1964). (as Ellis Peters) *A Nice Derangement of Epitaphs* (1965; in the U.S. as *Who Lies Here?*). *The Lily Hand and Other Stories* (1965). (trans.) *Maj,* by L. H. Macha (1965). (trans.) *The End of the Old Times,* by V. Vancura (1965). (as Ellis Peters) *The Piper on the Mountain* (1966). (as Ellis Peters) *Black is the Colour of My True-Love's Heart* (1967). (as Ellis Peters) *The Grass-Widow's Tale* (1968). (trans.) *A Close Watch on the Trains,* by B. Hrabal (1968). (as Ellis Peters) *The House of Green Turf* (1969). (as Ellis Peters) *Mourning Raga* (1969). (trans.) *Report on My Husband,* by J. Slanska (1969). (trans.) *A Ship Called Hope,* by I. Klima (1970). (as Ellis Peters) *The Knocker on Death's Door* (1970). (trans.) *Mozart in Prose,* by J. S. Seifert (1970). (as Ellis Peters) *Death to the Landlords!* (1972). (as Ellis Peters) *Bloody Field by Shrewsbury* (1972). (as Ellis Peters) *City of Gold and Shadows* (1973). (as Ellis Peters) *The Horn of Roland* (1974). *Sunrise in the West* (1974). *The Dragon at Noon Day* (1975). (as Ellis Peters) *The Hounds of Sunset* (1976). (as Ellis Peters) *Never Pick Up Hitch-hikers!* (1976). (as Ellis Peters) *Afterglow and Nightfall* (1977). (as Ellis Peters) *A Morbid Taste for Bones* (1977). (as Ellis Peters) *Rainbow's End* (1978). (as Ellis Peters) *One Corpse Too Many* (1979). *The Marriage of Meggotta* (1979). (as Ellis Peters) *Monk's Hood* (1980). (as Ellis Peters) *Saint Peter's Fair* (1980). (as Ellis Peters) *The Leper of Saint Giles* (1981). (as Ellis Peters) *The Virgin in the Ice* (1982). (as Ellis Peters) *The Sanctuary Sparrow* (1983). (as Ellis Peters) *The Devil's Novice* (1983). (as Ellis Peters) *Dead Man's Ransom* (1984). (as Ellis Peters) *The Pilgrim of Hate* (1984). (as Ellis Peters) *An Excellent Mystery* (1985). (as Ellis Peters) *The Raven in the Foregate* (1986). (as Ellis Peters)

The Rose Rent (1986). (as Ellis Peters) *The Hermit of Eyton Forest* (1987). (as Ellis Peters) *The Confession of Brother Haluin* (1988). (as Ellis Peters) *A Rare Benedictine* (1988). *The Brothers of Gwynedd* (1989). (as Ellis Peters) *The Heretic's Apprentice* (1989). (as Ellis Peters) *The Potter's Field* (1989). (as Ellis Peters) *First Cadfael Omnibus* (1990). (as Ellis Peters) *The Summer of the Danes* (1991). (as Ellis Peters) *The Dominic Felse Omnibus* (1991). (as Ellis Peters) *Second Cadfael Omnibus* (1992). (as Ellis Peters) *Third Cadfael Omnibus* (1992). (as Ellis Peters) *The Holy Thief* (1992). (as Ellis Peters) *The Benediction of Brother Cadfael* (1992). (as Ellis Peters) *The Detective Omnibus* (1992). (as Ellis Peters) *Fourth Cadfael Omnibus* (1994). (as Ellis Peters) *Fifth Cadfael Omnibus* (1994). (as Ellis Peters) *Brother Cadfael's Penance* (1994). (as Ellis Peters) *The George Felse Omnibus* (1994). (as Ellis Peters) *The Second George Felse Omnibus* (1995).

BIBLIOGRAPHY: Boyd, M. K. *Clues* (1988). Donohue, J. W. *America* (16 April 1994). Greeley, A. M. *ArmD* (1985). Herbert, R. *PW* (9 August 1991). Klein, K. G. *Great Women Mystery Writers* (1994).

For articles in reference works, see: *CA*. *IAWWW*. *Longman*. *TCC&MW*. *TCRGW*. *WA*.

Other references: *LonT* (16 October 1995).

Cheryl Forbes

Parker, Leslie: See *Thirkell, Angela (Margaret)*

Katherine (or Catherine) Parr

BORN: 1513, Westmoreland.
DIED: 1548, Sudeley, Wiltshire.
DAUGHTER OF: Sir Thomas Parr and Maud Green Parr.
MARRIED: Edward Brugh, Lord Brugh, 1525; Sir John Nevill, Lord Latimer, 1533; Henry VIII, King of England, 1543; Sir Thomas Seymour, later Lord High Admiral, 1547.

The sixth and surviving wife of King Henry VIII, P. proved a nurturing stepmother to his children, Mary (daughter of Catherine of Aragon), Elizabeth (daughter of Anne Boleyn), and Edward (son of Jane Seymour). A learned woman, inclined to study and to serious religiosity, she restored sobriety to Henry's court, surrounding herself with a coterie of like-minded noblewomen, and supported such religious reformers as Coverdale, Latimer, and Pankhurst. She sponsored a translation of the Bible into the vernacular and published two works emanating from her own religious experience. *Prayers, or Meditations* . . . (1545) is a collection of her own religious exercises and *The lamentation or complaynt of a sinner* . . . (1547) is a moving account of her own religious odyssey. Both works were extremely popular and both were reprinted several times within the century.

P. united learning, intelligence, and a personal sympathy that brought light into the tossled lives of her stepchildren, quiet and peace into the life of her difficult, invalid husband, King Henry, and encouragement to the religious scholars of her time. That she was able to persuade her Roman Catholic stepdaughter, Mary Tudor, to contribute a translation to the edition of the New Testament that she sponsored is a measure of her personal gifts. That Henry valued her is shown by his appointment of her as regent while he campaigned in France in 1544. She also overcame a plot laid against her by intriguing courtiers.

After Henry's death, P., then thirty-four, married the swashbuckling Thomas Seymour, a former suitor. Accounts of the success of this marriage vary, but it was, in any case, shortlived. P. died in September 1548, six days after the delivery of her only child, a daughter.

As J. Mueller has shown, P.'s *Prayers or Meditations*, the first original published work bearing the author's name to appear in the lifetime of an Englishwoman, thoroughly reworks Book 3 of a monastic work, Thomas à Kempis's *Imitation of Christ* (as translated by Richard Whytford), into a work accessible to pious persons of either sex.

P.'s moving *Lamentacion* is interesting in combining simple and humble statements of her perception of herself as a feeble individual, struggling to escape from the coils of sin and justified only by faith, with politically and personally astute (and possibly sincere) statements of support for Henry's leadership of the English church.

The admiration of her contemporaries for P. is attested to by the preface by William Cecil to the 1548 edition of her *Lamentacion*. It reads, in part, "Here mayest thou se one, if the kynde may moove the a woman, if degre may provoke thee a woman of highe estate, by byrthe made noble, by mariage mooste noble, . . . refusyng the worlde wherin she was loste, to obteyne heaven, wherin she may be saved; . . . remoovyng supersticion wherwith she was smothered, to enbrace [sic] true regilion [sic], wherwith she may revive."

WORKS: *Prayers, or Meditations, wherein the mynd is stirred, patiently to suffre all afflictions here, to set at nought the vaine prosperitie of this worlde, and always to longe for the everlasting felicitie: collected out of holy woorkes the most vertuous and gracious Princess Katherine qveene of Englande, Fraunce, and Irelande* (1545; in T. Bentley, *Monument of Matrones,* 1582). *The lamentation or complaynt of a sinner, made by the most vertuous Ladie, Quene Caterin, bewayling the ignorance of her blind life: set forth and put in print at the instant desire of the righte gracious ladie Caterin Duchesse of Suffoke, & the earnest requeste of the right honorable Lord, William Parre Marquesse of North Hampton* (1547; in T. Bentley, *Monument of Matrones,* 1582; in *Harleian Miscellany,* 1808). *Writings of Edward VI, William Hugh, Queen Catherine Parr, Anne Askew, Lady Jane Grey, Hamilton, and Balnaves* (1831). *Katherine Parr,* ed. J. Mueller (1996).

BIBLIOGRAPHY: Bainton, R. H. *Women of the Reformation in France and England* (1973). Beilin, E. V. *Redeeming Eve: Women Writers of English Renaissance* (1987). Devereaux, E. J. *BJRL* (1969). *DNB*. Foxe, J. *Actes and monuments of these latter and perillous dayes* (1563). Gordon, M. *A Life of Queen Katherine Parr* (1951). Haugaard, W. P. *RQ* (1969). Hays, M. *Female Biography, or, Memoirs of Illustrious and Celebrated Women, of All Ages and Countries* (1807). Hoffman, C. F. Jr. *HLQ* (1960). Hogrefe, P. *Tudor Women: Commoners and Queens* (1975). Hogrefe, P. *Women of Action in Tudor England* (1977). Hughey, R. *Library,* 4th Series (1934). King, J. N., in *Silent but for the Word,* ed. M. P. Hannay (1985). Levin, C. *International Journal of Women's Studies* (1980). McConica, J. *English Humanists and Reformation Politics under Henry VIII and Edward VI* (1965). *The Female Spectator: English Women Writers before 1800,* ed. M. R. Mahl and H. Koon (1977). Martienssen, A. *Queen Katherine Parr* (1973). Mueller, J. in *Historical Renaissance,* ed. H. Dubrow and R. Strier (1988). Mueller, J. *HLQ* (1990). Sessions, W. A. *ANQ* (1992). Strickland, A. *Lives of the Queens of England from the Norman Conquest* (1842). *Paradise of Women: Writings by Englishwomen of the Renaissance,* ed. B. Travitsky (1981). Warnicke, R. M. *Women of the English Renaissance and Reformation* (1983). Williams, J. *Literary Women of England* (1861).

For articles in reference works, see: *Allibone. Ballard. Bloomsbury. DNB. Europa. Feminist. IDWB. ToddBWW.*

Betty Travitsky

Parthenissa: See *Lennox, Charlotte Ramsay*

Margaret Paston

BORN: 1423, Norfolk.
DIED: 1482.
DAUGHTER OF: John Mauteby.
MARRIED: John Paston, c. 1440.

Prior to her marriage to John Paston, nothing is known of P.'s life except that she was the daughter of a wealthy landowner of Norfolk. From the day of her first meeting with her future husband, however, she became one of a handful of medieval women or medieval men whose individual experiences were recorded and preserved for future generations, in her case in a vast collection of Paston family correspondence and papers spanning almost a century. Had she married anyone else, P. might or might not have ever written a letter, but in either event her experience would have been completely lost to us; so, in a very real sense, the P. we now reconstruct epitomizes the extent to which a woman's life was determined by the particular role of wife to which she was assigned. As P.'s own words reveal, this role (for a woman of her class and times) was circumscribed and subordinate, but in no way was it marginal or powerless. Her central and formidable responsibility included and is manifest in her letter writing, but it may be misleading to think of P. as a "woman writer" without an initial word of qualification. There is no evidence that P. was in the least bit learned or interested in reading and writing in ways that we would understand; it is not even possible to be sure that she was able to write, since the 104 extant letters sent in her name were written in a number of different hands. It is most probable that she could and did write herself, but like most affluent men and women in the fifteenth century more often hired a scribe to take dictation. It is a voice rather than a hand, then, that speaks in her letters.

A single, not extraordinary circumstance (for the fifteenth century) occasioned both P.'s most remarkable activities and many of her letters: For a good deal of their married life, her husband was away from home. John Paston was a student at Cambridge University when he married and left his wife with his in-laws while he finished his studies there and then went on to the Inner Temple in London. Later he spent many months of each year in London, when the courts were in session, and on a few occasions he was detained in Fleet prison as a result of the vagaries of his complex property claims and political maneuvers. The nature of the disputes in which the Pastons were involved often left P. to defend, in a literal sense, their properties. One of the early struggles centered on a mansion in Gresham that they bought from Geoffrey Chaucer's son Thomas, to which a rival baron also laid claim. In 1449–50 John Paston seized the property and left his wife in charge while he went to London to take further legal action. The rival claimants soon retook the house with armed forces, physically removing P. from the premises and then looting and partially destroying the house. Similarly, a decade later, when the Pastons inherited Caister Castle from John Fastolf (Shakespeare's Falstaff, and apparently a distant relative of P.'s), they were subsequently sued and attacked by various claimants. P. was again left to fend off enemies for long periods of time, and no settlement of this private war took place until after her husband's death in 1466.

P. also bore at least eight children, six of whom survived, and even when her husband was at home planned for and orchestrated all the daily needs of a large household of family and servants. Modern biographers often comment on what is perceived by our standards as her harshness and lack of affection for her children, and her relationship with one of her daughters is often cited. When it became known that her daughter had secretly exchanged a vow of marriage with the Pastons' bailiff, P. attempted to block official sanction of the unapproved match. When her efforts failed, she formally refused to let her daughter back into her home, and the daughter was sheltered in a nunnery until the wedding took place.

Her function as mother and even as "housewife," in the broadest sense of the term, is not a dominant theme in P.'s writing, however, though occasionally she requested that her husband buy certain food or clothes for her and her family. Her letters center, instead, on her part in the public spheres of property management, politics, and local warfare; Virginia Woolf described them as "the letters of an honest bailiff to his master." Her writing was never an incidental part of her life, a leisure pastime, or a vehicle of self-expression; instead, it was an integral and essential part of the job she undertook. She acted repeatedly in her husband's place to manage his large estate and the complex affairs it entailed, buying and selling goods, negotiating with his tenants and enemies, holding courts, and pleading his cases. She reported on what she had done and agreed (or in some cases refused) to perform future services for him. She passed on appeals and information from others and kept him well advised on what was happening on the local front, since affairs of all sorts affected their family peace and prosperity. She sometimes asked for money and sometimes agreed to send him funds. In all this, she played a crucial advisory role, evaluating and proposing strategy and recommending action.

After her husband's death, most of P.'s extant letters were written to two of her sons, the eldest Sir John Paston (John II), and the younger John Paston (John III). While still carrying out Sir John's occasional orders and always acting and plotting on his behalf, she advised her sons more directly and authoritatively than she did their father on increasingly troublesome financial and political matters and even resorted to threats in her efforts to force the titular head of the family to act as she thought he should. Her letters to her eldest son are filled with reproaches for spending too much, failing to work hard, forgetting to write or come home, selling off family property to pay for personal indulgence, and neglecting to buy a tombstone for his father's grave. In the later letters, she spoke more and more openly with disappointment and bitterness as well as with characteristic anxiety, as her son failed to take the charge and care to which she, for his and his name's sake, devoted her entire life.

WORKS: *The Paston Letters and Papers of the Fifteenth Century,* ed. N. Davis (1971).

BIBLIOGRAPHY: Bennett, H. S. *The Pastons and Their England* (1932). Bennett, H. S. *Six Medieval Men and Women* (1955). Gies, F. and J. Gies *Women in the Middle Ages* (1978). Harding, W. *WS* (1992). Whitaker, E. E. *ELN* (1993). Woolf, V. *Collected Essays,* Vol. III (1925).

Elaine Tuttle Hansen

Pasture, de la, Edmée Elizabeth Monica: See *Delafield, E. M.*

Paton Walsh, Jill: See *Walsh, Jill Paton*

Pax: See *Cholmondeley, Mary*

Pembroke, Countess of: See *Sidney, Mary*

Pendarves, M.: See *Delany, Mary Granville Pendarves*

Percy, Charles Henry: See *Smith, Dorothy (Dodie) Gladys*

Percy, Elizabeth: See *Northumberland, Duchess of*

Perdita: See *Lennox, Charlotte Ramsay*

Perdita: See *Robinson, Mary Darby*

Anne Perry

BORN: (as Juliet Marion Hulme) 28 October 1938, London.

DAUGHTER OF: Henry Rainsford Hulme and Hilda Marion Reavley Hulme.

P. is the author of two series of Victorian mysteries, admired for their authentic period atmosphere and complex characterization, which have become popular successes as well: Three million of her books have been sold in the United States alone. P. is frequently mentioned in the same breath with Charles Dickens for her exposure of upper-class hypocrisy and insularity and for her exploration of the slums and criminal underworld. This community of victims and vultures, P. indicates, both results from and feeds on the upper-class world that pretends to ignore its existence: In her books, the estate and the gutter exist side by side.

Little was known about P. until, in 1994, a journalist discovered her connection with a decades-old New Zealand murder. P., formerly Juliet Hulme, was sent to recuperate in the Bahamas and then New Zealand after having been diagnosed with a chest complaint at the age of eight. Her parents joined her in New Zealand but left separately in the spring of 1954, when her father lost his position as president of Canterbury University, and her mother left the country with her eventual second husband. Fifteen-year-old P. was expected to leave the country as well; this would mean parting from her dependent best friend, Pauline Parker, whose mother refused to let her accompany P. P.'s judgment was impaired by medication and by the fear that Parker would commit suicide. According to a New Zealand court, together they murdered Parker's mother a few days later. The 1994 film *Heavenly Creatures* is based upon these events.

After her conviction and a five-and-a-half-year prison sentence, P. moved to Newcastle-on-Tyne to live with her mother and stepfather, Walter Perry, whose surname she took as her own. She worked at a variety of jobs, including property underwriter and assistant buyer. From 1967 to 1972, she lived in California, where she discovered and joined the Mormon church. Since 1990, she has lived in Scotland.

In 1979, she published *The Cater Street Hangman,* the first of her Victorian mysteries. The first in a series that takes place in the 1880s, it features Inspector Thomas Pitt and his well-born love interest, Charlotte Ellison, in subsequent books his wife. *The Face of a Stranger* (1990) inaugurated a new series, set in the mid-1850s, which features Inspector William Monk and nurse Hester Latterley. The second in this series, *A Dangerous Mourning* (1991), introduces barrister Oliver Rathbone, who becomes a major figure in later books; in this novel, Monk is dismissed from the police and embarks on a new career as a private investigator.

A trademark feature of P.'s novels, and one that has contributed to their great success, is their scrupulous historical detail. P. situates each series in the current events of the times, involving her characters in the political, social, and artistic climate. She is particularly adept at re-creating the sometimes subtle demarcations of Victorian social and class distinctions. P.'s period atmosphere is fresh and vivid, transforming the Victorian era from a distant, antiquated period into an immediate reality.

P.'s characterization is another strong point in her work, and her heroines Charlotte and Hester are particularly engaging: Frequently modern in attitude, they are, however, never anachronistic, and their outspokenness is appropriately checked by their more traditional elders. P. also allows her characters and their relationships to grow and change with the passage of time, a process that enhances the realism of her work. One such character is Inspector Monk: When he first appears in *The Face of a Stranger,* his memory has been destroyed by an accident, and throughout the series he gradually pieces together fragments of his past.

Since P. now recalls almost nothing of the Parker murder and trial, some critics have found the source of Monk's amnesia in her own memory loss. P. points out the flaws in the parallel, however, saying that she created the character because she wanted to explore looking for the monster outside and finding that "there are no monsters . . . only people, like oneself." The Pitt mystery *Traitor's Gate* (1995), while no more autobiographical than the Monk books, deals with an issue that P. notes has personal significance for her: The novel concerns conflicting loyalties, a type of dilemma P. faced when Parker proposed the murder.

The hidden presence of evil is a prominent theme of P.'s mysteries, which emphasize the dangerous hypocrisy of Victorian society. P.'s denouements usually turn on the sordid presence of an evil hidden by the superficial social fabric and display a devastating contrast between the era's would-be gentility and its often brutal truths. Her upper-class Victorians murder every bit as viciously as their social inferiors to hide sodomy, incest, even impotence—secrets that would be incompatible with, and lethal to, their social standing. P. vividly depicts a ruthlessly conformist society in which reputation is worth killing for, but in which a gentleman is by definition above such things. P.'s evocation of the Victorian period clearly indicates the dangers of some of its most dearly held tenets, while showing that many motives for murder have survived the era and are still present today.

WORKS: *The Cater Street Hangman* (1979). *Callander Square* (1980). *Paragon Walk* (1981). *Resurrection Row* (1981). *Rutland Place* (1983). *Bluegate Fields* (1984). *Death in the Devil's Acre* (1985). *Cardington Crescent* (1987). *Silence in Hanover Close* (1988). *Bethlehem Road* (1990). *The Face of a Stranger* (1990). *A Dangerous Mourning* (1991). *Highgate Rise* (1991). *Belgrave Square* (1992). *Defend and Betray* (1992). *Farrier's Lane* (1993). *A Sudden, Fearful Death* (1993). *The Hyde Park Headsman* (1994). *The Sins of the Wolf* (1994). *Cain His Brother* (1995). *Traitors Gate* (1995). *Pentecost Alley* (1996). *Weighed in the Balance* (1996). *Ashworth Hall* (1997). *The Silent Cry* (1997).

BIBLIOGRAPHY: Klein, K. G. *Great Women Mystery Writers* (1994).

For articles in reference works, see: *CA. TCC&MW. WD.*

Other references: Lambert, P. *People* (26 September 1994). Lyall, S. *NYT* (17 August 1994).

Amanda DeWees

Peter, Rhoda: See *Doolittle, Hilda (H. D.)*

Peters, Ellis: See *Pargeter, Edith Mary*

Emily Jane Davis Pfeiffer

BORN: 26 November 1827, Montgomeryshire, Wales.
DIED: 23 January 1890, Putney, London.
DAUGHTER OF: R. Davis.
MARRIED: Jurgen Edward Pfeiffer, 1853.

P. was the daughter of an army officer and Oxfordshire landowner. Although he encouraged P.'s early talent, unexpected financial problems prevented him from giving her a thorough education. When P. married J. E. Pfeiffer, a prosperous German merchant living in England, she acquired the financial means and leisure to educate herself. The result, despite constant bouts of ill health and insomnia, was ten volumes of poetry and two of prose. P. wrote sonnets, lyrics, dramatic monologues, Pre-Raphaelite ballads, and blank-verse closet drama as well as political essays, travelogues, and a few mixed-genre works.

In general, P. wrote about the pressures on women, their victimization, and ways they might escape it. She expressed solidarity with women unlike herself—single women, working-class women, "fallen" women, foreign women, and so forth. She was very conscious of being a woman artist and often wrote about the constraints on female aspiration and achievement in the nineteenth century as well as the social need for women's particular contributions to art, politics, and education.

In 1857, P. published *Valisneria; or a Midsummer's Day's Dream,* a prose fantasy comparable to Sara Coleridge's *Phantasmion* (1837), full of trembling female eroticism, fairy episodes, and Romantic nature imagery in miniature, with a realistic framing tale of female innocence, marriage, and disillusionment. *Margaret, or the Motherless* (1861), a modern romance in verse, can be read as a plea for more humane divorce laws in England. In 1873, P. published *Gerard's Monument,* a romantic poetic narrative of love and death set in medieval times. Here as elsewhere, P. characteristically portrayed the sexual passion of lovers as both a natural and a spiritual experience. On the other hand, "Childe Rupert, the White Ermingarde, and the Red Ladye," set in the Middle Ages, is a gorgeous Pre-Raphaelite ballad of innocence and faith triumphant over temptations of pride and sexuality.

"Childe Rupert" appeared in *Poems* (1876), which also established P.'s reputation for writing fine lyrics, especially sonnets, admired by A. C. Swinburne and Oliver Wendell Holmes, among others. Many of P.'s sonnets addressed the confusion and dismay that evolutionary science had wrought upon religious faith in the nineteenth century. P.'s religious inspiration is evident as she expresses her hopes for an egalitarian future for herself personally, for women in general, for the working poor, and indeed for the entire human race. "The Winged Soul"—an image P. returns to throughout her career—and other sonnets of 1876 portrayed the pain and frustration of the creative human spirit born into the captivity of class or gender.

P.'s poetry continued to appear throughout the 1880s: *Sonnets and Songs* (1880, revised and enlarged in 1886), *Under the Aspens: Lyrical and Dramatic* (1882), *The Rhyme of the Lady of the Rock* (1884), and *Flowers of the Night* (1889). This poetry evidences a mature, feminist perspective on women's lives and problems. P. sometimes speaks in her own voice (as in many of her sonnets) and sometimes in a metaphorical, dramatic, or historical/mythological mode. *The Wynnes of Wynhavod* (1881), though never staged, is a very readable full-length blank-verse drama of nineteenth-century life. "From Out of the Night" (1882) is a 600–line soliloquy of a seduced and abandoned working girl who is about to jump into a river.

The Rhyme of the Lady of the Rock (1884), structurally similar to Alfred Lord Tennyson's "The Princess" (1847), is a a complex narrative addressing various social issues, such as the marriage market, marital rape, domestic tyranny, and the nature of female heroism. The narrator's husband reads his wife's poetic retelling of a local legend to an audience of mixed class, gender, education, and political perspectives, pausing frequently to entertain their commentary on the morality of the action and the quality of the poetry. In the framing narrative, the poet heroine confides her anxieties regarding her poetic authority and competence.

In many ways, P. seems a "modern" poet; she addresses issues still alive today and with a markedly female focus and tonality. Yet she is also very much a woman of her own times, bound in many ways by nineteenth-century artistic and social norms. Among the writers she most admired were Jane Austen, Charlotte Brontë, George Eliot, and Elizabeth Barrett Browning, to whom she was often compared; she cited their literary achievements as evidence of women's equality with men in the area of creative thought and expression. "The Lost Light" (1880) is a moving eulogy for George Eliot. In general, the ideals that emerge from P.'s poetry are personal courage and integrity, faith, idealism, freedom, and achievement.

Besides poetry, P. also published political essays. In 1885, after completing an extensive tour of Asia and North America, she published *Flying Leaves from East and West,* a collection of political and artistic commentaries in travelogue form. Among the political topics she addressed in this volume were class and race relations in the United States and the degraded status of women in Turkish harems. Also during the 1880s, P. wrote most of her numerous articles on the subjects of women and education, work, suffrage, dress reform, wife beating, and trade unionism, published in periodicals such as the *Cornhill Magazine* and the *Contemporary Review.* In *Women and Work* (1887), she attacked the physiological, pseudoscientific theories that claimed women were not strong enough to work and called for more occupational opportunities and more competitive wages for women.

When her husband died in 1889, P. was devastated; she did not long survive him. During the last year of her life, she made plans to found an orphanage, which was opened after her death, and provided funds for a School of Dramatic Art for women. She also left £2,000 for higher education for women, which was used in 1895 to erect Aberdare Hall, the first dormitory for women students at University College, Cardiff, in South Wales.

WORKS: *The Holly Branch: An Album for 1843,* by Emily Davis (1843). *Valisneria; or a Midsummer Day's Dream* (1857). *Margaret, or the Motherless* (1861). *Gerard's Monument and Other Poems* (1873; enlarged 1878). *Poems* (1876). *Glan-Alarch: His Silence and Song* (1877). *Quarterman's Grace and Other Poems* (1879). *Sonnets and Songs* (1880; rev. and enlarged 1886). *The Wynnes of Wynhavod: A Drama of Modern Life* (1881). *Under the Aspens: Lyrical and Dramatic* (1882). *The Rhyme of the Lady of the Rock and How It Grew* (1884). *Flying Leaves from East and West* (1885). *Women and Work: An Essay* (1887). *Flowers of the Night* (1889).

BIBLIOGRAPHY:

For articles in reference works, see: *BA19C. DNB. EP. Feminist. Oxford. PPC. Victorian Poets,* ed. E. Stedman (1875, 1887, 1903).

Other references: *Academy* (1 February 1890). *Athenaeum* (1 February 1890). Hickok, K. *Representations of Women: Nineteenth Century British Women's Poetry* (1984). Hickok, K. *JPRS* (1988). Hickok, K. *VP* (1995). Sackville-West, V. in *The Eighteen Seventies,* ed. H. Granville-Barker (1929). *Western Mail* (8 October 1895).

Kathleen Hickok

Katherine Philips

BORN: 1 January 1632, London.
DIED: 22 June 1664, London.
DAUGHTER OF: John Fowler and Katherine Oxenbridge Fowler.
MARRIED: James Philips, 1648.
WROTE UNDER: Orinda; Mrs. K. P.; Katherine Philips.

Although P. seemed to fit easily into the Interregnum and early Restoration literary community, admired as a genteel and skilled poet, retrospectively she appears as a paradox. Her poems, dramatic translations, and letters give the picture of a royalist surrounded by parliamentarian family members, of a loyal wife devoted chiefly to other women, and of a self-deprecating poet who promoted herself efficiently.

Born to middle-class Puritan parents in London and educated at Mrs. Salmon's School, P. moved to Wales after her father's death, when her mother remarried. By the age of sixteen, verbally precocious P. had written two surviving poems, one setting her ideals of a husband (a "man of sence," loyal to the king), one skeptical of marriage generally, and she had married fifty-four-year-old James Philips, soon to be a member of Parliament under Oliver Cromwell's government. From her home in the Priory, Cardigan, Wales, she worked her way into the literary circles of the London and Welsh Royalists. Henry Vaughan, for instance, praised her verse in his 1651 *Olor Iscanus.* In that same year, her first poem appeared in print, one of many prefacing

William Cartwright's posthumous works. In 1655, two of her poems appeared in Henry Lawes's *Second Book of Ayres*.

Mostly, her poems circulated in manuscript among her friends and were very often written for specific acquaintances, particularly Anne Owen and Mary Aubrey, whom P. styled Lucasia and Rosania. She herself took the name of Orinda. To what degree the circle of friends centering on Orinda became formalized is debatable, but both Francis Finch (called Palaemon in P.'s poems) and theologian Jeremy Taylor wrote treatises on friendship addressed to her.

P.'s approximately 125 original poems (plus recent discoveries of a few additional poems) range in subject from philosophical speculations to epitaphs, including one for her own son, to rejections of worldliness to royalist encomia. Those on the subject of friendship constitute the most notable category. Her verses praise particularly her female friends for their goodness and beauty, express the devotion she feels, lament or console at partings, or rebuke these friends for betrayals. Some of these poems insist on the platonic nature of their affection, taking this theme from Metaphysical and Cavalier poets and French *précieuse* society, but adapting this to love between women. Other poems insist strongly on the passion Orinda and the objects of her adoration feel, and they show the pain occasioned by the intrusion of men and marriage into the bond.

In fact, the male-centered world frequently intrudes into P.'s poems. Besides a number of directly political verses, even some of those concerning women's love refer to current political affairs. "Nor Bridegroomes nor crown'd conqu'rour's mirth / To mine compar'd can be: / They have but pieces of this Earth, / I've all the world in thee" declares one poem, "To My excellent Lucasia." That stanza possibly glances at the conqueror, Cromwell, but such remarks as another poem's "The dying Lion kick'd by every asse" more clearly indicate P.'s royalist sympathies. These sentiments threatened to get her husband into trouble with the government during the Interregnum. James Philips (called Antenor), an M.P., was vulnerable because of his wife's poetry, as P.'s "To Antenor, on a paper of mine wch J. Jones threatens to publish to his prejudice" makes clear. P. insists her opinions are her own ("Nor let my follies blast Antenor's name") and should not be imputed to her husband. Given P.'s divided loyalties during Cromwell's regime, her celebrations of rural retirement away from political turmoil are not surprising. These poems include a fine translation of Saint-Amant's "Solitude." Nonetheless, at the Restoration, P. sprang into activity, traveling to Dublin and London, producing panegyrics on the returning royal family, translating Corneille's politically appropriate *Pompey* (and leaving a translation of his *Horace* unfinished at her death), and countering threats to her husband, whom she was now in a position to protect, especially through her friendship with the Master of Ceremonies for King Charles II, Sir Charles Cotterell (called Poliarchus).

An extensive set of *Letters from Orinda to Poliarchus* exists, which reveals not only P.'s attempts to protect her spouse but her concerns with the publication of her various works. They also discuss the production of *Pompey*, which opened at Dublin's Smock Alley during the 1662–63 season and was the first public performance of a play by an Englishwoman; there was probably also a London performance. Repeatedly in these letters, however, P. insists on the undeservingness of her verse and her reluctance for publication. When seventy-five of her poems were printed without her authorization in January 1664, she expressed horror that they had appeared at all and suppressed the edition, though a number of copies survive. In what spirit and with what sincerity such protests were made is hard to say.

Just as her reputation was rising fast, at the age of thirty-two she died of smallpox. Her death brought forth quantities of commendatory verse, one piece insisting that she and Abraham Cowley were the two greatest poets of the age. The rest of the century kept her fame high: In 1667 an edition of 116 poems was published, as well as her two plays and five translated poems from the French. Further editions came out in 1669, 1678, and 1710. In 1668, *Horace,* completed by John Denham, was performed at court and had its London theater run nearly a year later. Four of P.'s letters were anthologized in 1697, with 1705 and 1729 seeing editions of those written to Cotterell. Through her skillful handling of verse and of men in political and literary power, P. created a reputation that rode high through the end of the seventeenth century.

WORKS: (trans.) *Pompey,* by Pierre Corneille (1663). *Poems By the Incomparable, Mrs. K. P.* (1664). *Poems By the most deservedly Admired Mrs. Katherine Philips The matchless Orinda* (1667; partial facsimile rpt. 1992). *Letters from Orinda to Poliarchus* (1705; enlarged 1729). *Minor Poets of the Caroline Period,* ed. G. Saintsbury (1905). *The Collected Works of Katherine Philips, The Matchless Orinda,* 3 vols., ed. P. Thomas, G. Greer, and R. Little (1990–93). Poems discovered since 1993: P. M. Sant and J. N. Brown, *ELR* (1994).

BIBLIOGRAPHY: *An Annotated Bibliography of Twentieth-Century Critical Studies of Women and Literature, 1660–1800,* ed. P. Backscheider, F. Nussbaum, P. Anderson (1977). Gosse, E. *Seventeenth Century Studies* (1883). Hageman, E. H., in *Women Writers of the Renaissance and Reformation,* ed. K. Wilson (1987). Hageman, E. *ELR* (1988; updated in *Women in the Renaissance,* ed. K. Farrell, E. Hageman, A. Kinney, 1990). Hobby, E. *Virtue of Necessity: English Women's Writing, 1649–88* (1989). Morgan, F. *The Female Wits* (1981). Sant, P. M. and J. N. Brown. *ELR* (1994). Steen, S. *ELR* (1994). Souers, P. *The Matchless Orinda* (1931). Thomas, P. *Katherine Philips ("Orinda")* (1988). Tinker, N. P. *ELN* (1995). Williamson, M. *Raising Their Voices: British Women Writers, 1650–1750* (1990).

For articles in reference works, see: *Aubrey's Brief Lives* (1693, 1898). *Ballard. Bell. Bloomsbury.* Bush, D. *English Literature in the Earlier Seventeenth Century: 1600–1660* (1962). Cibber, T. and R. Shiels. *Lives of the Poets of Great Britain and Ireland to the Time of Dean Swift* (1753, 1968). Crawford (1983). *DLB. Europa. The First Feminists,* ed. M. Ferguson (1985). *The Whole Duty of a Woman,* ed. A. Goreau (1985). *Kissing the Rod: An Anthology of Seventeenth-Century Women's Verse,* ed. G. Greer et al. (1988). *IDWB. The Female*

Spectator: English Women Writers Before 1800, ed. M. R. Mahl and H. Koon (1977). *Oxford. Rowton. Todd-BWW.* Uphaus, R. and G. Foster, ed. *The "Other" Eighteenth Century* (1991).

Other references: Andreadis, H. *Signs* (1989). Backscheider, P. *Spectacular Politics* (1993). Beal, P. *EMS* (1993). Biester, J. *SEL* (1993). Brashear, L. *Anglo-Welsh Review* (1979). Brashear, L. *N&Q* (1985). Brashear, L. *Restoration* (1986). Canfield, D. *Corneille and Racine in England* (1904). Cotton, N. *Women Playwrights in England: c. 1363–1750* (1980). Easton, C. *Restoration* (1990). Elmen, P. *PQ* (1951). Faderman, L. *Surpassing the Love of Men: Romantic Friendship and Love Between Women from the Renaissance to the Present* (1981). Hageman, E. *SCR* (1994). Hagemann, E. *Library* (1995). Hageman, E. and A. Sununu *EMS* (1993). Hobby, E., in *What Lesbians do in Books*, ed. E. Hobby and C. White (1991). Libertin, M. *WS* (1982). Lilley, K., in *Women, Writing, History: 1640–1740*, ed. I. Grundy and S. Wiseman (1992). Limbert, C. *ELR* (1986). Limbert, C. *Restoration* (1989). Limbert, C., in *Women in the Renaissance*, ed. K. Farrell et al. (1990). Limbert, C. *ELN* (1991). Limbert, C. *PQ* (1991). Limbert, C. *SoAR* (1991). Loscocco, P. *HLQ* (1993). Lund, R. *Restoration* (1988). MacLean, G. *Text* (1987). Mambretti, C. *PBSA* (1977). Mambretti, C. *CL* (1985). McDowell, P. *Genre* (1993). Mermin, D. *ELH* (1990). Moody, E. *PQ* (1987). Mulvihill, M., in *Curtain Calls: British and American Women and the Theater, 1660–1820*, ed. M. Schofield and C. Macheski (1991). Mulvihill, M. *SECC* (1992). Norbrook, D. *EMS* (1993). Price, C. *Theatre Notebook* (1979). Pritchard, A. *SEL* (1983). Radzinowicz, M. *LIT* (1990). Roberts, W. *ELN* (1964). Roberts, W. *PQ* (1970). Røstvig, M. *The Happy Man* (1954). Stiebel, A., in *Renaissance Discourses of Desire*, ed. C. Summers and T. Pebworth (1993). Thomas, P. *Anglo-Welsh Review* (1976). Wheatley, C. *RECTR* (1992).

Sayre N. Greenfield

Philomela: See *Rowe, Elizabeth Singer*

Philomena: See *Miller, Florence Fenwick*

Pier, Florida: See *Scott-Maxwell, Florida*

Laetitia Pilkington

BORN: 1712, Dublin, Ireland.
DIED: 29 July 1750, Dublin, Ireland.
DAUGHTER OF: John Van Lewen and Elizabeth Corry Van Lewen.
MARRIED: Matthew Pilkington, 1730.
WROTE UNDER: Mrs. Meade; Laetitia Pilkington.

Although her *Memoirs* (1748–54) brought her fame, P. considered them to be a mere vehicle for her poetry. Beginning with the claim that, with Alexander Pope, she "lisped in numbers" as a child, the *Memoirs* chronicles a life seen completely in terms of literature and literary production. The daughter of a Dutch obstetrician and a mother distantly related, through the Meades, to the Irish nobility, P. married Matthew Pilkington, an impoverished parson twelve years her senior. Matthew himself had literary pretensions (his *Poems on Several Occasions* was published in 1730), and with his help and that of a few well-aimed verses, P. managed to gain admittance to the inner circle of Jonathan Swift, who had recently retired to Dublin. Her account of their unusual friendship has remained an important source for biographers of Swift from William Makepeace Thackeray to the present.

At this point, the "harmless household dove" disappears in favor of the "notorious prostitute" of the broadsides. Her love of learning, it seems, had caused her to be caught in her bedchamber at an "unseasonable hour" with a man who possessed the "attractive charms of a new Book, which the gentleman would not lend me, but consented to stay until I had read it through." Expelled from her husband's house, she set off for London in 1738 to become the first professional woman of letters after Aphra Behn.

Volume I of the *Memoirs*, like the other "scandalous memoirs" that began to proliferate at the time, was written both for vindication and profit. The true motivation for her break with her husband, she claimed, was his envy of her literary ability, samples of which are sprinkled liberally throughout the text. The verse often provides a gloss on the prose: P.'s 1739 poem "The Statues," for instance, is inserted at an earlier point in the narrative where it comments upon both Swift's peculiar relations with women and her own disintegrating marital relations. The book's popularity was assured by the paper wars following its publication in which P. cleverly acquitted herself against an army of pseudonymous detractors, many of whom were suspected to be Matthew himself.

Volume II tells of P.'s attempts to support herself by furnishing epithets and verses to fashionable London. For a time, she was successful; however, her virtue, she says, did not stand her in good stead, and she gradually sank on the social scale until she was imprisoned for debt and had to be bailed out by her friend Colley Cibber. With the money left over from this adventure, she opened a print and pamphlet shop.

Volume III was written while P. was on her deathbed to furnish a legacy for her son, with whom she had recently been reunited. The narrative breaks down into a random collection of ripostes, reminiscences, and poems—anything, Virginia Woolf remarked, "to fill a page and earn a guinea." It appeared four years after her death with a long postscript by her son on her final illness.

Despite the fact that she gained notoriety as the author of a "scandalous memoir," P. refused to accept the association of "publishing" and being a "public woman." Declaring herself "an heteroclite, or irregular verb, which can be neither declined or conjugated," she aspired to a realm of literary merit of which Swift, even after he had repudiated her, had been a symbol.

WORKS: *The Memoirs of Mrs. Laetitia Pilkington, Wife to the Rev. Mr. Matthew Pilkington. Written by Herself. Wherein are Occasionally Interspersed All Her Poems; With Anecdotes of several eminent persons, Living and Dead. Among others Dean Swift, Alexander Pope, Esq;*

&c., &c., &c., Vol. I (1748), Vol. II (1749), Vol. III (1754). *The Memoirs*... (1928; ed. I. Barry, with a bibliography by J. Isaacs). *The Poetry of Laetitia Pilkington (1712–1750) and Constantia Grierson (1706–1733)*, ed. B. Tucker (1996). *Memoirs*, ed. A. C. Elias, Jr. (1997).

BIBLIOGRAPHY: *Gentleman's Magazine* (1748–49). Elias, A. C., Jr., in *Walking Naboth's Vineyard: New Studies of Swift*, ed. C. Fox and B. Tooley (1994). Elias, A. C., Jr. *SStud* (1994). Hann, Y., in *TransAtlantic Crossings: Eighteenth Century Explorations*, ed. D. W. Nichol (1995). Nussbaum, F., in *The New Eighteenth Century: Theory/Politics/English Literature*, ed. F. Nussbaum and L. Brown (1987). "An Oxford Scholar" *The Parallel: Laetitia Pilkington and [Teresia Constantia] Phillips Compared* (1748). Relke, D. M., in *Gender at Work: Four Women Writers of the Eighteenth Century*, ed. A. Messenger (1990). Woolf, V. *The Common Reader* (1925).

For articles in reference works, see: *Allibone. Bloomsbury. DNB. Europa.*

Other references: *BDIW. DBPP. Dictionary of English Literature* (1972). *DIL. The Poets of Ireland.* Shumaker, W. *English Autobiography: Its Emergence, Materials, and Form* (1954). Stauffer, D. A. *The Art of Biography in Eighteenth-Century England* (1941). *ToddDBA.*

Susan Pavlovska

Pinter, Lady Antonia: See Fraser, Antonia

Hester Lynch Salusbury Thrale Piozzi

BORN: 16 January 1741, Bodvel, Carnarvonshire, Wales.
DIED: 2 May 1821, Clifton, Bristol.
DAUGHTER OF: John Salusbury and Hester Cotton Salusbury.
MARRIED: Henry Thrale, 1763; Gabriel Piozzi, 1784.
WROTE UNDER: An Old Acquaintance of the Public; Hester Lynch Thrale Piozzi; Mrs. Piozzi.

Informally educated in Bodvel by doting parents, P. showed early signs of intelligence and wit. She spent the earliest years of her twenty-one-year marriage to Henry Thrale at Streatham Park near London. Of twelve pregnancies, five daughters survived infancy, four to adulthood. Although her own children and her associates in the Bluestocking circle objected to her second marriage to an Italian singer and music teacher, she managed to reconcile family and society to some extent as she pursued a career as an author, at her best in characterizing through dialogue.

Long an enthusiastic diarist, P. kept her first diary as a record of the progress of her daughter Queeney. Gradually, the diary expanded to include commentary about her growing family. Encouraged by Samuel Johnson's suggestion and Thrale's gift of an empty volume as repository, she began the diary she called *Thraliana* on 15 September 1776. A rich collection of anecdotes and conversations occasionally unified by her narrative, *Thraliana* provides insight into English society. P. selects her materials carefully, recording the words of famous persons or the compelling comments of relatively unknown associates. A connoisseur of conversation, she supplements overheard, spontaneous dialogue with discussions she has herself prompted and guided, especially in her salon among the members of the Bluestocking circle and with Johnson, a constant companion during the years of her marriage to Thrale. It also shows that P. was concerned less with keeping a daily record in strict chronological order than with aligning the rhythm of historical event with personal circumstance. Posterity would inherit not historicity but vivid moments captured in their entirety. While her emphasis on the personal and individual makes her writing more colloquial than orderly or authoritative, it recalls the rich texture and variety of a domestic life made vibrantly intellectual by the vigilant diarist's search for materials.

Much of *Thraliana* recalls Johnson's extended visits, but the *Anecdotes* (1786) and *Letters to and from the Late Samuel Johnson* (1788) more consistently interest Johnson scholars. P.'s collections include Johnson's minor poetry as well as details of his daily life and sayings. When Johnson, disapproving her marriage to Piozzi, terminated a long and mutually inspirational relationship with P., he freed her to consider more objectively his personality and thought. Thus, she tells of a different Johnson than the man portrayed by James Boswell, with whom she had several battles during the publication of numerous early reminiscences of Johnson.

An innovative author, P. discovered subjects for research and writing throughout her lifetime. With Johnson, she began translating Boethius, and she began a discussion of art and philosophy, abandoning the project after writing more than 100 pages. Other writings chronicle travel to Wales and France. P.'s verse is effective as satire, if not as poetry, a judgment she makes of her own work when she compiles it in *Thraliana*. Her ability to create compelling dialogue has been noted in her imitation of Jonathan Swift's poems on his own death ("Three Dialogues on the Death of Hester Lynch Thrale") and in a two-act comedy. Readers note political commentary in *British Synonymy* (1794), a popularizing of travel literature in *Observations and Reflections* (1789), and the leavening of history with anecdote and commentary in *Retrospection* (1801).

WORKS: *Anecdotes of the Late Samuel Johnson, LL.D. During the Last Twenty Years of His Life* (1786). *Letters to and from the Late Samuel Johnson, LL.D. to Which Are Added Some Poems Never Before Printed* (1788). *Observations and Reflections Made in the Course of a Journey Through France, Italy, and Germany* (1789). *The Three Warnings* (1792). *British Synonymy; or an Attempt at Regulating the Choice of Words in Familiar Conversation. Inscribed, With Sentiments of Gratitude and Respect, to such of her Foreign Friends as Have Made English Literature their Peculiar Study* (1794). *Three Warnings to John Ball before He Dies. By an Old Acquaintance of the Public* (1798). *Retrospection: or a Review of the Most Striking and Important Events, Characters, Situations, and Their Consequences, Which the Last Eighteen Hundred Years Have Presented to the View of Mankind* (1801). *Autobiography, Letters and Literary Remains*, ed. A. Hayward (1861). *Thraliana*, *the Diary of Mrs. Hester Lynch Thrale, Later Mrs. Piozzi,* ed. K. C. Balderson (1942). *The Piozzi Letters: Correspondence of Hester Lynch Piozzi, 1784–1821,* 4 vols., ed. E. Bloom and L. D. Bloom (1989–96).

BIBLIOGRAPHY: *The Private Self: Theory and Practice of Women's Autobiographical Writings,* ed. S. Benstock (1988). *BJRL* (Spring 1985). *Dr. Johnson and Mrs. Thrale's Tour in North Wales 1774,* ed. A. Bristow (1996). Broadley, A. M. *Doctor Johnson and Mrs. Thrale* (1910). Brownley, M. W., in *Mothering the Mind: Twelve Studies of Writers and Their Silent Partners,* ed. R. Perry and M. W. Brownley (1984). Brownley, M. W. *BJRL* (1985). Clifford, J. L. *Hester Lynch Piozzi (Mrs. Thrale)* (1952). Ellison, J. *CentR* (1989). Grundy, I., in *Johnson after Two Hundred Years,* ed. P. J. Korshin (1986). Hyde, M. M. *The Impossible Friendship: Boswell and Mrs. Thrale* (1972). McCarthy, W. *Hester Thrale Piozzi: Portrait of a Literary Woman* (1985). Mangin, E. *Pioziana . . . Recollections by a Friend* (1833). McCarthy, W. *BB* (June 1988). McCarthy, W. *MLS* (1988). McCarthy, W. *AJ* (1989). Merritt, P. *The True Story of the So-Called Love Letters of Mrs. Piozzi* (1927). Nussbaum, F. A., in *The Private Self: Theory and Practice of Women's Autobiographical Writings,* ed. S. Benstock (1988). Ribeiro, A. *SVEC* (1992). Riely, J., in *Greene Centennial Studies: Essays Presented to Donald Greene in the Centennial Year of the University of Southern California,* ed. P. J. Korshin and R. R. Allen (1984). Riely, J., in *Johnson and His Age,* ed. J. Engell (1984). Thaddeus, J. *ECLife* (1990). Thomson, K. B. *Queens of Society* (1860). Vuliamy, C. E. *Mrs. Thrale of Streatham* (1939).

For articles in reference works, see: *Allibone. ArtWW. BAB1800. BCE. BDLA. Bloomsbury. Cassell. CBEL. Chambers. CinP. DBPP. DictEur. DLB. DNB. ELB. Feminist. Ireland. Marshall.NCHEL. OCEL. Oxford. PCWL. RE. STET. ToddDBA. Warner.*

Other references: Adelman, J. *Famous Women* (1926). *BJRL* (1974). DeMorny, P. *Best Years of Their Lives* (1955). Dorland, W. *The Sum of Feminine Achievement* (1917). Hammerton, J. A. *Concise Universal Biography* (1934). *MLR* (1972). *MR* (1942). *N&Q* (1943). *RES* (1946, 1948). Stanton, D. *English Women in History* (n.d.). Thomson, K. *The Queens of Society* (1860).

Mary Sauter Comfort

Ruth Pitter

BORN: 7 November 1897, Ilford, Essex.
DIED: 29 February 1992, Long Grendon, near Aylesbury, Buckinghamshire.
DAUGHTER OF: George Pitter and Louisa R. Murrell Pitter.

P.'s poetry is often compared to the work of such seventeenth-century poets as Vaughan, Traherne, and Carew, as well as the work of such others as Spenser, Blake, Clare, and Hopkins. Her lyrical verse deals with such traditional subjects as the natural world and religion, and her clear awareness of sensory stimuli and concern for metaphysics seem to derive at least in part from the influence of her friend C. S. Lewis; her long identification with and precise knowledge of the English countryside, the joys of gardening, and her long life of physical exertion, however, contribute uniquely to her verse.

Oldest of three children born to two London elementary school teachers, P. started writing poetry at the age of five and published her first poem at thirteen, in A. R. Orage's *New Age* (later renamed *New English Weekly*). She worked as a War Office clerk in World War I; after the war she mastered such crafts as woodworking and painting before operating, with a partner, a gift shop in London until 1945. She then retired to Aylesbury, Buckinghamshire, where she died.

Her poetic appeal is to both heart and mind, and her lyrics often seem deceptively simple though admittedly deeply felt and balanced. Many of her poems reflect what Hilaire Belloc called her "perfect ear and exact epithet," with some, such as "The Fishers" and "The Cygnet," typical of her contemplations on and celebrations of what she calls the "secret dynamism of life." "The Cygnet," for example, uses two swans as suggestive of the soul's victory over evil. Other contemplative poems include "Urania," "The Eternal Image," and "The Downward-Pointing Muse." But she was also capable of witty, satiric verse, as in *The Rude Potato* (1941) and *On Cats* (1947), the latter collection less "old-maidish" (her term) and rollicking than the similar volume by her acquaintance T. S. Eliot.

P. is not experimental, preferring instead to depend on traditional meters and forms. Nor does the frantic world around her throughout most of her life intrigue her to any appreciable degree, though her "The Military Harpist" offers a subdued, sardonic commentary on war. Rather, she celebrates silence and contemplation through an emphasis on natural splendor and on life itself as reflective of the contrast between mere daily existence and the Christian hope. Widely praised by other poets and by many critics—Belloc was one of her first supporters, and she has been praised by Louise Bogan, Louis Untermeyer, Gorham Munson, Walter de la Mare, Gilbert Murray, Osbert Sitwell, John Masefield, and others—P. had an enduring though unpretentious poetic career. She won such awards as the Hawthornden Prize (1937), the Heinemann Award (1954), and the Queen's Gold Medal for Poetry (1955); in 1979 she received the Commander of the British Empire honor. Never a fashionable or popular writer and a member of no poetic "school," P. lived in comparative though wholly unjustified obscurity.

WORKS: *First Poems* (1920). *First and Second Poems, 1912–1925* (1930). *Persephone in Hades* (1931). *A Mad Lady's Garland* (1934). *A Trophy of Arms: Poems 1926–1935* (1936). *The Spirit Watches* (1939). *The Rude Potato* (1941). *Poem* (1943). *The Bridge: Poems 1939–1944* (1945). *On Cats* (1947). *Urania* (1951). *The Ermine: Poems 1942–1952* (1953). *Still By Choice* (1966). *Poems 1926–1966* (1968; in the U. S. as *Collected Poems*). *End of Drought* (1975). *A Heaven to Find* (1987). *Collected Poems,* intro. E. Jennings (1996).

BIBLIOGRAPHY: Gilbert, R. *Four Living Poets* (1944). *Poetry Northwest* (special P. issue, winter 1960). *Ruth Pitter: Homage to a Poet,* ed. A. Russell (1969). Watkin, E. I. *Poets and Mystics* (1953).

For articles in reference works, see: *Bloomsbury. CA. CP. DLB. EWLTC. Feminist. Oxford. TCW. ToddBWW. TWA* and *SUP.*

Other references: Bogan, L. *Poetry* (1937). Kunitz, S. *A Kind of Order, a Kind of Folly: Essays and Conversations* (1975). Munson, G. B. *Commonweal* (1929). Scott-James, R. A. *Fifty Years of English Literature: 1900–1950* (1951). Shahani, R. G. *Poetry* (1942). Swartz, R. T. *Poetry* (1940). Wain, J. *Listener* (1969).

Paul Schlueter

Mary Pix

BORN: 1666, Nettlebed, Oxfordshire.
DIED: 1709, London (?).
DAUGHTER OF: Roger Griffith and Lucy Berriman Griffith.
MARRIED: George Pix, 1684.

Daughter of an Oxfordshire vicar, P. married a London merchant tailor at the age of eighteen; her only child died in 1690. In 1696, at the age of thirty, she became a professional writer, producing in that one year a tragedy, *Ihrahim,* which, according to a contemporary, made audiences weep; a successful comedy, *The Spanish Wives;* and a romantic novel, *The Inhumane Cardinal,* in which a cardinal disguises himself in order to seduce a young girl.

Her initial success, coupled with her association with two other new women playwrights, Delariviere Manley and Catherine Trotter, caused her to be satirized in an anonymous play, *The Female Wits* (1696), in which P. appears as Mrs. Wellfed—"a fat Female Author," a tippler, unlearned but amiable and unpretentious. In 1697–98, P. was involved in a plagiarism dispute with George Powell, an actor and sometimes playwright for the United Company at Drury Lane, who copied her play *The Deceiver Deceived* (1697) in his *The Imposture Defeated.* William Congreve and Thomas Betterton of the Lincoln's Inn Fields playhouse were partisans of P. Except for these two occasions, her public and personal life was inconspicuous.

A professional playwright of modest abilities and moderate success, P. wrote twelve plays—six comedies and six tragedies. Her tragedies, which continued the Fletcherian tradition, are undistinguished, written in inflated prose printed as blank verse. Her one overt attempt at stage reform, *The False Friend* (1699), was a muddle of melodrama and moralizing. Her tragedies point forward in the increasing prominence of the heroines and of fatal accidents to love; their popularity probably rested on her knack for alternating scenes of rant with melting love scenes in which a mighty hero languished at his lady's feet.

P.'s best works are her comedies, especially *The Spanish Wives* (1696) and *The Adventures in Madrid* (1706). *The Spanish Wives* is a lively, amusing farce skillfully double-plotted to contrast the situations of two young wives. The lady of the old governor of Barcelona is given unusual liberty by her husband; touched by this goodness, she resists the advances of a young English colonel. Elenora, kept locked up by a jealous and avaricious husband, escapes to marry her former fiancé. Music, song, dance, and disguise proved stage spectacle. In *The Adventures in Madrid,* two English gentlemen intrigue with and eventually marry two Spanish ladies in spite of the complications provided by the villainies of the supposed husband of one of the ladies.

P.'s comedies contain lively intrigues, much stage business, many surprises, and some pleasant songs. Her encomium of the English merchant in *The Beau Defeated* (1700) suggests Lillo and the bourgeois drama of the next generation. Forced or unhappy marriages appear frequently and prominently in the comedies. P. is not, however, writing polemics against the forced marriage but using it as a plot device and sentimentalizing the unhappily married person, who is sometimes rescued and married more satisfactorily. Occasionally, the unhappy wife or husband seems erring but is really virtuous. P.'s use of sentimentalized characters in intrigue comedies, while causing oddities of plotting, reflects the changing theatrical taste that called for less emphasis on cuckolding and more on virtuous love. P.'s attempt to write a mixture of hard and soft comedy is characteristic of playwrights under pressure for stage reform at the turn of the eighteenth century.

WORKS: *Ihrahim* (1696). *The Spanish Wives* (1696). *The Inhumane Cardinal* (1696). *The Innocent Mistress* (1697). *The Deceiver Deceived* (1697; reissued as *The French Beau,* 1696). *Queen Catherine* (1698). *The False Friend* (1699). *The Beau Defeated* (1700). *The Double Distress* (1701). *The Czar of Muscovy* (1701). *The Different Widows* (1703). *Violenta* (1704). *The Conquest of Spain* (1705). *The Adventures in Madrid* (1706). *Plays,* ed. E. Steeves (1982).

BIBLIOGRAPHY: Clark, C. *Three Augustan Women Playwrights* (1986). Cotton, N. *Women Playwrights in England c. 1363–1750* (1980). *The Female Wits, ed. L. Hook* (1967). Messenger, A. *Gender at Work* (1990). Morgan, F. *The Female Wits* (1988). *Curtain Calls: British and American Women and the Theatre, 1660–1820* ed. M. A. Schofield and C. Macheski (1991).

For articles in reference works, see: *Bloomsbury. Feminist. ToddBWW. ToddDBA.*

Other references: *ECLife* (1988). *MLN* (1933). *N&Q* (1994). *RECTR* (May 1976). *RES* (July 1930). *WS* (1980).

Nancy Cotton
(updated by Claudia Thomas Kairoff)

Sylvia Plath

BORN: 27 October 1932, Boston, United States.
DIED: 11 February 1963, London.
DAUGHTER OF: Otto Plath and Aurelia Schober Plath.
MARRIED: Ted Hughes, 1956.

Although P.'s poetry has gone in and out of vogue in literary circles, P. will best be remembered for the notorious relationship between her life and her art. P. sought to distance herself from the personal nature of her subject matter by assuming a sharply ironic and detached tone in her poetry. Yet P.'s reputation is that of a confessional poet, in part because Robert Lowell, in his introduction to *Ariel* (1966), observed, "Everything in these poems is personal, confessional, felt." Aficionados and critics of P. alike have long contended, even if occasionally in oversimplified terms, that the dark subject matter of P.'s work and the autobiographical accounts of her depression, suicide attempt, and eventually her accomplished suicide have contributed to a cult of both her personality and her poetry that often clouds objective analysis of her work.

Born on 27 October 1932 to the German immigrant scientist Otto Plath and his wife, P. grew up in the Great Depression and under a cloud of racism fueled by a widespread belief that Germany was responsible for World War I. In spite of a fairly placid childhood, the combination of her father's ethnicity, his death from diabetes when P. was eight years old, and the specter of World War II contributed to the immortalizing of her father in the sardonic poem "Daddy" (1962) as "A man in black with a Meinkampf look / And a love of the rack and screw."

P. began her foray into poetry at an early age, publishing poems in the *Christian Science Monitor* and *Seventeen* magazine. P.'s journals during her years at Smith College (1950–54) reflect a growing concern with feminist issues such as the education of women and the tension between career and family. A number of P.'s early poems, reprinted in *The Collected Poems* (1981) in an appendix of juvenilia, reflect these concerns about the role of women in society.

After P. returned from a student internship at *Mademoiselle* magazine during the summer of 1953, she suffered a nervous breakdown. Later, she attempted suicide but failed. P.'s journals reflect her insecurity: "I will have to be cheerful and constructive. I will learn about shopping and cooking." Her sense of failure and its subsequent depression landed P. in a psychiatric hospital. Her experience with electroshock treatment is chronicled in "The Hanging Man" (1960).

After graduating and being awarded a Fulbright scholarship, P. began graduate study at Cambridge University and tried continuously to publish her writing. Although it appeared in *Harper's* and various British magazines and periodicals, P. was devastated by rejections; one submission "was rejected . . . this morning with not so much as a pencil scratch on the black-and-white doom of the printed page rejection." Also at Cambridge, in the winter of 1956, P. met Ted Hughes, the young British poet she would marry later that year.

In the summer of 1957, P. and Hughes left England for the United States where her first manuscript of poems began to take shape. Psychotherapy in Boston helped her to become introspective, and a therapeutic visit to her father's grave produced "Electra of Azalea Path" (1959), a poem filled with insight and self-revelation: "Small as a doll in my dress of innocence / I lay dreaming your epic, image by image."

In the early summer of 1959, P. and Hughes were invited to the Yaddo artists' colony in Upstate New York, where Hughes suggested that P. abandon the manuscript that was troubling her and work on a second book of poems. This began a period of great productivity. After leaving Yaddo late in 1959, P., Hughes, and their newborn daughter, Frieda, returned to England and settled in London. Early in 1960, P. signed a much-coveted contract with Heinemann for a volume of poems, *The Colossus* (1960), the majority of which includes poems written for her first volume of poems while the remainder were written at Yaddo. After the volume was published, P. suffered a miscarriage, underwent an appendectomy, and suffered from anxiety about her and Hughes's finances. As a result, her depression returned, but with it a desire to write, and she signed a contract for *The Bell Jar* (1971), a fictionalized account of the period surrounding her attempted suicide. The novel received mixed reviews, but because of its status as autobiography, it has received great attention.

Following the birth of her second child, Nicholas, in 1962, P. began a prolific writing period. The poems from this period can be divided into three stages: (1) the beekeeping poems, a chronicle of the dissolution of P.'s and Hughes' marriage; (2) "Daddy" and "Lady Lazarus" (1962); and (3) those poems written after October 1962, when P. and Hughes had separated.

Following the bee sequence, P. returned to the black humor and sardonic wit that informs her body of poetry. In "Daddy," "Medusa," "Cut," "Ariel," "Nick and the Candlestick," and "Lady Lazarus" (all from 1962), P. hit a poetic stride. In "Daddy," perhaps her most famous poem, P. turns to her childhood, embellishes it with imaginary reminiscences, and creates a dark but witty revenge poem: "Daddy, I have had to kill you." A poem rich in both metaphor and alliteration—"I have always been scared of *you*, / With your Luftwaffe, your gobbledygoo. / And your neat mustache / And your Aryan eye, bright blue. / Panzer-man, panzer-man, O You"—P. compels the reader's attention to each sound, each image. The October poems, in a continuum of the "Daddy" and "Lady Lazarus" period, represent an exploration into the darkest and deepest recesses of P.'s mind.

The circumstances of P.'s last months have been much discussed: the crumbling of her marriage, the bitter winter in London, the illnesses she and her children suffered, her literal and figurative sense of isolation (P. had no telephone), and her suicide. While much of her work has been read as a long suicide note, P.'s work functions independently from autobiography as an eclectic and exceptional body of work.

WORKS: *The Colossus* (1962). *Ariel* (1966). *The Bell Jar* (1971). *Crossing the Water* (1971). *Winter Trees* (1972). *Letters Home by Sylvia Plath: Correspondence, 1950–1963,* ed. A. S. Plath (1975). *The Bed Book* (1976). *Johnny Panic and the Bible of Dreams: Short Stories, Prose, and Diary Excerpts* (1980). *Collected Poems,* ed. T. Hughes (1981). *The Journals of Sylvia Plath,* ed. F. McCullough and T. Hughes (1982). *The It-Doesn't-Matter-Suit* (1996).

BIBLIOGRAPHY: *Ariel Ascending: Writings About Sylvia Plath,* ed. P. Alexander (1985). Bassett, S. *Sylvia Plath* (1987). *Sylvia Plath,* ed. H. Bloom (1989). Broe, M. L. *Protean Poetic: The Poetry of Sylvia Plath* (1980). *Sylvia Plath: A Bibliography,* ed. G. Lane and M. Stevens (1978). *Sylvia Plath: New Views on the Poetry,* ed. G. Lane (1979). Malcolm, J. *The Silent Woman: Sylvia Plath and Ted Hughes* (1994). Meyering, S. L. *Sylvia Plath: A Reference Guide, 1973–1988* (1990). Rose, J. *The Haunting of Sylvia Plath* (1993). Saldivar, T. *Sylvia Plath: Confessing the Fictive Self* (1992). Stevenson, A.

Bitter Fame: A Life of Sylvia Plath (1989). *Sylvia Plath: An Analytical Bibliography,* ed. S. Tabor (1987). *Sylvia Plath: The Critical Heritage,* ed. L. Wagner (1988). Wagner-Martin, L. *Sylvia Plath: A Biography* (1987).

For articles in reference works, see: *Bloomsbury. CA. Cambridge. CLC. CP. DLB. Feminist. Longman. MAL. Oxford. WWTCL.*

Lisa Altomari

Pollack, Mary: See *Blyton, Enid*

Elizabeth Polwhele

FLOURISHED: probably mid-seventeenth century.
WROTE UNDER: Mrs. E. P.

P.'s name has been known to scholars since the seventeenth century, but, until the 1970s, nothing else was known of this young woman dramatist. Her name, usually followed by a query (e.g. "Is anything known regarding the authoress?"), appeared in sale catalogues, in reference books known primarily to theater historians, and once in a nineteenth-century citation in *Notes and Queries* (2nd ser., 7, 1859: 279–80). We are particularly fortunate, then, in having recently located the play to which all these references belong, because the date and some of the details appended to the manuscript version suggests that P. may indeed have been one of the first women to write for the professional stage in England.

The play is a lively romantic comedy entitled *The Frolicks, or the Lawyer Cheated* (1671). It was found, in manuscript, in the Rare and Manuscript Collections of Cornell University when a Cornell librarian, Donald D. Eddy, was moving some books in the basement of the library in the spring of 1974. Research in the library files confirmed that it had been part of a 1919 bequest from the book collector Benno Loewy. From the front matter of the manuscript, we learn that its author was a woman, as the manuscript is described as "the 'first Coppy' written by Mrs. E. P.," who in the dedication further describes herself as "an unfortunate young woman . . . haunted with poetic devils." Nevertheless, a reading of the play quickly establishes that however "young" and "haunted" Mrs. E. P. might have been, she clearly was no amateur. The play is a sophisticated and amusing romp through London life, led by its heroine, a thoroughly modern protagonist, whose wit and skillful repartée makes her more than a match for her male antagonists, including her lover, father, and admirers.

The front matter of that manuscript also supplies us with more data from which we can make some reasonable biographical inferences. Among the things we learn is that P. was the author of at least two other plays, one of which turns out to be the heretofore anonymous tragedy, *The Faithful Virgins,* which exists in manuscript in the Bodleian Library at Oxford (MS. Rawl. Poet. 195, ff. 49–78). The other play, titled *Elysium,* has not been located. It may well have been a religious masque. The variety of dramatic genres represented by P.'s three plays implies the versatility of this playwright. Furthermore, the dedication, directed to Prince Rupert, an aristocrat related to the reigning Stuart kings, suggests the kind of social circle with which P. might have been associated. That Prince Rupert was also a close friend of Thomas Killigrew, director of one of the two leading theatrical companies, and had as his mistress Margaret Hughes, the most distinctive seventeenth-century actress, implies that P. was calculating in her choice of dedicatee. The phrasing of her dedication, accentuating her youth and inexperience, might have been more artful than accurate.

P.'s earlier play, *The Faithful Virgins,* does not imply the dramatic expertise that her later comedy so vividly exemplifies. Instead, it is a rather tedious tragedy, taxed with too many undifferentiated characters and somewhat lacking in plot. Nevertheless, there is specific evidence that this play was indeed produced. The Bodleian's copy was most probably used as a prompt copy since it includes reference to which lines are to be cut or words to be altered, in accordance with the license permitting its production; on folio 49r is written: "This Tragedy apoynted to be acted by the dukes Company of Actors only leaving out what was Cross'd by Henry Herbertt M:R [i.e. Master of the Revels]." If *The Faithful Virgins* was indeed staged, as seems most likely from that evidence, then that staging is further verification of P.'s distinction as one of the first women professional dramatists.

If *The Faithful Virgins* is disappointing to read today, *The Frolicks,* by contrast, is strikingly modern both in its fast-paced scene shifting and in the creation of its main character, Clarabell. Her lively mind and her witty putdowns of her male comrades make her a distinguished ancestor, indeed a kind of seventeenth-century Katharine Hepburn, for the vivid young heroines of today's romantic comedies. The settings against which those skills are so deftly displayed include some of the first depictions of the night-life of London; P. even seems to be mocking some of the century-old conventions of romantic comedy in her staging of cross-dressing scenes, which pit Clarabell in male dress, jauntily triumphant, against some of her male admirers in female dress, clumsy and confused. In creating her heroine and designing the appropriate settings and actions (the "frolicks" of the title) for her, P. seems to have been revelling in the fact that, for the first time, female actresses were performing the parts of women on the London stage.

Delighted by the pleasures afforded by reading this play, scholars and theater historians have begun to sift the theatrical records of Restoration London to locate more biographical information on "Mrs. E. P." In spite of the tantalizing gaps in our knowledge of P., however, we can nonetheless be grateful to her, the woman who initiated the genre of London low comedy—exuberant, realistic, bawdy, and thoroughly entertaining.

WORKS: *The Faithful Virgins* (1660s?). *Elysium* (date unknown). *The Frolicks, or The Lawyer Cheated* (1671).
BIBLIOGRAPHY: *The Frolicks or The Lawyer Cheated,* ed. J. Milhous and R. D. Hume (1977).

Other references: Halliwell-Phillipps, J. O. *A Dictionary of Old English Plays* (1860). Harbage, A. and S. Schoenbaum, *Annals of English Drama 975–1700* (1964). Hazlitt, W. C. *A Manual for the Collector and Amateur of Old English Plays* (1892; rpt. 1966). *N&Q* (1859).

Nicoll, A. *A History of English Drama 1660–1900* (1959). Summers, M. *The Playhouse of Pepys* (1964).

Ann Hurley

Elizabeth Poole

BORN: before 1640.
DIED: after 1668.
DAUGHTER OF: possibly Robert Poole.

Exact dates are not known for P., but it would appear that she was a seamstress by trade and a prophet by calling. She was an active prophet during the late 1640s, publishing three tracts addressed to the army.

Her first published prophecy, *A Vision Wherein Is Manifested the Disease and Cure of the Kingdom* (1648), was delivered to the General Council of the Army. It purports to show not only what ails the country but also the cure for these problems. P. supports the army in its arrest of King Charles I, but she also reminds them of their responsibilities now that the "kingly power has fallen into [their] hands." P.'s support of Oliver Cromwell at this time gave rise to Royalist speculations that he had arranged P.'s appearance. A later pamphlet, *The English Devil: or, Cromwell and his Monstrous Witch* (1660), articulates this theory.

Although P.'s first prophecy was well received by the General Council of the Army, P.'s next utterance, *An Alarum of War Given to the Army* (1649), was highly critical of the army's action of executing King Charles. She denounces the regicides, likening them to "strumpets" who rejoice at the fall of the "husband." Shortly after her condemnation of the army's action, she was expelled from her church, the Particular Baptists, whose minister, William Kiffen, was a friend of Cromwell's.

WORKS: *A Vision: Wherein is Manifested the Disease and Cure of the Kingdome* (1648). *An Alarum of War Given to the Army* (1649). *A Prophecie Touching the Death of King Charles* (1649).

BIBLIOGRAPHY: Crawford, P. *Women and Religion in England 1500–1720* (1993). George, M. *Women in the First Capitalist Society: Experiences in Seventeenth-Century England* (1988). Hobby, E. *Virtue of Necessity: English Women's Writing 1640–88* (1988). Mack, P. *Visionary Women: Ecstatic Prophecy in Seventeenth-Century England* (1992).

For articles in reference works, see: *Bell. Feminist. WL17C.*

Other references: *FSt* (1982).

Jane Baston

Anna Maria Porter

BORN: 1780, Durham.
DIED: 21 September 1832, Bristol.
DAUGHTER OF: William Porter and Jane Blenkinsop Porter.
WROTE UNDER: A Young Lady Eighteen Years of Age; Anna Maria Porter; Miss A. M. Porter; Miss Anna Porter.

P. was the younger sister of two artists. Jane Porter, also a novelist, collaborated with P. on two works, *Tales Round a Winter Hearth* (1826) and *Coming Out and the Field of Forty Footsteps* (1828). Sir Robert Ker Porter, her brother, was a painter who designed the frontispiece of P.'s first published work, *Artless Tales* (1793). P. had a friendship with a third artist, Sir Walter Scott. Both writers of historical romances, they likely influenced each other's art.

A traditional writer without feminist interests, P. preferred male protagonists who suffer because of a deceitful woman before finding happiness with a selfless, beautiful woman. This plot is evident in three of her most popular novels, *Walsh Colville* (1797), *The Hungarian Brothers* (1807), and *Don Sebastian* (1809).

Walsh Colville is an early example of a *Bildungsroman*, as are *The Hungarian Brothers* and *Don Sebastian*. After leaving home, the title character of this romance, Walsh Colville, must learn to tell the difference between the duplicity and genuine affection of the men and women he encounters. The portrayal of the protagonist as a naïve, earnest young man is effective, but the reformation of his deceitful friend Stanhope is unconvincing. Moreover, P.'s narrative style is uneven, alternating between well-delineated and hastily described scenes.

The Hungarian Brothers, a historical romance, concerns two brothers who overcome poverty, war, unworthy women, and deceitful men until they at last marry the women they love. While the novel lacks vivid sensory detail and the plot is clumsily handled at times, the contrast between the two brothers is effective. Charles, the older brother, is the prudent, brave soldier, while Demetrius is delicate and thoughtless. It is the younger brother who reflects the moral stated in the novel's introduction: "to shew youth the destructive tendency of uncontrolled passions."

Don Sebastian or the House of Braganza, a romantic tale of palace intrigue, has two plots: Don Sebastian's efforts to regain the throne of Portugal and his adventures in love. Excessive pathos, anti–Roman Catholic sentiment, and repetitive episodes make this work unappealing to modern readers.

Plot and characterization are well executed in *Ballad Romances and Other Poems* (1811), although the language is unimaginative and trite. Two of the better poems, like P.'s novels, depict the duplicity of women. In "Eugene," a woman, after losing the man she loves to her sister, secretly murders her nephew. In "The Knight of Malta," a woman's lie leads the hero to kill his own brother.

A novelist, poet, and writer of short fiction, P. is best remembered today for making an early contribution to sentimental romances.

WORKS: *Artless Tales* (1793). *Original Poems on Various Subjects* (1789). *Walsh Colville, or a Young Man's First Entrance into Life* (1797). *Octavia* (1798). *Airs, Duets, Choruses, Etc.* (1803). *The Fair Fugitives* (1803). *The Lake of Killarney* (1804). *A Sailor's Friendship and a Soldier's Love* (1805). *The Hungarian Brothers* (1807). *Don Sebastian or the House of Braganza* (1809). *Bal-*

lad Romances and Other Poems (1811). *The Recluse of Norway* (1814). *Tales of Pity on Fishing, Shooting and Hunting* (1814). *The Knight of St. John* (1817). *The Fast of St. Magdalen* (1818). *The Village of Mariendorpt* (1821). *Roche-Blanche* (1822). *Honor O'Hara* (1826). (with J. Porter) *Tales Round a Winter Hearth* (1826). (with J. Porter) *Coming Out and the Field of Forty Footsteps* (1828). *The Barony* (1830).

BIBLIOGRAPHY: Elwood, A. K. *Memoirs of the Literary Ladies of England* (1843). Hall, A. M. *Pilgrimages to English Shrines* (1854). Hall, S. C. *A Book of Memories of Great Men and Women of the Age* (1871). Wilson, M. *These Were Muses* (1924).

For articles in reference works, see: *Allibone. BA19C. DLEL. ELB. Feminist. NCHEL. Oxford. ToddBWW.*

Other references: Ashfield, A. *Romantic Women Poets, 1770–1838: An Anthology* (1995).

Margaret Ann Graham
(updated by Natalie Joy Woodall)

Jane Porter

BORN: 1776, Durham.
DIED: 24 May 1850, Bristol.
DAUGHTER OF: William Porter and Jane Blenkinsop Porter.

Novelist and playwright, daughter of an army officer and sister of Dr. William, Anna Maria, and Sir Robert, P.'s Edinburgh education was enhanced by an avid interest in Scottish myths and legends, many narrated to her by a poor neighbor, Luckie Forbes.

In 1797, P. and Anna Maria assisted Thomas Frognall Dibdin in the publication of *The Quiz,* a short-lived periodical. Following its failure, the family moved to a London residence formerly owned by Sir Joshua Reynolds, where, it is believed, P. wrote her early biographical fiction. The first romance, *Thaddeus of Warsaw* (1803), was considered a product of her youthful exuberance and natural sympathy for the influx of Polish citizens seeking refuge. An equally vital source of inspiration was her brother Robert's description of a personal meeting with the Polish hero, Thaddeus Kosciuszko, during the general's visit to England. P. wrote that her first heroic tale was "founded on the actual scenes of Kosciuszko's suffering and moulded out of his virtues," though she masks her protagonist as a young descendant of John Sobieski. Many other characters are thinly disguised versions of various friends and family members. Acclaimed as a "work of genius" and later recognized as "the best and most enduring" of P.'s fiction, the novel achieved wide acceptance and was published in several translations.

The ninth edition of *Thaddeus of Warsaw* and the initial printing of *The Scottish Chiefs* occurred in 1810. The latter publication, a five-volume work, is based on the life of the Scottish patriot, William Wallace. This heroic romance incorporates the childhood legends P. loved as well as an old poem by Henry the Minstrel (Blind Harry) and bits of information on Wallace's life received from Campbell the Poet, who also supplied a list of recommended references. Wallace's career as an outlaw began when he killed an Englishman who had insulted him. As his band of brigands increased in number, they engaged the British army several times, notably at Stirling Bridge, and almost succeeded in liberating Scotland until a reinforced troop of British soldiers overpowered Wallace's men at Falkirk. Although he escaped capture, he was eventually arrested, tried, and executed as a traitor, but his death provided inspiration for the country's next hero, Robert Bruce, who successfully achieved Wallace's dream of independence. P.'s interpretation of this much-loved legend found instant favor with her readers, and its fame rivaled the predecessor, with numerous translations printed throughout Europe and in India. *The Scottish Chiefs* was dubiously "honored" by Napoleon who attempted to have its translation banned in France. It is considered one of the few historical novels printed prior to Sir Walter Scott's *Waverly* to have survived and has had several reprints.

After writing a three-volume novel dealing with the Stuart clan, *The Pastor's Fireside* (1815), P. wrote several plays. One, *Egwont: or the Eve of St. Alyne,* sent to Edmund Kean, famed Shakespearean tragedian, was denied production by his fellow actors, and it was never published. *Switzerland* (1819) and *Owen: Prince of Powys* (1822) were eventually presented at Drury Lane but considered "lamentable failures."

King George IV suggested the subject of her next novel, *Duke Christian of Lüneburg* (1824), which she dedicated to the monarch. Her final publication, *Sir Edward Seaward's Narrative of His Shipwreck and Consequent Discovery of Certain Islands in the Caribbean Sea* (1831), harbors the mystery of its origin. Purported to have developed from an actual diary account and edited by P., it was described by the *Quarterly* as a well-written work of fiction. P. insisted that the account was genuine and had been given to her by the writer's family, yet an inscription in Bristol Cathedral, supposedly placed there by P., cites her brother William as the actual author.

P., a strikingly good looking woman, received many honors and invitations, especially for her first two works. She was made a Lady of the Chapter of St. Joachim and given the gold cross of the order from Württemberg. In 1844, an organization composed of American authors, publishers, and booksellers sent a rosewood armchair "as an expression of admiration and respect," but these gifts did not alleviate the family's financial difficulties, a fact that she repeatedly noted in her unpublished diaries.

P. seriously regarded her literary skill as a "religious duty" and painfully extracted each word. She often envied her sister, Anna Maria, who had a facility for free expression and a more relaxed approach. P. insisted that the major changes in the English novel originated with her works, rather than with the creations of Sir Walter Scott—ironically, a childhood playmate—as her reputation was in its zenith long before his first novel reached publication. P. defended her ability to unite "the personages and facts of real history or biography with a combining and illustrative machinery of the imagination," although later critics deplored her manipulation of various events in order to secure the novel's development.

The public, however, is the final critic, and its delight in P.'s enthusiastic exaggerations cannot be denied. Scottish children, normally denied the reading of romantic stories, were encouraged to enjoy her tales, and P.'s unique blends of legend, myth, and reality remain landmark contributions to the art of fiction.

WORKS: *The Spirit of the Elbe* (1799). *A Defence of the Profession of an Actor* (1800). *The Two Princes of Persia, Addressed to Youth* (1801). *Thaddeus of Warsaw* (1803). *Sketch of the Campaign of Count A. Suwarrow Ryminski* (1804). *The Scottish Chiefs* (1810). *The Pastor's Fireside* (1815). *Switzerland* (1819). *Owen: Prince of Powys* (1822). *Duke Christian of Lüneburg* (1824). (with A. M. Porter) *Tales Round a Winter Hearth* (1826). (with A. M. Porter) *Coming Out and the Field of the Forty Footsteps* (1828). *Sir Edward Seaward's Narrative of His Shipwreck and Consequent Discovery of Certain Islands in the Caribbean Sea* (1831). *Young Hearts* (1834).

BIBLIOGRAPHY: Elwood, A. K. *Memoirs of the Literary Ladies of England* (1843). Hall, A. M. *Pilgrimages to English Shrines* (1854). Hall, S. C. *A Book of Memories of Great Men and Women of the Age* (1871). Hook, A. D. *Clio* (1976). Hume, R. D. *PMLA* (1969). Maclise, D. *The Maclise Portrait Gallery* (1873). Rogers, W. H. *PMLA* (1934). Vaughn, H. M. *From Anne to Victoria* (1967). Wagenknecht, E. *Cavalcade of the English Novel* (1954). Wilson, M. *These Were Muses* (1924).

For articles in reference works, see: *BA19C. Cambridge. Chambers. DNB. Feminist. Oxford. ToddBWW.*

Other references: *Scottish Review* (April 1897).

Zelda R. B. Provenzano

Porter, Miss A. M.: See *Porter, Anna Maria*

Porter, Miss Anna: See *Porter, Anna Maria*

Beatrix Potter

BORN: 28 July 1866, Bolton Gardens, Kensington.
DIED: 22 December 1943, Sawrey, Lancashire.
DAUGHTER OF: Rupert Potter and Helen Leech Potter.
MARRIED: William Heelis, 1913.

Born into a family whose fortune was already well established, P. led a carefully guarded childhood. Unlike her younger brother Bertram, P. was not sent to school and had virtually no friends. At an early age, P. showed a talent for illustration and was encouraged by her governess to practice her artwork. P. found subject material first at local museums and later in nature when her family took extensive summer vacations in Scotland and the Lake District.

P.'s attachment to nature was by no means sentimental; she often dissected dead animals when she found them and had a keen eye for ecological and biological detail. Her illustrations in W.P.K. Findlay's *Wayside and Woodland Fungi* (1967) are the work of a skilled and knowledgeable naturalist. P. maintained a tie with nature even in the austere home of her parents by keeping a small menagerie. Most notable among her pets, which included mice, bats, frogs, and snails, were two of her rabbits, Peter Rabbit and Benjamin Bunny, and her hedgehog, Mrs. Tiggy-Winkle.

In 1893, the son of one of P.'s former governesses took ill. To amuse the boy during his recovery, P. sent him illustrated letters that traced the adventures of her pets. The letters circulated among friends, and P. was encouraged to prepare the story of Peter Rabbit as a book. Failing to find a publisher, P. had *The Tale of Peter Rabbit* printed privately in 1900. A second private printing followed in 1902, and a private edition of *The Tailor of Gloucester* appeared in 1903. By this time, the firm of Frederick Warne & Co. offered to publish *Peter Rabbit* if P. would do color illustrations. The success of *Peter Rabbit* established P. as an important children's writer, and with each successive work, usually in the same miniature format as the first, her reputation and popularity grew.

The association between P. and Warne & Co. was a long and happy one that lasted over the publication of twenty-four of her books. P. was particularly close to Norman Warne, who worked in his father's firm. In 1905, Norman proposed and P., in spite of her parents' strenuous objections, accepted. Unfortunately, Warne died shortly after their engagement was announced. During this period, P. bought Hill Top, a farm near the village of Sawrey, using both the earnings from her books and a small legacy. Still under the rule of her parents, P. leased the farm, under generous terms, to a tenant farmer and visited it only occasionally. The legal concerns of her property brought P. into contact with William Heelis, a local solicitor, whom she married in 1913.

Although some books did appear after her marriage, P.'s career as a writer was essentially over. She immersed herself in the concerns of her farm and was respected enough to be elected president of the Herdwick Sheep-Breeders' Association shortly before her death. As Mrs. Heelis, P. shunned fame, and though she referred to accolades of her work as "great rubbish," there is no question of her stature or the extent of her influence in children's literature.

P.'s stories have a simplicity that is complemented by a sense of realism and of humor. Her characters, who live in a world that can be both comforting and threatening, learn to appreciate the former by experiencing the latter. The impact of her stories is consistently emphasized by the deft accuracy and subtle playfulness of her artwork.

WORKS: *The Tale of Peter Rabbit* (1902). *The Tale of Squirrel Nutkin* (1903). *The Tailor of Gloucester* (1903). *The Tale of Benjamin Bunny* (1904). *The Tale of Two Bad Mice* (1904). *The Tale of Mrs. Tiggy-Winkle* (1905). *The Pie and the Patty-pan* (1905). *The Tale of Mr. Jeremy Fisher* (1906). *The Story of a Fierce Bad Rabbit* (1906). *The Story of Miss Moppet* (1906). *The Tale of Tom Kitten* (1907). *The Tale of Jemima Puddle-Duck* (1908). *The Roly-Poly Pudding* (1908; later *The Tale of Samuel Whiskers,* 1926). *The Tale of the Flopsy Bunnies* (1909). *Ginger and Pickles* (1909). *The Tale of Mrs. Tittlemouse* (1910). *Peter Rabbit's Painting Book* (1911). *The Tale of Timmy Tiptoes* (1911). *The Tale of Mr. Tod* (1912). *The Tale of Pigling Bland* (1913). *Tom Kitten's Painting Book* (1917). *Appley Dapply's Nursery Rhymes* (1917).

The Tale of Johnny Town-Mouse (1918). *Cecily Parsley's Nursery Rhymes* (1922). *Jemima Puddle-Duck's Painting Book* (1925). *Peter Rabbit's Almanac for 1929* (1928). *The Fairy Caravan* (1929). *The Tale of Little Pig Robinson* (1930). *Sister Anne* (1932). *Wag-by-Wall* (1944). *The Tale of the Faithful Dove* (1956). *The Journal of Beatrix Potter, 1881–1887* (transcribed from her code writings by L. Linder; ed. H. L. Cox, 1966; new foreword by J. Taylor, 1990). *Wayside and Woodland Fungi* (illustrations only, 1967). *Letters to Children*, ed. J. Taylor (1992).

BIBLIOGRAPHY: Anderson, C. *Proceedings of the 7th Annual Conference of Children's Literature* (1980). Crouch, M. *Beatrix Potter* (1960). Davies, H. and C. Pemberton-Pigott. *Beatrix Potter's Lakeland* (1989). Foote, T. *Smithsonian* (1989). Greene, G. *Collected Essays* (1951). Grinstein, A. *The Remarkable Beatrix Potter* (1995). Hobbs, A. S. *Beatrix Potter's Art* (1990). Lane, M. *The Tale of Beatrix Potter* (1946). Lane, M. *The Magic Years of Beatrix Potter* (1978). Linder, L. *A History of the Writings of Beatrix Potter* (1971). MacAdam, B. *ARTnews* (Oct. 1988). Nesbitt, E. A. *Critical History of Children's Literature* (1953). Scott, C. *ChildL.* (1994). Sicroff, S. *ChildL* (1973). Taylor, J. *Beatrix Potter: Artist, Story-Teller, and Countrywoman* (1986). Whalley, J. I. *Natural History* (May 1988).

For articles in reference works, see: *CLR*. *DNB*. *YA*.

Other references: *IFR* (1977). Hamer, D. *N&Q* (1969). *Horn-Book* (1941, 1944, 1977, 1978). *LonSunT* (16 February 1997). Nere, C. *Country Life* (1972). Sicroff, S. *ChildL* (1973).

Alan Rauch

Poyntz, Albany: See Gore, Catherine Grace Frances Moody

Adelaide Anne Procter

BORN: 30 October 1825, London.
DIED: 2 February 1864, London.
DAUGHTER OF: Bryan Waller Procter and Anne Benson Skepper.
WROTE UNDER: Mary Berwick; Adelaide Anne Procter.

As the eldest child of Bryan Waller Procter (the poet "Barry Cornwall"), P. grew up in the company of William Wordsworth, Charles Lamb, William Hazlitt, C. K. D. Patmore, and other Romantic writers. Charles Dickens and William Makepeace Thackeray were among her regular correspondents. She published her first poem, "Ministering Angels," in *Heath's Book of Beauty* for 1843 when she was eighteen years old. In 1853, she sent Dickens a few poems under the pseudonym "Mary Berwick" so he would not be biased by knowing the identity of their author; her identity was revealed in December 1854. Dickens published them in *Household Words*, which he edited from 1850 to 1859, and P.'s career as a poet was launched. Her poetry continued to appear in *Household Words*, as well as in *All the Year Round*, the *Cornhill Magazine*, and *Good Word*; Anne Lohrli claims that a sixth of all the contributions to *Household Words* were by P. Before she died of tuberculosis at the age of thirty-nine, P. became Queen Victoria's favorite poet, at one time outselling all living poets except Alfred Lord Tennyson. In addition, she was very active in feminist social causes of the day, including employment for women and housing and education for the poor.

P. was educated at home, became fluent in French, Italian, and German, and excelled in mathematics as well as the usual requisites of a "lady's" education, playing the piano and drawing. In 1851, P., along with her two sisters, converted to Roman Catholicism; cathedrals, convents, angels, and Mary figure prominently in her poetry. In 1853, she visited her Catholic aunt, Emily de Viry, at the Turin court and became interested in legends of medieval Europe, seeing in the old stories metaphors for modern life. Her poetry collection, *Legends and Lyrics* (first series, 1858; second series, 1861), contained many fine poems of this kind, including "A Legend of Provence" addressing the dilemmas of fallen women; "A Legend of Bregenz," a tale of female heroism reminiscent of both Lady Godiva and Paul Revere; and "A Tomb in Ghent," a poem about exile, artistic expression, and sexual feeling. P.'s best known poem was "A Lost Chord," on the theme of idealistic striving after artistic and spiritual harmony; it compares with Robert Browning's "Abt Vogler." Several of P.'s poems became popular hymns or parlor songs, including "A Lost Chord," which was set to music by Sir Arthur Sullivan.

In addition to the legends and lyrics for which these volumes were named, P. also included numerous poems portraying modern life, many on feminist themes. "Philip and Mildred," for example, criticizes the doctrine of separate spheres for men and women, the inadequacy of women's education, the Victorian custom of long engagements made necessary by women's financial dependency, and the enervating idleness of middle-class women. The speakers of "A Warning" and "A Parting" are quite cynical about heterosexual love. "Three Evenings in a Life" cautions women against depending upon men for security, affection, self-respect, or meaningful work. P. never married, though she was reputed to have had several disappointing love affairs. Instead, she joined the Langham Place circle of women, some of whom formed intimate alliances with each other in preference over heterosexual marriage.

Legends and Lyrics was dedicated to one such woman, Matilda Hays, a feminist novelist and editor, the translator of George Sand, and the devoted companion of the actress Charlotte Cushman and, later, of the American sculptor Harriet Hosmer. With Bessie Rayner Parkes (later Belloc), Hays edited the *English Woman's Journal*, established in 1858 as a venue for promoting feminist causes. P. became the journal's most prominent poet and joined Hays, Parkes, and other women, including Barbara Bodichon (later Smith), Jessie Boucherett, and Emily Faithfull in agitating for expanded employment and educational opportunities for women. She also belonged, along with Jean Ingelow and Christina Rossetti, to the Portfolio Club, established by Bodichon and Parkes as a forum for women to share their poetry and art.

When Faithfull established the Victoria Press to provide printing jobs for women, P. edited an elegant miscellany to showcase the press, *Victoria Regia* (1861), which included poems and stories by Tennyson, Thackeray, Patmore, Matthew Arnold, George MacDonald, Caroline Norton, Harriet Martineau, Anna Jameson, James Russell Lowell, and many other prominent writers. This volume was dedicated (with special permission) to the queen; the profits benefited the Society for Promoting the Industrial Employment of Women, which the Langham Place women established and administered. P. donated the proceeds from her last volume of poetry, *A Chaplet of Verses* (1862), to a Roman Catholic charity, the Providence Row Night Refuge for Homeless Women and Children. This volume included "Homeless," "A Beggar," "The Homeless Poor," and other poems designed to secure public attention and sympathy for the predicament of indigent women and children.

P.'s struggle with consumption became desperate in 1862; she went to Malvern to try the cure but returned to her mother's home where, after being confined to bed for fifteen months, she died. She was buried at Kensal Green Cemetery. Dickens took a continuing interest in P. He was pleased to discover that "Mary Berwick" was his friend's daughter rather than the impoverished governess he had been imagining; when she died, he prefaced her collected poems with a sentimental tribute. But P. was an active feminist and a strong poet, not the fragile and modest saint of Dickens's characterization.

WORKS: *Legends and Lyrics*, 2 vols. (1858–61; with additions and intro., C. Dickens, 1866; with more additions, 1895). *A Chaplet of Verses* (1862, 1868). *Poetical Works* (1880). *Legends and Lyrics together with A Chaplet of Verses*, intro., C. Dickens (1905, 1914). *Selected Poems* (1911).

BIBLIOGRAPHY: Dickens, C. *Atlantic* (1865; repub. as preface to *Legends and Lyrics*, 1866). Faithfull, E., preface to *Victoria Regia* (1861). Hickok, K. *Representations of Women: Nineteenth Century British Women's Poetry* (1984). Fields, J. T. *Yesterdays with Authors* (1888). Kemble, F. *Records of a Girlhood* (1879). Kemble, F. *Records of a Later* Life (1882). *Victorian Women Poets: An Anthology*, ed. A. Leighton and M. Reynolds (1995). Lohrli, A. *Household Words: A Weekly Journal 1850–1859* (1973). Maison, M. *Listener* (29 April 1965).

For articles in reference works, see: *Allibone. BA19C. Catholic Encyclopedia. DLB. DNB. EP. Europa. Feminist.* Julian, J. *Dictionary of Hymnology* (1892). *NCBEL. Oxford. PPC.* Rogal, S. J. *Sisters of Sacred Song* (1981). *ToddBWW. VB.*

Other references: Armstrong, I. *Victorian Poetry: Poetry, Poetics and Politics* (1993). Belloc, B. R. (Parkes) *In a Walled Garden* (1895). Benson, E. F. *As We Were: A Victorian Peep Show* (1985). Leighton, A., in *New Feminist Discourse: Critical Essays on Theories and Texts*, ed. I. Armstrong (1992). Mermin, D. *Godiva's Ride: Women of Letters in England, 1830–1880* (1993).

Kathleen Hickok and Natalie Joy Woodall

Prowse, Anne: See Locke, Anne Vaughan

Barbara Pym

BORN: 2 June 1913, Oswestry, Shropshire.
DIED: 11 January 1980, Oxford.
DAUGHTER OF: Frederic Crampton Pym and Irena Thomas Pym.

After receiving her B.A. with honors in English Literature from St. Hilda's College, Oxford, P. served with the Women's Royal Naval Service in England and Italy from 1943 to 1946. She then began her long career working for the International African Institute where she became assistant editor of its journal, *Africa*, while writing novels in her spare time.

Her first six novels, published between 1950 and 1961, achieved critical recognition and a small but loyal following. These books established P. as the chronicler of a world small in scope but wide in relevance, the world of spinsters dedicated to the church and to more or less worthless curates; the world of small office workers, librarians, anthropologists, the Church of England clergy; and persons on the outskirts of academic life. This world of little people, especially women, leading quiet lives of compromise, resignation, and acceptance is recorded with compassion, irony, dry wit, an evocative attention to details, and an absolute absence of sentimentality.

Incredibly, P. could not find a publisher after 1961, although she continued to write fiction, seeing it increasingly as a personal and private exercise. Despite great fortitude, though, she began to question the value of her early work. In 1974, she retired from her editorial position and went to live with her sister in an Oxfordshire village.

In February 1977, responding to an invitation from the *Times Literary Supplement* to a number of literary figures to name the most underrated and overrated writers of the century, Lord David Cecil and Philip Larkin both named P. as underrated, suddenly catapulting her to fame and international publication after sixteen years of oblivion. Her frequently rejected novel, *Quartet in Autumn* (1977), a small ironic masterpiece on the theme of aging, was bought by Macmillan, while Jonathan Cape reissued all her out-of-print books. *The Sweet Dove Died* followed (in 1978), and *A Few Green Leaves* was published posthumously in 1980, after P.'s death from cancer.

A reserved person who described her avocations as "reading, domestic life and cats," P. was also a traditionalist in feeling that what mattered most to her in life were the Church of England and the English poetic tradition. Nonetheless, and despite a calm, conventional, though highly crafted, style, P.'s art is radical in that she insists on telling the truth about women's lives, albeit with gentle skepticism and satire. Typical is this comment in *Less Than Angels* (1955): "It would be a reciprocal relationship—the woman giving the food and shelter and doing some typing for him and the man giving the priceless gift of himself."

Her themes are consistent throughout her books: the (often unmet) need for an appropriate and responsive recipient of one's love; the necessity for humorous acceptance of a confining existence; and the pathos of lives being lived without affection or any other aesthetic framework to dignify, amplify, and explain their significance. These themes have made her work of interest to a growing number of feminist scholars; P.'s work has been the subject of almost a dozen dissertations and as many journal articles in recent years, primarily focusing on issues of gender. Her life, too, is attracting a great deal of scholarly attention.

WORKS: *Some Tame Gazelle* (1950). *Excellent Women* (1952). *Jane and Prudence* (1953). *Less Than Angels* (1955). *A Glass of Blessings* (1959). *No Fond Return of Love* (1961). *Quartet in Autumn* (1977). *The Sweet Dove Died* (1978). *A Few Green Leaves* (1980). *A Very Private Eye: An Autobiography in Diaries and Letters* (1985). *An Academic Question* (1986). *Civil to Strangers and Other Writings,* ed. H. Holt (1987). *An Omnibus* (1995). *À La Pym: The Barbara Pym Cookery Book,* ed. H. Pym and H. Wyatt (1995).

BIBLIOGRAPHY: Ackley, K. *The Novels of Barbara Pym* (1989). *Joinings and Disjoinings: The Significance of Marital Status in Literature,* ed. K. Ackley (1991). Allen, J. *Barbara Pym: Writing a Life* (1994). Brothers, B. and B. Bowers. *Reading and Writing Women's Lives: A Study in the Novel of Manners* (1990). Burkhart, C. *The Pleasure of Miss Pym* (1987). Cooley, M. *The Comic Art of Barbara Pym* (1990). *Old Maids to Radical Spinsters: Unmarried Women in the Twentieth Century Novel,* ed. L. Doan (1991). Holt, H. *A Lot to Ask: A Life of Barbara Pym* (1990). Little, J. *The Experimental Self* (1996). Long, R. E. *Barbara Pym* (1986). Rossen, J. *The World of Barbara Pym* (1987). Rossen, J. *Independent Women: The Function of Gender in the Novels of Barbara Pym* (1988). *The Life and Work of Barbara Pym,* ed. D. Salwak (1987). Sochen, J. *Women's Comic Visions* (1991). Weld, A. *Barbara Pym and the Novel of Manners* (1992). Wyatt-Brown, A. *Barbara Pym: A Critical Biography* (1992).

For articles in reference works, see: *Bloomsbury. CA. Cambridge. DLB. Feminist. Oxford. ToddBWW.*

Other references: Cooley, M. *TCL* (1986). Dobie, A. *ArQ* (1988). *Encounter* (May 1987). Fisichelli, G. *PLL* (1988). Gordon, J. *ELWIU* (1989). Griffin, B. *ELWIU* (1992). Kane, P. *SDR* (1986). Kaufman, A. *TCL* (1986). Kennard, J. *ConL* (1993). Little, J. *VWM* (1992). Macheski, C. *Barbara Pym Newsletter* (1988). Rubenstein, J. *MFS* (1986). Sadler, L. *WVUPP* (1986). Sadler, L. *BPN* (1988). Whitney, C. *ELWIU* (1989).

Carey Kaplan
(updated by Christina Root)

Quaker Authoress, The: See *Leadbeater, Mary*

Q. Q. See *Taylor, Ann and Jane*

Ann Ward Radcliffe

BORN: 9 July 1764, London.
DIED: 7 February 1823, London.
DAUGHTER OF: William Ward and Ann Oates Ward.
MARRIED: William Radcliffe, 1787.

The mysteries and ironies of R.'s life are somehow appropriate for the woman who perfected the Gothic suspense tale. Arguably the most popular writer of her time, she lived a reclusive life and stopped writing for publication altogether when her mother's will made her financially comfortable. Her best novels are set in a romanticized Italian landscape, but she never traveled to Italy. Although contemporaries and writers of the next generation told jokes at her expense, they also imitated her. She bequeathed more to the Romantic imagination in terms of sensibility and vocabulary than the Romantics would ever admit. By all accounts, she lived as a dutiful wife, daughter, and niece; her novels, however, are powerful explorations of female fantasy. In many of her tales, apparently supernatural events arouse suspense and terror, which are alleviated when the explanation is found to be purely natural; her own mind tended toward melancholy and outright depression, and perhaps even to madness near the end of her life.

R.'s family included famous physicians and scholars, but her father was a haberdasher, salesman, and businessman. She often visited her uncle, Thomas Bentley, who knew many eminent poets, scientists, and travelers. In her obituary, her husband wrote that these visits to her uncle were a major influence on her imagination. Otherwise, her education was standard. When living in Bath, R. may have been a student of Sophia Lee, who ran a school for "young ladies" there. If R. did not meet Lee, she certainly read and was deeply influenced by Lee's novel *The Recess,* which had marked a departure from the standard domestic sentimental novel. There is an interest in madness, passion, and mystery in the psychology of the romantic sensibility. What was new about Lee's novel was its freedom from the constraints of "realism," which in most cases meant the depiction of house, home, and duty expected in women's fiction. Female characters could now be placed in wild and unpredictable circumstances, and the depiction of their perils and emotions could be freer. Thus, fantasy of a powerful kind was given a new latitude. These developments, along with an interest in the dark and the macabre (R. frequently reread *Macbeth*), left its mark on R.'s subsequent literary work.

In 1787, R. married William Radcliffe, a law student turned journalist, who encouraged her to write and critiqued her work. Her novels were almost immediately popular, and by *The Romance of the Forest* (1791) she was a well-known literary figure. R. achieved true fame with *The Mysteries of Udolpho* (1794), a book that earned her the nickname "The Great Enchantress."

R.'s novels have been considered in several ways. Earlier critics, wishing to get around R. as quickly as possible, either dismissed her work as trash or praised it faintly as the precedent for much better novels, such as *Jane Eyre* and *Wuthering Heights.* Lately, however, critics have begun to attribute a great deal of importance to R. Her novels can be seen as the first perfection of an enduringly popular genre (witness the vogue for romance novels). R. also wrote the first novels whose main aim was to elicit emotions of terror, horror, and suspense. These later critics have recognized her as a writer whose main theme was female fantasy—specifically, the fantasy in which the virtuous and beleaguered heroine triumphs over insurmountable difficulties to achieve her own happiness and vindicate the essential goodness of the divine order.

Clearly, R. was a writer with a formula. John Keats was responding to R.'s depiction of nature when he lampooned her as a writer who will "cavern you and grotto you, and waterfall you and wood you, and immense-rock you." R. concocted a mixture of medieval and contemporary romance that brought ruined castles, houses with secret passageways, cryptic messages that explain everything, and dark, half-understood portents in nature into fiction; she also resurrected the apparatus of Renaissance romance, including the low-born heroine who discovers that she is nobly born, woods lushly responsive to the excesses of the heroine's emotions (as is the case with Adeline of *The Romance of the Forest*), and the reunion of deserving lovers after eventful separation. There is also a cast of characters that has become too familiar: a lonely maiden, an older authoritarian male figure who sooner or later becomes an out-and-out villain, a loyal servant, and a virtuous hero.

Yet R. deserves to be remembered for more than these clichés. Her writing reveals a genuine interest in the extremes of human psychology. She is acutely sensitive to the aspects of life that make us anxious and afraid. And there is a moral purpose to the excitation of terror in the reader, for terror is a test of reason, an index of the extent to which the reader trusts herself and her world. As mentioned above, the point of most of her novels is that all terror has a natural explanation. Her heroines are heroines because they triumph over great difficulties to discover this; her villains are villains because, like La Motte of *The Romance of the Forest,* they often know the secret and try to prevent the heroine from discovering it. These villains often enjoy tormenting the unknowing heroine over their half-understood world. The extent of their evil is revealed at the end, when the heroine understands that world more clearly and has a more complete control over her life. Thus La Motte keeps the true origin of Adeline's birth from her, and Montoni of *The Mysteries of Udolpho* tries to wheedle his dead wife's money out of her daughter Emily. Emily triumphs over Montoni and Adeline triumphs over La Motte because of self-reliance and inner strength.

One need not belabor the patterns that emerge so clearly from these novels—male figures denying female figures essential information and essential power, revelations that change the place of woman in the world. When in *Udolpho* the veil is lifted from over the mysterious picture, the key to it all, Emily faints; it is as if she, allowed to see the real truth, must escape somehow from its impact. Most important, R.'s heroines do it themselves: In the end they act to change their worlds and break free of the dark, often unconscious fetters of fear.

Part of all the fantasy is the undeniably attractive nature of some of the villains. Some readers have been quick to find Electra complexes throughout R.'s fiction. More to the point, her villains are brooding, isolated, full of a mysterious inner conflict. R. refined and refined this character until she perfected it in Father Schedoni of *The Italian* (1797). He has been recognized as the prototype of the aloof, preoccupied Romantic hero, a proto-Manfred: "there was something in [Schedoni's] air, something almost superhuman." Though Ellena triumphs over Schedoni in the end and marries the virtuous Vivaldi, it is Schedoni's character that remains the most striking element in a very striking novel.

The Italian was the last of R.'s novels to be published during her lifetime. A year later, her father died and her husband fell ill. In March 1800, her mother died, leaving R. alone, despondent, "the last leaf on the tree." Although she wrote one more novel, *Gaston de Blondeville* (1826), she had lost the desire to publish, possibly even to be read. According to her husband's obituary, she died in a delirium.

R. is a writer who has had a remarkable and enduring impact on fiction both serious and popular. Of her works, *The Romance of the Forest* and *The Italian* hold up the best. They are still enjoyable for their suspense and attractive for their substance. Though she wrote very little about her personal life, one imagines that she would have appreciated readers who could see the moral intent of all the wildness, the twists of plot, the romance, and the fantasy. She virtually discovered a form of myth that, however it may embarrass or distress us, is still very powerful.

Beginning in the 1980s, there was an astonishing explosion of scholarship about R., in parallel with an explosion in feminism and poststructuralism. Because R. explored the female subconscious, her concerns were those of many students of literature. This surge of interest derives also from the long-delayed realization that R. was a pivotal figure in literary history, exerting a quiet influence on Jane Austen, the Romantics (Samuel Taylor Coleridge once called *Udolpho* "the most interesting novel in the English language"), Charles Dickens, and many later novelists. At various times, various people have claimed her as one of the founders of many modern genres, including the suspense tale, the horror story, the romantic novel, the detective novel, even science fiction. Far from being a writer only of her own time, R. seems to have bequeathed to posterity a particular way of seeing life and making it into a story.

WORKS: *The Castles of Athlin and Dubayne* (1789). *A Sicilian Romance* (1790). *The Romance of the Forest* (1791). *The Mysteries of Udolpho* (1794). *A Journey made in the Summer of 1794 through Holland and the Western Frontiers of Germany, with a return down the Rhine, to which are added Observations during a tour to the Lakes of Lancashire, Westmoreland and Cumberland* (1795). *The Italian, or the Confessional of the Black Penitents* (1797). *Gaston de Blondeville, or the Court of Henry III Keeping Festival in Ardenne* (1826). *St. Alban's Abbey* (1826). *Posthumous Works* (1833). *Poetical Works* (1834).

BIBLIOGRAPHY: English, S. W. *The Hunger of Imagination* (1978). Frank, F. S. *Extrapolation* (1975). *Gothic Fictions: Prohibition/Transgression,* ed. K. W. Graham (1989). Grant, A. *Ann Radcliffe* (1920). *Listening to Silences: New Essays in Feminist Criticism,* ed. E. Hedges and S. F. Fishkin (1994). McIntyre, C. F. *Ann Radcliffe in Relation to Her Time* (1920). Murray, E. B. *Ann Radcliffe* (1972). Ware, M. *Sublimity in the Novels of Ann Radcliffe* (1963). Weiten, A. S. S. *Mrs. Radcliffe, Her Relation Towards Romanticism* (1926).

For articles in reference works, see: *Annual Biography and Obituary for 1824. Bloomsbury. Cambridge. Feminist. Oxford. ToddBWW. ToddDBA.*

Other references: Abdoulatief, S., in *Inter Action,* ed. L. Nas and L. Marx (1994). Adams, D. K. *Detection* (1972). Adickes, S. *The Social Quest* (1991). Allen, M. L. *ES* (1966). Anderson, H., in *The English Hero, 1660–1800,* ed. R. Folkenflik (1982). Bachelor, R. *ECF* (1994). Beatty, F. L. *PQ* (1963). Benedict, B. M. *PQ* (1989). Berglund, B. *LSE* (1993). Bernstein, S. *ELWIU* (1991). Blair, D., in *Reading the Victorian Novel: Detail into Form,* ed. I. Gregor (1980). Broadwell, E. P. *South Atlantic Bulletin* (1975). Bruce, D. W. *ContempR* (1991). Butler, M. *W&L* (1980). Castle, T., in *The New Eighteenth Century: Theory, Politics, English Literature,* ed. F. Nussbaum and L. Brown (1987). Christensen, M. *WC* (1971). Conger, S. M. *Gothic* (1987). Derry, S. *Persuasions* (1992). Durant, D. *ECent* (1981). Durant, D. *SEL* (1982). Ellison, J. A. *Mallorn* (1991). Epstein, L. *University of Hartford Studies in Literature* (1969). Fawcett, M. *SEL* (1983). Fitzgerald, L. *WC* (1993). Flaxman, R. L., in *Fetter'd or Free? British Women Novelists, 1670–1815,* ed. M. A. Schofield and C. Macheski (1986). Gamer, M. *WC* (1993). Garrett, J. *Sphinx* (1978). Greenfield, S. *ECent* (1992). Hagstrum, J., in *Centennial Studies,* ed. P. Korshin and R. Allen (1984). Haupt, A., in *Inter Action,* ed. L. Nas and L. Marx (1994). Hennelly, M. M., Jr. *StHum* (1987). Holland, N. N. and L. F. Sherman, in *Gender and Reading,* ed. E. Flynn and P. Schweikart (1986). Kahane, C. *CentR* (1980). Kahane, C., in *The (M)other Tongue: Essays in Feminist Psychoanalytic Interpretation,* ed. S. N. Garner, et al. (1985). Kelly, G. *ArielE* (1979). Kostelnick, C. *Mosaic* (1985). Krely, R. *The Romantic Novel in English* (1972). Leranbaum, M. *APS Proceedings* (1977). Lewis, P. *CLAJ* (1980). London, A. *ECLife* (1986). Macdonald, D. L. *JNT* (1989). Mellor, A., in *The Columbia History of the British Novel,* ed. J. Richetti, et al. (1994). Michasiw, K. I *ECF* (1994). Morrison, P. *TSLL* (1991). Murrah, C. *University of Windsor Review* (1984). Nicholas, N., in *The Female Gothic,* ed. J. E. Fleenor (1983). Nollen, E. *ELN* (1984). Novak, M. E., in *Probability, Time, and Space in the Eighteenth-Century Novel,* ed. P. Backscheider (1979). Poovey, M. *Criticism* (1979). Price, F. W. *N&Q* (1976). Rogers, D. *Extrapolation* (1991). Ronad, A., in *The Female Gothic,* ed. J. Fleenor (1983). Roper, D. *N&Q* (1972). Ruff, W., in *The Age of Johnson: Essays Presented to C. B. Tinker,* ed. F. W. Hilles (1949). Schmitt, C. *ELH* (1994). Scott, W., intro. to *The Novels of Ann Radcliffe* (1824). Sedgwick, E. K. *PMLA* (1981). Smith, N. C. *SEL* (1973). Snyder, W. C. *WS* (1992). Spacks, P. M., in *Rhetorics of Order/Ordering Rhetorics in English Neoclassical Literature,* ed. J. W. Canfield and J. P. Hunter (1989). Spencer, J. *The Rise of the Woman Novelist* (1986). Swigart, F. H., Jr. *StHum* (1969). Tamkin, L. E. *Heroines in Italy* (1985). Taylor, M. *ESC* (1991). Thomas, D. *ES* (1964). Thomson, J. *AUMLA* (1981). Todd, J. *W&L* (1982). Tomkins, J. M. S. *The Popular Novel in England: 1770–1800* (1932). Varma, D. P. *The Gothic Flame* (1957). Ware, M., in *A Provision of Human Nature,* ed. D. Kay (1977). Williams, A. *SEC* (1992). Winter, K., in *Misogyny in Literature,* ed. K. Ackley (1992). Wolff, C. G. *MLS* (1979). Wright, E. P. *Discourse* (1970).

John Timpane

Mary Ann[e] Radcliffe

BORN: 1745 or 1746, Scotland.
DIED: after 1810, Edinburgh, Scotland.
MARRIED: Joseph Radcliffe, 1760.

R. was not the author of the Gothic classic, *The Mysteries of Udolpho,* though some Gothic novels were attributed to her and she may have written in this genre. R. was in fact known as "the other Mrs. Radcliffe," as one critic called her, and she is best remembered for *Memoirs* (which tell us what is known of her life) and for a feminist document that deserves to be better known, *The Female Advocate* (1799).

She meant to publish her "Attempt to Recover the Rights of Women from Male Usurpation" (*The Female Advocate*'s subtitle) anonymously, but her publisher overruled her, probably wishing to capitalize on the similarity of her name with that of Ann Radcliffe, the famous Gothic novelist. This fairly standard marketing practice has led to some uncertainty about R.'s actual literary output. R. has also frequently been identified as another Mary Anne Radcliffe (fl. 1790–1809), also a Gothic novelist, who is sometimes credited with authorship of *The Female Advocate* in addition to several other high Gothic novels for the Minerva Press list. Very little is known about this "Mrs. Radcliffe," and it is unclear whether the two Mary Ann(e)s are one and the same or even whether the novelist is in fact the author of other works attributed to her. In 1802, the Minerva Press credited her with writing the epistolary *The Fate of Velina de Guidova* (1790); in 1814, it credited her (or the other Radcliffe) with *Radzivil* (1790), but this book's original Russian author (a "celebrated M. Wocklow"), its translator, and the translation's reviser were all said to be male. In 1809, J. F. Hughes published a Gothic novel titled *Manfrone; or, the One-Handed Monk* (1809) and attributed it to R. Hughes also published *The Mysterious Baron,* initially as by "Eliza Radcliffe," and in 1808 changed the attribution to "Mary Ann Radcliffe." R. offers no direct claim to writing Gothic fiction in her final work, *Memoirs of Mrs. Mary Ann Radcliffe: in Familiar Letters to her Female Friend* (1810), and, in fact, states explicitly that she always resisted "soaring into the airy regions of fiction." R. was also listed as the author of two numbers of *Radclife's* [sic] *New Novelist's Pocket Magazine* (1802), but she may not have written these or the novel *The Secret Oath* (also from 1802).

Only child of a thirty-year-old Roman Catholic mother and a seventy-year-old Anglican father, R. was to rue the day on which, at the age of fifteen, she ran off to London to marry the thirty-five-year old Joseph Radcliffe. She had stood to inherit a sizeable fortune, but due to her minority it was withheld. Shortly after her marriage, she realized that her husband, though kindly, was an ineffectual provider, and she was forced to find work in order to support their growing family (eight children in all).

Though she managed to send her sons to school, her life seems to have been an unrelieved struggle against penury. R. undertook many different jobs, none of which brought in much money; she ran a coffeehouse, took in lodgers, and kept a shop. She finally separated permanently from her husband after 1781, when she found work as governess to the children of a friend, Mary, Countess of Traquair, in Scotland. It was at the countess's home that she met Alexander Geddes (1737–1802), controversial Roman Catholic theologian, political liberal, and biblical scholar whose writings greatly influenced her.

Her husband's financial neglect led R. in 1792 to write *The Female Advocate,* a discourse on the inhumane economic conditions that led women into prostitution. R. criticizes the male-dominated market economy that has set the "grievous precedent of men usurping females' occupations" in such trades as millinery, sewing, and shopkeeping. Because of this "usurpation," women's only recourse for survival became prostitution. R.'s thesis, radical for its time, points out the constriction that women's roles suffered as a result of the Industrial Revolution. Moreover, she is one of the earliest social critics to theorize the connection between the personal and the political: "That political and private happiness are invariably connected, is beyond doubt," she writes.

The *Memoirs,* published by subscription, includes eleven "familiar letters to a female friend" and *The Female Advocate.* It is more intimate than the earlier work, but its feminist spirit, born out of painful personal experience, is the same. R. warns against hasty marriages, dating the start of her own troubles to her elopement. After years of financial and emotional struggle, housebound with rheumatism, her inheritance long since depleted, R. died in Edinburgh. Her life and works offer a valuable insight into the consequences of the Industrial Revolution for middle-class women who, deprived of their husbands' financial help, were forced into a restricted job market to earn a living. And though she attempted to distance herself from the "Amazon" Mary Wollstonecraft, R.'s writings contributed to the burgeoning feminist awareness of the 1790s.

WORKS: *The Female Advocate; or, An Attempt to Recover the Rights of Women from Male Usurpation* (1799; ed. G. Luria, 1974). *Memoirs of Mrs. Mary Ann Radcliffe: in Familiar Letters to her Female Friend* (1810). Possible attributions: *The Fate of Velina de Guidova* (1790). *Radzivil* (1790). *Radclife's* [sic] *New Novelist's Pocket Magazine* (2 issues, 1802). *Manfrone; or the One-Handed Monk* (1809). MSS. are preserved in Bar Convent (York), the Royal Literary Fund (London), the British Library, the Scottish Catholic Archives (Edinburgh); see also the Countess of Traquair's diary, Peebles House (Peebles).

BIBLIOGRAPHY: Adams, D. K., *Mystery and Detection Annual* (1962). Blakey, D. *The Minerva Press, 1700–1820* (1939). Evans, B. *Gothic Drama from Walpole to Shelley* (1947). *First Feminists: British Women Writers, 1578–1799,* ed. M. Ferguson (1985). Frederick, F. S. *The First Gothics: A Critical Guide to the English Gothic Novel* (1987). Fuller, R. C. *Alexander Geddes, 1737–1802: Pioneer of Biblical Criticism* (1984). Howells, C. A. *Love, Mystery, and Misery: Feeling in Gothic Fiction* (1978). Kloesel, C.J.W. *English Novel Explication. Supplement III* (1986). Mayo, R. D. *The English Gothic Novel in Magazines (1740–1815)* (1962). Rogers, K. *Feminism in Eighteenth-Century England* (1982). Summers, M. *A Gothic Bibliography* (1964). Spender, D. *Mothers of the Novel: 100 Good Women Writers Before Jane Austen* (1986).

For articles in reference works, see: *Feminist.* Grundy, I., *DNB: Missing Persons* (1993). *Oxford. ToddBWW. ToddDBA.*

Leonard R. N. Ashley and Samantha Webb

Raimond, C. E.: See *Robins, Elizabeth*

Kathleen Raine

BORN: 14 June 1908, Ilford, Essex.
DAUGHTER OF: George Raine and Jessie Raine.
MARRIED: Hugh Sykes Davies; Charles Madge.

R. has won many awards for her poetry and criticism, in particular for her many books on William Blake. Daughter of two London school teachers, R. received an M.A. in natural sciences from Girton College, Cambridge University, in 1929, and was briefly married to two Cambridge professors. R., along with her second husband and William Empson, were part of a group of Cambridge poets in the 1930s, though the group was less well known than a comparable group at Oxford University that included W. H. Auden, Stephen Spender, C. Day Lewis, and Louis MacNeice. R. has been a research fellow at Girton College; a lecturer at Morley College, London; and Andrew Mellon Lecturer at the National Gallery of Art, Washington, D.C., in the United States.

R.'s earliest verse was warmly praised for her precise observations of nature, which resulted at least in part from her scientific studies; all of her poetry is distinguished by her lucid, introspective awareness of the physical universe as this affects human life, by a use of diction that is sometimes archaic and intentionally unembellished, and by a persistent meditative attitude. She has self-consciously chosen to use the term "symbolic language" traditionally used by the British Romantic poets for her own work, and her neo-Platonic concern with such universal themes as birth and death, nature and eternity, distinguish her work from that of most other modern poets. In the introduction to her *Collected Poems* (1956), she said that "the ever-recurring forms of nature mirror eternal reality; the never-recurring productions of human history reflect only fallen man and are, therefore, not suitable to become a symbolic vocabulary for the kind of poetry I have attempted to write."

Her emphasis on the natural world's transcendence over mere human concerns has led to many volumes of what she calls "soul-poetry," traditional verse that reflects Platonic reality and objectivity. Unlike many modern poets, she has never emphasized wit or self-conscious confessionalism; rather, her smooth, graceful lyricism and precise diction subordinates what she calls "mere human emotion" to the "Perennial Philosophy" (i.e., to an expression of ancient truths in a modern world). Among the writers with whom she shares the greatest affinities are Blake, Edmund Spenser, Thomas Taylor, and William Butler Yeats.

Her major critical work, *Blake and Tradition* (1962), is an exhaustive analysis of Blake's visionary language and cosmology in which she shows how Blake's symbolic language derives from and is directly in the line of antimaterialistic philosophy dating from Plotinus and Plato. In *Defending Ancient Springs* (1967), R. argues that genuine poets "learn" a symbolic language as a means of grasping "the beautiful order of 'eternity'." Her three-volume autobiography—*Farewell Happy Fields* (1973), *The Land Unknown* (1975), and *The Lion's Mouth* (1978)—is important both for a detailed analysis of her literary theories and for vivid accounts of her rural youth, Cambridge in the 1930s, her marriages and other relationships, and her incessant seeking after transcendent truth, a search that led to a brief conversion to Roman Catholicism.

Both her verse and her criticism thus reflect a visionary attempt to return to the roots of modern experience and thought. Some of her best poems, such as "The Speech of Birds," are especially successful in depicting man's separation from nature. The universal, Jungian symbols and images she uses (as in her dream or meditational poems) are constant reminders of this separation. At her least effective, she relies too heavily on wistful, escapist, and self-consciously mystical experience; at her best she effectively reminds the reader of those poets she considers her masters.

WORKS: *Stone and Flower* (1943). *Living in Time* (1946). *The Pythoness and Other Poems* (1949). *William Blake* (1951; rev. 1965, 1969). *Selected Poems* (1952). *The Year One* (1952). *Coleridge* (1953). *Collected Poems* (1956). *Poetry in Relation to Traditional Wisdom* (1958). *Christmas 1960: An Acrostic* (1960). *Blake and England* (1960). *Blake and Tradition* (1962). *The Hollow Hill and Other Poems* (1965). *The Written Word* (1967). *Defending Ancient Springs* (1967). *Six Dreams and Other Poems* (1969). *Life's a Dream* (1969). *On the Mythological* (1969). *Poetic Symbols as a Vehicle of Tradition* (1970). *William Blake* (1971). *The Lost Country* (1971). *Faces of Day and Night* (1972). *Yeats, The Tarot, and the Golden Dawn* (1972, rev. 1976). *Hopkins, Nature, and Human Nature* (1972). *Farewell Happy Fields* (1973). *On a Deserted Shore* (1973). *Three Poems Written in Ireland* (1973). *Death-in-Life and Life-in-Death* (1974). *David Jones: Solitary Perfectionist* (1974). *A Place, A State* (1974). *The Land Unknown* (1975). *The Inner Journey of the Poet* (1976). *Waste Land, Holy Land* (1976). *Berkeley, Blake, and the New Age* (1977). *Blake and Antiquity* (1977). *The Oval Portrait and Other Poems* (1977). *Fifteen Short Poems* (1978). *From Blake to "A Vision"* (1978). *The Lion's Mouth* (1978). *David Jones and the Actually Loved and Known* (1978). *Blake and the New Age* (1979). *Cecil Collins: Painter of Paradise* (1979). *What is Man?* (1980). *The Oracle in the Heart* (1980). *The Celtic Twilight* (1981). *Collected Poems: 1935–80* (1981). *The Human Face of God: William Blake and The Book of Job* (1982). *The Inner Journey of the Poet and Other Papers* (1982). *The Chaldean Oracles of Zoroaster* (1983). *Blake and the City* (1984). *The Matter of Britain* (1984). *The Lipstick Boys* (1984). *Yeats the Initiate: Essays on Certain Themes in the Writings of W. B. Yeats* (1985). *The Presence: Poems 1984–87* (1987). *Selected Poems* (1988). *To the Sun* (1988). *India Seen Afar* (1989). *Golgonooza, City of Imagination* (1991). *Living with Mystery: Poems 1987–1991* (1992). *On a Deserted Shore: A Sequence* (1995). *For David Gascoyne* (1996). *Philip Sherrard, 1922–1995* (1996). *Lost Illusions* (1997).

BIBLIOGRAPHY: Aubrey, B. *SMy* (1986). Cavaliero, G. *PrS* (1985). Duncan, E. *BookForum* (1981). Duncan, E. *Unless Soul Clap Its Hands: Portraits and Passages* (1984). Grigson, G. *The Contrary View* (1974). Grubb, F. *A Vision of Reality* (1965). MacVean, J. *Agenda* (1988). Mills, R. J., Jr. *Kathleen Raine* (1967). Milne, W. S. *Agenda* (1988). Netterville, H. E. *Kathleen Raine: The Heart in Flower* (1981). Rosemergy, J.M.C. *Kathleen Raine, Poet of Eden: Her Poetry and Criticism* (1982). *Poetry and Prophecy* (*Lindisfarne Letter* #9, 1979, special issue).

For articles in reference works, see: *Bloomsbury. CA. Cambridge. CLC. CP. EWLTC. Feminist. MBL* and *SUP. Oxford. TCW. ToddBWW.*

Other references: *Book Forum* (1981). Disch, T. *TLS* (14 August 1981). *ES* (1961). Olney, J. *New Republic* (18 December 1976). *Poetry* (1952). *Spring 1982: An Annual of Archetypal Psychology and Jungian Thought* (1982). *Texas Studies in English* (1958).

Paul Schlueter

Marie Louise de la Ramée (Ouida)

BORN: 1 January 1839, Bury St. Edmunds, Suffolk.
DIED: 25 January 1908, Viareggio, Italy.
DAUGHTER OF: Louis Ramé and Susan Sutton Ramé.
WROTE UNDER: Ouida.

An only child, R. was left by the long and frequent absences of her French father to be raised almost entirely by her English mother and grandmother. The family liked to believe that the mysterious M. Ramé was involved in opposition politics in his native land and that he died during the days of the Commune in 1871. R.'s fierce pride in her French heritage soon combined with her fantasizing temperament to inflate her surname to de la Ramée.

Her fantasies having long outgrown the narrow provinciality of Bury St. Edmunds, R. welcomed the move to London with her mother and grandmother in 1857. After being introduced to Harrison Ainsworth, then editor of *Bentley's Miscellany*, she began her writing career as "Ouida" (her childhood mispronunciation of "Louise"). She followed up the success of her "Dashwood's Drag; or the Derby and What Came of It," which appeared in *Bentley's* for April and May 1859, with a series of similar tales of high society and sporting life, many collected in *Cecil Castlemaine's Gage, and Other Novelettes* (1867). *Granville de Vigne*, serialized in Ainsworth's *New Monthly Magazine* and reprinted as *Held in Bondage* (1863), typified R.'s early fiction. Its formula of dashing military life, extravagant luxury, tortuous romantic intrigue, and a hero of almost impossible beauty, courage, and style reached its epitome in *Under Two Flags* (1867).

The public attention (and financial rewards) such fiction attracted allowed R. to live out the fantasies otherwise denied by her lack of beauty and social status. Adorned in Worth gowns and surrounded by hothouse flowers, she held court to largely male audiences in the Langham Hotel during the late 1860s; in later years, she frequently dressed to resemble the heroines of her latest novel. Although essentially conventional in her own behavior, she flouted Victorian codes of respectability by encouraging people to smoke throughout dinner and by remaining with the men over brandy and cigars, collecting material for her novels from their conversation. *Tricotrin* (1869) and *Folle-Farine* (1871) added a new element to her fictional formulas: the peasant heroine who becomes tragically enmeshed in the snares of high society, a device she would exploit again in *Two Little Wooden Shoes* (1874).

In 1871, R. traveled to the Continent, producing *A Dog of Flanders and Other Stories* (1872) from her observations of the Belgian peasantry; she also wrote a series of novels set in Italy, among them *Pascarel* (1873), *Signa* (1875), *In a Winter City* (1876), and *Ariadne* (1877). She lived in the Villa Farinola outside Florence from 1874 to 1888. Of the several novels featuring fashionable members of Florentine society, the most notorious was *Friendship* (1878). Its main characters were recognized to represent R., the Marchese della Stufa (a gentleman-in-waiting to the Italian court whom she had pursued with unrequited passion), and Mrs. Janet Duff Gordon Ross, Stufa's avowed mistress. R.'s insistence that the novel was based on absolute truth made its idealization of her own role and its vilification of her rival all the more outrageous.

Her personal disappointments helped turn her attention from the glamor to the failings of polite society. *Moths* (1880), perhaps her most successful work, shows the social fabric being eaten away by the vice and hypocrisy of society's fashionable "moths." She would increasingly lament the upper class's failure to live up to the ideals of taste and breeding she set for them, as well as their surrender to the values of the vulgar and social climbing middle classes she had all her life detested. She sentimentalized the Italian peasantry as victims abandoned by the aristocracy to the tyranny of the bourgeois bureaucracy in *A Village Commune and Other Stories* (1881). *The Massarenes* (1897) most directly condemns the *nouveaux riches* and the "smart" set that collaborated with them.

As the 1880s waned, so, too, did R.'s popularity with an audience turning from three-decker romances to more realistic one-volume works. Her extravagant life-style continually outran her income, leaving unpaid bills and pending law suits behind her as she moved from place to place, her only companions after her mother's death being a faithful servant or two and the pack of spoiled dogs on which she lavished her affection. In her final years only a Civil List pension, awarded in appreciation for her contributions to literature, stood between her and real poverty. During the 1890s, she turned increasingly to criticism and commentary: Many of her analyses of British and European writers and her vendettas against publishers, plagiarists, cruelty to animals, female suffrage, Italian misgovernment, the Boer War, and the rising tide of vulgarity and ugliness brought on by the ascendancy of middle-class money and values were collected in *Views and Opinions* (1895) and *Critical Studies* (1900).

R. owed her considerable success in the 1870s and 1880s in part to her abundant imagination for sensational plotting, vivid detail, and local color, and in part to the expanding market for fiction created by lending libraries and railway bookstalls. Her eccentricity, her egotism, and her flamboyance were always straining against the prosaic and sometimes sordid reality of her life; her wish-fulfilling fictions fed her own and her audience's longing for the glamour, romance, and luxury forever beyond their reach.

WORKS: *Held in Bondage* (1863). *Strathmore* (1865). *Chandos* (1866). *Cecil Castlemaine's Gage, and Other Novelettes* (1867). *Under Two Flags* (1867). *Idalia* (1867). *Tricotrin* (1869). *Pock* (1870). *Folle-Farine* (1871). *A Dog of Flanders and Other Stories* (1872). *Pascarel* (1873). *Two Little Wooden Shoes* (1874). *Signa* (1875). *In a Winter City* (1876). *Ariadne* (1877). *Friendship* (1878). *Moths* (1880). *Pipistrello, and Other Stories* (1880). *A Village Commune and Other Stories* (1881). *Bimbi: Stories for Children* (1882). *In Maremma* (1882). *Wanda* (1883). *Frescoes: Dramatic Sketches* (1883). *Princess Napraxine* (1884). *Othmar* (1885). *A Rainy June* (1885). *Don Guesaldo* (1886). *A House Party* (1887). *Guilderoy* (1889). *Ruffino and Other Stories* (1890). *Syrlin* (1890). *Santa Barbara, and Other Tales* (1891). *The Tower of Taddeo* (1892). *The New Priesthood: A Protest against Vivisection* (1893). *Two Offenders and Other Tales* (1894). *The Silver Christ and A Lemon Tree* (1894). *Toxin* (1895). *Views and Opinions* (1895). *Le Selve, and Other Tales* (1896). *The Massarenes* (1897). *Dogs* (1897). *An Altruist* (1897). *La Strega, and Other Stories* (1899). *The Waters of Edera* (1900). *Critical Studies* (1900). *Street Dust, and Other Stories* (1901). *Helianthus* (1908).

BIBLIOGRAPHY: Beerbohm, M. *More* (1899). Bigland, E. *Ouida the Passionate Victorian* (1950). Elwin, M. *Victorian Wallflowers* (1934). Ffrench, Y. *Ouida: A Study in Ostentation* (1938). Lee, E. *Ouida: A Memoir* (1914). Schroeder, M. *TSWL* (1988). Stirling, M. *The Fine and the Wicked: The Life and Times of Ouida* (1958). Van Vechten, G. *Excavations* (1926). Yates, E. *Celebrities at Home*, 1st series (1877).

For articles in reference works, see: *BA19C*. *Bloomsbury*. *Cassell*. *Chambers*. *DLB*. *DNB*. *Europa*. Hays, F. *Women of the Day* (1885). *IDWB*. *JBA*. *Longman*. Myers, R. *Dictionary of Literature in English from Chaucer to 1940* (n.d.). *OCEL*. *Oxford*. Platt, V. *Men and Women of the Time* (1899). *ToddBWW*.

Other references: *Bulletin of Research in the Humanities* (1978). *LonT* (27 January 1908). *Publishing History* (1978). Street, G. S. *Yellow Book* (1895).

Rosemary Jann

Randall, Ann Frances: See *Robinson, Mary Darby (Perdita)*

Raymond, Henry Augustus: See *Scott, Sarah*

Rayner, Elizabeth: See *Lowndes, Marie Adelaide Belloc*

Redfern, John: See *Pargeter, Edith Mary*

Clara Reeve

BORN: 23 January 1729, Ipswich, Suffolk.
DIED: 3 December 1807, Ipswich, Suffolk.
DAUGHTER OF: William Reeve and Hannah Reeve.
WROTE UNDER: "The editor of *The Phoenix*"; Clara Reeve.

R. led a quiet and retired life; her birth and death took place in the same town where her forebears had long resided. Her mother was the daughter of the goldsmith and jeweler to King George I; her father was a clergyman, as was his father before him. R. was educated by her father (rather than by her mother or a governess), and her reading included parliamentary debates, Rapin-Thoyres' *History of England,* Cato's *Letters,* Plutarch, and Greek and Roman history. This was a more masculine and classical education than most of her female contemporaries would have received.

Not surprisingly, one of R.'s first literary endeavors was a translation from the Latin of John Barclay's romance *Argenis,* published as *The Phoenix* (1772). In 1777, she published semi-anonymously her most famous original work, *The Champion of Virtue,* and its title page identified her only as "the editor of *The Phoenix.*" A second edition appeared in 1778, revised by Mrs. Bridgen, Samuel Richardson's daughter, and renamed *The Old English Baron,* with R. now clearly identified as the author. (Subsequent editions have all borne this title.)

R. wrote five other romances. *The Two Mentors* (1783) and *The School for Widows* (1791) have contemporary settings; *The Exiles, or Memoirs of the Count de Cronstadt* (1788), *Memoirs of Sir Roger de Clarendon* (1793), and *Destination: or, Memoirs of a Private Family* (1799) are set in earlier periods. In addition, R. is known for her literary criticism, *The Progress of Romance* (1785), which, presented in the form of a conversation between fictional characters, comments on ancient and modern romances. In *Plans of Education, with Remarks on the Systems of Other Writers* (1792), R. offers her educational views under the guise of an exchange of letters between friends.

R. is most remembered for her first novel, *The Old English Baron,* however. A composite of three genres, this work blends the marvels of the medieval romance with the credibility of the novel of manners and the emotional appeal of sentimental fiction. R. takes Horace Walpole's *Castle of Otranto* as both her model and her point of departure. In her preface to the second edition, R. calls her work the "literary offspring of the Castle of Otranto," written to unite "the most attractive and interesting circumstances of ancient Romance and modern Novel." At the same time, R. criticizes *Otranto*'s violent supernatural machinery, claiming that the story should have been "kept within the utmost verge of probability." Her work seeks to use the marvelous to arrest the reader's attention and so direct it to some morally useful end.

While contemporary reviews awarded moderate praise to this endeavor, other writers found fault with her compromise between the rational and the supernatural. Walpole found the result an "insipid dull-nothing," and Mrs. Barbauld concurred that the manipulation of the supernatural should have been "more artful, or more singular." The reading public, however, was much taken with this tale of a young man's discovery of his noble origins and the restoration of his title and estates, despite the scheming efforts of envious kinsmen. Between 1778 and 1886, thirteen editions were published; in 1787, the book was translated into French; in 1799, it was dramatized (although never presented); and during this period it inspired several chapbooks as well.

Underlying R.'s works, both her didactic fiction and her fictionlike expository prose, is a profound conservatism. *The Old English Baron* presents a rigidly stratified society in which the hero's obscure but noble birth triumphs inevitably. *Plans of Education,* although published in the same year as Mary Wollstonecraft's *Vindication of the Rights of Women,* advocates an education for women less progressive than R.'s own: "There is no education for daughters equal to that which they receive under the eye of a good mother, who herself gives, or superintends it, according to her degree and station." The education that women receive should emphasize "virtue, modesty, and discretion," instill religious principles, and agree with their "gradations of rank and fortune." Like *The Old English Baron, Plans of Education* reveals a society in which each class must maintain its place in order to ensure the harmonious regulation of the whole.

R.'s ideological conservatism is of interest because it tells us of the historical context in which she wrote, but she is more properly appreciated for her role in the development of the Gothic novel. R. is credited with introducing the conventions of the haunted suite, the portentous dream, and the identifying token of jewelry. In her attempt to curb the supernatural powers that Walpole unleashed in full force, R. is an important precursor of Ann Radcliffe, whose novels of terror effect the consummate compromise between the marvelous and the probable by placing apparently supernatural occurrences within the framework of individual psychology and rational explanation.

WORKS: *Original Poems on Several Occasions* (1769). (trans.) *Argenis* by John Barclay (as *The Phoenix,* 1772). *The Champion of Virtue* (1777; reissued as *The Old English Baron,* 1778). *The Two Mentors* (1783). *The Progress of Romance* (1785). *The Exiles, or Memoirs of the Count de Cronstadt* (1788). *The School for Widows* (1791). *Plans of Education, with Remarks on the Systems of Other Writers* (1792). *Memoirs of Sir Roger de Clarendon* (1793). *Destination: or, Memoirs of a Private Family* (1799).

BIBLIOGRAPHY: Punter, D. *The Literature of Terror: A History of Gothic Fictions from 1765 to the Present Day* (1980). Scott, W., preface to Vol. 5 of *Ballantyne's Novelists' Library* (1823). Summers, M. *The Gothic Quest: A History of the Gothic Novel* (1938). Tompkins, J.M.S. *The Popular Novel in England 1770–1800* (1932). Trainer, J. *Introduction to The Old English Baron* (1967). Varma, D. *The Gothic Flame* (1957).

For articles in reference works, see: *BAB1800. Bloomsbury. Cambridge. Feminist. Oxford. ToddBWW. ToddDBA.*

Eileen Finan
(updated by Lisa Altomari)

Reid Banks, Lynne: See *Banks, Lynne Reid*

Reiner, Max: See *Caldwell, (Janet) Taylor*

Mary Renault (pseudonym of Eileen Mary Challans)

BORN: 4 September 1905, London.
DIED: 15 December 1983, Cape Town, South Africa.
DAUGHTER OF: Frank Challans and Clementine Baxter.

R. was the daughter of an English Puritan descendant and a medical doctor. She received her early education in Bristol; against her parents' wishes, she attended and graduated from St. Hugh's College, Oxford, and later completed nursing training at Radcliffe Infirmary, Oxford. Her youthful unpublished writings were heavily influenced by her interest in mythology and medieval history; she later encountered ancient Greek culture at the Ashmolean Museum in Sir Arthur Evans's replicas of his major discoveries at Knossos, especially the Cretan Bull-leaper. R. turned to nursing to observe human life first-hand since she noted that her earlier writings were purely derived from other people's books. Her first novel, *The Purposes of Love* (1939), published in the United States as *Promise of Love,* was drawn from R.'s hospital nursing experience; even at this early stage of her career, R. dealt ambiguously with homosexuality, proposing a broad potential of sexual relations. Her next three novels, love stories with well-drawn character portrayals, were written off-duty. The last of these, *Return to Night* (1947), described by one critic as "everything Hollywood could possibly want," earned her a prize of $150,000 from MGM in 1947. The story is told from the male doctor's point of view, leading T. Sugrue to comment in the *New York Herald Tribune Book Review* that "the objectivity of which she is so proud is a negation of feminine tenderness." This work established R.'s reputation in the United States.

After her nursing service during World War II, R. moved to Natal, South Africa, and began extensive travels through Italy, France, Greece, and the Aegean. She was most impressed with Greece, the setting for her first historical novel, *The Last of the Wine* (1956), a taut and absorbing narrative. In 1959, *The Charioteer* appeared in the United States, a book that, according to H. Saal in *Saturday Review,* enters "the shadowy world of the homosexual" and whose main character's "untiring delicacy becomes—like a steady diet of English lady writers, tiresome—and the intrusion of some good old-fashioned heterosexual vulgarity welcome." Other critics, however, praised her sensitive delineation of love among men. She also touched upon contemporary issues by introducing conscientious objectors and the subject of pacifism into the novel.

Her 1962 novel, *The Bull from the Sea,* is a sequel, dealing with the death of Theseus. The structure is episodic, held together by the presence of the hero. At this point, critics began to debate whether R. might best be considered a writer of historical novels or historical romances. In spite of her appended "historical notes" and scholarly bibliographies, much of R.'s writing, especially in the dialogues, is pure fiction. A unifying motif of a number of the novels is the sacrificial death of a king. R. makes the mythological personal and humanized through her use of the first-person narrative.

The Persian Boy (1972) received mixed reviews. A panoramic view of the Asian and African conquests of Alexander the Great, the tale is told from the point of view of a castrated Persian slave whose understanding of the historical moment is unbelievable. R. pursued her interest in the conqueror with a biography, *The Nature of Alexander* (1975). In *The Praise Singer* (1978), R. returned to her earlier formula of presenting a story from the point of view of an obscure but historically representative figure, Simonides the Poet, who laments the passing of traditional Greek values in the sixth century B. C. R. ended her Alexander trilogy with *Funeral Games* (1981), a complex story with a preface of forty-five "Principal Persons." An especially vivid character is the Amazonian Eurydice who fails as a "masculine" warrior. The presence of such a figure in R.'s final novel is an interesting one. While the theme of homosexuality is a frequently recurring one in R.'s works, the characters were usually masculine. Indeed, many critics reacted rapidly to these characters—one, Hugh Kenner, referred to R. as "a male impersonator"—in spite of the fact that homosexuality is always dealt with in a delicate, natural fashion throughout her work. Such attacks were perhaps directed at R. personally because of her lifelong relationship with Julie Mullard, a friend she had met during nurses' training. In spite of this kind of criticism, R.'s novels, especially *The Last of the Wine* and *The Mask of Apollo,* continue to enjoy popularity as novels of historical and entertaining value.

WORKS: *The Purposes of Love* (1939; in the U.S as *Promise of Love*). *Kind Are Her Answers* (1940). *The Friendly Young Ladies* (1944; republished as *The Middle Mist,* 1945). *Return to Night* (1947). *North Face* (1948). *The Charioteer* (1953). *The Last of the Wine* (1956). *The King Must Die* (1958). *The Bull from the Sea* (1962). *The Lion in the Gateway* (1964). *The Mask of Apollo* (1966). *Fire from Heaven* (1969). *The Persian Boy* (1972). *The Nature of Alexander* (1975). *The Praise Singer* (1978). *Funeral Games* (1981).

BIBLIOGRAPHY: Burns, L. C. *Crit* (1963). Dick, B. *The Hellenism of Mary Renault* (1972). Miller, D. M. *Arete* (1985). Wolfe, P. *Mary Renault* (1969).

For articles in reference works, see: *Bloomsbury. CA. Cambridge. Feminist. CN. MBL SUP. MCL. Oxford. ToddBWW. WA.*

Other references: *Atlantic* (December 1972). *BW* (6 November 1966, 23 November 1969). *CSM* (17 July 1958, 6 November 1975). *Commonweal* (1 August 1958). *Economist* (4 October 1975). *New Republic* (19 November 1966). *New Yorker* (19 April 1947). *NYHTBR* (20 April 1947, 14 October 1956, 13 July 1958, 18 February 1962). *NYT* (12 March 1939, 20 April 1947, 13 July 1958, 14 December 1983). *NYTBR* (18 February 1962, 30 October 1966, 14 December 1969, 31 December). *Saturday Review* (12 July 1958, 16 May 1959, 17 February 1962, 1 October 1966, 9 December 1972). *SR* (1973). *TLS* (25 February 1939, 29 June 1956, 19 September 1958, 16 March 1962, 15 December 1966, 11 December 1970, 3 November 1972). *VQR* (1973, 1976).

Carole M. Shaffer-Koros

Ruth Rendell

BORN: 17 February 1930, London.
DAUGHTER OF: Arthur Grasemann and Ebba Elise Kruse Grasemann.
MARRIED: Donald John Rendell, 1950; remarried Rendell, 1977.
WRITES UNDER: Ruth Rendell; Barbara Vine.

After completing her formal education at Loughton High School, Loughton, Essex, R. worked as a newspaper reporter and subeditor for the *Essex Express and Independent* from 1948 to 1952. In an interview with Diana Cooper-Clark, R. recounts how she had written a number of novels before her first one was accepted. After finally submitting one—a drawing room comedy—which was rejected, she sent in a detective story that she had written just for fun. This became her first published novel, *From Doon with Death* (1964). R. reports:

> It was quite successful for a first novel, and I was caught up really because of this success with the genre. Having now established for myself a means of livelihood, I was constrained to work within the detective genre and doing so I found that I preferred to deal with the psychological, emotional aspects of human nature rather than the puzzles, forensics, whatever most seem to come within the ambiance of the detective novel.

Since that first novel, R. has written more than thirty novels and collections of short stories under her own name, as well as eight novels and a collection of short stories under the pseudonym of Barbara Vine. Her novels fall into two groups: the Wexford series and the psychological thrillers, sometimes referred to as the non-Wexford novels. She has won several awards for her work, including the Mystery Writers of America Edgar Allan Poe Award in 1974, 1984, and 1986; the Gold Dagger from the Crime Writers' Association for *A Demon in My View* in 1977; the Arts Council of Great Britain book award for a genre novel in 1981; and an Arts Council bursary, also in 1981. She was named a Life Peer in the House of Lords following Tony Blair and the Labour Party's rise to power in 1997.

R.'s publisher refers to her as "The New First Lady of Mystery," and some critics have called her the new Agatha Christie. Although R. maintains that she writes in the classic detective tradition, she dislikes being compared to Christie or to P. D. James, another frequent comparison. In fact, R.'s development of her series character, Detective Chief Inspector Reginald Wexford, is more in the style of Ngaio Marsh's Roderick Alleyn. Inspector Wexford and his assistant Michael Burden are down-to-earth policemen with private lives and families. Both men have family problems that become subplots in many of the detective novels. In the early works there is a certain amount of antagonism between Wexford and the Chief Constable of Kingsmarkham. As a result of this conflict, Wexford sometimes goes off in the wrong direction following unproductive leads. Wexford is not an infallible Hercule Poirot. During the course of the novels, the reader becomes involved with Wexford's coming to terms with the marriage-vs.-career concerns of his two grown daughters and follows Burden's coping with the sudden death of his wife, problems of raising two adolescents on his own, and his own needs as a man. Both characters are drawn into sexual liaisons; Wexford's in *Shake Hands Forever* (1975) is more a suggestion than a reality. David Lehman in a review refers to Wexford as "sane, shrewd, a good family man, a reassuring father figure." In the same review, R. says, "I get letters from women who would like to marry him [Wexford] if his wife ever dies."

R.'s Wexford novels are classic detective stories only in the sense of the Sherlock Holmes and Dr. Watson type of relationship between Wexford and Burden as well as the need to follow a series of clues in order to solve a murder. Otherwise, R., despite her dislike of the comparison, is similar to P. D. James in her development of theme or social comment. In *A Sleeping Life* (1978), Wexford's married daughter Sylvia leaves her husband and brings her small sons home to live. The marital break occurs when Sylvia decides that she needs to be more than cook, housekeeper, and nursemaid, a subplot providing a brief examination of the women's liberation movement. Another timely theme appears in *Some Lie and Some Die* (1973), where the murder takes place during a rock music festival. Wexford's understanding and tolerant handling of a generation quite different from his own provides a subtle balance to Burden's stiff, heavy-handed, and more typical approach.

Family relationships, or relationships in general, could be said to be a theme in all of R.'s work. Arthur, the main character in *A Demon in My View* (1976), is an estranged child. In *Murder Being Once Done* (1972) and *The Best Man to Die* (1969), R. uses Wexford's relationship with his younger daughter Sheila as a contrast to the selfish attitudes of another family. The employee/employer relationship is the focal point of *A Judgement in Stone* (1977). R. says that family relationships are important to her. She comments in the interview with Diana Cooper-Clark: "Relationships in general interest me and I am always watching them and how people react to each other. The family relationship is very important as an impetus to murder."

Although R.'s Wexford novels are skillfully written, with ingenious plots and subtly handled themes, it is with her psychological thrillers that she creates her best work. Newgate Callendar calls R. "a master at bringing horror to ordinary situations." Similarly, David Lehman says that R. "communicates an almost palpable sense of impending disaster. Her novels are mesmerizing studies in psychopathology. The culprits, victims, and bystanders of crime are frequently ordinary people who slip (or are pushed) into madness."

All of the non-Wexford novels are disturbing. Arthur in *A Demon in My View*, for example, strangles a department store mannequin over and over in order to control his desire to kill for real. Dolly in *The Killing Doll* (1984) creates an effigy of her stepmother; after she persuades her brother Pup to disembowel it with satisfactory results, the stepmother is found dead after an accident with a syringe. *The Tree of Hands* (1984) focuses on a young single mother, Benet Archdale, whose baby dies suddenly while she is still suffering from postnatal depression. Benet's mother, also suffering from a mental illness, kidnaps a child briefly left alone on the street by his own single mother. Benet keeps the child and convinces herself it is her own. *Heartstones* (1987) is narrated by a disturbed sixteen-year-old girl, Elvira, who says, "In those days I had never given a thought to poisoning and I can be sure of this, that I had nothing to do with our mother's death." This is the only thing she and the reader can be sure of as she describes her obsession with her father, the sudden death of her father's fiancée, a time in a mental hospital, and the deteriorating mental state of her younger sister Despina. When asked about the main characters in her thrillers, R. replied, "I do think there are a lot of people in a sad psychotic state. . . . It seems that a number of people believe that most people that one encounters in this world were leading happy, rational, lucid and logical lives, but I don't find that." Certainly one does not find rational characters in R.'s novels.

Although not all of her novels have been universally applauded by the critics, R.'s expert characterization is widely admired. One critic sums up her accomplishment by saying, "Concern with character and its development is perhaps the greatest of her many strengths as a writer. Each personality is clearly drawn; each is believable because each is honestly motivated." In addition, R. is also acclaimed for her technique in building suspense. Newgate Callendar comments, "Nothing much seems to happen, but a bit here, a bit there, a telling thrust, and suddenly we are in a sustained mood of horror. Rendell is awfully good at this kind of psycho-suspense." If R. is not "The New First Lady of Mystery" or "The Queen of Crime"—another title she dislikes—she has certainly carved out her own place among crime writers. In the words of Callendar, "Her writing style is muted, purposely so, and that makes the extraordinary situations all the more biting. She has worked out a special field for herself, and she continues to pursue it with ingenuity."

WORKS: *From Doon with Death* (1964). *To Fear a Painted Devil* (1965). *Vanity Dies Hard* (1965; in the U.S. as *In Sickness and in Health*, 1966). *A New Lease of Death* (1967; in the U.S. as *Sins of the Fathers*, 1970). *Wolf to the Slaughter* (1967). *The Secret House of Death* (1968). *The Best Man to Die* (1969). *A Guilty Thing Surprised* (1970). *No More Dying Then* (1971). *One Across, Two Down* (1971). *Murder Being Once Done* (1972). *Some Lie and Some Die* (1973). *The Face of Trespass* (1974). *Shake Hands Forever* (1975). *A Demon in My View* (1976). *The Fallen Curtain and Other Stories* (1976). *A Judgment in Stone* (1977). *A Sleeping Life* (1978). *Make Death Love Me* (1979). *Means of Evil and Other Stories* (1979). *The Lake of Darkness* (1980). *Put on by Cunning* (1981; in the U.S. as *Death Notes*). *Master of the Moor* (1982). *The Fever Tree and Other Stories* (1982). *The Speaker of Mandarin* (1983). *The Killing Doll* (1984). *The Tree of Hands* (1984). *An Unkindness of Ravens* (1984). *The New Girlfriend* (1985). *Live Flesh* (1986). (as Barbara Vine) *A Dark-Adapted Eve* (1986). (as Barbara Vine) *A Fatal Inversion* (1987). *Heartstones* (1987). *Collected Short Stories* (1987; in the U.S. as *Collected Stories*, 1988). *Talking to Strangers* (1987, in the U.S. as *Talking to Strange Men*). *The Veiled One* (1988). (as Barbara Vine, with others) *Yes, Prime Minister: The Diaries of the Right Honourable James Hacker* (1988). *The Bridesmaid* (1989). (as Barbara Vine) *The House of Stairs* (1989). (with C. Ward) *Undermining the Central Line* (1989). (as Barbara Vine) *Gallowglass* (1990). *Going Wrong* (1990). *The Copper Peacock and Other Stories* (1991). (as Barbara Vine) *King Solomon's Carpet* (1992). *Kissing the Gunner's Daughter* (1992). (with photographs by P. Bowden) *Ruth Rendell's Suffolk* (1992). (as Barbara Vine) *Anna's Book* (1993). *The Crocodile Bird* (1993). (as Barbara Vine) *No Night Is Too Long* (1994). *Simisola* (1995). *Blood Lines* (1995). *The Keys to the Street* (1996). (as Barbara Vine) *The Brimstone Wedding* (1996). *Road Rage* (1997).

BIBLIOGRAPHY: Bakerman, J. *ArmD* (1978). Bakerman, J. *The Mystery Nook* (1977). Bakerman, J., in *Ten Women of Mystery*, ed. E. Bargainnier (1981). Barnard, R. *ArmD* (1983). Carr, J. C. *The Craft of Crime: Conversations with Crime Writers* (1983). Clark, S. L. *ArmD* (1989). Cooper-Clark, D. *ArmD* (1981). Giffone, T., in *Cultural Power/Cultural Literacy*, ed. B. Braendlein (1991). Hendershot, C. *Clues* (1994). Klein, K. G. *Great Women Mystery Writers* (1994). Marsden, M. *Clues* (1989). Miller, D. *The Mystery Nook* (1977). Stowe, W. W. *CE* (1986).

For articles in reference works, see: *Bloomsbury. CA. Cambridge. CLC. Feminist. Oxford. TCC&MW. ToddBWW.*

Other references: Callender, N. *NYTBR* (26 February 1978). Lehman, D. *Newsweek* (21 September 1987). *LonT* (1 September 1996). *NYT* (10 April 1995).

Alice Lorraine Painter

Jean Rhys (pseudonym of Ella Gwendolyn Rees Williams)

BORN: 24 August 1890, Roseau, Dominica, British West Indies.

DIED: 14 May 1979, Exeter.

DAUGHTER OF: William Rees Williams and Minna Lockhart Williams.

MARRIED: Jean Lenglet, 1919; Leslie Tilden-Smith, 1932; Max Hamer, 1947.

The daughter of a Welsh doctor and his Scottish-Dominican wife, R. was educated at a convent in Roseau, Dominica, until she left the island to attend the Perse School in Cambridge, England. She studied later at the Royal Academy of Dramatic Arts but was unable to continue after her father's death. Over her family's objections, she remained in England and worked as a chorus girl in a musical comedy company touring the provinces. Some later jobs included modeling, tutoring, translating, and ghostwriting a book on furniture. Her writing career began in earnest shortly after her first marriage in 1919. A member of the Royal Society of Literature, she received the Arts Council of Great Britain Award for Writers in 1967 and the W. H. Smith Award for the publication of *Wide Sargasso Sea;* Queen Elizabeth II honored R. with a Commander of the British Empire designation in 1978.

R. wrote for many years before Ford Madox Ford encouraged her to publish her first book, *The Left Bank and Other Stories,* in 1927. These stories, and most of her later works as well, depict her experiences as a child growing up in Dominica and as a young woman living in London and Paris. Although there is a fine line in her work between life and art, her prose transcends autobiography by capturing the impressions of an unrepresented class in literature, those cast out by society. In his preface to *The Left Bank,* Ford characterized R.'s innovation as "an almost lurid! [sic] passion for stating the case of the underdog." Ford also praised her sensitive ear for dialogue and her careful eye for form in fiction, stylistic qualities revealing her conviction that one must write from life in order to portray truth in fiction. As R. stated in a 1968 interview, "I am the only truth I know."

In the four novels written in the 1920s and 1930s, R. fashions similar protagonists, lonely women who are imaginative re-creations of her own moods and experiences at different stages of life. Yet R.'s life is transmuted in her work, for "she used and changed her own biography to fit the shape of her fiction," as Teresa O'Connor notes. In R.'s first novel, *Postures* (R. preferred the American title *Quartet*) (1928), she presents the *ménage à trois* of an English couple and Marya Zelli, a young married woman whose husband is imprisoned, as R.'s first husband, Jean Langlet, was. Seen by critics to be a *roman à clef* describing the difficult relationship of R., Ford, and Ford's common-law wife, Stella Bowen, the novel details the cruel treatment of the unprotected single woman by "respectable" people, a scenario that recurs frequently in R.'s works. In this case all "characters" published their own versions of events; see Ford's novel *When the Wicked Man,* Bowen's autobiography *Drawn From Life,* and Lenglet's novel, *Sous le Verrous* (later translated, cut, and edited by R. and published as *Barred,* 1932).

In R.'s second novel, *After Leaving Mr. Mackenzie* (1931), Julia Martin, the former mistress of the title character, has been pensioned off by her lover and ekes out a lonely existence in a Paris hotel room. The typical R. heroine, like Julia, ends up alone, friendless, and broke, without the protection of a man. R.'s own favorite of her early novels, *Voyage in the Dark* (1934), tells the story of Anna Morgan, a chorus girl who becomes the mistress of an older man only to be discarded by him when she asserts her independence. In R.'s fictional world, women who abhor the hypocrisy of respectability are always at odds with those, usually men, who have law and money on their side. Women of a certain type struggle desperately for financial security, but they lose or spend money freely when they have it. Although the aging Sasha Jansen in *Good Morning, Midnight* (1939) manages, through the generosity of a friend, to live well during a trip to Paris, she cannot let down her guard to trust a gigolo who eventually reveals himself to be as vulnerable as she is. Sasha's amorous experiences scar her and leave her emotionally bankrupt.

R.'s heroines do not think about the consequences of their behavior. Like her protagonists, R. suffered from her inability to care for herself, a characteristic that allowed her to become easily alienated from others; frequently her friendships with men and women ended in conflict. The biographical details of R.'s adult life produce a disturbing portrait: Her first child by Lenglet, William Owen, died at the age of three weeks after suddenly coming down with pneumonia; their second child, Maryvonne, was born in a period when Lenglet was a fugitive from the Hungarian police for trading currency on the black market. Around the same time (the fall of 1922), Lenglet was served with divorce papers by his first wife, Marie Pollart. Maryvonne rarely lived with both father and mother. After her parents separated, she lived for brief periods with each. But the greater part of Maryvonne's childhood was spent at school in Holland as she and her father desired, and the girl visited her mother only during vacations. According to biographer Carole Angier, at the age of eighty R. expressed some regret for not being more involved in raising her daughter but characteristically claimed that her inability to do so was nevertheless matched by her strong love and affection.

R.'s most successful fiction similarly works, despite the "gloom" that Rebecca West found in it, because it carefully delineates the reasons for both emotional ambivalence and defensively motivated emotional outbursts. R.'s fictional powers are strongest in depicting those who are marooned but fighting off any rescuers. As desperate as any of her protagonists, R. often lived in straitened circumstances that inhibited her writing and strained her mental condition. During her marriages to Leslie Tilden-Smith and Max Hamer, R. was arrested for being drunk and disorderly in public. On these occasions and others, her defensive streak would encourage her to criticize those around her in a very cruel way, thereby returning any contempt others might have for her drinking and dishevelment.

R. receded from public view in the 1940s and 1950s and lived in obscurity in Cornwall. During this period she was "rediscovered" twice. In 1949, when she awaited sentencing on an assault charge in Holloway Prison Hospital, she was contacted by Selma Vas Diaz who was working on a dramatization of *Good Morning, Midnight.* Later, in 1957, the BBC, producing a radio version of the same novel, placed an advertisement in the *New Statesman* seeking its author; R., who had been preoccupied in the interim by Hamer's imprisonment on check fraud, then renewed her relationship with Vas Diaz. Although this relationship, like so many others, ended in conflict, R. was able to return to writing with greater diligence because the editors Diana Melly and Francis Wyndham offered advice, encouragement, and practical assistance that helped R. organize her work.

R.'s early novels, re-issued after the successful reception of *Wide Sargasso Sea,* gained a wider audience in the 1960s and 1970s when critics pointed out that she had been a pioneer in addressing the difficulties faced by a single woman in a male-dominated society. Although in interviews R. revealed her opposition to strictly feminist readings, she raised the issue of the powerlessness of women in many fictions, most successfully in her last novel. She had worked for years on a number of short stories and on a novel based on the character of Antoinette Cosway, Rochester's mad wife in Charlotte Brontë's *Jane Eyre*. Revising the nineteenth-century interpretation of the West Indian woman and vindicating the madwoman in the attic, *Wide Sargasso Sea* is a painfully compelling story of violence and madness that questions how "primitive" Caribbean and English cultures might be. While R.'s earlier novels represent the alienated foreigner in European settings, her portrait of Antoinette centers on the distorted view of Caribbean culture held by the English and the ambiguous status of the white West Indian, who is not at home in either society.

In the last years of her life, R. published two volumes of short stories and worked on her autobiography. These collections are technically superior to her first book of stories, which R. felt did not merit republication, although she allowed selected stories to reappear in *Tigers Are Better Looking* (1968). The later stories in this collection are more polished, but all describe the unmarried woman struggling financially and the alienated West Indian enduring British prejudices. In her last book, *Sleep It Off, Lady* (1976), R. ordered the stories chronologically according to the stages of her life. Stories of the Caribbean are followed by stories treating her encounter with England, and the last story tells of an old woman reviled by the inhabitants of a small English village. In her unfinished autobiography, *Smile Please* (1979), R. described the real-life versions of some stories and revealed how closely, and painfully, her work is tied to her life. The *Collected Short Stories* (1985), a volume including some previously uncollected stories, was published posthumously, as was *The Complete Novels* (1987).

Called by A. Alvarez in 1974 "the best living English novelist," R. was able to portray sadness better than almost any other fiction writer, with the possible exception of Françoise Sagan. Although R. in her youth was a voracious reader of Lord Byron and Charles Dickens and as an aspiring writer became acquainted with a number of modernist writers who admired her work, she did not keep up with others' work and remained outside any literary movement. Her contribution to literature bridges two traditions, the British and the Caribbean, but she does not rest securely in either, as her work is at its best when it considers those who do not belong and who spit in the face of respectability.

While a number of R.'s critics analyze the psychology of the writer and her characters, others read her work as a harbinger of the contemporary critical interest in cultural critique. R.'s work has become especially popular during the multicultural 1980s and 1990s, for her fiction pointedly reviews political and social imperialism and offers numerous memorable examples of those who struggle to survive in a world in which race, gender, class, and sexual orientation become battlegrounds for writers and readers.

WORKS: *The Left Bank and Other Stories* (1927). (trans.) *Perversity*, by Francis Carco (1928). *Postures* (1928; in the U.S. as *Quartet*, 1929). *After Leaving Mr. Mackenzie* (1931). (trans.) *Barred*, by Edward de Neve (pseud. J. Lenglet) (1932). *Voyage in the Dark* (1934). *Good Morning, Midnight* (1939). *Wide Sargasso Sea* (1966). *Tigers Are Better-Looking, with a Selection from the Left Bank* (1968). *My Day* (1975). *Sleep It Off, Lady* (1976). *Smile Please: An Unfinished Autobiography* (1979). *The Letters of Jean Rhys*, ed. F. Wyndham and D. A. Melly (1984). *The Complete Novels* (1985). *Tales of the Wide Caribbean*, ed. K. Ramchand (1985). *The Collected Short Stories* (1987).

BIBLIOGRAPHY: Angier, C. *Jean Rhys* (1985). Angier, C. *Jean Rhys: Life and Work* (1990). Benstock, S. *Women of the Left Bank, Paris 1900–40* (1987). Davidson, A. *Jean Rhys* (1985). Emery, M. L. *Jean Rhys at 'World's End': Novels of Colonial and Sexual Exile* (1990). *Critical Perspectives on Jean Rhys, ed. P. Frickey* (1990). Gardiner, J. K. *Rhys, Stead, Lessing, and the Politics of Empathy* (1989). Gregg, V. M. *Jean Rhys's Historical Imagination: Reading and Writing the Creole* (1995). Harrison, N. R. *Jean Rhys and the Novel as Woman's Text* (1988). Hemmerechts, K. *A Plausible Story and a Plausible Way of Telling It* (1987). Hite, M. *The Other Side of the Story: Structures and Strategies of Contemporary Feminist Narrative* (1989). Howells, C. A. *Jean Rhys* (1991). James, L. *Jean Rhys* (1978). James, S. *The Ladies and the Mammies: Jane Austen and Jean Rhys* (1983). Joseph, M. P. *Caliban in Exile: The Outsider in Caribbean Fiction* (1992). Kloepfer, D. K. *The Unspeakable Mother: Forbidden Discourses in Jean Rhys and H. D.* (1989). Le Gallez, P. *The Rhys Woman* (1990). Mellown, E. *Jean Rhys: A Descriptive and Annotated Bibliography of Works and Criticism* (1984). Nebeker, H. *Jean Rhys, Woman in Passage: A Critical Study of the Novels* (1981). O'Connor, T. F. *Jean Rhys: The West Indian Novels* (1986). Plante, D. *Difficult Women: A Memoir of Three* (1983). Staley, T. *Jean Rhys* (1979). Wolfe, P. *Jean Rhys* (1980).

For articles in reference works, see: *Bloomsbury. CA. Cambridge. CB. CLC. Feminist. OCEL. Oxford. Todd-BWW. WA.*

Other references: *ArielE* (July 1977, October 1986, October 1991, April 1993, July 1993). *Atlantic* (January 1975, June 1980). *BW* (5 April 1970). *ChiR* (1981). *CollL* (June 1993, February 1995). *ConL* (1979, 1983, 1994). *Crit* (1985, 1990). *ELWIU* (1994). *GaR* (1981). *Guardian* (8 August 1968). *JRR* (1986–present). *MFS* (1986, 1988). *Ms.* (January 1976). *New Republic* (31 May 1980, 25 May 1987, 17 February 1992). *New Statesman* (15 February 1980, 30 November 1990). *New Yorker* (10 December 1984, 2 December 1991). *NYRB* (18 May 1972; 11 November 1976). *NYTBR* (17 March 1974, 25 May 1980). *Novel* (Winter 1989). *PLL* (1994). *Poetry Today* (1985). *Saturday Review* (1977). *SNNTS* (Summer 1984). *TCL* (1982, 1992). *TLS* (21 December 1979, 23 November 1990, 25 June 1993).

Carol Colatrella

Mary Boyle Rich, Countess of Warwick

BORN: 8 November 1625, Youghal, Cork, Ireland.
DIED: 12 April 1678, Leighs, Essex.

DAUGHTER OF: Richard Boyle, first Earl of Cork, and Catherine Fenton.
MARRIED: Charles Rich, 1641.

Renowned for her piety and philanthropy, R. began her life in the home of the powerful and wealthy Boyle family. She was the seventh daughter and the thirteenth child of the prominent Royalist family. Her brother was the eminent Robert Boyle. Less than three years old when her mother died in 1628, R. and her younger sister, Margaret, were brought up by the wife of Sir Randall Clayton. In 1638, Lord Cork tried to marry his young daughter to James Hamilton, the only son of James, first Viscount Clandeboye, later Earl of Clanbrassil. In the best-known gesture of her life, young R. rejected her suitor. Her father saw the twelve-year-old as an "unruly child."

R.'s early resistance to her father's authority took on a more serious tone when she permitted herself to be wooed and won by Charles Rich, the second son of Robert, third Earl of Warwick. Lord Cork disapproved of the match because the young man lacked a fortune; in contrast, his other six daughters had all arranged brilliant matches. He banished R. to the family's house in a little country seat near Hampton Court, where Rich secretly visited her. They were quietly married in 1641; after others intervened on her behalf, her father bestowed on her a generous dowry of £7,000 per year.

R. spent the rest of her life with her husband's family and on the Warwick estate at Leighs Priory. Within a short time, she bore two children, a girl who died in infancy and a son who lived until 1663. By 1671, R. was already recognized for her piety. Her life seemed to be devoted to meditation, works of charity, and the occasional entertainment of her husband's associates. In 1671, her husband inherited the Warwick title and lands. For twenty years he had suffered with painful and debilitating attacks from gout, and he died 24 August 1673, leaving his entire estate to R. The last five years of her life R. spent as she had spent most of her years of marriage—piously and privately.

Upon her death, she was hailed by Anthony Walker, her minister, as a generous and pious woman. Her "soul father" during her life, Walker fittingly preached the sermon, "The Virtuous Woman Found," at her funeral. It was published in 1686 in London along with three works by R.: "Rules for a Holy Life, in a Letter to George, Earl of Berkeley," "Occasional Meditations upon Sundry Subjects," and "Pious Reflections upon Several Scriptures." R.'s piety and the quality of her life are also revealed in the diary that she kept from July 1666 to November 1677. The thoughtfulness, religious fervor, and profound sense of guilt and suffering that defined R.'s adult life permeate each day's entry and each prayer. Of special interest is her need to control her emotions when she felt particularly burdened or punished. On 28 August 1671, for example, she writes:

> After dinner got an opportunity of speaking to my lord about his soul's concernments, and I did much beseech him to be more careful for his soul's good, and told him of his offending God by his passions, and the sad effects of it. Afterwards my lord in a dispute fell into a great passion with me, upon which I found in myself a sudden violent eruption of passion, which made me instantly go away, for fear it should break out, and by so doing I was kept from having my lord hear me say anything; but to myself I uttered some passionate words, which though no other heard yet, O Lord, thou didst; oh, humble me for it.

The diaries, like her meditations, were not published until after R. died. Given the title *Occasional Meditations*, the diaries passed into the hands of Thomas Woodroffe, R.'s personal chaplain. It is believed that he annotated the diaries after R.'s death. In 1847, the Religious Tract Society published selections from or an abridgement of R.'s diary by Woodroffe or a Mr. Barham entitled *Memoir of Lady Warwick: Also Her Diary, from A.D. 1666 to 1672, Now First Published: To Which Are Added, Extracts from Her Other Writings*. Then, in 1848, Thomas Crofton Croker collected "Some Specialties" that he published for the Percy Society under the title *Autobiography of Mary Countess of Warwick*. In 1866, the British Museum acquired the diaries (Additional MSS. 27351–58).

Although R. did not write for publication, she left an important document for her twentieth-century readers, particularly those who wonder about the life of a woman of spirit and intellect in the seventeenth century. Her accounts are vivid and effective. R. writes with simplicity and purpose, leaving her readers with a better understanding of those turbulent years and of an aristocratic woman's irreconcilable problems and her efforts to find peace.

WORKS: *A Funeral Elegy Upon the much lamented Death of . . . Mary, Lady Dowager, Countess of Warwick* (1678). *The Virtous Woman Found: (1) Rules for a Holy Life, in a Letter to George, Earl of Berkeley, (2) Occasional Meditations upon Sundry Subjects, (3) Pious Reflections Upon Several Scriptures* (1686). *Memoir of Lady Warwick: Also Her Diary, from A.D. 1666 to 1672, Now First Published; To Which Are Added, Extracts from Her Other Writings* (1847). *Autobiography of Mary Countess of Warwick*, ed. T. C. Croker (1848).

BIBLIOGRAPHY: Budgell, E. *Memoirs of the Lives and Characters of the Illustrious Family of the Boyles* (1737). Fell-Smith, C. *Mary Rich, Countess of Warwick (1625–1678): Her Family and Friends* (1901). Findlay, S. and E. Hobby. *Literature and Power in the Seventeenth Century* (1981). Mendelson, S. H. *The Mental World of Stuart Women: Three Studies* (1987). Palgrave, M. E. *Mary Rich, Countess of Warwick (1625–1678)* (1901).

For articles in reference works, see: Aubrey, J. *Brief Lives* (1898). *BAB1800*. *Bell*. *BioIn*. *Bloomsbury*. *DNB*. *Feminist*. Rogers, K. M. *Feminism in Eighteenth-Century England* (1982). *ToddBWW*.

Sophia B. Blaydes

Dorothy Richardson

BORN: 17 May 1873, Abington, Berkshire.
DIED: 17 June 1957, Beckenham, Kent.

DAUGHTER OF: Charles Richardson and Mary Taylor Richardson.
MARRIED: Alan Odle, 1917.

R.'s home life, outwardly conventional and prosperous, at least until R. was twenty and her father went bankrupt, was inwardly disrupted by pretension and madness: Her father urgently longed to transcend his merchant-grocer origins and be a gentleman; her mother, depressed for many years, killed herself in 1895 while on vacation with R. At the age of five, R. learned to read and spell, her only interests, at a small private school. Later she was educated, first at home by a governess whom she detested, then at Southborough House, London, an intellectually lively institution where R. particularly revelled in the study of logic. Poverty forced her to become a pupil-teacher in Germany in 1891 and a governess from 1891 to 1895, experiences treated in the first volumes of *Pilgrimage.* After her mother's death, longing for independence and freedom from what she perceived as the horrors of woman's lot in a middle-class domestic setting and having learned that teaching was far too confining for her, R. accepted a post as a dental assistant at £1 per week and began her long romance with London. At this time she met H. G. Wells, her friend for many years and lover for a few, husband of a school friend. Wells encouraged her to write, as did others. She began with journalism and went on to nonfiction and finally to her masterwork, *Pilgrimage.* In 1917, at the age of forty-four, she married Alan Odle, a talented but highly eccentric and unworldly artist sixteen years younger than she, with whom she lived amicably but maternally until his death in 1948.

From the publication of *Pointed Roofs* (1915), the first volume of *Pilgrimage,* R. received enthusiastic and awed critical recognition. Even Virginia Woolf, who felt competitive with her, acknowledged that R. had "invented . . . or developed and applied to her own use, a sentence which we might call the psychological sentence of the feminine gender." In histories of the novel, R. is consistently coupled with Marcel Proust, James Joyce, and Woolf as a major early innovator in technique and subject and an early practitioner of the stream-of-consciousness method. Many books and studies have been written about R., particularly in recent years. Remarkably, though, she remains a very nearly unread writer. Ford Madox Ford fulminated that she was "the most abominably unknown contemporary writer," and Elizabeth Bowen insists that "until Dorothy Richardson has been given her proper place, there will be a great gap in our sense of the growth of the English novel."

Pilgrimage, the work to which she devoted most of her life, is a twelve-volume (or twelve-chapter, as she preferred) work charting and capturing the flow of consciousness through Miriam Henderson as she grows and changes from adolescence to young womanhood. At the same time, without being remotely didactic, the work gives an incomparable portrayal of the consciousness of an era. Unlike Joyce, R. is faithful to the waking, coherent, rational mind, despite her record of the profusion of experience. And, unlike Proust, she records without attempting to analyze. Her constant low-key awareness of the specialness of the female mind and of complex issues confronting that mind at a period of rapid and radical emancipation is highly congenial to modern feminist readers. R.'s anti-Semitism, on the other hand, even if perceived as a reflection of the times, is unsympathetic since it is presented with no irony, detachment, or distance, particularly in the last chapter-volumes.

R. herself knew that her work was highly original and groundbreaking but contemptuously dismissed the critical attempt to define her technique: "What do I think of the term 'Stream of Consciousness' . . . ? Just this: that amongst the company of useful labels devised to meet the exigencies of literary criticism it stands alone, isolated by its perfect imbecility."

WORKS: *The Quakers Past and Present* (1914). *Gleanings from the Works of George Fox* (1914). *Pointed Roofs* (1915). *Backwater* (1916). *Honeycomb* (1917). *The Tunnel* (1919). *Interim* (1919). *Deadlock* (1921). *Revolving Lights* (1923). *The Trap* (1925). *Oberland* (1927). *John Austen and the Inseparables* (1930). *Dawn's Left Hand* (1931). *Clear Horizon* (1935). *Pilgrimage* (including *Dimple Hill*), 4 vols. (1938). *Pilgrimage* (including *March Moonlight*), 4 vols. (1967). *Windows on Modernism: Selected Letters of Dorothy Richardson,* ed. G. G. Fromm (1995).

BIBLIOGRAPHY: Blake, C. R. *Dorothy Richardson* (1960). Bluemel, K. *Experimenting on the Borders of Modernism: Dorothy Richardson's "Pilgrimage"* (1997). *Look Who's Laughing: Gender and Comedy,* ed. G. Finney (1994). *Breaking the Sequence: Women's Experimental Fiction,* ed. E. Friedman (1990). Fromm, G. *Dorothy Richardson: A Biography* (1977). Gevirtz, S. *Narrative's Journey: The Fiction and Film Writing of Dorothy Richardson* (1996). Gregory, H. *Dorothy Richardson: An Adventure in Self-Discovery* (1967). Hanscombe, G. *The Art of Life: Dorothy Richardson and the Development of Feminist Consciousness* (1982). Labovitz, E. K. *The Myth of the Heroine: The Female Bildungsroman in the Twentieth Century: Dorothy Richardson, Simone de Beauvoir, Doris Lessing, Christa Wolf* (1986). Rado, L. *Rereading Modernism: New Directions in Feminist Criticism* (1994). Staley, T. F. *Dorothy Richardson* (1976). Watts, C. *Dorothy Richardson* (1995). Wyatt-Brown, A. and J. Rossen *Aging and Gender in Literature: Studies in Creativity* (1993).

For articles in reference works, see: *Bloomsbury. BWW. CA. CWA. DLB. EWLTC. Feminist. Oxford. TCLC. ToddBWW.*

Other references: DeKoven, M. *SLitI* (1992). Egger, R. *CamObsc* (1994). Friedman, E. *MFS* (1988). Fromm, G. *PRev* (1990). Fromm, G. *LCUT* (1993). Hidalgo, P. *RAE* (1993). Kemp, S. *CritQ* (1990). Knowles, O. *Conradiana* (1986). Podnieks, E. *Frontiers* (1994). Poresky L. *VWM* (1990). Schyler, S. *Genders* (1990). Vanacker, S. *BeteN* (1988).

Carey Kaplan
(updated by Christina Root)

Charlotte Eliza Lawson Cowan Riddell

BORN: 30 September 1832, Carrickfergus, County Antrim, Ireland.
DIED: 24 September 1906, Hounslow, London.
DAUGHTER OF: James Cowan and Ellen Kilshaw.
MARRIED: James H. Riddell, 1857.
WROTE UNDER: Charlotte Riddell; F. G. Trafford.

R., the youngest daughter of the High Sheriff of Carrickfergus, Ireland, was self-educated and began her writing career at the age of fifteen with her first novel, *The Moors and the Fens* (1858), published under the pseudonym F. G. Trafford, which she used until 1864.

Throughout her life, R. suffered much misfortune, beginning in her youth with her father's lingering illness and eventual death, at which time she and her mother were forced to leave their old home. They lived for some while in County Down, where R. later set her four Irish novels *Maxwell Drewitt* (1865), *The Earl's Promise* (1873), *Berna Boyle* (1884), and *The Nun's Curse* (1888). Shortly after their arrival in London, R.'s mother became an invalid; R. tried desperately to sell her stories, and when at last she succeeded in selling *The Moors and the Fens,* her mother died. Her wanderings through London at this time gave her an intimate knowledge of the city, which is reflected in a number of her later novels.

After her marriage in 1857, R. frequently consulted her gifted civil-engineer husband on chemistry, engineering, and other topics she incorporated into her novels. His struggle to make a fortune in business led to severe financial difficulties, the business details of which R. incorporated into novels such as *The Race for Wealth* (1866) and *Mortomley's Estate* (1874). In spite of the struggles, R. had a large family and succeeded in making a profit with her novels. Her first major success was *George Geith of Fen Court* (1864); between 1864 and 1902, and under her own name, she wrote thirty novels, most of which went into second and third editions. Most had a background of city and commercial life, which was unusual for England in the 1860s when businessmen were looked down upon. R. tried to prove that "a man did not lose caste for engaging in business"; however, by 1902, the new generation conceded the point, making R.'s novels antiquated.

R.'s works are sensation novels, mostly in three volumes, that are carefully written and reflect much insight into character. Both male and female characters value passion and assertive action. *George Geith,* republished in 1886, was dramatized into a popular play in 1883 by W. Reeve. With time, however, the dramatic force of the reappearance of the "dead" wife was lost. R. also displayed a bright sense of humor in *A Mad Tour, or A Journey Undertaken in an Insane Moment through Central Europe on Foot* (1891). Some of her work, however, is spoiled by anti-Semitic diatribes.

R. cleverly retained her book copyrights. By 1867, she achieved a powerful and influential position as co-proprietor and editor of *St. James Magazine.* She also edited a magazine called *Home* and wrote fairly successful stories for the Christian Knowledge Society and Routledge's Christmas Annuals, but her short stories were never as popular as her novels.

WORKS: *Zuriel's Grandchild* (1855). *The Ruling Passion* (1857). *The Moors and the Fens* (1858). *Rich Husband* (1858). *Too Marsh Alone* (1860). *City and Suburb* (1861). *The World in the Church* (1863). *George Geith of Fen Court* (1864). *Maxwell Drewitt* (1865). *Phemie Keller* (1866). *The Race for Wealth* (1866). *Far Above Rubies* (1867). *The Miseries of Christmas* (1867). *Austin Friars* (1870). *A Life's Assize* (1871). *The Earl's Promise* (1873). *Home, Sweet Home* (1873). *Mortomley's Estate* (1874). *Frank Sinclair's Wife and Other Stories* (1874). *The Uninhabited House* (1875). *Above Suspicion* (1876). *Her Mother's Darling* (1877). *The Haunted River: A Christmas Story* (1877). *Fairy Water* (1878). *The Disappearance of Mr. Jeremiah Redworth* (1878). *The Mystery of Palace Gardens* (1880). *The Curate Lowood* (1882). *Daisies and Buttercups* (1882). *The Prince of Wales's Garden Party and Other Stories* (1882). *Idle Tales* (1882). *A Struggle for Fame* (1883). *Susan Drummond* (1884). *Weird Stories* (1884). *Berna Boyle: A Love Story of County Down* (1884). *Mitre Court* (1885). *For Dick's Sake* (1886). *Miss Gascoigne* (1887). *The Nun's Curse* (1888). *Princess Sunshine and Other Stories* (1889). *A Mad Tour, or a Journey Undertaken in an Insane Moment Through Central Europe on Foot* (1891). *The Head of the Firm* (1892). *The Rusty Sword* (1894). *A Silent Tragedy* (1893). *The Banshee's Warning and Other Tales* (1894). *Did He Deserve It?* (1897). *A Rich Man's Daughter* (1897). *Handsome Phil and Other Stories* (1899). *The Footfall of Fate* (1900). *Poor Fellow* (1902).

BIBLIOGRAPHY: Black, H. C. *Notable Women Authors of the Day* (1893). Ellis, S. M. *Wilkie Collins, Le Fanu, and Others* (1931).

For articles in reference works, see: *DNB. Feminist. Oxford. ToddBWW. VB.*

Other references: *LonT* (26 September 1906).

Carole M. Shaffer-Koros

Anne Ridler

BORN: 30 July 1912, Rugby, Warwickshire.
DAUGHTER OF: Henry Christopher Bradby and Violet Milford Bradby.
MARRIED: Vivian Ridler, 1938.
WRITES UNDER: Anne Bradby; Anne Ridler.

In fifty years, R. has amassed a substantial *oeuvre* in poetry, drama, and criticism. At Faber & Faber in the late 1930s, she was T. S. Eliot's secretary (see her "Personal Reminiscence" in *Poetry Review,* 1983), assisting in the editing of the *Criterion,* and a reviewer of manuscripts submitted for publication. Her own first collection, *Poems* (1939), was published by Oxford, but after she left Faber's Eliot urged her to submit a manuscript, and Faber's has since published four volumes of her poetry, four of plays, and three anthologies. She has received two prizes (1954, 1955) for work published in *Poetry* (Chicago).

Most of R.'s poems are distillations from ordinary experience. She writes with tenderness of married love, both beginning and grown over the years, of the pain of separation (her husband was an intelligence officer in the Royal Air Force during World War II), the awe of parenthood, the tensions and joys of family life, and, especially recently, aging and death. With great subtlety she observes human relationships in poems like the early "On Being Asked Pardon" and the late "A Pirated Edition." Places, associated with homes or holidays, often inspire her meditative insights; so also, in her 1951 collection, do works of music and art. A few poems address contemporary moral decay.

Tensions between doubt and faith inform "Deus Absconditus," a rare example of R.'s dealing directly with religious experience. More often, her antennae for epiphanies in the quotidian will draw profound theological insight from an astonishing range of everyday events: "For a Child Expected," "Blood Transfusion Centre," and "Corneal Graft" are salient examples. Such, she believes, is the function of poetry, whose "lifeblood" is symbolism; symbols are the "hiding places of power." In "Taliessin Reborn," she explores the power of poetry to awaken realizations of the "other world"; in a sonnet for Eliot's sixtieth birthday ("'I Who Am Here Dissembled'"), she explores its power to sound the depths of human emotion. Yet aware as she is of the tragic dimension of existence, for R. "still the raw material of pain / Is changed into joy" ("Exile"). "All art is not tragedy, and music / Cries of a haven, over the storm swell. / Where did they find their faith, the serene masters, / Their crazy word, that all shall yet be well?" ("Reading the News"). That echo of Eliot reveals one of R.'s formative influences, but the interrogative form is typical of her quietly honest balance of affirmation and doubt.

Contributing to the realization of epiphanies is R.'s gift for fresh description. An azalea indoors in winter is an "explosion of sunsets, archangels on a needle-point, / Red parliament of butterflies." To a loafing boy in summer, the river is "cool as lemon squash"; clouds are "the lazy yachts of the sky" ("Evenlode"). Fresh too in its effect is her deft word play, sometimes bilingual. In "Deus Absconditus" God "absconds from every promised land." The sea ("Mare Nostrum"), a "changeable beast with rumpled fur of foam," "plunges along the land, / Held by a moonstring, yet by solid rock / Hardly contained."

The heir of (among others) Sir Thomas Wyatt, the Metaphysical poets, Gerard Manley Hopkins, Charles Williams, and W. H. Auden, she commands great metrical variety and writes with polish, believing that "the poet will do his work better if he has his conscious mind occupied with technical problems."

At home from the start with dramatic forms ("Dialogue Between Three Characters and a Chorus" in *Poems* [1939]), R. has written several works for stage and radio performance. In 1945, she was one of three poets chosen for the "New Plays by Poets" series (Mercury Theatre). *The Trial of Thomas Cranmer* (1956) was commissioned for broadcast on the 400th anniversary of Cranmer's martyrdom; full performance followed in St. Mary's Church, Oxford, where Cranmer had been tried. Since 1970 all her dramatic writing has been for musical accompaniment, including libretti for productions of Italian opera in translation.

Most of R.'s original plays are religious in orientation. *Cranmer* is a tough-minded modern hagiography, *Cain* a reseeing of sacred myth, "For a Christmas Broadcast" (*The Golden Bird* [1951]) and *The Jesse Tree* festal observances. *The Missing Bridegroom,* like *Cranmer,* was originally designed for performance in a church. *The Shadow Factory* (1946), externally social satire—critics compare it to work by John Galsworthy or George Orwell—centers on a factory Christmas pageant and looks for social solutions first in personal, only then in structural, change. (Even that hope is extremely cautious: "We must make the best of a bad job"—a line that anticipates Eliot's *Cocktail Party.*) *The Mask, Henry Bly* (1950), and "The Golden Bird" develop folk tales to bring out religious overtones. "Evenlode," however (in *A Matter of Life and Death* [1959]), charmingly replays but does not christianize Greek myth. Recurrent themes in R.'s plays include the ultimate self-destructiveness of self-enthronement and self-indulgence and, related to that, the rarity of genuine relationships between selves difficult and costly at best and sometimes simply refused. Both these themes are central to *Cain;* the second is especially prominent in *The Shadow Factory, How Bitter the Bread* (1963), and—emphasizing frustrated love—*The Mask,* "Evenlode," and *Who Is My Neighbor?* (1963). The last of these also explores themes of responsibility, forgiveness, and the movement of souls after death, a theme found also in "The Departure" (in *Some Time After* [1971]). Alongside these themes is that of redemptive grace able to triumph even over perverse self-destructiveness. The delightful *Henry Bly* (produced 1947, published 1950) best exemplifies this vein. It is grace also that makes of Cranmer's death at the stake what his wife can credibly call "his happy ending." There and elsewhere, thanks to Williams's influence, the theme of substitution and exchange is also prominent.

R. has been much concerned with the relations of music and poetry and with the technical problems of verse drama. Her first play experimented with varied forms: blank verse for Adam and Abel, alliterative for Cain, commonsensical prose for Eve. In keeping with the rejection of naturalism that poetic drama implies, she employs such other devices as prologues and epilogues directly addressing the audience, choric characters who become part of the plot (Witness in *Cranmer,* Prompter in *The Mask,* Verger in *The Missing Bridegroom*), masquelike stylization (*The Jesse Tree*), and liturgylike incantation.

In her editorial work at Faber's, R. was known as a sensitive critic. Most of her published criticism is scattered in reviews, prefaces, and introductions, and letters to the *Times Literary Supplement.* In edited works, selection, of course, is implicit criticism; her most substantial explicit scholarship is in the editions of Thomson, Darley, Austin, and the first two of Williams.

WORKS: *Poems* (1939). *The Missing Bridegroom* (n.d.). *The Mask* (n.d.). *A Dream Observed and Other Poems* (1941). *The Nine Bright Shiners* (1943). *Cain* (1943). *The Shadow Factory: A Nativity Play* (1946). *Henry Bly* [produced 1947] *and Other Plays* (1950). *The Golden Bird and Other Poems* (1951). *The Trial of Thomas Cranmer*

(1956). *A Matter of Life and Death* (1959). *Selected Poems* (1961). *Who Is My Neighbour?* [produced 1961] *and How Bitter the Bread* (1963). *Olive Willis and Downe House: An Adventure in Education* (1967). *The Jesse Tree: A Masque in Verse* (produced 1970, pub. 1972). *Some Time After and Other Poems* (1972). (trans.) *Rosinda,* by F. Cavelli (1973, unpublished). *The King of the Golden River* (1975). (trans.) *Orfeo,* by C. Monteverdi (1975; rev. ed., 1981). (trans.) *Eritrea,* by F. Cavalli (1975). *Italian Prospect: Six Poems* (1976). *The Lampton Worm* (1979). (trans.) *Return of Ulysses,* by C. Monteverdi (1978, unpublished). (trans.) *Orontea,* by A. Cesti (1979, unpublished). (trans.) *Agrippina,* by G. Handel (1981, unpublished). (trans.) *Calisto,* by F. Cavalli (1984, unpublished). *Crucifixion* (1993, for cantata by B. Kelly). *Collected Poems* (1994; exp. 2nd ed., 1997). (trans.) *The Magic Flute,* by W. A. Mozart (1996, unpublished). (trans.) *Orfeo ed Euridice,* by W. Glück (1997, unpublished).

BIBLIOGRAPHY: *The Penguin Book of Contemporary Verse 1918–60,* ed. K. Allott (1962). Jennings, E. *Poetry Today* (1961). Kliewer, W. *Approach* (1964). Morgan, K. E. *Christian Themes in Contemporary Poets* (1965). Nicholson, N. *Man and Literature* (1943). Spanos, W. V. *The Christian Tradition in Modern British Verse Drama* (1967). Thwaite, A. *Contemporary English Poetry* (1959). Warr, T. *PoetryR* (1983). Weales, G. *Religion in Modern English Drama* (1961).

For articles in reference works, see: *CA. CD. CP. DLB. International Who's Who in Poetry,* ed. E. Kay (6th ed., 1982).

Other references: *Drama* (Autumn 1956). *Faber Book of Modern Verse,* 3rd ed., ed. M. Roberts; sup.. by D. Hall (1965). *New Statesman* (24 November 1951). *Poetry* (Chicago) (March 1963). Speaight, R. *Christian Theatre* (1960). *TLS* (10 June 1939, 6 November 1959, 21 April 1972, 9 June 1995).

Charles A. Huttar

Rigby, Elizabeth: See Eastlake, Lady, Elizabeth Rigby

Anne Thackeray Ritchie

BORN: 9 June 1837, Hyde Park, London.
DIED: 26 February 1919, "The Porch," Freshwater.
DAUGHTER OF: William Makepeace Thackeray and Isabella Shawe Thackeray.
MARRIED: Richmond Thackeray Ritchie, 1877.

The elder of the two Thackeray daughters, R. grew up in a thoroughly literary environment. Shortly after the birth of R.'s sister Minny (Harriet Marrion Thackeray, b. 1840), Mrs. Thackeray began to show signs of the mental instability that would result in lifelong institutionalization. The daughters were therefore sent to live with their grandmother and step-grandfather, the Charmichael-Smyths, in Paris. William Thackeray remained close to his daughters even when they were away, and in 1846 he brought them back to live with him in London. Although she had no rigorous education, R. showed an early awareness of contemporary culture and politics; by the age of fourteen she was assisting Thackeray as his amanuensis.

During Thackeray's tours of America his daughters returned to their grandmother in Paris. Although there was an effort by Mrs. Charmichael-Smyth to provide the girls with the moral and religious education she thought they were lacking, the sisters remained open and broadminded. Reminiscences of R.'s travels in Europe at this time, her friendship with the Dickens children (who were also in Paris), and her acquaintances in Paris are recounted in *Chapters from Some Memoirs* (1894). R. joined her father in London when he returned from America and continued to act as his secretary. Her London acquaintances included Alfred Lord Tennyson, the Carlyles, the Brownings and even, in her 1850 visit, Charlotte Brontë ("a tiny, delicate, serious, little lady, pale with fair straight hair and steady eyes").

When she was twenty-three, R.'s first story, "Little Scholars," was published (with the consent of publisher George Smith) in her father's new and prestigious *Cornhill Magazine.* According to Thackeray, the firm of Smith and Elder was "in raptures about Anny's style," and in 1862 R.'s first novel, *The Story of Elizabeth,* was serialized in the *Cornhill.* The novel (published in book form in 1863), a convoluted romance centered on an impetuous heroine, was an immediate success.

In 1863, on Christmas Eve, William Thackeray died—leaving his daughters well off but very much alone (their grandmother died within a year). Among the ever-increasing circle of friends who watched over the Thackeray sisters was the Stephen family, and in 1867 Minny was married to Leslie Stephen. R. lived with her sister and brother-in-law until 1875, when Minny died. This period was R.'s most productive in terms of fiction. In 1867, *The Village on the Cliff,* a novel in which a woman must come to grips with unrequited love, was published. It remained one of R.'s favorite works. Other works of fiction followed, including *Old Kensington* (1873), *Bluebeard's Keys and Other Stories* (1874), and *Miss Angel* (1875), as well as a collection of essays (*Toilers and Spinsters and Other Essays,* 1874).

Following Minny's death, R. and Stephen, who called her "the most sympathetic and sociable of beings," shared a residence at Hyde Park. Here she met and was courted by her cousin Richmond Thackeray Ritchie, who, though seventeen years her junior, proposed and was accepted. Although Ritchie had an "uneventful" career in the India Office, his work was solid enough to merit a knighthood in 1907 and appointment as permanent Undersecretary for India in 1909, three years before he died. The Ritchies had two children.

R. was active until her death. She wrote introductions to the works of Mary Russell Mitford, Elizabeth Gaskell, and Maria Edgeworth. Some of her later reminiscences are recorded in *Blackstick Papers* (1908) and *From the Porch* (1913). But the most consuming project of her later years by far were the introductions she prepared for her father's collected works.

Virginia Woolf, R.'s "niece," describes her aunt in the character of Mrs. Hilbery in the novel *Night and Day*

(1919). In the obituary she prepared for the *Times Literary Supplement,* Woolf praised R.'s work for its "surprisingly sharp edges." "It is Lady Ritchie," says Woolf elsewhere in the obituary, who "will be the un-acknowledged source of much that remains in men's minds about the Victorian age."

WORKS: *The Story of Elizabeth* (1863). *The Village on the Cliff* (1867). *Five Old Friends* (1868). *Old Kensington* (1873). *Bluebeard's Keys and Other Stories* (1874). *Toilers and Spinsters and Other Essays* (1874). *Miss Angel* (1875). *To Esther and Other Sketches* (1876). *Madame de Sévigné* (1881). *Miss Williamson's Divagations* (1881). *A Book of Sibyls* (1883). *Mrs. Dymond* (1885). *Little Esme's Adventure* (1887). *Records of Tennyson, Ruskin, and Robert and Elizabeth Browning* (1892). *Alfred Lord Tennyson and His Friends* (1893). *Chapters from Some Memoirs* (1894). *Lord Amherst and the British Advance Eastward to Burma* (1894). *Chapters from Some Unwritten Memoirs* (1895). *Blackstick Papers* (1908). *A Discourse on Modern Sibyls* (1913). *From the Porch* (1913). *From Friend to Friend* (1919). *The Two Thackerays: Anne Thackeray Ritchie's Centenary Biographical Introductions to the Works of William Makepeace Thackeray,* ed. P. L. Shillingburg and J. Maxey (1988). *Anne Thackeray Ritchie: Journals and Letters,* ed. A. B. Bloom and J. Maynard (1995).

BIBLIOGRAPHY: Puller, H. R. and V. Hammersley. *Thackeray's Daughter* (1951). Gerin, W. *Anne Thackeray Ritchie* (1981). Lewis, N. *A Visit to Mrs. Wilcox* (1957). Mackay, C. H. *WS* (1988). Ritchie, H. *Thackeray and His Daughter* (1924).

For articles in reference works, see: *Allibone. Bloomsbury. Cambridge. DNB. Feminist. Oxford. ToddBWW.*

Other references: Callow, S. *Virginia Woolf Quarterly* (1979). Woolf, V. *TLS* (6 March 1919). Zucherman, J. *Virginia Woolf Quarterly* (1973).

Alan Rauch

Michèle (Brigitte) Roberts

BORN: 20 May 1949, Gushey, Hertfordshire.
DAUGHTER OF: Reginald George Roberts and Monique Pauline Joseph Caulle.

R. is a prolific feminist writer, involved with the women's movement since 1970 as well as with women's communes and writing and publishing groups. She graduated from Oxford University with honors in English literature in 1970 and is trained as a librarian. She has co-edited and contributed to many poetry publications, such as *Licking the Bed Clean* (1978) and *Smile, Smile, Smile, Smile* (1980). She was the poetry editor of *Spare Rib* from 1975 to 1977 and *City Limits* from 1981 to 1983 and, according to the *Bloomsbury Guide to English Literature,* is "influential on the development and recognition of contemporary poetry." In 1988, she produced a play, *The Journeywoman,* which premiered in Colchester. Through the years, R. has worked as a librarian, creative-writing teacher, cook, cleaner, researcher, and writer-in-residence at Lambeth Borough, London (1981–82), and Bromley Borough, London (1983–84), to support herself and her writing.

R. has also written articles and essays on various topics, including the function of art for the women's movement ("Writing and (Feminist) Politics," 1979); a fictional interview with Christine of Pisan ("Write, She Said," 1986); the muse as a source of female inspiration ("Musing over Power," 1990); and Marina Tsvetayeva's work (1993).

In 1978, R. published her first novel, *A Piece of the Night.* Mixed reviews greeted this somewhat autobiographical work, which was a joint winner of the Gay New Book Award in 1979. While J. Cooke compared her to Colette and called her a "landmark in women's writing," V. Cunningham felt she was "too much given to a flatly generalised way with people, and language that tends to jargon." Julie, the protagonist, traces her journey through flashbacks from an education in an English convent to Oxford and a difficult marriage with a history don, the birth of her daughter and her discovery of the women's movement, living in a women's commune, and her lesbian affair. This is interspersed with her trip back to Normandy to her ailing French mother. R. continues this fascinating use of flashbacks and overlapping with other women's stories (sometimes in the historical past) in her later novels, *The Visitation, The Book of Mrs. Noah, In the Red Kitchen,* and *The Daughters of the House. The Visitation* (1983) explores the intricate meanings of twinship, sexuality, writing, male and female energy, mothers and grandmothers, and friendships among women through Helen's relationships with her twin brother, her mother and grandmother, her long-time friend, Beth, and the male lovers in her life. As M. Glastonbury writes, "this elaborate lyrical sequence . . . is all richly implicit in the mood of the moment."

In 1984, R. wrote her controversial and thought-provoking *The Wild Girl,* which is about the "gospel" of Mary Magdalene. Mary is the lover of Jesus, mother of his child, and chronicler of an early Christianity that believed in equality among sexes and the importance of the female and her spirituality. According to E. Fisher, "her rich use of symbols and metaphor transforms feminist cliché into something alive and moving."

R. collected her many poems into three books, *The Mirror of the Mother* (1986), poems from 1975 to 1985; *Psyche and the Hurricane* (1991), poems from 1986 to 1990; and *All the Selves I Was,* published in 1995. In *The Mirror of the Mother,* she writes mainly of mothers and daughters, drawing on mythology, such as the Persephone myth, and religious poetry and prose. According to M. Wandor, the poems "encompass a range of ways in which the woman's voice searches for its own identity." M. Horovitz points out that R. is "at once intellectually passionate and passionately lyrical." In *Psyche and the Hurricane,* R. explores language as the expression of myths in revisiting other places, love, and the death of her sister.

The Book of Mrs. Noah (1987) is the story of a woman librarian who finds herself in Venice wishing to have a child (though her husband does not) and dreams of herself on an ark with five sibyls (*des refusantes*) who tell their stories of outraged womanhood and their envisionings of a feminist future. It is, according to Brown, a "strange and interesting book, pouring the subject matter of Virginia Woolf into a form designed by Boccaccio."

R.'s love and use of color, as well as her knowledge and love of language (she knows French and Italian, though she writes only in English), is used effectively in all her works but most especially in *Piece of the Night* and in *In the Red Kitchen* (1990), a mystery story that again uses flashbacks and interweavings to tell the stories of four women from ancient Egypt, Victorian England, and contemporary London. As H. Brown writes, R. "establishes a sub-textual dimension for which the timeless spirit world is a metaphor, where the four women's experiences overlap in more significant ways." The central character is a Victorian medium, Flora Milk, and is based on the real story of nineteenth-century Florence Cook.

Daughters of the House (1992) won the W. H. Smith Award and was short-listed for the Booker Prize. It is, according to F. King, "a ghost story, a tale of visions and miracles, and a painful physical remembering of female adolescence" as Thérèse returns home to Normandy and her cousin, Leonie, in the family home where they experienced the tragedies of war, apparitions of Mary, and their own closeness and distance. *Flesh and Blood* (1994) tells of the narrator, Freddy, who believes she has murdered her own mother. Once again, there are time travels, convent educations, sixteenth-century religion, arranged marriages, French culture, eroticism, and lesbian sexuality. R.'s most recent novel, *Impossible Saints* (1997), focuses on a fictional Saint Josephine, who dies laughing at an ambiguous joke about sex and faith. In a chapel, Josephine and other women offer variations on father-daughter relationships that run from the comic to the blasphemous, from the violent to the fabulous.

R. is a "wild original," according to J. Cooke, using all aspects of her life, thought, emotions, and learning in her strongly feminist writings. As R. puts it, "My writing generally is fueled by the fact that I am a woman. I need to write in order to break through the silence imposed on women in this culture."

WORKS: (with others) *Licking the Bed Clean* (1978). *A Piece of the Night* (1978). (with A. Fell and others) *Tales I Tell My Mother* (1978). (with others) *Smile, Smile, Smile, Smile* (1980). (with Z. Pairbairns and others) *More Tales I Tell My Mother: Feminist Short Stories* (1987). (with M. Wandor and J. Kazantizis) *Touch Papers* (1982). *The Visitation* (1983). *The Wild Girl* (1984). *The Mirror of the Mother: Selected Poems, 1975–1985* (1986). *The Book of Mrs. Noah* (1987). *In the Red Kitchen* (1990). *Psyche and the Hurricane: Poems 1986–1990* (1991). *Daughters of the House* (1992). *During Mother's Absence* (1993). *Flesh and Blood* (1994). *All the Selves I Was: New and Selected Poems* (1995). *Impossible Saints* (1997).

BIBLIOGRAPHY: Alvarez, K. *TLS* (16 September 1994). Birch, H. *New Statesman* (30 March 1990). Broughton, T. *TLS* (22 October 1993). Brown, H. *New Statesman* (12 March 1993). Cooke, J. *New Statesman* (16 September 1994, 9 October 1992). Cunningham, V. *New Statesman* (3 November 1978). Doughty, L. *TLS.* (6 April 1990). Fisher, E. *TLS* (26 October 1984). Glastonbury, M. *New Statesman* (22 April 1983). Horovitz, M. *Punch* (12 November 1986). Hughes-Hallett, L. *LonSunTBks* (4May 1997). Kantaris, S. *PR* (1991). Kaveney, R. *TLS* (18 September 1992). Keitel, E. *A&E* (1994). King, F. *Spectator* (3 October 1992). McKay, J. *Listener* (10 September 1987). Morrison, B. *TLS.* (1 December 1978). Porter, P. *Observer* (9 March 1986). Rowland, S. *L&T* (1966). Showalter, E. *LRB* (2 October 1997). Vaux, A. *TLS* (24 July 1987). Wandor, M. *British Book News* (April 1986). White, R. *BeteN* (1993). Wills, C. *TLS* (10 July 1987). Wolitzer, M. *NYTBR* (16 April 1995).

For articles in reference works, see: *Bloomsbury. CA. Feminist.*

Jacquelyn Marie

Denise Naomi Robins

BORN: 1 February 1897, London.
DIED: 1 May 1985, Haywards Heath, Sussex.
DAUGHTER OF: Herman Klein and Denise Clarice Cornwell Klein.
MARRIED: Arthur Robins, 1918; O'Neill Pearson, 1939.
WROTE UNDER: Denise Chesterton; Ashley French; Harriet Gray; Hervey Hamilton; Julia Kane; Denise Robins; Francesca Wright.

R.'s autobiography, *Stranger Than Fiction* (1965), tells of her life as a neglected and unloved child, unwanted by either parent. Her father was a music critic and singing teacher; her mother eloped with an army officer younger than herself and turned to writing romances to support her second husband. R. was sent from school to school in the United States and England, apparently to keep her away from home. When she left school, she did some apprentice journalism in Dundee, Scotland, and at the outbreak of World War I qualified as a V.A.D. (Voluntary Aid Detachment) nurse. She met and married a wounded soldier and, in the hard times after the war, followed in her mother's footsteps by writing romances to help support her family. (Interestingly, one of her daughters also became a romance novelist.) Her marriage was not happy, but she and her first husband remained married until their three daughters were grown, at which time R. again followed her mother's example and married a second time, to a man a decade younger than herself.

R. wrote formula fiction in prodigious quantity, more than 200 novels in just under sixty years. Even when she first began writing, freelancing romantic stories and novelettes for magazines, she "wrote so much that it couldn't all be published under one name," according to her autobiography, and she began her practice of using several pseudonyms. At one time, her books were advertised on London buses with the slogan "Robins for Romance." By the time of her death, her novels had sold more than 100 million copies and had been translated into fifteen languages.

Her love stories deal with a variety of characters, themes, and settings and keep abreast of the changing social mores from the 1920s to the 1970s. Although pedestrian, her prose is clear and her plots fast-moving. Continuing reprints of her novels, some in large-type library editions, suggest that she remains popular with romance readers.

Her popularity as a writer of romances led to broadcast

work in radio and television, and in 1954 she became editor of an advice column for *She* magazine. In 1960, she founded the Romantic Novelists Association, of which she was president from 1960 to 1966.

WORKS (all published as Denise Robins except where specified): *The Marriage Bond* (1924). *Sealed Lips* (1924). *The Forbidden Bride* (1926). *The Man Between* (1926). *The Passionate Awakening* (1926). *Forbidden Love* (1927). *The Invitable End* (1927). *Jonquil* (1927). *The Triumph of the Rat* (1927). *Desire Is Blind* (1928). *The Passionate Flame* (1928). *White Jade* (1928). *Women Who Seek* (1928). *The Dark Death* (1929). *The Enduring Flame* (1929). *Heavy Clay* (1929). *Love Was a Jest* (1929). *And All Because* (1930). *It Wasn't Love* (1930). *Swing of Youth* (1930). (with R. Pertwee) *Heat Wave* (1930). *Love Poems and Others* (1930). *Crowns, Pounds, and Guineas* (1931). *Fever of Love* (1931). *Lovers of Janine* (1931). *One Night in Ceylon, and Others* (1931). *Second Best* (1931). *Blaze of Love* (1932). *The Boundary Line* (1932). *There Are Limits* (1932). *Gay Defeat* (1933). *Life's a Game* (1933). *Men Are Only Human* (1933). *Shatter the Sky* (1933). *Strange Rapture* (1933). *Brief Ecstasy* (1934). *Never Give All* (1934). *Slave-Woman* (1934). *Sweet Love* (1934). *All This for Love* (1935). *Climb to the Stars* (1935). *How Great the Price* (1935). *Life and Love* (1935). *Ivor Novello's Murder in Mayfair* (novelization of play, 1935). *Love Game* (1936). *Those Who Love* (1936). *Were I Thy Bride* (1936). *Kiss of Youth* (1937). *Set Me Free* (1937). *The Tiger in Men* (1937). *The Woman's Side of It* (1937). (as Hervey Hamilton) *Family Holiday* (1937). *Restless Heart* (1938). *Since We Love* (1938). *You Have Chosen* (1938). *Dear Loyalty* (1939). *Gypsy Lover* (1939). *I, Too, Have Loved* (1939). *Officer's Wife* (1939). *Island of Flowers* (1940). *Little We Know* (1940). *Sweet Sorrow* (1940). *To Love Is to Live* (1940). *If This Be Destiny* (1941). *Love Is Enough* (1941). *Set the Stars Alight* (1941). *Winged Love* (1941). *This One Night* (1942). *War Marriage* (1942). *What Matters Most* (1942). *The Changing Years* (1943). *Daughter Knows Best* (1943). *Dust of Dreams* (1943). *Escape to Love* (1943). *This Spring of Love* (1943). *War Changes Everything* (1943). *Give Me Back My Heart* (1944). *How to Forget* (1944). *Never Look Back* (1944). *Desert Rapture* (1945). *Love So Young* (1945). *All for You* (1946). (as Hervey Hamilton) *Figs in Frost* (1946). *Greater Than All* (1946). *Heart's Desire* (1946). *Separation* (1946). *The Story of Veronica* (1946). *Forgive Me, My Love* (1947). *More Than Love* (1947). *Could I Forget* (1948). *Khamsin* (1948). *Love Me No More!* (1948). *The Hard Way* (1949). *To Love Again* (1949). *The Uncertain Heart* (1949). *The Feast Is Finished* (1950). *Love Hath an Island* (1950). *Heart of Paris* (1951). *Infatuation* (1951). *Only My Dreams* (1951). *Second Marriage* (1951). *Something to Love* (1951). *The Other Love* (1952). *Strange Meeting* (1952). *The First Long Kiss* (1952). (as Francesca Wright) *The Loves of Lucrezia* (1953). *My True Love* (1953). (as Ashley French) *Once Is Enough* (1953). (as Ashley French) *The Bitter Core* (1954). (as Harriet Gray) *Gold for the Gay Masters* (1954). *The Long Shadow* (1954). *Venetian Rhapsody* (1954). *Bitter-Sweet* (1955). (as Denise Chesterton) *The Price of Folly* (1955). (as Denise Chesterton) *Two Loves* (1955). *The Unshaken Loyalty* (1955). (as Denise Chesterton) *When a Woman Loves* (1955). *All That Matters* (1956). (as Ashley French) *The Breaking Point* (1956). (as Harriet Gray) *Bride of Doom* (1956; as *Bride of Violence*, as by Denise Robins, 1966). *The Enchanted Island* (1956). (as Harriet Gray) *The Flame and the Frost* (1957). (with M. Pertwee) *Light the Candles* (dramatic adaptation of story by R., 1957). *The Noble One* (1957). *The Seagull's Cry* (1957). *Chateau of Flowers* (1958). *The Untrodden Snow* (1958). (as Harriet Gray) *Dance in the Dust* (1959). *Do Not Go, My Love* (1959). *Light the Candles: Stories* (1959). *We Two Together* (1959). *Arrow in the Heart* (1960). *The Unlit Fire* (1960). *I Should Have Known* (1961). (as Harriet Gray) *My Lady Destiny* (1961). *A Promise Is for Ever* (1961). (as Julia Kane) *Dark Secret Love* (1962). *Put Back the Clock* (1962). *Mad Is the Heart* (1963). *Nightingale's Song* (1963). *Reputation* (1963). *Meet Me in Monte Carlo* (1964). *Moment of Love* (1964). (as Julia Kane) *The Sin Was Mine* (1964). *Loving and Giving* (1965). *Stranger Than Fiction: Denise Robins Tells Her Life Story* (1965). *The Strong Heart* (1965). (as Julia Kane) *Time Runs Out* (1965). *The Crash* (1966). *Lightning Strikes Twice* (1966). *Love! O Fire!* (1966). *House of the Seventh Cross* (1967). *Wait for Tomorrow* (1967). *Laurence, My Love* (1968). *Love and Desire and Hate* (1969). *A Love Like Ours* (1969). (as Francesca Wright) *She-Devil: The Story of Jezebel* (1970, rev. as *Jezebel*, 1977). *Sweet Cassandra* (1970). *Forbidden* (1971). *The Snow Must Return* (1971). *The Other Side of Love* (1973). *Twice Have I Loved* (1973). *Dark Corridor* (1974). *Come Back Yesterday* (1976). *Fauna* (1978). *Love*, 12 vols. (1979–).

BIBLIOGRAPHY: Hughes, H. *The Historical Romance* (1993).

For articles in reference works, see: *CA. DNB. IAWWW. OCEL. TCRGW. TCW. WD.*

Other references: *ArmD* (1981). *Books and Bookmen* (July 1968). *LonT* (3 May 1985).

Nancy Cotton

Elizabeth Robins

BORN: 6 August 1862, Louisville, Kentucky, United States.
DIED: 8 May 1952, Brighton, Sussex.
DAUGHTER OF: Charles Ephraim Robins and Hannah Maria Crow Robins.
MARRIED: George Richmond Parks, 1885.
WROTE UNDER: C. E. Raimond.

R. established her reputation in the British theater as part of the Ibsen Circle, yet her talents went far beyond those of an actress. R. was in the forefront of breaking the actor-manager system and a leader of the women's suffrage movement in addition to being a recognized novelist and essayist.

Born to parents who were also first cousins, R. was the eldest of seven children. R. spent her early childhood on Staten Island, New York, but because of failed family fortunes and her mother's increased mental instability the family moved to Zanesville, Ohio, in 1872, where for seven years R. attended the Putnam Feminine Seminary. During that time, she acquired a love for acting and the habit of keeping a diary, an activity she pursued, with few gaps, throughout her long life.

Though R.'s father encouraged her to become a doctor, she wanted a career on the stage. At the age of eighteen, she moved to New York City, took the stage name of Claire Raimond, and toured with James O'Neill's troupe and with H. M. Pitt's company. In 1883, R. was recruited by the Boston Museum Company, where she met George Richmond Parks, an aspiring actor five years her senior. Though initially hesitant because of her family's history of mental illness, R. married Parks, but the marriage was unsuccessful. Parks was possessive, their frequent separations did little to quell his jealousy, his career did not equal hers, and, in 1887, he committed suicide.

After Parks's death, R. toured in *Macbeth* and *The Merchant of Venice* and accepted an invitation to visit Norway. On the way, she stopped in England and determined she might be able to find work in the British theater as the Ibsen craze was making its appearance. In 1891, R. translated Ibsen's *Hedda Gabler* and played the lead. So defining was the role that she once wrote: "I came to think of my early life as divisible into two parts: before and after *Hedda.*" Yet *Hedda Gabler* was important not merely because it established R.'s reputation as an actress. An equally significant fact is that R., together with Marion Lea, successfully circumvented the theater establishment by producing and directing the show themselves. Such a step was virtually unheard of, but R. was determined not to partake of the actor-manager system that effectively controlled actresses by determining which roles they would play. She produced, directed, and starred as Hilda in Ibsen's *The Master Builder* (1893), winning rave notices; in later years, she produced Ibsen's *Brand, Little Eyolf,* and *John Gabriel Borkman.* After leaving the stage, R. wrote *Ibsen and the Actress* (1928), in which she maintained that "no dramatist has ever meant so much to the women of the stage as Henrik Ibsen."

Because of the precarious financial nature of acting, R. turned to writing to supplement her income, turning out reviews, short stories, and novels. In 1893, she and Florence Bell wrote the play *Alan's Wife,* which shocked theatergoers with its theme of infanticide. In all, R. wrote fourteen novels and two series of short stories. She tackled the tough issues of the day: divorce, prostitution, women's suffrage. *George Mandeville's Husband* (1894) showed R.'s feminist leanings. This novel, as Angela John points out, can be read "as a wry exploration of role reversal. All that the husband has to endure is what is usually commonplace for wives: to live vicariously through the provider, to be denied even your own name, and to be valued, if at all, for your position as the spouse of the acclaimed."

In 1907, R. wrote and produced a suffrage play, *Votes for Women!,* which she later recast into a novel, *The Convert.* After her lover, George Stonor, refuses to marry her, Vida Levering, the pregnant heroine, has an abortion. Instead of succumbing to the status of victim, however, she becomes an ardent champion of women's rights, even converting her former lover's fiancée to the cause. Vida obtains her ultimate revenge when Stonor, as a member of Parliament, also agrees to support the movement.

Where Are You Going To? (1913) tackles the problem of the white slave trade. R. had long been interested in this problem, and the poet John Masefield provided her with first-hand knowledge that she incorporated into the story of two middle-class teenagers lured to London and then kidnapped. In the United States, where the novel was first serialized and then released in book form, it was said to have "startled a continent." It went into a fourth edition within a month of its release and sometimes sold more than one thousand copies a day.

Ancilla's Share (1924) was published anonymously. R. lashes out at the "sex antagonism" that erupted at the conclusion of World War I. Subtitled *An Indictment of Sex Antagonism,* this polemic details the failure of male-dominated governments to make peace following the war. It questions why women, "the strongest peace element in any civilised society," continue to be excluded from official public life. The text, presented as a legal brief, begins with "Indictment," then lays out the evidence to prove that women have been wrongly deprived of equal rights, receiving only the *ancilla*'s [handmaid's] share of prosperity. A reviewer, who misunderstood the book's purpose, took issue with R.'s style, complaining it was "clumsy and confused," often making it "difficult to see at once what the author is driving at, especially since her argument is split up into short paragraphs consisting of one sentence only." The reviewer also criticized her "obsession which traces every deficiency or failure of women to the wickedness of men." *Ancilla's Share* sold very poorly, partly because it was published anonymously. R.'s most popular novel was *Magnetic North* (1904), based on her trip to Alaska in 1900 to find her brothers, who had disappeared when they traveled to the Yukon in search of gold. So popular was this novel that it went through seven printings in four years.

Although R. remained an American citizen, she became actively involved in the British Women's Suffrage Movement, enlisted by the Pankhursts to speak at rallies and to write pamplets and letters. Among others, R. wrote "The Feminist Movement in England" (1907) and "Woman's War. A Defense of Militant Suffrage" (1913). She did not participate in the more militant activities such as firebombing and brickthrowing, possibly because of a fear of deportation, but her vast network of friends allowed her to apply informal pressure on politicians and governmental officials. R. helped organize the Actresses' Franchise League and the Women Writers' Suffrage League, of which she was the first president. She provided financial assistance to the cause by dividing the royalties of *Votes for Women!* between the two main suffrage organizations, the Women's Social and Political Union and the National Union of Women's Suffrage Societies.

Although R. never remarried, she counted many male admirers among her acquaintances, including Oscar Wilde and William Heinemann, whose repeated proposals of marriage she finally ended by threatening to shoot him with a pistol. When George Bernard Shaw made unwanted advances in a cab, she literally threw him out onto the pavement. She found his feminism suspect. She called H. G. Wells, Wyndham Lewis, and Aldous Huxley "this brace of minotaurs." William Archer and R. carried on a long, probably celibate, relationship, chronicled in letters, poetry, and diary entries. John Masefield became enamored of her after writing a fan letter (1909), though she was fifty at the time, old enough to be his mother. Masefield wrote R. an enormous number of letters, nine in one day alone, but R. slowly extricated herself from this affair; she wrote in the corner of one of Masefield's letters, "Oh dear! Why will he fantasticate like this; it spoils things. . . . These poets!" R. knew and corresponded with Henry James, eventually publishing a series of his letters (*Theatre and Friendship*, 1932). She was devoted to her brother Raymond and, towards the end of her life, wrote a memoir of him, *Raymond and I*, which he would not allow to be published until after his death.

In 1909, R. met Octavia Wilberforce. R. had by this time bought her home, Backsettown, and Wilberforce, whose family lived nearby, began riding her bicycle to visit R. on a regular basis. Wilberforce wanted to become a doctor. When she rejected a marriage proposal, her father cut her out of his will. R. encouraged Wilberforce in her studies and eventually the two women decided to live together, becoming lifelong companions.

Other neighbors were Virginia and Leonard Woolf. Virginia Woolf had reviewed R.'s *A Dark Lantern* (1905), faulting R.'s characterization of Dr. Garth Vincent but overall applauding the novel: "But there can be no doubt that few living novelists are so genuinely gifted as Miss Robins, or can produce work to match hers for strength and sincerity." She also reviewed *The Mills of the Gods* (1920): "Miss Elizabeth Robins must be used by this time to being told that she writes like a man." The Woolfs published *Ibsen and the Actress* and the posthumous *Raymond and I* (1956).

R. is important to theater history both for her performances of Hedda and Hilda, but equally for her insistence on equity for actresses. A living example of the New Woman and once called by Stella Campbell "the first intellectual I had known on the stage," R. demanded, through her fight for women's suffrage, that women also be acknowledged as equal partners in society at large. She even championed the cause of better race relations. Her plays, novels, memoirs, and diaries all reveal a strong, intelligent woman who refused to succumb to societal conventions and who was willing to deal openly with topics considered taboo by "polite society."

WORKS: (with F. Bell) *Alan's Wife* (1893). *George Mandeville's Husband* (1894). *Milly's Story, Or, The New Moon* (1895). *Below the Salt* (1896; in the U.S. as *The Fatal Gift of Beauty*). *The Open Question* (1898). *The Mirkwater* (1900). *The Silver Lotus* (1900). *Woman's Secret* (1900). *Magnetic North* (1904). *A Dark Lantern* (1905). *Woman's Search* (1905). *The Florentine Frame* (1907). *Votes for Women!* (1907; repub. as *The Convert*, 1907). *Under the Southern Cross* (1907). *Come and Find Me* (1908). *The Mills of the Gods and Other Stories* (1908). *Miss Cal* (1910). *Why?* (1910). *Where Are You Going To?* (1913; serialized in the U.S. as *My Little Sister*, 1913). *Way Stations* (1913). *What Can I Do?* (1914). *Camilla* (1918). *The Messenger* (1919). (with O. Wilberforce) *Prudence and Peter. A Story for Children About Cooking Out-of-Doors and Indoors* (1920). *Time Is Whispering* (1923). *Ancilla's Share* (1924). *The Secret That Was Kept* (1926). *Ibsen and the Actress* (1928). *Theatre and Friendship* (1932). *Both Sides of the Curtain* (1940). *Portrait of a Lady, Or, The English Spirit Old and New* (1941). *Raymond and I* (1956).

BIBLIOGRAPHY: Cima, G. G. *ThS* (1980). Gates, J. *Elizabeth Robins: Actress, Novelist, Feminist* (1994). Gates, J. *MD* (1985). John, A. *Elizabeth Robins: Staging a Life, 1862–1952* (1995). *LonT* (9 May 1952). *NYT* (9 May 1952).

For articles in reference works, see: *AWW. CA. DNB. 1890s. OCAL. Stanford. TCA. ToddBWW. Who Was Who.*

Other references: Babington Smith, C. *John Masefield: A Life* (1978). Marcus, J. *Art and Anger: Reading Like a Woman* (1988). *Essays of Virginia Woolf 1904–1912*, ed. A. McNeillie (1987). *Essays of Virginia Woolf, 1919–1924*, ed. A. McNeillie (1987). Mulford, W., in *Re-Reading English*, ed. P. Widdowson (1982). Powell, K. *Oscar Wilde, and the Theatre of the 1890s* (1990). Powell, K. *NCTR* (1993). Powell, K., in *Rediscovering Oscar Wilde*, ed. G. Sandalescu (1994). Spender, D. *Women of Ideas (And What Men Have Done to Them)* (1983). Stowell, S. *A Stage of Their Own: Feminist Playwrights of the Suffrage Era* (1992). Whitebrook, P. *William Archer: A Biography* (1993). *TLS* (29 May 1924). Wiley, C., in *Women in Theatre*, ed. J. Redmond (1989). Wiley, C. *TJ* (1990).

Natalie Joy Woodall

Agnes Mary Frances Robinson

BORN: 27 February 1857, Leamington Spa, Warwickshire.

DIED: 1944, Aurillac, France.

DAUGHTER OF: George T. Robinson and Frances Sparrow.

MARRIED: James Darmesteter, 1888; Émile Duclaux, 1901.

R. was the daughter of a Coventry architect who also served as a newspaper correspondent during the Franco-Prussian war; her early years were spent in Warwickshire and Lancashire. A cosmopolitan young woman, she was educated in Belgium and Italy and studied English and classical literature at University College, London. She had a busy career as a writer, producing poetry in a variety of genres as well as criticism, prose fiction, and biographies in both English and French from the age of twenty-one until her middle sixties. R. spent much of her life in France and was equally well known as a French literary and cultural historian and as an English poet of the late Victorian and Edwardian periods.

R.'s poetic career opened in 1878, when *A Handful of Honeysuckle* was privately published by her parents. This little book included a number of poems addressed to R.'s close friend, the writer "Vernon Lee" (Violet Paget), who herself had been publishing since the age of fourteen. R.'s first volume, Pre-Raphaelite in inspiration, was admired at Oxford and remarked upon by Alfred Lord Tennyson and by Robert Browning, who was a friend of R.'s parents and an occasional visitor in their home. Encouraged, R. began her writing career in earnest.

R.'s next publication was a translation of *The Crowned Hippolytus* by Euripides (1881), to which she appended some original verses of her own. That same year, she launched her career as a biographer with a life of Emily Brontë for the Eminent Women series. This proving successful, she went on to write literary portraits and biographies of Queen Margaret of Navarre (1886) and of numerous French literary and cultural figures, including Renan, Hugo, Pascal, Racine, and Froissart.

A novel, *Arden* (1883), portrays an orphaned young woman who marries a farmer much older and rougher mannered than she: "So they were married, and all her struggles over. At first, the bird beats wildly against the strange, confining bars, but soon it is reconciled and makes of the cage a home. The wife is pregnant at seventeen, miscarries, and begins an innocent flirtation with an old boyfriend. Her husband dies suddenly, and Arden realizes too late that she loved him after all." After *Arden,* R. left novel writing to her younger sister Frances Mabel (who wrote six of them), and turned her aspirations to write narratives honoring the poor toward poetry. *The New Arcadia* (1884) is a collection of poems (e.g., "The Wise-Woman," "The Scapegoat," "The Rothers") "drawn from human models," R. explained. "Most of the personages of the New Arcadia lived on a common in Surrey near my garden gates." Arthur Symons compared these poetical sketches, ballads, and dramatic monologues to Balzac's portrayals of tragic peasant life.

In 1888, after marrying James Darmesteter, a professor of Persian, and moving to Paris where she established a salon, R. never lived in England again. She turned her attention to France, publishing introductions to French-language editions of Robert Browning and other English writers, as well as editing Margaret of Navarre (1887), Renan (1914), and Marie de Sévigné (1927). She translated her husband's criticism into English (and translated some of her poetry into French), and she produced numerous critical, historical, and sociological articles about French culture. When Darmesteter died in 1894, R. remained in France. In 1901, she married Emile Duclaux and moved with him to Olmet in the Cantel region.

The Return to Nature (1904), published the year R.'s second husband died, concerns the cycles and seasons of nature, reflections on mortality and the spirit of life, and the celebration of natural beauty. R.'s desire to portray life in farm communities continues in this volume. A Wordsworthian ballad, "Too Busy," depicts a peasant girl who breaks her ankle in a field on the way home from her job in town. The "return to nature" becomes ironic as the girl dies of exposure to thirst and is subsumed into nature while rural life goes on all around her. *Images and Meditations* (1923) presents images of aging, mortality, and the disappearing self. It also contains numerous poems about World War I, including "The Submarine, January 1916," "The Wood at Sucy, July 1915," and "The Mourners, Paris 1917." It is a poignant final volume, dedicated to her sister Mabel, who, like R., was then about sixty-five years old.

R.'s poetic style is difficult to characterize; her artistic competence developed throughout her career. Her preferred forms were ballads and lyrics, including Italian forms like the rispetti and stornelli. Her voice was delicate, composed, and thoughtful. From first to last, R. was self-effacing about her gifts as a poet. In the preface to her collected poems (1902), R. wrote: "like all poets, I trust these little songs may find an audience tomorrow. . . . We cannot all be great poets; but the humblest, if they be sincere, may give a genuine pleasure."

WORKS: *A Handful of Honeysuckle* (1878). (trans.) *The Crowned Hippolytus of Euripides, with New Poems* (1881). *Emily Brontë* (1883). *Arden: A Novel* (1883). The *New Arcadia and Other Poems* (1884). *An Italian Garden: A Book of Songs* (1886). *Margaret of Angouleme, Queen of Navarre* (1886). *The Fortunate Lovers* (1887). *The Witching Time* (1887). *Songs, Ballads, and a Garden Play* (1888). *The End of the Middle Ages: Essays and Questions of History* (1888). *Lyrics Selected from the Works* (1891). *Retrospect and Other Poems* (1893). *Froissard* (1895). (trans.) *New English Studies,* by J. Darmesteter (1896). *The Life of Ernest Renard* (1897). *A Medieval Garland* (1898). *My Sister Henrietta* (1900). *Collected Poems, Lyrical and Narrative, with a Preface* (1902). *The Fields of France* (1903). *The Return to Nature: Songs and Symbols* (1904). *Songs from an Italian Garden* (1908). *The French Procession: A Pageant of Great Writers* (1909). *Heaven: What and Where?* (1909). *Casa Guidi Windows* (1911). *The French Ideal* (1911). *A Short History of France* (1918). *Twentieth-Century French Writers* (1919). *Victor Hugo* (1921). *Images and Meditations: Poems* (1923). *The Life of Racine* (1925). *Portrait of Pascal* (1925). *Our Lady of the Broken Heart* (1970). (with others) *Romantic Tales* (n.d.).

BIBLIOGRAPHY: Holmes, R.V.Z. *ELT* (1967). *Victorian Women Poets: An Anthology,* ed. A. Leighton and M. Reynolds (1995). Lynch, H. *Fortnightly Review* (February 1902). Watson, W. *Academy* (21 February 1891).

For articles in reference works, see: *EP. Feminist. PPC.*

Other references: Hickok, K. *Representations of Women: Nineteenth-Century British Women's Poetry* (1984).

Kathleen Hickok

Mary Darby Robinson (Perdita)

BORN: 27 November 1758, College Green, Bristol.
DIED: 26 December 1800, Englefield Cottage, Surrey.
DAUGHTER OF: Captain John Darby and Elizabeth Seys Darby.
MARRIED: Thomas Robinson, 1774.
WROTE UNDER: Tabitha Bramble; Mary Darby; Daphne; Echo; A Friend to Humanity; Julia; Horace Jevenal; Laura; Laura Maria; Louisa; Oberon; Perdita; Ann Frances Randall; Mrs. Robinson; Sylphid.

The daughter of a whaling-ship captain of Irish descent, R. became an actress, a playwright, a poet, and a novelist. She was also, for a brief time, the mistress of the Prince of Wales, later King George IV.

R. was introduced by the dancing-master at Mrs. Hervey's to David Garrick, who asked R. to play Cordelia to his Lear. Although R. served a period of internship at Drury

Lane Theatre, her acting debut was postponed by her marriage to Thomas Robinson, a law student. After a period of high living in London, Robinson, who proved to be a scoundrel, was sent to debtors' prison, where R. and her infant daughter, Maria, spent ten months with him.

Shortly after her marriage, R. began writing poetry. With the help of her patroness, Georgianna Cavendish, the Duchess of Devonshire, R. published her first collection of poems, *Verses*, in 1775. Cavendish was R.'s only female visitor in prison, a fact that led R. to develop a bitter dislike for members of her own sex. In her *Memoirs* (1801), R. said: "During my long seclusion from society . . . not one of my female friends even inquired what was become of me. . . . Indeed, I have almost found my own sex my most inveterate enemies; I have experienced little kindness from them, though my bosom has often ached with the pangs inflicted by their envy, slander, and malevolence."

Upon her husband's release from prison, R. resumed her acting career and enjoyed four highly successful seasons at Drury Lane, but her fourth season, 1779–80, was her last. On 3 December 1779, R. played the part of Perdita in *The Winter's Tale.* Her performance so captivated the Prince of Wales that he fell in love with her, and R. was permanently nicknamed "Perdita." R. shortly became the prince's mistress but was soon replaced. Humiliated by the prince's rejection, R. abandoned the stage and fled to France, where she was befriended by Marie Antoinette, in whose honor R. later composed "Monody to the Memory of the Late Queen of France." When R. returned to England, she formed a lasting liaison with Colonel Tarleton (Sir Banastre), an officer of the British army in America.

The early 1780s marked the high point of R.'s public fame. She regularly toured the fashionable sections of London in an "absurd chariot with a basket shaped like a coronet attached to the side," driven by her current "friend"; her husband and other hopeful admirers sat in the side-car. R.'s life changed drastically in 1784, however, when she contracted an "unknown" disease, probably rheumatoid arthritis or polio, that left her lower body weakened and partially paralyzed. R. remained an invalid for the rest of her life and devoted herself to her writing.

Though much of R.'s poetry now seems too affected and sentimental, with an over-abundance of eighteenth-century apostrophizing, a number of R.'s contemporaries, most notably Samuel Taylor Coleridge, had high praise for R.'s work and found her "a woman of undoubted genius." Coleridge not only admired R.'s poems but imitated one of them himself: His "The Snow-Drop" was originally entitled "Lines written immediately after the perusal of Mrs. Robinson's Snow Drop." Coleridge was also very much impressed with R.'s "Haunted Beach," a poem vaguely reminiscent of his own "Rime of the Ancient Mariner." As a final tribute, Coleridge's "The Stranger Minstrel" was subtitled: "Written [to Mrs. Robinson] a few weeks before her death." From 1788 to 1791, R. was part of the Della Cruscan movement led by Robert Merry. R. and other female followers of Merry (Hester Thrale Piozzi and Hannah Cowley) were viciously attacked, both personally and professionally, by literary critic William Gifford in his *Baviad.*

R. spent her last years in London, where she belonged to a circle of "radical" women that included Mary Wollstonecraft, Mary Hays, Charlotte Smith, and Helen Maria Williams, all of whom were accused by the Reverend Richard Polwhele, an anti-feminist, anti-"Jacobin" critic, of trying to "taint" their young female readers with the "demon democracy." It was due, in part, to the influence of the Wollstonecraft circle that R. published two feminist tracts, "Thoughts on the Condition of Women" and "A Letter to the Women of England on the Injustice of Mental Subordination, with Anecdotes by Ann Frances Randall," in 1799. R. was also a close friend of William Godwin, whose influence can be seen in R.'s most widely read novel, *Walsingham; or, The Pupil of Nature* (1797). *Walsingham,* basically a sentimental novel, though it does touch on political and ethical questions similar to those posed in Godwin's works, was especially popular in France. At the time of her death in 1800, R. was writing her autobiography. The work was completed by R.'s daughter and published posthumously in 1801 as *Memoirs of the Late Mrs Robinson, Written by Herself.*

WORKS: *Verses* (1775). *Poems* (1777). *The Lucky Escape* (1779). *Poems* (1791). *Vacenza; or the Dancers of Credulity* (1792). *Nobody* (1794). *The Widow* (1794). *Angelina* (1796). *The Sicilian Lover* (1796). *Sappho and Phaon* (1796). *Hubert de Sevrac* (1796). *Walsingham; or, the Pupil of Nature* (1797). *The False Friend* (1799). "A Letter to the Women of England on the Injustice of Mental Subordination, with Anecdotes by Ann Frances Randall" and "Thoughts on the Condition of Women" (1799). *Effusions of Love* (R.'s correspondence with the Prince of Wales, n.d.). *Lyrical Tales* (1800). *The Mistletoe* (1800). *Memoirs of the Late Mrs. Robinson, Written by Herself,* ed. M. Robinson (1801). *Poetical Works of the Late Mrs. Mary Robinson,* ed. M. Robinson (1806).

BIBLIOGRAPHY: Bass, R. *The Green Dragoon: The Lives of Banastre Tarleton and Mary Robinson* (1957). *Romantic Women Writers: Voices and Countervoices,* ed. P. Feldman and T. Kelley (1995). Hargreaves-Mawdsley, W. N. *The English Della Cruscans and Their Time 1783–1828* (1967). Luria, G., intro. to *Walsingham; or The Pupil of Nature* (1797, rpt. 1974). Makower, S. *Perdita [Mary Robinson]; A Romance in Biography* (1908). Robinson, M., preface to *Poetical Works of the Late Mrs. Mary Robinson* (1806, rpt. 1828). *Revisioning Romanticism: British Women Writers, 1776–1837,* ed. C. S. Wilson and J. Haefner (1994).

For articles in reference works, see: *DNB. Feminist. Oxford. ToddBWW. ToddDBA.*

Other references: *Drama* (Summer 1950). Pergus, J. and J. Thaddeus. *SECC* (1987). Labbe, J. *WC* (1994). Luther, S. *SIR* (1994). McGann, J. *MLQ* (1995). Miskolcze, R. *PLL* (1995). Pascoe, J. *WC* (1992). Reiman, D. *Criticism* (1984). Ty, E. *ESC* (1995).

Kay Beaird Meyers

Robinson, Mrs.: See *Robinson, Mary Darby (Perdita)*

Margaret More Roper

BORN: 1505, Bucklersbury (London).
DIED: 1544.
DAUGHTER OF: Sir Thomas More and Jane More.
MARRIED: William Roper, 1521.

Although recognized in her own day as an accomplished scholarly woman, R. has received little attention since then. Three of her father's early biographers—William Roper, R.'s husband (c. 1556), Nicholas Harpsfield (c. 1557), and Thomas Stapleton (1588)—singled out R. from among the four siblings as the most scholarly and virtuous of his children. By eighteen years of age, R. had excelled at Greek and Latin studies of classics and patristics, and Stapleton listed her accomplishments as Latin and Greek verse, "elegant and graceful" Latin speeches, a "clever" exercise in imitation of Quintilian's oratory, meditations on *The Four Last Thynges,* and "eloquent" Latin and English letters. Well aware of both her accomplishments and the predicament of a female scholar, her father writes, "the incredulity of men would rob you of the praise you so richly deserved . . . as they would never believe when they read what you have written that you had not often availed yourself of another's help."

Only a small elite circle knew R. as a scholar; however, her gentle personality and excellent scholarship did have a profound effect on several Renaissance humanists in their consideration of a classical education for women. Erasmus, after living with the More family for an extended period, specifically mentioned R.'s written work as the basis for his new belief in higher education of women, according to G. Bude. Richard Hyrde, in a dedicatory letter prefacing the *Devout Treatise,* speaks to a young woman, advocating a good education, referring to R. as "proof evident enough, what good learning can do, where it is surely rooted."

Few of her works are extant: several letters and the *Devout Treatise Upon the Pater Noster* (1526?). One of the letters written to her step-sister, Lady Alice Alington, and likely written in cooperation with her father when he was imprisoned in the Tower of London awaiting execution, is an artfully crafted dialogue patterned after Plato's *Crito.* Like the Platonic defense for Socrates's position shortly before his execution, R.'s dialogue provides the defense for her father's conscientious stand against the desires of King Henry VIII.

R.'s *A Devout Treatise,* though considered a translation of Erasmus's Latin meditations on the Lord's Prayer, is, in fact, an expression of her own voice and emphases. She goes well beyond a mere literal translation. Her sentence structure is independent of the original, with added phrases and clauses, and she creates parallel structures indicative of an expertise in composition not frequently found in the English prose of the early sixteenth century. But particularly in the sense of the work, R. has contributed her own expression, emphasizing the contrast between man's unworthiness and vileness against God's goodness and gentleness far more than the original work suggests.

WORKS: Letter found in *The Correspondence of Sir Thomas More,* No. 206, ed. E. F. Rogers (1947). *A Devout Treatise Upon the Pater Noster* (1526?; STC 10477; rpt. in *Erasmus of Rotterdam,* ed. R. L. De Molen, 1971).

BIBLIOGRAPHY: Kaufman, P. I. *SCJ* (1989). Maber, R. G. *Moreana* (1986). McCutcheon, E., in *New Ways of Looking at Old Texts,* ed. S. W. Hill (1993). McCutcheon, E., in *Women Writers of the Renaissance and Reformation,* ed. K. M. Wilson (1987). Reynolds, E. E. *Margaret Roper* (1960). Robineau, M. C., G. J. Donnelly, G. Marc'hadour, and E. E. Reynolds. *Moreana* (1966). Stapleton. T. *The Life and Illustrious Martyrdom of Sir Thomas More* (1588; trans. P. E. Hallett, 1928; ed. E. E. Reynolds, 1966). Verbrugge, R. M., in *Silent but for the Word: Tudor Women as Patrons, Translators, and Writers of Religious Works,* ed. M. Hannay (1985). Waithe, M. E., in *A History of Women Philosophers,* ed. M. E. Waithe and J. Gibson (1989). Wright, N. E., in *Creative Imitation,* ed. D. Quint et al. (1992).

For articles in reference works, see: *Bloomsbury. Feminist. Oxford. ToddBWW.*

Rita Verbrugge-Cunningham

Rosanna: See *Tighe, Mary*

Rosina: See *Bulwer-Lytton, Rosina Wheeler*

Ross, Martin: See *Somerville and Ross (Violet Florence Martin)*

Christina Rossetti

BORN: 5 December 1830, London.
DIED: 29 December 1894, London.
DAUGHTER OF: Gabriele Rossetti and Frances Polidori Rossetti.
WROTE UNDER: Ellen Alleyn; Christina Rossetti.

R., the foremost female poet of religious verse and orthodox Christianity in nineteenth-century England, has been ranked with John Donne, George Herbert, and Gerard Manley Hopkins as one of the great religious poets.

R. was the youngest of four children born into a gifted, literary Italian-English family; the Pre-Raphaelite poet and painter Dante Gabriel Rossetti was her oldest brother, and R.'s first book, *Verses* (1847), was printed by her grandfather on his own press when she was sixteen. R. suffered from chronic ill health throughout her life, a condition that allowed her to escape the odious work as a governess that her sister Maria undertook to help support the family. On two occasions, R. assisted her mother in conducting a day school, in 1851–52 and again in 1853, and from 1860 to 1870 she worked at a House of Charity for "fallen" women run by Anglican nuns.

Family and religion formed the dominant centers of R.'s life. She was strongly attached to her mother, with whom she lived most of her life. Like her mother and sister, R. was influenced by the Oxford Movement and became a fervent Anglo-Catholic. In 1850, R. broke her engagement to the Pre-Raphaelite painter James Collinson because of religious differences, and again in 1866 she refused to marry a close friend, the linguist Charles Bagot Cayley, ostensibly because he did not share her religious views.

Significantly, perhaps, R. served as the model for Mary in several of her brother's paintings.

In 1850, seven of R.'s poems appeared in the Pre-Raphaelite journal *The Germ,* all under the pseudonym of Ellen Alleyn. D. G. Rossetti eagerly promoted his sister's poems, sending them in 1861 to the Victorian critic John Ruskin, who judged that no publisher would take them because they were too full of "quaintnesses and offenses." In the same year, however, Macmillan accepted R.'s manuscript of *Goblin Market and Other Poems* (1862), the success of which established R. as a leading English poet. A moral allegory of sensual temptation, fall, and redemption through sisterly love and self-sacrifice, this work is considered by some critics to be R.'s major claim to literary immortality. The subject of sisters, who frequently embody contrasting states of mind, occurs in a number of R.'s poems from the 1850s and 1860s. The title poem of R.'s next collection, *The Prince's Progress and Other Poems* (1866), is a richly textured Pre-Raphaelite allegorical pilgrimage of a soul and the moral crisis that results from worldly self-indulgence. A mood of world-weariness echoes through many of R.'s poems. The themes of unhappy or unrequited love, renunciation, regret at a wasted life, and musings on death and eternal life are common. Rarely does a note of joyous exultation break through, as it does in her early and famous love poem, "A Birthday" (1857). Of her more than 1,000 poems, nearly half are devotional and nearly half deal with death, either as an end to suffering or as a prelude to the happier afterlife of the Christian resurrection. R. renounced the fulfillment of earthly love in devotion to an ideal of spiritual love. That R.'s love of heaven presented her with no easy consolation but with a difficult journey is apparent in her well-known poem "Uphill" (1858).

A different side of R. emerges in her poems for children, published as a collection in *Sing-Song: A Nursery Rhyme Book* (1872). These verses consist of light instructional rhymes; poems about animals, flowers, and the natural world; lullabies; Christmas carols; and a few nonsense rhymes. R.'s most famous poem for children, "Who has seen the wind?" is still widely anthologized, as is the carol "In the bleak mid-winter."

R.'s two collections of short stories, *Commonplace* (1870) and *Speaking Likenesses* (1874), were not popular and are of interest chiefly for their characterizations of people in the Rossetti circle. More successful as an autobiographical portrait is R.'s youthful novella (*Maude* (1897), written when she was nineteen but published posthumously. Maude, suffering from R.'s own character flaws of overscrupulousness and a very human and impenitent pride in her poetic accomplishments, dies when she falls out of a carriage. R. presents in the story several alternative female roles and fates, though Maude's own fate is clearly the most romantic.

"Monna Innominata," a sonnet sequence on the theme of unhappy love, was originally published in *A Pageant and Other Poems* (1881). Like Elizabeth Barrett Browning before her, R. intentionally reverses the male poetic tradition in these fourteen sonnets and lets the "unnamed lady" of so many love sonnets express her own love in her own voice. Another sonnet sequence published in *A Pageant and Other Poems* is "Later Life," twenty-eight poems that are essentially religious and hortatory in tone. Here, as in other poems, R. uses the cycle of nature to represent the cycle of despair and of hope for rebirth in the human spirit.

R.'s religious prose does not reveal the intensity of spiritual struggle shown in many of her poems and is often merely dutiful in tone. But works like *Annus Domini* (1874), *Called To Be Saints* (1881), and *The Face of the Deep* (1892) reflect her intimate knowledge of the Bible and the Apocrypha, and *Time Flies: A Reading Diary* (1885) is of interest for its reflections on incidents and details from R.'s life.

Although many readers have regarded R. as one of the world's finest religious poets, and some have called her the greatest English woman poet of the nineteenth century, her vision and power were limited by the restrictions of the Victorian world. The deep conflict between R.'s instinctive temperament and the demands of Victorian womanhood and authoritarian religion resulted in her withdrawal from direct experience of life into an intense and often anguished inner life. Thus, much of her poetry deals, as Ralph Bellas has said, with "the self-consciousness of buffering rather than the dramatic presentation of suffering itself." Yet from within her limited angle on the world, tidy, technical mastery, and expressive tenderness assure her of literary immortality.

WORKS: *Verses* (1847). *Goblin Market and Other Poems* (1862). *The Prince's Progress and Other Poems* (1866). *Poems* (1866). *Commonplace and Other Stories* (1870). *Sing-Song: A Nursery Rhyme Book* (1872, 1893). *Annus Domini: A Prayer for Each Day of the Year, Founded on a Text of Holy Scripture* (1874). *Speaking Likenesses, with Pictures Thereof by Arthur Hughes* (1874). *Goblin Market. The Prince's Progress, and Other Poems* (1875). *Seek and Find: A Double Series of Short Studies on the Benedicite* (1879). *A Pageant and Other Poems* (1881). *Called to be Saints: The Minor Festivals Devotionally Studied* (1881). *Letter and Spirit: Notes on the Commandments* (1883). *Time Flies: A Reading Diary* (1885). *Poems* (1890). *The Face of the Deep: A Devotional Commentary on the Apocalypse* (1892). *Verses: Reprinted from "Called to be Saints," "Time Flies," "The Face of the Deep"* (1893). *New Poems, Hitherto Unpublished or Uncollected* (1896). *Maude: A Story for Girls* (1897). The *Poetical Works of Christina Georgina Rossetti, with Memoir and Notes,* ed. W. M. Rossetti (1904). *Rossetti Papers 1862–1870,* ed. W. M. Rossetti (1903). *The Family Letters of Christina Georgina Rossetti,* ed. W. M. Rossetti (1908). *Three Rossettis. Unpublished Letters to and from Dante Gabriel, Christina, William,* ed. J. C. Troxell (1937). *Collected Poems of Christina Rosetti,* 3 vols., ed. R. W. Crump (1979–90). *Letters vol. 1, 1843–73,* ed. A. H. Harrison (1997).

BIBLIOGRAPHY: Addison, J. *BB* (1995). Battiscombe, G. *Christina Rossetti: A Divided Life* (1981). Bell, M. *Christina Rossetti* (1898). Bellas, R. A. *Christina Rossetti* (1977). Belsey, A. and C. Belsey. *TexP* (1988). Bishop, N., in *Reform and Counterreform/Women in Literature: Criticism of the Seventies* (1979). Fredeman, W. E. *The Victorian Poets: A Guide to Research* (1968). Garlick, B. *PMLA* (1955). Garlick, B., in *Virginal Sexuality and Textuality in Victorian Literature,* ed. L. Davis (1993).

Gilbert, P. K. *English* (1992). Hassett, C. W. *PQ* (1986). Hunt, H. W. *Pre-Raphaelitism and the Pre-Raphaelite Brotherhood* (1905). *The Achievement of Christina Rossetti,* ed. D. A. Kent (1987). Leder, S. and A. Abbott. *The Language of Exclusion: The Poetry of Emily Dickinson and Christina Rossetti* (1987). Leighton, A. *MP* (1990). Marsh, J. *Christina Rossetti: A Literary Biography* (1994; in the U.S. as *Christina Rossetti: A Writer's Life,* 1995). Marshall, L. E. *UTQ* (1994). Maxwell, C. *ES* (1995). Mayberry, K. J. *Christina Rossetti and the Poetry of Discovery* (1989). Mermin, D. *VP* (1983). Packer, L. M. *Christina Rossetti* (1963). Rosenblum, D. *VP* (1982). Smulders, S. *TSLL* (1992). Smulders, S. *Christina Rossetti Revisited* (1996). Thomas, F. *Christina Rossetti: A Biography* (1994). Thompson, D. A. *Mosaic* (1991). *VP* (special R. issues: 1993, 1994). Woolf, V. *The Second Common Reader* (1932).

For articles in reference works, see: *BA19C. Bloomsbury. Cambridge. DLB. DNB. Feminist. NCLC. Oxford. ToddBWW. VB.*

Other references: Keane, R. N. *Nineteenth-Century Women Writers of the English-Speaking World* (1986). Knoepflmacher, U. C. *NCF* (1986).

Jean E. Pearson

Elizabeth Singer Rowe

BORN: 1674.
DIED: 20 February 1737.
DAUGHTER OF: Walter Singer and Elizabeth Portnell.
MARRIED: Thomas Rowe.
WROTE UNDER: Philomela.

One of the most popular religious poets and epistolary writers of the first half of the eighteenth century, whose works were a staple of the press throughout Europe and America, R. was educated in the Ilchester, Somerset, household of a nonconformist minister. Following a correspondence with the bookseller John Dunton, R. began her career as a professional author in October 1693 by contributing poems to Dunton's *The Athenian Mercury* (1691–97). In 1696, at the age of twenty-two, she published her first collection, *Poems on Several Occasions,* by "Philomela." By the end of her life, she would be universally lauded as "saintly" for the fervor of her devotional poetry. During her long, productive career, she attracted the notice and praise of such figures as Matthew Prior, Isaac Watts, Alexander Pope, the Earl of Orrery, Elizabeth Carter, and Samuel Johnson, who in his typically backhanded fashion praised the purity of her sentiment and her fusion of religion and romance.

Poems on Several Occasions helped earn her the patronage of Lord Weymouth and the attention of Prior, who declared his admiration for her in print and published "Love and Friendship, a Pastoral" in one of his own collections. In 1710, she married Thomas Rowe (1687–1715), the product of a similar nonconformist upbringing, and a classical scholar and biographer of some renown. The elegy R. wrote upon the death of her husband on 13 May 1715 was appended by Pope to his second edition of *Eloisa and Abelard* (1720). With an inheritance from her father, she moved into a small home in Frome, Somerset, where she composed her best-known works. *Friendship in Death* (1728), employing the epistolary form to express her faith in the immortality of the soul, remained popular until the early nineteenth century. *Letters Moral and Entertaining* (1729) furthered her reputation for piety. She died on 20 February 1737, and Watts published posthumously her *Devout Exercises of the Heart* (1737), a series of "meditations" and "soliloquys" designed to inspire faith.

As Dunton's "Pindarick Lady," R. displays with great pride and erudition the "early products of a Female muse." She is both champion of her sex and one whose satiric pen will "lash the darling vices of the times." Her early verse typically articulates a conflict between her physical passions and her desire for independence from the "Slavery of Man." Her personae are ambitious, conscious of their own poetic power, in search of both glory and solitude.

Her later works are far more self-effacing, recasting the poet as rapturous mystic, a humble tool for inspiring the young or woebegone. It is in this later poetic incarnation that eighteenth-century critics memorialized her. Yet R.'s passionate imagery, her enthusiasm, the ecstatic confessional quality of her poetry unites both her early and later writing, her secular and devotional verse.

WORKS: *Poems on Several Occasions* (1696). *Friendship in Death* (1728). *Letters Moral and Entertaining* (1729). *The History of Joseph* (1736). *Devout Exercises of the Heart* (1737). *Miscellaneous Works in Prose and Verse* (1739). *The Poetry of Elizabeth Singer Rowe (1674–1737),* ed. M. F. Marshall (1987).

BIBLIOGRAPHY: *DNB.* Boswell, J. *Life of Johnson* (1791). *Kissing the Rod: An Anthology of Seventeenth-Century Women's Verse,* ed. G. Greer et al. (1988). *Eighteenth-Century Women Poets,* ed. R. Lonsdale (1990).

Richard C. Taylor

Susanna Rowson

BORN: c. 1762, Portsmouth, Hampshire.
DIED: 2 March 1824, Boston, Massachusetts, United States.
DAUGHTER OF: William Haswell and Susanna Musgrave Haswell.
MARRIED: William Rowson, 1786.
WROTE UNDER: Susanna Haswell; Mrs. Rowson of the New Theater, Philadelphia; Susanna Rowson.

Though born in England, R. achieved her fame in America: One of the first professional woman writers in the United States, she wrote the first American best-selling novel, *Charlotte: A Tale of Truth* (1791). Enormously productive and virtually self-supporting, she worked at various times as governess, novelist, dramatist, actress, poet, lyricist, editor, essayist, textbook writer, and mistress of one of the most successful American girls' boarding schools of her time.

Many reference works that mention R. classify her as an American author, but her early experiences were distinctly British. Her mother died in childbirth and R.—an only child—stayed in England when her father, a lieutenant in the Royal Navy, went to America to serve as a collector of Royal Customs. Having remarried and settled in Nantasket, Massachusetts, he returned to England in 1767 to bring his daughter to his new home. Because he was an officer of the Crown, his property was confiscated during the Revolutionary War; the family, impoverished, returned to England in 1778.

Already resourceful in her late teens, R. became a governess (eventually working for the Duchess of Devonshire) and began to write. She published *Victoria,* an epistolary novel interspersed with verse, in 1786. In that year, she married a hardware merchant, William Rowson, and continued writing at an impressive rate. The five novels she produced in England during the first six years of her marriage include the famous *Charlotte* as well as *Rebecca: or, The Fille de Chambre* (1792), a popular novel that drew on R.'s experiences in England and America during and after the war.

Reasonably popular in England, *Charlotte* was phenomenally successful in the United States and went through some 200 editions. A moralizing account of a fallen woman "for the perusal of the young and thoughtless of the fair sex," the novel was presented as being "not merely the effusion of Fancy, but . . . a reality" based on the true experience of acquaintances of the author's. Whether its appeal arose—as many critics have assumed—from its apparent veracity, from its scandalous story, from its metaphoric treatment of the themes of filial rebellion and paternal forgiveness (so close to the consciences of Americans), or from a literary merit that twentieth-century critics have been slow to ascribe to R.'s writing, *Charlotte* in many ways resembles Samuel Richardson's *Clarissa.* The story of the sixteen-year-old daughter of devoted British parents, it details her seduction by an army lieutenant whom her parents dislike. Corrupted by the influence of an immoral French teacher, Mlle. La Rue, Charlotte elopes to America with her lover, only to be disappointed in her expectation of marriage. Falsely convinced that Charlotte is unfaithful, her lover rejects her in favor of a respectable American girl; Charlotte dies in childbirth, in the arms of her forgiving father and to the regret of her penitent seducer. Following as it does the outlines of *Clarissa,* the novel is astonishingly short: only about 130 pages in modern editions. R.'s style is relatively terse, relying on dialogue and dramatic presentation of scenes and using comparatively little narrative intervention to underline her moral points. Nevertheless, *Charlotte* inspired many tears and led faithful readers for decades to place flowers on the grave of the heroine's supposed original in Trinity Churchyard in New York.

R.'s husband's business failed in 1792, and the couple took the unusual course of making their living on the stage, first in Britain, then in America; R. was the more successful actor of the two. In 1793, they joined the New Theatre in Philadelphia, for whom R. wrote plays in addition to acting character parts (she was, for example, Audrey in *As You Like It,* the Nurse in *Romeo and Juliet,* Mrs. Quickly in *The Merry Wives of Windsor,* Lady Sneerwell in *School for Scandal*). Her first play, *Slaves in Algiers* (1794)—a comedy promoting liberation of black slaves and equal rights for women—created a controversy in the American press; her subsequent plays were also topical. The Rowsons moved to the Federal Street Theater in Boston, where R.'s creditable acting career ended with her retirement in 1797.

R. opened a girls' school in 1797 that was to absorb much of her energy for twenty-five years. During this period, she nevertheless wrote the lyrics for about forty popular songs (with titles as diverse as "America, Commerce, and Freedom," "Will You Rise, my Beloved," "Orphan Nosegay Girl," and "He is not Worth the Trouble"). She also published textbooks, poems, religious writings, and several more novels, including a very popular sequel to *Charlotte,* known variously as *Charlotte's Daughter;* or *The Three Orphans* (1828); *Lucy Temple: One of the Three Orphans* (1842); and *Love and Romance: Charlotte and Lucy Temple* (1854). From 1802 to 1805, R. also edited and contributed to the *Boston Weekly Magazine.* As a writer and as an educator, R. can fairly be called one of the more productive and influential women of her age, in England or America.

WORKS: *Victoria* (1786). *The Inquisitor; or, Invisible Rambler* (1788). *Poems on Various Subjects* (1788). *A Trip to Parnassus; or, The Judgement of Apollo on Dramatic Authors and Performers* (1788). *The Test of Honour* (1789). *Charlotte: A Tale of Truth* (1791; as *The History of Charlotte Temple,* 1801). *Mentoria; or, The Young Lady's Friend* (1791). *Rebecca; or, the Fille de Chambre* (1792; as *The Fille de Chambre,* 1793). *Slaves in Algiers; or, A Struggle for Freedom* (1794). *The Female Patriot; or, Nature's Rights* (adapted from the play *The Bondman,* by P. Massinger, 1795). *Trials of the Human Heart* (1795). *The Volunteers: A Musical Entertainment* (1795). *The American Tar* (1796). *Americans in England; or Lessons for Daughters* (1797; as *The Columbian Daughters; or, Americans in England,* 1800). *Reuben and Rachel; or Tales of Old Times* (1798). *Miscellaneous Poems* (1804). *An Abridgement of Universal Geography, Together with Sketches of History* (1805). *A Spelling Dictionary* (1807). *Hearts of Oak* (1810). *A Present for Young Ladies, Containing Poems, Dialogues, Addresses* (1811). *Sarah; or, The Exemplary Wife* (1813; originally serialized in *Boston Weekly Magazine* as "Sincerity"). *Youth's First Step in Geography* (1818). *Biblical Dialogues Between a Father and His Family* (1822). *Exercises in History, Chronology, and Biography, in Question and Answer* (1822). *Charlotte's Daughter; or, The Three Orphans* (1828; as *Lucy Temple: One of the Three Orphans,* 1842; as *Love and Romance: Charlotte and Lucy Temple,* 1854).

BIBLIOGRAPHY: Adams, O. F. *Christian Register* (17 March 1913). Bowne, E. S. *A Girl's Life Eighty Years Ago* (1887). Brandt, E. B. *Susanna Haswell Rowson: America's First Best Selling Novelist* (1975). Cobbett, W. A. *Kick for a Bite* (1795). Dall, C.W.H. *The Romance of the Association; or, One Last Glimpse of Charlotte Temple and Eliza Wharton* (1875). Knapp, S. L. *Charlotte's Daughter* (1828). Nason, E. A. *Memoir of Mrs. Susanna Rowson* (1870). Parker, P. L. *SSF* (1976). Parker, P. L. *Susanna Rowson* (1986). Sargent, M.E. *Medford Historical Register* (7 April 1904). Swanwick, J. *A Rub from Snub* (answer to Cobbett) (1795). Vail, R. W. G. *PAAS*

(1932). Weil, D. *In Defense of Women: Susanna Rowson (1762–1824)* (1976).

For articles in reference works, see: *Allibone. American Authors 1600–1900. Bloomsbury. CHAL. Feminist. GWELN. Oxford.* Quinn, A. H. *A History of the American Drama from the Beginning to the Civil War* (1923). Seilhamer, G. O. *History of the American Theatre: New Foundations (1888–1891).*

Other references: Brown, H. R. *The Sentimental Novel in America, 1789–1860* (1940). Cherniavsky, E., in *Discovering Difference: Contemporary Essays in American Culture,* ed. C. K. Lohmann (1993). Cowie, A. *The Rise of the American Novel* (1948). Dauber, K. *Criticism* (1980). Davidson, C. N. *Reading in America: Literature and Social History* (1989). Dunlap, W. *History of the American Theatre and Anecdotes of the Principal Actors* (1963). Durang, C. *Philadelphia Dispatch* (15 October 1854). Fiedler, L. *Love and Death in the American Novel* (1969). Loshe, L. D. *The Early American Novel* (1907). Martin, W. *WS* (1974). Pattee, F. L. *The First Century of American Literature, 1770–1870* (1935). Petter, H. *The Early American Novel* (1971). Rourke, C. *The Roots of American Culture* (1942). Saar, D. A., in *Curtain Calls: British and American Women and the Theatre, 1660–1820,* ed. M. A. Schofield and C. Macheski (1991). Schofield, M. A., in *Modern American Drama: The Female Canon,* ed. J. Schlueter (1990). Spender, D. *Mothers of the Novel* (1986).

Robyn R. Warhol
(updated by Eve M. Lynch)

Bernice Rubens

BORN: 26 July 1928, Cardiff, Wales.
DAUGHTER OF: Eli Rubens and Dorothy Cohen.
MARRIED: Rudi Nassauer, 1947.

Prolific as both a novelist and short-story writer, R. is best known for her poignant depictions of marginal characters and colorful, offbeat portrayals of Jewish family life. Her fictions often center around a small group of eccentric and sometimes exaggerated characters involved in a farcical series of actions enlivened by epigrammatic narrative comment. One reviewer writes that "her characteristic territory is domestic and her usual subject is the point of crisis in an individual spirit aspiring to its fullness of life. . . . Her characters are most faceless and those on the periphery of the story are often sketched with the simple certainties of caricature, while those at the center exist as voices and sensibilities experiencing a depression."

R. is perhaps most highly esteemed for her more serious work, *The Elected Member* (1969), which was awarded the Booker Prize in 1970. This plain and direct novel deals with the inherited burden of Jewish suffering through the story of Norman, the infant prodigy of a close-knit Jewish family living in London's East End. By the age of forty-one, Norman is a brilliant and successful barrister, but his intellectual vitality gradually gives way to a solitary and nightmarish world of drug-induced hallucinations and paranoia brought on by the suffocating pressure of a series of emotional family disasters. Norman is typical of R.'s early protagonists: stifled, suffering, incompetent, unable either to give or to receive love, experiencing life as a relentless saga of pain. For some, redemption is a possibility; for others, affliction is thrown into relief only by the grimly comic nature of their emotional lives.

After graduating with honors in English from the University of Wales in Cardiff (which awarded her an honorary D. Litt. in 1991), R. began work as a schoolteacher and a director of documentary films for the United Nations and various charities; she was awarded the American Blue Ribbon Award for her documentary film *Stress* (1968) and describes how she became "something of a specialist in the making of documentary films about victims, the handicapped." Clearly, there is some linkage between her interest in disability and suffering and the issues raised in much of her early fiction. R. claims that she is primarily interested in "non-communication between people, the theme of all my novels," and "the links between sanity, madness, the ever changing meaning of these terms. I inhabit that limbo, no fixed abode, loitering there without intent." She was granted the Welsh Arts Council Award in 1976.

R.'s first works won her a reputation as a compassionate and intelligent novelist, described variously as "one of our finest Jewish writers," "compulsively readable," "deeply committed yet objectively truthful." These early tragicomedies of Jewish family life usually center around a small group of characters who are at the same time both stereotypes and oddities. Typical of this period is the popular *Madame Sousatzka* (1962). A film version, directed by John Schlesinger and starring Shirley MacLaine, was released in 1988, with the focus of the screenplay (by Ruth Prawer Jhabvala) shifted to a Bengali family. *Sousatzka* is the story of a possessive piano teacher in a household of bizarre, neurotic tenants and her young Jewish prodigy, Marcus Crominski. Marcus is stifled by the relentless emotional needs of both his teacher and his mother, who create in Marcus a numbing mixture of pity, affection, and repulsion. His musical talent is finally exploited by the commercial ambitions of a vulgar impresario. *Sousatzka* is one of R.'s many novels that focus on a monstrous mother figure whose remorseless devotion to her children is fatally compromised by her insatiable desire to be loved in return.

The literary success of *The Elected Member* marked a change in narrative direction and tone; R. began to turn increasingly to gentile settings with singularly grotesque, freakish protagonists. *Sunday Best* (1971) is the story of a bored suburban schoolmaster who turns transvestite on Sundays; *Birds of Passage* (1981) charts a journey into self-knowledge by a group of solitary people in late middle-age who meet on a cruise. Two elderly widows, Alice and Ellen, at first appear to have discovered some kind of liberty, but after both women are forced to deal with the violent attentions of a rapist waiter, it becomes clear that the liner is a confined and confining place where even their last privacies are void.

Go Tell the Lemming (1973) reports the lonely monologue of a betrayed and isolated wife. *The Ponsonby Post* (1977), an adventure of expatriate life in Java (where R. had spent time on location directing two films for the U.N.

on the problems of agricultural education in the Third World), contains such elements of the political thriller as the constant threat of guerrilla forces lurking in the hills. *I Sent a Letter to My Love* (1975), an absorbing, architectural story of human faith and love, has been made into a film (with Simone Signoret) and a stage play in the United States. R.'s ninth book, *A Five Year Sentence* (shortlisted for the Booker Prize in 1978), charts a lonely spinster's descent into madness impelled by a last, pathetic grasp at love. *Our Father* (1987) deals with a professional female explorer who has an encounter with God in the desert; and *Mr. Wakefield's Crusade* (1985, televised 1992) tells of catastrophe-prone Luke Wakefield, whose witnessing of an unexpected death leads to a crusade in search of truth and justice. These quirky, taut, blackly comic, sometimes obsessional tales speak to the pathos in human nature by centering the peripheral. At other times, the desperation of the lovelorn and the rejected is transformed into an intelligent comedy of manners through sly, verbal wit.

More recently, R. has been examining these and similar concerns on a broader, sometimes epic scale. This has been most successful in works such as *Brothers* (1983), a family saga of momentous geographical and historical range; *Kingdom Come* (1990), which fictionalizes a seventeenth-century self-appointed Messiah, later a convert to Islam; and *Mother Russia* (1992), a love story set against the turbulent background of Russian history (which received contradictory reviews). In these later works, morally recondite considerations fuse with narrative density to produce a less marginal, less grotesque examination of the pettiness of human emotions. These most recent works encompass complex and sweeping narrative that deal with suffering and endurance on an ambitious, intelligent scale. R. has also written for the stage and for television.

WORKS: *Set on Edge* (1960). *Madame Sousatzka* (1962, film by John Schlesinger, 1988). *One of the Family* (1964). *Mate in Three* (1965). *Call Us by Name* (1968). *The Elected Member* (1969). *Out of the Mouths* (1970). *Sunday Best* (1971). *Third Party* (1972). *Go Tell the Lemming* (1973). *I Sent a Letter to My Love* (1975). *The Ponsonby Post* (1977). *A Five Year Sentence* (1978). *Spring Sonata* (1979). *Birds of Passage* (1981). *Brothers* (1983). *Mr. Wakefield's Crusade* (1985, televised 1992). *Our Father* (1987). *Kingdom Come* (1990). *A Solitary Grief* (1992). *Mother Russia* (1992). *Autobiopsy* (1993). *Yesterday in the Back Lane* (1995). *The Waiting Game* (1997).

BIBLIOGRAPHY: Kossick, S. *UES* (1993). Parnell, M. *NWRev* (1990). White, H. C. *HEI* (1995). g

For articles in reference works, see: *Bloomsbury. CA. Collins. Feminist. ToddBWW. Who's Who (UK)* 1995.

Other references: *Jewish Quarterly* (1969). *New Statesman* (14 February 1969). *NYT* (27 May 1969, 28 November 1987). *NYTBR* (18 May 1969). *Saturday Review* (26 July 1969). *TLS* (11 September 1981, 16 September 1983, 23 July 1982).

Mikita Brottman

Elizabeth Russell

BORN: 1528, Gidea Hall, Essex.
DIED: 1609.
DAUGHTER OF: Sir Anthony Cooke and Anne Fitzwilliam Cooke.
MARRIED: Sir Thomas Hoby, 1558; John, Lord Russell, 1574.

Like her learned sisters, Mildred Cooke Cecil and Ann Cooke Bacon, R. put her Latin and Greek education to use in religious writings. She translated a Latin treatise on the Eucharist and wrote Latin, Greek, and English elegiac verse of some distinction. Her book, *A Way of Reconciliation of a good and learned man, touching the Trueth, Nature, and Substance of the Body and Blood of Christ in the Sacrament* (1605), is a translation of Bishop John Ponet's Latin *Diallacticon viri boni et literati, de veritate, natura, atque substantia corporis et sanguinis Christi in eucharistia.* Dedicating this work to her only surviving daughter, Lady Anne Herbert, R. calls it her "last Legacie" for the spiritual comfort of her "good sweet Nanne." Although she had apparently written the translation many years earlier, it was not published until R. was in her late seventies, for she feared that "after my death it should be Printed according to the humors of other, and wrong of the dead, who in his life approved my Translation with his owne allowance." Ponet, who died in 1556, wrote the treatise while a religious exile in Germany; perhaps it was he who approved the learned young woman's work. R.'s father, Sir Anthony Cooke, also an exile, published Ponet's Latin original in Strasbourg in 1557. If it was he who approved his daughter's work, she composed it before 1576, the year of his death. A French translation of Ponet, which R. notes in her dedication, appeared in 1566.

In the treatise, the doctrine of the Eucharist, one of the most contentious subjects of the Reformation, is expounded in order to reconcile diverse Protestant opinions and to bring peace to a Church riven by bitter fighting. Ponet gathers commentary from ancient and modern sources, demonstrates the common thread of doctrine, "wherefore, the seeds of contention and discord bee now taken away." R.'s translation of Ponet allowed her to contribute a significant "reconciliation" to the English church, much as her sister, Lady Anne Bacon, had contributed *An Apologie or aunswer in defence of the Church of England* (1564), a translation of Bishop John Jewel's seminal Latin work.

R. first married Sir Thomas Hoby, a linguist, diplomat, and scholar who apparently shared her active commitment to the English church; he translated the Reformist Martin Bucer's *Gratulation . . . unto the Churche of England for the restitution of Christes Religion* (1549). After Hoby's death in 1566, R. began to write elegies for the family tombs at Bisham, Berkshire, composing more than eighty lines in English and Latin to Sir Thomas and his half-brother, Sir Philip. She also wrote the brief, moving elegy inscribed on the tomb of her two little daughters who died in 1571. Later, she wrote Greek and Latin verses for the tomb of her sister, Katherine Killigrew; for the tomb in Westminster Abbey of her second husband, John, Lord

Russell, she wrote a series of Latin and Greek elegiac verses.

R.'s letters to her brother-in-law, William Cecil, Lord Burghley, and to his son, Sir Robert Cecil, demonstrate her persuasive style and her active involvement in managing her familial and legal business. She consulted Burghley over her problems with her son, Thomas Posthumus Hoby, who consistently disobeyed his mother, "though my naturall inclinacion have ben, by love and reason to procure my children to love, and feare me; yet I have not deserved thereby contempt, nor shewed myself simple, in being ignorant of my due, and valew of my desart." Her vigorously worded letters to her nephew, Robert Cecil, the Secretary of State, ask for Cecil's help in solving substantial difficulties, particularly her protracted and violent quarrel with the Lord Admiral over the possession of Donnington Castle. Consistent with her work to memorialize the dead, she commissioned her own monument at Bisham and wrote to Sir William Dethick, Garter King of Arms, to request that he would "set down advisedly and exactly, in every particular itself, the number of mourners due to my calling, being a Viscountess of birth."

WORKS: (trans.) *A Way of Reconciliation of a good and learned man touching the Trueth, Nature, and Substance of the Body and Blood of Christ in the Sacrament*, by John Ponet (1605, STC 21456).

BIBLIOGRAPHY: Lamb, M. E., in *Silent But for the Word*, ed. M. P. Hannay (1985). McIntosh, M. K. *Proceedings of the American Philosophical Society* (1975). Schleiner, L. *Tudor and Stuart Women Writers* (1994). Travitsky, B. *The Paradise of Women* . . . (1989). Wilson, V. *Society Women of Shakespeare's Time* (1924, 1970).

For articles in reference works, see: *Ballard. Bloomsbury. DNB* (under "Thomas Hoby"). *Feminist.*

Elaine V. Beilin

Russell, Mary Annette Beauchamp: See *Armim, Elizabeth von*

Russell, Sarah: See *Laski, Marghanita*

Sabrina: See *Havergal, Frances Ridley*

Vita (Victoria Mary) Sackville-West

BORN: 8 March 1892, Knole, Sevenoaks, Kent.
DIED: 2 June 1962, Sissinghurst, Cranbrook, Kent.
DAUGHTER OF: Lionel Edward Sackville-West and Victoria Sackville-West.
MARRIED: Harold Nicolson, 1913.

"I *will* get myself into English Literature." As S. herself might appreciate, her prominence therein relies upon a notoriously unconventional life as well as upon prodigious—if essentially non-"modernist"—literary works. Early in life, she imagined her name in histories of literature: "Sackville-West, V., poet and novelist." Excluding juvenilia (eight novels and five plays between 1906 and 1910), S. produced twelve novels, five biographies, two long poems, much other poetry, and assorted travel, garden/country, and critical writing.

Anomalous among her works is the short experimental novel *Seducers in Ecuador* (1924), which Virginia Woolf praised for its "fantasticallity." It remains a delightful and disconcerting text, probably intended as a complement to Woolf's style. In S.'s English Georgics, *The Land* (a poem that won the 1927 Hawthornden Prize), and superb novel, *The Edwardians* (1930)—both enormously popular—her literary conservatism triumphs: She sings the cycle of her country's year in rurally erudite verse and re-creates in brilliant, often satiric, prose the overblown *vie-en-rose* of aristocrats during her childhood. S.'s best writing treats the extremes of gentry life, fields, and salons alike. Her other work is less achieved artistically, betraying a lack of "central transparency" (in Woolf's phase) and giving "the effect of having been done from the outside" (in S.'s)—perhaps the aesthetic price for ingrained snobbery and indirect narcissism.

That her *oeuvre* should continue to intrigue readers is hardly surprising, however, if only for what it reveals about S. and her relations with both *beau monde* and Bloomsbury. "I am an incredible egoist, that's the long and the short of it"; fascinated by her own personality (or personalities) and sexuality (or sexualities), S. reflected creatively upon her forty-nine-year marriage to diplomat-politician Harold Nicolson and her lifelong series of love affairs with women, including Woolf. The "Author's Note" to *The Edwardians* advises, "No character in this book is wholly fictitious"; early S. novels such as *Challenge* (written in 1919) suggest psychobiographical readings of the author's fictionalized self-representation as either male or tellingly split between two characters of different gender.

S.'s mixed Spanish-English heritage also divided her. Born and raised on a colossal estate held by centuries of Sackvilles (one of whom co-authored *Gorboduc* [1561]and wrote the Induction to *A Mirror for Magistrates* [1559]), S. considered it her life's tragedy as an only daughter to watch her beloved Knole pass to an uncle and a cousin. The literary compensation for this loss was extraordinary: Woolf's *Orlando* (1928), which has been called the longest love-letter in history. Given an early copy (and later the manuscript, beautifully bound), S. read it on publication day, overwhelmed and flattered to be consoled for her father's death and identified with Knole for posterity.

S. was more ambivalent about her maternal past. She adored and feared her mother, by turns an impulsively generous "Bonne Maman" and cruelly imperious Lady Sackville (who called Woolf "that wicked Virgin Wolf"). At midlife S. wrote *Pepita* (1937), a biography of her grandmother, the Spanish dancer whose supposed gypsy blood S. associated with the wanderlust and passionate nature she was finally beginning to control in herself. Henceforth, "heart of darkness" themes—even latent sadomasochism, notably in *The Dark Island* (1934)—gave way to themes of leave-taking (partially suggested in 1931 by the splendid novel *All Passion Spent*), solitude (the title of a 1938 poem), and saints' lives (those of Joan and the two Teresas). S. would explore "the power of being alone," specifically, in her poetics of place, "the power of being alone with earth and skies."

A prolific correspondent, S. wrote daily to Nicolson for most of their lives. Her letters to Woolf alone fill a volume. She kept a rich diary, and a long autobiographical account about her traumatic affair with Violet (Keppel) Trefusis was published posthumously in *Portrait of a Marriage,* together with explanatory chapters by son Nigel amounting to a panegyric of his parents' marriage.

That relationship has been mythologized by all concerned, its ability to withstand both partners' series of homosexual lovers elevated to a principle of "caring without interference." S. and Nicolson spoke about marriage on the BBC and on tour in the United States; in transcripts (and elsewhere) one notes the slippage in S. between feminist and aristocratic/egoistic self-assertion, between rights for all women, as women, and independence for exceptional selves who transcend gender through personal privilege. S. became conservative with age and her experiences in World War II (like Woolf, she lived under the bombing path across southern England). She was surprised that one of her young female relatives wanted a career, for example. Yet in her last novel, *No Signposts in the Sea* (1961), S. speaks through a narrator, lower class in background, to challenge the wealth-based assumptions of a woman who prescribes against "squalour" in marriage by recommending separate bedrooms. *Signposts* also returns to the cruise-of-life metaphor of *Seducers.*

Not generally considered a professional writer, S. in fact wrote most deliberately for money: She supported herself, and often Nicolson; sent her sons to Balliol College, Oxford; paid for Long Barn and Sissinghurst Castle; and financed the creation of the celebrated Sissinghurst Garden. (She was nonetheless loyal to the Woolfs' Hogarth Press, ignoring in mid-career other publishers' lucrative offers.) Weekly *Observer* gardening columns brought S. more contemporary recognition than her poetry and novels put together, and she was awarded the Royal Horticultural Society's Gold Medal (which, in her words, "generally goes to old men over eighty, who have devoted the whole of their lives to horticulture").

Some find paradoxical S.'s devotion to "country notes," truth-in-platitude, and formal gardens after a nonconformist youth (the "splendid arson of my reckless days" [*The Garden,* 1946]). Hugh Walpole characterizes her as a romantic hedonist. Given British social history, however, S.'s defiant independence can be seen in a tradition of licensed aristocratic eccentricity. She took pains to avoid overt "scandal," keeping her lesbian affairs semi-secret and withdrawing *Challenge*—with its portraits of Trefusis as Eve, S. as Julian—from publication in the United Kingdom. Her "open" marriage had an Edwardian aspect: Members of the upper class, including S.'s parents, had always tolerated discreet adultery. Her literary works reflect a personal progress toward restraint, service, and reclusivity; the result is balanced prose of great beauty brought up to match her consistently decorous poetry. S.'s career joins together distinguished writing with an idiosyncratic life of struggle against sexual norms.

WORKS: Chatterton (1909). *Constantinople: Eight Poems* (1915). *Poems of East and West* (1917). *Heritage* (1919). *The Dragon in Shallow Waters* (1921). *Orchard and Vineyard* (1921). *The Heir* (1922). *Knole and the Sackvilles* (1922). *Challenge* (1923 in the U.S.; 1974 in the U.K.). *Grey Wethers* (1923). *Seducers in Ecuador* (1924). *The Land* (1926). *Passenger to Teheran* (1926). *Aphra Behn* (1927). *Twelve Days* (1928). *King's Daughter* (1929). *The Edwardians* (1930). *Sissinghurst* (1931). *Invitation to Cast Out Care* (1931). (trans.) *Rilke* (1931). *All Passion Spent* (1931). *The Death of Noble Godavary and Gottfried Kunstler* (1932). *Thirty Clocks Strike the Hour* (1932). *Family History* (1932). *Collected Poems,* Vol. I (1933). *The Dark Island* (1934). *Saint Joan of Arc* (1936). *Pepita* (1937). *Some Flowers* (1937). *Solitude* (1938). *Country Notes* (1939). *Country Notes in Wartime* (1940). *English Country Houses* (1941). *Grand Canyon* (1942). *The Eagle and the Dove* (1943). *The Woman's Land Army* (1944). (with H. Nicolson) *Another World Than This* (1945). *The Garden* (1946). *Nursery Rhymes* (1947). *Devil at Westease* (1947). *In Your Garden* (1951). *In Your Garden Again* (1953). *The Easter Party* (1953). *More for Your Garden* (1955). *Even More for Your Garden* (1958). *A Joy of Gardening* (1958). *Daughter of France* (1959). *No Signposts in the Sea* (1961). *Faces: Profiles of Dogs* (1961). *V. Sackville-West's Garden Book,* ed. P. Nicolson (1968). *Dearest Andrew: Letters from V. Sackville-West to Andrew Rieber, 1951–62,* ed. N. MacKnight (1979). *The Letters of Vita Sackville-West to Virginia Woolf,* ed. L. DeSalvo and M. A. Leaska (1984).

BIBLIOGRAPHY: Brown, J. *Vita's Other World: A Gardening Biography of Vita Sackville-West* (1985). Glendinning, V. *Vita: The Life of V. Sackville-West* (1983). Nicolson, N. *Portrait of a Marriage* (1973). *The Diaries and Letters of Sir Harold Nicolson,* ed. N. Nicolson (1966). Stevens, M. *V. Sackville-West: A Critical Biography* (1973; incl. definitive list of published works, index of reviews, some unpub. Sackville-West poems). Watson, S. R. *V. Sackville-West* (1972).

For articles in reference works, see: *Bloomsbury. CA. Cambridge. DLB. Feminist. Longman. MBL. Oxford. TCA* and *SUP. TCW. ToddBWW.*

Other references: Cohen, E. H. *ELN* (1981). DeSalvo, L. A. *VWM* (1979). DeSalvo, L. A. *Signs* (Winter 1982). DeSalvo, L. A., in *Women Writers and the City,* ed. S. M. Squier (1984). Edgar, S. *Quadrant* (March 1984). Fone, B.R.S., in *The Gay Academic,* ed. L. Crew (1978). Gindin, J. *SNNTS* (1980). Haight, G. S. *YR.* Heilbrun, C. *Ms.* (February 1974). Klaitch, D. *Woman + Woman: Attitudes towards Lesbianism* (1974). Miles, R. *The Fiction of Sex* (1974). Pomeroy, E. W. *TCL* (1982). Ruas, C. *Book Forum* (1979). Rule, J. *Lesbian Images* (1975). Schaefer, J. O. *Virginia Woolf Quarterly* (1976). Stimpson, C. R. *Nation* (30 November 1974). Tomalin, C. *New Statesman* (23 September 1977). Trautmann, J. *The Jessamy Brides: The Friendship of Virginia Woolf and V. Sackville-West* (1973).

Catherine Milsum

Mary Anne Sadlier

BORN: 31 December 1820, Cootehill, County Cavan, Ireland.
DIED: 5 April 1903, Montreal, Canada.
DAUGHTER OF: Francis Madden.
MARRIED: James Sadlier, 1846.

S. was well known in her lifetime for her didactic, romantic fiction, most of which centers around immigrant Roman Catholic culture in North America. She was a spirited, spiritual, and productive woman whose novels consciously explore the situations of women, particularly Irish Catholic immigrant women. Educated at home by private tutors, S.'s literary career began at an early age: By eighteen she was contributing poetry to *La Belle Assemblée* in London. At twenty-three, impoverished after the death of her merchant father, S. migrated with family members to Montreal, Canada, where her contributions to the *Literary Garland* helped to support her family. The 1845 publication of her first book, *Tales of Olden Times,* was also crucial to the economic survival of the Madden family. Her 1846 marriage to Irish immigrant James Sadlier relieved S.'s financial pressures and allowed her to write full time, no longer for monetary necessity but under the socially appropriate guise of didactic fervor and moral purpose.

S.'s fiction is characterized by a deeply abiding Catholicism and concern for the plight of the Irish immigrant. Her lifelong friend, Thomas D'Arcy McGee, whose poems she edited for publication, called her the unsurpassed author of "the romance of Irish immigration." Michelle Lacombe points out that "a characteristic blend of pious Catholic precepts and hard-earned awareness of the plight of unschooled immigrant girls, her American novels are particularly worth a second look." S.'s historical romances and her religious texts were well received and were largely responsible for the success of her husband's and brother-in-law's New York publishing firm, D. & J. Sadlier and Company.

The 1850 serialization of her novel, *The Blakes and the Flanagans,* in McGee's *The American Celt,* catapulted S. into popular fame and, from 1853 on, the Sadlier brothers published virtually all of her work. While generally unknown to today's audiences, her work was immensely popular in her day, and her works were regularly serialized and reprinted. Her fiction tends to attempt to provide rather false moral glosses, and unsatisfying happy endings abound, yet S. is adept at rendering the often-ignored situation of immigrant women, offering crucial information about the contemporary social climate. Her fiction, while often not particularly riveting in plot, explores and celebrates the values of working women.

S. and her husband lived in Canada for fourteen years before moving to New York City. During those years, S. gave birth to six children and published six novels. When McGee moved from New York to Canada in 1857, S.'s brother-in-law purchased the *American Celt,* changing its name to the *Tablet.* S. took over as editor, guiding the magazine according to her religious and nationalist objectives. After her husband's death in 1869, S. took over management of the publishing house until her brother-in-law's death in 1885. In the 1870s, she became actively involved in social and philanthropic works, establishing a foundling asylum, a home for the aged, and a home for friendless girls. In 1885, the death of her favorite son, Jesuit priest Francis Xavier Sadlier, and increasing financial difficulties combined to lead S. back to Montreal where she moved in with her daughter, Anna Teresa Sadlier, a novelist in her own right.

In 1895, S. lost control of the publishing house and all her copyrights to her nephew, William Sadlier. In response to her reduced circumstances, friends established a fund in her name and obtained for her, in light of her contributions to the Roman Catholic church, a blessing from Pope Leo XIII. For her literary contributions, S. received the Notre Dame University Laetare Medal. As Lacombe notes, after S.'s death, her "novels, like the publishing house associated with them, passed into obscurity."

WORKS: *Tales of Olden Times: A Collection of European Traditions* (1845). *The Red Hand of Ulster; or, the Fortunes of Hugh O'Neill* (1850). *Willy Burke; or, the Irish Orphan in America* (1850). *Alice Riordan: The Blind Man's Daughter* (1851). *New Lights; or, Life in Galway* (1853). *The Blakes and the Flanagans: A Tale Illustrative of Irish Life in the United States* (1855). *The Confederate Chieftains: A Tale of the Irish Rebellion of 1641* (1860). *Julia, or the Golden Thimble: A Drama for Girls* (1861). *Elinor Preston; or, Scenes at Home and Abroad* (1861). *Bessie Conway; or, the Irish Girl in America* (1862). *The Lost Son* (1862). *Old and New; or, Taste versus Fashion* (1862). *The Daughter of Tyrconnell: A Tale of the Reign of James the First* (1863). *The Fate of Father Sheehy: A Tale of Tipperary Eighty Years Ago* (1863). *The Hermit of the Rock: A Tale of Cashel* (1863). *The Talisman: A Drama in One Act; Written for the Young Ladies of the Ursuline Academy, East Morrisania* (1863). *Con O'Regan; or, Emigrant Life in the New World* (1864). *Confessions of an Apostate* (1864). *The Old House by the Boyne; or, Recollections of an Irish Borough* (1865). *Secret, A Drama Written for the Young Ladies of St. Joseph's Academy, Flushing* (1865). *Aunt Honor's Keepsake. A Chapter from Life* (1866). *A New Catechism of Sacred History* (1866). *The Heiress of Kilgoran; or, Evenings with the Old Geraldines* (1867). *MacCarthy More; or, The Fortunes of an Irish Chief in the Reign of Queen Elizabeth* (1868). *Maureen Dhu, the Admiral's Daughter* (1870). *The Invisible Hand: A Drama in Two Acts* (1873). *Purgatory: Doctrinal, Historical and Poetical* (1886). *Catholic School History of England* (1891). *Stories of the Promises* (1895?). *The Minister's Wife, and Other Stories* (1898). *O'Byrne; or, The Expatriated* (1898). *Short Stories* (1900).

BIBLIOGRAPHY: Lacombe, M. *ECW* (1984).

For articles in reference works, see: *DLB. Feminist.*

Kirsten T. Saxton

Dora (Doris) Jessie Saint

BORN: 17 April 1913, Surrey.
DAUGHTER OF: Arthur Gunnis Shafe and Grace Read Shafe.
MARRIED: Douglas Edward John Saint, 1940.
WRITES UNDER: Miss Read.

S., writing under the name "Miss Read," is the author of more than fifty books, mainly fiction, about life in the English countryside in the long, rich tradition of Izaac Walton, Gilbert White of Selborne, and James Woodforde. S. is clearly familiar with the particular wealth of country writers, both fictional and factual, between the world wars; she owes little to any of them, however, except Woodforde, whose *Diary of a Country Parson 1750–1852* was published between 1924 and 1931, and the humorist E. M. Delafield, author of *Diary of a Provincial Lady* (1930).

S., one of three daughters born to an insurance agent and his wife, was born in 1913 in Surrey; she describes her early life in *A Fortunate Grandchild* (1982). When she was seven, the family moved to Chelsfield, Kent, where S. attended the village school and developed a lifelong devotion to country life, the subject of much of her fiction; she describes this period in *Time Remembered* (1986). She attended Homerton College, Cambridge, in 1931–33 and subsequently taught at schools in Middlesex. In 1940 she married Edward John Saint, a schoolmaster who served in the Royal Air Force in World War II. During the war years, she lived at Wood Green (near the Oxfordshire village of Witney), the basis for the town of "Lulling" in the Thrush Green series, and began writing for *Punch*, the *Times Educational Supplement*, the BBC, and various Sunday newspapers. After the war, when her husband returned to teaching at a school in Newbury, the couple settled in a hamlet in the Berkshire Downs, the model for the fictional "Fairacre." Her publisher, Michael Joseph, suggested the name "Miss Read" for *Village School* (1955), and she has continued to use the pseudonym for her subsequent fiction. She and her family (she has one daughter) live in Berkshire, where she has served as a justice of the peace and maintains interests in theater, music, reading, and wildlife.

The fictional works are organized in two major series of "chronicles," one on the Cotswold village of Fairacre, the other on the village of Thrush Green, which is larger than Fairacre and blends imperceptibly into the neighboring country town of Lulling. The relationship between the two series is explained in *The World of Thrush Green* (1988):

> I think it was J. B. Priestley who said that there was no need to pity the novelists, as "they are only playing with their dolls." The time had come to find a new set of dolls for me to play with, and this time [i.e., as she skillfully adopts different authorial voices in the Thrush Green series] I was determined to write in the third person. It is advice I give to all budding authors of fiction. Trying to observe the verities of time and place, when acting as narrator, can be a traumatic experience, take my word for it.

S. has also written two novels in the "Chronicles of Caxley" series.

The language of these books is clear, precise, and deceptively simple, matching the apparent simplicity of the subject matter. S. deals easily and naturally with sentiment, but she is never sentimental. Her attitude toward her characters is warm and generous; a touch of irony comes from Jane Austen (with whom S. can sustain comparison) or Delafield. Her observations of the countryside are worthy of Gilbert White, her comments on the changing nature of country life and behavior over the forty years covered by these books always acute, her revelation of character by dialogue unusually apt. As Walter Harding wrote in the *Chicago Sunday Tribune*, S.'s "quiet methods . . . have achieved a sort of universality."

S. has been prolific and enormously successful, but with these handicaps she has received little critical or scholarly attention except in newspaper reviews and publishers' trade publications. Reviews, however, have been generous, as in the case of praise by Mary Ellen Chase in the *New York Times Book Review*, whose writing about country life in New England is similar to that of S.'s; Chase noted that *Village Diary* (1957), for instance, is "quite a lovely book from the pen of a wise, humorous, lively, and delightful writer who knows the use of language as well as she knows the persons, places, and problems she so accurately and vividly described." It has been noted by critics, too, that though her setting is usually a small English village, her treatment is far from parochial but rather universal; she enables readers to recall their own early lives through Dorothy Watson and Agnes Fogerty, her central characters in the Thrush Green series. As S. has aged, so her aging characters in this series also reflect concerns of the elderly.

WORKS: *Village School* (Fairacre series; 1955). *Village Diary* (Fairacre series; 1957). *Hobby Horse Cottage* (1958). *Storm in the Village* (Fairacre series; 1958). *Thrush Green* (1959). *Fresh from the Country* (1960). *Winter at Thrush Green* (1961). *Miss Clare Remembers* (Fairacre series; 1962). *Country Bunch* (1963). *Over the Gate* (Fairacre series; 1964). *Chronicles of Fairacre* (1964). *The Little Red Bus and Other Stories* (1964). *The New Bed* (1964). *No Hat!* (1964). *Plum Pie* (1964). *Hob and the Horse-Bat* (1965). *Cluck, the Little Black Hen* (1965). *The Little Peg Doll* (1965). *Village Christmas* (1966). *The Market Square* (Caxley series; 1966). *The Howards of Caxley* (1967). *The Fairacre Festival* (1968). *Miss Read's Country Cooking or To Cut a Cabbage-Leaf* (1969). *News from Thrush Green* (1970). *Emily Davis* (Fairacre series; 1971). *Tiggy* (1971). *Tyler's Row* (Fairacre series; 1972). *The Christmas Mouse* (1973). *Farther Afield* (Fairacre series; 1974). *Animal Boy* (1975). *Battles at Thrush Green* (1975). *No Holly for Miss Quinn* (Fairacre series; 1976). *Village Affairs* (Fairacre series; 1977). *Return to Thrush Green* (1978). *The White Robin* (Fairacre series; 1979). *Christmas Mouse and Village Christmas: Two Novels* (1979). *Village Centenary* (Fairacre series; 1980). *Gossip from Thrush Green* (1981). *A Fortunate Grandchild* (1982). *Affairs at Thrush Green* (1983). *Summer at Fairacre* (1984). *At Home in Thrush Green* (1985). *Time Remembered* (1986). *The School at Thrush*

Green (1987). *The World of Thrush Green* (1988). *Mrs. Pringle* (Fairacre series; 1989). *Friends at Thrush Green* (1990). *Changes at Fairacre* (1991). *Celebrations at Thrush Green* (1992). *Miss Read's Christmas Book* (1992). *Farewell to Fairacre* (1993). *Tales from a Village School* (1994). Early Days (1995). *The Year at Thrush Green* (1995). *A Peaceful Retirement* (Fairacre series; 1996).

BIBLIOGRAPHY: *BW* (7 November 1982). *Chattanooga Free Press* (29 December 1996). *Chicago Sunday Tribune* (9 September 1956). *CSM* (8 March 1962). *New Yorker* (28 March 1959, 23 January 1960, 21 March 1962, 11 May 1963). *NYHTBR* (9 September 1956). *NYT* (9 September 1956). *NYTBR* (8 March 1959, 8 January 1960, 4 June 1961, 11 March 1962, 2 January 1963, 9 September 1967, 8 March 1987). *Saturday Review* (8 September 1956, 26 October 1957). *TES* (30 September 1994).

For articles in reference works, see: *CA. DLEL. IAWWW. SATA. WA. WB.*

Other references: Chase, M. E. *NYT* (6 October 1957). *LJ* (15 September 1991). *PW* (12 October 1984, 21 October 1988, 9 December 1988, 6 October 1989, 15 August 1994, 27 September 1991).

Christine Trinh and Leslie J. Workman

Lisa St. Aubin de Terán

BORN: 2 October 1953, London.
DAUGHTER OF: Jan Rynveld and Joan St. Aubin Carew.
MARRIED: Jaime Terán, 1970; George MacBeth, 1981; Robbie Duff-Scott, 1989.

S. was born in London to a professor from Guyana, Jan Rynveld, and his wife, Joan St. Aubin, a teacher. She began to write when she was twelve, and by the time she was sixteen she had decided that she was going to be a writer by profession. She went to Italy and Venezuela, working as a farmer, as did her first husband, whom she married when she was seventeen. She lived abroad for ten years, writing constantly, until the marriage ended, after which she returned to England. She now divides her time between England and Italy.

Academic literary criticism has chosen largely to ignore S., whose body of work is now well into its second decade of publication. Perhaps the longing for a sense of normalcy in family life that the author's persona projects or the subtle character analyses that people her novels are not what some might expect of the emerging canon of female writing.

Much of what S. evokes is similar to a synthesis of Spain's Ana María Matute and Gloria Fuertes, for S. is like a midpoint between the former, as a novelist, and the latter, as a poet. War, especially World War II, is both theme and plot element in many of S.'s novels. It is a vital part of post-war Britain that she seeks to exorcise among her contemporaries who have lived through only the Cold War and the Falkland Islands War. As Fuertes and Matute are peninsular, S. is stubbornly insular. She seems engaged in a constant struggle to succeed in defining her self-identity as an alien in England, Venezuela, and Italy.

The pathos of S.'s *Nocturne* (1992) is hard-hitting. Hurt and suffering, the human condition, and the equality of the sexes under all conditions of stress and happiness are characteristic of her prose. With subject matter similar to Ernest Hemingway, *Nocturne* has turns of phrase and images as frank and poignant as *For Whom the Bell Tolls*. Unlike Hemingway's Robert Jordan, her protagonist, Alessandro Mezzanotte, is not engaged in war for idealistic motives. Yet he is perfectly credible as a World War II veteran who is everyman.

Joanna (1990) is a study of a woman's identity through three generations. When it comes to equality of the sexes, to the archetype of Saturn devouring his son (as interpreted by Goya), S. opposes the archetype of the *vagina dentata* that not only attracts and emasculates men but who also destroys her offspring and abuses her mother. *Joanna* compares well, thematically, to Federico García Lorca's *The House of Bernarda Alba*.

The High Place (1985) is a collection of poems based on people that S. met and lived with in her first husband's estate in Venezuela. It is a sympathetic portrayal of peasants and farmers far from S.'s experience in England. She makes her characters alive from looking at them and their difficult life from the perspective of an outsider who—although privileged by wealth, education, and marriage—still gives them a voice different from the customary British colonial experience precisely because it has nothing to do with the British Empire. For the Latin-American scholar, *The High Place* is a rich document to compare in its very foreign idiom to the writing of Spanish- and Portuguese-speaking women. It is a respectful look at the microcosm of a coffee plantation.

S. has dabbled in picture books and in the chronicle of the restoration of an Italian villa that she owns. She has encouraged the publication of new writers, and she has written about various literary classics. Her books, though not literary triumphs per se, are a couple of examples of what just about all great and not-so-great male and female authors have done since the printed word became a commodity.

WORKS: *The Streak* (1980). *Keepers of the House* (1982; in the U. S. as *The Long Way Home*). *The Slow Train to Milan* (1983). *The Tiger* (1984). *The High Place* (1985). *The Bay of Silence* (1986). *Black Idol* (1987). *The Marble Mountain and other Stories* (1989). *Off the Rails: Memoirs of a Train Addict* (1989). *Joanna* (1990). *Nocturne* (1992). *Venice: The Four Seasons* (1992; photos by Mick Lindberg). *A Valley in Italy: The Many Seasons of a Villa in Umbria* (1994; repub. with subtitle *Confessions of a House Addict*, 1995). *Santos to Santa Cruz with Lisa St. Aubin de Terán* (1994; coproduction of BBC-TV and WNET). *The Hacienda: My Venezuelan Years* (1997). *The Palace* (1997).

BIBLIOGRAPHY: *LJ* (August 1985, September 1993). *LonSunTMag* (4 December 1993). *New Statesman* (25 May 1990). *NYTBR* (26 June 1994). *TLS* (11 March 1983, 5 May 1989).

For articles in reference works, see: *Bloomsbury. CA. CN. Feminist.*

Nicolás Hernández, Jr.

Sanford, Nell Mary: See *Dunn, Mary*

Sapphira: See *Barber, Mary*

Sappho: See *Moody, Elizabeth*

Sarah, Duchess of Marlborough: See *Churchill, Sarah Jennings, Duchess of Marlborough*

Sartoris, Adelaide: See *Kemble, Adelaide*

Dorothy L. Sayers

BORN: 13 June 1893, Oxford.
DIED: 17 December 1957, Witham, Essex.
DAUGHTER OF: Henry Sayers and Helen Leigh Sayers.
MARRIED: Oswald Arthur Fleming, 1926.

S. is best known for her Lord Peter Wimsey detective novels, witty mysteries that portray English society between the wars. The only child of the Reverend Henry Sayers and Helen Leigh Sayers, she had an isolated childhood, largely in the Fens. She went to Somerville College, Oxford, in 1912; many of her male contemporaries at Oxford died in the trenches of World War I. In 1915, she won first class honors in modern languages but no degree because of her sex; in 1920, she was awarded both the B.A. and the M.A. with the first group of women to be granted degrees from the University of Oxford. Blackwell's published her first work, two volumes of poetry, *Op. I.* (1916) and *Catholic Songs* (1918); she worked at Blackwell's as an editor, taught at a boys' school in southern France, and then in 1922 joined Benson's Advertising Agency in London as a copywriter. In 1924, she managed to hide her pregnancy from her family and close friends; after her marriage to Captain Oswald Arthur (Mac) Fleming in 1926, she legally adopted her own son without revealing his parentage.

Whose Body?, a rather conventional detective puzzle, introduced Lord Peter Wimsey in 1923. Wimsey's flippant delight in the corpse was gradually replaced by an attitude of moral responsibility in the later books. In *Clouds of Witness* (1926), he saved his brother, the Duke of Denver, from a murder conviction by brilliant sleuthing that included a daring cross-Atlantic flight just prior to Charles Lindbergh's. *Unnatural Death* (1927; in the U.S. as *The Dawson Pedigree)* introduced Wimsey's resourceful ally, Miss Climpson. *Unpleasantness at the Bellona Club* (1928) concerns the effects of World War I on veterans, a theme that recurred in the series as Lord Peter's own war service and subsequent breakdown were gradually revealed. (S.'s own husband suffered psychologically from his war experience; she supported him for most of their marriage, which lasted until his death in 1950.) By 1928, Lord Peter had made her famous. In that year she published *Lord Peter Views the Body,* a collection of twelve short stories, and edited *Great Short Stories of Detection, Mystery and Horror* (in the U.S. as *The Omnibus of Crime*), supplying a significant essay analyzing the detective tradition.

When her father died in 1928, leaving her a small legacy, S. bought a home in Witham, Essex, a pleasant train journey from her London publishers. With Anthony Berkeley, G. K. Chesterton, and other mystery writers, she founded the Detection Club, complete with rituals such as swearing a sacred oath on a skull named "Eric." She also completed *Tristan in Brittany,* a translation of the twelfth-century *Romance of Tristan* (1929). The following year she collaborated on *The Documents in the Case* with "Robert Eustace" (a pseudonym, probably for Eustace Fraser Rawlins; see Trevor Hall's book on S.) and published *Strong Poison,* the novel that introduced Harriet Vane as a mystery writer suspected of poisoning her lover. In 1931, S. published *The Five Red Herrings,* edited another volume of detective stories, and collaborated on *The Floating Admiral,* a detective parody written by members of the Detection Club, including Chesterton and Agatha Christie. *Have His Carcase* (1932) was a less successful Wimsey/Vane story; leaving out the "love interest," S. wrote two masterful mysteries, *Murder Must Advertise* (1933), set in an advertising agency rather like Benson's, and *The Nine Tailors* (1934), set in the Fen country where she had spent her childhood.

After giving a speech at the Somerville College Gaudy (reunion) in 1934, she published *Gaudy Night* (1935), a Wimsey/Vane novel set in a fictional women's college at Oxford. Her best novel, it focuses on the theme of intellectual integrity and explores the conflict between head and heart. By telling the story from Harriet Vane's perspective, S. is able to present Wimsey as a fully rounded character, beset with fears about the European situation and about his own aging; the book ends with Wimsey's famous proposal in Latin on Magdalen bridge. In the following year, S. collaborated with her friend Muriel St. Clare Byrne to produce *Busman's Honeymoon* on stage (1936), portraying the start of Harriet's life as Lady Peter Wimsey; the subsequent novel version was appropriately subtitled "A Love Story with Detective Interruptions." That was the end of the published Wimsey saga, except for some short stories and a few wartime essays and advertisements. Later, her friend Wilfred Scott-Giles published *The Wimsey Family,* telling the history of the Wimseys since 1066, a saga that S. and her friends had made up as a game. An unfinished Wimsey/Vane novel, *Thrones, Dominations,* begins just after the honeymoon; the manuscript is in the Marion E. Wade Collection at Wheaton College, in Illinois.

In 1937, S. "turned from her life of crime," as one schoolboy put it, and devoted her writing to theological drama. *The Zeal of Thy House* followed her friend T. S. Eliot's *Murder in the Cathedral* at the Canterbury Festival (1937). Other dramas include *The Devil to Pay,* a reworking of the Faust legend for the Canterbury Festival (1939); *The Just Vengeance* (Litchfield Festival, 1946); *The Man Born to Be King,* a series of twelve radio dramas on the life of Jesus broadcast in monthly segments in 1941–42 and published in 1943; and *The Emperor Constantine* (Colchester Festival Play, 1951). She also wrote several radio plays for children; *Love All,* a farce staged in London (1940); several volumes of short stories featuring Lord Peter or her other detective, Montague Egg; a book on aesthetics, *The Mind of the Maker* (1941); a series of witty essays on theology and social issues, including feminism; a translation of *The Song of Roland* (1957); and an unfinished biography of Wilkie Collins (1977).

Her final years were primarily devoted to Dante. One night during World War II, on her way to the air raid shelter, she grabbed a copy of *The Divine Comedy* in the original Italian and was entranced. She subsequently translated *Hell* (1949) and *Purgatory* (1955) for Penguin classics in a lively *terza rime,* documented with erudite and witty notes. At the invitation of her friend Barbara Reynolds, S. gave a series of lectures at Cambridge, later published as *Introductory Papers on Dante* (1954) and *Further Papers on Dante* (1957). While at work on the *Paradiso,* she died suddenly in her home on 17 December 1957; the translation was completed by Reynolds.

Although she wrote in many genres, S.'s work is unified by a concern with craftsmanship, with the value of worthwhile work done well. Appropriately, her memorial tablet in Somerville College is inscribed, "Praise Him that He hath made man in His own image, a maker and craftsman like Himself."

WORKS: *Op. I* (1916). *Catholic Tales and Christian Songs* (1918). *Whose Body?* (1923). *Clouds of Witness* (1926). *Unnatural Death* (1927; in the U.S. as *The Dawson Pedigree*). *The Unpleasantness at the Bellona Club* (1928). *Lord Peter Views the Body* (1928). (trans.) *Tristan in Brittany* (1929). (with R. Eustace) *The Documents in the Case* (1930). *Strong Poison* (1930). *The Five Red Herrings* (1931). (with others) *The Floating Admiral* (1931). *Have His Carcase* (1932). *Murder Must Advertise* (1933). *Hangman's Holiday* (1933). *The Nine Tailors* (1934). *Gaudy Night* (1935). (as by "M. Wimsey, editor") *Papers Relating to the Family of Wimsey* (1936). *Busman's Honeymoon* (1937). *The Zeal of Thy House* (1937). *The Greatest Drama Ever Staged* (1938). *Double Death* (1939). *Strong Meat* (1939). *The Devil to Pay* (1939). *In the Teeth of the Evidence* (1939). *He That Should Come* (1939). *Begin Here* (1940). *Creed or Chaos?* (1940). *Love All* (prod. 1940, pub. 1984). *The Mysterious English* (1941). *The Mind of the Maker* (1941). *Why Work?* (1942). *The Other Six Deadly Sins* (1943). *The Man Born To Be King* (1943). *Even the Parrot* (1944). *The Just Vengeance* (1946). *Unpopular Opinions* (1946). *Making Sense of the Universe* (1946). *Creed or Chaos and Other Essays* (1947). *Four Sacred Plays* (1948). *The Lost Tools of Learning* (1948). (trans.) *The Comedy of Dante Alighieri the Florentine: Cantica I: Hell* (1949). *The Emperor Constantine* (1951). *The Days of Christ's Coming* (1953). *Introductory Papers on Dante* (1954). (trans.) *The Comedy of Dante Alighieri the Florentine: Cantica II: Purgatory* (1955). *Further Papers on Dante* (1957). (trans.) *The Song of Roland* (1957). (trans., with B. Reynolds) *The Comedy of Dante Alighieri the Florentine: Cantica III: Paradise* (1962). *The Poetry of Search and the Poetry of Statement* (1963). *Christian Letters to a Post-Christian World,* ed. R. Jellema (1969). *Lord Peter: A Collection of All the Lord Peter Wimsey Stories,* ed. J. Sandoe (1972). *Talboys* (1972). *A Matter of Eternity,* ed. R. K. Sprague (1973). *Striding Folly* (1973). *Wilkie Collins: A Critical and Biographical Study,* ed. E. R. Gregory (1977). *The Wimsey Family: A Fragmentary History Compiled from Correspondence with Dorothy L. Sayers,* ed. C. W. Scott-Giles (1977). *Letters, 1899–1936,* ed. B. Reynolds (1995). *Letters, 1937–43,* ed. B. Reynolds (1997).

BIBLIOGRAPHY: Brabazon, J. *Dorothy L. Sayers: A Biography* (1981). Dale, A. *Maker and Craftsman: The Story of Dorothy L. Sayers* (1978). Durkin, M. B. *Dorothy L. Sayers* (1980). Hall, T. *Dorothy L. Sayers: Nine Literary Studies* (1980). *As Her Whimsey Took Her: Critical Essays on the Work of Dorothy L. Sayers,* ed. M. Hannay (1979). Harmon, R. and M. A. Burger. *An Annotated Guide to the Works of Dorothy L. Sayers* (1977). Hitchman, J. *Such a Strange Lady* (1975). Hone, R. E. *Dorothy L. Sayers, A Literary Biography* (1979). Hull, T. *Dorothy L. Sayers, Nine Literary Studies* (1980). Kenney, C. *The Remarkable Case of Dorothy L. Sayers* (1990). Reynolds, B. *The Passionate Intellect* (1989). Tischler, N. *Dorothy L. Sayers: A Pilgrim Soul* (1980). Youngberd, R. T. *Dorothy L. Sayers: A Reference Guide* (1982).

For articles in reference works, see: *Bloomsbury. CA. Cambridge. CLC. DLB. DNB. Europa. Feminist. IDWB. Oxford. MBL* and *SUP. TCA* and *SUP. TCC&MW. TCLC. TCW. ToddBWW.*

Other references: Adams, P. *Somerville for Women: An Oxford College 1879–1993* (1996). *ArmD* (1990). Bander, E. *ArmD* (1977). Beach, S. *Mythlore* (1993). Brody, M. *Style* (1985). Campbell, S. E. *MFS* (1983). Christopher, J. *SayersR* (1981). Cook, R. F. *Olifant* (1981). Elliott, J. R., Jr. and D. L. Sayers. *Seven* (1981). Epperson, W. *Mythlore* (1979). Freeling, N. *ArmD* (1994). Gregory, E. R. *C&L* (1975). Gwilt, P. and J. Gwilt. *Clues* (1980). Hahn, S. *Renascence* (1989). Hannay, M. P. *Mythlore* (1979). Heilbrun, C. *AS* (Autumn 1982). Heilbrun, C., in *Reading and Writing Women's Lives,* ed. B. K. Bowers (1990). Heldreth, L. *Clues* (1982). Hone, R. *Seven* (1985). James, P. D., in *Ten Women of Mystery,* ed. E. Bargainnier (1981). Joyner, N. C., in *Ten Women of Mystery,* ed. E. Bargainnier (1981). Kenney, A. *Mythlore* (1984). Kenney, C., in *Old Maids to Radical Spinsters,* ed. N. Auerbach (1991). Klein, K. G., in *Ten Women of Mystery,* ed. E. Bargainnier (1981). Klein, K. G. *Great Women Mystery Writers* (1994). Lane, T. *Clues* (1980). Low, D. *British Radio Drama* (1981). Marsden, B. *Seven* (1987). Marshall, D. G. *Seven* (1983). Martin, J., in *Taste of the Pineapple,* ed. B. Edwards (1988). Mascall, E. L. *Seven* (1982). McDiarmid, J. *Clues* (1985). McFarland, T. *ArmD* (1988). Meredith, P. *Mythlore* (1982). Merry, B., *Art in Crime Writing: Essays on Detective Fiction,* ed. B. Benstock (1983). Morris, V. B. *MFS* (1983). Ohanian, S. *JPC* (1980). Oliver, E. J. *CRev* (1993). Patterson, N. *Mythlore* (1984, 1988, 1989, 1993). Pitt, V. *L&H* (1988). Pitt, V., in *Twentieth-Century Suspense,* ed. C. Bloom (1990). Price, M. *Mythlore* (1982). Ralph, G. *Seven* (1986). Reynolds, B. *Seven* (1980, 1985). Rossen, J., in *University Fiction,* ed. D. Bevan (1990). Sayers, D. L., and K. Nott. *Seven* (1982). Scott, W. M. *ArmD* (1979). Scowcroft, P. L. *Seven* (1984). Stock, A. *ABR* (1985). Taylor, D. J. *Seven* (1982). Urdang, L. *Verbatim* (1986). Wald, G., in *The*

Cunning Craft, ed. D. Anderson (1990). Watts, J. *SayersR* (1981). Webster, R. *Seven* (1981).

Margaret P. Hannay

Janet Schaw

BORN: c. 1730–37, Lauriston, Scotland.
DIED: c. 1801, Edinburgh, Scotland (?).
DAUGHTER OF: Gideon Schaw and Anne Rutherfurd.

In October 1774, S. set sail from Scotland with her brother Alexander, two servants, and the children of an American relation on her mother's side of the family. Before the letters documenting that journey begin, we know little of S.'s life: She was born near Edinburgh and can be traced there again in 1778, two years after her return to Scotland; she had five siblings and was a distant relative of Sir Walter Scott; she was a well-educated gentlewoman who could quote poets and natural philosophers easily and claim to know "all the descriptions that have been published of America."

The letters collected into S.'s *Journal of a Lady of Quality* compensate for our limited knowledge. Beautifully written, they offer lively descriptions of the four stages of S.'s journey: an arduous trip to the West Indies, the stay there, her subsequent residence in the Cape Fear colony in North Carolina, and her escape to Lisbon on the eve of the American Revolution. The first of these sections is tightly structured and novelistic, with vivid images of storms and shipboard conditions, the pathetic tale of an emigrant family on board, and occasional passages in the present tense reminiscent of Samuel Richardson's "writing to the moment."

S. enjoyed and romanticized her voyage, and her letters became less dramatic once she reached land. While Alexander Schaw prepared to assume the post of customs agent, S. relished the social life, the food, and the sights of Antigua and St. Kitts. Her racism and Presbyterian prejudices surface here, as do her loyalist feelings in America, but she nonetheless comes across as a witty and appreciative observer.

To return the young relations and to see their brother Robert, the Schaws soon sailed for North Carolina, where S.'s predictions were borne out: "people talk treason by the hour." Though able to mock her out-of-place British finery, S. could not forgive the rebellion brewing around her. She scoffs at American manners and agriculture, wishes for a few good British troops, and refuses to believe that landowners might support the revolutionaries. As tensions increased, Alexander returned abruptly to England, Robert and other loyalists were ordered to take up arms for the Americans, news came south of the battle of "Bunkershill," and S. managed to make her escape with her relations, the young Rutherfurds. A pet bear came with them: "We were afraid he would join his brethren of the [rebel] congress, and as he has more apparent sagacity than any of them, he would be no small addition to their councils." A pleasant trip to Lisbon returned S. to Scottish friends, and her final, least interesting, letters mingle description of Portugal with tales of balls and sightseeing tours.

S.'s *Journal* is frequently cited by historians of slavery, the American Revolution, and North Carolina crafts and culture. Loyalist prejudices apart, it has proven highly accurate. The comic touches and colorful images of S.'s account make exciting reading. The manuscript is written to a Scots friend, and was copied for private circulation, though not published during the author's lifetime.

WORKS: *Journal of a Lady of Quality: Being the Narrative of a Journey from Scotland to the West Indies, North Carolina, and Portugal, in the Years 1774 to 1776*, ed. E. W. Andrews in collaboration with C. M. Andrews (1921; rev. 1939). *Letters* (unpublished).

BIBLIOGRAPHY: Bohls, E. *ECS* (1994). Hubbell, J. *The South in American Literature, 1607–1900* (1926).

For articles in reference works, see: *Feminist.* Joint Committee of the North Carolina Teachers' Assn. and the North Carolina Library Assn. *North Carolina Authors* (1952). *ToddDBA.*

Marie E. McAllister

Schmidt, Evald: See *Smyth, Ethel Mary*

Schreiber, Lady Charlotte Elizabeth: See *Guest, Charlotte E. B.*

Olive Emilie Albertina Schreiner

BORN: 24 March 1855, Wittebergen, Basutoland (now Lesotho).
DIED: 11 December 1920, Wynberg, South Africa.
DAUGHTER OF: Gottlob Schreiner and Rebecca Lyndall Schreiner.
MARRIED: Samuel "Cron" Cronwright, 1894.
WROTE UNDER: Olive Cronwright-Schreiner; Ralph Iron; Mrs. S. C.; O. Schreiner; Olive Schreiner.

Well known in the early twentieth century for her feminist novel, *The Story of an African Farm* (1883), and for *Woman and Labour* (1911), the "bible" of the early-twentieth-century British women's suffrage movement, S. was the first white woman to write novels about the African colonial situation.

The ninth of her missionary parents' twelve children and named for three dead brothers, S. was often estranged from her religious family. She claimed that she became a mystical "free thinker" after the death of her younger sister and that this early impulse was further shaped by reading the works of Charles Darwin, Herbert Spencer, John Stuart Mill, Percy Bysshe Shelley, Goethe, and Ralph Waldo Emerson, from whose name she derived her pseudonym Ralph Iron. S. attended no schools but received some education from her parents. When her family's home broke up because of poverty, S. was shuttled between older siblings until she left to become a governess in 1870. It was at this time that S. began to write seriously. In seven years of loneliness and isolation, she wrote the bulk of three novels—*Undine* (1929), *The Story of an African Farm*, and *From Man to Man* (1926)—the manuscripts of which she took with her when she left South Africa for England in 1881.

The Story of an African Farm has two major sections, childhood and adulthood, which are separated by a long, meditative passage about the birth and growth of a mystical belief shared by the novel's central characters, Lyndall and Waldo. Lyndall understands Victorian culture—and particularly its construction of masculinity and femininity—in an empowering and almost spiritual way. Like the heroine Rebekah in *From Man to Man,* however, Lyndall is unable to act on her feminist impulses, choosing instead a brief, masochistic liaison that ends in her shame and death. While S.'s best male characters often incorporate Victorian women's tasks into their own sense of work—they nurture the women they love and think of their creations as offspring—her most unsympathetic characters are usually women. Many of her women characters, such as Em in *African Farm* and Bertie in *From Man to Man,* remain emotionally as well as economically tied to a system that treats them as commodities for men's exchange.

Soon after it was published, *The Story of an African Farm* pushed S. to the center of London's literary and intellectual circles. She was an early member of the Men and Women's Club, an elite group that met weekly to discuss sexual reform and "sex morality," and she became close friends with group members Edward Carpenter, Havelock Ellis, and Karl Pearson. S.'s intense and dependent relationship with Ellis in particular is traced in *The Letters of Olive Schreiner* (1924). S. chose to live among prostitutes while in London, but she seems to have had few close women friends, with the notable exceptions of Eleanor Marx and the suffragist Constance Lytton.

S. suffered from severe attacks of asthma that may have been psychological in origin and that often prevented her from writing, talking, or traveling. Although she struggled to finish *From Man to Man* and an introduction to Mary Wollstonecraft's *A Vindication of the Rights of Woman* (1792), the only works S. completed in England were short, allegorical pieces, collected in *Dreams* (1890), *Dream Life and Real Life* (1893), and the posthumous *Stories, Dreams and Allegories* (1923). Although her husband radically edited the original letters and destroyed what he did not publish, his *Letters* and *The Life of Olive Schreiner* (1924) remain important sources in understanding her work.

When she returned to South Africa in 1889, she turned her attention to political writing. In *Trooper Peter Halket of Mashonaland* (1897), the title character's activities and beliefs are a bitter parody of those of Cecil Rhodes; a Dutch soldier sacrifices his own life to free a black man who has been convicted and sentenced to death because of British racism. Here, as in *An English South African's View of the Situation* (1899) and *Thoughts on South Africa* (1923), S.'s criticism of antinative colonial policies was radical for her time. She claimed that blacks act as a laboring class on which the South African economy depends, that race is a metaphysical as well as a physical reality, and that women understand what unites the races better than men because of their common experience of mothering. On the other hand, S. tended to idealize her own culture, particularly the traditional beliefs and roles of Boer women, in her attempt to imagine an interracial South Africa. In her later years, S. remained in contact with the militant suffragists and with Mohandas K. Gandhi's nonviolent *satyagraha* movement. She broke with the Cape Colony Women's Enfranchisement League when it failed to endorse native men's and women's, along with white women's, suffrage.

Although it is no longer well known, S.'s *Woman and Labour* was read by thousands of women in pre–World War I England. *Woman and Labour* brought together S.'s allegorical and political impulses: She considered it her most significant work. Stories are told of suffragists reading *Woman and Labour* to each other in jail and of women's "conversion" to feminism from reading S.'s work. *Woman and Labour* addresses women's emotional complicity in their economic oppression, blaming "parasitic" upper-class women and prostitutes for civilization's decline. As its title suggests, *Woman and Labour* tends to merge women's labor in the work force with their reproductive labor, implying that the knowledge gained from mothering should both enable and transform other kinds of professional work. S. argues that both men and women would benefit from women's improved economic status and that equality would lead to improved sexual relations between women and men.

When S. married Samuel Cronwright in 1894, he changed his name to Cronwright-Schreiner, but for most purposes she did not. Because of her asthma and political involvement, she spent long periods of time away from her husband. A month after her fortieth birthday, S. gave birth to a child that lived less than a day. This dead daughter remained a haunting presence in S.'s life and later writing, and she chose to be buried next to the child overlooking the kopje that inspired *The Story of an African Farm.* S. has been an influence on numerous white African writers, including Doris Lessing and Nadine Gordimer.

WORKS: *The Story of an African Farm* (1883). *Dreams* (1890). *Dream Life and Real Life* (1893). (with S. C. Cronwright-Schreiner) *The Political Situation* (1896). *Trooper Peter Halket of Mashonaland* (1897). *An English South African's View of the Situation. Words in Season* (1899). *A Letter on the Jew* (1906). *Closer Union* (1909). *Olive Schreiner's Thoughts About Women* (1909). *Woman and Labour* (1911). *Thoughts on South Africa* (1923). *Stories, Dreams and Allegories* (1923). *The Letters of Olive Schreiner, 1876–1920,* ed. S. C. Cronwright-Schreiner (1924). *From Man to Man; or Perhaps Only . . .* (1926). *Undine* (1929). *A Track to the Water's Edge: The Olive Schreiner Reader,* ed. H. Thurman (1973). *An Olive Schreiner Reader,* ed. C. Barash (1987). *Letters, 1871–1899,* ed. R. Rive (1987). *My Other Self: The Letters of Olive Schreiner and Havelock Ellis, 1884–1920,* ed. Y. Draznin (1992).

BIBLIOGRAPHY: Barash, C., in *Speaking of Gender,* ed. E. Showalter (1984). Barsby, C. *PreTexts* (1984). Beeton, R. *Olive Schreiner, a Short Guide to Her Writings* (1974). Berkman, J. *The Healing Imagination of Olive Schreiner* (1989). Burdett, C. *Olive Schreiner: Hidden Motives* (1995). Clayton, C., in *Women and Writing in South Africa,* ed. C. Clayton (1989). Clayton, C. *English Academy Review* (1990). Cronwright-Schreiner, S. C. *The Life of Olive Schreiner* (1924). Davis, R. *Olive Schreiner 1920–1971: A Bibliography* (1972). First, R. and A. Scott *Olive Schreiner, A Biography* (1980). Friedmann, M.

Olive Schreiner: A Study in Latent Meanings (1955). Gorak, I. E. *ArielE* (1992). Haynes, R. D. *ELT* (1981). Horton, S. *Difficult Women, Artful Lives: Olive Schreiner and Isak Dinesen, In and Out of Africa* (1995). Jacobsen, D., intro. to *Story of an African Farm* (1971). *Feminism, Utopia, and Narrative,* ed. L. F. Jones and S. W. Goodwin (1990). LeFew, P. A. *ELT* (1994). Lenta, M. *ArielE* (1986). Lenta, M. *Theoria* (1987). Lessing, D., intro. to *Story of an African Farm* (1976). Lewis, S. *ArielE* (1996). McMurry, A. *ESC* (1994). Meintjes, J. *Olive Schreiner: Portrait of a South African Woman* (1965). Monsman, G. *ELT* (1985). Monsman, G. *TSLL* (1985). Monsman, G. *Olive Schreiner's Fiction: Landscape and Power* (1991). Monsman, G. *BuR* (1993). Pechey, G. *CArts* (1983). Scherzinger, K. *UES* (1991). Showalter, E. *A Literature of Their Own* (1977). *Speaking of Gender,* ed. E. Showalter (1989). *Olive Schreiner and After,* ed. M. Smith and D. Maclennan (1983). Steele, M., in *Gender Roles and Sexuality in Victorian Literature,* ed. C. Parker (1995). Verster, E. *Olive Emilie Albertina Schreiner* (1946). Visal, R. *RAL* (1990). Wilkinson, J. *CE&S* (1992). Winkler, B. *Victorian Daughters* (1980).

For articles in reference works, see: *Biography and Genealogy Master Index. DLB. MCL. TCA* and *SUP. TCLC.*

Other references: *ContempR* (1984). *Contrast* (1979). *DLN* (1976). *DR* (1979). *EinA* (1979, 1985, 1986, 1988). *English Academy Review* (1990). *History Workshop Journal* (1986). *JCL* (1977). *Journal of Southern African Studies* (1968, 1995). *Ms.* (1977). *Pretexts* (1989). *Quarterly Bulletin of the South African Library* (1977). *RAL* (1972, 1990). *SNNTS* (1972). *Standpunte* (1980). *Texas Quarterly* (1974, 1978). *TLS* (15 August 1980). *TSLL* (1988). *Women's Studies International Forum* (1986). *ZAA* (1984).

Carol L. Barash

Scott, Agnes Neill: See *Muir, Willa*

See Muir, Willa

Sarah Scott

BORN: 21 September 1723, West Layton, Yorkshire.
DIED: 30 November 1795, Catton, near Norwich, Norfolk.
DAUGHTER OF: Matthew Robinson and Elizabeth Drake Robinson.
MARRIED: George Lewis Scott, 1751.
WROTE UNDER: A Gentleman on His Travels; Henry Augustus Raymond; Sarah Scott.

Known best today for her feminist utopian novel, *A Description of Millenium Hall* (1762), S. also wrote four other novels, one translation, two historical works, and one biography. The most significant period in her life seems to have been the ten years during which she and her close friend, Lady Barbara Montagu, lived together. During these years, the two women established and ran a school for twenty-four working-class girls and boys, and S. wrote and published five of her works.

S. was the sixth child and second daughter of a family of twelve children, nine of whom survived to adulthood. The family was wealthy, socially prominent, and well educated. When S. was four, her mother inherited the family estate of Mount Morris in Kent, and the family moved there. Although the girls were not sent to school, Sarah and her elder sister Elizabeth read avidly, enjoying Shakespeare, Marivaux, Bacon, Sidney, and Virgil. When she was eighteen, she suffered an attack of smallpox, which left her face disfigured. Later, when describing a character in *Millenium Hall,* she wrote that the "features and complexion have been so in'ured by smallpox, that one can but just guess that they were uncommonly fine."

Sometime in her late teens or early twenties, S. began to take an active interest in politics, education, and economics, interests she continued all her life. Also during this period, she wrote and published *The History of Cornelia* (1750), a melodramatic novel in imitation of Marivaux's *Marianne.* As was every one of her books, *Cornelia* was published anonymously. At the age of twenty-two, S.'s sister Elizabeth married Edward Montagu, nearly thirty years her senior, and was later much admired for her Bluestocking parties and stylish, energetic letters; interestingly, letters from S. to Elizabeth often employ figurative language and humor, devices generally absent from her published works. In 1751, the twenty-eight-year-old S. married George Lewis Scott, with whom she had been friends for six years, but in April 1752 S. was "taken from her house and husband by her father and brothers." S. retained half her dowry and received £100 a year from her husband, from whom she remained separated. S. had met Lady Barbara (Bab) Montagu (no relation to Edward Montagu) in 1748 and the two had become such dear friends that Lady Barbara had accompanied S. and George on their wedding trip and had lived with them for a time. After separating from George, S. went to Bath, partly for her ill health and partly to be near Lady Barbara's home.

In 1754, S. and Lady Barbara began living together, in a "most charmingly situated farm house" in the village of Batheaston. That same year, S. published *A Journey Through Every Stage of Life,* thought possibly to be a translation, and *Agreeable Ugliness, or The Triumph of the Graces,* a translation of the French novel *La Laideur Aimable* by Pierre-Antoine de La Place. Of the latter, S. wrote to Elizabeth that even her publisher Dodsley could "have no guess at the translator." S. next wrote *The History of Gustavus Ericson, King of Sweden* (1761) and *The History of Mecklenburgh* (1762).

Millenium Hall, written in about one month's time, was also published in 1762. A didactic novel, it tells the story of five women who pool their resources and live together in the west of England, where they establish a charity school to educate both girls and boys; girls study reading, writing, arithmetic, and needlework and are taught household management. Millenium Hall also shelters the elderly and the deformed, offers work training for needy gentlewomen, and provides paid employment for disabled persons. S. next wrote *The History of Sir George Ellison* (1766), in which the narrator of *Millenium Hall* founds a school for boys. Her last two works, published in 1772, were an epistolary novel, *A Test of Filial Duty,* and a biography, *The Life of Theodore Agrippa D'Aubigné.*

Financial insecurity was part of the life that S. and Lady Barbara shared, as were recurring illnesses in each of the women. In 1765, Lady Barbara died. After her friend's death, S. seems to have wandered, living short periods in Hitcham, London, Tunbridge Wells, Canterbury, and Sandleford. She finally settled in 1787 in the village of Catton, near Norwich, where she continued to lead an active social and intellectual life. She died in 1795.

WORKS: *History of Cornelia* (1750). (trans.) *Agreeable Ugliness, or the Triumph of the Graces*, by Pierre-Antoine de La Place (1754). *A Journey Through Every Stage of Life* (1754). (as Henry Augustus Raymond, Esq.) *The History of Gustavus Ericson, King of Sweden* (1761). *The History of Mecklenburgh* (1762). *A Description of Millenium Hall. By a Gentleman on His Travels* (1762). *The History of Sir George Ellison* (1766; in abridged form as *The Man of Real Sensibility, or the History of Sir George Ellison*, 1797). *A Test of Filial Duty* (1772). *The Life of Theodore Agrippa D'Aubigné* (1772). Letters in Doran, J. *Lady of the Last Century* (1873). Letters in Climenson, E. *Elizabeth Montagu, Queen of the Blues* (1906). Letters in Blunt, R. *Mrs. Montagu, Queen of the Blues* (1923). Unpublished letters: Elizabeth Montagu Collection, Huntington Library.

BIBLIOGRAPHY: Beach, J. W. *JEGP* (1933). Carretta, V. *AS* (1992). Crittenden, W. M. *The Life and Writings of Mrs. Sarah Scott, Novelist (1723–1795)* (1932). Crittenden, W. M., intro. to *Millenium Hall* (1955). Cruise, J. *SEL* (1995). Dunne, L., in *Utopian and Science Fiction by Women*, ed. J. L. Donawerth and C. A. Kolmerten (1994). Elliott, D. W. *SEL* (1995). Faderman, L. *Surpassing the Love of Men* (1980). Gonda, C. *SEL* (1992). Grow, L. M. *Coronto* (1972). Haggerty, G. E. *Genders* (1992). Rabb, M. A. *MLS* (1988). Reynolds, M. *The Learned Lady in England, 1650–1760* (1920). Schnorrenberg, B. B. *WS* (1982). Stoddard, E. W. *SVEC* (1992).

For articles in reference works, see: *Bloomsbury. Feminist. Oxford. ToddBWW. ToddDBA.*

Other references: *TLS* (12 August 1955). *MLN* (1955). *Personalist* (1957).

Carolyn Woodward

Florida Scott-Maxwell

BORN: 24 September 1883, Orange Park, Florida, United States.
DIED: 6 March 1979, Exeter, Devonshire.
DAUGHTER OF: Charles Morse and Beth White Pier.
MARRIED: John Maxwell Scott-Maxwell, 1911.
WROTE UNDER: Florida Pier; Florida Scott-Maxwell.

S. was raised by her mother's family, the Piers, in Pittsburgh, Pennsylvania. Primarily self-educated, she attended Pittsburgh public schools from the ages of ten to thirteen, then art school for a time. At fifteen, she trained at a drama school in New York City and at sixteen began a career as a player of minor roles in the Edwin Mayo Theatre Company. In 1903, she began writing short stories published in *Harper's* and *Century* magazines and became the first woman staff member of the *New York Evening Sun* with a weekly column.

After emigrating, S. married in 1911 and lived at Ballieston House, near Glasgow, for the next sixteen years, bearing four children and working for women's suffrage. During this time she published only a feminist play, *The Flash Point* (1914). Divorced in 1929, she settled in London and again supported herself by writing: women's columns, short stories, fiction reviews, and a play, *Many Women*, produced at the Arts Theatre in 1933. She also collaborated on an autobiographical account of a White Russian nurse's experiences during World War I, *The Kinsmen Knew How to Die* (1931).

By 1935, she was involved in Jungian analysis and afterward trained as an analyst herself. In 1939, she published *Towards Relationship*, which examines the difficulties women must face in filling expected feminine roles and also existing as individuals. *Towards Relationship* anticipated such major feminist themes as woman as "other" and the crucial value of the "feminine" in a world too much concerned with achievement and progress, at great cost to human relationships. She did not, however, picture men taking on part of the "feminine" task of relating and thus feared that the necessity for women to develop as individuals would deprive society of valued skills.

S. spent World War II immersed in her analytic practice in Edinburgh; it was only at the war's end that she began to write again—an experimental play, *I Said to Myself*, produced at the Mercury Theatre in 1946. Critics agreed that the idea—different actors playing the parts of one personality—was exciting but questioned the play's ultimate stageability. After World War II, S. settled in Exeter, practicing as an analyst, writing, and giving broadcasts for the BBC on such subjects as aging, loneliness, and sex roles. Her second Jungian book, *Women and Sometimes Men* (1957), further explored the ideas of *Towards Relationship*. Though the book was praised for its wisdom and perceptiveness, critics felt that it included too many generalizations and questioned the value of the masculine-feminine categorizations as related to character traits.

After a writing career plagued by all the silences common to women writers, due to marriage, immersion in nurturing roles, discouragement at criticism, and feelings of lack of authority due to lack of education, S. at eighty-five published her oft-quoted journal, *The Measure of My Days* (1968), which has been praised as an honest, impassioned, and sentient view of the aging process.

WORKS: *The Flash Point* (1914). (with S. Botcharsky) *The Kinsmen Knew How to Die* (1931). *Many Women* (1933). *Towards Relationship* (1939). *I Said to Myself* (prod. 1946, pub. 1949). *Women and Sometimes Men* (1957). *The Measure of My Days* (1968).

BIBLIOGRAPHY:

For articles in reference works, see: *BioIn. Norton's Book of Women's Lives*, ed. P. Rose (1993). *Who's Who of American Women* (1958).

Other references: *New Statesman* (8 October 1932). *NYHTBR* (6 October 1957). *NYT* (22 September 1957). *Saturday Review* (26 October 1957). *Spectator* (11 July 1947). *Washington Post* (4 March 1972).

Katherine A. Allison

E[dith]. J[oy]. Scovell

BORN: 9 April 1907, Sharow, West Yorkshire.
DAUGHTER OF: Canon F. G. Scovell.
MARRIED: Charles Sutherland Elton, 1937.

A clergyman's daughter, S. was educated at Casterton School, Westmorland, and at Somerville College, Oxford, where she received her B. A. degree after studying classics and English. In 1930, the young graduate moved to London and supported herself with secretarial work while writing poetry and contributing occasional reviews to *Time and Tide,* a feminist weekly whose literary editor, Ellis Roberts, was among her employers. S. married the ecologist Charles Elton in 1937, later traveling with him as his field assistant on research trips to the Caribbean and South American rain forests. The couple has two children.

S.'s themes of motherhood, birth, aging, and nature led early critics to relegate her work to the domestic realm of "women's poetry." In *Poetry 1945–50* (1951), for example, Alan Ross described her poems as "about family life, children, and the small realities of contemporary living." Geoffrey Grigson, who admired her work enough to anthologize her in 1949, nonetheless called her "the purest woman poet of our time." S. published her first volume of poetry, *Shadows of Chrysanthemums and Other Poems* (1944), at the age of thirty-seven. *The Midsummer Meadow* (1946) soon followed. Her third book, *The River Steamer* (1956), did not appear, however, until a decade later. Between 1956 and 1982, S. published only a few poems and no full volumes. The subsequent *The Space Between* (1982) not only collected poems from the intervening years but also contained her translations of Italian writer Giovanni Pascoli. The publication of *Listening to Collared Doves* (1986) finally prompted a drive for critical reassessment. A writer in *Poetry Review* called her "probably the best neglected poet in the country," and Carol Rumens championed her "unemphatic, undeceived and honest observation." *Collected Poems* (1988), which won the Cholmondeley award, includes her complete set of Pascoli translations, and *Selected Poems* (1991) contains seven new poems.

Although others have seen her as a woman poet, a lyric poet, and a religious poet, S. herself has resisted pigeonholing. "I should like the surface to be entirely clear, and the meaning entirely implicit," she wrote of her work in 1956. Accordingly, some more recent critics have found a higher metaphysics in S.'s use of physical and familial detail. Comparing her style with that of Virginia Woolf, J. Poster has written (in *British Women Writers,* ed. Janet Todd) that S. "shares Woolf's visionary perception of the ways in which the small, the familiar, the domestic, may encapsulate or gesture towards a range of truths which are neither slender nor superficial." Philip Hobsbaum in *Contemporary Poets* has observed that S. has "a grasp of life that puts her among the authoritative poets of the age," adding that "this is a poet we frequent in the same spirit as that in which we ponder the classics of our language."

Despite such recent praise, S.'s subtle but powerful poetic gift remains underappreciated and her name too little known.

WORKS: *Shadows of Chrysanthemums and Other Poems* (1944). *The Midsummer Meadow* (1946). *The River Steamer* (1956). *The Space Between* (1982). *Listening to Collared Doves* (1986). *Collected Poems* (1988). *Selected Poems* (1991).

BIBLIOGRAPHY: Ross, A. *Poetry 1945–50* (1951).

For articles in reference works, see: *Cambridge. CP. Feminist. OxComp. Oxford. ToddBWW. WD.*

Other references: *Poetry of the Present,* ed. G. Grigson (1949). Logan, W. *Poetry* (1991). Mole, J. *PoetryR* (1986). *Making for the Open: The Chatto Book of Post-Feminist Poetry, 1964–1984,* ed. C. Rumens (1985).

Paula Harrington

Sempronia: See *Lamb, Mary Ann*

Anna Seward

BORN: 12 December 1742, Eyam, Derbyshire.
DIED: 25 March 1809, Lichfield, Staffordshire.
DAUGHTER OF: Thomas Seward and Elizabeth Hunter Seward.
WROTE UNDER: Benvolio; Anna Seward.

A minor celebrity who believed herself a major poet but never understood her own limitations, S. was the mistress of a kind of ornate verse that revealed the excesses of eighteenth-century sentimentalism. Hailed as the "Swan of Lichfield," this spirited, opinionated Bluestocking was the very model of a provincial English *précieuse.* That is, she had little judgment and limited talent but an unending capacity to feel and an intense desire to express those feelings. Her work was vivid enough to attract a coterie of admirers and a degree of fame. All that she lacked was genius.

A precocious child, she showed an early aptitude for poetry. When she was in her teens, her fledgling verse was encouraged and influenced by Erasmus Darwin, then practicing as a physician in Lichfield. Not yet famous as a scientist, Darwin, grandfather of the naturalist Charles Darwin, was a poet of the ornamental school, but S. would eventually surpass him in floridity.

As a young woman, she seemed as interested in her familial and social obligations as in her budding verse, but although she had suitors she never married. Instead, she busied herself with the romances of her sister Sarah (who died just before she was to wed) and her adopted sister Honora (who married a man S. detested) and poured out her grief in her poetry. When she fell in love with the married vicar choral of the Lichfield Cathedral, the hopelessness of the situation could only have sharpened her grief.

Grief, mistaken perhaps for sensitivity, made the elegy an appropriate form for S. to try. In 1780, she published an *Elegy on Captain Cook,* a well-received tribute to the slain explorer that may have been written in part by Darwin. The next year, S. offered a *Monody on the Death of Major André,* an elegy to the young Englishman hanged in the Benedict Arnold affair. Since S. had known and truly liked André, she managed to make her poem's sentiments sincere. The *Monody* made her famous as it reached Britons everywhere and provided an outlet for their frustration over the American Revolution. It was no wonder Darwin called S. the inventor of the epic elegy.

For the rest of her life, S. poured out numerous epitaphs and short verses for her friends. In 1784, she published something longer: *Louisa,* a poetical novel in epistolary form. The story of lovers whose virtues first separate then reunite them, *Louisa* exemplifies the sensibility that was seminal to its author. She called herself an enthusiast, and since *Louisa* finally went through five editions, others must have shared her enthusiasm.

Always confident of her own ability, S. published a series of Horatian imitations (*Odes*) in the *Gentleman's Magazine* of 1786 that were immediately controversial since their author, who knew no classical languages, had merely paraphrased prose translations of Horace. In that same year and the next, S. wrote and published a set of letters signed "Benvolio" in which she criticized the character of the late Samuel Johnson. A native of Lichfield, Johnson had been taught by S.'s grandfather and was remotely related to her mother. Nonetheless, S. did not care for him, and after James Boswell queried her for Johnsonian anecdotes, he rejected the material (mostly negative) that she offered. In the 1790s, the two became embroiled in a further and quite public series of disputes over Johnson, which showed neither S. nor Boswell to much advantage.

What S. lacked in discretion she made up for in emotionalism. Deeply affected by the Welsh retreat of two eccentric Irish spinsters, she wrote *Llangollen Vale* (1796), a stylized description of what she perceived as an exotic refuge for two sublime hermits. Her 100 *Sonnets* (1799), Miltonic in style, are structurally sound but somewhat cloying in tone. Though her circle admired them, even they had trouble admiring her prose *Memoirs of the Life of Dr. Darwin* (1804). Inaccurate at points and inarticulate throughout, the *Memoirs* did nothing for its author's reputation.

As the nineteenth century began, S. was losing touch with the times. Though she championed the early work of Robert Southey, Walter Scott, and Samuel Taylor Coleridge, what she liked in these first-generation Romantics were their most conventional aspects. She had no grasp of Romanticism as a movement that had broken with her school of ornate sentimentality. After her death, Scott performed the gentlemanly task of editing her poetical works, and Archibald Constable published her later letters (both acting on requests from S. before she died); but there was no great call for either poems or letters.

WORKS: *Elegy on Captain Cook* (1780). *Monody on the Death of Major André* (1781). *Poem to the Memory of Lady Miller* (1782). *Louisa: A Poetical Novel in Four Epistles* (1784). *Variety: A Collection of Essays* (1788). *Llangollen Vale, with Other Poems* (1796). *Original Sonnets on Various Subjects and Odes Paraphrased from Horace* (1799). *Memoirs of the Life of Dr. Darwin* (1804). *Poetical Works,* ed. W. Scott (1810; rpt. 1974). *Letters of Anna Seward Written Between the Years 1784 and 1807* (1811; rpt. 1975).

BIBLIOGRAPHY: Ashmun, M. *The Singing Swan* (1931). Lucas, E. V. *A Swan and Her Friends* (1907). Monk, S. H., in *Wordsworth and Coleridge: Studies in Honor of George McLean Harper,* ed. E. L. Griggs (1939). Woolley, J. D. *MP* (1972–73).

BIBLIOGRAPHY:

For articles in reference works, see: *Bloomsbury. DNB. Europa. Feminist. Oxford. ToddBWW. ToddDBA.*

Mary Pharr

Anna Sewell

BORN: 30 March 1820, Yarmouth, Norfolk.
DIED: 25 April 1878, Old Catton, near Norwich, Norwich.
DAUGHTER OF: Isaac Sewell and Mary Wright Sewell.

The obscure author of only one book, the classic horse story *Black Beauty,* S. experienced a typical Victorian upbringing in a strict Quaker family. Except for two sojourns at spas in Germany and several extended visits with relatives, she remained at home, never married, and was nursed during her slow decline and last illness by her devoted and domineering mother, the writer Mary Sewell. From earliest childhood, S. displayed a lively interest in horses and fierce outrage at any mistreatment of animals. At the age of fourteen she fell while running and seriously injured her ankles, which brought to an end her brief attendance at a local day school; inappropriate medical treatment caused her to become a semi-invalid for the rest of her life, and S. came to depend on horses for companionship as well as freedom of movement.

During S.'s year-long medical treatment in Boppard, Germany, in 1856, her mother began to write ballads for children and working people. S. helped her prepare several collections of verse and prose for publication, and two of Mary Sewell's ballads (including "Mother's Last Words") became unprecedented bestsellers. In the town of Wick, near Bath, where the family lived from 1858 to 1864, S. and her mother founded a library, a Temperance Society, a hall for Mothers' Meetings, and an Evening Institute for Working Men, where mother and daughter taught reading, writing, and natural history three times a week. S. liked to improvise little humorous stories in verse that were occasionally written down and kept by friends, but only one serious poem by her survives from this period.

At the age of fifty-one, S.'s health deteriorated to the point that she gave up her own horse. To repay her debt of gratitude to the many horses she had ridden throughout her adult life, she began to write a book that would show "what gentle and devoted friends horses can be." At first, she dictated the book to her mother, but gradually she felt strong enough to write the story of *Black Beauty* down in pencil, which her mother then transcribed. Between November 1871 and August 1877, only three entries in S.'s journal note her progress on her famous story. The book was published in 1877 and began to be widely and enthusiastically reviewed in January 1878. When S. died three months later, 91,000 copies had been sold and she was happily aware that her work was a success.

S. designated *Black Beauty* as "the autobiography of a horse" with herself as the translator "from the original equine," and wrote the book not for children but for working men who dealt daily with horses. Her aim was not to create a lasting work of literature but "to induce kindness, sympathy, and an understanding treatment of horses." The title character is a thoroughbred stallion who falls to lowest social station of hired cart-horse through no fault of his own but through human mistreatment. The book contains much technical information on the care and training of horses; so accurate were the descriptions of horse care that one expert horseman declared the book to be written by a veterinarian.

Black Beauty is an "improving" book of the kind that was popular in the Victorian era. That *Black Beauty*'s fame has survived while the vast majority of such books are now forgotten testifies to the originality and sincerity of S.'s storytelling. She wished particularly to portray the difficult situation of London cabmen; however, although she sought practical alleviation for the working class, S. subscribed to an inherently feudal, hierarchical ordering of the world, with the benevolent master at the head of both family and society. She considered it the duty of the lower classes to serve the upper, just as horses were created to serve men. It was the responsibility of the masters, in turn, to look after those beneath them and to prevent cruelty, wrongdoing, and suffering wherever they occurred. S. disliked the changes brought about by the Industrial Revolution and technology, and the city represents corruption and evil for Black Beauty. Of social evils, alcoholism is the worst, often the cause of cruelty to horses. The ethic of humaneness, however, is clearly heralded throughout the novel in the words and behavior of compassionate men, women, and children.

WORKS: *Black Beauty: His Grooms and Companions. The Autobiography of a Horse* (1877).

BIBLIOGRAPHY: Baker, M. J. *Anna Sewell and Black Beauty* (1956). Bayly, M. *The Life and Letters of Mrs. Sewell* (1889). Chitty, S. *The Woman Who Wrote Black Beauty* (1971). Montgomery, E. R. *Story Behind Great Books* (1946). Starrett, V., *Buried Caesars* (1923).

For articles in reference works, see: *Bloomsbury. Cambridge. Feminist. Oxford. SATA. ToddBWW. VB.*

Jean E. Pearson

Elizabeth Missing Sewell

BORN: 19 February 1815, Newport, Isle of Wight.
DIED: 17 August 1906, Bonchurch, Isle of Wight.
DAUGHTER OF: Thomas Sewell and Jane Edwards Sewell.

S. is often classified as a writer of children's books and devotional tracts, but in her best work, the High Church novelist skillfully depicts the position of the unmarried Victorian woman with poignancy and wry humor. S. was acquainted with prominent Tractarian leaders John Henry Newman and John Keble, and novels such as *Margaret Percival* (1847) illustrate High Church doctrine and offer spiritual guidance to adolescent girls. In addition, though, they stress the importance of female education and self-sufficiency.

S. was the seventh of twelve children born to a well-to-do Isle of Wight solicitor and his wife. Her mother resolved to educate her daughters as well as her sons, and S. attended school for ten years, beginning at the age of four. Her education served her well after her father's death in 1842, when bank failures left the family indebted. Her five older brothers—a solicitor, a government official, and three Oxford Fellows—only added to her burden. Their lack of business acumen left S. and her sisters with the responsibility of repaying their father's creditors as well as raising the children of two widowed brothers. With her sister Ellen, S. in 1852 opened a small school in the house she bought in Bonchurch; in 1866, she founded St. Boniface Diocesan School for girls in Ventnor, which she supervised until her death. These domestic difficulties are reflected in nonfiction works such as *The Principles of Education* (1865), in which S. argues for improving girls' education.

S. first achieved popularity with *Amy Herbert* (1844), a novel that depicts an adolescent High Church girl. After John Henry Newman's conversion to Roman Catholicism, her brother William wrote a rabidly anti-Catholic novel and urged her to do the same. *Margaret Percival* is S.'s response to Newman's defection, but even her propaganda includes a message about the marital difficulties caused by authoritarian men. The novel most accessible to modern audiences is *The Experience of Life* (1853), an autobiographical story that illustrates the difficulties faced by unmarried women while it celebrates their independence. The protagonist of *Experience* is savvy, tough, and supportive. Without sentimentality or stridency, the character of Aunt Sally teaches her nieces the importance of women's economic solvency and emotional self-reliance, making the prospect of singleness seem immensely attractive in the bargain. In addition to her novels, S. wrote numerous educational manuals, devotional books, and children's history books. These works reflect not only her piety and her interest in education but also her need to support her family.

Charlotte Yonge is perhaps the best-known High Church novelist, and her numerous texts offer a virtual encyclopedia of the Tractarian experience. S.'s novels offer the same rich depiction of Victorian religion and domesticity, but they bring to this depiction an increased awareness of single women's economic vulnerability. The result is not a diminution of her piety but rather an enhancement as we see her faith in a social context.

WORKS: *The Affianced One* (1832). *Amy Herbert* (1844). *Gertrude* (1845). *Laneton Parsonage* (1846–48). *Margaret Percival* (1847). *The Sketches: Three Tales* (1848). *The Child's First History of Rome* (1849). *Walter Lorimer, and Other Tales* (1849). *Was It a Dream?* (1849). *The Earl's Daughter* (1850). *Margaret Percival in America* (1850). *Stories Illustrative of the Lord's Prayer* (1851). *A First History of Greece* (1852). *A Journal Kept During a Summer Tour* (1852). *The Experience of Life* (1853). *Readings for a Month Preparatory to Confirmation* (1853). *Katherine Ashton* (1854). *Cleve Hall* (1855). *Ivors* (1856). *Thoughts for Holy Week* (1857). *Ursula* (1858). *History of the Early Church* (1859). *Self-Examination Before Confirmation* (1859). *Night Lessons from the Scripture* (1860). *Passing Thoughts on Religion* (1860). *Ancient History of Egypt, Assyria and Babylonia* (1862). *Impresssions of Rome, Florence and Turin*

(1862). *A Glimpse of the World* (1863). *Preparation for the Holy Communion* (1864). *Dictation Exercises* (1865). *The Principles of Education* (1865). *The Journal of a Home Life* (1867). *After Life* (1868). *Historical Selections* (1868). *Uncle Peter's Fairy Tale for the Nineteenth Century* (1869). *European History* (1870). *Thoughts for the Age* (1870). *Mrs. Britton's Letter Touching the Europa Troubles* (1871). *The Giant* (1871). *A Catechism of English History* (1872). *Grammar Made Easy* (1872). *A Catechism of Roman History* (1873). *What Can Be Done for our Young Servants?* (1873). *A Catechism of the History of Greece* (1874). *Readings for Every Day in Lent* (1875). *Some Questions of the Day* (1875). *Popular History of France* (1876). *Note-book of an Elderly Lady* (1881). *Private Devotions for Young People* (1881). *Stories on the Lord's Prayer* (1881). *Letters on Daily Life* (1885). *Outline History of Italy* (1895). *Conversations Between Youth and Age* (1896). *Greece* (1897). *Rome* (1897). *The Autobiography of Elizabeth M. Sewell* (1907).

BIBLIOGRAPHY: Colby, V. *Yesterday's Woman* (1974). Colombat, J. *CVE* (1994). Ferguson, M. *Women: A Cultural Review* (1994). Foster, S. *Victorian Women's Fiction: Marriage, Freedom and the Individual* (1985). Weedon, A. *N&Q* (1993).

For articles in reference works, see: *DNB. Europa. Feminist. NCBEL. OCCL. Oxford. Stanford. VB.*

Other references: *Dutch Quarterly Review* (1976). *PSt* (1986). *VN* (1984).

Colleen Hobbs

Anne, Margaret, and Jane Seymour

Ann

BORN: 1532–34 (?).
DIED: 1587.
DAUGHTER OF: Edward, Duke of Somerset, and Anne Stanhope.
MARRIED: John Dudley, son of the Earl of Warwick, 1550; Sir Edward Union, 1555.

Margaret

BORN: 1533–36 (?).
DAUGHTER OF: Edward, Duke of Somerset, and Anne Stanhope.

Jane

BORN: 1541.
DIED: 1560.
DAUGHTER OF: Edward, Duke of Somerset, and Anne Stanhope.

The three S. sisters, authors of the only Latin composition and the only encomium published by any sixteenth-century Englishwomen, were the daughters of Edward, Duke of Somerset, and Anne Stanhope. Relatively little is known of their lives. Anne was praised by John Calvin for her liberal education and married one of the Duke of Warwick's sons in a lavish ceremony recorded by their cousin, the young king, Edward VI. After her father's execution in 1551 and her husband's death in 1554, she remarried and spent her life far from court. In 1583 she was declared insane and lived in seclusion until her death in 1587. Margaret wrote an epigram on Marguerite de Navarre, included in the 1551 edition of the sisters' poem, and was singled out among the sisters for her poetic talents. She and Jane also wrote a letter to Edward VI. She never married and her death is unrecorded. Jane wrote in Latin to Martin Bucer and Paul Fagius, Protestant reformers and scholars, when only eight years old. She became one of Queen Elizabeth's Ladies of the Bedchamber and, despite her implication in the events surrounding her brother Edward's illicit marriage to Katherine Grey, remained at court until her death at age nineteen. She was buried with much pomp at Westminster Abbey in 1560.

Their parents employed two tutors, John Crane and Nicolas Denisot, to teach them Latin and French. Shortly following the death of Marguerite de Navarre in December 1549 and after Denisot had left for his native France, the girls composed a Latin elegy of 104 distichs honoring Marguerite, which they sent to him in Paris. He quickly published it in a *tumulus*, or collection of memorial verse, with twenty-two other Greek and Latin contributions by a number of well-known French poets, all praising either the sisters or Marguerite. The volume was entitled *Annae, Margaritae, Ianae, sororum virginum, heroidum Anglarum, in mortem Diuae Margaritae Valesiae, nauarrorum Reginae, Hecatodistichon* (1550).

One year later, the girls' poem was republished but in a very different kind of volume. The title was now French, *Le Tombeau de Marguerite de Valois, Royne de Navarre. Faict premierement en Distiques latins par les trois Soeurs Princesses en Angeleterre* (1551). The poem was translated into Greek, Italian, and French and followed by fifty-one poems in Greek, Latin, and French; many of the contributors were eminent poets like Jean Dorat, Joachim du Bellay, Jean-Antoine de Baif, and Pierre de Ronsard. Denisot dedicated the volume to another learned Frenchwoman, Marguerite, Duchesse de Berry.

The two volumes achieved immediate and widespread popularity, for the enterprise was unique in its time: a Latin composition by three young English girls praising and lamenting a beloved French queen; contributions by two other women; the dedication of the second edition to yet another woman; and poems and epistles praising feminine erudition, piety, and chastity.

The S.s' poem was the first encomium written in England by women for a woman. It utilizes feminine biblical imagery—the beloved in the Song of Songs, the ten wise virgins, the bride of Christ in the Marriage of the Lamb—yet stands squarely in the tradition of Classical and Renaissance encomium and funeral elegy, fulfilling the function and exploiting the topoi of both genres. In short, it is a fine product of humanist education that deserves a prominent place in any catalog of Renaissance writings by English "learned ladies."

WORKS: (with others) *Annae, Margaritae, Ianae, sororum virginum, heroidum Anglarum, in mortem Diuae Margaritae Valesiae, nauarrorum Reginae, Hecatodistichon*

(1550). *Le Tombeau de Marguerite de Valois, Royne de Navarre, Faict premierement en Distiques latins par les trois Soeurs Princesses en Angleterre. Depuis traduictz en Grec, Italien, & François par plusieurs Odes, Hymnes, Cantiques, Epitaphes, sur le mesme subject* (1551). *A Collection of Letters from the Original Manuscripts of Many Princes, Great Personages and Statesmen,* ed. L. Howard (1753; contains Margaret's and Jane's letter to Edward VI). *Original Letters relative to the English Reformation, written during the Reigns of King Henry VIII, King Edward VI, and Queen Mary. Chiefly from the Archives of Zurich,* 2 vols., ed. H. Robinson (1846–47; contains Jane's letter to Bucer and Fagius).

BIBLIOGRAPHY: Harris, M. *A Study of Theodose Valeninian's "Amant resuscite de las mort d'amour." A Religious Novel of Sentiment and Its Possible Connexions with Nicolas Denisot du Mans* (1966). Hosington, B. M. *SP* (1996). *Anne, Margaret, and Jane Seymour, Mortem Margaritas Valesiae; Le Tombeau,* ed. B. M. Hosington (1997). Hosington, B. M., intro. to *The Printed Writings of Early Modern Englishwomen, 1500–1640 Series* (1998).

For articles in reference works: *Ballard.*

Brenda M. Hosington

S.F.E.: See Egerton, Sarah Fyge Field

Jane Sharp

FLOURISHED: 1671.

The only details known about S.'s life are those she herself reveals in *The Midwives Book, Or the whole Art of Midwifry Discovered* (1671). A practitioner of the art of midwifery for more than thirty years, she was the first Englishwoman to write a book on childbirth and gynecology. If we take her at her word, S. was unusually well-read for a woman of the period, having read all the books on midwifery that she could find, including those in French, Dutch, and Italian, which she had translated at her own expense. She also seems to have had some knowledge of Latin.

At the time S. wrote her volume, the cries were already sounding to remove women from the practice of midwifery. In an attempt to keep medicine the exclusive domain of male practitioners, opponents of midwifery argued that women were contributing to the high infant mortality rates because they lacked a proper medical education. S.'s purpose in writing her *Midwives Book,* then, was twofold: to help prevent the "many Miseries Women endure in the Hands of unskilful Midwives" by educating women in the profession and, concomitantly, to keep midwifery under female control.

To achieve her goals, S. utilizes several effective strategies. First, she defends women's right to practice midwifery and even maintains women's superiority over men in this endeavor. Although she concedes that women are sometimes deficient in education because they have not received the benefits men have, "who are bred up in Universities, Schools of learning, or serve their Apprentiships for that end purpose," she nonetheless refuses to admit that this lack of education makes women unfit for practice. Citing examples of midwives from the Bible, she argues that "the holy Scriptures hath recorded Midwives to the perpetual honour of the female Sex." She notes that the Bible never mentions "Men-midwives," concluding that midwifery is "the natural propriety of women." What knowledge women might not have gleaned through their personal experience, they can gain through long and diligent practice and through communication with other women.

Second, S. seeks to make knowledge more accessible by writing in the vernacular and by explaining things as plainly and briefly as possible. She complains about the exclusive language used by medical textbooks, "as if none understood the Art that cannot understand Greek." Instead of the Greek and Latin terms favored by most physicians, she uses only common language. Thus in her description, for example, the womb is compared to a pear, its mouth is described as "open[ing] and shut[ting] like a purse."

Despite her desire to give precedence to female experience, S.'s treatise is largely traditional, following the ordering set forth in her primary source, Nicholas Culpeper's *A Directory for Midwives: Or, A Guide for Women, In Their Conception. Bearing; And Suckling Their Children* (1651). Although she does so rather grudgingly, S. follows convention by opening her discussion of anatomy with a description of the male body before she proceeds to the female body. The rest of the volume covers the standard range of topics for a book on obstetrics: fertility and pregnancy, infertility, miscarriage, childbirth, diseases of women during and after pregnancy, and diseases of children.

Although the book bears a strong similarity to other contemporary texts, S.'s genuine concern for the well-being of her fellow women is distinctive. In course of the volume, S.'s commitment and dedication take on the tone of a mission. Many of her remarks suggest that she seeks to establish a community of "sister" midwives by binding them together against a common enemy. She frequently achieves this community in flashes of anger at misogynistic arguments about female inferiority and through jokes told at men's expense. At one point, for example, she relates the story of a husband who complained that his wife's vagina had grown so slack through childbirth that his pleasure was reduced. S. comments, "Perhaps the fault was not the woman's but his own, his weapon shrunk and was grown too little for the scabbard." It is this sense of female authority that makes S.'s volume unique.

The Midwives Book was apparently popular during its time and went through several editions. During a period when it was not unusual for the woman or the child to die during childbirth, S.'s book sought to offer a remedy. Even more important, it hoped to reestablish midwifery as the natural providence of women. Unfortunately, S.'s goal of keeping midwifery in female hands met with little success. By the mid-eighteenth century, the devaluation of the midwife was virtually complete and the practice of obstetrics rested almost solely in the hands of male physicians.

WORKS: *The Midwives Book* (1671; as *The Compleat Midwives Companion,* 1725). *The Midwives Book* (facsimile, 1985; also available through Brown Women Writers Project).

BIBLIOGRAPHY: Hobby, E. *Virtue of Necessity: English Women's Writing 1649–88* (1989). Otten, C. *English Women's Voices 1540–1700* (1992).

For articles in reference works, see: *Bell. Feminist. ToddBWW.*

Susan C. Staub

Margery Sharp

BORN: 1905, Malta.
DIED: 14 March 1991, London.
DAUGHTER OF: J. H. Sharp.
MARRIED: Major Geoffrey L. Castle, 1938.

S., who was born to British parents and raised on the island of Malta, began to write novels after her graduation, with honors, from London University with a degree in French. For more than forty years she had a successful and prolific double career—as a writer of adult fiction and also as the creator of Miss Bianca and the Prisoners Aid Association of Mice. Miss Bianca, an engaging white mouse, beloved of Bernard the Brave, has ventured in subsequent volumes to the Salt Mines, the Orient, the Antartic, and elsewhere.

From 1930 to 1970, S. published more than twenty novels, many of which contain zany, unconventional, and offbeat characters (usually female) who must function in tradition-laden, socially stratified, and conservative English settings. Julia Packett, the protagonist of her seventh novel, *The Nutmeg Tree* (1937), is a typical product of S.'s angle of vision. Her theory, S. has said, is "that people often aren't bad but circumstances sometimes make them so. . . . Julia, particularly, [is] a warm-hearted and completely amoral person who was perfectly good in her way, but if placed in a completely conventional society she looked bad. In fact, she *was* bad for them because she broke up all their patterns."

Cluny Brown, published in 1944 and made into a motion picture in 1946, is, similarly, about a young, restless heroine, a plumber's niece. She is charming and predictably unpredictable; she likes pipes and tools more than feather dusters and aprons. Cluny is sent as a parlor maid to a family in Devon where everyone keeps reminding the reader that "the trouble with young Cluny is she don't know her place." This is, indeed, the case, since she ends up with a distinguished Polish professor for a husband.

Alice Bensen has pointed out in *Contemporary Novelists* that S.'s "satire of social assumptions lacks bitterness" and that the "off-beat characters . . . . are basically sound, and the conventional persons are basically kind." But there is still a wry edge to S.'s work. In *The Faithful Servants* (1975), for instance, she creates the Copstock Foundation, established in 1860 to help support "the honest and faithful superannuated maidservants in the City of Westminster." Predictably, it is the monied, educated, and sometimes titled trustees of the Foundation who become dependent on the very servants who apply for financial aid. The trust is named after Emma Copstock, the archetypal, faithful housekeeper of Jacob Arbuthnot, "a womanizer approaching eighty." As S. noted, Arbuthnot had "womanized for far longer than appears credible, let alone decent," and when "medical opinion [pronounced] him off the hooks [he] took the warning in good part, and sent for the lawyer." Emma Copstock becomes the first "superannuated maidservant" to apply to the Foundation and is followed in the next 100 years by a potpourri of saintly, corrupt, devious, immoral, and virtuous female servants, all, in the final analysis, shrewder and stronger than the masters and mistresses they have served.

This idea of reversal dominates *The Foolish Gentlewoman* (1948) as well. Here, Isabel Brocken, a daffy dowager type familiar in British novels, gives the family wealth over to her annoying and obnoxious second cousin, Tilly Cuff, much to the consternation of both her indignant brother-in-law and her heir. Every expectation of the reader is upset by the novel's end; nothing happens as S.'s audience would expect it to, and yet the overturned events are believable. The cloying, even repulsive, Tilly, for many years a paid companion to various gentlewomen, dominates the book. She is a precursor of the often devious, vulgar, and manipulative servants who emerge in the more recent fiction of Muriel Spark and Iris Murdoch.

S. will be remembered for her intelligent perceptions into the psyches and motivations of all classes of English people because, in her light and entertaining novels, there is insight as well as froth.

WORKS: *Rhododendron Pie* (1930). *Fanfare for Tin Trumpets* (1932). *The Nymph and the Nobleman* (1932). *Meeting at Night* (1934). *The Flowering Thorn* (1934). *Sophie Cassmajor* (1934). *Four Gardens* (1935). *The Nutmeg Tree* (1937). *Harlequin House* (1939). *Stone of Chastity* (1940). *Three Companion Pieces* (1941). *Lady in Waiting* (1941). *Cluny Brown* (1944). *Britannia Mews* (1946). *The Foolish Gentlewoman* (1948). *Lise Lillywhite* (1951). *The Gipsy in the Parlour* (1954). *The Birdcage Room* (1954). *The Tigress on the Hearth* (1955). *Eye of Love* (1957). *The Rescuers* (1959). *Melisande* (1960). *Something Light* (1960). *Martha in Paris* (1962). *Miss Bianca* (1962). *The Turret* (1963). *Martha, Eric and George* (1964). *Lost at the Fair* (1965). *The Sun in Scorpio* (1965). *Miss Bianca in the Salt Mines* (1966). *In Pious Memory* (1967). *Rosa* (1970). *Miss Bianca in the Orient* (1970). *Miss Bianca in the Antarctic* (1971). *Miss Bianca and the Bridesmaid* (1972). *The Innocents* (1972). *The Lost Chapel Picnic* (1973). *Children Next Door* (1974). *The Magical Cockatoo* (1974). *The Faithful Servants* (1975). *Bernard the Brave* (1977). *Summer Visits* (1978). *Bernard into Battle* (1979). *Miss Bianca: More Adventures of Miss Bianca and the Rescuers* (1991). *The Turret: Further Adventures of Miss Bianca and the Rescuers* (1991).

BIBLIOGRAPHY: Newquist, R. *Counterpoint* (1964).

For articles in reference works, see: *CA. CN. OCCL. SATA. TCA* and *SUP. TCCW. ToddBWW. Who's Who.*

Other references: *CSM* (4 May 1967). *Harper's* (August 1937). *National Review* (27 June 1967). *New Yorker* (22 June 1967). *NYTBR* (April 1967).

Mickey Pearlman
(updated by Abby H. P. Werlock)

Mary Wollstonecraft Shelley

BORN: 30 August 1797, London.
DIED: 1 February 1851, London.
DAUGHTER OF: William Godwin and Mary Wollstonecraft.
MARRIED: Percy Bysshe Shelley, 1816.
WROTE UNDER: The Author of Frankenstein; Mary Wollstonecraft Shelley.

Of his wife S., Percy Bysshe Shelley wrote in the dedication to *The Revolt of Islam,* "They say that thou wert lovely from thy birth, / Of glorious parents, thou aspiring child." William Godwin, radical philosopher, and Mary Wollstonecraft, author of *A Vindication of the Rights of Women,* were those "glorious parents." Wollstonecraft had died as a result of giving birth to S., and Godwin's remarriage to widow Mary Jane Clairmont four years later created bitter feelings and resentment for S. These feelings and her strong attachment to her father led to her removal to Scotland in 1812 at the age of fifteen to ease tensions in the family, which included S., Fanny Imlay (Wollstonecraft's "love child"), Charles, Jane (later Claire), and William.

In 1812, S. met the poet Shelley and his wife, Harriet Westbrook Shelley. S. was nearly seventeen when she and Shelley met again in May 1814; he and his wife were estranged by this time, and, almost immediately, S. and Shelley became lovers. By July, she was pregnant, and the couple eloped to the Continent. S.'s first book, *History of a Six Weeks' Tour,* published anonymously in 1817, describes the trip through France, Switzerland, and Germany that S., Shelley, and S.'s stepsister Claire Clairmont took following the elopement. S.'s earlier writing has all been lost, but with Shelley's aid and encouragement, her best-known work would be published the following year.

Frankenstein; or, The Modern Prometheus was published anonymously in 1818. Shelley, S., and Claire had taken residence in Geneva near Lord Byron (Claire's somewhat reluctant lover) and John Polidari. *Frankenstein,* a novel of the scientific creation of life severed from moral concerns and social affiliation, became a literary sensation in London. It apparently grew in S.'s imagination in response to a casual competition to create a ghost story as well as to a conversation about contemporary experiments with galvanic electricity on dead tissue. *Frankenstein,* according to Ellen Moers, "is most interesting, most powerful, and most feminine: in the motif of revulsion against newborn life, and the drama of guilt, dread, and fright surrounding birth and its consequences."

For S., the consequence of giving birth was tragedy. Before she reached twenty-two, she had given birth to three children, all of whom had died. These deaths separated her emotionally from Shelley. Her only surviving child, a boy, was born in 1819. In addition, her half-sister Fanny Imlay had committed suicide in 1816, as did Harriet Shelley (abandoned by Shelley earlier the same year and pregnant by an unknown lover). Harriet's death freed Shelley to wed S. two weeks later. Her greatest loss, however, was the death by drowning of Shelley himself in July 1822. Still somewhat emotionally estranged from him at this time, S., an impoverished widow at twenty-four, attempted through her grief and guilt to establish Shelley's literary reputation (against his father's express wishes) and to support her son through her writing.

S. wrote other novels, several biographies, and many stories, most of which were published in *The Keepsake;* some have elements of science fiction while others are Gothic. Among them is the novella *Mathilda* (1819), in which Shelley is fictionalized as Woodville. This largely autobiographical work explores the estrangement between S. and Shelley after their daughter Clara's death at age one.

Valperga (1823) and *The Last Man* (1826) are widely considered S.'s best work after *Frankenstein. The Last Man* represents a creative landmark in S.'s work. Though marred by overwriting and excessive length, the book commemorates her husband as she was unable to do in a biography. Her characterization of Adrian, second Earl of Windsor, is the only acknowledged portrait of Shelley: "I have endeavoured, but how inadequately, to give some idea of him in my last published book—the sketch has pleased some of those who best loved him." This idealized view of Shelley, a variation on the "Noble Savage" motif, is set in the future and describes the gradual destruction of the human race by plague; its narrator, Lionel Verney, begins life as a shepherd boy and after many years finds himself amid the ruined grandeur of Rome in the year 2100.

The same theme is found in *Lodore* (1835): The heroine Ethel is taken as a child by her father, Lord Lodore, to the wilds of Illinois, in America, and raised amid the grandest objects of Nature, after which she returns to a life of romance and penury in a London reminiscent of S.'s early years. S. also wrote *The Fortunes of Perkin Warbeck* (1830) and *Falkner* (1837) and another novella, *The Heir of Mondolfo* (published posthumously in 1877). In addition to her many stories, S. also wrote biographical and critical studies of continental authors and published several editions of her husband's work. She also worked on, but never completed, biographies of Shelley and her father. In short, S. spent her widowhood as a productive and successful woman of letters.

In 1844, S.'s father-in-law died, leaving his title and estate to S.'s son. Only then was she secure financially. The devotion of her son and his marriage to her friend Jane St. John made her last years comfortable. She died 1 February 1851, eight days after falling into a coma.

WORKS: (with P. B. Shelley) *History of a Six Weeks' Tour Through a Part of France, Switzerland, Germany, and Holland, with Letters Descriptive of a Sail round the Lake of Geneva and of the Glaciers of Chamouni* (1817). *Frankenstein; or, The Modern Prometheus* (1818). *Mathilda* (1819). *Valperga; or, The Life and Adventures of Castruccio, Prince of Lucca* (1823). *The Last Man* (1826). *The Fortunes of Perkin Warbeck. A Romance* (1830). *Lodore* (1835; ed. L. Vargo, 1997). (with others) *Lives of the Most Eminent Literary and Scientific Men of Italy, Spain, and Portugal* (1835–37). *Falkner: A Novel* (1837). (with others) *Lives of the Most Eminent Literary and Scientific Men of France* (1838). *Rambles in Germany and Italy in 1840, 1842, and 1843* (1844). *The Swiss Peasant* (in *The Tale Book,* with others, 1859). *The Choice. A Poem on Shelley's Death* (1876). *The Heir of*

Mondolfo (1877). *Tales and Stories,* ed. R. Garnett (1891). *The Romance of Mary W. Shelley, John Howard Payne, and Washington Irving (The Payne-Shelley Letters),* ed. F. B. Sanborn (1907). *Letters, Mostly Unpublished,* ed. H. H. Harper (1918). *Proserpine and Midas. Two Unpublished Mythological Dramas,* ed. A Koszuly (1922). *Letters,* ed. F. L. Jones (1944). *Journals,* ed. L. Robinson (1947). *My Best Mary: The Selected Letters,* ed. M. Spark and D. Stanford (1953). *Mathilde,* ed. E. Nitchie (1959). *Collected Tales and Stories,* ed. C. E. Robinson (1976). *Letters,* ed. B. T. Bennett (Vol. 1, 1980; Vol. 2, 1983; Vol. 3, 1988). *Journals 1814–44,* ed. P. R. Feldman and D. Scott-Kilver (1987). *Selected Letters,* ed. B. T. Bennett (1995). *Journals,* ed. P. R. Feldman and D. Scott-Kilver (1995). *Novels and Selected Works,* 8 vols., ed. N. Crook, et al. (1996). *The Frankenstein Notebooks: A Facsimile Edition,* ed. C. E. Robinson (1997).

BIBLIOGRAPHY: Bann, S. *Frankenstein, Creation, and Monstrosity* (1985). *Approaches to Teaching Shelley's Frankenstein,* ed. C. Behrendt (1990). Bigland, E. *Mary Shelley* (1959). Bloom, H., intro. to *Mary Wollstonecraft Shelley* (1986). Botting, F. *Making Monstrous: Frankenstein, Criticism, Theory* (1991). Church, R. *Mary Shelley* (1928). Clemit, P. *The Godwinian Novel: The Rational Fictions of Godwin, Brockden Brown, Mary Shelley* (1993). Fisch, A., et al. *The Other Mary Shelley: Beyond Frankenstein* (1993). Gerson, N. B. *Daughter of Earth and Water: A Biography of Mary Shelley* (1973). *The Female Body: Figures, Styles, Speculations,* ed. L. Goldstein (1991). Grylls, R. G. *Mary Shelley, A Biography* (1938). Hill-Miller, K. C. *My Hideous Progeny: Mary Shelley, William Godwin and the Father-Daughter Relationship* (1995). Hindle, M. *Mary Shelley: Frankenstein* (1995). *The Endurance of "Frankenstein": Essays on Mary Shelley's Novel,* ed. G. Levine and U. C. Knoopflmacher (1979). Lowe-Evans, M. *Frankenstein: Mary Shelley's Wedding Guest* (1993). Lyles, W. H. *Mary Shelley: An Annotated Bibliography* (1975). Marshall, D. *The Surprising Effects of Sympathy: Marivaux, Diderot, Rousseau, and Mary Shelley* (1988). *The Life and Letters of Mary Wollstonecraft Shelley,* ed. F. A. Marshall (1889). Mellor, A. K. *Frankenstein: A Feminist Critique of Science* (1987). Moore, H. *Mary Wollstonecraft Shelley* (1886). Nitchie, E. *Mary Shelley: Author of "Frankenstein"* (1953). Norman, S. *On Shelley* (1938). Small, C. *Ariel Like a Harpy: Shelley, Mary, and "Frankenstein"* (1972; in the U.S. as *Mary Shelley's "Frankenstein": Tracing the Myth*). Phy, A. S. *Mary Shelley* (1988). Spark, M. *Child of Light* (1952). Spark, M. *Mary Shelley: A Biography* (1987). St. Clair, W. *The Godwins and the Shelleys: A Biography of a Family* (1991). Sunstein, E. *Mary Shelley: Romance and Reality* (1989). Thornburg, M.K.P. *The Monster in the Mirror: Gender and the Sentimental/Gothic Myth in "Frankenstein"* (1987). Tropp, M. *Mary Shelley's Monster: The Story of "Frankenstein"* (1977). Walling, W. *Mary Shelley* (1972).

For articles in reference works, see: *Allibone. BA19C. Bloomsbury. Cambridge. DNB. Feminist. Moulton. Oxford. ToddBWW.*

Other references: Bennett, B. T. *Text* (1994). Bewell, A. *YJC* (1988). Bloom, H. *PR* (1965). Brewer, W. D. *PLL* (1994). Callahan, P. D. *Extrapolation* (December 1972). Cude, W. *DR* (1972). Favret, M. *Genders* (1992). Fleck, P. D. *SIR* (1967). Forry, S. E. *ELN* (1987). Goldberg, M. A. *KSJ* (Winter 1959). Gubar, S., in *Women and Men: The Consequences of Power,* ed. D. V. Miller and R. A. Sheets (1977). Harpold, T. *SIR* (1989). Hill, J. M. *American Imago* (1975). Jones, F. L. *PMLA* (1946). Kiely, R. *The Romantic Novel in England* (1972). Kmetz, G. *Ms.* (15 February 1975). Levine, G. *Novel* (1973). Mays, M. A. *SHR* (1969). Moers, E. *NYRB* (21 March 1974, 4 April 1974). Newman, B. *ELH* (1986). Norman, S. *Shelley and His Circle,* ed. K. N. Cameron (1970). Peck, W. E. *PMLA* (1923) Philmus, R. M. *Into the Unknown: The Evolution of Science Fiction from Francis Godwin to H. G. Wells* (1970). Pollin, B. R. *ConL* (1965). Reeve, H. *Edinburgh Review* (1882). Reiman, D. *Text* (1988). Roovey, M. *PMLA* (1980). Sherwin, P. *PMLA* (1981). Spark, M. *Listener* (22 February 1951). Veeder, W. *CritI* (1986). Waxman, B. F. *PLL* (1987).

Anne-Marie Ray
(updated by Jacqueline Dello Russo)

Frances Sheridan

BORN: 1724, Dublin, Ireland.
DIED: 26 September 1766, Blois, France.
DAUGHTER OF: Philip Chamberlaine and Anastasia Whyte Chamberlaine.
MARRIED: Thomas Sheridan, 1747.

S., forbidden by her father to learn to write, was educated in Latin and botany as well as in written English by her older brothers. When she was fifteen years old, she wrote her first novel, *Eugenia and Adelaide,* on paper given to her for the household accounts. In 1743, when she was nineteen, she entered the fray of a pamphlet war, defending a man whom she had not yet met but was later to marry. Both the pamphlet, "A Letter from a Young Lady to Mr. Cibber," and a poem, "The Owls," published in the *Dublin News Letter,* were in protest to the attacks of Theophilus Cibber on Thomas Sheridan, a popular actor and manager of the Theatre Royal, Smock Alley, Dublin.

In 1747, S. married Thomas Sheridan, but she did not again write for publication until 1759. During these years she was made intimately aware of birth and death. She bore six children, two of whom died, her beloved uncle died, both her parents died, and her close friend, Miss Pennington, died. S. herself was plagued with illness; lame since childhood, she was stricken in her early thirties with maladies that stayed with her until her death, variously described as rheumatism in the head, violent headaches, disorders of the stomach, and fainting seizures. Yet she was noted for her vivacity and charm, and from 1759 until her death she worked steadily at the profession of writing.

To get away from Dublin theater disturbances and from financial debts, S. and her husband settled in London in 1754. S. became friends with Samuel Johnson, David Garrick, and Samuel Richardson, and with several literary women, such as Hester Mulso Chapone, Sarah Fielding, and Catherine Macauley. Samuel Richardson read *Euge-*

nia and Adelaide, contemplated but decided against publishing it, and encouraged S. to begin writing again.

During the winter of 1759–60, busy with household management and with supervision of her children's education, grieving for Miss Pennington's death, and suffering from her own illnesses, S. wrote her novel *The Memoirs of Miss Sidney Bidulph.* It was published in March 1761 in both London and Dublin, and by July a second London edition came out. Her next effort was a comedy, *The Discovery,* which in late 1762 opened at Drury Lane, where it played to packed houses for seventeen nights. In the following year, she wrote another comedy, *The Dupe,* which opened in December at Drury Lane. Although it closed after only three performances, sales of the printed play were so brisk that she was paid £100 above the usual copyright fee.

In September 1764, in response to S.'s worsening health and to continuing financial distress, the family moved to France. Over the next two years, she wrote four works. For some time, her health seemed to improve, but in early September 1766 she was seized with fainting fits and a fever and died two weeks later. An autopsy revealed, as her husband wrote, that "all the noble parts were attacked, and any one of four internal maladies must have proved fatal." Two works were published posthumously in 1767: *The History of Nourjahad,* an exotic moral tale, and a two-volume continuation of *Sidney Bidulph;* a dramatic tragedy based on this continuation was lost in manuscript. A third comedy, *A Journey to Bath,* was refused by Garrick and not published until 1902, at which time a three-act fragment, credited to her, was included in W. Fraser Rae's edition of her son Richard Brinsley Sheridan's plays.

S.'s youthful effort, *Eugenia and Adelaide* (published 1791), depicts the Gothic adventures of two girlhood friends. *Sidney Bidulph,* noted by Johnson for its power of feeling, was immensely popular during the eighteenth century, running to five London editions and at least one Dublin edition. In translation, it was avidly read on the Continent: For instance, twenty years after its first publication, a French bookseller remarked that she had sold more copies of *Sidney Bidulph* than of any other novel. Here, S.'s interest is in exploring the passions, perhaps encouraged as much by grief for the deaths of loved ones as by the inspiration of Richardson's *Clarissa.* The plot is sentimentally tragic, but S.'s language is energetic and direct and comic interludes break the general air of sorrow. One such interlude, the story of a rich relation from the West Indies who disguises himself as a beggar in order to test the kindness of Sidney and her brother, was picked up by S.'s son Richard Brinsley in *The School for Scandal.* Themes in the novel are the powerlessness of women in a patriarchal society and the bonds of consolation formed among women. A destructive kindness exists between Sidney and her mother; oppression as women binds Sidney and the maidservant Patty Main, while class difference separates them; and romantic friendship offers solace but no hope for change. In the 1767 continuation, Sidney's powerlessness is destructive to her own daughters.

As early as mid-1763, *The Discovery* had been published in London, Dublin, and Edinburgh, with a second London edition printed before the year was out; the play saw repeated revivals during the eighteenth century, was anthologized and adapted well into the nineteenth century, and in 1924 Aldous Huxley offered a modern version. In this novel, women assure harmony through placating and indirectly guiding villainous or foolish men. Here, as in her other comedies, S. achieves effect through an awareness of language from which her son learned much. For instance, the contrasting personalities of Lord Medway and Sir Anthony are caught by the language they use: Lord Medway, "the shorter we make the wooing—women are slippery things—you understand me!" Sir Anthony, "Your Lordship's insinuation, though derogatory to the honour of the fair-sex (which I very greatly reverence) has, I am apprehensive, a little too much veracity in it." Aptly, Sir Anthony's nephew refers to him as "uncle Parenthesis."

The Dupe might have been a stage success half a century earlier, but in 1763 its satire offended the moral sensibilities of its bourgeois audience. The play closed to "an almost universal hiss" from the critics, who found it "low and vulgar" and who censured its author for "conduct so unbecoming, so unfemale." In the printed version, S.'s language was sanitized. For instance, "Spawn of a Chimney Sweeper" and "Cinder Wench" are expunged, and the description of the name of *wife* as worse "than ten thousand blistering Plaisters" dwindles to "worse than ten thousand daggers."

In *A Journey to Bath,* Mrs. Surface, a landlady whose parlor is "a Mart of Scandal," uses language hypocritically. S. had her most fun, however, with Mrs. Tryfort, who later metamorphosed into Mrs. Malaprop. Among her frequent linguistic manglings are these: "to teach my Lucy, and make her illiterate," "Oh in everything ma'am he is a progeny! a perfect progeny!" and "But my Lord Stewkly is so embelished, Mrs. Surface! No body can be embelished that has not been abroad you must know. Oh if you were to hear him describe contagious countries as I have done, it would astonish you. He is a perfect map of geography."

Nourjahad, which S. had planned as the first in a series of Oriental moral tales, is a whimsical fable with a complicated plot having a true surprise ending. In the story, a young man who values pleasure above all else is granted his desire for eternal youth and wealth; the world remains mortal, however, and he learns what loss is. Gradually he discovers new values. The tale was reprinted often in the eighteenth and nineteenth centuries and as recently as 1927.

Criticism of S.'s work focuses on what her son learned from her, which was significant, but S.'s work has more to offer than evidence of her son's comedic training. *Sidney Bidulph* is fascinating for the ways in which it questions how completely woman's life is bound by patriarchy. The comedies are lively explorations of the use and misuse of language. Finally, *Nourjahad* is a delight in its inventive plot, its finely sketched characterization, and its tone of poignant simplicity.

WORKS: "A Letter from a Young Lady to Mr. Cibber" (1743; in T. Cibber, *Cibber and Sheridan*). "The Owls: Fable" (1743; in *Dublin News Letter*). *The Memoirs of Miss Sidney Bidulph* (1761). *The Discovery* (1763). *The Dupe* (1764). *The History of Nourjahad* (1767). *Eugenia and Adelaide* (1791). "Letters and Ode to Patience" (1799; in *A Miscellany,* ed. S. Whyte). "A Journey to Bath"

(1902; in *Sheridan's Plays now Printed as He Wrote Them and His Mother's Unpublished Comedy, "A Journey to Bath,"* ed. W. F. Rae). "Verses on Thomas Sheridan" (1909; in *Sheridan, from New and Original Material,* ed. W. S. Sichel). *The Plays of Frances Sheridan,* ed. R. Hogan and J. C. Beasley (1984).

BIBLIOGRAPHY: Baker, E. A. *The History of the English Novel* (1924–36). Fitzgerald, P. *The Lives of the Sheridans* (1886). LeFanu, A. *Memoirs of the Life and Writings of Mrs. Frances Sheridan* (1824). Nicoll, A. *A History of Late Eighteenth-Century Drama, 1750–1800* (1925). Wilson, M. *These Were Muses* (1924).

For articles in reference works, see: *Biographica Dramatica. Cambridge. DIL. DNB. Feminist. Oxford. Todd BWW. ToddDBA.*

Other references: Baker, D. E. *The Companion to the Play-House* (1764). Burt, J. *The Mid-Eighteenth Century,* ed. G. Carnall (1979). Chew, S. P. *PQ* (1939). Doody, M. A., in *Fetter'd or Free? British Women Novelists, 1670–1815,* ed. M. A. Schofield and C. Macheski (1986). Horner, J. M. *Smith College Studies in Modern Languages* (1929–30). Russell, N. E. *Book Collector* (1964).

Carolyn Woodward

Helen Selina Sheridan, Lady Dufferin

BORN: 1807.
DIED: 13 June 1867, Dufferin Lodge, Highgate.
DAUGHTER OF: Tom Sheridan and Caroline Henrietta Callander.
MARRIED: Commander Price Blackwood, 1825; George Hay, Earl of Gifford, 1862.

Songwriter S.'s talent in versification may have been influenced by her literary lineage: Her great-grandmother was novelist and playwright Frances Sheridan, her grandfather was dramatist Richard Brinsley Sheridan, and her mother, Caroline Sheridan, was a novelist. S. began writing songs in childhood and, while she published only anonymously in her lifetime, she left a legacy of verse that reveals flashes of wit and talent. The family left England when S. was six, moving to the Cape of Good Hope where her father was a colonial treasurer. Upon his death in 1817, S. and her mother returned to England. She spent the rest of her girlhood in Hampton Court Palace by the hospitality of the Regent (later King George IV).

S. was the eldest of "the three beautiful Sheridan sisters"; her sisters were the brilliant Caroline Norton, made famous by her husband's unsuccessful adultery charge against Lord Melbourne, and the Duchess of Somerset. In their teens, S. and Caroline wrote a collection of songs, which was eventually published in 1829, earning them £100. When she was only eighteen, S. married Commander Price Blackwood, the young heir to the Irish title of Baron Dufferin and Claudeboye. Both families disapproved of the match as Blackwood had no income but his pay and S. had no family money. As a result of this disapproval, directly after their marriage service ended the young couple moved to Florence, Italy, for two years, where their son was born in 1826.

In 1827, they moved back to England and lived in a small cottage at Thames Ditton. S. was able to visit regularly with her sisters in London and was introduced to the world of wit and fashion in which they moved. While attending her sisters' salons and parties, S. became acquainted with such notables as Samuel Rogers, Henry Taylor, John Gibson Lockhart, Sydney Smith, and Benjamin Disraeli, the last of whom called her, in later years, his "chief admiration."

In 1839, Blackwood succeeded to the title and estates, but two years later he died aboard ship from an accidental overdose of morphia. After her husband's death, S. dedicated herself to the education of her son. When he came of age, she accompanied him on his travels. A trip they took up the Nile resulted in the 1863 publication of *Lispings from Low Latitudes; or, Extracts from the Journal of the Hon. Impulsia Gushington.* She also wrote the play *Finesse; or, a Busy Day in Messina,* which was first performed at Haymarket in 1863. S. did not acknowledge authorship, nor did she attend the play's performance.

On his deathbed, and at his earnest request, S. married George Hay, Earl of Gifford, and son and heir of the Marquis of Tweedale. He died the next month. She had refused to marry him until it became clear that his death was imminent. One wonders if the marriage was undertaken to ensure title and position for her son, for whom she wrote many verses.

WORKS: *A Set of Ten Songs and Two Duets. The Words and Music by Two Sisters* (1829). *The Charming Woman* (1835). *By-Gone Hours* (1840). *Terrence's Farewell* (1840). *The Lament of the Irish Emigrant* (1845?). *By-Gone Hours: A Romance* (1859). *To My Dear Son on His Twenty-First Birthday* (1861?). *Finesse; or a Busy Day in Messina* (1863). *Lispings From Low Latitudes: or, Extracts from the Journal of the Hon. Impulsia Gushington* (1863). *Songs, Poems and Verses* (1894).

BIBLIOGRAPHY: Dufferin, Lady. *Songs, Poems and Verses* [see *Memoir By Her Son, the Marquess of Dufferin, and Ava*] (1894).

For articles in reference works, see: *BA19C. DNB.*

Kirsten T. Saxton

Mary Martha Butt Sherwood

BORN: 6 May 1775, Stanford, Worcestershire.
DIED: 22 September 1851, Twickenham, Middlesex.
DAUGHTER OF: George Butt and Martha Sherwood.
MARRIED: Henry Sherwood, 1803.

S. is known primarily as a writer of stories and manuals for children and young people. Several of her works were published repeatedly in the nineteenth century and played an important role in making the Victorian mentality.

The daughter of a Church of England cleric, S. was educated first at home and then at the Abbey School in Reading, probably the best girls' school in England at that time.

She began to write while still at school. After her father's death in 1795, S., her mother, and her siblings settled in Bridgnorth, Shropshire. She occupied herself with charitable work and writing; in 1802 she published several tales designed for her Sunday School pupils, such as *Susan Gray*, which was widely admired and appeared in pirated editions.

In 1803, S. married her cousin, Henry Sherwood, an army officer. In 1805, his regiment was sent to India. S. followed, leaving her daughter, born the previous year, in England. In India, S. once again took up charitable works; she became especially concerned with soldiers' orphans, including those of mixed race. She is usually given credit for pushing the founding of the first British orphanage in the subcontinent. She was encouraged in her evangelical zeal by various churchmen in India; this zeal also served as consolation for the several children she lost there. Sympathetic to the Indians and their culture, while firmly convinced of the need for their conversion to Christianity, S. attempted to bridge the two cultures in her writing. One such effort was *The Indian Pilgrim* (1815), an adaptation of *Pilgrim's Progress* to Indian experiences. Her best known children's tale, *Little Henry and his Bearer* (1814), also reflected the two cultures. She herself learned some Hindustani; various of her works were translated into that language and other Asian tongues as well as into French and German.

In 1816, S. and her family returned to England, settling at Wick, near Worcester. Her household now consisted of five Sherwood children, the last born in 1818, and three orphans adopted in India. With her sister, Lucy Butt Cameron, S. set up a school that catered especially to children of men serving in India and that operated for several years. She also continued her charitable and religious work as well as her writing for young people. Her most famous and influential work, *The History of the Fairchild Family*, first came out in 1818, with a second part in 1842 and a third in 1847. Numerous editions, adaptations, and reworkings appeared throughout the nineteenth century. *The Fairchild Family* is a series of short stories about a family—parents and three children—and their daily life. The realistic portrayal of seemingly ordinary events, which include eating and playing as well as encounters with death, animals, and the poor, had great appeal to young readers despite the didactic tone of the work. The stories are usually so interesting that the moral and religious teaching can be ignored, though many later editions cut or eliminated this didactic material.

After 1830, S. and her husband engaged in a work of biblical scholarship that was never published. They traveled frequently to the Continent and in 1848 moved to Twickenham, where her husband died the following year. When S. herself died in 1851, she was survived by three children as well as her vast number of stories and tracts. Later writers have faulted her for the puritanical, evangelical tone of her works, but, despite the strong didactic flavor, there was much in them that appealed to young readers.

WORKS: *The Traditions* (1794). *Margarita* (1802). *The History of Susan Gray* (1802). *The Infant's Progress* (1814). *Little Henry and his Bearer* (1815). *The History of Lucy Clare* (1815). *The Indian Pilgrim* (1815). *The Lady and her Ayah* (1816). *Memoirs of Sergeant Dale* (1816). *An Introduction to Astronomy for Children* (1817). *The History of the Fairchild Family*, pt. 1 (1818); pt. 2 (1842); pt. 3, with S. Butt (1847). *The History of Theophilus and Sophia* (1818). *An Introduction to Geography* (1818). *The Hedge of Thorns* (1819). *The Governess, or the Little Female Academy* (1820). *Dudley Castle. A Tale* (1820?). *The Welsh Cottage* (1820). *The Infant's Progress from the Valley of Destruction to Everlasting Glory* (1821). *The Potter's Common* (1822). *The History of Henry Milner* (1822–37). *Mary Anne* (1823?). *The History of Mrs Catherine Crawley* (1824). *Waste Not, Want Not* (1824). *Juliana Oakley* (1825). *The Lady of the Manor* (4 vols., 1825–29). *My Uncle Timothy* (1825). *My Three Uncles and the Swiss Cottage* (1825?). *Two Dolls* (1826). *The Two Sisters* (1827). *The Lady in the Arbour* (1827?). *The Idiot Boy. A Tale* (1828). *The Rainbow. A Tale* (1828). *Home. A Tale* (1828). *My Aunt Kate* (1828). *Arzoomund* (1829). *The Orange Grove* (1829). *Roxobel* (1830). *The Oddingley Murders* (1830). *Sequel to the Oddingley Murders* (1830). *Obedience* (1830). *Maria and the Ladies and Other Tales* (1830). *Ermina* (1831). *The Little Morière* (1833). *Victoria* (1833). *The Nun* (1833). *Indian Orphans* (1836). *Biography Illustrated* (1836). *The Monk of Cimiés* (1837?). *Sea-Side Stories* (1838?). *The Flowers of the Forest* (1839). *The Druids of Britain* (1840). *The Christmas Carol* (1840?). *The History of John Milner. A Sequel to Henry Milner* (1844). *Caroline Mordaunt, or the Governess* (1845?). (with S. Butt) *The De Cliffords. An Historical Tale* (1847). (with S. S. Streeten Kelly) *The Golden Garland of Inestimable Delights* (1849). *The Two Knights, or Delancey Castle. A Tale of the Civil Wars* (1851). (with S. S. Streeten Kelly) *The Mirror of Maidens in the Days of Queen Bess* (1851). (with S. S. Streeten Kelly) *Boys Will Be Boys* (1854). *Works* (16 vols., 1855). *The Juvenile Library* (selection of tracts and stories, 1880, 1891).

BIBLIOGRAPHY: Cutt, M. N. *Mrs. Sherwood and her Books for Children* (1974). *The Life and Times of Mrs. Sherwood*, ed. F.J.H. Darton (1910). *The Life of Mrs. Sherwood*, ed. S. Kelly (1857). Royde-Smith, N. *The State of Mind of Mrs. Sherwood* (1946). Wilson, M. *Jane Austen and Some Contemporaries* (1838).

For articles in reference works, see: *Bloomsbury. Cambridge. DNB. Feminist. Oxford. ToddBWW. ToddDBA.*

Barbara Brandon Schnorrenberg

Elizabeth Shirley

BORN: c. 1568, Leicestershire (?).
DIED: 1 September 1641, Louvain, Flanders.
DAUGHTER OF: John Shirley of Leicestershire.

S. is known for her *Life of Margaret Clement* (1611), possibly the first known biography of an Englishwoman by a contemporary Englishwoman who personally knew her. Little is known of S.'s early life in England other than that at the age of twenty she became housekeeper to her unmarried brother, the Baronet Sir George Shirley, a post she remained in until he married six years later. A Roman Catholic, Sir George had tried unsuccessfully to persuade S. to convert, as he did others in her milieu; but S. made her own decisions by "reading books," converting later and almost immediately becoming a recusant (i.e., an English Roman Catholic who refused to attend Church of England services and therefore was guilty of a statutory offense) at Louvain, in Flanders.

In the biography, S. first describes the later life of Clement's mother, Margaret Giggs Clement, the adopted relative of Sir Thomas More. In England, she had married the tutor of the More children, Dr. John Clement, and had assisted Thomas More in the Tower. (She is shown next to Margaret Roper in the famous Hans Holbein painting of the More family.) Following More's execution by King Henry VIII, the Clements fled to Spanish-held Flanders to escape the same fate or imprisonment, as did many other family members (Ropers, Rastells) and close associates of More and others who in conscience could not conform to the renewed Oath of Allegiance, the (Religious) Uniformity Acts, and later the Treason Act. The primary subject of S.'s biography, Prioress Margaret Clement (1540–1612), was the English-born daughter of Margaret Giggs and John Clement, who had taught her Latin and Greek with the humanist education advocated by More. In 1557, Clement became a canoness regular of St. Augustine (Windesheim) at the Dutch Monastery of St. Ursula in Louvain, which traced its origins to Gerard Grote and the Devotio Moderna. In 1569, she became prioress, an office she held when S. was professed at St. Ursula's in 1596; S. writes that Clement had the ability to "keep love and ametye among us as the appell of her eie and so many sorts of nations, as Duch [Flemish], frinch, Inglish, Spanyard, garmons, all in one house, lived in great unity and concord."

S. portrays Clement's human nature, showing her courage in events such as floods and sewer inundations, plagues, wars, and slaughter by the invading Gueux; her intelligence and sense of justice in not listening to and requiring evidence for rumors; her compassion and patience in consoling and counselling those who came to her even for minor problems at all hours of the night, causing her loss of many nights' sleep; and her high opinion of human nature. The biography shows the influence of the writings of both St. Augustine and Grote's followers in the Devotio Moderna: humanity with sacred immanence, close to the thought of Thomas More.

So many English women recusants followed Clement to become canonesses at St. Ursula's that an affiliated but entirely English Monastery and school, St. Monica's, was founded in Louvain in 1606. Both Clement and S. were among its founders, and S. became acting superior, then subprioress for twenty-eight years. During S.'s aegis, St. Monica's Monastery "overflowed" with additional English women recusants joining the canonesses—including other relatives and descendants of Thomas More—and to accommodate them another entirely English affiliate, the Monastery of Nazareth, was founded at Bruges in 1623; it is still in existence as "The English Convent." A number of literary works were later composed at these two affiliated monasteries.

WORKS: *Excerpts from the Life of Margaret Clement*, in *The Chronicle of the English Augustininan Canonesses Regular at St. Monica's, Louvain, 1548–1625*, ed. A. Hamilton (1904). Durrant, C. S. *A Link Between the Flemish Mystics and English Martyrs* (1925). Canonesses Regular of St. Augustine (Windesheim). Critical edition of the MS. of the *Life of Margaret Clement* (forthcoming).

BIBLIOGRAPHY: Guilday, P. *The English Catholic Refugees on the Continent, 1558–1798* (1914). *Neglected English Literature, 16th–17th Century Recusant Writings: Collected Papers from the Recusant Sessions of the International Medieval Congress, Western Michigan University, 1990–1994*, ed. D. L. Latz (1997).

Other references: *DNB* (under "John Clement").

Dorothy L. Latz

Mary Sidney, Countess of Pembroke

BORN: 27 October 1561, Tickenhall, near Bewdly, Worcestershire.
DIED: 25 September 1621, London.
DAUGHTER OF: Sir Henry Sidney and Mary Dudley.
MARRIED: Henry Herbert, Earl of Pembroke, 1577.

S. was born to a family of power in Queen Elizabeth's court. Her mother was the daughter of John Dudley, Duke of Northumberland, who had died for his attempt to put Lady Jane Grey on the English throne. Northumberland's surviving sons—Robert Dudley, Earl of Leicester, and Ambrose Dudley, Earl of Warwick—were primary patrons for Protestant writings in England, supported Elizabeth against her Roman Catholic rivals, and advocated military intervention on the Continent on behalf of Protestants there. Northumberland's two daughters married men who strongly supported the Protestant cause: Katherine Dudley married the Earl of Huntington, Lord President of the Council in the North; Mary Dudley herself married Sir Henry Sidney, Lord President of the Marches of Wales and Lord Deputy of Ireland, who had been educated with the young King Edward VI. Among them, S.'s father and uncles ruled approximately two-thirds of the land under Elizabeth's rule.

After the death of her older sister, Ambrosia, S. went to Elizabeth's court at the queen's express invitation. Her uncle, Robert Dudley, Elizabeth's favorite and reputedly the most powerful man in England, arranged for her marriage at the age of fifteen as the third wife of one of the great Protestant lords, the middle-aged Henry Herbert, Earl of Pembroke, and contributed substantially to her dowry. As the Countess of Pembroke and the mistress of huge estates near Salisbury, in Wales, and in London, she used her money and influence to encourage such writers as Edmund Spenser, Abraham Fraunce, and Samuel Daniel.

Her brother, Sir Philip Sidney, was the hope of Protestants on the Continent. Endeavoring to influence Elizabeth to support the Huguenots against the Roman Catholic Valois in the French religious wars, the earls of the Dudley/Sidney alliance met at S.'s London home to plan a letter dissuading Elizabeth from marrying the Duc d'Anjou. Philip served as spokesman for the alliance, infuriating the queen, who forced him to leave the court. Philip spent his time of enforced idleness with S. at Wilton, her country estate. There he wrote the *Arcadia*, the most popular prose fiction in English for two centuries. After Philip died, S. supervised the publication of *Arcadia* (1593) as well as his sonnet sequence *Astrophil and Stella* (1598) and other works.

S. also helped to create a hagiography, virtually establishing Philip as a Protestant martyr. She apparently wrote two poems mourning his death, "The Doleful Lay of Clorinda," published with other elegies for Philip in Spenser's *Colin Clouts Come Home Again*, and "To the Angell Spirit of the most excellent Sir Philip Sidney," which exists in one manuscript copy, a presentation copy of her Psalms. Her other two original poems praise Elizabeth. "A Dialogue between two shepheards . . . in praise of Astrea" was written for the Queen's visit to Wilton; it is unfortunately undated. "Even now that care" dedicates the Sidneys' poetic paraphrase of the Psalms to Queen Elizabeth (1599).

In addition to these original poems, she translated four works in the 1590s: Robert Garnier's *Marc Antoine*, Philippe de Mornay's *A Discourse on Life and on Death*, Petrarch's *Trionfo delta Morte*, and the Psalms of David. The first three works deal with the theme of death, which was particularly appropriate to her at that time; her three-year-old daughter Katherine had died the same day her son Philip was born in 1584; her father, mother, and her brother Philip all had died in 1586; by 1595, her youngest brother Thomas and all her powerful uncles had died as well.

S.'s major literary achievement was her paraphrase of the Psalms. Philip had rendered the first forty-three Psalms into sophisticated English verse patterns modeled on the French psalter of Clemont Marot and Theodore de Bezel. After his death, S. revised some of those psalms and completed the rest. Rarely repeating a verse pattern, her work is a triumph of English prosody and consists more of meditations on the Psalms than of literal translations. John Donne praised her Psalms, saying "They tell *us why*, and teach us how to sing," a statement more accurate than hyperbolic, as recent studies of Donne, George Herbert, Aemilia Lanyer, and others have recognized.

The Psalms were never presented to the queen, and S.'s prestige waned with her husband's. Pembroke had long been plagued with ill health and in his physical weakness had lost most of his power in Wales. In January 1601, he died, leaving his widow the castle and town of Cardiff, Wales, along with some other properties. When he came of age, her son William, third Earl of Pembroke, assumed S.'s role as patron of writers; the first folio of Shakespeare, for example, is dedicated to her sons William and Philip. Although both William and Philip attained great wealth and power in the court of King James I, S. largely retired from court life after the accession festivities. She attempted to put down insurrections in Cardiff, continued her literary friendships, and spent much time taking the waters for her health in the fashionable Continental town of Spa. Her continued, although diminished, importance as a patron is seen in Aemilia Lanyer's dedication of *Salve Deus Rex Judaeorum* to her (and other women of her circle) in 1611. She died in 1621 at the advanced age of fifty-nine and was buried "in a manner befitting her degree."

Samuel Daniel had prophesied that by her Psalms S.'s name would live even when her great house at Wilton "lies low levell'd with the ground." In 1647, Wilton burned, destroying most of the records of her life and quite possibly some additional writings alluded to in contemporary correspondence. Nevertheless, her Psalms do stand as one of the most significant poetic achievements in Elizabeth's reign.

WORKS: (trans.) *A Discourse of Life and Death, by P. de Mornay; Antonius: A Tragoedie*, by R. Garnier (1592; *The Countess of Pembroke's Antonie*, ed. A. Luce, 1897). "A Dialogue Between Two Shepheards . . . in Praise of Astrea," in *A Poetical Rhapsody*, ed. F. Davison (1602). *Two Poems by the Countess of Pembroke*, ed. B. Juel-Jenson (1962). *The Psalms of Sir Philip Sidney and the Countess of Pembroke*, ed. J. C. A. Rathmell (1963). *Narrative and Dramatic Sources of Shakespeare 5*, ed. G. Bullough (1966). *The Triumph of Death and Other Unpublished and Uncollected Poems by Mary Sidney, Countess of Pembroke (1561–1621)*, ed. G. F. Waller (1977). *The Countess of Pembroke's Translation of Philippe de Mornay's Discourse of Life and Death*, ed. D. Bornstein (1983). *Collected Works of Mary Sidney Herbert, Countess of Pembroke*, ed. M. P. Hannay, N. J. Kinnamon, and M. G. Brennan (1997).

BIBLIOGRAPHY: Hannay, M. *Philip's Phoenix: Mary Sidney, Countess of Pembroke* (1990). Roberts, J. in *Women in the Renaissance*, ed. K. Farrell, E. Hageman, and A. Kinney (1988). Waller, G. *Mary Sidney, Countess of Pembroke: A Critical Study of her Writings and Literary Milieu* (1979). Young, F. B. *Mary Sidney, Countess of Pembroke* (1912).

For articles in reference works, see: *Bell. Bloomsbury. CLC. Europa. Feminist. IDWB. Oxford. W&D.*

Other references: Beauchamp, V. *Renaissance News* (1957). Beilin, E. *Redeeming Eve* (1987). Bornstein, D., in *Silent But for the Word: Tudor Women as Translators, Patrons and Writers of Religious Works*, ed. M. Hannay (1985). Brennan, M. G. *RES* (1982). Brennan, M. G. *N&Q* (1984). Brennan, M. G. *Wiltshire Archaeological and Natural History Magazine* (1986). Brennan, M. G. *Literary Patronage in the English Renaissance: The Pembroke Family* (1988). Eriksen, R. *CahiersE* (1989). Fisken, B. W., in *Silent But for the Word: Tudor Women as Translators, Patrons and Writers of Religious Works*, ed. M. P. Hannay (1985). Fisken, B. W. *TSWL* (1989). Fisken, B. W., in *The Renaissance Englishwoman in Print*, ed. A. M. Haselkorn and B. S. Travitsky (1990). Freer, C. *Music for a King: George Herbert's Style and the Metrical Psalms* (1971). Freer, C. *Style* (1971). Freer, C., in *Women Writers of the Renaissance and Reformation*, ed. K. M. Wilson (1987). Hannay, M. P., in *Silent But for the Word: Tudor Women as Translators, Patrons and Writers of Religious Works*, ed. M. P. Hannay (1985). Hannay, M. P. *SSt* (1985). Hannay, M. P. *ELR* (1989, 1994). Hannay, M. P., in *Sir Philip Sidney's Achievements*, ed. M.J.B. Allen et al. (1990). Hannay, M. P., in *Reading Mary Wroth: Representing Alternatives in Early Modern England*, ed. N.

Miller and G. Waller (1991). Hannay, M. P. *R&L* (1991). Hannay, M. P., in *Privileging Gender in Early Modern England,* ed. J. Brink (1993). Hannay, M. P., in *Attending to Women in Early Modern England,* ed. B. Travitsky and A. Seeff (1994). Hogrefe, P. *Women of Action in Tudor England* (1977). Jacobus, L. *MiltonS* (1987). Kay, D. *Melodious Tears: The English Funeral Elegy from Spenser to Milton* (1990). Kinnamon, N. J. *GHJ* (1978). Kinnamon, N. J. *SNew* (1981). Kinnamon, N. J. *ANQ* (1984). Kinnamon, N. J. *EMS* (1990). Kinnamon, N. J. *National Library of Wales* (1995). Krontiris, T. *Oppositional Voices: Women as Writers and Translator of Literature in the English Renaissance* (1992). Lamb, M. *YES* (1981). Lamb, M. *ELR* (1982). Lamb, M. *Gender and Authorship in the Sidney Circle* (1990). Lewalski, B. K. *Protestant Poetics and the Seventeenth-Century Religious Lyric* (1979). Martz, L. *Poetry of Meditation* (1962). May, S. *The Elizabethan Courtier Poets* (1991). Rathmell, J.C.A., intro. to *The Psalms of Sir Philip Sidney and the Countess of Pembroke* (1963). Roberts, J. A. *HLQ* (1983). Robertson, J. *RES* (1965). Schleiner, L. *Tudor and Stuart Women Writers* (1994). Sheppeard, S. *Texas College English* (1985). Sheppeard, S. *POMPA* (1988). Smith, H. *HLQ* (1946). Steppat, M., in *Shakespeare: Essays in Honour of Marvin Spevack,* ed. B. Fabian and K. Tetzelli von Rosador (1987). Todd, R. *TSLL* (1987). Todd, R. *HLQ* (1989). Wall, W. *The Imprint of Gender: Authorship and Publication in English Renaissance* (1993). Waller, G. *WascanaR* (1974). Waller, G., in *Silent But for the Word: Tudor Women as Translators, Patrons and Writers of Religious Works,* ed. M. P. Hannay (1985). Waller, G., in *The Renaissance Englishwoman in Print,* ed. A. M. Haselkorn and B. S. Travitsky (1990). Woods, S. *Natural Emphasis: English Versification from Chaucer to Dryden* (1984). Zim, R. *English Metrical Psalms* (1987).

Margaret P. Hannay

Catherine Sinclair

BORN: 17 April 1780, Edinburgh, Scotland.
DIED: 4 August 1864, London.
DAUGHTER OF: John Sinclair and Diane McDonald.

Born the fourth daughter of a baronet, Sir John Sinclair, S. is best known today as the author of *Holiday House* (1839), a pioneering children's book credited with ushering in the reign of the nonsense tale and marking the triumph of imaginative literature for children over pious moral tracts.

S.'s father was the first president of the Board of Agriculture, and she, too, took part in philanthropic life, serving as her father's secretary until his death in 1835. Although she never married, S. would often tell stories to her nieces and nephews, and this is considered the origin of many of her books.

Holiday House is a loosely connected series of episodic adventures that has as its genesis Sir Walter Scott's remark to S. that "in the rising generation there would be no poets, wits, or orators because all the play of imagination is now carefully discouraged and books written for young persons are generally a mere dry record of facts, unenlivened by any appeal to the heart or any excitement to fancy." Her sibling protagonists, Harry and Laura, get into various escapades: Harry almost burns down the house, and Laura cuts off all her hair. S. believes, however, that the scrapes can be forgiven because they are examples of children's careless naughtiness, not wicked wrong-doing. The villain of the piece is the governess, Mrs. Crabtree, who believes that one could make children good by whipping them; the author's mouthpiece is their grandmother, who declares, "Parents are appointed by God to govern their children as he governs us, not carelessly indulging their faults, but wisely correcting them." The tone of the book significantly alters towards the end and concludes with the death of one of the major characters.

The work is equally well known because it contains Uncle David's "Nonsensical Story About Giants and Fairies," which is often anthologized separately, most recently in Jack Zipes' collection *Victorian Fairy Tales: The Revolt of the Fairies and the Elves* (1987). Though this tale is considered one of the first nonsense stories in the language, the telling of it actually allows S. to engage in a disguised form of moralizing. Lewis Carroll reportedly gave a copy of *Holiday House* to the Liddell family as a Christmas gift in 1861.

S.'s other children's books include *Charles Seymour* (1832), which critics have found more sedate, and *Sir Edward Graham* (1849), a sequel to *Holiday House,* presenting many of the same characters (and reissued in 1854 under the title *The Mysterious Marriage*). The *Letters,* volumes begun in 1861, were a series of six stories in letter form with pictures by W. H. McFarlane printed in color. Advertised as "warranted to keep the noisiest child quiet for half an hour," they proved her most popular success.

Though remembered mostly as a children's writer, S. also wrote novels for adults, beginning with *Modern Accomplishments* (1836) and its sequel, *Modern Society* (1837). Both were commercially successful, but today critics see them as wordy and moralistic. S. also wrote travel literature, beginning with a descriptive tour of Wales, *Hill and Valley* (1840). In addition, she wrote stories that were issued separately between January and April 1853 under the title "Common Sense Tracts" and published as a collection, *London Homes.*

While successful in her day at all the forms she tried, in this century only *Holiday House* remains in print, most recently reissued in 1972. Though reacting against didacticism in children's literature, recent critics have pointed out that the work fails to fulfill its stated intentions. David Gryllis points out that S. does preach conventional morality by paying homage to the family and that her permissive attitude applies only to children of respected classes. Barbara Wall points out that the work vacillates between "pleasing children and pleasing adults," between "entertaining and instructing."

WORKS: *Charles Seymour; or the Good Aunt and the Bad Aunt* (1832). *Modern Accomplishments, or the March of Intellect* (1836). *Modern Society, or the March of Intellect* (1837). *Holiday House* (1839). *Hill and Valley* (1840). *Scotland and the South* (1840). *Shetland and the Shetlanders* (1840). *Modern Flirtations, or a Month at Harrowgate* (1841). *Jane Bouverie, or Prosperity and Adversity* (1846). *The Journey of Life* (1847). *Sir Edward Graham, or the Railway Speculators* (1849). *Lord and Lady Harcourt, or Country Hospitalities* (1850). *Beatrice, or the Unknown Relatives* (1852). *London Homes* (1853). *Cross Purposes* (1855). *The Picture Letter* (1861). *Another Letter* (1862). *The Bible Picture Letter* (1862). *The Crossman's Letter* (1862). *The Sunday Letter* (1862). *The First of April Letter* (1864).

BIBLIOGRAPHY: *Children and Their Books*, ed. G. Avery and J. Briggs (1989). Carpenter, H. *Secret Gardens* (1985). Darton, F.J.H. *Children's Books in England* (1962). Green, R. L. *A Teller of Tales* (1965). Gryllis, D. *Guardians and Angels* (1978). Hunt, P. *An Introduction to Children's Literature* (1994). Jackson, M. *Engines of Instruction, Mischief, and Magic: Children's Literature in England from the Beginning to 1839* (1989). *Romanticism and Children's Literature*, ed. J. H. McGavran (1991). Thwaite, M. *From Primer to Pleasure* (1963). Townsend, J. R. *Written for Children* (1975). Wall, B. *The Narrator's Voice: The Dilemma of Children's Fiction* (1991).

For articles in reference works, see: Bingham, J. and G. Scholt *Fifteen Centuries of Children's Literature* (1980). *Bloomsbury. DNB. Feminist. Oxford.* Sadleir, M. *19th Century Fiction: A Bibliographical Record* (1951). *ToddBWW. VB.*

Tony Giffone

Mary Amelia St. Clair Sinclair

BORN: 24 August 1863, Rock Ferry, Higher Bebington, Cheshire.

DIED: 14 November 1946, Aylesbury, Buckinghamshire.

DAUGHTER OF: William Sinclair and Amelia Hind Sinclair.

WROTE UNDER: Julian Sinclair; Mary Sinclair; M. A. St. C. Sinclair; May Sinclair.

S. wrote twenty-four novels and two major works of philosophy, as well as numerous poems, short stories, translations, and reviews. She was one of the most popular novelists of the early twentieth century and, speaking of Dorothy Richardson's *Pilgrimage* (1915), the first to apply William James's term "stream of consciousness" to the psychological force of modern literature.

All but ignored in England until *The Divine Fire* (1904) was successful in the United States, S. was the only daughter in a strictly religious Victorian family with five sons. When her shipowner father's business collapsed and he became an alcoholic, S.'s parents separated and S. cared for her ailing and dogmatic mother until the latter's death in 1901. She attended Cheltenham Ladies' College between 1881 and 1882 and began studying philosophy with the headmistress, Dorothea Beale. The autobiographical novel *Mary Olivier: A Life* (1919), which S. considered her best work and which was originally serialized beside James Joyce's *Ulysses* in the *Little Review*, reveals the competition and the orthodoxy that haunted S.'s childhood. The philosophies of Plato, Spinoza, and Kant became ways to resist Christian dogma and to search for a more universal truth. *Mary Olivier* is one of fiction's most sustained studies of the mother-daughter relationship.

S. began translating from the Greek tragedies while writing dense narrative and argumentative poems and abstract philosophical pieces for journals in the 1880s. Her first stories and novels bring together the strengths of these two genres: the compact, imagistic language of poetry and the hard, moral questioning of idealist philosophy. Several of S.'s early works—*Mr. and Mrs. Nevill Tyson* (1898), *The Helpmate* (1907), *The Judgement of Eve* (1908), and *Kitty Tailleur* (1908)—explore bad Victorian marriages and the ways disappointment in love leads to illness, brutality, and death. *The Helpmate* shocked many Edwardian readers with its scene of a husband and wife talking in bed. In *The Divine Fire* (1904) and *The Creators* (1910), S. depicts a variety of creative personalities; she shows sensory and sensual experiences inspiring creative work, and she portrays a variety of women choosing for and against marriage and family ties as they attend to their impulse to write.

In the 1910s and 1920s, S. was one of the few advocates of the younger modern writers. She and Arnold Bennett, who was probably the model for *Taskor Jevons* (1916), were the only two established writers to protest publicly the banning of D. H. Lawrence's *The Rainbow* (1915). In addition, S. introduced Ezra Pound to the editor Ford Madox Hueffer (Ford) in 1909 and wrote one of the first positive reviews of T. S. Eliot's *Prufrock and Other Observations* (1917). She published a poem, "After the Retreat," in the April 1915 Imagist number of the *Egoist*, and she encouraged the avant-garde writing of numerous women—Hilda Doolittle (H. D.), Dorothy Richardson, Violet Hunt, and Charlotte Mew—both privately and in print. Like these younger writers, S. strove to uncover the mysteries of the individual psyche and the differences between the individual woman and the individual man.

A member of the Women Writers Suffrage League, S. wrote a pamphlet, *Feminism* (1912), and several letters to the editor on behalf of women's freedom to work. In 1914, she traveled with a Red Cross ambulance corps to Belgium, from which she derived *Journal of Impressions in Belgium* (1915). *The Tree of Heaven* (1917) was one of the first novels to explore the psychological impact of World War I.

She tried, in her biography of the Brontë sisters, *The Three Brontës* (1912), to disentangle them from a web of hostile and often conflicting critical views. S., the first to see the relationship between Emily's Gondal poems and the novel *Wuthering Heights* (1847), also considered Anne's *The Tenant of Wildfell Hall* (1848) the first feminist novel. She praised Charlotte's *Jane Eyre* (1847) as a novel without precedent, and Lucy Snowe, the heroine of *Villette* (1853), as the forerunner of the psychological realism of George Meredith and Henry James. Also derived from S.'s fascination with the Brontës' family life in the Yorkshire moors, *The Three Sisters* (1914) breaks radically from her earlier works to show the ongoing psychological impact of women's social and political inequality.

S. was a member of both the Society for Psychical Research and Dr. Jessie Margaret Murray's Medico-Psychological Clinic, the first group to practice Freudian analysis in England. Various contemporary theories of "psychology"—from the individual's almost passive psychic development, to mysticism, to the spiritual responsibility to discover and to apply absolute truth—work against one another in S.'s works of fiction and philosophy. S. underwent at least partial analysis; she discusses the changes in her style and form resulting from the study of psychoanalysis in the introduction to *The Judgement of Eve and Other Stories* (1914).

In *A Defense of Idealism* (1917), S. uses Indian mysticism, through the poetry of Rabindranath Tagore, to challenge Bertrand Russell's reigning realism. *The New Idealism* (1922) distinguishes between primary and secondary consciousness (the self's knowing the objective world and the self's knowing that it knows) and the "ultimate consciousness" of order, unity, and presence. On the basis of her work in philosophy, S. was named a member of the Aristotelian Society for the Systematic Study of Philosophy in 1923.

Many of S.'s short stories, especially those in *Uncanny Stories* (1923), hinge on one character's ability to communicate with the spirit world, to perceive and to extend unity, or to link the living and the dead. *The Dark Night* (1924), a novel in blank verse, includes a powerful evocation in the "Grandmother" section. On the other hand, with the exception of *Life and Death of Harriett Frean* (1922) and *Arnold Waterlow: A Life* (1924), S.'s later novels became more hardened and satirical than the experimental, psychological works of her middle period. *Mr. Waddington of Wyck* (1921) tells of a provincial aristocrat, and *A Cure of Souls* (1923) tells of a lazy, materialistic rector who prefers not to mix the untidy death of the poor with the propriety and order of afternoon tea. Several of S.'s works were rewritten by others for the stage; *The Combined Maze* (1913) had a short run in London in 1927.

In the 1930s, S. retired from London with her nurse and companion, Florence Bartrop. She died of Parkinson's disease in 1946 after a long and painful illness.

WORKS: (as Julian Sinclair) *Nakiketas and Other Poems* (1886). *Essays in Verse* (1892). (trans.) *Outlines of Church History*, by R. Sohm (1895). *Audrey Craven* (1897). *Mr. and Mrs. Nevill Tyson* (1898; in the U.S. as *The Tysons*, 1907). (trans.) *England's Danger, The Future of British Army Reform*, by T. von Sosnosky (1901). *Two Sides of a Question* (1901). *The Divine Fire* (1904). (trans.) *Thoughts from Goethe* (1905). *The Helpmate* (1907). *The Judgement of Eve* (1908). *Kitty Tailleur* (1908; in the U.S. as *The Immortal Moment: The Story of Kitty Tailleur*). *The Creators: A Comedy* (1910). *Feminism* (1912). *The Flaw in the Crystal* (1912). *The Three Brontës* (1912). *The Combined Maze* (1913). *The Judgement of Eve and Other Stories* (1914). *The Three Sisters* (1914). *The Return of the Prodigal and Other Stories* (1914). *America's Part in the War* (1915). *A Journal of Impressions in Belgium* (1915). *Tasker Jevons: The Real Story* (1916; in the U.S. as *The Belfry*). *The Tree of Heaven* (1917). *A Defence of Idealism: Some Questions and Conclusions* (1917). *Mary Olivier: A Life* (1919). *The Romantic* (1920). *Mr. Waddington of Wyck* (1921). *Anne Severn and the Fieldings* (1922). *Life and Death of Harriett Frean* (1922). *The New Idealism* (1922). *A Cure of Souls* (1923). *Uncanny Stories* (1923). *Arnold Waterlow: A Life* (1924). *The Dark Night: A Novel in Verse* (1924). *The Rector of Wyck* (1925). *Far End* (1926). *The Allinghams* (1927). *History of Anthony Waring* (1927). *Fame* (1929). *Tales Told by Simpson* (1930). *The Intercessor and Other Stories* (1931).

BIBLIOGRAPHY: Aldington, R. *Life for Life's Sake* (1941). Allen, W. *The Modern Novel: in Britain and the United States* (1964). Boll, T. M. *Miss May Sinclair: Novelist* (1973). Brewster, D. and A. Birrell. *Dead Reckonings in Fiction* (1924). Chevalley, A. *The Modern English Novel* (1921). Cooper, F. T. *Some English Story Tellers* (1912). Cooper, H. et al. *Arms and the Woman: War, Gender, and Literary Representation* (1989). Doolittle, H. *Bid Me to Live* (1960). Fitzgerald, P. *Charlotte Mew and Her Friends* (1988). Frierson, W. *The English Novel in Transition 1885–1940* (1942). Gorsky, S., in *Images of Women in Fiction: Feminine Perspectives*, ed. S. Cornillon (1972). Gould, G. *The English Novel of Today* (1924). Kaplan, S. J. *Feminine Consciousness in the Modern British Novel* (1975). Kumar, S. *Bergson and the Stream of Consciousness Novel* (1963). Myers, W. *The Later Realism* (1927). Phelps, W. *The Advance of the English Novel* (1916). Radford, J., intro. *Mary Olivier: A Life* (1980). Radford, J., intro. to *The Three Sisters* (1982). Raikes, E. *Dorothea Beale of Cheltenham* (1908). Stevenson, L. *History of the English Novel* (1967). Swinnerton, F. *The Georgian Scene* (1934). Taylor, C. *A Study of May Sinclair* (1969). Tynan, K. *The Middle Years* (1916). Zegger, H. *May Sinclair* (1976).

For articles in reference works, see: *Bloomsbury. Cambridge. 1890s. Europa. Feminist. OCEL. Oxford. RE. SFW. TCA. TCLC.*

Other references: *Arts and Decoration* (July 1924). *Bulletin of the New York Public Library* (September 1970). *ConL* (1959, 1972). Harris, J. H. *PLL* (1993). Kemp, S. *CritQ* (1990). *Literary Digest International Book Review* (1924). Neff, R. K. *ELT* (1973, 1978, 1983). *Proceedings of the American Philosophical Society* (August 1962). *Psychoanalytic Review* (April 1923). Stark, S. *WS* (1992). *TCL* (1980). *University of Pennsylvania Library Chronicle* (1961).

Carol L. Barash
(updated by Bette H. Kirschstein)

Edith Sitwell

BORN: 7 September 1887, Scarborough, Yorkshire.
DIED: 11 December 1964, London.
DAUGHTER OF: Sir George Sitwell and Lady Ida Denison Sitwell.

S., a poet and public figure who provoked controversy, was associated with avant-garde styles and thought for fifty years. S. became a public figure because she not only read her poems on lecture tours but she also wrote and performed poetry designed to be accompanied to music.

A child of an aristocratic family, she and her younger brothers Osbert and Sacheverell were brought up in legendary elegance. S. was educated at home and was introduced to French symbolist poetry, especially Rimbaud's, through her governess, Helen Rootham, with whom she lived in the 1920s. When S. moved to London, she published at her own expense her first volume, *The Mother and Other Poems* (1915), and she edited the annual volumes of *Wheels* (1916–21). In S.'s poems through the 1910s and 1920s, her style is close to the experimental nonrepresentational style of Picasso and the cubists.

S. also became notorious by performing her poems in *Façade* (1922), set to music by William Walton, in a concert hall. Many of the titles of these poems were dance names such as "Waltz," "Polka," or "Fox Trot." S. not only explored the rhythms of word order but the sounds as well. In "Waltz," for example, the sound and rhythm create the 1–2–3 beat of the dance: "Daisy and Lily, / Lazy and silly, / Walk by the shore of the wan grassy sea— / Talking once more 'neath a swan-bosomed tree." Criticism, much of it hostile, responded to the seemingly meaningless poems and the theatricality of her performance. Other poems published in the 1920s also reflect her experimentation in synesthesia and the social disillusionment of the times; her friends of the period included T. S. Eliot, Aldous Huxley, Virginia Woolf, and W. B. Yeats.

In the 1930s, much of S.'s work was written to support herself, so there are several anthologies and general prose works: a study of Alexander Pope (1930), a book about Bath (1932), *English Eccentrics* (1933), *Aspects of Modern Poetry* (1934), a biography of Queen Victoria (1936), and a novel about Jonathan Swift's loves, *I Live Under a Black Son* (1937). She resumed writing poetry in 1938.

Poems written after World War II reflect a change in style and philosophies, as in *Green Song & Other Poems* (1944), *Song of the Cold* (1945), and *Shadow of Cain* (1947). In these poems, lines are longer, and her despair over the destruction of life through the bomb "rains" can be seen in her openly pacifist poems. "The Shadow of Cain," S. insists in her introduction to her *Collected Poems* (1954), shows her outrage at the bombing of Hiroshima: "This poem is about the fission of the world into warring particles, destroying and self-destructive."

Later poems are more metaphysical and spiritual. In 1955, S. was accepted into the Roman Catholic Church, and many poems of the late 1940s and 1950s seek to "give holiness to each common day." In her 1962 *The Outcasts*, S. called poetry the "deification of reality." S. took herself and her art very seriously, and she frequently complained of being called a lady poet or poetess because she rejected sentimental "women's poetry" as "floppy" and "whining" (see letter to M. Bowra, 24 January 1944).

In her last years, honors and praise made her well known. In 1948 and 1950, S. toured the United States reading her poems, which contributed to her reputation. In 1951, the University of Oxford gave her an honorary D.Litt., and in 1954 Queen Elizabeth made S. a Dame Commander of the Order of the British Empire. Most of her manuscripts, sold in auction at Sotheby's, were sent to the library of the University of Texas.

WORKS: *The Mother and Other Poems* (1915). (with O. Sitwell) *Twentieth-Century Harlequinade and Other Poems* (1916). *Clowns' Houses* (1918). *The Wooden Pegasus* (1920). *Façade* (1922). *Bucolic Comedies* (1923). *The Sleeping Beauty* (1924). *Troy Park* (1925). (with O. and S. Sitwell) *Poor Young People* (1925). *Poetry and Criticism* (1925). *Elegy on Dead Fashion* (1926). *Rustic Elegies* (1927). *Gold Coast Customs* (1929). *Alexander Pope* (1930). *Collected Poems* (1930). *Bath* (1932). *The English Eccentrics* (1933; rev. and enlarged, 1957). *Five Variations on a Theme* (1933). *Aspects of Modern Poetry* (1934). *Victoria of England* (1936). *Selected Poems* (1936). *I Live Under a Black Sun* (1937). *Poems New and Old* (1940). *Street Songs* (1942). *English Women* (1942). *A Poet's Notebook* (1943, 1950). *Green Song & Other Poems* (1944). *The Song of the Cold* (1945). *Fanfare for Elizabeth* (1946). *The Shadow of Cain* (1947). *The Canticle of the Rose* (1949). *Poor Men's Music* (1950). *Façade and Other Poems, 1920–1935* (1950). *Selected Poems* (1952). *Gardeners and Astronomers* (1953). *Collected Poems* (1954). *The Outcasts* (1962). *The Queens of the Hive* (1962). *Taken Care Of* (1965). *Selected Poems of Edith Sitwell*, ed. J. Lehmann (1965). *Selected Letters, 1919–1964*, ed. J. Lehmann (1970). *Fire of the Mind*, ed. E. Salter and A. Harper (1976). *The Early Unpublished Poems of Edith Sitwell*, ed. G. Morton and K. Helgeson (1974). *Collected Poems*, expanded ed., ed. S. Stevenson (1993). *Selected Poems*, ed. R. Greene (1997). *Selected Letters*, ed. R. Greene (1997).

BIBLIOGRAPHY: Bowra, C. *Edith Sitwell* (1947, 1973). Brophy, J. *Edith Sitwell: The Symbolist Order* (1968). Cevasco, G. *The Sitwells: Edith, Osbert, and Sacheverell* (1987). Daiches, D. *Poetry and the Modern World* (1940). Deutsch, B. *Poetry in Our Times* (1956). Elborn, G. *Edith Sitwell* (1981). Glendinning, V. *Edith Sitwell: A Unicorn Among Lions* (1981). Mills, R. *Edith Sitwell* (1966). Morton, G., in *Rossetti to Sexton*, ed. D. Oliphant (1992). National Portrait Gallery, London. *The Sitwells and the Art of the 1920s and 1930s*, ed. J. Skipwith and K. Bent (1994); ed. S. Bradford et al. (1996). Parker, D. *Sacheverell Sitwell* (1979). Pearson, J. *Sitwell: A Family's Biography* (1978). Pondrom, C., in *Influence and Intertextuality in Literary History*, ed. J. Clayton (1991). Salter, E. *Edith Sitwell* (1979). Singleton, G. *Edith Sitwell: The Hymn to Life* (1960). *A Celebration for Edith Sitwell*, ed. J. Villa (1948).

For articles in reference works, see: *Bloomsbury. BW. CA. CLC. Critical Survey of Poetry. DLB. English Poetry 1900–1950. EWLTC. Feminist. MBL* and *SUP. Oxford. Poetry Criticism. TCA.*

Other references: *ABR* (1976). *Agenda* (1983). *America* (28 February 1981). *BB* (1954, 1974, 1993). *British Museum Quarterly* (1965). *Catholic World* (1956). *CE* (1952). *ChiR* (1961). *Cithara* (1972). *CL* (1971). *Commonweal* (1959, 1965). *ContempR* (1959). *Criticism* (1967). *Encounter* (May 1966, November 1981). *Geneologists' Magazine* (1967). *LCUT* (1984). *MLN* (1959). *Month* (1960). *New Yorker* (9 November 1981). *NYRB* (17 December 1981). *Personalist* (1965). *Poetry* (June 1945). *PoetryR* (1965). *Renascence* (1951, 1974). *St. Louis Quarterly* (1965). *TCL* (October 1970). *TLS* (29 April 1965, 9 March 1990). *TPQ* (1991). *TSWL* (1985).

Marilynn J. Smith

Menella Bute Smedley

BORN: 1820, Wandsworth, Surrey.
DIED: 25 May 1877, London.
DAUGHTER OF: the Reverend Edward Smedley and Mary Hume Smedley.
WROTE UNDER: The author of *Lady Grace;* B.; M. S.; S. M; and others.

Details about S.'s life are sparse and much of what is known is contained in the memoir of her father that was written by her mother. S. had three siblings, Mary (b. 1816), Edward Hume (b. 1817), and Elizabeth Anna (b. 1822); another sister (b. 1819?) lived only a few months. On her mother's side, she was distantly related to Lewis Carroll. S., her sister Elizabeth, and their cousin, Francis Smedley, all became writers. Her grandfather, the Reverend Edward Smedley, was noted for a narrative poem *Erin,* and her father, also an Anglican clergyman with the same name, was a long-time editor of the *Encyclopedia Metropolitana.* He contributed to various periodicals and published several volumes of poetry. S. and her siblings learned Latin and Greek from their father and the daughters became his amanuenses when his health failed. In 1874, S. was an inspector for Mary Charlotte [Mrs. Nassau] Senior's investigations into the conditions at pauper schools, and she edited the reports that appeared in 1875. She wrote a lengthy article, "Workhouse Schools for Girls" (1874), criticizing current practices and offering suggestions to ameliorate conditions. S.'s interest in girls' education is further demonstrated in "The English Girl's Education" (1870), in which she deplores the extreme breadth and insufficient depth of the typical middle- and upper-class girl's educational experiences. Calling female education "desultory, imperfect, shallow, and unsystematic," S. argues for fewer subjects and more intensive study. She advocates a national, endowed educational system for girls similar to that for boys and justifies her proposal on the premise that all women, whatever their vocation, will benefit.

S.'s works were usually published anonymously or under variations of her initials. For example, she produced her popular *Lays and Ballads from English History* (1842) under her inverted first and last initials, "S. M." This collections was curiously classified as children's literature by a reviewer. Through the centrality of her female characters, including Duchess Matilda and Eleanor of Brittany, S. subtly points to the enforced passivity and the powerlessness of women, even those of noble or royal birth. The implication is that, at best, women are unrecognized supporters of male victories. At worst, they are expendable pawns in male power plays.

The Story of Queen Isabel (1863) was published under the initials "M. S." This fictionalized poetic account of the marriage of Isabel of Angoulême and King John of England explores the issue of marriage for wealth and rank rather than for affection, a question faced by many nineteenth-century women. Through her portrayal of Isabel, S. categorically affirms that marriage should be based solely on mutual affection.

As a lyric poet, S. enjoyed a certain amount of success. Two of her finest poems are "'Wind Me a Summer Crown,' She Said" and "The Little Fair Soul," both of which deal with perceptions of heaven and the afterlife.

S. also published several novels. One early effort, *Nina: A Tale for the Twilight* (1853), published under the pseudonym "S. M.," is quite engaging. Set in tenth-century Spain, Nina, the central character, is the kidnapped, orphaned daughter/heiress of Count Miro of Barcelona. S.'s description of Nina as a child is both touching and lively. This tale of damsel in distress, however, is unconventional in at least two ways. First, Nina resists her passivity, complaining at one point that woman's life is "sad, and tardy, and feeble." Secondly, the novel features a "fallen" damsel who uncharacteristically is not required to die to atone for the perceived sin of loving and marrying an infidel. That S. allows her to live and to be forgiven provides evidence of the author's own Christian charity.

The Use of Sunshine: A Christmas Tale (1852), also published under the pseudonym "S. M.," is set in Ireland where Horace Durward, an Anglican clergyman, and his sister Marion settle with two goals in mind: to find out more about their family and to "civilize" the local peasantry. About the latter Horace has firm opinions: "You must have a clothing-club, and there must be a regular system of prizes in the school, and I think of prizes for tidy cottages." S.'s portrayal of the Irish lower class as happily dirty (Horace vows to campaign against "animals in the house") and religiously "lost" to Roman Catholicism reveals the then-common bias among the British. Nevertheless, Horace and Marion exemplify Christian love through quiet devotion to all the people in the parish and they are eventually accepted by the entire community.

The Story of a Family (1850) is quite different, for it plays on the sin of greed. The heroine, Ida, is the heir to a fortune provided she marry one of her cousins upon reaching adulthood. When she chooses the "wrong" cousin, the other young man's father successfully contests the will that specifies the qualifications of Ida's inheritance. Reduced to straitened conditions, she is forced to seek employment as an embroiderer, an occupation that ultimately brings her a fair modicum of financial reward and much personal satisfaction. Ida eventually recovers her fortune, while the greedy relative dies a lonely and painful death.

S. also composed three closet-dramas, "Cyril" and "Blind Love" (*Two Dramatic Poems,* 1874) and *Lady Grace* (*Poems,* 1868), of which the last is the most significant. The widowed Lady Grace Aumerle offers financial assistance to a niece, the reckless Rosa Wilmot, and a nephew, the boorish Captain DeCourcy. When Lady Grace jeopardizes her own reputation to save Rosa's, DeCourcy betrays her. Only her attorney, Mr. Cranston, a man considered a social inferior, supports Lady Grace. The play exposes the opprobrium suffered by women in Victorian England who merely appeared to act immorally and, conversely, offers good insight into the not-so-proper activities of upper-class British males. On the other hand, two dramatic sketches, "Choice" (1869) and "Work" (1870), under the pseudonym "the author of *Lady Grace,*" focus on Cyril Vere, the brilliant young man forced to choose between a promising career in the government and a vocation as a clergyman. "Choice" recounts the temptations he faces while struggling to come to terms with his calling, and "Work" shows Cyril, having overcome the well-meaning tempters, faithfully carrying out his pastoral duties among the poor and the destitute.

S. is chiefly known for her adult writings, but she and her sister, Elizabeth Anna (Mrs. Thomas Barnard) Hart, also composed poetry for children. *Poems Written for a Child* (1868) was published with the pseudonym "by two friends." S. signed her poems with "B." and Hart with "A.," apparently representing their respective middle names. They later collaborated on *Child-World* (1869), in which they identified themselves as "the authors of *Poems Written for a Child.*" Hart, who has been erroneously confused with Fanny Wheeler (Mrs. Dudley) Hart, was particularly noted for her adult novel, *Mrs. Jerningham's Journal* (1869), which was so popular that it went into three editions. She was even more famous for her children's novel *The Runaway* (1872, 1936). Several works were serialized in children's periodicals. Her works were all published anonymously or with pseudonyms such as "the author of *Mrs. Jerningham's Journal.*" Her "A." poems, which originally appeared in *Aunt Judy's Magazine*, were signed "Eoinein."

It is ironic that reference books devote considerable space to Francis Smedley, S.'s and Hart's cousin, while completely omitting them or primarily giving them credit for inspiring their cousin in his literary efforts. In actuality, the output of the sisters and the variety of genres in which they worked vastly exceed what their male relative achieved.

WORKS: (as S. M.) *Lays and Ballads from English History* (1842). (as S. M.) *The Maiden Aunt* (1845?). (as M. B. Smedley) *A Very Woman,* in *Seven Tales by Seven Authors,* ed. F. Smedley (1849). (as the author of *The Maiden Aunt*) *The Story of a Family* (1850). (as S. M.) *The Use of Sunshine: A Christmas Tale* (1852). (as S. M.) *Nina: A Tale for the Twilight* (1853). (as Menella Bute Smedley) *Twice Lost* (186?). (as M. S.) *The Story of Queen Isabel and Other Verses* (1863). (as S. M., the author of *Twice Lost*) *Linnet's Trial* (1864). *A Mere Story* (1865; ascribed to S., but cannot be determined with certainty). (as Menella Bute Smedley) *Poems* (1868). (with E. A. Hart) *Poems Written for a Child* (1868). (with E. A. Hart) *Child-World* (1869). (as Menella Bute Smedley) *Other Folks' Lives* (1869). (as Menella Bute Smedley) *Two Dramatic Poems* ("Cyril" and "Blind Love") (1874). (as Menella Bute Smedley) *Boarding Out and Pauper Schools Especially for Girls* (1875). (as one of the authors of *Poems Written for a Child*) *Silver Wings and Golden Scales* (1877?).

BIBLIOGRAPHY:

For articles in reference works, see: *Allibone* (contains errors). *Bloomsbury. Boase. EP. Feminist. Miles. NCA* (article is inaccurate and skimpy). *NCBEL. Oxford. Poole. Stanford* (under "Smedley, Frank"; contains many errors).

Other references: *DNB* ("Smedley, Edward—1788–1836"). Ellis, S. M. *Mainly Victorian* (1925, 1969): see "Frank Smedley." Forman, H., in *Our Living Poets* (1871). Green, R. L. *TLS* (23 November 1956). *Literary Gazette* (28 June 1845). Smedley, E. *Poems by the Late Rev. Edward Smedley, with a Selection from His Correspondence and a Memoir of His Life* (1837).

Natalie Joy Woodall

Smith, Barbara Leigh: See *Bodichon, Barbara*

See *Bodichon, Barbara*

Charlotte Turner Smith

BORN: 4 May 1749, Sussex.
DIED: 28 October 1806, Surrey.
DAUGHTER OF: Nicholas Turner and Anna Towers Turner.
MARRIED: Benjamin Smith, 1765.

S. was one of England's most popular writers in a period when literary tastes mirrored the revolutionary changes taking place in the political and economic spheres of life in the western world. Her four volumes of poetry, ten novels, translations, and moralistic children's books made her one of the most prolific writers of the last years of the eighteenth century, and readers of the day were usually quite ready to support both critically and financially this woman who dared on the one hand to question the social structures under which she lived while on the other she challenged the already crumbling literary standards of a rationally prejudiced age.

S.'s first and most enduring literary success was a small volume, *Elegiac Sonnets and Other Essays* (1784), that she published at her own expense, hoping to earn a profit. Her financial motivation was both genuine and psychological, for her wastrel husband had been put in debtors' prison and it was legally impossible for her to collect either his inheritance or her own. Writing seemed the only career open to a woman who wished to support many children (she bore twelve) and still retain a semblance of rural gentility. *Elegiac Sonnets* was a novelty for an audience unaccustomed to Romantic poetry and to a form that had been, with a few random exceptions, out of style for nearly a century; it was only after S.'s death that the market for the book began to dwindle. By that time Samuel Taylor Coleridge's and William Wordsworth's "experimental" *Lyrical Ballads* had been published, with their careful perfection of the technique of transmitting a "true feeling for rural Nature" finally overshadowing S.'s tentative explorations of the revolutionary mode.

The Emigrants (1793), a two-volume narrative poem, presents much of the same tone of melancholy that the sonnets do within the context of a politically liberal depiction of the French Revolution. The power of S.'s literary innovations and her sympathies, however, is weakened by descents into domestic and legal complaints, which were real enough but hardly suited to the grandeur of her subject. *Beach Head, with Other Poems* (1807) was published posthumously; although it contains moments of lovely, almost transcendental identification of the self with Nature, it, like *The Emigrants,* was not a popular success.

Although S. hoped her future reputation would rest

upon her poetry, it is for her novels that she is best remembered. Her translations had only limited appeal, and she had found accomplishing them tedious if not (as with *Manon Lescaut,* 1786) socially dangerous. Novel writing offered her a way to earn a living that was only slightly less refined than poetry, and its domestic content was more appropriate to the concerns that constantly interrupted her. Four years after *Elegiac Sonnets,* she published her first novel, *Emmeline* (1788). Within the following nine years, she wrote and published eight more novels, making her average annual production one three-, four-, or five-volume novel. Unlike Fanny Burney, Elizabeth Inchbald, and Ann Radcliffe, S. never received more than £50 a volume, and she never at any time found writing novels more artistically rewarding than writing poetry. Despite her resentment at having to write, S. continued with the novels and later with the even-less-satisfying children's books, for each was popular enough when new to enable her to support the ever-increasing demands of her children and grandchildren and to challenge the circumstances that had once made her dependent upon a husband who was at his best unreliable and at his worst physically cruel.

Almost from the beginning, S.'s novels were criticized for their sentimentality and self-indulgent complaining. Often the accusations have been just, for the novels were written in haste and they exploited her carefully cultivated reputation as a "pathetic poetess." In the novels, as in the poetry, however, there is evidence of a genuinely innovative mind at work. The romantic mood of the poetry is carried over into the novels, and it often led the contemporary reader into new territories of genre and even feminism. *The Old Manor House* (1793), S.'s best novel, contains carefully structured scenes of Gothic terror and wilderness sublimity. *Desmond* (1792), her most severely criticized, uses the French Revolution not only to advance the plot and define the characters but to serve as a macrocosm of the chaos that arises out of unnatural patriarchal systems. S.'s often-overlooked feminist assertion can best be seen not in her stereotypically melancholy heroines but in her skillfully wrought, individually heroic minor characters, most notably the autobiographical Mrs. Stafford of *Emmeline* and Mrs. Denzil of *The Banished Man* (1794).

Through the sad voice of her poetry and through thinly disguised fictionalizations of her life's hardships, S. encouraged her public to believe in her mournful authorial persona. Her background of solitary leisure was prized for the opportunity it gave to develop a "superior understanding," but quite early in life she lost the right to function in such a refined milieu. In her maturity she moved in a society in which it was rarely respectable for a woman to go out into the world to earn a living, but she was forced by the circumstances of a large and almost completely irresponsible family to do just that. Her only possible solution to the problem offered a synthesis of old and current values and gave her a temporary opportunity for fame. Writing in a melancholy mood perhaps justified her unmerited fall from grace at the same time it saved her family from absolute poverty, but daring to attack the conventions of the day from any stronger position would have meant courting economic and social disaster. When other writers, more secure in their economic, social, and literary positions than S. could ever be, arrived upon the scene and expanded her narrow base of literary perspective, she was relegated to the ranks of minor and then forgotten writers. One of her greatest admirers, William Wordsworth, perhaps best described her place in literature when he called her "a lady to whom English verse is under greater obligations than is likely to be either acknowledged or remembered."

WORKS: *Elegiac Sonnets, and Other Essays* (1784; expanded to two volumes in 1797; further expanded through 1811). (trans.) *Manon Lescaut* by A. F. Prevost (1786). (trans.) *The Romance of Real Life* based on Gayot de Pitival's *Causes Celèbres* (1787). *Emmeline, The Orphan of the Castle* (1788). *Ethelinde, or the Recluse of the Lake* (1789). *Celestina. A Novel* (1791). *Dermond. A Novel* (1792). *The Old Manor House* (1793). *The Emigrants, a Poem, in Two Books* (1793). *The Wanderings of Warwick* (1794). *The Banished Man. A Novel* (1794). *Rural Walks: in Dialogues; Intended for the Use of Young Persons* (1795). *Montalbert, A Novel* (1795). *A Narrative of the Loss of the Catherine, Venus and Piedmont Transports* (1796). *Rambles Farther: a Continuation of Rural Walks* (1796). *Marchmont. A Novel* (1796; rpt. 1989, with intro. by M. A. Schofield). *Minor Morals, Interspersed with Sketches of Natural History, Historical Anecdotes and Original Stories* (1798). *The Young Philosopher: A Novel* (1798). *The Letters of a Solitary Wanderer: Containing Narratives of Various Description* (1802). *Conversations Introducing Poetry: Chiefly on Subjects of Natural History. For the Use of Children and Young Persons* (1804). *History of England, from the Earliest Records to the Peace of Amiens, in a Series of Letters to a Young Lady at School,* Vol. I and II (1806). *Beach Head, with Other Poems* (1807). *The Natural History of Birds, Intended Chiefly for Young Persons* (1807).

BIBLIOGRAPHY: Allen, W. *The English Novel* (1954). Baker, E. A. *The History of the English Novel* (1931). Bowstead, D., in *Fetter'd or Free? British Women Novelists, 1670–1815,* ed. M. A. Schofield and C. Macheski (1986). Bray, M. *WC* (1993). Brydges, E. *Censura Literaria* (1815). Curran, S. *Romanticism and Feminism* (1988). Elliot, P., in *Living by the Pen: Early British Women Writers,* ed. D. Spender (1992). Ehrenpreis, A. H., intro. to *The Old Manor House* (1969) and *Emmeline* (1971). Foster, R. *PMLA* (1928). Hilbish, F. *Charlotte Smith: Poet and Novelist* (1941). Kavanaugh, J. *English Women of Letters: Biographical Sketches* (1863). Kelly, G. *The English Jacobin Novel* (1976). Magee, W. H. *SNNTS* (1975). McKillop, A. D. *HLQ* (1951–52). Mei, H. *From Fanny Burney to Charlotte Brontë: The Transformation of a Dream* (1989). Phillips, R. *Public Characters* (1798–1809). *Before Their Time: Six Women Writers of the Eighteenth Century,* ed. K. M. Rogers (1979). Schofield, M. A., in *Living by the Pen: Early British Women Writers,* ed. D. Spender (1992). Scott, W. *Lives of the Novelists* (1905). Todd, J. *Women's Friendship in Literature* (1980). Todd, J. *Sensibility: An Introduction* (1986). Tompkins, J.M.S. *The Popular Novel In England 1770–1800* (1932). Ty, E. *TSWL.* Zimmerman, S. *PULC.*

For articles in reference works, see: *The British Female Poets,* ed. G. Bethune (1849). *Cambridge. DNB.*

Europa. Feminist. Hale, S. J. *Women's Record* (1855). *IDWB. Eighteenth-Century Women Poets,* ed. R. Lonsdale (1989). *Oxford.. The Meridian Anthology of Early Women Writers,* ed. K. M. Rogers and W. McCarthy (1987). *Rowton. ToddBWW. ToddDBA.*

Susan Hastings

Dorothy (Dodie) Gladys Smith

BORN: 3 May 1896, Whitefield, Lancashire.
DIED: 24 November 1990, The Barretts, Finchingfield, Essex.
DAUGHTER OF: Ernest Walter Smith and Ella Furber Smith.
MARRIED: Alec Beesley, 1935.
WROTE UNDER: C. L. Anthony; Charles Henry Percy; Dodie Smith.

S. was a prolific writer of plays, novels, children's stories, autobiography, and journals that she continued writing until the end of her life. She is perhaps best remembered for her chidren's story, *The Hundred and One Dalmatians,* and its sequel, *The Starlight Barking.* The creation of the heroic dalmatian Pongo and his adventures will be long remembered, notably for Walt Disney's 1961 cartoon feature and the 1996 live-action motion picture that inspired Valerie Grove to write S.'s biography.

After S.'s father died when she was eighteen months old, S. and her mother moved in with her mother's family, where S. was exposed to art, music, and drama. It was her uncle, an actor, who inspired S.'s love of the theater. By the time she was a student at the St. Paul Girls' School, she had already penned a screenplay, *Schoolgirl Rebels,* under the pseudonym Charles Henry Percy.

S. entered the Royal Academy of Dramatic Art and acted in several small parts as she toured with various repertory companies. Not finding success, she gave up acting for a time to work as a buyer at Heal & Son in London. Her love of the theater continued, however, and in 1931 her first play, *Autumn Crocus,* was produced under the pseudonym C. L. Anthony. S. continued to use this pseudonym, under which she produced three more plays—*British Talent* (1924), *Service* (1932), and *Touch Wood* (1934)—until 1935.

With the success of *Autumn Crocus,* S. was able to write full-time and began writing plays under her own name. But it was *Dear Octopus,* produced in 1938 and her only play still produced, that established S. as a writer.

In 1939, *Dear Octopus* opened on Broadway, and S. left England for the United States, where she lived for the following fifteen years. Shortly after arriving in New York City, she married her manager and self-proclaimed best friend, Alec Beesley, at the age of forty-three.

S. also wrote several novels. She said of her writing, "I have come to enjoy writing novels better than writing plays. . . . I find I can live right inside a novel." Her first and most famous novel, *I Capture the Castle* (1948), a Literary Guild selection, was written in the form of the diary of Cassandra, the main character, and set in a ruined castle where she lived with her eccentric family. Its fresh and original characterization and dialogue made it an immediate success. S. herself said, "Of all my books I think I like *Castle* best. I wrote myself into Cassandra." She also wrote four volumes of autobiography: *Look Back With Love* (1974), *Look Back With Mixed Feelings* (1978), *Look Back With Astonishment* (1979), and *Look Back With Gratitude* (1985).

The inspiration for S.'s children's book, *The Hundred and One Dalmatians* (1956), a dalmatian puppy named Pongo, arrived in May 1934 on her thirty-fourth birthday. S. was devoted to her pet and became a staunch champion of dogs, especially dalmatians, for the rest of her life. Other children's books include *The Starlight Barking* (1967), *More About the One Hundred and One Dalmatians* (1967), and *The Midnight Kittens* (1978).

In 1953, S. and her husband returned to England and to The Barretts at Finchingfield, a three-hundred-year-old country estate in a picturesque Essex village. S. continued to write—including personal journals—until her death at the age of ninety-four in 1990.

WORKS: (as C. L. Anthony) *British Talent* (1924). *Autumn Crocus* (1931). *Service* (1932). *Touch Wood* (1934). *Dear Octopus* (1938). (as Dodie Smith) *Lovers and Friends* (1943). *The Uninvited* (screenplay, 1944). *I Capture the Castle* (1948, as a novel; as a play, 1953). *Darling How Could You* (screenplay, 1951). *Letter From Paris* (1952). *The One Hundred and One Dalmatians* (1956) *These People: Those Books* (1958). *Amateur Means Lover* (1962). *The Little Moon with the Old* (1963). *The Town in Bloom* (1965). *It Ends With Revelations* (1967). *The Starlight Barking* (1967). *More About the One Hundred and One Dalmatians* (1967). *A Tale of Two Families* (1970). *Look Back With Love* (1974). *The Girl From the Candlelit Bath* (1978). *Look Back With Mixed Feelings* (1978). *The Midnight Kittens* (1978). *Look Back With Astonishment* (1979). *Look Back With Gratitude* (1985).

BIBLIOGRAPHY: Grove, V. *Dear Dodie: The Life of Dodie Smith* (1996).

For items in reference works, see: *CA. Chambers. Longman. NCHEL. RE. SATA. WA. WD.*

Other references: *Author's and Writer's Who's Who. Biographical Encyclopedia and Who's Who in American Theatre. Dictionary of Literature in the English Language. McGraw Hill Encyclopedia of World Drama. Who's Who in the Theater.*

Patianne DelGrosso Stabile

Stevie Smith (pseudonym of Florence Margaret Smith)

BORN: 20 September 1902, Hull, Yorkshire.
DIED: 7 March 1971, London.
DAUGHTER OF: Charles Smith and Ethel Spear Smith.

Author of whimsical, deceptively simple verse, S. also wrote three novels, ten short stories, a BBC radio play, and book reviews. She was given the nickname "Stevie," which she used for all her published work, for her resemblance to a small, popular jockey. S. and her older sister were raised by their mother and their aunt and then by the aunt alone after their mother's death during S.'s sixteenth year. Throughout her adult life, S. made her home with her aunt in a northern suburb of London, Palmers Green. Disguised under the names "Bottle Green" and "Syler's Green," Palmers Green became the setting for fiction and essays in which S. comments wryly on the community's "fairly harmless snobbery" and describes nostalgically the woods she and her older sister explored as children. She attended Palmers Green High School and North London Collegiate School for Girls, where the subjects she studied were those studied in boys' schools—an unorthodox curriculum that she appreciated. At school, she learned to love the musical rhythms of the poems she memorized, and she often built her own poetry upon quantitative musical measures. For thirty years, she worked as a secretary for two London magazine publishers, employment that gave her time to write poetry, fiction, and book reviews. Her literary reputation grew slowly from 1936 until 1957, when the publication of *Not Waving But Drowning* won her wider critical acclaim. Her lively, humorous letters to other writers, friends, and editors reveal her intelligence as witty, whimsical, serious, philosophical, and not morbid, though in many of her poems she considers death a welcome guest. When she died of a brain tumor in 1971, she had won a popular audience for her poems, which she read on BBC radio programs. The 1975 publication of her *Collected Poems* was welcomed with appreciative reviews; a movie, *Stevie,* based on a play by Hugh Whitemore and starring Glenda Jackson, appeared in 1978.

Placing herself within a cultural tradition and also challenging its values, S. wrote several poems in which she imaginatively re-creates the voice of legendary and literary characters. "I Had a Dream I Was Helen of Troy" offers a critique of the simpering, thoughtless, and inconsistent character in Homer's *Iliad.* "The Last Turn of the Screw" retells Henry James's tale from the perspective of the not-so-innocent child Miles. Other poems revise the characters of Hamlet's mother Gertrude and her new husband Claudius, of Dido, of Persephone, of Antigone, and of Phaedra (in which she criticizes Marcel Proust's interpretation of Jean Racine's tragic heroine).

In metaphysical poems, both serious and comic in tone, she questions Christian doctrine. "How Cruel Is the Story of Eve" explores the traditional interpretation of women as seducers, responsible for original sin. Her speaker notes that the legend has been employed to "give blame to women most / And most punishment." In another poem, "How Do You See," she questions the definitions given for the "Holy Spirit," adopting a style that echoes and mocks a catechism. The poem asks, quite seriously, whether Christianity may not have played out its role in human history. After an allusion to the armed nations ready to destroy each other, she concludes grimly, "we shall kill everybody."

S.'s novels are set during times of war, espionage, betrayal, and social unease, but she employs a narrator who breezes through these crises with a crooked smile and an acid tongue. Commenting on England's possible response to the Italian invasion of Abyssinia, the narrator in *Over the Frontier* (1938) notes of herself: "we do not so much like the peace-at-any-price people who go about today to apologise for England and to pretend that she hasn't really got so much of the earth's surface, it only looks that way on these jingo maps. . . . For if we are not nowadays the conquerors and pioneers, we are at least the beneficiaries under empire, and at least and basest we have cheap sugar." She deflates the self-righteous polemic of imperialists and pacifists, then knocks out from under herself any pretentious stand of moral superiority. Her novels sparkle with political insights that are human and funny.

Most critics focus on her nonsense verse, her poems built upon odd and charming patterns of sound. Although they share with children's nursery rhymes certain simple aural pleasures, these poems are only superficially simple in tone and attitude. (The doodling drawings that S. attached to her published poems also suggest a simplicity in attitude, but her cartoons work, as do James Thurber's, upon the fantasies and candid dream images of the unconscious.) Like T. S. Eliot, S. could use chiming rhymes for whimsical satire. Her "The Dedicated Water Bull and the Water Maid," written, her subtitle suggests, in response to a performance of Beethoven's Sonata in F. Opus 17, for Horn and Piano, wittily mocks self-important pomposity: "O I am holy, oh I am plump." Her "The Singing Cat" seems at first a transparent description of an amusing, inconsequential incident in a commuter train but develops a mild critique of those who transform others' pain into their own aesthetic pleasure.

S.'s subtitles often suggest that her verses were prompted by a brief experience, but the poems are not lightly occasional. After reading two paragraphs in a newspaper, she wrote "Valuable," which explores the complex moral and psychological situation of young girls who bear illegitimate babies because they lack a sense of their own worth. An unsympathetic speaker begins the poem in a self-righteous and superior tone of voice, but that stance is challenged both by the image of a panther in a cage and by the voice of one of the young girls, who protests that her low self-esteem merely reflects the community's evaluation of her. S.'s poem, hardly sentimental, implies that the illegitimate babies are the mutual responsibility of society and individuals.

By creating a fiercely comic persona for her poems, fiction, and essays, S. gave voice to her serious questions on Christian doctrine, contemporary morality, the abuse of power, and the literary tradition. In her eccentric voice, she ridiculed the perfect idiocy of much human behavior while revealing her compassion for fellow creatures caged in a prison.

WORKS: *Novel on Yellow Paper* (1936; retitled *Work It Out for Yourself,* 1969). *A Good Time Was Had by All* (1937). *Over the Frontier* (1938). *Tender Only to One* (1938). *Mother, What Is Man?* (1942). *The Holiday* (1949). *Harold's Leap* (1950). *Not Waving but Drowning* (1957). *Some Are More Human Than Others: Sketchbook by Stevie Smith* (1958). *Selected Poems* (1962). *The Frog Prince and Other Poems* (1966). *The Best Beast* (1969). *Two in One* (includes *The Frog Prince,* 1971). *Scorpions and Other Poems* (1972). *Collected Poems* (1975). *Me Again: Uncollected Writings of Stevie Smith,* ed. J. Barbera and W. McBrien (1981).

BIBLIOGRAPHY: Barbera, J. and W. McBrien., intro. to *Me Again: Uncollected Writings of Stevie Smith* (1981). Barbera, J. and W. McBrien, *Stevie: A Biography of Stevie Smith* (1987). Dick, K. *Ivy & Stevie: Ivy Compton-Burnett and Stevie Smith: Conversations and Reflections* (1971). Rankin, A. C. *The Poetry of Stevie Smith—"Little Girl Lost"* (1985). Severin, L. *Stevie Smith's Resistant Antics* (1997).

For articles in reference works, see: *Bloomsbury. CA. Cambridge. CLC. Feminist. MBL. Oxford. ToddBWW.*

Other references: *Antiquarian Bookman* (24 June 1971). *Books & Bookmen* (June 1971). Enright D. J. *Man Is an Onion* (1972). *Poetry* (August 1958, March 1965, December 1976). Sergeant, H. *PoetryR* (Spring 1967). *TLS* (14 July 1972).

Judith L. Johnston

Ethel Mary Smyth

BORN: 23 April 1858, Sidcup Place, Footscray, Kent.
DIED: 8 May 1944, Coign, Woking, Surrey.
DAUGHTER OF: Major-General John Hall Smyth and Nina Struth Smyth.
WROTE UNDER: Evald Schmidt; Ethel Smyth.

"I am the most interesting person I know, and I don't care if no one else thinks so" (*As Time Went On,* quoted in Nicolson and Trautman). Thus unabashedly wrote S., easily one of the most famous women of her time. Called the "stormy petrel" by her mother, with whom she shared a lifelong love-hate relationship, S. was the third daughter in a family of six girls and two boys. She described her childhood as unhappy, alleging that while she recognized her abilities and ambitions, she was "merely considered an exceptionally naughty, rebellious girl" by her family. Early in her life, she knew she was different from her sisters and brothers, but not until the age of twelve, when a governess who had studied music in Leipzig, Germany, played a piece of Beethoven on the piano, did S. conclude what her life must be. She announced that she too would travel to Leipzig, study music, and become a composer. Instead, S. and her sister Mary were packed off to boarding school at Putney (1872–75), after which she briefly studied harmony with Alexander Ewing. When her parents began discussing her coming-out parties, S. once again renewed her desire to study music in Germany. Her father in particular was against this venture, at one point saying he would prefer to see her "under the sod" than a professional musician. S. isolated herself from her family, refusing to attend church or parties or to perform for the family. Her father finally relented, and, at age nineteen, S. set out for Leipzig.

The original plan had been for S. to study at the Leipzig Conservatorium, but after meeting Heinrich von Herzogenberg, conductor of the Bach Verein, and his wife, Elisabeth ('Lisl'), S. decided to study with him. Through the von Herzogenbergs, S. met many of the musicians whose names would one day be famous: Grieg, Dvořák, Tchaikovsky. She was ambivalent toward Brahms, who could be supportive on one occasion and dismissive on another: "it angered me, as did also his jokes about women, and his everlasting gibes at any . . . who possessed brains or indeed ideas of any kind." Clara Schumann, though, saw great promise in S. and encouraged her in her studies.

As a woman and a composer, S. faced incredible prejudice. While music was thought to be essential to a "lady's" education, for a woman to consider making music a career was met with distinct disapproval. Not until 1890 were any of S.'s compositions performed in public—her *Serenade* in April and her *Overture to Antony and Cleopatra* in October, both at the Crystal Palace in London.

Perhaps S.'s greatest musical achievement was her *Mass in D* (1891). This work, consisting of orchestra, chorus, and soli, was performed 18 January 1893 by the Royal Choral Society. Despite a favorable reception, *Mass in D* would not be performed again for thirty-one years, something S. blamed on the male-dominated musical establishment. The power of this composition can be gauged by a comment made by George Bernard Shaw, who saw its revival in 1924. According to Shaw, this piece cured him forever "of the old delusion that women could not do men's work in art and other things."

S. made her biggest mark in the musical field with her six operas. Opera was a much-neglected genre in English music, but for a woman to attempt it was nothing short of revolutionary. *Der Wald* (1902), originally performed in Berlin and later at Covent Garden, became the first opera by a woman to be performed at the Metropolitan Opera in New York City. S., who was present for the first performance, enjoyed an ovation lasting ten minutes. Her most popular opera was *The Wreckers,* originally written in French, performed in Leipzig and Prague in 1906 and in London in 1909. Sir Thomas Beecham, who conducted the opera, praised it, saying it was "one of the three or four English operas of real musical merit and vitality." Another favorite with audiences was *The Boatswain's Mate* (1916), which showed S.'s feminist leanings.

Both public and private life was tumultuous for S. Even as a young girl she had developed what she termed "passions" for various women. One of her greatest "passions" was Lisl von Herzogenberg. Their long, devoted friendship was broken in 1882 when S. met Henry Brewster, husband of Lisl's sister, Julia. The two fell in love in 1883, but not until Julia died (1895) would S. permit their relationship to become intimate, though she refused to marry him. Despite repeated protestations of innocence, S. could not persuade Lisl to renew their friendship. Brewster collaborated with S. on several of her operas; when he died in 1908, she recalled that she "felt then like a rudderless ship aimlessly drifting hither and thither." Her symphony, *The Prison* (1930), was S.'s memorial to Brewster.

In spite of her love for Brewster, S. found her greatest friends among women. As she herself commented, "the people who have helped me most at difficult moments of my musical career, beginning with my own sister Mary, have been members of my own sex. Thus, it comes to pass that my relations with certain women, all exceptional personalities I think, are shining threads in my life." Among these "shining threads" were the former Empress Eugénie of France and Queen Victoria. S. became enamored of Lady Mary Ponsonby, to whom she dedicated *Impressions That Remained* (1919). Among other friends S. counted the Princesse de Polignac, Edith Somerville, and the Pankhursts; late in life she met Virginia Woolf, who had reviewed S.'s *Streaks of Life* (1921), calling S. "a lady of remarkable and original personality." The two women formed a close attachment, though Woolf was cautious: "An old woman of seventy-one has fallen in love with me. It is at once hideous and horrid and melancholy-sad. It is like being caught by a giant crab." After overcoming her early reservations, Woolf revealed to S. many things she had never before put on paper, such as her madness and ideas about sexuality. For S., the relationship was intense: "I don't think I have ever cared for anyone more profoundly. For eighteen months I really thought of little else." S. dedicated *As Time Went On* (1935) to Woolf, who in turn used S. as the pattern for the character of Miss La Trobe in her last work, *Between the Acts.*

S. became active in the women's suffrage movement after some initial reluctance. She vowed to devote two years to the campaign and did so with gusto. *Female Pipings in Eden* (1933) contains essays S. wrote at the time concerning the problems facing women composers and musicians. It also chronicles S.'s membership in the Women's Social and Political Union, which she joined in 1910. In 1911, she set to music Cicely Hamilton's poem, *The March of the Women,* which was first performed to welcome the release of twenty-one suffragists from prison and ultimately became the anthem of the women's movement. S. was arrested in 1912 for breaking the window of a house belonging to the antisuffragist Colonial Secretary, Lewis Harcourt. She was sentenced to two months at Holloway Prison but served only part of that term. Even in jail, she demonstrated her indomitable will. Beecham reported observing S. use a toothbrush for a baton to conduct *The March of the Women* from her cell window for a group of suffragists standing in the exercise yard.

In her later years, partially as a result of increasing deafness, S. turned from music to literature, writing several volumes of autobiography. Although Woolf initially discounted S. as a writer, she wrote of *Streaks of Life,* S.'s second book, "Her method appeared to consist of extreme courage and candour."

Many people have commented on S.'s outrageous behavior and appearance. Photographs show she was fond of wearing a man's tie. She smoked cigarettes for forty years and occasionally even smoked cigars. Sylvia Pankhurst called her "[i]ndividualized to the last point." In a letter to Lytton Strachey (30 November 1919), Woolf said, "I saw her at a concert two days ago—striding up the gangway in coat and skirt and spats and talking at the top of her voice." After S.'s death, Vita Sackville-West, who also knew her, wrote that S. "was often a nuisance but never a bore." In E. F. Benson's novel, *Dodo,* S. became the composer Edith Staines, who, according to the author, was the "one decent character in the book." And about herself, S. wrote that she remained undefeated because of "an iron constitution, a fair share of fighting spirit, and, most important of all, a small but independent income."

S.'s struggles for recognition were not unrewarded. She received honorary doctorates from the universities of Durham (1910), Oxford (1926), St. Andrews (1928), and Manchester (1930). The award she considered the most significant was given in 1922 when she was created a Dame of the British Empire. S. had predicted at the age of nine she would be made a peeress for her music and therefore accepted her DBE merely as her due.

S. never acknowledged defeat. In the conclusion of *A Final Burning of Boats* (1928), she wrote: "The exact worth of my music will probably not be known until naught remains of the writer but sexless dots and lines on ruled paper. . . . And should the ears of others, whether now or after my death, catch a faint echo of some such spirit in my music, then all is well, and more than well." She was tireless in her efforts to obtain for women musicians the opportunities denied them, and she could be as sharp with her own sex as with men when she thought women were contributing to their own troubles. As she once wrote to Henry Brewster: "I feel I must fight for *Der Wald,* also because I want women to turn their minds to big and difficult jobs; not just to go on hugging the shore, afraid to put out to sea."

WORKS (selected): *Musical Serenade* (1890). *Overture to Antony and Cleopatra* (1890). *Mass in D* (1891). *Fantasio* (1892). *Der Wald* (1902). *The Wreckers* (1903). *March of the Women* (1911). *Hey Nonny No* (1911). *The Boatswain's Mate* (1916). *Impressions That Remained* (1919). *Streaks of Life* (1921). *Fête Galante* (1923). *Entente Cordiale* (1925). *A Three-Legged Tour in Greece* (1927). *A Final Burning of Boats* (1928). *The Prison* (1930). *Female Pipings in Eden* (1933). *Beecham and Pharaoh* (1935). *As Time Went On* (1935). *Inordinate (?) Affections* (1936). *Maurice Baring* (1938). *What Happened Next* (1940).

BIBLIOGRAPHY: Beecham, T. *Musical Times* (1958). Bernstein, J., intro. to *Ethel Smyth. Mass in D* (1980). Bernstein, J., in *Women Making Music,* ed. J. Bowers and J. Tick (1986). Boughten, R. *Music Bulletin* (February 1923). Capell, R. *Monthly Musical Record* (July 1923). Dale, K. *Music and Literature* (1944). Dale, K. *Music and Literature* (1949). *LonT* (24 July 1912). McNaught, W. *Musical Times* (1944). St. John, C. [Christabel Marshall]. *Ethel Smyth: A Biography* (1959). Wood, E. *MR* (1983).

For articles in reference works, see: Arnold, D. *New Oxford Companion to Music* (1983). *Feminist.* Bohle, B. *The International Cyclopedia of Music and Musicians* (1985). *DNB.* Hussey, M. *Virginia Woolf A to Z* (1995). Kennedy, M. *Concise Oxford Dictionary of Music* (1980). Kester-Shelton, P. *Feminist Writers* (1996; contains errors). Sadie, S. *The New Grove Dictionary of Music and Musicians* (1980). *ToddBWW* (1989). *Who Was Who, 1941–1950. World of Music: An Illustrated Encyclopedia* (1963).

Other references: Groh, J. B. *Evening the Score: Women in Music and the Legacy of Frédérique Petrides* (1991). Howes, F. *The English Musical Renaissance* (1966). Lee, H. *Virginia Woolf* (1997). Marcus, J., in *New Feminist Essays on Virginia Woolf,* ed. J. Marcus (1981). Marcus, J., in *Mothering the Mind,* ed. R. Perry and M. W. Brownley (1984). *Essays on Virginia Woolf, 1919–1924,* ed. A. McNeillie (1987), Musgrave, M. *The Musical Life of the Crystal Palace* (1995). Neuls-Bates, C. *Women in Music* (1982). *Letters of Virginia Woolf, 1929–1931,* ed. N. Nicolson and J. Trautman (1975).

Raitt, S. *Critical Quarterly* (1988). Rhondda, Viscountess [Margaret Haig]. *This Was My World* (1937). Walker, E. *A History of Music in England* (1952). White, E. W. *The Rise of English Opera* (1972). Wood, E., in *Musicology and Difference*, ed. Ruth Solie (1993). Wood, E., in *Queering the Pitch: The New Gay and Lesbian Musicology*, ed. P. Brett, et al. (1994). Wood, E., in *En Travesti: Women, Gender Subversion, Opera*, ed. C. Blackmer and P. J. Smith (1995). Young, P. *A History of British Music* (1967).

Natalie Joy Woodall

Somers, Jane: See *Lessing, Doris*

Edith Œ: See *Somerville and Ross (Edith Œnone Somerville)*

Somerville and Ross (pseudonyms)

Edith Œnone Somerville

BORN: 2 May 1858, Corfu.
DIED: 8 October 1949, Castle Townshend, Ireland.
DAUGHTER OF: Thomas Somerville and Adelaide Coghill Somerville.
WROTE UNDER: Geilles Herring; Edith Œ. Somerville.

Violet Florence Martin

BORN: 11 June 1862, Ross House, County Galway, Ireland.
DIED: 21 December 1915, Cork, Ireland.
DAUGHTER OF: James Martin and Anna Selina Fox Martin.
WROTE UNDER: Martin Ross.

Writing during the time of the Irish Literary Revival, S. and R. depicted Ireland not mythically but realistically, evoking the era when changes in the Land Laws brought about the end of the Anglo-Irish Ascendancy.

Second cousins and members of prominent English families that had established themselves in Ireland in the twelfth and sixteenth centuries, S. and R. grew up in "big houses," and S. was to spend much of her energy trying to find money to maintain the Somerville House and her own pack of hounds, even introducing and successfully raising Friesian cattle in Ireland. When R. met her in 1886, S. had already established herself as a professional illustrator, studying art in Paris with Delécluse and Colarossi and sketching Pasteur in his clinic. The two then began a literary collaboration that was so successful that critics have found it almost impossible to separate their styles and that continued even after R.'s death; S. asserted that she remained in spiritual communication with her partner and signed both their names to the works she published.

Following in the tradition of Maria Edgeworth, a close friend of S. and R.'s great-grandmother, the two were particularly interested in language and dialect, first working together on a collection of phrases used by S.'s family, and throughout their lives collecting instances of the Irish use of English. William Butler Yeats praised the accuracy of the reported Irish speech in their work. These details of Irish life were the most effective aspect of S. and R.'s first novels, *An Irish Cousin* (1889) and *Naboth's Vineyard* (1891), both of which are burdened with Gothic and melodramatic plot devices. *The Real Charlotte* (1894) was S. and R.'s most effective novel and was honored as a World Classic by Oxford University Press in 1948. Set against the background of Anglo-Irish society as portrayed through the decaying Dysart family, it focuses particularly on two women, Francie, an uneducated but beautiful lower-class girl, and Charlotte, an unattractive, driven middle-class woman who is successful in her business dealings but fails in her personal relations. The novel, like many of S. and R.'s, is a study in frustrated desire and has been compared favorably with Jane Austen's novels, George Eliot's *Middlemarch*, and Honoré de Balzac's *Cousine Bette*. S. and R.'s subsequent novel, *The Silver Fox* (1898), was less successful, perhaps because it deals so intensely with Irish mysticism.

In order to support themselves, S. and R. also wrote, at the same time as their novels, a series of comic sketches of their travels through Ireland and Europe: *Through Connemara in a Governess Cart* (1893), *In the Vine Country* (1893), *Beggars on Horse-back* (1895), and *Stray-Aways* (1920). Many of these were first published in periodicals, as were the Irish R. M. stories, which first appeared in the *Badminton Magazine* in October 1898. S. and R.'s agent, J. B. Pinker, who also worked for Henry James and Arnold Bennett, suggested they work on a series of comic stories about hunting that led to the publication of *Some Experiences of an Irish R. M.* (1899). This work, depicting the adventures of a Resident Magistrate, Major Sinclair Yeates, trying to cope with the Irish peasants and his crafty landlord, Flurry Knox, brought its authors international fame. From then until R.'s death in 1915, the pair continued to write primarily hunting stories, *All on the Irish Shore* (1903), articles in *Some Irish Yesterdays* (1906), and a hunting novel, *Dan Russel the Fox* (1911).

After R.'s death, with the worsening situation in Ireland, S. wrote a series of novels that dwelt more specifically, though it had always been a concern of theirs, with the social and political problems of Ireland, particularly with how sectarianism was undermining Irish life. In *Mount Music* (1919), S. writes about religious schisms; in *An Enthusiast* (1921) about political ones. And in *The Big House of Inver* (1925), S. writes a novel, thought to be as effective as *The Real Charlotte*, about the decay and collapse of the "big houses" in Ireland, with the house modeled on Ross House, R.'s ancestral home.

S. and R. are interesting because, as Lord Dunsany said of the Irish R. M. stories, readers can get "more of Ireland from that book than from anything I can tell them" and because of the relation between the two women. As S. puts it, "the outstanding fact . . . among women who live by their brains, is friendship. A profound friendship that extends through every phase and aspect of life, intellectual, social and pecuniary."

WORKS: (S.) *The Kerry Recruit* (1889). (S. [as Geilles Herring] and R.) *An Irish Cousin* (1889). (S. and R.) *Naboth's Vineyard* (1891). (S. and R.) *In the Vine Country* (1893).

(S. and R.) *Through Connemara in a Governess Cart* (1893). (S. and R.) *The Real Charlotte* (1894). (R. and S.) *Beggars on Horseback* (1895). (R. and S.) *The Silver Fox* (1898). (S. and R.) *Some Experiences of an Irish R. M.* (1899). (R. and S.) *A Patrick's Day Hunt* (1902). (S. and R.) *All on the Irish Shore* (1903). (S.) *Slipper's ABC of Fox Hunting* (1903). (S. and R.) *Some Irish Yesterdays* (1906). (S. and R.) *Further Experiences of an Irish R. M.* (1908). (S. and R.) *Dan Russel the Fox* (1911). (S.) *The Story of the Discontented Little Elephant* (1912). (S. and R.) In *Mr. Knox's Country* (1915). (S. and, nominally, R.) *Irish Memories* (1917). (S. and, nominally, R.) *Mount Music* (1919). (S. and R.) *Stray-Aways* (1920). (S.) *An Enthusiast* (1921). (S. and, nominally, R.) *Wheel-Tracks* (1923). (S. and, nominally, R.) *The Big House of Inver* (1925). (S. and, nominally, R.) *French Leave* (1928). (S.) *The States Through Irish Eyes* (1930). (S. and, nominally, R.) *An Incorruptible Irishman* (1932). (S. and, nominally, R.) *The Smile and the Tear* (1933). (S. and, nominally, R.) *The Sweet Cry of Hounds* (1936). (S. and, nominally, R.) *Sarah's Youth* (1938). (S. and B. T. Somerville) *Records of the Somerville Family of Castlehaven and Drishane from 1174 to 1940* (1940). (S. and, nominally, R.) *Motions in Garrison* (1941). (S. and, nominally, R.) *Happy Days!* (1946). (S. and, nominally, R.) *Maria and Some Other Dogs* (1949).

BIBLIOGRAPHY: Barlow, J.E.M. *Country Life* (1916). Cahalan, J. M. *Eire* (1993). Collis, M. *Somerville and Ross: A Biography* (1968). Cronin, J. *Somerville and Ross* (1972). Cronin, J. *CJIS* (1985). Cummins, G. E. *Œ. Somerville: A Biography* (1952; contains R. Vaughan's "The First Editions of Edith Œnone Somerville and Violet Florence Martin"). Gwynn, S. *Edinburgh Review* (1921). *A Bibliography of the First Editions of the Works of E. Œ. Somerville and Martin Ross,* ed. E. Hudson (1942). Imhof, R., in *Ancestral Voices: The Big House in Anglo-Irish Literature,* ed. O. Rauchbauer (1992). Institute of Irish Studies, The Queen's University, Belfast. *Somerville and Ross: A Symposium* (1969). *Irish Writing* (1946). Lewis, G. *Somerville and Ross: The World of the Irish R. M.* (1985). *LonT* (10 October 1949). Lucas, E. V. *Cloud and Silver* (1916). McMahon, S. *Eire* (1968). Martin, D. *EI* (1982). Mooney, S. R. *CJIS* (1992). O'Brien, C. C. *Writers and Politics* (1965). Orel, H. *ELT* (1987). Orel, H., in *Anglo-Irish and Irish Literature: Aspects of Language and Culture,* ed. B. Bramsback (1988). Powell, V. *The Irish Cousins* (1970). Power, A. *Dubliner* (1964). Pritchett, V. S. *The Living Novel* (1946). Rauchbauer, O. *The Edith Œnone Somerville Archive in Drishane* (1995). Robinson, H. *Somerville and Ross: A Critical Appreciation* (contains bibliography of periodical articles by S. and R., 1980). Tillinghast, R. *NewC* (1995). Tynan, K. *Bookman* (1916).Williams, O. *Some Great English Novels* (1926).

For articles in reference works, see: *DIB. DIL. DNB. EBH. 1890s. Feminist. Hickey. NCBEL. TCA. Todd-BWW. VB.*

Other references: *ArielE* (1970, 1972). *CJIS* (1985). *EI* (1967, 1968, 1982). *Hermathena* (1952). *KR* (1966). *NCF* (1951). *Quarterly Review* (1913).

Elsie B. Michie
(updated by Natalie Joy Woodall)

Mary Fairfax Greig Somerville

BORN: 26 December 1780, Jedburgh Manse, Burntisland, Scotland.
DIED: 29 November 1872, Naples, Italy.
DAUGHTER OF: Vice-Admiral Sir William George Fairfax and Margaret Charters Fairfax.
MARRIED: Captain Samuel Greig, 1804; Dr. William Somerville, 1812.

Called at her death the "Queen of Nineteenth-Century Science," S. wrote four important books on physical science, mathematics, and astronomy. A largely self-taught mathematician, S. had a profound influence on the definition of physics ("physical sciences") and on the exchange and dissemination of major scientific theories and ideas.

Born to a British naval officer and his second wife, S. was the fifth of seven children and grew up in Burntisland, a small seaport on the Firth of Forth. For much of her childhood, her father was absent on foreign service, eventually rising to the rank of vice-admiral. She received fitful spurts of education in writing, reading, and the domestic arts but was discouraged from pursuing any formal education or even home study unrelated to domestic concerns. Her memoirs, written when she was more than ninety years old, recount many of the Scottish customs of her girlhood as well as good-naturedly detailing her many frustrations at not being allowed to pursue any kind of formal learning.

At the age of ten, she received one year of formal education when her father, returning home after a long absence, found her to be a "savage" unable to read or write and consequently sent her to a fashionable boarding school for young ladies at Musselburgh. Although it was to be the only formal full-time instruction she was ever to receive, this schooling turned out to be a tedious ordeal, involving mindless memorization coupled with a strict dress code that restricted free movement.

Her love of nature and her scientific curiosity were viewed by her family as inappropriate, irrelevant, eccentric, and dangerous for a girl. She was sent for lessons in needlework, dancing, piano, cookery, drawing, and painting but was also allowed to receive lessons on the use of terrestrial and celestial globes. Her thirst for knowledge, which her family found unladylike, incited surreptitious study; she quietly followed the course of study recommended by Hester Chapone's *Letters on the Improvement of the Mind.* At the age of thirteen, she spent a summer at the Manse, the home of her aunt, Martha Charters Somerville, and uncle, the Reverend Thomas Somerville, the only relative who did not disapprove of her studious inclination. She began to teach herself Latin and read for two hours every morning before breakfast with her uncle, who agreed to tutor her in Latin. She also began to teach herself the fundamentals of astronomy. When she was fifteen, she noticed algebraic symbols in a monthly fashion magazine and developed a strong ambition to learn higher mathematics. She took up the study of Euclid and Bonnycastle in the evenings, after her domestic chores were completed.

At twenty-four, S. married a distant cousin, Samuel

Greig. The couple moved to London, where S., left alone most of the day, could continue with her studies; like the members of S.'s family, however, Greig disparaged her studious and intellectual pursuits and had no knowledge of or interest in any kind of science. Nonetheless S. persevered, teaching herself plane and spherical trigonometry, conic sections, some astronomy, and French. The couple had two sons, the younger of whom died at the age of nine. Following the birth of their second son, Greig died.

S. returned to Burntisland as a widow but with some financial and social independence. S. wrote to William Wallace, mathematics master at the Royal Military College at Great Marlow, a self-taught mathematician who sympathized with anyone trying to master mathematics alone and who later became professor of mathematics at Edinburgh University. He encouraged S. and became her main advisor, helping her to outline a course of study in math and astronomical science and to select books for a small library. At the age of thirty-three, independent, she was openly able to pursue her interests. She met some of the men associated with the liberal-minded *Edinburgh Review*—such as Henry Brougham, the natural philosopher, and mathematics professor John Playfair—and became part of the Edinburgh intellectual scene. In 1811, having solved an algebraic problem in a mathematical journal, S. was awarded a silver medal.

In 1812, she married another cousin, the army doctor and surgeon William Somerville (the eldest son of her uncle, Thomas Somerville), a widower who had returned to Scotland after serving as inspector-general of hospitals and controller of the customs in Quebec, Canada. S. and her new husband shared an interest in the branches of natural history, botany, minerology, and geology, and she appreciated his knowledge of the world and his tolerant openmindedness, his emancipation "from Scotch prejudice," as S. put it. A true companion, William admired her talent and encouraged her studies. He shared many of S.'s scientific interests and assisted her studies in numerous ways, visiting, on her behalf, libraries that were closed to women, copying manuscripts, and proofreading. He encouraged her to systematize her studies and take up Greek, botany, geology, and minerology. She amassed a small but important collection of mathematical works, mostly French, that her daughters donated to the new women's college at Hitchin (now Girton College, Cambridge) after her death.

After a brief move to Portsmouth, they returned to Scotland, settling in Edinburgh for four years while William worked in his new post as head of the Army Medical Department of Scotland. With her husband's help, S. continued to study mathematics and began the study of Greek and minerology.

In 1816, the couple moved to Queen Square, London, in order for William to take up his new post as one of the two principal inspectors to the Army Medical Board. In London, S. attended lectures at the Royal Institution, meeting many of the leading thinkers and scientists, including Georges Cuvier, Sir Charles Napier, Charles Babbage, Thomas Babington Macaulay, William Lamb, Caroline Melbourne, Sir William and Sir John Herschel, and Sir Charles Lyell. Sir Edward Parry, a leading English astronomer, named a small island in the Arctic in her honor. On a visit to Paris, they met the mathematician and astronomer Marquis Pierre de Laplace, whose work S. had already read. Impressed with S.'s erudition, Laplace gave her an inscribed copy of the *Système du Monde.* He later said that S. was the only woman who understood his work. Back in London, S. met, among others, Maria Edgeworth, who became a close friend.

In 1826, her first published work, "On the magnetizing power of the more refrangible solar rays," an account of a study S. had made on the possible connection between sunlight and magnetism, appeared in *Philosophical Transactions of the Royal Society.* Although her husband read the paper on which it was based, entitled "The Magnetic Properties of the Violet Rays of the Solar Spectrum," to the Royal Society, the paper was published in the *Philosophical Transactions* under her name, the first experimental paper by a woman published in that journal. Although the theory presented in this paper was refuted by other scientists three years later, the work brought her significant recognition in the scientific community as an original, speculative, and ingenious thinker and established her credibility as a serious scientist.

In 1827, she was asked by her old acquaintance Henry (now Lord) Brougham to prepare an English version of Laplace's *Traite de mécanique céleste* for the Society for the Diffusion of Useful Knowledge, a society Brougham founded to help popularize scientific information by publishing inexpensive editions of worthy books for the general public. The work, which took S. three years to complete, included her explanatory preface, commentaries, mathematical calculations, explanation of the French analysis of mathematics, an account of the materials and methods of French physical astronomy, and her interpretive translation of the first four books of "Mécanique céleste." But the book, too long for the popular series for which it was intended, was published independently as *Mechanism of the Heavens* (1831), and brought her acclaim and placed her in the first rank of scientific writers. It was immediately adopted as a textbook for advanced mathematics at Oxford and Cambridge, even though at that time neither university admitted women. S.'s published work was one of only a few by women who wrote under their own names. She was invited to spend a week at Cambridge as the guest of the university, and her relations who had disparaged her ambitions as a girl now praised her. *Mechanism of the Heavens* remained a standard higher mathematics and astronomy textbook for the rest of the century.

Even higher praise was accorded her next book, *On the Connexion of the Physical Sciences* (1834), a summary of research into physical phenomena and a consideration of the "mutual dependence and connection in many branches of science." It incorporated the most recent scientific findings in physical and descriptive astronomy, matter, sound, light, heat, electricity, and magnetism. A comprehensive and authoritative description of the physical sciences, this work gave rise to the current meaning of the term "physics" and helped define the limits of physical science for more than a century. S.'s greatest work, it went through ten editions and several revisions, the last in 1877; it was translated into French, German, and Italian; a pirated edition was printed in the United States. A sentence in the 1842 edition, suggesting another planet behind Uranus, is credited by John Couch Adams with sparking the calculations from which he deduced the orbit of Neptune. This achievement won S. widespread recognition and numerous honors: S. was elected honorary member of several British and foreign learned societies, including the Royal Academy of Dublin (1834), the Société de Physique et d'Histoire Naturelle de Geneva (1834), and the British Philosophical Institution (c. 1835). The Royal Astronomical Society elected S. and Caroline Herschel, their first female honorary members, at the same time (1835), and she was elected to the Royal Irish Academy. In 1835, she was awarded an annual government pension of £200, increased to £300 two years later, and she wrote a lengthy review essay on comets for *Quarterly Review.* In 1836, her paper, "Experiments on the Transmission of Chemical Rays of the Solar Spectrum Across Different Media," appeared in *Comptes Rendus Hebdomadaires de Séances de L'Académie des Sciences.* While in London, she was asked by Lady Annabella Byron (the wife of poet Lord Byron) to direct the mathematical studies of her daughter, Ada Byron, later Lady Lovelace. Lovelace went on to work with inventor and scientist Charles Babbage (who became known as the father of modern computers), and she is considered the first computer programmer.

William's failing health forced a move to Italy in 1838, at the height of S.'s fame, where they remained for the rest of their lives. There S. continued to write important scientific papers and to conduct scientific experiments on the solar spectrum and the juices of plants. An extract of a letter she wrote to Sir John Hershel in which she described results of her experiments was published in the *Abstracts of Philosophical Transactions* in 1845. Her third book, the two-volume *Physical Geography,* was published in 1848. A pioneering effort at regional (as opposed to national) earth science, the book dealt with geology, topography, hydrography, meteorology, oceanography, and zoology. It went through seven editions and was used as a textbook by numerous schools.

In 1860, when her husband died at the age of ninety, S. remained in Italy. In 1869 when she was eighty-nine, S. published *Molecular and Microscopic Science,* a two-volume summary of the recent discoveries in chemistry and physics. Although it was already outdated at the time of its publication (S. excluded Darwinian ideas on evolution), it was received with deferential interest. In that year she was awarded the first gold medal given by the Italian Geographical Society; in 1870, she was awarded the Victoria Gold Medal of the Royal Geographical Society, and she was elected to the American Geographical and Statistical Society.

S. returned to pure mathematics late in life, working until her death on the unfinished *Theory of Differences.* She did complete a vivid and entertaining autobiographical memoir, *Personal Recollections,* before her death. Written in a friendly and engaging style, this work resonates with her enthusiasm for experimentation and the excitement of discovery. Edited by her daughter, Mary Charters Somerville, these memoirs appeared a year after she died (1873). She died within a month of her ninety-second birthday and was buried at the English Campo Santo at Naples.

S. wrote on scientific and astronomical subjects with simplicity and power, explaining complex matters with an unpretentious and energetic clarity so that even those unfamiliar with the subject could absorb difficult principles. Henry Morley claimed that she was the first woman to shake men's comfortable faith in the incapacity of women for scientific thought. Her prefaces to her works were published separately for the general public while the actual works were used as textbooks for university students and mathematics scholars. Her writings brought the newest and most authoritative scientific ideas to a wider public.

S. was a lifelong proponent of education for women. Her name headed John Stuart Mill's Women's Suffrage petition of 1868. Seven years after her death, she was commemorated in the foundation of Somerville Hall (later College) at Oxford (1879) and in the Mary Somerville scholarship for women in mathematics.

WORKS: *Philosophical Transactions of the Royal Society of London* (1826). *The Mechanism of the Heavens* (1831). *A Preliminary Dissertation on the Mechanism of the Heavens* (1832). *On the Connexion of the Physical Sciences* (1834). *Physical Geography* (1848). *Molecular and Microscopic Science* (1869). *Personal Recollections, From Early Life to Old Age of Mary Somerville with Selections from her Correspondence,* ed. M. C. Somerville (1873).

BIBLIOGRAPHY: Adams, P. *Somerville for Women: An Oxford College, 1829–1993* (1996). McKinlay, J. *Mary Somerville 1780–1872* (1987). Patterson, E. C. *British Journal for the History of Science* (1969). Patterson, E. C. *Bodleian Library Record* (1970). Patterson, E. C. *Mary Somerville and the Cultivation of Science 1815–1840* (1983). Patterson, E. C. *Proceedings of the American Philosophical Society* (1974). Tabor, M. E. *Pioneer Women,* 4th series (1933). Walford, L. B. *Four Biographies from "Blackwood"* (1888). Wilson, M. *Jane Austen and Some Contemporaries* (1938).

For articles in reference works, see: *Dictionary of Men and Women in the Sciences. DNB. Europa. Feminist. IDWB. Oxford. VB.*

Other references: Cooney, M.P. *A Celebration of Women in Mathematics and Science by Twenty Teachers* (1992). Mozans, H. J. *Women in Science.* (1991). Osen, L. M. *Women in Mathematics* (1974). Perl, T. H. *Math Equals: Biographies of Women Mathematicians and Related Activities* (1978). Rolke, G. M. *100 Women Who Shaped World History* (1994).

Gale Sigal

Joanna Southcott

BORN: 25 April 1750, Devonshire.
DIED: 27 December 1814, London.
DAUGHTER OF: William Southcott and Hannah Southcott.

Prophet, priestess, and mystic, S. wrote and published dozens of religious pamphlets from 1792 to 1814 and was the center of a large religious movement known as the Southcottians, which some have estimated as having up to 100,000 members.

Born the fourth daughter of a farmer, S. worked as a

domestic servant; she rejected numerous marriage proposals from farmers' sons, determined to remain single. She began writing down her prophecies in 1792 but did not publish any of them until nearly a decade later when, in 1801, she published her first work, *The Strange Effects of Faith,* financed by her own savings. It attracted a small group of followers, enabling her to move to London in 1802. In 1803, S. undertook a speaking tour of the north and west of England. From 1804 to 1814, S. lived in London in the house of the wealthy Jane Townely, who was her patron and secretary. S. believed that she heard the Lord's voice and received visions that permitted her to distribute an inscribed seal to her followers, and she believed that the millenium was exclusively available for her followers, the "seale people." In 1809, the movement ran into controversy when Mary Bateman, a member of the Yorkshire congregation of followers, was accused of being a witch and murderess. S. denied any contact or communication with Bateman. A second controversy followed in 1814, when S., then sixty-four, promised to give birth to the son of God. The majority of the doctors who examined her were convinced that she had all the signs of pregnancy. At the time of the expected birth, she suddenly died; an autopsy performed on her body revealed no pregnancy. After her death, the movement did not die out but persisted until the end of the nineteenth century. In the early twentieth century, Alice Seymour reissued S.'s writings, and there is still a small body of followers today.

The movement appealed strongly to women; reiterated throughout S.'s writings is the idea that just as a woman had been responsible for the Fall, so she would be for the salvation and redemption of mankind. The movement also appealed to the working classes adjusting to economic, agricultural, and military upheavals. It also included several Anglican clergy and the engraver William Sharp, who wrote the introduction to her pamphlet *Divine and Spiritual Communications* (1803). Critics have pointed out that her prophecies did not provoke her followers toward political action but instead emphasized personal salvation and thus was in the Methodist tradition. S. expected Methodist support but was rejected by the Exeter Methodist community and grew disillusioned. She considered herself a devout member of the Church of England, and most of her efforts were directed at persuading individual clergy and bishops to re-examine her prophecies. She is often associated with Richard Brothers, a religious leader who declared himself "King of the Hebrews and Nephew of God," but S. felt that he was a victim of self-deception. She believed that all religious sects were to be united with the Church of England. Her purpose was not to form a competing sect, but her followers eventually founded their own chapels and named them after her.

Just as S. perceived herself as a mere vehicle of God, so too she perceived her writings. They were not intended for any esthetic purpose but to spread her message. Critics have noted that her style is a mixture of the mystical and the literal in which biblical allusions and history are combined with autobiographical and dream references. She quotes frequently from scripture, often to rebuke what she sees as false interpretations. Her style is often ornate and verbose, given over to "mystical revelations," but the essays are also well organized, with a clear sense of intended audience and purpose. Her handwriting is often illegible, giving the sense of having been written in a moment of mystical revelation. The pamphlets later had to be dictated to her secretaries, Frances Taylor and Ann Underwood. The pamphlets, however, were not the only way that S. reached her audience; her actions were widely commented on and debated in the press, so that even those who never read any of her pamphlets were aware of her beliefs and activities.

S.'s writings have attracted commentators who are either fervent defenders or detractors. Among her contemporaries, John Keats, Robert Southey, and Lord Byron all refer to her negatively. Recent criticism has attempted to be more objective, seeing S. within the currents of her time and her radical religious fervor as part of Romanticism. J.F.C. Harrison likens the autobiographical aspects of her writings to the autobiographies of radical working men. Today, S. is rarely if ever read, but she provides an interesting footnote to the literary, religious, and social history of early nineteenth century England.

WORKS: *The Strange Effects of Faith* (1801). *A Continuation of the Prophecies* (1802). *Dispute Between the Woman and the Powers of Darkness* (1802). *Answer of the Lord to the Power of Darkness* (1802). *Books of Sealed Prophecies* (18–?). *Second Book of Visions* (1803). *A Word in Season* (1803). *A Word to the Wise* (1803). *Divine and Spiritual Communications* (1803). *Sound an Alarm in My Holy Mountain* (1804). *True Explanation of the Bible,* 7 vols. (1804–10). *A Warning to the World* (1804). *On the Prayers for the Fast Day* (1804). *Letters on Various Subjects* (1804). *Copies and Parts of Copies* (1804). *Letters and Communications* (1804). *The Trial of Joanna Southcott* (1804). *Answer to Garrett's Book* (1805). *Answer to the Five Charges in the Leeds Mercury* (1805). *True Explanation of the Bible* (1805). *Explanation of the Parables* (1805). *Kingdom of Christ Is at Hand* (18–?). *Answer to Rev. Folcy* (1805). *Controversy with Elias Carpenter* (1805). *An Answer to the World* (1806). *Full Assurance That the Kingdom of Heaven Is at Hand* (1806). *The Long Wished for Revolution* (1806). *Answer to Mr. Brother's Book* (1806). *Caution and Instruction to the Sealed* (1807). *An Account of the Trials on the Bills of Exchange* (1807). *Answer to a Sermon by Mr. Smith* (1808). *Answer to False Doctrines* (1808). *A True Picture of the World* (1809). *Controversy of the Spirit* (1811). *An Answer to Thomas Paine* (1812). *The Books of Wonders* (1813–14). *Prophecies Announcing the Birth of the Prince of Peace* (1814).

BIBLIOGRAPHY: Harrison, J.F.C. *Quest for a New Moral World* (1969). Harrison, J.F.C. *The Second Coming: Popular Millenarianism, 1780–1850* (1979). Hopkins, J. K. *A Woman to Deliver Her People* (1982). Johnson, D. A. *Women in English Religion* (1982). *Amazing Grace: Evangelicalism in Australia, Britain, Canada, and the United States,* ed. G. A. Rawlyck and M. A. Noll (1994). Smith, A. *The Established Church and Popular Religion, 1750–1850* (1971). Thompson, E. P. *Rise of the English Working Class* (1966). *Catalogue of the Joanna Southcott Collection at the University of Texas,* ed. E. P. Wright (1969).

For articles in reference works, see: *DNB. Europa. Feminist. IDWB. Oxford. ToddBWW.*

Tony Giffone

Southey, Caroline: See *Bowles, Caroline*

Ester Sowernam (pseudonym)

FLOURISHED: early 1600s.

S. is the author of *Ester hath hang'd Haman: Or An Answere To a lewd Pamphlet, entitled, The Arraignment of Women. With the arraignment of lewd, idle, froward, and unconstant men, and Husbands,* printed in 1617; it was the second published response to Joseph Swetnam's popular 1615 pamphlet, *The Arraignment of Lewde, idle, froward, and unconstant women: Or the vanitie of them, choose you whether.* The pseudonym "Ester Sowernam" both celebrates Esther, the biblical heroine who saved the Jewish people living in Persia from the attacks of Haman, and puns on the name Swe[e]tman.

It is likely that S. was a woman: Both Rachel Speght in *Moralities Memorandum* (1621) and Constantia Munda in the third response to Swetnam's pamphlet, *The Worming of a mad Dogge: Or, A Soppe for Cerberus The Jaylor of Hell. No Confutation But A sharpe Redargution of the bayter of Women* (1617), refer to S. as "she," and S. states that she is "neither Maide, Wife nor Widdowe, yet really all, and therefore experienced to defend all." S. is well educated in classics, history, and law. In her pamphlet, she arraigns and indicts Swetnam, the idea of which may have formed the basis for the anonymous comedy *Swetnam, the Woman-hater, Arraigned by Women,* acted at the Red Bull and printed in 1620. She states she is in London only for Michaelmas term, which may mean she was a barrister's wife. S.'s religion is unclear: She makes reference to both the Geneva Bible and the (Roman Catholic) Douai Bible, and she praises the Catholic Mary, Queen of Scots.

In *Ester hath hang'd Haman,* S. reinterprets Genesis to charge that Adam is more to blame than Eve because he, unlike Eve, continued to sin after she ate the forbidden fruit. In her catalogues of virtuous women, S. includes women noted for their brave deeds, not just for dying with their husbands, as was customary in many defenses of women. S. states that women are not superior to men but then develops arguments to prove that they are; she cites Aristotle's belief that "every thing by nature doth seeke after that which is good" and then concludes that the female must be superior because the male seeks after the female. She also points out the double standard of behavior applied to men and women concerning pregnancy out of wedlock and drunkenness.

Ester hath hang'd Haman was printed for Nicholas Bourne by T. Snodman, the same printer who had produced the 1616 and 1617 reprints of Swetnam's best-selling pamphlet.

WORKS: *Ester hath hang'd Haman: Or An Answere To a Lewd Pamphlet, entitled, The Arraignment of Women. With the arraignment of lewd, idle, froward, and unconstant men, and Husbands* (1617, STC 22974; rpt. J. Smeeton, 1807; rpt. M. Ferguson, 1985; ed. S. Shepherd, 1985; facsimile with intro. by S. O'Malley, 1995).

BIBLIOGRAPHY: Beilin, E. *Redeeming Eve* (1987). Jones, A. R., in *The Renaissance Englishwoman in Print,* ed. A. Haselkorn and B. Travitsky (1990). Shepherd, S. *Amazons and Women Warriors* (1981). Travitsky, B. *ELR* (1984). Woodbridge, L. *Women and the English Renaissance* (1984).

Susan Gushee O'Malley

Muriel Spark

BORN: 1 February 1918, Edinburgh, Scotland.
DAUGHTER OF: Bernard Camberg and Sarah Elizabeth Maud Uezzell.
MARRIED: S. O. Spark, 1938.

The wit and style of S.'s novels and short stories express vividly the many themes present in her work. The various genres in which she works range from translations of Horace, Catullus, and Guillaume Apollinaire to radio plays (*Voices at Play,* 1961), stage plays (*Doctors of Philosophy,* 1963), essays, literary criticism, children's stories, biography, poetry, short stories, and novels. Her sense of the comic is visible throughout her work although it is used most often to express serious themes. She is a genius at describing the surfaces of social situations in a way that is anything but flippant.

S. was born to a Presbyterian mother and a Jewish father. Educated at James Gillespie's Girls School, a Protestant school in Edinburgh, she started learning classical languages at the age of seven. She completed her schooling in 1936 and left the following year for Africa, living in Rhodesia and South Africa until 1944. While in Africa she married S.O. Spark, an Englishman, but soon after the birth of their son the marriage was dissolved. Returning to wartime London, S. worked in the Political Intelligence Department of the British Foreign Office until the war was over.

Her first writing job was on the staff of the *Argentor,* a jeweler's trade magazine, but she also worked as editor of *The Poetry Review* for two years; she put out two issues of her own journal, *Forum;* and she worked as a part-time editor at a publisher. During this time her main literary interests developed in the direction of poetry and criticism; she had been publishing her poetry since 1941 and was on the fringe of London's literary bohemia. Her poems in *The Fanfarlo and Other Verse* (1952) are of many types, the title poem influenced heavily by the Scottish border ballad form.

From 1950 to 1957, her attention was focused mainly on nonfictional work. She edited *The Brontë Letters* (1954) and, with Derek Stanford—her literary partner until 1957 and friend of many years who wrote a study of her entitled *Muriel Spark: A Biographical and Critical Study* (1963)—edited the *Letters of John Henry Newman* (1957) and those of Mary Wollstonecraft Shelley in *My Best Mary: The Selected Letters of Mary Wollstonecraft Shelley* (1953) as well as *Tribute to Wordsworth: A Miscellany of Opinion for the Centenary of the Poet's Death* (1950). She concentrated at this time on literary criticism, producing such diverse volumes as *Emily Brontë: Her Life and Work* (1953)—she wrote the biographical first section of this work and Stanford the critical second section—*John Masefield* (1953), and *Child of Light: A Reassessment of Mary Wollstonecraft Shelley* (1951).

S. turned seriously to fiction only after winning a short-story contest sponsored by *The Observer* in 1951 with her short story "The Seraph and the Zambesi." Macmillan, interested in her work, invited her to try novel writing, and she responded (with the additional help of a stipend from Graham Greene) with *The Comforters* in 1957, an experimental work, and the first of her many critically well-received novels. Her attitude toward the novel form has always been mistrustful. Commenting on her first novel, Spark explained that she wrote it in order to try out the form: "So I wrote a novel to work out the technique first, to sort of make it all right with myself to write a novel at all—a novel about writing a novel."

A major influence on S.'s life and her work was her conversion to Roman Catholicism in 1954. "All my best work has come since then," she reports. Religion, as well as the self-conscious craft of novel writing itself, is a major theme in her work; in *The Comforters*, for example, she heavily criticizes "professional" Catholics. Her second novel, *Robinson* (1958), is an adventure story and allegory, and her third, *Memento Mori* (1959), was adapted for the London stage in 1964.

The first collection of her short stories, *The Go-Away Bird and Other Stories* (1958), brought together much of the short fiction that S. had been placing in a variety of publications. Her further stories and poems were collected in separate volumes in 1967, including many that were first published in the *New Yorker.* Her stories reveal this talented writer's range, which moves easily from comedy and fantasy ("Miss Pinkerton's Apocalypse") to tragic experience ("Bang-Bang You're Dead"), to laying open, as delicately as a fine surgeon, the characteristic hypocrisy of human beings ("The Black Madonna").

The Prime of Miss Jean Brodie (1961), probably her best-known work, is the story of the influence of an unusually romantic teacher on her students in a girls' school in Edinburgh. Like many of S.'s works, this novel has been adapted for the stage (1964) and screen (1967) and even television (1978). Again, like most of her early works, this book focuses on a small society described in accurate detail, in a detached satiric tone that is often described by critics as that of a "dandy." Partly because of the success of this novel, S. left London to live first in New York City and then Rome, where she now makes her home. Along with this change in place has come a change in the tone of her novels, which are increasingly harsh and more virulent than her early work, although she is still often described as a writer of comedy. *The Abbess of Crewe: A Modern Morality Tale* (1974) is an example of a work combining these two elements. An allegory of Watergate set in a nunnery, it points out the pervasive influence of the mass media on the modern world.

S.'s work has been burdened by the insistence of traditional scholarship on labeling and categorizing any writer considered as a respectable member of the canon. Her changing styles and autobiographical bent have influenced critics who have overlooked her work on the basis of these "faults." Newer critical methods with more inclusive approaches, however, open her work to more extensive study, such as is shown by her inclusion in Judy Little's study *Comedy and the Woman Writer, Woolf, Spark, and Feminism.* Also examined recently in terms of her use of cinematic technique, psychological exploration of characters, and her quasi-detective fiction, S.'s innovative uses of time and form demand further attention.

WORKS: *Child of Light: A Reassessment of Mary Wollstonecraft Shelley* (1951). *The Fanfarlo and Other Verse* (1952). (with D. Stanford) *Emily Brontë: Her Life and Work* (1953). *John Masefield* (1953). *The Comforters* (1957). *The Go-Away Bird and Other Stories* (1958). *Robinson* (1958). *Memento Mori* (1959). *The Bachelors* (1960). *The Ballad of Peckham Rye* (1960). *The Prime of Miss Jean Brodie* (1961). *Voices at Play* (1961). *The Girls of Slender Means* (1963). *Doctors of Philosophy* (1963). *The Mandelbaum Gate* (1965). *Collected Poems I* (1967). *Collected Stories I* (1967). *The Very Fine Clock* (1968). *The Public Image* (1968). *The Driver's Seat* (1970). *Not to Disturb* (1971). *The Hothouse by the East River* (1973). *The Abbess of Crewe: A Modern Morality Tale* (1974). *The Takeover* (1976). *The Only Problem* (1984). *The Stories of Muriel Spark* (1985). *Mary Shelley: A Biography* (1987). *A Far Cry from Kensington* (1988). *Symposium* (1990). *Portabello Road and Other Stories* (1990). *Curriculum Vitae: Autobiography* (1992). *The French Window and the Small Telephone* (1992). *The Hanging Judge* (1995). *Reality and Dreams* (1996). *Harper and Wilton* (1996). *Open to the Public: New and Collected Stories* (1997).

BIBLIOGRAPHY: Barreca, R., in *New Perspectives on Women and Comedy,* ed. R. Barreca (1992). *Muriel Spark: An Old Capacity for Vision,* ed. A. Bold (1984). Bower, A. L. *MQ* (1990). Devoize, J. and P. Valette *JSSE* (1989). Edgecombe, R. S. *Vocation and Identity in the Fiction of Muriel Spark* (1990). Frankel, S. *PR* (1987). Glavin, J. *WS* (1988). Halio, J., in *British Novelists Since 1900,* ed. J. I. Biles (1987). Hoyt, C. A. *Muriel Spark: The Surrealist Jane Austen* (1965). Hynes, J., in *Contemporary British Women Novelists,* ed. R. E. Hosmer, Jr. (1993). Kane, R. C. *UMSE* (1990). Kemp, P. *Muriel Spark* (1974). Leonard, J., in *Foundations of Religious Literacy,* ed. J. V. Apczynski (1983). Leonard, J. *SLitI* (1985). Little, J. *Comedy and the Woman Writer: Woolf, Spark, and Feminism* (1984). Little, J., in *The British and Irish Novel Since 1900,* ed. J. Acheson (1991). Little, J., in *Old Maids to Radical Spinsters: Unmarried Women in the Twentieth-Century Novel,* ed. L. L. Doan (1991). Litvack, L. B., in *Literature and the Bible,* ed. D. Bevan (1993). McBrien, W., in *Twentieth-Century Women Novelists,* ed. T. F. Staley (1982). Malkoff, K. *Muriel Spark* (1968). Manning, G. F. *ArielE* (1987). Massie, A. *Muriel Spark* (1979). Monterrey, T. *SSL* (1992). Parrinder, P. *CritQ* (1983). Pyper, H. *L&T* (1993). Randisi, J. L. *On Her Way Rejoicing: The Fiction of Muriel Spark* (1991). Rankin, I. *JNT* (1985). Richmond, V. B. *Muriel Spark* (1985). Richmond, V. B. *MLQ* (1990). Rowe, M. M. *Crit* (1987). Shaw, V., in *The History of*

Scottish Literature, ed. C. Cairns (1987). Stanford, D. *Muriel Spark: A Biographical and Critical Study* (1963). Stevenson, S. *ArielE* (1993). Stubbs, P. *Muriel Spark* (1973). Todd, R., in *Essays on the Contemporary British Novel,* ed. H. Bock and A. Wertheim (1986). Whittaker, R. *The Faith and Fiction of Muriel Spark* (1982).

For articles in reference works, see: *Bloomsbury. CA. CB. CLC. CN. CP. DLB. Feminist. MBL SUP. Oxford. TCW. ToddBWW. WA.*

Other references: Coe, J. *LRB* (13 September 1990). Kermode, F. *The House of Fiction: Interviews with Seven Novelists* (1963). Keyser, B. *Arizona Quarterly* (1976). McBrien, W., in *Twentieth-Century Women Novelists* (1982), ed. T. Staley. Whittaker, R., in *The Contemporary English Novel,* ed. M. Bradbury and D. Palmer (1972).

Jan Calloway-Baxter

Rachel Speght

BORN: 1597 (?)
DIED: after 1630 (?)
DAUGHTER OF: James Speght.
MARRIED: William Procter, 1621.

A writer of considerable religious, rhetorical, and classical learning, S. published her first work before she was twenty. Her *Mouzell for Melastomus* (1617) contributed to the pamphlet war about women in the second decade of the seventeenth century; in it, she vigorously attacks Joseph Swetnam's *Arraignment of Lewde, idle, froward, and unconstant women* (1615) as "irreligious and illiterate" and defends women with a barrage of well-supported arguments based upon her own exegesis of Scripture. Her name appears on the title page, in contrast to two other defenses of women published in the same year by "Ester Sowernam" and "Constantia Munda." S.'s serious religious purpose perhaps reflects her upbringing in a strict Calvinist home by a father who was rector to two London churches and author of *A Briefe demonstration, who have, and of the certainty of their salvation, that have the spirit of Jesus Christ* (1613) and by a mother about whose death she wrote: "shee in glorie lives with Christ for aye; / Which makes me glad, and thankefull for her blisse, / Though still bewayle her absence, whom I misse."

As the title of *A Mouzell for Melastomus* implies, the muzzle is intended to silence the barking of Swetnam, the slanderer or "black mouth." In strong, vivid language S. attacks the "mingle mangle invective" of the "pestiferous enemy." By assailing Swetnam primarily for his blasphemy, S. reveals her own talent for religious disputation. She argues that he defames women by false interpretations of Scripture, for women "are highly esteemed and accounted in the eyes of their gracious Redeemer." S.'s own readings of biblical texts emphasize the spiritual equality of the sexes and a humane vision of "domesticall affaires" modeled on mutual responsibility. In her interpretation of Genesis, for example, she argues against traditional exegesis that apportions all the blame to Eve and insists that God subjected all creatures to both Adam and Eve, in this regard making "their authority equall." S. does not, however, praise all women or extend women's spiritual equality to their social circumstances as wives or citizens. Remarking S.'s apparent acceptance of women's lesser position, Ester Sowernam complains in *Ester hath hang'd Haman* (1617) that S. does not defend but "doth rather charge and condemne women." More favorable notice in the same year came in *The Worming of a mad Dogge,* in which Constantia Munda praises S. as "the first Champion of our sexe that would encounter with the barbarous bloudhound."

S.'s second work was *Mortalities Memorandum, with a Dreame Prefixed* (1621), a poem of more than 1,000 lines on the subject of human mortality. Some elements of this work appear to be autobiographical, since it was apparently occasioned by her mother's death, was dedicated to her godmother, Mary Moundford, and begins with a 300–line dream allegory of the poet's journey from Ignorance to "*Eruditions* garden" with the advice of Thought, Experience, and Industry. Her avowed purpose in publishing her poem is the "common benefit" that a work on the origin and nature of death would have for her pious readers. As a work of Christian—and specifically Calvinist—faith, the poem moves between the extremes of human mortality after the loss of Eden and Christian redemption and immortality. Its six-line stanzas of iambic pentameter verse are moderately skillful, with by far the best writing occurring in the *Dreame.*

Little is known about S.'s life. Records of her marriage in 1621 to a Calvinist minister, William Procter, and of the subsequent births of a daughter and son are extant. The date of her death is presently unknown.

WORKS: *A Mouzell for Melastomus, The Cynical Bayter of and foule mouthed Barker against Evahs Sex* (1617, STC 23057). *Mortalities Memorandum, with a Dreame Prefixed* (1621, STC 23058). *The Polemics and Poems of Rachel Speght,* ed. B. K. Lewalski (1996).

BIBLIOGRAPHY: *Redeeming Eve: Women Writers of the English Renaissance,* ed. E. Beilin (1987). *MLQ* (1990). Jones, A. R., in *The Renaissance Englishwoman in Print,* ed. A. Haselkorn and B. Travitsky (1990). Lewalski, B. *Writing Women in Jacobean England* (1993). Shepherd, S. *The Women's Sharp Revenge: Five Women's Pamphlets from the Renaissance 1580–1640* (1985). Travitsky, B. *ELR* (1984). Woodbridge, L. *Women and the English Renaissance* (1984).

For articles in reference works, see: *Bloomsbury. DNB. Feminist. Oxford. ToddBWW.*

Elaine V. Beilin

Speranza: See *Wilde, Jane Francesca*

Spindle, Penelope: See *Lennox, Charlotte Ramsay*

Lucy Hester Stanhope

BORN: 12 March 1776, Chevening, Kent.
DIED: 23 June 1839, Djoun, Lebanon.

DAUGHTER OF: Charles, Viscount Mahon, later third Earl Stanhope, and Hester Pitt.

Noted traveler to the Levant, mystic, and eccentric, S. drew to her mountain convent in Lebanon such visitors as the fabled literary voyagers Alexander Kinglake, Alphonse de Lamartine, and Eliot Warburton. She embodied the essence of that melancholy romanticism, aristocratic disdain, and extravagant temperament that fired the imagination of European writers of the early nineteenth century. Although her reputation today is wrapped in obscurity, in her heyday her forcefulness of character and the seductiveness of her glamor convinced the Arab tribes of Syria and Palestine among whom she lived of the essential truth of her many oracular pronouncements.

As the granddaughter of the first Lord Chatham, whom she resembled, and daughter of the third Earl Stanhope, the radical politician and famed experimental scientist, she possessed a very definite sense of her station in life. She quickly came to the attention of William Pitt the Younger, her uncle, whom she served as trusted confidant and private secretary. So closely did she identify with this role, a drawing room ornament of the first order, that she wished for nothing more than to be known as "Mr. Pitt's niece." Poorly educated by the standards of the day, having no instruction in the classics when such was the norm, her irrepressible wit and acerbic tongue nevertheless left their marks. With the ascension of William Pitt to the office of Prime minister in 1804, S. assumed enormous social importance, dispensing much patronage and arranging official banquets.

Proud, imperious, restless—a first-rate conversationalist and a fiery haranguer—she quit the Pitt household upon the Prime Minister's death in 1806. She retired to the solitude of Wales after the deaths of her favorite brother, Major Stanhope, and Sir John Moore, an admirer and one of her uncle's favorite generals. Subject to fierce bouts of dejection and contempt for a society that no longer recognized her worth, she renounced Europe for the Levant in 1810. In what would later become typical for the Victorian age, she traveled in the grand manner, her entourage growing as she moved east, taxing her financial resources to the limit. After entering Jerusalem and Damascus with great style, she struck east to the famed ruins of Palmyra, the first European woman ever to do so. She finally settled in a half-ruined convent in Djoun on the slopes of Mount Lebanon, eight miles from Sidon. Such was her sway over the neighboring Druses that the most fearsome tribal chieftains and their Turkish overlords came to respect her and heed her word. Not only did she make prodigal provision for her entourage, but she also provided a haven for fleeing Europeans after the battle of Navarino (1827) and compelled Ibrahim Pasha to solicit her neutrality when he sought to invade Syria. She was known to have given Pasha, the fierce lieutenant of Mehmet Ali, the Viceroy of Egypt, more trouble than all the insurgent tribes of Syria and Palestine combined.

For writers such as Kinglake, her name was almost as familiar as that of Robinson Crusoe; Kinglake, the author of *Eothen,* the most famous of English travelogues to the Near East and a minor masterpiece much beloved by Winston Churchill, wrote "both [Crusoe and S.] were associated with the spirit of adventure; but whilst the imagined life of the castaway mariner never failed to seem glaringly real, the true story of the Englishwoman ruling over the Arabs always sounded to me like a fable." Combining the charm and commanding temper of her aristocratic line and the melancholy of a stubborn recluse partially going to seed in the East, she could not help but fascinate literary travelers. Although many sought interviews with her, she was loath to grant them. Disgruntled with Europe, she barricaded herself against its influence, never consulting its books or newspapers but trusting to astrology alone. As a mimic of savage repute, she could obliterate any target of her choice. Lord Byron, with his many affected airs, was a natural favorite, and she was known to have attributed to the Romantic poet a "curiously coxcombical lisp." Among her other distinguished victims was Lamartine, whom she found overrefined, bearing himself, in her phrase, "like the humbler sort of English dandy."

In the Levant, S. came to be regarded as a seer and was respected as such; even sober westerners, with a healthy dash of skepticism, could not escape the magnetism of her personality. For the voyager with literary ambitions, she was an obligatory sight on a journey east. Kinglake, her most famous English visitor, characterized her religious beliefs as a curious melange of the different religions of the Ottoman empire, although he emphasized that she never lost her practical streak and her famed abhorrence for any display of exquisiteness.

Known by such sobriquets as "The Mad Nun of Lebanon" or such self-styled ascriptions as "Queen of the Arabs," S. died alone and abandoned in 1839, walled up in her half-ruined convent. Deeply in debt in her last years, she reacted with fury when Lord Palmerstone approved the appropriation of her pension to settle the insistent claims of her many creditors. Ever the aristocrat, she refused to accept any visitors and declined into hopeless indigence in her proud tower of Isolation.

WORKS: *Memoirs of the Lady Hester Stanhope, as Related by Herself in Conversations with Her Physician,* ed. C. L. Meryon (1845). *Travels of Lady Hester Stanhope, Forming the Completion of Her Memoirs Narrated by her Physician,* ed. C. L. Meryon (1846).

BIBLIOGRAPHY. Bruce, I. *The Nun of Lebanon* (1951). Haslip, J. *Lady Hester Stanhope* (1934). Hogg, J. *News from Lebanon: Lady Hester Stanhope's Autograph Letter to Michael Bruce* (1988). Kinglake, A. *Eothen* (1844). Newman, A. *The Stanhopes of Chevening* (1969). Roundell, C. *Lady Hester Stanhope* (1910). Warburton, E. *The Crescent and the Cross* (1845).

For articles in reference works, see: *Feminist. Oxford. ToddBWW. ToddDBA.*

Other references: Agress, L. *The Feminine Irony: Women on Women in Early-Nineteenth-Century English Literature* (1978).

Michael Skakun
(updated by Natalie Joy Woodall)

Henrietta Eliza Vaughn Palmer Stannard

BORN: 13 January 1856, York.
DIED: 13 December 1911, Putney, London.
DAUGHTER OF: the Reverend Henry Vaughn Palmer and Emily Catherine Cowling.
MARRIED: Arthur Stannard, 1884.
WROTE UNDER: H. Palmer; Violet Whyte; John Strange Winter.

S. descended from several generations of soldiers; her father had been an officer in the Royal Artillery before taking holy orders. Brought up on contemporary novels, S. was very well read by the time she entered school at the age of eleven. Her familiarity with army life inspired her at the age of eighteen to begin writing short stories and novels of military life that were at first contributed to the *Family Herald* and other journals. Her publishers urged her to adopt the masculine *nom de plume* "John Strange Winter" because "her military novels would stand a better chance as the work of a man." The rousing success of stories such as *Cavalry Life* (1881) and *Bootles' Baby* (1885) (2 million copies sold in ten years) led critics such as John Ruskin to describe S. as "the author to whom we owe the most finished and faithful rendering ever yet given to the character of the British soldier." Literary critics consistently referred to S. as a man until 1889, when her enormous popularity led the public to discover her true identity. Except for *The Old Love or the New* (1880) and *Broken Sixpence* (1881), written under the pseudonym "Violet Whyte," and a few articles written under "H. Palmer," S. used "John Strange Winter" throughout her life.

S. wrote and published more than ninety novels, with a majority set in "Blankshire." The protagonists of many novels reappear as minor figures in other novels; S. seems to enjoy cross-referencing to earlier novels. Her works are sensation novels dealing with the aristocracy and higher gentry. Whether dealing with murder (*A Born Soldier,* 1894) or a young woman's secret religious crisis (*The Soul of the Bishop,* 1893), S. artfully spins a tale that keeps the reader in suspense until the last page. She frequently fascinates the reader by contrasting a character's outward social conformity with his or her internal psychological turmoil, a conflict that must have been very real to Victorian readers. While dealing with typical Victorian topics such as morality, marriage, and religion, S.'s approaches are frequently not typical of the times. S. exhibits her wide-ranging literary knowledge by beginning every chapter of a work with an appropriate quote from numerous sources, including Euripides, Shakespeare, and Longfellow. While a moral lesson is generally intended, S.'s high-born characters are incapable of truly evil comportment.

In 1891, S. began publishing a penny weekly magazine, *Golden Gates,* subsequently changed to *Winter's Weekly.* She shows a real sense of humor, however, in her novel *Confessions of a Publisher, Being the Autobiography of Abel Drinkwater* (1892), in which she pokes fun at male publishers and their condescending attitudes toward female novelists. S. also took up women's issues, such as their lack of independence and the legal discrimination against them. In *A Blameless Woman* (1894), she presents a case in which a young woman is punished for unwitting adultery while the married man goes free. In her 1898 novel *The Price of a Wife,* S. argues for a woman's right to choose her husband. Besides expounding feminist themes,. S. also attacked religious hypocrisy in *The Truth Tellers* (1896) and *The Peacemakers* (1898).

In addition to her writing and domestic activities—she had one son and three daughters—S. was first president of the Writers Club, president of the Society of Women's Journalists (1901–03), and a Fellow of the Royal Society of Literature.

WORKS: *A Christmas Fairy* (1878). (as Violet Whyte) *The Old Love or the New* (1880). (as Violet Whyte) *Broken Sixpence* (1881). *Cavalry Life* (1881). *Nell's Story* (1881). *Koosje—A Study of Dutch Life* (1883). *Regimental Legends* (1883). *A Man's Man* (1884). *Hoop-la* (1885). *Bootles' Baby* (1885). *In Quarters with the 25th* (1885). *A Man of Honor* (1886). *Army Society* (1886). *Army Tales—Bootles' Baby* (1886). *Mignon's Secret: The Story of a Barrack Bairn* (1886). *On March* (1886). *Pluck* (1886). *Driver Dallas* (1887). *Garrison Gossip* (1887). *Her Johnnie* (1887). *A Siege Baby* (1887). *Mignon's Husband* (1887). *Sophy Carmine* (1887). *That Imp* (1887). *Beautiful Jim of the Blankshire Regiment* (1888). *Bootles' Children* (1888). *Princess Sarah* (1888). *A Little Fool* (1889). *Buttons* (1889). *Harvest* (1889). *Mrs. Bob* (1889). *My Poor Dick* (1889). *Dinna Forget* (1890). *Ferrers Count* (1890). *He Went for a Soldier* (1890). *The Other Man's Wife* (1890). *Goodbye* (1891). *In Luck's Way* (1891). *Lumley the Painter* (1891). *Confessions of a Publisher, Being the Autobiography of Abel Drinkwater* (1892). *Experience of a Lady Help* (1892) *Mere Luck* (1892). *Mr. Geoff* (1892). *Only Human, or, Justice* (1892). *A Soldier's Children* (1892). *Those Girls* (1892). *Aunt Johnnie* (1893). *The Soul of the Bishop* (1893). *A Born Soldier* (1894). *A Seventh Child* (1894). *A Blameless Woman* (1894). *Every Inch a Soldier* (1894). *The Stranger Woman* (1894). *A Magnificent Young Man* (1895). *I Married a Wife* (1895). *Private Tinker* (1895). *The Major's Favorite* (1895). *Crip* (1896). *The Strange Story of My Life* (1896). *The Same Thing with a Difference* (1896). *The Truth Tellers* (1896). *Everybody's Favourite* (1897). *Into an Unknown World* (1897). *Mary Hamilton's Romance* (1898). *The Price of a Wife* (1898). *The Peacemakers* (1898). *Wedlock* (1898). *A Mother's Holiday* (1899). *A Name to Conjure With* (1899). *A Summer Jaunt* (1899). *Heart and Sword* (1899). *Binks' Family* (1899). *Just as It Was* (1900). *Little Gervaise* (1900). *The Married Mrs. Binks* (1900). *The Money Sense* (1900). *A Self-Made Countess: Career of a Beauty* (1901). *The Magic Wheel* (1901). *Blaze of Glory* (1902). *The Soul of Honor* (1902). *A Matter of Sentiment* (1903). *Little Joan* (1903). *Marty* (1903). *Cherry's Child* (1904). *Countess of Mountenoy* (1904). *Little Vanities of Mrs. Whittaker* (1904). *Sly-boots* (1904). *That Little French Baby* (1906).

BIBLIOGRAPHY: Black, H. *Notable Women Authors of the Day* (1893).

For articles in reference works, see: *1890s. Longman. Oxford. Stanford. ToddBWW. Who Was Who in Literature 1906–1934* (rpt. 1979).

Carole M. Shaffer-Koros

Freya Stark

BORN: 31 January 1893, Paris, France.
DIED: 9 May 1993, Asolo, Italy.
DAUGHTER OF: Robert Stark and Flora Stark.
MARRIED: Steward Perowne, 1947.

An intrepid traveler and adventurer, World War II propagandist, photographer, and writer, S. traveled early with her artist parents but by 1901 moved permanently to Italy with her mother and younger sister, Vera. They lived first in Asolo near Venice, and two years later moved to Dronero in the Piedmont, where S.'s mother invested in Count Mario di Roscio's carpet factory. In 1906, just before her thirteenth birthday, an accident in the factory permanently disfigured S. and left her acutely aware of her appearance; for the rest of her life, her hairstyle and hats hid her scars. Discovering literature while visiting her father at Ford Park, Dartmoor, S. began independent reading, studying French, and teaching herself Latin. In 1911, her father emigrated to Canada; until his death, S. corresponded with him frequently and visited him twice. The next year, S. began reading English literature and then history at Bedford College, London, where she was influenced by W. P. Ker, whom S. came to consider her godfather. She claimed he taught her everything she knew about English literature.

At the outset of World War I, S. trained as a nurse in Bologna; her fluent Italian made her a valuable addition to George M. Trevelyan's Italian ambulance corps near Gorizia, where she witnessed the Italian retreat at Caporetto. In 1921, S. began learning Arabic while living at La Mortola, her refuge near Genoa purchased for her by her father. Two great personal losses affected S.: W. P. Ker was killed while mountain climbing with her; three years later her sister Vera died after childbirth.

In 1926, Herbert Young, her father's childless friend, left S. his Casa Freia in Asolo, where she took up permanent residence; the inheritance and wise investments allowed S. some freedom. She pursued Arabic by enrolling at the School of Oriental and African Studies and then departed for the East in November 1927 to spend the winter near Beirut improving her Arabic. The next spring she took the first of her "difficult" journeys, this one (with Venetia Buddicom) to Jebel Druze in the Syrian desert. Her first article, based on this trip, appeared in *Cornhill Magazine.*

Resolved to learn eastern languages, S. arrived in Baghdad and, at the age of thirty-six, set her personal tone for travel and life abroad. She lived in the native quarter, wore Arab dress, and developed her keen sense of observing and reporting. While mapping unknown, unprotected territory in The Valleys of the Assassins in western Persia, S. discovered two missing castles and gave names to the mountain ranges and villages she passed through. A return trip established a third castle. These daring expeditions brought her social approval in the British community in Baghdad, and she began writing for *The Baghdad Times,* which published her *Baghdad Sketches* (1932). She was awarded the Royal Geographic Society's Back Memorial Grant for her remarkable travels to Persia, recounted in *Beyond Euphrates* (1951), the second volume of her autobiography. During this period, she wrote weekly letters to her mother, despite their ambivalent relationship; these and letters to others such as Jock Murray, W. P. Ker, "Naps" Browning, Bernard Berenson, and Lord Wavell (Archibald Percival Wavell, first Earl of Wavell), and her diaries, formed the backbone of her books. Throughout her years, her letters recount adventures and illnesses, describe sites and native customs, and reveal her wit and devotion to friends.

After more than two years in the east, S. returned to London, where the War Office approved her map of the Assassins' Valley. She met Jock Murray, her lifelong publisher, and signed a contract for *The Valleys of the Assassins* (1934). That same year, S. was the first woman awarded the Burton Memorial Medal of the Royal Asiatic Society for her travels in Luristan, where she had gone in search of buried treasure.

In 1935, S. mapped and photographed the Hadhramaut, part of the old trade route in present day Yemen; on this trip, as on many others, she was plagued by illness. Nevertheless, S. returned three years later with Gertrude Caton Thompson on an archaeological dig financed by Lord Wakefield to establish whether there had been contact between Arabia and Africa during the Roman period; *A Winter in Arabia* (1940) gives a candid account of the project. After strained relations with Thompson, S. mounted an independent mapping and writing trip along a spice route. A year later, she visited crusader castles in Syria.

At the start of World War II, S. served as assistant information officer to Steward Perowne, whom she married in 1947. Her assignment was to summarize the news, which was then translated into Arabic and broadcast in town squares. In February 1940, S. began propaganda work for the Allies; she traveled to Yemen, where she showed Ministry of Information films in harems in an attempt to neutralize Italian and German activities. Her effectiveness in Yemen brought her a transfer to Cairo, where she established and recruited Egyptians for the "Brotherhood of Freedom," an organization of cells for antifascist, prodemocracy discussions. Her Egyptian success led to her establishing a Brotherhood in Iraq. Now recognized as a talented propagandist, although she preferred the term "persuasion," S. contributed articles to the *London Times.* In 1942, S. was awarded the Royal Geographical Society's Founder's Medal for the travels in Wadi Hadhramaut and, with the encouragement of Sir Sidney Cockerell, began the first volume of her autobiography, *Traveller's Prelude* (1950).

At the onset of the war, S. was recognized as an intrepid traveler and writer. By war's end, she had transformed herself into an Arabist and consultant to government officials. *Dust in the Lion's Paw* (1961), the fourth volume of her autobiography, covers this period. She had visited Lord and Lady Wavell in India in 1943 and, under the British government's auspices, traveled to the United States to defend British policy toward Palestine. She returned briefly to India to serve as assistant to Lady Wavell to garner support for the Empire among Indian women and inspected reading centers in Italy in an effort to improve Anglo-Italian relations.

At fifty-four, S. married Perowne, an unhappy liaison that lasted a scant five years. In 1948, she published *Perseus in the Wind,* a collection of essays about beauty, death, sorrow—"the things which are beyond our grasp yet visible to all." Glasgow University awarded her an honorary degree in 1951, and a 1952 trip to western Turkey allowed her to visit fifty-five ancient sites and to write *Ionia: A Quest* (1954). In 1953, she was awarded the Commander of the British Empire (C.B.E.) and published the third volume of her autobiography, *Coast of Incense.* Her other travels in the 1950s included trips to Syria, Turkey, Greece, Lebanon, Iran, and Kenya, as well as publication of her account of following Alexander the Great's path to the east. During the 1960s, she extending her travels to include Cambodia, China, Afghanistan, Samarkand, and, her lifelong dream, Nepal. Her writing now took on a more historical, meditative flavor rather than the fresh eye of the contemporary traveler.

S.'s war-work, travels, and writing brought her continuing fame and awards. In 1972, she was named Dame of the British Empire, lunched with Queen Elizabeth II, and visited her admirer, the Queen Mother. In 1977, she returned to Syria with a BBC crew, which filmed her floating down the Euphrates on a specially constructed raft conversing about life, history, and art; she revisited Nepal with another BBC crew in 1984. Three months after her one hundredth birthday, she died in Asolo, her adopted home; it had awarded her the keys to the city in 1985 with S., independent as ever, dressed in eastern costume at the grand ceremony.

WORKS: *Baghdad Sketches* (1932). *Valleys of the Assassins* (1934). *The Southern Gates of Arabia* (1936). (photographs) *Seen in the Hadhramaut* (1938). *Winter in Arabia* (1940). *Letter from Syria* (1942). *Perseus in the Wind* (1948). *Traveller's Prelude* (1950; autobiography, Vol. I). *Beyond Euphrates* (1951; autobiography, Vol. II). *Coast of Incense* (1953; autobiography, Vol. III). *Ionia: A Quest* (1954). *The Lycian Shore* (1956). *Alexander's Path* (1958). *Riding to the Tigris* (1959). *Dust in the Lion's Paw* (1961; autobiography, Vol. IV). *The Journey's Echo* (1963). *Rome on the Euphrates* (1966). *The Zodiac Arch* (1968). *The Minaret of Djam* (1970). *A Peak in Darien* (1976). *Letters,* ed. C. Moorehead and L. Moorehead (8 vols.; 1974–82). *Over the Rim of the World,* ed. C. Moorehead (1988, selected letters).

BIBLIOGRAPHY: Cardiff, M. *Friends Abroad: Memories of Lawrence Durrell, Freya Stark, Peggy Guggenheim and Others* (1997). Hogg, J. *News from Lebanon: Lady Hester Stanhope's Autograph Letter to Michael Bruce* (1988). Izzard, M. *Freya Stark: A Biography* (1993). Maitland, A. *A Tower in the Wall* (1982). Moorehead, C. *Freya Stark* (1986). Ruthven, M. *Traveller Through Time: A Photographic Journey with Freya Stark* (1986). Ruthven, M. *Freya Stark in Southern Arabia* (1994).

For articles in reference works, see: *Bloomsbury. CA. Cambridge. Feminist. IAWWW. IDWB. Longman. MBL. OCEL. Oxford. RE. TCA. TCW. ToddBWW. Who's Who. WD.*

Other references: *LonT* (11 May 1993).

Judith C. Kohl

Enid (Mary) Starkie

BORN: 18 August 1897, Killiney, Dublin, Ireland.
DIED: 21 April 1970, Oxford.
DAUGHTER OF: William Joseph Myles Starkie and Mary Walsh Starkie.

A scholar of French literature, S. wrote more than fifteen books on nineteenth- and twentieth-century writers. After receiving her undergraduate education at Alexandra College in Dublin, S. received her training in French literature at the Sorbonne, University of Paris, where she earned her doctorate in 1928. S. taught French literature at Exeter University, in several American universities on visiting appointments, and, for most of her career, at Oxford University starting in 1929. She described her childhood and college years in her only autobiographical book, *A Lady's Child,* in 1941.

S. used such biographical sources as manuscripts and correspondence to write her critical studies of French writers and was the first outsider allowed to use Arthur Rimbaud's papers for her 1938 study of the writer's life and works. She felt that better understanding of a work comes from knowing the artist's personality. As she wrote in her introduction to the 1957 edition of *Baudelaire,* "True, the intrinsic value of a work of art depends, from the artistic point of view, on itself alone, but those who enjoy it, responding to it sympathetically, will always be interested to discover all they can about the nature of the man who could produce it, and wish to come into contact deeply with his personality."

Always the scholar, S.'s studies of Rimbaud, Baudelaire, Petrus Borel, André Gide, and Gustave Flaubert are known for their careful documentation of sources and assimilation of biographical information into a critical analysis. S.'s studies provide what critics have called a "joy of continuous discovery." Her last book, published posthumously, was the second volume of her two-part study of Flaubert, a book called by Flaubert scholar and translator Francis Steegmuller "the most sympathetic, best written modern account in English, or in French, of Flaubert's complete later career. It is a worthy monument to the great novelist and to his indomitable biographer."

Honors in S.'s life include her election to the Irish Academy of Letters, being made Commander of the Order of the British Empire in 1967, and being made Chevalier of the French Legion of Honor in 1948. The Faculty of Modern Languages at the University of Oxford conferred on her the Doctorate of Letters in 1939.

S. was remembered for her individualistic personality, and her obituaries even included references to her touches of rebellious dress and behavior. She campaigned for her choices of candidates for Oxford's prestigious Chair of Poetry, a post decided in an election by the Masters of Arts of the university; through her efforts W. H. Auden was elected to the post in 1956. Among the French writers she knew well and was instrumental in bringing to Oxford for honors and lectures were Jean Cocteau and André Gide. S. also knew British writer Joyce Cary well.

S. spent several months in the United States teaching at Berkeley and Seattle in 1951. She was, however, so warmly received at Hollins College in Virginia during her term in 1959 that S. bequeathed her fortune to the college.

WORKS: *Baudelaire* (1933; rewritten in 1957). *Arthur Rimbaud in Abyssinia* (1937). *Arthur Rimbaud* (1938; rev. and enlarged, 1947). *A Lady's Child* (1941). *A Critical Edition of Baudelaire's "Les Fleurs du Mal"* (1947). (with others) *The God That Failed* (1948). *Arthur Rimbaud, 1854–1954* (1954). *Petrus Borel* (1954). *From Gautier to Eliot: The Influence of France on English Literature, 1851–1939* (1960). *Arthur Rimbaud* (1961). *Flaubert: The Making of the Master* (1967). *Flaubert: The Master* (1971).

BIBLIOGRAPHY: Davin, D. *Closing Times* (1975). Richardson, J. *Enid Starkie* (1973).

For articles in reference works, see: *CA. DIB. NYT Biographical Ed* (2 May 1970). *TCA. Who's Who* (1969).

Other references: *Books Abroad* (Spring 1971). *FS* (October 1970). Steegmuller, F. *NYTBR* (29 November 1971).

Marilynn J. Smith

Christina (Ellen) Stead

BORN: 17 July, 1902, Rockdale, Australia.
DIED: 31 March 1983, Sydney, Australia.
DAUGHTER OF: David George Stead and Ellen Butters Stead.
MARRIED: William Blake (b. William Blech), 1952.
WROTE UNDER: Christina Stead.

S. trained at the Sydney Teachers College and became a public school teacher, work for which she later considered herself unfitted. After studying typing and shorthand for a business career, she sailed from Australia in 1928. She worked in England and France as a grain clerk and a bank clerk; in the former position, she worked for a company whose manager was William Blake, a Marxist economist. They formed an alliance in 1928 and finally married in 1952. From 1937 to 1946, S. lived in the United States, publishing several novels and writing scripts for MGM in Hollywood. In 1946, she traveled to Europe with Blake, staying in numerous cities on the Continent, and then returned to England in 1953 to refresh her feel for the English language. Blake died in London in 1968. In 1974, S. returned to Australia to live with her brother and died in 1983.

Although S. is best known for her eleven novels, she began her writing career with a collection of short stories, *The Salzburg Tales* (1934), parables, allegories, and stories of the grotesque. *The Puzzleheaded Girl* (1967) is a collection of four novellas, exploring the figure of the young woman in the United States. In addition, S. wrote reviews and translated novels from French to English, and she edited two collections of short stories, one with William Blake. In 1974, S. received the Patrick White Award, recognizing her excellence as an Australian novelist.

The Man Who Loved Children (1940) is S.'s acknowledged masterpiece. Ignored for twenty-five years, the novel was reissued in 1965 with an introduction and afterword by Randall Jarrell, naming the novel great because it does one thing better than any other fiction—it makes the reader part of one family's day-to-day existence. The novel depicts three characters of mythic proportions: the father, Sam; the mother, Hetty; and the daughter, Louisa (Louie), a potential artist. It portrays elemental conflicts between parents and children for power and autonomy, between man and woman for identity and understanding, and between parents for the allegiances of their children. In a virtuoso performance, S. establishes personality through the distinctive languages of the three central characters with their obsessions and individual blindnesses. The woman's movement solidified the reputation of the novel and procured a new generation of readers for the depiction of a family tearing itself apart. *The Man Who Loved Children* can also be seen as a portrait of the artist as a young woman, with Louie declaring her resistance to Sam and Hetty in a play about tyranny. Miss Aiden, her teacher, is her muse and ego ideal. Louie is finally willing to kill both her parents and begin her own life in the world.

S.'s novel *House of All Nations* (1938) won both popular acclaim and critical success. This exploration of banking and international finance can be seen as S.'s greatest intellectual achievement because of its scope and complexity. This huge novel displays S.'s mature style, charting a world of avarice.

Dark Places of the Heart (1966), also titled *Cotter's England,* is a depiction of the poverty and ugliness of Britain's industrialized North. A central concern is the relationship between Nellie Cotter Cook and her brother Tom. Like Michael and Catherine Baguenault, the brother-sister pair in *Seven Poor Men of Sydney* (1934), Nellie and Tom seem too close to each other, engaged in a battle for power and personal survival. The dark places of Nellie's heart manifest themselves in a fascination with death, a compulsion to manipulate other people, and a dangerous desire to be more than human, to achieve a charismatic destiny. As in all of S.'s strongest fiction, the plot of the novel is subordinate to the drama of character.

Although recognition of her achievement has been slow, S. is now acknowledged to be a significant twentieth-century fiction writer. A realist novelist with a modern post-Freudian sensibility, S. depicts people's social connections, understanding the underlying economic forces that shape their lives. She is compared to Charles Dickens for her density of realistic detail, for her comic eye and her ear for exaggerated rhetoric, for her use of the grotesque, and for her commentary on social conditions. S. uses her characters' language to reveal their illusions and deceptions. S. has identified herself as a psychological writer, expressing the drama of the person.

WORKS: *The Salzburg Tales* (1934). *Seven Poor Men of Sydney* (1934). *The Beauties and the Furies* (1936). *House of All Nations* (1938). *The Man Who Loved Children* (1940). *For Love Alone* (1944). *Letty Fox: Her Luck*

(1946). *A Little Tea, A Little Chat* (1948). *The People with the Dogs* (1952). (trans.) *Colour of Asia,* by F. Gigon (1955). (trans.) *The Candid Killer,* by J. Giltene (1956). (trans.) *In Balloon and Bathyscape,* by A. Piccard (1956; also titled *Earth and Sky*). *Dark Places of the Heart* (1966; also titled *Cotter's England*). *The Puzzleheaded Girl* (1967). *The Little Hotel* (1974). *Miss Herbert: The Suburban Wife* (1976). *The Christina Stead Anthology,* ed. J. B. Read (1979). *Ocean of Story: The Uncollected Stories of Christina Stead,* ed. R. G. Geering (1986). *The Palace With Several Sides,* ed. R. G. Geering (1986). *I'm Dying Laughing: The Humorist,* ed. R. G. Geering (1987). *A Web of Friendship: Selected Letters (1928–73),* ed. R. G. Geering (1992). *Talking into the Typewriter: Selected Letters (1973–83),* ed. R. G. Geering (1992).

BIBLIOGRAPHY: Arac, J. *The New Historicism* (1989). Bennett, B., in *Perceiving Other Worlds,* ed. E. Thumboo (1991). Brydon, D. *Christina Stead* (1987). Carter, A., intro. to *The Puzzleheaded Girl* (1984). Clancy, L. *Christina Stead's "The Man Who Loved Children" and "For Love Alone"* (1981). Clancy, L., in *Who Is She?,* ed. S. Walker (1983). Edelson, P. F., in *International Literature in English* (1991). Eldershaw, M. B. *Essays in Australian Fiction* (1938). Gardiner, J. K., in *Daughters and Fathers,* ed. L. E. Boose and B. S. Flowers (1988). Gardiner, J. K. intro. to *The People With the Dogs* (1981). Gardiner, J. K. *Rhys, Stead, Lessing and the Politics of Empathy* (1989). Geering, R. G. *Christina Stead* (1969, 1979). Hardwick, E. *A View of My Own* (1962). Iseman, K., in *Australian Women: Feminist Perspectives,* ed. N. Grieve and P. Grimshaw (1981). Jarrell, R., introduction and afterword to *The Man Who Loved Children* (1965). Lidoff, J. *Christina Stead* (1982). Roderick, C. *Introduction to Australian Fiction* (1950). Rowley, H. *Christina Stead. A Biography* (1993). Sage, L., in *Women's Writing: A Challenge to Theory,* ed. M. Montieth (1986). Sheridan, S., in *Gender, Politics, and Fiction,* ed. C. Ferrier (1985). Sheridan, S. *Christina Stead* (1988). Sturm, T., in *Cunning Exiles: Studies of Modern Prose Writers,* ed. D. Anderson and S. Knight (1974). Wattie, N., in *Voices From Distant Lands* (1983). Williams, C. *Christina Stead: A Life of Letters* (1989).

For articles in reference works, see: *Bloomsbury. CA. Cambridge. CLC. Feminist. Oxford. TCA.*

Other references: Allen, B. *NewC* (October 1994). Anderson, R. F. *ArielE* (October 1985). Apstein, B. *IFR* (1980). Bader, R. *WLWE* (1984). Berry, R. *Landfall* (September 1986). Beston, J. B. *WLWE* (1976). Blain, V. *Southerly* (December 1993). Blake, A. *Meanjin* (Autumn 1988). Blake, A. *JCL* (1991). Blake, A. *Southerly* (December 1993). Blake, A. *Durham University Journal* (1994). Brown, D. *ALS* (October 1987). Brydon, D. *ArielE* (October 1986). Brydon, D. *ANZSC* (Fall 1989). Burns, D. R. *Meanjin* (September 1986). Carter, A. *LRB* (16 September–6 October 1982). Chisholm, A. *National Times* (29 March–4 April 1981). Clancy, L. *ALS* (October 1982). Dobrez, L. A. *RNL* (1982). Drewe, R. *Scripsi* (July 1986). Duffy, J. *Antipodes* (Spring 1990). Durix, J. P. *JCL* (1986). Evans, P. *SPAN* (April 1982). Fagan, R. *PR* (1979). Gardiner, J. K. *North American Review* (1977). Garner, H. *Scripsi* (July 1986). Geering, R. G. *Southerly* (1962, 1978, 1984, 1987, 1990, 1991). Green, D. *Meanjin* (1968). Gribble, J. *Southerly* (September 1987). Hardwick, E. *New Republic* (1 August 1955). Harris, M. *Meridian* (October 1989). Harris, M. *Southerly* (September 1989, December 1993). Howarth, R. G. *Biblionews* (January 1958). Kellaway, F. *Overland* (July 1986). Leggott, M. *WLWE* (Winter 1984). Lilley, K. *Southerly* (December 1993). Macainsh, N. *Westerly* (December 1987). Mansfield, N. *Southerly* (March 1992). McLaughlin, M. *Ball State University Forum* (1980). Mercer, G. *SPAN* (October 1985). Muncaster, T. *Southerly* (December 1993). Pybus, R. *Stand* (1982). Raskin, J. *London Magazine* (February 1970). Reid, I. *Literary Criterion* (1980). Richlin, A. *TSWL* (Fall 1992). Ross, R. *LCUT* (1988). Rowley, H. *Westerly* (March 1988). Rowley, H. *Meridian* (October 1989). Rowley, H. *ConL* (Winter 1990). Rowley, H. *Southerly* (December 1993). Segerberg, A. *Antipodes* (Spring 1989). Sheridan, S. *Southerly* (December 1993). Wetherell, R. *Overland* (1983). Whitehead, A. *ALS* (May 1974). Wilding, M. *ALS* (October 1983). Williams, C. *Southerly* (March 1993). Woodward, W. *Theoria* (December 1986). Woodward, W. *JLSTL* (March 1988). Woodward, W. *Southerly* (December 1993). Yglesias, J. *Nation* (5 April 1965).

Kate Begnal

Flora Annie Steel

BORN: 2 April 1847, Harrow, Middlesex.
DIED: 12 April 1929, Talgrath, Wales.
DAUGHTER OF: George Webster and Isabella Webster.
MARRIED: Henry Steel, 1867.

The bulk of S.'s work reflected a woman's view of the colonial experience. Altogether thirty-two of her books were published between 1884 and her death in 1929. S. had little or no formal education. Instead, she was allowed free run of her parents' library and the moors and woods surrounding her childhood home in Scotland. She was known in her family for her strong personality and indefatigable energy; when she married at the age of twenty, she left for India with her husband (a newly appointed district officer in the Punjab, now part of Pakistan) within twenty-four hours of the ceremony.

She spent the next twenty-two years as a tireless organizer of community enterprises wherever she or her husband were posted. During these years she acted as medical advisor to the local population, headed health and education committees, designed and sought funding for municipal buildings and improvements, and set up numerous schools for local children. She learned to speak the local language and displayed a genuine if somewhat paternalistic interest in the lives of the people of India, especially the women. S.'s experiences in India gave her a sense of self-sufficiency that encouraged her to take on all kinds of challenges but that also put her at odds with the patriarchal Raj authorities. She supported British rule in India but stated, "My considered opinion is that there is no greater mistake an honest man can make than to hold his tongue regarding error. It stops progress; it is the great curse which underlies democracy." Despite the fact that she was frequently a thorn in the side of the authorities, they appointed her an inspector of schools. Later, in an effort to terminate her tenure, they transferred her husband, but S., stalwart as ever, remained alone in the school district for a further year and a half.

S. began writing short stories reflecting her experiences and collecting Indian folk tales toward the end of her time in India, though only one book was published before she left in 1889. She had a long friendship and business association with the publisher William Heinemann. She wrote copiously and was well received by the British public, becoming somewhat of a literary celebrity and gaining equal popularity with Rudyard Kipling in the London publishers' lists.

Of the numerous novels and short stories she wrote, at least half were concerned with Indian or Anglo-Indian life. Her most famous novel, *On The Face of the Waters* (1896), depicted the so-called Indian Mutiny of 1858, which she felt compelled to write in order to clarify the events for the British public. Much of her writing concerning India was an attempt to educate the British about the culture and customs of the East. One of her themes was that, far from the eastern culture tainting westerners, the effect of western ways on easterners debilitated their traditional culture. She did try to interpret this very different culture by using its own criteria rather than relying on an ethnocentric world view.

S. was an ardent supporter of the suffragist movement, making numerous speeches on its behalf. Though much of her work seems dated to modern readers, repeatedly depending on her protagonists' untimely deaths, several of her novels stand out, notably *Mussamat Kirpo's Doll* (1894) and *The Reformer's Wife* (1903). She wrote several novels of British life, plus historical novels and nonfiction works on India, but she was at her best when depicting Indian life and the colonial experience.

WORKS: *Wide Awake Stories* (1884). *From the Five Rivers* (1893). *Miss Stuart's Legacy* (1893). *The Flower of Forgiveness* (1894). *Mussamat Kirpo's Doll* (1894). *The Potter's Thumb* (1894). *Tales of the Punjab* (1894). *Red Rowans* (1895). *On the Face of the Waters* (1896). *In the Permanent Way and Other Stories* (1897). *In the Tideway* (1897). *The Complete Indian Housekeeper and Cook* (1899). *Voices in the Night* (1900). *The Hosts of the Lord* (1900). *In the Guardianship of God* (1900). *The Reformer's Wife* (1903). *A Book of Mortals* (1905). *India* (1905). *Sovereign Remedy* (1906). *India through the Ages* (1908). *A Prince of Dreamers* (1908). *The Gift of the Gods* (1911). *King Errant* (1912). *The Adventures of Akbar* (1913). *The Mercy of the Lord* (1914). *Marmaduke* (1917). *Mistress of Men* (1917). *English Fairy Tales* (1918). *A Tale of Indian Heroes* (1923). *A Tale of the Tides* (1923). *The Law of the Threshold* (1924). *The Builder* (1928). *The Curse of Eve* (1929). *The Garden of Fidelity* (1929). *The Indian Scene* (1933).

BIBLIOGRAPHY: Collins, J. P. *Bookman* (November 1917). Greenburger, A. *The British Image of India* (1969). Hennessy, R. and R. Mohan. *TexP* (1989). Parry, B. *Delusions and Discoveries* (1972). Patwardham, D. *A Star of India* (1963). Paxton, N. L. *Women's Studies International Forum* (1990). Paxton, N. L., in *The New Nineteenth Century: Feminist Readings of Underread Victorian Fiction*, ed. B. Harman and S. Meyer (1996). Powell, V. *Flora Annie Steel* (1981). Saunders, R., in *Women's Writing in Exile*, ed. M. L. Broe and A. Ingram (1989).

For articles in reference works, see: *Chambers*. *Feminist*. *Longman*. *NCHEL*. *OCEL*. *TCA*. *ToddBWW*.

Other references: *Bookman* (July 1914, June 1923, May 1924).

Hilary Pursehouse

Stella: See *Johnson, Esther*

Stella: See *Johnson, Esther*

Julia Prinsep Stephen

BORN: 7 February 1846, Calcutta, India.
DIED: 5 May 1895, London.
DAUGHTER OF: John Jackson and Maria Pattle Jackson.
MARRIED: Herbert Duckworth, 1867; Leslie Stephen, 1878.
WROTE UNDER: Julia Duckworth Stephen; Mrs. Leslie Stephen.

Best known as the wife of Leslie Stephen, editor of *The Dictionary of National Biography* (*DNB*), and as the mother of Vanessa Bell and Virginia Woolf, S.'s literary career is easily overshadowed by those of her personal relations. As a teenager, S.'s visits to her aunt Julia Cameron's home at Freshwater introduced her to Alfred Lord Tennyson, William MakepeaceThackeray, George Frederic Watts, Holman Hunt, Edward Burne-Jones, William Gladstone, and Benjamin Disraeli. There she served as a model for countless photographs and paintings, such as Burne-Jones's famous *The Annunciation*. Until her writings were compiled by D. F. Gillespie and E. Steele in 1987, however, the importance of S. as a writer, and not just as a model, was not apparent. Arguing with authority on the current issues of her day, from child rearing to nursing the sick, S.'s works discount the voiceless image portrayed by her family and friends.

As the mother of seven children, S. naturally gravitated to children's stories. Although none of these were published during her lifetime, Leslie Stephen's illustration and submission of them to Routledge attests to S.'s view of her enterprise as a professional venture. S. wrote her tales in the heyday of Victorian children's stories. Not surprisingly, her stories share many similarities with Lewis Carroll's "Alice" stories—most notably talking animals, fantastic events, and mischievous children. Furthermore, S.'s stories clearly identify themselves as products of the nineteenth century by their well-plotted schemas and their didactic content.

Among S.'s published items are her entry on Julia Margaret Cameron for her husband's *DNB* (1882) and a tract on nursing the sick, *Notes From Sick Rooms* (1883). Written in response to debates in journals such as *Cornhill* and *Nineteenth Century*, S.'s unpublished essays are of interest to both literary and historical scholars. On issues such as the treatment of servants, agnostic women, and the running of a home, S.'s essays paint a vivid picture of the situation and life-style of the upper-middle-class woman. Although clearly not a feminist (in 1889 S. signed a petition against women's suffrage that appeared in *Nineteenth Century*), S.'s essays argue for the dignity and equality of women's work. S.'s *Notes From Sick Rooms* attempt to professionalize women's activities and serve as a precursor to her daughter Virginia Woolf's "Professions for Women" fifty-nine years later.

The majority of S.'s letters remain unpublished, although some of them are included in *Leslie Stephen's Life in Letters* (1993), and portions of other letters can be glimpsed in Stephen's posthumous tribute to his wife, *The Mausoleum Book* (1977). That Woolf followed in her mother's literary footsteps, writing both children's stories and essays, proves her claim that "we think back through our mothers if we are women" and demonstrates the importance of S.'s influence on both her daughters.

WORKS: "Tommy and His Neighbours"; "The Monkey on the Moor"; "Emlycaunt"; "The Mysterious Voice"; "[Dinner at Baron Bruin's]"; "The Black Cat or the Grey Parrot"; "The Wandering Pigs"; "Cat's Meat"; "The Duke's Coal Cellar" (all between 1880 and 1884). *Notes From Sick Rooms* (1883). "[Agnostic Women]" (1893). "[The Servant Question]" (1893). "[Domestic Arrangements of the Ordinary English Home]" (1893). "Julia Margaret Cameron" (1917). *Selections,* ed. D. F. Gillespie and E. Steele (1987).

BIBLIOGRAPHY: *Julia Duckworth Stephen,* ed. D. F. Gillespie and E. Steele (1987). Maitland, F. W. *The Life and Letters of Leslie Stephen* (1906). Marcus, J., in *Virginia Woolf: Centennial Essays,* ed. E. K. Ginsberg and L. M. Gottlieb (1983). Spalding, F. *Vanessa Bell* (1983). Stemerick, M., in *Virginia Woolf: Centennial Essays,* ed. E. K. Ginsberg and L. M. Gottlieb (1983). Stephen, L., in *The Mausoleum Book,* ed. A. Bell (1977). Stephen, L. *Leslie Stephen's Life in Letters,* ed. G. Fenwhich (1993). Woolf, V. *Moments of Being* (1985).

For articles in reference works, see: *Allibone SUP. BioIn.*

Geneviève Sanchis Morgan

Stephen, Virginia: See *Woolf, Virginia*

Catherine (Catharine), Lady Stepney

BORN: 1785, Grittleton, Wiltshire.
DIED: 14 April 1845, London.
DAUGHTER OF: the Reverend Thomas Pollok and Susannah Palmer Pollok.
MARRIED: C. Russell Manners, 1799 (?); Sir Thomas Stepney, 1813.
WROTE UNDER: Mrs. Manners; Lady Stepney.

S.'s long association with London society found expression in her novels belonging to the "silver-fork" or "fashionable novel" genre that flourished during the first half of the nineteenth century and then reappeared late in the century as part of the "dandy" movement fostered by Oscar Wilde.

According to the anonymous "Memoir of Lady Stepney," S. and her sister, identified only as Mrs. Scottowe, defied their father's attempts to prevent them from becoming "Bluestockings," the latter going so far as to climb in the window of his locked library to read forbidden books. S. reportedly began writing at a very early age.

S. possibly married C. Russell Manners in 1799, since her only child, Russell Henry, was born 30 January 1800. The same anonymous article cited above says she "was married when a mere child [going] from the nursery to the altar." Manners died before 1813, for on 8 June of that year she married Sir Thomas Stepney, who died on 12 September 1825. For the next twenty years, the "pretty, accomplished, and fashionable" S. entertained authors and artists at her home in Cavendish Square, London.

S.'s first two literary efforts were Gothic horror tales. Novels published between 1833 and 1841, however, belong to the genre derisively labeled "Silver-Fork" by William Hazlitt in 1827 and are similar to those being produced at the same time by Catherine Grace Gore, the acknowledged queen of the genre, Benjamin Disraeli, and Edward Bulwer-Lytton, among others. Noted for "the delineation of the gilded absurdity that during the thirties and forties was known as the *ton*" (Sadleir, 1951), these novels described the lives and habits of the nobility and are characterized by extensive use of French phrases, noblemen who appear to be laws unto themselves, and ladies who perpetuate the medieval "damsel in distress" motif. The women are laden with jewels, and caskets filled with priceless gems lie carelessly open. S.'s *The Three Peers* (1841) is a good example of the formula. Lady Beatrix appears at a party, her hair decorated with a headdress composed of expensive pearls. Gwenderline Clairvil, the central figure, waits patiently for her eventual husband, Lord Haldane, to propose. When she is kidnapped by agents of the wicked Duke of Dorringden, Haldane does not seek the aid of the authorities to search for her. Instead, he, Beatrix, and a company of personal retainers rescue her. A curious departure from the formula, however, may be seen in the finely drawn portrayal of Teresa Ibarra, who "had all the daring courage of a man." Teresa's crossdressing, her assertive, even dangerous, nature, and her bravery contrast starkly with the behavior of Gwenderline Clairvil, the alleged heroine, whose most assertive act is to refuse to marry a man she does not love.

S.'s novels provide insights into how and why upper-class marriages were concluded. In *The Three Peers,* for example, Lady Beatrix is in love with her cousin but is encouraged to marry the handsome, debt-ridden Duke of Dorringden, who is willing to marry her (even though he would prefer to marry the penniless Gwenderline) because he needs her wealth to extricate himself from his financial difficulties. Gwenderline adores Lord Haldane, but her grandmother, the dowager countess, insists she marry Prince Herman of Waltenburg, a man she has never met, because of the countess's own familial ties.

Marriage might also be contracted for purposes of revenge and greed. Lady Villetta Delainey, in *The New Road to Ruin* (1833), endures her family's persecution for four years before agreeing to marry Lord Darmaya, a much older man, whose sole motivation for this marriage is to prevent his heir from inheriting his wealth. (It is worth noting that at his death, Sir Thomas Stepney was sixty-five years old, twenty-five years older than his wife.) The stigma attached to marrying "beneath one's station" is expressed in *The Three Peers* in the description of Gwenderline Clairvil's mother, "an obscure and unknown person." The fact that her mother was well-educated, respectable, and devoted to her husband means little to Gwenderline's noble relatives who have long since disowned her father for his folly.

Despite an early review (1806) that pronounced *Castle Nuovier* "tolerably well written," S. had a reputation as a careless author. Barbara Hofland and Mary Russell Mitford both commented in correspondence that Letitia Elizabeth Landon had to rewrite S.'s manuscripts. Concerning *The Heir-Presumptive* (1835), Hofland wrote to Mitford on 6 July 1835: "I find Miss Landon wrote Lady Stepney's book. . . . She had a hundred pounds and grumbles much, as she says it took her more time than writing a new one would" (quoted in Sadleir, 1951). Mitford, in a letter to Elizabeth Barrett three years later, made a similar remark about *The Courtier's Daughter* (1838): "The things that go under Lady Stepney's title were all written by Miss Landon, or the grammar and spelling would have disgraced a lady's maid. This is a want of self-respect which one can not pardon; and, coupled with other facts of a similar nature, they explain my distaste toward her as a sister authoress" (29 [?] September 1838; quoted in Kelly and Hudson, 1984). *Bentley's Private Catalogue* confirms Landon's participation by acknowledging that she edited *The Heir-Presumptive* and *The Courtier's Daughter.*

Copies of S.'s books today are difficult to obtain, yet, if considered according to the genre to which they belong, they possess a certain charm and are quite entertaining.

WORKS: *Castle Nuovier, Or Henry and Adelina* (1806). *The Lords of Erith* (1809). (as Lady Stepney) *The New Road to Ruin* (1833). *The Heir-Presumptive* (1835). *The Courtier's Daughter* (1838). *The Three Peers* (1841).

BIBIOGRAPHY:

For articles in reference works, see: *Allibone*. Block, A. *The English Novel, 1740–1850* (1939, 1963). *Boase* (under "Russell Henry Manners"). *DNB. OCEL.* Sutherland, J. *The Standard Companion to Victorian Fiction* (1989; under "Mrs. Catherine Manners"). *VB* (under "Silver-Fork Novel").

Other references: *Athenaeum* (12 December 1840). *Bentley's Private Catalogue* (1835). *Gentleman's Magazine* (September 1825, July 1845). *The Brownings' Correspondence, Vol. 4,* ed. P. Kelly and R. Hudson (1984). *Literary Gazette* (19 April 1845). *Literary Journal* (June 1806). "Memoirs of Lady Stepney" (n.d.). *Monthly Literary Recreations* (August 1806). *New Monthly Magazine* (1837). Rosa, M. W. *The Silver-Fork School* (1936). Sadleir, M. *XIX Fiction: A Bibliographical Record* (1951).

Natalie Joy Woodall

G[ladys]. B[ertha]. Stern

BORN: 17 June 1890, London.
DIED: 19 September 1973, Wallingford, Berkshire.
DAUGHTER OF: Albert Stern and Elizabeth Schwabacher Stern.
MARRIED: Geoffrey Lisle Holdsworth, 1919.

The reprinting in the 1980s of such novels as *The Matriarch, A Deputy Was King,* and *The Ugly Dachshund* may signal a renewed interest in this prolific and once-popular writer.

The second daughter of Albert and Elizabeth Stern, S. later changed her middle name to Bronwyn but was known in her writing career as G. B. Stern and to her friends as Peter. After leaving Notting Hill High School at the age of sixteen (the family had suffered financial losses two years earlier), she traveled with her parents and attended schools in Germany and Switzerland; she also studied acting for two years at the Academy of Dramatic Art in London. In 1919, S. married Geoffrey Lisle Holdsworth, a New Zealander; in his memoir, *Present Indicative,* Noël Coward claims indirect responsibility for the marriage (which ended in divorce): He introduced Holdsworth to some of S.'s books and letters.

Although she called herself a "thoroughly lazy person," S. produced a large body of work, including short stories, plays, novels, memoirs, and critical studies, dictating to a secretary and working regularly from 10 A.M. until 1 P.M, and sometimes after tea, but never at night.

S. began writing while young and published her first novel, *Pantomime,* in 1914; *Twos and Threes* (1916) was her first book to draw notice. Her reputation rests largely on a series of novels about the Rakonitz family, loosely based on her own Jewish relatives. The first two novels, *Children of No Man's Land* (1919; in the U.S. as *Debatable Ground,* 1921) and *Tents of Israel* (1924; in the U.S. as *The Matriarch,* 1925), were adapted in 1929 for a stage production, *The Matriarch,* featuring Mrs. Patrick Campbell. *Tents of Israel, A Deputy Was King* (1926), and *Mosaic* (1930) were later published as *The Rakonitz Chronicles* (1932). In 1935, S. published another in the series, *Shining and Free,* which was later included with the three previously collected Rakonitz novels in an omnibus volume titled *The Matriarch Chronicles* (1936). *The Young Matriarch* (1942), dedicated to that other chronicler of family life, John Galsworthy, continued the Rakonitz saga. In spite of *The Matriarch*'s popularity, S. declared that she was not particularly fond of the novel, because her great-aunt, Anastasia Schwabacher, the inspiration for the title character, was "too despotic" for S.'s tastes. She preferred *No Son of Mine* (1948), her novel based on the life of Robert Louis Stevenson, a writer she admired, and also declared her satisfaction with *The Rueful Mating* (1932), *Ten Days of Christmas* (1950), and her later memoirs.

S.'s dramatic works include *Debonair* (1930), written with Frank Vosper, an English actor, and based on her 1928 novel of the same name, and *The Man Who Pays the Piper,* a play consisting of a prologue and three acts, which was produced at London's St. Martin's Theatre in 1931;

she also assisted Noël Coward in choosing the songs used in *Cavalcade*. S.'s theatrical interests extended to film: Her novels *Long-Lost Father* (1932), *The Ugly Dachshund* (1938), and *The Woman in the Hall* (1939) were made into feature films, and S. herself worked on screenplays for *Little Women, The Last Days of Pompeii*, and *Men Are Not Gods*. In addition to numerous short stories and novels (some, like *The Dark Gentleman*, 1927, featuring animal characters), S. wrote critical studies of Robert Louis Stevenson and Somerset Maugham, edited works of Stevenson and Jane Austen, and, with her friend Sheila Kaye-Smith, produced *Talking of Jane Austen* (1943; in the U.S. as *Speaking of Jane Austen*, 1944) and *More About Jane Austen* (1949; in the U.S. as *More Talk of Jane Austen*, 1950).

S.'s chatty memoirs—*Monogram* (1936), *Another Part of the Forest* (1941), *Trumpet Voluntary* (1944), *Benefits Forgot* (1949), and *A Name to Conjure With* (1953)—depict an active life among the London literati. Her conversion to Roman Catholicism in 1947 inspired two more memoirs, *All in Good Time* (1954) and *The Way It Worked Out* (1957).

In her obituary, the *Times* (London) declared S. "a fluent, animated and accomplished writer" whose later writing "did not quite live up to the promise of her work in the early 1920s." Still, S.'s works are often bright, witty, and sophisticated. Her Rakonitz novels continue to engage readers in part because of the increasing independence of the novels' female protagonists. S.'s short stories often make use of clever twists of plot, and her memoirs command the attention of readers interested in S.'s spiritual pilgrimage and her lifelong friendships with prominent Londoners.

WORKS: *Pantomime: A Novel* (1914). *See-Saw* (1914). *Twos and Threes* (1916). *Grand Chain* (1917). *A Marrying Man* (1918). *Children of No Man's Land* (1919; in the U.S. as *Debatable Ground*, 1921). *Larry Munro* (1920; in the U.S. as *The China Shop*, 1921). *The Room* (1922). *Smoke Rings* (1923). *The Back Seat* (1923). *Tents of Israel: A Chronicle* (1924; in the U.S. as *The Matriarch: A Chronicle*, 1925). *Thunderstorm* (1925). *A Deputy Was King* (1926). (with G. Holdsworth) *The Happy Meddler* (1926). *Jack a' Manory* (1927; in the U.S. as *The Slower Judas*, 1929). *The Dark Gentleman* (1927). *Bouquet* (1927). (with F. Vosper) *Debonair: The Story of Persephone* (1928). *Petruchio* (1929; in the U.S. as *Modesta*). *Mosaic* (1930). *The Shortest Night* (1931). *The Man Who Pays the Piper* (1931). *The Rakonitz Chronicles* (1932). *Little Red Horses* (1932). *The Rueful Mating* (1932). *Long-Lost Father: A Comedy* (1932). *The Augs: An Exaggeration* (1933). *Summer's Play: An Exaggeration* (1934). *Pelican Walking: Short Stories* (1934). *Shining and Free: A Day in the Life of the Matriarch* (1935). *The Matriarch Chronicles* (1936). *Monogram* (1936). *Oleander River* (1937). *The Ugly Dachshund* (1938). *The Woman in the Hall* (1939). *A Lion in the Garden* (1940). *Another Part of the Forest* (1941). *Dogs in an Omnibus* (1942; contains *The Dark Gentleman, Toes Unmasked, The Ugly Dachshund*). *The Young Matriarch* (1942). (with S. Kaye-Smith) *Talking of Jane Austen* (1943; in the U.S. as *Speaking of Jane Austen*, 1944). *Trumpet Voluntary* (1944). *The Reasonable Shores* (1946). *No Son of Mine* (1948). *A Duck to Water* (1949). (with S. Kaye-Smith) *More About Jane Austen* (1949; in the U.S. as *More Talk of Jane Austen*, 1950). *Benefits Forgot* (1949). *Ten Days of Christmas* (1950). (with R. Croft-Cooke) *Gala Night at "The Willows": A Comedy in One Act* (1950). *Thunderstorm* (1951). *Robert Louis Stevenson* (1952). *He Wrote "Treasure Island": The Story of Robert Louis Stevenson* (1954; in the U.S. as *Robert Louis Stevenson, The Man Who Wrote "Treasure Island": A Biography*). *The Donkey Shoe* (1952). *A Name to Conjure With* (1953). *Johnny Forsaken* (1954). *All in Good Time* (1954). *For All We Know* (1956). *The Way It Worked Out* (1957). *And Did He Stop and Speak to You?* (1957). *Seventy Times Seven, A Novel* (1957). *Unless I Marry* (1959). *One Is Only Human* (1960). *Dolphin Cottage* (1962). *Promise Not to Tell* (1964).

BIBLIOGRAPHY: Showalter, E. *A Literature of Their Own*.

For articles in reference works, see: *Bloomsbury*. *Feminist*. *LA*. *Oxford*. *TCA* and *SUP*. *Webster's Biographical Dictionary*. *WWWiL*. *Who Was Who in the Theatre*.

Anita G. Gorman

Anne Stevenson

BORN: 3 January 1933, Cambridge.
DAUGHTER OF: Charles Leslie Stevenson and Louise Destler Stevenson.
MARRIED: R. L. Hitchcock, 1955; Mark Elvin, 1962; Michael Farley, 1984; Peter Lucas, 1987.

S. was born in Cambridge in 1933 when her father, the American philosopher C. L. Stevenson (*Ethics and Language*), was studying there. Her birthplace appears to have been determinative. Like Henry James and H. D. (Hilda Doolittle), she has become an American writer unable to live in America. Although educated in Ann Arbor, Michigan, she has lived all of her adult life in England, Scotland, and Wales. She settled for ten years near Durham in an ex-mining village before moving to North Wales in 1992. Her present choice of rural life, trying, as she says, "to keep away from 'fame' and 'personalities,'" manifests values evidently formed during childhood summers in Vermont: personal reticence and appreciation of natural locale while perceiving its multiple significations. These qualities characterize her poetry from early and late.

S. began writing poetry with Donald Hall when she was a graduate student at the University of Michigan (B.A. 1954, M.A. 1962). Her first book of poems, *Living in America*, appeared in 1965. Of the recognition of her abilities, she says: "I won three Hopwood Awards in Poetry at the University of Michigan in the 1950s, but not many awards since, apart from three grants from the British Arts Councils in Scotland, Wales and the South. I am a Fellow of the Royal Society of Literature . . . was on the Arts Council Advisory Board for Literature and on the Poetry Book Society's Board of Management. Have been Northern Arts Literary Fellow at Durham and Newcastle Universities,

1981–82 and 1984–85." She was a Fellow at the Radcliffe Institute for Independent Women in 1970–71, Fellow (in arts) of Lady Margaret Hall, Oxford, in 1975–77, and recipient of the Athena (alumnae) Award from the University of Michigan in 1990. She has a daughter from her first marriage and two sons from her second.

Tension between domesticity and need for larger scope is strong in her early volume, *Reversals* (1969), which includes poems from *Living in America.* Marriage, pregnancy, and motherhood claustrophobically enclose the poet but also force her "outside" those parameters. Yet joy often prevails over negativity, as in "The Victory," written after childbirth: "Snail! Scary knot of desires! / Hungry snarl! Small son. / Why do I have to love you? How have you won?" In "On Not Being Able to Look at the Moon," she warns herself against pathetic fallacy, "a mania for / stealing moonlight and transforming it into my own pain." Here she defines the poetic stance that continues throughout her career: The world is self-existent, to be observed with accuracy and delight, not to be appropriated by ego. Therefore, the poem itself, she notes in "Morning," is "not made but discovered."

S.'s major strength lies in this discovery of the poem in the place. She persistently finds the natural world a rich "objective correlative" for both her emotions and her intelligence. In her poems, therefore, description and commentary subtly blend, as in "England": "The paths are dry, the ponds dazed with reflections. A pearly contamination strokes the river / As the cranes ride or dissolve in it." Contrapuntal to "England" is "Sierra Nevada," a poem evoking that very American mountain range: "Landscape without regrets whose weakest junipers / strangle and split granite, whose hard, clean light / is utterly without restraint." Like her close contemporary, Sylvia Plath, she adheres to rhyming forms, often self-designed, flexible, and slant, and to intense metaphor, modalities that pay homage to the similarly stringent forms of the world. Her poems are tight yet detailed, even explanatory in her use of her favored syntactic form, the declarative sentence. She is honest, working hard not to mislead or be misunderstood.

In the 1970s, her formal concerns expanded to include more experimentation. Ambition to combine prose and poetry produced *Correspondence: A Family History in Letters* (1974). Tracing evolution of attitudes through six generations, these poem-epistles reveal interrelationships between members of the Chandler family of Clearfield, Vermont. The revelations of this family, which resembles S.'s own, paint a broad historical portrait of nineteenth-century America's influence on the twentieth century. The ancestors' greed, intolerance, sexual repression, and misplaced religion have bred broken family ties, anger, uncertainty, and death-consciousness in the modern descendents. *Travelling Behind Glass: Selected Poems 1963–1973* (1974) emphasizes "glass" as both barrier between self and world and transmitter of light to see that world, although glass is what also shatters and cuts one open, admitting mingled hope and pain. In *Enough of Green* (1977), she grapples with difficult experiences by presenting the stark landscapes of Scotland where "salt-worried faces" and "an absence of trees" abound. Loneliness and transience continue as themes, expressed by indicative titles: "Temporarily in Oxford," "Hotel in the City," "Goodbye! Goodbye!" Darkness, ruins, and abandoned houses preoccupy her; to live amid greenery and comfort appears a suspect luxury.

The contrast—even struggle—betweeen "green" and "black" also dominates *Minute by Glass Minute* (1982), written after the poet had moved to Hay-on-Wye in Wales; these colors take on personal symbolic meanings. "Green Mountain, Black Mountain" is an elegy, cantata-like in form, to her dead parents, especially to her father, who had made music central in the family. The poem resolves in a coda uniting the United States, the New World of the private past—Vermont's green mountains—with the Old World and its collective myths, signified by the black mountains of Wales and the harsh beauties of its wind, soil, and birdsong. "Like *Correspondences,*" she says of this book, "it was an attempt to come to terms with the present, make the Atlantic crossing."

In S.'s 1985 volume, *The Fiction-Makers,* elegies to the dead also appear. Although informed by sadness and loss, these poems become celebration; wreckage and energy coexist in them. On the damaged terrain of old mine-pits she observes that lush wildflowers have grown; thus the breakdown of her illusions has rejuvenated her psychic landscape. This book, she says, "is an effort to disencumber myself of the illusion of believing in my own 'story.'" The themes of doubt in her own "story," relentless self-evaluation, and meditations re-creating the past in present places closely observed deepen in her 1990 collection, *The Other House.* She increasingly opposes present-day degraded ideas and artifacts of "The Mass, The Media, the Market," as her poem by that title shows in its satiric despairing defiance. In "Journal Entry: Impromptu in C Minor," Schubert's piano piece takes her back to childhood, when she played it on the piano. She looks at herself as that young girl who "died . . . to make room for the woman I am now. / . . . She doesn't know yet she will be deaf. / She doesn't yet know how deaf she's been." Increasing deafness has come on her as she grows older, a highly ironical loss for a poet and musician.

Despite her self-accusation, however, there is no moral "deafness" or insensitivity to others in her work. Her handicap has sharpened her consciousness of pain, which leads her to sympathetic re-creation of the sufferings of old age in *Four and Half Dancing Men* (1993). In several poems, she adopts the personae of helpless memoryless women in nursing homes, as in "Mrs. Meredith," who knows her name only because she reads it on her medical tag. In "A Sepia Garden," S.'s own voice registers her torn feelings as she pushes the wheelchair of her old and very ill mother-in-law, Mary Lucas, to whom the book is dedicated. The poem's italicized sections quote the old woman and testify to her admirable qualities while also revealing her irritating habits as well. After leaving the old woman weeping in the nursing home, S.'s emotions as she witnesses such profound loss of "self" are almost unbearable. The title poem of this book, by contrast, focuses on youth in the person of S.'s small grandson, whom one knows she loved as she loved her infant son in her early poem. The grandson is sick in bed: "So cross. So bored. For / all that, a little blond god, / with the shifting realm / of his risen knees to govern." His mother cuts out for his entertainment a paper chain of five dancing men. He tears one of them in half, an act that pleases him: "the same / can be done with the rest. / Four blind men, and a half unafraid, unafraid." These final lines suggest symbolic overtones to the innocently unsocialized child's act of governance over his "realm." They symbolically suggest an ominous future for the world: To many national leaders, the millions of human beings whom they govern exist only as paper playthings that caprice can destroy and forget.

This poet has maintained from the beginning of her career a formal integrity and remarkable personal commitment, aspects of the "genuine" praised by T. S. Eliot in Marianne Moore. Now S.'s steadfast mirroring of the world and her own mind has added another dimension: prophetic vision. Her poetry altogether represents one of the most solid achievements in contemporary British letters.

WORKS: *Living in America* (1965). *Elizabeth Bishop* (1966). *Reversals* (1969). *Correspondence: A Family History in Letters* (1974). *Travelling Behind Glass: Selected Poems 1963–1973* (1994). *Correspondences* (radio play, 1975). *Child of Adam* (radio play, 1976). *Enough of Green* (1977). (with others) *A Morden Tower Reading 3* (1977). *Cliff Walk* (1977). *Minute by Glass Minute* (1982). *The Fiction-Makers* (1985). *Winter Time* (1986). *Selected Poems* (1987). *Bitter Fame* (biography, 1989). *The Other House* (1990). *Four and a Half Dancing Men* (1993). *Collected Poems 1955–1995* (1997).

BIBLIOGRAPHY:

For articles in reference works, see: *Bloomsbury*. *CA* (mistakenly attributes to Stevenson three novels by another author with the same name). *Cambridge*. *CLC*. *CP*. *Feminist*. *International Who's Who in Poetry*, ed. E. Kay (1972). *WD*.

Other references: *Encounter* (December 1974). *Five Modern Poets* (1993). *Lines Review* (1974). *Listener* (28 November 1974). *London Magazine* (October-November 1974). *KR* (1987). *MQR* (1966, 1971, and 1995). *The New Review* (London, October 1974). *Open Places* (Spring/Summer 1976). *Ploughshares* (Autumn 1978). *PNR* (1993, 1994). *Poetry* (February 1971, November 1975). *PoetryR* (1994). *Poetry Wales* (1990).

Jane Augustine

Mary (Florence Elinor) Stewart

BORN: 17 September 1916, Sunderland, County Durham.
DAUGHTER OF: Frederick Albert Rainbow and Mary Edith Matthews Rainbow.
MARRIED: Frederick Henry Stewart, 1945.

Educated at the University of Durham, S. received her B. A. with first class honors in 1938, a teaching diploma in 1939, and her M. A. in 1941. In 1945, she married Frederick H. Stewart, a lecturer in geology, and continued her own teaching career. She began writing in 1949 but did not give up her university career in favor of fulltime writing until 1956, at which time she moved to Edinburgh, Scotland, where her husband became Regius professor of geology at the University of Edinburgh.

Her first book, *Madam, Will You Talk?*, was an instant success at its appearance in 1955. In this work, she found her original formula for popular romantic thrillers, which she repeated with variations in her next several novels, all of which exhibit an appealing combination of mystery, adventure, romance, and poetic description. Each novel is narrated by the feminine protagonist, a young woman, independent and self-supporting, usually traveling abroad either on vacation or on business when she finds herself caught up in a dangerous criminal intrigue. Each novel is set in a vividly depicted locale, often somewhere on the Continent. Both *Madam, Will You Talk?* and *Nine Coaches Waiting* (1956) are set in France, the first related by a young widow on vacation, the latter by a governess assuming a post, an orphan whose plight recalls that of Jane Eyre. *My Brother Michael* (1959), winner of the British Crime Writers Association Award, is set in Greece, and *The Moon Spinners* (1962), which was made into a Hollywood film, is set in Crete. *This Rough Magic*, winner of the Mystery Writers of America Award for 1964, is set in Corfu, which functions in the novel as the assumed island setting of William Shakespeare's *The Tempest*. S.'s interest in Shakespeare is also reflected in *Touch Not the Cat* (1976), which is sprinkled with subtly relevant references to *Romeo and Juliet*.

In 1970, S. deviated from the Gothic romance format with *The Crystal Cave*, a work of historical fiction with elements of fantasy. This novel was the first of a trilogy based on the life of the legendary medieval wizard Merlin, who also serves as first-person narrator. The second volume, *The Hollow Hills* (1973), continues Merlin's account to the coronation of Arthur, while the final volume, *The Last Enchantment* (1979), completes the wizard's career, ending with his magically induced sleep at the hands of the enchantress Nimue. Throughout the trilogy, the emphasis is on an historically accurate depiction of life in fifth-century Roman Britain. The central figure of Merlin is, in effect, demythologized from his traditional role as archetypal wizard to the portrayal of a complex, sympathetic human being, gifted only with skills of prophecy. A sequel to the trilogy, *The Wicked Day* (1983), focuses on the Arthurian villain, Mordred.

S. has also written two children's books, *The Little Broomstick* (1971) and *Ludo and the Star Horse* (1974), which won the Scottish Arts Council Award. Her most recent works of adult fiction are *Thornyhold* (1989) and *Stormy Petrel* (1994).

Almost all of S.'s novels have been best sellers. They have also been serialized, broadcast, and translated into sixteen languages, including Finnish, Portugese, Hebrew, and Icelandic. Distinguished by their literary quality, these highly successful novels elude classification among the popular genres they so skillfully blend.

WORKS: *Madam, Will You Talk?* (1955). *Nine Coaches Waiting* (1956). *Wildfire at Midnight* (1956). *Thunder on the Right* (1957). *My Brother Michael* (1959). *The Ivy Tree* (1961). *The Moon Spinners* (1962). *This Rough Magic* (1964). *Airs Above the Ground* (1965). *The Gabriel Hounds* (1967). *The Crystal Cave* (1970). *The Little Broomstick* (1971). *The Hollow Hills* (1973). *Ludo and the Star Horse* (1974). *Touch Not the Cat* (1976). *The Last*

Enchantment (1979). *The Wicked Day* (1983). *Thornyhold* (1989). *Stormy Petrel* (1994).

BIBLIOGRAPHY: *Signs de Roman, Signes de la Transition,* ed. J. Bessiere (1986). *Comparative Studies in Merlin from the Vedas to C. G. Jung,* ed. J. Gollnick (1991). Kobler, T. S., in *The Arthurian Myth of Quest and Magic: A Festschrift in Honor of Lavon B. Fulwiler,* ed. W. E. Tanner (1993).

For articles in reference works, see: *CA. CLC. SATA. TCC&MW. TCRGW. TCW. WA.*

Other references: Watson, J. *Arthurian Studies* (1987).

Charlotte Spivack

Stickney, Sarah: See *Ellis, Sarah Stickney*

Agnes Strickland

BORN: 19 August 1796, London.
DIED: 13 July 1874, Southwold, Suffolk.
DAUGHTER OF: Thomas Strickland and Elizabeth Homer.

S. is best known as the historian of the queens of England, although she wrote a number of other volumes of history as well as tales and poetry. She was the first female British historian to be widely respected both at home and abroad. S.'s biographical works reflect both the strengths and weaknesses of nineteenth-century history writing and interpretation.

S. was the second of six daughters; she and her older sister Elizabeth were educated by their father, a landed gentleman of Suffolk. He forbade their reading plays or novels; instead he taught them mathematics and organized reading history and poetry in English, Latin, Greek, French, and Italian. Her father died in 1818, having lost most of his fortune; the daughters, who had already begun to write, turned more seriously to this means of increasing their income. Four of S.'s sisters also published, but she was the best known.

S.'s first published work was *Monody on the Death of the Princess Charlotte,* which appeared anonymously in the *Norwich Mercury* in 1817. She and her sisters Elizabeth, Jane Margaret, and Susanna produced several short works for children. S. contributed to various magazines and in 1827 published two volumes of verse. Elizabeth, who was editor of *The Court Magazine,* and S. collaborated on several volumes of historical tales for children in the 1830s; S. by herself wrote another, *The Pilgrims of Walsingham* (1835).

The attractions of history and royal biography led the sisters to write *The Lives of the Oueens of England* (1840–48). Although they shared the authorship nearly equally, only S.'s name appeared on the title page. In 1840, she also published a brief biography of Queen Victoria, based on inaccurate gossip. The queen was not at all pleased, despite earlier permission to dedicate *The Lives of the Queens* to her. S.'s real interest was in the years before 1800; she was especially devoted to the Stuarts. Her partisanship is evident in *Letters of Mary Stuart* (1842–43) and *Lives of the Queens of Scotland* (1850–59). In addition, S. and her sister published volumes on the bachelor kings of England (1861), the *Seven Bishops* (1866), and the Tudor and Stuart princesses (1867 and 1870). The sisters lived and worked together in London and after 1864 in Southwold. S. predeceased Elizabeth by only a year.

S. seemed to have been responsible for most of the research for the works on the queens and other royal personages. Though in no way sympathetic to the usual aims of feminists, she saw no reason she should not be allowed to use the public, royal, and private archives along with male researchers. After some initial resistance to the idea of a woman historian, various collections both in Britain and on the Continent were opened to S. The success of the first volumes of the *Queens* made work on later publications easier. The methods and results of S.'s research were as good as those of other historians of the time. They relied as much as possible on manuscript material and contemporary records of various kinds, and their volumes of biography went through a number of editions. S. was criticized by contemporaries primarily for her devotion to the Stuarts, her Tory interpretation, and for including gossip and domestic detail. Later readers may find the volumes burdened with more political information than modern social history regards as necessary. They remain an easily accessible repository for details and facts.

WORKS: *Monody on the Death of the Princess Charlotte* (1817). *Guthred: The Widow's Slave* (1821). *The Tell-Tale* (1823). *Prejudice Reproved or the Young Emigrants* (1825). *The Juvenile Forget-Me-Not* (1827). *Worcester Field or the Cavalier* (1827). *The Seven Ages of Woman* (1827). (with E. Strickland) *Historical Tales of Illustrious British Children* (1833). *The Pilgrims of Walsingham* (1835). (with E. Strickland) *Tales and Stories from History* (1836). *Queen Victoria from her Birth to her Bridal* (1840). (with E. Strickland) *The Lives of the Queens of England,* 12 vols. (1840–48). *The British Captive* (1841). *Letters of Mary Stuart* (1842–43). *The Royal Sisters* (1849). (with E. Strickland) *Lives of the Queens of Scotland,* 8 vols. (1850–59). *Historic Scenes and Poetic Fancies* (1850). *Old Friends and New Acquaintances* (1860). (with E. Strickland) *Lives of the Bachelor Kings of England* (1861). *Althea Woodville or How Will it End?* (1864). *Seven Bishops* (1866). (with E. Strickland) *Lives of the Tudor Princesses* (1867). *Lives of the Last Four Princesses of the House of Stuart* (1870). *St. Edmund, the last King of East Anglia* (1871).

BIBLIOGRAPHY: Peterman, M. *CanL* (1989). Pope-Hennessy, U. *Agnes Strickland, Biographer of the Queens of England, 1796–1894* (1940). Smith, B. G. *American Historical Review* (1984). Strickland, J. M. *Life of Agnes Strickland* (1887).

For articles in reference works, see: *DNB. Oxford.*

Barbara Brandon Schnorrenberg

Jan Struther

BORN: 6 June 1901, London.
DIED: 20 July 1953, New York City, United States.
DAUGHTER OF: Henry Torrens Anstruther and Eva Anstruther.

MARRIED: Anthony Maxtone Graham, 1923; Adolf Kurt Placzek, 1948.

WROTE UNDER: Maxtone Graham, Joyce Anstruther, Jan Struther

Known almost exclusively as the author of one book, *Mrs. Miniver* (1939), S. was married first to the son of a senior member of an Edinburgh law firm and then, following her move to the United States in 1940 with two of her three children, to a librarian at Columbia University in New York City. She lectured extensively in the United States during World War II for the British War Relief fund and appeared on the radio program "Information Please."

Mrs. Miniver was a phenomenon: a Book-of-the-Month selection, a bestseller, and in 1942 an Academy Award-winning movie. The sketches about English family life just before the onset of World War II that comprise *Mrs. Miniver* were first published in the *London Times* and remain a charming evocation of country houses, leather engagement books, drawing rooms, and parlor maids, a world largely gone from both the United States and Great Britain. It captured the mundane, day-by-day events in a typical middle-class household in England that included Nannie, Mrs. Adie (a Scots cook), Gladys (the house parlormaid), and, on occasion, Mrs. Burchett (to help with the "washing-up" at dinner parties). Mrs. Miniver herself, beguiling and charming, lives in a world of appointment books and drawing rooms and a country house named "Starling"; her sons attend Eton; she drives up to Scotland in the summer. Yet her perceptions are as apt today as when the book was published, suggesting that the book has a timeless quality unlike that of many other bestsellers.

S. was also a poet with a darker, grimmer vision that she displayed effectively in *The Glass Blower* (1940). Stephen Vincent Benét observed that S. preferred to write poetry in possible reaction to the public's inability to distinguish S.'s own life from that of Mrs. Miniver. Indeed, S. grew so "heartily sick" of *Mrs. Miniver* that when a contest was announced for the best parody of the book, she wrote a "cruel" parody, submitted it under a pen-name, and won the prize, subsequently donating the prize money to an organization for "distressed gentlewomen."

S. also wrote essays for *Punch* and *The Spectator*, which were collected in *Try Anything Twice* (1938), and several collections of light verse. She never escaped the fame of her best character and best-known work, however, and will always be identified more for *Mrs. Miniver* than for any of her other books.

WORKS: *Betsinda Dances and Other Poems* (1931). *Sycamore Square and Other Verses* (1931). *The Modern Struwwelpeter* (1936). *When Grandmamma Was Small* (1937). *Try Anything Twice* (1938). *Mrs. Miniver* (1939). *The Glass Blower and Other Poems* (1940). *Pocketful of Pebbles* (1946).

BIBLIOGRAPHY:

For articles in reference works, see: *Authors' and Writers' Who's Who*. *CB*. *Feminist*. *Longman*. *Oxford*. *TWA* and *SUP*.

Other references: *Book-of-the-Month Club News* (July 1940). *LonT* (21 July 1953). *New York Herald-Tribune* (25 July 1940). *NYHTBR* (13 October 1940, 2 August 1953). *NYT* (21 July 1953). *NYTBR* (25 August 1940). *Spectator* (24 July 1953). *Time* (4 August 1940). Van Gelder, R. *Writers and Writing* (1946).

Mickey Pearlman
(updated by Abby H. P. Werlock)

Louisa Stuart

BORN: 1757, London.

DIED: 1851, London.

DAUGHTER OF: John, third Earl of Bute, and Mary, Countess of Bute.

Born the eleventh child of an embittered and repudiated politician, S. spent a lonely childhood in the isolated country house at Luton, where her father retired from public life to botanize in solitude. As an adult she made regular visits to Scotland to visit friends in the country outside Edinburgh and Glasgow. Her grandmother was the famous (or infamous) Bluestocking Lady Mary Wortley Montagu. Although S. never knew this grandmother, she was subjected to cruel remonstrances from her brothers and sisters whenever she displayed any signs of intellectual or literary inclinations; the family decidedly did not wish to foster any real or fancied inherited tendencies. Thus S. learned to read surreptitiously and to write in secret.

Fascinated by the political and literary worlds barred to her by class and gender, S. read widely but willingly adhered to the code of conduct for an aristocratic lady, which prohibited publishing one's work or participating publicly in literary or political controversy. To find an outlet for these interests, she developed a wide correspondence with various men of influence and discussed national affairs with a large group of friends and relatives spanning several generations. Consistent with those loyalties to family and class that she cherished throughout her long life, her political views remained steadfastly Tory, although she balanced political conservatism with an instinctive human sympathy for people of all classes so long as they remained well-behaved.

Until Lady Bute died in 1794, S. served as companion to her mother. Then she made her home in London, leaving frequently for prolonged visits to various country houses from which she wrote many of her finest letters. Financially secure although far from wealthy, S. never married; she lived the leisured life of an independent gentlewoman, enlivened by an extraordinary genius for friendship and an all-embracing intellectual curiosity. She died at the age of ninety-four, afflicted by deafness and rheumatism but otherwise in full possession of her faculties.

S. is best known through her connection with Sir Walter Scott. Their correspondence reveals a friendship founded in mutual esteem and affection and shows her to be a brilliantly perceptive literary critic whose opinions Scott highly regarded. There are also two volumes of letters to Louisa Clinton (written 1817–34, published 1901–03), a younger woman whose character and opinions S. nurtured. Always conscious of the need for self-discipline, especially in women, she counsels Clinton against reverie and the excesses of self-consciousness and repeatedly urges her pupil to acquaint herself with all sides of a given issue. Although she did not regard herself as a feminist, S. laments woman's "natural dependence" on man and expresses considerable contempt for the male preference for silly women of weak intellect. An earlier collection of letters to her favorite sister (Lady Portarlington) shows her rapid intellectual growth and the strategies she employed to reconcile herself to the limitations imposed on her life by class and gender.

Although her letters are engaging and at times exceedingly funny, S. is at her best as a writer of memoirs. Her *Memoir of John, Duke of Argyll* includes a hilarious portrait of her father's cousin, Lady Mary Coke, whose ridiculous self-dramatizations and imaginary conspiracies rendered her the dread of the entire family and the object of their scorn. Even while deftly sketching Lady Mary's bizarre behavior, however, S.'s sympathy remains active, and the finished character's frailties emerge as both devastatingly funny and frighteningly human. The "Introductory Anecdotes" to *The Letters and Works of Lady Mary Wortley Montagu* and the *Memoire of Frances, Lady Douglas* further demonstrate S.'s talent to be simultaneously respectful and candid in a memoir. This approach also informs her "Notes" to J. H. Jesse's *George Selwyn and His Contemporaries,* which she drew from her customary sources of personal recollection and remembered ancedotes. S.'s letters, which include a large collection of unpublished material at the Bodleian Library at Oxford, memoirs, and short moral fables, combine incisive analysis of current events, polished literary criticism, and witty social satire. She demands of herself high standards of taste, intellectual honesty, stylistic elegance, and human charity. That the products of this vibrant mind remained unpublished in her own day was a significant loss, one that remains not yet wholly rectified.

WORKS: "Introductory Anecdotes" to *The Letters and Works of Lady Mary Wortley Montagu,* ed. J.A.S. Wharncliffe (1837). *Gleanings from an Old Portfolio,* ed. Mrs. Godfrey Clark (1895–98). *Selections from the Manuscripts of Lady Louisa Stuart,* ed. J. A. Home (1899). *Letters of Lady Louisa Stuart to Miss Louisa Clinton,* ed. J. A. Home (1901–03). *The Letters of Lady Louisa Stuart,* ed. R. B. Johnson (1926). *Memoire of Frances, Lady Douglas,* ed. J. Rubenstein (1985).

BIBLIOGRAPHY: Buchan, K. J. *Some Eighteenth Century Byways* (1908) Buchan, S. C. *Lady Louisa Stuart: Her Memories and Portraits* (1932). Graham, H. *A Group of Scottish Women* (1908). MacCunn F. *Sir Walter Scott's Friends* (1909). Rubenstein, J. *PSt* (1986). Rubenstein, J. *WC* (1988). Simpson, R. *TRB* (1984).

For articles in reference works, see: *Feminist.*

Other references: *Scottish Literary Journal* (1980). *WC* (1981).

Jill Rubenstein
(updated by Natalie Joy Woodall)

Stuart, Mary: See *Mary, Queen of Scots*

Surbiton: See *Moody, Elizabeth*

Alice Sutcliffe

BORN: c. 1600.
DIED: presumably after 1634.
DAUGHTER OF: Luke Woodhouse.
MARRIED: John Sutcliffe, 1624 or before.

S. is the author of *Meditations of Man's Mortalitie. Or, A Way to True Blessednesse,* which survives only in a "Second Edition, enlarged" (title page) printed in 1634. She was born into a family with court connections: Her father, Luke Woodhouse of Kimberly, Norfolk, was of the family of Sir Thomas Woodhouse, attendant to Prince Henry in the court of James I. She also married a man with court connections: Her husband is described on the title page of the *Meditations* as "John Sutcliffe Esquire, Groom of his Maiesties most Honourable Privie Chamber"; he was a nephew of Dr. Matthew Sutcliffe, who had been a chaplain in the court of James I.

For all its spiritual dimension as a guide to the "way of true blessednesse," S.'s *Meditations* is also very much a creation designed to promote, or at least consolidate, her and presumably her husband's position at court. The work is dedicated to Catherine Villiers (wife of George Villiers, first Duke of Buckingham, whom John Sutcliffe may have served) and to Susan(na) Villiers (Buckingham's sister and hence Catherine's sister-in-law), two of the most powerful women of the court of Charles I; an encomiastic acrostic is dedicated to Philip, Earl of Pembroke and Montgomery, who was Lord Chamberlain of the Household and hence her husband's superior. Another sign of S.'s (or her husband's) desire to make her volume a court event is the testimonial poems from Ben Jonson, Thomas May, George Withers, Peter Heywood, and Francis Lenton; most of these were prominent writers in the Court.

The first and main part of S.'s *Meditations* consists of six prose meditations organized somewhat loosely around the subject of the subtitle, namely "a way to true blessednesse." That way consists, simply, of first acknowledging one's mortality and weakness (under the old law) and then accepting God's mercy (of the new law). The meditations resemble sermons, and the best way of describing them might be as devotional sermons; they are composed of strings of biblical quotations and paraphrases interspersed with moral and exegetical reflections.

The second part of the work is a poem of eighty-eight six-line stanzas (ababcc) on "our losse by Adam, and our gayne by Christ." Curiously, though the poem takes up a third of the volume, it is not mentioned on the title page or in the table of contents. It is possible that the poem was added to make "the Second Edition, enlarged," but one cannot be certain, nor can one be certain whether the poem was designed as a poetic reprise of the prose meditations or as a separate work. Like the prose meditations, however, the poem is structured around an argument for "a way to true blessedness": It begins as a meditation on the corruption of our fallen nature (by way of an introductory address to and rebuke by Eve) and progresses to a meditation on the blessedness obtainable through Christ's sacrifice.

WORKS: *Meditations of Man's Mortalitie. Or, A Way to True Blessednesse* (1634).

BIBLIOGRAPHY: Cullen, P., intro. to *Meditations of Man's Mortalitie*, in *The Early Modern Englishwoman: A Facsimile Library of Essential Works*, Part One, Vol. 7 (1996). Hughey, R. *RES* (1934). Medoff, J., intro. and notes to "Alice Sutcliffe," in *Kissing the Rod: An Anthology of Seventeenth-Century Women's Verse*, ed. G. Greer et al. (1988).

For articles in reference works, see: *Feminist*.

Patrick Cullen

Sylphid: See *Robinson, Mary Darby (Perdita)*

Catherine Talbot

BORN: May 1721, Berkshire.
DIED: 9 January 1770, London.
DAUGHTER OF: Edward Talbot and Mary Martyn.

Often associated with the first circle of Bluestockings, T. published little during her lifetime but developed a literary reputation for a virtuous cleverness on the basis of letters, essays, and poems circulated in manuscript. Her father, son of a Durham bishop, died of smallpox shortly before she was born. Taken into the household of Thomas Secker, a well-known scholar who became Archbishop of Canterbury in 1758, T. studied the Bible, literature, and languages, including some Latin but no Greek. T. knew Elizabeth Montagu, Samuel Richardson (she corresponded with him regarding the writing of his novels), and Samuel Johnson, but she developed her most intense and sentimental friendship with Elizabeth Carter beginning in 1741. Although the friendship was conducted mostly through correspondence, the two exchanged locks of hair, and Carter rhapsodized, probably ironically, that "Miss Talbot is absolutely my passion: I think of her all day, dream of her all night." Whatever the private meaning of their friendship, T. was instrumental in persuading Carter to publish her translation of Epictetus. In 1758, T. reluctantly refused an offer of marriage from the much younger George Berkeley, son of the philosopher and Bishop of Cloyne. They remained close friends throughout his life, even prompting the jealous anger of Berkeley's wife, Eliza. In 1768, Secker's death brought T. and her mother the income from an investment of £13,000; this enabled them to move to London, where T. died of cancer on 9 January 1770 at the age of forty-nine. A portrait engraved by C. Heath is owned by the British Museum.

T. wrote regularly, placing her work in a "green book" and saving it in what she called her "considering drawer." A *Rambler* essay called "Sunday" (30 June 1750) was the only work to appear during her lifetime. Here she creates a personified "Sunday" who wishes people to spend the day attending church in plain clothes, eating together, taking walks, and reading religious books. More entertaining, perhaps, is T.'s posthumously published correspondence with Carter in which T. complains humorously about the "small dominion" she regulates: "a foolish dog, a restive horse, and a perverse gardener." Throughout her life, T. seems to have suffered from ill-health and depression. She commented often on the limitations society imposed on genteel women, complaining particularly of the monotony of a purposeless life of trivial duties in which she had "the appearance, without the reality, of being quite at my own liberty to do just what I please."

After T.'s death, Carter prompted the publication of T's religious work, *Reflections on the Seven Days of the Week* (1770), which went through several editions its first year and sold more than 25,000 copies between 1770 and 1809. In 1772, *Essays on Various Subjects,* a collection of poems, dialogues, allegories, Ossianic imitations, and other works appeared. Although T. was known to have complained bitterly about Pericles' advice to ladies "to keep themselves quiet, and make themselves as little talked of as possible," T. speaks often in the essays on the value of resignation, inventing the term "accommodableness" to describe those fortunate enough to be able to adjust their mood to their circumstances. She dwells as well on the ephemeral nature of all achievement, including those "brittle monuments of Female Diligence in Pye-Crust."

T.'s daily life was dominated by domestic duties; she cared for the archbishop, managed a household of forty people, and dealt with numerous visitors. The poignancy of a cultural milieu that discouraged her from developing her abilities was recognized even by her contemporaries, one of whom wrote after her death that "so diffident was she of her own powers, that her elegant and refined taste was sometimes nipped in the bud."

WORKS: "Sunday" *Rambler* (30 June 1750). *Reflections on the Seven Days of the Week* (1770). *Essays on Various Subjects* (1772). *The Works of the Late Miss Catherine Talbot* (1780), *The Works of Miss Catherine Talbot* (1809), *A Series of Letters between Mrs. Elizabeth Carter and Miss Catherine Talbot 1741–1770* (1809).

BIBLIOGRAPHY: Myers, S. *The Bluestocking Circle: Women, Friendship, and the Life of the Mind in Eighteenth-Century England* (1990). Rogers, K. M. *Feminism in Eighteenth-Century England* (1982). *The Other Eighteenth Century,* ed. R. W. Uphaus and G. M. Foster (1991).

For articles in reference works, see: *DNB. Feminist. Oxford. ToddBWW. ToddDBA.*

Kathryn D. Temple

Ann and Jane Taylor

Ann

BORN: 30 January 1782, London.
DIED: 17 December 1866, Nottingham.
DAUGHTER OF: Isaac Taylor and Ann Martin Taylor.
MARRIED: Joseph Henry Gilbert, 1813.

Jane

BORN: 23 September 1783, London.
DIED: 12 April 1824, Ongar, Essex.
DAUGHTER OF: Isaac Taylor and Ann Martin Taylor.
WROTE UNDER: Q. Q.

Born into a poor but intellectually active and creative nonconformist family, the T. sisters became known in literary circles in their early twenties for fresh, original, and sprightly verse, tales, short stories, and essays for children and young people. Although their writing was to change the nature of children's literature, their impact was even broader. Iona Opie writes of them: "No two young women aroused more affection in the 19th century through their work," an appreciation emanating from the new middle class and authors now in the literary canon. Sir Walter Scott praised their work; Lord Byron parodied it; and Robert Browning, who read their works as a child, later developed one of Jane's tales into a poem.

Ann's "Meddlesome Matty" as a poem may be dated, as is Jane's "Busy Idleness," but, as phrases, they have entered into the language. In spite of inherent moralizing in all their works, the sisters' influence can be traced in late-nineteenth- and early-twentieth-century writers such as Browning, Lewis Carroll, Robert Louis Stevenson, and Hilaire Belloc. Kate Greenaway illustrated a selection of the sisters' poems, including "The Cow" and "Meddlesome Matty," in 1883; Edith Sitwell and Amy Lowell read them and owned, as adults, copies of their works.

The T.s' father and grandfather bore the same name, Isaac, and practiced the same profession, engraver and illustrator; the T.s' father was ordained later in his career. In 1786, the family moved from London to Lavenham, in Suffolk, where they remained for ten years. During these years, the T.s were taught at home and allowed to develop their talents. Ann says of her sister that she lived in "a world entirely of her own creation" and invented her extended imaginative games, verse, and stories while watching her spinning top for hours on end. Precocious and lively, Jane was willingly put on display for family friends both in Lavenham and in Colchester, where the family moved in 1796.

When the Napoleonic Wars reduced the volume of engraving work, the teenaged girls were apprenticed to their father as engravers. The engraving demanded careful attention, and the hours of work were long but not rigidly arduous. The girls' friends came visiting into the workroom, and ideas for poems and tales were scribbled on scraps of paper; there was also time for dancing lessons, evening literary reading and discussion parties, and competing for prizes offered by *Minor's Pocket Book.* After some five years of submitting verses and puzzle solutions, the publisher asked them to write "some easy poetry for young children. . . . [W]hat would be most likely to please little minds." The sisters produced *Original Poems for Infant Minds* (1805–06), an instant critical and popular success with reviews in several nonconformist periodicals; the general tenor of the reviews was that the verse was more poetic than moral, yet very moral.

The early 1800s also saw the publication of *Rural Scenes* (1805) and *City Scenes* (1809), readers with many engravings; both were noticed in the *Eclectic Review. Original Poems* was followed by *Rhymes for the Nursery* (1806), which contains Jane's "The Star" ("Twinkle, twinkle, little star"), the basis of Lewis Carroll's parody in *Alice in Wonderland,* and their joint "The Cow," later used by R. L. Stevenson. *Limed Twigs* (1808); a reader, Ann's *The Wedding Among the Flowers* (1808); and her *Signor Topsy-Turvy's Wonderful Magic Lantern* (1810) did not distract from their more serious joint venture, *Hymns for Infant Minds* (1810), for which Ann also did the engravings and which was nearly as popular as *Original Poems,* winning immediate acceptance in the burgeoning Sunday schools and necessitating forty-eight editions. Most remembered today is Ann's "I thank the goodness and the grace, / Which on my birth has smiled." Thomas Arnold wrote of Ann: "The knowledge and love of Christ can nowhere be more readily gained by young children than from the hymns of this most admirable woman."

The T. family moved to Ongar in 1811, Isaac being called to the meeting house there, a move that was to be the last for the family. The three oldest children, Ann, Jane, and their older brother Isaac, spent more time away from home; Ann and Jane spent the winter of 1811–12 with Isaac in Cornwall, where they were able to pursue the arts unhampered. Ann and Isaac would marry, but otherwise the home at Ongar would remain until the death of their parents.

Until the volume of publication proved otherwise, their father insisted that the two young women regard writing as secondary to the security of engraving as a way of earning their living. When writing proved so successful, their mother also began to publish; her first work, *Maternal Solicitude,* appeared in 1814. She and Jane collaborated on *Correspondence Between a Mother and Her Daughter at School* (1817). Before Ann's marriage in 1813, she and Jane collaborated heavily on much of their writing for children, with some contributions from the three younger members of the family.

Ann's marriage to Joseph Henry Gilbert, a Congregationalist minister known for his liberal views, was happy, busy, and successful, leaving little time for writing, given the demands of raising eight children. She did find time for reviewing for the *Eclectic Review,* however. A somewhat negative review of Hannah More's *Christian Morals* angered More, who objected to such a tone being taken by an obscure writer. The intervening years saw little writing, and what was written was often in support of Parliamentary reform, abolition, or disestablishment, with some occasional verse. Ann returned to her pen in the 1860s to write her *Autobiography,* used by Virginia Woolf in her essay "Lives of the Obscure" to evoke forgotten nonconformists who lived lives of such high purpose.

Ann's contribution to children's literature included the poem "My Mother," published in volume one of the two-volume *Original Poems* (1805), which became one of the most popular, imitated, and parodied poems in the nineteenth century. Inspired by William Cowper's poem "My Mary," these sentimental verses were parodied by Byron and by a sixteen-year-old Bertrand Russell, among many others, in the latter half of the nineteenth century, in reaction to the serious imitations of the first half. "My Mother" was described in the *Athenaeum* (12 May 1866) as "one of the most beautiful lyrics in the English language" except for the final verse: "For God, who lives above the skies, / Would look with vengeance in His eyes, / If ever I should dare despise / My Mother." This verse, it was suggested, should be replaced with one made by the poet laureate, Alfred Lord Tennyson. Ann replied in the 19 May issue, defending her ending of the poem. She cited Isaac Watts as her mentor in theology for children and suggested an alternative: "For could our Father in the skies / Look down with pleased or loving eyes / If ever I could dare despise / My Mother?" The anonymous editor ends this communication with the statement: "While the author is living, no one can be heard except herself on the subject." The section on fragments in Christopher Ricks's edition of Tennyson's poems (1969, 1987) contains no lines that suggest they were penned for this purpose.

In 1817, Jane began to write for *Youth Magazine* under the pseudonym of Q. Q.; these poems and essays were published posthumously in book form as *Contributions of Q. Q.* (1824), and, with demand stimulated by praise from Sarah Hale, in book and tract form in the United States. In this collection is printed "How It Strikes a Stranger," which uses a visitor from a small planet to provide perspective on living for earthlings, and "A Day's Pleasure," which describes a group of young people's adventures as they visit a stately house.

Both sisters were influenced in their literary development by their close-knit family and the religious value they placed on the imaginative life. To the adult Jane, lyrical and reflective where Ann was concrete and dramatic, unbridled imagination, however tempting, was worldly and hence unacceptable; the irresolution of this matter is detailed in a letter she wrote to a friend on the vexed subject of novel reading, which, although coming down triumphantly on the side of the novel as a moral instrument, was insufficiently convincing to move Jane to use her gifts in this way. Choosing instead the tale as her vehicle, she created honest, sound psychological sketches. *Display*, written in Cornwall in 1815, was considered by herself and others her major work. Seeming to echo Jane Austen's *Emma* and *Mansfield Park* (but written independently), the novel is a Bildungsroman of Emily and Elizabeth, who seek happiness in upward mobility, only to find more modest contentment. Broadly reviewed, *Display* went into three editions in six months. Jane, like Maria Edgeworth, shaped her characters to fit her moral, sacrificing the richness of texture characteristic of the true novel.

Jane once described herself as two people—a morning self, busy, pedestrian in thought, even brusque; and an evening self, imaginative and gay. This latter literary self, fascinated by space, stars, and the night sky—"I used to roam and revel 'Mid the stars'"—produced her two most enduring works, the children's poem "The Star" and the short story "How It Strikes a Stranger," the theme of which Browning used in "Rephan," attributing it to her and perhaps forgiving the strong moralistic tone by which she justified her imagination.

In addition to the works discussed here, Jane also collaborated with her mother on works of social advice, such as *Correspondence Between a Mother and her Daughter at School*.

Jane died of cancer in 1824 at home in Ongar but Ann outlived her husband, traveled in England, and wrote her *Autobiography* (1874), dying at the age of eighty-eight.

WORKS: (Ann and Jane T.) *Rural Scenes* (1805). *Original Poems for Infant Minds*, 2 vols. (1805–1806). *Rhymes for the Nursery* (1806). *Limed Twigs to Catch Young Birds* (1808). *City Scenes* (1809). *Hymns for Infant Minds* (1810). (Jane T. and Ann Martin T.): *Correspondence Between a Mother and her Daughter at School* (1817). (Jane T.): *Display, a Tale* (1815). *Essays in Rhymes* (1816). *The Contributions of Q. Q.* (1824). *Writings* (1832). *Jane Taylor, Prose and Poetry*, ed. F. V. Barry (1925). (Ann T.): *The Wedding Among the Flowers* (1808). *Signor Topsy-Turvy's Wonderful Magic Lantern* (1810) *Autobiography* (1874).

BIBLIOGRAPHY: Armitage, D. M. *The Taylors of Ongar: Portrait of an English Family of the Eighteenth and Nineteenth Centuries* (1939). Curran, S., in *Romanticism and Feminism*, ed. A. K. Mellor (1988). Kastner, J. *Smithsonian* (October 1983). Kent, M. *English* (1935). Opie, I. *Three Centuries of Nursery Rhymes and Poetry for Children* (1973). Stewart, C. D. *The Taylors of Ongar: An Analytical Bio-bibliography* (1975). *Ann Taylor Gilbert's Album*, ed. C. D. Stewart (1978). Taylor, I., Jr. *Memoirs and Poetical Remains of Jane Taylor* (1826). Walford, L. *Four Biographies from "Blackwood's."* (1888). Woolf, V. *The Common Reader* (1925).

For articles in reference works, see: *Bloomsbury*. *Oxford*. *ToddBWW*.

Eleanor Langstaff

Elizabeth Taylor

BORN: 3 July 1912, Reading, Berkshire.
DIED: 19 November 1975, Grove's Barn, Penn, Buckinghamshire.
DAUGHTER OF: Oliver Coles and Elsie Fewtrell Coles.
MARRIED: John Kendall Taylor, 1936.

Fine ironies and a polished style, a retiring life and a dedicated readership have caused some critics to mention in the same breath Jane Austen and the modern Englishwoman T.

T. was born Elizabeth Coles in Berkshire in 1912, and she worked as a governess and a librarian before her marriage in 1936. Having had two children and started to bring them up, she turned in 1945 to fulltime authorship after the success of her first novel, *At Mrs. Lippincote's*. She dedicated herself to the short and not-so-simple annals of the British middle class, which she viewed with a penetrating eye and a gentle but not wholly uncontemptuous amusement.

She was especially good at catching the individuating gesture and in penetrating the often-elaborate disguises that stockbrokers and other middle-class suburbanites put on those actions that they think are beneath them but nevertheless perform for some real or imagined advantage. She was not at all surprised to discover in the group of people who "had advantages"—and were typically anxious always to "take advantage" in order to increase that "superiority"—startling inconsistencies; she was able to render these carefully without ever creating characters who were merely puzzling bundles of contradictions. She was able to get right to the heart of characters who were, deep down, at war with the surfaces they deliberately and ingeniously adopted or unfortunately and uncomfortably were compelled by society to adopt.

She chronicled in novels and exquisite short stories (said

to be so subtle as to be an acquired taste) the incongruous situations in which perfectly ordinary middle-class people were to be observed doing the most extraordinary things. Hers was the world of human foibles and contradictions that Logan Pearsall Smith, in 1931, described as inhabited by "meat-eating vegetarians" and similar strange but everyday people.

Eschewing the sensational, T. opted for plots that permitted her sometimes improbable characters to exhibit themselves without attracting undue attention to the machinery of the fiction. At the same time she was completely aware that even a pillar of the middle-class Establishment is, on occasion, liable to appear among the respectable in an outrageously loud tie, or kick over the traces and run away with someone's wife, or do in a rich and elderly relative, or take off with the most unpredictable and "unsuitable" companion to some place impossibly distant or déclassé. Her characters inhabited a world of modulated voices and clichéd emotions, a world in which only a few "advanced" or "artistic" persons were expected to be eccentric in manner or extravagant in speech and gesture. T. made it perfectly credible for the momentous to interrupt the mundane.

In character, plot, and dialogue she added a seasoning of malice, a dash of censure or contempt (but never toward the reader, who was invited to be on the side of the Right). We are shown how, in their genteel and fundamentally British hypocrisy, the characters sometimes fool even themselves, and we are invited to sit in judgment of what fools such mortals can be.

T.'s work is quintessentially British in its shrewd tolerance and its "superior" correction, in its admixture of snobbery with morality, in its skillful combination of the delicious secret guilt of gossip with the properly public stance of "sorting things out." Along with her feminine intuition and village-scandalmonger cattiness—admittedly frequently leavened by a sincere sympathy for characters one might have thought deserved nothing but condemnation—she has an unflinching dedication not only to *setting* things right but also to *getting* things right. Her glance is penetrating. Her work is highly crafted, deliberate in every effect, calculated when it seems the most casual. Telling us all about her subjects, also, she wastes little or nothing, except perhaps some compassion on a few wayward people who ought to have known better. All of her people we recognize. Some of them we ought not to like as much as her kindness and art makes us like them.

T.'s wit is the kind vaguely described as "dry," which is to say that it prompts smiles, not guffaws, even at the outrageous. Margaret Willy (in *Great Writers of the English Language, Novelists,* the best brief estimate of T.'s achievement) notes that T.'s ironies have been compared with Austen's and then cleverly adds: "Another attribute shared by these tolerantly amused, intensely feminine delineators of human foible was a distaste for sensational subject-matter and personal publicity alike. This perhaps in part accounts for the comparatively limited recognition, in favour of flashier fictional attractions, accorded to one of the most quietly distinguished talents of our time."

Arguably the simplest explanation of why a dozen novels from *At Mrs. Lippincote's* to the posthumous *Blaming* (1976) have been so "quietly" received by critics is that most book reviewers over that period were men, and T. writes best about and for women. Men may not be able to feel to the same extent the "shock of recognition" at her economical and precise depiction of a young girl's dreams and embarrassments, at a middle-aged woman's hypocrisies and insecurities, at an old woman's disappointments and forced adjustments. Male critics have to acknowlege T.'s art; female critics keep telling us of her heart.

Her skill is evident in her novels and her collections of short stories; these latter prove that she is also the mistress of the briefer form, but here the influence of her favorite writer (Jane Austen) is perhaps less.

WORKS: *At Mrs. Lippincote's* (1945). *Palladian* (1946). *A View of the Harbour* (1947). *A Wreath of Roses* (1949). *A Game of Hide-and-Seek* (1951). *The Sleeping Beauty* (1953). *Hester Lilly and Other Stories* (1954). *Angel* (1957). *The Blush and Other Stories* (1958). *In a Summer Season* (1961). *The Soul of Kindness* (1964). *A Dedicated Man and Other Stories* (1965). *Mossy Trotter* (1967). *The Wedding Group* (1968). *Mrs. Palfrey at the Claremont* (1971). *The Devastating Boys* (1972). *Blaming* (1976). *Elizabeth Takes Off: Autobiography* (1988). *Dangerous Calm: Selected Stories,* ed. L. Knight (1995).

BIBLIOGRAPHY: Bailley, P. *New Statesman* (10 August 1973). Gillette, J. B. *TCL* (1989). Liddell, R. *Review of English Literature* (April 1960). Luere, J. *SAD* (1988). Macheski, C. *Barbara Pym Newsletter* (1988). Wyatt-Brown, A. M. *Gerontologist* (1986).

For articles in reference works, see: *CA. CLC. GWELN. SATA. TCA. TCW.*

Other references: *BuR* (1993). *RMS* (1991). Smith, L. P. *AfterThoughts* (1931).

Leonard R. N. Ashley

Elizabeth Taylor (Wythens)

FLOURISHED: 1685.
DIED: 1708.
DAUGHTER OF: Sir Thomas Taylor.
MARRIED: Sir Frances Wythens, 1685; Sir Thomas Colepeper, 1704.
WROTE UNDER: Olinda; Mrs. Taylor; Lady Wythens.

Poems by T. appear in several anthologies from the period, most notably in Aphra Behn's *Miscellany, Being a Collection of Poems By Several Hands* (1685). Two of the poems from Behn's collection also appear in John Dunton's *The Muses Magazine, or: Poeticall Miscellanies* (1705), but these are identified only as "by a timorous Lady." As "Lady Wythens" T. also contributed to Henry Playford's *Banquet of Music* (1688). Her "Ode" beginning "Ah poor Olinda never boast" is printed with variations in at least two songbooks of the period and reappears in Mary Delarivière Manley's *Secret Memoirs from the New Atlantis* (1709) along with a brief story of its author, here referred to as "Olinda." It is likely that "Olinda" and T. are the same person.

Calling her "the *witiest* Lady of the *Age,*" Manley explains that Olinda fell in love with a "Country Chevalier," "the only Man of Honour in Atlantis, as to Amour." Unfortunately, the two lovers soon parted when Olinda's father forced her to marry an "Old, Infirm, and Humourous" judge. Quickly finding it impossible to live away from the man she really loved and with the one she hated, Olinda withdrew to the country, first to a house near her lover's villa and finally to the villa itself. Her husband, apparently fearing a scandal, aided the affair, frequently visiting his wife and even granting her a separate allowance. At length the old husband obligingly died and the two lovers married. Manley expresses amazement at this turn of events, describing the author as jealous and revengeful, "so little Mistress of her Passions, or so defective of the Art of concealing 'em, that they often made her, (with all her distinguishing Wit,) both the Object of his Pity and Contempt." *The Dictionary of National Biography* entry on Sir Francis Wythens offers a similar view of T., crediting her with being "clever and witty" but noting that she "brought no comfort to her husband, and acquired for herself a very bad reputation."

T.'s poems, in ballad stanza, are all love songs. "Ah poor Olinda never boast" describes a woman so irresistibly drawn to the man she loves that it costs her both her freedom and her reputation: "In vain I do his *Person* shun, / I cannot from his *Glory* run, / 'Tis universal as the *Sun*." Another poem warns against love and begins, "Ye Virgin Pow'rs defend my heart / From Amorous looks and smiles, / From sawcy Love, or nicer Art / Which most our Sex beguile." Still another tells of a woman agreeing to help the man she loves woo another woman. Although witty and light, T.'s poems all speak of the betrayal and pain of love.

Manley's assessment of her still seems valid today: "The Muses took up their Habitation in Olinda's lovely Breast: All she wrote was *Natural, Easy, Amorous* and *Sparkling!*"

WORKS: Poems in several anthologies: "Ode: Ah poor Olinda never boast," "Song, Made by Mrs. Taylor: Ye Virgin Pow'rs defend my heart," "Song. by Mrs. Taylor: Strephon has Fashion, Wit and Youth," "To Mertill who desired her to speak to Clorinda of his Love."

BIBLIOGRAPHY: *Kissing the Rod: An Anthology of Seventeenth-Century Women's Verse*, ed. G. Greer et al. (1988). Manley, M. Delarivière. *Secret Memoirs from the New Atlantis*, Vol. II (1709; facsimile, 1972).

For articles in reference works, see: *Bell. DNB* (under "Sir Francis Wythens"). *ToddDBA.*

Susan C. Staub

T. B.: See *Haywood, Eliza Fowler*

Temple, Ann: See *Mortimer, Penelope Ruth*

Tennant, Emma Alice Margaret: See *Asquith, Emma Alice Margaret Tennant*

Emma Tennant

BORN: 20 October 1937, London.
DAUGHTER OF: Christopher Grey, second Baron Glenconner, and Elizabeth Lady Glenconner.
MARRIED: Sebastian Yorke, 1957; Mr. Cockburn; Mr. Dempsey.
WROTE UNDER: Catherine Aydy; Emma Tennant.

Shortly after T. was born, her family moved to Scotland, where she lived for nine years before moving back to London. T. attended a village school in Scotland, St. Paul's Girls' School in London, and a finishing school in Oxford, where she was inspired to learn more about art. At the age of fifteen, T. traveled to Paris to study art history at the École de Louvre. When she returned to England, T. became a debutante and was presented at Court in 1956.

In 1961, T. began to contribute occasionally to the *New Statesman.* Two years later she became travel correspondent for *Queen.* Her first novel, *The Colour of Rain,* was published pseudonymously in 1964. In 1966, T. became features editor for *Vogue.* When *The Time of the Crack* (1973) was published, T. became a fulltime novelist. Since then she has written many novels and children's books, edited two anthologies, and contributed to various publications.

T. was the founding editor of *Bananas,* a literary magazine of the British Arts Council, from 1975 to 1978. In 1978, T. began writing book reviews for the *Guardian,* to which she still contributes. She also became general editor of *In Verse* in 1982 and *Lives of Modern Women* in 1985. T. became a Fellow of the Royal Society of Literature in 1982.

Novelist, critic, and editor, T. cannot be pigeonholed. Three of her novels—*The Time of the Crack* (1973), *The Last of the Country House Murders* (1975), and *Hotel de Dream* (1976)—are science-fiction publications. The rest of her novels contain varying amounts of realism. T. herself does not believe that prose literature has an obligation to be realistic. She has said, "I would like to feel that I can go off in any direction that seems right." Consequently, her novels cannot be categorized. T. does, however, admit that "a lot of my books have actually been a blend of Calvinism and romanticism—having to do with murder and morals." By some critics she has been called a "woman writer" as opposed to a "writer"; that is, she does treat the feminist viewpoint, examining it and at times exhorting it, in most of her works. Nevertheless, she says about feminism, "the theory must never stand in the way of creativity."

After *The Colour of Rain* (1963), a realistic and critical view of English upper-class society, there was a ten-year hiatus in publishing, mainly because of T.'s loss of confidence resulting from a disparaging remark reportedly made about her book during judging for the Prix Formentor. T. reentered the publishing market by way of the science-fiction genre, whose writers gave her support and confidence, with *The Time of the Crack.* In this novel, a huge crack opens unexpectedly in the Thames, separating the North from the South and throwing into chaos the strict separation between social classes that had existed before. The plot also involves two analysts who attempt to cure their patients by regression; the novel is an early example of T.'s criticism of the theories of "experts" in trying to explain a world that includes myth, imagination, and unexplainable phenomena. The *Times Literary Supplement* called the novel "Lewis Carroll technique applied to H.G. Wells material."

The Last of the Country House Murders is set in an England with a "Big Brother" government some time in the near future. In this parody of an English murder mystery, the murder of a remaining decadent aristocrat, Jules Tanner, is going to be staged by the government for the entertainment of tourists. His only freedom: He gets to choose his murderer. In *Hotel de Dream,* fantasy and reality intermingle as inhabitants of a boarding house enter each other's dreams, spending much of their time escaping reality by sleeping. These three novels, which T. has called "political satire-fantasy," received fairly good reviews that noted her skill at describing settings and feelings, her intelligent humor, and her satire of modern society.

In *The Bad Sister* (1978), T. broke away from fantasy and returned to a more realistic mode, using "documents" to make up the novel. The bulk of this murder mystery consists of "The Journal of Jane Wild," sandwiched by comments from the "editor" of this journal. Here, T. explores the theme of doubles, coupled with a critical look at both patriarchal tradition in society as well as its confrontation by militant revolutionary movements and militant feminism. As the clergyman Stephen remarks in the novel: "'It's the modern evil, I believe, this jumble of Marxism and Tantrism and anything else thrown in, which is used to persuade people to kill each other.'" This novel is based on James Hogg's *The Private Memoirs and Confessions of a Justified Sinner* (1824).

In her next two novels, *Wild Nights* (1979) and *Alice Fell* (1980), T. was less interested in plot and more in perception. Both novels, she has said, were "intended to be short works of poetic prose." *Wild Nights* is a first-person, "fictional childhood memoir" set in the Tennants' family home in Scotland. T. has described *Alice Fell* as a novel about "the fall of a girl, using the myth of Persephone." These two novels, along with her next, *Queen of Stones* (1982), use the theme of childhood. All three were inspired by her daughters' growing up.

Queen of Stones, a female version of William Golding's *Lord of the Flies,* uses documents to reconstruct a fictional event. Besides presenting the lives of adolescent girls, the novel also satirizes society's official interpretation of adolescence, particularly Freudian analysis. The narrator pontificates: "Thus, perhaps, will the psychopathology of the developing female be more fully comprehended; as also the mythology sustaining our concept of the feminine in society." The narrator, whom T. has described as "pretty stupid," ends by blaming all the sinister events in the novel on the arrival of the first menstrual period of one of the main characters.

In *Woman Beware Woman* (1983; in the U.S. as *The Half-Mother*), T. tried to evoke character more strongly than in her previous novels. Each of the three women in this story must beware of the others after the famous husband of one has been found dead. T. says that the book is about "the horrors of the 'perfect' family, and what in fact goes on underneath, the entrapments and tensions." She emphasizes that the characters do not represent women in our time.

Black Marina (1985), another mystery, brings the left-wing politics and feminism of the Portobello Road area in London to St. James, a tiny Caribbean Island. The book is also about the search for identity—not only for Marina, a young girl searching for her "roots," but for the entire island. T.'s evocation of place is superb. She describes the library of the last of the white colonial landowners as a place "where the peeling-off spines of the books hang like moths half out of their cocoons." This is a perfect metaphor for the entire island, which is stuck halfway between its colonial past and the modern world of resorts and condominiums—not to mention revolutions and invasions.

T.'s novel *The Adventures of Robina by Herself,* "edited" by T. (1986), is a picaresque, autobiographical novel using eighteenth-century idiom but set in the 1950s. It traces the adventures of an incredibly naive young woman from Oxford to Paris to London and is based on the premise that "the ways and manners of a certain section of the society in which we live are virtually unchanged since the early eighteenth century."

The House of Hospitalities (1987; Book I of the "Cycle of the Sun" series) chronicles the lives of a group of friends from a girls' school and the changes in their lives as they move through their teenage years during the 1950s. The emptiness and decay of upper-class life is realized by the narrator as she glimpses life at Lovegrove, the estate of Amy Rudd, her school friend.

A Wedding of Cousins (1988; Book II of the "Cycle of the Sun" series) continues the story of the girls' lives as Amy Rudd prepares for and marries her cousin, Crispin. The novel points out the limitations placed on young women's lives by their frightingly few options. The narrator's dreamlike inability to act creates a passivity that functions to record others' lives without, apparently, influencing them.

As other postmodern novelists have done, T. has used myths and plots from literary history as frameworks for her own novels, reworking them into more modern versions with a feminist perspective. In *Two Women of London: The Strange Case of Ms. Jekyll and Mrs. Hyde* (1989), she uses the Jekyll/Hyde transformation, applying it to a woman who experiences the oppression of society as a poor single mother while living a parallel life as an upper-crust art-gallery manager. The novel proceeds with fragments of various documents, voices, and points of view as the "editor" tries to piece together the events leading up to a murder.

The Magic Drum: An Excursion (1989) is an intriguing murder mystery recounted in Catherine Treger's diary. Treger, a journalist who visits a writing workshop at the home of a famous poet, becomes involved in the playing-out of old emotions, family tensions, and jealousies that lead, eventually, to murder. The ending is ambiguous; did a murder even take place? Treger ends up having a mental breakdown.

Faustine (1991) reworks the myth of Dr. Faustus, only this time a woman makes her pact with the devil. In using this myth, T. exposes society's obsession with youth and beauty in women. Ella, the abandoned grand-daughter of Muriel, the woman who has bargained with Satan, narrates the story as she tries to recover and understand the stories of her mother and grandmother and, in the end, herself. The last narrator here is the devil.

The ABC of Writing (1992) is an alphabetical listing of words and phrases having to do with being a writer, with bitingly satirical definitions, some from historical figures, some written by T. herself: "Word processor: A machine which produces long, repetitive, meandering novels."

In *Tess* (1993), using Thomas Hardy's *Tess of the D'Urbervilles* as a context, T. transforms the story into a myth of love and betrayal that visits women of all times, all countries. The shock at the end provides an answer to the question of why women cannot seem to break away from this destructive pattern. This is a brilliant narration of the power issues that prevent women from leading their own lives.

In *Pemberley, or Pride and Prejudice Continued* (1993) and *An Unequal Marriage, or Pride and Prejudice Twenty Years Later* (1994), T. again uses other works of literature to fashion her own. This time, instead of creating a new work, T. writes two novels with straightforward continuations of Jane Austen's novel. The first picks up with Darcy's marriage to Elizabeth Bennet, chronicling their first year together, the second chronicling their twentieth year of marriage. T. has subsequently written two additional "continuations" of Austen's *Emma* (1995) and *Sense and Sensibility* (1996).

Although T. has said, "I think, in most writers, there's some sort of pattern," her own writing exemplifies another of her statements: "Every different thing demands its own expression."

WORKS: (as Catherine Aydy) *The Colour of Rain* (1963). *The Time of the Crack* (1973). *The Last of the Country House Murders* (1975). *Hotel de Dream* (1976). *The Bad Sister* (1978). (with M. Rayner) *The Boggart* (1979). *Wild Nights* (1979). *Alice Fell* (1980). *The Search for Treasure Island* (1981). *Queen of Stones* (1982). *Woman Beware Woman* (1983; in the U.S. as *The Half-Mother*). *Black Marina* (1985). *The Ghost Child* (1984). *Adventures of Robina by Herself* (1986). *The House of Hospitalities* (1987; Book I of the "Cycle of the Sun" series). *A Wedding of Cousins* (1988; Book II of the "Cycle of the Sun" series). *Two Women of London: The Strange Case of Ms. Jekyll and Mrs. Hyde* (1989). *The Magic Drum: An Excursion* (1989). *Faustine* (1991). *The ABC of Writing* (1992). *Tess* (1993). *Pemberley, or Pride and Prejudice Continued* (1993). *An Unequal Marriage, or Pride and Prejudice Twenty Years Later* (1994). *Emma in Love* (1995). *Elinor and Marianne: A Sequel to "Sense and Sensibility"* (1996).

BIBLIOGRAPHY: Anderson, C., in *The Scottish Novel Since the Seventies*, ed. G. Wallace and R. Stevenson (1993). Connor, S., in *Liminal Postmodernisms: The Postmodern, the (Post-) Colonial, and the (Post-) Feminist*, ed. T. D'haen and H. Bertens (1994). Indiana, G. *VLS* (May 1991). Roe, S., and E. Tennant, in *Women's Writing: A Challenge to Theory*, ed. M. Monteith (1986). Widdowson, P. *CrSurv* (1995).

For articles in reference works, see: *CA. CLC. DLB. SFW.*

Other references: *New Yorker* (20 May 1985). *NYT* (4 May 1995). *NYTBR* (12 May 1985). *TES* (23 February 1986). *TLS* (15 June 1973, 19 November 1982, 21 June 1985, 24 January 1986, 29 October 1993).

Carol Pulham

Terán, Lisa St. Aubin de: See St. Aubin de *Terán, Lisa*

Ellen Terry

BORN: 27 February 1847, Coventry, Warwickshire.
DIED: 21 July 1928, Small Hythe, Kent.
DAUGHTER OF: Ben Terry and Sarah Ballard.
MARRIED: George Frederick Watts, 1864; Charles Wardell, 1877; James Carew, 1907.

T. was born into the second generation of a large theater family that would include her elder sister Kate; her son, Edward Gordon Craig; and her great-nephew, Sir John Gielgud. T. made her debut at the age of nine as Prince Mamillius in *The Winter's Tale* with Charles Kean. She continued to play minor roles while her sister Kate took center stage until 1864, when she married George Frederick Watts, a portrait artist thirty years her senior. Attracted by his wealth and sophisticated life-style, T. retired from the stage to marry him, but the couple separated ten months later.

The next three bleak years were enlivened for T. by friendship and photo sessions with Charles Dodgson, better known as Lewis Carroll. In one of the one-line but perceptive character sketches that fill her writing, T. described her shy friend: "He was as fond of me as he could be of anyone over the age of ten." In 1867, T. appeared with Henry Irving in a one-act travesty, *Katherine and Petruchio,* an inauspicious beginning to what was to be one of the most influential partnerships in British theater history. T.'s career was once again interrupted in 1868, when she met Edward Godwin, an architect and designer, and retired to live with him (though still legally married to Watts) and raise their two children, Edith (b. 1869) and Edward Gordon Craig (b. 1872); Edward was to be one of the most important theatrical designers and theorists of the twentieth century.

In desperate need of money by 1875, T. broke with Godwin and was lured back to the stage by Charles Reade, her dearest friend and most dedicated teacher. Under his guidance, T. began to develop her own theory of dramatic style, which is recorded in her memoirs, letters, lectures, and acting notes. Filled with detailed directorial notes, careful explorations of all aspects of a role, and recollections of emotional memories that might be used to create appropriate moods, T.'s writings at this time show that she was developing independently what would later be systematized by Stanislavsky at the Moscow Art Theatre. Rather than relying on instinct, as many actresses of her day did, T. relied on intellect and technique to produce a more natural acting style, free of bombast or presentational theatricality. Using these techniques, T. had her first major success as Portia in *The Merchant of Venice* and claimed the Shakespearean heroines as her own for the next thirty years.

In 1877, finally divorced from Watts, T. married a fellow actor, Charles Wardell (stage name Charles Kelly), primarily to give her family respectability, and initiated a financially and stylistically profitable twenty-two-year partnership with Irving. Together, the two revolutionized Victorian theatrical style, researching the plays they produced to ensure historical and psychological verisimilitude.

T.'s writings at this time provide perhaps the most detailed and intelligent records of style from the Victorian period. For her role as Ophelia, T. visited an asylum, but concluded that "it is no good observing life and bringing the result to the stage without selection, without a definite idea. The idea must come first, realism afterward." T.'s acting texts are filled with copious notes on delivery, tone, pace, gesture, and motivation, as well as research about how others had performed or misperformed roles. Although her forte was voice and expressive movement, T. did not ignore other aspects of staging; she advised Irving about sets, costumes, and, in particular, lighting design.

From 1878 to 1901, T. and Irving reigned in public and in private as the chief theatrical couple, for T. had by now separated from Wardell. Together, the two played almost all of Shakespeare and began to infuse the world of theater with intellectual and social respectability, for which Irving was rewarded in 1894 with the first knighthood to be granted to an actor. While she was busy breaking away from Victorian melodramatic style, however, T. almost missed the significance of the Ibsen invasion. Her 1891 "Stray Memories" in the *New Review* dismissed Nora and Hedda as "silly ladies . . . extraordinarily easy to act," a sentiment that earned her George Bernard Shaw's severe criticism and that she was intelligent enough to omit from her memoirs in 1908.

T.'s letters, memoirs, and notes preserve brilliant sketches of remarkable people, a fascinating record of the Victorian age, and a priceless historical document about the development of modern acting and staging styles. Of chief interest among the letters is her famous and spirited correspondence with Shaw (1892–1922), whom she counted as her second-best friend, and her letters to her son, in which she is by turns scolding and supportive, lamenting always over Craig's profligacy and infidelity but ever confident that his genius would be recognized. T.'s letters and memoirs also record intimate portraits of and communications from Alfred Lord Tennyson, Oscar Wilde, Matthew Arnold, Henry James, Winston Churchill, Sarah Bernhardt, Eleanora Duse, Virginia Woolf, Edith Sitwell, William Gladstone, and Vita Sackville-West, among others.

Interestingly, one of the greatest actresses of the late nineteenth-century is also one of the greatest theatrical historians and theorists. Her writings allow contemporary historians to reconstruct exactly the performance of yesterday and to eavesdrop at the formation of modern acting style. Before Stanislavsky, before Ibsen, before "Method" acting, before Freud, T. began to set down for herself, her age, and her son the scaffolding upon which contemporary theatrical style would be built.

WORKS: *The Story of My Life* (1908). *The Russian Ballet* (1913). *The Heart of Ellen Terry* (1928). *Ellen Terry and Bernard Shaw: A Correspondence*, ed. C. St. John (1931). *Four Lectures on Shakespeare* (1932). *Memoirs*, with preface, notes, and additional biographical chapters by E. Craig and C. St. John. (1933).

BIBLIOGRAPHY: Adland, E. *Edy, Recollections of Edith Craig* (1949). Auerbach, N. *Ellen Terry: A Player in Her Time* (1987). Craig, E. G. *Ellen Terry and Her Secret Self* (1931). Craig, E. G. *Index to the Story of My Days* (1957). Manvell, R. *Ellen Terry* (1968). Nicoll, A. *A History of Late Nineteenth-Century Drama* (1949). Prideaux, T. *Love or Nothing: The Life and Times of Ellen Terry* (1975). Shaw, G. B. (attributed) *Lady Wilt Thou Love Me?*, ed. J. Warner (1980). Steen, M. *A Pride of Terrys* (1962).

For articles in reference works, see: *1890s. IDWB. Longman. VB.*

Suzanne Westfall

Tey, Josephine: See *Mackintosh, Elizabeth*

Gertrude Aston Thimelby

BORN: c. 1617, Tixall, Staffordshire.
DIED: 1668, Louvain, Flanders.
DAUGHTER OF: Walter, first Baron of Forfar, and Gertrude Sadler Aston.
MARRIED: Henry Thimelby, Esq.
WROTE UNDER: Gertrude Aston Thimelby; Mrs. Henry Thimelby, Esq.

T. wrote poetry influenced by John Donne and other poets who were favorite writers of members of both the Aston and Thimelby families, as we know from the manuscripts of poetry and letters collected and published by their descendant, Arthur Clifford, in the nineteenth century. The members of both prominent families were Roman Catholic recusants (i.e., Catholics who refused to attend Church of England services and therefore were guilty of a statutory offense) who had close relatives living on both sides of the English Channel. Family members often traveled to and from the Continent for religious study, despite the English penal laws, thus often risking their lives as well as imprisonment or crippling fines for those who lived on the families' estates in Staffordshire and Lincolnshire. The preserved letters to the family in England written by T.'s sister-in-law in Louvain, prioress Winifred Thimelby (1618–90), trace almost the entire history of the family from approximately 1655 to 1690.

Particularly noteworthy are T.'s poems "No Love Like That of the Soule, Contented Poverty" and "To My Husband, H. T.," written in the tradition of seventeenth-century English metaphysical poetry, and with an Augustinian outlook possibly heightened by the influence of her two writing sisters-in-law. Upon the deaths of her husband (c. 1655) and almost simultaneously of her only child, an infant, T. joined Winifred as an Augustinian canoness regular at the English recusant monastery of St. Monica's in Louvain, a convent founded by exiled relatives and associates of Sir Thomas More. Winifred was sister of T.'s husband and of Katherine Thimelby Aston (1614–58), wife of T.'s brother Herbert; Katherine wrote *The Golden Mean*, a noteworthy poem in the style of the English metaphysical poets. When T. was professed a few years later, Winifred described the ceremony in a 1658 letter to the family. It does not seem that anything written by T. outside of England has been preserved.

Winfred's work is of theological importance, for her spiritual letters to her family illustrate an integrated love of God and neighbor beyond the Jansenism of her century to which she alludes as she writes to request news from the family in England: "Do not suppose me . . . dead to the world for . . . I am alive and as nearly concerned for those I love as if I had never left them, and must share in all their fortunes, whether good or bad"; and again, "Age summons me quickly to the grave and I thank God I feel no unwillingness to die, but whilst I live, I must love; God forbid my love should die with life." Her letters are permeated with the influence of the Devotio Moderna of her order's founder, Gerard Grote, as well as with the writings of the medieval Flemish mystics and of St. Augustine, all of whom were read and imitated at St. Monica's.

WORKS: *Tixall Poetry* (1813) and *Tixall Letters* (1815), ed. and intro. Arthur Clifford.

BIBLIOGRAPHY: Durrant, C. S. *A Link Between the Flemish Mystics and English Martyrs* (1925). Guilday, P. *The English Catholic Refugees on the Continent, 1558–1798* (1914). *The Chronicle of the English Augustininan Canonesses Regular at St. Monica's, Louvain*, ed. A. Hamilton (1904, 1906). Latz, D. L., in *Neglected English Literature, 16th–17th Century Recusant Writings—Collected Papers from the Recusant Sessions of the International Medieval Congress, Western Michigan University, 1990–1994* (1997). Latz, D. L., in *Festschrift for James Hogg, Univ. Salzburg* (forthcoming).

Dorothy L. Latz

Angela (Margaret) Thirkell

BORN: 30 January 1890, London.
DIED: 29 January 1961, Bramley, Surrey.
DAUGHTER OF: J. W. Mackail and Margaret Burne-Jones.
MARRIED: James Campbell McInnes, 1911; George Thirkell, 1918.
WROTE UNDER: Leslie Parker; Angela Thirkell.

Born into a milieu of learning, culture, and creativity, T. was the daughter of the classicist and Oxford Professor of Poetry, J. W. Mackail, and of Margaret Burne-Jones, herself the daughter of the famous painter Edward Burne-Jones and Georgiana Macdonald Burne-Jones, an aunt of Rudyard Kipling. The Burne-Jones household, where T. and her sister Clare spent much of their early years, was the haunt of such late nineteenth-century notables as George Eliot, Beatrix Potter, Henry James, John Ruskin, and William Morris and was the subject of her first book, *Three Houses* (1931). At home, there was much reading of Charles Dickens, Anthony Trollope, Elizabeth Gaskell, George Eliot, Charles and Henry Kingsley, and George Macdonald (no relation), all of whose works are reflected in her work.

In 1911, she married James Campbell McInnes; the novelist Colin McInnes is her son. After divorcing McInnes in 1917, in 1918 she married George Thirkell, an Australian by whom she had a son, Lance, the prototype of Tony Morland in her Barsetshire novels.The Thirkells left England for Australia in 1920 on board a troopship, a harrowing adventure that was the subject of *Trooper to the Southern Cross* (1934), written under the name "Leslie Parker." The troopship was crowded with army prisoners, many deserters, and some hardened criminals who organized a near-mutiny. The mayhem and destruction, the first T. experienced in her sheltered life, may have contributed to her lack of confidence in the lower classes that is continually expressed in her novels, at first in Dickensian humor, later in bitterness.

Always homesick for England, T. made a long visit in 1928 and returned permanently in 1929, her marriage having failed. As she had in Australia, T. began to write for magazines on literary topics, drawing on her family contacts and her own interests, and published her first novel, the popular autobiographical *Ankle Deep* (1933). During this time she was also reader for a British publisher, using her French and German to good effect.

The first of the "Barsetshire" novels (although not so planned) was *High Rising* (1933) whose heroine was Laura Morland, a valiant lady novelist who wrote to support her family. This book was dismissed as mere "feminism" by the *London Times* but led to *The Demon in the House* (1934), in which Barsetshire (modelled on Trollope) was first mentioned as T.'s imaginary world. After a break in 1935, when she published another autobiographical novel, *O These Men, These Men!,* and a children's book, *The Grateful Sparrow,* the "Barsetshire" novels continued yearly until 1960.

The Barsetshire novels have been called both social history (by Elizabeth Bowen) and social documentary (by Richard Church), and as such have engendered controversy as to whether they are valuable as descriptions of a lost middle class or to be condemned for false values. A good deal of the appreciation of her work is due to her unabashed debt to Trollope, the Kingsleys, George Meredith, and Dickens. These nineteenth-century writers gave not only rich allusive texture but plots and parts of plots as well. *Miss Bunting* (1945), for instance, has heroines and a plot very similar to Trollope's *The Two Heroines of Plumpington,* a design for the T. material that worked very well until the last tired novels, which are essentially pastiche. Her point of view, if dated carefully, is that of an upper-middle-class observer of a decade or so before her birth and owed much to her early Burne-Jones exposure as well as her academic home. Her perspective, seen by critics as reactionary, was in fact nostalgic; she regretted not knowing a world that had never been hers but through hearsay.

Other writings of note include *The Fortunes of Harriette* (1936) and *Coronation Summer* (1937), which utilized her love of research, the first a biography of Harriette Wilson, the intellectually liberated eighteenth-century courtesan, and the second a fictionalization of Queen Victoria's coronation festivities in 1837. During her career she also wrote short stories and novelettes for various magazines; these she deprecated and they have never been collected.

WORKS: *Three Houses* (1931). *Ankle Deep* (1933). *High Rising* (1933). *The Demon in the House* (1934). (as Leslie Parker) *Trooper to the Southern Cross* (1934). *Wild Strawberries* (1934). *The Grateful Sparrow and Other Stories* (1935). *O These Men, These Men!* (1935). *August Folly* (1936). *The Fortunes of Harriette* (1936). *Coronation Summer* (1937). *Summer Half* (1937). *Pomfret Towers* (1938). *Before Lunch* (1939). *The Brandons* (1939). *Cheerfulness Breaks In* (1940). *Northbridge Rectory* (1941). *Marling Hall* (1942). *Growing Up* (1943).

The Headmistress (1944). *Miss Bunting* (1945). *Peace Breaks Out* (1946). *Private Enterprise* (1947). *Love Among the Ruins* (1948). *The Old Bank House* (1949). *County Chronicle* (1950). *The Duke's Daughter* (1951). *Happy Returns* (1952). *Jutland Cottage* (1953). *What Did It Mean?* (1954). *Enter Sir Robert* (1955). *Never Too Late* (1956). *A Double Affair* (1957). *Close Quarters* (1958). *Love at All Ages* (1959). (with C. A. Lejeune) *Three Score and Ten* (1961).

BIBLIOGRAPHY: Bowen, E., intro. to *An Angela Thirkell Omnibus*, ed. M. F. Gilbert (1966). McInnes, G. *The Road to Gundagai* (1965, includes reminiscences of his mother). *Journal of the Angela Thirkell Society* (1981–). Kenny, V., in *Aspects of Australian Fiction*, ed. A. Brissenden. Lee, H. *New Yorker* (7 October 1996). Strickland, M. *Angela Thirkell: Portrait of a Lady Novelist* (1977).

For articles in reference works, see: *Bloomsbury. CA. Feminist. Longman. MBL. Oxford. TCA* and *SUP. TCW. ToddBWW.*

Eleanor Langstaff

Elizabeth Thomas

BORN: 1675, Surrey.
DIED: 5 February 1731, London.
DAUGHTER OF: Emmanuel Thomas and Elizabeth Osborne Thomas.
WROTE UNDER: Corinna.

Born to gentility, T. faced poverty, illness, the loss of loved ones, and isolation most of her life. From her birth, T. was subject to unfortunate conditions that shaped her life. The first was the fact that her mother, Elizabeth, was only a teenager when T. was born, and her father, Emmanuel, was sixty years old. Despite their gentility—Elizabeth was from an old Kent family and Emmanuel was an eminent London lawyer—they quickly faced difficult times. Within two years of T.'s birth, her father died, leaving the family in poverty. With her mother and grandmother, T. settled in Dyott Street, Bloomsbury.

In 1700, T. met Richard Gwinnett, a barrister and heir to a Gloucestershire estate, who courted her despite his family's objections. For almost seventeen years they exchanged poems, letters, and literary criticism. Meanwhile, in 1711 she became seriously ill after swallowing a bone. When Gwinnett was finally free to marry, having come into some money, T. was forced to postpone their union because her mother was dying of breast cancer. Gwinnett died in 1717 in T.'s home on Dyott Street. He left her £600, but eight years of litigation took all but £213, and that was used to pay creditors after her mother's death the following January.

Self-educated, T. showed early aptitude for learning, claiming that by the age of five she had read the Bible three times. In 1699, T. sent two poems to John Dryden, who compared her to Katherine Philips and the Theban poetess Corinna. The name stuck. Her first volume of poetry was published in 1722. Titled *Miscellany Poems on Several Subjects,* then reissued as *Poems on Several Occasions* four years later. T. offers her readers some satires, views on platonic love, and feminist views on the limitations of women's education and marriage. T. early recognized her kinship with women, especially her friends Mary Astell and Lady Mary Chudleigh.

By 1726, to alleviate her poverty, she resorted to selling twenty-five letters by Alexander Pope that her friend Henry Cromwell had given her. She sold them for ten guineas to Edmund Curll, who published them. Two years later, Pope retaliated in *The Dunciad* with the harsh portrait of T. as "Curll's Corinna." In 1727, she invented an account of Dryden's death and funeral, which Curll published three years later in *Memoirs of Congreve.* That same year, T. was sent to debtor's prison where she wrote with Curll *Codrus, or The Dunciad Dissected,* which he published in 1728. The following year, 1729, she was to be released from prison, but, unable to pay the jailer's fees, she was not freed. To raise funds, T. published letters from Henry Norris of Bemerton and asked other friends for money. She was released from prison the following June. In 1731, again needing money, T. published *Pylades and Corinna,* her autobiography and letters that she and Gwinnet exchanged during their courtship. She died destitute on 5 February 1731 in her room on Fleet Street. Lady Margaret de La Warr paid for her burial in the churchyard of St. Bride's.

One could say that T. was unlucky from her birth. Born to gentility and endowed with literary aspirations, T. should have had a more satisfying life. Instead of literary fame and respect, she is defined today by her notorious controversy with Pope. Yet, like other women of her time, T. wrote for herself and her friends with whom she exchanged letters and poems about reason, science, and platonic love. Many, even Pope at first, enjoyed her good sense, wit, and decorum.

WORKS: *Miscellany Poems on Several Subjects* (1722). *Poems on Several Occasions* (1726). *Codrus; or the Dunciad Dissected. To which is added Farmer Pope and his Son* (1728). *The Metamorphoses of the Town; or, a View of the Present Fashions. A Tale: after the Manner of Fontaine* (1730). *Pylades and Corinna; or Memoirs of the Lives, Amours, and Writings of Richard Gwinnet, Esquire, and Mrs. Elizabeth Thomas, junior . . . To which is prefixed the Life of Corinna written by herself* (1731). *Pylades and Corinna . . . Richard Gwinnet, Esq. of Great Shurdington in Gloucestershire, and Mrs. Elizabeth Thomas, of Great Russell Street, Bloomsbury: Consisting of Letters, and Other Miscellaneaous Pieces, in Prose and Verse, Which Passed Between Them during a Courtship of Above Sixteen Years,* 2nd ed. (title of Vol. II: *The Honourable Lovers, or, The Second and Last Volume of Pylades and Corinna: Being the Remainder of Love Letters, and Other Pieces, (in Verse and Prose) which Passed Between Richard Gwinnett . . . and Mrs. Elizabeth Thomas . . . to which is added, a Collection of Familiar Letters, Between Corinna, Mr. Norris, Capt. Hamington, Lady Chudleigh, Lady Pakington, &c.*; appended to Vol. II with separate title page and pagination: *The Country Squire, or, Christmas Gambol; A Comedy, Written by Pylades*) (1732).

BIBLIOGRAPHY: Ayre, W. *Memoirs of Alexander Pope* (1745). Cibber, T. *The Lives of the Poets* (1753). Curll, E. *Mis-*

cellanea (1727). Dilke, C. W. *Papers of a Critic* (1875). Dryden, J. *Critical and Miscellaneous Prose Works,* ed. E. Malone (1800). Dryden, J. *Works,* ed. W. Scott (1808). Dryden, J. *Letters,* ed. C. E. Ward (1942). Guerinot, J. V. *Pamphlet Attacks on Alexander Pope* (1969). Lipking, J. *ECLife* (1988). Lonsdale, R. *Eighteenth-Century Women Poets* (1989). Pope, A. *Dunciad* (1743). Pope, A. *The Works of Alexander Pope,* ed. W. Elwin and J. W. Courthope (1871–89). Rogers, K. *Feminism in Eighteenth-Century England* (1982). *The Correspondence of Alexander Pope,* ed. G. Sherburn (1956). Steiner, T. R. *N&Q* (1983). Thomas, W. M. *N&Q* (1855). *Memoirs of William Congreve,* ed. C. Wilson (1730).

For articles in reference works, see: *Bell. DNB. Feminist. ToddBWW.*

Sophia B. Blaydes

Thompson, A. C.: See *Meynell, Alice*

Thompson, A. C.: See *Meynell, Alice*

Alice Wandesford Thornton

BORN: 13 February 1626, Kirklington, Yorkshire.
DIED: Winter 1706/1707, East Newton, Yorkshire.
DAUGHTER OF: Christopher Wandesford and Alice Osborne.
MARRIED: William Thornton, 1651.

The life of T. is worth our attention, but, ironically, it comes down to us because her autobiography was valued in the late nineteenth century as "a kind of family history," a reconstruction of several small manuscript volumes, all written by T. Despite the necessity of reading it at second hand, the autobiography today reveals the conditions of life during mid-seventeenth-century England and the particular circumstances and character of an exceptional woman. T.'s lot is one that attracts our attention because of the many trials and losses she endured. It also becomes a testimony to the strength and resilience T. derived from the memory of her mother and from her faith.

T. memorialized her father, Christopher Wandesford, a man of good estate, domestic virtue, and strict religious principles best known as a statesman. He had accompanied his cousin, the Earl of Strafford, to Ireland, where Wandesford became Lord Deputy with a considerable estate and nobility. He died at an early age, however, leaving his widow with three young children. She settled in Hipswell and raised her children according to those principles instilled in her by her own father and honored by her husband, especially the lessons of piety. It is those lessons that sustained T.

T.'s husband was of the minor gentry of Yorkshire, from a family that had been Roman Catholic until the early seventeenth century. During the few years they were married, Thornton was weak and careless; when he died, he left T. with few resources other than those that were a part of her heritage and her character. She remained alone in their home until her death. During those years, T. wrote of her youth, a time she recalled with some contentment—especially the days before her marriage when she lived with her mother.

T.'s autobiography, however, is not a pleasant remembrance of things past; it is, instead, a vindication of her name and her actions. With as much evidence as she could gather, T. reveals, point by point, how she was cheated and slandered and how she was forced to endure extreme poverty from the time she married until her death. She was cheated by her brother, she was humiliated by her husband's limitations, and she was slandered by those who stood to benefit from her struggles. Although T.'s autobiography ends in 1669, additional material about her later years comes from the diary and letters of her son-in-law, Dean Comber, and from her last will and testament. From the first pages, T. recounts her gratitude to God, even while she is describing some awful events, such as, for example, when she fell and almost died. The view that she survives to remember God's mercy becomes one of the forces in T.'s life, infusing her autobiography with its power and purpose.

A number of first-hand accounts of the Civil War—the Wandesfords were Royalists—bring to life the confrontations between the religious and the political factions. Her account of the beheading of King Charles I testifies to the despair and righteousness of many in England who suffered at the hands of the parliamentarians. When the Wandesfords' property was sequestered in 1651 and when her oldest brother died, T. suffered even more—this time, however, at the hands of her younger brother, Christopher, who became the heir. To escape his greed, T.'s mother urged T. to marry. T. writes, however: "I was exceedingly sattisfied in that happie and free condittion, wherein I injoyed my time with delight abundantly in the service of my God, and the obedience I owed to such an excelent parent." She marries, but on her wedding day she is so ill that she fears that God does not want her to wed. She writes: "It highly concerned me to enter into this greatest change of my life with abundance of feare and caution, not lightly, nor unadvisedly, nor, as I may take my God to witnesse that knowes the secretts of hearts, I did it not to fulfill the lusts of the flesh, but in chastity and singleness of heart, as marrieing in the Lord."

The problems with her marriage, childbirth, and her widowhood are rich sources for those who want to know more about the condition of women during the seventeenth century. No richer source exists, despite its being secondhand. T.'s patience, goodness, and endurance endear her to her readers, who admire and learn what it was to be a woman at that time.

WORKS: *The Autobiography of Mrs. Alice Thornton, of East Newton, Co. York,* ed. C. Jackson (1875).

BIBLIOGRAPHY: Fraser, A. *The Weaker Vessel* (1984; provides commentary on hundreds of women of the seventeenth century, frequently referring to T.). Rose, M. B., in *Women in the Middle Ages and the Renaissance: Literary and Historical Perspectives,* ed. M. B. Rose (1986).

For articles in reference works, see: *Bell. BioIn. DNB. Feminist.* Stirling, A.M.W. *Odd Lives* (1959).

Sophia B. Blaydes

Thrale, Hester: See *Piozzi, Hester Lynch Salusbury Thrale*

Mary Tighe

BORN: 9 October 1772, Dublin, Ireland.
DIED: 24 March 1810, Woodstock, County Kilkenny, Ireland.
DAUGHTER OF: the Reverend William Bla[t]chford and Theodosia Tighe.
MARRIED: Henry Tighe, 1793.
WROTE UNDER: M. T.; Rosanna; Mary Tighe; Mrs. Tighe; Mrs. Henry Tighe.

Though she led a sad, short, and sickly life and found little pleasure in a strained and childless marriage, T. was one of the most celebrated Irish women poets of her day. At the height of her vogue, T.'s "wild, witching tales" and Irish ballads thrilled readers well beyond her native Wicklow. Her volume of collected works (1811) was reissued in Dublin, London, Edinburgh, and, in 1812, Philadelphia; her work remained in print until the mid-nineteenth century. The fact that T. sat for George Romney, one of London's most fashionable portraitists, further attests to her celebrity and prestige.

In spite of personal unhappiness and illness, T. led a privileged life that emphasized the joys of learning. She was introduced in girlhood to classical studies and foreign languages, and she was conversant with English, French, German, Irish, and Scottish literatures. T.'s manuscripts display a lovely aristocratic hand and an obvious familiarity with literary manuscripts and manuscript formatting. Her father, the Reverend William Bla[t]chford, a Protestant cleric and bookman, was the librarian at Marsh's Library, Dublin, formerly rector at St. Werburg's, and chancellor of St Patrick's Library, Dublin. T. also had an accomplished mother, Theodosia Blan[t]chford (née Tighe), whose guidance is acknowledged in T.'s "Sonnet. Addressed To My Mother," which prefaces T.'s *Psyche:* "to thee belong / The graces which adorn my first wild song." In 1793, at the age of twenty, T. reluctantly married her first cousin, Henry Tighe, of Woodstock, County Wicklow, who represented the borough of Inistioge, Kilkenny, in the Irish Parliament. This union was neither felicitous nor fruitful, and T. evidently found a happier relationship with her husband's brother, William Tighe, also a poet.

Owing to the great success of her signature poem, *Psyche; or, The Legend of Love,* (1795), T. was a major contributor to the early flowering of Romantic poetry. Her major influence on John Keats and the Romantic School was first brought to notice in 1861 by Charles Cowden Clarke in *The Atlantic Monthly* and was then examined at length in 1928 by Earle Vonard Weller. His comparative study identified "nearly four hundred parallel passages" in T. and Keats. Hence it is astonishing that T. could be accused of having "plagiarized Keats," notably by Germaine Greer in *Slip-Shod Sibyls* (1995), when it was Keats who drew from T.

Like many Irish writers of her time, T. was a dual-language author who often composed in her native tongue but published in English (and in England) to attract a broader market and reputation. Her writings demonstrate the strong influence of new aesthetic and literary values that dominated the latter half of the eighteenth century and the first quarter of the nineteenth century. These new values, discussed in Edmund Burke's *Philosophic Enquiry into the Origin of Our Ideas of the Sublime and Beautiful* (1756), promoted sublimity, the past, the supernatural, and strong emotion. For a while T.'s verse enjoyed a robust popularity, but with the decline of Romanticism and the rise of the Victorians her verse fell into relative obscurity. Only in the twentieth century, with the resurgence of interest in Irish literature and in women writers, has T. found an appreciative, second audience. T.'s material derived from two sources: her native Rosanna, County Wicklow, whose pastoral beauty held compelling transformative power for her; and the world of myth and faerie. In her allegorical tales and romantic narratives, T. proved herself a capable imitator of Apuleius, Ovid, and especially Edmund Spenser.

Due to her husband's political engagements, T. spent the first eight years of her marriage in London, where her literary interests were further stirred by exposure to prominent English and Anglo-Irish writers. It was during these years that T. launched her chief work, *Psyche.* When she returned to Ireland, T. began circulating her writings, then publishing them for private distribution. She soon became the darling of the Dublin *literati,* evidently seeing herself as a modern-day pastoral and greeting friends and visitors in pastoral garb (wearing a chaplet of roses about her head, for example). She became known as "Rosanna," after her beloved home in County Wicklow whose natural beauty she both celebrated and personified. With profits from her popular verse, T. built an addition to the orphan asylum in County Wicklow, "The Psyche Ward." She also contributed to the Methodist Home of Refuge in Dublin, which her mother had founded. In about 1803, T. became seriously ill with consumption. A note in the 1811 edition of her works, signed "W. T." (probably William Tighe, her brother-in-law), indicates that T. died "after six years of protracted malady." She succumbed in her thirty-seventh year at her brother-in-law's home in Woodstock.

T.'s small but diversified canon consists chiefly of poetry and light verse. She exercised her muse in the descriptive, supernatural, and sentimental modes. Her diverse poetic forms include the tale, ballad, sonnet, verse-epistle, and biblical imitation. T.'s principal work, *Psyche,* is a loose, allegorical imitation of Apuleius's version of the Cupid and Psyche legend. In the opening verse, T. writes that her poem will "tell of goodly bowers and gardens rare, / Of gentle *blandishments* and amorous play, / And all the *lore of love,* in courtly verse essay." This substantial first effort consists of six long cantos in Spenserian stanza, running just over 200 pages; it was originally written in Irish and completed in 1795. The poem was issued for private circulation in English in 1805 but not in a commercial edition, introduced by her brother-in-law, until a year after her death. T.'s preface to this volume had been written shortly after the 1805 edition. William Tighe was wise to include these important pages in the 1811 posthumous issue, for they reveal something of T.'s artistic principles and temperament. In her preface, T. responds to a minority of critics of her 1805 version, who had churlishly charged her with plagiarism, obscenity, and bad writing, as was predictable at this time. In a bold, confident voice, she asserts that her poem is a tasteful representation of love. She also defends her "method of perplexing allegory" and her (florid) style, which, she emphasizes, does not retain "such obsolete words as in Spenser and his imitators." As for plagiarism, T. boasts of eclectic reading habits and states that *Psyche* (her "first wild song") is the "fruit of a much indulged taste."

T.'s work was generally praised, and her literary reputation during her lifetime was high and unblemished. Sir James Mackintosh, in a diary entry of 27 January 1812, judged the last three cantos of *Psyche* as poetry "of surpassing beauty, and beyond all doubt the most faultless series of verse ever produced by a woman" (though still inferior to his favorites, Madame de Staël and Joanne Baillie). William Howitt, in his popular *Homes and Haunts of the Most Eminent British Poets* (1847), judged that "None but Spenser has excelled Mrs Tighe in allegory." G. W. Bethune, in *British Female Poets* (1848), considered T. "unequalled in classical elegance by any English female. . . . She has the rare quality for a poetess of not sparing the *pumice-stone,* for her verse is polished to the highest degree." T.'s collected works, an immediate best-seller, was reprinted into the mid 1850s. In no contemporary edition was T. identified on the title page as anyone other than "Mrs Henry Tighe."

In addition to *Psyche,* T. wrote a privately printed thirty-five page memoir, *Mary: A Series of Reflections during 20 Years* (1811). She also wrote an unpublished autobiographical novel, *Selena* (five volumes in manuscript). This little-known text was completed in 1809 but lost to the public until 1940, when it was "found." Some uncollected verses of T.'s appeared in the *Amulet* (1827–28). Sections of her (destroyed) diary were reportedly copied by a relative.

Much of T.'s poetry is an indigenous Irish poetry, to the extent that it was originally written in Irish, drew upon Irish lore, and celebrated the prospects of Wicklow, but her work does not address such timely Irish issues as the Rising of 1798 or the Act of Union in 1800, nor does it allude to contemporary feminist issues. T.'s was not an intellectual or polemical poetry but rather a poetry of sensibility and imagination. Yet, as her preface in the 1811 edition revealed, T. was a proud writer who could be contentious in the face of criticism. Her short career was successful, and T. was significantly promoted by her kin and admirers in Wicklow, Dublin, and London. The 1812 Philadelphia edition of her works resulted in a T. vogue in the United States. Though postmodern readers are apt to find T. more charming than impressive, she was an inspired imitator of classical and Renaissance verse, and she produced an interesting and appealing range of writings over a short period of time, writings that won large numbers of readers. The greatest testament to T.'s literary achievement is her resonance in Keats, whose genius was evidently nourished on occasion by T.'s exotic material and vivid imagery.

WORKS: *Psyche; or, The Legend of Love, written in Irish* (1795; circulating in MS. for about a decade; first ed., London, 1805, private printing, fifty copies; second ed., 1811, first public printing, *Psyche, with Other Poems,* quarto, with preface, notes, and Romney frontispiece). *Selena* (unpublished autobiographical novel, 5 vols. in MS., c. 1809, "found" 1940). *Mary: A Series of Reflections during 20 Years* (T.'s memoir, 1811, privately printed by William Tighe). Miscellaneous verse: *The Amulet* (T.'s diary, reportedly destroyed but copied in sections by a relative, 1827–28). *Works of Mary Tighe, Published and Unpublished,* ed. P. Henchey (1957). *Psyche; or, The Legend of Love,* ed. D. H. Reiman (1978). Anthologies with selections: *The Field Day Anthology of Irish Writing, Vol. IV: Women,* ed. S. Deane (1997). *Pillars of the House: An Anthology of Verse by Irishwomen from 1690 to Present,* ed. A. Kelly (1987). *New Oxford Book of Irish Verse,* ed. T. Kinsella (1986).

BIBLIOGRAPHY: Bethune, G. W. *British Female Poets* (1848). Cruikshank, C. H. *Memorable Women of Irish Methodism* (1882). Hamilton, C. J. *Notable Irishwomen* (1904). Howitt, W. *Homes and Haunts of the Most Eminent British Poets* (1847). Mackintosh, J. *Diary* (1812). Weller, E. V. *Keats and Mary Tighe* (1928; identifies some 400 parallel passages; collates *Psyche,* includes 1811 ed. of T.'s works and photo of T. holograph). *The Orlando Project: An Integrated History of Women's Writing in the British Isles* (U. of Alberta, Canada, forthcoming).

For articles in reference works, see: *DLB* (unreliable). *British Women Poets of the Romantic Era,* ed. P. R. Feldman (1997). *Feminist. Woman's Record,* ed. S. J. Hale, 2nd ed. (1855).

Other references: Clarke, C. C. *Atlantic* (1861). Elmes, R. M. *Catalogue of Engraved Irish Portraits* (NLI). *Irish Booklover* (1912). Kucich, G. *KSJ* (1995). *Manuscript Sources for the History of Irish Civilisation* (1970–). Mulvihill, M. E. *International Irish Literatures Conference Proceedings: Hofstra University, 1996, New York* (forthcoming). *PBSA* (1957). Sutton, D. C. *Location Register of English Literary Manuscripts & Letters* (1995). Weekes, A. O., ed. *Unveiling Treasures: The Attic Guide to Published Writings of Irish Women Literary Writers: Drama, Fiction, Poetry* (1993). Databases: *Eighteenth-Century Short-Title Catalogue* (*ESTC*). *Irish Literary Records* (University of Ulster, Coleraine, County Derry).

T.'s papers and manuscripts are preserved in several British libraries. Autographs of *Psyche* are preserved at the National Library of Ireland, The National Library of Wales, Cambridge University Library, and Edinburgh National Library. The Wicklow Papers and an autograph of *Selena* are at the National Library of Ireland. T.'s extensive correspondence (fifty-seven letters, c. 1802–09?) to Joseph Cooper Walker, an Irish antiquary, is preserved at Trinity College Library, Dublin. Other correspondence of T.'s is at the National Library of Ireland, the British Library, Christ Church Library (Oxford), and the University of Birmingham Library. Romney's half-length portrait of T. (engraver E. Scriven; miniature by Comerford after Romney) is at the National Library of Ireland. A half-length vignette of T. by Emma Drummond (engraver J. Hopwood, Jr.) was published in the *Ladies Monthly Magazine* (February 1818).

Maureen E. Mulvihill

Gillian Tindall

BORN: 4 May 1938, London.
MARRIED: R. G. Lansdown.

T. is noted for her fiction, but she has also written books on literary biography (George Gissing) and urban history (Bombay and a London suburb). She received a master's degree with first class honors at Oxford and published her first book when she was twenty-one. She regularly contributes essays and reviews to the *London Times*, the *Sunday Times*, *New Society*, *The Guardian*, *The Observer*, and *The New Statesman*, as well as other publications. T., whose range of interests is wide, has been described as "insatiably curious" about topics that interest her. She has won a number of prizes for her books, including the Mary Elgin Prize (1970) and the Somerset Maugham Prize (1972, for *Fly Away Home*). Though she has been compared to other writers, such as Margaret Drabble, her flat journalistic style and distinctive approach to her characters make her unlike other women writing in Britain at the end of the twentieth century.

Her first book, *No Name in the Street* (1959; in the U.S. as *When We Had Other Names*, 1960) received respectable reviews, as did the several books that followed: *The Water and the Sound* (1961), *The Edge of the Paper* (1963), and *The Israeli Twins* (1963). Most of her protagonists in these, and her other works, are women who have compromised their own values and independence for the security that comes from stable relationships; there comes a time, however, when, due to death, war, or other calamity, these relationships are no longer open to them. Reviewers have noted the frequency with which T.'s central characters seem to accept their lives until such unexpected events occur, after which they move on to evaluate their options, whether renewed relationships with others, a return to their families, or independence. In most cases, acquiescence to conventionality dilutes their individuality and makes them less interesting, but T. evidently intends to suggest that there are relatively few options open and that some of these options carry a price, namely conformity and compromise.

T.'s openness with her characters' lives is evident in her first two novels and is frequently illustrated thereafter. Both *No Name in the Street* and *The Water and the Sound* present young, self-consciously "emancipated" women exploring new worlds, not only physically (Paris) but even more the freedom of choice suddenly thrust upon them. Hence, their self-conscious sexual initiation and awareness of such related activities as miscarriage, a lover's secret homosexuality, and even incest serve only to make them more determined to find their places in life and to do so with drive and tenacity. *The Water and the Sound* is especially effective in showing how the young Nadia gradually discovers the truth about her wild, bohemian father and mother, both of whom had lived fast, romantic lives in Paris and died before Nadia was able to piece together their lives when she too moves to Paris.

These characters' relative impotence in the face of overwhelming forces takes a curious turn, however; when they opt for marriage and conventionality, their determination ceases. The wife in *The Edge of the Paper*, for example, has all that a woman might conventionally desire in a mate, including wealth and good looks, but when her husband's psychotic cruelty is revealed she increasingly feels trapped and threatened but does nothing. The wife in *Someone Else* (1969) reacts intensely to her husband's death, having sublimated all her inner resources to her husband; all she can do is passively accept the support and vicarious emotional protection offered by other men.

T. often balances such ordinary, unassuming people as these wives and other characters against forces that seem disproportionate to the effect they have on the characters; her novels are filled with fiery accidents, infanticide, abortion, murder, incest, and infant deformity, as if to suggest that the reality her characters experience is somehow thrown into relief by the terrors they encounter. All the stories in *Dances of Death: Short Stories on a Theme* (1973) deal with death in some way, but even here T.'s concern seems to be the inadequate reaction of respectable middle-class people to death. In this and in some novels, characters are dispatched with seeming indifference because, as T. notes in her foreword to *Dances of Death*, "It is not the extra-ordinary possibility of life after death which interests me at the moment but, rather, the ordinariness of death, the awkward mystery, within the context of daily life."

Though T.'s fictions have been dismissed as "Bourgeois Hausfrau" novels, she has shown growth as a writer. Her protagonist in *Fly Away Home* (1971), Antonia Boileau, reflects self-consciously about the changes in her life since adolescence and especially her French husband's inability to grapple with his Jewish origins; only after she goes to Israel to see a former lover does she realize that she cannot restore the past. The same necessary acceptance of what is can be found in *The Traveller and His Child* (1975), about a divorced man's grief for his son.

Her later novels have focused on her protagonists' efforts to capture the all-but-forgotten past. *The Intruder* (1979) tells of an English woman's memories of being caught with her son in occupied France during World War II and her attempt in the present to find the truth regarding the past; it has been compared favorably to such novels as Elizabeth Bowen's *The Heat of the Day*. Her 1987 novel, *To the City*, also describes an attempt to recapture the past, in this case in the person of a Nazi Holocaust survivor who returns some forty-five years later, as a successful publisher, to the Europe of the war years and to a former mistress. Though this novel was received less favorably (it was called "self-indulgent and turgid" in the *Times Literary Supplement*), it does suggest T.'s continuing fascination with her characters' traumatic pasts.

T. has also written well-received works of nonfiction, notably *The Born Exile: George Gissing* (1974), which has been uniformly praised for its intelligence, sensitivity, and care; it reflects a thorough awareness of conventional scholarship on Gissing and is sufficiently detailed and documented to warrant its being called (in the *Times Literary Supplement*) the "best critical study of Gissing yet written." T.'s interest in the development of cities has led to her writing *The Fields Beneath: The History of One London Village* (1977), about Kentish Town, a run-down part of the metropolis that was founded in the eleventh century, and *City of Gold: The Biography of Bombay* (1982), both of which have received acclaim from specialists and general readers alike for their vivid re-creation of the cities' lives and for her scholarship.

Though T. has not been accorded the quantity or kind of criticism received by other contemporary writers concerned with middle-class women's struggles to find themselves in a world of change and insecurity, she has established a niche with her fiction for the kind of novel that seems on the surface to be little more than a conventional exploration of the same issues that more exciting writers, such as Lessing or Drabble, have made into metaphysical or psychological territory.

WORKS: *No Name in the Street* (1959; in the U.S. as *When We Had Other Names*, 1960). *The Water and the Sound* (1961). *The Edge of the Paper* (1963). *The Israeli Twins* (1963). *A Handbook on Witches* (1965). *The Youngest* (1967). *Someone Else* (1969). *Fly Away Home* (1971). *Dances of Death: Short Stories on a Theme* (1973). *The Born Exile: George Gissing* (1974). *The Traveller and His Child* (1975). *The Fields Beneath: The History of One English Village* (1977). *The Intruder* (1979). *The China Egg* (1981). *City of Gold: The Biography of Bombay* (1982). *Looking Forward* (1983). *Rosamund Lehmann: An Appreciation* (1985). *To the City* (1987). *Celestine: Voices from a French Village* (1995).

BIBLIOGRAPHY: Schulz, M. F. *Crit* (1992).

For articles in reference works, see: *CA*. *CLC*. *CN*. *WD*.

Other references: *Books and Bookmen* (September 1973, March 1974, September 1979, July 1983, February 1984, September 1984, March 1985). *Economist* (2 February 1974, 17 September 1977). *Encounter* (July 1975, September 1975). *History Today* (October 1980). *Listener* (5 July 1973, 19 June 1975, 13 September 1979, 14 May 1981, 11 March 1982). *LRB* (16 November 1995). *New Statesman* (17 August 1973, 1 February 1974, 27 June 1975, 16 September 1977, 14 September 1979, 16 April 1982, 8 February 1985, 25 January 1991, 14 April 1995). *NYTBR* (8 September 1974, 1 December 1974, 28 April 1996). *Observer* (8 July 1973, 3 February 1974, 15 June 1975, 11 September 1977, 9 September 1979, 12 April 1981, 4 April 1982, 21 August 1983, 16 October 1983, 3 February 1985). *PR* (Winter 1976). *Punch*, (27 February 1980). *Spectator* (9 February 1974, 21 June 1975, 2 May 1981, 10 April 1982, 2 March 1985). *TES* (19 March 1982, 15 February 1985). *TLS* (20 July 1973, 22 February 1974, 20 June 1975, 23 November 1979, 27 March 1981, 16 April 1982, 15 February 1985, 8 May 1987, 8 February 1991, 28 April 1995).

Paul Schlueter

Annie Turner Tinsley

BORN: 1808, Preston, Lancaster.
DIED: 1885.
DAUGHTER OF: Thomas Milner Turner and [given name unknown] Carruthers.
MARRIED: Charles Tinsley, 1833.

T. was a poet and a novelist whose best work addresses the hope that work ignored in its own day might be read and appreciated in the future. Her life was a difficult one: When T. was eight, her father decided to pursue an unsuccessful acting career and continuously relocated his family in search of his dream. T. published her first book of poems, *The Children of the Mint*, at a loss when she was still a teenager (1826 [7?]) and, as a result, she was arrested for debt (although her youth made the arrest technically illegal). She was saved from Fleet Street Prison by the solicitor Charles Tinsley, whom she eventually married in 1833.

T.'s foray into fiction was motivated by financial necessity. Like her father, her husband was financially irresponsible. T's description of her husband both reveals her dry wit and hints at her sense of despair at her marital situation. She comments that "Charles had industry, rectitude and worthiest purpose [but] one fatal obstacle—incapacity." The two had six children and, while her first love was always poetry, T. began regularly to publish fiction in order to support her family, stating that her "married life soon knocked the poetry out of me."

Her first novel, *The Priest of the Nile* (1840), was published during the heyday of sensational fiction and played upon the contemporary fascination with the Eastern "other." After 1840, she wrote numerous short stories, many of which were published in magazines such as *Blackwood's*. She also wrote several other novels, including *Margaret* (1853) and *Women as They Are, by One of Them* (1854). The latter, published anonymously, is the first person narration of a young girl's solitary and emotional childhood and displays imaginative and descriptive talents that outshine its somewhat lackluster plot. *Women* was accused of imitating both *Uncle Tom's Cabin* and *Villette*, charges that were rebutted in an "Advertisement" that claims the novel was written before the publication of either Harriet Beecher Stowe's or Charlotte Brontë's works.

T. did produce a second and final book of poetry, publishing *Lays for the Thoughtful and Solitary* in 1848 as Mrs. Charles Tinsley. The collection is considered T.'s strongest work. The poems express the bitterness and loneliness of a woman poet whose most cherished words fall on unheeding ears. In "Dreams of the Future," T. writes of work neglected by its contemporaries and of hopes that perhaps some future audience will be moved by this work "as our own hearts have thrill'd to the words of the dead." In the excellent poem, "The Grave of L. E. L." about Letitia Elizabeth Landon, T. issues a biting comment on the gendered status of literary success, a comment that speaks to the difficulty of her own life as a writing woman. The line reads: "'Fame,' cold cheat of woman still."

WORKS: *The Children of the Mint* (1826 [7?]). *The Priest of the Nile* (1840). *Lays for the Thoughtful and Solitary* (1848). *Margaret* (1853). *Women as They Are, by One of Them* (1854).

BIBLIOGRAPHY: Peet, H. *Mrs. Charles Tinsley, Novelist and Poet: A Little Known Lancashire Authoress* (1930).

For articles in reference works, see: *Feminist*.

Kirsten T. Saxton

Elizabeth Tipper

FLOURISHED: 1690s.
DAUGHTER OF: William Tipper and Elizabeth Tipper (?).

Virtually nothing is known about T.'s life. One of her poems indicates that she was a country recluse, living unmarried in an "uncouth cottage" for years until she was convinced by friends to try life in the city. She lived as "servant one day, and mistress another," as another poem relates, teaching ladies "Writing and Accompts" on one day and keeping shop-books, "in which business I am a hired servant," on the next. Germaine Greer uses T.'s dedication to Anne, Countess of Coventry, to suggest that T. taught at a Gloucestershire charity school supported by Anne; T.'s reference to teaching "ladies," however, suggests her pupils were of higher social standing. A prefatory poem by John Torbuck, a Ludgershall, Wiltshire, rector, may connect T. with that area. An Elizabeth Tipper was christened in Seend, about twenty-three miles from Ludgershall, in 1640.

T.'s only work, *The Pilgrim's Viaticum, or, The Destitute, but not Forlorn* (1698), is a collection of poems on mainly religious subjects. A series of prefatory poems praises T.'s verse; one offers that "Phillips and Behn, whose praise fame still rehearse, / In all their works don't paralel thy verse." She takes as her theme "the Oracles of God" and writes on, among other subjects, biblical texts and the loss of friends—through marriage as well as death: "But cease, my muse, cease, lest I now despair, / To think how I lost her, that was so dear; / Marriage, which fixes lovers in one state, / Divides us two to places separate."

WORKS: *The Pilgrim's Viaticum: or, The Destitute, but not Forlorn* (1698).

BIBLIOGRAPHY:

For articles in reference works, see: *EWW. Feminist.*

Other references: *Kissing the Rod: An Anthology of Seventeenth-Century Women's Verse,* ed. G. Greer et al. (1988).

Rebecca P. Bocchicchio

Margaret Georgina Todd

BORN: 1859, Glasgow, Scotland.
DIED: 3 September 1918, London.
DAUGHTER OF: James Cameron Todd.
WROTE UNDER: Margaret Todd; Graham Travers.

"New Woman" novelist T. is best known for her participation in the Medical Woman Movement in late-nineteenth century Britain. Her first and most popular novel, *Mona Maclean, Medical Student* (1892), is a charming and loosely autobiographical work advocating the medical education and employment of women. T.'s final and perhaps best literary work was the 1918 biography of her friend and mentor, Sophia Jex-Blake.

Polished and intellectual, T.'s writings reflect the high degree of education attained by the author. T. first prepared for a teaching career by studying at Edinburgh, Glasgow, and Berlin, Germany. In 1888, she enrolled at Jex-Blake's newly opened Edinburgh School of Medicine for Women, from which she graduated in 1894, having passed the M.D. examination at Brussels, Belgium. T. became Jex-Blake's assistant physician at the Edinburgh Hospital and Dispensary for Women and Children, but then effectively retired from medicine a year later when Jex-Blake, who was older, retired. T. had been living in Jex-Blake's Edinburgh home since 1888; in 1895, the two women moved into a house they named Windydene in Sussex, where they lived until Jex-Blake's death in 1912. T.'s few surviving letters indicate that she spent much time after 1895 doctoring friends and family members, but she seems to have returned to active medical duty only briefly during World War I, when domestic hospitals found it difficult to staff themselves adequately.

In retirement, T. maintained a quietly productive literary career. After *Mona Maclean,* she published *Fellow Travellers* (1896), a collection of short stories featuring literal travelers whose lives cross aboard ship or on trains. *Windyhaugh* (1898), T.'s second full-length novel, is a Bildungsroman about a creative Scottish heroine from a religiously repressive home who undergoes a crisis of faith as an adult. *The Way of Escape* (1902) is a fallen-woman novel whose pessimism shows the influence of literary naturalism upon T.'s work. T.'s final novel, *Growth* (1906), again takes up medical themes and even uses for one of its settings the Edinburgh School of Medicine for Women. T.'s novels are fast paced, with sparkling prose and particularly well-developed characters. Her works are solid examples of New Woman fiction, which treat "modern" themes such as marriage, women's education, and sexuality from a strong feminist perspective.

T.'s artistic skill and feminist politics came together wonderfully in her *Life of Sophia Jex-Blake* (1918), a meticulous and engaging labor of love that integrates many of Jex-Blake's now-lost personal papers. Only months after the biography was published, T. committed suicide. Jex-Blake's most recent biographer, Shirley Roberts, speculates that before taking her own life, T. burned Jex-Blake's papers in accordance with instructions in the latter's will. In all likelihood, T. burned her own at this time as well.

WORKS: (as Graham Travers) *Mona Maclean, Medical Student* (1892). (as Graham Travers) *Fellow Travellers* (1896). *Windyhaugh* (1898). *The Way of Escape* (1902). *Growth* (1906). *The Life of Sophia Jex-Blake* (1918).

BIBLIOGRAPHY: Roberts, S. *Sophia Jex-Blake* (1993). Thompson, C. *NCC* (1991).

For articles in reference works, see: *Feminist. Longman.*

Kristine Swenson

Tomson, Graham R.: See *Watson, Rosamund Marriott*

Charlotte Elizabeth Tonna

BORN: 1 October 1790, Norwich, Norfolk.
DIED: 12 July 1846, Ramsgate, Kent.
DAUGHTER OF: Michael Browne.
MARRIED: George Phelan, 1813; Lewis Henry Joseph Tonna, 1837.
WROTE UNDER: C. E.; Charlotte Elizabeth.

T. was a prolific and popular Protestant evangelical editor of religious periodicals, including *The Christian Lady's Magazine* and *The Protestant Magazine,* and writer of social-protest fiction, religious historical novels, political songs, children's stories, poems, travel narratives, and an autobiography; her centerpiece is her religious conversion to evangelicalism. T. is best known for her social-protest works, including the anonymously published *Perils of the Nation* (1843) and novels focusing on women workers, especially *Helen Fleetwood* (1841) and *The Wrongs of Woman* (1843–44). These novels provided a model for "the condition of England" writers including Elizabeth Gaskell, Benjamin Disraeli, Charles Kingsley, and Charles Dickens. *Helen Fleetwood,* which focused on the decline of a family forced from the country to a manufacturing town, was influential in passing the 1844 Factory Bill, which limited female factory workers' days to twelve hours. *The Wrongs of Woman,* prose fiction in four parts, personalizes findings from the parliamentary "Blue Books" investigations into the oppressive work conditions in female-dominated nontextile work such as dressmaking in sweatshops and lace running, a cottage industry. T. reflects the very real degradation of women who were overworked, paid starvation wages, and prone to early blindness and death. Unable to earn a living by sewing, many of these women turned to prostitution. Consistent with commonplace contrasting figures in sketches like John Tenniel's "The Haunted Lady, or 'The Ghost in the Looking-Glass'" in *Punch,* T. calls upon the leisured woman wearing expensive clothing to acknowledge that she and the destitute needlewoman who stitched the garments are "sisters in nature." Industrialization and the accompanying moral decay, T. argued, had robbed many women of their natural role as nurturing, moral guide in the home and had turned others into unknowing oppressors. Both *Helen Fleetwood* and *The Wrongs of Woman* argued that the spiritual breakdown of individuals, especially women, was woven inextricably with the breakdown of the nation.

T.'s father, Michael Browne, was a rector. Reading widely as a child, T. also enjoyed a freedom of movement with her brother that was unusual for the times. She was hearing impaired, if not deaf, by age ten. She married an abusive army officer, George Phelan, in 1813 and lived with him in Nova Scotia, Canada, and then in Ireland. She thereafter crusaded to improve the living conditions of the Irish. When the couple separated around 1824, T. moved in with her brother at Clifton, where she met Hannah More. She published under "Charlotte Elizabeth" in order to protect her income from her husband's claims. Phelan died in 1837, and T. married L.H.J. Tonna, also a religious writer, in 1841. She died of cancer five years later.

T. was a fervent Low Church Evangelical, and many of her religious essays and religious-historical novels like *The Rockite* (1829) are fiercely anti-Catholic. Many of her contemporaries found her "extreme opinions, strongly expressed and perniciously adhered to" disturbing, even though they may have been sympathetic to her goals. In her introduction to T.'s collected works in 1845, Harriet Beecher Stowe, who also valued domesticity and religion, diplomatically praised T.'s autobiography, *Personal Recollections* (1841), as evidence of a "woman of strong mind [and] powerful feeling" committed to moral causes. L.H.J. Tonna brought out *Personal Recollections of Charlotte Elizabeth, Continued to the Close of her Life* in 1848, after her death. Although many of her religious writings seem as harsh today as they did 150 years ago, these pieces and T.'s social-protest fiction have provided historians and literary scholars with valuable insights into the intersections of gender, social class, work, and religion in Victorian England.

WORKS: *The Shepherd Boy; and The Deluge* (1823). *Zadoc, the Outcast of Israel* (1825). *Perseverance: or Walter and His Little School* (1826). *Osric: A Missionary Tale; with The Garden and Other Poems* (1826). *Anne Bell: or, the Faults* (1826; rev. by D. P. Kidder, 1847). *Consistency* (1826). *The Grandfather's Tales* (1826). *Izram, A Mexican Tale and Other Poems* (1826). *The Net of Lemons* (1826). *Rachel. A Tale* (1826; in the U.S. as *The Flower of Innocence; or, Rachel. A True Narrative: With Other Tales,* 1841). *Allen M'Leod, The Highland Soldier* (1827). *The Bird's Nest* (1827). *Edward, The Orphan Boy; A Tale, Founded on Facts* (1827). *The Hen and Her Chickens* (1827). *Little Frank, The Irish Boy* (1827). *The System: A Tale of the West Indies* (1827). *A Visit to St. George's Chapel, Windsor, on the Evening Succeeding the Funeral of His Late Royal Highness the Duke of York* (1827). *A Friendly Address to Converts from the Roman Catholic Church* (1828). *The Willow Tree* (1828). *The Fortune Teller* (1829). *The Rockite: An Irish Story* (1829). *The Swan* (1829). *The Burying Ground* (1830). *Little Oaths* (1830). (as C. E.) *Maternal Martydom: A Fact, Illustrative of the Improved Spirit of Popery, In the Nineteenth Century* (1830?). *A Respectful Appeal to the Primates and Prelates of the Church, on the Present Crisis* (1830?). *Tales and Illustrations,* 2 vols. (1830; enlarged as *The Works of Charlotte Elizabeth,* 1844). *An Address to the Christian Friends and Supporters of the British and Foreign Bible Society, on the Connexion between Socinians and Arians and that Institution* (1831). *The Baby* (1831). *The Fragments* (1831). *The Glowworm* (1831; rev. by D. P. Kidder, 1848). *A Letter to a Friend, Containing a Few Heads for Consideration, on Subjects that Trouble the Church* (1831). *"Try Again"* (1831). *The Wasp* (1831). *The Bible the Best Book* (1832). *The Bow and the Cloud* (1832). *Combination: A Tale, Founded on Facts* (1832). *The Dying Sheep* (1832). *The Girl's Best Ornament: With Other Sketches* (1832). *Ireland's Crisis* (1832). *The Museum* (1832; repub. as *Pleasure and Profit, or Time Well Spent,* 1835; repub. as *Glimpses of the Past,* 1839). *Short Stories for Children,* 2 vols. (1832). *Derry: A Tale of Revolution* (1833; in the

U.S. as *The Siege of Derry; or, Sufferings of the Protestants: A Tale of the Revolution,* 1841). *The Happy Mute; or, the Dumb Child's Appeal* (1833; in the U.S. as *Happy Mute,* 1842). *The Oak-grove* (1833). *White Lies* (1833; in the U.S. as *White Lies; Little Oaths and The Bee,* n.d.). *Good and Bad Luck* (1834). *Grumbling* (1834). *A Few Words on the Eightieth Psalm* (1835). *The Mole* (1835). *The Newfoundland Fisherman. A True Story* (1835; rev. by D. P. Kidder as *The Newfoundland Fisherman,* 1846). *Chapters on Flowers* (1836; in the U.S. as *Floral Biography; or Chapters on Flowers,* 1840; enlarged as *The Flower Garden; or Chapters on Flowers,* 1840). *The Deserter* (1836). *The Industrious Artist* (1836). *Letter Writing* (1836). *Alice Benden, or, The Bowed Shilling* (1838). *Letters from Ireland* (1838). *Passing Thoughts* (1838). *The Lady Flora Hastings. A Brief Sketch* (1839). *The Simple Flower* (1840). *Conformity: A Tale* (1841). *Dangers and Duties. A Tale* (1841). *Falsehood and Truth* (1841). *Helen Fleetwood* (1841). *A Peep Into Number Ninety* (1841). *Personal Recollections* (1841; repub. by L.H.J. Tonna as *Life of Charlotte Elizabeth, as Contained in her Personal Recollections* and as *Personal Recollections, with Explanatory Notes,* 1848). *Philip and His Garden: and Other Tales Suitable for Sabbath Schools* (1841). *Backbiting* (1842; repub. as *Backbiting Reproved, The Visit, and Other Sketches,* 1860s). *The Bee* (1842). *"Principalities and Powers in Heavenly Places"* (1842). *The Glory of Israel; or, Letters to Jewish Children on the Early History of Their Nation* (1843). *Israel's Ordinances. A Few Thoughts on Their Perpetuity Respectfully Suggested in a Letter to the Right Rev., the Bishop of Jerusalem* (1843). *Judah's Lion* (1843). *Perils of the Nation; an Appeal to the Legislature, the Clergy, and the Higher and Middle Classes* (1843). *Promising and Performing. A True Narrative* (1843). *Second Causes; or, Up and Be Doing* (1843). *The Wrongs of Woman,* 2 vols. (1843). *The Church Visible in All Ages* (1844). *The Female Martyrs of the English Reformation* (1844). *Kindness to Animals* (1844; in the U.S. as *Kindness to Animals; or, The Sin of Cruelty Exposed and Rebuked,* 1845). *Mesmerism. A Letter to Miss Martineau* (1844). *Ridley, Latimer, Cranmer, and Other English Martyrs* (1844). *The Yew-tree, and Other Stories* (1844). *The Convent Bell; and Other Poems* (1845). *Judaea Capta. An Historical Sketch of the Siege and Destruction of Jerusalem by the Romans* (1845). *Works of Charlotte Elizabeth,* ed. H. B. Stowe (1845). *Posthumous and Other Poems* (1846). *Richard and Rover* (rev. by D. P. Kidder, 1846). *The Snow-Ball* (rev. by D. P. Kidder, 1846). *Days of Old* (1847). *The Minor Poems of Charlotte Elizabeth, Written Especially for Juvenile Readers* (1848). *War with the Saints* (1848). *Humility Before Honor, and Other Tales and Illustrations. With a Brief Memoir of the Author by William B. Sprague* (1849). *James Orwell, the Mountain Cottager* (1840s?). *Stories from the Bible; to Which is Added, Paul, the Martyr of Palestine* (1840s). *Memoir of John Britt, the Happy Mute Compiled from the Writings Letters, and Conversation of Charlotte Elizabeth* (1850). *Bible Characteristics* (1851). *The Peep of Day* (1852). *Wants and Wishes* (1854). *Stories for Children* (1854). *Juvenile Stories for Juvenile Readers* (1858). *The Red Berries* (1850s?). *Juvenile Tales for Juvenile Readers* (1861). *Little Tales for Little Readers* (1861). *The Boat* (n.d.). *The Star* (n.d.). *The Two Carpenters* (n.d.). *The Two Servants* (n.d.).

BIBLIOGRAPHY: Brantlinger, P. *The Spirit of Reform* (1977). Cazaman, L. *The Social Novel* (1973). Corbett, M. *WS* (1990). Fryckstedt, M. *BJRL* (1980). Fryckstedt, M. *VPR* (1981). Kaplan, D. *Mosaic* (1985). Kestner, J. *Protest and Reform: The British Social Narrative by Women, 1827–1867* (1985). Kestner, J. *TSWL* (1983). Kovacević, I. and S. Kanner. *NCF* (1970). Kowaleski, E. *TSWL* (1982).

For articles in reference books, see: *DNB. Feminist. ToddBWW. VB.*

Carol Shiner Wilson

Sue (Susan Lilian) Townsend

BORN: 2 April 1946, Leicester.
DAUGHTER OF: John Johnstone and Grace Johnstone.
MARRIED: Keith Townsend, 1964; Colin Broadway, 1986.

Playwright and humorist T. became the best-selling author in Britain in the 1980s for her creation of Adrian Mole, a teenager beleaguered with acne, straying parents, and intellectual pretensions. The original book, *The Secret Diary of Adrian Mole, Aged 13 3/4* (1982), was followed by *The Growing Pains of Adrian Mole* (1984), which brought the hero to age sixteen. These two books have been translated into more than twenty languages, to worldwide acclaim. T.'s musical adaptation (with Ken Howard and Alan Blaikley, 1984) was followed by *The Secret Diary of Adrian Mole Songbook* (1985), and the television series began in 1986. T. continued the diaries in a column in *Women's Realm* magazine and published three further volumes of diary entries that carry Adrian into adulthood.

Adrian Mole grows up in Leicester (T.'s home town) in a dispirited working-class neighborhood. His diaries record the dismal state of the National Health Service, the Department of Social Services, the public comprehensive school, and the services for old-age pensioners. When hot school lunches are eliminated, Adrian ponders, "Perhaps Mrs Thatcher wants us to be too weak to demonstrate in the years to come." Adrian's travails are more personal than political, however. His mother runs off with a neighbor, while his father has a fling with a woman Adrian names "the Stick Insect." Adrian moons over the elusive, socially superior Pandora, tries to avoid the local bully, and befriends a surly octogenarian. He notes his passing intellectual fancies in his diary and records his poetry and sections of his dreadful novel, *Lo! The Flat Hills of My Homeland,* alongside his disappointing correspondence with publishers, agents, and the BBC. Adrian never gives up, declaring "I feel it incumbent upon me to promote artisticness wherever I tread."

T. created another best-selling sensation with *The Queen and I* (1992), which she also adapted into a radio series and a musical play (1994, with Ian Dury and Mickey Gallagher). In the book, a republican government has ousted the monarchy and rehoused the royal family in a council estate aptly named Hell Close, where they meet the locals and begin to adapt to their new lives. The Queen learns to fasten her own brassiere and to make soup, while the Queen Mother supplements her pension by betting on the horses, and Princess Diana tries to cope as the single mother of her hooligan son. Although the plot is largely static, there are many funny and occasionally touching scenes, as when the ex-queen wrangles with bureaucrats for an emergency welfare payment. The juxtaposition of the wealthy figureheads and the squalid council life hit a nerve with the British public in the early 1990s, and the book was another enormous success for T.

T. grew up in a working-class family in Leicester and left school at the age of fifteen to work in various unskilled jobs before marrying at eighteen. When her husband left her with three small children, T. took on part-time jobs working in community services. These experiences would later inform her writing and her politics, although she says, "I can't bear proselytizing."

At Leicester's local writing group, T. met director Sue Pomeroy, who staged several of her early plays. T.'s first play, *Womberang* (1979), takes place in the waiting room of a gynecology clinic where the assembled women gather strength and joy from one another. T. continued to write about the decline of health services in *Dayroom* (1981), which was rewritten as *Ear, Nose and Throat* (1988) for a production sponsored by two health service unions. *Bazaar and Rummage* (1982) and *Groping for Words* (1983) each explore the bonding relationships within unlikely groups; the former play treats a group of agoraphobics, and the latter describes the progress of an adult literacy class. *The Great Celestial Cow* (1984), created in collaboration with the Joint Stock theatre company, celebrates the friendship among Asian women facing the difficulties of living in Leicester.

T.'s most sophisticated drama, *Ten Tiny Fingers, Nine Tiny Toes* (1990), is set in a future Britain with codified social classes. Ralph and Lucinda, Class Three, have government approval to have a baby girl, while Dorothy and Pete, Class Five, become "unlawfully pregnant." When Lucinda's unborn child is discovered to have a missing toe, officials inform her that "no child of Government parents can be born with the slightest defect. . . . We are aiming for perfection in our governing class." While Lucinda and Dorothy become unlikely friends, Ralph buys the healthy baby from Pete. In *Ten Tiny Fingers, Nine Tiny Toes*, T. achieves new levels of suspense and narrative tension, while her social satire takes on a sinister edge.

T.'s picaresque novel *Rebuilding Coventry: A Tale of Two Cities* (1988) follows the adventures of Coventry Dakin, a Midlands housewife, who accidentally kills her loathsome neighbor and flees into London "without my handbag." There Coventry encounters the exigencies of homelessness, becoming a prostitute, a maidservant, a bag lady, and an emigrant in quick succession. As ever, T.'s social observations are witty and astute, but the novel's straying plot lines never quite reunite, and individual episodes are more satisfying than the novel as a whole.

Although her work has received little scholarly attention, T. has made a profound impact on British culture of the 1980s and 1990s. Adrian Mole has become a household name, and N. Andrews in 1985 predicted that "when the social history of the 1980s comes to be written, the *Mole* books . . . will probably be considered as key texts." T. has contributed to many periodicals, including *The Times, The Guardian, The Observer, New Statesman,* and *Marxism Today.* In 1993, she was awarded membership into the Royal Society of Literature.

WORKS: *Womberang* (1979). *Dayroom* (1981). *The Ghost of Daniel Lambert* (1981). *Bazaar and Rummage* (1982). *The Secret Diary of Adrian Mole, Aged 13 3/4* (1982). *Groping for Words* (1983). *The Great Celestial Cow* (1984). *The Growing Pains of Adrian Mole* (1984). *The Secret Diary of Adrian Mole, Aged 13 3/4: The Play* (1984, with songs by K. Howard and A. Blaikley). *The Secret Diary of Adrian Mole Songbook* (1985, with songs by K. Howard and A. Blaikley). *The Adrian Mole Diaries* (contains *Secret Diary of Adrian Mole, Aged 13 3/4* and *The Growing Pains of Adrian Mole,* 1985). *Rebuilding Coventry: A Tale of Two Cities* (1988). *Ear, Nose, and Throat* (1989). *The True Confessions of Adrian Albert Mole, Margaret Hilda Roberts, and Susan Lilian Townsend* (1989). *Mr. Bevan's Dream* (1990). *Disneyland It Ain't* (1990). *Ten Tiny Fingers, Nine Tiny Toes* (1990). *Adrian Mole: From Minor to Major* (1991). *The Queen and I* (1992). *Adrian Mole: The Wilderness Years* (1993). *Adrian Mole: The Lost Years* (contains *Adrian Mole: The Wilderness Years,* and selections from *Adrian Mole: From Minor to Major* and *True Confessions of Adrian Albert Mole,* 1994). *The Queen and I: The Play with Songs* (1994, with songs by I. Dury and M. Gallagher). *Ghost Children* (1997).

BIBLIOGRAPHY:

For articles in reference works, see: *CA. Feminist.*

Other references: Andrews, N. *Listener* (1985). *LonT* (28 November 1984, 30 September 1988). *New Statesman* (18 September 1992, 17 June 1994). *New York* (27 September 1993). *NYTBR* (22 April 1990, 12 September 1993). *People* (23 May 1994). *Spectator* (22 February 1992, 4 September 1993). *TES* (23 December 1983, *Washington Post* (24 May 1986, 3 May 1990).

Julia Matthews

Honor (Lilbush Wingfield) Tracy

BORN: 19 October 1913, Bury St. Edmunds, East Anglia (some sources use 19 December 1915).

DIED: 13 June 1989, Oxford.

DAUGHTER OF: Humphrey Wingfield and Christabel May Clare Miller Tracy.

T. was the daughter of a British surgeon, Humphrey Wingfield, and it is probably not stretching the analogy to say that she spent her own career dissecting and eviscerating the natives of Ireland, Spain, and the Caribbean. Most of the unwilling patients die on the table, "hapless victims," according to T. A. McVeigh, "[of] totally uneven contests and nasty little stories of victim and victimizer."

Many of T.'s fictional efforts—*The Straight and Narrow Path* (1956), *The Prospects Are Pleasing* (1958), *The First Day of Friday* (1963), *The Quiet End of Evening* (1972), *In a Year of Grace* (1975), *The Man from Next Door* (1977), and *The Battle of Castle Reef* (1979)—deal with the foibles and failings of the Irish among whom T. lived for the better part of ten years. Ironically, her name and the Irish settings of these novels convinced many readers that she was Irish. Her usual retort was that her ancestor, Beau Tracy, lived in Ireland until 1775. When he later attempted to have the family reinstated as citizens of Ireland, he was imprisoned for debt in Fleet Prison in England and the Irish turned down his petition.

When T. was sent to Ireland in 1950 by the *London Sunday Times* as a special correspondent, she became embroiled in a libel suit filed against her by a country priest who felt insulted by one of her articles; this legal action was her introduction to the convoluted and labyrinthine paths of Irish justice. In *Mind You, I've Said Nothing! Forays in the Irish Republic* (1953, a collection of essays), she explains how her own solicitor managed to defend and betray her in the same courtroom. A somewhat fictionalized account of this same case was the basis for *The Straight and Narrow Path,* in which an English anthropologist, Andrew Butler (who speaks for T.), is sued by a canon. The canon is, of course, represented in court by the same charming and devious Irishman who precipitated the legal battle in the first place.

In typical T. style, this canon is cheated by a plumber who builds him an upstairs bath. Unfortunately for the priest, water does not flow to the second story in houses in Patrickstown, the scene of the novel; but, as T. points out, the priest ordered a tub—he never mentioned water. Like all the Irish plumbing in T.'s novels, it doesn't work and we don't expect it to. The constant reader of her fiction is not surprised when Sabrina Boxham's bathtub in *The Quiet End of Evening* is delivered without faucets or a plug and that the old bathtub has already been removed.

T.'s novels are peopled with silly, annoying, and devious types running naked through the gardens and pell-mell through the books. They usually serve as counterpoint to one sensible character with whom the reader can identify. In *The Prospects Are Pleasing,* he is Felix Horniman, and in *A Number of Things* (1960), set not in Ireland but in Trinidad, he is Henry Lamb, who is entranced by three Indian women, Mummee, Grannee, and Auntee. He is followed in *A Season of Mists* (1961) by Ninian Latouche, only superficially sane, who is surrounded not by Irishmen but by Siamese cats, Italian servants, and the jarring noise of jet planes. This book is a dissection of life in modern anachronistic England.

The First Day of Friday is again set in Ireland, but it is a more bitter book replete with madness, tormented souls, and melancholia. As Walter Allen has noted in the *New York Times Book Review,* this novel "verges on the comedy of despair." It was followed by several happier novels (particularly *The Quiet End of Evening*) and in 1977 by *The Man from Next Door.* The reasonable, sensible type surfaces in Caroline Bigge, a schoolfriend of Penelope Butler's around whom the novel revolves. Ms. Butler is a recently rich heroine (courtesy of the football pools) who is being victimized by her next-door neighbor, Johnny Cruise, and his Indian cohorts, the Khans; Cruise's motive seems to be one thousand years of his Irish ancestors' anger at the English, represented by Ms. Butler. His character is so shady and shallow, and hers so silly and gullible, that the reader has trouble feeling empathy with either of them.

This is perhaps the most glaring fault in the work of T.; as Jill Neville in the *London Sunday Times* has noted, "some of the jokes are too hoary" and the caricatures are a bit heavyhanded to be believable. The reader is usually amused because T. is funny, clever, and even devilish. But there is always a sense of laughing at the characters, who are immersed in their own smug, nonsensical folly. In her works, T. doesn't have much patience for the delusions of these people, and she is an ardent enemy of the superstitions and hypocrisy that permeate twentieth-century life.

In any case, her books have been translated into several languages and she is read and admired from Budapest to New York City. The critics have consistently praised her travel books, particularly *Winter in Castile* (1973), and in this genre she is considered to be without peer.

WORKS: (trans.) *The Conquest of Violence,* by B. deLigt (1937). *Kakemono: A Sketch Book of Post-War Japan* (1950). *Mind You, I've Said Nothing! Forays in the Irish Republic* (1953). *The Straight and Narrow Path* (1956). *Silk Hats and No Breakfast: Notes on a Spanish Journey* (1957). *The Prospects Are Pleasing* (1958). *A Number of Things* (1960). *A Season of Mists* (1961). *The First Day of Friday* (1963). *Men at Work* (1966). *The Beauty of the World* (1967; in the U. S. as *Settled in Chambers*). *De l' Angleterre; or Miss Austen Provides a Footnote; The Sorrows of Ireland* (1967). *The Butterflies of the Province* (1970). *The Quiet End of Evening* (1972). *Winter in Castile* (1973). *In a Year of Grace* (1975). *The Man from Next Door* (1977). *The Ballad of Castle Reef* (1979). *The Heart of England* (1983).

BIBLIOGRAPHY: Gindin, J. *Postwar British Fiction* (1962).

For articles in reference works, see: *CN. DIL. DLB.*

Other references: *BW* (28 April 1968). *LonT* (15 July 1989). McVeigh, T.A. *America* (4 March 1978). *National Observer* (10 August 1968). Neville, J. *LonSunT* (22 August 1975). *NYT* (26 December 1979). *NYTBR* (24 November 1963, 10 March 1968, 8 May 1977). *Time* (5 April 1980).

Mickey Pearlman
(updated by Abby H. P. Werlock)

Trafford, F. G.: See *Riddell, Charlotte Eliza Lawson Cowan*

See Riddell, Charlotte Eliza Lawson Cowan

Anna Trapnel

FLOURISHED: 1642–60.
DAUGHTER OF: William Trapnel.

T. was the most important prophet of the radical millenarian sect the Fifth Monarchists. Among the religious movements of the English Revolution (1640–60), the Fifth Monarchists were distinguished for advocating the use of force to usher in the "Kingdom of Christ" on earth and for prospectively identifying themselves as the governors of the "New Jerusalem." Her coreligionists held T.'s prophecies, all of which affirmed the Fifth Monarchist agenda, in such high esteem because she delivered her divinely inspired messages while fasting for long periods of time. They understood her extraordinary capacity for fasting as a sign of divine possession.

Outside of the information provided in her prophetic treatises, little is known about her. In *The Cry of a Stone* (1654), she tells us that her father, William Trapnel, was a shipwright who lived in Poplar (London). She describes both her mother and father as "living and dying in the profession of the Lord Jesus." Her mother's death (c. 1645) appears to have profoundly influenced the direction of T.'s spiritual life. She records her mother's dying wish that God would particularly bless her daughter: "Lord! Double thy spirit upon my child, These words she uttered with much eagerness three times, and spoke no more" (quoted in Burrage, 1911).

According to her spiritual autobiography, *A Legacy for Saints* (1654), T. received God's "free grace" in 1642 while attending a sermon on Romans: "Suddenly my soul filled with joy unspeakable, and full of glory in believing, the spirit witnessing in that word, Christ is thy wel-beloved, and thou art his." In 1647, she attended the bedside of the prophet Sarah Wight. A young girl of fifteen, Wight became something of a celebrity among Baptists and members of "gathered churches" (now called Congregationalists) when she fasted for seventy-six days and delivered prophecies about her experiences of divine grace. Henry Jessey's account of Wight, *The Exceeding Riches of Grace* (1647), claims that T., also in 1647, fasted and prophesied in a manner akin to Wight's: "About the same time . . . one [T.] . . . then had great enjoyments of God, and could not take in a crumme or sip of the creatures, for full six dayes together."

In 1654, T. emerged as the leading oracle of the Fifth Monarchists. At that time, the Fifth Monarchists were furious with Oliver Cromwell because he had dissolved the Barebones Parliament and declared himself Protector. Just weeks after Cromwell had asserted his authority, T. was "seized upon by the Lord" and fell into a trancelike state that lasted for some eleven days. During this period, she fasted and delivered prophecies, in prose and verse, on topics ranging from God's promise that the Fifth Monarchists would rule the nation to what she believed to be the misguided policies of Cromwell. Her words were transcribed by an anonymous amanuensis and published in 1654 as *The Cry of a Stone*.

In that same year, T. claimed that she was persuaded "by the secret whisperings of the Spirit" to travel from London to Cornwall in order to "do good to poor souls" by relating the "variety of experiences God hath given" her. There, she was accused of being a witch and brought before the Assizes for questioning. Ten days later, she was arrested by the "Souldiers of the Fox" and transported back to London where, much to her chagrin, she was confined to the notorious prison of prostitutes, Bridewell. Her account of her journey to and from Cornwall and her imprisonment was published as *Report and Plea* (1654).

We hear of T. again in 1658 when two collections of her prophecies—*A Voice for the King of Saints* and 1,000-page treatise (untitled and found only in the Bodleian Library at Oxford)—were published. In particular, these texts denounced the members of another sect, the Quakers, as "instruments" of the "Devil." The historian B. S. Capp suggests that T. may have been the "A. T. who was married at Woodbridge, Suffolk" in 1661.

WORKS: *The Cry of a Stone* (1654). *A Legacy for Saints* (1654). *Report and Plea* (1654). *Strange and Wonderful Newes From White-Hall* (1654). *A Voice for the King of Saints* (1658).

BIBLIOGRAPHY: Burrage, C. *English Historical Review* (1911). Capp, B. S. *The Fifth Monarchy Men* (1972). Hobby, E. *Virtue of Necessity* (1988). Mack, P. *Visionary Women* (1992). Smith, N. *Perfection Proclaimed* (1989). Watkins, O. C. *The Puritan Experience* (1972).

For articles in reference works, see: *Bloomsbury. DNB. Feminist. Oxford.*

Teresa Feroli

Travers, Graham: See *Todd, Margaret Georgina*

P[amela]. L[yndon]. Travers

BORN: (as Helen Lyndon Goff) 9 August 1899, Queensland, Australia.
DIED: 23 April 1996, Chelsea, London.
DAUGHTER OF: Robert Travers and Margaret Goff Travers.
WROTE UNDER: P. L. Travers.

T.'s name will forever be linked with that of Mary Poppins, the heroine of her popular series of magical books. Vain, sharp-tongued and fiercely proper, Mary Poppins denies the existence of a magical realm even though she is among its elite. The Poppins *oeuvre,* which extends to nine books, has captivated children from its first volume, *Mary Poppins* (1934), which has been translated into twenty-five languages and has sold millions of copies. Although some elements of the mercurial nanny were clearly derived from T.'s own family, scholars are focusing increasingly upon the antecedents of Mary Poppins in mythic and spiritual sources.

The mythic flavor of T.'s work has been ascribed in part to a childhood steeped in Celtic mythology: Her father was Irish, her mother Scotch-Irish, and T. was brought up by a succession of Irish nannies. She worked as an actress and reporter in Australia and in England, where she moved when she was seventeen. The poet AE (George Russell), editor of the *Irish Statesman,* became her friend and mentor; at his suggestion she submitted poetry to the journal and became a regular contributor during the 1920s. Starting in 1933 she wrote for the *New English Weekly* as drama critic until its demise in 1949. She also contributed poetry, travel pieces, essays, and book and film reviews, and she was a contributing editor for *Parabola: The Magazine of Myth and Tradition* from 1976 until her death.

While recovering from an illness in 1934, she wrote *Mary Poppins,* which was inspired by stories she had invented to amuse two children; in the same year she visited the Soviet Union and published an account of her experiences, *Moscow Excursion.* During World War II, she lived in the United States and worked for the British Ministry of Information, at which time she visited various Pueblo, Hopi, and Navajo reservations. As well as adding to the Mary Poppins series, she wrote New Year's gift books for private circulation: *Happy Ever After* (1940), *Aunt Sass* (1941), *Ah Wong* (1943), and *Johnny Delaney* (1944). A book for children, *I Go By Sea, I Go By Land* (1941), describes the wartime experiences of two British children evacuated to the United States.

She returned to the United States as writer-in-residence at Radcliffe College (1965) and Smith College (1966) and as a guest lecturer at Scripps College in California (1970). In 1977, she was awarded the Order of the British Empire, followed the next year by an honorary doctorate from Chatham College, Pittsburgh. She died in 1996.

Although Mary Poppins has become a cultural icon and her books are classics of children's literature, she did not bring uninterrupted gratification to her author. T. found herself labelled a children's writer although she vigorously resisted the tendency to classify books as "children's" or "adult." The 1963 Disney film, for which T. served as consultant, offered a sugar-coated version of the heroine, reducing her mystery and complexity. *Mary Poppins* has also come under attack for the purported racism of the ethnic characterization in the "Bad Tuesday" chapter, which T. revised in 1972 to remove "pickaninny" language, and again, more drastically, in 1981, when she replaced all the ethnic characters with animals. The continuous theme underlying the Poppins books, however, is one of harmony among all things, and every episode in *Mary Poppins*'s history attests to this cosmic connectedness.

T.'s continuing interest in mythology and religion, including Zen and Taoism, surfaced not only in the *Poppins* books but also in *The Fox at the Manger* (1963), as well as *Friend Monkey* (1971), which was based on the Hindu myth of Hanuman. Discussions of Mary Poppins have attempted to identify her mythic and spiritual roots, tracing her ancestry to such figures as Artemis and Kali, the Hindu Terrible Mother. That T. drew on such complex and ancient sources for her "children's" books is evident from her continued insistence on the relevance of myth and fairy tale to everyday life, a theme that was her frequent topic in interviews and lectures. For T., the world of the fairy tale was not limited to children but was an eternal and enveloping experience.

WORKS: *Mary Poppins* (1934; rev. 1972, 1981). *Moscow Excursion* (1934). *Mary Poppins Comes Back* (1935). *Happy Ever After* (1940). *Aunt Sass* (1941). *I Go by Sea, I Go by Land* (1941). *Ah Wong* (1943). *Mary Poppins Opens the Door* (1943). *Johnny Delaney* (1944). *Mary Poppins in the Park* (1952). *Mary Poppins from A to Z* (1962). *The Fox at the Manger* (1963). *A Mary Poppins Story for Coloring* (1969). *In Search of the Hero* (1970). *Friend Monkey* (1971). (trans., with R. Lewinnek) *The Way of Transformation,* by K. D. Montmartin (1971). *George Ivanovitch Gurdjieff* (1973). *About the Sleeping Beauty* (1975). *Mary Poppins in the Kitchen: A Cookery Book with a Story* (1975). *Two Pairs of Shoes* (1980). *Mary Poppins in Cherry Tree Lane* (1982). *Mary Poppins and the House Next Door* (1988). *What the Bee Knows* (1989).

BIBLIOGRAPHY: Bergsten, S. *Mary Poppins and Myth* (1978). Cott, J. *Pipers at the Gates of Dawn* (1983). Demers, P. *P. L. Travers* (1991).

For articles in reference works, see: *CA. Feminist. Longman. Newsmakers Cumulative Index,* ed. L.M. Collins and F. V. Castronova (1996). *OCCL. Oxford. SATA. TCCW. WD.*

Amanda DeWees

Violet Keppel Trefusis

BORN: 6 June 1894, Wilton Crescent, London.
DIED: 29 February 1972, l'Ombrellino, Florence.
DAUGHTER OF: the Hon. George Keppel and Alice Edmonstone Keppel.
MARRIED: Denys Trefusis, 1919.

T. was born into the last golden age of the English aristocracy, not as an aristocrat herself but as the daughter of King Edward VII's mistress. Alice Keppel was one of the great ladies of the Edwardian period, known for her discretion and tact in one of the most public, yet guarded, liaisons in English history. Because of this connection to the court, T.'s childhood was one of fairytale proportions. In later life, T. hinted that she was indeed Edward's daughter, but the king first met Mrs. Keppel four years after T.'s birth. Much evidence does support the idea that T.'s father was not George Keppel but William Beckett, a member of London society, acquaintance of the then Prince of Wales, and named Lord Grimthorpe in 1905. T.'s early history accounts for her lifelong interest in both personal and historical myth making.

One other major event of T.'s life must be mentioned: her friendship and love affair with Vita Sackville-West. They met in 1904, when Vita was twelve and T. ten, and despite the storms and separations that typified their relationship, some degree of devotion appears to have remained until Vita's death in 1962. This very complicated segment of Vita's and T.'s lives is thoroughly treated by Vita's son, Nigel Nicolson, in his *Portrait of a Marriage* (1973). At Sissinghurst, Nicolson found a manuscript written by his mother that detailed the history of Vita and T., as well as a hoard of letters from T. Unfortunately, those sent from Vita to T. were burned by Denys Trefusis in July 1920, a low point of their marriage. T. and Denys married despite T.'s professed desire to be with Vita. Denys died of tuberculosis in the summer of 1929, and T. seemed genuinely saddened by his death, but T.'s attraction to Vita and their fantasy of running away together can be regarded as the real passion of her life. Thwarted lovers that could represent Vita and T. figure in several of her books.

T. became a Francophile early on and was able to write fluently in French, an ability much admired by other writers, and she moved in circles that included Colette, Marcel Proust, and Jean Cocteau. As an adult, she lived exclusively in France, except during wartime. One of T.'s autobiographical works, *Don't Look Round* (1952), points out T.'s admiration for anything French. In *Echo* (1931), probably T.'s most successful novel, a young woman from Paris visits her Scottish cousins, the inseparable twins Malcolm and Jean. Jean kills herself when she wrongly believes that the Parisian has become Malcolm's lover. This novel is an excellent example of T.'s ability to weave her personal memories of childhood holidays in Scotland and her adult life in France into literature.

Because of her comfortable financial situation, T. never depended on writing for a living, and this independence may account for T.'s apparent lack of concentrated attention to the development of her literary skills. Her novels' settings usually seem more important than the characters. T.'s real talent lay in creating images, scenes from the society that revolved around her. Even if her writing lacks real brilliance, T. is vitally important for her role as observer of the small but fascinating Edwardian and twentieth-century worlds she inhabited.

WORKS: *Sortie de Secours* (1929). *Echo* (1931). *Tandem* (1933). *Broderie Anglaise* (1935). *Hunt the Slipper* (1937). *Les Causes Perdue* (1941). *Prelude to Misadventure* (1942). *Pirates at Play* (1950). *Don't Look Round* (1952). (with Philippe Julian) *Memoirs of an Armchair* (1960). *From Dusk till Dawn* (1972).

BIBLIOGRAPHY: Julian, P. and J. Phillips. *Violet Trefusis: A Biography* (1976). *Violet to Vita: The Letters of Violet Trefusis to Vita Sackville-West, 1910–21*, ed. M. Leaska and J. Phillips (1989). Nicolson, N. *Portrait of a Marriage* (1973). Sharpe, H. *A Solitary Woman: A Life of Violet Trefusis* (1981). *The Last Edwardians: An Illustrated History of Violet Trefusis and Alice Keppel* (1985).

For articles in reference works, see: *Bloomsbury*. *Feminist*. *Location Register of Twentieth Century English Literary Manuscripts and Letters*, Vol. II (1988). *ToddBWW*.

Michelle Q. Hill

Rose Tremain

BORN: 2 August 1943, London.
DAUGHTER OF: Keith Nicholas Home and Viola Mabel Dudley Thomson.
MARRIED: Jon Tremain, 1971; Jonathan Dudley, 1982.

T. lived in the Chelsea section of London until her parents divorced when she was ten, after which her father, a writer, refused to have anything more to do with his children. T. went to boarding school, then to the Sorbonne, where she received a diploma in 1963, and then to the University of East Anglia, taking the B.A. in 1967. During 1967–69, she was an elementary school teacher of French and history in London. In 1970–71, she was an editor for British Printing Corp. Publications. In 1971, she married for the first time and had a daughter, Eleanor Rachel; she married a second time in 1982. She presently shares her life with Coleridge biographer Richard Holmes. For a number of years, she has taught creative writing at the University of East Anglia; in 1987, she taught one semester at Vanderbilt University in Nashville, Tennessee. T. began writing nonfiction when Ballantine Books commissioned her to do an illustrated history of the women's suffrage movement, which appeared in 1971. A few years later, she wrote an illustrated life of Joseph Stalin, also for Ballantine. In addition to these histories, she has written plays for radio and television, children's books, and criticism. She is best known, however, for her fine novels and short stories.

Her first novel, *Sadler's Birthday* (1976), demonstrates her polished craftsmanship and some of her characteristic themes. Dealing with an elderly butler who has inherited his employers' estate, the novel typifies T.'s creation of characters remote from her own circumstances and her exploration of loneliness, isolation, and lovelessness. She followed up with *Letter to Sister Benedicta* (1978) in which an elderly woman re-examines her life after her husband has suffered a stroke. *The Cupboard* (1981) was more ambitious and generated conflicting opinions of the vibrant elderly writer Erica and the bland journalist Ralph.

T.'s ability was recognized early: In 1983, she was selected as one of the Twenty Best of Young British Novelists and was made a fellow of the Royal Society of Literature. The following year she won the Dylan Thomas Short Story Prize (her first collection of short stories appeared that year under the title *The Colonel's Daughter*) and the Giles Cooper Award for best play (for her radio play *Temporary Shelter*). In 1985, her novel *The Swimming Pool Season* portrayed a large cast of characters in a French provincial town and won the Angel Literary Award.

After another volume of short stories, *The Garden of the Villa Mollini* (1987), T. published her best novel to date, *Restoration* (1989). Typical of her work in being both funny and sad, the book uses the reign of King Charles II to imply a critique of our own time. The protagonist, Robert Merivel, rises to the height of the king's favor (as he thinks) and falls to heart-tearing drudgery in an isolated rural bedlam, or mental hospital; he grapples with plague, fire, and his own identity as the novel reaches its powerful and moving conclusion. T. has commented several times on the connections she sees between the 1660s and the 1980s, remarking on a similarity in state of mind "which finds it difficult to confront not only the wider world, social issues, but also more universal facts like our own mortality. We're into diversion in a significant way. We only want to see the surfaces of things." *Restoration* was shortlisted for the Booker Prize, won the Sunday Express Book of the Year Award (1989), was included on the *Publishers Weekly* list of the Best Books of the Year (1990), and has been made into a movie.

Sacred Country (1992) is another powerful study of characters caught in the ceaseless interplay of desire, necessity, and identity. Mary, the main character, realizes when she is six that she is really a boy born by mistake in a girl's body. In the same village, Walter is reared to take his father's place as a butcher but yearns to be an American country singer in Nashville. The novel deals with their struggles to transform themselves, in particular Mary's determination to be a transsexual. T. chose gender as a way to deal with the fluidity of identity. She explains: "The transsexual person is a metaphor for all of us: someone who has this better, brighter self *inside*."

WORKS: *Freedom for Women* (1971). *Stalin, an Illustrated Biography* (1974). *Sadler's Birthday* (1976). *The Wisest Fool* (1976). *Dark Green* (1977). *Blossom* (1977). *Don't*

Be Cruel (1978). *Letter to Sister Benedicta* (1978). *Leavings* (1978). *Down the Hill* (1979). *Mother's Day* (1980). *Half Time* (1980). *Hallelujah Mary Plum* (1980). *The Cupboard* (1981). *Findings on a Late Afternoon* (1981). *A Room for the Winter* (1982). *Yoga Class* (1984). *Temporary Shelter* (1984). *The Colonel's Daughter and Other Stories* (1984). *The Swimming Pool Season* (1985). *The Kite Flyer* (1985). *Journey to the Volcano* (1985). *The Garden of the Villa Mollini* (1987). *Restoration* (1989). *Sacred Country* (1992). *Music and Silence* (1992). *Evangelista's Fan and Other Stories* (1994). *The Way I Found Her* (1997).

BIBLIOGRAPHY:

For articles in reference works, see: *Bloomsbury*. *CA*. *CLC*. *DLB*. *Feminist*.

Other references: *LJ* (15 June 1985, 1 February 1990, 1 March 1993). *LonT* (25 February 1989, 25 September 1989, 14 July 1994). *LRB* (9 November 1989, 8 October 1992). *New Statesman* (15 March 1985, 29 September 1989, 15 April 1992). *NYTBR* (27 May 1984, 1 September 1985, 15 April 1990, 11 April 1992). *PW* (5 April 1993). *TLS* (17 February 1984, 12 April 1985, 29 February 1989, 4 September 1992).

Nancy Cotton

Trifler, Mrs.: See *Lennox, Charlotte Ramsay*

Sarah Kirby Trimmer

BORN: 1741.
DIED: 4 January 1811, Brentford, Middlesex.
DAUGHTER OF: Joshua Kirby.
MARRIED: James Trimmer, 1762.

T. was born into a middle-class family of some limited professional accomplishment—her father later became drawing instructor to the Prince of Wales—and a decidedly religious cast of mind. At the age of twenty-one, she married a prosperous brickmaker in the parish of Brentford, west of London, set about bearing his children (ten of whom lived to adulthood), and by degrees discovered a vocation that linked her nursery to a wider world. With her husband's encouragement, T. began to write stories for the instruction of her own children, introducing them to the world around them and publishing them in 1780 as *An Easy Introduction to the Knowledge of Nature*. Thus was launched the career of one of the earliest and most prolific children's authors in our language.

T. seems instinctively to have been a teacher and to have recognized the efficacy of the narrative form for making important moral points for children. In the 1780s she published lessons and prints to assist children in learning English history, scriptural history, and Roman history, sets that became enduring classics for home instruction of middle-class children; these were reissued and expanded well into the nineteenth century, and the two volumes on scriptural history (one for each testament) were translated into French. In 1786, she wrote her most famous work, *Fabulous Histories*, more widely known by its familiar title (and most popular story), *The History of the Robins*. It is this book, dedicated to promoting kindness to animals, on which T.'s enduring fame rests; it was translated into French and German, and new editions were being published as late as 1912.

Buoyed by her success and encouraged by friends and reviewers to turn her attention to the legions of children living in poverty and squalor, in 1787 she quickly wrote a pair of exemplary tales (*The Servant's Friend* and *The Two Farmers*) intended to show them the way to grow. (Most of the credit for inventing and popularizing this genre has gone to her friend and contemporary, Hannah More, but T. also deserves recognition.) More importantly, she set about establishing Sunday schools in Brentford, modeled upon those of Robert Raikes in Gloucester, since she believed that the poor were most desperately in need of moral regeneration and that it would take the combined efforts of many like herself to effect any change for the better. Consequently, she published in 1787 *The Œconomy of Charity*, an extensive discourse intended to show English ladies how they could help the poor and help themselves at the same time by starting Sunday schools and schools of industry for children of the poor. Recognizing that poor people who had been taught to read would need something wholesome upon which to practice their skills, T. began in 1788 to publish *The Family Magazine*, a monthly journal issued for a year and a half and filled with discourses, poems, reprinted religious tracts, columns of news from foreign parts, tips on domestic economy, and exemplary tales by the editor herself. These tales were collected and issued under the title *Instructive Tales* in 1812 by the Society for Promoting Christian Knowledge (S.P.C.K.). Since T. was the first woman to be published by the Society, it was clear that her way of talking to the poor had found favor with the Anglican establishment.

In the last two decades of her life, T. wrote more for her wider audience on social questions than for children; those things she wrote for children were not marked by the generosity of spirit that had characterized her early works and never achieved any reputation. She became much more interested in practical theology than she had been before and wrote several books on the sacraments and offices of the church. Clearly, however, her energies were being absorbed by the great social crisis in England attendant upon the Revolution of 1789 in France. In common with many reputable churchmen, she believed there was a great anti-Christian conspiracy abroad in Europe, of which the Revolution was only the greatest manifestation. Her piety, which had been tolerant if not ecumenical before 1789, became markedly more narrow and intolerant of dissent. Her charity was strained by fear of the unregenerate masses, and her publications in the 1790s are more concerned with controlling the poor than regenerating them.

The final chapter of T.'s public career centers around her second venture into periodical publication, *The Guardian of Education*, which she began in May 1802 and which had as its purpose nothing less than the screening of all publications on education and the censoring of those ideas that did not measure up to a proper Christian standard. Education is quite widely defined here to include anything bearing upon the nurture of children, indeed, one of the most interesting features of the publication is the extended essay on Christian child raising by T. herself, which was posthumously published by the S.P.C.K. She became embroiled in the famous Lancaster-Bell controversy over monitorial education in 1805, when she published her *Comparative View of the New Plan of Education....* Having come under fire from Sydney Smith in the *Edinburgh Review* for those efforts, she ceased publication of *The Guardian* and retired to her study in 1806. She had served notice, however, of the need for a genuinely national, church-based approach to the education of the poor and has been given credit for inspiring the National Society, formed in 1812 to accomplish those ends.

WORKS: *An Easy Introduction to the Knowledge of Nature* (1780). *Description of a Set of Prints of English History* (1785). *Description of a Set of Prints of Scripture History* (1786). *Fabulous Histories* (1786). *The Œconomy of Charity* (1787). *The Servant's Friend* (1787). *The Two Farmers* (1787). *The Family Magazine* (1788–89). *Description of a Set of Prints of Ancient History* (1789). *Comment on Dr. Watt's Divine Songs for Children* (1789). *Explanation of the Office of Public Baptism... and Confirmation* (1791). *Reflections upon the Education of Children in Charity Schools* (1792). *Charity School Spelling Book* (1799). *An Attempt to Familiarize the Catechism* (1800). *Abridgement of Scripture History* (1804). *Help to the Unlearned in the Study of Holy Scripture* (1804). *The Guardian of Education* (1802–06). *A Comparative View of the New Plan of Education Promulgated by Mr. Joseph Lancaster... and of the System of Christian Education Founded by Our Pious Forefathers...* (1805). *Concise History of England* (1808). *Essay on Christian Education* (1812). *Instructive Tales* (1812).

BIBLIOGRAPHY: (Anon.) *Some Account of the Life and Writings of Mrs. Trimmer, with Original Letters and Meditations and Prayers, Selected from Her Journal* (1814). Balfour, C. L. *A Sketch of Mrs. Trimmer* (1854). Meigs, C. *A Critical History of Children's Literature* (1953).

For articles in reference works, see: *CBEL. Feminist. Oxford. ToddBWW. ToddDBA.*

Other references: Silver, H. *The Concept of Popular Education* (1965). Start, M. *The Education of the People* (1967).

Robert Bonner

Frances Milton Trollope

BORN: 10 March 1779, Stapleton, near Bristol.
DIED: 6 October 1863, Florence, Italy.
DAUGHTER OF: William Milton and Frances Gresley.
MARRIED: Thomas Anthony Trollope, 1809.

Although the author of thirty-four novels, T. has been more widely recognized as the mother of Anthony Trollope and as the author of a popular travel book, *Domestic Manners of the Americans,* than for her fictional achievements. Yet her controversial social-reform novels and her recurring use of a new, strong heroine makes T. a significant pioneer in nineteenth-century fiction. Her use of fiction to advocate legal reform and attack social abuses and her development of complex feminine characters influenced the work of many of her contemporaries.

T. was a Bristol clergyman's daughter who lost her mother early and who was educated by her father in languages, the classics, and the arts. When her father remarried, she went to London with her brother and sister for five years, not marrying until she was nearly thirty. T.'s marriage was somewhat of a surprise to those who knew her well, for her husband, by whom she had seven children (four sons and three daughters) in eight years, was a serious and retiring barrister. After eighteen years in London and Harrow, where the family built a stately home, the Trollopes found themselves on the brink of bankruptcy.

Faced with destitution, T. decided to join an experiment in utopian living in the United States. The venture was a disappointment, however, and T. went on to Cincinnati, Ohio, where she tried to find work. Here her life alternated between plans for grandiose business and cultural schemes and devastating failure. At the age of fifty-two, destitute again, she returned to England and published her first book, *Domestic Manners of the Americans* (1832), an instant and controversial bestseller. Exposing "the lamentable insignificance of the American woman" and attacking many of America's most prized beliefs, the book generated some of the harshest criticism of its time, yet it went through many editions in America, England, and the Continent.

Domestic Manners of the Americans, which achieved an almost unheard-of success for a first work, is a chronological account of her experiences during her almost four-year stay in America. The book's appeal lies in T.'s brilliant selection of detail and the way she transformed her material into representative and amusing vignettes of nineteenth-century American life. According to Mark Twain, her work was accurate enough to be called "photography." The most original part of the book is T.'s underlying thesis that the sins and flaws of America stem mainly from the exclusion of women from the mainstream of American life, a situation resulting, she believed, from male preference, not economic necessity. Throughout the work, she documents a hostility toward women lurking beneath the surface of American life.

Thus, at fifty-three, T. was launched on a writing career, but even the earnings from her subsequent travel books on Germany and Paris and several popular novels failed to keep the family afloat. They were forced to abandon their home and flee to Belgium, where Trollope could not be sued by his creditors. For several years, the Trollopes lived in rented lodgings in Brussels while T. wrote frantically to support the family. At the same time, she nursed several of her children who were dying of tuberculosis; she often spent her time alternating between caring for the mortally ill and grinding out fiction.

She continued to make tours, however, hoping to repeat the success of *Domestic Manners of the Americans.* She soon realized, though, that much of what she earned was spent in transporting herself and her family to the places she needed to see. Thus for economic as well as domestic reasons, T. turned primarily to writing fiction.

Through her concentration on social abuses she became one of the first novelists to bring unpleasant subject matter squarely into what had been aptly called "the fairy land of fiction." Her first social-reform novel, *The Life and Adventures of Jonathan Whitlaw* (1836), grew out of her strong revulsion against American slavery. Telling the story of a cruel overseer, T.'s work anticipated the more famous Harriet Beecher Stowe's *Uncle Tom's Cabin* by fifteen years. T.'s next contribution to social-reform fiction was *The Vicar of Wrexhill* (1837), an attack upon evangelical excesses and their unfortunate effects upon women.

In the course of her literary career, T. was twice prompted to write a novel advocating legislative reform. In 1839, she began publishing *Michael Armstrong, the Factory Boy* to dramatize the need for passage of a ten-hours bill, and in 1843 she published *Jessie Phillips: A Tale of the Present Day* to demonstrate the weaknesses of the New Poor Law, particularly the bastardy clauses. Both works met with only mediocre popular success and both were harshly criticized, although for different reasons. As far as most critics were concerned, *Michael Armstrong* revealed nothing about child labor that the 1832 republication of John Brown's *Memoir of Robert Blincoe* and the 1837–38 publication of Charles Dickens's *Oliver Twist* had not already shown. Yet, despite the charge that it all had been said before and that reform was on the way, T.'s novel was very much of its time. She investigated factory conditions herself, finding that while some changes had been made, many abuses still existed; the Ten Hours Bill was not passed until 1847.

Jessie Phillips was also often criticized as a second-rate novel dealing with a topic, the New Poor Law, already portrayed in more finely executed works, particularly *Oliver Twist* and Thomas Carlyle's *Past and Present*, published in 1843, the same year as *Jessie Phillips*. Much of the criticism was leveled at T. for having "sinned grievously against good taste and decorum" by dealing with the bastardy clauses of the New Poor Law; yet precisely because it deals with the bastardy clauses *Jessie Phillips* is unique. T. was by no means a first-rate novelist, but her weakness is in her presentation, not her subject matter. Stereotypical and exaggerated characterization and intrusive narrators are her major weaknesses, although significant improvements can be seen when later novels are compared with earlier ones.

After her daughter Cecilia's death in 1848, T. moved to Florence where she embarked upon her last fictional innovation: a group of novels in which the heroines are triumphant, whose most obvious quality is an aggressive independence, and whose most frequent trials are confrontations with tyrannical fathers or marriages to weak or evil men. In her last novel, *Fashionable Life; or, Paris and London* (1856), T. moves from these dominant ladies to a vision of a community of females living in peace, harmony, and cooperation—happier than they had ever been with the men in their lives.

While never becoming a novelist of special distinction, T. did develop as a writer. Her growing understanding of how the structures of the novel—such as characterization, parallelism, and continuity—work to form a whole made her a popular novelist during her lifetime and an interesting figure for study in light of her influence both on society and on other writers.

WORKS: *Domestic Manners of the Americans* (1832; ed. P. Nevill-Sington, 1997). *The Refugee in America: A Novel* (1832). *The Mother's Manual; or, Illustrations of Matrimonial Economy: An Essay in Verse* (1833). *The Abbess: A Romance* (1833). *Belgium and Western Germany in 1833* (1834). *Tremordyn Cliff* (1835). *Paris and the Parisians in 1835* (1836). *The Life and Adventures of Jonathan Jefferson Whitlaw; or, Scenes on the Mississippi* (1836). *The Vicar of Wrexhill* (1837). *Vienna and the Austrians* (1838). *A Romance of Vienna* (1838). *The Widow Barnaby* (1839). *The Life and Adventures of Michael Armstrong, the Factory Boy* (1839–40). *The Widow Married: A Sequel to The Widow Barnaby* (1840). *One Fault: A Novel* (1840). *Charles Chesterfield; or, The Adventures of a Youth of Genius* (1841). *The Ward of Thorpe Combe* (1841). *The Blue Belles of England* (1842). *A Visit to Italy* (1842). *Jessie Phillips: A Tale of the Present Day* (1842–43). *The Barnabys in America; or, Adventures of the Widow Wedded* (1843). *Hargrave; or, The Adventures of a Man of Fashion* (1843). *The Laurringtons; or, Superior People* (1844). *Young Love: A Novel* (1844). *The Attractive Man* (1846). *The Robertses on Their Travels* (1846). *Travels and Travellers: A Series of Sketches* (1846). *Father Eustace: A Tale of the Jesuits* (1847). *The Three Cousins* (1847). *Town and Country: A Novel* (1848). *The Young Countess; or, Love and Jealousy* (1848). *The Lottery of Marriage: A Novel* (1849). *The Old World and the New: A Novel* (1849). *Petticoat Government: A Novel* (1850). *Mrs. Mathews; or, Family Mysteries* (1851). *Second Love; or, Beauty and Intellect: A Novel* (1851). *Uncle Walter: A Novel* (1852). *The Young Heiress: A Novel* (1853). *The Life and Adventures of a Clever Woman. Illustrated with Occasional Extracts from Her Diary* (1854). *Gertrude; or, Family Pride* (1855). *Fashionable Life; or, Paris and London* (1856).

BIBLIOGRAPHY: Ellis, L. A. *Frances Trollope's America* (1993). Heineman, H. *Mrs. Trollope: The Triumphant Feminine in the Nineteenth Century* (1979). Heineman, H. *Frances Trollope* (1984). Heineman, H. *Three Victorians in the New World: Interpretations of the New World in the Works of Frances Trollope, Charles Dickens, and Anthony Trollope* (1992). Johnson, J. *Fanny Trollope* (1979). Kissel, S. S. *In Common Cause: The "Conservative" Frances Trollope and the "Radical" Frances Wright* (1993). Neville-Sington, P. *Fanny Trollope* (1997). Pope-Hennessy, U. *Three English Women in America* (1929). Ransom, T. *Fanny Trollope: A Remarkable Life* (1995). Sadleir, M. *Anthony Trollope* (1927, 1945). Stebbins, L. P. and R. P. Stebbins. *The Trollopes* (1946). Trollope, A. *Autobiography* (1883). Trollope, F. E. *Frances Trollope: Her Life and Literary Works from George III to Victoria* (1895). Trollope, T. A. *What I Remember* (1887). Wilson, M. *These Were Muses* (1924).

For articles in reference works, see: *Allibone. BA19C. DLB. DNB. OGEBWW.*

Other references: Ar, P. M. *ATQ* (1993). Chaloner, W. H. *VS* (1960). Giltrow, J. *Mosaic* (1981). Kissel, S. S. *SNNTS* (1988). Kissel, S. S. *KPR* (1989). Lackey, K. *AmerS* (1991). Heinemann, H. *AQ* (1969). Heinemann, H. *International Journal of Women's Studies* (1978). *LonSunT* (2 November 1997). Super, R. H. *MLS* (1986).

Lynn M. Alexander

Joanna Trollope

BORN: 9 December 1943, Gloucestershire.
DAUGHTER OF: Arthur George Cecil Trollope and Rosemary Hodson Trollope.
MARRIED: David Roger William Potter, 1966; Ian Bayley Curteis, 1985.
WRITES UNDER: Caroline Harvey; Joanna Trollope.

Known in England as the Queen of "Aga-Sagas" after a type of fashionable upper-middle-class kitchen stove, T. is an important figure in British fiction whose reputation rests on the novels she has published since 1988. These novels focus on women in contemporary provincial settings who must assess the relative weights of their relationships and their self-respect. After the BBC televised *The Rector's Wife* in 1994 (subsequently shown in the United States on PBS), T. became a household name.

Educated at St. Hugh's College, Oxford, T. worked in the British Foreign Office for two years (1965–67) and then took a variety of teaching positions, including various secondary school jobs, adult education, and English as a Second Language. Her first novel, *Elizabeth Stanhope,* was published in 1978, and for the next ten years she published magazine articles, historical novels, and a study of women in the British Empire, *Britannia's Daughters* (1983). In 1988, she changed her focus from historical to contemporary novels, although until financial success accompanied the reception of *The Rector's Wife* (1991) she published four romances under the pseudonym "Caroline Harvey" to supplement her income. Her second husband, Ian Curteis, is a playwright; the couple lives in Gloucestershire.

The Rector's Wife explores the tensions in the life of Anna Bouverie, who must run a home and provide for her children on the meager salary earned by her husband, the rector of a provincial church. Issues of class and economics figure strongly in T.'s work; they help define each female protagonist's need for self-identity. Anna's frustration is exacerbated by her husband's inability to see beyond "duty"; he assumes they can live by faith alone, and he disapproves of her struggles toward independence, which include taking a menial job to pay for her daughter's private school. Having thus rebelled against her circumstances because she has felt increasingly "invisible," Anna begins to fall in love with the archdeacon's brother. T. has been criticized for the *deus ex machina* solution to Anna's ensuing moral dilemma: Peter Bouverie is killed in a car accident, which leaves Anna technically and morally free. Like many of T.'s heroines, however, Anna refuses to fall back into another relationship that will subsume her identity. *The Rector's Wife* analyzes the connection between economics and independence and suggests the repressions imposed by living within a community. Anna's refusal to conform to the norms of her class may seem a minor rebellion, but T.'s novels, as she has said, reveal "how limited the options for escape are for provincial, rural women."

The theme of community also underlies *A Village Affair* (1989), which establishes the boundaries of provincialism even more narrowly in its examination of a lesbian affair and its effects on a marriage and on a village. The novel abounds in richly sensuous description, from the details of the protagonist's kitchen to the glories of her mother-in-law's garden. Again, T. shows women making choices and living with the consequences; Alice Meadows is tempted from her rather banal marriage by the blandishments of Clodagh Unwin, daughter of the local squire. Ultimately, Alice rejects both the affair and the marriage in order, like Anna Bouverie, to establish her own identity and, important to all T.'s characters, her own home, chosen and decorated independently.

Although T. has been criticized for being "smug," especially about her characters' social standing, her novels' dissection of women's choices reflect the legacy of Jane Austen and George Eliot. She has said, "I believe passionately in narrative, even if it's the narrative of the heart rather than a complicated plot." The vicissitudes of the heart, in T.'s work as in Austen's, allow female characters to recognize themselves and to define their identities in relation to their communities.

WORKS: *Elizabeth Stanhope* (1978). *Parson Harding's Daughter* (1979: in the U. S. as *Mistaken Virtues,* 1980). (as Caroline Harvey) *Charlotte, Alexandra* (1980). *Leaves from the Valley* (1980). *The City of Gems* (1981). *The Steps of the Sun* (1983). *Britannia's Daughters: A Study of Women in the British Empire* (1983). *The Taverners' Place* (1986). *The Choir* (1988). *A Village Affair* (1989). *A Passionate Man* (1990). *The Rector's Wife* (1991). (as Caroline Harvey) *Legacy of Love* (1992). *The Men and the Girls* (1992). (as Caroline Harvey) *A Second Legacy* (1993). (as Caroline Harvey) *A Castle in Italy* (1993). *A Spanish Lover* (1993). *The Best of Friends* (1995). *Next of Kin* (1996).

BIBLIOGRAPHY:
For articles in reference works, see: *CA. TCRGW. WD.*
Other references: *Guardian* (11 March 1995). *LonSunT* (12 March 1995). *LonSunTMag* (5 May 1996). *LonT* (31 March 1995).

Helen Clare Taylor

Catharine Trotter

BORN: 16 August 1679, London.
DIED: 11 May 1749, Northumberland.
DAUGHTER OF: David Trotter and Sarah Ballenden Trotter.
MARRIED: Patrick Cockburn, 1708.

The resurgence of interest in all things female has brought attention to T., who was relegated to oblivion after her death despite an extraordinary and celebrated career. T. may well have been a darling of her day because of her precocity and her beauty; George Farquhar was one of many smitten by her. Perhaps because she outlived those youthful qualities, T. was forgotten after her death at the age of sixty-nine, even though she was known in her later years as a philosophical and religious disputant and commentator.

Born to an aristocratic Scottish family, T. suffered from poverty for most of her life. Harsh conditions began in

1683 when T.'s father died. Her father, the second son in his family, had been a captain in the navy and had served King Charles II so well that the king dubbed him "Honest Dave." When Captain Trotter died, however, his wife and two daughters were left penniless. For two years, until the king's death in 1685, the family lived on a pension. For the next seventeen years, until the pension was resumed by Queen Anne in 1702, the family depended upon relatives and friends.

From her childhood, T. impressed her family with verses in English and French and her mastery of logic and Latin grammar. Early in her life, she converted to Roman Catholicism, only to return to the Anglican Church in 1707. Meanwhile, she had embarked on a successful career. In 1693, while only thirteen, T. published a poem anonymously for a friend who was ill with smallpox. Later that year, she published her novel *Olinda's Adventures,* again anonymously. While the poem is of interest because of the sex and age of its writer, the novel is another matter. It reveals much about love, marriage, and infidelity in the late seventeenth century. Surprising is the skill with which the thirteen-year-old drew characters, scenes, and actions, especially the strong young Olinda and her money-grasping mother.

Not so surprising is the transposition of those skills to the theater. T.'s dramatic success came at sixteen when her first play, the blank-verse tragedy *Agnes de Castro,* was performed at the Theatre Royal in Drury Lane. It was published the next year. Both were offered anonymously, but her authorship was an open secret. In her dedication, T. refers to her "early Muse." In the poem that follows, Mary Delariviere Manley declares that the playwright is heir to the throne vacated by Katherine Phillips and Aphra Behn. Then, in his prologue, William Wycherley begs readers to be kind to "Our Female Wit." Finally, in her epilogue, T. asks the audience to "judge aright" for the "New Author . . . is Virtuous, Young, and Fair." Christopher Rich had high expectations for T.'s first work, for it was his theater's competition with Thomas Betterton's production of William Congreve's *Love for Love* at Lincoln's Inn Fields. The play itself continued T.'s emphasis on strong women who determine the plot and action.

In 1696, three years after the success of *Agnes de Castro,* Lincoln's Inn Fields presented T.'s next play, the tragedy *Fatal Friendship.* Again, T.'s name is not on the title page, but the dedication is signed. Probably T.'s best known play, *Fatal Friendship* was followed four years later with her only comedy, *Love at a Loss.* It premiered in Drury Lane on 23 November 1700 with Colley Cibber and Anne Oldfield. The play failed. Disappointed by its failure, T. nonetheless published it, and, years later revised it as *The Honourable Deceiver; or, All Right at the Last.* The revised play was never performed or published. Even before the failed comedy was printed, T.'s next blank-verse tragedy, *The Unhappy Penitent,* was performed at Drury Lane. It was published in 1701, and for the first time T.'s name is on the title page.

In the midst of her theatrical activity, in 1702 T. published a treatise defending John Locke's *Essay on Human Understanding.* It was published anonymously because T. feared that Locke would be criticized if people knew his defender was a woman.

Five years passed before T.'s final play appeared in 1706. While writing *The Revolution of Sweden,* T. consulted Congreve, who offered revisions. When it appeared in the Haymarket at the Queen's Theatre, the play had Thomas Betterton and Elizabeth Barry in its cast. Even so, it was not well-received, and T. attacked her critics in its published version and blamed the audience.

By 1707, T. had left the theater. Soon after, in 1708, she married Patrick Cockburn, a clergyman whose first positions were in Nayland, Suffolk, and St. Dunstan's in Fleet Street, London. Beginning in 1714, the family suffered twelve years of poverty because Cockburn refused to take the Oath of Abjuration. Finally, in 1726, he took the oath and was appointed to St. Paul's Episcopal Church in Aberdeen, Scotland, and then to Long Horsley, Northumberland, where the Cockburns resided with their two daughters and one son until her husband's death in 1748, followed by her own death a few months later in 1749.

From 1708 to 1726, T. did not write or publish. Her silence was broken by another defense of Locke, this one in response to Dr. Winch Holdsworth's attack six years earlier, but T. had been silent so long that she could not find a publisher. Her defense did not appear until 1743 in *History of the Works of the Learned,* and it carried her dedication to Alexander Pope. Four years later, T. responded to Rutherforth's *Essay on the Nature and Obligations of Virtue.* Its preface was by Pope's friend, William Warburton. At the time of her death, T. was preparing an edition of her work, giving materials to Thomas Birch who used them in the two-volume *Works* (1751).

T.'s works and life provide lessons today. Her career proves that women could succeed as playwrights and that Aphra Behn was not alone. Furthermore, she offers in her novel and plays examples of strong women who determine the action and plots. Moreover, she demonstrates that women could discuss and defend philosophical and religious positions. Finally, she demonstrates most clearly that women writers of the seventeenth and eighteenth centuries warrant more attention.

WORKS: *Olinda's Adventures; or, The Amours of a Young Lady,* in *Letters of Love and Gallantry* (1693). *Agnes de Castro, A Tragedy* (1696). *Epilogue,* in *Queen Catharine or, The Ruines of Love* by Mary Pix (1698). *Fatal Friendship, A Tragedy* (1698). "Calliope: The Herock Muse: On the Death of John Dryden," in *The Nine Muses* (1700). *Love at a Loss, or, Most Votes Carry It. A Comedy* (1701). *The Unhappy Penitent. A Tragedy* (1701). *A Defence of Mr. Locke's "Essay of Human Understanding"* (1702). *The Revolution of Sweden. A Tragedy* (1706). *A Discourse concerning a Guide in Controversies, in Two Letters, Written to One of the Church of Rome, By a Person late Converted from that Communion* (1707). *A Letter to Dr. Holdsworth, Occasioned by His Sermon Preached before the University of Oxford: On Easter-Monday, Concerning the Resurrection . . . By the Author of "A Defence of Mr. Locke's Essay"* (1726). "Poetical Essays: May 1737: Verses, occasion'd by the Busts in the Queen's Hermitage," in *Gentleman's Magazine* (1737). *Remarks upon the Principles and Reasonings of Dr. Rutherforth's "Essay on the Nature and Obligations of Virtue"* (1747). *The Works of Mrs.*

Catharine Cockburn, Theological, Moral, Dramatic, and Poetica, Several of them now first printed, ed. T. Birch (1751).

BIBLIOGRAPHY: Carter, H. *Bookman's Journal* (1925). Clark, C. *Three Augustan Women Playwrights* (1986). Cotton, N. *Women Playwrights in England: c. 1363–1750* (1980). Day, R. A., intro. to *Olinda's Adventures* (1969). Doran, J. *Their Majesties' Servants: Annals of the English Stage from Thomas Betterton to Edmund Kean* (1865). Duncombe, J. *The Feminead, or Female Genius, A Poem* (1754). Finke, L. A. *Restoration* (1984). Gosse, E. W. *Transactions of the Royal Society of Literature* (1916). Hodges, J. C. *Congreve's Letters and Documents* (1964). *The Female Wits,* ed. L. Hook (1967). Maison, M. *RES* (1978). Morgan, F. *The Female Wits: Women Playwrights on the London Stage 1660–1720* (1981). Reynolds, M. *The Learned Lady in England, 1650–1760* (1920). *Scots Magazine* (1940). Sorelius, G. *Annales Societatis Litterarum Humaniorum Regiae Upsaliensis* (1977–78). Steeves, E. L., intro. to *The Plays of Mary Pix and Catharine Trotter* (1982). Thornton, G. *Poems by Eminent Ladies* (1755). Whincop, T. *A Compleat List of all English Dramatic Poets* (1747). Williams, J. *Literary Women of England* (1861). " Mr. W.M." *The Female Wits; or, The Triumvirate of Poets at Rehearsal, A Comedy* (1697).

For articles in reference works, see: Adburgham, A. *Women in Print* (1972). Baker, D. E. *The Companion to the Playhouse* (1764). Ballard. *Biographica Dramatica. Bell. BioIn. BCE. Cambridge Guide to World Theater. CBEL* (1971). Didbin, C. *A Complete History of the English Stage* (1800). *DLB. DNB* (under "Cockburn"). Doran, J. *Annals of the Stage* (1835). Genest, J. *Some Account of the English Stage* (1832). Hale, S. J. *Women's Record, or, Sketches of All Distinguished Women, from Creation to A.D. 1854* (1855). Hays, M. *Female Biography* (1807). *Index to Women of the World (Supplement).* Jacob, G. *The Poetical Register* (1723). Langbaine, G. *The Lives and Characters of the English Dramatic Poets* (1699). Pilkington, M. *Memoirs of Celebrated Female Characters* (1804). *Rowton.* Stenton, D. M. *The English Woman in History* (1957). *ToddBWW.*

Sophia B. Blaydes

Tudor, Elizabeth: See *Elizabeth I*

Tudor, Mary: See *Mary I*

Jane Turner

BORN: before 1640.
DIED: after 1660 (?).
MARRIED: John Turner.

T. participated in several religious groups before becoming a Baptist; she describes these experiences in her only published work, *Choice Experiences of the Kind Dealings of God before, in, and after Conversion* (1653). This lengthy tract documents her Presbyterian beginnings, her brief involvement with the Quakers, and her eventual entry into the Baptist church.

Choice Experiences is one of a number of spiritual autobiographies produced by women during the Interregnum (e.g., Anne Venn). Such texts were an important opportunity for women writers, for they presented a "legitimate" channel through which to publish. Although reluctant to publish, she was encouraged to do so by her husband, John Turner, who wrote a preface to the work.

T.'s account of her experiences as a Quaker was seen as anti-Quaker, for in 1654 Edward Burrough, an eminent Quaker, issued a reply, *Something in answer to Jane Turner.*

WORKS: *Choice Experiences of the Kind Dealings of God before, in and after Conversion; laid down in six general heads. Together with some brief observations upon the same. Whereunto is added a description of the experience* (1653).

BIBLIOGRAPHY: *Her Own Life: Autobiographical Writings by Seventeenth-Century Englishwomen,* ed. E. Graham, et al. (1989). Hobby, E. *Virtue of Necessity: English Women's Writing 1646–1688* (1988). Mack, P. *Visionary Women: Ecstatic Prophecy in Seventeenth-Century England* (1992).

For articles in reference works see: *Bell. Feminist. WL17C.*

Jane Baston

Turnley, Christopher: See *Ellis-Fermor, Una Mary*

Margaret Tyler

BORN: 1530s–1540s (?).
DIED: 1595, Castle Camps, near Cambridge.
MARRIED: John Tyler (?).

In her preface and letter to the reader in her translation of Diego Ortunez de Calahorra's *Espejo de principes y cavalleros,* T. formulated what is probably the first woman-authored defense in English of women's reading and writing. *The First Part of the Mirrour of Princely Deedes and Knighthood* (1578), the *Espejo*'s English title, with its preface and letter to the reader, are her only extant texts. In many ways, T. remains an anonymous voice since she conveys little information about herself and no irrefutable external records survive. She certainly worked for the Howard family previous to the *Mirrour*'s publication, she may well have been Roman Catholic, and her financial situation was such that mentioning the small payment from a publisher for her translation seemed a possible rationale for a woman to publish. Her birth and death dates, the identifications of her husband as John Tyler and her two children as Robert and a daughter with a married name of Ross rests on plausible but nonetheless circumstantial evidence (see L. Schleiner).

The *Mirrour*'s publication occurred as the popularity of romance in Elizabethan England was increasing and consequently was very successful. Two more editions of T.'s translation appeared in 1580 and 1599; the remaining books of the *Espejo* were entirely translated into English—although not by T.—by 1601; and the *Mirrour* eventually was criticized for being a bad influence on youthful readers. The defensive tone T. adopts in her preface constitutes her response to a climate antagonistic to a woman writing, especially in a genre as secular as romance. Although T. may appropriate some of the language of romance—she describes her translation as an adventure—she also differentiates her translation from composition: "The invention, disposition, trimming & what else in this story, is wholly another man's, my part none therein but the translation, as it were only in giving entertainment to a stranger, before this time unacquainted with our country guise." As well as comparing the act of translation to the feminine virtue of hospitality, T. emphasizes that friends have encouraged her to publish her work. By examining what happens to texts that are dedicated to women readers, she further defends herself by suggesting that a translation might be seen as an elaborate act of reading rather than of writing.

Despite these disclaimers, T. ultimately argues for women's rights to authorship and treats her work as more than mere translation. It is "all one for a woman to pen a story, as for a man to address his story to a woman." Her comments inserted into the romance itself reveal how she distinguishes her ideas from those of Ortunez; for instance, she parenthetically notes in a story depicting pride as a characteristically feminine downfall that she is not the originator of this story. Her voice again emerges when the character Rosicleer muses on interpreting a confusing text; his reading is discussed as an unsuccessful act of translation. She includes several patriotic notes about England—English knights take the field in one of the plot's most important tournaments—that probably do not come from the Spanish text. T.'s creative translation deserves a critical comparison to Ortunez's original so that we can more fully perceive her construction and feminization of romance and her revisions of cultural mores of authorship.

WORKS: (trans.) *The First Part of the Mirrour of Princely Deedes and Knighthood,* by Diego Ortunez de Calahorra (1578, 1580, 1599; ed. K. Coad, 1995).

BIBLIOGRAPHY: Krontiris, T. *ELR* (1988). Krontiris, T. *Oppositional Voices* (1992). Perott, J. *RR* (1913). Schleiner, L. *ELN* (1992).

For articles in reference works, see: *Feminist. Todd-BWW.*

Other references: *First Feminists,* ed. M. Ferguson (1985). *N&Q* (1946). Thomas, H. *Spanish and Portuguese Romances of Chivalry* (1920). *Paradise of Women,* ed. B. Travitsky (1981). Warnicke, R. M. *Women of the English Renaissance and Reformation* (1983).

Kathryn Coad Narramore

Katharine Tynan

BORN: 23 January 1861, Dublin, Ireland.
DIED: 2 April 1931, London.
DAUGHTER OF: Andrew Tynan and Elizabeth Reity Tynan.
MARRIED: Henry Albert Hinkson, 1893.

T. was a prolific Irish novelist and poet who published some eighty novels, twenty books of poetry, and six books of reminiscences; she also edited ten collections of works by other writers.

T. was the fourth of her parents' eleven children; her father was a moderately successful farmer and businessman. In 1867, T.'s eyesight began to fail, and within a short time she became blind. After nearly two years of suffering, the cause of T.'s blindess was found to be ulcers on her eyes; once these were removed, T.'s sight returned, but it was never fully restored.

After attending an infant school in Dublin until 1871, T. was sent to the convent of St. Catherine of Siena at Drogheda, where, as Ann Fallon suggests, her experiences were a major influence on her work: "Tynan found the convent school a place of peace and contentment, and, as a result, developed in three short years a lifelong respect and affection for the life of the convent and the nuns who lived there. This love, and her knowledge of the inner workings of convent life, especially the order and cleanliness, inform many passages in her later novels." T. left the convent in 1874, after the death of her mother, to care for her father and siblings.

T. published her first poem in 1878. In 1879, she joined the Ladies Land League and became friends with Anna Parnell, sister of the Irish political leader Charles Parnell. The year 1885 was extremely important for T., for she published her successful first volume of poetry, *Louise de la Valliere and Other Poems,* and she met William Butler Yeats, with whom she remained close; their friendship cooled somewhat in later years, however, because Yeats disapproved of T.'s determination to write prose and journalism solely for money.

Yeats and T. worked together in 1888 on a project that Marilyn Gaddis Rose calls, along with Yeats' *The Wandering of Oisin* (1889), "the publishing event inaugurating the Irish Renaissance." T. and other young Irish writers, working out of the home of John O'Leary, the Fenian leader, put together a volume entitled *Poems and Ballads of Young Ireland,* which included the work of T., Yeats, Douglas Hyde, T. W. Rolleston, John Todhunter, and Rose Kavanagh.

Shortly after her marriage, T. published the first of her "formula" novels, *The Way of a Maid* (1895). Fallon describes that formula:

> A young, inexperienced poor girl from a good family of either a noble line in declining circumstances or an old family line which has suffered because of religious reasons . . . loves, and is loved by, a young, refined, often wealthy, and high-born young man. The course of this romance does not run smoothly because of the interference . . . of the families and because of misunderstandings on the part of the lovers themselves. . . . These romances invariably end happily with the marriages of the major and minor characters.

After her husband's death in 1919, T. traveled extensively throughout Europe and settled for several years in Cologne,

Germany, where she wrote a memoir, *Life in the Occupied Area* (1925), in which she suggests unrealistic ways of returning European society to its prewar structure.

At the end of her career, T. turned to a more realistic form of novel writing, She realized that her female audience had changed: They came from all social classes and some were career women. T. was sympathetic to the shop girl, the office or factory worker, the single woman, and tried to provide "remedies for [the] harsh reality" of their lives. Though these novels had more realistic characters, they still followed the old formula—they still ended in marriage.

T. died in 1931 in London. She will undoubtedly be remembered far more for the poetry of her early years and for her memoirs, which are of significant literary/historical value (due to T.'s careful recording of her meetings with Yeats, as well as other writers of her era—Christina Rossetti, for example), than for the basically trite romantic novels of her later years. Whatever the quality of her work (and how much its quality may have been diluted by its quantity), T. did manage to publish, and to make money, when such accomplishments were difficult for women.

WORKS: *Louise de la Valliere and Other Poems* (1885). *Shamrocks* (1887). (with others) *Poems and Ballads of Young Ireland* (1888). *Ballads and Lyrics* (1891). *A Nun: Mother Mary Xavier Fallon* (1891). *Irish Love-Songs* (1892). *Cuckoo Songs* (1894). *Miracle Plays* (1895). *The Way of a Maid* (1895). *An Isle in the Water* (1896). *A Lover's Breast-Knot* (1896). *The Wind in the Trees* (1898). *The Golden Lily* (1899). *The Queen's Page* (1900). *The Sweet Enemy* (1901). *Poems* (1901). *The Handsome Quaker and Other Stories* (1902). *The Great Captain* (1902). *The French Wife* (1904). *A Daughter of Kings* (1905). *Dick Pentreath* (1905). *For the White Rose* (1905). *Innocencies* (1905). *Julia* (1905). *A Little Book of Twenty-Four Carols* (1907). *Her Ladyship* (1907). *The Story of Baron* (1907). *Twenty-One Poems* (1907). *The Lost Angel* (1908). (with F. Maitland) *The Book of Flowers* (1909). *A Little Book for John O'Mahony's Friends* (1909). *Peggy the Daughter* (1909). *Mary Gray* (1909). *Ireland* (1909, 1911). *Betty Carew* (1910). *Her Mother's Daughter* (1910). *Freda* (1910). *New Poems* (1911). *Paradise Farm* (1911). *Princess Katharine* (1911). *The Story of Cecilia* (1911). *A Midsummer Rose* (1913). *A Misalliance* (1913). *Twenty-five Years: Reminiscences* (1913). *Miss Pratt of Paradise Farm* (1913). *Rose of the Garden* (1913). *The Wild Harp* (1913). *The Honourable Molly* (1914). *Irish Poems* (1914). *The Flower of Peace* (1915). *Flower of Youth* (1915). *The Curse of Castle Eagle* (1915). *The Holy War* (1916). *The Middle Years* (1916). *Lord Edward* (1916). *Late Songs* (1917). *The Rattlesnake* (1917). *Herb O'Grace* (1918). *Miss Gascoigne* (1918). *Love of Brothers* (1919). *The Man from Australia* (1919). *The Years of the Shadow* (1919). *The House* (1920). *Denys the Dreamer* (1921). *The Second Wife* (1921). *The Wandering Years* (1922). *Evensong* (1922). *Mary Beaudesert* (1923). *Pat, the Adventurer* (1923). *They Loved Greatly* (1923). *The Golden Rose* (1924). *The House of Doom* (1924). *Memories* (1924). *Life in the Occupied Area* (1925). *Miss Phipps* (1925). *The Moated Grange* (1926; as *The Night of Terror* in later editions). *The Respectable Lady* (1927). *The Face in the Picture* (1927). *Twilight Songs* (1927). *Castle Perilous* (1928). *The House in the Forest* (1928). *Lover of Women* (1928). *The Rich Man* (1929). *A Fine Gentleman* (1929). *The Most Charming Family* (1929). *The River* (1929). *Collected Poems* (1930). *Grayson's Girl* (1930). *The Admirable Simmons* (1930). *The Forbidden Way* (1931). *The Pitiful Lady* (1932). *The Playground* (1932). *An International Marriage* (1933). *A Lad Was Born* (1934). For a more extensive listing, see below: A. Fallon (182–85) or M. G. Rose (94–96).

BIBLIOGRAPHY: Fallon, A. *Katharine Tynan* (1979). Gibbon, M. intro. to *Poems of Katherine [sic] Tynan* (1963). Rose, M. *Katharine Tynan* (1974). Russell, G. (AE). foreword to *Collected Poems*, by K. Tynan (1930).

For articles in reference works, see: *Bloomsbury. CA. Cambridge. DIL. DIW. Feminist. IAWWW. Oxford. ToddBWW.*

Other references: *A Round Table of the Representative Irish and English Catholic Novelists* (1897). Atkinson, F. *N&Q* (1977). Boyd, E. *Ireland's Literary Renaissance* (1916). Brown, S. *Ireland in Fiction: A Guide to Irish Novels, Tales, Romances, and Folklore* (1915). D'Amico, D. *VP* (1994). Gatton, J. *ELN* (1989). Holdsworth, C. *Yeats Annual* (1983). Hone, J. *W. B. Yeats, 1865–1939* (1943). McFadden, J. *Yeats* (1990). Maguire, C. E. *Bookman* (June 1931). Marcus, P. *Yeats and the Beginning of the Irish Renaissance* (1970). Revie, L. *The Little Red Fox, Emblem of the Irish Peasant in Poems by Yeats, Tynan, and Ni Dhomhnall* (1993). Yeats, W. B. *Autobiography* (1936). Yeats, W. B. *Letters to Katharine Tynan* (1953).

Kay Beaird Meyers

Evelyn Underhill

BORN: 6 December 1875, Wolverhampton, Staffordshire.
DIED: 15 June 1941, Hampstead, London.
DAUGHTER OF: Sir Arthur Underhill and Alice Lucy Ironmonger.
MARRIED: Hubert Stuart Moore, 1907.
WROTE UNDER: John Cordelier; Evelyn Underhill.

A prolific religious writer, authority on mystical theology, and spiritual director, U. began as an agnostic who turned to theism and ultimately in 1921 to the Church of England. Although she had an explicit conversion to Roman Catholicism in 1907, she never joined that church largely because of its position on modernism. She was educated at King's College for Women, London. Although she received numerous honors—she was a Fellow of King's College, London; honorary Doctor of Divinity at the University of Aberdeen, in Scotland; the Upton Lecturer on religion at Manchester College, Oxford, in 1921; and the first female retreat leader in the Anglican church—she had no affiliation with an academic institution. Instead, for more than forty years, she wrote from her home. Her marriage to a childhood friend, a barrister, was affectionate but childless.

U.'s works include poetry, novels, devotional works, editions of mystical writings, book reviews, biography, essays, and major historical and analytical studies. She wrote a book of poetry and three novels, among other works, before she produced *Mysticism: A Study in the Nature and Development of Man's Spiritual Consciousness* (1911), a pioneering work in which mysticism and its relationship to vitalism, psychology, theology, symbolism, and magic are explored as well as the inner processes of the mystical experience.

Mysticism went through twelve editions and has remained in print continuously. As a result of its publication, U. met Baron Friedrich von Hügel, the lay Catholic theologian to whom she said she owed her whole spiritual life. From 1921 to 1925, he served as her spiritual director. U. contends that mysticism, an essential element in all religion, is available to everyone. While this is a major theme of her writing, particularly in *Practical Mysticism* (1914), U. does not neglect the great mystics. She introduced the lives and contributions of these "pioneers of humanity" to the English reading public through the biographies of Jan van Ruysbroeck and Jacopone di Todi; through translations, editions, and introductions to the writings of Ruysbroeck, Jakob Böhme, Walter Hinton, Richard Rolle, and Nicholas of Cusa; and through numerous essays on the mystics.

U.'s efforts to examine the spiritual life are best realized in her Oxford lectures published as *The Life of the Spirit and the Life of To-day* (1922). In these, she brings the experience of the spiritual life into line with the conclusions of psychology. By the late 1920s U. began to give retreat addresses; *Concerning the Inner Life* (1926), *The Golden Sequence* (1932), *Fruits of the Spirit* (1942), and *Light of Christ* (1944) were all first presented in this form. These devotional writings, as well as *House of the Soul* (1929), *The School of Charity* (1934), *The Spiritual Life* (1937), *The Mystery of Sacrifice* (1938), and *Abba* (1940), were well received, and the *The Spiritual Life,* first delivered as a series of broadcast talks, was the most popular. All of these works are characterized by an elegant simplicity and homeliness that made them particularly appealing to women and to preachers.

U.'s last major book was *Worship* (1936), a study of the human response to the Eternal. In it, she examined the basic characteristics of worship—ritual, symbol, sacrifice, and sacrament—and then explored the various traditions of Christian worship. It remains a classic study of the subject.

Although U.'s writing focused on the spiritual life, she construed that topic broadly. Her many lectures and essays, collected in three anthologies—*Essentials of Mysticism* (1920), *Mixed Pastures* (1933), and *Collected Papers* (1946)—illustrate her breadth. She wrote on topics as far-reaching as the vocation of the teacher, the basis of social reform, and the ideals of the ministry of women. As theological editor of the *Spectator* and as a reviewer for *Time and Tide,* U. kept the literature on the spiritual life before the twentieth-century reader.

While a prodigious writer, the last part of U's life was given over increasingly to spiritual direction. Her letters, which were published posthumously, reveal her deep and sensitive care for souls. Never a political partisan, U. in 1938 became a pacifist and subsequently wrote *The Church and War* for the Anglican Pacifist Fellowship. This piece must be understood as the fruit of her deepening incarnational theology. U. believed that pacifism was a corollary of the doctrine of universal charity, a personal vocation to speak truth in dark times and give witness to the power of a loving God. As such, it clearly illustrated U.'s final position that it was not one's mystical experience but one's love that counted most.

WORKS: *A Bar-Lamb's Ballad Book* (1902). *The Grey World* (1904). *The Miracles of Our Lady Saint Mary* (1906). *The Lost Word* (1907). *The Column of Dust* (1909). *The Path of the Eternal Wisdom* (1911). *Mysticism: A Study in the Nature and Development of Man's Spiritual Consciousness* (1911). *Immanences, A Book of Verses* (1913). *The Mystic Way, A Psychological Study in Christian Origins* (1913). *Practical Mysticism* (1914). *Ruysbroeck* (1915). *Theophanies, A Book of Verses* (1916). *Jacopone da Todi, Poet and Mystic, 1228–1306. A Spiritual Biography* (1919). *Essentials of Mysticism and Other Essays* (1920). *The Life of the Spirit and the Life of To-day* (1922). *The Mystics of the Church* (1925). *Concerning the Inner Life* (1926). *Man and the Supernatural* (1927). *Life as Prayer* (1928). *House of the Soul* (1929). *The Golden Sequence, A Four-Fold Study of the Spiritual Life* (1932). *Mixed Pastures, Twelve Essays and Addresses* (1933). *The School of Charity* (1934). *Worship* (1936). *The Spiritual Life* (1937). *The Mystery of Sacrifice, A Meditation on the Liturgy* (1938). *Eucharistic Prayers from the Ancient Liturgies* (1939). *The Church and War* (193–?). *Abba, Meditations Based on the Lord's Prayer* (1940). *Fruits of the Spirit* (1942). *Letters of Evelyn Underhill,* ed. C. Williams (1943). *Light of Christ* (1944). *Collected Papers,* ed. L. Menzies (1946). *Meditations and Prayers* (1948). *Shrines and Cities of France and Italy* (1949). *Evelyn Underhill: Modern Guide to the Ancient Quest for the Holy,* ed. D. Greene (1988). *The Ways of the Spirit,* ed. G. A. Brame (1990). *Fragments from an Inner Life: The Notebooks of Evelyn Underhill,* ed. D. Greene (1993).

BIBLIOGRAPHY: Allchin, A. M. and M. Ramsey *Evelyn Underhill: Two Centenary Essays* (1971). Armstrong, C. *Evelyn Underhill* (1975). Cropper, M. *Evelyn Underhill* (1958). Greene, D., in *The Spark in the Soul: Four Mystics on Justice,* ed. T. Tastard (1989). Greene, D. *Evelyn Underhill: Artist of the Infinite Life* (1990). Greene, D., in *Spiritual Guides for Today,* ed. A. Callahan (1992). Wyon, O. *Desire for God* (1966).

For articles in reference works, see: *Dictionary of Christian Spirituality* (1983). *DNB. Feminist. Oxford Dictionary of the Christian Church* (1958).

Other references: *America* (August 1976). *Anglican Theological Review* (April 1978). *The Month* (July 1959). *Theology* (October 1953).

Dana Greene

V.: See *Clive, Caroline; Currie, Mary (Montgomerie) Lamb Singleton; Vardill, Anna Jane*

Anna Jane Vardill

BORN: 19 November 1781, London.
DIED: 4 June 1852, Skipton, Yorkshire.
DAUGHTER OF: John Vardill.
MARRIED: James Niven, 1822.
WROTE UNDER: A.J.V.; V.

V. is best known for having published a sequel to "Christabel" before Samuel Taylor Coleridge's poem was in print. Her "Christabel" appeared in the *European Magazine* and *London Review* in April 1815 over the signature "V.," but it was not until 1907 that William E. A. Axon identified V. as the author and discovered how she had managed this strange feat. On 19 December 1814, Henry Crabb Robinson had read the manuscript of "Christabel" to a small group of friends, including V. Already an accomplished, published poet and a regular contributor of verse to the *European Magazine,* she relied on her memory of Coleridge's poem and set to work on her sequel almost immediately and then sent it off to the *European* in March the next year.

V. was the daughter of the Reverend John Vardill, an American Loyalist with literary ambitions who wrote political satires, miscellaneous verse, and at least one play. V., his only child, was born in London in 1781 and spent her childhood first in Galloway, Scotland, and then Lincolnshire, where her father held rectorships. She was educated in the classics by him at home, and through him she may have made acquaintance with literary and artistic figures such as Robinson and John Flaxman. Thus, like many English women writers of this period, V.'s status as the daughter of a clergyman gave her access to an education otherwise not available, to the leisure time in which to write, and to the connections that might lead to publication. V. must have begun writing at a very early age indeed: Her first volume of verse, *Poems and Translations from the Minor Greek Poets and Others* (1809), announces on the title page that its author wrote the contents between the ages of ten and sixteen.

Her translations of Anacreon, Sappho, Theocritus, Horace, and others are conventional but accomplished enough to testify to her linguistic ability. (The book went through three editions in one year.) The original verses in her second volume of verse, *The Pleasures of Human Life* (1812), tend toward the more contemporary "romantic" mode, with subjects like sublime landscapes, gypsies, and ancient legends as well as conversation pieces. All display the talent of a reader thoroughly immersed in contemporary verse who could adopt and imitate a variety of poetic forms and voices in her own work.

Her father died in 1811; by 1813 V. was apparently living in London and had already begun her long (1813–22) association with the *European Magazine,* including "A Fragment Found in a Skeleton Case," a popular anthology piece. Indeed, so impressive were her published verses that several correspondents to the *European* wrote to inquire if they were not extracts from Walter Scott, Robert Southey, or Lord Byron. Her continuation of "Christabel" is of greater interest than most because of its illustrious inspiration and for its ingenious solution of the problem of the identity of Geraldine, who is revealed to be the Witch of the lake who has temporarily escaped Merlin's spell.

Many of her magazine contributions form series of loosely linked verse and prose narrative tales, including "Legends of the Hermitage," "Traditions of Tabby Hall," "Tales of To-day," and "Annals of Public Justice." Several later contributions were written as "Fragments of the Attic Chest," named after a cedar box owned by Eleanor Anne Porden, a young friend of V.'s who later married Sir John Franklin, the polar explorer; they were intended to amuse Porden's infirm mother. Another series was titled "Extracts from a Lawyer's Portfolio," somewhat prophetic in that V. herself later was involved as defendant in a monumentally lengthy lawsuit begun by John Birtwhistle in 1823 to recover properties bequeathed to V. by her father. Birtwhistle's parents had married in Scotland six years after his birth, thereby making him legitimate under Scottish law; in England, however, illegitimacy was permanent and barred inheritance. Thus, property left to Birtwhistle by his father had passed instead to John Vardill as residuary legatee. Birtwhistle's claim that his legitimacy in Scotland carried into England dragged on for years until it was concluded (in V.'s favor) in August 1840. V. was also in the curious situation of being a ward of the Court of Chancery until the age of fifty-two as a result of a clause in her father's will that left her inheritance in trust until she passed that age.

V. stopped writing—or at least publishing—in 1822, when the *European* changed hands and when she married James Niven and moved to her husband's estate in Scotland. Her only child, Agnes, was born in 1825, and Niven died in 1830. At this time, V. began writing again. Perhaps it was her husband's death and her own peculiar experience with the law that inspired V. to write a letter to her young daughter in December 1830. In this letter, she announces her intention to collect for the child all her writings, published and in manuscript, particularly several recent ones written "to preserve in remembrance facts which seemed to prove that many evils in a woman's life might be prevented by an early knowledge of the laws which regulate her place and property." These are listed in an accompanying inventory as "A Little Girl's Law-book," "A Young Lady's [Law-book]," and "An Old Lawyer's Legends." Only parts survive in manuscript, principally a long tale that is Part II of the "Legends." It is a rambling tale of a Scottish lord, Henry Stewart, and his bride, Marianne, both of whom take on various identities and suffer great hardships (mainly in pre-revolutionary France) that derive from their experiences with the law. Marianne as a child, in fact, had been deprived of an inheritance under circumstances that recall the Birtwhistle suit. In the last section, "L'Envoi," V. indicates that but for her failing sight and other illnesses she had planned a series of tales "shewing the greivous [sic] dependence & total sacrifices which women might escape by knowing the rights & protection given to them by the laws of their country."

V.'s uncompleted final project presages the period of public attention to the condition of women under English law that began with the publication of Caroline Norton's *A Plain Letter* in 1839. There is no evidence that V. wrote after 1830, although there are very brief notes dated 1840,

1847, and 1848 at the end of the manuscript of her unfinished book on the law and women. She lived in England again from 1830 with her daughter (who never married and died in 1872), dividing her time between Skipton and London. She was a friend of Mary Russell Mitford and is mentioned frequently in Mitford's correspondence. She was an inveterate traveler even in old age; she was in France in 1845 and 1847, and in that latter year in Scotland again. Through Mitford, she was known to Elizabeth Barrett, who thought her travel letters worthy of publication and once sent her a book of her own, but they apparently never met. V. died in 1852 at Skipton.

WORKS: *Poems and Translations from the Minor Greek Poets and Others* (1809). *The Pleasures of Human Life* (1812). Approximately 150 poems, short stories, and essays in *European Magazine* (1813–22).

BIBLIOGRAPHY: Axon, W. E. A. *Transactions of the Royal Society of Literature* (1908). Haven, R. *WC* (1976). Reiman, D. H. *WC* (1975).

For articles in reference works, see: *Feminist*.

Fredric S. Schwarzbach

Varley, Isabella: See *Banks, Isabella Varley*

Anne Venn

BORN: 1626 (?).
DIED: 1654.
DAUGHTER OF: Colonel John Venn and Margaret Langley.

V.'s conversion narrative, *A Wise Virgins Lamp Burning* (1658), is a selection of her writings published posthumously. The text includes a lengthy description of V.'s religious beliefs that first developed when she was nine years old, a personal account of her search for spiritual consolation, and discussions of doctrinal matters.

V.'s work was found and published by V.'s parents after her death. Thomas Weld, V.'s Presbyterian minister, wrote a rather unfortunate preface to the work in which he expressed the hope that it would serve as a model of ideal female behavior although "to thy knowledge it should not add much." In fact, much of the text shows V. to be quite different from the meek and biddable woman Weld's preface suggests. V. describes the effect of her beliefs in graphic, physical terms that made her "arched heart . . . like a wild thing ready to break out," and the struggle of the soul "that cries out as the infant after the breast and is not satisfied with anything without it."

WORKS: *A Wise Virgins Lamp Burning* (1658).

BIBLIOGRAPHY: Crawford, P. *Women and Religion in England 1500–1720* (1993). Hobby, E. *Virtue of Necessity: English Women's Writing 1649–88* (1988).

For articles in reference works see: *Bell*. *Feminist*. *WL17C*.

Jane Baston

Elizabeth Vesey

BORN: c. 1715, Ireland.
DIED: 1791, London.
DAUGHTER OF: Sir Thomas Vesey and Mary Muschamp Vesey.
MARRIED: William Handcock, n.d.; Agmondesham Vesey, before 1746.

V. was born in Ireland about 1715. Sometime before 1746, she married her second husband, her cousin Agmondesham Vesey, accountant-general of Ireland, amateur architect, and womanizer. Dividing her time between the family home in Ireland and a house in London, V. attracted many friends, and from 1770 until 1786 she was a leading Bluestocking. Of her letters, Lord Lyttleton wrote to David Garrick, "You will be charmed (as I am) with the lively colouring and fine touches in the epistolary style of our sylph, joined to the most perfect ease." V.'s letters reflect the sprightly wit and good humor by which she inspired convivial talk among the continental and British literati, philosophers, and scholars who gathered regularly in her "blue room" during the London winter season.

In 1751, Mary Delany dubbed her "the Sylph." Elizabeth Montagu praised the "musick" of her voice and the "gentle vivacity" of her wit. Horace Walpole asked, "What English heart ever excelled hers?" Her witty sallies were commonly aimed at herself, as when, denouncing second marriages, she seemed to overlook her own, finally exclaiming, "Bless me, my dear! I had quite forgotten it." Even when ill, she kept up her self-mockery, once remarking that her only happy moment in fourteen days had been a fainting fit, another time fearing for the loss of "seven or eight" of her senses.

This fascination with her own illnesses suggests a dark side to V. She herself said she had "a mind formed for doubt." Her friend Elizabeth Carter believed that because V. scarcely ever enjoyed "any one object, from the apprehension that something better may possibly be found in another," she lived in "a perpetual forecast of disappointment." Once V. told Carter of the sublime thrill of reading the agnostic Abbé Raynal during violent thunderstorms. Carter, who saw in her friend "coral groves and submarine palaces," was alarmed, writing back, "'Tis a dangerous amusement to a mind like yours.'"

When she was forty-seven years old, V. captivated Laurence Sterne, who for five years sought her out and wrote her love letters. Sterne's appreciation must have been a joy, for Mr. Vesey's peccadillos were unceasing. When V.'s husband died in 1785, he left her hardly anything out of an income of £4,000 except their London house, while settling on his mistress a legacy of £1,000. Although reportedly the nephew and heir "acted with great kindness and liberality," assuring V. of at least a "competency," this double stroke—her husband's death, and evidence of his neglect of her—blasted her already skeptical and apprehensive mind. From the age of seventy until her death at seventy-six, she was in a state of decline, from uncontrolled weeping to passivity, violent outbursts, and, finally, childlike vulnerability.

While Bluestocking gatherings derived from French salons, the name seems to have been inspired by V.'s assurances, "Pho, Pho, don't mind dress! Come in your blue stockings!" Through studied informality, V. created a casual atmosphere for her conversations; Fanny Burney noted that "she pushed all the small sofas, as well as chairs, pell-mell about the apartments." Her ability to render her guests "easy with one another" (Burney) was often noted. V.'s aim was to draw together the most exciting thinkers in various realms and to get them talking, sometimes stimulated by a reading from a new work. In this way, ideas were kept in motion. Additionally, such literary arts as letter writing and biography owe much to Bluestocking conversations in which the real social world and the world of ideas met in talk that was at once gossipy, thought provoking, and artful.

V.'s letters sometimes reveal the excesses of imagination that worried her friends: When ill in 1779, she wrote to Montagu, "I find the lamp of the mind sinking in its socket and had I courage to face the World unknown I should wish the flame quite extinct." This same letter, however, also reveals the value she placed on civilized conversation between friends, for she went on to create solace for herself through her communication of news events, gossip, and political analysis, ending abruptly and wittily with, "here is Ann come with the dressing basket how I hate to look at my own face when I can talk to you." V.'s letters primarily show her delight in language play. They are full of sharp sensuous detail, often in surprising combinations, as in a series that closes her thanks to Lord Lyttleton for his concern while she was ill: "& since you set any value upon my life I don't regret the blisters bleedings & the Boluses they cram'd down my throat." And sometimes her bright details are used in a game of self-mockery, as when she teases Lyttleton, in 1768, about his supposed proposition that they elope.

Her language play often involves comic hyperbole, and active verbs keep her reader rushing along. For instance, she creates a picture of ridiculous extravagance in the preparations she and Mr. Vesey are making for a party to be held in Lyttleton's honor:

> half a dozen oaks stript of their bark, the bed of the River dug up for rustick Stones the bogs and Heaths uncover'd of their Moss the Labourer taken from Harvest the Housekeeper robb'd of her Bread and barley to tempt the Birds to build their nests in Malvina's Bower—and there they are now—such a flight—whistling and singing the fish leaping the Farmer scolding and I almost crying to give up all hopes of seeing you there till next year which is to me for ever.

The "whistling and singing" series, dashing from comedy to pure affection, is typical of V.'s prose style. Through her letters one can appreciate the bright spirit that for fifteen years created conversation and good humor among a richly diverse group of friends.

WORKS: Selected letters in the following: *A Series of Letters Between Mrs. Elizabeth Carter and Miss Catherine Talbot 1741–70 . . . Letters from Mrs. Elizabeth Carter to Mrs. Vesey 1763–87*, ed. M. Pennington (1809). *Memoirs of the Life and Correspondence of Mrs. Hannah More*, ed. W. Roberts (1834). *Mary Hamilton at Court and at Home, from Letters and Diaries 1756 to 1816*, ed. E. Anson and F. Anson (1925). *Bluestocking Letters*, ed. E. B. Johnson (1926).

BIBLIOGRAPHY: *Mrs. Montagu, "Queen of the Blues," Her Letters and Friendships from 1762 to 1800*, ed. R. Blunt (1923). Huchon, R. L. *Mrs. Montagu and Her Friends, 1720–1800* (1907). Wheeler, E. R. *Famous Bluestockings* (1910).

For articles in reference works, see: *DNB*. *OCEL*.

Other references: *The Diary and Letters of Madame d'Arblay*, ed. A. Dobson (1904–05). *Edinburgh Review* (October 1925). *Horace Walpole's Correspondence*, ed. W. S. Lewis (1961). *Letters from Mrs. Carter to Mrs. Montagu 1755–1800*, ed. M. Pennington (1817). Tinker, C. *The Salon and English Letters* (1915). Wheatley, H. B. *The Historical and Posthumous Memoirs of Sir Nathaniel William Wraxall, 1772–1784* (1884).

Carolyn Woodward

Victoria

BORN: 24 May 1819, Kensington Palace, London.
DIED: 22 January 1901, Osborne House, Isle of Wight.
DAUGHTER OF: Edward, Duke of Kent, and Princess Mary Louisa Victoria of Saxe-Coburg.
MARRIED: Prince Albert of Saxe-Coburg-Gotha, 1840.

V., Queen of the United Kingdom of Great Britain and Ireland, Empress of India, was her whole life an indefatigable letter writer, addressing her voluminous correspondence to royal friends and relatives throughout Europe, to the ministers of the realm, and to loyal subjects (like Alfred Lord Tennyson) for whom she developed varying degrees of fondness and respect. John Raymond, editor of V.'s *Early Letters* (1963), remarked of her writing that "Queen Victoria was no verbal artist, as her journals and diaries show. Yet, in her letters, we can hear her authentic voice—rebuking, consoling, confirming, cajoling, upbraiding—in accents unlike those of any British sovereign (Queen Elizabeth I not excepted)." The letters, as well as her highly descriptive diaries and journals, afford us a remarkably rich record of her daily activities and observations—a record that may be of even greater interest to future historians than it has been to past ones.Their hasty dismissal of the literary interest of V.'s writing and their strictly factual consideration of her prose mostly overlooks its value as historical evidence of a more subtle sort concerning her womanly and often unheeded moral stance on a vast number of such pressing social questions as slum clearance, civil discontent, and the responsibilities of empire.

V. of the House of Hanover—conceived expressly to provide her fifty-two-year-old father (Edward, Duke of Kent, fourth son of King George III) with an heir to the British throne—was born at Kensington Palace on 24 May 1819 and was reared properly for her royal destiny by a strict and protective mother and a sagacious maternal uncle, Leopold of Saxe-Coburg (later elected King of Belgium).

Upon learning that she would some day be queen, V. at age twelve prophetically pronounced, "I will be good." Her remarkably detailed journal—a delightful source of information about her education—dates from that year. In 1837, on the very day of her accession, with amazing political acumen, the eighteen-year-old queen effected a polite but clean break from the nearly total control the Coburgs (mother, uncle, and governess) had held up to that point over her life. The young queen shouldered the responsibilities of her new position, devoting many hours each morning to state, then to personal correspondence. As the editors noted in the preface to the first series of *The Letters of Queen Victoria*, "nothing comes out more strongly in those documents than the laborious patience with which the Queen kept herself informed of the minutest details of political and social movements in both her own and other countries." Throughout her life, V. sought to influence history through her communications to political rivals like Lord Melbourne (Whig) and Sir Richard Peel (Conservative), Lord Palmerston (Foreign Office), and Lord John Russell (Prime Minister). The personal letters that V. wrote to her daughters and granddaughters reveal, as Richard Hough puts it in his introduction to *Advice to a Grand-daughter* (1975), "a sharply prophetic eye and highly developed intuition" that permitted her "to perceive the dangers that lay ahead."

Of course, none of V.'s correspondence was published during her lifetime. V.'s contemporaries were acquainted with only two of the many collections of her writings now in print: *Leaves from the Journal of Our Life in the Highlands* celebrates the joys of family life with Prince Albert, the Royal Consort; *More Leaves* poignantly evokes the void that the untimely death of Albert left in V.'s personal life. Even these popular volumes would not have appeared had Arthur Helps been less persuasive than he was in urging their publication, for V. protested "that she had no skill whatever in authorship, that these were, for the most part, mere homely accounts of excursions near home; and that she felt extremely reluctant to publish anything written by herself." Since by her own admission the collection referred "to some of the happiest hours" of her life, *Leaves from the Journal of Our Life in the Highlands* provides an important key to the complex story of Great Britain's most influential monarch.

Still, she would have enjoyed having even greater influence. Near the end of her sixty-four-year reign and after a lifetime of exerting unceasing epistolary pressures upon the governments of the realm, V. avowed in despair to her granddaughter, Princess Victoria of Hesse: "I feel very deeply that my opinion & my advice are never listened to & that it is almost useless to give any." Unequivocally honest, V.'s letters provide rare insights into the personal and political motives of thousands of her contemporaries—as well as into her own.

WORKS: *The Letters of Queen Victoria*, First Series, ed. A. C. Benson and R.B.B. Esher (1907); Second Series, ed. G. E. Buckle (1926–28); Third Series, ed. G. E. Buckle (1930–32). *The Girlhood of Queen Victoria: A Selection from Her Majesty's Diaries Between the Years 1832 & 1840*, ed. R.B.B. Esher (1912). *Letters of Queen Victoria, from the Archives of the House of Brandenburg-Prussia Between Victoria & Her Foreign & Prime Minister, 1837–1865*, ed. H. Bolitho (1938). *Leaves from a Journal: A Record of the Visit of the Emperor and Empress of the French to the Queen, & of the Visit of the Queen and H.R.H., the Prince Consort, to the Emperor of the French, 1855*, ed. R. Mortimer (1961). *Early Letters*, ed. J. Raymond (1963). *Dearest Child: Letters Between Queen Victoria and the Princess Royal, 1858–1861*, ed. R. Fulford (1964). *Dearest Mama: Letters Between Queen Victoria and the Crown Princess of Prussia, 1861–1864*, ed. R. Fulford (1968). *Dear and Honoured Lady: The Correspondence Between Queen Victoria & Alfred Tennyson*, ed. H. Dyson and C. Tennyson (1969). *Your Dear Letter: Private Correspondence of Queen Victoria and the Crown Princess of Prussia, 1865–1871*, ed. R. Fulford (1971). *Advice to a Grand-daughter: Letters from Queen Victoria to Princess Victoria of Hesse*, ed. R. Hough (1975). *Darling Child: Private Correspondence of Queen Victoria and the Crown Princess of Prussia, 1871–1878*, ed. R. Fulford (1976). *Queen Victoria's Highland Journals*, ed. D. Duff (1980). *Queen Victoria in her Letters and Journals*, ed. C. Hibbert (1985).

BIBLIOGRAPHY: Benson, E. F. *Queen Victoria* (1935). Besant, W. *The Queen's Reign 1837–1897* (1897). Creston, D. *The Youthful Queen Victoria* (1952). Dickson, J., in *Virginia Woolf: Themes and Variations*, ed. T. V. Neverow and M. Hussey (1993). Erickson, C. *Her Little Majesty: The Life of Queen Victoria* (1997). Fulford, R. *Queen Victoria* (1951). Gernsheim, H. *Victoria R.: A Biography with 400 Illustrations* (1959). Hardie, F. *The Political Influence of Queen Victoria 1861–1901* (1935). *Remaking Queen* Victoria, ed. M. Homans and A. Munich (1997). Huff, C. *ABSt* (1988). Longford, E. *Victoria R. I.* (1983). Looker, M. S. *VPR* (1988). May, J. *Victoria Remembered* (1983). Mullen, R. and J. Munson. *Victoria: Portrait of a Queen* (1987). Munich, A. A. *TSWL* (1987). Munich, A. *Queen Victoria's Secrets* (1996). Plowden, A. *The Young Victoria* (1981). Potts, D. M. and W.T.W. Potts. *Queen Victoria's Gene* (1995). Ricks, C. *VP* (1987). Rosenbaum, D. *CLAJ* (1992). Sinclair, A. *The Other Victoria* (1981). Sitwell, E. *Victoria of England* (1936). Strachey, L. *Queen Victoria* (1921). Warner, M. *Queen Victoria's Sketchbook* (1979). Woodham-Smith, C. *Queen Victoria: Her Life and Times* (1972).

For articles in reference works, see: *Allibone. Bloomsbury. CinP. DNB. Dole. Everyman's. Feminist. Oxford. Warner.*

Other references: Gosse, E. *Quarterly Review* (1901).

R. Victoria Arana

Vine, Barbara: See *Rendell, Ruth*

von Arnim, Elizabeth: See *Arnim, Elizabeth von*

Ethel Lilian Boole Voynich

BORN: 11 May 1864, Cork, Ireland.
DIED: 27 July 1960, New York City, United States.
DAUGHTER OF: George Boole and Mary Everest Boole.
MARRIED: Wilfrid Michael Voynich, 1891.
WROTE UNDER: Lily Boole; E.L.V.; E. L. Voynich.

V. is remembered primarily for her first novel, *The Gadfly* (1897), a romantic philosophical melodrama set in Italy during the Risorgimento. An idealistic revolutionary, betrayed and disillusioned, redoubles his political efforts, transforms his cynicism into a weapon, and ultimately forces his former spiritual advisor—a priest who is also his unacknowledged father—to face the truth about himself and his corrupt church. This novel was admired by D. H. Lawrence, adapted for the stage by George Bernard Shaw, and acclaimed by Bertrand Russell as "the most exciting novel I have read in the English language." It went through eight printings in its first four years and was popular worldwide in English and in translation; it was particularly popular in Russia, where it was published in more than 100 editions and, assigned as required reading in schools, read by more than 250 million young people. V.'s four other novels—two of which deal with characters from *The Gadfly*—achieved neither popular nor critical success; they address similar political and psychological themes, but with reduced balance and insight. V. also published several translations, and, for twenty-five years, composed choral music.

She was the last of the five daughters of George Boole, a mathematician and logician who died the year she was born, and of Mary Everest Boole, a speculative thinker (and an influence on the novelist Dorothy Richardson) who wrote on philosophy, physiological perception, and mathematical education. Educated in Ireland and in Germany, she became involved in revolutionary politics and spent two years in Russia. Through her work with Sergei M. Stepniak, she met not only Shaw and Friedrich Engels but also her future husband, Habdank Woynicz, a Polish nationalist of aristocratic background who escaped political imprisonment in Siberia. He anglicized his name to Wilfrid Michael Voynich and became a British citizen; they married in 1891. He was an internationally known dealer in antiquarian books, based first in England, later in New York City, where they lived after the first world war. V., inaugurating her literary career with translations of Russian fiction and of Sergei Stepniak's book on nihilism, achieved instant renown with her first novel.

The Gadfly begins with the sheltered youth of Arthur Burton, devoted to his mother (an Italian widow, who dies when he is sixteen), his guardian and mentor (the priest Montanelli, who is also his biological father), and his sweetheart Gemma, his partner in amateur political activities. The idyl ends when Montanelli betrays his political secrets; at the same time, Arthur discovers his true parentage and loses all trust in Montanelli and the church. Feigning suicide, Arthur sails for South America; as Felice Rivarez, he is mutilated, lamed, and disgraced. Years later, he returns to Italy, as the Gadfly, to serve as satirist for the revolutionary struggle. When Cardinal Montanelli, forced to condemn him to death, tries secretly to rescue him, the Gadfly refuses to be saved unless Montanelli admits that he and his church are frauds.

Dramatic surprises and intensely emotional confrontations won immediate acclaim and popularity for the novel. The Soviets and other readers were shocked, however, to learn in 1968 that the Gadfly, adopted as a Soviet hero, may have been based on an anti-Russian spy. The Gadfly—with his mysterious antecedents, cynical temperament, and satirical manner—may be V.'s version of Sidney Reilly, an enigmatic international spy who plotted to assassinate V. I. Lenin and is reported to have died at the hands of the Secret Police in 1925. According to Robin Bruce Lockhart, Reilly claimed that V. had a romance with him in 1895 and drew the character from his shrouded origins (Reilly too was the product of an affair between his mother and an admired family friend) and his years of suffering in Brazilian plantations and jungles. Given Reilly's propensity for inventing rumors, it is possible that some of the adventures he reported about his life were based on V.'s novels rather than vice versa.

Jack Raymond (1901) and *Olive Latham* (1904) illustrate the power of emotional and intellectual sympathy to heal spirits wounded by cruelty and shocked by loss. Raised by his uncle, a sadistic minister, Jack Raymond survives a variety of tortures—including severe beatings and unfounded accusations of "perversion"—largely because of his inner resources and the support of a schoolmate's mother, the widow of a Polish political activist who had died in Siberia. Olive Latham is driven to mental collapse by the persecution and death of her lover, a Russian anarchist; she recovers through the love of a Polish revolutionary, himself a survivor of spinal paralysis. Like the Gadfly, the protagonists of both novels suffer intensely, yet prevail; both novels, too, appear to be drawn on V.'s husband's experiences as a political prisoner in Siberia.

An Interrupted Friendship (1910) deals with events in South America during the time of *The Gadfly,* years at which the original novel only hints. After Arthur's innocent trust is shattered, he becomes Felice Rivarez; sometimes a plantation laborer, sometimes a circus clown, he joins a British jungle expedition posing as a Portuguese cook and ultimately saves the lives of several officers. The novel's protagonist is not the Gadfly himself but Rene, one of the men whose life he saves. Rene loves Rivarez for his courage and dignity. The relationship ends suddenly because Rivarez wrongly believes that Rene has revealed his secrets. Years later, Rene tells his son that it is a privilege to have known "one of the rare spirits that go through the world like stars, radiating light," but it is "a dangerous thing to love them too much." Whether or not *The Gadfly* had constituted a revelation of a lover's secrets, V.'s 1910 novel, thirteen years after *The Gadfly,* shows that those who are once betrayed are forever suspicious and never forgiving.

More than thirty years later, after a second career in music, V. returned to fiction with the novel *Put Off Thy Shoes* (1945). In a lengthy, multigenerational chronicle focusing mostly on the Gadfly's British grandparents and great-grandparents, she endeavors, as she explains in the foreword, to make plausible the apparent contradictions in the Gadfly's nature. This novel retains the emotional pain of *The Gadfly* while lacking its narrative concentration.

Although V. remains a writer known for a single novel, that novel may be the best-selling title in Russia of all novels written in English. *The Gadfly* was initially interpreted as a echo of the idealist Decembrist movement of 1825; it became even more popular after the Bolshevik Revolution. *The Gadfly* was eventually translated into twenty-two Slavic languages; it was required reading in schools; and the Gadfly became a Soviet hero to generations of young people. Adapted as three operas and as two films (one with a scenario by formalist critic Viktor Shklovsky, the other with a score by Shostakovich), it has remained an official classic; the Russians rank her with Charles Dickens, Mark Twain, and Theodore Dreiser. When a Soviet editor, a fan of the novel, discovered in 1955 that V. was still alive, half a century after the novel, "Voynich Lives in New York!" was a front-page story in *Pravda.*

The Gadfly, although often described as a precursor of the gallant Scarlet Pimpernel, is remarkable in several respects: the specifically intellectual quality of his revolutionary activities, the anticlerical animus that inspires his condemnation of Montanelli (who is both a Father and his father), and the psychological struggle, in his nature, between his cynical bitterness and radiant love for his sweetheart, his cause, and the earth. The character V. devised (whether entirely invented or based on Sidney Reilly) dominated her fiction for half a century and fascinated generations of readers, not only in Russia but worldwide.

WORKS: (trans.) *Stories from Garshin* (1893). (trans.) *Nihilism as It Is by Stepniak* (1895). (trans.) *The Humour of Russia* (1895). *The Gadfly* (1897). *Jack Raymond* (1901). *Olive Latham* (1904). *An Interrupted Friendship* (1910). (trans.) *Six Lyrics from the Ruthenian of Taras Schevchenko* (1911). (trans.) *Chopin's Letters* (1931). *Put Off Thy Shoes* (1945).

BIBLIOGRAPHY: Bernhardt, L. *PULC* (1966). Courtney, W. L. *The Feminine Note in Fiction* (1904). Fremantle, A. *History Today* (1975). Kennedy, J. G. *ELT* (1970). Kettle, A. *EIC* (1957). Lockhart, R. B. *Ace of Spies* (1967). MacHale, D. *George Boole* (1978). Orioli, G. *Adventures of a Bookseller* (1937). Sowerby, E. M. *Rare People and Rare Books* (1967).

For articles in reference works, see: *CA. 1890s. Grimes. Longman. NCBEL. NCHEL. OCEL. Oxford. RE. Todd-BWW. VB. WN.*

Other references: *A.L.A. Booklist* (10 April 1910, 1 June 1945). *Athenaeum* (19 March 1910). *Bookman* (10 April 1910). *Dial* [Chicago] (1 April 1910). *Independent* [New York] (19 May 1910). *LJ* (15 May 1945). *Look* (8 July 1958). *New Yorker* (26 May 1945). *NYT* (13 March 1957, 1 June 1959, 29 July 1960). *NYTBR* (5 June 1897, 26 June 1897, 20 August 1898, 1 June 1901, 4 June 1904, 26 March 1910, 20 September 1931, 31 March 1957, 27 May 1945). *Outlook* (2 April 1910). *PW* (8 August 1960). *Saturday Review* (26 May 1945). *Time* (8 August 1960).

Shoshana Milgram Knapp

Helen Jane Waddell

BORN: 31 May 1889, Tokyo, Japan.
DIED: 5 March 1965, London.
DAUGHTER OF: the Reverend Hugh Waddell and Jane Martin.

W. was an author, translator, lecturer, and scholar whose numerous books in the 1920s and 1930s helped to bring the Latin poetry of the Middle Ages into the mainstream of intellectual life. The daughter of an Irish Presbyterian missionary, W. attended Victoria College and Queen's University, Belfast, from which she received the B.A. degree in 1911 and the M.A. in 1912. For the next seven years she cared for her ailing stepmother in Ulster while writing *Lyrics from the Chinese* (1913), articles, reviews, children's devotional stories, and a play, *The Spoilt Buddha* (1919).

She entered Somerville College, Oxford, in 1920, where she gave a series of lectures on medieval mime. After a brief teaching stint at Bedford (1922–23), she studied in Paris under a Susette Taylor Travelling Scholarship from Lady Margaret Hall (1923–25). At Paris she completed the original reading of medieval Latin poets that she had begun at Oxford. She published the results of this inquiry as *The Wandering Scholars* (1927) and *Medieval Latin Lyrics* (1929). In the rush of popularity that followed these publications, W. became a much-loved personality in the social circles of London. She gave frequent lectures and addresses and was awarded a stream of honorary degrees. Her friends included G.E.B. Saintsbury, AE (George Russell), Max Beerbohm, George Bernard Shaw, Siegfried Sassoon, and William Butler Yeats.

Her best work combines the thorough knowledge of the medieval scholar with the expressive energy of the creative writer. She was significant in raising modern consciousness of the medieval spiritual world. Her novel *Peter Abelard* (1933) was the ideal vehicle to combine both her love for the twelfth century and her creative imagination, and it is widely considered her best work. While working on her novel, she also produced *A Book of Medieval Latin for Schools* (1931), an edition of *Cole's Paris Journal* (1931), a translation of *Manon Lescaut* (1931), and a play, *The Abbé Prevost* (1931). A translation of Rosweyde's *Vitae Patrum* (1615) appeared as *The Desert Fathers* (1936).

W. planned and had begun work on a study of John of Salisbury, but the onset of World War II diverted her energies. Fiercely patriotic, she wrote and translated poems relating to Britain's struggle. She assumed greater responsibilities at Constable's (her publisher) and became assistant editor of *The Nineteenth Century.* Her translations from this period have been collected by Felicitas Corrigan in *More Latin Lyrics from Virgil to Milton* (1976). Throughout her life, she wrote fascinating letters to her sister, Margaret Waddell, in Kilmacrew House, Banbridge, Northern Ireland, and many of these are quoted in Monica Blackett's *The Mark of the Maker* (1973). After the war, W. suffered from intermittent amnesia. Her last achievement was the W.P. Ker Lecture at Glasgow University in 1947, published as *Poetry in the Dark Ages* (1948). She died in London on 5 March 1965.

WORKS: *Lyrics from the Chinese* (1913). *The Spoiled Buddha* (1919). *The Wandering Scholars* (1927). *Medieval Latin Lyrics* (1929). *A Book of Medieval Latin for Schools* (1931). *Cole's Paris Journal* (1931). (trans.) *Manon Lescaut,* by Abbé Prevost (1931). *The Abbé Prevost* (1931). *Peter Abelard* (1933). (trans.) *The Desert Fathers,* by Rosweyd (1936). *Beasts and Saints* (1934). *Poetry in the Dark Ages* (1948).

BIBLIOGRAPHY: Blackett, M. *The Mark of the Maker: A Portrait of Helen Waddell* (1973). Cooper, A. *Agenda* (1982–83). *More Latin Lyrics from Virgil to Milton,* ed. F. Corrigan (1976). *TLS* (17 June 1977).

For articles in reference works, see: *CA. Cambridge. DNB. Feminist. Longman. TCA* and *SUP. TCW.*

Richard Poss

Priscilla Wakefield

BORN: 31 January 1751, Tottenham, Middlesex.
DIED: 12 September 1832, Ipswich, Suffolk.
DAUGHTER OF: Daniel Bell and Catharine Barclay.
MARRIED: Edward Wakefield, 1771.

Philanthropist and writer, W. was known for her commitment to the improvement of people's lives through education. She developed her theories and practical applications in numerous books on science and travel, many written for children, essays on social conditions and behavior, one biography, and an influential conduct manual. Her publications were reprinted well into the 1850s.

The granddaughter of Quaker apologist Robert Barclay, W. was early committed to education and social action through the Society of Friends. In 1791, she established a maternity hospital. She was also among the earliest promoters of savings banks, called "frugality banks," and established several during her lifetime. Although following religious practices of Quakers, W. did not observe their restrictions on dress or entertainments. W. and her husband, a Quaker merchant, had three children.

W., knowledgeable in botany and natural history, believed that scientific studies were an important dimension of both boys' and girls' education. Like Maria Edgeworth and Richard Lovell, she believed in the child's capacity to wonder, inquire, and learn through conversation and experimentation. *An Introduction to Botany* (1796) teaches Linnaeus's system of taxonomy through a series of letters between two sisters. Her popular *The Juvenile Travellers* (1801) and *A Family Tour through the British Empire* (1804) examine the value of travel in a child's education.

W.'s most notable contribution to the dialogue about women's education was *Reflections on the Present Condition of the Female Sex, with Suggestions for its Improvement* (1798). It stresses the importance of a practical education for women of all social classes. Women, like men, ought to contribute their labor to the good of society, but they had been impeded from doing so by limited education, custom, and a devaluation of their abilities. If a woman married, her solid education and preparation for work would make her a better companion to her husband and a valuable co-worker in his enterprise. If she did not marry, W. believed, her preparation would enlarge the opportunities for gainful employment in a variety of areas not usually open to women: writing, engraving, book illustration, bookkeeping, sales-clerk, and numerous other careers. Moreover, *Reflections* condemns the pay inequities of men and women in the same field, such as stay-maker or hairdresser, and in comparable fields, such as footman and cook-maid. W. believed that opening more careers to women would reduce many social problems, including prostitution. W. also outlines the educational content for women of each of four classes, and *Reflections* includes a proposal for a Female College.

W.'s works remain remarkable for their wide range of subjects, their combination of theory and practice, and the striking anticipation of modern concerns about women and their opportunities for education and employment.

WORKS: *Leisure Hours, or Entertaining Dialogues* (1794–96). *Juvenile Anecdotes, founded on Facts* (1795; 1798). *An Introduction to Botany, in a Series of Familiar Letters* (1796). *Mental Improvement, or the Beauties and Wonders of Nature and Art; conveyed in a Series of Instructive Conversations* (1797). *Reflections on the Present Condition of the Female Sex, with Suggestions for its Improvement* (1798; rpt. 1974). *The Juvenile Travellers* (1801). *A Family Tour through the British Empire* (1804). *Domestic Recreation, or Dialogues illustrative of Natural and Scientific Subjects* (1805). *Excursions in North America* (1806). *Sketches of Human Manners* (1809). *Variety, or Selections and Essays* (1809). *Perambulations in London and its Environs* (1810). *Instinct Displayed, or Facts Exemplifying the Sagacity of Various Species of Animals* (1811). *The Traveller in Africa* (1814). *An Introduction to the Natural History and Classification of Insects, in a Series of Letters* (1816). *A Brief Memoir of the Life of William Penn* (1817). *A Catechism of Botany* (1817). *The Traveller in Asia* (1817).

BIBLIOGRAPHY: Riddenhough, G. *DR* (1958).

For articles in reference works, see: *DNB. Feminist. Oxford. ToddBWW. ToddDBA.*

Carol Shiner Wilson

Lucy (Bethia) Walford

BORN: 17 April 1845, Portobello, near Edinburgh.
DIED: 11 May 1915, London.
DAUGHTER OF: John Colquhoun and Frances Sara Fuller-Maitland.
MARRIED: Alfred Sanders Walford, 1869.

W. was raised in a socially well-connected, strict Presbyterian family. Her grandfather was a baronet, her aunt was the novelist Catherine Sinclair, and her father was a well-known sportsman, author, and former army officer. She was educated at home by a series of foreign governesses and states that she was an avid reader from the age of seven. W. contextualized her work within a female literary tradition: She cites Charlotte Yonge as an early influence and states that, after reading Jane Austen for the first time in 1868, the author was to "exercise an abiding influence over all my own future efforts." Her continued interest in women's writing is demonstrated by her 1888 publication of *Four Biographies from Blackwood's* in which she focuses on the lives and works of women writers Elizabeth Fry, Hannah More, Mary Somerville, and Jane Taylor.

W. began to write after her marriage, secretly working on stories and sketches when she could find the time. She published her first novel, *Mr. Smith, a Part of His Life,* in 1874, incurring the strong disapproval of her mother's family. In spite of her family's displeasure, the novel was a resounding and immediate popular success, earning the praise of none other than Queen Victoria, whose enjoyment of the novel led to W.'s presentation at court. *Mr. Smith's* success also led to regular contributions in *Blackwood's* and other periodicals, where many of W.'s novels eventually appeared as serials. Her first novel is typical, in both subject and tone, of much of W.'s fiction: The light-hearted story recounts the social and romantic adventures of its heroine, the charming and flirtatious Helen Tolleton. The novel's breezy look at domestic life reveals a talent for comedy which runs throughout many of W.'s novels. Her witty attention to the familiar, feminine, and social world is best reflected in the following books: *Pauline* (1877), *The Baby's Grandmother* (1884), *Cousins* (1885), *The History of a Week* (1886), *A Mere Child* (1888), *A Stiff-necked Generation* (1889), *The Havoc of a Smile* (1890), *The Mischief of Monica* (1892) and *Sir Patrick the Puddock* (1899). Her novel *The Matchmaker* (1894) is notable for being the last three-decker accepted by Mudie's Circulating Library.

W. served as London correspondent for the New York *Critic* from 1889 to 1893 and published a total of some forty-five books, including *Recollections of a Scottish Novelist* (1910), which centers on memories of her early life, and *Memories of Victorian London* (1912), a treasure trove of contemporary literary and social gossip. Her prolific career continued into her seventieth year with the 1914 publication of her final novel, *David and Jonathan on the Riviera.* W. was a multitalented and energetic woman whose fictions, like those of her literary foremother Jane Austen, foregrounded the feminine world of manners and the domestic, pointedly characterizing the social codes that ruled Victorian women's lives.

WORKS: *Mr. Smith, a Part of His Life* (1874). *Nan and Other Tales* (1875). *Pauline* (1877). *Troublesome Daughters* (1880). *The Baby's Grandmother* (1884). *Cousins* (1885). *The History of a Week* (1886). *Four Biographies from Blackwood's* (1888). *A Mere Child* (1888). *A Stiff-necked Generation* (1889). *The Havoc of a Smile* (1890). *A Pinch of Experience* (1891). *The Mischief of Monica* (1892). *A Question of Penmanship* (1893). *The Matchmaker* (1894). *A Bubble: A Story* (1895). *Successors to the Title* (1896). *Leddy Margaret* (1898). *Sir Patrick the Puddock* (1899). *The Archdeacon* (1899). *One of Ourselves* (1900). *A Dream's Fulfillment* (1902). *Charlotte* (1902). *The Enlightenment of Olivia* (1907). *Lenore Stubbs* (1908). *Celia: And the Parents* (1910). *Recollections of a Scottish Novelist* (1910). *Memories of Victorian London* (1912). *David and Jonathan on the Riviera* (1914).

BIBLIOGRAPHY:

For articles in reference books, see: *Bloomsbury. Feminist. Oxford. ToddBWW.*

Kirsten T. Saxton

Jill Paton Walsh

BORN: 29 April 1937, London.
DAUGHTER OF: John Llewellyn and Patricia Dubern Bliss.
MARRIED: Antony Edmund Paton Walsh, 1961.
WRITES UNDER: Gillian Paton Walsh; Jill Paton Walsh.

Known more for her children's books than for her adult novels, W. writes with an intellectual depth and complexity unusual in either genre, creating works that explore with lyrical rhythmic precision such basic themes as love, death, courage, and the human spirit. Her ability to create deeply evocative settings is one of her strongest points; another is the high value she places on intellectual discourse, creating texts that interweave deep examinations of profound issues throughout well-crafted fictional frameworks.

After reading English at St. Anne's College, Oxford, W. taught at Enfield Girls' Grammar School in Middlesex from 1959 to 1962. She married Antony Edmund Paton Walsh in 1961, quickly became "bored frantic" with life as a housewife, and began to write. Her first book, she says, was "dreadfully bad" and was not published, but with encouragement from an editor at Macmillan she wrote *Hengest's Tale,* published in 1966. Since then, she has written more than thirty books, many of which have earned awards and honors, including the Boston Globe–Horn Book Award for *Unleaving* (1976). She lectured at the Library of Congress in Washington, D.C., in 1978 and was a visiting faculty member at the Center for the Study of Children's Literature at Simmons College in Boston from 1978 to 1986. In 1986, she and John Rowe Townsend founded Green Bay Publishers.

Hengest's Tale, a historical novel set in the fifth century, centers around a character who appears in *Beowulf.* A number of her other works also demonstrate W.'s interest in narrating the past; among these are *The Emperor's Winding Sheet* (1974), which chronicles the fall of Constantinople; *Wordhoard* (1969), a collection of Anglo-Saxon tales; and *The Dolphin Crossing* (1967) and *Fireweed* (1969), both set during World War II. Told from the adult perspective of the narrator, Bill, *Fireweed* is one of her best books—a hard-hitting and unsentimental, yet moving, depiction of young love amid the bombed-out ruins of London. Slightly less successful in its execution, *A Chance Child* (1978) is a mixture of horrifying reality and strange fantasy. Creep, a young abused boy, escapes his twentieth-century life to flit almost ghostlike through a nineteenth-century world where children struggle to stay alive by working under terrible conditions. The book is an effective indictment of child abuse past and present, saturated with W.'s vivid descriptions, but at times her didactic intent overshadows the story as it falters into what feels like a guided tour of the horrors of nineteenth-century industries and labor abuses.

Vivid, lyrical descriptions predominate in *Goldengrove* (1972) and *Unleaving* (1976), both set on the Cornish Coast, in which the sea and land almost seem to become characters themselves. By tracing the maturation of Madge from young girlhood through old age, W. literally examines issues of life and death in these two novels; although bordering on the morbidly depressing in *Unleaving,* the message is ultimately life affirming. W.'s use of the present tense and multiple subject viewpoint add to the complexity and rhythm of the novels, giving them an unusual and at times disconcerting edge that grows more disturbing as the climax approaches.

In *A Parcel of Patterns* (1983), W. employs first-person narration, complete with seventeenth-century inflections and vocabulary, to unfold the true story of Eyam, a small town in England whose inhabitants were decimated by the plague in 1665 and 1666. By voluntarily closing their town borders, the inhabitants kept the plague from spreading locally, as 267 out of some 350 of them died in the course of the year. The story, heart-rending in its exploration of human dignity in the face of appalling circumstances, is also a vehicle for examining the personal resonances of the theological shifts taking place just five years after the reinstallation of the Church of England upon King Charles II's return to the throne. W. deftly weaves theological issues into the body of the story through her characterizations of Puritan and Anglican parsons who minister to the townspeople when the plague strikes.

W. also tackles knotty theological problems in a number of her other books, including one of her adult novels, *Lapsing* (1986), which traces a young woman's struggle to fit her desires within Roman Catholic precepts and her growing disillusionment with her faith. Set in the 1950s, the novel contains pointed (and sometimes cynical) interjections about the incredible innocence and naïveté that marks this transitional historical period.

A difficult writer to categorize, W. has more recently published *The Wyndham Case* (1993) a straightforward and thoroughly enjoyable murder mystery set in the Cambridge University milieu—which is also, in part, a not-*too*-biting satire of the vagaries of academic life—as well as *Knowledge of Angels* (1994), an unsettling and unusual exploration of the nature of faith and religious belief. It is impossible to forecast exactly where she will go next, but one thing is probably true: Whatever books she writes will likely be complex explorations of human nature, filled with lyrical descriptions and permeated by a quiet intelligence.

WORKS: *Hengest's Tale* (1966). *The Dolphin Crossing* (1967). *Fireweed* (1969). (with Kevin Crossley-Holland) *Wordhoard: Anglo-Saxon Stories* (1969). *Farewell, Great King* (1972). *Goldengrove* (1972). *Toolmaker* (1973). *The Dawnstone* (1973). *The Emperor's Winding Sheet* (1974). *The Butty Boy* (1975; also published as *The Huffler*). *The Island Sunrise: Prehistoric Britain* (1975; in the U.S. as *The Island Sunrise: Prehistoric Culture in the British Isles* (1976). *Unleaving* (1976). *Crossing to Salamis* (1977). *The Walls of Athens* (1977). *Children of the Fox* (1978; contains trilogy: *Crossing to Salamis; The Walls of Athens;* and *Persian Gold*). *Persian Gold* (1978). *A Chance Child* (1978). *Babylon* (1981). *The Green Book* (1981; also published as *Shine,* 1988). *A Parcel of Patterns* (1983). *Gaffer Samson's Luck* (1984). *Lost and Found* (1984). *Five Tides* (1986). *Lapsing* (1986). *Torch* (1987). *Birdy and the Ghosties* (1989). *A School for Lovers* (1989). *Can I Play Farmer, Farmer* (1990). *Can I Play Jenny Jones* (1990). *Can I Play Queenie* (1990). *Can I Play Wolf* (1990). *Grace* (1991). *Matthew and the Sea Singer* (1992). *When Grandma Came* (1992). *The Wyndham Case* (1993). *Knowledge of Angels* (1994). *Pepi and the Secret Names* (1994). *A Piece of Justice* (1995).

BIBLIOGRAPHY: *Triumphs of the Spirit in Children's Literature,* ed. F. Butler and R. Rotert (1986). Egoff, S. A. *Thursday's Child: Trends and Patterns in Contemporary Children's Literature* (1981). *Celebrating Children's Books,* ed. B. Hearne and M. Kaye (1981). Lenz, M. *CLAQ* (1988). *The Voice of the Narrator in Children's Literature,* ed. B. Otten and G. D. Schmidt (1989). Stanek, L. W. *A Study Guide to the Novels of Jill Paton Walsh* (1978).

For articles in reference works, see: *CA. CLC. CLR. OCCL. SATA. TCCW.*

Other references: *Booklist* (15 June 1992, 1 November 1992, 15 April 1993, July 1993). *Childhood Education* (1993). *Horn Book* (August 1967, June 1970, August 1976). *LJ* (15 February 1994). *LonT* (18 September 1986). *NYTBR* (9 April 1967, 5 November 1972, 8 August 1976, 16 June 1985, 24 January 1988, 14 June 1992).

Jackie E. Stallcup

Barbara Ward (Jackson)

BORN: 23 May 1914, York, Yorkshire.
DIED: 31 May 1981, Lodsworth, Sussex.
DAUGHTER OF: Walter Ward and Teresa Mary Burge Ward.
MARRIED: Robert G. A. Jackson, 1950.

An internationally known economist, journalist, broadcaster, and writer on international affairs, W. was the author of many books and the recipient of many awards, including a Life Peeress of the House of Lords in 1976. Born to a Quaker solicitor and a Roman Catholic mother, W. was raised a Catholic near Ipswich and studied in France (including the Sorbonne) and Germany before entering Somerville College, Oxford, where she graduated with highest honors in politics, philosophy, and economics. She then studied abroad for three years and lectured at Cambridge University and to worker groups. Deeply influenced by a papal encyclical that warned against dividing the world into have and have-not nations, she began an illustrious career as a writer defending this principle and working toward developing Third World nations.

Throughout her life, W. was a noted teacher and administrator, as well as a prolific writer, turning out, for example, an unpublished 200,000-word novel when she was fourteen. She published her first book when she was twenty-six, *The International Share-Out* (1938), then joining *The Economist* the year after and becoming foreign editor in 1940. She was also a governor of the BBC from 1946 to 1950 and regularly served on broadcasts of the "Brains Trust" program as well as American interview programs. She lived for several years in Gold Coast (now Ghana) with her husband, an economist and a former Assistant Secretary General of the United Nations. For seven years, she was president of the International Institute for Environment and Development, and she also taught for a number of years in the United States at Radcliffe College and Harvard and Columbia universities.

At the heart of her writing is W.'s conviction that richer nations must aid poorer nations in order for international peace and the security of the West to be maintained, a concept now accepted as gospel. She wrote for both popular and scholarly audiences and was especially skillful at synthesizing complex ideas for the broadest possible audience.

Her ideas, however, were not accepted uniformly, and she was sometimes criticized for alleged oversimplification. Reviews of *Five Ideas that Change the World* (1959), for example, claimed that she was blind to the economic realities governing investment and political stability.

A firm believer in international order and cooperation, W. proposed (as in *Nationalism and Ideology,* 1966) that the world economy would be better apportioned through the creation of federations above the level of nation and below the level of the United Nations. The "sense of humanity" and "responsibility of power" she described in this work was necessary, she felt, because of the increased rise of nationalism. Critics here, too, faulted her wishful thinking, and even supporters such as Robert L. Heilbroner saw the inconsistency in her asking for "faith" in poorer nations, on the one hand, and documenting the "terrible actualities facing these countries," on the other hand.

She consistently tried to defend environmental issues as well, though here, too (as in reviews of *Only One Earth,* written with René Dubos in 1972), she predictably received criticism. John Kenneth Galbraith, among others, saw that W.'s penultimate book, *Progress for a Small Planet* (1979), was written out of her conviction that a total cooperative effort among nations was necessary to solve the many problems facing "Spaceship Earth" (as she called it in her 1966 book of the same title) but that her optimism and, as some saw it, her inability to see the reality around her was a welcome antidote to the prevailing cynicism.

W. was a brilliant synthesizer of complex economic and political issues, and her influence was great; she served as adviser to U. N. Secretary General U Thant and U.S. presidents John F. Kennedy and Lyndon B. Johnson. With evangelical zeal, she warned prophetically of matters that today are accepted worldwide as true, particularly the necessary interdependence of all nations, rich or poor, and the corresponding close integration of economic and ecological priorities. She moved easily and competently through history for her arguments, and she was equally adept at offering sensitive, humane, well-reasoned solutions to the world's ills. Her reliance on her religious faith served as foundation for her thinking, and her "compelling" vision (as it was called in the *Times Literary Supplement*) acted as a form of political conscience for some forty years.

WORKS: *The International Share-Out* (1938). (with others) *Hitler's Route to Bagdad* (1939). *Russian Foreign Policy* (1940). *Italian Foreign Policy* (1941). (with others) *A Christian Basis for the Post War World* (1941). *The Defence of the West* (1942). *Turkey* (1942). *Democracy, East and West* (1947; 1949). *The West at Bay* (1948). *Policy for the West* (1951). *Are Today's Basic Problems Religious? [and] Moral Order in an Uncertain World* (1953). *Faith and Freedom* (1954). *Britain's Interest in Atlantic Union* (1954). *The Interplay of East and West: Points of Conflict and Cooperation* (1957, 1962; in the U.K. as *The Interplay of East and West: Elements of Contrast and Co-operation*). *My Brother's Keeper* (1957). *Herbert Lehman at 80: Young Elder Statesman* (1958). *Five Ideas that Change the World* (1959). (with others) *The Legacy of Imperialism: Essays* (1960). *The Unity of the Free World* (1961). *India and the West* (1961; 1964). *The Rich Nations and the Poor Nations* (1961). *The Plan under Pressure: An Observer's View* (1963). (with M. Zinkin) *Why Help India?* (1963). *Women in the New Asia: The Changing Social Roles of Men and Women in South and South-East Asia* (1963). *Spirit of 76—Why not Now?* (1963) *Towards A World of Plenty* (1964). *The Decade of Development: A Study of Frustration* (1965). (with P. T. Bauer) *Two Views on Aid to Developing Countries* (1966). *Spaceship Earth* (1966). *Nationalism and Ideology* (1966). *World Poverty—Can It Be Solved?* (1966). (author of commentary) *Populorum Progressio,* by Pope Paul VI (1967). *The Lopsided World* (1968). *A New History* (1969). *Urbanization in the Second United Nations Development Decade* (1970). *The Widening Gap: Development in the 1970's, A Report on the Columbia Conference on International Economic Development* (1971). *An Urban Planet* (1971). *The Angry Seventies: The Second Development Decade—A Call to the Church* (1972). (with R. Dubos) *Only One Earth: The Care and Maintenance of a Small Planet* (1972). (with others) *Who Speaks for Earth?,* ed. M. F. Strong (1973). *A New Creation? Reflections on the Environmental Issue* (1973). *The Age of Leisure* (1973). *Human Settlements: Crisis and Opportunity* (1974). *A "People" Strategy of Development* (1974). *Habitat 2000* (1975). (with G. Ward) *The John Ward House* (1976). *The Home of Man* (1976). (with W. R. Ward) *The Andrew-Safford House* (1976). (with G. Ward) *Silver in American Life* (1979). *Progress for a Small Planet* (1979). *Peace and Justice in the World* (1981).

BIBLIOGRAPHY: Lean, G., et al. *Tribute to Barbara Ward, the Lady of Global Concern* (1987).

For articles in reference works, see *BCathA. CA. CB. TCA SUP.*

Other references: *Atlantic* (April 1959, August 1972). Bellringer, A. W. *PSt* (1986). *CSM* (12 March 1959, 7 June 1972, 1 June 1976, 7 November 1979). *Commonweal* (14 January 1955). Galbraith, J. K. *BW* (2 September 1979). Heilbroner, R. L. *BW* (5 June 1966). *LonT* (1 June 1981). *Natural History* (October 1972). *New Statesman* (26 May 1972). *Newsweek* (7 April 1947, 2 March 1959, 15 June 1981). *New Republic* (13 April 1959, 27 October 1979). *New Yorker* (29 October 1979). *NYT* (1 March 1959, 1 June 1981). *Saturday Review* (20 November 1954). *Spectator* (20 March 1959). *Time* (19 May 1947, 15 June 1981). *TLS* (30 June 1966). *Washington Post* (1 June 1981).

Paul Schlueter

Ward, Maisie: See *Ward, Mary Josephine*

Mary Augusta Arnold Ward

BORN: 11 June 1851, Tasmania, Australia.
DIED: 24 March 1920, London.
DAUGHTER OF: Thomas Arnold and Julia Sorell Arnold.
MARRIED: Thomas Humphry Ward, 1872.
WROTE UNDER: Mrs. Humphry Ward.

W.'s life as a novelist, journalist, and philanthropist carried on a family tradition of intellectual inquiry, service, and leadership. The granddaughter of Thomas Arnold of Rugby and Matthew Arnold's niece, W. was motivated by their spirit of conservative reform. She came to grips with the relativism of modern thought but never surrendered her faith in unchanging moral laws and inflexible moral duties.

W.'s most famous novel, *Robert Elsmere* (1888), was shaped in part by her own experience with Victorian religious crisis. Her father, Thomas Arnold's second son, showed no sign of wavering from his father's Broad Church Christianity when he went out to homestead in New Zealand in 1847 and married the staunchly Protestant Julia Sorell in 1850. W. was five when her father's conversion to Roman Catholicism rocked the family and cost him his job as school inspector in 1856. The family returned to Britain and faced a life of relative privation for the next ten years, despite John Henry Newman's help in getting the younger Thomas Arnold employment in Catholic schools. As was usual with interfaith marriages, the daughters remained Protestant like their mother and the sons were raised as Catholics. When W. was fifteen, her father returned to Anglicanism. His new position as tutor moved the family to Oxford, where W. was able to repair the large gaps left in her girls' school education by concentrated study at the Bodleian Library. She married Thomas Humphry Ward, a fellow of Brasenose College, in 1872. The second of their three children had just been born when Thomas Arnold went back to Roman Catholicism in 1876. Despite her lifelong loyalty to her father, she keenly felt the sufferings of her mother, who this time refused to follow her husband to the Catholic University in Dublin.

Although W.'s publishing career began officially when *The Churchman's Companion* accepted "A Westmoreland Story" in 1870, her bent for more serious work came out in the many articles on literature and history that soon followed in such periodicals as *Macmillan's*, the *Saturday Review*, the *Oxford Spectator*, the *Times*, the *Fortnightly*, and the *Pall Mall Gazette*. In 1877, she began to contribute entries based on her early studies in Spanish history to *The Dictionary of Christian Biography*. She published a children's story, "Milly and Olly," in 1881; *Miss Bretherton*, her first novel, in 1884; and a translation of Frederic Henri Amiel's *Journal Intime* in 1885. Long devoted to the Brontës' novels, she wrote a series of introductions to the Haworth edition of their works between 1899 and 1900.

When W. began work on *Robert Elsmere* in 1885, she had already been thinking for many years about the religious issues it raised. Her own historical studies had convinced her to see the Bible as a fallible cultural record. She was confirmed in a liberal, antidogmatic theology by such Oxford intellectuals as Benjamin Jowett, Mark Pattison, J. R. Green, and T. H. Green. When she heard the Reverend John Wordsworth attack such liberal theology as sinful in 1881, she responded with "Unbelief and Sin," a pamphlet arguing that intellectual honesty, not weak morality, led men to question dogmatic faith. *Robert Elsmere* recounts the "deconversion" of just such an intellectual. An Oxford philosopher modeled on T. H. Green introduces the first doubts about Christian dogma into the mind of its eponymous hero, a young Anglican clergyman; reading *The Origin of Species* and contradictory church histories further erodes his orthodoxy. Skeptical continental scholarship completes the task, and Elsmere, causing much pain to his strictly evangelical wife, leaves the ministry. He continues to serve his fellow man as a social worker and teacher, however, carrying a secularized Christianity into the London slums, where he ultimately dies of tuberculosis.

The tremendous success of *Robert Elsmere*, which by 1889 had sold more than 300,000 copies in England and 200,000 in the United States, suggests how topical were the issues it raised. Its combination of serious intellectual questions, didactic uplift, and human interest was typical of W.'s later fiction. The strains of religious doubt were again her subject in *The History of David Grieve* (1892) and *Elsmere's* sequel, *The Case of Richard Meynell* (1911). The Roman Catholic hero of *Helbeck of Bannisdale* (1898), torn between his faith and the nonbeliever he loves, offers the closest analogies with W.'s own family.

W.'s essential conservatism where both liberalism and feminism were concerned comes out in her social and political novels, in which the most effective form of social conscience is always allied with a respect for wealth and tradition. She found her ideals in women who fulfilled themselves through subordination to duty, like the self-sacrificing heroine of *Eleanor* (1900), and in reform-minded aristocrats like Aldous Raeburn of *Marcella* (1894) and the title character of its sequel, *Sir George Tressady* (1896). Women who transgressed the bounds of traditional wifely duty, no matter what the provocation, were routinely punished in W.'s novels; Lady Rose in *Lady Rose's Daughter* (1903), Kitty Ashe in *The Marriage of William Ashe* (1905), and Daphne in *Marriage à la Mode* (1909) are cases in point. Believing that direct involvement in political life would "blunt the special moral qualities of women," W. steadfastly opposed the vote for women. In 1908 she organized the Women's Anti-Suffrage League, dedicated to "bringing the views of women to bear on the legislature without the aid of the vote." The subversive potential W. feared in feminism is made clear in *Delia Blanchflower* (1915), where the suffragist is a neurasthenic fanatic who burns down a country home to dramatize her cause. Notwithstanding W.'s skill in combining sensation and melodrama with bracing moral lessons, her attempts to adapt works like *Eleanor* and *The Marriage of William Ashe* for the stage were neither financially nor artistically successful.

W. herself was a tireless if traditional worker for social reform. At Oxford she helped found a lecture series for women in the early 1870s and played an instrumental role in founding Somerville Hall, one of the university's first women's colleges. After relocating to London in the 1880s, she became active in planning the Passmore Edwards Settlement; the Settlement House later named after her opened in 1897 to serve the poor of the Bloomsbury community. In later years, she was instrumental in gaining government support for child-care centers and schools for handicapped children. In 1908, she toured Canada and the United States, where she was entertained by President Theodore Roosevelt. Later, during World War I, at Roosevelt's request she undertook a series of works dramatizing the British war effort for American audiences; these were later collected as *England's Effort* (1916), *Towards the Goal* (1917), and *Fields of Victory* (1919). As a tribute to both her patriotism and her journalistic skill, the British War Ministry allowed her to visit the front and other military installations as a war correspondent. In 1920, she was awarded an honorary degree by Edinburgh University and was selected as one of the first women magistrates of England. Her unfinished autobiography, *A Writer's Recollections,* appeared in 1918.

Although updated with twentieth-century concerns, W.'s writing remains quintessentially Victorian in its peculiar blend of moral seriousness and sentimentality. If bounded by Victorian conceptions of a woman's sphere, her life and work were animated by high standards of intellectual and social responsibility that gave both a far-reaching effect.

WORKS: *Milly and Olly, or A Holiday among the Mountains* (1881). *Miss Bretherton* (1884). (trans.) *Journal Intime,* by Frederic Henri Amiel (1885). *Robert Elsmere* (1888). *The History of David Grieve* (1892). *Marcella* (1894). *The Story of Bessie Costrell* (1895). *Sir George Tressady* (1896). *Helbeck of Bannisdale* (1898). *Eleanor* (1900). *Lady Rose's Daughter* (1903). *The Marriage of William Ashe* (1905). *Fenwick's Career* (1906). *The Testing of Diana Mallory* (1908). *Daphne, or Marriage à la Mode* (1909). *Canadian Born* (1910). *The Case of Richard Meynell* (1911). *The Mating of Lydia* (1913). *The Coryston Family* (1913). *Delia Blanchflower* (1915). *Eltham House* (1915). *A Great Success* (1916). *England's Effort* (1916). *Lady Connie* (1916). *Towards the Goal* (1917). *Missing* (1917). *A Writer's Recollections* (1918). *The War and Elizabeth* (1918). *Fields of Victory* (1919). *Cousin Philip* (1919). *Harvest* (1920).

BIBLIOGRAPHY: Colby, V. *The Singular Anomaly* (1970). Coulter, M. *DownR* (1989). Gwynn, S. L. *Mrs. Humphry Ward* (1917). Higdon, D. L. *ELT* (1987). Huws Jones, E. *Mrs. Humphry Ward* (1973). Peterson, W. *Victorian Heretic* (1976). Phelps, W. L. *Essays on Modern Novelists* (1921). Smith, E. M. *Mrs. Humphry Ward* (1980). Sutherland, J. *Mrs. Humphry Ward: Eminent Victorian, Pre-Eminent Edwardian* (1990). Thesing, W. and S. Pulsford. *Mrs. Humphry Ward: A Bibliography* (1987). Trevelyan, J. P. *The Life of Mrs. Humphry Ward* (1923). Walters, J. S. *Mrs. Humphry Ward, Her Work and Influence* (1912).

For articles in reference works, see: *Allibone. DLB. DNB. ELB. Europa. Feminist. IDWB.* Platt, V. *Men and Women of the Day* (1917). *TCA* and *SUP. ToddBWW.*

Other references: Bellringer, A. W. *PSt* (1985, 1986). Collister, P. *ES* (1985). *Living Age* (January 1902). *Nation* (3 April 1920). *New Statesman* (19 August 1947). *NCF* (1951). *North American Review* (April 1903). Otte, G. *ClioI* (1990). *Quarterly Review* (July 1920). Sutton-Ramspeck, B. *VS* (Autumn 1990). *TLS* (15 June 1951).

Rosemary Jann

Mary (Joan Mary) Ward

BORN: 23 January 1585, Mulwith, Yorkshire.
DIED: 30 January 1645, Osbaldswick, Yorkshire.
DAUGHTER OF: Marmaduke Ward and Ursula Wright Ward.

Daughter of a wealthy Yorkshire family of Roman Catholic recusants (i.e., Catholics who refused to attend Church of England services and therefore were guilty of a statutory offense) who were related to the nobility, W. is well known as an educator but less known for her writings: her two-part autobiography with essays on her mystical experiences (completed in c. 1626), and her letters and personal papers describing in detail her ideas and motives in founding schools for girls of all economic classes throughout Europe. Certain aspects of her life explain her writings.

First assisted in Channel crossings by a descendant of Sir Thomas More, and later accompanied by likeminded women of the English gentry and nobility, W. founded her first school in 1609 at St. Omer (then in Spanish-held Flanders). The school was destined for English girls who were voluntary exiles fleeing persecution for their Catholicism in Britain, as a result of renewals of the Oath of Allegiance first promulgated by Henry King VIII as well as the Treason Act. Because of the penal laws in effect, those leaving Britain to live or study in Roman Catholic countries abroad also were subject to heavy fines, imprisonment, and/or execution. Nevertheless, with her first English school in Flanders, W. also founded a free school for local girls. The double foundation, under the patronage of the Infanta Isabella of Spain and the local bishop, became the prototype for the schools W. initiated elsewhere, in Germany, Austria, Czechoslovakia, and Hungary under the patronage of Emperor Maximilian and his brother Ferdinand, and in Rome and Naples with papal permission. W.'s followers Winifred Wigmore and Mary Poyntz wrote in their biography of W. (c. 1650) that in the schools girls of all nationalities were taught reading, writing, languages (including Latin), "public exhortation," sewing and embroidery to earn a living, and theology so that the English girls "may be either Religious in these parts or returning to marry in England, may there maintain what they have learned" (W.'s letter to Isabella, 1612).

Often called "Jesuitesses" because they derived many of their ideas from the English Jesuits, W. evoked the fury of the English diocesan clergy secretly practicing in England, for by 1621 W. had obtained preliminary approval from the Vatican both for her schools and for her attempt to found an unenclosed religious congregation for women for the "conversion of England" and for "works of charity . . . that cannot be undertaken in convents" (W.'s letter to Pope Paul V, 1616). This was extraordinary so soon after the Council of Trent's edict ordering enclosure of women religious. The English diocesan clergy denounced W. and her followers at the Vatican as "Galloping Gurls," "a scandal," with "boldness and rashness" "unbecoming to their sex." Rumors about W.'s educational efforts ensued and her schools were suppressed by Vatican cardinals, but Pope Urban VIII personally vindicated W., permitting her to restore the Munich school and a boarding home in Rome and then to return to England with letters of introduction to Queen Henrietta Maria in order to establish schools there (1639). W. died of natural causes during the English Civil War before accomplishing her goal. Her followers, after establishing schools on the Continent, founded a school in York in 1686 that still exists as the York Bar Convent. W.'s congregation was approved in 1707 as the Institute of the Blessed Virgin Mary, but W. was officially recognized as founder only in 1909.

In her writings, W. affirms "women's dignity" and equality with men in ability, including to "apprehend God" and to do "great matters." "And I hope in God . . . that women in time to come will do much," she wrote. W. describes her spirituality of Divine Love and "labour[ing] without reward," not seeking praise for her honors and success which she attributes to "God's work." Excerpts of W.'s writings appear especially in E.C.E. Chambers and M. E. Orchard. For the forthcoming canonization process of W. at the Vatican (official declaration of sainthood), Immolata Wetter has prepared six volumes of documents and manuscripts (1993; to date not in English).

WORKS: Chambers, E.C.E. *The Life of Mary Ward, 1645*, 2 Vols. (1882; 1885). Orchard, M. E. *Till God Will—Mary Ward Through Her Writings* (1985). *Maria Ward: Missverständnisse und Klärung*, ed. I. Wetter (1993).

BIBLIOGRAPHY: Guilday, P. *The English Catholic Refugees on the Continent, 1558–1798* (1914). Latz, D. L. *"Glow-Worm Light," Writings of 17th Century English Recusant Women*, with excerpts from W. (1989). Littlehales, M. M. *Mary Ward: A Woman for All Seasons* (1974). Littlehales, M. M. *Mary Ward: Pilgrim and Mystic* (forthcoming). (trans. by H. Butterworth) Peters, H. *Mary Ward: A World in Contemplation* (1994). Phillip, M. *Companions of Mary Ward* (1939).

For articles in reference works, see: *DNB*.

Dorothy L. Latz

Mary Josephine Ward

BORN: 4 January 1889, Isle of Wight.
DIED: 28 January 1975, New York City, United States.
DAUGHTER OF: Wilfrid Ward and Josephine Ward.
MARRIED: Francis Joseph Sheed, 1926.
WROTE UNDER: Maisie Ward.

W. was a woman of diverse interests: publisher, biographer, and Roman Catholic activist. One of five siblings, she was raised in a literary family; her father was the biographer of cardinals John Henry Newman and Nicholas Wiseman and editor of the *Dublin Review*, and her mother was a novelist.

During World War I, W. served as a nursing aide in military hospitals. When the war ended she joined the Catholic Evidence Guild, street-corner speakers who lectured on Catholicism, where she met her future husband, Frank Sheed, an Australian. In 1926, they started the publishing house of Sheed and Ward, specializing in Catholic books and with a goal of publishing works of literary as well as religious merit. The enterprise prospered, and in 1933 a branch was opened in New York City. From then on they lectured extensively on both sides of the Atlantic. Two children were born—a daughter, Rosemary, and a son, Wilfrid Sheed, the novelist.

When World War II began, W. went to the United States with her children and worked on her best-known book, *Gilbert Keith Chesterton* (1943); she was asked to write the book about her friend by Chesterton's wife, but, as Graham Greene said, "Mrs. Ward, however, is too fond of her subject and too close to it to reduce her material into a portrait for strangers." Nine years later, *Return to Chesterton* appeared, presenting his family life. W. assembled all the odds and ends of Chestertoniana she could find by visiting his old haunts and cronies, with the result that this book has an intimacy and immediacy that the biography lacked.

W. also believed that the early years of Newman had been neglected. *The Young Mr. Newman* (1948) portrays the childhood and university years of Newman as fully as her father had presented the second half of his life. And *Robert Browning and His World* (1967) was written because W. was incensed at a contemporary biography subjecting Browning to Freudian theories. W. stresses his masculinity and denies the allegation that he was seeking a mother rather than a mate. "I ended my research believing more than ever in the idyllic love story of Browning," she claimed. *The Tragi Comedy of Pen Browning* (1972) is the sad story of the poets' only child, an indulged son forever overshadowed by his famous parents.

Quite different from these nineteenth-century subjects is *Caryll Houselander, That Divine Eccentric* (1962). Houselander—artist, writer, therapist of disturbed children and "mystic"—became known to W. as a writer of spiritual books. Sheed and Ward also published *This War Is the Passion*, Houselander's best-known book, written at the time of the London blitz.

Unfinished Business (1964), W.'s autobiography, recalls the life of a remarkably energetic woman. W., christened Mary Josephine, was called Maisie in childhood and wrote under that name. Her family knew many of the leading literary figures of the time; Alfred Lord Tennyson, Hilaire Belloc, and Chesterton, among others, were friends. A cradle Catholic, W. remained a faithful daughter of the church, which did not prevent her criticizing what she believed to be its defects. Her interest in the worker-priest movement in France resulted in a book, *France Pagan* (1949). Despite her conservative upbringing, W. came to espouse radical social views reinforced by her association with Dorothy Day of the Catholic Worker and Baroness Catherine de Hueck, founder of Friendship House in Harlem in New York City.

A sense of optimism, engendered by her strong religious faith, permeated W.'s life and writing. In *To and Fro on the Earth* (1973), a sequel to her autobiography written in her eighties, W. crisscrossed four continents. She delighted in finding pockets of people performing good works amid the spreading chaos of civilization; she herself, as a young woman, had been engaged in volunteer work for social causes, and in later years she founded subsidized housing for the needy in England and the United States. Writing books was only one of the many activities of this multifaceted woman.

WORKS: *Father Maturin* (1920). *The Wilfrid Wards and the Transition* (1934). *The Oxford Group* (1937). *Insurrection versus Resurrection* (1937). *This Burning Heat* (1941). *Gilbert Keith Chesterton* (1943). *The Young Mr. Newman* (1948). *France Pagan* (1949). *St. Jerome* (1950). *St. Francis of Assisi* (1950). *Return to Chesterton* (1952). *Be Not Solicitous* (1953). *They Saw His Glory* (1956). *The Rosary* (1957). *Saints Who Made History* (1960). *Caryll Houselander, That Divine Eccentric* (1962). *Unfinished Business* (1964). *Robert Browning and His*

World (1967). *To and Fro on the Earth* (1971). *The Tragi-Comedy of Pen Browning* (1972).

BIBLIOGRAPHY: Coulter, M. *DownR* (1989). Higdon, D. L. *ELT* (1987). Sheed, W. *Frank and Maisie: A Memoir with Parents* (1985).

For articles in reference works, see: *CA*.

Other references: *Commonweal* (16 February 1968). Greene, G. *Collected Essays* (1969). *New Yorker* (15 March 1952). *New York Herald-Tribune* (9 March 1952). *TLS* (1 October 1964). *YR* (1968).

Joan Ambrose Cooper

Ward, Mrs. Humphry: See *Ward, Mary Augusta Arnold*

Marina Sarah Warner

BORN: 9 November 1946, London.
DAUGHTER OF: Esmond Pelham Warner and Emilia Terzulli Warner.
MARRIED: William Shawcross, 1971; John Dewe Mathews, 1981.

An interest in women characterizes the diverse writings of W.: great women of mythic stature, from Joan of Arc to the Empress Dowager of China; women as storytellers and the objects of storytelling, from Mother Goose to the Queen of Sheba; women as symbols, from the Virgin Mary to the Little Old Lady of Threadneedle Street; and ordinary women, from the middle class to the marginalized, who inhabit the world of her fiction. W.'s publications include critical and historical works, novels and short stories for adults as well as children, articles in scholarly and popular journals, film scripts, and opera librettos. Her novels, described by reviewers as "bookish," "erudite," "mythopoeic and iconoclastic," have been received to wide critical acclaim; *The Lost Father* (1987) was the winner of the Regional Commonwealth Writers' Prize and the PEN/Macmillan Silver Pen Award and was shortlisted for the Booker Prize. Her works have been translated into numerous languages and she has held a series of prestigious visiting-scholar chairs at universities around the world. W. was made a Fellow of the Royal Society of Literature in 1985 and has served on a number of civic councils including the National Council for One-Parent Families, the Advisory Council of the British Library, and the Arts Council of Great Britain.

W. was born in London of an Italian mother and English bookseller father, and her training, interests, and publications reflect this cosmopolitan and learned childhood. W. was educated at Les Dames de Marie in Brussels (1953–59) and then at St. Mary's convent in Berkshire (1959–63). She was runner-up for the W. H. Smith Children's Poetry Prize in 1964. She studied at Lady Margaret Hall, Oxford, taking her B.A. there in 1967 and her M.A. in modern languages (French and Italian) in 1968.

While W. was at Oxford she was editor of the university magazine, *Isis*. She continued her work in journalism following graduation, working freelance for the *Daily Telegraph Magazine* (1967–70) and later as features editor for *Vogue* (1970–72); she published articles in a number of journals and newspapers during this period. From 1970 to 1975, W. worked in broadcasting as well. In 1971, she was named Young Writer of the Year by *The Daily Telegraph*. In that same year, she married William Shawcross, by whom she had one son.

W.'s first books to be published were works of cultural criticism. *The Dragon Empress: The Life and Times of Tz'u-hsi, Empress Dowager of China 1835–1908* (1972) is a richly embroidered portrait of the woman who began as concubine and outlived both the emperor and her royal son to figure as an international player in the maelstrom of competing French, English, and Chinese interests over political power, religion, and opium. This book was followed by the work for which she is perhaps best known, *Alone of All Her Sex: The Myth and the Cult of the Virgin Mary* (1976). Here W. argues that, despite the significance of Mary as archetypal symbol for women in the history of the Christian West, she serves as a poor model for women because she has been used as a tool against them for the aggrandizing of the church's authority and power and because the myth she embodies is dead. In 1979 W. contributed *The Crack in the Teacup: Britain in the Twentieth Century* to the "Mirror of Britain" histories for young readers. The book is rich in the material detail and anecdotes of everyday life and provides an indictment of the racism inherent in empire and of the class structure that organized the political life of Britain in the twentieth century. That same year, W. edited *Queen Victoria's Sketchbook*, the first edition ever of the queen's private journals with their lively watercolors chronicling her extraordinary life.

During the late 1970s, the first of W.'s novels appeared. *In a Dark Wood* (1977) and *The Skating Party* (1982) were followed by numerous works for children: *The Impossible Day, The Impossible Night, The Impossible Bath, The Impossible Rocket* (1981–82), and *The Wobbly Tooth* (1984). The 1980s also saw publication of *The Lost Father*, a tour-de-force postmodern novel that moves fluently between decades, narrators, and genres as it seeks to fix the truth about the death of W.'s grandfather.

W. also kept up an impressive schedule of scholarly publication during the 1980s, placing dozens of essays and articles in a wide variety of learned journals and collections. In 1981, she published *Joan of Arc: The Image of Female Heroism*. W.'s book examines the history of the image of the heroine in the context of "the intellectual and emotional tradition of thought concerning women." In 1984, W. wrote the script for the film *Joan of Arc. Monuments and Maidens: The Allegory of Female Form* (1985) continued W.'s exploration of woman as sign and symbol. There she examines the disjunction between the ideal female figures, who represent entities as diverse as justice, naval ships, and the Bank of England, and "the actual order, of judges, statesmen, soldiers, philosophers, inventors" inhabited almost solely by men. The book was winner of the Fawcett Prize. In 1987–88, she was Getty Scholar at the Getty Center for the History of Art and the Humanities, in Los Angeles, California.

This era also inaugurated her work with fairy tales. In 1986, W. wrote two more film scripts, for *Cinderella* and

Imaginary Women, and in 1992 she wrote the libretto for a children's opera, *The Queen of Sheba's Legs.* (The Queen of Sheba has a complex history connecting her to Mother Goose.) Work begun during her tenure as "Tinbergen Professor" at Erasmus University in Rotterdam in 1991 culminated with the publication of *From the Beast to the Blonde: On Fairy Tales and Their Tellers* (1994). In that study, she explores the many roles of women in fairy tales, from archetypal Mother Goose storyteller to enchantress to stepmother to lover. In 1994, she edited *Wonder Tales: Six Tales of Enchantment.*

The 1990s have seen publication of more fiction. *Indigo, or Mapping the Waters* (1992) is an imaginative novel based on William Shakespeare's *Tempest* that blurs the boundaries of time while it rewrites the myths of western culture and literature. It was followed by *Mermaids in the Basement* (1993), a collection of short stories that shows W.'s confidence in many voices as she explores the pressures and the possibilities of women's lives in a wide range of situations.

W. continues her impressive pace of research and publication, which includes numerous reviews of books and exhibitions in many international journals. *Cinema and the Realms of Enchantment* (1993) includes three essays based on seminars offered by the British Film Institute, where W. was a Visiting Fellow. She also continues to publish widely on contemporary art and artists, including *Richard Wentworth* (1993) and *David Nash* (1996). W. was awarded an honorary D. Litt from the University of Exeter in 1995. She recently collaborated with composer John Woolrich on the opera *In the House of Crossed Desires* (1996), based on Apuleius's *The Golden Ass.* W.'s *Donkey Business, Donkey Work: Magic and Metamorphosis in Contemporary Opera* (1996) is a meditation on that experience. She has taken a research fellowship at Trinity College, Cambridge, for 1998 to complete a new novel. The year should also see the publication of a new cultural study, *No Go the Bogeyman: On Scaring, Lulling and Making Mock.*

WORKS: *The Dragon Empress: The Life and Times of Tz'u-hsi, Empress Dowager of China, 1835–1908* (1972). *Alone of All Her Sex: The Myth and the Cult of the Virgin Mary* (1976). *In a Dark Wood* (1977). *The Crack in the Teacup: Britain in the Twentieth Century* (1979). *Joan of Arc: The Image of Female Heroism* (1981). *The Impossible Day* (1981). *The Impossible Night* (1981). *The Skating Party* (1982). *The Impossible Bath* (1982). *The Impossible Rocket* (1982). *The Wobbly Tooth* (1984). *Joan of Arc* (film script; 1984). *Monuments and Maidens: The Allegory of Female Form* (1985). *Cinderella* (film script; 1986). *Imaginary Women* (film script; 1986). *The Lost Father* (1988). *Into the Dangerous World: Some Reflections on Childhood and its Costs* (1989). *The Absent Mother, or, Women against Women in the Old Wives' Tale* (1991). *"Tell Me More"* (film script; 1991). *The Queen of Sheba's Legs* (1992). *Indigo, or Mapping the Water* (1992). *Mermaids in the Basement* (1993). *Richard Wentworth* (1993). *Towards a Democratic Culture* (1993). *Cinema and the Realms of Enchantment: Lectures, Seminars and Essays by Marina Warner and Others,* ed. D. Petrie (1994). *L'Atalante* (1994). *Managing Monsters: Six Myths of Our Time* (1994; in the U.S. as *Six Myths of Our Time,* 1995). *From the Beast to the Blonde: On Fairy Tales and Their Tellers* (1994). *Lost Souls, Stolen Shadows* (1995). *The Book of Signs and Symbols* (1996). *David Nash* (1996). *Donkey Business, Donkey Work: Magic and Metamorphosis in Contemporary Opera* (1996). (with J. Woolrich) *In the House of Crossed Desires* (opera libretto) (1996). *The Trial of Joan of Arc* (1996). *The Inner Eye: Art Beyond the Visible* (1997).

BIBLIOGRAPHY:

For articles in reference works, see: *Feminist. CN. Who's Who.*

Kari Boyd McBride

Sylvia Townsend Warner

BORN: 6 December 1893, Harrow, Middlesex.
DIED: 1 May 1978, Maiden Newton, Dorset.
DAUGHTER OF: George Townsend Warner and Eleanor Mary Warner.

W. was the daughter of a schoolmaster at Harrow but was educated privately, first by her mother and then by a governess and tutors. Given free run of her father's library, she read widely on her own and can thus be considered largely self-educated. She originally aspired to a career in music and at one point intended to study composition with Arnold Schönberg, but the intervention of World War I turned her to musicology. As a young woman, she was the only female editor of the monumental *Tudor Church Music* (10 vols., 1925–30); however, the encouragement of David Garnett and T. F. Powys helped her decide in favor of literature. In a career spanning more than fifty years, she produced poems, novels, short stories, biographies, and translations. For these accomplishments she was elected a fellow of the Royal Society of Literature and was an honorary member of the American Academy of Arts and Letters.

From an early age, W. showed an interest in the supernatural, which is evident in works throughout her career. Her first novel, *Lolly Willowes* (1926), the first book selected by the Book-of-the-Month Club, chronicles the life of a woman who rejects traditional roles and turns to witchcraft. Stories written over many years deal in various ways with supernatural themes, while her novel *The Corner That Held Them* (1948) shows an intimate knowledge of the occult and herbal medicinal lore in its portrayal of life in a fourteenth-century convent. *The Kingdoms of Elfin* (1977) is a collection of *New Yorker* stories, all of which treat the world of elves, fairies, werewolves, and other such creatures as ordinary inhabitants of the planet that mortals think of as exclusively their own. W. never exploits the supernatural for its own sake or for cheap effects. Her interest is primarily in extending the limits of vision or in using the extraordinary as a means of exploring human psychology.

In her novels, W. is less interested in social and political themes than in the interior struggles of her characters. Lolly Willowes chooses witchcraft after a lifetime of searching for a fulfilling alternative to the sterile and boring life that Victorian society permits her; even so, witchcraft is more a symbol of individual freedom than an indictment of social policies. *Mr. Fortune's Maggot* (1927) takes its main character, an innocent missionary, to the tropical island of Fuana where he is sorely tempted by the delights of the pagans he is sent to convert. Far more complex, and often considered W.'s masterpiece, is *The Corner That Held Them.* Its roguish and picaresque central character, Ralph Kello, enters Oby convent during the days of Black Death, claiming to be a priest, and spends the rest of his life wrestling with the moral consequences and complications of this sin. Others at Oby are similarly torn between worldly temptations and the demands of the church. Complex, detailed, learned, and spirited, this novel has been called a "sustained delight." Similar in theme though Victorian in setting is *The Flint Anchor* (1954), in which John Barnard is moved by experiences as a student to strive for moral perfection only to find that the everyday concerns of business and family life frustrate his lofty ideals. Moreover, idolatry toward his daughter Mary leads to neglect of other family members, each of whom is warped by Barnard's tyranny and inability to love. *Summer Will Show* (1936) resembles *The Flint Anchor* in period, but the struggles of its heroine are for identity and purpose in a male-dominated culture that permits little scope or assertiveness for its women.

W. is best known and most highly regarded for her short stories, which range broadly over the British cultural scene but focus mainly on the middle classes. The majority of her characters are women. Often written in the "plotless" vein pioneered by Anton Chekhov, her stories range from brief impressionistic sketches to novella-length studies and, like the novels, focus on character and situation, frequently exploring with wit and irony the follies and foibles of ordinary people. A master of technique and storycraft, W. never settled into a pattern or formula. "The Phoenix" can be construed as a sophisticated joke or as an allegory; "A Garland of Straw" is a disturbing excursion into madness and thwarted love; "The Museum of Cheats" requires only forty pages to satirize the greed and vanity of two and a half centuries; "Winter in the Air" is a realistic portrayal of a woman whose husband has rejected her for another; "The One and the Other" intertwines the "material world with the immaterial" in a tale at once fantastic and realistic.

In all her fiction, W. is an acute observer of manners, morals, the minutiae of daily existence, and the secret ways of the human heart. Her concern with appearance and reality is humane and liberal; she seldom condemns, preferring to look instead for the secret beneath the surface that enlivens and even ennobles her humblest characters.

W. belongs to the broad mainstream of British fiction and has often been compared to Jane Austen and Katherine Mansfield. Her style exhibits clarity, restraint, precision, and simplicity in both poetry and prose. Wit, grace, humor, subtlety, and charm are frequently noted characteristics, but her special quality resides in a precise yet original use of language. She has a genius for metaphor, drawing on art, music, and nature as the sources of her imagery. Although sometimes criticized for writing with more attention to style than substance, W. is never boring or trite. Readers are required to look carefully, for her effects are often subtle and demand an alert and sensitive audience. These qualities will probably deny her a large following, but critical appreciation of her work is growing and a place for her in twentieth-century letters is assured.

WORKS: *The Espalier* (1925). *Lolly Willowes* (1926). *Mr. Fortune's Maggot* (1927). *Time Importuned* (1928). *The Tree Heart* (1929). *Some World Far from Ours* and *Stay, Corydon, Thou Swain* (1929). *Elinor Barley* (1930). *A Moral Ending and Other Stories* (1931). *Opus 7: A Poem* (1931). *Rainbow* (1932). *The Salutation* (1932). (with Valentine Ackland) *Whether a Dove or a Seagull* (1933). *More Joy in Heaven and Other Stories* (1935). *Summer Will Show* (1936). (with Graham Greene and James Laver) *Twenty-four Stories* (1939). *Cat's Cradle Book* (1940). *A Garland of Straw: Twenty Eight Stories* (1943). *Portrait of a Tortoise: Extracted from the Journals of Gilbert White* (1946). *The Museum of Cheats: Stories* (1947). *The Corner That Held Them* (1948). *Somerset* (1949). *Jane Austen: 1775–1817* (1951; rev. ed. 1957). *The Flint Anchor* (1954). *Winter in the Air and Other Stories* (1955). *Boxwood* (1958; rev. ed. 1960). *A Spirit Rises: Short Stories* (1962). *Sketches from Nature* (1963). *Swans on the Autumn River: Stories* (1966). *A Stranger with a Bag and Other Stories* (1966). *T. H. White: A Biography* (1967). *King Dufus and Other Poems* (1968). *The Innocent and the Guilty* (1971). *The Kingdoms of Elfin* (1977). *Scenes from Childhood and Other Stories* (1982). *Letters,* ed. William Maxwell (1983). *Collected Poems,* ed. C. Harman (1983). *One Thing Leading to Another: And Other Stories,* ed. S. Pinney (1984). *Selected Poems,* ed. S. Pinney (1984). *Selected Stories* (1988). *Diaries,* ed. C. Harman (1994). *Sylvia and David: The Townsend Warner/Garnett Letters,* ed. R. Garnett (1994).

BIBLIOGRAPHY: Ackland, V. *For Sylvia: An Honest Account* (1985). Daiches, D. *The Present Age in British Literature* (1958). Harmon, C. *Sylvia Townsend Warner: A Biography* (1989). Mulford, W. *This Narrow Place: Sylvia Townsend Warner and Valentine Ackland: Life, Letters, and Politics 1930–1951* (1988).

For articles in reference works, see: *Bloomsbury. CA. DLB. NCBEL. Oxford.*

Other references: Allen, W. *The Short Story in English* (1981). *Women's Writing in Exile,* ed. M. L. Broe and A. Ingram (1989). *Rewriting the Good Fight: Critical Essays on the Literature of the Spanish Civil War,* ed. F. S. Brown, et al. (1989). *Crazyhorse* (Fall 1986). *Old Maids to Radical Spinsters: Unmarried Women in the Twentieth-Century Novel,* ed. L. L. Doan (1991). *The English Short Story 1880–1945: A Critical History,* ed. J. M. Flora (1985). *London Magazine* (November 1979). *New Republic* (5 March 1966). *New Yorker* (27 August 1979). *NYT* (19 May 1978). *PNR* (1981). *The Gender of Modernism,* ed. B. K. Scott (1990). *Women Writers and the City,* ed. M. Squier (1984). *SSF* (1973). *TLS* (23 May 1980). Updike, J. *Hugging the Shore* (1983).

Dean R. Baldwin

Rosamund Marriott Watson

BORN: 6 October 1860, Hackney, London.
DIED: 29 December 1911, Shere, Surrey.
DAUGHTER OF: Benjamin William Ball and Sylvia Good Ball.
MARRIED: George Francis Armytage, 1879; Arthur Graham Tomson, 1887.
WROTE UNDER: Mrs. G. Armytage; R. Armytage; Graham R. Tomson; Rosamund Marriott Watson.

W. was a female aesthete active at the *fin de siècle;* her work endorsed the unity of the arts, actively shaped sensory or lived experience into the materials of art, and publicly appropriated cultural authority to pronounce on matters of taste, beauty, or social principles. A talented poet, editor, and prose stylist who authored literary essays on *belles lettres,* art, fashion, interior decoration, and gardening, she was also a beautiful woman who aestheticized her own body through artful dress.

Born Rosamund Ball, she was thwarted by parental opposition from becoming a painter and married a wealthy young colonial, George F. Armytage, when she was nineteen; she later gave birth to two daughters. As Mrs. G. Armytage, she published an essay on artistic principles of dress in *Fortnightly Review,* an anonymous volume of poetry (*Tares,* 1884), and poems and reviews signed "R. Armytage" in other magazines. Armytage divorced her when she eloped with Arthur Tomson, a member of the New English Art Club; she married Tomson in 1887, a month before their son was born. Andrew Lang "discovered" "Graham R. Tomson" when she submitted poems to a magazine and promoted her in *Longman's Magazine.* W. was soon active in literary and artistic circles; her connections included Alice Meynell, Amy Levy, Elizabeth Pennell, Lang, Oscar Wilde, and Thomas Hardy, whose character Mrs. Pine-Avon in *The Well-Beloved* she may have inspired; her photograph is the subject of Hardy's late poem "An Old Likeness (Recalling R. T.)." From 1887 to 1895, she published two volumes of poetry, and she edited anthologies and a woman's magazine, *Sylvia's Journal* (1893–94). She contributed a literary fashion column to W. E. Henley's *Scots Observer;* columns on interior decoration to the "Wares of Autolycus" feature written entirely by women in the *Pall Mall Gazette;* and poems, reviews, and occasional short stories to prominent journals. She was active in the Literary Ladies, founded in 1889, and served as its president in 1892.

In 1894, her second marriage collapsed because of her affair with Australian-born novelist H. B. Marriott Watson, one of Henley's "regatta." She eloped a second time in 1895, pregnant once more (bearing a son that year), and began publishing under the signature "Rosamund Marriott Watson." Tomson divorced her in 1896, and though she stayed with Marriott Watson until her death they never married. From 1895 to 1911, she published two more volumes of poems with John Lane, a leading publisher of "aesthetic" and decadent titles, a book on interior design, a volume of prose meditations and poems on her garden, an unsuccessful children's novel, and poems and reviews in such periodicals as the *Yellow Book* and *Athenaeum.* In 1902, she suffered a nervous breakdown from which neither her career nor her poetry ever entirely recovered. She died at the age of fifty-one from uterine cancer.

From the first her verses displayed deft auditory effects and rhythm, command of rhyme and verse forms, and a fascination with the evanescent moments of life—traits common to aesthetes and decadents. As well, her poems inscribe female experiences that anticipate Modernist work: agnosticism, troubled marriages, disillusionment, even divorce. Most frequently her explorations of sexuality and marriage are staged in mythological or supernatural material, another anticipation of twentieth-century women poets. "Nirvana" in *Tares* (1884), her first volume, repudiates Christian notions of an afterlife. "Ballad of the Bird-Bride" (1889) and "Ballad of the Werewolf" (in which the werewolf is a farmer's wife [1895]) represent strife within marriage, while "Vespertilia" (1895) is a revenant poem fruitfully read in the context of divorce and remarriage. Lyrics such as "An Enchanted Princess" and "Resurgam" (both 1891) reflect the influence of Christina Rossetti, while her ballads and occasional poems of political protest (e.g., "Hymn to Labour," 1889) are indebted to Algernon Swinburne and the Pre-Raphaelites. Her fascination with the ballade and triolet in her 1889 volume indicates the vogue of verse forms in the 1880s and 1890s as well as her friendship with Austin Dobson; impressionist urbanscapes like "In the Rain" (1891) sound a distinctly modern note. Her most frequent themes are the brevity of youth and the fragility of human connections.

Her prose is notable for its wit and poetic plangency, her poetry for its technical mastery and ability to modulate from wistful lyric to scenes of violence and devastation. It is such unpredictability that gives her work enduring interest.

WORKS: *Tares* (1884). *The Bird-Bride, and Other Poems* (1889). *A Summer Night and Other Poems* (1891). *The Patch-Work Quilt* (1891). *Vespertilia, and Other Poems* (1895). *The Art of the House* (1897). *An Island Rose* (1900). *After Sunset* (1904). *The Heart of a Garden* (1906). *The Poems of Rosamund Marriott Watson* (1912).

BIBLIOGRAPHY: Archer, W. *Poets of the Younger Generation* (1902). Hughes, L. *VP* (1994). Hughes, L. *TSWL* (1995). *Victorian Women Poets: An Anthology,* ed. A. Leighton and M. Reynolds (1995). Millgate, M. *N&Q* (1973). Mix, K. *A Study in Yellow* (1960). Pennell, E. *Nights* (1916).

For articles in reference works, see: *1890s. NCBEL.*

Other references: *JENS* (1992). *VPR* (1996).

Linda K. Hughes

Anna [Anne] Weamys [Weames]

FLOURISHED: 1650s.
WROTE UNDER: Mrs. A. W.

By tradition, W. is the author of *A Continuation of Sir Philip Sydney's [sic] "Arcadia"* (1651), identified on the title page only as "Mrs. A. W." Almost nothing is known about the identity of "A. W.," but evidence to support the ascription of the work to W. can be found in a letter by James Howell, "To Dr. Weames" (*Epistolae Ho-elianae* [IV.xx]). Howell thanks the father for sending him a copy of his daughter's "continuance of Sir Philip Sidney's *Arcadia,*" and he offers him "a few lines" to be used as one of the volume's commendatory poems. Howell does not, however, give the first name of Dr. Weames's daughter. Dr. Weames may have been a doctor of divinity, probably a clergyman in the Church of England (possibly Dr. Ludowick Weames, who was among those Anglican clergymen whose livings were sequestered and given to Puritan ministers in the 1640s). His academic title suggests that W. was born into an educated family, but not an aristocratic or noble one. What else is known about W. is discovered in the introductory material to her volume, where she is described as being young, precocious, unmarried, and a gentlewoman. The background of most of the people involved with the production of her volume is royalist, and indeed authors of romances during the Interregnum were generally royalist in their sympathies.

Sidney's *Arcadia* was one of the most popular works of the seventeenth century. The version that W. knew was, in all likelihood, the *Arcadia* Sidney's sister had published in 1593; this version attempted to make a coherent whole out of Sidney's revised narrative (the "New Arcadia," left a fragment upon his death and first published in 1590) by appending to it the last books of his earlier draft (the "Old Arcadia," not published in its entirety until it was rediscovered early in the twentieth century). Even this combined text, however, left certain narratives fragmented or undeveloped: Plangus's love of Erona; Helen's love of Amphialus; Claius's and Strephon's love of Urania; the tale of Mopsa; and the love of Philisides (Sidney's pseudonym). W.'s Sidney is clearly the romantic Sidney; accordingly, she chooses to have her continuation climax with five marriages: Erona's, Helen's, and Urania's, in addition to Pamela's and Philoclea's (Sidney's two central heroines). Moreover, Mopsa's comic tale also focuses on romantic love, and Philisides dies of a broken heart. At the same time, the character who is most W.'s own invention, the shepherdess Urania, is very much a woman who prizes the independence chastity gives her and who is in constant flight from the rapacity of male desire. Moreover, one must always remember that the choice of a mate was one of the few choices available to many early modern women, and it should not be surprising that an early modern female author should make it her focus, even more than had Sidney.

W.'s *Arcadia* is a work easily underestimated as a mere "continuation" and thus a reflection of the docile subservience of a female author to a male author. But just as the work's central focus on marriage is more complicated than it might seem, so is the issue of its being a continuation. W.'s decision to continue Sidney can be seen as an act of daring: She was, in effect, stepping arcadian with a male author who was probably, for W.'s era, the most famous and widely read of the Elizabethan authors. W.'s relation to Sidney contrasts with that of W.'s female precursor (whom she apparently did not know), Mary Sidney Wroth, Sidney's niece and the author of the first English prose romance by a woman. Wroth chooses a different tack in her relation to Sidney: She alludes to her uncle in the title of her work (*The Countess of Mountgomery's "Urania"*), but her narratives do not continue his. W.'s relation to her male precursor by way of continuation could not be more different from Wroth's, but it does not make her less her own writer; her decision to create by way of a continuation entails, by its very nature, her assuming a direct relationship with this powerful male precursor, and in so doing she takes on to herself the power of completing his stories.

WORKS: *A Continuation of Sir Philip Sydney's [sic] "Arcadia": Wherein is handled the Loves of Amphialus and Helena Queen of Corinth, Prince Plangus and Erona. With the Historie of the Loves of Old Claius and Young Strephon to Urania* (1651).

BIBLIOGRAPHY: *A Continuation of Sir Philip Sidney's "Arcadia"*, ed. P. C. Cullen (1994). Hobby, E. *Virtue of Necessity: English Women's Writing, 1649–88* (1989). MacCarthy, B. G. *Women Writers: Their Contribution to the English Novel, 1621–1744* (1944). Salzman, P. *English Prose Fiction, 1558–1700* (1985). Spender, D. *Mothers of the Novel* (1986).

For articles in reference works, see *Bloomsbury. Feminist.*

Patrick Cullen

Beatrice Potter Webb

BORN: 22 January 1858, Standish House, Gloucestershire.
DIED: 30 April 1943, Passfield Corner, Hampshire.
DAUGHTER OF: Richard Potter and Laurencina Heyworth Potter.
MARRIED: Sidney James Webb, 1892.

W., reformer, researcher, and Fabian Socialist, was the eighth of nine daughters born to Richard Potter, a wealthy and cultivated merchant. Although frequent childhood illnesses limited her formal education, her father encouraged all his daughters to read widely and independently. She had frequent contact with such free-thinking family friends as T. H. Huxley, John Tyndall, and James Martineau, and she developed a close relationship with Herbert Spencer.

Intensely introspective, W. grew up haunted by her lack of a meaningful faith and a useful purpose in life. The socialism that finally provided her with alternatives to both religion and profession opposed Spencer's laissez-faire philosophies, but his scientific investigation of social institutions exercised a lasting influence upon her. Her early involvement with the Charity Organisation Society and the Octavia Hill housing projects in London left her dissatisfied because such philanthropic efforts did nothing to reach the roots of poverty. She welcomed the opportunity to investigate working-class labor for Charles Booth's *Inquiry into the Life and Labour of the People of London,* and her essay on "Dock Life in the East End of London" first appeared in *The Nineteenth Century* in 1887. She disguised herself as a seamstress to gather data on the East

End tailoring trade later that same year. The articles based on her experiences resulted in her being called to testify before a House of Lords Commission on the Sweating System in 1888. There she made clear her growing conviction that such exploitation was endemic in capitalism itself.

In an effort to develop a more systematic criticism of capitalism, she turned her attention in 1889 to co-operative societies and trade unionism. Research for *The Co-operative Movement in Great Britain* (1891) first introduced her to Sidney Webb, the Fabian Socialist she married, over the objections of friends and family, in 1892. For the next fifty years they formed an intellectual, political, and emotional partnership devoted to furthering Fabian policies of gradual reform, collectivism, and administration by an intellectual elite. Their home at 41 Grosvenor Road in London became the salon of Fabian thinkers and the workshop for the methodical and meticulously researched studies of social phenomena that were their trademark. Their first joint effort was *The History of Trade Unionism* (1894), followed by *Industrial Democracy* in 1897. In 1895, they used a £10,000 bequest to the Fabian Society to found an institution for the study of political economy that later became the London School of Economics.

In 1905, W. was appointed to a Royal Commission on the Poor Law, which she induced to sponsor many investigations into the impact of government policies on the poor. Although she was unsuccessful in moving the commission toward changes that might prevent rather than cure poverty, as outlined in her Minority Report of 1909, she had the satisfaction in later years of seeing many of her recommendations adopted. The Webbs' hopes of organizing an Independent Socialist Party in the years before World War I were disappointed by infighting among those who disagreed with their gradualist and collectivist policies and resented their domineering personalities. A project of more lasting effect was their founding of *The New Statesman* in 1913, dedicated to the furthering of Fabian Socialism and the scientific study of social problems.

During and after the war, W. served on the McLean Committee on the reform of local government, the Reconstruction Committee, and the War Cabinet Committee on Women in Industry. Her defense of equality in *The Wages of Men and Women—Should They Be Equal?* (1919) suggests a sensitivity to sexual discrimination missing in her early attitudes toward female suffrage and protective factory legislation. She was highly successful with the Seaham Harbour constituency that her husband represented in Parliament from 1919 to 1928, promoting a regular series of educational activities for its members and writing a monthly "News Letter to the Women of Seaham." The useful activities of the Half-Circle Club, which she organized in London to bring together the wives of other Labour Party M.P.s, were somewhat undercut by members' resentment about W.'s often unsubtle attempts to make them more socially presentable. During the 1920s she and Sidney published *English Prisons* (1922), *Statutory Authorities* (1922), revised studies of trade unionism and the cooperative movement, and *English Poor Law History* (2 vols., 1927–29). *The Decay of Capitalist Civilisation* (1923) presented their strongest indictment of the economic and moral bankruptcy of the prevailing system, and *A Constitution for the Socialist Commonwealth of Great Britain* (1920) their impracticably utopian alternatives. In 1929, she gave a series of talks for the BBC on their research techniques, which appeared in 1932 as *Methods of Social Study*. Between 1924 and 1926, W. composed *My Apprenticeship*, her autobiography up to her marriage. Like the diaries it is based upon, this work gives compelling testimony to her own literary gifts. Its projected two-volume sequel, *Our Partnership*, was begun in the late 1920s; the only completed volume (1892–1911) appeared after her death in 1948.

In 1929, the Webbs moved from London to Passfield Corner in Hampshire. Sidney chose the title "Baron Passfield" when granted a peerage in 1929, although W. herself disliked having to share the title with him. Despite their earlier skepticism about Soviet Russia and their continued awareness of its many repressive policies, a visit in 1932 made them "fall in love" with this society, which seemed to embody so many of their most cherished ideals: production for use rather than for profit, centralized planning and collective ownership, party support for "the vocation of leadership," an intense spiritual commitment to political ideals. They recorded their views in *Soviet Communism: A New Civilisation?* (1935) and remained staunch defenders of the Soviet Union to the ends of their lives. W. resigned from the executive committee of the Fabian Society in 1933 and published her farewell address to it in the *Fabian News* for 1941. Before her death from kidney disease in 1943, she had received honorary degrees from the universities of Manchester, Edinburgh, and Munich, and she had become the first woman ever elected to the British Academy. After her husband's death in 1947, their ashes were moved to Westminster Abbey.

W. found her vocation in social science and public service. What struck some observers as arrogance resulted from her confidence in her own vision of the social good and her urgency about making it a reality. She dedicated her life to defining and promoting a society in which economic justice would foster moral and social progress.

WORKS: (most written with S. Webb) *The Co-operative Movement in Great Britain* (1891). *The History of Trade Unionism* (1894). *Industrial Democracy* (1897). *The Webbs' Australian Diary* (1898). *The Problems of Modern Industry* (1902). *The History of Liquor Licensing in England* (1903). *London Education* (1904). *The Parish and the County* (1906). *The Manor and the Borough* (1908). *Minority Report to the Royal Commission on the Poor Law* (1909). *The State and the Doctor* (1910). *English Poor Law Policy* (1910). *The Prevention of Destitution* (1911). *Grants in Aid* (1911). *The Story of the King's Highway* (1913). *An Appeal to Women* (1917). *The Wages of Men and Women—Should They Be Equal?* (1919). *A Constitution for the Socialist Commonwealth of Great Britain* (1920). *The Consumer's Co-operative Movement* (1921). *English Prisons Under Local Government* (1922). *Statutory Authorities for Special Purposes* (1922). *The Decay of Capitalist Civilisation* (1923). *My Apprenticeship* (1926). *English Poor Law History: The Old Poor Law* (1927). *English Poor Law History: The Last Hundred Years* (1929). *Methods of Social Study* (1932). *Soviet Communism, A New Civilisation?* (1935). *Soviet Communism: Dictatorship or Democracy?* (1936).

The Truth about Soviet Russia (1942). *The Constitution of the USSR* (1942). *Our Partnership* (1948). *Diaries, 1912–24*, ed. D. A. Shannon (1952). *Diaries, 1924–32*, ed. M. I. Cole (1956). *American Diary, 1898* (1963). *The Diaries of Beatrice Webb*, ed. N. MacKenzie and J. MacKenzie, Vol. I, 1873–92 (1982); Vol.II, 1892–1905 (1983); Vol. III, 1905–24 (1984); Vol. IV, 1924–43 (1985).

BIBLIOGRAPHY: Caine, B. *Destined to Be Wives: The Sisters of Beatrice Webb* (1986). Cole, M. *Beatrice Webb* (1945). *The Webbs and Their Work*, ed. M. Cole (1949). Cole, M. *The Story of Fabian Socialism* (1961). Hamilton, M. A. *Sidney and Beatrice Webb* (1933). Hynes, S. *The Edwardian Turn of Mind* (1968). Hynes, S. *Edwardian Occasions* (1972). Letwin, S. *The Pursuit of Certainty* (1965). MacKenzie, J. A. *Victorian Courtship: The Story of Beatrice Potter and Sidney Webb* (1979). *The Letters of Sidney and Beatrice Webb*, ed. N. MacKenzie (1978). Muggeridge, K. and R. Adam *Beatrice Webb: A Life, 1858–1943* (1967). Nord, D. *The Apprenticeship of Beatrice Webb* (1985). Radice, L. *Beatrice and Sidney Webb* (1984). Seymour-Jones, C. *Beatrice Webb: A Life* (1992). Spacks, P. *The Female Imagination* (1972).

For articles in reference works, see: *Bloomsbury. CA. DNB. ELB. Europa. Feminist. IDWB. Longman. TCA* and *SUP. ToddBWW. VB.*

Other references: Ardis, A. L. *WS* (1990). Caine, B. *VS* (1983). Crick, B. *Essays on Politics and Literature* (1989). *LonT* (1 May 1943). *Proceedings of the British Academy* (1943). *Scrutiny* (1949). *TLS* (20 October 1940).

Rosemary Jann

(Gladys) Mary Webb

BORN: 25 March 1881, Leighton, Shropshire.
DIED: 8 October 1927, St. Leonards-on-Sea, Sussex.
DAUGHTER OF: George Edward Meredith and Sarah Alice Scott Meredith.
MARRIED: Henry Bertram Law Webb, 1912.

A transitional novelist between Victorianism and Modernism, W. lived most of her life in her native county of Shropshire, whose nature she apotheosized in her writings. The eldest of six children born to a Welsh schoolmaster and a distant relative of Sir Walter Scott, W. was educated at home by her governess and lifelong friend, Miss E. M. Lory. W. also attended a finishing school in Southport, Lancashire, for three years. Upon returning from school, she was expected to supervise the education of her younger siblings. At the age of twenty, W. suffered a collapse from Graves' disease, which left her with a disfiguring goiter. During her long convalescence, she devoted herself to writing essays and poems.

From the beginning, nature was W.'s central subject. As her brother recalled, "Her God was Nature." W.'s first completed work was a collection of nature essays, written between the time of her father's illness and death in 1909 and her marriage in 1912 to Henry Webb, a Shropshire schoolmaster. First published in 1917 as *The Spring of Joy*, these essays, though rather old-fashioned in tone, contain the core of W.'s pantheistic nature mysticism and reveal her precise, minute observation of natural phenomena. They express her faith that health and divine vitality are to be found in "the spiritual ties between man and nature."

At the time of her marriage, W. received a substantial allowance from her mother. With this W. and her husband were able to establish a modest home near Shrewsbury. For several years they worked as market gardeners, an activity that provided more material for W.'s future novels than income. In the spring of 1915, in three weeks' time, W. wrote her first novel, *The Golden Arrow* (1916). Spasmodic and rapid writing was typical of her manner of composition, and she seldom revised her work.

All six of W.'s novels are love stories; all but one end happily for the lovers. Yet it is nature that seems to be the true hero and heroine of her novels. W.'s nature mysticism acts as a vital, transforming force in her characters' lives. Deborah in *The Golden Arrow* experiences this force in her "apocalypse of love" as a presence "behind light and shadow, under pain and joy . . . —too intangible for materialization into words, too mighty to be expressed by any name of man's." Prue Sarn in *Precious Bane* (1924) experiences the mystical union as "a most powerful sweetness that had never come to me afore. It was not religious, like the goodness of a text heard at a preaching. It was beyond that." W. may be described as a "transcendental realist," portraying human characters and the natural world with the vision of a poet and the eye of a naturalist.

W.'s most pantheistic work is her memorable tragic novel, *Gone to Earth* (1917), which also marks an impressive technical advance over her earlier writing. Rebecca West, in her review of this work, declared it the novel of the year and pronounced its author "a genius." Here the landscape and its myriad lives are active presences, taking sides in the drama surrounding Hazel Woodus, a wild and graceful child of nature who "can never adjust herself to the strait orbit of human life." Like Catherine in Emily Brontë's *Wuthering Heights*, Hazel "did not want heaven; she wanted earth and the green ways of earth." The fate of the girl who wants only to "be her own" is determined by the conflict between her two lovers, the cruel sensualist, Reddin, and the tormented idealist, Marston. Hazel, more truly spiritual and attuned to the spirit of nature than the conventionally religious world that condemns her, is literally hounded to death by hunters as she chooses to die with her pet fox rather than sacrifice it to the "death pack." Written in the dark days of World War I, the novel echoes "the keening—wild and universal—of life for the perishing matter that it inhabits."

In 1917, W. and her husband moved into "Spring Cottage," a small bungalow they had built according to W.'s own design. Her next novel, *The House in Dormer Forest* (1920), takes for its theme the destructive influence of lifeless tradition on the inheritors of an entailed estate. W. often pits her visionary characters against those whose lives and souls have been stifled by rigid codes of behavior.

The success of *Gone to Earth* had paved the way for greater recognition of W.'s gifts, and she began to receive advance royalties for her novels. In 1921, W. and her husband moved to London. Though ultimately disappointed in the literary life there, W. met writers and editors, wrote reviews for *Bookman* and the *Spectator*, and had several short stories published in the *English Review*. She made the acquaintance of Walter de la Mare, who published three of her poems in his anthology *Come Hither*. In London, W. wrote *Seven for a Secret* (1922), for which Thomas Hardy's novels served as model. She asked and received permission from Hardy to dedicate the book to him.

Precious Bane, her last completed work, was the novel W. and many of her critics considered her best work. Here nature mysticism is offset by dominant Christian symbolism. Set in England at the end of the Napoleonic wars, *Precious Bane* is a first-person retrospective narrative of the life of a "hare-shotten" young woman. Prue Sarn's harelip is viewed as a sign of witchcraft, the "devil's mark," by the highly superstitious villagers. At the end of the novel, an angry mob nearly drowns Prue on a ducking stool, but she is rescued by the ideal man and her ideal lover, the weaver Kester Woodseaves. W.'s knowledge of the dark side of human nature is balanced here by her passionate faith in the healing power of love. Her portrayal of female sexual feeling is surprisingly bold rather than sentimental. As in her other novels, W.'s prose style reaches heights of lyrical intensity, especially in her descriptions of the landscape. *Precious Bane* was awarded the Prix Femina for the best English novel of 1924–25.

W.'s last novel, *Armour Wherein He Trusted* (1928), remained a fragment and was first published posthumously in a collection of her short stories. Her essays were reissued posthumously, together with some of her poems, as *Poems and the Spring of Joy* (1928), for which Walter de la Mare wrote the introduction, and a final collection of *Fifty-One Poems* was published posthumously in 1946.

W.'s genius as a novelist remains obscure. Her use of dialect, local traditions, and folklore has led to her being classified as a regional or rural writer by some critics, while others have regarded her as a "hierophant" of the "cult of the primitive." Charles Sanders, who compiled an excellent annotated bibliography on W. (*ELT*, 1966), finds that in spite of her rhapsodic treatment of nature, her novels are essentially modern in their probing of the fear and insecurities of twentieth-century humanity and in their analysis of the "herd instinct" of conventional society.

WORKS: *The Golden Arrow* (1916). *The Spring of Joy* (1917; reissued as *Poems and the Spring of Joy*, 1928). *Gone to Earth* (1917). *The House in Dormer Forest* (1920). *Seven for a Secret* (1922). *Precious Bane* (1924). *Armour Wherein He Trusted* (unfinished novel, together with ten short stories, 1928). *Fifty-One Poems* (1946). *Collected Prose and Poems*, ed. G. M. Coles (1977).

BIBLIOGRAPHY: Addison, H. *Mary Webb* (1931). Armstrong, M., intro. to *The Essential Mary Webb* (1949). Barale, M. A. *Daughters and Lovers: The Life and Writing of Mary Webb* (1986). Byford-Jones, W. *The Shropshire Haunts of Mary Webb* (1948). Cavaliero, G. *The Rural Tradition in the English Novel, 1900–1939* (1977). Coles, G. M. *The Flower of Light: A Biography of Mary Webb* (1978). Cusick, E. *NWRev* (1991). de la Mare, W., intro. to *Poems and the Spring of Joy* (1928). Duncan, E., intro. to *Gone to Earth* (1979). Duncan, E. *Unless Soul Clap its Hands: Portraits and Passages* (1984). Hannah, B. *Striving Toward Wholeness* (1971). Moult, T. *Mary Webb: Her Life and Works* (1932). Paterson, J. H. and E. Paterson, in *Humanistic Geography and Literature*, ed. D. C. D. Pocock (1981). Sykes, M. *Anglo-Welsh Review* (1981). Wandor, M., preface to *Precious Bane* (1978). Wrenn, D.P.H. *Goodbye to Morning* (1964).

For articles in reference works, see: *DLB*. *TCA*.

Other references: Davis, W. E. *ELT* (1968). Sanders, C. *ELT* (1966). Sanders, C. *ELT* (1967).

Jean E. Pearson

(Julia) Augusta Davies Webster

BORN: 30 January 1837, Poole, Dorset.
DIED: 5 September 1894, Kew, London.
DAUGHTER OF: George Davies and Julia Augusta Hume.
MARRIED: Thomas Webster, 1863.
WROTE UNDER: Cecil Home; Augusta Webster.

W. was the daughter of Vice-Admiral George Davies, who held several Coast Guard commands; as a consequence she spent her girlhood on various islands and ships. In her youth she studied modern languages and classical authors, particularly the Greek dramatists, and in her twenties she published translations of Aeschylus and Euripides. At the age of twenty-six, she married Thomas Webster, Fellow of Trinity College, Cambridge, and a practicing solicitor; they had one daughter. From 1860 until her death, W. wrote plays, poems, and essays on contemporary and classical themes.

Having moved with her husband to London in 1870, W. published in the following decade numerous essays on women's issues in the *Examiner* (collected in 1879 as *A Housewife's Opinions*). She viewed with alarm the growing expectation that middle-class women should do their own housework, anticipating that women's time for study, art, or music would be drastically curtailed; instead, she recommended increased wages and respect for domestic servants. She supported clothing reform, work opportunities for single women, full university privileges for women students, and women's suffrage. An ardent feminist, W. believed that gaining suffrage for women was only a matter of time despite the six parliamentary defeats she personally witnessed in her lifetime. She had a strong commitment to advancing women's educational opportunities and was twice elected to the London School Board, in 1879 and 1885, where she also advocated technical training for working-class children.

W.'s dramas—*The Auspicious Day* (1872), *Disguises* (1879), *In a Day* (1882), and *The Sentence* (1887)—were praised by contemporaries for their "concentrated strength." William Michael Rossetti pronounced *The Sentence* (about Caligula) to be "one of the masterpieces of European drama." *In a Day* was produced at a matinee in 1890 at Terry's Theatre in London, with W.'s adult daughter appearing as the heroine; it was the only one of her plays to be staged. In 1864, W. published her only novel, *Lesley's Guardians*, under the pseudonym Cecil Home.

W.'s most lasting work is her poetry, beginning with the 1866 volume *Dramatic Studies*, which included the widely admired poem "Snow-Waste," and culminating in the unfinished sonnet sequence, *Mother and Daughter*, published the year after her death. Christina Rossetti valued only Elizabeth Barrett Browning's poetry above W.'s. Showing the influence of her acknowledged mentor, Robert Browning, W. wrote many dramatic monologues in blank verse, often on social themes pertaining particularly to women. These pieces are especially interesting for their rendering of female consciousness and are much more psychologically convincing than most contemporary poems on similar subjects. Outstanding examples include "By the Looking-Glass" (1866), about spinsterhood; "The Heiress's Wooer," "A Woman Sold," and "A Mother's Cry" (1867), about the marriage market and parental matchmaking; and "A Castaway" (1870), about a fallen woman.

"A Castaway," a 600–line poem ranging widely over the whole complicated issue of prostitution in the nineteenth century, compares favorably with Dante Gabriel Rossetti's "Jenny," which appeared in the same year. "A Castaway" was greatly admired by both Browning and Rossetti, although some contemporary critics complained that the subject matter was unsuitable for a woman poet. Likewise, "Circe" (1870), a psychological character study of the mythological figure, is notable for its sexual imagery and erotic tone as well as its persuasive representation of the heroine's inner life.

W. also composed numerous studies of Christian saints, addressing the glory and the difficulty of asceticism and submission to God, as in "Jeanne d'Arc" and "Sister Annunciata" (1866). In other poems, such as "Pilate" and "A Soul in Prison" (1867), her characters wrestled with religious doubts.

In *A Book of Rhyme* (1881), W. introduced into English poetry an Italian form of peasant song known as "rispetti" or "stornelli." Her final volume of poetry, *Mother and Daughter* (1895), is at once a personal expression of maternal love and a commentary on the varying moods and experiences of motherhood in the nineteenth century.

W.'s ethical leadership was widely recognized in her lifetime. At her death in 1894, Theodore Watts-Dunton placed W. in the moral company of George Eliot and Frances Power Cobbe. Yet Victorian commentators were often uneasy about the realism and directness of W.'s poetry. Some complained of W.'s eccentricity in printing her blank verse without capitals at the beginning of the lines; others found her diction inadmissibly vulgar, particularly for a woman writer. Mackenzie Bell, in *The Poets and the Poetry of the Nineteenth Century,* while comparing W. favorably with Elizabeth Barrett Browning, Christina Rossetti, and Jean Ingelow, nevertheless remarked, "the other women poets of England must yield to her [W.] in that quality which, as it is generally deemed the specially masculine quality, is called virility." However ambivalent contemporary critics may have been about the characteristic strength and force of W.'s poetry, these are the very qualities that make her work readable today.

WORKS: *Blanche Lisle, and Other Poems* (1860). *Lilian Gray* (1864). (as Cecil Home) *Lesley's Guardians* (1864). *Dramatic Studies* (1866). *A Woman Sold, and Other Poems* (1867). *Portraits* (1870; enlarged 1893). *The Auspicious Day* (1872). *Yu-Pe-Ya's Lute* (1874). *Parliamentary Franchise for Women Ratepayers* (pamphlet) (1878). *A Housewife's Opinions* (1879). *Disguises* (1879). *A Book of Rhyme* (1881). *In a Day* (1882). *Daffodil and the Croäxaxicans: A Romance from History* (1884). *The Sentence* (1887). *Selections from the Verse of Augusta Webster* (1893). *Mother and Daughter,* ed. W. M. Rossetti (1895).

BIBLIOGRAPHY: Leighton, A. *Victorian Women Poets: Writing Against the Heart* (1992).

For articles in reference works, see *BA19C. DNB. 1890s. EP.* Evans, B. I. *English Poetry in the Later Nineteenth Century* (1933). *Feminist.* Forman, H. B. *Our Living Poets* (1871). *Oxford. PPC. VB.*

Other references: Armstrong, I. *Victorian Poetry: Poetry, Poetics and Politics* (1993). Brown, S. *VR* (1991). Brown, S. *VP* (1995). Hickok, K. *Representations of Women: Nineteenth-Century British Women's Poetry* (1984). Leighton, A., in *New Feminist Discourse: Critical Essays on Theories and Texts,* ed. I. Armstrong (1992). *Victorian Women Poets: An Anthology,* ed. A. Leighton and M. Reynolds (1995). Mermin, D. *Godiva's Ride: Women of Letters in England, 1830–1880* (1993). Sackville-West, V., in *The Eighteen Seventies,* ed. H. Granville-Barker (1929). Watts-Dunton, T. *Athenaeum* (15 September 1894).

Kathleen Hickok

Ciceley Veronica Wedgwood

BORN: 10 July 1910, Stocksfield, Northumberland.
DIED: 9 March 1997, London.
DAUGHTER OF: Sir Ralph Wedgwood and Iris Veronica Pawson Wedgwood.

Born in Northumberland, the daughter of a railway chairman, Sir Ralph Wedgwood, and the author of books of history and topography, Iris Veronica Pawson Wedgwood, W. was a lineal descendant of the famous Staffordshire potter, Josiah Wedgwood, whose biography she later wrote. At an early age, W. moved with her family to London, where she was educated, first privately, and then at Norland Place School in Kensington. In a famous passage in her autobiographical fragment, "The Velvet Study," W. recalled her "electrifying discovery of the document" and the revelation that "immediate contact could be made with these dead." The call to write was immediate and compelling; her first compositions, now all destroyed, were a play and three novels written when a child. At the age of twelve, she essayed a history of England, also consigned to the wastebasket. The study of history at school was followed in 1927 and 1928 by courses at the University of Bonn and the Sorbonne, where she perfected her knowledge of German and French. Returning to England, she received a scholarship to study at Lady Margaret Hall, Oxford, where her tutor was A. L. Rowse. W. earned her A.B. with first class honours in Modern History in 1931 and was soon appointed to work for the Commission on the History of Parliament, making the civil war and commonwealth period her specialty.

The first product of this work was her biography of Thomas Wentworth, the first Earl of Strafford, published when she was twenty-five. This was followed in 1939 by her popular narrative, *The Thirty Years' War*, based on extensive research in German, French, Dutch, and Swedish documents, written under the gathering clouds of another great European war. Her attraction to the depictions of the human personality, so evident in that work, is also manifest in her short biography *Oliver Cromwell* (1939) and her first major translation, an English version of Karl Brandl's massive life in German of the Emperor Charles V. In 1944 she published her study of the Dutch Stadtholder William the Silent, which won the James Tait Black Memorial Prize from the University of Edinburgh. This was followed in 1946 by a volume of essays, *Velvet Studies*, which gathered many pieces written as literary editor of the British weekly *Time and Tide* and for other journals. In 1949 she published a study on *Richelieu and the French Monarchy* in the "Teach Yourself History Series" edited by her former tutor, A. L. Rowse.

From 1948 to 1958, she served as director of *Time and Tide* and from 1952 to 1978 as a member of the Royal Commission on Historical Manuscripts. The 1950s were spent on the research and writing of what was to be her masterpiece, a narrative history of the English civil war, a projected trilogy entitled *The Great Rebellion*. The first volume, *The King's Peace, 1637–1641*, appeared in 1955, and the second, *The King's War, 1641–1647*, followed in 1958. Though acclaimed for the power and skill of the historical narrative, W.'s account was widely criticized for its lack of concern with historical causation. Such criticism probably caused W. to abandon completion of her trilogy in favor of other projects. The seventeenth century, however, remained W.'s subject of special study. In 1950, she published a short book on English literature in the seventeenth century, and in 1952 a biography of the Marquess of Montrose, the Scottish aristocrat chosen by King Charles I to quell a rebellion in Scotland.

Her distinction as a stylist, popularity as a writer, and evident skill in administration led to election to several offices and the receipt of many honors. W. served as president of the English Association in 1955–56, and her presidential address on *Literature and the Historian* was published as a pamphlet in 1956. She was president of the English Centre of the International PEN Club in 1956–57 and president of the Society of Authors in 1972–77. She was early elected a fellow of the Royal Historical Society, the Scottish Historical Society, and the Royal Society of Literature. She was later elected a fellow of the British Academy, the American Academy of Arts and Letters, and the American Philosophical Society. In 1962 she was elected an honorary fellow of her old college, Lady Margaret Hall, Oxford, and in 1978 Honorary Bencher of the Middle Temple. In 1956, the Crown recognized her service to history and literature when she was made a Commander of the Order of the British Empire. In 1968, she was made Dame of the British Empire and the next year awarded the Order of Merit. Several colleges and universities bestowed honorary doctorates: Sheffield, Oxford, Keele, Sussex, Liverpool, Smith, and Harvard. W. was the Clark Lecturer at Cambridge in 1957–58; the Northcliffe Lecturer at London in 1959; and special lecturer at University College, London, from 1962 to 1970. She was a member of the Institute for Advanced Study at Princeton from 1953 to 1968, the advisory council of the Victoria and Albert Museum from 1959 to 1969, and the Art Council Literature Panel from 1965 to 1967. W. served as a trustee of the National Gallery in London from 1962 to 1976.

In 1960, W. collected many of her published lectures and occasional pieces in *Truth and Opinion, Historical Essays*, and in 1964 she published her stunning account of the trial and execution of Charles I under the title *A Coffin for King Charles*. In 1967, she collaborated with other scholars to produce an illustrated volume on the world of the artist Peter Paul Rubens. There followed brief studies on *Milton and His World* (1969) and *The Political Career of Peter Paul Rubens* (1975). The major project of W.'s later years was a history of the world begun in the 1960s. The first volume of this unfinished series, *The Spoils of Time*, covering from earliest times to the sixteenth century, appeared in 1984. In the words of a reviewer, she "eschews broad interpretations and relies almost exclusively on her very considerable narrative gifts." In 1986 W. was honored with a festschrift, *For Veronica Wedgwood These: Studies in Seventeenth-Century History*. The next year, W. issued another collection of her essays, *History and Hope*.

Befriended and deeply influenced by two superb narrative historians, G. M. Trevelyan and A. L. Rowse, W. was perhaps the last representative of that hearty species of British writer—the private scholar who commanded a large, enthusiastic readership while making great contributions to British culture. Though largely living as an independent writer without a permanent academic post, W. won wider recognition from the universities, her government, and the literary public than any academic historian of her generation. That many of her books have been often reprinted attests both to the enduring appeal of biography and narrative history and the felicity of her style.

WORKS: *Strafford* (1935; rev. as *Thomas Wentworth, First Earl of Strafford*, 1961). *The Thirty Years' War* (1939). *Oliver Cromwell* (1939). (trans.), *The Emperor Charles V: The Growth and Destiny of a Man and a World-Empire*, by K. Brandl (1939). *William the Silent, William of Nassau, Prince of Orange, 1533–1584* (1944). *Velvet Studies* (1946). *Richelieu and the French Monarchy* (1949). *Seventeenth Century English Literature* (1950; rev. 1977). *The Last of the Radicals, Josiah Wedgwood, M.P.* (1951). *Montrose* (1952). *The King's Peace, 1637–1641* (1955). *Literature and the Historian*, Presidential Address, The English Association (1956). *The Sense of the Past*, Leslie Stephen Memorial Lecture (1957). *The King's War, 1641–1647* (1958). *Truth and Opinion, Historical Essays* (1960). *Poetry and Politics under the Stuarts*, Clark Lectures (1961). *A Coffin for King Charles: The Trial and Execution of Charles I* (1964). *Milton and the World* (1969). *The Political Career of Peter Paul Rubens* (1975). *The Spoils of Time, A Short History of the World, I. From Earliest Times to the Sixteenth Century* (1984). *History and Hope, Collected Essays* (1987).

BIBLIOGRAPHY:

For articles in reference works, see: *Blackwell Dictionary of Historians* (1988). *CA. Cambridge. CB. Major Twentieth-Century Writers*, ed. B. Ryan (1991). *Who's Who. International Who's Who. WD.*

Other references: Kenyon, J. *History Men* (1984). *LonT* (11 March 1997). Mehta, V. *The Fly and the Fly Bottle: Encounters with British Intellectuals* (1963). *For Veronica Wedgwood These: Studies in Seventeenth-Century History*, ed. J. Ollard and P. Tudor-Craig (1986).

Benjamin G. Kohl

Fay Weldon

BORN: 22 September 1933, Alvechurch, Worcestershire.
DAUGHTER OF: Frank T. Birkinshaw and Margaret Jepson Birkinshaw.
MARRIED: Ron Weldon, 1960.

"It took me a long time to believe that men were actually human beings," W. writes. Brought up in New Zealand and raised by her mother and sister after her parents' divorce, she attended a convent school. In the 1950s, she completed her M.A. in economics and psychology at St. Andrews University and was an unmarried mother—"a solitary experience," as she has written. The result of her early life was a unique perspective on the world: "I believed the world was female, whereas men have always believed the world is male. It's unusual for women to *suffer* from my delusion." W.'s subject has largely been the generation of women who grew up after World War II; her theme is how these women survive being human.

To read a W. novel is to encounter a densely truthful depiction of the claims people make on one another. Each of W.'s novels traces the complex interweavings of human relations and how these inevitably constrain women. *Down among the Women* (1971) follows a group of women of W.'s generation as they variously fight, deny, and fail to transcend the label of "woman." In *Praxis* (1978), the expectations forced on women figure in the fate of Praxis Duveen, in prison for infanticide. *Puffball* (1980) is part supernatural parody, part autobiography about Liffey, who is going through a pregnancy while separated from the father; he has a full and busy life in London while Liffey comes to term amid witches and hauntings in Somerset. *Female Friends* (1975), one of W.'s best novels, records how the concatenation of personal failings and male exploitation defeat even the most modest dreams.

W. has both claimed and disclaimed the feminist viewpoint. She has written that she belongs to the last prefeminist generation: women without power, without theory, often aware of their impotence and oppression, often angry, frustrated, and despairing but also trying to make a life of it. Thus the last words of *Down among the Women* are "We are the last of the women." One feels that the last two words might be enclosed in their own quotation marks.

W.'s best work is less didactic than it is moral; it seeks less to draw a lesson than to depict the truth. Readers have sensed a distance between W.'s fictional practice and the strident moralism that mars other feminist writing. W. has acknowledged the strong, even lopsided, moral intention in her fiction. She has admitted that she intentionally rounds out her female characters more fully than her male characters: "I just make [male characters] behave, talk, and I don't add any justification for their behaviour. Whereas my women characters are all explained." Male behavior is so well established that it hardly needs explication; male domination is such an accomplished fact that it hardly needs mention. Fiction becomes a way of "redressing a balance so far tilted as to be all but unworkable." Though W. accords her women a fuller explanation, she does not idealize them. Throughout her fiction and drama there is a refusal to invest women characters with unusual courage, resources, or integrity. Lily of *Remember Me* (1976), Chloe of *Female Friends*, Ruth of *Life and Loves of a She-Devil* (1983)—all are women with failings, all dole out their share of hurt and disappointment, and all contribute to their respective fates. All we have is what happens: the ironies of relationships with men; the successes and failures of friendships between women; the demands of motherhood; the coming to terms with menstruation, pregnancy, the physical aspects of being a woman; the lack of an alternative to male-defined roles; and always, isolation. W.'s women often end neither better nor wiser than before. In place of great expectations, they have a clearer view of themselves and of their chances for happiness. Indeed, this final clarity verging on optimism rescues W.'s work from what some readers find is a tragic pessimism relieved only by black humor. Chloe of *Female Friends* searches for some parting wisdom to give the reader, and her conclusions are characteristically concrete: "Take family snaps, unashamed. Dress up for weddings, all weddings. Rejoice at births, all births. For days can be happy—whole futures cannot."

W. may be an even better writer for the stage than she is a novelist; much of her best fiction has been adapted from her dramatic works. Her best single piece of writing, "Polaris" (1978) has succeeded equally well as drama, radio play, and short story. Dramatic technique often surfaces in the experimental aspects of her fiction: staccato sentences, short paragraphs, jagged alternations between chronologies and points of view. A novel like *Female Friends* may be rendered largely in stage dialogue, exploiting the inherent irony of the dramatic situation. Her best work delivers what good drama delivers: the impression of voiceless objectivity combined with that of an unmistakable voice.

W. writes about a sharply delimited, claustrophobic world, which may lead some readers to the impression of sameness from work to work. In the 1980s and 1990s, a productive period for this very productive writer, she has sought to widen her scope, with her adaptation of and reflections on Jane Austen (1980 and 1984), her book on Rebecca West (1985), and novels such as *The Hearts and Lives of Men* (1987) and *The Rules of Life* (1987). Of the novels, the former is a mock fairy tale and the latter a vicious satire on religion. *The Shrapnel Academy* (1986) explores a theme that has always been in her work: the obsolescence and brutality of war. In these as in all her other writings, W. struggles against the sermonizing impulse, the desire to bash the reader over the head with the moral import of the tale. She sometimes gives in to this impulse, however. In the 1990s, W. further explored her two characteristic modes: the contemporary fairy tale and the realistic novel of manners. *Life Force* (1992), *Affliction* (1993; in the U. S. as *Trouble*), and *Splitting* (1994) form a devastating trilogy about marriage—the first concerning adultery, the second the turbulence of unhappy marriage, and the third divorce. Increasingly she has become a voice in the political and cultural debate in the English-speaking world.

As one of the most industrious and professional of writers, she has given a growing number of interviews about just how she manages to do it all. As much as feminist theorists enlist her viewpoint—and she does see the world from a woman's perspective—she cannot be enlisted as a radical feminist or an advocate. Her tales are too tough on women for that. She refuses to let us see her women either as heroines or as victims; she wants us to see women as they are, in the world as it is.

WORKS: *Wife in a Blonde Wig* (1966). *The Fat Woman's Tale* (1966). *The Fat Woman's Joke* (1967; in the U.S. as . . . *And the Wife Ran Away,* 1968). *What About Me* (1967). *Dr. De Waldon's Therapy* (1967). *Goodnight, Mrs. Dill* (1967). *The 45th Unmarried Mother* (1967). *Fall of the Goat* (1967). *Ruined Houses* (1968). *Venus Rising* (1968). *The Three Wives of Felix Hall* (1968). *Hippy Hippy Who Cares* (1968). *£13038* (1968). *The Loophole* (1969). *Smokescreen* (1969). *Poor Mother* (1970). *Office Party* (1970). *Permanence* (1970). *Upstairs Downstairs* (1971). *On Trial* (1971). *Down among the Women* (1971). *Old Man's Hat* (1972). *A Splinter of Ice* (1972). *Hands* (1972). *The Lament of an Unmarried Father* (1972). *A Nice Rest* (1972). *Time Hurries On,* in *Scene Scripts,* ed. M. Marland (1972). *Spider* (1973). *Comfortable Words* (1973). *Housebreaker* (1973). *Desirous of Change* (1973). *In Memoriam* (1974). *Mr. Fox and Mr. First* (1974). *Words of Advice* (1974). *The Doctor's Wife* (1975). *Poor Baby* (1975). *Friends* (1975). *Female Friends* (1975). *The Terrible Tale of Timothy Bagshott* (1975). *Aunt Tatty* (1975; from the story by E. Bowen). *Moving House* (1976). *Remember Me* (1976). *Words of Advice* (1977; in the U.K. as *Little Sisters,* 1978). *Act of Rape* (1977). *Married Love* (1977). *Act of Hypocrisy* (1977). *Chickabiddy* (1978). *Mr. Director* (1978). *Polaris* (radio and stage drama, 1978). *Praxis* (1978). *Weekend* (1979). *All the Bells of Paradise* (1979). (with P. Anderson and M. Stott) *Simple Steps to Public Life* (1980). *Action Replay* (1980). *Puffball* (1980). *Pride and Prejudice* (1980; from the novel by J. Austen). *Honey Ann* (1980). *Life for Christine* (1980). *Watching Me, Watching You* (television drama, 1980; novel, 1981). *I Love My Love* (radio drama, 1981; stage play, 1984). *After the Prize* (1981). *Woodworm* (1981). *The President's Child* (1982). *Little Mrs. Perkins* (1982; from the story by P. Mortimer). *Redundant! or, The Wife's Revenge* (1983). *Life and Loves of a She-Devil* (novel, 1983; television serial, 1986). *Letters to Alice: On First Reading Jane Austen* (1984). *The Western Women* (1984). *Bright Smiler* (1985). *Rebecca West* (1985). *Polaris and Other Stories* (1985). *Jane Eyre* (1986; drama, from the novel by C. Brontë). *Face at the Window* (1986). *A Dangerous Kind of Love* (1986). *The Shrapnel Academy* (1986). *The Heart of the Country* (television serial and novel, 1987). *The Hole in the Top of the World* (1987). *The Good Woman of Setzuan* (1987; adapted from B. Brecht). *Scaling Down* (1987). *The Hearts and Lives of Men* (1987). *The Rules of Life* (1987). *Polaris and Other Stories* (1989). *The Leader of the Band* (1989). *The Cloning of Joanna May* (1989). *Darcy's Utopia* (1991). *Wives and Husbands* (1991). *Life Force* (1992). *So Very English* (1991). *Moon over Minneapolis* (1992). *Affliction* (1993; in the U.S. as *Trouble). Bram Stoker's Dracula* (screenplay, 1993). *Splitting* (1994). *Angel, All Innocence and Other Stories* (1995). *Wicked Women* (1995). *Worst Fears* (1996).

BIBLIOGRAPHY: Bailey, D. *The Lady is a Tramp* (1995). Barreca, R. *Fay Weldon's Wicked Fictions* (1994). Haffenden, J. *Novelists in Interview* (1985). Haffenden, J. *New Women and New Fiction* (1986). Haffenden, J. *Contemporary British Women Novelists* (1987). Kenyon, O. *The Writer's Imagination* (1993). Lodge, D. *The Art of Fiction: Illustrated from Classic and Modern Texts* (1993). Pearlman, M. *Listen to Their Voices: Twenty Interviews with Women Who Write* (1993). Salzmann-Brunner, B. *Amanuenses to the Present: Protagonists in the Fiction of Penelope Mortimer, Margaret Drabble, and Fay Weldon* (1988). *Short Story Criticism: Excerpts from the Criticism of the Works of Short Story Writers,* ed. D. Segal (1992). Winter, N., in *Interview with the Muse: Remarkable Women Speak about Creativity and Power,* ed. N. Winter (1978).

For articles in reference works, see: *Bloomsbury. CA. Cambridge. CD. CLC. CN. DLB. Feminist. Oxford. ToddBWW.*

Other references: Alexander, R., in *Inter Action,* ed. N. Loes and L. Marx (1994). Bird, L. and J. Eliot, in *British Television Drama in the 1980s,* ed. G. W. Brandt. *Crit* (1978). Ford, B. *WVUPP* (1993). *London Telegraph Sunday Magazine* (16 December 1979). *LonT* (17 February 1980). *Manchester Guardian* (20 February 1979). Marshall, D. *VWM* (1992). *MSpr* (1979). *NYT* (28 February 1988, 1 December 1991, 8 January 1992). *NYTBR* (2 October 1977, 26 April 1987). *Observer* (18 February 1979). Smith, P. J. *Expl* (1993). Reman, A. *Presumptuous Girls; Women and Their World in the Serious Woman's Novel* (1977). *Time* (22 February 1973). *TLS* (22 February 1980, 13 February 1987, 11 September 1987). *On Gender and Writing,* ed. M. Wandor (1983). Wilde, A. *ConL* (1988). Wright, K. G. *THJ* (1992). Young, P. *Folklore in Use* (1994).

John Timpane

Timberlake (Lael Louisiana) Wertenbaker

BORN: 1946, New York City, United States.
DAUGHTER OF: Charles Christian Wertenbaker and Lael Tucker Wertenbaker.

"When I am asked where my plays come from, I am always stuck for an answer," W. reflected in the introduction to a collection of her plays (1996). "There are so many sources, a mishmash of autobiography, obsession, chance encounters, reading and conversations. And yet, when I try to retrace the roads to individual plays, I am always intrigued by the landscapes on the way." Poised in mid-career as an original and incisive voice in British theater, both as a writer of original plays and an adept translator of

French and ancient Greek plays, W. eludes attempts to group her into narrow stylistic or ideological camps. American by birth, raised in France, living and writing in London since the 1970s, W. brings her own cosmopolitan, multicultural upbringing to her work. Her dramatic writing tends to situate crises of personal experience or contemporary social issues within circumscribing themes of classical, literary, and historical references. She braids issues of individual search for identity with discursive concerns pertaining to a broad social consciousness; and she depicts restlessness, adventure, philosophical questioning, and a desire to delimit boundaries of national and cultural identity. Her scripts roam through confines of naturalistic settings and dialogue, then into open spaces of thought composed into monologue. Her recent work rejects tracking the unifying arc of a central protagonist's quest in favor of pursuing parallel progression among multiple characters. In structures that seem to meander along twisted paths, W. dramaturgically constructs purposeful explorations of uncertain journeys.

"The whole thing about being a writer is that you can have a floating identity anyway," W. has mused while maintaining a somewhat guarded reticence about her own past. Some details may be pieced together. The second child of urbane Americans born in New York City, W. grew up in the Basque region of France, near St. Jean-de-Luz, attending French schools. Her father worked for *Time* magazine throughout World War II. Her mother reported from Berlin, Germany, for *Time* during 1940–41. The family spent time both in France and in Sneden's Landing, New York. In September 1954, when W. was eight years old, her father was diagnosed with colon cancer. Following an exploratory operation in New York, during which W. was left in France with her older brother Christian, her father decided to end his life on his own terms. W.'s mother's moving, courageous, and pioneering story of his last months and of the assisted suicide at their home in France was published as *Death of a Man* in 1957. It was later adapted for the stage by Garson Kanin as *Gift of Time* and was produced on Broadway in 1962 with Henry Fonda and Olivia de Havilland as the Wertenbakers. W. attended St. John's College in Annapolis, Maryland, where she cultivated her appreciation of a "great works" approach to learning. She graduated in 1966 with a degree in philosophy. Following college, W. worked as a writer for Time-Life Books in New York City and London. While teaching French and English in Greece for a year, she began writing and producing children's plays.

The 1978 Ring's Head production of *This is No Place for Tallulah Bankhead* (unpublished) was the first London production of a W. play. *New Anatomies* was performed at the Edinburgh Theatre Festival by the Women's Theatre Group in 1981. Translations from the French of Pierre Marivaux's eighteenth-century mannered comedies *False Admissions* and *Successful Strategies* premiered in 1983 at the Lyric (Hammersmith) Studio Theatre. These drew attention to her skill as a translator and gave her valuable experience working with a theater ensemble, Shared Experience, directed by Mike Alfreds.

The Grace of Mary Traverse, which opened in October 1985 during W.'s second year as resident writer for the Royal Court Theatre, continued *New Anatomies*' theme of women dressing as men. Living in Brixton during the riots of the early 1980s, W. set *Grace* during the Gordon riots of the 1780s. W. admits that the principal character's restlessness is autobiographical. The play follows Mary Traverse on what W. describes as "her quest for experience and knowledge and eventual political power and the price attached to this Faustian pact." Mary is led by Mrs. Temptwell along an odyssey of encounters with corruption and malice. Epiphany follows but, echoing the Sophoclean precept, Mary comes to knowledge only through suffering. This stands as a recurrent motif in W.'s work.

Although she does not march in the front rank of the feminist regiment, W.'s original plays do explore the construction of gender and the function of language as a tool of oppression and a lever to redemption. Themes of personal silencing, dispossession and limitation of potential, and probing questions of stability, multiplicity, and fracture of identity are located in her plays both in modern and mythological settings. A woman playwright who has moved from the radical fringe to higher-profile theaters, identified within the feminist lexicon, W. speak to issues of social philosophy in general, not just in her plays.

As W. matured as a playwright, her plays continued to explore thematic dimensions of personal silence and the value of language. *The Love of the Nightingale,* produced by the Royal Shakespeare Company (RSC) in 1988, offers a refashioning of the Philomel myth to reflect, as W. notes, upon "the violence that erupts in societies when they have been silenced too long. Without language, brutality will triumph." In *Three Birds Alighting in a Field* (1991), a woman defining herself through her husband educates herself ironically at her husband's request, and in the process moves toward self-enlightenment through her experience with art. In *Break of Day* (1995), feminist women at mid-life equate motherhood and their rediscovery of their sexual nature with self-fulfillment. The one character in *Break of Day* who achieves motherhood through adoption is then set free to rediscover her voice and language as a singer-songwriter.

Her most frequently produced script, *Our Country's Good* (1988), probes the worth of language in a society that has been silenced and the power of theater to regenerate the voice of the spirit. An astutely crafted work, the play developed from an intense workshop collaboration with the Royal Court's artistic director, Max Stafford-Clark, and a group of Royal Court actors. W. based *Our Country's Good* on Thomas Keneally's historical novel *The Playmaker,* "converting" features of the novel into the medium of theater. The drama metatheatrically celebrates "the redemptive value of art" through its reenactment of the first theatrical production to take place in the convict colony of Australia in 1787, Farquhar's eighteenth-century play *The Recruiting Officer.* The original production opened at the Royal Court Theatre in September 1988, alternating in repertory with Farquhar's play.

W. herself embodies the cross-border children passionately described in the last act of *Break of Day:*

> Now it will be in the hands of the children, possibly most of all, these cross-border children I have helped to get out. Born in one country, loved and raised in another, I hope they will not descend into narrow ethnic

identification, but that they will be willfully international, part of a great European community. I hope they will carry on history with broad minds and warm hearts. They have the complexity for their childhood: change, migration and indifference and uncertainty came to them early. Now, cherished, secure, educated. Is it unfair of me to place the responsibility of history onto them? We must not go into the next century with no ideal but selfishness.

W.'s own adopted child, Dushka Wertenbaker-Man, and her own experience in cross-border adoption no doubt inspired the eloquence of the speech and informed other dramatic translations into the play.

Of her work as a translator, W. has acknowledged that "No translation has the quality of writing that the original has" and that she "always feel(s) uncomfortable with translations that transpose from one culture to another." The deftness of her Marivaux work in conveying a sense of "Marivaudage"—an idiosyncratic style of prissy banter—earned her critical praise. Other translations include plays by Maurice Maeterlinck (*Pelléas and Mélisande,* 1988), Jean Anouilh (*Leocadia,* 1987), and Luigi Pirandello (*The Way You Want Me,* n.d.). Her reworkings of the Greeks—"another passion of mine"—venture into adaptation. W.'s idiomatic, "plain-spoken" version of Sophocles' Oedipus cycle for the RSC, directed by Adrian Noble, premiered as a seven-hour trilogy titled *The Thebans* in the Swan Theatre, Stratford-upon-Avon, in October 1991.

In addition to her appointments as resident writer with Shared Experience (1983) and with the Royal Court Theatre (1984–85), W. has been the recipient of several honors. She won the All London Playwrights Award in 1983 for *The Third* (1980), and *Plays and Players* Most Promising Playwright Award in 1985 for *The Grace of Mary Traverse. Our Country's Good* earned her the Laurence Olivier Play of the Year Award (1988), the John Whiting Award (1989), and the New York Drama Critics' Circle Award (1990). In 1991, she received the Susan Smith Blackburn Prize for *Three Birds Alighting on a Field,* followed by the London Theatre Critics' Circle Award and Writers Guild Award.

W.'s output has not been prolific but it has been steady. She says:

> I like to work on my plays in rehearsals and even well into their run as I watch them performed in front of an audience. It's part of the travelling you do. Then suddenly, one day, there is no more you can do and the play becomes a part of your past, a country you won't revisit. I suppose I keep writing because there's always somewhere else to go.

Where she will go in her work should compel continuing critical attention.

WORKS: *This is No Place for Tallulah Bankhead* (King's Head Theatre, London, 1978, unpublished). *The Third* (King's Head Theatre, London, 1980, unpublished). *Second Sentence* (Brighton, 1980). *Case to Answer* (Soho Poly Theatre, London, 1980). *Breaking Through* (Women's Theatre Group, London, 1980). (trans.) *The House of Bernarda Alba,* by Garcia Lorca (1980). *New Anatomies* (London, 1981, 1984). *Inside Out* (Stoke-on-Trent, 1982). *Home Leave* (Ipswich, Suffolk, 1982). (trans.) *False Admissions,* by P. Marivaux (Shared Experience, London, 1983, 1989). (trans.) *Abel's Sister,* by Yolande (Bourcier Royal Court Theatre Upstairs, 1984). *The Grace of Mary Traverse* (Royal Court, 1985). (trans.) *Leocadia,* by Jean Anouilh, in *Five Plays,* by J. Anouilh (1987). (adaptation) *Mephisto* (1986; from *Mnouchkine,* by Klaus Mann). *Our Country's Good* (Royal Court, 1988, rev. 1989; from *The Playmaker* by T. Keneally). *The Love of the Nightingale* (Royal Shakespeare Company, 1988, 1989). (trans.) *Pelléas and Mélisande,* by M.-P.-M.-B. Maeterlinck (broadcast 1988, produced 1989). (trans.) *False Admission, Successful Strategies and La Dispute,* by P. Marivaux (1989). *Three Birds Alighting on a Field* (Royal Court, London, 1991). (trans.) *The Thebans,* by Sophocles (Royal Shakespeare Company, 1991). *Do Not Disturb* (television play, 1991). *The Children* (screenplay from. E. Wharton novel, 1992). *Break of Day* (Royal Court, London, 1995). (trans.) *The Way You Want Me,* by L. Pirandello (n.d.). (trans.) *Hecuba,* by Euripides (American Conservatory Theater, San Francisco, 1996). (trans.) *Agamemnon's Daughter* (*The Orestia,* by Aeschylus, unproduced, n.d.).

BIBLIOGRAPHY: Bayley, C. *New Statesman* (1 December 1995). Brustein, R. *New Republic* (10 June 1991). Carlson, S. *JDTC* (1989). Carlson, S. *NTQ* (1993). Chaillet, N., intro. to *False Admissions, Successful Strategies and La Dispute: Three Plays by Marivaux* (1989). Coen, S. *American Theatre* (March 1994). Cook, R. *TJ* (October 1993). McDonough, C., in *British Playwrights: 1956–1995: A Research and Production Sourcebook,* ed. W. W. Demastes (1996). *Platform Papers: 1. Translation* (a booklet published by the Royal National Theatre, 1992). Rabey, D. I. *MD* (1990). Sullivan, E. B. *TJ* (1993). Wertenbaker, L. T. *Death of a Man* (1957). Wilson, A. *MD* (1991). Winston, J. *MD* (1995).

For articles in reference works, see. *Bloomsbury. CD. Feminist. OCTCL.*

Other references: *TES* (9 October 1991). *TLS* (20 September 1991, 22 December 1995).

Paul D. Nelsen and Mary Lou Nelsen

Mary Wesley

BORN: 24 June 1912, Englefield Green, near Windsor, Berkshire.

DAUGHTER OF: Colonel Harold Mynors Farmar and Violet Dalby Farmar.

MARRIED: Charles Eady, Lord Charles Swinfen, 1937; Eric Siepmann, 1952.

W. was born into a military family that could trace its ancestry to the Duke of Wellington's eldest brother. W.'s father attained the rank of colonel, her grandfather that of general. Hers was not, however, a close family, and she was raised essentially by governesses and her maternal grandmother, Lady Dalby, who died when W. was thirteen. After being schooled at home by a succession of governesses, she attended Queen's College, London, from 1928 to 1930 and the London School of Economics, in 1930–31. In January 1937, she married Lord Charles Swinfen, a London barrister ten years her senior, primarily, as she has admitted, to escape her home life. The marriage produced two sons.

With the outbreak of World War II, she joined the War Office and worked for two years at Bletchly Park. In 1941, however, she took her children to Kent, away from the Blitz, leaving her husband in London; they did not live together after this and were divorced in 1944. That same year she met Eric Siepmann, who was still married to a woman he had not lived with for years and could not locate. They were finally married in 1952, however, and subsequently had one son. The postwar years were lean ones for England generally and for W. in particular, as her husband often changed jobs. Siepmann died of Parkinson's disease in 1970. Through his illness, W. managed on Social Security, and after 1970, until her novels became best-sellers, on a meager widow's pension.

W.'s first attempts as writer were two children's books published in 1969; her first novel was *Jumping the Queue*, published in 1983 when she was seventy years old. It was an almost instant success with the public, and in the years following she has produced a succession of best-sellers. In 1995, she was made a Commander of the British Empire.

W.'s novels of England's upper-middle-class life can provoke comparisons with the novel-of-manners tradition in general and Jane Austen in particular. Her central characters are almost always women in search of emotional and sexual fulfillment. Their problem is not liberation—they are liberated already—but using their freedom to avoid the twin traps of passion on the one hand and economic and social security on the other. In this sense, they are certainly modern novels, dealing with issues of identity, sexuality, and happiness in ways that modern readers find familiar and congenial. W.'s novels are not merely romantic froth, however, for she is not afraid to face the threat of death or even the possibility of despair and suicide.

Jumping the Queue is her most serious novel. Matilda Poliport is a middle-aged widow, comfortably off, with apparently everything to live for. Yet at the beginning of the novel we see her on the coast, preparing to commit suicide by swimming out to sea. She changes her mind, however, when she meets Hugh, also about to kill himself before the police can arrest him for murder. Too predictably, perhaps, Matilda dissuades Hugh from suicide, hides him from the police, and eventually takes him to her bed. As their relationship progresses, we learn some of the sordid secrets of Matilda's past, most notably of a husband who dealt in drugs and probably committed incest with their daughter. The novel ends when Hugh is finally arrested and Matilda returns to the seaside, this time successfully completing the suicide that was interrupted in the first chapter.

W.'s second novel, *The Camomile Lawn* (1984), is more ambitious in plot and characterization and less somber in theme. The book follows the lives of five cousins—Oliver, Polly, Calypso, Walter, and Sophy—over forty years, from an August afternoon in 1939 at the home of Helena and Richard Cuthburtson on the Cornish coast to the day of Max Ernstweiler's funeral at the same home in 1979. This house on the coast, and its camomile lawn, serves as a touchstone of normality for the disruptions brought on by World War II. Not all of these disruptions are unwelcome, however. During the war, sex is liberation, and not just for the beautiful and amoral Calypso. Polly has affairs with twin brothers, either of whom could be the father of her children. Helena springs to life as Max's mistress, and even Richard rouses from his self-pitying torpor to find new purpose as a lover and as a reactivated warrior.

Indeed, the novel focuses on the hedonistic pleasures of food, drink, and sex as experienced against the backdrop of war and its attendant privations and miseries—bombing raids, concentration camps, and the ever-present threat of death. W. does not dwell on the horrors or war or even its inconveniences of rationing, nightly blackouts, and chaotic train schedules; rather, she depicts the period as a cultural broom, sweeping out musty conventions and prejudices and allowing new light and air into British society. At times, the balance seems to tip too much in the direction of rosy-tinted nostalgia, but on the whole there are enough chilling details—like Walter's death at sea and Calypso's giving birth in the basement of her bombed-out home—to remind us that the war was indeed deadly and destructive.

The theme of sexual liberation is very much at the heart of W.'s third novel, *Harnessing Peacocks* (1985). As a teenager, its protagonist, Hebe Rutter, fled the home of grandparents who wanted her to abort the child she is carrying. Twelve years later, Hebe has established herself in two professions: highly paid cook and call girl. Hebe pursues these two traditionally confining female roles with shrewd independence. She cooks only for women who can both appreciate and afford her services, just as she bestows her sexual favors only on those men willing to accept her terms and who give her pleasure in bed. She is so successful at her chosen professions that her young son can attend an expensive boarding school. As the plot unfolds, we learn not only about Hebe's checkered past and present but also about the family lives of three other couples, each of which represents a different style of family life. In this sense, the novel is less about Hebe than about the contemporary problem of raising children both within and outside of wedlock. W.'s thesis (perhaps inevitable from a writer who was herself a single mother) is that marriage itself confers no particular advantages: What matters is the degree of love and commitment that parents bring to the marriage and to the raising of their children.

The Vacillations of Poppy Carew (1986) illustrates the strengths and weaknesses of W.'s fiction. The novel is W.'s version of Jane Austen's *Emma;* its central character is a young woman of wealth, beauty, and intelligence whose main focus is to find the right man. Predictably, there is no shortage of contenders, each offering something attractive. In the end, Poppy chooses the man her late father would have approved of—a pig farmer named Willy Gutherie (nephew of Calypso Grant of *The Camomile Lawn*). Poppy's adventures are narrated with zest and energy. The novel sparkles with bright dialogue, clever insights, humorous asides, and interesting minor characters. Entertaining as the novel is, however, there remains a certain moral hollowness. Poppy's only criteria for a suitable mate seem to be sexual compatibility and a modicum of unselfishness. Willie Gutherie, for all his charms and his environmentally friendly farming methods, is merely a decent young man. Good manners and good coupling seem to exhaust W.'s moral universe—and not only in this novel. *Not That Sort of Girl* (1987), for example, uncritically applauds its heroine for being "faithful" to two men throughout her life—her husband and her lover. What does fidelity mean in such an instance? *A Sensible Life* (1990) returns to World War II, again asserting its liberating effects on middle class women and the joys of independent, late middle age.

W. excels in the craft of story-telling. Her plots move along swiftly, smoothly, almost effortlessly. She has a knack for moving the story forward even while pausing to describe a scene or record dialogue. Subplots hum along on noiseless gears, and everything is suffused in genuine wit. The style is a model of clarity and urbanity. Characters major and minor spring immediately to life; and, as suggested above, there can be genuine moral and social seriousness behind the brisk dialogue, frisky sex, and compelling characters. At the same time, it can be fairly argued that her plots depend too heavily on coincidence and a small, closed society in which everyone knows or is related to everyone else. There is something too cozy and neat in W.'s polite, urbane, well-heeled world. It is easy, in this heady atmosphere, to gloss over the serious issues that do arise.

W. is unlikely to emerge as a major novelist, but as an accomplished entertainer with her fingers on the pulse of late-twentieth-century Britain she will continue to give pleasure and enlightenment and to offer lively insights into the manners and mores of her time.

WORKS: *Speaking Terms* (1969). *The Sixth Seal* (1969). *Jumping the Queue* (1983). *Haphazard House* (1983). *The Camomile Lawn* (1984). *Harnessing Peacocks* (1985). *The Vacillations of Poppy Carew* (1986). *Not That Sort of Girl* (1987). *Second Fiddle* (1988). *A Sensible Life* (1990). *A Dubious Legacy* (1992). *An Imaginative Experience* (1994). *Part of the Furniture* (1997).

BIBLIOGRAPHY:

For articles in reference works, see: *CA. Cambridge. CN. Feminist. RGTCW.*

Other references: *Literary Review* (October 1988). *LonSunTMag* (12 April 1997). *LonT* (27 January 1994, 7 January 1995). *NYTBR* (30 April 1995). *TLS* (17 June 1983, 13 April 1984, 28 June 1985, 27 June 1986, 25 June 1987, 14 October 1988, 16 March 1990, 7 February 1992, April 1994).

Dean R. Baldwin

Jane West

BORN: 30 April 1758, London.
DIED: 25 March 1852, Little Bowden, Northamptonshire.
DAUGHTER: John Iliffe and Jane Iliffe.
MARRIED: Thomas West, c. 1780.
WROTE UNDER: Prudentia Homespun; Jane West.

W.'s conservative educational tracts and didactic novels were well received by late eighteenth- and early nineteenth-century readers. She was ninety-four when she died, and her writing covers a period of fifty-three years. During this time, she was active as a writer, wife, mother, property owner, and spokeswoman for the Anglican Church.

W. was self-taught and began writing early in her life. Some of her youthful compositions appeared in her first work, *Miscellaneous Poetry,* published in 1786. Around 1780, she married Thomas West, a yeoman farmer, and moved to Little Bowden where she was to live for the rest of her life and where she raised her three sons. During this time W. published poetry, plays, and her first novel, *The Advantages of Education* (1793), an attempt to capitalize on the craze for novels.

W. hoped to advance her family through her novels. In 1800, she wrote to Bishop Percy, "Though a sentiment inherent in my character will ever preserve me from any degrading meanness, yet a just sense of the wants and claims of a rising family inspires me with an anxious wish to procure these emoluments which have sometimes resulted from literary *efforts.*" Her very popular novels and conduct books for young men and women brought her some measure of celebrity.

W. always presented herself first and foremost as a wife and mother. In a letter published in *Gentleman's Magazine* in January 1802, one of her admirers praised her because she "pays the greatest care and attention to her farm, manages her dairy, and even carries her butter to market." The next month, another of her admirers in rebuttal pointed out that W. was too much of a gentlewoman ever to carry her goods to market. Rather, she supervised the sending of the cheeses to market "while knitting stockings for her husband and sons."

W.'s *A Gossip's Story* (1796) has often been seen as a source or starting point for Jane Austen's *Sense and Sensibility.* Her early novels are narrated by Prudentia Homespun, an elderly spinster whose observations are as much ironic and humorous as instructive. However, in the introduction to *The Refusal* (1810), W., through another narrator, announces the "demise of that inimitable author." W. explained in an 1811 letter to Bishop Percy that "the wings of my gaiety have been clipped, the history of the times I date in, and the moral purposes of my work, preclude jocularity. . . . Mrs. Prudentia Homespun . . . is dead and buried."

At this time, W. turned her attention to historical fiction. Her historical romance *Alicia de Lacey* (1814) begins with a justification not only of developing fictions around historical characters but also of "making past heroes and heroines talk in the language of common life," perhaps setting a direction for Walter Scott's historical fiction.

She outlived her celebrity, her husband, and all her sons. In her later years she suffered from a growing feeling of isolation and described herself as "an old Q in a corner whom the rest of the world has forgotten." The last image of herself that she left is of a lonely woman who saved all the letters from her sons and her friends, "valuable Scripts . . . reserved as bon bons to gratify" her old age, but "failing eyesight" denied her even this enjoyment.

Although W.'s didacticism eventually overwhelmed her

fiction, she explored new issues and fictional forms in her work. She was an early advocate of education for women, and her early works recognized the role that an educated mother could play in a daughter's life. She believed that the past determined the present, and, as a result, her fiction attempted to capture women's lives lived over decades rather than weeks. It is a disappointment that in her fiction these women's lives had to become more circumscribed in order for them to survive.

WORKS: *Miscellaneous Poetry* (1786). *The Humours of Brighthelmstone: A Poem* (1788). *Miscellaneous Poems and a Tragedy* (1791). *The Advantages of Education* (1793). *The Gossip's Story* (1796). *Elegy on Edmund Burke* (1797). *Poems and Plays, Volumes I and II* (1799). *A Tale of the Times* (1799). *Letters To a Young Man* (1801). *The Infidel Father* (1802). *The Sorrows of Selfishness* (1802). *Poems and Plays, Volumes III and IV* (1805). *Letters To a Young Lady* (1806). *The Mother: A Poem in Five Books* (1809). *The Refusal: A Novel* (1810). *The Loyalists: An Historical Novel* (1812). *Select Translations of the Beauties of Massillon* (1812). *Alicia de Lacey: An Historical Romance* (1814). *Scriptural Essays adapted to the Holy Days of the Church of England* (1816). *Ringrove; or Old Fashioned Notions* (1827).

BIBLIOGRAPHY: Butler, M. *Jane Austen and the War of Ideas* (1975). Lloyd, P. *N&Q* (1984). London, A., in *Tradition in Transition*, ed. A. Ribiero (1996). Mayer, V. G. *N&Q* (1982). Moler, K. *Jane Austen's Art of Allusion* (1968). Nelson, B. *KSJ* (1994). Pedley, C. *N&Q* (1989). Spacks, P. M., in *Fetter'd or Free: British Women Novelists, 1670–1815*, ed. M. A. Schofield and C. Macheski (1986). Ty, E. *1650–1850: Ideas, Aesthetics, and Inquiries in the Early Modern Era* (1994).

For articles in reference works, see: *Allibone*. *BDLA*. *CinP*. *Feminist*. *Oxford*. *ToddBWW*. *ToddDBA*.

Other references: *N&Q* (1984). *RES* (1940).

Pamela Lloyd

Rebecca West (pseudonym of Cicily Isabel Fairfield)

BORN: 25 December 1892, London.
DIED: 15 March 1983, London.
DAUGHTER OF: Charles Fairfield and Isabella MacKenzie Fairfield.
MARRIED: Henry Andrews, 1930.
WROTE UNDER: Corinne Andrews; Rebecca West.

By voicing her ideas memorably in prose that could be raucous, elegant, and precise, and by remaining an active writer for more than seventy years, W. earned a unique position in twentieth-century British letters. Working as a novelist, journalist, biographer, historian, and commentator on the morality of her time, W. demonstrated a brilliant fusion of rational analysis and spirited engagement.

W. published under the pseudonym "Rebecca West," chosen for Henrik Ibsen's defiant character in *Rosmersholm*, and she proclaimed herself a radical feminist not only in her political essays but also in her fictional characters and plots, in her biography of St. Augustine, in her historical analyses, and in her literary criticism.

Autobiographical writing by W. conceals as much personal information as it reveals, and she chose to publish only one autobiographical fiction. Since her death, four more have been edited and published. These incomplete revelations have intrigued literary biographers. A disguised self-portrait may be found in a fictional trilogy: *The Fountain Overflows* (1956), *This Real Night* (1985), and *Cousin Rosamund* (1985). In *The Fountain Overflows*, the novel W. chose to publish, her childhood is partially represented in the story of a poor family of three sisters, one brother, and a mother who manages their affairs despite their periodic financial reverses caused by their impractical father; their overflowing love gives them the strength not only to suffer genteel poverty but also to offer shelter and support to others. The unfinished autobiographical novel *Sunflower* (1986) treats a love affair between a younger woman and an older man, a character based on two different lovers of W. Her posthumously published *Family Memories* (1987) adds little information to her own life; it is focused on other members of her family.

W.'s imaginative grasp of abstract theories—whether Hegel's dialectic or Jung's unconscious or the Manichean myth of good and evil—enabled her to create characters and narrative structures embodying those concepts she believed essential to understanding twentieth-century history. That she could command a forceful rhetoric to connect disparate concepts and events is evident in *Black Lamb and Grey Falcon* (1941), as she wryly comments on D'Annunzio's seizure of Fiume: "All this is embittering history for a woman to contemplate. I will believe that the battle of feminism is over, and that the female has reached a position of equality with the male, when I hear that a country has allowed itself to be turned upside-down and led to the brink of war by its passion for a totally bald woman writer." Her satire of individual or cultural imbecility combines ruthlessness and wit.

As a literary critic, W. praised the achievements and deplored the inadequacies of her fellow authors. Her literary judgment in *Henry James* (1916) is both irreverent and astute, for, without idolizing the master of psychological insights, she acknowledges his class-conscious aversion to vulgarity and his limited imaginative grasp of women's characters; hers is the first feminist study of James's fiction. She admired James Joyce's "Marion Bloom, the great mother who . . . lies in a bed yeasty with her warmth and her sweat," and she compared Molly's monologue to the "unified beauty" of Beethoven's Fifth Symphony, but she also noted that Joyce "pushes his pen about noisily and aimlessly as if it were a carpet-sweeper, whose technique is a tin can tied to the tail of the dog of his genius." W. wrote a sensitive, appreciative sketch of D. H. Lawrence but brazenly called his genius eccentric.

As a fiction writer, W. chose to adopt a different pattern with each book, but she always created characters in conflict, wrestling with ideas that symbolize real forces in history. W.'s most radical fiction was a short story, "Indissoluble Marriage," published in the first issue (June 1914) of *Blast* (and reprinted in 1982 in *The Young Rebecca*). W. draws upon Jungian symbolism to explore the sexual politics of a marriage. The dramatic tale, narrated by an unsympathetic husband, depicts his wife's powerful sensuality, evident in her body and her voice, and her self-determined spirit, evident in her advocacy of woman's suffrage. She is indestructible; he nearly drowns. W., affirming the power of female sexuality, undermines the aggressive misogynistic assumptions of Vorticist and Futurist theory.

Her two novels about World War I are unequal in literary quality. *The Return of the Soldier* (1918) imaginatively fleshes out a Freudian interpretation of neurosis, in this case shell shock induced by war. The love triangle contrasts the natural, passionate, lusty, erotic drives with the repressive, materialistic, and tyrannical, death-loving drives, both competing for the psyche of the soldier. The shell-shocked soldier, suffering amnesia, remembers only his prewar lover, a common woman whom his family would never have accepted into their class; he has forgotten his family obligations, his proper, cold wife, and his dutiful participation in the war. W. in her exposition of the story links war's aggression with society's class-consciousness, both exemplary of patriarchal tyranny over the individual. Prompted by the memory of his young son who had died, the soldier regains his memory and returns to his wife and to the war. By contrast with this brilliant fiction, her anonymous fictional memoir, *War Nurse: The True Story of a Woman Who Lived, Loved and Suffered on the Western Front* (1930), ostensibly written by "Corinne Andrews," seems an attempt to earn easy money quickly by competing with the war novels and films of the time.

The Judge (1922) explores the familial triangle of an independent, self-determined woman, her weakling husband, and his domineering tyrannical mother. The power struggle between daughter-in-law and mother-in-law reveals aspects of W.'s rebellion against and respect for her own mother. *Harriet Hume: A London Fantasy* (1929) oddly combines a moral parable with a romantic comedy in an episodic plot that turns on the artistic heroine's ability to read the thoughts of her beloved, an ambitious politician. At the end, the lovers unite, as if two halves of a personality are finally reconciled.

Of the four short novels published under the title *The Harsh Voice* (1935), the most impressive creates a memorable character, Alice Pemberton, who is *The Salt of the Earth.* Alice carefully controls her life, repressing her own and her husband's desires, smothering her family's love for her, and expecting incompetence, carelessness, and inconsiderateness from all around her. As she rubs salt into wounds, she believes herself to be acting sensibly and selflessly in the best interests of her victim. The husband's decision to poison Alice provides a satisfying fictional conclusion.

A partial definition of the happy marriage between female and male power occurs in *The Thinking Reed* (1936) in a dialogue where each spouse admits admiring the other as superior. Isabella, the rational heroine, widowed at the beginning of the novel, rejects an aristocratic French lover because he is a tyrant (she compares him to the Arc de Triomphe, embodying male patriotic glory), then marries a kind-hearted, intuitive Frenchman who has peasant ancestors but who now owns profitable automobile factories. He can behave like an ass, and she can behave like a maenad, but together they are morally superior to both the imbecilic ruling class and the envious, mean-spirited politicians. She saves her husband's career from disaster, but her action destroys their child she is carrying; Isabella and her husband heal their estrangement, but W. clearly signals the loss of their wealth in the stock market crash.

During World War II, W. published a short, propagandistic novel, *"Thou Shalt Not Make Any Graven Images"* (1943), depicting the courage of a Danish actress during the Nazi occupation of Copenhagen. The actress develops from a self-centered coward into a self-aware martyr, who chooses solidarity with victims of Nazi policies knowing that she is sacrificing her life. In this fiction, W. warns her readers that the concentration camps are death camps, a fact disputed by or unknown to other writers at that time.

In *The Birds Fall Down* (1966), W. creates a fiction about expatriate Russians before the 1917 Revolution, pairing a young woman, daughter of an English aristocrat and a Russian emigrée, with a double agent for the tsar and the Revolutionaries. Each character is formed by two antithetical forces at work within: political forces for the double agent, cultural forces for the young woman. The death of the young woman's tsarist grandfather provides the crisis that brings these two characters in contact. The double agent passionately explains to the Russian-English woman Hegel's "theory of the dialectic," combining thesis and contradictory antithesis into a new synthesis; the reader realizes, as the young woman does not, that he loves her. In her eyes, the double agent threatens her life, and she arranges for his assassination.

W.'s fascination with the mind divided against itself, with the formation of nationalist loyalty and the betrayal of that loyalty, may also be seen in her essays on the Nuremberg trials reprinted in *A Train of Powder* (1955) and her essays on the trial of a British fascist, on the Profumo affair, and on other "sordid and undignified" crimes: *The Meaning of Treason* (1947) and *The New Meaning of Treason* (1964).

The most famous of W.'s books is her *Black Lamb and Grey Falcon,* a two-volume narrative based on her travels in Yugoslavia in 1937 and 1938. She mixes travelogue, history, fiction, autobiography, and political analysis in a compelling, entertaining, informative work that explains the cultural differences among the peoples, narrates a history of violent insurrection against tyranny, and exposes the origins of a passionate, cruel nationalism. She wrote down her evaluation of Yugoslavian, Austrian, and German motives, "convinced of the inevitability of the second Anglo-German war." Of all her works, *Black Lamb and Grey Falcon* best exemplifies her intellectual range, her ability to move and inform, her imaginative grasp of philosophical, political, and historical movements, her brilliant rhetorical style, and her self-assured judgment.

WORKS: *Henry James* (1916). *The Return of the Soldier* (1918; 1987). *The Judge* (1922). *The Strange Necessity* (1928). *Harriet Hume: A London Fantasy* (1929). (as Corinne Andrews) *War Nurse: The True Story of A Woman Who Lived, Loved and Suffered on the Western Front* (1930). *D. H. Lawrence: An Elegy* (1930). *A Letter to a Grandfather* (1930). *Ending in Earnest: A Literary Log* (1931). *St. Augustine* (1933). *The Harsh Voice: Four Short Novels* (1935). *The Thinking Reed* (1936).

Black Lamb and Grey Falcon: A Journey through Yugoslavia (1941). *"Thou Shalt Not Make Any Graven Images,"* in *The Ten Commandments: Ten Short Novels of Hitler's War against the Moral Code,* ed. A. L. Robinson (1943). *The Meaning of Treason* (1947). *A Train of Powder* (1955). *The Fountain Overflows* (1956). *The Court and the Castle* (1957). *The New Meaning of Treason* (1964; in the U.K. as *The Meaning of Treason,* rev. ed., 1965). *The Birds Fall Down* (1966). *1900* (1981). *The Young Rebecca: Writings of Rebecca West, 1911–1917,* ed. J. Marcus (1982). *This Real Night* (1984). *Cousin Rosamund* (1985). *Sunflower* (1986). *Family Memories,* ed. F. Evans (1987).

BIBLIOGRAPHY: Deakin, M. *Rebecca West* (1980). Glendinning, V. *Rebecca West: A Life* (1987). Hutchinson, G. *A Preliminary List of the Writings of Rebecca West, 1912–1951* (1957). Hynes, S., in *Rebecca West: A Celebration,* ed. S. Hynes (1977). Orel, H. *The Literary Achievement of Rebecca West* (1986). Packer, J. G. *Rebecca West: An Annotated Bibliography* (1991). Ray, G. *H. G. Wells and Rebecca West* (1974). Rollyson, C. *Rebecca West: A Life* (1995). Weldon, F. *Rebecca West* (1986). Wolfe, P. *Rebecca West: Artist and Thinker* (1971).

For articles in reference works, see: *Bloomsbury. CA. CLC. CN. DLB. MBL. TCA* and *SUP.*

Other references: Adcock, St. J. *Bookman* (September 1958). Chamberlain, L. *ContempR* (1986). Colquitt, C. *SoAR* (1986). Davies, A. P. *New Republic* (8 June 1953). Davis, H. *Canadian Forum* (June 1931). Dinnage, R. *NYRB* (12 August 1982). Ellmann, M. *Atlantic* (December 1966). Enright, D. J. *New Statesman* (4 November 1966). Feld, R. C. *NYTBR* (11 November 1923). Ferguson, M. *MinnR* (1980). Haley, W. *ASch* (Winter 1978). Halper, N. *PR* (1949). Kalb, B. *Saturday Review* (19 March 1955). Kobler, T. S. *Crit* (1971). Marcus, J., in *Women Writers and the City: Essays in Feminist Literary Criticism,* ed. S. M. Squier (1984). Panter-Downes, M. *New Yorker* (3 December 1977). Pritchett, V. S. *New Yorker* (3 December 1966, 19 July 1982). Rainer, D. *Commonweal* (10 May 1968). Scott, B. K.*TCL* (1991). Stetz, M. *ArQ* (1987). Stetz, M. *TSWL* (1989). Thompson, C. P. *New York Herald-Tribune Magazine* (7 February 1934). Walpole, H. *Bookman* (May 1925). Webster, H. C. *Saturday Review* (8 December 1956).

Judith L. Johnston

Westmacott, Mary: See *Christie, Agatha*

Elizabeth Jane Weston

BORN: 2 November 1581/2 (?), Chipping Norton, Oxon.
DIED: 23 November 1612, Prague, Bohemia.
DAUGHTER OF: John Weston and Jane Cooper Weston.
MARRIED: Johannes Leo, 1603.

At the beginning of the seventeenth century, the Anglo-Latin poet W. enjoyed a fame on the Continent unequalled by any other English writer who was not (like Philip Sidney or Thomas More) of other than purely literary interest. Her presentation of herself as "Virgo Angla"—an orphaned English maiden seeking patronage at the court of Rudolph II—elicited extravagant praise from neo-Latin poets throughout Europe, and she received a laurel wreath from Paul Melissus of Heidelberg. Poems and letters by and to her were collected in two editions by her principal patron, Georg Martinus von Baldhoven; numerous other poems exist in occasional pamphlets and in the collections of her correspondents.

Czech scholars recognized as early as 1928 that W.'s presence in Prague, and her dire personal straits, were owed to the fact that she was the stepdaughter of Rudolph's alchemist, Edward Kelley, who had married the recently widowed Jane Cooper Weston in 1582 before leaving England for Bohemia. His subsequent disgrace and death in prison in 1597 left his family penniless and reliant on the support of a few aristocratic friends. W.'s skill in Latin verse, especially her mastery of personalized laments and begging poems in elegiac distichs, enabled her to define a role in the neo-Latin republic of letters as a helpless virgin whose support by the emperor and his subordinates would confirm their own positions in the classic hierarchy of imperial patronage. Her identity as an English virgin named Elizabeth probably helped as well to suggest that she could serve as an unofficial ambassador from distant Britain: Her admirers repeatedly allude to her nobility as a "Weston," when in effect any such title she might possess derived from the knighthood Rudolph had granted her stepfather in happier times.

Although her marriage in 1603 to a German jurist, Johannes Leo, to whom she would bear seven children over the next nine years, put an end to her career as English maiden and to her need to write appeals for support, she continued to write poetry until her death, including appeals to King James I of England and to Rudolph's successor, the Emperor Matthias. Nevertheless, Baldhoven published an expanded edition of her writings around 1607 as "Parthenica," virginal works. A manuscript poem by her in two copies of the volume expresses her dissatisfaction with this exclusive focus on her as a maiden as well as with other forms of editorial manipulation; she expresses a hope for a future edition that will display her correctly and fully, but this was never realized.

WORKS: *Poemata* (1602). *Parthenicon,* ed. G. M. von Baldoven (c. 1607–10). Individual poems listed in Truhlar, A., et al., ed. *Enchiridion. . .* (1966–82), rev. ed., ed. and trans. D. Cheney and B. Hosington (forthcoming).

BIBLIOGRAPHY: Bassnett, S. *CahiersE* (1990). Binns, J. W. *Intellectual Culture in Elizabethan and Jacobean England* (1990).

For articles in reference works, see: *Ballard. Bell. DLB. DNB. Oxford.*

Donald Cheney

Anne Lee Wharton

BORN: June 1659, Spelsbury. Oxfordshire.
DIED: 29 October 1685, Adderbury, Oxfordshire.
DAUGHTER OF: Sir Henry Lee and Anne Danvers Lee.
MARRIED: Thomas Wharton, 1673.

While only one of her poems appeared in print duing her lifetime, W. was among the most highly praised women poets of the Restoration. In the years immediately following her death, two songs (one is in three corrupt versions), a biblical paraphrase of "The Lamentations of Jeremiah," a translation of the Ovidian epistle "Penelope to Ulysses," and a handful of occasional poems appeared, scattered through poetic miscellanies. Several of her poems remained in manuscript; most of her poetry has probably been lost. W. herself has been systematically misrepresented as an elderly, pious, and conventional poet when, in fact, she died at the age of twenty-six, and the most important influence in her life was her uncle, the notorious libertine poet, John Wilmot, Earl of Rochester.

Orphaned only days after her birth, W. was co-heiress with her sister (John Dryden's "Eleanora") to the extensive and disputed estates of their grandfather, Sir John Danvers, and their great uncle, Henry, Earl of Danby. She was raised by her grandmother, Anne St. John Lee Wilmot, Countess of Rochester and mother of John, Earl of Rochester. W. spent her childhood at Ditchley and Adderbury in Oxfordshire and at court at Whitehall, where her grandfather was Groom of the Stole to the Duchess of York. In 1673, when W. was fourteen, a marriage with Thomas Wharton—twenty-six-year-old son of the Puritan Lord Philip Wharton, an established rake, and a future Whig leader—was quickly and quietly arranged. A month before the complex marriage settlement was signed, another suitor, John Arundel, challenged Wharton to a duel, wounding him, then yielding him "his life and Mistresse too since he had courage to fight for her." Despite objections from the king, W.'s guardians succeeded in carrying through the marriage, though Lord Wharton had to mortgage the futures of his younger sons in the hope of gaining control of W.'s fortune. Wharton and his young wife went to live at Winchendon in Buckinghamshire, and while he acquired a reputation as a horseman, swordsman, and promising young politician, she maintained friendships with the wives and daughters of courtiers, among them Lady Anne Coke and Dorothy Mason, whose reputations were bandied about by satirists. Within a year of the wedding, the clergy reported to Lord Wharton that "Religion is gone from Winchingdon . . . they have brought the court into the country."

W. probably composed her songs, her classical paraphrases of "Penelope to Ulysses" and "Dido to Aeneas," and her play "Love's Martyr," about Ovid's love for the princess Julia, during the first years of her childless marriage. In 1680, after a spectacular deathbed repentance of his profligate life, Rochester died, and she mourned his death in her most celebrated poem "An Elegy on the Earl of Rochester." At the same time, W.'s own health was deteriorating: she suffered serious attacks in 1678 and 1680, and in March 1681 her husband took her to Paris for medical treatment. In Paris, W. wrote affectionate, mostly unanswered, letters to Wharton, and a poem, "On the Storm between Gravesend and Dieppe," in which she looked forward to death as a release from her personal storm. W. returned to England in July 1681, bringing with her her verse paraphrase of the "Lamentations of Jeremiah," which she sent to the nonconformist clergyman, Samuel Clark. He replied, "I am chiefly pleas'd with ye Subject you have chosen . . . which will turn to better account & afford more comfortable reflections at a dying hour, than conversing with what belong only to, or is fit for ye Theatre."

Within a few months of her return, both Rochester's widow and his son were dead. W. mourned the young heir's death in "Elegie on Charles Earle of Rochester"; in "Thoughts occasioned by her retirement in the countrey," she resigned herself to a life of increasing pain without the surety of heaven. She was in London in the summer of 1682 and met Bishop Gilbert Burnet, who had orchestrated not only the conversion of Rochester but also the publicity surrounding it. When she returned to Winchendon in July, Burnet began writing letters to W., determined to perform the same service for her. When W. remained unconvinced by his exhortations to religion, he turned literary critic, correcting the poems she sent him and circulating them among the friends who met at Catherine Jones's (Lady Ranelagh) house in London. W.'s biblical paraphrases earned poetic praise from Edmund Waller and William Atwood, members of the circle, and W. responded to them in kind. The correspondence with Burnet ended in January 1683 after he compounded his error of relaying the gossip that she was "upon parting with Mr. Wharton" with rapturous praise of the Earl of Mulgrave's "Essay Upon Poetry," a poem that attacked her uncle Rochester.

In the last years of her life, W. was committed to preserving Rochester's reputation as a poet. In "To Mrs. Behn on what she Writ of the Earl of Rochester," she thanked Aphra Behn for her continuing defenses of Rochester. She may also have helped Behn and Rochester's friends Robert Wolseley and John Grubham Howe revive his tragedy *Valentinian* in 1684. W.'s poem on Wolseley's "Preface" to the printed version of *Valentinian* encourages him to "clear the Injur'd and Instruct the Town." Behn, Howe, and Wolseley wrote poems to W., all consoling her for the loss of her uncle, and Wolseley's in particular praised her as Rochester's "sole Executrix in Wit."

In May 1685, with her fortune finally settled, W. signed a paper that broke the entail upon her property and made a deed of gift of her entire fortune to her neglectful and unfaithful husband. A bequest of £3,000 to Rochester's bastard daughter was charged against the estate, but with the Lees effectively disinherited, Thomas Wharton was at last given the means of financing his political career. On 15 August 1685, W. left Winchendon for Adderbury where Rochester had died and where, two months later, unrepentant and torn by "convulsions" apparently caused by "the pox," she too died. She was buried at Upper Winchedon ten days later in a funeral noted only for its meanness.

Only two dozen of W.'s poems can be identified, and of those only eighteen were printed in the years following her death. Others remained in manuscript collections belonging to the Waller family and the Earls of Leicester. Among W.'s editors were some of the most influential poets of the era: Nahum Tate, John Dryden, and Aphra Behn. An entry in the Stationers' Register for February 1686 is a caveat preventing anyone from entering a book containing her play "Love's Martyr and other Poems." Despite evidence that much of what she wrote was either edited or suppressed, W.'s surviving poetry bears the marks of a conscientious poet who, like her uncle and many of her class, experimented with a range of forms, from spiritual exercise to heroic tragedy. The most moving of her poems are autobiographical, many of them bitterly melancholy and angry: In lines omitted from the first publication of "Elegy on the Earl of Rochester," she tells how she taught her "Infant Muse . . . all Desire and all Despair." The themes of her poetry—disillusionment with love and society, loneliness, illness, and the very tedium of life—are Rochester's, but in the dignified poise of her presentations she lacks the light and seemingly easy grace that have made his poems accessible for so many generations.

WORKS: Poems published in *Poems by Several Hands, and on Several Occasions. Collected by N. Tate* (1685). *Vinculum Societatis* (1687). *The Idea of Christian Love* (1688). *Lycidus: Or the Lover in Fashion* (1688). *Miscellany Poems on Several Occasions* (1692). *The Gentleman's Journal: Or the Monthly Miscellany* (July 1692). *A Collection of Poems, by Several Hands: Most of them Written by Persons of Eminent Quality* (1693). *The Temple of Death* (1695, 1701, 1702, 1716). *Examen Miscellaneum* (1702). *Ovid's Epistles, Translated by Several Hands* (1712, 1716, 1725). *Whartoniana, or Miscellanies in Verse and Prose by the Wharton Family and Several Other Persons of Distinction* (1727, 1731, 1740). *The Gentleman's Magazine* (June 1815). *The Surviving Works of Anne Wharton*, ed. G. Greer and S. Hastings (1995).

BIBLIOGRAPHY: *The General Dictionary* (1741). Gould, R. *A Funeral Eclogue to the Pious Memory of the Incomparable Mrs. Wharton* (1685). *Kissing the Rod: An Anthology of Seventeenth-Century Women's Verse*, ed. G. Greer et al. (1988). Greer, G. *The Slipshod Sybils* (1995). *Rochester: The Critical Heritage*, ed. D. Farley-Hills (1972). Malcolm, J. P., ed. *Letters of the Reverend James Granger* (1805). [Steele, R.] *Memoirs of the Most Noble Thomas Late Marquess of Wharton* (1715). Verney, F. P. and M. M. Verney. *Memoirs of the Verney Family* (1892). Waller, E. *The Poems of Edmund Waller*, ed. G. Thorn Dury (1893). Walpole, H., in *A Catalog of the Royal and Noble Authors*, ed. T. Park (1806).

For articles in reference works, see: *Bell. Bloomsbury. DNB. Specimens of British Poetesses*, ed. A. Dyce (1825). *Europa. Feminist. Rowton. The Cavalier Poets*, ed. R. Skelton (1970). *ToddDBA*. White, G. *The Complete Peerage* (1959).

Susan Hastings

Anne Wheathill

FLOURISHED: late sixteenth century.

What little is known about W. derives from the single publication attributed to her, a book of prayers and meditations entitled *A handfull of holesome (though homelie) hearbs*. She presumably flourished around the date of publication (1584), and the introductory material of the volume portrays her as an unmarried Protestant gentlewoman. W.'s Protestantism manifests itself throughout the volume, especially in her emphasis on the redemptive power of faith; her religious attitudes are not sufficiently pronounced to define with confidence her particular kind of Protestantism, however.

A handfull belongs to the history of the English Reformers' efforts to revise the Roman Catholic devotional books, specifically the primers and the *Books of Hours*, to satisfy the devotional needs of a Protestant middle class. W.'s devotions, like most other Protestant books of private devotion, has a more informal structure than the Roman Catholic primers (it is not, for example, organized around the Hours of the Blessed Virgin Mary); her prayers and meditations are largely constructed as pastiches of prayers scattered throughout the Old and New Testaments. There is a possible suggestion in the introductory material (notable in W.'s dedication of her work "To all Ladies, Gentlewomen, and others . . .") that she may have intended her work largely for a female audience, but there is little, if anything, in the work itself to suggest gender as a dominant concern.

A handfull does not seem to have found a large audience in its time (it had only one edition), and it is almost unknown now, but it merits attention. Its prose, immersed as it is in the cadences of the prose of translators of the Bible and especially of the Psalms, can rise to genuine excellence; at the very least, it is an important document for any examination of the role women played in the early development of English prose.

WORKS: *A handfull of holesome (though homelie) hearbs, gathered out of the goodlie garden of Gods most holie word; for the common benefit and comfortable exercise of all such as are deuoutlie disposed* (1584).

BIBLIOGRAPHY: Beilin, E. V. *Redeeming Eve: Women Writers of the English Renaissance* (1987). Cullen, P., intro. to *A handfull of holesome (though homelie) hearbs . . .*, in *The Early Modern Englishwoman: A Facsimile Library of Essential Works*, Part One, Vol. 9 (1996). Warnicke, R. M. *Women of the English Renaissance and Reformation* (1983).

For articles in reference works, see: *Bell. Bloomsbury*.

Patrick Cullen

Anna Doyle Wheeler

BORN: 1785, Clonbeg Parish, County Tipperary, Ireland.
DIED: 7 May 1848, London.
DAUGHTER OF: Archdeacon Doyle and Anna Dunbar Doyle.
MARRIED: Francis Massy Wheeler, 1800.

Born to an Anglican family of Clonbeg Parish in Tipperary, W. was a beautiful and headstrong youngest daughter. Her father, a mid-level Church of Ireland cleric, died when she was not yet two years old. Her godfather was the great Irish nationalist, Henry Grattan, but she was brought up mostly by her mother's family. When she was only fifteen, W. was noticed at the races by nineteen-year-old Francis Massy Wheeler, a young inheritor of his family's estate at Ballywire. Wheeler proposed to her at a ball. Over family objections, she married Wheeler the same year. In twelve years, she bore six children, the first four of whom were girls. Only Henrietta and Rosina (later the novelist Rosina Bulwer-Lytton) survived infancy. The marriage became unbearable, and W. took refuge from her inebriated husband by reading Mary Wollstonecraft and the French *philosophes*.

Finally, W. was able to arrange to escape. In August 1812, she fled with her children, her sister, and her brother to the Isle of Guernsey, where her uncle Sir John Doyle was governor. Francis made no attempt to persuade her to return but refused her any allowance for the rest of his life; predictably, he left her no maintenance in his will when he died in 1820.

After a peripatetic decade with moves to London, Caen, Dublin, and Paris, W. settled in London. She had met both Jeremy Bentham and Charles Fourier in Paris and had worked with a Saint-Simonian group in Caen. She always claimed that Fourier's system was essentially the same as those of Robert Owen and the Saint-Simonians. In all three, cooperation is central, men and women are entitled to equal education and employment opportunities, and marriage and divorce laws are changed to abolish the double standard and to give women equal rights. For the rest of her life, she attempted to bring these three versions of socialism into union. To that end, she arranged for Fourier to meet Robert Owen, introduced Saint-Simonian missionaries to Owenites in England, translated Fourieriat and Saint-Simonian articles for the Owenite press, sent young people to France with letters of introduction to Fourier, and persuaded Owenites in England that Saint-Simonian doctrines were similar to theirs. W. was connected to the Saint-Simonian women's journal, *Tribune des Femmes,* and she translated articles for the Owenite newspaper, *The Crisis.* She became a well-known lecturer at a time when women were not often allowed to speak to mixed-sex groups.

Through her friendship with Jeremy Bentham, she met William Thompson, whose socialist economic theory so impressed Robert Owen. Thompson, also Anglo-Irish (a large landowner from Cork), formed a close relationship with W. Together, they wrote *The Appeal of One Half the Human Race, Women, Against the Pretensions of the Other Half, Men, to Restrain Them in Political and Thence in Civil and Domestic Slavery* (1825) as a reply to James Mill's essay on government in the *Encyclopaedia Britannica.* Mill, in less than a sentence, had dismissed women's rights as unnecessary, since their interests were represented or "covered" by their husbands or fathers.

The Appeal of One Half the Human Race, Women . . . bears only Thompson's name, but the long introductory letter makes the fact of co-authorship clear. It begins with the proposition that a social system cannot provide for the greatest happiness for the greatest number if one-half that number is removed from consideration. In Part II, the first question asks whether there is indeed an identity of interest between women and men: single women without fathers, adult daughters living in fathers' houses, and wives. As one might expect, the essay especially critiques marriage: "All women, and particularly women living with men in marriage . . . having been reduced . . . to a state of helplessness, slavery . . . and privations, . . . are more in *need* of political rights than any other portion of human beings."

The essay as a whole is an unequivocal appeal for votes for women, the first to be cogently argued (Wollstonecraft had only hinted at it). The conclusion is a long "Address to Women" in which Thompson and W. exhort women to awaken to their degraded state and join with a system of cooperation in intentional community such as that espoused by Owen's followers.

W. soon became a well-known lecturer on women's rights and the various forms of the inoperative movement. A famous address in 1829 at Finsbury Square lecture chapel was directed particularly to women. Entitling it "Rights of Women," she set out to demolish the main arguments given by men to justify their claim of superiority over women.

She called on women to press for "a sound and liberal education" for their daughters, not being content to wait for others. Women must, she said, form groups of like-minded people, "the ultimate object of which will be to obtain, by all legal means, the removal of the disabilities of women, and the introduction of a national system of *equal education* for the Infants of both sexes." This call for an *organization* of women, demanding equal education and equal property and political rights, marks W. as one of the earliest and most radical of feminists.

When Thompson died in 1833, he assigned an annual annuity of £100 to W.; most of the rest of his estate he willed to the Owenite cooperative movement for the building of an intentional community. The will, however, was contested by his relatives on the grounds that Thompson was insane, and W. never received the money. She was invalided for her last years but lived to hear of the beginning of the 1848 Revolution in Paris.

WORKS: (with W. Thompson) *The Appeal of One Half the Human Race, Women, Against the Pretensions of the Other Half, Men, to Restrain Them in Political and Thence in Civil and Domestic Slavery* (1825). *Rights of Women,* in *The British Co-operator* (1830). (trans.) "Appel aux femmes," by Jeanne-Victoire [pseud.], in *The Crisis* (1833). (trans.) "The Women of the Future," in *The Crisis* (1833).

BIBLIOGRAPHY: Dooley, D. *Equality in Continuity: Sexual Equality in the Writings of William Thompson and Anna Doyle Wheeler* (1996). McFadden, M. *Hypatia* (1989). Pankhurst, R.K.P. *Political Quarterly* (1954).

For articles in reference works, see: *Biographical Dictionary of Modern British Radicals* (1979). Hamilton, S., in *British Reform Writers, 1789–1892,* ed. G. Kelly and E. Applegate (1996).

Other references: Burke, S. *Studies in Labor History* (1976). Spender, D. *Women of Ideas* (1982). Stenton, D. *The English Woman in History* (1957). Taylor, B. *Eve and the New Jerusalem* (1983).

Margaret McFadden

Antonia White

BORN: 31 March 1899, London.
DIED: 10 April 1980, London.
DAUGHTER OF: Cecil George Botting and Christine Julia White Botting.

MARRIED: 1921; 1929; H. Tom Hopkinson, 1930 (first two marriages annulled; husbands' names unknown).

Though perhaps best known as a translator from the French of works by Colette and others, W. also wrote a number of well-received novels. Her central concern in much of her fiction is Roman Catholicism, to which faith she was twice converted: first at the age of seven, when her father converted and brought her mother and W. with him, and later during World War II, after a number of lapsed years. Her first novel, *Frost in May* (1933), closely parallels her own experiences as a child. She was a boarding student at a convent school but never felt wholly accepted because she was, as she says, a "middle-class convert among aristocratic 'born' Catholics." When she was fifteen, she planned to write a novel, thinking its emphasis on Catholicism would appeal to her father. With only five chapters written and with forbidden behavior hinted at, the manuscript was confiscated by the nuns and W. was expelled. W.'s sense of guilt, occasioned by her father's shock, made it impossible for her to write fiction for almost twenty years.

After completing her schooling, W. attended the Royal Academy of Dramatic Art (1919–20) and acted for a year with a touring company. She also worked as a governess, a teacher at a boys' school, and a civil servant. Finally, she began writing again, this time as a freelance magazine and advertising copywriter. In her thirties, she was variously a theater critic, fashion editor, copywriter for an advertising agency, and teacher at an acting studio; when World War II started, she worked first for the BBC and then for British intelligence in the French section of the British Foreign Office.

W.'s first two marriages were annulled and her third ended in divorce. Following a breakdown during the first (described in *Beyond the Glass*, 1954), she spent nine months in an asylum. During her third marriage, to Tom Hopkinson, also a journalist, she discovered the partial manuscript of her schoolgirl novel and gradually completed it; between 1933, when *Frost in May* was published, and 1950, W. wrote no novels, and a gap of fifteen years exists between the beginning and ending of *The Lost Traveller* (1950).

W. had recurrent spells of mental illness and breakdown, ultimately recovering, she says, through a "remarkably successful" Freudian analysis. Her reconversion to Catholicism in 1940 is reflected in *The Hound and the Falcon* (1965), a series of letters written to a fellow Roman Catholic. Following the war, she translated two or three works a year from the French and found that she could again write fiction; her initial endeavor was the "Clara Batchelor" trilogy—*The Lost Traveller, The Sugar House* (1952), and *Beyond the Glass*—based on her life after the convent school. Even though the heroine's name is changed from Nanda Grey in *Frost in May*, the trilogy is clearly a sequel to W.'s first book.

Hence W.'s major writing, four novels, is centered on her life from childhood to her mid-twenties. The central focus in *Frost in May* is on W.'s attempt to answer such questions as why people become Catholic and how one can subjugate one's will to God's. The trilogy, by contrast, explores successively W.'s traumatic childhood, her marital failures, and her mental illness. Samuel Hynes has noted that these four novels "came out of urgent psychic needs rather than out of a strict creative impulse," out of a need to "testify" so as to free herself from the past.

Frost in May covers W.'s heroine's life from the age of nine through age thirteen and is, as Elizabeth Bowen has noted, characterized by an objective quality that allows all events, whether emotionally disturbing ones or the mundane activities of school, to be given relatively similar emphasis. The girls learn that every action in the closed atmosphere of the convent school fits into a structured belief system that they only slowly accept as the standard by which they must live. Though that system equates individual achievement with pride, as with Nanda's writing or with another girl's acting in a school play, the girls nonetheless strive to develop their talents, personalities, values, and friendships.

In *The Lost Traveller,* adolescence with all its bewildering traumas is explored. Clara's confusion about sex and love receives special attention: Her parents hold opposing viewpoints about such volatile matters, and although Clara deeply loves her father, it is her mother who understands Clara's approaching womanhood. When Clara considers marriage, it is her mother, not her religious and strict father, who can best advise her. *The Sugar House* tells of Clara's unfortunate relationship with an actor and an unhappy marriage to the man she considered marrying in the previous novel; Clara and her alcoholic husband gradually grow apart and the marriage ends. *Beyond the Glass,* generally acknowledged as the best of the three, focuses on a more "perfect" match, as Clara and a young officer, Richard, communicate telepathically; even so, Clara suffers a breakdown, with her psychic trauma offered in the barest but most vivid terms. Clara's Catholicism, like W.'s, underlies her visions, perceptions, memory lapses, fears, and reactions, and her recovery is simply stated.

Novel writing was continually a problem for W., as she seemed unable to separate life from art. Her Catholicism was undoubtedly the single greatest influence on her work, as her work is often therapeutic. W. once observed that "'Creative joy' is something I haven't felt since I was fourteen and don't expect to feel again," suggesting that her attempts to purge herself of her youthful traumas through writing were compulsive, not liberating. Yet her books remain fascinating accounts of the impact of religious obsession on a woman in a constant but unsuccessful struggle to free herself from that obsession.

WORKS: *Frost in May* (1933). *Three in a Room* (1947). (trans.) *A Woman's Life,* by G. de Maupassant (1949). *The Lost Traveller* (1950). *The Sugar House* (1952). (trans.) *A Pathway to Heaven,* by H. Bordeaux (1952). (trans.) *Reflections on Life,* by A. Carrel (1952). (trans.) *Gigi* and *The Cat,* by Colette (former work trans. by R. Senhouse, latter by W.) (1953). (trans.) *A Sea of Troubles,* by M. Duras (1953). *Beyond the Glass* (1954). *Strangers* (1954). (trans.) *A German Officer,* by S. Groussard (1955). (trans.) *The Wind Bloweth Where It Listeth,* by P. A. Lesort (1955). (trans.) *Claudine at School,* by Colette (1956). (trans.) *I Am Fifteen and I Do Not Want to Die,* by C. Arnothy (1956). (trans.) *God Is Late,* by C. Arnothy (1957). *Minka and Curdy* (1957). (trans.) *The Branding Iron,* by P. A. Lesort (1958). (trans.) *Clau-*

dine in Paris, by Colette (1958). (trans.) *It Is Not So Easy to Live*, by C. Arnothy (1958). (trans.) *The Stories of Colette* (1958). (trans.) *The Swing*, by F. Rouget (1958). (trans.) *Thou Shalt Love*, by J. M. Langlois-Berthelot (1958). (trans.) *The Charlatan*, by C. Arnothy (1959). (trans.) *Children in Love*, by C. France (1959). (trans.) *I Will Not Serve*, by E. Mahyere (1959). (trans.) *The Tortoises*, by L. Masson (1959). (trans.) *Claudine Mamed*, by Colette (1960). (trans.) *Till the Shadow Passes*, by J. Storm (1960). (trans.) *The Serpent's Bite*, by C. Arnothy (1961). (trans.) *Claudine and Annie*, by Colette (1962). (trans.) *The Trial of Charles de Gaulle*, by A. Fabre-Luce (1963). (trans.) *Advocate of the Isle* by L. Masson (1963). (trans.) *The Captive Cardinal*, by C. Arnothy (1964). (trans.) *St. Michel and the Dragon*, by P. Laulliette (1964). (trans.) *The Shackle*, by Colette (1964). *The Hound and the Falcon: The Story of a Reconversion to the Catholic Faith* (1965). (trans.) *The Candle*, by T. de Sainte Phalle (1968). (trans.) *The Innocent Libertine*, by Colette (1968). *Living with Minka and Curdy: A Marmalade Cat and His Siamese Wife* (1970). (trans.) *Memoirs of the Chevalier d'Eon*, by F. Gaillardet (1970). (trans.) *The Glass Cage*, by G. Simenon (1973). (trans.) *The Novels of Smollett*, by P.-G. Bouce (1975). (trans.) *The Complete Claudine*, by Colette (1976). (trans.) *The History of Charles XII, King of Sweden*, by Voltaire (1976). (trans., with others) *The Collected Stories of Colette*, ed. R. Phelps (1983). *As Once in May: The Early Autobiography of Antonia White and Other Writings*, ed. S. Chitty (1984). *Diaries, 1926–1957*, ed. S. Chitty (1992–).

BIBLIOGRAPHY: Beusen, J. *L&T* (1993). Bowen, E., intro. to *Frost in May* (1948). Callil, C., intro. to Virago rpt. of *The Lost Traveller, The Sugar House*, and *Beyond the Glass* (1979). Flood, J. A. *Crit* (1983). Hynes, S. *TLS* (3 July 1969). O'Mara, P. F. *Cithara* (1988). Palmer, P., in *Feminist Criticism: Theory and Practice*, ed. S. Sellers, et al. (1991). Rose, E. C. *LIT* (1991).

For articles in reference works, see: *BCathA. Bloomsbury. CA. Cambridge. CN. Feminist. Oxford. ToddBWW. WA.*

Other references: *Books and Bookmen* (January 1984). *Crit* (Spring 1983). *Economist* (17 December 1983). *Harper's* (April 1981, December 1982). *LonT* (31 August 1991, 7 September 1991, 13 June 1992). *LRB* (26 September 1991). *New Statesman* (27 April 1984). *Newsweek* (26 January 1981). *NYTBR* (5 October 1980, 28 June 1992). *Observer* (23 July 1978). *TES* (23 January 1981, 7 May 1982, 25 November 1983). *Time* (13 July 1981). *VV* (17 May 1983).

Paul Schlueter

White, Babington: See *Braddon (Maxwell), Mary Elizabeth*

Isabella Whitney

FLOURISHED: 1567–73.

While increasing critical attention has been paid to W. for her poetry, especially her "Wyll and Testament," little definite biographical information remains. By connecting names and initials in W.'s verse with names in Geoffrey Whitney's will, R. J. Fehrenbach has identified W. as the sister of Whitney, author of *A Choice of Emblems* (1586). From her relationship with Geoffrey Whitney, named for his father, it follows that her father was also named Geoffrey Whitney and that she was raised near Coole Pilate in Cheshire, although her "Wyll and Testament" describes her as "bred" in London, and mentions that at one time her parents had lived in Smithfield. Apparently, she spent her youth in service, perhaps as a gentlewoman attendant in London, for in *A Sweet Nosegay* (1573) she refers to herself as out of service ("servicelesse") and expresses her respect for "a vertuous Ladye . . . / The losse I had of service hers, / I languish for it still." This event, which caused her to be "weake in Purse," seems to have precipitated the unwilling departure from London described in her "Wyll and Testament," the concluding poem of *A Sweet Nosegay*. Since W. was not mentioned by her maiden name in her brother's will in 1600, she may have died by that date, or she may have been mentioned by a married name, either Eldershae or Evans.

W.'s first work, *The Copie of a Letter* (1567 ?), consists of two of her verse letters, one to "her unconstant Lover" now engaged to another woman, and the other to "al yong Gentilwomen: And to al other Maids being in Love." These were then joined to two letters by male writers in similar circumstances, the first by W. G. to his unconstant mistress and the second by R. W. to young men, warning them against the "fained Fidelytie of unconstant Maydens." W.'s first poem expresses her continued desire to wed her lover, her disappointment in his falsehood, her hope that his new love may prove as chaste as she, and finally her good wishes for his contentment and wealth. Her second letter advises young maidens to test their suitors before trusting them. Both letters reread classical literature from her own perspective as a jilted maiden; the first presents epic heroes such as Aeneas and Jason as unfaithful lovers, and the second exposes deceitful strategies recommended to male suitors in Ovid's *Art of Love*.

A Sweet Nosegay versifies and occasionally expands 110 *sententiae* from Seneca as translated in Hugh Plat's *Floures of Philosophie* (1572). This section is followed by "Certain familiar Epistles and friendly Letters by the Auctor: with Replies," for the most part to and from family members. The work concludes with her "Wyll and Testament," a rich and witty poem that figuratively appoints London as her executor of all she possesses of London in her imagination: its many commodities, its streets, its people, and its buildings. W.'s "Wyll and Testament" is simultaneously a will and a survey mapping this urban world with lively detail. Her request to London for a shrouding sheet continues the preoccupation with illness characterizing this "nosegay" of poetic flowers offered to prevent or to cure readers' spiritual or emotional disease.

W.'s verse is particularly significant because of the paucity of extant poetry written by women from the middle class towards the middle of the sixteenth century. Her ready use of classical allusions, her representation of her own reading of various texts, and her fluency of writing all demonstrate access to some form of education by a woman who was in service, probably as a gentlewoman attendant.

The social embeddedness of her verse letters suggests the formative presence of a network of writers exchanging work with each other. W's poetry reveals her mastery of the mid-century verse style characterized by regular fourteeners and earnest morality. Most discussed, however, is the *persona* W. creates for herself in her poetry: confident, sensible, and able to express desire, anger, and longing without compromising her level and self-contained tone.

WORKS: *The Copie of a Letter* (1567 ?). *A Sweet Nosegay* (1573). Both in *The Floures of Philosophy (1572) by Hugh Plat and A Sweet Nosegay (1573) and The copie of a Letter (1567) by Isabella Whitney,* ed. R. Panofsky (1982). Travitsky, B. *ELR* (1980). *Paradise of Women,* ed. B. Travitsky (1981). (R. J. Fehrenbach argues that W. may also have contributed anonymous verses to the poetic miscellanies *A Gorgeous Gallery of Gallant Inventions* [1578] and *A Handful of Pleasant Delights* [1566?; 1584]).

BIBLIOGRAPHY: Beilin, E. *Redeeming Eve: Women Writers of the English Renaissance* (1987). Beilin, E. *MLQ* (1990). Fehrenbach, R. J. *CahiersE* (1981). Fehrenbach, R. J. *ELN* (1983). Jones, A. R., in *Ideology of Conduct,* ed. N. Armstrong and L. Tennenhouse (1987). Jones, A. R. *The Currency of Eros* (1990). Krontiris, T. *Oppositional Voices* (1992). Schleiner, L. *Tudor and Stuart Women Writers* (1994). Travitsky, B. *ELR* (1984). Wall, W. *ELH* (1991). Wall, W. *The Imprint of Gender* (1993).

For articles in reference works, see *Bloomsbury. Feminist. Oxford. ToddBWW.*

Mary Ellen Lamb

Whyte, Violet: See *Stannard, Henrietta Eliza Vaughn Palmer*

Anna Wickham

BORN: 1884, Wimbledon, Surrey.
DIED: 30 April 1947, Hampstead, London.
DAUGHTER OF: Geoffrey Harper and Alice Whelan Harper.
MARRIED: Patrick Hepburn, 1906.
WROTE UNDER: Edith Harper; John Oland; Anna Wickham.

Born Edith Alice Mary Harper, W.—English poet and vocalist—was not yet a teenager when she adopted her *nom de plume* (and stage name) after Wickham Terrace, Brisbane, where her father, on a momentous day in her tenth year, had made her promise to be a poet. She had begun writing verse when she was six—to the delight of her self-cultivated, misogynous father and to hoots of derision from her gypsy-like mother. Not surprisingly, W. kept her passion for writing quite to herself—that is, until she was well into adulthood. According to her friend and editor R. D. Smith, W. "wrote compulsively, producing over 1400 poems in her lifetime." The greater part of these, unpublished during the poet's life, remain unpublished still, although many have been preserved in her own typescript. Smith added approximately 100 previously unpublished poems to the works in print (and his Virago Press edition includes *Fragment of an Autobiography* as well as selected prose pieces). So private is much of W.'s poetry that its publication, given the circumstances, is almost a miracle, and the delay, therefore, unavoidable.

W. had been writing verse for twenty-eight years before the public saw any of it. Even after her marriage in 1906, W. did not "for years" tell her husband that she wrote poetry. In fact, when she published her first volume in 1911, it bore not her "singing name" but a male pseudonym, John Oland. While Patrick Hepburn, a lawyer and an astronomer, was apparently not opposed to his wife's musical activity, he considered public shows of private emotion contemptible. He had, in fact, known of, and himself secretly subsidized, W.'s brief career as an opera singer in Paris. Discovering his anonymous generosity, W. had dropped another lover and married Patrick—a form of passionate impulsiveness that had flattered the young husband. But W.'s poetry was something else: powerful, erotic, searing in its radical antidomesticity. It seemed especially objectionable to Patrick and his strait-laced family, and it is no wonder that W. poured her intense and wayward emotions into essentially private poems, meant in the beginning primarily as personal release. Smith reports that a jealous Patrick, when he finally did read her work, strenuously opposed its publication, angry to learn the nature of what had been diverting W.'s attention from him: "their bitterest clash" was caused by W.'s insistent will to write herself out of her intolerable feelings of oppression and to publish her feelings. Her poems "Woman and Artist" and "Genius" best express her sentiments concerning the risks she took and the risks she did not take.

Before Harold Monro and Alida Klemantaski (the renowned owners of the Poetry Bookshop) printed nine of W.'s poems in their collection *Poetry and Drama* (1914), her work received virtually no public acclaim. Two early dramatic pieces, *The Seasons* and *Wonder Eyes,* were printed privately in Sydney, Australia, when she was seventeen; *Songs of John Oland,* first published by a feminist vanity press in 1911, had not even been associated with W.'s (or Mrs. Patrick Hepburn's) name until they were reprinted some time later. The Poetry Bookshop published W.'s second volume of verse, *The Contemplative Quarry,* in 1915; Grant Richards published *The Man with a Hammer* in 1916; and, in 1921, these two volumes were published together, through Louis Untermeyer's intervention, in New York City. Suddenly, W. had a name; but 1921 (the year of her son Richard's death) marked for a time the end of her efforts to publish, although she did not cease to write. On Christmas Day, 1929, Patrick died in a mountaineering accident eerily like one his wife had previsioned in the poem "The Homecoming" (written in 1921). It took W. several years to wind up her husband's law practice. By then, her reputation as a poet was well established.

Untermeyer early identified W.'s originality, associating the poet's artistic probity with that of novelists May Sinclair, Virginia Woolf, Rebecca West, Willa Cather, and Dorothy Richardson; he praised W.'s "vigorous self-examination" and found her "in many ways the best of these seekers and singers." By 1932, Humbert Wolfe had written of her poetry in the *Encyclopaedia Britannica,* 14th Edition; she was in *International Who's Who;* she had joined P.E.N. and was giving readings regularly. Through her close friendship in the 1920s and 1930s with Natalie Barney, the Sapphic American expatriate in Paris, W. was moving in the same literary circles as Rainer Rilke, Paul Valéry, Gabriele D'Annunzio, Colette, Ezra Pound, Marcel Proust, and Gertrude Stein. John Gawsworth included her work in his two now-famous collections, *Edwardian Poetry and Neo-Georgian Poetry* (both 1937). Malcolm Lowry and Dylan Thomas were friends. Along with seven feminist activists (on 16 June 1938), W. founded The League for the Protection of the Imagination of Women. Slogan: World's Management by Entertainment. Among its supporters were Olivia Manning, J.B.S. Haldane, and Gwen le Gallienne. Not surprisingly, the league's manifesto and program were consistent with the tenor of W.'s life and verse.

Through most of W.'s best poetry runs the obsessive concern to achieve utter freedom of expression and so to create, spontaneously, a poetry as perfect as that for which others labored. That spontaneity seems fully achieved in satirical pieces like "The Housemaid," in lyrics like "The Little Love," in caustic verses like "The Tigress" and "The Sick Assailant," and in strong poems like "The Mill." In "Examination," W. wrote, "If my work is to be good, / I must transcend skill, I must master mood. / For the expression of the rare thing in me / Is not in *do,* but deeper, in *to be.*" What she in fact had managed to achieve she phrased another way: "The tumult of my fretted mind / Gives me expression of a find; but it is faulty, harsh, not plain— / My work has the incompetence of pain." Humbert Wolfe nevertheless admired it, saying that her poems "should be lived with like a great picture rather than caught like the colour of flowers." In 1947, lonely and tired, W. committed suicide by hanging herself. She was survived by three grown sons, to whose morale she had been ministering all through their active service in World War II.

We do not know whether or not W. meant her autobiography to be published. Candid, socially and psychologically insightful, and concise, her *Fragment of An Autobiography: Prelude to a Spring Clean* (written in 1935) served the poet as a repository for family history, self-revealing anecdotes, and Lawrentian vignettes about the volatile relations among the members of her family: the dramatic Whelans on her mother's side, the bookish Harpers on her father's side, the snobbish Hepburns into whose bosom she was never taken when she married Patrick, and their respective circles. From the fast-paced narrative emerges the self-portrait of a moody, untidy, often violent woman who at times wrestled mightily with her wild impulses and frequently lost to them. The self-deprecating, slapdash, critical tone of *Fragments* is counterbalanced by R. D. Smith's objective account of W.'s reputation and artistic accomplishments and by his fine critical essay on the poems themselves, in his introduction to the 1984 collection of the poet's writings.

WORKS: *The Seasons—Speaking Tableaux for Girls (100 Performers)* (1901?). *Wonder Eyes—A Journey to Slumbertown (For 80 Little People)* (1901?). *Songs of John Oland* (1911). *The Contemplative Quarry* (1915). *The Man with a Hammer* (1916). *The Contemplative Quarry & The Man With a Hammer,* intro. L. Untermeyer (1921). *The Little Old House* (1921). *Thirty-Six New Poems,* ed. J. Gawsworth (1936). *Selected Poems,* intro. D. Garnett (1971). *The Writings of Anna Wickham: Free Woman and Poet,* ed. and intro. R. D. Smith (1984).

BIBLIOGRAPHY: Holland, M. *PoetryR* (1988). Untermeyer, L. *Lives of the Poets* (1959).

For articles in reference works, see: *Bloomsbury. Feminist. Longman. Oxford. TCA. TCW. ToddBWW. WWWAEEA. World Authors,1900–1950,* ed. M. Seymour-Smith and A. C. Kimmens (1996).

Other references: *Bookman* (December 1921). *New Republic* (27 April 1921). *Picture Post* (27 April 1946). Wolfe, H. "Modern Developments in British Poetry." *Encyclopaedia Britannica,* Vol. 18 (1956).

R. Victoria Arana

Wife of a Beneficed Clergyman: See *Besant, Annie Wood*

Jane Francesca Wilde

BORN: 27 December 1821, Dublin, Ireland.
DIED: 3 February 1896, London.
DAUGHTER OF: Charles Elgee and Sarah Kingsbury.
MARRIED: Sir William Wilde, 1851.
WROTE UNDER: John Fanshawe Ellis; Speranza.

A fervor to celebrate imagination inspired W. to rebel against history's facts. Although she was the daughter of Charles Elgee, a Dublin solicitor from a family of Irish Protestant ecclesiastics and landowners with ancestral roots in Counties Down and Wexford, W. claimed that the name "Elgee" had its etymological origins in the Italian "Algiati," and that she was, by a sonorous variation of that name, the descendant of the Florentine poet Dante Alighieri. No proof exists, however, to support the literary verve with which W. translated her middle name from Frances to Francesca.

She did possess genealogical literary connections. W. was the great-granddaughter of Jonathan Swift's friend Dr. Thomas Kingsbury, and the popular novelist the Reverend Charles Maturin was her uncle by way of his marriage to W.'s mother's sister, Henrietta. Her literary heritage provided W. with courage to address the gruesome facts of her time. She wrote poems identifying the epidemic typhus, dysentery, and cholera, as well as the broadcast starvation that accompanied Ireland's famines of the 1840s. This poverty and pestilence, combined with the death of the Young Ireland Movement's founding advocate, Thomas Davis, provoked W. to compose political poems and essays. She adopted the pen name "Speranza," Italian for "hope," to distinguish herself as a rebel poet during the 1840s. *Dublin University Magazine, The Nation,* and *The United Irishmen* published her verse under this pseudonym, though her essays were signed "John Fanshawe Ellis," a name with her initials.

W.'s poems took the form of political ballads that inveighed against the injustices of British rule. When her editor, Charles Gavan Duffy of *The Nation,* was imprisoned and tried for sedition, she assisted Margaret Callan in taking over the editorship of the magazine. While Duffy was in prison for treason, W. printed "The Challenge to Ireland" in the 22 July 1848 issue. In this poem, she cross-examines the people of Ireland: "are there no men in your Fatherland / To confront the tyrant's stormy glare / With scorn as deep as the wrongs ye bear— / With defence as fierce as the oaths they swear, / With vengeance as wild as the cries of despair / That rise from your suffering Fatherland?" During the long ensuing litigation, W. went so far as to attend and interrupt Duffy's trial by announcing that she had written the seditious statements for which he was being prosecuted.

W.'s translations of Johann Wilhelm Meinhold's *Sidonia the Sorceress* and Alphonse de Lamartine's *Pictures of the First French Revolution* were published respectively in 1849 and 1850. The former is a Gothic tale set in Pomerania about a witch's exploits, trial, and beheading. The latter represents a polemical decision to remind readers in English, particularly those in Ireland, of the uprisings that led to the French Revolution.

When W. married Dr. William Wilde in 1851, she moved from the affluence of Dublin's Leeson Street to the socially elite Merrion Square. Her husband was knighted in 1864 for his innovations in eye surgery and for his achievements in caring for Ireland's sick and poor. He shared W.'s love of literature. He was the author of *Irish Popular Superstitions* (1852), which he dedicated to Speranza. His native Ireland was a lifelong theme in other work. When he died in 1876, W. inherited the handwritten stories that he had accepted as payment from his indigent Irish patients. She gathered and edited these legends into *Ancient Legends, Mystic Charms, and Superstitions of Ireland* (1888) and *Ancient Cures, Charms, and Usages of Ireland* (1890), collections of oral traditions that provided W. B. Yeats and his generation of the Irish literary revival with a prolific source for Ireland's culture and psyche.

W. and William had three children—William (1852–99), Oscar (1854–1900), and Isola (1859–67)—with whom W. shared her enthusiasm for languages and literatures. She made Walt Whitman's *Leaves of Grass* available to the youngsters in 1868, the year of its publication. She read her letters aloud as she corresponded with American poet Henry Wadsworth Longfellow and the Irish novelist William Carleton.

W. had moved from Dublin to London in 1879 and continued the tradition that she had begun in Dublin of holding extravagant parties in her home that included such guests as George Bernard Shaw and Yeats. From her new home, she published *Driftwood From Scandinavia* (1884), an account of her travels in 1858 to Sweden. In addition to producing the book *Social Studies* during this phase of her life, she contributed articles to the London magazine *The Woman's World* between 1887 and 1889, when her son Oscar served as editor. Her 1888 poem, "Historic Women," was featured in *Woman's World,* which ran a column by her entitled "Irish Peasant Tales." While living in London, she became a charter member of the Irish Literary Society.

In a letter to Oscar in 1891, W. compared her son's success with that of Sir Walter Pater. Implicit in this parallel is her wish that Oscar might have been knighted for his literary accomplishments, just as his father had been knighted for medical research and service. A fast-paced fall to disgrace was the Wilde family's defining note by 1896, however, as a series of trials indicted Oscar Wilde for sodomy and found him guilty of the lesser crime of what Victorian law termed "indecent behavior with men." W.—recalling histrionic trials from her earlier life in Dublin—insisted throughout the legal proceedings that her son would gain public support and be exonerated. She died in 1896, while Oscar Wilde was serving his sentence of two years at hard labor.

WORKS: (trans.) *Sidonia the Sorceress,* by J. W Meinhold (1849). (trans.) *Pictures of the First French Revolution,* by A. de Lamartine (1850). (trans.) *The Wanderer and his Home,* by A. de Lamartine (1851). (trans.) *The Glacier Land,* by A. Dumas (1852). (trans.) *The First Temptation,* by W. Canz (1863). *Poems* (1864). *Driftwood from Scandinavia* (1884). *Ancient Legends, Mystic Charms and Superstitions of Ireland* (1888). *Ancient Cures, Charms and Usages of Ireland* (1890). *Notes on Men, Women and Books* (1891). *Social Studies* (1893).

BIBLIOGRAPHY: Amor, C. *Mrs Oscar Wilde* (1983). Ellmann, R. *Oscar Wilde* (1987). Hyde, H. M. *Oscar Wilde* (1976). Lambert, E. *Mad With Much Heart: A Life of the Parents of Oscar Wilde* (1967). Melville, J. *Mother of Oscar Wilde: The Life of Jane Francesca Wilde* (1994). Page, N. *An Oscar Wilde Chronology* (1991). White, T. D. *The Parents of Oscar Wilde* (1967).

For articles in reference works, see: *Bloomsbury. Cambridge. DIL. DIW. Oxford.*

John Lavin

Helen Maria Williams

BORN: 1762, London.
DIED: 1827, Paris, France.
DAUGHTER OF: Charles Williams and Helen Hay Williams.

Novelist, essayist, poet, translator, and historian, W. is best remembered for her chronicles of France in the wake of the French Revolution. With the vivid detail of a skilled novelist and self-consciousness as a spectator of high drama, W. records and analyzes the intersection of personal and public life in a dangerous, turbulent age. Her work is increasingly important in studies of women writers and politics.

When her father, a Welsh army officer, died in 1769, the family moved to Berwick-upon-Tweed. Educated by her Scots mother, W. returned to London in 1781. The following year, with the assistance of the dissenting minister Dr. Andrew Kippis, W. published *Edwin and Eltruda,* her first long poem. Soon joined by her family, W. continued to publish her poetical works, well-received and financially profitable, over the next eight years. The subscription list for her two-volume *Poems* (1786) numbered more than 1,500. *Peru* (1784), her poem about European exploitation of South America, and *Poem on the Bill Lately Passed for Regulating the Slave Trade* (1788) mark early on a liberal commitment to human liberty. Her 1790 novel *Julia* rewrites Jean-Jacques Rousseau's *La Nouvelle Héloise,* weaving Republicanism into the depiction of a sensitive heroine in a love triangle. Valued in the popular cult of sensibility, W.'s sentimental descriptions of victims of misfortune moved hundreds of readers to tears. William Wordsworth wrote a sonnet celebrating the poignant scene of her weeping over a tale of distress. Gregarious, articulate, and generous, W. developed a wide circle of literary acquaintances, including Fanny Burney, Elizabeth Montagu, Anna Seward, William Hayley, Samuel Johnson, Hester Piozzi, Samuel Rogers, and Charlotte Smith.

W. was one of many intellectuals, including Mary Wollstonecraft, Wordsworth, and Smith, who were optimistic about the possibilities of benevolence and human liberty at the outset of the French Revolution in 1789. For most, the dream was shattered by the realities of anarchy and blood-letting during the 1793–94 Reign of Terror, which contrasted with the dearly held English myth of the Glorious or Bloodless Revolution of 1688. W. maintained a loyalty to the French people and to the principles of the French Revolution, rupturing relations with friends and supporters in England and subjecting her to scathing reviews in the English press. Her relationship with John Hurford Stone, a literary collaborator and divorced man considered a traitor to England, intensified her vilification in the press. Their connection, which may have resulted in marriage, ended with Stone's death in 1818.

W. wrote *Letters Written from France in the Summer of 1790* during a visit to the du Fossé family, whom she had befriended in England. The work celebrates the progress in human liberty marked by the joyful first anniversary of the fall of the Bastille and includes the powerful story of her friends, whose suffering at the hands of M. du Fossé's tyrannical father emblemizes the repressive, legally sanctioned privilege of the French aristocracy. Particularizing human experience within the larger context of explosive and political events became a hallmark of W.'s histories. The next three decades of her chronicles were to combine realistic observation of detail, astute political commentary, poignant scenes of individual suffering and heroism, and a continued struggle to affirm faith in human goodness and the progress of history. Although her volumes do not address in detail the economic and class dimensions of the French struggle, she is sensitive to the important roles of women. She often notes shared values of the French and English to elicit sympathy for the French.

The second volume of *Letters from France,* still optimistic, appeared in 1792, the year that W. moved with her mother and sisters to Paris. Her residence became a center of intellectual and political life, and guests included Wollstonecraft, Thomas Paine, Crabb Robinson, Joel Barlow, Lady Morgan, Gilbert Imlay, and, early on, both Girondists and Jacobins. By the summer of 1793, the Jacobins had defeated the moderate Girondists. Madame Roland, whom she immortalized as a heroine, was one of many Girondist friends arrested and later guillotined. W. and her family were arrested with other British subjects and imprisoned 11 October 1793. The family was released three months later through the intervention of a nephew of Madame du Fossé. In danger of the "knife of the guillotine" for her political sympathies, W. fled to Switzerland with Stone and returned when Robespierre's associates deposed him in July 1794. Her six months in Switzerland are described in *A Tour of Switzerland* (1798).

The mood shifts dramatically in volumes 3–6 of the *Letters* as W. depicts the increasing violence, confusion, and brutish lust for power under the Jacobins, French wars abroad, and misconceptions of the French Revolution in England. Conspiracies and political factions compound as the despotism of the monarchy is replaced by a Jacobin despotism "more hideous than history has ever presented." Marie Antoinette and Louis XVI, misguided by their privilege, are attentive parents, calm and dignified in adversity. Prison life, which W. knew first-hand, tests the decency of prisoner and guard, providing opportunities for selfless community created by shared calamity. The last two volumes conclude with the establishment of the Directory in 1795. W., hopeful at first about Napoleon's leadership, came to see him as yet another ruthless dictator. He had her arrested briefly for sentiments in her verses on the Peace of Amiens. Articulating her own shortcomings as eyewitness and partisan, W. has nonetheless provided important documents for understanding this period and for challenging the concept of historical objectivity.

In 1798, W. assumed responsibility for bringing up two nephews orphaned by the death of her sister, Cecilia Williams Coquerel, who had married a nephew of the du Fossés. Athanase, Jr., was to become a Protestant pastor in Amsterdam and Paris, and Charles founded the *Annales protestantes* and *Revue Britannique.* In desperate need of money to support her family, W. translated seven volumes of travel narratives by Alexander von Humboldt and wrote *Sketches of the State of Manners and Opinions in the French Republic,* which included a popular tale about a bellows-mender that provided the model for Edward Bulwer-Lytton's *The Lady of Lyons.* In 1803, she edited a volume of the correspondence of Louis XVI, later proved forgeries, which drew sharp criticism from English reviewers and an order by Napoleon to seize all copies of the French and English editions. With the exile of Napoleon in 1815, she resumed publication of books on contemporary French politics. She was naturalized as a French citizen in 1817.

W. continued her celebrated salon, sought after by another generation of intellectuals, including Percy and Mary Shelley. In 1820, W. met with Wordsworth, whose poem had celebrated her sensibility in 1787. Many of the Romantics, including Wordsworth, had long before retreated from the liberal ideal of the French Revolution. W. had remained in the fray, loyal to friends and ideals, writing to salvage the principles and possibilities of the dream gone wrong.

WORKS: *Edwin and Eltruda* (1782). *An Ode on the Peace* (1783). *Peru* (1784). *Poems* (1786, expanded 1791). *Julia* (1790). *A Poem on the Bill Lately Passed for Regulating the Slave Trade* (1788). *Letters from France: Letters Written from France in the Summer of 1790; Letters from France Containing Many New Anecdotes Relative to the French Revolution and the Present state of French Manners; Letters from France Containing a Great Variety of Interesting and Original Information . . . Particularly Respecting the Campaign of 1792; Letters Con-*

taining a Sketch of the Politics of France; Letters Containing a Sketch of the Politics of France from the Twenty-first of May 1793 till the Twenty-eighth of July 1794 and of the Scenes which have passed in the Prisons of Paris; Letters Containing a Sketch of the Politics of France from the Thirty-first of May 1793 till the Twenty-eighth of July 1794; Letters Containing A Sketch of the Scenes which passes in Various Departments of France during the Tyranny of Robespierre, and of the Events which took place in Paris on the 28th of July 1794; Letters Containing a Sketch of the Politics of France from the Twenty-eighth of July 1794 to the Establishment of the Constitution in 1795 (1790–97; facsimile 1975). (trans.) *Paul and Virginia* by B. Saint-Pierre (1795). *A Tour of Switzerland* (1798). *Sketches of the State of Manners and Opinions in the French Republic towards the Close of the Eighteenth Century* (1801). *Perourou, the Bellows-Mender* (1801). (trans.) *Personal Narrative of Travel*, by A. Von Humboldt, 7 vols. (1814–29). *A Narrative of Events Which Have Taken Place in France from the Landing of Napoleon Bonaparte . . . till the Restoration of Louis XVIII* (1815). *On the Late Persecution of the Protestants in the South of France* (1816). *Letters on Events Which Have passed in France since the Restoration in 1815* (1819). *Poems on Various Subjects* (1823).

BIBLIOGRAPHY: Adams, M., in *Wordsworth and Coleridge: Studies in Honor of G. M. Harper*, ed. E. Griggs (1939). Adams, M. *Political Radicalism in England: A Study in Literary Backgrounds* (1940). Adickes, S. *The Social Quest* (1991). Bray, H. *ECLife* (1992). Ellison, J. *SECC* (1990). Favret, M. *SIR* (1993). Forsyte, C. *EA* (1989). Jones, C. *PSt* (1989). Jones, V. *HEI* (1993). Jones, V., in *Beyond Romanticism*, ed. S. Copley and J. Whale (1991). Kelly, G. *Women, Writing, and Revolution, 1790–1827* (1993). Kennedy, D. *WC* (1990). Kennedy, D. *Lumen* (1991). Kennedy, D. *Man and Nature* (1991). Kennedy, D. *PQ* (1994). Kurtz, B. and C. Autrey *Four New Letters of Mary Wollstonecraft and Helen Maria Williams* (1937). Rigby, B., in *The French Revolution and British Culture*, ed. C. Crossley and I. Small. Scheffler, J. *WC* (1988). Todd, J., intro. to *Letters from France* (facsimile, 1975). Todd, J. *Sensibility: An Introduction* (1986). Watson, N. *WC* (1992). Watson, N. *Revolution and the Form of the British Novel, 1790–1825* (1994). Ty, E. *Unsex'd Revolutionaries: Five Women Novelists of the 1790s* (1993).

For articles in reference works, see: *Bloomsbury. Cambridge. DNB. Oxford. ToddBWW.*

Carol Shiner Wilson

Catherine Winkworth

BORN: 13 September 1827, London.
DIED: 1 July 1878, Monnetier, Savoy, France.
DAUGHTER OF: Henry Winkworth and Susanna Dickenson Winkworth.

The daughter of a well-to-do silk manufacturer, W. devoted her life to reform: in various social causes, especially having to do with education and careers for women, and above all in English hymnody. Most of her writings were translations from German; her hymns enjoyed great popularity and made a lasting impact.

On her early life there were strong and varied religious and literary influences. One grandfather was a deacon in a nonconformist chapel in Tunbridge Wells for fifty years; the other, William Winkworth, was a prominent Evangelical minister in the Church of England. Educated at home in Manchester, she had as successive tutors two scholarly Unitarian clergymen, William Gaskell and James Martineau. Family friends included the novelists Charlotte Brontë and Elizabeth Gaskell, her tutor's wife. Through the latter, in 1849 W. and her elder sister Susanna met the Prussian ambassador, Baron C.K.J. von Bunsen, a man of many connections and many projects. The association with Bunsen was to shape both sisters' careers.

Already well versed in German language and culture through study and a year's residence in Dresden (1845–46), W. did some translating to help Susanna with the three-volume biography of B. G. Niebuhr that Bunsen had urged her to undertake. After its appearance in 1852, W. turned to translating hymns from Bunsen's 1833 collection, *Versuch eines allgemeinen evangelischen Gesang- und Gebetbuchs*. One hundred and two of these, carefully chosen to connect with the scripture readings assigned throughout the church year in the English liturgy, were published as *Lyra Germanica* in 1855 as an aid to private devotion. The book sold out within two months; by Christmas there was a second edition, with revisions; soon W.'s translations were appearing in anthologies on both sides of the Atlantic, and there was a demand both for more translations and for versions suitable for singing. In 1858, W. published a "second series" of 121 hymns, including some from sources other than Bunsen. She then secured the services of William Sterndale Bennett and Otto Goldschmidt, husband of the singer Jenny Lind, as musical editors; in 1863 she published *The Chorale Book for England*, containing 72 new translations in addition to revised versions of 130 from the two *Lyra Germanica* volumes. Her only original published work, *The Christian Singers of Germany*, was published in 1869; it was an historical survey of the German religious lyric from the eighth to the nineteenth century, with some 130 examples, including nearly 100 newly translated by W. for the purpose.

In a busy age of translation—there were some twenty Victorian collections of German hymns, three fourths of them by women—W.'s work was remarkable for both quantity and quality. In volume and range (more than 170 authors representing all schools—Minnesingers, Luther and his followers, Hussites, Pietists, Moravians, Roman Catholics, etc.), it far surpassed that of other translators. Many of her hymns—among them "Now thank we all our God," "Praise to the Lord, the Almighty," and "Lift up your heads, ye mighty gates"—remain in modern hymnals. E. Routley writes that she "gave a very strong impetus towards raising the standards of translation." She combined accuracy and respect for the spirit of her originals, even to the point of reproducing such devices as alliteration, with sensitivity to English idiom and graceful expression. Many of her early translations involved slight metrical adaptation for the sake of a smoother English rendering; later, however, when producing singing versions for the *Chorale Book*, she retranslated to fit the German tunes. In a few cases she omitted or altered stanzas she considered offensive in doctrine or taste; however, she disapproved of editorial habits of free alteration that resulted in "correct and tiresome flatness."

As her personal religious views developed, W. became critical of both liberal Christianity and Tractarianism and returned to a position closer to her Evangelical heritage. Her *Chorale Book,* especially with its 1865 supplement of English hymns, may have been an effort to compete with the influential Anglo-Catholic *Hymns Ancient and Modern* (1861). On the other hand, her hymn writing had an avowed ecumenical purpose, "to make us feel afresh what a deep and true Communion of Saints exists among all the children of God in different churches and lands" (Preface to *Lyra Germanica,* 1855).

W. was also active in various religious and social causes. Before the age of twelve she was teaching in the church school; on returning from a trip to Switzerland in 1853, she added duties in the District Visiting Society. After the family moved in 1862 to Clifton, a suburb of Bristol, her activities reflect a growing interest in social work and especially in promoting both the welfare of women and the role of women in social ministry. She was the authorized translator from German of biographies of Amelia Wilhelmina Sieveking (1863), founder of the Female Society for the Care of the Sick and Poor in Hamburg, and Theodor Fliedner (1867), who founded a lunatic asylum for women, a normal school for training infant-school mistresses, and an order of deaconesses, with houses in several countries, called to the care of the sick, the poor, and the young. Following the example of such reformers, W. assumed a host of responsibilities, such as helping to organize, in 1868, the Committee to Promote Higher Education of Women, of which she became secretary in 1870. This group helped women prepare for university entrance examinations and led the way in establishing England's first coeducational institution, University College, Bristol. W. was also a delegate in 1872 to a conference on women's work in Darmstadt, Germany; a promoter of the Clifton High School for Girls; and a board member of the Red Maids' School, Bristol, and Cheltenham Ladies College.

Troubled from youth by periods of ill health, W. died of heart disease at the age of fifty while on a trip to France. In her memory, scholarships were endowed at University College, Bristol, and a tablet erected in Bristol Cathedral praising her "clear and harmonious intellect and gift of true poetic insight and expression."

WORKS: (trans.) *Lyra Germanica: Hymns for the Sundays and Chief Festivals of the Christian Year, by Baron von Bunsen* (1855; 2nd ed., 1855; more than twenty other editions, some with alternate title *Songs for the Household* or *Songs, Sacred and Devotional*). (trans.) *Lyra Germanica, 2nd series: The Christian Life* (1858; more than ten other editions; combined edition, 1879 and later). *A Selection of Hymns from the Lyra Germanica of Catherine Winkworth,* ed. A. Ewing (1859). (assemb. and trans.) *The Chorale Book for England* (1863). (trans.) *Life of Amelia Wilhelmina Sieveking* (1863). (ed.) *Supplement to the Chorale Book for England Containing English Hymns with Appropriate Tunes* (1865). (trans.) *Life of Pastor Fliedner of Kaiserswerth* (1867). *The Christian Singers of Germany* (1869; rpt. 1972). (trans.) *Prayers from the Collection of the Late Baron Bunsen* (1871). *Letters and Memorials of Catherine Winkworth,* ed. S. Winkworth (1883; incorporated in Shaen, 1908).

BIBLIOGRAPHY: Leaver, R. A. *Catherine Winkworth: The Influence of Her Translations on English Hymnody* (1978). Routley, E. *The Hymn Society of Great Britain and Ireland Bulletin* (1958, 1963). *Memorials of Two Sisters: Susanna and Catherine Winkworth,* ed. M. J. Shaen (1908). Skrine, P. N. *Susanna and Catherine Winkworth* (1992).

For articles in reference works, see: *Allibone. BA19C. DNB.* Julian, J. A. *A Dictionary of Hymnology* (1891). *Miles.* Routley, E. *An English Speaking Hymnal Guide* (1979). Routley, E. *A Panorama of English Hymnody* (1979).

Other references: *Historical Companion to Hymns Ancient & Modern,* ed. M. Frost (1962). *LonT* (16 July 1878). Miles, A. H. *Sacred, Moral, and Religious Verse* (1897).

Charles A. Huttar

Winter, John Strange: See *Stannard, Henrietta Eliza Vaughn Palmer*

Jeanette Winterson

BORN: 27 August 1959, Manchester.
DAUGHTER OF: adopted by John William Winterson and Constance Brownrigg Winterson.

W. was adopted into the Lancashire home of Pentecostal evangelists and attended Accrington Girls' Grammar School. Active as a child preacher from the age of eight, W. left home at fifteen when she discovered that her love for another woman made her an outcast in her family and church. Before reading English at St. Catherine's College, Oxford (B.A. 1981), W. studied at Accrington College of Further Education and took a number of unusual parttime jobs (ice-cream-van driver, make-up artist in a funeral parlor, etc.), detailed in her autobiographical first novel, *Oranges Are Not the Only Fruit.* After Oxford, W. moved to London and worked at the Roundhouse Theatre as a general assistant (1981–82) and in publishing (Brilliance Books and Pandora Press, 1983–87). Since the publication of *Oranges,* W.'s literary output has been steady. W. shared her Hampstead home (the ground floor of which houses her own literary agency, Great Moments Ltd.) with her partner, scholar/writer Margaret Reynolds, but in 1994 they moved to an isolated farm in Gloucestershire to escape intense media interest (one critic charges that W. has fans, not readers) and controversy; she also has a house in Spitalfields, London. W. has been severely chastized by London critics for her ostensible self-promotion ("No one working in the English language now comes close to my exuberance, my passion, my fidelity to words"), although W. argues that false modesty is the greater transgression.

W. delights in blurring the lines between established biographical fact and invention in her first novel, *Oranges Are Not the Only Fruit* (1985), written for money in just two months. W. claims "I genuinely don't know what I made up and what was reality. It's become a story to me." This comic *Bildungsroman* received wide critical acclaim (Whitbread Prize for a First Novel), and her BBC screenplay adaptation (1990) was awarded the BAFTA Best Drama and Prix Italia. Quickly named a rising star in the British literary establishment, W. was included in a list of "Best Young British Writers." The novel is an exuberant and witty coming-of-age and coming-out novel set in Northern England. Drawing upon the stylistic devices of historiographic metafiction and magic realism, W.'s adolescent protagonist, Jeanette, rejects the missionary vocation planned by her mother. Instead, Jeanette decrees that heterosexuality is beastly and confusing, and she ponders why her passionate involvement with members of her own sex causes so much disruption: "It all seemed to hinge around the fact that I loved the wrong sort of people. Right sort of people in every respect except this one; romantic love for another woman was a sin." Ironically, in forging a lesbian identity in a hostile world, Jeanette, ever her mother's daughter, simply reverses her mother's bold, absolutist binary thinking: heterosexuality is abnormal and homosexuality is normal. The novel celebrates lesbian desire and concludes with a sophisticated critique of the church and masculine hegemony as the narrator enters into self-imposed exile to attend the university.

In many respects, W.'s second work, *Boating for Beginners* (1985), is another version of her first, which might account for W.'s attempt (so far unsuccessful) to expunge it from the list of her publications; the title appears on the dust jackets under a separate heading, "comic novel," as opposed to "fiction." W. playfully revises the biblical tale of Noah to insert a feminist critique of capitalism, advertising, and romance novels as the young protagonist searches for the meaning of life.

W. returns to "serious" fiction with two novels that fuse the fantastic with history: *The Passion* (1987), awarded the John Llewellyn Rhys Prize, and *Sexing the Cherry* (1989), the winner of the E. M. Forster Award from the American Academy of Arts and Letters. *The Passion,* a richly textured, poetic work, takes as its central concern the multiple meanings of the word "passion," described as "somewhere between fear and sex . . . passion is not so much an emotion as a destiny." The narrative progresses through France, Russia, and Venice during the Napoleonic Wars and traces the journeys of the two narrators: Henri, a chicken cook to Napoleon, and Villanelle, a woman whose webbed feet constitute androgyny in the culture of gondoliers and who, disguised as a boy, works in a Venetian casino. Venice, a beguiling postmodern city par excellence in its mutability and capacity to disguise, is the ideal domain for an exploration of the ambiguities of gender and sexuality, the intensity of passionate love, and the dangers of obsession, while the grim backdrop of war invites an analysis of Henri's hero-worship of Napoleon. The novel also probes the nature of narrative, cleverly unravelling and reconstructing itself, as seen in Henri's repetitive and mesmeric invitation to "Trust me, I'm telling you stories." Upon reading *The Passion,* Gore Vidal pronounced W. the "most interesting writer I have read in twenty years," while Muriel Spark observed that W. is "a master of her material, a writer in whom great talent abides." In *Sexing the Cherry,* W. returns to some familiar themes and narrative devices, but the result continues to be fresh and inventive: the rewriting of history, the imprecision of language, sexual ambiguity, the nature of truth and narrativity, the expansion of the dimensions of space and time, an antilinear plot, feminist revision of the fairytale, character as metaphor, and so on. The two narrators, the giantess Dog-Woman and her adopted foundling, Jordan, roam a fantastic version of seventeenth-century London, complete with Puritans, Royalists, the plague, and the Great Fire.

Written on the Body (1992) seems a rather more conventional story of a love triangle, although W. claims it is her "most profound and profoundly misunderstood book. A fiction which dismantles the scaffolding of the nineteenth-century novel, replacing time, place, situation, even gender, with an intense consciousness. An exaltation of love. An exultation of language. Words unclothed." The narrator, whose gender is undisclosed, moves from lover to lover—of both genders—until finally forming an intensely erotic and passionate attachment to Louise, a red-headed Australian married to Elgin, a cancer specialist. Louise's leukemia diagnosis gives Elgin an opportunity to reclaim his wife by informing the narrator that Louise's survival hinges on the narrator's immediate departure. Imagining exile from the beloved as an act of selflessness, the narrator leaves for northern England, though her/his love intensifies rather than diminishes. The final passages shift from a lengthy reflection on the physicality of Louise's body, "the cells, tissues, systems and cavities," to loss and mortality.

In *Art & Lies* (1994), W. abandons plot completely. Three characters, all bearing some resemblance to their namesakes, Handel, Picasso, and Sappho, share a compartment on a train bound for the coast. W.'s most philosophical and rhapsodic work to date turns to a modernist style with a narrative that builds around key images and concepts (trains, light and lightness, words and language, music and art, and so on); as one narrator states: "Words beyond information. Words done with plot."

With a zealousness reminiscent of her childhood training, W.'s lean, experimental prose appropriates and exploits the full range of metafictional techniques (parody, frame breaks, pastiche, self-conscious aphorisms, self-reflexivity) in order to negotiate a space for lesbian feminism in a postmodern culture.

WORKS: *Oranges Are Not the Only Fruit* (1985; screenplay, 1990). *Boating for Beginners* (1985). (ed.) *Passion Fruit: Romantic Fiction with a Twist* (1986). *Fit for the Future* (1986). *The Passion* (1987). *Static* (radio play, 1988). *Sexing the Cherry* (1989). *Written on the Body* (1992). *Art & Lies: A Piece for Three Voices and a Bawd* (1994). *Great Moments in Aviation* and *Oranges Are Not the Only Fruit* (film scripts, 1994). *Art Objects: Essays on Ecstasy and Effrontery* (1995). *Gut Symmetries* (1997).

BIBLIOGRAPHY: Doan, L., in *The Lesbian Postmodern,* ed. L. Doan (1994). Duncker, P. *Sisters and Strangers: An Introduction to Contemporary Feminist Fiction* (1992). Hinds, H., in *New Lesbian Criticism: Literary and Cul-*

tural Readings, ed. S. Munt (1992). O'Rourke, R., in *Feminist Criticism: Theory and Practice*, ed. S. Sellers, L. Hutcheon, and P. Perron (1991). Suleiman, S. R., in *Femmes Frauen Women*, ed. F. van Rossum-Guyon (1990).

For articles in reference works, see: *Bloomsbury. Chloe Plus Olivia: An Anthology of Lesbian Literature from the Seventeenth Century to the Present*, ed. L. Faderman (1994). *Feminist.*

Other references: *LonSunTMag* (4 January 1997).

Laura L. Doan

Jane Wiseman

FLOURISHED: c. 1700.
MARRIED: (?) Holt.
WROTE UNDER: Jane Holt; Jane Wiseman.

Little is known about the author of the remarkable tragedy *Antiochus the Great*, which was first performed at the New Theatre, Lincoln's Inn Fields, around November 1701 (the precise date of the premiere is unknown) and published 25 November 1702. G. Jacob's *Poetical Register* (1719) describes W. as being a servant in the family of William Wright, Recorder of Oxford, in which capacity she had access to a library and the leisure to read extensively and begin her play. She later became the wife of a vintner named Holt. She apparently retired from the stage and used the profits of her playwrighting to help set up a tavern in Westminster. Although the precise number of initial performances *Antiochus* received is unknown, Kendall speculates that the play must have run at least three nights, for which its author would have received a benefit, and perhaps six nights (entailing a second benefit) to have produced profits substantial enough for W. to set up a new business.

Around 1700, a "Mrs Wiseman" inherited the part of Roxolana in the Earl of Orrery's *Mustapha* from Mrs. Betterton, so it is possible that W. the tragedian was also a tragic actress. She was also a poet, as Roger Lonsdale demonstrates in reprinting her "To Mr. Wren, my Valentine Six Year Old," an affectionately didactic poem included in her collection that was published in 1717. Her business career did not completely preclude her authorship, therefore, and she turned her talents to children's verse.

Included in Kendall's *Love and Thunder, Antiochus* is in some respects typical of the affective "she-tragedies" in vogue at the time: didactic heroicism with rich displays of formalized grief, sustained pathetic appeal, female distress, rivalry, suicide, revenge, and the punishment of evildoers. It also presents, as did contemporaries such as Mary Pix and Susanna Centlivre, portraits of female friendship and agency. Kendall notes that the conclusion is unique in presenting a "virtuous female couple, Irene and Berenice, heading off for a life in the wilderness together."

J. Genest dismisses the tragedy as "poor" and complains that "Mrs. Wiseman has taken great liberties with the story on which she has founded her play." It was a play, however, that W., in the preface to the published text, called the "first Fruits of a Muse, not yet debas'd to the Low Imployment of Scandal or Private Reflection," and the product of a self-taught servant; its blank verse quite effectively conveys the mercurial emotion that typifies the genre. While it is certainly "excessive" in its pathos, it is also witty, ironic at times, and affecting—clearly stageworthy, as its returns in 1711, 1712, and 1721 would indicate. With the burgeoning critical interest in the productions of servant and working-class women, W. looms large as an early eighteenth-century tragedian and poet even though details of her life will likely remain enigmatic.

WORKS: *Antiochus the Great* (1702). *A Fairy Tale . . . With Other Poems* (1717).

BIBLIOGRAPHY: Downes, J. *Roscius Anglicanus* (1708). Genest, J. *Some Account of the English Stage from the Restoration in 1660 to 1830* (1832). *A Biographical Dictionary of Actors, Actresses, Dancers, Managers, and Other Stage Personnel in London, 1660–1800*, ed. P. H. Highfill,. Jr., et al. (1993). Jacob, G. *Poetical Register* (1719). Kendall [sic]. *Love and Thunder: Plays by Women in the Age of Queen Anne* (1988). Lonsdale, R., ed. *Eighteenth-Century Women Poets* (1990).

Richard C. Taylor

Mary Wollstonecraft (Godwin)

BORN: 27 April 1759, London.
DIED: 10 September 1797, London.
DAUGHTER OF: Edward Wollstonecraft and Elizabeth Dickson.
MARRIED: William Godwin, 1797.

W. was the second child and first daughter of seven children born to Edward Wollstonecraft, an unsuccessful farmer and brutal, drunken father. In 1775, W. met Fanny Blood, a painter two years older than she, who became a powerful influence and friend and who later died in childbirth in W.'s arms. *Mary, A Fiction* (1788), W.'s only complete novel, depicts Blood's situation and conveys W.'s literary and life theme of distrust of marriage.

W. wrote *Thoughts on the Education of Daughters* in 1787 following the failure of a school at Islington that she had established with her sister Eliza and Fanny Blood. In *Thoughts,* W. counseled women to seek tranquility through reason and self-discipline; she questioned the underlying purposes of education and concludes: "In a comfortable situation, a cultivated mind is necessary to render a woman contented, and in a miserable one, it is her only consolation."

Following her dismissal as governess to the daughters of Lord and Lady Kingsborough, she became involved in the radical publication *Analytical Review,* edited by Joseph Johnson. Johnson published her *Original Stories from Real Life* (1788), *The Female Reader* (1789), and *Extract of The Cave of Fancy,* in *Posthumous Works* (1798). At Johnson's home, she met Thomas Holcroft, Henry Fuseli, William Blake, Anna Laetitia Barbauld, Thomas Paine, and William Godwin, and she wrote translations and reviews revealing her increasing awareness of women's secondary status.

In answer to Edmund Burke, W. wrote *A Vindication of the Rights of Man* (1790), first published anonymously and in her name in a second edition. In this, she set herself up as the voice of reason (although she argues emotionally) and spoke out for the rights of the poor, the oppressed, and the degraded of either sex.

A Vindication of the Rights of Women, W.'s best known work, was published in 1792. W. has been called the first major feminist because of this work, in which she discussed all aspects of women's education, status, and position in society and dramatically argues that true freedom necessitates equality of men and women.

Following the uproar caused by this publication, W. left for Paris, traveling first with the Fuselis, then alone. There she met Gilbert Imlay, observed the French Revolution, conceived her first child (fathered by Imlay), and wrote *An Historical and Moral View of the Origin and Progress of the French Revolution, and the Effect it Has Produced in Europe* (1794). Her daughter Fanny was born 14 May 1795. Imlay's subsequent indifference led to two suicide attempts, the first in May and the second in October. To rid himself of her, Imlay sent W. on a business trip to Scandinavia, which resulted in *Letters Written during a Short Residence in Sweden, Norway, and Denmark* (1796).

Her parting from Imlay was softened by the renewal of her acquaintance with William Godwin, then at the height of his fame as a philosopher and writer; they proved to be a match politically, intellectually, and emotionally. Pregnant since December 1796, W. married Godwin on 29 March 1797, despite both having been opposed to marriage. While pregnant, she wrote *The Wrongs of Woman* (1798) and led an unconventionally separate marriage.

W.'s daughter Mary (who later married Percy Bysshe Shelley), was born 30 August 1797. On 10 September, W. died of septicemia, the result of the placenta remaining in her for several days and becoming gangrenous. Her death, then, reflected her life: The constraints that held her sex won her final struggle.

WORKS: *Female Reader* (1787). *Original Stories from Real Life* (1788). *Thoughts on the Education of Daughters; with Reflections on Female Conduct, in the More Important Duties of Life* (1787). *Mary, A Fiction* (1788). *Original Stories from Real Life; with Conversations, Calculated to Regulate the Affections, and Form the Mind to Truth and Goodness* (1788). (trans.) *On the Importance of Religious Opinions*, by J. Necker (1789). *The Female Reader: or Miscellaneous-Pieces, in Prose and Verse; Selected from the Best Writers, and Disposed Under Proper Heads; for the Improvement of Young Women* (1789). *A Vindication of the Rights of Man, in a Letter to the Right Honourable Edmund Burke* (1790). (trans.) *Young Grandison*, by Mme. de Cambon (1790). (trans.) *Elements of Morality for the Use of Children*, by C. G. Salzmann (1790). *A Vindication of the Rights of Women with Strictures on Political and Moral Subjects* (1792). *An Historical and Moral View of the Origin and Progress of the French Revolution, and the Effect it Has Produced in Europe* (1794). *Maria, or The Wrongs of Woman* (1795; as *The Wrongs of Woman; or Maria*, part of *Posthumous Works*, 1798). *Letters Written During a Short Residence in Sweden, Norway, and Denmark* (1796). *Posthumous Works of the Author of "A Vindication of the Rights of Woman"* (1798). *The Wrongs of Woman* (part of *Posthumous Works*, 1798). *Extract of Cave of Fancy* (part of *Posthumous Works*, 1798). *Mary Wollstonecraft's Original Stories with Five Illustrations by William Blake*, ed. E. V. Lucas (1906). *The Love Letters of Mary Wollstonecraft to Gilbert Imlay, with a Prefatory Memoir*, ed. R. Ingpen (1908). *Memoirs of Mary Wollstonecraft*, ed. W. C. Durant (1927). *Four New Letters of Mary Wollstonecraft and Helen Maria Williams*, ed. B. P. Kurtz and C. C. Autrey (1937). *Letters*, ed. F. L. Jones (1944). *Journal*, ed. F. L. Jones (1947). *Godwin and Mary: Letters of William Godwin and Mary Wollstonecraft*, ed. R. M. Wardle (1966). *Collected Letters of Mary Wollstonecraft*, ed. R. M. Wardle (1979).

BIBLIOGRAPHY: Conger, S. M. *Mary Wollstonecraft and the Language of Sensibility* (1994). Detre, J. *A Most Extraordinary Pair: Mary Wollstonecraft and William Godwin* (1975). *Feminist Interpretations of Mary Wollstonecraft*, ed. M. J. Falco (1996). Ferguson, M. and J. Todd. *Mary Wollstonecraft* (1984). Finke, L. A., in *The Philosopher as Writer: The Eighteenth Century*, ed. R. Ginsberg (1987). Flexner, E. *Mary Wollstonecraft: A Biography* (1972). George, M. *One Woman's "Situation": A Study of Mary Wollstonecraft* (1970). Godwin, W. *Memoirs of Mary Wollstonecraft*, ed. W. C. Durant (1927). Grylls, R. G. *William Godwin and His World* (1953). *A Short Residence in Sweden and Memoirs of the Author of 'The Rights of Woman,'* ed. R. Homes (1987). Hoock-Demarle, M. C., in *Woman as Mediatrix: Essays on Nineteenth Century Women Writers*, ed. A. H. Goldberger (1987). James, H. R. *Mary Wollstonecraft: A Sketch* (1932). Jebb, C. *Mary Wollstonecraft* (1912). Kelly, G. *Revolutionary Feminism: The Mind and Career of Mary Wollstonecraft* (1992). Linford, M. *Mary Wollstonecraft (1759–1797)* (1924). Myers, M., in *The Private Self: Theory and Practice of Women's Autobiographical Writings*, ed. S. Benstock (1988). Nixon, E. *Mary Wollstonecraft: Her Life and Times* (1971). Pennell, E. R. *Mary Wollstonecraft Godwin* (1885). Preedy, G. R. [pseud. for G. C. Long] *This Shining Woman: Mary Wollstonecraft Godwin* (1937). Rauschenbusch-Clough, E. *A Study of Mary Wollstonecraft and the Rights of Woman* (1898). Robinson, V. *William Godwin and Mary Wollstonecraft* (1907). Sapiro, V. *A Vindication of Political Virtue: The Political Theory of Mary Wollstonecraft* (1992). Sunstein, E. W. *A Different Face: The Life of Mary Wollstonecraft* (1975). Taylor, G.R.S. *Mary Wollstonecraft: A Study in Economics and Romance* (1911). Tomalin, C. *The Life and Death of Mary Wollstonecraft* (1974). Wardle, R. *Mary Wollstonecraft: A Critical Biography* (1966). Warnock, K. *Mary Wollstonecraft* (1991).

For articles in reference works, see: *Allibone. BAB100. Bloomsbury. Cambridge. Cassell. DLB. Feminist. Oxford. ToddBWW. ToddDBA.*

Other references: Barker-Benfield, G. J. *JHI* (1989). Blodgett, H. *WStu* (1990). Bowerbank, S. *SVEC* (1992). Burns, L. *Woman and Earth* (1993). Conger, S. M. *SVEC* (1992). Corfield, P. J. *TLS* (31 March 1997). Gubar, S. *FSt* (1994). Homans, M. *Narrative* (1994). Jones, V. *HEI* (1993). Maurer, S. L. *ELWIU* (1992). Michaelson, P. H. *JNT* (1991). Michaelson, P. H. *WS* (1993). Moskal, J.

MLQ (1991). Rajan, T. *SIR* (1988). Trouille, M. *SVEC* (1991). Wilson, A. *Genders* (1989).

Anne-Marie Ray
(updated by Jacqueline Dello Russo)

Ellen Price Wood

BORN: 17 January 1814, Worcester.
DIED: 10 February 1887, London.
DAUGHTER OF: Thomas Price and Elizabeth Evans Price.
MARRIED: Henry Wood, 1836.
WROTE UNDER: Mrs. Henry Wood.

W. was the author of the Victorian best seller *East Lynne* (1861) and nearly fifty other works of fiction. From 1865 until her death, she owned and edited the periodical *Argosy,* which serialized the novels of popular writers like Anthony Trollope and Charles Kingsley as well as many of her own works. The daughter of a glove manufacturer, W. was a lifelong invalid who wrote in a reclining chair, yet she demonstrated the resilience and devotion to work and family characteristic of other well-known women novelists such as Frances Trollope and Dinah Mulock Craik.

W. became an author fairly late in life. Her first fictional work, a tale called *Danesbury House* that had won a £100 prize offered by a temperance society, appeared anonymously in *New Monthly Magazine* in 1860. The W. family had been prosperous; her husband, whom she married in 1836, was a member of a banking and shipping firm who had consular duties that required him and his wife to settle in France, where they lived for twenty years. Yet there is speculation that by 1856, when her husband retired and the W.s and their children returned to London, she had to supplement their income and turned to writing.

East Lynne, W.'s first full-length novel, was enormously successful, selling 500,000 copies by the end of the century. It was paid the dubious compliment of being pirated by American publishers and was adapted numerous times for the stage, although W. received no royalties. The book was a quintessential sensation novel (a form popular in the 1860s that featured mysterious and shocking deeds, guilty family secrets, and, often, unconventional feminine behavior). *East Lynne* told the story of Isabel Vane, who marries from duty, mistakenly suspects her husband of infidelity, runs off with a rake, and is punished by disfigurement and the loss of her illegitimate child. Crushed by life, she returns to her husband's house disguised as a governess to do penance and be near her children. Her husband has by this time divorced her and married her bitter rival, and Isabel learns too late the wages of abandoning home and children.

East Lynne was a novel whose anti-heroine was, in the popular phrase of the day, more to be pitied than scorned. Misunderstood, treated as an invalid (a cause for identification on her creator's part?), and shut out from running her own home by her spiteful sister-in-law, Isabel Vane must have earned sympathy from the feminine domestic readership that provided a large part of W.'s market. Indeed, much of the novel's appeal issued from its rather subversive sympathy for an adulteress, even though W. ultimately applauds middle-class virtues and punishes her "fallen woman."

W.'s other popular novels include *The Channings* (1862), a work with a wealth of detail about the lives of the professional classes of a middle-class rural English town. It was the story of a solid, loyal family shaken by accusations about a favorite son. "How God was trying them!" exclaims the aptly named sister Constance. Like most of W.'s work, it combined realistic rendering of middle-class life with suspense and mystery. Other works that were particularly notable for their mystery elements were *Lord Oakburn's Daughters* (1864), *Elster's Folly* (1866), and *Roland Yorke* (1869).

For *Mrs. Halliburton's Troubles* (1862) and *A Life's Secret* (1867), W. drew on memories of her Worcester birthplace and the labor disputes that, as a manufacturer's daughter, she witnessed there. Both works are unsympathetic to strikers. *Mildred Arkell* (1865) explores another source of uneasiness for W., the vulgar infusion of "new money" into the quiet serenity of genteel provincial life.

W. was compared favorably to Wilkie Collins in her 1860s heyday, but by the time of her death in 1887 her reputation had declined. One critic lamented that she had gone from being "overpraised" to "unduly depreciated." There is justice in this: Her work, while melodramatic and didactic, is cleverly plotted and immensely readable. Equally important, it remains an index to prevailing attitudes about marriage and gentility—and to its Victorian readership's fantasies of rebellion and flight.

WORKS: *Danesbury House* (1860). *East Lynne* (1861). *The Golden Casket* (1861). *Mrs. Halliburton's Troubles* (1862). *The Channings* (1862). *The Shadow of Ashlydyat* (1863). *The Foggy Night at Offord* (1863). *Verner's Pride* (1863). *William Allair: or Running Away to Sea* (1864). *Lord Oakburn's Daughters* (1864). *Oswald Cray* (1864). *Trevlyn Hold: or Squire Trevlyn's Heir* (1864). *Mildred Arkell* (1865). *St. Martin's Eve* (1866). *Elster's Folly* (1866). *Lady Adelaide's Oath* (1867). *A Life's Secret* (1867). *Orville College* (1867). *Mixed Sweets from Routledge's Annual* (1867). *Castle Wafer: or the Plain Gold Ring* (1868). *The Red Court Farm* (1868). *Anne Hereford* (1868). *Roland Yorke* (1869). *Bessy Rane* (1870). *George Canterbury's Will* (1870). *Dene Hollow* (1871). *Within the Maze* (1872). *The Master of Greylands* (1873). *Johnny Ludlow* (1874–89). *Told in the Twilight* (1875). *Bessy Wells* (1875). *Adam Grainger* (1876). *Edina* (1876). *Parkwater* (1876). *Our Children* (1876). *Pomeroy Abbey* (1878). *Court Netherleigh* (1881). *About Ourselves* (1883). *Lady Grace and Other Stories* (1887). *The Story of Charles Strange* (1888). *Featherston's Story* (1889). *The Unholy Wish and Other Stories* (1890). *Edward Burton* (1890). *Summer Stories from the Argosy* (1890). *The House of Halliwell* (1890). *Ashley and Other Stories* (1897).

BIBLIOGRAPHY: Elwin. M. *Victorian Wallflowers* (1934). Hughes, W. *The Maniac in the Cellar: Sensation Novels of the 1860's* (1980). Sergeant, A., in *Women Novelists of Queen Victoria's Reign,* ed. M. Oliphant (1897). Showalter, E. *A Literature of Their Own* (1977). Spencer, S. D. *Nurturing in the Novels of Fanny Burney, Ann Radcliffe, and Ellen Price Wood* (1994).

For articles in reference works, see: *CBEL*. *DLB*. *DNB*.

Other references: Auerbach, N. *Woman and the Demon* (1982). Mitchell, S., intro. *East Lynne* (1984). Mitchell, S. *VS* (1976).

Laura Hapke

Virginia Woolf

BORN: 25 January 1882, London.
DIED: 28 March 1941, Monk's House, Rodmell, Sussex.
DAUGHTER OF: Sir Leslie Stephen and Julia Jackson Duckworth Stephen.
MARRIED: Leonard Woolf, 1912.
WROTE UNDER: Virginia Stephen; Virginia Woolf.

W. survives as several distinct and familiar voices. Her most public voice during her lifetime, the voice in her book reviews and essays on literature, is calm, witty, rational, and candid. The voice in her letters to friends and family is sometimes defensive, sometimes caustic, but nearly always clever, charming, and warm. In her diaries, though, the voice seems stricken cold with terror—dread of potential public and critical rejection of her work and fear of the physical and emotional collapses that recurred throughout her life, finally driving her to suicide. As widely read as all these voices have been, however, W. earned her fame with her artist's voice, the voice that speaks in her stories and novels.

From childhood, W. knew that she would become a novelist. Her heritage certainly suggested a literary career: Her father, Sir Leslie Stephen, literary critic, frustrated philosopher, and original editor of the *Dictionary of National Biography,* was married to one of William Makepeace Thackeray's daughters before he married W.'s mother; the Stephenses' friends included Henry James, George Meredith, James Russell Lowell, and Edward Burne-Jones. W. has preserved an evocative though fictionalized version of her family's life in *To the Lighthouse.* W. modelled the characters of Mr. and Mrs. Ramsay in the novel so closely on her own late parents' personalities that her sister Vanessa, in reading the novel, felt her mother had been "raised from the dead" and said she was shattered to find herself "face to face with those two again."

As a child in London and in Cornwall, W. read voraciously, studied languages, and wrote articles for a weekly family newspaper. When her mother died of influenza in 1895, it was, as W. later remarked, "the greatest disaster that could happen," and a few months later W. had her first breakdown, hearing voices, avoiding food, and suffering from the physical symptoms of extreme anxiety. Her grief over her mother's loss may have been exacerbated by the sexual fondlings of her half-brother, George Duckworth, which certainly upset her during her adolescence and may have contributed to her lifelong inability to respond sexually to men.

Her father's death marked a change in the children's lives; emerging from under his depressed and inhibiting influence, W. and her siblings began "a voyage out" from their eminently Victorian background. Resisting George Duckworth's attempts to introduce them into polite society, they began associating with her brother Thoby's Cambridge friends, the Apostles, a group greatly influenced by the rationalist philosopher G.E. Moore. Clive Bell (later Vanessa's husband), Saxon Sidney-Turner, Lytton Strachey, Desmond MacCarthy, and Leonard Woolf became frequent visitors, first at the Stephens' Gordon Square home and then at the house in Bloomsbury that W. and her brother Adrian rented in 1907. Though the group was diminished by Thoby's death in 1906, it later expanded to include John Maynard Keynes, Duncan Grant, Roger Fry, and—more peripherally—Bertrand Russell, E. M. Forster, and T. S. Eliot. The Bloomsbury Group, bound by no particular philosophy or discipline, came to represent a high level of intellectual discourse; an intense interest in current literary, philosophical, historical, and artistic issues; and a commitment to destroying "all barriers of reticence and reserve."

Associated with new ideas, artistic experimentation, homosexuality, and a certain degree of class snobbery, Bloomsbury was a controversial but nevertheless fertile atmosphere for W.'s writing. In 1907, during that autumn when Bloomsbury began meeting in Fitzroy Square, W. started *Melymbrosia,* which was to become her first novel, *The Voyage Out,* accepted for publication in 1913 after extensive revisions. The six years of labor indicate the difficulties that novel writing always presented to W. Her habitual reaction to stress persisted in her professional life: Upon completing each of her major novels, she would collapse in more or less serious breakdowns and, after recovering, would pursue less demanding writing projects to build her strength toward the next important novel.

W.'s most serious breakdown—and her first attempt at suicide—came after her marriage to Leonard Woolf in 1912. Six months after their marriage, W.'s condition deteriorated from severe headaches into the violent ravings that her friends and biographers have called "madness," and she tried to overdose on sleeping pills. One of Leonard Woolf's inspirations was to found and operate the Hogarth Press at their London home. W. worked as a reader and typesetter for the press from 1917 until 1937, when she sold her half of the concern to John Lehmann. W.'s first Hogarth publication, *The Mark on the Wall* (1917), is a miniaturized model of her experiments in fiction. Having no action, it can hardly be called a "story," but at the same time it is too fanciful to be called an "essay." It is a highly controlled, brief "stream of consciousness," tracing a narrator's thoughts as she observes a spot on the wall across the room from her chair. When in the end her companion makes a complaint about World War I, remarking in passing that there is a snail on the wall, the narrator reacts only to the dissolution of her reverie and the mention of the snail. The relative unimportance of the war typifies W.'s characteristic treatment of the world of politics and events. She criticized the "materialist" novelists of the previous generation—Wells, Galsworthy, and Bennett—for focusing too exclusively on externalities of setting, costume, and behavior; her fiction depicts instead her characters' inner realities, or that "life" that W. calls in her essay "Modern Fiction" (1925) "a luminous halo, a semi-transparent envelope surrounding us from the beginning of consciousness to the end."

Each of W.'s novels takes a different approach in depicting that reality through those "moments of being" when her characters become fleetingly conscious of their memories, their emotions, their perceptions, their constantly shifting selves. Her experiments in narrative technique seldom involve a literal "stream of consciousness" but venture instead into forms of free indirect discourse, following the thoughts of various characters from an external point of view and shifting frequently from observing one character's mind to another's. In *Mrs. Dalloway* (1925), the narrator depicts the inner lives of two very different Londoners: Clarissa Dalloway, a lovely, unhappy, successful socialite whom W. had originally created in *The Voyage Out*, and Septimus Warren Smith, a mad, miserable, "seedy" man who—the novel's structure suggests—has much more in common with Clarissa than is immediately obvious. Touching upon shared public experiences (for instance, watching a sky-writer over London), W. makes transitions among the overtly separate external worlds in the novel.

To the Lighthouse (1927) takes the experiment a step further, ranging among the consciousnesses of many characters but focusing especially on Mr. and Mrs. Ramsay, W.'s portraits of her parents. The novel explores their modes of thinking: Mr. Ramsay's egocentric, intellectual, self-pitying, and ambitious grapplings with philosophy; Mrs. Ramsay's maternal, emotional, manipulative, and affectionate attempts to achieve connections among the members of her extended family circle. We observe them from their own points of view as well as through the eyes of their children and friends, especially Lily Briscoe, an unmarried painter who tries simultaneously to come to terms with the Ramsays' relationship and with the frustrations of being a woman artist.

The novel is rich with symbolic significances, though W. herself claimed she couldn't "manage Symbolism except in this vague, generalised way . . . directly I'm told what a thing means, it becomes hateful to me." Though some early critics, particularly those of the *Scrutiny* school under the influence of F. R. Leavis, condemned W.'s novels as too ethereal, rarefied, and amoral, sympathetic readers have found that her symbolism and narrative structure are not at all vague but rather poetically suggestive.

W.'s most ambitious and unconventional novel, *The Waves* (1931), is still more poetic than *To the Lighthouse.* Following the internal lives of a group of friends from schooldays to adulthood as they come to terms individually and collectively with one friend's death, the novel alternates articulations of each character's thoughts with passages describing a seascape in meticulous, almost impersonally observed, densely symbolic detail. Inspired by a recurring mental image of a shark's fin emerging from beneath a wave, this novel most graphically explores the darker corners of consciousness that were such a perpetual source of terror, as well as inspiration, for W.

Self-consciously experimental, W. is also very emphatically a *woman* writer. In essays and lectures like *A Room of One's Own* (1929) or "Professions for Women" (published posthumously in 1942), W. enunciates the difficulties of any woman who wishes to overcome cultural expectations; to throttle the specter of "the Angel in the House" who insists that she maintain charming, unassertive domesticity; and to write. Highly amusing and influential, *A Room of One's Own* explores the traditional barriers to women artists—from family expectations to educational segregation to self-doubt—and concludes that women can write if they can achieve certain conditions: privacy (represented by their own rooms), independence (represented by a minimum annual income), and an ability to use "the androgynous mind." A crux in W.'s feminism, the androgynous mind would—like Shakespeare's—draw on both its "masculine" and "feminine" creative powers while writing without any self-consciousness of gender or any sense of grievance against the opposite sex. If a woman writer were to achieve this, she would be free to write her vision of life whole and undistorted, finding "a woman's sentence" and new fictional forms in which to express herself. Whether or not the argument is theoretically consistent, it certainly provides insight into W.'s view of the uncharted literary ground that she was to explore so courageously and at so high a cost to her emotional equilibrium.

In March 1941, discouraged by the ominous progress of World War II and its implications for her pacifist Jewish husband, dreading the critical reception of her last novel, *Between the Acts,* and faced with yet another emotional collapse, W. gave in to her despair and drowned herself in the River Ouse near her home. As an artist, critic, diarist, and literary theoretician, it is unlikely that she could possibly have made a greater contribution than in fact she did make to English literature and to women's literature at large.

WORKS: *The Voyage Out* (1915). *The Mark on the Wall* (1917). *Kew Gardens* (1919). *Night and Day* (1919). *Monday or Tuesday* (1921). *Jacob's Room* (1922). *Mr. Bennett and Mrs. Brown* (1924). *The Common Reader* (1925). *Mrs. Dalloway* (1925). *To the Lighthouse* (1927). *Orlando: A Biography* (1928). *A Room of One's Own* (1929). *The Waves* (1931). *Letter to a Young Poet* (1932). *The Common Reader: Second Series* (1932). *Flush: A Biography* (1933). *Walter Sickert: A Conversation* (1934). *The Years* (1937). *Three Guineas* (1938). *Roger Fry: A Biography* (1940). *Between the Acts* (1941). *The Death of the Moth and Other Essays* (1942). *A Haunted House and Other Short Stories* (1943). *The Moment and Other Essays* (1947). *The Captain's Death Bed and Other Essays* (1950). *Letters and Diaries: A Writer's Diary,* ed. L. Woolf (1953). *Virginia Woolf and Lytton Strachey: Letters,* ed. L. Woolf and J. Strachey (1956). *Granite and Rainbow* (1958). *Contemporary Writers* (1965). *Collected Essays* (4 vols., 1966–67). *Mrs. Dalloway's Party: A Short Story Sequence by Virginia Woolf,* ed. S. McNichol (1973). *The Letters of Virginia Woolf,* ed. N. Nicolson and J. Trautmann, 6 vols. (1975). *The Waves: The Two Holograph Drafts,* ed. J. W. Graham (1976). *Freshwater. A Comedy.* ed. L. P. Ruotolo (1976). *The Diary of Virginia Woolf,* ed. A. Oliver Bell (1977). *Books and Portraits: Some Further Selections from the Literary and Biographical Writings of Virginia Woolf,* ed. M. Lyon (1978). "Virginia Woolf's *The Journal of Mistress Joan Martyn,*" ed. S. M. Squier and L. DeSalvo. *TCL* (1979). *The Complete Shorter Fiction of Virginia Woolf,* ed. S. Dick (1985). *Essays,* ed. T. A. McNeillie (Vol. I, 1986; Vol. 2, 1987). For a complete bibliography of Virginia Woolf's writings, including reviews, see B. J. Kirkpatrick *A Bibliography of Virginia Woolf* (1980).

BIBLIOGRAPHY: Abel, E. *Virginia Woolf and the Fictions of Psychoanalysis* (1989). Alexander, J. *The Venture of Form in the Novels of Virginia Woolf* (1974). Alexander, P. F. *Leonard and Virginia Woolf: A Literary Partnership* (1992). *Virginia Woolf: Lesbian Readings*, ed. E. Barrett and P. Cramer (1997). Bazin, N. T. *Virginia Woolf and the Androgynous Vision* (1973). *Virginia Woolf: To the Lighthouse: A Case Book*, ed. M. Beja (1970). Bennett, J. *Virginia Woolf, Her Art as a Novelist* (1945). *Clarissa Dalloway*, ed. H. Bloom (1990). Bond, A. H. *Who Killed Virginia Woolf? A Psychobiography* (1989). *Virginia Woolf*, ed. R. Bowlby (1992). Bowlby, R. *Feminist Destinations and Further Essays on Virginia Woolf* (1997). Brewster, D. *Virginia Woolf* (1963). Brosnan, L. *Reading Virginia Woolf's Essays and Journalism: Breaking the Surface Silence (1997).* Caramagno, T. C. *The Flight of the Mind: Virginia Woolf's Art and Manic-Depressive Illness* (1992). Caws, M. A. *Women of Bloomsbury: Virginia, Vanessa, and Carrington* (1990). Chambers, R. L. *The Novels of Virginia Woolf* (1947). Daiches, D. *Virginia Woolf* (1945). Delattre, F. *The Psychological Novel of Virginia Woolf*, trans. C. Hungin (1994). De Salvo, L. *Virginia Woolf: The Impact of Childhood Sexual Abuse on Her Life and Work* (1989). DiBattista, M. *Virginia Woolf's Major Novels: The Fables of Anon* (1980). Dusinberre, J. *Virginia Woolf's Renaissance: Woman Reader or Common Reader?* (1997). Fleischman, A. *Virginia Woolf: A Critical Reading* (1975). Forster, E. M. *Virginia Woolf* (1942). *The Multiple Muses of Virginia Woolf*, ed. D. F. Gillespie (1993). Goldman, M. *The Reader's Art: Virginia Woolf as Literary Critic* (1976). Gorsky, S. R. and K. E. Roby. *Virginia Woolf* (1989). Guiguet, J. *Virginia Woolf and Her Works* (1965). Hafley, J. *The Glass Roof: Virginia Woolf as Novelist* (1954). *A Concordance to the Novels of Virginia Woolf*, ed. J. M. Haule and D. H. Smith, Jr. (1991). Hawthorn, J. *Virginia Woolf's "Mrs. Dalloway": A Study in Alienation* (1975). *Virginia Woolf: Emerging Perspectives*, ed. M. Hussey and V. Neverow (1994). Johnston, J. K. *The Bloomsbury Group: A Study of E. M. Forster, Lytton Strachey, Virginia Woolf, and Their Circle* (1954). Kelley, A.V.B. *The Novels of Virginia Woolf: Fact and Vision* (1973). Kettle, A. *Mrs. Dalloway* (1973). *Critics on Virginia Woolf*, ed. J. E. Latham (1970). Laurence, P. O. *The Reading of Silence: Virginia Woolf in the English Tradition* (1991). Leaska, M. A. *The Novels of Virginia Woolf: From Beginning to End* (1978). Lee, H. *The Novels of Virginia Woolf* (1977). Lee, H. *Virginia Woolf* (1996). Lehmann, J. *Virginia Woolf and Her World* (1975). *Virginia Woolf*, ed. T.S.W. Lewis (1977). Little, J. *The Experimental Self: Dialogic Subjectivity in Woolf, Pym, and Brooke-Rose* (1996). Love, J. O. *Worlds in Consciousness: Mythopoetic Thought in the Novels of Virginia Woolf* (1970). Majumdar, R. *Virginia Woolf: An Annotated Bibliography of Criticism, 1915–1974* (1976). *Virginia Woolf: The Critical Heritage*, ed. R. Majumdar and A. McLaurin (1975). *New Feminist Essays on Virginia Woolf*, ed. J. Marcus (1981). *Virginia Woolf: A Feminist Slant*, ed. J. Marcus (1983). Marder, F. H. *Feminism and Art: A Study of Virginia Woolf* (1968). McLaurin, A. *Virginia Woolf: The Echoes Enslaved* (1973). Mepham, J. *Virginia Woolf* (1992). Mepham, J. *Virginia Woolf* (1992). Moody, A. D. *Virginia Woolf* (1968). Morris, J. *Time and Timelessness in Virginia Woolf* (1977). Naremore, J. *The World Without a Self: Virginia Woolf and the Novel* (1974). *Virginia Woolf's Themes and Variations*, ed. V. Neverow-Turk and M. Hussey (1993). *Recollections of Virginia Woolf by Her Contemporaries*, ed. J. R. Noble (1972). Novak, J. *The Razor Edge of Balance: A Study of Virginia Woolf* (1978). Paul, J. M. *The Victorian Heritage of Virginia Woolf: The External World in Her Novels* (1987). Pippett, A. *The Moth and the Star: A Biography of Virginia Woolf* (1955). Poresky, L. A. *The Elusive Self: Psyche and Spirit in Virginia Woolf's Novels* (1981). Rantavaara, L. *Virginia Woolf and Bloomsbury* (1953). Reid, P. *Art and Affection: A Life of Virginia Woolf* (1996). Richter, H. *Virginia Woolf: The Inward Voyage* (1970). Rose, P. *Woman of Letters: A Life of Virginia Woolf* (1978). *Virginia Woolf/Women and Fiction*, ed. S. P. Rosenbaum (1992). Rosenthal, M. *Virginia Woolf* (1979). Ruddick, L. *The Seen and the Unseen: Virginia Woolf's "To the Lighthouse"* (1977). Schaefer, J. O. *The Three-Fold Nature of Reality in the Novels of Virginia Woolf* (1965). Schlack, B. A. *Continuing Presences: Virginia Woolf's Use of Literary Allusion* (1979). Scott, B. K. *Refiguring Modernism* (1995). Spater, G. and L. Parsons *A Marriage of True Minds: An Intimate Portrait of Leonard and Virginia Woolf* (1977). Spilka, M. *Virginia Woolf's Quarrel with Grieving* (1980). *Virginia Woolf: A Collection of Critical Essays*, ed. C. Sprague (1971). *Virginia Woolf: Interviews and Recollections*, ed. J. H. Stape (1995). Sugiyama, Y. *Rainbow and Granite: A Study of Virginia Woolf* (1973). Thakur, N. C. *The Symbolism of Virginia Woolf* (1965). Trautmann, J. *The Jessamy Brides: The Friendship of Virginia Woolf and V. Sackville-West* (1974). Trombley, S. *All That Summer She Was Mad: Virginia Woolf, Female Victim of Male Medicine* (1982). Verga, L. *Virginia Woolf's Novels and Their Analogy to Music* (1945). Vogler, T. A. *Twentieth-Century Interpretations of "To the Lighthouse": A Collection of Critical Essays* (1970). Woodring, C. *Virginia Woolf* (1966).

For articles in reference works, see: *Bloomsbury. CA. Cambridge. CLC. Longman. Feminist. MBL* and *SUP. Oxford. TCA* and *SUP. TCW. ToddBWW.*

Other references: Cecil, D. *Poets and Story Tellers* (1949). Dahl, L. *Linguistic Features of the Stream-of-Consciousness Techniques of James Joyce, Virginia Woolf, and Eugene O'Neill* (1970). Daiches, D. *The Novel and the Modern World* (1939). Elert, K. *Portraits of Women in Selected Novels by Virginia Woolf and E. M. Forster* (1979). Fleischman, A. *The English Historical Novel: Walter Scott to Virginia Woolf* (1971). Gill, R. *The English Country House and the Literary Imagination* (1972). *The Representation of Women in Fiction*, ed. C. G. Heilbrun and M. R. Higgonet (1983). Kaplan, S. J. *Feminine Consciousness in the Modern British Novel* (1975). Little, J. *Comedy and the Woman Writer: Woolf, Spark, and Feminism* (1983).

Robyn R. Warhol

Dorothy Wordsworth

BORN: 25 December 1771, Cockermouth, Cumberland.
DIED: 25 January 1855, Rydal Mount, Cumberland.
DAUGHTER OF: John Wordsworth and Anne Cookson.

The early loss of both parents bound W. closely to her brothers John and especially to William. In 1795, W. and William took up residence together at Racedown in Dorset, and two years later they moved to Alfoxden to be near Samuel Taylor Coleridge at Nether Stowey. After the publication of *Lyrical Ballads* (1798), W. and William spent a winter in Germany, after which they settled at Dove Cottage in Grasmere. When William married Mary Hutchinson, W.'s long-time and intimate friend, in 1802, W. lived on with her brother and his wife, taking an active interest in their domestic life and their children. The last twenty years of W.'s life were spent as an invalid, afflicted in both body and mind. She survived William by five years.

Despite her literary gifts, W. never became an author in her own right during her lifetime. Yet family and friends, including some of the finest literary minds of the period, recognized her abilities. In one journal entry, W. speaks of a scene making her "more than half a poet," but elsewhere she insists, "I should detest the idea of setting myself up as an Author." She wrote fewer than twenty poems, only five of which were published during her lifetime, and these were incorporated into her brother William's work, as were short extracts from her journals and letters. And although her *Narrative Concerning George and Sarah Green* was meant to be part of the public record of Grasmere Vale, she refused to have it published. Only her *Recollections of a Tour in Scotland,* although actually published posthumously in 1874, was ever intended for publication.

It is for her journal writing that W. is now praised, especially for the journals kept at Alfoxden (January–May 1798) and Grasmere (May 1800–January 1803); she also kept a journal during her stay in Germany (1798) before her residence at Grasmere. After Grasmere, the intimate record of daily life stops, but W. continued to keep a number of journals about various expeditions: a Scotland tour in 1803; excursions on the banks of Ullswater and up Scawfell Pike in 1805 and 1818, respectively; an 1820 tour of the Continent; a second tour of Scotland in 1822; and an 1828 tour of the Isle of Man.

The Alfoxden and Grasmere journals are characterized by a naturalness and spontaneity that seem to bridge the prosaic and poetic details of everyday life with effortlessness and ease. Throughout her writing there is evidence of what Coleridge described as "her eye watchful in minutest observation of nature" and what Thomas De Quincey called her quick and ready "sympathy with either joy or sorrow, with laughter or with tears, with the realities of life or the larger realities of the poets." In her journals, W. tells of making shoes, weeding the garden, copying her brother's poems, packing mattresses, reading Shakespeare, gathering firewood, walking with Coleridge, ironing linen. The poetic and the prosaic, the ready sympathy for the unfortunate, and the keen observation of nature are all brought together in her 18 May 1800 entry. In this representative entry, W. begins with a passing mention of church-going and the weather, moves on to an appreciation of the surrounding valley and mountains with their bare ashes and emerging corn, and follows with a tale of a beggar girl turned out of doors overnight by her stepmother.

W. clearly influenced and inspired some of her brother's poetry: She continued her journal at Grasmere "because I shall give Wm Pleasure by it," and he sometimes had her read aloud journal passages to revive his memory. His poems "I wandered lonely as a cloud," "Beggars," and "Resolution and Independence," among others, all owe a profound debt to W.'s prose descriptions. Not only did her journals give William poetic inspiration but her daily attention to the responsibilities of domestic life (as her journal readily attests) freed him to pursue his poetry. Her ready concern in her brother's labors, illnesses, and achievements provided an important source of emotional support, for which he remembers her in *The Prelude:* "She, in the midst of all, preserved me still / A Poet" (Book XI). For W., in her modesty, it seems to have been enough to have inspired her brother as a poet rather than to have emerged as one herself.

WORKS: *George and Sarah Green: A Narrative* (1808; as *A Narrative Concerning George and Sarah Green of the Parish of Grasmere Addressed to a Friend,* ed. E. De Selincourt, 1936). *Recollections of a Tour in Scotland* (1874). *The Early Letters of William and Dorothy Wordsworth,* ed. E. De Selincourt (1935). *The Letters of William and Dorothy Wordsworth: The Middle Years (1806–1820),* ed. E. De Selincourt (1937). *The Letters of William and Dorothy Wordsworth: The Later Years (1821–1850),* ed. E. De Selincourt (1939). *The Journals of Dorothy Wordsworth,* ed. E. De Selincourt (1941). *The Grasmere Journal,* rev. ed., ed. J. Wordsworth (1987). *Letters of William and Dorothy Wordsworth,* 8 vols., ed. A. G. Hill (1967–93). *Selections from the Journals,* ed. P. Hamilton (1992).

BIBLIOGRAPHY: Alexander, M. *WS* (1988). Bond, A. *ChLB* (1984). Cole, L. and R. G. Swartz, in *At the Limits of Romanticism,* ed. M. A. Favret and N. J. Watson (1994). Cook, K. K. *ABSt* (1990, 1995). Curtis, J. *BuR* (1992). De Selincourt, E. *Dorothy Wordsworth: A Biography* (1933). Fay, E. A. *Becoming Wordsworthian: A Performative Aesthetic* (1995). Heinzelman, K. *ABSt* (1986–87). Heinzelman, K., in *Romanticism and Feminism,* ed. A. K. Mellor (1988). Homans, M. *Women Writers and Poetic Identity: Dorothy Wordsworth, Emily Brontë, and Emily Dickinson* (1980). King, F. *WC* (1987). Kramer, L. *VP* (1986). Lawrence, B. *ChLB* (1995). Levin, S. M. *Dorothy Wordsworth and Romanticism* (1987). Levin, S. M. *PSt* (1987). Liu, A. *Criticism* (1984). McCormick, A. H. *PQ* (1990). McGavran, J. H., Jr. *MLQ* (1981). McGavran, J. H., Jr., in *The Private Self: Theory and Practice of Women's Autobiographical Writings,* ed. S. Benstock (1988). McGavran, J. H., Jr. *SoAR* (1988). McGavran, J. H., Jr. *PLL* (1990). MacLean, C. M. *Dorothy and William Wordsworth* (1927). Meiners, K. T. *CentR* (1993). Powell, R. *Neophil* (1995). Robinson, J. C. *PQ* (1985). Snyder, W. C. *WS* (1992). Soderholm, J. *NLH* (1995). Taylor, E. R. *BB* (1983). Thomson, D. H. *SEL* (1987). Tyler, L. *UDR* (1995). Vegler, T. A., in *Mothering the Mind,* ed. R. Perry and M. W. Brownly (1984). Walker, J. R. in *A Handbook to English Romanticism,* ed. J. Raimond and J. R. Waters (1992). Wilinsky, J., in *The Educational Legacy of Romanticism,* ed. J. Wilinsky (1990). Willy, M. *Three Diarists* (1964). Wolfson, S. J., in *Romanticism and Feminism,* ed. A. K. Mellor (1988). Woof, P. *WC* (1986, 1989, 1991). Woof, P. *ChLB* (1989). Woof, P. *BuR* (1992). Woolsey, L. M. *TPB* (1990).

For articles in reference works, see: *BA19C. Bloomsbury. Cambridge. Feminist. Oxford. ToddBWW.*

Other references: Agress, L. *The Feminine Irony: Women on Women in Early-Nineteenth-Century English Literature* (1978). Bawer, B. *NewC* (January 1986). Freeman, N. *TLS* (28 June 1985). Huftel, S. *ContempR* (1986).

Eileen Finan
(updated by Natalie Joy Woodall)

Frances Wright

BORN: 6 September 1795, Dundee, Scotland.
DIED: 13 December 1852, Cincinnati, Ohio, United States.
DAUGHTER OF: James Wright and Camilla Campbell Wright.
MARRIED: Guillaume Phiquepal D'Arusmont, 1831.
WROTE UNDER: Frances Wright D'Arusmont; Madam D'Arusmont; Frances Wright.

A radical woman espousing racial integration, free love (i.e., state-sanctioned marriage vows are unnecessary), working-class rights, birth control, and opposition to the stranglehold of organized religion on human freedom and thought, W. remains one of the most unusual and enigmatic of early feminists. Throughout her life, she advocated complete universal suffrage—for blacks, for women, for the working class—and education as the means of achieving equality between male and female, black and white, rich and poor. She was more democratic in her beliefs than any feminist for the next hundred years.

A charismatic leader, orator, and writer, her life and writings reflect her concerns. From an early age she demonstrated her facility with the English language, the influences of the Enlightenment, and the egalitarian rhetoric of the American and French revolutions. Born in Scotland, W. was daughter to a devotee of Thomas Paine but was orphaned at the age of two. She speaks in her third-person autobiography, *Biography, Notes, and Political Letters of Frances Wright D'Arusmont* (1844), of being immediately entranced as a young woman with the democratic experiment in the United States. In 1818, at the age of twenty-three, she and her sister sailed to New York City. The letters she wrote home for the next two years to her friend, Mrs. Rabina Millar—accounts of her travels, meetings, and observations on American character, institutions, and morals—were published in 1821 as *Views of Society and Manners in America.* This volume, a sensation in England and France, brought W. to the attention of the aging Marquis de Lafayette, hero of the American Revolution. The essays show a vivid sense of detail and enthusiasm for America as well as insight into such institutions as education, the position of women, and slavery, areas that were to occupy W. for the rest of her life.

Her youthful passions for drama and Byronic verse found outlet in *Altorf,* a verse drama about Swiss independence, first performed and printed in Philadelphia (1819); interest in the example of Greece as the first democracy led to her writing a Socratic dialogue, *A Few Days in Athens* (1822). Thereafter, most of W.'s work was written not primarily for book publication but as lectures and journalism. Her greatest influence was as an orator and lecturer, and all her charisma and leadership were vented in the persuasive arts.

When she returned to the United States, she quickly modified her earlier enthusiasms. In particular she began worrying over the institution of slavery, having seen a slave ship and auction in Virginia and the wretched condition of freed blacks. She advocated a scheme of gradual emancipation whereby slaves would work off their freedom on productive farms (the land set aside by Congress), participate equally in the affairs of the farm with whites, be educated, and eventually earn their freedom. The idea, she felt, would not pose an economic hardship to southern land owners because they would be given the profits of the blacks' labor for several years. W. published this utopian scheme in 1825 as *A Plan for the Gradual Abolition of Slavery in the United States, Without Danger of Loss to the Citizens of the South;* various leaders encouraged her in this scheme, including Thomas Jefferson and Robert Owen, who had just purchased the Rappite community of New Harmony (Indiana) for his own communal experiment. In December 1825, W. purchased 640 acres east of Memphis, Tennessee, bought a number of slaves, and set out to carve a utopia from the mosquito lowlands and pine forests on the Wolf River, calling the community "Nashoba," Chickasaw for "wolf." Nashoba ultimately failed after four years when an abolitionist paper published the community's negative views on intermarriage and miscegenation. W. published a manifesto in the Memphis *Advocate* restating her compensated-emancipation plan and went on to attack segregation in education and sexual relations, organized religion, and marriage itself, which led to attacks by both dedicated abolitionists and southern slave owners.

To her credit, W. kept her promise to the slaves working on their "gradual emancipation" at Nashoba. She and Phiquepal D'Arusmont, a French doctor with whom she had become intimate in New Harmony, took the slaves by boat down the Mississippi and across the Gulf of Mexico to Haiti, the only black republic in the New World. There they were given land and freedom.

W. returned to New York City, where she had begun work in education and agitation for the working class by publishing and editing the *Free Enquirer,* founding the Workingmen's Institute in an old church on the Bowery, and continuing her lecture circuit. Some of the lectures were collected and published in *Course of Popular Lectures* (1829; 1836). In these, "Of Free Enquiry" for example, W. is much more critical of America than she was in *Views of Society and Manners.* She sees education as the key to equality for all and advocates a system of collective cooperation with a Kantian view of individual rights bounded only by other human beings. She considers children to be human beings and advocates the development of all their faculties. She holds that it is in the interest of all to enlighten females more than males; society can never be perfected with half the population remaining uneducated. She was one of the first to equate women with other subjected classes (blacks, working class), and her use of the term "humankind" predated twentieth-century nonsexist language by 150 years.

W. was so influential in the nascent working-class political movement that the election of 1829 won her group a seat in the New York legislature and the nickname "the Fanny Wright party." Soon, though, she returned to Europe with her dangerously ill sister Camilla, settling in Paris near Phiquepal D'Arusmont, whom she married in 1831. She gave birth to a daughter, Sylva, in 1832. By 1835, W. was again lecturing in America, her family sometimes with her and sometimes remaining in Paris.

After W. inherited the family fortune in Scotland, she and her husband were divorced while she continued lecturing and writing. Her last work, *England the Civilizer* (1848), presents an apocalyptic vision of a new egalitarian society, the instigators being science, industry, and women. At the same time, she had become disenchanted with much of the American "experiment"—critical of attitudes toward women, blacks, and the working class, and particularly hostile toward the hold that evangelical religion had on the Midwest and South.

Called "The Priestess of Beelzebub" and her followers dubbed "Fanny Wright Free Lovers," W.'s influence waned after her death from a fall at the age of fifty-seven, in 1852. Although Elizabeth Cady Stanton paid tribute to her in *The History of Woman Suffrage* (1881), most other contemporary works on nineteenth-century women (such as Phoebe A. Hanaford's *Daughters of America, or Women of the Century* [1883]) failed to mention W. For more than a century her life and works were essentially forgotten until the second wave of feminism began in the 1960s.

WORKS: *Altorf, a Tragedy* (1819). *Views of Society and Manners in America* (1821). *A Few Days in Athens* (1822). *A Plan for the Gradual Abolition of Slavery in the United States, Without Danger of Loss to the Citizens of the South* (1825). *Course of Popular Lectures* (1829; 1836). *Biography, Notes, and Political Letters of Frances Wright D'Arusmont* (1844). *England the Civilizer* (1848).

BIBLIOGRAPHY: Bartlett, E. *Liberty, Equality, Sorority: The Origins and Interpretation of American Feminist Thought* (1994). Boyer, P. S., in *Notable American Women*, ed. E. T. James et al. (1971). Eckhardt, C. *Frances Wright: Rebel in America* (1984). Ferguson, M. *ECent* (1986). Kissell, S. *In Common Cause: The "Conservative" Frances Trollope and the "Radical" Frances Wright* (1993). Lane, M. *Francis Wright and the Great Experiment* (1972). Mullen, R. *Birds of Passage: Five Englishwomen in Search of America* (1994). Perkins, A.J.G. and T. Wolfson. *Frances Wright: Free Enquirer* (1939). Stiller, R. *Commune on the Frontier: The Story of Frances Wright.* (1972). Waterman, W. *Frances Wright.* (1924).

For articles in reference works, see: *Feminist.* James, E. T. et al. *Notable American Women* (1971). *IDWB.*

Other references: Rossi, A. *The Feminist Papers* (1973). *SoQ* (1972). Spender, D. *Women of Ideas and What Men Have Done to Them* (1982). *WS* (1974).

Margaret McFadden

Wright, Francesca: See *Robins, Denise Naomi*

Mary (Sidney) Wroth

BORN: 1586 or 1587.
DIED: 1651 or 1653.
DAUGHTER OF: Robert Sidney and Barbara Gamage.
MARRIED: Sir Robert Wroth, 1604.

W. was the eldest daughter of Barbara Gamage, a Welsh heiress, and Robert Sidney, Earl of Leicester, the younger brother of Sir Philip Sidney and Mary Sidney, Countess of Pembroke. Robert Sidney's letters frequently mention "my daughter Wroth" with particular affection, and he often visited her after her marriage in 1604. In that year W. became part of the court and acted in masques, including Ben Jonson's *The Masque of Blackness.* Contemporary writers such as Nathaniel Baxter, Joshua Sylvester, and George Chapman praised her poetry. Ben Jonson said that reading her sonnets had made him "a better lover and much better Poet." Jonson also praised her as "a Sidney, though unnamed," dedicated *The Alchemist* to her, and, although he told William Drummond that she was "unworthily maried on a Jealous husband," wrote a poem (possibly ironic) in praise of Sir Robert Wroth.

A month after her first child, James, was born, her husband died (1614), leaving her with a staggering debt of some £23,000. Two years later, James died, whereupon most of the estate went to her husband's brother, John Wroth; W. was in financial difficulties throughout the rest of her life. She never remarried, but she bore two illegitimate children to her cousin, William Herbert, third Earl of Pembroke.

She wrote a pastoral tragicomedy, *Love's Victorie*, for manuscript circulation and possibly for performance with her friends, but only one of her works was published in her lifetime, *Urania* (1621), an intricate romance modeled on her uncle's *Arcadia.* The first full-length work of fiction by an Englishwoman, its central tale concerns the love of Queen Pamphilia, the image of Constancy, for Amphilanthus ("Lover-of-two"). Despite the presence of some constant male lovers, such as Pamphilia's brother Rosindy, inconstancy is frequently, and sometimes comically, presented as a male attribute: "Being a man, it was necessary for him to exceede a woman in all things, so much as inconstancie was found fit for him to excell her in, hee left her for a new." Like Queen Elizabeth, Pamphilia swears that she will never marry since she is married to her kingdom. A second major plot strand is the friendship of Pamphilia and Urania. The romance opens with Urania seeking her true identity. Although she has been raised as a shepherdess, she is revealed to be the sister of Amphilanthus and the cousin of Pamphilia. Both women eventually marry; in the second part, which W. never published, the story continues into the next generation.

Urania, which intermingles transparent references to W. herself and to other contemporary figures with its fictions, offended powerful figures at court. W. was forced to apologize and withdraw the book from sale; it was not reprinted until 1995.

In addition to poems scattered through the text in the manner of Sidney's *Arcadia,* a series of nineteen songs and eighty-three sonnets entitled *Pamphilia to Amphilanthus* is appended to the text, presenting the Petrarchan courtly love traditions from a female perspective. Significantly, W. wrote in an Elizabethan mode like her father's *Rosis and Lysa* and her uncle's *Astrophel and Stella.* The poems have a melancholy tone; Pamphilia is constant in her love to the faithless Amphilanthus. Much of the imagery is Petrarchan, but the tone of suffering seems from the heart. Pamphilia finally turns from love of Amphilanthus to the love of God. The concluding poem speaks of Venus's praise as proper to "young beeginers"; Pamphilia vows to progress now to "truth, which shall eternal goodnes prove; / Injoying of true joye, the most . . . The endles gaine which never will remove."

W. was the first English woman to write a full-length work of prose fiction and the first to write a significant body of secular poetry, but she was castigated for that achievement. Lord Denny admonished her to imitate her "vertuous & learned Aunt, who translated so many godly bookes, & especially the holy Psalms of David," rather than creating "lascivious tales & amarous toyes"; translation, not creation, was the province of a learned woman. W. gave a spirited reply to Denny, but she apparently was forced to learn the womanly virtue of silence; if she did write more after she withdrew her *Urania,* it has not survived.

WORKS: *Love's Victorie* (MS., n.d.). *Urania* (1621, including *Pamphilia to Amphilanthus,* a series of 19 songs and 83 sonnets; ed. J. A. Roberts, 1995). *Pamphilia to Amphilanthus,* ed. G. Waller (1977). *The Power of Lady Mary Wroth,* ed. J. A. Roberts (1983). *Lady Mary Wroth's Love's Victory,* ed. M. G. Brennan (1988). *Poems: A Modernized Edition,* ed. R. E. Pritchard (1997).

BIBLIOGRAPHY: Beilin, E. V. *SSt* (1981). Beilin, E. V. *Redeeming Eve* (1987). Carrell, J. *SEL* (1994). Hannay, M. P., in *Women Writers of the Renaissance and Reformation,* ed. K. Wilson (1987). Hannay, M. P., in *Reading Mary Wroth,* ed. N. Miller and G. Waller (1991). Hannay, M. P., in *Attending to Women in Early Modern England,* ed. B. Travitsky and A. Seeff (1994). Hanson, E., in *Homosexuality in Renaissance and Enlightenment England,* ed. D. J. Summers (1992). Jones, A. R. *The Currency of Eros* (1990). Krontiris, T. *Oppositional Voices: Women as Writers and Translator of Literature in the English Renaissance* (1992). Lamb, M. E., in *Reading Mary Wroth,* ed. N. Miller and G. Waller (1991). Lewalski, B., in *Reading Mary Wroth,* ed. N. Miller and G. Waller (1991). Lewalski, B. *Writing Women in Jacobean England* (1993). MacArthur, J. *ESC* (1989). McLaren, M., in *The Renaissance Englishwoman in Print,* ed. A. Haselkorn and B. Travitsky (1990). Masten, J., in *Reading Mary Wroth,* ed. N. Miller and G. Waller (1991). Miller, N. *SEL* (1989). Miller, N. J. *Changing the Subject: Mary Wroth and Figurations of Gender in Early Modern England* (1996). *Reading Mary Wroth,* ed. N. Miller and G. Waller (1991). O'Connor, J. J. *N&Q* (1955). Parry, G. *PLPLS-LHS* (1975). Paulissen, M. N. *PMPA* (1978). Paulissen, M. N. *The Love Sonnets of Lady Mary Wroth: A Critical Introduction* (1982). Pigeon, R. *N&Q* (1991). Quilligan, M., in *Soliciting Interpretation: Literary Theory and Seventeenth-Century English Poetry,* ed. E. Harvey and K. Maus (1990). Quilligan, M., in *Unfolded Tales: Essays on Renaissance Romance,* ed. G. Logan and G. Teskey (1989). Quilligan, M., in *The Renaissance Englishwoman in Print,* ed. A. Haselkorn and B. Travitsky (1990). Roberts, J. A. *N&Q* (1977). Roberts, J. A. *Journal of Women's Studies in Literature* (1979, 1982). Roberts, J. A. *HLQ* (1983). Roberts, J. A., in *The Renaissance Englishwoman in Print,* ed. A. Haselkorn and B. Travitsky (1990). Roberts, J. A. *WS* (1991). Roberts, J. A., in *New Ways of Looking at Old Texts,* ed. S. Hill (1993). Salzman, P. *RES* (1978). Salzman, P. *English Prose Fiction* (1985). Salzman, P. *Southerly* (1989). Schleiner, L. *Tudor and Stuart Women Writers* (1994). Shapiro, M. *MRDE* (1989). Shaver, A. *MLS* (1991). Swift, C. *ELR* (1984). Wall, W. *The Imprint of Gender: Authorship and Publication in the English Renaissance* (1993). Waller, G., in *Silent But for the Word: Tudor Women as Translators, Patrons and Writers of Religious Works,* ed. M. Hannay (1985). Waller, G. *The Sidney Family Romance: Mary Wroth, William Herbert, and the Early Modern Construction of Gender* (1993). Wynne-Davies, M., in *Gloriana's Face,* ed. S. P. Cerasano and M. W. Davies (1992).

For articles in reference works, see: *Bell. Bloomsbury. Europa. Feminist. Oxford. ToddBWW. Wives and Daughters.*

Other references: *Women Writers of the Renaissance and Reformation,* ed. K. M. Wilson (1987).

Margaret P. Hannay

Wynman, Margaret: See *Dixon, Ella Nora Hepworth*

Wythens, Lady: See *Taylor, Elizabeth (Wythens)*

Frances Amelia Yates

BORN: 28 November 1899, Portsmouth, Hampshire.
DIED: 19 September 1981, London.
DAUGHTER OF: James Alfred Yates and Hannah Malpas Yates.

When she died, Y. left behind a body of work that kept commentators grasping for sufficiently high praise. They sounded almost surprised to find that her work had become so important, so indispensable. That it was both is a testament to her talent and originality.

She was that rarest of things, the semiprivate scholar

who went her own way and convinced others to come as well. As a writer and scholar, she started somewhat late, earning her first degree at the age of twenty-five and writing her first book ten years later. She took her B.A. and M.A. at the University of London, and she managed to support herself as a private scholar and sometime teacher, working as a research assistant at the Warburg Institute until the outbreak of World War II. From 1939 to 1941, she worked with the ambulance corps in London, after which she became a lecturer in Renaissance culture at the Warburg.

Her great topic was the Renaissance—but a side of the Renaissance that, until her work, had been less studied than it should have been. *Esoterica* would be a good word for it, a word of the highest praise. After her first book, a biography of John Florio, she became interested in Giordano Bruno, a philosopher, writer, and mystic. In 1947, she wrote an essay entitled "Queen Elizabeth as Astraea," which discussed a cult of the virgin queen, not only in England but throughout Europe. And she was drawn to the revival of interest in Plato in late sixteenth-century France.

Her sixties and seventies saw an astonishing production of controversial, brilliant, and ground-breaking works. She was more and more interested in mystical ideas, the interplay of the supposedly rigid Christian culture with the enduring fascination with magic, mysticism, and alternative ways of imagining the universe. Scholars had known about these lines of thought, but few had really investigated them, perhaps believing that the Renaissance was dominated by the familiar mainstream ethic.

Incredibly learned, Y. crossed disciplines to forge new ways of studying literature and culture. Her approach was a kind of history mixed with a kind of sociology, always illustrated with wide-ranging references that included industrial processes, linguistics, psychology, medicine, economics, and garden-variety literary studies. She was likely to juxtapose unfamiliar things—sonnets with smelting, rituals of initiation with village feasts, alchemy with foreign policy—to create new ways of seeing old certainties. Peter Burke is right in pointing out that her great talent was to "suggest connections between fields too often studied in isolation."

Y.'s great contribution was to show how much tributaries can drive the main stream. Bruno, a figure who, while well known, had been relegated to the outskirts of Renaissance scholarship, stepped front and center in her book *Giordano Bruno* (1964), as was the huge underground culture of hermetic thought in Renaissance Europe. As she showed in that book, hermetic philosophy infiltrated standard Christian culture and pervaded painting, poetry, philosophy, and the arts. This kind of thinking transcended national and linguistic boundaries and created, if not exactly a counterculture, a parallel culture across Europe. Y. showed that the Renaissance was much more diverse and complex than had been previously imagined, and she argued so convincingly for the importance of Bruno that few books today on Renaissance thought or philosophy fail to mention him or hermeticism.

Nothing seemed too recondite, nothing too oddball. Her book *The Art of Memory* (1966) was perhaps her best. Again, it seemed as if Y. had tackled a strange and idiosyncratic topic: how medieval and Renaissance methods of memorization and learning affected views of the psyche and the mind. The book encapsulated a neglected chapter in cultural and philosophical history, and within a few years it became obligatory reading for any student of the Renaissance. *Theatre of the World* (1969), though criticized for applying her findings too broadly, added a new layer of knowledge about how astrology, alchemy, and other branches of mysticism affected the way the Renaissance theater grew up. Her critics charged that she too often connected marginal thinkers with mainstream cultural productions, such as when she argued that the shape of Elizabethan theaters had been influenced by contemporary mysticism. Her findings left their impact, however, and most Renaissance scholars acknowledge the truth of her discoveries. Her book on *The Rosicrucian Enlightenment* (1972) demonstrated once again how a supposedly off-center minority religio-mystical brotherhood could disseminate its ideas into the productions of canonical authors, artists, and thinkers. By the time her last books appeared, the mystical and the occult had become industries unto themselves in Renaissance studies. During her life, Y. never ceased to be the leader and creator of that industry. She made the terms "hermeticism," "the occult," and "the Cabalistic tradition" familiar to Renaissance scholars everywhere.

Her way of doing things, once considered maverick, has influenced scholars in other fields, particularly sociology, anthropology, folklore, and popular culture—any humanist field in which it is important to measure art against its social, economic, and cultural environs. She was not alone (one can argue that scholars such as Rosalie Colie, Ernst Gombrich, Natalie Zemon Davis, and Gertrude Himmelfarb, all in very different ways, were operating by similar lights), but she certainly showed the way in a series of densely learned and resonantly written books. She was guided by a quirky, personal intuition, combined with an intense and detailed regard for the documents she was reading. Renaissance studies, and humanist studies in general, will never be the same.

WORKS: *John Florio: The Life of an Italian in Shakespeare's England* (1934). *A Study of Love's Labor's Lost* (1936). *The French Academies of the Sixteenth Century* (1947). *The Valois Tapestries* (1959). *Giordano Bruno and the Hermetic Tradition* (1964). *The Art of Memory* (1966). *Theatre of the World* (1969). *The Rosicrucian Enlightenment* (1972). *Astraea: The Imperial Theme* (1975). *Shakespeare's Last Plays* (1975). *The Occult Philosophy in the Elizabethan Age* (1979). *Collected Essays*, Vol. 1: *Lull and Bruno* (1982); Vol. 2: *Renaissance and Reform: The Italian Contribution* (1983); Vol. 3: *Ideas and Ideals in the North European Renaissance* (1984).

BIBLIOGRAPHY: Gombrich, E. *The Evaluation of Esoteric Currents: A Commemoration of the Work of Frances A. Yates (1899–1981)* (1984). Vickers, B. *Frances Yates and the Writing of History* (1979). *Frances A. Yates 1899–1981* (1982).

For articles in reference works, see: *CA*. *IAWWW*. *ToddBWW*.

Other references: Burke, P. *History Today* (1982). Burke, P. *Bulletin for the Society of Renaissance Studies* (1984). Jacob, M. and E. Gosselin. *Isis* (1982). Richards, B. *N&Q* (1988). Rowland, B. *Poetica* (1993). Sicari, S. *Cross-Currents* (1988).

John Timpane

Ann Cromartie Yearsley

BORN: 1752, Clifton, near Bristol.
DIED: 8 May 1806, Melksham, Wiltshire.
DAUGHTER OF: John Cromartie and Ann Cromartie.
WROTE UNDER: Lactilla.

Born to working-class parents, Y. was only minimally educated. Like her mother, she delivered milk from door to door, thus gaining membership in the society of "heaven-taught" poets as "Lactilla," or the poetical milkwoman.

In 1784, Hannah More's cook, one of Y.'s customers, told her employer about this remarkably gifted poet victimized by dire poverty and grinding toil. More attempted to fill in some of the gaps in Y.'s education and then set about editing her poetry and seeking subscriptions for its publication. The first published volume, *Poems on Several Occasions* (1784), earned some £600. More and Elizabeth Montagu took charge of the profits as trustees for the author. Y. strenuously objected to this arrangement, quarreled publicly with her two patronesses, and demanded editorial and financial control of her work. Using the money earned by the first volume, she opened a circulating library at Bristol Hot Wells, but it soon failed. She subsequently published three more volumes of poetry, an unfinished historical novel, an unsuccessful tragedy, and several occasional poems.

Perhaps because of her sporadic education, Y.'s poetry is highly derivative in both form and content. She relished the role of untutored poetess deprived by the cruelty of circumstances, and her poetry is infused by a tone of woe, self-pity, and general lamentation. Most of Y.'s poems are occasional, commemorative, or meditative lyrics, liberally endowed with the formulae and conventions of eighteenth-century verse. At her best, she employed simple metrical and stanzaic forms within a structured narrative whose chronological sequence countered her tendency toward expansiveness.

Given the deplorable conditions of the earlier parts of her life, it is not surprising that Y. cultivated melancholy and meditated frequently upon death. She sought resignation to God's will and wrote elegies that proffered the traditional consolation of the soul's union with loved ones in a better and happier afterlife. Although Y. yearned for the spiritual tranquility of untroubled faith, her speculative nature disturbed the serenity of her religious contemplations.

Y. found consolation in friendship, which she glorified as the highest earthly value; she tried in many poems to distinguish it from self-serving hypocrisy, a concern that probably originated in the quarrel with More. Friendship must be kept uncontaminated by the relationship between dependent and superior, which will destroy both friendship and poetic inspiration. Y. protested in verse More's charges of ingratitude and retaliated with her own accusations of "guilty blandishment."

Y. held a conventional concept of woman's proper role: While men fight the world's battles and do the world's work, the mother should stay home to nurse her child and satisfy its intellectual needs. In the persona of a parent, she expresses her strongest emotions; a successful example is the poem entitled "On Jephtha's Vow," wherein she mixes revulsion and sympathy for the father who exchanged his daughter's life for a promise of victory in battle. Y.'s fondness for parenthood was not accompanied by a similarly conventional view of marriage. In "Lucy, A Tale for the Ladies," she suggests that worldly interests often preclude marriage for love. Women thus become victims of cruel and unloving husbands, but men, too, suffer from the wiles of silly and flirtatious women.

In writing about public events, Y. combined conservative political views with humanitarian sympathies. Her "Ode to the Genius of England," for example, extols the virtues of the social order, while the "Bristol Elegy" mourns the slaughter of a group of demonstrators (whose numbers she grossly exaggerates) protesting unjust bridge tolls. Even while lamenting the murder of innocent victims, however, the poet advises their families to set aside the desire for vengeance and to find solace in "contemplation." Y.'s "Poem on the Inhumanity of the Slave Trade" has a more convincing effect because she replaces abstract morality with humanized narrative, focusing on the disruption of social and domestic bonds as the primary evil of slavery. The poet places her faith in the power of the sympathetic imagination to make us respond to the misery of our fellow creatures.

Y. was delighted to play "Lactilla," and thus many of her poems praise the power of "Nature" as source of the most intense emotions and the finest sensibility. Despite the derivative nature of her verse, she purported to reject both "Rule" and "Education" as trammels upon natural inspiration. In her elegy on Thomas Chatterton, the spirit of the dead poet disdains the praise of the traditional Muses but values the tribute of "some rustic Muse, in Nature drest," who bears a singular resemblance to herself. She thought of herself as "unadorned by art, unaccomplished by science" and proudly acknowledged writing "in the short intervals of a life of labour, and under every disadvantage which can possibly result from a confined education." A woman very much of her time, Y. entered into the spirit of Lactilla with considerable enthusiasm and absolutely no discernible sense of irony.

WORKS: *Poems on Several Occasions* (1784). *Poems on Various Subjects* (1787). *Earl Goodwin* (performed 1789, pub. 1791). *Stanzas of Woe* (1790). *The Royal Captives*, 4 vols. (1795). *The Rural Lyre* (1796).

BIBLIOGRAPHY: Cole, L. and R. G. Swartz, in *At the Limits of Romanticism*, ed. M. A. Favrat and N. J. Watson (1994). Demers, P. *HLQ* (1993). Ferguson, M. *TSWL* (1993). Ferguson, M. *Eighteenth-Century Women Poets: Nation, Class, and Gender* (1995). Landry, D., in *Approaches to Teaching Pope's Poetry*, ed. W. Jackson and R. P. Yoder (1993). Waldron, M. *AJ* (1990). Waldron, M. *SVEC* (1992). Waldron, M. *"Lactilla," Milkwoman of Clifton* (1996). Wordsworth, J., in *Centre and Circumference: Essays in English Romanticism*, ed. K. Kamijima and Y. Deguchi (1995). Zionkowski, L. *ESLife* (1989).

For articles in reference works, see: *Allibone*. *Bloomsbury*. *DNB*. *Feminist*. *Oxford*. *ToddBWW*.

Other references: Cottle, J. *Early Recollections*. Ferguson, M. *Eighteenth Century* (1986). *Horace Walpole's Correspondence*, 43 vols., ed. W. S. Lewis, et al. (1937–

83). *Memoirs of the Life and Correspondence of Mrs. Hannah More*, ed. W. Roberts (1834). Southey, R. *The Lives and Works of the Uneducated Poets* (1836). Tompkins, J.M.S. *The Polite Marriage* (1938).

Jill Rubenstein

Charlotte Mary Yonge

BORN: 11 August 1823, Otterbourne, Hampshire.
DIED: 20 March 1901, Otterbourne, Hampshire.
DAUGHTER OF: William Crawley Yonge and Frances Bargus Yonge.

Born the eldest of two children to High Church, upper-middle-class parents, Y. passed her entire life in Otterbourne, the village where she taught Sunday school for seventy of her seventy-eight years. Beloved by school girls and the Victorian reading public alike, she published more than 200 works, including nearly 100 novels and more than 30 histories, as well as stories of village life, biographies, books of religious instruction, natural histories, editions, and translations. *The Heir of Redclyff* (1853), an enormous success in its day, has proved to be the most enduring of her novels. Y. created several fictional families, and the sagas of the Mays, in *The Daisy Chain* (1856) and *The Trial* (1864), and the Underwoods, in *The Pillars of the House* (1873), were among her most popular. In her last novel, *Modern Broods* (1900), various Mays, Underwoods, Mohuns, and Merrifields make their final appearances. Over the course of fifty years, Y. also edited and contributed to three journals: the *Monthly Packet* (1851–94), the *Monthly Paper of Sunday Teaching* (1860–75), and the *Mothers in Council* (1890–1900). Y. perceived herself as an "instrument for popularizing Church views," views that were molded by her parents and, more significantly, by John Keble, one of the founders of the Oxford Movement and vicar of the neighboring parish of Hursley. Hers is certainly edifying fiction; nonetheless, her best novels offer lively portraits of Victorian family life, well-delineated characters, and skillful dialogue.

While her upbringing strikes the modern reader as unduly harsh, Y. spoke of her childhood as a happy one and remained devoted to her parents, particularly to her father. Fearful lest they spoil their spirited, pretty, intelligent daughter, the Yonges imposed strict controls on the child. She was given a diet of dry bread and milk for both breakfast and supper, and her mother discouraged vanity and selfishness by minimizing Y.'s attractiveness and by chastising her for selfish, though typically childish, desires. Her home education, supervised entirely by her father, was a rigorous affair. From the time she was seven, she rose for an hour of math before breakfast, followed by lessons in Greek, science, and history. Evenings were devoted to an hour of Bible reading, followed by an hour of history. Y.'s many "romantic" histories were written as by a teacher attempting to provide adequate texts for young people.

The necessity of submission and self-sacrifice is both the theme that informs her novels as well as the precept by which she lived her life. In Y.'s world, moral obligation is clear: Children must submit to the wisdom of their parents; women must submit to the superior judgment of men; mankind must submit to the will of God. Y. drew support for her belief in the inferiority of women from the biblical account of the fall of man. When her maternal grandmother objected to writing as a suspicious and unfeminine occupation and nearly prevented the publication of *Abbey Church*, Y. agreed to donate the profits from her works to the missions. She submitted her writing for criticism to her father and to Keble; Keble read to assure that "delicacy and reverence" were observed. Not unexpectedly, then, characters in her novels are judged and dealt with according to the degree to which they submit to and obey those wiser than themselves, and female characters who act independently are often made to suffer quite severely.

The life of the shy, socially awkward, spinster "Aunt Charlotte," who is said to have remained fixed in adolescence, was possibly uneventful; nonetheless, the sheer volume and variety of her writing bespeak a rich and active imaginative life. Her first novel, *Abbey Church* (1844), was a frankly Tractarian work. Over the following decade, she published several works; however, it was *The Heir of Redclyff* (1853) that earned her a wide and devoted audience. The tale of Sir Guy Morville, heir to Redclyff and to an ancestral curse that blights the happiness of all the Morvilles, was admired by Dante Gabriel Rossetti, William Morris, and Henry James, who praised the novel and called Y. a writer with "a force of genius." By 1868, *Heir* was in its seventeenth edition. Even Jo, in *Little Women*, wept over Sir Guy's death. The novel centers on Guy's struggle to subdue his self-destructive temper and to suffer patiently the false attacks of his cousin, Philip. Though Guy is vindicated by the truth and wed to his beloved Amy, his is the ultimate self-sacrifice; on their honeymoon he nurses the intolerable Philip through a terrible fever that he then catches and from which he dies. Amy later gives birth to a daughter, whereupon Redclyff is passed on to Philip, now a grief-stricken, guilt-ridden man.

As is often noted, Y.'s characters are punished for their transgressions of the moral code as Y. herself perceived it. In *The Clever Woman of the Family* (1865), Rachel Curtis tries to ameliorate the working conditions of girls in the lacemaking trade, but, by ignoring the advice of others, she ends up placing the girls in homes where they are mistreated and loses the money she has collected for them to an embezzler. In *Magnum Bonum* (1879), Janet Brownlow studies medicine in order to continue her father's discoveries, but her carelessness and poor judgment bring about the deaths of several people, including her child. Her own death, a result of her work to control an epidemic, serves as a penitential act of self-sacrifice, a pattern reflecting Y.'s deeply held religious convictions, convictions apparently shared by many of her readers. Yet her novels offered those readers more than a series of didactic plots, for much of her appeal lay in her characters and depictions of life in the Victorian hearth and home.

After 1875, Y. wrote fewer novels and a greater number of children's books and school texts. In her lifetime, she was much admired, and devoted readers would make pilgrimages to her home, to her dismay. In the 1940s, her novels enjoyed a revival in England, but today her novels are discussed chiefly in terms of their religious sentiments and their conservative response to the Victorian crisis of faith, of the patterns and concerns characteristic of the fiction of nineteenth-century women novelists, and of their domestic realism.

WORKS: *Le Chateau de Melville* (1838). *Abbey Church* (1844). *Scenes and Characters* (1847). *Kings of England* (1848). *Henrietta's Wish* (1850). *Kenneth* (1850). *Langley School* (1850). *Landmarks of History* (1852–57). *The Two Guardians* (1852). *The Heir of Redclyff* (1853). *The Herb of the Field* (1853). *The Castle Builders* (1854). *Heartsease* (1854). *The Little Duke* (1854). *The History of the Life and Death of the Good Knight Sir Thomas Thumb* (1855). *The Lancer of Lynwood* (1855). *The Railroad Children* (1855). *Beechcroft at Rochstone* (1856). *Ben Sylvester's Word* (1856). *The Daisy Chain* (1856). *Harriet and her Sister* (1856?). *Leonard the Lionheart* (1856). *Dynevor Terrace* (1857). *The Instructive Picture Book* (1857). *The Christmas Mummers* (1858). *Friarswood Post Office* (1860). *Hopes and Fears* (1860). *The Mice at Play* (1860). *The Strayed Falcon* (1860). *Pigeon Pie* (1860). *The Stokesley Secret* (1861). *The Young Stepmother* (1861). *Biographies of Good Women*, 2 sers. (1862–65). *The Chosen People* (1862). *Counters Kate* (1862). *Sea Spleenwort and Other Stories* (1862). *A History of Christian Names* (1863). *The Apple of Discord* (1864). *A Book of Golden Deeds of All Times and All Lands* (1864). *Historical Dramas* (1864). *Readings from Standard Authors* (1864). *The Trial* (1864). *The Wars of Wapsburgh* (1864). *The Clever Woman of the Family* (1865). *The Dove in the Eagle's Nest* (1866). *The Prince and the Page* (1866). *The Danvers Papers* (1867). *A Shilling's Book of Golden Deeds* (1867). *The Six Cushions* (1867). *Cameos from English History*, 9 vols. (1868–99). *The Chaplet of Pearls* (1868). *Historical Selections* (1868–70). *New Ground* (1868). *The Pupils of St. John the Divine* (1868). *A Book of Worthies* (1869). *Keynotes of the First Lessons for Every Day in the Year* (1869). *The Seal* (1869). *The Caged Lion* (1870). *A Storehouse of Stories*, 2 sers. (1870–72). *Little Lucy's Wonderful Glove* (1871). *Musings over the Christian Year and Lyra Innocentium* (1871). *A Parallel History of France and England* (1871). *Pioneers and Founders* (1871). *Scripture Readings for Schools* (1871–79). *A History of France* (1872). *In Memoriam Bishop Patterson* (1872). *P's and Q's* (1872). *Questions on the Prayerbook* (1872). *Aunt Charlotte's Stories of English History for the Little Ones* (1873). *Life of John Coleridge Paterson* (1873). *The Pillars of the House* (1873). *Aunt Charlotte's Stories of French History for the Little Ones* (1874). *Lady Hester* (1874). *Questions on the Collects* (1874). *Questions on the Epistles* (1874). *Questions on the Gospels* (1874). *Aunt Charlotte's Stories of Bible History for the Little Ones* (1875). *My Young Alcides* (1875). *Aunt Charlotte's Stories of Greek History for the Little Ones* (1875). *Eighteen Centuries of Beginnings of Church History* (1876). *The Three Brides* (1876). *Aunt Charlotte's Stories of German History for the Little Ones* (1877). *Aunt Charlotte's Stories of Roman History for the Little Ones* (1877). *The Disturbing Element* (1878). *A History of France* (1878). *The Story of the Christians and Moors of Spain* (1878). *Burnt Out* (1879). *Magnum Bonum* (1879). *Short English Grammar for Use in Schools* (1879). *Byewords* (1880). *Love and Life* (1880). *Nelly and Margaret* (1880?). *Verses on the Gospel for Sundays and Holy Days* (1880). *Aunt Charlotte's Evenings at Home with the Poets* (1881). *Cheap Jack* (1881). *Frank's Debt* (1881). *How to Teach the New Testament* (1881). *Lads and Lasses of Langley* (1881). *Practical Work in Sunday Schools* (1881). *Questions on the Psalms* (1881). *Wolf* (1881). *Given to Hospitality* (1882). *Historical Ballads* (1882). *Langley Little Ones* (1882). *Pickle and his Page Boy* (1882). *Sowing and Sewing* (1882). *Talks about the Laws We Live Under* (1882). *Unknown to History* (1882). *Aunt Charlotte's Stories of American History* (1883). *English Church History* (1883). *Landmarks of Recent History 1770–1883* (1883). *Langley Adventures* (1883). (with others) *The Miz Maze* (1883). *Shakespeare's Plays for School* (1883). *Stray Pearls* (1883). *The Armourer's Prentices* (1884). *The Daisy Chain Birthday Book* (1885). *Higher Reading-book for Schools, Colleges and General Use* (1885). *Nuttie's Father* (1885). *Pixie Lawn* (1885). *The Two Sides of the Shield* (1885). (with M. Bramston, C. Coleridge, and E. Stuart) *Astray* (1886). *Chantry House* (1886). (with others) *Just One Tale More* (1886). *The Little Rick-burners* (1886). *A Modern Telemachus* (1886). *Teachings on the Catechism* (1886). *Victorian Half-Century* (1886). *Under the Storm* (1887). *What Books to Lend and What to Give* (1887). *Womankind* (1887). *Conversations on the Prayer Book* (1888). *Deacon's Book of Dates* (1888). *Hannah More* (1888). *Nurse's Memories* (1888). *Our New Mistress* (1888). *Preparation of Prayerbook Lessons* (1888). *The Cunning Woman's Grandson* (1889). *Neighbor's Fare* (1889). *The Parent's Power* (1889). *A Reputed Changeling* (1889). *Life of HRH the Prince Consort* (1890). *More Bywords* (1889). *The Slaves of Sabinns* (1890). *The Constable's Tower* (1891). *Old Times at Otterbourne* (1891). *Seven Heroines of Christendom* (1891). *Simple Stories Relating to English History* (1891). *Twelve Stories from Early English History* (1891). *Twenty Stories and Biographies from 1066 to 1485* (1891). *Two Penniless Princesses* (1891). *Westminster Historical Reading Books* (1891–92). *The Cross Road* (1892). *The Hanoverian Period* (1892). *That Stick* (1892). *Chimes for the Mothers* (1893). *The Girl's Little Book* (1893). *Grisly Grisell* (1893). *The Strolling St. Lo* (1894). *The Story of Easter* (1894). *The Carbonels* (1895). *The Long Vacation* (1895). *The Release* (1896). *The Wardship of Steepcomb* (1896). *The Pilgrimage of the Ben Beriah* (1897). *Founded on Paper* (1898). *John Keble's Parishes* (1898). *The Patriots of Palestine* (1898). *Scenes with Kenneth* (1899). *The Herd Boy and His Hermit* (1900). *The Making of a Missionary* (1900). *Modern Broods* (1900). *Reasons Why I Am a Catholic and Not a Roman Catholic* (1901).

BIBLIOGRAPHY: Avery, G. *Nineteenth-Century Children* (1965). Battiscombe, G. *Charlotte Mary Yonge: The Story of an Uneventful Life* (1943). *A Chaplet for Charlotte Mary Yonge*, ed. G. Battiscombe and M. Laski (1965). Brownell, D., in *The Worlds of Victorian Fiction*, ed. J. Buckley (1975). Colby, V. *Yesterday's Woman: Domestic Realism in the English Novel* (1974). Coleridge, C. R. *Charlotte Yonge: Her Life and Letters* (1903). Demoor, M. *CVE* (1994). Foster, S. and J. Simons. *What*

Katy Read: Feminist Re-Readings of "Classic" Stories for Girls (1995). Hayter, A. *Charlotte Yonge* (1996). Mare, M. and A. C. Percival *Victorian Best-Sellers: The World of Charlotte M. Yonge* (1947). Romanes, E. *Charlotte Mary Yonge: An Appreciation* (1908). Showalter, E. *A Literature of Their Own* (1977). Sturrock, J. *VRev* (1922). Tillotson, K. *Mid-Victorian Studies* (1965). Waugh, H. *The Chaplet of Pearls* (1997).

For articles in reference works, see: *Bloomsbury. Europa. Feminist. IDWB. OCCL. VB.*

Other references: *Durham University Journal* (March 1973, December 1900). *EA* (1980). *Mary Wollstonecraft Journal* (May 1974). *Scrutiny* (Summer 1944).

Patricia A. O'Hara
(updated by Virginia Zimmerman)

E[mily]. H[ilda]. Young

BORN: 1880, Northumberland.
DIED: 8 August 1949, Bradford-on-Avon, Wiltshire.
DAUGHTER OF: William Michael Young and Frances Jane Young.
MARRIED: J.A.H. Daniell, 1902.
WROTE UNDER: E. H. Young.

The third of seven children, Y. was born into a comfortable middle-class home where she received a good education, first at Gateshead Grammar School and then at Penrhos College in Wales. Y. married J.A.H. Daniell, a solicitor, in 1902 and went to live with him in the comfortable Clifton district in Bristol (which, renamed Radstowe, was to be the setting of most of her major novels). The marriage lasted until 1917, when Daniell was killed fighting at Ypres. During her marriage, Y. wrote her first three novels. After her husband's death, Y. moved to London where she shared a home with her lover, Ralph Henderson, and his wife. This arrangement, though apparently amenable to Mrs. Henderson, who enjoyed Y.'s company, was made even more unusual in that Henderson was head master of Alleyn's London public school, and a revelation of the true nature of the *ménage à trois* would have ruined his career. The relationship between the lovers was never publicly divulged, however, and the household remained together for some twenty years. In 1940, following his wife's death, Henderson retired to Bradford-on-Avon in Wiltshire to live with Y. until her death in 1949 of lung cancer. During this entire period of Y.'s later life, she continued to write, authoring two books for children in addition to eleven adult novels.

Because her stories play out against the backdrop of conventional bourgeois life with its parties, concerts, and afternoon calls, and because her subjects are so often concerned with the intricacies of class distinctions and social propriety, Y. is sometimes compared in critical discussions to Jane Austen or George Eliot. Beneath the quiet provincial lives of her characters, however, Y. reveals deeper concerns with such serious issues as loneliness, illness, disgrace, and death. Known for her sardonic wit and unsentimentalized style, Y. writes with a lightly comic tone that belies the controversial issues brewing under the surface of her novels, subjects that subtly challenge the conventional social structures they outwardly uphold. While Y.'s novelistic form does not embark on any of the modernist experiments that so many of her counterparts of the era were exploring, her characters themselves are often quite contemporary in their private attitudes and beliefs.

Y.'s most successful novel, *William* (1925), helped establish her reputation in her lifetime, but it seems less sophisticated today than some of her later works. The story deals with the emotional estrangement of a husband and wife who discover late in their marriage that they have been existing in separate, increasingly incompatible worlds, highlighted most dramatically by their opposing reactions to their married daughter's elopement with another man. Y.'s marriages are often depicted as limited and lacking in communication, but, like most of her couples, the pair in *William* make their way together in the end. *Miss Mole* (1930), winner of the James Tait Black Memorial Prize for fiction that year, is considered Y.'s most accomplished novel. In the story, a spinster housekeeper goes to work for a pompous and difficult minister from whom she must keep her own secret of disgrace. Y. deftly constructs a character whose independence and individuality make her a lively, fun, and provocative heroine whose double life ironically imitates her creator's. It is, in fact, Y.'s remarkably outspoken and even subversive female characters that make her worthy of consideration today. Toward the close of *Chatterton Square* (1947), the wife of tyrannical Herbert Blackett speaks her mind after many difficult years of marriage, finally revealing to her husband that his self-centeredness is abominable and that her love for him has been an incredible deception. While this extraordinary disclosure ends, as most of Y.'s confrontations do, in reconciliation, the honesty with which Y. confronts marital and family relationships makes her relative obscurity today seem unjustified.

Though Y. is no longer widely read, she was quite popular and successful in her lifetime, and a renewed interest in the novelist has come with the reissue of six of her major novels by Virago Modern Classics.

WORKS: *A Corn of Wheat* (1910). *Yonder* (1912). *Moor Fires* (1916). *The Bridge Dividing* (1922; repub. as *The Misses Mallett*, 1927). *William* (1925). *The Vicar's Daughter* (1928). *Miss Mole* (1930). *Jenny Wren* (1932). *The Curate's Wife* (1934). *Celia* (1938). *Caravan Island* (1940). *River Holiday* (1942). *Chatterton Square* (1947).

BIBLIOGRAPHY: Lawrence, M. *We Write as Women* (1937). Also see introductions by J. Bayley and S. Beauman in Virago editions.

For articles in reference works, see: *Oxford. Feminist.*

Karen Castellucci Cox

Young Lady, A: See *Lennox, Charlotte Ramsay*

Young Lady Eighteen Years of Age, A: See *Porter, Anna Maria*

Zoide: See *Havergal, Frances Ridley*

Contributors and their Entries

Timothy Dow Adams (West Virginia Univ.)
Ruth Fainlight

Lynn M. Alexander (Univ. of Tennessee)
Jane Austen, Anne Brontë, Charlotte Brontë, Emily Brontë, Maria Edgeworth, Elizabeth Gaskell, Frances Milton Trollope

Katherine A. Allison (late of the Univ. of Washington)
Maureen Duffy, Florida Scott-Maxwell

Lisa Altomari (Vermont Technical College)
Sylvia Plath, Clara Reeve (update only)

R. Victoria Arana (Howard Univ.)
Esther Johnson, Naomi Mitchison, Victoria, Anna Wickham

Leonard R. N. Ashley (Brooklyn College, C.U.N.Y.)
Charlotte Brooke, Charlotte Cibber Charke, Agatha Christie, Richmal Crompton, Clemence Dane, Daphne du Maurier, Pamela Hansford Johnson, Ngaio Marsh, Nancy Mitford, Mary Ann[e] Radcliffe (co-author), Elizabeth Taylor

Jane Augustine (Pratt Institute)
Bryher, Mina Loy, Charlotte Mew, Anne Stevenson

Brett Averitt (Westfield State College)
Carol Ann Duffy, Penelope Ruth Mortimer

Sonja Bagby (State Univ. of West Georgia)
Mary Carey

Dean R. Baldwin (Behrend College, Pennsylvania State Univ.)
Sylvia Townsend Warner, Mary Wesley

Carol L. Barash (independent scholar)
Vera Brittain, Eliza Fowler Haywood, Olive Emilie Albertina Schreiner, Mary Amelia St. Clair Sinclair

Jane Baston (Pennsylvania State Univ.)
Hester Biddle, Mary Cary, Priscilla Cotton, Elizabeth Poole, Jane Turner, Anne Venn

Anna Battigelli (Plattsburgh State Univ., S.U.N.Y.)
Henrietta Maria

Tracy W. Beck-Briggs (independent scholar)
Charlotte Bury

Linda Hunt Beckman (Ohio Univ.)
Jane Austen (update only), Constance Clara Black Garnett (update only), Amy Levy (update only)

Kate Begnal (Utah State Univ.)
Angela Carter, Ivy Compton-Burnett, Patricia Moyes, Christina Stead

Elaine V. Beilin (Framingham State College)
Anne Dowriche, Elizabeth Russell, Rachel Speght

Temma F. Berg (Gettysburg College)
Charlotte Ramsay Lennox

Kathleen Collins Beyer (Framingham State College)
Eliza Fay

Nandini Bhattacharya (Valparaiso Univ.)
Anna Maria Bennett, Bithia May Croker, Sarah Fyge Field Egerton

Sophia B. Blaydes (West Virginia Univ.)
Sarah Jennings Churchill, Mary Evelyn, Celia Fiennes, Anne Murray Halkett, Frances Norton, Dorothy Osborne, Mary Boyle Rich, Elizabeth Thomas, Alice Wandesford Thornton, Catharine Trotter

Rebecca P. Bocchicchio (Univ. of California, Davis)
Joanna Baillie (update only), Elizabeth Blower, Anne Fuller, Delariviere Manley (update only), Mary Meeke, Elizabeth Tipper

Robert Bonner (Carleton College)
Sarah Kirby Trimmer

Philip Bordinat (West Virginia Univ.)
Mary Berry, Elizabeth Burnet, Hannah Parkhouse Cowley, Susanna Harvey Hopton, Henrietta Hobart Howard

Mikita Brottman (Univ. of East London, U. K.)
Julie Burchill, Jilly Cooper, Candia McWilliam, Bernice Rubens

Kate Browder (Seattle, WA)
Elizabeth Griffith, Sydney Owenson

Jan Calloway-Baxter (Tulsa Community College)
Storm Jameson, Muriel Spark

Kitti Carriker (Community College of Philadelphia)
Stella Benson

G. A. Cevasco (St. John's Univ.)
Olive Custance, Ada Leverson

Laurie Champion (Sul Ross State Univ.)
Shena Mackay

Miriam Quen Cheikin (Nassau Community College)
Monica Dickens

Donald Cheney (Univ. of Massachusetts)
Elizabeth Jane Weston

Lorna J. Clark (Ottawa, Ontario, Canada)
Frances Burney (update only), Sarah Harriet Burney

Carol Colatrella (Georgia Institute of Technology)
Jean Rhys

Jane Collins (Pace Univ.)
Susan Du Verger

Mary Sauter Comfort (Moravian College)
Jean Adam(s), Mary Granville Pendarves Delaney, Hannah Glasse, Mary Wortley Montagu, Hester Lynch Salusbury Thrale Piozzi

Paula Connolly (Univ. of North Carolina)
Georgette Heyer

Joan Ambrose Cooper (independent scholar)
Phyllis Bentley, Mary Josephine Ward

Nancy Cotton (Wake Forest Univ.)
Aphra Behn, Elizabeth Cary, Susanna Centlivre, Liz Lochhead, Emma . . . Orczy, Mary Pix, Denise Naomi Robins, Rose Tremain

Karen Castellucci Cox (Bronx Community College, C.U.N.Y.)
Juliana Horatia Ewing (update only), Mary Russell Mitford (update only), Deborah Moggach, E[mily]. H[ilda]. Young

Adriana Craciun (Loyola Univ.)
Charlotte Dacre

Lisa Plummer Crafton (State Univ. of West Georgia)
Mary Alcock

Joanne Creighton (Mount Holyoke College)
Margaret Drabble

Margaret L. Cruikshank (Univ. of Maine)
Barbara Bodichon

Patrick Cullen (Graduate Center, C.U.N.Y.)
Alice Sutcliffe, Anna Weamys, Anne Wheathill

Mary R. Davidson (Univ. of Kansas)
Caryl Churchill, Pam Gems

Marcia M. Davis (independent scholar)
Dorothy Kempe Leigh

W. Eugene Davis (Purdue Univ.)
Henrietta M. Batson

Jennie Dear (Ft. Lewis College)
Damaris Masham

Jacqueline Dello Russo (Univ. of California, Davis)
Mathilda Betham-Edwards, Mary Wollstonecraft Shelley (update only), Mary Wollstonecraft (update only)

Dolores De Luise (John Jay College of Criminal Justice, C.U.N.Y.)
Adelaide Kemble

Amanda DeWees (Univ. of Georgia)
Elizabeth von Arnim, Dinah Maria Mulock Craik, Anne Perry, P[amela]. L[yndon]. Travers

Laura L. Doan (State Univ. of New York, Geneseo)
Sara Maitland, Jeanette Winterson

Josephine Donovan (Univ. of Maine)
Brilliana Harley, Lucy Apsley Hutchinson, Delariviere Manley, Mary Russell Mitford

Angela G. Dorenkamp (Assumption College)
A[ntonia]. S[usan]. Byatt

Priscilla Dorr (Clovis Community College)
Joanna Baillie, Anna Laetitia Barbauld, Elizabeth Carter, Anna Kavan, Ethel Mannin

Peter Drewniany (Germantown Academy, Ft. Washington, Pennsylvania)
Julia O'Faolain

Valerie Kim Duckett (independent scholar)
Harriet Martineau

Angela Emanuel (late of University College, Univ. of London, U.K.)
Cecilia Mary Ady, Julia Cartwright

Robert C. Evans (Auburn Univ.)
Martha Molesworth

Teresa Feroli (Univ. of Tulsa)
Eleanor Audeley Davies, Margaret Fell, Anna Trapnel

Eileen Finan (Cambridge, MA)
Sara Coleridge, Sophia Lee, Clara Reeve, Dorothy Wordsworth

Lucretia Anne Flammang (U. S. Coast Guard Academy)
Josephine Butler

Rhoda Flaxman (Brown Univ.)
Fanny Kemble, Alice Meynell

LuAnn McCracken Fletcher (Cedar Crest College)
Anne Brontë (update only), Elizabeth Rigby

Robert P. Fletcher (West Chester Univ.)
Emily Brontë (update only), Mary Lamb Singleton Currie

Cheryl Forbes (Hobart and William Smith Colleges)
Edith Mary Pargeter

Kathleen L. Fowler (Ramapo College)
Mary Balfour Brunton, Eliza Fenwick, Susan Edmonstone Ferrier, Elizabeth Hamilton, Mary Ann Hanway, Laetitia Matilda Hawkins

Elizabeth M. Fox (Massachusetts Institute of Technology)
Hilda Doolittle

Richard C. Frushell (Pennsylvania State Univ., McKeesport)
Catherine Clive

Tony Giffone (State Univ. of New York, Farmingdale)
Mary Golding Bright, Maria Charlesworth, Catherine Sinclair, Joanna Southcott

Steven J. Gores (Northern Kentucky Univ.)
Sophia Lee (update only)

Anita G. Gorman (Slippery Rock Univ.)
Isobel Pagan, Julia Pardoe, G[ladys]. B[ertha]. Stern

Margaret Ann Graham (Iowa State Univ.)
Margaret Blessington, Juliana Horatia Ewing, Anna Maria Porter

Joseph A. Grau (Richmond, VA)
Frances Burney

Katherine S. Green (Western Kentucky Univ.)
Mary Mitchell Collyer, Susannah Minifie Gunning, Elizabeth Simpson Inchbald

Dana Greene (St. Mary's College)
Evelyn Underhill

Sayre N. Greenfield (Univ. of Pittsburgh, Greensburg)
Elizabeth I, Katherine Philips

Margaret P. Hannay (Siena College)
Dorothy L. Sayers, Mary Sidney, Mary Wroth

Elaine Tuttle Hansen (Haverford College)
Elizabeth Elstob, Margaret Paston

Laura Hapke (Pace Univ.)
Rhoda Broughton, Alice Mona Caird, Marie Corelli, Florence Marryat, Ellen Price Wood

Tori Haring-Smith (Brown Univ. and American Univ. of Cairo, Egypt)
Ariadne, George Ann Bellamy, Isabella Lucy Bird Bishop, Eleanor Farjeon, Mary Henrietta Kingsley

Paula Harrington (Univ. of California, Davis)
Jessica Mitford, E[dith]. J[oy]. Scovell

Susan Hastings (College of New Jersey and Fairleigh Dickinson Univ.)
Grisell Hume Baillie, Margaret Cavendish, Charlotte Turner Smith, Anne Lee Wharton

Nicolás Hernández, Jr. (Russell Sage College)
Anne Barnard, Emily Lawless, Harriet Lee, Lisa St. Aubin de Terán

Kathleen Hickok (Iowa State Univ.)
L[ouisa]. S[arah]. Bevington, Caroline Bowles, Eliza Cook, Michael Field, Dora Greenwell, Jean Ingelow, Letitia Elizabeth Landon, Emily Jane Davis Pfeiffer, Adelaide Anne Procter (co-author), Agnes Mary Frances Robinson, Augusta Davies Webster

Michelle Q. Hill (North Carolina State Univ.)
Violet Keppel Trefusis

Colleen Hobbs (Austin, TX)
Elizabeth Missing Sewell

Ernest Hofer (Univ. of Massachusetts)
Susan Hill

Brenda M. Hosington (Univ. of Montreal, Quebec)
Anne, Margaret, and Jane Seymour

Robert Ellis Hosmer, Jr. (Smith College)
Fleur Adcock, Anita Brookner, Isabel Colegate, Eva Figes, Penelope Fitzgerald, Pam Gems (update only), Penelope Gilliatt, Molly Keane (co-author)

Evelyn A. Hovanec (Pennsylvania State Univ., Uniontown)
Marie Adelaide Belloc Lowndes

Elizabeth Huberman (Kean Univ.)
Jacquetta Hawkes, Willa Johnstone Anderson Muir

Linda K. Hughes (Texas Christian Univ.)
Rosamund Marriott Watson

Ann Hurley (Wagner College)
Ann Collins, Elizabeth Polwhele

Charles A. Huttar (Hope College)
Sarah Lynes Grubb, Sarah Tuke Grubb, Frances Ridley Havergal, Susan Howatch, Anne Vaughan Locke, Elizabeth Mackintosh, Anne Ridler, Catherine Winkworth

Sherrie A. Inness (Miami Univ.)
Angela Brazil

Rosemary Jann (George Mason Univ.)
Mary Elizabeth Braddon, Helen Maud Cam, Margaret Gatty, Marie Louise de la Ramée, Mary Augusta Arnold Ward, Beatrice Potter Webb

Judith L. Johnston (Rider Univ.)
Valerie Bloom, Elizabeth Bowen, Frances Crofts Darwin Cornford, Amryl Johnson, Stevie Smith, Rebecca West

Claudia Thomas Kairoff (Wake Forest Univ.)
Aphra Behn (update only), Elizabeth Cary (update only), Susanna Centlivre (update only), Mary Pix (update only)

Carey Kaplan (St. Michael's College)
Margery Allingham, Elizabeth Jane Howard, Rosamond Lehmann, Barbara Pym, Dorothy Richardson

Bette H. Kirschstein (Pace Univ.)
Ella D'Arcy, Ella Nora Hepworth Dixon, Violet Hunt (update only), Violet Paget (update only), Mary Amelia St. Clair Sinclair (update only)

Shoshana Milgram Knapp (Virginia Polytechnic Institute and State Univ.)
Victoria Cory, Gillian Freeman, Ethel Lilian Boole Voynich

Benjamin G. Kohl (Vassar College)
Cecilia Mary Ady (update only), Julia Cartwright (update only), Ciceley Veronica Wedgwood

Judith C. Kohl (Dutchess Community College, S.U.N.Y.)
Mary Bateson, Christine Brooke-Rose, Eleanor Mary Carus-Wilson, Elspeth Josceline Grant Huxley, Frieda Lawrence, May McKisack, Beryl Markham, Freya Stark

Gail Kraidman (late of Rutgers Univ.)
Grace Aguilar, Amy Levy, Margaret Oliphant

Mary Ellen Lamb (Southern Illinois Univ.)
Margaret Hoby, [A]emelia Lanier, Isabella Whitney

Eleanor Langstaff (Baruch College, C.U.N.Y.)
Mary Victoria Cowden Clarke, Lucy Lane Clifford, Alicia Cockburn, Mary St. Leger Harrison, Geraldine Ensor Jewsbury, Maria Jane Jewsbury, Julia Kavanagh, Leonora Blanche Alleyne Lang, Mary Dolling O'Malley, Ann and Jane Taylor, Angela Thirkell

Elizabeth K. Larsen (West Chester Univ.)
Frances Moore Brooke

Dorothy L. Latz (independent scholar)
Anne and Lucy Cary, Catherine Holland, Agnes More, Helen Gertrude More, Jane Owen, Elizabeth Shirley, Gertrude Aston Thimelby, Mary Ward

Ellen Laun (Pennsylvania State Univ., Uniontown)
Margaret Forster, Ruth Prawer Jhabvala

John Lavin (St. Joseph's Univ.)
Eva Gore-Booth, Estelle Sylvia Pankhurst, Jane Francesca Wilde

Pamela Lloyd (independent scholar)
Jane West

Eve M. Lynch (Univ. of California, Davis)
Catherine Ann Cookson, Elizabeth Hands, Susanna Rowson (update only)

Marie E. McAllister (Mary Washington College)
Margaret Steuart Calderwood, Anna Maria Falconbridge, Anna Riggs Miller, Duchess of Northumberland (Elizabeth Percy), Janet Schaw

Kari Boyd McBride (Univ. of Arizona)
Eliza Acton, Theodosia Alleine, Monica Furlong, Anna Hume, Anne King, Mary MacLeod, Elizabeth Middleton, Marina Sarah Warner

Margaret McFadden (Appalachian State Univ.)
Rosina Wheeler Bulwer-Lytton, Harriet Hardy Taylor Mill, Anna Doyle Wheeler, Frances Wright

Raymond N. MacKenzie (Univ. of St. Thomas)
Cynthia Asquith, Catherine Carswell, Ivy Litvinov, Viola Meynell

Sylvia McLaurin (Univ. of Georgia)
Mildred Cable, Caroline Clive, Mary Crawford Fraser

Glenda K. McLeod (Gainesville College)
Jane Anger, Augusta Gregory, Katherine Mansfield

Loralee MacPike (California State Univ., San Bernardino)
Isabella Mary Mayson Beeton, Emily Eden, Stella Gibbons

Susan Garland Mann (Indiana Univ. Southeast) *and David D. Mann* (Miami Univ.)
Grace Norton Gethin (co-authors)

Jacquelyn Marie (Univ. of California, Santa Cruz)
Buchi Emecheta, Michèle Roberts

Carol A. Martin (Boise State Univ.)
Mary Botham Hewitt

Edward Marx (independent scholar)
Adela Florence Nicolson

Julia Matthews (Kennesaw State Univ.)
Sarah Daniels, Margaretta Ruth D'Arcy, Louise Page, Sue Townsend

Cynthia A. Merrill (Univ. of California, Los Angeles)
Catherine Grace Frances Moody Gore

Kay Beaird Meyers (Oral Roberts Univ.)
Susanna Blamire, Phyllis Bottome, Nancy Cunard, Elinor Glyn, Anne Killigrew, Bathsua Reginald Makin, Kate O'Brien, Mary Darby Robinson, Katharine Tynan

Karen Michalson (independent scholar)
Charlotte E. B. Guest

Elsie B. Michie (Louisiana State Univ. & A&M College)
Mathilde Blind, Violet Paget, Somerville and Ross

Catherine Milsum (independent scholar)
Vita Sackville-West

JoAnna Stephens Mink (Mankato State Univ.)
Barbara Hardy

Geneviève Sanchis Morgan (Marlborough School, Los Angeles)
Dora de Houghton Carrington, Julia Prinsep Stephen

Joanne Stafford Mortimer (Muhlenberg College)
Annie Wood Besant

Maureen E. Mulvihill (Princeton Research Forum)
Ephelia, Mary Leadbeater, Elizabeth, Countess of Longford, Eileen O'Connell, Mary Tighe

Kathryn Coad Narramore (Graduate Center, C.U.N.Y.)
Judith Man, Margaret Tyler

Mary Lou Nelsen (Dummerston, VT)
Timberlake Wertenbaker (co-author)

Paul D. Nelsen (Marlboro College)
Shelagh Delaney, Nell Dunn, Ann Jellicoe, Timberlake Wertenbaker (co-author)

Shondel J. Nero (St. John's Univ.)
Abena P. A. Busia, Grace Nichols

Jennifer Poulos Nesbitt (Emory Univ.)
Mary Manning, Winifred Langford Mantle

Laura Niesen de Abruña (Ithaca College)
Maud Bodkin, Una Mary Ellis-Fermor, Helen Louise Gardner

Patricia A. O'Hara (Franklin and Marshall College)
Elizabeth Barrett Browning, Mary Cholmondeley, Mary Lavin, Charlotte Mary Yonge

Susan Gushee O'Malley (Kingsborough Community College, C.U.N.Y.)
Constantia Munda, Ester Sowernam

Alice Lorraine Painter (independent scholar)
Antonia Fraser, P[hyllis]. D[orothy]. James, Marghanita Laski, Ruth Rendell

Ruth Panofsky (Ryerson Polytechnic Univ., Toronto)
Edna Lipson

Louis J. Parascandola (Long Island Univ., Brooklyn)
Anne Beresford, Barbara Burford, Mary Elizabeth Coleridge, Radclyffe Hall, Molly Holden

Susan Pavlovska (Doshisha Univ., Kyoto, Japan)
Laetitia Pilkington

Mickey Pearlman (independent scholar)
Rumer Godden, Margery Sharp, Jan Struther, Honor Tracy

Jean E. Pearson (independent scholar)
Christina Rossetti, Anna Sewell, Mary Webb

Mary Pharr (Florida Southern College)
Hannah More, Anna Seward

Marjorie Podolsky (Behrend College, Pennsylvania State Univ.)
Molly Keane (co-author)

Richard Poss (Univ. of Arizona)
Elizabeth of York, Helen Jane Waddell

Anne Prescott (Hunter College, C.U.N.Y.)
Mary Astell

Zelda R. B. Provenzano (Drexel Univ.)
Joan Aiken, Helen Brodie Cowan Watson Bannerman, Barbara Cartland, Anne Fanshawe, Pamela Frankau, Caroline Glyn, Jane Porter

Carol Pulham (Cedar Crest College)
Sarah Grand, Emma Tennant

Hilary Pursehouse (Tucson, AZ)
Flora Annie Steel

Alan Rauch (Georgia Institute of Technology)
Jane Welsh Carlyle, Jane Wells Webb Loudon, Beatrix Potter, Anne Thackeray Ritchie

Anne-Marie Ray (Jamestown Community College)
Germaine Greer, Emmeline Goulden Pankhurst, Mary Wollstonecraft Shelley, Mary Wollstonecraft

James Reibman (Lafayette College)
Ellis Cornelia Knight

Jeannette E. Riley (Kent State Univ.)
Eavan Aisling Boland, Gillian Clarke, Medbh McGuckian

Christina Root (St. Michael's College)
Margery Allingham (update only), Elizabeth Jane Howard (update only), Rosamond Lehmann (update only), Barbara Pym (update only), Dorothy Richardson (update only)

Jill Rubenstein (Univ. of Cincinnati)
Louisa Stuart, Ann Cromartie Yearsley

Kirsten T. Saxton (Mills College)
Margaret Oliphant (update only), Mary Anne Sadlier, Helen Selina Sheridan, Annie Turner Tinsley, Lucy Walford

Nancy E. Schaumburger (Manhattanville College)
Monica Dickens (update only)

Phyllis J. Scherle (Indiana Univ.-Purdue Univ.)
Isabella Varley Banks, Anna Eliza Bray, Rosa Nouchette Carey, Frances Power Cobbe, Jessie Fothergill, Anna Maria Fielding Hall, Margaret Hamilton Wolfe Hungerford

Paul Schlueter (independent scholar)
Beryl Bainbridge, Sybille Bedford, Anne Cluysenaar, Pearl Craigie, Elaine Feinstein, Elizabeth Goudge, Winifred Holtby, Elizabeth Jennings, Jennifer Johnston, Sheila Kaye-Smith, Margaret Moore Kennedy, Doris Lessing, Olivia Manning, Iris Murdoch, Kathleen Nott, Ruth Pitter, Kathleen Raine, Gillian Tindall, Barbara Ward, Antonia White

Barbara Brandon Schnorrenberg (Birmingham, AL)
Elizabeth Bonhote, Anne MacVicar Grant, Mary Hays, Sarah Lennox Bunbury Napier, Mary Martha Butt Sherwood, Agnes Strickland

Fredric S. Schwarzbach (Kent State Univ.)
Anna Jane Vardill

Carole M. Shaffer-Koros (Kean Univ.)
Ada Ellen Bayly, Annie French Hector, Mary Renault, Charlotte Eliza Lawson Cowan Riddell, Henrietta Eliza Vaughn Palmer Stannard

Robin Sheets (Univ. of Cincinnati)
Catherine Anne Crowe, Emily Davies, Sarah Stickney Ellis, Felicia Dorothea Browne Hemans, Anna Brownell Jameson, Anne Marsh-Caldwell, Florence Nightingale

Gale Sigal (Wake Forest Univ.)
Amelia Ann Blanford Edwards, Octavia Hill, Eliza Lynn Linton, Mary Fairfax Greig Somerville

Anne B. Simpson (California State Univ., Pomona)
Emma Alice Margaret Tennant Asquith

Michael Skakun (independent scholar)
Brigid Brophy, Lucie Duff-Gordon, Q[ueenie]. D[orothy]. Leavis, Amelia Opie, Lucy Hester Stanhope

Marilynn J. Smith (Head Librarian, U.S. Navy base at Yokosuka, Japan)
A[udrey]. L[ilian]. Barker, Taylor Caldwell, Kate Greenaway, Caroline Lamb, Mary Ann Lamb, Edith Sitwell, Enid Starkie

Charlotte Spivack (Univ. of Massachusetts)
Vera Chapman, Edith Nesbit, Mary Stewart

Robert Spoo (Univ. of Tulsa)
Rose Macaulay

Patianne DelGrosso Stabile (Pace Univ.)
Dorothy Gladys Smith

Jackie E. Stallcup (Univ. of California, Riverside)
Jill Paton Walsh

Susan C. Staub (Appalachian State Univ.)
Jane Sharp, Elizabeth Taylor (Wythens)

Loretta Stec (San Francisco State Univ.)
Katharine Penelope Burdekin

Kristine Swenson (Univ. of Missouri)
Margaret Georgina Todd

Helen Clare Taylor (Louisiana State Univ.)
Enid Blyton, E. M. Delafield, Joanna Trollope

Richard C. Taylor (East Carolina Univ.)
Frances Boothby, Elizabeth Boyd, Mary Collier, Elizabeth Cooper, Mary Davys, Mary Monck, Elizabeth Singer Rowe, Jane Wiseman

Fran Teague (Univ. of Georgia)
Ann Bacon, Anne Clifford, Elizabeth Colville, Elizabeth Grymeston, Elizabeth Jocelin, Grace Sherrington Mildmay

Kathryn D. Temple (Georgetown Univ.)
Penelope Aubin, Catherine Talbot

Ann ter Haar (independent scholar)
A[ntonia]. S[usan]. Byatt (update only), Katherine Mansfield (update only)

John Timpane (independent scholar)
Elizabeth Craven, Elizabeth Daryush, Anne Kingsmill Finch, Edna O'Brien, Ann Ward Radcliffe, Fay Weldon, Frances Amelia Yates

Betty Travitsky (Graduate Center, C.U.N.Y.)
Anne Askew, Elizabeth Knevet Clinton, Joanna Fitzalan Lumley, Mary, Queen of Scots, Katherine Parr

Christine Trinh (Hope College)
Dora Jessie Saint (co-author)

Linda V. Troost (Washington and Jefferson College)
Mary Chandler, Hester Chapone

Bernard Tucker (Univ. of Southampton New College, U. K.)
Mary Barber, Constantia Grierson

Rosemary T. Van Arsdel (Univ. of Puget Sound)
George Eliot, Florence Fenwick Miller

Rita Verbrugge-Cunningham (independent scholar)
Margaret More Roper

Elizabeth Wahl (Stanford Univ.)
Jane Barker (co-author)

Robyn R. Warhol (Univ. of Vermont)
Constance Clara Black Garnett, Violet Hunt, Susanna Rowson, Virginia Woolf

Susan Waterman (Rutgers Univ.)
Ethelind Frances Colburn Mayne

Samantha Webb (Univ. of Montevallo)
Anne Lister, Mary Ann[e] Radcliffe (co-author)

Jane Weiss (Hunter College, C.U.N.Y.)
Lynne Reid Banks, Nina Bawden

Jan Wellington (Univ. of New Mexico)
Elizabeth Moody

Abby H. P. Werlock (St. Olaf College)
Rumer Godden (update only), Margery Sharp (update only), Jan Struther (update only), Honor Tracy (update only)

Suzanne Westfall (Lafayette College)
Enid Bagnold, Mrs. Patrick Campbell, Ellen Terry

Annemarie Koning Whaley (East Texas Baptist Univ.)
Mary I

Carol Shiner Wilson (Mulhenberg College)
Lucy Aikin, Anna Laetitia Barbauld (update only), Jane Barker (co-author), Elizabeth Ogilvy Benger, Anne Dudley Bradstreet, Penelope Lively, Charlotte Elizabeth Tonna, Priscilla Wakefield, Helen Maria Williams

Katharina M. Wilson (Univ. of Georgia)
Julian of Norwich, Katherine of Sutton, Margery Kempe, Marie de France

Sharon A. Winn (Northeastern State Univ.)
Ann Raney Thomas Coleman, Jane Ward Lead[e], Mary Leapor, Carolina, Baroness Nairne

Natalie Joy Woodall (independent scholar)
Emma Alice Margaret Tennant Asquith (update only), Margaret Blessington (update only), Mathilde Blind (update only), Elizabeth Carter (update only), Sara Coleridge (update only), Dinah Maria Mulock Craik (update only), Lucie Duff-Gordon (update only), Emily Eden (update only), Mary Anne Everett Wood Green, Charlotte E. B. Guest (update only), Jane Ellen Harrison, Emily Henrietta Hickey, Jenefer Ruth Joseph, Fanny Kemble (update only), Anne Manning, Alice Meynell (update only), Amelia Opie (update only), Violet Paget (update only), Anna Maria Porter (update only), Adelaide Ann Procter (co-author), Elizabeth Robins, Menella Bute Smedley, Ethel Mary Smyth, Somerville and Ross (update only), Lucy Hester Stanhope (update only), Catherine, Lady Stepney, Louisa Stuart (update only), Dorothy Wordsworth (update only)

Carolyn Woodward (Univ. of New Mexico)
Sarah Fielding, Elizabeth Montagu, Sarah Scott, Frances Sheridan, Elizabeth Vesey

Leslie J. Workman (Editor, *Studies in Medievalism*)
Juliana Berners, Dora Jessie Saint (co-author)

Virginia Zimmerman (Univ. of Virginia)
Elizabeth Barrett Browning (update only), Mary Cholmondeley (update only), Mary Lavin (update only), Charlotte Mary Yonge (update only)

Index

This index is necessarily selective. All references to subjects of entries, of course, are included, with names and page numbers for main entries given in **bold face**. Cross-references, including pseudonyms and significant variant names used for publication (for example, titles, birth names, or married names), are followed by "See" and the name for the main entry. In most cases, entries are included by authors' full personal names instead of, for example, by pseudonyms that may be better known; but since all such alternate names are included in the index, it is easy to determine if a particular author is the subject for an entry and to locate that entry. In general, names are cited as they are found in such reference works as the *Encyclopædia Britannica*; hence Vincent van Gogh is indexed as "Gogh, Vincent van" and the Marquis de Sade as "Sade, . . . marquis de." A quick glance at the index will also turn up numerous quaint and intriguing names for authors (for instance, Aunt Belinda, Exploribus, Galesia, Justicia, Lactilla, The Mad Nun of Lebanon, The Matchless Orinda, An Old Acquaintance of the Public, Perdita, The Queen of the Arabs) that will lead a curious reader to specific entries.

Names mentioned in passing, such as those of other writers and critics, are included since they generally reflect influences, friendships, contexts, or comparisons for the subjects; if subjects' family members who are mentioned in passing offer independent interest or importance, they are also included. Specific topics about which various authors have written are cross-referenced to related topics; thus a reader looking up "slavery" will also be directed to look for "abolitionism" and vice versa. Pertinent categories (such as professions) in which a number of authors are represented (acting or journalism) are also indexed. Major literary genres are analyzed, with fiction, for instance, divided into such categories as "romance," "mystery/detective," and "science fiction/fantasy."

We have not indexed such common categories as autobiography, diaries, memoirs, correspondence, devotional meditations, essays, and most poetry of a conventional sort simply because such headings would merely provide long, indiscriminate lists of names. We have also excluded names and other kinds of information in headnotes; names of authors in the various bibliographies unless they are also mentioned in the text; titles of books and other publications cited in the entries or in the bibliographies; most geographical entities; cathedrals and other religious edifices; and literary, biblical, or mythical characters. We have also excluded "Anonymous" from this index, as we have in the headnote terms "Writes under" or "Wrote under," though such a byline as "The author of . . ." is included since it refers to a single writer and in some cases was an author's sole byline.

abolitionism, 67, 235–36, 243, 300, 366, 463, 499, 692 (*see also* race relations/racism; slavery)
abortion, 17, 83, 112, 466, 541
A. C. *See* Bacon, Ann
Acton, Eliza, 1
actresses, writers as, 25, 44, 62–63, 76, 119–20, 190, 291, 312, 313, 316, 338, 365, 414, 433, 434, 540–42, 543–44, 547–48, 582, 615–16, 629, 676, 685
Adam(s), Jane. *See* Adam(s), Jean
Adam(s), Jean, 1–2
Adams, John Couch, 588
Adcock, (Karen) Fleur, 2–4
Addams, Jane, 321
Addinsell, Richard, 189
Adler, Alfred, 72 (*see also* psychoanalysis/psychiatry)
advertising, 6, 556, 676
Ady, Cecilia Mary, 4, 132
Aeschylus, 98, 661
Aesop, 8, 43, 93, 200
Africa, writing about, 61–62, 111–12, 229–30, 235–36, 337, 370–71, 392, 432, 451–52, 476–77, 520, 558–59
Agard, John, 475
agriculture, 400, 474
Aguilar, Grace, 4–5
Aiken, Conrad, 6
Aiken, Joan (Delano), 5–7
Aikin, John, 32
Aikin, Lucy, 8, 45
Ainsworth, Harrison, 407, 525
A. J. V. *See* Vardill, Anna Jane
A. L. *See* Locke, Anne Vaughan
Alcock, Mary, 8–9
alcoholism, 563–64, 576
Alcott, Louisa May, 64
Aldington, Richard, 204, 205, 381
Alexander, George, 119
Alexander the Great, 102, 528, 597
Alexander, Mrs. *See* Hector, Annie French
Alfreds, Mike, 666
Algarotti, Francesco, 127, 460
Ali, Hyder, 238
Ali, Mehmet, 594
Alington, Alice, 545
Alleine, Theodosia, 9–10
Allen, George, 441
Allen, Grant, 174
Allen, Ralph, 139, 245
Allen, Walter, 427, 481, 628
Allenby, G. *See* O'Malley, Mary Dolling (Sanders)
Alleyn, Ellen. *See* Rossetti, Christina
Allingham, Margery, 10–11, 341, 434
Altick, Richard, 152
Alton, Delia. *See* Doolittle, Hilda (H. D.)
Alvarez, A., 532
American Indians, 342, 630
Ames, Richard, 220
Amiel, Frederic Henri, 651

Amis, Kingsley, 346
Anacreon, 127, 641
Anastasia, Clara, 151
Andersen, Hans Christian, 266, 319, 331
Anderson, Elizabeth Garrett, 196
Anderson, Lindsay, 199
Andreas, Bernard, 225
Andrews, Corinne L. *See* West, Rebecca
Andrews, Miles, 180
Andrews, N., 627
Anger, Jane, 11–12
Angier, Carole, 531
Anglo-Irish Ascendancy (gentry, "big house"), 72–74, 355, 362–63, 586–87, 675, 679–87 (*see also* Irish Literary Renaissance)
Anglo-Saxon, study of, 228–29
animal rights, 337 (*see also* vivisectionism/ anti-vivisectionism)
Anne, Countess of Winchelsea. *See* Finch, Anne Kingsmill, Countess of Winchelsea
Anodos. *See* Coleridge, Mary Elizabeth
Anouilh, Jean, 354, 467, 667
Anspach (Ansbach), Margravine of. *See* Craven, Elizabeth (Berkeley)
Anstey, Christopher, 140
Anstey, F. (Thomas Anstey Guthrie), 474
Anstruther, Joyce. *See* Struther, Jan
Anstruther-Thompson, Kit, 498
Anthony, C. L. *See* Smith, Dorothy (Dodie) Gladys
Anthony, Susan B., 451, 499
anthropology, 309, 375, 520
anti-semitism, 243, 395, 534 (*see also* Holocaust; religion, Judaism)
Apollinaire, Guillaume, 591
Appignanesi, L., 419
Apuleius, 620, 655
Arabian Nights, 85
Aragon, Louis, 185
Arblay, d', Frances Burney. *See* Burney, Frances (Fanny)
Arbuthnot, John, 138, 329
Arcasia. *See* Boothby, Frances
archeologists, writers as, 304–05, 309, 402
Archer, William, 177, 541
Ardelia. *See* Finch, Anne Kingsmill, Countess of Winchelsea
Arden, John, 193–94, 345
Aretina. *See* Moody, Elizabeth
Ariadne, 12–13
Aristophanes, 173
Aristotle, 591
Arlen, Michael, 184, 256
Armytage, Mrs. G. *See* Watson, Rosamund Marriott
Armytage, R. *See* Watson, Rosamund Marriott
Arnim, Elizabeth von, 13–14
Arnold, Benedict, 562
Arnold, Matthew, 23, 98, 155, 158, 197, 315, 445, 520, 626, 651
Arnold, Thomas, 610, 651
art: cubism, 578; Dada, 184, 409; Futurism, 409; surrealism, 184 (*see also names of individual artists*)
artists or art critics, writers as, 31, 68–69, 93–96, 123–24, 131, 202, 215, 216, 226, 268–69, 274, 284, 285, 287, 295, 304–05, 306, 320, 342–43, 359–60, 367–68, 368, 394, 402–03, 407, 409, 414, 425, 426, 427, 444, 456, 492, 498, 500, 516, 518, 538, 561, 586, 657
Arthur, King, 140, 193, 257, 294, 431, 605
Ascham, Roger, 224
Ashby, George, 38
Asia, writing about, 58, 474–75
Askew, Anne (Kyme), 14–15
Asquith, Anthony, 160
Asquith, Cynthia, 15–16, 381
Asquith, H. H., 17, 171, 330, 500
Asquith, Emma Alice Margaret Tennant, 16–17
Astell, Mary, 17–19, 220, 440, 460, 618
Astor, John Jacob, 258
Astor, Nancy, 405
Astrea. *See* Behn, Aphra
astrology, 594, 695
astronomy, 587–88
Ataturk, Kemal, 489
Atwood, Margaret, 125
Atwood, William, 673
Aubin, Penelope, 19–20, 291
Aubrey, Mary, 509
Auden, W. H., 185, 303, 346, 451, 524, 536, 597–98
Augustine, 324, 346, 358, 462, 465, 573, 617, 670
Aunt Belinda. *See* Braddon (Maxwell), Mary Elizabeth
Austen, Jane, 20–22, 63, 72, 94, 100, 108, 109, 143, 199, 216, 217, 243, 246, 296, 303, 317, 338, 361, 377, 378, 418, 454, 488, 491, 494, 508, 522, 554, 586, 603, 611, 612, 615, 635, 647, 648, 656, 664, 668, 669, 699
Austin, Alfred, 339, 536
Austin, John, 327
Austin, William, 447
Austria, writing about, 424
Author of *David Simple*. *See* Fielding, Sarah
Author of *Elizabeth and Her German Garden*. *See* Arnim, Elizabeth von
Author of *The Female Quixote*. *See* Lennox, Charlotte Ramsay
Author of *Frankenstein*. *See* Shelley, Mary Wollstonecraft
Author of *John Halifax, Gentleman*. *See* Craik, Dinah Maria Mulock
Author of *The Ladies of Bever Hollow*. *See* Manning, Anne
Author of *Lady Grace*. *See* Smedley, Menella Bute
Author of *Little Black Sambo*. *See* Bannerman, Helen Brodie Cowan Watson
Author of *The Magic Lantern*. *See* Blessington, Margaret (Marguerite)
Author of *Mary Powell*. *See* Manning, Anne
Author of *Mrs. Leicester's School*. *See* Lamb, Mary Ann
Author of *IX Poems by V*. *See* Clive, Caroline
Author of *Paul Ferroll*. *See* Clive, Caroline
Author of *Phyllis*. *See* Hungerford, Margaret Hamilton Wolfe
Author of *The Proposal to the Ladies*. *See* Astell, Mary
Author of *Sketches and Fragments*. *See* Blessington, Margaret (Marguerite)
Avellaneda, Alonzo F. de, 385

Avoos. *See* Coleridge, Mary Elizabeth
A. W., Mrs. *See* Weamys [Weamers], Anna [Anne]
Axon, William E. A., 641
Aydy, Catherine. *See* Tennant, Emma
Ayer, A. J., 481

B. *See* Smedley, Menella Bute
Babbage, Charles, 588–89
Babthorpe, Grace Birnand, 325
Bacon, Francis, 23, 77, 212, 270, 311, 560
Bacon, Ann, 22–23, 550
Bagnold, Enid, 16, **23–24**
Bahn, Paul, 310
Baif, Jean-Antoine de, 565
Bailey, Paul, 341
Baillie, Grisell (Grizell) Hume, 24–25, 26
Baillie, Joanna, 8, 24, **25–26**, 32, 33, 45, 300, 325, 621
Bainbridge, Beryl (Margaret), 26–28
Baker, Augustine, 462, 464
Baker, Harold, 16
Baker, Ida, 428
Baldhoven, Georg Martinus von, 672
Bale, John, 15
Ballantyne, R. M., 64
Ballard, George, 107, 229, 270, 368, 439
Ballin, Rosetta, 387
Balzac, Honoré de, 76, 93, 394, 543, 586
Bampfield, Joseph, 297
Bancroft, Anne, 466
Banks, Isabella Varley, 28–29
Banks, Lynne Reid, 29–30
Bannerman, Helen Brodie Cowan Watson, 30–32
Bannon, Barbara, 341
Barbauld, Anna Laetitia, 8, 26, **32–33**, 45, 91, 242, 461, 527, 685
Barber, Frances, 268
Barber, Mary, 34, 290
Barclay, John, 421, 527
Barclay, Robert, 647
Baring, Maurice, 23
Barker, A[udrey]. L[ilian]., 34–35
Barker, Jane, 35–37
Barlow, Joel, 681
Barnard, Anne, 37
Barnes, Djuna, 102
Barnes, Joshua, 220
Barney, Natalie, 679
Baron, Elizabeth, 190
Barrett, Elizabeth Barrett. *See* Browning, Elizabeth Barrett
Barrie, James M., 16, 82, 119
Barrow, Isaac, 311
Barry, Elizabeth, 43, 636
Barstow, Montague, 492
Bartas, Guillaume de Salluste, Seigneur de, 77
Barthes, Roland, 92
Bartrop, Florence, 577
Baryshnikov, Mikhail, 260
Bashkirtseff, Marie, 60
Basse, William, 135
Bateman, Mary, 590
Bateson, F. W., 385
Bateson, Mary, 37–38
Batson, Henrietta M., 38–39
Batten, Mabel Veronica (Mrs. George), 299
Baudelaire, Charles, 597
Bauhaus, 102
Bawden, Nina (Kark), 39–40
Bax, Clifford, 441
Baxter, Nathaniel, 693
Bayard, Chevalier, 163
Bayley, John, 125, 470
Bayly, Ada Ellen, 40
BBC. *See* British Broadcasting Corporation
Beale, Dorothea, 576
Beale, Mary, 42
Beardsley, Aubrey, 97, 187, 394
Beaton, Cecil, 185
Beauchamp, Mary Annette. *See* Arnim, Elizabeth von
Beauman, Sally, 104
Beaumarchais, Pierre-Augustin Caronde, 291
Beaumont, Francis, and John Fletcher, 227, 513
Beaverbrook, Maxwell A., 128
Beckett, Samuel, 92, 185, 248, 426
Beckford, William, 278, 372
Bedford, Brian, 345
Bedford, Sybille, 40–41
Beecham, Thomas, 184, 584–85
Beerbohm, Max, 23, 189, 203, 394, 646
Beethoven, Ludwig van, 307, 583, 584, 670
Beeton, Isabella Mary Mayson, 41–42
Behn, Aphra, 12, **42–44**, 71, 142, 156, 176, 220, 231, 291, 510, 612, 636, 673
Behrman, S. N., 23
Bekassy, Bert, 173
Belhaven, Lord (John Hamilton, Lord Belhaven and Stenton), 479
Bell, Acton. *See* Brontë, Anne
Bell, Clive, 84, 86, 88, 123, 688
Bell, Currer. *See* Brontë, Charlotte
Bell, Ellis. *See* Brontë, Emily
Bell, Florence, 541
Bell, Mackenzie, 662
Bell, Vanessa, 123, 600
Bellamy, George Ann, 44–45
Bellarmine, Robert, 494
Bellas, Ralph, 546
Bellay, Joachim du, 565
Bellini, Vincenzo, 364
Belloc, Hilaire, 408, 512, 610, 653
Benét, Stephen Vincent, 607
Benger, Elizabeth Ogilvy, 8, **45**, 241
Bennett, Anna Maria (Evans), 45–46
Bennett, Arnold, 48, 171, 192, 206, 207, 326, 576, 586, 688
Bennett, Louise, 61
Bennett, William Sterndale, 682
Bensen, Alice, 567
Benson, E. F., 585
Benson, Stella, 46–47
Bentham, Jeremy, 675
Bentley, Phyllis, 47–49, 243
Bentley, Richard, 311
Bentley, Thomas, 521

Benvolio. *See* Seward, Anna
Beran, J. *See* Doolittle, Hilda (H. D.)
Berenson, Bernard, 132, 596
Beresford, Anne, 49
Bergson, Henri, 305
Berkeley, Anthony, 556
Berkeley, Elizabeth, 609
Berkeley, George, 533
Berkeley, George (the younger), 609
Berman, Al, 267
Berners, Juliana, 49–50
Bernhardt, Sarah, 119, 616
Berry, Mary, 50–51
Berryman, John 303
Bertie, Susan, 376
Berwick, Mary. *See* Procter, Adelaide Anne
Besant, Annie Wood, 51–55
Besant, Walter, 397
Betham-Edwards, Mathilda, 55–56
Bethune, G. W., 21
Betjeman, John, 405, 412
Betterton, Mary, 685
Betterton, Thomas, 42, 513, 636
Bevington, L[ouisa]. S[arah]., 56–57
Bezel, Theodore de, 574
Bibesco, Emmanuel, 23, 24
Bicknell, Alexander, 44
Biddle, Hester (Esther), 57
Binch, Caroline, 476
biography, writing of, 45, 79, 101, 115, 128–29, 131–32, 405–06, 408, 423, 487, 528, 551, 572–73, 576, 578, 591, 647, 653, 654, 662, 682
Birch, Thomas, 389, 636
birth control, 52, 288, 451, 692
Birtwhistle, John, 641
Bishop, Isabella Lucy Bird, 57–58
Bismarck, Otto von, 60
Bjornson, Bjornstjerne, 119
Black, Clementina, 395
Black, C[onstance]. C[lara]. *See* Garnett, Constance Clara Black
Black, Helen, 398
Black, Kitty, 354
Black Mountain Group, 239
Black, Tom Campbell, 432
black writers, 61–62, 105–06, 111–12, 185, 229–30, 475–76
Blackett, Monica, 646
Blackwood Publishers, 488
Blades, William, 50
Blagdon Controversy, 464
Blaikley, Alan, 626
Blair, the Rev. David. *See* Fenwick, Eliza
Blair, Robert, 243
Blake, William, 9, 90, 274, 445, 524–25, 685
Blake, William [not the writer], 598
Blamire, Susanna, 58–59
Blanch, Lesley, 477
Bland, E. *See* Nesbit, Edith
Bland, Fabian. *See* Nesbit, Edith
Blavatsky, Petrovna, 52
Blencowe, John, 384
Blencowe, Samuel, 301
Blessington, Margaret (Marguerite), 59–60, 407
Blind, Mathilde, 60
Blixen, Karen (Isak Dinesen), 432
Blond, Anthony, 159
Blood, Fanny, 685
Bloom, Valerie (Wright), 61–62
Bloomsbury, 123, 551, 651, 688
Blosius, Franciscus Ludovicus, 135
Blower, Elizabeth, 62–63
Bluestockings, 108, 127, 141, 201, 459, 463, 511, 560, 562, 601, 607, 609, 642–43
Blunt, Wilfrid Scawen, 15, 406
Bluth, K. T., 360
Blyton, Enid, 63–67
Boccaccio, Giovanni, 125, 431, 538
Bodichon, Barbara, 55, **67–68**, 196, 319, 332, 519
Bodkin, (Amy) Maud, 68–70
Boethius, Anicius, 224, 511
Bogan, Louise, 512
Bogan of Bogan, Mrs. *See* Nairne, Baroness Caroline
Bogus, Diane, 106
Böhme, Jakob, 381
Boland, Eavan Aisling, 48, **70**
Bolingbroke, Henry, 329
Bonaparte, Joseph, 258
Bonaparte, Napoleon, 35, 108, 190, 517, 681, 684
Bonhote, Elizabeth, 71
Bonifas, G., 105
Bonnecorse, Balthasar, 43
Bonner, Edward, 14
Bonnycastle, John, 587
book clubs, 341, 414, 607, 655
Boole, Lily. *See* Voynich, Ethel Lilian Boole
Booth, Charles, 658
Boothby, Frances, 71
Boscawen, Frances, 201
Boskin, Joseph, 31
Boswell, James, 109, 127, 155, 479, 511, 563
Botticelli, Sandro, 132
Bottome, Phyllis, 71–72
Boucher, Anthony, 340
Boucherett, Jessie, 519
Boufflers, Mme. S.-J. de, 479
Boulton, Matthew, 387
Bourne, Nicholas, 591
Bow, Clara, 275
Bowen, Elizabeth (Dorothea Cole), 72–74, 114, 321, 368, 388, 534, 617, 622, 676
Bowen, Stella, 531
Bowles, Anne, 109
Bowles, Caroline, 74–75, 286
Bowra, Maurice, 405, 578
Boyd, Elizabeth, 75
Boyer, Charles, 367
Boyle, Robert, 533
Bracegirdle, Anne, 12, 43
Bracegirdle, Elizabeth, 220
Braddon, Mary Elizabeth (Maxwell), 75–77, 97, 433, 488
Bradford, David, 148
Bradlaugh, Charles, 40, 52, 55

Bradley, Katharine Harris. *See* Field, Michael (Katharine Harris Bradley)
Bradstreet, Anne Dudley, 77–79, 121
Brahms, Johannes, 584
Brandl, Karl, 663
Bray, Anna Eliza (Kempe), 79–80
Bray, Charles and Cara, 221
Bray, R., 229
Brazil, Angela, 80–81, 260
breastfeeding, 154, 172–73
Brecht, Bertolt, 147, 191, 193, 403
Brel, Petrus, 597
Bremer, Fredrika, 331–32
Brereton, Humphrey, 225
Breton, André, 359, 409
Brett, Dorothy, 381
Brewster, Henry, 584–85
Bridge, Ann. *See* O'Malley, Mary Dolling (Sanders)
Bridges, Robert, 162, 163, 194, 443
Brien, Alan, 378
Bright, Mary Golding, 81–82
Brink, J. R., 420
Brinkelow, Henry, 404
British Broadcasting Corporation (BBC), 49, 61, 96, 104, 148, 150, 151, 190, 193, 200, 252, 261, 267, 337, 357, 403, 414, 427, 531, 552, 561, 582–83, 597, 626, 635, 649, 659, 676, 684 (*see also* television)
Brittain, Vera, 48, **82–84**, 325, 326, 368
Broch, Hermann, 468–69
Brome, Richard, 326
Bronowski, Jacob, 481
Brontë, Anne, 84–85, 86, 88, 189, 576
Brontë, Branwell, 84, 85, 87, 88, 212, 264
Brontë, Charlotte, 48, 82, 84, **85–87**, 88, 183, 215, 226, 264, 360, 398, 436, 508, 537
Brontë, Elizabeth, 84, 85
Brontë, Emily, 84, 85, 86, **87–89**, 303, 385, 543, 576, 592, 660
Brontë, Maria, 84, 85
Brontë, Patrick, 85
Brontë sisters, 30, 110, 178, 190, 255, 281, 365, 591, 651
Brook, Peter, 193
Brooke, Charlotte, 89–91
Brooke, Frances Moore, 91–92
Brooke, Henry, 90
Brooke, Rupert, 172, 173
Brooke-Rose, Christine, 92
Brookner, Anita, 93–96
Brooks, Gwendolyn, 475
Brophy, Brigid, 96–97, 260
Brophy, John, 96
Brothers, Richard, 590
Brougham, Henry, 588
Broughton, Rhoda, 97–98, 144
Brown, Georgina, 269
Brown, H., 539
Brown, John, 634
Brown, Norman O., 96
Brown, Samuel, 183
Browne, Felicia. *See* Hemans, Felicia Dorothea Browne
Browne, Thomas, 311
Browning, Elizabeth Barrett, 56, 74, **98–101**, 155, 168, 186, 187, 258, 286, 315, 343, 395, 445, 454, 508, 537, 546, 602, 642, 662
Browning, Naps, 596
Browning, Robert, 98–99, 114, 153, 158, 162, 187, 244, 285, 318, 319, 334, 343, 366, 441, 445, 498, 519, 537, 542, 543, 610, 653, 662
Bruce, Margaret, 100
Bruchet, Max, 134
Brueghel, Pieter the Elder, 148
Bruno, Giordano, 695
Brunton, Mary Balfour, 100–01, 243
Bryher (pseudonym of Annie Winifred Ellerman), 101–03, 204
Bucer, Martin, 550, 565
Büchner, Georg, 268
Buddicom, Venetia, 596
Bude, G., 545
Buffon, G.-L., 180
Bulwer-Lytton, Edward, 76, 103, 372, 601, 675, 681
Bulwer-Lytton, Rosina Wheeler, 103
Bunbury, Sarah. *See* Lennox Bunbury Napier, Sarah
Bunsen, C. K. J. von, 682
Bunyan, John, 82, 85, 207, 261, 307
Burchill, Julie, 103–04
Burdekin, Katharine Penelope, 104–05
Burford, Barbara, 105–06
Burgess, Anthony, 272, 353, 354, 427
Burgess, Jackson, 29
Burke, Edmund, 201, 382, 383, 620, 685
Burke, Peter, 695
Burleigh, William Cecil, 387
Burlington, Richard Boyle, 139
Burma, writing about, 424
Burnaud, Francis, 394
Burne-Jones, Edward, 119, 132, 203, 251, 334, 600, 617, 688
Burnet, Elizabeth, 106–07
Burnet, Gilbert, 18, 107, 673
Burnett, Frances Eliza, 377
Burney, Charles, 108, 109
Burney, Frances (Fanny), 31, 46, 91, 101, **107–09**, 141, 146, 201, 229, 243, 246, 296, 449, 450, 484, 561, 643, 681
Burney, Sarah Harriet, 109–10
Burns, Robert, 25, 51, 59, 85, 124, 243, 460, 473, 496
Burnside, Helen Marion, 122
Burrage, C., 629
Burrough, Edward, 637
Bury, Charlotte, 110–11
Bush, Douglas, 494
Bushnell, N., 242
Busia, Abena P. A., 111–12
Bute, Mary Ellen, 426
Butler, Josephine (Elizabeth Grey), 112–13, 286, 321
Byatt, A[ntonia]. S[usan]., 113–14, 125, 207
Bynner, Witter, 381
Byrne, Charlotte Dacre. *See* Dacre, Charlotte
Byrne, Mrs. *See* Dacre, Charlotte
Byrne, Muriel St. Clare, 556
Byron, Ada, 589
Byron, Annabella, 343, 442, 589

Byron, George Gordon, Lord, 188, 212, 226, 251, 278, 315, 331, 365, 372, 374, 385, 403, 406, 441–42, 454, 495, 532, 568, 589, 590, 594, 610, 692

C. *See* Bowles, Caroline
Cable, (Alice) Mildred, 115
Cadogan, Mary, 182
Caird, Alice Mona, 115–16, 202
Calcraft, John, 44
Caldecott, Randolph, 234
Calderwood, Margaret Steuart, 116–17
Caldwell, (Janet) Taylor, 117–18
Callan, Margaret, 680
Callendar, Newgate, 529–30
Calman, Mel, 456
Calvin, John, 404, 565
Cam, Helen Maud, 118–19
Cambridge University, 32, 93, 137, 253, 305, 384, 480, 505, 514, 649; Emmanuel, 448; Girton, 118, 196–97, 388, 418, 524, 588; Homerton, 554; New Hall, 93; Newnham, 37, 113, 206, 239, 244, 263, 287, 304, 309, 395; St. John's, 37; Trinity, 9, 655
Cambry, Jeanne de, 462
Cameron, Julia Margaret, 600
Campbell, Joseph, 25–26
Campbell, Mrs. Patrick (Beatrice Stella Tanner Campbell Cornwallis-West), 119–20, 542, 602
Campbell, Roy, 185
Campbell, Susan, 213
Campbell, Thomas, 517
Camus, Jean Pierre, 214
Canfield, Bennet de, 465
Capp, B. S., 629
Caravaggio, 491
Carco, Francis, 428
Cardinale, S., 224
Carey, Mary, 120–21
Carey, Rosa Nouchette, 121–22
Caribbean, writing about, 61–61, 351–52, 475–76, 530–32, 558, 628
Carleton, William, 680
Carlisle, Charles Howard, Earl of, 141
Carlyle, Jane Welsh, 122–23, 183, 200, 347, 348, 537
Carlyle, Thomas, 60, 122, 183, 208, 347, 492, 634, 537
Caron, Leslie, 29
Carossa, Hans, 469
Carpenter, Edward, 559
Carr, George, 298
Carrington, Dora de Houghton, 123–24 (*see also* Bloomsbury)
Carroll, Lewis (C. L. Dodgson), 98, 189, 266, 394, 575, 579, 600, 610, 613, 615
Carson, Murray, 177
Carswell, Catherine, 124–25, 400
Carter, Angela (Olive Stalker), 125–27
Carter, Elizabeth, 9, **127–28**, 141, 371, 459, 547, 609, 642
Cartland, Barbara, 128–131
Cartwright, Julia, 4, **131–32**
Cartwright, William, 509
Carus-Wilson, Eleanor Mary, 132–33
Cary, Anne and Lucy, 133–34
Cary, Elizabeth, Viscountess Falkland,133, **134–35**
Cary, Henry, 376
Cary, Joyce, 368, 598
Cary, Mary, 135–36
Casson, Lewis, 190
Castiglione, Baldassare, 131–32
Cather, Willa, 114, 678
Catherine, 346
Catherine of Genoa, 462
Catherine of Siena, 465
Cato, 527
Catt, Carrie Chapman, 451
Catullus, Gaius Valerius, 591
Cave, Edward, 127
Cavendish, Georgianna, 544
Cavendish, Margaret, Duchess of Newcastle, 136–38, 214, 316, 335, 389, 494
Cavendish, William, 136–37
Caxton, William, 225
Cayley, Charles Bagot, 545
C. C. *See* Cookson, Catherine Ann
C. E. *See* Tonna, Charlotte Elizabeth
Cecil, David, 520
Cecil, Mildred Cooke, 550
Cecil, Robert, 551
Cecil, William, 23, 504, 551
Centlivre, Susanna, 138–39, 156, 176, 220, 685
Cervantes de Saavedra, Miguel, 385, 386
Cézanne, Paul, 346
Challans, Eileen Mary. *See* Renault, Mary
Chamberlain, Joseph, 405
Chamberlain, Neville, 405
Chambers, Colin, 267
Chambers, E. C. E., 653
Chambers, Robert, 183
Chandler, Mary, 139–40
Channing, William Ellery, 8, 33
Chapin, Ruth, 377
Chaplin, Charlie, 27, 273
Chapman, George, 227, 693
Chapman, John, 68, 221
Chapman, Maria Weston, 437
Chapman, Vera, 140
Chapone, Hester (Mulso), 33, **140–41**, 459, 569, 587
Charke, Charlotte Cibber, 141–42
Charles, Gerda. *See* Lipson, Edna
Charlesworth, Maria, 142–43
Charleton, Walter, 137
Charlotte, Elizabeth. *See* Tonna, Charlotte Elizabeth
Charteris, Hugh, 15
Chase, Mary Ellen, 554
Chatterton, Thomas, 190, 696
Chaucer, Geoffrey, 92, 140, 152, 237, 248, 384, 385–86, 505
Chaucer, Thomas, 505
Chekhov, Anton, 255, 264, 268, 345, 428, 446, 656
Chernaik, Warren, 231
Chesterfield, Philip D. S., 150, 329
Chesterton, Denise. *See* Robins, Denise Naomi
Chesterton, G. K., 346, 556, 653
child abuse, 311
child labor, 98, 286

child-raising, 288, 350–51, 651
children's literature: animal stories, 285, 518, 563–64, 632; anthologies, 15, 376; drama, 15–16, 121, 237–38, 289, 434, 556; fiction, 5–7, 8, 15–16, 29–30, 30–32, 32–33, 39, 61–62, 63–67, 76, 79, 80–81, 97–98, 121, 125–26, 142–43, 151, 153–54, 166, 170, 178, 183, 201–02, 213, 217, 229–30, 233–34, 237–38, 242, 245, 249, 261, 266–67, 277, 281, 285–86, 289, 307–08, 323–24, 331–32, 339, 348, 373, 375–76, 383, 401, 407, 430, 434, 456, 474, 475, 518, 564, 567, 571–72, 575, 580–81, 581, 582, 591–92, 600, 605, 606, 609–11, 613–15, 625, 629–30, 631, 632, 646, 648, 657, 668, 651, 697; illustrations in, 233–34, 285; poetry, 32–33, 121, 163–64, 237–38, 285, 347, 373, 546, 578, 581, 610–11 (*see also* fairy tales)
Chimaera. *See* Farjeon, Eleanor
China, writing about, 490
Cholmondelay, Alice. *See* Arnim, Elizabeth von
Cholmondeley, Mary, 143–44
Chomsky, Noam, 309
Christian Socialism, 305–06, 319 (*see also* Fabian Society; International Labour Party; Socialism)
Christie, Agatha, 10, **144–47**, 182, 340–41, 433, 434, 529, 556
Christie, Julie, 200
Christine of Pisan, 538
Chudleigh, Lady Mary, 618
Church, Richard, 617
Churchill, Caryl, 147–49, 191
Churchill, Charles, 155
Churchill, Jennie, 177
Churchill, Sarah Jennings, Duchess of Marlborough, 149–50, 313, 422
Churchill, Winston, 147, 149, 187, 405, 490, 594, 616
Cibber, Colley, 141, 198, 510, 636
Cibber, Susanna Mary Anne, 155
Cibber, Theophilus, 141, 569
Cicero, Marcus Tullius, 330
Clairmont, Claire, 568
Clairmont, Mary Jane, 568
Clairvaux, Bernard de, 462
Clanchy, Kate, 210
Clare, John, 323, 512
Clarendon, Edward Hyde, 311
Clarinda. *See* Egerton, Sarah Fyge Field
Clarke, Charles Cowden, 51, 311, 620
Clarke, Coningsby, 299
Clarke, Gillian, 150–51
Clarke, Mary Victoria (Novello) Cowden, 151–52
Clarke, Maude, 416
Clarkson, Thomas, 300
Clavering, Charlotte, 243
Clement, Margaret Giggs, 573
Clementia (or Clementina), Dame. *See* Cary, Anne
Clifford, Anne, 152–53
Clifford, Arthur, 616
Clifford, Lucy Lane, 153
Clifford, Margaret, 376
Clinton, Elizabeth Knevet, 154
Clinton, Louisa, 607
Clive, Caroline, 154–55
Clive, Catherine (Kitty), 155–56
Clive, Mrs. Archer. *See* Clive, Caroline
Cluysenaar, Anne (Alice Andrée), 157
Cobbe, Frances Power, 157–58, 197, 662
Cobbett, William, 463
Cockburn, Alicia (or Alison), 159
Cockerell, Sydney Carlyle, 446, 596
Cocteau, Jean, 598, 630
Codron, Michael, 147
Coffeteau, Nicolas, 421
Coffey, Charles, 155
Coffin, William Sloane, 453
Cohen, M., 243
Coke, Anne, 673
Coke, Mary, 608
Colarossi, F., 586
Colburn, Henry, 109, 407
Colby, Robert, 100
Colby, V., 300
Cole, Mary, 175
Colegate, Isabel, 159–61
Coleman, Ann Raney Thomas, 162
Coleman, Olive, 133
Coleridge, Henry Nelson, 74
Coleridge, Mary Elizabeth, 162–63
Coleridge, Samuel Taylor, 33, 46, 114, 162, 163, 373, 445, 454, 464, 522, 544, 563, 580, 641, 691
Coleridge, Sara, 163–64, 507
Colette, Sidonie-Gabrielle, 93, 630, 676, 679
Colie, Rosalie, 695
Collier, Jane, 245, 246
Collier, Mary, 164–65, 301
Collins, Ann, 165–66
Collins, Wilkie, 76, 98, 145, 155, 212, 433, 557, 687
Collinson, James, 545
Collyer, Mary Mitchell, 166
Colman, George, 290, 386
Colquhoun, Mrs. Campbell, 473
Colum, Padraic, 280
Colville, Alexander, 167
Colville, Elizabeth, 166–67
Comber, Dean, 619
Comber, George, 183
communism, 115, 453, 500 (*see also* Lenin, V. I.; Marx, Karl; Marxism; Stalin, Joseph; Trotsky, Leon)
Compton-Burnett, Ivy, 167–68
computers, 589
Comte, Auguste, 209, 449
conduct books, 225–26, 312, 350, 647 (*see also* cookbooks and recipes; household advice books)
Conelly, Joseph, 104
Congreve, William, 24, 220, 270, 461, 480, 513, 618, 636
Connolly, Cyril, 359
Connolly, James, 193
Connolly, Sybil, 363
Conquest, Robert, 346
Conrad, Joseph, 171
Constable, Archibald, 563
Constable, Thomas, 286
Constant, Benjamin, 93, 372, 491
Constantine, Murray. *See* Burdekin, Katharine Penelope
Conti, Louis François Joseph, 479
Cook, Eliza, 168–69, 407
Cook, Florence, 539

Cook, John Douglas, 397
cookbooks and recipes, 1, 41–42, 273–74, 304, 363, 448
  (*see also* conduct books; household advice books)
Cooke, Anthony, 22
Cooke, J., 538, 539
Cooke, Rose Terry, 454
Cookson, Catherine Ann, 169–70
Cookson, William, 49
Cooper, Edith Emma. *See* Field, Michael
Cooper, Elizabeth, 170
Cooper, James Fenimore, 109, 217, 434
Cooper, Jilly, 170–71
Cooper-Clark, Diana, 529
Cope, Esther S., 195
copyright reform, 332
Cordelia, John. *See* Underhill, Evelyn
Corelli, Marie (pseudonym of Mary Mackay), 171–72
Corinna. *See* Thomas, Elizabeth
Corio, Silvio, 500
Corneille, Pierre, 509
Cornell, Katherine, 190
Cornford, F. M., 304
Cornford, Frances Crofts Darwin, 172–74
Correggio, 478
Corrigan, Felicitas, 646
Corvo, Baron (Rolfe, Frederick William), 354
Cory, Annie Sophie. *See* Cory, Victoria
Cory, Victoria (pseudonym of Annie Sophie Cory), 174–75
Cory, William, 162
Cotterell, Charles, 509
Cotton, Priscilla, 175
Couldrey, Jack, 432
Council of Trent, 495
Cournos, John, 204
Courtenay, T. P, 493
Courtney, W. L., 306
Courville, C., 111
Cousin, Victor, 209
Cousins, James H., 280
Coventry Lady, 18
Coverdale, Miles, 504
Coward, Noël, 24, 174, 177, 362, 602–03
Cowden Clarke, Mary Victoria. *See* Clarke, Mary Victoria (Novello) Cowden
Cowley, Abraham, 43, 231, 232, 509
Cowley, Hannah Parkhouse, 176, 544
Cowper, William, 9, 50, 445, 610
Crabbe, George, 382, 383
Crackenthorpe, Blanche, 477
Crackenthorpe, Hubert, 192
Craig, Edward Gordon, 615
Craigie, Pearl, 176–78
Craik, Dinah Maria Mulock, 178–79, 687
Craik, W., 243
Crane, John, 565
Crane, Stephen, 356
Cranmer, Thomas, 536
Craven, Arthur, 409
Craven, Elizabeth (Berkeley), Baroness Craven, 179–81
Crawford, Archibald, 2
Crawford, Francis Marion, 258
Crawford, R., 476
Creak, Edith, 263, 395
Creeley, Robert, 239
Creighton, Mandell, 37–38
Crespigny, Champion de, 45
Cressy, Serenus, 465
Crisp, Samuel, 107
Crispin, Edmund, 145
Croker, Bithia May (or Mary), 181
Croker, John Wilson, 328, 495
Croker, Thomas Crofton, 533
Crompton, Richmal (Lamburn), 182–83
Cromwell, Elizabeth, 135
Cromwell, Henry 493, 618
Cromwell, Oliver, 177, 240, 249, 257, 336, 417, 493, 508–09, 516, 629, 663
Cronwright-Schreiner, Olive. *See* Schreiner, Olive Emilie Albertina
Crosland, M., 275
crossdressing, 142, 260, 297, 419, 549
Cross(e), Victoria, *See* Cory, Victoria
Crousaz, Jean Pierre de, 127
Crowder, Henry, 185
Crowe, Catherine Anne, 183–84
Cruikshank, George, 218, 234, 407
Cudworth, Ralph, 440
Cullen, L. M., 485
Culpeper, Nicholas, 566
Culross yonger, Ladie. *See* Colville, Elizabeth
Cunard, Nancy, 184–85
Cunningham, Valentine, 456, 538
Curll, Edmund, 460, 618
Currie, Mary (Montgomerie) Lamb Singleton, Lady Currie, 186–87
Curtin, Philip. *See* Lowndes, Marie Adelaide Belloc
Curzon, George, 177
Curzon, Mary, 177
Curzon, Nathaniel, 177
Cushman, Catherine, 168, 519
Cushman, Charlotte, 454
Custance, Olive, 187–88
Cuvier, Georges, 491, 588
Czechoslovakia, writing about, 502

Dacre, Charlotte, 188–89
Dame Clementia (or Clementina). *See* Cary, Anne and Lucy
Dame Lucy Magdalena. *See* Cary, Anne and Lucy
Dane, Clemence, 189–91
Daniel, Samuel, 170, 573
Daniels, Sarah, 191
D'Annunzio, Gabriele, 670, 679
Dante Alighieri, 4, 434, 557, 679
Danvers, John, 673
Daphne. *See* Hands, Elizabeth; Robinson, Mary Darby (Perdita)
d'Arblay, Frances Burney. *See* Burney, Frances (Fanny)
Darby, Mary. *See* Robinson, Mary Darby (Perdita)
D'Arcy, Ella, 192–93, 441
D'Arcy, Margaretta Ruth, 193–94
Darley, George, 536

Darling, Grace, 453
Darmesteter, A. M. F. (Mary). *See* Robinson, Agnes Mary Frances
D'Arnaud, Baculard, 386, 387
Dart, Helga. *See* Doolittle, Hilda (H. D.)
D'Arusmont, Frances Wright. *See* Wright, Frances
D'Arusmont, Madam. *See* Wright, Frances
D'Arusmont, Phiquepal, 692
Darwin, Charles, 42, 56, 60, 93, 158, 159, 172, 173, 266, 309, 558, 562–63, 589 (*see also* evolution)
Darwin, Erasmus, 462, 562
Daryush, Elizabeth, 194–95
Daudet, Alphonse, 408
Daughters of the American Revolution, 117
Davenport, Fanny, 176
Davie, Donald, 239
Davies, Eleanor Audeley (Douglas), 195–96
Davies, Emily, 68, **196–97**
Davies, Gordon. *See* Macintosh, Elizabeth
Davies, John, 135
Davies, P. *See* Godden, (Margaret) Rumer
Davies, Rhys, 381
Davies, Thomas, 155
Daviot, Gordon. *See* Macintosh, Elizabeth
Davis, Natalie Zemon, 695
Davis, Thomas, 679
Davy, Humphrey, 42
Davys, Mary, 197–98
Day, Dorothy, 653
Day Lewis, Cecil, 524
Dean, Basil, 367
Deane, Samuel, 484
Dedmon, Emmett, 377
Deffand, Marie de Vichy-Chamrond, marquise du, 51
Defoe, Daniel, 8, 17, 18, 19, 29, 142
de Havilland, Olivia, 666
de Hueck, Catherine, 653
Dekker, Thomas, 227
Delafield, E. M. (pseudonym of Edmée Elizabeth de la Pasture), 198–99, 554
de la Mare, Walter, 163, 237, 411, 443, 512, 661
Delaney, Patrick, 290
Delaney, Shelagh, 199–200, 345
Delany, Mary Granville Pendarves, 201, 229, 642
de la Warr, Margaret, 618
Délécluse, Etienne-Jean, 586
Dell, Ethel M., 128
della Cruscan movement, 176, 188, 544
Della Stufa, Marchese, 526
Deniosot, Nicolas, 565
De Quincy, Thomas, 464, 691
Dering, Anna. *See* Locke, Anne Vaughan
d'Este, Beatrice, 131
d'Este, Isabella, 4, 131
Dethick, William, 551
Devereaux, Robert, 23, 323
Devine, George, 345
dialects, 61–62, 167, 288–89, 351–52, 403, 661 (*see also* linguistics)
Dibdin, Thomas Frognall, 517
Dickens, Charles, 6, 11, 26, 51, 93, 122, 151, 183, 201, 208, 222, 234, 264, 264, 278, 303, 319, 370, 385, 394, 396, 414, 450, 455, 474, 492, 506, 519, 510, 522, 532, 537, 598, 617, 625, 634, 646
Dickens, Monica, 201–02
Dickinson, Emily, 114, 239
Dickinson, Violet, 216
Diderot, Denis, 386
Dietrich, Marlene, 268, 269
Dignam, Augustis, 444
Dimant, Penelope. *See* Mortimer, Penelope Ruth
Dingley, Rebecca, 353
Dinnis, Enid, 318
Disch, Thomas M., 418
Disney, Walt, 582, 630
Disraeli, Benjamin, 186, 571, 600, 601, 625
Dixon, Ella Nora Hepworth, 202–03
Dixon, Mrs., 386
D. M. M. *See* Craik, Dinah Maria Mulock
Dobrizhoffer, Martin, 163
Dobson, Austin, 657
Dodd, James, 338
Dodsley, Robert, 560
Dodwell, Henry, 18
Donne, John, 152, 231, 232, 262, 263, 303, 368, 411, 462, 464, 545, 574, 616
Donoghue, Denis, 485
Doody, Margaret, 46, 389
Doolittle, Hilda (H. D.), 102, **203–06**, 576, 603
Doorn, Helga. *See* Doolittle, Hilda (H. D.)
Dorat, Jean, 565
Dorn, Ed, 239
Dörpfeld, Wilhelm, 305
Dostoyevsky, Fyodor, 264
Douglas, Alfred, 187, 394
Douglas, Norman, 185
Douglas, William, 333
Dowding, Hugh, 205
Dowland, John, 173
Dowriche, Anne, 206
Doyle, Arthur Conan, 10, 145, 433, 434
Doyle, John, 675
Drabble, Margaret, 113, **206–08**, 622, 623
Drake, Francis, 387
drama, 12–13, 24, 25–26, 42–43; allegorical/symbolic, 22, 166–67; closet, 579; comedy, 12–13, 19, 42–43, 92, 138–39, 155–56, 167, 176, 180, 289, 338, 344–46, 385, 386, 422, 511, 513, 515, 548, 569–70; criticism and theory, 227–28, 271–73, 338, 344–46, 426–27, 540–41, 616, 629, 676; experimental/improvisational, 25, 344–46, 497, 511, 561; historical, 90, 227–28, 365–66, 386, 414–15, 454, 498, 517, 536, 661–62; humorous, 156; melodrama, 107, 516; musical, 148, 189; nationalistic/regional, 279–80, 288–89, 298; production and staging, 434, 540–42, 615–16; religious, 10–11, 358, 536, 556; romantic/sentimental, 180, 386, 693; social/political, 148, 189, 199–200, 279–80, 355–56; study and teaching, 9–10, 540–42; tragedy, 25–26, 70, 135, 189, 245–46, 289, 315, 384, 386, 422, 454, 463, 491, 513, 515, 569–70, 636, 673; tragicomedy, 71, 693; verse, 636; writing of, 22, 25–26, 81–82, 147–48, 189–90, 267–69, 271–73, 278, 291, 312–13, 354, 377–78, 386, 434, 483–84, 508–09, 664–65, 665–67 (*see also* actresses, writers as)

Drayton, Michael, 135
Dreiser, Theodore, 646
Drummond, William, 333, 693
Dryden, John, 85, 220, 231, 368–69, 384, 618, 673
Dubos, René, 650
Du Bourg, Anne, 206
Duchess, The. *See* Hungerford, Margaret Hamilton Wolfe
Duclaux, Mary. *See* Robinson, Agnes Mary Frances
Duckworth, George, 688
Dudley, Ambrose, 573
Dudley, John, 573
Dudley, Robert, 573
Duff-Gordon, Lucy, 208–09
Duffy, Carol Ann, 209–10
Duffy, Charles Gavan, 679–80
Duffy, Maureen, 97, **211**
du Fossé family, 681
Dumas, Alexandre *fils*, 268
Dumas, Alexandre *père*, 365
du Maurier, Daphne, 211–13
du Maurier, George, 211
Dundee, John Graham, 415
Dunn, Nell (pseudonym of Nell Mary Sandford), 213–14
Dunne, Mary Chavelita. *See* Bright, Mary Golding
Dunsany, Edward John M. D. P., 379, 586
Dunton, John, 547, 612
Duperron, Jacques Davy, 135
Durand, Lionel, 205
Durkheim,Émile, 305
Durrell, Lawrence, 347, 428
Dury, Ian, 626
Duse, Eleanora, 616
Du Verger, Susan, 214–15
Dvořák, Antonín, 584
Dzhagarov, Georgi, 354

Eager, Edward, 474
Eagleton, Terry, 346
Eastlake, Lady, Elizabeth Rigby, 215–16
EBB. *See* Browning, Elizabeth Barrett
Echo. *See* Robinson, Mary Darby (Perdita)
Eco, Umberto, 503
economics, 132–33, 649–50, 680
Eddy, Donald D., 515
Eden, Anthony, 216
Eden, Eleanor (Lena), 216
Eden, Emily, 216–17
Eder, David, 400, 401
Eder, Edith, 400
Edgeworth, Maria, 33, 90, 108, 109, **217–18**, 243, 296, 298, 300, 380, 382, 383, 454, 491, 537, 586, 588, 611, 647
Editor of *The Phoenix*, The. *See* Reeve, Clara
Edkins, Joshua, 383
Edmondes, Sara, 447
Edmonds, Helen Wood. *See* Kavan, Anna
educational theory and planning, 68, 71, 196–97, 217, 291, 293, 300, 311, 320, 350, 376, 388–89, 423, 436–37, 440, 449, 457, 459, 527, 548, 560, 564, 572, 579, 632–33, 647, 661, 669, 685–86 (*see also* schools, establishment of)
Edwards, Amelia Ann Blanford, 218–19
Egerton, George. *See* Bright, Mary Golding
Egerton, Sarah Fyge Field, 202, **219–21**, 231
Egypt, writing about, 218–19, 401–02, 539
E. H. *See* Haywood, Eliza Fowler
Einstein, Albert, 260
Elford, William, 454
Elias, A. C., 290
Eliot, George, 38, 48, 55, 60, 68, 110, 113, 114, 117, 153, 178, 189, **221–23**, 234, 303, 315, 320, 326, 327, 348, 360, 377, 384, 396, 397, 398, 445, 446, 471, 508, 586, 617, 635, 662, 699
Eliot, T. S., 69, 262, 263, 346, 385, 394, 481, 512, 535–36, 556, 576, 578, 583, 605, 688
Eliza. *See* Carter, Elizabeth; Moody, Elizabeth
Elizabeth. *See* Arnim, Elizabeth von
Elizabeth I, 8, 78, 113, 141, 152, 163, 190, 206, **224–25**, 227, 258, 323, 376, 387, 388, 403, 438, 439, 447–48, 504, 565, 573–74, 578, 643, 693, 695
Elizabeth, Charlotte. *See* Tonna, Charlotte Elizabeth
Elizabeth of York, 225
Elizabethan Society of Antiquities, 410
Ellerman, Annie Winifred. *See* Bryher
Elliott, Jean, 159
Ellis, Havelock, 185, 299, 559
Ellis, John Fanshawe. *See* Wilde, Jane Francesca
Ellis, John Harvard, 78
Ellis, Sarah Stickney, 225–27
Ellis-Fermor, Una Mary, 227–28
Eloise. *See* Boyd, Elizabeth
Elstob, Elizabeth, 228–29
E. L. V. *See* Voynich, Ethel Lilian Boole
Elwood, Anne Katharine, 91
Elys, Edmund, 368
E. M. D. *See* Delafield, E. M.
Emecheta (Florence Onye), Buchi, 229–31
Emerson, Ralph Waldo, 183, 347, 558
Emmet, Robert, 382
Empson, William, 303, 524
Engels, Friedrich, 264, 645
Ephelia, 231–33
Epictetus, 127, 141, 371, 609
Erasmus, Desiderius, 42, 239, 438, 545
Erskine, Thomas, 462
Escher, M. C., 147
Esmond, H. V., 190
Esten, Harriet Pye, 46
Etherege, George, 198, 231, 232
Euclid, 587
Euripedes, 148, 411, 543, 595, 661
Eusebia. *See* Hays, Mary
Evans, Arthur, 528
Evans, Mary Ann. *See* Eliot, George
Evaristi, Marcella, 403
Evelyn, John, 17, 233, 342, 484, 493
Evelyn, Mary, 233
Everett, Mary Anne. *See* Green, Mary Anne Everett Wood
evolution, 56, 60, 159 (*see also* Darwin, Charles)
Ewing, Alexander, 584
Ewing, Juliana Gatty, 266
Ewing, Juliana Horatia, 233–34, 377

Exploribus. *See* Haywood, Eliza Fowler
Eyre-Todd, George, 496

Fabian Society, 52, 264, 429, 474, 499, 658–59 (*see also* Christian Socialism; International Labour Party; socialism)
fables, 249, 250, 431 (*see also* fairy tales; legends; myth; parables)
Fagius, Paul, 565
Fainlight, Ruth, 234–35
Fairbaird, Zöe, 419
Fairbanks, Douglas, Jr., 432
Fairfield, Cicily Isabel. *See* West, Rebecca
fairy tales, 9, 46, 125, 153, 163–164, 178, 246, 289, 293, 324, 333, 342, 376, 403, 431, 444, 465, 488, 492, 575, 630, 654–55, 655, 664 (*see also* Andersen, Hans Christian; fables; legends; myth; parables)
Faithfull, Emily, 519
Falconbridge, Anna Maria, 235–36
Falkland, Viscountess. *See* Cary, Elizabeth
Fallon, Ann, 638
Fane, Violet. *See* Currie, Mary (Montgomerie) Lamb Singleton, Lady Currie
Fanshawe, Anne, 236–37
Fanshawe, Catherine, 26
Farjeon, Eleanor, 237–38
Farjeon, Herbert, 237
Farmer, Thomas, 231
Farnol, Jeffrey,190
Farquhar, George, 19, 198, 635, 666
Farrell, M. J. *See* Keane, Molly
fascism, 72, 105, 343, 455, 500 (*see also* Hitler, Adolph; Mussolini, Benito; Nazism)
Fastolf, John, 505
Faulkner, William, 282
Fay, Eliza, 238–39
Fehrenbach, R. J., 677
Feinstein, Elaine, 239–40, 418
Fell, John, 106
Fell, Margaret, 240–41
Fellowes, Anne. *See* Mantle, Winifred Langford
Felton, Elizabeth, 231
feminist theology, 112, 418, 419, 477–78
Fénelon, François, 292
Fenwick, Eliza, 241–42
Ferber, Michael, 453
Ferguson, Helen. *See* Kavan, Anna
Fernandez, Benjamin Diaz, 5
Ferrier, Susan Edmonstone, 183–84, **242–44**
Feuerbach, Anselm Ritter von, 208
Feuerbach, Friedrich von, 208
fiction: allegorical, 359, 368, 446, 559, 577; *Bildungsromane*, 39, 124, 391, 400, 516, 611, 624, 684; comic/satiric, 97–98, 239, 243, 252–53, 254, 265, 270–71, 272–73, 299, 300, 313, 325, 334, 349, 363, 377, 411–12, 415, 422, 471–72, 495, 567, 577, 592, 611–12, 628, 656, 699; didactic/religious, 106–07, 261–62, 243; domestic, 13–14, 435, 491, 648; epistolary, 20, 107–08, 166, 245–46, 275, 291, 296, 312, 386, 422, 425, 548, 560; experimental/metafictional, 24–27, 93–95, 207–08, 245–46, 248, 275, 282, 334, 355, 359, 363, 388, 419, 429, 466, 471–72, 531, 534, 551–52, 576–77, 654, 684, 688–89; gothic/horror/ghost/occult, 6, 14, 20, 39, 46, 97, 110, 169, 171–72, 183, 186, 188–89, 211–12, 218, 246, 271, 296, 329, 334, 335, 362, 365, 377, 387, 392, 442, 433, 471, 521–22, 523–24, 527, 539, 568, 570, 581, 586, 601, 605, 655, 680; historical, 6, 40, 103, 117–18, 159–61, 189, 281, 300, 451, 483, 489–90, 502, 528, 648, 669; manners, 20, 108, 278, 291, 302, 306, 313, 527, 544, 562; melodrama, 211–12, 291, 335, 361, 408, 560, 586; mystery/detective, 6, 10–11, 32–31, 39, 144–47, 257, 317, 337, 340–41, 401, 408, 414–16, 433–35, 467, 489–90, 502–03, 506–07, 529–30, 556–57, 592, 605, 614, 687; naturalistic, 76, 96, 203, 306, 518; picaresque, 10, 246, 296, 386, 412, 495, 614; political/social, 72, 272–73, 356, 391–92, 422, 424, 483, 495, 586, 625, 633–34, 670–71; psychological, 10, 76, 81–82, 96–97, 265, 272, 305, 340–41, 354, 359, 391–93, 534, 576–77, 598, 610–11; regional/local color/nature, 13–14, 217, 218, 243, 270–71, 281, 300, 321–22, 325–26, 334, 360, 361, 363, 379, 453–54, 495, 518, 526, 535, 563–64, 580, 597, 617, 632, 660–61; religious, 106–07, 261–62, 625, 676, 697; *Roman fleuve*, 428; romances (historical), 6, 60, 80, 93, 128–31, 170, 226, 281, 312, 317–18, 430, 433, 458, 489–90, 495, 501, 516, 526–27, 539–40, 553, 635, 638–39; science fiction/fantasy, 37, 105, 125, 136, 140, 147, 161, 239, 377, 391, 392, 377, 407, 474, 568, 613, 655; sensation, 97, 433, 535, 595, 623, 687; "Silver Fork," 278, 601; stream-of-consciousness/interior monologues, 27, 248, 334, 444, 534, 576, 688–89; technique, 23–24, 34–35, 42–43, 48, 339, 569–70, 583, 687; theory and criticism, 6–7, 113–14, 306, 482, 655–56; utopian/dystopian, 104–05, 174–75, 252–53, 259, 423–24, 455, 480, 560, 633, 659, 692
Fidelia. *See* Barker, Jane
Field, Michael, 244–45
Field, Mrs. *See* Egerton, Sarah Fyge Field
Fielding, Henry, 46, 139, 155, 245, 310, 312, 313, 389, 461
Fielding, Sarah, 245–47, 459, 569
Fiennes, Celia, 247
Figes, Eva, 247–50
Fildes, Luke, 218
film, writing for or about, 102, 120, 123, 129, 145, 161, 181, 190, 200, 203, 212, 213, 259, 259–60, 271–73, 277, 275, 281, 325, 326, 337, 344, 349–50, 367, 377, 426–27, 456, 465, 466, 467, 477, 482, 528, 549–50, 567, 582, 592, 596, 598, 603, 629, 630, 631, 645–46, 654–55
Finch, Anne Kingsmill, Countess of Winchelsea, 138, **250–51**, 368
Finch, Francis, 509
Finch, Isabella, 389
Finch, Peter, 466
Finden, Woodesforde, 299
Firbank, Ronald, 96, 97
Firminger, W. R., 238
Fischer, Loth, 381
Fisher, E., 538
Fisher, Samuel R., Jr., 382
FitzGerald, Edward, 366
Fitzgerald, Penelope (Knox), 251–53
Fitzgerald, Rose, 427

Flanner, Janet, 40
Flaubert, Gustave, 101, 394, 597
Flaxman, John, 641
Flecker, James Elroy, 476
Fleetwood, Charles, 142, 156
Fletcher, John Gould, 204
Fletcher, Loraine, 243
Fliedner, Theodor, 683
Flint, F. S., 204
Flint, Kate, 203
Florio, John, 695
Flower, Eliza, 448
Flower, Sarah, 448
folklore, 283, 389, 375, 484
Fonda, Henry, 666
Fontaine, Joan, 367
Fontenelle, Bernard Le Bovier, 43, 180
Fool, Tom. *See* Farjeon, Eleanor
Forbes, Luckie, 517
Forbes, Peter, 210
Forbes-Robertson, Johnston, 119
Ford, Ford Madox, 102, 192, 204, 334–35, 384, 441, 531, 534, 576
Ford, John, 227
Forman, Simon, 376
Forster, E. M., 13, 69, 113, 238–39, 253, 397, 490, 688 (*see also* Bloomsbury)
Forster, John, 306, 374–75
Forster, Margaret, 254
Foscolo, Ugo, 372
Fothergill, Jessie, 254–55
Foucault, Michel, 148
Fouque, Friedrich Heinrich Karl de la Motte, 132
Fourier, Charles, 675
Fowles, John, 161
Fox, Charles James, 391
Fox, George, 56, 240
Fox, Margaret. *See* Fell, Margaret
Fox, William Johnson, 448
Fox-Strangways, Susan, 390
Frakes, James B., 213
France, writing about, 206, 218, 364, 501, 543, 681, 686
France, Anatole, 408, 498
Frances. *See* Griffith, Elizabeth
Francis of Assisi, 281
Francis, Dick, 467
Franco, Francisco, 185
Frankau, Gilbert, 256
Frankau, Julia, 256
Frankau, Pamela, 255–56
Franklin, John, 641
Fraser, Antonia (Lady Antonia Pinter), 257–58
Fraser, Flora, 405
Fraser, Kennedy, 288
Fraser, Lovat, 23
Fraser, Mary Crawford, 258–59
Fraunce, Abraham, 573
Frazer, James, 304
Frazier, Cary, 231
Freedman, Richard, 117
Freeman, Gillian, 259–60
Freeman, Samuel, 502
Freemantle, W., 320
French, Ashley. *See* Robins, Denise Naomi
French Revolution, writing about, 680–81
Freud, Sigmund, 68, 96, 153, 203, 204, 205, 303, 305, 400, 576, 598, 614, 653, 671, 676 (*see also* psychoanalysis/psychiatry)
F. R. H. *See* Havergal, Frances Ridley
Friedenberg, Edgar Z., 213
Friel, Brian, 363
Friend, A. *See* Lennox, Charlotte Ramsay
Friend to Humanity. *See* Robinson, Mary Darby (Perdita)
Froissart, Jean, 543
Frost, Robert, 347
Froude, John A., 122, 220
Fry, Elizabeth, 226, 647
Fry, Roger, 123, 132, 688
Fuertes, Gloria, 555
Fuller, Anne, 260–61, 387
funeral industry, 453
Furlong, Monica, 261–62
Furnivall, Frederick, 318
Fuseli, Henry, 685–86

Gabrieli. *See* Meeke, Mary
Gaddis, Marilyn, 638
Gaitskell, Hugh, 405
Galbraith, John Kenneth, 650
Galesia. *See* Barker, Jane
Gallagher, Mickey, 626
Gallagher, Willie, 148
Galsworthy, John, 326, 327, 329, 361, 536, 602, 688
Galt, John, 243
Galton, Francis, 209
Gandhi, Mohandas K., 52, 423, 559
Garbo, Greta, 190
García Lorca, Federico, 185, 555
gardening/horticulture, 38, 307, 552
Gardner, Helen Louise, 262–63
Garibaldi, Giuseppe, 60
Garnett, Constance Clara Black, 263–64, 395
Garnett, David, 123, 263, 381, 655
Garnett, Edward, 177, 263–64
Garnett, Richard, 184, 395
Garrett, Elizabeth, 320
Garrick, David, 9, 139, 155, 176, 179, 291, 384, 385, 450, 463, 543, 569–70, 642
Gaskell, Elizabeth, 82, 85, 86, 255, **264–66**, 303, 331, 343, 348, 454, 537, 617, 625, 682
Gaskell, William, 682
Gaster, Moses, 377
Gatty, Margaret, 233, **266–67**
Gaudier-Brzeska, Henri, 23
Gawsworth, John, 679
Gay, John, 138, 176, 250, 328, 329, 460
Geddes, Alexander, 524
Gems, Pam, 267–69
Genast, J., 685
Genlis, Felicite de, 15, 491
Gentleman on His Travels, A. *See* Scott, Sarah
Gentlewoman, A. *See* Ephelia
Gentlewoman in Culros. *See* Colville, Elizabeth

Gentlewoman from Those Parts, A. *See* Bradstreet, Anne Dudley
George, Anita, 501
George, Eliot. *See* Freeman, Gillian
Germany, writing about, 218, 424, 429, 638–39
Gessner, Salomon, 166
Gethin, Grace Norton, 270, 480
Gibbon, Edward, 26, 315
Gibbons, Stella, 270–71
Gibbs, Cecil Armstrong, 231
Gide, André, 597, 598
Gielgud, John, 161, 362, 414, 615
Gifford, William, 176, 544
Gilbert, John, 275
Gilchrist, A., 373
Gill, Brendan, 268
Gillespie, E. F., 600
Gilliatt, Penelope, 271–73
Gilman, Charlotte Perkins, 104
Giovanni, Michiel, 438
Gissing, George, 192, 203, 622
Gladstone, William, 40, 76, 97, 154, 171, 177, 600, 616
Glanville, Brian, 398
Glanville, Mary, 290, 329
Glass, Philip, 392
Glasse, Hannah, 273–74
Glastonbury, M., 538
Glyn, Anthony, 275
Glyn, Caroline, 274–75
Glyn, Elinor, 128, 274, **275–76**
Godden, (Margaret) Rumer, 276–77
Godiva, Lady, 190, 519
Godolphin, Margaret, 233
Godolphin, Mary. *See* Aikin, Lucy
Godwin, Edward, 615
Godwin, Mary. *See* Wollstonecraft, Mary Godwin
Godwin, William, 9, 188, 241, 300, 311, 385, 407, 491, 544, 568, 685–86
Goethe, Johann Wolfgang von, 263, 315, 491, 495, 558
Goethe, Ottilie von, 343
Gogh, Vincent van, 113–14, 346
Gold, Sylviane, 214
Golding, William, 354, 614
Goldman, Emma, 254, 424
Goldoni, Carlo, 289, 291
Goldschmidt, Otto, 682
Goldsmith, Oliver, 9, 59, 155, 300, 339
Gombrich, Ernst, 695
Goncharov, Ivan, 264
Goncourt, Edmond de, 408
Goodbody, Buzz, 267
Goodman, Mitchell, 453
Goodwin, Jo-Ann, 357
Gordimer, Nadine, 559
Gordon, I., 429
Gordon, William, 390
Gore, Catherine Grace Frances Moody, 278–79, 601
Gore, Isabel, 249
Gore-Booth, Eva, 279–80
Gorki, Maxim, 428
Gosse, Edmund, 177, 202, 231, 480
Goudge, Elizabeth (de Beauchamp), 281–82
Gould, Robert, 220
Gow, Nathaniel, 473
Gow, Neil, 473
Goya, Francisco, 555
Graham, Henry Grey, 496
Graham, Maxtone. *See* Struther, Jan
Graham, Viva. *See* Somerville and Ross
Grand, Sarah (pseudonym of Frances Elizabeth [Clarke] McFall), 202, **282–83**, 397
Grant, Anne MacVicar, 283–84
Grant, Duncan, 123, 688
Grant, Ulysses S., 258
Granville, Mary. *See* Delaney, Mary Granville Pendarves
Grattan, Henry, 674
Graver, Bruce, 110
Graves, Robert, 82, 185
Gray, Cecil, 204
Gray, Edith. *See* Doolittle, Hilda (H. D.)
Gray, Effie, 215
Gray, Harriet. *See* Robins, Denise Naomi
Gray, Jacqueline, 110
Gray, John, 187, 394
Gray, Thomas, 74
Greatheed, Bertie, 301
Greece, writing about, 528, 692
Green, J. R., 651
Green, Mary Ann Everett Wood, 284–85
Green, T. H., 651
Greenaway, Kate, 285–86, 610
Greene, Graham, 354, 481, 489, 592, 653
Greene, Robert, 11
Greenham, Richard, 323
Greenwell, Dora, 286–87
Greer, Germaine, 121, 231, **287–88**, 368, 447, 457, 620, 624
Gregg, Frances, 204
Gregory, Augusta, 227, **288–90**
Gregory, Saint, 357
Greimars, Algirdas Julien, 92
Greville, Fulke, 227
Grief, J., 479
Grieg, Edvard, 584
Grierson, Constantia, 289
Griffin, Gerald, 383
Griffin, Heneage, 174
Griffin, V. G. *See* Cory, Victoria
Griffith, Elizabeth, 291
Griffiths, Emily, 247
Griffiths, Ralph, 461, 462
Grigson, Geoffrey, 562
Grindal, William, 224
Grosse, Helen, 211
Grote, Gerard, 573, 617
Grove, Valerie, 582
Grubb, Sarah Lynes, 291–92
Grubb, Sarah Pim, 291
Grubb, Sarah Tuke, 291, **293–94**
Grundy, Isobel, 46, 241–42
Gryllis, David, 575
Grymeston or Grimston, Elizabeth, 294
Guest, Charlotte E. B., 294–95

Guggenberger, Louisa S. *See* Bevington, Louisa Sarah
Guizot, François, 208
Gunn, Thom, 346
Gunning, Susanna Minifie, 295–96
Gurney, Joseph John, 292, 491
Gussow, Mel, 257, 258
Guyon, Jeanne-Marie Bouvier de La Motte, Mme., 292

Habberton, John, 7
Hadrian, 498
Haight, Gordon, 221
Haldane, J. B. S., 679, 451
Hale, Sarah, 502, 611
Hales, John, 369
Halkett, Anne (or Anna) Murray, 296–98
Hall, Anna Maria Fielding, 298–99, 407
Hall, Donald, 603
Hall, Joseph, 270
Hall, Radclyffe, 83, **299**, 388
Hall, S. C., 454
Halliwell, Leslie, 190
Hals, Frans, 492
Hamburger, Michael, 49
Hamilton, Cicily, 585
Hamilton, Elizabeth, 45, 243, **300–01**, 310, 312
Hamilton, Emma, 249, 371, 386
Hamilton, George Rostrevor, 446
Hamilton, Hervey. *See* Robins, Denise Naomi
Hamilton, William, 371
Hamilton-King, Harriet, 318
Hampton, Christopher, 123
Hamsun, Knut, 81
Hanaford, Phoebe A., 693
Handel, George Frideric, 155, 201, 307, 684
Hands, Elizabeth, 301
Hands, Rachel, 50
Hanway, Jonas, 302
Hanway, Mary Ann(e), 302
Harcourt, Frances Vernon, 304
Harcourt, Lewis, 585
Hardenberg, Friedrich von (Novalis), 253, 315
Hardie, James Keir, 500
Harding, Walter, 554
Hardinge, George, 461
Hardy, Barbara, 242, **303**
Hardy, E., 353
Hardy, G. H., 253
Hardy, Thomas, 38, 39, 48, 81, 153, 175, 177, 249, 303, 361, 397, 443, 446, 476, 477, 488, 615, 657, 661
Hare, David, 147
Hargreaves, Tamsin, 483
Harington, John, 447
Harland, Henry, 192, 441
Harland, John, 29
Harley, Brilliana, 303–04
Harley, John Pritt, 298
Harley, Mrs. M., 387
Harper, Edith. *See* Wickham, Anna
Harpsfield, Nicholas, 545
Harris, Frank, 23
Harrison, Jane Ellen, 172, **304–05**
Harrison, J. F. C., 590
Harrison, Mary St. Leger (Kingsley), 305–06
Harston, Edward, 339
Hart, Elizabeth Anna, 580
Hart, F. R., 243
Hart, Fanny Wheeler, 580
Harte, Bret, 285
Hartl, Karl, 190
Hartley, David, 436
Hartley, L. P., 16, 361, 368
Harvey, Caroline. *See* Trollope, Joanna
Harvey, William Henry, 267
Harwood, Edward, 290
Hastings, Henry, 323
Hastings, Lady Elizabeth, 17, 18
Hastings, Lucy, 410
Hastings, Warren, 300
Haswell, Susanna. *See* Rowson, Susanna
Hatchett, Richard, 312
Hathaway, Anne, 189
Hatton, Denys Finch, 432
Hatton, G. Noel. *See* Caird, Alice Mona
Hauffe, Frederike, 184
Hauptmann, Gerhart, 469
Havergal, Frances Ridley, 306–08
Hawkes, (Jessie) Jacquetta (Hopkins), 309–10
Hawkesworth, John, 141, 311
Hawking, Stephen, 331
Hawkins, Laetitia Matilda, 310–11
Hawthorne, Nathaniel, 343
Haydn, Franz Joseph, 307
Hayes, Laurence, 470
Hayley, William, 90, 681
Hays, Mary, 241, 300, **311–12**, 544
Hays, Matilda, 519
Hayward, John, 262
Haywood (or Heywood), Eliza Fowler, 19, 291, **312–14**, 386
Hazlitt, William, 373, 519, 601
H. D. *See* Doolittle, Hilda (H. D.)
Heaney, Seamus, 363, 413, 485
Hearne, G. R. M., 10
Hearst, William Randolph, 275
Heath, C., 609
Hebbel, Friedrich, 189
Hector, Annie French, 314–15
Hegel, Friedrich von, 640
Hegel, Georg Wilhelm Friedrich, 670, 671
Heger, Constantin, 86, 265
Heilbroner, Robert L., 650
Heine, Heinrich, 208
Heinemann, William, 541, 600
Helforth, John. *See* Doolittle, Hilda (H. D.)
Heller, John, 126
Hemans, Felicia Dorothea Browne, 26, **315–16**, 348
Hemingway, Ernest, 102, 427, 555
Hénault, Charles Jean François, 180
Henderson, Ralph, 699
Henley, W. E., 657
Hennell, Charles, 221
Henri, Adrian, 213
Henrietta Maria, 134, 135, 136, 214, 284, **316–17**, 652
Henry, Earl of Richmond, 225

Henry the Minstrel, 517
Henty, G. A., 101
Hepburn, James, 439
Hepburn, Katharine, 252, 515
Heraclitus, 294
Herbert, Elizabeth Somerset, 325
Herbert, George, 121, 152, 307, 545, 574
Herbert, Henry, 515
Herbert, John Alexander, 400
Herbert, Lucy, 325
Herbert, Mary. *See* Sidney, Mary
Herbert, Philip, Earl of Pembroke and Montgomery, 608
Herbert, William, 693
hermeticism, 220
Hern, Anthony, 405
Herodotus, 209
Heron, Liz, 476
Herrick, Robert, 307, 411, 445
Herring, Geilles. *See* Somerville and Ross (Edith Œnone Somerville)
Herschel, Caroline, 589
Herschel, John, 588, 589
Herschel, William, 588
Hertford, Countess of, 139
Hervey, John, 460
Herzogenberg, Elisabeth ("Lisl") von, 584
Herzogenberg, Heinrich von, 584
Hett, F. P., 386
Hewat, Sybil, 157
Hewlett, Maurice, 361
Heydon, John, 220
Heydt, Eric, 205
Heyer, Georgette, 114, **317–18**
Heywood, Peter, 608
Hichens, Robert, 394
Hickes, George, 229, 327
Hickey, Emily Henrietta, 318–19
Highmore, John, 156
Highmore, Susanna, 141
Hill, Aaron, 328
Hill, D. A. *See* Doolittle, Hilda (H. D.)
Hill, James. *See* Jameson, Storm
Hill, Jane, 123
Hill, Octavia, 319–21, 332, 658
Hill, Susan, 321–23
Hillerman, Tony, 467
Hilton, Walter, 262, 465
Himmelfarb, Gertrude, 695
Hinton, Walter, 640
history, writing about, 38, 118–19, 131–33, 257–58, 284, 367–68, 405, 411, 416, 425, 427–28, 435, 451, 456, 490, 495, 498, 501, 542, 606, 631, 632, 648–49, 662–63, 695
Hitchcock, Alfred, 248, 415
Hit-Him-Home Joan, 12
Hitler, Adolph, 27, 48, 94, 185, 247, 452 (*see also* fascism; Nazism)
Hobbes, John O. *See* Craigie, Pearl
Hobbes, Thomas, 137
Hobby, E., 231
Hobsbaum, Philip, 562
Hoby, Margaret, 152, **323**
Hoby, Thomas, 550
Hofland, Barbara, 602
Hogan, Michael, 190
Hogarth, William, 243
Hogg, James, 614
Holbein, Hans, 573
Holcroft, Thomas, 212, 241, 685
Holden, Molly, 323–24
Holdsworth, Winch, 636
Holland, Barbara, 238
Holland, Catherine, 324–25
Holmes, Oliver Wendell, 507
Holocaust, 27, 235, 248, 622 (*see also* anti-semitism; religion, Judaism)
Holt, Jane. *See* Wiseman, Jane
Holtby, Winifred, 48, 82, 83, **325–26**
Home, Cecil. *See* Webster, (Julia) Augusta Davies
Homer, 42, 101, 305, 471, 583
Homespun, Prudentia. *See* West, Jane
homosexuality, 83, 142, 148, 151, 261, 273, 312, 394, 418, 422, 528 (*see also* lesbianism)
Hood, Thomas, 407
Hooke, Nathaniel, 149–50
Hooker, Richard, 311
hooks, bell, 106
Hope, Anthony, 330, 394
Hope, Laurence. *See* Nicolson, Violet (Adela Florence)
Hopkins, Frederick Gowland, 309
Hopkins, Gerard Manley, 96, 194, 195, 309, 346, 512, 536, 545
Hopton, Susanna Harvey, 326–27
Horace, 139, 224, 245, 563, 591, 641
Horne, R. H., 168
Horovitz, M., 538
Hoskyns, Katharine, 357
Hosmer, Harriet, 519
Hough, Orlando, 148
Hough, Richard, 644
Houghton, Richard Monckton Milnes, 209
Houldsworth, A. E., 406
household advice books, 1, 41–42, 388–89, 447–48, 505–06, 611 (*see also* conduct books; cookbooks and recipes)
Houselander, Caryll, 653
housing reform, 319–20, 519
Houston, Sam, 162
Howard, Brian, 185
Howard, Elizabeth Jane, 327–28
Howard, Henrietta Hobart, 328–29
Howard, John, 338
Howard, Ken, 626
Howard, Leslie, 492
Howard, Thomas, 297
Howatch, Susan, 329–31
Howe, John Grubham, 673
Howe, Julia Ward, 258
Howell, James, 369, 658
Howitt, Mary Botham, 226, 315, **331–33**
Howitt, William, 621
Hoylake, Tabitha, 293

Hoyle, Fred, 309
Hughes, J. F., 523
Hughes, Joanna, 9
Hughes, Langston, 185
Hughes, Margaret, 515
Hughes, Ted, 514
Hugo, Victor, 318, 542
Hulme, Juliet, 506
Humboldt, Alexander von, 681
Hume, Alexander, 166–67
Hume, Anna, 333
Hume, Cyril, 190
Hume, David, 159, 333
humor: black, 514; satire, 46, 97–98; wit and wordplay, 471
Hungerford, Margaret Hamilton Wolfe, 333–34
Hunt, Holman, 285, 600
Hunt, Leigh, 151, 152, 176
Hunt, Margaret, 286
Hunt, Violet, 334–35, 441, 576
Hunter, John, 310
Huntington, Grace, 16
Huntley, Frances E. *See* Mayne, Ethelind Frances Colburn
Hurston, Zora Neale, 185
Hutchinson, Lucy Apsley, 8, **335–36**
Hutchinson, Mary, 691
Huxley, Aldous, 23, 40, 41, 123, 184, 337, 381, 451, 498, 541, 570, 578
Huxley, Elspeth Josceline Grant, 337–38
Huxley, Julian, 23, 309, 337
Huxley, Thomas Henry, 658
Hyde, Douglas, 90, 289, 638
Hyde, Richard, 545
Hyman, Stanley Edgar, 68, 69, 304
Hynes, Samuel, 676

Ibsen, Henrik, 81, 116, 119, 120, 162, 227, 249, 326, 345, 540–41, 616
Imagism, 203–04
Imlay, Fanny, 568
Imlay, Gilbert, 681, 686
incest, 457, 466, 472
Inchbald, Elizabeth Simpson, 338–39, 462, 581
India, writing about, 181, 216, 238–39, 300, 349–50, 424, 476, 477–78, 572, 596–97, 599–600
Industrial Revolution, 463, 524, 564
Ingelow, Jean, 268, 286, **339–40**, 445, 519, 662
International Labour Party, 423 (*see also* Christian Socialism; Fabian Society; socialism)
Ireland, writing about, 90, 193, 217, 362–63, 382–83, 484–85, 486–87, 495, 586, 620–21, 628, 670
Ireton, Bridget, 135
Irish Literary Renaissance, 227–28, 279, 288, 380, 586 (*see also* Anglo-Irish Ascendancy)
Iron, Ralph. *See* Schreiner, Olive Emilie Albertina
Irving, Edward, 122
Irving, Henry, 119, 615–16
Irving, Washington, 454
Isherwood, Christopher, 367
Italy, writing about, 218, 450, 498, 555
Ivory, James, 349

Jackson, Elaine. *See* Freeman, Gillian
Jackson, Glenda, 583
Jackson, J. H., 377
Jackson, Tommie, 111
Jacob, E. F., 4
Jacobi, Derek, 503
Jaff, Michael, 406
Jakobson, Roman, 92
James, Henry, 24, 68, 72, 76, 92, 93, 94, 95, 98, 150, 153, 207, 234, 303, 306, 366, 388, 441, 471, 487, 498, 542, 576, 583, 586, 603, 616, 617, 670, 688, 697
James, P[hyllis]. D[orothy]. (White), 145, **340–41**, 529
James, Stalie, 111
James, Thomas, 301
James, William, 69, 153, 378, 576
Jameson, Anna Brownell, 226, **342–43**, 365, 520
Jameson, Storm, 343–44, 588
Jamie, Kathleen, 210
Japan, writing about, 424
Japp, Alexander, 286
Jarrell, Randall, 354, 598
Jeaffreson, J. Cordy, 501
Jefferson, Thomas, 692
Jeffrey, Francis, 51, 183, 283, 300, 325
Jellicoe, (Patricia) Ann, 344–46
Jenkins, Elizabeth, 372, 377
Jennings, Elizabeth (Joan), 346–47
Jerdan, William, 407, 374
Jerrold, Douglas, 435
Jesse, J. H., 608
Jewel, John, 22, 550
Jewett, Sarah Orne, 379, 454
Jewsbury, Geraldine Ensor, 122, **347–48**
Jewsbury, Maria Jane, 315, 347, **348–49**
Jex-Blake, Sophia, 320, 450, 624
J. F. *See* Fothergill, Jessie
Jhabvala, Ruth Prawer, 349–50, 549
J. H. G. *See* Ewing, Juliana Horatia
Joan of Arc, 478, 552, 654
Jocelin, Elizabeth, 350–51
John, Angela, 541
John, Augustus, 123, 184, 367
John Birch Society, 117
John of the Cross, 346, 462, 465, 570, 609, 681
John of Salisbury, 646
Johnson, Amryl, 351–52
Johnson, Augustine, 143
Johnson, Esther ("Stella"), 352–53
Johnson, Joseph, 311, 382, 383, 685
Johnson, Lyndon B., 650
Johnson, Pamela Hansford, 353–55
Johnson, Paul, 257
Johnson, Samuel, 32, 91, 107, 108, 109, 127, 141, 155, 156, 179, 180, 290, 302, 310, 311, 371, 389, 454, 460, 463, 479, 511, 547, 563, 569
Johnston, George, 167
Johnston, Jennifer, 200, **355–57**
Jones, Dan, 213
Jones, David, 347
Jones, Inigo, 317
Jones, Lady Catherine, 17, 18

Jones, Roderick, 23
Jonson, Ben, 152, 224, 369, 377, 390, 421, 608, 693
Jordan, Dorothea, 176
Joseph, Jenefer Ruth, 357
Josepha, Maria, 456
Josephus, Flavius, 35
Jourdain, Margaret, 167
journalists, writers working as, 34, 75, 83, 103–04, 124–25, 128, 170, 171–72, 177, 190, 198–99, 201, 202, 215, 218–19, 221, 256, 261, 271, 312, 325, 347, 357, 377, 394, 396, 405, 418, 423, 433, 437, 441, 445, 446, 450, 452–53, 456, 475, 483, 488, 529, 539, 542–43, 561, 595, 596, 638, 650–52, 654, 670, 676
Jowett, Benjamin, 17, 477, 478, 651
Joyce, James, 96, 102, 249, 303, 363, 380, 409, 426, 427, 481, 534, 576, 670
Julia. *See* Robinson, Mary
Julian of Norwich, 357–58, 367, 465
Jung, Carl Gustav, 58, 69, 305, 309, 330, 391, 525, 561, 670 (*see also* psychoanalysis/psychiatry)
Justicia. *See* Haywood, Eliza Fowler
Juvenal, Horace. *See* Robinson, Mary Darby (Perdita)

Kadar, Judit, 501
Kael, Pauline, 271
Kafka, Franz, 34, 248, 249, 360, 468–69
Kane, Julia. *See* Robins, Denise Naomi
Kanin, Garson, 666
Kant, Immanuel, 576, 692
Karl, Frederick, 167
Karsavina, Tamara, 423
Katherine of Sutton, 358–59
Katz, Ephraim, 190
Kauffman, Angelica, 310
Kavan, Anna (Helen Woods Edmonds), 359–60
Kavanagh, Julia, 360–61
Kavanagh, Rose, 638
Kay, Jackie, 106
Kaye, M. M., 239
Kaye-Smith, Sheila, 361–62
Kean, Charles, 615
Kean, Edmund, 517
Keane, Molly (Mary Nesta Skrine Keane), 362–64
Keaton, Buster, 239, 273
Keats, John, 74, 151, 328, 331, 332, 365, 413, 445, 522, 590, 620, 621
Keble, John, 564, 697
keening, 484–85
Kemble, Adelaide, 364–65
Kemble, Charles, 454
Kemble, Fanny (Frances Anne), 51, 162, 343, 364, **365–66**
Kemble, John Mitchell, 26, 364
Kemble, John Philip, 338, 365
Kempe, Alfred John, 79
Kempe, Margery, 358, **366–67**
Kendall, 685
Keneally, Thomas, 666
Kennedy, John F., 650
Kennedy, M. F., 257
Kennedy, Margaret Moore, 367–68
Kenner, Hugh, 528
Ker, W. P., 596, 646
Kermode, Frank, 95
Kerner, Justinus, 184
Kerouac, Jack, 261
Kelley, Edward, 672
Key, Thomas, 438
Keynes, John Maynard, 123, 253, 688 (*see also* Bloomsbury)
K. G. *See* Greenaway, Kate
Kiffen, William, 516
Killeen, J. F., 486
Killigrew, Anne, 231, **368–69**
Killigrew, Katherine, 550
Killigrew, Thomas, 515
Kilty, Jerome, 120
King, Anne, 369–70
King, Charlotte. *See* Dacre, Charlotte
King, Francis, 252, 539
King, Henry, 369, 445
King, Sophia, 188
Kinglake, Alexander W., 208, 594
Kingsbury, Thomas, 679
Kingsley, Charles, 305–06, 617, 625, 687
Kingsley, Henry, 617
Kingsley, Mary Henrietta, 337, **370–71**
Kipling, Rudyard, 23, 234, 476, 600, 617
Kippis, Andrew, 680
Kirkland, Caroline, 454
Kirwin, Patrick, 190
Klemantaski, Alida, 678
Klopstock, Gottlieb, 166
Knight, Ellis Cornelia, 371–72
Knoblock, Edward, 190
Knoepflmacher, U. C., 89
Knox, John, 404
Knox, Ronald, 251
Knyphausen, Wilhelm, 381
Korda, Alexander, 190
Kosciuszko, Thaddeus, 491, 517
Koteliansky, S. S., 381, 428
Kotzebue, August von, 338
Krantz, Judith, 104
Krishna, Bal. *See* Cory, Victoria
Kristeva, Julia, 92
Kropotkin, Peter, 164
Kuhn, Sophie von, 253

L. *See* Landon, Letitia Elizabeth
Lab, Louis, 231
labor conditions, relations, and unions, 280, 499, 500, 559, 625, 634, 658, 687, 692–93
Lacan, Jacques, 68
Lacombe, Michelle, 553
Lacordaire, Henri, 286
Lactilla. *See* Yearsley, Ann Cromartie
Ladie Culross yonger. *See* Colville, Elizabeth
Lady, A. *See* Fielding, Sarah; Finch, Anne Kingsmill, Countess of Winchelsea; Glasse, Hannah; Hanway, Mary Ann
Lady Ann Bacon. *See* Bacon, Ann
Lady Eleanor. See Davies (Douglas), Eleanor Audeley
Lady Stepney. *See* Stepney, Lady Catherine

Lafayette, Marie-Joseph-Paul-Yves-Roch-Gilbert du Motier, marquis de, 692
Lafayette, Marie-Madeleine Pioche de la Vergue, Mme., de, 456, 491
Laing, R. D., 391
Lake, Claude. *See* Blind, Mathilde
Lam, Henry, 123
Lamartine, Alphonse de, 594, 680
Lamb, Caroline, 372–73, 374
Lamb, Charles, 45, 151, 241, 373–74
Lamb, Mary Ann, 373–74
Lamb, William. *See* Jameson, Storm
Lan, David, 148
Landon, Letitia Elizabeth, 315, 348, **374–75**, 602, 623
Landor, Walter Savage, 396, 397
Landry, Donna, 164, 301
Lane, Hugh, 289
Lane, John, 192, 657
Lang, Andrew, 280, 375–76, 657
Lang, Frances. *See* Mantle, Winifred Langford
Lang, Leonora Blanche Alleyne, 375–76
Langford, Jane. *See* Mantle, Winifred Langford
Langham Place group, 519–20
Lanier (Lanyer), [A]emelia, 376–77, 574
La Place, Pierre-Antoine de la, 560
Laplace, Pierre-Simon, marquis de, 588
Lapotaire, Jane, 268
Larkin, Philip, 210, 346, 520
La Rochefoucauld, François VI, duc de, 43, 422
Laski, Harold, 377
Laski, Marghanita, 377–78
Latimer, Hugh, 504
La Tourette, Aileen, 419
Latter, Mary, 301
Laud, William, 195–96
Laura. *See* Robinson, Mary Darby (Perdita)
Laura Maria. *See* Robinson, Mary Darby (Perdita)
Lavery, Bryony, 148
Lavin, Mary, 378–80
Lawes, Henry, 509
Lawick, Hugo van, 337
Lawless, Emily, 380
Lawrence, D. H., 16, 41, 113, 123, 124–25, 204, 303, 335, 347, 380–81, 400, 423, 428, 446, 451, 576, 645, 670, 679
Lawrence, Frieda (von Richthofen), 204, **380–81**, 400
Lawrence, Thomas, 387
Lawton, Marianne, 399
Layard, Austen Henry, 295
Lea, Marion, 541
Leacock, Stephen, 145
Lead[e], Jane Ward, 381–82
Leadbeater, Mary, 300, **382–84**
League of Nations, 325
Leapor, Mary, 164, 301, **384**
Leary, Timothy, 261
Leavis, Frank Raymond, 384–85, 689
Leavis, Q[ueenie]. D[orothy]., 384–85, 487
Lee, Francis, 381
Lee, Harriet, 385–86, 387
Lee, Henry, 135
Lee, Sophia, 385, **386–87**, 521
Lee, Vernon. *See* Paget, Violet
le Fanu, Sheridan, 97
le Fanu, William P., 383
le Gallienne, Gwen, 679
le Gallienne, Richard, 187
legends, 680 (*see also* Arthur, King; fables; fairy tales; myth; parables; Robin Hood)
Lehman, David, 529
Lehmann, Beatrix, 190
Lehmann, John, 185, 388, 688
Lehmann, Kisa, 299
Lehmann, Rosamond, 387–88
Lehmann-Haupt, Christopher, 258, 341
Leigh, Arbor. *See* Bevington, Louisa Sarah
Leigh, Arran. *See* Field, Michael (Katherine Harris Bradley)
Leigh, Dorothy Kempe, 388–89
Leigh, Isla. *See* Field, Michael (Edith Emma Cooper)
L. E. L. *See* Landon, Letitia Elizabeth
Leland, Thomas, 387
Lely, Peter, 42
lending libraries, 526 (*see also* Mudie's Circulating Library)
Lenglet, Jean, 531
Lenin, V. I., 264, 645 (*see also* communism; Marxism)
Lennox, Charlotte Ramsay, 389–90, 458
Lennox, Sarah Bunbury Napier, 390–91
Lenton, Francis, 608
Leonardo da Vinci, 287
lesbianism, 112, 148, 167, 191, 203–04, 244–45, 260, 299, 388, 395, 399–400, 401, 422, 428, 483, 498, 528, 538–39, 542, 551–52, 584–85, 630, 635, 683–84 (*see also* homosexuality)
Lessing, Doris, 114, **391–94**, 559, 623
Lester, Richard, 344
Leverson, Ada, 394–95
Levey, Michael, 96
Levin, Martin, 117
Levy, Amy, 263, **395–96**, 657
Lewes, Charles, 320
Lewes, George Henry, 55, 221, 320, 347, 348, 398, 396, 398
Lewis, C. S., 23, 64, 481, 512
Lewis, Maria, 221
Lewis, Matthew G., 188, 243
Lewis, Teresa, 51
Lewis, Wyndham, 123, 184, 204, 394, 498, 541
librarians, writers working as, 42, 48, 61, 229, 264, 346, 538, 611
Lilley, J., 502
Lillo, George, 513
Linacre, Thomas, 438
Lind, Jenny, 162, 682
Lindbergh, Charles, 556
linguistics, study of, 55, 157, 228–29, 695 (*see also* dialects)
Linnaeus, Carolus, 42, 647
Linton, Eliza Lynn, 115, 314, **396–98**
Lipson, Edna, 398–99
Lister, Anne, 399–400

literary critics, writers as, 68–70, 92, 96, 226, 227–28, 262–63, 271, 303, 318–19, 347, 348, 384–85, 389, 397, 416, 427, 444, 458, 462, 487, 526, 527, 536, 591–92, 597–98, 631, 646, 670–71
Little, Judy, 592
Littlewood, Joan, 199–200
Litvinov, Ivy (Low), 400–01
Litvinov, Maxim, 401
Lively, Penelope, 401–02
Lloyd, Harold, 273
Lloyd George, David, 203
Loach, Kenneth, 213
Lochhead, Liz, 402–03
Locke, Anne Vaughan, 403–05
Locke, John, 436, 440, 636
Lockhart, John Gibson, 243, 571
Lockhart, Robin Bruce, 645
Lodge, David, 92
Loewy, Benno, 515
logical positivism, 481
Lohrli, Anne, 519
Lok, Henry, 404
Lollardy, 367
Lomas, Sophia Crawford, 284
London, University of, 47, 182, 219, 227, 303, 349, 567, 695; Bedford, 227, 596; Birkbeck, 303; King's, 93, 211, 305, 343, 378, 639; Morley, 524; Queen Mary, 247; Queen's, 196, 271, 668; Royal Holloway, 118–19, 167, 303; School of Oriental and African Studies, 596; University College, 92, 113, 177, 261, 343, 542; Westfield, 132–33, 416
Longfellow, Henry Wadsworth, 40, 258, 339, 366, 595, 680
Longford, Elizabeth (Pakenham née Harman), Countess of Longford, 257, **405–06**
Lonsdale, Roger, 9, 34, 685
Lonsdale, Henry, 59
Lorimer, James, 435
Lory, E. M., 660
Loudon, Jane Wells Webb, 406–08
Louisa. *See* Boyd, Elizabeth; Robinson, Mary Darby (Perdita)
Loveday, John, 301
Lovell, Richard, 647
Lovibond, Edward, 461
Lowell, Amy, 101, 204, 610
Lowell, James Russell, 152, 520, 688
Lowell, Robert, 513
Lowndes, Marie Adelaide Belloc (Mrs. Belloc Lowndes), 408–09, 441, 490
Lowndes, Susan, 490
Lowry, Malcolm, 679
Loy, Mina, 409–10
Lubbock, Percy, 144
Lucas, Mary, 604
Lucretius, 336
Lucy Magdalena, Dame. *See* Cary, Lucy
Luhan, Mabel Dodge, 381, 409
Lumley, Joanna (Jane) Fitzalan, 410–11
Luria, Gina, 302
Lurie, Alison, 153
Luther, Martin, 682
Luxemburg, Rosa, 267
Lyall, Edna. *See* Bayly, Ada Ellen
Lyell, Charles, 588
Lyly, John, 11, 12, 224
Lyttleton, George, 642–43
Lytton, Constance, 559

McAlmon, Robert, 102, 204
Macauley, Catherine, 569
Macauley, (Emilie) Rose, 73, **411–12**
Macauley, Thomas Babington, 51, 122, 442, 493, 588
McBurney, W. H., 197
MacCarthy, B. G., 75
MacCarthy, Desmond, 16, 23, 688
McCarthy, Mary, 354
McClellan, George B., 258
McCorquodale, Barbara. *See* Cartland, Barbara
MacDiarmid, Hugh, 185
McDiarmid, Ian, 268
Macdonald, Edwina, 212
MacDonald, George, 286, 339, 520, 617
McDonald, John, 50
McElroy, Joseph, 92
McFall, Frances Elizabeth [Clarke]. *See* Grand, Sarah
McFarlane, W. H., 575
McGee, Thomas D'Arcy, 553
McGuckian, Medbd, 412–13
Machiavelli, Niccolò, 206, 302
McIlvanny, Liam, 210
McInnes, Colin, 617
Macintosh, James, 33, 491
Mack, Phyllis, 241
Mackail, J. W., 617
Mackay, Charles, 171
McKay, Claude, 185
Mackay, Mary. *See* Corelli, Marie
Mackay, Shena, 413–14
Mackenzie, Henry, 26, 243
Mackintosh, Elizabeth, 414–16
Mackintosh, James, 621
McKisack, May, 416
Macklin, Charles, 156
Maclaine, Shirley, 549
Maclean, George, 375
MacLeod, Mary, 417, 484
MacMillan, Kenneth, 160
MacNeice, Louis, 524
Macpherson, Kenneth, 102, 204
MacRae, Lindsay, 106
Macready, William Charles, 454
McVeigh, T. A., 627
McWilliam, Candia, 417–18
Mad Nun of Lebanon, 594
Madam D'Arusmont. *See* Wright, Frances
Maeterlinck, Maurice, 119, 667
Magid, Marion, 200
Maginn, William, 374
Mailer, Norman, 287
Maitland, F.W., 38, 118
Maitland, Sara, 106, **418–20**
Majeski, Jane, 257
Makin, Bathsua Reginald, 77, **420–21**

Makower, Frances, 405
Malet, Francis, 438
Malet, Lucas. *See* Harrison, Mary St. Leger (Kingsley)
Mallock, W. H., 186
Mallowan, Agatha Christie. *See* Christie, Agatha
Malory, Thomas, 152
Malthus, Thomas, 51
Man, Judith, 421
Manley, (Mary?) Delariviere, 150, 220, 313, **421–23**, 513, 612–13, 636
Mann, Heinrich, 268
Manners, Diana, 184
Manners, Mrs. *See* Stepney, Lady Catherine
Mannin, Ethel, 423–25
Manning, Anne, 425–26
Manning, Mary, 426–27
Manning, Olivia, 427–28, 679
Mansfield, Katherine, 14, 23, 271, 394, 412, **428–30**, 484, 656
Mantle, Winifred Langford, 430–31
Mar, Frances, Countess of, 460
Marcet, Jane, 436
Marchant, Catherine. *See* Cookson, Catherine Ann
Marchef-Girard, Mlle., 499
Marguerite, Duchesse de Berry, 565
Marie de France, 431
Marie de Sévigné, 543
Marinda. *See* Monck, Mary
Marinetti, Filippo Tommaso, 409
Marivaux, Pierre, 166, 386, 460, 560, 666
Markandaya, Kamela, 349
Markham, A. H., 279
Markham, Beryl, 432
Markievicz, Constance, 280
Marlborough, Sarah, Duchess of. *See* Churchill, Sarah Jennings, Duchess of Marlborough
Marlowe, Christopher, 227, 275
Marmontel, Jean-François, 291
Marot, Clemont, 574
Marryat, Ellen, 52
Marryat, Florence, 433
Marryat, Frederick, 433
Marsh, Anne. *See* Marsh-Caldwell, Anne
Marsh, Edward, 172
Marsh, Mrs. *See* Marsh-Caldwell, Anne
Marsh, Ngaio, 433–35, 529
Marsh-Caldwell, Anne, 435–36
Marston, John, 227
Martin, Frances, 178
Martin, John, 407
Martin, Stella. *See* Heyer, Georgette
Martin, Violet Florence. *See* Somerville and Ross (Violet Florence Martin)
Martineau, Harriet, 8, 50, 86, 343, 435, **436–38**, 448, 478, 491, 520
Martineau, James, 658, 682
Martines, Lauro, 486
Marvell, Andrew, 239
Marx, Eleanor, 395, 559
Marx, Karl, 55
Marxism, 423, 614 (*see also* communism; Lenin, V. I.; Marx, Karl; Stalin, Joseph; Trotsky, Leon)
Mary I (Mary Tudor), 316, 404, **438–39**, 494, 504
Mary, Queen of Scots (Mary Stuart), 45, 114, 224, 257, 387, 403, **439–40**, 591
Masefield, John, 405, 443, 512, 541, 592
Masham, Damaris, 440
Mason, Dorothy, 673
Mason, James, 161
mastectomy, 70
masturbation, 2 (*see also* sexuality)
Matchless Orinda. *See* Philips, Katherine
mathematics, 587–89
Mather, Cotton, 77
Matilda, Anna, 176
Matilda, Rose. *See* Dacre, Charlotte
Matisse, Henri, 114
matricide, 373, 506
Maturin, Charles, 679
Matute, Ana Maria, 555
Maugham, W. Somerset, 82, 394, 603
Maupassant, Guy de, 23, 192, 344
Mauriac, François, 490
Maurice, F. D., 196, 319
Maurois, André, 192
Maxwell, John, 75–76
Maxwell, Patrick, 59
May, Thomas, 608
Mayne, Ethelind Frances Colburn, 441–42
Mayne, Jasper, 369
Mazzini, Giuseppe, 60
M. B. *See* Lamb, Mary Ann
Meade, Mrs. *See* Pilkington, Laetitia
Meads, D., 323
Medici, Catherine de, 206
Medici, Marie de, 316
medicine, writing about, 115, 196, 297–98, 320, 450–51, 453, 460, 542, 624, 679–80, 695 (*see also* nurses; women's health)
Medieval Academy, 118
Medoff, Jeslyn, 219, 220, 221
Medwin, Thomas, 372
Meeke, Mary, 442–43
Meinhold, Johann Wilhelm, 208, 680
Melbourne, Caroline, 588
Melbourne, William Lamb, 644
Melissus, Paul, 672
Melly, Diana, 531
Melvill, Elizabeth. *See* Colville, Elizabeth
Melville, Herman, 86
Melville, Lewis, 329
Mendelssohn, Felix, 307
Mendoza, Ana de, 483–84
menopause, 288
menstruation, 70, 614, 664
Merchant, Ismail, 349
Meredith, George, 208, 244, 306, 339, 444, 576, 617, 688
Merry, Robert, 544
Merton, Thomas, 261
metaphysical poets, 537
Metternich, Klemens, Fürst von, 128–29
Mew, Charlotte, 443–44, 576
Meynell, Alice, 203, **444–46**, 657

Meynell, Viola, 16, 400, 445, **446–47**
Michelangelo di Lodovico Buonarroti Simoni, 347
Middleton, Elizabeth, 447
Middleton, Thomas, 227
Mideast, writing about, 594, 596–97 (*see also* Egypt; Morocco; Palestine; Persia; Turkey)
midwifery, 290, 566–67
Milbanke, Anne Isabella, 372
Mildmay, Grace Sherrington, 152, **447–48**
Miles, A. H., 56, 74
Mill, Harriet Hardy Taylor, 448–49
Mill, James, 675
Mill, John Stuart, 158, 196, 197, 448–49, 477, 478, 558, 589
Millais, John Everett, 285, 334, 339
Millar, Andrew, 389
Millar, Rabina, 692
Miller, Anna Riggs, 449–50, 479
Miller, Florence Fenwick, 450–51
Miller, George, 462
Miller, Henry, 172
Miller, J. M., 311
Miller, James, 155
Millet, Jean-François, 132
Mills, Cotton Mather, Esq. *See* Gaskell, Elizabeth
Milman, Henry Hart, 332
Milton, John, 77, 85, 173, 226, 245, 249, 262, 263, 307, 315, 328, 345, 389, 411, 425, 563, 663
Miner, Valerie, 419
Minifie, Miss. *See* Gunning, Susannah Minifie
Mira. *See* Haywood, Eliza Fowler
Mirrlees, Hope, 305
Miss A. M. *See* Porter, Anna Maria
Miss G. *See* Moody, Elizabeth
Miss Minifie. *See* Gunning, Susannah Minifie
Mitchison, Naomi, 451–52
Mitford, Diana, 452
Mitford, Jessica, 452–53, 455
Mitford, Mary Russell, 278, 364, 425, **453–55**, 537, 602, 642
Mitford, Nancy, 40, 452, **455–56**
Mitford, Unity, 452
Mix, Katherine, 192
Mlle. V. P. *See* Paget, Violet
M[istres] M[elvill]. *See* Colville, Elizabeth
Moers, Ellen, 568
Moggach, Deborah, 456–57
Molesworth (Moulsworth), Martha, 377, **457–58**
Molière, 177, 180, 289, 403
Moltmann, Jurgen, 331
Monboddo, James Burnett, 159
Monck (Monk), Mary, 458–59
Monet, Claude, 162, 248
Monro, Alida, 443
Monro, Harold, 443, 678
Montagu, Barbara, 560
Montagu, Edward, 560
Montagu, Elizabeth, 141, 201, 246, **459–60**, 542–43, 609, 681, 696
Montagu, Mary Wortley, 17, 32, 149, 201, 400, **460–61**, 501, 607–08
Montagu, Walter, 317
Montaigne, Michel de, 245
Montesquieu, Charles-Louis de Secondat, baron, 180
Monte, Lola, 258
Montrose, Marquess of, 663
Moody, Elizabeth, 461–62
Moore, G. E., 688
Moore, George, 76, 177, 184–185, 192, 244, 394
Moore, Harry T., 381
Moore, Henry, 309
Moore, John, 594
Moore, Marianne, 102, 204, 409, 605
Moore, T. Sturge, 244
Mordaunt, Charles, third earl of Peterborough, 329
Mordaunt, Elizabeth, 297
More, Agnes, 134, **462–63**, 464
More, Anne, 462, 464
More, Bridget, 134, 464, 465
More, Cresacre, 462
More, Hannah, 9, 33, 176, 300, 310, 342, 459, **463–64**, 610, 625, 632, 647, 696
More, Helen Gertrude, 134, 462, **464–65**
More, Thomas, 425, 438, 462, 464, 573, 616, 652, 672
Morgan, Henry, 415
Morgan, Lady. *See* Owenson, Sydney
Morley, Henry, 589
Morocco, writing about, 424
Morrell, Ottoline, 123, 441
Morris, Abraham, 485
Morris, Christopher, 247
Morris, John, 325
Morris, William, 56, 251, 339, 617, 697
Morrison, Toni, 114
Mortimer, Penelope Ruth, 465–67
Moser, Thomas C., 335
Mosley, Oswald, 452, 455
Motion, Andrew, 3
Motteux, Peter Anthony, 12
Moundford, Mary, 593
Moyes, Patricia, 467–68
Mozart, Wolfgang Amadeus, 96
Mrs. Alexander, *See* Hector, Annie French
Mrs. Bogan of Bogan. *See* Nairne, Carolina, Baroness
Mrs. Byrne. *See* Dacre, Charlotte
Mrs. Ellis. *See* Ellis, Sarah Stickney
Mrs. K. P. *See* Philips, Katherine
Mrs. Manners. *See* Stepney, Lady Catherine
Mrs. Meade. *See* Pilkington, Laetitia
Mrs. Piozzi. *See* Piozzi, Hester Lynch Salusbury Thrale
Mrs. Robinson. *See* Robinson, Mary Darby (Perdita)
Mrs. Rowson of the New Theatre, Philadelphia. *See* Rowson, Susanna
Mrs. S. C. *See* Schreiner, Olive Emilie Albertina
Mrs. Tighe. *See* Tighe, Mary
M. S. *See* Smedley, Menella Bute
M. T. *See* Tighe, Mary
Mudie's Circulating Library, 97, 100, 648 (*see also* lending libraries)
Mueller, J., 504
Mugabe, Robert, 62
Muir, Edwin, 346, 360, 468–69
Muir, Kenneth, 228

Muir, Willa (Wilhelmina or Williamina) Johnstone Anderson, 468–70
Muldoon, Paul, 210, 413
Mullard, Julie, 528
Mulock, Dinah Maria. *See* Craik, Dinah Maria Mulock
Mulock, Mrs. *See* Craik, Dinah Maria Mulock
Mulso, Hester. *See* Chapone, Hester Mulso
Mulvihill, Maureen E., 231
Munda, Constantia, 470, 591, 593
Munson, Gorham, 512
Murdoch, (Jean) Iris, 35, 113, 417, **470–72**, 567
Murphy, Arthur, 155
Murray, Gilbert, 119, 173, 512
Murray, Jock, 596
Murry, J. Middleton, 23, 124, 381, 429
music composers, performers, or critics, writers as, 299, 364, 394, 473, 477, 492, 577, 584–86, 645, 655, 678, 682–83; ballads and songs, 24–25, 37, 155, 159, 339, 375, 468–69, 473, 484, 507, 516, 563, 579, 591, 620, 638; criticism, 539; hymns, 167, 286, 307, 682–83; opera, 155, 271, 279, 313, 364, 386, 392, 454, 584–86, 645, 655, 678; reggae, 62; rock, 103–04; singing/songwriting, 58–59, 364–65, 496, 507–08, 539, 571 (*see also names of individual composers*)
Mussolini, Benito, 48, 500 (*see also* fascism; Nazism)
Mutanta, Constantia, 12
MWM. *See* Montagu, Mary Wortley
mysticism, 307, 357–58, 366–67, 381–82, 462, 464–65, 473, 477, 594, 616–17, 639–40, 652, 660, 695
myth, 77, 173, 203–05, 240, 246, 268, 304, 368, 419, 478, 485, 528, 536, 538, 556, 614–15, 629–30, 630, 654, 662, 666 (*see also* fables; fairy tales; legends; parables)

Nabuco, Carolina, 212
Nairne, Carolina, Baroness, 473
Napier, Charles, 588
Napier, Sarah Lennox Bunbury. *See* Lennox, Sarah
Naylor, Eliot. *See* Frankau, Pamela
Nazism, 71–72, 73, 83, 102, 259, 343, 451, 456, 622, 671 (*see also* fascism; Hitler, Adolph; Mussolini, Benito)
Neill, A. S., 423
Nelson, Frances, 249
Nelson, Horatio, 190, 249, 266, 371, 386
Neruda, Pablo, 185
Nerval, Gérard de, 76
Nesbit, Edith, 101, 234, **474–75**
Nettleby, Randolph, 161
Neville, Jill, 628
New, Cabel, 422
New, Melvyn, 395
Newall, Mike, 200
Newbolt, Henry, 162
Newby, P. H., 354
Newby, Thomas Cautley, 84, 86, 88
Newcastle, Duchess of. *See* Cavendish, Margaret
Newman, John Henry, 478, 564, 591, 651, 653
Newton, Charles, 304
Newton, George, 9
Newton, Isaac, 127, 345
"New Woman," 81, 116, 174, 192, 202–03, 282, 395, 397–98, 441, 542, 624
New Zealand, writing about, 428–29, 433–34
Ni Chonaill, Eibhlin Dubh. *See* O'Connell, Eileen
Nichol, John Pringle, 183
Nicholas of Cusa, 640
Nicolas, N. Harris, 236
Nichols, Grace, 61, 106, **475–76**
Nichols, Mike, 345
Nichols, Peter, 254
Nicolson, Harold, 551
Nicolson, Nigel, 552, 630
Nicolson, Victoria, 476
Nicolson, (Violet) Adela Florence, 174, **476–77**
Niebuhr, B. G., 682
Niebuhr, Georg, 208
Nightingale, Benedict, 148
Nightingale, Florence, 249, 254, 321, 450, **477–79**
Nijinsky, Vaslav, 260
Noble, Adrian, 667
Nolbandov, Sergei, 190
Norman, Charles Bath-Hurst, 432
Norman, Sylvia, 377
Norris, Frank, 428
Norris, Henry, 618
Norris, John, 220, 440
North, Christopher, 348
Northumberland, Duchess of (Elizabeth Percy), 479–80
Norton, Andrews, 315
Norton, Caroline, 74, 520, 571, 641
Norton, Frances (Freke), 270, **480**
Nott, Kathleen (Cecilia), 480–81
Novalis. *See* Hardenberg, Friedrich
Novello, Ivor, 190
Nugent, Jim, 57–58
Nunn, Trevor, 268
nurses, writers as, 82, 154, 411, 436, 451, 477–79, 528, 539, 596 (*see also* medicine; women's health)
Nussey, Ellen, 85

Oberon. *See* Robinson, Mary Darby (Perdita)
O'Brien, Edna, 481–83
O'Brien, Frances, 378
O'Brien, Kate, 483–84
O'Brien, William, 390
O'Carolan, Turlogh, 90
O'Casey, Sean, 289
occult, 171, 204, 271, 334–35, 655, 695 (*see also* Rosicrucianism; spiritualism; theosophy)
O'Connell, Daniel, 484
O'Connell, Eileen, 484–86
O'Connell, Mary Ann Biancoli, 485
O'Connell, Maurice, 484
O'Connor, Frank, 427
O'Connor, Teresa, 531
O'Day, Marc,125
O'Faolain, Julia, 486–87
O'Grady, Standish, 90
Ojaide, Tanure, 111
O'Keeffe, Adelaide, 310
Okyay, Tarik, 403
Oland, John. *See* Wickham, Anna
Olcott, Henry Steel, 52

Old Acquaintance of the Public, An. *See* Piozzi, Hester Lynch Salusbury Thrale
Oldfield, Anne, 43, 636
O'Leary, Art, 485
O'Leary, John, 638
Oliphant, Margaret, 226, 435, **487–89**
Oliver, Edith, 147
Oliver, William, 139
Olivier, Laurence, 414
O'Malley, Mary Dolling (Sanders), 489–91
O Muirithe, Diarmid, 484
Opie, Amelia, 436, **490–91**
Opie, John, 491, 610
Orage, A. R., 512
Orchard, M. R., 653
Orczy, Emma Magdalena Rosalia Maria Josefa Barbara, 492–93
Orinda. *See* Philips, Katherine
Orrery, Earl of (Charles Boyle), 547, 685
Orris. *See* Ingelow, Jean
Orton, Joe, 147
Ortunez de Calahorra, Diego, 637–38
Orwell, George, 105, 536
Osborne, Charles, 96
Osborne, Dorothy, 493–94
Osborne, John, 147, 200, 311, 345
Ossian, 90
Ossory, Lady, 50
Ostrovsky, Aleksandr Nikolayevich, 264
O Tuama, Sean, 485
Ouida. *See* Ramée, Maria Louisa de la
Ovid, 43, 152, 620, 673, 677
Owen, Anne, 509
Owen, Jane, 494–95
Owen, John, 494
Owen, Robert, 692, 675
Owen, Wilfred, 356
Owenson, Sydney, Lady Morgan, 342, 380, **495–96**, 681
Oxford University, 9, 32, 41, 137, 470–71, 480, 489, 524, 538, 597, 617; All Souls, 272; Balliol, 552; Bedford, 646; Christ Church, 405; Lady Margaret, 4, 140, 147, 257, 262, 405, 430, 604, 646, 654, 662; Manchester, 639; St. Anne's, 346, 401, 418, 648; St. Antony's, 111, 401; St. Catherine's, 683; St. Hilda's, 262, 357, 520; St. Hugh's, 4, 96, 528, 635; St. John's, 36; Somerville, 39, 82, 92, 113, 219, 227, 251, 254, 325, 367, 377, 411, 416, 556–57, 562, 589, 646, 649, 651

pacifism, 11, 82, 105, 280, 305, 343, 423, 444, 640
Pagan, Isobel, 496
Page, Gilbert H. *See* D'Arcy, Ella
Page, J. A., 231
Page, Louise, 496–98
Paget, Violet, 244, 395, **498–99**, 542
Paine, Thomas, 9, 681, 685, 692
Pakenham, Antonia. *See* Fraser, Antonia
Pakenham, Elizabeth. *See* Longford, Countess of, Elizabeth (Pakenham neé Harman)
Pakenham, Frank, 405
Pakistan, writing about, 456–57
Palestine, writing about, 424
Palmer, Barbara, 421
Palmer, H. *See* Stannard, Henrietta Eliza Vaughn Palmer
Palmerstone, Henry John Temple, 594, 644
Pankhurst, Adela, 500
Pankhurst, Christabel, 499, 500
Pankhurst, Emmeline Goulden, 499–500, 541, 585
Pankhurst, Estelle Sylvia, 500–01, 541, 585
Pankhurst, Sylvia, 585
Papini, Giovanni, 409
parables, 359 (*see also* fables; fairy tales; legends; myth)
Paracelsus, 239
Pardoe, Julia, 501–02
Parfitt, George, 121
Pargeter, Edith Mary, 502–04
Parker, Leslie. *See* Thirkell, Angela (Margaret)
Parker, Matthew, 23
Parker, Pauline, 506
Parker, William M., 243
Parkes, Bessie Rayner, 519
Parnbell, Ryan "Buster," 432
Parnell, Anna, 638
Parnell, Charles, 638
Parr, Katherine (or Catherine), 14, 15, **504–05**
Parry, E. A., 493
Parry, Edward, 588
Parsons, Tony, 104
Parthenissa. *See* Lennox, Charlotte Ramsay
Pascal, Blaise, 543
Pascoli, Giovanni, 562
Pasha, Ibrahim, 594
Paskin, Sylvia, 106
Passavant, Johann David, 215
Pasta, Guidetta, 364
Pasternak, Boris, 347
Pasteur, Louis, 586
Paston, George, 179
Paston, Margaret, 505–06
Pasture, de la, Edmée Elizabeth Monica. *See* Delafield, E. M.
Patai, Daphne, 105
Pater, Walter, 498, 680
Paterson, Don, 210
Paterson, James, 496
Patmore, Coventry, 339, 444, 445, 519, 520
Paton Walsh, Jill. *See* Walsh, Jill Paton
Pattison, Mark, 98, 651
Paulson, Ronald, 166
Pax. *See* Cholmondeley, Mary
Paxton, N., 243
Peabody, Andrew, 315
Pearse, Gabriel, 106
Pearson, Karl, 559
Pearson, Norman Holmes, 205
Peel, Richard, 644
Peel, Robert, 163
Pelissier, Anthony, 190
Pembroke, Countess of. *See* Sidney, Mary
PEN International, 343–44, 663, 679
Pendarves, M. *See* Delany, Mary Granville Pendarves
Pennell, Elizabeth, 657
Pepys, Samuel, 484, 493

Percy, Thomas, 90, 186, 669
Percy, Charles Henry. *See* Smith, Dorothy (Dodie) Gladys
Percy, Elizabeth. *See* Northumberland, Duchess of
Perdita. *See* Lennox, Charlotte Ramsay; Robinson, Mary Darby
Pericles, 609
Perkins, William, 323
Perowne, Steward, 596–97
Perry, Anne, 506–07
Perry, John, 362
Perry, W. C., 101
Perse, St.-John, 347
Persia, writing about, 400
Pestalozzi, Johann Heinrich, 300, 319
Peter, Rhoda. *See* Doolittle, Hilda (H. D.)
Peterborough. *See* Mordaunt, Charles
Peters, Ellis. *See* Pargeter, Edith Mary
Peters, Maureen, 339
Petitpierre, M., 371
Petrarch, Francesco, 224, 325, 333, 342
Petre, Edward, 151
Petrie, Martin, 132
Pfeiffer, Emily Jane Davis, 507–08
Philip, Earl of Pembroke and Montgomery. *See* Herbert, Philip
Philippart, John, 502
Philips, James, 509
Philips, Joan, 231
Philips, Katherine, 36, 71, 231, **508–10**, 618, 636
Phillips, Sian, 269
Philomela. *See* Rowe, Elizabeth Singer
Philomena. *See* Miller, Florence Fenwick
philosophy, study of, 481, 576–77
Philpotts, Bertha, 132
Phipps, Sally, 363
Piaf, Edith, 268
Picasso, Pablo, 578, 684
Pickford, Mary, 477
Pier, Florida. *See* Scott-Maxwell, Florida
Pilkington, Laetitia, 290, **510–11**
Pinero, Arthur Wing, 119, 189, 203
Pinker, J. B., 586
Pinney, Charles, 42
Pinter, Harold, 167, 248, 257, 345, 405, 466
Pinter, Lady Antonia. *See* Fraser, Antonia
Piozzi, Hester Lynch Salusbury Thrale, 107, 328, 329, 386, 387, 450, **511–12**
Piramus, Denis, 431
Pirandello, Luigi, 667
Pitt, William the Elder, 150
Pitt, William the Younger, 594
Pitter, Ruth, 512–13
Pix, Mary, 513, 685
Place, Frances, 241
plagiarism, 137, 167, 526
Plat, Hugh, 677
Plath, Sylvia, 114, 220, 235, **513–15**, 604
Plato, 40, 69, 524–25, 545, 576
Playfair, John, 588
Playford, Henry, 612
Plotinus, 525
Plutarch, 224, 527
Poe, Edgar Allan, 145, 433
poetry, 545, 546, 578, 580, 583, 604, 662, 696; autobiographical/biographical, 35–36, 60, 296, 352–53, 372, 374–75, 409–10, 543–44, 678–79; blank verse, 25–26, 662; children's, 546; dramatic monologues, 661–62; elegies, 42–43, 420, 491, 562–63, 573–74, 580–81, 603–05, 607, 673–74, 696; experimental, 239–40, 409–10, 577–78, 603–04; heroic couplets, 98–99, 139–40; humorous/light/nonsense, 237, 582–83, 607–08; narrative, 431, 580–81; nationalistic and regional, 9, 60, 139–40, 279–80, 603–04, 673; religious/didactic, 1–2, 9, 98–99, 166–67, 168, 184–85, 250–51, 307–08, 315, 346–47, 368–69, 374–75, 388–89, 443–44, 444–45, 480–81, 510, 512, 524–25, 536, 545–46, 551–52, 573–74, 577–78, 582–83, 673–74, 696; romantic/pastoral, 84–85, 85–86, 87–89, 157, 168, 235, 244, 250, 279–80, 299, 323, 331–32, 339, 346–47, 384, 454, 502, 507–08, 524–25, 543–44, 545–46, 551–52, 562–63, 580–81, 673, 691, 696; satiric, 49, 384, 460–61, 511, 678–79; sonnets, 67–68, 98–99, 539, 572–73, 580–81, 693–94; symbolist, 578
Polidari, John, 568
Polignac, Winnaretta Singer, Princesse de, 585
Pollack, Mary. *See* Blyton, Enid
Pollitt, Katha, 310
Polwhele, Elizabeth, 515–16
Polwhele, Richard, 312, 544
Pomeroy, Sue, 627
Pompadour, Jeanne-Antoinette Poisson, Mme. de, 456
Ponet, John, 550
Ponsonby, Mary, 584
Poole, Elizabeth, 516
Poole, Reginald Stuart, 219
Pope, Alexander, 90, 127, 138, 139, 149, 245, 250, 313, 328, 329, 384, 460, 461, 510, 547, 578, 618, 636
Popes: Leo XIII, 553; Paul V, 652; Pius X, 319; Urban VIII, 652
Pordage, John, 381
Porden, Eleanor Anne, 641
Porter, Anna Maria, 241, **516–17**
Porter, Jane, 241, 243, 516, **517–18**
Porter, Mary, 142
Porter, Miss A. M. *See* Porter, Anna Maria
Porter, Miss Anna. *See* Porter, Anna Maria
Porter, Peter, 3
Porter, Robert Ker, 516
Poster, J., 562
Potter, Beatrix, 31, 273, **518–19**, 617
Pound, Ezra, 92, 102, 184, 185, 203–04, 409, 576, 679
Poussin, Nicolas, 287
Powell, David, 477
Powell, George, 513
Power, Eileen, 132, 133
Power, Tyrone, 298
Powis, Elizabeth Somerset, 214
Powis, William Herbert, 214
Powys, T. F., 655
Poyntz, Albany. *See* Gore, Catherine Grace Frances Moody
Poyntz, Mary, 652

pre-Raphaelite movement, 285, 334–35, 339, 498, 507, 542, 545–46, 657
Prescott, Peter, 257
Prévost, Antoine-François, Abbé, 87
Priestley, J. B., 28, 309, 554
Priestley, Joseph, 33, 408, 462
Pringle, Thomas, 226
Prior, Matthew, 220, 547
prison reform, 143, 453, 499
Pritchett, V. S., 213
Procter, Adelaide Anne, 519–20
Procter, William, 593
Profumo, John, 671
prophets, writers as, 135–36, 195–96, 516, 589–90, 628–29
prostitution, 112, 126, 524, 541, 559, 627, 647
Proud, Anne Phillips, 231
Proud, Mary, 293
Proust, Marcel, 72, 95, 354, 394, 402, 534, 583, 630, 679
Prowse, Anne. *See* Locke, Anne Vaughan
Pryce, Jonathan, 123
Prynne, William, 316, 458
Przybyszewska, Stanislawa, 268
psychic research, 52, 576
psychoanalysis/psychiatry, 68–69, 72, 96, 203–04, 346, 359, 466, 514, 561, 576–77, 614 (*see also* Adler, Alfred; Freud, Sigmund; Jung, Carl Gustave)
publishers, writers working as, 184–85, 519–20
Puccini, Giacomo, 394
Purcell, Henry, 151
Purslowe, G., 470
Pye, Thomas, 46
Pym, Barbara, 14, 114, **520–21**

Q. Q. *See* Taylor, Ann and Jane
Quaker Authoress, The. *See* Leadbeater, Mary
Queen of the Arabs, 594
Quiller-Couch, Arthur, 212
Quin, James, 44
Quintilian, 545

race relations/racism, 61–62, 111–12, 184–85, 235–36, 325, 351–52, 382, 405–06, 452, 457, 692–93 (*see also* abolitionism; slavery)
Racine, Jean, 543, 583
Radcliffe, Ann Ward, 20, 212, 387, 450, **521–23**, 523, 527, 581
Radcliffe, Mary Ann[e], 523–24
Rae, W. Fraser, 570
Raffalovich, André, 394
Raimond, C. E. *See* Robins, Elizabeth
Raine, Kathleen, 524–25
Raleigh, Walter, 275, 336
Ralph, James, 150
Ramée, Marie Louise de la (Ouida), 525–26
Randall, Ann Frances. *See* Robinson, Mary Darby (Perdita)
Ranke, Leopold von, 209
rape, 112, 403, 419, 508
Raphael, 132
Raphael, Frederick, 398
Rapin-Thoyres, Paul de, 527
Raskin, Marcus, 453
Rathbone, Basil, 190
Rattigan, Terence, 199
Ravagli, Angelo, 381
Ray, Man, 185
Raymond, Diana, 256
Raymond, Henry Augustus. *See* Scott, Sarah
Raymond, John, 643
Raynal, Guillaume-Thomas, abbé de, 642
Rayner, Elizabeth. *See* Lowndes, Marie Adelaide Belloc
Reade, Charles, 76, 155, 615
recusancy, 133–34, 294, 324, 462, 464, 494–95, 573, 616, 652–53 (*see also* religion, Roman Catholicism)
Redfern, John. *See* Pargeter, Edith Mary
Redgrave, Vanessa, 104
Reed, Henry, 163
Reeve, Clara, 387, **527**
Reeve, W., 535
Rehan, Ada, 176
Reid Banks, Lynne. *See* Banks, Lynne Reid
Reilly, Sidney, 645–46
Reiner, Max. *See* Caldwell, (Janet) Taylor
religion: agnosticism, 56, 255, 304, 639, 657; atheism/freethinking, 40, 52, 56, 396, 558; Baptists, 221, 516, 629, 637; Calvinism, 124, 165, 221, 304, 361, 447, 593, 613; Christianity (general), 40, 112, 171; Church of England, 10, 17, 18, 22–23, 32, 35, 52, 57, 85, 90, 97, 133, 140, 175, 182, 204, 261, 276–77, 281, 286, 319, 326–27, 330, 359, 361, 396, 397, 412, 418, 448, 462, 478, 494, 502, 520, 523, 545, 571, 573, 579, 590, 616, 632, 636, 639, 649, 652, 658, 669, 674, 682; Church of England, Broad or Low Church, Evangelical, 463–64, 625, 651; Church of England, High Church/Anglo-Catholicism/Oxford Movement/Tractarian Movement, 4, 361, 348, 545, 564, 683, 697; Church of Ireland, 90, 674; Congregationalists, 68, 629; cults, 104; Deism, 18, 158; Dissenters/Nonconformists, 8, 139, 177, 264, 381, 547, 673, 682; Evangelicalism, 304, 306–08, 605; Fifth Monarchists, 135, 628–29; Huguenots, 206, 361, 383, 573; Hussites, 682; Islam, 501, 550, 568; Judaism, 5, 41, 93–94, 162, 188, 215–16, 223, 239–40, 247, 259–60, 349, 377–78, 394, 395–96, 398, 400–01, 409, 480, 549–50, 591, 602, 622; Methodist, 222, 286, 464, 590; Minnesingers, 682; Moravians, 682; Mormons (Church of Jesus Christ of Latter-Day Saints), 68, 506; Pentecostal, 683; Pietists, 682; Presbyterianism, 24, 135, 558, 591, 637, 642, 647; Protestantism, 5, 9, 14, 90, 402, 403, 438, 439, 447, 448, 478, 485, 550, 625, 674, 679, 681; Puritanism, 77–78, 247, 248, 206, 388, 323, 324, 336, 389, 403–04, 447, 483, 493, 528, 649, 658, 684; Quakers (Society of Friends), 47, 56, 57, 175, 207, 225, 240–41, 254–55, 261, 286, 291–94, 331, 382–84, 423, 491, 563, 629, 637, 647, 649; Roman Catholicism, 5, 14, 17, 22, 27, 36, 41, 78, 90, 106, 108, 112, 133–134, 134–135, 177, 187, 196, 201, 206, 214–15, 236, 244, 247, 256, 257, 268, 276–77, 286, 288, 294, 300, 306, 316, 318, 324, 326–27, 332, 338, 346, 348, 356, 357–58, 361, 405, 407, 408, 413, 418–19, 438, 439, 444, 445, 446, 447, 462–63, 473, 478, 481, 483, 485, 490, 494–95, 495, 501, 504, 516,

religion (*continued*)
519–20, 523, 525, 550, 553, 564, 573, 578, 579, 591, 592, 603, 616, 619, 625, 637, 638, 639–40, 636, 649, 649, 651, 652–53, 653, 674, 675, 682; Southcottians, 589–90; Taoism, 630; Theism, 52, 158; Unitarianism, 8, 67, 264, 311, 332, 682, 448; Zen, 630
Rembrandt van Rijn, 346, 491
Renaissance, writing about, 131, 695
Renan, Ernest, 543
Renault, Mary, 159, **528–29**
Rendel, Ellie, 249
Rendell, Ruth, 341, **529–30**
Rennie, George, 122
Renoir, Auguste, 162, 346
Repyngdon, Philip, 367
Revere, Paul, 519
Reynolds, Barbara, 557
Reynolds, Frances, 371
Reynolds, Joshua, 9, 107, 127, 179, 371, 382, 383, 491, 517
Reynolds, Margaret, 693
Reynolds, Myra, 368, 420
Rhodes, Cecil, 559
Rhondda, Margaret, 83, 325
Rhys, Jean, 530–32
Rich, Christopher, 636
Rich, Frank, 268
Rich, John, 44, 156
Rich, Mary Boyle, Countess of Warwick, 532–33
Richards, I. A., 498
Richardson, Dorothy, 102, **533–34**, 576, 645, 678
Richardson, Maurice, 378
Richardson, Samuel, 46, 100, 101, 127, 141, 166, 242, 246, 296, 297, 313, 527, 548, 558, 569, 570, 609
Richardson, Tony, 200
Ricketts, Charles, 244
Ricks, Christopher, 611
Riddell, Charlotte Eliza Lawson Cowan, 535
Riding, Laura, 185
Ridler, Anne, 535–37
Rigby, Elizabeth. *See* Eastlake, Lady, Elizabeth Rigby
Riley, Robert, 377
Rilke, Rainer Maria, 679
Rimbaud, Arthur, 192, 578, 597
Ritchie, Anne Thackeray, 144, **537–38**
Ritterhaus, Rudi von, 72
Roach, Richard, 381
Robbe-Grillet, Alain, 92
Roberts, Ellis, 562
Roberts, Michèle (Brigitte), 419, **538–39**
Roberts, Shirley, 624
Robertson, Duncan, 473
Robertson, Robin, 210
Robeson, Paul, 102, 204
Robespierre, Maximilien-François-Marie-Isadore de, 268, 681
Robin Hood, 75, 262
Robins, Denise Naomi, 539–40
Robins, Elizabeth, 540–42
Robinson, Agnes Mary Frances, 542–43
Robinson, Henry Crabb, 33, 109, 241, 641, 681
Robinson, J. A. T., 331
Robinson, Mary Darby (Perdita), 46, 241, 310, 461, 498, **543–44**
Robinson, Mrs. *See* Robinson, Mary Darby (Perdita)
Robinson, Robert, 311
Robson, Flora, 190
Roche, Henri-Pierre, 385
Rogers, Katharine M., 494
Rogers, Samuel, 9, 33, 51, 571, 681
Roland, Jeanne-Marie, 60, 681
Role, Margaret, 135
Rolland, Romain, 306
Rolle, Richard, 640
Rolleston, T. W., 638
Rolo, Charles J., 377
Romantic movement, 1, 3, 9, 60, 188, 374, 409, 454, 463–64, 521, 524, 563, 613, 620
Romilly, Rosmond, 453
Romilly, Samuel, 284
Romney, George, 9, 620
Ronsard, Pierre de, 565
Roosevelt, Theodore, 651
Rootham, Helen, 578
Roper, Esther, 280
Roper, Margaret More, 425, **545**, 573
Roper, William, 545
Rosanna. *See* Tighe, Mary
Roscio, Mario de, 596
Roscoe, William, 33
Rosicrucianism, 220, 221, 695 (*see also* occult; spiritualism; theosophy)
Rosina. *See* Bulwer-Lytton, Rosina Wheeler
Ross, Alan, 562
Ross, Janet Duff Gordon, 526
Ross, Martin. *See* Somerville and Ross (Violet Florence Martin)
Ross, Robert, 394
Rossetti, Christina, 114, 286, 334, 339, 444, 445, 445, 519, **545–47**, 639, 657, 662
Rossetti, Dante Gabriel, 99, 545–46, 285, 334, 394, 662, 697
Rossetti, William Michael, 56, 99, 315, 334, 661
Rostand, Edmond, 189
Rosweyde, Héribert, 646
Rousseau, Jean-Jacques, 188, 201, 217, 242, 300, 681
Roussin, André, 456
Routley, Eric, 682
Rowe, Elizabeth Singer, 19, 139, 250, **547**
Rowe, Nicholas, 142, 250
Rowe, Thomas, 547
Rowse, A. L., 4, 662
Rowson, Susanna, 547–49
Rowton, Frederic, 59
Royal Academy, 137, 491
Royal Historical Society, 118
Rubens, Bernice, 549–50
Rubens, Peter Paul, 663
Ruby, Jack, 41
Rule, Jane, 299
Rumers, Carol, 562
rural life, writing about, 444, 454
Rushdie, Salman, 419
Ruskin, John, 99, 122, 162, 163, 215, 244, 285, 320, 334, 339, 445, 546, 595, 617

Russell, Bertrand, 23, 123, 253, 381, 423, 481, 577, 610, 645, 688
Russell, Elizabeth, 323, **550–51**
Russell, George (AE), 280, 629, 646
Russell, John, 644
Russell, Margaret, 152
Russell, Mary Annette Beauchamp. *See* Arnim, Elizabeth von
Russell, Lady Rachel, 139
Russell, Sarah. *See* Laski, Marghanita
Russia, writing about, 198, 400, 423, 477–78, 681
Rutherforth, Thomas, 636
Ruysbroeck, Jan van, 465

Saal, Hubert, 528
Sabor, P., 46
Sabrina. *See* Havergal, Frances Ridley
Sachs, Hans, 102
Sackville, George, 9, 55
Sackville-West, Vita (Victoria Mary), 23, 60, 185, 216, **551–52**, 585, 616, 630
Sade, Donatien-Alphonso-François, marquis de, 123, 125, 188
Sadlier, Mary Anne, 553
sadomasochism, 551
Sage, Lorna, 125, 303
Said, Edward, 186
Saint, Dora (Doris) Jessie, 554–55
St. Aubin de Terán, Lisa, 555
St. Hilaire, Barthelmy, 209
St. John, Jane, 568
Saint-Amant, Antoine Girard, 509
Saint-Exupéry, Antoine de, 347, 432
Saintsbury, G. E. B., 646
Saint-Simonians, 675
Salinger, J. D., 200
Salmon, V., 420
Salt, Samuel, 373
Salzman, Paul, 421
Sand, George, 347, 348, 379, 519
Sanders, Charles, 661
Sanford, Nell Mary. *See* Dunn, Mary
Sapphira. *See* Barber, Mary
Sappho, 244, 641, 684
Sappho. *See* Moody, Elizabeth
Sarah, Duchess of Marlborough. *See* Churchill, Sarah Jennings, Duchess of Marlborough
Sardou, Victorien, 119
Sargent, John Singer, 498
Sarraute, Nathalie, 92, 167
Sartoris, Adelaide. *See* Kemble, Adelaide
Sartre, Jean-Paul, 470
Sassoon, Siegfried, 356, 646
Savage, Richard, 312
Savonarola, Girolamo, 222
Sayers, Dorothy L., 10, 145, 258, 368, 434, **556–58**
Schaw, Janet, 558
Schiff, Sydney, 394
Schiller, Friedrich von, 60, 180, 190, 253, 315, 365, 380
Schleiner, Louise, 637
Schlesinger, John, 549
Schliemann, Heinrich, 304–05
Schmideberg, Walter, 205
Schmidt, Evald. *See* Smyth, Ethel Mary
Schönberg, Arnold, 655
Schoolcraft, Henry, 342
schools, establishment of, 18, 68, 196–97, 548, 564, 572, 632 (*see also* educational theory and planning)
Schreiber, Lady Charlotte Elizabeth. *See* Guest, Charlotte E. B.
Schreiner, Olive Emilie Albertina, 82, 202, 395, **558–60**
Schubert, Franz, 210, 604
Schumacher, Raoul, 432
Schumann, Clara, 584
Schurman, Anna Maria von, 420
Schuyler, Mrs. Philip, 283
Schwabacher, Anastasia, 602
science and technology, writing about, 137, 309–10, 535, 587–89, 647
Scotland, writing about, 302, 451, 604, 691
Scott, Agnes Neill. *See* Muir, Willa
Scott, David, 183
Scott, Paul, 399
Scott, Sarah, 246, 459, **560–61**
Scott, Walter, 25, 26, 33, 37, 46, 76, 79, 85, 109, 159, 162, 217, 234, 243, 283, 300, 315, 365, 386, 387, 484, 491, 495, 516, 517, 558, 563, 575, 607, 610, 641, 660
Scott, William Bell, 286
Scott-Giles, Wilfred, 556
Scott-Maxwell, Florida, 561
Scovell, E[dith]. J[oy]., 562
Scudèry, Madeleine de, 228
Secker, Martin, 446
Secker, Thomas, 127, 609
Secor, Marie and Robert, 335
Sedgwick, Catherine, 454
Segal, George, 345
Ségur, Comtesse Sophie de, 491
Séjourné, Philippe, 389
Selassie, Haile, 500
Sempronia. *See* Lamb, Mary Ann
Seneca, 677
Serres, Jean de, 206
Sévigné, Marie de Rabutin-Chantal, Marquise de, 304
Seward, Anna, 301, 450, **562–63**, 681
Sewell, Anna, 563–64
Sewell, Elizabeth Missing, 564–65
Sewell, Mary, 226, 563
sexuality, writing about, 35, 81, 83, 112, 124, 174, 399, 313, 400–01, 409, 444, 476, 481–82, 486–87, 497, 507, 624, 657, 668–69 (*see also* masturbation)
Seymour, Alice, 590
Seymour, Anne, Margaret, and Jane, 565–56
Seymour, Thomas, 448
S.F.E. *See* Egerton, Sarah Fyge Field
Shakespear, Dorothy, 204
Shakespeare, William, 2, 3, 60, 77, 79, 85, 96, 101, 110, 111, 119, 126, 145, 151, 163, 189, 190, 224, 226, 227, 228, 234, 244, 245, 248, 248, 249, 262, 263, 287, 288, 291, 303, 315, 318–19, 342, 345, 365, 366, 373, 389, 403, 414, 458, 498, 505, 517, 560, 574, 595, 605, 615–16, 655, 689, 691
Shannon, Charles, 244

Sharp, Jack, 88
Sharp, Jane, 566–67
Sharp, Margery, 567
Sharp, William, 590
Shaw, George Bernard, 23, 24, 52, 82, 86, 97, 119, 120, 177, 283, 326, 498, 541, 584, 616, 645, 646, 680
Sheed, Frank, 653
Sheed, Wilfrid, 653
Shelley, Harriet Westbrook, 568
Shelley, Mary Wollstonecraft, 151, 212, 403, 407, **568–69**, 591–92, 681, 686
Shelley, Percy Bysshe, 60, 74, 151, 188, 192, 251, 315, 403, 413, 445, 491, 558, 568–89, 681, 686
Sher, Antony, 269
Sheridan, Caroline, 571
Sheridan, Frances, 386, **569–71**
Sheridan, Helen Selina, Lady Dufferin, 571
Sheridan, Richard Brinsley, 9, 107, 386, 570, 571
Sheridan, Thomas, 290
Sherman, William Tecumseh, 258
Sherwood, Mary Martha Nutt, 571–72
Shiel, M. P., 192
Shirley, Elizabeth, 324, **572–73**
Shklovsky, Viktor, 646
Shostakovich, Dmitry, 646
Showalter, Elaine, 478
Siddal, Lizzie, 335
Siddons, Sarah, 26, 338, 365, 386, 387
Sidgwick, Henry, 304
Sidney, Dorothy, 132
Sidney, Mary, Countess of Pembroke, 323, 387, **573–75**, 658, 693
Sidney, Philip, 77, 78, 231, 232, 323, 387, 457, 560, 573–74, 657–58, 672, 693
Sidney-Turner, Saxon, 688
Sieveking, Amelia Wilhelmina, 683
Signoret, Simone, 550
Sigourney, Lydia, 315
Sillitoe, Alan, 235
Simpson, Helen, 190
Sinclair, Catherine, 575–76, 647
Sinclair, Mary Amelia St. Clair, 83, 204, 443, 678, **576–77**
Singh, Ranjit, 216
Sitwell, Edith, 184, 394, **577–78**, 610, 616
Sitwell, Osbert, 184, 394, 423, 512, 577
Sitwell, Sacheverell, 577
Skeel, Caroline, 132
Skipworth, Thomas, 422
slavery, 8, 68, 310, 351, 366, 463, 491, 548, 558, 634, 680–81, 692 (*see also* abolitionism; race relations/racism)
Smart, Annie, 148
Smedley, Edward, 579
Smedley, Francis, 579–80
Smedley, Menella Bute, 579–80
Smiles, Samuel, 178
Smith, Barbara Leigh. *See* Bodichon, Barbara
Smith, Charlotte Turner, 108, 544, **580–82**, 681
Smith, Dorothy (Dodie) Gladys, 582
Smith, George, 86, 264, 537
Smith, H., 214, 220
Smith, Logan Pearsall, 612
Smith, R. F., 678–79
Smith, Stevie (pseudonym of Florence Margaret Smith), 582–84
Smith, Sydney, 51, 571, 633
Smollett, Tobias, 116, 243
Smyth, Ethel Mary, 584–86
Snodman, T., 591
Snow, C. P., 353–54, 481
Snow, Moses, 231
Sobieski, John, 517
Society of Authors, 663
social problems and social work, writing about, 108, 168, 319–20, 658–59, 661
socialism, 405, 658, 675 (*see also* Christian Socialism; Fabian Society; International Labour Party)
Society for the Promoting of Christian Knowledge (S.P.C.K.), 131, 535, 632–22
Socrates, 395, 545
Soltau, Henrietta, 115
Somers, Jane. *See* Lessing, Doris
Somerset, Lady Henry, 451
Somerville and Ross (pseudonyms), 585, **586–87**
Somerville, Mary Charters, 589
Somerville, Mary Fairfax Greig, 587–89, 647
Sophocles, 497, 667
Sorelli, Guido, 501
Souline, Evguenia, 299
Southcott, Joanna, 589–91
Southey, Caroline. *See* Bowles, Caroline
Southey, Robert, 33, 74–75, 79, 90, 109, 163, 247, 563, 590, 641
Southwell, Robert, 294, 447
Sowernam, Ester (pseudonym), 12, **591**, 593
Spark, Muriel, 253, 567, **591–93**, 684
S.P.C.K. *See* Society for the Promoting of Christian Knowledge
Speght, Rachel, 12, 350, 470, 591, **593**
Spencer, Herbert, 56, 221, 558, 658
Spencer, Jane, 197
Spencer, Stanley, 123, 268–69
Spender, Stephen, 185, 524
Spenser, Edmund, 77, 152, 224, 318, 524, 573, 620
Speranza. *See* Wilde, Jane Francesca
Spiess, Christian Heinrich, 387
Spinckes, Nathaniel, 326
Spindle, Penelope. *See* Lennox, Charlotte Ramsay
Spinoza, Benedict de, 222, 241, 576
spiritualism, 183, 205, 298, 332, 433, 539 (*see also* occult; Rosicrucianism; theosophy)
Spock, Benjamin, 453
Stabb, Charles, 446
Staël-Holstein, Anne-Louise-Germaine Necker, baronne de, 45, 51, 243, 315, 342, 348, 372, 621
Stafford-Clark, Max, 147, 666
Stalin, Joseph, 264, 401, 631 (*see also* communism; Marxism)
Stanford, Derek, 591–92
Stanhope, Lucy Hester, 400, **593–94**
Stanislavsky, Konstantin, 615
Stannard, Henrietta Eliza Vaughn Palmer, 595–96
Stanton, Clara, 162

Stanton, Elizabeth Cady, 254, 451, 693
Stapleton, Thomas, 545
Stark, Freya, 596–97
Starkie, Enid (Mary), 597–98
Stead, Christina (Ellen), 598–99
Stead, W. T., 52, 202, 408
Stearn, Jess, 117
Steegmuller, Francis, 597
Steel, Flora Annie, 599–600
Steele, E., 600
Stein, Gertrude, 102, 409, 670
Stella. *See* Johnson, Esther ("Stella")
Stephen, Fitzjames, 158
Stephen, Julia Prinsep, 600–01
Stephen, Leslie, 150, 153, 537, 600, 601, 688
Stephen, Virginia. *See* Woolf, Virginia
Stepney, Catherine (Catharine), Lady, 601–02
Stepniak, Sergei M., 264, 645
Stern, G[ladys]. B[ertha]., 361, **602–03**
Sternberg, Josef von, 268
Sterne, Laurence, 116, 642
Stevens, Wallace, 239, 346
Stevenson, Anne, 603–05
Stevenson, C. L., 603
Stevenson, Lionel, 374
Stevenson, Robert Louis, 27, 76, 162, 602–03, 610
Stewart, Dugald, 154
Stewart, Henry, 641
Stewart, Mary (Florence Elinor), 605–06
Stewart, Neil, 354
Stickney, Sarah. *See* Ellis, Sarah Stickney
Stoker, Bram, 403
Stone, John Hurford, 681
Storey, David, 147, 190
Stothard, Thomas, 79
Stowe, Harriet Beecher, 226, 454, 623, 625, 634
Strachey, Lytton, 123, 405, 406, 585, 688 (*see also* Bloomsbury)
Stratemeyer, Edward L., 182
Strauss, David Friedrich, 60, 221
Street, G. S., 394
Strickland, Agnes, 284, **606**
Strickland, Elizabeth, 606
Strickland, Jane Margaret, 606
Strickland, Susanna, 606
Strindberg, August, 81
Struther, Jan, 606–07
Stuart, Arabella, 300
Stuart, Louisa, 607–08
Stuart, Mme., 318
Stuart, Mary. *See* Mary, Queen of Scots
Stuart, née Villiers, Mary, 231
Stubbs, William, 118
Sturgis, Howard, 144
Sturgis, Julian, 280
Sudermann, Hermann, 119
suffrage, 40, 46–47, 55, 68, 112, 115, 158, 196, 219, 279, 282, 286, 305, 321, 395, 400, 444, 450–51, 499–501, 540–42, 558–59, 561, 576, 585, 589, 600, 601, 631, 651, 659, 661, 671, 692–93 (*see also* women's rights/emancipation)
Sugrue, T., 528
suicide, 202, 477, 514, 534, 540, 679, 689
Sullivan, Arthur, 519
Surbiton. *See* Moody, Elizabeth
surrogate motherhood, 457
Suso, Heinrich, 465
Sutcliffe, Alice, 608–09
Sutcliffe, Matthew, 608
Sutherland, Donald, 200
Sutherland, James, 297
Swanson, Gloria, 275
Swartley, Ariel, 160
Swetnam, Joseph, 470, 591, 593
Swift, Jonathan, 9, 34, 197, 201, 229, 250, 290, 328, 329, 352–53, 377, 410, 422, 494, 510, 578, 679
Swinburne, Algernon, 99, 188, 397, 507, 657
Switzerland, writing about, 79, 239
Sykes, Christopher, 40
Sylphid. *See* Robinson, Mary Darby (Perdita)
Sylvester, Joshua, 77, 693
Symons, Arthur, 244, 543
Symons, Julian, 145, 341
Synge, John Millington, 227, 289
Szladits, Lola L., 502

Tagore, Rabindranath, 577
Talbot, Catherine, 127, **609**
Tallemant, des Réaux, 43
Tassie, Franz, 190
Tasso, Torquato, 325
Tate, Nahum, 220, 673
Tattlewell, Mary, 12
Tauler, Johann, 465
Taylor, Ann and Jane, 339, **609–11**
Taylor, Coleridge, 299
Taylor, Elizabeth, 321, **611–12**
Taylor (Wythens), Elizabeth, 612–13
Taylor, Frances, 590
Taylor, Henry, 571
Taylor, Jane, 647
Taylor, Jeremy, 509
Taylor, John Russell, 199, 345, 346
Taylor, Mary, 86
Taylor, Thomas, 524
T. B. *See* Haywood, Eliza Fowler
Tchaikovsky, Peter Ilich, 584
Tchaykovsky, N., 264
Tcherkessov, Prince, 264
Tedlock, E. W., 381
television, 97, 230, 321, 327, 398, 434, 492, 540, 626 (*see also* British Broadcasting Corporation)
Temple, Ann. *See* Mortimer, Penelope Ruth
Temple, William, 311, 352–53, 493–94
Tennant, Emma, 613–15
Tennant, Emma Alice Margaret. *See* Asquith, Emma Alice Margaret Tennant
Tenniel, John, 625
Tennyson, Alfred, 17, 50, 122, 158, 162, 208, 226, 339, 445, 508, 519, 520, 537, 542, 600, 610, 616, 643, 653
Terán, Lisa St. Aubin de. *See* St. Aubin de Terán, Lisa
Teresa of Avila, 307, 346, 462, 465, 483, 552
Terry, Ellen, 82, 119, 120, 176, 177, **615–16**
Terry, Fred, 492

Tey, Josephine. *See* Mackintosh, Elizabeth; 145
Thackeray, William Makepeace, 51, 76, 86, 110, 183, 208, 217, 254, 278, 302, 303, 394, 510, 519–20, 537, 600, 688
Thant, U, 650
Thatcher, Margaret, 3, 210, 626
Theocritus, 204, 641
theosophy, 52 (*see also* occult; Rosicrucianism; spiritualism)
Thérèsa of Lisieux, 261
Thimelby, Gertrude Aston, 616–17
Thimelby, Winifred, 616
Thirkell, Angela (Margaret), 16, **617–18**
Thomas à Kempis, 504
Thomas, Brandon, 394
Thomas, Dylan, 92, 679
Thomas, Edward, 237, 323
Thomas, Elizabeth, 220, **618–19**
Thompets, Mesdames, 371
Thompson. A. C. *See* Meynell, Alice
Thompson, Emma, 123
Thompson, Gertrude Caton, 596
Thompson, William, 675
Thomson, James, 536
Thorndike, Sybil, 190
Thornton, Alice Wandesford, 421, **619**
Thornton, Bonnell, 290
Thrale, Hester. *See* Piozzi, Hester Lynch Salusbury Thrale
Thurber, James, 583
Tickell, Richard, 386
Tighe, Mary, 620–21
Tilley, Vesta, 419
Tilly, John, 422
Tindall, Gillian, 622–23
Tindall, William York, 381
Tinsley, Annie Turner, 623
Tipper, Elizabeth, 624
Titian, 287
Tochatti, James, 56
Todd, Janet, 242, 305, 562
Todd, Margaret Georgina, 624
Todhunter, John, 638
Todi, Jacopone di, 640
Todorov, Petko, 92
Tolkien, J. R. R., 92, 140
Tolstoy, Leo, 163, 252, 264, 498
Tolstoy, Sonya, 16
Tomalin, Claire, 242
Tompkins, J. M. S., 46
Tomson, Graham R. *See* Watson, Rosamund Marriott
Tonna, Charlotte Elizabeth, 625–26
Torbuck, John, 624
Tosti, Paolo, 186
Tourneur, Cyril, 227
Townely, Jane, 590
Townsend, Sue (Susan Lilian), 626–27
Toynbee, Philip, 453
Tracy, Honor (Lilbush Wingfield), 627–28
Trafford, F. G. *See* Riddell, Charlotte Eliza Lawson Cowan
Traherne, Thomas, 512
translators, writers as, 22–23, 32, 43, 60, 91, 92, 127, 135, 166, 178, 179–80, 183, 203–04, 208–09, 214, 215, 221–22, 224, 228, 235, 239–40, 263–64, 266, 288–89, 290, 291, 294–95, 300, 318, 331–32, 333, 336, 347, 375–76, 383, 386, 390, 395, 403, 404, 411, 421, 435, 438, 441–42, 442, 444, 460, 462–63, 467, 468–70, 476–77, 480, 486, 487, 501, 502, 504, 508, 509, 511, 519, 527, 531, 543, 545, 550, 556–57, 560, 562, 563, 565, 566, 574, 576, 580–81, 591, 596, 598, 637–38, 640, 641, 645, 646, 651, 655, 663, 666–67, 673, 674, 675, 676, 680, 680–81, 682–83, 685, 694
transsexualism, 631
Trapnel, Anna, 628–29
Trasquair, Mary, Countess of, 524
travel writing, 47, 55, 57–58, 60, 115, 116–17, 158, 180–81, 208–09, 215–16, 218–19, 235–36, 247, 258–59, 337, 370–71, 380, 412, 423, 424, 427, 433, 436, 449–50, 468, 479, 482, 484, 487, 495, 498, 501, 508, 511, 571, 575, 594, 596–97, 613, 629, 633, 641–42, 647, 671, 680, 686, 691 (*see also names of specific countries or continents*)
Travers, Graham. *See* Todd, Margaret Georgina
Travers, P[amela]. L[yndon]., 629–30
Tree, Herbert Beerbohm, 119
Tree, Iris, 184
Trefusis, Violet Keppel, 552, **630–31**
Tremain, Rose, 631–32
Trench, Melesina, 382
Trevelyan, G. M., 247, 663, 596
Trifler, Mrs. *See* Lennox, Charlotte Ramsay
Trilling, Diana, 41
Trimmer, Sarah Kirby, 462, **632–33**
Trollope, Anthony, 162, 330, 401, 617, 633, 687
Trollope, Frances Milton, 633–34, 687
Trollope, Joanna, 635
Trotsky, Leon, 264 (*see also* communism; Marxism)
Trotter, Catherine, 513, **635–37**
Troubridge, Una, 299
Tsvetaeva, Marina, 239–40, 538
Tudor, Elizabeth. *See* Elizabeth I
Tudor, Mary. *See* Mary I
Tuke, Esther, 293
Turbeville, Henry, 327
Turgenev, Ivan, 217, 264
Turkey, writing about, 460, 501–02, 597
Turner, Jane, 637
Turner, Kathleen, 268, 269
Turner, Reginald, 394
Turner, William, 231
Turnley, Christopher. *See* Ellis-Fermor, Una Mary
Twain, Mark, 7, 283, 370, 633, 646
Tyler, Evan, 333
Tyler, Margaret, 637–38
Tymme, Thomas, 206
Tynan, Katharine, 280, **638–39**
Tynan, Kenneth, 24, 200, 345
Tyndale, William, 404
Tyndall, John, 658
Tzara, Tristan, 185

Udall, Nicholas, 438
Ulster Poets, 412

Underhill, Evelyn, 464, **639–40**
Underwood, Ann, 590
UNESCO, 309–10
United Nations, 6, 549, 650
United States, criticism of/writing about, 57–58, 68, 162, 198, 436–37, 558, 604, 633–34, 692–93
Untermeyer, Louis, 443, 512, 678
Updike, John, 466
Urquhart, Lawrence, 124
Ustinov, Peter, 467

V. *See* Clive, Caroline; Currie, Mary (Montgomerie) Lamb Singleton; Vardill, Anna Jane
Valásquez, Diego, 491
Valentino, Rudolph, 275
Valéry, Paul, 679
Van Eerde, K., 284
Vardill, Anna Jane, 641–42
Varley, Isabella. *See* Banks, Isabella Varley
Vas Diaz, Selma, 531
Vaughan, Henry, 508, 512
Veevers, Erica, 317
Vega, Lope de, 315
Venn, Anne, 637, **642**
Vere, Aubrey de, 445
Verlaine, Paul, 408
Verne, Jules, 408
Vesey, Elizabeth, 642–43
Victoria, 174, 215, 249, 257, 272, 320–21, 339, 406, 478, 484, 578, 584, 606, 617, **643–44**, 647–48, 654
Vidal, Gore, 684
Viguy, Alfred de, 209
Villiers, Catherine, 608
Villiers, George, 155, 608
Vine, Barbara. *See* Rendell, Ruth
Virgil, 245, 383, 560
Viry, Emily de, 519
Vivaldi, Antonio, 522
Vives, Juan Luis, 438
vivisectionism/anti-vivisectionism, 115–16, 116–17, 158, 286 (*see also* animal rights)
Volkhovsky, Felix, 264
Voltaire, 310, 456, 459, 479
von Arnim, Elizabeth. *See* Arnim, Elizabeth von
Vonnegut, Kurt, 92
Vosper, Frank, 602
Voynich, Ethel Lilian Boole, 644–46

Waddell, Helen Jane, 646–47
Wagner, Richard, 279
Wailly, Leon de, 209
Wakefield, Gilbert, 33, 311
Wakefield, Priscilla, 647
Wales, writing about, 150–51, 294–95
Walford, Lucy (Bethia), 425–26, **647–48**
Walker, Anne, 400
Walker, Anthony, 533
Walker, John, 18
Walkowitz, J. R., 112
Wall, Barbara, 575
Wall, Thomas, 289
Wallace, Michele, 106
Wallace, William, 25, 26, 517, 588
Waller, Edmund, 132, 673
Walpole, Horace, 13, 14, 34, 50–51, 155, 179, 180, 201, 212, 313, 328, 329, 387, 450, 460, 463, 479, 527, 642
Walpole, Hugh, 441, 443, 552
Walpole, Robert, 149
Walsh, Jill Paton, 648–49
Walton, Izaak, 310, 311, 369, 554
Walton, William, 578
Wandesford, Christopher, 619
Wandor, Michelene, 148, 419, 538
Warburton, Eliot, 594
Warburton, William, 311, 636
Ward (Jackson), Barbara, 649–50
Ward, Maisie. *See* Ward, Mary Josephine
Ward, Mary Augusta Arnold, 23, **650–52**
Ward, Mary (Joan Mary), 495, **652–53**
Ward, Mary Josephine, 653–54
Ward, Mrs. Humphry. *See* Ward, Mary Augusta Arnold
Ward, Stephen, 41
Wardle, Irving, 268, 346
Warne, Frederick, 518
Warne, Norman, 518
Warner, Charles Dudley, 5
Warner, Marina Sarah, 654–55
Warner, Sylvia Townsend, 655–56
Warnock, Mary, 378
Waters, Lucy, 281
Watson, H. B. Marriott, 657
Watson, Rosamund Marriott, 657
Watt, Ian, 36
Watt, James, Jr., 387
Watts, Alan, 261
Watts, Alaric A., 348
Watts, Arthur, 198
Watts, George Frederic, 132, 600
Watts, Isaac, 547, 610
Watts-Dunton, Theodore, 662
Waugh, Auberon 254, 327
Waugh, Evelyn, 40, 405, 456
Wavell, Archibald Percival, 596–97
Weamys [Weames], Anna [Anne], 657–58
Webb, A., 241
Webb, Beatrice Potter, 118, 321, 395, **658–60**
Webb, (Gladys) Mary, 660–61
Webb, Richard David, 382, 383
Webb, Sidney, 659
Webster, (Julia) Augusta Davies, 661–62
Webster, John, 227
Wedgwood, Ciceley Veronica, 662–64
Wedgwood, Josiah, 662
Weekley, Ernest, 380
Weld, Thomas, 642
Weldon, Fay, 664–65
Weller, Earle Vonard, 620
Wellington, Arthur Wellesley, 257, 406, 667
Wells, H. G., 13, 14, 23, 203, 400, 498, 534, 541, 613, 688
Wentworth, Anne, 421
Wentworth, Thomas, 662
Wertenbaker, Timberlake (Lael Louisiana), 665–67

Wesker, Arnold, 345
Wesley, John, 484
Wesley, Mary, 667–69
West, Benjamin, 491
West, Jane, 669–70
West, Mae, 239
West, Rebecca (pseudonym of Cicily Isabel Fairfield), 23, 172, 299, 531, 660, 664, **670–72**, 678
Westbrook, Harriet, 491
Westmacott, Mary. *See* Christie, Agatha
Weston, Elizabeth Jane, 672
Weston, Jane Cooper, 672
Wetter, Immolata, 653
Weymouth, Thomas Thynne, 547
Wharton, Anne Lee, 672–74
Wharton, Edith, 379, 384, 498
Wharton, Thomas, 673
Wheathill, Anne, 674
Wheatley, H. B., 231
Wheeler, Anna Doyle, 674–75
Wheeler, Mortimer, 310
Whibley, Charles, 16
White, Antonia, 212, 377, **675–77**
White, Babington. *See* Braddon (Maxwell), Mary Elizabeth
White, Edward, 110
White, Gilbert, 141, 554
White, Jean, 340
White, Patrick, 354
Whitemore, Hugh, 583
Whitman, Alden, 257
Whitman, Walt, 96, 680
Whitney, Geoffrey, 677
Whitney, Isabella, 677–78
Whittier, John Greenleaf, 40
Whyte, Violet. *See* Stannard, Henrietta Eliza Vaughn Palmer
Whytford, Richard, 504
Wickham, Anna, 678–79
Wife of a Beneficed Clergyman. *See* Besant, Annie Wood
Wight, Sarah, 629
Wigmore, Winifred, 652
Wilberforce, Octavia, 542
Wilberforce, William, 463
Wilde, Jane Francesca, 679–80
Wilde, Kim, 104
Wilde, Oscar, 3, 76, 119, 171, 175, 177, 187, 202, 244, 394–95, 396, 409, 428, 498, 541, 601, 616, 657
Wilkes, John, 479
Wilkinson, Tate, 91
Wilks, W. H., 314
Willard, Frances, 451
Williams, Anna, 371
Williams, Charles, 536
Williams, Emlyn, 190
Williams, Helen Maria, 310, 461, 544, **680–82**
Williams, William Carlos, 185, 204, 239
Williamson, M., 231
Willy, Margaret, 612
Wilmot, John, Earl of Rochester, 43, 186, 232, 673
Wilson, C. H., 290
Wilson, Edmund, 145, 385, 434
Wilson, Harriette, 617
Wilson, John, 305
Winchelsea, Countess of. *See* Finch, Anne Kingsmill, Countess of Winchelsea
Winkworth, Catherine, 682–83
Winslow, W. C., 219
Winter, John Strange. *See* Stannard, Henrietta Eliza Vaughn Palmer
Winter, T. B., 40
Winters, Yvor, 194, 195
Winterson, Jeanette, 106, **683–85**
Winthrop, John, 77
Wiseman, Jane, 685
Wiseman, Nicholas, 653
Wister, Owen, Jr., 366
Withers, George, 608
Wittgenstein, Ludwig, 471
Wittig, Monique, 114
Wocklow, M., 523
Wodehouse, P. G., 145
Woffington, Peg, 43, 156
Wolfe, Humbert, 678–79
Wollstonecraft (Godwin), Mary, 9, 103, 241, 311–12, 382, 396, 463, 491, 524, 527, 544, 559, 568, 675, 681, **685–87**
Wolseley, Robert, 673
women's health, 626–27 (*see also* medicine; nurses)
women's rights/emancipation, 128, 396, 449, 450–51 (*see also* suffrage)
Wood, Ellen Price, 687–88
Woodbridge, John, 77
Wooddeson, Richard, 461
Woodforde, James, 554
Woodforde-Fuinden, Amy, 477
Woodhouse, Thomas, 608
Woodring, Carl, 286
Woodroffe, Thomas, 533
Woods, S., 376
Woodward, Harry, 155–156
Woodward, Henry, 44
Woolf, Leonard, 23, 123, 172, 185, 428, 542, 552, 688
Woolf, Virginia, 16, 23, 47, 83, 95, 99, 123, 137, 185, 216, 248, 299, 303, 325, 332, 348, 378, 388, 402, 428, 443, 482, 505, 510, 537–38, 534, 538, 542, 551–52, 562, 578, 585, 600, 601, 610, 616, 678, **688–90** (*see also* Bloomsbury)
Woolley, Leonard, 309
Woolman, John, 286, 292, 293
Woolrich, John, 655
Worde, Wynkyn de, 49
Wordsworth, Dora, 348
Wordsworth, Dorothy, 123, 277, 373, **691–92**
Wordsworth, John, 651
Wordsworth, Mary, 436
Wordsworth, William, 1, 3, 33, 61, 85, 109, 110, 163, 251, 274, 303, 315, 319, 331, 347, 348, 373, 394, 402, 435, 445, 454, 464, 519, 580, 591–92, 681, 691
Wordworth, Paddy, 356
Wright, Frances, 692–93
Wright, Francesca. *See* Robins, Denise Naomi
Wright, Jules, 191

Wright, William, 685
Wrightson, Aldborough, 382
Wroth, Mary (Sidney), 231, 351, 421, **693–94**, 658
Wyatt, Thomas, 536
Wycherley, William, 636
Wyndham, Francis, 145, 531
Wyndham, Mary, 15
Wyngard, Diana, 190
Wynman, Margaret. *See* Dixon, Ella Nora Hepworth
Wythens, Francis, 613
Wythens, Lady. *See* Taylor, Elizabeth (Wythens)

Yates, Frances Amelia, 694–95
Yates, Mary Ann, 91
Yearsley, Ann Cromartie, 301, **696–97**
Yeats, W. B., 23, 119, 203, 204, 227, 244, 279, 280, 288–89, 303, 346, 347, 363, 380, 426, 524, 578, 586, 638, 646, 680
Yonge, Charlotte Mary, 197, 233, 307, 308, 377, 564, 647, **697–99**
York, Peter, 104
Young, Arthur, 55
Young, E[mily]. H[ilda]., 699
Young, Herbert, 596
Young Lady Eighteen Years of Age, A. *See* Porter, Anna Maria
Yugoslavia, writing about, 490

Zimmerman, Paul, 277
Zipes, Jack, 575
Zoide. *See* Havergal, Frances Ridley
Zola, Emile, 72, 76, 192, 408, 428